California
Riparian Systems

CALIFORNIA RIPARIAN SYSTEMS

Ecology, Conservation, and Productive Management

Edited by

Richard E. Warner *and* Kathleen M. Hendrix

UNIVERSITY OF CALIFORNIA PRESS
Berkeley   Los Angeles   London

University of California Press
Berkeley and Los Angeles, California

University of California Press, Ltd.
London, England

Library of Congress Cataloging in Publication Data

Main entry under title:

California riparian systems.

   1. Riparian ecology—California—Congresses.
2. Conservation of natural resources—California—
Congresses. 3. Natural resources—California—
Management—Congresses. I. Warner, Richard E.
II. Hendrix, Kathleen M.
QH105.C2C36   1984   333.91′62′09794   83-47665
ISBN 0-520-05034-7
ISBN 0-520-05035-5 (pbk.)

Printed in the United States of America

1   2   3   4   5   6   7   8   9

TO

A. STARKER LEOPOLD, 1913-1983

Scientist

Conservationist

Mentor

Colleague

Friend

ALOHA NUI LOA, AND GODSPEED

IN MEMORIAM

Rick Warner has died since completing this book. He finished it with the last of his ebbing great strength. He was a remarkable field scientist and activist who could be counted on to get things done correctly regardless of the difficulties. He was a strong moral force that will be sadly missed in the ongoing struggle to maintain a semblance of environmental quality.

Huey Johnson

CONTENTS

9. NATIONAL AND REGIONAL RIPARIAN TRENDS: TOWARD A BROADER PERSPECTIVE

10. RIPARIAN RESTORATION: PROBLEMS AND OPPORTUNITIES

11. RIPARIAN SYSTEMS AND WATER DIVERSION PROJECTS:
CAN THE CONFLICTS BE RESOLVED?

A PICTORIAL OVERVIEW OF CALIFORNIA RIPARIAN SYSTEM CHARACTERISTICS

California riparian systems exhibit, in both structure and function, a mixture of regional uniqueness and global universality. An understanding of the nature and consequences of these characteristics can be very useful in interpreting observed field conditions and in designing and implementing management programs. Many of these characteristics are best described using on-site photography. The adage "one picture is worth a thousand words," is especially true here, where the diversity of species, topography, biogeography, climate, and geology found in California is so great. The set of photographs described below was selected to demonstrate and to assist in interpreting some of the more pervasive elements of structure and function in riparian systems both in California and elsewhere.

Frontispiece.--Valley oak (Quercus lobata) forest on the lower floodplain of the Cosumnes River, San Joaquin County. The wild grape (Vitis californica) draping the branches in areas exposed to the sun gives this magnificent forest a cathedral-like aspect. (Photograph © 1983 by R.E. Warner.)

Page 1.--A stand of black cottonwood (Populus trichocarpa) at about 4,000 ft. elevation along the Yuba River, Nevada County. This species is replaced at lower, drier, and warmer elevations by Fremont cottonwood (P. fremontii), and at higher elevations by the quaking aspen (P. tremuloides). (Photograph © 1983 by R.E. Warner.)

Page 45.--A stand of black willow (Salix gooddingii var. variabilis) along the American River Parkway, Sacramento. Willows vary greatly in form, depending upon species. Some are small, prostrate shrubs; others robust shrubs and small trees; and others, like that illustrated here, are capable of developing into a dense forest, 50 ft. or more in height. (Photograph © 1983 by R.E. Warner.)

Page 109.--The California sycamore (Platanus racemosa), here growing on the floodplain of the Sacramento River about 12 miles north of Sacramento, Yolo County. This species is strictly limited to streamside corridors and riverine floodplains, where it provides an attractive and ecologically valuable element to the riparian vegetation. Its tendency to produce cavities in trunks and major branches following limb loss makes it especially valuable to hole-nesting species of birds and mammals. (Photograph © 1983 by R.E. Warner.)

Page 159.--Valley oak forest in Caswell State Park, San Joaquin County. This area has been protected from human-use damage for several decades and is one of the most intact and ecologically diverse riparian systems in California. Even here, however, recent studies have demonstrated that tree size/frequency ratios and other determinants of vegetation structure are unusual. Thus, while valley oak forests of Caswell State Park are among the most intact of California riparian systems, even they are not "primeval," further supporting the growing suspicion that because of ubiquitous, long-term, human use impacts, there are essentially no pristine riparian systems left in the state. (Photograph © 1983 by R.E. Warner.)

Page 189.--A large specimen of the California buckeye (Aesculus californica) near the 100-year floodzone line on the Cosumnes River, Sacramento County. Less obligate a riparian species than the cottonwoods and willows, it is found concentrated in some riparian zones, especially riverine floodplain riparian systems, in the Central Valley. One finds, for example, a well-defined band of California buckeye in the lower floodplains of such rivers as the American, Cosumnes, Stanislaus, and Tuolumne. This band intermixes at its upper boundary with a broad band of valley oak and at its lower boundary with mixed cottonwood/Oregon ash (Fraxinus latifolia) forest. During earlier, less disturbed times this California buckeye zone must have been even more pronounced, as some of the largest, most massive specimens of the species are still present where human-use impacts have been limited. The species is also concentrated along perennial and intermittent streams of the Coast Ranges, often well above the riparian zone, but where local circumstances produce shaded slopes and enhanced soil moisture conditions. (Photograph © 1983 by R.E. Warner.)

Page 215.--Seeps are an inconspicuous but important type of riparian system, being essentially diminutive wet meadows. Studies of them have been neglected until recently. It is now becoming clear that they are often refugia for unique, riparian-dependent species of plants and animals. Like desert oases, seeps provide a special, insular biogeographical circumstance. This seep is located at about 1,520 ft. elevation near Placerville in El Dorado County. (Photograph by Cheryl Lemming Langley, with permission.)

Page 241.--Along mountainous streams the banks and floodplains may be so steep, rocky, fractured, and/or unstable that the riparian zone is difficult to recognize. This segment of the upper Van Duzen River below Dinsmore (part of the state Wild and Scenic River System) illustrates this very well. Small pockets of riparian woodlands and meadows can be found where hydrologic and geologic circumstances permit. Other reaches may have only an occasional willow, alder, or other mesophyte growing amongst boulders and in the rocky, uneven streamside zone. (Photograph courtesy of Kerry J. Dawson, with permission.)

Page 287.--Yosemite Valley, Merced County, the floor of which contains grand and magnificent riparian systems. Carved from granite by glacial processes, the valley is a broad, nearly flat floodplain partially dammed by lateral and terminal moraines, where imported waters are delivered via a series of majestic waterfalls and cataracts. (Photograph © 1983 by R.E. Warner.)

Page 383 (upper).--Wet meadows comprise a significant part of the Yosemite Valley riparian zone. High soil moisture levels from the imported water supplies provide the necessary water for mesic riparian plants, while at the same time excluding the more xeric upland species found on adjacent slopes and higher sites. (Photograph © 1983 by R.E. Warner.)

Page 383 (lower).--Meadows constitute a major riparian resource wherever they occur, as the combination of high light intensity, soil moisture, nutrient availability, and amenability to fish and wildlife render them highly productive. They may be thought of as small riparian islands in the far less productive uplands. This meadow, at about 4,500 ft. elevation in the transition forest near Strawberry, Yuba County. Despite periodic meadow-hay cutting, grazing, and livestock yarding operations, it still retains much of its original structure and provides habitat for many wildlife species. (Photograph © 1983 by R.E. Warner.)

Page 437 (upper).--Vernal pools are another type of seasonal wetland with a strong riparian component. Precipitation is captured during winter rains in these impermeable-bottomed lowlands, creating shallow seasonal pondlets or "pools." As spring arrives and the imported water evaporates, concentric bands of wildflowers and other vegetation develop along the riparian zones of the pools. Many of these plant species are especially adapted to vernal pool circumstances. This vernal pool in the Vina Plains Preserve of The Nature Conservancy is just beginning to dry out with the onset of spring. (Photograph by Hella Hammid and The Nature Conservancy, with permission.)

Page 437 (lower).--Greater and Lesser Sandhill Cranes rising from the riparian floodplain grasslands of the Mokelumne River. For some five million years Sandhill Cranes have been flying south each winter to use this riparian resource for foraging and roosting. Recently, however, a strong trend to convert the riverine bottomlands to vineyards and other land uses incompatible to the cranes has developed. These land-use practices are so damaging to the native Sandhill Cranes that whole regional crane populations could be decimated. (Photograph © 1983 by R.E. Warner.)

Page 481 (upper).--Saratoga Springs is a unique type of desert riparian system in the southern end of Death Valley National Monument. Its imported water source is a series of springs emerging from the base of some rocky hills to the right. The encompassing sand dune ridges are maintained by the interaction of wind and stabilizing shrubs and grasses. The inner riparian zone is lush and green, being protected from wind by the dune barrier. The area receives less than five inches precipitation per year. (Photograph © 1983 by R.E. Warner.)

Page 481 (lower).--In this palm oasis the native riparian palm Washingtonia filifera finds adequate moisture in a surface-emergent aquifer on the desert floor of Anza-Borrego Desert State Park. In such riparian systems water may appear only very rarely--or not at all-- at ground level, sometimes limiting the ability of riparian shrubs and groundcover species to survive. Digging at the base of these trees produced wet, sandy soil. During wet years water has been recorded at ground level. (Photograph © 1983 by R.E. Warner.)

Page 537 (upper).--In the drier, warmer, more southerly portion of its range, the red alder (Alnus rubra) is closely associated with and dependent upon riparian systems, occurring as a streamside species. In this photograph of a stream in the Coast Ranges about five miles south of Point Reyes Station, the species can be seen as relatively riparian-dependent, the trees closely following the watercourse. (Photograph © 1983 by R.E. Warner.)

Page 537 (lower).--Further north, as climate tempers and precipitation increases, the species abandons its riparian dependency and is regularly found on moist, open slopes and along roadside berms. Here the species is growing vigorously in roadside gravels on coastal Vancouver Island, British Columbia. Precipitation in this region is between 100 and 200 inches per year. This varying dependency upon the riparian zone, resulting from changes in climatic circumstances, is seen in many riparian species. (Photograph © 1983 by R.E. Warner.)

Page 577 (upper).--A mature grove of Fremont cottonwood on the floodplain of the South Fork Kern River, Kern County. One of the finest remaining cottonwood/willow riparian systems in southern California, the area has now been preserved by The Nature Conservancy, and efforts are underway to rehabilitate portions that have been most seriously affected by grazing, clearing for agriculture, and other human-use impacts. (Photograph © 1983 by R.E. Warner.)

Page 577 (lower).--The floodplain riparian wetlands of the South Fork Kern River riparian system illustrate very well one of the major geologic principles in the formation and development of these unique systems. As can be seen here, there are large expanses of meadow as well as cottonwood/willow forest. The South Fork Kern River canyon was initially cut down several hundred feet below its present level, and at one time was a relatively steep-walled canyon. Subsequent downstream faulting and earth movement created a barrier across the watercourse. Today the canyon is filled with unconsolidated alluvial sediments and the resulting aquifer filled, raising water table height to at or near ground level. (Photograph © 1983 by R.E. Warner.)

Page 633 (upper).--It is easy to see how riparian systems can be major contributors to ecological diversity and productivity in arid and semi-arid regions. Little Panoche Creek provides a ribbon of mesic summer vegetation and shade through the otherwise arid, treeless uplands. This narrow band of riparian vegetation is heavily used by both wildlife and domestic livestock. (Photograph © 1983 by R.E. Warner.)

Page 633 (lower).--The world's second largest tree (the largest is found in similar circumstances), a coast redwood (Sequoia sempervirens), in the Rockefeller Grove of Redwood State Park, Humboldt County. This immense specimen is growing on the floodplain riparian zone of Bull Creek and is one of the largest living beings on the face of the earth. Note from the photograph that its dimensions are: tree circumference--53 ft.; diameter--17 ft.; and height 346.5 ft. (Photograph © 1983 by R.E. Warner.)

Page 687 (upper).--An example of a very important but poorly understood riparian phenomenon common in the Central Valley. This "lake" or "slough" is formed by runoff erosion in upland areas immediately above the floodplain. The lower ends of these lakes empty onto the floodplain itself, and are at times blocked off and isolated from the floodplain by silt plugs, beaver dams, and other barriers. These lakes are generally perennial and host large populations of waterfowl, wading birds, and other wildlife. When left undisturbed by man, they are often exquisitely beautiful. The site illustrated here is along the lower Cosumnes River, Sacramento County. No special effort has been made to preserve these sites, and they are rapidly being lost to overgrazing, drainage, and forest clearing. (Photograph © 1983 by R.E. Warner.)

Page 687 (lower).--As the lowest-lying area of the Central Valley floodplain is reached, the character of the watercourses changes. Rivers and streams become slower moving, and sloughs, oxbows, lakes, and other secondary waterways with warm, nutrient-rich waters become prominent. Shortly before its confluence with the Mokelumne River, the lower Cosumnes River, shown here, becomes a series of slow-moving, warm water, high nutrient waterways. Wildlife is abundant here at all seasons. Indeed, this zone appears to be one of the most productive in the entire Central Valley ecosystem. (Photograph © 1983 by R.E. Warner.)

Page 721 (upper).--One of California's more remarkable watercourses, with its attenuated riparian zone. This small, perennial freshwater stream derives from springs and seeps in the mountains forming the western boundary of Death Valley in Death Valley National Monument. The water is fresh enough to support a population of the native (and endangered) species of pupfish, as it passes through the salt flats comprising the floor of Death Valley. (Photograph © 1983 by R.E. Warner.)

Page 721 (lower).--A closer view of the riparian zone of the small stream illustrated above. The narrow, dark line at the edge of the crystalline salt concretions is the riparian zone, a growth zone for several species of algae. This riparian algal growth zone, and algal mats on the bottom of the streambed, are the two major sites of primary production for this peculiar stream ecosystem. (Photograph © 1983 by R.E. Warner.)

Page 747 (upper).--As a result of nearly two centuries of diverse, unplanned, and often destructive land-use practices, thousands of miles of smaller streams, creeks, and sloughs throughout California have been largely divested of their riparian resources. This is especially pronounced and observable in the San Joaquin Valley, where precipitation rate is low and the rate of natural recovery of riparian vegetation is slow. This small watercourse bordering Sandy Mush Road, San Joaquin County, formerly had a corridor woodland of Fremont cottonwood, willow, and riparian shrubs. Systems such as this have been variously grazed, burned, and cleared, until today little riparian vegetation remains. From an ecological point of view, the value of these systems is often reduced 90-95%. (Photograph © 1983 by R.E. Warner.)

Page 747 (lower).--Subsiding water tables are responsible for the loss of large areas of riparian vegetation. The willow-lined sloughs shown here are part of the formerly massive natural drainage system connecting the Kern River with Kern, Buena Vista, Goose, and Tulare lakes. Historically, overflow water moved via this system to the San Joaquin River for discharge to the Pacific Ocean. The terrestrial component of this extensive wetland system comprised a major riparian resource for that region and provided essential habitat for the endangered tule elk as well as many other species. Diversions for agricultural irrigation in the late 1800s, intensive groundwater pumping from agricultural wells in the early 1900s, and finally construction of Isabella Reservoir and further diversion of the Kern River water supplies removed so much water from the system that it dried up and its dependent riparian vegetation died. The photograph shows one of these dry sloughs in what is now the Tule Elk State Reserve. The trees are today but dead carcasses bordering the now-dry slough. (Photograph © 1983 by R.E. Warner.)

Page 783 (upper).--Rock riprap on the western bank of the Sacramento River north of Sacramento. This controversial structural erosion control measure is aesthetically defacing, ecologically damaging, expensive, and subject to failure. Yet it is one of the few structural bank erosion protection devices that has proven relatively effective over the years. Over time, as alternate bank protection strategies--e.g., river meander zones, integrated pest control on levees, integrated floodplain management, riparian vegetation reestablishment-- become available and are accepted at policy and administrative levels, use of rock riprap and other controversial structural erosion control will diminish. Until then, because one of the principal mandates upon the Corps of Engineers remains the protection of life and property from flood damage, riprapping will continue to be used despite its well known negative values. (Photograph © 1983 by R.E. Warner.)

Page 783 (lower).--Rafting and other forms of boating recreation are developing into important uses of California's river systems. Here a group prepares to run the Merced River immediately below Yosemite National Park. Maintenance and restoration of riparian system values is very important to these user groups, as both the ecological and aesthetic values of the sport depend upon the health of the riparian zone. On such excursions, much time is spent picnicking, resting, and camping in the riparian zone. It is this type of recreational activity, in addition to recreational fishing, that feels most keenly the impact of structural bank protection measures such as riprapping. (Photograph © 1983 by R.E. Warner.)

Page 825 (upper).--Cattle foraging for food in the riparian zone of Little Panoche Creek. Note the absence of groundcover and shrubcover vegetation and presence of prominent browse lines on the Fremont cottonwood. Cattle are attracted to the riparian zone by the shade, (usually) high moisture, palatable vegetation, and (usually) free water. (Photograph © 1983 by R.E. Warner.)

Page 825 (lower).--Human disturbance has caused the cattle to leave immediate area. Note complete absence of cottonwood regeneration even though adult plants are present. In due course the remaining, heavily browsed trees will die, and this reach of stream will become devoid of tree cover. This pattern of gradual decline of ecological diversity and quality through livestock-induced destruction of riparian vegetation is common throughout the arid and semi-arid regions of California. (Photograph © 1983 by R.E. Warner.)

Page 867 (upper).--Many human-use riparian impacts are subtle and not readily apparent for many years. The effects of two different livestock management programs on adjacent reaches of the same watercourse are illustrated here. This photograph, looking west immediately upstream from the property line fence, shows a young, recovering riparian system with vigorous ground- and shrubcover growth. This vegetation, while deriving from a previously more heavily degraded riparian system and hence in no way "pristine," none-the-less indicates the regeneration potentials for such small streams. (Photograph © 1983 by R.E. Warner.)

Page 867 (lower).--Looking downstream from the fenceline dividing the two properties, one sees denuded streambanks, remnant trees with browselines, and an almost complete absence of vegetation regeneration of any kind. This latter pattern of denudation from long-term overuse of the riparian zone is one of the more common riparian land-use patterns seen throughout California. (Photograph © 1983 by R.E. Warner.)

Page 905 (upper).--Some symptoms of hydrologic and vegetative instability damaging to riparian values: 1) cut or eroded streambanks, where roots are showing and the bank faces are unstable; 2) lack of ground- and shrubcover vegetation (grasses will often remain throughout a sequence of severe erosion damage); 3) grossly uneven size classes of trees. Here only a few decadent cottonwoods, willows, and sycamores remain after decades of overuse. (Photograph © 1983 by R.E. Warner.)

Page 905 (lower).--Some further symptoms of riparian erosion problems: 1) widening and shallowing of watercourse; 2) reduction in streamside vegetation cover, with reduced amounts of shade and increasing water temperatures; 3) significant numbers of dead and dying trees. Healthy streamside forests and woodlands have low rates of tree mortality, and tree carcasses are present but uncommon. Here dead mature willows are abundant; 4) lack of regeneration of dominant tree species; 5) loss of palatable mesic groundcover and shrubcover plants. (Photograph © 1983 by R.E. Warner.)

Page 957 (upper).--A good, relatively non-destructive use of riparian zones where competing human use interests exist. This golfcourse near Galt, Sacramento County, makes use of the aesthetic values of the Dry Creek riparian zone, while retaining intact most of its ecologic and hydrologic values. Golf carts trundle across bridges, making both sides of the system accessible for recreational use. (Photograph © 1983 by R.E. Warner.)

Page 957 (lower).--Some riparian systems are especially attractive and uniquely suited for dispersed recreation activities which, if properly designed, can protect and restore the systems while making them accessible for non-consumptive uses. Shown here is Orestimba Creek where it crosses Interstate 5 near Stockton. The floodplain supports a unique and beautiful stand of mature California sycamore. Unfortunately, the sycamore stand has been continuously grazed for several decades, the inevitable result being no sycamore or other riparian tree reproduction and loss of vegetative diversity and plant cover. If the present land-use practices prevail, the sycamore woodland will ultimately be destroyed. A park has been proposed for the site, which, if effectively implemented, could lead to long-term protection and recovery of the system. Presently the concept has low priority because the intrinsic riparian values and the potential symbiosis of park and natural system have not been fully factored into the planning process. (Photograph © 1983 by R.E. Warner.)

FOREWORD

In the semi-arid environment that characterizes most of California, the narrow riparian strip of moist soil bordering watercourses, seeps, and springs supports the maximum abundance and variety of plant and animal life. This, of course, is most obvious in the desert or on the sagebrush flats in the Great Basin where the surrounding uplands are extremely dry. But apparently it was equally true of the Central Valley in 1844 when Colonel John Fremont traveled southward from Sutter's Fort on the American River, skirting the western foothills of the Sierra Nevada. With each river crossing he eulogized the beauties of the riparian vegetation: "We traveled for 28 miles over the same delightful country as yesterday, and halted in a beautiful bottom at the ford of the Rio de los Mukelemnes. ...The bottoms on the stream are broad, rich, and extremely fertile. ...A showy lupinus of extraordinary beauty, growing four to five feet in height, and covered with spikes in bloom, adorned the banks of the river, and filled the air with a light and grateful perfume." Not only did Fremont have a keen eye for rich soil and bright blossoms, but he commented as well on the numbers of deer and elk seen in the oak parklands and along the edges of the lowland tulares, or marshes. In the South Coast Ranges, the Spanish traveled the broad valleys and established most of their missions in riparian situations. Only in the wet and rugged North Coast Ranges did travelers shun the watercourses, largely because the valleys were V-shaped, with scant bottomlands.

In the process of settlement, the riverbottoms and alluvial terraces were the first areas to be homesteaded and adapted for tillage. Today virtually every acre of the Central Valley bottomlands has been cleared, drained, diked, leveled, or otherwise altered for cultivation. As reported in this volume, less than 10 percent of the original riparian vegetation remains, and over half of this remnant forest and woodland has been logged and otherwise degraded. Similarly, many other major California river valleys have been turned by the plow—the Russian, Napa, Salinas, Santa Maria, Santa Ana, and on—to take advantage of the fertile soils wherever they occur. Thousands of miles of diversion canals have permitted extension of cultivated fields and pastures to areas far removed from streamsides, even well into the desert. At the same time, these diversions have removed large amounts of water from the streams and rivers of origin, often greatly modifying their character. Today there are few arable acres left that are not producing crops or livestock.

The agricultural conquest has made a great contribution to the economy of California, but in the process some natural values have been sacrificed, at times unnecessarily. Riverine ecosystems often are unique, supplying habitats for animal and plant species that are narrowly restricted in their requirements. For example, the Yellow-billed Cuckoo and Bell's Vireo are two birds that nest exclusively in riparian thickets in the Central Valley and adjoining arid areas. The original, uncountably large populations of waterfowl and other wetland-dependent birds have been reduced to a pittance. Those that remain are still associated with and dependent upon the remnant wetlands. Many, like the large herons and egrets, colonize mature riparian trees. Others, like the Greater and Lesser Sandhill Cranes both feed and breed in riparian wetlands.

Aquatic mammals including the otter, beaver, and muskrat frequent streams and billabongs. According to Williams and Kilburn (this volume), of the 502 native species and subspecies of land mammals in California 25 percent (133 taxa) are limited to or largely dependent upon riparian systems. Of these, 21 species and subspecies are especially vulnerable to loss of habitat and are facing potential threats of extinction, principally through destruction of habitat.

Of the 120 species of reptiles and amphibians that occur in California, half of the reptiles and three-fourths of the amphibians are closely associated with riparian situations. And even the fishes in streams are sheltered by streamside vegetation and obtain much food from the insects that live on the banks and indirectly from the leaves and woody materials provided by riparian vegetation.

When riparian vegetation is stripped away and the soil is seeded to monotypic crops, the native riparian ecosystem is effectively destroyed. Water impoundment or diversion can accomplish the same end. Logging and road building have exposed many streams to erosion and desiccation of the bank areas. Perhaps the most subtle but still highly degrading influence on riparian vegetation is unrestricted grazing by domestic livestock. All of the above forms of land exploitation are justifiable within limits. Yet it would seem both desirable and quite possible to preserve shelter strips along streams, wide enough to protect the riverbanks and riparian flora and fauna, but narrow enough to minimize loss of production. Rigorous protection of desert riparian systems, so few in number and so vital to wildlife, would also seem reasonable, especially because of their extreme vulnerability to human-use impacts.

Fortunately, there is an awakening public appreciation of the beauty, interest, and productive values of riverine forests, streamside woodlands, desert washes and oases, and their richly endowed ecosystems. Some of the most appreciated public parks are situated in old-growth riparian stands along the Sacramento and San Joaquin Rivers, Bidwell Park near Chico being an outstanding example. The stimulus of the California Riparian Systems Conference and this resultant volume of thoughtful and informative reports on many aspects of the problem is evidence of that new interest and concern. Hopefully, from this auspicious beginning there will emerge enduring public and private determination to perpetuate the rich values of riparian systems throughout California.

A. Starker Leopold
13 June 1983

PREFACE

This volume had its origin in the California Riparian Systems Conference, held at the University of California, Davis, 17-19 September 1981. The conference, one year in development and execution, was organized as a means of bringing together the wide range of riparian interests which have been evolving throughout California (and indeed throughout America) over the last decade. From the arid southern deserts to the rainy northcoast forest country, development and other land-use pressures have been destroying and degrading riparian systems at unprecedented rates. Field observations and inquiries throughout the state indicated that virtually every city and county has its own set of urgent riparian problems. Planners, city councils, boards of supervisors, local, state, and federal resource managers, developers, lawyers, conservationists, to mention a few, were all coping with riparian issues. Many of these issues were markedly similar in character, despite their disparate geographical locations.

The main goals of the conference were: a) to define major riparian concepts, problems, and opportunities; b) to promote discussion and information exchange among riparian interests; and c) to establish the technical and communicative base for a long-term, statewide riparian planning, management, and conservation strategy.

Seven hundred and eleven people, from not only California, but at least 10 other states and Washington, D.C., registered as conference participants, attesting both to the intensity and the wide geographical extent of interest in this subject. Sixteen federal and state agencies and two private organization (listed in the Acknowledgments) provided the funding and in-kind support necessary for a gathering of this size and complexity. Three plenary and 21 concurrent sessions permitted the presentation of approximately 150 technical papers.

Of these papers, 128 were ultimately accepted for publication, and then subjected--as required--to intensive post-conference technical and general editorial review. This review often involved extensive consultation with authors. Following editorial review, all manuscripts were retyped, proofread twice, and subjected to a final editorial review. It will be noted that there are two general formats, one for broadly scientific papers, the other for legal and related papers. This protocol facilitated most efficient reporting of reference material in the various disciplines.

The goals of the editors throughout were to provide a final product that is technically sound, accurate, and as free from jargon, imprecise terminology, and confusing graphics as possible. Our ultimate goal--which we believe we have achieved, but leave the reader to be final arbiter--has been a document of significantly higher professional quality than the usual conference proceedings, falling perhaps midway between that and rigorously peer-reviewed, heavily edited technical journals and monographs.

The task proved far more time consuming and costly than had been anticipated. In retrospect this is understandable, as the material derived from some 175 widely scattered authors and exceeded the equivalent of 3,000 manuscript pages in length. It is our hope that the combined efforts of authors, editors, and dedicated support staff have resulted in a document that will materially advance the long-term interests of riparian systems--both throughout California and in other areas where similar issues are being addressed.

SOME RIPARIAN DEFINITIONS

The following definitions and the conceptual frame they provide were used both in the design of the conference and the preparation of this volume. While the editors did not attempt to achieve absolute uniformity of definition in order to accommodate strong author terminological preferences, considerable effort was made to minimize ambiguity and approach standardization of the most widely used descriptors. While all readers may not agree or be comfortable with all definitions, all will at least understand what the authors are trying to say.

It is important to discern at the outset that the "riparian" concept has had a specific ecological context for well over two thousand years. The present day riparian concept and its derivative terms (riparian, riparial, riparious) all come from the Latin <u>Riparius</u>, which itself derives from the Latin <u>Ripa</u> (Pl. <u>Ripae</u>) meaning bank or shore, as of a stream or river. The original meaning has been largely retained through subsequent history, i.e., pertaining to the terrestrial, moist soil zone immediately landward of aquatic wetlands, other freshwater bodies, both perennial and intermittent watercourses, and many estuaries.

While the original Latin usage apparently related to freshwater/upland and estuarine/upland interfaces, the term has occasionally been applied to coastal shore zones. There is presently no clear concensus as to its applicability to coastal shorelines, but a conservative interpretation (which we prefer) would probably exclude them.

Despite numerous attempts, no single purely descriptive definition embracing riparian systems—that is, one that attempts to define by listing all the different types of riparian phenomena—has proven successful. There are far too many types of riparian systems to be encompassed in a single descriptive statement. Such all-inclusive descriptive definitions have inevitably proven both too unwieldy and less than totally encompassing of all significant riparian phenomena.

Last, it is useful to recognize that the term "riparian" <u>is an adjective</u>. The term, once defined, can thus usefully modify a multitude of other well-accepted terms. This process leads in a straight-forward manner to a set of riparian definitions that is functional and easily understood. The linch-pin or common denominator is of course the term "riparian." Once that has been adequately defined, everything else falls into place. Proceeding in a sequence that builds logically, the following definitions are offered.

RIPARIAN: pertaining to the banks and other adjacent terrestrial (as opposed to aquatic) environs of freshwater bodies, watercourses, estuaries, and surface-emergent aquifers (springs, seeps, oases), whose transported freshwaters provide soil moisture sufficiently in excess of that otherwise available through local precipitation to potentially support the growth of mesic vegetation.

AQUATIC: growing or living in or frequenting water; taking place in or on water.

ZONE: an area surrounde by boundary lines; a region or area set off as distinct from surrounding or adjoining parts.

WETLAND: a zone that is periodically, seasonally, or continuously submerged or which has high soil moisture; which may have both aquatic and riparian components, and which is maintained by transported water supplies significantly in excess of those otherwise available through local precipitation.

UPLAND: the ground above a floodplain; that zone sufficiently above and/or away from transported waters as to be dependent upon local precipitation for its water supplies.

POPULATION: a group of individuals of the same species inhabiting a specific zone or system.

HABITAT: the ecological and/or physical place determined and bounded by the needs and the presence of a specific plant or animal population, which contains a particular combination of environmental conditions sufficient for that population's survival. Similar or equivalent to "niche".

VEGETATION: the total plant cover or plant life of a zone or area.

FAUNATION: the total animal life of a zone or area; the animal equivalent of vegetation.

ASSOCIATION: a collection of units or parts into a mass or whole (e.g., a group of animals, plants, or both). A statement of physical proximity or grouping, without necessarily requiring or implying interactions between units of the group, in contrast to "community", which does. Similar or equivalent to "aggregation."

COMMUNITY: an association of living organisms having mutual relationships among themselves and to their environment and thus functioning, at least to some degree, as an ecological unit.

SYSTEM: a group of related natural objects and/or forces within a defined zone; a regularly interacting or interdependent group of items forming a unified whole; a more general and less rigorous term than "ecosystem".

ENVIRONMENT: the complex of factors that act upon an organism or an ecological community and ultimately determine its form and survival.

ECOSYSTEM: the interacting complex of a community and its environment functioning as an ecological unit in nature. Differs from "system" in being a more rigorous definition that encompasses and requires assumptions of energetics, ecological interactions, species adaptations, and so forth.

A **RIPARIAN ZONE** is thus a delimited of riparian (moist soil) substrate, within whose boundaries may grow a **RIPARIAN VEGETATION**, which in turn may support a **RIPARIAN FAUNATION**. The riparian vegetation and riparian faunation in turn comprise one or more plant, animal, or biotic **RIPARIAN ASSOCIATIONS**, which, if the populations are known to interact and to have mutual relationships among themselves and their environments, constitute a **RIPARIAN COMMUNITY**. Each **POPULATION** of plant or animal so involved has its own population-specific **HABITAT**, determined and delimited by the specific physiological and ecological requirements of that population. All are part of and exploit a **RIPARIAN ENVIRONMENT**, and in so doing become parts of a **RIPARIAN ECOSYSTEM**. A **RIPARIAN SYSTEM** denotes, in a generalized way, a site-specific set of riparian phenomena without necessarily connoting an entire riparian ecosystem. Where the riparian plant and aminal life has been stripped off or otherwise destroyed, the remnant riparian system may consist of only the remaining geologic riparian zone. The riparian zone in turn may be reduced or even destroyed by the diversion or other loss of its transported water supplies.

Applying this terminology with respect to wetlands, there are permanently inundated **AQUATIC WETLANDS** (having water depths of two meters or less) with saturated soils and hydrophytic plants; and less frequently to never inundated **RIPARIAN WETLANDS** with moist soils and mesophytic plants. Riparian wetlands are bounded on their outer or drier sides by yet more xeric **UPLANDS**, which are usually higher in elevation and still further removed from the transported water supplies.

ACKNOWLEDGMENTS

The enterprise resulting in the present volume spanned three years and involved the support and dedicated assistance of a wide array of organizations, institutions, and individuals. While space does not permit the enumeration of all to whom we are indebted, some must be identified because of their especially important contributions to the success of the venture.

Conference Organization and Execution

The funding and in-kind support of the following co-sponsors (listed alphabetically) was indispensible to the success of the California Riparian Systems Conference.

Conference Co-sponsors

California Department of Boating and
  Waterways
California Department of Conservation
California Department of Fish and Game
California Department of Food and
  Agriculture
California Department of Forestry
California Department of Parks and
  Recreation
California Department of Water
  Resources
California Resources Agency
Friends of the River

Natural Resource Biologists' Association
  (Friend of the Conference)
Riverlands Council
State Water Resources Control Board
The Reclamation Board
University of California (Davis) Water
  Resources Center
US Army Corps of Engineers
USDA Soil Conservation Service
USDI Bureau of Reclamation
USDI Fish and Wildlife Service
US Water Resources Council

Their confidence in the value of the enterprise and in our ability to bring it to fruition is deeply appreciated; without their support there could have been neither the conference nor the present volume.

During the year of organization preceeding the conference, day-to-day guidance was provided by the Conference Steering Committee. Committee members served as interested individuals rather than official agency representatives and gave unstintingly of their time and professional expertise as issues of planning and organization were dealt with. They also provided liason with their respective organizations, facilitating involvement and better understanding of the riparian interests and needs of these organizations.

Conference Steering Committee

Dana Abell*
Michael Aceituno*
Betty Andrews
E. Lee Fitzhugh
Randy Gray*
Glen Holstein
Joanne Jackson

Peter Moyle*
Anne Sands*
Ronald Schultze*
Kevin Shea*
John Speth*
Richard Warner (Chairman)*

* also served as conference session convener

The unwavering commitment to the success of the conference, and the significant professional and personal investments of effort each of these people made toward that end were impressive. Again, the conference could not have succeeded without this invaluable assistance. Some Steering Committee members also served as session conveners. They, and the other session conveners listed below had the important and difficult tasks of helping to formulate and then chairing specific sessions.

Session Conveners

Dana Abell	Peter Moyle
Mike Aceituno	Bob Potter
Harriet Allen	John Renning
Bertin Anderson	Hal Salwasser
Gary Bullard	Anne Sands
James Burns	Ronald Schultz
Mark Capelli	Lauren Scott
Randy Gray	Kevin Shea
Bruce Jones	Kent Smith
Don Kelley	John Speth
John Kramer	Charles Van Riper III
Philip Meyer	Richard Warner

Promotion and execution of the conference itself was undertaken through the auspices of University Extension, University of California, Davis. Bill Hilden, then Assistant Dean for Business and Finance, was a bastion of sympathetic support and guidance. Promotion was handled with creativity and skill by Vicki Hines. Garrett Jones and Extension staff coordinated registration, facilities, and other on-site conference needs.

Betty Brandon and the staff of the USDA Soil Conservation Service Communication Center, Davis, provided unflagging and sympathetic help with various, often urgent, printing projects.

Roberta Walters, then Director of the Davis Art Center, took very able command of the riparian art exhibit and competition. Her professional skill was largely responsible--excepting, of course, the splendid participation of the contributing artists--for the success of that part of the conference.

Field Studies Center staff and interns Barbara Ott, Karin Van Klaveren, and Mary Tappel covered many bases with patience and unfailing good spirits throughout organization and execution of the conference. JoAnn Wildenradt lent her skill and grace as coordinator and hostess for food and drink.

The Present Volume

Bob Hamre, USDA Forest Service, Fort Collins, Colorado, kindly provided editorial counsel and copies of format and protocols used by that organization for manuscript preparation. These were utilized with but few modifications.

The University of California (Davis) Water Resources Center, in addition to being a conference co-sponsor, was responsible for the initial suggestion and the subsequent meetings which led to publication of this volume by the University of California Press. This and other assistance by Herbert Snyder, Otto Helwig, and the Water Resources Center staff is remembered with appreciation.

With very few exceptions, manuscript authors responded with understanding and often with appreciation to our editorial efforts. Their responses encouraged us in our negotiations with the prickly or unresponsive few who objected to proposed modifications of run-on sentences and dangling participles, or who sat in ruminative silence upon our requests for clearer graphics and more complete literature citations.

A significant number of authors also provided page costs to help defray the expense of putting their manuscripts into final camera-ready form. Readers should know of and appreciate--as we do--this additional contribution of the authors to the successful completion of this volume.

The Field Studies Center, Davis, provided overall coordination, logistic support, technical and support staff, office and library facilities, and materials and supplies throughout both phases of the enterprise. The Center also provided computer hardware and software for word processing, as well as secretarial and proofreading staff under the supervision of the assistant editor. Ronnie James, Carol Van Alstine, and Lisa Steinmann contributed patience and good humor as well as word-processing and proofreading skills. Melanie Minor and Nancy Gooch, interns from the University of California, Davis, helped with bibliographies, word processing, and other important chores.

Throughout the enterprise, from initial conference concept to completion of the present volume, colleagues, friends, and family have provided unflagging guidance, support, and encouragement. One spouse and three children in particular made no material contribution, but without their loving understanding and tolerance for thrown-together meals, consultations into the wee hours of the morning, and enforced absences from home to accommodate their wife/mother's bizarre work schedule, we would be laboring still.

Finally, special acknowledgment is due the late A. Starker Leopold, who first called attention to the problem of riparian system decline nearly a decade ago, and who saw more clearly than most the ominous implication of this decline to our fish and wildlife resources. It is an enduring regret of the editors that he did not live to see the publication of this volume, which he so consistently encouraged.

To all those who helped bring this volume to publication, whether mentioned here or not, we express our most sincere thanks.

Richard E. Warner
   Editor
   Technical Coordinator, California Riparian Systems Conference

Kathleen M. Hendrix
   Assistant Editor
   Assistant Coordinator, California Riparian Systems Conference

CALIFORNIA RIPARIAN FORESTS:

DECIDUOUS ISLANDS IN AN EVERGREEN SEA[1]

Glen Holstein[2]

Abstract.--California riparian forests are dominated by deciduous trees and are thus anomolous in a state where most dominant woody plants are evergreen. Riparian zones provided refuges where riparian elements of the Arcto-Tertiary Geoflora could survive when its upland elements were decimated by the development of California's mediterranean-type climate. Water and nutrients imported to California's dry lowlands from wetter mountains by perennial streams permit high summer primary productivity in riparian communities while adjacent upland vegetation is severely drought stressed. High riparian productivity makes the cost of annual replacement of deciduous foliage affordable because such foliage is more photosynthetically efficient than that of evergreen upland dominants. Bird abundance and diversity in riparian communities are related to this high riparian productivity.

INTRODUCTION

Much of California has a mediterranean-type climate. In such climates rainfall and snowfall are maximal in winter, when minimal solar radiation limits plant growth. When the long days of summer potentially maximize growth, rainfall is minimal or nil and many plants are dormant or under severe drought stress. Thus moisture and solar radiation, two necessities for plant growth, are exactly out of phase (Major 1977).

Even near the moist northwest coast of California, fields of annual grasses in the hills above Redwood National Park (Humboldt County) are dead by late summer. Summer drought is also a major factor contributing to the uniqueness of California's alpine flora (Chabot and Billings 1972). Only at a few desert localities in California do some summer months have more rain than any single winter month, but here rainfall is so scanty and unpredictable at all times that vegetation is sparse and the flora limited to specialized drought resisters or evaders.

Most California vegetation is maximally productive in spring, when days are longer and warmer than in winter, and some moisture is still available. Stressful winter and summer conditions are thus both avoided. Productivity is less,

however, than in ecosystems where light, warmth, and water are all simultaneously available in abundance. The productivity potential which is frequently unfulfilled in California because of summer drought stress is revealed by the increase in crop yield obtained there with irrigation, and by the productivity of the riparian vegetation which lines or once lined perennial streams. These streams carry the part of the winter water surplus which is slowly released from deep aquifers and melting mountain snow, making it available to lowland riparian vegetation in summer when little water is provided by the local climate. The resultant greater productivity and biomass of this vegetation is frequently obvious when contrasted with that of nearby communities which lack imported water. Riparian forests in central Asia ecologically similar to those of California's Central Valley are among the world's most productive natural ecosystems (Major 1977). When the current vacuum in California riparian research is filled, it is likely that riparian systems here will be found to be comparably productive.

BIOGEOGRAPHY OF RIPARIAN FOREST COMPONENTS

Axelrod (1973) has provided compelling paleobotanical evidence that California's mediterranean-type climate is a relatively late phenomenon which first appeared in the upper Pliocene. This and other climatic perturbations caused the Arcto-Tertiary Geoflora, a zone of rich and diverse forest which was once continuous around the Northern Hemisphere, to retreat and become impoverished. Destructive impoverishment

[1]Paper presented at the California Riparian Systems Conference. [University of California, Davis, September 17-19, 1981].
[2]Glen Holstein is Lecturer, Botany Department, University of California, Davis.

of the Arcto-Tertiary Geoflora by spreading drought and cold was severe in western North America and Europe, but many of its elements survived in major refuges in eastern Asia, the Pontic region of southwest Asia, the Mexican highlands, and the southeastern United States. California's expanding mediterranean-type climate caused the replacement of many Arcto-Tertiary communities by drought-resistant vegetation known as the Madro-Tertiary Geoflora, which had long been adapted to local dry habitats (Axelrod 1975).

Riparian forests, as ecosystems in but not under the control of a mediterranean-type climate, seem likely refuges for Arcto-Tertiary elements within California, and Robichaux (1977) has shown in a review of their fossil record that most dominant California riparian forest taxa have modern ranges reduced from more widespread Tertiary distributions. These dominants all have relatives which are common in the Arcto-Tertiary derived deciduous forests of eastern North America (Axelrod 1960), and their dominance by deciduous trees and shrubs gives these vegetation types a similar aspect. Examination of the evolution and biology of the taxa dominant in California riparian forests provides further clues to the origin, evolution, and relationships of western North American riparian vegetation.

Acer (Maple)

This large genus, with 200 species of mostly deciduous trees, is one of the most important components of the temperate deciduous forests of the Northern Hemisphere, and its modern range coincides closely with those communities which are predominantly derived from the Arcto-Tertiary Geoflora (Hora 1981). It is by far the largest of the two genera in the Aceraceae and is the only one occurring naturally in North America, where it includes major upland dominants such as A. saccharum and widespread riparian species such as A. saccharinum and A. negundo.

The Aceraceae are part of the Sapindales (Cronquist 1968; Dahlgren 1975) or the essentially equivalent suborder Sapindineae of Thorne (1976), taxa which are otherwise largely dominated by entomophilous, evergreen, or drought-deciduous tropical to subtropical woody plants with compound leaves. The Hippocastanaceae are probably the closest relatives of the Aceraceae, and both of these families are unusual within the Sapindales because of their winter dormancy and largely north temperate distributions.

Acer consists mostly of winter-deciduous trees, but it is otherwise quite diverse and includes morphoclines both from compound to simple leaves and from flowers which are corollate and entomophilous to those which are reduced, apetalous, and wind pollinated. In both cases these clines reflect a shift from the primitive Sapindalean condition to a derived condition typical of the majority of dominant north temperate forest trees.

The four California species of Acer, A. glabrum, A. circinatum, A. macrophyllum, and A. negundo var. californicum, all can occur along streams, but only A. negundo (box elder) is primarily riparian. The other species are more common in mesic upland sites in the wetter parts of montane and coastal California, where gradients between riparian and upland vegetation are much more diffuse and less distinct than in the drier areas of the state.

A. macrophyllum is a particularly common and important tree throughout much of coastal and montane California, and it is listed by Roberts et al. (1977) along with Sequoia sempervirens, Umbellularia californica, and several more strictly riparian species as one of the common trees of California's north coastal riparian forests. In this region A. macrophyllum, S. sempervirens, and U. californica all occur from streambanks to the shaded, moist upland sites where they are most abundant.

A. negundo is frequent in riparian zones throughout the Mississippi basin and the Great Plains. Locally, it extends to the Atlantic coast and occurs along scattered streams and rivers in the southern Rocky Mountains, the Southwest, and California (fig. 1). Few other North American trees are transcontinental.

Within California A. negundo is locally common in riparian communities in the drier parts of the Coast Ranges and in the lower parts of the Sacramento and San Joaquin Valleys, where marine airflow through the Carquinez Straits somewhat moderates summer temperatures. Virtually nowhere in California, however, is it dominant. It is

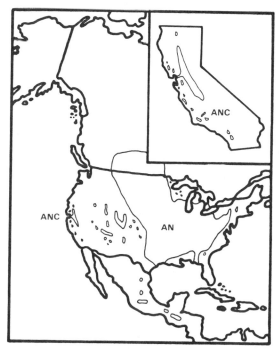

Figure 1.--Range of Acer negundo (AN) including A. negundo var. californicum (ANC) (after Little 1971).

normally a shade-tolerant subordinate tree in dense riparian vegetation dominated by Populus fremontii, P. trichocarpa, Salix goodingii, S. laevigata, S. lasiandra, or S. lasiolepis. Association with P. fremontii is especially frequent.

Dispersal of A. negundo is by wind dispersed samaras, but these are produced in smaller quantities and are less easily dispersed than the lighter, comose seeds of Salix and Populus. As a result, box elder is less efficient at colonizing the new riparian habitats which are frequently created on sandbars and along ditches and canals.

A. negundo appears to be in decline in California since it is a relatively poor competitor which has been restricted to the most highly competitive riparian zones. It may now be at an early stage of the process by which climatic vicissitudes eliminated (e.g., A. saccharinum and Ulmus americana) (Axelrod 1977) or almost eliminated (e.g., Juglans hindsii) other riparian taxa from California whose relatives are still common in the much more extensive riparian systems of eastern North America, which receive summer rain.

A. negundo is taxonomically isolated among North American maples since it is the only member of section Negundo on this continent. This section is distinct enough to be segregated as the genus Negundo Boehm. by some (Willis and Airy Shaw 1973). Its other species are Asian, and it combines the putatively primitive character (within Acer) of compound leaves with dioecy and inflorescences which are apetalous and anemophilous in A. negundo but corollate in at least some Asian species (Rehder 1940).

Alnus (Alder)

Alnus is a morphologically homogeneous genus of 35 species of deciduous trees and shrubs of the Northern Hemisphere and the Andes, and it has monoecious, anemophilous catkins and nutlets which vary among species in the degree of development of marginal wings and the resultant relative importance of wind, water, and gravity dispersal (Sudworth 1908; Fowells 1965).

It shares a distinctive pattern of ecological adaptation with some other important California riparian genera like Salix. These consist primarily of large, obligately riparian trees in warm temperate climates but are increasingly dominated by widespread shrubs which are only facultatively riparian in colder boreal and montane regions. Unlike other genera with large California riparian trees, however, Alnus contributes no important trees to North America's eastern deciduous forest. The commonest alder there is the shrubby A. serrulata. The adaptations needed by alders which are temperate riparian trees and those which are boreal and montane shrubs may not be greatly different since snowmelt frequently saturates soils of cold regions during the brief growing season and

creates conditions similar to those found only along streambanks and lakeshores in warmer climates. Alders can symbiotically fix nitrogen, which otherwise may be limiting in forest environments and elsewhere (Spurr and Barnes 1980).

Alnus is a member of the Betulaceae, a family of mostly north temperate deciduous and anemophilous trees and shrubs which is in the Fagales (Cronquist 1968; Dahlgren 1975; Thorne 1976), an order it shares with the Fagaceae, to which it is linked by several intermediate genera (Corylus, Carpinus, Ostrya, and Ostryopsis) sometimes placed in Betulaceae and sometimes in the segregate families Corylaceae and Carpinaceae (Willis and Airy Shaw 1973). The Fagales are the most important single order of angiosperm trees in temperate regions and most member taxa have Arcto-Tertiary distributions.

Alnus has four California species: A. sinuata, A. tenuifolia, A. rubra, and A. rhombifolia. The first two are largely shrubs of the boreal/montane type mentioned previously, but they can occasionally grow large enough along streams to be riparian trees (Sudworth 1908). The second two are among California's most important riparian trees. All California alders are in subgenus Alnus except A. sinuata which is in Alnaster.

Alnus rubra (A. oregona), the red alder, is associated with the North Coastal Coniferous Forest (Munz 1959) from the Alaska panhandle to the coast of San Luis Obispo County (Little 1971; Griffin and Critchfield 1972). Within its range (fig. 2) it is frequently the dominant riparian tree. This largest of American alders (Elias 1980) is also very common on moist slopes, especially after conifers have been removed by logging operations, but it is much more likely to form dense and distinctive riparian gallery forests which it overwhelmingly dominates than are trees such as Acer macrophyllum, which are also found from moist slopes to streamsides. A fine example of such a gallery forest is protected along Prairie Creek in Humboldt County at Prairie Creek Redwoods State Park.

Alnus rhombifolia (white alder) forms similar gallery forests throughout much of the rest of California south and east of the range of A. rubra (fig. 2), but it much more obligately restricted to streamsides than its coastal relative. As a result, it is the most reliable indicator of permanent water among California's riparian trees (Jepson 1910). A. rhombifolia is the usual dominant in California's montane riparian forests up to about 1,600 m., but it also is dominant near sea level along Alameda Creek in Alameda County's Niles Canyon and numerous other similar places. It is most common along fast-flowing mountain streams west of the crest of the Sierra Nevada and near the coast south of Sonoma County (Griffin and Critchfield 1972). White alders are absent from much of the Central Valley floor but are common along the Sacramento River in Shasta County (ibid.) and further south (Conard et al. 1977). Such

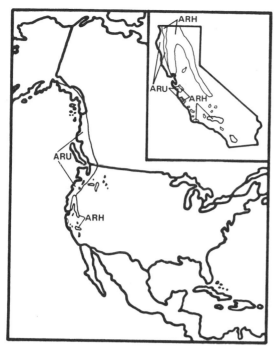

Figure 2.--Ranges of Alnus rubra (ARU) and A. rhombifolia (ARH) (after Little 1971, 1976).

montane-coastal distributions suggest intolerance for summer heat (e.g., Populus trichocarpa), but this is unlikely in the case of A. rhombifolia since it is common in the vicinity of Redding, where summer temperatures are as high or higher than in most of the area where it is absent. The ecological factor which most controls the distribution of A. rhombifolia seems to be a need for constant saturation of its root zone by cool, well-aerated water.

The total range of A. rhombifolia extends from southern California to central Washington in the Peninsular, Transverse, Coast, Sierra Nevada, Klamath, and Cascade ranges, with an extension through the Columbia River Basin to northwestern Idaho (Little 1976). It is most common and its range most continuous in the Sierra Nevada, Klamath Mountains, and northern Coast Ranges of California. A. rhombifolia and A. rubra are morphologically similar and closely related, but hybrids between them do not seem to have been reported. They apparently diverged from a common ancestor at an unknown time in the Tertiary or Quaternary Periods and adapted to wet and riparian sites within the Sierran-Klamath and north coastal forests, respectively.

Betula (Birch)

Betula is the second genus in the Betulaceae when that family is narrowly defined to exclude the Corylaceae and Carpinaceae (Willis and Airy Shaw 1973). Its characters are similar to those of its sister genus, Alnus, which it resembles in its deciduous habit, its anemophilous catkins, its north temperate range, and

its nutlets, which are more consistently winged and wind dispersed than those of Alnus. Betula also shares a similar range of adaptations with Alnus since it includes both temperate zone trees and arctic and montane shrubs, but Betula contributes many more important upland trees to the deciduous forests of eastern North America than Alnus, which is more important as a source of dominant trees in western riparian forests than Betula.

California has two species of Betula: B. occidentalis (B. fontinalis) and B. glandulosa, but only the former reaches tree size. B. occidentalis (water birch) is a large shrub or small tree of riparian sites which is widespread in the cordilleran region of western North America (Little 1976) but is restricted to just a few parts of California. It is relatively frequent in the Klamath Mountains and on the east slope of the southern Sierra Nevada, but much less so in the Warner, White, and Panamint Mountains (fig. 3). The Klamath and Warner Mountains have an abbreviated summer drought because of their northern locations, and the southern Sierra Nevada's east slope and the White and Panamint Mountains all regularly receive summer thunderstorms of tropical origin. As a result, all California populations of B. occidentalis receive quantities of summer rain which are unusual for that state and which approach the greater amounts received by the much larger populations in states to the east and north. Consequently, lack of summer rain must be suspected as an ecological factor limiting the range of this species despite its adaptation to riparian zones. Non-riparian Pinus balfouriana and other taxa have similar distributions for similar reasons (Raven and Axelrod 1978). Seedlings can be much more sensitive than mature

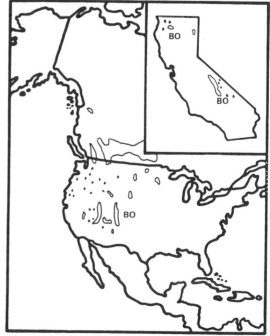

Figure 3.--Range of Betula occidentalis (BO) (after Little 1976).

plants to environmental stresses like summer drought (Grime 1979).

B. occidentalis is in series Albae within Betula (Rehder 1940) and is thus a close relative of the white birches such as B. papyrifera, B. pendula, and B. pubescens, which are very important early successional trees throughout the upland boreal forests of North America and Eurasia.

Cephalanthus (Button Bush or Button Willow)

Cephalanthus occidentalis, an obligately riparian small tree or shrub, is the single California representative of this genus of 17 species which is widespread in the warm regions of the world and is one of only three California genera in the very large (500 genera and 7,000 species) family Rubiaceae, best known in temperate regions for the large and usually herbaceous genus Galium. Most of the Rubiaceae, however, are understory trees and shrubs in tropical forests. The family is clearly of tropical derivation and its placement in the Gentianales by Dahlgren (1975) and Thorne (1976) and in the related Rubiales by Cronquist (1968) reflects considerable consensus cocerning its evolutionary relationships. Cephalanthus is in the subfamily Cinchonoideae, which is largely woody and tropical, rather than in the Rubioideae, which includes most of the family's temperate herbs and its other California genera.

C. occidentalis is primarily a deciduous shrub and only rarely reaches tree size in California. Its flowers are small but corollate and probably entomophilous like those of most Rubiaceae, and the fruit is a dry schizocarpic mericarp which lacks obvious adaptations for dispersal.

Like A. negundo, C. occidentalis is found naturally in both Atlantic and Pacific coast states (fig. 4). It is widespread in the East and ranges south through Mexico to Honduras, but it is restricted to a few Arizona stations and to the floor and adjacent watershed of California's Central Valley in the West (Little 1976). In California and in most of the rest of its range it is limited to areas with mean July temperatures above 20°C where most of the root zone is reliably saturated with water throughout the year. Relatively poor dispersal has made it an inefficient colonizer of the banks of artificial ditches and canals, but it is still common along many permanent natural streams. In backwaters where still, poorly oxygenated water stands throughout the year, C. occidentalis is best developed and can be dominant (Conard et al. 1977), but such habitats in California have been almost entirely destroyed by water resource and agricultural development. Their Button Bush Swamp Forest vegetation type is thus among the rarest and most endangered in the state. A particularly fine example of this vegetation is still extant along the Cosumnes River in southern Sacramento County west of Galt, and its continued preservation should receive high

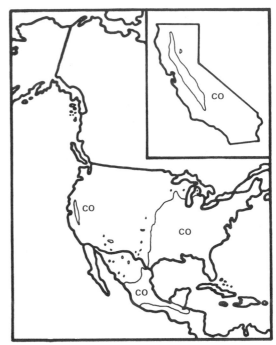

Figure 4.--Range of Cephalanthus occidentalis (CO) (after Little 1976).

priority from California's conservation community.

It is clear that C. occidentalis in California is a relict which has survived the loss of a warmer and wetter climate because of the fortuitous juxtaposition of the hot Central Valley and the high mountains which surround it and keep it continuously supplied with abundant water.

Fraxinus (Ash)

This genus has a range which matches almost exactly that of the Arcto-Tertiary Geoflora, and it shows a range of adaptations including deciduousness, anemophilous catkins, and wind-dispersed samaras which is typical of the flowering trees in the modern forests derived from it. Fraxinus clearly evolved these characters by convergence, however, since its probable ancestors had few if any of them.

It is a member of the Oleaceae, whose placement in the Oleales by Dahlgren (1975) and Thorne (1976) and in the Scrophulariales by Cronquist (1968) only hints at the lack of consensus among plant evolutionists about its origin. Most other members of the family have entomophilous flowers with well-developed corollas, and many are tropical species with evergreen leaves and fleshy fruits adapted to internal dispersal by birds. Fraxinus itself includes a floral reduction series which suggests the mode of evolution of its apetalous, wind pollinated catkins since several species along the southern periphery of its range, including F. cuspidata in the southwestern United States and northern Mexico and F. ornus in southeastern Europe, have

6

fragrant entomophilous flowers with conspicuous corollas. Evergreen leaves are less common, but they occur in F. gooddingii of southern Arizona and northern Sonora (Elias 1980).

Most ash species like F. cuspidata and F. ornus which have primitive characters typical of the Oleaceae are included in section Ornus. Section Fraxinaster, however, includes many species of upland (F. americana, F. excelsior, F. quadrangulata) and riparian (F. nigra, F. pennsylvanica) trees which are important in north temperate deciduous forests and share many characters with the trees most highly adapted to that ecosystem in other families (Rehder 1940).

California is usually considered to have four Fraxinus species (F. dipetala, F. anomala, F. latifolia, and F. velutina) (Munz 1959). F. dipetala is interesting among these as a Fraxinaster species with a corolla (Rehder 1940) and F. anomala for its frequently simple leaves, but only F. latifolia and F. velutina are important riparian trees in California (F. anomala is a riparian species of the Colorado Plateau with a few relict populations in the mountains of the eastern Mojave Desert). These are only nominally species, however, since the riparian ashes of California (fig. 5) are part of an attenuated but essentially continuous cline between more important ash populations in Arizona (F. velutina) and in Oregon and Washington (F. latifolia) along which species can be separated only artificially and arbitrarily (Griffin and Critchfield 1972).

The Pacific Northwest has a relatively short summer drought because of its northerly latitude, and Arizona regularly receives heavy summer thunderstorms of tropical origin, so both areas have much more summer rain than California. There ashes must rely almost entirely on riparian water during the growing season, and probably as a result, they are a very subordinate component of the state's riparian forests except near its northern border, where F. latifolia becomes more important as the climate becomes more like that of Oregon. In the rest of California F. latifolia/F. velutina occurs sparsely as a non-dominant riparian tree in the northern Coast Ranges, the Central Valley, the west slope of the Sierra Nevada, and in southern California, but it is rare or absent in the southern Coast Ranges, where summer drought is especially strongly developed and very few streams are naturally permanent. The Tehachapi Mountains and the western Transverse Range are conventionally used to separate these "species" in California (Griffin and Critchfield 1972).

The biology and distribution of California's riparian ashes suggest that they are declining relicts like Acer negundo var. californicum which are probably somewhat more tolerant of heat and low humidity but less tolerant of summer soil moisture deficits than that taxon. On a larger scale, Arizona and the Pacific Northwest

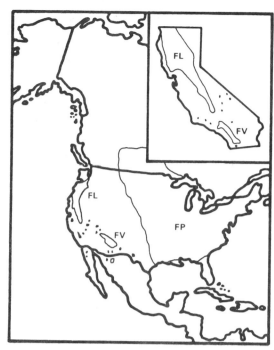

Figure 5.--Ranges of Fraxinus latifolia (FL), F. velutina (FV), and F. pennsylvanica (FP) (after Little 1971, 1976).

appear to be relict nodes where populations of a once more widespread (Robichaux 1977) and probably continuously transcontinental riparian ash have successfully survived Quaternary climatic perturbations that eliminated it in much of the West and greatly reduced it in California. F. velutina and F. latifolia are, in fact, both similar enough to riparian F. pennsylvanica of the eastern United States (fig. 5) to be considered its subspecies (Miller 1955).

Juglans (Walnut)

This genus of deciduous trees has a largely Arcto-Tertiary distribution like many of the other important California riparian genera, but its distribution within the Arcto-Tertiary zone is incomplete because of its absence from large areas, including much of Europe. It is best developed along the southern margins of this zone and extends far south of it to Argentina along the Andes.

Juglans and Carya are the only genera in their family, the Juglandaceae, which still include widespread and important north temperate forest trees. Both have distributions which suggest reductions from formerly more complete Arcto-Tertiary ranges. The other genera of the family, Pterocarya, Engelhardtia, Oreomunnea, Platycarya, and Alfaroa, are all restricted to much smaller warm temperate to tropical Arcto-Tertiary refuges in Middle America or Asia.

The Juglandaceae have often been treated as a distinctive order, the Juglandales, and associated (in the subclass Hamamelidae or Amentiferae) with other families of temperate trees which share their characters of large-seeded woody fruits and anemophilous catkins (Cronquist 1968), but much current opinion (Dahlgren 1975; Thorne 1976) interprets these similarities as convergence and places the Juglandales close to or in the Sapindales/Rutales, the order of compound-leaved tropical trees from which the Aceraceae were also derived through a separate lineage.

The United States has six of the world's 15 species of Juglans, but J. cinerea is the only strongly distinctive species among these six. The other five include J. nigra, an important upland to weakly riparian forest tree of the eastern deciduous forest (Fowells 1965), and four species of various refuge areas in the West (fig. 6). The western species closely resemble J. nigra and suggest the same pattern of Late Tertiary to Quaternary reduction in the range of a formerly transcontinental species which we have seen in Fraxinus. These four include the two California species of Juglans, J. californica and J. hindsii, both of which are endemic to the state.

J. californica is a mostly non-riparian tree of southern California which is depauperate relative to J. nigra and J. hindsii but is not greatly different from them morphologically. It is restricted to deep, friable Tertiary marine shales with high water-holding capacity which permit it to survive as a local dominant on upland sites since the warm spring temperatures of southern California allow summer-

wet conditions to be simulated earlier in the year wherever soil storage capacity is adequate to hold surplus water from winter rains.

J. hindsii was apparently restricted to a very few sites in central California when European settlement began there, and at least some of these sites were riparian (Griffin and Critchfield 1972). Since this species was probably derived from ancestors which were adapted to a summer-wet climate and were only weakly riparian, it is likely that J. hindsii was escaping a mediterranean-type climate to which it was completely unadapted in a riparian zone to which it was poorly adapted. Its large, nutrient-rich seeds in heavy nuts with little obvious capacity for dispersal are a more appropriate adaptation for reproduction in a stable forest (Grime 1979) than in the highly unstable, frequently flood-prone riparian environment that existed in California before most of its streams were dammed.

J. hindsii was clearly on the verge of natural extinction when California was first settled by Europeans and was at the midpoint on a continuum between those taxa with similar histories such as Nyssa and Ulmus which are now known only from California's fossil record (Axelrod 1973) and those such as Acer negundo and Fraxinus latifolia which survived until the settlement period with greater but still declining ranges and abundances (Robichaux 1977). Ironically, since European settlement, J. hindsii has been widely planted and subsequently commonly naturalized in California's now largely stabilized riparian systems at a time when its once much more abundant congener J. californica is declining rapidly because of the urban expansion of Los Angeles.

Platanus (Sycamore)

Platanus, even more than Juglans, is an example of an old, declining Arcto-Tertiary genus, since it is now largely restricted to warm temperate to tropical refuges along the southern periphery of the Arcto-Tertiary zone despite an extensive and diverse fossil record from as far north as Greenland (Engler and Melchior 1964). Only P. occidentalis of the eastern United States is still an important forest tree in a major north temperate forest biome.

Platanus is traditionally placed in the monotypic family Platanaceae, which is widely agreed to belong in the order Hamamelidales (Cronquist 1968; Dahlgren 1975; Thorne 1976), a relationship which links it to several other old families of Arcto-Tertiary trees and shrubs. The Hamamelidales show ancient tendencies toward the deciduous tree habit, unisexual wind pollinated flowers, and wind dispersed fruits, characters which are typical of the modern dominants of north temperate forests and of all 10 living species of Platanus, a taxon which culminates one of probably several floral reduction series within the order and its relatives (Thorne 1976).

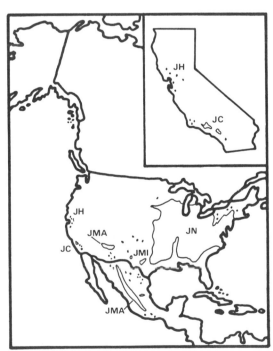

Figure 6.--Ranges of Juglans hindsii (JH), J. californica (JC), J. major (JMA), J. microcarpa (JMI), and J. nigra (JN) (after Little 1971, 1976).

Platanus in the United States includes P. occidentalis and two closely related species of the Southwest, P. wrightii of Arizona, New Mexico, and northwestern Mexico, and P. racemosa of California (fig. 7). All three species are strongly riparian, but the two southwestern species are more similar to P. orientalis, a riparian tree native from southeastern Europe to the Himalayas, than to the geographically closer P. occidentalis (Hsiao 1973). This may reflect ancient relationships and patterns of extinction within Platanus, but the very close relationship between P. racemosa and P. wrightii suggests they were separated relatively recently when expanding deserts separated woodlands that were continuous between Arizona and California in the Miocene (Axelrod 1975; Raven and Axelrod 1978).

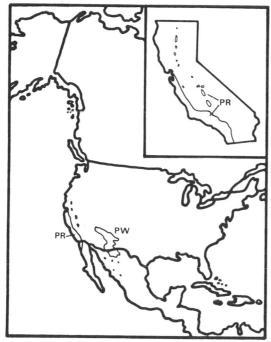

Figure 7.--Ranges of Platanus racemosa (PR) and P. wrightii (PW) (after Little 1976).

P. racemosa is a common riparian tree in northwestern Baja California, southern California, the southern Coast Ranges, the southern Sierra Nevada foothills, and the Sacramento Valley, but it is scarce in the San Joaquin Valley and absent from the northern Coast Ranges, where much seemingly suitable habitat occurs (Griffin and Critchfield 1972). P. racemosa is an important secondary component of the mixed riparian forests of the Sacramento Valley, where it is often associated with sites higher and drier than those where dominant Populus fremontii is found (Conard et al. 1977), but it is particularly conspicuous as frequently the single dominant tree along the intermittent streams of the southern Coast Ranges and southern California. Very large sycamores form an open woodland along such streams, and fine examples of this distinctive vegetation-type can be seen along Pacheco Creek in southern Santa Clara

County and along Orestimba Creek in Stanislaus County.

Intermittent streams are general in southern California and the southern Coast Ranges because of their mediterranean-type climate and lack of extensive highland snowfields to provide summer runoff, and sycamore woodlands are particularly characteristic of those with beds of coarse, porous sand and gravel. Such substrates are common in the region where sycamore woodlands occur because it has been subjected to very rapid and recent Plio-Pleistocene uplift which may still be continuing and to massive erosion which has inevitably followed (Page 1981). The small, comose achenes of P. racemosa are easily carried long distances by wind, enabling the rapid reestablishment of these woodlands after the flood damage which was frequent before California streams were dammed.

The obligate restriction of P. racemosa to riparian zones indicates a need for access to groundwater within its root zone, but its preference for dry, porous sites within riparian zones suggests that for a riparian species it also has a rather high requirement for aeration of at least part of its root zone. The reasons for its complete absence from the northern Coast Ranges are not obvious since seemingly suitable intermittent streams with coarse beds are fairly common there. Along some of these streams on the dry east slope of the northern Coast Ranges native riparian trees are replaced by halophytic graminoids and an introduced Tamarix species, probably because their flows are made brackish by salts leached from the Cretaceous marine sediments which dominate their watersheds,[3] but many other northern Coast Ranges streams have fine riparian gallery forests along their banks. The clay-rich Franciscan Formation dominates the northern Coast Ranges, but the same formation yields enough sand and gravel to support major stands of sycamore woodland in parts of the southern Coast Ranges. Temperature does not provide a simple explanation for the absence of sycamores from the northern Coast Ranges because summers there are not necessarily hotter or cooler nor winters colder or milder than those at places well within the range of P. racemosa.

A possibly significant factor limiting the capacity of sycamores to invade the northern Coast Ranges is that region's cool, wet spring. The collective mean precipitation for May is 43 mm. among the climatic stations of both the northern Coast Ranges and the Sacramento Valley, but that month is 1°C warmer at the Valley sta-

[3] A high Mg/Ca ratio may be important in these streams as well since many have much serpentinite in their watersheds. This ratio is 1.6 in Cache Creek, which has many tributaries which have always lacked riparian trees. The Mg/Ca ratio, electrical conductivity, and dissolved Na are, respectively, 87%, 628%, and 975% greater in Cache Creek than in the Sacramento River into which it flows.

tions. In the southern Coast Ranges the collective May mean temperature is also 1°C warmer than in the northern Coast Ranges, but the collective mean precipitation for that month is 28 mm. less (US Department of Commerce 1970). Anthracnose (Gnomonia platani) is a very serious and prevalent disease which can cause complete spring defoliation of Platanus species including P. racemosa, and it is known to be promoted by cool and wet spring weather (Fowells 1965; Collingwood et al. 1974; Pirone 1970). This fungus is currently severely stressing wild populations of P. racemosa in Alameda and Contra Costa Counties at the northwestern limit of the range of that species, and it must be suspected of limiting the further expansion of sycamores northwestward in California.

Populus (Cottonwood)

Populus is the most important riparian genus in California, and one of the two major genera of the Salicaceae, probably the most important riparian family in the world. This family was traditionally placed close to the Hamamelidales and Fagales in the artificial taxon Amentiferae because of its unisexual catkins, but it is now recognized to be misplaced there. Its characters, which include capsular fruit with many seeds, suggest a much closer relationship to the small, largely halophytic Tamaricales and to the large and diverse assemblage of plants variously known as the Violales or Cistales. It is distinctive enough, however, to be retained in its own monotypic order, the Salicales (Cronquist 1968; Dahlgren 1975; Thorne 1976).

The Salicaceae, which include the large and widespread genus Salix and the monotypic East Asian Chosenia in addition to Populus, are deciduous woody plants which are dioecious and have very light and easily wind dispersed comose seeds. They share the pattern seen in the Betulaceae of adaptation to riparian zones in temperate climates (as well as tropical in the case of Salix), with much wider extension into upland habitats in boreal, montane, and arctic climates where late snowmelt saturates the soil during part or all of the growing season. Unlike Alnus, Betula, and Salix, however, Populus consists entirely of trees. Unlike Salix, which is secondarily entomophilous (Thorne 1976), it is entirely wind pollinated.

Populus consists of 35 species and ranges throughout the North Temperate Zone into parts of the Arctic. Four species (P. tremuloides, P. trichocarpa, P. fremontii, and P. angustifolia) are native to California. P. tremuloides (aspen) is a largely upland species which is widespread in the boreal and montane parts of North Amnerica, and extends south to some of the higher California mountains. P. angustifolia is a riparian species of the Rocky Mountains, which occurs in a few colonies in the area east of the southern Sierra Nevada crest where summer thunderstorms of tropical origin also permit larger but still relict populations of Betula occidentalis to survive.

P. tremuloides is the most taxonomically distinctive Populus species in California, and is set off from the others in section Leuce. P. trichocarpa and P. angustifolia are close enough to share placement in section Tacamahaca, but even though P. fremontii is set off from these species in section Aegeiros (Rehder 1940), it can hybridize with P. trichocarpa (Little 1953). Such hybrids seem to be rare in California, but hybrids between P. angustifolia of Tacamahaca and P. sargentii of Aegeiros are abundant in the Great Plains (Elias 1980).

P. fremontii (Fremont cottonwood) and P. trichocarpa (black cottonwood) are the two principal riparian species of Populus in California, and P. fremontii is the single most important riparian species in the state since it dominates the great riparian forests of the Central Valley (Conard et al. 1977) as well as many of those elsewhere in cismontane and transmontane California (Roberts et al. 1977). Most of these magnificent forests have been destroyed (Thompson 1977), but small good examples have been preserved by the Nature Conservancy on the Kern River, by the California Department of Parks and Recreation at Caswell State Park, and by a few other groups and agencies elsewhere. Because of their great ecological significance (Sands 1977; Hehnke and Stone 1978) every effort should be made to preserve what remains of these rapidly vanishing natural communities. Particular attention should be given to those in the Sacramento and lower San Joaquin Valleys, where preservation opportunities are greatest, and to what remains of those along the Colorado River, where destruction has been most complete.

P. trichocarpa is one of the largest broad-leaved trees in North America, but it is a less conspicuous riparian tree than P. fremontii in California because it is most common in the cooler, wetter parts of the state, where it frequently associates with highly competitive riparian species such as Alnus rhombifolia, and often grows near upland forests dominated by giant conifers. Magnificent riparian forests dominated by P. trichocarpa do occur in coastal and montane California, however, and a fine example remains along the Carmel River in Monterey County.

The California ranges of P. trichocarpa and P. fremontii overlap (Griffin and Critchfield 1972), and individuals of the two species frequently grow sympatrically without hybridization. P. trichocarpa is essentially limited to those parts of California with July mean temperatures cooler than 25°C, while California populations of P. fremontii grow at sites with a range of July means approximately between 17°C and 36°C. The cooler P. fremontii sites are limited to coastal areas around San Francisco Bay and from San Luis Obispo County south where winters are mild and the growing season long.

The total ranges of these species and their closest relatives outside California (fig. 8 and 9) reflect a pattern similar to that of their ecological relationships in the state. P. trichocarpa is common throughout the cool, wet Pacific Northwest north to southern Alaska and east to the northern Rocky Mountains (Little 1971), and its closest North American relatives are P. angustifolia of the Rocky Mountains and P. balsamifera, a frequently upland

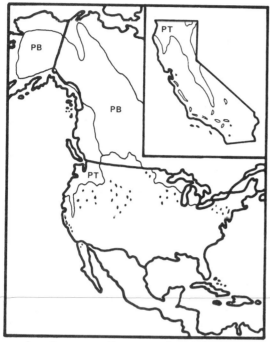

Figure 8.--Ranges of P. trichocarpa (PT) and P. balsamifera (PB) (after Little 1971).

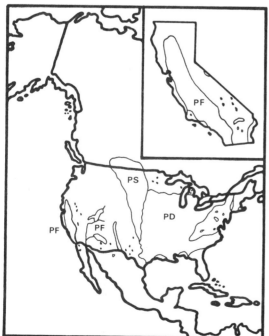

Figure 9.--Ranges of Populus fremontii (PF), P. deltoides (PD), and P. sargentii (PS) (after Little 1971).

species which is widespread in the continent's boreal regions (Rehder 1940). P. trichocarpa is considered conspecific with the latter by Eckenwalder (1980).

P. fremontii, in contrast, is found east to Trans-Pecos Texas in riparian sites throughout the Southwest, and it is most closely related to the riparian species P. arizonica of the Southwest, P. deltoides and P. sargentii of warm temperate eastern North America, and P. nigra of warm temperate Europe (Axelrod 1975). Macrofossils intermediate between P. fremontii and P. deltoides are known from the then warmer and wetter Miocene Ellensburg Flora of Washington, where neither species occurs today (Robichaux 1977).

These relationships suggest that both P. trichocarpa and P. fremontii are western derivatives of formerly transcontinental Arcto-Tertiary entities within Populus. P. trichocarpa and its relatives within section Tacamahaca are derivatives of a cool temperate to boreal species complex, and P. fremontii and the other species of section Aegeiros are of warm temperate ancestry.

Quercus (Oak)

This huge genus of 450 species dominates the upland deciduous forests of the North Temperate Zone, but it also includes many riparian, shrubby, and evergreen species, and extends south through the American tropics as far as the Colombian Andes. Quercus is in the Fagaceae, which it shares with several other major tree genera, and thus in the Fagales, which it shares with the Betulaceae, Corylaceae, and Carpinaceae (Willis and Airy Shaw 1973).

Quercus and other Fagaceae are wind pollinated and frequently deciduous like the Betulaceae, but their heavy, nutrient-rich fruits, like those of Juglans, are poorly dispersable and better adapted to germination in mature forests than in the regularly disturbed riparian zones to which the light, easily wind dispersed fruits of Alnus and Betula are well adapted (Grime 1979).

The 16 California species of Quercus include most of the range of morphological diversity in the genus, and all of its three subgenera (Quercus, Erythrobalanus, and Protobalanus), but Q. lobata (valley oak) is the state's only major riparian oak. The other species are primarily or exclusively upland trees and shrubs, and even Q. lobata is somewhat more common in upland than in riparian zones. In the upland oak woodlands of the Coast Ranges it is common in sites which have heavy, poorly aerated soils with high water-holding capacity. Such ecological conditions are similar to those of the riparian sites where it occurs since these tend to be both drier and less well aerated than sites dominated by the other principal riparian trees.

In addition to its occasional dominance of upland oak woodland in the Coast Ranges when ecological conditions are suitable, Q. lobata can dominate two kinds of riparian communities: 1) riparian forest adjacent to streams when aeration is too poor for Populus fremontii, the typical riparian forest dominant. Q. lobata can form gallery forests in a matrix of treeless grassland in such situations, which were once common in the area of excessively heavy soil in the Sacramento Valley where rice is now extensively grown. The grasslands have almost entirely been converted to rice fields in this area, and many gallery forests of Q. lobata lost as well, but a fine example is still extant along Honcut Creek in northern Yuba County; 2) forest, woodland, and savanna on alluvial plains and terraces, usually above and toward the upland edge of typical riparian forest dominated by Populus fremontii (Conard et al. 1977). In these communities oaks must have access to water throughout the growing season, and their field relationships suggest that the accessibility of their water supply determines their density. Closed forests overwhelmingly dominated by Q. lobata can occur where water is abundant at relatively shallow depths, but progressively more open woodland and savanna communities in which oaks are scattered in a matrix of grassland are found as water apparently becomes more limiting. One of the very few field studies of the water relations of California oaks was done at such a Q. lobata community in Monterey County. It suggested that while Q. lobata had access to a reliable water table, Q. douglasii of adjacent uplands probably did not (Griffin 1973). However, since Q. lobata can also occur on upland sites similar to those of Q. douglasii (Griffin 1977), it should not be assumed that all its populations have the ready access to groundwater of its alluvial communities.

California's alluvial Q. lobata communities were once fairly common in parts of the Central Valley and in many Coast Ranges valleys as well, but since they were indicators of some of the world's best agricultural soils, most have long since been converted to farmland (Rossi 1980). A very few small but good examples of California's alluvial Q. lobata forests are still extant in Mendocino, Butte, Yolo, and Sacramento Counties, and perhaps elsewhere. Every effort should be made to permanently preserve them while the opportunity still exists.

All oaks need water, and several other upland species share some of Q. lobata's tolerance of poor soil aeration, so it is not surprising that they occasionally dominate riparian communities as well. Riparian Q. douglasii occurs along Mitchell Creek in Contra Costa County; riparian Q. engelmannii is found along Pala and other similar creeks in San Diego County; and Q. agrifolia forms a fine but very unusual riparian forest along the lower Mokelumne River on the floor of the Central Valley. Since the latter species is ordinarily restricted to the Coast Ranges and southern California, it must be assumed that marine airflow through the Carquinez Straits permits its survival in this part of the lower San Joaquin Valley. It is hoped that this rare and unstudied natural community will also soon receive adequate protection.

Q. lobata is a distinctive species endemic to California (fig. 10) of subgenus Quercus, the only one which extends to Eurasia (Tucker 1980). This subgenus is quite diverse and includes many large deciduous and evergreen trees as well as a number of evergreen shrubs in the Southwest and northern Mexico, but Q. lobata does not seem to be particularly closely related to any of these. As a large deciduous tree it is superficially similar to Q. garryana, but it stands somewhat apart from the series of increasingly drought-adapted species which Q. garryana forms with Q. douglasii and Q. engelmannii. It can occasionally hybridize with each of these, however. Surprisingly, it naturally hybridizes most abundantly with the shrub Q. dumosa (ibid.), and it is interesting but perhaps not significant that several other small white oaks of the Southwest have similarly elongated acorns with shallow cups. Since it is not particularly close to any of the eastern North American white oaks either, it is perhaps best to view Q. lobata as a distinctive derivative of subgenus Quercus which shares a complex pattern of interrelationships with other species of that taxon, and which has been a recognizable entity at least since the Miocene, when it was more widespread in western North America (Robichaux 1977).

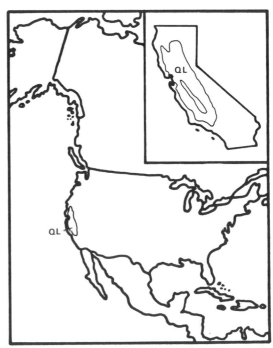

Figure 10.--Range of Quercus lobata (QL) (after Little 1971).

12

Salix (Willow)

Salix, the second major genus of the Salicaceae and Salicales, consists of about 500 species of trees and shrubs. The trees are very important components of riparian communities of the North Temperate Zone, and have invaded similar habitats in the tropics and South Temperate Zone as well, but the shrubs are largely restricted to the Northern Hemisphere and tend to be smaller and more associated with upland zones as high latitudes and altitudes are approached, a pattern of adaptation similar to but more well-developed than that seen in Alnus and Betula. Willows are typically deciduous and share the dioecious catkins and easily dispersed comose seeds of other Salicaceae, but they are usually secondarily entomophilous (Thorne 1976), and can be almost evergreen in the tropics (e.g., S. bonplandiana).

California has about 32 Salix species (Munz 1959, 1968); the exact number is uncertain because of the difficult and controversial taxonomy of the genus. Which of these species should be considered trees is almost as controversial since the state's willow species are a continuum between large trees and dwarf shrubs, and several of the species which are usually shrubs can develop into small trees when conditions are favorable. The California willows which most frequently reach tree size are S. exigua, gooddingii, hindsiana, hookeriana, laevigata, lasiandra, lasiolepis, rigida (mackenziana), scouleriana, sitchensis (coulteri), and tracyi. All of these are riparian, but S. hookeriana, rigida, scouleriana, and tracyi are small local or northern species largely limited to riparian zones within montane or northwest coast coniferous forests, and are of little importance in the riparian communities of the rest of California.

Salix gooddingii is the most important willow of the great riparian forests of California's Central Valley, and it frequently shares dominance there with Populus fremontii, particularly at intermediate successional stages. It is a better pioneer than P. fremontii, if not as good as S. hindsiana, and it usually dominates the new riparian forests which often form in the Valley along neglected ditches and canals. Since it is generally more weedy and tolerant of stress than P. fremontii as long as water is abundantly available, it is particulaly important in the depauperate riparian forests along the lower San Joaquin River, where high salinity and poor development of natural levees have probably long limited maximal riparian community development (Kahrl 1979). S. gooddingii is limited to riparian zones of the Central Valley, southern California, and the desert Southwest (Little 1976; Elias 1980), a distribution which suggests a need for long, hot growing seasons as well as abundant groundwater (fig. 11). The relationships of this species are not in doubt since it is so similar to S. nigra, the most important large willow of eastern North America, that it is still some-

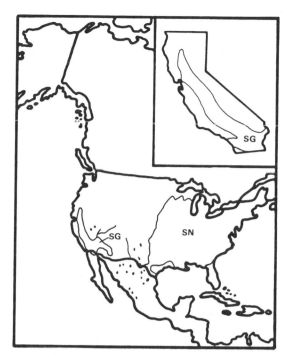

Figure 11.--Ranges of Salix gooddingii (SG) and S. nigra (SN) (after Little 1971, 1976).

times included within it as S. nigra var. vallicola (Little 1953, 1976).

S. lasiandra and S. laevigata are similar enough to one another that Hoover (1970) doubted their distinctness. Their ecological niche seems similar as well since both are large riparian willows which grow along streams in the Coast Ranges and the lower foothills of the Sierra Nevada. S. laevigata is reported to prefer well-aerated, rapidly flowing streams (Elias 1980), and it has been mapped as absent from most of the Central Valley by Little (1976), who also excludes S. lasiandra from most of the San Joaquin Valley. Conard et al. (1977) and Roberts et al. (1977) report both species to be common components of Central Valley riparian forests, however. What is clear about these two species at this time is: 1) they are more common along streams in the highlands surrounding the Valley than along the Valley floor; 2) they occur on the Valley floor; and 3) the details of their distribution and ecological relationships in California need to be much better understood. S. lasiandra may have less tolerance for habitats along intermittent streams than S. laevigata and thus may have a greater need for permanent water, but this observation needs verification.

The total ranges of these species do suggest that S. laevigata may be the more drought-adapted of the two since S. lasiandra extends down the mountains and coast of California from a wide range in the cool and wet parts of the Pacific Northwest, the northern Rocky Mountains, western Canada, and central Alaska while S. laevigata is restricted to mediterranean California and a few relict stations in Arizona, Nevada, and Utah (fig 12 and 13) (Little 1976). S. lasiandra is reported to be closely related to S. lucida of the boreal forests of eastern North America (Rehder 1940), and S. laevigata is similarly reported to be related to S. bonplandiana, a semi-evergreen species of southern Arizona and tropical western Mexico (Elias 1980), but a critical reexamination of their relationships to each other and to other species which they resemble would be desirable.

S. hindsiana and S. exigua (fig. 14) are largely shrubs, but they are both major components of California riparian vegetation because they are usually the first woody plants to colonize sandbars and other newly-formed riparian habitats when these are relatively fine-grained and shallow to groundwater. The dominance of such sites by these willows produces a distinctive and common riparian shrub community (Conard et al. 1977), but Baccharis viminea and B. glutinosa can become more important when alluvium is coarser and the water table deeper.

S. hindsiana is largely cismontane and endemic to the California Floristic Province while S. exigua is mostly transmontane in California and widespread in the rest of North America (fig. 14) (Little 1976). Both are ecologically and morphologically similar, however, and difficult to distinguish when sympatric (Hoover 1970; Smith 1970). They are part of a complex of closely related and ecologically similar western willows which also includes S. fluviatilis, S. sessilifolia, and S. melanopsis.

S. lasiolepis is a common small willow of much of the California Floristic Province, and it also occurs at scattered, possibly relict stations throughout the West (fig. 15) (Little 1976). It becomes an important vegetation component in the fog belt of the California coast, however, because there it dominates a distinctive forest community on alluvial bottomlands and in dune slacks. Myrica californica is an important associate in these forests, and a rare thistle, Cirsium loncholepis, is entirely restricted to them. Most of this apparently previously undescribed community was lost early

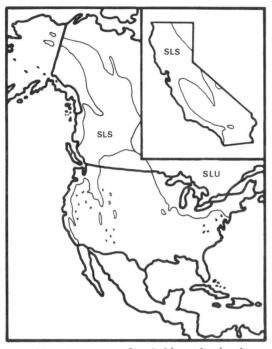

Figure 12.--Ranges of Salix lasiandra (SL) and S. lucida (SLU) (after Little 1976).

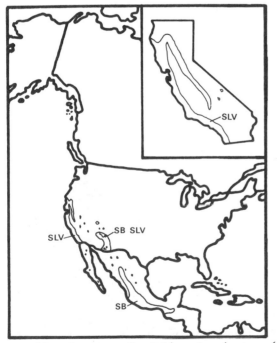

Figure 13.--Ranges of Salix laevigata (SLV) and S. bonplandiana (SB) (after Little 1976).

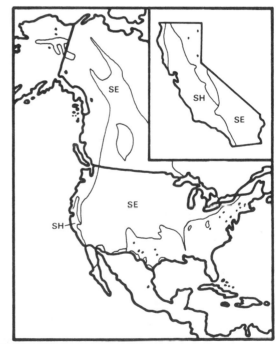

Figure 14.--Ranges of Salix hindsiana (SH) and S. exigua (SE) (after Little 1976).

14

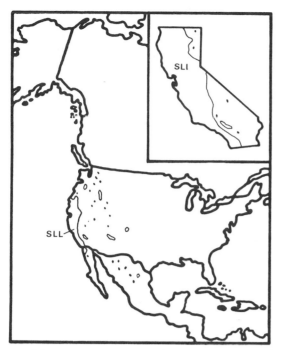

Figure 15.--Range of <u>Salix lasiolepis</u> (SLL) (after Little 1976).

to agriculture since it frequently dominated wide coastal plains in the Arroyo Grande, Oso Flaco, and Santa Maria Valleys, which are now rich vegetable districts. A small remnant of it is now protected at Pismo State Beach in San Luis Obispo County, and a larger stand, which includes critical habitat of the endangered Unarmored Three-spine Stickleback (<u>Gasterosteus</u> <u>aculeatus</u> <u>williamsoni</u>), could be saved along San Antonio Creek in Santa Barbara County.

<u>S. lasiolepis</u> is closely related to <u>S. hookeriana</u> and <u>S. tracyi</u> (Elias 1980), two small trees of north coastal riparian communities, and probably to a number of northern and montane shrubs as well. It is less close to <u>S. sitchensis</u>, a small tree which also grows along fog belt streams as far south as Santa Barbara County (Smith 1976) but seldom forms extensive forests.

RIPARIAN ORIGINS

When the Arcto-Tertiary Geoflora was decimated throughout western North America in the Late Tertiary and Quaternary by spreading drought and cold, it is clear that some of its elements which were already strongly adapted to riparian conditions were able to survive along California's permanent and intermittent streams (Axelrod 1977). Their descendents dominate the state's riparian forests today. Some Arcto-Tertiary elements which were weakly adapted to riparian conditions such as <u>Juglans hindsii</u> were also able to precariously survive to the present in riparian refuges. Riparian forests are not among California's major refuges for Arcto-Tertiary and other relicts, however (Stebbins and Major 1965). This is partly because most riparian taxa are still too successful to be considered relictual but primarily because riparian environments are too competitive and frequently disturbed to promote high plant species richness and thus the survival of many marginal, relict species. Grime (1979) has shown that plant species density is highest in environments of intermediate productivity in which neither competition nor stress are excessive.

Before California streams were dammed, floods periodically disturbed riparian communities, renewing nutrients and understory light in an environment where warmth and soil moisture were already ideal for maximal productivity. Such conditions of regular but relatively infrequent disturbance when resources are not limiting are conducive to maximum plant competition and thus low species richness (<u>ibid.</u>). In contrast, California's concentrations of relictual species are in areas of intermediate productivity where plant species density is not limited by extremes of either stress or competition.

RIPARIAN DOMINANCE AND ENVIRONMENT

<u>Populus fremontii</u> is the most common dominant of central California's riparian forests, but as discussed previously, environmental factors can shift dominance to other species. The most obvious of these factors are frequency of disturbance, air temperature, root zone aeration, and depth to groundwater, but others are probably important as well. It has been shown that when disturbance is high, dominance is shifted to <u>Salix hindsiana</u> and when somewhat less severe to <u>S. gooddingii</u>. Cool growing seasons favor <u>P. trichocarpa</u>, and hot environments sites with a high water table and low root aeration promote <u>Cephalanthus occidentalis</u>, but when turbulent, well-aerated water is close to the surface, <u>Alnus rhombifolia</u> can become dominant. When water tables are relatively deep, <u>Platanus racemosa</u> is the usual dominant when aeration of the intervening soil is high and <u>Quercus lobata</u> when it is low.

<u>Q. lobata</u>, the only major California riparian tree which is probably not of riparian origin, is most frequently dominant in riparian systems when two stressing factors, deep groundwater and low soil oxygen, are both present. This suggests that it is a relatively more stress-tolerant competitor than other riparian dominants. It is interesting that this species is probably derived from drought-stressed upland climax forests and woodlands, where trees with the stress-tolerant competitor adaptive strategy would be expected to dominate, rather than from riparian communities, which are more frequently dominated by trees with a simply competitive strategy (Grime 1979).

15

DECIDUOUSNESS AND PRODUCTIVITY

Mediterranean-type climates, with their mild, wet winters and dry summers, are well known for their sclerophyllous evergreen vegetation (Mooney et al. 1977; Cody and Mooney 1978; Walter 1979), but the presence of seemingly anomalous winter-deciduous riparian vegetation well within such a climate in California has generated relatively little comment. Air temperature obviously does not exclude evergreens from the Central Valley since they are common there in non-riparian zones. This led Stebbins (1974) to suggest that winter-deciduousness is favored when a highly productive growing season alternates with a cool season which is much less favorable but not necessarily extremely cold. He further postulated that it arose in riparian zones because wet roots aggravate winter cold stress and thus deciduousness.

The first hypothesis is undoubtedly correct, but the second is unlikely since evergreen woody angiosperms are more common in riparian than in upland zones on the Atlantic Coastal Plain in South Carolina, where summers are hot, wet, and highly productive, and winters are about as cold as those of the Central Valley. Evergreen angiosperm trees common in some riparian zones on the South Carolina Coastal Plain include Gordonia lasianthus, Ilex cassine, I. coriacea, I. myrtifolia, I. opaca, I. vomitoria, Magnolia virginiana, Myrica cerifera, M. heterophylla, Persea borbonia, P. palustris, and Quercus laurifolia (Elias 1980).

In January Columbia, South Carolina, at the inner edge of the coastal plain, has a mean temperature of 7°C and a mean minimum temperature of 1°C. Sacramento in January has the same mean temperature and a mean minimum of 3°C. Despite the similarity of these temperatures, however, Sacramento has a mean frost-free growing season of 307 days and Columbia of only 248. Charleston, on the coast at the outer edge of the coastal plain, has milder winters than Columbia or Sacramento since it has a January mean of 9°C and mean minimum of 3°C, but even here the mean frost-free growing season is only 285 days, fully 22 days shorter than at Sacramento (US Department of Agriculture 1941).

The shorter growing season and greater spread between winter mean and mean minimum temperatures of these South Carolina cities relative to Sacramento are caused by the much more frequent penetration of outbreaks of cold arctic air to the coastal plain than to the Central Valley, which is usually protected from them by the Rocky Mountains and the Sierra Nevada and Cascade Ranges. The riparian evergreens of South Carolina must cope with these regular cold outbreaks as well as with their mean winter climate, so it is unlikely that the winter-deciduousness of the California riparian community is a general phenomenon which occurs wherever winter cold and wet soil interact.

Rundel (1980), in a comparative study of the adaptive strategies of mediterranean-climate oaks, supported Stebbins' view that winter-deciduousness is favored when highly productive summers alternate with winters which are much less productive but not necessarily highly stressful. Rundel assembled evidence which showed that deciduous oak leaves are considerably more photosynthetically efficient than those of evergreen oak species. For this extra efficiency to be profitable, however, a growing season which is sufficiently long, warm, and stress-free must be predictably present to compensate for the energetic cost of producing a new crop of leaves each year.

There is every reason to believe that Rundel's generalizations about the adaptive strategies of oaks apply equally well to those of other taxa. Deciduousness is clearly an example of the ability to rapidly respond to environmental change, a characteristic which Grime (1979) considered central to the competitive adaptive strategy. As discussed above, riparian environments, with their high productivity, minimal stress, and regular but infrequent disturbance, provide just the conditions which Grime predicted would most favor this strategy.

Major (1963) has shown that the activity of upland plant communities can be estimated from readily obtainable climatic data by using Thornthwaite's water balance concept (Thornthwaite 1948; Thornthwaite and Mather 1955). Thornthwaite's potential evapotranspiration (PE) is a function of temperature and day length and thus of warmth and light. His actual evapotranspiration (AE) predicts the evapotranspiration which can take place at a site if no more water is available to it than that received from precipitation. Since AE is a function of warmth, light, and precipitation (as well as soil water storage) and these are three of the most essential ingredients of plant productivity, Rosenzweig (1968) pointed out that AE can provide a reasonably good estimate of this as well.

In mediterranean-type climates AE is depressed far below PE because lack of summer rain causes severe drought stress and suppresses plant productivity just at the time when warmth and light are maximal. At Sacramento, for example, in the heart of California's mediterranean-type climate, annual PE is 815 mm. but annual AE is only 458 mm. (Mather et al. 1964). AE and PE are both 15 mm. in January, but while PE climbs as high as 140 mm. in July, AE peaks at 72 mm. in May and then declines because of summer drought. If less soil moisture storage were assumed than the 300 mm. used to calculate these figures, AE would peak even earlier and its annual sum would be even less.

Grassland is the dominant upland vegetation type at Sacramento. Upland broad-leaved trees are sparse and consist almost entirely of two species, evergreen sclerophyllous Quercus wislizenii and deciduous but semi-sclerophyllous Q. douglasii.

16

At Columbia, South Carolina, however, summer rain is abundant, and the annual AE of 915 mm. almost matches the annual PE of 952 mm. Both AE and PE are 13 mm. in January, and both rise to similar peaks in July, when PE is 172 mm. and AE is 162 mm. Columbia is surrounded by a rich upland forest which can be dominated by pines or by several species of deciduous broad-leaved trees.

When rivers flowing from distant mountains import far more water to an area than would be available from local precipitation, keeping soil saturated at shallow depths throughout the year, AE, in effect, becomes equal to PE. This is exactly what happens in the riparian forests of California's Central Valley. As a result their de facto AE, their activity cycle, their productivity, and even their physiognomy are all very similar to those of the upland deciduous forests of South Carolina's coastal plain.

It can be seen that a gigantic natural experiment has confirmed Stebbins' and Rundel's hypothesis. Deciduousness is promoted wherever a long, very productive growing season is paired with a minimally productive but not necessarily very stressful cool or cold season. Like human beings with high incomes and low expenditures, deciduous trees can afford to rest during the season when their income would otherwise be lowest. The poorer evergreens do not have this luxury.

Quercus kelloggii (black oak) is found from San Diego County to central Oregon and is one of California's most abundant broad-leaved trees (Bolsinger 1980). Since Q. kelloggii is a non-riparian tree with deciduous, non-sclerophyllous leaves, theory predicts that it should occur where the local climate promotes maximal productivity during a well-defined growing season. Table 1 validates this prediction. Maximum monthly AE, and thus seasonal productivity, is considerably higher within the black oak's California range than in those parts of the state where it does not occur.

Table 1.--Maximum monthly actual evapotranspiration (AE) in mm. (water balance data from Mather et al. 1964; Q. kelloggii range from Griffin and Critchfield 1972).

California climatic stations (N)	$\bar{x} \pm$ SE
Outside Q. kelloggii range (43)	47.9 ± 3.66
Inside Q. kelloggii range (14)	83.1 ± 1.66

AE is high within the range of Q. kelloggii because this species is limited to mountain slopes too low and too far inland to have cool summers but of relief sufficient for high orographic precipitation. Summers are dry, but where soil storage is good, surplus water from winter and early spring rains can promote high productivity during the warm days of late spring and early summer and thus favor this upland tree's deciduous habit.

MINERAL NUTRITION

Monk (1966) found that forests in north-central Florida are much more likely to be dominated by evergreen than deciduous trees when mineral nutrients and pH are low, and he generalized that relative soil sterility promotes evergreenness. Rundel (1980) also noted that evergreen leaves are more nutrient-use efficient. It is clear that nutrient losses from the regular shedding of deciduous leaves represent a cost which can only be made up during a long and productive growing season in a reasonably fertile environment. Since nutrient deficiencies lower productivity (Kramer and Kozlowski 1979) they, in effect, lower AE and promote evergreenness indirectly as well as directly.

California riparian forests receive imported nutrients as well as water from their rivers and streams (or did before dams stopped floods and became nutrient traps). Thus their productivity and deciduousness are doubly promoted. It is interesting that the Sacramento and the Stanislaus, the two Central Valley rivers with the most limestone in their watersheds and thus the most calcium, are also those with the best developed riparian forests along the banks of their lower reaches.

It was noted earlier, however, that some riparian communities on the Atlantic Coastal Plain are evergreen while surrounding upland communities are deciduous. These riparian communities occur because the low relief of the Coastal Plain does not permit rapid drainage of the heavy precipitation which it receives. They are nutrient-poor because their water is of local, meteorological origin, and can only leach and carry away mineral nutrients, not deposit them (Wharton and Brinson 1979). In this climate, where abundant summer rain makes AE maximal, the water available to riparian communities can not raise their productivity much above that of adjacent upland vegetation. It can only lower it through leaching. The result is evergreen vegetation in riparian communities on the Coastal Plain when the water is of local origin, but deciduous riparian forests dominated by species of Salix, Populus, Quercus, Platanus, and Fraxinus similar to those of California occur along the major rivers. These flow out of the Appalachians and import nutrients to the Coastal Plain to replace those lost by local leaching (Braun 1950; Hosner 1962; Wharton and Brinson 1979).

PRODUCTIVITY AND COMMUNITY ECOLOGY

California's riparian communities are its most productive because they receive abundant water during hot, cloudless summers which are ideal for maximum photosynthesis. Their high PE thus becomes a high AE. Everywhere else in California except on the highest mountain summits summer drought suppresses AE below PE and plant productivity below its potential. Outside of alpine areas AE approaches PE most closely among California's upland communities in the coastal redwood belt of Del Norte and northwestern Humboldt Counties, but summers are too cool and cloudy there for productivity and either AE or PE to be extremely high. Crescent City, in the center of this area, has an AE of 597 mm. and a PE of 650 mm. while Davis, in the Central Valley, has an upland AE of 420 mm. and a PE and thus riparian AE of 810 mm. (300 mm. soil storage assumed).[4]

The riparian systems of California are clearly far more productive than any of that state's communities which are dependent on their local climate can be. Maximal riparian productivity more closely approaches that of eastern deciduous forests in summer and of tropical rain forests throughout the year. It is not surprising, then, that California's riparian forests share some features with exotic ecosystems which are absent, rare, or poorly developed elsewhere in the state.

Herbs with tropical affinities, such as _Hibiscus californicus_ and _Fimbristylis vahlii_, occur in California riparian communities, and riparian _Vitis californica_ is a well-developed liana, a growth form 90% confined to tropical forests (Walter 1979) and very poorly developed in upland California. Abundant warmth and water are apparently essential to large lianas, and the inability to tolerate even a brief winter rest period is probably what confines most taxa to the tropics. Notoriously high root pressures have undoubtedly helped _Vitis_ cope with this problem and survive in seasonally highly productive temperate habitats like California riparian zones (Kramer and Kozlowski 1979).

Despite their small overall area California's riparian forests are especially well known for the abundance and diversity of their bird fauna (Small 1974; Gaines 1977). Their breeding avifauna is particularly important because it includes many species which occur in virtually no other California habitat. Gaines (_ibid._) has shown that these birds are very frequently insectivorous foliage gleaners which winter in tropical forests and have vicariant populations in eastern deciduous forests, two habitats which share the high productivity of western riparian communities.

Insects, as poikilotherms which are largely primary consumers, are expected to increase in abundance with increasing warmth and primary productivity, and in California upland vegetation

insect biomass does, in fact, peak in spring and closely fluctuate with primary productivity throughout the year (Cody et al. 1977). Comparable data do not seem to be available for any California riparian community, but the extremely high summer productivity of such communities undoubtedly induces similarly high summer peaks of insect biomass. These in turn act as magnets for insectivorous migratory birds. Gaines (1977) was ambivalent about this since at more than one point he noted the connection between riparian insect and insectivorous bird abundance but also yielded to Willson's (1974) view that bird density is not dependent on habitat productivity. Willson reached this conclusion after field work in what were apparently mostly various successional stages of upland forest and woodland vegetation within a single local climate in east central Illinois. Her studies showed that avian biomass was similar at all these successional stages and bird density greatest at intermediate ones. Willson concluded that her data showed these parameters of bird populations are unrelated to either plant or insect productivity since she assumed plant productivity is highest in early successional stages and insect productivity highest in late stages. Her first assumption ignored the very important stem and root components of primary productivity, however, and the second was the result of a literature review which, in effect, assumed that vegetation in different climates--and thus productivity regimes--can represent stages of and thus show the ecological effects of a single successional sequence. Her data do not support her conclusion that bird populations are unrelated to community productivity, but they do suggest that bird density may be highest at intermediate successional stages. These are just the successional stages when primary productivity is greatest (Larcher 1975).

Bird abundance does appear to be positively related to community productivity, and riparian bird populations can be expected to be augmented most relative to those of upland habitats when contrasts between upland and riparian productivity are greatest. Such contrasts occur whenever perennial streams reliably bring water to arid or semiarid lands. In deserts with summer rainy seasons, however, vegetation along ephemeral streams which merely carry away the floodwaters of rare storms may actually be less productive of plants and animals than nearby uplands which are less disturbed and no drier (Wauer 1978). The biotic effects of riparian environments are much less conspicuous in areas such as the Atlantic Coastal Plain where upland vegetation is highly productive, but even here the variety of drainage conditions typical of riparian zones produces edaphic diversity and resultant habitat and species diversity. (Hosner 1962; Hair et al. 1974).

Bird populations are not simply a function of primary productivity, however, since highly productive irrigated cropland supports bird populations which are less diverse and frequently less abundant than those of natural riparian

---

[4]Major, J. No date. Water balances for California climatic stations. Unpublished manuscript.

communities within the same local climate (Hehnke and Stone 1978). MacArthur and MacArthur (1961) demonstrated that bird species diversity is greatest in tall, highly stratified vegetation, and this can only occur when community phytomass is high. High phytomass is not universal in productive environments, but it is limited to them (Walter 1978).

It is tragic that the rich bird fauna of California's riparian communities has declined drastically within just the last few decades. Gaines (1977) cited reports which attribute this decline to brood parasitism by the recently introduced Brown-headed Cowbird, but he also noted that its introduction to Arizona occurred long before a similar decline in the riparian avifauna there. The cowbird has been especially frequently linked to the virtual extirpation of the riparian and insectivorous Bell's Vireo from California and Arizona, and yet these two species coexist in abundance in the less agricultural Rio Grande Valley of Texas (Wauer 1977). The riparian communities of Califorina and Arizona are frequently surrounded by agricultural areas where massive quantities of insecticides are used, but there seems to have been little comment about or investigation of their potential impact on a largely insectivorous riparian avifauna.

LITERATURE CITED

Axelrod, D. 1960. The evolution of flowering plants. p. 227-305. In: S. Tax (ed.). Evolution after Darwin. Volume 1: the evolution of life. 629 p. University of Chicago Press, Chicago, Ill.

Axelrod, D. 1973. History of the mediterranean ecosystem in California. p. 225-277. In: F. diCastri and H. Mooney (ed.). Mediterranean type ecosystems: origin and structure. 405 p. Springer Verlag, New York, N.Y.

Axelrod, D. 1975. Evolution and biogeography of Madrean-Tethyan sclerophyll vegetation. Ann. Missouri Bot. Garden 62:280-334.

Axelrod, D. 1977. Outline history of California vegetation. p. 139-193. In: M. Barbour and J. Major (ed.). Terrestrial vegetation of California. 1002 p. John Wiley, New York, N.Y.

Bolsinger, C. 1980. Oaks in California's commercial forests--volume, stand structure, and defect characteristics. p. 101-106. In: T. Plumb (tech. coord.). Proceedings of the symposium on the ecology, management, and utilization of California oaks. [Claremont, Calif., June 26-28, 1979]. USDA Forest Service GTR-PSW-44. 368 p. Berkeley, California.

Braun, L. 1950. Deciduous forests of eastern North America. 596 p. Hafner, New York, N.Y.

Chabot, B., and W. Billings. 1974. Origins and ecology of the Sierran alpine flora and vegetation. Ecol. Monog. 42:163-199.

Cody, M., E. Fuentes, W. Glanz, J. Hunt, and A. Moldenke. 1977. Convergent evolution in the consumer organisms of mediterranean Chile and California. p. 144-192. In: H. Mooney (ed.). Convergent evolution in Chile and California mediterranean climate ecosystems. 224 p. Dowden, Hutchinson & Ross, Stroudsburg, Penn.

Cody, M., and H. Mooney. 1978. Convergence versus nonconvergence in mediterranean climate ecosystems. Ann. Rev. of Ecol. and Syst. 9:265-321.

Collingwood, G., W. Brush, and D. Butcher. 1974. Knowing your trees. 374 p. American Forestry Association, Washington, D.C.

Conard, S., R. MacDonald, and R. Holland. 1977. Riparian vegetation and flora of the Sacramento Valley. p. 47-55. In: A. Sands (ed.). Riparian forests in California: their ecology and conservation. Institute of Ecology Pub. No. 15. 122 p. University of California, Davis.

Cronquist, A. 1968. The evolution and classification of flowering plants. 396 p. Houghton Mifflin, Boston, Mass.

Dahlgren, R. 1975. A system of classification of the angiosperms to be used to demonstrate the distribution of characters. Bot. Notiser. 128:119-147.

Eckenwalder, J. 1980. Populus. p. 420-421. In: J. Kartesz and R. Kartesz (ed.). A synonymized checklist of the vascular flora of the United States, Canada, and Greenland. Volume II: the biota of North America. 500 p. University of North Carolina Press, Chapel Hill, N.C.

Elias, T. 1980. The complete trees of North America: field guide and natural history. 948 p. Van Nostrand Reinhold, New York, N.Y.

Engler, A., and H. Melchior. 1964. Syllabus der pflanzenfamilien, Band II. 666 p. Gebruder Borntraeger, Berlin-Nikolassee.

Fowells, H. 1965. Silvics of forest trees of the United States. USDA Forest Service Agriculture Handbook No. 271. 762 p.

Gaines, D. 1977. The valley riparian forests of California: their importance to bird populations. p. 57-85. In: A. Sands (ed.). Riparian forests in California: their ecology and conservation. Institute of Ecology Pub. No. 15. 122 p. University of California, Davis.

Griffin, J. 1973. Xylem sap tension in three woodland oaks of central California. Ecology 54:152-159.

Griffin, J. 1977. Oak woodland. p. 383-415. In: M. Barbour and J. Major (ed.). Terestrial vegetation of California. 1002 p. John Wiley, New York, N.Y.

Griffin, J., and W. Critchfield. 1972. The distribution of forest trees in California. USDA Forest Service Research Paper PSW-82. 114 p.

Grime, J. 1979. Plant strategies and vegetation processes. 222 p. John Wiley, New York, N.Y.

Hair, J., G. Hepp, L. Luekett, K. Reese, and D. Woodward. 1979. Beaver pond ecosystems and their relationships to multi-use natural resource management. p. 80-92. In: R.R. Johnson and J.F. McCormack (tech. coord.). Strategies for protection and management of floodplain wetlands and other riparian ecosystems. [Callaway Gardens, Georgia, December 11-13, 1978]. USDA Forest Service GTR-WO-12. 410 p. Washington, D.C.

Hehnke, M., and C. Stone. 1979. Value of riparian vegetation to avian populations along the Sacramento River system. p. 228-235. In: R.R. Johnson and J.F. McCormack (tech. coord.). Strategies for protection and management of floodplain wetlands and other riparian ecosystems. [Callaway Gardens, Georgia, December 11-13, 1978]. USDA Forest Service GTR-WO-12. 410 p. Washington, D.C.

Hoover, R. 1970. The vascular plants of San Luis Obispo County, California. 350 p. University of California Press, Berkeley.

Hora, B. (ed). 1981. The Oxford encyclopedia of trees of the world. 288 p. Oxford University Press, New York, N.Y.

Hosner, J. 1962. The southern bottomland hardwood region. p. 296-333. In: J. Barrett (ed.). Regional silviculture of the United States. 610 p. Ronald, New York, N.Y.

Hsiao, J. 1973. A numerical taxonomic study of the genus Platanus based on morphological and phenolic characters. Amer. Journ. Bot. 60:678-684.

Jepson, W. 1910. The silva of California. University of California Mem. Vol. 2. 480 p. University of California, Berkeley.

Kahrl, W. 1979. The California water atlas. Prepared by the Governor's Office of Planning and Research in cooperation with the California Department of Water Resources. 118 p. Sacramento, Calif.

Kramer, P., and T. Kozlowski. 1979. Physiology of woody plants. 811 p. Academic Press, New York, N.Y.

Larcher, W. 1975. Physiological plant ecology. 252 p. Springer Verlag, New York, N.Y.

Little, E., Jr. 1953. Check list of native and naturalized trees of the United States (including Alaska). USDA Forest Service Agriculture Handbook No. 41. 472 p.

Little, E., Jr. 1971. Atlas of United States trees. Volume 1: conifers and important hardwoods. USDA Forest Service, Misc. Publ. No. 1146. 9 p., 200 maps.

Little, E., Jr. 1976. Atlas of United States trees. Volume 3: minor western hardwoods. USDA Forest Service, Misc. Publ. No. 1314. 13 p., 210 maps.

MacArthur, R. and J. MacArthur. 1961. On bird species diversity. Ecology 43:594-598.

Major, J. 1963. A climatic index to vascular plant activity. Ecology 44:485-498.

Major, J. 1977. California climate in relation to vegetation. p. 11-74. In: M. Barbour and J. Major (ed.). Terrestrial vegetation of California. 1002 p. John Wiley, New York, N.Y.

Mather, J., D. Carter, and F. Hare. 1964. Average climatic water balance data of the continents. Part VII: United States. C.W. Thornthwaite Associates Lab. Climatol. Pub. Climatol. 17:419-615.

Miller, G. 1955. The genus Fraxinus, the ashes in North America, north of Mexico. Cornell Agri. Exp. Sta. Mem. 335. 64 p.

Monk, C. 1966. An ecological significance of evergreenness. Ecology 47:504-505.

Mooney, H., J. Kummerow, A. Johnson, D. Parsons, S. Keeley, A. Hoffman, R. Hays, J. Giliberto, and C. Chu. 1977. The producers--their resources and adaptive responses. p. 85-143. In: H. Mooney (ed.). Convergent evolution in Chile and California mediterranean climate ecosystems. 224 p. Dowden, Hutchinson & Ross, Stroudsburg, Penn.

Munz, P. 1959. A California flora. 1681 p. University of California Press, Berkeley.

Munz, P. 1968. Supplement to a California flora. 224 p. University of California Press, Berkeley.

Page, B. 1981. The southern Coast Ranges. p. 329-417. In: W. Ernst (ed.). The geotectonic development of California. 706 p. Prentice-Hall, Englewood Cliffs, N.J.

Pirone, P. 1970. Diseases and pests of ornamental plants. Fourth edition. 546 p. Ronald, New York, N.Y.

Raven, P., and D. Axelrod. 1978. Origin and relationships of the California flora. University of California Publ. in Botany. Volume 72. 134 p. University of California Press, Berkeley.

Rehder, A. 1940. Manual of cultivated trees and shrubs. Second edition. 996 p. Macmillan, New York, N.Y.

Roberts, W., J. Howe, and J. Major. 1977. A survey of riparian forest flora and fauna in California. p. 3-19. In: A. Sands (ed.). Riparian forests in California: their ecology and conservation. Institute of Ecology Pub. No. 15. 122 p. University of California, Davis.

Robichaux, R. 1977. Geologic history of the riparian forests of California. p. 21-34. In: A. Sands (ed.). Riparian forests in California: their ecology and conservation. Institute of Ecology Pub. No. 15. 122 p. University of California, Davis.

Rosenzweig, M. 1968. Net primary productivity of terrestrial communities: prediction from climatological data. Amer. Nat. 102:67-74.

Rossi, R. 1980. History of cultural influences on the distribution and reproduction of oaks in California. p. 7-18. In: T. Plumb (tech. coord.). Proceedings of the symposium on the ecology, management, and utilization of California oaks. [Claremont, Calif., June 26-28, 1979]. USDA Forest Service GTR-PSW-44. 368 p. Berkeley, California.

Rundel, P. 1980. Adaptations of mediterranean-climate oaks to environmental stress. p. 43-54. In: T. Plumb (tech. coord.). Proceedings of the symposium on the ecology, management, and utilization of California oaks. [Claremont, Calif., June 26-28, 1979]. USDA Forest Service GTR-PSW-44. 368 p. Berkeley, California.

Sands, A. (ed.). 1977. Riparian forests in California: their ecology and conservation. Institute of Ecology Pub. No. 15. 122 p. University of California, Davis.

Small, A. 1974. The birds of California. 310 p. Collier, New York, N.Y.

Smith, C. 1976. A flora of the Santa Barbara region, California. 331 p. Santa Barbara Museum of Natural History, Santa Barbara, Calif.

Spurr, S., and B. Barnes. 1980. Forest ecology. Third edition. 687 p. John Wiley, New York, N.Y.

Stebbins, G. 1974. Flowering plants: evolution above the species level. 399 p. Belknap Harvard, Cambridge, Mass.

Stebbins, G., and J. Major. 1965. Endemism and speciation in the California flora. Ecol. Monog. 34:1-35.

Sudworth, G. 1908. Forest trees of the Pacific Slope (1967 reprint of 1908 edition). 455 p. Dover, New York, N.Y.

Thompson, K. 1977. Riparian forests of the Sacramento Valley, California. p. 35-38. In: A. Sands (ed.). Riparian forests in California: their ecology and conservation. Institute of Ecology Pub. No. 15. 122 p. University of California, Davis.

Thorne, R. 1976. A phylogenetic classification of the Angiospermae. p. 35-106. In: M. Hecht, W. Steere, and B. Wallace (ed.). Evolutionary biology. Volume 9. Plenum, New York, N.Y.

Thornthwaite, C. 1948. An approach toward a rational classification of climate. Geogr. Rev. 38:55-94.

Thornthwaite, C., and J. Mather. 1955. The water balance. Drexel Inst. Technol. Pub. Climatol. 8:1-104.

Tucker, J. 1980. Taxonomy of California oaks. p. 19-29. In: T. Plumb (tech. coord.). Proceedings of the symposium on the ecology, management, and utilization of California oaks. [Claremont, Calif., June 26-28, 1979]. USDA Forest Service GTR-PSW-44. 368 p. Berkeley, California.

US Department of Agriculture. 1941. Climate and man: yearbook of agriculture. 1248 p. US Department of Agriculture, Washington, D.C.

US Department of Commerce. 1970. Climate of California. In: Climates of the states: climatography of the United States, 60-4. 57 p. US Depatrment of Commerce, Washington, D.C.

US Department of Interior, Geological Survey. 1977. Water resources data for California. Water year 1977. Volume 4. USGS Water-data Report CA-77-4.

Walter, H. 1979. Vegetation of the earth and ecological systems of the geo-biosphere. Second edition. 274 p. Springer Verlag, New York, N.Y.

Wauer, R. 1977. Significance of Rio Grande riparian systems upon the avifauna. p. 165-174. In: R.R. Johnson and D.A. Jones (tech. coord.). Importance, preservation, and management of riparian habitat: a symposium. [Tuscon, Ariz., July 9, 1977]. USDA Forest Service GTR-RM-43. 217 p. USDA Forest Service Range and Experiment Station, Fort Collins, Colorado.

Wauer, R. 1978. The breeding avifauna of Isla Tiburon, Sonora, Mexico. Unpublished manuscript. 75 p. USDA Fish and Wildlife Service, Washington, D.C.

Wharton, C, and M. Brinson. 1979. Characteristics of southeastern river systems. p. 32-40. In: R.R. Johnson and J.F. McCormack (tech. coord.). Strategies for protection and management of floodplain wetlands and other riparian ecosystems. [Callaway Gardens, Georgia, December 11-13, 1978]. USDA Forest Service GTR-WO-12. 410 p. Washington, D.C.

Willis, J., and H. Airy Shaw. 1973. A dictionary of the flowering plants and ferns. Eighth edition. 1245 p. Cambridge University Press, London.

Willson, M. 1974. Avian community organization and habitat structure. Ecology 55:1017-1029.

A BRIEF HISTORY OF RIPARIAN FORESTS

IN THE CENTRAL VALLEY OF CALIFORNIA[1]

Edwin F. Katibah[2]

Abstract.--Riparian forests once occupied substantially greater areas in the Central Valley of California than they do today. This paper explores the hydrologic influences which allowed the original riparian forests to establish themselves, the extent and reasons for the decline of the pre-settlement forests, as well as an estimate of the extent of today's remaining forests.

INTRODUCTION

One hundred and fifty years ago, California's Central Valley was endowed with a natural environment the scope and magnitude of which it is difficult, if not impossible, to fully comprehend today. Two major river systems, the Sacramento and the San Joaquin, drained the Valley. Flooding in the winter and spring, these rivers and their tributaries formed vast flood basins and huge, shallow seasonal lakes. Marsh vegetation (primarily Scirpus spp. and Typha spp.) occupied these wetter sites. Extensive perennial grassland (Stipa spp.) and scattered valley oak (Quercus lobata) woodlands were found on the drier uplands, while the southern end of the Valley had large areas of saltbush (Atriplex spp.) desert. Through all of these vegetation communities, along the major river and stream systems, were strips of dense forest. These riverine, or riparian, forests developed on the natural levees of river-deposited silt, lining most of the Valley's drainages.

Riparian forests are structurally and floristically complex vegetation communities. These forests are difficult to characterize, for they occur in many different forms throughout the Valley. Under ideal conditions, these forests consist of several layers with dense undergrowth, similar in some cases to tropical jungles (Holmes et al. 1915). Fremont cottonwood (Populus fremontii), California sycamore (Platanus racemosa), willow (Salix spp.), and valley oak are common upper canopy species found throughout the Valley. Such species as box elder (Acer negundo subsp. californicum), Oregon ash (Fraxinus latifolia), and various species

of willow generally occur in intermediate layers. Vines (lianas) are characteristic of many riparian forests, with wild grape (Vitis californica), poison oak (Rhus diversiloba), Dutchman's pipe vine (Aristolochia californica), and wild clematis (Clematis spp.) growing through the various layers. Riparian forest undergrowth has a very diverse flora which varies widely throughout the Valley. Too many characteristic undergrowth plant species occur to mention but a few: mugwort (Artemisia douglasiana), mulefat (Baccharis viminea), wild rose (Rosa californica), and blackberry (Rubus spp.).

Riparian forests have been greatly reduced or eliminated throughout much of the Valley. Ecologically they continue to play an important role with many plant and animal species dependent on them. Riparian forests are popular recreation sites, providing a wide range of beneficial values for the Valley's populace. These facts, among others, have recently aroused an interest in riparian forest ecology and management by both the general public and various Federal, State, and local agencies. This new interest has prompted questions as to why these forests occurred more along some river systems than others; how extensive the pre-settlement forests were; what caused their decline; and how many of these forests remain today. This paper attempts to provide a brief, informative look into these questions.

HYDROLOGY OF THE CENTRAL VALLEY

There is significant hydrologic diversity throughout the Central Valley, and it was this diversity which was in part responsible for differences between individual riparian forests. For example, the Valley has two major riverine hydrologic systems: that of the Sacramento Valley component in the north and of the San Joaquin Valley component in the south. The influences of these major hydrologic systems on the nature of

[1]Paper presented at the California Riparian Systems Conference. [University of California, Davis, September 17-19, 1981].
[2]Edwin F. Katibah is an Associate Specialist, Department of Forestry and Resource Management, University of California, Berkeley.

23

the riparian forests associated with them were profound. Figure 1 depicts the Central Valley and its major surface hydrology as it may have appeared under pre-settlement conditions.

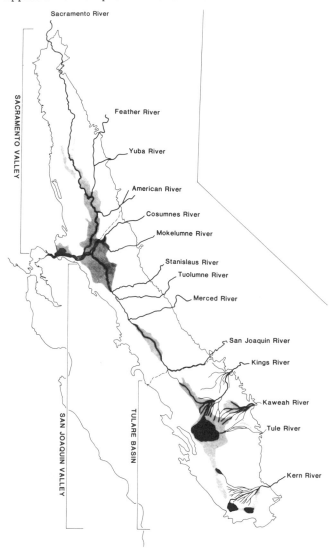

Figure 1.--Surface hydrology of the Central Valley as it may have appeared around 1850. Areas in black within the Tulare Subbasin represent seasonal lakes. Shaded areas, shown throughout the Valley, indicate flood basins and freshwater marshes.

Hydrology of the Sacramento Valley

The Sacramento Valley is bordered by the mountains of the Coast Ranges to the west, the Klamath and Cascade Ranges to the north, and the Sierra Nevada to the east. To the south, the Sacramento Valley joins the San Joaquin Valley at the Sacramento/San Joaquin River Delta. The comparatively dry interior Coast Range mountains have no large rivers draining into the Valley, only streams, some of the larger being Stony, Cache, and Putah Creeks. The Sacramento River originates in the Klamath Mountains and is joined by two rivers, the McCloud and the Pit, in what

is now Shasta Lake. The Sierra Nevada mountains to the east provide the greatest number of rivers and major streams draining into the Sacramento Valley--the Feather, Yuba, Bear, and American Rivers, and Butte and Big Chico Creeks.

Numerous other streams also flowed into the Sacramento Valley from the surrounding mountains. Not all of these streams actually reached the Sacramento River. Historically, natural levees and naturally occurring flood basins prevented some streams from reaching the main rivers. Instead, these streams spread out "through a welter of distributaries" (Thompson 1961) on the Valley floor. These distributaries typically ended in "sinks" of tule marsh. Putah, Cache, and Butte Creeks are among those streams which never joined the main river network in the Sacramento Valley.

The Sacramento Valley and its surrounding foothills, unlike the San Joaquin Valley region, receive substantial rainfall in the winter and early spring. This resulted in Sacramento Valley rivers experiencing maximum flows from December through March instead of May and June as is characteristic of most western rivers, including those in the San Joaquin Valley (Fortier 1909). Snowmelt fortified the river flow in the Sacramento Valley through the late spring. Annual summer drought brought the low flow rates found in these rivers through late fall.

During the peak flows of the Sacramento Valley rivers, the flood basins were filled by sediment-carrying waters. The natural levees dividing the flood basins from the major rivers were initially developed and then augmented by this annual flood cycle. Impressive natural levees along the Sacramento River, "...from 5 to 20 feet above the flood basins..." and 1.6-16 km. (1-10 mi.) in width, averaging 4.8 km. (3 mi.), "...formed corridors of generally dry land during times of flooding..." (Thompson 1961). The other major Sacramento Valley rivers and streams also formed well-developed natural levees.

Hydrology of the San Joaquin Valley

The San Joaquin Valley is bounded by the flat relief of the Sacramento/San Joaquin River Delta to the north, the mountains of the Sierra Nevada to the east, the Coast Ranges to the west, and the Tehachapi Mountains to the south.

The Coast Ranges and the Tehachapi Mountains bordering the San Joaquin Valley are very arid. Thus, the streams which originate from these mountains were characteristically intermittent in flow. Probably the most notable of these intermittent streams was Los Gatos Creek, whose alluvial fan helped form the Tulare Subbasin, a major influence in the hydrology of the San Joaquin Valley.

Numerous Sierra Nevada rivers and streams flowed into the San Joaquin Valley, including the Cosumnes, Mokelumne, Calaveras, Stanislaus, Tuolumne, Merced, Chowchilla, Fresno, San Joaquin, Kings, Kaweah, Tule, White and Kern Rivers.

The San Joaquin Valley is itself divided into two distinct hydrologic subbasins: the San Joaquin and the Tulare. The San Joaquin Subbasin is drained by the San Joaquin River; the Tulare Subbasin has no perennial surface outlet.

The Tulare Subbasin was formed at the south end of the San Joaquin Valley by the merging of alluvial fans from the Kings River to the east and Los Gatos Creek to the west (Cone 1911). Water originating from the major Tulare Subbasin rivers—the Kings, Kaweah, Tule, White, and Kern—flowed into this subbasin and found no normal outlet to the sea. Instead, large inland lakes formed—the Tulare, Buena Vista, Kern, and Goose. These largely temporary lakes, extremely shallow as they flooded the nearly flat landscape, rose dramatically as winter and spring runoff filled them. As the seasonal lakes filled beyond capacity they flowed into one another, finally rising above the natural alluvial barriers which divided the Tulare and San Joaquin Subbasins, sending tremendous quantities of water down the Fresno Slough into the San Joaquin River.

Later in the season, after the overland flow of water had ceased, substantial quantities of water were still drained from the Tulare Subbasin into the San Joaquin River via subsurface flow. This underground accession may have doubled the San Joaquin River's volume (Irrigation in California 1873). This undoubtedly helped to maintain the flow of the San Joaquin River in its southern reaches during the long, dry California summers.

The San Joaquin Valley rivers, whose waters were primarily snowmelt, tended to reach maximum flow in May and June. In contrast, peak flow of the Sacramento was usually in March, although some of the major peak flow rainfloods have occurred much earlier in the winter (1955-56 flood—December and January; 1964-65 flood—December and January; 1970 flood—January). In addition, the San Joaquin River's flow into the Delta in its peak flow period was less than one-half the discharge rate of the Sacramento River during its usual peak flow period in March. Despite this difference in peak flow timing, the two rivers discharged approximately equal amounts of water into the Delta.

San Joaquin Valley rivers and streams in some instances did not produce the large, natural levees characteristic of the Sacramento Valley. Peak water flows in San Joaquin Valley rivers and streams were typically less than those in the Sacramento Valley, thus limiting their ability to pick up and carry sediment for great distances. Natural levees did form along the major northern San Joaquin Valley rivers—the Tuolumne, Stanislaus, Merced, Mokelumne, Cosumnes, and northern San Joaquin.

The southern (upper) reaches of the San Joaquin River developed natural levees only poorly, and only as the river entered the Valley floor. Never a particularly big river, it ranked third in peak flow after the Tuolumne and Kings Rivers (Cone 1911). Relatively low-energy peak flows resulted in suspended sediment deposition and natural levee formation only where it first entered the Valley. From there until it reached Fresno Slough, the San Joaquin River received no surface tributaries. At that point it received the surface floodwater flows through the Fresno Slough from the Tulare Subbasin and the underground flow through the extensive Tulare Subbasin aquifer.

Both of these flows were substantial, but both lacked significant sediment content. The overland flow through Fresno Slough had already deposited its sediment load in the shallow Tulare Subbasin lakes. The subsurface waters had been filtered of any sediment long before they joined the San Joaquin River. Thus while the southern San Joaquin River gained a large water accession, especially during the peak spring flood, it was unable to build any significant natural levees because of the low sediment load. With no natural levees to contain its waters, the San Joaquin River spread out over the flat Valley floor, sustaining the large freshwater marshes still found there today. The first major sediment-carrying waters to reach the San Joaquin River for many miles occurred at its confluence with the Merced River. From here to the Delta, substantial natural levees were built along the San Joaquin River.

The Tulare Subbasin rivers developed natural levees where these rivers first entered the Valley. The shifting courses of these rivers undoubtedly allowed many miles of levees to be formed, though they were quite narrow and confined compared to the levees of the Sacramento Valley rivers.

EXTENT OF PRE-SETTLEMENT RIPARIAN FORESTS

While the largest and most diverse riparian forests occurred on rivers having natural levees, well-developed riparian systems were found along virtually all watercourses in the Central Valley. Most riverine floodplains supported riparian vegetation to about the 100-year flood line. Virtually all watercourses supported dense vegetation from the water's edge to the outer edge of the riparian (moist soil) zone, whether or not natural levees were present. The overall pre-settlement riparian vegetation pattern was one of stringers or corridors of dense, mesic, broadleaf vegetation of varying widths bounding the watercourses, the widths being determined by local hydrologic and landform characteristics.

According to various accounts, the Sacramento Valley had approximately 324,000 ha. (800,000 ac.) of riparian forest remaining after 1848 (Smith 1977; Roberts et al. 1977). No comparable estimate for riparian forests is available for the San Joaquin Valley. However, based on a map compiled by J. Greg Howe (ibid.) showing presumptive original riparian forest distribution, and estimates by this author, it is conservatively estimated that the Central Valley had greater than 373,000 ha. (921,000 ac.) of riparian forest under pre-settlement conditions.

Howe's map is based on early soil maps and covers an area in the Central Valley from the Sacramento River at Redding in the north to the Merced River in the south. I measured for areal extent the presumptive riparian forests shown on Howe's map. This estimate, presented in table 1, yields a value of 312,400 ha. (771,600 ac.) of pre-settlement riparian forest. This value must be considered conservative for that area, as Howe's map depicts only the large, contiguous riparian forests. The many smaller areas of riparian-indicator soil-types were below the mapping level of the historic soil maps used in the presumptive-riparian-forest map preparation.

In addition, Howe's map excluded the southern rivers of the San Joaquin Valley--the San Joaquin below its confluence with the Merced; and the Kings, Kaweah, Tule, and Kern. The above figure reflects that exclusion. I judged the riparian systems associated with those rivers to have totalled an estimated 20,200 ha. (50,000 ac.) (table 1). Furthermore, I estimated approximately 40,500 ha. (100,000 ac.) to account for the riparian forest vegetation present along the small streams, sloughs, lakes, ponds, and marsh borders throughout the entire Central Valley (table 1). These estimates are undoubtedly quite conservative and subject to considerable refinement.

Table 1.--Estimates of areal extent of pre-settlement riparian forests in the Central Valley of California.

Forest name	Description	Estimated size ha. (ac.)
Central Valley Riparian Forest Area Estimated From Howe Map		
Upper Sacramento River	Sacramento River from Table Mountain to near Redding (includes forests along Cottonwood, Stillwater, and Cow Creeks).	17,500 (43,200)
Big Bend	Sacramento River in the vicinity of Big Bend.	800 (2,000)
Antelope Creek	Antelope Creek east of Red Bluff.	300 (700)
Sacramento River	Sacramento River from below Sacramento to above Red Bluff (includes Elder, Mill, Thomes, Deer, Rice, Stony, Pine, Rock, Big Chico, Little Chico, Butte, Honcut, and Cache Creeks; Feather, Yuba, Bear, and American Rivers).	206,000 (508,800)
(Near) Knight's Landing	An area near Knight's Landing	500 (1,300)
Putah Creek	Putah Creek from above Winters to the Putah Creek Sinks.	8,900 (22,000)
Dixon	An area in the vicinity of Dixon.	2,200 (5,400)
Lower Sacramento River	Sacramento River below Courtland.	1,100 (2,600)
Cosumnes/Mokelumne Rivers	Upper reaches of Cosumnes and Mokelumne Rivers to below their confluence.	23,400 (57,800)
Calaveras River	Calaveras River north of Stockton.	9,500 (23,500)
Upper San Joaquin River	San Joaquin River west of Stockton.	300 (700)
San Joaquin River	San Joaquin River from its confluence with Merced River to just outside Stockton (includes Merced River, parts of Stanislaus and Tuolumne Rivers).	36,700 (90,600)
Middle Tuolumne River	Middle Tuolumne River near Modesto.	3,100 (7,700)
Upper Tuolumne River	Upper Tuolumne River from where it enters the Valley downstream.	2,100 (5,300)
Total		312,400 (771,600)

Table 1.--Estimates of areal extent of pre-settlement riparian forests in the Central Valley of Califor- nia (cont.).

Additional Riparian Forest Area Based On Estimates By Katibah

South San Joaquin Valley	Series of forests along major southern San Joaquin Valley rivers (includes upper San Joaquin, Chowchilla, Fresno, Kings, Kern, and Tule); and the alluvial floodplains from these rivers.	20,200 (50,000)
Miscellaneous	Riparian forest present along small streams and sloughs; and lake, pond, and marsh borders throughout the entire Central Valley.	40,500 (100,000)
Total		60,700 (150,000)
Total Estimated Pre-Settlement Central Valley Riparian Forest Area		373,100 (921,600)

[1]Based on a map by J. Greg Howe (Roberts et al. 1977) and estimates by E. Katibah.

DECLINE OF CENTRAL VALLEY RIPARIAN FORESTS

"No natural landscapes of California have been so altered by man as its bottomlands" (Bakker 1972). The once-lush riparian forests, forming natural vegetation corridors along many of the Central Valley's watercourses, are mostly gone today. These forests were, in Thompson's words, "...modified with a rapidity and completeness matched in few parts of the United States" (Thompson 1961).

The reasons for the rapid decline of this once extensive ecosystem are not hard to find; one needs only to review the cultural history of the Central Valley for the last 150 years.

Prior to 1822 the land known as California was claimed and ruled by Spain. Little development occurred during this period, and at the cessation of Spanish rule in 1822 only about 30 ranches or farms had been granted in California (Fortier 1909). Mexico assumed control of California until 1848. By "... 1846 no less than eight hundred large tracts containing some of the best land in the State had been given away" (ibid.). The character and size of the large Mexican land grants had a profound influence on the social, commercial, and agricultural development of the Central Valley (ibid.), development which would ultimately and adversely affect riparian vegetation.

With the annexation of California to the United States in 1848, rapid development of the Central Valley began. The Gold Rush, beginning in 1849, exerted enormous land use pressures and led to rapid and often unplanned development of the Valley.

Riparian vegetation removal was one of the first significant losses in the natural environment. The large number of immigrants seeking their fortunes in the gold-bearing Mother Lode rivers and streams soon found that agriculture provided a much more stable and practical existence. The riparian forests, often the only significant woody vegetation on the Valley floor, were utilized by the growing agricultural community for fencing, lumber, and fuel (Thompson 1961). Steamships using the Sacramento River were also heavy users of local wood fuel. Knight's Landing on the Sacramento River was a site where cordwood was loaded onto these ships. It has been speculated that this wood came from the Cache Creek and Sacramento River riparian forests because Knight's Landing is adjacent to the treeless Yolo flood basin (ibid.). This supplying of fuel wood to the numerous woodburning vessels on the Sacramento River must have made a significant contribution to the early destruction of the local riparian forests (ibid.).

As early as 1868 the general scarcity of woody vegetation was noted in the Valley by some of its inhabitants (ibid.). The pressures on riparian forest vegetation continued as farmers found that the soil on the natural levees was highly fertile, easily managed, and not subject to the seasonal flooding of nearby lower-lying ground (ibid.). As agriculture expanded in the Central Valley, water demand began to exceed water supply. Farmers also found that the Valley had too much water in the winter and spring and not enough in the summer. Water development and reclamation projects were started, primarily for agriculture and community flood protection, and rapidly eliminated many of the Valley's native wetland systems.

With agricultural expansion, cities grew to support the new industry. Many Valley towns and cities were built in flood basins and upon active floodplains, and were subject to seasonal flooding. The city of Sacramento suffered a tremendous flood in 1850, and its response, the builing of levees around the town, "...set the course for Valley development over the next several generations" (Karhl 1979). To promote the reclamation of the tule marsh and floodplain lands, the Arkansas Act of 1850 was applied in California. This act gave the State of California millions of acres of federally owned floodplains, provided that the State drain and reclaim these lands. The Arkansas Act of 1850 stipulated that all manmade levees were to be constructed along natural drainage systems. The Green Act of 1868, passed by the California Legislature, however, freed the reclamation process of most controls. The effects of the Green Act were devastating to riparian forests. Levees were built for the convenience of landowners with little or no regard for the natural hydrologic systems. Remaining riparian forests, occupying natural levees along river courses, were destroyed in the quest to protect lands from flooding.

As in the Sacramento Valley, artificial levees were built along major San Joaquin Valley rivers. San Joaquin Valley agriculture faced different water-related problems. Winter and spring rainfall there is substantially less than in the Sacramento Valley, thus San Joaquin Valley land needed to be irrigated if it was to reliably produce crops. With the Green Act as guiding legislation, more than 1,600 km. (1,000 mi.) of irrigation canals were developed by 1878 in Fresno County alone (ibid.).

In the following years, and continuing up to the present time, numerous and controversial water projects have been the hallmark of Central Valley development. The demand for water, so tied to the agricultural, commercial, and urban development of the Valley, was, at least indirectly, responsible for the degradation of many of the remaining riparian forests. Artificial levees, river channelization, dam building, water diversion, and heavy groundwater pumping were among the factors which reduced the original riparian forest to the small, scattered remnant forests found today.

PRESENT EXTENT OF REMNANT RIPARIAN FORESTS

In 1979, the Geography Departments of California State University, Chico, and California State University, Fresno, under contract to the California Department of Fish and Game, compiled riparian vegetation distribution maps for the Central Valley (Nelson and Nelson 1983). This mapping effort provided an essentially complete inventory of all extant riparian vegetation (not just mature forest) in the Central Valley.[4]

_____

[4]Central Valley riparian mapping project. 1979. Interpretation and mapping systems. Report prepared by the Riparian Mapping Team, Geography Department, California State University, Chico, with the Department of Geography, California State University, Fresno. Unpublished report to the Califronia Department of Fish and Game, Planning Branch, Sacramento. 24 p.

Using these maps, the areas and lengths of riparian systems were calculated on an individual map and county basis.[5] Even though there is no explicit riparian forest category on these maps, applicable classifications were determined which should represent riparian forests. Using this approach, it was determined that approximately 41,300 ha. (102,000 ac.) of riparian forest remain in the Central Valley today (Katibah et al. 1983). Of the 41,300 ha. of forest, approximately 19,800 ha. (49,000 ac.) are in a disturbed and/or degraded condition based on the riparian mapping category code. Approximately 21,500 ha. (53,000 ac.) were identified as mature riparian forest, with no indication of condition. However, based on recent research findings (Katibah et al. in press), it can be surmised that the majority of these 21,500 ha. of mature riparian forest have been and are currently being heavily impacted by human activities.

CONCLUSIONS

The complex hydrologic systems found in the Central Valley of California under pristine conditions are gone. The original riparian forests, dependent on the diverse Valley hydrology, are likewise gone for the most part. Today's riparian forests are in a precarious position as the demand for greater land utilization by the agricultural industry and the spread of urbanization threaten the remaining forest tracts.

Offsetting this trend, however, is a greater apreciation of the values (economic and noneconomic) of riparian forests by Valley landowners and the general public. Riparian forests are present in some of the finest and most popular parks in the Central Valley. These forests provide habitat for many of the Valley's wildlife species. They also contain numerous and diverse native plant species.

These values, among others, must compete with the most complex and controversial issue of all: water. In California as in the rest of the West, water equals development, and California does not have adequate water to meet its anticipated future demands. How the remaining riparian forests will fare in the future is not known. As interest in and knowledge about this resource develops, and as hindsight provides an understanding of the past, it is hoped that a reasonable compromise can be achieved between this unique and valuable resoure and the needs of society.

_____

[5]Katibah, E.F., N.E. Nedeff, and K.J. Dummer. 1980. The areal and linear extent of riparian vegetation in the Central Valley of California. Final report to the California Department of Fish and Game, Planning Branch. Remote Sensing Research Program, Department of Forestry and Resource Management, University of California, Berkeley.

LITERATURE CITED

Bakker, Elna S. 1972. An island called California. 357 p. University of California Press, Berkeley, California.

Cone, Victor M. 1911. Irrigation in the San Joaquin Valley, California. USDA Office of Experiment Stations, Bulletin 239. 62 p. Government Printing Office, Washington, D.C.

Fortier, Samuel. 1909. Irrigation in the Sacramento Valley, California. USDA Office of Experiment Stations, Bulletin 207. 99 p. Government Printing Office, Washington, D.C.

Holmes, L.C., J.W. Nelson, and party. 1915. Reconnaissance soil survey of the Sacramento Valley, California. USDA Publication. Government Printing Office, Washington, D.C.

Irrigation in California: the San Joaquin and Tulare Plains, a review of the whole field. 1873. 22 p. Record Steambook and Job Printing House, Sacramento, California.

Kahrl, William L. 1979. The California water atlas. Prepared by the Governor's Office of Planning and Research in cooperation with the California Department of Water Resources. 113 p. Sacramento, California.

Katibah, Edwin F., Nicole E. Nedeff, and Kevin J. Dummer. 1983. A summary of the riparian vegetation areal and linear extent measurements from the Central Valley riparian mapping project. In: R.E. Warner and K.M. Hendrix (ed.). California Riparian Systems. [University of California, Davis, September 17-19, 1981]. University of California Press, Berkeley.

Katibah, Edwin F., Kevin J. Dummer, and Nicole E. Nedeff. In press. Evaluation of the riparian vegetation resource in the Central Valley of California using remote sensing techniques. Proceedings of the ASP and ACSM fall technical meeting. [San Francisco, California, September 9-11, 1981].

Nelson, Charles W., and James R. Nelson. 1983. Central Valley riparian mapping project. In: R.E. Warner and K.M. Hendrix (ed.). California Riparian Systems. [University of California, Davis, September 17-19, 1981]. University of California Press, Berkeley.

Roberts, W.G., J.G. Howe, and J. Major. 1977. A survey of riparian forest flora and fauna in California. p. 3-19. In: A. Sands (ed.). Riparian forests in California: their ecology and conservation. Institute of Ecology Publication No. 15. 122 p. University of California, Davis.

Smith, F.E. 1977. A short reveiw of the status of riparian forests in California. p. 1-2. In: A. Sands (ed.). Riparian forests in California: their ecology and conservation. Institute of Ecology Publication No. 15. 122 p. University of California, Davis.

Thompson, K. 1961. Riparian forests of the Sacramento Valley, California. Annals Assoc. of Amer. Geog. 51:294-315.

THE IMPORTANCE OF RIPARIAN SYSTEMS

TO AMPHIBIANS AND REPTILES[1]

John M. Brode and R. Bruce Bury[2]

Abstract.--California has a rich herpetofauna, including about 120 native species. Riparian systems provide habitat for 83% of the amphibian and 40% of the reptile species. Amphibians and reptiles utilize these systems to varying degrees and can be classified according to the type of use. Riparian systems provide corridors for dispersal and also allow certain species to use otherwise unsuitable environments. Amphibians and reptiles may be abundant in riparian systems where they may outnumber other taxa. Harvesting timber and creating reservoirs are detrimental to amphibians and reptiles in the zone of influence of such activities. These activities have their greatest effects upon reptiles and amphibians whose entire life histories occur in the riparian zone.

INTRODUCTION

California has a rich herpetofauna, including about 120 native species. Amphibians and reptiles represent important ecological components of riparian communities, where they may reach high densities. In California, we estimate riparian systems provide habitat for 83% of the amphibians and 40% of the reptiles. Many species are permanent residents of the riparian zone, while others are transient or temporal visitors.

In many (if not most) natural communities, nongame species constitute the greatest portion of vertebrate species, individuals, and biomass; and they are energetically critical elements in the functioning of ecosystems (Bury et al. 1980). Based on figures compiled by Bury et al. (ibid.) 88% of the vertebrate species (fish excluded) in California are nongame.

Much emphasis has been placed on the loss of California's Central Valley riparian forests (Sands 1977). However, there are many other riparian systems in California that have suffered substantial degradation. Logging has proved detrimental to certain animal species that depend on cool, shaded streams. Reservoirs have been

created on many streams in California, eliminating the original riparian environment and much of the herpetofauna, while providing habitat for nonnative species which are usually managed more intensely than the original fauna. Many of the species lost, especially the amphibians and reptiles, are endemic to California.

In this paper, we present background information on species diversity and abundance, review the habitat requirements of California amphibians and reptiles, and suggest use classifications for species using riparian systems. Lastly, we review the effects of logging on selected species and discuss the effects of reservoirs on amphibians and reptiles, presenting preliminary data from two preimpoundment studies.

SPECIES DIVERSITY AND ABUNDANCE

Species diversity and abundance of amphibians and reptiles may be dramatic in riparian systems. For example, the riparian system of Corral Hollow Creek, San Joaquin County (fig. 1), supports 7 species of amphibians and 21 species of reptiles, including 13 species of snakes (Stebbins 1966; Sullivan 1981). Burton and Likens (1975) estimated there were 2,950 salamanders per ha. within the Hubbard Brook Experimental Forest, New Hampshire, and concluded there were more salamanders than either birds or small mammals. In biomass, salamanders were 2.6 times greater than birds and approximately equal to mammals. Burton and Likens were surprised at this result as most ecologists have ignored amphibians in ecosystem energy flow and nutrient cycling studies while considering birds and mammals in detail.

[1] Paper presented at the California Riparian Systems Conference. [University of California, Davis, September 17-19, 1981].

[2] John M. Brode is a Herpetologist, Endangered Species Program, California Department of Fish and Game, Rancho Cordova, Calif. R. Bruce Bury is a Research Zoologist, Ecology Section, Denver Wildlife Research Center, USDI Fish and Wildlife Service, Fort Collins, Colo.

Figure 1.--Corral Hollow Creek, San Joaquin County, California. This riparian system supports 7 species of amphibians and 21 species of reptiles. Photo by John E. Hummel.

Other workers have obtained similar results regarding amphibian abundance. Nussbaum[3] estimated the density of the Siskiyou Mountain salamander (Plethodon stormi) to be 0.27 per m^2 (2,700 per ha.) in optimal habitat. Murphy and Hall (1981) reported in certain streams, Pacific giant salamander (Dicamptodon ensatus) was the dominant vertebrate in both biomass and frequency of occurrence and made up as much as 99% of the total predator biomass in some sites. The population density of an eastern stream sala-

mander (Desmognathus fuscus) was estimated at 0.4 to 1.4 per m^2 (400 to 1,400 per ha.) (Spight 1976); in certain areas, male D_2 ochrophaeus occur at densities of 4.4 per m^2 (Tilley 1974). Western pond turtle (Clemmys marmorata) may reach densities of 425 per ha. in California ponds and streams (Bury 1979). Fitch (1975) estimated densities of 1,000 to 1,500 ringneck snakes (Diadophis punctatus) per ha. Sullivan (1981) reported a density of 22.4 snakes per km. along an 11-km. road transect in Corral Hollow.

---

[3]Nussbaum, R.A. 1974. The distributional ecology and life history of the Siskiyou Mountain salamander, Plethodon stormi, in relation to the potential impact of the proposed Applegate Reservoir on this species. 52 p. Report submitted to the US Army Corps of Engineers, Portland, Ore.

USE OF RIPARIAN SYSTEMS BY AMPHIBIANS AND REPTILES IN CALIFORNIA

Amphibians that utilize riparian systems in California can be placed in one of three classifications, according to their dependency upon aquatic environments and the extent to which they utilize terrestrial riparian systems (table 1). All amphibians in California, except lungless salamanders of the family Plethodontidae, require aquatic environments to complete their life cycle. Certain frogs (Rana, Ascaphus) and salamanders (Rhyacotriton, some Batrachoseps) frequent the riparian zone throughout their lives. Other salamanders and newts (Ambystoma, Taricha) and some toads (Bufo) utilize riparian systems primarily for breeding, spending most of their adult life in upland areas. Lungless salamanders are more generalized in their habitat requirements, but many species utilize

Table 1.--Use classification of amphibians occurring in California riparian systems.

Constant[1]	Breeding[2] Type of use	General[3]
Northwestern salamander Ambystoma gracile	Long-toed salamander Ambystoma macrodactylum	Del Norte salamander Plethodon elongatus
Pacific giant salamander Dicamptodon ensatus	Rough-skinned newt Taricha granulosa	Siskiyou Mountain salamander Plethodon stormi
Olympic salamander Rhyacotriton olympicus	California newt Taricha torosa	Ensatina Ensatina eschscholtzi
Dunn's salamander Plethodon dunni	Red-bellied newt Taricha rivularis	Pacific slender salamander Batrachoseps pacificus
Desert slender salamander Batrachoseps aridus	Colorado River toad Bufo alvarius	California slender salamander Batrachoseps attenuatus
Inyo Mountains salamander Batrachoseps campi	Western toad Bufo boreas	Black salamander Aneides flavipunctatus
Tailed frog Ascaphus truei	Yosemite toad Bufo canorus	Clouded salamander Aneides ferreus
Red-spotted toad Bufo punctatus	Woodhouse's toad Bufo woodhousei	Arboreal salamander Aneides lugubris
Black toad Bufo exsul	Southwestern toad Bufo microscaphus	Limestone salamander Hydromantes brunus
California treefrog Hyla cadaverina	Great Plains toad Bufo cognatus	Shasta salamander Hydromantes shastae
Red-legged frog Rana aurora	Pacific treefrog Hyla regilla	Mount Lyell salamander Hydromantes platycephalus
Spotted frog Rana pretiosa		
Cascades frog Rana cascadae		
Foothill yellow-legged frog Rana boylei		
Mountain yellow-legged frog Rana muscosa		
Leopard frog Rana pipiens		

----

[1] Species that occur in the riparian zone throughout their lives.
[2] Species that utilize riparian systems primarily for breeding, but may leave the riparian zone as adults.
[3] Species that utilize riparian systems as well as other systems throughout their range.

riparian systems. Wide-ranging plethodontid salamanders (Ensatina) have generalized habitat requirements in the mesic environments of northern California, but tend to associate with riparian systems in xeric environments.

Reptiles that utilize riparian systems in California can also be placed in one of three categories (table 2). Turtles (Clemmys) and most garter snakes (Thamnophis) depend on aquatic environments and occur primarily in the riparian zone throughout their lives. Some lizards (Gerrhonotus) and snakes (Contia) have rather general habitat requirements but become riparian obligates in arid portions of their range. The remaining reptiles that occur in riparian systems (Cnemidophorous, Pituophis, Lampropeltis) are more generalized in their habitat requirements, but they frequent ecotones and water bodies associated with riparian areas.

The riparian zone also provides corridors of dispersal and islands of habitat for many species of amphibians and reptiles, especially in arid climates. The Gilbert's skink (Eumeces gilberti) and ringneck snake (Diadophis punctatus) are foothill species that extend their ranges into the Central Valley along the American River and other riparian corridors. The desert slender salamander (Batrachoseps aridus) and Inyo Mountains salamander (B. campi) are restricted to the narrow riparian zones of desert seeps and springs.

Historically, riparian corridors probably facilitated the maintenance of genetic continuity between populations. Now, due to habitat disruption, certain populations are isolated. The wide-ranging California slender salamander (Batrachoseps attenuatus) was probably once common in the southern Sacramento Valley. Now, in the Valley this species is restricted to a few isolated remnants of valley oak woodland while still common elsewhere. Ultimate consequences of habitat disruption include local extinctions, reduction in species diversity, and loss of population heterogeneity.

EXAMPLES OF ACTIVITIES DETRIMENTAL TO AMPHIBIANS AND REPTILES IN RIPARIAN SYSTEMS

Timber Harvest

The tailed frog (Ascaphus truei), the most primitive frog in North America, is highly specialized for life in cool, fast-flowing waters. The southern terminus of the species in the United States is in small streams along the north coast and in the North Coast Range of California (Bury 1968). Larval Ascaphus prefer temperatures at or below 15°C., and avoid waters over 22°C. (deVlaming and Bury 1970); such behavior is unlike any other native frog, and underscores the dependence of Ascaphus on a cool, shaded habitat. Removal of timber by lumbering or fire results in the disappearance of tailed frogs, apparently due to increased temper-

atures of the exposed stream-bed (Noble and Putnam 1931; Bury 1968).

Similarly the Olympic salamander (Rhyacotriton olympicus) frequents cool ravines and rivulets in northwestern California. This species is absent in open (postlogging) habitat; logging apparently eliminates populations even in wet, coastal redwoods (Bury in prep.).

The Siskiyou Mountain salamander (Plethodon stormi) inhabits shaded talus slopes in canyons and along stream courses above the floodplain. Nussbaum[3] considered the gradual elimination of the overstory vegetation by clearcutting to be a serious threat to this species.

Reservoirs

Barrett and Cordone (1980) counted 1,272 reservoirs in California. Out of these, 926 (73%) are "mixed" or "warm water" types, those most commonly found on foothill and mid-elevation streams and rivers. Reservoirs have adverse effects on amphibians and reptiles by flooding their habitats. They often result in bodies of water with fluctuating levels, which prevents reestablishment of natural riparian communities. In addition, reservoirs are usually managed for human activities.

Specific examples of the effects of reservoirs on amphibians and reptiles are few. Nussbaum[3] estimated that the Applegate Reservoir in Oregon and California would cover 1.06% of the total known range and 2.1% of the estimated total population of the Siskiyou Mountain salamander. He further stated that although the construction of Applegate Reservoir in itself will pose no threats to the continued existence of P. stormi, the effects of Applegate Reservoir added to numerous other man-caused effects could seriously threaten the existence of the species.

We do not have data regarding the numbers of individual amphibians and reptiles that may have been affected by previous reservoir construction in California, but information on two proposed reservoir projects will serve as examples of what may be lost.

Los Vaqueros Reservoir

The primary effect of the proposed Los Vaqueros Reservoir will be on Kellogg Creek, Contra Costa County. Preliminary investigations by the Department of Fish and Game (DFG) indicate that the Kellogg Creek area supports at least 6 species of amphibians and 12 species of reptiles. The reservoir, as proposed, would inundate 12 km. of tributaries. An additional 6.4 km. of Kellogg Creek would be affected below the dam due to changes in streamflow.

A species of special concern that occurs in Kellogg Creek is the red-legged frog (Rana aurora--fig. 2), which is well adapted for living in arid environments with intermittent or temporary aquatic habitat. However, it has

Table 2.--Use classification of reptiles occurring in
California riparian systems.

Type of use

Constant[1]	Arid[2]	General[3]
Western pond turtle _Clemmys marmorata_	Western skink _Eumeces skiltonianus_	Western fence lizard _Sceloporus occidentalis_
Sonoran mud turtle _Kinosternon sonoriense_	Gilberts skink _Eumeces gilberti_	Sagebrush lizard _Sceloporus graciosus_
Common garter snake _Thamnophis sirtalis_	Panamint alligator lizard _Gerrhonotus panamintinus_	Long-tailed brush lizard _Urosaurus graciosus_
Western aquatic garter snake _Thamnophis couchi_	Northern alligator lizard _Gerrhonotus coeruleus_	Western whiptail lizard _Cnemidophorus tigris_
Checkered garter snake _Thamnophis marcianus_	Ringneck snake _Diadophis punctatus_	Southern alligator lizard _Gerrhonotus multicarinatus_
	Sharp-tailed snake _Contia tenuis_	California legless lizard _Anniella pulchra_
	Western terrestrial garter snake _Thamnophis elegans_	Western blind snake _Leptotyphlops humilis_
		Rubber boa _Charina bottae_
		Racer _Coluber constrictor_
		Striped racer _Masticophis lateralis_
		Gopher snake _Pituophis melanoleucus_
		Common kingsnake _Lampropeltis getulus_
		California mountain kingsnake _Lampropeltis zonata_
		Northwestern garter snake _Thamnophis ordinoides_
		Western black-headed snake _Tantilla planiceps_
		Night snake _Hypsiglena planiceps_
		Western rattlesnake _Crotalus viridis_

----

[1]Species that occur primarily in the riparian zone throughout their lives.
[2]Species that depend on riparian systems in the arid parts of their range.
[3]Species that utilize riparian systems as well as other systems throughout their range.

34

little tolerance for habitat disturbances or competition from exotic species. Approximately 18 km. of red-legged frog habitat, virtually the entire Kellogg Creek population, could be adversely affected if Los Vaqueros Reservoir impoundment project is built.

Thomes-Newville Reservoir

The primary effect of the proposed Thomes-Newville Reservoir will be on the North Fork Stony Creek, Glenn and Tehama Counties. Preliminary investigations by DFG indicate that the North Fork Stony Creek area supports at least 4 species of amphibians amd 14 species of reptiles. The proposed reservoir will inundate about 14 km. of perennial stream and about 40 km. of intermittent stream. In addition, about 13 km. of Thomes Creek may be affected by water diversion. Another species of special concern, the foothill yellow-legged frog (Rana boylei) occurs in North Fork Stony Creek and its tributaries. These frogs are adapted to rocky foothill streams. Salt Creek, on the project site, supports an excellent population of yellow-legged frogs. The majority of the yellow-legged frog population will be affected adversely if this project is completed.

CONCLUSIONS

Amphibians and reptiles represent important ecological components of riparian communities. Many species are permanent residents of the riparian zone, while others are transient or temporal visitors.

Amphibians and reptiles may be abundant in riparian systems where they can outnumber other taxa. Riparian systems provide important corridors of dispersal for many species. Disruption of these corridors can cause isolation and may lead to local extinctions.

Figure 2.--Adult red-legged frog (Rana aurora). Photo by Robert L. Livezey.

Activities which affect riparian systems adversely have their greatest effects on those amphibians and reptiles that occur in the riparian zone throughout their life. There is critical need for more quantified studies on how these activities directly affect riparian herpetofaunas; and a need for research on the relation of amphibians and reptiles to structural diversity of riparian vegetation.

ACKNOWLEDGEMENTS

We thank Kimberly A. Nicol and David P. Muth for assistance in preparing the tables. Stephen J. Nicola and Larry L. Eng reviewed an early draft.

LITERATURE CITED

Barrett, John G., and Almo J. Cordone. 1980. The lakes of California. Inland Fish. Admin. Rep,. 80-5. 10 p. California Department of Fish and Game.

Burton, Thomas M., and Gene E. Likens. 1975. Salamander population and biomass in the Hubbard Brook experimental forest, New Hampshire. Copeia 1975:541-546.

Bury, R. Bruce. 1968. The distribution of Ascaphus truei in California. Herpetologica 24:39-46.

Bury, R. Bruce. 1979. Population ecology of freshwater turtles. In: Marion Harless and Henry Morlock (ed.). Turtles: perspectives and research. 695 p. John Wiley and Sons, Inc., New York, N.Y.

Bury, R. Bruce, Howard W. Campbell, and Norman J. Scott, Jr. 1980. Role and importance of nongame wildlife. Trans. 45th North Amer. Wildl. Nat. Res. Conf. 1980:197-207.

deVlaming, Victor L., and R. Bruce Bury. 1970. Thermal selection in tadpoles of the tailed frog, Ascaphus truei. J. Herpetol. 4: 179-189.

Fitch, Henry S. 1975. A demographic study of the ringneck snake (Diadophis punctatus) in Kansas. Univ. Kansas Mus. Nat. Hist. Publ. 62. 53 p.

Murphy, Michael L., and James D. Hall. 1981. Varied effects of clear-cut logging on predators and their habitat in small streams of the Cascade Mountains, Oregon. Can. J. Fish Aquat. Sci. 38:137-145.

Noble, G.K., and P.G. Putnam. 1931. Observation on the life history of Ascaphus truei Stejneger. Copeia 1931:97-101.

Sands, Anne (ed.). 1977. Riparian forests in California: their ecology and conservation. Institute of Ecology Pub. 15. 122 p. University of California, Davis.

Spight, T.M. 1967. Population structure and biomass production by a stream salamander. Amer. Midl. Nat. 78:437-447.

Stebbins, Robert C. 1966. A field guide to western reptiles and amphibians. 279 p. Houghton Mifflin Co., Boston, Mass.

Sullivan, Brian K. 1981. Distribution and relative abundance of snakes along a transect in California. J. of Herp. 15:247-248.

Tilley, S.G. 1974. Structure and dynamics of populations of the salamander _Desmognathus ochrophaeus_ Cope in different habitats. Ecology 55:808-817.

SOME IMPLICATIONS OF POPULATION GROWTH

TO CALIFORNIA'S RENEWABLE RESOURCES[1]

Judith Kunofsky[2]

Abstract.--Efforts at better management of riparian systems will ultimately fail unless zero population growth is achieved. The increasing population in the United States, often overlooked as a causal factor, has contributed to the significant deterioration of riparian resources in this country. Advocates of riparian protection can be a vital link between proponents of population stabilization and the public and political leaders capable of effecting reversal of present population trends.

INTRODUCTION

This paper is a presentation that is not of original research. Nor am I a researcher. Rather, its perspective is that of advocate, and I hope it will be regarded as welcome diversity to other technical presentations, rather than as an aberration.

The organization I represent, Zero Population Growth (and, in particular, its California arm), is a political and educational non-profit membership organization founded in 1969 to advocate a rapid end to human population growth in this country and around the world. We have active programs in Washington, D.C; in Sacramento; and in communities around the state and the country. In addition, my position as director of the Population and Growth Policy Program of the national Sierra Club enables me to represent that organization on this issue as well.

The case I will make is that efforts at better management of riparian resources will ultimately fail unless the population stops increasing--unless we achieve zero population growth.

For those unfamiliar with the concept, zero population growth (zpg) occurs globally if the number of births each year equals the number of deaths. In a limited geographical area such as the United States or California or this room, population change is more complicated. Popula-

tion change equals the number of births plus the number of people moving in (immigrants), minus the number of deaths and the number of people moving out (emigrants). If these balance, if the population remains roughly constant from year to year, we achieve a state of zero population growth, also known as population stabilization.

Most people now believe that the population of the United States has stopped growing or is well under way toward stabilization. This is not true. The country's population is increasing by two and a half million people per year, the result of roughly 3.6 million births, 2.0 million deaths, and 800,000 net immigration (immigrants minus emigrants). While the goal is much closer than it was a decade ago in terms of the birth rate, zpg is neither here nor is it assured. Despite the decrease in the number of births per woman, continued population growth is resulting from the combination of an "echo" of the post-war baby boom and immigration to this country. Growth could continue for several decades or perhaps far into the distant future. The US population could increase from today's 228 million to 260 million in 50 years and stop increasing, or it could reach 350 million or more by the year 2030, depending on the future course of fertility in and migration to the United States. Here in California, the state's population of 24 million is increasing by almost half a million people per year (more precisely, 479,000). We are far from achieving zero population growth.

CURRENT STATUS OF RIPARIAN SYSTEMS

It is useful to briefly review the status of this country's riparian systems, i.e.: "...the vegetation and associated animal life found in close proximity to streams and other watercourses, around lakes, and adjacent to springs, seeps, and desert oases" (Warner 1979). According to Dr. Warner, riparian systems are:

---

[1]Paper presented at the California Riparian Systems Conference. [University of California, Davis, September 17-19, 1981].

[2]Judith Kunofsky is past National President of Zero Population Growth (1977-1980) and continues to serve on its board of directors. She also heads the Population Growth Policy Program of the Sierra Club.

"...perhaps the most important of all ecosystems to fish and wildlife," determining the health of associated aquatic environments, enhancing erosion control, and improving water quality (ibid.). They constitute important agricultural lands and sources of timber. Riparian vegetation is the source of nutrients for streams, of diverse recreational opportunities, of clean water, fuel, and shade.

However, America has in the last 150 years destroyed between 70% and 90% of her indigenous riparian resources and badly damaged much of the rest (US Council on Environmental Quality 1978). Examples of that destruction:

1) In 1977 the USDI Bureau of Land Management concluded that 83% of the riparian systems under its control were "...in unsatisfactory condition and in need of improved management, largely because of the destruction caused by excessive livestock grazing, road construction, and other damaging human activities" (Almand and Krohn 1979).

2) "On the 2.3 million acres of riparian lands and wetlands within the National Forest System, livestock grazing...timber harvest and associated road construction and silvicultural practices, recreation, public highway construction, and mining...all...continue to exert destructive pressures requiring prompt and concerted corrective measures (USDA Forest Service 1979).

3) In California: "...riparian systems are now so decimated as to be in jeopardy as a productive ecological resource" (Warner 1979).

WHAT IS THE SOURCE OF THE PROBLEM?

Our riparian resources are in such terrible shape because of human impact. This impact is increasing because of continued conversion of riparian lands to other uses—agriculture, forestry, livestock grazing, water control, highways, recreation, and housing. Directly or indirectly: "...all the dominant impacts are human ones" (ibid.).

ZPG maintains that the role of sheer human numbers cannot be ignored, and an end to population growth, the achievement of zpg, is an integral part of any serious, long-term plan for rehabilitating and sustaining riparian systems. To the extent that researchers, planners, regulators, and concerned Americans ignore this issue, they are dooming their work to ultimate failure.

This appraisal of the effect of population growth is applicable to any ecosystem or natural feature. This is part of the difficulty of the population concept; the impact of the size and growth of the human population is relevant to all resources, exclusive to none, and therefore, unfortunately, too often overlooked or considered such a general problem as not to be worth mentioning in any specific context.

PROTECTION OF RIPARIAN SYSTEMS

Returning to the discussion of riparian systems, since the source of the problems is human impact, we clearly need to change human activity. What does this mean?

First, we need specific management protections for riparian systems. However, even the best management will eventually be overwhelmed by continued population growth. When the pressure of human demands is great enough, any scheme of resource management or protection will go out the window. This is not a law of biology, but one of politics. When short-term human needs conflict with the long-term maintenance of the carrying capacity of an ecosystem, unfortunately we, as a society, as a world, seem to always sacrifice the long-term goal for the short-term need.

Resource management alone, however well-done, is simply not enough to protect riparian systems. These specific protections must be coupled with a reduction in demand for those services provided by riparian systems. This reduction requires a change in patterns of consumption (e.g., conservation and adoption of more environmentally sound technologies). It also necessitates a change in the quantity of consumption, which means, for example, fewer people directly enjoying the benefits of recreation along rivers, or fewer people relying on the products of riparian environments.

A decade ago, the Science and Technology Advisory Council of the California Assembly held a forum at the University of California, Davis, to analyze the nature and consequences of population change in the state. At that conference, demographers Kingsley Davis and Frederick G. Styles observed:

If any state in the United States epitomizes the dilemmas of advanced technology, it is California; and if any one of its problems embodies the dilemmas, it is rapid population growth... The productivity of its economy makes it a prime target for interstate and international migration, causing it to be...the most populous state in the union... Although it has been subject to temporary lulls in growth...its population increase has been remarkably persistent... The resulting environmental damage is greater than that found almost anywhere else in the United States....

If advanced societies are to solve their environmental problems, not to mention other questions concerned with the quality of life, they cannot indulge in continued rapid population growth. No sensible planning, no satisfactory management of land use, no long-run solution to urban problems is possible in the State of California if it continues to add half a million to its population each year (Davis and Styles 1971).

Zero population growth will be reached eventually. I have no doubt of this, nor do I think it is a matter of opinion. In the long run, the population of the earth will be no greater than its carrying capacity, that being a function of the level and style of consumption of humans, the quality of natural systems at the time, and the population size.

We still have a long way to go in convincing some people of this. Last year I was being interviewed by a member of the press for a story on California's population growth. "Tell me," he said, "does California have a carrying capacity?" "Of course," I responded, "but that is not a matter of my opinion, that is a biological fact." I pointed out to him that people might disagree about what California's carrying capacity for humans actually was, but I had no doubt at all that there certainly was one! I suspect he remained skeptical.

It is my opinion that the earth is probably well beyond its carrying capacity now. One device for generating a sense of the earth's carrying capacity is to list the countries one thinks could support populations twice their current numbers for the next 1,000 years. Assume, for the purpose of this exercise, that those population levels are reached within 100 years. If your sense of the world is anything like mine, your list will be very short. If it is, you believe the world is close to or beyond its carrying capacity.

Are any of these statements new? Not really. A decade ago, these same observations could have been made about the effect of population growth on riparian systems. Scientifically, little remains to be done except to document the degradation of natural resources that has occurred in the past ten years. This relative lack of "new" scientific research is another reason it is sometimes difficult to focus attention on population growth.

California might try to manage its riparian resources despite increasing population in a number of ways. Here are some theoretical examples. We could encourage a smaller fraction of the population to utilize the systems. Each person could, on the average, visit them less often. Californians could decide to visit other ecosystems (or use timber from other ecosystems). Or we could expand the number of riparian systems open for human recreation—or for timber production. However, this merely postpones the inevitable day of reckoning with growth. Already more than one million people are

turned away annually from over-booked state campgrounds, whether riparian or not.

No, this will not be enough. A concerted effort over time to limit California's numbers must be part of all of our efforts to protect riparian systems.

This is not to assert that any particular resource "runs out" or becomes totally degraded overnight. To the contrary, change is most often gradual, as the choices and our future options become ever more limited.

Of course, achievement of zero population growth alone will not solve our problems. It will not by itself protect any ecosystem, preserve the quality of human life or the wellbeing of the economy. It is not a substitute for wise management and stewardship of resources, but it is an essential complement to and component of such management.

ANALYZING POPULATION'S EFFECT ON RIPARIAN SYSTEMS

Before I tell you what has been done and what needs to be done, let me point out some dilemmas in analyzing the problem and developing solutions.

First, the local population in and around a riparian system is not self-regulating with respect to the carrying capacity of that system, because resources to sustain the population are imported from outside the system. For example, the number of people living near a riverbank is not related to the carrying capacity of that riverbank, because the population can bring in outside resources to satisfy its needs.

Second, the demands on a riparian system are not limited to the demands of the people living near it because resources produced by riparian systems are exported from the system. For example, agriculture responds to demands for goods from outside that system where the goods originate. According to the National Agricultural Lands Study, the harvest of one-third of the cropland in the United States is exported from the country (US Department of Agriculture and Council on Environmental Quality 1981).

Another example of this phenomenon is the National Forest Management Act, which calls for the Executive Branch to establish national targets for timber, wildlife, recreation, and wilderness. These are then apportioned to particular national forests and finally to particular ecosystems or parcels of land. This is not the kind of approach likely to match resource demands with the carrying capacities of natural systems.

Third, population growth comes from two sources, fertility and immigration. Fertility is only indirectly influenced by the public will, through social pressure and some government actions. Immigration is influenced directly only at certain geographic levels, specifically, by national governments, and only very indirectly at lower levels such as states or communities. Regions wanting to slow or end their population increases have few strong legal foundations on which to do so.

Fourth, those most motivated to be aware of the problems of population growth in its biological dimensions are not the ones best situated to affect policy. It is not surprising that the political leader in California most sensitive to the problems of population growth is Huey Johnson, Secretary of the Resources Agency for the State—someone who has no jurisdiction whatsoever over those factors influencing fertility and migration.

Fifth, the effects of population are gradual and cumulative, just as the degradation of riparian systems is gradual. The expression "population bomb" is an inappropriate metaphor. In a particular crisis, population growth is never seen as the proximate cause and therefore is often ignored completely.

A fine discussion of this problem—population being overlooked as a causal factor—was contained in a recent editorial in "Science" by demographer Kingsley Davis (Davis 1981).

Seldom are public policies constrained only by scientific and engineering limitations; they are also limited, consciously and unconsciously, by social norms. Solutions to the energy problem, for example, usually take one of two forms: to conserve energy, or to increase or at least maintain the total supply... A third approach—stopping or reversing population growth—is seldom treated as a part of energy policy...

(S)topping or reversing population growth could play a major role in solving the energy problem. When we take into account the environmental problems that heroic efforts to increase the total energy supply will entail, or the human problems that reducing average per capita consumption throughout the world will bring, we conclude that population control is not only a desirable but also a necessary part of any effective energy policy. To "solve" the energy problem otherwise is like fixing a leaky roof by putting more containers on the floor...

(W)e still construe energy policy as producing or saving energy for however many people there are, not as producing fewer people so as to give each one as much energy as he or she needs...

Yet it is people who use energy. With fewer people, less energy is needed. This may seem obvious, but so far we

have tragically postponed acting on it....

My sixth, and final observation, is that the decisions which cause population growth, namely fertility and migration decisions, whether of individuals or governments, are virtually never seen as environmental decisions at all.

Fertility decisions are matters of individual choice. Public policy aspects are the protection of those rights, ensuring (theoretically) that every child is a wanted child, and protecting the health of women and children.

Immigration decisions are made because the individual believes, in most cases correctly, that his or her life will be bettered by the move. Immigration policies are seen as labor policies, components of international relations, fulfillment of commitments to family reunification, and service to refugees.

Still further, migration within the country is seen as a response to economic growth or economic stagnation. Many cities in the Northeast or Midwest see their current population stability or decrease not as a welcome sign of balance but rather as a symptom of serious economic problems.

RESPONSE TO THESE DILEMMAS

One response to the problems posed by population growth, and a common one, is to try to "buy time". Journalist Hall Gilliam addressed the problem of "Finding Space for All the People".[4] He considered tradeoffs among population growth, urban open space (within cities and as farmland at the fringes), and density, and concluded that those concerned about environmental protection must endorse higher densities of housing. He then broadened his observations with a conclusion paralleling some of my own. To make it more relevant to this discussion, read "riparian system protection" where he uses "open space protection."

... (G)reater urban density is no guarantee that regional open-space lands will remain open, even with legal protection. Open-space laws can be changed, and if population pressure becomes intolerable, they will be.

That brings us to the unanswered question: How can unlimited population growth be accommodated in a limited area?

Probably the best we can do now is to buy time to find an answer. Meanwhile, we can house more people in existing urban areas, keep the farmlands intact

---

[4]Earthwatch column, San Francisco Sunday Examiner/Chronicle, August 30, 1981.

to feed the cities, and pray for insight.

I do not believe that "buying time" is all we can do. The evidence of the last decade is that much can be done to slow population growth, as indicated by these gains:

1) the establishment of Federal and state programs to fund family planning services;

2) the conclusion of the 1972 Commission on Population and the American Future that the nation should welcome and plan for an end to population growth (Commission on Population and the American Future 1972);

3) the 1973 Supreme Court decisions legalizing abortion throughout the country;

4) the rapid and continuing proliferation of movements to control growth in individual communities (whose motives range from the very best to the very worst);

5) the decrease in the number of children born to American couples and the decrease in the number of children they desire;

6) the turnaround in public attitudes towards population as evidenced by a 1977 Gallup poll that found 87% of those polled would rather that the US population not increase any more;

7) the increase in attention given to immigration as a source of half of our country's population growth.

In early 1981, a Governmental task force prepared recommendations for the (Carter) Administration on how to respond to the Global 2000 Report (US Council on Environmental Quality and Department of State 1980). The task force's findings included this recommendation (US Council on Environmental Quality and Department of State 1981):

Population growth in richer countries, though much slower (than in less developed countries), is of concern because consumption of resources per capita... is very much higher... The United States should develop a national population policy.

In fact, in 1974 then-Governor Reagan stated:

Our country...has a special obligation to work toward the stabilization of our own population so as to credibly lead other parts of the world toward population stabilization.

RECOMMENDATIONS

What is needed now is a way to articulate goals linking policies on fertility and immigration with the overall need to end population growth. We need a national population policy.

H.R. 907, introduced into the House of Representatives by Richard Ottinger of New York, declares a policy of comprehensive and coordinated planning for demographic change and establishes the goal of eventual stabilization of the population of the United States by voluntary means. The bill has been co-sponsored by more than two dozen representatives.[5]

Researchers, scientists, and managers of government programs to protect riparian systems do not have direct or indirect control of programs influencing the numbers of people in the country. They can, however, serve as a vital link between those who best understand why we need population stabilization, and those political leaders who can articulate such policies and bring zpg about. I offer as a model the policy statement issued by the Society of American Foresters:[6]

If human populations continue to increase substantially, insatiable demands on forestland resources will occur. The United States has the capacity to provide leadership in this global population challenge—as it has done in the conservation movement. Our legislative measures...have established a world standard. Yet these measures treat only the symptoms of uncontrolled population growth. This primary conservation issue has yet to be seriously addressed by the nation...

The best science and technology we can devise will not extricate us from the absolute limitations of the carrying capacity of our environment.

Therefore the Society of American Foresters supports a national policy of population stabilization and establishment of an office to coordinate its implementation. While recognizing that

---

[5]More recently, in October 1981, Senator Mark O. Hatfield of Oregon introduced S.B. 1771, the Global Resource, Environment, and Population Act of 1981. That bill, co-sponsored by Senators Alan Cranston (California), Charles Mathias (Maryland), Slade Gorton (Washington), and Spark Matsunaga (Hawaii), is a stronger version of H.R. 907.

[6]Excerpted from "Statement of the Society of American Foresters" submitted to the Subcommittee on Census and Population, Committee on Post Office and Civil Service, US House of Representatives, May 12, 1981, re: HR 907, to establish a national population policy and Office of Population Policy.

the technical aspects of such a policy are peripheral to the expertise of professional land managers, we also recognize that the long-term effectiveness of our management and conservation efforts depends on the resolution of this major domestic and global challenge.

In this context I wish to offer several recommendations. As scientists, managers, administrators, planners, and concerned public, you are in an advantageous position to define population problems and provide guidance in their solution.

First, professional organizations to which you belong should pass resolutions supporting population stabilization for the United States, endorsing the Ottinger and Hatfield bills or, if the latter is prohibited by your organization's tax status, calling for hearings on the two bills.

Second, you must continue to teach each new generation of Americans about the need to end population growth, because what is obvious to one generation may be forgotten by the next. Population education is not sex education, just as learning how to build, control, and put out a campfire is not the same as learning about the (positive and negative) effects of fire on forest ecosystems.

Third, you must expand research on the carrying capacity of particular ecosystems and on the concept of carrying capacity in general. It is important that you continually stress that "proper management" cannot possibly be enough; stabilization of the demands on a system must accompany management.

Fourth, use the language of goals. You need to say "when we reach zpg..." or "the ultimate population of this area will..." You must stress the tradeoffs between numbers of people and their consumption or lifestyles.

Fifth, in your professional lives, make recommendations for population stabilization. Raise this theme of the need for zpg in government service, on committees to which you belong, in reports you write to or for government agencies, and in testimony you prepare. Every time there is developed a set of recommendations for action, make sure action on population is among them. Remember that acknowledgment of the need for rapid achievement of zpg will come because those who think about resources point it out.

Sixth, take a public stand endorsing an end to population growth for the country and for the state. The latter is important because we experience the impacts of growth primarily at state and local levels. The former is important because immigration policy, critical in controling growth, is a national concern. Population policy therefore must be established at the national level.

And last, request that the State conduct an analysis of California's long-term carrying capacity, as has been suggested by Secretary of Resources Huey Johnson. You should also examine what the optimum population for California might be. The Resources Agency's report, "Investing for Prosperity" (California Resources Agency 1981), is an excellent model, having specific goals for enhancing California's resources by the year 2000. If only it had had a section on population goals for the state!

Overall, we must all use our commitment to the protection of natural systems to be public leaders in making the link between our concerns and the need for population stabilization.

CONCLUSION

The problem of controlling California's growth, or that of any state, is a difficult one because the state does not directly control migration across its borders. We in California get much more than our share of foreign immigration to the country and our currently healthy economy attracts migrants from other states. To some extent we still need to take Hal Gilliam's advice to accommodate growth as best we can, thereby buying time to find a real solution.

In welcoming participants to the previously-mentioned conference on California's growth held in 1971, Bob Moretti, Speaker of the Assembly, stated that the Assembly was interested in developing:

... some aproaches to legislation which will influence state population growth and distribution. Even though the personal decisions of individuals will always govern where they live...I do not agree that we are powerless to influence them through legislation.... (F)ederal and state legislation in this field...has contributed significantly to changed attitudes and population distribution.

We can no longer accept the proposition that all growth is good. In fact the quality of our life and our economic well-being may in the future depend to a great extent on more effective management of growth. What we need to seek is a balance between our resources of air, water, and open space and our population growth.

These are tough problems, and we are not so naive as to believe that there are any simple answers. I believe, however, that unless we deal with them, our efforts to control smog, clean up our waters, and open spaces [and here one might add 'protect and enhance the state's riparian systems'] will become mere stopgaps.

Mr. Moretti's comments are as true today as they were ten years ago when he said them.

LITERATURE CITED

Almand, J.D., and W.B. Krohn. 1979. Position paper: the position of the Bureau of Land Management on the protection and management of riparian ecosystems. p. 359-361. In: R.R. Johnson and J.F. McCormack (tech. coord.). Strategies for protection and management of floodplain wetlands and other riparian ecosystems. [Callaway Gardens, Georgia, December 11-13, 1978]. 410 p. USDA Forest Service GTR-WO-12, Washington, D.C.

California Resources Agency. 1981. Investing for prosperity: enhancing California's resources to meet human and economic needs. California Resources Agency, Sacramento.

Commission on Population and the American Future. 1972. Population and the American future. Report of the Commission on Population Growth and the American Future. US Government Printing Office.

Davis, Kingsley. 1981. It is people who use energy. Science 211(4481):439.

Davis, K., and F.G. Styles (ed.). 1971. California's twenty million: research contributions to population policy. Population Monograph Series, No. 10. 349 p. Institute of International Studies, University of California, Berkeley.

US Council on Environmental Quality. 1978. The Ninth Annual Report of the Council on Environmental Quality. 599 p. US Government Printing Office, Washington, D.C.

US Council on Environmental Quality and the Department of State. 1980. The global 2000 report to the President: entering the Twenty-first Century. US Government Printing Office.

US Council on Environmental Quality and the Department of State. 1981. Global future: time to act. Report to the President on global resources, environment and population. US Government Printing Office.

US Department of Agriculture and Council on Environmental Quality. 1981. National agricultural lands study. US Government Printing Office.

USDA Forest Service. 1979. Report of a USDA Forest Service riparian study task force on riparian policies and practices in the National Forest system. 15 p. Unpublished manuscript.

Warner, R.E. 1979. California riparian study program. 177 p. California Department of Fish and Game, Planning Branch, Sacramento, Calif.

SUMMARY OF RIPARIAN VEGETATION

AREAL AND LINEAR EXTENT MEASUREMENTS

FROM THE CENTRAL VALLEY RIPARIAN MAPPING PROJECT[1]

Edwin F. Katibah, Nicole E. Nedeff, and Kevin J. Dummer[2]

Abstract.--This paper summarizes the areal and linear extent measurements of riparian vegetation on the floor of the Central Valley of California, based on the maps produced by the Central Valley Riparian Mapping Project. Results are presented by riparian vegetation category for the applicable counties, and for the depositional bottomland or floor of the Central Valley as a whole.

INTRODUCTION

In 1978, the California Legislature, responding to the need for information on riparian resources in the state, appropriated $150,000 to the Department of Fish and Game (DFG) for a study of riparian resources in the Central Valley and California Desert (AB 3147, Fazio). A portion of this money was allocated for the mapping of riparian vegetation in the Central Valley.

In June, 1979, riparian mapping teams from the Geography Departments of California State University, Chico, and California State University, Fresno, completed mapping of the riparian vegetation on the floor of the Central Valley. The Department of Water Resources (DWR) made available 35mm. color slides of aerial photographs of those parts of the Central Valley (principally the irrigated and non-irrigated agricultural zones) for which it had photocoverage. Surrounding foothills and higher slopes were not included in the mapping project. The teams transferred riparian vegetation distributional data onto standard USDI Geological Survey (GS) 1:24,000 topographic quadrangle maps (quads). Riparian vegetation was mapped on fade-out blue copies or mylar overlays for each quad. A total of 465 individual map sheets, covering 388 unique quads, were compiled.

AREA AND LIMITS OF MAPPING COVERAGE

While the enabling legislation called for the study of Central Valley riparian resources up to the upper edge of the blue oak/digger pine zone (about 760 m. (2,500 ft.) elevation in the mountains surrounding the floor of the Central Valley) (Küchler 1977), only the depositional bottomlands of the Central Valley were mapped in this project. This was because the available DWR aerial photography was limited to those portions of the Central Valley where patterns of water use (principally agricultural) were being monitored.

Thus, the data on areal and linear extent reported here must not be construed either as the total amount of riparian vegetation for the entire Central Valley, which includes upland slopes as well as depositional bottomlands, or for the listed counties. As indicated in figure 1, only the depositional bottomland portions of the listed counties were mapped. As a result, summaries for Central Valley counties having only small amounts of depositional bottomlands (e.g., Nevada, Amador, Napa, Shasta) reflect only a small portion of these counties' total riparian resources.

Figure 1 indicates the actual mapping coverage by quad, within the relevant counties. Quads are identified by an index numbering system commonly used by California state agencies. A complete list of 388 individual quads, mapped for riparian vegetation, and the respective length and area measurements derived for each quad, are presented in the final report to DFG (Katibah, Nedeff, and Dummer 1980).

---

[1] Paper presented at the California Riparian Systems Conference. [University of California, Davis, September 17-19, 1981].

[2] Edwin F. Katibah is Associate Specialist, Remote Sensing Research Program, Department of Forestry and Resource Management, University of California, Berkeley. Nicole E. Nedeff is a Graduate Student, Department of Geography, and affiliated with the Remote Sensing Research Program, Department of Forestry and Resource Management, University of California, Berkeley. Kevin J. Dummer is Staff Research Associate, Remote Sensing Research Program, Department of Forestry and Resource Management, University of California, Berkeley.

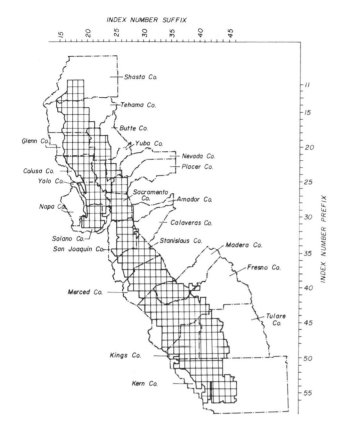

Figure 1.--Locations of 1:24,000 quads in which
riparian vegetation was mapped. Quads only
partially mapped are included.

MAPPING PROCEDURES

For the actual mapping of riparian vegetation, the teams used a physiognomic mapping category system, with vegetative life-form as the
basic criterion: trees, shrubs, and herbaceous
cover. These three basic lifeform categories
were further refined by certain "modifiers", and
by hybridizing the primary categories. Table 1
is a summary of the riparian mapping category
codes developed by the mapping teams. The table
does not include hybridized vegetation categories
(i.e., R1/R2, R1/R3) developed and used by the
teams. A more complete description of the riparian mapping project methodology may be found in
Nelson and Nelson (1983).

Table 1.--Summary of riparian vegetation mapping
category codes (adapted from Central Valley
Riparian Mapping Project 1979).

Code   Category and description

R1--Large woody vegetation.
    Tall mature forests with significant woody
    understory.
R1v*--Valley oak woodland.
    Mature, well-spaced stands of valley oaks
    (Quercus lobata) without woody under-
    story.
R2--Low woody vegetation.
    Low dense stands of young trees and shrubs.
R3--Herbaceous vegetation.
    Low herbaceous growth occurring along stream
    channels or in natural clearings among other
    riparian vegetation categories.
R3p*--Perennial seeps.
    Herbaceous vegetation occurring near peren-
    nial springs and seeps.
M--Marsh.
    Herbaceous emergent vegetation of perennial-
    ly moist areas.
S--Sandbars and gravelbars.
    Exposed sand, gravel, or rock areas.
W--Open water.
    Standing or moving waters.
A--Agricultural land.
    Cultivated lands completely or nearly sur-
    rounded by riparian vegetation.
U--Urban land.
    Built-up areas nearly or completely surroun-
    ded by riparian vegetation.
c**--Channelized.
    Irrigation canals and highly channelized
    streamcourses so altered as to no longer
    show natural stream characteristics.
d**--Disturbed.
    Areas readily identified as severely altered
    by human activities.
i**--Intermittent.
    Used to designate spottiness or non-consis-
    tent occurrence of any given vegetation
    category.

---

    * Subcategory
    ** Modifier

CENTRAL VALLEY RIPARIAN VEGETATION

Table 2 is presented to give the reader some
idea of the actual plant species found within
Central Valley riparian systems. Typical riparian trees and shrubs are listed, along with an
indication of their relationship to the mapping
category codes used in the project.

Table 2.--Riparian vegetation of the Central Valley, California (adapted from Roberts et al. 1977).

1. Typical native riparian trees (potential R1 when mature, R2 when young.

Acer negundo subsp. californicum	box elder
Aesculus californica*	California buckeye
Alnus rhombifolia*	Sierra alder
Fraxinus latifolia	Oregon ash
Juglans hindsii	black walnut
Platanus racemosa	California sycamore
Populus fremontii	Fremont cottonwood
Quercus agrifolia*	coast live oak
Quercus lobata	valley oak
Quercus wislizenii*	interior live oak
Salix goodingii var. goodingii*	Gooding willow
Salix laevigata	red willow
Salix lasiandra	Pacific willow

2. Typical riparian shrubs (potential R2).

Artemisia douglasiana	mugwort
Atriplex lentiformis*	quail-bush
Baccharis douglasii*	false-willow
Baccharis glutinosa*	seep-willow
Baccharis viminea	mulefat
Cephalanthus occidentalis	button willow
Cornus glabrata*	brown dogwood
Cornus occidentalis*	red osier dogwood
Heteromeles arbutifolia*	toyon
Hibiscus californicus*	wild hibiscus
Lonicera involucrata*	twinberry honeysuckle
Nicotiana glauca*,**	tree tobacco
Phylostachos bambosoides**	bamboo
Ptelea crenulata*	hop tree
Rosa california	wild rose
Salix hindsiana	sandbar willow
Salix lasiolepis	arroyo willow
Salix melanopsis	willow
Sambucus mexicana	elderberry
Symphoricarpos rivularis	snowberry
Tamarix parviflora	tamarisk

3. Typical riparian vines (potential R2).

Aristolochia california	Dutchman's pipe vine
Clematis lasiantha	wild clematis
Clematis ligusticifolia	western clematis
Lonicera hispidula var. vacillans*	wild honeysuckle
Rhus diversiloba	poison oak
Rubus discolor*	Himalayan blackberry
Rubus ursinus	wild blackberry
Rubus vitifolius	wild blackberry
Similax californica	greenbrier
Vitis californica	wild grape

---

* Uncommon
** Exotic

MEASUREMENT METHODS

Upon completion of the Central Valley Riparian Mapping Project, the DFG contracted with the Remote Sensing Research Program, Department of Forestry and Resource Management, University of California, Berkeley, to calculate the lengths and areas of each category of riparian vegetation by individual quad and by county.

Riparian vegetation on each overlay for each quad, comprising a network of polygons and linear features (with representative mapping category codes), was measured using a flat bed digitizer.[3] The digitizer has a resolution of 1,000 points per inch and 1,000,000 points per square inch. Areas and lengths of riparian vegetation were calculated in digitizing units and converted to acres and miles, as appropriate. At a map scale of 1:24,000, the digitizer conversion factors were:

lines:
number of digitizing points/2,640 =
    length in miles

areas:
number of digitizing points/10,890 =
    area in acres.

RESULTS

The riparian length and area results were tabulated by county and by quad overlay. An example of the county riparian vgetation tabulations is presented in figure 2. The complete set can be found in Katibah et al. (1980). In virtually all cases, the applicable counties did not have complete mapping coverage (see figure 1).

Table 3 gives an aggregated summary of the riparian vegetation mapping category measurements for the entire mapped portion of the Central Valley study area. Mapping categories were consolidated by combining all hybridized categories by their principal components (e.g., R1/R2 and R1/R3 would be included in the aggregated category R1 hybrid). Also included in the hybridized categories were categories where the modifiers "c", "d", and "i" were combined with a major riparian vegetation category (e.g., R3d would be included in R3 hybrid). The "miscellaneous" category refers to categories where the principal component in a hybridized category does not represent riparian vegetation (e.g., M/R3, where M designates marsh). Additionally, categories for valley oak are given under the codes R1v and R1v hybrid, even though this is a subcategory.

---

[3]Talos Series 6000 high resolution digitizer.

Table 3.—Aggregated summary, by category, of area and length measurements for Central Valley depositional bottomland riparian vegetation.

Code	ha. (ac.)	km. (mi.)
R1	20,725 (51,191)	773 (480)
R1 hybrid	18,157 (44,849)	1,248 (775)
R1v	9,204 (22,734)	151 (94)
R1v hybrid	1,294 (3,195)	227 (141)
R2	5,341 (13,193)	683 (424)
R2 hybrid	10,256 (25,332)	1,315 (817)
R3	14,737 (36,400)	369 (229)
R3 hybrid	8,168 (20,174)	214 (133)
Miscellaneous	5,882 (14,528)	55 (34)
Total	(231,596)	5,035 (3,127)

AUTHORS' NOTE

The results presented in this paper are based on a report submitted to the DFG (Katibah, Nedeff, and Dummer 1980). This report, containing more detailed information than is presented here, is filed with the original riparian vegetation maps (compiled by the Central Valley Riparian Mapping Project) at the California Natural Diversity Data Base, DFG, Sacramento.

LITERATURE CITED

Central Valley Riparian Mapping Project. 1979. Interpretation and mapping systems. Report prepared by the Riparian Mapping Team, Geography Department, California State University, Chico, in cooperation with the Department of Geography, California State University, Fresno. 24 p. California Department of Fish and Game, Planning Branch. Unpublished manuscript.

Katibah, Edwin F., Nicole E. Nedeff, and Kevin J. Dummer. 1980. Areal and linear extent of riparian vegetation in the Central Valley of California. Final report to the California Department of Fish and Game, Planning Branch. Remote Sensing Research Program, Department of Forestry and Resource Management, University of California, Berkeley.

TEHAMA COUNTY

COUNTY MAPPING COVERAGE

CLASS. CODE	AREA (ACRES)	LENGTH (MILES)
R1	10,574.7	10.9
R1c	7.3	
R1d	4.0	
R1i	2913.1	35.3
R1vi	658.8	32.8
R1v	7115.0	5.7
R1v/A	161.2	
R1i/W		5.9
R1/R2	157.8	
R1/R2i	18.7	
R2	1433.0	3.3
R2c		1.0
R2i	1443.2	8.8
R2ic	6.4	.4
R2id	42.5	
R2/R1	551.9	
R2/R1i	48.7	
R3	4995.5	25.4
R3c		1.5
R3d	456.0	
R3p	20.1	
R3/S	173.0	
R3/R1	238.4	
R3/R1v	13.7	
R3/R1vi	29.3	
R3/R2	26.5	
W/R1vi		20.6
S/R1i	62.7	1.3
W/R1i		5.5

TEHAMA COUNTY : CONTINUED

COUNTY MAPPING COVERAGE

CLASS. CODE	AREA (ACRES)	LENGTH (MILES)
S/R2i	20.5	
M/R2	15.8	
S/R3	87.2	

TULARE COUNTY

COUNTY MAPPING COVERAGE

CLASS. CODE	AREA (ACRES)	LENGTH (MILES)
R1	398.3	22.6
R1c	1.0	3.0
R1i	849.8	58.8
R1v	557.4	9.0
R1/R2	145.7	3.6
R1/R2i	23.0	
R1/R3	5.0	
R1v/R3	25.9	
R1/W	7.7	
R2	472.8	54.8
R2c	18.6	3.7
R2i	315.4	36.5
R2/S	93.6	.5
R2/W	17.3	.6
R2/R1	114.2	8.7
R2/R1i	16.7	
R2/R3	27.0	5.4
R2/R3d		22.7
R3	1906.9	19.4
R3d	22.8	
R3/M	44.7	.8
R3/S	20.4	
R3i		1.2
R3/R2	53.2	
S/R2	34.2	
UNLABELED	346.0	1.7

Figure 2.—Example of a county summary tabulation for bottomland floodplain, riparian and aquatic wetlands.

Küchler, A.W. 1977. Map of the natural vegetation of California. 1:1,000,000 + 31 p. A.W. Küchler. Department of Geography, University of Kansas, Lawrence.

Nelson, C.W., and J.R. Nelson. 1983. The Central Valley riparian mapping project. In: R.E. Warner and K.M. Hendrix (ed.). California Riparian Systems. [University of California, Davis, September 17-19, 1981]. University of California Press, Berkeley.

Roberts, W.G., J.G. Howe, and J. Major. 1977. A survey of riparian forest flora and fauna in California. p. 3-19. In: A. Sands (ed.). Riparian forests of California: their ecology and conservation. Institute of Ecology Pub. No. 15. 121 p. University of California, Davis.

AN HISTORICAL OVERVIEW OF THE SACRAMENTO RIVER[1]

Lauren B. Scott and Sandra K. Marquiss[2]

Abstract.--This paper summarizes an analysis of two
aspects of the history of the Sacramento River: the fluvial
process; and man's development of the floodplain over the
last 130 years. The analysis was made to trace the origins
of problems--seepage, loss of riparian vegetation, and
limited public access--occurring in the riparian zone, and
to establish a perspective from which to study these problems. Significant historical aspects of these problems must
be considered in a comprehensive study of the river.

INTRODUCTION

This paper presents an historical overview
of the Sacramento River, shown in figure 1, to
trace the origins of some of the problems occurring in its riparian zone, and to provide a
perspective from which these problems can best be
studied. The overview focuses on: 1) the
fluvial process of the river itself, and 2) the
principal activities of man over the last 130
years which have affected the river.

The Sacramento River has played a significant role in the history of the Central Valley
and the State. The first humans occupying
northern California chose to live along the banks
of the Sacramento River as did later settlers who
populated the floodplain, reclaiming the river's
lands and diverting its waters. Today the river
continues to provide a means of sustenance to the
people of the Valley and the State.

[the Missis-
the Columbia
the Sacra-
of any other
iver system,
e north and
the State's
ps of Engi-
irrigation,
needs. The
an increas-
particularly
a haven for
dlife which
rian system

California
iversity of
81].
ngineer, and
iter-Editor,
, Calif.

Long before man came in contact with the
river, natural processes that develop and shape
rivers were creating the Sacramento River man
would have to live with when he entered the
Valley. The problems that we struggle with today
have their roots in the early, pre-settlement
development of the river.

Over the last 130 years, dams, dikes,
levees, drainage works, bypasses and bank
protection systems have been built to control the
river and to protect people living in the floodplain. These facilities, often built years
apart, to varying standards, and for different
purposes, have greatly altered the river system.
Built to solve a variety of problems, they
created other problems. Among these problems are
seepage of river water into adjacent agricultural
lands, loss of riparian vegetation to urban and
agricultural encroachment, and restriction of
public access to the river. The many uses of the
river have also resulted in diverse and sometimes
conflicting views on how and by whom these problems should be resolved and how future development of the river should or should not proceed.

The overview presented here identifies
significant historical aspects of these problems
showing how the changes inherent in the fluvial
process itself, together with the changes caused
by man, have resulted in the river as we know it
today.

FLUVIAL MORPHOLOGY

Fluvial morphology can be defined as the
science of the forms created by the action of
flowing water (Lane 1955). The relationships
among the many factors operating in this process
are complicated and not completely understood.
Two concepts from fluvial morphology--equilibrium
and evolutionary development of rivers--have been
chosen to show the importance of the fluvial
process in understanding some of the problems of
the Sacramento River.

51

Figure 1.--Location map.

Equilibrium

Alluvial rivers are among the most dynamic of all geomorphic forms. All changes in the river, however, whether occurring over geologic eons, or within a human lifetime, are governed by the principle of equilibrium; that is, although the river continually changes, only those changes leading to equilibrium, or stability, persist (Maddock 1976).

The principle of equilibrium is based on the assumption that all variables influencing the form of a river are interrelated in such a way as to represent a predictable system (Leopold and Maddock 1953). Since morphology and form of a river are primarily determined by the nature and quantity of sediment and water moving through the channel, the river's configuration is the result of a relationship among four variables: quantity of sediments, size of sediments, water discharge, and channel slope. The relationship among these variables is expressed as $Q_s d \mathrel{\mathcal{N}} Q_w S$. By the theory of equilibrium, changes in any one of these variables will be compensated for by corresponding changes in the other three, thus tending to change toward stability. For example, a decrease in sediment load is compensated for by a decrease in water discharge or slope, or by an increase in the sediment diameter.

A result of the dynamic properties of the fluvial process operating on a portion of the Sacramento River is illustrated in figure 2, which shows the configuration of the Sacramento River in 1874 and again in 1974. Some of the changes are notable: for example, the creation of a slough.

Evolutionary Development of Rivers

The variables of the fluvial process working to create a river valley have been characterized by some geomorphologists as an evolutionary process, a progression from youth to old age. There is no sharp division between the ages and no general agreement as to when one age ends and another begins (Johnson 1932).

By the time a river is old, as is the Sacramento River, the features of its valley are well developed and distinct. In the case of the Sacramento, floodplains are wide with low relief, and the river follows a broad, meandering course. Its channel is graded; that is, its energy and slope are just sufficient to carry away the material delivered to it from the uplands. Natural levees occur along its banks, with low-lying poorly drained swamp areas or flood basins on either side (Simmons and Senturk 1977). Two of these features--natural levees and meandering--are keys to not only understanding problems along the river but formulating their solutions.

Natural levees are the result of repeated overflows of sediment-laden river water onto adjacent lands, and occur where the valley slope is lowest and the duration of overbank flow is highest. The coarse, sandy material deposited close to the channel gradually builds up forming broad slopes which fall gently away from the river. Because they are comprised of coarse sediment, these levees are extremely porous and transmit water readily.

Natural levees along the Sacramento River occur discontinuously from Red Bluff downstream, and are most extensively developed in the river's middle reach from Ord Ferry to Sacramento. This is the same reach where the most extensive seepage problems occur. Here the river has adjusted to the lower slope of the Valley floor by annually overflowing its banks and emptying its water into the adjacent lateral flood basins. Near the city of Sacramento, levee heights range from 3.0-4.6 m. (10-15 ft.) above the adjacent low basin lands. Levee widths range from 3.2-4.8 km. (2-3 mi.).

Another important feature of the Sacramento River is its meandering. Meandering results from the constant and sometimes rapid changes in the form of a river and is the configuration taken by most alluvial rivers.

Meandering is thought to be caused by the direction of currents in the channel. These currents, in essence, cause a constant process of erosion of the riverbank and deposition of this

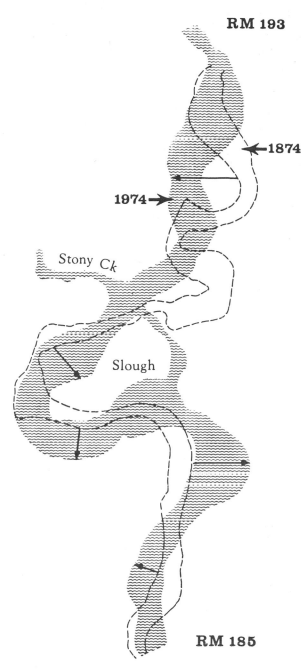

RM 193

←1874

1974→

Stony Ck

Slough

RM 185

Figure 2.--Sacramento River, 1874 and 1974 (from Brice 1977).

material at a point farther downstream. The material deposited downstream accumulates as a point bar which builds out from the bank, constricting the channel and subsequently forcing the channel to move in a lateral direction. In such a way meander loops are thought to form and "move," or migrate down the valley (Simmons and Senturk 1977). The loops move unequally however, and may occasionally be cut off and abandoned as the river changes its course.

When a cutoff occurs, the part of the river bypassed forms an oxbow lake, which gradually begins to fill in with sediment. The lower end of the oxbow, receiving the relatively impermeable finer silts and clays, eventually forms what is, in effect, a clay plug between the old meander loop and the main channel. Because of its impermeability this plug is essentially a semipermanent geologic control which can affect river geometry. Natural levees deposited from overflow and point bar, oxbow, and alluvial deposits laid down in meandering create complex soil structures along the river. It is through these soils that groundwater flows between the mountains and the river. Some deposits are very permeable and transmit water readily; others are impermeable, but influence the possible directions, horizontal and vertical, that water can travel.

A major factor in the fluvial process is the interrelation of all reaches of an alluvial river. Although specific changes in a river may originally be local, the effects of the changes can extend to all parts of the river (Burkham 1981). This characteristic is important when assessing the impact of man's activities on a river basin. Since the effects of a development on the river cannot be isolated to the reach in which it occurs, the net result of any change can be a greater departure, along the whole river, from equilibrium than that which was originally present.

DEVELOPMENT OF THE SACRAMENTO RIVER BY MAN

Beginning with the discovery of gold at Coloma on the American River in 1848, man became another variable in the fluvial process. Principal activities of man affecting the river were urban settlement and agricultural development on the floodplain, and hydraulic mining of the surrounding foothills. The combined effect of these activities on the regime of the river was profound and far-reaching; the problems of seepage, loss of riparian vegetation, and restricted public fishing access may be cited as consequences. The effects of hydraulic mining were so immediate and so drastic as to influence the course of all other development on the floodplain.

Hydraulic Mining

Hydraulic mining began in 1852 with the discovery that water under pressure could easily and economically remove the layers of lava and sediment covering the gold deposited in the ancient stream channels of the Sierra Nevada. Eventually, giant machines operated from considerable distances could tear apart a bank several hundred feet high in a very short time.

The machines that removed gold from the hills deposited millions of tons of silt and gravel in the nearby streams. Erosion that would have occurred naturally over hundreds of years occurred literally overnight. In one analysis of the amount of sediment in the rivers resulting from hydraulic mining, it was concluded that the 35 years of hydraulic mining tripled for about 100 years the average annual amount of sediment passed from the Sacramento Basin into San Francisco Bay under natural conditions. Over 1,000,000 acre-feet of debris has been deposited throughout the valley or passed into the Bay.[3]

The effect on the valley below was enormous. As river channels filled with more and more debris, the rivers rose. It is estimated that in some reaches the elevations of the Sacramento, Feather, Yuba, Bear, and American Rivers, the rivers most affected by sediment deposition, rose as much as 6 m. (20 ft.) (State of California 1978). With higher streambeds, capacities to carry water were greatly diminished. During a series of floods in 1861-62, 1875, and 1878, the debris washed out of the mountains and into the streams. The rivers overflowed their banks, inundating farms and homes with muddy polluted water.

By 1880, fertile land lost to hydraulic mining totaled more than 17,400 ha. (43,000 ac.).[4] The State Engineer, speaking to the State Legislature in 1880, described the effect of debris on farmland adjacent to the Yuba and Bear Rivers:

> ...the bottom lands were submerged... with sand and clay sediment, to such depths that in places orchards, gardens fields, and dwellings were buried from sight...and the course of the devastating flood was marked out by broad commons of slimes and sands.[3]

Antagonism between farmers and miners grew, culminating in a series of suits filed against the mining companies, in which the farmers at first sought damages, and eventually sought the complete abolition of hydraulic mining. In 1884, the State Supreme Court in the case of Woodruff v. North Bloomfield et al. prohibited the discharge of any mining debris into the streams. This decision, known as the Sawyer Decision, ended hydraulic mining.

---

[3]Jones, G.H. January, 1967. Alteration of the regimen of the Sacramento River and tributary streams attributable to engineering activities during the past 116 years. Prepared for the Historical Records of Sacramento Sector, American Society of Civil Engineers.

[4]Hagwood, J.J. 1970. From North Bloomfield to North Fork: attempts to comply with the Sawyer Decision. Unpublished draft thesis for completion of Master of Arts degree, California State University, Sacramento.

The most adverse effects of hydraulic mining were on the rivers. Debris had choked and clogged some channels and completely obliterated others. With their equilibria destroyed, the rivers readjusted by overtopping their banks, depositing large quantities of debris in the valleys and carrying the remainder to San Francisco Bay.

Transport of the debris from hydraulic mining downstream took many years. Fluctuations in the low water levels, or streambed elevations, for the mouth of the Yuba River at Marysville and for the Sacramento River at Sacramento, shown in figure 3, indicate the length of time, depth of deposition of mining debris in riverbeds, and rate of erosion back to original stream elevations. The changes illustrated for the Yuba and Sacramento Rivers would occur in a similar manner in other streams in the Sacramento River system which experienced hydraulic mining.

Although the bed of the Sacramento River returned to its original elevation, the plan view of the river was permanently altered. Before the river established a new pattern of stability, dams and levees were built to control floods.

Development of the Floodplain

One of the most important impacts of hydraulic mining on the Valley came when mining was stopped. By the late 1800's development of the Valley's resources had come to an impasse. The interests of farming and mining appeared incompatible; one could continue only at the expense of the other. The Sawyer Decision in 1884, which ended the hydraulic mining era, signaled the beginning of the agricultural era, and also determined the course of future development of the Sacramento River. With the growth of agriculture and commerce as the Valley's principal economic activities, the Sacramento River system would be extensively developed for irrigation supplies and for flood control.

Urban settlement of the floodplain began with the Gold Rush and was concentrated around the city of Sacramento. The city's population of about 150 in 1848 exploded to 12,000 by 1852 (Sacramento Magazine 1976). With its favorable location at the juncture of the American and Sacramento Rivers, the city was an important port and supply center, linking the coast and the city of San Francisco with the goldfields. Upstream, the city of Marysville, also at the juncture of two rivers—the Feather and the Yuba—was another population center in the Valley.

In the decade following the Gold Rush many settlers turned to farming, and within a few years agriculture had become the principal use of land in the Valley. Agricultural development began on the natural levees, called rimlands

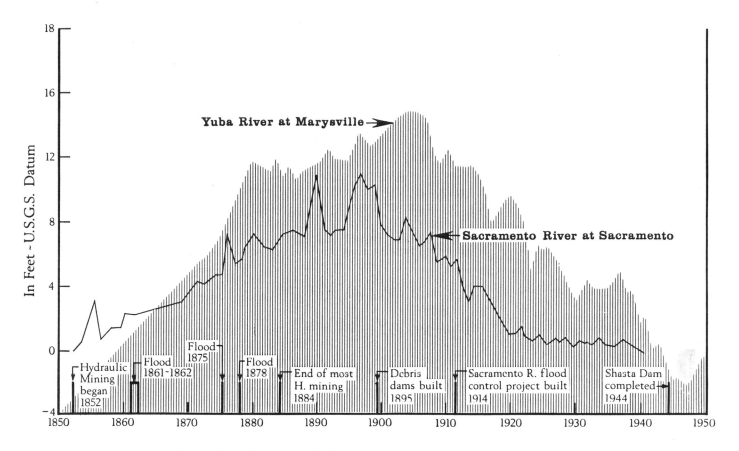

Figure 3.--Changes in bed elevation for portions of the Yuba and Sacramento Rivers, 1850-1950 (from G.H. Jones[4]).

because of their higher locations, which supported dense stands of riparian forests. It is estimated that in 1842, nearly 324,000 ha. (800,000 ac.) along the Sacramento River were forested, sometimes extending 8 km. (5 mi.) from the river.[5]

After the rimlands, the overflow, or tule. lands, comprising approximately 200,000 ha. (500,000 ac.) were developed (State of California 1976). Impetus for large-scale reclamation of the tule lands came in 1850 when the passage of the Arkansas Act transferred ownership of all such swamp and overflow lands from the Federal Government to the State on the condition that the lands be drained. The State in turn made these lands available for private ownership on the same condition of reclamation. This conditional transfer of ownership is significant because it determined that much of the land along the river would be used for agriculture and that ownership would be private, which has resulted in the problem of restricted public access to the river.

_____

[5]Michny, F. 1980. Causes for the loss of riparian forest along the Sacramento River. Unpublished report. USDI Fish and Wildlife Service.

Levee Construction

As tule lands were reclaimed, the number of towns and farms increased, as did the need for flood protection. During very large storms the volume of water delivered to the river could be from four to eight times greater than the capacity of the channel, depending on the section of the river. The Sacramento River, particularly in its middle reaches over the flat valley floor. could not contain the volumes of water resulting from winter storms and spring runoff, and overflowed its banks almost annually. In the lower portion of the river the severity of these floods was amplified during the hydraulic mining period. For much of the year the floodplain was an inland sea, as vast quantities of water moved slowly down the valley through the flood basins to reenter the river in its lower reaches.[4]

At first, levees were constructd piecemeal by individuals or small groups with little or no consideration given to the effects on other areas along the river or the natural tendency of the river to meander. Natural drainage boundaries were ignored, with the result that some natural drains were closed off and marshes created in places which had previously been well drained. Levee wars began as landowners on one side of the river raised their levees to force the floodwaters onto the opposite side of the river.

The configuration of the river changed rapidly and radically. Some levees eventually measured 7.6 m. (25 ft.) high and 61 m. (200 ft.) wide at the base. As levees were built higher, the water levels rose higher, and water that had previously overflowed into natural flood basins was now confined to a channel between the levees. As a result, during floods, the surface of the river water was often well above the level of the surrounding land.

Levee construction was accelerated when debris from hydraulic mining raised the riverbeds, decreasing the capacities of the river channels, including the Sacramento, which even under natural conditions could not contain its floodwaters. By the 1870's the beds of the Yuba and the Feather Rivers, tributaries to the Sacramento River, were higher than the town of Marysville, whose citizens responded by building better and even higher levees to protect the city. The city of Sacramento, inundated by a series of floods during the 1850's and 1860's, had by 1870 literally been raised by as much as 3.8 m. (12 ft.) to prevent future flooding of the city (Sacramento Magazine 1976).

Ultimately, efforts by individuals and small reclamation districts to prevent extensive flooding were ineffective. As the century closed, the complications from mining debris, a series of floods, and the inefficient and, in some cases, even detrimental levee system amply demonstrated the need for a Valley-wide flood control system.

Flood Control

The first centralized flood control plan was the Sacramento River Flood Control Project, formulated by the California Debris Commission. This project in essence rearranged the landscape to allow the river to revert to its natural regime during floods. The changes in regime enabled floodwaters overflowing into the adjacent flood basins to be conveyed slowly down the valley and returned back into the river in its lower reaches.

Authorized in 1914, the project was essentially in place in 1944 and is now about 90% complete. From the Sacramento River, water flows east into Butte Basin, thence to Sutter Bypass where it flows across the river into Yolo Basin, then through Yolo Bypass back into the river.

Foundation and composition of the man-made levees are part of the seepage problem. Man-made levees were built on top of the natural levees which were extremely porous. For economic reasons, the levees were often constructed from soils adjacent to or within the channel. These coarse, silty soils, which were deposited on the natural levees, were also extremely porous.

Levee construction and reclamation of levee lands destroyed large amounts of riparian vegetation and began the conversion of riparian lands to croplands which continues today. Levee

systems often evolve into bank protection systems. This results in further loss of vegetation because the use of riprap and rock revetment to control erosion requires stripping the land of vegetation.

The Central Valley and State Water Projects

The Central Valley Project, begun in the 1940's, and the State Water Project, begun in 1960, were also constructed as part of the Valley-wide flood control system. Their purpose was in part to alleviate the imbalance in water supply between the northern and southern parts of the State. Both projects store and transfer water from the north to the central and southern parts of the State for irrigation and domestic use. The Sacramento River and its tributaries are the principal conveyors of this water to collection points in the Delta, where it is distributed south by a series of canals and holding reservoirs.

Key features of the Central Valley Project are Shasta Dam and Reservoir, which are operated for flood control and which modify the flow of the entire river downstream from the dam. Overall, this development has resulted in substantially higher summer flows, and intensified problems of erosion and sediment deposition. Because of the high flows, the streambanks never dry out and are more susceptible to erosion. Substantial amounts of sediment formerly deposited in flood basins are now deposited in the downstream overflow and bypass areas adjacent to the river and in the navigation and flood control channels.

CONCLUSIONS

This historical overview of the river points up two conditions as the basis for seepage, loss of riparian vegetation, and limited public access along the river. These conditions are: a) the location, composition, and foundation of flood control levees, resulting both from fluvial morphology and the activities of man; and b) the nature of land ownership and control along the river, laid out by the Arkansas Act.

Seepage problems were an inevitable consequence of agricultural development of levee lands and construction of man-made levees on top of the natural ones. Permeable complex soils deposited along the river are a major part of the problem. And although the impermeable deposits do not transmit water, they do influence the direction the seepage water can flow.

Construction of levees began and then accelerated the conversion of riparian lands to croplands. The riparian vegetation which remains today is essentially limited to thin strands along the river.

Land ownership patterns are directly related to both the loss and preservation of riparian vegetation, and directly affect the most popular recreational use of the river--fishing. Public access for recreation in general and fishing in particular is very limited and in some reaches almost nonexistent, a problem which will become more acute in the future.

A final value of an historical overview is the awareness of a continuing theme in the river's development--that of perspective. The levee building of the late 1800's was the result of piecemeal solutions to what was a Valley-wide problem of flooding. The broad and unified planning approach ultimately required to solve the flooding problem, is required again today to study the problems existing in the riparian zone. The fragmentary nature of land use and ownership patterns along the river has resulted in the creation of several publics, each competing to control some aspect of the river. Agreement on a common perspective of the river is difficult to achieve.

An overview suggests that an agreement on such a perspective could begin with the recognition that the river at any given time is the result of a continuing process among interrelated variables, of which the activities of man is but one. Planning from this point of view would seek to reinforce the natural tendency of the river toward equilibrium, and hence offer more satisfactory solutions to problems existing in the riparian zone.

LITERATURE CITED

Brice, James. 1977. Lateral migration of the middle Sacramento River, California. USDI Geological Survey, Water Resources Investigations 77-43. Menlo Park, Calif.

Burkham, D.E. 1981. Uncertainties resulting from changes in river form. J. Hydraulics Division, Proceedings of American Society of Civil Engineers 107(HY5):593-610

California Department of Water Resources. 1955. Report to the Water Project Authority on seepage conditions in the Sacramento Valley.

California Resources Agency. 1978. Sacramento River Environmental Atlas. Prepared by the Upper Sacramento River Task Force for the California Resources Agency. Sacramento, Calif.

Johnson, Douglas. 1932. Streams and their significance. p. 78-96. In: S.A. Schumm (ed.). Benchmark papers in geology: river morphology. Dowden, Hutchinson, and Ross, Inc., Pennsylvania.

Lane, E.W. 1955. The importance of fluvial morphology in hydraulic engineering. p. 180-201. In: S.A. Schumm (ed.). Benchmark papers in geology: river morphology. Dowden, Hutchinson, and Ross, Inc., Pennsylvania.

Leopold, L.B., and T. Maddock, Jr. 1955. The hydraulic geometry of stream channels and some physiographic implications. USDI Geological Survey Professional Paper 252.

Maddock, T., Jr. 1976. A primer on floodplain dynamics and water conservation. J. Soil and Water Conservation 31(2):44-47.

Sacramento Magazine. 1976. Special Bicentennial issue. p. 21-25. July-August, 1976.

Simmons, D.B., and Fuat Senturk. 1977. Sediment transport technology. Water Resources Publication, Fort Collins, Colorado.

U.S. Army Corps of Engineers. 1978. Reconnaissance report on Sacramento River and tributaries bank protection and erosion control investigation, California. U.S. Army Corps of Engineers, Sacramento District, Sacramento, Calif.

REGENERATION OF RIPARIAN FORESTS OF THE CENTRAL VALLEY[1]

Jan Strahan[2]

Abstract.--Riparian forests of the Sacramento River have an overstory and a regeneration pattern corresponding to the successional stage and fluvial landform associated with the forest stands. Cottonwood/willow forests form initially on gravelbars. With development of the floodplain and maturation of the forest, other species enter. Floodplain forest regeneration is primarily box elder, black walnut, and valley oak with few sycamore and ash. Riverside floodplain forests differ from oxbow lake forests in species diversity, density, and reproduction. Land use and water development projects alter fluvial landforms and fluvial events to create changes in forest composition and regeneration.

INTRODUCTION

Riparian systems provide an excellent opportunity to study the effects of landform and fluvial processes on vegetation distribution and forest regeneration. Erosion, deposition, and lateral channel migration regulate both the distribution and development of vegetation in the riparian zone. With continual changes in landforms as a result of seasonal and catastrophic fluvial events, vegetation dynamics remain in a state of "perpetual succession" (Campbell and Green 1968).

The generalized patterns of vegetation zonation resulting from fluvial processes have been described and illustrated by Conard et al. (1977) for the Sacramento Valley region. The Sacramento River Atlas (Upper Sacramento River Task Force 1978) illustrates the pattern of zonation as well as the successional stages found in riparian forests. McGill (1975, 1979) has also correlated the existing riparian vegetation with fluvial landforms. Gaines (1974) has noted that the more extensive remaining riparian forests occur on islands, along bends in the river, and adjacent to oxbow lakes and other areas subject to flooding. As such, the remaining forests are a result of the most dynamic interplay between the fluvial system and riparian vegetation.

---

[1] Paper presented at the California Riparian Systems Conference. [University of California, Davis, September 17-19, 1981].

[2] Jan Strahan is a Graduate Student, Wildland Resource Science, Department of Forestry and Resource Management, University of California, Berkeley.

OBJECTIVES

The primary objective of this study was to develop regeneration data for the dominant tree species in the riparian forests of the Sacramento River. The information compiled can be used to assess present conditions and future trends of the forests. Work by Conard et al. (1977) and Michny et al. (1975) illustrates the variety of plant community structure and composition encountered in the riparian zone. Recognizing this, information was gathered at two levels to gain a more comprehensive picture of the structure and composition than previously developed. A detailed quantitative study was undertaken at three sites near Princeton, Glenn County, where disturbance to the fluvial system and vegetation is relatively minimal. At these sites, regeneration was examined relative to landform in different successional stages: a young forest (less than 30 years) associated with a gravelbar; an established forest (less than 70 years) located on the floodplain along the current river channel; and a mature forest (greater than 85 years) adjacent to an oxbow lake. To understand the larger patterns occurring along the length of the river, a broad survey of the river as a fluvial system was undertaken. This survey relates the effects of land use and water resource development projects to regeneration potential and stand development. The survey included a review of the geomorphic and ecological literature as well as air and ground reconnaissance.

METHODS

Floodplain vegetation was sampled using the point-centered quarter method of Cottam and Curtis (1956). Transects were located perpendicular to the water course at 50-m. intervals.

Points were centered at 10-m. intervals. At each point-center a 1-m. circular plot was used to tally the number of tree seedlings by species and a 10-m² circular plot was used for saplings. Seedlings were defined as having become established this season, and saplings were classed as other size-classes less than 10-cm. diameter-at-breast-height (DBH). Saplings were further classified into seven size-classes: (1) less than 0.3-cm.; (2) 0.3- to 1-cm.; (3) 1- to 1.5-cm.; (4) 1.6- to 2.4-cm.; (5) 2.5- to 5-cm.; (6) 5- to 7.5-cm.; and (7) 7.5- to 10-cm. Vegetative reproduction was not distinguished from seed reproduction as part of this tabulation, but was recorded wherever observed. Composition and cover of the shrubs and groundcover were also recorded. On gravelbars, seedling establishment was sampled through the use of 1-m² plots. Five-m. by 20-m. belt transects were used in the young forests on gravelbars and for levee sampling.

PHYSIOGRAPHY

Fluvial processes result in a number of characteristic landforms. Floods contribute to overbank deposition and aid in the building of floodplains. Lateral channel migration results in progressively building point bars which account for much of the existing natural topography of the Sacramento River riparian zone (Leopold 1973; Brice 1977). A cross-section through the riparian zone may have the following landforms: cut bank, point bar, natural levee, floodplain, oxbow lakes, meander scars, and islands. Variable surface features occur on these landforms, depending on the type of aggradation and frequency of flooding. The microtopography of the floodplain, consisting of ridges and swales, was formed by flows of old channels and is periodically altered by flood channel flows (Nanson and Beach 1977). These slight variations in elevation lead to considerable differences in soils and drainage conditions which provide the opportunity for tree species with different flood tolerances to occupy different elevations of the floodplains (Hosner and Minckler 1960). Vegetation, once established, also plays an active role in the depositional environment by acting as a sediment collector. Erosional bowls frequently form around trees and shrubs in the active channel.

Distinct landform changes occur in the downvalley progression of the Sacramento River. Brice (1977) describes the following features which change in the reach between Chico Landing and Colusa. As with most rivers, there is a downward progression in gravel size as one moves downvalley. The Sacramento River is classified as a gravel-bed stream from Red Bluff to Glenn. Below Glenn, it is a sand-bed stream. (Note: This shift was noted by Bryan in 1923, prior to the construction of Shasta Dam.)

Natural levees are composed of coarser materials deposited as floods flowed over the top of channel banks. Beginning at Hamilton City, the levees form a strip 4.8 to 8 km. (3 to 5 mi.) wide between Hamilton City and Colusa. Levees are discontinuous for several miles south of Stony Creek and continuous from near Butte City southward.

Brice (1977) also reviews the changes in the river which have occurred since white settlement, using the "natural" river of 1870 as a baseline. According to Brice, channel sinuosity has decreased while channel width has increased. Morphologic changes have been attributed to both clearing of riparian vegetation and the effect of levees in reducing overflow areas. These changes have caused the main river channel to be scoured deeper and wider and water velocities to increase. Meander loops from Butte City to Colusa are confined by artificial levees and tend to be distorted and unstable. Flow regulation by Shasta Dam has resulted in an increase in mean monthly flows at Red Bluff for June, July, and August from 6,190 ft³/sec. (1889 to 1944) to 10,520 ft³/sec. (1945 to 1970). Maximum observed flood peaks at Red Bluff before regulation attained about 250,000 ft³/sec. with subsequent peaks of 140,000 ft³/sec.

The California State Department of Water Resources (McGill 1979) identified 29,352 ha. of riparian zone from Butte Creek to Keswick Dam in 1977. This includes 3,828 ha. high terrace riparian vegetation (rarely flooded), 3,395 ha. low terrace (frequently flooded), 2,096 ha. gravelbars, 162 ha. oxbow lakes, and 3,942 ha. water surface, for a total of 13,423 ha. undeveloped lands. Agricultural lands comprise 14,852 ha. of the zone and 1,097 ha. are in other developed uses. Of particular significance in this study is the reduction of high terrace lands by 15% in the five years between 1972 and 1977, mostly through agricultural conversion. Erosional losses from bank undercutting are not concurrently offset by building processes.

These variations in physiography have major ecological significance in the riparian zone. Lindsey et al. (1961) attributed the different plant communities to the differences in soil-water relationships resulting from physiographic variation. The amount of floodplain activity and influence of the river on landforms results in different degrees of community stability. Wilson (1970) found stabilized forest communities developed along the Missouri River floodplain after the river had been stabilized by a series of dams and reservoirs. Campbell and Green (1968) link "perpetual succession" to rivers which actively meander over their floodplains. They found the frequent shifting of landforms and channels resulted in early successional stages occupying the majority of the floodplain. Everitt (1968) and Fonda (1974) attributed spatial distribution of the riparian plant communities primarily to the meandering pattern of the river.

Along the Sacramento River, physiographic variation was sampled through the use of transects perpendicular to the river. The three main landform categories sampled were: gravelbar, floodplain adjacent to the riverside, and floodplain adjacent to oxbow lakes. These three categories are representative of a sequence of landform and soil development which led to progressively older forests with distance away from the channel.

FOREST ESTABLISHMENT AND COMPOSITION

Establishment and distribution of species in riparian forests is controlled by the interaction between fluvial events and ecological requirements of the species.

Fluvial Processes

The water regime of the river influences distribution through both seasonal fluctuations and catastrophic occurrences (Sigafoos 1964; Bell and Johnson 1974). Both the low-flow regime and high flows or floods causing inundation influence distribution. The low-flow regime, which provides freshly exposed surfaces, is the most important factor for successful seedling establishment and is critical for survival of young trees.

Whether the result of flooding is an adverse or beneficial effect on the plant is dependent on the frequency, duration, and depth of inundation (Teskey and Hinckley 1978). Susceptibility to flooding affects species location on the floodplain relative to the height of the water table. Tolerance to flooding may also vary between young and old trees of the same species (Lindsey et al. 1961). Inundation may result in the death of young or established plants through mechanical abrasion or through lack of sufficient soil oxygen. For established dormant plants, floods deposit soil nutrients necessary to maintain high productivity rates (Johnson et al. 1976). Time between major disturbances determines the amount of forest stands that will be in early, middle, or late successional stages throughout the floodplain. Both scour and fill processes, resulting from high flows, determine vegetation patterns: a flood may eliminate a portion of a mature forest through bank undercutting with the undercut material forming new depositional surfaces for seedling establishment further downstream. Aside from being the agent of plant mortality, flooding can also cause topping or "flood-training" (Sigafoos 1964) of both young and mature trees, resulting in the formation of sprout groups.

Ecological Characteristics

Ecological characteristics of the dominant tree species are important determinants of successional events in the riparian zone. Of particular importance are the light-weight seeds of the pioneer species dispersed by wind or water. Seed disperal at the time of a falling water level is essential for successful establishment of the pioneer species. These characteristics result in the initial colonization of a

site by the pioneer species cottonwood (Populus fremontii) and willow (Salix spp.). Shade intolerance of cottonwood and willow has been noted to be the limiting factor in preventing their establishment in mature forests as well as the need for a mineral seedbed for germination (Sigafoos 1964; Johnson et al. 1976; Lindsey et al. 1961). Mid-successional stages have species with both light-weight seeds (box elder, ash) and heavy seeds (black walnut, oak). However, they all are able to germinate through litter and under the canopy of a cottonwood/willow forest.

Results

The interaction of fluvial events, landforms, and autecological requirements has led to the development of heterogeneous forest stands along the Sacramento River. The following tree species were encountered frequently in the floodplain forests: box elder (Acer negundo ssp. californicum), Fremont cottonwood (Populus fremontii), willow (Salix spp., including S. hindsiana, S. laevigata, S. goodingii, S. lasiandra, and S. lasiolepis), and black walnut (Juglans hindsii). Sycamore (Platanus racemosa), valley oak (Quercus lobata) and ash (Fraxinus latifolia) occurred less frequently.

Overstory composition associated with each landform in the intensive survey is shown in table 1. This mixed riparian forest (of the species listed above) is found in different successional stages along the majority of the floodplain. As shown by the table, early stages are usually pure cottonwood/willow. Mid- and late-successional stages frequently have a cottonwood/willow overstory and oak and sycamore ocasionally. Box elder, black walnut, and ash comprise the second canopy layer in these later stands. The broad survey also revealed different types of forest stands than encountered in the intensive survey of the river. There are several older groves of pure oak or oak/sycamore on high terraces. Within the later stages of the mixed forest, small stands of pure box elder or box elder/black walnut, approximately $200/m^2$ or less, were encountered in several locations. In the pure box elder stands average densities were 100 stems per 100 m^2. In these stands, saplings from 2.5 to 7.5 cm. were most frequent with no stems greater than 15 cm. found. Several standing dead stems and many small stems on the ground were evidence of an even higher density at one time. Shade was sufficient to prevent groundcover but a few Prunus sp. and valley oak seedlings were in the stand.

REGENERATION

Establishment and survival of riparian species are related to landforms and a sequence of fluvial events (table 2). Most seedling establishment occurs along the newly exposed surfaces of gravelbars and is significantly

Table 1.--Riverside and oxbow lake riparian forests: overstory density and composition. (n = 178)

RIVERSIDE FORESTS

	Density (trees/ha)	Relative density	Basal area (m^2/ha)
Acer negundo	1.04	1%	0.03
Ficus carica	-	-	-
Fraxinus latifolia	-	-	-
Juglans hindsii	1.04	1%	0.01
Platanus racemosa	-	-	-
Populus fremontii	53.8	52%	6.52
Quercus lobata	-	-	-
Sambucus mexicana	-	-	-
Salix lasiolepis	-	-	-
Salix spp. (tree)	48.6	47%	2.83
Total	104.4	100%	9.38

OXBOW LAKE FORESTS

	Density (trees/ha)	Relative density	Basal area (m^2/ha)
Acer negundo	42.1	13%	0.83
Ficus carica	16.2	4.8%	0.17
Fraxinus latifolia	6.4	1.9%	0.39
Juglans hindsii	40.4	12%	3.07
Platanus racemosa	16.2	4.8%	8.63
Populus fremontii	57.2	17%	38.99
Quercus lobata	74.1	22%	10.56
Sambucus mexicana	9.8	3%	0.22
Salix lasiolepis	3.4	1%	0.03
Salix spp. (tree)	70.7	21%	13.07
Total	336.5	100%	75.96

different in species composition than regeneration in the established forests.

Gravelbar Regeneration

Seasonal variation in flow regimes greatly influences establishment and survival of the pioneer species on gravelbars. During the winter, streamflows must remove humus and freshly fallen leaf litter from the surface so that the seeds land on mineral soil. A receding water level in late spring and early summer must coincide with cottonwood and willow seed dispersal. As establishment is directly related to the low-flow line (McBride and Strahan 1983), a 1-m. wide band of seedlings and saplings is often found along the river's edge. Prior to further flooding, seedlings must achieve sufficient size to withstand mechanical injury. The subsurface of bars must remain moist throughout the summer in order for the seedlings to withstand late summer drought. Late summer desiccation results in the death of many seedlings (McBride and Strahan ibid.). Winter floods often wash away or bury many seedlings. While density in the initial stages of establishment on bars is extremely high (table 3), the latter two factors account for significant mortality.

Floodplain Regeneration

Within the mature riparian forests of the floodplain, the link between regeneration and the flow regime of the river is not as direct. The most influential flows here are the floods which may remove seedlings established for a season or longer and at the same time prepare seedbeds. While low flows have less direct influence on these species than on those of pioneer species, McGill (1979) attributed some losses on high terraces of riparian vegetation to the lack of occasional flooding during the drought of 1976 and 1977.

In the mature forest, young cottonwoods and willows are rare while box elder and black walnut are common (table 2). The latter two species enter at a later successional stage, establishing through litter and under the shade of a cottonwood/willow canopy. While regeneration in the floodplain is currently occurring primarily in swales or on the banks of swales, young trees are much more scattered throughout the forest and much less dense (table 2), than on gravelbars. Some riverside forests 30-40 years old have little reproduction. Thus, distinct compositional differences exist between reproduction in the riverside floodplain forests and the oxbow lake forests with an increase in seedling density occurring in the oxbow lake forests. Factors limiting successful seedling establishment in the floodplain forests appear to be associated primarily with extremely dense groundcover. Grape vines were noted entwined around many dead saplings.

Succession

The successional progression of forest stands in the riparian zone begins with seedling establishment on gravelbars. The amount of available soil moisture may be an important factor governing these zonal sequences, with the younger land surfaces significantly drier than the older ones. Vegetation establishes on fresh surfaces of the point bar when sufficient sediment accumulates above summer low-water levels. Young cottonwood and willow stands do not form a continuous protective cover on the gravelbar because of the river cutting across point bars during floods. Providing floods do not alter the bar significantly, plant colonization creates additional deposits. Several inches of soil may be deposited by a single flood. As the bar builds higher, it is less frequently flooded. This deposition, in combination with channel migration, results in a stabilized floodplain developing from a shifting gravelbar.

If bars remain relatively undisturbed for a number of years, deposition gradually occurs until the floodplain supports mature cottonwood/willow forests. Eventually an understory of shade tolerant species enters the forests. Should the forests be missed by flood scouring

Oxbow Lake Forests

Species	Seedlings	Saplings (stem diameter classes in cm.)						
		0.3	0.4-1	1.1-1.5	1.6-2.4	2.5-5	5.1-7.5	7.5-10
Acer negundo	385	10	-	154	144	29	-	19
Ficus carica	289	-	-	58	135	29	39	-
Fraxinus latifolia	-	-	-	-	-	-	10	-
Juglans hindsii	-	-	29	29	154	39	29	-
Platanus racemosa	-	-	-	-	77	10	10	-
Quercus lobata	866	-	19	29	10	-	-	19
Sambucus mexicana	-	-	-	10	-	10	-	-
Salix lasiolepis	-	-	-	10	10	-	-	-
Prunus sp.	-	-	-	19	19	-	-	-

Riverside Forests

Species	Seedlings	Saplings (stem diameter classes in cm.)						
		0.3	0.4-1	1.1-1.5	1.6-2.4	2.5-5	5.1-7.5	7.5-10
Acer negundo	96	-	-	-	-	-	-	-
Juglans hindsii	-	-	-	-	29	29	19	-

for many years, the cottonwood/willow may be replaced by these understory species. In places where the river has moved progressively across the floodplain in a uniform direction, a sequence of stand ages is produced, chronologically arranged in the direction of bend migration with the youngest stands nearest the river.

A broad perspective of Sacramento River successional stages is available through aerial reconnaissance. Bands of vegetation of successive ages can be found to occupy the floodplain (Murray et al. 1978). Channel lateral migration studies (Brice 1977) show the maximum ages of the forests in the intensive survey to be 32 years for the developing forest, 73 years for the riverside forest, and >85 years for the oxbow lake forest. Everitt (1968) noted similar findings for the Little Missouri River with germination and growth of cottonwood intricately related to the discharge of the river, movement of the channel, and development of the flood-plain. Tree age increases both upvalley and away from the channel according to Everitt (ibid.) and is the result of the rise of sapling thickets along gravelbars.

Physiognomy

The forest structure and physiognomy differ considerably according to the age of forests and landforms on which they develop. Young cotton-wood/willow forests are dense with many small trees, but have few other woody species. These gravelbar forests develop in progressive bands, each associated with a rise in elevation of the ridge-swale topography. In the older cottonwood/willow forests, the trees are tall and widely spaced, allowing sufficient light for shrub and herb development. Lianas are prominent in some stands and non-existent in others. Older forests have a two-layer tree canopy and are denser than

Table 3.—Characteristics of progressive bands of cottonwood on gravelbars.

Type	Species	Density (/m^2)	Age Range (yrs)	Aver. Dia. (cm)	Max. Dia. (cm)	Aver. Ht. (m)	Aver. Stand Width (m)
Seedlings at stream edge	cottonwood	124.0	-	-	-	0.3	1
	sandbar willow	32.0	-	-	-	-	-
	tree willow	28.0	-	-	-	-	-
1st Sapling Band: beginning of ridge-swale topography	cottonwood	23.6	1-3	0.9	2.5	2.1	2
	sandbar willow	17.2	-	0.5	1	-	-
	tree willow	4.0	-	-	-	-	-
2nd Sapling Band: swale	cottonwood	64.0	1-3	1.3	5.5	3.6	3
	sandbar willow	72.0	-	-	-	-	-
	tree willow	4.0	-	-	-	-	-
3rd Sapling Band: swale banks	cottonwood	76.0	1-4	4	8	6	4
	sandbar willow	20.4	-	1.6	3.1	-	-
	tree willow	14.4	-	1.8	3.5	-	-
4th Sapling Band: ridge	cottonwood	10.4	2-4	1;7.5	12	8	13
	sandbar willow	4.0	-	1.8	3.5	-	-
	tree willow	2.0	-	2.5	4	-	-
5th Sapling Band: ridge and banks of swales	cottonwood	2.0	2-11	8	15	10+	20
	sandbar willow	3.4	-	2	5	-	-
	tree willow	1.0	-	7	11	-	-

the mid-successional stage forests. Forests adjacent to cut banks are more frequently composed of alder, oak, or sycamore than are the forest edges that develop behind bars. Young oaks and sycamores were only found in mixed species stands, while old oaks and sycamores are found in groves without the associates. Diameter-classes (table 4) of the oxbow lake and riverside forests show the difference in species composition and structure of the two forests.

Reproductive Strategies

The most common method of reproduction is by seed. However, throughout the floodplain vegetative reproduction is also common. Sandbar willow (Salix hindsiana) was frequently observed sprouting on higher portions of the gravelbars. This was explained by Wilson (1970) who noted an adaptive value of vegetative reproduction on sandy soils where seedling establishment is limited by surface soil moisture availability. Sprouting was also recorded on the floodplain in areas infrequently flooded: older sycamore trees frequently had basal sprouts. In areas which undergo severe mechanical abrasion from flows (banks downstream from reservoir flow releases or banks receiving a high degree of wave action from boats), vegetative reproduction was as common as seedling establishment.

Survival

In the developing cottonwood/willow forests, survival is reduced by both drought and winter flooding as well as shade and competition from groundcover. Significant attrition occurs for different stages of cottonwood development (compare tables 2 and 3). Floodplain forests had many dead trees, probably a result of the 1976-1977 drought (McGill 1979).

DISCUSSION

Initial Establishment

The study indicates that the initial establishment of riparian forests is along point bars. Cottonwood and willow can be regarded as classic pioneer species; within this region, their seeds germinate almost exclusively on fully exposed alluvium recently deposited by the river. Not a single seedling of these species was found in any of the floodplain samples (table 3). This indicates that neither functions as a gap-phase species (Watt 1947) by establishing seedlings in forest openings following disturbance. Smaller stems of cottonwood/willow in the floodplain forests (table 4) appear to result from suppression or sprouting (Note: the two size-classes in table 3, plot 4 had all established at the same time). In areas with sufficient light, flood deposits of fresh alluvium may provide areas for a younger age class to develop. Other dominant tree species, such as box elder and black walnut, all have the ability to germinate and grow under the cottonwood/willow overstory. Without disturbance, they in time could replace the cottonwood/willow overstory.

Table 4.--Riverside and oxbow lake forests: diameter size-
classes of dominant species. (Stems/ha; all size-
classes in cm.).

Riverside Forests

Species	Seedling	Sapling	10-20	21-30	31-40	41-50	51-60	61-70	71-80	81-90	91-100	101-110	111+
Acer negundo	96	-	1.5	-	-	-	-	-	-	-	-	-	-
Juglans hindsii	-	77	1.5	-	-	-	-	-	-	-	-	-	-
Populus fremontii	-	-	10.4	11.8	14.8	5.9	8.8	5.9	-	-	-	-	-
Salix spp. (tree)	-	-	19.4	20.7	5.9	1.5	3.0	-	-	-	-	-	-

Oxbow Lake Forests

Species	Seedling	Sapling	10-20	21-30	31-40	41-50	51-60	61-70	71-80	81-90	91-100	101-110	111+
Acer negundo	385	356	35.6	3.2	-	-	-	-	-	-	-	-	-
Juglans hindsii	-	280	22.7	3.2	6.5	6.5	3.2	-	-	-	-	-	-
Platanus racemosa	-	97	-	-	-	-	-	3.2	-	3.2	3.2	-	6.4
Populus fremontii	-	-	-	3.2	3.2	3.2	9.7	3.2	3.2	6.4	6.4	3.2	16.4
Quercus lobata	866	77	22.6	9.7	22.6	3.2	9.7	3.2	3.2	3.2	-	-	-
Salix spp. (tree)	-	20	3.2	12.9	16.2	12.9	13.0	3.2	9.7	-	-	-	-

Structure and Composition

The data also show that the structure and composition of the overstory are strongly related to stand age and horizontal and vertical position of the floodplain. For example, cottonwood and willow predominate in young stands on low terraces near the river. Ash, box elder, and black walnut enter cottonwood/willow stands over time and predominate in stands away from the river. Oak and sycamore are found in old stands on high terraces with the other dominants and along banks high above the river. Reproduction in these stands is very limited (table 5). Thus, species diversity initially increases as stands age, reaches a maximum in stands with mixtures of both pioneer and later successional species, and may decline slightly in oldest stands.

The high frequency of sapling box elder and black walnut in cottonwood/willow forests suggsts that the next successional stage will consist predominantly of these two species. However, although box elder was found in small pure patches, there is no evidence available at this time that large scale replacement of the cottonwood/willow type along the Sacramento River by these two species is occurring. Despite the establishment of cottonwood only on point bars, mature cottonwoods remain throughout the floodplain. Lateral channel migration occurs frequently enough to retain cottonwoods and willows in most stands except the few high terraces where only oak and sycamore remain.

Cultural Impacts on Regeneration

The Sacramento River riparian system is much altered both in its natural flow regime and floodplain characteristics. Land use and water resource development projects may have a significant effect on the current regeneration situation and on the future regeneration potential. While further research into these areas is necessary to provide quantitative data for the Sacramento River, correlation with other major rivers provides us with clues to changes caused by alteration of the riparian zone. Historical research, although qualitative, provides a picture of the riparian forests of the past upon which we may also draw.

Table 5.--Riparian oak woodland: stem diameter-classes.
(Stems/ha; diameter-classes in cm.)

Species	Seed. Sapl.	10-20	21-30	31-40	41-50	51-60	61-70	71-80	81-90	91-100	101-110
Acer negundo	-	3.6	-	-	-	-	-	-	-	-	-
Platanus racemosa	-	-	-	-	-	3.6	-	-	-	-	-
Populus fremontii	-	-	-	-	-	3.6	-	-	-	-	-
Quercus lobata	-	-	7.3	-	14.6	14.6	21.8	7.3	10.9	14.5	10.9
Salix spp.	-	-	-	3.6	-	-	-	-	-	-	-

Land Clearing

Removal of all but the frequently flooded areas of the riparian forests has had obvious impacts on the reduction of certain species such as oak and sycamore in the Sacramento Valley. Thompson (1961) cites several descriptions of the riparian forests prior to extensive clearing which speak of forests of oak, cottonwood, and sycamore. While the oak is found in large groves in several areas along the upper river, individual sycamores are scattered very infrequently throughout the forests. Ongoing reduction of the high terrace lands (McGill 1979) will contribute to a further reduction of these two magnificent species.

Introduced Species

The introduction of exotic species in the area has also changed species composition. For example, figs (Ficus carica) in patches in the forest create such a dense shade that reproduction under them is limited to sprouting figs. While these patches are fairly small in extent (100 m^2), they have created a major change in the localities in which they are found by their high reproduction (table 2). Prune seedlings (Prunus sp.), and tree of heaven (Ailanthus altissima) are also found in many areas along the river.

The native black walnut (Juglans hindsii), now so common in the riparian forests, appears to have become widespread in the forest through the use of its rootstock for commercial propagation of the English walnut (Juglans regia). The only population noted along the Sacramento River prior to the arrival of European man was between Freeport and Rio Vista (Fuller 1978). This was discovered by Richard Brindsley Hinds of the Sulphur Expedition in 1837 (Thomsen 1963).

Grazing

Grazing of the forest may lower reproduction densities in floodplain areas. When grazed, forests are kept clear of groundcover and young trees. When grazing is excluded, the regrowth of a thick understory which may prevent seedlings from establishing has occurred in the riparian forests. Thus, grazing could be responsible for the lack of establishment of certain age-classes in the flood-induced age structure through seedling elimination. Further work is necessary to substantiate the degree to which this has affected the Central Valley riparian forests. Carothers (1977) had shown it to be a major cause of reduction in reproduction in the Southwest riparian forests.

Water Resource Development

Levees: Aerial photography of the river reveals a large-scale change resulting from the artificial levees. Above Colusa, artificial levees are either non-existent or are far away from the channel. This allows lateral migration to form point bars at most bends and provides new surfaces for cottonwood and willow establishment. Below Colusa, the levees are adjacent to the river channel preventing point bar formation. Aerial photography (Murray et al. 1978) depicts 18 bars forming in a 20-river-mile (RM) reach above Colusa and only four bars forming in a 20-RM reach below Colusa. Bars below Colusa are much smaller in size than those above Colusa. Without the initial landform on which to colonize, riparian forest formation and regeneration will not continue in the same pattern.

New Landforms: Development of man-made levees has caused a disruption of gravelbar formation thereby limiting reproduction. However, the levees themselves could provide new habitats for the development of new forests, providing current management practices were discontinued. The following species were common on levees: alder, ash, fig, cottonwood, valley oak, sandbar willow, and tree willow. Densities for saplings ranged from $3/100m^2$ for most species up to $85/100m^2$ for willows and cottonwood <2.5 cm. stem diameter. Regeneration density was partially dependent on levee management. Survival in burned areas was mainly in swales with sandbar willow and a few sapling oaks near the top of the levee. Species zonation is very noticeable with oaks often lining the tops of the levees; alder, ash, and cottonwood near the water level; and willows in swales. Weirs also provide a place where seasonal water flows and abundant light have created an oak phase of riparian forests along their levees.

Flow Regulation: The impacts of controlled flows on seedling establishment and survival have two effects. On certain rivers, willow encroachment on the streambanks has occurred as a result of controlled flows (Pelzman 1973). Pelzman (ibid.) attributed this to a prolonged soil moisture which allowed greater establishment and survival. McGill (1979) and Brice (1977) have also noted an increase in vegetated bar surfaces for the Sacramento River. They both attributed this to the moderating effect of Shasta Dam which has resulted in the lack of scour. The data for seedling establishment for the Sacramento River as a controlled stream reveals a lower density of seedlings (table 3) than similar data collected for a non-controlled stream (McBride and Strahan 1983). This suggests that the annual falling of the water level that coincided with seed dispersal and allowed abundant germination on the non-controlled stream did not occur on the Sacramento River. Daily flow data (USDI Geological Survey 1978, 1979; 1980 and 1981 data not available) for the Butte City gauging station reveal a wide fluctuation of streamflow with high flows following low flows frequently during the months of May-September. Thus, the absence of a continual lowering of the water level could have resulted in a limited amount of seedling establishment this year. However, the controlled flows may result in a higher survival percentage through lack of scouring. Also, a continual provision of moisture throughout the summer would reduce losses from desiccation for those seedlings which do become established.

Land and Water Effects: Forest composition for the entire Sacramento River riparian zone must differ from the earlier forests because only frequently flooded areas remain to be sampled. Thus our results probably show a more flood-tolerant community dominating the area than we once had. With the decrease in bank stability of the river (Brice 1877), bank erosion has caused the loss of high terrace lands resulting in further decrease of sycamore and oak forests. Infrequent flooding and higher stands due to controlled flows and levees has probably resulted in the development of a greater proportion of older trees, since flooding of the areas does not clear out the undergrowth and provide bare areas for establishment to occur. As the rate of meandering is a major factor in determining the proportion of the floodplain in pioneer, transi-tional, and later successional stages, changes in meandering noted by Brice (1977) would suggest different proportions of forest stands in these stages may occur in the future than we had in the past.

SUMMARY

Existing riparian forests have been shown to have an overstory and regeneration that corresponds to landforms and fluvial processes as well as successional stages. Establishment, growth, maturation, and death of floodplain trees are merged with the complete flow regime of the river and the erosion and deposition of sediment. The heterogeneity of forests is an indicator of a dynamic fluvial system. Establishment of the forests begins on gravelbars with the development of a cottonwood/willow type, making bars a critical landform in forest development. With deposition and time, the forests develop and mature, with understory species of box elder and black walnut becoming frequent. While regeneration on the bars is almost totally cottonwood and willow, regeneration on the floodplain is predominantly box elder and black walnut, especially on the low terraces. High terraces have minor amounts of oak, sycamore, and ash establishing. Forests surrounding oxbow lakes are older and have higher densities of reproduction than riverside floodplain forests. Water resource development projects and land uses have significant impacts on regeneration potential of riparian forests.

LITERATURE CITED

Bell, D.T., and F.L. Johnson. 1974. Flood-caused mortality around Illinois reservoirs. Trans. Ill. State Acad. Sci. 67(1):28-37.

Brice, James. 1977. Lateral migration of the Middle Sacramento River, California. USDI Geological Survey Water-Res. Investigations 77-43. 51 p.

Bryan, Kirk. 1923. Geology and ground-water resources of Sacramento Valley, California. USDI Geological Survey Water-Supply Paper 495. 285 p.

Campbell, C.J., and Win Green. 1968. Perpetual succession of stream-channel vegetation in a semiarid region. J. Ariz. Acad. Sci. 5:86-98.

Carothers, S.W. 1977. Importance, preservation, and management of riparian habitat: an overview. p. 2-4. In: R.R. Johnson and D.A. Jones (tech. coord.). Importance, preservation, and management of riparian habitat. USDA Forest Service General Technical Report RM-43. Fort Collins, Colo.

Conard, S.G., R.L. MacDonald, and R.F. Holland. 1977. Riparian vegetation and flora of the Sacramento Valley. In: A. Sands (ed.). Riparian forests in California: their ecology and conservation. Institute of Ecology Pub. 15. 122 p. University of California, Davis.

Cottam, Grant, and J.T. Curtis. 1956. The use of distance measures in phytosociological sampling. Ecology 37(3):451-460.

Dietz, R.A. 1952. The evolution of a gravel bar. Missouri Bot. Garden Annals 39:249-254.

Everitt, B.L. 1968. Use of the cottonwood in an investigation of the recent history of a flood plain. American J. of Sci. 266:417-439.

Fonda, R.W. 1974. Forest succession in relation to river terrace development in Olympic National Park, Washington. Ecology 55: 927-942.

Fuller, T.C. 1978. *Juglans hindsii* Jepson ex. R.E. Smith. Northern California black walnut. Rare plant status report. California Native Plant Society.

Gaines, D. 1974. Review of the status of the Yellow-billed Cuckoo in California: Sacramento Valley populations. Condor 76: 204-209.

Hosner, J.F., and L.S. Minckler. 1960. Bottomland hardwood forests of southern Illinois--regeneration and succession. Ecology 44(1):29-41.

Johnson, W.C., R.L. Burgess, and W.R. Keammerer. 1976. Forest overstory vegetation and environment on the Missouri River floodplain in North Dakota. Ecol. Mono. 46:59-84.

Leopold, L.B. 1973. River channel change with time: an example. Geol. Soc. Amer. Bull. 84(6):1845-1860.

Lindsey, A.A., R.O. Petty, D.K. Sterling, and W. Van Asdall. 1961. Vegetation and environment along the Wabash and Tippecanoe Rivers. Ecol. Mono. 31(2):105-156.

McBride, J.R., and Jan Strahan. 1983. Influence of fluvial processes on patterns of woodland succession along Dry Creek, Sonoma County, California. In: R.E. Warner and K.M. Hendrix (ed.). California Riparian Systems. [University of California, Davis, September 17-19, 1981.] University of California Press, Berkeley.

McGill, R.R., Jr. 1975. Land use changes in the Sacramento River riparian zone, Redding to Colusa. California Dept. of Water Resources, Northern Dist. Report. 23 p.

McGill, R.R., Jr. 1979. Land use change in the Sacramento River riparian zone, Redding to Colusa. An update--1972 to 1977. 34 p. California Department of of Water Resources, Sacramento.

Michny, F.J., D. Boos, and F. Wernette. 1975. Riparian habitat and avian densities along the Sacramento River. California Dept. of Fish and Game Adm. Report 75-1.

Murray, Burns, and Kienlen. 1978. Retention of riparian vegetation. Sacramento River, Tisdale Weir to Hamilton City. California Dept. of Water Resources, The Reclamation Board.

Nanson, G.C., and H.F. Beach. 1977. Forest succession and sedimentation on a meandering-river floodplain, northeast British Columbia, Canada. J. Biogeog. 4:229-251.

Pelzman, R.J. 1973. Causes and possible prevention of riparian plant encroachment on anadromous fish habitat. California Dept. of Fish and Game. Adm. Report 73-1.

Sigafoos, R.S. 1964. Botanical evidence of floods and floodplain deposition. USDI Geological Survey Prof. Paper 485-A. 35 p.

Sudworth, G.B. 1908. Forests trees of the Pacific slope. USDA Forest Service. 441 p.

Teskey, R.O., and T.M. Hinckley. 1978. Impact of water level changes on woody riparian and wetland communities. Vol. 1: Plant and soil responses to flooding. USDI Fish and Wildlife Service. 30 p.

Thompson, Kenneth. 1961. Riparian forests of the Sacramento Valley, California. Ann. Assoc. Amer. Geog. 51(3):294-315.

Thomsen, H.H. 1963. *Juglans hindsii*. The Central California black walnut, native or introduced? Madrono 19(1):1-10.

USDI Geological Survey, 1978, 1979. Water resources data for California. Vol. 4: Northern Central Valley basins and the Great Basin from Honey Lake to Oregon state line.

Upper Sacramento River Task Force. 1978. Sacramento River environmental atlas. California Dept. of Water Resources.

Watt, A.S. 1947. Pattern and process in the plant community. J. Ecol. 35(1&2):1-22.

Wilson, R.E. 1970. Succession in stands of *Populus deltoides* along the Missouri River in southeastern South Dakota. Amer. Midl. Nat. 83(2):330-342.

PLANT SUCCESSION ON MERCED RIVER DREDGE SPOILS[1]

Thomas H. Whitlow and Conrad J. Bahre[2]

Abstract.--One hundred and nine species of vascular plants were collected from 22 stands at six sites in the 2,800 ha. (7,000 ac.) of dredge spoils along the Merced River near Snelling, California. Five sites were dredged, one per year, in 1910, 1928, 1938, 1941, and 1950; one was not dredged. Association analysis of the stand data identified four species groups closely related to dredge-spoil topography and moisture availability. In addition, the program ordinated stand data according to floristic affinities. The ordination showed no age-dependent patterns.

INTRODUCTION

Nearly 24,000 ha. (60,000 ac.) of flood-plains and terraces in the northeastern part of California's Central Valley were mined by huge gold dredges from 1898 to 1968 (fig. 1). In all, 12 major gold fields were dredged between Butte Creek and the Merced River (Clark 1970; Wagner 1970). The dredge spoils consist of wormlike ridges of unsorted boulders and cobbles with intervening swales of fine-textured soils and standing water (fig. 2). Except for a few areas of limited extent leveled for housing or used as a source of aggregate, the spoils now serve as little more than poor grazing lands and wildlife habitat. Nevertheless, they offer plant ecologists a novel means of studying plant succession because the spoils are of similar structure and can be dated to the week of deposition as far back as 70 years. Summarized here is a preliminary investigation of successional patterns in the Snelling dredge field (fig. 3).

The Snelling dredge field, mined between 1907 and 1951 (Aubury 1910; Davis and Carlson 1952; Clark 1970), consists of 2,800 ha. (7,000 ac.) of spoils paralleling the Merced River near the town of Snelling (fig. 4). Snelling (79 m. [259 ft.] above sea level) has an average annual precipitation of 840 mm. (33.2 in.), most of which falls between November and April (California Department of Water Resources 1980). Local vegetation is valley oak woodland (sensu Griffin 1977), grassland (sensu Heady 1977),

[1] Paper presented at the California Riparian Systems Conference. [University of California, Davis, September 17-19, 1981].

[2] Thomas H. Whitlow is Research Associate, Urban Horticulture Institute, Cornell University, Ithaca, N.Y. Conrad J. Bahre is Assistant Professor, Department of Geography, University of California, Davis.

Figure 1.--Yuba Dredge No. 2. This dredge, once owned by Yuba Goldfields, was brought to Snelling from Montana in 1935. Only 23 m. (75 ft.) long, it was one of the smallest dredges ever used at Snelling. It was dismantled in 1939 and taken to Chico.

Figure 2.--Dredge spoil mound tops. Note cobbles and boulders as well as sparse vegetation cover. Trees in the swales are Salix spp. and Populus fremontii.

and riparian forest (sensu Conard et al. 1977).

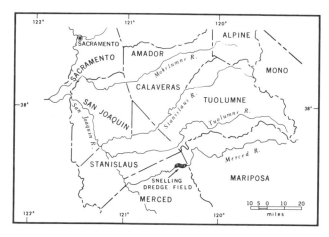

Figure 3.--Map of east-central California. Note the Snelling field.

The gold is mostly flour gold derived from the pocket belt of the Mother Lode in Mariposa County, which is traversed by the upper course of the Merced River. It is found in the Quaternary gravel deposits of the modern river which range in depth from 5.4 to 11 m. (18 to 36 ft.).

Bucket-line gold dredges, constructed chiefly of steel, were so heavy and cumbersome they had to be assembled in a dry pit. Water from a canal was turned into the pit, allowing the dredge to float (Aubury 1910). The dredges were only capable of digging 7.6 to 9.1 m. (25 to 30 ft.) below the surface of the dredge pond. Their earth-moving capacity, depending on their size, ranged from 153,000 to 260,000 cu. m. (200,000 to 340,000 cu. yd.) per month.

Individual dredge piles usually differ in slope and elevation. Fines may or may not be found on the surfaces. Whereas some dredge piles are in neat rows, most are rather haphazard. Differences in spoil topography reflect dredging depths, the particular ways in which the tailing

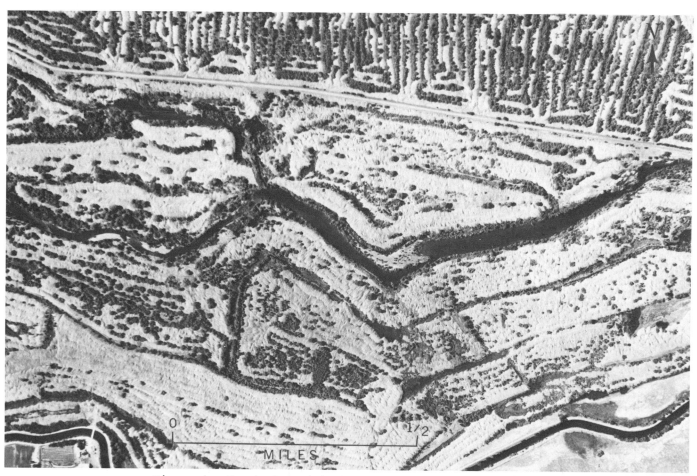

Figure 4.--Vertical aerial photograph of part of the Snelling dredge field. Note tree-lined swales and sparsely vegetated spoil tops. The oldest spoils do not necessarily have tree-lined swales. In some cases, the spoils were stacked so that no swales were left for trees to colonize (photograph taken in 1959).

69

stackers were operated, and whether overburden was sent directly to the stacker without sorting.

METHODOLOGY

Five study-sites in the Snelling dredge field were selected and dated using USDI Geological Survey 1:24,000 topographic maps, large-scale aerial photographs, mining progress maps, interviews with local residents, and records in the Merced County Recorder's Office (table 1). These sites were dredged, one per year, in 1910, 1928, 1938, 1941, and 1950. One undredged site was selected as a control.

Stands on mound tops, high swales, and low swales at each dredge site were subjectively chosen to conduct a complete floristic inventory. This inventory was needed to detect floristic distinctions between sites of different ages. The sharp gradients and irregular depositional patterns of the spoils made random and systematic sampling techniques impractical and highly sensitive to artifacts of sample location. Edge effects were minimized by placing the stands no closer than 100 m. (300 ft.) from the edges of the spoils. The stands, which varied in size and shape, were inventoried using the Braun-Blanquet relevé method (Mueller-Dombois and Ellenberg 1974). High swales were inventoried in toto, while mound tops and low swales were inventoried along belt transects whose lengths were designed to include all species in a particular habitat. The sampling method was designed to eliminate minimum area problems arising from the use of discrete sample sizes, to represent the total flora, and to establish within-stand homogeneity while maximizing the possibility of between-stand differences.

The stand data were analyzed using the association analysis program of Ceska and Roemer (1971). This program, which identifies associational relationships between species using pre-established phyto-sociological criteria, arranges species into groups of co-occurrence and ordinates stands according to floristic similarities. Of the program's five different "inside-outside" rules, the 50%-inside:20%-outside rule was chosen because it included the highest percentage of the entire flora and hence accounted for more variations than the other rules. According to this rule, a species belongs to a species group if it occurs in 50% of the stands in its group and does not occur in more than 20% of the stands outside of its group. A stand belongs to a species group when it contains 50% of the species in the group. Field work was carried out between March and May 1980, during the peak bloom of the annual flora.

RESULTS AND DISCUSSION

One hundred and nine species of vascular plants were collected from 22 stands at the six study-sites in the dredge field. The association

Table 1.--Age and location of sites and topography of stands in the Snelling dredge field.

A. Site age—1928
   Location—SNESE Sec. 6,
            T. 5 S., R. 15 E.

Stand number	Topography
1	Low swale
2	High swale
3	Mound top
4	High swale
5	High swale

B. Site age—Undredged site
   Location—SENWSE Sec. 5,
            T. 5 S., R. 15 E.

Stand number	Topography
6	River terrace top

C. Site age—1950
   Location—ESWSW Sec. 6,
            T. 5 S., R. 15 E.

Stand number	Topography
7	Mound top
8	High swale
9	Mound top
10	High swale
11	High swale

D. Site age—1941
   Location—NWSWSE Sec. 7,
            T. 5 S., R. 14 E.

Stand number	Topography
12	High swale
13	Mound top
14	High swale
15	Low swale
16	Mound top

E. Site age—1938
   Location—NESWSE Sec. 9,
            T. 5 S., R. 14 E.

Stand number	Topography
17	Mound top
18	High swale
19	Low swale

F. Site age—1910
   Location—WNENE Sec. 9,
            T. 5 S., R. 14 E.

Stand number	Topography
20	Mound top
21	High swale
22	Low swale

analysis program organized the stand data into four species groups (table 2). Only 36 of the 109 species were sufficiently well associated to be included in these groups. From left to right in table 2, the stands range from dry mound tops with sparse annual grass and herbaceous cover, to high dry swales dominated by thickets of Salix spp., to low mesic swales with forests of Salix spp. and Populus fremontii surrounding

Table 2.--Stand ordination and species groups on the Snelling dredge field summarized in a species-by-stand matrix using the association analysis program of Ceska and Roemer (1971). Cover values are: − = not present; R = single individual; + = <1%; 1 = 1-5%; 2 = 6-25%; 3 = 26-50%; 4 = 51-75%; and 5 = 76-100% (Mueller-Dombois and Ellenberg 1974). Date of deposition: A--1928; B--undredged site; C--1950; D--1941; E--1938; F--1910.

	Xeric mound tops									Semi-xeric high swales				Mesic swales					Misc. swales			
Date of deposition	A	A	B	C	C	D	D	E	F	C	D	D	E	D	E	F	A	A	A	C	C	F
Stand number	2	3	6	7	9	13	16	17	20	10	12	14	18	15	19	22	1	5	4	8	11	21
Group 1 Species (Cover values)																						
Bromus mollis	+	−	2	1	1	+	1	1	1	1	−	−	−	−	−	−	−	+	−	+	−	−
Bromus diandrus	1	−	1	−	+	+	−	1	1	+	−	−	−	−	−	R	−	−	−	−	1	−
Avena barbata	−	2	−	1	1	1	1	1	1	−	−	−	−	−	−	−	1	−	−	−	−	−
Vulpia myuros	−	−	1	+	1	1	+	1	1	+	−	−	−	−	−	−	−	−	−	1	−	−
Lotus purshianus	−	1	−	1	−	1	1	+	1	1	−	−	−	−	−	−	−	−	−	−	1	−
Vulpia megalura	−	1	2	+	−	+	−	1	1	+	−	−	−	−	−	−	−	−	−	+	−	−
Hypochoeris glabra	+	+	−	+	+	−	−	+	R	R	−	−	−	−	−	−	−	+	−	−	−	−
Bromus rubens	1	2	+	1	−	−	−	1	+	−	−	−	−	−	−	R	−	−	−	−	−	−
Group 2 Species (Cover values)																						
Salix lasiandra	4	−	−	−	−	−	−	−	−	3	4	2	3	2	2	2	−	−	−	−	−	−
Salix hindsiana	−	−	−	−	−	−	−	−	−	3	−	2	3	2	2	1	−	−	3	−	−	4
Populus fremontii	−	−	−	−	−	−	−	−	−	3	−	2	1	1	−	2	3	−	−	3	2	−
Quercus lobata	R	−	−	−	−	−	−	−	−	R	R	1	−	1	−	1	−	−	−	−	−	R
Salix gooddingii	−	−	−	−	−	−	−	−	−	−	3	2	−	2	2	−	3	2	−	1	−	−
Group 3 Species (Cover values)																						
Rubus procerus	−	−	−	−	−	−	−	−	−	−	−	−	−	2	2	2	−	−	−	−	−	−
Oxalis pilosa	−	−	−	−	−	−	−	−	−	−	−	−	−	−	+	+	−	−	−	−	−	−
Alnus rhombifolia	−	−	−	−	−	−	−	−	−	−	−	−	−	1	−	1	−	−	−	−	−	−
Vitis californica	−	−	−	−	−	−	−	−	−	−	−	−	−	2	−	2	−	−	−	−	−	−
Typha latifolia	−	−	−	−	−	−	−	−	−	−	−	−	−	2	2	−	−	−	−	−	−	−
Juncus effusus	−	−	−	−	−	−	−	−	−	−	−	−	−	+	−	+	−	−	−	−	−	−
Group 4 Species (Cover values)																						
Lythrum californicum	−	R	−	−	−	−	−	−	−	−	−	−	−	−	−	−	−	+	R	−	R	−
Geranium pilosum	−	+	−	−	−	−	−	−	+	−	−	−	−	−	−	−	−	+	R	−	−	−
Melilotus indicus	−	−	−	−	−	−	−	−	−	−	−	−	−	−	−	R	−	−	+	−	1	−
Hordeum geniculatum	−	−	−	−	−	−	−	−	−	−	−	−	−	−	−	−	−	+	+	−	−	−
Rumex crispus	−	−	−	−	−	−	−	−	−	−	−	−	−	−	−	R	−	−	R	−	−	−
Eleocharis macrostachya	−	−	−	−	−	−	−	−	−	−	−	−	−	−	−	−	−	1	1	−	−	−
Centaurea melitensis	−	−	−	−	−	−	−	−	+	−	−	−	−	−	−	−	−	−	3	−	−	−
Juncus balticus	−	−	−	−	−	−	−	−	−	−	−	−	−	+	−	−	+	−	−	−	−	−
Medicago arabica	−	−	−	−	−	−	−	−	−	−	−	−	−	−	−	−	−	−	+	−	−	+
Lactuca sp.	−	−	−	−	−	−	−	−	−	−	−	−	−	−	−	−	−	−	R	−	−	+
Rumex conglomeratus	−	−	−	−	R	−	−	−	−	−	−	−	−	−	−	−	R	−	−	−	−	−
Alisma sp.	−	−	−	−	−	−	−	−	−	−	−	−	−	−	−	−	R	−	−	−	−	−
Marsilea vestita	−	−	−	−	−	−	−	−	−	−	−	−	−	−	−	−	−	+	−	−	−	−
Briza minor	−	−	−	−	−	−	−	−	−	−	−	−	−	−	−	−	−	−	R	−	−	−
Cynodon dactylon	−	−	−	−	−	−	−	−	−	−	−	−	−	−	−	−	R	−	−	−	−	−
Cyperus alternifolius	−	−	−	−	−	−	−	−	−	−	−	−	−	−	−	−	−	+	−	−	−	−
Vicia sativa	−	−	−	−	−	−	−	−	−	−	−	−	−	−	−	−	−	−	1	−	−	−

shallow ponds. The four high-swale stands at the far right of the table do not fit within the topographic-moisture gradient of the rest of the ordination or within any single species group. This fact, plus their affinities to Groups 1, 2, and 4, are due to small-scale habitat variation. Stand 2, a high swale covered by grass, also falls within the xeric mount tops, whereas Stand 10, another high swale, contains two species groups.

The nesting of the species groups according to moisture availability and topography is readily apparent in table 2. Group 1, composed primarily of introduced annual species, grows exclusively on mound tops and corresponds floristically and physiognomically to the "California annual type", a climax annual grassland described by Heady (1956, 1958, 1977). Heady's climax annual grassland depends on the development of organic mulch; here it has developed on largely unweathered dredge spoil and completely lacks a litter layer.

Group 2, made up entirely of native tree species, occupies the bottom of nearly every swale with fine-textured soils. It overlaps little with Group 1; only Stand 10 includes extensive representation from both groups. Group 2 species are common pioneers in disturbed riparian zones in the Central Valley, and except for Quercus lobata all have wind-dispersed seeds (Munz and Keck 1959; Thompson 1961; Conard et al. 1977). Except for two large individuals at the 1910 site, the oaks are seedlings growing in the shade of willows. Since no parent oaks grow nearby, the oaks probably germinated from acorns dispersed by animals.

Group 3, consisting of woody perennials and emergent aquatics, occupies the edges of forested sites and shares most of the low mesic swales with Group 2. Group 3 reflects the greater habitat diversity of the low swales because of the presence of perennial ponds and a forest canopy. Vitis californica and Rubus procerus occupy the landward margins, whereas Typha latifolia and Juncus effusus occupy the pond margins.

Group 4 is made up largely of herbaceous annuals growing in semi-shaded, moist places in the swales containing standing water. The species in this group range from emergent and floating aquatics (Cyperus alternifolius, Alisma sp., and Marsilea vestita) to plants usually found in open, droughty habitats (Centaurea melitensis, Briza minor, and Cynodon dactylon). Group 4, like Group 3, is also associated with a forest canopy.

Sixty-two percent of the species collected in the dredge field are native, 38% are introduced. According to Heady (1977), the percentage of native plants in species lists for individual stands in California's annual grassland ranges between 71% at Hastings Reservation (White 1967) and slightly less than 20% at Hopland (Heady

1956). Our findings indicate that the Snelling dredge field has a relatively high proportion of native species.

In addition to identifying associational groups, the Ceska and Roemer program ordinated the stand data according to floristic affinities (table 2). However, the ordination shows no age-dependent patterns. In some cases, closer affinities occur between stands of the oldest and youngest sites than between stands of the same age.

Seventy-three species were not included in any of the four species groups because they were too frequent (>66% is the threshold value of the program) or non-faithful. Although we lack the quantitative data to fully interpret the significance of these rare species, two conclusions are drawn. First, our sampling was adequate because it included so many rare species. Large stands usually include a high proportion of rare species (Preston 1948). Secondly, rare species are continually being added to the flora for at least 50 years after spoil deposition.

Table 3 summarizes the percentage of rare species in proportion to the total flora of the six study sites. Vicia benghalensis was excluded because its occurence exceeded the 66% threshold of the program. The other species had frequency values of 18% or less. Note that the rare species made up 55% or more of the total species in the undredged and 1910 sites, and only 30-39% of the species in the other sites. A similar trend has been documented by Bazzaz (1975) in his study of old field succession in Illinois. There, he found that species diversity increased most rapidly during the first 15 years after field abandonment and that the species colonization curve maintained a positive slope for at least 40 years. Since the youngest spoils at Snelling are 30 years old, we have probably missed the rapid colonization phase that occurred shortly after dredging. White (1966) in his studies of abandoned fields at Hastings Reservation noted that only 18 to 28 years were needed after initial disturbance for the dominant species of the climax grassland to re-establish themselves.

Changes in species diversity were not quantifiable because the stands were of different sizes. Nevertheless, the 1910 and 1928 sites were floristically richer than the other sites (table 3). Of particular interest is the fact that Chlorogalum grandiflorum, Brodiaea californica, and B. multiflora, all native perennials, were only found at the 1910 site. The occurrence of these perennials and greater species diversity at this site may not be entirely age-dependent. The site, which is periodically flooded by the Merced River, has some alluvium and is exposed to flood-borne propagules. The undredged grassland site contained most of the Group 1 species plus three native perennials: Stipa pulchra, Brodiaea hyacinthina, and Calochortus luteus. In general, species

Table 3.--Percent of rare species for each age-class.

	Undredged control	1910	1928	1938	1941	1950
Total number of species	12	56	57	29	41	54
Total number of outliers	7	31	17	9	13	21
Percent outliers	58	55	30	31	32	39

diversity was highest in the forests of the mesic swales and lowest in the grasslands of the mound tops.

CONCLUSIONS

Only small changes in species composition were noted in the dredge-spoil sequence investigated at Snelling. The dominant species probably colonized rapidly after spoil deposition. The four species groups identified by the Ceska and Roemer (1971) program occur on all sites regardless of age. The groups correlate most closely with dredge-spoil topography and moisture availability. In general, the slow weathering of the dredge spoil has not resulted in enough soil development to affect the vegetation. Only in a few swales with moist, shallow soils and standing water is the vegetation very diverse or structurally complex. Several immature Quercus lobata in the swales and a Quercus wislizenii at the 1910 site are the only evidence of direct species replacement in the study-sites. The data suggest that species richness increases with successional age and that 50 years or more are required for the accumulation of well-developed flora. Structural changes will be much slower, correlating with the slow development of soil.

ACKNOWLEDGMENTS

Financial support was provided by a Faculty Research Grant from the University of California, Davis. We thank the following residents of Snelling for their assistance and information: Robert Peirce, H.G. Kelsey, Ed Romero, and Kermit Robinson. Thanks must be extended also to Jack Major and Marlyn Shelton who read and commented on the manuscript.

LITERATURE CITED

Aubury, L.E. 1910. Gold dredging in California. California State Mining Bureau, Bull. 57. 312 p. California State Printing Office, Sacramento, Calif.

Bazzaz, F.A. 1975. Plant species in old-field successional ecosystems in southern Illinois. Ecology 56:485-488.

California Department of Water Resources. 1980. California rainfall summary: monthly total precipitation 1849-1979. Various pages. California Department of Water Resources, Sacramento, Calif.

Ceska, A., and H. Roemer. 1971. A computer program for identifying species-relevé groups in vegetation studies. Vegetatio 23:255-277.

Clark, W.B. 1970. Gold districts of California. 180 p. California Division of Mines and Geology, San Francisco, Calif.

Conard, S.G., R.L. MacDonald, and R.F. Holland. 1977. Riparian vegetation and flora of the Sacramento Valley. p. 47-55. In: A. Sands (ed.). Riparian forests in California: their ecology and conservation. Institute of Ecology Pub. 15, University of California, Davis. 122 p.

Davis, F.F., and D.W. Carlson. 1952. Mines and mineral resources of Merced County. Calif. J. Mines Geol. 48:207-251.

Griffin, J.R. 1977. Oak woodland. p. 383-415. In: M.G. Barbour and J. Major (ed.). Terrestrial vegetation of California. 1002 p. John Wiley and Sons, New York, N.Y.

Heady, H.F. 1956. Changes in a California annual plant community induced by manipulation of natural mulch. Ecology 37:798-812.

Heady, H.F. 1958. Vegetational changes in the California annual type. Ecology 39:402-416.

Heady, H.F. 1977. Valley grassland. p. 491-514. In: M.G. Barbour and J. Major (ed.). Terrestrial vegetation of California. 1002 p. John Wiley and Sons, New York, N.Y.

Mueller-Dombois, D., and H. Ellenberg. 1974. Aims and methods of vegetation ecology. 547 p. John Wiley and Sons, New York, N.Y.

Munz, P.A., and D.D. Keck. 1959. A California flora. 1689 p. University of California Press, Berkeley, Calif.

Preston, F.W. 1948. The commonness, and rarity of species. Ecology 29:254-283.

Thompson, K. 1961. The riparian forests of the upper Sacramento Valley. Ann. Assoc. Am. Geogr. 51:294-315.

Wagner, J.R. 1970. Gold mines of California. 259 p. Howell-North Books, Berkeley, Calif.

White, K.L. 1966. Old-field succession on Hastings Reservation, California. Ecology 47:865-868.

White, K.L. 1967. Native bunchgrass (Stipa pulchra) on Hastings Reservation, California. Ecology 48:949-955.

HISTORICAL VEGETATION CHANGE IN
THE OWENS RIVER RIPARIAN WOODLAND[1]

Timothy S. Brothers[2]

Abstract.--This study evaluates human-caused vegetation change in the riparian woodland of Owens River (Inyo Co., Calif.). The greatest change has occurred below the intake of the Los Angeles Aqueduct, where drying of the channel has eliminated most native riparian cover and allowed invasion by salt cedar (Tamarix ramosissima) and Russian olive (Elaeagnus angustifolia). Fire, water management, and other factors may have reduced tree cover above the aqueduct intake and encouraged proliferation of weedy native shrubs. The present scarcity of tree seedlings suggests that one or more of these factors continues to inhibit tree regeneration.

INTRODUCTION

Owens River has long been an important source of water for an otherwise arid region. Since settlement of Owens Valley by Europeans in the 1860's it has supported a mix of farming, mining, stock raising, and other economic activities common in the West. Its waters have been diverted for agriculture within Owens Valley and for export to Los Angeles. This study examines how these activities have changed the character and extent of the riparian woodland bordering Owens River.

PHYSICAL SETTING

Owens River runs from just south of Mono Lake through Owens River Gorge to the head of Owens Valley, and from there the length of Owens Valley to Owens Lake. This study was limited to Owens Valley.

Below Owens River Gorge, Owens River is a meandering, low-gradient stream (fig. 1), winding over a floodplain whose width varies from less than 100 m. to more than 1 km. The floodplain lies at a lower elevation than the rest of the valley floor and is bounded by abrupt bluffs along much of the river. The floodplain surface is crisscrossed in many places by abandoned river meanders, but is otherwise fairly level. The river channel is relatively deep and narrow, bor-dered in many places by steep banks composed of fine-textured, cohesive alluvium.

The Owens River system is fed almost entirely by runoff from the Sierra Nevada, but even before man altered the hydrologic regime only about a third of its Sierra tributaries maintained perennial flow to the river. The rest normally disappeared short of the river channel as a result of percolation and evaporation. Much Sierra runoff thus reaches the river as subsurface flow. South of the Poverty Hills, however, the 1872 earthquake fault (fig. 1) restricts eastward groundwater movement (Los Angeles Department of Water and Power 1966). No groundwater reaches the river channel where it lies well east of the fault, but seepage increases gradually above the intersection of river and fault near Manzanar Road. From there south to Lone Pine many small springs occur in and along the channel, probably the combined result of channel entrenchment, proximity of the earthquake fault, and inflow from the alluvial fan of Lone Pine Creek.

Under natural conditions, maximum monthly discharge of Owens River normally occurred in June or July with melting of the Sierra snowpack; minimum discharge usually came in August or September. River flow was comparatively regular: the ratio of maximum to minimum monthly discharge at Pleasant Valley from 1919 through 1940 was 2.8 to 1[3]--much lower than, for example, the Kings River at Piedra (46.4 to 1); the Kern at Bakersfield (13.4 to 1); and the Kaweah at Three Rivers (53.6 to 1) (USDI Geological Survey 1959). Factors responsible for this low variation may

---

[1]Paper presented at the California Riparian Systems Conference. [University of California, Davis, September 17-19, 1981].

[2]Timothy S. Brothers is a Graduate Student in the Department of Geography, University of California, Los Angeles, Calif.

---

[3]Unpublished streamflow records, Los Angeles Department of Water and Power (LADWP).

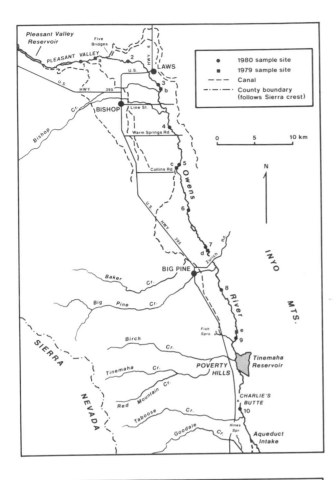

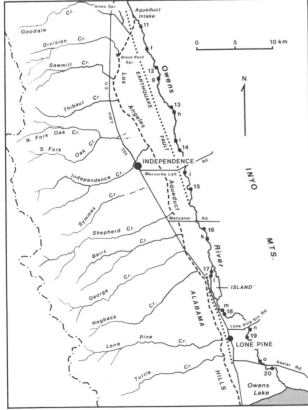

Figure 1.--Owens Valley.

have included the gentle gradient of the river channel; low precipitation east of the Sierra crest and regulation of the discharge by the Sierra snowpack and groundwater. River regime and channel morphology suggest that most floods were relatively mild events, causing little disturbance of the floodplain surface.

PRESENT VEGETATION

Sampling Methods

Field sampling of the present riparian woodland was carried out in August, 1979, and in April, May, and June, 1980. (Only data from 1980 are included here.) At each of 20 systemically spaced sites, three parallel 1-m.-wide belt transects were extended 20 m. apart at right angles to the river channel. Presence of woody perennial species was noted in each meter of the transect. At sites below the aqueduct intake, transects extended across the channel and 35 m. outward from the bank top on each side. Above the intake, water in the channel limited sites to one side of the river; transects at these sites extended 35 m. from the bank top.

Trees were counted at each site within a plot 50 m. wide, ending 50 m. from the bank on each side of the river (one side only at sites 1-10). Plots thus measured 50 m. by 50 m. above the bank on each side, but area of the channel section at sites 11-20 varied with channel width. Trees less than 2 m. tall were counted as a subset of the total tree population at each site to provide a rough measure of recent reproduction from seed.

Species Composition and Patterning

The Owens River riparian woodland is somewhat species-poor compared to many other riparian areas in California (Roberts, Howe, and Major 1977). Of the 17 woody perennials observed in 1980 (tables 1 and 2), only 10 are primarily members of the riparian woodland: valley willow (_Salix gooddingii_), black willow (_S. laevigata_), and cottonwood (_Populus fremontii_), which make up the tree stratum; and the shrubs narrowleaf willow (_Salix exigua_), _Rosa woodsii_, rabbitbrush (_Chrysothamnus nauseosus_), Nevada saltbush (_Atriplex torreyi_), salt cedar (_Tamarix ramosissima_), Russian olive (_Elaeagnus angustifolia_), and desert olive (_Forestiera neomexicana_). The remaining species are found more often as members of desert scrub communities bordering the floodplain. Of these ten, all except rabbitbrush and Nevada saltbush grow mostly near the present river channel. The latter two also grow down to the water's edge, but they are more abundant on higher ground and are the only woody species present on much of the floodplain outside the immediate vicinity of the river.

Herbaceous species form an understory throughout the riparian woodland. Areas that remain wet most of the year support marsh vegeta-

76

Table 1.--Percentage frequency of riparian woodland species above channel banks.[1]

Site	1	2	3	4	5	6	7	8	9	10	11	12	13	14	15	16	17	18	19	20
Bank	W	W	E	E	W	E	E	W	W	E	W/E	W/E	W/E	W/E	W/E	W/E	W/E	W/E	W/E	W/E
Artemisia spinescens	-	-	-	-	-	-	-	-	7	-	-	-	-	-	-	-	-	-	-	-
Atriplex canescens	-	-	-	-	-	-	-	-	-	-	-	-	3/	-	-	-	-	-	-	-
Atriplex confertifolia	-	-	-	-	-	-	-	-	14	-	/31	-	-	-	-	-	-	-	-	-
Atriplex parryi	-	-	-	-	-	-	-	-	26	-	/3	-	-	-	-	-	-	-	-	-
Atriplex torreyi	-	-	-	44	11	13	19	-	+	-	38/9	18/11	28/41	17/38	30/16	11/44	47/43	15/27	15/	+/
Chrysothamnus nauseosus	27	46	-	53	18	44	31	-	-	11	5/10	-	-	/3	56/21	11/18	8/	23/15	15/	+/
Populus fremontii	-	1	-	-	-	-	-	-	-	-	-	-	-	-	-	-	-	-	-	-
Rosa woodsii	11	22	+	6	2	1	-	-	-	16	-	-	-	-	-	-	-	-	-	-
Salix exigua	-	22	93	8	2	1	2	-	-	19	-	-	-	-	-	-	-	-	2/2	-
Salix gooddingii	-	-	-	-	-	21	5	85	+	44	-	-	-	-	/2	1/1	2/9	1/1	1/13	31/6
Salix laevigata	-	-	5	-	-	-	16	-	-	-	-	-	-	-	-	-	-	-	-	-
Sarcobatus vermiculatus	-	2	-	7	-	-	14	-	37	-	/+	-	-	-	-	-	-	/+	-	1/38
Tamarix ramosissima*	-	-	-	-	-	+	-	-	-	+	-	/6	14/	-	-	5/	-	/+	/3	-
Tetradymia axillaris	-	-	-	-	-	-	-	-	-	-	/2	-	-	-	-	-	-	-	-	-

[1] Frequency is expressed as percentage of meters transected (105 m. per bank) in which species is present.

* Introduced species.

+ Present on site but not on transect.

Table 2.--Percentage frequency of riparian woodland species in channel.[1]

Site	11	12	13	14	15	16	17	18	19	20
No. of m. transected	76	90	79	168	115	174	97	119	115	83
Artemisia tridentata	-	-	-	-	-	-	-	+	-	-
Atriplex canescens	-	-	-	2	-	-	-	-	-	-
Atriplex confertifolia	1	1	-	-	-	-	-	-	-	-
Atriplex torreyi	4	10	30	8	2	5	5	6	-	10
Chrysothamnus nauseosus	-	-	-	5	5	4	2	9	-	-
Elaeagnus angustifolia*	-	-	-	+	-	-	-	-	-	-
Forestiera neomexicana	-	-	-	-	-	2	-	+	-	+
Rosa woodsii	-	-	-	-	-	-	+	+	-	-
Salix exigua	-	-	-	-	-	-	-	-	2	-
Salix gooddingii	-	-	13	7	42	24	25	42	26	61
Tamarix ramosissima	-	14	18	4	17	3	-	-	-	-

[1] Frequency is expressed as percentage of meters transected in which species is present.

* Introduced species.

+ Present on site but not on transect.

tion dominated by _Typha_, _Scirpus_, _Carex_, and _Juncus_. On much of the floodplain, however, the herb layer is a dense perennial sod of _Distichlis spicata_, _Sporobolus airoides_, and _Juncus balticus_.

At the boundary between floodplain and valley floor, vegetation on both sides of the river changes in most areas to a desert scrub dominated by _Sarcobatus vermiculatus_, _Atriplex confertifolia_, and _A. parryi_. Less frequently encountered are _Artemisia spinescens_, _A. tridentata_, _Atriplex canescens_, _A. polycarpa_, _Dalea fremontii_, _D. polyadenia_, _Tetradymia glabrata_, and _T. axillaris_.

Species turnover along Owens River is low: eight of the ten most common riparian woodland species occur at least sporadically throughout the study area. The exceptions are desert olive, not observed north of Manzanar Road, and Russian olive, encountered only between the aqueduct intake and Mazourka Canyon Road. Nevertheless, the character of the woodland varies greatly from one end of Owens Valley to the other because of differences in the abundance of the few species present, as shown in tables 1 and 2. (Sites 11-20 are separated into above-bank and channel sections to allow better comparison with sites 1-10, where transects did not extend into the channel.)

North of Bishop, the woodland consists mostly of dense stands of _Rosa woodsii_, narrowleaf willow, and rabbitbrush that extend well back from the river on low ground (fig. 2). Tree cover (mostly valley willow) increases below Bishop, and the frequency of _R. woodsii_ and narrowleaf willow declines, though both remain common to the aqueduct intake. Rabbitbrush and Nevada saltbush are abundant everywhere; both were observed at or near all sites north of the intake.

Below the intake an immediate change occurs. Few trees grow on the floodplain surface south to Mazourka Canyon Road; woody vegetation above the

banks consists almost entirely of Nevada saltbush and rabbitbrush, with salt cedar scattered along dry washes (fig. 3). The dry channel bottom is lined with _Atriplex_ and _Tamarix_, though trees become more frequent southward. Russian olive grows sparsely on the floor of the channel for several kilometers north of Mazourka Canyon Road. Narrowleaf willow and _R. woodsii_ were observed only in the channel, at places where damp soil indicated a shallow groundwater table.

Below Mazourka Canyon Road, tree cover continues to increase both in the channel and along the banks (fig. 4). Salt cedar becomes less frequent and rabbitbrush more so; _Rosa woodsii_ and narrowleaf willow are also more common, but for the most part do not occur in the large stands found in the Bishop region.

Like the woody overstory, most herbaceous species become less abundant along the dry channel. In contrast to the thick sod present in other areas, much of the floodplain surface in this section is bare except for _Salsola iberica_, _Bassia hyssopifolia_, and other weedy annuals.

Few tree seedlings were seen north of the aqueduct intake except at site 8 (table 3). Seedlings are also absent in most of the dry section below the intake, but become more common from site 14 south in the channel bottom.

HUMAN IMPACT

Early Descriptions of the Riparian Woodland

Descriptions of the riparian woodland as it appeared before European settlement are few and somewhat contradictory. Expeditions escorted by Joseph Walker passed through Owens Valley in 1834, 1843, and 1845 (Goetzmann 1966; Davidson 1976), but apparently none left a first-hand account of vegetation along the river. The 1845 expedition was directed, but not accompanied, by

Figure 2.--Owens River north of Bishop.

Figure 3.--Salt cedar lining dry bed of Owens River near Independence.

Table 3.--Riparian tree density.[1]

											Above banks									
Site	1	2	3	4	5	6	7	8	9	10	11	12	13	14	15	16	17	18	19	20
Bank	W	W	E	E	W	E	E	W	W	E	W/E	W/E	W/E	W/E	W/E	W/E	W/E	W/E	W/E	W/E
Salix gooddingii																				
Taller than 2 m.	-	-	-	-	-	-	29	2	71	1	9	-	-	-	-	1/1	2/13	/1	4/38	10/4
Less than 2 m.	-	-	-	-	-	-	2	-	44	-	-	-	-	-	-	-	-	-	-	-
Salix laevigata																				
Taller than 2 m.	-	-	-	-	-	-	-	9	-	-	-	-	-	-	-	-	-	-	-	-
Populus fremontii																				
Less than 2 m.	-	2	-	-	-	-	-	-	-	-	-	-	-	-	-	-	-	-	-	-

	In channel									
Site	11	12	13	14	15	16	17	18	19	20
Salix gooddingii										
Taller than 2 m.	-	-	1	19	24	26	7	48	4	8
Less than 2 m.	-	-	-	2	-	2	9	4	3	1

[1]Area sampled above banks at each site is 2500 m^2 (0.25 ha.) per bank. Area sampled in channel varies between 1200 and 2900 m^2.

John C. Fremont, who later described Owens River as "wooded with willow and cottonwood" (Fremont 1849), perhaps on the basis of descriptions furnished him by members of the expedition. Much of Owens Valley was surveyed by A.W. von Schmidt in 1855, but his field notes only mention riparian vegetation near Lone Pine, where von Schmidt encountered willows along the river.[4] A cor-

Figure 4.--Owens River near Keeler Road.

---

[4]USDI Bureau of Land Management. Surveyor General of California. 1855. Unpublished surveyor's field notes, books 115, 203, 296. On file at Bureau of Land Management, Sacramento, Calif.

respondent accompanying a military expedition through Owens Valley in 1859 described it as untimbered except for a few small cottonwoods (Davidson 1976). William Brewer, of the California Geological Survey, encountered no trees at all in the valley in 1864 (Brewer 1930). An 1886 settler's tract states that before settlement there was "no timber of any kind" in Owens Valley; the river was bordered by "grassy plains" dotted with occasional shrubs (Anon. 1886). An early inhabitant of the valley, however, recalled large willows lining the river east of Independence (Earl 1976).

These accounts suggest that tree cover has always been sparse along Owens River, though it seems unlikely that trees were ever entirely absent. Early explorers may have kept mostly to the west side of the valley, where travel is easier but the river is often hidden from view. Although no clear picture of the presettlement riparian woodland emerges from these descriptions, examination of the history of land use and water management in Owens Valley provides indirect evidence of the changes that may have occurred since settlement.

Mining

Between 1860 and 1864 numerous claims were located in the Inyo and White Mountains, and four mining towns were established near Owens River (Chalfant 1922). Reduction works were built at five sites near the river, at least two of them requiring wood or charcoal for operation (Raymond 1869). Although additional discoveries were made in the valley after 1864, the early excitement died out rapidly. By 1870, three and perhaps all four of the small mining towns were deserted, and most of the mills were idle (California State Mining Bureau 1888). The impact of this short-lived mining boom on the riparian vegetation of Owens River was probably small. Canals were dug from the river to at least two mills, but their construction entailed little disturbance of the riparian zone. Trees may have been cut near the river to supply the mills, but most wood no doubt came from the mountain slopes flanking Owens Valley.

Browsing

Livestock

Livestock were driven through the valley as early as 1859; by 1861 permanent ranches were established near present-day Bishop (Chalfant 1922; Davidson 1976). Local stock were wintered on the meadows of the Owens River floodplain and other shallow-groundwater areas on the valley floor, then moved to mountain pastures in summer (Earl 1976). In addition, large herds of sheep were driven through Owens Valley to mountain ranges each spring (Anon. 1886), and in dry years cattle and sheep were driven into the valley to take advantage of its subirrigated grasslands (California State Mining Bureau 1888).

Stock raising suffered along with the rest of the valley economy as Los Angeles bought up land for the Los Angeles Aqueduct. The greatest decline took place after 1923, when the city began to buy land in the Bishop-Big Pine region. Collapse of the industry was averted by Los Angeles' decision to lease some land back to ranchers. Expansion of the lease program was encouraged by a series of wet years beginning in 1936 and by completion of the aqueduct extension to Mono Lake in 1940 (Los Angeles Department of Water and Power 1966). Most of the valley floor, including the floodplain of Owens River, is now occupied by large grazing leases devoted almost entirely to cattle production. Animals are still moved seasonally to mountain range, but some ranchers keep stock in the valley year-round. In general, stock graze the river lands from October or November to March or April, and are absent the rest of the year.

Without detailed historical records, the impact of livestock on the riparian woodland must largely be surmised. The river grasslands provide a perennial water supply and abundant forage, and have probably always been used more heavily than the surrounding desert range. Grazing pressure may have become severe in dry years before institution of the present lease program, but if overgrazing occurred it seems not to have been recorded. Creation of large leases reduced fluctuations in the size of the valley's livestock population, and probably also reduced summer grazing intensity near the river. Determination of range carrying capacity has been left

to leaseholders, however, and some overstocking may have occurred since leasing began.

Regardless of past stocking levels, livestock have probably exercised selective pressure on the composition of the riparian woodland. All of the shrub species in the woodland are browsed, but some are of low palatability or have weedy characters that enable them to persist despite browsing. Narrowleaf willow spreads by means of root suckers, in some areas forming dense stands that appear to exclude livestock. Rabbitbrush is well known as an invader of overgrazed rangeland and other disturbed areas in the West. Presence of livestock in the riparian zone may have favored these shrubs at the expense of other species. Livestock browse mature willow trees very lightly, according to local ranchers—perhaps partly because most animals are removed from bottomland pastures when the trees are in leaf. Browsing does not appear to injure mature trees greatly, though some have browse lines. Damage to seedlings may be greater: many of those observed during field work appeared to have been cropped by browsing animals.

Tule Elk

An initial herd of 54 tule elk (Cervus elaphus nannodes Merriam) was released north of Independence in 1933 and 1934. The herd multiplied to 189 head by 1943, but has since fluctuated between 150 and 500 because of hunts held to control population size (McCullough 1969). At least four herds of elk now browse near Owens River. Although seasonal movements vary from one herd to the next, elk may use most of the bottomland from Owens Lake to the bend north of Bishop in the course of a year (Curtis et al. 1977).

The elk subsist on browse plants, particularly on willows, to a much greater degree than do livestock (McCullough 1969). They may have contributed to development of browse lines on some trees, but like livestock are more likely to have damaged seedlings than mature trees. Nevertheless, the elk population is small in relation to the livestock population, and its effect on the riparian woodland is probably small by comparison.

Beaver

Beaver were introduced to Owens Valley by the California Department of Fish and Game at Baker Creek in 1948.[5] They have since spread to Owens River, both above the aqueduct intake and in the spring-fed section below it.

Beaver feed on cottonwood and on both willow tree species. They often gnaw willows completely through, but the willows are able to stump-sprout if not further disturbed. Large cottonwoods are often girdled and completely killed. Beaver are

_____

[5]Unpublished records, California Department of Fish and Game.

80

found the entire length of the upper river, but their activity is localized. In some areas almost all trees have been affected; in others they remain untouched. Approximately 24% of the trees at sites 1–10 showed signs of gnawing by beaver. Despite the presence of beaver in the lower river, none of the trees at sites 16–20 appeared to have been damaged.

Crop Cultivation

Cultivation of crops began in the 1860's, largely as an adjunct to the livestock industry. Farms were at first clustered along creeks on the west side of the valley, but later spread onto the valley floor following construction of large irrigation canals from Owens River. Expansion of irrigated cropland was greatest near Bishop and Big Pine, where approximately 17 canals began operation between 1872 and 1890.[6]

Los Angeles' acquisition of valley lands halted irrigation of cropland from Owens River by about 1930.[7] Although Los Angeles began to make water available again in the late thirties for irrigation of pasture and fodder crops on grazing leases, local irrigation allotment has depended on annual runoff and cultivated acreage has remained small (Los Angeles Department of Water and Power 1979).

Land-use maps compiled for most of the valley floor early in this century[8] suggest that, despite the extensive canal system, little land was ever farmed near Owens River. A few fields were cultivated on the floodplain at Big Pine and Bishop, but there as elsewhere most of the bottomland was left in native pasture, probably because of its shallow water table and salt-affected soils.

Agricultural land clearing thus caused no wholesale reduction of the riparian woodland in Owens Valley. Cultivation and abandonment of the few fields on the floodplain may have encouraged the growth of rabbitbrush—a frequent invader of abandoned fields in the Bishop area—but the maps cited above show vegetation patterns approximating those of today: the floodplain largely covered by herbaceous growth, with willows confined to the river and other runoff channels.

---

[6] Los Angeles Department of Water and Power [n.d.]. History Owens Valley irrigation ditches. Unpublished report by J.L. Graham.
[7] Unpublished canal discharge records, LA DWP.
[8] Los Angeles Department of Water and Power. Map of Bishop region in Owens Valley [unpublished]. Prepared under the direction of C.H. Lee. 6 sheets. Scale 1:12,000.
Los Angeles Bureau of Water Works and Supply [n.d.]. Detail map of a portion of Owens Valley near Lone Pine, California [unpublished]. 2 sheets. Scale 1:6000. On file at LADWP.

Fire

Intentional burning has been practiced at one time or another along most of Owens River. Ranchers probably burned the bottomland pastures occasionally in pre-aqueduct days, and present leaseholders say that intentional burning occurred on many leases from shortly after institution of the lease system until about 1970. During the sixties, for example, the floodplain was burned between Lone Pine Station Road and Mazourka Canyon Road, and between Pleasant Valley Reservoir and Five Bridges (north of Bishop). The latter area has been burned several times, and part of it sprayed with herbicides, to improve livestock access to the river.

The incidence of wildfires has probably increased along the upper river with greater use of the riparian zone by campers and fishermen in the last 30 years. Local residents recalled several recent wildfires on the floodplain, including a large one northeast of Bishop in about 1968. I found evidence of burning at 12 of the 20 sites sampled in 1980 (sites 1–3, 6, 12, and 14–20).

The riparian woodland may have been affected most by fire north of Bishop. Repeated burns there could have eliminated willow and cottonwood trees and favored faster-maturing shrubby species like rabbitbrush and narrowleaf willow, which resprout readily after fire. The impact of burning is difficult to assess, however, without better information about the post-fire responses of the other woodland species.

Plant Introductions

Two Eurasian shrubs, Russian olive and salt cedar, have become established in the riparian woodland as an indirect result of human dispersal. Both were probably introduced to the Southwest as ornamental plants in the nineteenth century, but have since become naturalized along many southwestern watercourses (Christensen 1963; Robinson 1965). Earliest evidence I have found of Russian olive in Owens Valley is a 1942 collection from naturalized plants growing along Lone Pine Creek,[9] but it had probably been introduced in cultivation long before then. Russian olive appears to have become established on Owens River only in the Independence region, where it is scattered along the bottom and sides of the dry channel. Salt cedar reached Owens Valley at least by 1944, when aerial photographs show it growing along the 1872 earthquake fault near Mazourka Canyon Road.[10] It too may first have been introduced as an ornamental, but has now become naturalized throughout Owens Valley and is a notable element of the riparian woodland

---

[9] Constance, Lincoln. 1980. Personal communication.
[10] Los Angeles Department of Water and Power. 1974. Vegetational resource inventory and potential change assessment, Owens Valley, Calif. Unpublished report by Earth Satellite Corporation.

south of the aqueduct intake. Establishment of salt cedar and Russian olive along Owens River appears related to alteration of the river's natural regime by the Los Angeles Aqueduct system (discussed below).

Water Management

Irrigation

Most irrigation diversions in Owens Valley began before 1890; by 1904 it was estimated that over 75% of the annual runoff in the valley was diverted for irrigation.[11] These diversions reduced the total discharge of Owens River and altered its natural regime: maximum and minimum flows were both reduced downstream by large summer irrigation diversions, but winter flow was almost doubled by agricultural drainage.[12] Flood frequency and magnitude doubtless diminished as well.

These changes may have affected regeneration of willows and cottonwoods, whose reproduction is tied to the natural runoff regime. Reduction of maximum and minimum flows could have decreased the area of freshly exposed alluvium available for colonization during the growing season or shifted the zone of seedling establishment downward in the channel, where young plants would be more susceptible to damage by the increased winter discharge. Consumptive use of water by agriculture would also have decreased the total water supply to riparian vegetation downstream. The effects of irrigation have since been obscured, however, by changes associated with more recent water management practices.

The Los Angeles Aqueduct System

Operation of the Los Angeles Aqueduct system began with completion of the aqueduct in 1913. The aqueduct had little effect on Owens River above the intake until 1929, when Tinemaha Dam began to regulate flow to the aqueduct at the Poverty Hills. The rest of the upper river remained unregulated until 1941, when Long Valley Dam was completed at the head of Owens River Gorge. Pleasant Valley Dam was added in 1957 to smooth out fluctuations caused by powerplants below Long Valley Dam.

Natural river discharge has been increased above the intake by interbasin transfers and groundwater pumping. The Mono Basin extension of the aqueduct system began diverting water to Owens River at Long Valley in 1941, and diversions increased following construction of the Second Los Angeles Aqueduct (located outside the study area) in 1970. These increases can be seen in the record of annual river discharge at Pleasant Valley (fig. 5).

---

[11]U.S. Reclamation Service. 1904. Report on the Owens Valley, California. Unpublished report by J.C. Clausen. On file at the Los Angeles Public Library, Water and Power Branch.
[12]Unpublished streamflow records, LADWP.

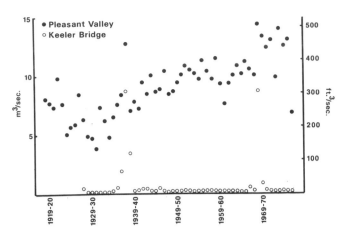

Figure 5.--Annual discharge of Owens River at Pleasant Valley and Keeler Bridge. Source: unpublished streamflow records, LADWP.

During a prolonged dry period in the twenties and thirties, Los Angeles drilled approximately 170 wells in Owens Valley to increase supply to the aqueduct (Los Angeles Department of Water and Power 1966). Many of these wells were located north of the intake and discharged water into the river channel rather than the aqueduct. Pumping occurred from 1919 through 1935, then halted until the dry years 1960-62 (Los Angeles Department of Water and Power 1979). More wells were drilled after completion of the Second Aqueduct, and pumping now occurs every year.

South of the aqueduct intake, Owens River and most other streams have been diverted by the aqueduct since 1913, though some water continued to flow down the lower channel past the intake in most years until Tinemaha Dam provided a means of storing high flows. Since then water has been shunted downstream on just a few occasions, mostly when runoff has exceeded system capacity: in 1936-39 (before completion of Long Valley Dam), then again in 1967, 1969, and 1975.[13] The 1938 and 1969 flows were exceptionally large, as can be seen from the record at Keeler Bridge east of Lone Pine (fig. 5).

Groundwater seepage has maintained some surface flow in the lower channel south of its intersection with the 1872 earthquake fault. This discharge has been quite small, often dropping to almost nothing from July through September, but relatively constant from year to year when no water is released past the intake.

Vegetation change associated with operation of the aqueduct system should be greatest in the section of channel between the aqueduct intake and the river-fault junction, which has remained dry since 1929 except for scattered seeps and irregular flood discharges. Field data (tables 1

---

[13]Unpublished streamflow records, LADWP.

and 2) support this conclusion: diversion of surface flow appears to have eliminated most of the native riparian woodland from this area, except for the species least closely associated with riparian zones. Riparian taxa persist mainly in the channel bottom just north of the fault, where groundwater is most readily available. South of the fault, the small surface flow provided by spring discharge has evidently been sufficient to maintain much of the original riparian cover.

Establishment of salt cedar and Russian olive in the woodland is also best explained as a consequence of aqueduct system operation. Although salt cedar was perhaps naturalized near the river by 1944, local residents say that it became common only after flooding of the lower river in 1967 and 1969. The shrub spread rapidly into flooded areas, becoming especially dense in the dry section below the intake. Salt cedar is similar to the native willows and cottonwoods in being adapted for establishment after such fluvial disturbances, but here as elsewhere in the Southwest it has been better able than the native flora to colonize a habitat created by alteration of the natural runoff regime. Its success may be partly attributable to such inherent ecological advantages as more prolonged annual seed production and lower moisture requirement than the native riparian species (Horton 1977), Water was released down the old channel during the entire summer of both 1967 and 1969, perhaps delaying most seedling establishment until only salt cedar was still dispersing seed. On the other hand, willow and cottonwood seedlings may have been present initially but failed to survive without a permanent water supply.

When Russian olive reached the river is not certain, but the small size of all individuals observed during field work suggests that it too may have become established since 1969. It has not become as widespread as salt cedar, perhaps because its olive-like fruits are not wind dispersed.

Above the aqueduct intake, operation of the aqueduct system has changed the natural regime of Owens River (fig. 6): instead of cresting early in summer and falling rapidly to a late-summer minimum, the river now remains high from spring through fall, and maximum monthly discharge often occurs at the time of former low water. Flood magnitude and frequency have decreased, because flood discharge can be diverted or stored upstream. Similar changes in natural river regime have been found to hinder reproduction of riparian species elsewhere by eliminating the substrate necessary for seedling establishment (Johnson et al. 1976), and may partly account for the scarcity of young cottonwood and tree willow seedlings along the upper river channel. (The single exception, at site 8, is difficult to explain since other, apparently similar sites are devoid of young trees, but it does show the potential for seed reproduction where favorable conditions exist.) Seed reproduction appears

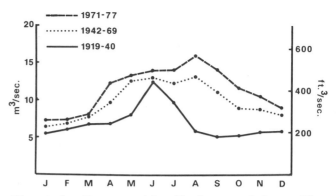

Figure 6.--Mean monthly discharge of Owens River at Pleasant Valley. Source: unpublished streamflow records, LADWP.

more active in the channel itself below the earthquake fault, the only area in which river discharge still rises and falls more or less naturally.

Since 1970, tree regeneration along the upper river may also have been reduced by erosion associated with increased import for the Second Aqueduct. Bank slumping has in many areas produced vertical, unstable channel sides on which seedlings are unable to take root.

CONCLUSIONS

The most obvious human-caused changes in the Owens River riparian woodland have stemmed from diversion of the river by the Los Angeles Aqueduct. Elimination of much of the native riparian vegetation between the intake and the earthquake fault has created an open niche that has been partly filled by salt cedar and Russian olive with recent flooding of the old channel. Both species will probably continue to spread in the future because of the need to waste water from the aqueduct system in very wet years.

Below the fault, native riparian vegetation has been maintained by spring flow, and has in fact spread into the channel with reduction of river discharge. The riparian woodland may be as dense now in some parts of the lower river as it was before completion of the aqueduct.

North of the intake, the combined effects of browsing, burning, clearing, and water management may have caused a reduction in the tree cover and an increase in such weedy shrubs as rabbitbrush and narrowleaf willow--especially near Bishop, where human impact has been most concentrated. Lack of seed regeneration by native tree species along the upper river may be due to browsing or the disruption of the natural river regime. Nevertheless, sexual regeneration of riparian species could be naturally uncommon along Owens

River. Historical records suggest that the river's unusually small annual discharge range, together with a shallow groundwater table and relatively erosion-resistant floodplain material, allowed development of a dense growth of herbaceous perennials that covered much of the floodplain and often extended, as at present, right to the water margin. Competition from this herbaceous cover could have limited most seedling establishment to areas of intense fluvial disturbance, perhaps present only after infrequent major floods. In this regard the dynamics of the riparian zone along Owens River may have differed from those of many other western streams, which annually rework a much wider expanse of alluvium because of their greater discharge range and might provide greater opportunity for seed regeneration. Comparison of the relative success of vegetative and seed reproduction in relation to discharge regime in other riparian systems might clarify processes in the Owens River woodland.

Regardless of whether tree regeneration is being artificially suppressed or is naturally uncommon, the present scarcity of young trees along the upper river may portend further decline of the tree cover. Management of the river discharge for aqueduct operations will no doubt continue to prevent most flooding, and tree establishment may be increasingly confined to the immediate river channel, which is now near bankful stage much of the time.

LITERATURE CITED

Anon. 1886. Inyo County, its resources and attractions for settlers. Inyo Independent Printers, Independence, Calif.

Brewer, W.H. 1930. Up and down in California in 1860-1864. F.P. Farquhar (ed.). Yale University Press, New Haven, Conn.

Chalfant, W.A. 1922. The story of Inyo. Published by the author.

Christensen, E.M. 1963. Naturalization of Russian olive (Elaeagnus angustifolia L.) in Utah. American Midland Naturalist 70:133-137.

Curtis, B. et al. 1977. Owens Valley tule elk habitat management plan. 2 sections.

Davidson, J.W. 1976. The expedition of Capt. J.W. Davidson from Fort Tejon to the Owens Valley in 1859. In: P.J. Wilke and H.W. Lawton (ed.). Publications in archaeology, ethnology, and history, No. 8. Ballena Press, Soccorro, N.M.

Earl, G.C. 1976. The enchanted valley and other sketches. Arthur H. Clark Co., Glendale, Calif.

Fremont, J.C. 1849. Notes of travel in California. James M'Glashan, Dublin, Ireland.

Goetzmann, W.H. 1966. Exploration and empire: The explorer and the scientist in the winning of the American West. Alfred A. Knopf, New York, N.Y.

Goodyear, W.A. 1888. Inyo County. p. 224-288. In: Eighth annual report of the state mineralogist. California State Mining Bureau.

Horton, J.S. 1977. The development and perpetuation of the permanent tamarisk type in the phreatophyte zone of the Southwest. p. 124-127. In: R.R. Johnson and D.A. Jones (ed.). Importance, preservation and management of riparian habitat. USDA Forest Service General Technical Report RM-43.

Johnson, W.C., R.L. Burgess, and W.R. Keammerer. 1976. Forest overstory vegetation and environment of the Missouri River floodplain in North Dakota. Ecological Monographs 46:59-84.

Los Angeles Department of Water and Power. 1966. Report on water supply management in Inyo and Mono Counties. Prepared by R.V. Phillips et al.

Los Angeles Department of Water and Power. 1979. Final environmental impact report: Increased pumping of the Owens Valley groundwater basin. 2 volumes.

McCullough, D.R. 1969. The tule elk: Its history, behavior, and ecology. University of California publications in zoology, Vol. 88. University of California Press, Berkeley, Calif.

Raymond, R. 1869. Statistics of mines and mining in the states and territories west of the Rocky Mountains. First annual report of the U.S. commissioner of mining statistics. Government Printing Office, Washington, D.C.

Roberts, W.G., J.G. Howe, and J. Major. 1977. A survey of riparian forest flora and fauna in California. p. 3-21. In: A. Sands (ed.). Riparian forests in California: Their ecology and conservation. Institute of Ecology Pub. 15. 122 P. University of California, Davis, Calif.

Robinson, T.W. 1965. Introduction, spread and areal extent of salt cedar (Tamarix) in the western states. U.S. Geological Survey Professional Paper 491-A.

USDI Geological Survey. 1959. Compilation of records of surface waters of the United States through September, 1950. Part 11-B. Pacific slope basins in California, Central Valley. Water-Supply Paper 1315-A.

THE TRANSITIONAL NATURE OF

NORTHWESTERN CALIFORNIA RIPARIAN SYSTEMS[1]

R. Chad Roberts[2]

Abstract.--Within the region between the Sacramento Valley and the northwestern California coast, riparian vegetation undergoes a change in species composition apparently related to floristic history, climate, and local conditions. While forest areas appear structurally convergent, there may be significant regional taxonomic differences. Each plant species shows an individualistic response. Broad-niched nonriparian species may constitute the riparian forest in some sites. The vegetation type is used by many bird species distributed throughout the area; northcoast forests appear to have more resident species, but lack oak tree specialists.

INTRODUCTION

This paper presents a first look at biogeographic patterns in northwestern California riparian systems. Sacramento Valley riparian studies were just being planned a decade ago, motivated by the imminent demise of the native forests. To many northwestern California residents, riparian forests are a nuisance, an income source from logging, or a hindrance to agriculture. At best, the riparian strips are known to provide flood protection, and may be considered picturesque. Given these local viewpoints, it is not surprising that no studies similar to those of the last decade in the Sacramento River system have been done.

The 1980's should see such studies; northwestern California riparian systems are both different from those in the Sacramento Valley, and are subject to similar conversion pressures. These attributes raise a plea for attention from academic scientists, conservation biologists, and agency personnel. This paper is motivated to extend the concern that has developed for riparian systems elsewhere to include northwestern California. I show here how the biogeographic face of riparian forest changes within this region, and suggest preliminary explanations for the changes.

Interested readers are encouraged to investigate the area for themselves.

METHODOLOGY

Because this was a preliminary survey, no attempt was made to be quantitative or to rigorously test alternative hypotheses. These actions are logically deferrable to more detailed second-level studies. Information used herein was derived from field sampling and literature descriptions. Field sampling involved recording tree species, most shrub species, and common herbaceous species at sample sites within the study area. In most cases, notes were made of adjacent nonriparian vegetation. Additionally, (given my training and long-standing predilection) I recorded all bird species encountered.

Sample site choice was decidedly nonrandom. The coastal areas in Humboldt and Del Norte Counties are better covered than interior areas, and these counties are better sampled than inland counties. The Eel River's South Fork, the lower Mad River, and the Trinity River drainage are better sampled than are other basins.

The area covered by this survey extends from the lower Sacramento Valley (Yolo County; see figure 1) north to western Siskiyou County. West of that transect, the study area includes Del Norte, Humboldt, Trinity, northern Mendocino, Lake, and eastern Napa Counties. The area from southern Mendocino County to San Pablo Bay and nearby areas is specifically excluded.

Numerous literature sources proved useful, including descriptions accompanying mapping, planning documents and agency descriptions, published papers, and textbook descriptions. Some of these are cited below; others will be cited in subsequent papers.

---

[1] Paper presented at the California Riparian Systems Conference. [University of California, Davis, September 17-19, 1981].
[2] R. Chad Roberts is a Staff Environmental Analyst with Oscar Larson & Associates, P.O. Box 3806, Eureka, Calif.

Figure 1.--County outline map of northern California, showing study area and its relationship to other areas. Adapted from Griffin and Critchfield (1972).

RESULTS

Plant Biogeography

Species

Certain tree and shrub species are often considered characteristic of riparian systems, due either to requirements for high soil water content or to a tolerance of it. In this paper I assume that this requirement and/or tolerance is the criterion of riparian species in general. Other factors (light intensity, flood-scour potential, seed-source proximity, history, and competition) are likely to affect species distribution as well. Two distinct species groups comprise riparian forests in the study area. The following summaries deal only with tree species, but shrubs and herbaceous plants show similar (or even greater) regional differentiation.

Southern Group.--The study area includes parts of the Central Valley Riparian Forest region and most of the North Coast Riparian Forest region of Roberts et al. (1980). The entire west side of the Sacramento River Valley below elevations of 914 to 1218 m. (3000 to 4000 ft.) contains Foothill Woodland (Munz and Keck 1959), the riparian face of which includes species such as valley oak (Quercus lobata), interior live oak (Q. wislizenii), blue oak (Q. douglasii), California buckeye (Aescu- (lus californica), Fremont cottonwood (Populus fremontii), and digger pine (Pinus sabiniana). In the study area's southern end, Hind's walnut (Juglans hindsii) is a conspic- uous element, and larger creeks may have Oregon ash (Fraxinus latifolia) and box elder (Acer negundo).

The small creeks draining the inner Coast Ranges largely lack the extensive and diverse flora found beside major rivers (Conard et al. 1980). Larger creeks (Putah Creek, for example) have riparian forests containing many typical riparian species, but these disappear from riparian systems to the northwest. Cache Creek resembles the smaller creeks in its ripar- ian borders. Figure 2 shows a typical riparian section from a southern creek.

Northern Group.--As a useful generaliza- tion, the opposite extreme of southern group creeks is the small coastal streams of Del Norte and Humboldt Counties. Elk Creek in Del Norte County has a relatively undisturbed, second- growth riparian forest, with red alder (Alnus rubra), Pacific wax-myrtle (Myrica califor- nica), California bay (Umbellularia cali- fornica), and madrone (Arbutus menziesii) the most abundant hardwoods. North coast riparian forests contain a significant conifer element; Elk Creek includes Sitka spruce (Picea sitchensis), Douglas-fir (Pseudotsuga men- ziesii), redwood (Sequoia sempervirens), and several other conifer species (Del Norte County Planning Dept. 1979). The same species are characteristic of small, coastal stream- channel forests from southern Oregon as far south as Ft. Bragg in Mendocino County. Since most coastal streams have been logged at least once, however, the conifer element is often less conspicuous, or is missing entirely.

Figure 2.--Riparian vegetation bordering Chicka- hominy Slough, Yolo Co. Blue oak, interior live oak, and digger pine are evident.

86

North coastal riparian forests also contain diverse shrub and understory floras, including several willow (Salix) species, several berry (Rubus) species, two huckleberry (Vaccinium) species, Pacific red elder (Sambucus callicarpa), cascara (Rhamnus purshiana), and a number of others (Del Norte County Planning Dept. 1979; Roberts et al. 1980; McLaughlin and Harradine 1965). Most of these species are equally characteristic of other nonriparian zones near the streams, suggesting that they may not be obligate riparian species. This appears to be true of most riparian tree species listed above, though the species appear to achieve their best growth in riparian situations.

South or inland of coastal Del Norte County, additional species occur which are characteristic of the northern species group. Bigleaf maple (Acer macrophyllum) is an important redwood forest understory component, reaching maximum growth as a riparian species. Bigleaf maple occurs from the coast to the Sierra Nevada foothills (Griffin and Critchfield 1972); in eastern Shasta County it is often a shrub restricted to stream vicinities. Figure 3 shows a typical north coastal riparian forest.

Inland from the coast, additional riparian species are encountered that appear to be part of the northern species group. Oregon ash is a major riparian component in the Klamath River region of eastern Humboldt County, as well as in the upper Eel basin in northern Mendocino County. It occurs throughout the Trinity River basin and is still prominent in the Cottonwood Creek basin southwest of Redding. Oregon ash is present, but not prominent, in the North Fork, Cache Creek drainage, Lake County.

White alder (Alnus rhombifolia) replaces red alder away from the coast, assuming the riparian alder role. It is present in the upper Eel River basin of southern Humboldt, where its range overlaps the red alder (A. rubra), and is common throughout the Klamath, Trinity, and

upper Sacramento River basins. I have noted it in the upper Russian River drainage in eastern Mendocino County, but am uncertain of its abundance south and east of Clear Lake.

A major northern group species is the black cottonwood (Populus trichocarpa). It is largely restricted to riparian zones, and forms the dominant structural component in floodplain forests in the lower Eel, Klamath, and upper Trinity River systems. It is not common in coastal areas, per se, reaching the Pacific only in the Eel, Mad, and Klamath River floodplains (fig. 4). The same gallery forests in the Eel (and probably the Klamath) River valley contain large willow trees, up to 24 m. (80 ft.) tall. At least Pacific willow (Salix lasiandra) is present as a tree, along with black cottonwood and red alder. These riparian gallery forests are impressive for their luxuriance and structural diversity (fig. 4).

A third group of species exists which is technically related to the northern group. Generally part of the mixed evergreen association, it is composed of species found in the Klamath and Siskiyou Mountains and the interior Coast Ranges. Several species in this group occupy the riparian zone along creeks or rivers throughout much of the study area, in much the same way foothill woodland species do in the southern group. The most prominent facultative

Figure 3.--Riparian forest, Mad River, Humboldt Co.; including red alder, bigleaf maple, and Pacific elderberry.

Figure 4.--Riparian gallery forest, Eel River, Humboldt Co. Red alder, Oregon ash, black cottonwood, and willow constitute the dominant vegetation.

riparian species appear to be canyon live oak (<u>Quercus</u> <u>chrysolepis</u>), tanoak (<u>Lithocarpus</u> <u>densiflorus</u>), and to a lesser extent black oak (<u>Q. kelloggii</u>) and garry or Oregon white oak (<u>Q. garryana</u>). Riparian species such as white alder, bigleaf maple, and dogwood may or may not be present, as is true for Douglas-fir, redwood, madrone, and other facultative riparian species noted above. Figure 5 shows a typical area where these ecologically eurytopic species occupy riparian zones.

Physiography

The words "riparian forest" usually evoke an image of a floristically and structurally diverse community growing by a large river. It is immediately clear that most northwestern riparian forests do not fit that mold. The following three community types appear to reflect on-the-ground conditions.

<u>Headwaters Areas</u>.--Throughout the study area, the uppermost stream reaches have a border mostly comprised of the common species in the region. Southeastward in the region, chaparral species are prominent in this role; northward and westward, mixed-conifer forest species fill the role. In the Sacramento, Trinity, and Eel River headwater reaches, white alder, bigleaf maple, and various riparian shrubs are usually present.

The small headwaters streams are often actively eroding their channels at or close to bedrock. It appears that a significant physical parameter affecting the plants is the ability to find a foothold and nourishment in the thin alluvial soils of these mountain canyons. In most cases, the streamflow regime provides adequate year-round water.

<u>Midlevel Areas</u>.--As the stream grade flattens, most north coast rivers show gravel-bars and sand flats supporting riparian vegetation. Often these are narrow strips squeezed between the river and bedrock hillslopes (fig. 5). Fluctuating water levels and flood scour may

leave relatively little riparian vegetation in these areas. Where a valley is wide enough terraces form, which often support riparian groves.

Community composition on the terraces appears to result from a dynamic process of elimination, colonization, and exploitive competition. There communities typically have "non-riparian" canyon live oaks, tanoaks, or madrones growing in the riparian corridors, with or without alders, Oregon ashes, and other species. Apparently, individuals are eliminated from the community through bank scour or competitive death. Recolonization depends on seed source proximity and dispersal factors. In the midlevel Eel and Trinity River drainages, the result is a mosaic of riparian community types. Throughout much of northwestern California, the characteristic riparian species are white alder, canyon live oak, and Douglas-fir. The same process apparently leads to dominance of foothill woodland species in the Sacramento Valley area riparian communities.

<u>Broad-Valley Floodplain Areas</u>.--Deposition of a thick sediment layer near abundant water leads to the formation of riparian gallery forests. In the Sacramento River drainage, this is the community primarily addressed in Sands (1980), which is present in this study area only in a few major, interior Coast Range channels. In the westward drainages, the broad floodplains are largely confined to the lower reaches (except in the Weaverville and Scott Valley areas where they are in large part due to gold dredging). Apparently, these areas once supported mixed conifer/deciduous redwood communities such as that on Elk Creek. Those riparian plant communities still present for the most part lack conifers, and consequently resemble deciduous gallery forests in interior river basins (fig. 6).

Figure 5.--Midlevel riparian zone, upper Eel River, Mendocino Co. Canyon live oak, white alder, and Douglas-fir are the major riparian species.

Figure 6.--Floodplain gallery forest, Eel River near Miranda, Humboldt Co. Black cottonwood and willow have reached large sizes on terrace probably dating from 1964 flood.

Colonization processes on the major flood-plains appear to occur very rapidly. However, these floodplain areas are the primary agricultural areas in the north coast, and barring effective land use regulation, many of the gallery forests are likely to be cleared for agricultural purposes or in flood-control projects.

Bird Biogeography

Several Sacramento Valley studies have catalogued riparian bird use (Gaines 1980, and included references; Motroni 1979; Hehnke and Stone 1979). No studies have been done to date specifically on riparian birds in northwestern California. Gaines (1980) noted 69 species during the breeding season and 66 wintering species in Central Valley riparian forests. Motroni (1979) observed 71 species. Hehnke and Stone (1979) apparently recorded 90 species. By contrast, Harris (1974) listed 142 species for mid-Humboldt County riparian systems, and (1979) 157 species for this type of system in the "North Coast/Cascade Zone" that includes this study area. Taken as a whole, northwestern riparian forests are apparently used by more species than are Central Valley riparian forests.

Gaines (1980) recorded 26 migrant species in the 69-species breeding avifauna (38%), and 30 migratory or sporadic visitors among the 66 wintering species (45%). Harris' (1974) list contains 36 summer visitors and 27 wintering species of the 142 total species, the remainder being residents. After the appropriate adjustments, 31% of the 115 summer species are visitors and 25% of the 106 wintering species are not permanent residents. As initial hypotheses, north coastal riparian forests appear to support more total bird species and more resident bird species than do the Sacramento River forests.

In comparing Harris' (1979) listing with Gaines (1980) the Falconidae, Rallidae, Hirundinidae, Strigidae, and Charadriidae are better represented in northwestern forests. Very likely, recent habitat simplification in the Central Valley is the basis for the difference. However, one ecological (but not taxonomic) group, namely oak woodland birds, appears to be under-represented in the north. Throughout the Sacramento River basin, the Plain Titmouse (Parus inornatus), White-breasted Nuthatch (Sitta carolinensis), Scrub Jay (Aphelocoma coerulescens), Nuttall's Woodpecker (Picoides nuttallii), and Acorn Woodpecker (Melanerpes formicivorus) are common resident riparian species. Of these only the Scrub Jay and Acorn Woodpecker regularly occur in Humboldt County, and use systems other than riparian forests (Harris 1974, 1979; personal observation). A likely hypothesis to account for this is the lack of riparian valley oaks north of northern Mendocino County.

DISCUSSION

Geofloristic History

When Axelrod (1958, 1959) postulated the Arcto-Tertiary and Madro-Tertiary Geofloras, he separated northwestern California from the Central Valley and its fringes. The former was called the Border-Redwood Forest (Axelrod 1959: 7); this association apparently dates to Pliocene age and represents a combination of floristic elements from Arcto- and Madro-Tertiary backgrounds.

As Robichaux (1980) showed, elements in the present riparian flora can be linked to fossils within both these geofloristic associations. Oregon ash and Pacific willow appear to be Arcto-Tertiary in origin and California sycamore (Platanus racemosa) and arroyo willow (S. lasiolepis) are more likely to have come from the southeast. Nonetheless, since the several species are all adapted to conditions near streams, they can be found intermixed to greater or lesser degree. For example, Fremont cottonwood is a Madro-Tertiary species now found along Central Valley watercourses, including those in the southeastern part of the sample area. Black cottonwood is an Arcto-Tertiary species; in the sample area, it is both coastal and higher elevation. Nonetheless, the two species overlap in the Trinity River basin at least from Douglas City to west of Weaverville. This site is in a drainage where black cottonwood are expected. Even if the present overlap were an artifact, there are dense stands of Fremont cottonwood along Cottonwood Creek, less than 33 air km. (20 air mi.) from the Trinity River stands, over a low ridge.

Axelrod (1977) discussed the range alterations induced in California vegetation by climatic change. In northwestern California there is little to impede north-south range shifts induced by changing temperature and rainfall regimes. The Franciscan Formation, the major geological substrate for the region, is faulted in a north-westward-trending direction; the north coastal rivers have followed the faultblock alignment (fig. 7). It appears that this alignment would be conducive to riparian species mixing, if species showed differential climatic responses along this north-south transect.

Substrate availability within the river channel should modify the pattern induced by climate. Narrow, rocky canyons could prove an obstacle to species requiring thick sediment deposits. Extreme channel scouring through high runoff during winter rainy periods could prevent seedling establishment and remove parent trees. Conversely, high erosion levels (typical of north coast rivers) could provide alluvial sediment deposits favoring riparian growth.

Present Communities

Given the origins shown in geological records, combined with other factors affecting

Figure 7.--Raised relief map of northern California. Note northwest-trending mountain blocks. Modified from Griffin and Critchfield (1972).

plant evolution in California (Raven 1977), it follows that present riparian communities reflect species' tolerances of recent geoclimatic conditions. As an hypothesis, communities along a southeast-to-northwest transect show decreasing cold (or wetness) tolerance toward the southeast end.

Riparian plant associations at opposite ends of the transect appear quite different in species composition, though there are great structural similarities. However, the changes along the transect appear gradual; species composition changes by percentages, rather than in sharp discontinuities. Both the lower Sacramento and lower Eel Rivers have forests dominated by broad-leaved deciduous trees; the forests are structurally similar but taxonomically different. Between those endpoints, tree taxa respond to local ecological conditions, and one finds conifers mixed with broad-leaved riparian species (both evergreen and deciduous). The forest composition at a particular site within the sample area depends on ecofloristic factors reflecting species ranges, and on physical conditions at the site. Hence, one expects to find an isolated Fremont cottonwood among the white alder, Oregon ash and canyon live oak in the upper Eel River drainage in Mendocino County; or sparse-foliaged Oregon ash among the oak and digger pine in Chickahominy Slough in Yolo County; or California buckeye within three kilometers of the Pacific Ocean in the lower Mattole River in Humboldt County.

It is time that biologists and conservationists interested in riparian forests investigated these northwestern sites. This holds for

zoologists as well as botanists. The absence of oak forest birds from Humboldt County riparian forests suggests it may be profitable to consider the evolutionary association of birds such as Nuttall's Woodpecker and Plain Titmouse with such California endemics as the blue oak (Quercus douglasii) and valley oak. I am unaware of California studies of riparian small mammal communities, such as that by Geier and Best (1980) in Iowa, or those of the Lower Colorado River Project. Comparisons between the structurally similar but taxonomically distinct forests in the Sacramento Valley and the lower Eel or Klamath River basins could serve to test biogeographic habitat-diversity models. These studies should be initiated soon, however, for the north coast riparian forests, like those elsewhere, are under duress, and the situation will likely get worse rather than better.

LITERATURE CITED

Axelrod, D.I. 1958. Evolution of the Madro-Tertiary Geoflora. Bot. Rev. 24:433-509.

Axelrod, D.I. 1959. Geological history. p. 5-9. In: P.A. Munz and D.D. Keck, A California Flora. 1681 p. University of California Press, Berkeley, Calif.

Axelrod, D.I. 1977. Outline history of California vegetation. p. 139-193. In: M.G. Barbour and J. Major (ed.). Terrestrial vegetation of California. John Wiley & Sons, New York, N.Y.

Conard, S.G., R.L. MacDonald, and R.F. Holland. 1980. Riparian vegetation and flora of the Sacramento Valley. p. 47-55. In: A. Sands (ed.). Riparian forests in California--their ecology and conservation. Institute of Ecology Pub. 15. 122 p. University of California, Davis, Calif.

Del Norte County Planning Department. 1979. Elk Creek wetland special study; Del Norte County Local Coastal Program. 51 p.

Gaines, D.A. 1980. The valley riparian forests of California; their importance to bird populations. p. 57-85. In: A. Sands (ed.). Riparian forests in California--their ecology and conservation. Institute of Ecology Pub. 15. 122 p. University of California, Davis, Calif.

Geier, A.R., and L.B. Best. 1980. Habitat selection by small mammals of riparian communities: evaluating effects of habitat alterations. J. Wildl. Manage. 44:16-24.

Griffin, J.R., and W.B. Critchfield. 1972. The distribution of forest trees in California. USDA Forest Service Research Paper PSW-82. 114 p. Pacific Southwest Forest and Range Experiment Station, Berkeley, Calif.

Harris, S.W. 1974. No title. p. II-94- II-105. In: Eureka-Arcata Regional Sewage Facility Project Environmental Impact Report. Environmental Research Consultants, Inc.

Harris, S.W. 1979. Bird narratives. In: B. Marcot (ed.), California Wildlife/Habitat Relationships Program--North Coast/Cascades Zone, Vol. 2. USDA Forest Service. Washington, D.C.

Hehnke, M., and C.P. Stone. 1979. Value of riparian vegetation to avian populations along the Sacramento River system. p. 228-235. In: R.R. Johnson and J.F. McCormick (ed.). Strategies for protection and management of floodplain wetlands and other riparian ecosystems. USDA Forest Service GTR-WO-12. Washington, D.C.

McLaughlin, J., and F. Harradine. 1965. Soils of western Humboldt County, California. 85 p. Department of Soils and Plant Nutrition, University of California, Davis, with Humboldt County, Calif.

Motroni, R.S. 1979. Avian density and composition of a riparian forest--Sacramento Valley, California. 172 p. M.S. Thesis, Sacramento State University.

Munz, P.A., and D.D. Keck. 1959. A California Flora. 1681 p. University of California Press, Berkeley, Calif.

Raven, P.H. 1977. The California flora. p. 109-137. In: M.G. Barbour and J. Major (ed.). Terrestrial vegetation of California. John Wiley & Sons, New York, N.Y.

Roberts, W.G., J.G. Howe, and J. Major. 1980. A survey of riparian forest flora and fauna in California. p. 3-19. In: A. Sands (ed.). Riparian forests in California--their ecology and conservation. Institute of Ecology Pub. 15. 122 p. University of California, Davis, Calif.

Robichaux, R. 1980. Geological history of the riparian forests of California. p. 21-34. In: A. Sands (ed.). Riparian forests in California--their ecology and conservation. Institute of Ecology Pub. 15. 122 p. University of California, Davis, Calif.

Sands, A.(ed.) 1980. Riparian forests in California--their ecology and conservation. 122 p. Institute of Ecology Pub. 15. University of California, Davis, Calif.

CLASSIFICATION AND DYNAMICS OF SUBALPINE MEADOW

ECOSYSTEMS IN THE SOUTHERN SIERRA NEVADA[1]

Nathan B. Benedict[2]

Abstract.--Subalpine meadow ecosystems are an important high elevation riparian vegetation type in the Sierra Nevada. The study of meadows has proceeded in two directions: classification; and studies of meadow dynamics. This paper reviews current research on these two topics in the southern Sierra Nevada.

INTRODUCTION

At high elevations in the southern Sierra Nevada, California, one of the most frequently referred to riparian systems is meadow ecosystems. Although there are other high elevation riparian systems, meadows are often chosen for study due to their visual attractiveness and importance for grazing and camping. High elevation meadows, though, are not exclusively riparian in that they can occur in any area with a sufficient amount of moisture, e.g. spring-fed meadows. This correlation between meadow ecosystems and moisture suggests that meadows play an important role in the hydrology of high elevation watersheds. As a result, a discussion of meadow classification and dynamics is vital to a thorough understanding of Sierran high elevation watersheds and riparian systems. This paper reviews current research on the classification and dynamics of southern Sierran meadow ecosystems.

CLASSIFICATION

Until recently, the classification of Sierran meadows was based on a simplistic scheme first suggested by Sumner[3] and subsequently followed and modified by Sharsmith[4], Benedict (1965), and Strand (1972). The classification consists of three basic meadow types: 1) wet; 2) short-hair; and 3) woodland. Harkin and Schultz[5] proposed a topographic classification of meadows in the Rock Creek drainage, Sequoia National Park which consists of three meadow types: 1) level meadows; 2) hanging meadows; and 3) elongated stringers. More recently three meadow classifications have been presented for the southern Sierra Nevada (Benedict 1981; Benedict and Major 1980, 1981; Ratliff 1979). These three recent classifications look at meadows from three different and complementary points of view. Vegetation studies in other parts of the Sierra contain scattered descriptions of additional meadow communities and those described in the southern Sierra are discussed by Benedict (1981).

Ratliff (1979) presents a classification of meadow sites based on floristic composition. A meadow site is an area of meadow homogenous within itself and having a general species composition which is visually different from that of the adjacent areas (Ratliff _ibid._). The classification was derived using various cluster analysis procedures until a final optimum classification was developed. Fourteen "site-classes" were described (table 1). Ratliff (_ibid._) notes several problems with the classification. He states that the current site-classes are at least two levels above the individual meadow site. This increases the variability between sites within one site-class making it difficult to assign sites in the field to a given site-class. Another problem is that the actual number of sites in the classes is small in most cases. A total of 82 meadow sites were sampled for the classification and only 71 of over 200 species present were selected for use in the analysis proceedures.

[1]Paper presented at the California Riparian Systems Conference. [University of California, September 17-19, 1981].

[2]Nathan B. Benedict is with the Biology Department, University of Nevada, Reno, Nevada.

[3]Sumner, E.L. 1941. Special report on range management and wildlife protection in Kings Canyon National Park. Unpublished report. Sequoia National Park, Three Rivers, Calif.

[4]Sharsmith, C.W. 1959. A report on the status, changes, and ecology of back country meadows in Sequoia and Kings Canyon National Parks. Unpublished report. Sequoia National Park, Three Rivers, Calif.

[5]Harkin, D.W., and A.M. Schultz. 1967. Ecological study of meadows in Lower Rock Creek, Sequoia National Park. Unpublished report. Sequoia National Park, Three Rivers, Calif.

Table 1.--Site-classes of Sierran meadows (Ratliff 1979).

Association	Series (Site-class)
Dry Meadow	B -- Kentucky bluegrass
	F -- tufted hairgrass
Moist Meadow	B -- Kentucky bluegrass
	E -- longstalk clover
	F -- tufted hairgrass
	G -- Nebraska sedge
	I -- pullup muhly
	J -- bentgrass
	K -- carpet clover
Wet Meadow	A -- beaked sedge
	C -- ephemeral lake
	D -- hillside bog
	H -- fewflowered spikerush
Subalpine/Alpine Dry Meadow	N -- short-hair sedge
Subalpine/Alpine Moist to Wet Meadow	L -- short-hair
	M -- gentian/aster

Table 2.--Meadow plant associations. Sequoia National Park (Benedict 1981).

Meadow Type	Associations
Hydric	Carex rostrata
	Eleocharis pauciflora
	Eleocharis pauciflora/ Mimulus primuloides
	Carex rostrata/ Mimulus primuloides
	Calamagrostis canadensis/ Dodecatheon redolens
	Deschampsia caespitosa/ Cardamine breweri
Mesic	Calamagrostis breweri/ Aster alpigenus
	Calamagrostis breweri/ Vaccinium nivictum
	Calamagrostis breweri/ Oryzopsis kingii
	Calamagrostis breweri/ Trisetum spicatum
	Deschampsia caespitosa/ Senecio scorzonella
	Deschampsia caespitosa/ Senecio scorzonella/ Achillea lanulosa
	Juncus orthophyllus
	Penstemon heterodoxus/ Achillea lanulosa
	Carex heteroneura/ Achillia lanulosa
Xeric	Artemisia rothrockii
	Carex exserta
	Muhlenbergia richardsonis
	Eriogonum/Oreonana clementis

Benedict (1981) presents a classification of meadow plant communities based on floristic composition of stands. Stands are defined as homogenous units of vegetation of variable size. Sampling was done using the Braun-Blanquet releve technique (Mueller-Dombois and Ellenberg 1974). The classification was derived using tabular association analysis of the 134 stands sampled. All species present (141) were used in the analysis procedure (Benedict 1981). Three main meadow types were described on the basis of floristic composition: 1) hydric; 2) mesic; and 3) xeric (table 2). Within each of these larger units, 19 plant associations were described with more narrowly defined species composition (table 2). The plant associations are at the stand or "site" (Ratliff 1979) level thus making them readily useable in the field. The geographic distribution of these plant associations is not known at present, but is thought to include most of the southern Sierra. Other meadow plant associations remain to be described (Benedict 1981).

Benedict and Major (1980, 1981) present a classification of whole meadows on the basis of physiographic characteristics (table 3). Two major physiographic meadow types are described: Type I meadows with predominately vegetated margins (fig. 1), and Type II meadows with predominately sandy margins (fig. 2). Type I meadows occur in areas glaciated relatively recently and are usually surrounded by forests composed mainly of Pinus contorta subsp. murrayana. Type II meadows typically occur in areas of relatively more ancient glaciation or in areas that have not been glaciated, and are surrounded by forests composed of either pure Pinus balfouriana or a mixture of P. balfouriana and P. contorta subsp.

murrayana. Both major types have a variety of subtypes distinguished by topographic position and rock type (Benedict and Major 1980, 1981; table 3). The geographic distribution of the different physiographic types is not completely

Figure 1.--Rock Creek Meadow #3, Sequoia National Park. Example of physiographic Type I subalpine meadow.

known. Type II meadows, though, are correlated with the southern boundary of mountain glaciation in the Sierra Nevada (Benedict and Major 1980, 1981).

MEADOW DYNAMICS

The dynamic description of meadows until recently was based largely on inferences from spatial patterns and on the presence or absence of decreasers, increasers, and invaders (Shar-smith[4]). Recently Wood (1975) has described long-term changes in seven montane meadows based on the soil stratigraphy revealed in deep erosion gullies. DeBenedetti (1980) and DeBenedetti and Parsons (1979a) have been following meadow recovery after a natural wildfire in 1977. Benedict (1981) has initiated a study of the long-term development of subalpine meadows as revealed in the stratigraphy of soil cores collected in the Rock Creek drainage, Sequoia National Park, which will be directly comparable with Wood (1975).

Table 3.--Physiographic meadow types, Sequoia National Park (Benedict 1981, Benedict and Major 1980, 1981).

Code	Type Description	Example	Elev.
I	Predominately vegetated margins		
A	Topographic basin		
1	Bedrock	Lower Crabtree Meadow	3148
		Rock Creek Meadow #1	3185
		Rock Creek Meadow #2	3145
2	Moraine	Upper Crabtree Meadow	3184
		Rock Creek Meadow #3	3048
		Wright Creek Meadows	3292-3353
B	Slope		
1	Lateral moraine	Rock Creek Meadow #4	2426
		Lower Rock Creek	2804-2126
2	Bedrock	Trail Crew Stringer, Rock Creek	3195
C	Stream	Army Pass Creek Meadows	3292-3414
II	Predominately sandy margins		
A	Basin	Siberian Outpost	3292
		Big Whitney Meadow	2450
		Guyot Flat	3243
B	Stream	Sandy Meadow	3200-3231

Figure 2.--Siberian Outpost, Sequoia National Park. Example of physiographic Type II subalpine meadow.

Classically meadows have been viewed as a seral stage in the hydrosere of a lake developing into a forest (Oosting 1956, and many others). Recent evidence suggests that this interpretation of meadow dynamics may be too restrictive (Benedict 1981). Two other possible hypotheses are: 1) meadow ecosystems, like any ecosystem, have changed through time as the climatic factors influencing meadows have changed; and 2) meadow ecosystems have changed the same amount or less than the surrounding forest vegetation over a given period of time. These two hypotheses are not necessarily alternatives to each other (Benedict 1981).

Evidence in support of the first hypothesis comes from three sources. Wood (1975) describes a generalized montane meadow stratigraphic sequence as: 1) a basal layer of alluvium deposited by pre-Holocene streams; 2) a paleosol dated at between 8,705 and 10,185 years B.P. developed under a mesic montane forest; 3) stratified sandy deposits dated at between 8,700 and 1,200-2,500 years B.P. and deposited under a fir, yellow pine, and lodgepole pine forest; and 4) stratified sedge peat, loams, and grus deposited since 2,500-3,000 years B.P. in a meadow environment. Based on this stratigraphic evidence, Wood (1975) suggests that meadow ecosystems can develop from, and develop to forest ecosystems, and that this is a result of climatic changes.

The second source of evidence for the first hypothesis comes from the widespread invasion of forest trees into meadows throughout the western United States (Dunwiddie 1977; Franklin et al. 1971; DeBenedetti and Parsons 1979b; Vale 1981 a,b). It has been suggested that this widespread tree invasion has resulted from excessive meadow grazing and climatic changes. It is only infrequently suggested that this is the result of successional processes. This implies that meadow ecosystems are in dynamic equilibrium with their total environment and that it is an oversimplification to view meadows only as stages in a hydrosere.

The third source of evidence that meadows are dynamically adjusted to their environment and climate comes from a man-induced experiment at Osgood Swamp near South Lake Tahoe, California (Benedict 1981). Osgood Swamp occupies a wet basin formed behind a morainal dam (Physiographic Type IA2, Adam 1967). When the morainal dam was artificially breached, the basin became drier simulating a dramatic change in climate. Subsequently, there was a massive invasion of Pinus contorta subsp. murrayana into the meadow. This indicates that meadow vegetation changes not only as a result of successional processes but as a result of climatic and environmental changes. These changes can be either man-induced or natural.

Evidence for the second hypothesis that meadows are as stable as the surrounding forest has been discussed previously by Benedict (1981). Two sources of evidence support this hypothesis. Adam (1967) presents pollen diagrams from Osgood Swamp, and Soda Springs (near Tuolumne Meadows). These diagrams suggest that meadow vegetation is as stable or more stable than the surrounding forest vegetation. The second source of evidence comes from Wood (1975). From his stratigraphic work, seven of the meadows studied have been in existence since 1200-3000 years B.P., and two since 7700-9800 years B.P. This suggests that these meadows have been unstable over the past 10,000 radiocarbon years. In a similar manner, the forest vegetation at these same sites has also been unstable over the past 10,000 radiocarbon years (Wood 1975).

CONCLUSIONS

Meadows are variable in space and time. Spatial variation can be described from a static viewpoint and has resulted in both floristic and physiographic classifications. Temporal variation can be described from a dynamic viewpoint. Current evidence suggests that meadows have variable development patterns. The classic dynamic description of meadows as a seral stage in a hydrosere may apply to some meadows. Other meadows, though, may have developed in areas previously occupied by forest vegetation while still other meadows may be developing into forest as a result of climatic changes. Some meadows may have been in existence for the entire Holocene and are as stable or more stable than the surrounding forest vegetation. More studies are needed to determine if there are other as yet undescribed meadow development patterns.

LITERATURE CITED

Adam, D.P. 1967. Late-Pleistocene and recent palynology in the Central Sierra Nevada, Calif. p. 275-301. In: Quaternary paleoecology. 433 p. Yale University Press, New Haven, Conn.

Beguin, C., and J. Major. 1975. Contribution a l'etude phytosociologique et ecologique des marais de la Sierra Nevada (Californie). Phytocoenologia 2:349-367.

Benedict, N.B. 1981. The vegetation and ecology of subalpine meadows of the southern Sierra Nevada, California. 128 p. Ph.D. Thesis, University of California, Davis.

Benedict, N.B., and J. Major. 1980. A physiographic classification of subalpine meadows of the Sierra Nevada, California. p. 323-336. In: Proceedings of the conference on scientific research in the national parks (2nd.). [San Francisco, Calif., November 26-30, 1979]. Volume 4: Resource analysis and mapping. 363 p. N.T.I.S., US Department of Commerce, Springfield, Va.

Benedict, N.B. and J. Major. 1981. A physiographic classification of subalpine meadows of the Sierra Nevada, California. Madrono [in press].

Bennett, P.S. 1965. An investigation of the impact of grazing on ten meadows in Sequoia and Kings Canyon National Parks. 164 p. M.S. Thesis, San Jose State College.

Burke, M. 1980. The flora and vegetation of the Rae Lakes Basin, southern Sierra Nevada: an ecological overview. 166 p. M.S. Thesis, University of California, Davis.

DeBenedetti, S.H. 1980. Establishment of vegetation following fire in a subalpine meadow of the southern Sierra Nevada: one year post-burn. p. 325-336. In: Proceedings of the conference on scientific research in the national parks (2nd). [San Francisco, Calif., November 26-30, 1979]. Volume 10: Fire ecology. 403 p. N.T.I.S., US Department of Commerce, Springfield, Va.

DeBenedetti, S.H., and D.J. Parsons. 1979a. Natural fire in subalpine meadows: a case description from the Sierra Nevada. Journal of Forestry 77:477-479.

DeBenedetti, S.H., and D.J. Parsons. 1979b. Mountain meadow management and research in Sequoia and Kings Canyon National Parks: a review and update. p. 1305-1311. In: Proceedings first conference on scientific research in the national parks. Volume 2. 1325 p. National Park Service Transactions and Proceedings. Series no. 5.

Dunwiddie, P.W. 1977. Recent tree invasion of subalpine meadows in the Wind River Mountains, Wo. Arctic and Alpine Research 9:393-399.

Franklin, J.F., W.H. Moir, G.W. Douglas, and C. Winberg. 1971. Invasion of subalpine meadows by trees in the Cascade Range, Washington and Oregon. Artic and Alpine Research 3:215-224.

Klickoff, L.G. 1965. Microenvironmental influence on vegetational pattern near timberline in the central Sierra Nevada. Ecological Monographs 35:187-211.

Mueller-Dombois, D., and H. Ellenberg. 1974. Aims and methods of vegetation ecology. 547 p. John Wiley and Sons, New York, N.Y.

Oosting, H.J. 1956. The study of plant communities: an introduction to plant ecology. 440 p. W.H. Freeman and Co., San Francisco, Calif.

Pemble, R.H. 1970. Alpine vegetation in the Sierra Nevada of California as lithosequences and in relation to local site factors. 247 p. Ph.D. Thesis, University of California, Davis.

Ratliff, R.D. 1979. Meadow sites of the Sierra Nevada, California: classification and species relationships. 288 p. Ph.D. Thesis, New Mexico State University.

Strand, S. 1972. Investigation of the relationship of pack stock to some aspects of meadow ecology for seven meadows in Kings Canyon National Park. 125 p. M.S. Thesis, San Jose State University, California.

Taylor, D.W. 1976. Ecology of the timberline vegetation of Carson Pass, Alpine County, California. 124 p. Ph.D. Thesis, University of California, Davis.

Vale, T.R. 1981a. Tree invasion of montane meadows in Oregon. American Midland Naturalist 105:61-69.

Vale, T.R. 1981b. Ages of invasive trees in Dana Meadows, Yosemite National Park, California. Madrono 28:45-47.

Wood, S.H. 1975. Holocene stratigraphy and chronology of mountain meadows, Sierra Nevada, California. 180 p. Ph.D. Thesis, California Institute of Technology, Pasadena.

COMPOSITION AND TREND OF RIPARIAN VEGETATION ON

FIVE PERENNIAL STREAMS IN SOUTHEASTERN ARIZONA[1]

Michael G. Rucks[2]

Abstract.--Composition and trend of 78 km. (49 mi.) of riparian vegetation on five watercourses was determined. Aravaipa Creek has been excluded from cattle since 1973 and was the only study area with a dominant broadleaf riparian community and a trend towards maintaining this community.

INTRODUCTION

There are only 1119 km^2 (437 mi^2) of riparian vegetation in Arizona of which 404 km^2 (158 mi^2) are within the Gila River drainage (Babcock 1968; Minckley and Sommerfeld[3]). It is imperative we assess the composition and trend of these remaining riparian areas.

The Gila River, San Francisco River, Bonita Creek, Mescal Creek and Aravaipa Creek were chosen for study because they are the major riparian areas on public lands administered by the USDI Bureau of Land Management's Safford District. There are also numerous smaller riparian areas associated with short perennial stream reaches and springs not discussed in this paper.

The five riverine riparian systems were studied in the summer of 1980 to establish baseline data to be used for management decisions and future monitoring.

METHODS

A point-sample pace-transect with 10- to 20-pace interval (approx. 18-36.5 m. (60-120 ft.)) was used to sample the selected riparian systems.

Riparian System	Pace Interval	Distance Sampled km. (mi.)	Total Sample Points
Gila	20	20.6 (12.9)	570
San Francisco	20	14.0 (8.75)	370
Aravaipa	12	15.4 (9.6)	737
Mescal	10	4.3 (2.7)	290
Bonita	20	23.8 (14.9)	624

A zig-zag pace route was followed to distribute sample points across the width of the riparian community from terrace to terrace. No sample points were established in the river itself.

Relative abundance of woody species for delineation of the riparian vegetation into mappable vegetation types was determined by recording the nearest woody species in a 180°-arc in front of each sample point. If the nearest woody species was not a broadleaf riparian species, the nearest broadleaf riparian species was recorded. This method maximized the amount of data collected on the broadleaf riparian species. Species recorded were designated as belonging to one of four plant communities: broadleaf riparian, riparian scrub, adjacent desert, and higher elevation. A 20-point running mean of the frequency of the members of each community was plotted to depict the mappable community at each point along the reach.

Relative abundance of herbaceous perennials was determined by recording the herbaceous perennial species closest to the sample point, expressed as a percent of the total points.

Population data on all tree species were obtained by recording the diameter-at-breast-height (DBH), or the diameter below the lowest branch of each tree recorded at each sample point. Diameters were estimated using a Biltmore scale and recorded to the nearest inch. Tree height was recorded for each tree under 1-in. diameter.

Canopy coverage, density, and frequency of perennial species were determined using a line-

---

[1]Paper presented at the California Riparian Systems Conference. [University of California, Davis, September 17-19, 1981.]

[2]Michael G. Rucks is a Wildlife Biologist, Bureau of Land Management, Safford, Ariz.

[3]Minckley, W.L., and M.R. Sommerfeld. 1979. Resource inventory for the Gila River complex, eastern Arizona. Unpublished report to USDI Bureau of Land Management. Contract No. YA-512-CT6-2166. Arizona State University, Tempe, Ariz. XXV + 570 p.

plot method. From each 10th sample point on the pace transect, a 43.56-foot tape was stretched as close to the ground as possible in a predetermined direction roughly parallel to the channel. Canopy coverage of all woody species whose canopy intercepted a vertical plane above the tape was recorded by distance on the tape to the nearest 0.1-foot by species. Canopy coverage of a species is expressed as the percent of the total length of line.

The 43.56-foot tape also served as the center of rectangular 0.01-acre plot (435.6 ft^2) in which species density was determined. Each plant with at least 50% of its basal area within 5 ft. of either side of the tape was tallied by species. Because of the difficulty of determining actual plant number of the sod-forming Bermuda grass (Cynodon dactylon), density of this species was recorded as one (1) when it was present in the plot.

Frequency of a species is expressed as the percent of 0.01-acre plots in which it occurs.

An importance value was determined for each woody species. This value incorporates three parameters of a species in relation to its community. Relative coverage (size or biomass), relative density (number), and relative frequency (ubiquitousness) of each species are combined in one value for comparative purposes. The importance value is determined as:

$$\text{Importance Value} = \frac{\text{Coverage of a species}}{\text{Coverage of all species}} + \frac{\text{Density of a species}}{\text{Total density of all species}} + \frac{\text{Frequency of a species}}{\text{Total frequency of all species}}$$

The maximum importance value of a species would be 300 if it were the only species present.

Utilization of a plant species by browsing wildlife or domestic livestock was recorded at each sample point.

The following is a summary of the amount of line intercept and number of 0.01-acre plots recorded on each riverine riparian system.

Riparian System	Line Intercept (ft.)	Number of 0.01-acre plots
Gila	2482.92	57
San Francisco	1568.16	36
Aravaipa	3179.88	73
Mescal	1263.24	29
Bonita	2700.72	62

RESULTS AND DISCUSSION

Table 1 lists perennial species recorded in the riparian inventory described in this paper. Plant common names are from the USDA Soil Conservation Service National Plant List (May 1980).

Table 1.--Scientific and common names, occurrence of plants, and community classification of woody species.

BR: broadleaf riparian   AD: adjacent desert
RS: riparian scrub   HE: higher elevation

Scientific Name	Common Name	Aravaipa Creek	San Francisco River	Mescal Creek	Bonita Creek	Gila River	Community Classification
Acacia constricta	Whitethorn	X		X			AD
Acacia greggii	Catclaw acacia	X			X		AD
Acer negundo	Box elder	X			X		BR
Agave palmeri	Century plant	X					AD
Agrostis sp.	Bent grass				X		--
Allionia incarnata	Trailing allionia				X		--
Alnus oblongifolia	Arizona alder	X					HE
Artemisia ludoviciana	Wormwood	X			X		AD
Baccharis glutinosa	Seep willow	X	X	X	X	X	RS
Baccharis sarothroides	Desert broom			X			AD
Berberis haematocarpa	Red mahonia			X			HE
Brickellia spp.	Brickellia	X		X			AD
Celtis pallida	Desert hackberry				X	X	RS
Celtis reticulata	Netleaf hackberry	X		X	X	X	RS
Cercidium microphyllum	Yellow palo verde				X		AD
Chilopsis linearis	Desert willow		X		X		RS
Chrysothamnus nauseosus	Rubber rabbit-brush			X			RS
Condalia spp.	Greythorn	X	X	X	X	X	RS
Crossosoma bigelovii	Bigelow crossosoma			X			AD
Cynodon dactylon	Bermuda grass	X	X	X	X	X	--
Datura meteloides	Jimson weed	X		X	X	X	--
Dodonaea viscosa	Aalii			X			AD

Scientific name	Common name						Community
Eriogonum fasciculatum	California buckwheat			X			AD
Fraxinus velutina	Velvet ash	X		X	X	X	BR
Gutierrezia spp.	Snakeweed	X		X	X	X	AD
Hymenoclea monogyra	Burro brush	X	X	X	X	X	RS
Juglans major	Arizona walnut	X		X	X	X	BR
Juniperus monosperma	Juniper			X	X		HE
Larrea divaricata	Creosote bush			X	X	X	AD
Lycium spp.	Wolfberry		X	X	X	X	AD
Marrubium vulgare	Horehound			X			--
Melilotus sp.	Sweet clover			X			--
Mentzelia sp.	Stickleaf		X	X	X		--
Mimosa biuncifera	Catclaw mimosa			X		X	RS
Mimulus guttatus	Common monkeyflower			X			--
Morus microphylla	Texas mulberry				X		RS
Nicotiana glauca	Tree tobacco		X	X	X	X	RS
Nicotiana trigonophylla	Desert tobacco			X	X		--
Nolina microcarpa	Bear grass			X			--
Opuntia spp.	Prickly pear/cholla	X					AD
Penstemon	Penstemon				X		--
Platanus wrightii	Arizona sycamore	X		X	X	X	BR
Populus fremontii	Fremont cottonwood	X	X	X	X	X	BR
Prunus serotina	Chokecherry	X					HE
Prosopis juliflora	Mesquite	X	X	X	X	X	RS
Quercus arizonica	Arizona white oak	X					HE
Rhus radicans	Poison ivy	X					RS
Rumex spp.	Dock	X	X	X	X		--
Salix bonplandiana	Bonpland willow	X		X	X		BR
Salix gooddingii	Goodding willow	X	X	X	X	X	BR
Senecio longilobus	Threadleaf groundsel				X		--
Sphaeralcea spp.	Globe mallow			X	X		--
Stephanomeria pauciflora	Wire lettuce			X	X		--
Tamarix pentandra	Salt cedar	X	X	X		X	RS
Vitis arizonica	Arizona grape	X			X		RS

Community Classification of Woody Species

Occurrence on each system studied and the assignment of woody species to one of four plant communities (broadleaf riparian, riparian scrub, adjacent desert, higher elevation) is also shown in table 1.

Figures 1, 2, 3, 4, and 5 depict the relative abundance of the woody species communities in each

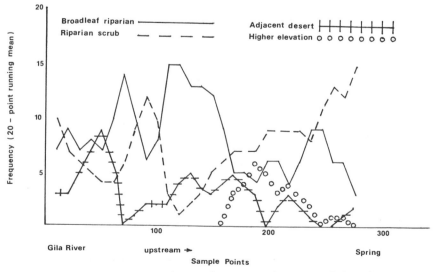

Figure 1.--Community classification of woody species and photograph of Mescal Creek.

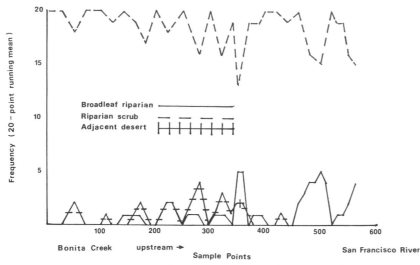

Broadleaf riparian ————————
Riparian scrub — — — —
Adjacent desert ┼┼┼┼┼┼

Frequency (20 – point running mean)

100   200   300   400   500   600

Bonita Creek   upstream →   San Francisco River
Sample Points

Figure 2.--Community classification of woody species and photograph of the Gila River.

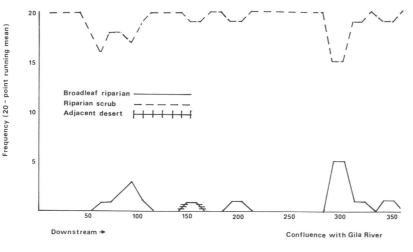

Broadleaf riparian ————
Riparian scrub — — — —
Adjacent desert ┼┼┼┼┼

Frequency (20 – point running mean)

50   100   150   200   250   300   350

Downstream →   Confluence with Gila River

Sample Points

Figure 3.--Community classification of woody species and photograph of the San Francisco River.

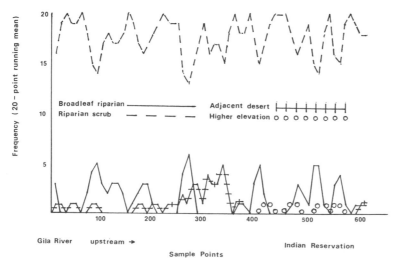

Broadleaf riparian ————   Adjacent desert ┼┼┼┼┼┼
Riparian scrub — — — —   Higher elevation o o o o o o o

Frequency (20 – point running mean)

100   200   300   400   500   600

Gila River   upstream →   Indian Reservation
Sample Points

Figure 4.--Community classification of woody species and photograph of Bonita Creek.

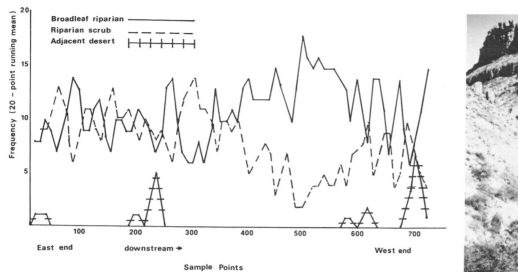

Figure 5.--Community classification of woody species and photograph of Aravaipa Creek.

riparian system, expressed as a running mean of the woody species per 20 sample points. Also included are photographs of the watercourses. A good distribution of mature broadleaf riparian trees without successful reproduction in the open areas made it more likely for riparian scrub, adjacent desert, or higher elevation species to be the nearest woody species to the sample point. Mescal Creek was found to be an example of fluctuation in community type caused by seedling absence. The Gila River and San Francisco River showed a very clear dominance of the riparian scrub community type. Bonita Creek also showed a riparian scrub community type with a slightly greater broadleaf riparian component.

Aravaipa and Mescal Creeks were the only systems with a dominant broadleaf riparian component. No apparent correlation appeared to exist between broadleaf riparian dominance and channel or terrace width. Broad areas on the watercourse might be expected to correspond to broadleaf riparian dominance, but this was not always the case.

Since no broadleaf riparian species was recorded if one was not present before the next sample point, the percent of sample points on each watercourse where broadleaf riparian species were recorded illustrates the ubiquity of these species. Broadleaf riparian species were recorded at the following percentages of sample points on the watercourses: Aravaipa Creek 99.5%; Mescal Creek 84.9%; Bonita Creek 73.1%; Gila River 22.5%; San Francisco River 21.1%.

Relative Abundance of Woody Species

Table 2 shows the relative abundance of woody species occurring at a frequency over 1.0%. Aravaipa Creek had a high percentage of broadleaf riparian species as would be expected from the community classification in figure 1. The San

Francisco and Gila Rivers had a very high percentage of riparian scrub species. Salt cedar, burro brush, mesquite and seep willow account for 90% of the woody species recorded on the San Francisco River.

Relative Abundance of Herbaceous Perennials

Table 3 shows the relative abundance of the principal species of herbaceous perennials recorded. Bermuda grass is clearly the dominant herbaceous perennial on each of the watercourses. All the herbaceous perennials in table 3 are grazing-resistant with the exception of bent grass, a minor component of Bonita Creek.

After seven years of cattle exclusion on Aravaipa Creek, palatable grasses other than bermuda grass still occurred at negligible frequencies. Trend plot photos for Aravaipa Creek show bermuda grass in sparse clumps extending to form a solid mat after the cattle were removed. This extensive sod formation by bermuda grass has apparently limited establishment of other grasses.

Table 2.--Relative abundance of woody species.

Species	Occurrence (%)	Species	Occurrence (%)
Gila River		Aravaipa Creek	
Burro brush	28.5	Fremont cottonwood	22.35
Seep willow	28.1	Seep willow	14.67
Mesquite	23.9	Velvet ash	12.34
Salt cedar	6.0	Willow (Salix)	10.97
Fremont cottonwood	3.7	Burro brush	10.83
Snakeweed	3.2	Mesquite	8.09
Desert broom	3.2	Arizona sycamore	4.66
		Salt cedar	3.70
Mescal Creek		Snakeweed	2.74
		Netleaf hackberry	1.78
Fremont cottonwood	17.0	Arizona walnut	1.64
Burro brush	10.0	Catclaw acacia	1.23
Velvet ash	9.0	Box elder	1.09
Seep willow	9.0		
Arizona sycamore	6.9	Bonita Creek	
Willow (Salix)	5.9		
Mesquite	5.5	Burro brush	34.5
Snakeweed	4.5	Mesquite	23.5
Red mahonia	4.5	Seep willow	12.9
Desert broom	4.2	Wolfberry	5.8
Salt cedar	4.1	Greythorn	3.4
Netleaf hackberry	4.1	Desert hackberry	3.2
Tree tobacco	3.8	Sycamore	3.2
Wolfberry	2.1	Netleaf hackberry	2.7
Whitethorn	1.7	Willow	1.4
Arizona walnut	1.7	Fremont cottonwood	1.3
Juniper	1.1	Arizona walnut	1.3
		Creosote	1.3
		Brickellia	1.1
San Francisco			
Salt cedar	26.7		
Burro brush	25.6		
Mesquite	23.0		
Seep willow	15.4		
Tree tobacco	3.8		
Fremont cottonwood	3.2		

Table 3.--Relative abundance of herbaceous perennials.

Species	Occurrence (%)	Species	Occurrence (%)
Aravaipa Creek		Bonita Creek	
Bermuda grass	73.94	Bermuda grass	55.0
Dock	14.05	Dock	8.3
Jimson weed	7.77	Tree tobacco	7.3
		Threadleaf groundsel	7.1
Gila River		Stickleaf	4.1
		Desert tobacco	3.2
Bermuda grass	88.6	Globe mallow	2.6
Tree tobacco	8.9	Horehound	2.5
Stickleaf	2.6	Trailing allionia	1.7
Jimson weed	1.9	Penstemon	1.2
		Brickellia	1.2
		Bent grass	1.0
		Jimson weed	1.0
		Wire lettuce	1.0

Table 3.--Abundance of herbaceous perennials (cont.).

Species	Occurrence (%)	Species	Occurrence (%)
Mescal Creek		San Francisco River	
Bermuda grass	35.21	Bermuda grass	85.1
Tree tobacco	18.66	Alfalfa	5.4
Desert tobacco	13.38	Tree tobacco	3.7
Jimson weed	11.26	Stickleaf	2.7
Common monkeyflower	4.22	Dock	1.6
Globe-mallow	2.46		
Wire lettuce	2.46		
Brickellia	1.76		
Bear grass	1.76		
Dock	1.40		

Population Data

Figures 6-9 depict the size-class data for broadleaf riparian trees and mesquite on the five watercourses.

Aravaipa Creek

Aravaipa Creek (fig. 6) has been excluded from cattle since 1973 and shows a high percent-age of seedlings in every species population. The survival of seedlings to the 1- to 3-inch size-class is good for the broadleaf trees with the exception of sycamore and walnut. Sycamore seed production and establishment is sporadic and sycamores often rely on sucker sprouts for reproduction. It would require a follow-up study to determine the number of sycamore seedlings surviving to the 1- to 3-inch size-class. The absence of walnuts in the 1- to 3-inch size-class may be due more to the small walnut sample (31 trees) than to ecological factors.

Gila and San Francisco Rivers

The Gila River and San Francisco River (fig. 7 and 8) show virtually no successful broadleaf riparian reproduction. The only trees in the 1- to 3-inch size-class are cottonwoods on the Gila River, and they comprise only 2% of the cotton-wood sample. The low percentage or absence of 1- to 3-inch size-class trees indicates low seedling survival. On the San Francisco River, 82% of the cottonwood seedlings were browsed by cattle. On the Gila River, 62% of the cottonwood and willow seedlings were browsed, resulting in seedlings 6-10 in. tall with up to 0.6 in. diameters indicating the seedlings had been browsed for more than one growing season. Mesquite, however, is reproducing successfully on both of these rivers.

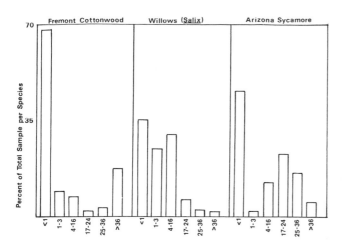

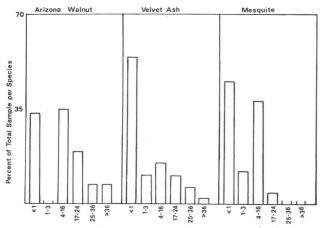

Figure 6.--Size-class data for Aravaipa Creek (DBH size-classes in inches).

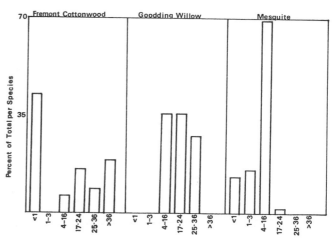

Figure 7.--Size-class data for the San Francisco River (DBH size-classes in inches).

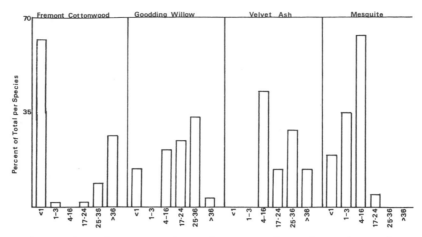

Figure 8.--Size-class data for the Gila River (DBH size-classes in inches).

Very poor broadleaf riparian tree establishment and successful mesquite establishment will eventually lead to the replacement of the broadleaf riparian community by mesquite and other riparian scrub species. This trend is already well established on the Gila and San Francisco Rivers (figs. 2, 3, 7, and 8).

Mescal Creek

All the broadleaf species on Mescal Creek (fig. 9) showed good representation in the seedling size-class. However, willows, sycamore, and walnut showed a total absence of 1- to 3-inch size-class trees. Cottonwood had 1.5% in this size-class and ash 5.5%. This strongly indicates seedlings were not surviving. Cottonwood seedlings were 70% browsed by cattle, willows 9%, sycamores 62%, ash 1%, and no walnut seedlings were recorded as browsed. Mesquite is reproducing successfully on Mescal Creek.

Poor broadleaf riparian establishment and successful mesquite establishment will eventualy lead to the replacement of the broadleaf riparian community on Mescal Creek. A good distribution of mature broadleaf riparian trees on Mescal Creek results in a dominant broadleaf riparian community (fig. 1). However, poor reproduction will not maintain this broadleaf riparian community over time.

Bonita Creek

Data from Bonita Creek (fig. 9) indicated poor reproductive success of all broadleaf riparian species:
1) only 4% of the cottonwoods were in the seedling size-class and all of these seedlings were browsed by cattle. The 1- to 3-inch size-class represented only 2% of the sample;
2) only 1.5% of the willows were in the seedling size-class and 67% of these were browsed. No 1- to 3-inch size-class willows were recorded;

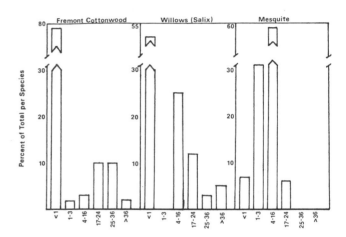

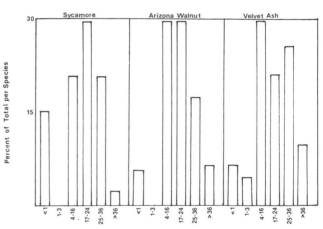

Figure 9. Size-class data for Mescal Creek (DBH size-classes in inches).

3) only 1.5% of the sycamores and no velvet ash were in the seedling or 1- to 3-inch size-class.

Grazing has occurred on Bonita Creek for over 100 years. The palatability of broadleaf riparian seedlings in descending order of

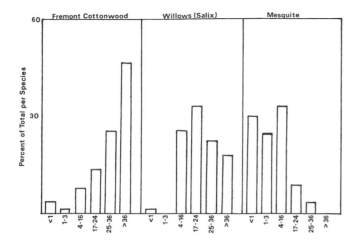

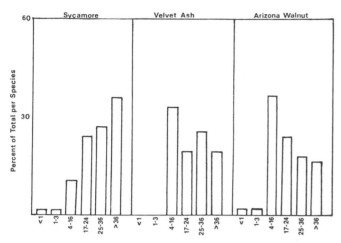

Figure 10.—Size-class data for Bonita Creek (DBH size-classes in inches).

preference is: cottonwood, willow, sycamore, ash, and walnut.[4] Prior to 1972, grazing pressure on Bonita Creek was perhaps severe enough to affect the most palatable species, but not severe enough to affect ash and walnut. Since 1972, grazing pressure has apparently increased sufficiently to affect the less palatable ash and walnut seedlings.

Sycamore, willow, and cottonwood populations indicate a size-class distribution the reverse of one needed to maintain these species in the community.

Arizona walnut and velvet ash are slow growing species. On Bonita Creek, size-classes for these trees show a normal size-class distribution from 4- to 16-in. and larger. This indicates successful seedling reproduction prior to about 8-10 years ago to establish the 4- to 16-in. trees. The grazing allotment history on Bonita Creek indicates a change in grazing allottees in 1972. The change in grazing

allottees corresponds to the downward trend in successful reproduction of walnut and ash.

The trend on Bonita Creek is toward replacement of the broadleaf riparian community by mesquite and other riparian scrub species. This trend is already well established as illustrated in fig. 4 (community classification).

Summary

Aravaipa Creek is the only system where the trend is not toward replacement of the broadleaf riparian community by riparian scrub. Aravaipa is also the only system where cattle have been excluded.

Flooding

Flooding is another factor that influences reproductive success. In the winter of 1978-79, all five watercourses experienced severe floods. Mesquite is not damaged by cattle browsing, but is as susceptible to flooding as the broadleaf species. In each of the systems, mesquite indicated successful reproduction. Mesquite trees were recorded in all parts of the riparian systems from high on the upper banks to within feet of the water. Mesquite seedlings and 1- to 3-inch trees were found under mature broadleaf riparian species and in habitats suitable for broadleaf riparian reproduction.

Aravaipa Creek experienced severe flooding, yet did not indicate poor broadleaf riparian reproduction. Flooding does have adverse effects on tree seedlings, but is not, apparently, as detrimental to the broadleaf riparian communities as cattle browsing upon seedlings.

Importance Values

Table 4 shows the importance values for the major woody species on the five systems. An analysis of these data confirm the inferences drawn from the population analysis.

Aravaipa Creek

High coverage, density, and frequency of the cottonwoods indicate a mature population evenly distributed along the river with very successful reproduction. High coverage indicates large mature trees. High frequency indicates uniform distribution and high density indicates numerous seedlings and small trees. Walnut is the only broadleaf riparian tree with a low importance value, but Aravaipa Creek is the only system in the study where walnut is recorded in the 0.01-acre samples. High density relative to frequency of seep willow indicates clump-like concentrations. Nearly equal density and frequency of burro brush indicates a fairly uniform linear distribution.

---

[4]Steve Bingham. Personal communication.

Table 4.--Importance values.

Species	Relative Coverage	Relative Density	Relative Frequency	Importance Value
Aravaipa Creek				
Fremont cottonwood	29.06	20.81	9.36	59.23
Seep willow	8.72	37.41	8.99	55.12
Velvet ash	14.42	5.37	6.74	26.53
Willows (Salix)	10.62	4.98	6.74	22.34
Mesquite	11.02	3.40	6.37	20.79
Arizona sycamore	14.68	2.54	3.37	20.59
Burro brush	1.72	7.14	5.62	14.48
Arizona walnut	6.28	1.10	1.87	9.25
Netleaf hackberry	2.17	1.82	3.37	7.36
San Francisco River				
Mesquite	59.3	7.9	8.1	75.3
Salt cedar	15.1	42.4	11.1	68.6
Seep willow	5.8	17.6	13.2	36.6
Burro brush	2.0	6.2	9.1	17.3
Fremont cottonwood	9.1	2.4	3.0	14.5
Goodding willow	5.1	-	-	5.1
Desert willow	3.5	0.6	0.9	5.0
Gila River				
Mesquite	58.1	8.4	9.0	75.5
Seep willow	12.8	37.2	17.0	67.0
Tree tobacco	7.8	17.6	7.0	32.4
Burro brush	0.4	17.8	14.0	32.2
Fremont cottonwood	18.7	2.1	2.0	22.8
Salt cedar	0.8	3.9	6.0	10.7
Mescal Creek				
Velvet ash	32.48	0.79	1.87	35.14
Fremont cottonwood	10.69	9.71	5.61	26.01
Arizona sycamore	15.62	2.70	4.67	22.99
Seep willow	0.21	17.83	3.74	21.78
Netleaf hackberry	5.05	8.58	7.47	21.10
Tree tobacco	-	12.07	8.41	20.41
Mesquite	13.16	2.37	4.67	20.20
Willows (Salix)	8.05	5.08	1.87	15.00
Burro brush	0.43	8.13	5.61	14.17
Arizona walnut	11.42	-	-	11.42
Bonita Creek				
Burro brush	11.8	48.27	13.3	73.37
Mesquite	27.0	5.15	13.3	45.45
Arizona sycamore	26.1	0.34	1.8	28.24
Seep willow	8.6	15.01	4.1	27.71
Netleaf hackberry	4.9	3.53	6.0	14.43
Willows (Salix)	4.6	0.30	0.9	5.8
Fremont cottonwood	4.7	0.09	0.5	5.29
Arizona walnut	3.4	-	-	3.4
Desert willow	1.0	0.85	0.9	2.75
Velvet ash	1.9	-	0.5	2.4

San Francisco River

The two broadleaf riparian species recorded on the San Francisco River have very low importance values compared to the riparian scrub species. High coverage and low but fairly equal density and frequency of the cottonwoods indicate large mature trees growing singly and sparsely along the river with very few seedlings. Low coverage of willows with none recorded in the

0.01-acre samples indicate very sparse distribution of mature trees with no successful reproduction. Very high coverage of mesquite and nearly equal, but high frequency and density indicate mature mesquite and successful reproduction. Extremely high density of salt cedar relative to its coverage indicates an abundance of young plants. The frequency is also high indicating uniform distribution and strongly suggesting salt cedar will become dominant.

Gila River

High coverage of cottonwood relative to its frequency indicates large mature trees sparsely distributed along the river. Low density of cottonwoods indicates few seedlings. Willow was recorded in only one of the 57 0.01-acre samples and this was a browsed seedling. Very high coverage of mesquite and nearly equal, but high frequency and density indicate mature mesquite and successful reproduction.

Mescal Creek

Data from Mescal Creek show a predominantly broadleaf riparian community (fig. 1). The very high coverage of ash relative to its density indicates large mature trees without successful reproduction. The low frequency value indicates these large trees are sparsely spread along the creek. The density of cottonwoods relative to frequency indicates good tree establishment. The coverage value for cottonwood is not disproportionately high indicating seedlings are fairly numerous. However, coverage, density, and frequency of cottonwoods on Mescal Creek are much lower than cottonwoods on Aravaipa Creek. Successful reproduction and establishment of the broadleaf riparian community on Mescal Creek is apparently less than on Aravaipa Creek.

Bonita Creek

Very high coverage of sycamore relative to its density and frequency indicates large mature trees distributed sparsely along the creek with very few seedlings. Sycamore was third in importance only because of its relatively high coverage. Riparian scrub species are clearly dominant. Willows, cottonwood, walnut, and ash all have low density compared to their coverage indicating a mature broadleaf riparian vegetation which is not successfully maintaining itself.

General Conclusions

Aravaipa Creek is the only system of the five studied with a dominant broadleaf riparian community and successful reproduction. Mescal Creek is also dominated by a broadleaf riparian community, but has poor reproductive success. The Gila River, San Francisco River, and Bonita Creek all show a well established trend toward replacement of the broadleaf riparian community by riparian scrub.

Cattle browsing appears to be the major contributing factor to the downward trend of broadleaf riparian communities. The only system in this study with an upward trend in the broadleaf riparian community is Aravaipa Creek, where cattle have been excluded since 1973.

SUMMARY

Riparian vegetation along five perennial watercourses in the USDI Bureau of Land Management's Safford District was studied. Community classification of woody species, relative abundance of woody and herbaceous perennial species, and size-class data were recorded using a pace-transect. Coverage, density, and frequency were determined for each species.

These data were analyzed to determine condition and trend of the five riparian vegetation communities. Aravaipa Creek, where cattle have been excluded since 1973, was the only system with a dominant broadleaf riparian community and successful reproduction.

ACKNOWLEDGEMENTS

I appreciate the guidance of Steve Bingham, Botanist, Eastern Arizona College, Thatcher, Arizona, for the design of this study and identification of plant specimens. I would also like to thank Cindy French for her assistance with the field work.

LITERATURE CITED

Babcock, H.M. 1978. The phreatophyte problem in Arizona. Arizona Watershed Symposium, Proceedings 12:34-36.

USDA Soil Conservation Service. 1980. National Plant List (May, 1980). USDA Soil Conservation Service. Washington, D.C.

3 HYDROLOGIC AND HYDRAULIC CONSIDERATIONS IN THE STRUCTURE, FUNCTION, AND PROTECTION OF CALIFORNIA RIPARIAN SYSTEMS

FLUVIAL PROCESSES AND WOODLAND SUCCESSION

ALONG DRY CREEK, SONOMA COUNTY, CALIFORNIA[1]

Joe R. McBride and Jan Strahan[2]

Abstract.--Fluvial processes, as they relate to the formation of riffle bars and point bars, and banks, terraces, and swales of the floodplain terrace are examined in the context of Dry Creek, Sonoma County, California. These processes control seedling establishment and survival on riffle bars, point bars, and the banks of floodplain terraces. Autogenic forces were found to be more important in determining successional patterns on older, more stable portions of the floodplain terrace. Mule fat (Baccharis viminea), sandbar willow (Salix hindsiana), red willow (S. laevigata), and Fremont cottonwood (Populus fremontii) are dominant species in the pioneer stages on bars and at the base of the floodplain terrace. Hinds walnut (Juglans hindsii), California box elder (Acer negundo ssp. californicum), coast live oak (Quercus agrifolia), and California bay (Umbellularia californica) dominate the climax woodlands of the undisturbed floodplain terrace.

INTRODUCTION

Dry Creek, a tributary of the Russian River, drains some 562 sq. km. (217 sq. mi.) along its 50-km. (31-mi.) course through the Coast Ranges in Sonoma and Mendocino counties of northern California. The lower 22.5 km. (14 mi.) of Dry Creek pass through a broad valley where fluvial geomorphic processes have created and destroyed environments for riparian woodland species. The purpose of this paper is to identify the influence of those processes upon the pattern of succession in the riparian zone.

Dry Creek is a fourth-order stream which forms with its tributaries a palmate, dendritic pattern. An overall channel gradient of 1.5% occurs from its headwaters to the Russian River. The lower reaches, in Dry Creek valley, follow a gradient of 0.2% and drop 1.9 m. per km. (10 ft. per mi.). Average annual precipitation over the Dry Creek watershed varies from 1,016 mm. (40 in.) near Healdsburg to 1,524 mm. (60 in.) in Mendocino County. Stream discharge ranges from average annual flood peaks of about 1,000 cubic feet per second (cfs) to 0 cfs when the stream dries

up each year by late August. The maximum recorded flood occurred in December 1964 with a discharge of 32,400 cfs. The 100-year frequency flood is calculated to be 52,000 cfs. (US Army Corps of Engineers 1981).

The vegetation of the riparian zone along Dry Creek is typical of streams in the North Coast Ranges which drain eastward to the Eel and Russian rivers. A mosaic of woodland stands dominated by various mixtures of Fremont cottonwood (Populus fremontii), Hinds walnut (Juglans hindsii), red willow (Salix laevigata), white alder (Alnus rhombifolia), California box elder (Acer negundo ssp. californicum), and Oregon ash (Fraxinus latifolia) occur on the banks of these streams. Within the stream channels one finds patches of sandbar willow (Salix hindsiana) and mule fat (Baccharis viminea), as well as white alder, cottonwood, and red willow.

Fluvial Processes

Fluvial geomorphic processes, first described by Davis (1909), have recently been reviewed by Leopold et al. (1964) and Keller (1977). These processes determine the characteristics of a stream channel and its adjacent floodplain terrace(s). They also create substrates for the establishment of plants, as well as destroy areas of existing vegetation. As water moves across the land surface in response to gravity, it loses its potential energy as it loses elevation. This potential energy is dissi-

[1] Paper presented at the California Riparian Systems Conference. [University of California, Davis, September 17-19, 1981].

[2] Joe R. McBride is Associate Professor of Forestry and Landscape Architecture, Jan Strahan is Research Assistant in Forestry; both are at the University of California, Berkeley.

pated where the water is in contact with the ground surface or a streambed.

The amount of energy loss per unit area is referred to as the bed shear stress. Transportation of material by a stream occurs when the bed shear stress exceeds the gravitational forces acting upon materials in the streambed. Water velocity and particle size determine the threshold of shear stress required to transport material. Water velocity varies in different parts of a stream channel and, therefore, the potential for transporting materials also varies. In straight sections the greatest velocity occurs in the middle of the stream, just under the water surface. In bends of the channel the flow quickens, and the greatest velocity occurs near the outside of the bend.

Sediments are thus picked up on the concave sides of the stream and tend to be deposited on the convex sides. Along these convex sides the bank is gradually extended streamward by the deposition of a point bar. Along the concave sides the bank is eroded to form a cut bank. The result of these processes is a meandering of the stream, which causes the channel to move laterally. This lateral movement cuts back valley walls to form floodplain terraces. Once formed, the floodplain terrace will serve as a surface for the deposition of smaller particles carried by the stream when it overflows. Deposition on the floodplain terrace combined with scouring of the stream channel leads to an incision of the stream channel into the floodplain terrace. Deposition also occurs at the backs of the point bars. This deposition allows for the extension of the floodplain terrace as the stream moves laterally.

In relatively straight sections of a stream channel, the streambed will follow a somewhat sinuous path. Riffle bars tend to form in these straight sections on alternate sides of the channel. The pattern of riffles and pools tends to be maintained due to the greater bed shear stress in the pools during high flows. However, during peak flows the streambed may be shifted within the stream channel in these straight sections. Braiding of the streambed may also occur where the stream gradient is very low and the channel is wide.

Individual pieces of gravel are moved over the surfaces of both point and riffle bars when the bed shear stress overcomes the gravitational and frictional forces holding them in place. They are carried along the surface of the bar and redeposited as the potential energy of the water is dissipated. Smaller-diameter and lighter pieces are more easily lifted by the bed shear stresses and will be carried farther. Scouring of both the stream channel and the plants growing in the channel can occur during the movement of this material.

In addition to the fluvial processes which create and destroy surfaces for the establishment of riparian species, one must also consider streamflow characteristics which influence seedling establishment and survival in various substrates along the stream and across the stream channel. The fluctuation of water level in the channel both provides moisture to and excludes oxygen from seeds and roots of plants.

Previous Work

Publication of research into the dynamics of riparian vegetation in relation to fluvial processes in California has been limited. Conard et al. (1977) described the distribution of vegetation-types along the Sacramento River. They suggested idealized toposequences of riparian vegetation and indicated that the time interval between major disturbances was related to locations along the toposequence. Their work did not, however, specifically relate species establishment and replacement to fluvial processes.

Pelzman (1973) examined the causes of riparian plant encroachment into streambeds along streams below dams in northern California. Pelzman's field observations and laboratory experiments demonstrated the significance of fluctuations in stream height to successful establishment of common willows and mulefat. He concluded that their establishment was limited by declining spring and summer flows under natural streamflow regimes in California's Mediterranean climate. Pelzman's work is basic to an understanding of the initial stage of succession on newly created substrates in the riparian environment.

Outside of California a number of studies have investigated fluvial processes as they relate to riparian vegetation and succession. Some general concepts can be derived from this body of research; however, climatic differences and different floras limit the transfer of specific findings to the California situation. Swanson and Lienkaemper's (1979) research on the South Fork Hoh River in Washington is an outstanding study of the influence of fluvial processes upon the distribution of riparian and adjacent coniferous forest types. They were able to correlate the age of stands with the creation of various geomorphic surfaces in cross-sections of the South Fork Hoh River valley. They identified four distinctive floodplain terrace environments in the valley which were related to the geomorphic process and which described the character of the vegetation in each environment. They did not, however, examine successional trends on the various terraces.

Fonda (1974), working in the same area, did address the question of succession on the four floodplain terrace environments. He suggested a sequence of Alnus rubra to Picea sitchensis/Acer macrophyllum/Populus trichocarpa to Picea sitchensis/Tsuga heterophylla to Tsuga heterophylla. Soil profile development as it influenced moisture-holding capacity was proposed as a major factor controlling forest succession. Fonda demonstrated that an ability to tolerate soil moisture stress was a significant feature of plants in the early successional stages.

Nanson and Beach (1977) examined forest succession and sedimentation on a meandering-river floodplain in northwestern British Columbia. They used the changing age structure of dominant tree species to describe successional changes within the floodplain forest. The direction of channel migration and the earlier position of the channel's convex bank were accurately preserved in the form of ridges and swales on the floodplain terrace. This pattern allowed Nanson and Beach to establish a chronosequence of plots across the floodplain. The successional change from balsam poplar to white spruce occurred following the decline in overbank sedimentation on surfaces approximately 50 years old. Annual sedimentation during this initial 50 years destroyed any spruce seedlings beneath the balsam poplar crown canopy. The balsam poplar survived each increment of sediment by developing a new root crown near the surface of the deposition.

Research in the mid-western and eastern parts of the United States has identified successional patterns which could be linked to fluvial geomorphic processes (Hefley 1937; Ware and Penfound 1949; Shelford 1954; Wistendahl 1958; Lindsey et al. 1961; Everitt 1968; Wilson 1970; Johnson et al. 1976). Generalizations drawn from these papers suggest that sediment size on point bars controls the species composition of the pioneer stands. Willows are more commonly observed on finer-textured deposits, while cottonwoods develop on the more coarsely textured deposits. As floodplains extend over the back of point bars, the willows and cottonwoods are replaced by species adapted to mesic environments with somewhat reduced soil moisture, such as box elders, elms, ashes, and oaks. Major factors influencing species composition of the riparian forests on the floodplain are depth to water table and moisture-holding capacity of the soil. It would appear from a review of the previous research that initial patterns of succession on point bars are allogenic in character, while subsequent successional changes on the stabilized floodplain are autogenic.

METHODS AND RESULTS

To study the influence of fluvial processes upon succession on Dry Creek, we selected three physiographic locations representative of the various consequences of fluvial geomorphic processes. These locations were: 1) riffle bars; 2) point bars; and 3) the hydrologically active, stream-adjacent floodplain terrace.

Stream Channel

Riffle Bars

Riffle bars in the relatively undisturbed portions of lower Dry Creek are characterized by low elevations. The highest elevations on these bars are seldom more than 2 m. above the lowest point in the channel cross section. The gradient across these bars, normal to streamflow, is generally very low, although some bars had slopes approaching 45° at the edge of the streambed.

Vegetation on these bars consists of occasional strips of basket sedge (Carex barbarae), mulefat, sandbar willow, or sandbar willow/ cottonwood. At the back of some riffle bars, adjacent to the floodplain bank, we encountered a narrow secondary streambed which carried water only during higher flows. A lagoon was formed at both the upstream and downstream ends of this streambed. Red willow thickets were common on the floodplain side of these secondary stream banks, while mulefat, sandbar willow, and cottonwood were more commonly found on the riffle bar side.

To determine the pattern of seedling establishment and survival on riffle bars, we measured species density of seedlings and young saplings (plants less than 1 m. tall, assumed to be 1 year old in June 1981) in June and September, 1981. Twenty one-quarter-square-meter quadrats were established in strips of germinating seedlings near the stream edge during the last two weeks of June. Separate sets of 20 quadrats each were located in areas which appeared to be dominated by: 1) basket sedge; 2) mulefat; 3) sandbar willow; 4) cottonwood; and 5) red willow. A similar set of 20 quadrats was established in a zone of young saplings in which mulefat, sandbar willow, cottonwood, and red willow were present.

Results of these measurements suggest there are correlations between 1) species seedling establishment and gravel size; and 2) mortality during the first growing season and depth to groundwater. The transient viabilities of riparian species limit their germination to a moist zone adjacent to the receding stream in late spring. Floating seeds are concentrated on this moist zone. Successful establishment depends upon gravel size in the moist zone. Establishment of some species is limited by larger sizes of gravel. Our results indicate a close correlation between occurrence of particles less than 0.2 cm. and the establishment of sandbar willow (fig. 1.) Available moisture is present for a longer period of time in the fine-textured portions of riffle bars. The transient viability of sandbar willow prevents its establishment on the rockier and drier portions of the bars.

Seedling survival depends upon the availability of soil moisture through the summer months. Among tree species, mortality ranged from 65% to 100% on those plots adjacent to the section of the stream which dried out by September 1, 1981 (table 1). Weekly observations indicated mortality began during the third week in July. Mortality ranged from 6% to 88% for these same species on plots adjacent to water. The depth to water was about 20 cm. on these plots, while it exceeded 1 m. on the former plots by September 1, 1981.

In addition to drought-induced mortality, direct heat injury may kill seedlings during the summer months. Differences in survival among trees may be due to root growth capacity. Cottonwood roots for 1981 seedlings were three times

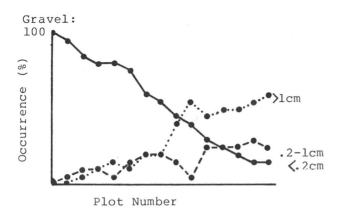

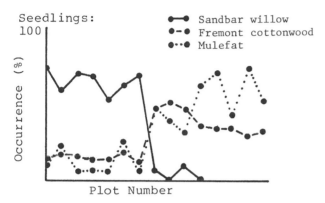

Figure 1.—Percentage occurrence of gravel sizes and seedlings on riffle bar plots along lower Dry Creek.

Table 1.—Average density of seedlings (number/m^2) on riffle bars in June and September, 1981 along lower Dry Creek.

Species	Average density June	Sept.	Mortality (%)
Riffle bars adjacent to sections of stream which dried out by September 1			
Mulefat	50	33	34
Basket sedge	44	0	100
Fremont cottonwood	23	8	65
Sandbar willow	4	0	100
Red willow	41	0	100
Riffle bars adjacent to sections of stream which were not dried out be September 1			
Mulefat	81	74	9
Basket sedge	9	0	100
Fremont cottonwood	67	63	6
Sandbar willow	141	17	88
Red willow	8	3	62

as long as those of the willows. No mortality was recorded on the sapling plots. It is assumed that the seedlings on sapling plots produced sufficient root growth to remain in contact with

a water supply during the summer of 1980. Furthermore, these plants survived the winter period of peak discharge. The absence of saplings from many areas on riffle bars suggests that winter scouring of the bars often removes seedlings which survive the first summer. Older saplings on point bars frequently have basal scars on the upstream side of their stems which are the result of scouring away of the bark, phloem, and cambium.

Examination of a series of aerial photographs of Dry Creek dating from the 1940s indicates a shifting of the locations of riffle bars. The streambed may move completely across the stream channel and obliterate a riffle bar with any seedlings and saplings growing upon it. The temporary nature of the riffle bar prevents the development of the riparian woodland beyond the pioneer stage.

Point Bars

The environment of the point bar shares certain characteristics with that of the riffle bar; however, since the point bar is built outward as the stream meanders, it is more stable over time and provides an environment for further development of the riparian woodland. Point bars along Dry Creek had a more significant increase in elevation as one moved away from the streambed than did riffle bars. They were also characterized by more vegetative cover. Seedling establishment at the margin of the streambed followed the same pattern as was observed on the riffle bars. Large numbers of seedlings became established in June only to succumb to heat and drought. Those which survived the rigors of summer, as well as winter scouring, produced linear stands ranging in length from a few to as many as 30 m. in length.

Plants in these strips reduced the velocity of water during high-flow periods and, therefore, caused gravels and smaller-sized particles to accumulate. As a result, point bars often had the appearance of ridges and swales as one moved from the streambed to the bank of the floodplain terrace. The pattern of sediment-trapping depended upon the density of the vegetation and the distance water travelled over the bar. Plant stems often trap larger-sized gravels at the upstream end of point bars and along the edge of the streambed. Finer sediments are deposited toward the downstream end of the bar and the floodplain terrace bank.

To study woodland succession on point bars we conducted a reconnaissance of several point bars along Dry Creek. Vegetative cover on these bars appeared to be closely tied to gravel size distribution and location relative to the streambed. Our reconnaissance indicated that point bars could be divided into five environments as follows: 1) point bar bank; 2) first ridge and swale; 3) interior ridges and swales; 4) lagoons; and 5) base of the floodplain terrace. Not all point bars exhibited all five of these environments along Dry Creek. Smaller point bars sometimes lacked areas of interior ridges and swales. Lagoons were also not found on all point bars.

A typical point bar exhibiting all five environments was chosen for a detailed analysis of its vegetation and gravel size distribution. The vegetation on the point bar was mapped and four transects were chosen to cut across the various environmental zones and vegetation-types. Along each transect ten adjacent one-quarter square meter plots were established parallel to the streambed in the point bar bank, first ridge and swale, and base of the floodplain terrace environments. In the area of interior ridges and swales, 10 similar plots were established at the top of each ridge and the bottom of each swale along the transect lines. Plants occurring on each plot were tallied as seedlings or, if they were older, their basal diameter and height were recorded. A point frame was also used to determine the distribution of gravel size on each plot.

The data collected along these transects suggested that an autogenic pattern of succession followed the establishment of seedlings along the point bar bank (table 2). Initial seedling establishment along these banks appeared to follow the pattern observed on the riffle bars. Numerous seedlings became established as water receded in the spring. Species success depended upon gravel size. The absence of any seedlings in the 1 cm. size-class suggested that none of last year's cohort survived. The occurrence of plants in the 1-5 cm. and >5 cm. size-classes indicated establishment had been successful in previous years.

On the first ridge and swale, current seedling establishment was dominated by cottonwood and red willow as evidenced by the 1981 seedlings and plants under 1 cm. in diameter. These ridges and swales were dominated by older sandbar willow and mulefat. It would appear that these pioneers established a footing on an earlier streambank and have trapped gravel to produce a ridge as the point bar advanced. The larger gravel sizes trapped by these plants, combined with the higher elevation of the seed beds, have not provided a suitable environment for the continued establishment of sandbar willow and mulefat. Cottonwood and red willow can become established here as evidenced by the data in table 2.

In the zone of interior ridges and swales, gravel size was associated with the distribution of the dominant species. Alder was found on areas of the smallest-sized particles, while sandbar willow and cottonwood occurred on sandy and gravelly sites. Many point bars along Dry Creek lacked extensive areas of smaller-sized particles and did not support alder. No current or recent seedling establishment was observed on any of the plots on the interior ridges and swales. Light intensities were reduced in this zone due to the crown canopy, which may have prevented successful establishment. More important, the elevation

Table 2.--Average density of plants (number/m^2) by size-class (S--seedling; size-classes in cm.) and gravel size distribution on point bars along lower Dry Creek.

Bank

Species		Density		
	S	<1	1-5	>5
White alder	0	0	0	0
Mulefat	85.9	0	0.9	0.13
Fremont cottonwood	2.8	0	1.6	0
Sandbar willow	38.4	0	0.7	0.4
Red willow	12.7	0	0.2	0
Arroyo willow	0	0	0	0
Gravel size	<0.2	0.2-1	1-3	3-6	>6
	32%	20%	15%	20%	13%

First Ridge and Swale

Species		Density		
	S	<1	1-5	>5
White alder	0	0	0	0
Mulefat	0	0.7	1.7	0.8
Fremont cottonwood	0.2	2.7	2.2	0
Sandbar willow	0.3	0.2	0.3	0.2
Red willow	3.7	0.4	0.2	0
Arroyo willow	0	0	0	0
Gravel size	<0.2	0.2-1	1-3	3-6	>6
	26%	5%	34%	22%	13%

Interior Ridges and Swales--Alder

Species		Density		
	S	<1	1-5	>5
White alder	0	0	1.2	2
Mulefat	0	0	0	0
Fremont cottonwood	0	0	0	1.8
Sandbar willow	0	0	0	0
Red willow	0	0.6	0	0
Arroyo willow	0	0	0	0
Gravel size	<0.2	0.2-1	1-3	3-6	>6
	67%	20%	10%	3%	0%

Interior Ridges and Swales--Cottonwood

Species		Density		
	S	<1	1-5	>5
White alder	0	0	0	0
Mulefat	0	0	0.7	0
Fremont cottonwood	0	0	0.3	0.6
Sandbar willow	0	0	0.6	0.4
Red willow	0	0	0.2	0
Arroyo willow	0	0	0	0
Gravel size	<0.2	0.2-1	1-3	3-6	>6
	11%	15%	35%	24%	14%

Base of Floodplain Terrace

Species		Density		
	S	<1	1-5	>5
White alder	0	0	0.2	0
Mulefat	0	0	0	0
Fremont cottonwood	0	0	0	1.8
Sandbar willow	0	0	0	0
Red willow	0	0.6	0	0
Arroyo willow	0	0	2.4	0
Gravel size	<0.2	0.2-1	1-3	3-6	>6
	45%	30%	13%	5%	7%

of this zone was above the elevation where the stream appeared to have deposited vast numbers of seeds during the spring. Seed beds in the interior ridges and swales zone may have been too dry for successful germination during this period of seed dispersal. Vegetative reproduction by layering may have been very important in this zone. Many alder sprouts were growing from buried trunks.

At the base of the floodplain terrace, a gulley occurred across the back of most of the point bars along Dry Creek. Bed shear stress is high at this location during periods of peak runoff. The larger percentage of smaller particle sizes reduces the bed shear stress necessary to transport material. The gulleys were higher in elevation than the bank of the streambed and dried out much earlier. The more xeric character of these gulleys was responsible for the presence of arroyo willow (Salix lasiolepis) and the absence of mulefat and sandbar willow. No seedling establishment was observed on the plots measured in these gulleys at the base of the floodplain terrace. Periodic establishment would be expected to occur in years of higher streamflow later in the spring. Winter scour may also be a factor in the dynamics of plants in this zone.

The lagoons supported a margin of mulefat or cattail (Typha latifolia) and basket sedge, depending upon the gravel size distribution. Mulefat occurred on coarser gravels, while the cattail and basket sedge grew on sediments less than 0.2 cm. Red willow also occurred above the lagoon margin on the finer sediments.

The conclusion drawn from investigation on point bars is that a type of autogenic succession is occurring in which the initial trapping of coarser sediments by mulefat, willows, and cottonwood produces a ridge of gravel along the outer edge of the point bar. This ridge is a more favorable environment for further cottonwood establishment. As the ridge is built up, finer sediments are deposited between it and the base of the floodplain terrace, toward the downstream end of the point bar. New ridges form adjacent to the stream as the point bar extends laterally. With the growth of cottonwood and willows in the interior ridges, more smaller-sized sediments are trapped, and the swales between ridges begin to fill in.

The increasing height of the bars also contributes to the trapping of smaller-sized particles. The decreased particle size of this substrate results in a more favorable soil-moisture regime for plant growth; however, seed bed conditions are less favorable for willows because of their transient viability. Alder becomes established on the finer sediments of these interior swales and grows up to form a dominant canopy. Shade-intolerant willows and cottonwood cannot survive beneath this canopy. With time, alder dominates the interior downstream portions of the point bars, reproducing primarily by layering.

More gravelly areas remain dominated by cottonwood and willow. Floodplain terrace building during unusually high floods may eventually make the ground surface too high and therefore too dry for continued layering of the alder. As the point bar advances laterally, the distance from the streambed to the root systems of alders near the base of the floodplain terrace will become too great for effective water transport. Under these conditions alder will be replaced by species with better adaptations for the floodplain terrace environment.

Floodplain Terrace Environment

To investigate the structure and reproduction of woodlands occurring on the floodplain terrace, we first classified these woodlands into 10 types based on percent cover of dominant species (table 3). These types were mapped on aerial photographs, and their areal contributions to the total riparian woodland along lower Dry Creek were calculated. Types were considered to be dominated by a single species when over 80% of the crown canopy visible on aerial photographs was made up of that species. These types were given the name of the dominant species (e.g., cottonwood). In types where crown-cover dominance was shared by two species, the names of both species were applied using the name of the tallest species first (e.g., cottonwood/willow). Shared dominance was defined as two species making up 80% of the crown cover of an area, but neither species contributing less than 30% of the cover. The type name "mixed riparian woodland" was used for the commonly occurring stands in which several species occurred but none had a crown cover in excess of 30%.

In addition to the classification based on dominant species, the woodlands could also be divided into two broad categories on the basis of width. Narrow woodlands, seldom more than two crown diameters wide, occurred where channel erosion and land clearing had reduced the original riparian woodland. All woodland-types, based on dominant species, occurred in these narrow strips. Wider woodlands, up to 120 m. wide made up the second category. Only the mixed riparian type was observed to occur in this wider category. These wider woodlands were often situated behind point bars and were characterized by irregular surfaces. Distinct swales often cut 3-4 m. into the floodplain terrace surface, carrying water during periods of overbank flow. This characteristic may have prevented them from being cleared for agriculture.

Sampling for tree density, basal area, and regeneration was done in the mixed riparian woodland using the point quarter method with 10 square meter and one square meter plots at point centers for measuring saplings and seedlings. Nested rectangular plots (5 m. x 20 m. for trees; 2 m. x 20 m. for saplings; 1 m. x 20 m. for seedlings) were used in the narrow willow and cottonwood/willow types. Other woodland-types were not sampled because of their limited distribution.

115

Table 3.--Woodland-types occurring on the flood-plain along lower Dry Creek and their percent of the total riparian woodland.

Type	Dominant species	% of total
Mixed riparian	Hinds walnut Coast live oak Valley oak Red willow California box elder Fremont cottonwood	40.2
Willow	Red willow	23.5
Cottonwood/ willow	Fremont cottonwood Red willow	22.3
Oak	Coast live oak or Valley oak	8.0
Cottonwood	Fremont cottonwood	2.3
Alder	White alder	2.0
Walnut/willow	Hinds walnut Red willow	0.6
Walnut	Hinds walnut	0.5
Bay	California bay	0.4
Oak/bay	Coast live oak or Valley oak California bay	0.2

The mixed riparian woodlands were divided into three environments: 1) bank; 2) terrace; and 3) swale. Sample-points were located at 10-m. intervals along transects normal to the stream in each environment. Eleven transects with a total of 85 points were used in the sample. Eight rectangular plots were used to sample the narrow woodland-types.

Bank

Results from the survey of the mixed riparian woodland show a dominance of alder, cottonwood, and red willow in the bank environment (table 4). It should be noted that these two species were not uniformly distributed along the bank. Alder dominated at the upstream and downstream ends of the point bars where the streambed was adjacent to the bank. Cottonwood and red willow were dominant where the banks were in contact with point bars. Size distribution data (table 4) suggest that these dominant species were not regenerating by seed in this environment. Only current-year seedlings of box elder were observed. Stems under 2.5 cm. in diameter of alder and red willow may have been the products of layering or earlier seedling establishment. No cottonwood regeneration was observed.

Table 4.--Average density of plants (number/100 m^2) by size-class (in cm.) in floodplain environment, mixed riparian woodland-type, along Dry Creek. S--seedling.

Bank

Species	S	<2.5	2.5-5.0	5.0-7.6	7.6-10
California box elder	1.4	0	0	0	0.1
Buckeye	0	0	0	0	0
Red alder	0	1.5	0.1	0.1	0
Oregon ash	0	0.1	0	0	0
Hinds walnut	0	0	0	0	0
Fremont cottonwood	0	0	0	0	0
Coast live oak	0	0	0	0	0
Valley oak	0	0	0	0	0
Sandbar willow	0	0	0	0	0
Red willow	0	0.3	0	0.1	0
Arroyo willow	0	0.4	0.3	0.1	0.1
Elderberry	0	0	0	0	0
California bay	0	0	0	0	0

Terrace

Species	S	<2.5	2.5-5.0	5.0-7.6	7.6-10
California box elder	0	1.8	0.9	0.1	0.3
Buckeye	0	0	0.3	0.3	0
Red alder	0	0	0	0	0
Oregon ash	1.4	0	0	0	0
Hinds walnut	0	0.5	0	0.3	0.1
Fremont cottonwood	0	0	0	0	0
Coast live oak	0	0	0	0	0
Valley oak	0	0	0	0	0
Sandbar willow	0	0	0	0	0
Red willow	0	0	0	0	0
Arroyo willow	0	0	0	0	0
Elderberry	0	0.3	0.3	0.1	0.1
California bay	0	0.2	0	0	0

Swale

Species	S	<2.5	2.5-5.0	5.0-7.6	7.6-10
California box elder	0	2.4	0.3	0.1	0.4
Buckeye	0	0	0	0	0
Red alder	0	0	0	0	0
Oregon ash	0	0.7	0.1	0.3	0
Hinds walnut	0	0.1	0.1	0	0.1
Fremont cottonwood	0	0	0	0	0
Coast live oak	1.4	0	0	0	0
Valley oak	0	0	0	0	0
Sandbar willow	0	0	0	0	0
Red willow	0	0	0	0	0.1
Arroyo willow	0	0	0	0	0
Elderberry	0	0	0	0	0
California bay	0	0	0	0	0

Terrace

On the floodplain terrace, the mixed riparian woodland exhibited a large basal area of both coast live oak and valley oak (table 5). However, the relative densities of these species were low compared to that of Hinds walnut and willow. Sandbar willow, alder, and cottonwood showed significantly reduced relative densities in the floodplain terrace environment. The pattern of regeneration suggested Hinds walnut, bay, and Oregon ash were successfully establishing seedlings in this environment. Seedbeds in this environment were dominated by herbaceous cover (often _Vinca major_) or leaf litter. Following peak floods, deposits of silt may temporarily provide mineral seedbeds. The data collected in this portion of the study reflects establishment on non-mineral seedbeds where competition from herbaceous species may be intense.

Swale

The swale environment tended to be dominated by a mixture of Hinds walnut, box elder, coast live oak, and red willow (table 5). Hinds walnut exhibited the largest basal area, while box elder had the highest relative density. Coast live oak showed a large basal area but a much lower relative density than the other dominants; it was found at the upper edge of the swales, while the other species were more common on the lower portion of the swale slopes or in the swale bottoms. Reproduction in the swale environment was dominated by box elder, although regeneration of Hinds walnut, coast live oak, and Oregon ash was evident. Seed beds in the swales tended to be less dominated by herbaceous plants and leafy litter. The swales are more frequently flushed out by winter storms than are the higher surfaces of the floodplain terrace.

The densities of various stem diameter size-classes in the narrower willow and cottonwood/willow types suggests the invasion of more shade-tolerant Hinds walnut and box elder into these types (table 6). With time, stands of willow and cottonwood/willow occurring on the floodplain

terrace can be expected to succeed to the mixed riparian woodland. Increment cores taken from larger cottonwood trees in the cottonwood/willow type suggest that these stands are of relatively recent origin (within the last 20 years). At some locations, these types had arisen on fresh deposits of silt following major floods. These deposits were laid down where the floodplain was extended into the stream channel behind newly formed point bars. The two types also appeared to arise at the base of the freshly eroded floodplain banks where gravel rather than the streambed was in contact with the bank. Although initial establishment occurred at the base of the bank, both cottonwood and red willow colonized the lower portions of the floodplain bank.

CONCLUSIONS

To summarize the pattern of succession in the environments of the floodplain, one must start with the deposition of silt at the back of the point bar or the exposure of silt on cut banks in the concave sections of streams. Initial colonization of these environments occurs by seedling establishment of red willow and cottonwood. In some cases, cottonwood which is partially buried by the silt deposit may be capable of developing new root systems in the deposit and continuing its growth. Alder may also become established at the base of banks in contact with the streambed. Sandbar willow does not become established in these situations because of the very fine texture of the floodplain silts. Subsequent seedling establishment of more shade-tolerant species occurs in willow and cottonwood/willow stands on the upper slope and top of the floodplain bank. Establishment of additional

Table 5.--Density, relative density, and basal area of tree species in floodplain environments along lower Dry Creek. D--density (number/100 m^2); RD--relative density (%); BA--basal area (cm^2/100 m^2).

Species	Bank			Floodplain			Swale		
	D	RD	BA	D	RD	BA	D	RD	BA
California box elder	0.32	3.8	27	0.26	12	112	0.76	28	281
Buckeye	0	0	0	0.11	5	13	0.05	2	8
Red alder	2.13	25	11.76	0.02	1	12	0.05	2	27
Oregon ash	0.15	1.8	34	0.06	3	17	0.08	3	12
Hinds walnut	0.64	7.6	337	0.53	25	650	0.70	25	630
Fremont cottonwood	1.45	17	2830	0.06	3	323	0.03	1	145
Coast live oak	0	0	0	0.26	12	864	0.16	6	519
Valley oak	0	0	0	0.11	5	904	0	0	0
Sandbar willow	1.02	12	200	0.04	2	7	0.05	2	12
Red willow	2.64	31	459	0.40	19	160	0.46	17	263
Arroyo willow	0	0	0	0.02	1	2	0.11	4	21
Elderberry	0.15	1.8	49	0.11	5	29	0.22	8	77
California bay	0	0	0	0.01	7	24	0.05	2	127
Total	8.50	100	5112	2.13	100	3117	2.70	100	2122

Table 6.--Average density (number/100 m^2) of tree species by size-class (in cm.) in narrow willow and cottonwood/ willow floodplain woodlands along lower Dry Creek.

Species	Seedling	Sapling	Willow woodland 10-15	16-20	21-25	26-30	31-35	36-40	41-50	90
California box elder	0	10.0	1.0	0	0	0	0	0	0	0
Red willow	0	0	2.0	1.0	0	0	1.0	1.0	1.0	0

Species	Seedling	Sapling	Cottonwood/Willow Woodland 10-15	16-20	21-25	26-30	31-35	36-40	41-50	90
California box elder	0	9.2	0.3	0.3	0	0	0	0	0	0
White alder	0	0	0.3	0	0	0	0	0	0	0
Oregon ash	0	0	0.3	0	0	0	0	0	0	0
Hinds walnut	0	5.8	1.3	0	0	0	0.3	0	0	0
Fremont cottonwood	0	0.8	1.0	1.0	1.0	0.7	0.7	0.7	0	0
Red willow	0	7.3	4.7	3.7	2.0	0.3	0	0	0	0
Elderberry	0	4.2	1.0	0.3	0	0	0	0	0	0

species at the base of the bank is somewhat limited by the periodic inundation of this environment. Alder stands established here appear to be self-perpetuating as long as the streambed is in contact with the bank.

Left undisturbed by man, the cottonwood/ willow floodplain woodland will undergo succession to a mixture of Hinds walnut, box elder, oak, and bay, with significant variations in basal area and relative density in relation to swales and floodplain terrace locations. As the floodplain terrace builds in height or extends into the stream channel, one can anticipate an increase in the importance of the more drought-tolerant species such as the oaks and bay. These species will dominate the higher elevations in portions of the floodplain woodland and those sites most removed from the stream channel. This steady state is achieved only for brief intervals because of the continuous migration of the stream channel. This migration either destroys the woodland or isolates it from the streambed and the groundwater it needs for the existence of its various species.

LITERATURE CITED

Conard, S. G., R.L. MacDonald, and R.F. Holland. 1977. Riparian vegetation and flora of the Sacramento valley. p. 47-55. In: A. Sands (ed.). Riparian forests of California: their ecology and conservation. Institute of Ecology Pub. 15, University of California, Davis. 122 p.

Davis, W.M. 1909. Geographical essays (reprinted in 1954). 777 p. Dover Publications, New York, N.Y.

Everitt, B.L. 1968. Use of the cottonwood in an investigation of the recent history of a flood plain Amer. Jour. Science 266: 417-439.

Fonda, R.W. 1974. Forest succession in relation to river terrace development in Olympic National Park, Washington. Ecol. 55: 927-942.

Hefley, H.M. 1937. Ecological studies on the Canadian River floodplain in Cleveland County, Oklahoma. Ecol. Monog. 7(3): 345-484.

Johnson, W.C., R.L. Burgess, and W.R. Keammerer. 1976. Forest overstory vegetation and environment of the Missouri River floodplain in North Dakota. Ecol. Monog. 46:59-84.

Keller, E.A. 1977. The fluvial system: selected observations. p. 39-46. In: A. Sands (ed.). Riparian forests of California: their ecology and conservation. Institute of Ecology Pub. 15, University of California, Davis. 122 p.

Leopold, L.B., W.G. Wolman, and J.P. Miller. 1964. Fluvial processes in geomorphology. 522 p. W.H. Freeman and Company, San Francisco, Calif.

Lindsey, A.A., R.O. Petty, D.K. Sterling, and W.V. Asdall. 1961. Vegetation and environment along the Wabash and Tippecanoe rivers. Ecol. Monog. 31(2):105-156.

Nanson, G.C., and H.F. Beach. 1977. Forest succession and sedimentation on a meandering-river floodplain, northeast British Columbia, Canada. Jour. Biogeography 4:229-259.

Pelzman, R.J. 1973. Causes and possible prevention of riparian plant encroachment on anadromous fish habitat. California Department of Fish and Game Environmental Services Branch, Administrative Report No. 73-1. Sacramento, Calif. 26 p.

Shelford, V.E. 1954. Some lower Mississippi Valley floodplain biotic communities: their age and elevation. Ecol. 35(2):126-142.

Swanson, F.J. nd G.W. Lienkaemper. 1979. Interactions among fluvial processes, forest vegetation, and aquatic ecosystems, South Fork Hoh River, Olympic National Park, Washington. Proceedings of the Second Conference on Scientific Research in the National Parks. [San Francisco, Calif., Nov. 26-30, 1979]. Vol. 7:23-34.

US Army Corps of Engineers. 1981. Channel improvements. Design Memorandum No. 18. Warm Springs Dam and Lake Sonoma Project. 25 p. US Army Corps of Engineers, San Francisco, Calif.

Ware, G.H., and W.T. Penfound. 1949. The vegetation of the lower levels of the floodplain of the South Canadian River in central Oklahoma. Ecol. 30(4):478-484.

Wilson R.E. 1970. Succession in stands of *Populus deltoides* along the Missouri River. Am. Midl. Nat. 83:330-342.

Wistendahl, W.A. 1958. The flood plain of the Raritan River, New Jersey. Ecol. Mono. 28(2):129-153.

RIPARIAN VEGETATION PLANTING FOR FLOOD CONTROL[1]

J. Fred Chaimson[2]

Abstract.--The area around Murphy Slough on the Sacramento River near Chico is critical in the operation of the Sacramento River Flood Control Project. Erosion at this location threatens the proper function of the area with potentially catastrophic results. This paper describes a planting plan intended to alleviate some of these problems.

INTRODUCTION

Usually flood control maintenance is much more involved in clearing riparian vegetation than in planting it. However, in some cases erosion and wave wash protection are of greater concern than channel capacity. This paper describes an instance of planting riparian vegetation on a site previously cleared for agriculture where erosion control and deposition of sediment is considered desirable.

BACKGROUND

The area around Murphy Slough on the Sacramento River southwest of Chico, Butte County, is a key element in the Sacramento River Flood Control Project. It is the beginning of the overbank flow of excess water from the river to the Butte Sink and Sutter Bypass. It is also an area of considerable river dynamism, with areas of almost one section (259 hectares) each having changed sides of the river (and ultimately ownership) as late as 1921 (fig. 1).[3]

A review of the current USDI Geological Survey 7.5' quadrangle map dated 1949, and photo-revised in 1969, shows a surprising amount of vitality; with the river continuing to erode laterally, narrowing the neck of the oxbow between river mile (RM) points 187.5 and 189.5 in that 20 years. Subsequent erosion has opened the mouth of Murphy Slough to the full force of the Sacramento River (reversing the direction in which it once flowed in this channel).

The problem with this is that when an excessive amount of water is directed into Murphy Slough, some of it returns to the river, across the narrow neck to RM 187 (fig. 2). With the energy of 4.8 km. (3 mi.) of river concentrated in .4 km. (.25 mi.) of cutoff, erosion is inevitable. If the river were to cut off almost 4.8 km. of channel at this location, the headward erosion of the river bottom would lower the water surface upstream of the cutoff, reducing or eliminating entirely the overbank flow at the Chico weir site and carrying the additional water down the channel with the streambed gravels and sands.

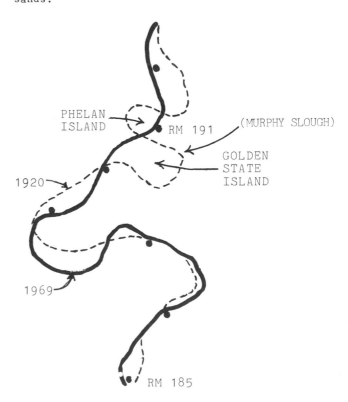

Figure 1.--Centerline meanders of the Sacramento River near Golden State Island, 1920 and 1969 (from Brice, 1977).

[1]Paper presented at the California Riparian Systems Conference [University of California, Davis, September 17-19, 1981].

[2]J. Fred Chaimson is Chief of the Flood Control Maintenance Branch for the State Department of Water Resources, Sacramento, California.

[3]George Carter, Manager of the M&T Ranch, Chico, California. Personal communication.

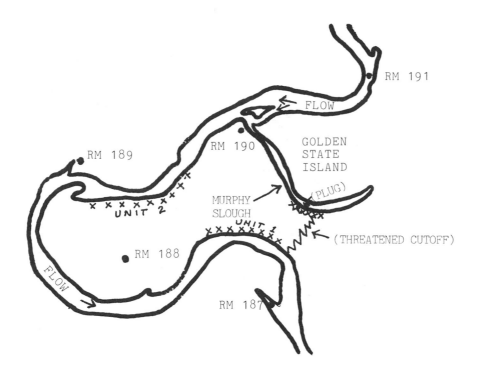

Figure 2.--Bank lines, Sacramento River, 1980, RM 187 to RM 191 (from Sacramento River Aerial Atlas, September 1980, Sacramento District, US Army Corps of Engineers).

There are three alternative scenarios to this.

1. The resulting increased flow and debris would stay in the river channel and overtax the levees downstream.

2. The increased velocity and flow, coupled with a rising river bottom (caused by the adjustment of the eroding river bottom upstream), would cause the river to complete eroding of its natural levees somewhere between Sidds Landing (RM 178) and Kimmelshew Bend (RM 186.5), diverting the Sacramento River into Butte Basin (Brice 1977). This would cause widespread flooding in Butte Basin, possible failure of the levees of the Sutter Bypass, and loss of usefulness of the levees of the Sacramento River from Ord Ferry to Verona.

3. The third alternative is similar to the second except that the breakout would be to the west, flooding the nearby towns of Colusa and Princeton. This alternative is considered much less likely, however.

To forestall these possibilities, in 1974-75 the US Army Corps of Engineers (CE), with the usual State participation, constructed two revetment areas on the narrow waist of the peninsula and built an embankment or plug at the cutoff on Murphy Slough. The embankment was outflanked in high water of 1978 with some damage and again in 1980 with considerable damage, including erosion of the unit three revetment at the return to the river. Using emergency funds, the CE repaired and extended the embankment at the cutoff in 1980.

FLOOD CONTROL VEGETATION STUDIES

Recognizing the value of riparian vegetation in preventing flood damage under some circumstances, the Reclamation Board commissioned the firm of Murray, Burns, and Kienlen to identify areas of riparian vegetation of value to the stability of the river. Of the 38 sites identified, three of them are in this area and two of these, sites 35 and 36 (fig. 3), are pertinent to the problems of the division of flows at Murphy Slough.

FLOOD CONTROL PLANTING ON GOLDEN STATE ISLAND

In 1980, the Department of Water Resources and the Reclamation Board entered into an agreement with the Department of Fish and Game and M&T Ranch (the landowners) to provide for revegetation of the riverside slope of Golden State Island. The landowner agreed to provide right-of-entry for the revegetation and agreed not to remove or cause the removal of any resulting vegetation. In addition, he provided irrigation for the first planting and has agreed to do so for the replanting this year.

The planting plan includes:
1. grading of the riverside slope of Golden State Island to a three-to-one or four-to-one slope to prevent rain-caused gullying,
2. planting a mixture of Bermuda grass and rye grass on the slope face, and,
3. planting willow and cottonwood cuttings in the lower part of the slope in the fall season

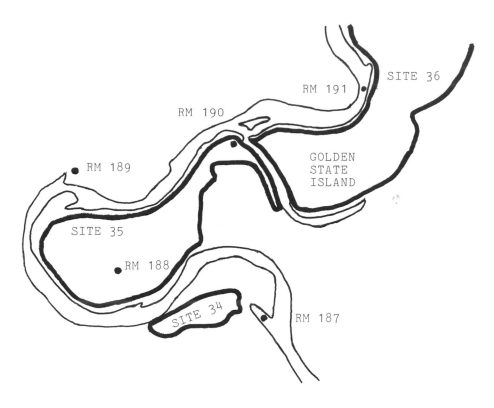

Figure 3.--Proposed riparian vegetation retention sites in vicinity of Murphy Slough (from Murray, Burns, and Kienlan 1978).

in accordance with the availability of moisture, and extending the cuttings up the slope in succeeding years as appears necessary or desirable.

In late summer/early fall of 1980, the initial planting of the Bermuda/rye grass mixture was made. Unfortunately, before it was sufficiently established, high water in the relatively mild winter of 1980-81 washed out most of the lower part of the slope (fig. 4). This year, with the promise of irrigation sprinkling being available after mid-August, we will get an earlier start and have better growth before winter (fig. 5). Also, when the California Conservation Corps crews are available, after the fire season in the fall of 1981, we will have the willow/cottonwood plantings made.

One purpose of these plantings, in addition to obvious ones of habitat replacement and erosion control, is to encourage deposition of river-borne materials. Figure 6 shows the deposition of sediments downstream of a willow clump.

The plan is to promote a growth of willows and cottonwoods along the slope of Golden State Island, so that deposition will eventually reclose the mouth of Murphy Slough, reducing the flow of water into it and the resulting pressure on the Murphy Slough Cutoff.

Figure 4.--Eroded bank of Golden State Island.

Figure 5.--Re-sloped bank of Golden State Island.

Figure 6.--Depositions downstream of willow bush.

CONCLUSIONS

While flood control maintenance at times involves removal of riparian vegetation to maintain channel capacity, there are selected areas where vegetation is beneficial for wave wash control, erosion control, and in this case sediment deposition, velocity reduction, and the redirection of flows.

LITERATURE CITED

Brice, James. 1977. Lateral migration of the Middle Sacramento River, California. U.S. Geological Survey, Water Resources Investigation 77-43. 51 p. Menlo Park, Calif.

Murray, Burns, and Kienlen. 1978. Report to the Reclamation Board, Sacramento, California, on retention of riparian vegetation. February, 1978.

THE ROLE OF RIPARIAN VEGETATION IN CHANNEL BANK STABILITY:

CARMEL RIVER, CALIFORNIA[1]

G. Mathias Kondolf and Robert R. Curry[2]

Abstract.--A narrow channel with well-vegetated banks developed on the lower 15 km. of the Carmel River by 1939, and by 1960 this condition had extended to the entire lower 24 km. of river channel. Noticeable die-off of riparian trees near water supply wells began in the 1960s and intensified during the 1976-1977 drought. Substantial bank erosion occurred during the winters of 1978 and 1980 along reaches which had suffered loss of bank-stabilizing riparian trees.

SETTING

The Carmel River, Monterey County, drains a 660-sq. km. (255-sq. mi.) basin. Rising in the rugged Santa Lucia Mountains and passing through the 24-km. (15-mi.) long alluvial Carmel Valley, it ultimately discharges into the Pacific Ocean near Carmel, Monterey County (fig. 1 and 2). This alluvial reach is sub-divided by a bedrock constriction and narrowing of the valley (the "Narrows") into a lower 16-km. (10-mi.) reach (the "Lower Carmel"), and a middle 8-km. (5-mi.) reach (the "Middle Carmel"), with "Upper Carmel" indicating the segment above San Clemente Dam (fig. 3). Average annual rainfall ranges from 1,040 mm. (41 in.) in the mountainous headwaters to 430 mm. (17 in.) in the lower valley. While the upper river is perennial, the lower river is intermittent, with flows typically from December through June. Near the river mouth, average discharge is 2.7 cms (97 cfs), and the bankfull discharge (here, the 2.4-year flow) is 79.2 cms (2,800 cfs).

Two water supply dams, the Los Padres and San Clemente dams (fig. 2), together impound about 3,000 acre-feet (AF). The Carmel basin supplies most of the water for the Monterey Peninsula cities of Monterey, Pacific Grove, Seaside, and Carmel. As these areas have grown, demand for water has risen substantially. To meet demand over the past two decades, California-

[1]Paper presented at the California Riparian Systems Conference. [University of California, Davis, September 17-19, 1981].

[2]G. Mathias Kondolf is in the Department of Geography and Environmental Engineering, Johns Hopkins University, Baltimore, Maryland. Robert R. Curry is a member of the Board of Environmental Studies, University of California, Santa Cruz, Calif.

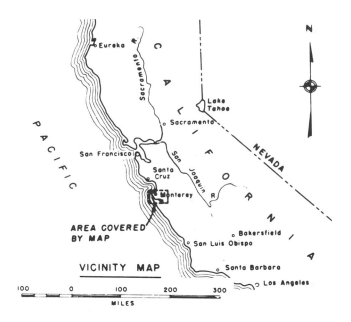

Figure 1.--Vicinity map of the Carmel River basin (US Army Corps of Engineers 1967).

American Water Company (Cal-Am), a private utility, has drawn increasingly upon water supply wells in the alluvium along the Lower and Middle Carmel. Of the total 13,000 AF exported from the basin in 1980, 9,000 AF was diverted from reservoirs, and 4,100 AF was extracted from streamside wells.

In the late 1960s, residents began complaining that vegetation was dying off near the wells in the region near Robinson Canyon Road (Lee 1974). The Carmel Valley Property Owners Association hired a forestry consultant to study the vegetation problem; he concluded that lowered water tables near the wells had killed the vegeta-

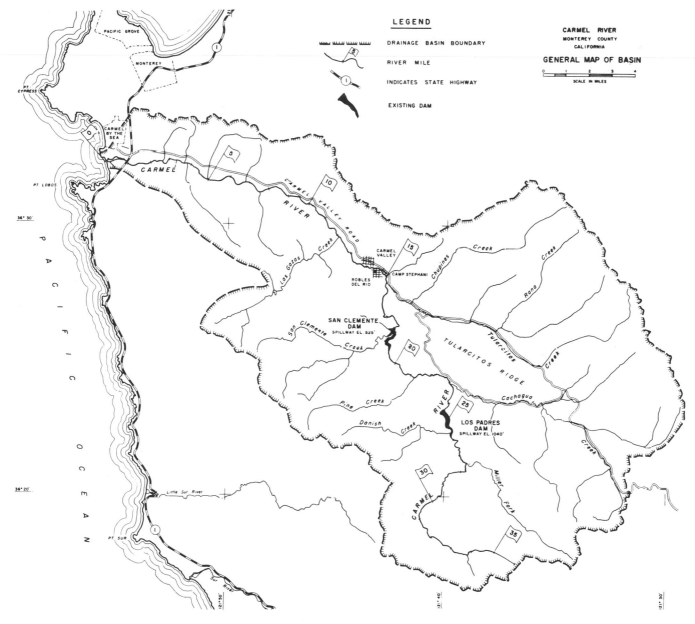

LEGEND

≈≈≈≈≈ DRAINAGE BASIN BOUNDARY

RIVER MILE

INDICATES STATE HIGHWAY

EXISTING DAM

CARMEL RIVER
MONTEREY COUNTY
CALIFORNIA

GENERAL MAP OF BASIN

SCALE IN MILES

Figure 2.--General map of the Carmel River basin (US Army
Corps of Engineers 1967).

tion (Zinke 1971). Cal-Am hired another consultant; he acknowledged that lowered water tables near the wells affected vegetation, but stated that the effect was simply to accelerate the "natural succession" of plants (Stone 1971).

The drought of 1976-1977 imposed additional demand on streamside wells. The die-off of mesic riparian plants was significant between Schulte and Robinson Canyon roads and above the Narrows-- two areas of substantial groundwater withdrawal. The high flows of 1978 and 1980 resulted in severe bank erosion, primarily in areas where bank-stabilizing vegetation had been affected.

RIVER HISTORY

River course and pattern changes were documented by comparing maps of the Carmel River from 1858 to 1945 and aerial photos of the river from 1939 to 1980.

Changes in Course

Historical changes in the Carmel River from Garland Ranch to the mouth are plotted in figures 4 and 5. The 1858 and 1882 channels were determined from boundary surveys. The 1911 course appears on the Monterey 15' USDI Geological Survey topographic map (quad) of 1913 (based on surveys in 1911-12), and the 1945 course is taken

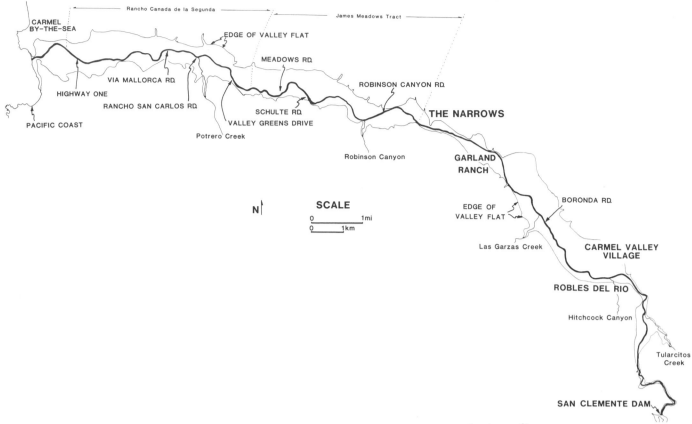

Figure 3.--Location map, Middle and Lower Carmel River (base
from Monterey, Seaside, and Carmel Valley 7.5' quads).

from the Monterey and Seaside 7.5' quads of 1947 (based on aerial photography in 1945). The 1947 maps were photorevised in 1968, but the only mapped revision in the river's course was down-stream of Garland Ranch, where a northward bend of the river was eliminated by highway construc-tion.

Comparison of these maps reveals nine locali-ties where lateral channel migrations of 250-500 m. (820-1,640 ft.) occurred during the 87 years between 1858 and 1945. Except for the change near Garland Ranch Park, since the survey of 1911-1912, changes in course have been modest, generally less than 0.2 km. These migrations were gradual changes from 1911 to 1945, unlike the dramatic shifts that were wrought by floods in the preceding years. This is consistent with the observation that most major shifts take place during large floods. No floods comparable to the 1911 event occurred between that year and 1945, nor have they since.

Figures 4 and 5 show changes in the channel reach from San Clemente Dam downstream to Las Gar-zas Creek. The 1917 channel is plotted from the Jamesburg 15' quad of 1918 (from surveys in 1917). The 1954 course is from the Carmel Valley 7.5' quad of 1956 (compiled from 1954 aerial photography). The lack of dramatic changes com-parable to those seen downvalley may be attribut-

ed to: 1) the lack of record prior to the 1860 and 1911 floods; and 2) bedrock confinement along much of this reach.

Flood History

The earliest flood on record along the Car-mel River was the great statewide deluge of 1862. While no records exist to document the exact magnitude of this flood, it was severe enough to induce the few valley residents to move to higher ground.[3] Most of the great changes in channel course visible between the 1858 and 1882 channels in Rancho Canada de la Segunda probably occurred during this flood.

The next great flood occurred in 1911. An account in the "Monterey Cypress" of 11 March 1911 reported that Fannie Meadows and Roy Martin lost 10 acres and a pear orchard due to lateral migration of the river. Their adjacent proper-ties extended downstream from the present Schulte Road to Meadows Road. The channel shift that consumed their land can be seen by comparing the river course of 1858 with that of 1911 (fig. 4).

---

[3]Roy Meadows. Personal communication of family history.

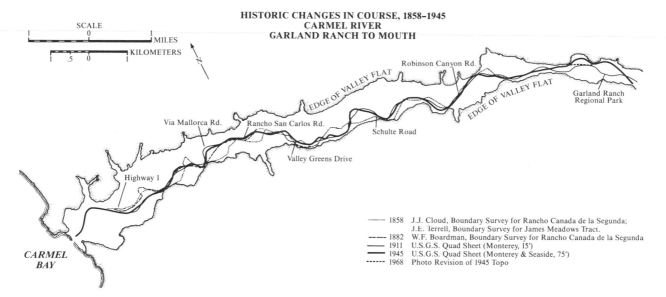

SCALE

MILES
KILOMETERS

Robinson Canyon Rd.

EDGE OF VALLEY FLAT

EDGE OF VALLEY FLAT

Garland Ranch
Regional Park

Via Mallorca Rd.

Rancho San Carlos Rd.

Schulte Road

Valley Greens Drive

Highway 1

CARMEL
BAY

.... 1858   J.J. Cloud, Boundary Survey for Rancho Canada de la Segunda;
                J.E. Terrell, Boundary Survey for James Meadows Tract.
– – – 1882   W.F. Boardman, Boundary Survey for Rancho Canada de la Segunda
———— 1911   U.S.G.S. Quad Sheet (Monterey, 15')
━━━━ 1945   U.S.G.S. Quad Sheet (Monterey & Seaside, 75')
------ 1968   Photo Revision of 1945 Topo

Figure 4.--Course changes of the Carmel River, Garland Ranch
to mouth.

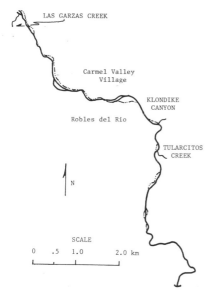

LAS GARZAS CREEK

Carmel Valley
Village

KLONDIKE
CANYON

Robles del Rio

TULARCITOS
CREEK

N

SCALE

0   .5   1.0   2.0 km

Figure 5.--Course changes of the Carmel River
channel, San Clemente Dam to Las Garzas
Creek. Key: dashed--1917 channel from 1918
edition Jamesburg 15' quad; solid--1954 channel, from 1956 edition Carmel Valley 7.5'
quad.

The flood of 1911 was a big flood indeed.
Before it was swept away, a staff gauge at the
site of the San Clemente Dam indicated a discharge of 480 cms (17,000 cfs). The peak flow
has been estimated at 708 cms (25,000 cfs). In
1914 another major flood occurred, but this one
was far less destructive. It is not known
whether this flood was significantly smaller than
the 1911 event, or if it simply caused less dis-

ruption because it flowed through a channel pre-
adjusted to the large 1911 flow.

No comparable floods occurred in the following decades. The absence of large floods, together with the drop in sediment load resulting from
construction of the San Clemente Dam in 1921,
served to permit channel narrowing, increased
sinuosity, and bed degradation.

Changes in Sinuosity and Gradient

Sinuosity, defined as the ratio of stream
channel length to valley length, was computed for
several sequential channels. From 1911 to 1945,
the reach of river from Garland Ranch to the
mouth increased in sinuosity from 1.11 to 1.18.
The reach from Sleepy Hollow to Las Garzas Creek
experienced an overall increase in sinuosity of
1.05 to 1.09 from 1917 to 1954. Map slopes computed for the 1911 and 1945 channels from Garland
Ranch to the mouth show a decrease from 0.0034 in
1911 to 0.0029 in 1945. The overall increase in
sinuosity and decrease in gradient suggest that
the Carmel River stabilized in the aftermath of
the 1911 flood.

Changes in Channel Pattern and Form

Channel pattern (pattern in plan view, e.g.,
meandering, braided) and form (cross sectional
shape, e.g., narrow, wide) of the Lower and Middle Carmel River have changed dramatically since
the last major flood and construction of the
dams. No doubt, the entire Lower and Middle
Carmel were strongly modified by the 1911 and
1914 floods. The resulting channel is probably
well represented by the historical photos (ca.
1918) from the Slevin Collection (University of
California, Berkeley). These photos of the

127

river, at and downstream of the Narrows (fig. 6 and 7), show a wide, sandy channel, reflecting the recent passage of a major flood.

By 1939, the Lower Carmel had developed a narrower, more sinuous channel while the Middle Carmel retained much of its braided character, as evidenced by aerial photography of 1939. Figure 7 shows the area pictured in figure 6 as it subsequently appeared in the 1930s. By this time, a riparian forest had developed along virtually all of the Lower Carmel River, narrowing the channel. Aerial photographs taken in 1965 show further development of vegetation and narrowing of the channel.

This change in channel pattern occurred concurrently with the increase in sinuosity and decrease in gradient apparent by 1945. Together, they indicate that the Lower Carmel had adjusted to the absence of major floods and the cut-off of 60% of its previous sediment load (based on drainage area upstream of San Clemente Dam). These adjustments included channel narrowing with encroaching vegetation, an increase in sinuosity, and reduction of gradient through incision.

Figure 7.--Carmel River channel, 1930s, viewed from right bank upstream from location of present Robinson Canyon Road bridge. View upstream. Contrast this with figure 6, essentially the same view, taken in 1918. (Pat Hathaway Photograph Collection, Pacific Grove, California.)

Similar adjustments have been documented in other rivers in response to the absence of floods or the construction of upstream dams (Leopold et al. 1964).

By 1939, the Lower Carmel had incised about 4 m. into deposits of the 1911 flood, leaving a 4 m. terrace. Some of this incision is visible when figures 6 and 7 are compared. The flat surface of sand and gravel to the right of the river in figure 6 is the 1911 channel floor. By 1918 (when figure 6 was taken), the channel had cut down about 2 m., and willows had begun to invade the low terrace. By the 1930s (when figure 7 was taken), the channel had incised about 4 m. The 1911 channel floor appears as the terrace in figure 7, with a farmed field and small building on it. This 1911 terrace can be confidently traced along much of the Lower Carmel on the basis of morphology and historic changes in course. Figure 8 shows the 1911 terrace (Qt1) and higher terraces. There is evidence that Qt2A may be the 1862 flood terrace, but otherwise the higher terraces are of unknown age.

Above the Narrows along the Middle Carmel, similar adjustments took place, but they occurred later. The aerial photos taken in 1939 show the scars of numerous anastamosing channels in the Middle Carmel. By 1971, most of these scars no longer appeared, as exemplified by the reach from Boronda Road to Robles del Rio (fig. 9). Accompanying this change in pattern was degradation of the bed. Sequential cross sections show 1.5 m. (5 ft.) of degradation under the Boronda Road bridge from 1946 to 1980.

By the 1960s, most of the Lower and Middle Carmel had developed a narrow, sinuous, well-vegetated course. It bears repeating that these

Figure 6.--Carmel River channel, 1918, viewed from right bank upstream from location of present Robinson Canyon Road bridge, looking upstream. (Slevin Collection, Bancroft Library, University of California, Berkeley.)

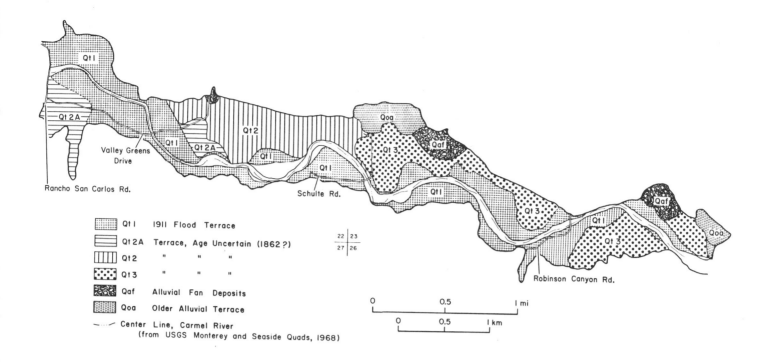

Qt 1   1911 Flood Terrace

Qt 2A   Terrace, Age Uncertain (1862?)

Qt 2   "   "   "

Qt 3   "   "   "

Qaf   Alluvial Fan Deposits

Qoa   Older Alluvial Terrace

–·–·–   Center Line, Carmel River
(from USGS Monterey and Seaside Quads, 1968)

Figure 8.—1911 flood terrace and other Quaternary deposits
of the Carmel River, from the Narrows to Rancho San
Carlos Road. (Based on reconnaissance-level study of
aerial photographs, historic ground photographs, and
historic changes in course.)

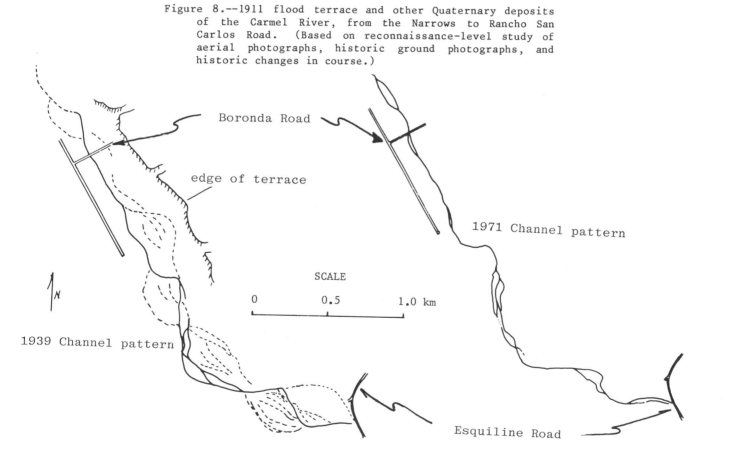

Figure 9.—Pattern changes, Middle Carmel River, from
Boronda Road to Esquiline Road at Robles Del Rio.
(Data from aerial photographs of 1939 and 1971, Map
Library, University of California, Santa Cruz.)

129

conditions developed only in the absence of major floods and, further, may have depended upon a cut-off of upstream sediment by the dams.

Additionally, before their suppression by European settlers, fires occurred regularly in the upper Carmel basin, periodically leading to vastly greater sediment yields. The accumulation of sediment in the Los Padres Reservoir after the Marble-Cone fire of 1977 was dramatic. The capacity of this reservoir decreased from 3,200 AF upon closure in 1947 to 2,600 AF in 1977, a loss of storage of 600 AF in 20 years. Consequent to the Marble-Cone fire and the high flows in the ensuing winter, the reservoir's capacity decreased to 2,040 AF by the end of 1978. Thus, in one year the reservoir lost 560 AF of storage.[4] This post-fire sedimentation rate was nearly 20 times greater than the pre-fire rate.

Prior to dam construction, all this sediment passed through to the Middle and Lower Carmel. It is probable that a wide, sandy channel would have developed in order to transport these high sediment loads. However, it is notable that the sediment contributed by the recent bank erosion has passed through the lowermost reaches of the Carmel (Valley Greens Drive downstream) without destabilizing that narrow channel. The stability of this lowermost reach may be due, in part, to the automobile bodies and riprap emplaced within the banks or to the extensive irrigating of streamside golf courses. Without these stabilizing influences, the channel might have widened in response to the higher load. Alternatively, such a narrow channel in its natural state, protected only by bank vegetation, may be able to pass these high loads without disruption of its existing geometry. In this latter case, the observed changes in channel pattern, form, gradient, and sinuosity may best be ascribed to recovery from the major floods of 1911 and 1914.

RECENT BANK EROSION

Peak discharges over the winters of 1978 and 1980 were 208 cms (7,360 cfs) and 168 cms (5,920 cfs) respectively. These flows resulted in massive bank erosion along parts of the Middle and Lower Carmel. Most severely affected was the region upstream of Schulte Road Bridge. Here the channel at bankfull discharge (defined as the flow with a recurrence interval of 2.4 years on an annual maximum series) increased in width from 13 m. (43 ft.) to 35 m. (115 ft.) in two years. This increased the width:depth ratio from 15 to 113. Aerial photographs show the changing aspect of this reach from 1939 to 1980. In 1939 and 1965, a narrow channel fringed by dense riparian vegetation is visible (fig. 10a and b). The 1977 photo indicates no obvious change in the channel, but does show a marked thinning of streamside trees (fig. 10c). The 1980 photo exhibits a

---

[4]B. Buel. 1981. Monterey Peninsula Water Management District. Personal communication.

major widening of the channel, most of which occurred during one storm in the winter of 1980 (fig. 10d).

Throughout the Middle and Lower Carmel, the river banks are composed of unconsolidated sands and gravels, which lack cohesive strength in the absence of binding vegetation. These banks offered no resistance to lateral erosion. A comparison of surveys and aerial photographs of 1965 and 1980 from Schulte Bridge upstream 0.6 km. (0.4 mi.) indicates that 100,000 cu. m. of bank material was consumed by the river, mostly during the winter of 1980. The resulting channel is wide and floored by sand and gravel (fig. 11).

The die-off of bank vegetation and consequent lateral erosion appear to be coincident with lowering of water tables below the root zone of trees. Downstream of Valley Greens Drive, where no producing wells were located, the riparian vegetation remained largely unaffected during the drought of 1976-77. The channel there remained stable during both the 1978 and 1980 winters. A plot of water table elevations for the drought, i.e., drawdown (October 1977), and post-drought, fully recharged conditions (April 1978) shows far less drawdown in this lowermost reach of the Carmel (fig. 12). Figure 12 shows that along much of the Middle and Lower Carmel the water table was drawn down about 10 m. This is generally considerd to be below the root zone of riparian willows (Zinke 1971). The depression of the water table upstream of Schulte Road is due to the drawdown created by wells in the highly permeable alluvium of the Carmel Valley. While the drought of 1976-1977 certainly exacerbated the drawdown problem, the drought alone cannot explain the fact that severe drawdown, vegetation die-off, and subsequent bank erosion affected certain areas only.

EROSION MITIGATION

Individual efforts to control bank erosion along the Carmel range widely in cost and effectiveness. Riprap has been used with mixed results. Among the materials used for riprap on the Carmel are ornamental dolomite, concrete blocks, and rubble from Cannery Row. Gabions and pervious fences with rock fill have been used successfully. Some landowners are attempting to establish willows on their eroding banks, but many of these seedlings are not adequately irrigated and die. One of the most popular revetment strategies is emplacement of automobile bodies in the eroding banks (fig. 13). The individual bank protection efforts thus far are uncoordinated and may, in some cases, have deleterious downstream effects. The government agency charged with managing the area's water resources, the Monterey Peninsula Water Management District, is now considering an integrated management plan for the Carmel River.

a. 1939.

b. 1965.

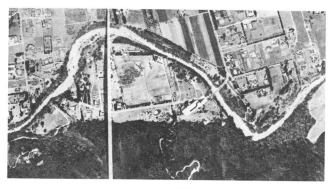

c. 1977.

d. 1980.

Figure 10.--Aerial photographs of the Carmel River near Schulte Road bridge. Arrows point to bridge. (Aerial photograph collection, Monterey County Flood Control, Salinas.)

Figure 11.--Channel of the Carmel River upstream of Schulte Road bridge, November 1980. View downstream from about 0.5 km (0.3 mi.) upstream of bridge (photograph by the authors).

REDESIGNING THE CARMEL RIVER

The "river-training" experience of New Zealand engineers provides a possible model for restoring unstable reaches of the Carmel (Nevins 1967). Their procedure is to determine "design geometries" from stable reaches of a river and to reengineer unstable reaches to these design geometries. Cross-sectional geometry, sinuosity, and gradient of the stable reaches are duplicated as closely as possible in the unstable reaches. Initially, bank protection works are used to stabilize the banks and willows are planted; once fully established, the willows are expected to become the principal bank-stabilizing agent. The reengineered channels in New Zealand have remained stable in all but very high flows. If large discharges disrupt the design channels, these reaches can be reengineered to design specifications at a lower cost than the initial work (ibid.).

For the Carmel River, the stable reaches downstream of the disturbed reaches can serve as design geometries. In figure 14, cross sections are plotted for an eroded reach upstream of

131

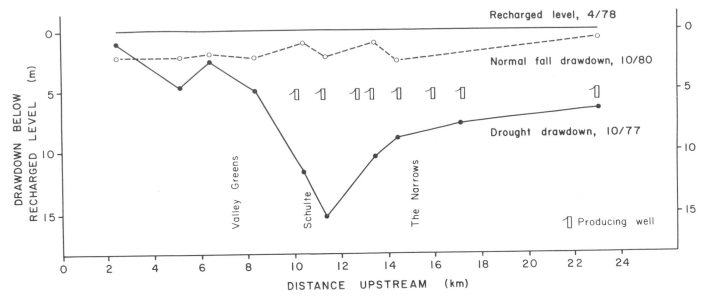

Figure 12.—Water table elevations, drought and recharged conditions. (Date from Monterey County Flood Control well level records.)

Figure 13.—Automobile bodies used as bank revetment, downstream of Meadows Road (photograph by the authors).

Schulte Road (section 37) and for a stable reach about 1.5 km. (1 mi.) downstream (section 45). No tributaries enter between these sections, so discharge remains essentially constant. Yet the present-day geometries are vastly different. Surveys by the US Army Corps of Engineers in 1965 (US Army Corps of Engineers 1967) indicate that the reach encompassing section 37 was characterized by a geometry closely resembling that of the present-day section 45. Thus, a design-stable geometry for section 37 could be drawn largely from the existing geometry at section 45. Certain corrections would have to be made for difference in gradient, sinuosity, and bed material size between these reaches. Fortunately, many of these parameters are well documented for the stable, pre-disturbance Carmel River.

The success of a river-training program depends, in part, on a favorable flow regime in the years following channel redesign. A major flood (e.g., a 20- to 30-year event) in the first few years following the redesign may take out the new banks before they have been stabilized by vegetation. A catastrophic flood (e.g., a 75- to 100-year event) will probably carve a new channel for itself regardless of how well vegetated the existing banks might be (Nevins 1967). Applying these concepts to the Carmel, we might expect that a flow comparable to the 1980 event within the first five-to-ten years following channel redesign could take out the design banks. A flow comparable to the 1911 flow could take out the design banks whether vegetated or not.

SUMMARY

The lower 24-km. (15-mi.) reach of the Carmel River is alluviated and is divided by a bedrock constriction into a lower 16-km. (10-mi.) reach and a middle 8-km. (5-mi.) reach. This alluvial reach of the river has experienced major changes in channel course, pattern, and form over the past 130 years. Major floods in 1862 and 1911 changed the river's course by up to 500 m. (1,640 ft.). After 1914, the absence of severe floods, coupled with dam construction upstream, led to a change from a wide, braided channel to a narrow, more sinuous channel. Accompanying this change was a decrease in overall gradient in the lower reach from .0034 to .0029 between 1911 and 1945.

By 1939, the date of the first coverage by aerial photography, the lower reach had developed a narrow, sinuous channel with well-vegetated banks that remained stable for most of the next four decades. The middle reach of the river, however, displayed a predominantly wide, braided

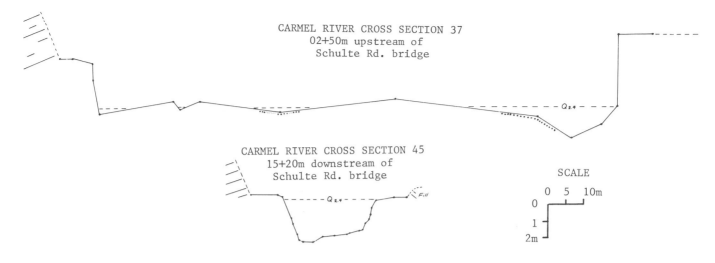

Figure 14.—Channel cross sections of the Carmel River near Schulte Road bridge. Section 37: 250 m. (820 ft.) upstream of bridge; section 45: 1,520 m. (5,000 ft.) downstream of bridge. Discharge is essentially constant. (From field surveys by the authors).

pattern. Between 1939 and 1971, this middle reach developed a single thread channel and downcut up to 1.5 m. (5 ft).

As groundwater withdrawal from streamside wells increased in the 1960s, residents began complaining that riparian trees were dying near the wells. During the 1976-1977 drought, lowered water tables were associated with substantial die-off of riparian trees. The death of these bank-stabilizing trees is associated with significant lateral erosion that occurred during the winters of 1978 and 1980. Upstream of the Schulte Road bridge, the river's bankfull channel increased in width from 13 m. to 35 m., increasing the width:depth ratio from 15 to 113. Downstream, the channel remained stable despite passage of the sediment derived from the eroding reaches.

Individual efforts to control bank erosion have included planting of willows and emplacement in banks of automobile bodies and riprap. The mixed success of these efforts demonstrates that a coordinated program is needed to manage the river. Most promising as a model for the Carmel is the experience of New Zealand engineers in "river training." Their procedure is to determine design geometries from stable reaches and then redesign disturbed reaches to the design geometry. After initial stabilization using engineering works, planted willows are expected to serve as the primary stabilizing agents.

ACKNOWLEDGMENTS

This study was supported by a contract with the Monterey Peninsula Water Management District. Our thanks to the District staff for generous assistance in every phase of the study. We are also grateful for the invaluable cooperation of Monterey County Flood Control, the California Department of Fish and Game, Monterey Office, and the US Army Corps of Engineers, San Francisco District. To the friends who helped with the field work, our thanks.

LITERATURE CITED

Lee, E.B. 1974. A summary report of facts, analysis, and conclusions relating to the Monterey Peninsula water supply problems. Public Utilities Commission Case 9530. 23 p. Unpublished report.

Leopold, L.B., W.G. Wolman, and J.P. Miller. 1964. Fluvial processes in geomorphology. 522 p. W. Freeman and Company, San Francisco, Calif.

Nevins, T.H. 1967. River training—the single-thread channel. New Zealand Engineering 24 (Dec. 15, 1967):367-373.

Stone, E. 1971. The dynamics of vegetation change along the Carmel River. Unpublished report to the California-American Water Company, March, 1971. 54 p.

US Army Corps of Engineers. 1967. Flood plain information on Carmel River, Monterey County, California. 36 p. US Army Corps of Engineers, San Francisco District, San Francisco, Calif.

Zinke, P. 1971. The effect of water well drawdown on riparian and phreatophyte vegetation in the Middle Carmel Valley. Unpublished report to the Carmel Valley Property Owners Association, Carmel Valley, Calif. February, 1971. 27 p.

SEQUENTIAL CHANGES IN BED HABITAT CONDITIONS

IN THE UPPER CARMEL RIVER

FOLLOWING THE MARBLE-CONE FIRE OF AUGUST, 1977[1]

Barry Hecht[2]

Abstract.--Runoff following a major fire filled the upper Carmel River, Monterey County, California, with sediment. Repeated measurements of four habitat descriptors were made in riffles during three years following the fire. Habitat values were largely restored by the end of the first winter, with virtually complete recovery after three years.

INTRODUCTION

The importance of episodic or unusual events in the management of riparian systems in montane areas is increasingly being recognized. Wildfires are one of the major recurring disturbances affecting biologic and geomorphic processes in these watersheds. This is especially true in basins with significant areas of steep, chaparral-covered slopes.

Many resource managers consider the canyon bottoms--the channels, riparian zones, and valley flats--the most biologically significant zones in these watersheds. The bottomlands commonly remain unburned during fires which otherwise affect much of the drainage area. The primary physical changes in these corridors are frequently those associated with erosion, deposition, and channel instabilities induced by post-fire storm runoff. While numerous studies of fire-related increases in runoff and debris load have been made, relatively little is known of their effects on habitat values.

This report is a preliminary summary of an ongoing study addressing one aspect of the larger management problem--the indirect effects of fires on bed conditions affecting aquatic habitat values. The upper Carmel watershed in Los Padres National Forest, Monterey County, California was chosen for this study for three reasons. First, the drainage is used primarily for recreational, habitat, and watershed purposes; the alluvial corridor is central to all three uses. Second, direct human disruption of soil and vegetation in the basin is minimal, limited primarily to ridge-

tops far removed from the channels. Third, the watershed is in the size range of smaller basins capable of sustaining an anadromous fishery, commonly considered to be from about 10-100 km^2 (4-40 mi^2).

There were two significant limitations on this study imposed by the choice of the upper Carmel watershed. First, there are no stream gauges in the basin. Synthesis of a flow-record for each site will be required to establish the relationship of the observed sequential changes to runoff. Data needed to develop the synthetic flow-record are presently not fully available. Secondly, access to the sites required a hike of about 8 km. (5 mi.) over damaged trails with backpacks and survey gear, limiting both the equipment which could be used and the number of sites which could be monitored during a given weekend.

REGIONAL SETTING

The Carmel River drains the northern slopes of the Santa Lucia Mountains (fig. 1). The upper portion of the basin is a rugged area of approximately 161 km^2 (62 mi^2) above Los Padres Dam, a municipal water-supply source for the Monterey Peninsula urban area about 50 km. (30 mi.) to the north.

The watershed is underlain by faulted crystalline rocks, primarily schists, gneisses, and metasomatic granitic rocks ranging in composition from granodiorite to gabbro (Wiebe 1970). Weathering of these rocks produces a large amount of medium-grained sand and a disproportionately small percentage of fine gravel. The courses of the main channels are structurally-controlled, primarily by faults and fractures. The channels are unusually steep for watersheds of comparable size in the region.

[1]Paper presented at the California Riparian Systems Conference. [University of California, Davis, September 17-19, 1981].
[2]Barry Hecht is Senior Hydrologist, HEA, a Division of J.H. Kleinfelder and Associates, Berkeley, California.

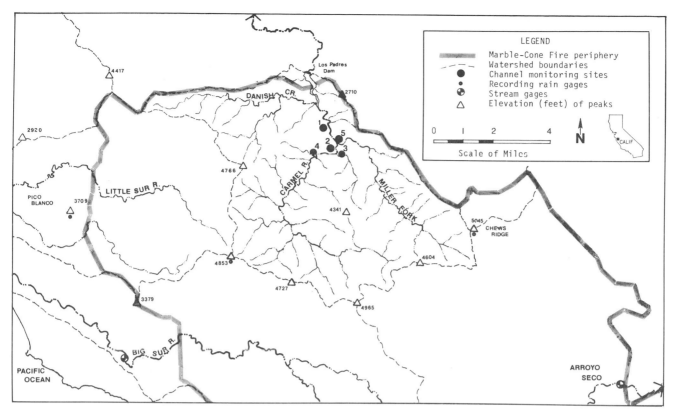

Figure 1.-- Upper Carmel watershed and vicinity. Monitoring sites on the Carmel River are at Bluff Camp (1), Carmel Camp (2), below Bruce Fork (3), at Sulphur Springs Camp (4), and on Miller Fork above its mouth (5).

Rainfall ranges from an average of 610 mm. (24 in.) per year at Los Padres Dam to an estimated 1150-1270 mm. (45-50 in.) at the drainage divide with the Big Sur watershed. This supports a vegetative mosaic with chamise/chaparral on steeper exposed slopes, oak/madrone woodland community on more protected slopes and terraces, and mixed hardwood/coniferous forest at the highest elevations.

The Marble-Cone Fire

The Marble-Cone Fire burned approximately 72,000 ha. (178,000 ac.) in the Santa Lucia Mountains during August, 1977 (fig. 1). Virtually all of the Carmel watershed above Los Padres Reservoir was affected by the fire. The USDA Forest Service staff estimated remaining canopy cover to be less than 10% in 42% of the upper Carmel basin; 11-50% over an additional 20% of the watershed; and more than 51% over the remaining 38% of the area.[3] No extensive fires had occurred in the watershed during the previous 50 years. Much of the basin had remained unburned for 76 years or more (Griffin 1978).

---

[3]USDA Forest Service. Undated. Marble-Cone fire: remaining vegetative cover. Unpublished staff report. Los Padres National Forest.

Two unusual occurrences contributed to the severity of the burn, and particularly to its impact on the canyon floor areas. Fuel levels were abnormally high due to an extreme amount of limb breakage sustained during a wet and sticky snowfall on January 3, 1974. The effect on fuel loadings was especially large in the riparian zone and on the terraces and lower slopes, areas seldom affected by snowfall. Secondly, conditions were also unusually dry following the severe drought of 1976 and 1977. Rainfall at Big Sur, the nearest long-term station, during each of these years was less than that measured for any of the previous 58 years.

Post-Fire Runoff

Rainfall during the 1977-78 and 1979-80 winter seasons was 40-50% above normal at many stations in the region; rainfall during 1978-79 was generally slightly below average. Runoff in the Carmel and nearby watersheds was markedly above normal during this 3-year period, reflecting both the above-average rainfall and the altered runoff characteristics (table 1). The duration of high flows was also much above normal. One measure of this duration is the number of days that flow exceeded bankfull conditions. In the Monterey Bay area (as in many other regions), this corresponds roughly to the flood with a recurrence of 1.5 years. The Big Sur River is the nearest gauged stream, and is consisidered most representative of the upper Carmel River. The 1.5-year flood discharge on the Big Sur River is approximately 1,600 cubic feet per second (cfs). Based on preliminary records, this discharge was exceeded for a total of about 10 days in 1978 and about 6 days in 1980, compared with an annual average of 1.1 days for the period prior to the fire.

Table 1.--Post-fire runoff at gauges in the vicinity of the upper Carmel watershed.

USGS gage no.	11143000	11143200	11151870
Stream	Big Sur R.	Carmel R.	Arroyo Seco
Location	Big Sur	Robles del Rio	nr. Greenfield
Period of record	1950-pres.	1957-pres.	1961-pres.
Drainage area (sq. mi.)	46.5	193	113
Mean annual runoff (cfs)	89.6	71.3	121
Runoff			
1978 (cfs)	246	206	378
(% of mean[1])	275	289	312
1979 (cfs)	97.9	63.5	163
(% of mean[1])	109	89	135
1980 (cfs)	200	192	295
(% of mean[1])	223	269	243

[1]Mean annual runoff through Sept. 30, 1977, excluding period of post-fire runoff.

More specific data are available on the effect of the fire on sediment yields of the upper Carmel watershed (table 2). Deposition in Los Padres Reservoir during the three years following the fire was about equal to that during the previous 30 years. In addition, a large but undetermined amount of debris has accumulated in the channels of the Carmel River and Danish Creek above the spillway elevation.[4]

SEQUENTIAL CHANGES IN BED HABITAT CONDITIONS

Habitat in the streams of the upper Carmel system is generally evaluated by its suitability for salmonid production. The local resource includes both steelhead and resident trout. Availabilities of suitable spawning and rearing habitats are considered factors limiting both populations, a common situation in streams of central California.

In riffles of boulder-bedded streams such as the upper Carmel River, both spawning and rearing occur in spaces or openings between the larger bed-forming rocks. Spawning occurs in bars and accumulations of gravels which form between the

[4]Bloyd, R.M. 1981. Letter of March 18 to Robert F. Blecker, hydrologist for Los Padres National Forest, which summarizes USDI Geological Survey studies of post-fire sedimentation in Los Padres Reservoir.

Table 2.--Sequential sediment accumulation in Los Padres Reservior (source--R.M. Boyd[4]).

Survey date	Reservoir capacity[1] (acre-ft.)	Loss in capacity (acre-ft.)	Annual rate of capacity loss (acre-ft.)
Nov 1947[2]	3200	–	–
Nov 1977	2592.7	607.3	20.2
Sep 1978	2037.6	555	555
Oct 1980	1996.3	41.3	20.6

[1]Below spillway elevation of 317.2 m. (1040.8 ft.) above mean sea level.
[2]From pre-construction capacity curves developed by California Water and Telephone Company.

boulders or in their lees, locations partially protected from scour.

The epicycle of massive fill and scour following fires in this environment temporarily buries most of the limited habitat with finer material, largely sand. For this reconnaissance study, descriptors chosen to define the extent of burial and subsequent uncovering of habitat include:

1. net fill and scour, as measured by level-surveys following each major group of storms;
2. particle-size distribution of the bed surface, measured by censusing particles at the intersections of a grid;
3. percentage of bed area occupied by sand and finer material, also sampled on a grid; and
4. percent of the bed covered by material of sizes suitable for spawning, determined as above.

Net Fill and Scour

Minimal spawning or rearing habitat was available in the upper Carmel channels during the period of maximum fill. Habitat availability increased as the stored sediment was gradually scoured. A useful measure of these sequential changes is net mean fill or scour, determined from the change in mean bed elevation of the channel during each storm period. This change was quantified using repeated level-surveys of monumented cross-sections.

The sequence of fill and scour was recorded at six cross-sections in three riffles. The riffles were chosen shortly after the fire on the basis of observable habitat values for both spawning and rearing, their general alluvial character, absence of major unusual hydraulic properties, and presence in a long and straight reach. The last three criteria were necessary to meet the hydraulic requirement of the indirect discharge measurements used to determine the peak flows during each storm period. The sections were established in early November, 1977, following the fire but prior to any measurable run-off. Cross-sections were resurveyed after each significant flood event during the winter of 1977-78, and again following the wet season of 1979-80. An example of data collected at one section describing the sequential changes in elevation and configuration of the bed is presented in figure 2.

The fill and scour cycle observed at each riffle is summarized in table 3. Fill occurred immediately after the first storms in December, 1977, and continued at some sections through the major storm period in January, 1978. By the end of the first winter, the bed was being scoured at all six sections, a process which continued through the second and third rainy seasons. The

final column in table 3 traces the proportion of maximum net fill removed during each period.[5] By the end of the first season, 57-102% of the maximum observed net fill had been scoured. "Re-covery percentages" of 80-151% were recorded by the end of the third year. At four of the six sections, 80-90% of the maximum observed fill had been removed by the end of the third year. Mean scour exceeding the mean maximum fill was limited to the riffle at Carmel Camp, where about half of the mean scour is attributable to lateral erosion of the lower bank area on one side of the channel.

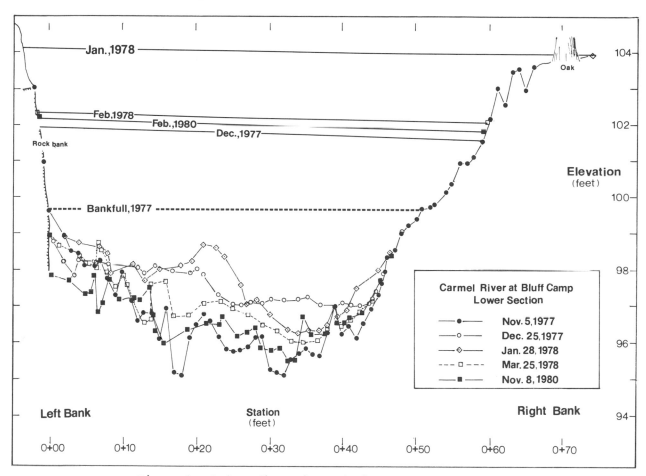

Figure 2.--Bed configuration and high-water marks during the fill and scour cycle following the Marble-Cone fire, looking downstream. Some high-water profiles slope toward the right bank, discussed below in the text.

[5] Maximum fills may have been greater during one of the storm periods. Ephemeral bed conditions during storm crests may not have great importance in defining spawning or rearing habi-tat value; thus the methodology is appropriate for the purposes of this study. The reader is cautioned that recovery percentages in table 3 may underestimate the removal of within-storm fill maxima.

Table 3.—Sequential changes in net fill and scour.

		Mean Bed Elevation (ft.)	Net Fill(+) or Scour(-) (ft.)	Percent[1] Recovery
Carmel River at Bluff Camp				
Lower Section	11/05/77	96.82	-	-
	12/25/77	97.72 [2]	+0.90	-
	01/28/78	97.83	+0.11	0
	03/25/78	97.25	-0.58	57
	11/08/80	96.93	-0.32	89
Upper Section	11/05/77	99.48	-	-
	12/25/77	100.49 [2]	+1.01	0
	01/28/78	99.89	-0.60	59
	03/25/78	99.68	-0.21	80
	11/08/80	99.68	0.00	80
Carmel River at Carmel Camp				
Lower Section	11/06/77	93.82	-	-
	12/26/77	94.23 [2]	+0.41	0
	01/28/78	94.00	-0.23	56
	03/25/78	93.81	-0.19	102
	11/09/80	93.61	-0.20	151
Upper Section	11/06/77	95.24	-	-
	12/26/77	95.48 [2]	+0.24	0
	01/29/78	95.40	-0.08	33
	03/26/78	95.30	-0.10	75
	11/09/80	95.15	-0.15	138
Miller Fork above Carmel R.				
Lower Section	11/06/77	91.50	-	-
	12/26/77	91.56 [2]	+0.06	0
	01/29/78	91.56 [2]	0.00	0
	03/26/78	91.52	-0.04	67
	11/09/80	91.51	-0.01	83
Upper Section	11/06/77	94.18	-	-
	12/26/77	94.29	+0.11	-
	01/29/78	94.53 [2]	+0.24	0
	03/26/78	94.27	-0.26	74
	11/09/80	94.23	-0.04	86

[1]Defined as whole channel change in mean bed elevation (MBE) by the relation $100(MBE_m-MBE_i)/(MBE_m-MBE_o)$, with subscripts m, i, and o identifying maximum net fill, measured, and original post-fire conditions, respectively.

[2]Maximum net fill.

Size Distribution of Bed Material

The particle-size distribution of bed material is commonly quantified in the course of habitat assessments, either by a visual estimate or by a grid-by-number census. The latter approach was used in this study.

Particle-size distributions of bed-surface material were determined by measurement made at the same five riffles in the early fall months of each year, prior to the onset of rains. This is the season in which rearing habitat is most likely to be constrained by sediment. An area-stratified random sample of the entire riffle bed was drawn by stretching cloth measuring tapes between rows of eight to ten iron pins at the top and base of each riffle. Lengths of intermediate axes of particles immediately beneath preselected points on the tapes were measured and grouped in standard size-classes. This procedure is an adaption for use in boulder-bed channels of Wolman's (1954) now-standard methodology. A sample of 50 to 100 rocks is generally considered sufficient to describe bed-surface populations; larger samples were drawn following the 1978 storms as a wider range of size-classes were observed.

Sequential changes in the size distribution of bed material are shown in table 4. Sizes at the key descriptive percentiles generally decreased following the fire, then subsequently have increased. Relative changes were more pronounced at the 16th and 50th percentiles than in the larger materials, as might be expected.

Much, and probably most, of the change in particle-size distribution occurred during the first year following the fire. It was not feasible to recensus the bed between storms due to the unusually high flows of the winter of 1978. In most cases, the minimum sizes probably were associated with the December, 1977, or January, 1978 storm periods. Had no more storms occurred during the winter of 1978, a much greater effect on habitat conditions would have been observed during the summer and fall of 1978.

Sand-Covered Bed Areas

Aquatic biologists have often identified percent bed area covered by sand (or finer material) as a significant influence on the distribution of species in the channel, and as a factor affecting salmonid egg viability. The distribution of sand and finer material on the bed of mountain stream riffles appears to be controlled by different geomorphic processes than those governing the coarser sizes. In this study, sand is considered as a separate population, one whose variability is also best described by the percentage of the riffle bed which it covers. In this study, the sand-and-finer percentage of the bed surface was determined in the course of the particle-size measurements. Intermediate axial lengths of particles smaller than 4 mm. could not be readily measured under field conditions; these were grouped in a single class informally labelled "fines."[6]

---

[6]Most standard classifications divide sands and gravels at 2 mm. In the upper Carmel environment, which is deficient in very fine gravels, any interpretive difficulty introduced by including 2-4 mm. material with the sands is minor.

Table 4.--Sequential changes in particle-size of bed material, upper Carmel watershed.

Site No.		1				2				3				4				5	
Stream / Location		Carmel River at Bluff Camp				Carmel River at Carmel Camp				Carmel River below Bruce Fork				Carmel River at Sulphur Springs Camp				Miller Fork above mouth	
Month/Year → Lower limit of size class ↓		10/77	10/78	10/79	11/80	10/77	10/78	10/79	11/80	10/77	10/78	10/79	11/80	10/77	10/78	10/79	11/80	10/77	10/78
Boulders	2050 mm.	1	1	1	1														
Boulders	1450	1	2	3	5		1		1	1	1	1	5						1
Boulders	1024	3	2	3	8	4	5	1	1	3	1	1	3					3	3
Boulders	725	6	2	11	9	10	6	2	3	6	3	2	8					8	6
Boulders	512	8	5	17	9	13	17	19	15	8	6	12	11	2	2	2	5	8	6
Boulders	360	7	6	14	12	18	13	17	23	6	7	14	12	7	14	13	8	6	7
Boulders	256	11	7	12	13	16	10	16	23	6	15	10	18	10	16	18	11	14	7
Cobbles	180	7	7	14	9	6	13	14	14	7	17	17	16	2	16	15	20	12	9
Cobbles	128	6	10	18	9	2	7	19	12	6	9	11	16	10	14	14	15	12	12
Cobbles	90	4	9	18	12	1	5	12	14	3	5	13	11	7	12	14	10	12	9
Cobbles	64	1	7	15	10	2	4	12	9	3	9	5	7	5	10	4	12	9	7
Pebbles	45	3	7	11	13	2	5	3	2	–	9	7	4	–	7	8	7	3	4
Pebbles	32	2	6	10	6	1	5	2	2	1	3	9	3	1	3	6	–	1	5
Pebbles	22.6	1	6	7	7	1	3	2	2	–	5	4	1	1	3	1	1	–	4
Pebbles	16	2	4	3	5	2	1	2	2	1	3	2	2	4	1	2	2	–	4
Fine Gravels	11.3	2	1	3	2	1	–	1	2	2	1	2	1	1	1	1	–	2	3
Fine Gravels	8	2	1	4	1	1	–	3	1	1	1	–	1	1	–	2	–	1	–
Fine Gravels	5.6	2	3	1	–	1	1	–	1	–	–	1	–	1	–	1	1	1	–
Fine Gravels	4	1	2	2	–	–	–	–	–	–	1	–	–	–	1	–	–	–	1
	<4 mm.[1]	1	6	9	2	5	9	3	3	2	3	2	3	3	5	7	0	5	6
Totals[2]		70+1	88+6	167+9	130+2	81+5	96+9	125+3	127+3	54+2	96+3	111+2	119+3	60+3	118+5	113+7	112+0	82+5	89+6
Percentile size (mm.)[3]	d_{84}	710	494	606	783	751	676	531	510	984	412	490	658	499	502	468	482	541	587
	d_{50}	273	118	154	184	395	294	213	266	304	188	187	242	175	206	196	212	231	174
	d_{16}	39	27	40	45	151	66	78	88	97	48	45	64	67	68	56	80	98	40
Fines abundance[4] (% bed area)		1.4	6.8	5.1	1.5	5.8	8.6	2.4	2.4	3.6	3.0	1.8	2.5	4.8	4.1	5.8	0.0	5.7	6.3
Spawning material abundance[5] (% bed area)		23	39	32	35	13	18	20	16	14	32	28	16	22	22	21	20	13	20

[1] 4 mm. is considered the lower limit for size class discrimination under field conditions. Division between sand and gravel usually taken at 2 mm.

[2] Expressed as total rocks + total sand and finer material (<4 mm.).

[3] Size, in millimeters, of material, coarser than 84, 50, and 16 percent of the sample.

[4] Percentage of bed area covered by material finer than 4 mm.; in the upper Carmel basin, this is mainly medium sand.

[5] Percentage of bed area occupied by material of 4 - 90 mm. (see text).

[6] Bed-surface distribution clearly altered by large limb from diseased oak which fell into channel during 1979. Monitoring discontinued.

Sequential changes in the sand-covered portion of the bed are shown in figure 3. The abundance of fines increased markedly with the first storms after the fire. At the Bluff Camp riffle, the percentage of bed area covered by sand or finer debris on December 25, 1977, was visually estimated to be 40% in the riffle and 95% in the pool beneath it. By the end of the first year, the fines abundance at the five sites averaged only very slightly greater than at the time of the fire. As with the particle-size changes, the sequential variations in fines abundance were greatly accelerated by the unusually high runoff conditions of the 1978 water year.

Availability of Spawning-sized Material

Salmonid spawning habitat in the upper Carmel watershed may be limited by the availability of material of suitable sizes in riffles. The relative abundance of this material can be quantified for the Carmel channels as the percentage of the bed surface occupied by rocks within the range of suitable sizes, as no appreciable armoring of the bed was observed. For this study, it is assumed that the range of 4 mm. to 90 mm. defines the bulk of material found in and above freshly-constructed redds in streams of comparable size, slope, and underlying rock types (e.g., Orcutt et al. 1968, Platts et al. 1979).[7]

The availability of spawning-size material increased markedly at four of the five riffles in the first year after the fire. The percentage of the bed occupied by this size-range has remained slightly elevated, although depletion has probably occurred since 1978, particularly in the smaller sizes. To an appreciable degree, the increase has been manifested as expanded bars in

[7] Percentages of bed area occupied by material of other ranges may be computed from table 4 by those who would prefer to consider different sizes.

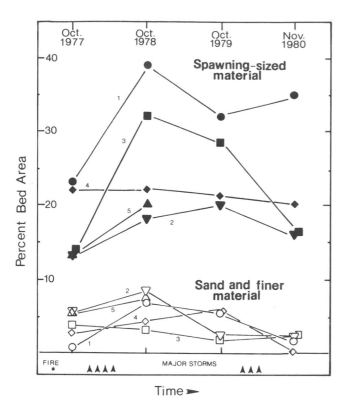

Figure 3.--Sequential changes in bed area occupied by spawning-sized material and sand-and-finer debris following the Marble-Cone fire. Runoff events substantially exceeding bankfull discharge are considered major storms. Sites are numbered as on figure 1 and table 4.

the lees of larger boulders, a location preferentially used for spawning in boulder-bedded channels. The role of fires in the supply of gravels in high-gradient streams merits study.

SUPPLEMENTAL OBSERVATIONS

Other processes related to post-fire sedimentation also affected the channels and riparian corridors. These were observed in a more general way.

1. The fill and scour cycle in pools and glides (or "runs") was greater in absolute magnitude than in riffles. Several traditional swimming holes were completely filled during the December and January storms following the fire. The relative rates of recovery in pools and glides seemed to be similar to or slightly slower than those in the riffles of this boulder-bedded channel.

This study was limited to describing sequential changes in riffles, where indirect discharge estimates and bed-material census are custo-

marily made. Equally important in this decision was the historical emphasis placed on riffles by aquatic biologists. Subsequent research has clarified and quantified the importance of rearing habitat within pools and glides in salmonid production (e.g., Bjornn et al. 1977; Kelley and Dettman 1979). Future studies of post-fire changes in habitat should include pools and glides.

2. Few secondary slope instabilities were induced by the fire. Landslide-related sediment delivery to the main channels was probably of negligible magnitude; this presumably contributed to the rapid rate of sediment depletion in the channels. The relative stability of the slopes is considered to be primarily a function of bedrock type.

3. Interception of sediment on the lowermost terrace was widespread, particularly at the mouths of ravines, chutes, and small tributaries. Much of this material is of gravel or pebble size. Relative to the volume of coarse material deposited in and above Los Padres Reservoir since the fire, the volume of debris intercepted on the terrace was small, perhaps 1-3%. This is a smaller amount, but somewhat similar to the fire-related sediment still stored in the main channels at least above the tailwater areas of Los Padres Reservoir. Delayed delivery of coarse material stored in these debris cones may be a factor in maintaining the supply of spawning-sized material during extended periods between major fires and floods.

4. Floods following the fire removed much of the organic matter which had accumulated in the channel. Most fallen trunks and limbs on or spanning the streambed were dislodged, then either washed through to Los Padres Reservoir or wedged between the trunks of larger riparian trees distributed along the banks. These small debris jams generated significant eddies during flood periods. As an example, the high-water marks of the December, 1977, February, 1978, and February, 1980 floods indicate that the water-surface profile sloped toward the right bank, the result of a small debris jam 12 m. (40 ft.) upstream. Nearly continuous lines of broken twigs and other fine organic matter accumulated in these eddies during each storm. Each line contained an appreciable amount of material, generally 0.5 to 5 cm. thick. Partial incorporation of this material into the soil was clearly visible by November, 1980. Post-fire additions of organic material to soils at or slightly above the active floodplain may be an appreciable factor in the development of soils in the riparian zone.

CONCLUSIONS

1. Sequential changes in riffle conditions in the upper Carmel watershed following the Marble-Cone fire were observed using four physical descriptors of salmonid habitat:

a. mean fill and scour;

b. particle-size distribution of the bed surface;

c. percent of the bed surface covered by sand and finer debris;

d. percent of the bed surface occupied by material of sizes suitable for spawning.

2. Riffles in the master channels of the upper Carmel watershed filled up to 0.3 m. (1 ft.) during the first storms following the Marble-Cone fire, primarily with sand. By the end of the first year, most of the fill had been scoured; much of what remained was of pebble and cobble size. By the end of the third year, all descriptors had returned to within 20% (relative to the maximum measured disruption) of their pre-fire conditions. Other on-going watershed processes were probably more important than residual effects of the fire as influences on habitat conditions by the end of the third year.

3. Effects of the fire on runs and pools were not measured. Maximum mean channel fill was generally observed to be several times greater than in riffles. Recovery of habitat values appears to occur at relative rates similar to or slightly slower than those in the riffles.

4. A substantial volume of sediment, primarily gravels and cobbles, was intercepted in the riparian and terrace areas. Delayed delivery to main channels is likely to be an important factor in maintaining the availability of spawning-sized material between major disruptive events.

ACKNOWLEDGMENTS

This study was conducted in cooperation with the USDA Forest Service, Pacific Southwest Forest and Range Experiment Station, as part of the Chaparral Management Research and Development Program. Suggestions and assistance were contributed by Wade G. Wells and C. Eugene Conrad of the station; Robert F. Blecker (Los Padres National Forest); Gene H. Taylor (Monterey County Flood Control and Water Conservation District); and Vincent Piro and Randal Benthin (California Department of Fish and Game). Special thanks are extended to friends and colleagues who assisted in the field work, often under wet and cold conditions: Robert Herman, David F. Hoexter, Mark Jansen, G. Matt Kondolf, Yane Nordhav, Mark Springer, and Philip B. Williams. Wade Wells, David Hoexter and Nicholas M. Johnson reviewed the report in draft form.

LITERATURE CITED

Bjornn, T.C., M.A. Brusven, M.P. Molnau, J.H. Milligan, R.A. Klamt, E. Chacho, and C. Schaye. 1977. Transport of granitic sediment in streams and its effects on insects and fish. University of Idaho Forest, Wildlife, and Range Experiment Station Bull. No. 17. 43 p.

Griffin, J.R. 1978. The Marble-Cone fire ten months later. Fremontia 6(2):8-14.

Kelley, D.W., and D.H. Dettman. 1980. Relationships between streamflow, rearing habitat, substrate conditions, and juvenile steelhead populations in Lagunitas Creek, Marin County. Report to the Marin Municipal Water District. 36 p. D.W. Kelley and Associates, Newcastle, California.

Orcutt, D.R., T.R. Pulliam, and A. Arp. 1968. Characteristics of steelhead trout redds in Idaho streams. Trans. Amer. Fish Soc. 97(1):42-45.

Platts, W.S., M.A. Shirazi, and D.H. Lewis. 1979. Sediment particle sizes used for spawning, with methods for evaluation. US Environmental Protection Agency Pub. 3-79-043. Cincinnati, Ohio. 32 p.

Wiebe, R.A. 1970. Relations of granitic and gabbroic rocks, northern Santa Lucia Range, California. Geol. Soc. Am. Bull. 81(1): 105-116.

Wolman, M.G. 1954. A method of sampling coarse river-bed material. Trans. Am. Geophys. Union 35(6):951-956.

FLOOD CONTROL AND RIPARIAN SYSTEM DESTRUCTION:

LOWER SAN LORENZO RIVER, SANTA CRUZ COUNTY, CALIFORNIA[1]

Gary B. Griggs[2]

Abstract.--A 1959 flood control project on the lower San Lorenzo River in Santa Cruz County, California, involved levee construction and excavation below the river's natural grade. Subsequent siltation has greatly reduced the channel's capability to contain flood waters. Annual dredging has destroyed the riparian corridor and has not significantly increased flood protection.

INTRODUCTION

The San Lorenzo River drains 357 km^2 of the central California Coast Ranges (fig. 1). Annual rainfall in the redwood-forested basin averages 150 cm., and flooding has been common within the communities which occupy the river's floodplain. Steep slopes, landslides, and unstable soils combined with high-intensity precipitation have led to severe erosion in certain parts of the basin. Logging, quarrying, and the grading and vegetation removal that accompany urban and rural developments have compounded the erosion and sediment-production problem.

Excluding the population of the city of Santa Cruz at the river's mouth, the watershed is home to 33,000 people. Most of the population is concentrated along the stream bottoms of the river and its tributaries.

As a result of disastrous flooding within the city of Santa Cruz during December 1955, the US Army Corps of Engineers (CE) proposed a flood-control project along the lower San Lorenzo River. The project consisted of levee construction and channel dredging for 4 km. upstream from the river mouth. Changes in channel equilibrium have produced heavy siltation which has greatly reduced the project's flood control capacity. For the past four years the city has annually removed all river-bottom vegetation and bulldozed the accumulated sediment into windrows in the hope that the river would scour out its bed. Scouring has not taken place, but loss of riparian system has occurred.

[1] Paper presented at the California Riparian Systems Conference. [University of California, Davis, September 17-19, 1981].
[2] Gary B. Griggs is Professor of Earth Sciences, University of California, Santa Cruz.

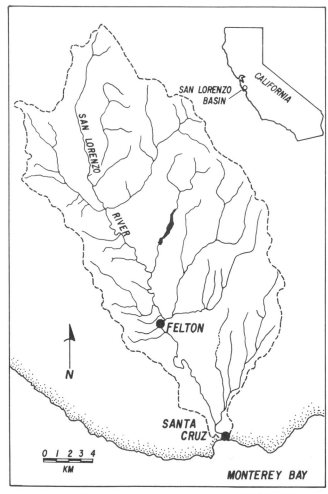

Figure 1.--Index map showing the San Lorenzo River watershed and its location in California.

FLOODING

Flooding is the most widespread geologic hazard in the United States, accounting for greater annual property loss than any other single hazard. Despite the construction of ever-increasing numbers of dams, channels, and levees for "flood control" purposes, losses from flooding have continued to increase primarily due to expanded use, re-occupation, and development of downstream floodplains.

There is little doubt that river control works accelerate floodplain development. Once a sense of security from flooding has been established, the conversion of open space to densely populated areas has become commonplace. Although flood control projects do offer protection from all events smaller than the design flood, if properly designed, they will not be effective against the infrequent larger events. In other words, all flood control ends somewhere; we simply cannot afford to provide protection from the 500- or 1,000-year flood. Thus, as "protected" floodplain areas are more intensively developed, the potential damage from a great or catastrophic flood, which cannot be contained, continues to rise.

Developments located in the floodplain are not only more susceptible to damage, but also reduce the capacity of the floodplain to transport and store floodwaters, and may actually increase the depth and areal extent of inundation. Virtually the entire downtown portion of Santa Cruz lies within the 100-year floodplain of the San Lorenzo River, as do certain residential areas along the river's upper reaches.

Logging and land clearing activity can contribute to flooding problems. Logjams can form as logs and other debris are swept downstream during high flows. Considerable damage during past floods in the densely wooded and heavily logged San Lorenzo basin was apparently caused by logjams occurring at bridges, followed by river back-up and over-bank flooding.

Continued heavy rainfall during December, 1955, led to severe flooding throughout the San Lorenzo basin. Fifty centimeters of rain fell between 15 and 28 December at Boulder Creek, with almost half of that (23 cm.) falling on 22 December. The gauging station at Big Trees in Felton recorded a 6.88-m. stage with a discharge of 861 cu. m. per second (30,400 cfs). Overflow occurred from the headwaters to the mouth, resulting in the maximum flood on record. Numerous logjams and other channel obstructions diverted the floodflows, causing streams to change from their normal alignments and undercut and scour out numerous bridges, road fills, and private developments (US Army Corps of Engineers 1973). Seven persons lost their lives, 2,830 people were displaced from homes, and damages amounted to $8.7 million; most of this was within the city of Santa Cruz itself.

FLOOD CONTROL

Almost two years before the 1955 flood, in the spring of 1954, the CE applied to Congress for $2.265 million for the construction of a flood control project on the lower 4 km. of the San Lorenzo River and lower Branciforte Creek in the city of Santa Cruz (fig. 2). Preliminary designs had already been completed using discharge from a 1940 flood.

The December 1955 flood apparently interrupted work and necessitated a re-evaluation of the "standard project flood" (the 150-year event), but it also provided the CE with even stronger justification for proceeding with the project. Construction began in 1957, after the following revisions in the discharge capacities of the project: a 25% increase for the San Lorenzo, and a 110% increase for Branciforte Creek, to 1,303 cu. m. per second (46,000 cfs) and 238 cu. m. per second (8,400 cfs) respectively (US Army Corps of Engineers 1957).

The CE project consisted of the construction of levees for 4 km. upstream from the mouth, and the excavation of about 590,000 cu. m. of sediments from the existing channel, to increase the slope and capacity of the new channelized reach. The "design" channel bottom was lowered as much as 2.1 m. below the natural or original river-bottom (fig. 3). In conjunction with the excavation, the CE design utilized flow velocities of 2.4-7.5 m. per second (7.9-24.7 ft. per second) to move the necessary water volumes through the various design cross sections.

In July of 1959 the project was completed and was deeded to the City of Santa Cruz by the CE. The city agreed to maintain the channel to design specifications and was provided with a maintenance plan and procedure. Annual maintenance costs were estimated by the CE at $25,000. Total project cost at the time of completion was $6,466,000. The CE departed at this point, absolved of all further responsibility. Considering the awesome reputation of the CE and the docile mentality of the times, it is not surprising that no one questioned the wisdom of dredging the channel and altering the gradient, the velocities used in the design, or the size of the channel. Because the CE presumably had the most experience in the field, it was assumed that the project as planned was the best long-term solution.

Flood protection assured, Santa Cruz intensively redeveloped the "former" floodplain of the

Figure 2.--The city of Santa Cruz and the San Lorenzo River Flood Control Project in 1971. Dashed line delineates the floodplain. Numbers refer to individual bridges-- 1) Highway 1, 2) Water Street, 3) Soquel Avenue, 4) Riverside Avenue. Arrow indicates point where Branci-forte Creek enters San Lorenzo River.

now-tamed San Lorenzo River over the next 10 years. A shopping mall became the showpiece of a downtown renovation project. The early 1970s, however, brought some threatening revelations about the safety of downtown Santa Cruz and the condition of the channel. A 1975 channel center-line survey showed that at least 306,000 cu. m. of sediment had accumulated, significantly reduc-ing the project's capacity. Annual dredging to project depth was not performed by the city, as public works officials felt that high winter flows would scour the accumulated sediments out to sea.

In an effort to aid this process, the city began to utilize a bulldozer with ripper blades to uproot all river-bottom vegetation along the entire 4-km. length of the flood control project, believing that the roots held sediment in place, thereby preventing scour. Scour, however, still did not occur. Subsequent surveys have shown only minor variation in the amount of channel fill, which now stands at about 350,000 cu. m. (figs. 3 and 4).

The California Department of Water Resources (DWR) discovered the situation in 1976. DWR threatened to assume responsibility for clearing the channel and charge the City of Santa Cruz for the dredging later. Responding to these official warnings, the city began to bulldoze sediment up into windrows within the last four years, again, hoping for winter scour to remove the sand (fig. 5). The city also started to remove sediment on a small scale; as of June 1981 less than 40,000 cu. m. had been removed. This has led to nearly total destruction of the riparian vegetation on an annual basis, as well as an unsightly downtown river channel. However, the city is unable to

144

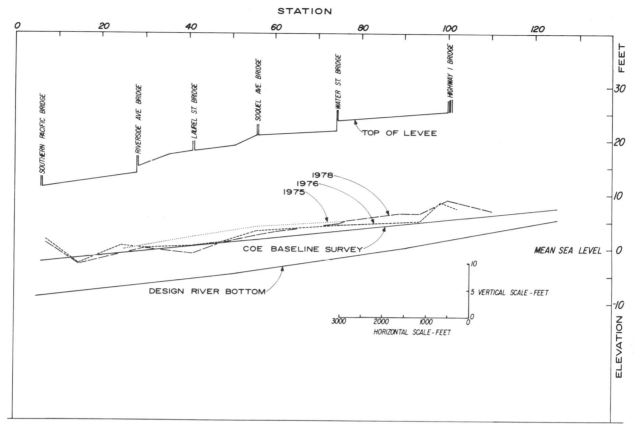

Figure 3.--Changing gradient of the San Lorenzo River as it passes through Santa Cruz. Note the contrast between original or design river bottom after dredging and surveys taken in the late 1970s. Baseline survey refers to channel condition prior to commencement of flood control project in 1959. Station numbers refer to distance upstream from the river mouth in hundreds of feet (Station 20 = 2,000 feet).

finance the total removal of the accumulated sediments, with the cost estimated to be as much as $3 million initially and at least $200,000 annually to maintain. These are considerably different figures (even allowing for inflation) than the CE estimated in 1959 ($25,000/year). As a result, the city is concerned both about the cost of removing sediment and the potential flood hazard of leaving the sediment in the channel.

With no scouring during a large storm, it has been determined that some individual cross sections could only contain the 25- to 30-year flood. This is of immediate concern because the city is now hydrologically, as well as legally, back within the 100-year floodplain, as it was prior to the construction of the "flood control" project. No federal monies should thus be available for projects in the area; flood insurance coverage is also in question. Santa Cruz is

stuck with a poorly designed project, a difficult dilemma, and a financial and ecological disaster. Why has this happened? Are there any solutions? And can we learn something from this expensive mistake?

THE EFFECT OF ALTERING THE NATURAL CHANNEL GRADIENT

Stream equilibrium is a dynamic process that is continually reacting to changing hydraulic conditions and basin sediment production. Water velocity, channel slope, and sediment transport capacity are adjusted in response to variations in discharge, channel morphology, and sediment availability.

In removing 590,000 cu. m. of sediment during construction of the flood control project,

145

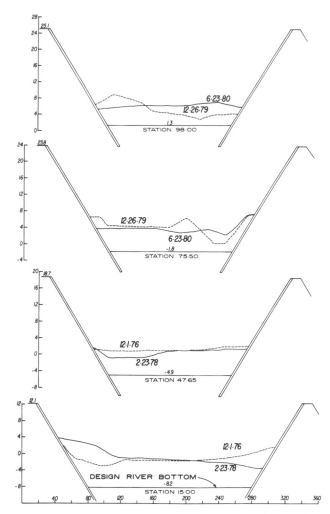

Figure 4.--Selected channel cross sections along San Lorenzo River in Santa Cruz showing extent of channel fill above original design channel bottom. Station locations refer to Figure 3. All elevations are in feet relative to mean sea level.

the CE increased the channel slope 32% over its last 4 km. and upset the equilibrium conditions established over thousands of years. Sea level is the ultimate base level for the San Lorenzo and most other rivers; however, due to channel excavation, high tides could extend 4 km. inland to the Highway 1 bridge. During a spring tide of 2 m. (mean sea level), 1.7 m. of standing water would occur at the bridge.

The anticipated hydrologic response of flowing water upon entering a standing body of seawater would be a reduction in velocity with accompanying deposition of sediment load. The "improved" channel was actually a sink that would eventually be filled in with sediment from the watershed, much like a dam or reservoir traps sediment. This process would continue until the channel returned to an equilibrium slope. Periodic surveys of the channel centerline and various cross sections indicated that equilibrium was gradually reestablishing, and it has now been reached.

However, the new equilibrium channel has a different profile than either the original or the design channel in the reach between Soquel and Highway 1 bridges (see fig. 3). The increased channel width and an increase in river sediment load have created a new equilibrium gradient in this reach. The channel bottom is now 2 m. above the initial design bottom and 0.9-1.2 m. above the original natural channel.

The estimated quantity of sediment that must now be removed in order to restore the design channel is about 350,000 cu. m. The CE made no mention of deposition problems in their design manual except to note frequent dredging would be required to maintain the channel grade. Effects of the sediment removal on the river's aquatic system and riparian vegetation were also not discussed. The basis for the CE estimate of annual dredging cost is unknown, but no sediment discharge measurements from the watershed had been made at the time the project was initiated.

SEDIMENT YIELD AND TRANSPORT

Sediment yield within the San Lorenzo watershed is high and volumes of material transported by major runoff events can be very large. The natural basin conditions (steep and unstable slopes, highly erodible soils, and high intensity precipitation) combined with the vegetation removal and soil disturbance accompanying logging, quarrying, road-building and construction activities have all contributed to high erosion rates and the production of large volumes of sediment. Much of the construction and population growth in the watershed (the population tripled from 1960 to 1979, from 11,600 to 33,000 people) has occurred in areas with soils which are particularly erosion-prone. The San Lorenzo River Watershed Management Plan estimates that the two- to four-fold increase in sediment production during these years is directly attributable to human disturbance of the basin's soils.

Suspended sediment and limited bedload measurements have been intermittently collected at two stations within the basin since 1973. Using the sediment transport curves, flood frequency distribution, and particle size breakdown, projections can be made for the magnitude of sediment transport under various flood conditions as the river passes through

Figure 5.--San Lorenzo River channel immediately downstream from the Water Street bridge showing efforts by the City of Santa Cruz Department of Public Works to pile up sediment in hopes of flushing by high flows.

Santa Cruz (table 1). For example, the 10-year flood can carry over 800,000 metric tons per day (520,000 cu. m.) of sand-sized or larger material in suspension. Bedload would increase this by 5% to 10%. If a sink (as was created in the "flood control" project) or tide water was encountered by material of this size in transit, it seems probable that much of it would be deposited. Again, although flood conditions would not normally persist for 24 hours, even eight hours of the 10-year storm could produce 173,000 cu. m. of sediment. Significant volumes of sediment can be transported by the two- or five-year events. Even if the channel were to be dredged to original project design, sediment carried by one large floodflow (or even the cumulative effect of several years of moderate flow conditions) could soon fill the channel back to an equilibrium grade. This raises serious questions about the effectiveness of annual dredging as a solution to the flood control problem.

The unavoidable conclusions are the following. 1) The San Lorenzo River channel is now at equilibrium grade, and the sediment fill appears from all evidence to be stable. 2) The channel can no longer carry the 100-year event, and in fact cannot, in all probability, hold the 30- to 40-year flood. 3) Downtown Santa Cruz is endangered and has far less protection than is required by the Federal Flood Insurance Act. The $6.5 million flood control project designed by the CE grossly underestimated the sediment load being carried by the river and also failed to account for the changes in channel equilibrium gradient which would be produced by the alteration of channel morphology.

147

Table 1.—Sediment transport capacity of the San Lorenzo
River below Branciforte Creek in Santa Cruz.

Event (Recurrence interval)	Discharge (cfs)	Suspended Sediment (Tons/Day)	Suspended Sediment (>Sand Size-Tons/Day)	Suspended Sediment (Sand Size-Cu. Yds./ Day @ 100 lbs/ft^3
2 years	7,528	175,000	56,000	41,000
5	16,864	1,000,000	320,000	237,000
10	24,375	2,600,000	832,000	616,000
25	34,317	5,000,000	1,600,000	1,185,000
50	41,698	7,000,000	2,240,000	1,659,000
100	48,862	12,000,000	3,840,000	2,844,000

FUTURE OPTIONS

There are no simple solutions to the flood hazard which the city of Santa Cruz is currently faced with, but any solution clearly involves the riparian corridor and the life it supports and the natural beauty it can present. This problem is not unique to Santa Cruz and the San Lorenzo River, but develops anywhere major "flood control" projects have been carried out. Through dams and reservoirs, aquatic systems are totally flooded; through "channel improvements" (levees, dredging, and channel straightening) these same systems are destroyed or eliminated, temporarily if not permanently. Thus, the price of flood control using engineering works is riparian corridor elimination in most cases. The San Lorenzo River is an extreme example in that the annual river-bottom vegetation removal and sediment shuffling has not even produced the anticipated protection from flooding.

Two important factors to consider in any proposal dealing with Santa Cruz and the San Lorenzo River are: 1) is the solution permanent and does it deal with the root cause, or is it simply a temporary stopgap approach; and 2) how will it ultimately affect the riparian corridor?

We invariably select engineering rather than planning solutions because these are more visible, more impressive, and they are also driven by institutional inertia. In addition, once the engineering structure is in place, additional engineering is the usual solution to shortcomings or flaws in the original design. (The reality is, however, that large natural systems, such as rivers and the ocean, simply can never be totally controlled by man-made structures).

A number of possibilities exist or have been proposed.

Option 1.—Dredging and removal of all the accumulated sediment from the channelized reach of the river would cost about $3 million today. Although this would reduce the immediate flood threat to the city, it would offer only temporary protection. At average annual sand transport rates of 40-80,000 cu. m., either channel capacity would soon be reduced or expensive (estimated $100-200,000) yearly dredging would be required, thereby producing annual riparian corridor destruction. The city currently is using this dredging approach, but has only been removing sediment from the channel on a very modest scale. Channel surveys indicate that upstream sand input from winter flows is keeping pace with the sand removal operations.

Option 2.—A combination of erosion control measures and sediment or debris basins could be used to reduce downstream sediment transport in the San Lorenzo River. This effort would have to be accompanied by initial dredging of the channel reach through Santa Cruz in order to provide the required flood protection. Although any erosion control measures in the watershed would be beneficial, the costs of land acquisition and maintenance, and biological effects of a number of large sediment traps on the San Lorenzo River or major tributaries are serious negative factors. For comparison, costs for 20 such structures, each impounding one square mile watershed, would approximate the initial outlay and annual costs of maintaining the downtown channel.

Option 3.—A single large dam on the San Lorenzo itself or several smaller dams on major tributaries could reduce flood peaks by 20,000 cfs, such that the present channel could convey the reduced floodflows. No suitable site exists on the San Lorenzo for a dam of this sort without producing major inundation of populated areas. Construction costs and environmental impacts of the number of smaller dams required make this alternative an unattractive one.

Option 4.—The levees and bridges could be raised in order to increase the channel capacity such that the 100-year flood could be effectively contained. This option essentially enables the channel gradient to remain at its equilibrium position and allows for increased flood capacity through raising the banks. The costs for the replacement of four bridges and a six-foot increase in levee heights is estimted to be $20 million, over three times the cost of the original project (Jones-Tillson and Associates 1979). Any engineering solution of this sort has an obvious economic limitation, and the 100-year flood may well occur and top the banks despite the expenditure of $20 million. Should a flood large enough to breach the levees occur, the height of the floodwaters above the channel floor would provide a hydraulic head that could quickly erode the levee and inundate downtown Santa Cruz.

Perhaps the all too obvious solution is not to have built our cities on floodplains to begin with. History is against us however, and it is senseless to blame our ancestors for settling on the fertile flatlands adjacent to our rivers and streams. Although it may be cheaper and safer in the long run to relocate many floodplain communities, this is unlikely to ever occur without the occurrence of major floods which totally destroy those communities.

A compromise of sorts may be obtained by allowing a river to develop some sort of natural course, within the broader confines of a flood control structure. In the case of the San Lorenzo, a width increase of 18-34 m. would increase the channel capacity to original design conditions (approximately accomodating the 100-year flood). This proposal presents some challenges and opportunities in allowing the river to reconstruct some of its natural meanders and retain its natural gradient (both eliminated by the present levee system).

Utilizing a meandering pattern would only require rebuilding one of the levees at any particular location. A survey of land adjacent to the river shows that streets, parking lots, used car lots, parks, and tennis courts occupy much of the 18 to 34 m. of land in question. These uses could be continued after excavation occurs. The widening of the river could be designed such that a smaller pilot channel could hold perhaps the five- to 10-year event. Much of the remaining channel could be vegetated as a downtown park and green belt such as the recessed park which presently exists between Soquel and Water streets adjacent to the river. Other higher floodplain land could be used for the previously mentioned parking and streets except during and immediately after major flood events. The pilot channel could also provide an adequate flow depth for anadromous fish migration.

Existing bridges could probably be extended, obviating the complete bridge replacements necessitated by Option 3. Some houses and small commercial buildings may have to be removed, but initial investigation indicates that displacement need not be extensive. Much of the required land is city property which would lower acquisition costs.

CONCLUSIONS

In any attempt to control a natural system, we must realize that we are usually going to disturb a delicate equilibrium. By excavating the San Lorenzo River's bed to increase its slope and capacity to transmit floodwaters, we also created a disequilibrium to which the river had to adjust. As a result of the river aggrading its channel back to an equilibrium gradient, flood control capacity has been significantly reduced. Because the channel can no longer contain the 100-year event, the entire downtown area of Santa Cruz is apparently no longer covered by the Federal Flood Insurance Act. The stopgap bulldozer approach presently being used has led to yearly destruction of the riparian corridor and no significant alleviation of the flood hazard.

We must begin to focus our efforts on controlling our own activity, rather than persisting in the ineffective historical approach of an increasingly expensive system of dams, levees, and channels. All flood protection ends somewhere. We can never afford complete flood protection, as a community, a state, or a nation. The continued increase in annual flood losses despite the construction of an ever-increasing number of "flood control" structures is clear testimony to the failure of this approach.

LITERATURE CITED

US Army Corps of Engineers. 1973. Flood plain information--San Lorenzo River, Felton to Boulder Creek. US Army Corps of Engineers, San Francisco, Calif.

US Army Corps of Engineers. 1957. General design memorandum--San Lorenzo River flood control project. US Army Corps of Engineers, San Francisco District, San Francisco, Calif.

Jones-Tillson and Associates and Water Resources Engineers. 1979. San Lorenzo River reconnaissance study. US Army Corps of Engineers, San Francisco, Calif.

PHOTODOCUMENTATION OF VEGETATION AND LANDFORM CHANGE

ON A RIPARIAN SITE, 1880-1980:

DOG ISLAND, RED BLUFF, CALIFORNIA[1]

Stephen A. Laymon[2]

Abstract.--This study used ground and aerial photos taken over the past 100 years to trace the development of the present riparian vegetation. The photos show the changes in the Sacramento River channel which have led to the present configuration of the area. Principles illustrated by these photos are: 1) the dynamic nature of the riparian system showing rapid and dramatic changes at this site; 2) the rapidity with which riparian vegetation develops; and 3) the use of historic and present day photography to document changes in a riparian environment.

INTRODUCTION

During the course of my 5-year study at Dog Island, Tehama County, I became interested in the development of the present day landforms and riparian vegetation at this site. I was able to follow up on this interest in connection with a job as archivist at the Tehama County Library and in a physical geography seminar at California State University, Chico.

Little or no work has been done to document changes at riparian sites. This study was undertaken to show the changes at this particular site, but more importantly to show the potential resources available to document land use, landforms, and vegetation pattern changes, and to show the dynamic nature of the riparian system. The use of ground photos to compare past with present conditions is a common practice in forest and rangeland situations. Problems were encountered in this study when an attempt was made to apply this technique to a flat Sacramento Valley site with tall riparian vegetation.

METHODS

Research Techniques

Early ground photos were obtained from the collection of the Tehama County Library and several longtime local residents. Attempts to rephotograph these views of the study area met with limited success since the vegetation had grown so much in the ensuing 100 years, blocking the view from most angles.

The aerial photos were obtained from the United States Soil Conservation Service, US Army Corps of Engineers, and the California Department of Water Resources. Overlay projection using a photographic enlarger was used to document boundary changes.

STUDY AREA

Dog Island, or Walton's Pasture, as it was known in the early days, has long been a favorite picnic spot for the people of Red Bluff. Now a small island in the Sacramento River, the site's amenities included an area of still water, where the land sloped gently to the river, in contrast to the high, steep bluff for which the city is named. Here the city had its waterworks, which originally consisted of a horse and wagon delivering water door to door. Later, the city pumped water directly from the river, and still later from deep wells.[3] Here also, local youths spent their days cutting school classes, and in the early days this is where most of the local people learned to swim.

In the mid-1960's the area was donated to the city of Red Bluff by the Samuel Ayers family for use as a city park and natural area. The city has kept development at a fairly low level, with a footbridge to the island, a parking lot

[1] Paper presented at the California Riparian Systems Conference. [University of California, Davis, September 17-19, 1981].

[2] Stephen A. Laymon is a Graduate Student in the Department of Forestry and Resource Management, University of California, Berkeley.

[3] Walton, T. 1956. Tehama County centennial oral history interview. Tehama County Library oral history tape.

with landscaping, two restrooms, and trails. One loop road which was put in on the mainland portion has since been closed to vehicles due to a high level of vandalism.

The origin of the name Dog Island remains a mystery since long time residents say that the area was always called Walton's Pasture, and that the dairy cattle from Walton's Dairy on the bluff to the south grazed there. One story has it that an old man ran a kennel on the island in the 1880's, but since no island existed at that time, this is impossible. A more plausible explanation is that park officials asked some local truants what they called the area and "Dog Island" was the answer.

Landforms and Topography

The Dog Island study area consists of the river, the island, the channel around the island, the mainland plain, the red bluff, Brewery Creek, and the gently sloping area from the parking lot to the footbridge (see fig. 1). The entire study area has a remarkably narrow elevation range, with 95% lying between 77.1 m. and 79.2 m. above sea level. On the northwest side, the red bluff known as Duncan Hill rises almost vertically to a height of 97.5 m., or 20.4 m. above the river level. The parking lot at the west edge of the area is between 82.3 and 85.3 m. elevation. From there the land slopes in two terraces to the side channel 76 m. away. The highest point on the island is not more than 3 m. above the gross pool level of the Red Bluff diversion dam.

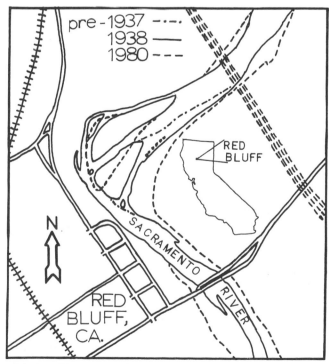

Figure 1.--Map of Dog Island study area and environs.

Despite having such a narrow elevation range, the area is not level, having many channels which have waterflow during flood stage. The three most prominent are old river channels that have been silted in over the years. One of these lies east of the bluff near the north boundary of the park, and was the 1850 river channel. Another lies near the east end of the footbridge. The third is found on the southeast side of the island, and was the main river channel prior to the 1937 flood.

The Sacramento River at Dog Island ranges from 170 m. to 250 m. in width. As a result of the diversion dam below Red Bluff, it is kept at a constant 77.1 m. above sea level. This is 2.4 m. higher than the river level would be without the influence of the dam. The water level is lowered slightly to 76.5 m. in the winter when no water is being diverted for irrigation. During flood stage the waters at times rise to 81 m. covering the entire area except the bluff and the parking lot. The river channel that separates the island from the mainland ranges in width from 20 m. to 41 m.

Brewery Creek is an intermittent stream which flows into the study area from the west. It was named for the brewery which was located along it near here in the 1880's. The creek has two main branches, the longer of which is 4.8 km. in length. It drains 8-10 km^2 of highly eroded impermeable soils. During heavy local rains the runoff is great and the creek runs high, carrying with it heavy bedloads of rock, gravel, and soil. This is building up a delta in the side channel which may in the future connect the island to the mainland. The creek has cut a deep channel on the north side of the parking lot, and is responsible for the gently sloping gap between the red bluffs of Duncan Hill to the north and the city to the south.

Soils

Soil is the base for the vegetation of any area. Ninety percent of the soils in the study area are fertile loams, so the dense vegetation found here is not surprising.

Five types of soils are found on or near Dog Island. The island itself is an alluvial soil known as Red Bluff loam. It consists of up to 15% gravel, and has both high available water and high moisture-holding capacity (USDA Soil Conservation Service 1967).

The low area to the north of the island is made up of the Columbia loam complex, ranging from mixed soils of silt and gravels to fine sandy loams. These soils generally lie above all but the highest floods, are well drained, and have moderate permeability. They are brown to pale brown in color and are neutral to slightly acid. These are very fertile soils, favored for farming (ibid.).

The soil in the sloping area to the south of Brewery Creek is an Arbuckle gravelly loam. It is an easily channeled soil with poor water-holding characteristics, very slow permeability, and a clay substrate (ibid.).

Duncan Hill, the bluff on the northwest side, is made up primarily of Newville gravelly loam. This soil is yellowish-brown on the surface and is slightly acidic. The subsoil is a reddish-brown gravelly clay. It is made up of sediment from conglomerate and silt stone of the Tehama formation. In addition, a portion of the hill consists of a mixture of Corning-Redding gravelly loams, a medium acidic, reddish-brown soil with a red clay subsoil. This soil has low permeability and high runoff (ibid.).

Vegetation

The vegetation-types that are found in the study area are floodplain riparian woodland, blue oak woodland, cattail marsh, and landscape plantings. Of the aforementioned vegetation-types, the latter three are the least important since they form such a small portion of the total area. The blue oak woodland found on the hill north of Brewery Creek covers only 1% of the land area. Scattered blue oaks (Quercus douglasii) form the canopy here, reaching up to 10 m. There is no understory, and the shrub layer consists of scattered buckbrush (Ceanothus cuneatus). The groundcover primarily consists of introduced grasses.

The landscape plantings are found around the main parking lot, restrooms and waterworks facilities. They consist mainly of several introduced cedars and pines, a border of live oaks (Quercus sp.) along the highway, several pyracantha (Pyracantha coccinea) hedges, scattered introduced flowering shrubs, and approximately 0.25 ha. of lawn. These are planted around several native blue oaks.

The two marsh areas are the most important of the minor vegetation-types. They cover about 1% of the area. The marsh on the southern part of the island has a thick growth of cattail (Typha sp.) with a border of willows (Salix spp.). The water is up to 0.3 m. in depth at this spot. The open areas of water are thick with small aquatic plants such as duckweed (Azolla filiculoides). The land area around the pond that is not covered with cattail and willows is grown up with dense stands of grasses. The marsh on the mainland is just north of the mouth of Brewery Creek. It is higher than river level and only contains water after a flood or heavy rain. The cattail here is much more scattered and intergrown with grasses, herbs, shrubs, and willows, a pattern that has accelerated over the past seven years.

The primary vegetation-type in the study area is riparian woodland. Various forms of this plant community cover 95% of the land. It is an exceptional vegetation-type in the arid West. The riparian vegetation in the study area is quite diverse. Various species of trees are dominant on different portions of the area, often forming stands of clumps or bands of a single species. The western border of the island, facing the slough, is primarily old-growth cottonwood (Populus fremontii) reaching 40 m. in height, with scattered willows (fig. 2). An understory of box elder (Acer negundo), willows, black walnut (Juglans hindsii), and elderberry (Sambucus mexicana), and bands of shrubcover and groundcover layers of wild blackberry (Rubus ursinus and R. vitifolius), and the introduced Himalayan blackberry (R. discolor) are found. The central part of the northern third of the island is the most open. It has a cottonwood canopy with a scattered understory of box elder, valley oak (Quercus lobata), blue oak, and buckeye (Aesculus californica), and a groundcover of mugwort (Artemisia douglasiana) sometimes reaching 2.5 m. The northern tip of the island is a white alder (Alnus rhombifolia) and willow thicket with no groundcover, surrounded by a blackberry thicket. The northeastern side of the island also has a cottonwood canopy with an understory of box elder, willow, and elderberry, and a shrub and groundcover of blackberry and herbaceous growth. The border of vegetation closest to the water is a dense mixture of white alder, Oregon ash (Fraxinus latifolia), and willows. Further south this band of alders and willows widens to about 30 m.

Cottonwoods are absent from the southeast quarter of the island. This area has a very dense canopy of alder, box elder, and willow reaching to 15 m. The trees are closely spaced, allowing very little light penetration. Groundcover is lacking in the thickly forested areas, but bands of blackberry and herbaceous growth are found in the more open spots. One alder thicket of almost 0.75 ha. is especially interesting; the trees have grown to 18 m. and many are now dying. There is no groundcover, but an understory of sycamores (Platanus racemosa) and Oregon ash is developing. At the southern tip of the island there is a willow thicket reaching 8 m. in height and 30 m. across.

The vegetation on the mainland, south of Brewery Creek, is similar to the western part of

Figure 2.--Footbridge to Dog Island showing dense vegetation along side channel, looking north (August, 1979).

the island, with a cottonwood canopy to 40 m., a well-developed understory of box elder, alder, and willow, and a groundcover of blackberry. This type of growth also extends along the northwest side of the slough, from 50 m. north of Brewery Creek to the freeway bridge. Also found in this area, in the slightly lower and more open spots near the slough, are several dense willow thickets reaching 7 m. in height and up to 30 m. across.

Along Brewery Creek the vegetation also has a canopy of scattered cottonwoods reaching 25 m., but the understory is much less typically riparian, with live oaks, blue oaks, toyon (Heteromeles arbutifolia) mixed with the willows, Oregon ash, and box elders. The groundcover is a mix of grasses, blackberries, and herbaceous growth.

Black walnut is the dominant tree in the area just north of Brewery Creek and along the base of the bluff. The trees are not large, reaching only 20 m., and do not form a closed canopy. This allows light penetration and the formation of a dense ground layer of blackberries with patches of willows and elderberries. Also in this area are a number of introduced species such as mulberry (Morus sp.), black locust (Robinia pseudoaccacia), osage orange (Maclura pomerifera), plum (Prunus sp.), fig (Ficus carica), and pyracantha.

At the north end of the bluff the dominant tree species is valley oak. The largest of these trees reaches 35 m. in height, and some are at least 100 years old. This site has a groundcover of grasses and a scattered understory of box elder and black walnut. The valley oak area borders the field to the north for about 300 m. and merges into an area with a canopy of black walnut and cottonwoods. In this location there is also a dense osage orange thicket of about 1 ha. which is devoid of groundcover.

The center of the mainland portion is the most open of the entire study area. Until 1975 it was a large, grassy meadow with a few scattered clumps of box elder, plum trees, and two dense box elder thickets. When the park loop road was constructed, the grass in the meadow was mowed to cut down on fire danger and provide a more "park-like" atmosphere. The meadow instantly became a de facto parking lot, the gathering place for the local teenagers, which totally denuded large areas of it. Due to reduction of competition from the grasses, the box elders began to grow rapidly and now are large trees reaching 15 m. and covering a much more extensive area. The tall rye and Johnson grasses that previously covered the meadow provided a vegetation-type that is now missing. More information on this area can be found in Laymon (1983).

RESULTS

As static as the scene appears today at this bend in the river, as little as 40 years ago the island was very different in appearance, and as recently as 100 years ago the entire study area was litte more than a sandbar, devoid of vegetation. With the use of maps, aerial photographs, ground photos, and local legend, I was able to reconstruct the development of Dog Island over the past 100 to 130 years.

Two basic types of geologic formations are found in the study area. They are the recently formed alluvial deposits of the island and low regions to the east, and the red bluffs consisting of Pleistocene and Pliocene nonmarine sedimentary deposits to the west (USDA Soil Conservation Service 1967). This hard, red soil has been an effective barrier to westward river movement for many thousands of years. One can picture the river migrating without restraint eastward across the valley many times, always to return to the west and to stop at this 23-m. bluff.

In the early 1850's when the first settlers came to Red Bluff, they found the river flowing against these bluffs from the center of the study area to 3.2 km. (2 mi.) south of town.[3] Maps from 1850 to 1900 show no evidence of even a sandbar in the river at this location. A photo taken in 1881 from the bluff adjacent to the study area looking south toward Red Bluff (fig. 3) shows a bare bluff with the river running at its base. On the right (west bank) a small delta from Brewery Creek was beginning to build up. The closest brick building on the right was the city waterworks. The building is still located at the site.

Another photo (fig. 4) taken from Red Bluff, looking north, circa 1900, shows the sides of the bluff and the rest of the study area, devoid of vegetation except for a few low willows on the sandbar in the river, a valley oak at the far right, and scattered blue oaks on top of the bluff. The amount of deposition at the foot of the bluff can be seen by comparing figures 3 and 4. Alluvial deposits had built out 30 to 50 m. in 20 years.

The next photo (fig. 5), taken in 1912, shows the area from the west, looking past the waterworks toward the Tuscan Buttes to the east. This photo illustrates the lack of vegetation and shows the river flowing towards the waterworks building (today the main flow is directed 350 m. south of that point due to deflection by Dog Island). No sandbars are seen in the river, but the west bank above the Brewery Creek outlet is in the same position as it is today. The area appears to be much lower than at present, indicating continued deposition on the mainland since the picture was taken. The first band of trees to the west of the river is very likely the 1850 river channel.

Figure 6 shows the river, looking towards Red Bluff, circa 1910, with the waterworks building on the right. One interesting feature is the amount of vegetation that has grown on the bank between 1881 and 1910.

Figure 3.--Dog Island area from bluff looking south toward Red Bluff, 1881 (courtesy of Tehama County Library collection).

Figure 4.--Dog Island from bluff at Red Bluff looking north, _circa_ 1900 (courtesy of Tehama County Library collection).

Figure 5.--Dog Island from Garrett home looking east toward Tuscan Buttes, 1912 (courtesy of the Wetter collection).

Figure 6.--Dog Island area from bluff looking south toward Red Bluff, 1910 (courtesy Tehama County Library).

I found it impossible to rephotograph any of the four historic photos of the area. The vegetation had grown up so much that the scenes were not repeatable. An oblique aerial photo (fig. 7), taken in 1979, was an attempt to duplicate figure 4. This photo illustrates the dramatic growth of vegetation at the site. Any photo taken at the point from which the photo in figure 4 was taken would today show only the first row of cottonwoods on the south end of the island.

Figure 5 was taken from an upstairs balcony of the Garrett house, a 1900 Victorian, on the west side of Main Street. I was not able to attempt a photo from this spot, but did try one from the front porch. All that could be seen from this point was the live oaks along Main Street. From the balcony, possibly the first row of cottonwoods along the slough could have been seen. I was able to take figure 8 from a point on the bluff, along the river, two blocks to the south. This photo, with Tuscan Buttes in the background, again shows how strikingly the area has changed.

Figure 7.--Oblique aerial photo looking north, 1979.

Figure 8.--Dog Island area looking east from Red Bluff with
Tuscan Buttes in the background, 1981.

The aerial photos (fig. 9, 10, 11, and 12) were taken in 1942, 1956, 1970, and 1980. This sequence illustrates the increase in riparian vegetation at the site during the 38-year period. In 1942 only 15% of the island was covered with riparian vegetation. This had increased to 50% by 1956; to 90% by 1970; and to 100% by 1980. The mainland portion shows a similar pattern with the most dramatic increase between 1970 and 1980, when the box elders filled in the center of the mainland plain.

The first aerial photos of the Sacramento Valley were taken in 1938. I was able to study the photo of the Red Bluff area. In Figure 13 the 1938 land boundaries, the pre-1937 flood boundary, and the present boundaries are shown. From this composite map one can see the recent changes in the area. Prior to the 1937-38 flood, the land that later became the eastern portion of Dog Island was part of the mainland on the east side of the river. During the floodwaters, 65 m. of bank were carved off. The end of the penin-

sula was cut off, forming an island.[4] By 1952 this channel had widened to about three times the 1938 width, and the channel between it and the other island had filled in, leaving the area with its present shape.

DISCUSSION

It is unfortunate that aerial photo coverage of the study site and the Sacramento River only go back as far as 1938. Quantitative land use changes can only be derived using these photos as a baseline. At Dog Island I was fortunate to find historic photos dating back 100 years. At most sites one would not be so lucky. Also, without the use of geographic and man-made landmarks, as I had at this site, it would be very difficult to tell where the early photos were

_____

[4]Wetter, Judge Curtis E., Red Bluff, California. Personal communication, September, 1978.

Figure 9.--Aerial photo, Dog Island, 1942 (courtesy of the US Army Corps of Engineers).

Figure 11.--Aerial photo, Dog Island, 1970 (courtesy of the US Army Corps of Engineers).

Figure 10.--Aerial photo, Dog Island, 1956 (courtesy of the US Army Corps of Engineers).

Figure 12.--Aerial photo, Dog Island, 1980 (courtesy of the US Army Corps of Engineers).

taken. Areas where photos would be most readily available would be near towns.

The technique of rephotographing a scene to document vegetation changes on a site appears to have limited usefulness in a riparian setting of low relief. Even at Dog Island where the 20 m. bluffs were available, it was not successful since the vegetation had grown so much and views were blocked from all previously photographed angles.

157

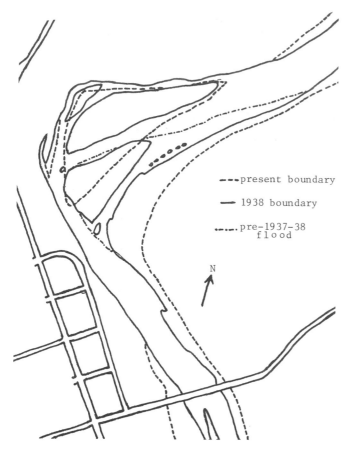

---present boundary

— 1938 boundary

-··-··pre-1937-38
flood

N

Figure 13.--Geographical changes at Dog Island, 1937-1980.

Significant changes have occurred at this site and the reasons are not obvious. I believe that the deposition at Dog Island is part of the normal east-west migration of the Sacramento River. When the early settlers arrived in the late 1840's, the river had reached the red bluffs on the west. Gradually, since then, it has been moving back to the east. This process was accelerated by the 1937-38 flood which cut off the tip of the peninsula on the east side of the river. This stabilized the west side at Dog Island by deflecting the main force of the water away from the island area, such that it hit a full 1.5 blocks farther south on the red bluff. This process has slowed again since the mid-1960's when the Red Bluff diversion dam was built and some attempt was made to stabilize the banks on portions of the pool by limited use of riprap.

The increase in vegetation is a natural process as new land is being formed, but it is likely that man has accelerated the process here. The first of these factors is the construction of Shasta Dam. This dam controls the level of flow on the Sacramento River throughout the year by storing the winter floodwater and releasing it for agricultural use during the summer and fall. This creates much higher flows in the summer than would normally occur and gives more free water to the riparian vegetation than would normally be available during this period of water stress.

Possibly the most significant reason for this increase in vegetation is the raised water table created by the Red Bluff diversion dam. This dam created Lake Red Bluff which is held at a constant water level throughout the growing season. This provides the vegetation with an unlimited supply of water. At no place on the area (except the bluff itself) is water a limiting factor to plant growth.

It will be interesting in the years to come to see what landform and vegetational changes take place on the island. It is doubtful, with the bank stabilization that has taken place near the area, that major changes in the shape of the site will occur. The most significant change that is now taking place is the silting in of the side channel. Riparian vegetation will be growing here within 20 years if this process continues. Young valley oaks and black walnuts are found on higher portions of the area and these species will likely become more dominant as the years pass.

When considering the study area and the riparian woodland system in general, two concepts must by held foremost in one's mind when making management decisions. The first concept is that change is the essence of the riparian zone. In 120 years, major changes have taken place here and the current vegetation structure is a product of this change. If man insists on a stagnant situation through the use of channelization, the riparian community will not survive.

The second concept is that of the rapid growth and resistance of this vegetation-type. In a period of 40 years this area has been transformed from a gravelbar to a mature cottonwood/ willow riparian woodland. The successional changes are still taking place, and in another 40 years a valley oak/black walnut riparian woodland will have taken its place. The land is the important resource, and if man can refrain from plowing, grazing, or riprapping it, the forest will return in a very short time.

LITERATURE CITED

Laymon, Stephen A. 1983. Riparian bird community structure and dynamics: Dog Island, Red Bluff, California. In: R.E. Warner and K.M. Hendrix (ed.). California Riparian Systems. [University of California, Davis, September 17-19, 1981.] University of California Press, Berkeley.

USDA Soil Conservation Service. 1967. Soil survey, Tehama County, California. U.S. Department of Agriculture.

THE IMPORTANCE OF RIPARIAN VEGETATION

TO STREAM ECOSYSTEMS[1]

Allen W. Knight and Richard L. Bottorff[2]

Abstract.--Riparian vegetation is very important in determining the structure and function of stream ecosystems. Most aquatic organisms, both invertebrates and fish, are directly or indirectly dependent on inputs of terrestrial detritus to the stream for their food. Natural changes in riparian vegetation and the biotic processing of detritus, as well as other factors, determine the kinds and abundance of aquatic invertebrates living in streams, from headwaters to large rivers. Removal of riparian vegetation will significantly affect stream organisms by: 1) decreasing detrital (food) inputs; 2) increasing the potential for primary production in aquatic plants; 3) increasing summer water temperatures; 4) changing water quality and quantity; and 5) decreasing terrestrial habitat for adult insects.

INTRODUCTION

The manner in which riparian systems are managed and protected is commonly related to their value as buffer strips, stream bank stabilizers, and fish and wildlife habitat. These strips of streamside vegetation may be the only habitat remaining for some wildlife species. As riparian vegetation is modified or destroyed by grazing, logging, urbanization, road construction, water development, mining, and recreation, interest in its importance is increasing. Our objective is to briefly review the role of riparian vegetation in the structure and function of stream ecosystems, especially headwater streams. We also explore the possible effects of vegetation modification or destruction in headwater streams. Whenever possible, our review emphasizes conditions found in Sierra Nevada streams.

HEADWATER STREAMS

Headwater streams are greatly influenced by riparian vegetation since they function as processors of natural organic matter coming from the watershed (Cummins and Spengler 1978). These small streams are characteristically shaded and kept cool by overhanging riparian vegetation,

which also contributes dead organic matter (detritus) to the stream. Shading not only affects water quality but influences the activities of primary producers such as algae and aquatic macrophytes. Riparian vegetation supplies organic matter in the form of dead leaves, needles, twigs, branches, logs, bud scales, fruit, droppings of terrestrial animals (frass), and dissolved organic matter (DOM).

The direct input of organic matter from riparian vegetation is substantial: annual values range from about 100 gm. per m^2 to more than 1,000 gm. per m^2 (Bray and Gorham 1964; Anderson and Sedell 1979), and values for standing crops can be much higher (Naiman and Sedell 1979). The addition of this organic matter is fundamentally important to the stream biota since this is often its major energy source, which is supplemented by lesser amounts of autochthonous production (Hynes 1963; Cummins 1974). Dead organic matter may contribute as much as 99% of the annual energy input to headwater streams covered by a dense forest canopy (Fisher and Likens 1973). Particulate detritus accounted for 53% of the annual energy input to Bear Brook, New Hampshire, and DOM input accounted for 47%; autochthonous primary production by mosses contributed very little. These streams are termed "heterotrophic", because in effect they consume organic matter produced by adjacent terrestrial systems.

Although allochthonous detrital input to streams continues throughout the year, seasonal pulses do occur. Detritus is added in autumn from deciduous leaf-fall and plant die-off. In winter and spring it is washed in by higher runoff (Minshall 1968; Fisher and Likens 1973;

[1] Paper presented at the California Riparian Systems Conference. [University of California, Davis, September 17-19, 1981].
[2] Allen W. Knight is Professor of Hydrobiology, University of California, Davis. Richard L. Bottorff is Research Assistant, Department of Land, Air, and Water Resources, University of California, Davis.

Hobbie and Likens 1973). Additional pulses may include bud scales in spring and frass in summer. Tree branches broken by wind and snow may drop into streams in winter. Rainstorms periodically wash in DOM exuded from plants or collected on leaves from arboreal animals, while groundwater continuously brings in DOM.

Although the heterotrophic nature of headwater streams enclosed in forests has been well emphasized by recent research (Fisher and Likens 1973; Cummins 1974), headwater streams in unforested or sparsely-forested regions can be autotrophic, receiving most of their energy from primary production of aquatic macrophytes and algae (Minshall 1978). Autotrophy has been documented in desert streams lacking riparian vegetation and shading (Naiman 1976; Minshall 1978; Busch and Fisher 1981) and has been suggested for high-altitude streams (Cummins and Klug 1979), especially in western montane regions (Wiggins and Mackay 1978). Headwater streams within forests can also change seasonally from heterotrophy to autotrophy, depending upon natural variations in light intensity, nutrients, hydrologic factors, and detrital input (Naiman and Sedell 1980).

Data are currently lacking to classify Sierra Nevada headwater streams as either heterotrophic or autotrophic. The vegetation, climate, and geology of Sierra Nevada mountains vary substantially from location to location. Thus headwater streams may vary widely in their heterotrophy/autotrophy balance. The extensive forests and chaparral on the western slope of the Sierras do suggest that detritus from riparian vegetation is very important to stream energetics. Even above the timberline, dense growths of willow, alder, grasses, and herbs overhang the small stream channels, supplying detritus and shading the water. Only at high elevations when streams flow over granite bedrock is riparian vegetation sparse and the stream unshaded.

ORGANIC MATTER PROCESSING

The importance of organic matter contributions from riparian vegetation to stream ecosystems has been fully appreciated for only about 10 years (Cummins 1974). The manner in which aquatic organisms utilize and process organic matter at different seasons and locations along streams is a current research topic (Cummins 1973, 1975; Cummins and Klug 1979; Anderson and Sedell 1979; Hawkins and Sedell 1981). We briefly summarize here the role of aquatic organisms in continually processing and transforming organic matter from the time it enters the stream (fig. 1).

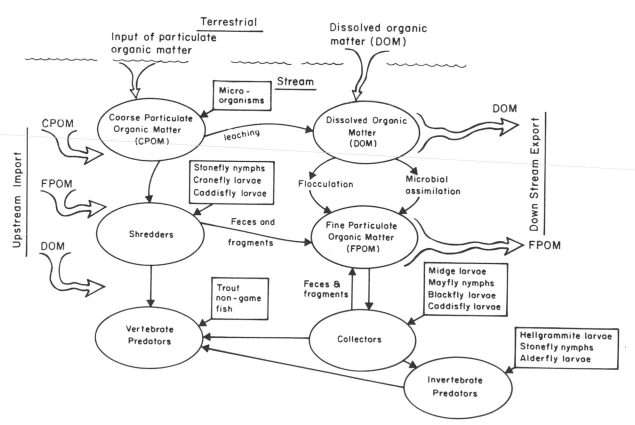

(Redrawn from data in Figures 2, 3 and 4 of Cummins and Spengler, 1978)

Figure 1.--Schematic diagram depicting the processing of dead organic matter in headwater streams (redrawn from data in Cummins and Spengler 1978).

Coarse particulate organic matter (CPOM: > 1 mm. diameter), such as leaves, starts leaching DOM once it enters the water. Up to 30% of dry weight may be leached in the first day; deciduous leaves leach faster than coniferous needles (Cummins 1974; Hynes et al. 1974). Fungi and bacteria rapidly colonize the leaves undergoing leaching. Although most of these microbes can metabolize cellulose, only some can use lignin (Cummins and Spengler 1978). Certain aquatic insects such as some stonefly nymphs, midge larvae, cranefly larvae, and caddisfly larvae shred or break down leaves (CPOM) during feeding and are called "shredders" (Cummins 1973). The microorganisms that colonize the leaves are an important source of shredder nutrition.

Shredder and microorganism feeding eventually breaks down CPOM into fine particulate organic matter (FPOM: < 1 mm. diameter). However this process is only one source of FPOM. FPOM may result from: 1) shredder and microorganism feeding on CPOM; 2) physical abrasion of CPOM by stream turbulence; 3) fine particles eroded from streambed algae; 4) fine material washed or blown in from the surrounding watershed; and 5) conversion from DOM by chemical and microbial activity (Cummins 1974). Dissolved organic matter leached from CPOM, plus DOM entering from the watershed, aquatic plants, and microbial excretions, can be partially converted into FPOM. This conversion is accomplished by physical flocculation and microbial assimilation, processes dependent on water turbulence, temperature, pH, and various ionic concentrations (Lush and Hynes 1973).

FPOM is the food for aquatic organisms known as "collectors". These animals obtain FPOM either by gathering it from stream substrate deposits or by filtering it from the flowing water. Deposit feeders include certain midge larvae and mayfly nymphs. Filter feeders have diverse ways of capturing FPOM from the passing water (Wallace and Merritt 1980). Blackfly larvae possess fan-shaped structures on their heads for filtering FPOM and transferring it to their mouths. Some caddisfly larvae construct detailed silk nets capable of sieving out FPOM. The net is often held between small twigs or stones exposed to the current, and the larva hides in a tube just behind. The collected FPOM contains bacteria on its surfaces, which increases the quality of the food for the collector. Particle size is very important to collectors since their mouthparts and sieving devices have specific shapes and openings for obtaining and handling FPOM.

A thin film of algae covers most stream substrates and contributes to instream primary production, especially when light intensity and nutrient concentrations are high. Microscopic diatoms are often the most abundant algal group, but larger filamentous green and blue-green algae are also common. Aquatic organisms known as "scrapers" have well-adapted mouthparts for scraping up and consuming this algal film, which

also includes some FPOM and microscopic animals. Scrapers in Sierra streams include many mayfly nymphs, water penny beetles, riffle beetles, and some midge larvae.

Some aquatic invertebrates and vertebrates prey on shredders, collectors, scrapers, and each other; they are known as "predators". Predators in Sierra streams include many stonefly nymphs, dragonfly nymphs, some midge larvae, alderfly larvae, and dobsonfly larvae. Most aquatic insects in streams, even those that are predatory, are potential prey for trout and many nongame fish species.

The amount, kind, and timing of riparian vegetation additions to the stream and the shading provided by streamside plants will determine which feeding groups (shredders, collectors, scrapers, predators) prosper at any site. Thus, the population abundance of stream animals and community composition of the stream ecosystem are dependent on riparian vegetation.

THE RIVER CONTINUUM CONCEPT

The structure and function of aquatic communities along a river system have recently been organized into the River Continuum Concept (Cummins 1975; Vannote et al. 1980). This concept involves several stream factors--temperature, substrate, water velocity, stream morphology, and energy inputs from allochthonous and autochthonous sources--which interact to influence the availability of food for stream animals. These factors should vary in a predictable fashion from headwaters to downstream locations, and should produce predictable distributions of the four feeding groups along the continuum (fig. 2).

Since headwater streams (orders 1-3) are often heavily shaded and receive large amounts of organic matter from riparian vegetation, these streams are heterotrophic. Their ratio of gross photosynthesis (P) to respiration (R) will be less than one. Coarse substrates predominate, since stream gradients and erosive power are high. Shredders reach maximum abundance in these upper stream sections because of the abundant CPOM. FPOM and DOM are used and exported downstream. Because many Sierra headwater streams originate within coniferous forests, they may differ from typical headwater streams originating within deciduous forests of the eastern United States in detrital input and lighting conditions.

Organic matter input and shading are less important in medium-sized rivers (orders 4-6) because of the greater widths and more open canopy. Increased primary production shifts these streams from heterotrophy into autotrophy, and a P:R ratio greater than one. Increased algal production allows scrapers to be abundant. Collectors are also common, and a few shredders are still present. FPOM and DOM are again used and exported downstream.

162

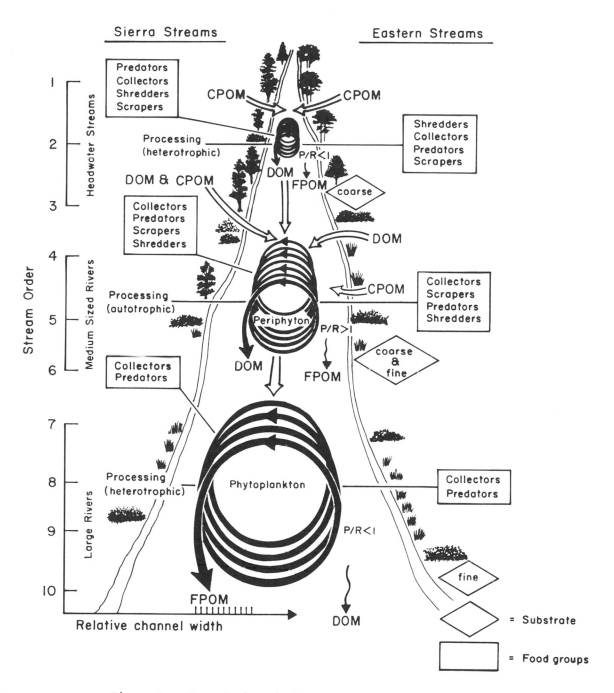

Figure 2.--The relationship between stream size and the progressive shift in structural and functional components of streams. Box graphs of feeding groups are provided to compare Sierra streams with eastern streams. The relative number of organisms in each feeding group is indicated by rank-ordered lists, from large to small (from Cummins 1975; Vannote et al. 1980).

Riparian vegetation has little direct influence on large rivers (orders > 6) since the wide channels are open to sunlight, and the input of terrestrial detritus relative to water volume is small. However, FPOM from upstream sources is very important, and for this reason collectors are the predominant aquatic organisms of large rivers. Although these rivers are open to sunlight, increased turbidity restricts both light penetration and primary production by algae on the fine river substrates. Instead, phytoplankton may be important primary producers in the upper water layers, although turbidity may restrict the depth of their production. Therefore, large rivers are thought to be heterotrophic and have a P:R ratio less than one.

Shredders and scrapers are essentially absent because their food resource and coarse substrate are lacking.

Streams on the western slope of the Sierra Nevada typically pass through several plant communities—subalpine forests (conifers), red fir forests, mixed conifer forests, oak woodlands, chaparral, and grasslands—each of which contributes different organic matter inputs and shading effects. In addition, alpine tundra, montane meadows, and montane chaparral may be locally important. It is not known if all aspects of the river continuum concept apply to Sierra streams.

It is possible to summarize predictions of the river continuum concept (Vannote et al. 1980), especially as they are thought to be true for many streams in forested regions. Exceptions are known to occur for desert streams (Minshall 1978), and possibly for western montane streams (Wiggins and Mackay 1978). Some of these predictions have recently been tested in four Oregon streams, and shown to support the river continuum concept (Naiman and Sedell 1980; Hawkins and Sedell 1981).

Width, depth, and discharge increase as stream order increases. Substrate size changes from coarse to fine going from headwaters to large rivers. Diel changes in water temperature increase to a maximum in medium stream orders (3-5), then decrease downstream.

CPOM and riparian vegetation shading decrease in importance downstream, and FPOM increases in importance. This causes the CPOM:FPOM ratio to decrease as stream order increases. The particle size of detritus decreases downstream.

DOM diversity decreases downstream as labile components are used by microorganisms, causing refractory components to accumulate.

P:R ratio < 1 for stream orders 1-3—heterotropic condition.
P:R ratio > 1 for stream orders 4-6—autotrophic condition.
P:R ratio < 1 for stream orders > 6—heterotrophic condition.

Shredders decrease downstream as CPOM becomes less abundant.

Collectors increase downstream as FPOM becomes more important.

Scrapers increase to a maximum abundance in medium-sized rivers (orders 4-6) as the canopy opens and admits light to the substrate, but then decrease in larger rivers (orders > 6) because turbid water shades algae on the stream substrate.

Predators maintain approximately constant abundance along the continuum.

Biotic diversity is low in the headwaters, increases to a maximum in medium stream orders (3-5), and decreases in larger rivers.

EFFECTS OF RIPARIAN VEGETATION REMOVAL

Some of the major inputs of riparian vegetation to instream systems are shown in figure 3. Effects on stream invertebrates of disruptions to five of these inputs will be discussed: 1) decrease of detrital inputs; 2) loss of shade as it affects primary production; 3) loss of shade as it affects stream temperature; 4) water quality and quantity alterations; and 5) loss of terrestrial habitat. The intensity of these effects is related to the degree of modification of the vegetation.

Decrease of Detrital Inputs

Riparian vegetation often supplies large amounts of organic matter (energy) to the stream, forming a dependable food base for stream invertebrates year after year. Many of these animals have complex structures, behaviors, and life cycle events which are specially adapted for using different kinds and sizes of detritus as food. Decrease of detritus will cause decreased populations of these species, although instream production may still maintain some at lower densities.

Loss of Shade: Effect on Primary Production

Riparian vegetation is a major control on light intensities reaching algae and macrophytes in headwater streams, and therefore on the level of primary production that can occur. Shade removal has been demonstrated to increase primary production and cause algal mats in small streams, both in the field (Brown and Krygier 1970; Likens et al. 1970; Granoth 1979), and in the laboratory (McIntire and Phinney 1965; Brocksen et al. 1968). For example, vegetation removal along a small stream in Kansas changed it from heterotrophy to autotrophy (Gelroth and Marzolf 1978). Also, in laboratory streams exposed to two different light levels, the stream receiving twice as much light had twice the gross plant production (Brocksen et al. 1968). If nutrients or other factors are not limiting, increased illumination due to shade removal will increase primary production and the food resources used by scrapers.

Loss of Shade: Effect on Stream Temperature

Shade from riparian vegetation moderates stream temperatures, often preventing excessive summer temperatures that may be lethal to invertebrates or fish. Field studies have demonstrated significant increases in summer water temperatures and decreases in winter temperatures when shade is removed from small streams (table 1).

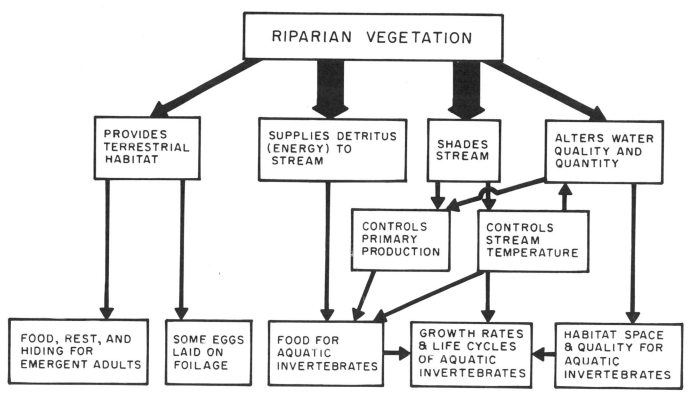

Figure 3.--Relationships between riparian vegetation and stream components.

Table 1.--Water temperature changes in small streams caused by riparian vegetation removal, in relation to undisturbed conditions.

Location	Forest type	Temperature change		References
		Summer[1]	Winter	
Oregon	Coniferous	+8(a)	--	Brown and Krygier (1970)
		+15(b)	--	
		+8(a)	0	Levno and Rothacher (1967,1969)
Alaska	Coniferous	+5(a)	0	Meehan et al. (1969)
Kansas	Deciduous	+5(c)	--	Gelroth and Marzolf (1978)
New Hampshire	Deciduous	+5(c)	+	Likens et al. (1970)
		+4(d)	--	
West Virginia	Deciduous	+8(a)	-2	Aubertin and Patric (1974) Lee and Samuel (1976)
North Carolina	Deciduous	+7(a)	-2	Greene (1950)
		+13(e)	--	
		+7(e)	--	Swift and Messer (1971)
New Zealand	Mixed coniferous and deciduous	+4(a)	-2.5	Graynoth (1979)
		+7(b)	--	

[1]Summer increase in water temperature based on:
    (a) mean monthly maximum water temperatures,
    (b) instantaneous water temperatures recorded for one year,
    (c) instantaneous water temperatures recorded for only one summer day,
    (d) mean weekly water temperatures,
    (e) weekly maximum water temperatures.

Studies on clear-cut watersheds show that when riparian buffer strips are used, stream temperatures remain essentially the same as in undisturbed watersheds (Brown and Krygier 1970; Swift and Messer 1971; Graynoth 1979), and stream macroinvertebrate diversities remain high (Erman et al. 1977).

Water temperature affects numerous important stream functions, such as processing rates of organic matter, chemical reactions and concentrations, metabolic rates of stream invertebrates, and cues for life cycle events. Because of these complex interactions it is very difficult to assess the ultimate effects of shade removal and water temperature changes on stream animals. Stream invertebrates have different tolerances for water temperature variations, but most species in headwater streams are narrowly adapted for cool temperatures and may use dormant strategies to survive natural warm periods (Hynes 1970). Some stoneflies in Sierra streams survive summer temperatures lethal to mature nymphs by being in the egg stage or by diapausing as young nymphs. Although some survival strategies can be used whenever conditions become unfavorable, other strategies are closely timed to natural stream temperature cycles and might not be useable during abnormal temperature patterns.

Water Quality and Quantity Alterations

Riparian vegetation affects water quality not only by moderating water temperature and influencing chemical reactions, but also by contributing DOM and nutrients to the stream. Riparian vegetation also protects streambanks from excessive erosion, minimizing the input of fine sediments which can fill the numerous cracks, crevices, narrow channels, and openings that ramify through the upper substrate layers that form the invertebrate habitat of normal headwater streams. Removal of riparian vegetation may increase the annual amount of stream runoff, increase peak discharges after rainstorms, and change the timing of peak flows. Change in runoff quantity will cause the stream channel to readjust its velocity patterns, channel dimensions, frequency of pools and riffles, and substrate composition, all of which are important for the amount and quality of invertebrate habitat. Since invertebrate species vary in their habitat requirements, some species may benefit while others are harmed. Nonetheless, disturbances that add fine sediment to streams decrease the species diversity.

Loss of Terrestrial Habitat

Most aquatic insects, including those in Sierra streams, emerge into terrestrial ecosystems as adults with wings for dispersing and searching for mates. Riparian vegetation is an important habitat used by these adult insects for feeding, resting, and hiding. Use of this foliage is heavy in spring and somewhat less in summer and autumn. Some use occurs even in winter. Without this vegetation, predation by birds, terrestrial insects, and mammals would

undoubtedly be much greater. Some insect adults lay eggs on riparian vegetation overhanging the stream so that upon hatching the young larvae will drop back into the stream for the aquatic life stages. This method of egg laying is used by the alderfly _Sialis_ in Sierra streams. Stoneflies signal and find mates by drumming with their abdomens on streamside vegetation.

LITERATURE CITED

Anderson, N.H., and J.R. Sedell. 1979. Detritus processing by macroinvertebrates in stream ecosystems. Ann. Rev. Entomol. 24:351-377.

Aubertin, G.M., and J.H. Patric. 1974. Water quality after clearcutting a small watershed in Western Virginia. J. Environ. Qual. 3:243-249.

Bray, J.R., and E. Gorham. 1964. Litter production in forests of the world. p. 101-157. In: J.B. Cragg (ed.). Advances in ecological research, Vol. 2. 264 p. Academic Press, New York, N.Y.

Brocksen, R.W., G.E. Davis, and C.E. Warren. 1968. Competition, food consumption, and production of sculpins and trout in laboratory stream communities. J. Wildl. Mgmt. 32:51-75.

Brown, G.W., and J.T. Krygier. 1970. Effects of clear-cutting on stream temperature. Water Resources Res. 6:1133-1139.

Busch, D.E., and S.G. Fisher. 1981. Metabolism of a desert stream. Freshwat. Biol. 11: 301-307.

Cummins, K.W. 1973. Trophic relations of aquatic insects. Ann Rev. Entomol. 18: 183-206.

Cummins, K.W. 1974. Structure and function of stream ecosystems. Bioscience 24:631-641.

Cummins, K.W. 1975. The ecology of running waters: theory and practice. p. 277-293. In: Proceedings of Sandusky River Basin symposium. International Joint Commission of the Great Lakes. Heidelberg College, Tiffin Ohio.

Cummins, K.W., and G.L. Spengler. 1978. Stream ecosystems. Water Spectrum 10:1-9.

Cummins, K.W., and M.J. Klug. 1979. Feeding ecology of stream invertebrates. Ann. Rev. Ecol. Syst. 10:147-172.

Erman, D.C., J.D. Newbold, and K.B. Roby. 1977. Evaluation of streamside bufferstrips for protection aquatic organisms. Water Resources Center Contract No. 165. 48 p. University of California, Davis.

Fisher, S.G., and G.E. Likens. 1973. Energy flow in Bear Brook, New Hampshire: an integrative approach to stream ecosystem metabolism. Ecol. Monog. 43:421-439.

Gelroth, J.V., and G.R. Marzolf. 1978. Primary production and leaf-litter decomposition in natural and channelized portions of a Kansas stream. Am. Midl. Nat. 99:238-243.

Graynoth, E. 1979. Effects of logging on stream environments and faunas in Nelson. New Zealand J. Mar. Freshwat. Res. 13:79-109.

Greene, G.E. 1950. Land use and trout streams. J. Soil Wat. Cons. 5:125-126.

Hawkins, C.P., and J.R. Sedell. 1981. Longitudinal and seasonal changes in functional organization of macroinvertebrate communities in four Oregon streams. Ecology 62:387-397.

Hobbie, J.E., and G.E. Likens. 1973. Output of phosphorus, dissolved organic carbon, and fine particulate carbon from Hubbard Brook watersheds. Limnol. Oceanogr. 18:734-742.

Hynes, H.B.N. 1963. Imported organic matter and secondary productivity in streams. Proc. XVI Int. Congr. Zool. 4:324-329.

Hynes, H.B.N. 1970. The ecology of running waters. 555 p. University of Toronto Press, Toronto, Canada.

Hynes, H.B.N., N.K. Kaushik, M.A. Lock, D.L. Lush, Z.S.J. Stocker, R.R. Wallace, and D.D. Williams. 1974. Benthos and allochthonous organic matter in streams. J. Fish. Res. Bd. Can. 31:545-553.

Lee, R., and D.E. Samuel. 1976. Some thermal and biologial effects of forest cutting in West Virginia. J. Environ. Qual. 5:362-366.

Levno, A., and J. Rothacher. 1967. Increases in maximum stream temperatures after logging in old-growth douglas fir watersheds. USDA Forest Service Research Note PNW-65. 12 p. Pacific Northwest Forest and Range Experiment Station.

Levno, A., and J. Rothacher. 1969. Increases in maximum stream temperatures after slash burning in a small experimental watershed. USDA Forest Service Research Note PNW-110. 7 p. Pacific Northwest Forest and Range Experiment Station.

Likens, G.E., F.H. Bormann, N.M. Johnson, D.W. Fisher, and R.S. Pierce. 1970. Effects of forest cutting and herbicide treatment on nutrient budgets in the Hubbard Brook Watershed-Ecosystem. Ecol. Monog. 40:23-47.

Lush, D.L., and H.B.N. Hynes. 1973. The formation of particles in freshwater leachates of dead leaves. Limnol. Oceanogr. 18:968-977.

McIntire, C.D., and H.K. Phinney. 1965. Laboratory studies of periphyton production and community metabolism in lotic environments. Ecol. Monog. 35:237-258.

Meehan, W.R., W.A. Farr, D.M. Bishop, and J.H. Patric. 1969. Some effects of clearcutting on salmon habitat of two southeast Alaska streams. USDA Forest Service Research Paper PNW-82. 45 p. Pacific Northwest Forest and Range Experiment Station.

Minshall, G.W. 1968. Community dynamics of the benthic fauna in a woodland springbrook. Hydrobiol. 32:305-339.

Minshall, G.W. 1978. Autotrophy in stream ecosystems. Bioscience 28:767-771.

Naiman, R.J. 1976. Primary production, standing stock, and export of organic matter in a Mohave Desert thermal stream. Limnol. Oceanogr. 21:60-73.

Naiman, R.J., and J.R. Sedell. 1979. Benthic organic matter as a function of stream order in Oregon. Arch. Hydrobiol. 87:404-422.

Naiman, R.J., and J.R. Sedell. 1980. Relationships between metabolic parameters and stream order in Oregon. Can. J. Fish. Aquat. Sci. 37:834-847.

Swift, L.W., and J.B. Messer. 1971. Forest cuttings raise temperatures of small streams in the southern Appalachians. J. Soil Wat. Cons. 26:111-116.

Vannote, R.L., G.W. Minshall, K.W. Cummins, J.R. Sedell, and C.E. Cushing. 1980. The river continuum concept. Can. J. Fish. Aquat. Sci. 37:130-137.

Wallace, J.B., and R.W. Merritt. 1980. Filter-feeding ecology of aquatic insects. Ann. Rev. Entomol. 25:103-132.

Wiggins, G.B., and R.J. Mackay. 1978. Some relationships between systematics and trophic ecology in Nearctic aquatic insects, with special reference to Trichoptera. Ecology 59:1211-1220.

THE ROLE OF STREAMSIDE BUFFERSTRIPS IN THE ECOLOGY

OF AQUATIC BIOTA[1]

Don L. Mahoney and Don C. Erman[2]

Abstract.--Riparian vegetation is important as a source of food to stream organisms, as shade over small-order streams, and as a bank-stabilizing force to prevent excessive sedimentation and to intercept pollutants. Logging may significantly affect each of these factors unless proper protective measures are employed. Current research is underway on the recovery of small northern California streams after logging. Analysis of algal samples from 30 streams shows light intensity and chlorophyll concentrations are major factors related to logging intensity that affect instream primary production. Transportable sediment from 24 streambeds has shown that this measure of sediment is higher (P = .001) in logged and narrow buffered streams than in controls 7 to 10 years after logging.

INTRODUCTION

Streamside vegetation is a source of food, provides shade which prevents excessive water temperatures, provides cover, and gives stability to the soil along the stream. If land-use activity on the slopes around a stream creates erosion or pollution hazards, streamside vegetation can intercept and filter sediments and contaminants before they enter the stream. Several studies have examined the value of streamside vegetation (bufferstrips) in protecting streams from timber management activities; we will emphasize these studies in this paper. In addition, preliminary results from our study of the recovery of logged streams in northern California will be presented.

STREAMSIDE VEGETATION AS A SOURCE OF FOOD

Streams are often classified according to the predominant source of energy used as a base for their food chains. Some streams receive energy primarily from leaffall and litter entering the stream, while others receive energy primarily from instream plant production. These two sources of energy can vary over the course of a year and from one section of stream to another. Recent emphasis has been placed on the role of outside energy sources to stream macroinvertebrates (Cummins 1974). Numerous studies (see Erman 1983; Knight and Bottorff 1983) have focused on the feeding habits of individual species of invertebrates, both as larvae and as adults. Much of this work has examined the functional aspects of the aquatic animals or the way that they obtain their food, rather than the origin of the food, the taxonomic nature of the species, or the trophic level they might occupy (Cummins 1973).

In a recent study, for example, Hawkins and Sedell (1981) have shown that the relative abundance of each functional group depends on the kind of food inputs into the stream system. They studied a relatively undisturbed stream system, from headwaters to lowlands, in the Oregon Cascades and found that shredders of large organic particles dominated upper shaded reaches; collectors of fine organic particles increased in abundance from the headwaters down; filterers of fine organic particles were only locally important; predators became equally distributed in the summer and fall, increasing in the lower reaches from a spring minimum; and algal scrapers became an important part of the fauna once the stream became wider and more open to light through the middle reaches. Obviously, if riparian vegetation is destroyed and a stream changes from a food web based on outside inputs to one based on internal production, then the various types of invertebrates will change in abundance also.

Another effect of streamside vegetation removal, although more indirect, is to alter

[1] Paper presented at the California Riparian Systems Conference. [University of California, Davis, Sept. 17-19, 1981].

[2] Don L. Mahoney is Ph.D. Candidate in Wildland Resource Science; Don C. Erman is Professor of Wildlife-Fisheries, both are in the Department of Forestry and Resource Management, University of California, Berkeley.

predation pressure from fish. Insects falling from the riparian zone are significant sources of food for stream fishes (Hunt 1975; Cadwallader et al. 1980), and when vegetation is removed, fish switch to feeding predominantly on instream invertebrates as the aerial source is diminished (Hess 1969; Cadwallader et al. 1980).

A compensating effect of the removal of the streamside shade is to increase the growth of certain algae, especially diatoms and filamentous green algae. Increased algal growth has been associated with increased biomass of some invertebrates and fish (Lyford and Gregory 1975; Murphy and Hall 1981), and may mask detrimental effects of increased sedimentation (Murphy et al. 1981), especially if adequate spawning sites for fish are available in nearby undisturbed sections of stream and if adequate care has been taken of the streambed. An increase in the amount of algae, however, may be at the expense of mosses and vascular macrophytes (Mahoney and Erman, unpublished), organisms which have been used as indicators of good water quality in Europe (Empain 1978; Wiegleb 1981).

TEMPERATURE EFFECTS OF STREAMSIDE VEGETATION

Streamside vegetation has a marked effect on the temperature of stream water (Hall and Lantz 1970; Meehan 1970; Swift and Messer 1971; Brazier and Brown 1973). Temperature increases after removal of streamside vegetation can be expected to be greater where stream discharges are smaller, as in low-order, headwater mountain streams. Methods are now available for quantifying the relationship between the amount of streamside vegetation and the change in stream temperature (Brown 1972). Temperature change is related to the amount of solar radiation at critical periods that is intercepted by the canopy, the surface area of the stream, and stream discharge. In some cases the annual maximum temperature has increased 12°C by complete canopy removal in small streams (Brown and Krygier 1970). By way of comparison, the average increase in water temperature caused by once-through cooling of electric generation stations was 10-11°C a few years ago (Mittursky et al. 1970; Levin et al. 1972).

There are detrimental effects of temperature increases on fish survival (e.g., Paladino et al. 1980) including those caused by riparian vegetation removal (Swift and Messer 1971; Ringler and Hall 1975). But Hunt (1979) intentionally cleared upper-story vegetation from along a small Michigan stream in order to recreate a meadow environment and reported that temperature increases were ameliorated once meadow vegetation began overhanging the stream.

While many of these studies have shown that temperature increases affect fish populations, there have been fewer studies to determine the effect of temperature increases on invertebrates. The change in fish production would by itself

change the predation pressure on the invertebrate community. Burton and Likens (1973) discussed possible changes in stream macroinvertebrate communities due to temperature increases from vegetation removal, and a number of other studies have demonstrated significant changes in populations and decreased diversity of macroinvertebrates in waters heated by power plant cooling systems (Howell and Gentry 1974; Ward 1976).

STREAMSIDE VEGETATION AS A PROTECTION FROM EROSION AND POLLUTION

One benefit of the herbaceous growth (including mosses and liverworts) along the banks of streams is to provide stability to the banks and thus prevent streambed erosion due to undercutting (e.g., Pfankuch 1975; Cederholm and Koski 1977). Taller, more woody growth along streams can prevent the debris produced by human activities or natural landslides from entering the channel (Benoit 1978). There are many reports of changes in the invertebrate biota that occur with increases in sedimentation (Cordone and Kelly 1961; Chutter 1964; Nuttal 1972; Rosenberg and Weins 1978). The exact mechanisms responsible for these changes are complex, involving smothering, loss of food or space, and substrate instability (Cederholm et al. 1978; Lenat et al. 1978; Williams and Mundie 1978).

When streams are buffered from the effect of road-building and logging by strips of vegetation, they have much lower increases in suspended sediment than comparable streams that are not protected by bufferstrips (Burns 1972; Moring 1975). Table 1 gives data from the Alsea watershed study in Oregon (Moring 1975), covering a period of 15 years; it clearly demonstrates the protective value of streamside vegetation. Similarly, in another study (Aubertin et al. 1974) only slight increases in stream turbidity occurred after clearcutting a 34-ha. watershed in West Virginia. The success in maintaining water quality was attributed to the retention of a 10- to 20-m. forest strip along the stream.

Table 1.--Average percentage of change in suspended sediment in the Alsea watershed seven years before and seven years after logging (Moring 1975).

Control	0.1
Clear-cut with bufferstrip	54
Clear-cut	205

Other studies, chiefly in the Midwest, have examined the value of vegetative bufferstrips as a protection from agricultural pollution. Vegetative strips around feedlots substantially reduced runoff, total solids, total nitrogen, and total phosphorus (Young et al. 1980). Asmussen et al. (1977) found that vegetative buffer-strips effectively reduced pollution from agricultural chemicals. An extensive review of the impact of nearstream vegetation on water quality and stream biota (Karr and Schlosser 1977) concluded that "proper management of nearstream vegetation and stream morphology may produce substantial improvement in water quality and the stream biota of agricultural watersheds." A summary of this report is available in Karr and Schlosser (1978),

The exact extent of bufferstrip that is necessary to protect water quality has been calculated for some situations. Based on soil stability ratings and slope, Haupt (1959) developed guidelines for the width of bufferstrips necessary to protect streams from road-building activities. Benoit (1978) has done the same for timber management activities based on data from a number of streams in Oregon. Federal regulations for national forests, and the Forest Practices Act regulations on private lands in California, limit the extent of timber harvesting activities near watercourses, but they do not dictate specific buffer widths.

A major study of macroinvertebrates in streams in northern California was undertaken at the University of California, Berkeley, to see if macroinvertebrates could indicate water quality in streams associated with logging activities (Erman et al. 1977; Roby et al. 1977; Newbold et al. 1980). A total of 65 buffered, unbuffered, and control streams was sampled, mostly on national forest land. These investigations showed that invertebrate communities of logged or disturbed streams had a lower diversity index and higher populations (primarily of Chironomidae, Baetis, and Nemoura) than streams in unlogged areas. Streams with bufferstrips wider than 30 m. had invertebrate communities no different than control streams; whereas, if bufferstrips were less than 30 m., some differences in communities were detected. The relationship between diversity and various land-use practice (no buffer, narrow buffer, wide buffer, control) is summarized in figure 1.

Similar work in New Zealand found changes in invertebrate abundances and diversity after streamside vegetation was cleared during logging operations (Graynoth 1979). Where a buffer of vegetation was left along the stream, changes in invertebrate populations did not occur.

A major concern of regulatory policy is whether fixed widths of vegetation along the streamside should be specified or land managers should make site-specific recommendations to balance resource use and stream protection. A fixed width (or some range of values) is appealing because of its simplicity of application and its provision of at least minimum stream protection. Site-specific recommendations theoretically allow for more precise adjustments to local risks (or lack of risks) and permit resource use (timber harvesting) to the limit of sound forest prac-

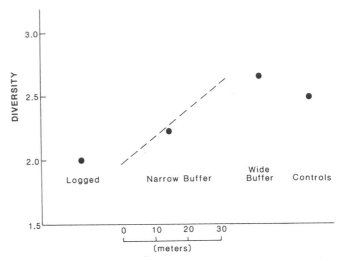

Figure 1.--Diversity of macroinvertebrate communities in streams in northern California as affected by varying forestry practices.

tices. Evidence is available to support either approach (Burns 1972; Erman et al. 1977). In the long run, we believe, use and protection must be balanced by the land manager, who needs to view land and water systems with equal concern.

ONGOING STUDY OF POST-LOGGING RECOVERY

While the previous study of logging and bufferstrips in California demonstrated significant reductions in invertebrate diversity in unbuffered and narrow buffered streams, causal mechanisms were not investigated thoroughly. As a follow-up study, 30 of the streams in the original investigation are currently being studied to see the recovery rate of narrow and unbuffered streams and to investigate possible causal mechanisms. Data on invertebrate distributions and abundances, algal production, and transportable sediment stored in the substrate have been collected. Invertebrate analysis is not yet complete; preliminary data on algal production and sediment storage will be presented here.

Algae Production

As mentioned earlier, one of the effects of removing the stream canopy is to alter the instream algal community. There are many methods to quantify this community, and comparisons between methods have been attempted (e.g., Bott et al. 1978). While oxygen evolution methods may provide a more accurate measure of primary production under some circumstances, the ease with which chlorophyll and biomass estimates can be made has assured these methods a place in the literature, even though extraction methods for chlorophyll remain uncertain (Rai 1980). But before chlorophyll analyses can be used as indicators of perturbations, factors affecting differences in chlorophyll concentration must be fully understood.

We used an approach similar to that of Bannister (1974), where the amount of chlorophyll was weighted by the amount of available light. Higher chlorophyll concentrations are usually present in shade plants (Brown and Richardson 1968; Boardman 1977), but they do not necessarily mean higher production; this method takes that relationship into account in making estimates of potential production. The presence of more chlorophyll in shade plants has been known for some time to plant physiologists, but apparently is not appreciated by limnologists (Naiman and Sedell 1980). A full description of the methods used in this study will be available in a later publication.

Algae for this study was removed from constant rock sizes (2-4 cm.), size-classes that are moved by moderate storms. No noticeable differences were detected between logged, buffered, and control streams. In those streams that were not light-saturated (i.e., did not receive 10% of full sunlight), there was a relationship between the amount of chlorophyll per unit area and the amount of radiant energy--the less energy received the more chlorophyll present (fig. 2). Potential production for these streams was inversely related to the chlorophyll concentration present (fig. 2). Streams that were not light-limited had a wide range of chlorophyll concentrations and production estimates. This range is due to a number of factors, the most prominent being the place in the bloom-dieoff cycle that was sampled. High values were obtained if samples were taken as a particular species of algae (usually filamentous) reached bloom proportions in streams modified to receive full sunlight. Low values were obtained from the same stream-types if samples were taken after a bloom of algae had begun to senesce. These results indicate some of the difficulties with, and hence limitations to, interpretation of algal chlorophyll data in evaluating stream perturbations.

Changes in Transportable Sediment

The amount and size of sediments in stream substrates is a result of many processes. Inputs may come from human activities such as logging or road-building, or from natural causes such as landslides. How fast sediment is moved through the stream depends on such things as slope, instream vegetation, instream sediment traps, and the frequency of large storms for the period in question. It may easily take five years or more for a pulse of sediment to flow completely through a stream system (Dunn and Leopold 1978). Thus the amount of sediment that is currently in the process of being moved through a stretch of stream (including that temporarily stored) is a summation of all the land-use activity and weather patterns that have prevailed in the basin in question for the preceding several years.

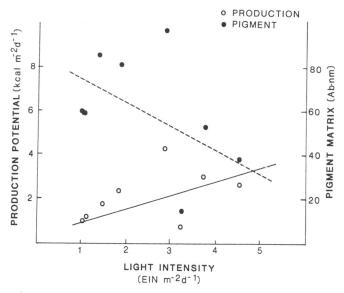

Figure 2.--Potential algal production and total pigment concentration for 8 light-limited streams in northern California.

For this study we measured the sediment that was present in a stream and could be easily moved (transportable sediment) by summer low flows. We stirred a small area of streambottom to a depth of 10 cm. and placed cylindrical containers into the substrate downstream to collect sediment (Beschta and Jackson 1979; Blomqvist and Hakanson 1981; Blomqvist and Kofoed 1981).

Figure 3 shows the percentage change in transportable sediment in logged or narrow-buffer treatment streams when compared with control streams. Each treatment (either logged or buffered) is compared with each control within that block of streams (a group of treatment and control streams from the same area). Transportable sediment was higher in 17 out of 20 comparisons of treatment to control (sign test: P = .001), even though several of the control streams were degraded by recent road-building activity. Figure 4 shows the change in transportable sediment, transportable detritus, and the ratio of the two for each block of streams. The average of treatment streams is compared against the average of control streams for each block. Comparisons between blocks are not completely analyzed. In all blocks, transportable sediment was higher in treatments than in controls (fig. 4). Transportable detritus was higher in five of the six blocks, while the ratio of detritus to sediment was lower in four of six blocks. These findings indicate that seven to ten years after logging, in unprotected streams and streams protected by buffers less than 30 m. wide, more sediment is being transported than in comparable controls. Detritus (from either out-of-stream or in-stream sources) is also higher in treatment streams, but this increase is not as great as the increase in sediments.

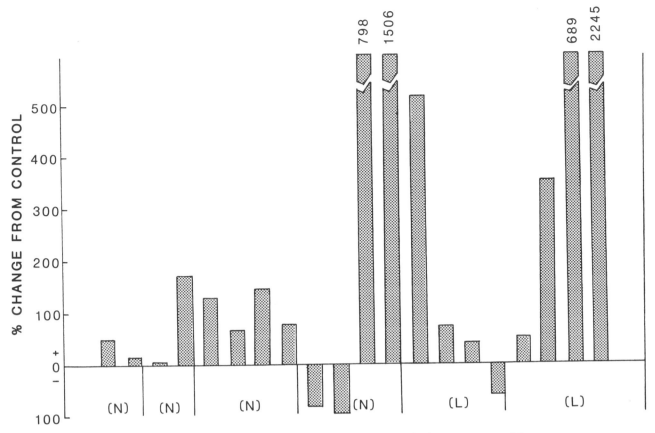

Figure 3.--Percentage change from control in transportable sediment in narrow-buffered (N) and logged (L) streams in northern California.

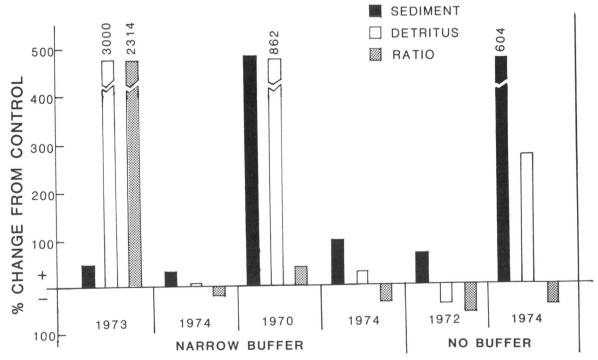

Figure 4.--Percentage change from control in transportable sediment, detritus, and the detritus:sediment ratio in narrow-buffered and unbuffered streams in northern California (dates are year of initial logging).

CONCLUSION

Streamside vegetation has been shown to play an important role in the ecology of aquatic plants, macroinvertebrates, and fish. The sources cited in the review sections of this paper are meant solely as an introduction to a greater body of literature available on many aspects of the subject. Perhaps the best way to summarize the importance of streamside vegetation is to place it in the context of the river continuum concept (Vannote et al. 1980). In this concept, the biotic community is shaped by both the immediate physical environment and by inputs from further upstream. Furthermore, the stream biota, after an extended period of time, reaches a dynamic equilibrium with the physical environment which itself undergoes periodic fluctuations.

It is in the headwaters of a stream that riparian vegetation plays its most important role in the ecology of invertebrates, both as a predictable annual source of food and as protection from excessive heating. The influence of this vegetation, however, is felt not only in the headwaters but also further downstream, where much of it eventually drifts. In the middle reaches of stream systems, the immediate riparian vegetation becomes less important as food, relative to the instream algal production, and in the lowest reaches, in large rivers, it plays an even lesser role as food. In these lower reaches riparian vegetation has its greatest importance as a soil-stabilizing force. This bank stabilization role is of course doubly important in the headwaters, as any sediment produced there will eventually find its way downstream.

Bufferstrips of vegetation left along streams affected by human activities have been shown to protect the integrity of stream systems. This vegetation is important in protecting not only the stream immediately adjacent to it, but also in protecting the biota further downstream since it prevents excessive sediment pulses from being flushed downstream. This downstream protective benefit of bufferstrips is usually not included in economic analyses of the costs and benefits of not harvesting the timber immediately adjacent to a stream (e.g., Gillick and Scott 1975). These downstream effects of riparian vegetation need more study so that they can be more realistically evaluated.

It is presently questionable how much riparian vegetation can be removed from a stream system without affecting the stability of the system. Natural resilience (e.g., increased algal blooms) may temporarily mask detrimental effects of this practice, but there is increasing evidence that decades may be necessary for the stream biota to return to normal. Since so much of the riparian vegetation in California has already been destroyed, it becomes even more imperative that what remains be managed wisely so that this important natural resource with all its diversity is not lost to posterity.

ACKNOWLEDGMENTS

We wish to thank Nancy Erman for her help in preparing the manuscript and Brian Plant for help in collecting field data. This work has in part been funded by the University of California, Water Resources Center as part of Water Resources Center Project UCAL-WRC-W-586.

LITERATURE CITED

Asmussen, L.E., A.W. White, Jr., E.W. Hauser, and J.M. Sheridan. 1977. Reduction of 2,4-d load in surfce runoff down a grassed waterway. J. Environ. Qual. 6:159-162.

Aubertin, G.M., and J.H. Patric. 1974. Water quality after clearcutting a small watershed in West Virginia. J. Environ. Qual. 3:243-249.

Bannister, T.T. 1974. Production equations in terms of chlorophyll concentration, quantum yield, and upper limit to production. Limnol. Oceanogr 19:1-12.

Benoit, C. 1978. Fluvial sediment delivery as percent of erosion. The relationship between landslope and effective streamside bufferstrip width. USDA Forest Service, Portland, Ore. Typescript.

Beschta, R.L. and W.L. Jackson. 1979. The intrusion of fine sediments into a stable gravel bed. J. Fish. Res. Board Can. 36:204-210.

Blomqvist, S. and L. Hakanson. 1981. A review on sediment traps in aquatic environments. Arch. Hydrobiol. 91:101-132.

Blomqvist, S. and C. Kofoed. 1981. Sediment trapping--a subaquatic in situ experiment. Limnol. Oceanogr. 26(3):585-590.

Boardman, N.K. 1977. Comparative photosynthesis of sun and shade plants. Ann. Rev. Plant Physiol. 28:355-377.

Bott, T.L., J.T. Brock, C.E. Cushing, S.V. Gregory, D. King, and R.C. Petersen. 1978. A comparison of methods for measuring primary productivity and community respiration in streams. Hydrobiologia 60:3-12.

Brazier, J.R., and G.W. Brown. 1973. Bufferstrips for stream temperature control. Research Paper 15, Forest Res. Lab., School of Forestry, Oregon State University, Corvallis. 9 p.

Brown, G.W. 1972. An improved temperature prediction model for small streams. 20 p. Dept. of For. Eng., Oregon State University, Corvallis, Water Resources Research Institute-16.

Brown, G.W., and J.T. Krygier. 1970. Effects of clear-cutting on stream temperature. Water Resour. Res. 6:1131-1139.

Brown, T.E., and F.L. Richardson. 1968. The effect of growth environment on the physiology of algae: Light intensity. J. Phycol. 4:38-54.

Burns, J.W. 1972. Some effects of logging and associated road construction on northern California streams. Trans. Amer. Fish. Soc. 101(1):1-17.

Burton, T.M., and G.E. Likens. 1973. The effect of strip-cutting on stream temperatures in the Hubbard Brook Experimental Forest, New Hampshire. Bioscience 23:433-435.

Cadwallader, P.L., A.K. Eden, and R.A. Hook. 1980. Role of streamside vegetation as a food source for Galaxias olidus Gunther (Pisces: Galaxiidae). Aust. J. Mar. Freshwater Res. 31:257-262.

Cederholm, C.J., and K.V. Koski. 1977. Effects of stream channelization on the salmonid habitat and populations of lower Big Beef Creek, Kitsap County, Washington 1969-1973. 31 p. Washington Cooperative Fish. Res. Unit, College of Fisheries, University of Washington, Seattle.

Cederholm, C.J., L.C. Lestelle, B.G. Edie, D.J. Martin, J.V. Tagart, and E.O. Salo. 1978. The effects of landslide siltation on the salmon and trout resources of Stequaleho Creek and the main Clearwater River, Jefferson County, Washington, 1972-1975. 53 . University of Washington, College of Fisheries, Fish. Res. Institute.

Chutter, F.M. 1969. The effects of silt and sand on the invertebrate fauna of streams and rivers. Hydrobiologia 34:57-76.

Cordone, A.J. and D.W. Kelley. 1961. The influences of inorganic sediment on the aquatic life of streams. Calif. Fish and Game 47:189-228.

Cummins, K.W. 1973. Trophic relations of aquatic insects. Ann. Rev. Entomol. 18:183-206.

Cummins, K.W. 1974. Structure and function of stream ecosystems. Bioscience 24(1):631-641.

Dunn, T. and L.B. Leopold. 1978. Water in environmental planning. Freeman Company, San Francisco, Calif. 818 p.

Empain, A. 1978. Quantitative relationships between populations of aquatic bryophytes and pollution of streams. Definition of an index of water qualtity. (In French) Hydrobiologia 60:49-74.

Erman, D.C., J.D. Newbold, and K.R. Roby. 1977. Evaluation of streamside bufferstrips for protecting aquatic organisms. Contribution No. 165, California Water Resources Center, University of California, Davis. 48 p.

Erman, N.A. 1983. The use of riparian systems by aquatic insects. In: R.E. Warner and K.M. Hendrix (ed.). California Riparian Systems. [University of California, Davis, September 17-19, 1981]. University of California Press, Berkeley.

Gillick, T. and B.D. Scott. 1975. Bufferstrips and the protection of fishery resources: an economic analysis. Report No. 332, Washington Department of Natural Resources, Olympia. 30 p.

Graynoth, E. 1979. Effects of logging on stream environments and faunas in Nelson. New Zealand Journal of Marine and Freshwater Research 13(1):79-109.

Hall, J.D., and R.L. Lantz. 1970. Effects of logging on the habitat of Coho salmon and cutthroat trout in coastal streams. Technical Paper No. 2570, Oregon Agricultural Experiment Station, Corvallis. 21 p.

Haupt, H.F. 1959. A method for controlling sediment from logging roads. USDA Forest Service Intermountain Forest and Range Experiment Station Miscellaneous Paper 22, Ogdon, Utah. 22 p.

Hawkins, C.P., and J.R. Sedell. 1981. Longitudinal and seasonal changes in functional organization of macroinvertebrate communities in four Oregon streams. Ecol. 62(2):387-397.

Hess, L.J. 1969. The effects of logging road construction on insect drop into a small coastal stream. M.S. Thesis, Humboldt State College, Arcata, Calif. 58 p.

Howell, F.G., and J.B. Gentry. 1974. Effects of thermal effluents from nuclear reactors on species diversity of aquatic insects. In: J.W. Gibbons and R.R. Scharitz (eds.). Thermal Ecology. U.S.A.E.C. Technical Information Center.

Hunt, R.L. 1975. Use of terrestrial invertebrates as food by salmonids. p. 137-151. In: A. D. Hasler (ed.). Coupling of land and water systems. Springer-Verlag, Berlin.

Hunt, R.L. 1979. Removal of woody streambank vegetation to improve trout habitat. Technical Bulletin No. 115, Wisconsin Department of Natural Resources, Madison. 36 p.

Karr, J.R., and I.J. Schlosser. 1977. Impact of nearstream vegetation and stream morphology on water quality and stream biota. Environ. Research Laboratory EPA-600/3-77-097, US Environmental Protection Agency, Athens, Georgia. 91 p.

Karr, J.R., and I.J. Schlosser. 1978. Water resources and the land-water interface. Science 201:229-234.

Knight, A.W., and R.L. Bottorff. 1983. The importance of riparian vegetation to stream ecosystems In: R.E. Warner and K.M. Hendrix (ed.). California Riparian Systems. [University of California, Davis, September 17-19, 1981]. University of California Press, Berkeley.

Lenat, D.R., D.L. Penrose, and K.W. Eagleson. 1981. Variable effects of sediment addition on stream benthos. Hydrobiologia 79: 187-194.

Levin, A.A., T.J. Birch, R.E. Hillman, and G.E. Raines. 1972. Thermal discharge: ecological effects. Env. Science and Technology 6(3):224-232.

Lyford, J.H., Jr., and S.V. Gregory. 1975. The dynamics and structure of periphyton communities in three Cascade mountain streams. Verh. Int. Verein. Theor. Angew. Limnol. 19:1610-1616.

Meehan, W.R. 1970. Some effects of shade cover on stream temperature in southeast Alaska. USDA Forest Service Pacific Northwest Forest and Range Experiment Station Research Note 113, Portland, Ore. 9 p.

Mittursky, J.A., A.J. McErlean, and V.S. Kennedy. 1970. Thermal pollution, aquaculture and pathobiology in aquatic systems. Journal of Wildlife Diseases 6:347-355.

Moring, J.R. 1975. The Alsea watershed study: effects of logging on the aquatic resources of three headwater streams of the Alsea River, Oregon. Part II. Fishery Research Report No. 9., Oregon Department of Fish and Wildlife, Corvallis. 39 p.

Murphy, M.L., and J.D. Hall. 1981. Varied effects of clear-cut logging on predators and their habitat in small streams of the Cascade mountains, Oregon. Can. J. Fish. Aquat. Sci. 38:137-145.

Murphy, M.L., C.P. Hawkins, and N.H. Anderson. 1981. Effects of canopy modification and accumulated sediment on stream communities. Trans. Amer. Fish Soc. 110:469-478.

Naiman, R.D., and J.R. Sedell. 1980. Relationships between metabolic parameters and stream order in Oregon. Can. J. Fish. Aquat. Sci. 37:834-847.

Newbold, J.D., D.C. Erman, and K.B. Roby. 1980. Effects of logging on macroinvertebrates in streams with and without bufferstrips. Can. J. Fish. Aquat. Sci. 37:1076-1085.

Nuttal, P.M. 1972. The effects of sand deposition upon the macroinvertebrate fauna of the River Camel, Cornwall. Freshwat. Biol. 2:181-186.

Paladino, F.V., J.R. Spotila, J.P. Schubauer, and K.T. Kowalski. 1980. The critical thermal maximum: a technique used to elucidate physiological stress and adaptation in fishes. Rev. Can. Biol. 39:115-122.

Pfankuch, D.J. 1975. Stream reach inventory and channel stability evaluation. USDA Forest Service, Northern Region, Missoula, Mont. 26 p.

Rai, H. 1980. (ed.). The measurement of photosynthetic pigments in freshwaters and standardization of methods. Arch. Hydrobiol. Beih. Ergebn. Limnol. 14. 106 p.

Ringler, N.H., and J.D. Hall. 1975. Effects of logging on water temperature and dissolved oxygen in spawning beds. Trans. Amer. Fish. Soc. 104:111-121.

Roby, K.B., D.C. Erman, and J.D. Newbold. 1977. Biological assessment of timber management activity impacts and bufferstrip effectiveness on National Forest streams of northern California. Earth Resources Monogr. 1, USDA Forest Service, Region 5, San Francisco, Calif. 170 .

Rosenberg, D.M., and A.P. Weins. 1978. Effects of sediment addition on macrobenthic invertebrates in a northern Canadian river. Water Research 12:753-763.

Swift, L.W., Jr., and J.B. Messer. 1971. Forest cuttings raise temperatures of small streams in the southern Appalachians. Jour. of Soil and Water Conservation 26:111-116.

Vannote, R.L., G.W. Minshall, K.W. Cummins, J.R. Sedell, and C.E. Cushing. 1980. The river continuum concept. Can. J. Fish. Aquat. Sci. 37:130-137.

Ward, J.V. 1976. Effects of thermal constancy and seasonal temperature displacement on community structure of stream macroinvertebrates. p. 302-307. In: G.W. Esch and R.W. McFarlane (ed.). Thermal ecology II, ERDA Symposium Series (Conf-740425).

Wiegleb, G. 1981. Application multiple discriminant analysis on the analysis of the correlation between macrophyte vegetation and water quality in running waters of Central Europe. Hydrobiologia 79:91-100.

Williams, D.D., and J.H. Mundie. 1978. Substrate size selection by stream invertebrates and the influence of sand. Limnol. Oceanogr. 23:1030-1033.

Young, R.A., T. Huntrods, and W. Anderson. 1980. Effectiveness of vegetated bufferstrips in controlling pollution from feedlot runoff. J. Environ. Qual. 9:483-487.

THE USE OF RIPARIAN SYSTEMS

BY AQUATIC INSECTS[1]

Nancy A. Erman[2]

Abstract.--Nearly all aquatic insects spend some portion of their lives in riparian zones. Many examples are given of terrestrial stages and activities of aquatic insects. The examples are divided into the areas of feeding, pupation, emergence and mating, and egg laying. Special emphasis is given to recent studies on caddisflies (Trichoptera) in riparian systems of the Sierra Nevada. The examples illustrate the point that knowledge of life cycles is essential for predicting the effect of disturbance in riparian areas on populations of aquatic insects.

INTRODUCTION

Most aquatic insects are either directly or indirectly dependent on riparian vegetation at some stage in their life cycles. This dependence has two aspects. The first is that the riparian system affects the aquatic system. The second is that nearly all aquatic insects are terrestrial at some stage in their life cycle and many at several stages in their life cycle (table 1). These terrestrial stages are usually spent close to the water in the riparian zone. It is the second aspect of riparian use that will be covered in this paper, but a brief review of the first is relevant to the theme of this symposium.

Riparian systems act on streams to produce shade and maintain cool summer stream temperature, to provide leaf fall, and to prevent soil erosion (Ross 1963). The smaller the stream, the greater is the effect of the riparian system on it and the more restricted to terrestrial biomes are the aquatic insects (Ross ibid.). In small streams in upper watersheds, terrestrial leaf litter is an important part of the diet of aquatic insects (Cummins 1973). Indirectly, insects farther downstream depend on the same food source when they eat fine particulate organic matter chewed and egested by those upstream. Carnivorous insects are indirectly dependent on riparian vegetation because their prey feed on it. Insects feed also on food produced within the aquatic system--algae and aquatic macrophytes (Merritt and Cummins 1978).

The relative importance of allochthonous and autochthonous food sources continues to be discussed (Kaushik and Hynes 1971; Hynes 1975; Minshall 1978; Vannote et al. 1980), but there is no doubt that the riparian zone contri-

Table 1.--Use of terrestrial vegetation (usually riparian) by aquatic insects. Orders in which nearly all members have an aquatic stage are all capitals. Orders in which only some families are aquatic are in lowercase type.

ORDER	LIFE STAGE		
	Egg	Nymph	Adult
EPHEMEROPTERA	A[1]	A	T[2]
ODONATA	A/t[3]	A	T
PLECOPTERA	A	A	T/a[4]
Hemiptera	A/T[5]	A/T[6]	A[7]/T

	Egg	Larva	Pupa	Adult
MEGALOPTERA	T	A	T	T
Neuroptera	T	A	T	T
TRICHOPTERA	A/t	A/t	A/t	T
Lepidoptera	A/t	A	A	T/a
Coleoptera	A/t	A/t	T/a	A/T
Diptera	A/t	A	A/T	T

[1] A--all members aquatic.
[2] T--all members terrestrial.
[3] A/t--most members aquatic, a few members terrestrial.
[4] T/a--most members terrestrial, a few members aquatic.
[5] A/T--many members aquatic, many members terrestrial.
[6] Insects live on surface film, adjacent banks, and at aquatic margins.
[7] Insects may leave water to migrate.

[1] Paper presented at the California Riparian Systems Conference. [University of California, Davis, September 17-19, 1981].
[2] Nancy A. Erman is Staff Research Associate in freshwater ecology, Department of Forestry and Resource Management, University of California, Berkeley, Calif.

butes a large part of the food base to any stream system.

Detailed studies of aquatic insect food habits have shown that many insects are omnivorous and that food needs change with instars (Chapman and Demory 1963; Winterbourn 1971; Mecom 1972; Anderson and Cummins 1979; Erman 1981). Therefore, an insect that may exist on algae produced within the stream in the early instars, may later shred decaying leaves from the riparian zone and later still become carnivorous.

The second aspect of riparian use by aquatic insects, that of their terrestrial stages, can be divided into four areas--feeding and, in the Trichoptera, case building; pupation; emergence and mating; and egg laying. Table 1 is a general representation of life stages of aquatic insects. Many exceptions have been omitted for simplification. It is particularly difficult to classify an order aquatic or terrestrial in any given stage when some orders (Hemiptera, Lepidoptera, Coleoptera, Diptera) have so many semiaquatic members. These members should be kept in mind, because although they are not covered in this paper, they are undoubtedly important in riparian zones. Special emphasis is given here to recent studies on caddisflies (Trichoptera) in riparian systems of the Sierra Nevada.

FEEDING ON STREAMSIDE VEGETATION

Most feeding by aquatic insects occurs in the nymphal or larval stage and, as discussed above, in the water. However, one caddisfly, Desmona bethula (Trichoptera:Limnephilidae) leaves the water to feed on several species of semiaquatic plants (Erman 1981). The life cycle is shown in figure 1. The larvae live in slow, unshaded stretches of small spring-streams in the Sierra Nevada and were studied at the Sagehen Creek Field Station (Nevada County). In most instances the larvae are in sections of spring-streams associated with fens or minerotrophic peatlands, described elsewhere (Erman and Erman 1975). Larvae leave the water at night to feed on Carex nebraskensis, C. praegracilis, C. rostrata, Calamagrostis canadensis (leaves and developing flowers), Veronica americana, Saxifraga oregana, Dodecatheon alpinum (developing fruits only), and Polygonum bistortoides. In all but the species indicated, larvae strip the tenderest tips and edges of the leaves (fig. 2). Such feeding is typical of many herbivores, probably because of richer nutrient concentrations in those portions of the plants.

Population estimates of Desmona bethula revealed that 14-16% of the population migrated on any one night but that a different segment migrated the following night. All or nearly all of the population may depend on terrestrial feeding at a critical stage in its life cycle. Fifth instar larvae had high densities, $1220/m^2$ and $1662/m^2$ in optimum stream sections. It may be that D. bethula reaches high numbers

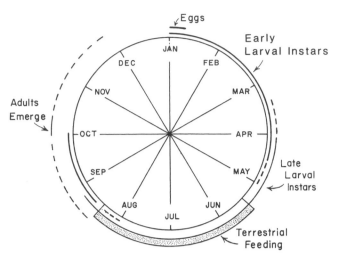

Desmona bethula (larvae terrestrial)

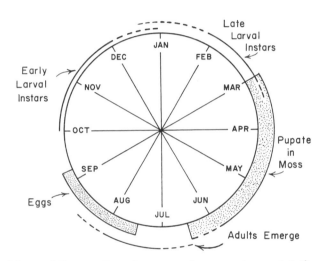

Limnephilus peltus (eggs and pupae terrestrial)

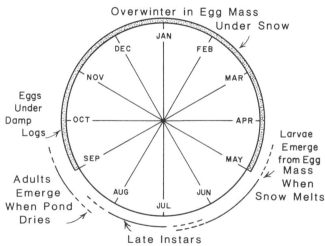

Lenarchus rillus (eggs terrestrial)

Figure 1.--Life cycle of three Trichoptera (Limnephilidae) in the Sagehen Creek basin (Nevada County, Calif.) showing aquatic and terrestrial periods.

178

Figure 2.--The caddisfly larva, <u>Desmona</u> <u>bethula</u> (Trichoptera:Limnephilidae) feeding at night on emergent vegetation (<u>Carex</u> spp.). Photo by Jerry Morse.

because it can leave the stream and use a food source unavailable to other aquatic insects.

Another group of caddisfly larvae, <u>Crypto</u><u>chia</u> spp. (Limnephilidae) has been found on wet wood and leaves at the water's edge as well as in the water (Wiggins 1977). <u>Psychoglypha</u> spp. (Limnephilidae) have been observed at the edge of spring-streams in the Sagehen Creek basin, Sierra Nevada, feeding on <u>Veronica</u> <u>americana</u> (N.A. Erman unpublished).

Some species of <u>Lepidostoma</u> (Trichoptera: Lepidostomatidae) are found only along the very edges of streams in the roots of sedges and other aquatic plants. These species are rarely if ever collected in open water. They use root material in their cases and may feed on it (N.A. Erman unpublished). Also <u>Onocosmoecus</u> spp. (Trichoptera:Limnephilidae) live along stream edges and feed on decaying grass that bends into the stream (Wiggins 1977).

There are other caddisflies, particularly in the family Limnephilidae, that live in springs, seeps, temporary streams, and along the edges of larger streams in California, and probably use the riparian zone as a food source. The Limnephilidae is a highly diverse family, important in California because it is dominant at higher ele-

vations in the Nearctic region. The above are only given as examples and should not be considered an inclusive list.

Many of the aquatic and semiaquatic Lepidoptera larvae feed on cattail (<u>Typha</u> spp.), bulrush (<u>Scirpus</u> spp.) or other vascular hydrophytes (Lange 1978). Also some of the aquatic Diptera larvae and some of the aquatic Coleoptera feed on living vascular plant tissue (Doyen and Ulrich 1978; Merritt and Schlinger 1978) though usually the plants are hydrophytes and might not be strictly riparian.

Adult stoneflies (Plecoptera) live on streamside vegetation where species of several families (Taeniopterygidae, Nemouridae, Capniidae, Chloroperlidae, some Perlodidae) feed on epiphytic algae or young leaves and buds (Harper 1978; Jewett 1963; Brinck 1949).

PUPATION OUTSIDE THE WATER

All the Megaloptera and aquatic Neuroptera leave the water to pupate on land, usually very close to the water. The alderflies (Megaloptera: Sialidae) burrow into soil along the bank (Azam and Anderson 1969). The dobsonflies and fishflies (Megaloptera:Corydalidae) pupate either in the soil or in decaying shoreline trees or stumps. And the spongillaflies (Neuroptera: Sisyridae) spin silk cocoons usually located in protected terrestrial sites near shore (Evans 1978).

In the Trichoptera terrestrial pupation is the exception but seems to have evolved as an adaptation to life in intermittent streams. Caddisfly larvae leave the water in the final instar and pupate on land as the water evaporates. Examples are <u>Ironoquia</u> <u>parvula</u> (Limnephilidae) (Ross 1944; Flint 1958), <u>I.</u> <u>punctatissima</u> (Williams and Williams 1975), and <u>I. lyrata</u> (Mackay unpublished).

<u>Limnephilus</u> <u>peltus</u> (Limnephilidae) leave spring-streams shortly after snowmelt in the Sagehen Creek basin and burrow into moss along the stream edges in the fens (fig. 1). In dry years when spring flow recedes and moss dries out early, some pupae die befor emerging (N.A. Erman upublished).

Nearly all aquatic Tipulidae (Diptera) leave the water to pupate in nearby soil, moss or litter (Byers 1978), and pupation is terrestrial in almost all species of aquatic Coleoptera (Leech and Chandler 1956; Pennak 1978). Usually they pupate in cells excavated by larvae under stones or logs. The Gyrinidae make mud cells on aquatic vegetation (Doyen and Ulrich 1978).

ADULT EMERGENCE AND MATING
IN THE RIPARIAN ZONE

By the very fact of emerging from the water most aquatic insects "use" the riparian zone, at least for resting, but in some the use is more specific than in others.

The mayflies (Ephemeroptera) emerge from the water as subimagoes (winged adults but sexually immature). They may perch on streamside vegetation for only a few minutes or for as long as 48 hours (about 24 hours for most species) before molting to the imago (Day 1963; Edmunds et al. 1976).

Adults of the dragonfly genus Aeshna (Odonata:Aeshnidae) tend to hang in the shade on the underside of leaves of trees in hot weather (Smith and Pritchard 1963).

Males of some Plecoptera wait on the shoreline for females to emerge. They drum on dry leaves, rocks, and moss by striking their abdomen on the substrate apparently to attract females. Mating takes place on the ground (Brinck 1949).

Adult caddisflies, Desmona bethula, fly up into lodgepole pines (Pinus contorta) along streams and peatlands immediately upon emerging from the water (Erman 1981). This same behavior has been observed in Heteroplectron californica (Trichoptera:Calamoceratidae), and Limnephilus peltus is known to mate on lodgepole pines near wetlands (N.A. Erman unpublished).

Several families of aquatic Diptera fly in mating swarms above vegetation, and most adults of aquatic Diptera use riparian vegetation or ground near the water as resting sites (Merritt and Schlinger 1976).

EGG LAYING IN THE RIPARIAN ZONE

Eggs of aquatic insects laid outside the water must have a mechanism for entering the water either as an egg or as a newly hatched larva. Therefore, they must be close to the water, often on overhanging vegetation.

Some species of Odonata attach their eggs onto plant stems, while others deposit them in plant tissue above drying ponds where they do not hatch until the ponds are refilled (Westfall 1978). Certain damselflies use emergent vegetation in another way during egg laying. The male clings to a plant, grasps the female by the prothorax with his terminal abdominal appendages, and lowers her into the water while she deposits eggs (Smith and Pritchard 1963).

All of the Megaloptera and aquatic Neuroptera lay their eggs out of water, often on leaves or branches overhanging the water. Eggs hatch and larvae fall or crawl into the water (Gurney and Parfin 1959; Azam and Anderson 1969).

Several Trichoptera species lay eggs outside the water, and as in the case of terrestrial pupation, it seems often to be another adaptation to drying conditions. Eggs are laid along the

edges of drying streams and ponds, often under damp logs. Larvae hatch but remain in the gelatinous egg mass until the stream or pond is reflooded (Novak and Sehnal 1963; Wiggins 1973; Wiggins et al. 1980). An example of this adaptation is known for Lenarchus rillus in the Sierra Nevada (N.A. Erman unpublished), shown in figure 1.

In other Trichoptera species the gelatinous egg masses are laid on stems above the water. When the larvae hatch and become active the gelatinous matrix thins, liquifies, and flows down the stem into the water (Wiggins 1973).

The female of Yphria californica (Trichoptera:Phryganeidae) swims underwater and attaches egg masses to the underside of over-hanging moss in small streams in the Sierra Nevada (N.A. Erman unpublished).

It is highly likely that as caddisfly behavior is studied in more specific detail, other species with aquatic/terrestrial adaptations may be revealed because Trichoptera is an order in which several members have reinvaded the land as larvae (Tomaszewski 1973; Mackay and Wiggins 1978; Erman 1981).

Beetles of some of the aquatic and semi-aquatic families, i.e. Dytiscidae, Helodidae, Georyssidae, Heteroceridae, Hydraenidae; oviposit in wet, shoreline places (Leech and Chandler 1963; Doyen and Ulrich 1978).

Aquatic Diptera often attach eggs to rocks or aquatic vegetation (Teskey 1978). Some of the Simuliidae oviposit on wet surfaces such as grass trailing in the water (Peterson 1978), and Chironomidae deposit gelatinous egg masses on emergent substrates or vegetation (Coffman 1978). The aquatic Diptera, like the Trichoptera, is an ecologically diverse and understudied group that will no doubt reveal more aquatic/terrestrial interactions when it is further investigated.

MANAGEMENT IMPLICATIONS

It is evident from the foregoing discussion that disturbance in the riparian zone will ultimately affect the large and varied group of aquatic insects present in any reasonably healthy stream or lake. Aquatic insects have intricate life cycles which if interrupted at any point may mean the disappearance or reduction of a given species in a given area. While many insects have life cycles with great flexibility, enabling them to respond to environmental conditions, i.e. diapause which delays development of an egg, larva, pupa, or adult until conditions are favorable, it must be remembered that such flexibility has evolved over long periods in response to gradually changing conditions. Such activities as channeling streams, logging, building dams, grazing livestock, drawing water out of streams, and putting in riprap have the potential for sudden interference with life cycles.

Dams are so disruptive to all stream life that there is no point in discussing them in this context. The effects of logging on stream life are being considered elsewhere (Mahoney and Erman 1981).

An insect that needs soil along a bank for a pupation chamber will not find it in a channelized stream or one with riprapped banks. Larvae that must immediately drop into water upon hatching may be eliminated if vegetation is destroyed because adults will not find suitable egg-laying sites. It is worth noting that Desmona bethula, the first caddisfly larva known to migrate daily from the water to feed, was found in a study area where grazing has been eliminated for many years. Its habitat, spring-stream in peatlands, is also a favorite of livestock in the Sierra Nevada. It may be no coincidence that these larvae have never been reported from any other area.

The more we know about life cycles, behavior, and feeding habits of individual species of aquatic insects, the more accurate can be our predictions on the effects of changes in the riparian zone. It is already clear that the riparian zone and aquatic insects are connected in an inseparable and intricate web of relationships.

ACKNOWLEDGEMENTS

I thank Don C. Erman for reviewing the manuscript and Jerry Morse for photographic work.

LITERATURE CITED

Anderson, N.H., and K.W. Cummins. 1979. Influences of diet on the life histories of aquatic insects. J. Fish. Res. Board Can. 36:335-342.

Azam, K.M., and N.H. Anderson. 1969. Life history and habits of Sialis rotunda and S. californica in western Oregon. Ann. Ent. Soc. Am. 62:549-558.

Brinck, P. 1949. Studies on Swedish stoneflies. Opusc. Ent. Suppl. 11:1-250.

Byers, G.W. 1978. Tipulidae. p. 285-310. In: R.W. Merritt and K.W. Cummins (ed.). An introduction to the aquatic insects of North America. 441 p. Kendall/Hunt Publ. Co., Dubuque, Iowa.

Chapman, D.W., and R.L. Demory. 1963. Seasonal changes in the food ingested by aquatic insect larvae and nymphs in two Oregon streams. Ecology 44:140-146.

Coffman, W.P. 1978. Chironomidae. p. 345-376. In: R.W. Merritt and K.W. Cummins (ed.). An introduction to the aquatic insects of North America. 441 p. Kendall/Hunt Publ. Co., Dubuque, Iowa.

Cummins, K.W. 1973. Trophic relations of aquatic insects. Ann. Rev. Ent. 18:183-206.

Day, W.C. 1963. Ephemeroptera. p. 79-105. In: R.L. Usinger (ed.). Aquatic insects of California. 508 p. University of California Press, Berkeley, Calif.

Doyen, J.T., and G. Ulrich. 1978. Aquatic Coleoptera. p. 203-231. In: R.W. Merritt and K.W. Cummins (ed.). An introduction to the aquatic insects of North America. 441 p. Kendall/Hunt Publ. Co., Dubuque, Iowa.

Edmunds, G.F., Jr., S.L. Jensen, and L. Berner. 1976. The mayflies of North and Central America. 330 p. University of Minnesota Press, Minn.

Erman, D.C., and N.A. Erman. 1975. Macroinvertebrate composition and production in some Sierra Nevada minerotrophic peatlands. Ecology 56:591-603.

Erman, N.A. 1981. Terrestrial feeding migration and life history of the stream-dwelling caddisfly, Desmona bethula (Trichoptera: Limnephilidae). Can. J. Zool. 59:1658-1665.

Evans, E.D. 1978. Megaloptera and aquatic Neuroptera. p. 133-145. In: R.W. Merritt and K.W. Cummins (ed.). An introduction to the aquatic insects of North America. 441 p. Kendall/Hunt Publ. Co., Dubuque, Iowa.

Flint, O.S. 1958. The larva and terrestrial pupa of Ironoquia parvula (Trichoptera: Limnephilidae). J. New York Entomol. Soc. 66:59-62.

Gurney, A.B., and S. Parfin. 1959. Neuroptera. p. 973-980. In: W.T. Edmondson (ed.). Freshwater biology (2nd ed.). 1248 p. Wiley, New York.

Harper, P.P. 1978. Plecoptera. p. 105-118. In: R.W. Merritt and K.W. Cummins (ed.). An introduction to the aquatic insects of North America. 441 p. Kendall/Hunt Publ. Co., Dubuque, Iowa.

Hynes, H.B.N. 1975. The stream and its valley. Verh. Internat. Verein. Limnol. 19:1-15.

Jewett, S.G., Jr. 1963. Plecoptera. p. 155-181. In: R.L. Usinger (ed.). Aquatic insects of California. 508 p. University of California Press, Berkeley, Calif.

Kaushik, N.K., and H.B.N. Hynes. 1971. The fate of dead leaves that fall into streams. Arch. Hydrobiol. 68:465-515.

Lange, W.H. 1978. Aquatic and semiaquatic Lepidoptera. p. 187-201. In: R.W. Merritt and K.W. Cummins (ed.). An introduction to the aquatic insects of North America. 441 p. Kendall/Hunt Publ. Co., Dubuque, Iowa.

Leech, H.B., and H.P. Chandler. 1963. Aquatic Coleoptera. p. 293-371. In: R.L. Usinger (ed.). Aquatic insects of California. 508 p. University of California Press, Berkeley, Calif.

Mackay, R.J., and G.B. Wiggins. 1979. Ecological diversity in Trichoptera. Ann. Rev. Entomol. 24:185-208.

Mahoney, D., and D.C. Erman. 1983. The role of streamside bufferstrips in the ecology of aquatic insects. In: R.E. Warner and K.M. Hendrix (ed.). [University of California, Davis, September 17-19, 1981]. University of California Press, Berkeley.

Mecom, J.O. 1972. Feeding habits of Trichoptera in a mountain stream. Oikos 23:401-407.

Merritt, R.W., and K.W. Cummins. 1978. An introduction to the aquatic insects of North America. 441 p. Kendall/Hunt Publ. Co., Dubuque, Iowa.

Merritt, R.W., and E.I. Schlinger. 1978. Aquatic Diptera. Part two: adults of aquatic Diptera. p. 259-283. In: R.W. Merritt and K.W. Cummins (ed.). An introduction to the aquatic insects of North America. 441 p. Kendall/Hunt Publ. Co., Dubuque, Iowa.

Minshall, G.W. 1978. Autotrophy in stream ecosystems. BioScience 28:767-771.

Novak, K., and F. Sehnal. 1963. The development cycle of some species of the genus Limnephilus (Trichoptera). Cas. Csl. Spol. Ent. 60:68-80.

Pennak, R.W. 1978. Freshwater invertebrates of the United States, second edition. 803 p. John Wiley & Sons, New York.

Peterson, B.V. 1978. Simuliidae. p. 331-344. In: R.W. Merritt and K.W. Cummins (ed.). An introduction to the aquatic insects of North America. 441 p. Kendall/Hunt Publ. Co., Dubuque, Iowa.

Ross, H.H. 1944. The caddis flies, or Trichoptera, of Illinois. Bull. Ill. Nat. Hist. Survey 23(1):1-326.

Ross, H.H. 1963. Stream communities and terrestrial biomes. Arch. Hydrobiol. 59:235-242.

Smith, R.F., and A.E. Pritchard. 1963. Odonata. p. 106-153. In: R.L. Usinger (ed.). Aquatic insects of California. 508 p. University of California Press, Berkeley, Calif.

Teskey, H.J. 1978. Aquatic Diptera. Part one: larvae of aquatic Diptera. p. 245-257. In: R.W. Merritt and K.W. Cummins (ed.). An introduction to the aquatic insects of North America. 441 p. Kendall/Hunt Publ. Co., Dubuque, Iowa.

Tomaszewski, C. 1973. Studies on the adaptive evolution of the larvae of Trichoptera. Acta Zool. Cracoviensia 18:311-398.

Vannote, R.L., G.W. Minshall, K.W. Cummins, J.R. Sedell, and C.E. Cushing. 1980. The river continuum concept. Can. J. Fish. Aquat. Sci. 37:130-137.

Westfall, M.J., Jr. 1978. Odonata. p. 81-98. In: R.W. Merritt and K.W. Cummins (ed.). An introduction to the aquatic insects of North America. 441 p. Kendall/Hunt Publ. Co., Dubuque, Iowa.

Wiggins, G.B. 1973. A contribution to the biology of caddisflies (Trichoptera) in temporary pools. Life Sci. Contr., Roy. Ont. Mus. 88:1-28.

Wiggins, G.B. 1977. Larvae of the North American caddisfly genera (Trichoptera). 401 p. University of Toronto Press, Toronto.

Wiggins, G.B., R.J. Mackay, and I.M. Smith. 1980. Evolutionary and ecological strategies of animals in annual temporary pools. Archiv. fur Hydrobiologie Suppl. 58:97-206.

Williams, D.D., and N.E. Williams. 1975. A contribution to the biology of Ironoquia punctatissima (Trichoptera:Limnephilidae). Can. Ent. 107:829-832.

Winterbourn, M.J. 1971. An ecological study of Banksoila crotchi Banks (Trichoptera: Phryganeidae) in Marion Lake, British Columbia. Can. J. Zool. 49:637-645.

THE INFLUENCE OF RIPARIAN VEGETATION ON STREAM

FISH COMMUNITIES OF CALIFORNIA[1]

Donald M. Baltz and Peter B. Moyle[2]

Abstract.--The direct and indirect interactions between native stream fishes and riparian vegetation of central California are reviewed. The relationships between riparian vegetation and temperature and cover are shown to have a number of effects on the composition of stream fish communities.

INTRODUCTION

Fishes are not usually considered as part of riparian communities. Yet they interact directly with such communities in many ways, such as feeding on terrestrial insects, using overhanging plants as cover, or using flooded vegetation for spawning. Even more important are indirect interactions through nutrient cycling and through effects of riparian vegetation on flows and temperatures. Since the human impact upon riparian systems is still increasing, knowledge of the relationship between riparian systems and fish communities is needed to permit effective management of the fish communities.

A fish community is defined broadly here as the assemblage of fishes generally associated with a given geographic location. In central California such assemblages in undisturbed situations show considerable annual fluctuation in composition, yet show a long-term persistence in structure (Moyle et al. in press). However, the composition at any given time (or place) is determined in a good part by the differential response of each species to variation in the physical characteristics of the habitats. The most important physical parameters to fish are generally identified as stream depth, current velocity, substrate composition, cover, and temperature. All of these factors, and some others as well, can be changed when the riparian community is altered. Consequently the fish communities are likely to change as well. Riparian systems affect instream fish communities because they are the parts of stream ecosystems that tie together the aquatic and terrestrial components, through energy exchange, interaction with flow regimes, and impact on temperature regimes. The purpose of this paper is to review these interactions and to demonstrate how alteration of riparian systems can cause changes in the fish communities of California streams.

ENERGY EXCHANGE

While the energy input in streams is ultimately photosynthetic in origin, it can enter the stream either from the surrounding vegetation or from producers within the stream. The relative importance of these two sources of energy varies from stream to stream and is the subject of some debate (Naiman and Sedell 1980). Regardless of source, this input eventually reaches fishes directly as detritus or indirectly through the aquatic food chain (Cummins 1974). In low-order streams the immature stages of aquatic insects, together with microbes, process coarse particulate organic matter (CPOM) into consumer biomass which becomes available to predators and fine particulate organic matter (FPOM) which is exported downstream where it is further processed. Other important energy inputs to the stream include aquatic insects that graze on riparian vegetation (Erman 1981) and terrestrial insects that are consumed by fish. In low-order streams the canopy decreases light penetration and temperature, and provides the CPOM in the form of leaves, twigs, and branches which form snags or packs. Overhanging vegetation, submerged root masses, aquatic macrophytes, and debris (CPOM) provide cover for fishes (Hynes 1970; Westlake 1975).

Flow regime and solar radiation interact with riparian canopy to determine stream temperature; reduction or removal of the canopy increases stream temperature, reduces the input of CPOM and increases the importance of primary producers within the stream. Generally, increased temperature and increased primary production in a small stream are likely to increase

---

[1] Paper presented at the California Riparian Systems Conference. [University of California, Davis, September 17-19, 1981].

[2] Donald M. Baltz is a Postdoctoral Research Associate in Wildlife and Fisheries Biology, University of California, Davis. Peter B. Moyle is Associate Professor of Wildlife and Fisheries Biology, University of California, Davis.

aquatic insect production and consequently fish production. The increase in fish production is most likely to be in nongame fish, such as the native minnows and suckers, which have higher temperature tolerances. However, Burns (1972) indicates that salmon and trout production in California streams may increase in some situations where the riparian forest is thinned by careful logging.

FLOW REGIME

Variation in stream flow may affect fish populations directly by changing the amount and quality of instream habitat available to fishes, or indirectly through interactions with the riparian community. Indirect effects of natural or unnatural variation in stream flow include changing the temperature, substrate, or availability of cover. At flood stage the water flowing through the riparian vegetation is slowed enough to provide refuge to fishes from excessively high velocities. During low flow, the riparian vegetation may further reduce flows through water removal via transpiration. Transpiration rates by riparian vegetation along small streams at low elevations may be high enough that flows become intermittent during late summer, confining the fish to isolated pools. Natural variation in stream flow strikes a long-term balance in riparian communities, whereas reduced and stabilized flows often result in drastically modified systems. In small, regulated streams the encroaching riparian vegetation may reduce stream width and shade the stream enough to significantly reduce production. The best known local example of riparian modification resulting from stabilized flows is the Trinity River, Trinity County. Following completion of the Lewiston Dam in 1965, the salmonid fishery in the Trinity River declined drastically due to low stabilized streamflow. This unnatural flow regime increased sedimentation and permitted riparian vegetation encroachment into the stream-bed, including areas once important for salmon spawning (Fraser 1972; Hoffman 1980). The negative effects of water diversion by Lewiston Dam were accentuated by logging and road construction in the drainage below the dam.

COVER

One of the more important ways variation in flow regulates fish populations is by moderating the availability of cover needed for protection against predators. Quantifying the importance of cover is difficult, however, because each species and each life history stage within a species is likely to have different cover requirements. For many fishes, but especially adult life history stages of larger species, instream cover is usually adequate: deep pools, the irregular surface of a riffle, or large boulders. However, the complex cover provided by overhanging or submerged riparian vegetation, including dead trees, or by beds of aquatic macrophytes seems to

be particularly important to young-of-year fish, to small active species, and to life history stages of larger fishes that need special protection from predators. Thus the small (3-5 cm. standard length (SL)) threespine stickleback (Gasterosteus aculeatus) are absent from pools containing Sacramento squawfish (Ptychocheilus grandis) unless complex cover is available to them (Smith in press). Similarly, the poor reproductive success of many fishes during low-water years may be due to the absence of suitable rearing habitat for their young when the riparian edge of a stream, which provides most of the complex cover, is dry. For larger fish, the importance of riparian vegetation as cover lies not only in the physical refuges created but in the shade. Helfman (1980) has demonstrated that fish holding in shaded areas are not only less visible to underwater predators, but can usually see the predators before the predators see them. However, too much shade by tall trees can have a negative effect on fishes by reducing the complex cover created by smaller riparian plants.

The importance of complex cover to fishes is reflected in the life history adaptations of the tule perch (Hysterocarpus traski), a species we have studied intensively (Baltz 1980; Baltz and Moyle 1981). The tule perch is a viviparous fish endemic to central California. Three subspecies have been recognized. Each of these has different life history characteristics which reflect the relative predictability of availability of complex cover for parturating females and for young. Essentially, female longevity and length at first reproduction vary directly with environmental predictability, while the number of young produced per female varies inversely.

In Clear Lake, Lake County, the subspecies H. t. lagunae has the longest life span; is largest when reproducing for the first time; and has the fewest young per female (but the young are larger than those of other subspecies). This seems to be largely the result of the constant availability of cover for pregnant females (which have reduced swimming abilities due to their distended abdomens) and for their young. This cover consists of submerged riparian vegetation and tule beds during high-water years, and beds of aquatic macrophytes in low-water years.

In contrast, the tule perch of the Russian River drainage (H. t. pomo) has the shortest life span, produces young at the smallest adult size, and produces comparatively large numbers of small young per female. This reflects the highly unpredictable nature of the flow regime of the Russian River, a coastal stream whose water level rises and falls with the seasonal rains and is not buffered (as are streams draining the Sierra) by snowmelt. As a consequence, adequate cover for females and young--mainly submerged trees and bushes--is available only on an irregular basis. Thus it is advantageous for each female to produce as many young as possible to exploit those times when the cover is available.

The third subspecies (H. t. traski) is found in the streams, rivers, and sloughs of the Sacramento Valley. As might be expected, its life history characteristics are intermediate between those of the Clear Lake and Russian River populations, reflecting the less extreme nature of the fluctuations in flows than in the Russian River and the more consistent availability of the complex cover they need for successful reproduction. Curiously, this subspecies seems to benefit from the stabilization of flows characteristic of the lower Sacramento and American Rivers, presumably because complex cover is consistently available. Even so, in the lower American River, tule perch are a major prey of striped bass (Morone saxatilis), an exotic species (Dehaven 1978).

TEMPERATURE

The shade created by riparian vegetation is effective in reducing summer maximum temperatures and in diminishing daily temperature variation. The importance of this phenomenon to the fish communities of central California is illustrated by two of our recent studies of species interactions: one on sculpins and dace, and one on suckers and trout.

Temperature modifies interactions between riffle sculpin (Cottus gulosus) and the speckled dace (Rhinichthys osculus) in Deer Creek, Tehama County, California.[3] Deer Creek is a western slope Sierra foothill stream. After leaving a steep-sided canyon, Deer Creek flows 12.5 km. (8 mi.) through low rolling hills to the Sacramento River. However, temperature differences between the upper and lower riffles in this section are substantial (fig. 1). Between the canyon and the river, the stream warms rapidly during the warm season. Just 9.7 km. (6 mi.) from the canyon mouth, the riffles are occupied exclusively by speckled dace. But only 6.4 km. (4 mi.) upstream, riffle sculpin occupy the riffles exclusively and the speckled dace are displaced to slower waters. Within this study area there are no significant differences in the microhabitat parameters (mean water column velocity, stream depth, and substrate) utilized by dace and sculpin.

Between the lower and upper riffles there is a highly significant negative correlation between the relative abundances of the two species (r = -0.86, P < 0.01). Warm summer temperatures exceed the tolerance of riffle sculpin in the lowermost reaches, but where temperatures are cooler riffle sculpin apparently aggressively force dace out of their preferred habitat. The riparian vegetation in the study area is only a relict of its historical expanse (Roberts, Howe,

---

[3]Baltz, D.M., P.B. Moyle, and N.J. Knight. Competitive interactions between benthic stream fishes, riffle sculpin, Cottus gulosus and speckled dace, Rhinichthys osculus. Unpublished manuscript.

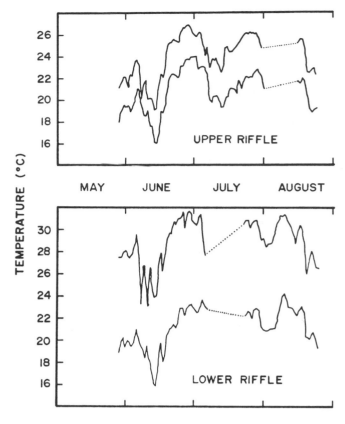

Figure 1.--Daily minimum and maximum stream temperatures in two reaches of Deer Creek, Tehama County, California, 1981.

and Major 1977), and the downstream range of riffle sculpin has probably been restricted by the resulting warmer stream temperatures.

The second example involves two rather similar Sierra streams which differ physically mainly in temperature regimes.[4] Eleanor Creek, Tuolumne County, is controlled by an older dam which discharges warm water from the epilimnion during the summer, whereas Cherry Creek, Tuolumne County, is controlled by a newer dam which discharges cooler water from the hypolimnion. Cherry Creek is also more shaded by riparian vegetation than Eleanor Creek. Summer temperatures in Eleanor Creek are higher and less variable than in Cherry Creek (fig. 2). Both streams have healthy rainbow trout (Salmo gairdneri) populations, but Sacramento suckers (Catostomus occidentalis) are found only in Eleanor Creek and in Cherry Creek below its confluence with Eleanor Creek. Suckers are absent from the cold upper sections of Cherry Creek, despite their presence in a reservoir above the section. Both the sculpin/dace example and the sucker/trout example demonstrate how relatively minor changes in temperature can cause major changes in fish communities. The temperature changes studied are well within the changes

---

[4]Moyle, P.B. and D.M. Baltz. Unpublished data.

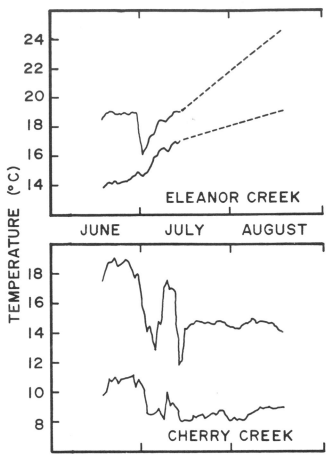

Figure 2.--Daily minimum and maximum stream temperatures in comparable reaches of Eleanor and Cherry Creeks, Tuolumne County, California, 1981.

possible on a stream through removal of a dense canopy.

FISH COMMUNITIES

Recent studies of the distribution patterns of central California fishes indicate that distinct habitat conditions are usually associated with distinct fish communities (see review in Moyle et al. in press). These studies indicate that both the type and amount of riparian vegetation often have a strong association with different fish communities. For example, Taylor et al. (in press) studied fish communities in streams of the Clear Lake drainage. The fish communities dominated by rainbow trout were found mainly in densely shaded streams surrounded by coniferous forest, while communities dominated by native nongame species were associated with chaparral or foothill woodland plant communities, where cottonwood and sycamore are common riparian trees.

In the Pit River drainage, Shasta County, Moyle and Daniels (in press) found that fish communities dominated by non-native fishes were associated with streams in which the riparian canopy was small or absent. The absence of a significant canopy was generally an indication of a degraded stream. Similarly, Moyle and Nichols (1973, 1974) studied the zonal distribution of Sierra foothill fishes in the San Joaquin Valley. The Introduced Species association (mainly centrarchids and cyprinids) has apparently displaced the Native Cyprinid-Catostomid association (mainly hardhead, Sacramento squawfish, and Sacramento sucker) from low-level streams which have been extensively modified by man. The introduced association was typically found in pools in reaches which lacked shade, had large amounts of aquatic vegetation, and had muddy-sandy bottoms. The native association persisted in reaches which were often sparsely shaded but contained little evidence of human modification. The rainbow trout was found mainly by itself in the densely shaded upper reaches of these streams.

GENERAL DISCUSSION

Although we have treated energy flow, cover, and stream temperature as separate topics, they are intricately interrelated. Seemingly harmless modifications in one aspect of the riparian or stream ecosystem may have severe repercussions elsewhere. There is a large literature on the effects of human disturbance of riparian and stream ecosystems by logging (Hansmann and Phinney 1973; Newbold, Erman, and Roby 1980); road building (Burns 1972); water diversion and impoundment (Ward and Stanford 1979); channelization and bank stabilization (Moyle 1976; Stern and Stern 1980a,b); clearing and snagging (Marzolf 1978; Bilby and Likens 1980); and grazing (Cope 1979). The alterations of the natural systems reviewed in these studies (and here) clearly result in changes in fish habitats, changes generally recorded as negative. These habitat changes, even seemingly minor changes, can have major effects on the composition of fish communities. It is also clear, however, that our understanding of the interactions between fishes and riparian communities is incomplete and that more attention needs to be paid to them in the future.

LITERATURE CITED

Baltz, D.M. 1980. Age-specific reproductive tactics and reproductive effort in the tule perch (Hysterocarpus traski). Ph.D. dissertation, University of California, Davis. 85 p.

Baltz, D.M., and P.B. Moyle. 1981. Morphometric analysis of tule perch (Hysterocarpus traski) populations in three isolated drainages. Copeia 1981(2):305-311.

Bilby, R.E., and G.E. Likens. 1980. Importance of organic debris dams in the structure and function of stream ecosystems. Ecology 61(5):1107-1113.

Burns, J.W. 1972. Some effects of logging and associated road construction on northern California streams. Trans. Amer. Fish. Soc. 101(1):1-17.

Cope, O.B. (ed.). 1979. Proceedings of the forum: grazing and riparian stream ecosystems. Trout Unlimited, Inc. 94 p.

Cummins, K.W. 1974. Structure and function of stream ecosystems. Bioscience 24(11):631-641.

Dehaven, R.W. 1978. An angling study of striped bass ecology in the American River, California. Annual Progress Report No. 3. P.O. box C, Davis, California. 36 p.

Fraser, J.C. 1972. Regulated discharge and the stream environment. p. 263-285. In: R.T. Oglesby, C.A. Carlson, and J.A. McCann (ed.). River ecology and man. Academic Press, New York.

Hansmann, E.W., and H.K. Phinney. 1973. Effects of logging on periphyton in coastal streams of Oregon. Ecology 54(1):194-199.

Helfman, G.S. 1981. The advantage to fishes of hovering in the shade. Copeia 1981(2):392-399.

Hoffman, J.P. 1980. Trinity River instream flow study. Lewiston Dam to the North Fork. Final report of the USDI Fish and Wildlife Service. Sacramento, California. 48 p.

Hynes, H.B.N. 1970. The ecology of running waters. Univ. Toronto Press, Toronto.

Marzolf, G.R. 1978. The potential effects of clearing and snagging on stream ecosystems. Biological Services Program FWS/OBS-78/14. 31 p.

Moyle, P.B. 1976. Some effects of channelization on the fishes and invertebrates of Rush Creek, Modoc County, California. Calif. Fish and Game 62(3):179-186.

Moyle, P.B., and R.A. Daniels. (in press). Studies on the distribution and ecology of stream fishes of the Sacramento-San Joaquin drainage system, California. I. Fishes of the Pit River system, McCloud River system, and Surprise Valley region. University of California Pub. Zool.

Moyle, P.B., and R.D. Nichols. 1973. Ecology of some native and introduced fishes of the Sierra Nevada foothills in Central California. Copeia 1973(3):478-490.

Moyle, P.B., and R.D. Nichols. 1974. Decline of the native fish fauna of the Sierra Nevada foothills, Central California. Am. Mid. Nat. 92(1):72-83.

Moyle, P.B., J.J. Smith, R.A. Daniels, and D.M. Baltz. In press. Studies of the distribution and ecology of stream fishes of the Sacramento-San Joaquin drainage system, California. IV. A review. University of California Pub. Zool.

Naiman, R.J., and J.R. Sedell. 1980. Relationships between metabolic parameters and stream order in Oregon. Can. J. Fish. and Aquatic Sciences 37(5):834-847.

Newbold, J.D., D.L Erman, and K.B. Rody. 1980. Effects of logging on macroinvertebrates in streams with and without buffer strips. Can. J. Fish. and Aquatic Sciences 37(7):1076-1085.

Roberts, W.G., J.G. Howe, and J. Major. 1977. A survey of riparian forest flora and fauna in California. p. 3-19. In: A. Sands (ed.). Riparian forests in California: their ecology and conservation. Inst. of Ecology Publ. 15, University of California, Davis. 122 p.

Smith, J.J. In press. Studies on the distribution and ecology of stream fishes of the Sacramento-San Joaquin drainage system, California. II. Fishes of the Pajaro River system. University of California Pub. Zool.

Stern, D.H., and M.S. Stern. 1980a. Effects of bank stabilization on the physical and chemical characteristics of streams and small rivers: an annotated bibliograhy. Biological Services Program FWS/OBS-80/11. 77 p.

Stern, D.H., and M.S. Stern. 1980b. Effects of bank stabilization on the physical and chemical characteristics of streams and small rivers: a synthesis. Biological Services Program FWS/OBS-80/11. 42 p.

Taylor, T.L., P.B. Moyle, and D.G. Price. In press. Studies on the distribution and ecology of the stream fishes of Sacramento-San Joaquin drainage system, California. III. Fishes of the Clear Lake basin. University of California Pub. Zool.

Ward, J.V., and J.A. Stanford (ed.). 1979. The ecology of regulated streams. Plenum Press, New York.

Westlake, D.F. 1975. Macrophytes. p. 106-128. In: B.A. Whitton (ed.). River ecology. University of California Press, Berkeley. 725 p.

RIPARIAN BIRDS IN THE RIPARIAN/AGRICULTURAL INTERFACE[1]

Bertin W. Anderson, Robert D. Ohmart,
and Hubert A. Allen, Jr.[2]

Abstract.--The interface between riparian and agricultural systems supports relatively large numbers of bird species and individuals because it offers a variety of food and structural resources that are especially apparent in winter. The interface can be used to compensate effectively for loss of natural habitats by interspersing agricultural lands with native vegetation.

INTRODUCTION

Conflict between a growing demand for more agricultural land and the need to maintain natural riparian systems is occurring all along the lower Colorado River. As valuable wildlife habitat continues to be converted to agricultural land, an urgent need exists to identify and preserve representative riparian systems and to determine how agricultural management might mitigate losses of natural habitats. This paper addresses the second point through a study of avian populations along the interface between riparian vegetation and cultivated lands.

We tested to see if the riparian/agricultural interface, hereafter referred to simply as "interface", is a distinct ecological community. Four avian community parameters were examined quantitatively in interface situations: 1) species richness (number of species); 2) avian densities; 3) species turnover (stability of species composition); and 4) relative proportions of different feeding guilds. Significant differences in these four parameters between agricultural land and riparian areas were used to indicate "distinctiveness." Finally we identify the unique attributes of the interface that define its value to riparian wildlife.

[1]Paper presented at the California Riparian Systems Conference. [University of California, Davis, September 17-19, 1981].

[2]Bertin W. Anderson is Faculty Research Associate, Center for Environmental Studies, Arizona State University, Tempe, Arizona. Robert D. Ohmart is Associate Director, Center for Environmental Studies, Arizona State University, Tempe, Arizona. Hubert A. Allen, Jr. is Field Biologist, Center for Environmental Studies, Arizona State University, Tempe, Arizona.

METHODS

We censused each of eight riparian areas bordering agricultural cropland areas for two to three years between 1978 and 1980 using a modified Emlen technique (Emlen 1971, 1977; Anderson et al. 1977). Transects were located where relatively homogeneous stands of riparian vegetation adjoined agricultural fields. The interface transects had agricultural areas paralleling the transects on one side and riparian vegetation on the other. Two transects were located near Yuma, Arizona; two were on the Cibola National Wildlife Refuge near Palo Verde, California; and four were on the Colorado River Indian Reservation, between Ehrenberg and Parker, Arizona. Transects varied in length from 610 m. to 1,524 m.

Each transect was censused two or three times every month; results were averaged to obtain seasonal density estimates. Five seasons were considered: winter (December-February); spring (March-April); summer (May-July); late summer (August-September); and fall (October-November). These seasons reflect differences in the avian community as well as general climatic changes. The averaging of six to nine censuses minimized random variation inherent in the censusing method (Engel-Wilson et al. 1981).

Data for riparian vegetation were taken from Anderson and Ohmart (in preparation). Measurements in those vegetation-types of foliage density and diversity (MacArthur and MacArthur 1961), horizontal patchiness (Anderson et al. 1978), and tree and shrub densities were used to quantitatively characterize the vegetation of the transects. Crops in adjacent agricultural fields were noted when censuses were taken.

Bird species were classified as riparian if they occurred in riparian vegetation with some regularity (Conine et al. 1978). Riparian bird species were grouped into several feeding guilds based on general dietary habits. This grouping allowed us to examine the avian community in terms of a few functional components.

Changes in guild dominance within and between seasons indicated changes in community organization.

To calculate bird species turnover, a species list was compiled for each season by transect for each year. All riparian bird species were included except raptors, swallows, swifts, hummingbirds, very rare species, birds usually associated only with agricultural areas, and migrants. "Migrants" refers to those species which did not spend at least one of the five seasons; they were strictly transient in the area. These groups were excluded because they occurred rarely or inconsistently in riparian areas and their effects on the community were not clear. The resultant species list provided a conservative basis from which to calculate bird species turnover. A bird species "turned over" on a transect in a particular season if it was present one year and absent the next year, or vice versa. The species turnover rate was calculated as the mean number of turnovers per season divided by the mean number of species present per season.

The G-test and Mann-Whitney U-test were used in this analysis. These techniques were used to compare frequency ratios and nonparametric t-tests, respectively. Because the probability distribution function of avian species abundance is unknown, nonparametric analysis is recommended if values are to be compared (Siegel 1956; Sokal and Rolhf 1969). Mann-Whitney U-tests were used to compare numbers within each guild over the seasons. When using the Mann-Whitney U-test, two sets of abundance data were rank-ordered in a single array from highest to lowest. A test statistic was determined based on the ordering of the two samples. This statistic was compared to a theoretical distribution and a significance level was determined.

G-tests were used to test the goodness-of-fit of frequency ratios. The hypothesis tested is that frequency ratios between replicate samples are homogeneous. We determined which season was consistently the richest by ranking seasonal richness values on each transect. Seasons then formed replicate samples. A five-part ratio of highest to second highest, etc., richness was compiled for the seasons, and a G-statistic was calculated. A significant value indicated that richness ratios were not equal among seasons.

RESULTS

Riparian vegetation along the transects was composed primarily of salt cedar (Tamarix chinensis), arrowweed (Tessaria sericea), and quail bush (Atriplex lentiformis). Athel tamarisk (Tamarix aphylla), a tall, evergreen species, was dominant at Yuma; salt cedar, a smaller deciduous species occurred in the other areas. Honey mesquite (Prosopis glandulosa) and screwbean mesquite (Prosopis pubescens)

trees were present on Cibola National Wildlife Refuge (CA) and Colorado River Indian Reservation (CRIR) transects. CRIR transects had high densities of shrubs other than arrowweed. Major crops in agricultural fields adjacent to transects included alfalfa, wheat, cotton, and pasture; in some seasons fields were fallow or plowed.

Bird species richness in interface was similar to that reported by Conine et al. (1978). Bird species richness was higher in interface than in either salt cedar vegetation or agricultural areas in all seasons except spring (fig. 1). Species numbers in cottonwood/willow (Populus fremontii/Salix gooddingii) vegetation, usually the richest riparian system, were higher than in interface in every season except winter, when the two systems had similar numbers of bird species. Honey mesquite vegetation averaged more bird species than interface in all seasons except late summer.

Bird species richness in interface varied significantly between seasons ($P < 0.05$). In interface, species richness values for late summer, fall, and winter were similar; they were higher than for spring and summer (fig. 1).

Interface bird densities were higher than those in either riparian or agricultural systems in all seasons except spring. Spring also averaged a higher turnover rate (32%) than other seasons in interface (fig. 2). Approximately 24% of bird species turned over between years (table 1). Except for spring, seasonal turnover rates were similar.

Table 1.--Mean seasonal turnover rates in riparian/agricultural interface.

Season	N	Mean percent turnover	Standard deviation
Winter	8	23	6.4
Spring	4	32	13.4
Summer	4	24	6.7
Late summer	8	24	9.3
Fall	8	25	8.7
All seasons	8	24	6.6

Each avian guild showed distinct seasonal patterns of abundance (fig. 3). Numbers of resident insectivores were not significantly different from summer to winter, but spring densities were always lower ($P < 0.05$). Visiting insectivore densities showed a pattern similar to that of resident insectivores with significantly ($P < 0.05$) higher densities in fall and winter.

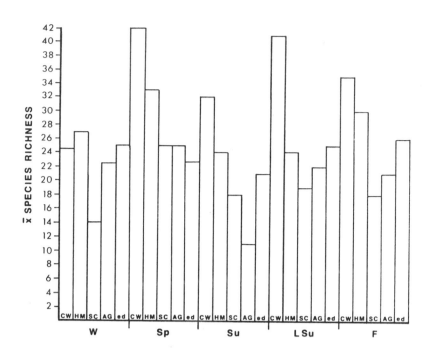

Figure 1.--Average species richness in riparian and agricultural (AG) systems of the lower Colorado River Valley. CW = cottonwood/willow; HM = honey mesquite; SC = salt cedar; ed = riparian/agricultural interface.

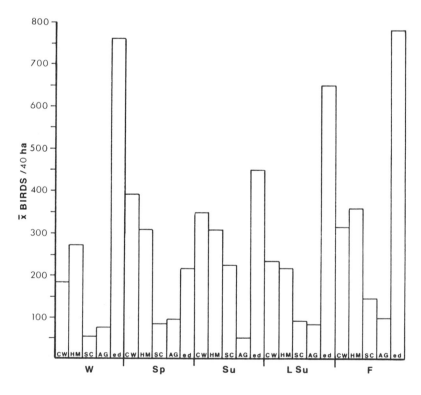

Figure 2.--Average densities in riparian and agricultural systems of the lower Colorado River Valley. Abbreviations as in figure 1. W = winter; Sp = spring; SU = summer; LSu = late summer; and F = fall.

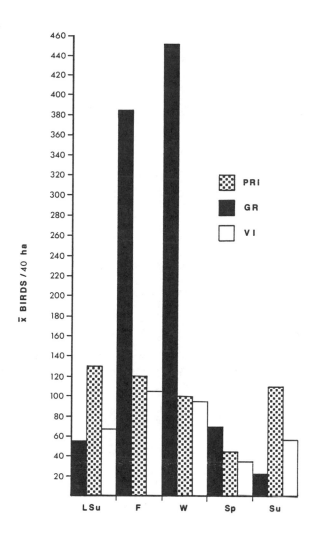

Figure 3.--Average densities in each feeding guild in the riparian/agricultural interface. PRI = permanent resident insectivores; VI = visiting insectivores; GR = granivores. Season abbreviations as in figure 2.

The relative proportion of individuals belonging to each feeding guild in interface also changed from season to season (fig. 4). Granivores were always proportionately dominant, but densities of species making up this group varied between seasons. The numbers of doves were highest in summer. Gambel Quail (Lophortyx gambelii) numbers were highest in late summer. Other granivores, which were mostly sparrows, had peak densities during winter. The proportion of visiting insectivores was relatively stable, constituting about 15% of total individuals throughout the year. Resident insectivores were proportionately fewer in winter.

DISCUSSION

Vegetation in the riparian/agricultural interface is often different from riparian vege-

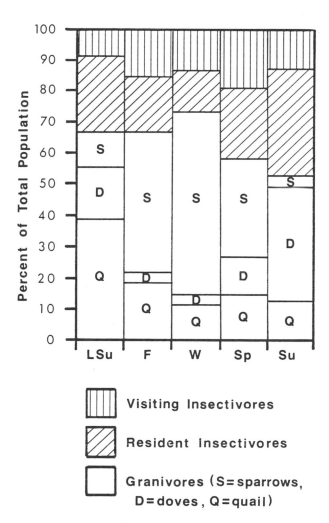

Visiting Insectivores

Resident Insectivores

Granivores (S = sparrows, D = doves, Q = quail)

Figure 4.--Proportion of total population in the riparian/agricultural interface belonging to each feeding guild in each season.

tation in both plant species composition and structure. Interface areas tend to be subject to change, and as a result are more heterogeneous than other vegetation-types. Shrubs, especially quail bush and inkweed (Suaeda torreyana), were more common in the interface than is usual in salt cedar stands. Quail bush shrubs have been shown to be related to increased bird densities in riparian systems (Anderson et al. 1978). These factors, as well as the juxtaposition of interface to agricultural fields, create a unique system.

Bird species richness and density comparisons indicate that when compared to salt cedar or agricultural systems, interface supported equal or greater numbers of birds in most seasons. Cottonwood/willow and honey mesquite vegetation-types are generally considered the most diverse and productive in the lower Colorado River Valley; interface was similar in richness to honey mesquite, but compared favorably to cottonwood/willow only in winter. Bird densities in interface exceeded those in all communities in every season except spring.

The primary factor accounting for relative species richness of interface compared to salt cedar or agriculture is probably related to the diverse resources that are available there. Agricultural lands provide a nearly constant supply of food in the form of seeds, plants, and insects. However, they provide relatively poor cover and offer few nest or perch sites. Trees and dense shrubs in interface supply abundant cover and vertical structure for nesting and other activities. Many bird species that reach high densities in interface, including Mourning Dove (Zenaida macroura), Gambel Quail, White-crowned Sparrow (Zonotrichia leucophrys), and Loggerhead Shrike (Lanius ludovicianus), forage in agriculture but return to interface for protection from predators, nesting, and perching. This situation is an example of "interface effect"; the interface between two systems (riparian and agricultural) is richer than either system alone because elements of both are combined.

Most riparian systems show avian density peaks between summer and fall, but interface supported greater numbers of birds in fall and winter. This is partly because many individuals disperse out of their preferred riparian areas after the breeding season (Anderson and Ohmart in press). However, the winter peak in bird densities in interface is probably most closely related to food resources, which are relatively high in agricultural areas during winter due to year-round growing of crops, and irrigation. Food resources in riparian areas are lowest in winter (ibid.).

The dominance of granivores in interface in all seasons indicates that large supplies of seeds are available throughout the year. Seed sources include shrubs and annuals in interface, weedy margins around fields, and agricultural crops. A significant portion of the avian community in interface in all seasons is insectivores, which indicates that insect food resources are abundant throughout the year.

All three feeding guilds showed decreased use of interface at some time during the breeding season, indicating that it may not be preferred when resources are abundant in other areas or when other considerations, such as nest sites, are important.

Not all riparian bird species reach higher densities in interface than in riparian areas (Conine et al. 1978), but some species clearly benefit from association with interface. This is demonstrated by the Greater Roadrunner (Geococcyx californianus) and the Loggerhead Shrike. Both species are top-level carnivores that eat rodents, reptiles, and small birds. Both species generally breed in areas other than interface or agriculture, but they are present in interface from fall through winter. At these seasons, Loggerhead Shrikes and Greater Roadrunners reached significantly (P < 0.05) higher densities in interface than in riparian vegetation. These high densities indicate that inter-face is particularly rich in resources compared to other areas. Rice et al. (in press) determined that approximately one-third of all bird species turned over between years in riparian vegetation; this turnover was statistically random across habitats. Our method was more conservative than that of Rice et al. (ibid.) because we eliminated some bird species from consideration. Had we used the same method, species turnover rates in riparian and interface areas would have been similar. Thus, the avian composition of interface communities is no more stable than that of riparian communities. Species turnover rates of over 20% suggest that there is some opportunism in the use of interface. Some bird species may use interface only when conditions in preferred areas are limiting.

CONCLUSIONS

The interface between agricultural areas and riparian vegetation supports relatively large numbers of bird species and individuals, presumably because it offers a variety of food and structural resources. This is especially apparent in winter, when resources in riparian areas decline. Because interface accommodates large bird populations at a time when resources in other areas may be scarce, interface may be critical in maintaining avian populations that normally inhabit riparian areas or migrate into the lower Colorado River Valley.

Interface can be used effectively to mitigate loss of natural habitat components by interspersing agricultural lands with native vegetation. This will benefit many bird species which utilize food resources associated with agricultural areas but require cover or other features provided by natural vegetation. Interface could also be important in integrated pest management to help reduce pesticide use and costs in agriculture, although there are strong feelings opposing this idea. Maintenance of interface will not compensate for habitat loss for species that are riparian specialists, such as Summer Tanager (Piranga rubra) or Yellow-billed Cuckoo (Coccyzus americanus). Protection of these species requires preservation or recreation of habitat in native riparian vegetation.

ACKNOWLEDGMENTS

The authors wish to thank Marcelett Ector for typing various drafts of the manuscript and Cindy D. Zisner for typing the final draft. Susan M. Cook and Jane R. Durham provided editorial assistance. Elaine Hassinger prepared the figures. We are grateful to the many field biologists who assisted in collecting data. The project was funded by the USDI Bureau of Reclamation through Contract Number 7-07-30-V0009.

LITERATURE CITED

Anderson, B.W., R.W. Engel-Wilson, D. Wells, and R.D. Ohmart. 1977. Ecological study of southwestern riparian habitats: techniques and data applicability. p. 146-155. In: R.R. Johnson and D.A. Jones (tech. coord.). Importance, preservation and management of riparian habitat: a symposium. [Tuscon, Arizona, July 9, 1977]. USDA Forest Service GTR-RM-43. 217 p. Rocky Mountain Forest and Range Experiment Station, Fort Collins, Colorado.

Anderson, B.W., and R.D. Ohmart. In preparation. Vegetation management. Annual report, 1981. USDI Bureau of Reclamation, Boulder City, Nevada.

Anderson, B.W., and R.D. Ohmart. In press. Evidence for social regulation in some riparian bird populations. Am. Nat. 120.

Anderson, B.W., R.D. Ohmart, and J. Disano. 1978. Revegetating the riparian floodplain for wildlife. p. 318-331. In: R.R. Johnson and J.F. McCormick (tech. coord.). Strategies for protection and management of floodplain wetlands and other riparian eco-systems: proceedings of the symposium. [Callaway Gardens, Georgia, December 11-13, 1978]. USDA Forest Service GTR-WO-12. 410 p. Washington, D.C.

Emlen, J.T. 1971. Population densities of birds derived from transect counts. Auk 88:323-342.

Emlen, J.T. 1977. Estimating breeding season bird densities from transect counts. Auk 94:455-468.

Engel-Wilson, R.W., A.K. Webb, K.V. Rosenberg, R.D. Ohmart, and B.W. Anderson. 1981. Avian censusing with the strip method: a computer simulation. p. 445-449. In: C.J Ralph and J.M. Scott (ed.). Estimating numbers of terrestrial birds. [Asilomar, California, October 26-31, 1980]. Studies in Avian Biology No. 6.

MacArthur, R.H., and J.W. MacArthur. 1961. On bird species diversity. Ecology 42:594-598.

Rice, J.C., R.D. Ohmart, and B.W. Anderson. In press. Rates of change in species composition of avian communities in contiguous riparian habitats. Ecology.

Siegel, S. 1956. Nonparametric statistics for the behavioral sciences. 312 p. McGraw-Hill, New York, N.Y.

Sokal, R.R., and R.J. Rolhf. 1969. Biometry. 776 p. W.H. Freeman and Company, San Francisco, California.

ALDER, COTTONWOOD, AND SYCAMORE DISTRIBUTION AND
REGENERATION ALONG THE NACIMIENTO RIVER, CALIFORNIA[1]

Allan N. Shanfield[2]

Abstract.--Distribution and regeneration of alder, cottonwood, and sycamore was assessed for much of the Nacimiento River (Monterey County, California). Alder, abundant along narrow reaches, had well-distributed height-classes. Cottonwood, now rare along the river, exhibited low numbers of saplings; overgrazing of cattle is believed primarily responsible for the decline. Sycamore had good regeneration along narrow reaches and poor regeneration on broader bottomlands. It appears unlikely that sycamore status is threatened for it exerts strong clonal regeneration.

INTRODUCTION

In recent years the many important values inherent in riparian systems have been recognized (Menke in press; Thomas et al. 1979; Warner 1979; and others). In response, the California Department of Fish and Game (DFG) conducted a riparian vegetation survey of the Nacimiento River, upstream from the Nacimiento Dam (Shanfield 1979). Available literature reveals that little is known of this region, outside of the inventory by Gerdes (1976). This paper draws from Shanfield (1979) and assesses the distribution and regenerative status of alder (Alnus rhombifolia), cottonwood (Populus fremontii), and sycamore (Platanus racemosa). In addition, the effects of cattle browsing upon these species are considered.

THE STUDY SITE

The Nacimiento River flows out of the Santa Lucia Mountains in central coastal California. It and the San Antonio River have parallel courses, and each is a major tributary to the north-flowing Salinas River. The study areas are located from the Los Padres National Forest and Fort Hunter Liggett (FHL) borders south to the Monterey County line (fig. 1).

---

[1]Paper presented at the California Riparian Systems Conference. [University of California, Davis, Sept. 17-19, 1981].

[2]Allan N. Shanfield was formerly with the California Department of Fish and Game, Wildlife Management Branch, Monterey, Calif; his present address is in Los Angeles, Calif.

Figure 1.--Location of study areas along the Nacimiento River.

Climatically, the area has hot, dry summers and cool, rainy winters. At FHL, the maximum and minimum temperature averages 37.5°C. and 15.8°C. for July, and 15.6°C. and 1.3°C. for January. Annual precipitation has ranged from 58.4 cm. to 73.5 cm. Temperature extremes have ranged from -9.2°C. to 46.8°C. (ibid.).

Much of FHL is periodically disturbed by US Army used each year to reduce fire hazard. An estimated 50% of areas surveyed show evidence of fire effects. Also, cattle grazing is a significant activity that has been modifying the landscape since the early 1800s. In recent years, including the 1976-1977 drought, cattle concentrations were excessively high and the range condition deteriorated. However, in recognition of riparian vegetation as a sensitive resource, the Directorate of Facilities Engineers at the Fort Ord Complex instituted a seasonal grazing program in lieu of a continuous grazing regime, concomitantly lowering animal unit months (AUMs).[3]

Other disturbances include ground squirrels, whose populations had increased because of overgrazing, and an infectious fungus, Anthracnose. This plant pathogen has been reported to hinder sycamore regeneration to an unknown degree (discussed further in Shanfield ibid.).

The Nacimiento River's riparian vegetation typically contains sycamore, willow (Salix spp.), and mulefat (Baccharis viminea) stands with grasses growing on broader floodplains. In canyons, there are higher densities of alder, willow, and mulefat with an understory of wild rose (Rosa californica), snowberry (Symphoricarpos spp.), poison oak (Rhus diversiloba), and herbaceous vegetation. The vegetation of the uplands bordering the riparian zone is typically a mosaic of blue oak (Quercus douglasii)/digger pine (Pinus sabiniana) woodland and oak-savannah grassland interdigitating with chaparral stands. Upstream of the FHL border, the oak-madrone (Arbutus menziesii) association becomes important, and bigleaf maple (Acer macrophyllum) occurs close to the water as the riparian zone assumes a more highly mesic character.

METHODS

The riparian zone defined in this study includes areas from the late-spring waterline outward to the furthest mesic riparian species (e.g., willow, sycamore). Five representative study segments, 3.2 km. (2.0 mi.) long, were selected for study in spring 1979. Black-and-white aerial photographs with transparent overlays[4] were used to type-map the vegetation. The ground survey was conducted during spring and summer of 1979.

Sampling units, subsegments having varying lengths, and site selection were predicated upon field-identifiable landmarks (e.g., bend in river, roadways). Within most subsegments the following information was recorded: 1) plant cover as estimated by Daubenmire's (1968) cover-classes utilizing midpoints; 2) census of rela-

---

[3]Langford, J. 1981. Range Conservationist, Division of Facilities Engineers, Fort Hunter Liggett, Jolan, Calif. Personal communication.
[4]Aerial photographs available at USDA Soil Conservation Service, Salinas, Calif.

tive ages of individual plants; and 3) other observations and photo-documented information.

Censused trees were categorized into height-classes as: seedlings (<1.5 m.); saplings (1.6-9 m.), poles (10-17 m.), or mature trees (>17 m.). Cottonwood seedlings were not counted as they were ubiquitous, wherever they did occur, on freshly exposed alluvium and within the river channel. Subsequent to sampling, younger-aged cottonwood and sycamore trees were censused, and trunk cores were taken to determine logical dbh-height bounds for each class. Reported bounds (Stone 1971) for cottonwood ages were used here. A more detailed description of the methods can be found in Shanfield (1979).

RESULTS AND DISCUSSION

Census results for size/age groups are presented in table 1. Before any interpretations are made regarding these data, it is appropriate to consider that two populations were present: 1) the population regenerating by clonal spread, wherein stand size/age structures of aboveground stems are different than belowground parts; and 2) the population regenerating from seed (Harper 1977). What appeared to be genetically individual plants (genets) were counted. However, such attempts yield little information regarding the true multiple age-structures of plants having clonal tendencies. This problem is especially inherent in riparian plants. Sycamore and alder exhibited considerable cloning, where an estimated 60-70% of mature and pole-sized trees had either root or trunk sprouts. All censused cottonwoods were individual trees showing slight to zero sprouting, suggesting that cottonwood regeneration is predominantly by seed along the Nacimiento River. This contrasts with Irvine and West's (1979) data showing that cloning is the predominant means of cottonwood regeneration along the Escalante River, Utah.

Species with low levels of regeneration have either: 1) naturally poor regeneration creating an uncertainty as to the "equilibrium" situation; or 2) been subjected to an increase in relative mortality in recent years; or both (Harper 1977; Johnson et al. 1976). Any interpretations, therefore, regarding the regenerative status of the study species are tempered by the fact that only the aboveground populations were sampled. However, both species exhibited a wide range of stem sizes.

Harper (1977) suggested that investigators study and characterize species' ecologies rather than perform statistics on broad age-class averages. Furthermore, an historic approach is necessary to determine riparian vegetation change, and Hastings and Turner's (1965) investigation serves as an excellent model.

Alder Distribution and Regeneration

Alder was most abundant along narrow reaches of study segments 2 and 5. These sites were

Table 1.--Numbers of seedlings, saplings, poles and mature trees along censused reaches of the Nacimiento River. Approximate age-classes for cottonwood and sycamore are shown. Length of river censused:total length of study segment is given in kilometers. Stream segment 2 is broken into northern (2a) and southern (2b) subsegments as it covers different regions. (See Shanfield 1979 for subsegment information).

	Stream segment						
Age-class	1	2a	2b	3	4	5	Total
Alder							
Seedlings	0	15	20	16	3	13	104
Saplings	0	4	35	19	26	14	98
Poles	0	25	7	14	7	10	56
Mature trees	0	75	14	10	8	12	119
Cottonwood							
Saplings (3-15 years)	0	1	0	3	2	3	9
Poles (16-29 years)	10	4	3	20	3	7	47
Mature trees (30-100 years)	41	9	6	17	12	7	92
Sycamore							
Seedlings (0-9 years)	12	8	26	7	35	60	148
Saplings (10-26 years)	8	2	27	3	41	11	92
Poles (27-63 years)	61	26	70	46	59	22	284
Mature trees (64+ years)	182	50	42	59	109	11	453
Length censused: length study segment	2.8/5.7	2.0/5.6		3.5/3.5	2.9/2.9	1.0/1.9	

characterized by year-round water, low browsing pressure, and 75-95% cover of alder (fig. 2). Alder was rare along broader floodplains and usually had less than five percent cover. Here, it was usually restricted to east-facing, more mesic streambanks.

Table 1 shows that alder had well-distributed height-classes for all areas except the northern reach of Segment 2. Outside of censused

areas, alder had good regeneration both clonally and from seed.

Cottonwood Distribution and Regeneration

Cottonwood was rare along the Nacimiento River and had less than five percent cover in all subsegments. Trees were distributed close to the water and on higher terraces. Seedlings were ubiquitous, especially on freshly exposed alluvium and in the river bed in summer months.

Most cottonwoods were in older age-classes, and very few saplings were present (table 1). Trees tended towards older ages along wider floodplains (such as Segment 1), while younger age-classes were more common along narrower reaches (Segments 2 and 5). One site of abundant regeneration in Segment 2 (uncensused) had 15-20 saplings on a bank approximately 15 m. long.

Areas of good regeneration typically had the following site characteristics for cottonwood (as well as sycamore) regeneration: 1) narrow riparian corridors (canyons); and 2) low grazing pressure based upon hoofprints, scat evidence, and reduced high-lining, presence of herbaceous vegetation at the water's edge, and ownership information. Glinski (1977) reported excellent regeneration by seed (586 saplings per 0.8 km. of stream edge) along ungrazed reaches in his study areas. Irvine and West (1979) reported that cottonwood was limited to broad flood terraces and regenerated almost exclusively by suckering.

Figure 2.--Typical alder stand along Nacimiento River, Study Segment 2, looking north.

Sycamore Distribution and Regeneration

Sycamore occupied sites closest to the water as well as on outer terraces. It was common on all reaches; its cover values ranged from 19-32% along the riparian zone. Seedlings were present here, contrasting with Griffin's[5] observation that seedlings are absent on Hastings Reserve, which is approximately 55 km. north. Similarly, Glinski (1977) reported an absence of seedlings and only one sapling along 14.4 km. of Sonoita Creek, Arizona, which included both grazed and ungrazed reaches.

Most sycamore stands tended toward older ages in segments 1, 3 (fig. 3), and part of 4 (fig. 4). Narrower, canyon-like sites, such as in segments 2, part of 4, and 5, had younger

Figure 3.--Mature sycamore and cottonwood trees along river. Location: segment 1.

Figure 4.--Mature sycamore stands in wash. Location: segment 4, looking south.

---

[5]Griffin, J.R. 1981. Curator and Plant Ecologist, Hastings Reservation, University of California, Carmel Valley.

age-classes. Two sites of active regeneration were found in segments 2 and 5 (fig. 5); these areas had site characteristics similar to those for excellent cottonwood regeneration.

Figure 5.--Typical site of sycamore regeneration in segment 2. Note bunchgrasses at water's edge.

Effects of Cattle Grazing

Direct Effects

Overgrazing by cattle has probably limited cottonwood sapling establishment along much of the Nacimiento River. Sources elsewhere (Glinski 1977; Reed 1979) indicate that cottonwood is a preferred food, and Glinski has provided strong correlations between sapling establishment and levels of grazing pressure. Locally, the sapling (3- to 15-year) class has been most affected, a timeframe synchronous with periods of heavy grazing and drought along the Nacimiento River. Saplings appeared to be locally restricted to areas of slight to zero cattle impact, such as drainage ditches along the Jolon Road, Salinas River at King City; study sites along segments 2 and 5; and within Mission Creek.

The Mission Creek site (fig. 6 and 7) provides a fenceline comparison that illustrates the degree of vegetation modification attributed to cattle grazing. Similar effects have been noted in the inter-mountain region (Keller et al. 1979; Storch 1979).

Upstream from the fenceline along Mission Creek, where cattle had been excluded, were countless cottonwood (as well as mulefat and willow) saplings which colonized an alluvium bed deposited about 1975 as a result of a dam break. Here, alder and sycamore regeneration was minimal, suggesting that these species occupy separate niches or are very poor interspecific competitors. This stand also suggests that cottonwood has strong potential for sapling establishment when proper seedbed conditions exist in conjunction with reduced grazing pressure.

Figure 6.—View north, ungrazed and fenced portion of Mission Creek. Rocks at lower left serve as landmark.

Figure 7.—View looking south of grazed portion of Mission Creek. Rocks in foreground are the same as in figure 5. Cattle have not been excluded, and regeneration is greatly reduced.

If grazing were the primary factor limiting tree establishment, then there should be a consistent increase in cottonwood and sycamore regeneration on a larger scale in areas with reduced grazing pressure (segments 2 and 5), but that is not the case. Cottonwood is naturally rare in narrower reaches, along both the Nacimiento and Escalante rivers (Irvine and West 1979), for where there is channelization, there is increased inundation and mechanical damage from water and sediment, fluvial erosion and deposition. Such fluctuations may wash out or bury young plants (ibid.).

Sycamore, in contrast, appears less affected by direct grazing pressure. It is reported to be an unpalatable browse species (Glinski 1977; Martin 1979). Sycamore saplings were absent in areas of reduced grazing pressure (e.g., Hastings Reserve, Mission Creek and those reaches studied by Glinski). It may be that the regenerative success of sycamore is largely independent from grazing pressure. It seems reasonable that other factors may contribute to poor sapling establishment; or sycamore may normally regenerate only by cloning, and once lost from an area may not reestablish itself.

Indirect Effects

Cottonwood and sycamore regeneration and the presence of understory species were typically limited to the water's edge along wide, braided floodplains. Segment 1, for example, had predominantly older, possibly even-aged trees widely dispersed on benches (fig. 3).[6] Much of this area has been burned frequently, and grazing levels were high, as exemplified by the degree of high-lining on trees. The soils are reported to be nutrient-poor, and bedrock is often exposed.[6]

Glinski (1977) and Irvine and West (1979) observed that trees rarely occurred on higher ground in their study areas, and it is believed that poor lateral water flows, in conjunction with other factors, have contributed to a "desertification" of riparian terraces. It appears reasonable that seedling establishment in such locales is a tenuous possibility, for young plants must quickly extend their root systems to survive desiccation, fires, and cattle grazing.

In mountain meadow situations, Platts (1981) found that cattle grazing initiated multiple effects upon riparian soils; where livestock trample and compact the soil, the range favors species that exist in areas of lowered water tables. As soils compact and groundcover diminishes, infiltration of water into deep soils becomes poor, surface runoff is increased, and rich topsoil is lost by water and wind erosion.

Much of the Nacimiento River had poor instream cover by comparison to the fenced Mission Creek site (figs. 6 and 7). Where there was less impoundment due to less overhanging vegetation and debris along the stream, there would be reduced lateral flows to deposit nutrient-rich alluvium and recharge water capacities on higher terraces.

CONCLUSIONS AND RECOMMENDATIONS

In the study area, alder had good regeneration as exemplified by high relative numbers of

[6] Summers, W.J. 1981. Range Conservationist, Natural Resources Management Branch, Naval Facilities Engineers, San Bruno, Calif. Personal conversation.

saplings. Its multiple-stemmed, clonal nature and relative lack of grazing use should ensure its existence.

Cottonwood may be declining along the Nacimiento River because of low recruitment levels. Cattle grazing has probably limited its regeneration and distribution on potentially suitable sites, both directly and indirectly.

Sycamore had various levels of regeneration which are correlated with specific site conditions. Cattle grazing may have indirectly affected sycamore distribution and regeneration along broader bottomlands; however, these data concur with Glinski (1977). Sycamore status will be unthreatened because it can exert strong clonal regeneration, that is, a large percentage of mature trees have root and trunk sprouts that should ensure its survival.

Large-scale regeneration of cottonwood and sycamore along the Nacimiento River could occur as pulses resulting from massive flooding and deposition cycles and coupled with a cessation of limiting factors (e.g., disease, grazing, etc.). This sequence is comparable to Harper's (1977) contention that regeneration occurs in waves rather than as a continuous process.

It is suggested that, where feasible, research and demonstration areas be created along the Nacimiento River where cattle are excluded (Platts 1981). This could provide a control situation where researchers could isolate the many habitat factors affecting riparian vegetation ecology (see Westman [1981] for list of habitat factors). Some suggested areas of research are: 1) what is the recovery time for riparian areas from cattle grazing, and what successional changes occur (see Platts [1981] for discussion of needed riparian/grazing research); 2) what are the effects of fire upon riparian vegetation; 3) how can "normal" regeneration of the studied species be characterized; 4) what is the autecology of the study species; 5) how much outbreeding does sycamore exhibit, and what levels are necessary to ensure its stability over time; and 6) what grazing strategies are most compatible with riparian resources in the California Coast Ranges.

ACKNOWLEDGMENTS

I express my gratitude to Drs. Menke and Bartolome for their thoughtful and incisive comments. Also, special thanks to Bruce Elliott for permission to use these data, and to Will Summers, Tim Brothers, and Kris Preston and John O'Leary for their generous input into this paper.

LITERATURE CITED

Daubenmire, R.F. 1968. Plant communities: a textbook of plant synecology. 300 p. Harper and Row Co., New York, N.Y.

Gerdes, G. 1976. A study of the Salinas River and its selected tributaries, California. Unpublished report on file with Department of Fish and Game, Wildlife Management Branch, Monterey, California.

Glinski, R.L. 1977. Regeneration and distribution of sycamore and cottonwood trees along Sonoita Creek, Santa Cruz County, Arizona. p. 116-123. In: R.R. Johnson and D.A. Jones (tech. coord.). Importance, preservation and management of riparian habitats: a symposium. [Tuscon, Arizona, July 9, 1977.] USDA Forest Service GTR-RM-43, Rocky Mountain Forest and Range Experiment Station, Fort Collins, Colo. 217 p.

Harper, J.L. 1977. Population biology of plants. 829 p. Academic Press, New York, N.Y.

Hastings, J.R., and R.M. Turner. 1965. The changing mile. 317 p. University of Arizona Press, Tucson, Arizona.

Irvine, J.R. and N.E. West. 1979. Riparian tree species distribution and succession along the lower Escalante River, Utah. Southwestern Naturalist 24(2):331-346.

Johnson, W.C. et al. 1976. Forest overstory vegetation and environment on the Missouri River floodplain in North Dakota. Ecol. Monog. 46(1):59-84.

Keller, C.C., L. Anderson, and P. Tappel. 1979. Fish habitat changes in Summit Creek, Idaho, after fencing the riparian area. p. 46-52. In O.B. Cope (ed.). Proceedings of the forum on grazing and riparian/stream ecosystems. 94 p. Trout Unlimited, Inc., Washington, D.C.

Martin, S.C. 1979. Evaluating the impacts of cattle grazing on riparian habitats in the national forests of Arizona and New Mexico. p. 35-38. In: O.B. Cope (ed.). Proceedings of the forum on grazing and riparian/stream ecosystems. 94 p. Trout Unlimited, Inc., Washington, D.C.

Menke, J.W. (ed.). in press. Symposium on livestock, wildlife, fisheries relationships in the Great Basin. [Sparks, Nevada, May, 1977.] USDA Forest Service Pacific Southwest Forest and Range Experiment Station, Berkeley, Calif.

Platts, W.S. 1981. Influence of forest and rangeland management on anadramous fish habitat in western North America--effects of livestock grazing. Intermountain Forest and Range Experiment Station, Boise, Idaho.

Reed, J. 1979. Resources-use, abuse, and management. p. 64. In: O.B. Cope (ed.). Proceedings of the forum on grazing and riparian/stream ecosystems. 94 p. Trout Unlimited, Inc., Washington, D.C.

Shanfield, A.N. 1979. Nacimiento River study. District Administrative Report 2. Unpublished report on file with Department of Fish and Game, Wildlife Management Branch, Monterey, California.

Stone, E.C. 1971. The dynamics of vegetation change. Unpublished report prepared for Cal-American Water Company. May be obtained through Department of Forestry and Resource Management, University of California, Berkeley.

Storch, R.L. 1979. Livestock/streamside management programs in eastern Oregon. p. 56-60. In: O.B. Cope (ed.). Proceedings of the forum on grazing and riparian/stream ecosystems. 94 p. Trout Unlimited, Inc., Washington, D.C.

Thomas, J. W., C. Maser, and J.E. Rodiek. 1979. Riparian zones in managed rangelands - their importance to wildlife. p. 21-30. In: O.B. Cope (ed.). Proceedings of the forum on grazing and riparian/stream ecosystems. 94 p. Trout Unlimited, Inc., Washington, D.C.

Warner, R.E. 1979. The California riparian study program phase I: background study and program design for phase II. 177 p. California Department of Fish and Game, Sacramento, Calif.

Westman, W.E. 1981. Factors influencing the distribution of species of Californian coastal sage scrub. Ecology 62(2):439-455.

HISTORICAL AVIFAUNAL CHANGES IN THE RIPARIAN ZONE

OF THE TRUCKEE RIVER, NEVADA[1]

Donald A. Klebenow and Robert J. Oakleaf[2]

Abstract.--Comparisons of populations of the present avifauna with observations made during 1868 along the lower Truckee River show species changes in abundance. The most noticeable changes in the avifauna involved species that require the dense understory of woody riparian vegetation, wet meadow, and marsh. Numerous species have declined in abundance; many not found in recent counts were abundant or common in 1868. The apparent population declines can be related to the compounding effects of farmland development, river channeling operations, and overgrazing.

INTRODUCTION

Gallery stands of riparian cottonwoods (Populus spp.) have been identified as important habitat for birds in Arizona (Carothers and Johnson 1975) and Colorado (Butorff 1974). Greater population densities and species diversity were reported for this vegetation-type than others in the western United States. Carothers and Johnson (1975) noted that over 50% of the species breeding in homogeneous cottonwood (Populus fremontii) stands along the Verde River, Arizona were exclusively dependent upon this vegetation-type for reproduction. Working in riparian vegetation of the Truckee and Carson Rivers, Ridgeway (1877) found that both the numbers of bird species and individuals were much greater when compared to sightings in other vegetation-types in Nevada.

Avifauna was observed during five years in the 1972-1981 period and compared with observations made during 1868 along the lower Truckee River (Ridgeway ibid.). The purpose of this comparison was to identify species and habitat situations that may be in need of additional study or special management attention.

[1]Paper presented at the California Riparian Systems Conference. [University of California, Davis, September 17-19, 1981]. It is contribution number 356 of Nevada Agricultural Experiment Station Journal series and Nevada Department of Wildlife Federal Aid, Project W-53-R.

[2]Donald A. Klebenow is Professor, Wildlife Management, University of Nevada, Reno. Robert J. Oakleaf is Biologist, Wyoming Game and Fish Department, Lander, Wyoming, formerly Nongame Biologist, Nevada Department of Wildlife, Reno.

STUDY AREA

Riparian cottonwood vegetation is relatively scarce in Nevada; we estimate that less that 1% of the state is comprised of this vegetation-type. The Truckee River is one of the principal areas supporting this vegetation-type. Ridgeway described riparian vegetation of the lower Truckee River as consisting of extensive groves of large cottonwoods forming dense thickets. A greater part of the shrub understory consisted of buffalo-berry (Shepherdia argentea) and willow (Salix spp.). However, they were associated with numerous other species of shrubs.

The riparian vegetation along the Truckee today is significantly different than the description provided by Ridgeway. Only a thin, discontinuous ribbon of cottonwoods extends along the river. Tree removal to expand fields and pastures has reduced the width of the native riparian vegetation in many areas (fig. 1). In

Figure 1.--Agricultural development has reduced the width of the native riparian vegetation.

the early 1960s, the Truckee River from Reno to Nixon was channelized and streamside vegetation eliminated (fig. 2, 3). Commercial logging and gravel operations have also reduced the amount of riparian cover. Much of the riparian vegetation is severely overgrazed, resulting in the elimination of cottonwood reproduction and most of the deciduous shrub understory (fig. 4). The few portions of the river that can be protected from grazing are limited to areas where fenced fields extend to the banks of the river. Cattle graze most of these fenced areas, but on one ungrazed area, willow and cottonwood have been reestablished by planting or natural reseeding (fig. 5).

Figure 2.--Riparian vegetation along the lower Truckee River prior to channeling operations.

Figure 3.--Lower Truckee River after channeling operations. Note the elimination of streamside vegetation.

METHODS

Ridgeway surveyed the lower Truckee River from 15 May through 6 June 1868. The survey was conducted with the objective of identifying as large a percentage of the breeding avifauna as possible. Relative abundances of most species were recorded as rare, common, or abundant. However, Ridgeway did not define these terms.

Figure 4.--Heavy grazing has eliminated cottonwood reproduction and shrub understory in much of the riparian vegetation along the Truckee River.

Figure 5.--Willows and cottonwoods can be expected to recover in areas protected from livestock grazing.

During the months of May through August, 1972, 1975, and 1976, bird counts were conducted along the lower Truckee River on two transects established in riparian vegetation. Each transect was counted eight times during this period. During June, 1980 and July, 1981, five additional counts were conducted on the transect located on the University of Nevada S-S Field Laboratory. On this area, the remaining riparian vegetation has been fenced and protected from grazing since 1975.

The transects were located in the river floodplain in the vicinity of the river. Each transect was approximately 2 km. in length. Distance from the river varied from a few meters to 50 m. Agricultural fields now occupy portions of the floodplain. Where they were located close to the river, the transects were run between the fields and the river's edge.

Counts were started approximately 30 minutes before sunrise and normally lasted until about two hours after sunrise. All birds seen and/or heard for a five-minute period were counted at a sample location. The observer then moved 150 paces along a line paralleling the river and again recorded all birds for five minutes. A total of 10 stops were made for each count, and the results were then tallied as to species frequency and total number.

In 1974, 1976, and 1980, complete surveys were made of the 25 km. of river between Wadsworth and Little Nixon. These surveys were to determine if our transect samples were representative of the entire area.

Ratings were developed for the species encountered during our counts to simplify comparisons with the information reported by Ridgeway. The categories of rare, common, and abundant were used. These categories were defined as follows:

Rare—less than or equal to three sightings total for all counts.
Common—more than three sightings but not abundant.

Abundant—sightings made consistently throughout all transects.

It was not possible to deduce the methods used by Ridgeway to determine the species present and their abundance. We assume his abundance ratings were subjective. Others may have aided in identification and collection of specimens, but that was not possible to ascertain.

RESULTS

All species observed during both Ridgeway's and our 1972-76 studies are presented in table 1. This includes 108 species total. Ridgeway reported 91 species associated with this riparian vegetation; we observed a total of 65 species, 17 of which were not on Ridgeway's list.

Table 1.—Comparative species richness and abundance ratings, lower Truckee River, 1868 and 1972-76. A = abundant, C = common, R = rare.

Species	Abundance 1868	1972-76
White Pelican (Pelecanus erythrorhynchos)	A	C
Double-crested Cormorant (Phalacrocorax auritus)	A	R
Great Blue Heron (Ardea herodias)	A	C
Snowy Egret (Egretta thula)	R	C
Black-crowned Night Heron (Nycticorax nycticorax)	R	—
Least Bittern (Ixobrychus exilis)	R	—
American Bittern (Botaurus lentiginosus)	C	—
Canada Goose (Branta canadensis)	C	C
Mallard (Anas platyrhynchos)	A	C
Gadwall (Anas strepera)	A	—
Pintail (Anas acuta)	R	R
Blue-winged Teal (Anas discors)	—	C (1 flock of 10)
Cinnamon Teal (Anas cyanoptera)	C	R
American Widgeon (Anas americana)	A	—
Shoveler (Anas clypeata)	C	—
Wood Duck (Aix sponsa)	R	C
Hooded Merganser (Lophodytes cucullatus)	R	—
Common Merganser (Mergus merganser)	—	C
Turkey Vulture (Cathartes aura)	A	—
Red-tailed Hawk (Buteo jamaicensis)	C	C
Swainson's Hawk (Buteo swainsoni)	C	R (2 observations)
Golden Eagle (Aquila chrysaetos)	R	—
Marsh Hawk (Circus cyaneus)	A	—
Osprey (Pandion haliaetus)	R	—
Prairie Falcon (Falco mexicanus)	—	R (active nest)
Peregrine Falcon (Falco peregrinus)	1 pr.	—
American Kestrel (Falco sparverius)	A	C
California Quail (Lophortyx californicus)	—	C
Sandhill Crane (Grus canadensis)	R	—
Virginia Rail (Rallus limicola)	R	—
Sora (Porzana carolina)	C	—
Killdeer (Charadrius vociferus)	C	A
Long-billed Curlew (Numenius americanus)	C	—
Spotted Sandpiper (Actitis macularia)	C	R (3 observations)
Solitary Sandpiper (Tringa solitaria)	R	—
Willet (Catoptrophorus semipalmatus)	C	—
Dunlin (Calidris alpina)	R	—
Western Sandpiper (Calidris mauri)	—	R (1 observation)
American Avocet (Recurvirostra americana)	C	—
Black-necked Stilt (Himantopus mexicanus)	C	—

Species	1868	1972-76
Herring Gull (Larus argentatus)	–	R
California Gull (Larus californicus)	A	C
Ring-billed Gull (Larus delawarensis)	–	C
Mourning Dove (Zenaida macroura)	A	A
Yellow-billed Cuckoo (Coccyzus americanus)	Not rated; several seen in July	–
Great Horned Owl (Bubo virginianus)	C	R (2 observations)
Long-eared Owl (Asio otus)	C	–
Common Nighthawk (Chordeiles minor)	C	C
Vaux's Swift (Chaetura vauxi)	C	–
White-throated Swift (Aeronautes saxatalis)	R	–
Black-chinned Hummingbird (Archilochus alexandri)	A	–
Rufous Hummingbird (Selasphorus rufus)	Not rated; but reported	C (4 observations)
Belted Kingfisher (Megaceryle alcyon)	C	C
Common Flicker (Colaptes auratus)	A	C
Hairy Woodpecker (Picoides villosus)	C	R (1 observation)
Downy Woodpecker (Picoides pubescens)	–	C
Western Kingbird (Tyrannus verticalis)	A	A
Ash-throated Flycatcher (Myiarchus cinerascens)	R	–
Say's Phoebe (Sayornis saya)	R	R (2 observations)
Willow Flycatcher (Empidonax traillii)	A	–
Gray Flycatcher (Empidonax wrightii)	–	C (8 observations)
Western Wood Pewee (Contopus sordidulus)	A	R (1 observation)
Violet-green Swallow (Tachycineta thalassina)	C	C
Tree Swallow (Iridoprocne bicolor)	A	C
Bank Swallow (Riparia riparia)	A	–
Rough-winged Swallow (Stelgidopteryx ruficollis)	A	C
Barn Swallow (Hirundo rustica)	C	C
Cliff Swallow (Petrochelidon pyrrhonota)	A	–
Purple Martin (Progne subis)	R	–
Black-billed Magpie (Pica pica)	A	A
Red-breasted Nuthatch (Sitta canadensis)	–	C (9 observations)
House Wren (Troglodytes aedon)	A	A
Bewick's Wren (Thryomanes bewickii)	–	C
Long-billed Marsh Wren (Cistothorus palustris)	A	–
Sage Thrasher (Oreoscoptes montanus)	C	R (1 observation)
American Robin (Turdus migratorius)	C	C
Western Bluebird (Sialia mexicana)	Not rated; noted a few families	
Loggerhead Shrike (Lanius ludovicianus)	C	–
Starling (Sturnus vulgaris)	–	A
Warbling Vireo (Vireo gilvus)	A	R (1 observation)
Orange-crowned Warbler (Vermivora celata)	–	R (3 observations)
Nashville Warbler (Vermivora ruficapilla)	–	C
Yellow Warbler (Dendroica petechia)	A	C (12 observations)
Audubon's Warbler (Dendroica coronata)	–	C
MacGillivray's Warbler (Oporornis tolmiei)	–	R (3 observations)
Yellowthroat (Geothlypis trichas)	C	–
Yellow-breasted Chat (Icteria virens)	C	–
Wilson's Warbler (Wilsonia pusilla)	Observed; not rated	C (5 observations)
House Sparrow (Passer domesticus)	–	C
Western Meadowlark (Sturnella neglecta)	A	C
Yellow-headed Blackbird (Xanthocephalus xanthocephalus)	A	C
Red-winged Blackbird (Agelaius phoeniceus)	A	C
Northern Oriole (Icterus galbula)	A	C
Brewer's Blackbird (Euphagus cyanocephalus)	Not rated; reported a large breeding colony nearby in the Pah Rah Mountains	A
Brown-headed Cowbird (Molothrus ater)	R	C
Western Tanager (Piranga ludoviciana)	C	–
Black-headed Grosbeak (Pheucticus melanocephalus)	C	–
Lazuli Bunting (Passerina amoena)	R	R (1 observation)
House Finch (Carpodacus mexicanus)	C	C
American Goldfinch (Carduelis tristis)	R	–
Rufous-sided Towhee (Pipilo erythrophthalmus)	C	–

Table 1.--Comparative species richness and abundance ratings, lower Truckee River, 1868 and 1972-76 (cont.).

Savannah Sparrow (<u>Passerculus sandwichensis</u>)	C	−
Lark Sparrow (<u>Chondestes grammacus</u>)	A	R (1 observation)
Black-throated Sparrow (<u>Amphispiza bilineata</u>)	C	−
Sage Sparrow (<u>Amphispiza belli</u>)	A	R (1 observation)
Chipping Sparrow (<u>Spizella passerina</u>)	A	R (1 observation)
Brewer's Sparrow (<u>Spizella breweri</u>)	A	C (7 observations)
Song Sparrow (<u>Melospiza melodia</u>)	A	−
Totals	91	66

We recorded 65 bird species during the 1972-76 period. We did not find 42 species that Ridgeway reported. In addition, 26 species that were present in 1868 have declined in abundance.

Of the species which have disappeared or declined in abundance, 42, or 62%, are associated with riparian vegetation including wet meadow, and marsh. Twenty-one species were selected to demonstrate this change, and to show the degree of recovery brought about by riparian shrub vegetation restoration through protection from grazing (table 2).

Table 2.--Abundance comparisons of species associated with riparian shrub vegetation, wet meadows, and marshes along the lower Truckee River. A = abundant, C = common, R = rare.

Species	Abundance		
	1868	1972-76	1980-81[1]
Riparian Shrub Vegetation			
Yellow-billed Cuckoo	not rated; several seen	−	−
Black-chinned Hummingbird	A	−	−
Willow Flycatcher	A	−	−
Western Wood Pewee	A	R	R
Warbling Vireo	A	R	−
Yellow Warbler	A	C	R
MacGillivray's Warbler	−	R	R
Yellow-breasted Chat	C	−	−
Wilson's Warbler	not rated; but observed	C	R
Black-headed Grosbeak	C	−	R
Song Sparrow	A	−	R
Wet Meadows and Marshes			
American Bittern	C	−	−
Marsh Hawk	A	−	−
Sora	C	−	R
Long-billed Curlew	C	−	−
Spotted Sandpiper	C	R	C
Willet	C	−	−
American Avocet	C	−	−
Black-necked Stilt	C	−	−
Long-billed Marsh Wren	A	−	−
Yellowthroat	C	−	−

[1] 1980-81 samples only include the University of Nevada, Reno, S-S Field Laboratory, the only location on the study site with the remnant riparian vegetation fenced from grazing. It has been protected since 1975.

Most of these bird species were common or abundant in 1868. Nearly all declined in numbers and many were not seen on any of our counts or surveys. Shrub and thicket inhabitants that were completely missing from the recent surveys included the Yellow-billed Cuckoo, Black-chinned Hummingbird, Willow Flycatcher, and Yellow-breasted Chat. Others were not entirely lost and some, like the Black-headed Grosbeak and Song Sparrow, were showing signs of recovery. Eight of the 10 species associated with wet meadows and marshes were not seen on our surveys. Of those seen, the Sora was a carcass found in 1980 in the area of the only slough that remains on the lower Truckee River. The Spotted Sandpipers were located where newly established cottonwoods grew on the riverbank--two broods were discovered in 1981 on the area of the river protected from grazing.

DISCUSSION

Vegetation

When Ridgeway (1877) saw the lower Truckee River, he reported:

"Along the bank of the river and surrounding the sloughs connected with the stream, were exceedingly dense willow-jungles, the sloughs themselves being filled with rushes, flags and other aquatic plants; but most of the valley consisted of meadowlands, interspersed with velvety swards of "salt-grass" and acres of beautiful sun-flowers (<u>Helianthus giganteus</u>), studded with fine large cottonwood trees (<u>Populus monilifera</u> (sic) and <u>P. trichocarpa</u>), which were here and there grouped into delightful groves, sometimes unencumbered, but generally with a shrubby undergrowth, amongst which the "buffalo-berry" (<u>Shepherdia argentea</u>) was conspicuous.

This description no longer fits. Missing are the "dense willow-jungles", the sloughs "...with a shrubby undergrowth, amongst which the "buffalo-berry" (<u>Shepherdia argentea</u>) was conspicuous."

The sloughs and moist meadowlands were, in part, converted to agricultural farmlands with settlement of the area. Meanders and additional sloughs were eliminated by the river channeling efforts for flood control, which also resulted in a straighter and faster-moving river. Trees and shrubs were removed to expand the fields and pastures, which further reduced the width of riparian vegetation in the farmed areas.

Severe overgrazing further reduced the willow and buffalo-berry thickets. Beaver (Castor canadensis) attacked the mature trees and grazing cattle prevented their reestablishment. Grazing by cattle has essentially prevented the reestablishment of cottonwood trees and shrub understory species since the river was channeled.

These changes in vegetation structure and condition set the stage for the changes in bird presence and abundance. Today there are fewer species, and many are less abundant than they were in 1868. Especially affected were the species associated with the riparian shrub vegetation and marshes and wet meadows (table 2).

Yellow-billed Cuckoo

Ridgeway saw several Yellow-billed Cuckoos along the lower Truckee River. We found none, and specific surveys statewide during 1974 and 1975 have failed to produce any sightings (Oakleaf[3]).

Gaines (1974) described preferred breeding habitat of the Yellow-billed Cuckoo as consisting of thick riparian growth occurring in minimum stands 300 m. long and 100 m. wide. Standing or slow-moving water associated with the riparian vegetation was preferred. Riparian zones containing these preferred characteristics no longer exist along the Truckee River.

Black-chinned Hummingbird

Ridgeway found the Black-chinned Hummingbird abundant during the breeding season. He also noted that the species was replaced in August by migrating Rufous Hummingbirds. No Black-chinned Hummingbirds were identified during the present study. However, two sightings of unidentified hummingbirds were made and four Rufous Hummingbirds were observed.

The lack of thickets in the riparian zone of the Truckee River probably explains the decline or loss of Black-chinned Hummingbirds from this area.

Willow Flycatcher

Ridgeway classified the Willow Flycatcher as abundant. The species was not recorded during the surveys in the 1970's and 1980's, indicating a significant population decline.

[3]Oakleaf, R.J. 1975. Population surveys, species distribution, and key habitats of selected nongame species. Nevada Department of Fish and Game. Job Progress Report W-35-R. 42 p.

Linsdale (1951) noted that the Willow Flycatcher: "...is a summer resident (in Nevada); occurs mainly in willow thickets bordering larger streams and in lower portions of the mountains." This vegetation-type no longer exists in a form suitable for this species on our study area.

Yellow-breasted Chat

The Warbling Vireo and several of the warblers have declined. The Yellow-breasted Chat is a species Ridgeway recorded as common; we did not observe it during any of our recent counts. Linsdale (ibid.) reported the Yellow-breasted Chat as a summer resident being most numerous in moist brushy areas close to bases of mountains. Apparently it prefers dense shrub tangles for cover and nesting, while feeding in wet meadows (Linsdale 1938). This habitat situation is presently almost completely lacking along the river.

Marsh Hawk and Long-billed Curlew

What once were wet meadows are now probably irrigated fields and pastures. The change probably led to the loss of nesting and hunting areas for the Marsh Hawk. The Long-billed Curlew also is gone.

Livestock Grazing and Vegetation Recovery

Control of livestock grazing pressure is one practice that can be achieved along the lower Truckee River. Other practices such as channeling will, it is hoped, never be repeated. However, the river will probably never be allowed to recover from the impact of the channeling. The fields and pastures that the channeling benefitted will be protected by bank stabilization efforts at all costs. The meandering nature that once existed on this lowest reach of the Truckee River would be too wasteful of space, now that it is parcelled to the present occupants.

Grazing of the riverbank portion of the riparian zone has been controlled on the University of Nevada S-S Field Laboratory. The banks were fenced in 1975, preventing cattle grazing adjacent pastures from reaching the riverbanks. The first efforts were only relatively successful. While cattle grazing adjacent pastures were kept from the riverbank, livestock from unfenced adjacent lands moved upstream and downstream into the protected zone. Driving off the trespassing stock, using barriers to prevent access along the banks, and constant monitoring were necessary to protect the area. This has been effective, and cottonwood and willow reproduction is occurring.

Numerous willow plantings were made from 1974 to the present, and the protection from livestock has permitted their establishment. Currently, this University of Nevada property is the only area on the lower Truckee River with any marked cottonwood and willow regeneration. While much regeneration is occurring, the dense willow thickets described by Ridgeway have not had time to develop. Thus, the recovery of species that require dense thickets has still not occurred.

Some recovery seems evident. The Black-headed Grosbeak and Song Sparrow are two species that were seen during the 1980-81 period, although they were rare.

Future prospects are good that the protection occurring on the University of Nevada property will be expanded to the Pyramid Lake Indian Reservation lands that encompass most of the lower Truckee River. The Tribe is attempting to raise the funds necessary to fence all the river within the reservation. If this is achieved, grazing within the immediate zone of the river will be controlled and some of the original vegetation should be restored. It is expected that the avifauna will respond according to the amount and type of habitable riparian vegetation that is permitted to develop.

ACKNOWLEDGMENTS

The authors appreciate the help of K. Giezentanner, L. Teske, D. Stinnett and G. Herron for their field assistance.

LITERATURE CITED

Butorff, R.L. 1974. Cottonwood habitat for birds in Colorado. Amer. Birds 28(6): 975-979.

Carothers, S.W., and R.R. Johnson. 1975. Water management practices and their effects on non-game birds in range habitats. p. 190-209. In: D.R. Smith (tech. coord.). Proceedings of the symposium on management of forest and range habitats for nongame birds. USDA Forest Service GTR-WO-1. Washington, D.C.

Gaines, D. 1974. Review of the status of the Yellow-billed Cuckoo in California. Condor 76(2):204-209.

Linsdale, J.M. 1938. Environmental responses of vertebrates in the Great Basin. Amer. Midland Nat. 19(1):1-216.

Linsdale, J.M. 1951. A list of the birds of Nevada. Condor 53(5):228-249.

Ridgeway, R. 1877. Ornithology. p. 303-669. In: C. King. Ornithology and paleontology. US Geological Explorations 40th Parallel 4.

PRONGHORN, CATTLE, AND FERAL HORSE USE

OF WETLAND AND UPLAND HABITATS[1]

Hal Salwasser and Karen Shimamoto[2]

Abstract.--Developed wetlands play a critical role in habitat quality for pronghorn, domestic cattle, and feral horses in Great Basin range-types. Wetlands provide abundant summer forage for pronghorn when cattle and horse grazing has removed coarse grasslike plants, making forbs available. Wetland creation should be balanced with needs for existing habitats on ranges.

INTRODUCTION

The Modoc Wetlands study began in October 1976 as a cooperative effort by the USDA Forest Service Pacific Southwest Region, Pacific Southwest Forest and Range Experiment Station, and Modoc National Forest; the California Department of Fish and Game, Region 1; and the Department of Forestry and Resoure Management, University of California, Berkeley. Local assistance and cooperation were also provided by the USDA Soil Conservation Service, USDA Fish and Wildlife Service Modoc National Wildlife Refuge, and the University of California Cooperative Agricultural Extension. The overall study goal was to assess the population responses of selected wildlife species to wetlands developments on the Devil's Garden plateau of the Modoc National Forest. Study efforts focused on pronghorn antelope (Antilocapra americana), sage grouse (Centrocercus urophasianus), puddle ducks (Anatidae), Canada goose (Branta canadensis), mule deer (Odocoileus hemionus), other wetland birds, domestic livestock, and feral horses.

Wetland development began on the Modoc National Forest in the 1920s, initially for runoff storage within Pit River Valley irrigation districts. Damming of major drainages, such as Rattlesnake Creek to create Big Reservoir, was the early mode of altering hydrologic patterns. Subsequently, over a period of 50 years, lesser drainages and internally drained basins were modified for irrigation, livestock forage, and wildlife purposes. An obvious result of these actions was that existing vegetation cover-types, dominated by big sagebrush (Artemisia tridentata), low sagebrush (A. arbuscula), silver sagebrush (A. cana), western juniper (Juniperus occidentalis), and riparian-associated willows (Salix spp.) and herbaceous vegetation, were converted to wetlands characterized by varying proportions of open water and hydrophytic plants; e.g., spike-rush (Eleocharis palustris), rushes (Juncus spp.) and a diverse flora of vernal forbs.

The effects of these ecosystem changes on wildlife populations have been the subject of much speculation. With the proposed and actual development of new wetlands in identified pronghorn and sage grouse habitat in the 1970s (Modoc National Forest Wetlands Development Plan), the issue of impacts on these and other wildlife species became a major concern to land managers. This study was initiated to assess those impacts. In addition, the issue of livestock and feral horse use of wetlands as factors in waterfowl, pronghorn, and sage grouse population dynamics was incorporated into the study.

Field investigations and literature studies dealt with four principal questions.

1. What are the characteristics of existing wildlife and livestock habitats?
2. How are wildlife, livestock, and feral horses currently utilizing and interacting with existing plant communities and with each other?
3. How do wetland development and management change the characteristics of plant communities and animal use of those communities?
4. How are pronghorn, sage grouse, waterfowl, mule deer, and other wetland birds responding to these changes and management strategies?

[1]Paper presented at the California Riparian Systems Conference. [University of California, Davis, September 17-19, 1981].

[2]Hal Salwasser is Regional Wildlife Ecologist, USDA Forest Service, Pacific Southwest Region, San Francisco, Calif. Karen Shimamoto is Forest Ecologist, Modoc National Forest, Alturas, Calif. Research reported in this paper was conducted while both authors were Research Associates at the University of California, Berkeley.

This paper reports on the use and preference of wetlands and surrounding upland habitats by pronghorn, cattle, and feral horses during the summers of 1978-1979.

STUDY AREA

Sampling on the entire area of the Modoc National Forest affected by wetland development was not within personnel and budget capabilities of this study. Therefore, a study area on the Devil's Garden Ranger District, covering roughly one-third of the Devil's Garden Plateau, was selected (fig. 1). The study area encompassed approximately 145,749 ha. (360,000 acres), and included all cover-types within which forest wetlands are being developed. Elevations range from 1,320 m. (4,400 ft.) to 1,680 m. (5,500 ft.). Terrain is generally flat and marked by numerous rimrocks and small block faults.

Soils in the study area are derived from basaltic lava flows, mud flows, and wind-blown ash. Alluvial soils are common in the numerous basins. Vegetation, fauna, and climate of the study area are all typical of the Great Basin environment. In fact, the area lies on the western margin of the Great Basin geomorphic province within what would be a natural extension of the Basin and Range Physiographic Province of southern Oregon (Franklin and Dyrness 1973). Young et al. (1977) placed it within the Great Basin Floristic Province.

Precipitation ranges from 51 to 610 mm. (2 to 24 in.) per year, averaging 305 to 356 mm. (12 to 14 in.). Extreme high or low precipitation years are more common than are "normal" years. Winter snow is the main source of precipitation. The frost-free growing season is 80 to 100 days.

Cover-types are described in detail by Salwasser and Shimamoto (in prep.). The bulk of the study area, 69.6%, was in Juniper/Sagebrush and Low Sagebrush cover-types (table 1). These two types were highly intermixed, but occurred in sizable distinct patches as well. Dense Juniper stands and the ecotonal Juniper/Pine/Shrub cover-types comprised 12.1% of the area. Ponderosa pine, which covered 5.3% of the area, was common on the northern and western fringes of the area. Remaining uplands were minor components.

Table 1.--Area of cover-types on the Modoc Wetlands Study area.

Habitat Cover-type	Area ha. (ac.)	Proportion of Study Area (%)
Ponderosa Pine	7,710 (19,040)	5.3
Pine Plantation	110 (270)	tr.
Montane Shrubs	60 (160)	tr.
Juniper/Pine/Shrub	8,870 (21,900)	6.1
Juniper	8,700 (21,500)	6.0
Juniper/Sagebrush	58,890 (145,450)	40.4
Low Sagebrush	42,490 (104,950)	29.2
Seeded Grassland	200 (490)	.1
Agricultural	190 (480)	.1
Other	310 (760)	.2
Subtotal	127,530 (315,000)	87.4
Dry Meadow	860 (2,120)	.6
Wet Meadow	1,110 (2,750)	.8
Vernal Wetland	1,060 (2,610)	.7
Silver Sagebrush	5,050 (12,480)	3.5
Emergent Wetland	4,920 (12,150)	3.4
Reservoir/Lake	4,790 (11,830)	3.3
Riparian	430 (1,060)	.3
Sub-total	18,220 (45,000)	12.6
TOTAL	145,750 (360,000)	100.0

Basins and wetlands in the study area were dominated by three types: Reservoir/Lake, Silver Sagebrush, and Emergent Wetland. There are 23 reservoirs, ranging in size from less than 4 ha. (10 ac.) to over 2,429 ha. (6,000 ac.). Seventy-four percent of the reservoirs are 8.1 ha. (20 ac.) to 81 ha. (200 ac.) in size. The 276 Silver Sagebrush basins ranged in size from .4 to 259 ha. (1 to 640 ac.). However, 96% of them were under 16 ha. (40 ac.). The 57 Emergent Wetlands ranged from .4 to 1,134 ha. (1 to 2,800 ac.); 81% of these were in the under 32-ha. (80-ac.) category. Thus, there are only a few very large reservoirs, silver sagebrush basins or emergent wetlands on the study area. This results in a fairly good distribution of smaller basin and wetland sites over the whole area. Eighty-three percent of all basin and wetland sites are less than 16 ha. (40 ac.) in size.

As a result of the upland conversions to wetlands, over 1,619 ha. (4,000 ac.) of Emergent Wetlands and Vernal Wetlands have been created. This has most certainly diversified the mosaic of cover-types on the study area.

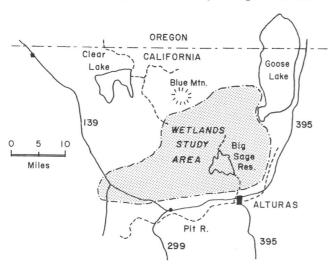

Figure 1.--Location of the Modoc Wetlands Study.

The loss of riparian vegetation has been largely mitigated by enhancement of streamside vegetation due to more consistent water flows from the reservoirs. All riparian areas continue to be heavily grazed by cattle.

The area of Low Sagebrush and Juniper/ Sagebrush lost to wetlands conversion is insignificant as a portion of the total area. We did not attempt an exact estimate of this loss, but it certainly amounts to less than 10% of the original area. While the size of the area affected by these changes is not significant, and not likely to ever become so, there is a distinct possibility that key pronghorn or sage grouse habitat areas could be lost through inundation.

METHODS

Fixed-wing and helicopter flights were used to census the animals: eight fixed-wing flights in 1978 and two in 1979, and five helicopter flights in 1979. Flights began at daybreak, usually between 06:00 and 07:00. Flights were made at approximately 190 kph (120 mph), 60 m. (200 ft.) above the ground, on north to south transects 0.8 to 1.61 km. (0.5 to 1 mi.) apart. Helicopter flights were made at 160 kph (100 mph), 150 m. (500 ft.) above the ground, on transects 3.2 to 4.8 km. (2 to 3 mi.) apart. All flights had two observers who recorded the number of animals seen, the cover-type, and location.

No attempt has been made to adjust data for differing observability of animals in different habitats. Habitat use is the number of animals observed in each cover-type as a proportion of the total number observed on each flight. Habitat preference is estimated by the index:

$$\frac{\text{Preference}}{\text{Index (PI)}} = \frac{\text{\% use of habitat} - \text{\% availability}}{\text{\% use of habitat} + \text{\% availability}}$$

This yields PI values that range from -1 to 1. When habitats are used in proportion to availability, PI = 0. PI values greater than zero imply preference while values less than zero imply lack of preference.

RESULTS

Wetlands

Developed wetlands were extremely important habitats to all three animals considered in the study. Use and preference for wetlands increased toward mid-summer with a peak depending on annual water conditions. In 1978, pronghorn use of wetlands peaked at 80% (PI = .86) on August 9 and remained over 40% through October 11; in 1979, use peaked at 71% (PI = .85) on September 14, after having exceeded 50% since August 31. Horse use peaked at 78% (PI = .86) on July 11 and remained over 40% through August 9 in 1978, and at 49% (PI = .78) on July 19 in 1979. Cattle use in 1978 peaked at 80% (PI = .86) on August 9 after exceeding 50% since June 22, and at 85% (PI =

.87) in 1979 on September 28 after exceeding 54% since May 22. Both pronghorn and horse exhibited a definite peak in wetland use in mid- to late summer; cattle use exceeded 50% of all observations from mid-June in both 1978 and 1979.

Emergent wetland vegetation, spikerush, and a diverse understory of succulent forbs was highly preferred for forage. Pronghorn appeared to lag about two weeks behind cattle and horses in using wetlands, perhaps needing the larger herbivores to remove coarse, grasslike forage and make forbs accessible.

Silver Sagebrush

Silver Sagebrush basins were also important to all three mammals. They were the first cover-type containing wetland forbs to dry each summer. Their use and preference preceded wetlands by two to four weeks. All three animals maintained a relativly high preference for Silver Sagebrush throughout the summer. Pronghorn use peaked at 23% on June 22 and 24% on July 25 (PI = .77) in 1978, and at 48% (PI = .88) on June 22 and 35% (PI = .84) on July 19 in 1979. Horse use peaked at 35% (PI = .84) on June 22, 1978, and at 44% (PI = .87) on May 25, 1979; cattle use never exceeded 31% of observations, but preference was high throughout the summer of both years.

Low Sagebrush

Low Sagebrush was used in the spring and early summer while its grasses and forbs were succulent. It was very important to pronghorn: 37% to 84% of all observations from April 27 to July 25, 1978 (PI = .11 to .48), and 19% to 66% of all observations from May 25 to August 31, 1979 (PI = .21 to .39). Horses and cattle used the Low Sagebrush type much less than its availability throughout the summer in both years; it is probably important in spring.

Juniper/Sagebrush

The Juniper/Sagebrush type was not a preferred summer habitat by any of the three animals. Only horses showed a slight positive PI on two flights. We suspect horses may use the cover-type for thermal cover on hot, sunny days. It could also be an important winter thermal cover habitat for horses.

DISCUSSION

Pronghorn vary their use and preference of habitat-types. Low Sagebrush is important in spring while forbs are palatable. As soils dry, Silver Sagebrush basins are preferred and may be especially important during drought or low-forage years, as in 1979. As wetland waters recede and horses and livestock remove coarse forage, pronghorn move to the drawdown zone. Wetlands appear to provide a significant source of green forage when uplands are dry. We believe wetlands must be drawn down and grazed by cattle to have maximum forage value to pronghorn.

Horses also vary their habitat use and preference, their pattern being similar to pronghorn. They do appear to rely on the Juniper cover-type more than pronghorn do.

Cattle prefer wetlands and Silver Sagebrush for summer grazing. They use Low Sagebrush when first put on the range, but rapidly move to the wetter sites. The presence of wetlands on a grazing allotment may relieve uplands of excessive use, and thus allow a natural improvement in condition.

It must be noted that all observations were made during the feeding period. Animals probably use habitats differently for resting cover during summer midday.

CONCLUSIONS

A variety of cover-types offering cover (thermal and security), seasonal forage, and water are used by large herbivores. Each cover-type appears to play a significant role for each animal. While wetlands are highly preferred, they are most often created by converting a Silver Sagebrush basin which itself is important to the animal in early summer. Land managers should try to achieve a representative balance among all possible habitats within allotments or wildlife home ranges. This study shows that a variety of cover-types may be a key to range capacity and condition.

LITERATURE CITED

Franklin, Jerry F., and C.T. Dyrness. 1973. Natural vegetation of Oregon and Washington. USDA Forest Service GTR-PNW-8. 417 p. Pacific Northwest Forest and Range Experiment Station, Portland, Oregon.

Salwasser, Hal, and Karen Shimamoto. In preparation. Modoc wetlands study: final report. University of California, Berkeley.

Young, James A., Raymond A. Evans, and Jack Major. 1977. Sagebrush Steppe. In: M. A. Barbour and J. Major (ed.). Terrestrial vegetation of California. 1002 p. John A. Wiley and Sons, New York, N.Y.

ECONOMIC AND SOCIAL VALUES IN RIPARIAN SYSTEMS[1]

Philip A. Meyer[2]

Abstract.--This paper identifies three progressively larger spatial and functional boundaries for riparian issues: 1) the riparian system, defined as the area adjacent to flowing fresh water, with its moist soils and associated biota and environment; 2) the riparian-use zone, where the riparian system and man interact and where riparian and non-riparian systems may interrelate with each other; and 3) the area of riparian influence, where "products" of the riparian-use zone (often water) are exported to impact on other ecological, social, and economic systems.

Riparian systems have value--and this value is generally recognized by Californians. But the prevalence of technologies of large scale finds "smaller" riparian systems and their direct dependents at a disadvantage. Forces of scarcity, of natural limits, and of political decentralization place large scale at present risk, however, and sustenance of the riparian-use zone may present important co-productive opportunity for balance and diversity--as insurance for California's larger productive systems.

Finally, such a co-productive approach to risk-spreading for California relies on the ability and willingness to exclude from decisional dialogue those whose allegiances are outside the state--for nomadic resource management will not be concerned with production or living conditions in California in the future and will consequently have little interest in protecting riparian systems or riparian-use zones.

RIPARIAN SYSTEMS AND RIPARIAN ZONES

Delineation of a riparian system seems an important point of departure for this discussion. In general, biological and physical sciences characterize riparian systems by the presence of fresh water in excess of that available locally, moist soils derived from that transported water, and the biota and environment associated with them. At any point in time, each single stream may be said to support such a system--to be observed in relatively dry valleys as distinct slashes of green along watercourses. In wetter areas, where soils are moister and vegetation more mesic, separation of one system from another is less distinct. Streams meander, fill channels, dry them up, and fill them again, giving riparian systems a distinctly dynamic character. Some would have us stop our definition of the system there, posing a major issue. Is man to be

treated as an integral part of the riparian equation--or is he to be considered an intruder? If one argues the latter, then one needs to proceed along the track of riparian system value for its own sake, and of public sentiment for preservation and against endangerment. Alternatively, if human use is considered part of riparian system dynamics, then approaches emphasizing community of interest, cooperative planning, and joint use become more feasible.

To be meaningful in an economic, social, or political sense, I suggest that riparian systems must encompass abutting human interest--to create what might be termed a riparian-use zone. Such a zone would encompass the spatial dynamics of meandering streams--but would not distinguish between the relative roles of nature and man in causing such meanderings. It would, in effect, recognize all plants, animals, and human activity found within the range of moist soils associated with riverine meanderings as part of the riparian-use

[1]Paper presented at the California Riparian Systems Conference. [University of California, Davis, September 17-19, 1981].

[2]Philip Meyer is Vice-President, Meyer Resources, Inc., Davis, Calif.

zone.[3] Within such an expanded definition, riparian-use zones remain small relative to total terrestrial area. But the definition would seem to encompass a breadth of alternative adjacent use and viewpoint--and thus offer compromise as well as confrontation as a viable policy tool.

Man is, of course, a riparian creature--having been attracted to and living near streams since earliest time. Thus, any systemic treatment of riparian systems must consider the people who are found in the riparian zone. These people may farm, fish and hunt, recreate non-consumptively, or carry on other activities, or they may do all of these. In early times, man did not often stray from his riparian zone of residence. Today, people are able to move from zone to zone, and to identify with particular zones at will. This matter of choice seems a critical issue for riparian systems in the 1980s.

As noted, riparian systems are dynamic. They change over time and are changed by man. In extreme cases--where, for instance, a river is dewatered and the water transferred to another area--a new riparian system may be established wherever the flows emerge. A major point at issue is, therefore, not whether riparian systems will exist, but where and for whom. This question is essentially economic, social, and--if one prefers--political. For man is not ambivalent between "self," "neighbor" and "others" nor between "now" and "later;" he will safeguard and nurture areas where he feels proprietary interest, while using and consumptively exploiting areas where he doesn't. Again, this would seem to render consideration of riparian systems within the broader context of riparian-use zones as imperative.

Finally, the influence of contemporary man and his technology have tended to extend and/or blur the boundaries of riparian-use zones. A further definition useful in this discussion is therefore advanced--the "area of riparian influence." While the riparian-use zone (as here defined) is bounded by adjacent water systems and their users, transmittal of Sacramento River water south, for instance, extends the Sacramento's hydrologic area of influence far beyond the riparian-use zone itself. In fact, hydrologic extension of riparian-use zones has been characteristic of water development in California. Similarly, human residents of riparian-use zones exert "influence" on matters beyond their zone--and influence is exerted on them by residents from other zones. This concept of zone of riparian influence may prove useful in bounding the definition of a riparian-use zone, and in separating riparian-use sources from destinations.

_____

[3]It is important to distinguish between a meander which leaves the mainstream but eventually returns (at least residually) and an export channel.

SOCIO-ECONOMIC PRODUCTIVITY OF RIPARIAN SYSTEMS

A second major issue affecting riparian systems may concern what role, if any, riparian systems and zones play in the larger economic, social and political processes of California.

Across a broad range of "products," the productivity of the riparian-use zone might be assessed by the equation:

$$RZ_p = WPHT,$$

where,

RZ_p = the productivity of the riparian zone.
W = quantity of water.
P = human population.
H = associated habitat.
T = available technology.

Of course, this equation is extremely simplified. In essence, however, it lays out the problem issues we face. Traditionally, P has expanded and T has been increased apace to alter habitat and "increase" water supply. Or has water supply increased? I think not. Our ability to control, husband, and reuse W has increased, but W has not. In the final sense, water constrains all but technology, and by constraining the production function RZ_p, eventually controls the usefulness of T, as well. If this is true, it may be that riparian systems will, in their full ecologic, social, and economic sense, be productivity controllers in California. Further, where riparian systems are in net decline, a decline in range of influence may follow, promising adverse conditions for a larger area. Productivity in the area of riparian influence may thus depend in some fundamental way on the continued viability of the riparian source.

RIPARIAN SYSTEMS AND VALUE

From a socio-economic perspective are riparian systems valuable? It is characteristic to answer such a question by "commissioning a study," "developing a survey," "establishing a valuing methodology," and so on. In fact, if you limit the concept of riparian to the narrow systems level, that is about all you can do; no effective method of dealing positively with users, let alone alternative users, will exist. But studies have been done. In 1979, Bollman (1979) used extremely conservative estimates of instream economic values to demonstrate a water management imbalance to the detriment of instream-related natural systems in California. In 1980, Meyer (1980) determined that 60% of the residents in California's Central Valley were unwilling to see fish and wildlife destroyed "at any price"--while the demands from those who would consider monetary compensation for destroyed fish and wildlife exceeded $2 billion annually. In 1982, similar findings were obtained for the riparian resources on the upper Sacramento River (Meyer Resources 1982). The values are there—but they have not been considered by decision-makers. Thus, it appears that we need to look elsewhere for the answer.

BIG IS VALUABLE—
IS SMALL UN-VALUABLE OR IN-VALUABLE?

It will be recalled that riparian-use zones are relatively small. Herein may lie several of the problems just referred to. First, economic models assume that valuation is applied to small units--a gallon of water, a bushel of wheat, a fishing day--that each unit of each product is valued separately. In this way, economists can demonstrate that the value of individual units of water applied to grow a crop, breed a fish, or support a water skier may increase for initial gallons used, but will progressively decrease as successive gallons are added. This principle of declining marginal value would suggest that where available water is in decline in the riparian-use zone, the water left for riparian uses would be increasingly productive--increased economic value for these remaining gallons or cubic feet per second would become evident--and progressive decline of the riparian water supply would stop due to this economic feedback loop.

This is what the economic model predicts, but such a reversal is not evident. One possible explanation of this "failure" of the market system is that the destruction of riparian systems in California is subsidized. In earlier times, it was reasoned that with markets still undeveloped, financial assistance was needed to transport water to arid areas to render soil productive and to support new populations and new crops. Today, subsidies continue. In consequence, the gap between value returns from subsidized large terrestrial zones and smaller riparian-use zones, which must demonstrate value unaided, has been large--and is only now beginning to close.

Second, while economic calculus operates in small incremental units, political calculus seems to operate in the largest available aggregates. Rhetoric about the risk to "$3 billion of crops" if "sufficient" water is not provided seems to largely obliterate questions of economic efficiency--and the riparian-use zone, with its relatively small area and limited number of residents, farmers, fishermen, and recreationists, finds itself with diminished political influence. As was noted earlier, there is also no guarantee that any given individual found in a riparian-use zone will feel particular allegiance to it.

Finally, the broad advance of technology has proceeded well beyond a scale appropriate to the riparian-use zone. Dialogue concerning this advance is well established in California--and poses two generalizable problems. First, while technology[4] is still able to increase its scale, the riparian-use zone does not seem well suited to assimilate the latest "big break-throughs" in the production of crops (via large-scale farming practice), fish (via hatcheries), or recreation (via people-intensive park experience). Of course, there is little assurance that such increases in scale will continue. The impacts of large-scale agriculture on employment and lifestyle, and on progressive deterioration of soil and water quality are at present being debated--as is vulnerability to variability in markets, seasons, and climatic conditions. Hatcheries, while a potential source of mitigation, are mistrusted by many fishery biologists--and there is no assurance that they will provide an effective replacement for natural stream habitat. Concerns over quality of experience and rising transportation costs now limit both the decision and the capability of recreationists to concentrate beyond immediate urban areas. But even if these concerns become realities, heavy investments at large scale have taken place--and the predictable response of most will be to plunge ahead, knowing "you're damned if you do, but it's too expensive to change."

These expenses, dealing with changing the momentum of larger scale, are termed frictional costs by economists. They are among the most serious challenges presently facing the riparian-use zone and will demand the fullest inventiveness of planners if they are to be dealt with.

RIPARIAN SYSTEMS--WHAT HOPE?

The foregoing analysis seems rather bleak. It suggests the riparian systems have value but that everybody knows that. Consequently, "documentation" of the obvious may do little to improve decisional result. What may then be needed is not documentation of value, but a strategy for survival. One such strategy is offered here.

Let us begin by recalling two basic features of California riparian-use zones: they are relatively small, and they are the source of extended benefits to a much larger area of California--principally through the transportation of their water. It seems that little is to be gained by conflict with development at large scale. When small confronts big, small usually loses. Consequently, decisions concerning the course of large-scale agriculture, urban development, fishery production, recreation, etc. will largely be determined in those respective arenas. This author believes that forces to curb expansion in scale are already at work--in cities, on the farm, in nature-based production. Some of these forces are economic and involve the increasing costs of "adding more" at the margin. Some are social and involve negative feedback from pollu-

---

[4]The word is here used to encompass the full range of applications of modern society to produce "products.

218

tion and other quality-of-life variables. Some are political and involve the major effort currently underway to reduce large scale in government and in decision-making. All these developments entail increased costs and risks for large systems.

It is my suggestion that concerns for riparian systems will be best advanced not through the adversarial challenge to furthering of such costs--but by presentation of riparian systems as a hedge against risk for overall productive systems in California. In agriculture, for instance, if technology at large scale is not fully effective and some significant level of damage is incurred by large-scale farming, it would seem desirable for agricultural policy to have alternative scaled-down systems of production available. Similarly, if difficulties arise in areas of riparian influence, it would seem important to have viable primary productive zones from which to reestablish effective agricultural systems. In fisheries, if hatchery production, transplant, and replant fall short of the required production, as they may, it may again be of benefit to maintain a diversified system offering alternative production possibilities. As noted, by focussing such a strategy upon riparian systems, this policy would not only provide a smaller-scaled hedge against production risks, but would also provide protection to the riparian system source of most of the extended benefits enjoyed at large scale by California. It would thus seem to offer an effective strategy across all productive levels.

RIPARIAN SYSTEMS FOR WHOM?

The foregoing preferred survival scenario is offered as a beneficial policy for all Californians. It would be naive, however, to suggest that all who presently produce in the state--or who speak out on resource issues--proceed from the perspective of a single riparian-use zone or of California as a whole. "Magnamobility" enables an individual's body to reside alongside the Sacramento River, while his/her voice is transmitted to Hong Kong, his bank account is in Switzerland, and his political allegiances are fixed in Kuwait, for example. Thus, magnomobility introduces a new concept of scale: scale in decision-making. Not only does this offer new expanded potential for strategic manipulation, but it involves us immediately in a resource management issue of consistent concern through history.

In early times, Indian bands, for example, were sometimes nomadic--following resources, depleting them, and moving on to a more productive area. As non-Indians came to North America and as populations increased, this nomadic style of resource use became less appropriate; sustained-yield treatment of production from land and waters has become the generally preferred mode of harvest. In fact, however, nomadism is not extinct. In commercial fishing, for example,

large Soviet-bloc fleets roam the seas, moving from depleted areas to more productive ones. At a lower level of aggregation, scallop fishermen from America's East Coast could be observed in the summer of 1981 "fishing out" scallops off southern Oregon, to the dissatisfaction of local fishermen who seek to sustain year-to-year resource capability.

The perspective of resource users with regard to resource capability in California is therefore critical to the dialogue on riparian system production, and, in fact, overall production in the state. If the present owners and users of agricultural, fishery, and other resources generated directly or indirectly from California's riparian systems are nomadic in their approach to resource use, they will have already hedged their production risks elsewhere, either in the United States or abroad. At the first sign of real trouble they can logically be expected to "take their money and run." Such individuals are unlikely to be much interested in hedging risk "for California," and consequently, little interested in the continued viability of California's riparian systems.

If such a resource-use style prevails in California (and it may), the co-productive scenario suggested here will not apply. Then, perhaps, humans cannot be treated as co-users--but might be more appropriately considered intruders. In such a case, initiatives based on a single interest or a single riparian-use zone would in fact seem to be the only viable way to preserve or maintain riparian systems. In this author's view, however, such approaches may hold little promise in the years ahead.

SUMMARY

In this introductory paper, I have not attempted to document the social and economic value of riparian systems, nor proposed more documentation. I contend that riparian value exists, is significant, and, for the vast majority of Californians, is self-evident. Rather, I have speculated as to why these values have not been fully reflected in resource policy. In so doing, I have posed three main issues.

The first is whether man is inside or outside the riparian system--for this decision will seriously influence the structure and scope of economic, social, and political value.

Second, harsh treatment of the relatively small riparian systems and their direct dependents by the relatively larger-scaled in agriculture, urban development, fish production, and so on, may have had an adverse impact. Such treatment follows from a societal commitment to large-scale technology and to production intensity that is beyond the aggregate scope of riparian productivity. It is not suggested here that riparian systems be forwarded as an alternative productive mode, but rather as an element of stability and diversity in California's productive plan—to act as an insurance policy should the future go well, and as lifeboats in the event of disaster.

Finally, it is suggested that those with boats on other seas will have little use for lifeboats in California—and the above proposal will have little interest for them. All that can be said here is that if California is going to develop her own effective resource policy, it will have to exclude or downplay from consideration those whose allegiance is elsewhere or who practice a nomadic style of resource management. Only then will concern for co-production within individual riparian-use zones—a principal preoccupation of many present planning efforts—be effective. If this cannot be achieved, it would seem better to return to the old style of single issue protective advocacy, fire the resource planners and coordinators, let research on social and economic values abound, and get on with the infighting.

LITERATURE CITED

Bollman, F. H. 1979. Instream values, a memorandum for the Governor's Commission to review California water rights law, State of California, Sacramento. 78 p. plus appendices.

Meyer, P. A. 1980. Recreational/aesthetic values associated with selected groupings of fish and wildlife in California's Central Valley. Center for Natural Areas, report of contract to USDI Fish and Wildlife Service, Sacramento, Calif. 56 p.

Meyer Resources. 1982. Economic evaluation of river projects—values for fish, wildlife, and riparian resources. Volume III. California Resources Agency, Sacramento. 56 p.

ECONOMIC ANALYSIS AND THE MANAGEMENT OF

RIPARIAN RESOURCES[1]

Frank H. Bollman[2]

"The age of chivalry is gone; that of the sophisters, economists, and calculators has succeeded."
Edmund Burke, circa 1770

INTRODUCTION

The management of riparian resources, including their development for other uses and their retention for present uses, is a political and social process and consequently is rooted in our social institutions. Public and private measures affecting the course of riparian resource development extend far beyond water resources development per se, whether by Federal, state, or local agencies. Apart from direct Federal regulation of navigable channels, state regulation of public water supplies and waste discharge, floodplain regulations, and county and city regulation of land use and drainage are but a few of the institutional means which exercise constraints on or stimuli to the conversion of riparian resources.

Legal rights to water, the essential resource in the many resources comprising riparian resources, play an important role in determining their respective uses. The whole fabric of water law rules on water transfers and allocations. The preservation of natural stream courses can even rest on the kind and terms of technical and financial assistance available to cities, towns, and individuals for water and land investments. Cost-sharing and reimbursement provisions of Federal, state and local authorities are important in shaping the use of one or more of the water and land resources comprising riparian resources. Nonstructural alternatives to structural measures for managing riparian resources, especially in floodplains, are eliminated by the cost-sharing arrangements which encourage local authorities to settle for engineering structures.

Water quality is as important as water quantity in maintaining a stream's fish and wildlife productivity and its aesthetic and recreational dimensions. The standard for water quality management is determined on the basis of public health, sanitary engineering, and other applied natural sciences.

The complexity and variety of the many laws and regulations pertaining to riparian resources suggest its management be construed as an administrative task carried out in response to laws and regulations which adopt certain criteria and standards. Where, therefore, does economic analysis enter the scene? How can the logic of policical economy prevail to ensure that riparian resources do produce the greatest welfare for society?

I propose in this paper to show that conservation and its converse, depletion, are highly significant economic problems. Thus, economic concepts and logic have a vital role in establishing policy objectives for managing riparian resources. My aim is to demonstrate the usefulness of economic concepts and principles in coping with two fundamental and interrelated problems in the economics of conservation of riparian resources, indeed of all natural resources. The two problems I am referring to are: 1) that of valuing the present and future flow of benefits and costs that emanate from any of several alternatives for managing the resource; and 2) that of dealing with uncertainties created by the changes in peoples' preferences, in technology, and in the institutions which directly or indirectly are responsible for managing riparian resources.

Man's overriding economic problem is to make the most of the resources we have. This involves picking the best allocation of resources among competing uses. Any such allocation involves the valuation of those competing uses, whether they be for riparian resources or any other single or bundle of natural resources. Economics is the systematic analysis involved in choosing alternative courses of action.

The economics of conservation of natural resources is the study of choice between different distributions in time of the use of natural resources. It is on these common grounds that the focus of the conservationist and the economist converge; the central issue for both being the relationship of past and present to fu-

[1]Paper presented at the California Riparian Systems Conference. [University of California, Davis, September 17-19, 1981].
[2]Frank H. Bollman is Consultant with Natural Resources Economics, Sacramento, Calif.

ture use of natural resources (Ciriacy-Wantrup 1963).[3]

FULL-ALTERNATIVE PLANNING

Economic analysis can provide aid where problems of choice present alternative courses of action in riparian resource management. Planning for water resources, as well as related land, vegetation, and fish and wildlife planning can benefit from application of the full-alternative method. When this method is not adopted and institutionalized, the value of economic analysis is greatly diminished.

The water resources planning process in policy and practice should not limit consideration of alternatives to those which are developed around the production of market products—irrigation, municipal and industrial water supplies, power, navigation, etc., to the exclusion of nonmarket uses—scenery, fish and wildlife, recreation, historic sites—social values which now cannot be easily expressed in monetary terms.

Water resources planning was in the past considered the appropriate method of appraising the development of natural resources at individual sites or in specific areas, designing feasible projects, and determining economic benefits and costs of the market products produced. The transition to full-alternative planning where all practicable alternatives, including market and nonmarket benefits and costs, are presented to the decisionmakers, has not yet been made in the area of water resources planning. In my judgment, state and Federal water resources planning still lack the facility to account for the nonmarket values intrinsic in the use of riparian resources.

If the avowed water policy thrust of the new Federal administration is any indication, future prospects for consideration of a broader range of alternatives to account for nonmarket uses seem to have narrowed. According to William R. Gianelli, Secretary, Civil Works, US Army Corps of Engineers, the tentative guidelines (for evaluating Federal water projects) being sent to Congressional committees, states, and interested

_____

[3]In 1941, Professor S.V. Ciriacy-Wantrup defined conservation and its corollary—depletion—in terms of changes in the intertemporal distribution of physical rates of resource use involving the comparison of at least two actual or hypothetical time distributions. To compare the distributions, a weighting system, using distance in time as weight, is devised. The optimum state of conservation refers to an economic optimum in time distribution of physical rate of resource use. (See S.V Ciriacy-Wantrup, 1942. Private enterprise and conservation. Journal of farm economics, February, 1942. Paper presented before the Annual Meeting of the American Farm Economic Association, New York City, December 27-30, 1941.)

parties for comment provide that, in analyzing whether a proposed water project should be built, environmental quality will no longer be an objective. That would mean "there will be only one objective which will be the basis for evaluation of projects. That will be the national economic development objective."[4]

The attempts in the recent past by the US Water Resources Council, to be disbanded September 30, 1981 by the present Administration, recognized that the social objectives of water and related land planning considered desirable by society had increased, and that attaining these objectives may not be consistent with the most economically profitable use (market products only) of these natural resources. Society's interest in recreation, aesthetics, quality of the environment, scenery, etc., indicates a willingness to have public monies spent in a way which does not satisfy the highest benefit:cost ratio computed for market goods. In other words, society is willing to pay for the nonmarket services provided by these natural resources, including riparian resources. On the other hand, society should know what nonmarket services are available and at what cost. Society can then determine what it is willing to pay (including foregone benefits for those nonmarket services).

The water and related land resources planning process should identify and present all valid alternative courses of action including nonmarket and market benefits and costs. The planning process must be designed, organized, and operated to find ways of realizing values held in different degrees by different people in different places.

New institutional arrangements, rather than elimination or reduction of the present arrangements, appear necessary to deal with the increasingly complex nature of water and land use planning. These new arrangements will have to account for the nonmarket as well as the market objectives.

THE VEXING PROBLEM OF VALUATION

The "best" allocation of resources is that which results in a maximum of net social value over time. This is an objective which unfortunately eludes quantification.

Riparian resources produce both market and nonmarket benefits. The former, expressed in monetary terms, are readily measurable; the latter still defy transformation into dollar terms entirely comparable with their market counterparts. This situation prevails although economists have devised, and are continuing to devise, innovative and ingenious methods of measurement. In my judgment, many of the proxies and surrogates are derived by methods employing

_____

[4]"The Sacramento Bee", September 14, 1981. p. B1-B2.

precise measurement and founded on sound economic demand theory with the added virtue that they are based on the consumer's actual behavior, not his hypothetical behavior. They are useful especially in providing insight as to the minimum values involved.

It is regrettably true that despite such progress in measuring nonmarket values, in the absence of objective criteria for evaluating nonmarket effects, they can be overvalued or undervalued. Devotees of natural riparian systems might claim they are continually underestimated.

Nonmarket benefits stemming from riparian resources are real; they are not zero nor are they infinite. Because they may be diffuse, as in the case of streams and ponds providing feeding and overwintering grounds for migratory waterfowl, they are not necessarily negligible. That the beneficiaries are difficult to identify, much less number, does not mean nonmarket benefits do not exist. As in the case of other natural resources, there is an urgent need to explore methods for explicitly weighing nonmarket benefits (measured in whatever units possess some relevance—miles of spawning gravels, acres of streamside vegetation, preferably in dollars of willingness to pay) together with dollar market benefits for riparian resources. The shortcoming of relying solely on market values must be effaced if we are to obtain "full value" from riparian resources.

Notwithstanding the difficulty of valuing nonmarket effects, economic logic and concepts provide insight to and resolution of other aspects of the valuation problem.

ALLOCATION OF RESOURCES

In the allocation of riparian resources, economic reasoning can be employed in several ways to support informed decisions. For example, a timbered streamside strip of land is considered valuable habitat for wildlife, while the stream itself has pristine spawning gravels. The competing use would initially be logging the timber stands, and subsequently clearing and cultivating to the water's edge, with the certain destruction of the wildlife habitat and the likely silting of the gravel beds ensuing. The strip of land can be purchased as a recreation or conservation easement.

The common sense economic approach is to find out how great the costs are before prejudging whether or not it is worth letting the wildlife habitat and spawning gravel be lost. If it would cost, for example, $100 per fish produced, $500 per deer produced, one may conclude there are better alternatives for this expenditure. But, if the cost would amount to only a fraction of a dollar per fish, perhaps less than a hatchery-produced fish, and especially if the costs of production for the logger and the farmer for a different production site are raised only

slightly, one might rationally conclude it would be a wise action to preserve the strip of timbered land as wildlife habitat.

For riparian lands, some uses are compatible. Where water quality is maintained, agriculture and fishing can coexist. Even game and cattle are not always direct rivals for riparian resources. The combination of uses—fishing with farming, wildlife with cattle grazing and forestry, panning for gold in the streams, summer camps, even homesites makes the task of valuing the joint products of the riparian resource exceedingly difficult, but also highly desirable. For example, when urbanization encroaches on a riparian sanctuary, it is essential to know what amenity and recreational values are being forfeited as a result of the encroachment. It is important to know when these values are sufficiently high to justify "buying off" further encroachment or even extending the area of the riparian sanctuary by buying out existing residents.

The attitudes of people toward preservation and maintenance of species is subject to change. As a species grows scarcer, it becomes more valuable in both monetary terms and public regard as basic to man's environment. Likewise, as the wilderness has receded and its proportion of the land area continually diminished, society has come to value it more highly. In Gold Rush days, large tracts of "riparian wilderness" could be hypothesized as having negative values. The change in attitude toward a resource is directly proportional to the availability of that resource.

Where large numbers of people are living in areas in which a considerable portion of the riparian resources is used for other purposes, there is a gradual change in attitude as to the value of preserving what little remains in its original use (or state). To maintain wildlife habitat, the State of California is buying very expensive land; the wildlife protection argument is now strongly supported by many sectors of the populace. It is just such a situation that creates a political climate which welcomes cogent economic argument as a useful aid to policy decisions for preservation of riparian resources.

Economic analysis has to cope with defining economic and technological irreversibility—i.e., what unique resources to maintain today, tomorrow, and in the future? Quite probably society can afford the first yard, the first mile, with much less loss in fish and wildlife and amenity resources than that involved in taking a subsequent segment. But to determine the point at which the values foregone are greater than those gained is extremely difficult, demanding a good knowledge of the total ecosystem and its overall production possibilities. In the next section, dealing with the problem of uncertainty, a useful policy objective is proposed for managing riparian lands, reduced to a marginal state, for the production of one or another or its nonmarket services.

What is lost as a result of not converting riparian lands to homesites as against leaving them as producing habitats for fish and wildlife? There is a balance; if we give up too much riparian resource, the loss of future benefits can be very great. Where the line of demarcation is to be drawn is difficult to gauge, but economic analysis can give useful insights. If the destruction of the riparian resource results in complete destruction of the species supported by that riparian system, and the system is extremely difficult to replace, the administrator should place a great deal of weight on keeping options for that system open.[5]

In making a decision as to how much, if any, of a riparian system is to be given up for the development of homesites, the administrator should take into account the relative scarcity of this resource or the relative scarcity of the wildlife and fish it supports and the amenities and recreation it makes available, and compare this with the relative scarcity of homesites in this vicinity or close by. Are there substitute opportunities for such homesites?

Where the riparian resource is unique, or very scarce, appreciating or increasing future values should be considered; the rarer something becomes relative to other things, the more valuable it becomes. Unique recreation experiences are worth a great deal to many people, and it is this future income stream which is important to assess.

One argument which has been proposed for the preservation of rare phenomena in the natural environment is that advances in technology permit society to provide an ever-increasing flow of goods and services from our agricultural and industrial bases at lower costs. However, the relatively scarce natural phenomena are not reproducible; and, even if tastes were not changing in society in favor of more natural environment, the cost of preserving it is rising. The natural environment is tending to become more valuable in terms of goods and services produced in the agricultural and industrial sectors.

Another variant of this argument which should be subjected to critical appraisal is that we don't really need the products of riparian systems--the timber, grass, or minerals; that the need for such commercial products from riparian lands and waters is very low. Society gives up very little in setting aside areas of natural riparian systems for there are more accessible and better (lower cost) places for obtaining these raw materials. This argument, should it hold, cautions the economist and wildlife administrator to examine carefully society's need for

---

[5]The discussion developed in this section follows closely the reasoning presented in Frank H. Bollman, "Some basic considerations in satisfying the demand for water in its natural environment" (Sackler 1971).

the natural environmental resource and check to see if it is a "sector" with appreciating values relative to those of other sectors. The value which poor farming land has in recreation as sites for week-end and vacation homes is quite high as gauged by the prices paid for such land. The community isn't losing very much in terms of the corn and timber foregone as a consequence of the new owner--the recreationist--not farming or logging the land. The cost of producing recreation in terms of the lumber and corn foregone is very low. Some classes of riparian lands fall into such a category.

Riparian resources, in addition to the joint products mentioned previously, also provide recreational services such as white-water canoeing, rafting, swimming, hiking, and in the case of the American River Parkway, other types of recreation--cycling, jogging, etc., which are ends in themselves. However, riparian systems provide wildlife resources which in Anthony Scott's terminology have a "state" value as well as a "use" value (Scott 1976). Riparian lands purchased as conservation easements for animal and bird sanctuaries and refuges may never be visited by those financing the easement. Unvisited resources are not therefore valueless, indeed the value is that of the purchase price.

THE PROBLEM OF UNCERTAINTY

The uncertainty of future demands for riparian resources and the effects in the future of past and present water and land resource developments on these resources cautions a need for flexibility that will foreclose as few alternatives as possible. Maintaining flexibility for the future is wise in a society with rapidly changing tastes and preferences which are impossible to forecast, and where technology provides many alternatives for the supply of water. In addition, it is presently very difficult to predict the consequences of changes in flows upstream upon a specific riparian resource downstream. Specific natural riparian environments in California are finite in number, irreplaceable, and increasingly scarce; decisions to change one or other of those systems' components, once implemented, can be irreversible. The ecological balance may be upset severely enough to set in motion a chain reaction which is irreversible. The siltation of streams and the disappearance of streamside vegetation are two examples of this. Often such results are caused as much by ignorance of the ecology of an area as by deliberate action to effect the change.

Ciriacy-Wantrup (1963) has proposed that a "safe minimum standard" of resource management be adopted so as to practically preclude the possibility of irreversible change.

For a certain class of flow resources such as fish and wildlife species threatened with extinction due to human action, a relevant management policy objective is to avoid the irreversible change entailed in that extinction.

This necessitates the recognition that there are "critical zones" in resource management--and to exceed these critical thresholds will mean the irreversible change cannot be averted. A safe minimum standard is adopted as a base level for maximizing social welfare. Ciriacy-Wantrup (ibid.) compares this objective of resources management with the objective of an insurance policy against serious losses that resist quantitative measurement; the objective being not to maximize a statistically computable net gain, but to adjust premium payments to pay out possibilities in such a way that maximum possible future losses are guarded against with minimum present costs.

Where policy action is taken in sufficient time, there is the likelihood that the costs of a course of action (i.e., the insurance premium) to guarantee the safe minimum standard are small in relation to the maximum posible losses which would result from not enforcing the standard.

The aesthetic resources of riparian systems--for example the scenic river gorges with their unique combinations of sights, sounds, and scents--and the gene pools of the many species of flora and fauna that have evolved in riparian circumstances, are resources which fall into the class of flow resources[6] where such a management objective is applicable.

SUMMARY

The planning for development and use of water and related land resources should give increased attention to alternative approaches and courses of action that minimize unintended effects on the amenity and fish and wildlife resource values of riparian systems. Economic analysis is a powerful aid to identifying and evaluating practicable alternatives. However, the planning process has to include all alternatives which should incorporate nonmarket as well as market uses of such systems. The appraisal of social costs and benefits should not be relegated to a "tack on" to satisfy Federal and state environmental assessments.

The present institutional framework for decisions in the State, and the process of planning in this field, although revised in recent years, still leave much to be desired. It might be fairly stated that economic analysis, including the employment of recognized useful methods of valuing amenity and recreational services of riparian sites, is undertaken, if at all, at a low level of sophistication. The organization of planning should permit balanced consideration of the choices and the values involved.

The difficulty of incorporating nonmarket effects should not blind us to the usefulness of economic logic in supplying insights as to the overall valuation of these resources.

The demands upon water and land in California necessitate sound planning and efficient management.

Management beneficial to the already greatly reduced riparian systems in the State depend on sound planning. Sound planning depends on sound economic analysis and accurate prediction of the consequences of natural resources development on the riparian system.

For "marginal" riparian systems, a safe minimum standard of management as a policy objective has been proposed, and if effectively applied could expand the State's ability to manage riparian systems for the public good.

LITERATURE CITED

Ciriacy-Wantrup, S.V. 1963. Resource conservation economics and politics. Second edition. Division of Agricultural Sciences, University of California.

Sackler, David W. (ed.). 1971. California water: a study of resource management. University of California Press, Berkeley.

Scott, Anthony. 1976. The valuation of game resources: some theoretical aspects. Canadian Fisheries Reports, number 4. Department of Fisheries of Canada.

---

[6]After a fashion, the State of California, in setting water quality standards for the Delta, has adopted in principle the safe minimum standard; maintenance of striped bass productivity has been elected as the key standard.

PUBLIC VALUES AND RIPARIAN SYSTEMS[1]

James W. Burns[2]

Abstract.--Because the benefits derived from riparian systems are provided by nature without cost, it is difficult to compare the real economic worth of riparian systems with activities--such as agriculture and grazing--that have well-defined market values. In addition, these more easily quantified activities receive subsidies that increase their value and encourage their development. The protection of riparian systems will not be won simply by the passage of a law by a county board of supervisors or the State Legislature. Pressures for development will continue to increase and an effective lobby for protecting riparian systems will be needed to balance the political influence of industrial and development lobbies.

Riparian systems accomplish many functions that are valuable to the public. These functions include fish and wildlife production, bank erosion protection, flood control, water quality maintenance, timber production, fuel production, sound absorption, air quality maintenance, recreation, and scenic barriers to upland development. The protection of these public values is primarily the responsibility of government. Some may disagree with me regarding government's role, especially in these times when so many people claim we have too much government interference in our lives. But because riparian systems are so often on or closely associated with public lands, government is the logical agency to look to for their preservation. The way government administers this responsibility depends upon the public's concern at all levels--Congress, state legislatures, boards of supervisors, city councils, and special districts--for the resource values of riparian areas as well as other variables such as market economics and politics.

The work performed by riparian systems--fish and wildlife production, flood and erosion control, and water quality maintenance, to name a few examples--is nature's free work. Because the work is free and there is no commonly accepted market value for this work, it is difficult to arrive at the economic value of a riparian system in conventional, dollars and cents, terms. Too often, decisionmakers resolve this problem by assigning a real estate value to it, that is, the selling price of a comparable acre of land.

If you are not guided by an environmental ethic, it may be difficult to accept an alternative economic value based upon the value of nature's free work, the dollar value that environmental groups or biologists might use, or a value derived from the energy accounting method developed by Odum. Although these methods can provide strong arguments that the system does have significant economic value, the data may be too subjective for the decisionmaker to accept. The market value of an agricultural crop, cattle grazing, or a condominium tend to win most of the battles in this economic value war.

Public opinion and scientific information, however, do play an important role in deciding the value of riparian systems. Public opinion and scientific information are most influential when dealing with public lands--the national parks, national forests, Bureau of Land Management lands, and state lands--since it is accepted that these lands belong to the public and agencies that manage them are guided by mandated multiple-use doctrines in addition to a recognized stewardship responsibility. For private lands there is another variable that weighs heavily in the decisionmaking formula--that variable is private property rights. Even for areas where the public concern is strong, decisions often favor the landowner at the public's expense. Prime examples of this are coastal wetlands and wild and scenic rivers. Because of public concern, laws were enacted to protect these resources. But now, because of strong industrial lobbies or the political influence of developers, these laws are being threatened by amendments that diminish the protections these public resources were previously afforded. The immediate needs of the landowner and the economic value of marketed resources are being emphasized over the long-term public values provided free by nature.

---

[1]Paper presented at the California Riparian Systems Conference. [University of California, Davis, September 17-19, 1981].

[2]James W. Burns is Assistant Secretary for Resources, The Resources Agency, State of California, Sacramento, Calif.

Even though decisionmakers may understand the important functions carried out by a river, a wetland, or a riparian system, they have not been told how much of the system needs to be preserved to carry out the functions. The decisionmakers may ask: "How much of the system do you need to preserve?" The environmentalist's answer to this question may be: "Everything that remains." This is unacceptable to a decisionmaker who is looking for a compromise.

Remember, it may be political suicide for a government decisionmaker to say "no" to development. Consequently, compromises are made and damage occurs in increments small or large. The debate may focus on a site-specific consideration--"Is the area that will be damaged critical to the functioning of the whole system?" Although scientists have not defined how much of the area must remain for a system to function, they have warned us that the systems are critical to the survival of important resources, and incremental damage has led to severe impacts. For example, king salmon populations in California have declined 60% from historic levels, wetlands have declined 90%, and riparian woodlands have declined over 90%. The trend for California is not unique. The Nation has lost 70-90% of its riparian woodlands and the rate of loss exceeds 6% per year. Although these statistics have some shock value, they still do not tell the decisionmaker that he has to say "no" to the proposed development. He may think: "If we have lost so much already how can a little more hurt?" Or: "If you don't want the development, then buy the land."

Often we look to purchasing the land or the owner's development rights as a solution. Even when funds are available to purchase development rights, the landowner may be unwilling to sell at a reasonable price. The development rights may be too valuable because public subsidies have lessened the landowner's costs and in turn have increased his profits. For agriculture, subsidized water supplies, subsidized erosion control, and subsidized flood control have decreased the risks of crop damage and have made it profitable to plant within the floodplain to the detriment of native riparian vegetation and the public resources it supports.

Even on public lands, a private user may develop an economic interest that has adverse impact on the public's resources. Because of this private economic interest, the public land manager may be unable politically to control the private use of the public's resource. For example, as a result of the political effectiveness of livestock interests, grazing fees on public lands have historically been below fees on comparable private lands. Thus, grazing fees on most public lands do not reflect the market value of similar forage on private lands, the costs of controlling erosion, restoring vegetation, improving water supplies, fencing, and generally managing the allotment. The public subsidizes the cattleman's use of the land and the public pays for the repair of the damaged riparian system-- the lost wildlife, erosion, etc. However, when decisions regarding management of public lands are made, emphasis is given to the economic impacts on the cattleman, not on the lands and other resources. I could cite other examples of how logging, mining, and concessionaires impair the public's resources on public lands without adequate compensation.

The point I want to make is that there is more to protecting and managing riparian systems than the government buying a strip of land along a river, or enacting laws controlling the removal of native vegetation within floodplains. A strong political influence is paramount. Riparian systems will always be threatened, regardless of ownership and laws, and government decisions will always be critical to the protection of the riparian system. Concerned citizens cannot focus all of their attention on any single solution to the problem. They must identify how government decisions are made and what will influence future decisions. They must consider how a proposed public acquisition, a law, a subsidy, or other government actions affect riparian systems. In order to idenfify and monitor these actions there must be a division of labor within a group of citizens sharing the common interest of protecting riparian sytems. The interest group must be active and must develop political influence to balance the lobbying of the private sector that uses and impacts the public's resources.

A FARMER'S VIEW OF RIPARIAN SYSTEMS[1]

E.M. Faye, Jr.[2]

"One impulse from a vernal wood
　May teach you more of man,
　Of moral evil and of good,
Than all the sages can."
　　Wordsworth--The Tables Turned

We can only imagine the spot William Wordsworth had in mind when he wrote those lines, but I can think of several places on my own farm where those words have special meaning to me.

Four generations of my family have worked the land along the Sacramento River that I call home. And I can empathize with everyone who would like to share with me the special feeling one gets in a spot where nature remains pretty much undisturbed. Visitors often seem to envy me--just the same way, I suspect, that I occasionally envy someone who lives within walking distance of a school or who doesn't have to call long distance to order a pizza to go.

Richard Warner invited me to add my thoughts to this discussion. I wasn't certain whether it was because I sit on the State Reclamation Board, whose job it is to keep the Central Valley river systems from flooding, or as Deputy Director of the Department of Food and Agriculture, whose job it is to promote and protect California agriculture in the interest of public health, safety, and welfare. Or perhaps because I farm along one of the great riparian systems in the State, the Sacramento River, and thus have more than a passing interest in the subject. I'd like to believe it is for all three reasons.

I must first confess to a built-in bias on the subject at hand as it relates to me. My first impulse is to advise everyone to stay away from the riparian systems. People either tromp them down, close them off, trash them, or set fire to them. They may even catch poison oak. I hope they do.

After all, many people in this land are still strongly influenced by the ownership ethic--the dream of having one's own place in the country, away from the hustle, the hassle, the "have to", and the "have not." The fact that it becomes more and more difficult as population and mobility increase, to find a spot where someone

else didn't arrive first, only augments the urge. And furthermore, the guy who got there first often has altered the scene, either with stuff he brought in or by taking something away.

As one who, in this particular case, got there first, I tend to be a strong defender of private property rights.

My problem is that I can see a little of the view perceived by the outsider who would like to get in--the "have not" who wants. I, too, lament each solitary oak tree removed from a tomato field that I have passed for years--a lone sentinel in a vast flat field, a spot of shade for horses to stop 50 or 60 years ago when it meant little to leave a few spots uncultivated in a 40-acre field. I, too, love to stop my car at the side of the road next to a lush coastal stream that empties into the ocean less than a thousand feet away. I would like better access to the vast untrafficked foothill lands covered with scrub oak and manzanita that characterize both sides of these great flat valleys--great country for horseback riding.

But I am compelled to defend that built-in bias I mentioned a moment ago, because I think my main message is in that arena. I suspect there will be sufficient voice represented here for the point of view of those who want more public access to private lands or to close off more land altogether.

In today's competitive economic climate, the owner of that tree standing alone in a tomato field has to weigh its value to him in terms of more than its beauty. It costs him extra to plant, irrigate, and harvest around it. It is a hazard to safe application of fertilizer and pesticides or herbicides. He's trying to stay in business and there is no economic reward for inefficiency. The tree goes.

The tree may be an isolated event, standing by itself, so to speak. But it represents the same principle applied to some riparian systems. There are isolated spots, sometimes many acres in area, that stand in the middle of or jut out into otherwise developed agricultural lands. Examples would include old sloughs and finger lakes or cut-off river bends along a meandering stream such as are found along the Sacramento River. Years ago when farm equipment permitted little more than cutting trees, clearing brush, and plowing, little could be done to include these spots into a farm. We simply worked around them and accepted the inefficiencies. As a matter of

---

[1]Paper presented at the California Riparian Systems Conference. [University of California, Davis, September 17-19, 1981].

[2]E.M. Faye is Deputy Director, Department of Food and Agriculture, Sacramento, California.

fact, we don't have a single field on our farm that has four square corners.

We have three or four places on our farm that could be defined as riparian systems. We keep them because we love them. So far, our devotion to them has outweighed the demands upon us to require their soil to help support the rest of our operation.

I submit to you the notion that most of the riparian forests that remain around us will continue to remain. Their demise, if it occurs, will happen no faster than their replacement. The development of our county, state, and Federal parks, preserves, forests, and even private parks continually brings land back into preservation. One need only to fly from here to New York to be impressed with the vast area of riparian systems that blesses this land. We have great wilderness areas already dedicated to long-term preservation.

Consider the Sacramento River for a moment. When commerce along the river was at its peak and the river itself was the principal transportation medium through the Valley, the big boats operated on steam. The steam resulted from water heated by burning wood. Where do you think that wood came from? The era ended or at least changed, before the trees were all gone, but there was a time, about 80-100 years ago, when there were few trees over a foot in diameter within a half-mile of the river. Nearly all the oaks and sycamores, the ash and cottonwood we glorify today, are second growth, or at least were too small to cut in the heyday of the steam era. But the era passed and our resilient nature bounced back. I don't think we're worse off for the experience.

It is my position today that the concern of some for the changing scene need not turn to excessive zeal to conserve or protect what remains. It will still be here long after we're gone. Rather I would encourage you to concentrate on improving the quality of life while we're here.

Make friends with a farmer. Pick up a bottle or a plastic beer holder or a rubber-thonged slipper that some thoughtless klutz left on the bank of the river. But don't legislate access or prohibition from access.

I believe we have a far greater problem with waste material, if you'd like to consider working for a better environment.

I should comment, however, that I'm not really too worried about the environment as a whole. While we do mess up our own nest as an animal--the cities are outrageous, roadways an embarrassment, and waterways undrinkable--it usually only hurts ourselves. It only takes one incident like Mt. St. Helens to demonstrate how inconsequential our projects like roads and houses can be. It only takes one good Pacific storm to clean up the air. It only takes one good wind-whipped lightning-started brushfire to clean up a mountainside. Then begins the time-worn process of rain, erosion, silting, germination, and regrowth that has provided us this vast and treasured agricultural valley in the first place.

The durability of the Medfly should demonstrate how adaptable various life forms are to changes in their original habitat.

The fact that a few species pass by to extinction while we happen to be watching does not mean we should feel responsible for a general degradation of the earth. Sure, we help some to extinction, but many have gone that we had nothing to do with. New ones come along too.

So I am recommending that you not be overly zealous. That you not try to save all sinners or cure all ills with a flurry of activity which may make you more satisfied while you're here, but may not really add to the best interests of everyone.

Seek soft solutions, if you will.

Provide economic incentives if you can figure out how. Buy land or let people give it when they want, but don't take it away either in toto or in the form of restrictions.

Our system of private enterprise, with its incentives built on an individual's ability to make the best use of the resources available to him, has served all of us well. We have come to the point where less than 5% of our population provides the food for the rest of us. It is only now in our evolution that people are free enough from the demands of food gathering to have the luxury of telling the food producers that they don't like what the producers are doing.

DIVERSE INTERESTS IN RIPARIAN SYSTEMS AND THE POTENTIAL

FOR COALITION[1]

William M. Kier[2]

Abstract.—The role of state government in flood control project financing is examined, considering the effect of such projects on riparian systems. Changes in state policy, and the unlikely coalition that brought them about, are discussed. The need for comprehensive policy analysis as a foundation for protection of riparian values is emphasized.

POLICY PROBLEM

The message of this paper is a simple one: There are public policies, including public investment programs, at work today destroying riparian systems. People concerned with the protection of riparian systems have demonstrated their inability to deal effectively with these policies. There is a demonstrated potential for a coalition to alter these destructive policies. The members of that potential coalition need to understand the problem. The California Riparian Systems Conference has provided a means to further that understanding.

California policy deems it appropriate to spend state general funds on local flood control projects.[3] I do not agree with that policy any more than I agree with the policy that states areas which are subject to being submerged by water are blighted areas and should be redeveloped.[4]

The state's flood control policies were enacted in 1945. The California Legislature had a problem in 1945. It had to decide what to do with an enormous budget surplus which had accumulated during the war. It decided to spend the money on a scatter of capital improvement projects, mostly local government programs. Flood control was one of the lucky winners.

The federal government plans, funds, and constructs local flood control projects, primarily through the US Army Corps of Engineers (CE) and the USDA Soil Conservation Service (SCS). Long ago, and far from California, the CE was embarrassed by local politicians profiteering by selling land to public agencies for flood control projects. The CE and the US Congress adopted a policy requiring the local sponsors of flood control projects to provide the necessary lands, easements, and rights-of-way necessary for its flood control projects. California's 1945 policy relieved local taxpayers of that burden and placed it, instead, on state taxpayers, arguing, in effect, that the people of Redding have a stake in the flood-proofing of Palm Springs.

The Redding-Palm Springs connection made sense, in a convoluted way. The greatest flood control needs in 1945 were those of the burgeoning urban communities, particularly in and around Los Angeles. As Los Angeles' needs were met from the new state program, there would be funds for the next burgeoning area, and the next. Eventually, there would be money for Redding—Redding need only be patient.

As it turned out, however, the problems of Los Angeles in 1949 and Redding in 1969 were different. Those communities which grew earlier did so under lax development rules. Floods did considerable damage to homes and businesses; those earlier projects were largely for the purpose of preventing further damage.

As state flood control funds became available to the smaller communities—desert and seashore resorts and the growth areas of the Central Valley and foothills—the project purpose was increasingly stated in terms of making land flood-proof to enable future development, rather than safeguarding existing development from further flood damage. This "land enhancement" flood control project purpose had the misfortune of making

---

[1] Paper presented at the California Riparian Systems Conference. [University of California, Davis, September 17-19, 1981.]

[2] William M. Kier is Environmental Policy Specialist, Senate Office of Research, State Capitol, Sacramento, California.

[3] California Water Code, especially Sections 12579 and 12583, State Water Resources Law of 1945.

[4] California Health and Safety Code, especially Sections 33030 and 33032, Community Redevelopment Law.

its first major appearances at the dawning of the "Environmental Decade," thus setting the stage for a riparian conservation-fiscal conservatism coalition—which had a feeble, but fruitful, life between 1969 and 1975.

DEFINING THE ISSUE

Three local flood control projects with major land enhancement benefits were reviewed by the California Resources Agency and its constituent departments in 1965 and 1966. Of these, the Jack and Simmerly Sloughs project, on lands north of Marysville, was found most objectionable by the Resources Agency, due to the loss of waterfowl habitat projected by the Department of Fish and Game (DFG).

In an unprecedented move, the California Secretary for Resources officially informed the CE that because the land enhancement benefits figured so heavily in the project justification, it would not be appropriate to use state funds for the purchase of lands, easements, and rights-of-way for the Jack Slough project. The Secretary did so only after consultation with the State Senator who represented Yuba County. That senator indicated privately that he understood the equity issue involved and would ask for a policy review of the state's role in flood control project financing.

A report prepared jointly by the Department of Water Resources (DWR), Department of Finance, and the Reclamation Board (RB) was submitted to the Legislature in December 1966, just as the "Pat" Brown administration was giving way to the Reagan Administration. That report noted that California was the only state in the nation which provided 100% of the non-federal costs of local flood control projects and recommended the policy be changed to require that an appropriate share of those costs come from local governments or landowner beneficiaries. In a minority report, the RB repudiated the main report's finding that unjust enrichment could result from local flood control projects and argued against the recommendation that the local interests share in the land, easement, and right-of-way costs.

At this point, it should be spelled out what has always seemed obvious, but may not in fact be. That is, during the years the 1945 policy applied, there was virtually no way local officials could say no to a local flood control project. It did not cost them a cent and it made developers and other boosters happy. The planning was done—and still is done—by the federal agencies. The California Legislature authorizes each project for state assistance. The local agency proceeds to buy the necessary lands, relocate railroads and pipelines, raise street and highway bridges, periodically billing the DWR for reimbursement. When the project is completed, local government planners and developers attack what was once a riparian system and produce residential, commercial, and industrial properties

which, in turn, produce the tax revenues necessary to maintain and operate the flood control project.

What seemed equally obvious, therefore, was that any substantive local government front-end cost, any earnest money, would cause enough discomfort that community leaders might first ask any of several pertinent questions, including: "Is this the best use of our scarce fiscal resources?", or even, "Is this the best use for this floodplain land?" It was this tiny bit of responsible question-asking that some have sought through legislation.

There was no interest in the report in the Legislature in 1967. The new Director of Water Resources disagreed with his predecessor's recommendations; flood control expenditures were the furthest thing from the new Department of Finance Director's mind. Conservationists, to the extent they existed at all in Sacramento, were blissfully ignorant of the report and its implications for riparian systems.

One spark remained, however. One person who had been involved in the review of those less-than-urgent projects—and troubled by their potential for destroying riparian systems—remained close to the policy buttons and levers.

COALITION DEVELOPMENT AND PERFORMANCE

In March, 1969, Sacramento County's fast-growing environmentalist community was seized with paroxysms of rage and indignation at news that a politically connected builder would undertake a satellite community development on the floodplain of Morrison Creek, 24 km. (15 mi.) south of the Capitol—and that the flood problems which had endowed the area with a remarkable oak forest and a rich fauna would be addressed through the Morrison Creek Stream Group Project, courtesy of the CE. Here was the fuel to which the spark should be applied.

Senate Bill 1018 was introduced on 8 April, 1969, by Senator Robert Lagomarsino, Chairman of the Senate Natural Resources Committee. Lagomarsino, a conservative from Ventura County, was willing to at least ask whether it was proper to spend state general funds to pave the way for a Sacramento County developer who, as far as anyone could tell, directed campaign funds largely to Democrats. Because of the local news angle, the bill, which would have withheld state assistance to the extent any project was justified by land enhancement, enjoyed wide publicity—that is, in the Sacramento Bee's circulation area. Beyond that, the bill was known only—and loathed—by county and district flood control engineers.

It was the best of years and the worst of years. The bill was opposed by the DWR, ignored by the Sierra Club, and, somehow, adopted by the Senate in its original form—only to die a lingering death in the Assembly Water Committee at the hands of the County Supervisors' Association's water and flood control committee lobbyists.

To his great credit, Senator Lagomarsino reintroduced the bill each year, which provided adequate opportunity to pit the Finance Director against the Water Resources Director. The fiscal conservatism of the Reagan Administration finally prevailed. Governor Reagan announced he would seek no funds for new state commitments to local flood control projects until the Legislature had sent him a policy which adequately recognized the local interest in these projects.

The bill succeeded, finally, in 1973. It had been watered down, of course, but a bit of its original spirit still showed through. The important thing is that the Water Code was amended to require a slight local cost-sharing for lands, easements, and rights-of-way, and, as predicted, the new policy had a chilling effect on local flood control projects.

This would be a swell little story, even somewhat instructive about coalition potentials, but it does not end there. In June 1978, California voters approved Proposition 13 and cut their property taxes in half. In January 1979, Senator Alfred Alquist of Santa Clara County introduced Senate bill 139, a bill to repeal the 1973 amendments to the flood control assistance statutes; that is, to restore the 1945 full state funding policy.

Senator Alquist's bill was completely appropriate. His flood control district had lost property tax income, and the state cost-sharing policy only added to the district's problems. What was not appropriate was the response from our conservation/conservative coalition. There was none. The bill cleared the first committee without dissent and the Senate floor without a discouraging word. The DFG, at that time in the midst of its riparian systems survey, did not know the bill existed.

One lone conservationist took it on himself to pester the DWR until it sluggishly advised the author of of the bill of its opposition. Slowly, ever so slowly, DWR—not DFG—alerted Assembly Water Committee members to its problems with SB 139.

Senator Alquist was fighting an uphill battle. Key tax-cutting legislators had taken stances againt further state bail-outs of troubled local government programs. Local government should tighten its belt in the spirit of Proposition 13. Thirteen months after its introduction, SB 139 was narrowly defeated in the Assembly policy committee—not by friends of riparian systems, but by champions of "cut, squeeze and trim."

CONCLUSION

That, then, is the story: a story about a 1945 policy that was entirely appropriate for the protection of California's burgeoning communities and entirely inappropriate for the protection of California's threatened riparian systems. We have learned how that policy came under attack by a strange alliance of resource conservation and fiscal conservative interests—and just how ephemeral that coalition proved to be.

We may even have noted how the right hand of state government was blithely out surveying riparian systems—one supposes because they have value—while the left hand was ready once more to smite them with renewed flood control subsidies.

It is not enough, then, to understand riparian systems, nor to share that understanding with others that they may also appreciate the value of such systems. If these systems have value, that value must not only be stated explicitly in public policy, but all the little policies and public practices which implicitly contravene positive policy must be dealt with as well. What is the sense of government saying on the one hand: "Riparian systems are valuable," and on the other: "Here's a permit and $10 million in tax receipts—go obliterate a riparian system"?

The agenda developed by the California Riparian Systems Conference must include a sophisticated analysis of laws and regulations affecting riparian systems and determination of which of them work against the protection of these systems. Then, I would suggest, look to the fiscal conservatives for coalition building. The conservation lobbies may figure out what their stake in your campaign is—but it will be late in the day when they finally do.

THE VALUE OF RIPARIAN ECOSYSTEMS:

INSTITUTIONAL AND METHODOLOGICAL CONSIDERATIONS[1]

Reuben C. Plantico[2]

Abstract.--Failures in our institutional mechanisms for allocating society's resources may, in many cases, favor the alteration of natural ecosystems such as riparian areas. Where this is true, decisionmakers may have a critical role to play in correcting such misallocations. This in turn requires that values be placed on resources so that appropriate allocation decisions can be made. This is an interdisciplinary task in which economics must play a central role.

INTRODUCTION

Numerous land and water uses affect the character and vitality of riparian systems throughout the United States. The examples are familiar ones. To accomplish a variety of public and private purposes, rivers are dammed and large amounts of land are inundated; streams are channelized and otherwise altered; the vegetation of riparian lands is cleared; and large quantities of water are withdrawn from rivers and streams. In many cases, the result of such practices is the physical alteration of riparian systems and the elimination of the natural functions performed by them.

However, another look at the same examples tells us that such alterations are "improvements" which benefit people through increased water supply and hydroelectric power, new flood protection, enhanced navigation, increased agricultural production, and more sites for homes and commercial activities. Yet, both views of the problem beg more basic questions. In the case of alteration, do the social benefits of these developments exceed the social costs? For that matter, are all of the benefits and costs even considered? In the case of preservation, is not society denying itself significant benefits by failing to exploit rivers, streams, and related land resources? Therefore, a central issue for decisionmakers--public and private--concerns the value of riparian resources in different and often competing uses.

In recent years there has been a growing awareness that riparian systems provide many useful goods and services to humans. These include natural flood-storage capacity, water quality maintenance, recreational opportunities, habitat for fish and wildlife, groundwater recharge, and various aesthetic and scientific values. Riparian systems also have the potential of providing goods and services that are available through their alteration. However, identifying goods and services that can be derived from natural or altered riparian areas is relatively simple when compared with the task of specifying the relative value of these goods and services.

The purpose of this paper is to provide an overview of the key issues concerning the valuation of nature's goods and services, particularly those associated with riparian areas. In addressing this topic, it is necessary to come to grips with two aspects of the valuation problem--one institutional and the other methodological. The institutional aspect concerns the manner in which different institutions approach valuation. Resources are allocated through the marketplace, by regulated markets (i.e., those controlled by significant regulatory constraints), and by agencies with public resource management authority; all these institutions may approach the task of resource valuation somewhat differently. This paper will review features of these institutions which cause such differences.

The second aspect of the valuation problem actually includes a bundle of issues all related to the selection of valuation methodologies. In the riparian wetland and floodplain literature, the term "value(s)" has been used to refer to many different things. Frequently, values are considered to be attributes such as flood storage capacity, groundwater recharge, water quality maintenance, habitat for fish and wildlife, and

---

[1]Paper presented at the California Riparian Systems Conference. [University of California, Davis, September 17-19, 1981].

[2]Reuben C. Plantico is Research Associate, Natural Resources Law Institute, Portland, Oregon.

others associated with natural or unaltered ecosystems (Greeson et al. 1978). Having identified these "values," one can proceed to determine the extent to which an area supports or exhibits these values. This is typically accomplished through "valuation" procedures, some of which will be mentioned later in the paper.

Value and valuation, however, take on a more comprehensive meaning when viewed from a social perspective. This approach, most frequently associated with the discipline of economics, not only asks what values are supported within an area, but also what uses of that area, new or existing, are most valuable to society. This approach requires an abundance of information, including ecological data. It also requires that methods be designed to make ecological information meaningful to people--especially the decisionmakers who actually make the choices about resource utilization (Comptroller General 1979). Therefore, in the socio-economic and socio-political spheres, one cannot end with a recitation and ranking of ecological values. An attempt should be made to ascertain the importance of those values to society, whether through enlightened benefit:cost analysis or some other form of analysis.

VALUATION: AN INSTITUTIONAL PERSPECTIVE

Overview

It is likely that resource valuation would not be a problem if resources were available in unlimited quantities. In that ideal situation, resources could be consumed for some purposes without making them less available for others. However, it is generally accepted that society possesses scarce resources which must be used to satisfy the unlimited wants and needs of people. This is true of environmental resources as well. As Freeman et al. (1973) note, "managing the environment can be viewed as a problem of allocating the services of scarce environmental resources among competing ends or uses."

While all uses of resources are not necessarily "mutually exclusive," trade-offs do result when resources are used for one or a combination of purposes. The choice of using a resource for one purpose has a cost--the foregone opportunity for another use. Activities in riparian areas provide a telling illustration of this situation. Yet, for reasons to be explained in this paper, the characteristics of resource values emanating from natural environments make accurate assessment of these trade-offs difficult in many circumstances.

Environmental Problems as Economic Problems

Economics provides one useful approach to analyzing land- and water-use practices which affect the extent and vitality of riparian areas. Basically, economics is a study of choice in a world of resource scarcity. Central to this field of study is the criterion of economic performance called "efficiency." Reduced to its simplest form, economic efficiency is achieved when resources are gravitating to their most valuable uses at the least possible cost to society (ibid.). All institutions which perform the function of allocating scarce resources can be evaluated against this criterion.

One institutional approach to resource allocation is the private market, where individuals own and exchange goods and services. Here, private resource owners are guided by incentives to use resources in particular ways, including the production of goods and services. Consumers, on the other hand, make individual choices regarding what combination of goods, services, and other amenities will satisfy their needs and wants. The price system, in theory, reflects the relative values of that which is being produced, consumed, or devoted to a specific purpose. In other words, prices result from the interaction of individuals making choices about what is or is not valuable.

Another method for allocating resources is a variation of the market where market activities are regulated by public bodies. These bodies perform any number of functions including determining prices, issuing permits and licenses, specifying land uses appropriate for certain areas, and setting standards of quality for land, air, and water. Finally, another approach is public ownership of resources where public bodies invest in, manage, and dispose of resources. We find all of these institutional approaches at work in the economy, interacting to perform the allocative function. The manner in which these institutions "value" resources--either explicitly or implicitly--will affect the way resources are used.

The Performance of Institutions

Tracing real world accounts of environmental degradation to flaws in the institutions which allocate resources is frequently a rather subjective exercise. Usually, the analysis begins and ends by pointing an accusing finger at the industrialist who discharges waste into open water, the farmer who clears and drains wet areas for agricultural production, or the developer who mars a scenic vista with rows of condominiums.

In many cases, the high value which consumers place on specific goods and services may well account for these alterations of natural systems. For example, it is believed that demand for soybean production causes conversion of bottomland hardwood areas in the southeastern United States to agricultural production. However, it is not unreasonable to suspect that in other cases, failures within both private and public institutions create significant incentives to ignore environmental values and therefore cause a misallocation of resources. In other words, the polluter, land clearer, and developer may be merely reacting to the incentives with which they are faced. The end result of these failures is the over- or under-production of specific goods and services.

Stated another way, existing scarce resources are not being used efficiently, in that they are not being put to more valued uses.

Valuation Problems in the Private Sector: Market Failure

For markets to allocate resources efficiently, economists generally agree that a few basic requirements must be satisfied. These include: 1) markets must be competitive (i.e., no monopolies); 2) there must be information about present and future prices and about alternatives available to producers and consumers; 3) there must be no externalities or, in other words, the costs and benefits of an activity must be realized only by those participating in a market exchange or transaction; and 4) there must be mobility (transferability) of resources so that they may be moved from less valuable to more valuable activities. Of these four requirements the third—"externalities"—presents the most persistent obstacle to the proper valuation of environmental resources (ibid).

Externalities, quite simply, are the costs and/or benefits of an activity that are not or cannot be restricted to the individuals making the resource-use decisions. In other words, the costs or benefits of an activity become "external" to those making resource-use decisions. In these situations, the price system is not allowed to perform its critical function of placing accurate values on resources put to various uses.

In riparian areas, potential examples of externalities can be identified. Several are given below.

1. A farmer clears, ditches, drains, and dikes his land located adjacent to a river in order to capitalize on a lucrative soybean market. Such actions by individual farmers along a watercourse frequently involve stream channelization as well.[3] These land-use practices tend to direct floodwaters downstream, subjecting individuals located there to greater flood risk. Also, the negative impact of these practices on fish and wildlife species has been well documented. Those who derive pleasure from these activities will realize (that is, ultimately pay both directly and through loss of value) the costs of such activities (Brown 1975).
2. Appropriators along a western stream place increasing demands on the supply of water available in the stream. Gradually, the demands become so severe that river flows are too low to support a fishery during some periods of the year. In addition, the low flows result in

damage to streamside vegetation critical to wildlife species.
3. Landowners fill in wetlands along a river to build attractive homesites. Replacement of the wetland area along a significant portion of the river results in several unintended effects. A sudden decline in the river's fishery is detected. Monitors of water quality notice an increase in sediment and pollutants in the municipal water supply requiring increased treatment costs.

These are but a few examples of what might happen when riparian areas are altered. The point is not that the uses resulting from alteration are not valuable, but that the other existing benefits derived from the natural environment are not valued. A look at the causes of externalities reveals the institutional basis of the problem.

Causes of Resource Misallocations

Externalities are symptoms of more fundamental institutional failures. For markets to allocate resources efficiently, property rights must be defined, assigned, and enforced (Posner 1977). With full ownership, the owner can prevent others from using, benefiting from, or damaging the resource without making compensation. However, some environmental resources are not easily appropriated as private property.

> ...many environmental resources are still unpriced and remain outside the market. Because ownership rights have not been assigned to them, or because they are not easily broken up into units that can be bought and sold, such valuable environmental assets as watercourses, the air mantle, landscape features, and even silence are 'used up' but their use is not accurately reflected in the price system. (Anderson et al. 1977)

If exclusion cannot be implemented through the assignment and enforcement of legal rights, no market will form to provide or maintain such services (Krutilla 1979).

Some environmental resources are held in the public domain. But where the public has not defined and exercised its right to exclude certain uses and users of these resources, the effect is the same as if no right of exclusion existed at all. For many years, watercourses, the atmosphere, and some public land resources were considered standard examples of this (Dales 1970). Recent attempts to define and enforce the rights of the public to specific resources through legislation represent attempts to correct this institutional void. Whether these are effective responses is a separate issue for analysis.

Some environmental resources possess characteristics which prevent the assignment of private ownership rights and efficient allocation in the marketplace. Economists refer to these as "pub-

---

[3]Such activities are often performed with the assistance of public subsidies. In these situations, it might be argued that a double subsidy is involved—the assistance from a government agency and the uncompensated use of or damage to other resources.

lic goods." Individuals cannot be economically excluded from the benefits of a public good once it is produced. Therefore, private entities have little or no incentive to produce and market these resources, goods, or services.

In some cases, riparian systems display convincing examples of public goods. A landowner who maintains his riparian lands for natural flood storage, water quality maintenance, and fish and wildlife habitat cannot sell the service to one buyer without making it available to others.[4] Potential buyers of the service cannot exclude others from benefiting as well. In essence, nonbuyers can take a "free ride" on the buyer's investment. Given this dilemma, maintenance of these services from the natural sector is extremely difficult (Krutilla and Fisher 1975). There is little incentive for landowners to maintain their riparian lands for these purposes because they receive no return on this type of use. On the consumer side, there is little incentive for one person to invest in or buy these services from landowners because he cannot exclude others from taking a "free ride" on his purchase. It might be argued that the public should try to organize and negotiate with riparian landowners to maintain these services where it seems appropriate. However, the costs of organizing people, devising a legal agreement, and enforcing the contract (i.e., transaction costs) are sometimes so high that such activity is impractical. Coercive arrangements created through public laws have generally been used as a substitute for this approach.

Valuation in the Public Sector: Opportunities and Problems

Opportunities for valuing resource uses arise in every situation where government makes decisions about resource allocation. Whether resource valuation is compelled by legislative mandate or whether it results from an internal agency decision to follow such a procedure is a separate issue. Also, the specific approach to be used in evaluating decisions may vary among and even within public agencies.

Examples of agencies at the state level that conduct some form of resource assessment before granting permits for development of wetlands are reviewed by Kusler (1978). Similar reviews of state water allocation procedures for granting permits for new water uses and transfers can be found in Clark (1972). At the federal level, the US Army Corps of Engineers (CE) conducts a "pub

lic interest review"[5] when deciding whether to permit activities that affect waters of the United States (pursuant to Sections 9 and 10 of the Rivers and Harbors Act of 1899 and Section 404 of the Clean Water Act). This is perhaps one of the more celebrated attempts to consider all possible variables in determining the highest and best use of water and related land resources. Economic values of resource uses are not the only factors considered in the public interest review. Arguably, however, the items for consideration under the review procedures are broad enough so as not to be inconsistent with the goal of economic efficiency. As another example, the Federal Energy Regulatory Commission (FERC) is required to consider alternative uses of a waterway before deciding to grant or deny licenses for hydroelectric power projects. FERC must consider the effects of the project on commerce, water power development, recreation, and other beneficial uses of the waterway.[6]

The CE, the USDI Bureau of Reclamation (BR), and the USDA Soil Conservation Service (SCS) invest in and provide technical assistance for projects which result in navigation improvements, flood control, hydropower development, irrigation, watershed development, and recreation. For many of the projects, Congress requires an analysis of project costs and benefits before considering the project for authorization. For example, the Watershed Protection and Flood Prevention Act[7] requires SCS to perform a cost: benefit analysis for its small watershed programs. Similarily, the Flood Control Act of 1936 requires the CE to conduct an analysis for many of its public works projects. In addition, the National Environmental Policy Act (NEPA)[8], the Water Resources Council's Principles and Standards (P & S) for Water and Related Land Resource Planning (developed in accordance with the Water Resources Planning Act[9]), and the Fish and Wildlife Coordination Act[10] have established broad requirements for the evaluation of the pros and cons of project development, including impacts on the environment.

Public land managers are faced with similar opportunities for resource valuation in their land and water management decisions. Legislation concerning wilderness preservation, national forest land management, and management of other public lands all encourage, if not require, resource valuation as a prerequisite for land and water management. In addition to the requirements of the public land management statutes such as the Forest and Rangeland Renewable Resources Planning Act of 1974 as amended by the National Forest Forest Management Act of 1976,[11] the Multiple-

---

[4]One possible exception here is the property owner who maintains his land as a game or fish preserve and then sells rights to hunt and fish. Some measure of exclusion is possible to make such a use of land profitable in a financial sense. However, once a species strays from the confines of the preserve, there is nothing except state hunting regulations to prevent the capture of the animal by an outsider.

---

[5]33 C.F.R. 320.
[6]16 U.S.C. 803(a).
[7]P.L. 83-566.
[8]42 U.S.C. 4321-4361.
[9]42 U.S.C. 1962-1962-s.
[10]16 U.S.C. 661-667e.
[11]16 U.S.C. 1600-1676.

Use Sustained-Yield Act of 1960[12], the Federal Land Policy and Management Act of 1976,[13] and the Wilderness Act of 1964,[14] NEPA, and P & S may require resource valuation as a prerequisite to specific land management decisions.

Problems with "Implicit" Valuation

Several studies have suggested that government programs involving taxes and subsidies encourage some uses of land and water over others. There is nothing unique about tax and subsidy programs, per se, as a form of government activity. They have been used to achieve environmental and developmental goals (Anderson et al. 1977). However, careful evaluation of the side effects on land and water use is important before any program involving taxes and subsidies is adopted.

Analysis of wetland drainage programs in the upper Midwest by Leitch and Danielson (1979) and Goldstein (1971) have identified a relationship between these land-use practices and government subsidies to agriculture. In a similar vein, Shabman (1980) suggests a correlation between subsidies to agriculture in the form of price supports and insurance and the clearing of ecologically valuable bottomland hardwood areas in the southeastern United States.

The National Flood Insurance Program (NFIP) has been criticized as a major contributor to floodplain development resulting in the alteration of riparian systems and increased flood hazard (Plater 1974). Through attractive insurance premiums, the NFIP subsidizes the cost of risk associated with locating in a floodplain. Although the goal of flood insurance is a noble one--to spare flood victims any economic disaster--it may tend to encourage floodplain development. The Federal Emergency Management Agency now requires communities to adopt floodplain management programs as a prerequisite for membership in the NFIP. The success of this program in encouraging wise use of floodplains is yet to be evaluated.

Brown (1975) conducted an economic analysis of government subsidies for stream channelization projects and concluded that federal subsidies for such projects should be terminated. Because the benefits of channelization projects are generally very localized, such projects should be financed at that level. Only where the effects of these projects extend beyond local jursidictions should federal intervention be considered.

Other Variables Affecting Public Evaluation

There is no question that resource valuation, even when conducted with skill and objec-

---

[12] 16 U.S.C. 528-531.
[13] 43 U.S.C. 1701-1782, as amended.
[14] 43 U.S.C. 1131-1136.

tivity, provides only one set of data for agencies and legislative bodies to consider before making decisions about resource allocation. Certainly, water resource projects with unattractive cost:benefit ratios have been approved and implemented. This should not be surprising. Once the function of resource allocation shifts from the private to the public sector, a whole new set of variables may affect the outcome. An influential politician, vocal constituents, and effective lobbying groups may all pave the way for approval of questionable projects. Indeed, it may be very rational conduct for a local concern to demand that a project providing very limited and localized benefits be subsidized by federal funds (Comptroller General 1980).

Even where cost:benefit analysis plays a significant role in decision-making, methodological flaws could reduce its overall value as a decision-making tool. Problems associated with the use of cost:benefit analysis in federal decision-making have been reviewed by the Comptroller General (1978). As Haveman (1972) pointed out in his study of navigation improvement, hydroelectric and flood control projects, preproject estimation of benefits by development agencies at times bears little resemblance to the actual accounting of benefits once the projects are in place. The same could be said for cost estimates. Whether discrepancies were the result of faulty methodology, uncertain information, or inappropriate application, significant questions about the careful use of such analysis must be addressed.

A METHODOLOGICAL PERSPECTIVE ON VALUATION

The Basis for Resource Valuation

Resource valuation becomes an important exercise at both a theoretical and practical level. In theory, where markets fail to produce efficient results, resources are not being valued at appropriate levels. The implication of this is that costs and benefits of resource use are not properly reflected and, therefore, are not providing the appropriate incentives to resource users. The theoretical purpose of non-market allocation (or government intervention) is to allocate the resource in question as if an efficient market were allocating it.

The practical implications of the theoretical ambitions of non-market allocation are numerous. One central task of public resource allocators (regulators, permit grantors, lease grantors, public land managers) is to assess the costs and benefits of various competing resource uses. To perform this analysis, the value of resources in different uses must be identified. Where market prices do not exist for reasons discussed earlier, the necessary dollar values for such analysis are not available. Methods of obtaining surrogate values for resources must be found so that an attempt at valuation can be made. However, the methodological problems are significant and may, in many circumstances, impede evaluation of all those potential costs and benefits of resource use.

During the past several years, substantial efforts have been made to develop methods of valuing natural systems and/or their outputs so that they might receive more careful attention in the decision-making process. Many assert that new methods are necessary because traditional cost:benefit analysis does not accurately reflect the value of natural outputs which are inherently difficult to value in an economic sense. Others argue the need for "quick and dirty" methods of valuation because public officials have neither the time nor money to conduct full-blown analyses of natural systems.

Stimulated, in part, by this kind of reasoning and by the environmental quality procedures of P & S established by the US Water Resources Council, new approaches have come about. For example, approaches developed by Reppert et al. (1979) and Larson (1976) for evaluating wetland resources begin with a comprehensive survey of functions, characteristics, and values associated with wetland areas. These values are generally the same as have been mentioned throughout this paper. The approaches then detail suggested procedures for documenting necessary information, compare the resource values with other wetlands in a given area, and rank the overall value of the wetland (i.e., usually by employing a simple numerical ranking or a descriptive "high," "moderate," or "low" value approach). While these methods are attractive, they do not address the critical question of what is the value of the resource to society. Having identified a wetland with levels "x, y, and z" flood storage, wildlife habitat, and water purification characteristics will not help decisionmakers compare the use of wetlands for these purposes with developmental or other uses. This does not mean that the approaches are not useful for what they were designed. It simply means that they can provide answers for only a limited number of decision-making questions.

On another front, Odum (1977) has argued that the true value of natural systems must be represented in terms of the energy flow patterns associated with ecosystem primary productivity. He suggests that energy, measured in units of calories, could be used in much the same way money is used. Decisions using least-cost alternatives would be made on the basis of the useful work performed by the whole ecosystem, which is assumed to contribute to the economic vitality of a region. Economists, while recognizing the importance of energy flows to ecosystems, assert that this is not an accurate approach for putting a social value on natural outputs. They point out that the market forces of supply and demand, not energy, determine the social value of ecosystems (Shabman and Batie 1978).

Another approach is based on the assumption that ecosystem valuation must be an interdisciplinary effort relying on biology, ecology, and economics. The critical problem is in understanding how information from each of the disciplines can contribute to a unified and coherent approach to valuation. The remainder of this paper will focus on this problem.

Ecological Outputs: Identifying and Organizing Information for the Valuation Process

Because water and other materials from the landscape converge in riparian zones, a given area of riverine/riparian ecosystem tends to support a greater production of natural goods and services than an equivalent area of upland in the same geographic region. Many ecological functions in riparian ecosystems, such as primary productivity and nutrient cycling, are accelerated because of greater fertility and the higher availability of water than in adjacent upland areas. In addition, riparian ecosystems have a profound influence on the condition of aquatic ecosystems to which they export material and energy (Brinson et al. 1981).

A number of valuable goods, services, and amenities result from the natural functions performed by riparian systems. These include production of fish and wildlife, recreational opportunities, natural flood storage, water purification, and various aesthetic and scientific values. Not all riparian ecosystems generate all of these outputs nor do all provide the same quantity of value for each category. For that matter, it is difficult to say, given our present state of knowledge on the subject, whether all natural functions of riparian areas and their resulting benefits are recognized. For example, in considering ecosystems from a global perspective, there is no question that they function to control levels of atmospheric gases, are essential to the circulation of water, and regulate the movement of nutrients. Similar functions in life support have been demonstrated on smaller scales. While the benefit of some of these functions appears immediate and direct, others may seem remote or marginally applicable to human well-being and survival. They are, nevertheless, present and part of the life-support system.

Rather than relying on one discipline in developing a method of ecosystem valuation, an interdisciplinary process in which economics plays a central role is preferred. Drawing from Freeman (1979), three sets of information are required to make these evaluations: 1) information about ecological processes and functions which ultimately result in benefits to humans; 2) specific information about the nature of these goods and services and the manner in which changes in land- and water-use practices will lead to changes in the flow of environmental goods and services; and 3) how changes in levels of environmental services lead to changes in economic welfare. The first set is almost entirely derived from biological and physical sciences.

The third set is largely within the realm of economics. The second set represents the interface between social and natural sciences.

Many of the natural functions mentioned earlier can occur simultaneously in natural and partially altered riparian ecosystems. However, some may conflict with each other. For example, normal agricultural practices require forest removal and flood protection activities which preclude perpetuation of many of the other values. Activities that alter the geomorphic and hydrologic characteristics of riparian ecosystems are most likely to have a lasting and irreversible effect on the natural services provided by riparian ecosystems.

The ultimate purpose of developing studies based on the information described by Freeman is to trace the relationship between individual land-/water-use activities and the flow of goods and services from the natural environment that contribute to human welfare. For example, a study might examine: 1) how do riparian functions result in natural flood storage; 2) how do alterations in the riparian zone affect the provision of this natural service; and 3) how can we measure changes in economic welfare that result from such changes? It seems as though most of our efforts in recent years have been focused on the first question. Approaches to answering the remaining two questions, including valuation techniques (question 3), are in early stages of development.

There is no question that numerous and complex questions of method and theory pervade attempts to use economics in the valuation of ecosystem services and outputs. These questions, as well as specific studies, have been reviewed by Brinson et al. (1981). For now, it suffices to say that there are essentially two general approaches to obtaining estimates of values for natural goods and services: the use of "market techniques," which analyze the relationship between marketed goods and services and those that are not marketed, and the use of non-market techniques. The first approach attempts to draw inferences about the value of natural environments from their relationship to marketed (priced) goods and services. The second approach is called a "non-market" mechanism because actual prices and buying behavior are not used as such. Rather, individuals are asked to reveal their preferences through questionnaires, voting, interviews, and other means. These general approaches are surveyed and critiqued by Freeman (1979). In addition, Dwyer et al. (1977), Thomas et al. (1979), and Krutilla and Fisher (1975) provide a thorough review of existing quantitative economic techniques for valuing goods and services of natural environments including wetland areas and other valuable habitats. These sources should be consulted for an appreciation of state of the art techniques in this field.

CONCLUSION

The valuation of riparian systems, or for that matter any ecosystem, is an interdisciplinary task in which economic analysis must play a central role. Since many outputs of riparian systems are not allocated efficiently by markets because of the institutional failures discussed earlier, careful study of the typical values associated with these natural areas must be performed. Once the goods, services, and other functions of an area have been established, natural resource and environmental economics specialists should be consulted. Since economic methods of valuation are complex and the pitfalls on the road to sound analysis are many, the need for a trained specialist is apparent. Trained economists should be consulted to ensure that the methods employed reflect state of the art techniques.

The need for site-specific studies is especially important. Ambitious studies attempting to make gross generalizations about the value of natural riparian areas are probably doomed to failure. Studies of this sort must recognize and utilize information from the natural sciences to affirm the relationships between the natural environment and the resulting benefits realized by humans (Freeman 1979, Shabman et al 1979).

ACKNOWLEDGMENTS

This paper is an abbreviated version of a study prepared for the Office of Biological Services, USDI Fish and Wildlife Service, Washington, D.C. The author wishes to thank Dr. Mark Brinson, Professor of Ecology at East Carolina University for helpful comments on this article.

LITERATURE CITED

Anderson, F., A. Kneese, P. Reed, S. Taylor, and R. Stevenson. 1977. Environmental improvement through economic incentives. Johns Hopkins University Presses, Baltimore.

Brinson, M., B. Swift, R. Plantico, and J. Barclay. in press, 1981. Riparian ecosystems. FWS/OBS 81/. USDI Fish and Wildlife Service, Kearneysville, West Virginia.

Brown, J. 1975. Stream channelization: the economics of a controversy. Natural Resources Journal 14:557-576.

Clark, R.E. 1972. Waters and water rights. Vol. 5, 6, and 7. The Allen Smith Company, Indianapolis, Indiana.

Comptroller General. 1978. An overview of benefit-cost analysis for water resource projects. US General Accounting Office, Washington, D.C. August 7, 1978.

Comptroller General. 1979. Better understanding of wetland benefits will help water bank and other federal programs achieve wetland preservation objectives. US General Accounting Office, Washington, D.C. February 8, 1979.

Comptroller General. 1980. Congressional guidance needed on federal cost share of water resource projects where project benefits are not widespread. US General Accounting Office, Washington, D.C. November 13, 1980.

Conservation Foundation. 1980. Cost-benefit analysis: a tricky game. Conservation Foundation Letter, December. Washington, D.C.

Dales, J.H. 1970. Pollution, property and prices. University of Toronto Press, Toronto, Canada.

Dwyer, J.F., J.R. Kelley, and M.O. Bowes. 1977. Improved procedures for valuation of the contribution of recreation to national economic development. Research Report No. 128, Water Resources Center, University of Illinois, Urbana.

Freeman, A.M. 1979. The benefits of environmental improvement: theory and practice. Johns Hopkins Univesity Press, Baltimore, Maryland.

Freeman, A., R. Haveman and A. Kneese. 1973. The economics of environmental policy. John Wiley and Sons, Inc., New York, N.Y.

Goldstein, J. 1971. Competition for wetlands in the Midwest: an economic analysis. Johns Hopkins Univer. Press, Baltimore, Maryland.

Greeson, P.E., J.R. Clark, and J.E. Clark. 1978. Wetland functions and values: the state of our understanding. American Water Resources Association, Minneapolis, Minn.

Haveman, R. 1972. The economic performance of public investments. Johns Hopkins University Press, Baltimore, Maryland.

Kemp, W.M., W.H.B. Smith, H.N. McKellar, M.E. Lehman, M. Homer, D.L. Young, and H.T. Odum. 1977. Energy cost-benefit analysis applied to power plants near Crystal River Florida. p. 508-543. In: C.A.S. Hall and J.W. Day, Jr. (ed.). Ecosystem analysis in theory and practice: an introduction with case histories. John Wiley and Sons, Inc., New York, N.Y. 684 p.

Krutilla, J. 1975. The use of economics in project evaluation. p. 374-381. In: Transactions of the 40th North American wildlife and natural resources conference. Wildlife Management Institute, Washington, D.C.

Krutilla, J. 1979. Economics and the environment: a time for taking stock. p. 5-12. In: G. Gorrie (ed.). Environmental economics: papers presented at the National Conference. [Canberra, Australia, May 29-30, 1978.] Department of Science and the Environment, Canberra, Australia.

Krutilla, J., and A. Fisher. 1975. The economics of natural environments: studies in the valuation of commodity and amenity resources. Johns Hopkins University Press, Baltimore, Maryland. 292 p.

Kusler, J. 1978. Strengthening state wetland regulations. FWS/OBS-78/98. USDI Fish and Wildlife Service, Washington, D.C.

Larson, J. 1976. Models for assessment of freshwater wetlands. Pub. No. 32. University of Massachusetts, Amherst.

Leitch, J., and L. Danielson. 1979. Social, economic and institutional incentives to drain or preserve prairie wetlands. Economic Report ER 79-6, Institute of Agriculture, Forestry and Home Economics, University of Minnesota, St. Paul, Minnesota.

Odum, H.T. 1977. Energy, value, and money. p. 174-196. In: C.A.S. Hall and J.W. Day, Jr. (ed.). Ecosystem modeling in theory and practice: an introduction with case histories. 684 p. John Wiley and Sons, New York.

Plater, Z. 1974. The takings issue in a natural setting: floodlines and the police power. Texas Law Review 52:201-256.

Posner, R. 1977. Economic analysis of law (second edition). Little, Brown, and Company, Boston, Massachusetts.

Reppert, R.T., W. Sigleo, E. Stakhiv, L. Messman, and C. Meyers. 1979. Wetland values: concepts and methods for wetlands evaluation. Research Report 79-R1, Institute for Water Resources, US Army Corps of Engineers, Fort Belvoir, Virginia.

Shabman, L. 1980. Economic incentives for bottomland conversion: the role of public policy and programs. Paper presented to the 45th North American Wildlife Conference. [Miami Beach, Florida, March 22-26, 1980.]

Shabman, L., and S. Batie. 1978. Economic value of natural coastal wetlands: a critique. Coastal Zone Management Journal 4:232-247.

Shabman, L., S. Batie, and C. Mabbs-Zeno. 1979. The economics of wetland preservation in Virginia. Virginia Polytechnic Institute and State University, Blacksburg, Virginia.

Thomas, M., B. Liu, and A. Randall. 1979. Economic aspects of wildlife habitat and wetlands. Midwest Research Institute, Kansas City, Missouri.

IS THERE A NATIONAL INTEREST IN WETLANDS:

THE SECTION 404 EXPERIENCE[1]

John R. Kramer[2]

Abstract.--Section 404 of the Federal Water Pollution Control Act requires a permit from the US Army Corps of Engineers for the placement of dredge or fill material in the waters of the United States. As interpreted by the courts, this law provides significant federal protection for wetlands and similar sensitive aquatic ecosystems. Recent court decisions have used detailed analysis of biologic, hydrologic and edaphic information in defining the scope of Section 404 jurisdiction. These decisions demonstrate that Section 404 can prevent the destruction of wetlands and the species they support. Yet, Section 404 has been the subject of substantial controversy since the first court decisions interpreting its scope. Federal protection of wetlands would be severely curtailed if legislation now pending in Congress is enacted.

INTRODUCTION

Controversy and litigation over regulatory programs which affect land development have always been the cutting edge of environmental law. The controversy which has attended the development of Section 404 of the Federal Water Pollution Control Act[3] (FWPCA) has been no exception to this. Section 404 began as a program narrowly defined by the US Army Corps of Engineers (CE) to regulate fills in traditionally navigable waters and disposal of dredge spoil at designated dumping sites. It has evolved into a major federal regulatory program charged with protecting the nation's wetlands and sensitive aquatic ecosystems from further unnecessary loss or damage.

Section 404 requires a permit from the CE for any activity that results in the disposal of dredge material, or the placement or disposal of dredge material, or the placement of any fill or structure in the waters of the United States.[4] Certain activities, like normal farming, silviculture and ranching activities are exempt from this permit requirement.[5] However, the purpose of Section 404 is not the direct regulation of land-use activities. Its objective, like the other provisions of the Clean Water Act,[6] is to restore and maintain the chemical, physical and biological integrity of the nation's waters.[7]

When Congress enacted the FWPCA in 1972, it knew that "water moves in hydrologic cycles" and declared that the purpose of the act is to control the discharge of pollutants of the source.[8] Since that time, the knowledge of hydrology has increased significantly, and it is

---

[1] Paper presented at the California Riparian Systems Conference. [University of California, Davis, September 17-19, 1981].

[2] John R. Kramer is Attorney, California Department of Water Resources, Sacramento. The views and opinions expressed are exclusively those of the author and do not necessarily reflect the official policies and views of the State of California or the Department of Water Resources.

[3] PL 92-500, 86 Stat. 884, 33 U.S.C. Sec. 1344, as amended by the Clean Water Act of 1977, PL 95-217, 91 Stat. 1566 (1977).

[4] Section 404(a), 33 U.S.C. Sec. 1344(a).
[5] Section 404(f)(1), 33 U.S.C. Sec. 1344(f)(1).
[6] See note 3, supra. The 1977 amendments indicated that the entire act, formerly known as the Federal Water Pollution Control Act (FWPCA), may be referred to as the Clean Water Act. This paper will refer to the act as amended as the Clean Water Act. Reference to the FWPCA refers to the act as it was prior to the 1977 amendments.
[7] Ibid., Section 101(a), 33 U.S.C. Sec. 1251(a).
[8] See S. Rep. No. 414, 92d Congress, 1st Session 77, reprinted in Volume 2, Congressional Research Service, "A Legislative History of the Water Pollution Control Act Amendments of 1972," 1495 (1973) (hereinafter cited as "Legislative History").

apparent that all parts of an aquatic ecosystem are interconnected. It is recognized that wetlands are important in biologic functions including food chains, habitats, spawning and nursery areas, and resting sites for aquatic and terrestrial species. Wetlands also shield other areas from wave and storm erosion. They moderate the effects of flood by absorbing and moderating the rush of floodwaters; they also moderate the effects of drought by slowly releasing their stored water.[9] One court summarized the value of a wetland to the biological and physical integrity of the water this way:

> Most of us are accustomed to defining a river by the width of its flowing waters, just as we mark the edge of the sea by the shore where its waves meet the land. In fact, the boundaries of these waters are much more elusive. The neighborhood of the river, the transition area between flowing water and dry land, is as important as the river itself to the continued productivity of both land and water.[10]

The broad scope of Section 404 has brought the Clean Water Act's objective of restoring and maintaining the integrity of the nation's waters into direct conflict with traditional land-use approaches to wetlands. In traditional approaches to land use, wetlands are allowed to be filled and converted to uses such as waste disposal, development, or agriculture. Controversy has raged unabated over the scope of Section 404 jurisdiction since 1975, when a court ordered broad national protection from the adverse effects of dredge and fill activities to the maximum extent permitted under the Constitution.[11]

This paper summarizes the development of Section 404 into a major federal regulatory program which now affords significant protection to wetlands. It also discusses how recent judicial interpretations of the Clean Water Act have used the word "wetlands" as a jurisdictional term[12] to include protection of some riparian systems. Finally, the paper considers several controversial problem areas with Section 404 jurisdiction which have brought about calls for legislation which could seriously curtail the present scope of protection.

It should be noted that there are many other federal laws, beyond the scope of this paper,

that may also afford protection to wetlands and riparian systems, including Section 10 of the Rivers and Harbors Act of 1899,[13] the Fish and Wildlife Coordination Act,[14] the Wild and Scenic Rivers Act,[15] the Endangered Species Act,[16] the Coastal Zone Management Act,[17] the National Historic Preservation Act of 1966,[18] and the National Environmental Policy Act of 1969.[19]

SECTION 10: THE PRECEDENT

Following enactment of the Rivers and Harbors Act of 1899,[13] the CE became the guardian of the nation's navigable waterways.[20] Section 10 of that act makes it unlawful without the prior permission of the CE to:

1) create an obstruction to the navigable capacity of the waters of the United States; or
2) build any structure in any navigable water outside of established harbor lines; or
3) excavate, fill, or otherwise alter or modify the course, location, or capacity of any navigable water of the United States.[21]

As the United States Supreme Court further defined the scope of permissible regulation under the commerce power in the Economy Light[22] and Appalachian Power[23] cases, CE jurisdiction under the Rivers and Harbors Act attained what is fundamentally its present scope. This is fre-

---

[9] For a summary of wetland values considered by the CE in determining whether a permit is in the public interest, see 33 C.F.R. Sec. 320.4(b).

[10] United States v. Weisman, 489 F. Supp. 1331, 1347 (M. Dist. Fla., 1980).

[11] Natural Resources Defense Council v. Calloway, 392 F. Supp. 685 (DC, 1975).

[12] See, e.g., Avoyelles Sportsmen's League v. Alexander, 511 F. Supp. 278 (W.D.La. 1981).

[13] 33 U.S.C. Sec. 402. This paper will briefly compare the scope of jurisdiction under Section 10 and Section 404. For a detailed analysis of Section 10, see Barker (1976).

[14] 16 U.S.C. Sec. 661-666(c). See Shipley (1974).

[15] 16 U.S.C. Sec. 1271-1287.

[16] 16 U.S.C. Sec. 1531-1543.

[17] 16 U.S.C. Sec. 1451-1464. Where a state has an approved coastal zone management program, a Section 404 permit must be consistent. See 33 CFR Sec. 320.3(b) and Sec. 325.2(b)(2).

[18] 16 U.S.C. Sec. 470-470(t). See also 33 CFR part 305 (preservation and mitigation of cultural resources in Corps permit procedures).

[19] 42 U.S.C. Sec. 4321-4327.

[20] Navigable waters subject to federal authority in 1899 were defined in The Daniel Ball case (77 U.S. [10 Wall] 557, 563 [1870]), as those which are "used or susceptible of being used in their ordinary condition as highways for commerce..."

[21] 33 U.S.C. Sec. 403.

[22] Economy Light and Power Co. v. United States, 256 U.S. 113 (1921). A waterway once navigable in interstate commerce retains its identification as navigable regardless of subsequent modifications.

[23] United States v. Appalachian Power Co., 311 U.S. 377 (1940). If "reasonable improvements" can make a waterway suitable for navigation in interstate commerce, it is subject to federal jurisdiction.

243

quently referred to as "traditional navigability." The touchstone for federal jurisdiction is navigability--the physical ability (or the potential) of a waterway to carry interstate commerce. The shoreward boundary of federal authority under the Rivers and Harbors Act is the ordinary high-water mark of rivers and lakes[24] and the mean high-tide line of tidal areas.[25]

The CE has almost always asserted the high-water mark as the basic limit of Section 10 jurisdiction. Projects beyond the point of traditional navigability or outside the high-water mark are subject to jurisdiction only if they affect the course, location, or condition of the waterbody in such a manner as to impact on the navigable capacity of the waterbody.[26] Within this jurisdictional boundary, however, the CE has discretion to consider impacts beyond navigable capacity. Its mandate to consider ecological impacts stems from the National Environmental Protection Act and the Fish and Wildlife Coordination Act.[27]

The CE's jurisdiction over traditionally navigable waters had a major impact on the development of Section 404. The presence of this in-place regulatory program influenced Congress' decision to avoid regulatory redundancy when it structured and strengthened the weak national water pollution laws by enacting the Federal Water Pollution Control Act Amendments of 1972.[3] Traditional Section 10 jurisdiction has also been used by the opponents of the present Section 404 program as a model of the appropriate limits of federal jurisdiction.

SECTION 404 EMERGES

The 1972 amendments to the FWPCA created a complex and comprehensive array of administrative procedures which were consolidated in a new federal agency--the Environmental Protection Agency (EPA). Section 404, however, which was a part of these amendments, placed the CE in charge of permits for the disposal of dredged or fill material; Congress, in effect, recognized the CE's historic role in protecting the nation's navigable waterways.[28]

The legislative history of Section 404 is contradictory.[29] Most of the debate over Section 404 was concerned with designating sites for the dumping of dredge spoil. In several instances, Senator Muskie, the prime architect of the FWPCA, indicated that the purpose of Section 404 was to recognize the CE jurisdiction over traditionally navigable waters.

> The conferees were uniquely aware of the process by which dredge and fill permits are presently handled and did not wish to create a burdensome bureaucracy in the light of the fact that a system to issue permits already existed. At the same time, the Committee did not believe that there could be any justification for permitting the Secretary of the Army to make determination as to environmental implications of either the site to be selected or the specific spoil to be disposed of in a site. Thus, the conferees agreed that the Administrator of the Environmental Protection Agency should have the veto over the selection of the site for dredge spoil disposal and over any specific spoil to be disposed of in any selected site.[30]

Muskie apparently held to the view that the main purpose of Section 404 was regulation of dumping sites. During 1976 hearings he said:

> Section 404 is designed to require the Corps, because of their existing authority, to maintain navigation, to regulate the dumping of polluted dredge spoil at specific

[24]United States v. Rands, 389 U.S. 121 (1967).

[25]Borax Consol. Ltd. v. City of Los Angeles, 296 U.S. 10 (1935). The CE, for a while, asserted Section 10 jurisdiction to mean the higher high-tide line on the West Coast. Citing Borax Ltd., the Ninth Circuit Court of Appeals held this to be beyond the scope of jurisdiction under the traditional navigational authority (Leslie Salt Co. v. Froehlke, 578 F. 2d 742 [9th Cir. 1978]).

[26]33 C.F.R. Sec. 322.3(a). See also United States v. Rio Grande Irrigation Co., 174 U.S. 690 (1899) (diversions from non-navigable portion of the river affect its navigable capacity downstream); United States v. Sexton Cove Estates, Inc., 526 F. 2d (5th Cir. 1976) (work above high-tide line alters course and capacity). The CE has proposed a regulation requiring a permit for work which alters the physical capacity, but it has not been adopted. See 45 Fed. Reg. 62744.

[27]Zabel v. Tabb, 430 F. 2d 199 (5th Cir. 1970). Cert. denied, 401 U.S. 910 (1971).

[28]The Senate version of the 1972 amendments called for regulating dredged and fill material within the NPDES system with a CE certification that a disposal site is reasonably available. The House version established a separate permit system administered by the CE. The conference committee adopted the basic approach of the House version, but with a veto power in the administration of the EPA over any Section 404 permit issued by the CE. See 1 Legislative History: 324; also Sec. 404(c), 33 U.S.C. Sec. 1344(c). Another reason for giving the program to the CE may have been the strong support of the dredging industry for the House version (Caplin 1977).

[29]For a good review of the legislative history of the 1972 and 1977 amendments, see Myhrum (1979).

[30]Exhibit to remarks of Senator Muskie, Debates on Senate Consideration of Conference Committee Report, October 4, 1972, reprinted in 1 Legislative History: 177.

disposal sites, the EPA having veto power over the selection of the sites. This was the intent precisely and specifically stated.[31]

The final language of Sections 404(a) and (b) enacted by Congress appeared at first glance to be consistent with this purpose. It read:

a) The Secretary of the Army, acting through the Chief of Engineers, may issue permits, after notice and opportunity for public hearings for the discharge of dredged or fill material into the navigable waters at specified disposal sites.

b) Subject to subsection (c) of this subsection [the EPA permit veto], each such disposal site shall be specified for each such permit by the Secretary of the Army: 1) through the application of guidelines developed by the Administrator, in conjunction with the Secretary of the Army, which guidelines shall be based upon criteria comparable to the criteria applicable to the territorial seas, the contiguous zone, and the ocean under Section 403(c); and 2) in any case where such guidelines under clause 1) alone would prohibit the specification of a site, through the application additionally of the economic impact of the site on navigation and anchorage.[32]

Interestingly, Section 404 did not refer specifically to wetlands (it still does not). In the early days of the FWPCA, the CE interpreted Section 404 as not enlarging its historic jurisdiction under the 1899 Rivers and Harbors Act. It promulgated regulations defining "navigable waters" for all purposes, including the FWPCA, as "those waters of the United States which are subject to the ebb and flow of the tide, and/or ar presently or have been in the past, or may be in the future, susceptible for use for the purposes of interstate or foreign commerce."[33]

This traditional definition of "navigable waters" did not prevail. While there is some legislative history, such as Muskie's statements, supporting a traditional definition, Section 404 uses words defined elsewhere in the act in a substantially more expansive manner. It was the intent of Congress, with respect to the FWPCA as a whole, that ultimately prevailed when the courts had to construe the scope of Section 404.

To accomplish the objective of the act—namely, the restoration and maintenance of the chemical, physical, and biological integrity of the nation's waters[7] --the discharge of a pollutant from any "point source" into the nation's waters is forbidden unless authorized under Section 402[34] or 404.[35] "Discharge of a pollutant" is defined in part as "any addition of a pollutant to navigable waters from any point source."[36] The act defines "pollutant" and "point source" very broadly.

The term "pollutant" means <u>dredged</u> <u>spoil</u>, solid waste, incinerator residue, sewage, garbage, sewage sludge, munitions, chemical waste, biological materials, radioactive materials, heat, wrecked or discarded equipment, <u>rock</u>, <u>sand</u>, <u>cellar</u> <u>dirt</u>, and industrial, municipal, and agricultural waste discharged into water[37] (emphasis added).

The term "point source" means any discernible confined and discrete conveyance, including but not limited to any pipe, ditch, channel, tunnel, conduit, well, discrete fissure, container, rolling stock, concentrated animal feeding operation, or vessel or other floating craft from which pollutants are or may be discharged. This term does not include return flows from irrigated agriculture.[38]

Finally, the act defines "navigable waters" as "the waters of the United States, including the territorial seas."[39]

Section 404 uses the phrase "navigable waters" without any qualification to indicate that any different meaning of the term is intended. The joint statement of the Conference Committee explained the act's definition.

The Conferees fully intend that the term "navigable waters" be given the broadest possible constitutional interpretation unencumbered by any agency determinations which

---

[31]Section 404 of the Federal Water Pollution Control Act Amendments of 1972, hearings before the Committee on Public Works, United States Senate, 94th Congress, 2d. Session (1976). Cited hereafter as "404 Hearings."

[32]PL 92-500 Sec. 404(a) and (b). The 1977 amendments defined the phrase "secretary" to mean the Secretary of the Army and dropped the repeated reference to the Army. Also, a provision was added to 404(a) requiring the CE to issue a public notice within 15 days after an application is submitted, (33 U.S.C. Sec. 1344[a] and [b]).

[33]39 Fed.Reg.12115 (1974).

---

[34]33 U.S.C. Sec. 1342. Section 402, the National Pollutant Discharge Elimination System (NPDES) requires permits for discharges of liquid effluent (or solids in some instances) from the EPA or from a state to which the program has been delegated.

[35]Sec. 301(a), 33 U.S.C. Sec. 404(f)(1) exempts certain discharges, e.g., from normal farming, silviculture, and ranching, from the act.

[36]Sec. 502(12), 33 U.S.C. Sec. 1362(12).

[37]Sec. 502(6), 33 U.S.C. Sec. 1362(6).

[38]Sec. 502(14), 33 U.S.C. Sec. 1362(14).

[39]Sec. 502(7), 33 U.S.C. Sec. 1362(7).

have been made or may be made for administrative purposes.[40]

In debates on the Conference Report in the House, Representative Dingell quoted this explanation and said:

> Thus, this new definition clearly encompasses all water bodies, including main streams and their tributaries, for water quality purposes. No longer are the old, narrow definitions of navigability, as determined by the Corps of Engineers going to govern matters covered by this bill.[41]

Representative Dingell's statement proved to be prophetic. It was the legislative history of the act's broad definitions and the declaration of its purpose[42] that controlled judicial interpretation of Section 404. Section 301(a), which forbids discharges of pollutants without a permit, makes the act's definitions of "pollutant," "point source," and "navigable waters" specifically applicable to Section 404. Judicial construction of Section 404 in the context of these other provisions made it inevitable that Section 404 would apply beyond the boundaries of traditional navigability.

NRDC v. CALLOWAY: THE CE TAKES 404 UP THE PROVERBIAL CREEK

The first judicial construction of the scope of Section 404 was United States v. Holland.[43] The case involved an enforcement action brought by the EPA against a land-fill project in a mangrove wetland in Florida. The project was beyond the ordinary high-tide line. The court reviewed the legislative history of the act (including the definition of "navigable water") and concluded that the FWPCA defined away the traditional test of navigability. It noted that the legislative history "manifests a clear intent (of Congress) to break from the limitations of the Rivers and Harbors Act to get at the sources of pollution."[44] Comparing Sections 101(a) and 404, the court concluded:

What these sections do is reveal a sensitivity to the value of a coastal breeding ground. Composed of various interdependent ecological systems (i.e., marshes, mudflats, shallow open water, mud and sand bottom, beaches and dunes), the delicately balanced coastal environment is highly sensitive to human activities within its confines... The FWPCA embodies the realization that pollution of these areas may be ecologically "fatal."[45]

The Holland case is the seminal interpretation of Section 404. The case clearly establishes that:

1. wetlands are a part of the nation's aquatic ecosystem, and they are necessary to the quality and biological productivity of the nation's waters;
2. the discharge of fill materials which causes damage to wetlands is a source of pollution regulated by the act;
3. loss of wetlands has serious effects on interstate commerce, and Congress is not limited by traditional definitions of navigability in regulating these impacts; and
4. while the high-water line may be relevant for other purposes, "it has no rational connection to the aquatic ecosystems which the FWPCA is intended to protect.[46]

While the Holland case clearly established that Section 404 is not limited by the traditional definitions of navigability, it did not involve the CE regulations limiting their jurisdiction to traditional navigability. The CE did not change its interpretation following the decision.[47]

In late 1974, the Natural Resources Defense Council brought a declaratory judgment action seeking to compel the CE to rescind its regulation limiting Section 404 jurisdiction to traditionally navigable waters.[48] On March 27, 1975, the District Court granted the plaintiff's motion for partial summary judgment, ordering the CE to propose new regulations "clearly recognizing the full regulatory mandate of the Water

---

[40] Conference Report, S. Rep. No. 92-1236 (1972) reprinted in 1 Legislative History. This explanation is quoted in many cases.
[41] 1 Legislative History.
[42] Sec. 101(a). The report of the House Committee on Public Works, which accompanied the House version of the bill referred to the phrase "integrity of the nation's waters"; the word "integrity," as used, is intended to convey a concept that refers to a condition in which the natural structure and function of ecosystems is maintained (H. Rep. No. 92-911, 92d Congress, 2d Session (1972), reprinted in 1 Legislative History.
[43] 373 F. Supp. 665 (M.D.Fla. 1974).
[44] Ibid., at 673.

[45] Ibid., at 624-625.
[46] Ibid., at 676.
[47] Leslie Salt Co. v. Froehlke, 403 F. Supp. 1292 (N.D.Calif. 1974). Modified, 578 F. 2d 742 (9th Cir. 1978), also held that Section 404 jurisdiction extends beyond traditionally navigable waters. Compare United States v. Ashland Oil and Transportation Co., 364 F. Supp. 349 (W.D.Ky. 1973)--EPA definition of "navigable waters."
[48] The EPA had also criticized the limited CE definition and had urged the CE to expand its definition. See 3 Env. L. Rep. 1240 (1973) and letter of June 19, 1974, from John Quarles to Lt. Gen. W.C. Gribble, reprinted in 404 Hearings.

Act."[49] The court specifically noted the conference report conclusion that "navigable waters should be given the 'broadest constitutional interpretation'."[40]

In response to the court's order, the CE published four alternative regulatory scenarios on May 6, 1975.[50] Two of the proposed definitions extended regulatory jurisdiction to most waters touched by interstate commerce. The other two were slightly broader than the traditional definition.[51] At the same time, the CE issued an infamous press release.

The press release, which basically described the alternative scenarios, began as follows:

Federal authority to regulate the disposal of dredged or fill material in the waters of the United States will be greatly expanded under proposed regulations published in the Federal Register today and would include practically all lakes, streams, rivers, and wetlands in the United States.

Under some of the proposed regulations, Federal permits may be required for the rancher who wants to enlarge his stock pond or the farmer who wants to deepen an irrigation ditch or plow a field, or the mountaineer who wants to protect his land against stream erosion.[52]

The infamous press release provoked a storm of protest. It united the opponents of expanded jurisdiction. No mere notice in the Federal Register could provoke as much controversy. The CE received over 14,000 pages of public comment.[53] The EPA protested the press release,[54] and from the floor of the Senate Senator Muskie demanded a retraction.[55] Further, the outraged comments of the agricultural and forest products interests impelled some Congressmen to act. Legislation attacking 404 jurisdiction has been introduced in almost every session of Congress since.[56]

_____

[49]Natural Resources Defense Council v. Calloway, 392 F.Supp. 685, 686 (D.D.C. 1975), reprinted in 404 Hearings.
[50]40 Fed. Reg. 19766-94 (1975).
[51]See "Wetlands Protection Under the Corps of Engineers' New Dredge and Fill Jurisdiction" 28 Hastings L.J. 223 (1976).
[52]Press release. May 6, 1975. Department of the Army, Office of the Chief of Engineers. Reprinted in 404 Hearings.
[53]Statement of Victor Vesey, Assistant Secretary of the Army for Civil Works, July 29, 1976, in 404 Hearings.
[54]Letter of May 16, 1975, from Russel Train to General Gribble. Reprinted in 404 Hearings.
[55]121 Congressional Record 17347 (1975). Reprinted in part in 404 Hearings.
[56]See discussion of Breaux, Wright and Tower Amendments below.

NRDC v. Calloway elicited two responses from the CE which have had ongoing impacts on federal wetlands protection. First, the infamous press release helped to galvanize the act's opponents. Second, the CE drafted a well thought-out, orderly and reasonable regulation in response to the court's order.[57] The July 25, 1975, "Interim Final" regulations[57] established that Section 404 could be administered to protect wetlands without the unreasonable intrusions suggested in the press release.

The Interim Final regulations accommodated the broad jurisdiction mandated by NRDC v. Calloway by incremental expansion in three phases over a period of two years.[58] Phase I, which took effect immediately, asserted jurisdiction over traditionally navigable waters plus adjacent wetlands. Phase II added primary tributaries to traditionally navigable waters plus all lakes greater than 4 ha. (10 ac.). Phase III included all other waters. The regulations defined "navigable waters" to include coastal and freshwater wetlands. The definition of "navigable waters" was very similar to the definition developed by EPA in 1974 for Section 402 NPDES jurisdiction.[59] The regulations also included separate definitions for coastal and freshwater wetlands, defining both as areas periodically inundated by water and normally characterized by vegetation that requires saturated (or salty) conditions.[60]

The regulations defined "dredged material" and "fill material," which were not defined in the FWPCA. The definitions of both terms exempted materials resulting from normal farming, ranching and silviculture activities.[61] Materials used in emergency reconstruction were also exempted.

To avoid the mass of permit applications inherent in broad jurisdiction (since Section 301(a) forbids discharges without a permit), the regulations authorized CE District Engineers to issue "general permits." A general permit authorized general categories of work found to have insignificant environmental impacts.[62] The general permit remains a significant feature of the CE regulatory process. It allows the permit

_____

[57]40 Fed. Reg. 31, 322-43 (1975). For a detailed analysis of the 1975 and 1977 regulations see Myhrum (1979).
[58]33 C.F.R. Sec. 209.120(e)(2).
[59]40 C.F.R. Sec. 125.1(p) (1975). The CE definition included traditionally navigable waters, interstate waters, and intrastate waters affecting interstate commerce (e.g., used by travellers in interstae commerce). See 33 C.F.R. Sec. 209.120(d)(2)(i) (1975).
[60]Compare 33 C.F.R. Sec. 209.120(d)(2)(i) (b) with Sec. 209.120(d)(2)(i)(h) (1975).
[61]Compare 33 C.F.R. Sec. 209.120(d)(4) and (d)(6) (1975).
[62]33 C.F.R. Sec. 209.120(i)(2)(ix)(a) (1975).

process to focus on controlling major projects and preventing damage to wetlands.[63]

During Phase I of the 1975 Interim Final regulations, the CE held hearings around the nation to encourage further public comment. The Interim Final regulations were to be made final in 1977 after Phase III of jurisdiction was implemented. Partly in response to public confusion over the 1975 regulations, and partially to stave off congressional attacks on Section 404, the CE in 1977 revised the regulations into their present form, making several significant changes.

The 1977 regulations dropped the complicated definition of "navigable waters" which had been taken from the EPA regulations.[57] Instead, the regulations referred to "waters of the United States," the FWPCA term.[64] This avoided confusion between waters subject to the CE 404 jurisdiction and their traditional Section 10 jurisdiction. The definition of waters of the United States dropped the illogical distinction between coastal and freshwater wetlands. The definition of wetlands also was modified in a manner that would better apply Section 404 to riparian systems. The 1975 regulations had defined a freshwater wetland as one "characterized by the prevalence of vegetation that <u>requires</u> saturated soil conditions" (emphasis added).[60] The 1972 regulations defined "wetland" as follows:

> The term "wetlands" means those areas that are inundated or saturated by surface or groundwater at a frequency and duration to support, and that under normal conditions do support, a prevalence of vegetation typically adapted for life in saturated soil conditions. Wetlands generally include swamps, marshes, bogs and similar areas...[65]

The 1977 regulations also provided an additional mechanism for excluding activities from individual permit review. The "nationwide permit" permitted certain activities in the regulations themselves. For example, discharges into certain identified waters under specified conditions are permitted for utility line crossing, bank stabilization, and minor road crossings.[66] If an activity described in the nationwide permit categories may have significant individual or cumulative effects on the aquatic environment, an individual permit can still be required.[67]

The scope of federal authority required by Section 404 and the Calloway case required an effective program to avoid an avalanche of individual permit applications and yet carry out the

purposes of the FWPCA. The CE effectively met this challenge by placing regulatory emphasis on larger projects that adversely affect wetlands, while avoiding individual review of all activities that may individually or cumulatively affect water quality.[68] The regulations made it possible for the CE to provide effective protection to sensitive aquatic ecosystems within their manpower and budgetary constraints. More important, however, the reasonable approach taken by the regulations probably saved Section 404 from legislative attack in 1976 and 1977.

CONGRESS CONSIDERS <u>CALLOWAY</u>: WETLANDS OR SHIP CHANNELS?

Congressional response to the controversy caused by <u>NDRC</u> v. <u>Calloway</u> and the CE press release was inevitable. Once Section 404 attracted the attention of Congress, that attention never waned. Congressional efforts in 1976 almost succeeded in returning Section 404 jurisdiction to traditionally navigable waters.

On April 13, 1976, the House Committee on Public Works amended a bill dealing with pollution control authorizations. The amendment, offered by Representative Breaux of Louisiana, would have added two subsections to Section 404:

> (d) the term "navigable waters" as used in this section shall mean all waters which are presently used, or are susceptible to use in their natural condition or by reasonable improvement as a means to transport interstate or foreign commerce shoreward to their ordinary high water mark, including all waters which are subject to the ebb and flow of the tide shoreward to their mean high water mark (mean higher high water mark on the west coast);

> (e) the discharge of dredged or fill material in waters other than navigable waters is not prohibited by or otherwise subject to regulation under this Act, or section 9, section 10, or section 13 of the Act of March 3, 1899.[69]

The approach taken by the Breaux amendment would have had serious effects on federal protection of wetlands, which go beyond the issue of

_____

[63]33 C.F.R. Sec. 209.120(g)(2)(iv) provides that projects in wetlands will not be approved unless required by the public interest.
[64]Sec. 502(7), 33 U.S.C. Sec. 1362(7). See 40 C.F.R. Sec. 323.2(a).
[65]33 C.F.R. Sec. 323.2(c).
[66]See 33 C.F.R. Sec. 323.4-323.4-3.
[67]33 C.F.R. Sec. 323.4-4.

_____

[68]Some commentators have noted that the CE regulatory approach avoids the cumulative effects of smaller discharges. See, e.g., Blumm (1980) (a good detailed analysis of the CE' procedures). Yet, that approach was sanctioned by the 1977 Clean Water Act amendments which statutorily exempted certain activities.
[69]H.R. 9650, 94th Congress, 2d Session (1976), Sec. 17. Substantially similar language appears in several bills pending [at the time of this writing] before Congress. See, e.g., S. 777 (Tower) and H.R. 3083 (Hall), 97th Congress, 1st Session (1981).

Section 404. The amendment deleted historical navigability from the traditional Section 10 jurisdiction.[22] Furthermore, it would have removed Section 10 jurisdiction from discharges in wetlands outside traditionally navigable waters, but which affect the course, condition, or physical capacity of such waters.[70] The Breaux amendment was defeated in the House on June 3, 1976, in favor of an amendment offered by Representative Wright of Texas. The Wright amendment would have added adjacent wetlands to the Breaux definition.[71] It also would have allowed the CE to regulate additional areas with the consent of a state. The Wright amendment passed in the House 234 to 121.[72]

When the Wright amendment was referred to the Senate, Senators Baker and Randolph substituted language for the Wright amendment. It limited CE jurisdiction to traditionally navigable waters and regulated other point source discharges under Section 402.[73] The Senate Committee on Public Works approved the Baker-Randolph amendment. On the floor, Senator Tower offered the Wright amendment in lieu of the Baker-Randolph amendment and won the first vote 39 38.[74] Senator Baker then succeeded in getting reconsideration, and on the second vote the Wright amendment failed 39-40.[75] Had the Wright amendment passed, it is very likely that Section 404 and Section 10 jurisdiction would have been severely curtailed in 1976. As it was, a joint conference committee was unable to work out a compromise, and Section 404 remained unaffected.

THE 1977 CLEAN WATER ACT AMENDMENTS

In 1977, the Wright amendment became a part of the House version of amendments to the FWCPA,[76] which the House quickly passed.[77]

The Senate passed amendments to the FWPCA which included the Baker-Randolph amendment.[78]

This time the conferees were able to agree on a compromise which resulted in the Clean Water Act Amendments of 1977.[6]

Section 404 jurisdiction was not curtailed. Section 404(e), added by the amendments, authorizes the issuance of general permits on a regional, state, or nationwide basis. The term of these permits cannot exceed five years.[79] This section confirmed the previously questionable authority for general permits and nationwide permits.

Subsection (f) dealt with the major subject of debate during 1976 and 1977: exemption of farming and silviculture. Discharges from normal farming, silviculture and ranching activities, emergency construction, construction of stock ponds and farm and forest roads, and maintenance of drainage ditches are not subject to regulation under Section 404.[80] Discharges incidental to such activities, which change the use of a waterbody, or impair its flow or circulation are not exempted.[81] In addition, discharges authorized by an approved state Section 208 plan are exempt.[82]

The conferees gave great importance to state assumption of dredged and fill material regulation.[83] While the CE must retain jurisdiction over traditionally navigable waters and adjacent wetlands, a state may apply to the Administrator of the EPA for certification of its regulatory program to issue permits for other water in a manner similar to 402 NPDES programs.[84]

While the legislative history of the 1972 FWPCA Section 404 contains no reference to wetlands, the 1977 Clean Water Act legislative history is replete with references to wetlands and the purposes they serve.

> Implementation of the 404 decision-making process is essential if we are to achieve that goal [restoration of the physical, chemical and biological purity of the nation's waters]. Section 404 represents an essential tool for moderating the degradation and sometimes the irrevocable destruction of aquatic areas that naturally control the

---

[70] See United States v. Sexton Cove Estates.
[26]

[71] 122 Congressional Record H. 5267 (June 3, 1976). For a detailed comparison of the Wright and Breaux amendments, see 404 Hearings.

[72] 122 Congressional Record H. 5280. The Wright amendment was renumbered as S. 2710 when it was referred to the Senate.

[73] See 122 Congressional Record at 15167-8, 94th Congress, 2nd Session (1976).

[74] Ibid., at S. 15183.

[75] Ibid., at S. 15184. For a detailed account of the efforts to pass the Wright amendment, see Caplin (1977).

[76] H.R. 3199, 95th Congress, 1st Session (1977), Sec. 16. See "A Legislative History of the Clean Water Act of 1977; A continuation of the Legislative History of the Federal Water Pollution Control Act (1978), Volume 4, Congressional Research Service. Cited as "4 (or 3) Legislative History."

[77] The vote was 361-43; 123 Congressional Record H. 3063 (April 5, 1977); 4 Legislative History: 1363-65.

---

[78] S. 1952, 95th Congress, 1st Session (1977).

[79] Sec. 49, 4 Legislative History: 619-630.

[80] 33 U.S.C. Sec. 1344(e).

[81] 33 U.S.C. Sec. 1344(f)(1).

[82] 33 U.S.C. Sec. 1344(f)(2).

[83] 33 U.S.C. Sec. 1341(f)(1).

See Conference Report No. 95-830, 95th Congress, 1st Session at 101-105. Reprinted in 3 Legislative History.

[84] Sec. 404(g)-(1), 33 U.S.C. Sec. 1344(g)-(1).

quality of water, including those vital areas of shallow water known as wetlands.[85]

Even Senator Muskie, who had not been enthusiastic about expansion of Section 404 jurisdiction[30] said:

First there is the problem of protecting wetlands, that is one of national interest... There is no question that the systematic destruction of the nation's wetlands is causing serious ecological damage ... The wetlands and bays, the estuaries and deltas are the nation's most biologically active areas... They are a principal source of food supply. They are the spawning grounds for much of the fish and shellfish which populate the oceans and they are passages for numerous upland game fish. They also provide nesting areas for a myriad of species of birds and wildlife.[86]

The presence of a clear and unambiguous legislative history directly linking Section 404 with protection of aquatic systems has not been lost on the courts. They have since utilized the intent of Congress, as expressed in the 1977 amendment, defining the boundaries of Section 404 jurisdiction in biological and hydrological terms.[87] Furthermore, the 1977 amendments have buttressed the CE administrative interpretations which have focused mainly on wetlands. This is further indication, perhaps, of the unusual evolution of the Section 404 program, since the amendments occurred after the 1977 regulations were effective.

JUDICIAL INTERPRETATION AND ENFORCEMENT

Section 404 has evolved through the dynamic interaction of all three branches of government. The FWPCA was enacted and amended by Congress; it was interpreted (narrowly at first), expanded, and implemented by the CE through its regulations. However, the role of the federal courts has been fundamental to the expansion and ongoing usefulness of Section 404. Section 404 became a major environmental program because in NRDC v. Calloway a court, interpreting the intent of Congress, ordered the CE to make it into one.

The evolution of Section 404 has not stopped with the 1977 amendments. It is the recent decisions of federal courts that fully illustrate the

extent to which Section 404 can prevent irreversible damage to sensitive aquatic ecosystems.

The[88] definitions of terms such as "point" source,[89] discharge of[90] dredged or fill material, or "wetland"[90] have an importance beyond questions of scientific precision. The courts interpret these definitions with reference to the purpose of the Clean Water Act and its history. These defined phrases are jurisdictional terms which answer a public policy need as well as a scientific one. They determine whether particular activities[91] or locations fall within federal protection.[91] Examples of several recent cases illustrate how the courts have construed terms used in the act to apply to a wide diversity of activities that harm aquatic systems.

IS A DAM A "POLLUTANT"?

In Minnehaha Creek Watershed Dist. v. Hoffman,[92] the Eighth Circuit Court of Appeals was confronted with the question of whether construction of dams and riprap are "pollutants" regulated by the Clean Water Act. The case involved issues of traditional navigability and Clean Water Act jurisdiction over Lake Minnetonka and Minnehaha Creek in Minnesota.

The lower trial court held that the CE had no jurisdiction over the lake and creek under Section 10 and Section 104.[93] With respect to Section 10 jurisdiction, the trial court held that while the lake itself was navigable, its outflow did not form a highway over which commerce could be conducted with other states. With respect to Section 404 jurisdiction, the trial court held that since there was no evidence that dams or riprap significantly affect water quality, "...there is no federal interest under the [Clean Water Act] in the activity."[94] The court declared that the CE regulations defining "discharge of dredged and fill material" invalid insofar as they regulated the construction of dams and riprap.[95]

The Eighth Circuit Court of Appeals affirmed the trial court's holding on Section 10 jurisdiction, but it reversed the holding on Section 404, noting that the court had interpreted the scope of the act too narrowly. Section 301(a) requires

---

[85] Remarks of Senator Baker during debate on S. 1952, 123 Congressional Record S. 13561, 95th Congress, 1st Session (1977), 4 Legislative History.
[86] 123 Congressional Record S. 13564, 95th Congress, 1st Session (1977). Reprinted in 4 Legislative History.
[87] See, e.g., Avoyelles Sportsmen's League v. Alexander.[12]

[88] Sec. 502(14), 33 U.S.C. Sec. 1362(14).
[89] Sec. 502(16), 33 U.S.C. Sec. 1362(16).
[90] The act does not define "dredged" or "fill" material. See C.F.R. Sec. 323.2(j) and (m), respectively.
[91] Much as the definition of "navigable waters" determined the scope of jurisdiction in 1975.
[92] 597 F. 2d 617 (8th Cir. 1979).
[93] Minnehaha Creek Watershed Dist. v. Hoffman, 449 F.Supp. 876 (D.Minn. 1978).
[94] Ibid., at 896.
[95] Ibid., see 33 C.F.R. Sec. 323.2(n).

a Section 404 or 402 permit for the discharge of pollutants. The Court of Appeals noted that the act's definition of "pollutant" includes "rock, sand and cellar dirt."[44] it concluded:

> We believe that the construction of dams and riprap in navigable waters was clearly intended by Congress to come within the purview of Sections 301 and 404 of the Act. By including rock, sand and cellar dirt in the list of polluting substances, Congress recognized that the addition of these substances could affect the physical as well as the chemical and biological integrity of the waterbody.[96]

The court held that this interpretation is buttressed by the 1977 Clean Water Act amendments. Since Section 404(f)(1)(B)[97] specifically exempts maintenance of such structures, it is obvious that such an exemption is necessary if the structures are subject to permit requirements.[96]

A related issue is whether the water quality effects of storage of water in the reservoir constitutes a "pollutant." The issue was raised in South Carolina Wildlife Federation v. Alexander.[98] The court found that loss of dissolved oxygen and increase of metallic substances could constitute the "addition of a pollutant into navigable waters" if the plaintiffs prove that the dam caused water quality degradation. The decision only considered the United States' motions to dismiss for which the court deemed plaintiffs' allegations to be true. No federal decision on the merits of dam-induced water quality degradation has been rendered. If included within the Clean Water Act, dam-induced degradation would be regulated under Section 402--NPDES permits.

Construction of a dam is subject to Section 404 jurisdiction even if it is placed across an artificial canal and is privately owned.[99]

Section 404 jurisdiction over construction of dams continues to be controversial. Most western states, except perhaps California, have seen Section 404 as an unjustified federal intrusion into their sovereign powers to grant and regulate water rights.[100] Furthermore, the states and local jurisdictions have objected to the possibility that a Section 404 permit to construct a dam may include conditions affecting the way it is constructed or operated.

---

[96] 597 F.2d at 625-626.
[97] 33 U.S.C. Sec. 1344(f)(1)(B).
[98] 457 F. Supp. 118 (D.S.C. 1978).
[99] United States v. DeFelice, 641 F. 2d 1169 (5th Cir. 1981).
[100] California and Florida have supported broad federal jurisdiction under Section 404 since NRDC v. Calloway.

DOES CLEARING A RIPARIAN FOREST INVOLVE A "DISCHARGE OF DREDGED OR FILL MATERIAL"?

Much agriculture in California and the southern states is conducted on land which was originally riparian forest or freshwater wetland (Kahrl 1979). In Louisiana, over 22 million acres of wetlands in the Mississippi River alluvial plain have been cleared; only 3 million acres of riparian woodland remain.[101]

In Avoyelles Sportsmen's League v. Alexander,[87] Judge Nauman Scott was faced with the question of whether clearing of riparian forest in Louisiana, to convert the land to soybean production, was covered under Section 404. The land involved in the case consists of 8,100 ha. (20,000 ac.) within an area generally known as the Lake Long Tract. It is in the Bayou Natchitoches Basin, which is an overflow area of the Red River. The land subject to the clearing operation represented one-quarter of the remaining forest in the basin.

The land was being cleared by bulldozers equipped with shearing blades, which cut off the trees just above ground level. After shearing, the felled trees were bulldozed into windrows where they were burned. Soil and leaf litter were also pushed into the windrows as a result of the clearing operation.

The plaintiffs sought to compel the CE to regulate this activity under Section 404. In response to a court order, the CE surveyed the area and designated portions of the tract as wetland. The CE also determined that:

> [a] Section 404 permit is not required for the shearing of trees, where no earth, (other than de minimis) is moved in the process and the trees are promptly removed through burning or other means. However, under the facts as they are known to the government, a Section 404 permit will be required for the construction of drainage ditches in the wetland area...[102]

The court bifurcated the trial, determining first whether the land clearing activities came within Section 404. Next, the validity of the CE wetland determination was to be litigated.[103]

To determine whether land clearing involved the disposal of dredged and fill material, the court had to determine: 1) whether a point source discharge was involved; 2) whether the activity would result in a discharge of dredged

---

[101] See Louisiana State University Sea Grant Legal Program, "Louisiana Coastal Law," July, 1980.
[102] 473 F. Supp. 529.
[103] The court's second opinion on the wetland determination is reported in Avoyelles Sportsmen's League v. Alexander, 511 F. Supp. 278 (W.D.La. 1981).

or fill material; and if so, 3) whether the activity was a normal farming and silviculture activity exempt under Section 404(f).

The point source issue was simple. Several previous decisions held that bulldozers are point sources.[104] The second issue, whether sheared trees, scraped soil, and leaf litter constitute dredged or fill material, had no precedents. The court first turned to the CE definition of a wetland, namely those areas which are periodically inundated and which "support a prevalence of vegetation typically adapted for life in saturated soil conditions."[65] The court noted that "[a] basic policy of the FWPCA is the protection of our nation's wetlands and the important functions they serve."[105] The court then reviewed the important functions that wetlands perform, and it found that each function was served by the riparian woodland involved in the case.[106] The functions include production of forest detritus, an important link in the aquatic food chain, fish spawning and nursery, and wildlife habitat. If the wetland were cleared, sedimentation and erosion would increase, and greater runoff would occur from cleared farmland. The court concluded that:

> The FWPCA would be emasculated insofar as wetlands are concerned were we to conclude that the permanent removal of the wetland's vegetation in the process of converting it to agricultural land was not subject to the Section 404 program. .... [W]etlands are important to the public interest because of the important functions they perform. If one destroys a wetland's ability to perform these functions, he has in effect destroyed the wetland insofar as the public interest is concerned.[107]

> Common sense dictates that an activity that results in the destruction of a wetland resource should be subject to regulation under an Act that has as its purpose the restoration and maintenance of the "chemical, physical and biological integrity" of our nation's wetlands."[108]

The court found that the clearing activity did not constitute normal farming or silvicultural activities exempt under Section 404(f)(1), because that section only exempts ongoing activities. Furthermore, the clearing activity would not be exempt because Section 404(f)(2) denies the exemption to activities that convert a wetland to another use where the flow or circulation of the water may be impaired.[108] The court

rejected the CE statement that no permit was required for land clearing that only moves a "de minimis" amount of earth.

> If you clear the wetland where no earth (other than de minimis) is moved; you can clear and destroy every acre of wetlands in the United States with impunity and without applying for a permit.[109]

Interestingly, the CE does not follow the decision in the Avoyelles case outside the district where it was decided. The decision does not appear to reflect current CE policy. The following is from a memorandum to all Division Engineers from the Chief of Engineers' Office:

> The Corps will continue to determine what activities will constitute a discharge of dredge or fill material in the waters of the United States. Specifically, land clearing may or may not constitute a discharge depending on how it is conducted. That decision shall be made by the District Engineer. The rationale of Avoyelles Sportsmen's League v. Alexander...shall not be used for authority under Section 404 outside the Western District of Louisiana. This issue is also being discussed at the Washington level between the Corps and EPA.[110]

It should be noted that federal district court decisions generally are not binding precedents outside the circuit where they are decided, though they are persuasive authority.

The CE reluctance to embrace the Avoyelles rationale may be politically motivated. The case would seem to cut dangerously close to the politically forbidden area—regulating agricultural practices. Yet the case is well reasoned and distinguishes routine agricultural practices from activities which result in the permanent destruction of wetlands. Its rule that land clearing is subject to Section 404 (when performed in a wetland to change existing wetland uses) is clearly consistent with Section 404(f)(2) and should be followed nationwide. The decision reflects the maturation of Section 404 into an environmental program designed to prevent the loss of wetlands.

WHAT IS A WETLAND?
THE IMPORTANCE OF EXPERT TESTIMONY

Both the opinion in the second Avoyelles case[103] and United States v. Weisman[10] illustrate the importance of expert professional opinions in the areas of soils, hydrology, and biology. The courts rely on expert testimony to determine whether an area is a wetland and thus subject to Section 404.[111]

---

[104]See, e.g., United States v. Fleming Plantations, 12 E.R.C. 1705 (E.D.La. 1978) (marsh buggies and draglines), United States v. Weisman[10] (bulldozers).
[105]473 F. Supp. at 533.
[106]473 F. Supp. at 533-535.
[107]Ibid., at 534.
[108]Ibid., at 535.

[109]Ibid., at 536.
[110]Memorandum from Major General E.R. Heiberg III, to Division Engineers, May 26, 1980.
[111]See, e.g., Avoyelles, 511 F. Supp. at 288.

The CE 1975 Interim Final regulations defined a freshwater wetland as one which, in effect, supports vegetation that requires saturated soil conditions.[60] The 1977 regulations changed this to an area that supports "a prevalence of vegetation typically adapted for life in saturated soil conditions."[65] This change was critical to the result of the second Avoyelles opinion. The court undertook a detailed review of the plant species that occur in the Lake Long Tract and their relative tolerance to periodic saturation.[112] The 1977 definition of wetland phrase "typically adapted for life in saturated conditions" was construed to include those plant species that can tolerate periodic saturation, rather than just vegetation that must spend its life in saturated conditions. The court held that the definition of wetland includes all vegetation which is capable of and does adapt to saturated conditions.[113] Thus, a wetland is characterized by the "dominance of tolerant species to the virtual exclusion of purely upland intolerant or nonaquatic species."[114]

The court clearly saw that "wetlands are transition areas lying between the aquatic and the terrestrial zone."[115] Thus, the analysis to determine whether an area is a wetland requires expert testimony on the type of soils in the area, the degree and frequency of inundation, and the type of vegetation.[115]

Expert testimony is also important in determining whether an illegally filled wetland will be restored. The CE regulations provide for court-ordered restoration as a civil remedy when it is in the public interest.[116] The courts have required illegally filled wetlands restored to their natural conditions.[117] In United States v. Weisman,[10] an illegal road fill that destroyed 0.9 ha. (2.2 ac.) of wetland was ordered removed, and the natural wetland forest replanted at an estimated cost of $19,600. The court found that the natural wetland forest performed substantial natural functions essential to adjacent tidal waters.

The wetland forest on the Weisman property is like productive farm land producing a crop which is harvested not by man but by the natural action of the seasons and the tides... The detrital material [produced by the forest], according to testimony, forms the base of the food chain and is relied upon by many aquatic organisms. Though shrimp are the first to profit from this

bounty[18] man is the ultimate beneficiary.[118]

The court found that the continuation of these natural functions was essential to the biological health of the adjacent tidal slough and bay.

In the Avoyelles case, no restoration was ordered because the defendants had cleared some wetland areas in good faith reliance on an initial determination by the CE that the land was not wetland.[119]

The Avoyelles opinions are probably the most significant decisions insofar as protection of riparian forests are concerned, because the court clearly recognized that transition zones between inundated areas and uplands may come within the Section 404 definition of wetlands. However, the last chapter of Avoyelles has not been written. The determination that clearing activities were subject to Section 404 was appealed to the Fifth Circuit in 1979, but review of the case was held up pending a decision on the wetlands issue. Thus, both issues are, at the time of this writing, before the Court of Appeals.

THE FUTURE OF SECTION 404:
SOME PROBLEMS THAT MUST BE RESOLVED

In 1980, Senator Tower and Representative Paul of Texas introduced legislation which would limit CE jurisdiction under Section 404 and Section 10 to traditionally navigable waters. The bill was similar to the Wright Amendment considered by Congress in 1976 and 1977.[120] The bills failed to be heard in their respective public works committees. In 1981 Senator Tower and Representative Hall of Texas again introduced legislation restricting 404 jurisdiction.[121] The legislation is closer to the Breaux amendment of 1966[69] in that it limits jurisdiction strictly to traditionally navigable waters. Adjacent wetlands would not be protected. If either of these bills or similar proposals were to become law, the scope of federal protection of wetlands outlined in this paper would be lost. The opponents of Section 404 have exploited two major federal-state issues in their efforts to thwart jurisdiction. These are the issues of state water rights and state assumption of Section 404 jurisdiction.

State Water Rights and Minimum Streamflow Requirements

The relationship between Section 404 and state water rights permit systems is important

112 Ibid., at 283-4.
113 Ibid., at 290.
114 Ibid., at 291.
115 Ibid., at 289.
116 33 C.F.R. Sec. 326.4.
117 See, e.g., United States v. Fleming Plantations;[104] Parkview Corp. v. Corps of Engineers, 490 F. Supp. 1278 (E.D.Wis. 1980); United States v. Holland.[43]

118 489 F. Supp. at 1346.
119 See 473 F. Supp. at 536-537.
120 The bills were numbered S. 2970 and H.R. 7245, respectively (96th Congress, 2d Session 1980).
121 S. 777 and H.R. 3083 (97th Congress, 1st Session 1981).

and often controversial. A major undecided issue is the extent to which the CE can condition a Section 404 permit to construct diversion works on maintaining minimum streamflows. The 1977 amendments to the Clean Water Act included Section 101(g), which reads:

> (g) It is the policy of Congress that the authority of each state to allocate quantities of water within its jurisdiction shall not be superseded, abrogated or otherwise impaired by this chapter. It is the further policy of Congress that nothing in this chapter shall be construed to supersede or abrogate rights to quantities of water which have been established by any state. Federal agencies shall cooperate with state and local agencies to develop comprehensive solutions to prevent, reduce and eliminate pollution in concert with programs for managing water resources.[122]

This section would appear to prohibit conditioning Section 404 permits where conflicts with state water rights allocations would result. However, the legislative history indicates that this section is only declaratory of existing law and not intended to prohibit Section 404 or 402 permit conditions that may incidentally affect water rights.[123]

The CE has taken the position that Section 101(g) does not prohibit conditioning or denying a Section 404 permit where necessary to protect the national interest. Rather, it is interpreted to be consistent with Senator Wallop's statement as prohibiting unnecessary interference with state water rights entitlements.[124] Actually, the CE rarely imposes conditions such as minimum streamflows on its own motion. Rather, it responds to comments received during its public interest review and attempts to meet the concerns of commenting agencies, particularly the USDI Fish and Wildlife Service and state fish and game agencies.[125]

---

[122] 33 U.S.C. Sec. 1251.

[123] Senator Wallop, the sponsor of the Conference Report, stated that Section 101(g) was "not intended to change present law" and that "the requirements of Section 402 and 404 permits may incidentally affect individual water rights ... It is not the purpose of this amendment to prohibit those incidental effects" (3 Legislative History).

[124] Letter from Major General Charles McGinnis to Brigadier General Richard Wells, April 6, 1979. The CE regulations provide that, where a state has approved a proposed project, a Section 404 permit will be denied only where there are "overriding national factors of the public interest that necessitate denial." 33 C.F.R. Sec. 320.4(j)(4).

[125] The Fish and Wildlife Coordination Act requires the CE to consult with federal and state wildlife agencies and identify mitigation measures to be adopted. 16 U.S.C. Sec. 662.

The scope of the CE authority to condition permits in a way that interferes with state water rights entitlements is argued in a case pending at the time of this writing before the Tenth Circuit Court of Appeal. In _Riverside Irr. Dist. v. Stipo_,[126] two local water districts have argued that the CE cannot regulate operation of a dam because their jurisdiction extends only to construction activities, and because regulation of operation would interfere with water rights granted under state law. The public agencies were informed that an individual permit was required for a dam and reservoir project in Morgan County, Colorado, because the project could have a significant impact on Whooping Crane habitat 402 km. (250 mi.) downstream. Rather than apply for the permit, the plaintiffs brought suit for declaratory, injunctive, and mandatory relief. The district court dismissed all claims, and the districts appealed. They argue that the CE cannot abrogate allocations of water made in an interstate compact and granted pursuant to state law. They also argue that the CE decision that an individual permit is required violates Section 101(g).[126]

Federal compliance with state substantive water law requirements has been a major issue with the western states, particularly since the United States Supreme Court decided _California v. United States_[127] and _United States v. New Mexico_.[128] They interpret these decisions to mean that the United States must comply with state substantive law, except where a federal reserved water right, the federal navigation servitude, or clear congressional directives to the contrary are involved. Many states see Section 404 permit conditions as a violation of this principle, particularly where a permit requires minimum flows.

The conflict between state water rights and Section 404 has not been lost on supporters of the Tower bill[120], who have urged substantial reduction of Section 404 jurisdiction as a means of dealing with the water rights problem. At recent meetings of the National Governors' Association (NGA) and the Interstate Council on Water Problems (ICWP), efforts to obtain resolutions specifically endorsing the Tower bill were defeated. The majority of NGA and ICWP members (including California and Florida) voted instead for a position which supports retention of broad Section 404 jurisdiction. However, the positions adopted by both organizations state that Section 404 should be amended so that a permit cannot be denied or conditioned in derogation of state water allocation decisions.[129] While this position does not urge Congress to restrict the scope

---

[126] Nos. 80-2142, 2141 and 2142 (10th Cir.)

[127] See E.L.R. Pending Litigation at 65682-3.

[128] 438 U.S. 645 (1978).

[129] 438 U.S. 696 (1978).

See The Clean Water Act, National Governors' Association, policy position adopted August 1981.

of Section 404, introduction of any amendments to the Clean Water Act offers an opportunity for the supporters of the Tower Bill, as the 1976-77 legislative maneuvers have shown.

One way to reduce the controversy over water rights would be administrative interpretation of Section 101(g) by the CE in regulations. While the CE regulations give deference to state approvals of a project, there are no specific standards interpreting Section 101(g). Adopting such standards could provide clear guidelines and procedures for resolving potential conflicts over water rights with no or minimal disturbance to the basic water right. In general, the policies should defer to state water rights law, except where such deference would clearly frustrate the purposes of the Clean Water Act, namely (for Section 404) the protection of wetlands from unavoidable loss or damage. Furthermore, the procedures could require that a decision affecting water rights should be made at a higher level than the District Engineer, and after an oppportunity for the affected state water rights agency to present its views. While such an approach would limit the ability of Section 404 to require minimum streamflows, particularly at existing facilities, hard choices need to be made. Section 404, as interpreted by the courts, has been demonstrated effective in protecting wetlands. To the degree that Section 404 is expanded into a minimum streamflow law, its chance of being curtailed increases. Such limitation would, of course, include curtailing the protection of wetlands under Section 404.

State Assumption of Section 404 Jurisdiction

Although most provisions of Section 404 have worked well, an exception occurs in Section 404(g)(1), providing for state assumption of Section 404 jurisdiction of all except traditionally navigable waters, have not worked. While the 1977 Conference Report stated that the assumption provisions in Section 404 would minimize federal-state conflicts,[130] no state has taken over a Section 404 permit program. This is probably due to several factors. The procedures for state assumption are very complicated, and the act provides a mechanism for an EPA veto of a proposed state permit.[131] A state could not assume jurisdiction over traditionally navigable waters and adjacent wetlands, so most states (especially coastal states) would have jurisdiction over only a portion of the activities that may affect the state's wetlands. While Section 404 provides for state assumption, no source of funding is available for setting up and operating a state program. Finally, in most coastal states the CE is already operating a permit program effectively, and there is little incentive to take the program over at additional cost to the state.

Many multi-state organizations have adopted positions urging that Section 404 be amended to provide for simiplified assumption of Section 404 jurisdiction. For example, the NGA position asks Congress to amend Section 404 to permit the CE (instead of the EPA) to approve a state proposal. Once assumed, federal agencies could comment on a proposed permit, but could not veto it.[132]

It is likely that legislative proposals will be introduced to modify the existing procedures for state assumption. Unlike the water rights issue, there is little the CE can do about the assumption issue.

CONCLUSION

The title of this paper asks, somewhat rhetorically, whether there is a national interest in wetlands. There clearly is one, as recognized by almost every court that has construed Section 404. However, while Section 404 has evolved into a major national regulatory program to protect wetlands, it remains a captive of its past history.

Section 404 is the fortuitous product of its inclusion in the FWPCA, the initial reluctance of the CE to administer the program, and a citizens' suit that precipitated expansion of the program to the full extent of FWPCA jurisdiction. In some respects, the fact that Section 404 is the product of this interaction makes it more vulnerable to change today, notwithstanding the 1977 amendments which confirmed its scope.

The various forces that brought Section 404 to its present point continue to interact. Those who oppose federal regulation of local activities in wetlands are still seeking an amendment like the original Breaux amendment. Environmental organizations and fish and wildlife agencies continue to seek strict enforcement of its requirements. Some states, buoyed by stirrings of new federalism, see Section 404 as an unwarranted invasion on state sovereignty. Now the CE itself is suggesting legislative modifications. In a speech in San Francisco in August 1981, Assistant Secretary of the Army for Civil Works, William Gianelli, told the American Society of Civil Engineers that Section 404 has "gone far beyond its originally envisioned scope, and more importantly beyond the appropriate role of the federal government in regulating the development of public and private resources involving our nation's water and wetlands."[133] Gianelli indicated that he

---

130 See 3 Legislative History.
131 Sec. 404(j), 33 U.S.C. Sec. 1342(j).

---

132 The Western States Water Council has also taken a similar position. See "Position Statement of the Western States Water Council Concerning Section 404 of the Clean Water Act and Section 10 of the Rivers and Harbors Act of 1899," (January 15, 1981). California did not vote for the WSWC position.
133 Water Information News Service 6(9) (August 21, 1981):1-3.

would like to see wetlands legislatively defined and designated "rather than to try the piecemeal, back-door approach applicable to the land fill areas under CE programs."[133] So the old arguments continue with the CE entering the fray.

How Section 404 will survive in the current anti-regulatory atmosphere of the Reagan administration is far from clear. Section 404 became what it is largely because of a citizens' suit in 1975. Several other major judicial interpretations of Section 404 (e.g., the Avoyelles case) are also due to citizen involvement. While the policy and purpose of Section 404 is perfectly clear to courts enforcing the act, that policy is less clear in the political arena. The survival of Section 404 may depend to a large extent on continued public involvement in identifying preservation of wetlands as a national priority.

LITERATURE CITED

Barker. 1976. Sections 9 and 10 of the Rivers and Harbors Act of 1899: Potent tools for environmental protection. 109 p. 6 Ecology L.Q.

Blumm. 1980. The Clean Water Act's Section 404 program enters its adolescence: an institutional and programmatic perspective. Ecology L.Q. 8:419-436.

Caplin. 1977. Is Congress protecting our water? The controversy over Section 404, Federal Water Pollution Control Act Amendments of 1972. 445 p. U. Miami L. Rev.

Karhl, W. (ed.). 1977. The California water atlas. Prepared by the Office of Planning and Research. 117 p. California Department of Water Resources, Sacramento.

Myhrum. 1979. Federal protection of wetlands through legal process. 567 p. 7 Boston College Env. Affrs. Rev.

Shipley. 1974. The Fish and Wildlife Coordination Act's application to wetlands. p. 2-49 to 2-59. In: Reitze. Environmental planning: law of land and resources.

THE CLEAN WATER ACTS AND THE PRINCIPLES OF

THE PUBLIC TRUST DOCTRINE: A DISCUSSION[1]

Felix E. Smith[2]

Abstract.--Congress passed PL 92-500 and PL 95-217, referred to as the Clean Water Acts. These acts provide for restoration and maintenance of the chemical, physical, and biological integrity of the nation's waters. The acts also enable states, upon meeting certain criteria, to assume the authority to regulate dredge and fill activities and discharges into non-traditional navigable waters and wetlands. The development of aggressive state programs would give the states an opportunity to affirm their stewardship responsibilities for the management of water, streams, wetlands, and associated resources consistent with the Public Trust.

INTRODUCTION

The nation's rivers and streams, from their headwater springs and adjacent wetlands to their receiving waters (estuaries or the oceans) are one of our most valuable natural resources and are held in trust. These unique resources are part of our natural heritage. Much of our water for agriculture, industrial purposes, drinking, and other domestic use comes from these waterways. Watercourses, from major rivers to small streams, are habitats for salmon, steelhead, trout, black bass, catfish, and numerous other fishes. Aquatic and riparian wetlands with their respective vegetations are habitats for numerous waterfowl species and other migratory and resident species of wildlife.

These rivers, streams, and wetlands also provide recreational, scenic, and aesthetic enjoyment; are natural drainage and floodway systems; are used to generate electricity; are conduits for supply of groundwater recharge; are transportation corridors for goods and services; and are of historic and scientific value. However, we have not managed these waters and lands with sufficient care to allow them to provide continuing and long-term values to society, either as functioning ecosystems or as a resource. Rivers were dammed and their waters diverted; wetlands were drained or otherwise reclaimed; streams were channelized, stripped of their riparian vegetation, mined of their gravels, and otherwise modified. Sediments and pollutants entered what remained of these same streams, further reducing their capacity to support valuable fish and wildlife resources, or to provide for the restorative needs of our minds and bodies.

HISTORICAL BACKGROUND

Over the years laws were passed which emphasized the need for stewardship of our waters, waterways, and adjacent wetlands. The Rivers and Harbors Act of 1899 was designed to regulate activities which could obstruct the navigability of the nation's waterways. All activities were prohibited unless permitted by the US Army Corps of Engineers (CE). Regulated activities included the placement of fills; construction of such structures as bridges, piers, docks, levees, etc.; and deposition of industrial or urban waste, oils, pollutants, or refuse of any kind. However, this act was administered as a development act, **not** as a conservation act (Morris 1978). The nation was rushing to become an industrialized power. Industries needed water, so rivers were dammed. Wetlands, bays, and rivers were convenient places to dump waste or to place fill. In this rush, little meaningful thought was given to conserving natural resources, including the water in lakes, rivers, and estuaries. There was little, if any, balance in the administration of the Rivers and Harbors Act and little real effort to protect the quality of the nation's waters or the resources in those waters, both of which are held in trust and belong or are "common" to the people.

Freedom to develop or use lakes, rivers, streams and wetlands--which can be considered "commons" or property belonging to the people-- and the administration of the Rivers and Harbors

---

[1]Paper presented at the California Riparian Systems Conference. [University of California, Davis, September 17-19, 1981.]
[2]Felix E. Smith is Senior Staff Specialist, USDI Fish and Wildlife Service, Sacramento, Calif.

Act of 1899, parallel the "tragedy of the commons" described by Garrett Hardin (1968). Hardin illustrates the tragedy of the commons by describing a pasture open to use by a number of herdsmen. Each herdsman seeks to maximize his own gain and does so by trying to raise as many cattle as possible on public commons, i.e., the pasture. A question faced by each herdsman is: what is the utility to me of increasing my herd by one animal? Since each herdsman receives all the proceeds from the sale of each animal, the positive component of this utility is nearly equal to the value of one animal. The negative component of this utility is a function of the additional overgrazing of the commons due to the additional animal. The effects of overgrazing, however, are distributed among all the herdsmen, and thus the negative component of the utility for the single herdsman is considerably less than the positive component. Because the net utility to the individual is positive, the practical herdsmen will conclude that the rational decision for him is to add the additional animal. Each herdsman sharing the public pasture reaches the same conclusion.

> Therein is the tragedy. Each man is locked into a system that compels him to increase his herd without limit in a world that is limited. Ruin is the destination toward which all men rush, each pursuing his own best interest in a society that believes in the freedom of the commons. Freedom in the commons brings ruin to all...the individual benefits as an individual...even though society as a whole, of which he is a part, suffers. (ibid.)

A "common resource" or "common pool resource" as described by Baden (1977) is a resource for which there are multiple owners (or where a number of people have rights to use the resource) and where one or a set of users can have adverse effects upon the interests of other users. In the situation where there is no agency with the power to coordinate, restrict, or ration use, or an agency so empowered fails to do so, actions which are individually rational can be collectively disastrous. This is the central point of the tragedy of the commons.

The tragedy of the commons can be identified in the administration of past and present permit systems regulating the use of water, waterways, their shorelines, and associated resources. This is comparable to a society allowing the exploitation or use of the common resources, the resources held in trust--"...the air, running water and the sea and hence the shores of the sea" (Althaus 1978), without guidance or regulation. The developer or user profits, with the costs in lost public resources and opportunities assessed against present and future generations, as a social cost of such development or use. A society without the knowledge or awareness to formulate and implement controls or restrictions on the use or exploitation of the commons will destroy the commons, and itself as well (Hardin 1968; Hickle 1971).

By the 1950s and 1960s, people were aware of the adverse impacts that unregulated, as well as regulated, activities and uses were having on the nation's waters. The adverse impacts were widespread and of increasing concern to the public. Drainage had destroyed a considerable portion of the nation's wetlands. Filling of estuaries and lakes was occuring at an alarming and ever-accelerating rate. Dams and diversions had altered many streams and even dried some of the nation's rivers, destroying them as functioning ecosystems. Some were degraded to the point that they no longer supported significant fish and wildlife resources of previous regional, national or international importance, or significant public use or contact. In addition, evidence of water pollution, as well as land pollution, was now widespread. Few if any of the nation's waters were spared the impacts of water diversion, sedimentation, or pollution.

CONGRESSIONAL ACTION AND ITS IMPLEMENTATION

Public concern alerted the Congress to what was happening to the nation's waters and wetlands. The Congress requested documentation. The National Estuarine Pollution Study (U.S. Department of Interior 1969) and National Estuary Study (U.S. Department of Interior 1970) were prepared. These reports alerted the Congress to what was really happening to the nation's waters and waterways and the resources in and industries dependent upon those waters and their associated resources. The future was not bright if the status quo of laws and their enforcement was maintained. In addition, it was being realized with much chagrin that restoring quality to a damaged environment was far more costly than retaining the quality of the original environment. This applied particularly to efforts to restore fish and wildlife resources and the integrity of their habitats.[3]

While the evidence was being gathered and reports prepared, Congress passed the Wild and Scenic Rivers Act[4] in 1968. In this act's declaration of policy, Congress stated that the established national policy of permitting dams and other construction at appropriate sections of the rivers of the United States needed to be complemented by a policy of preserving other selected rivers or sections thereof in their free-flowing condition. The goals of the latter policy were to protect the water quality of such rivers and to permit them to fulfill other vital conservation purposes for the benefit of present and future generations.

---

[3]Ketchum. 1969. Panel on ecology and the environment, National Water Commission.
[4]PL 90-542.

In response to the evidence and the national concern to protect the quality and resources of the nation's waters, Congress passed the Federal Water Pollution Control Act Amendments of 1972[5] and the Clean Water Act of 1977.[6] Congress recognized its stewardship responsibilities for restoring and maintaining the integrity of the nation's waters in a declaration of goals and policy:

1) It is the national goal that the discharge of pollutants into the navigable waters be eliminated by 1985;
2) It is the national goal that wherever attainable an interim goal of water quality which provides for the protection and propagation of fish, shellfish and wildlife and provides for recreation in and on the waters be achieved by July 1, 1983;
3) It is the national policy that the discharge of toxic pollutants in toxic amounts be prohibited;
4) It is the national policy that Federal financial assistance be provided to construct publicly owned waste treatment works;
5) It is the national policy that area-wide waste treatment management planning processes be developed and implemented to assure adequate control of sources of pollutants in each State and;
6) It is the national policy that a major research and demonstration effort be made to develop technology necessary to eliminate the discharge of pollutants into the navigable waters, waters of the contiguous zone and the ocean.[7]

These activities would be accomplished in cooperation with all the states.[8]

Congress recognized its stewardship responsibilities and left no doubt in anyone's mind about its concern for the chemical, biological and physical integrity of all the nation's waters, including streams and groundwater aquifers. It made it clear that due regard shall be given to improvements necessary to conserve such waters for: a) the protection and propagation of fish, shellfish and other aquatic life and wildlife; b) recreational purposes; and c) the withdrawal of these waters for public water supply, agricultural, industrial and other purposes. Congress clearly recognized that protecting the integrity of water as a resource and an ecosystem was a national concern and in the long-term public interest.

The goals stated and policy language used are definitely those of a "trustee"; a nation concerned with stewardship and management of its waters, wetlands, and associated resources and environmental needs.

With passage of the Federal Water Pollution Control Act amendments, Congress created new permit programs, outlined in Section 402, the National Pollutant Discharge Elimination System (NPDES), and Section 404 to control the many activities and impacts associated with dredging and placing fill. The permit programs were formulated by the Environmental Protection Agency (EPA) and the CE. The discharge of any pollutant is regulated by the NPDES (Section 402) permit, which basically replaced Section 10 of the Rivers and Harbors Act of 1899. In California this program has been delegated to and administered by the State Water Resources Control Board (SWRCB) and the Regional Water Quality Control Boards (RWQCB). The intent of the program was to reduce the amount of toxic material and other waste entering lakes, rivers, or coastal waters. It was by then realized that reliance on "dilution as the solution" to rendering innocuous all our wastes was, for our society, no longer possible.

The CE proceeded to administer the Section 404 program in traditional navigable waters, as it had the permit program under Section 10 of the Rivers and Harbors Act of 1899. In consequence, the Natural Resources Defense Council filed suit against the CE alleging that the CE definition of the nation's waters was too restrictive and not within the meaning of the Clean Water Act. The court, in Natural Resources Defense Council, Inc. v. Callaway[9] ordered the CE to include virtually all the nation's waters under Section 404. With the court's ruling and implementation of new permit regulations and penalties for violations came the needed police powers to protect and preserve wetlands and the beds and bottoms of streams and lakes. These latter are as important to the health and integrity of aquatic environments as the quality of the water itself.

The basic philosophy and intent of the laws and regulations concerning the nation's waterways and associated ecosystems are clear. They are to protect the public interest from harm or degradation; to foster stewardship in resources management; and to protect resources from being degraded or destroyed, while providing for uses consistent with sound policies of stewardship and public use. There is, for example, a theoretical prohibition against all degradations or encroachments into, across, or upon all waters of the United States under both the Rivers and Harbors Act of 1899 and the Clean Water Act. The Section 10 permit system was established to provide a variance to this prohibition so that works or activities supposedly consistent with aiding navigation; aiding, fostering or protecting fishery or ecosystem functions; or assisting or

---

[5] PL 92-500.
[6] PL 95-217.
[7] PL 92-500; 86 Stat. 816, codified at 33 U.S.C. 1251 (a).
[8] 33 U.S.C. 1251 (b).

---

[9] 392 F. Supp. 685 (1975).

providing for the movement of commerce (i.e., goods or services); and in the public interest, could be constructed and operated.

The Rivers and Harbors Act prohibits unreasonable obstruction or use of the nation's waters. Some idea of just what the term unreasonable encompasses can be found in a statement made by then-Assistant Secretary of the Interior Stanley Cain, testifying in a hearing before Brigadier General Ray T. Dodge (CE) regarding a fill and intake proposal of Bethlehem Steel Corporation in Lake Michigan:

> Section 10 and the related provisions of the Rivers and Harbors Act of 1899 embrace affirmatively and positively the proposition that the people of the United States are to be protected against all unreasonable occupancies of navigable waters of the United States. Those occupancies may be unreasonable because they pollute, or because they offend our sense of aesthetics or natural beauty, or because they interface with the right of the public to enjoy a natural resource of national significance, or because they threaten in a harmful way to upset the ecological balance of nature, or simply--if you please--because to permit the occupancy would confer a valuable privilege without either necessity therefore or a fair return to the public in whose name the privilege would be bestowed. Stating the matter somewhat differently, it is the applicant who must establish that the public interest will be served by bestowing this privilege.[10]

This testimony of about 15 years ago provides practical guidelines for managing the nation's waters, associated lands, and their ecological components, whether under the Rivers and Harbors Act of 1899 or the present Clean Water Act.

A CE permit is issued when works or activities are deemed consistent with the public interest. When a permit is issued, the general public's right to utilize the permit area, its resources, or other benefits are restricted, altered, or withdrawn for the benefit of the permit holder. In essence, public rights and interests are subordinated when permits are issued allowing placement of fill in a lake, river, or estuary; construction of a restaurant, homesite, wharf, pier, or bulkhead; construction of a dam on a river to generate electrical energy; impoundment or diversion of water; or riprapping or channelizing of a stream. As a result, permits confer an extremely valuable privilege or concession to the permit recipient, allowing the recipient to develop or utilize one or more aspects of public property or a public resource, all too frequently, for the personal use or gain of the permit holder or a few individuals at the most.

IMPLICATIONS OF THE PUBLIC TRUST DOCTRINE

Sax (1970) indicated that the Public Trust Doctrine, of all the concepts in American law, seems to have the breadth and substantive content to make it a useful tool for general application in developing a comprehensive legal approach to resource management problems. Others such as Cohen (1970), Dunning (1980), Johnson (1980), Stevens (1980), and Wilkinson (1980) are also very supportive of the Public Trust Doctrine and its principles in the management of natural resources. The Clean Water Act provides federal and state governments with opportunities to affirm the principle of stewardship and to become trustees in the administration of water resources for the benefit of present and future generations.

Public Trust Doctrine concepts have persisted in European, English, and American law throughout history. Their roots trace back to Roman times. The Institutes of Justinian in the sixth century stated: "...by the law of nature these things are common to mankind--the air, running water, the sea and consequently the shores of the sea." This was also considered the "law of nations." The Justinian complications were a restatement of a law which was already considered ancient at the time (Althaus 1978). The reference to "...things ... common to mankind..." implies that such things were common property, that is public property, held in trust for all the people and for future generations. This definition is similar to the common pasture described in "Tragedy of the Commons" (Hardin 1968) and the common pool reources of Baden (1977).

The Pubic Trust Doctrine generally imposes upon the states a trust obligation for publicly owned resources on behalf of all the people. For example, under the trust principles, resources or objects in which the public has a special interest are held, subject to the duty of the states not to impair the resources, even if private interests are also held. In a traditional sense, the Public Trust Doctrine imposes a trust in favor of public rights and uses of navigable waters, publicly owned bottoms or beds of such waters, including submerged land and submersible tidelands, shorelands, and stream channels, and fish and wildlife resources. The doctrine has been interpreted by some states to apply to waters over privately held beds when the waters are considered navigable under state motor boat or pleasure craft tests. Public rights are considered superior to private rights. The trust is generally considered inalienable. If title is conveyed to private use, the property is still subject to the trust and paramount state interests (Althaus 1978; Stevens 1980).

---

[10]Letter of Frank J. Berry, U.S. Department of the Interior, Officeof the Solicitor, to Henry Wright, Oil and Gas Association. 8 December 1966.

260

Over the years courts have broadened the scope of the Public Trust Doctrine to meet contemporary situations and changing public needs. The California Supreme Court in Marks v. Whitney[10] helped redefine the scope of the state's interest in navigable waters and tidelands. It recognized and clarified the uses encompassed within the tidelands trust. It held that in addition to the traditional purposes of navigation, fishery, and commerce, the trust also includes the preservation of those lands in their natural state for their value as open space and as environments which provide food and habitat for birds and marine life and which favorably affect the scenery and climate of the area. The court recognized that tidelands, with their plant and animal life, water over and in the sand, and gravel or mud substrate all interacting, are a valuable ecosystem having high attendant values and uses.

There is no doubt that there is great public interest in the water, instream flows, stream channels, riparian vegetation, and the fish and wildlife resources associated with water, stream, and wetland ecosystems. Research findings from agriculture, forestry, and hydrology indicate that riparian and near-stream vegetation can: a) reduce temperature-associated water quality problems; b) reduce undesirable nutrient and sediment transport from the upland to the aquatic ecosystem; and c) reduce bank erosion. In addition, maintaining a more natural riparian vegetation and channel morphology results in a more productive, diverse, and stable stream biota, which includes fish and wildlife resources (Karr and Schlosser 1978).

The broadened public trust definition and the knowledge and concern for tidelands ecosystems expressed in Marks v. Whitney could easily be applied to a stream, including the streambed with its water-, sand-, and gravel-associated vegetation and aquatic life. Thus, for the state to exercise the maximum public trust responsibilities for its rivers, streams and wetlands (and their associated fish and wildlife), state management jurisdiction should include the water in a stream to at least the headwater springs and the streambed to at least the ordinary within-bank or bankful high water mark. Similar conditions now apply to lakes (in California v. Superior Court [Lyon][11] and California v. Superior Court [Fogerty][12]). In California both water and the fish in the water are public resources held in trust by the state in its sovereign capacity (Robie 1974, Schneider 1978). In addition, for protection of the stream ecosystem, state jurisdiction should include the riparian vegetation corridor adjacent to the stream as well as the stream channel itself.

---

[10] 6 Cal. Report 790, 491 P. 2d 374 (C1971).

[11] 29 Cal. 3d 210 (1981).

[12] 29 Cal. 3d 240 (1981).

In 1892, the close of the nineteenth century and some thirteen centuries after the Institute of Justinian, the United States Supreme Court decided the leading American public trust case. In Illinois Central Railroad Company v. Illinois[13], the court held that state ownership of lands under the waters of Lake Michigan could not be surrendered or delegated except for public purposes:

It is a title held in trust for the people of the State that they may enjoy the navigation of the water, carry on commerce over them, and have liberty of fishing therein freed from the obstruction or interference of private parties--The Trust devolving upon State for the public, and which can only be discharged by the management and control of property in which the public has an interest, cannot be relinquished by a transfer of the property. The control of the State for the purposes of the trust can never be lost, except as to such parcels as are used in promoting the interests of the public therein, or can be disposed of without any substantial impairment of the public interest in the lands and waters remaining.

The Court further stated:

A grant of all the lands under the navigable waters of a State has never been adjudged to be within the legislative power; and any attempted grant of the kind would be held, if not absolutely void on its face, as subject to revocation. The State can no more abdicate its trust over property in which the whole people are interested, like navigable waters and soils under them, so as to leave them entirely under the use and control of private parties except in the instance of parcels mentioned for the improvement of the navigation and use of the waters, or when parcels can be disposed of without impairment of the public interest in what remains, than it can abdicate its police powers in the administration of government and the preservation of peace. In the administration of government, the use of such powers may for a limited period be delegated to a municipality or other body, but there always remains with the State the right to revoke those powers and exercise them in a more direct manner, and one more comfortable to its wishes. So with trusts connected with public property, or property of a special character, like lands under navigable waters; they cannot be placed entirely beyond the direction and control of the State. (emphasis added)

---

[13] 146 U.S. 387, 36 Led 1018 (1892).

The Court recognized that it is the public ownership of the water over the bed of Lake Michigan that gave the lakebed special character. The beds and bottoms of all lakes, streams, and rivers are also special in character relative to the chemical and biological integrity of the nation's waters.

The Oregon Supreme Court[14] in Morse v. Oregon Division of State Lands recognized the special character of the waters and bottom of Coos Bay. Regarding a permit to fill 13 ha. (32 ac.) of Coos Bay for an airport runway, which it found to be inconsistent with the public trust, it wrote:

> Because the trust is for the public benefit, the State's trustee obligation is commonly described as the protection of specified public usages, e.g., navigation, fishery and, in more recent cases, recreation. The severe restriction upon the power of the State as trustee to modify water resources is predicated not only upon the importance of the public use of such waters and lands but upon the exhaustible and irreplaceable nature of the resources and its fundamental importance to our society and to our environment. These resources, after all, can only be spent once. Therefore, the law has historically and consistently recognized that rivers and estuaries once destroyed or diminished may never be restored to the public and, accordingly, has required the highest degree of protection from the public trustee. (emphasis added)

Not only was the navigation servitude of Coos Bay involved, but the integrity of the physical aspects and biological components of an estuary and tributary rivers were at stake.

The statement by the Oregon Court is a clear indication that it realizes the ecosystem nature of Coos Bay waters and their resources, uses, and values to society. It also seems clearly understood by the Court that rivers are an integral system from their headwaters to their estuary, and, once destroyed or greatly diminished in a physical and ecological sense may never be restored. As such they deserve the highest degree of protection from the state as public trustee.

It must be remembered that in many instances governmental agencies, the trustees of public resources and interests, are the ones primarily responsible for excessive degradation of the physical, chemical, and biological components of the nation's waters and associated resources. By issuing permits for road construction, tideland fillings, discharges into public waters, spoil disposal, dam construction, factory or industrial park construction, riprapping, and stream channelization, and myriad seemingly minor land/water interface intrusions (e.g. bulkheads, piers, and docks), all too often in the name of progress and necessity, public trust values are progressively and irrevocably lost.

While each individual action seems rational, evidence indicates the collective result of these actions can be disastrous. This is the central point of the tragedy of the commons. In addition, the impact of the fill or project construction, made possible by the issuance of the permit, lasts into perpetuity. The permit results in the loss forever of a piece of tideland, marshland, stream reach, or shoreline with its associated resources, public uses, and economic and non-economic values.

The Clean Water Act, the Rivers and Harbors Act of 1899, the Fish and Wildlife Coordination Act of March 10, 1934, as amended, the Fish and Wildlife Act of 1956, and, of course, the National Environmental Policy Act should be read with the principles and obligations of the Public Trust Doctrine in mind. In these legislative acts, Congress fully intended to protect, preserve, and manage resources of great national wealth, such as fish and wildlife resources, water, and aquatic ecosystems, for the well-being of its people, in a manner similar to that of a trustee, not as a proprietor.

The Clean Water Act rests in the middle between the preservation and protection provided by the Wild and Scenic Rivers Act and the development/exploitation made possible in a multitude of acts for constructing dams, dredging waterways, channelizing streams, draining wetlands, or otherwise modifying the nation's wetlands, streams, rivers, and waterways. The Clean Water Act provides federal and state governments an opportunity to affirm their stewardship responsibilities and support the principles of the Public Trust Doctrine in the administration and management of water and related resources, for the benefit of the present and future generations to whom these resources belong. For example, in California the State has the obligation to protect and promote the public trust and public uses of its waters, the beds of such waters, and adjacent lands, as an ecosystem consistent with, but not limited to, navigation, fisheries, recreation, fish and wildlife, water quality and quantity, and aquatic ecosystem maintenance and renewability.

The obligation on the state, as trustee, should be to protect and promote these water-related resources as property held in trust. This is based not only upon the importance to the public of such waters, but upon the exhaustible and irreplaceable nature of these complex ecosystems and their associated resources, and their fundamental importance to our society and our total environment. The implementation of an aggressive state/federal Section 10/404 program is a logical step in restoring and maintaining the chemical, physical and biological integrity of the nation's waters.

---

[14] 285 Or. 197, 590 P. 2d 709. Affirmed 34 Or. App. 853 P. 2d 520.

Under a program built on Public Trust principles, public resources and associated interests would be treated as property to be maintained and protected for the benefit of present and future generations. They would be subject to infringement only: a) when it could be demonstrated that some other need is paramount (i.e., public health and safety); b) when the activity could be carried out in a manner consistent with the public trust, with minimum unavoidable harm; and c) when it can be shown that harmful effects would be offset to the greatest degree reasonably possible.

In the Section 10/404 program, it is the protection of public health, public uses, and the vitality and renewability of aquatic and related land ecosystems and associated resources that is at stake. The public trust responsibility must be given priority when considering the demands of other users with respect to other available alternatives, existing and potential technology, and the possibility of less harmful methods or locations of the development or activity.

The state, as trustee, and the permitting and reviewing agencies, as an integral part of their stewardship responsibilities, should stress the following during review of Section 10/404 permit applications.

1. Does the proposed activity conflict or interface with the paramount policy of state and federal agencies to protect, preserve, and promote the uses of its water, waterways, and adjacent lands, as biological and/or ecological resources, for fish, fishing, wildlife, navigation, and numerous recreational activities?

2. Is the proposed activity consistent with resource conservation policies?

3. Does the proposed activity interface with or endanger public use, health, or safety in the area?

4. Could significant external costs be incurred by an entity other than the project sponsor as a result of the proposed activity?

5. Is the proposed activity consistent with any existing comprehensive plan for the use of the waters of the basin, sub-basin, or planning area?

6. How will public resources and uses be protected from any adverse effects of the proposed activity?

7. Has the applicant adequately described how the proposed use of public land and/or water is in the overall public interest and how the proposed activity adequately provides for the protection of public uses and resources affected by the proposed activity?

8. Could the cumulative impacts of similar activities lead to the degradation of the resources held in stewardship by the Public Trust Doctrine?

9. Are public uses, resources, and opportunities being protected and promoted in a manner consistent with the public trust?

10. Are the mitigation and compensation measures feasible and capable of accomplishing the desired results?

11. Have practical alternatives to the proposed activity been considered and the least damaging alternative selected for permit processing?

If the state, acting as trustee, is lacking in understanding of the resources and ecosystems protected by the Public Trust Doctrine, it cannot possibly be a responsible steward.

For projects which the permitting agencies find acceptable, the formulation of permit terms and conditions should include measures to prevent or minimize adverse impacts to the values, functions, resources, and opportunities of the area. Where adverse impacts are unavoidable, resource compensation or mitigation measures should be required as an integral part of the proposed activity. These measures, needed to protect one resource, should not be developed at the expense of another. We have been forcibly reminded from our past experience of trying to clean up or protect our environment, of having to pick up after past resource management decisions that it is the consumer who eventually pays the bill. Society might as well include the cost of protecting, repairing, or restoring the environment in the price of today's project, rather than deferring it to future generations. Their environmental and resource protection costs will be high enough without having to shoulder today's costs as well.

The concept of the public trust puts the cost of protecting and stewarding resources such as those under the Clean Water Act on a pay-as-you-go basis. The costs for protecting the public interest in such resources should be included as a cost of doing business, just as the rent and electric bill, and workers wages are included in the cost of producing goods and services.

The states, in partnership with the federal government, should develop a conservation program for the nation's waters and wetlands which is consistent with trustee obligations and responsibilities of the states. The overall intent of an aggressive commenting, reporting, and monitoring program is to protect the public and its interests from ruin or degradation, to permit reasonable resource uses consistent with sound management practices, and to prevent or severely restrict uses or practices harmful to the land, water, or the beds or bottoms of such waters. The beneficiaries of this vigilance will be future generations of Americans.

The reduction or relaxation of enforcement of public trust responsibilities and obligations in any section of the Clean Water Act (e.g., 208, 402, or 404, or Section 10 of the Rivers and Harbors Act) could lead to the degradation or loss of part or all of the chemical, physical or biological components necessary for the integrity of the nation's waters or wetlands. To protect resources or ecosystems under one rule or law only to lose them because of another is pure folly in the administration and management of the nation's waters.

CONCLUSIONS

In managing the nation's waters, wetlands and associated resources, it is clear that society must not make or perpetuate the mistakes of the past. We no longer have the margin for errors that we once had. The concepts of the Public Trust Doctrine provide a tool for the management of natural resources by the state, for all the people. However, does the absence of broad public support for the public trust in natural resources management and in efforts to protect the public equity account for our seeming failure to protect such resources from loss or degradation?

Does the lack of public awareness that lakes, rivers, streams, wetlands, and fish and wildlife are resources held in trust account for what has happened to these resources as administered under past laws and regulations designed to protect them? Can we expect future generations to believe that we could not find alternatives to the continued degradation of our environment nor the funds to correct past mistakes and restore the physical, chemical and biological integrity of the nation's waters?

The future of the Public Trust Doctrine as a tool to protect the quality of water in streams, the ecological integrity of those streams, the beds of lakes and streams, and the riparian vegetation associated with them will be dependent upon the creativity and assertiveness with which it is applied. The states must recognize and aggressively meet their trust obligations and the needs of future generations to whom, in the final analysis, the waters and associated resources belong. The states in partnership with the federal government can do this through an aggressive action program of evaluation and monitoring, developed under provisions of the Clean Water Act and consistent with the principles of the Public Trust Doctrine.

LITERATURE CITED

Althaus, H.F. 1978. Public trust rights. 421 p. U.S. Department of Interior, Office of the Solicitor under contract for the USDI Fish and Wildlife Service, Portland, Ore.

Baden, J. 1977. A primer for the management of common pool resources. In: G. Hardin and J. Baden. Managing the commons. 421 p. W.H. Freeman and Co, San Francisco.

Cohen, B.S. 1970. The Constitution, the Public Trust Doctrine, and the environment. Utah Law Review 3:388-394.

Dunning, H.C. 1980. The significance of California public trust easements for California's water rights law. U.C.D. Law Rev. 14(2): 357-398.

Hardin, G. 1968. The tragedy of the commons. Science 162:1243-1248.

Hickle, W.J. 1971. Who owns America? 398 p. Prentice-Hall, Inc., Englewood Cliffs, New Jersey.

Johnson, R.W. 1980. Public trust protection for stream flows and lake levels. U.C.D. Law Rev. 14(2):233-267.

Karr, J.R., and I.J. Schlosser. 1978. Water resource and the land-water interface. Science 201:229-234.

Morris, J.W.. 1978. The Corps of Engineers and the American environment: Past, present, and future. EP-360-4-15. Office of the Chief Engineer.

Robie, R.B. 1974. Modernizing state water rights laws: some suggestions for new directions. Utah Law Review 4:760-784.

Sax, J.L. 1970. The public trust doctrine in natural resources law: effective judicial intervention. Michigan Law Review 68:471-566.

Schneider, A.S. 1978. Legal aspects of instream water uses in California. Staff Paper No. 6, Governor's Commission to Review Water Rights Law, State of California, Sacramento. 131 p.

Stevens, J.S. 1980. The public trust: a sovereign's ancient prerogative becomes the people's environmental right. U.C.D. Law Rev. 14(2):195-232.

U.S. Department of the Interior. 1969. National estuarine pollution study. Pursuant to Public Law 89-753.

U.S. Department of the Interior. 1970. National Estuary Study in Response to Public Law 90-454.

Wilkinson, C.F. 1980. The public trust doctrine in public land law. U.C.D. Law Rev. 14(2): 269-316.

THE PUBLIC TRUST AND RIPARIAN SYSTEMS:

A CASE FOR PRESERVATION[1]

David B. Anderson[2]

Abstract.--The Public Trust Doctrine may be a strong tool for preserving riparian systems when competing human interests are few. But where they are many and established, the public trust is particularly unsuited for use as a preservation or management rationale, because it remains a vague and purist doctrine with little integration into the positive law. Its utility, or even its own preservation, requires that limits on it be advanced in a timely manner by those interested in resource protection.

It is natural to look to the Public Trust Doctrine as a vehicle for protecting riparian systems. In the 1971 case of Marks v. Whitney, the California Supreme Court noted that preserving tidelands in their natural state for ecological study, open space, or aesthetic value was a proper and protectible trust purpose.[3] This case broke clearly with the traditional requirement that the protected public uses of trust waters relate to navigation or the "incidents" of navigation.[4] The California Supreme Court in the Lake Tahoe case (decided early in 1981) focused heavily on the ecological importance of the shorezone of navigable lakes in deciding that the area between ordinary high and low water is impressed with a public trust servitude, which the State has not been equitably estopped to assert.[5] And in the City of Berkeley case,[6] the Court set forth a balancing test under which the public trust remains impressed on alienated tidelands as long as they have not been filled, i.e., as long as they remain in their natural state.

These cases emphasizing the natural integrity of the trust resource may betoken a departure from prior cases which have held that the promotion of any kind of commerce, whether through the construction of freeway bridges[7] or tidelands oil drilling,[8] is a proper exercise of trust power by the State, notwithstanding the impairment of use of the trust resource in its natural state. It has always been considered proper for the state as trustee to impair or eliminate portions of the resource where the effect was to improve the remainder for its natural uses. Navigation and harbor improvements are examples of this. But this is far different from an impairment which does not redound to the benefit of the resource itself, but instead serves the same class of purpose though in a manner not related to the exercise of trust rights by the public. The proposition that the furtherance of commerce, for example, is a proper trust purpose does not support the corollary that everything done to advance commerce falls within the state's powers and duties under the trust.

Of these recent cases, the Lake Tahoe and Clear Lake[9] cases have the most importance for riparian systems. By expanding the recognized trust area to include the shorezone, these cases bring a portion of the riparian environment directly under legal protection. In addition, because of the very sensitivity of this area to landward influences this protection may be extended beyond the high-water mark to protect the more terrestrial reaches of the natural riparian system. Carried by the momentum of recent judicial successes, even more profound and creative

---

[1] Paper presented at the California Riparian Systems Conference. [University of California, Davis, September 17-19, 1981].

[2] David B. Anderson is Attorney with the California Department of Water Resources, and serves as Legal Counsel to the Reclamation Board, Sacramento, Calif.

[3] Marks v. Whitney, 6 Cal. 3d 251 (1971).

[4] Ibid. at 259; Bohn v. Albertson, 107 Cal. App. 2d 738 (1951).

[5] State of California v. Superior Court (Fogerty), 29 Cal. 3d 240 (1981).

[6] City of Berkeley v. Superior Court, 26 Cal. 3d 515 (1980).

[7] Colberg, Inc. v. State of California ex rel. Department of Public Works, 67 Cal. 2d 408 (1967).

[8] Boone v. Kingsbury, 206 Cal. 148 (1928).

[9] State of California v. Superior Court (Lyon), 29 Cal. 3d 210 (1981).

theories may be put forward to liberalize the application of the doctrine to California's riparian environments. But the point of this paper is not to urge expansion of the doctrine, which seems often to attend discussions of the public trust's potential. Its point is to advise caution and the need to limit the Public Trust Doctrine.

Where the natural riparian system is remote from competing human needs and development, the public trust, as it exists today, may well be a suitable tool. But where the riparian system includes residential and agricultural pressures for land and water--and this is where these pressures naturally gravitate--the Public Trust Doctrine appears today to be particularly ill-suited to the protection of environmental values. Such consumptive water and land uses may include using a river as a source or a conduit; flood control structures such as levees, dams, weirs, pumps, and bypasses; forest harvesting; sand and gravel extraction; sewage disposal; or any of the variety of things that are "useful to commerce".

Addressing a similar point, the Final Report of the Governor's Commission to Review California Water Rights Law[10] remarked:

The California Wild and Scenic Rivers Act does provide direct and substantive protection for natural stream resources. But it... is essentially an 'all-or-nothing' approach. This approach, while appropriate for the rivers included under the Act, is unsuited for the protection of many streams which must accommodate both instream and off-stream uses and equities, which vary widely from stream to stream.

The reason which underlies the need for caution is that the Public Trust Doctrine is fundamentally ill-defined and has remained a general political concept rather than a developed body of positive law. Its definition in the positive law, in actual controversies decided by courts, is burdened with a unique and vague terminology, of "jus publicum" and "jus privatum", of "imperium" and "dominium", which aid very little in integrating the public trust into the traditional and familiar legal framework. Furthermore, the California Legislature, in whom trust powers formally reside, has done almost nothing to define or implement the trust.

The basic question remains: does the public trust rest on the police power or does it derive from state property power? On the one hand, the argument has been made that it is a species of police power.[11] But property notions, imparted in its very name, run throughout the public trust cases in this state and elsewhere: public trust "easements" and "servitudes"; the idea that navigable waters are "owned" by the people; the division of legal and equitable title, as in the first Ivanhoe case;[12] the application of private trust law principles in Mallon v. City of Long Beach;[13] the coincidence of the public trust in tidelands with the original state ownership of the underlying land; and a burdening of private property interests beyond the accepted scope of the police power.

It has been said that the public trust easement is a "type of public property right" (Dunning 1980). Even commentators on the federal navigation servitude, derived from the Commerce Clause of the U.S. Constitution, describe it as being of a "proprietary" nature (Morreale 1963). Others argue the public trust arises from the original state ownership of the underlying soil. But if state property in the beds is the source of the public right to use the water, then what is the source of the public right to use waters whose beds are in private ownership, i.e., those "non-navigable" under the federal test and for which is recognized a state "navigation servitude"?

In fact, California cases have consistently mixed the language of public trust and navigation servitude, and cited these cases interchangeably as authority.[14] As far as "ownership" of the water goes, it has been repeatedly declared that private ownership of running water is impossible; and public "ownership," finding no correspondence in the private law, either means nothing or must denote some significant sovereign interest uniquely associated with the trust resource. But then, ownership would not be the source of the public trust, it would be the public trust (Trelease 1957).

It is possible that the association of trust rights and powers with ownership of the underlying land has been evolved as a convenient physical limitation on a government power and public right which is virtually absolute. On its face, "trust" connotes a property relationship, and we may have fallen into a problem of unfortunate nomenclature, just as public and private nuisance law has tended over time to be confused.[15] Finally, the property concept is useful in the cases where private property rights are abridged by the assertion of the trust. The idea of subordinating one property right to a superior property right is readily understood and accepted, and this device may serve the objective of property law to preserve expectations, or at least to "forestall outrage" when those expectations are violated (Michelman 1967).

---

[10] December 1978.
[11] See Sax (1970).

[12] Ivanhoe Irr. Distr. v. All Parties, 47 Cal. 2d 597 (1957).
[13] 44 Cal. 2d 199 (1955).
[14] See, for example, the Colberg case.
[15] See Restatement of the Law, Second, Torts 2d Comment, Sec. 821, 13, p. 85-87, 93 (1979).

Certainly, the concurrent state ownership of the beds underlying navigable waters can give greater scope of action to the state as trustee, and to the public, under the Public Trust Doctrine than might otherwise be socially tenable. But this proposition does not support the converse that property in the state is a necessary pre-condition to public trust rights and powers. In the end, neither the police power nor state property rights theories explain what has been the most traditional aspect of the trust: the limitation on governmental power, in favor of the public, to terminate or impair the trust in a particular resource.

The danger in this lack of definition in the public trust is not that its authority is diminished. The danger is that its ostensible authority as a potential tool and as a proposition of positive law is practically unrestrained. State power to administer the trust has been broadly expanded, as have been the public rights of use. It has been stated that, when the state so elects, it may enter and take possession of resources subject to the trust and exercise its absolute power over them, regardless of the legal title in a private person.[16] The doctrine itself brooks no limits, whether competing interests are asserted by individuals or by public entities in furtherance of other social policies.

But nothing in political reality or positive law is absolute. Even the most valuable of civil rights must have its limits, such as those which have been painstakingly evolved for freedom of speech. And principles which are not founded in constitutional law are especially at risk. Limitation may well mean attenuation, but it is also the key to effectiveness, if not to preservation.

The invocation of equitable estoppel in City of Long Beach v. Mansell[17] corresponds to the observation in the City of Berkeley case, that long reliance or the development of trust lands conveyed into private ownership will effect the termination of the trust easement otherwise retained by the state upon alienation of the property. This is an attempt by the courts to preserve substantial private expectations and values, in essence, to place limits on the trust in terms of the constraints and duties it imposes on government activity. But notably, even this type of limitation is an all-or-nothing approach: trust and competing values are not balanced, accommodated, or mutually compromised; either the trust exists or it is completely terminated.

The Mono Lake case[18] is an excellent example of the danger to the present trust doctrine. Water law and water rights cases have evolved a

solid and elaborate legal doctrine in this state. Considerable investment, as well as social and economic growth and development patterns have occurred in reliance on property rights established under this doctrine. Furthermore, water law has, primarily through the constitutional principles regarding waste and unreasonable use of water and through administrative consideration of the "public interest"--which as has been noted "spreads a large tent"[19]--developed the capacity to embrace and reconcile or to interact with myriad social values. The public trust, on the other hand, remains largely a purist doctrine, with little integration into the positive law and consequently with essentially no capacity to accommodate other values.

The property claims of Los Angeles to the waters feeding Mono Lake are firm and well established, over 40 years old. The economic benefit derived from power generation is substantial. There nonetheless may well be room for adjustment and compromise. Unfortunately, the Public Trust Doctrine does not suffer compromise. The State Attorney General has urged, and the trial court has agreed, that the public trust is "subsumed" in the administration of water rights and the State Water Resources Control Board (SWRCB) unreasonable-use authority.

Although this holding does not dispose of the central question of whether and to what extent the public trust uses and values of Mono Lake will prevail, it does represent a defeat for the National Audubon Society by the trust's loss of equal doctrinal dignity with and subordination to the more flexible water rights system. It may be going too far at this point to say that the Audubon society setback resulted from its failure to demonstrate how the public trust and property values could coexist at Mono Lake, or how, if the trust prevailed at Mono Lake, this would not have cataclysmic implications for all water development throughout the state. But the result, given this perspective, is not at all unexpected.

If the SWRCB is found to have continuing jurisdiction to consider and enforce public trust values over Los Angeles' water rights, the Audubon Society will still have the opportunity to make its case on the central issue, despite whatever disadvantages it may feel in a water rights administration forum. It still, therefore, has the opportunity to fashion some flexibility--some limitations--for the public trust to obtain as favorable a decision as possible from the SWRCB.

One may say that Mono Lake is such a special resource that its protection must be unyielding. But the hazard is that when significant competing values are arrayed against the trust theory, in the Mono Lake case, with implications for the state's entire water rights system, the result may well be the evisceration of the trust. The

---

[16]People v. California Fish Co. 166 Cal. 576 (1913).
[17]3 Cal. 2d 462 (1970).
[18]National Audubon Society, et al. v. Department of Water and Power, et al., County of Alpine, Civil No. 639.

---

[19]Duprey. 1977. Unpublished paper on F.E.R.C. permits, May, 1977.

lawyer's role is to provide courts or administrative boards in such circumstances with limitations on the trust that can preserve the trust's strong role in resource protection while assuring that competing values, while diminished, will not be destroyed. If limitation is inevitable, then it is in the definite interests of those who wish to advance trust objectives to control or influence the limitations which are bound to be devised in any case.

The public trust remains perhaps the closest thing to "natural law" in the field of resources law. The role of natural law or its functional counterparts is to legitimize the exercise of power. But power itself in a republic resides in the domain of positive law. As there is great need so is there great room for the translation of the public trust into the positive law and into the day-to-day decisionmaking of judicial, managerial, and regulatory bodies. At the very least, trust values may be more readily injected into the existing public interest authority of these bodies. But even this first step will require managers and regulators, as well as those challenging governmental action, to devise limitations for the implementation of these values so that they may reasonably coexist with competing social concerns.

LITERATURE CITED

Dunning, H. 1980. The significance of California's public trust easement for California water rights law. UCD L. Rev. 19:357-364.

Michelman. 1967. Property, utility, and fairness: comments on the ethical foundations of "Just Compensation" Law. Haw. L. Rev. 1165.

Morreale, E. 1963. Federal power in western waters: the navigation power and the rule of no compensation. Nat. Res. J. 3:1.

Sax. 1970. The Public Trust Doctrine in natural resource law: effective judicial intervention. Mich L. Rev. 68:473.

Trelease. 1957. Government ownership and trusteeship of water. Cal. L. R. 45:638.

THE STATE AS PUBLIC TRUSTEE:

NEUTRAL UMPIRE OR ACTIVIST GUARDIAN?[1]

Jan Stevens[2]

Abstract.--The public trust doctrine has been commonly characterized as an inhibition on the power of legislatures to deal with navigable waters and the lands underlying them. However, it may also impose affirmative duties on government to consider trust values and to engage in positive planning for the protection of trust uses. Such responsibilities may be expressed in state constitutions or statutes.

INTRODUCTION

The Public Trust, like the Ten Commandments, has historically been phrased in prohibitory terms. "Thou shall not abdicate the State's general control over its navigable waters," the courts have said. "Such abdication is not consistent with the exercise of that trust which requires the government of the State to preserve such water for the use of the public".[3]

The public trust doctrine in this country has traditionally been expressed as follows: With the Revolution, the thirteen colonies received all the rights of the Crown in the beds of navigable waters. These waters are held in trust for the common use of the people; the states have no power to make wholesale grants of them, and a grant of these waters, if effective at all, passes only bare title, subject to public trust rights. Our navigable waters were, in the words of the Northwest Ordinance and innumerable later acts of statehood (including California's), to be "common highways, and forever free." The sovereign power itself "...cannot, consistently with the principles of the law of nature and the constitution of a well ordered society, make a direct and absolute grant of the waters of the state, divesting all the citizens of their common right."[4] "It would be a grievance," said the court, "which never could long be bourne by a free people."

The public trust played a valuable role in the settlement of the frontier and the development of commerce. In 1842, Justice Taney was observing that:

> (T)he men who first formed the English settlements, could not have been expected to encounter the many hardships that unavoidably attended their emigration to the new world, and people the banks of its bays and rivers, if the land under the water at their very doors was liable to immediate appropriation by another as private property; and the settler upon the fast land thereby excluded from its enjoyment, and unable to take a shellfish from its bottom, or fasten there a stake, or even bathe in its waters without becoming a trespasser upon the rights of another.[5]

For, as the Court said 74 years later, "...the public authorities ought to have entire control of the great passageways of commerce and navigation to be exercised for the public advantage and convenience."[6]

Thus as it evolved in this country the trust was characterized in terms of commerce: the public trust for commerce, navigation, and fisheries, and it developed in terms of a limitation on the right of a sovereign state to divest itself of the lands underlying such waters, thus impairing the people's right to use these great passageways of commerce and depriving future legislatures of the opportunity to regulate and develop them.[7]

---

[1]Paper presented at the California Riparian Systems Conference [University of California, Davis, September 17-19, 1981].

[2]Jan Stevens (A.B., LL.B., University of California) is Deputy Attorney General, State of California. The views expressed are those of the author and do not purport to represent those of the Attorney General.

[3]Illinois Central Railroad Co. v. Illinois, 146 U.S. 387, 452-453 (1892).

[4]Arnold v. Mundy 6 N.J.L. 1, 78 (1821).

---

[5]Marten v. Waddell, 41 U.S. (16 Pet.) 367, 414 (1842).

[6]Barney v. Keokuk, 94 U.S. 324 (1876).

[7]E.g., Illinois Central Railroad v. Illinois, supra.

Two factors began to complicate this equation: the extension of trust uses to recreation and environmental protection, and the concurrent recognition that coping with the pressures of growth--whether in a police power or a public trust context--requires more than a passive or negative role on the part of government.

MARKS v. WHITNEY:
ENVIRONMENT AND THE FOUR-DAY WEEKEND

In its traditional common law form, the public trust was designed to prevent improvident kings or legislatures from disposing of the great public waterways. The doctrine was based on the protection of commerce. The 1821 New Jersey court in Arnold v. Mundy found no problem in the legislature's erecting "ports, harbours, basins, docks, and wharves..." from banking off the waters and reclaiming the land upon the shores, and from building dams, locks, and bridges "for the improvement of the navigation and the ease of passage ..."[8] And to this day, there are jurisdictions that stubbornly adhere to the proposition that the historic rights of the public to use of the foreshore are limited to fishing and bathing, and certainly do not include lying on the beach.[9] Not so in most American courts. By 1893, the Minnesota court had pointed out: "There are innumerable waters--lakes and streams--which will never be used for commerce, but which have been, or are capable of being used for sailing, rowing, fishing, fowling, bathing, skating and other public purposes, and... it would be a great wrong upon the public for all time to deprive the public of these uses merely because the waters are either not used or not adaptable for commercial purposes."[10]

A California appellate court identified the rationale: "With our ever increasing leisure time (witness the four- and five-day weekend), and the ever increasing need for recreational areas (witness the hundreds of camper vehicles carrying people to areas where boating, fishing, swimming and other water sports are available), it is extremely important that the public not be denied use of recreational water by applying the narrow and outmoded interpretation of 'navigability.'"[11]

The penultimate statement of public trust uses came from the California Supreme Court in 1971. The court made it clear that the public trust encompassed such recreational purposes as bathing, swimming, fishing, hunting, boating and general recreation, as well as use of the bottom for anchoring, standing or similar purposes. But that was not all:

> The public uses to which tidelands are subject are sufficiently flexible to encompass changing public needs... (T)he state is not burdened with an outmoded classification favoring one mode of utilization over another.... There is a growing public recognition that one of the most important public uses of the tidelands--a use encompassed within the tidelands trust--is preservation of these lands in their natural state, so that they may serve as ecological units for scientific study, for open space, and as environments which provide food and habitat for birds and marine life, and which favorably affect the scenery and climate of the area.[12]

IMPLEMENTATION OF THE PUBLIC TRUST OR,
CAN DEFEAT BE SNATCHED FROM
THE JAWS OF VICTORY

The public trust, then, comes to us in the shape of an elephant described by each interest group in terms of its own needs and desires. To the petroleum engineer, who, as Doonesbury points out, has just as much of a right to enjoy the environment as the Sierra Clubber, the public trust encompasses exploration and extraction of oil from the tide and submerged lands. To the port of Oakland, it represents the ability to develop docks and industrial parks. And government, representing as it presumably does, all the people, finds itself in the ambivalent position of weighing the competing needs of seagulls and urban consumers of water.

The interesting questions then arise: can it weigh such needs? Must it? And if it must, what is the role to be given to public trust considerations in the application of complex statutory schemes affecting the welfare of millions of people?

This is the next chapter in the developing law of public trust, and it is presently being played out in courts all over the country--from the Mono Lake litigation in Sierra County to 2.1 Million Acres of Trees v. Bert L. Cole, a superior court action filed in Thurston County, Washington, against the Commissioner of Public Lands for injunctive relief against threatened acts that will be left to your imaginations. However, we have been given a few clues from some recent past decisions. These decisions suggest that the public trust is most valuable when it is

---

[8]Arnold v. Mundy, supra, 6 N.J.L. 1, 78.
[9]Cf. Tucci v. Salzhauer, 69 Misc. 2d 226, 329 N.Y.S. 2d 825 (S. Ct. 1972), modified 336 N.Y.S. 2d 721, affd. 352 N.Y.S. 2d 198; cf. Blundell v. Catteral, 106 Eng. Rep. 1190 (Ex. 1821)
[10]Lamprey v. State, 52 Minn. 181, 199, 53 N.W. 1139, 1143 (1893).
[11]People ex rel Baker v. Mack, 19 Cal. App. 3d 1040, 1044, 97 Cal. Rptr. 448, 451 (1971).

---

[12]Marks v. Whitney, 6 Cal. 3d 251, 259-260; 491 P. 2d 374, 380, 98 Cal. Rptr. 790, 796 (1971).

applied as part of a statutory scheme for regulation of a valuable resource. Because it involves the enforcement of rights the public always had, it avoids the objection of taking with which police power regulations are invariably met. And because it is a doctrine that cries for reasoned legislative judgements, it acts admirably well as a device to compel planning for the present and future.

One of the famous examples of this is the justly celebrated case of Just v. Marinette County,[13] a decision from the Supreme Court of one of the states longest concerned with the public trust--Wisconsin. Acting pursuant to legislative direction, Marinette County adopted a model shoreland zoning ordinance requiring a permit for projects on lands within 305 m. (1,000 ft.) of the normal high-water elevation of navigable lakes, ponds or flowages, 91 m. (300 ft.) from a navigable river or stream or to the landward side of the floodplain, whichever distance is greater.[14] The purpose of the state law pursuant to which the ordinance was adopted was to "aid in the fulfillment of the state's role as trustee of its navigable waters and to promote public health, safety, convenience and general welfare."[15] Under the ordinance the filling, drainage or dredging of wetlands[16] required a permit.

Before the ordinance was passed, the Justs had purchased 14.7 ha. (36.4 ac.) of land on the south shore of Lake Moquebay, with a lakefront frontage of 386.1 m. (1,266.7 ft.). After selling five parcels, the Justs retained property with a frontage of 111.8 m. (366.7 ft.), half with a stand of cedar, pine, and various hardwoods (birch and red maple); and the half closer to the lake largely populated with "various plant grasses and vegetation including some plants which N.C. Fassett in his manual of aquatic plants... classified as 'aquatic.'" Six months after the ordinance became effective, Ronald Just, without the benefit of a permit, filled more than 500 square feet of wetlands contiguous to the water and with surface drainage toward the lake. When the trial court found he had violated the ordinance, he claimed that his land had been taken by Marinette County and the State of Wisconsin without compensation.

The Supreme Court disagreed. The regulation was valid, it was held, in part because "(l)ands adjacent to or near navigable waters exist in a special relationship to the state... and are subject to the state public trust powers."[17]

The state of Wisconsin under the trust doctrine has a duty to eradicate the present pollution and to prevent further pollution in its navigable waters. This is not, in a legal sense, a gain or a securing of a benefit by the maintaining of the natural status quo of the environment. What makes this case different from most condemnation or police power zoning cases is the interrelationship of the wetlands, the swamps and the natural environment of shorelands to the purity of the water and to such natural resources as navigation, fishing, and scenic beauty. Swamps and wetlands were once considered wasteland, undesirable, and not picturesque. But as the people became more sophisticated, an appreciation was acquired that swamps and wetlands serve a vital role in nature, are part of the balance of nature and are essential to the purity of the water in our lakes and streams. Swamps and wetlands are a necessary part of the ecological creation and now, even to the uninitiated, possess their own beauty in nature... An owner of land has no absolute and unlimited right to change the essential natural character of his land so as to use it for a purpose for which it was unsuited in its natural state and which injures the rights of others. The exercise of the police power in zoning must be reasonable and we think it is not an unreasonable exercise of that power to prevent harm to public rights by limiting the use of private property to its natural uses... the active public trust duty of the state of Wisconsin in respect to navigable waters requires the state not only to promote navigation but also to protect and preserve those waters for fishing, recreation, and scenic beauty.[18]

"The active public trust duty of the state," said the Court. But the traditional common law trust was a prohibition; a shield rather than a sword. And only lately has it been suggested that the existence of the public trust alone justifies the imposition of permit requirements on shorezone or wetlands developments.[19]

It is a short distance from Just v. Marinette County to the policy decision of the California Resources Agency that wetlands should be preserved in perpetuity, and that no state authorization or approval of projects detrimental to wetlands will be made unless, among other

---

[13] 56 Wis. 2d 7, 201 N.W. 2d 761 (1972).
[14] Ibid., 201 N.W. 2d 764 (1972).
[15] Ibid., at 765.
[16] Wetlands are defined as "areas where groundwater was at or near the surface much of the year or where any segment of plant cover is deemed an aquatic according to N.C. Fassett's 'Manual of Aquatic Plants.'"
[17] Ibid., at 769.

---

[18] Ibid., at 768 (emphasis added by author).
[19] Cf. T. McKnight, Title to Lands in the Coastal Zone, 47 Calif. State Bar J. 408, 471 (1972).

things, the public trust is not adversely affected.[20]

This "active duty" it appears, is most active when it is implemented by the people through constitutional amendment or statute. And even then, of course, the plaintiffs don't always win. The enactment of Pennsylvania's constitutional provision guaranteeing the people "a right to clean air, pure water, and to the preservation of the natural, scenic, historic and esthetic values of the environment," and describing the Commonwealth as "trustee" of the state's public natural resources,[21] nevertheless did not provide absolute protection against the widening of a street in an historical section:

> We hold that Section 27 was intended to allow the normal development of property in the Commonwealth, while at the same time constitutionally affixing a public trust concept to the management of public natural resources of Pennsylvania. The result of our holding is a controlled development of resources rather than no development.[22]

Courts do not file actions. They preside over them and attempt to resolve the controversies of determined adversaries. While they may describe the public trust as an active one, the activity must come from the parties. The framework in which the courts most successfully operate is provided by statutes reflecting recognition of and respect for the public trust, and determined efforts to reconcile competing trust uses with social and political realities.

When the Legislature enacted a statute modifying, by implication, a previous grant of tidelands to the City of Emeryville in the interests of greater protection for the San Francisco Bay, the court saw to it that its intent was carried out.[23]

When the Legislature empowered a state agency to reject the construction of dams when they did not serve "the public good," it permitted a finding that their effects on sports fishing, white water canoeing and streambed outweighed the alternate recreational and financial benefits accruing from a 21-acre reservoir.[24]

Where an historic state trust interest in wild game is threatened by the failure of a diverter of water to construct adequate fish screens, the diverter will be compelled to stop diverting until greater protection is provided,[25] notwithstanding his water rights. And even where a modern water pollution statute provides for statutory penalties, a polluter may be held equally liable under common law principles for the destruction of fish.[26]

Again, when the City of Madison proposed a plan to fill portions of a lake as part of a general plan for improvement of a city park, the court declined to apply the trust as a mechanistic prohibition. Finding that overall, more area would be made available for beach and related recreational uses, the court upheld the City's plan. In doing so, it observed:

> (I)t is not the law, as we view it, that the state, represented by its legislature, must forever be quiescent in the administration of the trust doctrine to the extent of leaving the shores of Lake Michigan in all instances in the same condition and contour as they existed prior to the advent of the white civilization in the territorial area of Wisconsin.[27]

It has long been recognized that application of the public trust involved the balancing of public trust uses and the extinguishment of the trust in small and isolated parcels at times when it is necessary to futher overall public trust uses. Thus, the court was impressed by the fact that notwithstanding part of the lakebed would be filled for a parking area and appurtenant highway, "(1) public bodies will control the use of the area; (2) the area will be devoted to public purposes and open to the public; (3) the diminution... will be very small as compared to the whole of Lake Windgra; (4) none of the uses of the Lake as a Lake will be destroyed or greatly impaired; (5) the disappointment of those members of the public who may desire to boat, fish, or swim in the area to be filled... is negligible when compared to the greater convenience to be afforded those members of the public who use the City Park."[28]

Again, in approving the exchange of land between the City of Milwaukee with a steel company, with city harbor development in mind, the court took and affirmative position:

> The trust reposed in the state is not a passive trust; it is governmental, active, and administrative. Repre-

---

[20]"Policy for Preservation of Wetlands in Perpetuity," September 19, 1977, as modified July 30, 1980.
[21]Art. I, sec. 27, Pennsylvania Constitution.
[22]Payne v. Kassab, 11 Pa. Cmwlth. 14, 312 A. 2d 86, 94 (1973).
[23]People ex rel S.F. Bay etc. Com. v. Town of Emeryville, 69 C. 2d 553, 549, 72 Cal. Rptr. 790, 446 P. 2d 790 (1968).
[24]Appl'n of Hemco, Inc. (Vt. 1971) 283 A. 2d 246; see, also, Muench v. Public Service Commission, 261 Wis. 492, 53 N.W. 2d 514 (1952).

[25]People v. Glenn-Colusa Irr. Dist., 127 Cal. App. 30 (1932).
[26]State v. Jersey Central P&L Co., 125 N.J. Super. 97, 308 A. 2d 671 (1973).
[27]State v. Public Service Commission, 275 Wis. 112, 120, 81 N.W. 2d 71, 74 (1957).
[28]Ibid., 81 N.W. 2d at 73 (1957).

senting the state in its legislative capacity, the legislature is fully vested with the power of control and regulation. The equitable title to those submerged lands vests in the public at large, while the legal title vests in the state, restricted only by the trust, and the trust, being both active and administrative, requires the law-making body to act in all cases where action is necessary, not only to preserve the trust, but to promote it.[29]

One final example will suffice to illustrate the extent to which the public trust can compel appropriate planning: the case of United Plainsmen v. North Dakota State Water Conservation Commission.[30] There, the United Plainsmen sought to restrain the State Engineer from issuing water permits for coal-related power and energy production facilities until a comprehensive short- and long-term plan for conservation and development of the State's natural resources had been developed. It was contended that such planning was required by a statutory declaration that accruing benefits from land and water resources could best be achieved through such planning. Second, the United Plainsmen contended that the discretionary authority of state officials to allocate such vital state resouces was circumscribed by the public trust doctrine. The court agreed. It held that in performance of the statutory duty to allocate resources consistent with the public interest:

> (T)he Public Trust Doctrine requires, at a minimum, a determination of the potential effect of the allocation of water on the present water supply and future water needs of this State. This necessarily involves planning responsibility... Confined to traditional concepts, the Doctrine confirms the State's role as trustee of the public waters. It permits alienation and allocation of such precious state resources only after an analysis of present supply and future need.[31]

This is not to say that such decisions will or should be left to the governmental guardians of our environment. Effective application of the obligations imposed by any doctrine as rich and ambiguous as the public trust requires participation from all segments of the environmental spectrum. It is clear in California that members of the public, as well as concerned organizations and individuals with a direct stake in controversies, may sue to enforce the trust (Marks v. Whitney, supra). An analogous example of what can happen in such cases arose under federal law in the recent Redwood Park cases.[32] There the federal district court found that the Secretary of the Interior had both general and specific obligations to preserve the Redwood Park from damage threatened by logging operations on lands adjacent to and upstream of the park, and ordered the National Park Service to use all of its powers to protect the lands, to attempt to negotiate contracts with the private loggers, to consider acquisition of the private adjacent lands, and even to lobby Congress for funds to buy out some of the private landowners.

The public trust is more effectively enforced through such statutory and constitutional foci than by lawsuits seeking to vindicate the deeply felt but evanescent rights of thousands of trees, rocks and jellyfish. When Margaret Fuller's inspirational statement, "I accept the universe," was brought to the attention of Thomas Carlyle, his reaction was said to have been, "She'd better!"

Or, as the Pennsylvania court said in more directly applicable form:

> We must recognize... that decision makers will be faced with the constant and difficult task of weighing conflicting environmental and social concerns in arriving at a course of action that will be expedient as well as reflective of the high priority which constitutionally has been placed on the conservation of our natural scenic, esthetic, and historic resources.[33]

---

[29]Milwaukee v. State, 193 Wis. 423, 214 N.W. 820, at 830, 54 ALR 419 (1927).
[30]247 N.W. 2d 457 (N.D. 1976).
[31]Ibid., at 462-463.

[32]Sierra Club v. Department of the Interior, 376 F. Supp. 90 (N.D. Cal. 1974); Sierra Club v. Department of the Interior, 398 F. Supp. 284 (N.D. Cal. 1975); Sierra Club v. Department of the Interior, 424 F. Supp. 172 (N.D. Cal. 1976).
[33]Payne v. Kassab, supra, 312 A. 2d at 94.

RIPARIAN REGULATIONS: RANDOM, REDUNDANT, OR RATIONAL?[1]

Sari Sommarstorm[2]

Abstract.--New approaches to riparian regulation will be necessary in the 1980s if past legal gains are to be maintained and new ones achieved. An evaluation of the present local, state, and federal regulatory framework for riparian system protection is presented to identify under- and overlapping authorities and possible areas of improvement.

INTRODUCTION

Regulation is like medication. Too little a dose may not cure the problem and too much may kill off the patient. In the 1960s and 70s, we were in an era of concern about too little environmental regulation; now in the 80s, rightly or wrongly, we are in an era of concern about over-regulation. Although California's riparian systems are still vulnerable to destruction, the use of regulation to protect them is being seriously challenged. To respond to this challenge, those of us concerned about the health of our riparian systems should seek to find the proper regulatory dosage before we lose the patient.

The purposes of this paper are several:

1. to identify the primary local, state, and federal regulatory agencies and laws responsible for conserving riparian systems on private lands;

2. to analyze these regulatory responsibilities from the perspective of the regulators as well as those regulated;

3. to propose some improvements in the current regulatory approach; and

4. to stimulate discussion regarding our traditional assumptions about environmental regulation as a conservation tool.

The riparian systems to be emphasized in this paper are mainly the riparian resources along inland rivers and streams rather than aquatic wetlands or lakes. This paper also takes a statewide perspective rather than that of a single geographical area. Of course some bias cannot be helped. I am partly approaching this subject from the perspective of a resource planner in a rural county which is innately resistant to any new regulations. The county is also extremely reluctant to accept or enforce mandatory directives from the state or federal level. The burden of proof is on me to justify any new local regulations to protect riparian vegetation when the county's decisionmakers feel there are too many regulations already.

The basic questions we need to ask ourselves and to honestly try to answer are the following.

1. Can we justify any new regulations for riparian zones?

2. Are riparian systems already overregulated?

3. Can we streamline the present regulatory process without stripping streams of their riparian vegetation?

A RECONNAISSANCE OF RIPARIAN REGULATIONS

A review of environmental laws reveals that the term "riparian" does not have to be explicitly stated for a law to include the riparian zone. Implicit regulations of activities in the riparian zone appear in the permit process for projects in a variety of ways. The scope of such permits involves: a) project location; b) project activities; and c) resources affected by the project (California Office of Planning and Research 1980). Table 1 illustrates the wide range of concerns in these three categories which can pertain to the riparian zone.

Identifying the range of concerns is the first step toward analyzing the specifics of regulation. Each item listed in table 1 has a unique set of regulations, or lack thereof, associated with it. Some of these will be explored later on in this paper.

---

[1]Paper presented at the California Riparian Systems Conference. [University of California, Davis, September 17-19, 1981].

[2]Sari Sommarstrom, Ph.D., is Natural Resource Policy, Planning and Management Consultant, Covelo, Calif.

Table 1.--Scope of riparian regulations.

Location

Navigable water	Coastal zone
Wild and scenic rivers	Central Valley rivers
Floodplain	

Project Activities

Timber harvesting	Water diversion
Timberland conversion	Channelization
Dredging/filling	Grazing
Grading/excavating	Road construction
Gravel extraction	Road maintenance
Streambed alteration	Dam construction
Vegetation removal	Subdivision
Stream crossing	Bank alteration
Riprapping	Groundwater extraction

Affected Resources

Endangered species	Commercial timber
Fish habitat	Vegetation
Wildlife habitat	Aesthetics
Water quality	Open space
Water supply	Land use
Streamflow	Land stability
Soils	Aquatic habitat

Before describing the pertinent regulatory agencies, it is important to note that they all reflect the scope of the laws establishing their existence. Most began as governmental entities designed to carry out a single purpose: water quality control; water rights control; game protection; timber harvest regulation. Because of new public concerns, some have evolved to add other purposes: endangered species protection; soil erosion control; nongame wildlife habitat concern. In addition, some agencies, particularly state and local, have had to reflect hierarchical directives for implementation from the federal level. New environmental laws are not necessarily reviewed, prior to passage, for their overlap or conflict with existing laws or agency responsibilities. All of the above factors add up to creating the regulatory bureaucracy we have today, for better or worse.

An exhaustive survey of every local, state, and federal riparian regulation in California is beyond the scope of this paper. Other papers (e.g., Jones 1983; Kramer 1983) provide a more indepth examination of the present legal framework. Focusing instead on the primary regulations and agencies allows an examination of the basic "who, what, where, why questions."

Local Regulations

Local government can use its police powers for protecting public health, safety, and welfare in establishing regulations. Several mechanisms are available which can be applied to regulating uses in streamside areas. These ordinances are briefly described below, from most to least common and in a general sense, rather than as specifically used in one locality. In most cases, the planning agency is the one responsible for administering the applicable ordinances, but sometimes public works, building, flood control, or water departments are also involved.

Zoning Ordinance

This measure is the most common form of local land-use regulation. It establishes the types of uses permitted on all private land within the city's or county's borders and can thereby influence riparian land use. Each zoning district establishes a list of permitted uses (e.g., single family residential; agricultural); prohibited acts (e.g., mineral extraction); and conditional-use procedures. Special requirements may be added, within reason, to use and conditional-use permits to ensure conformity to general plan policies. Floodplain regulations are assumed in this analysis to be administered as a floodplain overlay zone.

Grading Ordinance

Most local governments have adopted at least the minimal excavation and grading regulations established by Chapter 70 of the Uniform Building Code (International Conference of Building Officials 1979), which is mainly concerned with safeguarding private property. Others have either amended the zoning or subdivision ordinance or established a separate ordinance to minimize erosion or sedimentation from a project (Thurow et al. 1975). Grading controls can be used to minimize or prevent disturbance of riparian vegetation and "drainage channels."

Mining Ordinance

In addition to zoning controls on mining operations, counties were required by the California Surface Mining and Reclamation Act of 1975 (SMARA)[3] to adopt ordinances which require the reclamation of mining lands. Counties may either adopt the state model ordinance or a stricter one. Gravel extraction is the most common mining operation with the potential to affect riparian resources.

Riparian Ordinance

Also referred to as a watercourse or stream environment protection ordinance, this site-specific regulation is the least commonly used. It may be typified for scope and authorities by the "Model Riparian Ordinance" developed by the California Department of Fish and Game (1980). While specifically designed to protect riparian vegetation, the model ordinance also encompasses riparian lands not fringed by plant species.

---

[3]Section 2710-1793 Public Resources Code.

California Permit Handbook

The California Permit Handbook (California Office of Planning and Research 1980) provides a concise description of the "who, what, where, how" of the various state regulatory requirements for development projects. Based on this source, only four state agencies may require permits for projects affecting riparian resources. Two of these agencies, the Coastal Commission and the Reclamation Board, are eliminated from the following discussion because their jurisdictions are not statewide in scope.

Department of Fish and Game

Department of Fish and Game (DFG) Code Sections 1601-1603 require a Stream Alteration Agreement for any work undertaken below the mean high-water mark of a body of water containing fish or wildlife resources or where the project will use material from the streambed. While technically not a permit, the agreement includes specific conditions which must be met by the applicant to mitigate potential problems.

Department of Forestry

Timber harvesting of commercial species requires a Timber Harvest Plan to be approved by the Department of Forestry (DF). The plan must conform to the rules and regulations of the Board of Forestry, the Forest District, and the Z'berg-Nejedly Forest Practice Act of 1973 (as amended).[4] A small number of riparian forest trees, mostly in the north coast, are included as "commercial species": red alder, white alder, coast redwood, pepperwood, and others. A "Watercourse and Lake Protection Zone" is now established in the rules which requires a certain minimum width for special protection measures. No approval is required for timber operations on less than 1.2 ha. (3 ac.). Conversion of private commercial timberland to a use other than growing commercial timber requires a Timberland Conversion Permit.

State Water Resources Control Board - Division of Water Rights

According to the California Water Code, a Permit to Appropriate Water must be obtained from the State Water Resources Control Board (SWRCB) by any person or public agency who proposes to divert water from a surface stream for use on non-riparian land. Conditions are attached to such permits to assure that permittees prevent waste, practice water conservation, and put the water to the "fullest beneficial use". Water diversion under a riparian claim only requires a Statement of Water Diversion and Use, which is for informational purposes only. The SWRCB jurisdiction for issuing permits and licenses for

underground water is limited to "subterranean streams flowing through known and definite water channels" which will be applied to nonoverlying land. In general, most groundwater use does not require such a permit.

Regional Water Quality Control Boards

The nine regional water quality control boards (RWQCB) are delegated permit-issuing authority by the SWRCB for waste discharges into any surface waters or groundwater. Both point (e.g. from a pipe or confined channel) and non-point (e.g. erosion from soil disturbance) sources of water pollution may require a permit or waste discharge requirements, based upon the water quality standards adopted in the regional board's Basin Plan. Logging, construction, or associated activities in the riparian zone would be affected. Legal authority for the regional boards is derived from the Porter-Cologne Water Quality Control Act[5] and other related Water Code sections,[6] and the Federal Clean Water Acts.[6]

California Environmental Quality Act

Without belaboring the specifics, this discussion of regulation must at least note that agencies other than the above may have to review a project under the California Environmental Quality Act (CEQA)[7] referral process. These non-permit issuing agencies can make their own comments concerning a project's impacts. An example of a CEQA Referral List is provided in Table 2, a case study of gravel extraction permits. For the majority of private projects, the lead agency is usually a local rather than a state agency. The lead agency must determine whether the project will have a significant effect on the environment. This "significant effect" includes riparian concerns, such as the substantial reduction of habitat for fish, wildlife or plants. Exempted from CEQA requirements are "minor alterations to land."

Federal Regulations

Most federal laws which pertain directly or indirectly to riparian systems are administered at the state or local level. Only one federal regulatory agency is potentially involved with private projects.

US Army Corps of Engineers

Under the authority of Section 404 of the Clean Water Act (as amended), the US Army Corps of Engineers (CE) may require a permit for projects involving the location of a structure in or on, or the excavation or discharge of dredge or fill material into "navigable waters". This

---

[4] Section 4511-4628 Public Resources Code.

---

[5] Section 13000-13998 Water Code.
[6] 86 Stat. 816; 91 Stat. 1566.
[7] Section 21000-21178 Public Resources Code.

Table 2.--CEQA referral agencies for gravel extraction in Mendocino County. R = responsible agency; ** = always involved; * = often involved; L = lead agency; T = trustee agency.

Federal
*R   US Army Corps of Engineers

State
**T   Department of Fish and Game
**   Division of Mines and Geology
*R   Regional Water Quality Control Board,
       North Coast Region
*   Department of Forestry
*   CalTrans

Local
**L   Planning Department
**R   Air Pollution Control District
**   Environmental Health Department
**R   Public Works Department
       Building Inspection Department
*   Local water and flood control
       districts
**R   Archaeological Commission

Other
**   Sonoma State University
       Anthropological Studies Center
       Northwestern Pacific Railroad

---

jurisdiction now includes wetlands, rivers, and intermittent streams below the ordinary high-water mark. Although the riparian zone appears to be excluded, certain activities affecting riparian resources are covered by this permit (e.g. riprap, levees). [See Kramer (1981) and F. Smith (1981) for a thorough discussion of the Section 404 process and scope.]

REDUCTIONISTIC REFLECTIONS

Regulated Activities

Comparing the primary regulations just described with a representative sample of project activities from table 1 can lead to some useful insights. Such a comparison is facilitated by table 3. A slightly different description is offered for the local ordinances. Since these local regulations are not uniform throughout the state, it seems necessary to distinguish between an existing situation and a potential one. For each ordinance type, the left-hand symbol represents the present Mendocino County regulatory situation, which may be typical of rural counties. The symbol to the right indicates the potential authority which such a local ordinance might assume within its scope. This potential authority is based on "model" ordinances where possible (Thurow et al. 1975; California Department of Fish and Game 1980).

As one can see from table 3, the number of permits potentially required range from zero or

Table 3.--Riparian activities versus regulating agencies and ordinances. X--agency or ordinance with permit authority for given activity; †--agency is concerned with activity but may have only review authority; O--activity beyond present permit or agency review authority or interest. For local ordinances, left of /--present Mendocino County regulatory situation; right of /--potential authority an ordinance might assume within its scope.

	Federal	State				Local			
	CE	DFG	RWQCB	DF	SWRCB	Zoning	Grading	Mining	Riparian
Grazing	O	O	†	O	O	o/o	o/o	o/o	o/x
Groundwater extraction	O	†	O	O	†	o/o	o/o	o/o	o/†
Water diversion-- riparian	O	†	†	O	†	o/o	o/o	o/o	o/†
Vegetation removal	O	†	†	O	O	o/o	x/x	o/o	o/x
Deposition of materials	X	†	†	O	O	o/o	x/x	o/o	o/x
Water diversion-- approp.	O	†	†	O	X	o/o	o/o	o/o	o/x
Streambank alteration	X	†	†	O	O	o/o	x/x	o/o	o/x
Timber harvesting	O	†	X	X	O	o/x	o/x	o/o	o/x
Gravel extraction	X	X	X	O	O	x/x	o/o	x/x	o/x
Streambed alteration	X	X	X	O	O	o/o	x/x	o/o	o/x

277

one for grazing to four or five for streambed alteration. Both under- and overlapping authorities become apparent: groundwater use, water diversion based on riparian rights, and vegetation removal (non-timber) are essentially unregulated; timber harvesting and gravel extraction are regulated by two or more agencies. The implications of this observation depend upon one's point of view.

The regulated individual, or the applicant who wants to carry out a project in the riparian zone, will be concerned that, for example, he may need as many as five permits for a gravel extraction operation. He may have to deal with the time-consuming permit process of each federal, state, and local agency. The separate permit requirements may also be contradictory, for example, one agency demanding cross-sections every 50 ft. for a gravel operation, another requesting them every 75 ft., and a third stating the stream impacts are not important enough for a cross-section requirement. Such confusion, which is not unusual, may cause the applicant to take out his frustrations in the political arena, which can lead to poor publicity and possible weakening or loss of the law (Sommarstrom 1981).

Regulators should observe from this table which other agencies have overlapping authorities. The need for good coordination between regulators becomes obvious. Without consistency between the agencies' recommendations, the applicant may exploit the communication gap and play one agency against the other. The different expertise and enforcement powers of the various agencies need to work together and complement one another where possible. Aside from the overlap, certain agencies have the sole responsibility for regulating an activity, such as the appropriation of stream water by the SWRCB or the control of vegetation removal by a local agency through a riparian ordinance. Protection of the resource in these cases is dependent upon the ability of that particular agency to carry out its duties.

Regulatory Objectives

Another way to analyze regulations is to contrast the legal concerns or objectives of each of the agencies, as shown in table 4. CEQA has been added in order to compare its mandates.

Table 4 reveals that land-use regulation is solely a responsibility of local government while water quality is addressed at all three levels. These objectives only come into play, it should be noted, if a permit is required from the agency. The CE, for instance, is only concerned about protecting endangered species if a project occurs within its jurisdiction.

Several interpretations can be made of this table. Under- and overlapping objectives become obvious, as with table 3, and the problems and needs are similar to the preceding discussion. In addition, CEQA requires the lead agency to address each of the listed concerns through the environmental review process.

The column under each agency/regulation presents another set of information. The RWQCB, for instance, is primarily a single-purpose agency for water quality, although it is required to take other issues into consideration. Following much controversy, DF is now required to protect both the productivity of timberland and water quality through its timber harvest plan review.

Riparian regulatory programs are criticized by Kusler (1978) for having limited objectives which handicap their effectiveness. For example, floodplain regulations are directed to minimize flood hazards but not to protect wildlife, he states. The local zoning ordinance column in table 4 illustrates this criticism for the present situation; it also shows that zoning ordinance has the potential to address broader concerns and objectives.

The bottom line of this entire discussion on regulations is, of course, enforcement. Without adequate enforcement, one might as well place zeros in all of the columns in tables 3 and 4.

Table 4.--Some riparian concerns and objectives versus regulating agencies and ordinances. X--major objective or legal mandate (i.e., "shall protect"); †--limited objective (i.e., "should protect") of a less difinitive nature; O--little or no concern in criteria for regulation.

| | Federal | State | | | | Local | | | | |
	CE	DFG	RWQCB	DF	SWRCB	Zoning	Grading	Mining	Riparian	CEQA
Land use	O	†	†	†	†	x/x	o/o	†/†	o/x	X
Timberland	O	†	†	X	O	x/x	o/o	o/o	o/o	X
Wildlife habitat	†	X	†	†	X	†/x	o/x	†/†	o/x	X
Endangered species	X	X	†	†	†	o/x	o/x	†/x	o/x	X
Fish habitat	X	X	†	†	X	o/x	o/x	†/x	o/x	X
Water quality	X	X	X	X	†	†k/x	o/x	x/x	o/x	X

"Adequate" enforcement means the proper exercise of executive or police power when permit conditions are violated, as well as an effective "disincentive" penalty for violations.

REPACKAGING THE RULES

Repackage is defined in the dictionary as to put into a more efficient or attractive form. It certainly can be argued from the above analysis that the current approach toward riparian regulation could be made more efficient if the rules are to be productive of desired effects. With the array of single-purpose agencies and overlapping laws described, the present system is vulnerable to criticism despite the legal gaps also present. We must try to clean up our regulatory act while, at the same time, striving to improve riparian protection.

Reforming the Overlap

The public's perception of being "over-regulated" is directly related to the number of agencies involved, the number of permits required, the time it takes for approval, the expense of the permits, and the reasonableness and number of conditions on the permits. These concerns can be at least partly remedied in a variety of ways.

Streamlining the Permit Process

Streamlining is now a state directive under AB 884, which requires standardized procedures and strict time limits for state permits. Accomplishing this mandate will take some time and quite a bit of creativity. Several handbooks which describe successful techniques, such as a common application form and a one-stop permit center, are available on the subject (Vranicar et al. 1980; Bosselman et al. 1976).

Inter-agency Communication

Permit administrators need to meet and confer on mutual concerns more often. When the "bureaucrats" remain faceless to one another, the rapport necessary to make the system flow smoothly does not usually develop. Obtaining organizational charts and permit-processing flow charts of each agency can improve one's understanding of how each agency functions (theoretically, at least). Informal or formal inter-agency agreements may also facilitate permit review responsibilities, by coordinating field inspections, consolidating data-collection efforts, and strengthening enforcement, for example.

Intra-agency Communication

Any agency employee knows how frustratingly difficult it often is to adequately communicate within one's organization. Large, decentralized agencies, such as DFG, must especially learn to bridge the communication gap, or else biologists, enforcement officers, engineers, planners, and environmental specialists may end up working at cross-purposes. Despite problems inherent to the structure of governmental institutions, there are means of overcoming internal inertia (Downs 1967; Henning 1974).

Re-evaluating the Rules

Cleaning up the language of regulation goes a long way toward making friends, or at least fewer enemies. The CE learned this lesson in its "Section 404" program, which started out using unintelligible jargon but later switched to simpler terms and diagrams. One cannot expect people to comply with all the rules if they cannot understand them.

Rectifying the Underlap

The lack of authority or responsibility to protect certain riparian resources remains a problem. Concerned citizens may look at tables 3 and 4 and conclude that more regulations are definitely needed, especially to prevent the removal of riparian vegetation. Several options are recommended.

Expand the Scope of Existing Regulations

Instead of creating a new agency or commission, it would seem more prudent to expand the authority of the present regulators to cover the jurisdictional gaps. This could be accomplished by either adding new objectives or extending the jurisdiction of an agency. For instance, a state mandate to protect riparian vegetation could be assigned to the DF. While its current scope is limited to commercial tree species or the stream protection zone associated with a timber harvest plan, DF authority could be expanded to control all vegetation removal in the riparian zone. At the local level, existing zoning and grading ordinances could be amended as shown in tables 3 and 4.

Create Incentives

Like legislating morality, the establishment of regulations which are not supportable or realistic is doomed to failure. The requirement to fence streams from grazing livestock, as proposed in the DFG model riparian ordinance, is one such example. Even if a rancher is sympathetic, he may be unable to afford the cost of the fencing, if he is typical of most land-rich but cash-poor ranchers in rural California. Instead, concerned citizens and government should encourage the use of cost-share programs (e.g., California Forest Improvement Program, Agricultural Conservation Program) to help get the job done. We must remember that the purpose of environmental programs is not to penalize people but to protect resources. When regulations will not work, incentives may be the answer.

Use-performance Standards

Environmental performance standards attempt "to preserve or maintain the natural performance of the land already there", as opposed to controlling man-made features (Thurow et al. 1975). They are an improvement over traditional zoning by providing more equity in land controls and reducing the administrative problems of ordinances. As the result, impacts on the riparian system from both on- and offsite sources may be more successfully mitigated.

CONCLUSIONS

Yes, riparian regulations are random. They have evolved from many different sources for a variety of purposes and have followed no master plan. Not all of the resources associated with the riparian zone are protected by governmental controls. Riparian regulations are also redundant, however. They overlap in both permit authorities and regulatory objectives, with some project activities requiring as many as five permits. Whether riparian regulations are rational or not depends upon one's perspective and expectations. Certainly improvements can be made in the present regulatory system to assist both the regulators and those regulated.

This analysis is not intended to be a comprehensive examination of riparian regulations. It is intended to stimulate a greater understanding of how we can make the regulatory process work to meet its real purpose--not to kill the patient but to keep it healthy.

LITERATURE CITED

Bosselman, Fred, D. Feurer, and C. Siemon. 1976. The permit explosion: coordination of the proliferation. 86 p. Urban Land Institute, Washington, D.C.

California Department of Fish and Game. 1980. Model riparian ordinance. 6 p. Region 3, Yountville. Unpublished.

California Office of Planning and Research. 1980. California permit handbook. 270 p. California Office of Planning and Research, Sacramento.

Downs, Anthony. 1967. Inside bureaucracy. 292 p. Little, Brown, and Company, Boston, Mass.

Henning, Daniel H. 1974. The environmental administrative process. p. 36-52. In: Environmental policy and administration. 205 p. American Elsevier Company, New York, N.Y.

International Conference of Building Officials. 1979. Uniform Building Code. 734 p. I.C.B.O., Whittier, Calif.

Jones, Bruce. 1983. A state mandate for riparian wetland system preservation. In: R.E. Warner and K.M. Hendrix (ed.). California Riparian Systems. [University of California, Davis, September 17-19, 1981]. University of California Press, Berkeley.

Kramer, John. 1981. Is there a national interest in wetlands: the Section 404 experience. In: R.E. Warner and K.M. Hendrix (ed.). California Riparian Systems. [University of California, Davis, September 17-19, 1981.] University of California Press, Berkeley.

Kusler, Jon A. 1978. Regulating critical riparian lands: a challenge in intergovernmental cooperation. p. 332-335. In: R.R. Johnson and J.F. McCormick (ed.). Strategies for the protection and management of floodplain wetlands and other riparian ecosystems. [Callaway Gardens, Georgia, December 11-13, 1978]. USDA Forest Service GTR-WO-12. Washington, D.C. 410 p.

Sommarstrom, Sari. In press. Local-state coordination for gravel management in spawning streams. In: Proceedings of the symposium on habitat disturbance and recovery. [San Luis Obispo, Calif., January 29, 1981.] California Trout, San Francisco, Calif.

Smith, Felix. 1981. The Clean Water Acts and the principles of the public trust doctrine: a discussion. In: R.E. Warner and K.M. Hendrix (ed.). California Riparian Systems. [University of California, Davis, September 17-19, 1981.] University of California Press, Berkeley.

Thurow, Charles, W. Toner, and D. Erley. 1975. Streams and creeks. p. 7-20. In: Performance controls for sensitive lands: a practical guide for local administrators. Planning Advisory Service Report Nos. 307, 308. 156 p. American Society of Planning Officials, Chicago, Ill.

Vranicar, John, W. Sanders, and D. Mosena. 1980. Streamlining land use regulations: a guidebook for local governments. 74 p. US Department of Housing and Urban Development, Washington, D.C.

PROTECTION OF RIPARIAN SYSTEMS

IN AN ANTI-REGULATORY ERA[1]

Gary Weatherford, Barbara Andrews, and Kim Malcolm[2]

Abstract.--The twin objectives of this paper are to speculate about the longevity of the present "anti-regulatory era" and its effect on current efforts to protect riparian systems. We conclude that the legal and institutional means for riparian protection will not be lost--if sound strategies for their maintenance and expansion are developed and efforts to popularize riparian values can be increased.

THE ANTI-REGULATORY FIX: POLITICAL TRENDS AND IMPLICATIONS FOR FUTURE LEGAL TOOLS

The political environment of the 1980s may be changing the scope and nature of governmental policies related to environmental protection. For those concerned with the preservation and rehabilitation of riparian systems, the current political mood elicits two major questions. First, what will future attitudes of the public be with respect to environmental management? The anti-regulatory sentiment may be ephemeral or enduring; the current administration's objectives may have short-term or long-term effects. Second, what impact will these attitudes have on programs and regulations in the area of riparian system protection? The pace and extent of future changes will depend on a variety of legal and institutional considerations.

This paper explores ways in which the current anti-regulatory mood may affect future policies for protecting riparian systems at the federal, state, and local levels. We review generally how various legal tools have been and may be used in pursuit of riparian protection, against a backdrop of a number of possible political futures. We conclude by speculating as to the political environment over the next decade and offering some strategies for maintaining or expanding current efforts at riparian protection.

CURRENT STATUS OF THE ANTI-REGULATORY MOVEMENT

Political attitudes that will affect environmental policies are changing at all levels of government; the change is perhaps most visible at the federal level. The Reagan administration is seeking to eliminate many regulatory controls, to champion private sector interests, and to cut budgets by cutting programs. Secretary of the Interior Watt is pressing for mineral development in wilderness areas, an end to additional national park acquisitions, and the relaxation of fish and wildlife conservation policies (Mosher 1981). Already caught in the net of regulatory review are the Fish and Wildlife Coordination Act, the Endangered Species Act, and the US Army Corps of Engineers Section 404 permitting system for dredging and filling.[3]

Perhaps the clearest expression of anti-regulatory sentiment by the administration thus far is Executive Order 12291,[4] which requires new regulations to be subjected to cost:benefit analysis. This analytical technique has aroused a great deal of controversy in recent years, because its method of use is not standardized and its use cannot address conditions of uncertainty or redistributive effects.[5] Environmental programs and regulations could be jeopardized by the requirement because environmental values frequently defy quantification, which is the basis for

---

[1]Paper presented at the California Riparian Systems Conference. [University of California, Davis, September 17-19, 1981].

[2]Gary Weatherford is Director, Water Management Program, and Barbara Andrews and Kim Malcolm are Research Assistants; all are at the Center for Natural Resource Studies, Berkeley, Calif.

[3]Remarks of Vice President George Bush from a press release on regulatory relief, August 12, 1981.

[4]Executive Order No. 12291, Weekly Compilation of Presidential Documents 121-126. February 23, 1981.

[5]See Rodgers, W.H., Jr. Benefits, Costs, and Risks: Oversight of Health and Environmental Decisionmaking. Harvard Environmental Law Rev. 4:191.

cost:benefit analysis. The benefit side of environmental protection often accrues to future generations. Many environmental values are aesthetic or recreational and are therefore personal and subjectively determined. Further, many benefits of environmental programs are extremely difficult to isolate for purposes of measurement.

Besides the requirement for cost:benefit analysis, the executive order deals another possible blow to environmental policymaking by limiting public participation and access to information (Eads 1981). Soliciting public involvement in environmental policymaking has been important to efforts aimed at environmental protection, because often the economic incentives which promote the formation of special interest lobbies in other issue areas are absent.

It is difficult to gauge how this executive order will affect particular policies or regulations at this early date. The courts have thus far hesitated to impose rigorous cost:benefit requirements on environmental and health concerns (Miller et al. 1981). Many federal policies aimed at protecting riparian systems take the form of legislated programs, and the abolition of such programs will test the administration's ability to build consensus in Congress. The impact of the executive order by itself may be limited, but it is illustrative of the changing attitudes toward governmental involvement in environmental affairs, and how such attitudes may become institutionalized.

In this political context, a focus on efficiency and market values may determine the degree to which private lands are managed and public lands are managed properly. Programs aimed at protecting riparian systems may be particularly vulnerable because they often place restrictions on the use of private property. Decreasing budget outlays for managing public lands and promises by the "sagebrush rebellion" for stepped up exploitation of mineral resources in the West will also take their toll. Further, riparian issues may not have attained a high enough ranking in governmental priorities. They had not commanded the visibility of other environmental concerns, such as air quality, nor had they acquired strong public support or a well-established constituency by the time pro-environmental sentiment crested in the late 1970s. With the greater interest in private property, only the most compelling environmental values are going to gain and retain governmental support at the federal level.

On the other hand, the bark of current politicial attitudes may be worse than its bite. Anti-regulatory rhetoric is a symbolic expression of a broader political debate, and the actual implementation of decontrol policies may be limited. Notwithstanding the political mood in Washington, the scope of environmental protection will depend on longer-term social values. On the positive side, many environmental concerns are already institutionalized and protected by statutes and judicial review. Furthermore, most Americans have recognized the need for environmental protection and accepted government's inherent role in that undertaking. Riparian issues are public-interest issues which will be of increasing concern as the intensity of land and water resource management increases.

In the nearer-term, the Reagan administration may be, in many cases, hitting its head against the wall of a resistant federal bureaucracy. The federal government is not, by and large, inclined to rapid or dramatic change: "incrementalism" used to be defined as "last year's budget plus 10%;" since January, 1981, it has been redefined as "last year's budget minus 10%." After policy decisions have been made, implementation is usually slow and affected by pre-existing agency objectives and viewpoints. No matter how lasting the anti-regulatory fervor is generally, one can still expect anomalies. Some areas will escape regulatory scrutiny during this period because they are not highly politicized. In fact, the specific issue of "decontrol" may not even apply to riparian protection, since the existing regulatory controls are so few, and are, in some cases, indirect.

To the extent that the current administration is successful in narrowing the role of the federal government in environmental policy, environmental quality will depend on the activities of the private sector and lower levels of government. Such a situation carries with it some problems. In the case of local jurisdictions, region-wide problems need to be addressed by the coordinated efforts of many governmental bodies, since a single agency has no incentive to subsidize another by paying for solutions to problems of the larger area. State and local governments are also inhibited by budget cutbacks and decreased federal funding. Similarly, private sector interests are not likely to internalize the costs of environmental protection voluntarily in cases where private activities produce costs to the larger community. In spite of the difficulties associated with the programs at lower levels of government and with private voluntary action, there will be important areas that will have to be addressed by programs that are not federally sponsored.

AVAILABLE LEGAL TOOLS FOR RIPARIAN PROTECTION

Future political attitudes will determine not only who will be doing the protecting, but which legal tools will be used as well. Broadly speaking, the legal tools for riparian protection can be grouped under three headings: 1) public ownership and management; 2) public regulation and subsidy; and 3) private controls and voluntary cooperation. We will first survey the legal tools, existing and contemplated. We will then speculate as to their relative roles and utility in a variety of political settings.

Public Ownership and Management

The fullest range of protection is generally provided by public ownership of the riparian zone--if the capabilities and resources of the governmental agency involved are adequate, and provided that the agency's objectives correspond to its statutory duties. Lawful public agency actions along publicly owned riparian corridors have done their share of damage in the past.

With respect to public lands, enabling legislation usually provides administering agencies with ample legal authority to protect riparian values, although conflicting "multiple purpose" mandates in statutes and regulations can and do compromise riparian protection in practice. Specific riparian protection guidelines for planning and on-the-ground activities can be found in the manuals of the various land management agencies.[6]

Ownership interests in hitherto private lands acquired by the government (acquired lands) generally involve the same implicit legal authority for managing riparian areas that exists for public lands. The interest acquired can be a fee title or an easement, whether negative or affirmative. The acquisition may be through negotiated purchase, donation or dedication by gift, or condemnation (eminent domain). The purchase or condemnation of all types of easements has proven to be very costly, approaching the full fee value of the land in many cases.

Public Regulation and Subsidy

Governmental constraints and incentives directed at private landowners may be designed to prevent or halt harmful practices or to promote helpful practices. Carrots and sticks frequently appear together in government programs. They may be used by any level of government. Regulation can take many forms, but usually requires permits as a pre-condition to activities, such as removal of trees, which might disturb riparian values. The regulatory scheme can control single elements of the riparian system, such as species protection (e.g., the Endangered Species Act), stream alteration (e.g., Section 1601 et seq., California Fish and Game Code), or timber harvesting in streamside zones (e.g., California Administrative Code, Title 14, Article 6, Stream and Lake Protection, Coast Forest District). Or it can control general impacts or changes in critical areas (e.g., permit systems of coastal management programs, such as the State of Washington's Shoreline Management Act of 1971 or California Coastal Act of 1976).

The open space elements of general plans, zoning regulations, erosion and drainage control ordinances, and other development controls of local government can offer different levels of riparian protection, usually in terms of streamside set-backs, zones in which the drainage pattern, soil, and vegetation are not to be disturbed. Mitigation measures, including the rehabilitation of riparian values, can be required as permit conditions in land-use development approvals. The disclosure and analysis of potential impacts, as legally required by environmental impact reports, statements, or assessments, is an important phase of both development and protection.

Subsidy can take many forms. Income tax deductions for the donation of perpetual conservation easements to governments or qualified non-profit organizations, such as the Nature Conservancy, are popular (e.g., Internal Revenue Code, Section 170). Property tax reductions, through favorable assessment policies or reassessment after development values have been donated in conservation easements, can provide an incentive for protecting riparian areas. Cash payment to landowners to encourage certain land and water management practices is another approach that has been adopted, partially to provide an offset for economic losses resulting from not cultivating certain areas (e.g., USDA Agricultural Conservation Program, Rural Clean Water Program, and Water Bank Program). Technical advice and assistance to landowners concerning on-the-ground practices can be offered as part of such cash benefits or cost-sharing programs, or may be provided independently of them.

Private Controls and Voluntary Cooperation

Land-use restrictions aimed at protecting riparian systems can be applied in covenants running with the land, as part of grant deeds which are enforceable by other local property owners. In practice, these private controls are often prompted by public agency pressure. Private initiative can also take the form of riparian protection associations of landowners and interested persons, possibly with contractual commitments to preservation objectives.

Private legal action, under nuisance or trespass theories, can enjoin or restrain some practices having adverse effects on riparian zones, for example those producing increased sedimentation. Private interests and organizations are also turning to the Public Trust Doctrine for broader protective rulings by the courts.[7]

Finally, private associations such as the Nature Conservancy and the Trust for Public Lands provide legal information and assistance for a variety of land-use activities. They are also important fund-raisers for the private purchase and management of environmentally significant lands.

---

[6] See, for example, USDA Forest Service Manual, Title 2500, Watershed Management and USDI Bureau of Land Management Manual, Section 6740, Wetland-Riparian Protection and Management.

[7] See Public Trust Doctrine in natural resources law and management: A Symposium. UCD Law Rev. 14.

FUTURE SCENARIOS AND THE LEGAL TOOLS FOR RIPARIAN PROTECTION

Which of these various legal mechanisms are used, by whom, and to what extent will be determined by social, political, and economic environments. The following presents a number of possible future scenarios which range from greatly diminished to very high levels of governmental activity. It also discusses the types of legal tools most likely to be used for riparian protection in each of the alternate futures.

Dysfunctional Bureaucracy

In this scenario, federal agencies would experience heightened levels of internal conflict, resulting from unclear political conditions and agency responsibilities, coupled with a greatly diminished role of government. In the absence of a capable bureaucracy, management and protection of publicly owned riparian corridors would be ineffective. A highly deregulated condition would permit uncontrolled manipulation of privately owned lands. Under these conditions, courts would not be useful institutions for the enforcement of public or private arrangements aimed at environmental protection. Some private efforts might be undertaken to protect particular riparian areas, but little could be accomplished without some area-wide coordination and general public concern.

Despite such dire predictions, over the next ten years the absence of a government concerned with protecting the natural resource base is unlikely.

Low Bureaucracy

This situation would present major long-term reductions in governmental programming and personnel, which would curtail public resource management. Regulatory tools would not be as reliable as previously, and public apathy would reinforce government non-interference. New public acquisitions of riparian areas would be rare. Regulations and guidelines would be either revoked or discounted. Efforts to encourage the exploitation of natural resources for economic reasons would aggravate environmental conditions spawned by neglect. And technical assistance and cost-sharing, even though designed to strengthen private control and management, would probably be viewed as too intrusive and as requiring too much bureaucracy in this laissez-faire state. The most appropriate management tools would be tax loopholes and private covenants. Supporting revenue services and courts, necessary for the employment of these tools, would be maintained.

This condition of governmental non-involvement in environmental protection would probably only be reversed in the case of an environmental health crisis, bringing about a public reaction and a re-establishment of public confidence in government's role in the protection of natural systems. Subsequent clean-up efforts and the re-establishment of a bureaucracy to undertake those efforts would be very costly.

Moderate Bureaucracy

In this scenario, current levels of government programming would be sustained though not expanded. Fiscal conservatism would limit attention to environmental protection at all levels of government, although some state and local efforts might be developed. In general, new public acquisitions of riparian areas would be very selective. Field personnel in resource management would be overextended and unable to implement management guidelines or enforce regulations to the degree intended in the statutes and programs. But the guidelines and regulations for public lands and for a few privately owned critical areas, such as coastal zones, would be retained. Tax incentives for conservation easements would continue. Cost-sharing and technical assistance would remain authorized, but underfunded. Effective local government ordinances for riparian protection would be the exception rather than the rule in the near term, but could finally prevail under this scenario.

Private covenants and initiatives could increase; the environmental lobby could marginally stimulate more private action in response to the decline in government spending and programming. The extent of decreased governmental activity would depend mostly on the economic effects resulting from environmental degradation. Damage to private property by polluters or developers would inspire legal action and political pressure driving government at all levels toward renewed efforts at environmental protection.

High Bureaucracy Scenario

This scenario indicates a higher degree of both public ownership and regulation than presently exists, or has ever existed in peacetime in this country. It could mean national economic planning and/or the nationalization of certain private property interests. Or it could be an evolutionary growth in public ownership and public regulation, while retaining the mixed economy mode. Whether privately owned riparian corridors would ever be as highly placed on the public acquisition agenda as other productive elements of the economy is doubtful. However, an expansion of the public ownershp of riparian corridors over today's baseline could probably be expected. Increased police power regulation of private property would be permitted. Private covenants would diminish in importance, but some private initiatives to bring selective pressure to bear on bureaucracies probably would persist. In short, riparian values would probably, but not necessarily, be better protected than they are today, but the price paid in other legitimate values might be high.

FUTURE STRATEGIES FOR RIPARIAN PROTECTION
IN AN ANTI-REGULATORY ERA

Anti-regulatory sentiment will manifest itself as a coat of many colors in the coming decades. Although we cannot predict precisely what the outcomes will be, it would be naive to assume that the regulatory approach will not be relaxed at least to some extent. Advocates of riparian protection must reassess institutional options in light of this likelihood and carefully choose the most effective tools to fit the prevailing anti-regulatory mood.

In a broad sense, advocates of riparian systems will have to adjust their tactics to a growing emphasis on the private sector. Within the public sector, state and local governments will become more important relative to the federal level. As regulations and compliance programs are cut, other mechanisms such as ownership, planning and technical assistance, education and political activity, and reliance on private economic incentives, will emerge to advance environmental goals. Finally, as the political branches of government respond to anti-regulatory sentiment, the courts will provide a forum for the defense of riparian values according to sources of law which are beyond the power of the agencies and legislatures to change.

The burden of riparian protection will fall on advocates in both the public and private sectors. Proponents in government should focus first on preserving existing programs to the extent possible. In those areas targeted for special anti-regulatory scrutiny, such as California's coastal zone program and the dredge-and-fill permit system under Section 404 of the Clean Water Act, agencies should concentrate on streamlining regulations and coordinating programs on an agency-specific or interagency basis. If anti-regulatory sentiment remains high, agencies should identify the most critical environmental problems and assign priorities to their protective agendas accordingly. In addition, agencies may, on their own or with legislative assistance, adopt alternative techniques, such as effluent taxes and pollution marketing systems, to achieve standards in a manner more palatable to regulated industry.

Advocates of governmental protection will have to resort to techniques not directly associated with controversial regulatory programs. For example, they could try to achieve regulation through other channels such as litigation: government attorneys could bring public nuisance suits to enjoin private interferences with navigable waters and could advance the Public Trust Doctrine to restrain or revoke governmental authorizations of uses of water and development in riparian areas.[7] Another important tool will be state water rights administrations. Although regulatory in effect, these agencies are fundamentally intact and the major arbiters for private property rights in western waters. The California State Water Resources Control Board, pro-

vided it remains sufficiently isolated from the politics of anti-regulation, could administer its statutory and constitutional mandates to deny, or to protectively condition or modify permits to appropriate water and acquire existing water rights.[8]

Advocates of protection within government will have to intensify their efforts outside of the regulatory rubric altogether. Ownership is one option. The purchase of land or of easements in land, as well as the appropriation or condemnation of water rights, could all be used to protect instream flows and riparian systems. A major obstacle will be cost. State or federal reliance on the "navigation servitude" could avoid the constitutional duty to compensate in some cases, but future courts may construe the doctrine strictly against the government.[9] The federal government and native American tribes could assert potentially extensive ownership claims under the Reserved Rights Doctrine, but here again, successful court challenges could be a significant long-term impediment.[10] Political resistance will also dampen the urge to press reserved rights claims in over-appropriated streams, at least where federal lands, as opposed to Indian reservations, are involved.

To the extent that agency budgets and political opposition thwart the ownership solution, advocates of protection should promote government functions in an array of nonregulatory roles. These roles could include planning and setting guidelines for riparian systems, coordinating public and private protective efforts, collecting data and inventorying uses, promoting innovative management schemes, encouraging conservation and mitigation, offering grants-in-aid to accomplish environmental goals, and instituting economic incentives toward voluntary compliance with protective policies. In some cases, these roles will be merely educational. In others, they will have a more or less coercive effect, particularly if grants and incentives are conditioned upon the adoption of regulatory standards or management plans. Tax breaks will constitute an important noncoercive form of incentive, as will the repeal of current code provisions such as the investment tax credit, which serve to encourage development in riparian areas.

---

[8]For an overview of these possibilities, see Schneider (1978).

[9]For the most recent U.S. Supreme Court case in this area, see Kaiser Aetna v. United States, 444 U.S. 164 (1979). One commentator remarks that "(t)his case may mark the beginning of judicially imposed limitations on the servitude which has been "an almost impregnable doctrine under the shelter of the commerce clause" (Stevens 1980).

[10]See, e.g., United States v. New Mexico, 438 U.S. 496 (1978), which denied reserved rights for instream flow purposes on the Gila National Forest in New Mexico.

As the public sector abandons existing programs or fails to advocate protective policies, private interests will become the focal point of riparian system protection efforts. Private advocates will be faced with a number of tasks—encouraging their public allies in the strategies just described, forcing agency response when it is not internally prompted, lobbying for legislative change, and promoting voluntary efforts throughout the private sector.

To the extent that political pressure does not cause government to act, litigation and voluntary efforts will become the critical tools in the environmental arsenal. Litigation may be undertaken against private individuals and organizations for violations of property or contract rights or on tort theories of nuisance and trespass, and against government on constitutional grounds on principles of administrative law or for violations of emerging doctrines such as the Public Trust.

In conjunction with such efforts, private interests could form protective arrangements such as land trusts, encourage financial donations and protective actions by industry and land developers, instigate negotiated solutions and compliance programs among riparian users, and forge cooperative schemes with local governments, special districts, planning commissions, and the states.

The disadvantages of private action are well known. Litigation is protracted and its results are too often spotty. Voluntary efforts are difficult to achieve and, once arranged, are of highly uncertain duration and scope. At the same time, if "grass roots" has a meaning in the context of the American political system, it is that action initiated from below can stand on a surer footing than that imposed from above. It is to this prospect that advocates of riparian protection in the private sector must direct their energies. Within the framework of a mature, yet evolving environmental movement, the techniques of the past must be fine-tuned into a strategy for a substantially different future.

CONCLUSION

We are facing a period of political uncertainty which could be of tremendous consequence to riparian systems. In this setting, different political orientations and moods will accommodate different groupings of legal tools and make some legal approaches more promising than others. At the same time, there may be a tendency on the part of conservationists to promote all legal tools for all purposes at all times.

In practice, however, the struggle to preserve and extend available protective tools must express itself mostly in case-by-case encounters, according to the financial resources, public and media support, and political opportunities at hand. The key to future success is strategy. Selectivity, ingenuity, persistence, and carefully ordered priorities are all indispensable ingredients. In a future dominated by regulatory restraint, protectors of riparian values will have to be quick-witted and tenacious, capable of seizing essential opportunities and adapting to unforeseen change and adverse conditions.

In the final analysis, whatever the political climate, riparian protection needs to become a more visible issue, commanding a greater sense of social responsibility than is currently the case. Political systems and responses can be nurtured under which contemporary and future generations of biological communities will live in health, with a minimum of harsh tradeoffs between economic and environmental values. It is crucial that, amidst the recurring shifts in political fashion, of which the present anti-regulatory fix is one, natural systems be maintained to the greatest possible extent, to preserve flexibility in the availability of resources and in biological options for the future.

LITERATURE CITED

Eads, George. 1981. Harnessing regulation: The evolving role of White House oversight. Regulation (May/June):19-26.

Miller, Taylor, Lisa Chang, and Gary Weatherford. 1981. Risk assessment and regulation: Federal statutory background. Center for Natural Resource Studies, Berkeley, Calif.

Mosher, Lawrence. 1981. Reagan and the GOP are riding the sagebrush rebellion. National Journal (March 21):476-481.

Schneider, A. 1978. Legal aspects of instream water uses in California: Background and issues. Staff Paper No. 6; Governor's Commission to Review California Water Rights Law, State of California, Sacramento.

Stevens, J. 1980. The public trust: A sovereign's ancient prerogative becomes the people's environmental right. UC Davis Law Rev. 14(68):195-209.

EVOLUTION AND RIPARIAN SYSTEMATICS[1]

David E. Brown[2]

Abstract.--Arizona's perennial streams and important marshlands have been mapped and a wetland classification system developed. To be effective and usable, a resource classification must be systematic, universal, and hierarchical, and must illustrate, or at least recognize, evolutionary relationships. Biogeography is therefore an important factor in the development of the taxonomy for any living (i.e., renewable) resource. Few renewable resources are as alive and dynamic as are our riparian ecosystems.

We have mapped Arizona's perennial streams and important wetlands at 1:1,000,000 (Brown et al. 1977, 1978, 1981). These maps show the potential for maximum riparian ecosystem development--various riparian communities are not illustrated per se. Riparian communities are too dynamic to present the same structure and composition for any length of time; similar communities may also occur along seasonal and even some ephemeral subterranean-fed waterways. This does not mean that riparian vegetation cannot be inventoried and mapped for study purposes and to document change.

We have developed a classification system that includes riparian and other wetland communities as well as upland ecosystems (see Appendix A) (Brown and Lowe 1974a, 1974b; Brown et al. 1977, 1979, 1980). Like the Linnean taxonomic system, this classification system is systematic in approach, universal in application, and hierarchical in arrangement. It is also digitized and therefore computer-compatible. Like other ecosystem classifications, this system uses vegetation, structure, climate, and vegetative components as criteria. However, an important distinction is that it is based on biogeography.

A classification based on this system for use in the Southwest has proven serviceable for classification, delineation, description, and data storage of that region's natural vegetation and biogeography. For examples of its application see Turner and Cochran (1975), Steenbergh and Warren (1977), Patton (1978), Martin (1979), Turner et al. (1980), and Volger (1980).

All classifications of vegetation consider structure (i.e., forests, woodlands, grasslands, etc.); the most successful employ phytogeographic descriptions (i.e., floodplain forest, montane forest, coastal scrub, etc.). Unfortunately, many of these same classifications rely on soil and/or chemical criteria which influence floristics only regionally. Soil-types or soil properties are of little use in describing vegetation on a worldwide or even continental basis. Some systems (e.g. Bailey 1976, 1978) use physiographic approaches that are wholly regional in scope and bear little relationship to biotic parameters. Few systems employ biogeography as it is used by biologists.

Biologists have long been developing systems of biographic realms, provinces, and districts (e.g., see Wallace 1876; Clements and Shelford 1939; Rasmussen 1941; Pitelka 1941; Dice 1943; Goldman and Moore 1945; Dansereau 1957; Darlington 1957; Lowe 1961; Shelford 1963; Walter 1973; Udvardy 1975; Cox et al. 1976; Dasmann 1976; Franklin 1977) to show the distribution of plants and animals. These distributions are the result of evolutionary origin and adaptation. The basic biogeographic unit is the biome (i.e., biotic community). The biome is also the primary component and mappable reality of any biotic classification system that attempts to illustrate evolutionarily significant plant and animal distribution. Distributions which are of evolutionary significance are of great importance to bird watchers, ornithologists, zoogeographers, mammalogists, herpetologists, phytogeographers, taxonomists, and wildlife managers. Biologists will generally not accept classifications and inventories that do not recognize the importance of biomes and biogeography. This is especially true of our riparian and other wetland resources, so valued for their biotic diversity.

---

[1]Paper presented at the California Riparian Systems Conference. [University of California, Davis, September 17-19, 1981].

[2]David E. Brown is Wildlife Biologist, Arizona Game and Fish Department, Phoenix; and Professor of Wildlife Management, Arizona State University, Tempe, Ariz.

LITERATURE CITED

Bailey, R.G. 1976. Ecoregions of the United States (map, scale 1:7,500,000). USDA Forest Service, Intermountain Region, Ogden, Utah.

Bailey, R.G. 1978. Description of the ecoregions of the United States. USDA Forest Service, Intermountain Region, Ogden, Utah.

Brown, David E., Neil B. Carmony, and Raymond M. Turner. 1977. Inventory of riparian habitats. p. 10-13. In: R.R. Johnson and D.A. Jones (tech. coord.). Importance, preservation and management of riparian habitat: a symposium. [Tuscon, Ariz., July 9, 1977]. USDA Forest Service GTR-RM-43. 217 p. Rocky Mountain Forest and Range Experiment Station, Fort Collins, Colo.

Brown, David E., Neil B. Carmony, and Raymond M. Turner. 1978. Drainage map of Arizona showing perennial streams and some important wetlands. Ariz. Game and Fish Department map.

Brown, David E., Neil B. Carmony, and Raymond M. Turner. 1981. Drainage map of Arizona showing perennial streams and some important wetlands. Ariz. Game and Fish Department map.

Brown, David E., and C.H. Lowe. 1974a. A digitized computer-compatible classification for natural and potential vegetation in the Southwest with particular reference to Arizona. J. Ariz. Acad. Sci. 9, Suppl. 2:1-11.

Brown, David E., and C.H. Lowe. 1974b. The Arizona system for natural and potential vegetation--illustrated summary through the fifth digit for the North American Southwest. J. Ariz. Acad. Sci. 9, Suppl. 3: 1-56.

Brown, David E., C.H. Lowe, and C.P. Pase. 1977. A digitized classification system for the natural vegetation of North America with hierarchical summary for world ecosystems. In: A. Marmelstein (ed.). Proceedings of the national symposium on classification, inventory, and analysis of fish and wildlife habitat. [Phoenix, Ariz., Jan. 24-27, 1977]. USDI Fish and Wildlife Service, Office of Biological Science, Washington, D.C.

Brown, David E., C.H. Lowe, and C.P. Pase. 1979. A digitized classification system for the biotic communities of North America, with community (series) and association examples for the Southwest. J. Ariz.-Nev. Acad. of Sci. Suppl. 1:1-16.

Dansereau, P. 1957. Biogeography. Ronald Press. New York, New York.

Darlington, P.J., Jr. 1957. Zoogeography. John Wiley and Sons. New York, New York.

Dansmann, R.F. 1976. Biogeographical provinces. Co-Evolution Q. Fall:32-35.

Dice, L.R. 1943. The biotic provinces of North America. University of Michigan Press. Ann Arbor, Mich.

Franklin, J.F. 1977. The biosphere reserve program in the United States. Science 195: 262-267.

Goldman, E.A., and R.T. Moore. 1945. The biotic provinces of Mexico. J. Mammal. 26:347-360.

Lowe, C.H. 1961. Biotic communities in the sub-Mongollon region of the inland Southwest. J. Ariz. Acad. Sci. 2:40-49.

Martin, P.S. 1979. A survey of potential natural landmarks, biotic themes, of the Mojave-Sonoran Desert Region. Heritage Conservation and Recreation, U.S. Department of the Interior. 358 p.

Patton, D.R. 1978. Runwild-a storage and retrieval system for wildlife habitat information. USDA Forest Service GTR-RM-51:1-8, Rocky Mountain Forest and Range Experiment Station, Fort Collins, Colo.

Pitelka, F.A. 1941. Distribution of birds in relation to major biotic communities. Amer. Midl. Nat. 25:11-137.

Rasmussen, D.I. 1941. Biotic communities of Kaibab Plateau, Arizona. Ecol. Monog. 11: 229-275.

Shelford, V.E. 1963. The ecology of North America. University of Illinois Press. Urbana, Ill.

Steenbergh, W.F., and P.L. Warren. 1977. Preliminary ecological investigation of natural community status at Organ Pipe Cactus National Monument. USDI Cooperative National Park Resources Studies Unit, University of Arizona Tech. Rep. No. 3:1-152.

Turner, D.M., and C.L. Cochran, Jr. 1975. Wildlife management unit-37B-pilot planning study. Arizona Game and Fish Department, Fed. Aid Prog. FW-11-R-8, J-1:1-128.

Turner, R.M., L.H. Applegate, P.M. Bergthold, S. Gallizioli, and S.C. Martin. 1980. Range reference areas in Arizona. USDA Forest Service GTR-RM-79:1-34. Rocky Mountain Forest and Range Experiment Station, Fort Collins, Colo.

Udvardy, M.D.F. 1975. A classification of the biogeographical provinces of the world. Internat. Union Conserv. Nature and Natural Resources (IUCN, Morges, Switzerland). Occas. Pap. 18:1-48.

Vogler, L.E. 1980. The Arizona State Museum archaeological site survey system. Ariz. State Mus. Arch. Ser. 128:1-190.

Wallace, A.R. 1876. The geographical distribution of animals, with a study of the relations of living and extinct fauna and as elucidating the past changes of the earth's surface. MacMillan and Co. London, England.

Walter, H. 1973. Vegetation of the earth in relation to climate and the ecophysiological conditions. Translated from the Second German edition by Joy Wieser. English University Press, London; Springer-Verlag, New York, New York.

A DIGITIZED CLASSIFICATION SYSTEM FOR THE BIOTIC COMMUNITIES OF NORTH AMERICA, WITH COMMUNITY (SERIES) AND ASSOCIATION EXAMPLES FOR THE SOUTHWEST[1]/

DAVID E. BROWN, Arizona Game & Fish Department, Phoenix

CHARLES H. LOWE, University of Arizona, Tucson

CHARLES P. PASE, USDA Forest Service

INTRODUCTION. — In previous publications on the North American Southwest System we have addressed primarily the North American Southwest region as outlined in Fig. 1 (Brown and Lowe 1973, 1974a,b). Responses to both the classification system and the classification have been favorable in both general interest and use: e.g., Lacey, Ogden, and Foster 1975; Turner and Cochran 1975; Carr 1977; Dick-Peddie and Hubbard 1977; Ellis et al. 1977; Glinski 1977; Hubbard 1977; Pase and Layser 1977; Steenbergh and Warren 1977; Patton 1978; BLM 1978a,b; Turner et al. 1979. In this report we expand the classification nomenclature at digit levels 1-4 to represent the North American continent.

The Southwest System is evolutionary in basis and hierarchical in structure. It is a natural biological system rather than primarily a geography-based one in the sense of Dice 1943; Bailey 1978; and others. The resulting *classifications* are, therefore, *natural hierarchies.*

Because of the open-ended characteristic of a natural hierarchical system, resulting classification provides for orderly change. The inherent accordion-type flexibility provides for expansion and contraction at all levels. It permits accommodation of new information into the classification — addition, transference, and deletion of both (a) ecological taxa, and (b) quantitative data on ecological parameters concerning taxa, as our knowledge accumulates on either or both. Digit levels 7 to n accommodate the latter and digit levels 1-6 accommodate the former (ecological taxa) on a world-wide basis.

The system's potential is the provision of a truly representative picture for biotic environment. It permits but does not require inclusion of any and all biotic criteria in a given classification — animals as well as plants. Thereby included in the system's uses are the mapping of wildlife habitats and the determination and delineation of natural areas on a local to world-wide basis (Brown, Lowe, and Pase 1977). On a local basis, overlapping soil mapping units can provide "habitat-types" with their implied biotic potential for land use planning purposes.

The digitation of hierarchy makes the system computer-compatible; e.g., a system or subsystem for storing and retrieving biotic resource data within or parallel to an overall management system. The Southwest System is currently in use in the RUNWILD program developed for field unit use on remote terminals by Region 3 of the Rocky Mountain Forest and Range Experiment Station, U.S. Forest Service (Patton 1978). The system and classification is similarly incorporated in the State of Arizona Resources Inventory System (ARIS). It is currently used by both industry and agencies for biological studies, resource inventories, and procedures for environmental analysis, for example as required by the National Environmental Policy Act.

The system is responsive to scale. The hierarchical sequence permits mapping at any scale, and various levels of the system have been mapped at 1:1,000,000 (1 inch represents ca. 16 miles). 1:500,000, 1:250,000, 1:62,500 (1 inch represents ca. 1 mile), and others. Moreover, the use of hierarchical sequence permits the needed flexibility for mapping those complex communities where more intensive levels are impractical or needlessly time consuming in a given investigation.

The classification has been expanded to include the major biotic communities of North America (Brown, Lowe, and Pase 1977, 1979). To facilitate communication with potential users, we provide, in addition to some structural modification of the original classification, a number of additional definitions and explanations. Our fourth level (biome) examples for North America are representative; they are not intended as either a definitive or final classification. Examples of the use of the system to the fifth (series = community) and sixth (association) levels are given here for those biomes located wholly or partially within the North American Southwest.

Incorporated in the present classification are contributions from approximately one hundred investigators, primarily biogeographers, wildlife biologists, and ecologists, all of which pertain to or are in general use in the Southwest today. Additional references are given in Brown and Lowe 1974a,b, 1977.

A DIGITIZED HIERARCHY OF THE WORLD'S NATURAL ECOSYSTEMS

Where:

1,000 = Biogeographic (Continental) Realm

  1,100 = Vegetation

    1,110 = Formation-type

      1,111 = Climatic (Thermal) Zone

        1,111.1 = Regional Formation (Biome)

          1,111.11 = Series (Community of generic dominants)

            1,111.111 = Association (Community of specific dominants)

              1,111.1111 = Composition-structure-phase

A number preceeding the comma (e.g., 1,000) refers to the world's *biogeographic realms* (see Table 1). Origin and evolutionary history are recognized as primary in importance in the determination and classification of natural ecosystems. The mapable reality of the world's biogeographic realms is interpretive in part and dependent on criteria used. In those regions where the components of one realm merge gradually with those of another and the assignment of biogeographic origin is difficult, we include such transitional areas (wide ecotones) in both realms. The following seven realms are adapted from Wallace 1876; see also Hesse et al. 1937; Dansereau 1957; Darlington 1957; Walter 1973; I.U.C.N. 1974; DeLaubenfels 1975; Cox et al. 1976:

[1]/A contribution of the Arizona Game and Fish Department (with publication funded by Federal Aid Project W-53R), The University of Arizona Department of Ecology and Evolutionary Biology, and the United States Forest Service, Rocky Mountain Forest and Range Experiment Station.

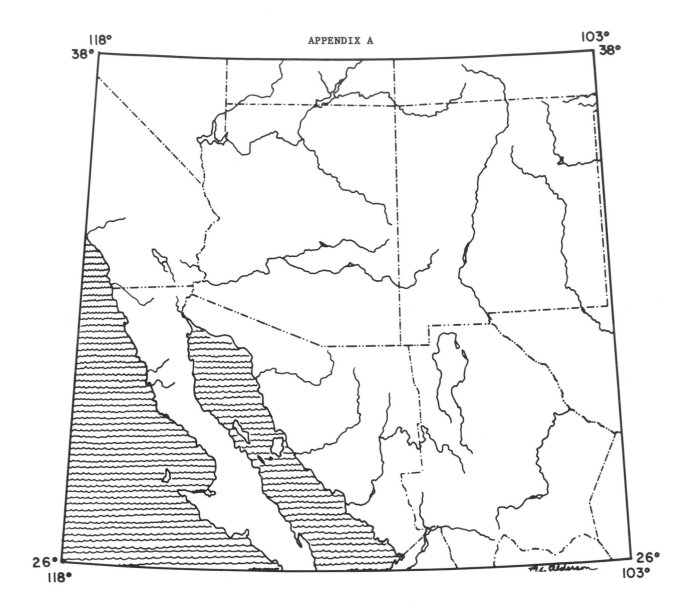

Figure 1. The Southwest. In delineating a *natural* Southwest region, approximately one half of the area falls in the Republic of Mexico and one half in the United States; the U.S. states of "Arizona and New Mexico" constitute less than half of the "American Southwest." Parts or all of the following states are included: Arizona, Baja California, California, Chihuahua, Coahuila, Colorado, Nevada, New Mexico, Sonora, Texas, Utah. All of Baja California and its associated islands (not completely shown) are included in our concept of a natural North American Southwest region; extreme northern Durango and Sinaloa are also included at Lat. 26° N.

1000 Nearctic	Continental North America exclusive of the tropics and certain highland areas south of the Tropic of Cancer. We include those tropic-subtropic regions in and adjacent to the North American Southwest and the Caribbean.	4000 Oriental	Southeast Asia, the Indian subcontinent; the Phillipines, Indonesia, etc.
		5000 Ethiopian	Africa south of the Sahara, Malagasy, and parts of the Arabian peninsula.
		6000 Australian	Australia and Tasmania.
2000 Palaearctic	Eurasia exclusive of the tropics. Africa north of the Sahel.	7000 Oceanic	Oceanic islands processing a high degree of endemism.
3000 Neotropical and Antarctican	Continental South America, Central America, and most of Mexico south of the Tropic of Cancer. Antarctica.		

First Level. — The first digit after the comma (e.g., 1,100) refers to vegetation, the structural and readily measurable reality of ecosystems. Included are all potential and/or existing plant communities that are presumed to be established naturally under existing climate and the cessation of artificially disruptive (man-caused) influences[2]/ (Table 1).

Table 1. Summary for the Natural Vegetation of the World to the First Digit level.

Biogeographic Realm	1. Upland Vegetation	2. Wetland Vegetation
1,000. Nearctic	1,100.	1,200.
2,000. Palaearctic	2,100.	2,200.
3,000. Neotropical-Antarctican	3,100.	3,200.
4,000. Oriental	4,100.	4,200.
5,000. Ethiopian	5,100.	5,200.
6,000. Australian	6,100.	6,200.
7,000. Oceanic	7,100.	7,200.

All existing and potential natural vegetation (PNV) is classified as belonging to uplands (1,100) or wetlands (1,200) as in Table 1. Cultivated lands are designated 1,300 (cultivated uplands) and 1,400 (cultivated wetlands). The evolutionary distinctions between plants and animals of terrestrial (upland) ecosystems and those of aquatic or hydric (wetland) ecosystems is recognized by this dichotomy (see Ray 1975).

As discussed here, wetlands include those periodically, seasonally or continually submerged ecosystems populated by species and/or life forms different from the immediately adjacent (upland) climax vegetation, and which are dependent on conditions more mesic than provided by the immediate precipitation. Certain ecosystems having both upland and wetland characteristics and components (e.g., riparian forests) could be properly considered as belonging to both divisions. They are treated in this report as wetlands (1,200).

Second Level. — The second digit after the comma (e.g. 1,110) refers to one of the following recognized ecological formations, which on a worldwide basis are the *formation-types* (biome-types); see Tables 2 and 3. On continents these are referred to as formations, which are vegetative responses (functions) to integrated environmental factors, most importantly plant-available moisture.

UPLAND FORMATIONS

Tundra[3]/ — Communities existing in an environment so cold that moisture is unavailable during most of the year, precluding the establishment of trees, and in which maximum vegetation development is of herbaceous root perennials, shrubs, lichens and mosses, with grasses poorly represented or at least not dominant.

Forest and Woodland

Forest — Communities comprised principally of trees potentially over 15 meters (50 ft) in height, and frequently characterized by closed and/or multilayered canopies.

Woodland — Communities dominated by trees with a mean potential height usually under 15 meters in height, the canopy of which is usually open — sometimes very open[4]/ — or interrupted and singularly layered.

Scrubland — Communities dominated by sclerophyll or microphyll shrubs and/or multi-stemmed trees, generally not exceeding 10 meters (31 ft) in height and usually presenting a closed physiognomy, or, if open, interspersed with other perennial vegetation.

Grassland — Communities dominated actually or potentially by grasses and/or other herbaceous plants.

Desertland — Communities in an arid environment — usually less than 300 mm (12 in) precipitation per annum — in which plants are separated by significant areas devoid of perennial vegetation.

Table 2. Summary for the Natural UPLAND Vegetation of the World to the Second Level (Formation-Type).

Biogeographic Realm	Formation Type					
	1. Tundra	2. Forest	3. Scrubland	4. Grassland	5. Desertland	6. Nonvegetated
1,000 Nearctic	1,110	1,120	1,130	1,140	1,150	1,160
2,000 Palaearctic	2,110	2,120	2,130	2,140	2,150	2,160
3,000 Neotropical-Antarctican	3,110	3,120	3,130	3,140	3,150	3,160
4,000 Oriental	4,110	4,120	4,130	4,140	4,150	4,160
5,000 Ethiopian	5,110	5,120	5,130	5,140	5,150	5,160
6,000 Australian	6,110	6,120	6,130	6,140	6,150	6,160
7,000 Oceanic	7,110	7,120	7,130	7,140	7,150	7,160

[2]/Our thinking on the complex question of determining climax, successional, and potential vegetation is to consider (and map) ecosystems on the basis of the existing or presumed vegetation of the foreseeable future.

[3]/The holistic integrity of a "Tundra" formation is not without question. Treated here, tundra may also be composed of grasslands, scrublands, marshlands (wet tundra), and desertlands in an Arctic-Boreal climatic zone (Billings and Mooney 1968; Billings 1973; and others).

[4]/The "savanna" formation (Dansereau 1957; Dyksterhuis 1957; and others) is here recognized (in North America) as an ecotone between *woodland and grassland*. Those homogeneous areas in which the crowns of trees normally cover less than approximately 15 percent of the ground space are classified as grasslands where grasses are actually or potentially dominant (= savanna grassland). Mosaics of grassland and smaller or larger stands of trees and shrubs are "parklands" and are composed of two or more ecologically distinct plant formations (Walter 1973).

293

Table 3. Summary for the Natural WETLAND Vegetation of the World to the Second Level (Formation-Type).

Biogeographic Realm	Formation Type					
	1. Wet Tundra	2. Forest[1]	3. Swamp-scrub, Riparian Scrub	4. Marshland	5. Strandland	6. Submergent Aquatic
1,000 Nearctic	1,210	1,220	1,230	1,240	1,250	1,260
2,000 Palaearctic	2,210	2,220	2,230	2,240	2,250	2,260
3,000 Neotropical-Antarctican	3,210	3,220	3,230	3,240	3,250	3,260
4,000 Oriental	4,210	4,220	4,230	4,240	4,250	4,260
5,000 Ethiopian	5,210	5,220	5,230	5,240	5,250	5,260
6,000 Australian	6,210	6,220	6,230	6,240	6,250	6,260
7,000 Oceanic	7,210	7,220	7,230	7,240	7,250	7,260

[1]/Swampforests, bog-forests and riparian forests.

WETLAND FORMATIONS

Wet Tundra[5]/	Wetland communities existing in an environment so cold that available plant moisture is unavailable during most of the year, precluding the establishment of trees and all but a low herbaceous plant structure in a hydric matrix.
Swampforest; Riparian Forest	Wetland communities possessing an overstory of trees potentially over 10 meters (31 ft) in height, and frequently characterized by closed and/or multilayered canopies.
Swampscrub; Riparian Scrub	Wetland communities dominated by short trees and/or woody shrubs, generally under 10 meters (31 ft) in height and often presenting a closed physiognomy.
Marshland	Wetland communities in which the principal plant components are herbaceous emergents which normally have their basal portions annually, periodically, or continually submerged.
Strandland	Beach and river channel communities subject to infrequent but periodic submersion, wind driven waves and/or spray. Plants are separated by significant areas devoid of perennial vegetation.[9]/
Submergent Aquatic	Aquatic communities comprised entirely or essentially of plants mostly submerged or lacking emergent structures.

Some localized upland and wetland areas are essentially without vegetation or are sparingly populated by simple organisms, e.g., on some dunes, lava flows, playas, sinks, etc. For purposes of classification certain of such areas could be considered as belonging to a *non-vegetated formation-type* (Tables 2 and 3).

Third Level. — The third digit beyond the comma (e.g., 1,11<u>1</u>) refers to one of four world *climatic zones* (c.f. Walter 1973; Ray 1975; Cox et al. 1976), in which minimum temperature remains a major evolutionary control of and within the zonation and the formation-types (Tables 4 and 5). All four of these broad climatic zones are found in North America and in the "Southwest."

Arctic-Boreal (Antarctic-Austreal)	Characterized by lengthy periods of freezing temperatures, with growing season of short duration (generally 60-150 days), occasionally interrupted by nights of below freezing temperatures.
Cold Temperate	Freezing temperatures of short duration although of frequent occurrence during winter months. Potential growing season generally 100-200 days and confined to spring and summer when freezing temperatures are infrequent or absent.
Warm Temperate	Freezing temperatures of short duration but generally occurring every year during winter months. Potential growing season over 200 days with an average of less than 125-150 days being subject to temperatures lower than 0 °C or to chilling fogs.
Tropical-Subtropical	Infrequent or no 24-hour periods of freezing temperatures, chilling fogs or wind.

Fourth Level. — *The fourth digit beyond the comma (e.g., 1,111.<u>1</u>)* refers to a subcontinental unit that is a *major biotic community* (= biome). Biomes are natural communities characterized by a distinctive vegetation physiognamy within a formation; accordingly, the natural geography of biomes is commonly *disjunctive*. A single biome is not to be confused with a single biotic (biogeographic) province; in distribution, a province is always a *continuous* (non-disjunctive) biogeographic area that may include several (e.g., five or more) biomes.[1]/

Our nomenclature at the biome (fourth) level incorporates useful geographic terms in the same sense of Weaver and Clements (1938). While such terms are also associated with biotic provinces (as in Fig. 2) we are classifying biomes, not biotic provinces. Biomes are characterized by a distinctive evolutionary history within a formation; thus they tend to be centered in, but are not restricted to particular biogeographic regions or provinces (e.g., see Weaver and Clements 1938; Clements and Shelford 1939; Pitelka 1941, 1943; Dice 1939, 1943; Odum 1945; Allee et al. 1949; Kendeigh 1954, 1961; Dansereau 1957; Shelford 1963; Daubenmire and Daubenmire 1968; Udvardy 1975; Dasmann 1976).

This fourth level and the fifth level (below) have provided the most successful and useful mapping of states, regions, and continents (e.g., in North America, Harshberger 1911; Shreve 1917, 1951; Shantz and Zon 1924; Bruner 1931; Morris 1935; Wieslander 1935; Brand 1936;

---

[5]/Treated here, tundra may also be composed of grasslands, scrublands, marshlands (wet tundra), and desertlands in an Arctic-Boreal climatic zone; see footnote 3.

[9]/Strand communities are situated in harsh physical environments that produce their characteristic physiognomy. Accordingly, strandland is treated as the wetland equivalent of desertland. While occurring in the usual sense on beaches and other seacoast habitats, freshwater (or interior) strands also occur in river channels, along lake margins, and below reservoir high water lines.

[1]/Originally termed *biotic provinces* by Lee Dice (1943) who developed this biogeographic concept in North America between 1922 (biotic areas) and 1943 (biotic provinces), they have been referred to variously in recent literature as "biotic provinces" (Dasmann 1972, 1974; IUCN 1973), "biogeograph provinces" (Udvardy 1975; Dasmann 1976), "ecoregions" (Bailey 1976, 1978), and "b gions" (Franklin 1977).

Table 4. Summary for the Natural UPLAND Vegetation of Nearctic and Adjacent Neotropical North America to the Third Level.

Formation	Climatic (Thermal) Zone			
	1. Arctic-Boreal	2. Cold Temperate	3. Warm Temperate	4. Tropical-Subtropical
1,110 Tundra	1,111			
1,120 Forest & Woodland	1,121	1,122	1,123	1,124
1,130 Scrubland	1,131	1,132	1,133	1,134
1,140 Grassland	1,141	1,142	1,143	1,144
1,150 Desertland	1,151	1,152	1,153	1,154
1,160 Nonvegetated	1,161	1,162	1,163	1,164

Table 5. Summary for the Natural WETLAND Vegetation of Nearctic and Adjacent Neotropical North America to the Third Level.

Formation	Climatic (Thermal) Zone			
	1. Arctic-Boreal	2. Cold Temperate	3. Warm Temperate	4. Tropical-Subtropical
1,210 Wet Tundra	1,211			
1,220 Forest[1]/	1,221	1,222	1,223	1,224
1,230 Swampscrub	1,231	1,232	1,233	1,234
1,240 Marshland	1,241	1,242	1,243	1,244
1,250 Strandland	1,251	1,252	1,253	1,254
1,260 Submergent Aquatic	1,261	1,262	1,263	1,264

[1]/Swampforests, bog-forests and riparian forests.

Nichol 1937; LeSueur 1945; Jensen 1947; Leopold 1950; Castetter 1956; Küchler 1964, 1977; Brown 1973; Franklin and Dyrness 1973; Brown and Lowe 1977). Biomes and biogeographic provinces are also the bases for the biosphere reserve program (MAB) in the United States and elsewhere (IUCN 1974; Franklin 1977).

A partial summary of the biotic communities (biomes) for Nearctic and adjacent Neotropical America is given in Tables 6 and 7.

Fifth Level. — The fifth digit beyond the comma (e.g., 1,111.1$\underline{1}$) refers to the principal plant-animal communities within the biomes, distinguished primarily on taxa that are distinctive climax plant dominants. Daubenmire and Daubenmire (1968) organized their data according to major dominants in climax communities referred to as *climax series.* "Series," or "cover-types" (sensu Society of American Foresters 1954), or "vegetation-types" (sensu Flores et al. 1971), are each composed of one or more biotic associations characterized by shared climax dominants within the same formation, zone, and biome (Oosting 1950; Lowe 1964; Franklin and Dyrness 1973; Pfister et al. 1977). For example, within Rocky Mountain montane conifer forest (122.3), the Pine Series (122.32) includes all of the Rocky Mountain forest associations in which *Pinus ponderosa* is a dominant.

Community diversity of tropical and subtropical upland climax dominants is inherently more complex than in boreal and temperate communities. Moreover, some taxa may exhibit polymorphism to the extent that the same species may be dominant — and ecotypically differentiated — in more than a single formation. As an extreme case in southwestern North America, mesquite *(Prosopis juliflora)* may be a dominant life-form in certain desertland, disclimax grassland, scrubland, woodland, and riparian forest communities, and exhibit phenotypic and presumably genotypic population differentiation across the complex gradient. Facultative growth-form is exhibited by dominant plant taxa in both cold and warm climatic zones.

The distribution of some plant dominants also may span more than a single climatic zone, as in *Larrea, Prosopis,* and the introduced

Tamarix. However, important plant and animal associates of these dominant species are usually encountered when passing from one formation or climatic zone to another. When specific and generic dominants are shared by more than one biome, closer investigation may reveal genetic geographic variation within the shared species, as in the chromosome races of creosotebush *(Larrea divaricata,* Yang and Lowe 1968; Yang 1970).

It is clear that the determination of fifth and sixth (below) level communities in particular will require modification and revision in the classification as field data accumulate. Some of the more widely distributed and commonly recognized series in the Southwest are given in Tables 6 and 7 under the appropriate biome.

Sixth Level. — The sixth digit beyond the comma (e.g., 1,111.11$\underline{1}$) refers to distinctive plant associations, and associes (successional associations), based on the occurrence of particular dominant species more or less local or regional in distribution and generally equivalent to habitat-types as outlined by the Daubenmires (1968), Layser (1974), Pfister et al. (1977), and others. While we give examples for certain communities within southwestern biomes, the enormous numbers of sets precludes presentation here for the treatments given in Tables 6 and 7. Associations may be added at length for regional studies by using a, b, c, sets as is also indicated in the tables in Brown and Lowe (1974a,b).

Seventh Level. — The seventh digit beyond the comma (e.g., 1,111.111$\underline{1}$) accommodates detailed measurement and assessment of quantitative structure, composition, density and other attributes for dominants, understories, and other associated species. This level and additional ones in the system provide the flexibility required for encompassing data for ecological parameters measured in intensive studies on limited areas (see e.g., Dick-Peddie and Moir 1970).

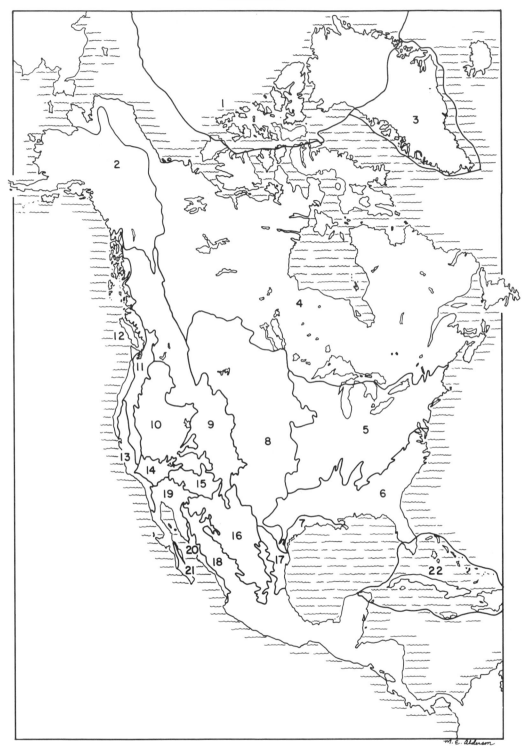

Figure 2. Biogeographic provinces of Nearctic and adjacent Neotropical North America (modified after Dice 1943, and Dasmann 1974), discussed in text under fourth (Biome) digit level.

1. Polar
2. Alaskan
3. Greenlandian
4. Canadian
5. Northeastern
6. Southeastern
7. Gulf Coastal

8. Plains
9. Rocky Mountain
10. Great Basin
11. Sierran-Cascade
12. Sitkan-Oregonian
13. Californian
14. Mohavian

15. Mogollon (Interior)
16. Chihuahuan
17. Tamaulipan
18. Madrean
19. Sonoran
20. Sinaloan
21. San Lucan
22. Carribean

Table 6. Nomenclature of UPLAND Biotic Communities of Nearctic and Adjacent Neotropical North America with Community (Series) and Association Examples for the North American Southwest.

1,100 Nearctic Upland Vegetation
  1,110 Tundra Formation
    1,111 Arctic Tundras
      1,111.1 Polar (High Arctic) Tundra
      1,111.2 Alaskan (Low Arctic) Coastal Tundra
      1,111.3 Canadian (Barren Ground = Low Arctic) Tundra
      1,111.4 Arctic Alpine Tundra
      1,111.5 Rocky Mountain Alpine Tundra
        1,111.51[1]/ Lichen-Moss Series*
          111.511 *Rhizocarpon geographicum* Association*
        111.52 Mixed Herb Series*
        111.53 Avens-Sedge Series*
          111.531 *Geum turbinatum* Association*
          111.532 *Geum turbinatum-Carex bella* Association*
        111.54 Woodrush Series*
          111.541 *Kobresia bellardi*-grass-forb Association*
      111.6 Sierran-Cascade Alpine Tundra
        111.61 Lichen-Moss Series*
        111.62 Mixed Herb Series*
          111.621 *Selaginella watsoni-Eriogonum umbellatum* et al. Association*
      111.7 Adirondack-Appalachian Alpine Tundra

120 Forest and Woodland Formation
  121 Boreal Forests and Woodlands
    121.1 Canadian Subarctic Conifer Forest and Woodland (North American Taiga)
    121.2 Appalachian Subalpine Conifer Forest
    121.3 Rocky Mountain Subalpine Conifer Forest and Woodland[2]/
      121.31 Engelmann Spruce-Alpine Fir Series*
        121.311 *Picea engelmanni-Abies lasiocarpa* Association*
        121.312 *Picea engelmanni* Association*
        121.313 *Abies lasiocarpa* Association*
        121.314 *Abies lasiocarpa arizonica* Association*
        121.315 *Picea pungens* Association*
        121.316 *Populus tremuloides* subclimax Association*
      121.32 Bristlecone Pine-Limber Pine Series*
        121.321 *Pinus aristata-Pinus flexilis* Association*
        121.322 *Pinus aristata* Association*
        121.323 *Pinus flexilis* Association*
    121.4 Sierran-Cascade Subalpine Conifer Forest
      121.41 Limber Pine-Lodgepole Pine Series*
        121.411 *Pinus flexilis-Pinus contorta murrayana* Association*
        121.412 *Pinus flexilis* Association*
    121.5 Madrean Subalpine Conifer Forest
  122 Cold Temperate Forests and Woodlands
    122.1 Northeastern Deciduous Forest
    122.2 Pacific Coastal (Oregonian) Conifer Forest
    122.3 Rocky Mountain (= Petran) Montane Conifer Forest
      122.31 Douglas-fir-White Fir (= Mixed Conifer) Series*

        122.311 *Pseudotsuga menziesi* Association*
        122.312 *Pseudotsuga menziesi-Abies concolor* Association*
        122.313 *Pseudotsuga menziesi*-mixed conifer (*Abies concolor, Pinus flexilis, Acer glabrum, Populus tremuloides, Pinus ponderosa*) Association*
        122.314 *Populus tremuloides* subclimax Association*
      122.32 Pine Series*
        122.321 *Pinus ponderosa* Association*
        122.322 *Pinus ponderosa*-mixed conifer Association*
        122.323 *Pinus ponderosa-Quercus gambeli* Association*
        122.324 *Pinus ponderosa-Quercus arizonica* Association*
        122.325 *Pinus ponderosa-Juniperus deppeana* Association*
        122.326 *Populus tremuloides* subclimax Association*
        122.327 *Pinus flexilis reflexa* Association*
        122.328 *Pinus ponderosa-Pinus leiophylla* Association*
      122.33 Gambel Oak Series*
        122.331 *Quercus gambeli* Association*
    122.4 Great Basin Conifer Woodland
      122.41 Pinyon-Juniper Series*
        122.411 *Pinus edulis-Juniperus scopulorum* Association*
        122.412 *Pinus edulis* Association*
        122.413 *Juniperus scopulorum* Association*
        122.414 *Pinus edulis-Juniperus monosperma* Association*
        122.415 *Juniperus monosperma* Association*
        122.416 *Pinus monophylla-Juniperus osteosperma* Association*
        122.417 *Pinus monophylla* Association*
        122.418 *Juniperus osteosperma* Association*
        122.419 *Pinus monophylla-Juniperus californica* Association*
        122.411a *Juniperus-californica* Association*
        122.412a *Pinus quadrifolia-Juniperus californica* Association*
        122.413a *Pinus quadrifolia* Association*
        122.414a *Pinus monophylla-Juniperus californica*-chaparral Association*
    122.5 Sierran-Cascade Montane Conifer Forest
      122.51 Mixed Conifer Series*
        122.511 *Abies concolor*-mixed conifer (*Pinus contorta murrayana, Pinus jeffreyi* et al.) Association*
      122.52 Pine Series*
        122.521 *Pinus ponderosa* Association*
        122.522 *Pinus ponderosa-P. jeffreyi* Association*
        122.523 *Pinus ponderosa-Quercus kelloggi* Association*
        122.524 *Pinus jeffreyi* Association*
      122.53 Black Oak Series*
        122.531 *Quercus kelloggi* Association*
    122.6 Madrean Montane Conifer Forest
      122.61 Douglas-fir-Mixed Conifer Series*
        122.611 *Pseudotsuga menziesi* Association*
        122.612 *Pseudotsuga menziesi-Pinus flexilis, Acer glabrum, Populus tremuloides, Pinus ponderosa* et al. Association*
      122.62 Pine Series*
        122.621 *Pinus flexilis ayacahuite* Association*
        122.622 *Pinus ponderosa* Association*
        122.623 *Pinus ponderosa*-mixed conifer Association*
        122.624 *Pinus ponderosa-Quercus* spp. Association*
        122.625 *Pinus ponderosa-Juniperus deppeana* Association*
  123 Warm Temperate Forests and Woodlands
    123.1 Southeastern Mixed Deciduous and Evergreen Forest
    123.2 Californian Mixed Evergreen Forest
      123.21 Mixed Mesophytic Series*

---

*Examples only.

[1]/The first "1" (in front of comma and representing the Nearctic Realm) is understood, and cropped for tabular convenience only, from this point onward.

[2]/Separation of this biotic community into Rocky Mountain and Great Basin units may be warranted.

123.211 Mixed hardwood Association*
123.212 *Quercus chrysolepis*-mixed hardwood Association*
123.22 Big-cone Spruce Series*
123.221 *Pseudotsuga macrocarpa* Association*
123.3 Madrean Evergreen Forest and Woodland
123.31 Encinal (Oak) Series*
123.311 Mixed *Quercus* (= *Quercus* spp.) Association*
123.312 *Quercus grisea* Association*
123.313 *Quercus emoryi* Association*
123.314 *Quercus chihuahuaensis* Association*
123.315 *Quercus arizonica* Association*
123.316 *Quercus* spp.-*Pinus cembroides*-*Juniperus* spp.
Association*
123.317 *Pinus cembroides* Association*
123.318 *Juniperus deppeana* Association*
123.32 Oak-Pine Series*
123.321 *Quercus hypoleucoides*-*Quercus rugosa* Association*
123.322 *Quercus* spp.-*Pinus leiophylla* Association*
123.323 *Quercus* spp.-*Pinus engelmanni* Association*
123.324 *Quercus* spp.-*Pinus* spp. Association*
123.325 *Quercus* spp.-*Arbutus xalapensis*-*Pinus* spp.
Association*
123.4 Californian Evergreen Woodland
123.41 Encinal (Oak) Series*
123.411 Mixed *Quercus* Association*
123.412 *Quercus agrifolia* Association*
123.413 *Quercus agrifolia*-*Juglans californica* Association*
123.414 *Quercus engelmanni* Association*
123.42 Walnut Series*
123.421 *Junglans californica* Association*
123.5 Relict Conifer Forest and Woodland
123.51 Closed-cone Pine Series*
123.511 *Pinus attenuata* Association*
123.512 *Pinus muricata* Association*
123.513 *Pinus torreyana* Association*
123.52 Cypress Series*
123.521 *Cupressus arizonica arizonica* Association*
123.522 *Cupressus arizonica glabra* Association*
123.523 *Cupressus arizonica stephensoni* Association*
123.524 *Cupressus arizonica montana* Association*
123.525 *Cupressus forbesi* Association*
123.526 *Cupressus forbesi*-*Pinus muricata* Association*
124 Tropical-Subtropical Forests and Woodlands
124.1 Caribbean Montane Rain Forest
124.2 Caribbean Cloud Forest
124.3 Caribbean Evergreen Forest
124.4 Caribbean Deciduous Forest
124.5 Tamaulipan Deciduous Forest
124.6 Sinaloan Deciduous Forest
124.61 Mixed Short Tree Series*
124.611 Mixed Deciduous Association*
124.612 *Lysiloma watsoni*-mixed deciduous Association*
124.613 *Conzattia sericea* Association*
124.614 *Ceiba acuminata*-mixed deciduous Association*
124.615 *Bursera inopinnata*-mixed deciduous
Association*
130 Scrubland Formation
131 Arctic-Boreal Scrublands
131.1 Alaskan (Low Arctic) Coastal Scrub
131.2 Canadian (Low Arctic, Barren Ground) Subpolar Scrub
131.3 Alaskan Alpine and Subalpine Scrub
131.4 Adirondack-Appalachian Alpine and Subalpine Scrub
131.5 Rocky Mountain Alpine and Subalpine Scrub
131.51 Willow Series*
131.511 *Salix brachycarpa* Association*

131.512 *Salix planifolia* Association*
131.513 *Salix nivalis* Association*
131.52 Spruce Elfinwood Series*
131.521 *Picea engelmanni* Association*
131.53 Bristlecone Pine Elfinwood Series*
131.531 *Pinus aristata* Association
131.6 Sierran-Cascade Alpine and Subalpine Scrub
131.61 Limber Pine-Lodgepole Pine Elfinwood Series*
131.611 *Pinus flexilis* Association*
132 Cold Temperate Scrublands
132.1 Great Basin Montane Scrub
132.11 Oak-scrub Series*
132:111 *Quercus gambeli* Association*
132.12 Mountain mahogany Series*
132.121 *Cercocarpus montanus* Association*
132.13 Maple-scrub Series*
132.131 *Acer grandidentatum* Association*
132.14 Serviceberry Series*
132.141 *Amelanchier alnifolia* Association*
132.15 Bitterbush Series*
132.151 *Purshia tridentata* Association*
132.16 Mixed Deciduous Series*
132.161 Mixed Scrub Association*
132.2 Sierran-Cascade Montane Scrub
132.21 Manzanita Series*
132.211 *Arctostaphylos glauca* Association*
132.212 *Arctostaphylos glandulosa* Association*
132.22 Mixed Scrub Series*
132.221 Mixed scrub Association*
132.3 Plains Deciduous Scrub
132.31 Oak-Scrub Series*
132.311 *Quercus harvardi* Association*
132.32 Sumac Series*
132.321 *Rhus lanceolata* Association*
132.33 Mixed Deciduous Series*
132.331 *Prunus americana* et al. Association*
133 Warm Temperate Scrublands
133.1 Californian Chaparral
133.11 Chamise Series*
133.111 *Adenostoma fasciculatum* Association*
133.112 *Adenostoma fasciculatum*-mixed sclerophyll
Association*
133.113 *Adenostoma sparsifolium* Association*
133.12 Scrub Oak Series*
133.121 *Quercus dumosa* Association*
133.122 *Quercus dumosa*-mixed sclerophyll Association*
133.123 *Quercus dumosa*-*Quercus wislizeni* Association*
133.13 Manzanita Series*
133.131 *Arctostaphylos glauca* Association*
133.132 *Arctostaphylos glandulosa* Association*
133.133 *Arctostaphylos glandulosa*-*Pinus coulteri*
Association*
133.134 *Arctostaphylos glandulosa*-mixed sclerophyll
Association*
133.14 Ceanothus Series*
133.141 *Ceanothus cordulatus* Association*
133.142 *Ceanothus* spp.-mixed sclerophyll Association*
133.2 Californian Coastalscrub
133.21 Sage Series*
133.211 *Artemisia californica* Association*
133.212 *Artemisia californica*-*Salvia* spp. Association*
133.22 Mixed Shrub Series*
133.221 *Eriogonum fasciculatum*-*Simmondsia chinensis*
et al. Association*
133.222 *Encelia californica*-Mixed shrub Association*

*Examples only.

298

133.3 Interior Chaparral
  133.31 Scrub Oak Series*
    133.311 *Quercus turbinella* Association*
    133.312 *Quercus turbinella-Cerocarpus breviflorus* Association*
    133.313 *Quercus turbinella-Cercocarpus betuloides* Association*
    133.314 *Quercus turbinella*-mixed sclerophyll Association*
    133.315 *Quercus intricata* Association*
    133.316 *Quercus intricata-Cercocarpus* spp. Association*
    133.317 *Quercus intricata-Quercus* spp. Association*
    133.318 *Quercus intricata*-mixed sclerophyll Association*
    133.319 *Quercus pungens* Association*
    133.311a *Quercus pungens*-mixed sclerophyll Association*
  133.32 Manzanita Series*
    133.321 *Arctostaphylos pringlei* Association*
    133.322 *Arctostaphylos pungens* Association*
  133.33 Ceanothus Series*
    133.331 *Ceanothus greggi* Association*
    133.332 *Ceanothus greggi*-mixed sclerophyll Association*
  133.34 Mountain mahogany Series*
    133.341 *Cercocarpus breviflorus* Association*
    133.342 *Cercocarpus montanus* Association*
  133.35 Silktassel Series*
    133.351 *Garrya wrighti* Association*
    133.352 *Garrya ovata* Association*
  133.36 Mixed Evergreen Sclerophyll Series*
    133.361 Mixed sclerophyll Association*
133.4 Southeastern Maritime Scrub
134 Tropical-Subtropical Scrublands
  134.1 Caribbean Thornscrub
  134.2 Tamaulipan Thornscrub
  134.3 Sinaloan Thornscrub
    134.31 Mixed Deciduous Series*
      134.311 Mixed scrub-*Fouquieria macdougali* Association*
      134.312 Mixed scrub-*Ipomoea arborescens* Association*
      134.313 Mixed scrub-*Lysiloma divaricata* Association*
      134.314 Mixed scrub-*Acacia cymbispina* Association*
      134.315 Mixed scrub-*Ceiba acuminata* Association*
      134.316 Mixed scrub-Mixed tree Association*
    134.32 Mesquite Disclimax Series*
      134.321 *Prosopis juliflora velutina*-mixed scrub Association*
140 Grassland Formation
141 Arctic-Boreal Grasslands
  141.1 Alaskan (Low Arctic) Coastal Grassland
  141.2 Canadian (Low Arctic) Grassland
  141.3 Appalachian Subalpine (Balds) Grassland
  141.4 Rocky Mountain Alpine and Subalpine Grassland
    141.41 Bunchgrass Series*
      141.411 *Festuca thurberi* Association*
      141.412 *Festuca arizonica* Association*
      141.413 Mixed grass-forb Association*
    141.42 Sedge-Forb-Grass Series*
      141.421 *Carex* spp.-mixed forb-grass Association*
  141.5 Sierran Cascade Alpine and Subalpine Grassland
    141.51 Bunchgrass Series*
      141.511 *Sitanion hystrix*-mixed forb Association*
      141.512 Mixed grass-forb Association*
    141.52 Sedge-Forb-Grass Series*
      141.521 *Carex* spp.-mixed forb-grass Association*
  141.6 Madrean Alpine and Subalpine Grassland
142 Cold Temperate Grasslands

142.1 Plains Grassland
  142.11 Bluestem "tall-grass" Series*
    142.111 *Andropogon scoparius* Association*
    142.112 *Andropogon* spp.-mixed tall-grass Association*
    142.113 *Andropogon* spp.-*Quercus harvardi* Association*
    142.114 Mixed tall-grass Association*
    142.115 *Artemisia filifolia*-mixed scrub disclimax Association*
  142.12 Grama "short-grass" Series*
    142.121 *Bouteloua gracilis* Association*
    142.122 *Bouteloua* spp. Association*
    142.123 *Bouteloua* spp.-mixed grass Association*
    142.124 *Bouteloua* spp.-mixed grass-mixed scrub Association*
  142.13 Buffalo-grass Series*
    142.131 *Buchloe dactyloides*-mixed grass Association*
  142.14 Mixed "Short-grass" Series*
    142.141 *Aristida* spp.-*Bouteloua gracilis-Buchloe dactyloides* Association*
  142.15 Shrub-Grass Disclimax Series*
    142.151 *Gutierrezia sarothrae* Association*
142.2 Great Basin Shrub-Grassland
  142.21 Wheatgrass Series*
    142.211 *Agropyron smithi* Association*
    142.212 *Agropyron smithi*-mixed scrub Association*
    142.213 *Agropyron smithi-Artemisia tridentata* Association*
  142.22 Mixed Bunchgrass Series*
    142.221 Mixed grass Association*
    142.222 Mixed grass-*Artemisia tridentata* Association*
  142.23 Ricegrass Series*
    142.231 *Oryzopsis hymenoides* Association*
  142.24 Sacaton Series*
    142.241 *Sporobolus airoides* Association*
    142.242 *Sporobolus airoides-Atriplex canescens* Association*
142.3 Pacific Coastal (Oregonian) Grassland
142.4 Rocky Mountain Montane Grassland
  142.41 Mixed Meadow Series*
    142.411 Mixed forb-grass Association*
  142.42 Rush Series*
    142.421 *Juncus* spp. Association*
  142.43 Fern Series*
    142.431 *Pteridium aquilinum* Association*
  142.44 Iris Disclimax Series*
    142.441 *Iris missouriensis* Association*
142.5 Sierran-Cascade Montane Grassland
  142.51 Mixed Meadow Series*
    142.511 Mixed forb-grass Association*
  142.52 Rush Series*
    142.521 *Juncus* spp. Association*
143 Warm Temperate Grasslands
143.1 Scrub-Grassland (Semidesert Grassland)
  143.11 Grama Grass-Scrub Series*
    143.111 *Bouteloua eriopoda-Yucca elata* Association*
    143.112 *Bouteloua eriopoda-Prosopis juliflora* Association*
    143.113 *Bouteloua eriopoda*-mixed grass-mixed scrub Association*
    143.114 *Bouteloua* spp.-mixed grass-mixed scrub Association*
  143.12 Tobosa Grass-Scrub Series*
    143.121 *Hilaria mutica* Association*
    143.122 *Hilaria mutica-Prosopis juliflora* Association*

*Examples only.

299

143.123 *Hilaria mutica*-mixed scrub Association*
143.13 Curleymesquite grass-scrub Series*
  143.131 *Hilaria belangeri*-mixed scrub Association*
143.14 Sacaton-Scrub Series*
  143.141 *Sporobolus wrighti* Association*
  143.142 *Sporobolus wrighti-Prosopis juliflora* Association*
143.15 Mixed Grass-Scrub Series*
  143.151 Mixed grass-*Yucca elata* Association*
  143.152 Mixed grass-*Prosopis juliflora* Association
  143.153 Mixed grass-*Acacia greggi* Association*
  143.154 Mixed grass-*Fouquieria splendens* Association*
  143.155 Mixed grass-mixed scrub Association*
143.16 Shrub-Scrub Disclimax Series*
  143.161 *Aplopappus tenuisectus* Association*
  143.162 *Aplopappus tenuisectus-Yucca elata* Association*
  143.163 *Aplopappus tenuisectus-Prosopis juliflora* Association*
  143.164 *Aplopappus tenuisectus*-mixed scrub Association*
  143.165 *Gutierrezia sarothrae-Prosopis juliflora* Association*
143.2 Californian Valley Grassland
  143.21 Annual Disclimax Series*
    143.211 Mixed annual grass Association*
    143.212 *Avena fatua* Association*
    143.213 *Bromus rubens* Association*
    143.214 Mixed forb Association*
144 Tropical-Subtropical Grasslands
  144.1 Caribbean Savanna Grassland
  144.2 Gulf Coastal (Tamaulipan) Grassland
  144.3 Sonoran Savanna Grassland
    144.31 Mixed Root-perennial Grass Series*
      144.311 *Heteropogon contortus-Bouteloua* spp.-*Aristida* spp.-mixed scrub Association*
    144.32 Grama Series*
      144.321 *Bouteloua rothrocki-Prosopis juliflora* Association*
      144.322 *Bouteloua* spp.-mixed scrub Association*
    144.33 Three-awn Series*
      144.331 *Aristida* spp.-*Prosopis juliflora* Association*
      144.332 *Aristida* spp.-mixed scrub Association*
150 Desertland Formation
  151 Arctic-Boreal Desertlands
    151.1 Polar Desertscrub
  152 Cold Temperate Desertlands
    152.1 Great Basin Desertscrub
      152.11 Sagebrush Series*
        152.111 *Artemisia tridentata* Association*
        152.112 *Artemisia tridentata*-mixed scrub-grass Association*
        152.113 *Artemisia nova* Association*
      152.12 Shadscale Series*
        152.121 *Atriplex confertifolia* Association*
        152.122 *Atriplex confertifolia*-mixed scrub Association*
      152.13 Blackbrush Series*
        152.131 *Coleogyne ramosissima* Association*
      152.14 Rabbitbrush Series*
        152.141 *Chrysothamnus nauseosus* Association*
      152.15 Winterfat Series*
        152.151 *Eurotia lanata* Association*
        152.152 *Eurotia lanata*-mixed scrub Association*
      152.16 Mixed scrub Series*
        152.161 *Ephedra viridis-Eriogonum* spp.-mixed scrub Association*
      152.17 Saltbush Series*
        152.171 *Sarcobatus vermiculatus* Association*
        152.172 *Atriplex canescens* Association*
  153 Warm Temperate Desertlands
    153.1 Mohave Desertscrub

153.11 Creosotebush Series*
  153.111 *Larrea divaricata* Association*
  153.112 *Larrea divaricata-Ambrosia dumosa* Association*
  153.113 *Larrea divaricata-Yucca* spp. Association*
153.12 Blackbrush Series*
  153.121 *Coleogyne ramosissima* Association*
  153.122 *Coleogyne ramosissima-Yucca* spp. Association*
153.13 Mesquite Series*
  153.131 *Prosopis juliflora torreyana* Association*
153.14 Bladdersage Series*
  153.141 *Salazaria mexicana* Association*
153.15 Joshuatree Series*
  153.151 *Yucca brevifolio-Acamptopappus sphaerocephalus-Larrea divaricata*-mixed scrub Association*
  153.152 *Yucca brevifolia-Coleogyne ramosissima* Association*
  153.153 *Yucca brevifolia-Larrea divaricata* Association*
153.16 Catclaw Series*
  153.161 *Acacia greggi*-mixed scrub Association*
153.17 Saltbush Series*
  153.171 *Suaeda torreyana* Association*
  153.172 *Atriplex* spp. Association*
153.2 Chihuahuan Desertscrub
  153.21 Creosotebush-Tarbush Series*
    153.212 *Larrea divaricata-Parthenium incanum*-mixed scrub Association*
    153.213 *Larrea divaricata-Flourensia cernua* Association*
    153.214 *Flourensia cernua* Association*
  153.22 Whitethorn Series*
    153.221 *Acacia neovernicosa* Association*
    153.222 *Acacia neovernicosa-Larrea divaricata* Association*
  153.23 Sandpaperbush Series*
    153.231 *Mortonia scabrella* Association*
    153.232 *Mortonia scabrella-Rhus microphylla* Association*
  153.24 Mesquite Series*
    153.241 *Prosopis juliflora glandulosa* (shrub hummock) Association*
    153.242 *Prosopis juliflora glandulosa-Artemesia filifolia* Association*
  153.25 Succulent Series*
    153.251 *Agave lecheguilla* Association*
    153.252 *Agave lecheguilla-Yucca* spp. Association*
    153.253 *Opuntia* spp.-*Agave* spp.-*Larrea divaricata* Association*
  153.26 Mixed Scrub Series*
    153.261 *Fouquieria splendens*-mixed scrub Association*
  153.27 Saltbush Series*
    153.271 *Suaeda torreyana* Association*
    153.272 *Atriplex canescens* Association*
    153.273 *Atriplex* spp.-*Artemisia filifolia* Association*
154 Tropical-Subtropical Desertlands
  154.1 Sonoran Desertscrub
    154.11 Creosotebush-Bursage ("Lower Colorado Valley") et al Series*
      154.111 *Larrea divaricata* Association*
      154.112 *Larrea divaricata-Ambrosia dumosa* Association*
      154.113 *Ambrosia dumosa* Association*
      154.114 *Prosopis juliflora torreyana* (shrub hummock) Association*
      154.115 *Cercidium floridum-Olneya tesota-Dalea spinosa* riparian Association*
      154.116 *Fouquieria splendens-Agave deserti* Association*

*Examples only.

300

154.117 *Opuntia bigelovi* Association*

154.12 Paloverde-Mixed Cacti ("Arizona Upland") Series*

154.121 *Ambrosia deltoidea-Cercidium microphyllum*-mixed scrub Association*

154.122 *Ambrosia deltoidea-Carnegiea gigantea*-mixed scrub Association*

154.123 *Simmondsia chinensis*-mixed scrub Association*

154.124 *Larrea divaricata-Canotia holacantha* Association*

154.125 *Larrea divaricata*-mixed scrub Association*

154.126 *Encelia farinosa*-mixed scrub Association*

154.127 Mixed shrub-*Cercidium microphyllum-Olneya tesota*-mixed scrub Association

154.13 Brittlebush-Ironwood ("Plains of Sonora") Series*

154.131 *Encelia farinosa-Olneya tesota* Association*

154.132 *Encelia farinosa*-mixed scrub Association*

154.133 Mixed shrub-mixed scrub Association*

154.134 Mixed shrub-*Prosopis juliflora velutina* Association*

154.135 Mixed shrub-*Forchammeria watsoni* Association*

154.14 Copal-Torote ("Central Gulf Coast") Series*

154.141 *Jatropha cinerea-Bursera microphylla* Association*

154.142 *Jatropha* spp.-*Bursera microphylla-Pachycereus pringlei* Association*

154.143 *Jatropha* spp.-*Idria columnaris*-mixed scrub Association*

154.15 Agave-Bursage ("Vizcaino") Series*

154.151 *Ambrosia chenopodifolia-Agave shawi* Association*

154.152 *Ambrosia* spp.-*Agave shawi-Pachycormus discolor-Idria columnaris*-mixed scrub Association*

154.153 *Ambrosia* spp.-*Agave shawi-Pachycereus pringlei*-mixed scrub Association*

154.154 Mixed shrub-*Agave shawi* Association*

154.155 *Eriogonum fasiculatum*-mixed scrub Association*

154.16 Paloblanco-Agria ("Magdalena") Series*

154.161 *Machaerocereus gummosus*-mixed scrub Association*

154.17 Saltbush Series

154.171 *Suaeda torreyana* Association*

154.172 *Allenrolfea occidentalis* Association*

154.173 *Atriplex* spp.-*Prosopis juliflora torreyana* Association*

154.174 *Atriplex polycarpa-Lycium* spp.-*Prosopis juliflora velutina* Association*

154.175 *Frankenia palmeri-Atriplex julacea* Association*

Table 7. Nomenclature of WETLAND Biotic Communities (Fourth Level) of Nearctic and Adjacent Neotropical North America with Some Community (Series) and Association Level Examples for the North American Southwest.

1,200 Nearctic Wetland Vegetation

1,210 Wet Tundra Formation

1,211 Arctic Wet Tundra

211.1 Polar (High Arctic) Wet Tundra[1]/

211.2 Greenlandian Wet Tundra

211.3 Alaskan (Coastal) Wet Tundra

211.4 Canadian (Low Arctic) Wet Tundra

220 Forest Formation

221 Boreal Swamp and Riparian Forests

*One or more examples only are given for these levels.

[1]/The first "1" (in front of comma and representing the Nearctic Realm) is understood, and cropped for tabular convenience only, from this point onward.

221.1 Canadian Swampforest

222 Cold Temperate Swamp and Riparian Forests

222.1 Northeastern Bog, Swamp and Riparian Forests

222.2 Plains and Great Basin Riparian Deciduous Forest

222.21 Cottonwood-Willow Series*

222.211 *Populus sargenti* Association*

222.212 *Populus sargenti-Salix amygdaloides* Association*

222.213 *Populus wislizeni* Association*

222.214 *Populus* spp.-*Salix* spp. Association*

222.215 *Salix exigua* Association*

222.3 Rocky Mountain Riparian Deciduous Forest

222.31 Cottonwood-Willow Series*

222.311 *Populus angustifolia-Salix* spp. Association*

222.32 Mixed Broadleaf Series*

222.321 *Acer negundo-Populus angustifolia*-mixed deciduous Association*

222.322 *Acer grandidentatum* Association*

222.4 Sierran-Cascade Riparian Deciduous Forest

222.41 Cottonwood-Willow Series*

222.411 *Populus trichocarpa-Salix* spp. Association*

222.42 Mixed Broadleaf Series*

222.412 *Acer macrophyllum-Populus trichocarpa-Alnus rhombifolia*-mixed deciduous Association*

223 Warm Temperate Swamp and Riparian Forests

223.1 Southeastern Swamp and Riparian Forest

223.2 Interior Southwestern Riparian Deciduous Forest and Woodland

223.21 Cottonwood-Willow Series*

223.221 *Populus fremonti-Salix* spp. Association*

223.212 *Populus fremonti* Association*

223.213 *Populus wislizeni* Association*

223.214 *Populus acuminata* Association*

223.22 Mixed Broadleaf Series*

223.221 *Platanus wrighti-Fraxinus velutina-Populus fremonti*-mixed deciduous Association*

223.222 *Platanus wrighti* Association*

223.223 *Fraxinus velutina* Association*

223.224 *Alnus oblongifolia* Association*

223.225 *Juglans major* Association*

223.3 Californian Riparian Deciduous Forest and Woodland

223.31 Cottonwood-Willow Series

223.311 *Populus fremonti-Salix* spp. Association*

223.32 Mixed Broadleaf Series

223.321 *Platanus racemosa*-mixed deciduous Association*

223.322 *Alnus rhombifolia* Association*

224 Tropical-Subtropical Swamp, Riparian and Oasis Forests.

224.1 Caribbean Interior Swamp and Riparian Forests

224.2 Caribbean Maritime Swampforest

224.3 Tamaulipan Interior Swamp and Riparian Forests

224.4 Sinaloan Interior Swamp and Riparian Forests

224.41 Mixed Evergreen Series*

224.411 *Ficus* spp.-mixed evergreen and deciduous Association*

224.412 *Taxodium mucronatum* Association*

224.413 *Populus* sp.-mixed evergreen and deciduous Association*

224.42 Palm Series*

224.421 *Sabal uresana* Association*

224.5 Sonoran Riparian and Oasis Forests

224.51 Palm Series*

224.511 *Washingtonia filifera* Association*

224.512 *Washingtonia filifera-Populus fremonti* Association*

224.513 *Washingtonia filifera-Brahea armata* Association*

224.514 *Brahea armata* Association*
224.515 *Phoenix dactylifera-Washingtonia filifera* Association*
224.52 Mesquite Series*
    224.521 *Prosopis juliflora velutina* Association*
    224.522 *Prosopis juliflora velutina*-mixed short tree Association*
224.53 Cottonwood-Willow Series*
    224.531 *Populus fremonti-Salix gooddingi* Association*
    224.532 *Populus fremonti* Association*
    224.533 *Salix gooddingi* Association*
230 Swampscrub Formation
  231 Arctic-Boreal Swampscrubs
    231.1 Polar (High Arctic) Swampscrub
    231.2 Greenlandian Swampscrub
    231.3 Alaskan Swampscrub
    231.4 Canadian Swampscrub
    231.5 Adirondack-Appalachian Alpine and Subalpine Swamp and Riparian Scrub
    231.6 Rocky Mountain Alpine and Subalpine Swamp and Riparian Scrub
    231.61 Willow Series*
      231.611 *Salix bebbiana* Association*
    231.7 Sierran-Cascade Alpine and Subalpine Swamp and Riparian Scrub
    231.71 Willow Series*
      231.711 *Salix* spp. Association*
  232 Cold Temperate Swamp and Riparian Scrubs
    232.1 Northeastern Deciduous Swampscrub
    232.2 Plains and Great Basin Swamp and Riparian Scrub
    232.21 Willow Series*
      232.211 *Salix* spp.-mixed scrub Association*
    232.22 Saltcedar Disclimax Series*
      232.221 *Tamarix chinensis* Association*
    232.3 Rocky Mountain Riparian Scrub
    232.31 Willow-Dogwood Series*
      232.311 *Salix* spp.-mixed deciduous Association*
    232.4 Sierran-Cascade Riparian Scrub
    232.41 Willow Series*
      232.411 *Salix* spp. Association
    232.5 Pacific Coastal (Oregonian) Swamp and Riparian Scrub
  233 Warm Temperate Swamp and Riparian Scrubs
    233.1 Southeastern Mixed Deciduous and Evergreen Swampscrub
    233.2 Interior Southwestern Swamp and Riparian Scrub
    233.21 Mixed Narrowleaf Series*
      233.211 *Cephalanthus occidentalis-Baccharis glutinosa*-mixed scrub Association*
    233.22 Saltcedar Disclimax Series*
      233.221 *Tamarix chinensis*-mixed deciduous Association*
    233.3 Californian Deciduous Swamp and Riparian Scrub
    233.31 Mixed Narrowleaf Series*
      233.311 *Salix lasiolepis* Association*
  234 Tropical-Subtropical Swamp and Riparian Scrub
    234.1 Caribbean Interior Swampscrub
    234.2 Caribbean Maritime Swampscrub
    234.3 Tamaulipan Interior Swampscrub
    234.4 Tamaulipan Maritime Swampscrub
    234.5 Sinaloan Interior Swamp and Riparian Scrub
    234.51 Mixed Evergreen Series*
      234.511 *Vallesia glabra-Baccharis glutinosa-Salix bonplandiana* Association*
    234.6 Sinaloan Maritime Swampscrub
    234.61 Mangrove Series*

      234.611 *Avicennia germinans* Association*
      234.612 *Rhizophora mangle* Association*
  234.7 Sonoran Deciduous Swamp and Riparian Scrub
    234.71 Mixed Scrub Series*
      234.711 *Prosopis pubescens-Prosopis juliflora torreyana-Pluchea sericea* Association*
    234.72 Saltcedar Disclimax Series*
      234.721 *Tamarix chinensis* Association*
      234.722 *Tamarix chinensis*-mixed scrub Association*
240 Marshland Formation
  241 Arctic-Boreal Marshlands
    241.1 Polar (High Arctic) Marshland
    241.2 Greenlandian Marshland
    241.3 Alaskan Maritime (Coastal) Marshland
    241.4 Canadian Interior Marshland
    241.5 Canadian Maritime (Coastal) Marshland
    241.6 Adirondack-Appalachian Alpine and Subalpine Marshland
    241.7 Rocky Mountain Alpine and Subalpine Marshland
    241.71 Rush Series*
      241.711 *Juncus balticus* Association*
    241.72 Manna Grass Series*
      241.721 *Glyceria borealis* Association*
    241.8 Sierran-Cascade Alpine and Subalpine Marshland
    241.81 Rush Series*
      241.811 *Juncus* spp. Association*
  242 Cold Temperate Marshlands
    242.1 Northeastern Interior Marshland
    242.2 Northeastern Maritime (Coastal) Marshland
    242.3 Plains Interior Marshland
    242.31 Rush Series*
      252.311 *Juncus tenuis* Association*
    242.32 Bur-reed Series*
      242.321 *Sparganium angustifolium* Association*
    242.33 Cattail Series*
      242.331 *Typha latifolia* Association*
    242.34 Bulrush Series*
      242.341 *Scirpus validus* Association*
    242.4 Rocky Mountain Montane Marshland
    242.41 Rush Series*
      242.411 *Juncus saximontanus* Association*
    242.5 Great Basin Interior Marshland
    242.51 Rush Series*
      242.511 *Juncus* spp. Association*
    242.52 Saltgrass Series*
      242.521 *Distichlis stricta* Association*
    242.6 Sierran-Cascade Montane Marshland
    242.61 Rush Series*
      242.611 *Juncus* spp. Association*
    242.7 Pacific Coastal (Oregonian) Interior Marshland
    242.8 Pacific Coastal (Oregonian) Maritime Marshland
  243 Warm Temperate Marshlands
    243.1 Southeastern Interior Marshland
    243.2 Southeastern Maritime Marshland
    243.3 Chihuahuan Interior Marshland
    243.31 Saltgrass Series*
      243.311 *Distichlis stricta* Association*
    243.4 Mohavian Interior Marshland
    243.41 Rush Series*
      243.411 *Juncus cooperi* Association*
    243.42 Saltgrass Series*
      243.421 *Distichlis stricta* Association*
    243.5 Madrean Marshland
    243.51 Rush Series*
      243.511 *Juncus mexicanus* Association*

*Examples only.

*Examples only.
**Our incomplete knowledge of these biotic communities precludes presentation of representative fifth (series) and sixth level (association) examples.

*Examples only.
**Our incomplete knowledge of these biotic communities precludes presentation of sixth level (association examples).

APPENDIX A   LITERATURE CITED

ALLEE, W. C., A. E. EMERSON, O. PARK, T. PARK, and K. P. SCHMIDT. 1949. Principles of Animal Ecology. W. B. Saunders Co., Philadelphia.

BAILEY, R. G. 1976. Ecoregions of the United States (map, scale 1:7,500,000). USDA Forest Serv., Intermtn. Region, Ogden, Utah.

_____. 1978. Description of the Ecoregions of the United States. USDA Forest Serv., Intermtn. Region, Ogden, Utah.

BARBOUR, M. G. and J. MAJOR (eds.) 1977. Terrestrial Vegetation of California. John Wiley and Sons, New York.

BILLINGS, W. D. 1973. Tundra grasslands, herblands and shrublands and the role of herbivores. *In* R. H. Kesel (ed.) Grassland Ecology. Louisiana St. Univ. Press, Baton Rouge.

_____ and H. A. MOONEY. 1968. The ecology of arctic and alpine plants. Biol. Rev. 43:481-529.

BRAND, D. B. 1936. Notes to accompany a vegetation map of northwestern Mexico. Univ. New Mexico, Biol. Ser. 4:5-27.

BROWN, D. E. 1973. The Natural Vegetative Communities of Arizona (map, scale 1:500,000). State of Arizona, Ariz. Resources Information System (ARIS), Phoenix.

_____ and C. H. LOWE. 1973. A proposed classification for natural and potential vegetation in the Southwest with particular reference to Arizona. Ariz. Game and Fish Dept., Fed. Aid Proj. Rep. W-53R-22-WP4-J1:1-26.

_____ and _____. 1974a. A digitized computer-compatible classification for natural and potential vegetation in the Southwest with particular reference to Arizona. J. Ariz. Acad. Sci. 9, Suppl. 2:1-11.

_____ and _____. 1974b. The Arizona system for natural and potential vegetation—illustrated summary through the fifth digit for the North American Southwest. J. Ariz. Acad. Sci. 9, Suppl. 3:1-56.

_____ and _____. 1977. Biotic communities of the Southwest. USDA Forest Serv., Rocky Mtn. Forest and Range Exp. Stn., Gen. Tech. Rep. RM-41:map, scale 1:1,000,000.

_____, _____, and C. P. PASE. 1977. A digitized classification system for the natural vegetation of North America with hierarchical summary for world ecosystems. *In* A. Marmelstein (1979) (ed.) Proc. National Symposium on Classification, Inventory, and Analysis of Fish and Wildlife Habitat, Jan. 24-27, 1977, Phoenix, Arizona. USDI Fish and Wildlife Serv., Off. Biol. Sci., Washington, D.C.

_____, _____, and _____. A Digitized Systematic Classification for Ecosystems with an Illustrated Summary of the Vegetation of North America. USDA Forest Service (in press).

BRUNER, W. E. 1931. The vegetation of Oklahoma. Ecol. Monogr. 1:99-188.

BUREAU OF LAND MANAGEMENT. 1978a. Draft Environmental Statement—Proposed livestock grazing program Cerbat/Black Mountain Planning Units. USDI, BLM Arizona State Office, Phoenix.

_____. 1978b. Upper Gila-San Simon Grazing environmental statement draft. USDI, BLM Arizona State Office, Phoenix.

CARR, J. N. 1977. Arizona Game and Fish Department comprehensive five year plan. Ariz. Game and Fish Dept., Fed. Aid Proj. FW-11-R-9, 1:1-12.

CASTETTER, E. F. 1956. The vegetation of New Mexico. New Mexico Q. 26:257-288.

CLEMENTS, F. E., and V. E. SHELFORD. 1939. Bio-ecology. John Wiley and Sons, New York.

COX, B. C., I. N. HEALY, and P. D. MOORE. 1976. Biogeography, an Ecological and Evolutionary Approach. 2nd ed. Blackwell Science Publ., Oxford.

DANSEREAU, P. 1957. Biogeography. Ronald Press, New York.

DARLINGTON, P. J., JR. 1957. Zoogeography. John Wiley and Sons, New York.

DASMANN, R. R. 1972. Towards a system for classifying natural regions of the world and their representation by national parks and reserves. Biol. Conserv. 4:247-255.

DASMANN, R. F. 1974. See I.U.C.N. 1974.

_____. 1976. Biogeographical provinces. Co-Evolution Q. Fall:32-35.

DAUBENMIRE, R. and J. DAUBENMIRE. 1968. Forest vegetation of eastern Washington and northern Idaho. Wash. Agric. Exp. Stn., Tech. Bull. 60:1-104.

DeLAUBENFELS, D. J. 1975. Mapping the world's vegetation. Syracuse Univ. Press., Geogr. Series 4:1-246.

DICE, L. R. 1922. Biotic areas and ecological habitats as units for the statement of animal and plant distribution. Science 55:335-338.

_____. 1939. The Sonoran Biotic Province. Ecology 20:118-129.

_____. 1943. The Biotic Provinces of North America. Univ. Mich. Press, Ann Arbor.

DICK-PEDDIE, W. A. and W. H. MOIR. 1970. Vegetation of the Organ Mountains, New Mexico. Colorado State Univ. Range Sci. Dept., Sci. Ser. 4:1-28.

_____ and J. P. HUBBARD. 1977. Classification of riparian vegetation. In Importance, Preservation and Management of Riparian Habitat: A Symposium. USDA Forest Serv., Rocky Mtn. Forest and Range Exp. Stn., Gen. Tech. Rep. RM-43:85-90.

DYKSTERHUIS, E. J. 1957. The savannah concept and its use. Ecology 38:435-442.

ELLIS, S. L., C. FALLAT, N. REECE and C. RIORDAN. 1977. Guide to land cover and use classification systems employed by Western governmental agencies. USDI Fish and Wildlife Service.

FLORES MATA, G., J. JIMENEZ LOPEZ, X. MADRIGAL SANCHEZ, F. MONCAYO RUIZ, and F. TAKAKI TAKAKI. 1971. Memoria del mapa de tipos de vegetacion de la Republica Mexicana. Secretaria de Recursos Hidráulicos, Subsecretaría de Planeacion, Direccion General Estudios, Dirección de Agrologia, Mexico, D. F. (manual and map, scale 1:2,000,000).

FRANKLIN, J. F. 1977. The biosphere reserve program in the United States. Science 195:262-267.

_____ and C. T. DYRNESS. 1973. Natural Vegetation of Oregon and Washington. USDA Forest Serv., Pac. Northwest Forest and Range Exp. Stn., Gen. Tech. Rep. PNW-8:1-417.

GLINSKI, R. L. 1977. Regeneration and distribution of sycamore and cottonwood trees along Sonoita Creek, Santa Cruz County, Arizona. In Importance, Preservation and Management of Riparian Habitat: A Symposium. USDA Forest Serv., Rocky Mtn. Forest and Range Exper. Stn., Gen. Tech. Rep. RM-43:116-123.

HARSHBERGER, J. W. 1911. Phytogeographic Survey of North America. G. E. Stechert, New York.

HESSE, R., W. C. ALLEE, and K. P. SCHMIDT. 1937. Ecological Animal Geography. John Wiley and Sons, New York.

HUBBARD, J. P. 1977. A biological inventory of the lower Gila River Valley, New Mexico. A report jointly prepared by Bureau of Land Management, Bureau of Reclamation, New Mexico Department of Game and Fish, Soil Conservation Service, U.S. Forest Service.

INTERNATIONAL UNION FOR CONSERVATION OF NATURE AND NATURAL RESOURCES (I.U.C.N.). 1973. A working system for classification of world vegetation. IUCN, Morges, Switzerland, Occas. Pap. 5:1-21.

_____. 1974. Biotic provinces of the world—further development of a system for defining and classifying natural regions for purposes of conservation. IUCN, Morges, Switzerland, Occas. Pap. 9:1-57.

JENSEN, H. A. 1947. A system for classifying vegetation in California. Calif. Fish and Game 33:199-266.

KENDEIGH, S. C. 1954. History and evolution of various concepts of plant and animal communities in North America. Ecology 35:152-171.

_____. 1961. Animal Ecology. Prentice-Hall, Englewood Cliffs, New Jersey.

KUCHLER, A. W. 1964. The potential natural vegetation of the conterminous United States. Amer. Geog. Soc., Spec. Publ. 36:1-116; map, scale 1:3,168,000.

_____. 1977. Natural vegetation of California (map, scale 1:1,000,000). In M. G. Barbour and J. Major (eds.) Terrestrial Vegetation of California. John Wiley and Sons, New York.

LACEY, J. R., P. R. OGDEN and K. E. FOSTER. 1975. Southern Arizona riparian habitat: spatial distribution and analysis. Univ. Arizona, Off. Arid Lands Studies Bull. 8:1-148.

LAYSER, E. F. 1974. Vegetative classification: its application to forestry in Northern Rocky Mountains. J. For. 72:354-357.

LEOPOLD, A. S. 1950. Vegetation zones of Mexico. Ecology 31:507-518.

LeSUEUR, H. 1945. Ecology of the vegetation of Chihuahua, Mexico, north of parallel twenty eight. Univ. Texas Publ. 452:1-92.

LOWE, C. H. 1961. Biotic communities in the sub-Mogollon region of the inland Southwest. J. Ariz. Acad. Sci. 2:40-49.

_____. 1964. Arizona's Natural Environment; Landscapes and Habitats. Univ. Ariz. Press, Tucson.

MORRIS, M. 1935. Natural Vegetation of Colorado (map). In R. E. Gregg (1963), The Ants of Colorado. Univ. Colo. Press, Boulder.

NICHOL, A. A. 1937. The natural vegetation of Arizona. Univ. Ariz. Agric. Exp. Stn., Tech. Bull. 68:181-222, with map.

ODUM, E. P. 1945. The concept of the biome as applied to the distribution of North American birds. Wilson Bull. 57:191-201.

OOSTING, H. J. 1950. The Study of Plant Communities. 2nd ed. W. H. Freeman and Co., San Francisco.

PASE, C. P. and E. F. LAYSER. 1977. Classification of riparian habitat in the Southwest. In Importance, Preservation and Management of Riparian Habitat: A Symposium. USDA Forest Serv., Rocky Mtn. Forest and Range Exper. Stn. Gen. Tech. Rep. RM-43:5-9.

PATTON, D. R. 1978. Runwild—a storage and retrieval system for wildlife habitat information. USDA Forest Serv., Rocky Mtn. Forest and Range Exper. Stn., Gen. Tech. Rep. RM-51:1-8.

PFISTER, R. D., B. L. KOVALCHIK, S. F. ARNO, and R. C. PRESBY. 1977. Forest habitat types of Montana. USDA Forest Serv., Intermtn. Forest and Range Exp. Stn., Gen. Tech. Rep. INT-34:1-174.

PITELKA, F. A. 1941. Distribution of birds in relation to major biotic communities. Amer. Midl. Nat. 25:11-137.

_____. 1943. Review of Dice's "Biotic Provinces of North America." Condor 45:203-204.

RAY, G. C. 1975. A preliminary classification of coastal and marine environments. Internat. Union Conserv. Nature and Natural Resources (IUCN, Morges, Switzerland), Occas. Pap. 14:1-26.

SHANTZ, H. L. and R. ZON. 1924. Natural Vegetation. USDA Atlas of Amer. Agric. Plt. 1, Sec. E (map). Washington, D.C.

SHELFORD, V. E. 1963. The Ecology of North America. Univ. Ill. Press, Urbana.

SHREVE, F. 1917. A map of the vegetation of the United States. Geogr. Rev. 3:119-125.

_____. 1951. Vegetation and Flora of the Sonoran desert. Vol. 1. Vegetation. Carnegie Inst. Wash. Publ. 591:1-192.

SOCIETY OF AMERICAN FORESTERS. 1954. Forest cover types of North America (exclusive of Mexico). Soc. Amer. Foresters, Washington, D.C.

STEENBERGH, W. F. and P. L. WARREN. 1977. Preliminary ecological investigation of natural community status at Organ Pipe Cactus National Monument. USDI Cooperative National Park

Resources Studies Unit, Univ. Ariz., Tech. Rep. No. 3:1-152.

TURNER, D. M. and C. L. COCHRAN, JR. 1975. Wildlife management unit—37B—pilot planning study. Ariz. Game and Fish Dept., Fed. Aid Prog. FW-11-R-8, J-1:1-128.

TURNER, R. M., L. H. APPLEGATE, P. M. BERGTHOLD, S. GALLIZIOLI, and S. C. MARTIN. Range reference areas in Arizona. USDA Forest Serv., Rocky Mtn. Forest and Range Exper. Stn., Gen. Tech. Rep. (in press).

UDVARDY, M.D.F. 1975. A classification of the biogeographical provinces of the world. Internat. Union Conserv. Nature and Natural Resources (IUCN, Morges, Switzerland), Occas. Pap. 18:1-48.

WALLACE, A. R. 1876. The Geographical Distribution of Animals, with a Study of the Relations of Living and Extinct Faunas and as Elucidating the Past Changes of the Earth's Surface. MacMillan and Co., London.

WALTER, H. 1973. Vegetation of the earth in relation to climate and the ecophysiological conditions. Translated from the 2nd German ed. by Joy Wieser. English Univ. Press, London; Springer-Verlag, New York.

WEAVER, J. E. and F. E. CLEMENTS. 1938. Plant ecology. 2nd ed. McGraw-Hill, New York.

WIESLANDER, A. E. 1935. A vegetation map of California. Madroño 3:140-144.

YANG, T. W. 1970. Major chromosome races of *Larrea divaricata* in North America. J. Ariz. Acad. Sci. 6:41-45.

_____ and C. H. LOWE. 1968. Chromosome variation in ecotypes of *Larrea divaricata* in the North American Desert. Madroño 19:161-163.

THE CENTRAL VALLEY RIPARIAN MAPPING PROJECT[1]

Charles W. Nelson and James R. Nelson[2]

Abstract.--The Central Valley Riparian Mapping Project was initiated in 1978 by the California Department of Fish and Game. Maps showing the occurrence of riparian vegetation on the depositional flatland or floor of the Central Valley were compiled from existing aerial photographs (35mm. color slides and high altitude, false-color infrared U-2). Special techniques devised to map from 35mm. color slides are described. Vegetation-types were divided into six riparian categories, two subcategories, and two nonriparian categories. Modifying characters were used to indicate unusual circumstances under which riparian vegetation occurred. These maps provide a record of this diminishing resource on the floor of the Central Valley as it appeared in 1976. This data base will permit the documentation of changes in this important riparian resource in the future.

INTRODUCTION

Project Background

The Central Valley Riparian Mapping Project (CVRMP) was the first attempt by the State of California to map, quantify, and monitor the distribution of riparian resources in the Central Valley. The distribution of riparian vegetation has been described by previous investigators using literature searches, early soil surveys, and personal communications (Conrad et al. 1977; McGill 1975; Roberts et al. 1977; Thompson 1961). Detailed mapping of riparian vegetation on the Sacramento River was recently completed by the California Department of Water Resources (DWR) (1978) and contributed significantly to the information on that riparian system. Work by the USDI Fish and Wildlife Service (FWS) (Cowardin et al. 1977) will provide a complete inventory of riparian vegetation in the Central Valley, but at a smaller scale. The CVRMP provided large-scale maps which record the distribution of riparian vegetation and provide a tool for quantifying the amount of this resource remaining in the Central Valley.

Legislation enacted in 1978 (AB 3147, Fazio) appropriated funding to the Department of Fish and Game (DFG) for a study of the riparian re-source of California's Central Valley up to the upper edge of the digger pine/ blue oak zone (Küchler 1977)--approximately 760-m. (2,500-ft.) elevational level--and the South Lahontan and Colorado Basins of the California Desert. This legislation was intended as a first step toward acquiring the data needed to properly care for this important and diminished resource.

The CVRMP was an element of the DFG's overall riparian study program and was designed to contribute to development of study recommendations for protection of the resource. In addition, the maps provide a record of the resource as it existed in 1976 (the average date of the aerial photographs). From this data base it will be possible to determine change in the riparian resource in the years to come. The maps can also be used to determine and analyze potential impacts of development upon the resource on a day-to-day basis.

The CVRMP was carried out by two mapping teams comprised of graduate and undergraduate students from California State University, Chico, and California State University, Fresno. While other mapping projects have mapped portions of the Valley's riparian resource, this is the only study that provides complete coverage of the entire Valley floor.

Project Objectives and Scope

The CVRMP was intended to provide a baseline assessment of existing riparian vegetation-types through their categorization and mapping. This study documented the extent and distribution of this resource and provided a basis for quantifying existing riparian vegetation (see Katibah, Nedeff, and Dummer 1981). The results of the

[1]Paper presented at the California Riparian Systems Conference. [University of California, Davis, September 17-19, 1981].

[2]Charles W. Nelson is Cartographic Technician/Lecturer in Geography at California State University, Chico. James R. Nelson is a Botanist with the California Energy Commission, Sacramento.

study have been incorporated into the DFG's fish and wildlife planning effort and are being used to direct riparian studies as well as preservation and restoration programs.

METHODS

Aerial photos depicting the Central Valley depositional flatland were used to produce maps of riparian vegetation categories and their spatial distribution. Methods were devised which allowed use of existing aerial photography in an accurate and rapid fashion at the lowest possible cost. A technique was devised to expedite the mapping task using available 35mm. photos. Project team members were trained in the recognition, interpretation, and mapping of riparian vegetation categories.

Imagery

Aerial photography served as the data base for the mapping process. Positive transparencies (35mm. color slides) taken by the DWR over a five-year period (average date 1976) were used as the primary information source for the project. These photos were taken at low altitude (ca. 1,525 m. (5,000 ft.)) and provided coverage for most of the study area. The large scale of this true color (Kodachrome) imagery made interpretation of vegetation-types relatively simple. The 35mm. format was easy to handle during the information transfer process using techniques described below.

For those areas not covered by DWR photography, high altitude, U-2, false-color infrared photography was used. Further coverage was provided by standard panchromatic (black-and-white) 9 x 9-in. photographs.

Interpretation

Interpretation of vegetation categories from aerial photographs was accomplished through careful evaluation of standard image characteristics (i.e., color, pattern, shape, association, size, shadow, and topographic location). A detailed description of the vegetation categorization appears below.

An initial field reconnaissance was conducted to familiarize all team members with the riparian vegetation categories. Discussions were held periodically during the mapping phase to ensure the correct interpretation of unusual photo-signatures and check the accuracy of completed maps. This routine procedure kept all mappers aware of various interpretive and cartographic problems and assured greater accuracy and consistency in the mapping effort. Ground-truth checks were conducted on most maps to further ensure map accuracy.

Data Transfer

The mapping of vegetation over large areas required the development of a system that would allow quick, accurate scale adjustment and adequate illumination of the image onto the base map. For this purpose, a transfer system was devised for the DWR 35mm. color slides.

Information from the 35mm. slides was traced onto mylar or blueline sheet overlays of 1:24,000 USDI Geological Survey (GS) quadrangle maps (quads) through the use of a system which projected the photo-image to the bottom of the map through a glass table. Figure 1 is a schematic diagram of this system. A Kodak Ektographic, high light-intensity slide projector (Model AF-2) with a 3-in. (f:3.5) close-up lens, was used to project the slides. The image was reflected up through the glass tabletop by means of a mirror which was mounted at a 45° angle. Slides were reversed when placed in the projector to allow for the reversal of the reflected image. Scale was adjusted either by moving the mirror toward or away from the projector (major-scale adjustments) or through the use of the projector's focus mechanism (minor-scale adjustments).

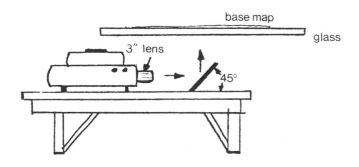

Figure 1.--Schematic of the data-transfer system. The image can be projected at the same scale as the base map, making transfer work accurate and efficient.

Cartographic Representation

Riparian vegetation categories were represented by polygons outlining each vegetation area. Each vegetation category polygon was labelled with a letter or letter/number code. Where vegetation strips were too narrow to outline (such as along a narrow stream or canal), the vegetation was indicated by a single solid line. Letter codes were placed within the polygon boundaries when space permitted. Where space was limited, they were placed outside, with an arrow drawn to the center of the area. Where the vegetation was indicated by a single line, an arrow was drawn from the category symbol to that line. Where more than one vegetation category occurred on a narrow (single-line) strip, a short perpendicular line indicated the boundary. When a single line intercepted a polygon or another single line, a label was placed on each line segment. Figure 2 is an example of the riparian vegetation map product.

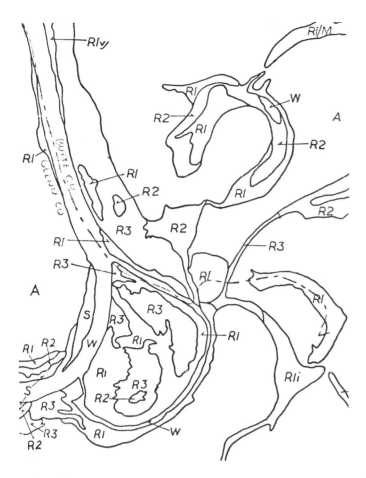

Figure 2.--A sample of the riparian vegetation map product. Scale = 1:24,000.

Mapping Criteria

The following criteria were used as the basis for mapping.

1) Areas with native or "wild" (nonagricultural) riparian vegetation which could be outlined were always mapped.

2) All continuous natural streamcourses associated wholly or in part with riparian vegetation were mapped. Where a natural stream had discontinuous riparian vegetation sections which were separated by short (e.g., 3.2-km. (2-mi.)) sections of vegetation-types not normally mapped, the entire streamcourse was shown.

3) Canals, discontinuous streams, or wet areas which appeared (from the imagery) to be dependent upon an artificial water source and devoid of woody riparian vegetation were not mapped.

4) Agricultural and urban areas were mapped only when they appeared as islands surrounded by riparian vegetation.

MAPPING CATEGORY SYSTEM

The major category system used in the CVRMP was based on structural differences (physiognomy) of vegetation units which could be readily discerned from aerial photography. Vegetation units were divided into six riparian or riparian-associated categories, two subcategories (for minor types occurring as part of major categories), and two nonriparian categories (used where nonriparian lands were surrounded by riparian vegetation). In addition, three modifying characters were used to indicate special circumstances under which riparian vegetation occurs. A "hybrid" system was devised to describe those areas which appear to be a mixture of more than one riparian vegetation category. In such cases, the codes of the two most predominant vegetation categories were indicated.

Riparian Mapping Categories

R1--Large Woody Vegetation

Large woody vegetation refers to the older, well-established riparian forests which are represented by tall (over 12 m.) woody vegetation. In the Central Valley bottomlands these areas are usually dominated by Fremont cottonwood (_Populus fremontii_), black walnut (_Juglans hindsii_), western sycamore (_Platanus racemosa_), Oregon ash (_Fraxinus latifolia_), and willow (_Salix gooddingii_ var. _gooddingii_ and other spp.). Accompanying these species is usually a dense understory of shrubs and vines; wild grape (_Vitis californica_), blackberry (_Rubus_ spp.), and mugwort (_Artemisia douglassiana_) are a few of these species. This vegetation category may cover large areas along broad undisturbed floodplains or very narrow (sometimes discontinuous) strips where human land-use practices have encroached upon the "wild" vegetation.

The R1 category may be discerned in true color aerial photography on the basis of distinct bright green color or mottled color combinations, the evident pattern of tree crowns, relative topographic location, and occasionally by the occurrence of tree shadows. The color of the R1 category is typically much lighter (at times almost yellow-green) than the R1v category (the only other tall-tree category). R1 often shows color or tonal mottling which results from the occurrence of numerous tree and shrub species. The crowns of individual large trees are usually evident when surrounded by different species. However, a dense even stand of large trees (usually tall cottonwoods) may appear homogeneous throughout; in such cases individual tree crowns are less discernible. However, the occurrence of long shadows or a comparison with associated vegetation usually is adequate to accurately identify the signature as R1.

R1v--Valley Oak Woodland

This subcategory of large woody vegetation (R1) refers to the Valley Oak woodland plant community. These are mature stands of well-spaced valley oak (Quercus lobata) without a well-developed woody understory. Valley grassland species dominate the areas between trees. This vegetation category is generally associated with high terrace portions of lower elevation Central Valley rivers.

Valley oak woodland may occur adjacent to other vegetation categories near streams or as discontinuous isolated patches away from streamcourses. Before extensive land clearing, these isolated patches would have been part of larger woodlands associated with the other riparian vegetation categories. Rlv can usually be discerned from R1 and R2 categories (large and low woody vegetation, respectively) on the basis of its dark green color. In addition, rounded, well-separated crowns often can be identified in older stands. As valley oaks are large, stately trees, shadows are also a good indicator.

R2--Low Woody Vegetation

This category represents an early successional stage of riparian forest development. Trees are younger, shorter (up to 12 m.), and may occur with shrub species. Willows and young cottonwoods usually dominate, although brush species occur in some areas.

Interpretation characteristics include nearly consistent coloration, an even photographic texture, and association with other vegetation categories. Low woody vegetation is generally light-green or gray-green in color. It usually appears as a consistently dense, closely spaced stand, although spottiness may occur. As an early successional type, this vegetation category can be expected to occur along sandbars, receding oxbow lakes and sloughs, and in disturbed areas such as canals and levees. It sometimes appears as an intermediate between open water (or sandbars) and the taller riparian forests. Also, it may occur alone, expecially along smaller streams in the lower foothills.

R3--Herbaceous Vegetation (Valley Grasslands)

Valley grasslands includes low (usually less than 1 m.), introduced and native herbaceous species which are mostly annual, although there are some perennial species. Occurrence may be natural (e.g., Valley Grassland plant community or perennially green herbaceous areas along streams) or the result of severe disturbance (constituting an early successional stage).

Two types of riparian-associated herbaceous vegetation were found in the Central Valley. Valley grasslands are treeless, low in stature, and brown during the summer months. In agricultural areas of the Central Valley they are almost exclusively located within a riparian corridor (i.e., uncultivated streamside lands) and may be surrounded by other kinds of riparian vegetation.

The other type of herbaceous riparian vegetation usually occurs along perennial streamcourses on Valley rangeland. It is low in stature, with little or no woody vegetation in evidence, but is green during the summer months, in contrast to the brown of the surrounding rangelands.

R3p--Perennial Seeps

This is a special subcategory of R3 referring to spring areas that are perennially green with herbaceous vegetation. This subcategory is not used for perennially green areas along streams and is differentiated by its patchiness and separation from streamside R3. Artificial seeps, such as those associated with irrigation canals, wells, or windmills, were not included in this subcategory.

M--Marsh

The marsh vegetation category includes intermittent or perennially wet areas with emergent herbaceous vegetation. These areas are characterized by dense stands of tall grass-like plants such as tules (Scirpus spp.), cattail (Typha spp.), sedges (Carex spp.), and rushes (Juncus spp.). These plants are found in, and sometimes interspersed with, continuously moist areas of mud, or standing or sluggishly-moving shallow water. Marsh areas are commonly associated with rivers, streams, lakes, canals, or depressions (sinks).

Marshes can be distinguished on aerial photographs on the basis of color, pattern, location, and association with other vegetation categories. On the photos, marsh appears as a mixed light- or dark-green color. The arrangement of marsh species varies from highly mixed stands (seen as mottled shades of green on the aerial photographs) to homogeneous bands around open pools (which appear as concentric rings around water areas). Marshes are usually found adjacent to or along canals, streams, sinks, and sloughs. They are often found adjacent to willows and herbaceous vegetation. Marsh occurring within channelized streams is often indiscernible. Where marsh occurs with taller mature forests, it is difficult to recognize except in instances where it covers very large areas. Since marsh vegetation was mapped only when it was found among or adjacent to other riparian vegetation categories, not all of the Central Valley marshland was mapped.

S--Sandbars and Gravelbars

Areas of sand and gravel or exposed rock are included in this mapping category. Vegetation is usually limited to very low willows, cottonwoods, and intermittent herbaceous growth undiscernible from the aerial photographs. Usually sandbars and gravelbars occur adjacent to a stream channel. Photographic signatures include white, gray, and brown colors.

W--Open Water

The open water classification includes standing or moving open waterways which are significantly free of vegetation. Sometimes these areas were difficult to interpret (especially where standing water was surrounded by tall, overhanging vegetation), as often this water displays a dull green color, flatness, and a very smooth, even texture, with occasional reflections evident on the aerial photographs. In other situations (particularly with moving water) the color may be darker. Where white areas occur, riffles or rapids may be present. Open water is usually apparent in stream and river channels. In areas where water cannot be seen on the photographs, even though it may be present, it was not mapped. Only water associated with riparian vegetation was mapped. For example, most manmade canals and reservoirs in the Central Valley were not mapped when devoid of significant riparian vegetation.

A--Agriculture

Agricultural lands partially or completely surrounded by riparian vegetation are included in this category. All cultivated and recently cleared lands are included. Agricultural areas which are adjacent to, but not surrounded by, riparian vegetation were not mapped.

U--Urban

The urban category includes those built-up areas which are completely surrounded by riparian vegetation. In practice, this mapping unit was seldom used. Any land cleared of its natural vegetation and put to industrial, commercial, or residential use would fall into this category.

Modifiers

The following modifying codes were used to signify special circumstances under which riparian vegetation might be found.

c--Channelized

This modifier was used where riparian vegetation exists along a watercourse which appears to have been modified by human activity to the point that natural stream contours are no longer visible.

d--Disturbed

Areas of severe man-caused soil disturbance were included within this modifier. Dredger tailings and gravel mining operations are the most common examples. Numerous ponds are found in some of these areas. Ridges of unvegetated gray rock occurring on the more recent sites indicate dredger tailings. At older locations, these ridges may be vegetated with a thin covering of herbaceous growth. Linear strips of R1 or R2 frequently occur between ridges. Most dredger tailings are ilustrated on GS 7.5 minute quads, confirming suspected identifications. Gravel

mining may be identified by the presence of vegetated or unvegetated ponds or pits, especially if they have an unnatural shape.

i--Intermittent

Intermittent was used to designate spottiness or nonconsistent occurrence of a given vegetation category. When used with a single code symbol, or both code symbols of a hybrid notation, the interspaced areas should be interpreted as either S, W, and/or R3.

Category Hybrids

Where any area of vegetation could not be classified clearly as one of the major categories or subcategories, a "hybrid" of two codes was used. This was intended to allow for the most accurate representation of areas which have a mix of vegetation categories occurring in spaces too small to map individually. The hybrid system identified only the two most common vegetation categories, even though other types may be present.

The hybrid code itself consists of codes from the two most prominent categories, separated by a slash. The first of the codes represents the category which, on the basis of general appearance, seems to cover the greatest area. The other portion of the hybrid code covers the second largest portion of the outlined area. For example, an area of 45% R1, 35% R2, and 20% of any other vegetation was labeled R1/R2.

Where modifiers were needed, they were placed at the end of the hybrid code (e.g., R1/R2c indicates a canal which is lined with mixed R1 and R2 vegetation). Where a modifier is used, it refers to both portions of the hybrid symbol (e.g., R1/R2ic would indicate a channelized stream lined with intermittent, mixed woody vegetation).

Table 1 presents a summary of the vegetation codes, their descriptions, and the characteristics by which they were identified on the aerial photographs.

Table 1.—Summary of mapping category codes used in the
CVRMP.

Mapping Category	Description	Signature
R1 Large woody vegetation	Older, well-established riparian forests with tall (< 12 m.) woody vegetation; dense understory usually present.	Bright green or mottled color combinations; pattern of tree crowns evident; lighter color than R1v.
R1v* Valley Oak Woodland	Mature well-spaced stands of valley oaks without understory.	Consistent dark-green coloration; tree crowns may be well separated with grassland understory visible.
R2 Low woody vegetation	Low dense stands of young trees and shrubs.	Smooth texture; light-green or gray-green coloration.
R3 Herbaceous vegetation	Low herbaceous growth occurring along stream channels or in natural clearings among other riparian vegetation categories.	Color ranges from bright-green to brown; appears as consistently treeless texture.
R3p* Perennial seeps	Herbaceous vegetation occurring near perennial springs and seeps.	Green, usually surrounded by brown grasslands; well separated from stream channels.
M Marsh	Herbaceous emergent vegetation on perennially moist areas.	Mottled or consistently colored (as concentric rings) with shades of green and brown; open water sometimes evident.
S Sandbars and gravelbars	Exposed sand, gravel, or rock areas.	Consistently textured areas typically white, gray, or brown; associated with deposited or disturbed areas.
W Open water	Standing or moving waters.	Color varies from green to near black; reflections, riffles, or rapids may appear white when present.
A Agricultural land	Cultivated lands completely or nearly surrounded by riparian vegetation.	Lacking natural vegetation; orchards, rowcrops, irrigation activity often visible.
U Urban land	Built-up areas nearly or completely surrounded by riparian vegetation.	
c** Channelized	Irrigation canals and highly channelized streamcourses no longer having natural stream characteristics.	
d** disturbed	Areas readily identified as having been severely altered by man.	
i** Intermittent	Designates spottiness or inconsistent occurrence of any given vegetation category.	

* Subcategory
** Modifier

LITERATURE CITED

Conrad, S.A., R.L. MacDonald, and R.F. Holland. 1977. Riparian vegetation and flora of the Sacramento Valley. p. 47-55. In: A. Sands (ed.). Riparian forests of California: their ecology and conservation. Institute of Ecology Pub. No. 15. 121 p. University of California, Davis.

Cowardin, L.M., V. Carter, F.C. Golet, and E.T. LaRae. 1977. Classification of wetlands and deep-water habitats of the United States (an operational draft). USDI Fish and Wildlife Service. Unpublished manuscript.

California Department of Water Resources. 1978. Sacramento River Environmental Atlas. California Resources Agency, Sacramento.

Katibah, E.F., N.E. Nedeff, and K.J. Dummer. 1983. Summary of riparian vegetation areal and linear extent measurements from the Central Valley Riparian Mapping Project. In: R.E. Warner and K.M. Hendrix (ed.). California Riparian Systems. [University of California, Davis, September 17-19, 1981]. University of California Press, Berkeley.

Küchler, A.W. 1977. Map of the natural vegetation of California. 1:1,000,000 + 31 p. A.W. Küchler. Department of Geography, University of Kansas, Lawrence.

McGill, R. 1975. Land use changes in the Sacramento River riparian zone, Redding to Colusa. 23 p. Resources Agency, Department of Water Resources, Sacramento, Calif.

Roberts, W.G., J.G. Howe, and J. Major. 1977. A survey of riparian forest flora and fauna in California. p. 3-19. In: A. Sands (ed.). Riparian forests of California: their ecology and conservation. Institute of Ecology Pub. No. 15. 121 p. University of California, Davis.

Thompson, K. 1961. Riparian forests of the Sacramento Valley, California. Annals of the Association of American Geographers 51:294-315.

CURRENT CONDITION OF RIPARIAN RESOURCES
IN THE CENTRAL VALLEY OF CALIFORNIA[1]

Edwin F. Katibah, Kevin J. Dummer, and Nicole E. Nedeff[2]

Abstract.--The riparian resources in California's Central Valley have been greatly reduced and altered in the last 150 years. This paper describes the current condition of the remaining riparian resources in the Central Valley as evaluated with the aid of low-altitude aerial photography. A discussion of several factors influencing riparian resources--grazing, stream channelization, intra-zone and adjacent land uses--is presented. Based on these influences, a qualitative evaluation of the current condition of the remaining riparian resources in the Central Valley is derived.

INTRODUCTION

California is a state of vast area and numerous environments, many of which are unique. Riparian vegetation was never a large resource from an areal standpoint, and yet it is a unique environment within the Central Valley, supporting a great variety of plant and animal life.

Most of the riparian vegetation formerly found in the Central Valley is gone today, a casualty of the great and rapid development of the valley. The small amount of riparian vegetation remaining takes on added significance when compared to the vast pristine forests of 150 years ago.

In the mid-1970s, the decline in the areal extent and quality of riparian vegetation was recognized by private conservation organizations. These organizations prompted the California Legislature to enact AB 3147 (Fazio) in August, 1978. This bill funded investigations into the current state of riparian vegetation and helped provide guidelines for the protection and preservation of this resource. The California Department of Fish and Game (DFG), through its Planning Branch, managed the riparian appropriations.

In 1980 the DFG contracted with the Remote Sensing Research Program, Department of Forestry and Resource Management, University of California, Berkeley, to investigate the condition of the riparian vegetation resource found in the Central Valley and adjacent foothills. The tremendous size of the area to be surveyed precluded conventional ground survey techniques from being the primary data source. The use of an aerial photography-aided approach allowed a substantial amount of data to be gathered with minimal expenditures of time and money.

METHODOLOGY

The project study area comprised the Central Valley of California, including portions of the surrounding foothills, to the approximate upper edge of the blue oak/digger pine zone (Küchler 1977) (fig. 1). It included all or part of 33 counties and covered 825,540 ha. (20,390,750 ac.).

Sample System Design

The sample system used for this study was comprised of two elements: 1) study area stratification; and 2) sample site allocation within study area strata.

Study Area Stratification

The objective of stratification, as used here, was to reduce the variability of the data collected for resource evaluation. In the case of riparian vegetation, stratification was used

---

[1] Paper presented at the California Riparian Systems Conference. [University of California, Davis, September 17-19, 1981].

[2] Edwin F. Katibah is Associate Specialist and Kevin J. Dummer is Staff Research Associate, both are with the Remote Sensing Research Program, Department of Forestry and Resource Management, University of California, Berkeley. Nicole E. Nedeff is a Graduate Student, Department of Geography, University of California, Berkeley and is affiliated with the Remote Sensing Research Program.

Figure 1.--Central Valley study area.

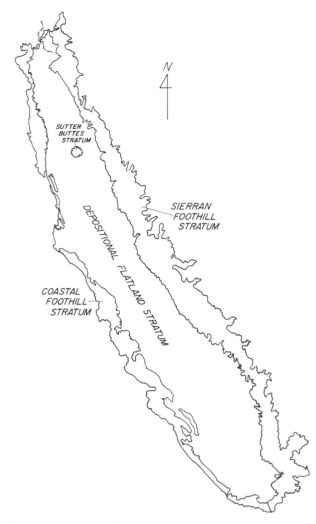

Figure 2.--Location of the major geo-physical strata within the study area.

to segregate the resource into zones (or strata) in which the relationships between samples of vegetation could be meaningfully compared for determining the basic condition of the resource. In order to accomplish this, the study area was stratified by major geo-physical differences, major land uses, and ancillary data pertinent to this investigation.

The geo-physical stratification divided the study area into seven distinct strata:

North Valley Depositional Flatland
North Valley Coastal Foothills
North Valley Sierran Foothills
North Valley Sutter Buttes
South Valley Depositional Flatland
South Valley Coastal Foothills
South Valley Sierran Foothills

The strata were developed from a 1:750,000-scale map of California geology published by the California Division of Mines and Geology. The locations of the geo-physical strata within the study area are shown in figure 2.

The land-use stratification recognized three major land-use practices. These three strata-- agricultural land use (generally irrigated), dry-land agricultural land-use (non-irrigated), and non-agricultural land-use (rangeland, wildland, urban, etc.)--were deemed important to the analysis of the riparian vegetation resource. The land-use strata were derived from the manual interpretation of 1:1,000,000 Landsat color composite imagery of the central California area (Wall et al. 1980).

Finally, a set of riparian vegetation maps (Central Valley Riparian Mapping Project 1979) was used to designate two more strata within the study area: areas mapped for riparian vegetation and areas not mapped for riparian vegetation. Of the 649 1:24,000 USDI Geological Survey (GS) quadrangle maps (quads) needed to cover the study area, 388 were mapped for riparian vegetation.

The final product of these three distinct stratifications yielded 39 unique combinations of geo-physical units, land use, and riparian map-

ping status. These strata were called primary
strata and were the basis for the sample allocation strategy. Figures 3 and 4 show the distribution of two primary strata in the study area:
Depositional Flatland; Agriculture, Mapped; and
Depositional Flatland, Non-agriculture, Mapped.

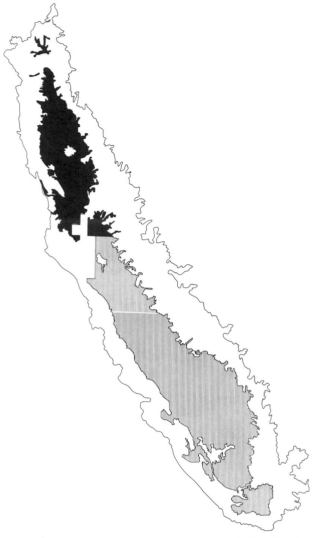

Figure 3.--Distribution of the Depositional Flatland, Agriculture, Mapped primary stratum in
the study area. The north and south valley
portions of this stratum are also identified. Darker shading indicates the north
valley stratum.

Sample-site Allocation

In order to gather information in a systematic and meaningful way, a sampling strategy was
developed. By evaluating the variables that
dictated the number of samples that could be
taken (aircraft availability, project time, available funds, etc.) it was determined that 188
sample sites could be overflown and photographed.

Next, the 188 potential sample-sites were
distributed among the primary strata. First,

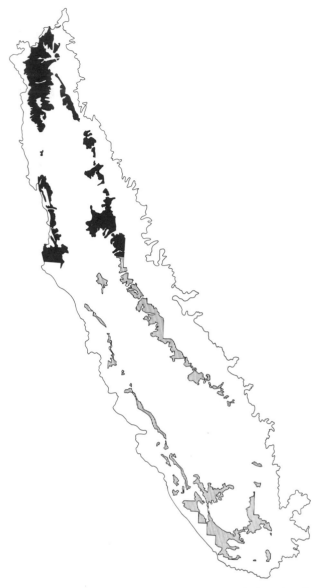

Figure 4.--Distribution of the Depositional Flatland, Non-agriculture, Mapped primary stratum in the study area. The north and south
valley portions of this stratum are also
identified. Darker shading indicates the
north valley stratum.

equal sampling weights were assigned to the north
and south valley strata, allocating 94 samples to
each. Secondly, the individual area for each
primary stratum was determined. Each area was
converted to a percentage of the total area for
the north or south valley strata, as appropriate.
The individual primary strata area percentages
were then multiplied by the total number of
sample sites possible (94 in each case).

Actual location of sample-sites within primary strata was done one of two ways, depending
on whether or not the area had been mapped for
riparian vegetation. For primary strata defined,
in part, by the occurence of riparian vegetation

mapping, samples were allocated as follows. All 1:24,000 quads covering a particular primary stratum were indexed and recorded. In each primary stratum, the set of GS quads was randomly ordered. The sample size value for each primary stratum dictated the number of GS quads selected from the randomly organized map set. Next, a 600-point grid was fitted to each map sheet (corresponding maps with riparian vegetation indicated were used in place of the GS quads). A grid point was randomly selected on each map sheet. If no riparian vegetation occurred under the point selected, the nearest riparian vegetation on the map sheet was selected. This process was continued until all sample sites were located for the primary strata occurring in previously mapped (for riparian vegetation) strata.

For those primary strata not having a previously mapped component, a different sample-site location system had to be employed. The 600-point grid was again fitted to a GS quad from a randomly ordered set, as before. This time the identifiable stream nearest to the randomly selected point was found. This stream was then located on 1:120,000 9- x 9-in., color infrared transparencies (flown by NASA-Ames Research Center in support of the University of California and DWR Irrigated Lands Project). Riparian vegetation and accessibility were quickly evaluated before final selection of the actual sample-sites. Only in a few cases (e.g., where streams were virtually inaccessible), was a potential sample-site rejected. Figure 5 shows the distribution of sample-sites in the study area.

With the sample-site selection completed, a full set of GS quads was compiled with the exact sample sites annotated on each appropriate map. Next, all sample-sites were located and plotted on county road maps. Based on the overall location of the sample-sites with relation to each other, flight plans were developed to facilitate the orderly photographing of each.

Aerial Photography

Camera System

The photographic system was comprised of cameras, camera mount, and supporting equipment. Two Hasselblad ELM (motorized) cameras were used for all photography. Both cameras were fitted with magazines capable of holding 15 ft. of 70mm. aerial film. Different lenses were used on the two cameras: a 100mm. f3.5 Zeiss Planar, fitted with an ultraviolet filter for natural color photography, and a 50mm. f4 Zeiss Distagon, fitted with a red (No. 25) filter for black-and-white infrared photography.

The camera mount was designed to hold the two cameras side-by-side in a vertical position. The mount was fitted with an auxiliary viewfinder etched with markings showing the approximate photo center and calibrated to give the desired overlap necessary for stereo photography. The mount was designed to rotate horizontally and to

Figure 5.--Distribution of sample-sites in the study area.

tip, allowing the photographer to correct for aircraft crab and tilt.

Both cameras were fitted with an intervelometer. The intervelometer was connected to a command unit which allowed the cameras to be triggered simultaneously. The time setting on the intervelometer was calibrated by comparing the firing rate of the cameras with the ground-glass image as seen in the camera mount viewfinder.

Film

Two film types were used for this study: 70mm. Kodak Ektachrome MS, Type 2448; and 70mm. Kodak Infrared Aerographic, Type 2424. The Ektachrome MS was intended to provide the main product used in the photo-interpretation, while the Infrared Aerographic was used primarily as a back-up.

Scale

Initially, a scale of 1:3,500 was used. However, the images produced lacked clear definition due to image motion. To remedy this, the forward speed of the aricraft was slowed and the scale changed to 1:6,000 by raising flight altitude.

The final photographic package used two different focal lengths with the two film/filter combinations. Since airplane altitude above the ground was fixed, two different image scales were acquired for each sample-site. The camera with the Ektachrome MS film, using the 100mm. lens, produced imagery at a nominal scale of 1:6,000. The camera, using the 50mm. lens and black-and-white infrared film, produced imagery at a scale of 1:12,000.

Stereo Imaging

In order to provide an adequate stereo model, a forward overlap of 60% between adjacent image frames was used. Because two different scales were being acquired simultaneously, both could not meet the same forward overlap specifications. Since the 1:6,000 scale natural color photography was intended as the primary interpretation data source, an intervelometer setting was used which gave it the desired forward overlap. The 1:12,000 scale black-and-white infrared photography was acquired at a forward overlap of 80% between adjacent frames.

Photographic Platorm

The platform used for all the photography acquired for this study was a Cessna 185 aircraft, provided by the DFG. The airplane was fitted with a camera port in the floor in which the cameras and mount were installed. Airspeed was kept as slow as practical for all photography, generally about 90 mi. per hour.

Image Characteristics

As mentioned above, the 1:6,000 scale for the natural color photography was chosen partially in an attempt to minimize apparent image motion. At this scale (1:12,000 for the black-and-white infrared), combined with a shutter speed of 1/500 second for each camera, the images were quite sharp and free of any apparent image motion.

Exposures were previously determined by a test flight. Exposures, calibrated to image vegetation properly, were 1/500 second at f5.6/8 for the natural color photography, and 1/500 second at f11 for the black-and-white photography (No. 25 filter).

Photographic Interpretation

The interpretation of the natural color photography was based on standard analysis procedures. Each sample-site was viewed in stereo by an interpreter who verbally noted the presence or absence of specific features and/or attributes of the sample-site. The interpreter's remarks were recorded by a second analyst.

Each sample-site was analyzed for a variety of features and attributes. A hierarchical interpretation system was used which divided the observations around a sample-site into four broad categories: 1) streamcourse, 2) streambank, 3) riparian vegetation, and 4) adjacent land. Within each one of these categories, subcategories were defined.

For recording observations on the streamcourse, the following categories and subcategories were used: artificially-channelized natural streamcourse; artificially-channelized artificial streamcourse; and natural streamcourse, with subcategories of flowing, pooled, rapids, riffles, and ephemeral recognized. For the artificially-channelized streams, stream lining was placed into concrete, dirt, or riprap subcategories. Finally, streamcourse width was measured.

Observations on the streambank were confined to vegetated and non-vegetated categories. Within the vegetated category, plants were recognized by species and placed into life-form groups: trees, shrubs, low herbaceous growth, vines, and grasses. The non-vegetated category was further described by bare rock, bare soil, sand, structures, and burned structures.

The riparian vegetation category was the most complex of all the major interpretation categories. Vegetation was identified by life form (tree, shrub, etc.). For individual tree species the following information was gathered: 1) dominance status, 2) age-class/height, 3) crown density, and 4) vigor. Where structures or other man-related activities occurred within riparian vegetation, detailed observations were recorded within the subcategory of intra-zone land use. Within this subcategory information regarding the status of livestock grazing was also noted.

The final category, adjacent land, provided for detailed recordings of observations regarding specific land-use practices: agriculture, urban, recreation, rangeland, etc. Vegetation was described in a manner similar to the method used in the riparian vegetation category. Grazing occurrence was recorded as well as observations on any fencing which would affect the distribution of cattle in or around the riparian zone.

RESULTS AND DISCUSSION

The data yielded by the photo-interpretation of the sample-sites were analyzed and described for six categories: 1) riparian vegetation, 2) intra-zone land use, 3) adjacent land use, 4) stream channelization, 5) livestock grazing, and 6) qualitative site condition. Each of the six categories was then further subdivided into six specific strata: depositional flatland, coastal foothill, Sierran foothill, agriculture, non-agriculture, and dryland agriculture. The results and discussion presented here are necessarily brief, as the full results would be too detailed to cover in this paper.

Riparian Vegetation

Riparian vegetation at each sample-site was described by a cover-type classification (Holstein 1980), which yielded dominant vegetation for each site. Any species found to be a constituent of the dominant vegetation at a sample-site was called a cover-type component. The percent occurrence of cover-type components as a relative percentage of all cover-type components found in the study area is presented in tables 1 and 2. an example of a cover-type is shown as follows:

Populus fremontii + Acer negundo

Both Populus fremontii and Acer negundo are cover-type components, individually. The cover-type components, determined from the cover-type classification for each sample-site, were aggregated into a list of all cover-type components found in the study area.

This method of analyzing the vegetation data allows a general description of diversity to be made. The non-agricultural strata (table 1) had the highest occurrence of riparian vegetation species. The dryland agricultural strata had the lowest riparian species occurrence, less than half that of the agricultural strata.

Table 1.--Occurrence of cover-type components by relative percentage of the total population of cover-type components within agriculturally-related strata.

	Agriculture	Non-agriculture	Dryland agriculture
North valley	43	79	25
South valley	57	64	14
Study area	61	96	29

Table 2.--Occurrence of cover-type components by relative percentage of the total population of cover-type components within geo-physical strata.

	Depositional flatland	Coastal foothill	Sierran foothill
North valley	65	53	67
South valley	56	35	63
Study area	74	60	81

Comparing geo-physical strata (table 2), the differences in vegetation species occurrence were not as great as in the agriculturally-related strata. Within the coastal foothill strata, the differences were the lowest overall. In the south valley coastal foothill stratum, the vegetation species occurrence was substantially below that of any other comparable stratum. The Sierran foothill strata were found to have greater species occurrence than counterpart depositional flatland strata, but the differences are probably not significant.

Intra-zone Land Use

An issue of critical importance to our understanding of the current condition or status of riparian systems is the degree to which they are being used for man-related purposes. The occurrence of nine major land-use categories was recorded for each sample-site. The categories included: 1) roads; 2) bridges; 3) structures; 4) commercial; 5) parks; 6) dumps; 7) farm related; 8) water related (water impoundment and pumping); and 9) marinas and docks (with attendant subcategories).

Roads, specifically dirt roads, constituted the single largest intra-zone land use, with bridges next. The effect of roads upon riparian systems can be substantial.

Road construction in riparian zones reduces their usefulness as wildlife habitat. Roads in riparian zones: 1) alter vegetative structure, 2) alter microclimate, 3) reduce the size of riparian zones, 4) disturb the wildlife, 5) impact water quality in the aquatic zone, and 6) destroy wildlife habitat. (Thomas et al. undated)

As would be expected, water-related uses of riparian zones were commonly found. Pooling of water in riparian zones was the most common water-related use. The purpose of the pooling ranged from livestock watering to water diversion, water pumping, gravel extraction operations, and non-specific uses. Pooling creates numerous adverse effects on the local riparian environment as well as on environments downstream. Locally, the water table is significantly raised, while it may be substantially lowered downstream. By altering the water table, gross changes can occur in the local environment thereby causing a shift in the species and structure of vegetation of the area. This destroys established wildlife habitat while creating habitat of unforeseeable capacity.

The other specific intra-zone land uses categorized in this study occurred only rarely throughout the study area. This infrequent occurrence may underestimate the potentially harmful environmental effects resulting from these categories (e.g., mining activities, dump sites, feedlots, etc.).

Adjacent Land Use

Areas adjacent to riparian systems were classified according to current land use. These classes were then used to assess potential impacts on riparian systems. Adjacent land-use categories were divided into six major groups: 1) agricultural; 2) residential; 3) commercial; 4) rangeland; 5) wildland; and 6) miscellaneous. Within each one of these groups, specific land uses were identified where practical.

The prevalent adjacent land use found throughout the study area was agriculture. This fact is noteworthy, especially in the so-called non-agricultural portions of the study area. The results indicate a correlation between riparian zones and agriculture, even within areas which overall have little agriculture. From an aesthetic and practical standpoint, riparian areas offer attractive features to agricultural practice; their wooded character in otherwise treeless expanses, the local availability of water, and the general fertility of the floodplain soils all contribute to the attractiveness of these areas.

Within the arid coastal foothills, rangeland was the dominant adjacent land use, while in the Sierran foothills, agricultural and rangeland adjacent land use were nearly equal in occurrence. Within the depositional flatland, agriculture land use dominated.

The other land-use categories occurred far less frequently within the sample-sites. They are nonetheless significant where they occur. For example, urbanization of the riparian zone is a problem wherever there are contiguous centers of population.

Stream Channelization

Channelization of the streamcourse was found to occur in 16.2% of the randomly-chosen sample-sites. This figure may be deceptive since only random sites within the study area were used. Thus, it is expected that a much larger percentage of streams in the survey area are actually channelized. Of the sample streams that were channelized, the overwhelming majority were perennial streams. As expected, channelizaton of streams was most common in the agricultural/ depositional flatland areas. An unexpected finding was in the dryland agriculture area, where a fairly large portion of the streams were channelized (20%). It was found that all dryland agriculture channelized streams occurred in the north valley depositional flatland, and only on perennial streams.

The vast majority of all major streams and rivers in the study area is affected either directly or indirectly by channelization. The location of channelization of a streamcourse yields much information on its potential fluvial effects. Channelization, especially by concrete lining or riprapping, tends to speed up the flow characteristics of the stream, giving the stream a higher potential cutting action on unprotected banks downstream. The increased flow rates also change the ecology of the stream itself, in addition to the apparent direct effects of channelization, for example by confining the streamcourse to predetermined configurations.

Livestock Grazing

Livestock grazing can have a large or small impact on riparian systems, depending on the amount of time livestock spend in a particular area. In many cases, the impacts are large, with the overall riparian area highly disrupted.

From the standpoint of livestock management, riparian zones offer several attractive features. They are usually well vegetated, offering forage for livestock. The tall vegetation provides shade, and is thus commonly used as a loafing area by cattle. Riparian zones also provide needed water for cattle in areas where it may be expensive to provide artificially (such as by pumping from wells).

Uncontrolled, heavy grazing in riparian zones will eventually lead to the total destruction of the riparian vegetation within them. Forage is then lost, shade is gone, and water, now exposed to the sun, evaporates more rapidly.

The sample-site aerial photography was used to determine the presence or absence of grazing on adjacent land and within riparian zones. The occurrence of livestock within each of these categories was determined by direct observation of livestock or by the presence of livestock trails. The occurrence of grazing in areas adjacent to riparian zones was included to give an indication of the number of situations where livestock were excluded from riparian zones. Only randomly-selected sample-sites were used in this portion of the study.

The occurrence of grazing within the riparian zone and on adjacent lands approached 60% for randomly-selected sample-sites. Those sample-sites falling in the agricultural stratum or conversely the depositional flatland stratum had the lowest grazing occurrence. The non-agriculture and dryland-agriculture strata had higher grazing occurrence with the coastal foothill stratum leading the way with 86.4%.

It is interesting to note that the occurrence of grazing in the north valley depositional flatland, agriculture stratum was substantially lower than its counterpart stratum in the south valley. Little can be surmised regarding this phenomenon except that there is probably more livestock grazing occurring in this south valley stratum than in the corresponding stratum in the north valley.

While most instances of grazing occurrence in riparian zones also showed grazing in the land adjacent to the riparian zones, it was observed that occasionally livestock would be grazed only in the riparian zone. This was especially true in the agricultural areas of the north valley. When grazing is allowed only in the riparian zone, it can be expected that the environmental effects of grazing would be accelerated.

Qualitative Site Condition Assessment

Taking into account all of the data gathered, a "qualitative" condition index was determined for each sample-site. Each site was placed into one of five categories: 1) apparently unaltered; 2) good; 3) disturbed; 4) degraded; and 5) severely degraded. An indication of condition trend was also estimated for each site--recovering, stable, degrading, and rapidly degrading. Tables 3 and 4 give an introductory illustration of the situation prevailing in riparian systems within the study area.

Table 3.--Current sample-site condition of riparian systems in the study area.

Apparently unaltered	2.5%
Good	12.4%
Disturbed	24.8%
Degraded	31.6%
Severely degraded	28.6%

Table 4.--Current condition trends in riparian systems for the study area.

Recovering	8.1%
Stable	25.5%
Degrading	37.9%
Severely degrading	28.6%

It is emphasized that this portion of the study was based on interpretation of the results and judgement by the investigators. All indications point to the fact that the riparian systems of the study area are substantially different in character today than they were in the recent past.

The nature of man's activities in the study area are typically insensitive to the ecology of the riparian resource. The maintenance of this resource is considered by many to be necessary for the integrity of the Central Valley by providing benefits both to man and to the environment. As our knowledge of this resource increases, solutions and compromises compatible with both human activity and the needs of riparian ecosystems will be found. Our increased awareness of the nature and direction of the quality of this resource must be applied to finding solutions to today's problems so that viable riparian areas are left for the future.

ACKNOWLEDGMENTS

The authors wish to thank the following individuals and organizations for their valuable contributions to the successful completion of the work reported: Dr. Robert N. Colwell, Principal Investigator, Department of Forestry and Resource Management, University of California, Berkeley; and Mr. John Speth, Planning Branch, DFG, Sacramento. A special recognition is made of Mr. Robert Cote and Mr. Carle Faist, both of the DFG, who provided the aircraft and camera system used in this study. Mr. Paul Lawrence of Genge Aerial Surveys, Sacramento, is also thanked for his help in purchasing and processing the aerial film.

LITERATURE CITED

Central Valley Riparian Mapping Project. 1979. Interpretation and mapping systems. Report prepared by the Riparian Mapping Team, Geography Department, California State University, Chico, in cooperation with the Department of Geography, California State University, Fresno. 24 p. California Department of Fish and Game, Planning Branch. Unpublished manuscript.

Holstein, Glen. 1980. California vegetation cover types. California Natural Diversity Data Base, The Nature Conservancy. Unpublished draft of March, 1980.

Küchler, A.W. 1977. Map of the natural vegetation of California. 1:1,000,000 + 31 p. A.W. Küchler. Department of Geography, University of Kansas, Lawrence.

Thomas, J.W., C. Maser, and J.E. Rodiek. Undated. Wildlife habitats in managed rangelands--the Great Basin of Southeastern Oregon riparian zones. USDA Forest Service GTR-PNW-80.

Wall, S.L., C.E. Brown, K.J. Dummer, T.W. Gossard, R.W. Thomas, R.N. Colwell, J.E. Estes, L. Tinney, and J. Baggett. 1980. Irrigated lands assessment for water management applications pilot test. Final report to NASA-Ames Research Center, Grant No. 2207. 156 p. University of California, Berkeley, and University of California, Santa Barbara, Space Sciences Laboratory, Series 21, Issue 5.

RIPARIAN SYSTEMS: DATA MANAGEMENT PROBLEMS AND

THE ROLE OF THE CALIFORNIA NATURAL DIVERSITY DATA BASE[1]

Deborah B. Jensen[2]

Abstract.--Uncounted and undocumented resources are lost daily by habitat destruction. Inventory systems are urgently needed to assess what natural resources require immediate attention. Management of natural resources data is complex. Using riparian systems as an example, inventorying problems and some solutions are explored in an examination of the California Natural Diversity Data Base.

INTRODUCTION

The worst thing that can happen (in the 1980s)...is not energy depletion, economic collapse, limited nuclear war or conquest by a totalitarian government. As terrible as these catastrophies would be for us, they can be repaired within a few generations. The one process ongoing in the 1980s that will take millions of years to correct is the loss of genetic and species diversity by the destruction of natural habitats. This is the folly our descendants are least likely to forgive us. (Wilson 1980)

Extinction is the usual fate of any species. However, current extinction rates are estimated at between 1,000 and 10,000 species per year and are expected to accelerate. This rate is far greater than the rate of speciation and could result in the loss of one million species within the next 30 years, or a 10 to 20% reduction in the total number of species on earth.

Species disappear when their habitats disappear, and at present habitat destruction is proceeding fastest where most of the world's species reside, in the tropics. But we in the temperate regions are no strangers to land conversion. In neither case is record kept of what is being lost. We are discarding, unexamined, resources of unknown aesthetic and practical value at a cost which has also been undetermined. Although most of the justifications for the indiscriminate exploitation of the world's resources are couched in the terms of economic need, no successful grocery store would tolerate such a poor accounting system. Even if we could, today, take an accounting of what exists, how much there is of each item, and what we are most likely to lose if we don't manage our inventory more carefully, we could not halt habitat destruction and species loss immediately.

HERITAGE PROGRAMS

There are an estimated 5 to 10 million species on earth. They occur in numerous different communities and species aggregations. To ensure the survival of the greatest number of natural communities and the species comprising them, we first need to know which communities and species are in greatest danger of disappearing. But the world with all its species is too large to try to organize in one inventory. It is much easier to work within geographic and political boundaries. Thus, The Nature Conservancy (TNC) has initiated projects known as "Heritage Programs" in 26 of the United States. The California Natural Diversity Data Base (CNDDB) is one such program.

These programs manage information about "elements of natural diversity." Elements of natural diversity are plant or animal species, natural communities, both terrestrial and aquatic, or geological features which occur in the inventory area. Information documenting the status and distribution of certain species and communities is used to identify significant natural areas, to re-evaluate decisions about the relative status of various elements, and to justify claims that particular elements need additional protection. The world-wide programs undertaken by TNC and UNESCO's Biosphere Reserve System also aim to preserve some of the world's natural diversity, although neither currently inventories elements. TNC's International Heritage Program is beginning a data management system which would track the preserves already in

---

[1] Paper presented at the California Riparian Systems Conference. [University of California, Davis, September 17-19, 1981].
[2] Deborah B. Jensen is Plant Ecologist at the California Natural Diversity Data Base, California Department of Fish and Game, Sacramento, Calif.

existence in the world and the elements of natural diversity protected within these preserves. State heritage programs complete this task as only one part of their inventory.

The basic steps in a heritage program like the CNDDB are quite simple (fig. 1). First an element list is made. The CNDDB is inventorying three types of "elements": plants, animals, and natural communities. The plant and animal lists come from floras, faunas, or check lists. The list of community elements is a revision of the "Annotated List of California Habitat Types" (Cheatham and Haller 1975).

Some elements are more endangered than others and therefore need immediate attention. So, the element list is ranked to create a list of critical elements in each of the three categories. There are already state and federal lists of rare and endangered species as well as inventories such as Smith et al. (1980). In addition, many agencies have lists of species of concern. Criteria used to rank species include range in California, total range, total number of occurrences which are protected, uniqueness (taxonomic distinctiveness), and endangerment. Thus, a species or community endemic to California and now rare in the state, occurring only at a few locations, which is also distinctive and found in an area quickly being converted by urban development would have a very high priority rank. Priority ranks indicate in what order information will be collected. Highest priority elements are inventoried first.

HERITAGE PROGRAM INVENTORY METHODS

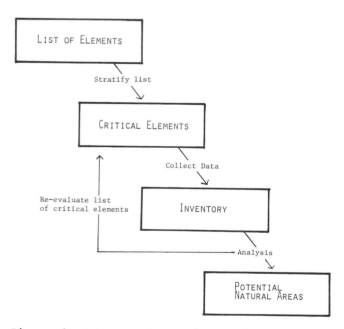

Figure 1.--Flow chart showing heritage program inventory methods. Step 1--list all elements. Step 2--rank the element list. Step 3--collect data. Step 4--analyze the data.

Next, information on locations where these critical elements are found, and their status and condition at these sites is collected. Since work is being done on many elements simultaneously, very little original research on the locations of various elements is being conducted. Rather, all available information is being collected so an up-to-date inventory can be begun. The data are from diverse sources: state and federal agencies, private corporations, and numerous knowledgeable professionals and laypersons.

The information is then analyzed. Knowing where critical elements occur, what their conditions are at each site, and whether or not they are protected makes it possible to draw some conclusions about the status of natural diversity in California. It is possible to analyze what elements are rare and endangered, what elements are rare but protected, and what sites (protected or not) contain the highest numbers of rare and endangered elements. Potential sites for designation as "significant natural area" status and other conservation activities can be identified and the question: "Are the best examples of the highest priority critical elements protected?" can be answered--thereby evaluating the endangerment and protection status of the elements in the system. This is an iterative process. Important natural areas are identified, and some areas protected. Then over time the priority ranks of different elements of diversity can be re-evaluated as the accuracy of inventoried information increases and/or the number of places where this element is protected changes.

Programs such as these can make effective use of limited financial and human resources to objectively identify those species and communities most in need of protection. The CNDDB and other programs like it inventory elements in the belief that by looking at the various species and communities in the state, important sites can be located. This approach should guarantee that the CNDDB does not simply identify pretty places for natural areas, but rather includes representative samples of all facets of California's natural heritage.

THE CNDDB INVENTORY SYSTEM

The CNDDB keeps manual and computerized files on the locations and biology of elements of natural diversity. The locations where an element, such as Valley Oak Riparian Forest, occurs are mapped on USDI Geological Survey 1:24,000 topographic quadrangle maps (quads) and labelled with an index code, a seven digit code which uniquely identifies each element. Plant index codes begin with SP for special plant, animal index codes begin with SA for special animal, and community element codes begin with NC for natural community. From the documents and information the CNDDB receives, a separate record is written for each location of the element in question. These records are referred to as element occurrence records (EOR's) and include element-specific information such as population size, areal extent, associated species, soil-type, and elevation range; as well as site-specific information such as site history, ownership, current management practices, and threats (see fig. 2).

INVENTORYING PROBLEMS

Data management is a byzantine hierarchy of problems. At the bottom is the problem of classification, converting communities into words that the computer can store and manipulate while retaining the essence of the community. Figure 2 is what the computer "thinks" a community looks like. Then there is a problem of too many types of data, and too many of them. Paradoxically, there is also the problem of too few data. Somewhere near the top of the hierarchy is the problem of how to organize the data to make them useful. Using riparian communities to illustrate CNDDB's solutions to some of these problems, we can thread our way through this data management maze.

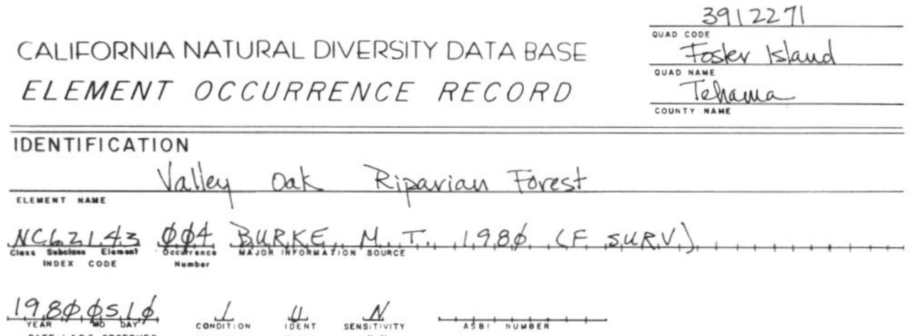
CALIFORNIA NATURAL DIVERSITY DATA BASE
ELEMENT OCCURRENCE RECORD

3912271
QUAD CODE
Foster Island
QUAD NAME
Tehama
COUNTY NAME

IDENTIFICATION
Valley Oak Riparian Forest
ELEMENT NAME
NCG2143 ØØ4 BURKE, M.T. 198Ø (F.SURV.)
INDEX CODE / Occurrence Number / MAJOR INFORMATION SOURCE
198ØØ51Ø J 4 N
DATE LAST OBSERVED / CONDITION 1-2-3-4-5 / IDENT Y-N-U / SENSITIVITY Y-N / ABBI NUMBER

LOCALITY
FOSTER ISLAND, NEAR MOUTH OF RICE CK., RIV MI 211
DIRECTIONS TO EO: LOCALITY & NEAREST LANDMARK

T23N R.Ø2W S.5 M ØØ2 S ØØ167 Y
T-R-S OF CENTROID / FRACTION / MERIDIAN / MARGIN NO. / PRECISION S-M-G / ELEVATION / ASSOC EL

DESCRIPTORS
CTA1.RZ9 QUERCUS LOBATA PCT. HIGH CROWN DENSITY
GENERAL DESCRIPTION: ELEVATION RANGE, STAND TRENDS, SOIL, SLOPE, ASPECT, MICROCLIMATE, ASSOCIATED SPECIES, AREAL EXTENT, DISTURBANCE
OLD GROWTH STAND. INTERGRADES W/ MIXED RIPARIAN FOREST TO S. ON HIGH TERRACE LAND

ADJACENT TO BLM FOSTER ISLAND PRESERVE.
COMMENTS: SITE HISTORY, LAND USE, SURROUNDING LAND USE, THREATS, OWNER AWARENESS

N 621ØØ D Y Y N N
PROTECTION Y-N-U / GENERAL HABITAT / BOUNDARY N-S-D / AREA / OWNER INFO / QUICK FIELD VISIT / INTENSIVE FIELD VISIT / PHOTO
BURSØFØ6 DWR78RØ1 DFG76MØ1
DOCUMENTS

TRANSCRIBER / MAPPER / FINAL QC/DATE / DATA ENTRY/DATE / UPDATE
DATE 8Ø1Ø08 DATE 81Ø6Ø9 KEB Jun.18.81

Additional Information on Reverse
REV 11-80

Figure 2.--Sample of an Element Occurrence Record (EOR), the CNDDB's computer-ready form containing all the textual information to be entered into the computer. (Shown reduced here.)

Classification and Information Sources

When inventorying communities, problems begin with the first step, the element list. There are myriad classification systems in California and throughout the country. Some systems classify only vegetation, some classify "habitat-types," while others have other classificatory paradigms or are hybrids. Classifications of "plant communities" use characteristics of the plant species present to distinguish between different "plant community-types." Criteria such as floristics, physiognomy, and seral stage are important in these classification systems. Other classification schemes categorize "habitat-types" or "natural communities." These are concerned with many more features of the ecosystem, not just vegetation, including climate, soils or substrate, geography and/or water regime.

Confusion results when systems called "vegetation classifications" rely on both vegetative and environmental features to distinguish community-types. This practice obscures the fact that these are not classifications of plant communities alone. The problem is exacerbated by the naming of community-types with plant species' names (often in Latin). Using plants to name community-types is not surprising since vegetation is such a dominant feature of most landscapes. However, it obfuscates the role of other criteria in identifying or naming communities in such systems.

The CNDDB initially used a classification system similar to that of the Society of American Foresters (Eyers 1980) and the Vegetation Type Map Survey (Jensen 1947). In these systems, homogeneous stands are named by the dominant species. Species with the highest relative crown cover are used to name the "cover-type". For example, pure stands of valley oak are Quercus lobata cover-type. Mixed stands where sycamore and cottonwood each comprise 20% or more of the cover, and no other species is as common, are Platanus racemosa - Populus fremontii cover-type.

Rigorous application of the naming criteria in vegetation classification systems results in a large number of different plant community-types. At the CNDDB a list of 2,700 cover-types was compiled in less than a year. It became clear that these well-defined "vegetation-types" were too finely divided to be of use as community elements. Examining the role of communities in a heritage program makes it clear why a larger natural community grouping should be used. In a heritage program, critical communities reveal what types of areas are most endangered. In contrast, critical species provide fine tuning to aid in the determination of which example of a critical community-type would include the greatest number of endangered elements (although at times sites are chosen solely because they harbor a rare plant or animal species). Since the CNDDB has incomplete information about how biological diversity is assorted in nature, the goal is to obtain representative samples of all types of communities. These samples are like black boxes; no one is certain of their exact contents, but most certainly this type of black box and the assortment of species within it was once more common than it is today.

Most other heritage programs use the nomenclature of a plant community classification system, but do not rigorously apply the naming criteria. A number of similar plant associations are lumped together and given the name of the two or three dominant species which are common to all the associations. The CNDDB chose to distinguish between plant communities which refer to only the vegetation and are tracked by cover-types, and "natural communities" which refer to the larger groupings defined by the interactions of vegetation, climate, soils and other abiotic features. As mentioned previously, the natural community list is a revision of Cheatham and Haller (1975). For more complete detail, cover-type information can be included in the description section of the EOR. Cover-types are one of the more important descriptors which enable careful comparison of sites. As knowledge of vegetation increases, and more detailed data become available, the CNDDB will obtain more complete information on the cover-types present at each location of the critical natural communities. Again, the CNDDB is attempting to identify blocks of habitat which are rare and/or endangered. This method makes it possible to inventory for species which occur in these habitats without following each separately or even knowing precisely what they are.

Even after compiling an element list, classification and nomenclatural problems remain to be confronted. Information comes from many sources, and each speaks its own dialect—it all needs to be translated into the CNDDB "dialect." Unfortunately, community names rarely correspond exactly to one another. For example, the CNDDB information on an element called Valley Oak Riparian Forest corresponds closely to the "Rlv category" used in the Central Valley Riparian Mapping Project (1979), but does not neatly fit the "Vl/H category" in the Sacramento River Atlas (California Resources Agency 1978) and has no equivalent in the system in Munz and Keck (1949). When detailed information on community composition is available, the associated plant species dominants at the site are recorded by indicating the cover-type(s) present. Successional stages and bank or soil characteristics are also recorded when possible. These details expedite translation from one nomenclature system to the next, and provide fine filter details for use when comparing two examples of the same natural community-type.

Not only is there a naming problem, but information arrives in many forms and with different levels of detail. CNDDB receives information from published articles, field surveys, aerial photos, vegetation maps, and various types of personal communication. All these must be combined into a single record for each site. Sometimes this seems akin to cleaning the Aegean stables in one night.

To make the task smaller the CNDDB staff decides what information can be left out of the computerized records. Generally information that briefly describes the site, plus locational information and a list of document codes indicating the sources for this information is included. One important question is: Should every location of a special element be entered into the data base? Some elements are so rare that all locations at which they occur should be carefully tracked. Other elements are common, but high quality examples are uncommon (or non-existent). Many natural communities, including riparian forests, fall within this latter category. The CNDDB's first purpose is to compile information which will facilitate identifying natural areas. With this purpose in mind it is not necessary to maintain detailed computerized records on all the riparian communities in the state or even all the riparian communities in the Central Valley. The types of vegetation and their areal extent have been mapped (Central Valley Riparian Mapping Project 1979; Katibah et al. 1980) and are currently housed at the CNDDB. There is no need to duplicate this effort. Rather, information is needed on how many high quality examples remain of each type of Central Valley riparian forest and how many are already managed for habitat protection by some organization. High quality sites should approximate pre-European riparian vegetation and be of an adequate size to harbor wildlife as a self-sustaining unit.

There are many hectares of riparian vegetation which are not suitable for natural areas because a) the parcel is too small; b) the site is highly disturbed, either by physical disruption or by the presence of non-native vegetation; or c) the area could not readily be managed to protect the riparian community. Only high quality sites are included for these elements in the first iteration of the inventory. Information on other sites is kept in manual files. The CNDDB policy is to inventory all locations of the most rare elements and high quality examples of more widely distributed types. In TNC jargon, it preserves "the last of the least and the best of the rest."

Mapping Criteria

Classification and mapping criteria are the features which make it possible to compare different studies documenting changes in vegetation over time and thereby determine the status of riparian communities and the locations of high quality examples. The locations of elements are represented in the computer graphics system by circles which indicate the approximate locations of the species or communities at these sites. Small circles (0.3 km. [0.2 mi.] radius) are used when very accurate locational information is available. Larger circles are used when the location information is more vague and it is not possible to pinpoint the location within 32 ha. (80 ac.).

Although circles are reasonable representations of the location of most species and communities, they are grossly inadequate portrayals of riparian communities which are long and narrow, usually traversing a band on either side of the watercourse. Our mapping criteria for riparian communities is therefore rather different than the criteria for other elements. Element occurrences can be represented in our graphics system by a polygon of any shape or size. The standard size circles are simply a matter of convenience. When there are maps detailing the boundaries of a community, the boundaries are entered as a polygon rather than a circle (fig. 3). Thus most riparian communities can be accurately portrayed. Linear stringers of vegetation, however, cannot easily be represented as polygons since their actual width may be narrower than the scaled width of the lines representing them on the map.

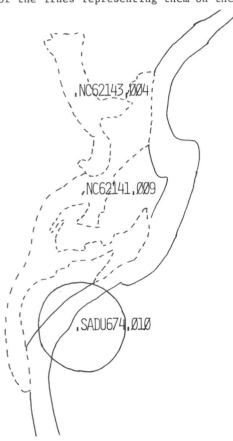

Figure 3.--A computer-generated map of element occurrences. Dotted lines indicate boundaries of the natural communities. The circle indicates an element occurrence of Yellow-billed Cuckoo. The river is also represented with solid lines. (Note: this is for demonstration only; we have no record of Yellow-billed Cuckoos at this site.)

Recognizing this problem, the Central Valley Riparian Mapping Project established mapping criteria which are well-suited to graphic execution and analysis, yet do not sacrifice biological reality. Riparian vegetation mapped on each of the quads was represented by either polygons or lines depending upon the width of the riparian vegetation. Vegetation less than approximately 18 m. (60 ft.) wide on the ground was mapped as a line (Katibah et al. 1980). The CNDDB intends to adopt similar criteria for mapping riparian vegetation in the belief that coordination and standardization of mapping criteria and classification systems among the various groups and individuals active in the area will simplify everyone's tasks and facilitate better-informed decisions about the future of these communities. At present the CNDDB can ignore this problem since no mapping of narrow strings of riparian vegetation is being done--they do not constitute high quality sites in terms of high levels of natural diversity.

Information Gaps

Though differences in nomenclature and study procedures are frustrating and make analysis particularly time consuming, information gaps are the most difficult problem to confront and solve. Basic information on the role of riparian communities in providing wildlife habitat and natural corridors is still being documented. We know that species diversity of vertebrates, especially birds, is extremely high in these communities (Gaines 1977, Hehnke and Stone 1978, Conine et al. 1978). Yet, we are poorly informed on other qualities of this ecosystem. With so few data available it is difficult to make well-informed decisions about what types of riparian systems to preserve, or how to manage a community which changes in quality and position with time as natural meanders of the watercourse modify the streambank. Nor can we adequately evaluate the values of riparian communities to society.

Much of the land surrounding riparian systems in the Central Valley has been converted to agriculture. What is the value of the remaining native vegetation? Some researchers have shown that hedgerows and other parcels of native vegetation have a beneficial effect on the control of crop pests by providing refuges for insect predators (Doutt and Nakata 1973; Alteri et al. 1977). Though it is likely that riparian communities provide an excellent refuge for beneficial insect predators (and their prey), we know little about the role of this native vegetation in providing habitat for these insect species. In an era when pesticide costs climb while their effectiveness decreases, this is not a negligible consideration.

CONCLUSION

Other papers presented at the California Riparian Systems Conference have discussed the extent of riparian vegetation remaining in the Central Valley. Unfortunately, no accurate figures on the historical extent of this community-type in California are available. It is clear, however, that only a fraction of the original area remains intact. An ongoing project to document the rate at which vegetation is being converted is needed. The CNDDB is inventorying high quality examples, but what percentage of the remaining area do these comprise? Such a project is currently being discussed within the Resources Agency. There is now some theory (and rather fewer data) on extinction rates for species in different ecological situations: on islands, in the presence or absence of competitors, etc. The acceleration of species extinction referred to by Wilson and others (e.g., Myers 1979; Soulé and Wilcox 1980) is primarily due to habitat destruction. Destruction of many hectares of habitat guarantees that the entire concert of species which occur there will be eliminated. It is not clear whether species losses will increase linearly in proportion with habitat loss or if there is a non-linear increase in species loss after some point.

Despite our lack of knowledge about riparian and many other communities, we cannot wait to make decisions about how to protect representative samples of our natural heritage. By the time we develop theories to predict how species losses will occur, there will no longer be samples of the communities left in which to test or document the validity of these theories. Coordinated efforts to collect information on endangered resources, and forums such as this to share the information we have collected, must be continued. This documentation must then be used as the impetus to ensure that representative examples of natural communities continue to exist throughout the world, so our descendants can forgive our folly...or at least know what they are missing.

ACKNOWLEDGMENTS

Many of the ideas presented here crystallized during long discussions about data management with colleagues at the CNDDB and in the National Office of TNC. Special thanks are due to Steve Buttrick for late Friday telephone conversations, Jack White for his perspective on natural communities, Patrick Foley and Jan Nachlinger for critical editing of the text and Jan Hunt for patience and typing. All errors and omissions are, of course, my own.

LITERATURE CITED

Alteri, M.A., A. VanSchoonhoven, and J. Doll. 1977. The ecological role of weeds in insect pest management systems: A review illustrated by bean (Phaseolus vulgaris) cropping systems. PNAS 23:195-205.

Central Valley Riparian Mapping Project. 1979. Interpretation and mapping systems. Report prepared by the Riparian Mapping Team, Geography Department, California State University, Chico, in cooperation with the Department of Geography, California State University, Fresno. 24 p. California Department of Fish and Game, Sacramento. Unpublished manuscript.

California Resources Agency. 1978. Sacramento River Environmental Atlas. 12 p. and appendices. Prepared by the Upper Sacramento River Task Force for the California Resources Agency, Sacramento.

Cheatham, N.H., and J.R. Haller. 1975. An annotated list of California habitat types. University of California Natural Land and Water Reserves System, Berkeley. 80 p. Unpublished manuscript.

Conine, K.H., B.W. Anderson, R.D. Ohmart, and J. R. Drake. 1979. Responses of riparian species to agricultural habitat conversion. p. 248-262. In: R.R. Johnson and J.F. McCormick (tech. coord.). Strategies for protection and management of floodplain wetlands and other riparian ecosystems: proceedings of the symposium. [Callaway Gardens, Georgia, December 11-13, 1978]. USDA Forest Service GTR-WO-12. 410 p. Washington, D.C.

Doutt, R.L., and J. Nakata. 1973. The Rubus leafhopper and its egg parasitoid: an endemic biotic system useful in grape management. Environ. Ent. 2:381-386.

Eyers, F.H. (ed.). 1980. Forest cover types of the United States and Canada. 148 p. and map. Society of American Foresters, Washington, D.C.

Gaines, D.A. 1977. The valley riparian forests of California: their importance to bird populations. p. 57-85. In: A. Sands (ed.). Riparian forests in California: their ecology and conservation. Institute of Ecology Pub. No. 15. University of California, Davis. 122 p.

Hehnke, M., and C.P. Stone. 1979. Value of riparian vegetation to avian populations along the Sacramento River system. p. 228-235. In R.R. Johnson and J.F. McCormick (tech. coord.). Strategies for protection and management of floodplain wetlands and other riparian ecosystems: proceedings of the symposium. [Callaway Gardens, Georgia, December 11-13, 1978]. USDA Forest Service GTR-WO-12. 410 p. Washington, D. C.

Holstein, G. 1980. California vegetation cover types. The Nature Conservancy, California Natural Diversity Data Base, Sacramento, California. Unpublished manuscript.

Jensen, H.A. 1947. A system for classifying vegetation in California. California Department of Fish and Game 33(4): 199-266.

Katibah, E.F., N.E. Nedeff, and K.J. Drummer. 1980. The areal and linear extent of riparian vegetation in the Central Valley of California. 151 p. Prepared for the California Resources Agency, Department of Fish and Game, Sacramento, California.

Munz, P.A., and D.D. Keck. 1949. California plant communities. El Aliso 2(1): 87-105.

Myers, N. 1979. The sinking ark. 307 p. Pergamon Press, New York, New York.

Smith, J.P., R.J. Cole, J.O. Sawyer. 1980. Inventory of rare and endangered vascular plants in California (second edition). In collaboration with W.R. Powell. California Native Plant Society Special Pub. No. 1, Berkeley, Calif. 115 p.

Soulé, M.E., and B.A. Wilcox (ed.). 1980. Conservation biology. 395 p. Sinauer Associates, Inc, Sunderland, Massachusetts.

Wilson, E.O. 1980. Critical 80s issue—species loss. Focus (published by the World Wildlife Fund) Vol. 2(2) spring.

THE NATIONWIDE RIVERS INVENTORY[1]

James R. Huddlestun[2]

Abstract.--The Nationwide Rivers Inventory is a data base that identifies the nation's best remaining natural and free-flowing stream resources. Approximately 63,000 mi. (101,400 km.) of rivers have been identified nationwide, of which 3,300 mi. (5,300 km.) on 70 rivers are located in California. This paper discusses the background, purpose, methodology, and applications of the inventory.

INTRODUCTION

The vast reaches of free-flowing rivers that comprised a part of the natural heritage of this nation in its early days have dwindled to a small remnant of streams that retain or even approach their original natural state. The advance of civilization, with its accompanying demands on river resources for agricultural and domestic water supplies, industrial development, and avenues of commerce, has greatly altered most of the nation's rivers.

In 1968, the Wild and Scenic Rivers Act[3] was passed by Congress for the purpose of placing some of the nation's best remaining free-flowing and natural river resources under permanent protection. While a number of rivers have been included in the National Wild and Scenic Rivers System, there has been no systematic approach to such designations. Also, there has been no identification of the universe of streams that could meet the criteria for national designation and no consideration of a balanced representation of streams (i.e., by physiographic divisions, provinces, sections, and stream-types) to comprise the system. Further, states, local governments, and private entities needed to be encouraged to consider river protection actions--federal action certainly is not the optimum or only solution in many instances--and a uniform data base was needed to guide such actions. These needs formed the basis for the Nationwide Rivers Inventory.

BACKGROUND AND PURPOSE

Background

Several years ago, the Heritage Conservation and Recreation Service (HCRS) began formulating a methodology for conducting an inventory of the nation's rivers.[4] The basic authority for conducting such an inventory is contained in Section 5(d) of the National Wild and Scenic Rivers Act, which provides that the Secretaries of the Interior and Agriculture make specific studies and investigations to determine which additional wild, scenic, and recreational river areas shall be evaluated in planning reports by all federal agencies as potential alternative uses of the water and related land resources involved. Additional authority is contained in Section 2(a) of Public Law 88-29,[5] which authorizes the Secretary of the Interior to, among other functions, prepare and maintain a continuing inventory and evaluation of outdoor recreation needs and resources in the United States.

The inventory process was initiated by the three HCRS eastern regions (Philadelphia, Atlanta, and Ann Arbor) and was divided into two phases. The first phase identified, by physiographic sections, those free-flowing and natural river segments which might qualify as wild or scenic rivers. The second phase identified potential recreational rivers. The eastern regions completed their first-phase processes by late 1978; the second-phase work in 1980. The western regions of HCRS (Albuquerque, Denver, San Francisco, and Seattle) initiated their inventories in early 1979 and, as of this writing, are at or

---

[1]Paper presented at the California Riparian Systems Conference. [University of California, Davis, September 17-19, 1981].

[2]James R. Huddlestun is River Program Manager, Division of Planning and Special Studies, Western Region, National Park Service, San Francisco, Calif.

[3]Public Law 90-542, as amended.

---

[4]In February, 1981, the HCRS was abolished by order of the Secretary of the Interior, and most of its functions, including river programs, were merged into the National Park Service. The merger was effected on 31 May 1981. Prior to 1978, HCRS was known as the Bureau of Outdoor Recreation.

[5]Enacted 28 May 1963.

near completion. While the western regions based their inventory processes on the experience gained and methodology developed in the eastern regions, some changes were dictated by the vast lengths of undeveloped streams in the West. Also, the western regions did not conduct a separate recreation rivers inventory. These differences are discussed below.

Purpose

In a broad sense, the Nationwide Rivers Inventory is intended to provide complete, consistent, and persuasive data on the nation's best remaining free-flowing and natural streams. It supplies the administration, Congress, states, local governments, and private interests with background data for their use in making informed decisions on a variety of river-related issues including, but not limited to, preservation, recreation, zoning, water supply, irrigation, hydroelectric power, and flood control. More specifically, the inventory is intended to: 1) provide baseline data on the condition and extent of the nation's free-flowing and natural river resources that can be monitored over time; 2) respond to Congress' mandate in Section 5(d) of the National Wild and Scenic Rivers Act; 3) provide a basis for recommending additional full-study authorizations to Congress and ensuring that the best candidate rivers are ultimately considered for inclusion within the national system by establishing an objective and systematic study nomination process; 4) identify potential water-use conflicts prior to heavy commitments of private or public funds, thus reducing the possibility of costly confrontations such as the Stanislaus River controversy in California and the Tellico Dam project in Tennessee; and 5) assist state, local, and private actions to preserve river resources.

An additional aspect of the inventory was contained in the President's Environmental Message of August 1979. This directive, implemented by the Council of Environmental Quality's "Memorandum for Heads of Agencies," dated 10 August 1980, requested that 1) federal land management agencies assess whether rivers located on their lands and identified in the inventory are suitable for inclusion in the national system and if so, that these agencies take prompt action to protect the rivers—either by preparing the recommendations for their designation or by taking immediate action to protect them; and 2) all federal agencies as part of their normal environmental planning and review processes, take care to avoid, or when necessary mitigate, adverse effects on rivers identified in the inventory.

It is important to understand that this directive does not absolutely prohibit an agency from taking an action which would adversely affect an inventory river. The inventory in itself does not impose or propose any permanent protective action which would preclude water resource development, restrict activities such as timber harvest or mining, or abrogate any existing land ownership and water rights. Instead, the inventory with its accompanying data base on natural stream values is intended to be used by decision-makers in order to ensure that these values receive due consideration in determining highest and best uses of river resources. Decisions as to whether rivers will be preserved or developed remain subject to the political process, compliance with applicable federal and state environmental statutes, and recognition of prior land ownership and water rights.

METHODOLOGY

The rivers inventory methodology described in the following sections is that used by the western regions of HCRS and more specifically, by the former Pacific Southwest Region, which included the states of Arizona, California, Hawaii, and Nevada. The Western Region of the National Park Service essentially covers the same states. The first phase of the inventory process applied only to rivers within Arizona, California, and Nevada. Hawaii rivers were not inventoried until the second phase.

Phase I

The principal objectives of the initial phase of the inventory process were to identify river segments which remained relatively free-flowing and undeveloped and to collect supporting data, including color videotape recordings, on the most outstanding 20% of the river mileage in each HCRS region. The 20% sample was considered the maximum mileage that could be recorded within HCRS budget and resource constraints. The river mileage universe consisted of all rivers and streams 25 mi. (40 km.) or longer. This both reduced the inventoried river mileage to a manageable level and reflected the minimum length stated in the existing "Guidelines for Evaluating Wild, Scenic, and Recreational Rivers under Section 2, Public Law 90-542."

However, there has been considerable opinion in favor of revising these guidelines to allow shorter streams or stream segments to be considered for inclusion in the national system. Also, as a result of the work conducted in the eastern regions' inventories, there was concern that important river segments were being eliminated under the 25 mi. limitation. Therefore, segments of the initially identified rivers as short as 5 mi. (8 km.) were considered in the western regions' inventories, and the eastern regions revised their inventories accordingly.

Another decision made at the onset of the first-phase process was that the rivers would be identified and compared by physiographic sections. Rivers within a given physiographic section tend to have a particular pattern of relief features or landforms which differ significantly from adjacent areas. Such rivers could be compared among themselves to identify the best rivers within a given section. Using physiographic

In the East, the earlier completion of the inventory process has permitted broader experience in practical applications. As examples, several states have utilized the inventory in developing state river systems. A number of Congressional requests have been received for guidance on the potential of certain inventory rivers for national system designation. Also, inventory data has been used by the power industry in developing mitigation packages and avoiding of possible confrontations on potential power sites.

The inventory is not intended to replace past studies or preempt future studies relating to preservation of river systems. Instead, it should be considered an overview that can guide and supplement more specific area studies that may be conducted by public agencies or private organizations. The infusion of any new data and conclusions from such studies will help to ensure that the inventory data base remains viable and useful.

SUMMARY AND CONCLUSIONS

The Nationwide Rivers Inventory is an extensive study that has resulted in the identification of nearly 63,000 mi. (101,400 km.) of the nation's best remaining natural and free-flowing streams that possess significant in-stream values. While these rivers and river segments have the baseline potential for inclusion in the National Wild and Scenic Rivers System, the suitability of such designation is yet to be determined for each river. This is now being accomplished, in part, by federal land-managing agencies, in response to President Carter's 1979 Environmental Message. Realistically, only a small portion of the inventory rivers will ever or should be included in the system. Instead, the inventory will serve as a guide to help ensure that only the best candidate rivers are considered for inclusion. Equally important, the inventory provid-

es an overview to guide state and local governments and private entities in river protection efforts and to ensure that decision-makers at all levels of government consider natural river values in determining the highest and best uses of river resources.

The inventory is not all-inclusive, and it is possible that rivers could be added or removed in the future as new information or changing conditions dictate. Therefore, the exclusion of a particular river from the inventory should not be interpreted to mean that its natural values are not worthy of protection. Also, it is important that the inventory and other present and future related river studies complement rather than compete with each other and that a mutual exchange of information continues. In California, the inventory process attracted considerable participation by all levels of government along with organizations and individuals. This resulted in a significant data base being compiled on the state's 3,300 mi. (5,310 km.) of inventory rivers. The data base is varied, ranging from information on natural river values to information on proposed water projects, conflicts on river use, and attitudes of landowners, local governments, and environmental groups. This data base should be an invaluable asset to present and future California riparian system study and management, and its use is encouraged.

LITERATURE CITED

Küchler, A.W., 1964. Potential natural vegetation of the conterminous United States. Am. Geogr. Soc. Spec. Publ. 36. 116 p. + map.

USDI Heritage Conservation and Recreation Service. 1980. Nationwide rivers inventory, phase 1. 55 p. Prepared by Pacific Southwest Region, USDI Heritage Conservation and Recreation Service, San Francisco, Calif.

sections also allowed identification of various types of rivers throughout the country. Physiographic sections were assigned as closely as possible to regional boundaries. However, if the bulk of one of these sections was within one region, the whole section was assigned to that region regardless of boundaries. In this manner the physiograhic sections were not divided and direct comparisons within a section could be made by one regional staff.

Following are descriptions of each step of the first-phase inventory process in the order of occurrence.

Inventory Filters

Length.--This filter identified all rivers or streams 25 mi. or longer from source to mouth. This was done nationwide by the HCRS Southeast Regional Office, which identified the qualifying rivers on USDI Geological Survey (GS) 1:500,000-scale maps. The maps and lists of rivers were turned over to each region according to assigned physiographic sections. Each regional staff then rechecked the river mileages on GS 1:24,000 and 1:62,500 quadrangle sheets (quads). This filter decreased the study universe to a manageable river mileage (for Arizona, California, and Nevada--30,000 mi. [48,300 km.] on approximately 700 rivers).

Water Resource Development.--This filter was designed to identify those river segments significantly affected by existing impoundments or other channel alterations such as channelization, straightening, dikes, and levees. This determination was based on US Army Corps of Engineers (CE) water resource booklets, USDA Soil Conservation Service (SCS) reports, USDI Bureau of Reclamation reports, state dam and reservoir listings, and GS 1:24,000 and 1:62,500 quads. Segments containing such water resource developments were eliminated from further consideration. Remnant segments between, above, or below developments were retained if they were 5 mi. (8 km.) or longer.

Cultural Development.--This filter served to identify river segments significantly affected by man-made developments other than water resource projects. The area of influence was considered to be 0.25 mi. (0.4 km.) on each side of the river. Cultural developments were plotted on GS quad sheets, scored according to an assigned point system; river segments over 100 points per mile were eliminated. Again, remaining segments over 5 mi. long were retained. The combination of the water resource and cultural development filters reduced the total inventory mileage for Arizona, California, and Nevada to 26,577 mi. (42,780 km.) or 88% of the original inventoried mileage.

Vegetation Map Analysis.--In the western regions, after completing the water and cultural development filters, it became evident that too many rivers were passing these filters to give a

clear indication of which rivers should be selected for further evaluation. This had not been a problem in the East--the water resources and cultural filters had effectively pared the list. For the western regions, an additional evaluation process was needed to cope with the sizeable undeveloped river mileage.

To accomplish this, each river segment that had passed the water and cultural development filters was plotted on 1:500,000 blow-ups of the Küchler (1964) map: Potential Natural Vegetation of the Conterminous United States. An effort was then made to have at least one and preferably two rivers representing each major vegetative zone. Within each vegetative zone, selection favored the longest continuous reaches of free-flowing river with an acceptably low level of cultural development intrusion. Preference was given to those rivers which traversed several vegetative zones--an expression of diversity. Where there were two or three rivers within a vegetative zone which met these criteria, the degree of cultural development intrusion identified became the deciding factor. In this manner, a preliminary first-phase rivers list was developed using positive factors such as representation and diversity. An additional factor in conducting this filtering process was that most intermittent streams were dropped (some regions never included these in the inventory universe) before undertaking the analysis. Also dropped after the cultural development filter were those rivers either included in the national system or under Section 5(a)[6] study for potential addition to the system. Considerable data had been or was being gathered for rivers either in or under study for addition to the system and any further evaluation would have been duplication.

Refinement

At this stage, the preliminary list developed through the four filtering processes was checked with information available through literature search and with existing state-protected river lists. Workshops were held in each state, with key agencies and river interest groups, to explain the process and enlist assistance in completing a mailing list of other public agencies, organizations, and individuals who were knowledgeable about natural river values in their respective areas of geographic interest.

The preliminary list was then circulated to these agencies, groups, and individuals to solicit comments and any nominations for additions to the list, including the reasons for nominations. Allowances were made for nominations of streams

[6] Section 5(a) of the National Wild and Scenic Rivers Act (Public Law 90-542, as amended) lists rivers designated, by Congress, as potential additions to the National System. These rivers are subjected to formal studies to determine their eligibility and suitability for inclusion in the system.

under 25 mi. long and of intermittent streams, provided there were compelling reasons for such additions. After nominations and comments were received from the mail-outs, the preliminary list was completed. For Arizona, California, and Nevada, it consisted of 6,298 mi. (10,140 km.) of streams and stream segments, 21% of the total mileage inventoried.

Videotape Process

Videotape helicopter flights were completed on as much of the preliminary inventory list mileage as the budget would allow. As a general rule, stream segments within national parks and those stream segments easily ground-accessible and/or known to have other photo-coverage were not flown. The rivers were flown from an altitude of 500-700 ft. (150-210 m.) and a 3/4-in. "U-Matic" type videotape format was used. All of the western regions conducted their flights in the summer and early fall of 1979. In the Pacific Southwest Region, approximately 4,950 mi. (7,308 km.) of stream were flown. Of this total, 4,539 mi. (1,383 km.) were selected for the final first-phase list for Arizona, California, and Nevada, comprising 83% of the stream mileage contained on the preliminary inventory list. In California, approximately 2,800 mi. (4,500 km.) on 65 streams were flown with approximately 87% of this mileage included on the list.

Post-flight Analysis

After the videotape flights were completed, all regions conducted some form of further analysis before finalizing their first-phase lists. In the Pacific Southwest Region, the results were reviewed; knowledgeable agencies, organizations, and individuals were consulted on specific rivers; and a proposed first-phase listing of rivers was compiled. This step involved dropping some of the rivers on the preliminary list and adding other river segment candidates. The proposed list, containing 5,433 mi. (8,747 km.) of streams and stream segments—18% of the total inventoried mileage—was then circulated to the mailing list established during the refinement stage for comment. Also, six workshops were conducted throughout the region to discuss the list, solicit comments, demonstrate the videotape product, and explain future phases and uses of the inventory. Upon conclusion of the workshops and receipt of comments on the proposed listing, necessary modifications were made and the final first-phase listing was published in the report "Nationwide Rivers Inventory - Phase I" (USDI Heritage Conservation and Recreation Service 1980) released in March 1980. The other HCRS regions released similar reports. The Pacific Southwest Region's list contained 5,157 mi. (8,303 km.) on 95 rivers and represented 17% of the original inventoried mileage. Of this total, approximately 3,000 mi. (4,830 km.) on 71 rivers were located in California.

The region distributed over 2,000 copies of its report, providing copies to diverse interests

such as water districts, timber companies, consulting firms, county supervisors, chambers of commerce, cattlemen's associations, mining companies, soil conservation districts, members of Congress and state legislatures, governors' offices, and individual property owners. All of these were in addition to the original established mailing list of agencies, organizations, and individuals knowledgeable on river resources.

Phase II

As stated in the Background section of this paper, the eastern regions of HCRS utilized a second-phase process of identifying potential recreational rivers. This was also considered as a possibility for the western regions. However, after the issuance of the President's 1979 Environmental Message and its directives to federal agencies regarding the inventory, HCRS determined that the official Nationwide Rivers Inventory list should contain only those rivers and river segments that could meet the baseline qualifications for the national system (i.e., mostly free-flowing and natural and containing either a singular potential outstandingly remarkable value or a combination of notable stream features). As a result of this determination, the eastern regions re-evaluated their second-phase lists and added only those streams meeting the baseline qualifications to the inventory. The western regions, for their second-phase processes, needed to further identify stream amenities for the rivers on their first-phase lists and to accept nominations for high-value streams that were either overlooked or did not meet the criteria in the first-phase process. This did allow for some of the more outstanding recreational rivers, eliminated by the water resource and cultural filters in the first phase, and other high-value rivers less than 25 mi. in length to be considered for inclusion in the inventory.

In the Pacific Southwest Region, the second-phase process was initiated with the distribution of the Phase I report. Each report contained a franked and return-addressed questionnaire which asked recipients whether or not they would be willing to provide stream values identification information and/or nominations for additional rivers for the inventory. Provision was also made for recipients to indicate if they wished to be retained on the mailing list. In this manner, the mailing list could be screened and potential sources of river value data and nominations could be identifed. Stream amenities identification and river nomination forms were then developed and distributed to the public agencies and organizations or individuals that had volunteered to provide this information. Also, an informational workshop was held in each state to explain the purpose and goals of the second phase.

At this point, the Hawaii component of the inventory was initiated. Since the methodology used for the mainland during the first phase was not suitable for Hawaii (i.e., few streams are 25 mi. in length, and the budget would not permit

videotape coverage), it was decided to explain the process; identify those agencies, groups, and individuals who could provide stream nominations; and obtain background data for researching Hawaiian streams. Nomination forms subsequently were distributed to those parties identifed both at the workshop and through other contacts.

The bulk of the stream amenities identification and river nomination forms were returned over a four-month period. After consideration of this material and regional staff research, it was determined that approximately 1,600 mi. (2,576 km.) of rivers included on the first-phase listing appeared to be sufficiently lacking in significant stream values to be retained on the list. Twenty-seven additional nominations were received for Arizona, California, and Nevada. Of these, 14 rivers or river segments, comprising 414 mi. (667 km.), were considered suitable for addition to the inventory. For California alone, 532 mi. (857 km.) were selected for deletion, 22 nominations were received, and 11 rivers or river segments, totaling 304 mi. (489 km.), were considered suitable for addition. In Hawaii, approximately 40 nominations were received, of which 12 rivers were selected as the proposed component and eight other streams were identified as potential additions or substitutions.

The proposed additions and deletions for the region's component of the inventory were circulated for comment in May 1981. The distribution pattern was similar to that used for the Phase I report with respect to the diversity of agencies, organizations, and individuals receiving copies. The circulation of these proposals represented the last formal step of the inventory process for the region. As of this writing, a considerable number of comments have been received and are being evaluated to determine the completed inventory listing. Although this task has not been completed, it can be estimated that the inventory for Arizona, California, and Nevada will include approximately 85 rivers totaling 4,500 mi. (7,245 km.) or about 14% of the original inventoried mileage. For California, the inventory is expected to include 70 rivers totaling approximately 3,300 mi. (5,313 km.).

This mileage is higher than the total stated for California at the end of the first phase and is due to the January 1981 designation by the Secretary of the Interior of five California rivers as components of the national system. While most of these rivers were included in the first phase of the inventory, approximately 500 mi. (805 km.) found eligible for the system were excluded. Under the designation, most of the inventory-excluded mileage was classified as "recreational," indicating a high degree of cultural development—a reason for exclusion from the first phase. Although components of the national system normally were excluded from the inventory, the current legal challenges to the California designation dictate the retention of these rivers until the issue is resolved. Therefore, the 500 mi. of excluded segments have been added to the inventory list.

In Hawaii, after receipt of comments proposed list, a meeting of federal and agencies and private groups was held to det. the optimum inventory listing. This result 18 streams totaling about 140 mi. (225 km.) selected for the Hawaii component.

INVENTORY APPLICATIONS

Experience has shown that as the exist of the inventory and its associated data l become known, the amount and types of reque for information and assistance increase. particular value are the videotape records t were made of the inventoried streams. These p vide a point of reference from which stream con tions can be monitored over time and provide visual display of the character and features stream corridors. In the Pacific Southwe Region, the entire videotape library has bee duplicated in order to permit loans for short term use or further duplication. To date, user of this service have included the USDA Fores Service, USDI Bureau of Reclamation, Federal High way Administration, State Water Resources Control Board, environmental interests, a consulting firm developing plans for hydroelectric projects, and a Nevada county agency evaluating a proposed park acquisition located along an inventoried river. In addition, the HCRS regional staff has utilized the tapes in two eligibility evaluations for national system designation and in the review of environmental impact statements prepared by other federal agencies.

The inventory data files on natural river values have proven useful for assisting in planning river protective actions, complementing other agency river-related studies, and determining possible impacts that could result from proposed water resource projects and other strea corridor development. Two examples of this us in the Pacific Southwest Region have been a re quest by a consulting firm for information on th natural values of an inventory river being consi ered for hydroelectric development and a reque by the State of Arizona for the available da base on Arizona inventory rivers for use in water-based recreation site survey. In addit to the data on natural stream values, the inv tory files contain information on proposed w resource development. Comments reflecting the attitudes of landowners and political ju dictions involved with the inventory rivers those of environmental groups supporting pr tive action and/or opposing water resource other development projects have also been in ed in inventory files. This information wa plied, during the course of the inventory cess, in the form of responses to comments s ted on the selection of rivers for the inve Such information will be useful in the identification and possible resolution of tial conflicts and in determining the suit and practicality of proposing individual for protective actions.

ENVIRONMENTAL DATA SYSTEM OF THE BUREAU OF RECLAMATION[1]

David E. Busch[2]

Abstract.--The Environmental Data System (EDS) of the USDI Bureau of Reclamation was begun in 1978 as a catalog for environmental conditions along the Colorado River. Currently in use in the Lower Colorado and Lower Missouri regions, EDS provides the capability to record data on a variety of riparian factors based on a river mile geographic location system.

INTRODUCTION

Compared to most land-managing government agencies, the USDI Bureau of Reclamation (BR) holdings are relatively minor. However, due to the nature of its activities there is a concentration of BR-withdrawn and fee-title lands along streams in the western United States. Because of this the BR exerts a measure of control over the destiny of a significant portion of the West's riparian systems of the West.

Background

In response to the environmental legislation of the 1960s and 1970s (e.g., the National Environmental Policy Act, Endangered Species Act, etc.), the BR became involved with a host of environmental compliance procedures. It soon became evident that these procedures were not always handled most efficiently if treated solely on a project-by-project basis. Thus, the BR began looking for means by which tasks could be combined. To date most environmental compliance activities are still handled in a project-specific manner. However, significant progress has been made toward consolidating tasks in the area of environmental data acquisition.

ENVIRONMENTAL DATA SYSTEM

Fundamental Concepts

The result of a number of developments over the intervening years is today's Environmental Data System (EDS). EDS has been most fully developed in the BR Lower Colorado Region for the Colo-

rado River; it is also in use in the Lower Missouri Region for the Platte River system.

EDS is particularly well suited to the Colorado River for a number of reasons.

1. Extensive involvement by government agencies at all levels often makes information exchange difficult. EDS provides an avenue by which certain data regarding riparian or riverine systems may be organized or summarized for inter-agency communication.

2. The BR, in conjunction with several other organizations, is involved with numerous projects along the river. With this ongoing work comes a continuing need for compliance with environmental statutes. In the several subject areas utilized in determining environmental compliance, EDS can provide relatively current data.

3. Because of the above data needs, extensive amounts of data have been and continue to be gathered on Colorado River ecosystems. EDS provides a means of managing data from the numerous studies of the BR and several other agencies.

4. The waters of the Colorado are heavily utilized. Although EDS will not provide a catalog of all appropriations or uses of the river, it does provide a data base for important instream uses by humans for recreation and by the river's biotic communities.

5. Finally, with the realization of the Colorado's importance as a mesic system surrounded by an extensive xeric upland, EDS provides a catalog for information on its sensitive riparian zone. Data from such studies as vegetation-type mapping or wildlife densities may be stored and retrieved with EDS.

System Philosophy

Considerations for specific projects still usually involve site-specific environmental compliance activities. However, comprehensive or

[1] Paper presented at the California Riparian Systems Conference. [University of California, Davis, September 17-19, 1981].
[2] David E. Busch is Biologist with the Bureau of Reclamation, Lower Colorado Region, Boulder City, Nevada.

definitive analyses would have required the system to be of such complexity to be impractical. Rather, this system is designed as a management tool to direct attention to potential impacts or conditions.

The system is not considered a model, as it does not pretend to arrive at a definitive result. Individual judgment exercised by professionals in the environmental sciences is required to evaluate data reported by EDS. Environmental values stored and reported by the system are often an approximation of a more definitive value. EDS is intended to serve as a "flag" to areas that require further specific analysis, but it can be used as a primary data source where a high level of resolution is not required.

Data Grouping

River Miles

Various techniques for storage of data by geographic location were considered, ranging from pinpoint accuracy to summarizing long river stretches into a single value for a given parameter. Traditional coordinate systems failed to adequately or simply describe the linear nature of riparian and aquatic systems. Instead, the river mile system in use for the Colorado River (Pacific Southwest Interagency Committee 1976) was adopted. Fundamentally, milepost numbering under this system starts with zero at the southerly International Boundary with Mexico and continues upriver.

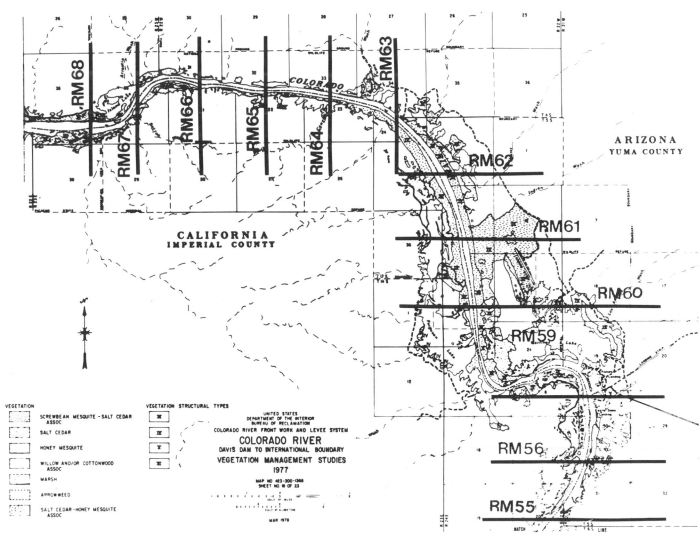

Figure 1.--River mile system used for mapping the Lower Colorado River's riparian vegetation (note combination of mileposts 57-59).

The river mile system works especially well for data tied closely to the aquatic zone (e.g., water quality or recreation). Consideration of subjects such as vegetation-types or cultural resource sites, more closely linked to the riparian zone, is not quite as simple. To handle these, river mile delineations are extended at a rough perpendicular to the river's axis. However, at sharper bends in the river such extended river miles could coincide, causing confusion. This is averted by combining river miles, as is depicted in figure 1 for Colorado River riparian vegetation-type and structure.

River Banks

Differentiation between left and right banks is made by the user visualizing he is facing upstream. On the lower Colorado River this means, of course, that the right bank is in Arizona while the left bank is in California or Nevada.

Summary

One particularly useful capability of EDS is the summary function. This option allows the user to add data over a given stretch to obtain a cumulative view. Thus, if concern is expressed for riparian vegetation adversely affected by a project, an estimate (by type and structure) of the amount of vegetation disturbed (by type and structure) of the amount of vegetation disturbed

may be obtained by milepost and also for the entire project area or convenient subdivision thereof.

Baseline

Because several major studies were scheduled for conclusion that year, 1976 was selected as baseline for the purposes of the EDS data base. Even though original data may actually have been collected in years subsequent to 1976, they are still derived from the year closest to 1976, and therefore still considered baseline information for comparative purposes. Data collected from later studies are used for modification of, or comparison to, the 1976 baseline. Historical information can be entered, as can conditions for the future derived from predictive models, if such data suit the user's purposes.

FUNCTIONAL DESCRIPTION

Data Input

A batch technique (punch-cards) was selected as the input mode for EDS. This method was found to be most reliable, with the consideration that most EDS data are developed by contractors. Problems with specifications for coding schemes were thought to make magnetic tape an unsuitable alternative. Likewise, online update methods were

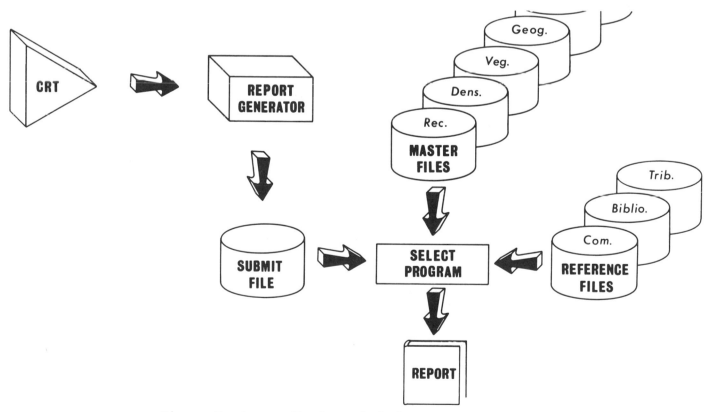

Figure 2.—Output flowchart depicting event sequence for producing an EDS report.

ruled out because of cost, the risk of unintentional alterations to the existing data base, and the difficulty of quality control.

Output/Report Production

The flowchart depicting EDS report production is found in figure 2. As an interactive system EDS is quite easy to access and use from a time-share terminal. Responding to the prompts of the Report Generator Program, the user creates the job control language and parameter records necessary to submit to the select program. This program then selects the data the user has requested from the previously created master file, disposing the appropriate report to a line printer.

Disciplines-Modules

Environmental compliance often requires input from a diverse range of expertise. Data for the EDS reside in one of the following modules, representing some of the various disciplines for which environmental studies are conducted.

1. Technical Modules:
Cultural resources   Fish abundance
Fish habitat   Geographic
Limnology   Recreation
Vegetation   Water quality
Wildlife density

2. Reference Modules:
Bibliography   Comments

Technical modules are designed to provide basic environmental data on a number of parameters within each module. Reference modules make up a data base supplementing or modifying information in the technical modules. The user works with only one technical module at a time, but may supplement a report with data from either of the reference modules.

Within each of these modules, the choice of the factors for which data could be recorded was made after an investigation by the appropriate professionals. Generally, the parameters, and the ranges thereof, are what might be considered "standard" or "accepted." Allowance was made, however, for the incorporation of data from other sources that were readily adaptable to EDS.

Currently, technical modules on-line in the Lower Colorado Region include recreation, vegetation (type and structure), wildlife (avian species) density, and geography. In the Lower Missouri Region, vegetation (community-type) data have been entered on EDS. What follows is a description of the existing data base for the Lower Colorado River and how it relates to the river's riparian zone.

Technical Modules

Vegetation

The vegetation module has much utility for riparian systems study. Some of its potential lies in its possibilities for interfacing with habitat-based biological evaluation methods. Data contained in this module can also be of interest to specialists dealing with aspects of stream hydrology.

Riparian vegetation data are entered on EDS using characteristics prescribed in Anderson and Ohmart (1976). Vegetation is recorded, by bank (left or right) and river mile, in acres. Plant community structural-type, based on foliage height density, may be superimposed on the vegetative community-type code if desired.

Wildlife Density

Data from wildlife surveys, conducted over any given river stretch, may be included on EDS in summary, or on a seasonal basis. Species occurrence may be recorded for specified river reaches. If more detailed studies have been performed, species densities, using number per 100 acres, may also be recorded. A five-season year is available in EDS, primarily to correspond to the avian yearly cycle.

Community- and structure-types (from the vegetation module) may be used to show habitat preference within any river mile(s) for which such data are available. Data for this type of utilization of the species density module were provided for Lower Colorado River avian species by Anderson and Ohmart (1977).

Recreation

Data pertaining to the recreational use of a stream are classed as either land-based or water-based for EDS. Such simplification was deemed necessary because the myriad recreational activities which could occur along a given river stretch defy adequate description by this type of system. Both land and water data are recorded for four seasons (spring, summer, fall, winter). Recreation data are in units of visitor-use days, with six-digit figures allotted for each river mile reach. Data developed for the Lower Colorado Region by Greey et al. (1980) include projections for the future in addition to the 1976 baseline.

Geographic

The geographic module was provided as an interface between the river mile descriptions of EDS and traditional legal descriptions or the Universal Transverse Mercator (UTM) system used in other geographic classifications. For example, a substantial data base on archaeological sites is available by geographic coordinates for the Lower Colorado Region. The geographic module will allow easy conversion of these site locations to

sections also allowed identification of various types of rivers throughout the country. Physiographic sections were assigned as closely as possible to regional boundaries. However, if the bulk of one of these sections was within one region, the whole section was assigned to that region regardless of boundaries. In this manner the physiograhic sections were not divided and direct comparisons within a section could be made by one regional staff.

Following are descriptions of each step of the first-phase inventory process in the order of occurrence.

Inventory Filters

Length.--This filter identified all rivers or streams 25 mi. or longer from source to mouth. This was done nationwide by the HCRS Southeast Regional Office, which identified the qualifying rivers on USDI Geological Survey (GS) 1:500,000-scale maps. The maps and lists of rivers were turned over to each region according to assigned physiographic sections. Each regional staff then rechecked the river mileages on GS 1:24,000 and 1:62,500 quadrangle sheets (quads). This filter decreased the study universe to a manageable river mileage (for Arizona, California, and Nevada--30,000 mi. [48,300 km.] on approximately 700 rivers).

Water Resource Development.--This filter was designed to identify those river segments significantly affected by existing impoundments or other channel alterations such as channelization, straightening, dikes, and levees. This determination was based on US Army Corps of Engineers (CE) water resource booklets, USDA Soil Conservation Service (SCS) reports, USDI Bureau of Reclamation reports, state dam and reservoir listings, and GS 1:24,000 and 1:62,500 quads. Segments containing such water resource developments were eliminated from further consideration. Remnant segments between, above, or below developments were retained if they were 5 mi. (8 km.) or longer.

Cultural Development.--This filter served to identify river segments significantly affected by man-made developments other than water resource projects. The area of influence was considered to be 0.25 mi. (0.4 km.) on each side of the river. Cultural developments were plotted on GS quad sheets, scored according to an assigned point system; river segments over 100 points per mile were eliminated. Again, remaining segments over 5 mi. long were retained. The combination of the water resource and cultural development filters reduced the total inventory mileage for Arizona, California, and Nevada to 26,577 mi. (42,780 km.) or 88% of the original inventoried mileage.

Vegetation Map Analysis.--In the western regions, after completing the water and cultural development filters, it became evident that too many rivers were passing these filters to give a

clear indication of which rivers should be selected for further evaluation. This had not been a problem in the East--the water resources and cultural filters had effectively pared the list. For the western regions, an additional evaluation process was needed to cope with the sizeable undeveloped river mileage.

To accomplish this, each river segment that had passed the water and cultural development filters was plotted on 1:500,000 blow-ups of the Küchler (1964) map: Potential Natural Vegetation of the Conterminous United States. An effort was then made to have at least one and preferably two rivers representing each major vegetative zone. Within each vegetative zone, selection favored the longest continuous reaches of free-flowing river with an acceptably low level of cultural development intrusion. Preference was given to those rivers which traversed several vegetative zones--an expression of diversity. Where there were two or three rivers within a vegetative zone which met these criteria, the degree of cultural development intrusion identified became the deciding factor. In this manner, a preliminary first-phase rivers list was developed using positive factors such as representation and diversity. An additional factor in conducting this filtering process was that most intermittent streams were dropped (some regions never included these in the inventory universe) before undertaking the analysis. Also dropped after the cultural development filter were those rivers either included in the national system or under Section 5(a)[6] study for potential addition to the system. Considerable data had been or was being gathered for rivers either in or under study for addition to the system and any further evaluation would have been duplication.

Refinement

At this stage, the preliminary list developed through the four filtering processes was checked with information available through literature search and with existing state-protected river lists. Workshops were held in each state, with key agencies and river interest groups, to explain the process and enlist assistance in completing a mailing list of other public agencies, organizations, and individuals who were knowledgeable about natural river values in their respective areas of geographic interest.

The preliminary list was then circulated to these agencies, groups, and individuals to solicit comments and any nominations for additions to the list, including the reasons for nominations. Allowances were made for nominations of streams

---

[6]Section 5(a) of the National Wild and Scenic Rivers Act (Public Law 90-542, as amended) lists rivers designated, by Congress, as potential additions to the National System. These rivers are subjected to formal studies to determine their eligibility and suitability for inclusion in the system.

under 25 mi. long and of intermittent streams, provided there were compelling reasons for such additions. After nominations and comments were received from the mail-outs, the preliminary list was completed. For Arizona, California, and Nevada, it consisted of 6,298 mi. (10,140 km.) of streams and stream segments, 21% of the total mileage inventoried.

Videotape Process

Videotape helicopter flights were completed on as much of the preliminary inventory list mileage as the budget would allow. As a general rule, stream segments within national parks and those stream segments easily ground-accessible and/or known to have other photo-coverage were not flown. The rivers were flown from an altitude of 500-700 ft. (150-210 m.) and a 3/4-in. "U-Matic" type videotape format was used. All of the western regions conducted their flights in the summer and early fall of 1979. In the Pacific Southwest Region, approximately 4,950 mi. (7,308 km.) of stream were flown. Of this total, 4,539 mi. (1,383 km.) were selected for the final first-phase list for Arizona, California, and Nevada, comprising 83% of the stream mileage contained on the preliminary inventory list. In California, approximately 2,800 mi. (4,500 km.) on 65 streams were flown with approximately 87% of this mileage included on the list.

Post-flight Analysis

After the videotape flights were completed, all regions conducted some form of further analysis before finalizing their first-phase lists. In the Pacific Southwest Region, the results were reviewed; knowledgeable agencies, organizations, and individuals were consulted on specific rivers; and a proposed first-phase listing of rivers was compiled. This step involved dropping some of the rivers on the preliminary list and adding other river segment candidates. The proposed list, containing 5,433 mi. (8,747 km.) of streams and stream segments—18% of the total inventoried mileage—was then circulated to the mailing list established during the refinement stage for comment. Also, six workshops were conducted throughout the region to discuss the list, solicit comments, demonstrate the videotape product, and explain future phases and uses of the inventory. Upon conclusion of the workshops and receipt of comments on the proposed listing, necessary modifications were made and the final first-phase listing was published in the report "Nationwide Rivers Inventory - Phase I" (USDI Heritage Conservation and Recreation Service 1980) released in March 1980. The other HCRS regions released similar reports. The Pacific Southwest Region's list contained 5,157 mi. (8,303 km.) on 95 rivers and represented 17% of the original inventoried mileage. Of this total, approximately 3,000 mi. (4,830 km.) on 71 rivers were located in California.

The region distributed over 2,000 copies of its report, providing copies to diverse interests such as water districts, timber companies, consulting firms, county supervisors, chambers of commerce, cattlemen's associations, mining companies, soil conservation districts, members of Congress and state legislatures, governors' offices, and individual property owners. All of these were in addition to the original established mailing list of agencies, organizations, and individuals knowledgeable on river resources.

Phase II

As stated in the Background section of this paper, the eastern regions of HCRS utilized a second-phase process of identifying potential recreational rivers. This was also considered as a possibility for the western regions. However, after the issuance of the President's 1979 Environmental Message and its directives to federal agencies regarding the inventory, HCRS determined that the official Nationwide Rivers Inventory list should contain only those rivers and river segments that could meet the baseline qualifications for the national system (i.e., mostly free-flowing and natural and containing either a singular potential outstandingly remarkable value or a combination of notable stream features). As a result of this determination, the eastern regions re-evaluated their second-phase lists and added only those streams meeting the baseline qualifications to the inventory. The western regions, for their second-phase processes, needed to further identify stream amenities for the rivers on their first-phase lists and to accept nominations for high-value streams that were either overlooked or did not meet the criteria in the first-phase process. This did allow for some of the more outstanding recreational rivers, eliminated by the water resource and cultural filters in the first phase, and other high-value rivers less than 25 mi. in length to be considered for inclusion in the inventory.

In the Pacific Southwest Region, the second-phase process was initiated with the distribution of the Phase I report. Each report contained a franked and return-addressed questionnaire which asked recipients whether or not they would be willing to provide stream values identification information and/or nominations for additional rivers for the inventory. Provision was also made for recipients to indicate if they wished to be retained on the mailing list. In this manner, the mailing list could be screened and potential sources of river value data and nominations could be identifed. Stream amenities identification and river nomination forms were then developed and distributed to the public agencies and organizations or individuals that had volunteered to provide this information. Also, an informational workshop was held in each state to explain the purpose and goals of the second phase.

At this point, the Hawaii component of the inventory was initiated. Since the methodology used for the mainland during the first phase was not suitable for Hawaii (i.e., few streams are 25 mi. in length, and the budget would not permit videotape coverage), it was decided to explain the process; identify those agencies, groups, and individuals who could provide stream nominations; and obtain background data for researching Hawaiian streams. Nomination forms subsequently were distributed to those parties identifed both at the workshop and through other contacts.

The bulk of the stream amenities identification and river nomination forms were returned over a four-month period. After consideration of this material and regional staff research, it was determined that approximately 1,600 mi. (2,576 km.) of rivers included on the first-phase listing appeared to be sufficiently lacking in significant stream values to be retained on the list. Twenty-seven additional nominations were received for Arizona, California, and Nevada. Of these, 14 rivers or river segments, comprising 414 mi. (667 km.), were considered suitable for addition to the inventory. For California alone, 532 mi. (857 km.) were selected for deletion, 22 nominations were received, and 11 rivers or river segments, totaling 304 mi. (489 km.), were considered suitable for addition. In Hawaii, approximately 40 nominations were received, of which 12 rivers were selected as the proposed component and eight other streams were identified as potential additions or substitutions.

The proposed additions and deletions for the region's component of the inventory were circulated for comment in May 1981. The distribution pattern was similar to that used for the Phase I report with respect to the diversity of agencies, organizations, and individuals receiving copies. The circulation of these proposals represented the last formal step of the inventory process for the region. As of this writing, a considerable number of comments have been received and are being evaluated to determine the completed inventory listing. Although this task has not been completed, it can be estimated that the inventory for Arizona, California, and Nevada will include approximately 85 rivers totaling 4,500 mi. (7,245 km.) or about 14% of the original inventoried mileage. For California, the inventory is expected to include 70 rivers totaling approximately 3,300 mi. (5,313 km.).

This mileage is higher than the total stated for California at the end of the first phase and is due to the January 1981 designation by the Secretary of the Interior of five California rivers as components of the national system. While most of these rivers were included in the first phase of the inventory, approximately 500 mi. (805 km.) found eligible for the system were excluded. Under the designation, most of the inventory-excluded mileage was classified as "recreational," indicating a high degree of cultural development—a reason for exclusion from the first phase. Although components of the national system normally were excluded from the inventory, the current legal challenges to the California designation dictate the retention of these rivers until the issue is resolved. Therefore, the 500 mi. of excluded segments have been added to the inventory list.

In Hawaii, after receipt of comments on the proposed list, a meeting of federal and state agencies and private groups was held to determine the optimum inventory listing. This resulted in 18 streams totaling about 140 mi. (225 km.) being selected for the Hawaii component.

INVENTORY APPLICATIONS

Experience has shown that as the existence of the inventory and its associated data bank become known, the amount and types of requests for information and assistance increase. Of particular value are the videotape records that were made of the inventoried streams. These provide a point of reference from which stream conditions can be monitored over time and provide a visual display of the character and features of stream corridors. In the Pacific Southwest Region, the entire videotape library has been duplicated in order to permit loans for short-term use or further duplication. To date, users of this service have included the USDA Forest Service, USDI Bureau of Reclamation, Federal Highway Administration, State Water Resources Control Board, environmental interests, a consulting firm developing plans for hydroelectric projects, and a Nevada county agency evaluating a proposed park acquisition located along an inventoried river. In addition, the HCRS regional staff has utilized the tapes in two eligibility evaluations for national system designation and in the review of environmental impact statements prepared by other federal agencies.

The inventory data files on natural river values have proven useful for assisting in planning river protective actions, complementing other agency river-related studies, and determining possible impacts that could result from proposed water resource projects and other stream corridor development. Two examples of this use in the Pacific Southwest Region have been a request by a consulting firm for information on the natural values of an inventory river being considered for hydroelectric development and a request by the State of Arizona for the available data base on Arizona inventory rivers for use in a water-based recreation site survey. In addition to the data on natural stream values, the inventory files contain information on proposed water resource development. Comments reflecting both the attitudes of landowners and political jurisdictions involved with the inventory rivers and those of environmental groups supporting protective action and/or opposing water resource and other development projects have also been included in inventory files. This information was supplied, during the course of the inventory process, in the form of responses to comments solicited on the selection of rivers for the inventory. Such information will be useful in the early identification and possible resolution of potential conflicts and in determining the suitability and practicality of proposing individual rivers for protective actions.

In the East, the earlier completion of the inventory process has permitted broader experience in practical applications. As examples, several states have utilized the inventory in developing state river systems. A number of Congressional requests have been received for guidance on the potential of certain inventory rivers for national system designation. Also, inventory data has been used by the power industry in developing mitigation packages and avoiding of possible confrontations on potential power sites.

The inventory is not intended to replace past studies or preempt future studies relating to preservation of river systems. Instead, it should be considered an overview that can guide and supplement more specific area studies that may be conducted by public agencies or private organizations. The infusion of any new data and conclusions from such studies will help to ensure that the inventory data base remains viable and useful.

SUMMARY AND CONCLUSIONS

The Nationwide Rivers Inventory is an extensive study that has resulted in the identification of nearly 63,000 mi. (101,400 km.) of the nation's best remaining natural and free-flowing streams that possess significant in-stream values. While these rivers and river segments have the baseline potential for inclusion in the National Wild and Scenic Rivers System, the suitability of such designation is yet to be determined for each river. This is now being accomplished, in part, by federal land-managing agencies, in response to President Carter's 1979 Environmental Message. Realistically, only a small portion of the inventory rivers will ever or should be included in the system. Instead, the inventory will serve as a guide to help ensure that only the best candidate rivers are considered for inclusion. Equally important, the inventory provides an overview to guide state and local governments and private entities in river protection efforts and to ensure that decision-makers at all levels of government consider natural river values in determining the highest and best uses of river resources.

The inventory is not all-inclusive, and it is possible that rivers could be added or removed in the future as new information or changing conditions dictate. Therefore, the exclusion of a particular river from the inventory should not be interpreted to mean that its natural values are not worthy of protection. Also, it is important that the inventory and other present and future related river studies complement rather than compete with each other and that a mutual exchange of information continues. In California, the inventory process attracted considerable participation by all levels of government along with organizations and individuals. This resulted in a significant data base being compiled on the state's 3,300 mi. (5,310 km.) of inventory rivers. The data base is varied, ranging from information on natural river values to information on proposed water projects, conflicts on river use, and attitudes of landowners, local governments, and environmental groups. This data base should be an invaluable asset to present and future California riparian system study and management, and its use is encouraged.

LITERATURE CITED

Küchler, A.W., 1964. Potential natural vegetation of the conterminous United States. Am. Geogr. Soc. Spec. Publ. 36. 116 p. + map.

USDI Heritage Conservation and Recreation Service. 1980. Nationwide rivers inventory, phase 1. 55 p. Prepared by Pacific Southwest Region, USDI Heritage Conservation and Recreation Service, San Francisco, Calif.

ENVIRONMENTAL DATA SYSTEM OF THE BUREAU OF RECLAMATION[1]

David E. Busch[2]

Abstract.--The Environmental Data System (EDS) of the USDI Bureau of Reclamation was begun in 1978 as a catalog for environmental conditions along the Colorado River. Currently in use in the Lower Colorado and Lower Missouri regions, EDS provides the capability to record data on a variety of riparian factors based on a river mile geographic location system.

INTRODUCTION

Compared to most land-managing government agencies, the USDI Bureau of Reclamation (BR) holdings are relatively minor. However, due to the nature of its activities there is a concentration of BR-withdrawn and fee-title lands along streams in the western United States. Because of this the BR exerts a measure of control over the destiny of a significant portion of the West's riparian systems of the West.

Background

In response to the environmental legislation of the 1960s and 1970s (e.g., the National Environmental Policy Act, Endangered Species Act, etc.), the BR became involved with a host of environmental compliance procedures. It soon became evident that these procedures were not always handled most efficiently if treated solely on a project-by-project basis. Thus, the BR began looking for means by which tasks could be combined. To date most environmental compliance activities are still handled in a project-specific manner. However, significant progress has been made toward consolidating tasks in the area of environmental data acquisition.

ENVIRONMENTAL DATA SYSTEM

Fundamental Concepts

The result of a number of developments over the intervening years is today's Environmental Data System (EDS). EDS has been most fully developed in the BR Lower Colorado Region for the Colo-

rado River; it is also in use in the Lower Missouri Region for the Platte River system.

EDS is particularly well suited to the Colorado River for a number of reasons.

1. Extensive involvement by government agencies at all levels often makes information exchange difficult. EDS provides an avenue by which certain data regarding riparian or riverine systems may be organized or summarized for interagency communication.

2. The BR, in conjunction with several other organizations, is involved with numerous projects along the river. With this ongoing work comes a continuing need for compliance with environmental statutes. In the several subject areas utilized in determining environmental compliance, EDS can provide relatively current data.

3. Because of the above data needs, extensive amounts of data have been and continue to be gathered on Colorado River ecosystems. EDS provides a means of managing data from the numerous studies of the BR and several other agencies.

4. The waters of the Colorado are heavily utilized. Although EDS will not provide a catalog of all appropriations or uses of the river, it does provide a data base for important instream uses by humans for recreation and by the river's biotic communities.

5. Finally, with the realization of the Colorado's importance as a mesic system surrounded by an extensive xeric upland, EDS provides a catalog for information on its sensitive riparian zone. Data from such studies as vegetation-type mapping or wildlife densities may be stored and retrieved with EDS.

System Philosophy

Considerations for specific projects still usually involve site-specific environmental compliance activities. However, comprehensive or

---

[1]Paper presented at the California Riparian Systems Conference. [University of California, Davis, September 17-19, 1981].

[2]David E. Busch is Biologist with the Bureau of Reclamation, Lower Colorado Region, Boulder City, Nevada.

definitive analyses would have required the system to be of such complexity to be impractical. Rather, this system is designed as a management tool to direct attention to potential impacts or conditions.

The system is not considered a model, as it does not pretend to arrive at a definitive result. Individual judgment exercised by professionals in the environmental sciences is required to evaluate data reported by EDS. Environmental values stored and reported by the system are often an approximation of a more definitive value. EDS is intended to serve as a "flag" to areas that require further specific analysis, but it can be used as a primary data source where a high level of resolution is not required.

Data Grouping

River Miles

Various techniques for storage of data by geographic location were considered, ranging from pinpoint accuracy to summarizing long river stretches into a single value for a given parameter. Traditional coordinate systems failed to adequately or simply describe the linear nature of riparian and aquatic systems. Instead, the river mile system in use for the Colorado River (Pacific Southwest Interagency Committee 1976) was adopted. Fundamentally, milepost numbering under this system starts with zero at the southerly International Boundary with Mexico and continues upriver.

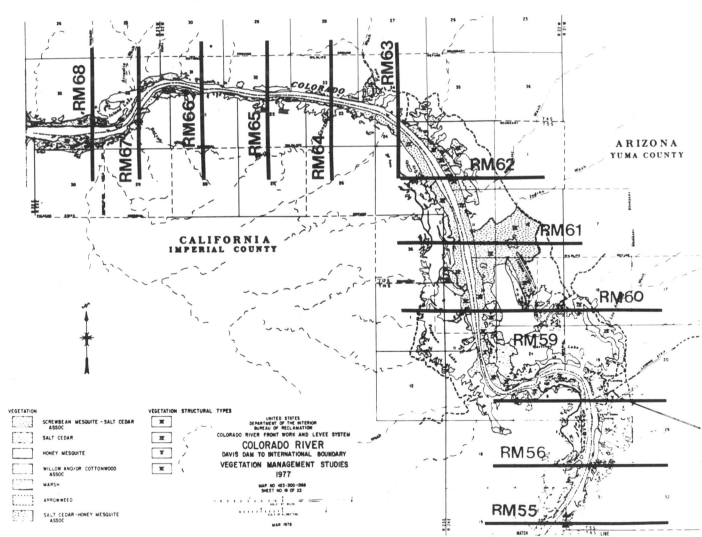

Figure 1.—River mile system used for mapping the Lower Colorado River's riparian vegetation (note combination of mileposts 57-59).

The river mile system works especially well for data tied closely to the aquatic zone (e.g., water quality or recreation). Consideration of subjects such as vegetation-types or cultural resource sites, more closely linked to the riparian zone, is not quite as simple. To handle these, river mile delineations are extended at a rough perpendicular to the river's axis. However, at sharper bends in the river such extended river miles could coincide, causing confusion. This is averted by combining river miles, as is depicted in figure 1 for Colorado River riparian vegetation-type and structure.

River Banks

Differentiation between left and right banks is made by the user visualizing he is facing upstream. On the lower Colorado River this means, of course, that the right bank is in Arizona while the left bank is in California or Nevada.

Summary

One particularly useful capability of EDS is the summary function. This option allows the user to add data over a given stretch to obtain a cumulative view. Thus, if concern is expressed for riparian vegetation adversely affected by a project, an estimate (by type and structure) of the amount of vegetation disturbed (by type and structure) of the amount of vegetation disturbed

may be obtained by milepost and also for the entire project area or convenient subdivision thereof.

Baseline

Because several major studies were scheduled for conclusion that year, 1976 was selected as baseline for the purposes of the EDS data base. Even though original data may actually have been collected in years subsequent to 1976, they are still derived from the year closest to 1976, and therefore still considered baseline information for comparative purposes. Data collected from later studies are used for modification of, or comparison to, the 1976 baseline. Historical information can be entered, as can conditions for the future derived from predictive models, if such data suit the user's purposes.

FUNCTIONAL DESCRIPTION

Data Input

A batch technique (punch-cards) was selected as the input mode for EDS. This method was found to be most reliable, with the consideration that most EDS data are developed by contractors. Problems with specifications for coding schemes were thought to make magnetic tape an unsuitable alternative. Likewise, online update methods were

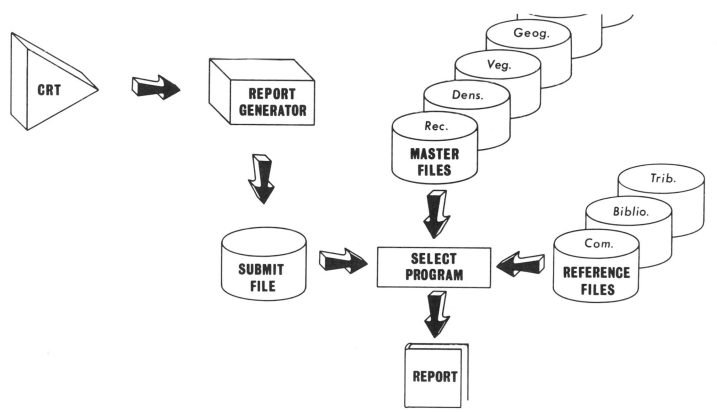

Figure 2.--Output flowchart depicting event sequence for producing an EDS report.

337

ruled out because of cost, the risk of
unintentional alterations to the existing data
base, and the difficulty of quality control.

Output/Report Production

The flowchart depicting EDS report production is found in figure 2. As an interactive
system EDS is quite easy to access and use from a
time-share terminal. Responding to the prompts
of the Report Generator Program, the user creates
the job control language and parameter records
necessary to submit to the select program. This
program then selects the data the user has requested from the previously created master file,
disposing the appropriate report to a line
printer.

Disciplines-Modules

Environmental compliance often requires input from a diverse range of expertise. Data for
the EDS reside in one of the following modules,
representing some of the various disciplines for
which environmental studies are conducted.

    1. Technical Modules:
    Cultural resources   Fish abundance
    Fish habitat   Geographic
    Limnology   Recreation
    Vegetation   Water quality
    Wildlife density

    2. Reference Modules:
    Bibliography   Comments

Technical modules are designed to provide
basic environmental data on a number of parameters within each module. Reference modules
make up a data base supplementing or modifying
information in the technical modules. The user
works with only one technical module at a time,
but may supplement a report with data from either
of the reference modules.

Within each of these modules, the choice of
the factors for which data could be recorded was
made after an investigation by the appropriate
professionals. Generally, the parameters, and
the ranges thereof, are what might be considered
"standard" or "accepted." Allowance was made,
however, for the incorporation of data from other
sources that were readily adaptable to EDS.

Currently, technical modules on-line in the
Lower Colorado Region include recreation, vegetation (type and structure), wildlife (avian species) density, and geography. In the Lower Missouri Region, vegetation (community-type) data
have been entered on EDS. What follows is a
description of the existing data base for the
Lower Colorado River and how it relates to the
river's riparian zone.

Technical Modules

Vegetation

The vegetation module has much utility for
riparian systems study. Some of its potential
lies in its possibilities for interfacing with
habitat-based biological evaluation methods.
Data contained in this module can also be of
interest to specialists dealing with aspects of
stream hydrology.

Riparian vegetation data are entered on EDS
using characteristics prescribed in Anderson and
Ohmart (1976). Vegetation is recorded, by bank
(left or right) and river mile, in acres. Plant
community structural-type, based on foliage
height density, may be superimposed on the vegetative community-type code if desired.

Wildlife Density

Data from wildlife surveys, conducted over
any given river stretch, may be included on EDS
in summary, or on a seasonal basis. Species
occurrence may be recorded for specified river
reaches. If more detailed studies have been performed, species densities, using number per 100
acres, may also be recorded. A five-season year
is available in EDS, primarily to correspond to
the avian yearly cycle.

Community- and structure-types (from the
vegetation module) may be used to show habitat
preference within any river mile(s) for which
such data are available. Data for this type of
utilization of the species density module were
provided for Lower Colorado River avian species
by Anderson and Ohmart (1977).

Recreation

Data pertaining to the recreational use of a
stream are classed as either land-based or water-
based for EDS. Such simplification was deemed
necessary because the myriad recreational activities which could occur along a given river
stretch defy adequate description by this type of
system. Both land and water data are recorded
for four seasons (spring, summer, fall, winter).
Recreation data are in units of visitor-use days,
with six-digit figures allotted for each river
mile reach. Data developed for the Lower Colorado Region by Greey et al. (1980) include
projections for the future in addition to the
1976 baseline.

Geographic

The geographic module was provided as an
interface between the river mile descriptions of
EDS and traditional legal descriptions or the Universal Transverse Mercator (UTM) system used in
other geographic classifications. For example, a
substantial data base on archaeological sites is
available by geographic coordinates for the Lower
Colorado Region. The geographic module will
allow easy conversion of these site locations to

to the river mile system used in most BR project work on the Colorado River.

Reference Modules

Bibliography

This module is designed to provide information on the authors of studies contributing to the data base in any of the other modules. The author's name, the study title, and date are all components of this module. Space is also reserved for government contract number and dates of the contract, if appropriate. The user, if he desires, may generate a bibliography list when in one of the data modules.

Comments

Similar to obtaining a bibliography list, comments pertaining to any of the other modules may be requested. Data contained in this module can be quite variable, and persons inputting data on EDS may use this module to suit their own needs.

EDS APPLICATIONS

In the past year, data from all existing EDS modules have been useful in the preparing several environmental assessments and environmental impact statements. BR hydrologists have referred to vegetative module data to assess transpiration "loss" of water. In addition, biologists from the California Department of Fish and Game have used both vegetation and avian species density information in special status species studies (e.g., Arizona Bell's Vireo) in the Colorado River's riparian zone.

Programmed additions will allow input and use of cultural resources inventory data, as well as data from a number of aquatic disciplines. Updates of existing wildlife species density and vegetation-type and structure modules will soon be possible as BR-contracted biological studies continue.

ACKNOWLEDGMENTS

The author wishes to acknowledge the assistance of Robert Adams of the BR Engineering and Research Center, without whom the Environmental Data System's development would not have been possible.

LITERATURE CITED

Anderson, B.W., and R.D. Ohmart. 1976. Vegetation type maps of the Lower Colordo River from Davis Dam to the southerly International Boundary. USDI Bureau of Reclamation, Boulder City, Nevada.

Anderson, B.W., and R.D. Ohmart. 1977. Wildlife use and densities report of birds and mammals in the Lower Colorado River Valley. 355 p. USDI Bureau of Reclamation, Boulder City, Nevada.

Greey, G.W., G.W. Cheatham, A.C. Jaten, and R.J. Virden. 1977. A comparison of study year data of divisional outdoor recreational use on the Lower Colorado River, 1976-1978. 388 p. USDI Bureau of Reclamation, Boulder City, Nevada.

Pacific Southwest Interagency Committee. 1976. Report of the Water Management Technical Subcommittee--River Mile Index. 70 p. USDI Bureau of Reclamation, Boulder City, Nevada.

SPATIAL VEGETATION UNITS USED WITH A DESCRIPTION METHOD

BASED ON TWO LEVELS OF RESOLUTION

TO PROVIDE THE REQUISITE STRUCTURAL INFORMATION

FOR VEGETATION PRESERVATION[1]

Edward C. Stone, Janet I. Cavallaro
and Laurence P. Stromberg[2]

Abstract.--Riparian system preservation requires information on vegetation structure as well as species composition. To produce sufficiently detailed structural descriptions, we have: (1) defined four new kinds of spatial
vegetation units; and (2) developed a description method
that has the capacity to produce a high resolution description using these spatial units which are not mapped but are
used in conjunction with aerial photos.

INTRODUCTION

Vegetation descriptions are fundamental to
the preservation of riparian systems. A description of the present vegetation provides baseline
data for evaluating the status of the resource
and making management decisions; and if the
vegetation has been described in the past, the
differences between earlier and present descriptions portray the changes that have occurred. A
description of the target vegetation specifies
the characteristics of the vegetation that are to
be maintained in the future following whatever
restoration may be required.

Not all descriptions, however, meet the
needs of those responsible for maintaining or
recreating a particular vegetation. Vegetation
managers require information on vegetation structure (Fosberg 1961)[3] as well as on species
composition because two vegetations, or vegetation units, with the same species composition
differ if the arrangement or distribution of the
plants in three-dimensional space differs. This
is analogous to the case where two chemical
compounds with the same elemental composition
differ if the arrangement of their atoms differ.

Since World War II, vegetation has been
described and mapped almost exclusively from
aerial photos. This has restricted the level of
resolution and, therefore, the homogeneity that
could be attained within vegetation units.[4] A
ramification of this low level of homogeneity is
that vegetation unit descriptions most often only
provide information on species composition, or
species-size composition; and not on structure,
even when the cover of each species is reported
by layer. Only when the unit is homogeneous can
the structure be inferred from a description of
species or species-size composition because only

[1] Paper presented at the California
Riparian Systems Conference. [University of
California, Davis, September 17-19, 1981].
[2] Edward C. Stone is Professor, Department
of Forestry and Silviculturist, Agric. Exp. Sta.,
University of California, Berkeley. Janet I.
Cavallaro is a graduate student and research
assistant, Department of Forestry, University of
California, Berkeley. Laurence P. Stromberg is a
vegetation management consultant with Larry
Seeman Associates, Berkeley, Calif.

[3] Fosberg, F.R. 1961. Fosberg defined
structure as the arrangement in space of the components of vegetation (i.e., the distribution of
the biomass in three-dimensional space). More
commonly, it has been defined by three components: vertical structure or stratification,
horizontal structure or pattern, and abundance
(Kershaw 1964). We prefer Fosberg's definition
because it does not restrict the way structure
can be analyzed.
[4] Homogeneity exists when there is uniformity throughout something. Resolution is the
degree to which something is divided into parts.
Consequently, resolution determines the homogeneity that can be attained in vegetation units.

then can the distribution of plants in three-dimensional space be predicted.

To increase the level of resolution at which the vegetation is described and thereby increase the homogeneity in the vegetation units recognized, a new method of vegetation description was developed for the USDA Forest Service for use in preparing stand[5] prescriptions (Stone 1977). The method, which was subsequently modified by Bonnicksen and Stone (in press), is based on two levels of resolution. At both levels, visual units are recognized using visual discontinuities present in the vegetation. At the first level, visual units referred to as "strata" are mapped on aerial photos. At the second, higher level of resolution, visual units referred to as "aggregations" are identified on the ground. These aggregations are homogeneous groups of plants of the same species or growth-form and size. Since they are not mapped, minimum-size constraints imposed by the scale of the aerial photo(s) do not prevent the vegetation from being resolved into homogeneous units.

Thus, the description has two parts. The first consists of an aerial photo on which all the recognized strata are outlined, and a family of proportions specifying the proportion of the area that is covered by each type of stratum. The second part (that at the second, higher level of resolution) is a family of proportions specifying the proportion of the area covered by each type of stratum that is covered by each type of aggregation. The aggregations are described by species composition, expressed in percent cover, of the plants in the largest size-class (fig. 1).

This description method proved useful in that homogeneous visual units could be recognized and used to describe vegetation structure by simply reporting species composition by height-classes. Using this method, Bonnicksen and Stone (ibid.) described vegetation in Sequoia and Kings Canyon National Parks in 1978, and that which existed prior to the parks' establishment in 1890. They then used the 1890 description as a baseline to show the changes that have occurred following the exclusion of fire. The description could also constitute a target description if

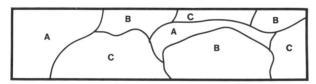

STRATUM A--35%	STRATUM B--35%	STRATUM C--30%
AGG TYPE 4--20%	AGG TYPE 13--40%	AGG TYPE 26--25%
AGG TYPE 1--15%	AGG TYPE 19--15%	AGG TYPE 30--20%
AGG TYPE 6--5%	AGG TYPE 16--5%	AGG TYPE 21--10%
ETC	ETC	ETC

Figure 1.--A hypothetical example of a vegetation description using aggregation.

_____

[5]As used here, a stand is a homogeneous vegetation unit, usually of the same species.

vegetation in the park, or portions thereof, is to be returned to its pre-settlement state, because the description provides the structural information that would be required.

The method suffers, however, from the subjectivity inherent in identifying visually determined units. An overwhelming number of visual discontinuities exists in any vegetation. Thus the development of a decision-rule that can specify which ones to use in identifying groups of plants is difficult if not impossible.

We have been able to circumvent the difficulties encountered in bounding homogeneous visual units by developing four new types of units which are based on the distance between plants of a given kind and size, rather than on visual discontinuities. Two of these unit types are unique while the other two are derived from them when the overlap among them is allocated.

All four kinds of units are defined by: a) a compound plant-descriptive-class consisting of a growth-form or species and a height- or stem-diameter-class and b) a spatial-class that includes a range of distances between plant stems. The compound plant-descriptive- and spatial-classes chosen to define these spatial units will vary, depending on the purpose for which the vegetation description is developed and the kind of vegetation being described.

In addition to overcoming the problems encountered in bounding homogeneous visual units, the identification of these spatial units can provide more information on the three-dimensional character of structure than can any other vegetation description system developed so far. The unit descriptions specify the size of the included plants together with the range of possible distances that separate them. The size (height, stem-diameter) of the included plants provides information on the vertical dimension of structure while the spatial-class provides information on the horizontal dimension.

SPATIAL UNITS

Structural-Groups and Single-Plants

"Structural-groups" and "single-plants" are the fundamental spatial units of this system. A structural-group consists of plants of the same compound plant-descriptive-class that are separated by distances that can be assigned to the same spatial-class (see A, fig. 2). When more than one spatial-class is used in conjunction with one compound plant-descriptive-class to define two or more kinds of structural-groups, however, a plant could belong to more than one structural-group. For example, a structural-group of 20- to 40-ft. tall alder (Alnus rhombifolia) with a spatial-class of 10-ft. can abut upon another alder structural-group containing plants of the same height which is defined by a wider spatial-class such as 10- to

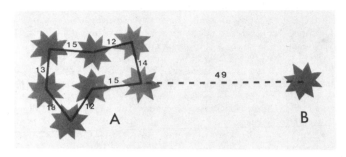

Figure 2.--A: A structural-group with plants of
a given kind and size that are all separated
by distances that fall within the spatial-
class. B: A single-plant that is separated
from other plants of the same kind and size
by a distance that exceeds the upper limit
of the spatial-class.

25-ft. The trees at the common margin can be
less than 10 ft. from alder on one side and
greater that 10 ft. from alder on the other side.
In such cases, a rule must be used to assign
plants of potential dual structural-group membership to one of the structural-groups. We assign
such plants to the group with the narrowest
spacing (see A, fig. 3).

Structural-groups are assigned trinomial
names consisting of a) the size-class; b) the
species or growth-form of the compound plant-
descriptive-class; followed by c) the spatial-
class. In the description, species names are
abbreviated by the first two letters of the genus
and the species. The species growth-form is
indicated by the combination of uppercase and

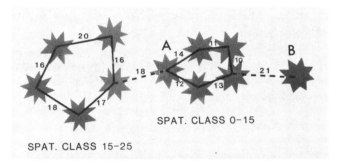

Figure 3.--A: A plant that could belong to more
than one structural-group because the
distance between it and one or more other
plants of the same kind and size falls
within one spatial-class while the distance
between it and one or more other plants
falls into another spatial-class. B: A
plant that is recognized as a single-plant
because the distance between it and another
plant of its kind and size exceeds the upper
limit of the spatial-class for the structural-group to which the other plant belongs
even though the distance between the plant
and the other falls within the spatial-class
used in defining another kind of structural-
group.

lowercase letters. For tree species, uppercase
is used for both the genus and species. For
shrub and vine species, uppercase is used for the
genus and lowercase for the species. For grami-
noid and forb species, lowercase is used for both
the genus and the species. A structural-group
consisting of 20- to 40-ft. tall cottonwood
(_Populus fremonti_) within 20 ft. of each
other, for example, is referred to as: 20-40'
POFR--0-20'.

In contrast to a structural-group, a single-
plant is: a) a plant that is separated from any
other plant in the same compound plant-descriptive-class, by a distance that exceeds the upper
limit of the spatial-class that is used to define
the structural-group with the widest spacing to
which plants in that compound plant-descriptive-
class are assigned (see B, fig. 2); or b) when
more than one spatial-class is used with one
compound plant-descriptive-class to define two or
more kinds of structural-groups, it can also be a
plant that is separated from any neighbor in the
same compound plant-descriptive-class by a
distance that exceeds the upper limit of the
spatial-class of the structural-group to which
its neighbor belongs (see B, fig. 3).

Single-plants are assigned a binomial name
consisting of the compound plant-descriptive-
class to which the plant belongs. For example, a
single 20- to 40-ft. tall cottonwood plant that
is more than 20 ft. from another is referred to
as: 20-40'POFR.

Bounding Structural-Groups
and Single-Plants

Structural-groups always have exterior
boundaries, and they have interior boundaries as
well when holes occur. These boundaries are
based on crown projection boundaries of selected
plants in the group. Since many projections are
irregular because branches protrude at odd angles
and differ in length, projections can be better
bounded with polygons than with circles. To
establish unequivocal boundaries for crown
projections, we always use the smallest possible
convex polygon[6] that has vertices located at
the tips of the longest branches (see A, fig. 4).

The first approximation of the exterior
boundary of a structural-group is a convex
polygon whose vertices are those of the crown
projection boundaries which when connected form
the smallest possible polygon that includes the
crown projections of all plants in the group (see
B, fig. 4). This approximation constitutes the
structural-group boundary unless the distance
between one or more pair of plants tangent to the
first approximation boundary exceeds the upper
limit of the spatial-class. Each new section of
the boundary is formed by connecting vertices of
crown projection boundaries to produce the

----

[6]A convex polygon is one in which all the
interior angles are less than 180°.

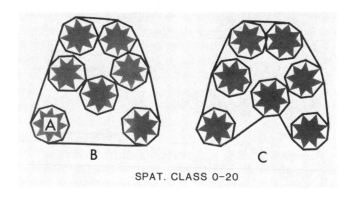

SPAT. CLASS 0-20

Figure 4.--A: The boundary of the crown projection of a plant. B: A structural-group
bounded by a convex polygon.

shortest boundary that includes the crown projections of all the plants in the group (see C, fig.
4). In the event that these criteria can be
satisfied by connecting more than one set of
crown projection boundary vertices for a section,
the boundary for the section is established by
connecting all the vertices that could be used to
establish new boundaries for the section.

A structural-group has one or more interior
boundaries when a hole(s) exists, giving the
structural-group a doughnut shape or swiss-cheese
appearance. A hole exists when the following two
conditions are met: a) an area exists between
plants that is large enough to accommodate a
circle with a diameter greater than the upper
limit of the spatial-class used in defining the
structural-group; and b) the area is not completely covered by the crown projections of
plants in the group (see C, fig. 4).

The boundary of a hole is a polygon which is
formed by connecting vertices of crown projection boundaries of plants on the perimeter of the
hole to produce the smallest possible polygon

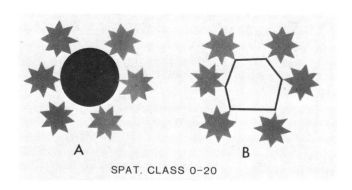

SPAT. CLASS 0-20

Figure 5.--A: A structural-group with a hole.
B: The boundary of a hole.

(see B, fig. 5). The polygon can be either
convex or concave.[7]

Bounding Single-Plants

The boundary of a single-plant is simply its
crown projection boundary (see A, fig. 4).

SPATIAL-AGGREGATIONS AND SOLITARY-PLANTS

Structural-groups and single-plants overlap
in such a wide variety of combinations in a
vegetation that few locations can be expected to
have the same combinations of structural-groups
and single-plants. Consequently, if a general
description of a vegetation were to be developed
on the basis of these combinations, classes to
which different combinations of structural-groups
and single-plants could be assigned would generally be so broad that the resolution obtained by
recognizing structural-groups and single-plants
would be lost and their recognition would have
served no useful purpose.

Therefore, instead of assigning different
combinations of structural-group and single-
plants to classes, we assign only those struc-
tural-group(s) and/or single-plant(s) present at
each location that include plants in the largest
size-class to classes. Our rationale for giving
priority to the largest plants at each location
is that they are the dominant structural components in the vegetation, and in addition they
occupy the largest part of the growing space and
to a large extent control the environments of the
plants growing beneath them.

All the structural-groups and single-plants,
or portions thereof, that have the highest priority at any location are referred to as "spatial-
aggregations" and "solitary-plants." Thus, a
spatial-aggregation is a structural-group or
portion thereof that is not overlapped by structural-groups or single-plants of higher priority;
and a solitary-plant is a single-plant or portion
thereof that is not overlapped by single-plants
or structural-groups of higher priority.

Plants in the understory are not ignored in
the description, however, when they are judged to
be significant. Information about them can be
collected in the inventory of spatial-aggregations and solitary-plants and included in the
description as a descriptive variable after the
spatial-class. Thereafter, the descriptive
variable is used to further define the classes to
which spatial-aggregations and solitary-plants
are assigned.

To identify spatial-aggregations or solitary-plants, the overlap among structural-groups
and single-plants must be allocated. This
allocation is based on the priority assigned to

---

[7]A concave polygon has one or more
interior angles that are greater than 180°.

these spatial units except when they have the same priority. Then the area of overlap is viewed as a mixture of spatial-aggregations and/or solitary-plants. The highest priority is assigned to structural-groups and single-plants that are defined, in part, by the largest size-class. Thereafter, successively lower priorities are assigned to structural-groups and single-plants that are defined, in part, by successively smaller size-classes.

These priorities are applied when allocating overlap as follows.
 (a) The overlap among structural-groups of different priorities is allocated to the structural-group with the highest priority (see A, fig. 6).
 (b) The overlap among single-plants of different priorities is allocated to the single-plant with the highest priority (see B, fig. 6).
 (c) The overlap among structural-groups and single-plants of different priorities is allocated to whichever one has the higher priority (fig. 7).
 (d) The overlap among structural-groups of the same priority is recognized as a mixture of spatial-aggregations (see A, fig. 8).
 (e) The overlap among single-plants of the same priority is recognized as a mixture of solitary-plants (see B, fig. 8).
 (f) The overlap among structural-groups and single-plants of the same priority is recognized as a mixture of spatial-aggregations and solitary-plants (see C, fig. 8).

The boundaries of spatial-aggregations, solitary-plants, or mixtures include boundaries of portions thereof of the spatial unit(s) from which they are derived. When the spatial-aggregation or solitary-plant is derived from a structural-group or single-plant that is not overlapped by one or more spatial units of higher priority, the boundary is that of the spatial unit from which the spatial-aggregation or solitary-plant is derived (fig. 6 and fig. 7). When the spatial-aggregation or solitary-plant is derived from a portion of a structural-group or

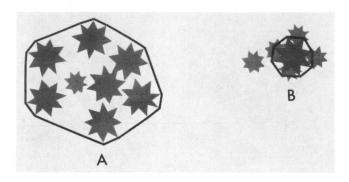

Figure 7.--A: A spatial-aggregation derived from a structural-group that has higher priority than the single-plant it overlaps. B: A solitary-plant derived from a single-plant that has higher priority than the structural-group it overlaps.

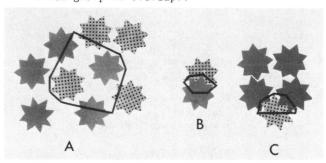

Figure 8.--A: A mixture of spatial-aggregations in the area of overlap of two structural-groups with equal priority. B: A mixture of solitary-plants in the area of overlap of two single-plants with equal priority. C: A mixture of a spatial-aggregation and a solitary-plant in the area of overlap of a structural-group and a single-plant with equal priority.

single-plant, the boundary consists of a portion of the boundary of the spatial unit from which it is derived plus portions of boundaries of other structural-groups and/or single-plants (fig. 9). When a mixture is recognized, the boundary consists of the portions of the spatial unit boundaries that define the area of overlap (fig. 8).

Spatial-aggregations, solitary-plants, and mixtures are all named after the spatial units from which they were derived.

DESCRIPTION METHOD

As discussed, the description method is based on the recognition of vegetation units at two levels of resolution; and therefore, the description has two parts. The first provides a delineation of the different types of strata on an aerial photo or vegetation map along with a family of proportions that specifies the proportion of the area that is covered by strata of

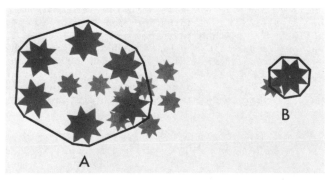

Figure 6.--A: A spatial-aggregation derived from the structural-group with the higher priority. B: A solitary-plant derived from the single-plant with the higher priority.

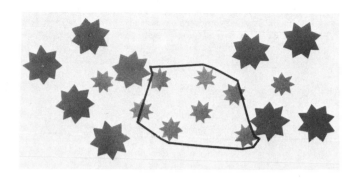

Figure 9.--The boundary of a spatial-aggregation that is derived from only a portion of a structural-group. It consists of portions of the boundary of the lower priority structural-group and an portion of the boundary of each of the two higher priority structural-groups.

each type. Unlike the description method presented by Bonnicksen and Stone (in press), however, the second part provides a family of proportions that specifies the proportion of the area covered by strata of each type that is covered by spatial-aggregations and solitary-plants of each type instead of visually determined aggregations.

PROCEDURE

1. Obtain stereo pairs of aerial photos. Most often, a scale of 1:15,000 or larger is required if the proportion of different kinds of spatial-aggregation and solitary-plants recognized within strata of each type are to differ significantly.

2. On the photos, identify strata based on plant growth-form, species, growth-form-size, species-size, or some combination of these plant-descriptive-classes.

3. Determine the proportion of the area occupied by the vegetation that is covered by strata of each type using a planimeter or by sampling on the photo. As part of the description, organize these proportions as a family of proportions of stratum types. When desired, include the confidence interval for each proportion in the family of proportions if the proportions were estimated by sampling.

4. Decide which compound plant-descriptive-classes and spatial-classes will be used to define different types of structural-groups and single-plants.

5. Decide if any descriptive variables will be used to redefine the spatial-aggregation and solitary-plant types.

6. Design an appropriate sampling procedure for inventorying spatial-aggregations and solitary-plants within strata of each type. The sampling method that is most efficient in strata of a given kind depends on their size, the sizes of aggregations belonging to the most common aggregation type, and the ease with which one can move through the vegetation (Stromberg 1980).

7. Conduct field sampling at which time the spatial-aggregation, solitary-plant, or mixture at each sample point is identified as follows:
   (a) Among the plants around or over the sample point, identify those that belong to the structural-group(s) and/or the single-plant(s) of highest priority that on first inspection appears to cover the sample point.
   (b) Bound only enough of each structural-group or single-plant to determine whether or not it covers the sample point. If none does, identify structural-group(s) of successively lower priority until one or more is found that covers the sample point.
   (c) Identify the spatial-aggregation(s) and/or solitary-plant(s) from among those structural-groups and/or single-plants that were found to cover the sample point by allocating any overlap or recognizing a mixture. If a descriptive variable is being used, collect the necessary information at each sample point.

8. Estimate the proportion of the area occupied by strata of each type that is covered by spatial-aggregations and solitary-plants of each type. As part of the description, organize these proportions as a family of proportions of spatial-aggregations and solitary-plant types. When desired, include the confidence interval for each proportion in the family of proportions.

REMARKS

In a subsequent paper, L.P. Stromberg and E.F. Katibah will present an example of the use of spatial units with this method to describe a riparian vegetation.

LITERATURE CITED

Bonnicksen, T.M., and E.C. Stone. In press. Reconstruction of a presettlement giant sequoia-mixed conifer forest community using the aggregation method. Ecology.

Fosberg, F.R. 1961. A classification of vegetation for general purposes. Trop. Ecol. 2:1-28.

Kershaw, K.A. 1964. Quantitative and dynamic ecology. 100 p. Edward Arnold Publishing Co. Ltd., London.

Stone, E.C. 1977. Timber management handbook. USDA Forest Service, Region 5, San Francisco, California, USA. Chapter 1. Stand management prescriptions. P. 1-40.

Stromberg, L.P. 1980. Relative cost-effectiveness of points, point clusters, and line transects in sampling vegetation for aggregation type proportions. Ph.D. Dissertation. 185 p. University of California, Berkeley.

AN APPLICATION OF THE SPATIAL-AGGREGATION METHOD

TO THE DESCRIPTION OF RIPARIAN VEGETATION[1]

Laurence P. Stromberg and Edwin F. Katibah[2]

Abstract.--The spatial-aggregation method is used to resolve complex riparian vegetation into a mosaic. A vegetation survey produced a mosaic of 65 spatial-aggregation and solitary-plant types, eleven of them covering half the area surveyed. This paper outlines the survey methods used and hypothesizes some dynamic relationships between and within selected types.

INTRODUCTION

This paper demonstrates an application of the spatial-aggregation method developed and described by Stone et al. (1983). It describes the steps taken to estimate the proportional (relative) areas within a selected riparian study area occupied by each of several tree- and shrub-dominated spatial-aggregation and solitary-plant types. To illustrate the use of the method in characterizing overstory-understory relationships, understory tree and tree reproduction data were collected in each spatial-aggregation type represented in the study area.

Change in any vegetation, including riparian vegetation, is the cumulative expression of changes that result from local deaths of some plants, establishment and growth of others, and associated plant and group replacement processes. Due to differences in: 1) the kinds, intensities, areal extent, and timing of disturbances; 2) the sources, amounts, and distribution of seed; 3) the successful establishment and subsequent growth of constituent species; and 4) other variables affecting vegetational development, a variety of overstory-understory relationships and species combinations normally exist in any riparian zone. Riparian vegetation is typically both compositionally and structurally heterogeneous. Therefore the change that takes place over the whole during a given time interval is likely to be a composite product of local changes proceeding at different rates and in different directions.

When data are combined, averaged, or otherwise synthesized across a vegetation which has in the past, or is in the future, likely to change along multiple successional (and other) pathways, two undesirable outcomes can result. First, the data summary or description may not portray the conditions that underlie the range and variety of types of changes possible. It may represent the full range of variation, a desirable feature, but it may not indicate that the heterogeneous whole is locally homogeneous, an undesirable feature if such homogeneity exists. Second, the data summary may obscure important differences in those overstory-understory and horizontal-spatial relationships between plants which partly drive and explain the multiple change potentials.

Under these conditions, the vegetational description has a low level of resolution, making it less useful than it could be as an analytical or management tool. Vegetational resources and processes are understood not on the basis of their actual character, but on the basis of information about that character gained from collecting data and generating descriptions. If the resource is very complex, patchy, or can be readily recognized as a mosaic, and if it changes in a non-uniform manner over space and time, data should be collected and organized to portray the mosaic and the associated various changes possible. Ecologically significant or substantial differences should be represented in the description--data should not be amalgamated across them.

The spatial-aggregation method allows users to arbitrarily but meaningfully and quantitatively treat vegetation as a mosaic, when that approach is warranted, and to describe the smaller, more homogeneous groups of plants which create the heterogeneous whole. The user incorporates the desired degree of resolution into data collection and description. This resolution is normally higher than that characteristic of most large-area vegetation surveys. By virtue of the focus on smaller homogeneous units, observations are

---

[1]Paper presented at the California Riparian Systems Conference. [University of California, Davis, September 17-19, 1981].
[2]Laurence P. Stromberg is Associate Project Manager with Larry Seeman Associates, Inc., Berkeley, Calif. Edwin F. Katibah is Associate Specialist, Department of Forestry and Resource Management, University of California, Berkeley.

directed into areas in which environmental variation and the plant responses to that variation
are relatively narrow. This focus simplifies
both analysis of the vegetation and the prediction of change.

STUDY AREA

The Las Trampas Creek study area is approximately 11.3 km. (7 mi.) east of Berkeley, Alameda
County, and 3.2 km. (2 mi.) south of Lafayette,
Contra Costa County. The area surrounding the
riparian zone was at one time farmed, grazed, and
planted in pear, plum, and walnut orchards.
Today the area is suburban-- much of the agricultural land has been converted to residential
development. At Las Trampas Creek, residential
development has occurred right into the riparian
zone, causing the partial elimination and local
destruction of the natural vegetation that once
lined the watercourse.

Las Trampas Creek is incised into alluvial
material mapped by the USDA Soil Conservation
Service (SCS) (1977) as Clear Lake clay. Currently, the channel bottom is 7.5-12 m. (25-40
ft.) below the level of the upper terrace. Locally, one or two minor intermediate terraces are
also present. These are distinguishable from
benches produced by slumping and oversteepening
of terrace banks.

The vegetation along Las Trampas Creek has
retained much of its natural character, but, at
the same time, the impacts of suburbanization and
associated disruptions were evident. Fremont cottonwood (Populus fremontii), white alder
(Alnus rhombifolia), and two willows (Salix
laevigata and S. lasiandra), all common
tree species in the central coast riparian forest
according to Roberts et al. (1977), were present in the overstory of the study area. Bigleaf
maple (Acer macrophyllum) and black walnut
(Juglans hindsii), both less common tree species, were also present. The walnut had, however, probably grown from seed produced in abandoned walnut orchards adjacent to the creek. At
one time in the Walnut Creek-Lafayette area,
English walnut (J. regia) was grafted onto
black walnut rootstock to improve the quality of
the walnut crop. When the walnut industry declined, the orchards were left untended and the
tree tops died or were overtaken by sprouts from
below. Subsequent seed produced was from the
black walnut rootstock--this was the likely
source of the walnut in the study area. Other
tree species present included California bay
(Umbellularia californica), coast live oak
(Quercus agrifolia), valley oak (Q. lobata), California buckeye (Aesculus californica), and box elder (Acer negundo).

Among the more abundant shrub species in the
study area were wild blackberries (Rubus ursinus and R. vitifolius), elderberries
(Sambucus spp.), wild rose (Rosa californica), gooseberries (Ribes menziesii and R.

divaricatum), and river snowberry (Symphoricarpos rivularis). Several willows not identifiable to species at the time of the field survey were also present in the study area. Common vines included Dutchman's pipe vine (Aristolochia californica), clematis (Clematis
ligusticifolia), poison oak (Rhus diversiloba), and the introduced and escaped English
ivy (Hedera helix).

METHODS

The essential steps in designing the field
survey were: a) choosing what kinds of structural groups would be recognized; and b) selecting
the types of sampling units to be used in estimating spatial-aggregation type proportions and
collecting understory tree and tree reproduction
data.

Structural Group Selection

Structural groups are basic building blocks
from which a mosaic of spatial-aggregations is
conceptually organized. In this study, they are
defined and recognized on the basis of species or
life form, plant height, and plant spacing.

Plant descriptive classes and spatial-
classes can be defined a several ways. Whenever
ecological information is available it can be
used; whenever objectives are clearly stated they
should be used as well. Growth data and estimates of the greatest attainable height for each
species given the site conditions within the
study area can be used to define height-classes.
These classes can be the same or different for
each species. Pattern studies or previous
investigations into the effects of density on
height or diameter growth can be used to set
spatial-class limits. In the absence of such
information, qualitative, semi-quantitative, or
fully quantitative methods can provide the means
for setting limits on spatial-classes.

An investigator can rely on past experience
to set the limits for height- and spatial-classes
and make no measurements at all. Such an approach would be acceptable if the product of the
investigation met the needs of the user. Qualitative and quantitative methods of any kind can be
used. One possible quantitative method uses a
distance measure such as the wandering quarter
method (Catana 1963) to obtain a sample of
nearest-neighbor distances for plants belonging
to the same compound plant descriptive class.
Height-classes could be established prior to or
during the distance sampling.

In this study, we relied upon the visual
discontinuities in the vegetation, that is, its
visible patchiness, as the basis for establishing
the structural groups we would recognize. During
two trips through the length of the study area,
tree heights and spacings in a large number of
visually recognizable plant groups were measured.
We chose to measure height rather than diameter

to facilitate a simpler portrayal of overstory-understory relationships. We used distance between stems rather than between crowns (an acceptable alternative, particularly in shrub-dominated vegetation types) because stem spacing is a visible and more easily measured variable.

We established at least two types of structural groups for each plant descriptive class and then conducted a trial run to determine how satisfactorily the structural groups we recognized resembled their "visual" counterparts in terms of plant membership. As expected, the match was imperfect, and a few minor adjustments in the height- and spatial-classes were made to improve the "fit". Partial coincidence between certain abrupt visual discontinuities and structural group and spatial-aggregation boundaries is normal, particularly when the visual mosaic is used to set height- and spatial-class limits, but some differences will persist. Plants that appear to warrant inclusion in a structural group because of their taxonomic identity are sometimes excluded because they are too tall, too short, or too far away from their nearest like neighbor to be included.

Imperfect registration or coincidence between visible patches in the vegetation and spatial-aggregations is unavoidable if the strict rules for deciding upon structural group membership and boundary location are followed. The user must accept the associated discomfort with the understanding that the consequences are repeatable sampling results and essentially identical boundary allocations, even by field survey teams working independently--the discrepancies should amount to no more than crown projection and measurement errors.

Table 1 contains the height- and spatial-classes used in recognizing structural groups and some examples of structural group trinomial names. By convention, plants whose heights placed them at height-class boundary limits were considered members of the "taller" of the two adjacent height-classes. In other words, the classes were handled in the field and in subsequent analyses to be 0.0-0.29, 0.3-0.89, 0.9-1.79, etc. The same convention was applied to plant spacing.

Non-overlapping, mutually exclusive height-classes were used to facilitate representation of overstory-understory relationships. The same height-classes apply to all species. Several of the species occurring in the study area, including cottonwood, the several willows, alder, and others, sprout; consequently some means had to be established to provide for unambiguous measurement of distances between multi-stemmed plants. By convention, distance was measured from the geometric center of the stem cluster. When required, a hole was dug to permit measurement.

Species were used to recognize all tree, shrub, and vine structural groups. However, forbs were not identified to species and forb

Table 1.--Structural group height- and spatial-classes.

Height-classes used for all species, in meters:

0.0 - 0.3	0.9 - 1.8	3.7 - 6.1	12.2 - 20.9
0.3 - 0.9	1.8 - 3.7	6.1 -12.2	20.9 +

Spatial-classes by species, in meters:

Species	Symbol	Spatial classes	
Salix lasiandra	SALA	0.0-2.6	2.6- 6.7
Salix laevigata		same	
Salix shrub species	SAsp.	same	
Alnus rhombifolia	ALRH	0.0-3.0	3.0- 8.7
Populus fremontii	POFR	0.0-6.1	6.1-12.2
Juglans hindsii	JUHI	0.0-6.1	6.1-11.2
Acer macrophyllum	ACMA	0.0-5.3	5.3-11.2
Umbellularia californica	UMCA	0.0-5.3	5.3-11.2
Aesculus californica	AECA	0.0-3.0	3.0- 6.1
Quercus lobata	QULO	0.0-8.7	8.7-12.2
Quercus agrifolia	QUAG	0.0-3.0	3.0- 6.1
Acer negundo	ACNE	0.0-2.6	2.6- 5.3
Baccharis pilularis	BApi	0.0-2.0	2.0- 3.0
Other shrub species		same	
All forbs	None used	0.0-0.3	0.3- 0.6

Representative trinomial names:

3.7-6.1 SALA 0.0-2.6	12.2-20.9 POFR 6.1-12.2
6.1-12.2 ACMA 0.0-5.3	20.9 + JUHI 6.1-11.2
1.8-3.7 ACNE 0.0-2.6	12.2-20.9 UMCA 0.0-5.3
0.0-0.3 Forbs 0.0-0.3	0.9-1.8 BApi 2.0-3.0

structural groups were recognized on the basis of life form.

Sample Survey Design

Approximate limits to the study area were set using color aerial photographs flown at a scale of 1:3,000. Three adjacent photographs from a single flight line provided complete coverage. Although we could have stratified the vegetation prior to sampling by coupling a minimal amount of photo-interpretation with ground verification, we chose not to because the study area is small and we did not intend to map the vegetation. For sampling purposes, we set the actual limits of the study area at 15.2 m. (50 ft.) from the edge of the upper terraces. The setback was used to include trees rooted above the terrace but belonging to spatial-aggregations containing trees rooted between the terraces.

Single points were used as the sampling units. They were randomly located to yield the largest possible sample size. By grouping points into clusters, total sampling time could be reduced. However, this would significantly decrease the precision possible in the estimated type proportions. Computer-generated random points were plotted onto mylar sheets. These sheets were placed over the three aerial photographs and points were transferred by pin from the mylar to the photographs. The point number, plotted beside the point on the mylar sheet, was marked on the back of the photograph to identify the point and insure that subsequent associations of field data with sampling locations would be correct.

During the field survey, points were thrown out of the sample whenever they fell in vegetation heavily modified by residential landscaping or local trash disposal. These points were replaced by others located elsewhere in the study area. The results are thus biased--dumpsite and unnatural vegetation are underrepresented in the sample. However, the number of points relocated was minor compared to the total sample size and the bias was therefore neglected.

Data on understory trees and tree reproduction were collected in square quadrats. Three-meter-square quadrats were used in tree-dominated aggregations, two-meter-square quadrats were used in shrub- and vine-dominated aggregations, and one-meter-square quadrats were used in forb-dominated aggregations. Quadrat size was reduced to insure that the quadrat could fit entirely within the limits of the spatial-aggregation recognized; smaller quadrats are necessary as the size of the dominants and the area of the associated spatial-aggregation decreased. In most instances, the quadrat was placed at the sample point location. Occasionally, however, when the point was near the boundary of the spatial-aggregation, it was relocated toward the center of the spatial-aggregation to avoid quadrat overlap. Whenever the spatial-aggregation was too small to contain the quadrat, the area of the spatial-aggregation was measured, and this was used in lieu of a quadrat--all trees and tree reproduction were counted within the spatial-aggregation boundary. Understory tree and tree reproduction data were collected using the same height-classes as for the structural groups.

Each quadrat was identified as to site and described by location (upper terrace, intermediate terrace, lower terrace, inter-terrace slope, slump, channel bottom, etc.). In addition, occular estimates of the total groundcover present in each quadrat were made using Daubenmire's (1968) cover classes, and the most abundant ground layer species were identified.

Sample Statistics

When sampling with randomly located points, the estimator for the proportion, P_i, of the "ith" spatial-aggregation or solitary-plant type is:

$$P_i = \frac{n_i}{n}$$

where n = the total number of points in the sample,

and n_i = the number of points in spatial-aggregations or solitary-plants of type i.

An unbiased estimator of the variance of p_i obtained from the sample is:

$$v(p_i) = \frac{p_i q_i}{n-1}$$

where $q_i = 1.0 - p_i$.

Confidence Limits

Placement of a confidence interval around a proportion with a stated alpha level, 0.05 for example, assumes reliance upon the normal approximation in the 95% confidence statement that the interval contains the true proportion. With an alpha level of 0.05 we accept that five out of 100 confidence intervals will not contain the true proportion and that we will have erred in those cases. As the number of estimates for which we produce confidence intervals increases, the overall error rate increases. With an alpha level of 0.05 for each of 10 intervals, the overall error will be somewhere between 0.05 and 0.50 but will be undefined. We can preserve an error rate with a definable upper limit of 0.05 by using simultaneous multinomial confidence intervals, each with an alpha level of 0.005. The result is wider confidence intervals.

Multinomial confidence limits to the intervals about estimates obtained for spatial-aggregation and solitary-plant proportions p_i, i = 1,2,3... c, using a sample of randomly located points are:

$$p_i \in \frac{X^2_{\frac{\alpha}{c}} + 2n_i \pm \sqrt{X^2_{\frac{\alpha}{c}}\left[X^2_{\frac{\alpha}{c}} + 4n_i(n-n_i)/n\right]}}{2(n + X^2_{\frac{\alpha}{c}})}$$

where $X^2_{\frac{\alpha}{c}}$ = chi square with one degree of freedom and a significance level of $\frac{\alpha}{c}$,

α = the overall acceptable error rate,

and c = the number of types over which the overall acceptable error rate is to be preserved.

RESULTS AND DISCUSSION

Table 2 shows the estimated spatial-aggregation and solitary-plant type proportions.

Table 2.--Estimated spatial-aggregation and solitary-plant type proportions (n = 192, number of points in each type shown in parentheses).

Spatial-aggregation or solitary-plant type		General type description						
Species or Life form	Spatial-class, meters	Tree seedlings and saplings, shrubs and forbs			Immature and small trees, large shrubs		Mature trees, large trees	
		Height-classes, in meters						
		0.0-0.9	0.9-1.8	1.8-3.7	3.7-6.1	6.1-12.2	12.2-20.9	20.9 +
SALA	0.0-2.5	-	-	-	.037(7)	.052(10)	.063(12)	.016(3)
SALA	2.5-6.7	-	-	-	-	.068(13)	.016(3)	.010(2)
SALA	(s)	-	-	-	.005(1)	.031(6)	.031(6)	.026(5)
ALRH	0.0-3.0	-	-	-	-	.0052(1)	.0312(6)	.0052(1)
ALRH	3.0-8.7	-	-	-	-	.0260(5)	.0156(3)	.0052(1)
ALRH	(s)	-	-	-	-	-	.0312(6)	.0104(2)
JUHI	0.0-6.1	-	-	-	.0052(1)	.0104(2)	.0104(2)	-
JUHI	(s)	-	-	-	.0052(1)	.0156(3)	.0208(4)	.0312(6)
AECA	0.0-3.0	-	-	-	.0156(3)	.0312(6)	-	-
AECA	3.0-6.1	-	-	-	-	.0052(1)	-	-
AECA	(s)	-	-	-	.0104(2)	.0052(1)	-	-
QULO	0.0-8.7	.0052(1)	-	-	.0052(1)	-	.0156(3)	.0052(1)
QULO	8.7-12.2	-	-	-	-	-	.0156(3)	.0104(2)
QULO	(s)	-	-	.0052(1)	-	-	.0052(1)	.0052(1)
UMCA	0.0-5.3	-	-	-	-	-	-	.0052(1)
UMCA	(s)	-	-	-	-	.0104(2)	.0260(5)	-
POFR	0.0-6.1	-	-	-	-	-	-	.0104(2)
POFR	6.1-12.2	-	-	-	-	-	-	.0104(2)
POFR	(s)	-	-	-	-	-	.0052(1)	.0104(2)
QUAG	0.0-3.0	-	-	-	-	.0052(1)	-	-
QUAG	(s)	-	-	-	-	-	.0104(2)	-
ACMA	0.0-5.3	-	-	-	-	.0104(2)	.0052(1)	-
ACMA	5.3-11.2	-	-	-	-	-	.0052(1)	-
BApi	0.0-2.0	.0104(2)	.0104(2)	.0521(10)	.0052(1)	-	-	-
Shrubs	0.0-2.0	.0104(2)	.0156(3)	-	.0052(1)	-	-	-
Forbs	0.0-0.3	.0104(2)	.0104(2)	.0052(1)	-	-	-	-
SALA 0.0-2.5/ALRH 0.0-3.0						.0052(1)		
SALA 0.0-2.5/ALRH (s)						.0052(1)		
QULO 0.0-8.7/QUAG 0.0-3.0/BApi 0.0-2.0				.0156(3)				

These proportions and the confidence intervals about the largest individual and combined type proportions shown in table 3 are based on a sample of 192 randomly located points. Together, the tables show the predominance of willow spatial-aggregation types; the three most abundant types contained either _Salix lasiandra_ or _S. laevigata_, and had a combined proportion of .182, indicating that these spatial-aggregation types occupied just over 18% of the study area. Figure 1 (left) shows a willow spatial-aggregation with 12.2- to 20.9-m. tall trees with nearest neighbor distances less than 2.5 m. Such spatial-aggregations were found on lower terraces and the thick sediment layers deposited during past floods.

The next two most abundant spatial-aggregation types were 1.8-3.7 BApi 0.0-2.0 and 3.7-6.1 SALA 0.0-2.5, with proportions of .052 and .037, respectively. The latter type is shown in figure 1 (right). These spatial-aggregation types occurred in quite different environments, the coyote brush primarily at the edge of the upper terrace and on slumps and in their scarps; the willow primarily along the stream channel and less than 1.5 m. (5 ft.) above it.

Alder, buckeye, black walnut, and willow spatial-aggregation and solitary-plant types were next in order of abundance and area covered. Each type accounted for slightly over 3% of the study area. Figure 2 shows a 12.2- to 20.9-m. tall solitary alder in the left foreground and two alder spatial-aggregations, 6.1-12.2 ALRH 0.0-3.0 in the left-center middleground and 12.2-20.9 ALRH 3.0-8.7 in the right middleground.

As table 3 shows, mature solitary alder, willow, and black walnut were common--in most cases the willow and alder standing alone because their neighbors had died or suffered crown damage

Table 3.—Confidence intervals for the most abundant spatial-aggregation and solitary-plant types and selected type combinations ($\alpha = 0.10$, c = 20).

Type or type combination	P_i	Confidence interval
Spatial-aggregation and solitary-plant types:		
6.1–12.2 SALA 2.5–6.7	.068	.032–.137
12.2–20.9 SALA 0.0–2.5	.063	.028–.131
6.1–12.2 SALA 0.0–2.5	.052	.022–.117
1.3– 3.7 BApi 0.0–2.0	.052	.022–.117
3.7– 6.1 SAsp. 0.0–2.5	.037	.013–.096
12.2–20.9 ALRH 0.0–3.0	.031	.011–.089
12.2–20.9 ALRH (s)	.031	.011–.089
20.9+ JUHI (s)	.031	.011–.089
6.1–12.2 AECA 0.0–3.0	.031	.011–.089
6.1–12.2 SALA (s)	.031	.011–.089
12.2–20.9 SALA (s)	.031	.011–.089
Subtotal proportion:	.458	
Type combinations:		
Other SALA, SAsp. types	.073	.036–.144
All QULO types	.073	.036–.144
Other JUHI types	.068	.032–.137
Other ALRH types	.068	.031–.137
All POFR types	.037	.013–.096
All QUAG, UMCA, and AMCA types	.078	.039–.150
Other shrub, vine, and forb types	.083	.043–.157
Remaining types	.026	.008–.081
Subtotal proportion:	.542	
Total:	1.000	

Figure 2.—A combination of a solitary alder 12.2–20.9-m. tall (left foreground) and alder spatial-aggregations, 6.1–12.2 ALRH 0.0–3.0 (left-center middleground) and 12.2–20.9 ALRH 3.0–8.7 (right middleground).

the sample occurred solitarily, even in the shorter height-classes.

Eleven of the 65 spatial-aggregation and solitary-plant types encountered in the survey have a combined proportion of .458 and cover just under one-half of the study area. Among the remaining types, willow tree and shrub types are most abundantly represented.

A mosaic of spatial-aggregations is formed when structural groups overlap one another. This is particularly true in multi-layered vegetation such as is commonly found in riparian zones. In the study area, this overlap is the rule. Most structural groups straddle spatial-aggregation boundaries and few spatial-aggregations do not contain parts of several shorter structural groups. The survey results nevertheless indicate that despite the overwhelming amount of structur-

which placed them in a shorter height-class. Black walnut, on the other hand, occured primarily as solitary, pre-mature individuals. In fact, three-quarters of the walnut trees represented in

Figure 1.—Willow spatial-aggregations abundant in the Las Trampas Creek riparian woodland. Left—12.2–20.9 SALA 0.0–2.5, a dense aggregation of mature trees. Right—3.7–6.1 SALA 0.0–2.5, a dense aggregation of immature trees.

al group overlap, over 97% of the study area consists of pure, single-species spatial-aggregations. This suggests that most of the overlap occurs between structural groups with different height-classes.

The relatively small proportion of the study area in mixed spatial-aggregations suggests that it is possible to recognize visually homogeneous patches and to use them as a basis for quantitatively organizing vegetation into a mosaic of distinguishable units. Of course a mosaic of spatial-aggregations is an artifact of height- and spatial-classes combined with species to define structural groups. Each particular combination will yield a unique mosaic. Nevertheless, the results indicate that the spatial-aggregation method can be used to partition even complex, heterogeneous riparian vegetation into definite, locally overstory-homogeneous units in a very simple manner. These units or spatial-aggregations then become the focal points of resource analysis and evaluation of past and potential future change.

Figure 3 diagrams some hypothetical dynamic relationships between several willow spatial-aggregation and solitary-plant types. The assumption of a relationship constitutes substitution of space for time. The arrows indicate possible trends from shorter, denser spatial-aggregations to taller, less dense spatial-aggregations. The structural transitions ultimately would terminate with solitary-plants. These developmental pathways are considered here without regard for past or future successional (compositional) changes which may be foreshadowed by understory trees and tree reproduction of other species.

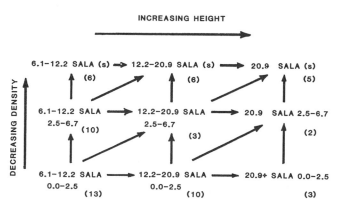

INCREASING HEIGHT

DECREASING DENSITY

| 6.1-12.2 SALA (s) → 12.2-20.9 SALA (s) → 20.9 SALA (s) |
| (6) (6) (5) |

6.1-12.2 SALA 2.5-6.7 → 12.2-20.9 SALA 2.5-6.7 → 20.9 SALA 2.5-6.7
(10) (3) (2)

6.1-12.2 SALA 0.0-2.5 → 12.2-20.9 SALA 0.0-2.5 → 20.9+ SALA 0.0-2.5
(13) (10) (3)

Figure 3.--Hypothetical relationships between willow spatial-aggregations and solitary-plants in a natural thinning process.

The several pathways suggest the kinds of essentially structural change in spatial-aggregations which could follow flooding--the abrasion, destruction, and/or removal of the previous cover, the deposition of a new unoccupied substrate, and the subsequent establishment and growth of willow from seed. Over time, the initially dense spatial-aggregations of shorter willow would undergo natural thinning. Some trees would die; growth would be transferred to the survivors which would eventually form taller, less dense spatial-aggregations. A decrease in the number of stems in each spatial-aggregation would accompany the losses through mortality. In the absence of disturbances severe enough to initiate this same developmental sequence elsewhere in the mosaic, a shift would occur in the areas occupied by spatial-aggregations representing early and later developmental stages. The taller, open spatial-aggregations would eventually occupy a greater proportion of the mosaic.

The ultimate transition to solitary trees could result from the death of some of the older willow in the mature spatial-aggregations. Since mortality would thin spatial-aggregations that already contained a reduced number of trees, the outcome could be a residual of several old, solitary individuals that together formed part of the same shorter spatial-aggregation several decades earlier, standing apart from each other.

These changes can be described a number of ways. Using the spatial-aggregation method, they are captured as the movements of groups of plants from one spatial-aggregation type to another. This suggests that structural group and spatial-aggregation membership and boundaries are transitory mosaic characteristics that change over time as plants grow in response to the environments they encounter. Groups form, spatial-aggregations coalesce and split apart, and type proportions increase and decrease, some to zero as types temporarily or permanently drop out of the mosaic.

In figure 3, the parentheses below each type contain the number of sample points that occurred in each type of spatial-aggregation, giving a relative indication of how much area is occupied by each representative of these hypothetically related developmental stages. If this scenario can be considered a realistic possibility for the study area, the data from the survey indicate that the relatively early stages are heavily represented and that very dense, mature willow spatial-aggregations are not very common.

The thinning processes hypothesized above are now evident in the study area. Several neighboring spatial-aggregations of the same type appear to have once formed a single larger predecessor. Dead and unhealthy trees slightly shorter than their live neighbors now separate these neighboring spatial-aggregations. This splitting has apparently accompanied the death or decline of the slowest-growing individuals in what were initially very dense spatial-aggregations.

During the field survey we recorded the number of trees in each spatial-aggregation sampled. Using the number of trees in a spatial-aggregation as a measure of its size, we found that although the sample of quadrats is too small

353

to permit a meaningful test of the statistical significance of the differences, trends in spatial-aggregation size tentatively support the above hypothesis. As the height-class increases, the average number of trees in willow spatial-aggregations decreases. For types with a spatial-class of 0.0-2.5 m., the decrease is from 12.3 to 8.2 to 6.1 trees per spatial-aggregation. Similarly, a decrease from 5.1 to 3.0 stems per spatial-aggregation was found between 6.1-12.2 SALA 2.5-6.7 and 12.2-20.9 SALA 2.5-6.7.

The trend in reduction in tree numbers is more evident between types that vary in spatial-classes. For 6.1- to 12.2-m. tall spatial-aggregations, those with 0.0- to 2.5-m. stem spacing average 12.3 trees, those with 2.5- to 6.7-m. stem spacing average 5.1 trees. In 12.2- to 20.9-m. tall spatial-aggregations, the average decreases from 8.2 to 3.0 trees as the spacing increases. This pair of trends better captures the thinning possible.

Although our data will be used to set several hypotheses for future work, the purpose here is not to test hypotheses about the above structural dynamics. Relationships are discussed here solely to indicate the ways in which vegetation dynamics can be tracked using the spatial-aggregation method.

Replacement processes whereby groups of plants belonging to one species replace those of another, either by mortality of the original species, or as the replacement species grows through them and assumes vertical dominance, can also be portrayed at a high level of resolution. The understory tree and tree reproduction data collected in each spatial-aggregation type suggest species replacement processes, including successional change. To illustrate the possibilities in mature alder spatial-aggregations we have combined data from the plots in 12.2-20.9 ALRH 0.0-3.0 and 12.2-20.9 ALRH 3.0-8.7 types (fig. 4). Black walnut, California bay, buckeye, alder, and willow are present in the understories of these types of spatial-aggregations. In some cases, we suspect that the alder became established later and grew through the trees now in the understory, in others that the understory trees became established after the alder. We would need to core both overstory and understory trees to confirm our opinions. Some of the understory trees such as box elder and buckeye normally attain a height of only 10 m. and would form an overstory only in the event that the taller trees die or are removed in some way. Bay, black walnut, and willow, however, can replace alder without reducing the height of the overstory canopy.

In some of the alder spatial-aggregations, shorter, younger alder is present in the understory, insuring that mature alder spatial-aggregations will remain in the mosaic in spite of future mortality. Of course, alder is also present under willow, cottonwood, and walnut spatial-aggregations and can replace the overstory trees in these too.

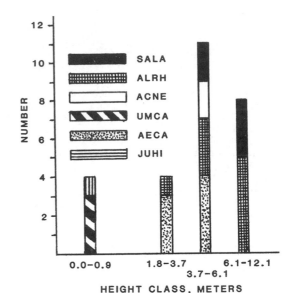

Figure 4.--Understory trees and tree reproduction in 12 3-m. x 3-m. quadrats in mature 12.2- to 20.9-m. tall alder spatial-aggregations.

Figure 5 illustrates tree reproduction in 6.1- to 12.2-m. tall buckeye spatial-aggregations. These buckeye spatial-aggregations generally occur above 1.5 m. (5 ft.) above the stream channel and are common on the minor intermediate terraces. Contrary to the situation in the alder spatial-aggregations, no alder or willow reproduction is present. Valley oak, walnut, bay, and buckeye are present--the last are by far the most abundant. Buckeye seedlings (0.0-0.9 m.) and saplings (0.9-1.8 m. and 1.8-3.7 m.) appear to have grown from seed produced by the trees in the overstory. The other species have, of course, become established from seed produced by trees in neighboring spatial-aggregations. In one case, a buckeye spatial-aggregation surrounds a solitary bay 12.2-20.9 m. tall; the four bay seedlings and saplings represented in figure 5 all occur just beyond the

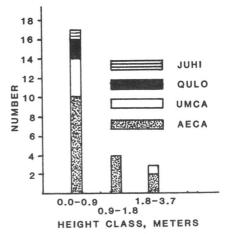

Figure 5.--Understory tree and tree reproduction in five 3-m. x 3-m. quadrats in 6.1- to 12.2-m. tall buckeye spatial-aggregations.

crown of the solitary bay and beneath the buckeye. Whether or not the buckeye seedlings will survive to replace the overstory buckeye is uncertain. No seedling survival information is available.

Ideally, projection of change in and maintenance of buckeye spatial-aggregations requires data on seedling survival and seedling and sapling growth in buckeye spatial-aggregations. Seedling survival and growth both vary with differences in light reduction and water consumption by trees in the overstory. These, in turn, vary with the height of trees, their density, and crown closure. Success of reproduction no doubt varies across spatial-aggregation types.

Reproduction alone may not be sufficient to maintain the existing buckeye spatial-aggregations, even when reproduction is adequate and both seedlings and saplings are present in large numbers in the understories. Buckeyes are quite short; often buckeye spatial-aggregations are surrounded by taller trees. Upon full height growth these surrounding trees may overtop the buckeye from the side. Buckeye may continue to survive in understory structural groups, as it appears capable of doing in the study area. But once a buckeye spatial-aggregation is overtopped, either from the side or by trees growing through it, it may no longer retain its status as a spatial-aggregation. Using this method, only overstory mosaics are characterized.

CONCLUSION

By keeping track of overstory-understory relationships and insuring that data on the understory are collected in plots entirely within the boundaries of particular spatial-aggregation types, the investigator is able to predict local successional and other replacement processes not possible when data are merged across several types of spatial-aggregations. Many more kinds of change are identifiable. As a result, exceptions to commonly accepted successional scenarios can be recognized. The exceptions are, however, a matter of resolution. Higher levels of resolution and recognition of departures from standard beliefs are valuable steps in the direction of improving our grasp of the mechanics of vegetation change.

Although the potential user may consider this approach to involve too high a level of resolution for a large area survey, the level of resolution can be flexibly set by the user. As with traditional data collection and descriptive methods, data are collected over the entire target vegetation or survey area using this method. However, with the spatial-aggregation method the user can accomodate the visible heterogeneity and structural variation in a way that more satisfactorily accounts for their influence on vegetation dynamics. Still, no more time need be spent collecting data than would be required with traditionally accepted methods. Therein lie the potential advantages of using the spatial-aggregation method.

LITERATURE CITED

Catana, A. J., Jr. 1963. The wandering quarter method of estimating population density. Ecol. 44(2):350-360.

Daubenmire, R. 1968. Plant communities, a textbook of plant synecology. 300 p. Harper & Row, New York, N.Y.

Roberts, W.G., J. G. Howe, and J. Major. 1977. A survey of riparian forest flora and fauna in California. p. 3-19. In: A. Sands (ed.). Riparian forests in California: their ecology and conservation. Institute of Ecology Pub. No. 15, University of California, Davis. 122 p.

Stone, E.C., J.I. Cavallaro, and L.P. Stromberg. 1983. In: R.E. Warner and K.M. Hendrix (ed.). California Riparian Systems. [University of California, Davis, September 17-19, 1981.] University of California Press, Berkeley.

USDA Soil Conservation Service. 1977. Soil survey of Contra Costa County, California. 122 p. plus maps. USDA Soil Conservation Service, Washington, D.C.

STRUCTURAL, FLORISTIC, AND CONDITION INVENTORY
OF CENTRAL VALLEY RIPARIAN SYSTEMS[1]

Richard E. Warner[2]

Abstract.--At the time of European settlement of the Central Valley in the mid-1800s, between two and three million acres of seasonally inundated floodplain supported vast areas of both aquatic and riparian wetlands. Over 90% of the valley's riparian systems are now gone. This paper reports a ground-based inventory of 51 riparian sites, some randomly selected, others chosen for their special structural or ecological values. Morphological structure, floristics, plant diversity, and site condition were quantified using an inventory methodology designed for that purpose. Stem diameter size-frequency curves for major canopy species indicate major reproductive problems in several species. Condition trends are assessed, and human-use impacts are discussed.

INTRODUCTION

History of the Problem

Since the first establishment of Spanish land grants in the early 1800s, the riparian systems of California's Central Valley have experienced an unremitting assault from cultivated agriculture, pasture and open-range grazing, dams and water diversions, groundwater pumping, flood control engineering, fuel wood cutting, and other consumptive uses and development activities.

Little note was taken of the cumulative impacts of these activities until the mid-1970s, when conservationists belatedly realized: a) the immense ecological importance of riparian systems; and b) the magnitude of their loss. In California, field studies of human-use impacts (e.g., McGill 1975, 1979) and riparian conferences in 1976 and 1977 (Sands 1977) brought these values and the extent of the loss into some perspective. During the same period, authoritative reports and the proceedings of important riparian conferences were emerging across the land, documenting the unusual importance of riparian systems as wildlife habitats, as protectors of the hydrologic and ecologic integrity of streams, as major recreation sites, and potentially as major forest product resources (e.g., Anderson and

Ohmart 1977; Carothers et al. 1974; Gaines 1977; Hubbard 1977; Jain 1976; Johnson et al. 1977; Johnson and Jones 1977; Korte and Frederickson 1977).

California Riparian Study Program

In 1978, goaded by now-alarmed conservationists, the California Legislature enacted legislation (AB 3147, Fazio) mandating and funding a study of Central Valley and California Desert riparian resources by the California Department of Fish and Game (DFG). The stated goal of DFG in mounting its California Riparian Study Program (CRSP) was: "to protect, improve, and restore the riparian resources of the state." Specific objectives were:

1. To determine the historical extent of the riparian resource in the Central Valley and California Desert and the causes of its destruction;

2. To determine the present status of the riparian resource;

3. To identify problems and threats to resource maintenance;

4. To recommend measures for riparian resource protection, improvement, and restoration."

The above goal and objectives were essentially the same as those which guided the Department's successful coastal wetland program. (Warner 1979)

---

[1] Paper presented at the California Riparian Systems Conference. [University of California, Davis, September 17-19, 1981.]

[2] Richard E. Warner is Director, Field Studies Center, Davis, Calif.

The CRSP studies began in 1979. The first, a riparian vegetation mapping project of Central Valley depositional bottomland, using California Department of Water Resources (DWR) 35mm. aerial photographs, was undertaken jointly by the Departments of Geography at California State University, Chico, and California State University, Fresno (Central Valley Riparian Mapping Project 1979). The second project was a problem analysis and research planning effort undertaken by the Field Studies Center, Davis (Warner 1979). The third project, a riparian mapping and inventory design study, was undertaken by the Remote Sensing Research Program, Department of Forestry and Resource Management, University of California, Berkeley (Bonner et al. 1979). These were followed in 1980 by a two-part, collaborative field inventory and condition assessment. Two research teams--Remote Sensing Research Program, University of California, Berkeley, and Field Studies Center, Davis--undertook, respectively, remote-sensing and ground-based inventories of selected Central Valley riparian systems. This paper reports some of the findings of the ground-based inventory component of the CRSP.

Objectives and Constraints

It was recognized at the outset that a definitive ground-based study was not possible, owing to: a) the vast size of the study area (8.3 million hectares); b) limited resources ($20,000, of which $15,000 was provided by the Denver Wildlife Research Center, USDI Fish and Wildlife Service [FWS]); c) limited time (four months field time for ground-based studies); and perhaps most important, d) lack of prior studies of Central Valley riparian systems. With the exception of Conard et al. (1977) and Roberts et al. (1977), virtually no quantitative studies of the morphological structure of riparian vegetation and its floristics had yet been undertaken. No quantitative information on regional differences had been developed. California riparian plant associations and communities were only partly defined. No riparian classification system had been developed. And no standardized field procedures specific to riparian systems had yet been developed.

Limited time and the need to develop and test quantitative procedures precluded extensive preliminary sampling to determine study site stratification possibilities. Thus, the CRSP ground-based study of the Central Valley was designed as a first, broad-brush effort, where the objectives were to:

1) develop, test, and deploy a quantitative riparian inventory methodology;
2) describe and quantify the diversity of riparian system morphological structure, floristics, and condition; and
3) determine the major causes of condition decline and recent overt loss of riparian systems throughout the study area.

Structural, floristic, and other riparian system variables were selected based on what appeared to be real intra-system relationships and which were at the same time universal; that is, they were common to many kinds of riparian systems in many places. Randomized sampling procedures, other than site selection, were not attempted owing to the complete absence of quantitative information on intra-site and inter-site variance. It seemed more naive to make the pretense of known normal distributions and variances of as yet undefined plant association types, than to admit our ignorance and start at "square one" with the most rudimentary quantitations. The present study thus lays the groundwork for later stratification and randomization in sampling procedures.

THE STUDY AREA

Physiography

The Central Valley of California is an immense, flat-bottomed trough averaging 160 km. wide and comprised of two principal subunits, the San Joaquin Valley south of, and the Sacramento Valley north of the Delta. It extends in a northwesterly direction from its southern end near Bakersfield, Kern County, for some 830 km. It is bounded by four landform provinces: on the east by the Sierra Nevada; the south and west by the Coast Ranges; and on the north and northeast by the Klamath Mountains and Cascade Range (Durrenburger and Johnson 1976).

The Fazio legislation prescribed that the boundary of the Central Valley study area be at the upper edge of the blue oak/digger pine zone of Küchler (1977). This vegetation boundary lies at about 1,060 m. elevation in the south, gradually lowering to about 760 m. elevation in the north. It encompasses an area averaging 110 km. E-W and 750 km. N-S, or a total land area of approximately 82,500 sq. km. (8.25 million hectares or 20.3 million acres). The bottom of the trough, i.e., the valley floor, is comprised largely of unconsolidated sediments, ranging from about 1,000 m. of depth in the north to as much as 17,000 m. of depth in the lower San Joaquin Valley. These sediments provide a permeable matrix for an aquifer or groundwater storage basin which is by far the largest in the state.

Climate

Climate ranges from desert in the south and south-central portion, through steppe in the center, to warm summer Mediterranean in the north. Precipitation on the valley floor is as low as 127 mm. per year in the south, increasing to 760 mm. per year in the north. Precipitation in the surrounding hills and mountains is significantly higher, up to 2,000 mm. per year in certain northerly Sierra and Cascade parts of the watershed (Durrenberger and Johnson 1976).

Temperature patterns are somewhat unusual, in that both the far northern and far southern ends experience 90-120 days per year above 32°C (90°F), while the central portion receives but 60-90 days per year in that temperature range. In contrast, the surrounding foothills have on average but 30-60 days per year above 32°C. Winters tend to be mild throughout the Central Valley, with low clouds and fog ameliorating winter cold. Freezing temperatures occur principally from the influx of cold air from Canada in January and February (ibid.).

Fluvial Systems and Surface Hydrology

The watersheds and their draining streams and rivers on both sides of the Central Valley have common patterns of sediment transport, although those of the east side (the west slope of the Sierra) carry much more water. Eroded materials are transported down in steeply sloped, incised channels from the higher mountains, ultimately to be deposited on the broad, gently sloping alluvial fans comprising the lower termini of the watersheds. These alluvial floodplains, found along both sides of the valley floor at the bases of the mountains, tend to coalesce at their lateral margins with adjacent fans. The valley floor is thus a centrally depressed surface, the center of which is a sink with permanent wetlands, whose topography is in a slow but constant process of change from sequential alluvial depositions and the continued slow subsidence of the valley floor itself. Many Central Valley towns and cities (e.g., Sacramento, Fresno, Marysville, Yuba City, Bakersfield) are built on these alluvial floodplains and have experienced chronic flooding problems as a result. A more thorough treatment of Central Valley hydrology can be found in Katibah (1983) and Warner and Hendrix (in press).

It is difficult to generalize about Central Valley fluvial systems. They vary from small, first-order ephemeral streams to large, mainstem bottomland rivers. Prior to extensive water development, between 0.8 to 1.2 million hectares (2 to 3 million acres) of the valley floor were seasonally flooded, creating vast areas of floodplain riparian forest, woodland, savannah, and meadow. Duration of seasonal flooding varied from a few days to several months, depending on topography and on the timing and magnitude of storms and snowpack (Zeiner unpublished; California Department of Public Works 1931a,b).

In 1850 the U.S. Congress passed the Arkansas Swamp Act, permitting these "swamp and overflow lands" to be turned over to the states. In 1871, after much quarreling over where boundaries should be, the U.S. Secretary of the Interior accepted the State's determination of 887,654 ha. (2,192,500 ac.) of "swamp and overflow lands" (Thompson 1957; Zeiner unpublished). Somewhat later, the then-California Division of Water Resources, in Bulletins 26 and 29 (California Department of Public Works 1931a,b) concluded that in the Central Valley there were some 1,262,753 ha. (3,119,000 ac.) of floodplain bottomland subject to "seasonal or permanent flooding." This figure did not include the extensive riparian zones along tributary streams and rivers, which if included would raise the figure by at least another 300,000 ha. (740,000 ac.).

The significance of this is apparent. First, virtually all these seasonally inundated floodplain bottomlands were riparian wetlands. Second, based on both federal and state determinations, the historical extent of Central Valley riparian wetlands (as of 1871) was far greater than recent estimates based on reviews of early vegetation maps and present vegetation patterns (Roberts et al. 1977; Smith 1977; Katibah, Nedeff, and Dummer 1983; Küchler 1977). The influence of this vast complex of riparian wetlands upon Central Valley ecology was profound.

Surface hydrology and native vegetation patterns of the Central Valley have been greatly and perhaps permanently altered by human activities. Dams now block the flows of most of the larger streams and rivers, and, in so doing have massively altered the hydrologic regimes of the watercourses and associated groundwater basins. In some cases, the water so dammed is diverted out of the watershed altogether. Overbank flooding, siltation, and natural revegetation of the riparian zone have been greatly reduced. Thousands of kilometers of diversion ditches and canals now remove water from the streams, transporting it elsewhere for agricultural and other purposes, reducing groundwater recharge rates in the floodplains. In some areas, especially in the San Joaquin Valley, groundwater pumping from wells has lowered the water table to below root zones, rendering large areas uninhabitable to native trees and shrubs. The construction of thousands of kilometers of levees for flood control purposes has isolated hundreds of thousands of hectares of riverine floodplain from the periodic flows which replenished their soils, nutrients, and soil moisture. And cultivated agriculture and fenced pasturage, both of which do especially well on floodplain soils, have directly replaced (often in concert with the flood control levees) over half a million hectares of former riparian forest, woodland, and floodplain grasslands.

Virtually all the foothill and lower mountain portions of the study area have been continuously or seasonally grazed. The century and a half of open-range and pasture grazing of domestic livestock has greatly altered distributional patterns and species composition of riparian vegetation, as cattle and other range animals are preferentially attracted to the riparian zone for its water and highly palatable mesic vegetation.

METHODS

The field team consisted of a senior scientist and a field assistant. The team was equipped with a recreational vehicle which permitted near-site camping the night prior to a riparian site inventory. Background and pilot studies testing the methodology took place in February and March 1980; full-scale field investigations commenced in April and continued until mid-July 1980. Field activities were broken into 10-day blocks, during which 10 sites were inventoried. After a four- to five-day break, an additional 10-day field period ensued.

A typical daily schedule was as follows:

1. hike to site at first light;
2. inventory until aproximately 13:00;
3. return to vehicles, review data collected, and drive to next site;
4. contact landowner to arrange trespass;
5. briefly survey site and camp for night.

This procedure required on average 12 hours per day. It was found that for complex or logistically difficult systems one day was insufficient. Two to three days per site would permit more detailed and in-depth study, would allow field personnel more time to check data and to rest, and is recommended if the riparian systems are at all complex and/or if additional study parameters are added. Increasing team size to four would permit adequate one-day site inventories for most systems. If sites are stratified into plant associations or other subsets, sampling will of course require additional time.

Data Collection Procedures

A principal objective of the field measurements was to provide a quantitative basis for determining site vegetation structure, floristics, and plant diversity, and for intersite comparisons. A second major objective was to determine the condition and condition trends of the sites with respect to human-use impacts. Groundcover, shrubcover, understory, and canopy components of the vegetation were quantified by height, providing the structural data. Ancillary observations on streambank condition, adjacent land use, etc., augmented structural and taxonomic data. Not enough is yet known about the floristics of riparian systems of the Central Valley to use them either comparatively or definitively as condition estimators. However, the distribution, abundance, size (and age), amount of reproduction (if any), and condition of indigenous riparian trees and other perennial woody vegetation are all useful indicators of cumulative human-use impacts and of the potentials for restoration of the systems.

Four specially designed data entry forms were used for recording measurements of riparian system variables used for quantifying vegetation composition, structure, floristics, size frequency, associated birds, etc. The design of the forms (standard column/row design) and the variables measured are illustrated in figures 1 and 2. The variables (see especially fig. 2) were selected after initial background studies of Central Valley and other riparian systems and a review of relevant literature.

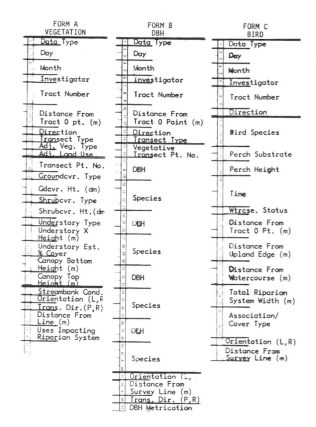

Figure 1.--Vegetation, diameter-at-breast-height (DBH), and bird data form heading layouts, indicating the riparian system structural, floristic, and condition variables measured.

Transverse (cross-sectional) transects were run across the riparian zone, from upland to upland if the watercourse was negotiable, from upland to watercourse if not. Transect endpoint locations were recorded in meters up- or downstream from a recorded "Site 0 (starting) Point", selected on the basis of permanence (e.g., a bridge) and visibility to aerial photography. A 2-m. pole marked off in decimeters was used locate transect points and to quantify groundcover and shrubcover vegetation height. Vegetation data (groundcover-type, groundcover height, shrubcover-type, shrubcover height, etc.) were recorded outbound; size frequency data were recorded inbound. Vegetation height and floristics were recorded at each 3-m. point along each transect. Size frequency data were recorded in a 6-m. belt along the same transect line. Bird observations were made while moving slowly through the site; species and location was recorded for each observation. Groundcover and shrubcover heights were measured in decimeters; understory (considered present only if a canopy was also present) and canopy bottom and top heights were estimated in meters by triangulation. Unknown species were collected for later identification. Stem size (DBH) of woody species with stems greater than 2 cm. was measured optically by holding a meter rule at arm's length against

VEGETATION TRANSECT SURVEY FORM: 1980 (DATA TYPE A)

Data Entry Descriptor Code

6. Investigator
   D. Dummer
   W. Warner
   A. _____
   B. _____

13. Direction
   U. Upstream
   D. Downstream

14. Transect Type
   A. 3 m Transverse
   B. 20x20m/3m Bird
   C. _____
   D. _____

15. Adjacent Vegetation
   Association/Cover Type
   (See List)

16. Adjacent Land Use
36. A. Undevel. Wildland
   B. Open Range Grazing
   C. Fenced Range Grazing
   D. Irrigated Pasture
   E. Dry Farming
   F. Irrigated Row Crops
   G. Irrigated Orchard
   H. Urban/Industrial
   I. Suburban Housing
   J. Commercial Forestry
   K. Forestry/Grazing
   L. Small Acreage Homesite
   M. _____
   N. _____
   O. _____
   P. _____

19. Groundcover Type
   A. Bare Ground
   B. Leafy Litter

   C. Woody Litter
   D. Grass
   E. Forbs
   F. Berries
   G. Shrubs
   H. Road
   I. Water
   J. Cattails
   K. Sedges
   L. Water/Veg.
   M. Rushes
   N. _____
   O. _____
   P. _____
   Q. _____
   R. _____

22. Shrubcover/Understory
25. Type
   A. Sambucus sp. (Elderberry)
   B. Salix sp. (Willow)
   C. Baccharis sp. (Coyote Bush)
   D. Eriogonum sp. (Buckwheat)
   E. Tamarix sp. (Tamarisk)
   F. Acer negundo (Box Elder)
   G. Rhus diversiloba (P. Oak)
   H. Rubus v. (Blackberry)
   I. Rosa c. (Wild Rose)
   J. Vitis c. (Wild Grape)
   K. Cephalanthus sp. (Buttonbush)
   L. Nicotiana g. (Tree Tobacco)
   M. Arctostaphylos sp. (Manzanita)
   N. Alnus sp. (Alder)
   O. Cornus s. (Creek Dogwood)
   P. Umbellularia c. (Calif. Bay)
   Q. Quercus lobata (Valley Oak)
   R. Quercus douglasii (Blue Oak)
   S. Quercus dumosa (Scrub Oak)
   T. Quercus sp. (Oak sp.)
   U. Heteromeles a. (Toyon)
   V. _____

22. Shrubcover/Understory
25. Type (Continued)
   W. _____
   X. _____
   Y. _____
   Z. _____

34. Streambank Condition
   A. Eroded/Bare
   B. Intermediate
   C. Vegetated/Stable
   D. Not Applicable

39. Present Impacting Uses
40. On Riparian System
   (See List)

Figure 2.--Data entry descriptors and entry codes for the vegetation form.

the stem and aligning the zero end at the left edge of the stem. The observed stem diameter was recorded in millimeters and later converted to actual diameter by a conversion equation. Very large tree trunks were measured circumferencially with a metal tape and the readings converted to millimeters DBH.

Random Sample Sites

A subset of 35 random sample sites was selected, using a randomized selection protocol based on USDI Geological Survey 1:24,000 quadrangles (quads). All perennial and intermittent watercourses shown on quads were candidate sites, from which the subset selected for study was drawn using stratified randomization procedures. Only 31 of these sites were ultimately used in the analysis. Randomized site selection procedures are described in greater detail in Katibah, Nedeff, and Dummer (1983) and Katibah, Dummer, and Nedeff (1983).

Nonrandom Sample Sites

It was important that selected riparian systems of special technical significance be included in the inventory. These included those known to be unique, to be relatively intact, and/or to be of special ecological importance. A subset of 20 nonrandom sites was selected based on available information and recommendations of field scientists with local knowledge. Because some of the nonrandom sites were relatively in-

tact (there are no pristine riparian systems left in California), they served as quasi-controls and as best-available baselines for comparative purposes.

Riparian Birds

Because of particular interest in the question of riparian system dependency and use by certain bird species, a special set of "bird" transects was run. Lists of "riparian-preferring" and "riparian-frequenting" birds were developed in consultation with the Denver Wildlife Research Center, FWS. While all bird species seen were recorded, a special watch was kept for these species and their precise locations noted when observed. At each such "bird" point, two 39-m. vegetation transects (13 transect points, each 3-m. apart, where point 7 fell at the point of bird observation) were run, one perpendicular (90°) to the other. These data were treated separately from the standard vegetation transect data. In simple and highly degraded riparian systems, bird species richness (i.e., the total number of bird species present) was determined. In large, complex systems, time and field staff limitations precluded such determinations, although many species were located. Findings from this part of the inventory will be reported elsewhere.

Data Processing and Descriptive Statistics

Computerized data management and analysis methods were utilized, with the assistance of the Statistical Resources Group of DFG, Menlo Park, Calif. The Statistical Package for the Social Sciences program (SPSS, Version 8.0, Vogelgack Computing Center, Northwestern University) was used for most data management and analysis needs. Special subroutines were written as necessary. These included data reduction and simple descriptive statistical procedures. Further description of field methodology, including that of the remote-sensing project, can be found in Warner and Katibah (1981) and Katibah et al. (ibid.).

RIPARIAN VEGETATION

Background Observations

The physical and biological makeup of any vegetation may be thought of in several ways. "Components" of morphological structure, floristics, spatial patterning, and intravegetation or "plant" diversity are the design determinants of any vegetation, whether our interest is in its value as timber, wildlife habitat, biomass, livestock forage, nature preserve, or any of a host of other attributes.

These site-specific components are in turn dependent upon other "factors" for their presence and expression. Climate, parent soil material, topography, accessibility of the site to potential inhabitants, length of time the site has been habitable, ecology of the plant species inhabitants (e.g., community interactions), external influences (primarily human-use impacts), and other factors all influence the floristics, structure, and spatial patterns of any plant association or community. Both Major (1951) and Mueller-Dombois and Ellenberg (1974) have developed vegetation-formation functions to describe this complex of factors. Major provides the following function for plant community.

Plant community = $f(o,c,p,r,t)$

$$\begin{array}{l} \text{where } o = \text{organisms} \\ \quad\quad c = \text{climate} \\ \quad\quad p = \text{parent soil material} \\ \quad\quad r = \text{relief or topography} \\ \quad\quad t = \text{time} \end{array} \Bigg] = \text{habitat}$$

Mueller-Dombois and Ellenberg offered a plant community formation function which is similar but has somewhat different emphases.

Plant community = $f(f,a,e,h,t)$

where f = flora
      a = accessibility factor
      e = ecological plant properties
      h = habitat
      t = time

However, many vegetations no longer have the "luxury" of untrammeled formation functions. Riparian vegetation especially has been subjected to violent human-use pressures which in many places all but obscure those factors responsible for their initial formation. Long-term livestock grazing can convert a forest to a grassland or a desert, as can damming and diversion of the water supply. Conversion to cultivated agriculture can efface entire vegetations.

Definition of Terms

To understand how structure, floristics, and spatial patterns relate to plant diversity and to vegetation formation factors, it is necessary first to define terms as used here. "Vegetation" is the plant life or total plant cover of an area. "Morphological structure" is the internal physical design of the vegetation—the brush, trunks, branches, canopies, and other vegetative materials that physically form its substance. "Floristics" is the biological component contributed by the different species of plants (the flora) making up that vegetation. "Spatial pattern" is the manner in which plants are aggregated. "Plant associations," where species are aggregated nonrandomly due to environmental factors, is one type of spatial pattern. "Plant diversity" is the internal heterogeneity of a vegetation created by structural and floristic nonuniformities in the plants which comprise it.

The term "plant diversity" was used deliberately to distinguish it from "species diversity" (a function of the number of species and their population sizes) and "vegetation diversity"

(differences between vegetations). Plant diversity includes species richness, population density, population demography, life form, spatial pattern, association (aggregation), and community (interacting association) components. For the present study the term was enlarged further to include certain human-use perturbations (e.g., roads) and absence of plants (e.g., bareground) as components because the frame of reference was the entire riparian system.

Thus—using one's own front lawn as an example—the vegetation is a simple one: a) composed of a single species of bermuda grass (its floristics); b) growing as a thin, dense, unbroken mat on the ground (its structure); and c) because of its uniformity and simplicity, having low plant diversity. In contrast, a gallery riparian forest may have: a) a luxuriant internal morphological structure, including up to four structural layers (groundcover, shrubcover, understory, canopy); b) be comprised of 50 or more species (i.e., have complex floristics); and c) have the entire array of species mixed heterogeneously, with gaps in the shrubcover and openings in the canopy so as to have a very high plant diversity.

Riparian Vegetations and the California Riparian Study Program

No two vegetations have the same structure, floristics, and plant diversity because each has a unique history and grows on a unique substrate (i.e., each has a unique formation function, in Major, and Mueller-Dombois and Ellenberg terminologies). Riparian vegetations, for example, are subject to being torn up and rearranged by floods. Each riparian system has a unique set of hydrologic conditions determining the amount and timing of the water it receives (hydroperiod), imposing site-specific conditions on presence/absence and growth rate of the various species comprising the vegetation. And each vegetation is growing on a substrate, whether a rocky streamside or an alluvial floodplain, that is in itself unique. Each, in addition, has an individual history of human-use impact. Some have been grazed by livestock, which alters the rates and patterns of plant reproduction and regrowth. Some have been selectively logged for timber or fuelwood, grossly changing both structure and floristics. Others may have at some time in the past been cleared for cultivation agriculture or burned and are at one stage or another of regrowth.

The study of these three major determinants of any vegetation—structure, floristics, and plant diversity—can thus tell us a great deal about the condition and condition trends of a vegetation (one might consider this the "health" of the vegetation) and provide useful insights into its human-use values and the best means of productive management.

Groundcover

"Groundcover" may be thought of as that layer of vegetation which actually covers the ground, for example grass, forbs (herbs other than grasses), leafy litter, etc. It is distinguished from "shrubs," the next higher layer, by the latter's having woody stems which hold the vegetation above the ground surface. In the present study, we have included "bare ground" and "road" as groundcover categories for practical reasons. Table 1 lists the principal groundcover-types occurring in the 51 ground-study sites for the entire Central Valley.

The data presented in table 1 are instructive in several ways. First, the major groundcover-types are indicated. Together with their frequencies of occurrence, they provide a quantitative picture of the nature of Central Valley riparian system groundcover-types. Second, the large ranges and standard deviations indicate that even though a groundcover-type may occur on several or many sites, the amount present varies widely between sites. Third, the large, highly varying coefficients of variation suggest that the factors responsible for the present groundcover-type patterns at any site are independent, that is each site probably has a unique vegetational history. This pattern of site individuality will be seen throughout, reinforcing the general observation that each riparian system is indeed unique, owing to the many independent variables discussed above, which create and modify them.

To give some idea of how these variables relate to any given riparian system, several sites are presented for comparative purposes. These are Caswell State Park (site no. 12, fig. 3), Kaweah River (site no. 24), Cantua Creek (site no. 16, fig. 4), and San Joaquin River at Frewert Road (site no. 4). Caswell State Park is a relatively intact, bottomland floodplain ripar-

Figure 3.--Floodplain riparian system at Caswell State Park. This area has been protected from disturbance for several decades. (Photograph by R.E. Warner.)

Figure 4.--Cantua Creek, a small perennial stream system in the Coast Ranges. Note the heavy growth of sedges and the scattered mature cottonwoods. (Photograph by R.E. Warner.)

Table 1.--Principal groundcover-types occurring in Central Valley riparian system study sites (N = 51). Number of sites = number of sites where groundcover-type occurred. Mean percent occurrence = mean percent occurrence for those sites where groundcover-type occurred.

Groundcover-type	Number of Sites	% of Sites	Mean % Occurrence	Range	Standard Deviation	Coefficient of variation
Grass	50	98	41.3	6.8-94.2	19.9	48.2
Bare ground	47	92	12.7	0.5-51.3	12.7	100.0
Forbs	45	88	13.7	0.3-43.9	11.9	86.9
Groundshrubs	33	65	8.6	0.4-29.5	8.5	98.8
Leafy litter	33	65	10.2	0.7-46.1	12.4	121.6
Woody litter	32	63	5.7	0.3-32.8	6.4	112.3
Road	21	41	4.2	0.4-9.4	2.5	59.5
Berry vines	18	35	7.7	0.5-26.5	6.8	88.3
Rushes	9	18	6.2	0.2-6.8	11.7	188.7
Sedges	7	14	6.9	0.8-24.6	8.2	118.8

ian system on the lower Stanislaus River, San Joaquin County; Kaweah River is a well-wooded, formerly grazed Sierra foothill stream near the town of Three Rivers, Tulare County; Cantua Creek is a heavily grazed, secondarily simplified system in the Coast Range foothills west of Fresno, Fresno County; and the San Joaquin River site is a vegetated levee on the floodplain near Stockton. Table 2 summarizes groundcover data for the four sites in terms of percent occurrence and mean height in decimeters, by groundcover-type.

Each site, as demonstrated here, had a unique set of groundcover characteristics reflecting its location, geophysical and hydrologic circumstances, land-use history, and present land-use patterns. Note, for example, the great difference in grass groundcover between Caswell (21.5%) and Cantua (70.6%) (table 2). Mean percent grass groundcover for all Central Valley sites combined was 41%; thus, Caswell was demonstrably below (19.5%) and Cantua well above (29.6%) the valley-wide average. Similarly, note the great disparity in forbs (non-grass herbs), where San Joaquin (25.0%) has over 16 times as many as Cantua (1.5%). The mean value for all Central Valley sites was 14%. Thus San Joaquin was well above the average value for forbs while Cantua was well below average. The high grass/low forb groundcover scores for Cantua reflect the long history of open-range grazing that particular riparian system has experienced. It also is linked to the reduced amount of tree canopy at that site, similarly the result of long-term open-range grazing. These figures can change very

markedly over time for any site, depending upon overall land-use practices, and can be used as quantitative elements to monitor the systems, if desired. Information on canopy structure and floristics is presented below to further illustrate the high degree of intersite diversity.

Groundcover Floristics

Conspicuously absent from this portion of the inventory are data on the plant species comprising the groundcover. The decision was made during project design to preclude collecting locational and floristics data on the many groundcover species because of the limited time available both for developing the inventory procedures and for acquiring field data. Grasses, forbs, herbs, mosses, ferns, lichens, and other groundcover plant species are important components of riparian system structure and plant diversity, and ideally should be included in riparian inventory and monitoring programs. They present special problems of location and taxonomy because of the intense seasonality of growth and flowering. Where time and resources permit, their inclusion into riparian inventory design is recommended.

Shrubcover, Understory, and Canopy

Each of these vegetation strata are potential structural components of riparian vegetations. In this study, plants were considered "shrubs" if they had woody stems supporting leafy

Table 2.--Groundcover-types for four different riparian systems in the Central Valley. Percent occurrence is as in table 1. Height--mean groundcover height in dm.; (Dev.)--standard deviation.

Groundcover-type	Caswell		Kaweah River		Cantua Creek		San Joaquin	
	% Occur.	Height (Dev.)	% Occur	Height (Dev.)	% Occur.	Height (Dev.)	% Occur	Height (Dev.)
Grass	21.5	4.1 (3.33)	34.7	3.0 (1.49)	70.6	2.8 (1.56)	59.4	3.9 (2.13)
Bare ground	5.1	– –	1.1	– –	11.0	– –	6.3	– –
Forbs	15.2	14.2 (6.35)	8.0	8.6 (3.13)	1.5	7.5 (2.12)	25.0	6.0 (3.12)
Groundshrubs	5.2	43.0 (24.05)	3.4	24.5 (5.75)	–	– –	–	– –
Leafy litter	8.3	0.9 (0.39)	27.3	1.9 (1.20)	0.7	1.0 0	–	– –
Woody litter	8.1	3.0 (4.56)	5.1	3.3 (1.41)	1.5	3.0 (1.41)	–	– –
Road	6.7	– –	6.8	– –	3.7	– –	9.4	– –
Berry vines	26.5	9.3 (5.48)	6.3	5.0 (1.61)	–	– –	–	– –
Sedges	–	– –	–	– –	7.4	5.7 (1.70)	–	– –

vegetation above ground level, but were no taller than 6 m. "Canopy" was the leafy vegetation produced by trees, and "understory" was that (rare, as it turned out) vegetation layer below and in the shade of an over-arching canopy, residing between it and the underlying shrubcover stratum. Normally, each vegetation stratum should be treated individually, as each contributes separately to the morphological structure, floristics, and spatial patterning of a vegetation. For reasons of space in this paper, these three vegetative components are not analyzed separately. Table 3 summarizes, by plant species and relative frequency of occurrence, the patterns of shrubcover, understory, and canopy for all 51 Central Valley sites studied on the ground.

A total of 50 plant species was recorded for the entire Central Valley. This does not, of course, mean that this is the total number of riparian species in the Central Valley, as the total sample size and sampling procedures did not permit identification of rarer species. However, the table clearly demonstrates the relative frequency and abundance of those species which are of major structural and ecological significance for riparian systems within the study area. Some are detailed below.

Table 3.--Principal shrubcover, understory, and canopy species found on 51 ground-study sites in the Central Valley. *--normally upland species sometimes found at the edges of riparian systems; SC--number of sites where species present as shrubcover; US--number of sites where species present as understory; C--number of sites where species present as canopy. % Occur.--mean percent occurrence. (s)--standard deviation (in parentheses).

	Number of sites where present	SC	% Occur. (s)	US	% Occur. (s)	C	% Occur. (s)
Willow (species) Salix spp.	35	35	8.6 (9.41)	3	1.2 (0.47)	32	36.9 (27.08)
Fremont cottonwood Populus fremontii	28	-	- -	-	- -	28	31.2 (34.93)
Valley oak Quercus lobata	20	2	0.6 (0.35)	-	- -	20	21.2 (18.49)
Oregon ash Fraxinus latifolia	18	-	- -	-	- -	18	7.7 (9.48)
Wild grape Vitis californica	17	5	1.4 (1.04)	13	1.3 (1.08)	-	- -
Poison oak Rhus diversiloba	13	13	5.3 (6.46)	-	- -	-	- -
Black walnut Juglans hindsii	13	-	- -	-	- -	13	15.2 (20.98)
White alder Alnus rhombifolia	13	2	1.6 (0.21)	1	4.7 (0)	10	10.6 (9.87)
Box elder Acer negundo	12	10	2.5 (2.56)	6	4.2 (4.49)	8	11.8 (13.88)
Button bush Cephalanthus occidentalis	12	7	2.9 (4.14)	1	0.9 (0)	-	- -
Blue elderberry Sambucus caerulea	11	9	6.8 (6.57)	1	6.3 0	2	2.5 (1.34)
Coyote bush Baccharis pilularis	10	9	3.5 (2.81)	-	- -	-	- -
Digger pine* Pinus sabiniana	10	-	- -	-	- -	10	13.4 (16.18)
Oak (species) Quercus spp.	10	10	3.1 (2.48)	-	- -	-	- -
Blue oak* Quercus douglasii	9	2	1.1 (0.33)	-	- -	9	33.9 (18.94)
California sycamore Platanus racemosa	8	-	- -	-	- -	8	22.2 (22.47)
Manzanita (species)* Arctostaphylos spp.	7	7	6.2 (7.40)	-	- -	-	- -

Table 3.--Continued.

	Number of sites where present	SC	% Occur. (s)	US	% Occur. (s)	C	% Occur. (s)
Wild rose	7	7	3.3	–	–	–	–
Rosa californica			(4.46)		–		–
Buckwheat	6	5	4.6	2	5.7	–	–
Eriogonum spp.			(2.65)		(2.48)		–
Interior live oak	6	–	–	–	–	6	31.8
Quercus wislizenii			–		–		(34.93)
Black oak	5	–	–	–	–	5	7.6
Quercus kelloggii			–		–		(4.19)
Toyon	4	4	2.1	–	–	–	–
Heteromeles arbutifolia			(0.90)		–		–
Tree tobacco	4	2	8.7	–	–	2	14.0
Nicotiana glauca			(8.45)		–		(11.67)
Scrub oak*	4	4	1.1	–	–	–	–
Quercus dumosa			(0.07)		–		–
Eucalyptus (species)	4	–	–	–	–	4	41.9
Eucalyptus spp.			–		–		(41.9)
Blackberry (species)	3	3	2.0	–	–	–	–
Rubus spp.			(1.23)		–		–
Tamarisk (species)	3	3	2.8	–	–	–	–
Tamarix spp.			(1.82)		–		–
California bay	3	3	0.8	1	1.1	1	13.3
Umbellularia californica			(0.38)		0		0
Ponderosa pine	3	–	–	–	–	3	41.4
Pinus ponderosa			–		–		(51.01)
Bigleaf maple	2	–	–	–	–	2	1.0
Acer macrophyllum			–		–		0
California buckeye	2	–	–	–	–	2	10.3
Aesculus californica			–		–		(5.02)
Red osier dogwood	2	2	0.6	–	–	–	–
Cornus occidentalis			(0.28)		–		–
California live oak	2	–	–	–	–	2	56.5
Quercus agrifolia			–		–		(9.12)
Fig (exotic)	2	–	–	–	–	2	7.3
Ficus carica			–		–		(8.49)
Oregon oak	2	–	–	–	–	2	31.4
Quercus garryana			–		–		(18.38)

Major Species

Shrubcover

As indicated in table 3, willow, poison oak, box elder, oak, elderberry, and coyote bush were the principal shrubcover plants, although at least 22 shrubcover species were identified.

Understory

Wild grape, box elder, and willow were the main constituents of understory, which was overall surprisingly scarce. For those sites where it did occur, it averaged only 2.9% occurrence, calling into question its ecological role (and indeed, its structural reality) in most Central Valley riparian systems.

Canopy

Again referring to table 3, various willow species (35, 36.9%), Fremont cottonwood (28, 31.2%), valley oak (20, 21.2%), Oregon ash (18, 7.7%), black walnut (13, 15.2%), and white alder (10, 10.6%) constitute the dominant riparian canopy species. The transect procedure scored as present at a transect point any canopy species which was either on or overhanging the transect point. Thus, for example, a valley oak whose trunk was 4 m. from the transect point was counted if some portion of its canopy was directly above the transect point. These figures can be treated as rough approximations of percent canopy cover by the different tree species.

There is a direct (though not linear) relationship between stem diameter and canopy size of most trees. Stem diameter data gathered from the 6-m. wide belt transects can thus be used to compute percent canopy cover by species once the stem:canopy diameter function has been determined. It is not reported here but mentioned to call attention to yet another analysis available with this methodology.

Reproduction and Size-class Patterns

Stem diameter (also called diameter-at-breast-height or DBH) data obtained by the 6-m. wide belt transects for the most frequently encountered riparian tree species were aggregated into 50 mm. size-classes. Figures 5 and 6 depict the resulting DBH size-frequency curves for six Central Valley riparian tree species. Figure 7, the DBH size-frequency curve for the giant sequoia (_Sequoia gigantea_) of the Sierra Nevada, is provided for comparative purposes. This population has been protected for many years from severe human-use impacts such as logging and grazing.

Figure 5 clearly shows the DBH size-frequency pattern differences between Oregon ash, on the one hand, and Fremont cottonwood and California sycamore on the other. These latter two species are clearly experiencing long-term perturbations to reproduction. Size(age)-classes smaller than about 40 cm. (16.3 in.) DBH are progressively less well represented. The decrement in the two smallest size-classes of Oregon ash is not yet understood. It may be real or may be an artifact of inadequate field procedures, where the smallest stems were undersampled.

Figure 6, DBH size-frequency curves for Hind's walnut, willow (species), and valley oak, again demonstrate a severe perturbation or disruption in the reproduction of valley oak. The Central Valley population of this species is clearly not maintaining itself. If one overlays the valley oak, Fremont cottonwood, and California sycamore DBH size-frequency curves, a strikingly similar curve shape will be noted. While it is not possible to deduce from these data what is causing the serious declines of these three species; it does appear that their patterns of decline are similar.

These size-frequency data also corroborate a similar inference which can be drawn from table 3 (discussion above), where these species were present in very low numbers as seedlings and saplings in the shrubcover and understory components of the vegetation.

The lack of continued recruitment into the riparian vegetation of these previously important canopy species indicates that: a) over time, as existing adult trees age and die (fig. 8), the systems are experiencing large structural and floristic shifts; b) the ecological values of the vegetations (e.g., their ability to support native riparian-dependent birds and other wildlife) are being progressively impaired; and c) suppression of riparian tree reproduction is a widespread phenomenon throughout the Central Valley.

Field studies have clearly demonstrated that open-range grazing of livestock and the lack of fencing protection for riparian systems within fenced pastures both result in selective removal of seedlings and saplings of broad-leaf deciduous riparian vegetation (fig. 9). Dams and water diversions are known to produce significant downstream changes in flow regimes, in the levels

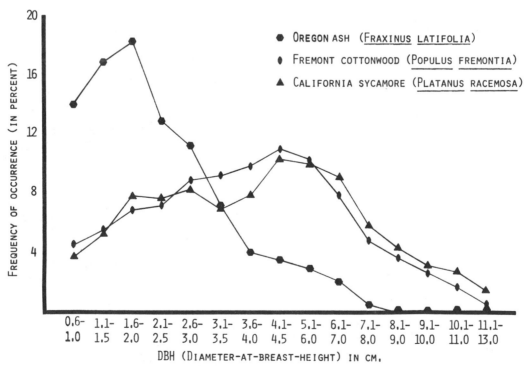

Figure 5.--DBH size-class curves (three-point moving means) for three species of Central Valley riparian trees, based on data from 51 sites.

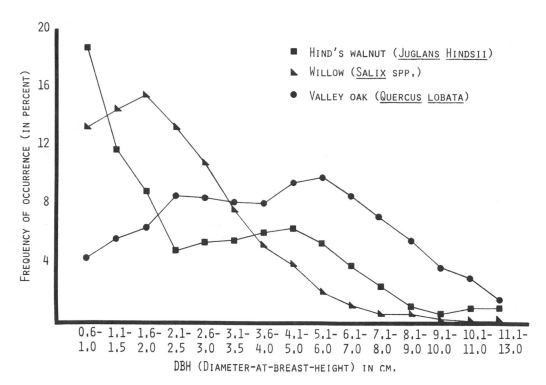

Figure 6.--DBH size-frequency curves (three-point moving means) for three species of Central Valley riparian trees, based on data from 51 sites.

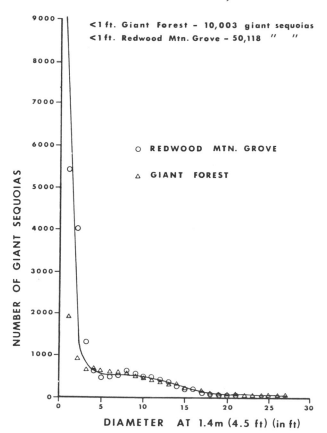

Figure 7.--DBH size-frequency curve for the giant sequoia (Sequoia gigantea) in the Sierra Nevada. (From Harvey et al. 1980.)

Figure 8.--Senescent cottonwood/willow riparian woodland on Dry Creek, near Academy, Fresno County. Note lack of reproduction.

of winter floodwaters, and in dry season flow rates (and riparian zone soil moisture) and thus to impact native vegetation reproduction. Cottonwoods and willows, for example, release their seeds in the spring during spring runoff. Both species germinate best in recently deposited, fine, moist silts, a trait of obvious adaptive value for riparian species, but one at risk if flow regimes are modified.

Figure 9.--Floodplain sycamore woodland by Orestimba Creek subjected to long-term fenced livestock grazing. Note complete absence of sycamore regeneration and lack of plant diversity.

In addition to being suppressed as seedlings and saplings by livestock browsing and other human-use pressures, cottonwoods of all sizes are a preferred food of the beaver (Castor canadensis), whose population density has increased in recent decades (fig. 10). Pocket gophers (Thomomys bottae) and ground squirrels (Citellus spp.) have been reported to feed on valley oak acorns and seedlings. Gopher and ground squirrel population densities are known to be greatly affected by land-use practices, increasing if ground- and shrubcover is removed through grazing, burning, or other means.

Floristics

Plant Species Richness

"Species richness" may be defined as the number of species in a plant association, in this case in a site of riparian vegetation. A cumulative total of 50 plant species was recorded by the ground study at 51 Central Valley riparian sites. Most are listed in table 3. As indicated earlier, there are considerably more than 50 riparian plant species in the Central Valley. The survey was not, however, designed to locate the rarer ones, nor any, common or rare, that were groundcover species.

There is no way of knowing with certainty what plant species were present, or in what numbers, during earlier periods, for measurements are lacking. One of the few comparative approaches presently available is to utilize species richness counts from the most intact of the remaining riparian systems. The selection of non-random sites in the study design was a conscious attempt to provide this quasi-natural kind of baseline information.

Figure 10.--Young cottonwood trees (15-18 years old) along Arcade Creek, Arcade Park, Sacramento County, being cut down by beaver.

Caswell State Park (site 12), San Joaquin County, and Sweetwater Creek (site 36), El Dorado County, both yielded 19 woody plant species using study procedures, the largest number. These were both relatively intact riparian systems with very high plant diversity indices and high riparian bird species richness. Wyman Ravine at Lower Wyandotte Road (site 41), Butte County, produced 18 species of woody plants. This site is a perennial stream floodplain that had been dredged for gold and is now vegetatively recovering. Its high species richness appeared to derive from the highly diverse nature of the substrate, where the floodplain and its ponds, swales, and dredge tailings are all watered by a small perennial stream. It also had one of the highest plant diversity indices.

Space does not permit a full discussion of species richness by site, although much can be learned from such evidence. There was a wide range of species richness between sites, indicating, as do the data on vegetation diversity, that there was very little similarity between the different riparian systems. The numbers of species (or species richness) in shrubcover, understory, and canopy of different sites are listed in table 4. The four "vegetation" columns list the number of sites where a given number of plant species (left column) occurs. The three sites where no (0) species occur had only a groundcover stratum.

Again the interesting fact emerges that on 35 sites there were no understory species at all (i.e., understory was absent). Where understory did occur, it was comprised of very few species. The wide range in species richness for canopy is also noteworthy.

Table 4.--Plant species richness by number of sites for shrubcover, understory, canopy, and total vegetation for 51 Central Valley riparian study sites.

Species Richness at site (no. species)	Shrubcover Vegetation (no. sites)	Understory Vegetation (no. sites)	Canopy Vegetation (no. sites)	Total Vegetation (no. sites)
0	7	35	3	3
1	8	6	3	3
2	11	4	6	6
3	4	2	2	2
4	5	0	5	5
5	5	3	3	3
6	4	0	4	4
7	2	0	2	2
8	2	0	5	5
9	0	0	2	2
10	1	0	6	6
11	2	0	1	1
12	0	0	3	3
13	0	0	0	0
14	0	0	1	1
15	0	0	0	0
16	0	0	1	1
17	0	0	0	0
18	0	0	1	1
19	0	0	2	2

Plant Diversity

"Plant diversity," as used here, is the total structural and floristic heterogeneity within a vegetation. In nature, plant diversity has many components, more than we can count and probably more than we can identify. For purposes of the present study, the following protocol for measuring plant diversity was used.

It will be recalled that four structural strata were identified by the inventory: ground-cover, shrubcover, understory, and canopy. In the site transect surveys where a transect sample-point was established every 3 m., each sample-point yielded information on the taxon, or structural type (when present), for each stratum. This taxon could be a species or a more general descriptor such as "grass." A vegetation such as a closed-canopy forest may have all four strata present; in this case there would be four scores--one for each stratum--at that transect sample-point. Thus groundcover, shrubcover, understory, and canopy taxa were recorded wherever present at each sequential sample-point along a transect, the aggregate of several transects providing a three-dimensional structural matrix.

For the purposes of the study, plant diversity resulted when one transect-point stratum reading was followed by a dissimilar one on either the vertical axis (vertical diversity component) or the horizontal axis (horizontal diversity component). For example, if for the ground-cover stratum a transect sequentially recorded: "grass - grass - forb - woody litter - berryvine - berryvine," the horizontal diversity score would be 1 (grass-forb) + 1 (forb-woody litter) + 1 (woody litter-berryvine) = 3 horizontal diversity points. If the vertical readings were: "grass - poison oak - elderberry - Fremont cottonwood," the vertical diversity score would be 1 (grass-poison oak) + 1 (poison oak-elderberry) + 1 (elderberry-Fremont cottonwood) = 3 vertical diversity points. This procedure, while a simplification of the real world complexity of natural vegetations, permits the development of a quantitative structural and floristic index of plant diversity in both horizontal and vertical axes.

The results of an analysis of plant diversity for the 51 ground-study sites are presented in figure 11. This is actually a scatter diagram, where the vertical diversity component is plotted on the vertical axis of the graph and the horizontal component plotted on the horizontal axis. The further to the right a point is, the greater the horizontal plant diversity component at that site; the higher on the y axis, the greater the site's vertical plant diversity component. Thus the higher and to the right that a point is, the larger that site's total plant diversity score.

Clearly, there is great variation in plant diversity between sites. Systems range in structural and floristic design (and hence plant diversity) from moist, grassy swales with a few sedges and no shrubs or trees, to narrow linear stringers of riparian vegetation along small spring-fed

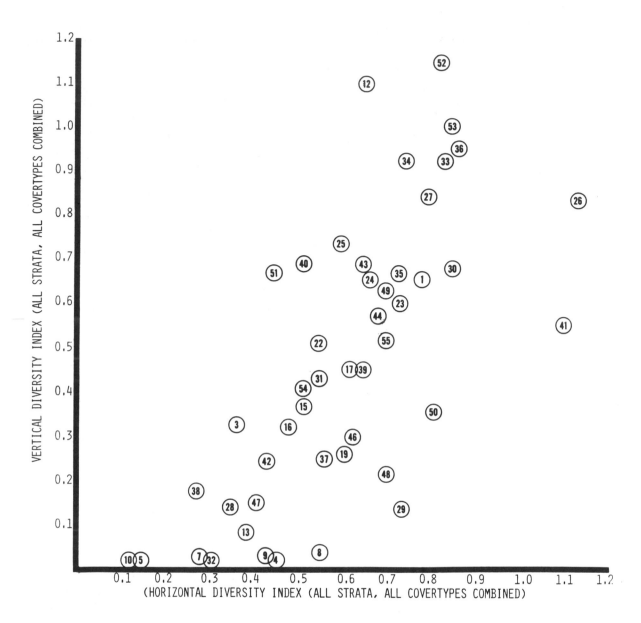

Figure 11.--Plant diversity scores for 51 Central Valley riparian sites.

creeks, to closed-canopy gallery forests. Surprisingly, the narrow stringer system often exhibited a high total plant diversity. This resulted from the intermixing of riparian and upland plant species. Another way of describing these narrow, perennial and intermittent stream riparian corridors or stringers is to say that they are almost pure ecotone; that is, they are so narrow that there is no inner core or "interior" of strictly riparian vegetation. Preliminary studies of riparian birds associated with these stringers suggests that despite this high plant diversity, narrow ecotonal riparian stringers do not support the greatest bird species richness. That is found in the larger systems having a combination of greater amounts of core or interior and more purely riparian vegetation conditions.

The great array of riparian system plant diversity illustrated in figure 11 reflects both the local geophysical and biogeographic circumstances of the systems and their individual histories of human-use impact. The three sites of highest plant diversity were: 1) Ladd Creek at Road 200 (site 26), Madera County, a small but complex perennial stream system below a small earthfill dam in the Sierra foothills; 2) Wyman Ravine at Lower Wyandotte Road (site 41), Butte County, a small perennial stream system on a broad floodplain with a partially closed canopy and well along in recovering from gold dredging, again in the Sierra foothills; and 3) Mooney Island on the Sacramento River (site 52), Tehama County, a mature cottonwood grove on the bank of the river. The two sites of lowest plant diversity were Dry Creek Swale at Academy (site 10), Fresno County, a grassy swale with perennial seepage and no woody vegetation; and Sandy Mush Road at Healy Road (site 5), Madera County, a small valley floor stream that has been channelized to carry runoff (and possibly agricultural) water.

At the Sandy Mush Road site, the cottonwood/willow stringer vegetation had been largely removed for channel clearance and other less obvious reasons. The Dry Creek Swale site has been exposed to livestock grazing since the latter 1800s, suppressing all but grazing-resistant groundcover plants such as grass, clover, and sedges.

HUMAN-USE IMPACT

The massive changes in surface hydrology and land-use practices since European settlement of the Central Valley were been briefly discussed earlier in this paper. The large areas of riparian vegetation displaced by cultivated agriculture are now so completely altered from their indigenous form that only the underlying substrate—the moist soil "riparian zone"—remains of the original system. For such grossly modified systems, it is impossible to assign a condition descriptor other than "completely altered." For those remnant systems still retaining riparian vegetation, most exhibited low plant diversity and other symptoms of chronic overuse such as lack of reproduction of woody species, low plant species richness, intrusion of xeric upland species, areas of bare ground, and unstable and eroding streambanks or continuing progressive encroachment of cultivated agriculture.

Condition and Condition Trend

Assessing condition and condition trend for Central Valley riparian systems presented several problems. The first was that of ownership pattern. Many riparian lands in the study area are privately owned. On some watercourses, there may be 10 or more riparian landowners per linear mile. Each parcel has a unique land-use history, and one often sees sharp differences in structure, floristics, plant diversity, and condition on sequential parcels. With such a linear mosaic, it is difficult even to set meaningful study site boundaries.

Second, actual condition trends are determined by human decisions on present and future land-use practices far more than on natural ecological patterns of reproduction and succession. A luxuriant riparian forest may be completely removed and replaced with cultivated agriculture or fenced pasture in a matter of days. Livestock numbers on open range change with market prices and precipitation-controlled forage production. Obtaining such data would require interviews with landowners and assessment of public policies and programs.

Third, surface hydrology changes are still taking place. Dams are still being built, more water being diverted, groundwater levels fluctuating more widely or being drawn down progressively further. For example, construction of the proposed dam on the Cosumnes and Tuolumne rivers would greatly alter the hydrology of thousands of hectares of downstream riparian zone. Flood control projects with their engineering works continue. These and other factors not readily discernible from single-visit field studies render condition-trend predictions from such studies somewhat speculative.

Because of these imponderables, only a simple condition-trend evaluation was undertaken. Study sites were rated for condition on the basis of present kind and intensity of human use, degree of disruption to the natural system, and apparent level of commitment to present land-use practices. Three scores were possible: 1) recovering; 2) stable; and 3) degrading. Table 5 presents the resulting condition scores.

Table 5.--Apparent condition trend evaluation expressed as percent of total for 53 Central Valley riparian sites. N = 15 publicly owned, 38 privately owned.

Ownership	Degrading	Stable	Recovering
Private	74	18	8
Public	67	13	20
All sites combined	72	17	11

It must be concluded that on both privately and publicly owned riparian lands, the overall condition pattern is one of continued degradation for most remnant riparian systems. The 20% recovering rating for public lands includes preserves owned by conservation organizations. These were considered public rather than private because of their communal nature. Were this not done, the two sets of scores would be almost identical.

These figures are quite similar to condition assessment values developed independently by Katibah, Dummer, and Nedeff (1983) for a larger set of 178 riparian sites, including the 53 sites reported here, from remote-sensing data. They found that for the CRSP Central Valley study area, 8.1% of riparian sites were recovering, 25.4% were stable, 37.9% were still being degraded, and 28.6% were so severely degraded that no assessment of possible recovery could be made.

Three conclusions concerning condition and condition trend seem inescapable. First, no Central Valley riparian system has escaped the destructive impacts of direct and/or indirect human-use practices. Over 90% have been so altered as to be unrecognizable as riparian systems, either structurally or ecologically. Second, of those remnant systems that are still sufficiently intact as to be assessable, all show significant perturbations due to human-use impacts. Third, about 8-11% of the remnant systems are recovering, 17-25% are stable, and 67-72% are still being degraded by ongoing destructive human-use impacts.

CONCLUSIONS

Central Valley riparian wetlands once occupied some 0.8-1.2 million hectares (2-3 million acres) of the Central Valley. Direct and indirect human-use impacts have reduced that amount by over 90%. Major causes of this decline have been changes in surface hydrology, displacement by cultivated agriculture, livestock grazing, and physical developments within the riparian zone. An inventory methodology developed for the CRSP demonstrated that quantification of structure, floristics, size-frequency, plant diversity, and other riparian system variables was possible and could be undertaken in a cost-effective and time-efficient manner. Some of the findings generated by the methodology as applied to 51 riparian sites are listed below.

1. Each riparian system is hydrologically, structurally and vegetatively unique.

2. This site-specific uniqueness derives from both environmental and human-use impact influences.

3. Groundcover-type and amount varied widely between sites.

4. Understory, as a functional component of Central Valley riparian systems, is uncommon and probably of limited ecological significance.

5. There is extreme variation in plant diversity between systems, with no evidence of natural types or categories of systems readily demonstrable on the basis of structure or plant diversity.

6. 50 species of woody plants were recorded, with willow (species) being the most common (35 sites), followed by Fremont cottonwood (28 sites), valley oak (20 sites), Oregon ash (18 sites), and wild grape, poison oak, and white alder (13 sites each).

7. Of these major riparian species, valley oak, Fremont cottonwood, and California sycamore all showed aberrant size-frequency patterns, indicating impaired reproduction and consequent lack of recruitment into their populations.

8. Observed major causes of these aberrant size-frequency patterns include livestock grazing and modification of surface and groundwater hydrology.

9. Condition trend assessment indicated that of the remnant riparian systems in the Central Valley, 8-11% are recovering, 17-25% are stable, and 67-72% are still being degraded by ongoing destructive human-use impacts.

There is both bad news and good news in this report. The bad news is that we have already lost most of our Central Valley riparian wetlands and the remainder are under heavy and unremitting siege by both private and public entities. The good news is that we: 1) are now finally alerted to the ongoing tragedy of their decimation; 2) are able to quantitatively inventory and monitor their most important variables; and 3) are thus prepared to embark on sound management and restoration programs capable of returning those still-remaining riparian wetlands to ecologic and economic productivity.

Some of the problems, such as the lack of reproduction in major riparian tree species, will require special study. Return to the presettlement landscape, with its vast and prodigiously productive immensity of riparian wetlands is of course neither possible nor desirable. But it is both desirable and possible to stop the continuing slide of this resource, and those species dependent upon it, toward extinction. Indeed, the laudable goal set by the California Legislature for our aquatic wetlands--doubling their size by the year 2000--is equally laudable, and attainable, for our remnant riparian wetlands.

ACKNOWLEDGMENTS

I thank Kevin Dummer for his willingness to thrash through poison oak thickets and blackberry brambles in the pursuit of field data. I thank Kathy Hendrix for her generous assistance in preparing this paper. Major support for the study was provided by the Denver Wildlife Research Center, USDI Fish and Wildlife Service; that financial support is gratefully acknowledged. Charlene Hensley, Sara Denzler, and Eda Lim provided valuable data reduction and processing. Philip Law and John Geibel of the Statistical Resources Group, DFG, Menlo Park, provided thoughtful consultation and computer facility support. Michael Barbour, Jack Major, Glen Holstein, and Tom Griggs contributed valuable botanical counsel, although they must not be held accountable for any aspect of this report. Stimulating planning sessions with Robert Colwell, Ed Katibah, Steve DeGloria, and others of the Remote Sensing Research Group, University of California, Berkeley, are remembered with pleasure. Thanks and gratitude to all of those, mentioned or not, who contributed toward this effort.

LITERATURE CITED

Anderson, B.W., and R.D. Ohmart. 1977. Vegetation structure and bird use in the lower Colorado River Valley. p. 23-24. In: R.R. Johnson and D.A. Jones (tech. coord.). Importance, preservation and management of riparian habitat: A symposium. [Tucson, Arizona, July 9, 1977.] USDA Forest Service GTR-RM-43, Rocky Mountain Forest and Range Experiment Station, Fort Collins, Colo. 217 p.

Bonner, K.G., L.D. Bowden, and R.R. Colwell. 1979. Riparian vegetation mapping and inventory design. (Draft.) Final report of work performed for the California Department of Fish and Game, Standard Agreement DFG-S-1729. Remote Sensing Research Program, Department of Forestry and Conservation, College of Natural Resources, University of California, Berkeley. 93 p.

California Department of Public Works. 1931(a). Sacramento Valley basin. Bull. No. 26, Division of Water Resources. California Department of Public Works, Sacramento.

California Department of Public Works. 1931(b). San Joaquin Valley basin. Bull. No. 29, Division of Water Resources. California Department of Public Works, Sacramento.

Carothers, S.W., R.R. Johnson, and S.W. Aitchison. 1974. Population structure and social organization of southwestern riparian birds. Amer. Zool. 14:97-108.

Central Valley Riparian Mapping Project. 1979. Interpretation and mapping systems. Report prepared by the Riparian Mapping Team, Geography Department, California State University, Chico, in cooperation with the Department of Geography, California State University, Fresno. 24 p. Unpublished manuscript on file with the Planning Branch, California Department of Fish and Game, Sacramento.

Conard, S.A., R.L. MacDonald, and R.F. Holland. 1977. Riparian vegetation and flora of the Sacramento Valley. p. 47-55. In: A. Sands (ed.). Riparian forests in California: Their ecology and conservation. Institute of Ecology Pub. No. 15, University of California, Davis. 122 p.

Durrenberger, R.W., and R.R. Johnson. 1976. California: Patterns on the land. 134 p. California Council for Geographic Education, Mayfield Publishing Company, Palo Alto, Calif.

Gaines, D. 1977. The status of selected riparian forest birds in California. A preliminary survey and review. Report to the California Department of Fish and Game, Sacramento. Unpublished manuscript. 72 p.

Harvey, H.T., H.S. Shellhammer, and R.E. Stecker. 1980. Giant sequoia ecology. Fire and reproduction. Scientific monograph Series No. 12, USDI, National Park Service, Washington, D.C. 182 p.

Hubbard, J.P. 1977. Importance of riparian ecosystems: Biotic considerations. p. 14-18. In: R.R. Johnson and D.A. Jones (tech. coord.). Importance, preservation and management of riparian habitat: A symposium. [Tucson, Arizona, July 9, 1977.] USDA Forest Service GTR-RM-43, Rocky Mountain Forest and Range Experiment Station, Fort Collins, Colo. 217 p.

Jain, S. 1976. Vernal pools—their ecology and conservation. Institute of Ecology Pub. No. 9, University of California, Davis. 93 p.

Johnson, R.R., L.T. Haight, and J.M. Simpson. 1977. Endangered species vs. endangered habitats: A concept. p. 68-79. In: R.R. Johnson and D.A. Jones (tech. coord.). Importance, preservation and management of riparian habitat: A symposium. [Tucson, Arizona, July 9, 1977.] USDA Forest Service GTR-RM-43, Rocky Mountain Forest and Range Experiment Station, Fort Collins, Colo. 217 p.

Johnson, R.R., and D.A. Jones (tech coord.) 1977. Importance, preservation and management of riparian habitat: A symposium. [Tucson, Arizona, July 9, 1977.] USDA Forest Service GTR- RM-43, Rocky Mountain Forest and Range Experiment Station, Fort Collins, Colo. 217 p.

Katibah, E.F. 1983. A brief history of riparian forests in the Central Valley of California. In: R.E. Warner and K.M. Hendrix (ed.). California Riparian Systems. [University of California, Davis, September 17-19, 1981.] University of California Press, Berkeley.

Katibah, E.H., K.J. Dummer, and N.E. Nedeff. 1983. Current condition of riparian resources in the Central Valley of California. In: R.E. Warner and K.M. Hendrix (ed.). California Riparian Systems. [University of California, Davis, September 17-19, 1981.] University of California Press, Berkeley.

Katibah, E.F., N.E. Nedeff, and K.J. Dummer. 1983. Summary of riparian vegetation areal and linear extent measurements from the Central Valley riparian mapping project. In: R.E. Warner and K.M. Hendrix (ed.). California Riparian Systems. [University of California, Davis, September 17-19, 1981.] University of California Press, Berkeley.

Korte, P.A., and L.H. Fredrickson. 1977. Loss of Missouri's lowland hardwood ecosystem. Contribution from the Gaylord Memorial Laboratory, University of Missouri, Columbia, and the Missouri Agricultural Experiment Station, Proj. 170. Journal Series No. 7766:1.

Küchler, A.W. 1977. The map of the natural vegetation of California. p. 909-938. In: M.G. Barbour and J. Major (ed.). Terrestrial vegetation of California. John Wiley and Sons, New York, N.Y. 1002 p.

Major, J. 1951. A functional, factorial approach to plant ecology. Ecology 32:392-412.

McGill, R.R., Jr. 1975. Land use changes in the Sacramento River riparian zone, Redding to Colusa. California Department of Water Resources, Northern District Report. 23 p.

McGill, Robert R., Jr. 1979. Land use change in the Sacramento River riparian zone, Redding to Colusa. An update--1972 to 1977. California Department of Water Resources, Northern District. 34 pp.

Mueller-Dombois, M., and H. Ellenberg. 1974. Aims and methods of vegetation ecology. 547 p. John Wiley and Sons, New York, N.Y.

Roberts, W.G., J. G. Howe, and J. Major. 1977. A survey of riparian forest flora and fauna in California: p. 3-19. In: A. Sands (ed.). Riparian forests in California: Their ecology and conservation. Institute of Ecology Pub. No. 15, University of California, Davis. 122 p.

Sands, A. (ed.). 1977. Riparian forests in California. Their ecology and conservation. Institute of Ecology Pub. No. 15, University of California, Davis. 122 pp.

Smith, F. 1977. A short review of the status of riparian forests in California. p. 1-2. In: A. Sands (ed.). Riparian forests in California: Their ecology and conservation. Institute of Ecology Pub. No. 15, University of California, Davis. 122 p.

Thompson, J. 1957. The settlement geography of the Sacramento-San Joaquin Delta, California. Ph.D. Dissertation, Stanford University, Palo Alto, Calif.

Warner, R.E. 1979. California riparian study program. Background information and proposed study design. California Department of Fish and Game, Sacramento. 177 pp.

Warner, R.E., and K.M. Hendrix. In press. Riparian resources of the Central Valley and California Desert: A report on their nature, history, status, and future. California Department of Fish and Game, Sacramento.

Warner, R.E., and Edwin F. Katibah. 1981. Measurement techniques for inventorying riparian systems. p. 487-494. In: H.G. Lund, M. Caballero, R.H. Hamre, R.S. Driscoll, and W. Bonner (ed.). Arid land inventories: Developing cost-effective methods. [La Paz, Mexico, November 30-December 6, 1980.] USDA Forest Service GTR-WO-28, Washington, D.C. 620 p.

Zeiner, D.C. 1983. A plan for protecting, enhancing, and increasing California's wetlands for waterfowl. Unpublished draft manuscript. California Department of Fish and Game, Sacramento. 80 p.

A RIPARIAN CLASSIFICATION SYSTEM[1]

R. Roy Johnson, Steven W. Carothers,

and James M. Simpson[2]

Abstract.--Riparian ecology, as one of the newest scientific disciplines, is developing a conceptual framework which includes new supportive terminology and classification schemes. This branch of ecology has developed largely in the arid western United States as an offshoot of wetlands ecology. This paper discusses important concepts, classifications, and interrelationships between riparian ecology and other disciplines. This new science is especially important to floodplain zoning and management, natural resource management, and recreation management.

INTRODUCTION

The word riparian is derived from the Latin ripa meaning "banks." Although a long-established word, it did not come into common usage until the early 1970s. Now the terms "riparian habitat" and "riparian system" are well known to wildlife and recreation managers. In the most restricted sense, the word riparian refers to the banks of a stream or river (Langbein and Iseri 1960; Oxford English Dictionary [Unabridged] 1979), although the Oxford Dictionary gives "riparial" for either a stream or lake. In its vaguest sense riparian refers to "the banks of a body of water" (American Geological Institute 1962) or bank of a river or other body of water (Random House Unabridged Dictionary 1967), and in its broadest sense riparian refers to "land bordering a stream, lake, or tidewater" (Hanson 1962).

It is not surprising, then, that some investigators would restrict riparian to streams or, at most, freshwater streams and lakes. However, it is often impossible to determine where a montane lake ends and the stream flowing from it begins. Similarly, at the junction of the stream's mouth with a gulf or seacoast, the point where the stream ends and the ocean begins depends on flow levels of the stream and tidal phases of the ocean. Thus, although some boundaries of particular watercourses or lakes are easily definable, their associated ecosystems are often continuous. This, in our opinion, justifies considering habitats associated with lakes, watercourses (temporary or permanent), and tidewater areas as part of a continuous wetland environment, although different segments may have their specifically recognizable riparian communities.

Little more than a decade ago, many resource managers and even scientists concerned with riparian areas were not familiar with the term riparian. Today, though technically an adjective, the word has been "elevated" to a noun (Johnson 1978a) in common usage allowing us to present a "Classification of Riparian."

In 1979 the USDI Fish and Wildlife Service (FWS) published a new system entitled "Classification of Wetlands and Deepwater Habitats of the United States" (Cowardin et al. 1979). This new improved system has synthesized most of the information from earlier, often antiquated, schemes designed for wetlands classification, inventory, and mapping. The foreword for that publication, written by the then-director of the FWS, calls on other federal and state agencies to adopt the system. In addition it states: "Congressional committees will be notified of this adoption action and will be encouraged to facilitate general adoption of the new system by amending any laws that reference the Circular 39 system [i.e., the previous FWS system]" (ibid.). Furthermore, classes to train personnel in the use of the system are now being conducted throughout the United States, not only for FWS personnel, but for those of other agencies as well.

---

[1]Paper presented at the California Riparian Systems Conference. [University of California, Davis, September 17-19, 1981].

[2]R. Roy Johnson is Unit Leader, Cooperative National Park Resources Study Unit, USDI National Park Service, University of Arizona, Tucson. Steven W. Carothers is Research Scientist, National Park Service, University of Arizona, and an ecological consultant, Flagstaff, Arizona. James M. Simpson is Associate, Museum of Northern Arizona, Phoenix, Arizona.

The implications of these actions are far-reaching. This is especially true when one considers that some of the most unappreciated, abused wetland areas of the United States are not considered wetlands under this new classification scheme. Among these excluded systems are some of the riparian wetlands in the more arid western half of the United States, where water is a premium resource. The rapid decline of these western riparian wetlands has been documented in detail, and the causes for the demise of these critical wildlife and recreational areas are at least partially known (Carothers 1977; Johnson and Jones 1977; Johnson and McCormick 1978; Johnson and Carothers 1982).

The system we outline in this paper represents an attempt to develop a riparian classification scheme that is compatible with the current FWS system.

RIPARIAN ECOSYSTEMS: DEFINITION OF TERMS

Wetlands Versus Drylands (Uplands)

The recently recognized field of riparian ecology is employing new terms, defining new conceptual phrases, and developing classification schemes. To demonstrate fully the inclusive scope of what may be identified as "riparian" and the complex and unique plant/animal interactions that contribute to the diversity of life forms within riparian ecosystems, a number of terms and concepts must, at the outset, be reviewed. The relationships among certain of these terms are indicated in table 1.

Terrestrial systems have traditionally been differentiated into two basic and mutually exclusive categories, "upland" and "wetland." These

are terms not to be confused with "highland" and "lowland," which simply denote elevational differences; uplands and wetlands may be differentiated on the basis of soil moisture. "Uplands" has been used in wildlife literature in opposition to "wetland," but uplands are also commonly thought of as "high ground," denoting an elevational context. To circumvent this problem, Cowardin (1978) used the term "dryland" in contrast to "wetland." We concur with Cowardin's choice in coining a much-needed technical term. The Oxford Unabridged English Dictionary (1979) defines dry land (two words!) as "land not submerged or under water; land as opposed to sea." Upland may be simply defined as "ground above the floodplain" (ibid.), whereas the term "wetland", referring to "land having wet or spongy soil," (Random House Unabridged Dictionary 1967) is not contained in the Oxford Dictionary.

By beginning with a classification system which categorizes systems as either uplands or wetlands, we would agree with other western authorities in considering virtually all riparian areas as wetlands (Brown et al. 1979, 1980). An outstanding discussion of wetlands in the arid Southwest appears in an extensive regional vegetation classification (Minckley and Brown 1982). This treatise characterizes wetlands as follows:

Wetlands are periodically, seasonally, or continuously submerged landscapes populated by species and/or life forms differing from immediately adjacent biotas. They are maintained by, and depend upon circumstances more mesic than those provided by local precipitation. Such conditions occur in or adjacent to drainageways and their floodplains (riparian zones) on poorly drained lands, along seacoasts,

Table 1.--Relationship of terms used to delineate wetland systems.

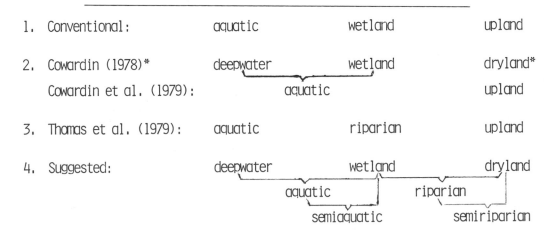

1. Conventional:	aquatic	wetland	upland
2. Cowardin (1978)*	deepwater	wetland	dryland*
Cowardin et al. (1979):	aquatic		upland
3. Thomas et al. (1979):	aquatic	riparian	upland
4. Suggested:	deepwater	wetland	dryland
	aquatic	riparian	
	semiaquatic	semiriparian	

*"Dryland" used by Cowardin (1978) as an antonym to wetland and thus as a synonym for upland.

and in and near other hydric and aquatic situations, i.e., springs and their outflows, ponds, margins of lakes, etc. The various wetland and riparian communities may be represented as forest, woodland or scrubland, marshland or strand, or be composed largely or entirely of submergent vegetation. [emphasis added]

One of the most perceptive, early characterizations of riparian communities was by Lowe (1964):

A riparian association of any kind is one which occurs in or adjacent to drainageways and/or their floodplains and which is further characterized by species and/or life-forms different from that of the immediately surrounding non-riparian climax. The southwestern riparian woodland formation is characterized by a complex of trees, and their plant and animal associates, restricted to the major drainageways that transgress the landscape of desert upward into forest. It is incorrect to regard this biotic formation as merely a temporary unstable, seral community. It is an evolutionary entity with an enduring stability equivalent to that of the landscape drainageways which form its physical habitat. That is, it is a distinctive climax biotic community. Moreover it is, as are all ecologic formations and their subdivisions, locally subject to, and often dissolved by, the vicissitudes of human occupation. In Arizona, the riparian woodlands have been rapidly dwindling just as the water table has been rapidly lowering. And its trees are now the native phreatophytes of the water-users. [emphasis added]

In their outstanding book on wildlife habitats, Thomas et al. (1979) did not use the term "wetland" for their work in Oregon and Washington. Instead, they used the term "riparian zone," which they defined as:

...an area identified by the presence of vegetation that requires free or unbound water or conditions more moist than normally found in the area.

In addition, we would add the barren, rocky, gravelly, or sandy banks along a body of water.

At the other extreme to the southwestern arid hydrological regime (e.g., the humid northwestern United States), the Oregon Coastal Conservation and Development Commission has a still different definition of wetlands (Metzger 1968 fide Akins and Jefferson 1973):

...areas on which standing water, seasonal or permanent, has a depth of six feet or less and where the wet soil retains sufficient moisture to support aquatic or semiaquatic life.

We offer here definitions for various terms, including "riparian wetlands," in full awareness of problems inherent in attempting to categorize and define riparian zones, since biological communities rarely have definitive boundaries. Indeed, the riparian community requires the moisture of the truly aquatic zones from one direction and the substrate of the terrestrial zones from the other. According to Cowardin (1978) "...wetland is part of a continuum of land types between deep water and dryland." Thus, as with all classification efforts, a subjective judgment must be made as to where to draw a boundary (where no clear boundary exists) between aquatic, terrestrial wetland, and dryland (upland) zones. The problem of specific definitions becomes even more complicated when certain transitional terms are included. For example, the term "semi-aquatic" is used in the extensive treatment of Oregon's coastal wetlands by Akins and Jefferson (1973); however, the term defies definition in their glossary. Semi-aquatic is obviously a term designed to identify vegetation or a zone of vegetation found in the area of transition between aquatic and terrestrial zones.

Semi-riparian and Pseudoriparian

Another transitional connotation is reflected by the term "semi-riparian zones." The term "semi-riparian communities" was used by Zimmerman (1970) and "semi-riparian habitat" by Hubbard (1971) in their work along the Gila River valleys of southwestern New Mexico, to describe vegetation consisting of "true" riparian species mixed with dryland species. Areas containing such vegetative mixtures are usually found on a gradient extending away from and upslope of the stream or watercourse. The semi-riparian zone, or semi-riparian vegetation, then, is an ecotonal transition between the terrestrial wetland (riparian) zone and the dryland (table 1). As with other ecotones (Johnson 1978b), the semi-riparian zone supports plant and animal species from both the bordering riparian type and the dryland type, as well as species that are almost exclusively specific to these transitional areas. It is important to emphasize here that we are attempting to categorize the various elements of the continuum between wet and dry zones, not merely for the sake of habitat or vegetation classification, but because we can often recognize distinct vegetation and wildlife communities within each of the vegetative types and subtypes.

In general, the semi-riparian community is on a soil substrate intermediate in moisture content between the riparian wetland and the dryland. In the semi-riparian community, where the typically upland species occur on soils containing moisture in excess of their typical habitat, these upland plants frequently attain a population density or size-class and vigor greater than that found in the uplands. When a dryland species migrates into the semi-riparian zone and as a result attains a greater density and rate of growth, it may be referred to as a "pseudoriparian" plant (Campbell and Green 1968).

"Pseudoriparian" plants have been described by Campbell and Green as "facultative" in contrast to "riparian" plants, which are "obligate." Unfortunately, the biological definition of facultative as able to live under more than one set of conditions does not indicate a preference for one situation or the other. Therefore, Campbell and Green (1968) have lumped three basic categories of plants under the term pseudoriparian: 1) species which may be best adapted to riparian zones but which will grow in drylands, e.g., velvet mesquite (Prosopis velutina); 2) species which are well adapted to either riparian or dryland zones, e.g., desert hackberry (Celtis pallida); and 3) species which are more common in dryland zones but which will grow in riparian zones, often attaining greater size and/or population densities, e.g., Arizona cypress (Cupressus arizonica). Table 2 demonstrates a classification scheme which further clarifies the concept of "pseudoriparian" in relation to a species' ability to grow in different zones.

Table 2.--Indicator assignments of plant species based on their relationship to the riparian zone (modified from Johnson et al. 1977; and Reed in press). Percent occurrence is defined as frequency with which individual plants occur in the riparian zone as compared to total population of the region.

Species category	Percent occurrence
Obligate riparian	91-100
Preferential riparian	76-90
Facultative riparian	26-76
Non-riparian	0-25

The classification scheme we present here is a refinement of an earlier system used by Johnson et al. (1977) composed of three categories: obligate, preferential, and non-riparian. This new, four-category system can be applied to plants or animals. By conducting a strip census or random count of individuals in a region and determining the percentage found in riparian zones compared to nonriparian zones, the species can be assigned to one of the four categories. Reed (in press) has developed a five-category system for wetland plants which would be more definitive, but is too sophisticated for our current level of information.

Perennial, Intermittent, and Ephemeral Riparian Zones

We have recently developed a new, simple, and inclusive classification system for riparian zones (Johnson et al. in press a). By combining standardized terms we have suggested: 1) Perennial Riparian; 2) Intermittent Riparian; and 3) Ephemeral Riparian for categorizing bank systems on streams, lakes, and tidewater areas. These three new riparian types may be applied to zones, vegetation-types, plant or animal communities, or ecosystems. These categories are not substitutes for various terms which have been used for plant species or vegetation communities in the past, including "desert riparian," "stream riparian" (Austin and Bradley 1971), "pseudoriparian," or "semi-riparian." Our three categories refer to zones occurring along and supported by perennial (permanent), intermittent, or ephemeral watercourses, lakes, or tidewaters.

A NEW RIPARIAN CLASSIFICATION

The aforementioned FWS classification system for wetlands and deep-water habitats (Cowardin et al. 1979) represents the current state of the art in official federal attempts to classify these habitat-types for inventory (in the National Wetlands Inventory), mapping, and protection of the systems. The coauthors of that important publication are eastern investigators and therefore used terms such as "bottomland hardwoods," "wooded swamps," and other regional terms, but riparian was never used. This, in effect, excluded many of the riparian wetlands in the vast region from the Great Plains westward (more than half the United States), with the possible exception of the lush Pacific Northwest. By the standards of some investigators in the wetter, more humid East, many of these areas are not considered wetlands. However, when compared to the surrounding drylands they are unquestionably wetlands, possessing inordinately high wildlife and recreational values and providing premium "living sites" for humans as well as plants and animals.

There are some obvious visual differences between most eastern and western wetlands, but there are also strikingly far-ranging similarities (Johnson et al. in press b). For example, western riparian wetlands are commonly highly visible, more heavily vegetated areas, contrasting sharply with the surrounding dry uplands. This is due largely to the fact that a high percentage of the woody species occurring in these western wetlands show different growth forms from those of surrounding dryland (upland) communities. By contrast, eastern riparian wetlands, along the bottoms of deciduous woodlands, are often not readily apparent because the vegetation growth forms of both habitats are very similar. Eastern investigators, however, have pointed out that the species composition in these eastern riparian woodlands is different from that of the surrounding upland communities (Shelford 1963).

A plethora of other publications have compared species richness and productivity of riparian with upland zones (Johnson and Jones 1977; Johnson and McCormick 1978). Although comparative differences between riparian wetlands and adjacent uplands may not be as extreme for the East as the West, reference to published papers quickly demonstrates that eastern and western riparian systems share a common factor of greater wildlife and recreational importance than surrounding uplands. In addition to the two aforementioned riparian symposia, other publications demonstrating the importance of eastern as well as western riparian systems include a series of national and regional nongame bird symposia conducted by the USDA Forest Service (FS) and bird censuses published quarterly in "American Birds." Johnson (1978b) has shown a differential dependency of avifaunas on riparian zones that is related to regional and local aridity in the Southwest.

Swift and Barclay (1980) demonstrate comparable riparian destruction for both the East and the West (commonly from 70 to 90%). For example, the Sacramento River drainage has an estimated riparian vegetation loss in excess of 98%, while that for southeastern Missouri is approximately 96%. The East apparently still has larger tracts of riparian vegetation left because there were more there originally.

Herein lies the crux of the matter, for in deleting western riparian wetlands from a national inventory, one of the main objectives of the inventory is not met. That objective is to provide practical and legal protection for these wetlands and their attendant ecosystems. Although other programs, such as floodplain zoning and policies of various agencies (see the position papers in Johnson and McCormick 1978), are providing some protection for riparian wetlands, all possible attempts must be made to properly manage these endangered riparian ecosystems.

The "riparian movement" to conserve riparian wetlands is often considered a western concern. However, we have just demonstrated why there is good reason for the East to be equally, or perhaps even more, concerned. Therefore, we present a classification scheme for riparian wetlands which is compatible with the FWS wetlands classification system (figs. 1 and 2). The palustrine system would be the point at which our riparian subsystems would be interfaced with that system (fig. 1). The complexity of these riparian ecosystems has previously defied assignment of subsystems. Table 3 provides our definitions for "riparian" and the subsystems, "hydroriparian," "mesoriparian," and "xeroriparian."

Previous to the 1970s, concerns were largely with clearing riparian zones to allow for "better utility." "Phreatophyte" was the word commonly used instead of riparian to describe vegetation (Johnson and Carothers 1982) for channelization, flood control, water and power projects, and other "water salvage" operations. Today,

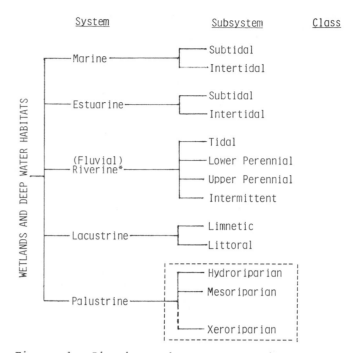

Figure 1.--Riparian subsystems superimposed on the National Wetlands Classification System (modified from Cowardin et al. 1979). * In more than 25 references checked (standard dictionaries; ecological, geological, and hydrological dictionaries; and scholarly works on aquatic ecosystems, the following consensus is established. Riverine: a) of or pertaining to a river (including the banks); b) located on or inhabiting the banks of a river. Fluvial: of, pertaining to, or inhabiting a river or stream. (See Reid and Wood 1976.)

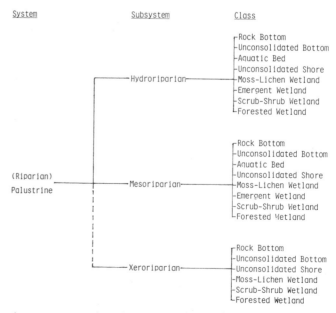

Figure 2.--Riparian subsystems and classes (modified after Cowardin et al. 1979).

Table 3.--Definitions of riparian wetland types.

Riparian: On or pertaining to land adjacent to riverine and estuarine channels, lacustrine beds, or oases and other sites where surface water and/or groundwater occurs in excess of on-site precipitation; occupied by biotic communities differing in species composition and/or population densities from those of the surrounding uplands due to the substrate: a) being or periodically covered with water; and/or b) having higher soil moisture; or c) in the case of rocky banks or cliffs, existing plant and animal species are dependent on a proximity to water.

Hydroriparian: Wetlands with hydric soils or whose substrates are never dry or are dry for only a short period; usually associated with perennial or intermittent water. Vegetation, when present, consists of a predominance of obligate and preferential wet riparian plants.

Mesoriparian: Wetlands with nonhydric soils and whose substrate is dry seasonally; usually associated with intermittent water or high-elevation ephemeral wetlands. Vegetation, when present, consists of a mixture of obligate, preferential, and facultative riparian plants.

Xeroriparian: Mesic to xeric habitat-type with average annual moisture higher than surrounding uplands, but provided with surface moisture in excess of local rainfall only on infrequent occasions (usually for less than one month per year). Vegetation, when present, consists of a mixture of preferential, facultative, and non-riparian plants.

---

however, the importance of riparian areas to regional ecosystem maintenance, complexity, and diversity has become evident. While there are still riparian areas to be protected from the insidious destruction that has already reduced this habitat-type to but a small portion of its original coverage, any classification system must consider the entire breadth of the riparian continuum. Our proposed system considers this breadth, extending from dry desert arroyos, and those plants and animals dependent upon their ephemeral water sources, to permanent bodies of water, and perennial marshes and streams.

CONCLUSION

Riparian systems have been in great demand during the exploratory, settlement, and developmental history of the United States. Riverine and lacustrine riparian zones were extremely useful as routes for exploration and travel; for building of forts, houses, and settlements; for grazing livestock and planting crops; for providing timber and firewood; and, finally, for the development of cities, greenbelts, and recreational facilities. Most reclamation projects and other rural and urban water resource development projects were undertaken prior to the 1960s. It was during the 1960s and 1970s that research documented the tremendous natural and sociological values of the riparian zone. Thus, much of the destruction to riparian ecosystems from these projects had occurred before there was an adequate understanding of the tremendous riparian wildlife and recreational values (Johnson and Carothers 1982). The process of developing the riparian zone for human use destroyed many of the values which had originally attracted humans to these areas. In too many situations, the riparian zone was converted from a lush, verdant "paradise" to a virtual desert (see Johnson and Haight 1983 for definition of desertification).

Insufficient baseline information, inadequate vocabulary, and general overuse and abuse all contributed to the rapid degradation and almost total demise of riparian zones. This was especially true in the arid and semi-arid West where water for human use is at a premium. This paper has mentioned a series of state of the art publications which were instrumental in developing a better understanding of these important riparian areas during the late 1970s. In addition, a vocabulary has developed (McCormick 1978; Warner 1979) and classification schemes have evolved (Lowe 1964; Brown et al. 1979, 1980; Minckley and Brown 1982). These works have demonstrated that riparian systems not only are important to those organisms and communities inhabiting the riparian zone, but also play a vital role in providing food and shelter to many upland and aquatic organisms. Now that the unique role played by riparian ecosystems has been recognized, steps are being taken to preserve and properly manage their fragmentary remains (see Johnson and Haight 1983).

Projects designed to provide water for agricultural, municipal, and industrial uses can now be developed without destroying the recreational and wildlife values of important riparian areas (Carothers and Johnson 1975). Through the use of recently gathered scientific information and application of sound principles of land-use planning, resource management agencies can even reestablish some of the riparian areas which have been destroyed through ignorance during past development projects. No other resource management task is so important to western ecosystems and to the living organisms they include, especially man.

LITERATURE CITED

Akins, G.J., and C.Q. Jefferson. 1973. Coastal wetlands of Oregon. 159 p. Oregon Coastal Conservation and Development Commission, Florence, Oregon.

American Geological Institute. 1962. Dictionary of geological terms. 545 p. Anchor Press, Garden City, N.Y.

Austin, G.T., and W.G. Bradley. 1971. The avifauna of Clark County, Nevada. J. Ariz. Acad. Sci. 6(4):283-303.

Brown, D.E., C.H. Lowe, and C.P. Pase. 1979. A digitized classification system for the biotic communities of North America, with community (Series) and association examples for the Southwest. J. Ariz.-Nev. Acad. Sci. 14(Suppl. 1):1-16.

Brown, D.E., C.H. Lowe, and C.P. Pase. 1980. A digitized systematic classification for ecosystems with an illustrated summary of the natural vegetation of North America. USDA Forest Service GTR-RM-73, Rocky Mountain Forest and Range Experiment Station, Fort Collins, Colo. 93 p.

Campbell, C.J., and W. Green. 1968. Perpetual succession of stream-channel vegetation in a semiarid region. J. Ariz. Acad. Sci. 5:86-98.

Carothers, S.W. 1977. Importance, preservation, and management of riparian habitats: an overview. p. 2-4. In: R.R. Johnson and D.A. Jones (tech. coord.). Importance, preservation, and management of riparian habitat: a symposium. [Tuscon, Arizona, July 9, 1977.] USDA Forest Service GTR-RM-43, Rocky Mountain Forest and Range Experiment Station, Fort Collins, Colo. 217 p.

Carothers, S.W., and R.R. Johnson. 1975. Water management practices and their effects on nongame birds in range habitats. p. 210-222. In: Proceedings of the symposium on management of forest and range habitats for nongame birds. USDA Forest Service GTR-1, Washington, D.C.

Cowardin, L.M. 1978. Wetland classification in the United States. J. Forestry. 1978 (Oct.):666-668.

Cowardin. L.M., V. Carter, F.C. Golet, and E.T. LaRoe. 1979. Classification of wetlands and deepwater habitats of the United States. USDI Fish and Wildlife Service FWS/OBS-79/31, Washington, D.C. 103 p.

Hanson, H.C. 1962. Dictionary of ecology. 382 p. Philosophical Library, New York, N.Y.

Hubbard. J.P. 1971. The summer birds of the Gila Valley, New Mexico. Nemouria (Occ. Pap. Del. Mus. Nat. Hist.) 2:1-35. Greenville, Del.

Johnson, R.R. 1978a. Foreword. p. ii. In: R.R. Johnson and J.F. McCormick (tech. coord.). Strategies for protection and management of floodplain wetlands and other riparian ecosystems: Proceedings of the symposium. [Callaway Gardens, Georgia, December 11-13, 1978]. USDA Forest Service GTR-WO-12, Washington, D.C. 410 p.

Johnson, R.R. 1978b. The lower Colorado River: a western system. p. 41-55. In: R.R. Johnson and J.F. McCormick (tech. coord.). Strategies for protection and management of floodplain wetlands and other riparian ecosystems: Proceedings of the symposium. [Callaway Gardens, Georgia, December 11-13, 1978]. USDA Forest Service GTR-WO-12, Washington, D.C. 410 p.

Johnson, R. R., and S. W. Carothers. 1982. Southwestern riparian habitats and recreation: interrelationships and impacts in the Southwest and Rocky Mountain region. Eisenhower Consortium Bull. 12, USDA Forest Service, Rocky Mountain Forest and Range Experiment Station, Fort Collins, Colo. 31 p.

Johnson, R.R., S.W. Carothers, and B.T. Brown. In press a. Perennial intermittent and ephmeral riparian habitats in the Southwest. J. Ariz.-Nev. Acad. Sci., Tempe, Ariz.

Johnson, R.R., S.W. Carothers, and N.H. Goldberg. In press b. Western riparian ecosystems: endangered natural communities. Burgess Publishing Company, Minneapolis, Minn.

Johnson, R.R., and L.T. Haight. 1983. Riparian problems and initiatives in the American Southwest: A regional perspective. In: R.E. Warner and K.M. Hendrix (ed.). California Riparian Systems. [University of California, Davis, September 17-19, 1981.] University of California Press, Berkeley.

Johnson, R.R., L.T. Haight, and J.M. Simpson. 1977. Endangered species vs. endangered habitats: a concept. p. 68-79. In: R.R. Johnson and D.A. Jones (tech. coord.). Importance, preservation, and management of riparian habitat: a symposium. [Tuscon, Arizona, July 9, 1977.] USDA Forest Service GTR-RM-43, Rocky Mountain Forest and Range Experiment Station, Fort Collins, Colo. 217 p.

Johnson, R.R., and D.A. Jones (tech. coord.). 1977. Importance, preservation and management of riparian habitat: a symposium. [Tuscon, Arizona, July 9, 1977.] USDA Forest Service GTR-RM-43, Rocky Mountain Forest and Range Experiment Station, Fort Collins, Colo. 217 p.

Johnson, R.R., and J.F. McCormick (tech. coord.). 1978. Strategies for the protection and management of floodplain wetlands and other riparian ecosystems: Proceedings of the symposium. [Callaway Gardens, Georgia, December 11-13, 1978]. USDA Forest Service GTR-WO-12, Washington, D.C. 410 p.

Langbein, W.B., and K.T. Iseri. 1960. General introduction and hydrologic definitions. USDI Geological Survey Water Sup. Pap. 1541-A. 29 p. US Government Printing Office, Washington, D.C.

Lowe, C.H. (ed.). 1964. The vertebrates of Arizona. 270 p. University of Arizona Press, Tucson.

McCormick, J.F. 1978. A summary of the National Riparian Symposium: A proposal for a national riparian program. p. 362-363. In: R.R. Johnson and J.F. McCormick (tech. coord.). Strategies for the protection and management of floodplain wetlands and other riparian ecosystems: Proceedings of the symposium. [Callaway Gardens, Georgia, December 11-13, 1978]. USDA Forest Service GTR-WO-12, Washington, D.C. 410 p.

Minckley, W.L., and D.E. Brown. 1982. Wetlands. In: D.E. Brown (ed.). Biotic communities of the American Southwest United States and Mexico. Desert Plants 4:223-341.

Oxford English Dictionary (Unabridged). 1979.

Random House Unabridged Dictionary. 1967.

Reed, P.B., Jr. In press. Differentiating between a classification system and a data base. Paper presented at "In-place Resource Inventories; principle and practice: a national workshop. [University of Maine, Arno, August 9-14, 1981]. USDA Forest Service.

Reid, G.K., and R.D. Wood. 1976. Ecology of inland waters and estuaries. 485 p. D. VanNostrand and Company, New York, N.Y.

Shelford, V.E. 1963. The ecology of North America. 610 p. University of Illinois Press, Urbana.

Swift, B.L., and J.J. Barclay. 1980. Status of riparian ecosystems in the United States. 29 p. USDI Fish and Wildlife Service, Kearneysville, W. Va. Unpublished manuscript presented at the 1980 American Water Resources Association National Conference, Minneapolis, Minn.

Thomas, J.W., C. Maser, and J.E. Rodiek. 1979. Riparian zones. p. 40-47. In: J.W. Thomas (tech. ed.). Wildlife habitats in managed forests: the Blue Mountains of Oregon and Washington. USDA Forest Service Agricultural Handbook No. 553, Washington, D.C. 512 p.

Warner, R.E. 1979. California riparian study program. 177 p. California Department of Fish and Game, Planning Branch, Sacramento.

Zimmerman, D.A. 1970. Birds of the Gila River Valley, New Mexico. Unpublished manuscript, Gila National Forest, Silver City. N.M.

CALIFORNIA RIPARIAN SYSTEMS:

A RENEWABLE RESOURCE AWAITING RENEWAL[1]

Huey D. Johnson[2]

Looking through the agenda of this conference I see a preponderance of papers reviewing the technical aspects of riparian systems. I charge that you may not be able to see the riparian forest in your enthusiasm for studying the individual trees. I am afraid if special care is not taken, this conference will be a funeral for the last vestiges of our once extensive riparian areas, instead of a rededication to the importance of preserving and enhancing our limited and constantly diminishing riparian resources.

Should the doctor spend his time studying a dying patient's condition, or should he concentrate on curing the disease and saving the patient's life? The answer is clear.

Our riparian systems are not merely sick or degraded, they are virtually destroyed. The systems did not cause their own destruction. Man caused the destruction through poor resource management unduly influenced by politics, policies, and economics. We can maintain and restore these systems using the same forces that helped in their destruction--enlightened politics, and forward-looking management policies which recognize cost:benefit ratios favoring natural systems and renewable resources.

Natural areas are imperative to our well-being. By saving riparian systems, we will save values badly needed in our urban society. These areas provide the recreation, open space, and aesthetics that we need to maintain our physical and mental health. The only place I know where I can guarantee that I can take you in only a short drive from Sacramento where you can hear the wildness of a coyote howling, or see the splendor of a wild Sandhill Crane, is a riparian area on the Cosumnes River. This spot is a remnant of what California once was, and it is needed as an escape from the congestion of urban living. And, ironically, or maybe just as history tends to repeat itself, Man wants to conquer the Cosumnes River, and destroy the riparian vegetation along this, the last undammed river in the central Western Sierra Nevada. There is a proposal for up to 11 dams. What good are these dams, and the

possible water and power they will provide, if we lose the aesthetics, the open space, and the ability to return to nature?

The concept of damming the Cosumnes is just a modern example of Man's greed and ignorance, destroying his environment as he has so often in the past. We can reflect on civilizations lost because of the overexploitation of resources: the Sumerians, Romans, Mayans, and Aztecs.

I also think of the Asazi Indians of New Mexico. A detailed account of their 12th century "conquest" of the Chaco Wash, a tributary of the Colorado River, can be found in "A River No More," by Phillip Fradkin (Knopf, 1981). This is a book I highly recommend. It gives a wonderful overview of the many problems faced by our river systems. The amenities of the location chosen by the Asazis included a meandering streambed which irrigated the canyon floor, and extensive pine forests. The native riparian vegetation was stripped for planting. Over 75,000 trees were felled to build structures. The massive disruption of vegetative cover and the denuding of the soil allowed Chaco Wash to become Chaco Canyon, a canyon 25 ft. deep and between 100 and 300 ft. wide. The riparian system, so complex and integrated, was destroyed. The Asazis moved on after destroying the amenities that attracted them to the spot in the first place. This is just one example of Man's tendency to ignore a system's carrying capacity and foul his nest. The Colorado River System alone gives numerous examples of poor resource management resulting from urbanization, water development, logging, grazing, agriculture, mining, and off-road vehicle use.

We now have an understanding of the problems we have created through poor resource management. The facts that over the last 150 years America has lost 70 to 90 percent of its indigenous riparian system--and over 90 percent in the Central Valley--and that salmon numbers, an indicator of the quality of our streams, have been declining steadily, until the point that we have now lost 65 percent, show us a trend of resource mismanagement. But we have really lost so much more than trees and salmon. There has also been a reduction in the quality of life and in the potential for recreational experiences. Many people use riparian and other forested areas as their way of returning to nature. John Muir's love for trees sent him around the world to write about them. In Muir's first book, "The Mountains of California," he describes the beauty of a

[1]Paper presented as a Keynote Speech at the California Riparian Systems Conference. [University of California, Davis, September 17-19, 1981].

[2]Huey D. Johnson is Secretary, The Resources Agency, State of California.

winter storm in the Sierra. He recounts the fragrance, the music, the colors, and the experience of climbing a 100-ft. Douglas fir to be a part of the tree traveling in the wind. We all need to be a part of nature, maybe not to this extent, but we all need that opportunity.

Laws and policies are helping us get a handle on some of these uses of riparian areas. In the North Coast, timber harvest regulations have tightened, and in the Central Valley we have learned about revegetation of levees. There is an increasing awareness of instream values, and we have been able to apply the Resources Agency wetlands policy to protect some riparian wetlands. But houses are still being built on the levees of the Sacramento River, and politicians are still serving special interests.

The Executive Orders which have protected our public lands from destruction by off-road vehicles have recently been attacked by James Watt. Wet meadows, and the highly fragile riparian systems which form the major basis for wildlife in California's arid and semi-arid areas, could have been open to an onslaught of off-road vehicles. But we fought, and we won the battle. However, the war goes on. And now there is a proposal to revise the grazing management regulations for Bureau of Land Management lands. The proposed change would undoubtedly accelerate desertification of our arid lands and destruction of sensitive riparian systems.

Just as we are getting somewhere, more problems arise. Just as we begin to understand an area, new mysteries unfold. We think we know the values of riparian systems, and are beginning to see the increased need for sustained yield use of all our renewable resources. Yes, riparian species can be beneficial for paper, fuel, and furniture, but what were we overlooking?

It brings to mind Azolla, a fresh-water fern, found here in Davis. When a rice farmer discovered it in his rice field, he called out crop dusters to apply aerial herbicides. Unbeknownst to him, this tiny fern is nitrogen-fixing and has been used in Asia for centuries to nourish rice in lieu of chemical fertilizers. In a world faced with a steadily increasing population and soaring fertilizer shortages and costs, this "green manure" has increased the productivity of food crops and saved us energy. Just a few weeks ago, an article in the "San Francisco Chronicle" described the discovery of a tree in China that yields an oil similar to diesel oil. These trees are rapidly disappearing. Will this renewable resource be wisely used, possibly with energy farms, or overexploited? It is embarrassing to think that we could destroy something this valuable when we need it so badly--for every energy equivalent of a barrel of oil we get out of our crops we invest the equivalent of eight barrels in fuel, fertilizers, and pesticides.

What unknown discoveries lie in riparian systems? What part of our gene pool will we lose if we sit by and watch the other 10 to 30 percent

be destroyed? The prime threat to species lies in loss of habitat. The economic exploitation of natural habitats must cease if we are to maintain the earth's stock of genetic material and preserve species diversity. Maybe some plant like Azolla, or a disease-curing insect, will be lost if we lose more of our riparian systems. Possibly the economic vitality of our nation depends upon riparian resources. It is up to the scientist to untangle the mysteries of riparian systems and to the managers and environmentalists to make sure that what we have left is preserved. And what can the politician and manager do to save these areas from destruction while the scientist ferrets out the secrets and develops methods for restoration and enhancement?

In response to problems such as those pointed out in the "Global 2000 Report," California has developed a program called "Investing for Prosperity." This 20-year plan states our resource management objectives. We can no longer sit back, watching the destruction of our natural systems. We need to restore our forests, renew our fisheries, reverse the loss of productivity of our farm and range soil, and make the wisest use of our energy resources. We have developed programs designed to achieve these goals. We have also included programs in urban areas to install awareness in the youth, the decision-makers of tomorrow. What good is rehabilitation of salmon habitat today if tomorrow's leaders have no appreciation for its values and allow it to deteriorate once again? We must continue to expand upon our programs and involve enough people who will demand needed, enlightened, long-term management. One good example we could follow is a United Nations program being implemented in India. They call it "for-every-child-a-tree". The government will supply trees to be planted, nurtured, and appreciated by the children. In India they will be fruit trees; why not riparian species here? We need programs like this if an awareness is to be instilled in future generations while restoring areas.

"Investing for Prosperity" is only a step in the direction we need to take if we are going to manage our resources properly to insure the future for not just the next few generations, but for hundreds of generations to come. In what other way can we save the Cosumnes River, or the finest riparian forest we have left along the South Fork of the Kern? How can we get the public and private sectors to come together? These are some of the challenges that lie before us.

The pioneering work found in many of the papers presented at this conference, and the research which follows, will be instrumental in helping us to find a new path. But each individual can do only so much alone. We must unite and put our ideas together, form task forces to fight the forces that want to dam our rivers and destroy our remaining riparian systems. Our energies must be focused to provide a direct path away from the destructive tendencies of "progress" which we have been following and toward responsible, farsighted use of our resources.

OVERVIEW: NATIONAL TRENDS IN FLOODPLAIN MANAGEMENT[1]

Frank H. Thomas and Gerald D. Seinwill[2]

Abstract.--The federal role in floodplain management expanded greatly between 1960 and 1980 as flood-loss reduction, environmental-loss reduction, and disaster assistance programs were united in a national floodplain management concept. In the 1980s, reduced federal funding and regulation will force the leadership role in floodplain management upon each of the individual states.

INTRODUCTION

The organizers of this conference, and especially Rick Warner, are to be commended for providing a timely opportunity to assess the current and future status of riparian systems management. The management of riparian systems faces the challenge of adjusting to a redefined federal role, as expressed through reduced federal budgets and through a revised concept of federalism which vests leadership in the states, with the federal government playing a supporting role.

In this paper, we shall first assess the trends and current status of floodplain management from a national perspective, but with a focus on the federal role. We shall discuss the new concept of federalism and some of its implications for floodplain management. Throughout, we shall consider floodplain management as generally encompassing riparian systems.

NATIONAL WATER POLICY 1960-1980: CONTEXT FOR FLOODPLAIN MANAGEMENT

The development of national water policy from 1960 to 1980 provides a context for understanding trends influencing floodplain management. This was a period in which the federal role expanded and specific federal programs were sorted out. There were repeated evaluations of water issues, first by the Senate Select Committee in 1961 and then by the National Water Commission, the National Commission on Water Quality, and more recently by the Carter administration.

National goals were revised. Environmental quality became a national objective; water quality maintenance became a high-priority; and disaster assistance expanded greatly. The number of federal programs increased accordingly, first emphasizing planning and later regulations to solve water resource problems.

This was also a period of sorting out responsibilities within the federal government and among federal, state, and local governments. Informal and formal coordination mechanisms, including the US Water Resources Council, were established. Some states waited and followed the lead of the "Feds" while other states, like California, aggressively led the federal government. Except for communities located in the more aggressive states, local governments tended to wait for the federal lead and thus became increasingly dependent upon federal funds and projects.

In general, during this period the major water resource issues of the nation were defined, and in most cases the direction of resolution for these issues was set. It was a sometimes painful, incremental process of sorting out a federal role and programs. Today, the question associated with most water resource issues is "how to do it," rather than "whether to do it."

DEVELOPMENT OF NATIONAL FLOODPLAIN MANAGEMENT

During the last two decades, the federal role in floodplain management also expanded, passing through the phases of reassessment, reconceptualization, and integration of related objectives. The reassessment was led by a 1966 task force on federal flood control policy, which concluded that more than 20 years of federal flood control had been inadequate to arrest rapidly rising flood losses (US 89th Congress 1966). The task force advocated greater reliance on nonstructural approaches to flood-loss reduction, including establishment of a National Flood Insurance Program. The task force recommended an executive

---

[1] Paper presented at the California Riparian Systems Conference. [University of California, Davis, September 17-19, 1981].

[2] Frank H. Thomas is Assistant Director for Policy and Gerald D. Seinwill is Acting Director; both are with the U.S. Water Resources Council, Washington, D.C.

order directing federal agencies to evaluate flood hazards before they located new federal installations.[3] The Presidential executive order issued immediately thereafter represented a first step for the coordination of federal flood-loss reduction activites.

In 1968, the Congress passed the National Flood Insurance Act,[4] which offered subsidized insurance in return for community regulation of future development in flood hazard areas. This quid pro quo arrangement brought local communities into direct contact with federal flood-loss reduction programs. This act also recognized the need for intergovernmental coordination and called for the President to prepare for the Congress "A Unified National Program for Floodplain Management," a task subsequently assigned to the US Water Resources Council.

In 1973 and 1974, Congress passed two acts strengthening federal flood-loss reduction efforts by linking flood insurance with federal disaster assistance.[5] Community participation in the flood insurance program was made a prerequisite for federal disaster assistance. State and local hazard mitigation and long-term disaster recovery were tied to the flood insurance program.

In 1977, Executive Order 11988--Floodplain Management, and its companion Executive Order 11990--Protection of Wetlands, directed federal agencies to avoid actions that would adversely affect floodplains and wetlands (US Water Resources Council 1978). The floodplain order states that if avoidance is not practical, agencies are to restore and preserve natural floodplain values as part of carrying out their action. It also cited the National Flood Insurance Act for its authority; from that act it established the insurance program's flood frequency standards as those to be used by all federal agencies. Thus, the floodplain management executive order became a significant mechanism for coordinating federal policies and programs. Since 1977, more than 50 federal agencies have issued procedures for implementing Executive Order 11988 at the field level.

In 1979, the Water Resources Council's "A Unified National Program for Floodplain Management" (US Water Resources Council 1979) was transmitted by the President to the Congress. Central

to the unified program is a holistic conceptual statement articulating the policy linkages that had evolved between 1960 and 1980. Floodplain management is a decision-making process. The management goal is the wise use of the nation's floodplains, subject to two constraints: satisfactory accommodation of flood-loss reduction and environmental-loss reduction. Loss reduction constraints include equal consideration of: 1) all structural and nonstructural approaches; 2) all upstream and downstream impacts; and 3) all pre-flood, during flood, and postflood disaster assistance actions. This concept also recognizes that authority for floodplain decisions is partitioned by law among federal, state, local, and nongovernmental entities, and that at each level of government authority is further fragmented. For example, 28 federal agencies have major floodplain management program authority. The unified program provides a framework for articulating policy relationships and coordinating floodplain decision-making authorities.

In 1980, the Office of Management and Budget issued a directive to 12 federal agencies to coordinate postflood disaster recovery programs with long-term basin planning programs (US Office of Management and Budget 1980). Subsequently, interagency hazard mitigation teams have been sent to flood disaster sites to work with state and local government officials to ensure that federal disaster recovery assistance does not result in reconstruction or new development in high-hazard areas. This coordination effort has produced promising results thus far.

CURRENT STATUS OF NATIONAL FLOODPLAIN MANAGEMENT

As we survey the scene in 1981, we find that progress has been made. First, we do have an adequate conceptual statement of national floodplain management in the US Water Resources Council's (1979) "Unified Program."

At the federal level, there are a number of useful coordinating mechanisms--the Office of Management and Budget directive, the executive orders, and the Floodplain Management Task Force of the Water Resources Council.

In the National Flood Insurance Program, a single program provides common floodplain delineation and risk standards used by all federal agencies, each of the 50 states, more than 17,000 communities, and over 2 million insurance policyholders. Indeed, the flood insurance program has become the backbone of national floodplain management.

We now face a major task in improving the effectiveness and coordination of existing programs. Few, if any, new programs are needed.

---

[3]President of the United States. 1966. Executive Order 11296. Evaluation of flood hazards in locating federally owned or financed buildings, roads, and other facilities, and in disposing of federal lands and properties. Federal Register 31(155). August 11, 1966.
[4]PL 90-448, 82 Stat. 572, 42 USCA 4001 et seq.
[5]Flood Disaster Protection Act (PL 93-234, 87 Stat. 980, 42 USC 4001 et seq.). Comprehensive Disaster Assistance Act (PL 93-288, 88 Stat. 163, 42 USC 5201).

NEW FEDERALISM IN THE 1980s

With the advent of the Reagan administration, the concept of federalism is again evolving. The new federalism is based upon three premises: 1) problems should be solved at the level of government closest to the problem; 2) the federal budget is bloated; and 3) federal programs are overexpanded and unduly burdensome.[6] Accordingly, the administration has three action strategies to change the federal role.

The first strategy is devolution or shifting of federal responsibility to the state and local levels. Federal agencies will bear the burden of proof to justify their programs by answering the questions: 1) Why isn't this function at the state level? and 2) Why isn't this function at the local level?

The objective of this evaluation of federal programs is to strengthen state government at the expense of federal government and to keep a status quo relation between state and local government. In order to insulate local government from the federal government, funds are to be channeled through states to local governments. The expected net result is a shift from federal leadership to that of federal assistance to support state and local initiatives.

The second strategy is to reduce the federal budget. The 1982 Budget Reconciliation Act[7] represents action by the Congress, with the support of the administration, to place a ceiling on federal budget expenditures. One major element of the act is an approximately $35 billion overall reduction in expenditures, primarily in program areas other than defense, the Social Security "net," and federal debt servicing. This translates into an estimated 20% reduction in the natural resource program category. Another major element in the act is the consolidation of individual grant programs into block grants in order to reduce administrative costs. Although no block grants were instituted in the natural resource program area in 1981-82, it is likely that some form of natural resource block grants to the states will be introduced in fiscal year 1983.

Apart from the Reconciliation Act, there is a clear trend toward full cost recovery in proposed legislation and in the federal role, as indicated by the Cabinet Council on Natural Resources and Environment. The federal role would be reflected in the principle that the cost of all services produced by water projects should be paid for by direct beneficiaries of the services. The implication is that we can expect new policies on discount rate financing and cost sharing for new water projects.

The third strategy, deregulation, is aimed at reducing the federal regulatory burden placed on local governments and private parties by simplifying regulations, terminating all regulations not explicitly required by legislation, and shifting responsibility for regulatory programs to state government. A Vice-Presidential task force has identified over 100 burdensome regulations, especially those affecting block grants. Three of these regulations directly affect riparian loctions: Executive Order 11988--Floodplain Management; Executive Order 11990--Protection of Wetlands; and the regulations of the National Flood Insurance Program. A final decision on whether block grants will be exempt from the requirements of these regulations is expected soon. To this point, congressional initiatives aimed at reducing the regulatory burden have been very limited. In the near future, it seems certain that the Congress will take up the Clean Water Act Section 404 permit program, and may redefine the relationship of the Environmental Protection Agency and the US Army Corps of Engineers (CE) and transfer program implementation to the states.

CONCLUSION

Based on our assessment of the current floodplain management status and the new federalism, significant adjustments will need to be factored into the state strategy for riparian system management in California. The following observations are offered for consideration in the development of the state strategy.

(1) Expanded state leadership and responsibility for grants and regulations will cause intensified lobbying at the state level and will decrease the relative importance of federal decisions made in Washington.

(2) States will be less able to avoid issues by saying "the Feds made me do it," especially when federal regulations are relaxed, as is expected in the case of Section 404 permits.

(3) Because of a reduced federal role, adjacent states may have more frequent conflicts over management priorities for interstate floodplains.

(4) Reduced federal budget and full repayment policies could mean few if any new water project starts and more emphasis on nonstructural solutions to flood problems. States and communities now waiting for federal flood control project funds will have to fund or forget their projects.

(5) More emphasis on economic evaluation will increase the importance of flood-loss reduction costs as a negative factor for floodplain development. Environmental-loss reduction may

---

[6] Carlson, Robert, and James Kelly. 1981. Comments presented at the Federal Executive Institute's seminar "Reagan Federalism." [Washington, D.C., August 12, 1981.]

[7] Omnibus Budget Reconciliation Act of 1981. PL 97-35, August 13, 1981.

have to be carried more frequently under the standards of the flood insurance program.

(6) More emphasis on economic evaluation and benefit:cost analysis will increase the pressure for dollar evaluation of floodplain and other riparian values such as wildlife habitat, biomass production, etc.

(7) Floodplain and other riparian system managers will have to obtain more of their funds from nongovernmental sources. They will also have to find inexpensive tools for accomplishing preservation.

Finally, there is a lack of explicit performance goals with completion deadlines. Targets are needed so that progress can be measured. In California:

(a) Can the losses of floodplain and other riparian natural resources be reduced by a fixed number of acres or units by the year 1990?

(b) Can a certain number of acres or units of riparian system be restored by 1990?

(c) Can the federal agencies with large land holdings in the state be formally brought into a state restoration and preservation program?

(d) Can the state establish and pursue finite performance goals for riparian systems management?

LITERATURE CITED

US 89th Congress, 2nd Session. 1966. A unified national program for managing flood losses. House Document 465. Government Printing Office, Washington, D.C.

US Office of Management and Budget. 1980. Nonstructural flood protection measures and flood disaster recovery. Executive Office of the President, Washington, D.C. July 10, 1980.

US Water Resources Council. 1978. Floodplain management guidelines (includes Executive Order 11988 and Executive Order 11990). Federal Register 43(29) February 10, 1978.

US Water Resources Council. 1979. A unified national program for floodplain management (revised 1976). Government Printing Office, Washington, D.C.

IMPORTANT RIPARIAN/WETLAND SYSTEMS

OF PENINSULAR BAJA CALIFORNIA: AN OVERVIEW[1]

Norman C. Roberts[2]

Abstract.--The peninsula of Baja California, Mexico, and its phytogeography are described. Climatological factors and their historical and present impact on the land and its inhabitants are noted. An inventory of peninsular wetlands and some of the dominant plants are provided. Some conclusions concerning the future of the peninsula are presented.

INTRODUCTION

Riparian/wetland systems, for the purposes of this paper, are defined as being periodically, seasonally, or continually submerged lands populated by species and/or life forms different from those of the immediately adjacent vegetation, maintained and dependent upon conditions more mesic than those provided by the immediate precipitation (Brown 1978).

While the original Latin usage of the term "riparian" apparently related to freshwater, the term has occasionally been applied to tidewater- and estuarine-adjusted zones (Warner 1979). Tidelands have been included in this study because of their critical importance to the future of both the peninsula and the adjacent seas of Baja California, Mexico.

GEOGRAPHY

Baja California is a jagged finger of land extending from the southern border of California to south of the Tropic of Cancer. It wanders irregularly south and east from latitude 32°30'N and longitude 117°W at the northern International Boundary and Tijuana, to terminate in the Pacific Ocean 1,300 km. further south at Cabo San Lucas (22°50'N, 110°W) after penetrating well past the Tropic of Cancer.

The peninsula is separated from mainland Mexico by a 160-km. wide body of water usually known as the Gulf of California or the Sea of Cortez. To the west and south lies the Pacific Ocean. Baja California varies in width from 250 km. at the International Border in the north to 135 km. at the Bahía de La Paz, 155 km. above its southernmost tip. Baja California comprises an area of 143,790 km^2, and has 3,240 km. of shoreline. Figure 1 illustrates the geography of the region and indicates locations of sites referred to in the following discussions.

GEOLOGY

The peninsula split off the mainland 25 million years ago and began moving northwest. It has continued to do so at the rate of 1.5-3 cm. per year ever since, widening the Gulf as it moves (Anderson 1971). In addition, most of the peninsula, with the exception of the northern mountains, those at the Cape, and a few peaks in between, underwent submergence during the Miocene period (ibid.; Murphy 1975).

The relatively recent geologic separation of the peninsula from the mainland has been a somewhat limiting factor in the development of endemic species of plants (Wiggins 1980). There is, however, a high degree of endemism, or near-endemism, of both floral and faunal elements on the peninsula (ibid.; Savage 1959).

CLIMATE

The climate is generally hot and dry over most of the peninsula. Average annual rainfall ranges from 250 mm. at Tijuana, 200 mm. at Ensenada, 125 mm. at San Quintín, 100 mm. at El Rosario, to 50 mm. mid-peninsula. The highest mountain ranges of both the north and south, however, each receive approximately 750 mm. of annual precipitation.

Most of the peninsula has a two-season rainfall pattern. In the northern mountains, 70% of the precipitation occurs in winter--some in the form of snow (particularly in the Sierra de San Pedro Mártir)--and 30% occurs in the summer. The Sierras de la Giganta and de la Laguna in the

[1]Paper presented at the California Riparian Systems Conference. [University of California, Davis, September 17-19, 1981].
[2]Norman C. Roberts is Staff Assistant, U.S. Department of Interior, Washington, D.C.

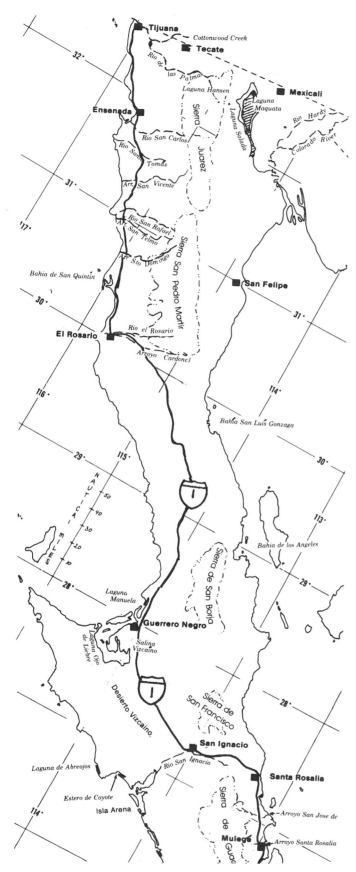

Figure 1.--Map of Baja California (northern portion).

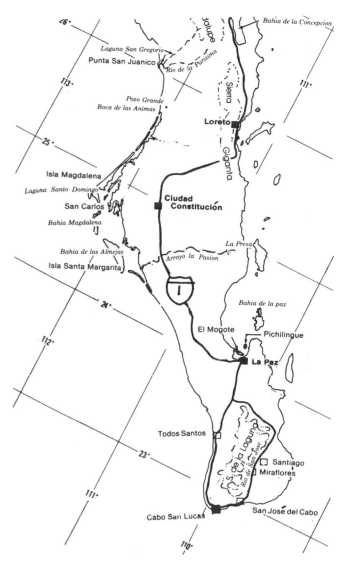

Figure 1 (cont.).--Map of Baja California (southern portion).

Cape Region receive 70% of their rainfall during the summer months (Hastings and Humphrey 1969). Both the Desert Region and the lower elevations of the Cape Region receive 50% or more of their precipitation in the summer.

Three general types of storms occur on the peninsula. Winter cyclonic storms moving south from the Gulf of Alaska bring rain to the north. These weaken as they move south, seldom reaching beyond the northern mountains. During the summer and fall, monsoon storms, also known as "Sonora storms", come across the Gulf of Baja California from the Mexican mainland. These are sometimes called "aquaceras" or "equipatas;" the former bring more rain to larger areas than the latter.

Tropical cyclonic storms that originate off Acapulco in the southeastern Pacific are known as "chubascos" by the natives of Baja California. Due to the violent nature of these storms and the winds accompanying them, the potential benefit of the rainfall is more than offset by the damage done as water rushes down the arroyos to the sea.

Normally chubascos do not make it as far north as California. However, on 10 September 1976, "Kathleen" reached the head of the Gulf and slammed into Southern California with winds of up to 160 km. per hr.[3] The storm caused at least 10 deaths and damage in excess of $10 million in San Diego and Imperial Counties. The northern peninsula was unaffected by "Liza" which followed "Kathleen" on 28 September 1976. The same cannot be said for La Paz; winds of up to 208 km. per hour and torrential rains burst a dam near the town and buried between 2,000 and 3,000 inhabitants.[4]

The San Diego Union reported the final chubasco of the season on 12 October 1972, "El Cardonoza de San Francisco", the shiplash of St. Francis. It dumped 250 mm. of rain on San Felipe in two days.[5] The average annual rainfall in San Felipe is only 55 mm. (Humphrey 1974).

In September, 1939, four chubascos struck Bahía de Magdalena, dumping a total of 570 mm. of rain. Between 1939 and 1962, the same area received an additional 750 mm., equal to 57 mm. annually.[6]

During the fall of 1978, in Arroyo de la Pasión, north of La Paz, one goat rancher measured 6 m. of water rushing past his house in what had been a dry stream bed the previous week.[7]

But there have been times when peninsula natives prayed for a chubasco. There have been periods of up to four years when not one drop of rain fell in some areas. During one dry period, or "seca," Antero Días of Bahía de Los Angeles fed viznaga (barrel cactus) (Ferocactus spp.) and cardóns (Pachycereus pringlei) to his livestock. The cacti were made more palatable by dousing them with kerosene and then lighting them to burn the spines.[8] During these dry years untold damage is done to the vegetation by overgrazing.

PHYTOGEOGRAPHIC REGIONS

There is considerable variation in the vegetative elements within the 1,300-km. peninsula. Additionally, the altitude goes from sea level to 3,096 m., and annual precipitation

varies between 50 and 750 mm. The phytogeography of the peninsula is best characterized as three more or less distinct vegetative zones: the California Region, the Desert Region, and the Cape Region (Wiggins 1959).

The California Region can be considered an extension of the southwestern California mountain ranges and their Pacific slopes. The Desert Region includes the eastern scarps of the northern mountain ranges, the central one-third of the peninsula, with the exception of the Sierra de la Giganta and the Cape Region. The Desert Region is generally divided into four subregions. The Cape Region includes the Sierras de la Laguna and de la Giganta ranges in addition to their drainages, and the southern mangrove forests on the seacoasts.

The California Region

The California Region includes the mountains and their western drainages to the Pacific Ocean from the International Border to the southern terminus of the Sierra de San Pedro Mártir. The transition to desert vegetative elements is gradual, becoming increasingly xeric from north to south coinciding with decreasing rainfall. On the Pacific slopes, this transition is well advanced at El Socorro (30°17'N), a few kilometers below Bahía San Quintín.[9]

There are two principal mountain ranges in the California Region. They are considered extensions of the peninsular ranges of Southern California and San Diego County. The northern-most, the Sierra Juárez, extends from the International Border south to Valle Trinidad, and has the highest representation of Southern California flora. Vegetation at the higher elevations consists of yellow pine forest and Jeffrey pine (Pinus jeffreyi), with a more or less typical chaparral group below, replaced by coastal sage scrub to the west as the elevation declines. The Sierra Juárez range average elevation is 1,400 m.

The Sierra San Pedro Mártir is the highest range in Baja California with an average elevation of 2,700 m. The forests are generally more open than those of the Sierra Juárez. Jeffrey pine is dominant, with sugar pine (P. lambertiana) occurring on the ridges. Lodgepole pine (P. murrayana) and quaking aspen (Populus tremuloides) are also found there, but not in the Sierra Juárez or in San Diego County. This range is a climatic island with the closest comparable plant community being the[10] Santa Rosa Mountains 250 km. to the north. The Sierra San Pedro Mártir lies at the southern

[3] San Diego Union, September 12, 1976.
[4] San Diego Union, October 3 and 4, 1976.
[5] San Diego Union, October 12, 1972.
[6] Schwenkmeyer, Richard. 1977. Baja California seminar, San Diego Natural History Museum, San Diego, California.
[7] Rancher at El Paso, in Arroyo de la Pasion, Baja California Sur. 1978. Personal communication.
[8] Dias, Antero. 1973. Personal communication, Bahía de Los Angeles.

[9] Moran, Reid. 1975. Plant life of Baja California, Baja California Seminar, San Diego Natural History Museum, San Diego, California.
[10] Moran, Reid. 1977. Plant geography of Baja California. Presented at Biogeography of Baja California Symposium, California State University, Fullerton.

extreme of the north temperate zone, influenced by both the Pacific and Gulf climates (Hastings and Turner 1965). This climatic interaction with the regional topography creates the greatest diversity of speciation and habitat to be found on the peninsula (Wiggins 1980).

The vegetation of the riverine corridors in the California Region is generally characteristic of comparable undisturbed riparian systems in Southern California. Riparian systems on the Pacific slopes of the peninsula all share many characteristics. At higher elevations and in the numerous deeper canyons, characteristic willow (Salix spp.), cottonwood (Populus fremontii), oak (Quercus spp.), and sycamore (Platanus racemosa) bosques remain with minimal disturbance. The streams are semi-perennial at lower elevations because of agriculture in the lower valleys and floodplains. None reach the sea except during heavy rains and flooding. With the exception of Río de Tia Juana, no major dams or water projects obstruct the arroyos of the peninsula.

Flooding during cyclonic storms from the north or south continues to discourage extensive human invasion in the canyons. In the valleys and on the coast, however, bridges, dikes, and flood channels are now being built to protect agricultural projects. When first constructed in 1973, trans-peninsular Highway 1 had few bridges along the 1,600+ km. stretch from the northern border to the tip of the peninsula. Truck and passenger traffic is increasing, and bridges are reconstructed after the roads are washed out during storms.

Although each riparian system exhibits individual characteristics, certain species are common in systems that have remained relatively pristine. The overstory may be open or closed, with willow the dominant tree comprising most of the overstory, along with sycamore, cottonwood, and oak. The understory is composed of Ceanothus spp., coffeeberry (Rhamnus californica), scrub oak (Quercus dumosa), chamise (Adenostoma fasciculatum), rose (Rosa minutifolia), arrowweed (Pluchea spp.) and Baccharis spp., as well as willow.

The Río de Tia Juana is the northernmost, and one of the more extensive riparian systems in the California Region. It is formed by the confluence of two major drainage systems, one on either side of the International Boundary. The mouth of the river is 135 km. from the most distant source. One of the two tributaries joining to form the Río de Tia Juana is the Río de las Palmas. A Baja California semi-perennial stream, during periods of drought it is dry over much of its course. Along the river where agriculture is not extensive, there are numerous stands of willow and sycamore. Farther east, cottonwoods and oaks join the riparian corridor. At lower elevations or in disturbed areas, Baccharis and arrowweed are found.

The second tributary of Río de Tia Juana is Cottonwood Creek. It drains a considerable area in southern San Diego County, becoming Arroyo del Alamar as it crosses into Baja California 9 km. east of the Pacific Ocean. It joins Río de las Palmas, then becomes Río de Tia Juana just east of the town of Tijuana. The river is being channelized through the city of Tijuana.

The sole major dam on the peninsula is Presa Rodriquez located 11 km. east of Tijuana. Constructed in 1937, it impounds water from Río de las Palmas. There are seven major dams in San Diego County alone draining a much smaller area of comparable mountain ranges. The lake impounded by the dam is now 7 km. long. The spillway was in use all during the spring of 1981. Five years ago however, the lake bed in its entirety was farmed. It was also a dry lake bed in the early 1960's.

Valle de las Palmas, 30 km. above the dam, has extensive olive and other fruit orchards in addition to variegated crops. The valley is so named because of a generous stand of California fan palms (Washingtonia filifera) that existed in previous years. Although common in the peninsular deserts, this was the only grove on the Pacific slopes of northern Baja California. Most of the trees fell to the machete long ago.

The Tia Juana River estuary is located on the American side of the International Border, its southern bank adjacent to the International Boundary marker at the Pacific Ocean.

"The Tia Juana Estuary of San Diego is recognized by ecologists as a model ecosystem, to be used in determining how to restore many modified coastal wetlands in the San Diego region. Its structure and function have been examined in detail and compared with other local wetlands, as well as more disturbed parts of Tia Juana Estuary itself, in order to establish how activities such as reduced tidal exchange, altered elevation, reduced species diversity, and altered channel morphology have changed southern California coastal wetlands."[11]

Río Guadalupe is the next important stream to the south. It flows west from its origin in the Sierra Juárez (32°5'N). Río Guadalupe is fed by springs and contains the only lake in the Sierra Juárez range, Laguna Hansen. Both the Río Guadalupe and Laguna Hansen sometimes go dry during long secas. The estuary at the mouth of the river is located at La Misión. This formerly rather extensive estuarine system has been drastically changed by the presence of several wells pumping water north 55 km. to the city of Tijuana. The estuary is now a salt water lagoon.

---

[11]Zedler, Joy. 1981. Personal communication.

Throughout most of its 100-km. course the river has been altered by heavy demands on the water table in the valleys through which it flows. Only at the higher elevations in the coniferous and chaparral zones of the mountains and in few steep canyons has the ecosystem remained relatively pristine.

Río San Carlos (31°45'N), another semi-perennial stream similar to Río Guadalupe, originates 30 km. to the south of Río Guadalupe. Its arroyo reaches the ocean at Estero Beach below Ensenada. There are at least three geothermal seeps along the river. The Río San Carlos corridor runs through chaparral for much of its course. Extensive dryland farming is practiced in the Ojos Negros Valley through which the river flows. For several kilometers at lower elevations, the river passes through an oak woodland with only subsistence farming to disturb the riparian system. The riparian corridors of this drainage include Tecate cypress (Cupressus forbesii) in some arroyos at lower elevations. A small population of western pond turtles (Clemmys marmorata), and introduced bullfrogs (Rana catesbeiana) occur above the resort of San Carlos, inland from Ensenada.

Río Santo Tomás (31°35'N), the next semi-perennial stream to the south, crosses Highway 1 approximately 40 km. south of Ensenada. Originating from a seep in the chaparral zone below the almost abandoned mining town of El Álamo, the riparian vegetation has remained relatively undisturbed for the first half of the corridor to the sea. For 25 km. the stream courses through one of the most beautiful arroyos in the northern peninsula.

Evidence of increasing xerification becomes apparent in this arroyo as northern riparian elements are joined by stands of cholla (Opuntia cylindropuntia), Our Lord's candle (Yucca whipplei), and "pitaya agria" (Machaerocereus gummosus), which nears the northernmost extension of its range in this arroyo. Western pond turtles and red-legged frogs (Rana aurora) are found in the river east of Highway 1.

Río San Vicente (31°30'N) (fig. 2) is the southernmost of the western-flowing streams originating in the Sierra Juárez drainage system. Like the others in this northern mountain chain, it remains relatively unaltered by humans wherever it passes thorough steep canyons. At lower elevations, or where subsistence farming is practiced, the native vegetation is substantially altered. Río San Vicente disappears into the sand during secas, leaving a dry stream bed with a few pools remaining. From its origin to the sea, it has one of the longest courses of any stream in the Sierra Juárez, nearly 100 km. Populations of Tecate cypress occur in the foothills and arroyos of this area.

Río San Rafael (31°07'N) is the northernmost drainage system of the Pacific slopes of the Sierra de San Pedro Mártir. It has few entering tributaries, and until recent years was little

Figure 2.--Arroyo San Vicente above the town.

disturbed over much of its course. Considerable water flows down this arroyo during storms (Welsh 1976). Arroyo San Rafael has a more direct corridor than other drainages to the north and is usually a permanent stream until it reaches the floodplain. Heavy willow bosques are dominant in the upper portion of Arroyo San Rafael. There is considerable agriculture for the final 20 km. of the river as the canyon opens into the floodplain and water sinks into the streambed.

The next large drainage system to the south is Arroyo San Telmo. It crosses Highway 1 in a broad valley at 30°55'N, 11 km. below Arroyo San Rafael. There is substantial agriculture along much of its course. The stream disappears in the upper San Telmo Valley 40 km. from the ocean. At higher elevations however, considerable undisturbed native woodland remains.

Continuing southward, Arroyo Santo Domingo (30°55'N) is located 15 to 25 km. south of Valle San Telmo. This stream has considerable pristine vegetation with few ranches because of the inaccessibility of the riparian corridor. At Mission Santo Domingo, the arroyo widens into a floodplain. For the remainder of its course to the sea, about 11 km., the arroyo intermittently carries water. Like most other streams of the California Region, it is characterized by heavy willow bosques along the streambed, joined by arrowweed and Baccharis at lower elevations and in agricultural areas.

In the arroyos of the California Region, the vegetation of the transition zones (upland to riparian) may include junco (Juncus acutus), oak, mountain mahogany (Cercocarpus betuloides), toyon (Heteromeles arbutifolia), Rhus spp., Ceanothus spp., and in some areas Tecate cypress.

Bahía de San Quintín (fig. 3) is the first salt water lagoon of major significance south of the International Boundary. The average annual

Figure 3.--Estero de San Quintín.

rainfall there is 120 mm. This relatively pristine salt marsh is located 275 km. south of Tijuana at 30°31'N. It is quite similar to the few remaining undisturbed Southern California salt marshes (Neuenschwander et al. 1979).

The bay itself is large, resembling an inverted J with the rounded base pointing towards the sea. From the entrance to the uppermost salt marsh is approximately 11 km. Much of the bay is shallow; the channel is tortuous and difficult to navigate even for small ocean-going fishing vessels.

The littoral marshes have dense stands of eelgrass (Zostera marina) in the channel bottoms. The channel banks are lined with cordgrass (Spartina foliosa), as well as glasswort (Salicornia bigelovii) and saltwort (Batis maritima) (ibid.). Three vegetation-types dominate the upper, middle, and lower littoral; they are salt cedar (Monanthochloe littoralis), pickleweed (S. virginica), and cordgrass, respectively (MacDonald and Barbour 1974).

The Desert Region

The Desert Region includes the eastern escarpment of the northern mountain ranges. The mountains are precipitous, dropping sharply between 1,000 and 2,000 m. to the desert floor. The Sierra de San Pedro Mártir escarpments in particular are spectacular, with the highest peak, Picacho del Diablo, rising abruptly to over 3,096 m. from the San Felipe Desert to the east.

The eastern scarp of the Sierra Juárez has several deep canyons cutting into the mountains. These narrow streambeds have steep gradients and are often relatively straight in their course to the desert, where they fan out sharply into large fans known as "bajadas" by the natives. Several of these canyons have water year-round and some also have geothermal seeps. In the Sierra Juárez all the larger arroyos, except the

northernmost, are palm-lined with California fan palm and the endemic blue palm (Brahea armata).

The largest and most beautiful of these canyons is called Tajo (Cantilles Canyon to early botanists). It usually carries water thoughout the year. Other picturesque palm canyons in the range are Carrizo, Guadalupe, and Palomar. During the summer and fall however, none have sufficient streamflow to reach their respective bajadas in the desert. These bajadas are littered with trunks of palms and large boulders washed down from higher elevations in the canyons during the often violent storms that occur in this region.

The eastern escarpment of the Sierra San Pedro Mártir also has several steep canyons cutting into its eastern face--Las Canada, del Diablo, Toledo, Oso, San Marcos, and San Luís. None have palms however, possibly because of their steep gradient (Rodriquez 1981). Like those of the Sierra Juárez, they have some water throughout the summer. In recent years, there has been considerable invasion of tamarisk (Tamarix spp.) in many of these arroyos.

The southwestern extension of the Colorado Desert, known as the San Filipe Desert, extends south along the eastern scarps of the northern mountains to join the Central Desert southwest of the town of San Felipe, above 30°N. The San Felipe Desert is considered the driest area on the peninsula--annual rainfall is 50 mm. One weather station in the northeast records 31 mm. of rainfall annually (Hastings and Humphrey 1969). In this region evaporation from a pan occurs at an estimated annual rate of 350 mm. per year during the summer.[12]

East of the Sierra Juárez, in an area formerly known as Laguna Salada, a new freshwater lake is now being formed. It is known as Laguna Maquata and extends from a few kilometers below the International Border south for 30 km. Laguna Maquata is being filled by a canal running north and west from the Río Hardy, a branch of the Río Colorado. It could become an important agricultural and vacation area for Mexicans in the future. The impact this lake will have on the surrounding desert is unknown.

Further east in the Colorado Desert lies the Mexicali Valley and the channelized Lower Colorado River. Both the Imperial and Mexicali Valleys are gradually being filled in by siltation from the Colorado River and peripheral canals. Because of irrigation and the canals involved, the Río Colorado no longer empties directly into the Gulf of California. However, the canals are dumping silt and salts into the upper Gulf, filling both it and the San Andreas

[12]Bloyd, Richard M. 1978. Water Resources talk presented at the California Desert Advisory Comm., USDI Bureau of Land Management public forum, Riverside, California.

Fault running down the middle of the Gulf. Ultimately this silt will raise the floor of the Gulf sufficiently to cause flooding of the entire adjacent low desert region.[13]

A detailed discussion of the Colorado River has been omitted. Originating far to the north, less than 200 km. of its long course to the Gulf of California winds through Mexico; it is not a Baja California river. Previous riparian symposia have adequately discussed the lower Colorado River (Ohmart et al. 1977; Johnson 1978).

Río El Rosario (30°5'N) is the last of the perennial streams with drainage from northern mountain ranges. It is formed by the confluence of two large arroyos, Rosario and Cardonal. The tributaries originate on either side of Cerro El Matomí (30°40'), a 1,500 m. desert peak 30 km. below the southern slope of the Sierra de San Pedro Mártir range, only 30 km. from the Gulf. In this area, the transition to Desert Region vegetation is nearly complete. Chaparral and coastal sage scrub have disappeared.

Both Arroyo El Rosario and Arroyo El Cardonal are pristine over much of their drainages and represent the first streams to be found in a "cardonal", a cardón (Pachycereus pringlei) forest. Arroyo El Rosario has been particularly subject to flooding during chubascos, and occasionally from northern storms in winter. In recent years, numerous wells have been drilled and crops are being raised where the arroyo widens 30 km. east of the ocean. In times of drought, both Río El Rosario and Río El Cardonal dry up, leaving only a few pools in protected areas. The average annual rainfall at El Rosario is 100 mm.

Laguna Manuela (28°10'N) is a substantial estuarine system. This narrow, shallow lagoon and the much larger adjacent Estero de San José (Guerrero Negro) are extensive and relatively untouched salt water estuarine marshes. They form part of the huge Ojo de Liebre (Scammons Lagoon) complex located in the region of 28°N, the state boundary between Baja California Norte and Baja California Sur. Laguna Ojo de Liebre extends nearly 60 km. into the Vizcaíno desert.

Much of the inland, or eastern, area of Scammons Lagoon is botanically rather sterile and is diked for salt production. These huge salt beds are known as Salina Vizcaíno. It is the largest seawater salt-producing facility in the world. Both Estero de San José and Laguna Manuela have rich biotas, however. Like many of the Pacific saltwater marshes they have beach barrier formations in which fine sandy sediments dominate (MacDonald and Barbour 1974). The species composition and zonal distribution in

Estero de San José are apparently quite similar to that of San Quintín with cordgrass, salt wort, glasswort, and salt cedar again succeeding one another as the elevation increases (ibid.).

No gray whales (Eschrichtius gibbosus) enter Laguna Manuela, but they winter and calve in adjacent Laguna Ojo de Liebre. Formerly a favorite visiting site for whale watching by boat, Scammons Lagoon has been closed by the Mexican Government to protect the whales. There is, however, a road off Highway 1 where visitors can watch whales from shore.

To the immediate south is the Laguna Abreojos/Estero del Coyote/San Ignacio group of marshes. San Ignacio (27°N) (fig. 4) is the largest of the three lagoons and extends into the Vizcaíno Desert 30 km. It is deep enough for large vessels. The Abreojos and Estero de Coyote lagoons are too shallow and narrow for ships. All three lagoons have extensive salt marshes with scattered mangrove shrubs and estuarine systems.

Figure 4.--Laguna San Ignacio, south side.

There are four species of mangrove-like plants occurring in Baja California: black mangrove or "mangle negro" (Avecennia germinans), white mangrove or "mangle blanco" (Laguncularia racemosa), "mangle dulce" (Tricerma phyllanthoides), and red mangrove or "mangle rojo" (Rhizophora mangle). Another bush tree in the family Combretaceae that occurs in this region is the button mangrove (Conocarpus erecta). It is sometimes called "mangle" by the natives.

Laguna Abreojos, also called Pond Lagoon, is the northernmost Pacific extension for white and red mangrove in the low marsh, with saltwort and glasswort dominating the littoral marshes at higher elevations.

---

[13]Jahns, Richard. 1978. Geological History talk presented at the California Desert Advisory Comm., USDI Bureau of Land Management public forum, Riverside, California.

Laguna San Ignacio has a 25-km. wide opening interrupted by a large, mostly sand barrier island known as Isla Arena, 15 km. long. South of the lagoon and island, shallow tidal lagoons extend for another 35 km., to 26°38'N. Gray whales winter in this lagoon and whale watching trips are popular. Vegetative elements in Laguna San Ignacio include white mangrove, red mangrove, and cordgrass in the low marsh; with glasswort, saltwort and salt cedar occurring in the high marsh.[14] The eastern and southeastern shore of the lagoon is called "La Laguna" locally. It is the largest marsh area of the complex. In the low marsh dominant vegetative elements are red mangrove followed by white mangrove with some cordgrass. The high marsh[15] is dominated by saltwort mixed with glasswort.

Río San Ignacio (fig. 5), located mid-peninsula between 27°N and 28°N at 113°W, is the first true river south of the northern mountains. It flows west from a long, narrow, spring-fed lake at the town of San Ignacio. The elevation is 165 m. at the lake and town. Annual rainfall of the area is slightly under 130 mm. At the river's origin and around the town, native vegetation has been replaced largely by date palms (Phoenix dactylifera), introduced by the missionaries. Dates are the only important industry of San Ignacio, there being no other agriculture with the exception of family gardens and a few cattle.

Figure 5.--Arroyo and Río San Ignacio

The geology of the San Ignacio region is similar to much of the Vizcaíno Desert: an ancient sea bed overlain with volcanic rocks, some of which are of recent geologic origin. Río San Ignacio winds its course west towards Laguna San Ignacio and the Pacific Ocean for approximately 30 km., disappearing into the sand as the shallow arroyo widens into the open Vizcaíno Desert. The river fails to reach Laguna San Ignacio by 20 km.

Río San Ignacio has been little disturbed by man; there are only two ranches located along the riparian corridor. These are both subsistence operations--one raising a few cattle and the other, goats. The riverbed itself is either lava rock, "caliche", or sandstone, affording little nourishment for plants. Below the palm grove and town of San Ignacio, a mesquite (Prosopis spp.) bosque follows the course of the river. There has been a considerable invasion of introduced tamarisk in some areas.

Bullfrogs have been introduced into the lake at the town of San Ignacio but they have not extended their range to the river below the date palm grove. Río San Ignacio is the northernmost extension of the range of pond slider (Chrysemys scripta) on the peninsula (Van Denburgh 1922; Roberts[16]).

Laguna San Gregorio (26°7'N) is a 10-km. long, narrow estuary just east of Punta San Juanico. Prior to 1958, the mouth of the lagoon was open and ships had navigated it for decades. A chubasco in 1958, followed by another in 1959 (a rare occurrence) caused extensive damage and several deaths in the area. The storm also closed the mouth of the laguna with a sand barrier.[16] It has remained shut to seagoing ships since then. The estuary is below the confluence of two of the larger Pacific drainage systems of the Sierra de la Giganta. The northernmost of these, Arroyo San Gregorio, has water over some of its riparian corridor only during wet periods.

Intertidal vegetation of Laguna San Gregorio includes some new elements in addition to the common high marsh species found at Laguna San Ignacio. Sea purslane (Sesuvium portulacastrum) and iodine bush (Allenrolfea occidentalis) are both found in the estuary. Other than red mangrove seedlings, there are no mangroves in this marsh. Dominant vegetative elements are saltwort and glasswort.[17]

The Río de la Purísima (fig. 6) is the next drainage system to the south of Río de San Gregorio; it empties into Laguna San Gregorio, flowing from the heart of the Sierra de la Giganta range from the region of 26°20' southwest to the lagoon. This is the largest perennial stream of the southern peninsula. It flows above ground for approximately 32 km. Midway a low dam, El Zacatón, about 300 m. long, blocks the arroyo, creating a shallow lake. There are numerous larger pools along the course of the

[14]Mudie, P.J., A. Johnson, J. Rutherford, and F.H. Wolfson. 1975. Shoreline vegetation of Baja California. Unpublished report prepared for Foundation of Ocean Research, San Diego, Calif.
[15]Mudie, Peta J. 1981. Personal communication.

[16]Roberts, Norman C. 1981. Unpublished manuscript.
[17]Mudie, Peta J. Diversity in the salt marsh floras of Southern California and western Baja California. Unpublished manuscript.

Figure 6.--Río de la Purísima.

Figure 7.--Boca de las Animas, upper end of Magdalena Bay.

river; many have apparently stable populations of pond sliders. Downstream from the dam two small towns, San Isidro and La Purísma, have subsistence agriculture using water from a dam flume. Several kilometers below the towns, the stream flows through limestone caliche and the water sinks into the stream bed.

Willow, "torote" (Bursera spp.), "palo verde" (Cercidium spp.), "palo colorado" (Colubrina viridis), "palo adan" (Fouquieria diguete), "lomboy" (Jatropha spp.), "garambullo" (Lophocereus schottii), mesquite, and cholla are all found in the riverine corridor.

The Cape Region

The southernmost phytogeographic region of the peninsula includes the Sierra de la Laguna (Cape Mountain Range) and the Sierra de la Giganta, a lesser range that extends northwest along the Gulf of California towards Bahía Concepcion. The Sierra de la Laguna extends nearly due north from 23°N to 24°10'N. This range consists primarily of granitic blocks, while the Sierra de la Giganta is volcanic in origin. Floristic elements of the two ranges are similar; both have semi-deciduous forests that share many species of plants not found in other regions of the peninsula (Carter 1980).

The vegetative elements of the region are widely diversified, generally dry and tropical, but with pine/oak woodland only at the higher elevations of the Sierra de la Laguna. At lower elevations is semi-deciduous forest prominent in leguminous trees and shrubs.

Southern peninsular coastal salt marshes and mangrove swamp forests have been included in the Cape Region flora (Wiggins 1980). These forests are extensive in the larger saltwater lagoons and estuaries. They are found from Laguna Abreojos (26°50') south around the Cape and north in the Gulf to Bahía de Los Angeles (29°N).

Bahía Magdalena (fig. 7, 8) is 960 km. south of San Diego. It is the third and southernmost of the gray whale mating grounds on

the peninsula. The bay area covers approximately 260 km^2 composed of quiet deep water with a network of uncharted small canals, islets and islands of estuarine character.

Bahía Magdalena (fig. 8) is the largest and most extensive saltwater lagoon on the peninsula, and contains a most impressive deep water harbor. The bay extends from the town of La Poza Grande (25°45'N) over 200 km. south in a dog-leg that terminates in a narrow shallow lagoon. Much of Bahía Magdalena is separated from the Pacific Ocean by narrow sand barriers that are often submerged during major storms.

Figure 8.--Magdalena Bay, south end.

The sea entrance to Magdalena Bay is protected by two large islands, Isla Magdalena and Isla Santa Margarita. Isla Magdalena, the northern island, is 100 km. long, low, narrow, and mostly sand. It protects the section of Magdalena Bay known as Laguna Santo Domingo and the port of San Carlos, used by ocean-going vessels for commerce. Isla Santa Margarita, to the immediate south, is mountainous and 40 km. long. The principal bay is 40 km. long and 25 km. wide.

The channel running between Puerto San Carlos and Puerto Lopez Mateos 45 km. to the north is known as the Hull Canal. This is a favorite playground for the gray whale. When the tides are favorable, smaller ocean vessels can navigate this canal north to the town of La Poza Grande from Puerto San Carlos.

Ciudad Constitución, located on Highway 1 in Valle Santo Domingo, is 58 km. inland from Puerto San Carlos. The valley, formerly a broad cardonal, has for the past decade been under intensive agricultural development. Hundreds of irrigation wells perforate an underlying fossil aquifer. Within a few years this irreplacable water supply will be depleted and saline. Rainfall in the area is replacing less than 10% of the groundwater being removed at present rates (Palacios 1978).

The wetland vegetative elements of Magdalena Bay include: red mangrove, cordgrass, and white mangrove in the low marshes; saltwort, salt cedar, and black mangrove in the high marshes. In the estuaries are iodine bush, a glasswort (_Salicornia subterminalis_) and mangle dulce.[15]

Dense beds of eelgrass occur in most of the lagoons but are absent from the estuaries. Ditchgrass (_Ruppia maritima_) is found in shallow open ponds in the salt marshes and mangroves. Red mangrove is the dominant mangrove species from Laguna Santo Domingo south. Black mangrove joins the other mangroves at Laguna Santo Domingo. It is much more common in the Gulf because of the warmer waters (MacDonald and Barbour 1974). Red mangrove increases in height southward from Laguna Abreojos and becomes the dominant mangrove species from the northern end of Laguna Santo Domingo.

Arroyo de la Pasión (fig. 9) is a shallow arroyo located below the 25th parallel. It meanders west for over 80 km., practically crossing the peninsula to terminate in Bahía Almejas at the southern end of Bahía Magdalena. This arroyo, located 250 km. north of La Paz, at 24°55'N and 111°W drains the low southern extension of the Sierra de la Giganta. It is semi-perennial with water remaining in the deeper pools during dry periods. Less than 30 km. of the arroyo has water. Pond slider turtles are found in many of these ponds at La Presa, Las Tinajitas and El Paso. This is the southernmost extension of this species, although they were formerly found in the Sierra de la Laguna drainages at the cape (Van Denburgh 1922, Roberts[16]).

The town of Todos Santos, on the west side of the peninsula south of La Paz, has little marsh, but button mangrove first occurs at Las Piedritas to the south. This appears to be the northernmost[15] extension of its range on the Pacific coast.

The Sierra de la Laguna Range of the Cape Region extends almost north/south in direc-

Figure 9.--Río de la Pasion.

tion, the drainages are east and west. The plant communities are oak/pinyon woodland above and semi-deciduous forest below. The Sierra de la Laguna weather station is in a meadow known as La Laguna. It is at approximately 1,900 m. elevation. Records indicate 350 mm. of rain falls in the summer months and about the same amount during the rest of the year. The average annual rainfall at the La Laguna station is 735 mm. (Hastings and Humphrey 1969).

The Sierra de la Laguna watershed empties into the tropical Pacific by several relatively straight canyons. None of the streams normally reach either the Gulf or the Pacific. The arroyos on the west scarp are precipitous and only carry water after rainfall. The larger and more gradual east-facing arroyos carry water much of the year and have considerable runoff during the summer months. There are subsistence farming or ranching operations on the lower slopes of the mountains, as well as in the arroyos.

Two of the largest arroyos have extensive drainages and pass through the towns of Santiago and Miraflores. Both streams are perennial in the mountains; even during periods of drought deep pools remain at the lower elevations. Both arroyos have bosques of willow (_S. taxifolia_) along their courses. The beautiful "zalate", a fig (_Ficus_ sp.), is common here.

The town of San José del Cabo (23°5'N) (fig. 10) at is at the middle of the peninsular tip. It overlooks the estuary and mouth of the broad valley through which the Río San José formerly flowed. The valley extends north for over 50 km. When Nelson visited the area there was extensive agriculture and a well-established town (Nelson 1922). The river no longer flows except during flood periods because of ever increasing agricultural and population demands. The valley has not suffered the damage of other areas because rainfall is sufficient to replenish the aquifers (Palacios 1978).

The Sierra de la Giganta range extends north roughly from Cerro Machado, a peak of 1,025 m. just north of Bahía La Paz (24°35'N) to about 30 km. northwest of Loreto (26°30'N). The

Figure 10.—San José del Cabo.

Figure 11.—Mulegé and Arroyo Santa Rosalea.

gable for small boats. It is surrounded by palms, both native Mexican fan palms (<u>Washingtonia robusta</u>) and introduced date palm. The wide valley, Arroyo Santa Rosalea, above Mulegé (fig. 11) has been under intensive cultivation for many years.

eastern escarpment of the Giganta range is precipitous and close to the Gulf. The western slopes decline more gradually to the Llano Magdalena.

There are several large mangrove lagoons on the west side of the Gulf between La Paz and Bahía de Los Angeles. Most of these areas have extensive salt marshes whose vegetative species include glasswort and saltwort. Bahía de La Paz (24°10'N) is well inside the Gulf of California and has the largest port on the Gulf side of the peninsula. Several areas in the bay have wetlands. Pichilingue in the outer bay has black, red and white mangrove at the lowest littoral zone. Saltwort dominates at higher elevations. Inside La Paz Bay and on the El Magote peninsula the same three mangroves are present, but glasswort replaces the saltwort at higher littoral zones.[15] The town of Loreto also has some mangrove and salt marsh vegetation.[16]

In the Sierra Giganta west of Loreto is an area known as Las Parras, a beautiful arroyo draining these mountains to the east. "Palma de taco" (<u>Brahea brandegeei</u>), an endemic palm, is found in abundance here (Coyle and Roberts 1975).

Mulegé and Bahía Concepción to the immediate south are rimmed with mangroves. Río Mulegé, in Arroyo Santa Rosalea (26°05'N) is actually a brackish water lagoon. It exists for only 3 km., running from below a bridge and dam in the town to the Gulf. The river is navi-

Río San José de Magdalena is one of the perennial streams in the Gulf drainage system. It is located just above 27°N. There is substantial subsistence farming in much of the arroyo and the willow overstory has been largely replaced by small agricultural plots. The stream disappears where the mouth of the canyon opens into the bajada leading to the Gulf. There is a large stand of the endemic "güeribo trees" (<u>Populus brandegeei</u>) in the arroyo above the town of San José de Magdalena. This is the northernmost population of this beautiful cottonwood species (Coyle and Roberts 1975). It is most common in the arroyos of the Cape, but a few trees are also found in the Sierra Giganta.

Farther north, San Lucas (27°30'N) has a relatively small bay, with red mangrove, black mangrove, and glasswort. There is also a <u>Suaeda</u> that resembles <u>Suaeda californica</u> but may be an undescribed species.[15]

Bahía de Los Angeles has a large salt marsh at the head of the bay with some red mangrove, also saltwort and glasswort. To the north, San Luís Gonzaga (29°42'N) has saltwort and glasswort in some areas of the bay.

With the exception of the California Region, the transition zones of vegetation over most of the peninsula are brief or absent in the riparian corridors. Species found in Desert Region transition zones include mesquite, palo verde, ironwood (<u>Olneya tesota</u>), creosote bush (<u>Larrea tridentata</u>), and lomboy (<u>Jatropha</u> spp.).

Much of the transition zone along both peninsular coasts is comprised of sand dunes or sea bluffs. The most common dune species in the northern and central sections of the west coast are sand verbena (Abronia maritima), ice plant (Mesembryanthemum chilense) and sea purslane (Sesuvium verrocosum) (Johnson 1973). Other coastal dune plants include species of Ambrosia, Oenothera, and Verbena. Sea bluff community plants are confined to the Pacific side of the peninsula. They include Dudleya spp., ice plant, marsh-rosemary (Limonium californicum), and Eriophyllum spp. (Wiggins 1959, 1980).

From Todo Santos south, sand verbena, ice plant, and sea purslane are replaced by the tropical grasses, dropseed (Sporobolus virginicus) and Jouvea pilosa. These grasses continue on the Gulf side of the Cape where sea purslane is absent and sand verbena is only found in scattered patches.

WHITHER THE PENINSULA

When the first dozen Europeans arrived at Loreto in 1697, there were probably 40,000 aborigines living a rather precarious existence on the entire peninsula (Aschmann 1967). Baegert, a German Jesuit missionary, returned to Europe after 20 years in Baja California and spent the remaining four years of his life writing an excellent account of the peninsula (Baegert 1772). In Chapter VIII entitled "The Vermin of California" he wrote:

To this group belong the snakes, toads, bats, wasps, ants and locusts. Of the first named there are twenty different kinds in California, and every year thousands of them are buried in the stomachs of the California Indians (ibid.).

The entire peninsula of Baja California could apparently only support 40,000 Indians in bare subsistence. It is difficult to imagine how long this fragile landmass, two-thirds of it desert, will sustain the rapidly expanding population of 2.25 million and the concurrent development. Since 1940, the average rate of population growth for Tijuana alone has been over 9% per year (Navarro 1976).

Last year, Baja California Norte produced nearly 300,000 tons of agricultural crops and shipped 152,000 head of cattle.[18] During the entire missionary period, the southern half of the peninsula never supported more than 1,000 ha. of agricultural crops, most of which were raised adjacent to or in riparian systems (Palacios 1978).

---

[18] Annual Report of the Sec. de Desarrollo, Dir. de Agricultura y Ganaderia, annual report of the state. 1979-1980.

Engineer Raul Palacios has provided the following critique of that situation:

It is estimated that from 1921 to 1930 the Magdalena plain of Baja California Sur did not cultivate more than 5,000 hectares. Cattle raising activity was more extensive. The limiting factor was water. At the present time, approximately 50,000 hectares are annually cultivated; in this same region, 600 wells are being used to furnish water.

Of the water removed by pumping from wells, 90.6% is coming from aquifers and only 9.3% is available from surface water. In all cases except the San José del Cabo region, this extraction is substantially higher than the new charge or recovery.

Due to over-exploitation, the resulting salt water intrusion, and new pumping areas, at least 100 wells will now have to be relocated farther away from the coast. The conception that underground waters are renewable resources must be changed by all means." (ibid.)

This headline appeared in the San Diego Union: NO WATER FOR 500,000 OF TIJUANA'S POOREST.

This city's antiquated water system and a sharp drop in reservoirs have left an estimated 500,000 of Tijuana's poorest residents without running water for two to six weeks. State officials said no water can be pumped to an estimated 80 affected neighborhoods until late 1982. That is when a new aqueduct from the Colorado River in Mexicali to Tijuana is scheduled to be completed.[19]

The California Region in the north has the greatest water resource potential, but it must be developed, and at prohibitive costs. At the present rate of growth in the north, it is doubtful that future water sources, including the new Colorado River aqueduct, will be capable of supplying the needs of the expanding population.

The northern mountain ranges and their riparian corridors have not yet suffered serious damage. Hydrologic development in the north, should it occur, will accelerate deterioration of the remaining riparian systems. The mid-peninsular Desert Region has no water available for development other than that supplied by depleting two fossil aquifers. The Vizcaíno Desert and the Magdalena Region will be forced to transport water from elsewhere or allow present agricultural projects to revert back to desert within a few years when the fossil aquifers are depleted. The Cape Region is growing less rapidly than the north and the government has not aggressively attempted to expand industry there.

---

[19] San Diego Union. August 22, 1981.

The Mexican Government is attempting to exploit marine resources at an accelerating pace throughout the peninsula. In most areas, shellfish beds have been so severely depleted that conservation efforts may prove futile. As the ports of Bahía Magdalena are developed, increasing pressures will cause further deterioration of the natural resources of this enormous wetland. The philosophy of the Mexican Government is oriented towards development of resources, not their conservation.

Scientists and others involved in natural resources programs are consequently charged with investigating possibilities for exploitation. Basic research or even long-range research is severely limited in favor of attempts to provide food and shelter for the rapidly expanding population.

Conservation programs, if initiated at all, are generally underfunded and understaffed. In Mexico, as in most Latin American countries, there is a very limited political constituency for the management of natural resources at the present time. However, in recent years both the USDI Fish and Wildlife Service and the Office of Environmental Services of the U.S. State Department have been working with Mexican officials to develop conservation programs applicable to Mexico.

LITERATURE CITED

Anderson, D.L. 1971. The San Andreas Fault. Scientific American 225(5): 52-68.

Aschmann, Homer. 1967. The central desert of Baja California: demography and ecology. p. 145-148. The Central Desert of Baja California: demography and ecology. Manessier Publshing Company, Riverside, Calif. 282 p.

Baegert, Johann Jakob. 1772. Observations in lower California. Second edition. Translated in 1952. University of California Press, Berkeley, California. 218 p.

Brown, David E. 1978. Southwestern wetlands--their classification and characteristics. p. 269-282. In: R.R. Johnson and J.F McCormick (tech. coord.). Strategies for protection and management of floodplain wetlands and other riparian ecosystems: proceedings of the symposium. [Callaway Gardens, Georgia, December 11-13, 1978]. USDA Forest Service GTR-WO-12. 410 p. Washington, D.C.

Carter, Annetta. 1980. The vegetation of the Sierra de la Giganta Baja California Sur: its scientific and potential economic importance. Presented at the eighteenth annual symposium of the Asociacion Cultural de Las Californias. [Loreto, Baja California Sur, Mexico, May, 1980]. 5 p.

Coyle, Jeanette, and Norman C. Roberts. 1975. A field guide to the common and interesting plants of Baja California. 206 p. Natural History Publishing Company, La Jolla, Calif.

Hastings, James R., and Robert R. Humphrey (ed.). 1969. Climatological data and statistics for Baja California. Technical report on meteorology and climatology of arid regions, No. 18. 85 p. University of Arizona, Tucson.

Hastings, J.R., and R.M. Turner. 1965. Seasonal precipitation regimes in Baja California, Mexico. Geografiska Annaler 47:204-223.

Humphrey, Robert R. 1974. The Boojum and its home. 214 p. University of Arizona Press, Tucson.

Johnson, Ann. 1973. A survey of the strand and dune vegetation along the Pacific coast of Baja California. Masters Thesis, University of California, Davis. 126 p.

Johnson, R. Roy. 1978. The lower Colorado River: a western system. p. 41-62. In: R.R. Johnson and J.F McCormick (tech. coord.). Strategies for protection and management of floodplain wetlands and other riparian ecosystems: proceedings of the symposium. [Callaway Gardens, Georgia, December 11-13, 1978]. USDA Forest Service GTR-WO-12. 410 p. Washington, D.C.

MacDonald, K.B., and M.G. Barbour. 1974. Beach and salt marsh vegetation of the North American Pacific coast. p. 175-233. In: R.J. Reimold and W.H. Queen. An ecology of Halophytes. 605 p. Academic Press, New York, N.Y.

Murphy, R.W. 1975. Two blind snakes (Serpentes: Leptotyphilopidae) from Baja California with a contribution to the biogeography of peninsular and insular herpetofauna. Proc. Calif. Acad. of Science series 4, 40:99-103.

Navarro, Gabriel Cuevas. 1976. Acueducto Rio Colorado-Tijuana, Baja California, Mexico. p. 3-22. In: J. Fernandez (ed.). Proceedings of XIV symposium of Baja California. [Tecate, Baja California, Mexico, May 1-2, 1976]. 59 p. Instituto de Investigaciones Esteticas de la U.N.A.M., Mexico.

Nelson, Edward W. 1922. Lower California and its natural resources. 194 p. Manessier Publishing Company, Riverside, Calif.

Neuenschwander, L.F., T.H. Thorsted, Jr., and R.J. Vogl. 1979. The salt marsh and transitional vegetation of Bahía de San Quintín. Bull. So. Calif. Acad. Sci. 78(3): 163-182.

Ohmart, R.D., W.O. Deason, C. Burke. 1977. A riparian case history: the Colorado River. p. 35-77. In: R.R. Johnson and D.A. Jones (ed.). Importance, preservation and management of riparian habitat: a symposium. [Tuscon, Arizona, July 9, 1977]. USDA Forest Service GTR-RM-43. 217 p. Rocky Mountain Range and Experiment Station, Fort Collins, Colorado.

Palacios, Raul Aviles. 1978. Evolution of the agriculture in south Californian desert. In: J.C. Agundez (ed.). Proceedings of the XVI Symposium de la Asociacion Cultural de las Californias. [San José del Cabo, Mexico, May 1978]. 254 p.

Rodriguez, Fernando. 1981. Baja California: its coast and highlands along the Sea of Cortez. p. C8-10. In: Kirchner, W.M. Mathes, D. Kerig, R. McFarlane (ed.). Proceedings of Baja California symposium XIX. [California State University, Los Angeles, May 16-17, 1981]. California State University, Los Angeles.

Savage, Jay M. 1959. Evolution of a peninsular herpetofauna. p. 184-212. In: J.S. Garth (ed.). Biogeography of Baja Califorina and adjacent seas: proceedings of the symposium. Part 3. [San Diego State College, San Diego, Calif., June 16-17, 1959]. 88 p. Society of Systemic Zoology, Washington, D.C.

Van Denburgh, John. 1922. Reptiles of western North America. 980 p. California Academy of Sciences, San Francisco.

Warner, Richard E. 1979. The California riparian study program: background information and proposed study design. 177 p. California Department of Fish and Game, Sacramento.

Welsh, Hartwell H., Jr. 1976. Ecogeographic distribution of herpetofauna of the Sierra de San Pedro Mártir region. Masters Thesis, California State University, Humboldt, Arcata, Calif. Unpublished. 169 p.

Wiggins, Ira L. 1959. The origin and relationships of the land flora. p. 148-165. In: J.S. Garth (ed.). Biogeography of Baja Califorina and adjacent seas: proceedings of the symposium. Part 3. [San Diego State College, San Diego, Calif., June 16-17, 1959]. 88 p. Society of Systemic Zoology, Washington, D.C.

Wiggins, Ira L. 1980. Flora of Baja California. 1025 p. Stanford University Press, Stanford, California.

RIPARIAN PROBLEMS AND INITIATIVES

IN THE AMERICAN SOUTHWEST: A REGIONAL PERSPECTIVE[1]

R. Roy Johnson and Lois T. Haight[2]

Abstract.--Southwestern riparian systems support some
of the world's most endangered ecosystems. These rich riparian areas are high-energy zones, supporting some of the richest biotas in North America, as well as being in great demand for human use. Estimated losses of these natural ecosystems range from approximately 70% to more than 95%. Associated problems include wildlife and recreational losses as
well as diminishing water quality.

INTRODUCTION

...For eons we dreamed of and labored
toward escaping from the anxieties and
hardships of a wilderness condition
only to find, when we reached the promised land of supermarkets and air conditioners, that we had forfeited something of great value. (Nash 1978)

The southwestern United States is drained by
two major river systems, the Colorado and the Rio
Grande. Both rivers drain large areas, but flow
levels are low due to sparse precipitation and
high evaporation rates. The region is generally
arid, except for some high montane areas and
scarce riparian wetlands. Warm weather and accompanying long growing seasons permit production of
semitropical crops and high-production food, forage, and fiber agribusinesses. Water withdrawal
for irrigation, mining, municipal, and industrial
uses results in heavy demands on both surface
water supplies (streams and lakes) and groundwater reserves (aquifers). Little water reaches
the Pacific Ocean from the Colorado or the Atlantic from the Rio Grande. Destruction of much of
the Southwest's riparian zone is the result of
two basic processes: 1) depletion of riverine
waters by consumptive uses; and 2) mechanical damage from grazing, mining, and engineering activities associated with railroad and road building
(Dobyns 1981), and more recently with suburban
and urban developments.

---

[1]Paper presented at the California Ripar-
ian Systems Conference. [University of Cali-
fornia, Davis, September 17-19, 1981].
[2]R. Roy Johnson is Unit Leader and Lois T.
Haight is Research Associate; both are with the
Cooperative National Park Resources Studies Unit,
USDI National Park Service, School of Renewable
Natural Resources, University of Arizona, Tucson.

CHARACTERISTICS AND VALUES OF SOUTHWESTERN
RIPARIAN ECOSYSTEMS

Recent investigations have demonstrated that
southwestern riparian zones support some of the
most productive ecosystems in North America (Johnson and Jones 1977; Johnson and McCormick 1978).
Characteristics which contribute to the ecological richness of southwestern riparian ecosystems
include the following.

1. As linear ecosystems, riparian systems
provide a maximum amount of edge per unit area.
The importance of this edge effect is discussed
by Johnson (1978) and Odum (1978).
2. The ecotonal nature of riparian systems
is due to their interfacing with adjacent aquatic
and terrestrial ecosystems.
3. As islands of mesophytic and hydrophytic
vegetation in the arid and semiarid West, riparian systems support a uniquely diverse fauna and
flora. Western riparian ecosystems are high energy systems due in part to "...high water tables
and alluvial soils from drainage and erosion of
adjacent uplands on the one side, or from periodic flooding from aquatic ecosystems on the other"
(McCormick 1978). As high-energy systems, riparian systems are in great demand by humans for
recreation and by both wildlife and humans for
food, water, dwelling sites, and a large variety
of other uses.

SOUTHWESTERN RIPARIAN SYSTEMS:
ENDANGERED ECOSYSTEMS

Southwestern riparian/wetland zones support
truly endangered ecosystems. This is especially
true of riparian zones of the arid and semiarid
lowlands. Johnson et al. (1977), for example, found that of 166 species of birds nesting
in the southwest lowlands, 47% are entirely dependent, and an additional 30% partially dependent,
on riparian and other wetlands. To date little

has been done to conserve the paltry remnants of our southwestern riparian ecosystems. Laws protecting riparian zones from destructive activities such as housing and business developments have been inadequate. A current strategy to protect prime riparian ecosystems is their purchase by groups such as The Nature Conservancy, Defenders of Wildlife, and the USDI Fish and Wildlife Service (FWS). Additional efforts in Arizona and New Mexico consist largely of attempts by governmental, scientific, and private groups to inventory and evaluate the miniscule remnants of what were often extensive riparian areas and to establish natural areas in what little remains (Smith 1974).

The overall result of riverine technological developments in the Southwest has been a diminished diversity of wildlife and vegetation-types. This constant erosion of ecological diversity has in turn resulted in a lack of recreational opportunities and a downward trend in the quality of human life itself. This downward trend does not refer just to the niceties of life. It refers to more than whether a reservoir is to be built to provide speedboating and water-skiing, in place of canoeing, camping, picnicking, and bird-watching. The concern is for subsistence— life itself—food and water.

Still, growth continues unchecked and with a lack of water resource planning in large southwestern cities. Populations continue to expand while surface water and groundwater supplies diminish. An example of a pending crisis brought on by river mismanagement is the effects on fisheries and the food and recreation they provide. Several papers presented by Paulsen and co-investigators in a recent symposium on aquatic resources of the Colorado River point out problems along the Colorado itself. Here, the construction of Glen Canyon Dam has degraded the fishery of downstream Lake Mead, important as a recreational fishery. We are all familiar with estuarine losses from water pollution. Less, however, is known of the rapid degradation of the important marine fishery further downstream in the Gulf of Lower California. Little attempt has been made to determine the influence of gargantuan dams upstream on the Colorado. The reservoirs behind these dams serve as gigantic sinks, trapping nutrients which formerly flowed into the Gulf, thereby providing an important energy source for these fisheries. And, if the fishery has deteriorated, (that is, the higher trophic levels are in "poor health,") then so has the rest of the ecosystem, (that is, the lower trophic levels on which the fish depend). Much of these aquatic nutrients originated in the riparian zone (Meehan et al. 1977). These same reservoirs have an annual evaporation rate of approximately one million acre-feet (AF) of water, enough for four million people (van Hylckama 1971; Jassby 1980), from a system already over-allocated by more than two million AF per year (Dracup 1977). The Colorado River is little more than a series of reservoirs and canals from Lake Powell to its delta, more than

1,287 km. (800 mi.) downstream. Even the world-famous Grand Canyon "whitewater" is at the mercy of Glen Canyon Dam releases. The Rio Grande has suffered a similar fate, with little more than 10% of its length flowing before the river is impounded.

Reclamation projects in the United States, instead of conserving water, may actually be "desertification projects." Sheridan (1981) recently wrote a treatise on "desertification," published by the US Council on Environmental Quality, which points out some startling commonalities between the results of many of our "reclamation projects" and the characteristics used to determine desertification. These characteristics include salinization of soil and water, diminishing groundwater supplies, high soil erosion, reduction of surface water, and loss of native vegetation. This technology of water salvage has misled us in two important ways. It has not provided an efficient, environmentally safe means of using our water resources and, in fact, has in the long run actually diminished the quality of our environment.

RIVERINE MANAGEMENT AND THE STATUS OF RIPARIAN SYSTEMS

In the same sense that riparian systems concentrate natural resources (e.g., energy, nutrients, plants, and animals), they also serve to concentrate cultural resources. This is true for agricultural, urban, and recreational factors. Unfortunately, in many cases the riparian characteristics which originally attracted humans are in turn destroyed by improper use and management. On the surface these management activities often sound respectable, even desirable or necessary. Many projects have led to the loss of riparian values and eventually even to desertification. Water management projects which have produced conditions resulting in desertification (ibid.) include reclamation, flood control, channelization, and phreatophyte control.

Primary, secondary, and even tertiary tributaries of major southwestern rivers have all been greatly affected by riverine management. The Gila-Salt-Verde River system is an example of a large riverine network which originally flowed into the Colorado. In the early 1900s, a series of storage dams was constructed on the three rivers. By the mid 1900s these rivers had been so greatly altered that less than one-half of the approximately 1600 km. (1000 mi.) of watercourse remained in a relatively free-flowing state. The remainder of the system had been converted to a series of storage reservoirs (above dams) and dry channels (below dams), greatly reducing the natural diversity of these riverine ecosystems. Today the Gila River flows into the Colorado River only during flood stage. In turn, water from the Colorado River is so heavily allocated that the last segment of this great river is dry, rarely debouching across its delta into the Gulf of Lower California.

Flood Control

The two basic means of flood control are a) construction of temporary holding reservoirs, and b) channelization. Each has advantages. The building of dams, often earth-filled and gravel types, has the advantage of requiring less maintenance than channelization. However, an interesting political problem has arisen recently with flood control dams in the Southwest, where water is such a scarce resource. Once floodwaters accumulate in the reservoir behind the dam, the local citizenry resists attempts to drain the reservoir in preparation for the next flood. Painted Rock Dam, on the Gila River near Gila Bend, is an example of this problem becoming a major local political issue. The draining of stored water represents a great resource loss to the people of arid areas, where water-based recreation such as fishing, water-skiing, boating, and swimming is at a premium. Orme Dam, a proposed dam associated with the Central Arizona Project, has been promoted by its backers as both a recreational and a flood control dam. The two uses are basically incompatible, for in order to fulfill their planned functions, reservoirs of flood control dams are best kept empty and those of recreational dams full.

Channelization has been advocated by numerous water salvage interests as a means of reducing vegetation, especially saltcedar, and thus allowing floodwaters to pass through an area with minimal damage. A major problem with the practice of channel clearing or ditching is continual expensive maintenance. Even worse, although it may reduce flooding in the area of channelization, the practice often increases flood damage downstream, since the floodwaters increase in velocity as they move through the channelized portion of the watercourse. Belt (1975) found that navigation works and levees caused significant rises in the stage of floods on the Mississippi and Missouri rivers. According to studies conducted on the Gila River and Tonto Creek, a tributary of the Salt River (Carothers and Johnson 1975), unchannelized areas supported approximately two to three times as many breeding bird species and individuals compared to channelized areas.

Phreatophyte Control

Many of the problems facing riparian systems today exist because the riparian zone has been so poorly understood. This may seem surprising for a widespread (but limited) zone of such great importance to both humans and wildlife. Until the 1970s, there was not a discipline which might be termed "riparian ecology." Up to that time, the term "phreatophyte" was often used, at least partially incorrectly, as a synonym for "riparian." As late as 1964, two well-known scientists, Campbell and Dick-Peddie (1964), published a paper in the prestigious journal Ecology entitled: "Comparison of phreatophyte communities on the Rio Grande in New Mexico." The paper is actually about riparian communities composed of a mixture of phreatophytes and non-phreatophytes.

Phreatophyte control has been one of the most damaging activities carried on by resource management agencies. Vegetation is usually removed from floodplains using chain saws or bulldozers, often in conjunction with stream channelization projects. Our own research findings indicate that removal of woody riparian vegetation drastically reduces wildlife usage of these disturbed areas. Proponents of these programs have suggested that phreatophyte removal may create open spaces, thereby increasing habitat diversity, and thus even improve wildlife values (Arnold 1972). On the contrary, our studies in the Verde Valley showed a linear relationship between the number of mature cottonwood trees per acre and the number of nesting birds (Carothers and Johnson 1971; Johnson 1971; Carothers et al., 1974); thus, the fewer the trees, the fewer the birds.

Phreatophyte clearing (control) has taken a heavy toll on southwestern riparian forests. Babcock (1968) estimated that there were 113,000 ha. (279,000 ac.) of "phreatophyte" (riparian) vegetation in Arizona, while Ffolliott and Thorud (1974) estimated approximately 121,500 ha. (300,000 [280,000-320,000] ac.). This comprises less than 0.4% of the total land area in Arizona. Swift and Barclay (1980)[3] estimated that "...at least 70% of the original area of riparian ecosystems has been cleared..." in the United States. We estimate that less than 5% of the original riparian vegetation remains in the southwestern lowlands.

Historically, the Pacific Southwest Interagency Committee (of federal and state agencies) established a Phreatophyte Subcommittee in 1951. This subcommittee was especially concerned with the spread of saltcedar (Tamarix chinensis) and associated problems (e.g., water usage through evapotranspiration [van Hylckama 1980] and clogging of river channels). The Subcommittee philosophy can be better understood by examining the proceedings of its third symposium, held in 1966, where only one of the eight papers addressed multiple-use values; the other seven being concerned only with water yield. Although early eradication programs were aimed largely at saltcedar, as time progressed more and more native riparian forests were also destroyed. In addition to the loss of shade and reduction in catchable fish (Stone 1970), high-value recreational sites apparently eroded more rapidly after the removal of trees (personal observation). Recent studies have shown that practices,

---

[3]Swift, B.L., and J.S. Barclay. 1980. Status of riparian ecosystems in the United States. Paper presented at 1980 American Water Resources Association National Conference, Minneapolis, Minn. 29 p. Unpublished manuscript. USDI Fish and Wildlife Service, Kearneysville, W. Va.

such as "phreatophyte control" and grazing, which degrade the natural riparian zone also commonly degrade associated aquatic ecosystems, including fisheries (Johnson and Jones 1977; Kennedy 1977; Cope 1979; Graul and Bissell 1978; Johnson and McCormick 1978; Boles and Dick-Peddie 1983). In addition to damaging and destroying riparian and aquatic ecosystems, it has not been shown that there is actually a net gain in water yield from areas where phreatophytes have been removed. Recent studies by USDI Geological Survey (GS) and other investigators on the Pecos River have failed to demonstrate increased river flows after removal of several thousand acres of saltcedar (Tamarix sp.).[4] Thus, phreatophyte control, like channelization, is a dubious method of flood control at best. In addition, these practices reduce plant and animal diversity in the riparian zone.

The year 1968, which appears so often in phreatophyte publications, is more than happenstance. This was the year during which activities peaked in phreatophyte control research, publications, and application. By 1970, only two years later, a drastic change in public attitude resulted in the following:

1) increased conservation activities in regard to rivers, culminating in the Sierra Club's fight with and victory over the Bureau of Reclamation (BR) in 1966, thereby preventing the construction of Marble Canyon and Bridge Canyon Dam on the Colorado River in Grand Canyon (Nash 1978);

2) a series of environmental laws and executive orders affecting riverine management including: a) the Wilderness Act of 1964; b) the Federal Water Project Recreation Act of 1965; c) the Wild and Scenic Rivers Act of 1968; and d) the National Environmental Policy Act (NEPA) of 1969; and

3) a growing body of knowledge regarding the values of riparian (phreatophyte) habitat to wildlife, water quality, and recreational activities. For example, the fact that southwestern riparian habitats support the highest density of noncolonial nesting birds in the United States was first presented by Carothers and Johnson at the annual American Ornithologists Union meeting in Fayetteville, Arkansas in 1969. The information was later published (Carothers et al. 1974).

In 1968, the Twelfth Annual Arizona Watershed Symposium featured a panel entitled "Phreatophyte Control Pro and Con." This was a definite change from past symposia where papers were almost all pro control. The paper on wildlife values was presented by Bristow (1968), now Director of the Arizona Game and Fish Department and an early leader in "wildlife rights for phreatophytes." Subsequent symposia often contained

---

[4]Personal conversation with investigators.

papers which discussed other watershed values in addition to water yield.

By 1970, the word phreatophyte was considered problematic enough that the Pacific Southwest Interagency Committee changed the name of its Phreatophyte Subcommittee to Vegetation Management Subcommittee, as though closing out the chapter on single-use value in watershed management.

RIPARIAN ECOLOGY--A NEW DISCIPLINE

At first glance it might seem contradictory that a science dealing with riparian systems would originate in the arid Southwest. But water resources, like gold, are most appreciated where they are scarcest. Thus, the rapid if belated growth of riparian ecology in the Southwest as one of the newest of the environment sciences is not as irregular as it might seem. It was here that early authors (Austin and Bradley 1971) first used the terms "stream riparian" and "desert riparian" (Lowe 1964) to differentiate between riparian system types. For example, cottonwood/willow is associated with flowing or intermittent streams, while mesquite/desert willow is associated with ephemeral watercourses.

Western riparian ecosystems differ strikingly from their eastern counterparts. The presence of water, scant though it might be, creates conditions that contrast sharply with those of the surrounding arid and semi-arid uplands. Because of this obvious, visible difference, a different terminology has developed from bottomland hardwoods, swamp forests, and similarly named eastern wetland types.

Previously, only a few scattered studies had addressed specific problems in riparian systems. The importance of these riparian areas had been recognized earlier, often in theses and dissertations (e.g., Arnold 1940; Beidleman 1948, 1954). Some of these early studies related to the bottomland hardwoods, or floodplains, of the eastern deciduous hardwood forests. An early outstanding treatment of these floodplain forests was presented in a chapter by Shelford (1963) in his book "The Ecology of North America." Shelford and others, such as Everitt (1968), were especially concerned with successional processes along streams and the associated plant species and communities. Most of these earlier riverine studies were conducted in the East, a few of them in the Great Plains of the Midwest. However, no attempt had been made to amalgamate these studies into a unified discipline.

By the late 1960s, a new focal point was evolving in the Southwest. Here, where water is a primary limiting factor, studies first focussed on phreatophytes and evapotranspiration. Although phreatophytes are not limited to riparian systems, they commonly occur along watercourses and around springs and lakes. A data base, methodology, literature, and terminology for riparian entities other than phreatophytes developed rapidly during the 1970s.

In 1974, Carothers _et al._ published a definitive paper dealing with the importance of southwestern riparian habitat to nesting birds. The conclusions in this paper were based on studies begun in 1969 (Carothers and Johnson 1971), which demonstrated that the highest concentrations of noncolonial nesting birds in North America occurred in cottonwood forests along western perennial streams (Johnson 1971). In addition to the fact that a large majority of the southwestern nesting lowland avifauna is dependent on perennial and intermittent riparian habitat, Raitt and Maze (1968) had earlier pointed out the vital importance of desert watercourses (arroyos) to nesting birds in creosotebush desert. Hensley (1954) had even earlier called attention to the importance of desert washes in Organ Pipe Cactus National Monument to nesting and migrating birds.

Although Carothers and Johnson's papers in the early 1970s provided the first published, scientifically documented proof of the importance of riparian systems to wildlife populations, numerous papers published since these early studies have reinforced those original findings (Johnson and Jones 1977, Johnson and McCormick 1978). While early studies documented the importance of these riparian ecosystems to birds, more recent studies suggest riparian systems are equally important to mammals, other vertebrates, and flowering plants. In addition, since a large percentage of southwestern riparian birds are insectivorous, it can be assumed that insect productivity is also very high in riparian systems (Stevens 1976).

EMERGING TRENDS IN RIPARIAN CONSERVATION

National Efforts

After decades of decimating riparian ecosystems, there are now good indications of a growing awareness of riparian values. Attempts are being made by some management agencies to lessen or prevent further destruction. A series of position papers addressing riparian issues was presented by several federal agencies concerned with riverine resource management in the Southwest at the first national riparian symposium (Johnson and McCormick 1978). These agencies included the US Environmental Protection Agency, USDA Forest Service, FWS, USDI Soil Conservation Service, and USDI Bureau of Land Management. In addition, papers were presented which discussed projects being conducted by other agencies involved in riparian resource management, including the US Army Corps of Engineers, BR, US Council on Environmental Quality, GS, National Recreation Service, Office of Water Research and Technology, Science and Education Administration, and Tennessee Valley Authority. All of these federal agencies were cosponsors of the symposium, along with 10 private organizations including the American

Forestry Association, Conservation Foundation, Environmental Law Institute, National Parks and Conservation Association, Nature Conservancy, National Wetlands Technical Council, Sport Fishing Institute, Oak Ridge Associated Universities, Wildlife Society, and Wildlife Management Institute.

Several projects, which have included local, state, and federal government and private organizations, have addressed the general problem of the demise of Southwestern riparian ecosystems. Foremost among those attempting to lessen riparian damages are several sections of FWS. Projects have included an unsuccessful attempt to develop a western riparian program. The results were an excellent draft by Robert Hays of the Western Energy and Land Use Team. His 63-page draft program was never initiated.

The efforts of the Eastern Energy and Land Use Team (EELUT), Kearneysville, West Virginia to develop a riparian program were also unsuccessful. However, efforts of this group resulted in outstanding synthesis draft manuscripts by Mark M. Brinson, Reubin Plantico, Bryan L. Swift, and John S. Barclay; a workshop by EELUT resulted in an important position paper (Warner 1979). Some of these scientists--e.g., Brinson and Barclay-- are cooperators from academic ranks. EELUT has recently been dismantled. So far these programs have been thwarted due to a lack of money and manpower. This lack is due largely to political maneuvering, since the "riparian movement" is considered by some to be competitive rather than complementary to the FWS National Wetlands program.

State and Local Programs

Several state and local programs have emphasized the protection and proper management of riparian ecosystems. The Arizona Natural Areas Program, a joint program of the Arizona Academy of Science and the Arizona Department of Planning and Development, was begun in 1973. The purpose of this program was to recommend outstanding natural areas in Arizona for protection for their research, educational, recreational, aesthetic, biotic, geologic, archaeologic, and other values (Bergthold 1978, Bergthold and Johnson 1980). A majority of these designated and suggested natural areas include riparian ecosystems.

Today this umbrella program involves coordinators from the Arizona State Parks, and Game and Fish departments, a Natural Areas Advisory Council appointed by the Arizona-Nevada Academy of Science, and a cooperative program between The Nature Conservancy and the state. In addition to encouraging landowners to properly mangage riparian zones, the program advises utility companies and highway and other construction groups on whether planned or existing projects may be detrimental to outstanding natural areas.

Another example of a cooperative program was undertaken in the Lower Gila River Valley, New Mexico by six state and federal agencies (Hubbard

1977). This project also included investigations by numerous scientists from research and educational institutions. The project was instrumental in establishing the outstanding biological importance of the Lower Gila River Valley. Interest generated by the information from the investigations led to the purchase of riparian lands by The Nature Conservancy and continuing efforts to establish a wildlife preserve.

A final example consists of a study along the San Pedro River, a tributary of the Gila River. The Office of Arid Land Studies, University of Arizona, financed by The Nature Conservancy, examined the feasibility of purchasing riparian areas along the San Pedro River. Negotiations to acquire and protect some of the outstanding riparian areas along the San Pedro River are continuing.

Numerous other activities have been conducted by groups concerned with riparian wetlands. A few which bear mentioning include: a FWS project along the Verde River where Orme Dam may be built for the Central Arizona Project (McNatt et al. 1980); a program for fencing riparian vegetation to exclude grazing along the Salt and Verde rivers (USDA Forest Service 1979); attempts to organize programs designed to prevent urban, suburban, and rural developments in floodplains and riparian zones (Kusler 1979; Clark 1980). Growing concern is being expressed by other agencies. The US Council on Environmental Quality (1978) stated in its ninth annual report "No ecosystem is more essential to the survival of the nation's fish and wildlife." The National Park Service, noted for its protection of outstanding natural areas, has conducted extensive research on riparian lands under its jurisdiction (Carothers et al. 1976; Schmidly and Ditton 1978; Johnson 1981; Carothers and Johnson 1983). Recent synopses regarding values and problems in riparian ecosystems have been prepared by the USDA Forest Service (Waldrip and Malespin 1979; Crumpacker et al.;[5] Johnson and Carothers 1982), the FWS (Swift and Barclay[3]), and even private organizations (American Fisheries Society 1980).

Much remains to be done. Numerous instances of unnecessary riparian destruction continue. Often they are the result of activities--or lack of preventative action--by the very agencies which are entrusted with the management of these important systems. Only by an increase in active, scientifically based management will we succeed in leaving even a viable remnant of Southwestern riparian ecosystems for posterity.

---

[5]Crumpacker, D.W., R. Roy Johnson, James O. Klemmedson, Paul A. Rechard, Robert G. Woodmansee. Effects of livestock grazing on resource values of western riparian ecosystems. 57 p. Unpublished manuscript.

ACKNOWLEDGMENTS

Thanks are due Lupe P. Hendrickson for editing and typing the manuscript. Bryan T. Brown, Kenneth J. Kingsley, and James M. Simpson aided in gathering information.

LITERATURE CITED

American Fisheries Society, Western Division. 1980. Management and protection of western riparian stream ecosystems. 24 p.

Arnold, J.F. 1972. Ecology and management of riparian vegetation (abstract only). J. Ariz. Acad. Sci. (Proc. Suppl. 16th Ann. Meeting) 7:20.

Arnold, L.W. 1940. An ecological study of the vertebrate animals of the mesquite forest. M.S. Thesis, University of Arizona, Tucson. 79 p.

Austin, G.T., and W.G. Bradley. 1971. The avifauna of Clark County, Nevada. J. Ariz. Acad. Sci. 6(4):238-303.

Babcock, H.M. 1968. The phreatophyte problem in Arizona. p. 34-36. In: Twelfth annual Arizona watershed symposium. 49 p. Arizona State Lands Department, Phoenix.

Beidleman, R.G. 1948. The vertebrate ecology of a Colorado Plains cottonwood river bottom. M.S. Thesis, University of Colorado, Boulder. 351 p.

Beidleman, R.G. 1954. The cottonwood riverbottom as a vertebrate habitat. Ph.D. Thesis, University of Colorado, Boulder. 358 p.

Belt, C.B., Jr. 1975. The 1973 flood and man's constriction of the Mississippi River. Science 189:681-684.

Bergthold, P.M. 1978. Arizona State Park's Natural Area Program. p. 243-247. In: R.R. Johnson and J.F. McCormick (tech. coord.). Strategies for the protection and management of floodplain wetlands and other riparian ecosystems: Proceedings of the symposium. [Callaway Gardens, Georgia, December 11-13, 1978]. USDA Forest Service GTR-WO-12, Washington, D.C. 410 p.

Bergthold, P.M., and R.R. Johnson. 1980. The relationship of natural areas on National Park lands to other natural areas. Proc. 2nd Conf. Sci. Res. in the Natl. Parks: Ecosystem Studies. Natl. Park Serv., Washington, D.C. 4:323-329.

Boles, P.H., and W.A. Dick-Peddie. 1983. Woody riparian vegetation patterns on a segment of the Mimbres River in southwestern New Mexico. SW. Nat. 28(1):81-87.

Bristow, B. 1968. Statement by Arizona Game and Fish Department of phreatophyte clearing project. p. 41-44. In: Twelfth annual Arizona watershed symposium. 49 p. Arizona State Lands Department, Phoenix.

Campbell, C.J., and W.A. Dick-Peddie. 1964. Comparison of phreatophyte communities on the Rio Grande in New Mexico. Ecology 45:492-502.

Carothers, S.W., and R.R. Johnson. 1971. A summary of the Verde Valley breeding bird survey. Project FW-16-10, Land and Water Project Investigations. 20 p. Arizona Game and Fish Department, Phoenix, Ariz.

Carothers, S.W., and R.R. Johnson. 1975. The effects of stream channel modification on birds in the southwestern United States. p. 60-76. In: R.V. Corning et al. (ed.). Stream Channel Modification: Proceedings of the symposium. [Harrisonburg, Virginia, August 15-17, 1975.] 172 p. Rt. 1, Box 312, Grottoes, Va.

Carothers, S.W., and R.R. Johnson. 1983. Status of the Colorado ecosystem in Grand Canyon National Park and Glen Canyon National Recreation Area. p. 139-160. In: V.D. Adams, and V.A. Lamarra (ed.). Aquatic resources management of the Colorado River ecosystem: Proceedings of the symposium. [Las Vegas, Nevada, November 6-18, 1981.] 697 p. Ann Arbor Science, Ann Arbor, Mich.

Carothers, S.W., R.R. Johnson, and S.W. Aitchison. 1974. Population structure and social organization of southwestern riparian birds. Amer. Zool. 14:97-108.

Carothers, S.W., Stewart W. Aitchison, Marin M. Karpiscak, George A. Ruffner, N. Joseph Sharber, Philip L. Shoemaker, Lawrence E. Stevens, Michael E. Theroux, and Dennis S. Tomko. 1976. An ecological survey of the riparian zone of the Colorado River between Lees Ferry and the Grand Wash Cliffs, Arizona. Colorado River Technical Report No. 10, Grand Canyon National Park, Ariz. 251 p.

Clark, J. (project director). 1980. Coastal environmental management. Guidelines for conservation of resources and protection against storm hazards. 161 p. The Conservation Foundation, Washington, D.C.

Cope, O.B. (ed.). 1979. Grazing and riparian/ stream ecosystems: proceedings of the forum. 94 p. Trout Unlimited Inc., Denver, Colo.

Dobyns, H.F. 1981. From fire to flood: Historic human destruction of Sonoran Desert riverine oases. 222 p. Ballena Press, Socorro, N.M.

Dracup, J.A. 1977. Impact on the Colorado River basin and southwest water supply. p. 121-132. In: J. Wallis (ed.). Climate, climatic change, and water supply. National Academy of Science, Washington, D.C.

Everitt, B.L. 1968. Use of the cottonwood in an investigation of the recent history of a flood plain. Amer. J. Sci. 266:417-439.

Ffolliott, P.F., and D.B. Thorud. 1974. Vegetation management for increased water yield in Arizona. Agricultural Experiment Station Bulletin 215. University of Arizona, Tucson. 38 p.

Graul, W.D., and S.J. Bissell (tech. coord.). 1978. Lowland river and stream habitat in Colorado: A symposium. [Greeley, Colorado, October 4-5, 1978.] 195 p. Colorado Chapter of the Wildlife Society and Colorado Audubon Council.

Hensley, M.M. 1954. Ecological relations of the breeding bird population of the desert biome in Arizona. Ecol. Monog. 24(2):185-207.

Hubbard, J.P. 1977. A biological inventory of the Lower Gila River Valley, New Mexico. 56 p. New Mexico Department of Game and Fish, Santa Fe.

Jassby, A.D. 1980. The environmental effects of hydroelectric power development. p. 32-43. In: Study of nuclear and alternative energy systems. Supporting paper 8: Energy and the fate of ecosystems. Rpt. Ecosystems Impact Res. Group. Risk and Impact Panel, Comm. Nuclear and Alt. Energy Sys. Natl. Res. Council, Natl. Acad. Press. Wash., D.C.

Johnson, R.R. 1971. Tree removal along southwestern rivers and effects on associated organisms. Amer. Phil. Soc. Yearbook 1970: 321-322.

Johnson, R.R. 1978. The lower Colorado River: a western system. p. 41-55. In: R.R. Johnson and J.F. McCormick (tech. coord.). Strategies for the protection and management of floodplain wetlands and other riparian ecosystems: proceedings of the symposium. [Callaway Gardens, Georgia, December 11-13, 1978]. USDA Forest Service GTR-WO-12. Washington, D.C. 410 p.

Johnson, R.R. 1981. Riparian resources and endangered ecosystems. Pac. Park Sci. 1(3): 1-2.

Johnson, R.R., and S.W. Carothers. 1982. Southwestern riparian habitats and recreation: interrelationships and impacts in the Southwest and Rocky Mountain Region. Eisenhower Consortium Bull. 12, USDA Forest Service Rocky Mountain Forest and Range Experiment Station, Fort Collins, Colo. 31 p.

Johnson, R.R., and D.A. Jones (tech. coord.). 1977. Importance, preservation, and management of riparian habitat: a symposium. [July 9, 1977, Tucson, Arizona.] USDA Forest Service GTR-RM-43. Rocky Mountain Forest and Range Experiment Station, Fort Collins, Colo. 217 p.

Johnson, R.R., and J.F. McCormick (tech. coord.). 1978. Strategies for the protection and management of floodplain wetlands and other riparian ecosystems: proceedings of the symposium. [Callaway Gardens, Georgia, December 11-13, 1978]. USDA Forest Service GTR-WO-12. Washington, D.C. 410 p.

Johnson, R.R., L.T. Haight, and J.M. Simpson. 1977. Endangered species vs. endangered habitats: a concept. p. 68-79. In: Johnson, R.R., and D.A. Jones (tech. coord.). 1977. Importance, preservation, and management of riparian habitat: a symposium. [July 9, 1977, Tucson, Arizona.] USDA Forest Service GTR-RM-43, Rocky Mountain Forest and Range Experiment Station, Fort Collins, Colo. 217 p.

Kennedy, C.K. 1977. Wildlife conflicts in riparian management: water. p. 52-85. In: Johnson, R.R., and D.A. Jones (tech. coord.). 1977. Importance, preservation, and management of riparian habitat: a symposium. [July 9, 1977, Tucson, Arizona.] USDA Forest Service GTR-RM-43. Rocky Mountain Forest and Range Experiment Station, Fort Collins, Colo. 217 p.

Kusler, J.A. 1979. Consultants' report. Summary: emerging issues in wetland/floodplain management. Report of a technical seminar, US Water Resources Council, Washington, D.C. 41 p.

Lowe, C.H. (ed.). 1964. The vertebrates of Arizona. 270 p. University of Arizona Press, Tucson.

McCormick, J.F. 1978. A summary of the National Riparian Symposium: a proposal for a national riparian program. p. 362-363. In: R.R. Johnson and J.F. McCormick (tech. coord.). Strategies for the protection and management of floodplain wetlands and other riparian ecosystems: proceedings of the symposium. [Callaway Gardens, Georgia, December 11-13, 1978]. USDA Forest Service GTR-WO-12. Washington, D.C. 410 p.

McNatt, R., R.J. Hallock, and A.W. Anderson. 1980. Riparian habitat and instream flow studies, lower Verde River: Fort McDowell Reservation, Arizona. Riparian Habitat Anal. Grp, USDI Fish and Wildlife Service, Albuquerque, N.M. 52 p.

Meehan, W.R., F.J. Swanson, and J.R. Sedell. 1977. Influences of riparian vegetation on aquatic ecosystems with particular reference to salmonid fishes and their food supply. p. 137-145. In: R.R. Johnson and D.A. Jones (tech. coord.). Importance, preservation, and management of riparian habitat: proceedings of the symposium. [July 9, 1977, Tucson, Arizona.] USDA Forest Service GTR-RM-43. 217 p. Rocky Mountain Forest and Range Experiment Station, Fort Collins, Colo.

Nash, R. 1978. Who loves a swamp? p. 149-156. In: R.R. Johnson and J.F. McCormick (tech. coord.). Strategies for the protection and management of floodplain wetlands and other riparian ecosystems: proceedings of the symposium. [Callaway Gardens, Georgia, December 11-13, 1978.] USDA Forest Service GTR-WO-12, Washington, D.C. 410 p.

Odum, E.P. 1978. Opening address: ecological importance of the riparian zone. p. 204. In: R.R. Johnson and J.F. McCormick (tech. coord.). Strategies for the protection and management of floodplain wetlands and other riparian ecosystems: proceedings of the symposium. [Callaway Gardens, Georgia, December 11-13, 1978]. USDA Forest Service GTR-WO-12. Washington, D.C. 410 p.

Raitt, R.J., and R.L. Maze. 1968. Densities and species composition of breeding birds of a creosotebush community in southern New Mexico. Condor 70:193-205.

Schmidly, D.J., and R.B. Ditton. 1978. Relating human activities and biological resources in riparian habitats of western Texas. p. 107-116. In: R.R. Johnson and J.F. McCormick (tech. coord.). Strategies for the protection and management of floodplain wetlands and other riparian ecosystems: proceedings of the symposium. [Callaway Gardens, Georgia, December 11-13, 1978]. USDA Forest Service GTR-WO-12. Washington, D.C. 410 p.

Shelford, V.E. 1963. The ecology of North America. 610 p. University of Illinois Press, Urbana.

Sheridan, D. 1981. Desertificaion of the United states. 142 p. US Council on Environmental Quality, Washington, D.C.

Smith, E.L. 1974. Established natural areas for Arizona. 300 p. Arizona Academy of Science and Arizona Office of Economic Planning and Development, Phoenix.

Stevens, L.E. 1976. Insect production of native and introduced dominant plant species. p. 129-135. In: S.W. Carothers, S.W. Aitchison, M.M. Karpiscak, G.A. Ruffner, N.J. Sharber, P.L. Shoemaker, L.E. Stevens, M.E. Theroux, and D.S. Tomko. 1976. An ecological survey of the riparian zone of the Colorado River between Lees Ferry and the Grand Wash Cliffs, Arizona. Colorado River Technical Report No. 10. 251 p. Grand Canyon National Park, Ariz.

Stone, J.L. 1970. Cottonwood clearance program on the Verde River and its tributaries. Completion report, FW16-10, Fisheries Eval. of Salt River Proj. 6 p. Arizona Game and Fish Department, Phoenix.

U.S. Council on Environmental Quality. 1978. Environmental Quality. Ninth Annual Report. 599 p. U.S. Council on Environmental Quality, Washington, D.C.

USDA Forest Service. 1979. Action program for resolution of livestock-riparian conflicts on the Salt River and Verde River. 129 p. Region Three, Arizona, Tonto, Prescott and Coconino National Forest. Albuquerque, N.M.

van Hylckama, T.E.A. 1971. Water resources. p. 135-155. Sinauer Associates, Stanford, Conn.

van Hylckama, T.E.A. 1980. Weather and evapotranspiration studies in a saltcedar thicket, Arizona. USDI Geological Survey Paper 491-F. 78 p. US Government Printing Office, Washington, D.C.

Waldrip, G., and M. Malespin. 1979. The importance of riparian habitats and their management of wildlife and fisheries: a current resumé of knowledge. 28 p. USDA Forest Service, Intermountain Region.

Warner, R.E. 1979. Proceedings of a workshop on fish and wildlife resource needs in riparian ecosystems. Natl. Water Res. Anal. Grp. Eastern Energy and Land Use Team. USDI Fish and Wildlife Service. 53 p.

REGIONAL RIPARIAN RESEARCH AND A MULTI-UNIVERSITY
APPROACH TO THE SPECIAL PROBLEM OF LIVESTOCK
GRAZING IN THE ROCKY MOUNTAINS AND GREAT PLAINS[1]

David W. Crumpacker[2]

Abstract.--A selected survey of Rocky Mountain/Great
Plains riparian research with emphasis on livestock grazing
impacts and management is presented. A multiuniversity plan
for studying interactions between livestock grazing and
riparian resources in the region is presented. The power of
an integrated, regionwide approach is compared with that of
one involving the conduct of numerous independent,
site-specific studies. An analogy is made to California,
considering the State as a region. The need for support of
long-term riparian research by traditional academic funding
sources is also stressed.

INTRODUCTION

This report is meant to serve three purposes: 1) provide a Rocky Mountain and Great
Plains regional perspective on riparian research
to complement similar reports at this conference
on the American Southwest and Intermountain
Region; 2) discuss relationships between livestock grazing and riparian resources; and 3) describe a regional, multi-university approach to
riparian research.

Status and Value of Western
U.S. Riparian Ecosystems

Recent estimates indicate that 70-90% of the
natural riparian ecosystems in the United States
have been lost to human activities (US Council on
Environmental Quality 1978; Warner 1979a; Swift

and Barclay[3]). Losses have been estimated at
98.5% in the Sacramento Valley of California
(Smith 1980) and 95% or more in Arizona (Warner
1979b). In the Rocky Mountain/Great Plains
region Johnson and Carothers (1981) believe that
90-95% of the cottonwood/willow riparian ecosystems of the plains and lower foothills have
been lost. Beidleman (1978) has stated that this
is unquestionably the most productive and highly
diversified ecosystem type in the Rocky Mountains
and Great Plains. Perhaps 80% of the publicly
and privately owned riparian areas that still
exist in the United States are in an unsatisfactory condition or are dominated by human
activities (Almand and Krohn 1978; Warner 1979b).

Western U.S. riparian ecosystems contain
disproportionately great concentrations of
wildlife species and populations compared to
adjacent uplands. This has been well documented
in the American Southwest (Davis 1977; Johnson
1971; Johnson and Carothers 1975; Johnson, Haight
and Simpson 1977; Stevens et al. 1977) and
the Pacific Northwest (see discussion and references cited in Thomas, Maser and Rodiek 1979).
The situation is similar in the Rocky Mountains

[1]Paper presented at the California
Riparian Systems Conference. [University of
California, Davis, September 17-19, 1981].
[2]David W. Crumpacker is Professor of
Environmental, Population and Organismic Biology,
University of Colorado, Boulder, Colo. He is
also President-Elect of the Eisenhower Consortium
for Western Environmental Forestry Research which
has its main office at 240 W. Prospect St., Fort
Collins, Colo.

[3]Swift, B.L. and J.S. Barclay. 1980.
Status of riparian ecosystems in the United
States. Unpublished manuscript. 29 p. USDI Fish
and Wildlife Service, Kearneysville, W. Va.
[Prepared for presentation at the 1980 American
Water Resources Association National Conference,
Minneapolis, Minn.] Cited in Johnson, R. Roy and
Steven W. Carothers. 1981. Southwestern
riparian habitats and recreation: interrelation-
ships and impacts in the Rocky Mountain Region.
Eisenhower Consortium Bulletin. [In press].
USDA Forest Service, Rocky Mountain Forest and
Range Experiment Station, Fort Collins, Colo.

and Great Plains. Beidleman (1978) estimated very conservatively that the cottonwood/willow ecosystem type contains at least 40% of the vertebrate species found in that region. The South Platte River Valley of northeastern Colorado in Weld and Morgan Counties has 151 vertebrate species of which 147 (97%) make at least seasonal use of the riparian and associated aquatic zones (Fitzgerald 1978). The mixed cottonwood/willow community type has the most species of birds and mammals, whereas the open-park, open-cottonwood, and aquatic types have the most reptilian and amphibian species (Fitzgerald 1978). The native trees and shrubs in the moist hardwood draws of northern plains grasslands comprise less than 1% of the regional ecosystems, but are believed to provide valuable, and possibly critical, wildlife habitat (Boldt, Uresk, and Severson 1978).

LIVESTOCK GRAZING AND RIPARIAN RESOURCES

Impacts

Livestock grazing is the most pervasive land use in the western United States. Eighty-three percent of the 11 conterminous western states is in forest and range and much of this is grazed by livestock. Nationwide, it has been estimated that 70% of the forests and rangelands are grazed (Platts 1979). Cattle derive great value from western riparian ecosystems. They strongly prefer them for a number of reasons (Ames 1977), the most important of which is access to water. This preference increases as summer progresses and the adjacent upland vegetation becomes depleted or desiccated (Dahlem 1979; Martin 1979).

The major direct impacts of livestock grazing are on vegetation and soils. This can cause severe indirect effects on wildlife. Grazing for only a few days or weeks has sometimes been observed to cause serious damage to woody regeneration (Ames 1977; Duff 1979). Extensive grazing can lead to virtually no reproduction of trees and a decadent riparian forest. If too much protective ground cover is removed, the soil becomes compacted, infiltration of precipitation decreases, and erosion of topsoil into the aquatic zone occurs (Moore et al. 1979; Thomas, Maser and Rodiek 1979; Platts 1979). Major detrimental effects to trout habitats and populations can then occur (Behnke and Raleigh 1978). Excessive use of the riparian zone by livestock also lowers its commercial grazing value. Soil compaction by trampling tends to favor shallow-rooted, herbaceous perennials or tap-rooted perennial shrubs in place of fibrous-rooted plants which are usually more palatable, nutritious and dependable on a year-round basis (Platts 1979).

Recovery under Livestock Exclosure or Withdrawal

Numerous observations on recovery of riparian and aquatic ecosystems following complete

exclusion of livestock have been reported in recent years. Many of the observations involved unreplicated comparisons and none included statistical analyses of the results. Nevertheless, the combined weight of this evidence suggests that there is considerable resilience in western U.S. riparian and aquatic systems. Platts (1979) and Keller, Anderson and Tappel (1979) reviewed a number of these studies that focused on streams and fisheries. Moderate to large percentage improvements were observed in riparian vegetation, streambank stability, channel morphology, substrate, water temperature, and trout number and biomass. A period of up to five years may be needed for reasonable recovery of an aquatic system, following removal of livestock (Behnke and Raleigh 1978; Moore et al. 1979; Skovlin[4]).

Some information is also available on the response of riparian trees and shrubs following livestock exclosure. Glinski (1977) observed large increases in cottonwood regeneration in an area of relatively abundant water and long growing season in southeastern Arizona, following eight years of exclosure. Davis (1977) has observed that young cottonwood, alder, and sycamore can grow 3-4.6 m. (10-15 ft.) in a few years in the American Southwest if protected from grazing. Crouch (1978) noted a doubling of woody understory in a cottonwood/willow community along the South Platte River in northeast Colorado, after seven years of exclosure. No further increases were observed during 18 additional years. Although the number of cottonwoods decreased in both the grazed and ungrazed areas that Crouch studied, the decline was 38% less for the ungrazed area. (The decline in the ungrazed area was attributed to other factors, one of the most important being managed stream flows which are detrimental to cottonwood germination and establishment.) A literature survey by Skovlin[4] led him to suggest that five to eight years may be required for acceptable recovery of riparian shrubs in most areas. A high-altitude willow community at 2650 m. in the North Park region of north central Colorado (46 frost-free days) was observed by Knopf and Cannon (1981) to recover at a slow rate following removal from chronic, heavy grazing pressure. They noted that their results lend quantitative support to Myers' estimate (1981) that: a) 10 to 12 years may be insufficient time for a southwestern Montana willow community to recover from prolonged, excessive grazing; and b) it is more difficult to improve a damaged riparian ecosystem by removing it from grazing than it is to maintain a good one while grazing it. These various observations suggest that riparian ecosystems do not undergo

---

[4]Skovlin. Impacts of grazing on wetlands and riparian habitat—the state of our knowledge. Unpublished draft manuscript, presented at National Academy of Sciences/National Research Council workshop: Impacts of grazing intensity and specialized grazing systems on use and value of rangelands. [March 16-17, 1981, El Paso, Tex.].

general recovery from overgrazing as rapidly as their aquatic counterparts, particularly in regions with short growing seasons.

Grazing Management Options

A number of grazing management options have been suggested for riparian/aquatic systems by wildlife and fishery researchers and managers (e.g. Behnke and Raleigh 1978; Benson 1979; Moore et al. 1979; Skovlin;[4] Storch 1979). These include alternatives such as the following: complete exclosure from grazing; management as a separate pasture in a grazing system; tailoring the management to specific flora, conditions, etc.; location of watering, salt, and supplement sites away from the riparian zone; intensive herding; reduction of stocking rates; seasonal deferments and/or yearly rests; specially designed grazing systems with six or more pastures instead of the standard two to five; changing the age and class of livestock; initial exclosures of five or more years to allow recovery of degraded riparian vegetation. There have been few suggestions from range scientists concerning riparian management under rangeland conditions. Their suggestions are also needed in order to achieve satisfactory solutions.

There has been considerable interest recently concerning the effectiveness of rest-rotation grazing systems in permitting adequate recovery and maintenance of riparian and aquatic ecosystems. There are many possible types of these grazing systems and they may include seasonal deferments in addition to the year-long rests for which they are named. Rest-rotation grazing was originally developed for upland ranges in ponderosa pine ecosystems (Stoddart et al. 1975) and is now commonly recommended by the Bureau of Land Management (BLM) in other grazing environments (Lea 1979).

Since rest-rotation systems were designed primarily for the maintenance of herbaceous range plants rather than woody riparian vegetation (Thomas, Maser and Rodiek 1979), it is certainly desirable to question their value for use in riparian recovery and maintenance. Wildlife and fishery biologists have been concerned that too much dependence on rest-rotatation systems will result in continued deterioration of riparian and aquatic systems (Armour 1979; Behnke and Raleigh 1978; Severson and Boldt 1978; Platts 1979). Although general observations and experience suggest this may be so, strong supporting evidence has not yet been produced. There is an obvious need for experimentally reliable tests of the effects of rest- and deferred-rotation grazing systems on riparian and aquatic ecosystems (Armour 1979; Platts 1979; Raleigh 1979a,b).

Furthermore, most previous observations have compared the effects of heavy, uncontrolled or unmanaged grazing to no grazing, whereas the more interesting comparisons involving light or moderate grazing have not been reported (Lea 1979; Skovlin[4]).

Several new investigations involving livestock-riparian interactions have been briefly described by Moore et al. (1979). Skovlin and Meehan are conducting a five-year study in the Blue Mountains of northeast Oregon. They are evaluating the effects of livestock grazing management strategies and effects of big game on soil, water quality and quantity, fish populations, benthic fauna, and productivity and utilization of herbaceous and woody vegetation.

According to Duff (as reported by Moore et al. 1979), effects of a three-pasture, rest-rotation system in southwest Utah will be monitored by exclosures in conjunction with BLM's Hot Desert Environmental Statement. Data will be obtained on recovery of vegetation and on fisheries and water quality in selected stream reaches.

According to Platts (as reported by Moore et al. ibid.) and Janes[5], a large 10-year study involving private (Saval Ranch) and Federal (BLM and USDA Forest Service (FS)) lands in Nevada is now underway. One aspect of this "Saval Ranch Study" will be to evaluate upland, riparian and aquatic responses to a new experimental grazing system which involves the use of a number of pasture units. Exclosures will also be maintained as controls. The Nevada Fish and Game Department will assist by conducting wildlife surveys and the USDA Science and Education Administration will perform hydrologic studies and inventories of soils and vegetation.

Various new Federal riparian research initiatives are either planned or underway in the Rocky Mountain/Great Plains region. Some of these will be described in order to indicate the current direction of riparian research.

USDI Fish and Wildlife Service

The Denver Wildlife Research Center of the USDI Fish and Wildlife Service (FWS) has recently initiated several studies of riparian ecosystems (Knopf[6]). Previous wildlife reports have indicated that higher elevation riparian systems have fewer species (Burkhard 1978; Schrupp 1978), as well as fewer stenotopic species (Burkhard 1978; Salt 1957), than lower riparian systems in the Rocky Mountains/Great Plains region. However, these observations have not been quantified within the different vegetation-types occurring along an altitudinal cline. Therefore, one of the projects will determine the significance of riparian vegetation to avian and mammalian communities on an altitudinal gradient. Faunal densities and vegetative parameters will be estimated in both

---

[5]Janes, Eric A. 1981. Personal communication. USDI Bureau of Land Management, Denver Service Center, Denver, Colo.
[6]Knopf, Fritz L. Personal communication. USDI Fish and Wildlife Service, Denver Wildlife Research Center, Fort Collins, Colo.

riparian and adjacent upland communities in north central and northeast Colorado as follows: willow vs. Engelmann spruce/subalpine fir at 2900 m.; willow and two stands of narrowleaf cottonwood/willow vs. ponderosa pine at 2100-2560 m.; open narrowleaf cottonwood/willow vs. mountain mahogany shrub at 2000-2200 m.; willow and plains cottonwood/willow vs. sagebrush steppe at 2650 and 1200 m. respectively; willow vs. aspen at 2600 m. Thus the significance of riparian vegetation to birds and mammals will be determined at each location as well as any changes in significance with altitude. Each of the study sites has been protected from livestock grazing for at least three years.

Research is in progress at the 2650 m. willow site mentioned above (Arapahoe National Wildlife Refuge) to monitor the effects of a three-year, rest-rotation grazing system on vegetation and avifauna.

The FWS in conjunction with the Colorado Division of Wildlife (Knopf[6]) also plans to assess vegetative and vertebrate responses to cattle grazing in a lowland, broadleaf cottonwood/willow community on the northeast plains of Colorado. The study site has been protected from livestock grazing for 30 years. This interesting experiment is essentially the reverse of those in which responses are observed in overgrazed riparian zones following removal of livestock. The effects of light to moderate grazing on a long-ungrazed riparian ecosystem will be determined. Interest will also be focused on identifying the most useful indicator species for the effects of grazing practices.

USDA Forest Service

The Rocky Mountain Forest and Range Experiment Station of the FS has a continuing interest in riparian studies in two parts of its region of responsibility. A southwestern section of the Station, with headquarters at Tempe, Arizona, is developing a comprehensive program that includes, or will include, studies on classification of plant communities, methods of artificial regeneration, effects of livestock on regeneration and maintenance of riparian systems, livestock behavior, and mammalian associations (Martin 1979; Smith[7]). A northern plains section of the Station, with headquarters at Rapid City, South Dakota, is conducting research on multiple-use management of woody riparian draws (e.g., see Boldt, Uresk and Severson 1978).

The Station has proposed in its 1980 Forest and Rangeland Renewable Resources Planning Act (RPA) program plan to expand both the southwestern and northern plains studies and to initiate new projects over the next 10 years as follows (Smith[7]; location of project headquarters in parentheses): management of riparian and asso-

ciated aquatic systems within rangeland environments (Laramie, Wyoming); marketing and silviculture of bottomland hardwoods, primarily cottonwoods (Lincoln, Nebraska); integrated management of riparian systems in forest environments (Fort Collins, Colorado). This last project will complement the existing effort at Tempe which deals with integrated management of riparian systems in rangeland environments. "Integrated management" refers in this context to managing riparian ecosystems without fencing the riparian zone or including it in a separate pasture of a grazing system.

USDI Bureau of Land Management

A very interesting, worthwhile effort is being made by the Rock Springs, Wyoming District of the BLM to provide information on recovery of overgrazed riparian/aquatic ecosystems by constructing and monitoring approximately 60 exclosures in southwest Wyoming (Smith[8]). Some of the exclosures will be maintained as controls while others will be used as experimental grazing units. The program was begun in 1976. It includes 20 exclosures, each 8 ha. (20 ac.) in size, and nine special grazing management units that will be located in the Big Sandy drainage. Sites will range from the lower sagebrush steppe area in the cold desert, which presently contains only sparse remnants of riparian vegetation, to willow communities in the foothills and aspen/willow communities in montane regions.

The Big Sandy system of exclosures is about 80% completed. Fenced plots already installed in the foothills zone of the Bear River drainage include five riparian/aquatic exclosures and eight riparian/aquatic special pasture units. Other exclosures have been set up in the Green River basin in the vicinity of Big Piney, Wyoming. Fenced plots have been constructd in the region south of Rock Springs, Wyoming to determine the feasibility of using beaver to restore the riparian water in a gulley-cut, eroded situation.

The immediate purpose of BLM's efforts in the Rock Springs District is to provide demonstrations of riparian/aquatic recovery. However, the potential clearly exists to utilize these exclosure systems for cooperative scientific investigations on a diverse group of riparian ecosystems and on the relation of riparian/aquatic resources to livestock grazing.

A PROPOSED MULTI-UNIVERSITY APPROACH

The tremendous concentration of natural diversity in western riparian ecosystems, which are rapidly shrinking in both quantity and quality, calls for an extensive program of research and development directed towards im-

---

[7]Smith, Dixie R. Personal communication. USDA Forest Service, Rocky Mountain Forest and Range Experiment Station, Fort Collins, Colo.

[8]Smith, Bruce H. Personal communication. USDI Bureau of Land Management, Rock Springs District, Rock Springs, Wyo.

proved multiple use management. Since livestock grazing is the most pervasive land use in much of the western U.S. and is acknowledged to have major impacts on riparian ecosystems, research on the relationship of livestock grazing management to riparian resources appears to have the greatest potential for maintaining and enhancing these resources. This situation led the Eisenhower Consortium for Western Environmental Forestry Research to develop a regional research plan for the states of Wyoming, Colorado, New Mexico, and Arizona (Crumpacker et al. 1981[9]).

The Eisenhower Consortium Plan

Study Design

The Eisenhower Consortium plan involves a long-term study to provide comparative information on the response of previously overgrazed riparian ecosystems to three kinds of experimental treatments:

1. a new rotation grazing system that includes one or more seasonal deferments and/or a year-long rest (e.g., a 3-pasture rotation with early- and late-season deferments or a 4-pasture rotation that also includes a year-long rest);
2. no grazing (achieved by fenced exclosures);
3. no grazing for several years (using exclosures) followed by the rotation grazing system used for (1), above.

The grazing systems described in treatment 1 are examples of systems which the BLM is actually recommending in their range improvement programs with the [10] primary intention of improving upland ranges. The treatments would be implemented by commercial operators on public grazing lands managed by one or more Federal or state agencies. A main purpose of the study would be to monitor the riparian responses in the setting of a commercial cattle operation.

The investigation should last 9-12 years, and preferably longer, in view of the evidence cited earlier on recovery of woody vegetation following exclosure, the expectation of even longer recovery periods associated with treatment 1, and the need to sample a representative set of climatic conditions. The riparian zone would not be treated separately, e.g., by separate fencing or designation as a separate pasture in the grazing system. Instead, each experimental plot

---

[9]Crumpacker, David W., R. Roy Johnson, James O. Klemmedson, Paul A. Rechard, Thomas A. Wesche, and Robert G. Woodmansee. 1981. Effects of livestock grazing on resource values of western riparian ecosystems. Research plan prepared for the Eisenhower Consortium for Western Environmental Forestry Research, 240 W. Prospect, Fort Collins, Colo.

[10]e.g., see USDI, Bureau of Land Management, Draft Environmental Impact Statement of Grazing Management in the Missouri Breaks of Montana.

would include portions of the riparian zone as well as the adjacent upland and aquatic zones. All plots would be included within one pasture of the grazing system.

A four-pasture, four-year, rest-rotation system of the following type appears preferable for experimental study in the Eisenhower Consortium region because it includes several components which are basic to many grazing systems:

1. early-season deferment (graze after flowering of upland range grasses)--protects young riparian vegetation during germination, sprouting, and early growth, and during maximum susceptibility of soils and stream banks to compaction and erosion;
2. early- and mid-season deferment (graze after seed ripening of upland range grasses)--extends the protection of 1, above, further into the riparian growing season;
3. mid- and late-season deferment (graze in spring until flowering of upland range grasses)--protects young riparian vegetation during warmest part of the year when less succulent upland vegetation is available and cattle tend to congregate more often in the riparian zone;
4. no grazing throughout the year.

The actual chronological sequence for a particular pasture might be 1, 3, 2, 4. A three-pasture, three-year, deferred-rotation could be obtained by the sequence 1, 3, 2, but would presumably be more likely to require a longer time for riparian improvement and be less likely to permit riparian recovery.

Half of the experimental plots would be closed by fencing to provide the comparison of riparian, aquatic, and upland responses to grazing vs. no grazing (treatment 1 vs. 2). Additional exclosed plots could be maintained until a decision was made to open them to grazing (treatment 3), after which a second comparison would be available (treatment 3 vs. 2). A more efficient means of obtaining treatment 3 might be to begin the experiment with double-sized closed plots (recording data from one-half of each closed plot) and then to open one-half of each such plot to grazing in order to create treatment 3.

Data Collection and Analysis

Data on basic soil, vegetative and aquatic parameters would be collected from the riparian, upland, and aquatic zones in each plot, as applicable. Several possible experimental designs could be used to provide the desired group of replicated plots. For example, a relatively large number of relatively small plots could be located at approximately equal distances along a drainage, half of them designated at random for fencing to provide exclosures. If there is extreme spatial heterogeneity of riparian vegetation, one alternative would be to locate a few relatively large, homogeneous main plots at strategic positions to include riparian vegetation, half of them open and half closed. A number of small subplots within each main plot could then be randomly assigned as replicates. In either case, a certain distance would have to be maintained between plots in order to minimize upstream effects on neighboring downstream plots. This would be a more serious source of bias in the aquatic than in the riparian and upland parts of each plot.

Since all experimental plots would be assigned to one pasture in a four-pasture, rest-rotation grazing system, the open plots would be exposed to each of the four components of the system described above only once every four years. Hence, comparisons such as the difference between grazed and ungrazed treatments when the grazing involved an early-season deferment vs. when it involved a mid- and late-season deferment would be confounded with years. However, this still appears to be one of the most satisfactory ways to obtain the desired information within the practical limitations of a commercial ranching operation.

The longer the period of study, the more opportunity there would be to overcome the confounding effects of individual years on comparisons involving different components of the rotation grazing system. The comparisons of most interest, viz. those of grazing vs. no grazing (1 vs. 2, see previous page) and grazing following an initial period of rest vs. no grazing (3 vs. 2, see previous page) for the entire system can be made once every four years at the completion of each full cycle of the rotation. A 12-year experiment would provide three such comparisons.

Tradeoffs

The sacrifice of an ideal experimental situation in which riparian and other responses to each grazing system component are studied each year must be weighed against the advantages of the Eisenhower Consortium scheme which utilizes public lands, public land managers, and commercial ranching operations. The cost of leasing fully experimental lands, combined with the considerably larger size of an ideal experiment, would be much greater. It might also be difficult to find a reasonably homogeneous site for such a large experiment. In addition, scientific results obtained under realistic conditions of operation are much more likely to be accepted by the livestock industry.

Another alternative approach would be to study individual grazing system components, such as early-season deferment, in completely separate experiments. However, the cumulative cost of a full set of such experiments might be as high as the holistic Consortium approach and the need would still exist to test certain combinations of the most effective components in a commercially applicable grazing system.

It is well known that cattle will utilize riparian areas rather intensely under any stocking rate or grazing system (Hormay, in Armour 1977). This has led a number of wildlife and fishery biologists to suggest that riparian zones must either be fenced or treated as separate rotational pasture units in a grazing system (e.g., see Ames 1977; Behnke and Raleigh 1978; Thomas, Maser and Rodiek 1979). However, these alternatives are not acceptable to the livestock industry (Swan 1979), and they create access problems for wildlife and recreationists. It is important, then, to determine if more realistic management techniques can be devised which will fit into commercial grazing systems and still provide for riparian maintenance or enhancement.

For these and other reasons, the Eisenhower Consortium plan includes a second level of experimentation that would be superimposed at some point on the basic design previously described. This would be tailored more to the site-specific conditions of the watershed and riparian ecosystem, as well as to the interests of local ranchers, public land managers, and university scientists. The secondary experiments might involve studies on such things as cultural aids to riparian recovery (fertilization, replanting, treatment of woody vegetation to discourage browsing); differences in palatability among woody riparian species; simulation by mechanical means of cattle grazing and trampling effects on vegetation and soils; placing of salt, supplements, shading structures, windbreaks, and alternative sources of water in the uplands; behavior of cattle in the riparian zone; and utilization of the riparian and aquatic zones by wildlife and fish.

Values of Broader Regional Application

Although the basic grazing study would be an independent experiment capable of producing results that could be extrapolated to other sites in the immediate vicinity, the potential for much more powerful generalizations exists if several similar experiments are conducted in widely different locations. The Eisenhower Consortium plan calls for a minimum of four such experiments, each in a region characterized by a different major watershed vegetation type of importance to the cattle industry. Since climatic factors are not expected to be constant over the Eisenhower Consortium region, there would be no urgent need to initiate these experiments simultaneously. Instead, they could be set up incrementally, depending on the availability of funding.

The four major watershed types suggested are as follows: sagebrush steppe of southwestern Wyoming; juniper/pinyon woodland of western Colorado; grama/galleta steppe of northern and central New Mexico; and grama/tobosa shrub steppe of southeastern Arizona. If careful attention were given to criteria such as elevation, aspect, and slope at each location, these four semiarid ecosystem types would form an interesting gradient along a north-south transect from Wyoming to Arizona. Differences among these ecosystems in amount of energy available for vegetative regeneration and growth would result primarily from differences in their characteristic length of growing season and daily temperatures during the growing season. Available energy would increase steadily from north to south, as would the general level of moisture stress in the ambient environment as measured by evapotranspiration potential. Data obtained from the different ecosystems on this transect could then be used to answer the following types of questions.

--Is the speed of recovery of woody riparian vegetation without grazing similar in the Colorado and New Mexico ecosystem types? Is recovery more rapid in these ecosystems than in those of Wyoming and Arizona where more severe limitations may exist as a result, respectively, of lower amounts of available energy and higher ambient moisture stress during seedling germination and establishment?

--Is exclosure from grazing for several years, followed by the rotation grazing system, a more effective way to stimulate recovery of herbaceous riparian vegetation in the Wyoming than in the Arizona ecosystem type?

--Do compacted riparian soils and unstable streambanks show some recovery over time in all ecosystems when subjected to the rotation grazing system from the start? Are there differences among ecosystems in these types of responses?

The extent to which these sorts of questions can be satisfactorily answered will depend on the maintenance of a reasonable amount of background constancy across locations for a group of important variables related to watershed, riparian communities, and grazing. For example, grazing management intensities (Laycock and Conrad 1981), stocking rates, and age-classes of cattle would need to be standardized as much as possible, in addition to the type and degree of previous overgrazing (Knopf and Cannon 1981), in order not to obscure effects of the different experimental grazing treatments and grazing system components. While the riparian and aquatic communities might differ considerably at each location, constancy could be maintained for factors such as number of vegetative layers, presence of obligate, woody, riparian vegetation, and size of the associated stream.

Cost

The set of four experiments suggested by the Eisenhower Consortium plan would be expensive. However, the total annual cost over all locations would not likely exceed that of the site-specific Saval Ranch study described above, in which the riparian studies are only one part. The costs of fencing and maintaining exclosures, and of payments to lease-holders for loss of production within exclosures and other inconveniences would be relatively small compared to those associated with salaries and travel of scientific personnel and technicians.

The Consortium Strategy

The regional nature of the Eisenhower Consortium makes it an effective vehicle for conducting this type of research. The Consortium could assemble by competitive means an interdisciplinary research team for each of the four experimental sites, drawing from the faculty pool of its nine member universities: Wyoming, Colorado State, Colorado, Texas Tech, New Mexico, New Mexico State, Northern Arizona, Arizona State, and Arizona. The tenth member of the Consortium is the Rocky Mountain Forest and Range Experiment Station of the FS. The researchers would be familiar with regional problems. Proximity of certain of the campuses to some or all of the experimental sites would decrease logistic problems and experimental costs. The Consortium would also have a "political" advantage resulting from previous contacts between its member universities and local ranchers and land managers.

THE CALIFORNIA ANALOGY

An analogy exists between the Eisenhower Consortium and its region, on the one hand, and the California system of state universities and colleges, on the other. It would appear desirable in California to integrate regionwide riparian research activities by means of some type of consortium structure. The University of California Natural Land and Water Reserves System might provide sites for a set of riparian projects. Alternately, a series of de novo sites could be selected as was in part done for the International Biological Programme Studies. One of the major advantages of an integrated regional approach is that it provides an opportunity to ask questions which, if properly framed, can provide more broadly generalizable answers. A less desirable alternative would be a series of completely independent, small projects springing up over time throughout the same region, involving more total cost, and providing less satisfying answers to important regional questions.

Once the initial investment has been made in a long-term, regional research project, the individual research sites have the potential of attracting funds for ancillary research. The longer the experimental sites are maintained and their baseline data accumulated, the more valuable they will become as locations for additional research efforts. Several workers have previously suggested that examples of different riparian communities should be protected over time as validation sites (Patton 1977), benchmarks (Moore et al. 1979) and places where, in general, concentration of efforts would produce maximum results (Claire and Storch 1977).

The Long-Term Ecological Research (LTER) program of the National Science Foundation should be considered as a potential source of funding for research on an integrated set of western U.S. riparian ecosystems. This program currently supports long-term studies on major ecosystem types such as northern lakes, coniferous and deciduous forests, tallgrass prairies, and estuaries. Support of riparian research might require some adjustment in the LTER programmatic philosophy since riparian ecosystmes are not organized at major levels such as biomes. Their mature successional stages are also less stable, more open to nutrient and energy fluxes, and less likely to contain a characteristic group of stenotopic species than are many other ecosystem types. Nevertheless, their biological value is so high that they are worthy of greatly increased consideration by traditional funding sources for ecological research.

LITERATURE CITED

Almand, J. David, and William B Krohn. 1978. The position of the Bureau of Land Management on the protection and mangement of riparian ecosystems. p. 359-361. In: R.R. Johnson and J.F. McCormick (tech. coord.). Strategies for protection and management of floodplain wetlands and other riparian ecosystems: Proceedings of the symposium. [Calloway Gardens, Ga., December 11-13, 1978] USDA Forest Service General Technical Report WO-12. 410 p. Washington, D.C.

Ames, Charles R. 1977. Wildlife conflicts in riparian management: grazing. p. 49-51. In: R.R. Johnson and D.A. Jones (tech. coord.). Importance, preservation and managment of riparian habitat: a symposium. [Tuscon, Ariz. July 9, 1977] USDA Forest Service Technical Report RM-43. 217 p. Rocky Mountain Forest and Range Experiment Station, Fort Collins, Colo.

Armour, Carl L. 1977. Effects of deteriorated range streams on trout. USDI Bureau of Land Management. 7 p. Idaho State Office, Boise Ida.

Armour, Carl L. 1979. Livestock management approaches and the fisheries resource. p. 39. In: O.B. Cope (ed.). Grazing and riparian/stream ecosystems: Proceedings of the forum. [Denver, Colo., November 3-4, 1978] Trout Unlimited Inc. 94 p. Denver, Colo.

Behnke, Robert J., and Robert F. Raleigh. 1978. Grazing and the riparian zone: impact and management perspectives. p. 263-267. In: R.R. Johnson, and J.F. McCormick (tech. coord.). Strategies for protection and management of floodplain wetlands and other riparian ecosystems: Proceedings of the symposium. [Calloway Gardens, Ga., December 11-13, 1978] USDA Forest Service General Technical Report WO-12. 410 p. Washington, D.C.

Beidleman, Richart G. 1978. The cottonwood-willow riparian ecosystem as a vertebrate habitat, with particular reference to birds. p. 192-195. In: W.D. Graul, and S.J. Bissell (tech. coord.). Lowland river and stream habitat in Colorado: a symposium. [Greeley, Colo., October 4-5, 1978] Colorado Chapter of Wildlife Society and Colorado Audubon Council. 195 p.

Benson, Patrick C. 1979. Land use and wildlife with emphasis on raptors. USDA Forest Service. 32 p. Intermountain Region.

Boldt, Charles E., Daniel W. Uresk, and Kieth Severson. 1978. Riparian woodlands in jeopardy on northern high plains. p. 184-189. In: R.R. Johnson and J.F. McCormick (tech. coord.). Strategies for protection and management of floodplain wetlands and other riparian ecosystems: Proceedings of the symposium. [Calloway Gardens, Ga., December 11-13, 1978] USDA Forest Service General Technical Riport WO-12. 410 p. Washington, D.C.

Burkhard, Walter T. 1978. Vertebrate associations in lowland versus high elevation river and stream habitat in Colorado. p. 52-55. In: W.D. Graul and S.J. Bissell (tech. coord.). Lowland river and stream habitat in Colorado: a symposium. [Greeley, Colo., October 4-5, 1978] Colorado Chapter of Wildlife Society and Colorado Audubon Council. 195 p.

Claire, E.W., and R.L. Storch. 1977. Streamside management and livestock grazing: an objective look at the situation. In: J.W. Menke (ed.). Livestock and wildlife-fisheries relationships in the Great Basin. [In press] USDA Forest Service. Pacific Southwest Forest and Range Experiment Station, Berkeley, Calif. (Cited in Moore, Elbert, Eric Janes, Floyd Kinsinger, Ken Pitney, and John Swainsbury. 1979. Livestock grazing management and water quality protection--state of the art reference document. U.S. Environmental Protection Agency, Seattle, Wash., and USDI Bureau of Land Management, Denver, Colo. 147 p.)

Crouch, Glenn L. 1978. Effects of protection from livestock grazing on a bottomland wildlife habitat in northeastern Colorado. p. 118-125. In: W.D. Graul and S.J. Bissell (tech. coord.). Lowland river and stream habitat in Colorado: a symposium. [Greeley, Colo., October 4-5, 1978] Colorado Chapter of Wildlife Society and Colorado Audubon Council. 195 p.

Dahlem, Eugene H. 1979. The Mahogany Creek watershed--with and without grazing. p. 31-34. In: O.B. Cope (ed.). Grazing and riparian/stream ecosystems: Proceedings of the forum. [Denver, Colo., November 3-4, 1978] Trout Unlimited Inc. 94 p. Denver, Colo.

Davis, Gary A. 1977. Management alternatives for the riparian habitat in the Southwest. p. 59-67. In: R.R. Johnson and D.A Jones (tech. coord.). Importance, preservation and management of riparian habitat: a symposium. [Tuscon, Ariz., July 9, 1977] USDA Forest Service Technical Report RM-43. 217 p. Rocky Mountain Forest and Range Experiment Station, Fort Collins, Colo.

Duff, Donald A. 1979. Riparian habitat recovery on Big Creek, Rich County, Utah--a summary of 8 years of study. p. 91-92. In: O.B. Cope (ed.). Grazing and riparian/stream ecosystems: Proceedings of the forum. [Denver, Colo., November 3-4, 1978] Trout Unlimited Inc. 94 p. Denver, Colo.

Fitzgerald, James P. 1978. Vertebrate associations in plant communities along the South Platte River in northeastern Colorado. p. 73-88. In: W.D. Graul and S.J. Bissell (tech. coord.). Lowland river and stream habitat in Colorado: a symposium. [Greeley, Colo., October 4-5, 1978] Colorado Chapter of Wildlife Society and Colorado Audubon Council. 195 p.

Glinski, Richard L. 1977. Regeneration and distribution of sycamore and cottonwood trees along Sonoita Creek, Santa Cruz County, Arizona. p. 116-123. In: R.R. Johnson and D.A. Jones (tech. coord.). Importance, preservation and management of riparian habitat: a symposium. [Tuscon, Ariz., July 9, 1977] USDA Forest Service Technical Report RM-43. 217 p. Rocky Mountain Forest and Range Experiment Station, Fort Collins, Colo.

Johnson, R.R. 1971. Tree removal along the southwestern rivers and effects on associated organisms. American Philosophical Society Yearbook, 1970. p. 321-323.

Johnson, R. Roy, and Steven W. Carothers. 1975. The effects of stream channel modifications on birds in the southwestern United States. In: Proceedings of symposium on stream channel modification. [Harrisburg, Va., August 15-17, 1975]

Johnson, R. Roy, and Steven W. Carothers. 1981. Southwestern riparian habitats and recreation: interrelationships and impacts in the Rocky Mountain Region. Eisenhower Consortium Bulletin. [In press] USDA Forest Service. Rocky Mountain Forest and Range Experiment Station, Fort Collins, Colo.

Johnson, R. Roy, Lois T. Haight, and James M. Simpson. 1977. Endangered species vs. endangered habitats: a concept. p. 68-74. In: R.R. Johnson and D.A. Jones (tech. coord.). Importance, preservation and management of riparian habitat: a symposium. [Tuscon, Ariz., July 9, 1977] USDA Forest Service Technical Report RM-43. 217 p. Rocky Mountain Forest Range Experiment Station, Fort Collins, Colo.

Keller, Charles, Loren Anderson, and Paul Tappel. 1979. Fish habitat changes in Summit Creek, Idaho, after fencing the riparian area. p. 46-52. In: O.B. Cope (ed.). Grazing and riparian/stream ecosystems: Proceedings of the forum. [Denver, Colo., November 3-4, 1978] Trout Unlimited Inc. 94 p. Denver, Colo.

Knopf, Fritz L., and Richard W. Cannon. 1981. Structural resilience of a willow riparian community to changes in grazing practices. In: J. Peek (ed.). Livestock-wildlife relationships symposium. [Coeur D'Alene, Idaho, April, 1981. In press.] University of Idaho, Moscow, Ida.

Laycock, W.A., and P.W. Conrad. 1981. Responses of vegetation and cattle to various systems of grazing on seeded and native mountain rangelands in eastern Utah. Journal of Range Management 34:52-58.

Lea, George D. 1979. BLM management and policy for riparian/stream ecosystems. p. 13-15. In: O.B. Cope (ed.). Grazing and riparian/stream ecosystems: Proceedings of the forum. [Denver, Colo., November 3-4, 1978] Trout Unlimited Inc. 94 p. Denver, Colo.

Martin, S. Clark. 1979. Evaluating the impacts of cattle grazing on riparian habitats in the national forests of Arizona and New Mexico. p. 35-38. In: O.B. Cope (ed.). Grazing and riparian/stream ecosystems: Proceedings of the forum. [Denver, Colo., November 3-4, 1978] Trout Unlimited Inc. 94 p. Denver, Colo.

Moore, Elbert, Eric Janes, Floyd Kinsinger, Ken Pitney, and John Swainbury. 1979. Livestock grazing management and water quality protection--state of the art reference document. U.S. Environmental Protection Agency, Seattle, Wash., and USDI Bureau of Land Management, Denver, Colo. 147 p.

Myers, L.H. 1981. Grazing management vs. riparian management in southwestern Montana. In: Proceedings on management of riparian ecosystems. [In press.] Montana Chapter of the Wildlife Society, Great Falls, Mont. (Cited in Knopf, Fritz L., and Richard W. Cannon. 1981. Structural resilience of a willow riparian community to changes in grazing practices. In: James Peek (ed.). Livestock-wildlife relationships symposium. [Coeur D'Alene, Idaho, April, 1981. In press.] University of Idaho, Moscow, Ida.)

Patton, David R. 1977. Riparian research needs. p. 80-82. In: R.R. Johnson and D.A. Jones (tech. coord.). Importance, preservation and management of riparian habitat: a symposium. [Tuscon, Ariz.. July 9, 1977] USDA Forest Service Technical Report RM-43. 217 p. Rocky Mountain Forest and Range Experiment Station, Fort Collins, Colo.

Platts, William S. 1979. Livestock grazing and riparian/stream ecosystems--an overview. p. 39-45. In: O.B. Cope (ed.). Grazing and riparian/stream ecosystems: Proceedings of the forum. [Denver, Colo., November 3-4, 1978] Trout Unlimited Inc. 94 p. Denver, Colo.

Raleigh, Robert F. 1979a. Introduction. p. 1. In: O.B. Cope (ed.). Grazing and riparian/stream ecosystems: Proceedings of the forum. [Denver, Colo., November 3-4, 1978] Trout Unlimited Inc. 94 p. Denver, Colo.

Raleigh, Robert F. 1979b. Closing remarks. p. 89-90. In: O.B. Cope (ed.). Grazing and riparian/stream ecosystems: Proceedings of the forum. [Denver, Colo., November 3-4, 1978] Trout Unlimited Inc. 94 p. Denver, Colo.

Salt, G.W. 1957. An analysis of the avifaunas in the Teton Mountains and Jackson Hole, Wyoming. Condor 59:373-393.

Schrupp, Donald L. 1978. The wildlife values of lowland river and stream habitat as related to other habitats in Colorado. p. 42-51. In: W.D. Graul and S.J. Bissell (tech. coord.). Lowland river and stream habitat in Colorado: a symposium. [Greeley, Colo., October 4-5, 1978] Colorado Chapter of Wildlife Society and Colorado Audubon Council. 195 p.

Severson, Kieth E, and Charles E. Boldt. 1978. Cattle, wildlife, and riparian habitats in the western Dakotas. In: Management and use of northern plains rangeland. Regional rangeland symposium. [Bismark, No. Dak., February 27-28, 1978].

Smith, Felix E. 1980. A short review of the status of riparian forests in California. p. 1-2. In: A. Sands (ed.). Riparian forests in California--their ecology and conservation: Proceedings of the symposium. [Davis, Calif., May 14, 1977] Division of Agricultural Sciences, University of California, Berkeley, Calif. 122 p.

Stevens, Lawrence E., Bryan T. Brown, James M. Simpson, and R. Roy Johnson. 1977. The importance of riparian habitats to migrating birds. p. 156-164. In: R.R. Johnson and D.A. Jones (tech. coord.). Importance, preservation and management of riparian habitat: a symposium. [Tuscon, Ariz., July 9, 1977] USDA Forest Service Techical Report RM-43. 217 p. Rocky Mountain Forest and Range Experiment Station, Fort Collins, Colo.

Stoddart, Laurence A., Arthur D. Smith, and Thadis W. Box. 1975. Range management. Third edition. 532 p. McGraw-Hill Book Co., New York, N.Y.

Storch, Robert L. 1979. Livestock/streamside management programs in eastern Oregon. p. 56-59. In: O.B. Cope (ed.). Grazing and riparian/stream ecosystems: Proceedings of the forum. [Denver, Colo., November 4-5, 1978] Trout Unlimited Inc. 94 p. Denver, Colo.

Swan, Bill. 1979. Riparian habitat--the cattlemen's viewpoint. p. 4-6. In: O.B. Cope (ed.). Grazing and riparian/stream ecosystems: Proceedings of the forum. [Denver, Colo., November 4-5, 1978] Trout Unlimited Inc. 94 p. Denver, Colo.

Thomas, Jack Ward, Chris Maser, and Jon E. Rodiek. 1979. Wildlife habitats in managed rangelands--the Great Basin of southeastern Oregon--riparian zones. USDA Forest Service General Technical Report PNW-80. 18 p. Pacific Northwest Forest and Range Experiment Station, La Grande, Ore. (Also published under the title "Riparian zones in managed rangelands--their importance to wildlife." 1979. p. 21-31. In: O.B. Cope (ed.). Grazing and riparian/stream ecosystems: Proceedings of the forum. [Denver, Colo., November 4-5, 1978] Trout Unlimited Inc. 94 p. Denver, Colo.)

US Council on Environmental Quality. 1978. Environmental quality. The Ninth Annual Report of the Council on Environmental Quality. 599 p. US Government Printing Office, Washington, D.C. [Stock No. 041-011-00040-8]

USDI Bureau of Land Management. Draft environmental statement on grazing management in the Missouri Breaks of Montana. Montana State Office.

Warner, Richard E. (recorder). 1979a. Fish and wildlife resource needs in riparian ecosystems: Proceedings of a workshop. [Harpers Ferry, W. Va., May 30-31, 1979] 53 p. National Water Resources Analysis Group, Eastern Energy and Land Use Team, USDI Fish and Wildlife Service, Kearneysville W. Va.

Warner, Richard E. 1979b. California riparian study program: background information and proposed study design. 177 p. Planning Branch, California Department of Fish and Game, Sacramento, Calif.

RIPARIAN SYSTEM/LIVESTOCK GRAZING INTERACTION RESEARCH

IN THE INTERMOUNTAIN WEST[1]

William S. Platts[2]

Abstract.--Research which identifies the influences livestock grazing has on riparian and aquatic ecosystems is limited. A research study initiated in 1975 by the USDA Forest Service is studing these influences and finding solutions so managers will have better information to evaluate range management alternatives. Preliminary findings on continuous and rest-rotation grazing systems are discussed.

INTRODUCTION

Research which identifies the influences livestock grazing has on riparian and aquatic ecosystems is limited. Even less research exists that offers corrective management alternatives should detrimental grazing practices occur. This necessary research has lagged because riparian zones have frequently been ignored in rangeland planning and management. They constitute only a small portion of the total range picture, and managers have difficulty meshing them into present management schemes. Skovlin and Meehan (1975) believe that streamside use problems evolved because of the lack of concrete information for judging how much of a resource can be utilized before that use infringes on the output of other resources. Utilization limits must be determined because world food demands make it essential that ranges come under multiple-use management, for both efficient red meat production and maintenance of the many other range resources.

Behnke (in press) believes rehabilitating riparian environments offers the most productive and efficient way to increase wild trout populations in the western United States. Thomas et al. (1977) believe riparian zones are the single most critical zones for multiple-use planning in the Blue Mountains of eastern Oregon. Riparian features such as shade, drinking water, gentle terrain, and higher production of more palatable forage lead to preferential use of this area by livestock. Armour (1977) quotes Hormay who, in personal communication, said:

---

[1]Paper presented at the California Riparian Systems Conference. [University of California, Davis, September 17-19, 1981].
[2]William S. Platts is Research Fishery Biologist, USDA Forest Service, Intermountain Forest and Range Experiment Station, Boise, Idaho.

Vegetation in meadows and drainageways is closely utilized (by livestock) under any stocking rate or system of grazing. Reducing the livestock or adjusting grazing seasons usually will not solve the problem.

Based on such discussions it is easy to see why Leopold (1974) and Platts (1979) have identified management of riparian systems as a national issue.

A research study initiated in 1975 by the USDA Forest Service (FS) identifies the type and magnitude of streamside impacts under different grazing strategies and classes of livestock. The purpose of the study is to give managers better information to evaluate alternatives for making grazing more compatible with riparian resources.

DEFINING THE PROBLEM

Riparian zones are often grazed more heavily than upland ranges (Holscher and Woolfolk 1953; Armour 1977). This grazing can affect the riparian environment by changing, reducing, or eliminating vegetation and by actually eliminating riparian areas by channel widening, channel aggradation, or lowering of the water table. Other literature indicates that streams modified by improper livestock grazing are wider and shallower (Marcuson 1977; Platts 1979; Van Velson 1979), contain more fine sediment and have more unstable streambanks, less bank undercut, and higher summer water temperatures than those of natural streams; therefore, fish populations are often reduced (Armour 1977; Behnke and Zarn 1976).

Despite extensive literature reviews, Meehan and Platts (1978), Gifford and Hawkins (1976), and Platts (1981) were unable to identify any commonly used grazing strategy compatible with all the environmental requirements of fish-producing streams. McGowan (1976) and Platts

(1978) expressed doubts that present grazing strategies are capable of solving the impacts of grazing on riparian systems. Also, because much former sheep range has been converted to cattle range and because cattle prefer to graze streamside environments, the deterioration of riparian systems may become even more significant. Sheep have the potential of converting forage to red meat without extensively affecting the riparian zone, but they are no longer utilized on many allotments.

For the land manager, then, insufficient information is available to determine alternate strategies when livestock are exerting stress on the fishery. To compound the problem, valid analytical techniques for assessing the magnitude of livestock impacts on riparian/stream environments have yet to be fully developed. Without these techniques, it is difficult to determine whether changes in existing grazing patterns are needed, and if so, what new strategies should be implemented.

ONGOING RESEARCH

This report principally addresses the research being conducted by the Intermountain Forest and Range Experiment Station of the FS. Methodology used in this study is described in Platts (1974, 1976) and Ray and Megahan (1978). To determine how sheep and cattle grazing interact with riparian/fishery habitats, 17 research sites in Idaho, Nevada, and Utah are being studied (fig. 1). The Idaho sites are in moist, high mountain meadows surrounded by forests, while the Utah and Nevada sites are in arid meadows surrounded by sagebrush. The Idaho studies test grazing effects on chinook salmon (Oncorhynchus tshawytscha [Walbaum]), steelhead rainbow trout (Salmo gairdneri [Richardson]), brook trout (Salvelinus fontinalis [Mitchell]), sculpin (Cottus spp.), resident rainbow trout (Salmo gairdneri [Richardson]), cutthroat trout (Salmo clarki [Richardson]), bull trout (Salvelinus confluentus [Suckley]), and mountain whitefish (Prosopium williamsoni [Girard]).

In the Idaho study areas, waters are low in mineral content because of the predominance of granitic bedrock in the Idaho Batholith. The study areas are in meadows at 1,890 to 1,950 m. (6,200 to 6,400 ft.) elevation, which were formed as an outwash train from extensive Pleistocene glacial deposits. The mountain meadows cover 1.62 million hectares (4 million acres) in the 11 western states (US Department of Agriculture 1972) and support more beef per hectare (acre) than any other range type (Skovlin in press).

The Utah-Nevada study areas are in the Basin-Range province in broad valley-type streams with relatively high mineral content. Riparian areas are much narrower than in the Idaho sites and are usually only thin ribbons along the borders of the streams. The Nevada studies evaluate grazing effects on the Humboldt cut-

IDAHO BATHOLITH

1 Lower Stolle
2 Cougar Stolle
3 Guard Stolle
4 Upper Stolle
5 Johnson Creek
6 Elk Creek
7 Lower Bear Valley
8 Upper Bear Valley
9 Lower Frenchman Creek
10 Upper Frenchman Creek
11 Horton Creek

HUMBOLDT RIVER BASIN

12 Gance Creek
13 Tabor Creek
14 Chimney Creek

BONNEVILLE BASIN

15 Lower Big Creek
16 Upper Big Creek
17 Otter Creek

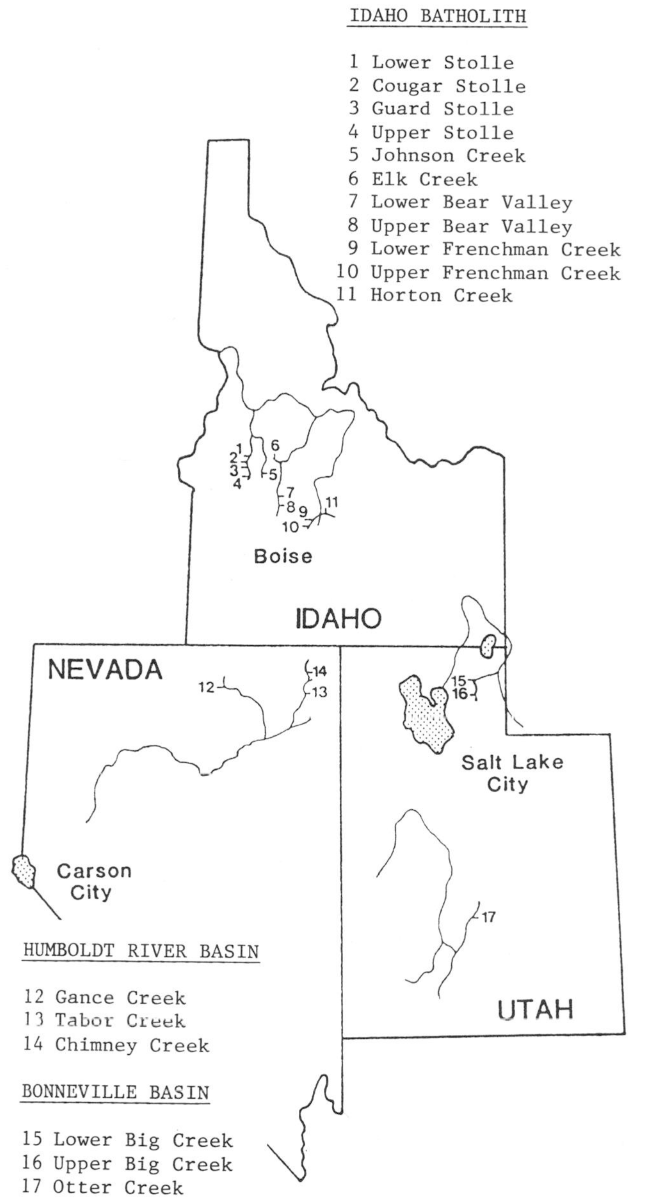

Figure 1.--General location of livestock-fishery study sites.

throat trout, a threatened and endangered species, as well as on rainbow trout and sculpin. The Utah studies evaluate grazing effects on rainbow trout and brown trout (Salmo trutta [Lineaus]).

The first stage of these studies will compare commonly used grazing strategies at different levels of herbage use in different riparian/fishery types. The second stage will develop and test those grazing strategies believed to be more compatible with riparian systems. The overall study objectives are:

1) to improve riparian/stream methodology so it will more accurately determine stream conditions and changes in these conditions;

425

2) to determine the potential of rehabilitating riparian/fishery environments altered by overgrazing;

3) to determine the difference in riparian/stream influences from grazing by different classes of livestock (sheep and cattle);

4) to determine the influences that different types of grazing strategies have on riparian/fishery environments; and

5) to determine the optimum mix of riparian forage utilization and fish needs.

Study sites have been established in grazed and nongrazed ranges. Historically grazed areas are being rested from grazing to determine rehabilitative processes and potentials. Previously nongrazed ranges are now being grazed to determine the effects and the processes that cause these effects on riparian/stream systems. All study sites may not yield immediate answers because environmental changes caused by livestock grazing may accumulate slowly over a long time.

Livestock/fishery research is difficult because in the early stage of degradation streams are often resilient and adaptable to change. Streams have a variety of ways of compensating for applied stress, a capacity which allows for assimilating and/or masking of small, short-term effects. These effects can accumulate until they reach the incipient lethal level for the fish population; then sudden collapse of the population can occur. Livestock grazing can each year cause microchanges in the environment, changes which can accumulate over many decades and thus be difficult to detect in short-term studies. Whether a stream suffers a catastrophic degrading event from a flood or the degradation of small events accumulating over a long period, the result for fish can be the same. In either case the stream and its fisheries have been altered, and, even once stress is relieved, recovery may take many years.

PRELIMINARY FINDINGS

Sheep Grazing

Different classes of livestock graze watershed in different ways. Sheep usually use slopes and upland areas, while cattle tend to use the lesser slopes or bottomlands that might have riparian zones. Because sheep grazing on public lands is usually controlled by herding, it is possible for sheep to graze a watershed without exerting direct significant influence on the riparian system. However, if sheep are not controlled properly impacts to riparian areas would be expected. Two types of sheep grazing systems are being studied: continuous grazing and rest-rotation.

Continuous Grazing

Statistically significant differences exist between reaches of the same stream on the Horton Creek site (fig. 1, site 11). One stream reach flowed through a heavily grazed meadow, but an adjacent downstream reach in the same meadow received light or no grazing each year (table 1). Although grazing intensity was insignificant in the fenced portion of the meadow, there was some trespass grazing in years when fences were not maintained properly. When the meadow was heavily grazed by sheep in large numbers, the stream reach became four times wider and only one-fifth as deep as the reach in the adjacent, lightly grazed meadow (fig. 2). In the heavily grazed meadow, streambanks were sloped sharply out, undercut banks were almost eliminated, the quality of riparian system decreased, and bank alteration was 15 times greater. In addition, four times as much stream surface was exposed to solar radiation, and streamside water depth was only one-thirteenth as deep as in the reach in the lightly grazed area. Fish density and biomass (annual average from 1978 through 1980) per unit area were 7.6 and 10.9 times greater, respectively, in the lightly grazed stream reach than in the heavily grazed stream reach (table 1). In the reach in the lightly grazed pastures, trout numbers per linear foot of stream were about 1.7 times greater than in the reach in the heavily grazed pasture. Fish density was much higher in the reach in the lightly grazed pasture, due in part to the narrower stream width there.

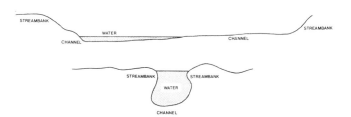

Figure 2.--A typical stream channel profile in the heavily grazed site (above) and the lightly grazed site (below).

Rest-Rotation

No significant changes in trends were found in environmental factors in that portion of Frenchman Creek that flowed through a series of meadows grazed by sheep using a herded rest-rotation system. On all of the sites grazed by sheep, the water column, stream channel, streambank, and riparian vegetation are exhibiting no detectable alterations from grazing. The stream is healthy; no significant artificial changes in the existing high fish populations could be detected. The herder has been able to graze the sheep lightly in the streamside zones, with

Table 1.--A comparison of environmental conditions in the heavily grazed and lightly grazed meadow with 95% confidence intervals in parenthesis.

	Heavy grazing (180-m. stream)	Light grazing (180-m. stream)
Stream width (m.)	2.4 (+0.2)	0.5 (+0.2)
Stream depth (cm.)	3.3 (+1.0)	15.7 (+1.0)
Bank-water depth (cm.)	1.0 (+1.3)	13.0 (+1.8)
Embeddedness (units)	4.8 (+0.3)	3.2 (+0.3)
Channel gravel (percent)	98.2 (+5.0)	69.3 (+0.5)
Streambank angle (degrees)	132.0 (+8.0)	82.0 (+0.3)
Streambank undercut (cm.)	1.5 (+1.0)	4.3 (+1.0)
Streambank alteration (percent)	86.1 (+4.0)	5.7 (+4.2)
Riparian habitat type (units)	14.0 (+0.2)	17.7 (+0.6)
Average fish numbers (brook trout)	17.0 (+0.5)	29.7 (+0.6)
Fish density per square meter	0.0387	0.2959
Fish density per linear stream meter	0.0929	0.1624
Fish biomass per square meter (grams)	2.0250	21.9795
Fish biomass per linear stream meter (grams)	4.8181	12.0636

riparian herbage utilization less than 5%. Sheep bedding has been offsite.

A rest-rotation grazing system that includes proper herding of sheep to control animal distribution and forage utilization apparently results in insignificant onsite impacts to this type of riparian/stream environment. This is a significant finding, and it sheds new light on statements by Skovlin (in press), Platts (1975, 1979), and McGowan (1976) that no known range management strategy has proven effective in adequately protecting riparian environments. The rest-rotation system should work well throughout the Rocky Mountain area where animal distribution is tightly controlled. It is possible, however, that a continuous, light-to-moderate grazing strategy under good herding could also give good results. This technique has not been tested.

Cattle Grazing

Rest-Rotation Strategy

Cattle have been grazing for two years (the early and late grazing phases of the three-stage rest-rotation cycle) on four Idaho sites in formerly ungrazed meadows (fig. 1, sites 1-4). Cattle grazing has also been introduced at two sites previously grazed lightly by sheep (fig. 1, sites 9 and 10). The riparian areas within these sites were grazed at different intensities, ranging from 25-80%.

After two years of cattle grazing, no significant changes could be detected in any water column or stream channel environmental conditions. The changes that were detected were some minor streambank instability and increased vegetation use. To date no detectable changes have occurred in fish population because of grazing influences.

It is too early to determine if these rest-rotation grazing systems with their different degrees of grazing intensity are compatible with the stream and its fisheries. A minimum of two grazing cycles (six years) will be needed before sufficient trend information will be available.

A key conclusion evolving during the early stages of the study is that when riparian systems are first grazed, initial adverse impacts will show on the streambanks and riparian vegetation. If this trend remains consistent, it may be possible to detect and correct livestock impacts occurring on good-conditioned riparian/ stream environments before the fishery is affected.

Continuous Grazing (Nevada and Utah)

Statistically significant differences in riparian/stream environmental condition measurements were observed over two years between continuously grazed pastures (60-100% utilization) and adjacent rested pastures (fig. 1, sites 12-14). The rest from grazing usually resulted in less streambank erosion and allowed streambanks to rebuild, with a corresponding decrease in stream width. Average stream depth and streamside water depth were usually greater in the rested areas. Vegetative overhang was usually much greater and streambank stability better in the rested areas. The studies have shown that continuous grazing with commonly used grazing intensities causes riparian/stream environment deterioration. In none of the study sites did improvements occur when a continuous grazing system was used.

FUTURE RANGE RESEARCH NEEDS

To date most rangeland research has been devoted to forage conditions, animal growth, and sediment movement off rangelands. Skovlin (in press) found abundant information on the effects of grazing systems and intensities on plant communities, livestock production, and watershed response (not including streams), but very little on riparian response. Clearly, there is insufficient information to assist land managers in determining if conventional grazing systems are causing stress to riparian/stream systems. It becomes imperative then that research determine those grazing strategies compatible with each of the riparian/stream habitat types, and find ways to modify those strategies that are not. To do this the following questions need better answers.

1. What grazing timing and intensity is most compatible with the ecological needs of riparian systems?

2. Can depleted riparian vegetative communities be restored using present grazing systems?

3. How do different classes of livestock affect the riparian environment?

4. What are the responses of fish and wildlife to different levels of riparian forage use?

5. How much riparian vegetation canopy is needed for optimum stream temperatures and overhead cover for fish?

6. What amount and type of riparian vegetation is needed to maintain streambank stability?

7. What environmental indicators first signal changes in the quality of riparian environment?

8. What techniques are available to rehabilitate degraded riparian systems?

To answer these questions research should be directed toward three targets.

Target I—Develop, test, and standardize methods to document the status and changing trend of riparian/stream systems.

Target II—Use these refined methods to evaluate all commonly used grazing management strategies to determine their potential for maintaining healthy riparian/stream systems.

Target III—Using the positive features found in these systems, design new grazing management strategies that are more compatible with riparian/stream systems.

After seven years of testing our methodology, we are not completely satisfied with the accuracy and precision of our environmental measurements. Consequently, we are having difficulty evaluating the commonly used grazing strategies. Researchers need to complete Target I before Targets II and III can be completed, but Target I is mostly ignored while researchers try to jump directly into II and III. Researchers must be able to measure small environmental changes and to differentiate between natural and artificially caused changes before valid results can be obtained.

Our methods, although crude in some aspects, have allowed us to do some evaluating of commonly used grazing strategies. This evaluation shows that successful management of riparian/stream systems requires the range manager to use or develop grazing strategies where timing, utilization, and **especially** animal distribution can be controlled within the entire allotment.

LITERATURE CITED

Armour, C.L. 1977. Effects of deteriorated range streams on trout. 7 p. USDI Bureau of Land Management, Idaho State Office, Boise, Idaho.

Behnke, R.J. (in press). Livestock grazing impacts on stream fisheries: problems and suggested solutions. In: John Menke (ed.). A symposium on livestock interactions with wildlife, fisheries and their environments. [Sparks, Nevada, May 1977]. USDA Forest Service Pacific Southwest Forest and Range Experiment Station, Berkeley, Calif.

Behnke, R.J., and M. Zarn. 1976. Biology and management of threatened and endangered western trouts. USDA Forest Service GTR-RM-28. 45 p. Rocky Mountain Forest and Range Experiment Station, Fort Collins, Colo.

Gifford, G., and R. Hawkins. 1976. Grazing systems and watershed management: a look at the record. Journal of Soil and Water Conservation 31(6):281-283.

Holscher, C., and E. Woolfolk. 1953. Forage utilization by cattle in the Northern Great Plains Range. US Department of Agriculture Circular No. 918. 27 p.

Leopold, A.S. 1974. Ecosystem deterioration under multiple use. p. 96-98. In: Proceedings of the wild trout management symposium. 103 p. USDI Fish and Wildlife Service, and Trout Unlimited, Denver, Colo.

McGowan, Terry. 1976. Statement on improving fish and wildlife benefits in range management. p. 97-102. In: Proceedings of a seminar on improving fish and wildlife benefits in range management [Washington, D.C., March 1976]. 118 p. USDI Fish and Wildlife Service, Biological Services Program, Washington, D.C.

Marcuson, Patrick E. 1977. The effect of cattle grazing on brown trout in Rock Creek, Montana. Project No. F-20-R-21-11-a. 26 p. Montana Department of Fish and Game, Helena.

Meehan, William R., and William S. Platts. 1978. Livestock grazing and the aquatic environment. Journal of Soil and Water Conservation 33(b):274-278.

Platts, W.S. 1974. Geomorphic and aquatic conditions influencing salmonids and stream classification with application to ecosystem classification. 200 p. USDA Forest Service, Surface Environment and Mining Project, Billings, Mont.

Platts, W.S. 1975. Livestock interactions with fish and aquatic environments: problems in evaluation. p. 498-504. In: Transactions of the Forty-third North American Wildlife and Natural Resources Conference. Wildlife Management Institute, Washington, D.C. 510 p.

Platts, W.S. 1976. Validity in the use of aquatic methodologies to document stream environments for evaluating fishery conditions. Instream Flow Needs Proceedings 2:267-284. American Fish Society, Bethesda, Md.

Platts, W.S. 1979. Livestock grazing and riparian/stream ecosystems: an overview. p. 39-45. In: O.B. Cope (ed.). Proceedings of the forum on grazing and riparian/stream ecosystems. [Denver, Colo., Nov. 3-4, 1978]. 94 p. Trout Unlimited, Inc. Vienna, Va.

Platts, W.S. 1981. Overview of the riparian/fish habitat issue in the western United States. p. 195-201. In: Proceedings of sixtieth annual conference of the Western Association of the State Game and Fish Commissioners. [Kalispell, Mont.]. 649 p.

Ray, G.A., and W.F. Megahan. 1978. Measuring cross sections using a sag tape: a generalized procedure. USDA Forest Service GTR-INT-47. 12 p. Intermountain Forest and Range Experiment Station, Ogden, Utah.

Skovlin, J. (In press.) The impacts of grazing on wetlands and riparian habitats. In: Impacts of grazing intenstiy and specialized grazing systems workshop. [El Paso, Texas, March 1981]. National Science Foundation, Washington, D.C.

Skovlin, J.M., and W.R. Meehan. 1975. Draft study plan--the influence of grazing on restoration of riparian and aquatic habitats in the Central Blue Mountains. USDA Forest Service, Pacific Northwest Experiment Station, LaGrande, Oregon.

Thomas, Jack Ward, Chris Maser, and John E. Rodiek. 1977. Riparian zones--their importance to wildlife and their management. 14 p. USDA Forest Service, Pacific Northwest Forest and Range Experiment Station, Corvallis, Oregon.

US Department of Agriculture. 1972. Western regional working conference--results of work group sessions--delegate ratings. National Program of Research for Forest and Associated Rangelands. 39 p. USDA Forest Service, Intermountain Forest and Range Experiment Station, Ogden, Utah.

Van Velson, R. 1979. Effects of livestock grazing upon rainbow trout in Otter Creek, Nebraska. p. 53-55. In: O.B. Cope (ed.). Proceedings of the forum on grazing and riparian/stream ecosystems. [Denver, Colo., Nov. 3-4, 1978]. 94 p. Trout Unlimited, Inc. Vienna, Va.

SENATE BILL 397:   A NEW APPROACH TO

RIPARIAN AREA PROTECTION IN OREGON[1]

Nancy E. Duhnkrack[2]

Abstract.--Legislation enacted by the State of Oregon
in August, 1981, established an innovative program for protection or rehabilitation of privately owned riparian lands
through use of tax incentives for property owners. This
voluntary incentive program has support from a diverse base
of interests in Oregon and could be an effective alternative
or companion to programs based on regulations or acquisition
in other states.

INTRODUCTION

The Legislative Assembly declares that
it is in the best interest of the State
to maintain, preserve, conserve and rehabilitate riparian lands to assure the
protection of the soil, water, fish and
wildlife resources of the State for the
economic and social well-being of the
State and its citizens.

So begins the preamble to Senate Bill 397,
legislation enacted by the State of Oregon during
the 1981 legislative session to encourage the
protection or rehabilitation of privately owned
riparian zones. With passage of SB 397, Oregon
took a major and much-needed step forward in
riparian area protection, setting in place a
cornerstone upon which to build a comprehensive
riparian system protection program. Passage of
SB 397 was due, in large part, to the design of
the bill and its consequent appeal to a broad
variety of interests. This paper will outline
the impetus for and content of SB 397. The paper
will also discuss the issues surrounding and
components of the legislative campaign which
resulted in its passage. But first I will give a
brief overview of efforts in Oregon to protect
riparian areas prior to passage of SB 397.

PAST RIPARIAN AREA PROTECTION IN OREGON

The Private Sector

There is no coordinated effort in Oregon to
inventory, study, or protect privately owned

riparian areas. A multitude of programs under
many jurisdictions have, to a greater or lesser
extent, recognized riparian areas and acted to
protect them. I will discuss two of the programs
unique to Oregon and some of their more notable
aspects.

Since 1973, the State of Oregon has had a
land-use planning program (codified as Oregon
Revised Statute [ORS] 197) which requires local
jurisdictions (cities and counties) to develop
comprehensive plans for land use in compliance
with 19 statewide planning goals. In the process
of developing these plans, the jurisdictions must
complete an inventory of resources within their
boundaries, establish land-use policies based on
these inventories and in compliance with the
goals, and develop ordinances to implement such
policies. One of the statewide goals, Goal 5,
specifically mentions the protection of scenic
and natural areas and fish and wildlife habitat.
To comply with Goal 5, local jurisdictions have
inventoried riparian areas and adopted a variety
of ordinances to protect them. These ordinances
include building setbacks, overlay zoning, "greenway" zoning, density transfers, and permit systems. The strength of these ordinances varies
greatly from jurisdiction to jurisdiction. At a
minimum, Goal 5 and the statewide land-use planning process have fostered an awareness among
local officials and planners of riparian areas
and their significance.

In 1970, Oregon established a Scenic Waterways program (ORS 390.805-390.925) very similar
in purpose to the National Wild and Scenic Rivers
System. Through the state program eight river
segments, totalling 510 river miles, are protected from adverse development. Private land use
along these rivers is regulated through a permit
system. Both Oregon's Scenic Waterways and land-
use planning programs have had far more success
in controlling construction and development
(e.g., houses, marinas, industrial parks) in

---

[1]Paper presented at the California Riparian Systems Conference. [University of California, Davis, September 17-19, 1981].
[2]Nancy E. Duhnkrack is Water Resources
Coordinator for the Oregon Wilderness Coalition,
Eugene, Oregon.

riparian areas than in regulating forest or agricultural practices.

Oregon has many additional programs, similar to those of other western states, which address management of riparian lands. The State Forest Practices Act (ORS 527.610-527.730), Agricultural Framework Plan, and efforts funded under Section 208 of the Clean Water Act are examples. Of these, the Forest Practices Act has done the most to promote wise management of riparian areas, particularly in western Oregon. However, the narrow focus of each of these programs has limited their effectiveness in riparian area protection. The Forest Practices Act, for example, only governs commercial forest operations. It does not regulate grazing in riparian areas on forestlands.

The Public Sector

The 52% of Oregon which is publicly owned consists primarily of lands managed by the USDA Forest Service (FS) and the USDI Bureau of Land Management (BLM). Here, in contrast to private lands, specific management direction for inventory, study, protection, and enhancement of riparian lands has been developed. In 1979 the Riparian Habitat Subcommittee of the Oregon/ Washington Interagency Wildlife Committee (composed of representatives of the FS, BLM, USDA Soil Conservation Service [SCS], USDI Fish and Wildlife Service [FWS], Oregon Department of Fish and Wildlife [ODFW], and Washington Department of Game [WDG]) prepared "Managing Riparian Ecosystems (Zones) For Fish and Wildlife in Eastern Oregon and Eastern Washington" (Oregon/Washington Interagency Wildlife Committee, Riparian Habitat Subcommittee 1979). This report outlines, in very basic terms, broad procedures for evaluating the present condition of riparian ecosystems, projecting potentials for enhancement, and establishing recommended habitat conditions for managing fish and wildlife within riparian ecosystems.

Other research available to public land managers in Oregon includes work coordinated by Dr. Jack Thomas of the Pacific Northwest Forest and Range Experiment Station, La Grande, Oregon, and published by the FS on wildlife habitats in managed forests and rangelands. Research has been completed for the Blue Mountains of eastern Washington and Oregon (Thomas 1979) and for the Great Basin of southeastern Oregon (Thomas et al. 1980). Preparation of similar reports for other geographic areas wthin the region is well underway. These reports provide valuable definitions of riparian areas, specify wildlife habitat needs met by riparian zones, and suggest specific management prescriptions for these zones.

Work done cooperatively by the USDC National Marine Fisheries Service, the FWS, and the ODFW on fish habitat restoration in eastern Oregon has added another dimension to research on riparian areas in Oregon. This work, begun in 1978 under a USDI Bureau of Reclamation (BR) authorization and nearing completion, has quantified the magnitude of streamflow augmentation possible when riparian areas are restored.

Region 6 of the FS (Washington and Oregon) has adopted the evaluation procedure for assessing the condition of riparian areas contained in the Interagency Wildlife Committee Report, (Oregon/Washington Interagency Wildlife Committee, Riparian Habitat Subcommittee 1979), a supplement to the Forest Service Manual. Following inventory and evaluation of riparian areas, each National Forest has been directed by the Regional Office to recommend habitat objectives for these areas and develop management prescriptions to meet these objectives. The FS mandates that development of these prescriptions include an analysis of the trade-offs involved and the cost-effectiveness of each management prescription, a time frame for implementation, and a monitoring procedure. This process will be part of the new land management planning process mandated by the National Forest Management Act (1976). Since no National Forest within the region has completed a draft Forest Plan under the new process it is difficult to assess the degree to which these guidelines will be implemented.

Rather than adopt the Interagency Wildlife Committee Report as agency policy, the Oregon State Office of BLM issued, in 1980, supplemental policy and procedures to BLM Manual 6740—Wetland-Riparian Area Protection and Management.[3] This supplement provides very specific direction to BLM district managers for the inventory and management of riparian areas. For example, the policy states, with regard to degraded riparian systems: "areas that are not currently classified as riparian habitats but have the potential for producing significant amounts of riparian vegetation should be considered for restoration; e.g., former wet meadows or marshes."

A preliminary judgement, at least, can be made of BLM's implementation of this supplemental policy as grazing management plans have been completed for several BLM districts in Oregon. In general, definitions of riparian areas are narrow, inventory is less than adequate (in one instance riparian areas were restricted to those adjacent to perennial streams and springs), evaluation procedures are not uniform, and management direction provides for protection or enhancement of a very small percentage of the total riparian area within the district (see Lakeview, Ironside, or Drewsey District Grazing Environmental Impact Statement[4]).

---

[3] Memorandum No. 8243, February 22, 1980. From the Oregon State Director, USDI Bureau of Land Management, to District Managers, Portland, Oregon.

[4] Lakeside grazing environmental impact statement, Portoand, Ore., 1981. Ironside grazing environmental impact statement, Portland, Ore., 1980. Drewsey grazing environmental impact statement, Portland, Ore., 1979.

Full implementation of both the BLM and FS riparian area management policies has been and will continue to be hampered by a number of factors, including the following.

1. Lack of an adequate inventory--neither BLM nor FS has a complete inventory on the lands they manage. The time constraints imposed by each agency's land-management planning process have forced both to make management decisions without full area inventories or inventories of resources in the riparian areas. This problem has been compounded by the absence of a common definition of riparian areas.

2. Lack of funding--neither BLM nor FS has funds adequate to restore or protect riparian areas. This has forced the agencies to pick and choose specific riparian areas for protection rather than to implement broad policies for the management and enhancement of all areas.

3. Pressure from other uses--as in other states, riparian areas in Oregon are subject to use pressures from livestock grazing, timber cutting, road construction, rock and gravel quarries, and recreational development. The most significant of these use pressures is from livestock grazing. Evidence of this is seen in the management of Malheur National Wildlife Refuge in southeastern Oregon. Established in 1908, primarily because of its value to migratory waterfowl, the area has been the focus of unabated controversy over cattle grazing. In 1948, 50,000 Mallards were counted in the refuge; in the early 1970s the number was 2,000. Again, in the early 1970s for two consecutive years, 230 nesting pairs of Sandhill Crane produced only two young. Destruction of habitat and increased predation stemming from overgrazing by cattle have been cited as the principal cause of the Mallard population decline and lack of Sandhill Crane nesting success. Since the early 1970s, cattle allotments have been reduced. The Mallard population now numbers close to 14,000, and the cranes succeeded in hatching 46 young in 1980. Nevertheless, this is an example of the kind of pressures land managers face in Oregon when determining the highest and best use of public riparian areas.

An unfortunate attitude was encountered among public land managers and land-use planners in interviews. Many of these professionals regarded the issue of riparian area management as unduly polarized and subject to ready compromise. Their attitude was generally expressed: "The environmentalists want to lock up these areas, the Cattlemen's Association wants to ravage them--we'll come down somewhere in the middle with 'multiple use' for some and 'single use' for others." This attitude, while making the planner's job easier ("I know I'm doing the right thing when nobody is happy with the decision") ignores the wide range of possibilities for creative management and education to meet many or all resource demands within the planning unit (e.g., seasonal grazing after full recovery in certain riparian zones). Most public land managers

in Oregon recognize the multiple benefits of healthy riparian zones, and most know what management techniques will protect or enhance riparian areas. Broad-based implementation of these techniques is the missing element.

Pilot Projects

The several experimental efforts to rehabilitate riparian areas on eastern Oregon rangelands (both public and private lands) are noteworthy examples of riparian area enhancement in Oregon. There, cooperative efforts have been conducted among state and federal agencies, private landowners, and other concerned organizations such as the Northwest Steelheaders. In these 10 or more pilot projects the level of stream corridor recovery has been phenomenal. The vegetative extremes between grazed and ungrazed stream reaches provide a vivid contrast. Adjacent landowners have removed livestock from the stream corridor after noting the revegetation of streambanks in the livestock exclosure and the corresponding increase in streambank stability.

The success of these experimental efforts provided much of the impetus for Senate Bill 397. The question arose: if these efforts have been so dramatically successful, why is there not more rehabilitation of riparian areas? The resistance of landowners to regulatory restrictions of commodity production on their lands without some form of compensation, the cost to landowners, the small return on their investment, the lack of incentives, and the perception of landowners that "things had always been that way" were all cited as factors. SB 397 was specifically designed to counterbalance these factors and provide constructive solutions to the problems of cost and lack of incentives. The bill emphasized enhancement, avoided the spectre of "bureaucratic regulation" by being voluntary, provided tax incentives directly to the person performing the work, and focused on the local nature, significance and solution to the problem. The remainder of this paper is devoted to the content of SB 397 and its legislative enactment.

SENATE BILL 397

Establishment of new government programs, particularly new programs based on tax incentives, is no easy task in years of revenue shortage. The mood in the Oregon Statehouse during the 1981 legislative session was far from festive as conservatives and liberals alike were forced to slash agency budgets and scrape for every penny. Yet, on August 1 the Legislative Assembly established a new program for riparian area protection, a program based on a property tax exemption and income tax credit.

What gave SB 397 the edge this session when everything from weatherization tax credits to farm deferrals came under attack? A broad base of support, a strong grass-roots network, the voluntary nature of the program, and a slide show that convinced even the most skeptical were a few of the elements that made SB 397 a winner.

The Legislation

SB 397 contains two mechanisms to encourage the maintenance or rehabilitation of privately owned riparian areas:

1. it provides an _ad valorem_ property tax exemption for riparian lands that are protected or enhanced; and

2. it grants a 25% personal or corporate income tax credit for costs incurred in fish habitat improvement projects (anything, for example, from spawning gravel enhancement or pool construction to streamside fencing).

Both programs are voluntary. The legislation makes no provision for public access to exempted properties, nor does it exclude all uses from the riparian area.

The programs are administered by the ODFW, the state agency responsible for fish and wildlife management. ODFW responsibilites, as spelled out in SB 397, and the responsiblities of the landowner and the local taxing authority, in this case the county assessor, are outlined below.

As defined in the legislation, designated riparian land includes "the beds of streams, the adjacent vegetative communities and the land thereunder, which are predominantly influenced by their association with water." Over the next year ODFW is required to develop standards and criteria for the designation of riparian areas. It must also develop a list of approved restoration practices which, when implemented, would result in the recovery of degraded riparian areas.

A landowner desiring a property tax exemption under the SB 397 program must first make an application to the county assessor. The application must describe the land for which the exemption is requested and the current use of the land. Once the county assessor notifies ODFW of an application, the ODFW field staff will make an on-site survey of the property and negotiate a signed management agreement with the landowner. The management agreement specifies allowed uses of the riparian area as well as the boundaries and size of the exempted property. No property may be exempted under the SB 397 program unless the activities specified in the management agreement are in compliance with ODFW standards and guidelines.

The ODFW must notify the county assessor and the applicant of its approval or disapproval of an application. If approved, the county assessor notes on the assessment roll that the land is exempt from taxation.

In addition to outlining this procedure, SB 397 sets up a penalty for withdrawal from the program in the form of a required payment of up to five times the amount of taxes due on the exempted property during the most recent tax year (the amount to be determined by the number of years the land was held in the program). The act authorizes assessors to request and receive land-use reports from owners of exempted lands. An assessor may also request ODFW to determine whether lands continue to qualify for the tax exemption, if there is reason to believe the management agreement has been violated.

Administration of the income tax credit portion of SB 397 follows a similar procedure. Over the next year, ODFW must develop rules and procedures for the tax credit program, specifying the criteria to be used to evaluate fish habitat improvement projects and the standards for project approval. The ODFW is required to make both a pre-project and a project-completion certification for each project.

Any resident individual is allowed a 25% income tax credit for funds expended on fish habitat improvement projects provided:

1. he/she is the person who actually expended the funds for construction or installation of the project, and

2. the project was not required by existing state or federal statute.

To receive the tax credit, an individual must apply for and receive a pre-project and project-completion certification. The pre-project application must include a description of the proposed project and its expected benefits, a drawing of the project and an estimate of project costs. After project completion, ODFW inspects the project and issues a final certification of the project costs, which can be no more than 10% in excess of the amount approved in the preliminary certification.

Enactment of SB 397

Passage of the two tax incentive programs reflected in SB 397 was a complex process which involved much compromise and negotiation. The issues raised by legislators were many; the bill went through three sets of comprehensive amendments before its final passage. The bill was heard by three committees—the Agriculture and Natural Resources and Revenue committees in the Senate, and the House Revenue Committee. Different versions of the bill were passed by the House and Senate and, ultimately, the bill had to go to a conference committee where a compromise, different than either of the two passed versions, was negotiated. This version passed both the House and Senate on the last day of the legislative session.

Revenue Impact

Chief among the concerns expressed by legislators was the impact of SB 397 on state revenues. Even those legislators most supportive of measures to protect the environment hesitated to support a bill that contained tax-exemption and tax-credit provisions. Two things were done to alleviate legislators' concerns: 1) SB 397 was amended to minimize its impact on revenue; and 2) an accurate assessment of the projected property tax revenue shift was made.

The point was continually made that the tax exemption portion of SB 397 was "a shift, not a gift," that is, those taxes foregone because of granted exemptions would be made up through slightly higher taxes on other lands within each taxing district. To minimize the property tax shift, limits were placed on the amount and types of riparian areas eligible for the property tax exemption. These limits are listed below.

1. Lands eligible must be designated forest- or farmlands (including rangelands) outside of adopted urban growth boundaries. This type of limitation was possible because of the comprehensive, statewide land-use planning and zoning process mentioned earlier.

2. Lands exempted can be no more than 33 m. (100 ft.) from the line of non-aquatic vegetation.

3. No more than 160 km. (100 mi.) of streambank can be exempted each year in any one county. Oregon has 36 counties, for a total limit of 5,760 km. (3,600 mi.) of newly exempted streambank each year.

Once these limitations were established, an accurate assessment of the maximum total property tax shift had to be made. Based on geography and land use, eight representative counties were selected. Supporters of the bill visited each county planning and assessor's office to obtain up-to-date land-use and tax lot maps of the county. Ten lots each in the forest and farm land-use zones were selected. Each lot contained or abutted a free-flowing stream.

Data were then compiled on each lot. These included: description, size, tax rate, lot valuation, current tax, and stream footage. These data were used to compute the riparian area valuation together with tax and tax rate, such that an average riparian area tax rate could be computed for each land-use category in each county. An overall average rate was determined and applied to the 28 other counties to give a total maximum tax shift under SB 397.

Based on an estimated 40-ft. average width of exempted properties, the total tax shift in Oregon, if the program is fully implemented, will be $215,000 statewide in 1983 (less than $6,000 per county) and $450,000 in 1984. This low figure went far to alleviate legislators' concerns. The true test of the methodology came when the bill came before a former tax assessor, now a legislator, in the House Revenue Committee. It held up under his scrutiny and won his support for the legislation, even though he hadn't voted for one other bill providing a tax break the entire session!

Resolving legislative concerns regarding the tax credit portion of SB 397 was somewhat easier. A limit was set on the total dollar amount of projects eligible annually for preliminary certification.

In addition to these limitations, tax credits and tax exemptions under SB 397 cannot be granted until 1983. This gives ODFW time to develop program guidelines and procedures, and, more important to legislators, it means no fiscal impact during this budget biennium.

A Small Investment With a Big Return

"Vote Yes on SB 397—A Small Investment With a Big Return" was the slogan when the bill went to the Senate floor for a vote on final passage. Supporting literature read: "Would you believe one mile of dry eroding gulch in Oregon can be transformed into a stable meadowland with year-round streamflow for less than $1,500?" Emphasis was placed on how little SB 397 would cost and the value of the benefits it would provide—from increased salmon and trout production, to bank stabilization, to increased late-season flows. Then the cost of providing these same benefits through alternate means—such as rock revetments, dams for water storage, fish hatcheries, and water treatment plants—was emphasized. The data provided to the committees and individual legislators covered subjects from the number of wildlife species found in a healthy riparian area, to the rate of silt deposition in healthy riparian zones during periods of peak spring runoff, to the value of the sport and commercial fishery in Oregon.

The message was: SB 397 is the most cost-effective means of providing all these benefits with a minimum of both regulation and public expenditure.

The Broad Base of Support

SB 397 was introduced at the request of the Oregon Chapter, American Fisheries Society (AFS). Even if AFS members could have convinced legislators on their own of the dollar-wise nature of SB 397, its passage would not have occurred without a broad base of supporters actively working for passage of the bill. The bill was designed to attract a wide spectrum of support. Its voluntary nature appealed to landowners who have repeatedly called for more incentives and less regulation. The bill also meshed well with existing state and federal efforts in Oregon, such as the ODFW Salmon, Trout Enhancement Program which works with volunteers to increase fish production through, for example, stream habitat improvement or egg-box installation.

For these and other reasons, farmers and ranchers, sport and commercial fishermen, members of the timber industry, hunters and wildlife enthusiasts, state agency representatives, and fish and wildlife biologists wrote or called their legislators in support of SB 397 and came to Oregon's state capitol to testify at hearings on the bill. This kind of support made it possible for a leading liberal Democrat from Portland to sign with a conservative Republican from eastern Oregon as chief sponsors of the legislation. This broad base kept the legislation from being stereotyped as one to which a legislator's response would be an automatic yes or no. Moreover, the bill did not become trading stock in the political marketplace and, instead, had to be judged on its own merits.

The Slide Program

A separate section of this paper is devoted to one very special, pivotal element of SB 397's legislative campaign: the slide program. The program was simple; it utilized two projectors and was narrated in person. It varied in length from five to 20 minutes. It was shown in semilit rooms and rooms where legislators had to crane their necks to see the screen. Committee staff people hated the idea of a slide program-- it was a struggle sometimes to set it up. But in every case it was well worth the struggle, for if any one element of the legislative campaign can be singled out as that which won the day, it was the slide show.

Professionals sometimes fail to realize just how foreign the word "riparian" sounds to a lay person. Many legislators, who are insurance salespersons, schoolboard members, or realtors during the off session, have never heard of riparian areas. "Is that something like artesian?" "You mean those bushes along the stream are good for something?" The slide program convinced legislators that riparian areas were indeed important, that their values were not some nebulous silver-lining pulled from the sky by a feverish biologist.

The slide program documented two areas in eastern Oregon where riparian rehabilitation has taken place. It began with a "before" slide, then traced the phenomenal regrowth of vegetation that occurred in the years after fencing to exclude livestock grazing. The program showed the eroded gulch filling in, the shoreline stabilizing, and year-round streamflow being restored. It showed the transformation of a dry, hot ditch to a cool stream shaded by lush, green trees in a period of five years. One slide sequence is shown in figure 1. After viewing the slide show, legislators knew what SB 397's purpose was, and they voted for its passage. The visual element of the legislative campaign was simple, inexpensive, and indispensible.

CONCLUSION

This paper has touched upon many of the existing methods of inventory and protection of riparian areas in Oregon. It has dealt in depth with SB 397--recently enacted legislation which provides incentives for rehabilitation or maintenance of privately owned riparian land. Results from implementation of SB 397 remain to be seen. Many compromises were made during the course of the bill's enactment. In particular, strict limitations were placed on the bill's application in order to minimize its fiscal impact. However, supporters of the legislation believe that those riparian areas in Oregon most in need of protection are in the farm- and forestlands eligible for the tax exemption program. SB 397 is an innovative approach to riparian area protection, an approach that supporters feel will work in Oregon and could work well in other states. The programs have already sparked a great deal of interest among landowners. Once implementation begins and results are produced, they will spark more.

LITERATURE CITED

Oregon/Washington Interagency Wildlife Committee, Riparian Habitat Subcommittee. 1979. Managing riparian ecosystems (zones) for fish and wildlife in eastern Oregon and eastern Washington. Oregon/Washington Interagency Wildlife Committee, Portland, Ore.

Thomas, J.W. (tech. ed.). 1979. Wildlife habitats in managed forests: The Blue Mountains of Oregon and Washington. USDA Forest Service Agriculture Handbook No. 553, Pacific Nortrhwest Forest and Range Experiment Station, Portland, Ore. 512 p.

Thomas, J.W., C. Maser, and J. Rodiek. 1980. Wildlife habitats in managed rangelands: The Great Basin of southeastern Oregon. USDA Forest Service, Pacific Northwest Forest and Range Experimental Station, Portland, Ore.

a. 1974.

b. 1975.

c. 1976.

d. 1978.

Figure 1.--This sequence of photos shows the dramatic recovery of a section of Fifteen-mile Creek, Wasco County, Oregon, following fencing to exclude livestock. Photos were taken from the same location in (from left to right) 1974, 1975, 1976, and 1978. Slide sequences similar to this one were used to convince legislators of the merits of SB 397.

MORTALITY AND GROWTH OF COTTONWOOD ON DREDGE-SPOIL[1]

Bertin W. Anderson, John Disano, Donald L. Brooks,
and Robert D. Ohmart[2]

Abstract.--Efforts to reintroduce cottonwood (Populus
fremontii) trees can be expected to be highly successful
at minimal costs. Trees grew 3-5 m. annually and survival
approached 100% when planting was accompanied by tillage to
a depth of 3 m. in sandy soil. Irrigation for five months
during the year of planting was adequate for maximum growth
and survival.

INTRODUCTION

Cottonwood (Populus fremontii) trees
were formerly a dominant riparian species along
the lower Colorado River (Ohmart et al.
1977). Their demise has paralleled construction
of major dams along the river and the encroachment of salt cedar (Tamarix chinensis). Dam
construction brought an end to the annual
flooding which was necessary to enrich and
moisten the soil in which cottonwood seeds could
germinate. The annual floods also flushed out
litter; incidence of fires has increased with
litter accumulation. Hot fires kill cottonwood
but not salt cedar. The latter species therefore
benefits from hot fires. Cottonwood seed germination has been reduced and hot fires have killed
many of the mature trees. Cessation of floods
combined with dredging has lowered the water
table; mature trees which once thrived with high
water tables and flooding are now growing over
layers of fine soil, left "perched" high and dry
as the water table has receded.

In January 1979 we began planting Fremont
cottonwood and other species of native riparian
trees (Anderson and Ohmart 1981) on a 30-ha.
dredge-spoil site. The site is located next to
the Colorado River about 8 km. southeast of Palo
Verde, Imperial County, California. One objective was to learn as much as possible about the
growth of cottonwoods under as wide a variety of

environmental conditions as logistically possible
on the 30-ha. plot. Another objective was to
determine the economic feasibility of reintroducing cottonwoods along the Colorado River.

METHODS

A total of 607 native Fremont cottonwood
tree cuttings were started in a nursery. Cutting
lengths were about 0.3 m. and diameters were
about 1.3 cm. All propagation materials came
from trees growing locally to assure the greatest
preadaptation to the planting site. Rooted cuttings were planted on the site beginning in late
January and extending through February 1979. At
planting the trees consisted of one or two shoots
about 0.6 m. tall and not over 1.3 cm. in diameter. All young trees were given about 85 gm.
of time-release fertilizer at the time of
planting.

Tillage

Tillage was accomplished by augering holes
to various depths to destroy the soil profile.
Holes 20 cm. in diameter augered to 1.2 m. were
provided for 125 young trees; an additional 340
holes 30 cm. in diameter were augered 3 m. deep.
As controls, 142 trees were planted without any
deep tillage. Holes 3 m. deep and 5 cm. in diameter were dug for these trees just prior to the
second growing season. Deep tillage facilitates
root and water penetration to the water table.
The water table was 3-4 m. beneath the soil
surface.

Irrigation

All trees were supplied with 121 l. of water
each day for a minimum of 150 days. Water was
then discontinued for 30 trees; every 15 days
thereafter water was terminated for 30 more trees
until November 1980, at which time irrigation
ceased. In March 1980 we randomly selected 161
trees which we watered for an additional eight
months.

[1] Paper presented at the California
Riparian Systems Conference. [University of
California, Davis, September 17-19, 1981].

[2] Bertin W. Anderson is Faculty Research
Associate, Center for Environmental Studies,
Arizona State University, Tempe, Ariz. John
Disano is Research Biologist, Center for Environ-
mental Studies, Arizona State University, Tempe,
Ariz. Donald L. Brooks is Field Biologist,
Center for Environmental Studies, Arizona State
University, Tempe, Ariz. Robert D. Ohmart is
Associate Director, Center for Environmental
Studies, Arizona State University, Tempe, Ariz.

Soil Type

The soil varied from sand to sandy loam to a depth of 3 m. to 3.7 m. with narrow clay layers at 0.9 m. and 1.5 m. below the surface. One hundred fifty-three trees were planted in the heavier soils, and the remainder were planted in sandy soil.

Competition From Other Plants

Shortly after drip irrigation began, Bermuda grass (Cynodon dactylon), Russian thistle (Salsola iberica), and smotherweed (Bassia hyssopifolia) germinated at various planting sites (almost exclusively in the areas with heavier soils). The potential for competition from other vegetation thus became an unanticipated additional variable.

Measurements

Trees were measured in May, late August, and late November 1979; each period included about 90 days of growth. The next measurements were taken in June 1980, after about 210 days of growth. Final measurements were made about 90 days later in October 1980. Measurements included the height of the tree from ground to tip. Crown measurements were the average of the north-south and east-west diameters. An index to total biomass was calculated as:

$$\text{Biomass Index} = (0.5 \text{ crown})^2 (\text{height})(1.047)$$

Analytical Methods

The mean growth for trees with varying deep tillage was compared using a two-tailed z-test. Interrelationships between variables were determined with Pearson product-moment correlations. The respective and collective contributions of environmental effects on growth were assessed with stepwise multiple linear regression analysis. In all cases, the accepted level of statistical significance was $P \leq 0.05$.

Sample sizes of trees grown under the various tillage depths, irrigation periods, soil types, and degrees of competition are presented in table 1.

RESULTS

Intercorrelations Between Growth Variables

All growth variables were highly intercorrelated (table 2). For this reason we present graphic and tabular material for height data only. Mention of other variables is included only where it is particularly significant or facilitates interpretation. Approximations for the other growth variables can be estimated from the equations in table 2. During the 630 days, over two growing seasons, the trees grew at an average rate of more than 0.007 m. per day (fig. 1). The fastest growth rate occurred during GP3 (August-October 1979), when the trees grew an average of 0.014 m. per day. The slowest growth

Table 1.--Number of Fremont cottonwood trees planted under various experimental conditions. A = absent, P = present, N = number of trees.

Depth of tillage (m.)	Other vegetation	Days of irrigation	N
0	A	150	5
0	A	165	4
0	A	180	8
0	A	195	6
0	A	210	2
0	A	225	6
0	A	240	18
0	A	480	3
0	P	150	1
0	P	165	1
0	P	180	1
0	P	195	7
1.2	A	150	1
1.2	A	165	2
1.2	A	180	1
1.2	A	195	2
1.2	A	210	1
1.2	A	240	24
1.2	P	150	6
1.2	P	165	9
1.2	P	180	5
1.2	P	195	1
1.2	P	210	3
1.2	P	225	4
1.2	P	240	67
3	A	150	16
3	A	165	15
3	A	180	16
3	A	195	16
3	A	210	21
3	A	225	14
3	A	240	177
3	A	480	60
3	P	225	1
3	P	240	3
3*	A	195	2
3*	A	480	79
		Total	607

*Tillage to 3 m. provided at beginning of second growing season.

Table 2.--Intercorrelation of growth variables for Fremont cottonwood trees planted on dredge-spoil. Correlations (r^2) are for the last growth period (GP).

Regression equation	r^2
-21.6 + 8.88 height = Biomass Index	0.804
-0.43 + 0.84 height = Crown Diameter	0.940
-17.3 + 10.62 Crown Diameter = Biomass Index	0.866

rate occurred during the 90 days immediately after planting; the next slowest growth rate was during GP4 (October 1979-July 1980). This was expected, since these periods included the winter

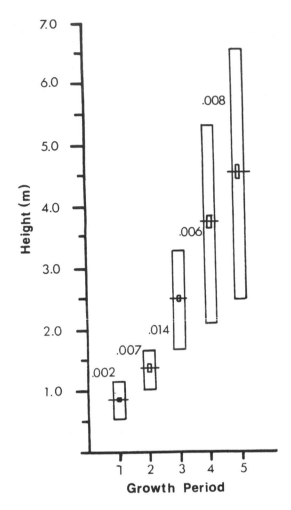

Figure 1.--Mean heights of Fremont cottonwood
trees planted on dredge-spoil. Mean growth
in m./growing period (GP) indicated by
three-digit numbers (1 m. = 3.28 ft.); horizontal line represents the mean; large
rectangle, one standard deviation; small
rectangle, two standard errors of the mean.
The measurements for the growing periods
were May, August, and October 1979, and July
and October 1980 for GP 1-5, respectively.

months when trees were dormant. While height of
trees from GP1 through GP5 increased about 600%,
biomass index increased by more than 1600% in the
same period. Estimates of growth are conservative relative to the maximum possible growth
rates, because some combinations of tillage and
irrigation proved to be greater stimulators of
growth than other combinations.

Effect of Environmental Variables on Growth

Extent of deep tillage was the overwhelmingly most important environmental variable
tested (table 3). Effect of deep tillage, although significantly correlated with growth in
GP1 and GP2, did not really become apparent until
GP3. This is reasonable because the effect of
breaking up the soil profile to a depth of 3 m.

does not become important until tree roots begin
to penetrate more deeply, a function of growth
and age. None of the other environmental variables explained more than 3% of the variance.

Collectively, the environmental variables
had little effect until GP3, when they accounted
for 49% of the variance in tree growth. By GP5,
the environmental variables accounted for 67%.
The rest of the variance is presumably due to
error introduced with measuring.

Effect of Deep Tillage on Growth

The dramatic effect of tillage to 1.2 m. and
3 m. is shown in figure 2. With no soil tillage,
the variance (4.41) is greater than with tillage
to 1.2 m. (2.07) or 3 m. (1.44). Although trees
initially planted without deep tillage, but which
received deep tillage at the beginning of the
second growing season, did not attain a significantly greater height than the controls, the
variance (0.49) was far less (all trees were
growing) than for those without augered holes
(some trees were growing and some were not). The
effect of deep tillage (fig. 3) demonstrates that
trees with tillage to 3 m. began to grow much
faster during GP3 than did the remainder. During
GP3 trees with tillage to 1.2 m. quickly exceeded
the height of those with no augered holes but
still did not grow as rapidly as those with tillage to 3 m. The biomass index at the end of GP5
was 32.3, 4.5, 1.2, and 0.9 for trees with tillage to 3 m., 1.2 m., 3 m. one year after planting, and no tillage, respectively. Those tilled
a year after planting almost immediately began to
grow faster than those with no tillage.

Effect of Deep Tillage on Survival

Effect of deep tillage on survival through
GP5 (table 4) was as dramatic as for growth.
With no tillage, 43% of the trees died. With
tillage to 1.2 m., mortality decreased to 12%;
there was no mortality of trees with deep tillage. Even among trees for which tillage to 3 m.
was delayed until a year after planting, none
died. Thus for 420 trees with tillage to 3 m.,
survival was 100%.

Table 2.--Correlation of environmental variables
with growth of Fremont cottonwood trees
planted on dredge-spoil. Tillage = depth
(m.) of tillage.

Growth period	First variable to enter analysis	R^2	P<	Total R^2 for all variables	P<
1	tillage	0.076	0.0001	0.093	0.0001
2	tillage	0.060	0.0015	0.066	0.0001
3	tillage	0.451	0.0001	0.487	0.0001
4	tillage	0.602	0.0001	0.602	0.0001
5	tillage	0.638	0.0001	0.669	0.0001

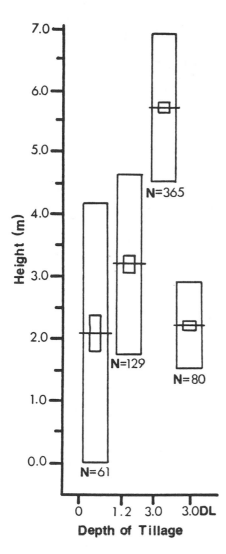

Figure 2.--Mean height after two growing seasons of Fremont cottonwood trees with tillage to various depths planted on dredge-spoil. Abbreviations and symbols as in figure 1. DL = tillage to 3 m. provided at beginning of second year.

Effect of Irrigation on Growth

Irrigating for different periods of time had little effect on growth (table 5). Trees with tillage to 3 m. that were watered for 165 days were significantly taller than those watered for 150 days. However, it is unlikely that this observation was biologically meaningful because none of the other irrigation periods produced trees of significantly greater height than those which were irrigated for the minimum amount of time.

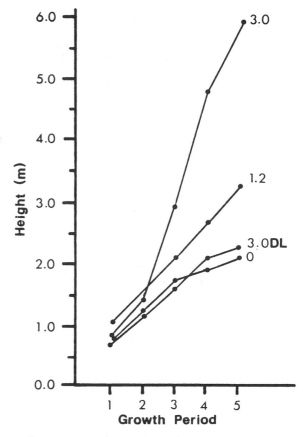

Figure 3.--Mean height for five growing periods with tillage to various depths, for Fremont cottonwood trees planted on dredge-spoil. The first three growing periods are for 1979 and the last two for 1980. Abbreviations and symbols as in figures 1 and 2.

Effect of Irrigation on Survival

For trees with tillage to 3 m., survival was not affected by length of irrigation period. When competition from other plants was a potential problem, however, there was significantly less mortality when trees with tillage to 1.2 m. received water for 240 days compared to those that received water for 159 days (table 4). This is the only evidence we have that irrigation in excess of the minimum 150-day period may significantly contribute to the survival of cottonwoods.

Deep tillage promoted growth and survival of cottonwood trees. Although deep tillage is an added initial expense, benefits are realized in terms of increased growth rates, survival, and reduced costs associated with prolonged irrigation. Faster growth rates are reflected in more rapid use of the area by wildlife. Use of irrigation minimizes water wastage. By learning precisely the minimum water requirements for the kind of growth desired, the full efficiency of drip irrigation can be realized. Data from table 5 indicate a 7.4% increase in mean height when trees were watered for 480 days. This amounts to 3 acre-feet (AF) per 40 ha. of trees. But by sacrificing the 7.4% of growth and irrigating for

Table 4.—Association of Fremont cottonwood tree mortality with environmental variables. GP = growth period: GP2 = June-July 1979; GP3 = August-October 1979; GP4 = November 1979-June 1980; GP5 = July-October 1980. Numbers in parentheses for GP's are the percent of the total mortality for each tillage depth; numbers in parentheses after total are the percent of the grand total mortality.

Depth of tillage (m)	Percent with grass	Days of irri- gation	N	Mortality					P*
				GP2	GP3	GP4	GP5	Total	
0	16	207	61	0	0	20(77)	6(13)	26(42.6)	
1.2	0	207	31	2(50)	2(50)	0	0	4(12.9)	<0.001
1.2	100	159	28	0	1(12.5)	7(87.5)	0	8(28.6)	NS
1.2	100	240	67	0	0	1(33.3)	2(66.7)	3(4.5)	<0.0001
3	1	240	339	0	0	0	0	0	<0.0001
3**	0	480	81	0	0	0	0	0	<0.0001
x̄ or Total 2.3	17.8	263	607	2(5)	3(7)	28(68)	8(20)	41(6.8)	

    * Probability that the difference in mortality between those trees with tillage and those with no tillage is due to chance.
    ** No hole the first year; a hole 3 m. deep and 5 cm. in diameter dug at beginning of second year.

Table 5.—Effect of length of irrigation time on growth of Fremont cottonwood trees planted on dredge-spoil. N = number of trees, SD = standard deviation.

Depth of tillage (m.)	Days of irrigation	N	Mean height (m.)	SD	P*
1.2	189	7	3.92	0.57	
1.2	240	24	3.27	1.61	NS
3	150	16	5.67	0.96	
3	165	15	6.32	0.61	NS
3	180	16	5.72	0.67	NS
3	195	16	5.89	1.01	NS
3	210	21	5.75	1.17	NS
3	225	14	5.71	0.76	NS
3	240	177	5.97	0.98	NS
3	480	60	6.09	0.76	NS

    * Probability that the difference in growth between those trees with shortest irrigation time and trees with longer periods of irrigation for a given tillage depth is due to chance. NS = nonsignificant.

only 150 days, the water requirements would be slightly less than 0.8 AF per year--a savings of 52,995,600 l. per 40 ha. In addition, maintenance and labor costs would be reduced. Use of light, portable irrigation systems would permit growing double the number of trees in the same time. This, of course, more than offsets any slight gain in productivity realized by irrigating for a longer period of time.

However, full irrigation efficiency can be realized only when we learn precisely the minimum amount of time irrigation is needed. Our field work, which spanned only 480 days after planting (excluding the dormancy period extending roughly from November 1979 through February 1980), was not long enough (150 days). By the time we realized that the shortest irrigation period in our experimental design still provided more than enough water for 100% survival, it was too late to plant more trees and water them for less time. We know that five months of irrigation is probably longer than necessary, but we do not know by how much. When we designed the study it seemed inconceivable that trees would survive with only five months of irrigation during one year. Every day that can be cut from the five months of irrigation means reduced water consumption and labor requirements, i.e., the total cost per acre of revegetating, will be reduced. A one-month reduction in irrigation time will reduce post-planting costs by 20%; a two-month reduction would cut costs by 40%.

Increased variance in growth among trees with no deep tillage is to be expected because in some places where trees were planted the soil was not as layered or compacted as in other places. Trees may thrive in such places even without deep tillage. In some places, even though soil layering may prevent roots from penetrating to the water table, the soil does not dry out to the depth to which the roots penetrate and the source of water is free of salts, so trees may thrive. Such conditions do occur on the dredge-spoil site. In some places, where the soil is layered at 1.5 m. or 1.8 m., the overlying layer is sand.

By backhoeing a hole along the side of trees that had no deep tillage, we were able to determine that their root systems were highly branched, penetrating the soil to a depth of only 1.2-1.8 m. The salt content of the soil was very low (<100 ppm). The overlying dredge-spoil, probably rich in nutrients, loses litle water through capillary action, contrary to capillary losses in heavier soil. The only source of water is rainfall, which contains no salts. Since the surrounding area is sand with low salt content, there is no runoff to carry salt into the roots. In heavier soils containing more salt, it is possible that irrigation would be required for more than five months. Until experimentation can be fully carried out on these points, we would not recommend extensive planting of Fremont cottonwoods anywhere except in sandy, relatively salt-free areas. We know that 121 l. of water per tree for five months is probably more than adequate.

PLANTING RECOMMENDATIONS

The following recommendations are based on conclusions drawn from planting under the range of conditions encountered on the dredge-spoil site. Our recommendations are conservative because they reflect a relatively narrow range of experimental conditions. We strongly discourage efforts to plant Fremont cottonwoods on a scale larger than about 2 ha. if any of the conditions included in the recommendations are not met. There is a high probability that failure to adhere to this recommendation would result in failure to establish trees and would be a waste of time and money. Money for revegetation projects outside the constraints listed below should be saved and put into a carefully planned and monitored experimental project. Such a project should be well funded, with adequate guarantees that funding will be available for completion of the project. This type of study would probably lead to a list of recommendations more liberal than those presented here. Our recommendations are based on facts that we learned from our experimental project.

1. Trees should be started from cuttings taken from local native stock. These cuttings should be allowed to take root and develop in a greenhouse for two or three months.

2. Planting should be done when the trees are small; the tallest shoot should not exceed 1 m.

3. The soil should be analyzed prior to planting. At this time we recommend planting only in sandy, relatively salt-free (<1200 ppm) soil.

4. The water table should be no more than 4.6 m. from the surface and the salt concentration in the ground water should not exceed 1200 ppm.

5. Deep tillage is of critical importance. Holes at least 20 cm. in diameter should be augered 3 m. deep or to the water table.

6. As a safeguard against salt damage to newly planted saplings, all holes should be leached 48 consecutive hours prior to planting.

7. Planting should be done only in January, February, and March.

8. Each tree should be supplied with 85 gm. of time-release fertilizer at planting.

9. Irrigation should begin no later than March and should extend for at least 150 consecutive days at about 114 l. per day. (This is not to be construed as meaning five days per week for 30 weeks. Such an interpretation could prove disastrous.)

10. Planting should not be done if Bermuda grass or a significant growth of any other vegetation is present.

11. Trees should be weeded regularly throughout the first summer to keep competition from other vegetation to near zero and to keep salt cedar from becoming established.

12. Rabbits, cotton rats, deer, burros, cattle, beavers, and perhaps other mammals will eat tree parts. At the first signs of damage, prompt action must be taken to protect the trees. Chicken wire placed around the saplings is adequate to keep small mammalian species from damaging the young trees. If weeds, such as Russian thistle, are present, the wind will blow them against the trees. On the dredge-spoil site, Russian thistle provided cover for cotton rats which ate the bark on the trees. We controlled the problem by piling the Russian thistle and burning it.

13. Trees with leaves, girdled by mammals, should be chopped down immediately. The tree will sprout from the root stock.

ACKNOWLEDGMENTS

We wish to thank Jeannie Anderson, Susan M. Cook, Jane R. Durham, Dr. Julie K. Meents, and Cindy D. Zisner for editorial assistance. Marcelett Ector and Cindy D. Zisner typed the numerous drafts of the manuscript. Rodney H. Ohmart prepared the illustrations. Kurt Webb carried out the computer work. We are grateful to Dr. F. Aljibury, Les Ede, and Jule Meyer from the University of California Agricultural Extension Service, Riverside, California, and to Wayne Flanagan and the late Charles Morris, District Conservationists, USDA Soil Conservation Service, for their advice and cooperation. We thank Louise Disano for assistance with data collection and handling. The work was supported by the USDI Bureau of Reclamation and the USDI Fish and Wildlife Service Contract No. 7-07-30-V0009.

LITERATURE CITED

Anderson, B.W., and R.D. Ohart. 1981. Revegetation efforts along the lower Colorado River. Final report, in preparation, to USDI Bureau of Reclamation, Boulder City, Nevada.

Ohmart, R.D., W.O. Deason, and C. Burke. 1977. A riparian case history: the Colorado River. p. 35-47. In: R.R. Johnson and D.A. Jones (ed.). Importance, preservation and management of riparian habitat: a symposium. [Tuscon, Ariz., July 9, 1977]. USDA Forest Service GTR-RM-43. 217 p. Rocky Mountain Forest and Range Experiment Station, Fort Collins, Colo.

RIPARIAN RESTORATION EFFORTS ASSOCIATED WITH

STRUCTURALLY MODIFIED FLOOD CONTROL CHANNELS[1]

Bernard H. Goldner[2]

Abstract.--For the past five years, the Santa Clara Valley Water District has revegetated flood control channels to benefit wildlife and provide aesthetic improvement. Drought-tolerant ornamental and native riparian species have been planted along the channel banks and levees with mixed results. The most important determinants of successful establishment are a fixed irrigation system and a well-managed weed abatement program. Densely planted, liner-size rooted cuttings irrigated by overhead sprinklers can reduce both installation and maintenance costs.

BACKGROUND

The semi-arid Santa Clara Valley is bounded on both sides by rolling hills and rugged mountainous uplands, the Santa Cruz Mountains to the west and the Diablo Range to the east. Drainage from both mountain ranges eventually empties into San Francisco Bay to the north and Monterey Bay to the south. The relatively flat valley floor is laced with a network of hundreds of miles of intermittently flowing streams originating in the surrounding foothills and mountain ranges. Because all the larger stream systems have been intercepted below their headwaters by water conservation dams, summer streamflows are enhanced by release of water from the reservoirs for groundwater recharge.

Many miles of riparian woodland streams are still in a relatively pristine or minimally disturbed condition, their banks lined with overstory vegetation of such trees as California sycamore (Platanus racemosa), Fremont cottonwood (Populus Fremontii), interior live oak (Quercus wislizenii), valley oak (Quercus lobata), box elder (Acer negundo var. californicum), coast redwood (Sequoia sempervirens), big-leaf maple (Acer macrophyllum), alders (Alnus spp.), California black walnut (Juglans hindsii), California bay (Umbellularia californica), and California buckeye (Aesculus californica). The understory of the streambanks consists of vines, shrubs, and herbaceous groundcover, including California blackberry (Rubus vitifolius),

poison oak (Rhus diversiloba), wild grape (Vitis californica), blue elderberry (Sambucus caerulea), coyote brush (Baccharis pilularis), toyon (Heteromeles arbutifolia), California wild rose (Rosa californica), willows (Salix spp.), and mulefat (Baccharis viminea).

The bottom freshwater marsh community of perennial streams includes cattails (Typha spp.), rushes (Scirpus spp.), sedges (Carex spp.), knotweed (Polygonum spp.), and watercress (Rorippa nasturtium-aquatica). The more disturbed streams are characterized by a mix of native, naturalized, and introduced species such as eucalyptus (Eucalyptus spp.), giant reed (Arundo donax), various orchard trees, and ornamentals escaped from yards.

In contrast, the freshwater habitat is modified by tidal influence in the baylands surrounding San Francisco Bay, where many of these streams support a distinctive levee or "eyebrow" salt-marsh plant community. Within a vertical distance of a few feet, the entire range of plants normally found in salt marshes typically occurs. Lowermost there is a thin line of cord grass (Spartina foliosa), backed by a few inches of pickleweed (Salicornia virginica), and finally a succession of salt grass (Distichlis spicata), brass buttons (Cotula cornopifolia), and mostly salt-tolerant, non-native upland grasses, herbs and shrubs.

The streams support a rich and varied assemblage of wildlife, some of which are wholly dependent upon the riparian environment for survival. Several of the larger streams still provide spawning grounds for the anadromous steelhead rainbow trout (Salmo gairdnerii). The streams also support a variety of native fish species.

---

[1]Paper presented at the California Riparian Systems Conference. [University of California, Davis, September 17-19, 1981].

[2]Bernard H. Goldner is Environmental Specialist, Santa Clara Valley Water District, San Jose, California.

On the heavily urbanized valley floor of north Santa Clara County and even in the rural/agricultural south county, streams provide virtually the only habitat remaining for wildlife; their stately trees also provide a greenbelt of visual relief from the surrounding urban setting. The Santa Clara County General Plan recognizes these stream systems as a unique scenic, wildlife, and recreational resource and includes policies designed to encourage their preservation. A number of the more scenic streams have been developed jointly as linear park chains with the cooperation of the county, cities, and Santa Clara Valley Water District (SCVWD); many more are designated in the General Plan as future park chains.

Of the nearly 1,130 km. (700 mi.) of streams within the jurisdiction of the SCVWD (which includes most of the streams in the county), only about one-half can carry the 1% (100-year) flood-flow. In the event of flooding of this magnitude countywide, over 32,800 ha. (81,000 ac.) of land would be flooded, with damages estimated in excess of $300 million. Consequently, as the flood management agency in the county, the SCVWD must continually plan and construct various types of flood damage reduction projects, many of which require that the hydraulic capacity of streams be substantially increased by excavation, i.e., widening the banks and deepening the channel bottom (channelization). Channelization results in major structural modification of natural streams by transforming them into flood control channels which include: 1) trapazoidal excavated earth channels; 2) concrete-lined channels; 3) trapezoidal earth channels lined with rock, concrete sack, or gabion (rock-filled wire baskets) riprap for slope stability; and 4) floodways enclosed with levees or floodwalls with or without channel bed excavation. Maintenance roads are located at the top of the channel bank or depressed near the bottom. Where there is sufficient land available, there is the option of excavating the stream from one bank to preserve high-quality riparian vegetation, or constructing a by-pass channel to avoid disturbing the stream. In most developed areas, however, the choice narrows down to removing adjacent homes and buildings or to channelizing the stream.

The types of modifications described above result in impacts on riparian vegetation ranging from slight disturbance to permanent removal with commensurate effects on dependent faunal communities and aesthetic values. While some channelized streams revegetate by natural succession, the extent and rate at which reestablishment occurs is unpredictable and depends upon a number of little-understood variables, including whether the channel slopes are concrete-lined or riprapped, the availability of upstream seed sources, soil temperature and moisture, streamflow regimen and velocities, steepness of the side slopes, fertility and compactness of fill material, and intensity of vegetation and sediment removal in the channel to maintain the constructed flow capacity.

HISTORY OF THE SANTA CLARA VALLEY WATER DISTRICT REVEGETATION PROGRAM

Early Projects

Partly as a response to the California Environmental Quality Act (CEQA) of 1970[3] and partly due to public concern, the Board of Directors of the SCVWD adopted a resolution in 1974 that set policy for landscaping of district projects.[4] Prior to 1974, landscaping associated with flood control channels was limited to screening highly visible street crossings. The resolution redefined and broadly expanded the purpose of the landscaping program to include the reestablishment of riparian vegetation and enhancement of aesthetic values for all new projects. The resolution also specified that the landscaping material be of a low-maintenance type, adapted to the climate and soil conditions of the flood control channel, and not require irrigation after a short establishment period. Thus, the plants selected would have to be drought-tolerant species, but not necesssarily California natives.

Following these guidelines, landscape projects were installed in 1976 in conjunction with four flood control projects. One of the landscape projects was installed along a rock-lined excavated earth channel located in a residential area (Randol Creek). A second was located along a partly excavated channel enclosed with levees and a floodwall (San Tomas Aquino Creek). The third was along an earth channel designated as a linear park chain, featuring a trail system and other recreational amenities (Los Gatos Creek). The fourth was located along the banks of a gabion-lined channel located next to an expressway (Guadalupe River).

Although the setting and type of channel varied, these projects shared a number of design features which are discussed below.

Plant Selection

Because of the dual purpose of enhancing aesthetic values of the flood control channels and providing vegetation of value to wildlife, the plants consisted of drought-tolerant species dominated by California natives, but including several introduced species, such as eucalyptus. Not all of the natives were riparian woodland species found in Santa Clara County, but they were considered to be compatible with the flood control channel environment. (Detailed information about the growth requirements and habits of drought-tolerant and California native plants can be found in Stiles [1975] and California Department of Water Resources [1979].)

The sizes of the plants used were 2-in. peat-pot liners and 1-, 5-, and 15-gal. container stock selected from commercial nurseries. The

---

[3] PRC Section 21000-21151.
[4] Resolution 74-40.

park chain project consisted almost exclusively of liners. A seed mix of annual flowers, perennials, and permanent groundcover species was applied to the bare soil between the planting basins by hydroseeding.

Native trees used included: big-leaf maple, box elder, California buckeye, white alder (Alnus rhombifolia), Pacific madrone (Arbutus menziesii), California sycamore, Oregon ash (Fraxinus latifolia), coast live oak (Quercus agrifolia), California black oak, valley oak, red willow (Salix laevigata), yellow willow (Salix lasiandra), blue elderberry, California bay, coast redwood, tanbark oak (Lithocarpus densiflora), Monterey pine (Pinus radiata), and mountain dogwood (Cornus nuttallii).

Native shrubs and vines used included: Parry manzanita (Arctostaphylos manzanita), coyote brush, toyon, scrub oak (Quercus dumosa), California coffeeberry (Rhamnus californica), sugar bush (Rhus ovata), California wild rose, purple sage (Salvia leucophylla), California huckleberry (Vaccinium ovatum), California wild grape, blue blossom (Ceanothus thyrsiflorus), flannel bush (Fremontodendron californicum), California blackberry, virgin's bowers (Clematis lasiantha), and California barberry (Berberis dictyota).

Not all of the plant species listed above were used for each project.

Design Concept

Because flood control channels are expected to maintain their designed flow capacity and remain hydraulically efficient, woody vegetative growth on the channel bottom which could lead to log jams, obstructions, or snags during high flows is removed. Such requirements dictate where plantings can remain and the types and number of plants that can be used. Flood control projects, if they are to be revegetated, should ideally be constructed with sufficient extra capacity to allow for the growth of a certain amount of mature trees and shrubs within the channel. Groundcover and smaller shrubs are acceptable along the lower portions of the channel side slopes, but trees must be placed near the top of the slopes or along the top of the banks or levees. Plants must be located so as to avoid interference with vehicle and equipment access along the maintenance roads.

These constraints preclude any attempt to simulate a terraced plant community characteristic of natural riparian ecosystems. Because the cross section of the channel bed is drastically altered by channelization, the land/water interface is affected. This in turn alters the complex relationships between the various vegetative zones that exist within riparian plant communities. Most of the plantings must be located along the upper channel slopes and the tops of

banks and levees, far above the saturated water zone. This not only modifies the natural conditions of indigenous riparian species, but increases their reliance on a source of supplemental water during the establishment period. However, in spite of these design limitations, revegetated channels can provide an "edge effect" attractive to wildlife and provide cover, food, and roosting and nesting opportunities for wildlife. Moreover, revegetation, whether with riparian species or not, enhances the aesthetic values of flood control channels and provides erosion protection for the banks.

Irrigation

Largely as an economy measure, none of the projects had a permanent irrigation system. The plants were truck-watered during the dry season with the aid of large watering basins constructed around each plant. The hydroseeded areas were not irrigated.

Maintenance

During the establishment period, maintenance activities were carried out either by SCVWD personnel, another public agency, or a landscape contractor. The program consisted of watering, basin repair, tree stake repair, pest and weed control, erosion repair, trash removal, replacement of diseased or dead plants, and protective fence repair. As expected, watering and weeding required the most labor.

Evaluation

Unfortunately, planting all four projects in 1976, at the beginning of one of the severest two-year droughts in California history, coupled with the lack of a permanent irrigation system, proved to be disastrous to the survival of the plants. A survey of survivors taken three years after installation showed that losses for three of the projects were about 75% on the average. The park chain project which relied mostly on liners suffered an almost total loss. The hydroseed mix either did not germinate or germinated poorly with only scattered California poppies, lupine, and a few daisies evident among the multitude of weeds.

It was apparent that the truck-watering regimen was not efficient or timely enough to compensate for the lack of adequate rainfall; competition from the profuse growth of weeds for water and nutrients contributed to the demise of the badly stressed plants. Disease organisms and insects probably took their toll as well. Aggravating the situation were complaints from public officials and citizens who viewed the projects as expensive weed patches with no aesthetic benefit to the community. Criticism was especially strong regarding the park chain project where the objective of revegetation was perceived by the public as primarily aesthetic improvement of the channel.

The most important lesson learned from the design of these projects was that natural rainfall cannot be relied upon to establish plantings. A fixed irrigation system is mandatory to ensure a high rate of survival until the plants are well established. The irrigation system can then be abandoned or possibly salvaged for use in other projects.

Intermediate Projects

The next two flood control channel revegetation projects were not installed until 1979, three years later. One project was installed along a realigned excavated earth channel with depressed maintenance roads. It was located in a commercial-industrial park; the primary objective of the project was replacing a riparian habitat lost just upstream due to channelization of the stream (Calabazas Creek). Due to its high visibility, aesthetic enhancement of the channel was an additional goal. California native riparian species were used, together with several native upland species. Trees (1- and 5-gal. size) consisted of California buckeye, Oregon ash, knobcone pine (Pinus attenuata), coast live oak, and California black oak. Shrubs (1-gal. size) and groundcover (liner size) were California sage brush (Artemisia californica), quail bush (Atriplex lentiformis), blue blossom, California buckwheat (Eriogonum fasciculatum), toyon, California coffeeberry, and dwarf coyote brush (Baccharis pilularis 'Twin Peaks').

The second project was installed along an excavated earth channel enclosed with levees in a developing area (Berryessa Creek). The purpose of revegetation in this case was not primarily to restore wildlife habitat, since the creek had low habitat value to begin with due to previous channelization. Rather, the purpose was to provide an aesthetic asset to the community. A citizen's committee assisted in developing the design concept of the landscape project. The plants selected were largely drought-tolerant species and included several California natives. Trees (5- and 10-gal. size) consisted of red horsechestnut (Aesculus carnea), Bailey acacia (Acacia baileyana), Sydney golden wattle (Acacia longifolia), coast redwood, California sycamore, allepo pine (Pinus halepensis), holly oak (Quercus ilex), and coast live oak. Shrubs (1-gal. size) were bearberry (Arctostaphylos uva-ursi), Point Reyes ceanothus (Ceanothus gloriosus), crimson spot rockrose (Cistus ladanifer), toyon, English lavender (Lavandula angustifolia), Pacific wax myrtle (Myrica californica), glossy privet (Ligustrum lucidum), California fuchsia (Zauschneria californica), Italian buckthorn (Rhamnus alaternus), and Japanese barberry (Berberis thunbergii).

Both projects included a drip irrigation system with an emitter head placed under the mulch of each watering basin. All irrigation pipe was buried.

Evaluation

In terms of plant survival, growth rate, and community acceptance, both projects are considered quite successful. Losses have amounted to only about 10-15%, with vandalism and predation by rabbits and squirrels responsible for most of the losses. Although the projects are fenced to discourage public entry, youngsters have repeatedly climbed or cut the chain link gates and fences to break tree stakes and destroy emitter heads and irrigation lines.

These projects have been well maintained, so that weed growth has not detracted from the appearance or overgrown the planted materials. Weed abatement was accomplished by hand labor and application of herbicides. Although the level of maintenance was higher than the earlier projects, the success achieved undoubtedly can be attributed to the advantages afforded by a fixed irrigation system. Figure 1 shows the projects two years after planting.

Figure 1.—Revegetated flood control channels two years after planting. Top: reach of Calabazas Creek. Note pedestrians on depressed maintenance road. Bottom: reach of Berryessa Creek. Note wide spacing of plantings on levees and freshwater marsh vegetation on channel bottom.

Recent Project

The drastic reduction in revenue engendered by the passage of Proposition 13 in 1978 required a reevaluation of all SCVWD programs, to determine where expenditures could be reduced. The landscape program evaluation led to the development of a new policy, formalized in a resolution adopted by the board of directors in 1979.[5] In contrast to the 1974 policy, which stated that all flood control projects would be landscaped for both aesthetic enhancement and environmental improvement, the new policy did not recommend revegetation if the impacts of channelization on existing habitat are minimal, or if it is likely that natural reestablishment of vegetation will occur in a reasonably short period. Under this policy, the loss of mature riparian woodland, for example, would be mitigated, but a freshwater marsh community dominated by willows and cattails would probably not be revegetated, due to their rapid regrowth. Planting primarily for aesthetic purposes would be carried out only if a flood control project resulted in significant visual impacts unacceptable to the community.

Thus, the emphasis of the program has shifted in focus to mitigation of substantial adverse impacts, in conformance with CEQA. The term "revegetation" is more descriptive of the current program than "landscaping" since the goal is to reestablish riparian habitat primarily for the benefit of wildlife. Obviously, as the plants mature, aesthetic benefits will accrue, but the public must now be educated to understand that the unique quality of streams is their natural appearance and that a park-like setting is not appropriate in most cases. Weeds will be allowed to coexist in spite of their unsightly appearance, as long as they do not gain a competitive advantage over the plantings or result in a fire hazard.

Between March and May, 1981, a revegetation project was installed along an excavated earth channel partially lined with gabions and located adjacent to the SCVWD administration building (Guadalupe River). The project was the first to follow the current revegetation policy; it also presented an opportunity to test some new concepts designed to reduce the costs of both installation and maintenance.

Plant Selection

The plants chosen were predominantly California natives associated with riparian communities in Santa Clara County and included three cultivated upland species (cultivars). Trees consisted of California buckeye, interior live oak, valley oak, and California black walnut. Shrubs and groundcover included California wild rose, blue elderberry, coyote brush, and the cultivars—dwarf coyote brush (Baccharis pilularis 'Pigeon Point'), ceanothus 'Frosty Blue,' and ceanothus 'Concha.' The plants were obtained by contract with the Saratoga Horticultural Foundation, which specializes in growing drought-tolerant and California native plants. This was done to ensure the availability of the large number of healthy plants that were required for

the project. The shrubs were started from stem cuttings; the tree species were collected as seeds. Except for the cultivars, cuttings and seeds were taken in the wild. The objective was to plant vigorously growing rooted cuttings (liner-size) of local genetic stock, rather than nursery-grown specimens that might be less adapted to the harsh conditions of the planting site. An additional advantage of liners and seeds over larger container stock is their considerably lower cost.

Unfortunately, due to a delay in completing the plans, the cuttings outgrew their containers and had to be repotted into 1-gal. size containers. All the buckeye and most of the valley oak seed sprouted and therefore were potted and planted as liners. Dwarf coyote brush was repropagated and also planted as liners. Instead of a more desirable early winter planting, planting occurred in late spring. Nevertheless, the plants were still vigorous and not rootbound, as might be the case for more mature 1-gal. size nursery stock.

Design Concept

Earlier irrigated projects spaced the plantings 3-6 m. (10-20 ft.) apart and depended upon a relatively high level of maintenance to control weeds in the unplanted areas. In this project, plants and seeds were installed on 1.5-m. (5-ft.) centers arranged in a random pattern to achieve a natural effect. Although such high density required a relatively larger number of plants, it was expected that they would rapidly fill in the voids, overgrow and suppress the weeds, and thereby reduce short- and long-term maintenance costs.

Low-growing shrubs were also placed in the occasional planting voids left between the gabions protecting the lower channel slopes.

Preparation of Planting Site

To reduce early weed competition and subsequent maintenance effort, the site was prepared first by mechanical weed removal. This was followed several months later by application of a contact herbicide to new weed growth, prior to planting. All planting holes were backfilled with a mixture of native soil, soil amendments, and a slow-release fertilizer.

Irrigation System

Because there were about 2,500 planting basins, it was far less expensive to install an overhead impact irrigation system rather than a drip irrigation system. The irrigation pipe, as in previous projects, was buried.

Maintenance

The installation contractor was awarded a 12-month contract to provide all maintenance necessary for survival of the plants. As an incentive to ensure good-quality work, the con-

---

[5] Resolution 79-76.

tractor was made responsible for a 70% minimum survival rate of all plants and germinated seeds. If after the 12-month period losses exceed 30%, the contractor must replace the plants in kind or pay a penalty of $4 per planting hole. This arrangement allowed the watering schedule and level of weed control to be left to the discretion of the contractor. A further incentive is the possibility of being awarded a follow-on 12-month maintenance contract. After a two-year period, the plants should be established, and only minimal maintenance should be required of the SCVWD maintenance crew which will assume responsibility for the project. The irrigation system will be left in place for a few additional years in case supplemental summer watering is required.

Evaluation

Although only three months have passed, judging by survival rate and vigor of the plants, the project is off to an excellent start. About 90% of the plantings have survived and most species have added 0.6-0.9 m. (2-3 ft.) of new growth. The liner-sized plants have grown especially vigorously and have proved their value. The blue elderberry has grown so profusely that it threatens to overgrow and suppress several slower-growing species. The one disappointment is the poor rate of seed germination. Only a few of the black walnut and interior live oak seeds have sprouted. It is probable that the seeds lost viability due to the long delay that occurred between gathering and planting. Replanting with fresh seed is being considered since this cost-saving technique deserves a fair trial.

Weed control has been accomplished by a combination of manual labor and use of a pre-emergence herbicide, Trifluralin, and a post-emergence herbicide, Diquat, applied between the planting basins. Because the irrigation system has worked effectively and the plants have grown rapidly, weed competition has been minimal even though the weeds, at times, have grown abundantly both in the voids between the plants and within the planting basins.

Resident ground squirrel and rabbit populations, feared at first to be a threat to the new plants, have not proven to be deterimental. A squirrel control program begun before installation was discontinued.

As might be expected, the project has suffered several incidences of vandalism, evidently from youngsters who frequent the area for various activities. The sprinkler heads, which are located at the top of the banks next to a maintenance road, have been damaged or stolen on several occasions. Brightly colored plastic markers placed in the seed planting basins promptly disappeared, but colored wooden stakes securely driven into the basins as replacements have remained in place. Unlike several previous projects, the plants themselves have escaped significant vandalism, possibly because their small size and the

large number of weeds makes them difficult for the untrained eye to identify.

Figure 2 shows the project three months after planting. Although the project is still in the very early stages of development, the indications are encouraging that this design concept will prove to be the most successful approach to revegetation attempted thus far.

Figure 2.--Revegetated reach of Guadalupe River flood control project three months after planting. Note plantings on slopes above depressed maintenance road.

SUMMARY

1. Even with the constraints that the design, operation, and maintenance of flood control channels place on revegetation with riparian woodland species, it is feasible to benefit wildlife and provide aesthetic improvement.

2. To ensure that most of the plantings survive through the establishment period, a fixed irrigation system must be provided. To reduce installation and maintenance costs, an overhead sprinkler system will provide effective irrigation, although exposed sprinkler heads may be more prone to vandalism than drip emitters hidden within the planting basins.

3. It is practical to establish plants from rooted cuttings (liners) rather than larger container stock as a significant cost-saving measure. Placing smaller-size plants at high densities, in contrast to widely spaced larger plants, appears to be a good method of reducing weed competition and rapidly providing cover for wildlife. An additional advantage is the vigorous growth of smaller plants.

4. The detrimental effects of weed competition during the establishment period can be minimized by installation of an effective irrigation system, as well as a weed management program com-

bining hand labor and the judicious use of selected herbicides.

5. Vandalism has been a serious and costly problem in all projects and is likely to increase. Fencing, posting with warning signs, and similar passive methods are generally ineffective. Some design suggestions to reduce vandalism are: 1) placement of sprinkler heads in less accessible areas, such as midway down the steep side slopes instead of at the top of the banks; 2) using liners or 1-gal. size trees that do not require staking; and 3) involving the surrounding neighborhood in the planning, implementation, and monitoring of revegetation projects.

ACKNOWLEDGMENTS

I am indebted to Steve Renfro, former District Landscape Architect, and Winthrop Stiles III, former District Assistant Environmental Specialist, who pioneered and contributed so much effort to the landscape and revegetation program of the SCVWD. They have left behind a living legacy.

Special thanks to Barrie Coate and the staff of the Saratoga Horticultural Foundation who provided invaluable advice about the cultivation of native plants.

LITERATURE CITED

California Department of Water Resources. 1979. Plants for California landscapes. Bulletin 209, California Department of Water Resources, Sacramento.

Stiles, W.A. 1975. A landscaping guide to native and naturalized plants for Santa Clara County. Prepared for the Santa Clara Valley Water District, San Jose, Calif.

STREAMBANK STABILIZATION TECHNIQUES USED BY
THE SOIL CONSERVATION SERVICE IN CALIFORNIA[1]

David W. Patterson, Clarence U. Finch,
and Glenn I. Wilcox[2]

Abstract.--Streambank protection techniques used by the
USDA Soil Conservation Service (SCS) have evolved over many
years of experience. Structural and vegetative protection
measures are generally used in combination. SCS designs are
based on national standards promoting protection measures
which are sound from environmental, economic, and engineering perspectives. The general principles for planning
streambank protection measures are presented as well as
brief descriptions and typical costs of several structural
and vegetative methods.

INTRODUCTION

Streambank protection techniques are technical conservation practices requiring the combined
planning efforts of engineers, biologists, plant
material specialists, and agronomists. The USDA
Soil Conservation Service (SCS) provides technical assistance through local resource conservation districts for the planning and design of
streambank stabilization systems on America's
smaller streams and rivers. It is fair to say
that the techniques SCS now uses for protecting
and revegetating streambanks have evolved over
many years of trial, error, and success.

The response of resource agencies and the
public to streambank protection projects has
often been emotional. However, those who have
closely evaluated SCS work are gaining confidence
in our approaches to streambank protection. In
several instances representatives from the USDI
Fish and Wildlife Service (FWS) have used SCS
methods for placement of natural rock riprap and
reestablishment of vegetation as examples for
streambank protection methods.

SCS is aware of its responsibility to design
conservation practices which are sound from both
environmental and engineering perspectives. Toward that end SCS has developed designs and techniques which serve as standards for streambank
protection work.

---

[1]Paper presented at the California Riparian Systems Conference. [University of California, Davis, September 17-19, 1981].

[2]David W. Patterson is Biologist, Red
Bluff, California; Clarence U. Finch is Agrono-
mist, Fresno, California; Glenn I. Wilcox is
Biologist, Salinas, California; all are with the
USDA Soil Conservation Service.

RESOURCES WORTH PROTECTING

Throughout this conference a great deal of
time and effort will be rightfully expended extol-
ling the many inherent values of riparian
systems. However, often overlooked, taken for
granted, or at least underemphasized, is the
value of soils and other substrates within riparian systems. Soils and other substrates located
within and adjacent to water bodies and waterways
provide the substrates on which riparian vegetation grows. In addition, deep alluvial soils of
high agricultural value are often found within
and immediately adjacent to riparian zones.

The erosion of riparian soils and substrates
acts as a double-bitted axe. Erosion within
riparian systems not only permanently removes
productive soils and substrates and associated
vegetation, but also results in a reduction in
downstream water quality (fig. 1). Streambank
erosion and associated stream meander and soil
loss are unacceptable to most private landowners,
especially for owners of high-value specialty
crops such as grapes, as well as in urban areas.
Streambank erosion and meander within private
lands can result in the loss of highly productive
and valuable agricultural soils, loss of or
damage to expensive irrigation systems, levee
failure, loss of real property, desiccation of
meadows, and loss of riparian vegetation (fig.
2). Head cutting (fig. 3) in streams and gullies
is another major source of erosion and sedimentation, leaving scars on the face of the earth that
are difficult and expensive to heal.

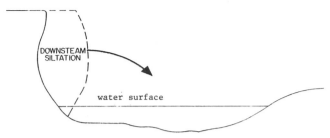

Figure 1.--Streambank erosion results in the loss of streamside soils, substrates, and associated riparian vegetation, which enter the waterway, resulting in siltation and reductions in downstream water quality.

Figure 2.--Active streambank erosion destroys valuable riparian vegetation.

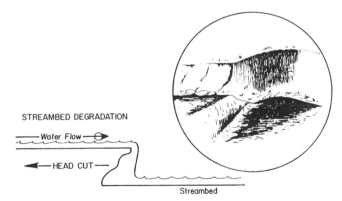

Figure 3.--Head cutting and streambed degradation are major causes of erosion and streambank sloughing in waterways.

SOME GENERAL PRINCIPLES

SCS recognizes and supports the need for proper land-use planning on land areas containing waterways. This is especially important in areas where inadequate planning has allowed urbanization up to the edges of eroding and meandering streams. SCS also encourages the practice of setbacks and appropriate use where agricultural lands contain or are traversed by riparian systems.

Several principles are observed by SCS in the design of streambank protection systems.

Channelization of waterways must be avoided, otherwise upstream repairs may create new problems downstream. As an example, adequate natural meander must remain to dissipate flow energy (fig. 4 and 5). Protection work must be carefully planned to avoid removing or damaging any more vegetation than is absolutely necessary. It is especially important to determine if apparent streambank erosion is actually a symptom of streambank degradation. Streambank protection efforts are doomed to failure if streambed degradation and undermining are creating ever-more critical angles of repose on associated streambanks (fig. 6).

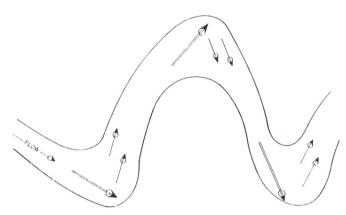

Figure 4.--Stream meanders dissipate flow energy naturally.

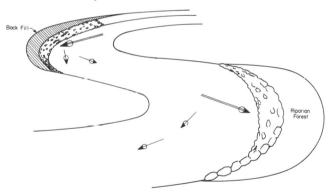

ALTERNATIVE OUTSIDE CURVE TREATMENTS

Figure 5.--Streambank protection measures for outside curves must retain adequate meander for energy dissipation.

The environmental attributes of streambank protection projects must be acceptable in the long-term. Too often people judge the environmental acceptability of projects immediately upon their completion. The streambank shown in figure 7 appears to be aesthetically undesirable, but protection measures were completed just before the photograph was taken. Figure 8 shows the same project five years later. In most cases it is five years before shrub and tree plantings achieve enough growth to reflect the total planning effort put into a typical project. It is important to keep this longer-term time frame in

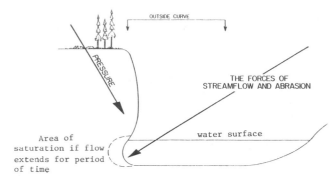

Figure 6.--The forces of streamflow and abrasion combined with streambed degradation and gravity are the key causes of streambank erosion.

Figure 7.--A riprapped outside curve on Anderson Creek, Mendocino County, just after construction was completed.

Figure 8.--The same riprapped outside curve on Anderson Creek, Mendocino County, five growing seasons after construction. Willow and alder are becoming well established. Before the project the streambank was a 3- to 6- m. (10- to 20-ft.) tall 90° cutbank threatening a schoolyard.

mind when commenting on proposed and newly completed projects.

SCS does not recommend the use of either car bodies or concrete slabs for streambank protection. Uncompressed car bodies are unsightly and unsound from an engineering standpoint. Concrete slabs are unsightly, often lack adequate density, and, because of the typical flat configuration of the material, are subject to tumbling in high flows.

SCS and landowners consider opportunities to create or re-create fish habitat. On many projects summer habitats for both game and nongame fish are actually improved over preproject conditions. Large riprap rocks which fall to the stream bottom during construction are generally left where they fall near the toe of the bank. Water working around the instream rock, and between the rock and the armored bank, creates pools which, when combined with reestablished overhanging vegetation, provide quality summer habitat. In comparison, "naturally eroding" 90° cutbanks not only have little to offer, but serve as sources of downstream pollution and sedimentation (fig. 9).

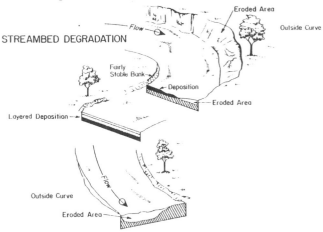

Figure 9.--Streambank erosion is a major factor in the loss of riparian vegetation and substrates, as well as sedimentation and water pollution.

DESIGN AND PLANNING CONSIDERATIONS

During project planning SCS engineers and planners consult SCS biologists and invite input from other agencies including the California Department of Fish and Game (DFG) and FWS. Cooperation during planning and design is now required under formal Channel Modification Guidelines (USDI Fish and Wildlife Service and USDA Forest Service 1978) which were jointly written by SCS and FWS. SCS conducts formal environmental evaluations for all streambank protection projects for which it provides designs. Both DFG and FWS are asked to participate in the evaluation process.

Landowners requesting SCS project designs are required to obtain all necessary permits before starting construction. Streambank protection work is carried out by cooperators during lowest flow periods or in dry streambeds when conditions for construction are best and the potential for downstream pollution is the lowest.

Streambank protection designs are normally limited to armoring outside curves, protecting instream structures, and protecting straighter reaches where loss of streamside resources is unacceptable. All designs must comply with appropriate SCS, state, and national conservation practice standards and specifications.

These design standards and specifications include:
1) channel vegetation;
2) critical area planting;
3) grade stabilization structure;
4) stream channel stabilization;
5) open channel;
6) streambank protection;
7) sediment basin.

Design criteria are also drawn from SCS engineering handbooks, engineering field manual, field office technical guides, and other technical resource material.

STREAMBANK PROTECTION TECHNIQUES

Although most often used in combination, SCS streambank protection techniques can be divided into two types: a) physical protection; and b) vegetative protection.

Physical Protection Techniques

Grade Stabilization

A dam, wall, or drop is used to reestablish or maintain streambed elevation (fig. 10). Maintenance of streambed elevation is necessary in stabilizing streambanks. Environmental considerations in designing grade stabilization measures include choice of construction materials, fish passage, plunge pools, number of structures used and their locations, and incorporation of vegetation.

Rock Riprap

Natural rock of appropriate size, density, and gradation is placed on shaped streambanks and in open-toe trenches. A gravel filter is placed under the rock to prevent erosion of soil material from beneath (fig. 11). Extensively eroded outside curves are generally realigned with enough "bend" left for necessary energy dissipation. Environmental considerations include impacts at sites where rock is obtained; preservation of as much existing streamside vegetation as possible during construction; construction during low-flow or dry stream conditions; preservation or enhancement of fish and wildlife habitat; fencing; and seep trenches. Stabilization of streambed grade may be an integral part of this measure.

Concrete grout may be incorporated where channel alignment problems and/or flow velocities require greater protection from the influence of scouring or high-energy flows. Environmental considerations include the use of vegetation,

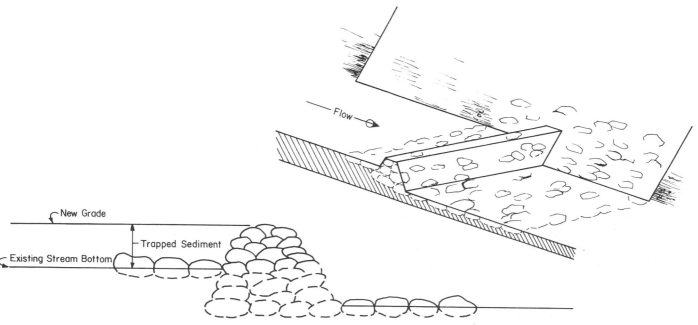

Figure 10.—Grade stabilization structures used to either maintain existing grade or raise streambottom by trapping sediment.

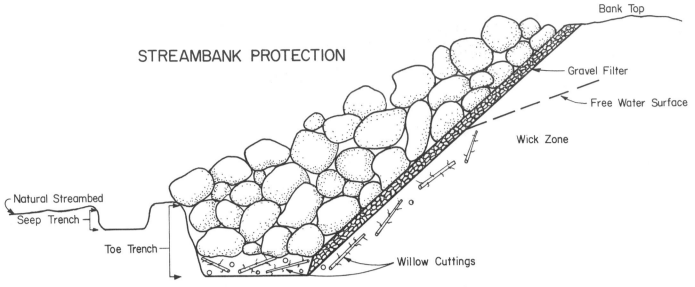

STREAMBANK PROTECTION

Figure 11.--A typical streambank in cross section protected with natural rock over gravel bedding and willow cuttings. The toe trench is used to trap bank seepage and encourage better growth of cuttings and natural vegetation.

visual impacts, aquatic life, and use of colored grout.

Post-and-Wire Revetment

Wire mesh strung on four-inch steel diameter or wooden posts, braced with steel cables along the top and bottom edges of the wire mesh, are used where flow, abrasion, and instream debris conditions will allow. Post-and-wire revetments are commonly used where rock is unavailable or not cost-effective in comparison. Riparian plantings immediately behind wire revetments are an integral part of revetment establishment and maintenance.

Figure 12.--A typical rail-and-cable revetment located on Rancharia Creek in Mendocino county.

Rail-and-Cable Revetment

Rail-and-cable revetments (fig. 12) are similar in general appearance and function to post-and-wire revetments but are usually taller and made of heavier material to withstand greater water velocity, more abrasion, and debris problems. The revetment is covered with wire mesh with cables strung along the bottom, middle and top of the revetment. Riparian plantings are important components of rail-and-cable revetments.

Rock-and-Wire Revetment

Rock-and-wire revetments are essentially a well-braced double post-and-wire revetment with rock or very coarse gravel placed between the revetment walls. Riparian plantings are an important component of this type of revetment. Although they are expensive, properly located and constructed rock-and-wire revetments are quite stable as long as the wire withstands abrasion.

Pilot Channels

Pilot channels are dug in streambed material and used to "train" water away from newly treated streambanks, keep water out of construction areas, and increase chances of establishing newly planted vegetation.

Gabion Baskets

Gabion baskets are rectangular, heavy-mesh wire baskets filled with coarse gravel, which are placed and then wired together in series. Gravel size must be large enough to prevent leakage through basket mesh. Abrasion may break the wire mesh, requiring periodic maintenance. Gabions are used where large rock is unavailable or not cost-effective. Plant material, generally in the form of willow cuttings, should be placed under, behind, and within baskets where moisture is adequate for growth.

8. Jacks and Cabled Trees

Past experience has shown these two methods to be less effective than many other methods. Cabled trees may be considered where ample trees are available and cost of other methods is absolutely prohibitive.

Vegetative Protection Techniques

Woody Cuttings

Cuttings are taken from locally adapted and locally growing plants when possible. Species which have been used include willow (<u>Salix</u> spp.), athel (<u>Tamarix aphylla</u>), and tamarisk or salt cedar (<u>Tamarix gallica</u>). Methods and procedures for taking and planting cuttings are provided in construction plans and specifications written for each project. In general, cuttings are laid horizontally in open-toe trenches and on shaped banks, as shown in figure 13, or planted vertically. If natural moisture is inadequate for growth, irrigation must be provided to insure establishment. Vertical plantings should be placed at a minimum depth of 1 m. (3 ft.) with 0.3 m. (1 ft.) of the cutting extending above the ground. The growing tip must extend aboveground. The best results have been obtained by augering holes for cuttings and watering cuttings in by washing soil material in around them. Watering in insures that cuttings are completely surrounded by soil which is devoid of air spaces. Immediate and generous irrigation should be provided at the time of planting. Water jetting can be used to both dig holes and water in plants where adequate water supply and pressure are available and soil texture allows.

Rooted Woody Plants

Rooted woody plantings are made on the bank side of revetments or on levees or streambanks above bank protection materials. Rooted plants can also be placed in planters set in concrete or gunnited rock. Unless natural seepage is adequate, plantings must be irrigated for at least two or three years for establishment. Plant species selection is influenced primarily by site conditions, soils, climate, plant availability, price, and wildlife habitat needs. Mulching is strongly recommended around and between plants. Herbaceous plants can be used in combination with rooted woody plants but should not create competition for the woody plants.

Herbaceous Plants

Perennial and annual grasses and forbs are seeded on sloping banks where mineral soil is exposed and on any disturbed areas on top of banks. Species selection, site preparation, timing, and seeding are all critical elements. If planted in combination with rooted woody plants, herbaceous seedings should be kept several feet away from establishing woody plants to avoid competition for space, moisture, and nutrients.

Mulching

Mulching around woody plants and over seedlings with straw and erosion control blankets

TYPICAL ROCK RIPRAP CROSS SECTION

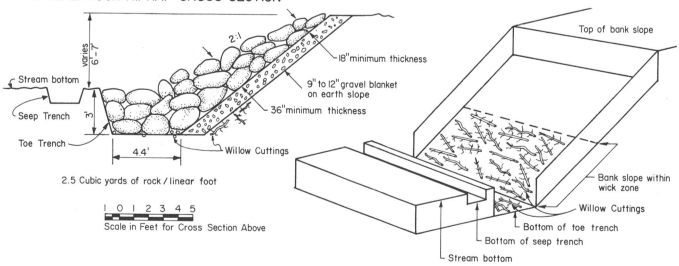

Scale in Feet for Cross Section Above

2.5 Cubic yards of rock / linear foot

<u>PLACING WILLOW CUTTINGS</u>
Willow cuttings will be placed in the toe trench and on the bank slope within the "wick" zone prior to laying gravel blanket or placing rock riprap.

Figure 13.--Placement of willow cuttings on bottom of toe trench and on moist areas (wick zone) of sloped banks.

457

made of jute, fiberglass, wood fiber, and other materials is recommended on steep and erosive streambanks and levees. Straw should not be chopped in lengths shorter than 15 cm. (6 in.) and should be anchored either mechanically or with fiber mulch and a tackifier. Fiber mulch should be wood cellulose fiber containing no germination- or growth-inhibiting properties. Fiber mulch should be hydromulched as a slurry containing tackifier at a rate of 1,500 pounds per acre. Seed can be either mixed with the slurry or the fiber slurry applied over the seeded area.

COSTS

Location, situation, type of contract, contractor, and project size greaty influence the price paid for a particular job. The price ranges of some common streambank protection methods are given below. When used in combination, the costs of each operation or structure type must be added together. Maintenance costs must also be taken into consideration.

Dumped rock (quarry run)--$20.00 or more per foot.

Livestock fence revetment (metal fence posts with braces and hogwire)--$0.40 to $0.60 per foot.

Four-inch by four-inch treated wood fence post-and-wire mesh revetment with braces--$12.00 to $15.00 per foot.

Four-inch double steel pipe, wire, and rock revetment with braces and ties--$15.00 to $30.00 per foot.

Rail-and-cable revetment (9-pound rail and one-inch or larger cable)--$30.00 per foot.

Combination seed, fertilizer, and mulch--$600.00 to 1,000.00 per acre with higher costs for smaller areas.

Planted woody cuttings--a) watered in--$2.00 to $3.00 per cutting; b) jammed in--$0.50 to $1.00 per cutting.

Planting one-year-old rooted woody plants--$2,400.00 to $2,700.00 per acre (includes materials).

Streambank protection projects are expensive in terms of dollars spent. Furthermore, riparian resources provide few direct benefits to private landowners relative to the cost of protecting and maintaining the resource. The conservation of streamside soils must be viewed as a long-term investment for the good of future generations. Values such as natural beauty, fish and wildlife habitat, and water quality enhancement directly benefit the public in both the short and long term. For this reason, the financial participation of the public in riparian conservation programs is strongly encouraged. In the Scott

Valley alone since 1968, over $1 million has been spent protecting streambanks along the Scott River. Approximately 70% of the cost has been provided by cost-shares under the USDA Agricultural Conservation Program (ACP). Much more work and much more cost-sharing are needed on the Scott River and throughout the state and nation.

CONCLUSION

For years SCS seemed to wear, and to some degree deserved, a black hat when it came to "doing its thing" in streams and waterways. Things have changed for a number of reasons. SCS has, through experience, learned some lessons and developed creative and feasible methods of streambank protection and conservation of riparian systems. Figure 14 shows an example of quality streambank protection work utilizing natural rock riprap designed by SCS. After 13 years the project is nearly mature, providing quality habitat. A woman who passes this site every day reported that she could not believe the riverbank had been shaped and riprapped. The SCS standards and specifications and other technical materials are available at local, area, and state SCS offices. Public participation in planning and evaluating streambank protection systems is always invited.

Figure 14.--A fully mature project creating quality terrestrial and aquatic habitat, as well as providing strong visual appeal. It takes time and money.

LITERATURE CITED

USDI Fish and Wildlife Service and USDA Soil Conservation Service. 1978. Channel modification guidelines. 15 p. Limited publication for agency use. Washington, D.C.

ENVIRONMENTAL RESOURCE CONSERVATION:

RIPARIAN SYSTEM ENHANCEMENT THROUGH WATER RECLAMATION[1]

Ronald LaRosa[2]

Abstract.--A proposed project would provide for the establishment of 2,000 native trees over 4 ha. (10 ac.) of floodplain. These public lands would be irrigated with wastewater from a planned water reclamation facility. The irrigation regime would be based on data from ongoing reclamation projects in the San Diego region.

INTRODUCTION

One of the most sensitive environmental resources in San Diego is the riparian or streamside woodland. Comprised of some five representative tree or tall shrub species, this plant community has been adversely affected by land-use development. Even where woodlands have been spared by open space easements or low-density development, environmental impacts include degradation through disturbances, clearing of understory vegetation, and interruption of continuous tree cover necessary for the systems' use as wildlife corridors.

Streamside vegetation occurs in areas subject to over- and/or underground water flows and can be seen in both inland and coastal drainages within the San Diego region. Species such as elderberry, willow and cottonwood (see table 1 for specific names) are common to woodlands occurring in these mesic or moist habitats (Sands 1977). Along the coast, sycamore and coastal oak replace species adapted to the montane climates of higher elevations.

One resource value of a dense woodland growing along a watercourse (intermittent or year-round) is in the habitat afforded various species of animals which live in, among, and under the vegetation. Where surface water is available year-round, an even greater diversity of fauna can be supported in addition to the trees and shrubs which provide food, nesting sites, and roosting cover.

These biological zones are so critical to diverse wildlife populations, for watersheds, and as aesthetic open spaces, that they have been the

Table 1.--Representative riparian woodland species in the San Diego region.

	Common name
Quercus agrifolia	Coast live oak
Platanus racemosa	California sycamore
Populus fremontii	Fremont cottonwood
Heteromeles arbutifolia	Christmasberry (Toyon)
Sambucus mexicana	Elderberry
Salix hindsiana	Sandbar willow

subject of extensive environmental legislation and local ordinances. In the San Diego region, the most effective measure yet developed to conserve these woodlands is the creation of open space easements and other withholding of development rights. To date no major effort has been made to create or enhance riparian woodland by establishing native trees and shrubs which would be irrigated until their root systems could utilize groundwater.

An environmental enhancement plan at the Naval Ocean Systems Center, Point Loma, resulted in the upland (not streamside) planting of 1,000 irrigated trees and shrubs. In addition, the USDI Forest Service in San Diego County annually installs thousands of seedlings without irrigation. However, these are not riparian system restoration efforts, as drought-tolerant species are planted in upland locations.

Water is a requisite for riparian woodland. Whether on or near the surface, soil moisture must be sufficient to carry the trees and shrubs through summer months and seasonal tropical dry winds. However, even with available water, continued intensive grazing by livestock, followed by repeated flooding can eliminate riparian vegetation and prevent recolonization of the woodland species. The trees give way to grasses which are in turn succeeded by weedy plants. In other

[1] Paper presented at the California Riparian Systems Conference. [University of California, Davis, September 17-19, 1981].
[2] Ronald LaRosa is Associate Water Quality Biologist, San Diego County Department of Public Works, San Diego, Calif.

instances, introduced tree species such as <u>Euca-lyptus</u> can out-compete native trees. This combi-nation of factors has led to the loss and degrada-tion of streamside vegetation along most of the Escondido Creek drainage and is particularly evi-dent on county-owned lands in the floodplain east of the San Elijo Lagoon, a regional park and eco-logical reserve (fig. 1).

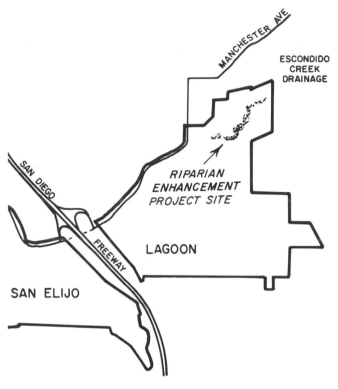

Figure 1.--Vicinity map and proposed project loca-tion, San Elijo Lagoon.

WATER RESOURCES AND RIPARIAN ENHANCEMENT

Although there are a number of drainages in San Diego County which could benefit from year-round reclaimed water flows[3] and a wild area landscape plan, Escondido Creek--one candidate area--will be discussed here for the following reasons.

1. The drainage system has the greatest potential to enhance wildlife habitats within an established public park and ecological reserve.

2. The drainage system could accommodate a woodland landscape without jeopardy from flood-ing.

3. The drainage system could receive surface water from existing and/or proposed wastewater facilities.

----

[3]Reclaimed water is the product of domes-tic wastewater treatment which is suitable for a beneficial/controlled use that would not other-wise occur.

4. The drainage system has extensive areas degraded by exotic vegetation, overgrazing, and erosion/sedimentation.

ENVIRONMENTAL DESIGN

Although this report discusses the environ-mental enhancement of a floodplain through water reuse,[4] the interdisciplinary considerations of water quality planning, landscape architecture, environmental planning, hydrologic engineering, and woodland management are recognized.

The plan for the proposed environmental enhancement project would call for the installa-tion of native shrubs and trees and provide year-round surface water to recreate the components of high-quality riparian systems. Figure 2 shows a conceptual schematic of the riparian woodland, including surface water and area subject to planned inundation.

Environmental design considerations in the enhancement plan include, but are not limited to,

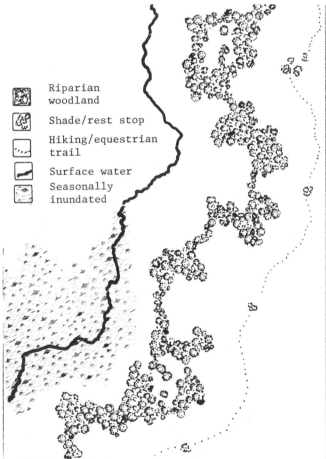

Riparian woodland

Shade/rest stop

Hiking/equestrian trail

Surface water

Seasonally inundated

Figure 2.--Conceptual schematic plan.

----

[4]Water reuse is the term used to describe the application of reclaimed wastewater for irri-gation, groundwater recharge, industrial uses, recreation, or wildlife habitats.

existing wildlife populations and ecological systems, water resources, health and water quality requirements, hydraulics, and fluvial conditions, as well as funding sources for capital expenditures and maintenance/management. The riparian woodland must satisfy specific biological parameters if it is to provide high-quality habitats for diverse wildlife species. In addition, the woodland must incorporate elements of visual resource management in order to have value as aesthetic open space and greenbelt zone. A summary of these design considerations follows.

Wildlife Habitats

A woodland must include trees and shrubs which provide food (nuts, fruit, nectar, insects), nesting sites (hollows, cavities, etc.), and roosting/perching cover (upper- and understory branches/foliage), as shown in figure 3. Vegetation must be sufficiently continuous, broad (deep), and dense to provide wildlife corridors or access routes (fig. 4). Trees and shrubs must be grouped to provide optimum habitat by providing a mixture of irregular edges and random openings in proximity to weedy sites and thickets. And last, plants must be irrigated for at least three growing seasons or until they can survive on groundwater and supplemental rainfall.

Figure 3.--Wildlife habitats provided by upper-story branches and understory cover of shrubs and small trees.

Figure 4.--Wildlife corridor provided by linear vegetative cover.

Visual Resource

Line, form, color, and texture must be provided by plant species; these should include evergreen and deciduous species with erect and procumbent forms, and columnar and round shapes (fig. 5). Groups of trees installed outside of the primary woodland to provide shade for hikers and equestrian riders are designed to encourage use of recreational trails away from sensitive habitats.

Figure 5.--Visual resource criteria include low-growing broad-leaved species, columnar evergreens, and deciduous round-headed trees.

Fluvial and Hydraulic Systems

In addition to planting trees and shrubs, a low dam is proposed to inundate a portion of the floodplain and create a marshland environment for diverse populations of wildlife including migratory and visiting birds, many of which are threatened species (table 2). Most of trees would be installed outside the floodway and further protected by an earthen bank or berm to avoid loss of irrigation systems and plants due to higher-than-normal flows (fig. 6).

Table 2.--Partial list of threatened species inhabiting Escondido Creek.

Rare/Endangered Species (federal and state statutes)	
California Least Tern	
Belding's Savannah Sparrow	

Declining Blue List Species (National Audubon Society)	
Marsh Hawk	Yellow Warbler
Sharp-shinned Hawk	Western Grebe
American Kestrel	Fulvous Duck
Cooper's Hawk	Bewick's Wren
Burrowing Owl	Bell's Vireo

Woodland Management

Water, in addition to nominal flows in Escondido Creek, will be required for the success of the proposed riparian enhancement project for the following reasons.

1. Seasonal runoff is subject to rainfall cycles and soil moisture would be insufficient to support the woodland during growing seasons.

Figure 6.--Landscape profile showing earthen berm to protect plants from high-water flows.

2. Aquatic systems are dependent upon year-round flows for the maintenance of pools and other surface water.

3. Vegetation "weaned" from irrigation would be augmented by the establishment of more plants.

4. The nutrients in wastewater would provide the vigor for vegetation to overcome the handicaps of characteristically poor soils.

WASTEWATER RE-USE

A possible source of water to enhance a riparian system and/or create a riparian woodland habitat is the liquid wastes (sewage) processed by a water pollution control facility (WPCF). In the San Diego region, facilities which process liquid wastes and produce an effluent of sufficient quality to be applied for irrigation, wetland replenishment, industrial make-up water, and other uses are called water reclamation plants. Wastewater can be reused if it meets state and local health and water-quality requirements. In the San Diego region, these regulatory agencies include the California Department of Health Services (DHS), State Water Resources Control Board (SWRCB), and San Diego County Department of Health Services. The fundamental intent of wastewater reclamation requirements is to provide guidelines to establish acceptable levels of constituents (chemical, physical, bacterial and other biological properties) and to prescribe processes which insure reliability, such that the reuse of wastewater for specified purposes does not impose undue risks to public health.

Federal and State Regulations

Laws have been enacted to establish requirements for adequate planning, implementation, and management of water quality control. Relevant portions of both federal and state laws, plans, and policies pertaining to water quality planning and control of wastewater discharges are summarized below.

Federal Water Pollution Control Act

The Federal Water Pollution Control Act: 1) sets forth the national strategy for controlling water pollution, including uniform effluent limitations, and requires states to set ambient water quality standards; 2) establishes various levels of water quality planning; and 3) sets up a National Pollutant Discharge Elimination System permit program.

National Environmental Policy Act of 1969

In general, this law directs the preservation of acceptable environments and the restoration of those that have been degraded.

Porter-Cologne Water Quality Control Act

The basic tenor of the Porter-Cologne Water Quality Control Act was set by a policy stating that the waters of the state shall be protected for use and enjoyment by the people of the state, and that activities and factors which may affect the quality of the waters of the state shall be regulated to attain the highest water quality which is reasonable; it further provides that the statewide program for water quality control can be most effectively administered regionally, within a framework of the SWRCB and the nine Regional Water Quality Control Boards (RWQCB). These agencies were established as the principal state agencies with primary responsibility for water quality control. SWRCB is responsible for formulating and adopting state policy for water quality control, including guidelines for long-range planning of groundwater and surface water and the use of reclaimed water. Each RWQCB must formulate and adopt, for its region, water quality control plans establishing such water quality objectives as in its judgment will ensure the reasonable protection of beneficial uses and the prevention of nuisance.

The Porter-Cologne Act addresses water reclamation and reuse through a policy in which the state has a primary interest in the development of facilities to reclaim water to supplement existing water supplies. Anyone proposing to reclaim or reuse wastewater must file a report with the RWQCB. After consulting with the DHS, the board may prescribe water reclamation requirements for either the individual reclaiming the water or the user, or both.

California Water Code

The California Water Code contains provisions controlling almost every consideration of water and its use.

California Environmental Quality Act of 1970

The California Environmental Quality Act of 1970 (CEQA) requires consultation with and comments from any governmental agency with jurisdiction or special expertise with respect to any environmental impact involved.

WATER RECLAMATION AND RIPARIAN SYSTEMS

A conventional wastewater system collects wastewater in sewers, transports it to a treatment plant, processes it, and then releases it into the ocean or evaporation ponds, or onto land. A reclamation facility instead treats the wastewater to a level suitable for reuse and then conveys it directly to the area of application.

The degree of treatment for reclaimed water depends on the intended use. Regulations covering this are issued by the DHS and are summarized in table 3. Most uses require at least second-level treatment, which is the minimum level required for discharge to surface waters. In addition, reclaimed water often must undergo coagulation and filtration to make it acceptable for many uses.

Although most reclaimed water in California is used to irrigate fodder crops, greenbelts, golf courses, orchards, and vineyards, its use in the creation of woodlands as part of a riparian system is the focus of this discussion.

SWRCB and RWQCB are encouraging reclamation projects which generally improve the beneficial use of water, e.g., those which create a new water supply, preserve recreational and aesthetic resources, or benefit fish and wildlife habitats (California Department of Water Resources 1979). However, reclamation is not universally feasible or practical. Even highly treated wastewater can contain more salts (defined as total dissolved solids [TDS] in milligrams per liter [mg/l] or parts per million [ppm]), nutrients, and other substances than freshwater. Water with high levels (1,000-1,500 mg/l) of dissolved salts or limiting constituents such as boron or heavy metals cannot be used to irrigate most crops. Although many species of riparian trees are salt-tolerant, water management plans for irrigation must consider salt build-up in root zones, changes in groundwater quality, and other impacts of wastewater reuse.

Reclaimed Water Irrigation Regime

Salts in irrigation water that can harm plants are classified as sodium-containing. Although these salts in wastewater can harm plants and be detrimental to the soil, they can also be removed. To prevent buildup in the root zone, enough water must pass through the soil profile to carry away dissolved minerals. The volume necessary to remove these salts--the leaching fraction, usually 5% to 20% of the applied irrigation--is beyond the quantity needed for plant growth. Although the problems of over-irrigation (loss of nutrients, saturated soils) can be alleviated by the additional nutrients in reclaimed water and the adaptability of most riparian species to water-logged soils, excess irrigation can create downstream impacts, in addition to being wasteful and costly (Dunne and Leopold 1978).

San Diego Case Studies

The San Diego County Department of Public Works has undertaken four limited water re-use projects which, among other objectives, provide reclaimed water to irrigate wild landscapes and woodlands. Although the circumstances of vegetative cover, irrigation volumes, and basin requirements differ among the sites, some general conclusions can be drawn.

Irrigation Uniformity.--More wastewater is generated, and therefore available, during summer months when plant growth and evapotranspiration are greatest. However, the problem of uniformly distributing reclaimed water to plants of varying size and water requirements must be overcome in order to avoid runoff (overwatering) or salt accumulation (underwatering).

Application Efficiency.--In San Diego, discharges of wastewater into moving water are not allowed due to regional health and basin plan requirements (Barry 1978). In some instances maximum use of wastewater is an objective; in every case, the irrigation regime has several goals, i.e., to fill the root zone for plant growth; to provide extra water for leaching salts; and to minimize poor distribution.

Table 3.--General water quality guidelines for uses of reclaimed water in California.

Beneficial Use	Criteria/Guidelines
Surface irrigation for orchards and vineyards	Primary plant effluent can be used provided that no fruit is harvested that has come in contact with the irrigation water or ground.
Nursery, golf course, freeway, wild landscape, woodland and landscape impoundment	An adequately disinfected, oxidized wastewater in which, at some location in the treatment process, the median number of coliform organisms does not exceed 23/100 ml. as determined from the bacteriological results of the last seven days for which analyses have been completed.

Salt Management.--Where the protection of groundwater is mandated by health and water quality objectives, irrigation regimes must take into account all sources of infiltration (rainfall, upstream sources, wastewater application) and losses (evaporation, plant transpiration, runoff). The water budget must consider TDS in wastewater, dilution from precipitation, and concentration of salts--in the area of application and downstream--both seasonally and in the long-term (Engineering Science and PRC Tours 1982).

Riparian Woodland Proposal

Project Costs

Expenses associated with the riparian enhancement proposal (table 4) include capital improvements of $82,000 and annual operation and maintenance costs of $18,000. Although conservation projects typically have high operational costs in the short-term, expenses decrease significantly after five years, since plant replacement and major maintenance will have been completed.

Woodland Specifications

The overall design and biological parameters of the riparian woodland have been previously discussed. Specifically, the proposed plan recommends that oak and pine species (see table 1) be

Table 4.--Project costs for riparian enhancement over 4 ha. (10 ac.) of public land.

Project Planning and Design	
Architecture and engineering	$9,500
Project review and environmental report	$3,500
Permits	$2,000
Total	$15,000
Construction	
Soil amendments and irrigation system	$7,500
Plant material	$26,500
Plant and irrigation installation	$33,000
Total	$67,000
Total capital cost	$82,000
Maintenance	
Irrigation system and water	$2,750
Plant material (replacement at average 10%)	$5,900
Labor (project management)	$9,650
Total operation and maintenance cost (first year)	$18,000
Total first-year project cost	$100,000

planted on higher ground in sandy soil, in odd, random groupings of five- and 15-gallon sizes in a ratio of 3:1 respectively. Cottonwoods and sycamores would be planted in both open and dense groupings (at an installation rate of 100 containers per 0.4 ha. [1 ac.]) with a minimum of three-trees width and maximum of 40-trees width in total planting area. Twenty percent of the trees planted should be planted on 1.5-m. (5-ft.) centers to allow crowns to grow into each other (fig. 7). Willows should be installed adjacent to watercourse/surface water. The plan recommends that other shrubs (5-gal. size) be mixed in among edges of tree areas in odd, irregular groupings. Openings in dense plantings would vary from 0.2 to 0.6 ha. (0.5-1.5 ac.).

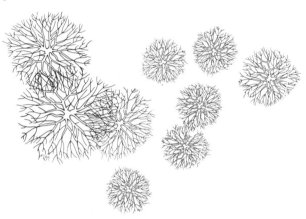

Figure 7.--Landscape specifications showing irregular groupings; plants installed to allow crowns to merge, shrubs mixed with trees.

LITERATURE CITED

Barry, Joseph N. 1978. San Diego City/County water reuse study report. 89 p. Department of Public Works, County of San Diego, San Diego, Calif.

California Department of Water Resources. 1979. Water reclamation: State-of-the-Art. Bulletin 189, California Department of Water Resources, Sacramento. 112. p.

Dunne, T., and L. Leopold. 1978. Water in environmental planning. 819 p. W.H. Freeman and Company, San Francisco, Calif.

Engineering Science and PRC Tours. 1981. Orange and Los Angeles Water reuse study. Issue paper on water quality. p. 7-13. In: Water Quality Workshop. [Orange, California, August 7, 1981]. 137 p. Engineering-Science and PRC Tours, Arcadia, Calif.

Sands, Anne (ed). 1977. Riparian forests in California: their ecology and conservation. Institute of Ecology Pub. 15, University of California, Davis. 122 p.

PLANTING DESIGN INVENTORY TECHNIQUES FOR MODELING

THE RESTORATION OF NATIVE RIPARIAN LANDSCAPES[1]

Kerry J. Dawson[2]

Abstract.--Inventory techniques for assessing vegetative distribution patterns in native riparian communities
are discussed along with their use and applicability in
formulating working drawings for planting design. Such techniques involve a review of historical context and the selection of comparable areas in which to inventory for distribution, community and soil patterns, canopy heights, and elevational transects in relation to streamflow.

INTRODUCTION

As native riparian landscapes are increasingly impacted by flood control and water resources
development projects, the need has grown for
restoration mitigation, not only along existing
streams but also on newly created floodways and
distribution canals. In the past, governmental
reclamation agencies have relied heavily on
planting design techniques dependent on exotic
plant materials to achieve simplistic goals of
erosion control, environmental tolerance (drought
tolerance and/or flooding tolerance, soil tolerance, browsing tolerance, etc.), and aesthetic
improvement. Today, the use of exotic plant materials is still entrenched in riparian projects.
But as more and more managers realize the value
and the increasing rarity of ecological diversity
that native riparian systems offer, it should be
expected that their use will grow.

Cost is more a factor of influence now than
ever before as governmental agencies are increasingly required to adhere strictly to cost:
benefit ratios. The greater the benefits and the
cheaper the cost, the better chance a project has
of proceeding. Native riparian communities are
certain to benefit from this phenomenon in that
the mitigation of habitat loss for endemic
species is a much-needed benefit. In addition,
native riparian species can reduce installation
costs because of their inherent ecological
tolerance, fast-growing character, and
regenerative efficiency, lacking in ornamentals.
Riparian vegetation has evolved under constraints

of erosion and streambed stabilization within
community associations which allow all species to
attain an optimum locale.

Perhaps, though, the largest influence on
riparian design philosophy has been a new attitude among the general populace and increasingly
among environmental designers toward the management of public lands. This new attitude places
less value on engineered landscapes and more
emphasis on the aesthetics of native landscapes.
This is especially true in the West where native
riparian plant communities provide landscape
patterning to otherwise homogeneous rangelands
and biological diversity to largely evergreen
forestlands.

Traditionally, the engineered or manicured
landscape used in riparian development projects
has represented design based on garden design
styles made popular along highways and in city
parks (fig. 1). The use of garden design style
reflects a concern that native riparian
vegetation is too vigorous and will clog channels, and in the first successional stages it contributes a weedy appearance. However, the realities of the engineered style now recognize that
as irrigation water grows scarce, the drought-
tolerant ornamentals used more and more frequently can rival any landscape for the weedy look.
While riparian landscapes can evolve rapidly to
lush, attractive woodland, this is definitely not
the case with ornamentals. Additionally, riparian landscapes can be installed and managed to
minimize channel clogging, while even the best of
the low-maintenance engineered landscapes require
some clearance management.

GENERAL DISCUSSION

There are two primary factors which presently impair full-scale implementation of vegetative
restoration for native riparian landscapes: 1)
lack of planting design techniques; and 2) lack
of management specifications. With the existing

[1] Paper presented at the California Ripar-
ian Systems Conference. [University of Califor-
nia, Davis, September 17-19, 1981].
[2] Kerry J. Dawson is Assistant Professor of
Landscape Architecture, University of California,
Davis, and Landscape Architect, University of
California Agricultural Experiment Station,
Berkeley.

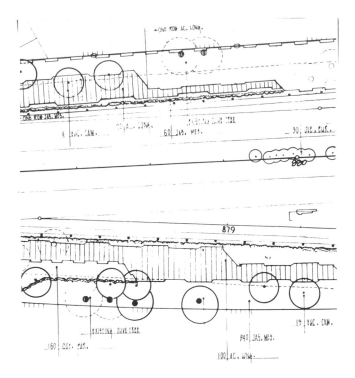

Figure 1.--A classic example of garden design as applied to planting design along State Highway 30 near Sterling Avenue in San Bernardino, California. This represents the static rather than the successional approach.

speed at which demands are being made for water resources development and the subsequently astonishing rate at which existing riparian systems are disappearing, the need for rapid growth in the development of restored riparian areas has become crucial for replacement habitat. This has meant that instead of relying primarily on downstream seed dispersal and natural succession, heavily disturbed riparian landscapes must be aided in their development by supplemental seeding or planting to speed succession. In the present construction industry, new types of planting plans and creative specifications in vegetative management to accompany them are called for. Unfortunately, neither concept has been adequately developed.

Planting plans for riparian restoration need to reflect all major components of the ecological system, including some representative water-edge and emergent zones. This means that either the overall engineering context has to be altered for differing circumstances, from small floodways relying heavily on rapid water movement with minimized vegetation in the channel, to larger floodways which temporarily store floodwaters; or the overall concept has to include a pool and channel concept where some areas have completely restored systems while others are partially restored. In either instance, coordinated research and implementation strategies amongst professionals are also necessary for informed, economical decision making.

Of the two factors above, planting design is most limiting in developing riparian restoration because of the uncertainty displayed by landscape architects and other environmental design professionals as to what procedures or guidelines to follow in developing planting design concepts for restoration. With disturbance dynamics as the population ecology norm for riparian systems, the question of what is the proper successional pattern for a severely degraded situation has always been difficult to answer. And, unlike the easily definable standards for ornamental design, standards have not been developed for simplifying riparian planting design criteria.

HISTORICAL CONTEXT

To begin to develop standards, it seems obvious that the historical contexts which have controlled the parameters of existence for native systems need to be investigated. First, the study site should be categorized in relation to to its physiographic province. Suppositions can then be made as to past plant community relationships and the respective ecological niches for species of special interest. This can be accomplished by studying relic evidence if the site has been historically riparian or, if adequate on-site information does not exist, by studying comparable areas.

In California, there are six basic "ecoregions" for riparian modeling (as adapted from Griffin and Critchfield 1972 and Walters et al. 1980). The first three can be thought of as "subregions" of the western Mediterranean or California physiographic region. They are the California grassland ecoregion, chaparral ecoregion, and the Sierran forest ecoregion. The fourth ecoregion is the northwest ecoregion associated closely with Oregon ash and the northern species. A miscellaneous or mixed community occupies the fifth ecoregion and occurs irregularly in isolated or eastern slope communities dominated by continentals. The sixth ecoregion is restricted to the low desert and is typified by the seasonal wash.

After physiographic classification by ecoregion, historic research into development patterns as they relate to the study site is essential. In "Riparian Forests of the Sacramento Valley" (Thompson 1961), a lengthy discussion on the pristine condition of the riparian lands of the Sacramento Valley is found. The vivid accounts of early fur-trappers, explorers, botanists, military expeditions, and surveyors are surprisingly detailed and site specific. For records before European settlement in California, researchers have had to rely heavily on fossil flora. In the "Geologic History of the Riparian Forests of California" (Robichaux 1977), such fossil records are combined to reveal specific information on the existence of riparian forests over the past 20 million years which remained basically unchanged until today.

During this century, the best historical records of land-use change in riparian communities have come with aerial photography and remote sensing. Accurate inventories of in-place resources can be made, and change through time can be assessed. A good example of application of this method is provided by the studies by McGill (1975, 1979) on land-use changes along the Sacramento River riparian zone from Redding to Colusa during the period 1952 through 1979.

ON-SITE AND COMPARABLE AREA INVENTORIES

In degraded situations where historical information is insufficient to formulate a design format, the use of comparable areas may be necessary to guide the planting plan. When relatively natural conditions exist upstream or downstream of a study site, these areas will prove valuable for comparison. This was the practice utilized by the Santa Clara Valley Water District in riparian revegetation completed on previously excavated earth channels where natural succession was encouraged. Comparative information for study sites came almost completely from upstream or downstream areas.

The best comparable areas are those that have been least disturbed and managed as natural areas. Such areas often have previous research which can save time and survey expenses. Examples of these areas include Caswell Memorial State Park on the Stanislaus River[3] and The Nature Conservancy's recently purchased Kern River Preserve. In comparable areas where previous research on community distribution is not available, studies to determine community and soil patterns, canopy heights, and elevational transects are necessary. These studies relate to the common formats of working drawings in landscape architecture by emphasizing the base (horizontal) plan and transect (vertical) elevation.

Base Plan Development

Base plan development first involves selecting a sample plot within the study site or a comparable area where homogeneous distribution of characteristic species occurs. Next, the designer must determine whether to utilize random or non-random species sampling for the distribution studies. Random sampling is usually used where the site is large[4] and/or statistical analysis is desirable. The random technique most commonly employed is the gridding of quadrants over the site with random sampling combinations used to ascertain sub-plots (fig. 2).

---

[3]Great Valley Museum. Undated. Flora and fauna of Caswell State Park, Ripon, Calif. Regional Biota Series, No. 1. Modesto, Calif.
[4]The site size is usually determined by enlarging the plot until the species list gets progressively shorter (fig. 3).

Figure 2.--The grid above is an example of random pairing of quadrants for the sampling and statistical analysis of spatial patterns. Frequency of species occurrence in the quadrants is the basis for the analysis (adapted from Goodall 1974).

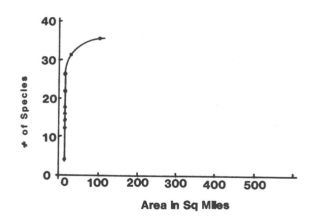

Figure 3.--When the curve in the graph begins to flatten, enlarging the study site area will result in fewer additional species. In the instance of riparian systems, so few species hold fidelity on the high terraces that sample plot expansion should be streamside (adapted from Kershaw 1964).

Non-random sampling implies the inventory of the whole plot and is used when ecological accuracy is the foremost consideration. If cost and time are major factors, statistical analysis difficult, and the plot size greatly enlarged due to limited species lists, carefully selected (but non-random) subplots might suffice.

Vegetative association is the primary classification arrangement for determining base-plan design patterns. The characteristics of an association rely primarily on the totality of homogeneous releves (lists) of species which relate floristically to one another in the plot. Associations should, however, also be characterized by geography, dynamics, and ecological niche (Kershaw 1964)(fig. 3).

The indicators for riparian associations depend primarily on one or two high-fidelity species. High fidelity can be thought of as faithfulness to a relatively narrow ecological niche. Other species may have wide ecological tolerance and occur in several associations, while still others may have such a limited tolerance that true consistency of association is not possible (plants on the limit of their range for example). Degree of faithfulness to a relatively narrow ecological niche is the key.

Patterns are drawn by placing an enclosing two-dimensional shape on the base map; this shape outlines individual species in primary association (fig. 4).[5] The actual location of the enclosing line is determined using either a multi-dimensional or hierarchical clustering method for correlation. The multi-dimensional method is controlled by positive associations detected between pairs of species, where distance is directly related to degree of association between them (ibid.). On the other hand, the hierarchical method relies on species clustering by descending order of importance (dominance rather than distance). Hierarchical clustering is generally considered an oversimplification (Webb 1954); while multi-dimensional clustering is considered the most applicable to patterning for design.

Soil types and topography can be mapped separately or as overlays to vegetative associations. Information usually comes from existing soil surveys or from field data collection. As with vegetative association, soil bores are also clustered by similarity and location.

Transect Elevation Development

Transect elevations can be placed randomly or non-randomly within the study site or comparable area. They profile the plot in representative locations for topography, soil depth, canopy height, and vegetative association. As with the base plan, the random selection of transects would apply mostly to a large plot where statistical analysis is desirable. Non-random sampling, on the other hand, would be most acceptable on smaller plots and where the quality of the base map has been sufficiently detailed.

_____

[5]An important point here is that the survey to locate individual species is the foundation for clustering. This information typically is accumulated through field work although remote sensing, especially with infra-red photography, is growing in popularity because of the time and expense involved in field work.

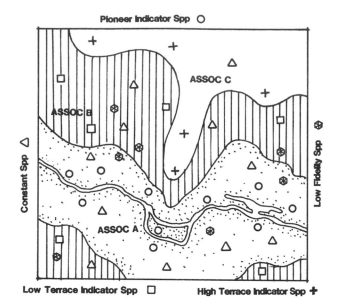

Figure 4.--After location symbols have been placed on the base map for all individual species locations, the enclosing line for an association should form a continuous and flowing line based on inclusion of only those individuals and species in close proximity to the key indicator species. Some species will occur constantly throughout all associations so judgments based on fidelity to ecological niche are essential.

Two basic forms of delineation are possible for transect elevations. The first is the histogram of occurrence for individual species; it compares percentage of cover to horizontal distribution along the transect (fig. 5). This inventory technique is very valuable for quantifying plants along the transect.

The second transect form is the profile diagram. The profile diagram identifies individual plants along the transect, shows stratification of canopy, which adds a third dimension to the base map, and delineates soil depths and topographical relationships (fig. 6). In addition, if wildlife habitat loss mitigation and ecological

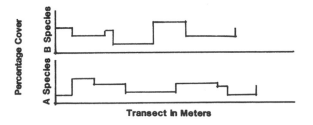

Figure 5.--An example of a histogram of occurrence (as adapted from Kershaw 1964).

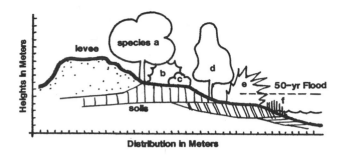

Figure 6.--Profile diagrams indicate a variety of design factors including canopy height, species niche, vegetative structure, and elevational relationships (topography, water levels, and soil depths).

stability are the foremost considerations for the project, crown density, basal area, vigor, and stand structure (age) should be added as inventory components (Davis 1977).

INTERPRETING PLANTING DESIGN

Design programs for developing a planting plan in riparian restoration usually include a number of structural decisions which are the true test of the designer. Included in these decisions are such program items as fire lane access, levee arrangements, channel alterations, and recreational facility locations. All of these program items should make use of planting as options in design. Unfortunately, this often does not often happen. As an example, gabions can often be combined with willow cuttings but are not, and willow mats will easily substitute for jute mats and nets. Normally, with either of these treatments (gabions and nets), vegetation has difficulty colonizing engineered channels because bare earth is not available. Most structural design decisions have to be made in relation to planting design. What erosion control is necessary, and what structures are appropriate (cribbing, bermed willow rolls, gabions, etc.)? Will recreation be non-structural or are facilities required, and if so, for what activities? The list of program needs can go on, and all will have some relationship to planting.

The basis for the planting plan must be successional pathways. Although highly statistical pathways can be established for most landscapes (Cattelino et al. 1979), riparian design can be simplified to three major successional stages. These are: a) the pioneer stage, usually associated with surface water and freshly exposed sand- and gravelbars dominated by willows; b) the low terrace, usually the moderately wet bottomland dominated by cottonwood; and c) the high terrace, the somewhat drier, infrequently flooded floodplain component, dominated by oak and other more drought-tolerant mesic species.

With succession as a primary design determinant, another determinant should be vegetative structure. Modelled vegetative structure designed into plans is crucial for habitat restoration. With western riparian systems serving as the principal corridors of biological diversity in an increasingly man-altered landscape, they offer the only habitat for both native wildlife and native plants (Dawson 1981).

As shown in figure 7, designers have been thinking about the evolving landscape since the English country gardens of the 1800s. What is new is the commitment to ecological integrity and the hopeful development of accurate native landscape survey methods to model design decisions. With a new commitment and tools available for

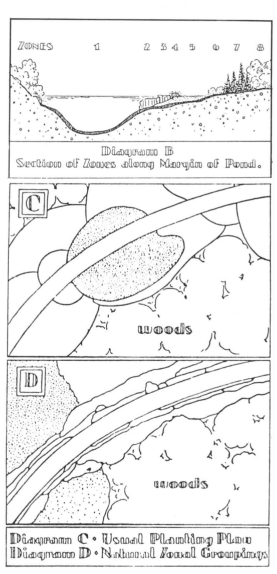

Figure 7.--These sketches represent early 20th century work in interpreting natural succession for design (Waugh 1931). Diagram B (upper drawing)--section of zones along margin of pond. Diagram C--usual planting plan. Diagram D--natural zonal grouping.

469

implementation, surely the minimum levels of mitigation measures necessary to satisfy CEQA are within our grasp.

Recently, methods outlined in this paper were used to complete planting design working drawings for riparian forest restoration along a two mile stretch of the Sacramento River near Interstate 5. In addition to vegetative modelling, endemic avian species were surveyed for preferred vegetative structure as a habitat restoration success indicator. The project will go to bid for installation in 1984. Copies of research methods will be available through the author during 1984.

ACKNOWLEDGMENTS

Special thanks to Landscape Architecture Magazine Archives for the use of the Waugh sketches.

LITERATURE CITED

Cattelino, Peter J., J.R. Noble, R.O. Slatyer, and S.R. Kessell. 1979. Predicting the multiple pathways of plant succession. Environmental Management 3(1):41-50. Springer-Verlag, New York, N.Y.

Davis, Gary A. 1977. Management alternatives for the riparian habitat in the Southwest. p. 59-67. In: R.R. Johnson and D.A. Jones (tech. coord.). Importance, preservation and management of riparian habitat: a symposium. [Tucson, Ariz., 9 July 1977.) USDA Forest Service GTR-RM-43. Rocky Mountain Forest and Range Experiment Station, Fort Collins, Colo. 217 p.

Dawson, Kerry J. 1982. Bioregional landscapes as frontier. p. 208-210. 1982-83 yearbook of the International Federation of Landscape Architects. IFLA Secretariat, Versailles, France.

Goodall, David W. 1974. A new method for the analysis of spatial pattern by random pairing of quadrats. Vegetatio 29(2): 135-146.

Griffin, James R., and William B. Critchfield. 1972. The distribution of forest trees in California. USDA Forest Service Research Paper PSW-82. (Reprinted with Supplement, 1976.) Pacific Southwest Forest and Range Experiment Station, Berkeley, Calif. 118 p.

Hackett, Brian. 1979. Planting design. McGraw-Hill Book Company, New York, N.Y. 174 p.

Kershaw, Kenneth A. 1964. Quantitative and dynamic ecology. Edward Arnold (Publishers) Ltd., London, England. 183 p.

McGill, Robert R., Jr. 1975. Land-use changes in the Sacramento River riparian zone, Redding to Colusa. 23 p. California Department of Water Resources, Northern District Report, Sacramento, Calif.

McGill, Robert R., Jr. 1979. Land-use change in the Sacramento River riparian zone, Redding to Colusa. An update—1972 to 1977. 34 p. California Department of Water Resources, Northern District, Sacramento, Calif.

Robichaux, Robert. 1977. Geologic history of the riparian forests of California. p. 21-34. In: A. Sands (ed.). Riparian forests in California: their ecology and conservation. Institute of Ecology Pub. 15, University of California, Davis. 122 p.

Thompson, Kenneth. 1961. Riparian forest of the Sacramento Valley, California. Ann. Assoc. Amer. Geogr. 51(3):294-315.

Walters, Alice M., R.O. Teskey, and T.M. Hinckley. 1980. Impact of water level changes on woody riparian and wetland communities. Vol. 3, FWS/OBS-78/93. USDI Fish and Wildlife Service, Washington, D.C. 55 p.

Waugh, Frank A. 1931. Natural plant groups. Landscape Architecture 21(3): 169-180. Landscape Architecture Publishing Co., Boston, Mass.

Webb, D.A. 1954. Is the classification of plant communities either possible or desirable? Saer. Dot. Tidssk. 51:362-370.

IRRIGATION SYSTEMS FOR RIPARIAN ZONE REVEGETATION[1]

John Disano, Bertin W. Anderson, and Robert D. Ohmart[2]

Abstract.--Revegetation of aridland riparian zones with native riparian species is feasible, but generally requires initial irrigation to maintain the plants while root systems are established. For most desert riparian revegetation work, the irrigation pump should be gasoline- or diesel-powered. Main irrigation lines should be PVC (polyvinyl chloride) buried about 31 cm. (12 in.). Laterals should be polyethylene tubing because this can safely lie on or near the surface. The water should be delivered to each tree through pressure-compensating emitters.

INTRODUCTION

We have been reintroducing native riparian species of trees and shrubs on an experimental basis along the lower Colorado River riparian zone since 1977. In this region, irrigation is a necessary prerequisite to any successful revegetation effort. Irrigation is critical in getting vegetation root systems established; it is also a major expense associated with revegetation efforts. In our work we have used two different systems. One was established in 1978 on a barren dredge-spoil area of about 30 ha. (75 ac.); the other was established on a 20-ha. (50-ac.) plot from which salt cedar (_Tamarix chinensis_) had been cleared. Both systems delivered water to 2,500 plantings and included about 19 km. (12 mi.) of pipe. In this report, we describe and evaluate the major systems with which we have had experience. Advantages and disadvantages of each system are noted and recommendations are made for designing irrigation systems for revegetation. English units of measurement are used in order to be consistent with units currently in use in the irrigation industry.

DREDGE-SPOIL SYSTEM

The irrigation system on the dredge-spoil revegetation site was assembled from polyvinyl chloride (PVC) irrigation pipe. A well was drilled that reached water at 3 m. (10 ft.); water from this well contained approximately 1100-1400 ppm total dissolved solids. A Worthington Model 8M-28 electric pump developing 20 hp at 1760 rpm was installed on the well (fig. 1). Pump bowls were set at 50 ft. The pump had a 5-in. suction pipe and a 6-in. discharge pipe. Water was delivered from the pump through an Olson-Filtomat Model FLT-3000 vacuum cleaning filter with a capacity of 250 gpm (fig. 1). This filter is an automatic backwash filter with a hydraulic controller which detects pressure differential between the intake and outlet valves of the filter. From the filter, water entered a pressure-regulating valve (fig. 1) which was set to maintain 35 psi in the irrigation system. Before entering the main line, water passed two pressure-sensitive electrical cutoff switches (fig. 1). One switch was set at a high pressure of 40 psi, the other was set at a low pressure of 30 psi. Any time the pump was running and the irrigation system control panel was set on automatic, an increase or decrease in pressure to the above settings automatically broke the electrical

Figure 1.--Dredge-spoil pump station.

[1]Paper presented at the California Riparian Systems Conference. [University of California, Davis, September 17-19, 1981].

[2]John Disano is Research Biologist, Bertin W. Anderson is Faculty Research Associate, and Robert D. Ohmart is Associate Director; all are with the Center for Environmental Studies, Arizona State University, Tempe, Arizona.

circuit and turned off the pump. These automatic cutoff switches protected the integrity of the irrigation system in the event of a failure of the pressure-regulating valve or a major break within the irrigation system.

The main body of the irrigation system consisted of a 750-ft. long, 6-in. PVC main line running from the pump station to the Colorado River (fig. 2). At the river a butterfly valve was installed along with a bypass pressure relief valve. The entire capacity of pumped water could be discharged into the Colorado River with the

butterfly valve open; there was no discharge if the valve was closed. The bypass pressure relief valve was a final safeguard to protect the irrigation system. If all other safeguards failed, the value would open at 50 psi and bleed water into the Colorado River, thereby relieving pressure on the system.

Seventeen laterals, each 2,000 ft. long, were installed north of the main line; 17 laterals, each 1,500 ft. long were installed south of the main line. The main line and all lateral lines were buried 15-20 in. Risers for irrigation were placed every 20 ft. along laterals (fig. 3).

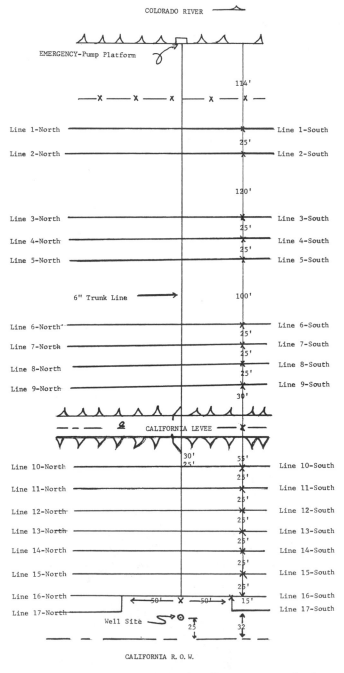

Figure 2.--Map of the irrigation system, dredge-spoil site.

Figure 3.--Riser with Subterrain Dual Flapper emitter and tubing.

The emitters used to deliver water to the trees were Subterrain Dual Flappers. These emitters are pressure-compensating and delivered 4 gal. per hour with a system pressure between 15-50 psi. Tubing was attached at each end of an emitter to deliver a point source of water to the base of a tree (fig. 3).

With the dredge-spoil irrigation system in full operation, the pump delivered 167 gal. per minute at a system pressure of 35 psi. This pressure was chosen because the last emitter along a 2,000-ft. lateral still delivered a pressure of 18-20 psi, while the first emitter near the main line had a pressure of 35 psi. Therefore, both emitters were within the recommended 15-50 psi, and each delivered 4 gal. per hour to its respective tree.

Another pertinent point concerning the irrigation system is that the main line could be opened or closed by a butterfly valve at the well or the river, thus permitting irrigation water to be supplied from the well or from the Colorado River by an auxiliary, trailer-mounted pump. Any one or more laterals could be shut off at the main line by turning a shutoff valve. Also, any one or more of the 2,500 emitters could be capped temporarily or permanently to prevent further irrigation of trees.

A major disadvantage of this system is that it is expensive to purchase and to install. Purchase and installation costs amounted to $34 per tree.

REFUGE SITE

The irrigation system on the refuge site received water from the lower Colorado River. This water contained 600-800 ppm total dissolved solids. The water was delivered to the revegetation site by the Cibola National Wildlife Refuge concrete-lined canal (fig. 4). A jack gate was installed (fig. 4) to divert water into two intake ports (fig. 5) of a holding pond (fig. 6). In addition to providing a seven day supply of water for irrigation, the pond also served as a settling basin. This was important because a drip irrigation system using microtubing or emitters with small orifices may be blocked or damaged by dirt or sand.

Water was pumped from the pond using an 8-hp., two-cycle Wisconsin-Robbins engine with a centrifugal pump (fig. 7). This pump delivered 90 gal. per minute at 20 psi to the main line.

A prescreen filter, made from a 3-ft. section of 6-in. PVC pipe with vertical slits and with the open ends covered with fine mesh wire, was fastened to the intake hose and suspended from a barrel float in the pond (fig. 8). The purpose of the prescreen filter was to prevent leaves, sticks, and other debris from being drawn into the pump. A Yardney Model-8 Free Flow manually cleaned filter was installed between the pump and main line (fig. 9). This filter had a capacity of 125 gal. per minute.

Figure 5.--Intake ports in canal.

Figure 6.--Holding pond at low-water level to show intake ports.

Figure 4.--Cibola National Wildlife Refuge, concrete-lined irrigation canal and jack gate.

Figure 7.--Engine and pump.

473

Figure 8.--Barrel float in pond.

Figure 9.--Free Flow filter.

The irrigation system on the refuge was assembled using regular 3-in. diameter aluminum sprinkler irrigation pipe for the main line transport of water. The laterals were flexible black polyethylene tubing with an inside diameter of 0.58 in. The maximum length of any lateral was 750 ft; none of the pipe was buried.

The site was divided into four 750- x 530-ft. sections (fig. 10). Water to each section was supplied by 17 lateral lines; each lateral supplied 38 trees. The main line of 3-in. diameter aluminum sprinkler pipe was 1,500 ft. long, with the pump located at the center. The north and south submains were both 530 ft. long.

The installation of two 3-in. gate valves (fig. 11) in the main line near the pump permitted the watering of either the north or south section separately or simultaneously. Further flexibility in design was incorporated by installing a ball valve (fig. 12) on each lateral so that any one or more laterals could be shut off during irrigation.

Each lateral valve assembly contained one Subterrain pressure regulator (fig. 12), which prevented main-line water from entering the lateral at more than 20 psi. This was to prevent bursting of laterals and blowing out of microtubes due to a pressure surge; it also assured equal distribution of water to all 68 laterals. The pressure at the beginning of a lateral was 20 psi; pressure at the end was 8-10 psi.

Each tree was watered by two microtubes (fig. 13), each delivering water at a rate of 1 gal. per hour. Any individual tree could be cut off from watering by removing the microtubing and installing "goof" plugs. In order to provide 1 gal. per hour delivery from each microtube, microtube length was varied as shown in figure 10. Appropriate microtube lengths were determined by a computer using the flow characteristics of the system.

Purchase of the system and installation costs associated with this system were much less than that for the dredge-spoil system, amounting to $3 per tree. However, maintenance costs ($16 per tree) were higher than for the dredge-spoil system ($11 per tree).

EVALUATION OF IRRIGATION SYSTEMS

In comparing the dredge-spoil irrigation system with the refuge irrigation system, there are several factors to consider. One important factor is the availability of electricity. In most areas along the lower Colorado River, electricity is not available. If a system based on electrical pumping is necessary, then revegetation efforts would have to be limited to areas where electricity is available. In most of these areas there is likely to be competition for land from farming or some form of urbanization. Cost of pumping with electricity is comparable to that for gasoline-powered pumping, but the cost of an electrical pump is about 20 times greater than for a gasoline pump. Locations for a gasoline or diesel-powered pump are limited only by the availability of free-flowing or well water.

A second important consideration is that flowing water is preferable for irrigation if total dissolved solids are low enough to permit plant growth. Water from a well has anaerobic bacteria; the combination of their chemical reactions with those of aerobic bacteria in irriga-

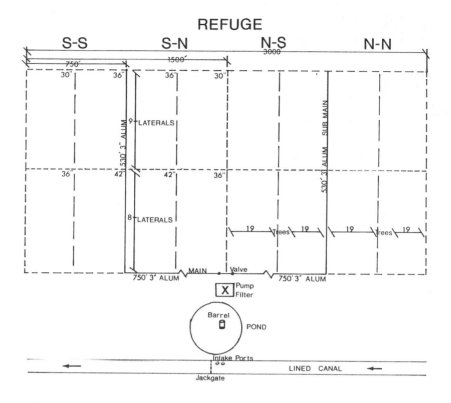

Figure 10.—Refuge site, map of irrigation system. Note: for 0.035 I.D. microtube, use various lengths as shown. North side of the field is the same as the south side.

Figure 11.—Gate valves.

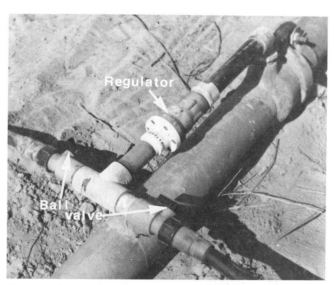

Figure 12.—Lateral valve assembly.

tion systems produces an orange or rust-colored precipitate that must be continuously flushed from lines and/or emitters. This problem usually does not occur when free-flowing river water is used for irrigation.

PVC pipe must be buried because of algae development and deterioration of the pipe when exposed to sunlight. Burying pipe is both labor-

Figure 13.--Microtubing at tree.

intensive and expensive (Anderson and Ohmart 1981[3]). Black polyethylene tubing accumulates very little algae and can be laid on the surface; in addition, it can be picked up and moved to another area relatively quickly. Also, if polyethylene tubing is damaged it can be repaired easily and cheaply on the surface. PVC pipe is about 10 times more costly than polyethylene tubing.

The decision of whether to use the very inexpensive microtubing or pressure-compensating emitters is more difficult. Although emitters would initially cost six to eight times more than microtubing, they last longer and provide more uniform water distribution over natural, sloping terrain. Also, the cost of labor for installation of emitters is about one-half that of microtubing.

RECOMMENDATIONS

For irrigating most desert riparian revegetation areas, the pump should be gasoline- or diesel-powered and should pump free-flowing water. For flexibility and durability, PVC pipe should be used in main irrigation lines; it must be buried in the soil about 12 in. Lateral lines should be polyethylene tubing with pressure-compensating emitters.

ACKNOWLEDGMENTS

We wish to thank Susan M. Cook, Jane R. Durham, Dr. Julie K. Meents, and Cindy D. Zisner for editorial assistance. Marcelett Ector and Cindy D. Zisner typed the numerous drafts of the manuscript. We are grateful to Dr. F. Aljibury, Les Ede, and Jule Meyer, University of California Agricultural Extension Service, Riverside, for their advice and cooperation. James Moore and Judy Huff prepared the figures. Our work was supported by USDI Bureau of Reclamation and the USDI Fish and Wildlife Service Contract No. 7-07-30-V0009.

---

[3]Anderson, B. W., and R. D. Ohmart. 1981. Chapter 5. In: Revegetation efforts along the lower Colorado River. Final report, in preparation, to USDI Bureau of Reclamation, Boulder City, Nevada.

HIGH MOUNTAIN MEADOW RESTORATION[1]

David H. Clay[2]

Abstract—A technique using a rock sill and vegetation to stabilize streams in high mountain meadows which will enable restoration of these riparian systems is discussed.

INTRODUCTION

The USDA Soil Conservation Service (SCS) believes strongly in the use of riparian vegetation for erosion control, wildlife habitat development, and improving the aesthetics of artificial and natural waterways.

From an engineering standpoint, the use of vegetation for an erosion control system has both advantages and disadvantages. Vegetation is not as predictable as concrete and other materials which engineers normally consider when they are designing waterways and erosion control systems. Since water velocities must be kept at lower levels when vegetation is used, greater channel cross-sectional areas are generally needed. This may be very costly where land values are high. Maintenance of the vegetation must be provided on a regular basis if channel capacities are to be maintained, and damaged sections must be cared for on an annual basis.

On the positive side, vegetation can provide channel stability which is aesthetically pleasing, provides wildlife habitat, recreational benefits, low initial cost, and maintenance which can be done by private landowners. The determination as to whether vegetation can be successfully used is dependent on the situation at the time of design and what is expected in the future. Some of the factors which should be considered are listed below.

1. Is there sufficient area available at a reasonable cost to provide adequate capacity at an acceptable level of maintenance?

2. Are climatic conditions suitable to establish and maintain the desired vegetation?

3. Are structural measures needed to provide an adequate level of protection and maintain the vegetation?

4. Has sufficient maintenance been provided for?

SOIL CONSERVATION SERVICE ROLE

The SCS works primarily with individuals and groups of landowners on their own lands. Cooperation between SCS and the landowners is on an entirely voluntary basis. In order for SCS to be effective, it must provide the landowner with a workable and economically feasible solution to his problems. In the case of developing stable waterways, the work proposed must be economically feasible and within the landowner's maintenance capability. Riparian vegetation often meets these requirements.

An example of this is demonstrated by the use of rock grade-control structures to establish vegetation along eroding natural channels in the arid areas of northeastern California and northwestern Nevada. Although the work is structural in nature when it is built, the long-term solution will be accomplished by vegetation. Recognition of this philosophy usually leads to success of the project.

WET MEADOW RESTORATION PROCEDURES

Historically, wet meadows have been drained, as a result of stream erosion (usually brought about by livestock grazing) forming gullies 1-2 m. (3-5 ft.) deep. These have eroded in an upstream direction through the meadows. Lowering of the water table changes the moisture regime so that native grasses and other meadow plants can no longer survive. With loss of vegetative cover, erosion is accelerated, and eventually the entire area will be converted to bare ground or brush.

The normal configuration of eroded gullies in the area is one with vertical sides and a relatively flat bottom. During spring runoff, the vertical banks are undercut, causing large

[1] Paper presented at the California Riparian Systems Conference. [University of California, Davis, September 17-19, 1981.]

[2] David H. Clay is Resource Conservation and Development Project Coordinator, Soil Conservation Service, Alturas, Calif.

portions of the bank to fall into the stream and wash away. The channel continues to deepen and widen until the meadow is entirely destroyed.

In order to bring this condition under control, the procedure described below has been very successfully employed.

1. Slots are cut across the channel using a bulldozer or backhoe. These slots extend into the bank approximately 3.3 m. (10 ft.) and into the bottom about 1 m. (3 ft.). Location of the slots is determined by channel gradient and configuration.

2. Large rock is dumped into the slots and then shaped so that it has a level crest and sides with slopes no steeper than 2:1 horizontal to vertical. This forms a sill across the channel. The rock should extend at least 0.3 m. (1 ft.) above the natural ground on each side of the channel.

3. Soil excavated from the trench is placed on the upstream side of the sill to prevent water from passing through the rock.

4. Low earth fills are placed a short distance out from each side of the rock sill to prevent water which exceeds the channel capacity from flowing overland immediately against the rock shoulder. Spillways are left at the end of each fill at ground level.

5. All disturbed areas are planted with suitable vegetation. It is desirable to plant willows or other woody shrubs into the rock on each abutment of the sills.

6. The entire area is fenced when necessary to prevent indiscriminate use by livestock. Such fencing should be designed to provide access to water by livestock and have a smooth bottom wire in areas where there are antelope. It is sometimes desirable to use controlled grazing of livestock inside the fenced areas to spread and cover seed when re-establishing sod along and in the waterway.

Generally two to three years after this work is completed deposition has filled the channel upstream from each sill to its crest, raising the channel bottom 0.7-1 m. (2-3 ft.). This raises the water table in the meadow, sometimes to original elevations. The sides of the channel develop a slope due to the action of the water. This slope is sufficiently flattened to let grass and shrubs become established. Sod forms on the low earth fills to a degree that prevents damage from the spring overflow. The sills themselves are almost unnoticeable.

Figures 1 through 4 illustrate this process as it occurred on Willow Creek near Adin, Modoc County, California.

Costs for installation of a typical loose rock grade-stabilization structure are $700 to $1,000.

Figure 1.--Willow Creek near Adin, Modoc County, before installation of rock sill. Note recent and continuing bank erosion.

Figure 2.--Willow Creek, May 1980, before erosion control device installed.

Figure 3.--Willow Creek one year after rock sills were installed.

Figure 4.--Willow Creek one year after rock sills were installed. Sediment has now filled eroded channels.

At this point the success of the program is dependent upon management. Under proper grazing management, the fencing can be removed and the meadow can be maintained in a stable condition for an indefinite period.

11 RIPARIAN SYSTEMS AND WATER DIVERSION PROJECTS:
CAN THE CONFLICTS BE RESOLVED?

THE SOUTH FORK (KERN RIVER) WILDLIFE AREA:

WILL THE COMMITMENT BE FORGOTTEN?[1]

Carolyn Fleshman and Darrell S. Kaufman[2]

Abstract.--This study reports the ecological effects of reservoir inundation on a portion of the floodplain riparian system of the South Fork, Kern River, Kern County, California. The South Fork Wildlife Area, lying within gross pool of Isabella Reservoir and administered by the US Army Corps of Engineers, constitutes the prime portion of one of the largest and healthiest riparian forests remaining in California. In spring, 1980, the entire sanctuary was inundated by Isabella Reservoir, drastically reducing its unusually high bird populations and contributing to a reduction in the overall habitat values of the forest.

INTRODUCTION

The South Fork Wildlife Area (SFWA) is an ecological reserve and wildlife management area established by the Sacramento District, US Army Corps of Engineers (CE), within the gross pool (the area subject to flooding when the reservoir fills to its highest level) of Isabella Reservoir, Kern County. While the reservoir dams both the North and South Forks of the Kern River (see fig. 1), the most luxuriant riparian forest (and the SFWA) occur on the floodplain of the South Fork.

The SFWA serves as a unique example of preservation and enhancement of an area of extremely rich biological diversity and productivity by the CE, an agency often criticized for its disregard for natural values. The SFWA project has won the CE, Sacramento District, several awards for excellence as a conservation initiative. However, a recent change in water management and a proposed water development project threaten to reverse all improvements the CE has made, and, if implemented, destroy the resource that it has striven to protect.

The first part of this paper presents background information on the ecology and management of the SFWA, and a description of Isabella Reservoir management policies affecting it. The second part details the results of bird censuses

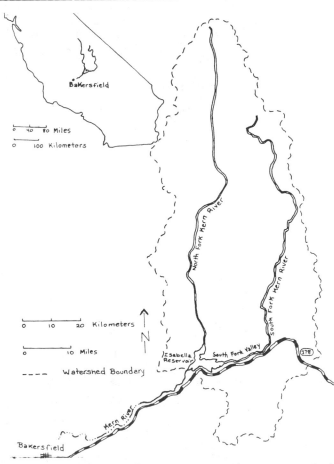

Figure 1.--Map of the Kern River watershed showing the South Fork Valley and the SFWA location.

and vegetative transects designed to assess the impacts of reservoir inundation on the SFWA.

---

[1] Paper presented at the California Riparian Systems Conference. [University of California, Davis, September 17-19, 1981].

[2] Carolyn Fleshman and Darrell S. Kaufman, Environmental Field Program, University of California, Santa Cruz. Co-authors in alphabetical order.

South Fork Valley

The South Fork Kern River (fig. 1) supports one of the largest contiguous riparian forests in the State, encompassing over 1,000 ha.[3] The forest is one of the best remaining examples of a native deciduous riparian system in California (USDI Fish and Wildlife Service 1980).

Hydrology and Geology

The South Fork, unlike most Sierran streams, flows through a broad, gently sloping floodplain. Draining a watershed of 1,370 km[2], the South Fork begins in the Golden Trout Wilderness and flows south, then east through the South Fork Valley. Originally it joined the North Fork, but now it empties into Lake Isabella, a reservoir created in 1954 by damming the North and South Forks of the Kern River at their confluence.

The South Fork once cut through a deeply incised canyon, into the underlying rocks of the Sierra Nevada basement complex at the time of the Sierra Nevada uplift. Changes in topography, probably the result of block faulting at or near the present dam site, raised the elevation of the Kern River drainageway. This in turn produced a sediment trap, causing the canyon to be partially filled with unconsolidated alluvial sediments, largely decomposed granite, carried down from the surrounding mountains. This accumulated material now forms the South Fork floodplain and is the substrate of the South Fork riparian system.[4]

The low hydraulic energy of the South Fork, and the gradual topography and porous soils of its floodplain provide aquifer storage and a high water table for the Valley throughout the year. These characteristics create optimum growing conditions for a luxuriant native riparian woodland (fig. 2).

Vegetation

Dominated almost entirely by a mature growth of various willows (<u>Salix gooddingii</u>, <u>S. lasiandra</u>, and <u>S. laevigata</u>) and Fremont cottonwood (<u>Populus fremontii</u>), some of them estimated to be up to 300 years old,[5] the South Fork forest forms a meandering vegetated corridor through nearly the entire length of the Valley. Its total length is about 16 km., its average width 0.75 km. At the eastern end, the cottonwoods and willows intergrade with a relict stand

Figure 2.--View of the lush cottonwood/willow forest of the South Fork Valley, looking east.

of Joshua trees (<u>Yucca brevifolia</u>). An extensive network of marshes weaves in and out of the forest for much of this length. The valley floodplain offers a distinct visual contrast to the sparse, xerophytic vegetation of the adjacent slopes.

Subjected to various land use practices, the structure of the forest reflects the activities of humans since the early settlers arrived following the Walker expedition of 1834. Portions of the forest were cleared for agricultural fields or cut for fuel (Powers 1971). Grazing, which continues today, has inhibited regeneration of the forest, resulting in areas of homogenous old growth with a dense understory of mulefat (<u>Baccharis viminea</u>) and stinging nettle (<u>Urtica</u> sp.). Areas where grazing has recently been eliminated are showing a remarkable recovery rate, with proliferous new growth of cottonwood and willow seedlings.

Wildlife

This unusually verdant valley supports an extraordinary abundance and diversity of wildlife. Singularly rich in avifauna, the South Fork riparian forest owes its diversity of birdlife to its location at the confluence of five distinct biogeographic regions, a situation which occurs nowhere else in North America north of Mexico. In the South Fork Valley, the Sierran Forest, Intermountain Sagebrush, California Grassland, American Desert, and California Chapparral provinces converge (Bailey 1978). Over 200 species, including songbirds, woodpeckers, waterfowl, raptors, and others, fill the South Fork forest with a jungle-like symphony of song in the breeding season. Riparian-dependent

---

[3]Gaines, D.A. 1977. Riparian cottonwood-willow forests in California, an inventory of potential preserves. Report prepared for The Nature Conservancy, Western Regional Office.

[4]Warner, R.E. 1980. Riparian vegetation/wildlife relationships in the South Fork Kern watershed. Unpublished field study prepared for the Kern County Wildlife Resources Commission. 26 p.

[5]Shevock, James. 1981. Personal conversation. Plant ecologist, USDA Forest Service, Sequoia National Forest, Calif.

species such as Wood Duck,[6] Red-shouldered Hawk, Yellow-breasted Chat, Blue Grosbeak, and Yellow Warbler, once common throughout California's riparian forests, but now absent from many of them, still inhabit the South Fork.

The cottonwood/willow forest is a haven for flycatchers, warblers, swallows, and other migrants on their flights over the mountains and deserts. Unusual species such as Indigo Bunting and Rose-breasted Grosbeak are also drawn to the forest.

The South Fork Valley supports an exceptionally high breeding bird population of 98 species, more than one third of the regular nesting species in California identified by Hehnke and Stone (1978). The largest population of the State Rare Yellow-billed Cuckoo outside of the Colorado River region, an estimated[7] 24 pairs, breeds in the South Fork forest. A pair of Osprey also nest in the Valley, one of only two[9] breeding pairs between Mexico and Sacramento. In addition, there are two Great Blue Heron rookeries with approximately 100 active nests.

The South Fork represents one of the last refuges for many species of birds threatened by habitat loss. Thirty-eight species found here are included on the 1981 Audubon Blue List for California, and the California Natural Diversity Data Base List of Special Animals.

Isabella Reservoir

Authorization

The CE Isabella Project was authorized by the Flood Control Act of 1944 to protect the city of Bakersfield, built on the floodplain of the Kern River, from floods. Project authorization included provisions for irrigation and recreation in addition to flood control. The Federal Government paid for approximately 70% of the project costs, with irrigation and hydroelectric power interests contributing 20% and 8% respectively.[8] The project, involving construction of a main and auxiliary dam, began in 1948 and was completed in 1954.

Normally, all water released from the main dam is used for irrigation of agricultural fields in Kern County. When flows are in excess of demand they can be diverted into the California Aqueduct via the Kern River/California Aqueduct Intertie, or to the Tulare and Buena Vista Lakebeds. Releases of floodwaters into the Lakebeds are usually damaging to crops, however.

---

[6] Scientific names of bird species mentioned in the text are included in Appendix A.

[7] Barnes, Robert. 1981. Personal conversation. President, South Fork Watershed Association, Calif.

[8] Schontzler, G. 1981. Politicians, farmers wrangle over who gets Kern River water. The Bakersfield Californian, Feb. 16, 1981. Sec. B2, p. 1.

South Fork Wildlife Area

Riparian System.--The creation of Isabella Reservoir resulted in the immediate loss of approximately 1,300 ha. of South Fork riparian forest.[9] An additional 1,417 ha. of riparian system lie within gross pool elevation (2,605.5 ft. msl). Of this additional area, only approximately 125 ha. are presently heavily forested, the remainder having been deforested by agriculture, woodcutting, grazing, and fire. The area is periodically inundated by the reservoir during years of especially high runoff. This portion of the forest, where the South Fork broadens into a braided delta, is the greatest in width and most dense (fig. 3).

In 1966, in a planning aid letter to the CE, the USDI Fish and Wildlife Service (FWS) recognized the superior value of the remaining cottonwood/willow forest as wildlife habitat. They recommended that grazing be eliminated in the forest because of its adverse impacts, and that the CE manage the area for the enhancement of wildlife values (US Army Corps of Engineers 1979a).

Management Plan.--In 1977, a wildlife management plan for what was to become the SFWA was developed by local CE rangers with professional training in wildlife management. The first phase of the plan called for restoration and wildlife improvement activities in 505 ha. of floodplain riparian zone, from the eastern boundary of the reservoir's gross pool line west to elevation 2,580 ft. msl. The major objective of the plan, to convert agricultural land within the riparian zone back to riparian forest by allowing agricultural leases to expire, has been partially achieved (ibid.) Leases have not been termi-

Figure 3.--Morning view of the South Fork Wildlife Area, looking southeast.

---

[9] Estimated from an aerial photograph taken in 1946, prior to construction of Isabella Dam.

nated, but have instead been placed on inactive status, allowing grazing or agriculture on an interim, short-term basis, as prescribed by the District Engineer.[10]

Other improvements under the SFWA plan have included construction of nesting structures for Mourning Dove, Wood Duck, and Osprey; and construction of a trail system for which an interpretive guide is being prepared. In addition, a riparian reforestation and habitat manipulation program is being implemented.

Because the SFWA lies within gross pool elevation of Isabella Reservoir, the management plan was designed to function under normal operations of the reservoir. Prior to 1978, the reservoir rarely inundated the riparian forest except in years of exceptionally high runoff, and then only for short durations (US Army Corps of Engineers 1978).

SFWA Awards.--In recognition of an outstanding demonstration of its knowledge and appreciation of the most important environmental values, the CE, Sacramento District, received a National Honor Award in the US Army Chief of Engineers Design and Environmental Awards competition for 1979. It also won a CE Divisional Award during the same year. In addition to numerous other commendations, the SFWA management plan earned the CE, Sacramento District, a National Audubon Society award, which was presented in a special on-site ceremony.

Reservoir Water Management.--The flood control function of the reservoir and, secondarily, irrigation demand dictate reservoir operation. According to the Lake Isabella Regulations Manual (ibid.), reservoir level should be drawn down to 170,000 acre-feet (AF) by 1 November each year and kept at this level until 1 February when snowmelt runoff predictions become available. This seasonal drawdown prepares the reservoir for both rain and snowmelt floodwaters. Any water remaining in the reservoir above this 1 November level, that is, within Flood Control Space, is called "winter carryover," and is dependent upon "prevailing conditions" (ibid.). Under no circumstances, however, is the storage of winter carryover permitted above 245,000 AF between 1 November and 1 March, as this minimum reservation is required to control rainfloods (ibid.).

To accomodate irrigation interests, since 1978 winter carryover has been substantially higher than the prescribed flood control capacity, as described in the Regulations Manual. In fact, since 1978 water has encroached on the rainflood reservation space of 325,000 AF (reservoir capacity above 245,000 AF) 40% of the time.[11] A comparison of historical reservoir operations shows that reservoir storage for the 1978-1981 period was substantially higher than ever before (fig. 4). First-of-the-month reservoir storage for the 1978-1981 period was an average of 40,000 AF higher than that of the 1967-1970 period when the total reservoir inflow was actually 13% higher.

The representative for the Kern County water districts maintains that the high winter carryover is the result of a CE reevaluation of the Kern River Basin hydrology.[12] However, the most recent hydrological study shows that the Probable Maximum Flood is actually higher than previously predicted (US Army Corps of Engineers 1979b).

The CE, Sacramento District, Operations Division claims that the completion of the California Water Project, making more water available to Kern County users and allowing more conservation of Kern River water, is responsible for the difference.[13]

Although both parties deny any connection, the Kern River/California Aqueduct Intertie was completed in 1977, reducing the flood hazard to Tulare Lake Basin--the ultimate destination for Kern River floodwaters--by absorbing floodwaters from the Kern River and transporting them south to the Los Angeles area (US Army Corps of Engineers 1978). The Intertie thus reduces the hazard of permitting encroachment into the Flood Control Space of Isabella Reservoir. It also results in the further diversion of water from the basin, which in the past had partially recharged the badly depleted groundwater aquifer.

Regardless of the reason for the change in reservoir storage, it has not been officially acknowledged, and thus no environmental assessment of its effects has been considered. Because of the high winter carryover, the reservoir fills earlier and to a higher elevation during the annual spring snowmelt runoff season, thus changing the timing and increasing the frequency, duration, and depth of reservoir inundation of the SFWA. With a reservoir storage increase of 40,000 AF (the minimum average increase since 1978 as compared to the 1967-1970 period) the reservoir is expected to inundate the lower boundary of the South Fork riparian forest once every four and one-half years, as compared to the 1977 calculation (ibid.) of once every six years. The entire sanctuary will be flooded every 20 years, as compared to once in 100 years.

Prior to 1980, the reservoir reached gross pool capacity only once in its history, in 1969. In 1980, as the result of high winter carryover

_____

[10]Slattery, Thomas. 1981. Personal correspondence. US Army Corps of Engineers, Sacramento District, Real Estate Division.
[11]Calculated from Isabella Project Office daily records.

_____

[12]Williams, Chuck H. 1981. Personal conversation. Kern River Watermaster, Bakersfield, Calif.
[13]Verke, Mark. 1981. Personal conversation. US Army Corps of Engineers, Sacramento District, Operations Division, Reservoir Control Section.

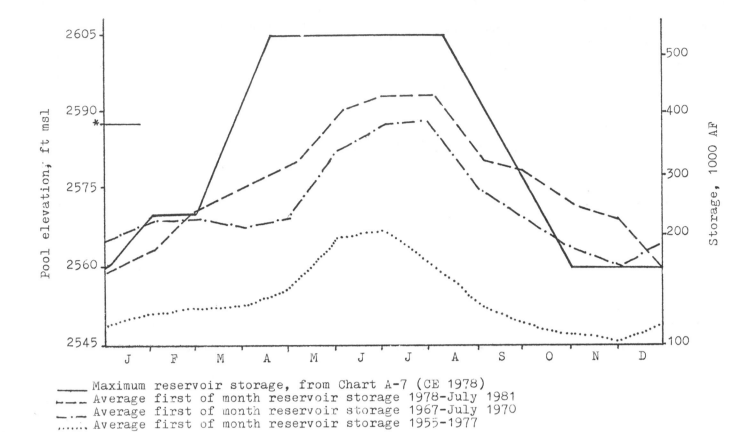

Pool elevation, ft msl
2605
2590
*
2575
2560
2545

Storage, 1000 AF
500
400
300
200
100

J F M A M J J A S O N D

———— Maximum reservoir storage, from Chart A-7 (CE 1978)
– – – Average first of month reservoir storage 1978–July 1981
– · – Average first of month reservoir storage 1967–July 1970
······ Average first of month reservoir storage 1955–1977

*Lower edge of forest (2588 ft msl).

Figure 4.--Comparison of Isabella Reservoir storage for three time periods.

(265,000 AF average from 1 November to 1 March) and high runoff (nearly 200% of normal), Isabella filled to gross pool again and rose an additional 0.46 m. (1.5 ft.) over the dam spillway, an unprecedented event. Encroachment of the riparian forest of the SFWA began in early April, peaked in early July when the entire sanctuary was inundated, and receded in September.

EFFECTS OF RESERVOIR INUNDATION

Identified by the FWS as the fourth preservation priority in the State, the importance and unique value of the South Fork forest has been widely recognized (see Gaines 1977, and Warner 1980, cited in footnotes 3 and 4), yet no systematic, baseline studies have been conducted in the area. Consequently, when Isabella Reservoir filled to gross pool capacity in 1980, the effects of reservoir inundation on the SFWA could not be predicted. The purpose of the present study was to monitor these effects on the avian community and to evaluate the overall effects of periodic inundation on the habitat values of the SFWA. Necessary to achieve this end, and important in itself, was the establishment of baseline data on bird population diversity and density in 1981.

Methods

Bird Censusing

A variable circular plot technique was used in estimating bird populations.[14] This method has been recommended for assessing the effects of habitat manipulation (Verner 1980).

In order to reduce variability, as suggested by Dawson (1980) and Verner (1980), the number of individuals of a species detected through time, rather than absolute densities, was used in measuring the responses of avifauna to flooding in 1980. Bird densities and diversities were calculated from 1981 data, when the high degree of disturbance from inundation was not a factor.

Fourteen observation stations, representative of five subhabitat-types, were established within the 160 ha. study area:
    4 along a forest/field ecotone where inundation is frequent;
    3 along a relatively undisturbed ecotone;

---

[14]Reynolds, R.T., J.M. Scott, and R.A. Nussbaum. 1980. A variable circular-plot method for estimating bird numbers. Unpublished report.

5 in closed-canopy forest;
1 in a dense grove of young trees; and
1 in an open stand of mature trees.
The bird censuses consisted of five "counts", each comprised of six "surveys", completed during April and May 1980 and 1981. A total of 360 person-hours was spent conducting bird surveys. An intensive search for active nests was conducted on the mornings of 22 and 23 May, 1981 at four stations within the closed-canopy forest.

Vegetative Transects

To characterize the difference in vegetative composition, structure, and condition at various frequencies of reservoir inundation, four 100-point transects, modified from Davis (1977), were conducted. The transects ran north to south along elevations corresponding to the 5-, 10-, and 25-year reservoir stage recurrence intervals taken from Chart 20 of the Reservoir Regulations Manual (US Army Corps of Engineers 1978). A control transect was run at the 300-year reservoir stage recurrence interval. Although not subjected to reservoir inundation, the control transect area was actively grazed.

Results and Discussion

Displacement of Birds

When the study period began on 7 May, 1980, Station 1, the lowest in elevation, was under 7.5 cm. (0.25 ft.) of reservoir water. The reservoir steadily rose, inundating five ecotonal stations by 30 May, 1980. In response to reservoir inundation, bird populations and species richness showed significant declines. Figures 5 and 6 depict the decline in these parameters in relation to water depth for the five stations subjected to inundation during the study period.

Because bird species have different habitat requirements, utilizing the riparian environment differently, their responses to inundation varied. Bird species were grouped into the fol-

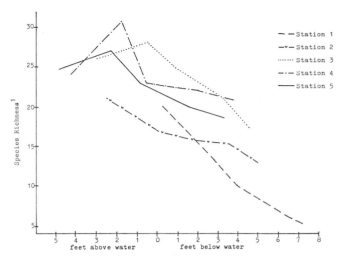

Figure 6.--Bird species richness and Isabella Reservoir inundation levels, 1980, at five stations.

[1]Number of bird species detected during a count period.

lowing four guilds based on their preferred nesting sites: 1) species which nest on the ground; 2) species which nest in shrubs; 3) species which nest among the foliage or branchwork of trees; and 4) species which nest in tree cavities.

The declines in bird populations and species richness are depicted for each guild in figure 7. The figure illustrates proportionately greater decline in ground and shrub nesters. The percent decline represents the average for the five stations once the reservoir level reached each station and assumes a linear decline. Data show, however, the decline in bird species abundance was roughly logarithmic, showing the greatest de-

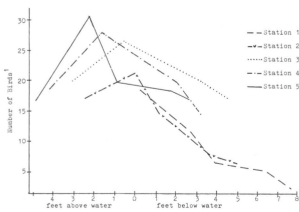

[1]Average number of birds detected per survey during each of the count periods.

Figure 5.--Bird populations and Isabella Reservoir inundation levels, 1980, at five stations.

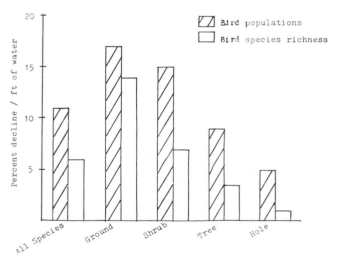

Figure 7.--Average decline of bird populations and species richness for four nesting guilds. The percent decline per foot of inundation once Isabella Reservoir water level reached each station was averaged for five ecotone stations.

cline during the first several feet of inundation, then leveling off.

As the water rose, birds utilizing the ground and shrubs for nesting and food sources were displaced to higher ground. Nests were destroyed and unfledged young were drowned. In general, tree nesting species stayed in flooded territory for a short time, but were eventually forced to leave because of reduction in available food and the threat to nests as the reservoir filled. The emigrating forest birds were temporarily replaced by shorebirds foraging along the shoreline of the advancing reservoir. Once inundation was complete, however, this habitat niche was also eliminated.

The influx of emigrating birds to unflooded regions, illustrated by increases in population densities and species richness just prior to inundation of a station, upset the balance of the entire avian community. There was a marked increase in agonistic activity, especially among the wrens and orioles, as competition for scarce unclaimed territories was heightened. The more aggressive species such as Starlings and blackbirds were observed to dominate perch sites previously shared by many species. Interspecific conflicts, indicative of lack of suitable nesting sites, were frequently observed. All of these factors cut into the parents' time and energy budgets. Smaller, more crowded territories, with a less abundant food supply, reduced nesting success and eliminated the opportunity for second and third broods.

Bird Census, 1981

Average aggregate bird densities, species diversity, and species richness for each count in each subhabitat-type are shown in table 1. Densities and diversities include only breeding populations. The highest average aggregate density was 3959 birds per 40 ha. in the closed-canopy forest. The low species diversity in the new-growth subhabitat-type is attributed to the predominance of Redwinged Blackbirds, which comprised over 60% of the total density; when this species is excluded, the new-growth subhabitat-type had the lowest density as well.

The exceptionally high bird densities of the South Fork forest well exceed the high density limits established by Peterson (1941), and are comparable even to worldwide maxima (Johnson et al. 1977). The intensive search for and location of 66 nests at four of the survey stations supports the high estimates obtained. Twenty-two active nests were found within a radius of 30 m. from Station 8 alone; the resulting breeding bird density would be over 6,000 birds per 40 ha. Bird densities for individual species within the SFWA are given in Appendix A.

When the rate of decline of bird populations observed in 1980 is applied to the high density estimates of 1981, the effects of reservoir inundation are clearly shown to be devastating.

Vegetation

Caution must be used in drawing conclusions about the effects of reservoir inundation on the condition of vegetation in the SFWA, as it has been affected by land use practices such as grazing, farming, and woodcutting as well (fig. 8). However, it is clear that prolonged inundation has significant immediate and long-term effects on vegetation. While some effects are readily observable after one season, others are not until some years later, when trees may die abruptly after a period of continued growth (Ewel 1978).

The immediate result of flooding, described by Teskey and Hinckley (1977), is the creation of an anaerobic environment around root systems, producing a variety of physiological plant stresses. The duration, depth, and rate of movement of floodwater are important factors controlling oxygen availability to the roots and hence the degree of stress produced. The time of year is also important; plants are much more susceptible to stress during the growing season (Walters et al. 1980).

Table 2 summarizes the data from four vegetative transects along the 5-, 10-, 25-, and 300-year reservoir stage recurrence intervals. Data show that total tree density, tree species diversity, average percent canopy cover, and average tree height all decrease with greater frequencies of reservoir inundation. The number of trees that died during the 1980 growing season (dead trees in 1981, with the previous year's leaves remaining), number of fallen trees, and degree of mistletoe (Phoradendron flavescens) infestation decreases with increasing elevation.

The decline in total tree density from 550 trees per ha. at transect 4 to 1 tree per ha. at transect 1 is dramatic. Although transect 2 appears to be more dense than transect 3, the filling in of a former open field with young black willow (Salix Gooddingii), of which 51% are more than 50% decadent, accounts for the high density figure.

Tree condition related to three age-classes for each tree species is shown in figure 9. The histogram illustrates a greater degree of decadence at lower elevations where inundation is most frequent.

Ewel (1978) concluded that the dependence of species composition on hydroperiod and depth of flooding is clearly the most sensitive characteristic of riparian ecosystems. Long periods of flooding eliminate the more sensitive species and generally favor the early successional stage species (Walters et al. 1980). The degree of decadence and mistletoe infestation were especially high among the cottonwoods along the lower elevation transects. In contrast, along the same transects, there was a high proportion of healthy black willow. These results indicate that Fremont cottonwood is least tolerant and black willow most tolerant of prolonged inundation in

Table 1.—Average breeding bird density, species richness, and species diversity for five subhabitat-types of the SFWA, 1981.

Count Period[1]	Disturbed Ecotone	Ecotone	Forest	Open Stand	New Growth
Breeding Bird Density[2]					
I	1327	1554	2481	605	1330
II	1594	2308	3174	1304	1880
III	1492	1324	3206	1199	1915
IV	688	2409	3417	1943	--
V	2126	2952	3959	2245	2178
Bird Species Richness[3]					
I	20	26	27	22	13
II	27	27	26	20	13
III	23	29	26	26	16
IV	24	33	30	28	--
V	27	31	27	32	18
Bird Species Diversity[4]					
I	2.15	2.17	1.95	2.09	0.08
II	2.50	2.17	2.08	1.91	0.98
III	2.52	2.28	2.01	2.23	1.34
IV	2.34	2.52	2.22	2.32	--
V	2.64	2.48	2.08	2.41	1.99

[1] Count periods: I) 15-17 April; II) 22-24 April; III) 29 April-1 May; IV) 17,18,21 May; V) 28-30 May.
[2] Density in birds/40 ha.
[3] Total number of species detected during a count period.
[4] Breeding bird species diversity =

$$-\sum_{i=1}^{n} p_i \ln p_i$$

where p_i equals the proportion of the i species to the total population and s equals the total number of species (Shannon and Weaver 1963).

the SFWA. Teskey and Hinckley (1977) classified Fremont cottonwood as "intermediately tolerant," that is, able to withstand one to three months of partial inundation during the growing season, and black willow as "tolerant," or able to withstand flooding for most of one growing season.

Figure 8.—Scattered willows and cottonwoods of the SFWA where the forest enters Isabella Reservoir.

Table 2.—Summary of vegetative transects at four Isabella Reservoir stage recurrence intervals, within the SFWA, 1981.

	Transect			
	1	2	3	4
Stage recurrence (years)	5	10	25	300
Elevation (ft msl)	2587	2596	2603	2609
Tree density (#/ha.)	1	346	178	550
Tree species diversity[1]	0.65	0.70	1.17	1.50
Ave. tree height (m.)	7.69	9.18	10.48	9.68
Ave. est. canopy cover (%)	5	20	35	42
% points with understory	0	8	25	40
Tree condition				
% fallen	9	7	2	0
% mistletoe infested	16	5	5	0
% est. 1980 deaths	27	25	3	1

[1] $-\sum p_i \ln p_i$

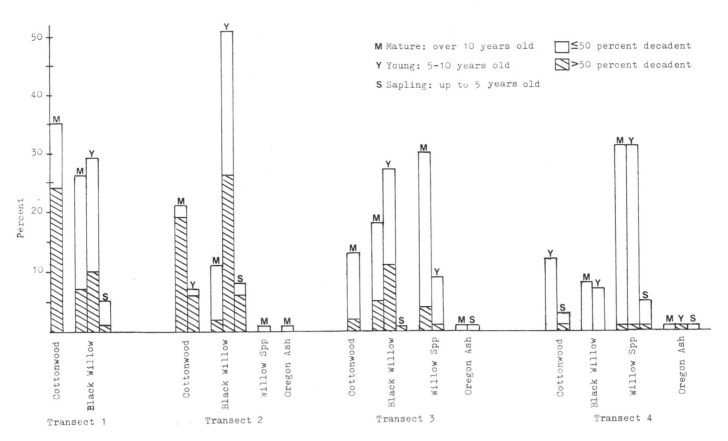

Figure 9.—Tree species composition, degree of decadence,
and age-class for four vegetative transects within the
SFWA, 1981.

The combined effects of grazing and inundation have retarded the regeneration of new trees, especially at lower elevations where large open fields have shown high potential for riparian reforestation. On transect 1, there were no seedling, sapling, or young cottonwoods. All seedling willows were concentrated in one narrow slough and had sprouted in 1981. Transect 2 had a high percentage of young willows concentrated in the interior forest, where aerial photographs show a former open field. This area was probably not easily accessible to cattle. Transect 4, an actively grazed area above gross pool, also had few seedlings or saplings of any species and was the only transect which showed a high percentage of mulefat—a shrub which is less palatable to cattle. The majority of the saplings, preferred food for cattle, were able to survive by growing through the protective center of a mulefat shrub.

The increase in percentage of fallen trees from transect 4 to transect 1 indicates that increased inundation also reduces soil stability, resulting in less support for root systems.

Another effect within the study area was the change in herbaceous vegetation in open fields. Prior to inundation, dominant plants were alfalfa (Medicago sativa), mustards (Rorrippa and Descurainia spp.), and various grasses (Graminae). When the water receded, the fields were recolonized by cocklebur (Xanthium) of little wildlife value and a nuisance to visitors.

The plant species composition also changed in a cattail (Typha) marsh of 4 ha. The cattails did not regenerate after inundation and were replaced with curly dock (Rumex spp.) and monkey flower (Mimulus guttatus).

Vegetation-Bird Relationships

The longer term effects of reservoir inundation on bird populations will be the result of an overall decrease of habitat value of the forest. Bird densities along ecotone stations are correlated with tree densities, both increasing with elevation. This correlation is also supported by the findings of Carothers and Johnson (1975) in a homogenous cottonwood forest. They found a linear relationship between bird density and tree density with a more rapid decline in bird populations if tree density fell below 25 trees/ha. Johnson (1970) also found that breeding bird populations in a cottonwood forest were reduced when tree density declined.

Tree species composition and age-class diversity also increased with elevation, showing an association between less diverse forest and lower bird densities at lower elevations.

490

The reduction in density of mature cottonwoods, in particular, has negative implications for bird populations. Nest site locations in the SFWA show that although mature Fremont cottonwood composed only 12% of the forest tree composition in the proximity of stations 8,10, and 13 (transect 3), they supported 89% of the 45 nests found at these stations. Willow species, constituting 83% of the trees, supported only 9% of the nests. Three percent of the nests were found in herbaceous understory. In a study of nesting birds of a cottonwood/willow community in California, Ingles (1950) also found that hole-nesting birds preferred cottonwood over other tree species.

Although new growth is essential to the continued viability of the forest and contributes to structural diversity, study results show that uniform stands of young trees are less favored habitat for birds than mature groves. Anderson et al. (1978) concluded that along the lower Colorado River, as trees mature they approach their full value to wildlife.

The elimination of the 4 ha. cattail marsh displaced a blackbird colony of several thousand breeding birds in 1980. Because the cattails failed to regenerate, the colony was reduced to less than 50 pairs in 1981.

As Best et al. (1978) has pointed out: "Birds with restricted habitat usage patterns are more vulnerable to changes in land use practices than those occupying a wider variety of environments." The high dependency of birds on riparian vegetation makes them especially susceptible to the effects of habitat degradation.

Additional Effects

Inundation also had important secondary impacts on wildlife and habitat improvements of the SFWA. Fishing activities, popular once the forest was under water, caused considerable disturbance to the Great Blue Heron rookery and to nesting Osprey. Because of the interference, no Osprey were hatched in 1980. Perch poles, necessary for successful utilization of nesting platforms, were washed away.

Reductions in mammals and other vertebrates were not quantified, but animals floating on debris or drowned were encountered daily during the study period in 1980. While mature birds were able to fly ahead of the advancing water level in the reservoir, many other terestrial animals were trapped. A prominent local naturalist has noted the absence of numbers and species of animals throughout the winter after inundation.[15] The recolonization rates for all species are unknown.

Inundation caused substantial damage to CE-constructed improvements in the SFWA. Artificial nesting boxes were inundated, many with occupants. All three footbridges were washed out and required reconstruction. Water control structures, including Waterman gates, levees, and ponds were destroyed, and cattle exclusion fences severely damaged. Repeated inundation will result in the destruction of the water system rebuilt in 1981, as well as other repairs and improvements; and damage or death to newly planted cottonwoods and willows.

Inundation also precluded visitor use of the SFWA for at least three spring and summer months during the season when visitation at Isabella Reservoir is highest.

CONCLUSIONS

Reservoir inundation has many adverse impacts on vegetation and wildlife in the SFWA. Flooding drastically reduces the unusually high bird populations of the SFWA by drowning and displacement. Prolonged flooding decreases tree density and diversity, which reduces the overall habitat value of the forest. The timing of inundation, during the spring nesting season of birds, and growing season of trees, amplifies these effects. Inundation is also destructive to CE structural and other improvements and significantly reduces the opportunity for visitor use of the area.

While high winter carryover is an immediate concern, enlargement of Isabella Reservoir, which is currently under consideration,[16] poses a more long-term threat of permanent inundation of part of the SFWA and more frequent inundation of the remainder.

Although the CE has made commendable habitat improvements, it maintains that it is helpless to prevent seasonal inundation of the SFWA. It has often been stated that because the SFWA is not one of the authorized purposes of Isabella Reservoir, it cannot be included in the determination of winter carryover. Failure to consider the management of the SFWA as a part of the management of the reservoir is a result of the lack of official recognition of the CE's responsibility to protect the values of the SFWA, and a lack of recognition of a change in winter carryover policy as a significant action requiring environmental impact assessment and mitigation.

If the CE's commitment to enhancement of natural values is to be honored, the South Fork Wildlife Area must be recognized as a legitimate concern and incorporated into reservoir operations and management.

ACKNOWLEDGEMENTS

This research was supported by a grant from the Environmental Field Program, University of California, Santa Cruz. We wish to thank Dr.

[15] Wilson, Lee. 1981. Personal conversation. Kernville, Calif.

[16] US Army Corps of Engineers, Sacramento District. 1977. Kern River Basin investigation.

Richard Warner for invaluable assistance throughout the study. Thanks also to the US Army Corps of Engineers, Sacramento District, and Isabella Project Office for providing information, logistic support, and other helpful assistance throughout the study.

LITERATURE CITED

Anderson, B.W., R.D. Ohmart, and J. Disano. 1978. Revegetating the riparian floodplain for wildlife. p. 318-333. In: R.R. Johnson and J.F. McCormick (tech. coord.). Strategies for protection and management of floodplain wetlands and other riparian ecosystems: Proceedings of the symposium. [Callaway Gardens, Ga., Dec. 11-13, 1978]. USDA Forest Service GTR-WO-12. 410 p.

Bailey, R.G. 1976. Ecoregions of the United States. U.S. Government Printing Office 777-124. USDA Forest Service Intermountain Region, Ogden, Utah.

Best, L.B., D.F. Stauffer, and A.R. Geier. 1978. Evaluating the effects of habitat alteration on birds and small mammals occupying riparian communities. p. 117-124. In: R.R. Johnson and J.F. McCormick (tech. coord.). Strategies for protection and management of floodplain wetlands and other riparian ecosystems: Proceedings of the symposium. [Callaway Gardens, Ga., Dec. 11-13, 1978]. USDA Forest Service GTR-WO-12. 410 p.

Carothers, S.W., and R.R. Johnson. 1975. Water management practices and their effects on non-game birds in range habitats. p. 210-222. In: Management of forest and range habitats for nongame birds: Proceedings of the symposium. [Tuscon, Ariz., May 6-9, 1975]. USDA Forest Service GTR-WO-1. 343 p.

Davis, G.A. 1977. Management alternatives for riparian habitat in the southwest. p. 59-67. In: R.R. Johnson and D.A. Jones (tech. coord.). Importance, preservation and management of riparian habitat: a symposium. [Tuscon, Ariz., July 9, 1977]. USDA Forest Service GTR-RM-43. 217 p. Rocky Mountain Forest and Range Experiment Station, Fort Collins Colo.

Dawson, D.G. 1981. The usefulness of absolute ("census") vs. relative ("sampling" or "index") measures of abundance. p. 554-558. In: C.J. Ralph and J.M. Scott (ed.). Estimating the numbers of terrestrial birds: Proceedings of the symposium. [Asilomar, Calif., Oct. 26-31, 1980]. Cooper Ornithological Society, Allen Press. Lawrence, Kansas.

Ewel, K.C. 1978. Riparian ecosystems: conservation of their unique characteristics. p. 56-62. In: R.R. Johnson and J.F. McCormick (tech. coord.). Strategies for protection and management of floodplain wetlands and other riparian ecosystems: Proceedings of the symposium. [Callaway Gardens, Ga., Dec. 11-13, 1978]. USDA Forest Service GTR-WO-12. 410 p.

Hehnke, M., and C.P. Stone. 1978. Value of riparian vegetation to avian populations along the Sacramento River system. p. 228-235. In: R.R. Johnson and J.F. McCormick (tech. coord.). Strategies for protection and management of floodplain wetlands and other riparian ecosystems: Proceedings of the symposium. [Callaway Gardens, Ga., Dec. 11-13, 1978]. USDA Forest Service GTR-WO-12. 410 p.

Ingles, L. 1950. Nesting birds of the willow-cottonwood community in California. Auk 67:325-333.

Johnson, R.R. 1970. Tree removal along southwestern river: effects on associated organisms. Amer. Phil. Soc., Yearbook 1970. p. 312-322.

Johnson, R.R., L.T. Haight, and J.M. Simpson. 1977. Endangered species vs. endangered habitats: a concept. p. 68-79. In: R.R. Johnson and D.A. Jones (tech. coord.). Importance, preservation and management of riparian habitat: a symposium. [Tuscon, Ariz., July 9, 1977]. USDA Forest Service GTR-RM-43. 217 p. Rocky Mountain Forest and Range Experiment Station, Fort Collins Colo.

Peterson, R.T. 1941. How many birds are there? Audubon 43:179-187.

Powers, R. 1971. South Fork Country. Western Cove Press, Los Angeles, Calif.

Shannon, C.E.; and W. Weaver. 1948. The mathematical theory of communication. University of Illinois Press. Urbana, Ill.

Teskey, R.O., and T.M. Hinckley. 1977. Impact of water level changes on woody riparian and wetland communities. Vol. I: Plant and soil responses to flooding. USDI Fish and Wildlife Service OBS-77/58. 30 p. National Stream Alteration Team, Columbia, Mo.

US Army Corps of Engineers, Sacramento District. 1978. Isabella Lake reservoir regulation manual.

US Army Corps of Engineers, Sacramento District. 1979a. Isabella Lake master plan. Design memorandum no. 5.

US Army Corps of Engineers, Sacramento District. 1979b. Kern River Basin hydrology. Office report. January, 1979.

USDI Fish and Wildlife Service. 1980. Important fish and wildlife habitats in California: an inventory. Portland, Oregon.

Verner, J. 1980. Measuring responses of avian communities to habitat manipulation. p. 543-547. In: C.J. Ralph and J.M. Scott (ed.). Estimating the numbers of terrestrial birds: Proceedings of the symposium. [Asilomar, Calif., Oct. 26-31, 1980]. Cooper Ornithological Society, Allen Press. Lawrence, Kansas.

Walters, A.M., R.O. Teskey, and T.M. Hinckley. 1980. Impact of water level changes on woody riparian and wetland communities. Vol. VII: Mediterranean region, western arid and semi-arid region. USDI Fish and Wildlife Service OBS-78/93. 84 p. National Stream Alteration Team, Columbia, Mo.

APPENDIX A

Species, Density, and Species Richness for Five Vegetation-Types

Species	Density[1]				
	Disturbed Ecotone	Ecotone	Forest	Open Stand	New Growth
Great Blue Heron / Ardea herodias	27	5	19	18	
Mallard / Anas platyrhynchos	79	78	101	94	+
Pintail / Anas acuta	+	15	72	+	
Cinnamon Teal / Anas cyanoptera		6			
Wood Duck / Aix sponsa	48	56	39	+	
Turkey Vulture / Cathartes aura	+	1	+	+	+
White-tailed Kite / Elanus leucurus	+	2	+	+	
Red-tailed Hawk / Buteo jamaicensis	+	+	4	+	+
Red-shouldered Hawk / Buteo lineatus	+	+	5	+	
Osprey / Pandion haliaetus			+		
American Kestrel / Falco sparverius	+	14	+	32	
California Quail / Lophortyx californicus			+		
Virginia Rail / Rallus limicola		+			
Sora / Porzana carolina		7			
American Coot / Fulica americana	+				
Killdeer / Charadrius vociferus	+	+	+		
Mourning Dove / Zenaidura macroura	110	73	195	37	64
Yellow-billed Cuckoo / Coccyzus americanus			+		
Barn Owl / Tyto alba			+		
Great Horned Owl / Bubo virginianus			+		
Vaux's Swift[2] / Chaetura vauxi		+	+		
White-throated Swift[2] / Aeronautes saxatalis			+		
Black-chinned Hummingbird / Archilochus alexandri	+		32		

Species	Density				
	Disturbed Ecotone	Ecotone	Forest	Open Stand	New Growth
Anna's Hummingbird / Calypte anna				+	
Belted Kingfisher / Megaceryle alcyon	+	+			
Common Flicker / Colaptes cafer	16	20	91	32	
Hairy Woodpecker[2] / Dendrocopos villosus		+	14		
Downy Woodpecker / Dendrocopos pubescens		+	28		
Nuttall's Woodpecker / Dendrocopos nuttallii	+	6	57	30	
Western Kingbird / Tyrannus verticalis	107	60	19	+	
Wied's Crested Flycatcher / Myiarchus tyrannulus					
Ash-throated Flycatcher / Myiarchus cinerascens	+	27	42	64	+
Olive-sided Flycatcher[2] / Myiarchus tuberculifer		+	21		
Black Phoebe / Sayornis nigricans		49	+	+	
Willow Flycatcher / Empidonax traillii			+		
Western Wood Pewee / Contopus sordidulus	71	121	224	142	+
Dusky/Hammond's Flycatcher[2] / Empidonax oberholseri/hammondii	+	+	+		71
Western Flycatcher[2] / Empidonax difficilis		14	+	+	
Horned Lark / Eremophila alpestris	16				
Violet-green Swallow[2] / Tachycineta thalassina			+		
Tree Swallow / Iridoprocne bicolor	142	64	155		
Rough-winged Swallow / Stelgidopteryx ruficollis	36				
Barn Swallow / Hirundo rustica		+	+		
Scrub Jay[2] / Aphelocoma coerulescens			+	+	
Common Raven / Corvus corax	16	7	5	18	+
Plain Titmouse / Parus inornatus		67	227	162	+

Species, Density, and Species Richness for Five Vegetation-Types (cont.)

Species	Density				
	Disturbed Ecotone	Ecotone	Forest	Open Stand	New Growth
Common Bushtit _Psaltriparus minimus_		14	108	+	94
White-breasted Nuthatch _Sitta carolinensis_			+		
House Wren _Troglodytes aedon_	162	508	1522	398	
Bewick's Wren _Thryomanes bewickii_		+	179	71	103
Robin _Turdus migratorius_	+	27	57	32	+
Hermit Thrush _Hylocichla guttata_			+		
Western Bluebird _Sialia mexicana_	+	6	35	103	
Ruby-crowned Kinglet[2] _Regulus calendula_		+	21	+	91
Cedar Waxwing[2] _Bombycilla cedrorum_	+	+	+		
Phainopepla[2] _Phainopepla nitens_		+	+		
Starling _Sturnus vulgaris_	132	151	456	103	
Hutton's Vireo[2] _Vireo huttoni_		14	14	+	
Solitary Vireo[2] _Vireo solitarius_			+		
Warbling Vireo _Vireo gilvus_		32	65		
Orange-crowned Warbler[2] _Vermivora celata_		+	+		
Nashville Warbler[2] _Vermivora ruficapilla_		+	+		
Yellow Warbler _Dendroica petechia_	36	102	171	98	71
Townsend's Warbler[2] _Dendroica townsendi_			+		
Yellow-rumped Warbler _Dendroica auduboni_	38	77	49	+	+
Black-throated Gray Warbler[2] _Dendroica nigrescens_			+		+
MacGillivray's Warbler[2] _Oporornis tolmiei_			+		
Wilson's Warbler _Wilsonia pusilla_		63	130	103	201
Common Yellowthroat _Geothlypis trichas_		16	+	32	
Yellow-breasted Chat _Icteria virens_				71	

Species	Density				
	Disturbed Ecotone	Ecotone	Forest	Open Stand	New Growth
Western Meadowlark _Sturnella neglecta_	16				
Tri-colored Blackbird _Agelaius tricolor_	71	32		+	
Red-winged Blackbird _Agelaius phoeniceus_	157	420	27	194	825
Northern Oriole _Icterus bullockii_	47	280	655	218	34
Brewer's Blackbird _Euphagus cyanocephalus_	110	19			
Brown-headed Cowbird _Molothrus ater_	71	234	198	291	71
Western Tanager[2] _Piranga ludoviciana_	+	14	85	+	
Summer Tanager _Piranga rubra_			+		
Rose-breasted Grosbeak _Pheucticus ludovicianus_					
Black-headed Grosbeak _Pheuticus melanocephalus_		6	61	+	
Blue Grosbeak _Guiraca caerulea_			+	+	
Indigo Bunting _Passerina cyanea_			2	32	+
Lazuli Bunting _Passerina amoena_	+	+	+	71	66
House Finch _Carppdacus mexicanus_	147	186	322	68	32
Lesser Goldfinch _Spinus psaltria_	+	123	199	142	
Lawrence's Goldfinch _Spinus lawrencei_		+	244	71	+
Brown Towhee _Pipilo fuscus_				+	
Savannah Sparrow _Passerculus sandwichensis_	36	6			
White-crowned Sparrow[2] _Zonotrichia leucophrys_	+	+	+		
Golden-crowned Sparrow[2] _Zonotrichia atricapilla_		+	+		
Fox Sparrow[2] _Passerella iliaca_		+			
Song Sparrow _Melospiza georgiana_	24	402	601	679	291
Species Richness[3] Total: 95	44	64	75	48	25

[1] Peak bird density over the five count periods (birds/40 hectares).
[2] Bird species which do not nest in the SFWA.
[3] Total number of species detected over the five count periods.

POTENTIAL EFFECTS OF SEWAGE EFFLUENT REMOVAL

ON THE LOWER SALINAS RIVER RIPARIAN SYSTEM[1]

Thomas T. Jones and Bruce W. Snyder[2]

Abstract.--The effects of summertime stream dewatering on the Salinas River and Lagoon due to removal of two waste-water treatment discharges were examined. It was found that there would be no adverse impact on the lagoon, but that the riparian vegetation may suffer from loss of water. A four-to six-year monitoring program is proposed to determine the precise effects.

INTRODUCTION

The Salinas River system is located in the intermontane valley of the Central Coast Ranges of California. From its headwaters in San Luis Obispo County, the river flows northwesterly through the Salinas Valley to its mouth in Monterey Bay. Almost all of the surface flow occurs from December through April as precipitation runoff.

Surface flow in the river is regulated by three dams and reservoirs on the upper reaches of the Salinas, Nacimiento, and San Antonio rivers. Santa Margarita Lake on the Salinas River is used as a municipal water supply for the city of San Luis Obispo. The Nacimiento Reservoir and the San Antonio Reservoir are used for flood control in the winter and spring and for groundwater recharge of the lower Salinas Valley aquifers in the summer and fall.

Proposed Project

In 1974, the Central Coast Basin Water Quality Control Plan Report (State Water Resources Control Board and Regional Water Quality Control Board, Central Coast Region 1975) called for removal from the Salinas River of the sewage effluent generated by the City of Salinas' two secondary wastewater treatment plants. This was to be accomplished by abandoning the treatment plants and pumping the wastewater to a new regional plant to be built on the Marina landfill site. This would result in the removal of about 0.28 m^3 per second (10 cfs) of effluent from the river. During the summer months this effluent

---
[1]Paper presented at the California Riparian Systems Conference. [University of California, Davis, September 17-19, 1981].
[2]Thomas T. Jones is Environmental Engineer with Engineering-Science, Inc., Berkeley, Calif. Bruce W. Snyder is Terrestrial Ecologist with Engineering-Science, Inc., Denver, Colo.

constitutes all or a major portion of the flow in the river below the Highway 68 bridge. The Basin Plan (ibid.) recognized this fact and recommended that a study of the effects of the effluent removal be conducted before project implementation.

The Monterey Regional Water Pollution Control Agency (MRWPCA) was the agency responsible for implementing the project. The Environmental Impact Statement (US Environmental Protection Agency and Monterey Regional Water Pollution Control Agency 1978) on the Final Facilities Plan (Engineering-Science 1978) also recommended that the effects on the river and lagoon of removal of effluent be studied. A task force composed of representatives from various concerned state and local agencies was formed to monitor and direct the study. The study was initiated in early 1979 with the objective of determining the effects of the flow reduction on the lower Salinas River. This paper summarizes the results of that study, completed in March 1981 (Engineering-Science 1980), and the actions which have followed.

ECOSYSTEM CHARACTERIZATION

Study Area Description

The area potentially affected by the proposed project includes riparian forest, freshwater marsh, saltwater marsh, and the lagoon near the river mouth. A map of the study area is shown in figure 1. The boundary farthest upstream is set by the City of Salinas Alisal wastewater treatment plant outfall, which discharges about 0.004 m^3 per second (1.5 cfs) about 200 m. (220 yd.) upstream of the Highway 68 bridge. The reach of river just upstream from Alisal is normally dry during the summer; water releases from the two reservoirs upstream are regulated such that all surface flow has percolated into the ground above this point. The City of Salinas' main treatment plant discharges about

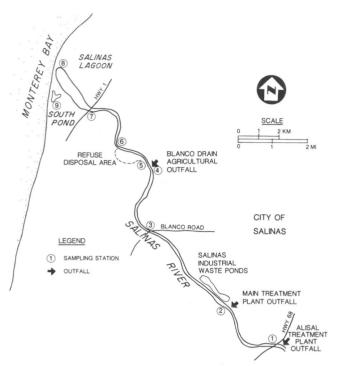

Figure 1.--Map of the study area showing sampling locations and significant point source discharges to the river.

0.24 m^3 per second (8.5 cfs) about 2.5 km. (2.5 mi.) downstream from Alisal.

Except for the riparian corridor, the land on both sides of the river has been extensively cleared for agricultural use. The land north of the river is uniformly flat for several miles; just south of the river and inland from Highway 1, the land rises sharply to elevations of 40 to 100 m. (125 to 330 ft.).

The lagoon at the mouth of the river is part of the 210 ha. (518 ac.) Salinas River Wildlife Refuge and serves as a feeding and breeding ground for large numbers of birds. During high flow periods, the lagoon is open to the bay, and the river discharges to Monterey Bay. During the summer, sand dunes close off the mouth, and the river discharges through Moss Landing Harbor about 6.5 km. (4 mi.) to the north via the old Salinas River channel.

Baseline Study Plan

The first phase of the monitoring program was a baseline study, initiated in 1979. Its objectives were to: 1) characterize the study area with respect to hydrology, water quality, and ecology; and 2) determine if there was a need for detailed impact analysis because of the proposed project. The study was conducted during the summer of 1979. Nine sampling stations, shown in figure 1, were established. At each station except Station 6, which proved to be inaccessible, the flow, electrical conductivity (EC), and temperature of the water were mea-

sured biweekly; in addition, at Stations 7 and 8 the dissolved oxygen (DO), ammonia, total organic nitrogen, nitrite, nitrate, phosphorus, and major cation and anion concentrations were measured monthly. This was done to better identify impacts on the water quality in the lagoon. The ecological portion of the study identified the dominant plant and animal species within the study area; it consisted of a literature review and two week-long field trips to the area.

Hydrology and Water Quality

Sources of Water Flow

A major effort of the baseline study was to identify the sources of summertime flow in the lower Salinas River. There are three major point sources of discharge within the study area; the two City of Salinas treatment plants and the Blanco Drain, which discharges an average of about 0.11 m^3 per second (4 cfs) approximately 8 km. (5 mi.) upstream from the mouth. This drain discharges agricultural irrigation water runoff from about 2,400 ha. (6,000 ac.) north of the river. In addition to these major point sources, there are numerous nonpoint sources of agricultural return water along both sides of the river and along the north side of the lagoon.

There are two other potential sources of water to the lagoon: groundwater inflow from the surrounding land, and seawater inflow from Monterey Bay. The magnitude of the groundwater inflow (or outflow) was measured by constructing groundwater wells around the periphery of the lagoon and calculating the magnitude and direction of flow based on soil permeability and water level difference in the wells. Seawater inflow was estimated by performing a salt balance on the lagoon water, and by a previous study which directly measured seawater inflow (Muckel et al. 1964).

Since it was impossible to measure the nonpoint flow into the river directly, it was calculated by performing a mass balance between the various sampling points on the river. The average nonpoint inflow between stations was estimated as the difference between the upstream flow and any known point source inflows within the reach. An average value for this flow per unit length of river was then computed and applied to the entire length of river and lagoon to give a total value for nonpoint inflow.

Using the data thus collected, an overall water budget for the river and lagoon was constructed. This is presented in figure 2. Surface flow into the lagoon accounted for about 92% of the inflow; of this, about 45% was from the treatment plants and the rest was from the Blanco Drain outfall and nonpoint sources. In the river, the quantity of flow from the treatment plants ranged from 100% in the upper reaches of the study area to about 45% at the head of the lagoon. Groundwater inflow from the periphery of the lagoon was negligible; seawater inflow was also very small. One source of water which was

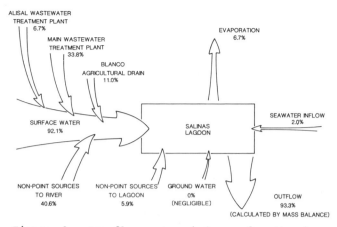

ALISAL WASTEWATER
TREATMENT PLANT
6.7%

MAIN WASTEWATER
TREATMENT PLANT
33.8%

BLANCO
AGRICULTURAL DRAIN
11.0%

EVAPORATION
6.7%

SURFACE WATER
92.1%

SALINAS
LAGOON

SEAWATER INFLOW
2.0%

NON-POINT SOURCES
TO RIVER
40.6%

NON-POINT SOURCES
TO LAGOON
5.9%

GROUND WATER
0%
(NEGLIGIBLE)

OUTFLOW
93.3%
(CALCULATED BY MASS BALANCE)

Figure 2.--Low-flow water balance for the lower Salinas River and Lagoon.

not measured was subsurface flow in the river channel.

Water Quality

Important water quality parameters which would be most affected by the proposed project were total dissolved solids (TDS), nutrients, ammonia, DO, pesticides, and coliform levels. TDS was measured at each station biweekly; nutrients, ammonia, and DO were measured monthly at Stations 7 and 8 to assess their effects on the lagoon. Pesticides and coliform levels were not measured, but data from other sources were reviewed. The significant findings for each parameter are discussed below.

Total Dissolved Solids.--TDS was determined indirectly by measuring electrical conductivity (EC) and temperature. The TDS values for the treatment plant effluents were generally less than half those for the Blanco Drain outfall, which is representative of agricultural runoff water. As expected, therefore, the TDS values generally increased downstream as more agricultural water entered the river. In particular, the TDS at the lower end of the lagoon (Station 8) was substantially higher than anyplace else in the river, due largely to seawater inflow through the sand dunes. The result of removing the sewage effluents would be to generally raise the TDS level in the river and lagoon by about a factor of two, from 1,000-1,500 mg. per l. at present to about 2,500-3,000 mg. per l.

Nutrients.--Nutrients in the form of total nitrogen and total phosphorus were measured at the upper (Station 7) and lower (Station 8) ends of the lagoon. Total phosphorus (as P) values ranged from 3.20 to 20.26 mg. per l. at Station 7 and from 0.72 to 5.56 mg. per l. at Station 8. Total nitrogen (as N) values ranged from 14.7 to 21.0 mg. per l. at Station 7, and from 4.4 to 11.2 mg. per l. at Station 8. The data indicated that nutrient removal in the lagoon was high. In addition, there was a shift in nitrogen speciation from predominantly ammonia nitrogen and nitrate to predominantly organic nitrogen and nitrate forms. These effects were undoubtedly due to algal activity in the lagoon. The treatment plant effluents are major contributors of these nutrients; mass balance calculations indicated that the two treatment plants contributed at least half and often virtually all of the nutrients found at Station 7. The Blanco Drain water (and most likely, nonpoint agricultural return water as well) occasionally had high nutrient levels, due to over-application of fertilizer, but generally it had low nutrient concentrations.

Ammonia.--Ammonia levels at Station 7 ranged from 3.09 to 16.0 mg. per l. and at Station 8 from 0 to 4.8 mg. per l. The levels of ammonia were directly correlated with high levels of ammonia in the treatment plant effluents. Mass balance calculations indicated that the plants consistently contributed most or all of the ammonia found at Station 7. Presumably, the ammonia levels upriver were even higher since less dilution water for the plant effluents was available. At the pH and temperatures encountered, these ammonia levels would lead to un-ionized ammonia--which is its toxic form--considerably in excess of the US Environmental Protection Agency EPA criterion of 0.02 mg. per l. Fish sensitivity to un-ionized ammonia varies widely among species and within the same species depending upon other environmental stress parameters (Willingham 1976).

Dissolved Oxygen.--DO levels at Station 7 ranged from 5.9 to 21.5 mg. per l. and at Station 8 ranged from 9.0 to 24 mg. per l. These generally high values were undoubtedly due to algae photosynthesis. All measurements were taken in the late morning or early afternoon when photosynthetic production of DO would be relatively high. Usually, in environments with high algal productivity, such as this, values drop substantially at night or in very cloudy weather, and can even be reduced to zero, due to algae decay.

Pesticides.--Historical pesticide data for the Salinas River, treatment plant effluents, and Blanco Drain water were examined. All the Salinas River levels were well below 1 ppm with the exception of one measurement of over 30 ppm of Diazinon at Stations 2 and 3 in October 1978. Diazinon was used to contol mosquitoes in the river and was undoubtedly the source of the high levels. A fish kill also occurred at this time, and was attributed to either the pesticide or the high ammonia levels, or a combination of both (Greenfield and Grunt 1978). A few pesticide analyses from Blanco Drain water also showed levels consistently less than 1 ppm. No pesticides have ever been detected in the effluents of either treatment plant.

Coliforms.--Coliform levels at various locations in the river have been periodically monitored by various agencies, (e.g., Bureau of Sanitary Engineering 1971; Irwin 1976). These studies have consistently shown much higher coliform levels below the treatment plant discharges than above them. Although coliforms can be contributed by agricultural runoff water, it is likely that most of the coliforms in the river were due to the treatment plant effluents. High coliform levels indicate a health hazard, and they were one of the main factors in the decision to remove the treatment plant discharges from the river. Chlorination by the treatment plants has been subject to periodic breakdown in the past, which led to very high coliform levels in the effluent.

ECOLOGY

The lower Salinas River ecological environment is composed of four major systems: salt marsh, freshwater marsh, riparian woodland, and river/lagoon. In the past, various water resource development activities have been responsible for significant degradation or loss of these once abundant systems throughout central California and elsewhere in the West. Because of the magnitude of past losses and the inherent biological values of these systems, they are now the focus of attention in ecological circles.

Salt Marsh

About 25 ha. (63 ac.), or seven percent of the study area, is salt marsh intermixed with mudflats and salt pans. The salt marsh system is located in the lower river sections near the confluence of the coast and lagoon environments. High concentrations of soil salts restrict the diversity of plants that can exist in the salt marsh. California coastal salt marshes are dominated by pickleweed and salt grass and receive only irregular salt water flooding. Pickleweed comprised about 90% of the salt marsh vegetation. Additional plant species appeared in localized areas along the lagoon/marsh interface where more frequent flooding reduces soil salinity.

The mixture of shallow water, mudflats, and vegetation in the salt marsh constitute an important wildlife area, especially for birds. The dense stands of pickleweed were heavily utilized by both resident and migrant waterfowl. Bird abundance and species diversity in the salt marsh and adjacent lagoon area were the highest in the study area. Over 127 species, both resident and migrant, have been observed in the general area. Major bird groups included gulls, terns, shorebirds, wading birds, and waterfowl. Figure 3 shows the lagoon and bordering salt marshes.

Inputs of soil moisture in the salt marsh come from both freshwater and saltwater sources. Saltwater comes directly from nearby Monterey Bay as salt spray or storm surges. High winds and tides send water around or over the dunes and onto low-lying marsh areas. Freshwater inputs are supplied primarily by rainfall. However during flood conditions, overbank flooding from the Salinas River is an additional source.

Land elevation has very important effects on salt marsh soil moisture and standing water dynamics. Elevation of the salt marshes isolates them and prevents their regular inundation by either saltwater from the bay or freshwater from the Salinas River. The salt marshes are perched

Figure 3.--Salinas River Lagoon, with salt marsh area in the foreground and sand dunes separating the lagoon from Monterey Bay in the background. Note the utilization of the lagoon by birds.

above the normal river channel and receive water from the river only during extremely high flow conditions. During normal flow conditions, water of the lower Salinas River Lagoon is channeled away from the salt marshes by high streambanks and therefore plays no significant role in the salt marshes' short-term hydroperiod. The water and salinity regime of the Salinas salt marshes are instead controlled by rainfall and by oceanic and evaporative processes not linked to normal river flows.

Freshwater Marsh

The freshwater marsh system is very limited in size and distribution; this system totals less than 0.8 ha. (2 ac.), less than 0.5% of the study area. Freshwater marshes occur as isolated, small stands rather than large, contiguous units. The dominant emergent plant was broad-leafed cattail. Small stands were scattered throughout the channel; they were most abundant below the Blanco Drain outfall, where water was constantly available.

The limited distribution and small size of this system precludes the development of any uniquely associated wildlife assemblage. Wildlife species present in freshwater marsh areas were also found in adjacent riparian woodlands.

The presence of standing water is the crucial parameter in this system. The depth of water and duration of submergence determine vegetative composition, zonation, and succession.

Riparian Woodland

Riparian woodland dominates the terrestrial areas, comprising approximately 93% of the upland portion of the study area. Riparian woodland extended almost continuously from the Highway 68 bridge to just east of the Highway 1 bridge. It formed an extremely narrow corridor, being confined to the Salinas River channel and occasional scattered waste places along the banks and floodplain that have not been converted to agricultural uses. Cottonwood and willow species were the important plant dominants. The relative abundance of these plants varied considerably along the river. Land elevation, local depth to groundwater, and, most importantly, the local land management techniques employed in adjacent areas determine the vigor, stature, and relative abundance of these species in the corridor.

The open floodplain bordering the Salinas River channel is frequently flooded by the natural rising of the river. Species growing in this habitat are adapted to flooding and constantly moist soil. Groundwater is continually recharged by overbank flows and subsurface seepage from nearby surface flows (Keller 1977; Johnson et al. 1976; Crouch 1979). Most species are low-growing annual or perennial herbs and grasses.

Wherever unstable soils accumulate to form slightly elevated gravelbars, dense stands of

shrubs up to 7 m. (24 ft.) tall have developed. The dominant shrub, sandbar willow, is the first species to colonize the gravelbars. Other dominant shrubs include arroyo willow and mule fat. Herbs usually grow towards the edge of the gravelbars. In time, the elevation of the gravelbar becomes higher and the gravelbar more distant from the river due to continual soil deposition. As a result, flood frequency decreases.

These new conditions favored the establishment of riparian forest, characterized by tall trees crowded and tangled with vines (Sands 1979). There were several vegetation layers within the forest along the Salinas River. Overstory trees attained heights up to 23 m. (75 ft.). The dominant overstory species was Fremont cottonwood. A subcanopy layer 4.6-13.7 m. (15-45 ft.) high was formed by red willow, black cottonwood, and box elder. Understory species consisted primarily of tall herbs and tangling vines.

This riparian forest or woodland corridor provides refuge for a large number of wildlife species unable to exist in adjacent agricultural areas. Bird population levels and species diversity were high. Common mammals included raccoon, deer, and cottontail rabbit. Coyote, grey fox, and bobcat were occasionally present.

River/Lagoon

For analytical and descriptive purposes, the river and brackish lagoon environments were combined into one functional ecosystem. This was done because of the intricate interdependencies, the absence of any distinct boundary between the two systems, and the functional similarity of the driving forces of the two systems.

The freshwater riverine zone extends roughly from the Alisal wastewater treatment plant outfall downstream approximately to the California Highway 1 bridge. At the bridge, a gradual transition from fresh to slightly brackish water occurs as the river merges imperceptibly into the lagoon itself. The position of the interface between these two zones shifts continually. Water salinity in the lagoon and upstream transitional zone fluctuates seasonally depending on river discharges, rainfall, and periodic saltwater influxes from Monterey Bay.

A larger sandbar forms across the river mouth during the summer and fall months, effectively sealing off the lower river from Monterey Bay and restricting regular tidal exchanges with bay waters. Sandbar development and maintenance are predominantly controlled by alongshore forces. Normal river discharges are too weak during the summer to counterbalance sandbar development. A water-control weir diverts summer streamflow from the lagoon to Monterey Bay through the old Salinas River channel which discharges through Moss Landing Harbor about 1.5 km. (1 mi.) to the north. The sandbar essentially excludes saltwater influences, making upstream freshwater discharges the system's sole driving force and the source of system energetics. Consequently, the hydrodynamics of the lower stream and lagoon areas during the summer and fall seasons are unlike classic river-influenced bays in which saltwater influxes and river discharges are physical forces of approximately equal importance regulating plant and wildlife populations.

Formerly, the Salinas River and Lagoon supported large populations of fish. Today, however, the populations have been significantly altered by major hydrologic changes in the watershed. Three groups of fish currently occur in the Salinas River: native, introduced, and marine visitors. Over the years, 23 fish species have been reported in the Salinas River; five are introduced, 16 are native, and two are anadromous. Among the native fish, populations of eight species have declined significantly in recent years. The other eight species have remained stable. Benthic invertebrates are also basic components of the Salinas River and Lagoon food chains.

IMPACT ANALYSIS

The proposed streamflow withdrawals represent major potential hazards to the basic integrity of some of the ecosystems on the lower Salinas River. An ecosystem-oriented impact analysis was conducted to assess the possible effects resulting from this periodic stream dewatering.

The most important objective of the impact analysis was to anticipate potential environmental changes arising from the proposed action which would threaten the preservation and perpetuation of the aquatic, wetland and riparian systems as they currently exist. The approach to achieving this objective was to: 1) identify and evaluate the critical ecological processes that maintain existing wetland, riparian, and aquatic systems in the study area; and 2) determine if and how the proposed action could cause changes in these processes, and thus possibly alter the functional stability of the riparian woodlands, salt marsh, freshwater marsh, and river/lagoon systems. An additional objective was to identify general mitigation measures for the anticipated ecosystem changes.

Impacts of the proposed project were considered beneficial if they enhanced biological productivity and diversity, and detrimental if they lowered productivity and diversity. The understanding implicit in this approach was that system characteristics such as biotic quality and quantity, species richness, species diversity, and overall biomass productivity are expressions of the overall stability and health of the ecosystem. Major disruptions of a system's functional integrity and stability would be expressed as shifts in plant composition, decreased plant vigor, loss of productivity, disappeance of certain wildlife species, or reduced animal abundance. These changes could be measured in the field.

In order to assess these complex ecosystems in an organized manner, an innovative analytical approach was used which utilized four ecosystem models. The models integrated and summarized a large amount of diverse ecosystem information and presented the information as diagrams showing the ecological interrelationships controlling the presence and development of plants and wildlife. Development of each model resulted from an extensive literature review and synthesis of diverse physical and biological data which established functional linkages between ecosystem components.

The analysis indicated that stability in each ecosystem was regulated by a different set of physical parameters. Even though all ecological processes are important to the integrity of a natural system, critical pathways become apparent through the large number and kinds of other system components they controlled. Ultimately, this control could be traced to vegetation and wildlife populations. Some of these ecological processes were linked to streamflow. Critical pathways for each system type were identified as follows.

Riparian Woodland: frequency, duration, and timing of stream flooding, and soil moisture.

Salt Marsh: soil moisture and soil salinity.

River/lagoon: freshwater stream discharge, stream velocity, and depth of standing water.

Freshwater Marsh: average depth of standing water and duration of soil submergence.

The hydrologic regime of the Salinas River was the pivotal issue of the analysis. The river's past and present flow characteristics provided important background information that was essential for assessing the future status of the biological systems.

The lower Salinas River possesses flow characteristics typical of other central California coastal systems. Streamflow varies seasonally and is often quite erratic between years, since flow is a function of annual rainfall patterns. Flows are heaviest following winter and spring storms and lowest during the long summer dry seasons.

Because riparian, wetland, and aquatic ecosystems are dependent on available water, the most critical phase of the annual hydroperiod is generally the summer low-flow period, when water availability is lowest and biological demand is highest. A dependable and adequate supply of soil moisture and water during these stress conditions is essential for the maintenance of these water-dependent systems.

The environmental analysis indicated that two aspects of the river's hydrologic character had major influences on the nature and quality of the riparian and other biological systems. These were: 1) timing, duration, and frequency of flooding; and 2) presence of perennial streamflow. A river's flood regime regulates riparian woodland regenerative capacity and also provides the mechanism for transporting upper watershed nutrients to downstream embayments and estuaries. Perennial streamflow helps maintain a permanent shallow water table within the root zones of the riparian and wetland vegetation which, in turn, sustains the vegetation through the summer. Removal of the wastewater treatment discharge presents no threats to the flooding regime of the river, although it does pose a significant potential hazard to the perennial flows in the channel.

Historical streamflow data indicate that, with few exceptions, constant but low flows were present in the river channel. The quantity of this low flow averages 0.03 to 0.06 m^3 per second (1 to 2 cfs). From the mid-1950s to the present, summer flows at the Highway 68 bridge have stabilized at a relatively constant level due to the Alisal treatment plant discharges. Daily average flow ranged consistently from 0.03 to 0.08 m^3 per second (1 to 3 cfs) during the July to September period. Sustained summer flows are important for maintaining standing water in the upper stream channel and probably for contributing to adequate soil moisture levels in adjacent riparian areas. Treatment plant flows have partially compensated for reductions in the annual streamflows caused by upstream impoundments.

The major environmental changes resulting from the proposed effluent removal project are summarized below by ecosystem. All anticipated significant impacts would result from manipulation of the existing hydrologic regime. The greatest effects would occur in the riparian woodland and river/lagoon systems, which are directly susceptible to flow reductions. The most significant effects would be caused by substantial lowering of the groundwater table beneath major sections of the nearby riparian woodland. In addition, in the upper stretches of the river, stream dewatering would eliminate the aquatic biota where the streambed dries out. Where wastewater flows provided major sources of water for freshwater marshes, there would be a moderate loss of wetland habitat and its associated wildlife benefits. The fact that most of this habitat-type is located downstream of other incoming water sources reduces the overall significance of this potential change.

All other environmental effects are generally expected to be of relatively small significance. Expected reductions in nutrient and detrital transport pathways were considered insignificant because other detrital sources are available, and the expected diversions would occur during minor transport periods. Major imports probably occur during winter and spring months. Specific ecosystem effects are summarized below.

Salt Marsh

No adverse or beneficial environmental impacts are anticipated for the salt marsh ecosystem. This system is apparently isolated hydrologically from the ecological processes which would be affected by the proposed project. The source of system energetics and critical regulatory processes is not controlled by the influences of wastewater flow reductions.

Freshwater Marsh

The freshwater marsh complex is a small system composed of discontinuous units of limited distribution. An assessment of the project effects on the entire ecosystem was complicated by its distributional characteristics. Some freshwater marsh areas are dependent upon wastewater treatment plant flows, while others are dependent upon agricultural return flows. Stands entirely dependent on agricultural return water would remain unchanged. Stands supported by treatment plant effluent would disappear. The ratio of these two types is unknown.

The total freshwater marsh ecosystem constitutes only about 0.5% of the entire study area. The proportion of this system which would be lost because of project activities represents an incremental decrease in overall habitat diversity, reduction in biological productivity, and loss of habitat for wetland-associated wildlife species, particularly waterfowl and wading birds. From the standpoint of the total freshwater marsh in the study area, the anticipated changes represent low to moderately significant changes. From the standpoint of the total ecosystem integrity of the study area, the anticipted changes would be of low significance.

Riparian Woodland

The greatest potential for significant adverse terrestrial impacts would occur in this ecosystem. Figure 4 shows a typical section of river with bordering riparian vegetation. Analysis of the best available hydrologic information suggested that the current treatment plant discharges constitute the major source of soil moisture for the riparian woodland. During the summer growing season, availability and abundance of adequate soil moisture is of paramount importance to the maintenance of system integrity. Removal of the water source could be expected to lead to the elimination or degradation of up to about 90% of the existing riparian woodland. It is essential that the existing water table not be lowered beyond the root zone (depths greater than 3.3 m. [10 ft.]) of the willows and cottonwoods. Given the degree of uncertainty associated with conclusively identifying the precise mechanism maintaining the present level of the water table, it was recommended that at least 0.042 m^3 per second (1.5 cfs), and preferably up to 0.28 m^3 per second (10 cfs) be maintained during the summer from the Alisal treatment plant downstream.

501

Figure 4.--Typical section of the Salinas River with bordering riparian vegetation.

One important mitigating consideration involved determining where the present water table is located within the riparian corridor and identifying its primary sources of recharge. If it could be conclusively shown that the primary source of soil moisture was either subsurface agricultural return water and/or shallow subsurface flows from upchannel recharge operations instead of existing surface flows from the treatment plants, the need for replacement surface flows would be less critical. However, this would not affect the adverse impacts on aquatic life from stream dewatering.

Lowering the water table would cause long-term, ecosystem-wide changes that would include major shifts in plant composition from cottonwood and willow probably to more drought-resistant brush and oak species; reduced ecosystem productivity; reduced quantities of riparian woodland; and reduced quality of riparian wildlife habitats, particularly for breeding bird species. The importance of riparian woodland to breeding birds is widely recognized. Local replacement breeding areas are not readily available; this impact could not be mitigated.

River/Lagoon

The greatest potential for significant adverse aquatic impacts exists in this ecosystem of flowing and standing water. The proposed project would remove a major source of summertime streamflow and initiate environmental changes ranging from complete dewatering in the upper stream reaches to little or no change at the extreme lower end of the lagoon. The magnitude of this change at any point would vary according to supplemental sources of stream inflows from agricultural return flows. The range of associated fish and wildlife impacts would vary accordingly. The most significant impacts would occur where dewatering was the most severe. Aquatic productivity would be completely eliminated in dewatered stretches. Available stream habitats and refuge areas for freshwater fishes would be significantly reduced, and the quality of the remaining fishery would be degraded by reduced flows and possibly by poorer water quality. Reduced streamflows might lead to higher concentrations of TDS and agricultural pesticides entering the lagoon system. This would be offset by lower dissolved nutrient and ammonia concentrations, and by the occasional DO depletion produced by treatment plant effluents. The resultant cumulative effect on the lagoon fish species is uncertain. The composition of fish species remaining after the project would be expected to consist of more stress-tolerant species, such as carp. In the long-term, the ratio of salt-tolerant species to freshwater species would probably increase, because of the reduction in upstream freshwater refuge areas.

Because the freshwater fishery in the upstream reaches of the study area is not substantial, and elimination of the discharges would improve a number of water quality parameters, this impact was considered less important than the potential impact on the riparian vegetation.

502

PROPOSED MITIGATION MEASURES

The results of the impact analysis indicated that the effect of the project on the lagoon would be minimal, but that serious adverse effects on the upstream riparian vegetation, which has value as a wildlife habitat, could occur. An adverse impact on the freshwater fishery would definitely occur, but since this fishery is not extensive and is considered of low value in the upstream reaches, this impact was not considered severe. It was concluded that to mitigate the known and potential impacts, some or all of the water lost due to removal of the wastewater treatment discharges should be replaced from another source.

Potential Water Sources

Seven alternatives were considered, and six possible sources of replacement water were identified. These alternatives were:

1. no action, allowing all flows to be diverted to the regional wastewater treatment plant with no Salinas River augmentation;

2. retaining and upgrading the quality of one or both of the City of Salinas treatment plants;

3. upgrading and pumping a portion of the effluent from the regional treatment plant back to Salinas and discharging it into the river during the summer;

4. developing a perched water aquifer wellfield and diverting pumped groundwater to the river;

5. developing a deep aquifer wellfield and diverting pumped groundwater to the river;

6. releasing additional quantities of water from the Nacimiento or San Antonio reservoirs; and

7. pumping effluent from the City of Salinas industrial waste lagoons to the Alisal discharge point.

Initial screening of the six flow replacement alternatives eliminated all but Alternative 4 from further consideration. Alternative 2 was prohibitively expensive due to the high level of treatment required. The net cost, assuming almost complete nitrogen and phosphorus removal, biochemical oxygen demand (BOD) and suspended solids limits of 5 mg. per l., and almost complete coliform kill, was estimated to be $1.7 million to retain just the Alisal plant, and $7.8 million to retain both plants.

Alternative 3 was also prohibitively expensive, costing $4.1 million to return 0.04 m^3 per second (1.5 cfs), and $12.7 million to return 0.28 m^3 per second (10 cfs) to the point of the Alisal plant discharge. Alternative 5 was also relatively expensive and had the additional

drawback of being an uncertain source of supply and a potential future source of municipal and irrigation water. Alternative 6 was not feasible because water rights for this purpose could not be obtained. Alternative 7 was rejected because of concerns about industrial pond effluent quality, and because of the likelihood that flow was already seeping from the ponds into the river. Alternative 4 was therefore the only feasible flow replacement alternative. However, there remained the question of whether or not sufficient water was indeed available from the aquifer. Water from this aquifer was too high in TDS for agricultural or municipal use, but was suitable for flow replacement. Developing wells and transporting it to the river would be relatively inexpensive because existing treatment plant outfalls could be used, and the annual operational cost would be low.

Consequently, in January 1981 several wells into the perched aquifer were dug and tested for their yields. It was found that insufficient water was available to make well development worthwhile. This eliminated the last potential source of inexpensive replacement water, and left the no action alternative as the only remaining choice.

Selected Alternative

At the August 5, 1981 meeting of the task force, it was agreed that because no easily developed replacement water was available, the precise effects of reducing or removing the effluent flow should be determined. A further study of the effects of flow removal on the riparian vegetation was proposed. It was the consensus of the group that if significant deterioration of the riparian vegetation should occur, replacement water should be obtained. If no significant harm to this vegetation occurred, stream dewatering would be permitted. A four- to six-year monitoring study would be conducted to determine what, if any, would be the effects on the riparian vegetation if some or all of the flow was removed.

The proposed study is to monitor depth to groundwater table across the river channel, and vegetation vigor, growth, and reproduction at five stations along the river. The first two years of the study will provide baseline data before any flow is removed. The following two years the 0.24 m^3 per second (8 cfs) flow from the Salinas main plant will be removed; the only effluent flow left will be the 0.04 m^3 per second (1.5 cfs) from the Alisal plant. If no effects are observed at this flow level, the Alisal plant flow will be removed for the last two years of the study. Criteria for determining what constitutes a "significant effect" will be set before the study begins. If a significant effect does occur due to the flow removal, some form of flow augmentation must then be developed by the MRWPCA.

503

CONCLUSIONS AND RECOMMENDATIONS

Although the monitoring program will be designed to answer specific questions about flow reduction in the Salinas River, the data and results generated should be widely applicable to other riparian systems. A better understanding of the dynamics of riparian systems should be gained from this effort.

The results of this study have made it clear that a regional project such as this can have a number of beneficial as well as adverse impacts which may not be perceived at the outset. Although the EIR/EIS process should identify most of the impacts, it is often impossible to accurately predict effects on complex hydrological and biological systems such as riparian systems. It is therefore critical that study of potential effects on complex systems begin very early in the planning stages of any project which may affect them.

LITERATURE CITED

Bureau of Sanitary Engineering. 1971. Sanitary engineering investigation of Salinas River, Reclamation Ditch and Blanco Drain. 23 p. California Department of Public Health.

Crouch, G.L. 1979. Changes in the vegetation complex of a cottonwood ecosystem on the South Platte River. In: Riparian and wetland habitats of the Great Plains: proceedings of the thirty-first annual meeting. Great Plains Agricultural Council, Fort Collins, Colorado.

Engineering-Science, Inc. 1978. Final facilities plan for North Monterey County (California). 283 p. Monterey Peninsula Water Pollution Control Agency, Monterey, Calif.

Engineering-Science, Inc., 1980. Lower Salinas River flow reduction impact report prepared for Monterey Regional Water Pollution Control Agency. 175 p. Monterey Regional Water Pollution Control Agency, Seaside, Calif.

Greenfield, H.R., and C.D. Grunt. 1978. Fish die-off in the Salinas River. Northern Salinas Valley Mosquito Abatement District.

Irwin, T. 1976. USDI Geological Survey, water quality investigation, Salinas River. California Water Resources Investigation (November) 76-100.

Johnson, W.D., R.L. Burgess, and W.R. Keammerer. 1976. Forest overstory vegetation and environment on the Missouri River floodplain in North Dakota. Ecology Monograph.

Keller, E.A. 1977. The fluvial system: selected observations. p. 39-46. In: A. Sands (ed.). Riparian forests in California: their ecology and conservation. Institute of Ecology Pub. No. 15. 122 p. University of California, Davis.

Muckel, D.C., K. Dyer, and J. Behnke. 1964. Report on salinity problems at the mouth of the Salinas River. U.S.D.A. Soil and Water Conservation Research Division, Agricultural Research Service.

Sands, A. 1979. Public involvement in riparian habitat protection: a California case history. p. 216-227. In: R.R. Johnson and J.F. McCormick (tech. coord.). Strategies for protection and management of floodplain wetlands and other riparian ecosystems. USDA Forest Service GTR-WO-12. 410 p. Washington, D.C.

State Water Resources Control Board and Regional Water Quality Control Board, Central Coast Region. 1975. Regional water quality control plan, Central Coastal Basin (3). State Water Resources Control Board and Regional Water Quality Control Board, Coastal Region, Sacramento, Calif.

US Environmental Protection Agency and Monterey Regional Water Pollution Control Agency. 1978. Final environmental impact statement and report, North Monterey County facilities plan. US Environmental Protection Agency and Monterey Water Pollution Control Agency, Monterey, Calif.

Willingham, W.T. 1976. Ammonia Toxicity, Control Tech. Branch, Water Division, US Environmental Protection Agency, Washington, D.C.

SOFAR: A SMALL-TOWN WATER DIVERSION PROJECT

ON THE SOUTH FORK, AMERICAN RIVER[1]

Russell D. Langley[2]

Abstract.--As designed, the SOFAR project would provide consumers with 30,000 acre-feet of water annually and a 1.2% increase in peak load capacity at 5 to 7 times the current price of power. Timberland, riparian and meadow communities, trout habitat, and a deer herd would be lost or jeopardized. Mitigation measures are few, and alternatives to the project have not been objectively considered. The author questions probable impact on future generations whose options such projects will have foreclosed.

INTRODUCTION

In its entirely, the South Fork American River (SOFAR) Project is described as the ultimate development of the South Fork of the American River. If built, it would consist of a series of powerhouses, reservoirs, and diversion dams extending from 66 km. (41 mi.) above Placerville to approximately 32 km. (20 mi.) below Placerville. Proponents advocate that the project is needed because of its ability to provide water for El Dorado County, to aid in this country's goal of energy self-sufficiency, and to provide recreational facilities.

A similar project was considered in 1969 by Ebasco Engineering Firm but was found to be not economically feasible at the time. In 1975, the project was re-evaluated by Tudor Engineering Company and shown to be feasible. Upon this finding, it was recommended to the El Dorado County Board of Supervisors, acting in their capacity as the County Water Agency, to seek a potential power purchaser.

GENERAL DESCRIPTION

The SOFAR Project consists of two sections located entirely within El Dorado County. The Lower Mountain Project is that section located below Placerville, while the Upper Mountain Project lies above Placerville.

The Upper Mountain Project would begin with two river diversions: the Forni Diversion Dam on

the South Fork of the American River and the Sherman Diversion Dam on the Silver Fork of the American River. Water would be diverted from these rivers to the proposed Alder Reservoir which is to be the primary storage reservoir. A major portion of seven small tributaries would also be diverted to the Alder Reservoir. Water released from Alder Reservoir would pass through two powerhouses, after which 30,000 acre-feet (AF) per year would flow through a third powerhouse and then be released into the South Fork of the American River, approximately 45 km. (28 mi.) below the Forni Diversion Dam. Water diverted to the Texas Hill Reservoir would be added to the El Dorado Irrigation District (EID) distribution system.

The Lower Mountain Project would be located solely along the South Fork American River and would be composed of two reservoirs. The Coloma Reservoir would be located above the gold discovery town of Coloma, while the Salmon Falls Reservoir would lie above Folsom Reservoir. Powerhouses would accompany both reservoirs.

PROJECT ALTERNATIVES

From 1975 to 1977 a total of 21 alternative plans for the development of the South Fork of the American River were reviewed and put into a summary by Frank B. Viller for EID. In 1977 a Technical Advisory Committee was formed to screen and evaluate the alternatives. The committee was given the following five criteria by the County Water Agency and EID to be used in their review:

1. control of sufficient water for storage and carryover;
2. control of sufficient water for consumptive use;
3. amount of power revenue required to construct, maintain, and operate the powerplant, and amortize their costs;

[1] Paper presented at the California Riparian Systems Conference. [University of California, Davis, September 17-19, 1981].

[2] Russell D. Langley is Chairman of Environmental Planning and Information Council of El Dorado County, Placerville, Calif.

4. amount of power revenue plus water revenue required on the less cost-effective plans; and

5. use only information from studies already made by engineers, updating to current costs (EDAW, Inc. 1979).

Thus, the evaluation and screening process was based both on cost effectiveness and on the amount of water made available to EID. New alternatives and the amount of environmental degradation caused by each alternative were not considered.

The Technical Advisory Committee recommended three alternatives which were ranked in order of their cost effectiveness. The preferred project design was the entire SOFAR Project. The second choice consisted of the Upper Mountain Project with the Salmon Falls Reservoir and powerhouse included. Ranking third in selection was the Upper Mountain Project. All three alternatives would provide the same amount of water for consumptive use.

On 12 August 1979 EID and the County Water Agency passed a joint resolution to undertake the Upper Mountain Project. Their decision to undertake the least preferred of the three alternatives rested on the knowledge that including any portion of the Lower Mountain area would interfere with a 32-km. (20-mi.) stretch of heavily used white-water. Thus, fearing strong opposition which promised to become statewide, advocates of SOFAR decided to pursue the Upper Mountain Project first and reserve the Lower Mountain Project for later.

Once the project design was chosen, environmental consultants were called upon to steer the project through the requirements of the California Environmental Quality Act and the National Environmental Policy Act. According to the draft Environmental Impact Report (EIR) the following concepts outline all options available to EID for additional water:

1. build a project for water supply only;
2. build a project for water supply and power generation;
3. buy an existing project and operate it for water and power generation (such as PG&E El Dorado Project, FERC 184);
4. purchase water from another agency (e.g., Sacramento Municipal Utilities District White Rock);
5. conserve existing water supplies (i.e., don't build a new project, but conserve the water supply, improve the present system, and control the demand for water instead); and
6. take no action (ibid.).

Taking no action was rejected because it was not considered realistic. Ideas involving building a project for water only, purchasing an existing project, or purchasing water from another agency were considered not economically feasible because the cost of the water would be too high.

The concept of improving the existing water distribution system was shelved. Currently, 40-46% of the water diverted for both domestic and irrigation purposes is lost from the EID distribution system (table 1). Most of this loss is due to leakage and evaporation; relining ditches or installing pipelines to reduce this loss would be expensive. System improvements could provide all needed water until approximately 1995, even taking into consideration projected growth rates. However, the expense of the improvements would have to be borne by the water consumers; no additional revenues would be generated by such an undertaking.

Table 1.--Consumption diversions of water and water consumption (total sales) within EID's service area. (Source: James Montgomery, Consulting Engineers, Inc.)

Year	Diversions for Consumption (AF)	Consumption (sales) (AF)	Loss (AF)	Percent not accounted for
1975	36,400	22,019	14,383	40
1976	38,545	22,576	15,969	41
1977	20,974	12,237	8,737	42
1978	25,188	--	--	--
1979	34,853	18,689	16,164	46
1980	34,133	--	--	--

With such high system losses, the actual need for the water to be delivered by the SOFAR project comes into question. If EID were to develop all of its existing water rights and reduce system losses to a reasonable level of 10%, the system could yield approximately 80,000 AF of water. In 1979, EID sold only 18,689 AF of water. Therefore, EID could easily double its water connections within the existing service area using currently available supplies. However, without system improvements, additional water would be needed to expand service into areas which are presently served by private wells.

Controlling the demand for water as an alternative was also shelved. According to the draft EIR, EID has determined its function is to "... furnish water for any beneficial purpose, not to discourage the use of water" (ibid.).

The only viable alternative remaining was the already decided upon concept of a project which produces power and, thus, subsidized water.

One alternative not given adequate consideration in the draft EIR was the Sly Park proposal. The original proposal was to enlarge the existing main water storage reservoir and to augment stream flows to the reservoir. Because this suggestion did not originally include a powerhouse, the proponents of SOFAR did not consider the expansion economically feasible.

It would seem feasibility is limited to a project which would generate sufficient revenues to pay for construction and maintenance of the facilities, deliver additional water for consumptive purposes, and possibly supply the county with additional income from power generation. This would put the cost of EID water on the consumers of the utility company which purchases the power. Current negotiations are with Sacramento Municipal Utility District (SMUD). The amount of power to be delivered to this purchaser by the SOFAR Upper Mountain Project is expected to be 1.2% of its summer peak load capacity, at a cost estimated to be five to seven times the present cost of power. Alternatives for this power exist.

Even without additional power, peak load demand could be reduced through electrical load management. A load management program could include shifting swimming pool filter pump use to periods of lower demand and installing remote load switches on air conditioners and water heaters. This would allow the utility company to turn off these appliances for a short period every hour during peak demand. Electrical load management does not reduce the overall demand for electricity, it just redistributes it.

Power consumption could be reduced by the use of solar water heaters, the application of additional house insulation, the reduction of transmission voltage levels, and requiring more efficient air conditioner and refrigerator motors. All of these improvements would not only save power but would also reduce peak load demand.

Additional power could be generated with small wind and solar units, but this type of development has been rejected:

> ...small decentralized solar and small decentralized wind generating systems have also been suggested. It is clearly not feasible for a utility to install, operate, and maintain such a vast array of scattered systems. (Federal Energy Regulatory Commission 1981).

But perhaps feasibility is not the real issue here. According to the final Environmental Impact Statement (EIS) issued by the Federal Energy Regulatory Commission (FERC) (ibid.), small wind and solar units would have to be owned and operated by private individuals. This is, for obvious reasons, simply not in the best interest of utility companies.

If SMUD contracts to purchase the power from the Upper Mountain Project to provide its consumers with the additional 1.2% peak load power, the cost will be between $560,000,000 and $750,000,000, not including interest on the bonds. The estimated cost of supplying and installing enough air conditioner remote control devices to save the same amount of peak load power would cost approximately 2% of that amount.

POLITICAL ASPECTS

Support for the SOFAR Project comes mainly from real estate development interests and others who stand to benefit immediately. To help foster the project, the SOFAR Council was formed. Membership donations provided for road signs, news releases, public information meetings, petitions, and advertising in local newspapers (fig. 1). Political support was gained from the area's Assemblyman Norm Waters.

Opposition to the project comes from rafting companies which fear that flow reductions in the white-water sections of the South Fork American River will inhibit river travel. They also fear that upon completion of the Upper Mountain Project, the Lower Mountain Project will be actively pursued; its completion would put an end to their livelihood.

Others who question or oppose the project include the Maidu Group of the Sierra Club, Friends of the River, the Environmental Planning and Information Council of El Dorado County (EPIC), Water and Power Resource Service, Pacific Gas and Electric, Sierra Kayak School, American River Canyon Association of West Sacramento, El Dorado Wine Grape Growers, California Department of Fish and Game (DFG), Concerned Citizens for Rural Resources, Environmental Council of Sacramento (ECOS), Central Valley Regional Water Quality Control Board, the owners of homes that would be inundated by the proposed project, and other concerned individuals and groups.

Figure 1.--One of three signs erected by proponents of the SOFAR projet. (Photo by Cheryl Lemming Langley.)

Public input meetings began in 1977, after the Technical Advisory Committee had made its recommendations. However, to those who raised questions and concerns, the project seemed set; they often found their questions ignored.

One concern repeatedly raised was that neither El Dorado County nor EID had comprehensive master plans to aid in deciding how much water would be needed and where growth should be directed. Many claimed the projected water needs shown in SOFAR's initial studies were too high. This claim was substantiated in 1981 when James Montgomery, Consulting Engineers, projected water needs for the year 2020 which were 46,000 AF less than the SOFAR-projected high and 16,000 AF less than the SOFAR-projected low water needs (fig. 2).

Other concerns voiced were that the SOFAR Upper Mountain Project would be growth inducing and public services would be further strained. The response by the SOFAR advisors was that water in itself does not ensure growth. Meanwhile, the paperwork for the project continued and a bond election for $560,000,000 was set for June 1980.

Fearing the bond would not pass by the required two-thirds majority, the SOFAR Council petitioned to bind EID to the bond if the measure was passed by a simple majority. As the election neared, the Council stirred up memories of the recent drought and predicted growth-related water shortages and building moratoria. They also implied that Los Angeles would obtain the water rights if the bond were not passed. As an added inducement it was promised the project would not

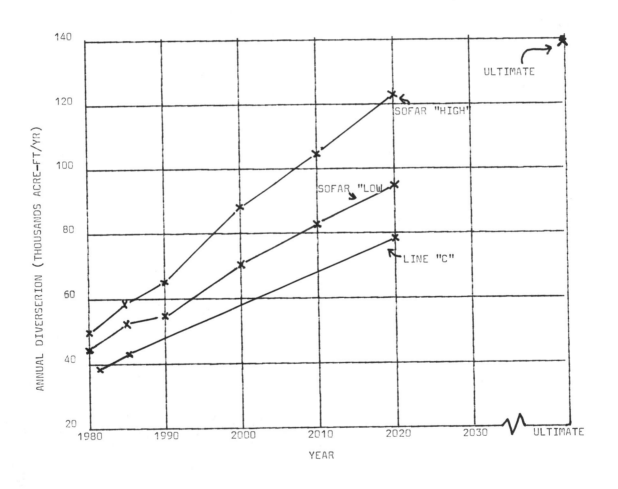

Figure 2.--EID's projected annual required water diversions for consumptive use from 1981 to ultimate. Lines for the SOFAR "High" and SOFAR "Low" represent the maximum and minimum projected requiremens as given by the applicants in the EIR. Line "C" represents new diversion requirements as projected by James Montgomery, Consulting Engineers, Inc.

cost the people of the county one cent in tax money. Only those within the EID service district were allowed to vote on the measure.

The bond election was a point of contention by some who felt the Upper Mountain Project was a county-wide concern. The reason for restricting the vote to EID's service district was reported in a local newspaper:

> Both the EID directors and the county Board of Supervisors discussed the issue of whether the election should be held within EID or county-wide at length last December... one of the main reasons for restricting the vote to the EID boundaries was that EID customers would have the greatest immediate benefit from the project.[3]

The bond measure for the Upper Mountain Project was approved by 65% of the voters.

Approximately six months after the bond was approved, the EIR was accepted by both the County Water Agency and EID. However, threats of a law suit by state agencies and the American River Recreation Association (ARRA) prompted them to withdraw the EIR for minor adjustments. The EIR was again approved in March 1981 and was again challenged, but this time only by ARRA, which brought suit. This action was countered by Assemblyman Norm Waters who introduced a resolution in the Assembly (Assembly Concurrent Resolution Number 6, 1981, Waters) directing the State Water Resources Control Board (SWRCB) to expedite the project and to consider "public interest" paramount for its consideration in granting water rights for the Upper Mountain Project.

Following filing of the law suit, the county Board of Supervisors came upon another stumbling block; the SWRCB requested the Sly Park alternative be thoroughly studied. The request was based on a letter from the Maidu Group of the Sierra Club and information in the final EIS which suggested that, in addition to expanding the capacity of Sly Park, a powerhouse could be added. According to the local newspaper, the Board of Supervisors approved funds begrudgingly:

> County officials decided Monday to spend another $19,000 on the South Fork of the American River project to deal with "people who are not rational" according to Supervisor Dub Walker.
>
> "How can they give credit to a completely irresponsible proposal?" asked Water Agency chairman Joe Flynn. SOFAR officials must now spend taxpayers' money to disprove the Maidu Group's suggestion, but the Sierra Club did not

have to provide any study to show that the alternative was feasible, he complained.[4]

The comments made by the supervisors cut into the heart of the problem. The SOFAR advocates have not been able to objectively consider alternatives to the 1975 proposal and feel they must disprove other proposals.

The first strong demonstration of public disapproval of this project was made at a SMUD Board of Directors meeting in April 1981. The SMUD board was considering advancing $6.2 million to begin the final engineering studies for the Upper Mountain Project. Those opposing the project brought in their concerns regarding the effects of this project on public services, agriculture, power rates, and the environment. The opposition asked SMUD not to grant any advances until the FERC had granted its license for power generation and the SWRCB had given EID the water rights. No funds were advanced.

Following the SMUD board meeting the SOFAR Council begin a mass media campaign for the project. People within the county were urged to write the SWRCB and then-Governor Brown to demonstrate their support for the project. A petition to the governor was circulated at the county fair. The petition was the subject of a press release written for the area's major newspaper:

> The SOFAR Council is circulating a petition to ask Governor Jerry Brown to "assist" the Water Control Board in processing the application for the proposed South Fork of the American River water and power project.
>
> The SOFAR Council will attempt to reach Governor Brown with the petitions in the near future, Combellack said, "in the hope that he will acknowledge our need and influence his agencies to recognize our rights."
>
> "We are a small county fighting for rights against the state bureaucracy," Flynn said. "It's a David and Goliath situation and all we have in our sling is the facts. We hope the governor realizes this is no medfly crisis—you can't spray to cure a drought."[5]

Besides the petition, the SOFAR Council used the county fair to pass out a pamphlet on the Upper Mountain Project. This pamphlet emphasized the drought of 1976-1977 and labelled those who

---

[3]Meyer, Marganne. 1980. Angry about SOFAR vote. Mountain Democrat, Placerville, California. 6 June 1980. p. A-14.

[4]Meyer, Marganne. 1981. Supervisors lament extra SOFAR costs. Mountin Democrat, Placerville, California. 15 April 1981. p. A-7.

[5]Press release. 1981. SOFAR Council circulates petition for governor. Mountain Democrat, Placerville, California. 23 August 1981. p. A-13.

opposed the project as self-interested "enviro-obstructionists."

At the time of writing, FERC has issued the Final EIS but has not granted a license for power generation. The water rights hearings are scheduled for early 1982 and the suit between ARRA and the project applicants has not been settled.

ENVIRONMENTAL CONCESSIONS

With completion of the Upper Mountain Project, approximately 1,154 ha. (2,850 ac.) of timber production land would be lost. This represents an estimated forest productivity loss of approximately 2.4 million board feet per year, with area losses evenly divided between the El Dorado National Forest and private lands. Additional timberland may be affected in the long term as recreational facilities are developed. Mitigation for the lost timberland will come with implementation of improved forest management techniques.

If the proposed recreational facilities for the project are fully developed, they would provide use for 4,118 people at one time. However, there would be a loss of existing recreational uses. Stream-flow reductions would eliminate kayaking along the South Fork American River from Kyburz to Riverton. Wild trout stream fishing would be reduced by 10.6 km. (6.6 mi.), and day users along Alder Creek would find their sites inundated. Eleven recreational residences would also be lost. SOFAR applicants have vowed to help provide relocation for the displaced residences and have proposed improving access and flows to three streams to mitigate for the loss in wild-stream fishing.

Air quality is also expected to suffer from the implementation of this project. The expected degradation would come from increased vehicular travel to recreational areas, campfires at new recreational facilities, and expected area population growth. Violations of state and federal air quality standards for ozone/oxidants and particulates are expected. No mitigation measures are offered.

The impacts of the construction of 24 km. (15 mi.) of tunnels, the deposition of tunnel sludge and rock, along with the erosion and sedimentation of topsoil from the construction of roads and conduit corridors, are potentially significant. Care in deposition of these materials and revegetation of stripped areas with fast-growing grasses and native plants are offered as mitigation.

Flows on the South Fork American River and Silver Fork American River would be reduced substantially once the project is under operation. Present flows in the South Fork show an average spring runoff of approximately 1,250 cubic feet per second (cfs) at a gauging station just below the proposed Forni Diversion Dam (fig. 3). The

Figure 3.--The South Fork of the American River in an area which will experience flow reductions between 30-37% during the summer. (Photo by Cheryl Lemming Langley.)

flow would be reduced to approximately 450 cfs, with summer flows being reduced 30-37%. For the South Fork just below the point of the proposed reentry, the average peak spring flow would be reduced from the present 2,200 cfs to an average peak of 1,700 cfs. However, due to water storage and release for power generation, the average late summer flow would be increased by approximately 25%.

For the Silver Fork of the American River, the average peak spring runoff would be reduced from the present 650 cfs to an average of 100 cfs, and summer flows would be reduced by 50%. All seven small tributaries would have summer flows of 1 cfs or less. There is no anticipated effect on water quality due to the reduction of the flows. However, the reduced peak spring streamflows would result in decreased streambed scouring, changes in riparian vegetation, increased water temperatures, and an alteration of streambed substrate materials; the quality of the aquatic habitat would be compromised. Mitigation for the reduced flows is to increase streamflow in three creeks which would become part of the SOFAR distribution system.

Because the project occurs within streamcourses and involves their inundation, the most significant vegetative communities affected will be riparian. It is estimated by the DFG that there would be a direct loss of 41.9 ha. (103.5 ac.) of riparian system. This estimate includes a small amount of wet-meadow land, but does not take into account potential losses which will occur due to stream flow reduction.

The riparian vegetation within the proposed Alder Reservoir and along Alder and North creeks are of particular interest. Vegetation along Alder Creek (fig. 4) consists of dense stands of lodgepole pine (Pinus murrayana) with patches of willow, alder, dogwood, and Sierra sweet-bay (Myrica hartwegii). Along North Creek are meadows of corn lily or skunk cabbage (Veratrum californicum), sedges, and grasses which alternate with stands of large black cottonwoods (Populus trichocarpa). These stands are unique within the El Dorado National Forest. Near Alder Creek is a lush wet meadow of grasses, rushes, perennial herbs, and sedges. This meadow provides important foraging for a number of wildlife species.

Figure 4.--Alder Creek at a site to be inundated by the proposed project. (Photo by Cheryl Lemming Langley.)

The riparian vegetation in the vicinity of the proposed Texas Hill Reservoir is typical for the area and includes Fremont cottonwood, willow, Oregon ash (Fraxinus latifolia), wild grape (Vitus californica), and blackberry (Rubus spp.). There is also a population of California holly fern (Polystichum lonchitis) within the riparian system of Texas Hill.

Riparian vegetation provides an extremely important habitat for wildlife. The DFG estimates less than 0.1% of El Dorado County is riparian system, with much of this being in private ownership. Considering that riparian systems are in critically short supply, any loss is to be considered significant. The joint applicants for the SOFAR Project consider the loss of riparian system a cost of the project and largely impossible to mitigate. However, they have proposed creation of artifical riparian systems and a wetmeadow community to help offset this loss. The procedure for creating such systems is considered experimental and unpredictable, without guarantee of any measure of success.

In addition to the impact to the riparian communities, there are, within the Upper Mountain Project construction area, six plant species which are considered rare. Two species are located within the Alder area, two within the Texas Hill area, and two within the Sherman and Forni areas. None of these species are considered endangered; however, the loss of these populations would represent a substantial impact to the species. The draft EIR states that while the SOFAR Project would limit their range, the loss of these populations would not significantly threaten the species' survival.

Both the Forni Diversion and the Sherman Diversion areas provide habitat for Bolandra californica and Juncus chlorocephalus. Though both are considered rare, they are relatively common at this elevation in the Sierra Nevada. The construction of the diversion dams is thought to simply limit the range of these plants; no mitigation measures are offered.

Within the Alder area are found woolly violet (Viola tomentosa) and Sierra sweet-bay The Sierra sweet-bay is a riparian type found along the banks of Alder Creek. The greatest impact to this species would occur at the dam site where the shrubs are most abundant. The woolly violet occurs at several locations within the proposed Alder Reservoir site, its habitat being among rock bluffs and in gravelly areas. The draft EIR states that the importance of the potential losses of the populations of both Sierra sweet-bay and woolly violet are "not well understood". Mitigation measures include seeking and protecting stands both above and below the proposed reservoir. If other populations are not found, then their loss would be considered impossible to mitigate.

Also within the Alder area are several species normally found at higher elevations. While none of these are considered rare, their presence at the Alder site "may represent their low altitude limits, and loss of these populations may reduce their range" according to the draft EIR. No mitigtion measures for their loss are offered.

Layne's butterweed (_Senecio layneae_) and California holly fern are two rare plant species found within the Texas Hill area. The California holly fern is uncommon in the Sierra Nevada as it is normally found within the mixed evergreen and redwood forests of the Coast Ranges. Because of its restricted range it is considered rare, but no mitigation for its loss is offered. Layne's butterweed is an endemic species found almost entirely within El Dorado County. Since two other populations exist and are being offered protection, the inundation of this species at the Texas Hill site is not considered threatening to its existence (fig. 5).

Not within the project's construction area, but just north of the South Fork of the American River, is a population of serrate-leaved Lewisia (_Lewisia serrata_), which is considered rare and endangered by the California Native Plant Society. The construction and immediate operation of the Upper Mountain Project is not expected to disturb this population. However, secondary effects such as the influx of people for recreational activity and its impact on this species were not considered in the EIS.

In addition to the project's impact on sensitive plant species, approximately 797 ha. (1,968 ac.) of pine/oak, mixed conifer, oak/grass, and oak brush land, considered critical wildlife habitat, would be lost. Mitigation offered for this loss is replacement of wildlife habitat at a ratio of two acres replaced for every acre lost.

Three deer herds within the immediate project area also may experience losses. These herds include the Placerville herd, the Pacific herd, and the Grizzly Flat herd. The Grizzly Flat herd would be the most significantly disturbed because of the construction of Alder Creek Reservoir. The Alder area not only serves as a spring holding site for this herd, but also provides an abundance of highly nutritious annual vegetation which is important for the survival of new fawns. Further, the proposed Alder Reservoir would cut through and inundate a major portion of the migratory path for this herd. Since deer will not deviate from their old migratory paths even though they are inundated, the danger of drowning and hypothermia from immersion in the cold reservoir exists. As a mitigation measure it was suggested that a deer fence surround the Alder Reservoir. However, applicants are reluctant to comply with this because the cost would be great and it would interfere with the ultimate development of Alder Reservoir as a recreational facility. Instead, the SOFAR proponents will work with the DFG to monitor the migration pattern of the Grizzly Flat herd and propose future

Figure 5.--Weber Creek at a point of inundation by the Texas Hill Reservoir. (Photo by Cheryl Lemming Langley.)

mitigation measures if they are found necessary. Also, a no hunting strip 183 m. (200 yd. wide) will be "encouraged" around the Alder Reservoir.

Further mitigation for the project's impact on wildlife comes in the form of implementation of a raptor program. The joint agencies for this project have proposed to introduce a pair of bald eagles in the Alder area. This program would be monitored by the DFG. If the program were successful, recreationoal development at Alder Creek would be held to a low use level, but if the raptor program were not successful, recreational facilities at Alder Reservoir would be expanded.

SOCIOECONOMIC FACTORS

Primary and secondary impacts of the SOFAR Project are not limited to wildlife and plant communities. The socioeconomic structure of El Dorado County would also be altered. There is a faction of the community which would benefit from the growth associated with the provision of additional water. The condensed summary for the Upper Mountain Project (El Dorado Irrigation District and El Dorado County Water Agency 1980) states: "This growth will be economically beneficial to some private sector groups in El Dorado County such as land owners, building contractors, real estate brokers, title insurance companies, and wholesale and retail businesses." However, this benefit would come at the expense of declining public services and decreased agricultural activity and open space.

El Dorado County's public services are presently experiencing severe problems. According to the final EIS:

> All public services in the West Slope are experiencing some strain because of the massive population expansion that has occurred in the last decade. Most of the schools in the West Slope are near or over capacity, with 12 elementary and three high schools in the West Slope now officially impacted. Six of the special fire districts in unincorporated areas have been officially declared impacted by the county.

Also, county police are requesting more manpower, and maintenance of less travelled roads is falling increasingly behind schedule. The development of the SOFAR Upper Mountain Project would further impact public services.

The migration of people working and looking for work on the project would also have an immediate adverse impact on public services offered by the county. More pressure would be placed on the rental market as competition increased for low-cost rentals. Currently the rental market is experiencing a vacancy factor of 1.2%; a healthy rate is considered 5%. The increased competition for rentals would not only lower the current vacancy factor, making rentals almost impossible

to find, but would cause rents to rise substantially. People on fixed and low incomes could possibly be forced out of their rented homes.

Secondary effects of the project would come from accelerated growth caused by new water distribution systems. As water distribution is expanded into areas of very low density, presently served by wells, new subdivisions of higher density would follow. This type of growth has already had an adverse effect on agriculture and open space in El Dorado County. Growth could be controlled by the county, but the present Board of Supervisors' philosophy is to not control growth. Consider, for example, a recent request made by the County Planning Department to implement interim zoning of a 40-acre minimum which would stop speculative land splits and medium density subdivision until the Somerset/Fairplay Area Plan (part of El Dorado County's Master Plan) is revised. The request was denied, and one of the board members is quoted by a local newspaper as saying: "This county was created on private enterprise... This is shooting holes right through the private plans of those who live in the area."[6] As more parcels are split and new subdivisions are developed, more water and services will be demanded. More open space will be consumed and increased pressure will be placed on agriculture, due to lack of buffer zones.

An example of the type of pressure felt in the agricultural community comes from a recent request for immediate cancellation of a Williamson Act contract for an 324-ha. (800-ac) agricultural preserve. The preserve is adjacent to a large subdivision, and the rancher complains of people cutting his fences and dogs chasing his cattle; he feels his agricultural preserve is no longer profitable. Once the Williamson contract is cancelled, either through immediate cancellation or through normal roll-out, a subdivision will follow.

SOFAR AND FUTURE WATER

If future water distribution systems are added to EID's service area, then consumptive water gained by the Upper Mountain Project would be quickly committed. It is conceivable that additional water will be needed to fulfill the accelerated demand which would follow the construction of new systems. EID would not be able to draw this additional water from the Upper Mountain Project because the cost of purchasing the water would be greater than the cost of constructing a new project. The reason for this, as presented by James Montgomery, Consulting Engineers, is that with an 8% inflation factor figured onto the price of energy, water used for energy produc-

---

[6] Bowker, Michael. 1981. Board clashes over south county zoning--no freeze. Mountain Democrat, Placerville, California. 129(59):A-1, A-11.

tion will have more value than water used for consumptive purposes (table 2). Because EID would only be able to afford 30,000 of the 200,000+ AF of water which would flow each year through the Alder Reservoir, the manager of EID claims two or three projects like the Upper Mountain plan would be required to satisfy EID's projected ultimate needs.[7]

Table 2.--Relative costs, using today's dollar, of five alternative projects for additional water after the 30,000 AF from SOFAR Upper Mountain has been committed. (Source: James Montgomery, Consulting Engineers, Inc.)

Supplementary water source	Present cost
SOFAR Project	$ 99,048,000
Slab Creek Reservoir	$ 85,549,000
Above Slab Creek Reservoir	$ 85,014,000
White Rock Reservoir	$ 91,035,000
Chili Bar	$112,723,000

CONCLUSIONS

Whenever a project is considered, there should always be a high dose of public input. This input should be allowed to begin early in project formation and follow the project all the way to completion. Input should be given objective consideration at all times. To aid in public response, all facts and data should be clearly presented.

When the present water distribution system was thought to be inadequate, EID should have brought in consultants to develop a water master plan. Then, while working with the county master plan and the public, the consultants could have helped determine where new water distribution systems could be located and how much additional water would be needed for the next 20-40 years. Ideally, a plan could then be developed to meet this anticipated need with first consideration given to system improvements and effective use of the existing facilities.

If, after a thorough evaluation, it was determined additional water supplies would be needed and a project would be in the best interest of the district and county, then a proposal based on the very least amount of environmental degradation could be considered. There is nothing wrong with maximizing a water project with powerhouses, but environmental considerations should supersede economic feasibility.

[7] Meyer, Marganne. 1981. Visiting SOFAR land two years later. Mountain Democrat, Placerville, California. 29 July 1981. p. C-3, C-8.

State and federal requirements regarding water projects should emphasize decentralization of power production, conservation, system improvements, and modification of present facilities before considering any new project. The EIR and EIS should be a joint full-disclosure document prepared by experts without bias. The political games played by the proponents of SOFAR, the changing of the requirements of the bond election, the creation of the SOFAR Resolution, and the petition to Governor Brown should have no part in the process.

Once the EIR/EIS has been prepared, the public should be given 90 days for unresolved concerns to be considered. The hearing for water rights and the granting of any licenses would then be a simple weighing and balancing of a project's gains versus its losses.

Unfortunately, governmental policy with respect to water development is not directed in a manner which works toward the ultimate good of the people. Current policy favors large, complex water and electrical companies over small power-producing units and individually owned wells or small service districts. When large projects are thoughtlessly undertaken, both the environment and the people are made to suffer in the long run. This writer questions why the people of this generation should consistently obtain low-cost water and high power production at the expense of the environment, and asks whether future generations will despise us for the way we have handled our resources.

LITERATURE CITED

EDAW, Inc. 1979. Applicants' environmental report and draft environmental impact report. 165 p. EDAW, Inc., San Francisco, Calif.

EDAW, Inc. 1980. Response to comments: final environmental impact report. 298 p. EDAW, Inc., San Francisco, Calif.

El Dorado Irrigation District, and El Dorado County Water Agency. 1980. Upper Mountain Project, condensed summary of license application exhibits. 44 p. Pioneer Press, El Dorado County, Calif.

Federal Energy Regulatory Commission. 1980. South Fork American River development: Upper Mountain Project, no. 2761. Draft environmental impact statement. Washington, D.C.

Federal Energy Regulatory Commission. 1981. South Fork American River development: Upper Mountain Project, No. 2761. Final environmental impact statement. Washington, D.C.

THE EFFECTS OF GROUNDWATER PUMPING

ON NATURAL SPRING COMMUNITIES IN OWENS VALLEY[1]

Deborah J. Perkins, Bruce N. Carlsen, Mike Fredstrom,
Richard H. Miller, Cindy M. Rofer, Gregory T. Ruggerone,
and Carolyn S. Zimmerman[2]

Abstract.--Attempts to return the marsh at Little Black Rock Spring to its pre-pumping condition have been unsuccessful. Runoff water does not adequately replace spring water in nutrient and groundwater levels. The lack of mitigation for water loss due to pumping the Springfield and Fish Springs Lake has resulted in the total loss of marsh habitats.

GENERAL INTRODUCTION

The purpose of this study was to determine the changes in water chemistry and plant and rodent distribution as a result of groundwater pumping at three historical spring sites. Since none of the affected sites were studied before pumping began, comparisons between affected and unaffected sites were made to estimate the extent of change that had occurred. The first section deals with Little Black Rock Spring as the subject of a mitigation effort to reestablish the marsh community lost as a result of nearby pumping. Water diverted from mountain runoff was introduced to the area to serve as a replacement for natural spring water. In this section, the water chemistries of a nearby well and two natural springs are compared with that of the diversion channel in an attempt to determine the differences between natural spring water and diverted water. The distributions of aquatic and marsh plants and rodents are included in the comparison. The second section compares the plant community structure in two former springs that have dried up due to water removal with that of a natu-

ral, free-flowing spring. The importance of vegetation structure to rodent distribution is also discussed.

STUDY SITES

Little Black Rock Spring

Little Black Rock Spring is located in Inyo County, California, approximately 14.5 km. (9 mi.) north of Independence and 1.6 km. (1 mi.) east of US 395. Prior to groundwater pumping, the spring flowed from the base of a fractured basaltic lava flow down a hill to a basin containing several ponds. Percolation from the ponds was minimal because the natural water table was high, approximately 1.0-2.4 m. (3-8 ft.) below ground level [Lee 1912]. The aquifer that supplied the spring was assumed to supply a nearby well, #351, water from which was used to estimate the chemical properties of the natural spring water at Little Black Rock Spring.

Groundwater pumping began in the early 1970s to supply water to the Little Black Rock Springs Fish Hatchery, because the volume of spring water was declining. Soon after pumping began, the spring ceased to flow. Water was then supplied to the spring area by Black Rock Ditch (fig. 1) which received water from two sources. The major source was Division Creek, a system of concrete-lined ditches and natural channels which receives water from Scotty Spring at the base of the Sierras. The second source was water diverted from Goodale Creek. Black Rock Ditch received water from the creek only when the damming action above the ditch intake caused an overflow; this seldom occurred.

Black Rock Ditch (site 1 for water chemistry) was a natural channel roughly 3-5 m. (10-15 ft.) wide and 0.6-0.9 m. (2-3 ft.) deep; it was

[1]Paper presented at the California Riparian Systems Conference. [University of California, Davis, September 17-19, 1981.]
[2]Deborah J. Perkins is Master's Candidate, California State University, San Diego. Bruce N. Carlsen received his B.S. from the University of California, Santa Barbara. Mike Fredstrom will receive his B.S. from California State University, Fullerton. Richard H. Miller is Master's Candidate, University of Utah, Salt Lake City. Cindy M. Rofer is Master's Candidate, Humboldt State University, Arcata, Calif. Gregory T. Ruggerone is Master's Candidate, University of Washington, Seattle. Carolyn S. Zimmerman is attending Arizona State University, Tempe.

Figure 1.--Black Rock Ditch which supplies water to the Little Black Rock Spring area.

lined with willows and other woody and herbaceous plants. Water flowed from the channel to the main pond (site 3) through a 12-in. diameter pipe. The main pond averaged 15 cm. in depth, contained at least three species of green algae, and was surrounded by three-square rush (<u>Scirpus americanus</u>) and the cat-tail <u>Typha domingensis</u>. A loose rock dam below the intake maintained a water level high enough to allow flow into the pipe. From the pipe, water flowed through a small channel and into the pond system (fig. 2). On occasion the rock dam deteriorated to the point that water could not reach the intake pipe. This situation occurred during our study and resulted in a significant drop in water level in the ponds from evaporation and percolation. During our study, the water table was measured at 11.3-11.5 m. (37-38 ft.) in a nearby observation well.

Fish Springs Lake

Fish Springs is located 8 km. (5 mi.) south of Big Pine (Inyo County) and 0.4 km (0.25 mi.) west of US 395. It is the site of a fish hatch-

Figure 2.--Main pond and marsh area at Little Black Rock Spring with <u>Anemopsis californica</u> in the immediate foreground.

ery run by the California Department of Fish and Game (DFG). Fish Springs Lake, the study site, is located several hundred meters south of the hatchery. The lake once occupied a depression below the face of a vesicular basaltic lava flow. Caliche deposits at the site suggest that the water level may have been 0.6-0.9 m. (2-3 ft.) deep at one time (fig. 3). Pumping at the fish hatchery was increased in 1971 to replace the dropping volume of spring flow. Flow from Fish Springs ceased in 1971 (Williams 1978), which corresponded with the increase in pumping at the hatchery. It is likely that the lake and the spring received water from the aquifer associated with the fractured lava flow. This source is not established due to lack of data at the study site. The lake has been noted as having water some years and being dry in others. The amount of water in recent years may be attributed to the accumulation of runoff.

Figure 3.--Fish Springs Lake, a dry bed covered with dead reeds. Note caliche deposits on rocks.

The Springfield

The Springfield is located 2.4 km. (1.5 mi.) east of Independence. The topography is essentially flat with the exception of broad, shallow

Figure 4.--Rabbit-brush (<u>Chrysothamnus nauseosus</u>), the dominant plant at the Springfield.

depressions. The spring area had been invaded by the desert shrub rabbit-brush (fig. 4). The five wells adjacent to the site pumped water from several different levels of a complex layering of sand, clay, and gravel. The deepest well pumped from 143 m. (468 ft.). Another well had artesian flow until 1971, after which the depth was approximately 4.6-7.6 m. (15-25 ft.). Pumping began in the early 1900s, which made this area the study site with the longest pumping history. A brush fire passed through the area in 1971 and destroyed most trees and marsh vegetation.

Fish Slough

Fish Slough is located 8 km. (5 mi.) north of Bishop in the southernmost extension of the volcanic tablelands. The slough is a marsh and pond area that extends 6.4 km. (4 mi.) back toward Bishop and empties into the Owens River. There are three primary springs within the slough, the northernmost of which is site 1. This spring issues near the base of a steep slope of volcanic tuff inside a circular pool constructed of rocks and cement. Overflow continues south through a system of channels and ponds into which the other springs flow. Site 3 was a pond located 4 km. (2.4 mi.) south of site 1. The pond was surrounded by three-square rush, and the bottom covered with a thick mat of macrophytes. The slough is bounded on the east by a faulted block of Bishop Tuff. Spring flow at the slough might have been caused by the impoundment of water from the drainage basin at the fault adjacent to it. If this was the case, then agricultural drainage and precipitation in the basin were major sources of spring flow at the slough.

Collins Warm Springs

Collins Warm Springs is located 13 km. (8 mi.) north of Big Pine and 8.6 km. (5.5 mi.) east of US 395 at the base of the Inyo/White Mountains. It has been designated part of the Owens Valley Pupfish Sanctuary. Springs issue from several sources at the base of a weathered and fractured marble outcrop that was probably exposed by faulting. The main group of springs (site 1) flows into a man-made pond (site 2), which was dammed to support the pupfish population. The pond was 0.9 m. (3 ft.) deep, and the bottom was partially covered with Oscillatoria sp. Water flowed from the pond through a pipe down to an extensive marsh area. Except for the building of the dam, the area had been undisturbed for some time.

ANALYSIS OF MITIGATION SUCCESS

Introduction

The purpose of this section is to analyze the success of mitigation at Little Black Rock Spring. The spring area has undergone significant biological changes since the natural spring flow ceased. Before cessation of spring flow,

flatworms (Dugesia or Planaria) were observed living near the spring source; other native aquatic organisms that require flowing spring water were also present.[3] The wetland plant yerba mansa (Anemopsis californica), which is known to thrive in unstable water conditions, was not a dominant plant in the basin.[4] When well #351 was drilled in the early 1970s, the water table dropped to the point that spring flow ceased. During the period when no water entered the basin, both aquatic and riparian plants were affected. The basin which lay directly beneath the spring lost large sections of vegetation, so that only bush stumps and dry grass clumps remained. In comparison to a 1947 aerial photograph of the area, the marsh was roughly one-third of its pre-pumping size. Yerba mansa became a dominant plant in the remaining marsh area.

No data were available on the pre-pumping condition of Little Black Rock Spring. In lieu of a direct comparison between pre- and post-pumping conditions, an indirect comparison was made. The water chemistry of well #351 was considered the closest to that of the original spring water. Well #351 and two natural springs, Fish Slough and Warm Springs, were used for the water chemistry comparison. Plant and rodent distributions at Little Black Rock Spring and Fish Slough were compared in an attempt to estimate the magnitude of changes that had occurred at Little Black Rock Spring since its source of water had changed.

Four aquatic plants were considered indicator species for dissolved ion levels. By comparing the ion levels at well #351 and Fish Slough, the potential for certain aquatic plants at the old Little Black Rock Spring could be established. The key word is "potential" since the composition of the pre-pumping plant community was unknown. Three assumptions were made regarding the plant species found at Little Black Rock Springs. 1) The plant species present following the transition were those able to tolerate the changes in water chemistry and availability. 2) New species had probably not had the time or the means to invade the area. 3) The absence of certain species could be explained either by their recent disappearance or by their never having been introduced.

Potamogeton crispus, a rooted vascular plant, showed optimal growth at 50 µg nitrogen per l. and 50 µg phosphorus per l. when grown in greenhouses (Mulligan and Baranowski 1969). More recently Mulligan et al. (1976) found that Potamogeton sp. grew well under conditions of high fertility (75,000 µg nitrogen per l. and 75,000 µg phosphorus per l.) in pond experiments. P. pectinatus cannot tolerate waters with a conductivity below 200 µmhos (Seddon

---

[3]Larson, E. 1977. Personal conversation. High school biology teacher, Bishop, Calif.
[4]DeDecker, M. 1977. Personal conversation. Local field botanist, Independence, Calif.

1972). Another rooted plant, aquatic buttercup (Ranunculus aquatilis), has a tolerance to low conductivity and can be found in waters as low as 60 μmhos.

Lemna is a genus of floating plants which must absorb all of its nutrients from the water. In the laboratory, Hicks (1932) studied the growth of Lemnaceae in buffered media lacking trace metals and set the pH range at from 4.5 to 8.0. McLay (1976) broadened the pH range for Lemna spp. to from 4 to 10, with optimal growth at pH 6.2 He used these results to support his findings in the field that the growth of Lemna perpusilla was poor at pH 8.23 (McLay 1974).

Littlefield and Forsberg (1965) found that Chara sp. absorbed phosphorus equally well through all of its parts, which indicates that water nutrients could have a profound effect on the distribution of Chara sp. It has been found that Chara sp. exists in waters that contain 20 μg total phosphorus per 1. or less, of which dissolved orthophosphates constitute a very small portion. A tolerance limit of Chara sp. to orthophosphates was reported by Forsberg (1965) to be 1 μg PO$_4$ phosphorus per 1. or less. The exclusion of Chara sp. was observed by Mulligan et al. (1976) by fertilizing experimental observation ponds. Chara succession was described by Wood (1950) and Crawford (1977), where three species of Chara and some Najas flexilis succeeded to a community of Najas, Potamogeton, and Typha in three years. The average alkalinity of waters in which Chara spp. are found was 2.55 milliequivalents per liter (Forsberg 1965), but some species were ubiquitous (Spence 1967).

According to Smith (1974), the alteration of one component in an ecosystem, such as lowered groundwater levels, often leads to changes in the community as a whole. Several ecological indices were used to estimate the degree of change in the distribution of marsh plants at Little Black Rock Spring. Species diversity, which combined the density and relative importance of all species found in a given area, was compared between sites. The assumption in this comparison was that undisturbed marshes in the area were expected to have comparable diversities, such that changes in the plant community at Little Black Rock Spring would be reflected in the species diversity of the site. Smith states that a greater number of vegetative life forms indicates a more complex ecosystem and that the biomass of total plant cover largely determines food resource availability. The number of life forms, as well as total plant cover, were compared between sites in an attempt to further delineate differences in the plant community and potential animal community between sites.

Within a freshwater marsh ecosystem, very slight alterations in environmental parameters often result in major changes in the riparian flora (Mason 1957). Typha domingensis, the common cattail, is classified as an early succes-

sional species (ibid.) and typically will invade newly flooded areas. Low salinity levels provide an advantage to the germination of Typha seeds over those of rushes (Scirpus spp.). Water salinity is a major determinant in the distribution of marsh vegetation (ibid.). The accumulation of organic matter is also important to distributions in that it is a necessary factor in the succession to other species (Spence 1967), such as those in the rush family.

Changes in food and water availability (Meserve 1974) and vegetation structure (Rosenzweig 1973; Beatley 1976) have been found to affect rodent populations. When a perturbation of water availability causes local habitats to change, the abundance of rodents, which are habitat specialists, is likely to change. Many rodent species seem to prefer one microhabitat over another (Price 1978). It has been suggested that body size and morphology determine which microhabitat is appropriate to maximize the seed collecting efficiency of a heteromyid (ibid). Each species is most dense where its preferred microhabitat is abundant (ibid.). Experimental augmentation of one microhabitat led to the increase in density of the appropriate microhabitat specialist. Thus, the availability of an appropriate microhabitat determines species abundance on a local scale (ibid.).

However, physical adaptation is not the only means of allocating separate microhabitats. Interspecific competition within a foraging habitat (ibid.) allows different species to coexist in the same area. Price has shown that removal or addition of a competitor results in a predictable shift in resource use by other species. For example, when Dipodomys merriami was removed from its open habitat, Perognathus amplus shifted its distribution to the open habitat (Wondolleck 1978). D. microps (a leaf eater) was replaced by D. merriami (a seed eater) when a disturbance reduced the amount of vegetation cover (Beatley 1976). Schroder and Rosenzweig (1975) found that two species of Dipodomys avoided competition by habitat selection. Cricetid rodents also compete for space (Crowell and Pimm 1976). Cricetid species with similar nutritional requirements also appear to coexist through the use of habitat selection (M'Closkey and Fieldwick 1975).

The reasons for selecting one microhabitat over another have been a subject of controversy for years. Originally, rodents were believed to partition food resources by seed size selection. More recently, rodents have been shown to collect different sizes of seeds whether they forage in the same habitat or not (M'Closkey 1980). M'Closkey went on to state that the seed sizes collected by one species of rodent are determined by the preferred microhabitat of that species, such that two of the elements involved in allowing heteromyid coexistence are reduced to one dimension—microhabitat selection. In addition, Rosenzweig and Winakur (1969) found that plant density, soil type, and bush height are all important parameters in habitat selection by _Dipodomys_ spp. Coexistence is probably maintained by a balance between habitat selection with its many parameters and interspecific competition.

Methods

Water Chemistry

Water samples were collected from Fish Slough, Little Black Rock Spring, well #351, and Warm Springs using a horizontal Van Dorn bottle. All filters and sample bottles were acid washed and rinsed with 10 megaohm water. In the field, concentrated sulfuric acid was added to the nitrate samples until pH 2 was reached. Then the nitrate, nitrite, and phosphorus samples were put into a deep freeze until analyzed. Nitrite, reactive phosphorus, and dissolved oxygen were analyzed using methods from Strickland and Parsons (1972). Nitrate was determined by the brucine method (American Public Health Association 1965). Field pH and alkalinity measurements were made with a Perkin-Elmer model Coleman 37A pH meter. Lab measurements were made with a Corning model 10 pH meter. Alkalinity titrations were done with concentrated HCl to a pH of 4.5. Specific conductance, which is directly proportional to the concentration of dissolved salts, was measured with a Lab-Line Lectro Mho-meter model MC-1 Mark IV.

Vegetation Sampling

The marshes were quite patchy in distribution and the methods employed in this study produced data that could be used only to approximate plant distributions. The line transect method (Smith 1966) was used to describe the plant community inhabiting the dried marsh at Little Black Rock Spring. Sixteen lines, 25 m. long, were placed at 10-m. intervals parallel to the old spring source. A random quadrat system was used in the area adjacent to standing water at Little Black Rock Spring and Fish Slough. Mean cover and species importance were calculated using techniques described by Mueller-Dombois and Ellenberg (1974). Species diversity was calculated using the Shannon-Wiener index (Krebs 1972). Plant species were divided into the following five life form categories: aquatic sedge; alkali grass and reed; alkali herb; shrub; and tree. The plant community within standing water was described from observations. Vegetation and terrain were characterized at Fish Slough by recording the three to five most dominant plant species and percent plant cover.

The effects of water table depth and some soil variables were estimated from the data gathered at 21 random grid points at each site. The grids were of equal area (100 m. x 70 m.) and were placed adjacent to the water channel at each site. The grid points were placed at 10-m. intervals and served as the loci of 1 sq. m. quadrats where soil was sampled. A water extraction pressure plate was used to determine soil moisture-holding capacity. Soil filtrates were measured for conductivity with a Yellow Springs model 31 Conductivity Bridge and pH with Hyrion pH paper.

Rodent Sampling

Rodents were captured in Sherman live-traps. Each study site was trapped for four consecutive nights and later for two consecutive nights. Trapping was adjusted to the lunar cycle so that each site had the same approximate amount of moonlight during its trapping period (Lochard and Owings 1974). The traps were placed on line transects with the traps 10 m. apart, 20-30 traps per transect, and three to five transects per site. The transects were arranged radially from the spring site.

Results

The water chemistry data presented in this paper were limited to those sites in each area that were located at the spring source (site 1) and the first major pond (sites 2 or 3). The natural spring waters at Fish Slough and Warm Springs had a higher alkalinity and specific conductivity than Little Black Rock Spring (table 1). Orthophosphates and nitrates were much higher at Fish Slough and well #351 than at Little Black Rock Spring (table 2). The data from Warm Springs showed that each spring had unique characteristics. However, the significant comparison lay between well #351 and Little Black Rock Spring. The water which originally supplied the spring was very different from the water that came from Black Rock Ditch. Orthophosphates had increased at site 3 in Fish Slough from <.004 µg PO_4 phosphorus per l. in 1973 to 4.70 to 10.23 µg PO_4 phosphorus per l. during the summer of 1978.

Table 1.--pH, alkalinity, and specific conductance at Fish Slough (FS), Little Black Rock Spring (LBR), and Warm Springs (WS). N = 1001-1400 hours, PM = 14:01-18:00 hours.

Site	Time	pH	Alkalinity (meq./l.)	Conductivity (µmhos/cm)
FS1	PM	7.8	2.08[1]	450
FS3	PM	8.6	1.96	430
LBR1	N	7.5	0.510	105
LBR3	N	8.9	0.494	120
WS1	PM	7.4	3.69	540
WS2	PM	7.8	3.56	550

[1]Well #351 had approximately the same alkalinity.

Figure 5 shows that diurnal water temperatures were more constant at the water source, which corresponded to site 1 at Fish Slough and Little Black Rock Spring. In both cases, site 3 was a pond where the flow rate had decreased; the

Table 2.--Mean dissolved nutrient concentrations at Fish Slough (FS), Little Black Rock Spring (LBR), well #351, and Warm Springs (WS).

Site	PO_4-P (μg P/1.)	NO_3-N (μg N/1.)	NO_2-N (μg N/1.)
FS1	24.04	663	1.53
FS3	6.98	302	2.00
LBR1	5.99	82	0.45
LBR3	6.98	31	0.21
#351	65.83	328	0.33
WS1	6.82	155	0.19
WS2	3.49	96	0.59

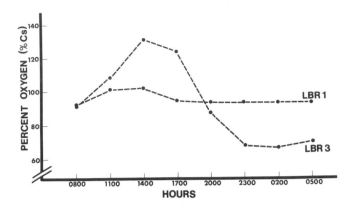

Figure 6.--Little Black Rock Spring diel oxygen study. (Note that the drop in oxygen before sunset resulted from a sudden cloud cover.)

water temperature increased during the day. The temperature change at Little Black Rock Spring was more drastic and required a greater range of tolerance from all aquatic organisms.

At Little Black Rock Spring and Fish Slough, site 1 showed little fluctuation in oxygen saturation (fig. 6 and 7). This indicated that the oxygen input from the water source was constant and there was little photosynthetic activity. In both cases, site 3 had a larger fluctuation due to the large standing crop of primary producers associated with each pond. Site 3 also had the largest change in pH, presumably due to the higher photosynthetic rate. The primary productivity of Fish Slough was higher at its peak than Little Black Rock Spring (185% versus 132% saturation). The slight increase in saturated oxygen in Black Rock Ditch (site 1) came from the macrophytes that lined the ditch.

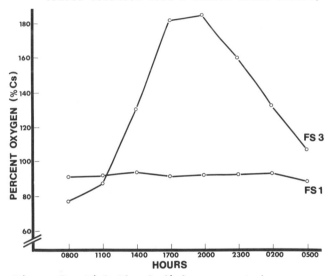

Figure 7.--Fish Slough diel oxygen study.

(table 3). The number of species present, species diversity, total cover, and number of life form categories were much lower. The marsh that survived the transition was slightly different than the Fish Slough marsh in that fewer species were present at Little Black Rock Spring, causing species diversity to decrease slightly.

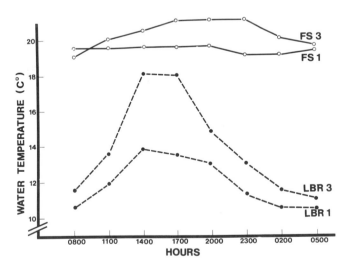

Figure 5.--Diurnal water temperature (°C) for sites 1 and 3 at Fish Slough and Little Black Rock Spring.

According to all of the community indices that were calculated, the dried marsh of Little Black Rock Spring has undergone marked changes

Table 3.--Plant community characteristics at Fish Slough (FS) and Little Black Rock Spring (LBR).

Site	Species Richness	Species Diversity	Total Cover	Life Form Number
FS	37	1.80	83%	5
LBR marsh	30	1.49	93%	5
LBR arid	9	0.80	17%	3

In comparing marsh areas, the dominant species were found to be quite different (table 4). The dominant plant at Fish Slough was a sedge, Eleocharis parishii. The most abundant herb was Glycyrrhiza lepidota, which covered less than half of the area of E. parishii. At Little Black Rock Spring, the most dominant plant was the invading herb Anemopsis californica, while E. parishii covered one-third of the area of A. californica. Another species of interest was wire grass (Juncus balticus), which had the same approximate cover area at both sites. Both Scirpus americana and Typha domingensis were present in the marsh at Little Black Rock Spring, but not at Fish Slough.

Unquantified observations of the entire marsh and pond areas revealed stands of marsh plants that were not sampled by the grids. Most of the waterways at Fish Slough were lined with

Table 4.--Mean cover and species importance of plant species at Fish Slough and Little Black Rock Spring in descending order.

Species	Mean Cover (%)	Species Importance
Fish Slough		
Eleocharis parshii	43.7	0.705
Glycyrrhiza lepidota	18.0	0.359
Juncus balticus	6.6	0.299
Distichlis spicata	4.3	0.165
Solidago spectabilis	2.4	0.048
Helianthus nuttallii	2.3	0.132
Equisetum hyemale var. affine	1.9	0.127
Cirsium mohavense	1.2	0.052
Sisyrinchium halophilum	0.63	0.046
Spartina gracilis	0.58	0.026
Asclepias speciosa	0.46	0.053
Sporobolus airoides	0.38	0.023
Iris missouriensis	0.33	0.013
Allenrolfea occidentalis	0.24	0.012
Little Black Rock Spring (marsh)		
Anemopsis californica	40.7	0.715
Scirpus americana	20.7	0.452
Eleocharis parshii	14.0	0.323
Typha domingensis	7.73	0.117
Juncus balticus	5.18	0.228
Melilotus albus	0.80	0.053
Polypogon monspeliensis	0.36	0.073
Little Black Rock (arid)		
Distichlis spicata	6.0	0.720
Conyza coulteri	4.0	0.269
Anemopsis californica	3.0	0.421
Artemesia tridentata	2.0	0.263
Sporobolus airoides	1.0	0.179
Elymus cinereus	1.0	0.263

dense stands of Scirpus americana, while Typha domingensis was sparse. In contrast, pure stands of T. domingensis were mixed with stands of S. americana at Little Black Rock Spring. The pond (site 3) at Fish Slough contained several macrophytes that had formed a mat on the floor of the pond. Of those species, the ones that were considered to be indicative of certain water characteristics were Najas marina, Potamogeton pectinatus, and Chara sp. At Little Black Rock Spring, the little channel that carried water from the source to the ponds contained Ranunculus aquatilis and Lemna sp. The main pond at Little Black Rock Spring (site 3) did not contain the same species as did site 3 at Fish Slough.

Some of the soil parameters were averaged for each site. Mean soil conductivity at Little Black Rock Spring was 616 mmhos, while Fish Slough had 2,717 mmhos. Mean soil pH was 6.6 at Little Black Rock Spring and 5.7 at Fish Slough. Soil moisture-holding capacity decreased linearly with increasing distance from the channel at Little Black Rock Spring (fig. 8). At Fish Slough, soil moisture-holding capacity was not dependent on distance from the channel. Depth to the water table at Fish Slough varied from 0.5 to 1.0 m. at a distance of 0-50 m. from the water channel. At Little Black Rock Spring, where the natural water table was at approximately 11.5 m., the artificial water table from the pond dropped off quickly. At the edge of the pond, the depth to water had dropped to the lowest limit of the soil auger, 1.8 m. At 20-50 m. from the channel, the water table was below 1.8 m.

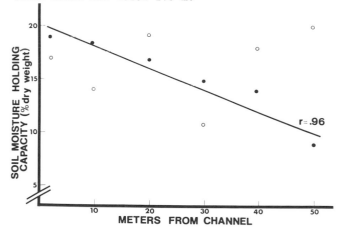

Figure 8.--Soil moisture-holding capacity as it varies with distance from the water channel. o--Fish Slough, o--Little Black Rock Spring.

The plant species present on the soil sample grids reflected the water table depth. On the line closest to the channel at Little Black Rock Spring, wire grass was abundant. Twenty meters away from the channel, drought-tolerant plants like rabbit-brush, Sporobolus airoides, and salt grass (Distichlis spicata) were present. At 50 m., Little Black Rock Spring had sparse vegetation cover consisting of rabbit-brush and annual weeds. At Fish Slough the plants found 20 m. from the channel were _Eleocharis parishii_, _Juncus balticus_, and _Glycyrrhiza lepidota_. At 50 m. the marsh plants were still abundant.

The rodent species common to both areas were the Heteromyids _Dipodomys microps_, _D. ordii_, and _Perognathus formosus_, and the Cricetids _Neotoma lepida_, _Peromyscus maniculatus_, _P. boylii_, _P. crinitus_, and _Reithrodontomys megalotis_. The additional species found at Fish Slough was _D. merriami_, for a total of nine species. Little Black Rock Spring had three additional species, _Neotoma fuscipes_, _Onychomys torridus_, and _Peromyscus truei_, for a total of eleven species.

Five hundred sixty-eight trap nights were used to calculate the rodent-habitat associations. These were considered preliminary results, since many more trap nights would be needed to make conclusive correlations. Positive associations were made with each rodent species and, in several cases, habitat overlaps existed between species (table 5). One of the patterns that emerged from these data was that none of the _Peromyscus_ spp. overlapped. _R. megalotis_ was found only in closed habitats where grass and tall plants were intermixed. _Dipodomys merriami_ and _D. ordii_ were found in different habitats, while _D. microps_ shared the habitats of the other _Dipodomys_ species.

Table 5.--Habitat associations from a Chi-squared analysis (p <0.001). Habitat descriptions: A--closed _Salix_ and grass; B--open _Chrysothamnus_; C--open _Atriplex_; D--open _Eriogonum_ and _Dalea_; E--closed _Chenopodium_; F--closed _Phragmites_.

Species	Habitat Description					
	A	B	C	D	E	F
Peromyscus maniculatus	X	X				
Peromyscus boylii			X			
Peromyscus crinitus				X		
Neotoma lepida			X	X		
Reithrodontomys megalotis	X					X
Dipodomys merriami		X				
Dipodomys microps		X		X		
Dipodomys ordii				X		
Perognathus formosus				X		

Discussion

A comparison of the chemical aspects of Fish Slough, Little Black Rock Spring, well #351, and Warm Springs showed that the water supporting the post-pumping marsh at Little Black Rock Spring was quite different from the water in the local aquifer and other natural springs. Alkalinity, salinity, and nutrients needed for primary production were all lower in the water supplied to the Little Black Rock Spring marsh from Black Rock Ditch. The low conductivity enabled _Ranunculus aquatilis_ to survive there. The low orthophosphate level would be suitable for _Chara_ sp., though it was not found at Little Black Rock Spring. Since the orthophosphate content of well #351 was extremely high, it is likely that _Chara_ was not present before pumping began. _Chara_ was not abundant at Fish Slough and might have been on the decline due to the recent increase in orthophosphates. The work done by Mulligan _et al._ (1976) showed that _Chara_ could be excluded with the addition of fertilizer. The successional pattern where a _Chara-Najas_ community changed to a _Najas-Potamogeton-Typha_ community observed by Woods (1950) and Crawford (1977) appeared to be in progress also. The increased agriculture in the drainage basin of Fish Slough could be affecting the ecological system of the slough.

The absence of _Lemna_ sp. in the ponds (both site 3s) was predictable because of the high daytime pH. _Lemna_ sp. was found in the intake channel at Little Black Rock Spring, which was well protected by tall brush, and probably survived there because shading prevented a high photosynthetic rate and the accompanying increase in pH. The absence of _Potamogeton pectinatus_ at Little Black Rock Spring was also predictable because of the low conductivity there. _P. pectinatus_ was found at Fish Slough where the conductivity was above the lower limit found by Seddon (1972). The conductivity of well #351 was probably above its lower limit too, since the alkalinity of well #351 and Fish Slough was similar. Considering these facts, _P. pectinatus_ may have been present before pumping and eliminated when the water source changed.

Primary production was higher at Fish Slough as demonstrated by the percent saturation of oxygen. The combination of more constant diurnal temperatures, a more constant water source, and higher nutrient concentrations probably supported more photosynthesis at Fish Slough than at Little Black Rock Spring.

The distribution of two major marsh plants, _Scirpus americana_ and _Typha domingensis_, was considerably different between the two areas and was probably due to the decrease in salinity at Little Black Rock Spring. Since _T. domingensis_ had been classified as an early successional species which germinates easily and thrives in water of low salinity, its high abundance at Little Black Rock Spring was predictable. _S. americana_ dominated the marsh at Fish Slough, a well-established marsh with a higher organic content in the soil and more saline water.

The marsh area at Little Black Rock Spring appeared to have sustained significant losses in area and, possibly, species richness. Before pumping, the water table was close to the surface and supported an extensive marsh. After pumping, the marsh ended abruptly at the edge of the pond where the water table dropped. Alkali deposits, remains of dead vegetation, and aerial photography supported the theory that the marsh once extended into the area later occupied by xeric vegetation. Species richness, diversity, and life form categories were lower in the desert area, which indicates that the losses occurred during the transition and that the surviving species were forced to retreat to the remaining marsh. Actual losses and gains in species composition at Little Black Rock Spring could not be estimated from our data. However, Little Black Rock Spring supported seven fewer species than Fish Slough within the sample grids. It was concluded that either species richness had always been lower there or species were actually lost during the transition.

The rodents at Fish Slough appeared to prefer different microhabitats and demonstrated possible rodent-habitat associations. For those species that appeared to be using the same microhabitat, other resource partitioning mechanisms might have been operating, although these mechanisms were not pursued further. Habitat preferences were determined only at Fish Slough, but were considered applicable to both sites.

More specifically, Dipodomys merriami and D. microps demonstrated the type of coexistence described in the literature. Within their common habitat, coexistence was possible because of their different food preferences. Another Heteromyid, Perognathus formosus, preferred a different habitat from the other Heteromyids. Each of the three Peromyscus species appeared to prefer a different habitat. Reithrodontomys megalotis was found only in wet places. Each species preferred one or two habitats. It has not been determined whether these habitats were preferred as a result of competitive exclusion or a physiological need to associate with that habitat.

It is clear, however, that changes in the number and type of habitats would influence the rodents that depend on them. In the case of Little Black Rock Spring, the mitigation to replace lost water maintained a set of moist habitats which probably supported most of the original species. The differences in species between the two areas could not be linked directly to the transition to ditch water since a similar census was not performed before pumping began. The differences in species present and species richness was attributed to artificial juxtaposition of desert and marsh, such that a transect that spanned the two major habitats produced a higher species composition than a transect that crossed the more homogeneous area of Fish Slough.

Conclusion

The water diverted into Little Black Rock Spring contained significantly lower concentrations of the components that influenced the structure of the biological community. The original spring probably had higher concentrations, as indicated by a nearby well. Comparison of the post-pumping marsh to an unaffected marsh showed definite differences in the water chemistries and

biological community. The low salinity at Little Black Rock Spring probably was the cause of the early successional marsh and the absence of certain aquatic plants. Low orthophosphate and nitrogen levels were probably the cause of the comparatively low primary productivity rates. The drop in groundwater and sharp percolation rate from the ponds caused an extensive marsh to evolve into a markedly dichotomous plant community. The most dominant plant species in the marsh were not the same as those in Fish Slough and were probably typical of the new habitat created after pumping began. The rodent community reflected some of the overall change, but the presence of water and moist habitats appeared to maintain a comparatively diverse population.

ESTIMATION OF BIOLOGICAL CHANGES

Introduction

The purpose of this section is to estimate some of the biological changes that resulted from unmitigated pumping in the vicinity of two natural spring areas. Fish Slough was used again as a source of comparison for changes in vegetation and rodent distributions. Warm Springs was also used for one comparison. The Springfield, once an artesian spring field and marsh, had been pumped for many years. Drought-tolerant shrubs and annuals had invaded the entire area. The observation that patches of these shrubs were dying indicated the need for a water stress study to determine whether these plants were mesic and would be affected by further reductions in the water table. Fish Springs Lake was considered an intermediate point between Fish Slough and the Springfield. The lake had dried out only a few years before the study, and the depression still caught surface runoff from time to time. More plant species were present there than at the Springfield, although they were mostly xeric species.

As in the previous section, the vegetation was sampled in order to estimate species richness and diversity, life form richness, and total cover. These indices were compared between the three areas to determine the vegetative differences produced by the pumping.

Plant water potential, according to Slatyer (1967) and Kramer (1969), is one of the best expressions of water deficit. Plants develop a water deficit as the soil water potential decreases (Slatyer 1967). Soil water potential was estimated from the pre-dawn measurement of plant water potential (Slatyer 1967; Merino et al. 1976). A plant was considered to be in equilibrium with the soil before it began to transpire during the day. The amount of transpiration was estimated by subtracting the pre-dawn water potential from the highest reading of the day. Pearcy (1974) found that excess water loss due to transpiration is controlled in some desert plants by stomatal closure. A decrease in water potential during the midday heat could indicate that stomatal closure has decreased the transpiration rate.

Atriplex torreyi was used to compare the water stress of plants at the Springfield and Warm Springs. In Owens Valley, it is found on the valley floor but not on the alluvial fans. The combination of this distribution and the close relation of this species to A. lentiformis, a mesophyte (ibid.), led to the hypothesis that A. torreyi is also a mesophyte. Since Merino et al. (1976) found that the annual range of plant water potential was directly associated with the annual water table depth, a mesophyte such as A. torreyi could be monitored to indicate changes in groundwater depth.

The absence of riparian systems and those defined by a more diverse vegetation structure was considered in relation to the rodent population. The first section presented the discussion on habitat preferences in rodents. Rodent home-range size and density were also considered in this study since the literature describes the dependence of those factors on vegetation density. Stickel (1960) found that Peromyscus leucopus had larger home ranges when the population density was small. She suggested that this relationship existed as a result of sparse vegetation. In a temporal study of desert rodent populations, Whitford (1976) found that most rodent species responded to fluctuations in rainfall and primary production by reductions in density during drought periods. Both Peromyscus spp. and Mus musculus responded to an increase in plant production with a relatively large population increase.

The comparison of affected and unaffected spring areas was the only method available to estimate the changes that had occurred as a result of pumping. The comparison should not be considered a statement of actual change involving a given species, but a statement of the potential change in magnitude of the physical and biological resources.

Methods

The vegetation at the Springfield and Fish Springs Lake was sampled with the line transect method (Smith 1966). At the Springfield, 10 lines 25 m. long were spaced at 10-m. intervals parallel to the spring source. Sixteen lines of similar length and orientation were placed at Fish Springs Lake. At Fish Slough, 24 random 4-sq. m. quadrats were sampled from a grid. From the data collected, mean cover, species importance (Mueller-Dombois and Ellenberg 1974), species diversity (Krebs 1972), species richness, and life form number were calculated.

The individual plants of Atriplex torreyi were sampled at the Springfield and Warm Springs by choosing those nearest to a center point on radial transects. At each reading, three twigs were cleanly severed from each of five to 10 plants. A Scholander Pressure Bomb was used to determine the xylem sap tension during three parts of the day: pre-dawn, mid-morning, and midday. Each plant was sampled on two different

days at each site. The results were averaged from each time period at each site.

Rodent species lists for the Springfield, Fish Springs Lake, and Fish Slough, and habitat associations at Fish Slough were determined by the same methods described in the first section. Home range data were collected at the three sites from a 10 m. x 10 m. grid on which each intersection was a trapping station. Two Sherman live traps were set at alternate stations every evening, using mixed birdseed as bait. Traps were inspected early the next morning, and captured rodents were identified and tagged by toe clipping. Rodents were released at the station where they were captured. Traps were set for 12 nights at Fish Springs Lake and 11 nights at Fish Slough and the Springfield. The first visit consisted of four consecutive nights, and thereafter each visit was two consecutive nights. Visits to each site were alternated so that each site was trapped during each phase of the moon. During the last two trapping sessions at each site, additional traps were added to the periphery of the grid. Home range areas were calculated using the exclusive boundary method (Stickel 1954). Rodents trapped only on the periphery were not used unless their home range area was equal to or larger than those inside the grid.

Since the number of trap nights was not sufficient to establish a constant home range size, a home range rate was developed. The relative home range rate was estimated by regressing the cumulative home range area against the number of recaptures, which should give the rate at which the home range size increases with each successive capture. The logic behind this technique is that a species with a larger home range will cover more area each successive night than a species with a smaller home range. Thus, the rate of increase or the home range rate should reflect the actual home range size. The null hypothesis H ; = 0 was tested for each slope at the 5% significance level. Slopes were then compared by using the Student t-test at the 5% significance level (Zar 1974).

Results

The structure of the plant communities at the Springfield and Fish Springs Lake was quite different from that of Fish Slough (table 6). Species richness, total cover, and life form number were all lower at the pumped sites. Diversity at Fish Springs Lake was still relatively high, because all of the species were accounted for even though the majority of the individuals were dead. Diversity at the Springfield was very low because the transect lines only touched one perennial. A couple of other perennials were present nearby and the annual Chenopodium berlandieri var. sinuatum was heavily intermixed with Chrysothamnus nauseosus, the dominant perennial. There was an obvious shift from marsh vegetation at Fish Slough (table 4) to drought-tolerant species at Fish Springs Lake and the Springfield (table 7).

Table 6.—Plant community characteristics at Fish Slough, Fish Springs Lake, and the Springfield.

Site	Species Richness	Species Diversity	Mean Cover	Life Form Number
Fish Slough	37	1.80	83%	5
Fish Springs	6	1.51	9%	1
Springfield	1	0.00	38%	1

Table 7.—Mean cover and species importance at Fish Springs Lake and the Springfield.

Species	Mean Cover	Species Importance
Fish Springs Lake		
Distichlis spicata	28%	.709
Phragmites communis	26%	.684
Sarcobatus vermiculatus	1.5%	.226
Sporobolus airoides	1.2%	.192
Elymus cinereus	0.7%	.191
The Springfield		
Chrysothamnus nauseosus	37.9%	1.379

The xylem sap tensions mesured on August 10 and 11 reflected the high ambient temperature, ranging from 13-45°C at the Springfield and 16-41°C at Warm Springs, respectively. The pre-dawn measurement, which reflected the soil water potential, was quite different between the sites (fig. 9). The water potential increased as the temperature rose, but dropped off in the afternoon. On August 24 and 25, the temperatures ranged from 10-31°C at Warm Springs and 13-35°C at the Springfield, respectively. The soil water potential was lower for both sites, although the Springfield maintained a higher potential. The diurnal changes in water potential showed the same pattern as those on August 10 and 11.

Fish Slough had nine species of rodents, while Fish Springs Lake had seven species, and the Springfield had six species. The three sites had only four species in common: _Dipodomys merriami_; _D. microps_; _Neotoma lepida_; and _Peromyscus maniculatus_. The other species found at Fish Slough are listed in the first section. Fish Springs Lake had _Perognathus formosus_, _Peromyscus boylii_, and _P. crinitus_. The Springfield had _D. ordii_ and _Onychomys torridus_.

Habitat preferences were calculated only at Fish Slough. Those results are presented in the first section. Habitat comparisons were possible between sites because the pumped sites had such distinct differences in vegetation structure. Fish Springs Lake had only one life form category, that is, alkali grass and reed, while the

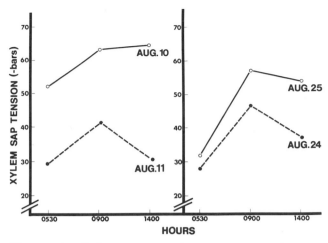

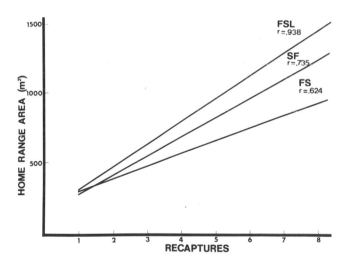

Figure 9.—Xylem sap tension at Warm Springs ● and the Springfield ○.

Springfield had only the shrub category. Fish Slough, on the other hand, had five categories, including aquatic sedge, alkali grass and reed, alkali herb, shrub, and tree.

Peromyscus maniculatus was the only species out of the four species in common with all three sites that had a home range rate that was significantly higher at the pumped sites (fig. 10). The lack of significance for the other species may have resulted from low capture rates.

Figure 10.—Home range rates of _Peromyscus maniculatus_ at Fish Springs Lake (FSL), the Springfield (SF), and Fish Slough (FS). (Rejected H_o : $\beta = 0$, $\beta_1 = \beta_2$, $\beta_2 = \beta_3$ at $p < .05$).

Discussion and Conclusion

The obvious effects of unmitigated groundwater pumping on marsh vegetation are a drop in the groundwater table and a loss of surface water. Marsh vegetation was lost entirely from

Fish Spring Lake and the Springfield, and plant diversity was ultimately reduced to include only those plants that could survive on ephemeral water or deep groundwater. A mesophyte such as Atriplex torreyi was subjected to further drops in the groundwater table, such that water could become inaccessible even to long tap roots. Areas which have been pumped to that extent and beyond can be expected to lose perennial vegetation and only support those annuals that grow as a result of precipitation accumulation. Rodents that lived in pumped areas such as the Springfield could not depend on free water except that which was contained within the leaves of annuals and perennials.

Water-dependent species did not remain in an area that was pumped to the extent of losing its marsh vegetation and standing water. Rodent species that depend on seeds are most adapted to the conditions prevailing at pumped sites. Those species that are physiologically adapted to such an environment would be further limited by the low diversity of vegetation structure which is necessary for the coexistence of some species. Those individuals that do inhabit the pumped sites must finally maintain a larger home range in order to gather enough food to exist. But home range size cannot be extended indefinitely because the energy budget of each species requires a balance between the energy expended and the energy gained in foraging.

GENERAL CONCLUSION

The attempts to mitigate the effects of pumping at Little Black Rock Spring have resulted in a marsh community that is probably quite different from the original marsh. The combination of nutrient-poor water and a lower water table have resulted in a smaller marsh area dominated by early successional marsh species. The area once inhabited by marsh vegetation has been invaded by more drought-tolerant perennials. The rodent community is still rather diverse, but the reduced marsh and encroaching desert have probably changed the overall structure of the rodent community.

Despite the serious loss of environmental quality at sites where water removal occurred, mitigation proved better than no mitigation at all. This was demonstrated in the cases of the Springfield and Fish Springs Lake. Both the plant and rodent communities were much less diverse than those found at natural spring sites. The reduction in plant diversity and the increase in water stress at the dewatered Springfield indicated that even the desert mesophytes that live there could be endangered if the water table drops further.

ACKNOWLEDGMENTS

This study was possible through the cooperative effort of eight people assembled by a National Science Foundation grant (SDI78-03663) in the Student Originated Studies program. The study was conducted during the summer of 1978 after seven of the participants had earned their bachelor degrees. Each participant was responsible for the experimental design and write-up of a particular subject. Bruce N. Carlsen handled the limnology section, while Mike Fredstrom wrote the hydrology section. Carolyn S. Zimmerman and Cindy M. Rofer were responsible for the vegetation sections. The rodent sections were handled by Gregory T. Ruggerone and Richard H. Miller. J. Michael Sanders assisted Deborah Perkins with a section on water stress which was not used in this report. Each person was indebted to the others for three months of assistance in his or her field research.

Dr. Richard E. MacMillen, our faculty advisor, gave us much needed advice and the room to experience the successes and pitfalls of such a study. Several residents of Owens Valley and the employees of the Los Angeles Department of Water and Power, the Caifornia Department of Fish and Game, and the Bureau of Land Management supplied important information about pre-pumping situations without which we could not have had a clear picture of the pumping issue.

LITERATURE CITED

American Public Health Association. 1965. Standard methods for the examination of water and wastewater (twelfth edition). 769 p. American Public Health Association, New York, N.Y.

Beatley, J.C. 1976. Environments of kangaroo rats (Dipodomys) and effects of environmental change on populations in southern Nevada. J. Mamm. 57:67-93.

Crawford, S.A. 1977. Chemical, physical, and biological changes associated with Chara succession in farm ponds. Hydrobiologica 55:209-217.

Crowell, K.L., and S.L. Pimm. 1976. Competition and niche shifts of mice introduced onto small islands. Oikos 27:251-258.

Forsberg, C. 1965. Environmental conditions for Swedish charophytes. Symbolae Botanicae Upsaliens 18:5-62.

Hicks, L.E. 1932. Ranges of pH-tolerance of the Lemnaceae. Ohio J. Sci. 32:115-131.

Kramer, P. J. 1969. Plant and soil water relationships. 482 p. McGraw-Hill, New York, N.Y.

Krebs, C. J. 1972. Ecology: the experimental analysis of distribution and abundance. 694 p. Harper and Row, New York, N.Y.

Lee, C. H. 1912. An intensive study of the water resources of a part of Owens Valley. USDI Geological Survey Water Supply Paper 294.

Littlefield, L., and C. Forsberg. 1965. Absorption and translocation of phosphorus-32 by Chara globularis Thuill. Physiol. Plantarum 18:291-296.

Lochard, R.B., and D.H. Owings. 1974. Moon-related activities of bannertail (Dipodomys spectabilis) and fresho (D. nitratoides) kangaroo rats. Anim. Behav. 22:262-273.

Mason, H.L. 1957. A flora of the marshes of California. 878 p. University of California Press, Berkeley.

McLay, C.L. 1974. The distribution of duckweed (Lemna perpusilla) in a small southern California lake: an experimental approach. Ecology 55:262-276.

McLay, C.L. 1976. The effect of pH on the population growth of three species of duckweed: Spirodela oligorrhiza, Lemna minor, and Wolffia arrhiza. Freshwater Biol. 6:125-136.

M'Closkey, R.T. 1980. Spatial patterns in sizes of seeds collected by four species of heteromyid rodents. Ecology 61:486-489.

M'Closkey, R.T., and B. Fieldwick. 1975. Ecological separation of sympatric rodents (Peromyscus and Microtus). J. Mamm. 56:119-129.

Merino, J., F. Garcia Nova, and M. Sanchez Diaz. 1976. Annual fluctuation of water potential in the xerophytic shrubs of the Donana Biological Reserve (Spain). Oecol. Plant. 11:1-11.

Meserve, P.L. 1974. Ecological relationships of two sympatric woodrats in a California coastal sage community. J. Mamm. 55:442-447.

Mueller-Dombois, D., and H. Ellenberg. 1974. Aims and methods of vegetation ecology. 547 p. John Wiley and Sons, New York, N.Y.

Mulligan, H.F., and A. Baranowski. 1969. Growth of phytoplankton and vascular aquatic plants at different nutrient levels. Vehr. Intern. Verein. Limn. 17:802-810.

Mulligan, H.F., A. Baranowski, and R. Johnson. 1976. Nitrogen and phosphorus fertilization of aquatic vascular plants and algae in replicated ponds. I. Initial response to fertilization. Hydrobiol. 48:109-116.

Pearcy, R.W. 1974. Comparative photosynthetic and respiratory gas characteristics of Atriplex lentiformis (Torr.) Wats. in coastal and desert habitats. Ecology 55:1104-1111.

Price, M.V. 1978. The role of microhabitat in structuring desert rodent communities. Ecology 59:910-921.

Rosenzweig, M.L. 1973. Habitat selection experiments with a pair of coexisting heteromyid rodent species. Ecology 54:111-117.

Rosenzweig, M.L., and J. Winakur. 1969. Population biology of a desert rodent community: habitat and environmental complexity. Ecology 50:558-572.

Schroder, G.E., and M.L. Rosenzweig. 1975. Perturbation analysis of competition and overlap in habitat utilizations between D. ordii and D. merriami. Oecol. 19:9-28.

Seddon, B. 1972. Aquatic macrophytes as limnological indicators. Freshwater Biol. 2:107-130.

Slatyer, R.O. 1967. Plant-water relationships. 366 p. Academic Press Inc., New York, N.Y.

Smith, R.L. 1966. Ecology and field biology. 686 p. Harper and Row, New York, N.Y.

Smith, R.L. 1974. Ecology and field biology. 850 p. Harper and Row, New York, N.Y.

Spence, D.H.N. 1967. Factors controlling the distribution of freshwater macrophytes with particular reference to the lochs of Scotland. J. Ecology 55:147-170.

Stickel, L.F. 1954. A comparison of certain methods of measuring ranges of small mammals. J. Mamm. 35:1-15.

Stickel, L.J. 1960. Peromyscus ranges at high and low population densities. J. Mamm. 41:433-441.

Strickland, J.D., and T.R. Parsons. 1972. A manual of seawater analysis (second edition). 310 p. Bull. Fish. Res. Bd. Canada No. 167.

Whitford, W.G. 1976. Temporal fluctuations in density and diversity of desert rodent populations. J. Mamm. 57:351-369.

Williams, P.B. 1978. Changes in the Owens Valley shallow groundwater levels from 1970 to 1978. Inyo County Board of Supervisors.

Wondolleck, J.T. 1978. Forage-area separation and overlap in Heteromyid rodents. J. Mamm. 59:510-518.

Wood, R.D. 1950. Stability and zonation of Characeae. Ecology 31:642-647.

Zar, J.H. 1974. Biostatistical analysis. 620 p. Prentice-Hall, Inc., Englewood Cliffs, N.J.

DESTRUCTION OF RIPARIAN SYSTEMS DUE TO WATER DEVELOPMENT

IN THE MONO LAKE WATERSHED[1]

Scott Stine, David Gaines, and Peter Vorster[2]

Abstract.--During the early decades of this century over 320 ha. (800 ac.) of marsh, wet meadow, and riparian woodland covered the Grant and Waugh Lake depressions and lined the banks of lower Rush, Parker, Walker, and Lee Vining Creeks. Construction of reservoirs and diversion of streams have destroyed virtually all of this wetland vegetation. Streamside riparian systems could be restored by allowing moderate amounts of water to flow down the creeks.

INTRODUCTION

Prior to the large-scale manipulation of streamflow in the Mono Basin, the lower reaches of Parker, Walker, Rush, and Lee Vining Creeks were bordered by riparian woodland, wet meadow, and marsh vegetation. The depressions now occupied by Waugh Lake and Grant Lake Reservoir supported extensive stands of marsh and wet meadow. This paper briefly describes the former extent of this wetland vegetation, and documents its destruction due to water impoundment and diversion.

FLOW REGIME UNDER NATURAL CONDITIONS

Rush, Parker, Walker, and Lee Vining Creeks head at the 3,200- to 3,960-m. (10,500- to 13,000-ft.) crest of the Sierra Nevada east of Yosemite National Park (fig. 1). The streams debouch from their bedrock canyons on the east side of the Sierra at elevations ranging from 2,130 to 2,440 m. (7,000 to 8,000 ft.), then flow 11 to 16 km. (7 to 10 mi.) across alluvial, lacustrine, and aeolian sediments on the floor of the Mono Basin to the shores of Mono Lake.

These streams, which under natural conditions account for approximately 75% of the surface inflow to Mono Lake, are fed primarily by snowmelt from the Sierra Nevada. Peak flows are usually attained in May, June, and July. By September of the average year, flows in the bedrock reaches of the streams have declined significantly. Along the basin floor, however, groundwater from the loose, unconsolidated sediments continues to feed the creeks.

The streams themselves constitute the main source of this groundwater. As they cross their alluvial fans and piedmont slopes, a substantial amount of flow percolates through the coarse sediments. The water is then slowly returned to the streams in their lower reaches. Streamflow in these basin reaches thus remains substantial during the dry months of late summer and fall. Even during prolonged (5- to 10-year) periods of drought, groundwater keeps the lower creek reaches flowing.

RIPARIAN SYSTEMS PRIOR TO WATER DEVELOPMENT

It was along these perennially flowing, lower reaches of Rush, Walker, Parker, and Lee Vining Creeks and in the Grant and Waugh Lake depressions that the most luxuriant wetland vegetation in the Mono Basin was found (fig. 2). Dense groves of aspen (Populus tremuloides), black cottonwood (P. trichocarpa), willow (Salix exigua, S. lutea, and probably others), Jeffrey pine (Pinus jeffreyi), and probably mountain alder (Alnus tenuifolia), interspersed with meadows and cattail marshes, formed riparian corridors that followed the streams practically to the shores of Mono Lake (fig. 3 and 4). Over 243 ha. (600 ac.) of this wetland mosaic laced 13 to 16 km. (8 to 10 mi.) of the river course. Early maps indicate that the Grant and Waugh Lake depressions supported 200 ha. (500 ac.) or more of wet meadow and marshland.

These riparian systems had considerable esthetic, recreational, and wildlife values.

[1] Paper presented at the California Riparian Systems Conference. [University of California, Davis, September 17-19, 1981].

[2] Scott Stine is a Graduate Student and Lecturer in the Department of Geography, University of California, Berkeley. David Gaines is an Independent Researcher and Author (P.O. Box 29, Lee Vining, Calif. 93541). Peter Vorster is a Consulting Hydrologist with Philip Williams and Associates, San Francisco, Calif.

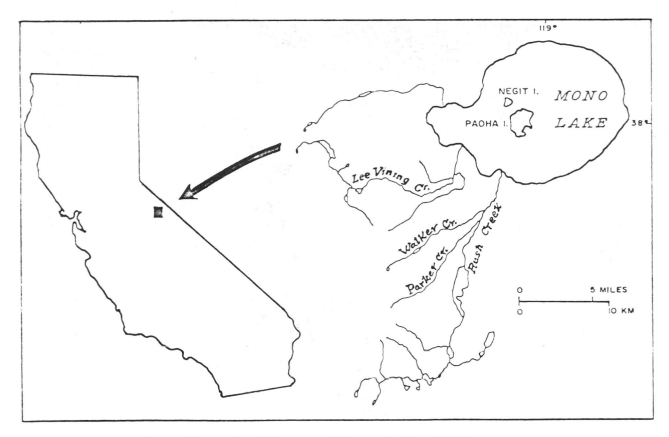

Figure 1.--Index map of Mono Lake (ca. 1953).

John Muir wrote glowingly of lower Rush Creek in 1894 (Muir 1894). In 1924 Joseph Grinnell pointed out the importance of the basin's cattail marshes to birds such as the Least Bittern

Figure 2.--A portion of the USDI Geological Survey Mariposa 1:250,000 sheet (1957) showing major riparian areas.

(Grinnell and Storer 1924). The alluvial reaches of Rush Creek are said to have supported the finest brown trout fishery in the eastern Sierra.[3] And until recently the riparian areas were used extensively by picnickers, hikers, and duck hunters.[4]

WATER DEVELOPMENT IN THE MONO BASIN

While small-scale stream diversions for irrigation, mining, and milling occurred in the Mono Basin as early as the 1850's, it was not until the early years of the twentieth century that water development escalated to significantly impact the region's riparian vegetation. Around 1915 a dam was constructed by the Cain Irrigation District to impound water in the Grant Lake depression. This small reservoir was enlarged in 1926. The Waugh Lake depression underwent similar modification in 1925 when the Southern Sierra Power Company built a small dam across upper Rush Creek.

In 1930 Los Angeles voters approved a $38-million bond issue to finance the extension of the City's aqueduct northward from the Owens Valley into the Mono Basin. By 1934 Los Angeles

----

[3]Johnson, Wes. 1981. Personal communication.
[4]Mathieu, Lily. 1981. Personal communication.

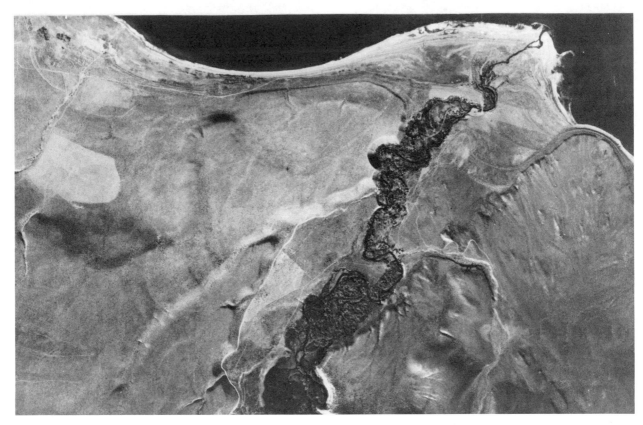

Figure 3.--1930 aerial photograph of lower Rush Creek, Mono
Lake at top. This was the most extensive area of
riparian vegetation in the Mono Basin.

Figure 4.--Rush Creek about 0.16 km. (0.1 mi.) southwest of
Highway 395, ca. 1920. (Courtesy of Enid Larson.)

had consolidated its rights to the basin's principal streams. Six years later workers completed a network of pipelines and impoundments; this included the further enlargement of Grant Lake Reservoir. The following year, in 1941, the first diversions of water from Mono Basin began (Gaines 1981).

During the next 30 years an average of 55,000 acre-feet (AF) of Mono Basin water per year was turned southward. An average of 40,000 AF per year, however, continued to flow down the creeks on an irregular basis (Los Angeles Department of Water and Power 1974).

In 1970, with the completion of a second Owens Valley aqueduct, the Los Angeles Department of Water and Power (LADWP) substantially increased its take of Mono Basin water (ibid.; Gaines 1981). During the past decade nearly the entire flows of Rush, Parker, Walker, and Lee Vining Creeks have been diverted southward. Effective groundwater replenishment has ceased. Except for brief periods in 1978 and 1980 the streams have remained essentially dry below the diversion dams (fig. 5).

IMPACT OF WATER DIVERSIONS ON RIPARIAN SYSTEMS

The early impoundment of water behind the Grant and Waugh Lake dams led to the immediate loss of some 140 ha. (350 ac.) of riparian system. Later enlargement of the Grant Lake reservoir by the LADWP flooded an additional 61 ha. (150 ac.) of marshland and meadow.

The destruction of streamside wetlands occurred more gradually. By the early 1950's the riparian vegetation along Lee Vining Creek was so desiccated that fire was able to consume some 40 ha. (100 ac.) of woodland.[5] During the early 1970's the arboreal vegetation along the lower creek reaches is said to have been brown and withered.[6] Photographs from 1978 show that little live vegetaton remained along the once-extensive Rush Creek wetlands (fig. 6 and 7).

Today the marshes and wet meadows that once lined the basin stretches of the streams have vanished entirely. Most of the deciduous trees have died (fig. 8). The few Jeffrey pines that remain are not establishing seedlings. Streambanks that were once clothed with mesic vegetation have been colonized by Great Basin xerophytes such as sagebrush (Artemisia tridentata) and rabbitbrush (Chrysothamnus nauseosus).

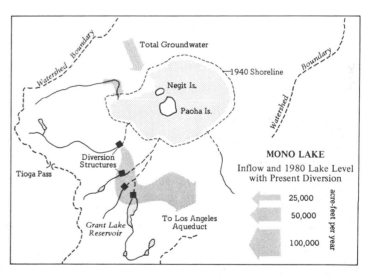

Figure 5.--Map of Mono Lake showing the major tributary streams and points of diversion. Since diversions began in 1941 the lower stretches of Rush, Parker, Walker, and Lee Vining Creeks have been transformed from perennial streams into abandoned washes. Mono Lake has fallen 13.7 vertical meters (45 vertical feet), its volume has been halved, its salinity has doubled, and Negit Island has become connected to the mainland.

_____

[5]Banta, Don 1981. Personal communication.
[6]Mathieu, Lily 1981. Personal communication.

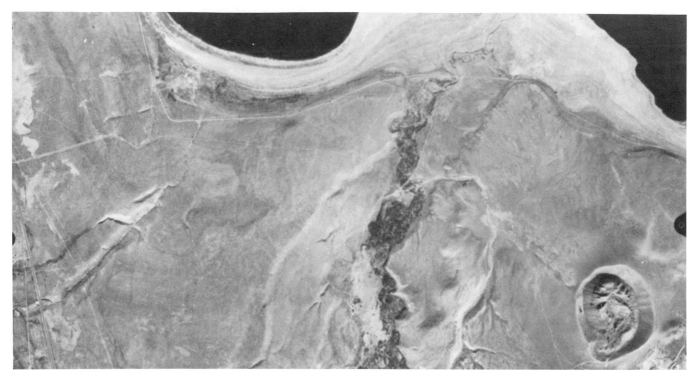

Figure 6.--1978 aerial photograph of lower Rush Creek.
Virtually no live riparian vegetation remains.

Figure 7.--The abandoned channel of lower Rush Creek in
1981. This photo was taken from the same point as
figure 4.

Figure 8.--All that remains of the once-extensive riparian woodland along lower Rush Creek.

RESTORATION POTENTIAL

Restoration of riparian vegetation along lower Rush, Parker, Walker, and Lee Vining Creeks would require a reduction in present diversions and maintenance of minimum streamflows throughout the year. Under these conditions it is thought that riparian vegetation would reestablish itself relatively rapidly.

The prospects for curtailing water diversions hinge on the outcome of current efforts to stabilize the level of Mono Lake. This unusual body of chloro-carbonate-sulfate water is shrinking and increasing in salinity due to the diversions, endangering a unique ecosystem and hundreds of thousands of nesting and migrating birds. Environmentalists and residents are attempting to preserve Mono Lake through legislation and litigation. They are opposed by the LADWP, which argues that diversions are critical to the City (Los Angeles Department of Water and Power 1974, Gaines 1981).

In December, 1979, an Interagency Task Force on Mono Lake, chaired by the California Department of Water Resources and consisting of representatives from Federal, State, and local agencies, recommended that Los Angeles reduce its diversions from the Mono Basin from an average of 100,000 AF to an average of 15,000 AF per year. The Task Force documented how the City could replace this water through an expanded program of conservation and waste-water reclamation (California Department of Water Resources 1979). Implementation of the Task Force Plan would also restore riparian vegetation along lower Rush and Lee Vining Creeks. To date, however, the opposi-

tion of the LADWP has blocked the Task Force Plan and prevented any reduction in diversions (Gaines 1981).

ACKNOWLEDGMENTS

We are indebted to Adreinne Morgan and Sharon Johnson for cartographic assistance, and to Mono Basin residents Don Banta, Lily Mathieu, and Wes Johnson for historical information.

LITERATURE CITED

California Department of Water Resources, Southern District. 1979. Report of the Interagency Task Force on Mono Lake. 140 p.

Gaines, David. 1981. Mono Lake guidebook. 113 p. Mono Lake Committee-Kutsavi Books, Lee Vining, Calif.

Grinnell, Joseph and Tracy I. Storer. 1924. Animal life in Yosemite. University of California Press, Berkeley, Calif.

Los Angeles Department of Water and Power. 1974. Los Angeles water rights in the Mono Basin and the impact of the Department's operations on Mono Lake.

Muir, John. 1894. The mountains of California. 381 p. T. Fisher Unwin, London.

INFLUENCING FUTURE EFFECTS OF WATER DEVELOPMENT

ON RIPARIAN SYSTEMS[1]

D. W. Kelley[2]

Abstract.--Making water development compatible with the protection of instream and riparian resources will require: a) more technical knowledge of the factors affecting those systems and how they are related; b) opportunities to use that knowledge in formulating or changing policy; c) project concept design and operation; and finally, d) public support. All are necessary; without one, the others are unlikely to succeed.

INTRODUCTION

A number of participants in the California Riparian Systems Conference reported on serious damage done to riparian systems by water development projects. The damage was caused by drowning underneath reservoirs, by elimination of streamflows, and by lowering groundwater tables through pumping. Despite the fact that the best damsites have been built upon and costs have risen, water development in California is expected to continue. It is driven by increasing population growth, much of it in coastal and foothill communities with limited water supplies; by the revitalized potential of hydropower generation; by economies that were developed by and are now threatened by overdrafting groundwater supplies; and by the momentum of a large water development industry that includes both private and government sectors of our society. Pumping from shallow groundwater basins and their increased use as reservoirs, to be emptied and filled like surface reservoirs, is especially important to the future of riparian systems and is sure to increase with escalating costs of surface water projects.

The essence of the California Riparian Systems Conference is that riparian systems are important and should be protected from these and other manmade and man-caused changes in our environment. But how? We have three basic needs.

1. Technical knowledge.
2. The opportunity to use it.
3. Public support.

[1]Paper presented at the California Riparian Systems Conference. [University of California, Davis, September 17-19, 1981].

[2]Don W. Kelly is Aquatic Biology Consultant, D.W. Kelley and Associates, Newcastle, Calif.

All three are necessary to influence water development.

Technical Knowledge: Understanding Riparian Systems

Consider the simple conceptual model in figure 1. Riparian vegetation is influenced directly by groundwater levels; by changes in the size, shape, and stability of the channel; and by the volume, frequency, and duration of the various streamflows throughout the year. Many groundwater levels are influenced by streamflow, and most are influenced by pumping from wells. As groundwater levels in alluvium decline, so, in many cases, do streamflows. In nearly all cases where groundwater levels decline, there is an increased demand for storage dams and diversions. These, of course, have a major impact on streamflows. Changes in streamflow affect channel size, shape, and stability. This in turn increases the demand for levees, channelization, and other kinds of flood control, including upstream storage reservoirs. The levees themselves encourage additional development in the floodplain which is often disastrous for riparian vegetation.

This model is much like one describing the factors influencing steelhead or most salmonid fishes, and steelhead have been added to it. Like riparian vegetation, steelhead are influenced primarily by streamflows and channel size, shape, and stability. Their third requirement is riparian vegetation to shade the stream and keep it cool. Steelhead are low-elevation salmonids, and in California they have a difficult time surviving the freshwater rearing period if long reaches are not about one-half (50%) shaded.

Steelhead, and many other fisheries resources, have been seriously damaged in California because biologists ignored the fact that all these variables are related. For instance, most

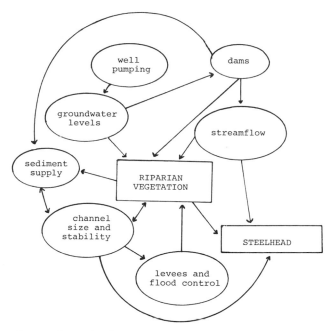

Figure 1.--Simple conceptual model of how water development affects riparian vegetation and steelhead.

"methodologies" for determining how much flow should remain in streams below dams are based on the erroneous assumption that the channels downstream will not change (Stalnaker and Arnett 1976; Stalnaker 1980). Yet it is well known that unless the dam is very small, all bedload sediment coming from erosion above the dam will be trapped in the reservoir and the frequency, magnitude, and duration of flows that have historically shaped the channel and affected its substrate will be very different after the project is built. A host of approaches have been used to "mitigate" the losses of fisheries resources caused by dams and diversions--instream flows, fish ladders, hatcheries, etc. They have not always worked well because few have been based upon a good understanding of even these simple variables.

Examining the model and thinking about various streams, fish populations, and riparian systems leads one to the obvious conclusion that no two systems are going to be alike. The relationship between riparian vegetation and streamflow, groundwater, fish habitat, and channel size, shape, and stability must be newly investigated on every project. Those investigations would, of course, be greatly expedited if principles and processes were understood as a result of basic research and objective review of past experience.

While that may seem obvious, agencies that regulate water development are under severe time constraints when making decisions. On instream flow matters they usually rely on reports and testimony from the California Department of Fish and Game (DFG) and the USDI Fish and Wildlife Service (FWS). Neither agency has adequate funds or staff to do the kind of thorough investigation needed on every water project. They should not have to. Applicants who propose a project should be required to conduct those studies; the fish and wildlife agencies should critique the results. More agency funds and energy should be devoted to basic investigations leading toward improved understanding of stream ecology and the effect of water development on it. Most project sponsors would prefer this approach.

Opportunities to Influence Water Diversion Projects

Unlike most people in the world, Americans have many opportunities to influence how much water development will occur, as well as where and when. We can influence our population size; our life styles; the drought risks we are willing to accept; what should and should not be subsidized; the philosophy and integrity of our decision-makers; and, ultimately, how much water development will occur, where, to what use it will be put, and who should pay for it. There are plenty of opportunities, but great lack of interest.

All individuals and organizations concerned with resource conservation, with protecting riparian corridors, streamflows, and fisheries resources in California should ask their elected representatives for written federal, state, and local government policies on water development. If no policies are available, the need should be pointed out, and constituents should urge their development and participate in their change or development.

In addition to influencing policy, we need to influence the concept, design, and operation of specific projects. In California, each water diversion project requires an application to the State Water Resources Control Board (SWRCB) in Sacramento, or, in the case of hydroelectric power projects, to the Federal Energy Regulatory Commission (FERC) in Washington, D.C. Copies of the applications are sent to all of the agencies responsible for environmental protection along with invitations to protest or intervene. Protesting an application to the SWRCB is easy and is not considered an hostile act. It simply opens the legal and institutional door to: a) discussions with the applicant; b) access to his various plans; and finally, c) to a public hearing in which all parties have their say and are subject to cross-examination. Intervening in a FERC licensing or relicensing is somewhat more complex, but not difficult.

The present administrative and legal system has evolved in the last decade to allow a more thorough consideration of environmental matters and is excellent if properly used. At best, it requires the project applicant to provide solid evidence that the proposed project has been carefully designed to avoid significant harm to instream resources. At worst, an inadequate agreement on streamflows is negotiated and accepted on the basis of "expert testimony." Post-project changes are rarely monitored or evaluated.

Making better use of the present system means requiring that it rely more on evidence and less on "experts"; and that post-project evaluations be made and "mitigation" features be modified if they are not working.

Public Support

The third requirement for making a water development project compatible with aquatic resources is public support. We need public support for better definition of goals and policies, more open planning and decision-making, more rigorous review of project plans, fairer pricing policies, and research on the geomorphology and ecology of streams and on groundwater basins.

In recent years, local groups and citizens concerned with the environment, with slowing growth, or with reducing taxes have become more involved in governmental processes. The present system encourages their serious involvement. Their critical evaluation of technical reports, and of what they may consider to be inappropriate conclusions of experts, is valuable. We need more of that. Public support for the protection of instream and riparian resources should not be limited to opposition. A project well conceived and designed to protect the environment should result in environmentalists supporting the project--not fading away once their concerns have been agreed to.

All government agencies are responsive to public input. Without it, knowledge and the opportunity to use it is of little value. Protection of public resources has not and will not be accomplished unless the public shows its concern.

Public support does not always require a lot of people. When I review the history of resources saved or destroyed there always seems to be one or two individuals--champions of the cause--who made the difference. As in most matters, it is persistence that counts. You must develop one or more champions for every riparian system you cherish. Identify them, cultivate them, educate them, support them, prepare them, and participate with them. They will make the difference.

LITERATURE CITED

Stalnaker, C.B., and J.L. Arnett (ed.). 1976. Methdologies for the determination of streamflow requirements: an assessment. Prepared for USDI Fish and Wildlife Service by Utah State University, Logan, Utah. 199 p.

Stalnaker, Clair B. 1980. The use of habitat structure preference for establishing flow regimes necessary for maintenance of fish habitat. p. 321-337. In: J.V. Ward and J.A. Stanford. The ecology of regulated streams. 398 p. Plenum Publishing Corp, New York, N.Y.

VEGETATION ON US ARMY CORPS OF ENGINEERS PROJECT LEVEES

IN THE SACRAMENTO/SAN JOAQUIN VALLEY, CALIFORNIA[1]

Michael F. Nolan[2]

Abstract.--The US Army Corps of Engineers' involvement with levees for flood control in the Sacramento/San Joaquin Valley is in cooperation with local interests. The integrity of a levee involves many factors, including structural stability and adequate maintenance. Trees and shrubs can be detrimental to the integrity of a levee, although there are opportunities for allowing vegetation on levees.

INTRODUCTION

This paper addresses the subject of vegetation on levees in the Sacramento/San Joaquin Valley which are part of Congressionally authorized flood control projects constructed by the US Army Corps of Engineers (CE). Levee design and maintenance criteria are explained, with emphasis on the importance of levee maintenance. Problems with and opportunities for vegetation on levees are presented, along with a discussion of multiple-purpose levees.

An evaluation of erosion control techniques is being made by the CE as part of a nationwide program authorized by the Streambank Erosion Control Evaluation and Demonstration Act of 1974.[3] The use of vegetation for erosion control is being investigated as part of that program, and therefore that subject is not addressed in this paper.

US ARMY CORPS OF ENGINEERS PROJECT LEVEES

The US Congress in the Federal Flood Control Act of 1936[4] declared a national interest in the prevention of flood damage. The act also set forth requirements for local cooperation. They provided that before any federal funds could be spent for constructing flood control improvements, states, political subdivisions thereof, or responsible local agencies would be required to to give assurances, satisfactory to the Secretary of the Army, that they would: a) provide without cost to the United States all lands, easements, and rights-of-way necessary for the construction of the project; b) hold and save the United States free from damages due to the constructed works; and c) maintain and operate all works after completion in accordance with regulations prescribed by the Secretary of the Army. The CE, on 16 August 1944, issued regulations governing the maintenance and operation by local interests of federal flood control projects.[5] These rules were designed as guides, to obtain a uniform standard of maintenance on all federal flood control projects.

At the request of local interests and with the authorization of the US Congress, the CE cooperates with local interests in planning, design, and construction of flood control projects in the Sacramento/San Joaquin Valley. The State of California has given the assurances required by the Federal Flood Control Act. The assurances are given by the State through the Reclamation Board. The California Water Code sets forth the duties and responsibilities of the Reclamation Board (RB), the California Department of Water Resources (DWR), and public districts and agencies with regard to construction, operation, and maintenance of these projects.

The Sacramento River Flood Control Project and the Lower San Joaquin River and Tributaries Project are two major flood control projects in the Sacramento/San Joaquin Valley which involve extensive levee systems. The extent of these levees is shown in the "Directory of Officials of Flood Control, Reclamation, Levee, and Drainage Districts, and Municipalities" (California Department of Water Resources 1982). Levee construc-

---

[1]Paper presented at the California Riparian Systems Conference. [University of California, Davis, September 17-19, 1981].

[2]Michael F. Nolan is Supervisory Civil Engineer, Sacramento District, US Army Corps of Engineers, Sacramento, California.

[3]Public Law 93-251 Section 32, as amended by Public Law 94-587, Section 155 and 161, October 1976.

[4]Public Law 738, Section 3 of Flood Control Act of 1936.

[5]Code of Federal Regulations, Section 208.10, Title 33. Flood Control Regulations.

tion on the Sacramento River Flood Control Project was basically completed in 1961, and on the Lower San Joaquin River and Tributaries Project, in 1968.

When local interests obtain land for local protection flood control projects, permanent easements are usually acquired obtaining the right to build, operate, and maintain a levee for flood control purposes. The landowner retains title to the land and all other land rights not encumbered by the easement. The local interest owns the easement and gives the CE permission to enter the land to construct and inspect a levee. For the Sacramento River Flood Control Project and the Lower San Joaquin and Tributaries Project, the RB purchased the flood control easements, although at times it has relied on the prescriptive rights of the responsible levee maintenance district. The local flood control interests have only acquired limited rights, and the landowner still owns the land and all remaining rights.

LEVEE DESIGN AND CONSTRUCTION

CE guidance for design and construction of flood control levees is contained in "Engineering and Design, Design and Construction of Levees" (US Army Corps of Engineers 1978). Levee design includes consideration of flow frequency, duration, and stages; erosion potential; seepage; soils; subsidence; maintenance and inspection requirements; and potential flood fight conditions. The guidance reflects the basic engineering considerations for design and construction of an earth embankment to retain water.

Aesthetics are of special concern from the standpoint of protecting the environment and blending levees with the surrounding environment. Vegetation on levees could serve purposes such as harmonizing a levee project with the surrounding environment, controlling dust and erosion, separating activities, providing privacy or screening of undesirable features, or providing habitat for wildlife. CE guidance on planting levees is contained in "Engineering and Design, Landscape Planting at Floodwalls, Levees and Embankment Dams" (US Army Corps of Engineers 1972) The guidance is to keep the basic levee structure free of roots and to provide a margin of safety of at least 1 m. (3 ft.) between the deepest expected penetration of plant roots and the face of the basic levee structure. If trees and shrubs are desired on a levee, the levee section must be overbuilt to accommodate the plant roots. This basic guidance is depicted in figure 1.

VEGETATION AND LEVEE MAINTENANCE

The detrimental effects of vegetation on flood control levees have been recognized for centuries. Printed below are excerpts from a rare

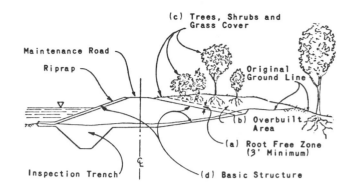

Figure 1.--Cross-sections of an urban levee showing: a) root-free zone; b) overbuilt area; c) trees, shrubs and grass cover; d) basic structure.

Spanish book, as translated by Amalio Gomez.[6] The book, "Hidrologia Historica del Rio Segura", deals with the struggles of the City of Murcia, Spain, from 1535 to 1879 against floods, droughts, and other calamities.

Murcia Levee Ordinance
1. It is hereby ordained that Murcia's levee shall not be swept by any person, with any type of broom, because the soil of which the levee is built will be blown away by the wind, and in the course of time the levee will lose height. Therefore, he who violates this ordinance shall be fined ... The city's share [of the fine] shall be used to pay the wage of a levee patrolman.
2. No person shall plant any trees, including mulberry bushes and fruit trees, within ten paces of the toe of the levee, along the entire length of the levee, and on both sides of the levee...
3. All trees (see 2. above) located within the ten pace strips described, should be pulled out within thirty days of the publication of this ordinance...
4. No person, for any reason, shall farm within the land occupied by the levee with a plow, hoe, or other implement...
5. No person shall accumulate a pile of manure within 100 paces of the toe of the levee all along its length...
6. It is ordained that no cattle of any kind shall be permitted to walk along the levee crown, with or without an attendant; such cattle must walk the road built parallel to the levee for that purpose. Cattle may cross the

[6]Former Chief, Engineering Division, Sacramento District, US Army Corps of Engineers.

levee only at the paved cattle crossings. Owners of cattle found violating this act shall be fined...

7. Grass grown on the levee crown and side slopes shall not be cut or pulled by any person...

8. The levee shall not be used as a playground; no person shall damage it by making holes or otherwise. No damage shall be done to any improvements on the levee crown, such as statues, paintings, stone seats, housewalls, stone pavements and hermitages. Violators shall be punished... It is further ordained that if the patrolman hired by the city to patrol the levee and enforce these ordinances does not apprehend the violators, he shall be removed from office and appropriately punished. (Gomez 1976)

Each prohibition of the ordinance carried a penalty. The usual procedure was to divide the fine, giving one-third to the judge, one-third to the accuser, and one-third to the city. The ordinance was enacted by the City of Murcia on July 25th, 1737. It was approved by the Royal Council of Castilla, August 30th, 1737.

Corps of Engineers Regulations

The Code of Federal Regulations contains the CE regulations for the operation and maintenance of local flood protection works.[7] These regulations, as written, apply to flood control projects throughout the nation and are of necessity general in character.

With regard to vegetation, the regulations require that measures be taken to promote the growth of sod, exterminate burrowing animals, and provide for routine mowing of the grass and weeds and removal of wild growth and drift deposits. The regulations also encourage planting willows and other suitable growth on the river side of levees to retard bank erosion; they discourage activities which retard or destroy the growth of sod, such as burning grass and weeds.

CE has several regulations which further address vegetation and the operation and maintenance of levees. Excerpts from "Project Operations, Levee Maintenance Standards and Procedures" (US Army Corps of Engineers 1968) are presented below.

Maintenance Standards
The levees will be maintained as necessary to insure serviceability against floods at all times. Standards for accomplishing the foregoing are as follows:

A good growth of sod will be maintained where feasible with grass height from 2 inches to 12 inches, substantially free of weeds.

All brush, trees, or other undesirable wild growth will be removed from the levee embankment. Vegetation specifically planted for aesthetics or recreation purposes may remain.

Maintenance Procedures
Maintaining sod growth--Maintenance of a sturdy sod growth on levee embankments is highly important as sod is one of the most effective means of protecting the levee against erosion from rain, current and wave wash. Periodic mowing is essential to maintaining a good sod growth, and should be done at such intervals as necesssary to keep down weeds and other noxious growth and to prevent the grass height from exceeding 12 inches. The grass should be mowed to a height of 2 inches or more. The number of mowings required each season will depend on local conditions, but experience has indicated that in most parts of the United States two or more mowings are necessary each season where pasturing is not used. The last mowing of the season should be accomplished under conditions which will allow the grass to obtain a height of approximately 8 to 10 inches going into the winter season. Mowing should be performed to a distance of at least 5 feet beyond the toe of the levee or berm.

Burning grass and weeds will not be permitted in the levee maintenance program, except during appropriate seasons when it will not be detrimental to the growth of sod.

"Project Operations, Inspection of Local Flood Protection Projects" (US Army Corps of Engineers 1973) addresses items to look for during inspections. Some excerpts from that regulation are presented below.

Are trees and other growth which might jeopardize the stability or watertightness of the structure removed at regular intervals?

Have trees and undesirable growth been cleared from the levees and along side floodwalls?

Does brush cover or other growth interfere with inspection?

Are there any obstructions to vehicular passage along the crown of the levee?

Is sod cover on levees being encouraged?

Is there any unauthorized burning of grass and weeds?

Is sod cover mowed regularly?

---

[7] Code of Federal Regulations Section 208.10, Title 33, Chapter II. Part 208--Flood Control Regulations. Corps of Engineers, Department of the Army.

Is sod or other desirable cover fertilized and reseeded as necessary?

Is there an effective program for control of burrowing animals?

"Project Operation, Maintenance Guide" (US Army Corps of Engineers 1967) also contains information on levee maintenance. Appendix I of the regulation, "Inspection Guide and Maintenance Standards," contains the following information:

Close inspection (should be made) for settlement, sloughing, slides, erosion, condition of ground drainage, the presence of burrowing animals, the presence of debris, need of mowing, encroachments that tend to weaken levees, rutting of crown, depressions or other defects.

Keep embankments sufficiently smooth to permit mowing by power equipment. Newly filled areas shall be sodded or seeded.

Levees should be mowed with tractor-operated equipment to a height of 2 inches or more when the grass reaches a height of 5 to 7 inches or when excessive uneven growth of grass or weeds becomes unsightly. Reseeding and fertilizing is limited to kind and weight necesssary to sustain vegetative cover for the control of erosion by wind and water.

Figure 2 is an example of a levee where vegetation interferes with inspection.

Figure 2.--Levee along Sutter Slough where dense vegetation interferes with levee inspection.

Title 33 of the Code of Federal Regulations[5] also requires the CE to furnish local interests with an operation and maintenance manual for each flood control project (e.g., US Army Corps of Engineers 1955, 1959). The manual assists the responsible authorities in carrying out their obligations by providing information

and advice on the operation and maintenance requirements of each project. Specific maintenance requirements that are applicable to an area are spelled out in special instructions in the manual for each project. This has been done, for example, in the special instructions contained in the "Standard Operation and Maintenance Manual for the Sacramento River Flood Control Project" (US Army Corps of Engineers 1955) which allow burning. Burning was allowed after the California Department of Public Works (DPW) in 1949 contended that due to the nature of the levee vegetation, burning weeds and brush during appropriate seasons should be allowed in order to determine danger to the levee such as slips and cracks and to permit the detection of holes caused by burrowing animals. Figures 3 and 4 present a good comparison between a burned levee and a mowed levee.

Figure 3.--Tractor-mounted hydraulically operated and controlled rotary mower as utilized by the American River Flood Control District (California Department of Water Resources 1973).

Figure 4.--Burned levee along the Sacramento River near Knights Landing.

Another example of special instructions in the "Standard Operation and Maintenance Manual for the Sacramento River Flood Control Project" (US Army Corps of Engineers 1955) deals with the provision in Title 33[5] which encourages growth riverward of the levees to retard bank erosion. The special instructions in the manual expand on this provision and allow retention of brush and small trees on the waterward levee slope where desirable for preventing erosion and wave wash. The manual contains the specific requirements for maintenance of each project.

Others besides the CE recognize that vegetation can be detrimental to levees. In December 1954, a year before the disastrous flooding of Yuba City and Nicolaus due to a levee break (fig. 5), the RB and the DPW expressed concern about trees on levees. The following is extracted from an 8 December 1954 letter from the RB to the District Engineer, CE, Sacramento:

> The Reclamation Board has through many years of experience found that the existence of trees on the river banks is a serious threat to the integrity of the levee system. In that respect the regulations of the Corps of Engineers require the removal of wild growth from levee banks and this agency is obligated to enforce these regulations. However, the Reclamation Board concurs in the view that trees constitute a menace to flood control works. Tree root systems penetrate levee sections, inducing seepage paths. Trees situated on the edge of the river banks that are uprooted by high winds, particularly when the banks are saturated, create craters in the sandy banks and levee sections rendering both of them susceptible to serious erosion during flood periods. Furthermore, the presence of trees on or adjacent to a levee often seriously interferes with routine maintenance operations such as slope dragging and control of weed cover.[8]

Figure 5.--Break in Feather River levee in Reclamation District 1001.

---

[8]California Reclamation Board. 8 December 1954. Letter to the District Engineer, CE, Sacramento, concerning tree removal along both banks of the Sacramento River between Sacramento and Rio Vista.

The following are excerpts from a letter dated 10 December 1954 from the DPW, Division of Water Resources, to the District Engineer, CE, Sacramento:

> Through the years, large trees became established on the levee slope and the heavy superimposed load produced slip-outs when the relatively unstable bank and levee section became saturated. Wind action on trees also tends to loosen the embankment and accelerates slippage when moisture is present. Trees overhanging the water's edge tend to pull out and drop into the stream when pressure is released from saturated banks. Trees which are of sufficient size to offer resistance to the flow of water are undesirable in a levee slope. Fallen trees and bared roots caused scour, silting and eventual diversion of the current with the result that banks became undercut, additional trees are dislodged and serious levee slippages ensue.
>
> Best maintenance practice dictates that the levee should be kept clear of trees and brush. However, in actual practice this condition is not fully obtained. In the sand levees below Sacramento, the presence of sod and light growth is not particularly objectionable and, in many instances, considered desirable. However, trees which attain large growth should never be permitted to become established on the levees. At locations where a wide berm exists between the bank of the river and the toe of the levee slope there is no objection to large trees if located in clear of the levee and riverbank.
>
> The assumption that the trees along the banks of the Sacramento River have provided a stabilizing effect is contrary to the experience of the engineers in the Division of Water Resources and others familiar with the conditions along the Sacramento River. Most severe slip-outs in levees of the Sacramento River can be directly attributed to the presence of large trees which place a superimposed load on the relatively unstable embankment, in excess of the ability of the levee material to resist when saturated.[9]

Figures 6 and 7 are examples of some of the problems cited by the RB and the DWR.

---

[9]California Department of Public Works, Division of Water Resources. 10 December 1954. Letter to District Engineer, US Army Corps of Engineers, Sacramento, concerning tree removal along Sacramento River channels downstream from Sacramento.

Figure 6.--Exposed roots and erosion around roots of tree along Sacramento River near Knights Landing.

Figure 7.--Exposed tree roots along Sacramento River near Cranmore.

The State maintains some portions of the Sacramento River Flood Control Project under the supervision of the DWR, with costs being defrayed by the State. The DWR also has exercised supervisory powers over maintenance performed by local districts on Sacramento River Flood Control Project levees. Such supervisory controls were accomplished generally in conformance with DWR "Standard Maintenance Procedures" (California Department of Water Resources n.d.) and "Guide for Levee Maintenance" (California Department of Water Resources n.d.). The following is taken from these manuals:

Clearing of the levee slopes of all growth, other than grass, should be accomplished at the earliest opportunity and once cleared the area should be maintained in that condition.
Burning of vegetation on levee slopes and shoulders should be performed annually.
Cut and pile brush, trees, and other obnoxious growths.

Clear brush, trees and wild growth, other than sod, from the levee crown and slopes. Herbicides applied with suitable equipment, under proper control and conditions, have been successfully employed in eradicating pernicious growth of vegetation.
Contrary to the often expressed belief that growth of trees and brush is beneficial for protection of the levee slopes, long experience has demonstrated that this is in error for the following reasons:
Under wind and wave action the larger growths tend to pull at their root systems, causing them to uproot themselves, disturb the soil or rock revetment and permit accelerated erosion to take place. Fallen trees may also cause harmful current deflection and accumulate drift, which can compound the erosive action. Roots of large trees also attract burrowing animals to the protective shelter afforded.
Removal of such growth promotes a growth of sod or grass, the pliable roots of which tend to provide a soil binding net.

Some detrimental effects of vegetation were pointed out again in "Findings and Recommendations Based on the Inspection of the Delta Levees During October 1980" (Department of Water Resources 1980a). Excessive wild growth was considered detrimental because it interfered with visual inspection of levee sections suspected of being inadequate. The DWR recommended some selective clearing to increase the capability for levee inspection and floodfighting.

The importance of levee maintenance has long been recognized. In 1925, in his report to the RB concerning revised plans for the Sacramento River Flood Control Project (California Department of Public Works 1925), the State Engineer stated: "This project will be incomplete and the expenditures largely wasted without adequate provisions for maintenance."

The importance of adequate levee maintenance is also recognized in "California Flood Management: An Evaluation of Flood Damage Prevention Programs" (California Department of Water Resources 1980b), which includes the statements:

Levees are...the method [of flood control] with the greatest potential risk of failure... Such failure can be caused by high waters overtopping a levee or eroding a portion of a levee, or by excessive seepage through a levee. Also, very large trees can be uprooted, leaving excessive voids in a levee, which can accelerate levee destruction... The effectiveness of any method of structural flood protection depends on the maintenance of the completed projects... Levees are the weakest part of a structural flood control program... Maintenance is a continuing responsibility with the objective of retaining the functional capability of the structures to store or carry storm flows according to their design... Levees are the most critical area in the maintenance of structural flood protection works.

The overriding concern of the CE, Sacramento District, has been ensuring the integrity of the flood control levees. Hence, adequate maintenance must provide a condition which will ensure the integrity of the systems when needed during flood periods. Encroachments which compromise the levee integrity or interfere with inspection, maintenance, and operation activities are detrimental to levee integrity.

MULTIPLE-PURPOSE LEVEES

Previous information on levee maintenance was focussed on flood control purposes. Multiple-purpose levees have also been investigated.

On 1 July 1962, the DWR initiated the Pilot Levee Maintenance Study. This five-year study was conducted to conceive and test alternative methods of levee maintenance that would provide for multiple use of levees. In 1967, when the Pilot Levee Maintenance Study (California Department of Water Resources 1967) was completed, all levee maintenance costs were borne by flood control beneficiaries. The results of the study indicated that levee maintenance costs increase significantly when efforts are made to work around and save vegetation. The report on the study included the statement that the introduction of uses other than flood control will require sharing of levee maintenance costs among flood control and the added users in some manner proportional to the value received from multiple-purpose maintenance.

Altering maintenance practices to reflect concerns of other interests was also addressed in the "Preliminary Report to the California State Legislature on a Multiple-Purpose Levee System for the Sacramento-San Joaquin Delta (California Department of Water Resources 1970) and "Sacramento River Levee Revegation Study Final Report, 1968-1973" (California Department of Water Resources 1973). The findings again were that it costs more to maintain levees for multiple purposes, and that some alternative methods of cost-sharing need to be developed for multiple-purpose levee maintenance.

In 1967, the CE, Sacramento District, approved the adoption of "Levee Encroachment: Guide for Vegetation on Project Levees" (The Reclamation Board 1967) as a guide in the consideration of vegetation encroachments. The

Sacramento District recognized fully that vegetation must be most carefully controlled in order to ascertain that the integrity of the levee system is not impaired.

In response to the findings of the DWR, AB 214 (Z'berg) was passed and became effective 1 January 1974. This bill[10] amended the California Water Code[11] to provide financial contributions from the state to local agencies for those costs associated with the operation and maintenance of project levees which are directly attributable to the planting or retention of controlled vegetative cover for wildlife, recreation, scenic, and aesthetic purposes, if the cost of maintenance is increased by such planting or retention. It has already been determined that vegetation was allowed on levees in accordance with the "Guide for Vegetation on Project Levees" (ibid.); this authority provided a method for funding the increased costs associated with preserving the vegetaion. Procedural requirements for this program were developed by DWR (The Reclamation Board 1974). The extent of implementation and funding of this program is unknown to the writer.

Continuous efforts are being made by DWR and RB to find and evaluate alternative construction methods and maintenance practices for flood damage reduction facilities which provide needed flood protection but are also responsive to environmental and aesthetic considerations. Some of these efforts are described in "Flood Control Project Maintenance and Repair 1980 Inspection Report" (California Department of Water Resources 1981).

One such effort involves using integrated pest management. The Center for the Integration of Applied Sciences of the John Muir Institute (JMI) has been working with the DWR since 1976 to develop and implement an integrated pest management program for the flood control levees of the Sacramento River (Center for the Integration of the Applied Sciences 1978). A major pest is the ground squirrel which is believed to weaken the levee structure by its burrowing. In assessing pest problems found on levees, particularly rodent control, the JMI has noted that lack of vegetation may enhance rodent populations. JMI is seeking to develop a vegetative management plan that would discourage rodent populations but not impede the ability of levee maintenance personnel to maintain the physical integrity of the levees. For investigation purposes, JMI selected vegetation which would not serve as a food source for ground squirrels or pocket gophers. JMI has also presented information on the movement of squirrels. Most squirrels remain within 33 m. (100 ft.) of their burrow entrances, although much farther movements have been observed. The ramifications of such selective

---

[10] Chapter 955, Statutes of 1973.
[11] Chapter 5, commencing with Section 8450, Part II, Provision 5 of the Calfornia Water Code.

plantings could be far-reaching if food sources for rodents are to be kept beyond the limits of the home range of squirrels.

OPPORTUNITIES FOR VEGETATION

The requirements for levee stability and the detrimental effects vegetation can have on flood control levees have been discussed. After taking these concerns into account, it is possible to outline the conditions under which, without reducing the flood protection provided by the levee systems, vegetation may be allowed on levees in the Sacramento/San Joaquin Valley. Such general guidelines are presented in the "Guide for Vegetation on Project Levees" (The Reclamation Board 1967), approved by CE, Sacramento District, in 1967. The basic guidance is that vegetation must be maintained in a controlled manner to ensure that it does not compromise the levee integrity or interfere with levee inspection, maintenance, operation, or flood-fight activities. The guide requires that the levee be oversized; this over-building provides for a root zone. The guide specifies minimum spacing intervals for trees and shrubs, the intent being to keep the levee slopes visible for inspection during low-flow and flood periods. The guide presents acceptable and unacceptable varieties of trees and shrubs—from the viewpoint of growth characteristics, impairment of inspection and maintenance, and potential impairment during flood-fight activities. The guide requires pruning of trees and shrubs so that inspection of the levees is possible.

There are opportunities for vegetation, including trees and shrubs, on project levees in the Sacramento/San Joaquin Valley. Vegetation is allowed, although the extent of vegetation that exists is often determined by the maintaining agencies and the underlying fee owners of the land. In cooperation with the RB, the CE, Sacramento District, has planted some vegetation on and adjacent to levees in the Sacramento/San Joaquin Valley. Where construction has been performed, the construction areas are seeded for dust and erosion control and aesthetic purposes with seed mixes suggested by fish and wildlife interests. Trees and shrubs have been planted where the levee is sufficiently oversized to provide a root zone, and riverward berm areas have also been planted. Figures 8, 9, and 10 show some of the planting that has been done.

There is presently significant emphasis on having vegetation on flood control levees. However, some levees are not suited to "riparian vegetation", when riparian vegetation is defined as that which requires free or unbounded water or conditions that are more moist than normal (Thomas 1979). Approximately 480 km. (300 mi.) of project levee are adjacent to the Sacramento River between Rio Vista and Ordbend. There are about 10,500 ha. (26,000 ac.) of land within the levee system along the Sacramento River in this reach. The levees occupy about 1,620 ha. (4,000 ac.) of land, the main river channel covers about

Figure 8.--Planting trees on levee, Sacramento River near Freeport.

Figure 9.--Various species of vegetation planted along Sacramento River levee near Elkhorn Park.

Figure 10.--Trees planted along Sacramento River levee near Sacramento Weir.

545

2,830 ha. (7,000 ac.), and the remaining 6,070 ha. (15,000 ac.) consist of berms, bars, banks, old oxbow channels and the like. Similar information listed by river reaches between Rio Vista and Ordbend is shown in table 1.

The area available within the levees for wildlife habitat or river aesthetics exceeds the area occupied by the levees almost four-fold. It is recognized that the levees along the Sacramento River downstream of Colusa (River Mile 144) are closely aligned to the main river channel. There are means available, consistent with good flood control practice, for allowing vegetation, including trees and shrubs, on these levees. Where the existing levees are sufficiently oversized, the "Guide for Vegetation on Project Levees" (The Reclamation Board 1967) in conjunction with the program authorized by AB 214 could be used to encourage vegetation on levees. In other areas, the levees could be overbuilt to accommodate such vegetation. Upstream of Colusa, there is ample land within the levees that could be acquired for development of vegetation areas. Such areas would also be better suited to riparian vegetation than the levee embankments which are most often set back from the river. The conditions along the lower San Joaquin River and Tributaries Project levees are similar to those along the Sacramento River levees.

The better levees are maintained, the less likely it is that problems will develop during flood periods; poor maintenance presents a much greater risk of levee failure. Regardless of vegetation, the primary concern in maintaining levees is to assure the flood protection. However, there is a feeling by some that some degree of risk associated with vegetation on levees can be tolerated when considering aesthetics and desires for wildlife habitat. The subject of risking the protection of lives and property that is presently provided by federal flood control projects goes beyond the scope of this paper. However, if such risks are to be taken, the degree of risk should be established and the concurrent liability determined.

LITERATURE CITED

California Department of Public Works. 1925. Sacramento River flood control project revised plans. 170 p. The Reclamation Board, State of California, Sacramento.

California Department of Water Resources. n.d. Standard maintenance procedures. 7 p. California Department of Water Resources, Sacramento.

California Department of Water Resources. n.d. Guide for levee maintenance. 8 p. Division of Design and Construction, California Department of Water Resources, Sacramento.

California Department of Water Resources. 1967. Pilot levee maintenance study, Sacramento-San Joaquin Delta. Bulletin No. 167, California Department of Water Resources, Sacramento. 24 p.

California Department of Water Resources. 1970. Preliminary report to the California State Legislature on a multiple-purpose levee system for the Sacramento-San Joaquin Delta. 21 p. California Department of Water Resources, Sacramento.

California Department of Water Resources. 1973. Sacramento River levee revegetation study, final report, 1968-1973. District Report, Central District, California Department of Water Resources, Sacramento. 19 p.

California Department of Water Resources. 1980a. Findings and recommendations based on the inspection of delta levees during October 1980. 23 p. California Department of Water Resources, Sacramento.

California Department of Water Resources. 1980b. California flood management: an evaluation of flood damage prevention programs. Bulletin 199, California Department of Water Resources, Sacramento. 277 p.

Table 1.--Lands within Sacramento River levee system between Rio Vista and Ordbend. Areas are approximate. (Source: Sacramento River, California Aerial Atlas, US Army Corps of Engineers, Sacramento District, September, 1980.)

	Reach (by River Mile)			Total
	15 to 80	84 to 144	144 to 176	
Land within levee system	2,800 ha. (7,000 ac.)	2,400 ha. (6,000 ac.)	5,300 ha. (13,000 ac.)	10,500 ha. (26,000 ac.)
Land occupied by levees	800 ha. (2,000 ac.)	600 ha. (1,500 ac.)	200 ha. (500 ac.)	1,600 ha. (4,000 ac.)
Other land between levees	400 ha. (1,000 ac.)	1,200 ha. (3,000 ac.)	4,500 ha. (11,000 ac.)	6,100 ha. (15,000 ac.)

California Department of Water Resources. 1981. Flood control project maintenance and repair 1980 inspection report. District Report, Central District, California Department of Water Resources, Sacramento. 35 p.

California Department of Water Resources. 1982. Directory of officials of flood control, reclamation, levee, and drainage districts, and municipalities. California Department of Water Resources, Sacramento.

Center for the Integration of the Applied Sciences. 1978. Making the transition to an integrated pest management program for ground squirrels on DWR levees. 114 p. Center for the Integration of the Applied Sciences, John Muir Institute, Berkeley, Calif.

Gomez, A. 1976. Hidrologia historica del Rio Segura. Information Bulletin, Sacramento District, US Army Corps of Engineers, Sacramento, California.

The Reclamation Board. 1967. Levee encroachment: Guide for vegetation on project levees. 4 p. California Department of Water Resources, Sacramento.

The Reclamation Board. 1974. Joint interim procedures for the administration of a state program of financial assistance for maintenance of controlled vegetation on project facilities. 9 p. California Department of Water Resources, Sacramento.

Thomas, J.W. (ed.). 1979. Wildlife habitats in managed forests: The Blue Mountains of Oregon and Washington. USDA Forest Service Agricultural Handbook No. 553, Washington, D.C. 512 p.

US Army Corps of Engineers. 1955. Standard operation and maintenance manual for the Sacramento River flood control project. 32 p. plus 62 supplements. South Pacific Division, Sacramento District, US Army Corps of Engineers, Sacramento, Calif.

US Army Corps of Engineers. 1959. Standard operation and maintenance manual for the lower San Joaquin River levees, Lower San Joaquin River and Tributaries Project, California. 32 p. plus 13 supplements. South Pacific Division, Sacramento District, US Army Corps of Engineers, Sacramento, Calif.

US Army Corps of Engineers. 1967. Project operation, maintenance guide. Engineering Regulation 1130-2-303. Department of the Army, Office of the Chief Engineer, Publications Depot, Alexandria, Va.

US Army Corps of Engineers. 1968. Project operations, levee maintenance standards and procedures. Engineering Regulation 1130-2-335. 4 p. Department of the Army, Office of the Chief Engineer, Publications Depot, Alexandria, Va.

US Army Corps of Engineers. 1972. Engineeering and design, landscape planting at floodwalls, levees and embankment dams. Engineering Manual 1110-2-301. 10 p. Department of the Army, Office of the Chief Engineer, Publications Depot, Alexandria, Va.

US Army Corps of Engineers. 1973. Project operations, inspection of local flood protection projects. Engineering Regulation 1130-2-339. 9 p. Department of the Army, Office of the Chief Engineer, Publications Depot, Alexandria, Va.

US Army Corps of Engineers. 1978. Engineering and design, design and construction of levees. Engineering Manual 1110-2-1913. 180 p. Department of the Army, Office of the Chief Engineer, Publications Depot, Alexandria, Va.

RIPARIAN VEGETATION ON FLOOD CONTROL PROJECT LEVEES:

CONSTRAINTS AND OPPORTUNITIES[1]

Lee W. Carter and Gene L. Anderson[2]

Abstract.--Efforts are being made to find and evaluate alternative construction methods and maintenance practices that are responsive to environmental and esthetic considerations in conjunction with flood control needs. Although some constraints on vegetation on levees are necessary, progress is being made to reach a compromise between the environmentalists and the flood control project builders and operators to allow riparian vegetation on and adjacent to flood control project levees.

INTRODUCTION

Can riparian vegetation on flood control project levees be managed differently in the future than it has been in the past? What constraints on vegetation are necessary to maintain the integrity of flood control project levees?

The answers to these questions are complex and controversial. This paper is primarily based upon experience with levees in the Central Valley of California.

BACKGROUND

Maintenance of flood control project channels and levees has come under considerable public criticism in the last several years. Some of this criticism can be attributed to the lack of environmental consideration on the part of the maintaining agencies. Some of the criticism is because the public fails to acknowledge the primary purpose of the levees. Public criticism is often triggered by removal of riparian vegetation and its replacement with rock bank protection.

In recent years, the California Reclamation Board and the Department of Water Resources (DWR) have advocated retention of a greater amount of riparian vegetation on and adjacent to flood control project levees. The US Army Corps of Engineers (CE) has resisted relaxation of present flood control project maintenance standards be-

cause of the high potential for loss of human life and property associated with levee failures. The CE has expressed particular concern about the increased wild growth developing in the rock revetment sites on the Sacramento River flood control project levees.

The differences between guidelines for allowable vegetation on levees proposed by the Reclamation Board and those in the operating manuals prepared by the CE have received considerable attention during the past three years. The staff of the CE and that of the DWR have jointly proposed a revised guide for allowable vegetation consistent with Title 33, Code of Federal Regulations. This revised draft of present guidelines was circulated for review within the DWR, CE, other interested State agencies, and local levee maintaining agencies. The local maintaining agencies and the South Pacific Division of the CE expressed opposition to relaxation of the CE's standards. The Department of Fish and Game expressed concern that the proposed guide does not adequately encourage the retention and protection of riparian vegetation.

The next step will be to submit the proposed guide to the Reclamation Board for its recommendations considering the comments that have been received.

CONSTRAINTS ON VEGETATION ON LEVEES

First, it is useful to discuss briefly the reasons for restricting vegetative growth on levees.[3] Most levees were constructed for one purpose--to protect the adjacent land from flooding. Early levees were constructed by local landowners. Later State and Federal governments

[1] Paper presented at the California Riparian Systems Conference. [University of California, Davis, September 17-19, 1981].
[2] Lee W. Carter is Chief, Data and Operations Branch, Central District, Department of Water Resources. Gene L. Anderson is Senior Engineer, Department of Water Resources, Sacramento, California.

[3] For more information on this subject, see Nolan (1981).

assisted in providing funds and expertise to up-grade the integrity of flood control projects. For the most part, the levees were considered single-purpose flood control structures. They were designed as dams to withstand the hydro-static pressure and relatively high velocities of flow exerted on the levees during high water.

The design, construction, and maintenance standards developed by the CE were designed to protect human life and property. The State of California gave assurances to the Federal govern-ment that the levees would be maintained to the standard outlined in the operation and mainte-nance manuals prepared by the CE for project levees. The most economical and efficient way to inspect the levees was to restrict the amount of vegetation so that the levee slopes could be inspected from the levee crown. Most inspections are made from an automobile moving along the levee at about 5 mi. per hr. or 1 mi. per 12 min. If the inspector were required to stop and spend time inspecting levee slopes on foot, the inspec-tion time could easily be tripled. Under the present inspection procedures, the State is spend-ing around $200,000 per year for inspections. Maintenance and flood fight activities also are easier to perform without wild growth on the slopes. Therefore, many maintaining agencies annually mow, burn, or spray vegetation. The maintaining agencies then fill eroded areas with soil or rock, exterminate burrowing rodents, and maintain levee heights to the design level.

In some cases, the local maintaining agencies have cleared more vegetation than is required by the CE standards; in other cases, they are doing less than is required by stan-dards. For example, the minimum-size levee on a major stream is 20-ft. minimum crown width, a design freeboard of 3 ft. to 5 ft., and slopes of 3:1 horizontal to vertical on the waterward levee slope, and 2:1 horizontal to vertical on the landward side of the levee. On smaller tribu-tary streams, the minimum crown width is 12 ft., freeboard 3 ft., and the same side slope require-ments. According to CE engineering manuals, this basic levee structure must be root-free except for grasses and low-growing, shallow-rooted groundcover plants. In certain areas, brush and small trees may be retained on the waterward levee slope to prevent erosion, wave wash damage, and for environmental values.

Unrevetted Levees

Although the Federal regulations still require the basic structure to be root-free, many levees are larger than the minimum standard levee. Where adequately overbuilt levees exist, trees and shrubs can be allowed to remain on the levee slope. However, to facilitate inspection of the levees and flood fighting efforts, spacing requirements are considered necessary. Selective clearing to satisfy spacing requirements is expensive.

The magnitude of the expense of retaining vegetation is difficult to evaluate. The expense would vary depending on the extent and type of vegetation and the present maintenance practices. Many local maintaining agencies contend they cannot provide for the additional expense required for selective clearing. No sources of funds, except for the unfunded Z'Berg Bill (Water Code Section 8450, et seq.), have been identified to subsidize local maintaining agencies for the increased cost of maintaining riparian vegetation.

Critics of the CE standards argue that the standards are too stringent and that vegetation can be a deterrent to erosion of the levee slopes. In some instances, their argument may be valid; however, the standards were developed to protect levees under adverse soil-type and founda-tion conditions, erosional forces, and problems associated with trees and shrubs.

The causes of levee failures are difficult to document. Failures have been attributed to levee subsidence because of foundation condi-tions, rodent activities, and caving of the levee from erosion. No levee failure has been attribut-ed directly to the existence of riparian vegeta-tion on the levee slopes. However, vegetation that hinders the local maintaining agency in performance of adequate maintenance increases the risk of levee failure. Consequently, frequent and adequate inspection of levee slopes is consid-ered imperative to a good maintenance program. Restrictions on vegetation species, spacing, and pruning are, therefore, considered necessary.

In general, unacceptable vegetation species either: 1) provide a food supply for rodents; 2) are detrimental or destructive and difficult to control or eradicate; or 3) are characteristical-ly thorny or intrusive, such as roses, black-berries, bamboo, and vines.

The proposed revised guidelines provide that spacing between trees or clumps of trees, shrubs, or clumps of trees and shrubs (up to 6 ft. in diameter), shall be no closer than 25 ft. The 25 ft. were considered an average inter-tree or inter-clump distance between trees on levees. Also, spacing encourages the tree to branch out rather than grow tall. Space requirements are for three general reasons: 1) to facilitate inspection of the levee; 2) to make flood fights and repairs less difficult; and 3) to encourage trees to develop a good root system and to branch out rather than grow tall. Tall trees have a greater tendency to be blown over.

Revetted Levees and Berms

The present CE guidelines prohibit growth of trees and shrubs in rock revetment on a standard levee section. Under the proposed revised guide, trees and shrubs are allowed in the revetment on either levees or berms when the distance from the landward shoulder measured at design freeboard level to the top of the revetment is 150 ft. or greater. When the stream velocity is less than 5 ft. per sec. and the channel is relatively straight, this distance can be reduced to 75 ft.

The rationale for this conservative guideline is: 1) revetment has been placed in areas where erosion has been a problem; and 2) flow pattern irregularities caused by trees and shrubs can cause displacement of the rock and failure of the revetment.

OPPORTUNITIES FOR VEGETATION ON LEVEES AND BERMS

As mentioned earlier, many levees along the major streams are large enough to accommodate vegetation under the proposed revised vegetation guidelines.

Unrevetted Levees

Most unrevetted levees that have two-lane surfaced roads on the crown exceed the 30-ft. width requirement at freeboard that is proposed in the revised vegetation guide for retention of vegetation. Also, the waterward slope of the basic levee under the proposed revision has been changed from 3:1 horizontal to vertical, to 2:1 horizonal to vertical. This change increases the area at the waterward base of the levee where roots are allowed. This would provide for considerably more trees and shrubs near the waterward toe of the levee.

Unrevetted Berms

The proposed vegetation guide provides that where a berm exceeds 10 ft. in width, vegetation is allowed with no requirement for species, spacing, height, or pruning unless special conditions require some restriction.

Low Rock Revetment

In the case of the Steamboat Slough bank protection work, the CE constructed a 10-ft. berm just above the normal low water level and placed rock on the face of the berm. This is an example of innovative design of a levee to provide a condition where vegetation can be allowed. This design is consistent with the criteria for vegetation on berms established in the proposed revised vegetation guide. It should be recognized that this special construction feature increased the cost of providing flood control. In this case the CE and the State provided the funds to pay the extra capital costs. The local maintaining agency will be responsible for maintenance.

Low rock was also placed by the CE in several reaches of the Sacramento River downstream from Sacramento as early as 1940. In many locations vegetation has grown in and above the rock. Normal deterioration of the rock has resulted in some areas and repairs are needed, but very few problems have been attributed to the vegetation. The rock has reduced erosion and has not been significantly displaced in 40 yrs., indicating that low rock has been successful under these flow and soil conditions.

FUNDING TO PROTECT RIPARIAN VEGETATION

Erosion of berms and levees is continuing at a high level, resulting in the loss of riparian vegetation at an alarming rate. Federal and State funds to protect levees and berms are decreasing. We will discuss briefly the status of two programs used in the past to help retain vegetation on levees and berms, the Sacramento River Bank Protection Program, and the 1973 Z'Berg Bill, codified as Section 8450, et seq., of the Water Code.

The Sacramento River Bank Protection Program began in June, 1963. Under this program, the CE repaired levees along the Sacramento River flood control project. Costs were shared, with the Federal Government paying two-thirds and the State paying one-third. Under Phase I of this program, a large amount of riparian vegetation was removed from the project levees. Due to environmental concerns, the CE (under Phase II of the program) received authorization to spend up to 10% of the project costs to mitigate the loss of streamside vegetation resulting from the bank protection work. The presently authorized work under Phase II is nearing completion. Work on Steamboat Slough, in Unit No. 36, is the last work authorized for construction under Phase II.

The continuation of Phase II bank protection is conditioned on Congressional authorization of mitigation for Phase I. Even though Phase II provides for environmental consideration, the Secretary for Resources has not authorized State participation with the CE on additional units of bank protection work under this phase until the replacement of wildlife habitat lost during construction of Phase I has been authorized.

CONCLUSION

We believe more vegetation can be retained on and adjacent to flood control levees if: 1) the levee section is designed as a multi-purpose structure, that is, enlarged to provide a zone for roots outside the basic structure required for flood control; and 2) if the levee and vegetation are adequately maintained. Both of these conditions require additional funding. The question arises: who is willing to pay? In this time of austere budgets, support will be required from many sectors to obtain the high priority necessary for funds to protect riparian vegetation on and adjacent to flood control levees.

LITERATURE CITED

Nolan, Michael F. 1981. Vegetation on Corps of Engineers' project levees in the Sacramento-San Joaquin Valleys, California. In: R. E. Warner and K.M. Hendrix (ed.). Proceedings of the California Riparian Systems Conference. [University of California, Davis, September 17-19, 1981]. California Water Resources Center Report No. 55. University of California, Davis.

THE ROLE OF VEGETATION IN AN INTEGRATED

PEST MANAGEMENT APPROACH TO LEVEE MANAGEMENT[1]

Sheila Daar, William Klitz, and William Olkowski[2]

Abstract.--Encouraging appropriate vegetation complexes on levee slopes maximizes levee safety, and improves wildlife habitat, recreational opportunities, and aesthetic amenities. This contrasts with standard levee maintenance practices which annually destroy vegetation on levees, thereby exacerbating a series of maintenance problems, and reducing environmental quality.

INTRODUCTION

Thousands of miles of levee systems border California's major riparian zones. Though constructed from engineered fill soils and designed to restrict floodwaters to designated channels, these levees nonetheless offer opportunities to protect and enhance the state's riparian ecosystems (Davis et al. 1967).

The extensive soil area represented by the levee system supports a considerable biomass of vegetation which in turn serves as potential harborage and food sources for many riparian wildlife species (Sands 1977). In addition, many levee reaches serve as buffers, separating waterside berms bearing remnant strands of riparian vegetation from landside agricultural and urban development. See figure 1 for illustrations of various levee configurations.

Standard levee maintenance practices, however, generally assume vegetation on levee slopes is a hindrance to the prime purpose of levees, namely flood protection (US Army Corps of Engineers 1955). Under such practices, vegetation is removed each year to permit inspection of the levee surface. This practice of yearly vegetation removal and frequent soil disturbance creates and aggravates a series of levee maintenance problems ranging from erosion to ground squirrels. These maintenance practices also severely limit the opportunity to utilize levees for such secondary functions as wildlife habitat,

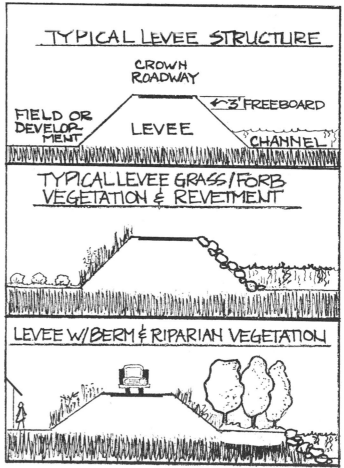

Figure 1.--Several possible levee and levee/berm configurations and their associated vegetations.

riparian vegetation enclaves, and aesthetic and recreational amenities.

[1] Paper presented at the California Riparian Systems Conference. [University of California, Davis, September 17-19, 1981].

[2] Sheila Daar is Staff Horticulturalist, William Klitz is Research Coordinator, and William Olkowski is Co-Director at the Center for the Integration of Applied Sciences, a division of the John Muir Institute, Berkeley, California.

This paper describes a vegetation management program for the levee system which not only has the potential for enhancing levee safety and improving maintenance cost-effectiveness, but which affords opportunities to bring levee maintenance practices more in line with needs to improve environmental quality and protect our dwindling riparian resources.

This approach to vegetation management has been a focus of the Integrated Pest Management (IPM) program under development for the Department of Water Resources (DWR) for the past four years by the Center for the Integration of Applied Sciences (CIAS), a division of JMI, Inc. IPM is a decision-making process for analyzing and solving pest problems and features mixes of tactics and strategies compatible with environmental quality.

Utilizing the IPM approach to problem solving, CIAS staff discovered a relationship between traditional levee maintenance practices and the onset and increase of weed and rodent pests, considered major problems by DWR.

TRADITIONAL LEVEE MAINTENANCE

The cornerstone of traditional levee maintenance practices is the mandate to remove levee vegetation annually in order to inspect levee slopes (ibid.). Inspections are designed to detect damage, such as cracks, slumps, seeps, erosion, or rodent burrows, which could weaken levees during periods of high water.

The major methods utilized in levee vegetation removal include burning, surface dragging, mowing, and applying herbicide. (Brush removal in channels to improve channel capacity is another major maintenance activity, but discussion of that topic is beyond the scope of this paper.)

The dominant role vegetation removal plays in levee maintenance is illustrated by budget figures compiled for the 523 km. (325 mi.) of levees and 24,300 ha. (60,000 ac.) of channels maintained by DWR Sacramento and Sutter Maintenance Yards. As detailed in figure 2, activities associated with vegetation removal consumed 57% of the 94,000 labor hours involved in maintenance in 1978. Activities included brush cutting (27,848 hours), spraying (14,315 hours), mowing (5,164 hours), burning (3,542 hours), fire guarding (1,872 hours), and tree management (582 hours). (Environmental costs due to pesticide residues in water, air pollution from burning, loss of wildlife habitat, and reduced recreational and aesthetic values are not available.)

Consequences to the Levee Plant Community of Vegetation Removal

One of the major effects of annual vegetation removal appears to be a shift in the species of plants growing on the levees. Plant ecology

Figure 2.--DWR labor hours involved in vegetation removal, 1977-78 (total maintenance budget $2.6 million.)

literature (Weaver and Clements 1938; Frenkel 1977) indicates that systematic yearly soil disturbance creates conditions favoring broad-leaf species over grasses.

Baseline vegetation transects in five levee study areas (Daar et al. 1979) showed that broad-leaf plant represented 76% of the total species present, although two annual grasses (Avena fatua and Bromis rigidis) sometimes dominated the stands. The competitive advantage which yearly soil disturbance accords broad-leaved species may explain the presence of dense stands of thistles and other weeds such as puncture vine (Tribulus terrestris) and field bindweed (Convolvulus arvensis) which are considered undesirable on levees because they are more difficult to remove than grasses.

Once established, these "weedy" species often maintain their presence and density over many years. Herbicides are applied to these broad-leaf plants (as well as to unwanted grasses such as Johnson grass [Sorghum halopensis]) to increase broad-leaf susceptibility to the annual burning and mowing operations. Table 1 shows the amount of herbicide (active ingredient) applied in 1979 and 1980, as well as projected use in 1981. The relationship of soil disturbance to presence of broad-leaf species indicates a cycle of maintenance practices which may be requiring an ever-increasing rate of herbicide use.

Routine use of herbicides on levee vegetation also promotes a shift in plant species composition--often in a direction not desired. For example, in many locations yearly application of triazine herbicides to levee crown roadways has

Table 1.--Herbicides used on levee and channel vegetation by Sacramento and Sutter Maintenance Yards, DWR (DWR Pesticide Use Plans 1980, 1981).

	1978-79 (actual)	1979-80* (actual)	1980-81 (proposed)
Pounds	2085	916	2900
Gallons	2564	1459	4402

*Amount of herbicide use was unusually low due to managerial reorganization as well as low rainfall which inhibited use of pre-emergents.

suppressed the relatively preferred wild oat (Avena fatua) which formerly populated the top of the levee slope. Removal of the wild oat has allowed establishment of perennial weed species such as Bermuda grass (Cynodon dactylon) and field bindweed, which are less susceptible to the herbicides (Frenkel 1977). Field bindweed is an important agricultural pest, and Bermuda grass encroaching on crown roadways is considered a major pest by levee maintenance personnel who feel it interferes with grading practices necessary to keep crown roadways clear and passable during the winter.

Relationship of Vegetation Removal to Presence of Erosion, Slumps, and Cracks in Levees

Most vegetation removal on levee slopes occurs during the summer and early fall, leaving levee surfaces relatively bare until germination of winter seedlings with the first rains. In areas treated with herbicides, soil sterilants may keep sections of slope bare for several seasons.

The ability of levee slopes to resist the erosive forces of wind and water is severely reduced in the absence of a densely rooted stand of vegetation (Enlow and Musgrave 1938). This is particularly true on the waterside slope where rainfall, wave wash, scouring, and other hydraulic forces place erosive pressure on levees.

The absence of vegetation on slopes during the heat of the summer may also exacerbate the development of cracks in the levee structure. Vegetation contributes to the even drying of soils after saturation by winter flows (Mathews and Cole 1938; Satterlund 1972). Removal of vegetation may alter that process, resulting in differential soil settling and drying, which can cause cracks.

GROUND SQUIRRELS AND LEVEE VEGETATION

Vegetation removal activities of levee maintenance cause changes in the plant composition and structure on the levees. These activities also have a major impact on ground squirrels, the most important animal pest on levees.

Ground squirrels can be significant pests on levees due to the extensive network of underground burrows these animals create. Their channeling may weaken levee structure during floods and increase the likelihood of a levee break. The population biology and behavior of rodents make them good candidates for control through habitat modification (Davis 1972), and ground squirrels may be susceptible to this strategy.

The relationship of ground squirrel population density to the degree of soil disturbance has long been noted. For example, Linsdale (1946) observed that ground squirrel numbers rose and fell with the extent of overgrazing on pasture lands. High squirrel populations are characteristically associated wih barren ground, outcrops, or elevated areas (Owings and Borchert 1975), and nearby food sources. Lack of vegetation permits high visibility for the squirrels, which aids in social communication and predator detection (Owings 1977). With the construction of levees and the traditional maintenance practices associated with them, people have inadvertently created prime ground squirrel habitat which is lacking only an enriched food source, often supplied by adjacent agriculture.

Figure 3 shows the results of a detailed study on a section of levee which demonstrated the relationship of ground squirrel density to vegetation and other environmental features. The number of burrows is indicative of the population size of squirrels and is a direct indication of the damage to levees caused by the squirrels.

Squirrel burrows on a 3.2-km. (2-mi.) stretch of levee encompassing various environments were counted in the late summer of 1980, after the levee had been burned. The squirrels' particular attraction to areas of barren ground was demonstrated by the high burrow densities observed in the area where overgrazed pasture extended up onto the side of the levee. Burrow numbers on the levee dropped where the fence line ended.

A second strong determinant of ground squirrel distribution is availability of food sources. Exceptionally high burrow densities were present near the walnut orchard. The area immediately adjacent to the walnut orchard, which had 583 holes per km. (932 per mi.), had been fumigated earlier in the season, so counts may actually have been depressed there. Areas within the squirrel foraging range of the walnuts on both sides of the levee also had very high burrow counts. (It was impossible to count burrows in the area of stone revetment on the water side opposite the orchard, although squirrel densities were clearly high there. The high counts in areas near the orchard showed the enhanced effect on squirrel densities produced by both disturbed slopes and nearby food.)

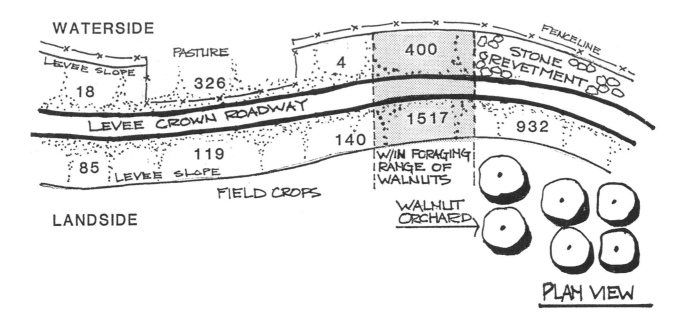

Figure 3.--Distribution of ground squirrels on 3.2 km. (2 mi.) of levee at East Yolo Bypass, Yolo County, California, August, 1980. Counts are in number of burrows per levee mile. Before burning, yellow star thistle (Centaurea solstitialis) and wild oat (Avena fatua) comprised the dominant vegetation on much of the otherwise undistinguished levee slope. The linear distance along the levee is not drawn to scale.

Areas lacking both nearby walnuts and the disturbed surface of the overgrazed pasture had lower burrow counts. In these areas, a weaker propensity of squirrels to burrow on land- versus water-side slopes may have been demonstrated. That is, there is a propensity to burrow on landside slopes, but that propensity is less pronounced in areas which are away from orchards and overgrazed pastures.

Vegetation on levee slopes during the summer and fall may be particularly important in habitat management of ground squirrels. During this period, young, first-year animals are actively dispersing, seeking new area in which to settle (Dobson 1979). Slopes covered with vegetation at this time of the year will be much less attractive to migrating squirrels than those freshly denuded by annual vegetation removal practices.

The traditional approach of annually burning levee slopes followed by dragging to obliterate burrow openings and smooth the levee surface improves the quality of ground squirrel habitat. In contrast, a program of deliberately maintaining certain vegetation on levee slopes may tend to discourage squirrel colonization. The tactic of revegetating levee slopes with appropriate plant species should be integrated into an active squirrel control program if permanent population reduction is to occur.

AN INTEGRATED PEST MANAGEMENT APPROACH TO LEVEE VEGETATION

An IPM approach to vegetation management offers a way out of the traditional dilemma of levee maintenance practices which exacerbate weed and rodent pests. Furthermore, this method shows promise as a means of achieving the objectives of maximum levee safety while simultaneously improving environmental quality of riparian areas.

Traditional approaches to levee maintenance have a single objective--that of flood safety. In contrast, the IPM approach recognizes flood safety as the primary maintenance objective but places high value on other goals including improvement of wildlife habitat and recreational opportunities, enhanced aesthetics, and reduced pesticide use. At the level of implementation, the main points at which the approaches differ are in the way in which vegetation is viewed and the process by which maintenance decisions are made.

Despite the wide variation in biotic and abiotic conditions of various levee reaches, traditional maintenance practices have tended to give all levee reaches equal attention and treatment. Thus, a uniform policy of slope clearing to facilitate inspection is implemented irrespective of characteristics of the levee vegetation. By contrast, the IPM approach gives more recognition to the uniqueness of each levee stretch in the belief that improved practices can be developed which both maximize flood safety and improve environmental quality.

When reduced to their basic structural forms, levees can be defined as "fill slopes." When viewed in this manner, both engineering (US Army Corps of Engineers 1978) and biological (Lines et al. 1978) expertise would agree that vegetation can and does play a key role in stabilizing these slopes against the erosive forces of wind, water, temperature fluctuation, and damage by animals, humans, or vehicles.

Damage to levees due to erosion, cracking, slumping, seeps, etc., may originate in soil type, construction techniques, seismic action, burrowing rodents, water pressure, maintenance practices, or other forces. Whatever the origin of the problem, the presence of vegetation holding the soil mass together can help reduce (and in some cases, prevent) the onset or impact of such problems.

Thus, protection and encouragement of certain vegetation-types on levee slopes can be seen as an important tool in maximizing the structural integrity--and therefore the safety--of these structures. Should a conflict appear to arise between the presence of vegetation and the need to inspect the levees, a site-intensive levee monitoring program offers a solution (fig. 4).

Under an IPM vegetation management system, information on current site or pest conditions is integrated with historical data on the construction and maintenance history of a levee reach. Site conditions are evaluated through use of a variety of monitoring techniques and record-keeping systems which vary in intensity, depending on a priority assigned to a given site. Utilizing the monitoring data, injury and action levels are established for the vegetation, and selective treatments are chosen. Spot treatments, selected from mechanical, cultural, biological, or chemical controls, are timed to minimize side effects on non-target organisms. Strategies and tactics are evaluated for long-term effectiveness and cost.

Utilizing this system, the maintenance manager has greater flexibility when it comes to the apparent conflict between vegetation and inspection of levees. By prioritizing sites to be monitored, those with no significant history of maintenance or other problems can receive a less intense level of monitoring, freeing maintenance personnel to focus major monitoring attention on areas with chronic flood history or maintenance problems. (This situation may occur de facto under the traditional approach but is not recorded, planned, or approached in a systematic manner.)

Ideally, levee inspections occur just before, during, and just after flood season (i.e., November-March each year). Under the IPM system, spring inspections (which detect damage from win-

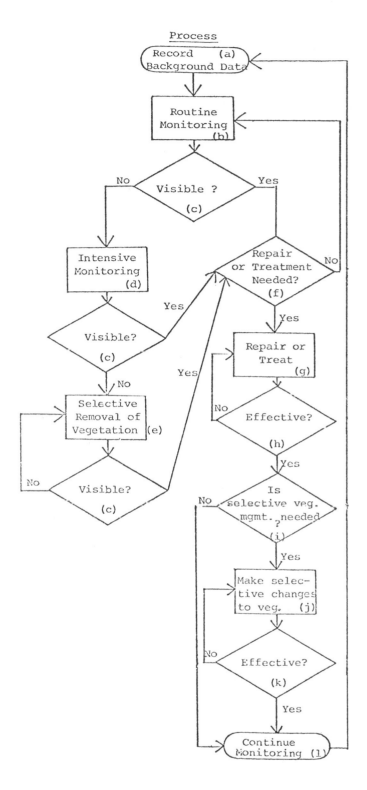

Figure 4.--Diagram showing a levee slope monitoring process. Key variable is slope visibility.

ter flows) should be timed to occur before spring grasses have grown more than one foot tall. By shifting existing maintenance personnel to inspection/monitoring roles in early spring, it should be possible to thoroughly monitor most sections of levee prior to dense growth of vegetation. If vegetative growth becomes too dense to detect potential levee damage, selective removal of that vegetation can occur. If damage is found, repairs can be made. If warranted, the vegetation at that site could be removed periodically, or vegetation more suited to the inspection and maintenance needs at that site could be encouraged.

Encouraging Appropriate Vegetation on Levees

A major strategy in an IPM program for levees is the development of practices which select for and encourage certain existing grass species and low-growing broad-leafed plants which reinforce the structural integrity of levees by reducing erosion and ground squirrel habitat. Examples of candidate species include salt grass (Distichlis spicata); creeping ryegrass (Elymus triticoides); perla grass (Phalaris tuberosa 'Hurtiglumis') and saltbush (Atriplex spp.).

Under some circumstances it may be appropriate to introduce new species to the levees (Daar et al. 1979), particularly in areas adjacent to residential subdivisions, where concerns about the relation of levee management to fire danger, recreation, and aesthetics are the focus of attention. Five candidate species for replacement vegetation in urban areas are showing promise as relatively low-growing, dense, low-maintenance slope covers in test plots at two levee locations near Sacramento. These species include: sage-leaf rockrose (Cistus salvifolius), Cleveland sage (Salvia clevelandii), Australian saltbush (Atriplex semibaccata), dwarf coyote brush (Baccharis pilularis 'Twin Peaks No. 2'), and Noel grevillia (Grevillia noellii).

Benefits of IPM Vegetation Management

The benefits of a selective vegetation-management system will be most evident during the flood season. The condition of levees at any given site will be known in intimate detail due to the data recorded by the monitoring program. This results in greater predictability of a given levee reach when under flood stress. At sites with chronic maintenance problems or flood histories, vegetation on the land side of the levee (the side visible during high water) will have been selectively managed to retain its rootmass while restricting its height, thus maximizing the stability of the slope as well as its visibility in case of a flood fight. Decisions regarding setting of priories and scheduling work, deployment of labor and materials, and evaluation of efficacy of maintenance efforts will be aided by the data collected by the monitoring process.

Other benefits of particular relevance to the riparian system would include reduction in the use of pesticides, more extensive wildlife habitat, enhanced recreational opportunities, and an increase in the aesthetic quality of the levee environment.

In conclusion, an IPM approach to managing levee vegetation shows promise as a method for achieving the dual objectives of maximum levee safety and improved environmental quality.

In recognition of this potential, the DWR is moving to implement new IPM practices including more intensive levee-monitoring and record-keeping systems, development of injury- and action-level concepts, and use of selective vegetation-management techniques to encourage the presence of certain grasses and other vegetation compatible with multiple-use management objectives. It is hoped that these and other IPM practices will become adopted Department-wide and serve as a model for the state's 7,000 local water districts, whose activities have a profound impact on California's dwindling riparian resources.

LITERATURE CITED

Daar, Sheila, Nancy Hardesty, Rhodes Hileman, Donna Michaelson, and William Olkowski. 1979. Vegetation checklist of potentially useful plant species for introduction into DWR level ecosystems. p. 42-59. In: Third IPM report to Division of Planning, Department of Water Resources. 120 p. Center for the Integration of Applied Sciences, John Muir Institute, Berkeley, Calif.

Davis, D.E. 1972. Rodent control strategy. p. 159-171. In: Pest control: strategies for the future. 376 p. National Academy of Sciences, Washington, D.C.

Davis, Larry C., Sam Ito, and Philip Zwanck. 1967. Pilot levee maintenance study. California Department of Water Resources, Bull. 167. Sacramento.

Dobson, F.S. 1979. An experimental study of dispersal in the California ground squirrel. Ecology 60:1103-1109.

Enlow, C.R., and G.W. Musgrave. 1938. Grass and other thick growing vegetation in erosion control. pp. 595, 623. In: Soils and men. Yearbook of Agriculture. US Department of Agriculture.

Frenkel, Robert E. 1977. Ruderal vegetation along some California roadsides. 163 p. University of California Press, Berkeley.

Lines, Ivan L. Jr., Jack R. Carlson, and Robert A. Corthell. 1978. Repairing flood-damaged streams in the Pacific Northwest. In: R.R. Johnson and J.F. McCormick (tech. coord.). Strategies for the protection and management of floodplain wetland and other riparian ecosystems. [Callaway Gardens, Georgia, December 11-13, 1978.] USDA Forest Service GTR-WO-12, Washington, D.C. 410 p.

Linsdale, J.M. 1946. The California ground squirrel. 475 p. University of California Press, Berkeley.

Mathews, O.R., and John S. Cole. 1938. Special dry-farming problems. p. 683. <u>In</u>: Soils and men. Yearbook of Agriculture. US Department of Agriculture.

Owings, D.H., and M. Borchert. 1975. Correlates of burrow location in Beechey ground squirrels. Great Basin Naturalist 35:402-404.

Owings, D.H., M. Borchert, and R. Virginia. 1977. The behavior of California ground squirrels. Animal Behavior 25:221-230.

Sands, Anne (ed.). 1977. Riparian forests in California: their ecology and conservation. Institute of Ecology Pub. No. 15., University of California, Davis. 122 p.

Satterlund, Donald R. 1972. Wildland watershed management. 279 p. Ronald Press, New York, N.Y.

US Army Corps of Engineers 1955. Standard operations and maintenance manual for Sacramento River flood control project. 32 p. US Army Corps of Engineers, Sacramento District, Sacramento, Calif.

US Army Corps of Engineers 1978. Interim report to Congress. The streambank erosion control evaluation and demonstration act of 1974. 41 p. US Army Corps of Engineers.

Weaver, John E., and Frederick E. Clements. 1938. Plant ecology. 320 p. McGraw-Hill Co., New York, N.Y.

EXPERIMENTING WITH LEVEE VEGETATION:

SOME UNEXPECTED FINDINGS[1]

Thomas H. Whitlow, Richard W. Harris, and
Andrew T. Leiser[2]

Abstract.--Vegetation has long been recognized as a component of levee systems which can be managed to protect and enhance the flood control function. The additional contribution of vegetation to the biological and recreational roles which levees perform make it an especially attractive component of the system to manipulate. Despite a lengthy history of experiments with levee vegetation, little progress has been made toward developing a management strategy which recognizes vegetation as a resource rather than a liability. It is suggested that scientific experimentation will not remedy the situation. Changes in current policy will be necessary before even existing information can be applied.

INTRODUCTION

"A functional, factorial approach to plant ecology" (Major 1951) is a conceptual design for field experiments in plant ecology which permits environmental factors to be isolated from one another and their relationships to the vegetation to be identified. Major identifies five independent variables as determinants of vegetation in the mathematical expression:

$$v = \int(cl,p,r,o,t)$$

where f = a measurable property of the
            vegetation
       cl = regional climate
       p = soil parent material
       r = topography or relief, including
            groundwater conditions
       o = organisms
       t = time

This general model is familiar to anyone engaged in experimentation. A problem or phenomenon is isolated (in this instance, vegetation) as a dependent variable, while independent variables are manipulated so that their effects on the dependent variable can be measured and evaluated.

Between July 1978 and July 1980 the authors, through the Department of Environmental Horticulture at the University of California, Davis, investigated the potential for using vegetation as an agent for erosion control in the tidal zone on levees in the Sacramento/San Joaquin Delta (Whitlow et al. 1979, 1980). As plant scientists, we focused on plant/environment interactions rather than engineering or policy considerations. In our experiments we strove to mimic the structural and floristic organization of the native riparian vegetation in Delta levees. In the terms of Major's model, we manipulated the topographic and organismal factors by deciding which species were to be planted and where they were to be planted in relation to tide levels. Additionally, we reviewed the pertinent literature to identify species which would be suitable components of levee vegetation.

This paper reviews the work we conducted for the California Department of Water Resources (DWR), identifies problems with current approaches, and suggests directions for future efforts to manage levee vegetation.

HISTORICAL OVERVIEW

Existing Delta Vegetation

Over the past 120 years the Sacramento/San Joaquin Delta has been converted from over 200,000 ha. of marsh and overflow lands to a dryland agricultural environment (Shlemon and Begg 1975). What remains of the natural vegetation is confined to narrow bands of marsh and riparian forest on levees and unreclaimed islands in the

[1] Paper presented at the California Riparian Systems Conference. [University of California, Davis, September 17-19, 1981.]

[2] Thomas H. Whitlow is Research Associate, Urban Horticulture Institute, Cornell University, Ithaca, New York; Richard W. Harris and Andrew T. Leiser are Professors, Department of Environmental Horticulture, University of California, Davis.

558

channels. Though in a highly modified environment very different from the pristine landscape, the natural vegetation has persisted or reconvened itself in a form that is remarkably like the original (Atwater 1980; Atwater et al. 1979; Thompson 1958). The constriction of a vast marsh to narrow, "riparian surrogate" communities (Dennis et al. 1983) increases the relative importance of the remaining vegetation to the present-day Delta ecosystem.

Two conspicuous environmental gradients are apparent in the natural Delta vegetation. The first is a small-scale flood gradient which exists in the vertical dimension on levee faces and other areas subject to tidal flux. The second is a large-scale salinity gradient which exists across the Delta. This second gradient fluctuates seasonally and from year to year, depending on freshwater inputs. The historic limits of this saltwater intrusion have been reduced and its gradient steepness increased by the construction of upstream dams (California Department of Water Resources, Central District 1981). While the salinity gradient is important to consider in long-range levee planning, the flood gradient is more immediately important to levee revegetation.

The natural vegetation on Delta levees may be arranged along a very apparent, though poorly understood, flood-tolerance axis (table 1). The nature of flood tolerance is complex and will not be discussed here. For present purposes it is adequate to recognize that frequency, depth, and duration of flooding decreases with increasing elevation, whether on a levee face or an island.

At the lower end of the intertidal zone is Scirpus californicus. Immediately uphill is Scirpus acutus. These two species are the familiar tules. Overlapping the tules but often extending well above the high-tide line are Typha spp. (three species of cattail are found in the Delta, with T. latifolia being the most common) and Phragmites australis (reed). Several species of rushes (Juncus spp.) and one

iris (Iris pseudacorus) are quite common and may dominate at the mean high-tide level.

It is at this level that woody species appear. Willows (Salix spp.), dogwood (Cornus stolonifera), and buttonbush (Cephalanthus occidentalis) form dense thickets at or just above the high-tide line. Above the zone of tidal flux but still within the reach of floods are species of the riparian forest: white alder (Alnus rhombifolia), cottonwood (Populus fremontii), sycamore (Platanus racemosa), California black walnut (Juglans hindsii), and valley oak (Quercus lobata).

Thompson (1957) has gleaned from the early chronicles that the natural levees in the pre-reclamation Delta were "stabilized" by the presence of vegetation. Though we cannot assess how stable these levees might have been, present-day evidence suggests that they might have been quite stable. Figure 1, taken on Medford Island facing south along the Stockton Deep Water Channel, illustrates a well-developed plant community whose structure and species composition closely resembles the preceding textual decription. The levee has withstood the same conditions which have breached nearby, intensively maintained levees in areas less exposed than the deep water channel. Interestingly, the DWR rates the Medford Island levee as "very poor," a category shared by Frank's Tract, which was never reclaimed after a flood in the 1930s (California Department of Water Resources, Central District 1981). Further, the Medford Island levee clearly violates Title 33 of the Federal Code because flood-fighting activities would be hampered by the presence of trees on the levee crown. Yet the levee appears to be quite stable.

Revegetation of Levees and Similar Sites

In the course of our investigations for DWR, we identified a number of information sources applicable to our levee revegetation interests. These often were not part of the published literature, and retrieval was therefore difficult. These sources are described elsewhere (Whitlow et al. 1979). However, a brief summary of

Table 1.--Organization of species of dominant plants and their relations to tidal flooding.

Increased Flooding Intertidal Zone				Decreased Flooding Supertidal Zone
Scirpus californicus	Scirpus acutus	Typha spp.	Salix spp.	Alnus rhombifolia
		Phragmites australis	Cephalanthus occidentalis	Populus fremontii
		Juncus spp.	Cornus stolonifera	Platanus racemosa
		Iris pseudacarus		Juglans hindsii
				Quercus lobata

Figure 1.--Well-developed plant community growing on a levee along the Stockton Deep Water Ship Channel, near Medford Island.

the kinds of sources available in 1979 is instructive. We identified four species lists specifically aimed at levee revegetation in California, compiled by various state and federal agencies or their consultants. Over 100 species were identified on these various lists as being suitable for use on levees.

In addition to these lists, seven experimental studies have been undertaken by the US Army Corps of Engineers (CE), DWR, USDA Soil Conservation Service (SCS), and the University of California, Davis, in collaboration with the US Department of Agriculture and various state and federal resource agencies. These studies identify an additional 100 species and also report on experimental outcomes, including survival, growth, and in some cases, costs. Two studies are especially worthy of mention because of their original scope and because they are extant and available for ongoing observation. These are the DWR Pilot Levee Maintenance Study (California Department of Water Resources 1967) and the CE Monument Bend planting on the Sacramento River (Morris 1976). Since our 1979 review, we have conducted three out-planting experiments, and the John Muir Institute has planted several experimental sites as well. We think it fair to conclude that an adequate, publicly available information bank exists which could serve as the basis for levee vegetation planning. It should also be noted that a companion literature for engineering treatments exists (Keown et al. 1977; US Army Corps of Engineers 1978) in which numerous applications of physical protection in conjunction with plant material are described.

Revegetation Research at Davis

Details of research conducted by the authors may be found elsewhere (Whitlow et al. 1979, 1980). Brief summaries are included here to indicate the scope and findings of the research.

Fall, 1978 Plantings

The objective of this planting was to identify species and planting techniques suitable for application in the intertidal zone of levees. The ultimate goal was a vegetative replacement for riprap. The DWR indicated that the engineering ideal would have the characteristics of aquatic "astroturf": dense, low-growing, and able to stabilize eroding banks without resorting to mechanical means. Accordingly, we utilized several native Eleocharis species (spikerush) (table 2) which had these characteristics. Tules, willows, and buttonbush were also planted in an attempt to generate basic information on native species normally occurring on levees. Such information could be used to tailor levee plantings to mimic natural vegetation. We planted two sites: 1) a freshly dredged and graded levee on Webb Tract, and 2) a series of eroding coves on Mandeville Island. We hoped to answer several specific questions:

1) which species survive?
2) at what depth of tidal inundation is optimum survival achieved?
3) is planting best conducted before or after refacing of levees?

We planted in the fall when water temperatures were warmest, on the assumption that root growth would be faster at this time than in the spring.

Survival was very low (table 2). The freshly faced levee on Webb Tract quickly changed from a 3:1 slope with neat planting rows to a steeply eroding headwall. What had been the lower edge of the intertidal zone washed away, and with it many of our plants.

The rooted woody cuttings and Eleocharis planting on Mandeville Island did not wash away. Instead, the local reclamation district riprapped the site, after observing no conspicuous growth in February 1979. (Our planting occurred in October, 1978.) We discovered this alteration during a periodic inspection and had had no prior notice that riprapping was scheduled. Indeed, site selection was done in collaboration with the reclamation district. Some quantitative survival data were salvaged and are included in table 2, but clearly the value of the experiment was compromised.

Despite the difficulties, several conclusions can be drawn and are worth stressing. First, small planting units like peat pots and gallon-can plants are not suitable for intertidal plantings, even if the material is rhizomatous and rapidly spreading, unless the material is well anchored. Second, there appears to be little advantage in planting rooted woody material. Again, this is partly related to the vulnerability of the planting unit. A 1-m. willow wand stuck into the mud has a better chance of establishment than a 0.2-m. rooted willow cutting in a pot. Third, a modicum of physical stability

Table 2.--1979 planting summary.

Species	Propagation Method	Planting Method	Percent Survival		
			Site 1	Site 2	Spot Plantings
Buttonbush Cephalanthus occidentalis	30-cm. softwood cuttings quick dipped in 4000 ppm IBA; rooted under mist in 50% vermiculite, 50% perlite	Rooted cuttings in 22-cm. tubes	N/A	0.51	0
Spikerush Eleocharis acicularis	1-cm.^{2} divisions, planted in peat pots under mist for 30 days	Peat pots	0	0	N/A
Spikerush Eleocharis coloradoensis	1-cm.^{2} divisions planted in peat pots under mist for 30 days	Peat pots	N/A	0	N/A
Spikerush Eleocharis macrostachys (=E. palustris)	10 x 10 cm. divisions planted in gallon cans and flooded in nursery benches	Gallon cans	N/A	2.5	15
Willow Salix gooddingii	1 30 cm. softwood cuttings quick dipped in 4000 ppm IBA; rooted under mist in 50% vermiculite 50% perlite	Rooted cuttings in 22-cm. tubes	N/A	N/A	0
	2) Direct transplant	Unrooted cuttings 0.5-m. long	7	N/A	N/A
	3) Direct transplant	Wattling	12	N/A	26
Common tule Scripus acutus	Direct transplant	0.5-m. segments of rhizome, shoots trimmed to 30 cm.	4	N/A	N/A

must exist on the levee bank before plants can be established. While we were able to establish some willows and tules which are extant on Webb Tract, this did not constitute an acceptable survival rate for practical use. Lastly, the importance of enlisting the active support of collaborators and their agents (reclamation districts, district engineers, and farm supervisors) was made very clear. These people are not used to experiments. They expect results and may not have the patience or understanding to coexist with an experiment on their property.

Spring, 1980 Plantings

Armed with the experience gained from our first round of experiments, we undertook a second experiment on Terminous Tract (Whitlow et al. 1980). The emphasis was on using locally harvested material (table 3, 4, and 5) in conjunction with erosion control fabrics to provide immediate stability and help anchor the plants (fig. 2). Again, the goal was to replace rock as the primary erosion control agent. Tules and willow cuttings were locally available and had the physical properties appropriate to the scale of the problem. We also experimented with spikerush (Eleocharis) again, this time using a sod mat contained within a polypropylene bag to facilitate anchoring. Observations in the Delta suggested that a naturalized iris was capable of rapid spreading in the tidal zone. Accordingly, a small number of these plants were installed. Finally, we seeded with alkalai bulrush (Scirpus robustus) and water grass (Echinochloa crusgalli) both on and under our fabric-protected plot and on adjacent, freshly laid riprap. The seeds are inexpensive and commercially available and have obvious advantages over vegetative propagules for large-scale applications.

The erosion control fabrics (Stabilenka and Enkamat, available from American Excelsior Company) were selected as a "soft" alternative to rock. We wanted the bank to stay in place during the period of establishment, and we also wanted our plants and seed held in place during high tides. These fabrics are far lighter than rock and thus easier to handle without heavy equipment; they may have the added advantage of being more available than rock in the future. While the fabric has been successfully applied in the Netherlands and the eastern United States, it has received little attention in California.

All of these details in our second experiment were modifications of our first approach in an effort to refine techniques and develop a practical demonstration. One last refinement was added: we enlisted the participation of the local

561

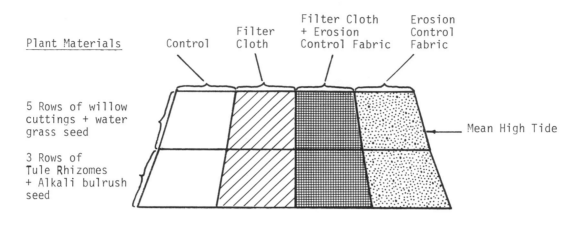

Physical Erosion Control Treatment

Figure 2.--Schematic diagram of main plot, 1980 planting.

Table 3.--Tule and willow establishment, spring 1980.

	Treatments							
	Control		Stabilenka		Stabilenka + Enkamat		Enkamat	
Material	#Sprouted/ #Planted	%Sprouted	#Sprouted/ #Planted	%Sprouted	#Sprouted/ #Planted	%Sprouted	#Sprouted/ #Planted	%Sprouted
Willow	10/60	17	2/145	1	8/160	5	8/180	4
Tule	6/10	60	11/30	37	4/30	13	29/30	97

Table 4.--Watergrass establishment, spring 1980.

	Treatments			
Location	Control % Cover	Stabilenka % Cover	Stabilenka + Enkamat % Cover	Enkamat % Cover
Top	44.66 + 19.55	8 + 5.19	3.66 + 1.52	23.00 + 18.52
Bottom	44.33 + 16.19	5 + 2.64	4.33 + 1.52	31.33 + 25.14

Table 5.--Survival of iris and spikerush, spring 1980.

	Iris			Spikerush		
Location	# Planted/# Survived	%		# Planted/# Survived	%	
Plot 1A	62/47	76		6/6	100	
Plot 1B	59/56	95		15/15	100	
Plot 1C	8/8	100		8/8	100	

reclamation board. With the help of the district engineer, a site was selected which could be used for at least two years without disturbance. The reclamation district contributed a backhoe and operator for site preparation.

The planting was undertaken in May, 1980, and establishment data were submitted to DWR in July (table 3,4,5). The more important data, however, were the long-term survival data to be collected in the spring and summer of 1981. Had we succeeded in establishing an erosion-resistant vegetation or had we merely put a few plants on a levee? The prospects for answering this question were promising: the levee was still there, and we had a viable cohort of survivors going into the second season. We were unable to assess second season performance, however, because in February the site was riprapped. There was a difference between this and our previous experience in that the reclamation district knew exactly what it was doing when the decision was made to install riprap revetment. It had not been part of the maintenance plan, but when long-awaited rock became available, the expedient choice was to take all that could be obtained. The authors were not contacted prior to the riprapping because the engineer in charge was uncomfortable about having to back out of his original agreement.

In view of our experiences with levee revegetation experiments, we conclude that the de facto policy practiced by reclamation districts is that rock is the preferred form of bank protection. It is not a matter of experimentation, it is a matter of preference, and in the absence of a clear, functional policy to the contrary coming from a public agency, this preference becomes policy.

DISCUSSION

The basic findings of our research are that while vegetation can be established on levees, these efforts do cost money and may not achieve the engineering goal of stopping erosion. This is especially true in the intertidal zone where severe conditions hinder plant establishment. Yet, experience indicates that even in the tidal zone, with proper anchoring several native species can be established. Whether this pattern would continue over the long run remains to be seen.

We began with an ecological model to identify factors affecting the establishment and survival of plants on levees. The unexpected finding was that this was not the right approach to the problem. While there are directions future research could take to overcome planting and survival problems, we question whether such research is appropriate at this time. Research models like ours which focus on environmental variables will continue to produce "results," but they will fail to deal with the real problem of levee maintenance.

Such models start with the wrong assumptions and therefore answer questions which skirt the central issue. Consider the following evidence. Both the work co-sponsored by DWR and the SCS, reported in Bulletin 167 (California Department of Water Resources 1967), and the Monument Bend study conducted by the CE have been neglected. When we inquired about touring these sites, no one in any of the organizations was familiar enough with the studies to even precisely locate the sites, much less assess the long-term performance. The studies were essentially forgotten, and there was no formal provision for follow-up to determine long-term survival, maintenance cost, and erosion protection at the sites. Such data are vitally important if policies are to be affected by research. Without a policy context, study results cannot be applied and are quickly forgotten.

From our own experience, it has been difficult to follow an experiment for even the first year owing to major site modifications undertaken by collaborating reclamation districts. We understand that experiments conducted by the John Muir Institute have suffered in similar fashion. The specific difficulties may range from benign neglect, through poor communication and misunderstanding of experimental goals, and ultimately to preemptive exercise of local management imperatives. The net effect, however, is the same: we never progress beyond a preliminary stage in solving the levee maintenance problem. If science and technology are not providing solutions, then what will?

We suggest that this problem is not amenable to scientific hypothesis testing, but rather falls into the policy arena. Scientific findings may contribute to an understanding of how ecosystem components interact, but may not provide clear-cut answers to complex issues of public administration. To paraphrase John Clark (1978) of the Conservation Foundation, science deals with verifiable **principles** based on natural laws, while resource administration deals with **policies** consistent with fiscal and political realities. The clear articulation of an ecological principle (for example, that riparian ecotones represent a large compartment in an energy flow model of an ecosystem) does not translate clearly into a policy. The policymaker may decide to conserve natural riparian systems or to substitute artificial systems, in the form of sewage sludge ponds covered with water hyacinth and populated by mosquito fish. Net energy flow may be the same in both cases, though the alternatives are radically different. "Science" contributes to the achievement of either alternative.

The general problem outline which emerges here is by no means unique to levees in California. McCarthy (1976) and Ranwell (1979) describe identical problems in coastal zone management in the United States and Great Britain. The difficulties they identify are:

1) the conflict between economic and environmental needs;
2) establishing common ground between administrators and ecologists;
3) gathering and handling large amounts of scientific and planning data; and
4) translating the results into field action (Ranwell 1979).

It appears we are not alone. Yet these difficulties are not insurmountable, and we are optimistic. For levee vegetation, items 2 and 3 have been accomplished to some degree already. The long history of levee vegetation research and the recent conference on the future of the Delta are positive indications that common ground has been established, and that it is extensive. The DWR has a capable professional staff equal to the task of assimilating existing information. This leaves us with items 1 and 4. These are **human** problems involving fiscal and logistic constraints. More data on tule mortality will not result in progress in these areas because they involve public policy. The time is upon us to develop a new policy for riparian zone management on levees.

This is especially true for the Delta, where if something is not done soon, we are going to lose the whole system. This process will be costly and frustrating to all involved, but then so is the existing status quo. Talking with the CE, DWR, the reclamation districts, and people in the Legislature leads us to conclude that no one is happy with the present situation. It would appear, then, that procrastination is not in anyone's best interest.

Although the following guidelines are not derived from our research, we offer them to facilitate the development of a new levee policy. We are adopting a "consider the problem solved" approach that vegetation on levees is desirable.

1. Retain existing vegetation wherever possible. It is much easier and cheaper to manage existing vegetation than to replant. This is especially true of intertidal plants.

2. Be realistic and flexible in deciding where and what to retain. A bramble patch may not be worth preserving if the consequence of preservation is probable levee failure or degradation of higher-quality habitat.

3. Especially in the Delta, this higher quality-habitat exists on unreclaimed channel islands. Protecting delta levees with rock and other mechanical means will help preserve these islands, first by ensuring that they remain islands in narrow channels rather than in a 200,000-ha. lake with enormous wind fetch, and second, by minimizing the need for constant channel dredging which literally pulls the foundation from under these islands.

4. Do a complete, thorough job of levee restoration. This includes removing vegetation such as blackberries the season before work is anticipated, as well as designating vegetation to be retained or planted.

5. Establish priorities for levee work. The present situation pits reclamation districts against one another for contract rock and dredgers. The result is less efficient use of resources.

6. Provide reliable, ongoing financial and planning assistance to levee maintenance districts. An uncertain, inadequate financial assistance program like the on-again-off-again Way Bill encourages mistrust, cynicism, and contempt of government by landowners.

7. Establish a native plant nursery for riparian species, especially tules. Provide this material free or at cost, along with planning expertise, to landowners.

8. Actively pursue revision of Title 33 of the Code of Federal Regulations, which sets the flood control standards followed by the CE. These regulations are more applicable to the Mississippi River and are internally confusing about the status of vegetation.

Until there is a clear mandate to manage levees as a multi-functioning resource, they will continue to be managed only as flood control structures. We believe that sufficient information presently exists to sustain a policy of multiple-use levees. Once this determination is made, the political and fiscal steps toward implementation will follow. Is this a simplistic approach to a complex, burdensome, expensive problem? We think not. Similar decisions in the past are models for our present conclusion. Consider the decision to landscape hundreds of miles of California highways for primarily aesthetic reasons. In addition to aesthetics, there are compelling biological and structural imperatives for levee maintenance. The decision should be an easy one to make. There is still the opportunity to make the decision; this luxury may not always be with us.

ACKNOWLEDGMENTS

This research was supported by grants from the DWR. Use of brand names is for identification purposes only and does not imply official endorsement.

LITERATURE CITED

Atwater, B.F. 1980. Attempts to correlate Late Quaternary climatic records between San Francisco Bay, the Sacramento-San Joaquin Delta, and the Mokelumne River, California. Ph.D. Thesis, University of Delaware, Newark. 277 p.

Atwater, B.F., S.G. Conard, J.W. Dowden, C.W. Hedell, R.L. MacDonald, and W. Savage. 1979. History, landforms, and vegetation of the estuary's tidal marshes. p. 347-385. In: T.J. Conomos (ed.). San Francisco Bay: The urbanized estuary. 493 p. Pacific Division, American Association for the Advancement of Science, San Francisco, Calif.

California Department of Water Resources. 1967. Pilot levee maintenance study: Sacramento-San Joaquin Delta. Bulletin 167, California Department of Water Resources, Sacramento. 24 p.

California Department of Water Resources, Central District. 1981. Delta water supply and quality. p. 30-37. In: The future of the Delta. [Sacramento, Calif., March 16-17, 1981.] Sponsored by the Resources Agency, California Department of Water Resources and University Extension, University of California, Davis.

Clark, J.R. 1978. Science and the conservation of riparian systems. p. 13-16. In: R.R. Johnson and J.F. McCormick (tech. coord.). Strategies for protection and management of floodplain wetlands and other riparian systems. [Callaway Gardens, Georgia, December 11-13, 1978.] USDA Forest Service GTR-WO-12, Washington, D.C. 410 p.

Dennis, N.B., D. Ellis, J.R. Arnold, and D.L. Renshaw. 1983. Riparian surrogates in the Sacramento/San Joaquin Delta and their habitat values. In: R.E. Warner and K.M. Hendrix (ed.). California Riparian Systems. University of California Press, Berkeley, Calif.

Keown, M.P., N.R. Orwalt, E.B. Perry, and E.A. Dardean, Jr. 1977. Literature survey and preliminary evolution of streambank protection methods. Technical Report H-77-9, US Army Engineer Waterways Experiment Station, Vicksburg, Miss. 258 p.

Major, J.M. 1951. A functional, factorial approach to plant ecology. Ecology 32:392-412.

McCarthy, J. 1976. Coastal conservation in the U.S.A., some experience from the eastern states. Winston Churchill Trust Fellowship Report.

Morris, R. 1976. Monument Bend plantings review. Internal document, US Army Corps of Engineers, Sacramento District, Sacramento, Calif. 99 p.

Ranwell, D.S. 1979. Strategies for the management of coastal systems. p. 515-527. In: Ecological processes in coastal environments. First European ecological symposium and 19th symposium of the British ecological society. Blackwell Scientific, Oxford.

Shlemon, R.J., and E.L. Begg. 1975. Late quaternary evolution of the Sacramento-San Joaquin Delta, California. p. 259-266. In: R.P. Suggate and M.M. Cresswell (ed.). Quaternary studies. 320 p. The Royal Society of New Zealand, Wellington.

Thompson, J. 1958. The settlement and geography of the Sacramento-San Joaquin Delta, California. Ph.D. Dissertation, Stanford University, Palo Alto, Calif. 551 p.

US Army Corps of Engineers, Sacramento District. 1978. Reconnaissance report. Sacramento River and tributaries bank protection and erosion control investigation. 64 p. US Army Corps of Engineers, Sacramento, Calif.

Whitlow, T.H., R.W. Harris, and A.T. Leiser. 1979. Use of vegetation to reduce levee erosion in the Sacramento-San Joaquin Delta. 4 p. plus appendices. California Department of Water Resources, Sacramento.

Whitlow, T.H., R.W. Harris, and A.T. Leiser. 1980. Use of vegetation to reduce levee erosion in the Sacramento-San Joaquin Delta. Annual progress report. 15 p. California Department of Water Resources, Sacramento.

RIPARIAN SURROGATES IN THE SACRAMENTO/SAN JOAQUIN DELTA

AND THEIR HABITAT VALUES[1]

Nona B. Dennis, Douglas Ellis, John R. Arnold,
and Diane L. Renshaw[2]

Abstract.--The distribution and condition of riparian vegetation in the Sacramento/San Joaquin Delta has been highly modified during 130 years of land reclamation, construction and maintenance of the present levee system, and conversion of the land to agricultural cultivation. A variety of vegetation complexes with partial riparian attributes exist under a few natural, but primarily induced conditions in the Delta, providing some of the wildlife values associated with historic Delta riparian vegetation. These examples of modified riparian communities suggest that compromises will be necessary to achieve wildlife values that are compatible with flood control requirements and agricultural land use in the Delta.

INTRODUCTION

In January, 1979, a team of individuals undertook a year-long study of wildlife habitats in the Sacramento/San Joaquin Delta. The study was funded by the USDI Fish and Wildlife Service (FWS) and co-directed by the California Department of Fish and Game (DFG) and the FWS. The study culminated in the Sacramento/San Joaquin Delta Wildlife Habitat Protection and Restoration Plan (California Department of Fish and Game 1980) whose principal objectives were to:

1. document the wildlife habitat resources of the Delta, based on a year-long avian census and mammal survey as well as on available data, and to describe the human demands and activities which affect them;

2. seek more effective ways--both technical and institutional—to protect and enhance existing wildlife habitats or restore those that have disappeared from the Delta; and

3. present the policies and interests of the DFG and FWS with respect to protecting the wildlife resources of the Delta.

This paper is an informal summary of information in the Sacramento/San Joaquin Delta Wildlife Habitat Protection and Restoration Plan. It also presents the senior author's observations concerning the circumstances under which "surrogate" riparian communities have developed in the Delta and are presently managed, and the opportunities for their protection and enhancement or restoration as partial but valuable riparian wildlife habitats.

The "legal Delta" (California Water Code Sec. 12220) encompasses 2,986 km^2 (1,153 mi^2) or 298,800 ha. (738,000 ac.) (fig. 1). Prior to 1850, when reclamation began, the Delta was largely a marshland of about 161,900 ha. (400,000 ac.) surrounded by approximately 121,500 ha. (300,000 ac.) of slightly higher lands and shallow backswamps behind natural alluvial levees (Thompson 1957). With the completion of reclamation in 1930, the Delta was transformed into 60 major leveed islands totalling 182,000 ha. (450,000 ac.) of primarily agricultural land, more than 800 islets, and 1,130 km. (700 mi.) of waterways lined with 1,709 km. (1,062 mi.) of levees. A number of urban settlements are situated on the periphery of the Delta, but the predominant land use is agricultural.

The Sacramento/San Joaquin Delta Wildlife Habitat Protection and Restoration Plan surveyed all of the evident wildlife habitat-types represented in the Delta, including agricultural, urban, and other "developed" habitats. Vegetation, physiography and land use were used as

---

[1]Paper presented at the California Riparian Systems Conference. [University of California, Davis, September 17-19, 1981].

[2]Nona B. Dennis is President, Madrone Associates, Environmental Consultants, Novato, Calif. Douglas Ellis is Field Ornithologist, Madrone Associates. John R. Arnold, PhD., is Professor Emeritus of Zoology, California State University, Sonoma, Rohnert Park, Calif., and Senior Consultant, Madrone Associates. Diane L. Renshaw is Senior Consultant, Madrone Associates.

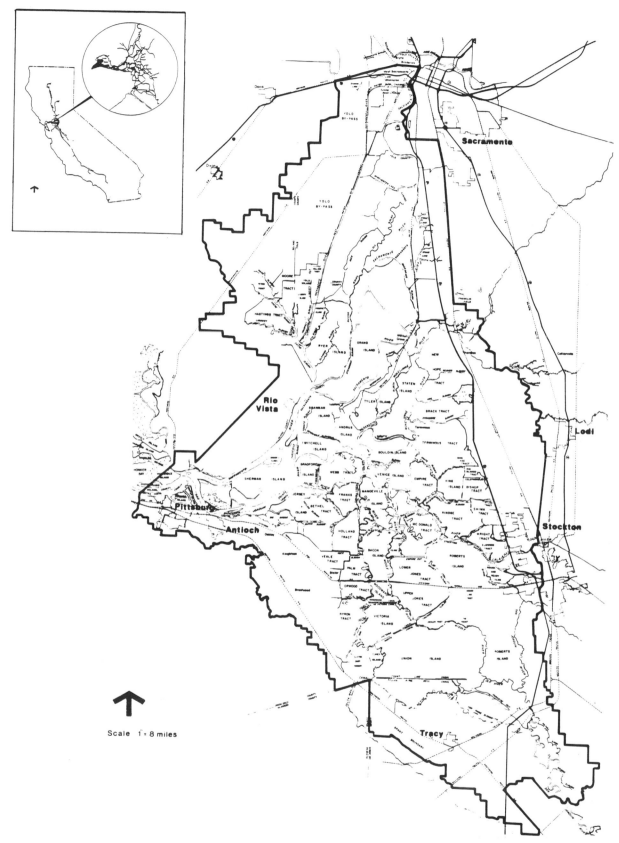

Figure 1.--The Sacramento/San Joaquin Delta.

567

bases for classifying habitats as they occur under present conditions, taking into account that agricultural practices (e.g.,crop selection, irrigation methods) can profoundly change habitat conditions from year to year.

During the study it was apparent that several Delta habitat-types, both on and off levees, have riparian attributes (terrestrial adjacency to free waters and/or substrate with high soil moisture). However, few areas in the Delta still support historic communities of riparian species (cottonwood, white alder, western sycamore, ash, valley oak) that can be classified as riparian woodland or forest according to conventional criteria. As with many managed waterway systems, riparian vegetation exists in the Delta under sufferance and in many variations. The variations (i.e., "surrogates") are nonetheless worthy of attention, since they demonstrate considerable wildlife value and, in an area managed principally for flood control and agriculture, may offer among the few opportunities in the Delta for useful terrestrial habitat for many wildlife species.

PREVIOUS WORK

Much attention in the past several decades has been focussed on the disappearance of riparian vegetation from many parts of the Delta, primarily in connection with levee construction and maintenance practices. There have been few ecological or floristic studies.

Most ecological investigations of riparian vegetation of the Sacramento River stop in the vicinity of Clarksburg, Yolo County, where the major native stands of Sacramento Valley riparian forest first appear (Thompson 1957). To our knowledge, only one analysis of structure and floristics of riparian vegetation of the Sacramento Valley extends study sites into the northern Delta, to include Stone Lake in the Sacramento River flood basin and Delta Meadows on Snodgrass Slough, as examples of relatively unmodified natural condition (Conard et al. 1977). The study characterizes riparian vegetation in terms of succession related to fluvial processes. This approach is generally valid but is not entirely useful when applied to Delta riparian vegetation. The extent of early vegetation and continuing manipulation of land, water, and vegetation in the Delta imposes an entirely new set of rules governing succession, even though familiar successional seres can still be seen throughout the Delta.

Whitlow et al. (1979) studied the role of natural and introduced riparian vegetation in retarding levee erosion. The research specifically addressed problems of establishing emergent species at the fluctuating water line. This study also provided an overview of the problems of maintaining vegetation on levees in the Central Valley (lower Sacramento River) and surveyed experimental levee planting projects conducted by the US Army Corps of Engineers

(CE) and the California Department of Water Resources (DWR). The study concludes that revegetation of Delta levees is technically feasible and can be compatible with flood control objectives, if species and location are carefully considered.

Jepson (1893) catalogued species growing on natural levees along the lower Sacramento River. Mason (1957) studied aquatic and emergent species in the Delta's tidal wetlands extensively. At-water (1979) reported on the distribution of dominant species and flora of six "pristine" Delta islets in pursuing the question of what vascular plants might have inhabited the freshwater reaches of Pleistocene estuaries. In so doing, he demonstrated the subtlety of the ecotone between "wetland" and "riparian" conditions in much of the prereclamation Delta, a condition which we feel bestows distinctive riparian attributes on the Delta.

The only complete and current mapping of wetland and terrestrial vegetation-types in the Delta was done by the CE (US Army Corps of Engineers 1979) at a scale of 1" to 1,000'. Delineation followed the FWS wetlands classification system (Cowardin et al. 1979). The system was based on a hierarchy of habitat variables: morphology (riverine, palustrine, lacustrine, etc.); vegetation-type (herbaceous, emergent, etc.); substrate (mud, sand, cobble, etc.); and salinity regime. Delta riparian vegetation under this classification falls primarily into one category: viz. "palustrine forested," or "riparian forest of broad-leaved deciduous vegetation, 6 m. or more in height" (ibid.). This riparian "type" compares with the R1 (large woody vegetation) and R1v (valley oak woodland) classifications used by the Central Valley Riparian Mapping Project (Central Valley Riparian Mapping Project 1979). A second category can be considered riparian, although CE maps do not specifically apply that term: viz. palustrine scrub/shrub, "dominated by woody vegetation less than 6 m. in height, with broad-leaved deciduous plants" (ibid.). This category compares with the R2 (low woody vegetation) used by the Central Valley Mapping Project (ibid.). The CE applies several other FWS categories to cover Delta "wetland" and "emergent" types. These generally compare with R3 (herbaceous vegetation) and M (marsh) used in the Central Valley Riparian Mapping Project.

The Sacramento/San Joaquin Delta Wildlife Habitat Protection and Restoration Plan adapted the FWS system, as used by the CE in mapping the Delta, to cover wildlife habitat designations which are more familiar and to express a wider range of riparian-like conditions.

A more detailed structural and floristic analysis of the diverse contemporary manifestations and wildlife use of riparian, or quasi-riparian, vegetation in the Delta would be useful and might provide guidance with respect to vegetation, given the apparent constraints of flood control and agricultural operations. The present paper does not fill this gap. It suggests, however, that the highly modified condition of the Delta, and its distinctive mixed estuarine and riverine origins and characters, have produced communities which have at least some if not all of the attributes of classic riparian zone vegetation, as well as many of the same plant species, and many of the same wildlife values.

PAST AND PRESENT DISTRIBUTION OF RIPARIAN VEGETATION IN THE DELTA

The Sacramento/San Joaquin Delta is an inland triangular network of waterways formed by the rising of sea level through the Carquinez Strait between 7,000 and 11,000 years ago to meet the alluvial fans and outflows of the Sacramento, San Joaquin, Cosumnes, and Mokelumne Rivers and smaller tributary streams (Atwater 1980) (fig. 1). Both rivers and tides have shaped the land and soils of the Delta (fig. 2). Peat soils derived from tule marshes occupy most of the level, low-lying central part of the Delta. Mineral-rich alluvial soils deposited by the rivers entering the Delta predominate on the periphery. Low natural alluvial levees defined the water courses throughout much of the Delta prior to reclamation, but today only vestiges of natural levees remain, the more massive man-made levee system having obscured these natural levees long ago.

Before reclamation, three-fifths of the Delta was awash with an ordinary tide, largely submerged by a spring tide and capable of being entirely overflowed by a river flood (Thompson 1957). There was little topographic relief, especially in the central and western Delta. The only features rising above the sea level swamp were the typical asymmetrical natural levees, narrow ridges of alluvium meandering into the backswamps, and occasional wind-deposited hummocks of sand, the highest of these 5 m. (17 ft.) in the western Delta near Knightsen-Oakley. Most features in the central Delta were less than 3 m. (10 ft.) high.

The prereclamation Delta "islands" were thus nothing more or less than backswamps partially or fully enclosed by alluvial levees, drained by meandering sloughs. The natural levees, both parallel and lateral to waterways, were composed of fine to sandy material carried in from surrounding Central Valley uplands by the rivers and their tributaries. The Sacramento River, with its greater volume and velocity, carried greater amounts of sediment toward the Delta than did the San Joaquin, and thus deposited more substantial natural levees.

Levee banks, shaped by tidal scour as much as by river deposition, were abrupt at the river face with the land side sloping inland, enclosing a saucer-like topography. As banks rose high enough above the mean tide level, water-tolerant

Figure 2.--The majority of Delta islands have been cut off from floods and tides. A few channel islands continue to be influenced by both.

569

vegetation could become established, checking the velocity of sediment-laden water. This would promote the accumulation of greater amounts of alluvium, encouraging more plant growth.

Generally, the height and breadth of natural levees increased with distance north, east, and south from the low tide, low water level at the western apex of the Delta. Thompson (ibid.) reconstructs an approximate gradient of increasing levee height northwest of Sherman Island, north of Isleton, north and east of Staten and Tyler Island, south and east of Roberts and Rough-and-Ready Islands, and southwest of the latitude of Rough-and-Ready Island. These natural levees beyond the central Delta might be as high as 3 to 5 m. (10 to 18 ft.), with the highest approaching 7 m. (24 ft.) at Sacramento. Natural levees averaged as much as 200 m. (660 ft.) wide along the (old) Sacramento River and 120 m. (400 ft.) wide along parts of Steamboat Slough (ibid.).

Prereclamation Riparian Vegetation

Hydric to mesic vegetation reflected the local microtopography of natural levees and hummocks and peripheral gradients in the otherwise unrelieved flat, generally wet terrain. Several investigators have reconstructed historic conditions by studying early illustrations as well as the few remaining sites which are relatively pristine. Thompson describes the conditions that were seen by travelers going up the Sacramento River:

The monotony of the green or brown canebrake-like vegetation was broken by channel and pond surfaces and by strips of alluvial land where woody shrubs and trees and herbaceous annuals grew. This natural levee cover consisted of coarse bunch grasses, willows, blackberry, and wild rose thickets, and galleries of oak, sycamore, alder, walnut, and cottonwood.

The shrubs appeared among the tules of Sherman, Lower Roberts, and other centrally located islands, but a continuity of woody growth probably did not develop until the latitude of Brannan Island and Stockton. This cover became a belt of heavy oak timber on the upper four miles of Union Island, and probably on Robert's Island. Fine groves occupied the more southerly San Joaquin distributary banks. Similar stands of woods occupied the Sacramento River levees upstream from about the lower end of Grand Island, in places so overhanging the river that it interferred with the rigging of passing ships (ibid.).

Levees and Reclamation

Levee building and reclamation of Delta lands irreversibly altered the physical appearance and function of the area. Perhaps nowhere in California have changes to the physiography and hydrography of an area been as profound as those that accompanied reclamation within the Delta. At the same time, throughout the major and minor drainages which feed into the Delta, major land-use changes significantly altered fluvial processes of erosion and deposition, ultimately affecting Delta waterways.

The history and techniques of levee construction in the Delta have been thoroughly documented and need only be reviewed briefly here. The early "shoestring" levees were hand-built from blocks of sod from island interiors; they were low earthen mounds, resembling natural alluvial levees, and afforded little protection from flooding. Later, clamshell dredges constructed higher, more substantial levees, using construction material from "borrow" ditches immediately external to the levee site. This practice created levees that were set back from an outer, waterside berm. When it was realized that levee survival was partly predicated on the flood-carrying capacity of adjacent channels, the interval between levee toe and borrow ditch was broadened. These residual berms also helped protect levees from rupture and wave attack (ibid.).

To some extent, the berm could accommodate a natural riverine system, the channel and narrow floodplain between levee and berm becoming part of a complementary system in which overland flow could be regarded as a natural process rather than an unnatural hazard. As levee construction techniques improved and conditions of channel alluviation and interior island subsidence dictated, artificial levees became more massive, as much as 61 m. (200 ft.) broad at the base and 9 m. (30 ft.) high, dominating the landscape. Natural levees and most of the artificial berms have either been removed in channel or levee improvements, concealed by reconstruction, or eroded away. The large levee structures which replaced them are so sloped and elevated above the natural floodplain level that with or without riprap they have lost the appearance of a natural floodplain and "riparian zone," except for obvious proximity to a waterway. Nevertheless, the levees introduced into the Delta many miles of topographic relief.

To the extent that "riparian" is an adjective that defines the topographic zone adjacent to fresh water (Warner 1979), the 1,600+ km. (1,000+ mi.) of man-made levees that now line 1,120 km. (700 mi.) of Delta channels and sloughs are riparian zones and hence existing and candidate substrates for woody riparian vegetation. The actual extent of this linear zone probably exceeds that of the prereclamation natural alluvial levees, particularly in the central Delta, which was largely a tidal marsh with little topographic variation.

"Riparian" as a concept also embraces other attributes—notably available soil moisture (high groundwater table), even distant from waterways. As reclamation proceeded, the backswamps of the Delta were drained and levees cut off their replenishment by flooding. But the water table has continued to be at or near the surface of the land, which is 3 to 6 m. (10 to 20 ft.) below mean sea level in many areas. These conditions would enable mesic vegetation to invade most of the Delta if the land were not regularly drained, cleared, and cultivated.

Changes to Riparian Vegetation Since Reclamation

It is ironic that humans--having built into the unrelieved flat landscape of the Delta hundreds of miles of "riparian zone" within or above the normal tide and floodplain level, sufficiently elevated to support luxuriant plant growth, and having drained the swamps--have been stripping, burning, plowing, or covering much of it ever since.

Some of the early land developers planted alfalfa or Bermuda grass on the waterside of levees in an attempt to reduce wave damage. Willows were used more commonly because they survived prolonged submersion better than alfalfa. Some reclamation interests thought that the roots of willow and other shrubs would reduce the tendency of peat levees to burst when subjected to prolonged river pressure. Unfortunately, willows tended to choke out the tule, depriving levee faces of the mass of sod and stems which were thought to break the force of wave action.

The protective role of berms left in early levee construction was enhanced by natural invasion of willow, cottonwood, and tule, which

formed a living defense against wave attack. The exterior borrow ditches served as alluvium traps and sites for succession from tule marsh to diverse riparian communities. Most of these berms are now gone; those remaining are restricted largely to a few reaches where setback levees have been deliberately reconstructed.

Since reclamation, the areal extent of all types of vegetation in the Delta has been steadily decreasing, becoming limited to narrow waterway margins and the outer edges of some levees, a few overflowed tracts, small unreclaimed islands and undeveloped lands outside levees, trapped sloughs and drainage ditches, some inner levee slopes, and whatever lands in island interiors have been left uncultivated or used as dredge spoil sites.

The Delta still contains remnant stands of riparian forest which, if they survived initial reclamation and subsequent clearing of land, continue to survive in spite of virtual isolation from the fluvial processes which induced and once sustained them (fig. 3). A few significant stands of riparian woodland can be found on the periphery of the Delta; there are examples near Thornton at the confluence of the Cosumnes and Mokelumne Rivers, isolated stands northwest of Stockton, and along the southern reaches of old Sacramento River and the San Joaquin River south of Stockton and Tracy. Other vestiges still exist on wooded islands, on a few remaining unleveed banks, and on occasional broad berms left on the waterside of levees.

Much of the adventitious riparian growth in the Delta still reveals itself as a series of hydric and mesic communities only partially

Figure 3.--Most stands of riparian forest have been cleared from the Delta floodplain, leaving stringers or small islands of cottonwood and associated species in a few uncultivated areas.

related to the dynamics of the waterways, dominated by emergent marsh species, with hummocks, older levees, highly modified levees, and miscellaneous interior areas supporting shrub thickets of woody and weedy species. The persistence of certain mesic species in springing up where ever the presence of groundwater, seasonal flooding, and benign neglect permit, is evidence of the natural propensity of the Delta to support riparian plant growth.

"Surrogate" Riparian Communities in the Delta

It is unlikely that levee construction and maintenance, with flood control as its main objective, and the prevailing agricultural land use, which is totally dependent on the levee system, will ever permit further manifestation in the Delta of the rich diversity of species and complex physiognomy that characterize a fully developed riparian plant association. Significant political, economic, technical, legal, and philosophical questions revolve around the maintenance of that system. Two perennial considerations that constrain riparian vegetation in the Delta are: 1) the degree to which vegetation on levees ("riparian" because of the obvious proximity of levees to waterways) is compatible with the primary flood control function and design specifications of the levee system; and 2) the degree to which "natural" vegetation in island interiors ("riparian" because of persistent high groundwater) is compatible with intensive crop cultivation. The levee and other riparian and quasi-riparian communities now found in the Delta are often natural in appearance but nonetheless are largely dependent on deliberate or inadvertent human actions.

Levee Riparian Vegetation

The four most common riparian-like communities associated with waterways on Delta levees are shrub-brush (scrub/shrub in the Sacramento/San Joaquin Environmental Atlas (US Army Corps of Engineers 1979)), brushy riprap (also designated scrub/shrub by the CE), herbaceous banks (labelled upland by the CE (ibid.)), and unvegetated riprap, now a common condition on most maintained and reconstructed levees. Other riparian-like communities found on levees might be called urban (landscaped) riparian; monospecific riparian with such species as willow or alder; and "discontinuous" riparian, evidenced by occasional isolated trees left standing in the wake of stripping, burning, or disking.

Riparian Shrub-Bush.--Riparian shrub-brush is characterized by broad-leaved woody growth less than 6 m. tall. The most common plants are shrubs such as blackberry, wild rose, young alder at the edge of the water, willow species, and herbaceous species such as mugwort and stinging nettle. Occasional small trees--usually willow, cottonwood, or sycamore--may be present. This is a highly variable community; if left undisturbed, as on natural berms on the margin of some of the channel islands, it would develop into woodland.

Periodic disturbance from levee maintenance practices generally discourages this long-term successional process, however.

One of two structural components typical of fully developed riparian vegetation may be absent. An upper stratum such as that provided by mature cottonwoods with snags is most often absent. There may or may not be a well-developed thicket and ground stratum, depending on how negligent levee inspection and maintenance have been.

Diversity of bird use of this habitat parallels its relatively lesser vegetative diversity and structural complexity. For example, hawks (e.g., Red-tailed, Red-shouldered, and Swainson's), woodpeckers (Downy and Nuttall's), and certain warblers are heavy users of wooded riparian areas and are largely eliminated from this community by the absence of an upper tree stratum. On the other hand, there is still sufficient vegetative diversity and cover to provide useful habitat for many common species of birds and mammals.

Other variables besides species composition influence wildlife use of this community; continuity (the linear distribution) is often interrupted at property lines or by periodic or partial maintenance; adjacent habitats (agricultural, urban, aquatic) in part determine the distribution of species in and extent of their dependence on this modified riparian vegetation-type.

Brushy Riprap.--Brushy riprap, one of the more common conditions on Delta levees, is valuable as wildlife habitat where riprapped banks have not been disturbed by inspection or maintenance for several years, or where riprapping has been limited to lower portions of the levee, allowing natural vegetation to remain on the upper levee. Vegetation here is less varied than in scrub-brush. Common wild blackberries predominate; other species include occasional shrubby alders at about mean water line, stinging nettles, wild radish, willows, and smartweed. Only when the vegetative cover on riprapped banks has grown almost out of the brush stage does the habitat appear to support wildlife comparable to shrub-brush banks.

Riprap which is exposed at low tides precludes bank burrowing by beavers, muskrats, and kingfishers. Hawks, woodpeckers, most warblers, and flycatchers are eliminated from this kind of substrate; ground foragers and swallows predominate. The yellow-throat, common on Delta freshwater marshes, uses the blackberry jungles of this community. Unvegetated, exposed riprap banks actually enhance striped and black bass habitat by providing substrate for crayfish, an important food source for bass.

Herbaceous Banks.--Herbaceous banks are most common on riprap or on banks where regular maintenance precludes all but summer annuals such as reed grass and giant reed (at the waterline), scouring rush, blackberry, and wild oats, brome, other introduced grasses, and a variable cover of thistles, poison hemlock, with occasional willow saplings. During the fall and winter, when cover is at a minimum, wildlife use is limited. Summer growth encourages use of the habitat by small seed-eating birds. The only bird species whose presence would qualify this as distinctively "riparian" are the Belted Kingfisher, which perches on small structures associated with the grassy banks, and the swallows flying low overhead. The most conspicuous inhabitant of herbaceous banks in spring and summer months is the ground squirrel, whose potentially destructive burrow colonies are actually favored by cutting and burning of vegetation to facilitate visual inspection of levees (John Muir Institute 1978 a,b).

<u>Unvegetated Riprap</u>.--Unvegetated riprap is similar to herbaceous banks in its absence of vegetative cover. At most, the habitat offers perches and resting areas for birds using the open water and nearby brushy areas.

Neither unvegetated riprap nor herbaceous banks can really be considered "riparian" except according to a broad topographic definition of the term. Yet the majority of levees lining Delta waterways are being managed to achieve this result (fig. 4). A variety of intermediate conditions exist throughout the Delta: old riprapped banks on which willow has formed a discontinuous cover; partially neglected levee faces on which alder saplings have sprung up at the waterline; miles of giant reed lining the water's edge on grass-covered levee banks; occasional trees left to stand alone because the surrounding bare levee slopes permit visual inspection of otherwise pernicious root systems; landscaped residential and recreational front-

Figure 4.--The safest levee from the perspective of flood control managers is free of vegetation and open to visual inspection. Habitat resources are virtually eliminated.

ages, notably deficient (for habitat purposes) in ground or brush stratum or liana. Each of these provides a limited habitat resource, always enhanced by the proximity of water and offering in return at least a narrow, if discontinuous, margin of vegetation or substrate to complement the aquatic environment.

Interior Riparian Vegetation

The most extensive remnants of native riparian woodland occur around the outer margins of the Delta, along those portions of natural floodplains which were either not leveed or not cleared for agricultural cultivation. In a few locations, woodlands extend well back from the rivers along with the alluvial soils on which they grow. Where alluvial soils still exist as narrow levees or margins bordering peat lands in the central Delta, riparian woodlands are minimal and display less deversity of species and structure. Small riparian woodlands occur in the interiors of small islands or on island tips which were all or partially leveed during dredging operations but never cultivated.

The Sacramento/San Joaquin Delta Wildlife Habitat Protection and Restoration Plan (California Department of Fish and Game 1980) did not limit its survey to more obvious manifestations of riparian vegetation on levees along waterways and on the periphery of the Delta. Even highly modified island interiors can reveal wildlife habitats with riparian characteristics. These include seasonally fallow or ruderal lands, dredge disposal areas, drainages and irrigation ditches, and seasonally or periodically flooded agricultural lands.

<u>Ruderal Lands</u>.--Ruderal lands are not widespread in the Delta, where most available land is cultivated. However, a few long-untended fields, abandoned homesites, and agricultural lands damaged by sandy sediments of past floods (e.g., a portion of Brannan Island following the 1972 flood) have been allowed to revert to an almost natural state and are characteristically early successional communities. Species such as sandbar willow, Goodding's willow, and arroyo willow and thick tangles of blackberry are evidence of sufficient year-round soil moisture to eventually support a more diverse riparian-like community behind the levees. Even narrow brushy margins between cultivated fields become important wildlife corridors or islands in the predominantly cultivated landscape.

Unfortunately, ruderal lands in the Delta are totally dependent on individual farming practices. These areas must presently be regarded as transitory, subject to burning, plowing, crop changes, and "clean" farming. They are heavily used by mammalian predators and raptorial birds such as White-tailed Kites and Short-eared Owls because they support large populations of prey species--rodents, reptiles, and ground birds.

Dredge disposal sites.--In the Delta these areas resemble ruderal lands in that they support early successional communities and are highly variable, depending on the underlying residual vegetation, depth of spoils, elevation, and recency and frequency of deposition. Vegetation varies particularly with the age of the spoils; it is not uncommon to find older areas supporting young willows and cottonwoods, as well as herbaceous and other woody species. As with ruderal lands, year-round soil moisture is probably sufficient to eventually sustain larger riparian species if disturbances were discontinued (fig. 5).

Figure 5.--Dredge material disposal sites in the Delta have demonstrated the ability to support adventitious riparian species, such as willow and cottonwood.

Drainage and irrigation ditches.--Drainage and irrigation ditches border and criss-cross agricultural fields and levees throughout the Delta. A few major ditches, such as the one which parallels 8-Mile Road northeast of Stockton, have well-established woody species such as willows and cottonwoods along their banks; others are little more than strips of tules and cattails with brushy margins. While these might be considered minimally "riparian", they are so numerous and widespread that they contribute a significant amount of aquatic and bankside wildlife habitat to the Delta, especially for common birds and amphibians.

The most useful agricultural wildlife habitats in the Delta, and the most "riparian-like", are fields of corn and grain stubble, flooded for several months during the winter for leaching or to create waterfowl habitat. These fields support far greater numbers of individuals (although fewer species) than do more typical riparian areas in the Delta, and closely resemble or at least substitute for ancestral wetland which, prior to reclamation, supported many thousands of the waterfowl wintering in the Delta and elsewhere in the Central Valley. Whistling Swan, Canada Goose, and Sandhill Crane in particular are dependent upon partially flooded fields for winter feeding and resting habitat.

Some fields are flooded briefly in late summer and early fall to control weeds and centipedes. These fields also provide temporary habitat for migrating geese, swans, ducks, and shorebirds. The number, area, and location of flooded fields in the Delta vary considerably from year to year, depending on weather and current leaching practices.

CONSTRAINTS AND OPPORTUNITIES FOR SURROGATE RIPARIAN VEGETATION IN THE DELTA

Constraining Factors

The numerous technical and economic factors responsible for restricting vegetation on Delta levees have been the subject of study and debate for more than two decades and are discussed in many other reports (e.g., California Department of Fish and Game 1980; Whitlow et al. 1979). Briefly, uncontrolled vegetation on levees presents a potential hazard to levee stability. Trees with laterally spreading root systems, such as some willow species, provide paths for piping of water. On the other hand, trees with shallow root systems, such as alder, are subject to wind throw, taking large chunks of the levees with them when they fall. Dense foliage or undergrowth obscures the levee face from easy visual inspection, impedes emergency operations, and, in the opinion of some, attracts burrowing animals.

Opinions vary concerning the contribution of vegetation to erosion control below the high water line: tules, for example, provide a natural breakwater in some situations but cause erosive eddy currents in others. There is general agreement that rock revetment (riprap) is the most reliable means of stabilizing eroding or incompetent banks. However, there is disagreement on the required height of riprap, that is, whether it should be placed below the mean water line, up to the mean water line, or up to the flood stage. The height of the riprap is critical to the amount of vegetation that can be supported on the waterface of the levee.

Riprap is an expensive treatment; its absence on older substandard levees which support some vegetation is often an indication not of preference for vegetation but of lack of sufficient funds or neglect. In all cases, economics are a major determinant in levee construction and maintenance methods. Riparian vegetation is viewed as a costly indulgence both to introduce following construction and to manage as part of ongoing levee maintenance, especially in a region in which agriculture is central to the economy and is dependent on a largely private levee system to separate land from water.

Opportunities

We have applied the term "surrogate" in this discussion to distinguish native riparian vegetation from variant forms of riparian vegetation and wildlife habitat that occur in the Delta. The term also reinforces the notion that protection of existing stands of riparian vegetation and reintroduction of riparian-like vegetation on or off levees under the evident constraints will involve some sacrifices and compromises.

At the outset, protection of existing riparian vegetation will require specific preservation programs that, through acquisition, easement, or other means, assure protection and management in perpetuity. A few of these areas are already publicly owned or have been earmarked for preservation. Certainly, all extant stands of riparian woodland in the Delta have been identified (US Army Corps of Engineers 1979; California Department of Fish and Game 1980). Encouraging expansion of riparian woodland (forest) would require identification of appropriate locations for reintroduction of species and protection through similar preservation programs.

Reintroduction or adoption of more sensitive maintenance practices of riparian-like vegetation will entail either acquisition, easements, subsidies, cost sharing, or a high degree of voluntary cooperation on private levees or in island interiors, to be coupled with one or more of the following management approaches.

Management and "Landscaping" of Permitted or Introduced Vegetation

Bulletin 192 titled "Plan for Improvement of Delta Levees" (California Department of Water Resources 1975) suggests that trees, shrubs, and grasses could be planted on levees between the top of riprap (1.5 ft. (0.5 m.) above mean high water level) and the crown (on a levee with adequate cross-section). Bulletin 192 also recommends that "desirable trees such as oak and crepe myrtle should be retained...(that there be) selective clearing of dead, diseased, and unwanted types of vegetatation...." (ibid.). The California Reclamation Board also recommends selecting tree species for maximum height (no more than 40 ft. (12 m.)), deep roots and clean trunks, deciduous foliage; placement of trees above the design floodplain, spacing (8 m. on centers), and limiting numbers (California State Reclamation Board 1976).

These recommendations, if followed throughout the Delta, would result in: 1) elimination of important and characteristic riparian vegetation strata, principally groundcover, brush, and liana; and 2) elimination of certain native species whose growth habit or other characteristics are incompatible with levee design specifications, and possible substitution of other non-native species according to specifications.

However, viewed positively, and notwithstanding the costs, a managed levee riparian community is better than none. Careful planning of revegetation projects and selective management can produce open, not brushy, growth; vegetation at the water's edge; topping of trees at maturity and removal of dead material; selection of species for non-pernicious root systems; and selective eradication of weedy or intrusive exotics.

Overconstruction of Levees

Where technically and economically feasible, overconstruction of levees to accommodate root zones of potentially damaging trees or construction of setback levees to recreate floodplains can be an ideal management practice to allow for growth of riparian vegetation. There is no question among engineers that, in the absence of structural armor (revetment), an overconstructed levee with berm is the only condition under which riparian vegetation can be fully tolerated within the floodplain of Delta waterways. There is sufficient evidence in limited situations to demonstrate that riparian vegetation under these circumstances aids in dissipating the energy of floodflows and waves against the main levee. The circumstances also permit a riparian forest that can safely reach the full maturity of an 18-m. (60-ft.) or higher upper canopy and favor the dense growth of vines and shrubs that are so important in niche differentiation.

Relocation of Riparian Vegetation

Riparian vegetation may be relocated off levees by creating suitable physiographic and hydrographic conditions not necessarily associated with the levees, at least not on their waterside. Many opportunities exist for permitting and encouraging riparian-like vegetation in the Delta so as not to compromise levee stability: on the landface of levees, in untended or uncultivated portions of agricultural lands, along drainage ditches, and on dredge material deposits. Vegetation even on the landface of levees will require a certain amount of landscaping to exclude "uncontrolled growth" and root systems. Ruderal lands, though limited in extent in the Delta, permit the "uncontrolled growth" that often provides the most diverse habitat niches. Their availability, however, is tenuous, varying from year to year.

Carefully managed dredge materials probably offer one of the best opportunities for partial riparian regrowth, because areas are acquired and deliberately set aside for that purpose. In the past, indiscriminate placement of spoils has eliminated or damaged valuable habitat. With proper location, timing, and management of spoils, new wetlands and riparian conditions can be simulated in island interiors, converting a liability to an asset.

LITERATURE CITED

Atwater, B.F. 1979. Generalized geologic map of the Rio Vista 15-minute triangle, California. USDI Geological Survey Open File Report 79-853, scale 1:62,500.

Atwater, B.F. 1980. Attempts to correlate late Quaternary climatic records between San Francisco Bay, the Sacramento-San Joaquin Delta, and the Mokelumne River, California. PhD. Thesis, University of Delaware. 214 p.

California Department of Fish and Game. 1980. Sacramento/San Joaquin Delta wildlife plan. 290 p. Madrone Associates, Novato, California.

California Department of Water Resources. 1975. Plan for improvement of the Delta levees. Bulletin 192, California Department of Water Resources, Sacramento. 26p.

California Reclamation Board. 1976. Levee encroachment: guide for vegetation on project levees. California Reclamation Board, Sacramento.

Central Valley Riparian Mapping Project. 1979. Interpretation and mapping systems. Report prepared by the Riparian Mapping Team, Geography Department, California State University, Chico, in cooperation with the Department of Geography, California State University, Fresno. 24 p. California Department of Fish and Game, Sacramento. Unpublished manuscript.

Conard, S.G., R.L. MacDonald, and R.F. Holland. 1977. Riparian vegetation and flora of the Sacramento Valley. p. 47-56. In: A. Sands (ed.). Riparian forests in California: their ecology and conservation. Institute of Ecology Pub. No. 15, University of California, Davis. 122 p.

Cowardin, L.M., V. Carter, F.C. Golet, and E.T. LaRoe. 1979. Classification of wetlands and deepwater habitats of the United States. USDI Fish and Wildlife Service Biological Services Program Report FWS/OBS-79/31. 103 p.

Jepson, W.L. 1893. The riparian botany of the lower Sacramento. Ethyreal (January): 238-246.

John Muir Institute. 1978a. Making the transition to an integrated pest management program for ground squirrels on DWR levees. 125 p. Center for the Integration of Applied Sciences (CIAS), John Muir Institute, Berkeley, California.

John Muir Institute. 1978b. Third written report from the Integrated Pest Management Project of the John Muir Institute to the California Department of Water Resources. 120 p. Center for the Integration of Applied Sciences (CIAS), John Muir Institute, Berkeley, California.

Mason, H.L. 1957. A flora of the marshes of California. 878 p. University of California Press, Berkeley.

Thompson, J. 1957. The settlement and geography of the Sacramento-San Joaquin Delta, California. PhD. Thesis, Stanford University, Palo Alto, California. 551 p.

US Army Corps of Engineers. 1979. Sacramento-San-Joaquin environmental atlas. 318 p.

Warner, R.E. 1979. California riparian study program: background information and proposed study design. 177 p. California Department of Fish and Game, Sacramento.

Whitlow, T.H., R.W. Harris, and A.T. Leiser. 1979. Use of vegetation to reduce levee erosion in the Sacramento-San Joaquin Delta. Prepared for the California Department of Water Resources, Sacramento, California. Contract No. B52830. 46 p. and appendices.

SEASONAL VARIATION OF BIRD NUMBERS IN A RIPARIAN FOREST,
SACRAMENTO VALLEY, CALIFORNIA[1]

Robert S. Motroni[2]

Abstract.--During the period 1 September 1976 to 30 August 1977, breeding and migratory birds were censused bi-weekly in a riparian system located 21 km. south of Yuba City, Sutter County, California. A significantly greater number of birds utilized the plant associations of the 174-ha. study area during the fall and winter (September to February) as opposed to the spring and summer (March to August). Forage substrates and food sources present on a seasonal basis were utilized by migratory species. The importance of early seral stage riparian growth to total bird numbers was significant. Habitat management in riparian systems of the Sacramento Valley should be directed toward wintering populations in addition to the requirements of breeding riparian bird species.

INTRODUCTION

Riparian systems are frequently considered one of the most productive forms of wildlife habitat in North America. Many bird species are wholly, or at least partially, dependent on riparian plant communities to perpetuate their kind. Johnson et al. (1977) found that of 166 breeding species in west Texas, southern Arizona, and southern New Mexico, 77% were partially dependent and 51% completely dependent upon riparian plant communities. Similar figures are available for California, where 43% of the species breeding in riparian zones dominated by cottonwood and willow exhibit a "primary affinity" to this vegetation-type (Gaines 1977). Cottonwood stands along the Verde River of Arizona provide the only breeding habitat for over 50% of the breeding species found there (Carothers and Johnson 1975).

Riparian systems are equally important to winter migrants and residents. Until recently however, the importance of wintering habitat has been neglected by researchers even though this season may be the critical one for bird populations. Anderson and Ohmart (1977, 1979) suggested that the mean niche breadth of all bird species along the lower Colorado River was narrowest with respect to use of vegetative structure in winter and was accompanied by reduced habitat overlap. This indicates that winter may be the period of greatest stress to bird populations in this area.

Riparian systems are clearly one of the most important types of wildlife habitat in North America. However, most of the significant literature on them has appeared only during the last 10 years. Of the 254 papers included in a recent bibliography on the importance of riparian systems to terrestrial wildlife, 85% were from the decade of the 1970's (Motroni 1980). The present paper deals with the seasonal variation of bird numbers within plant communities of a riparian system based on seral stage, total numbers, species composition, and foraging guild.

STUDY AREA AND METHODS

Study Area

The riparian system selected for study was the 174-ha. Bobelaine Audubon Sanctuary, located on the west bank of the Feather River directly opposite the confluence of the Feather and Bear Rivers. This riparian system is approximately 21 km. south of Yuba City, Sutter County, California (38° 35' 45" west longitude). The study area, located in a region dominated by agriculture, is bordered on the west by a slough that is the byproduct of a borrow pit created in the early 1900's during levee construction. The eastern edge of the study area abuts the Feather River for a distance of 3.25 km.

Five major plant associations were found on the study area and represent various stages of plant succession. Plant associations were iden-

[1]Paper presented at the California Riparian Systems Conference. [University of California, Davis, September 17-19, 1981].

[2]Robert S. Motroni is Wildlife Biologist, USDA Forest Service, Plumas National Forest, Blairsden, Calif.

tified based on the most abundant and dominant plant species present and are described below.

1. Riparian Shrub 1 (RS1)--composed primarily of California rose (Rosa californica), Mexican tea (Chenopodium ambrosioides), willow (Salix spp.), and blackberry (Rubus vitifolius).

2. Riparian Shrub 2 (RS2)--dominated by willow (Salix spp.), button bush (Cephalanthus occidentalis), and various species of annual and perennial grasses.

3. Cottonwood Forest (CF)--contains cottonwood (Populus fremontii), and valley oak (Quercus lobata) with an understory of Mexican tea, poison oak (Rhus diversiloba) and various grasses.

4. Riparian Forest (RF)--dominated, in contrast to the Cottonwood Forest association, by a dense stand of cottonwood with an understory of poison oak, blackberry, wild grape (Vitis californica), blue vervain (Verbena hastata) and other herbs and grasses.

5. Oak Woodland (OW)--on areas of high ground dominated by mature valley oak, sycamore (Platanus racemosa), and cottonwood. The understory is composed of widely separated shrubs such as poison oak and California rose, interspersed with grass. This association has an open, park-like appearance. A more complete quantitative description of the plant associations examined can be found in Motroni (1979).

Methods

Plot census techniques were utilized after the establishment of study plots in areas representative of the various plant associations of the study area. Plots of varying size depending on vegetation limits were established in each of the five plant associations: RS1--5 ha.; RS2--2.5 ha.; CF--3 ha.; RF--2 ha.; and OW--3 ha.

Plot censuses were conducted on alternate weeks from the initiation of the study on 1 September 1976 to its completion on 30 August 1977. Two methods of data collection and interpretation were utilized during the study. During the wintering and migratory periods, when little if any territoriality was evident in the avian population, a modified form of the summation method (originally a breeding bird census technique) was used. This method has been reported by Palmgren (1930) and Udvardy (1947), and was evaluated by Enemar (1959). The modified summation method entails recording the number and species of all birds encountered over the entire census plot. When the data were interpreted, an estimation of abundance and bird habitat preference on the day of the census was obtained.

During the breeding season, after territory establishment, the spot-map method described by Kendeigh (1944), and Enemar (1959), was utilized but modified such that all birds encountered, not only to territorial males or females, were marked on a plot map during each visit. Data collected in this manner were interpreted by compiling sightings of each species onto a separate species map. This facilitated an analysis of territory size, habitat preference, and recogninition of non-territorial transient birds. Also, as Williamson (1964) has pointed out, the mapping results provided information on the distribution and numbers of various species as well as on their interrelationships with the entire avian community. These spot-map censuses were initiated at the first sign of territorial activity and were made at regular intervals throughout the breeding season in order to cover the peak song periods of all species encountered. Data were collected only on fair days due to the adverse effects of wind and rain on the song and activity patterns of birds.

Bird species diversity was calculated with the Shannon-Wiener Diversity Index (Cox 1972) utilizing logs to the base e.

$$\text{Species Diversity} = -\sum_{i=1}^{s} P_i \log_e P_i$$

where Pi equals the decimal fraction of total individuals belonging to the ith species and s equals the total number of species. Maximum diversity (H maximum), an expression of the highest diversity value possible assuming equal numbers of all species, and evenness (E) were also obtained from the diversity formula. The seasonal distribution of the total number of birds observed was tested with the Kruskal-Wallis one-way analysis of variance by ranks described by Siegel (1956).

Bird species encountered during the fall/winter and spring/summer census periods were placed in foraging guilds based primarily upon the type of substrate and major food type utilized. A guild has been defined by Root (1967) as: "a group of species that exploit the same class of environmental resources in a similar way." The foraging guild taxonomy to which species were assigned was patterned after Bent (1923-1958), Gaines (1977), and field observations. Those species that belonged to two foraging guilds (e.g. Townsends Warbler (Dendroica townsendi) and Rufous-sided Towhee (Pipilo erythrophalmus)) were treated in the same manner as Gaines (ibid.), in that both guilds were weighted equally. All species were classified within the following foraging guilds: omnivore; ground seed; ground insect; ground mammal; bark insect; foliage seed; foliage insect; and air insect.

RESULTS

Plot Census of Avifauna

Fall/Winter

Fall/winter bird censusing was conducted from 12 September 1976 to 25 February 1977 on a bi-weekly basis, for a total of 12 census visits. Fifty-seven species of birds were observed.

The average density of birds ranged from 1,553 birds per 40 ha. in RS1 to 468 birds per 40 ha. in RS2. The high value obtained for RS1 was due primarily to the large numbers of White-crowned Sparrows (*Zonotrichia leucophrys*) and Golden-crowned Sparrows (*Zonotrichia atricapilla*) utilizing this plant association during the wintering period. Bird species diversity for the fall/winter period of all plots sampled varied from a high of 2.99 in the RF to a low of 1.36 in RS1 (table 1).

Spring/Summer

Breeding bird censuses were conducted from 11 March 1977 to 30 August 1977 on a bi-weekly basis for a total of 13 census trips. Sixty-two species of birds were observed during this time period. Twenty-six of these species were common enough that sufficient data could be collected to make a breeding bird density determination.

Non-breeding birds observed on the plots, and those not belonging to any established territory, were classified as surplus birds in the plot sample data. The total number of breeding birds per 40 ha. ranged from a high of 1,000 in RF to a low of 368 in RS1 (table 2). Breeding bird species diversity was calculated for this period in the same manner as the wintering bird species diversity. However, since wintering bird numbers were calculated from direct observations, and breeding bird numbers (aside from birds classified as transient) were based on numerous observations of territorial individuals, a reevaluation of breeding bird data was necessary so that the diversities from these two time periods could be compared. This reevaluation was accomplished by counting the total number of observations of birds exhibiting territorial behavior, including females and transients, noted on the composite plot map for each species. Thus, diversity figures were based on 257 birds observed in RF; 344 in CF; 447 in OW; 398 in RS1; and 133 in RS2. Although females, due to their secretive nature in this particular time period, were not encountered as frequently as during the

Table 1.--Wintering avifauna of the Bobelaine Audubon Sanctuary: September 1976-February 1977. RF--Riparian Forest; OW--Oak Woodland; CF--Cottonwood Forest; RS1--Riparian Shrub 1; RS2--Riparian Shrub 2.

	RF	OW	CF	RS1	RS2
Mean bird density/ 40 ha.	1,022	1,017	884	1,553	468
Species richness	32	35	35	39	28
Diversity (H)	2.99	2.59	2.69	1.36	2.63
H maximum	3.46	3.55	3.46	3.55	3.33
Evenness	0.858	0.724	0.770	0.381	0.778

Table 2.--Breeding and transient avifauna of the Bobelaine Audubon Sanctuary: March 1977-August 1977. RF--Riparian Forest; OW--Oak Woodland; CF--Cottonwood Forest; RS1--Riparian Shrub 1; RS2--Riparian Shrub 2.

	RF	OW	CF	RS1	RS2
Mean bird density/ 40 ha.[1]	1,000	749	750	368	416
Species richness	38	45	34	36	32
Diversity (H)	3.10	3.23	2.72	3.02	2.97
H maximum	3.64	3.83	3.53	3.58	3.46
Evenness	0.833	0.832	0.760	0.831	0.826

[1]Calculated as the number of territorial males x2 to account for males and females.

wintering period, the increased conspicuousness of active singing males was assumed to compensate in part for the lack of observation of females.

Bird species diversity values for the breeding period ranged from a high of 3.23 in OW to a low of 2.72 in CF (table 2). Evenness values ranged from a high of 0.833 in RF to a low of 0.760 in CF.

Total Numbers

The total numbers of wintering versus breeding birds actually encountered on the various census plots are depicted in table 3. The vast majority of birds were observed during the

Table 3.--Seasonal variation in total bird numbers observed in each of five plant associations surveyed. Count periods and percent of total bird numbers for each count period are shown for each plant association. RF--Riparian Forest; OW--Oak Woodland; CF--Cottonwood Forest; RS1-- Riparian Shrub 1; RS2--Riparian Shrub 2.

Plant Association	Wintering Birds				Breeding Birds			
	Sept.-Nov.	% of total	Dec.-Feb.	% of total	March-May	% of total	June-Aug.	% of total
RF	263	30	350	40	154	18	103	12
CF	337	30	459	40	202	18	142	12
OW	334	24	582	43	260	19	187	14
RS1	823	30	1,507	55	254	9	144	6
RS2	200	41	151	31	75	16	58	12

fall/winter census period (p < 0.05) with values ranging from 67% in the OW plot to 85% in the RS1 plot.

Foraging Guilds

The percentages of total breeding and wintering individuals in relation to their foraging guilds are depicted in table 4. Calculations of the total number of individuals in each foraging guild were done in the same manner as the diversity calculations for comparisons of breeding and wintering birds. This facilitated a more accurate comparison between fall/winter and spring/summer periods. Only those species known to forage in the plots sampled were included in the calculations.

During the fall/winter period, the majority of birds in each plant association fed primarily on the ground on seeds produced by shrubs and herbaceous vegetation, as well as on quiescent insect life. Bark insect guild birds were primarily permanent residents; the percentages of total numbers encountered during the census period were as follows: RF--75%; OW--77%; CF--66%; RS1--91%; and RS2--67%.

Conversely, migratory species (primarily wintering sparrows and the Dark-eyed Junco (Junco hyemalis), dominated the ground seed guild, with the exception of the RF birds: RF--19%; OW--81%; CF--80%; RS1--84%; and RS2--56%. The high percentage of resident birds in the ground seed foraging guild in RF (81%) was due in part to habitat selection. The high densities of permanent resident birds such as California Quail (Lophortyx californicus), Rufous-sided Towhee, and Brown Towhee (Pipilo fuscus) in this association overshadowed the presence of the migratory avifauna.

Resident species were again dominant in the ground insect foraging guild: RF--93%; OW--100%; CF--94%; RS1--99%; and RS2--100%. Similarly, species within the omnivore guild were composed entirely of resident birds in every plant association.

During the breeding period the utilization of insect life as forage increased markedly. Species found in the air insect guild were predominately migrants. The migratory composition of the foliage insect and air insect foraging guilds were, respectively, as follows: RF--71%, 100%; OW--43%, 96%; CF--27%, 100%; RS1--27%, 100%; and RS2--65%, 100%. The relatively low percentage of migratory birds in the foliage insect foraging guild was due in part to the presence of such residents as Bewicks Wren (Thryomanes bewickii), Common Bushtit (Psaltriparus minimus), and others that are flexible enough to change foraging guilds from the wintering to the breeding period.

If these species are excluded from foraging guild calculations then the percentages of migratory birds in the foliage insect guild ranged from 50-100% in the various associations surveyed. Gaines (1977) has shown that the foliage insect foraging guild is approximately equally divided between residents (53%) and migrants (47%) in a cottonwood/willow riparian forest. During the breeding period the bark insect guild continued to be dominated by resident birds: RF--98%; OW--89%; CF--100%; RS1--100%; and RS2--95%. As during the wintering period, the omnivore foraging guild was composed entirely of resident species in each plant association.

DISCUSSION

Density and Seral Stage

The relationships between breeding bird populations and various aspects of plant succession have been examined by Johnston and Odum (1956), and Bond (1957). Diversity values and the numbers of birds supported in any particular plant association during the breeding season have been related to the seral stage of the plant association examined, and to the structural complexity of the vegetation. Breeding bird densities have also been related to the distribution and volume of tree foliage (Balda 1969, 1970). It is noteworthy that OW supported a lower

Table 4.--Percentage of total birds observed related to foraging guilds during wintering and breeding periods for five plant associations. RF--Riparian Forest; OW--Oak Woodland; CF--Cottonwood Forest; RS1-- Riparian Shrub 1; RS2--Riparian Shrub 2.

Foraging Guild	RF Sept-Feb	RF Mar-Aug	OW Sept-Feb	OW Mar-Aug	CF Sept-Feb	CF Mar-Aug	RS1 Sept-Feb	RS1 Mar-Aug	RS2 Sept-Feb	RS2 Mar-Aug
Omnivore	18	15	15	15	36	32	8	15	13	15
Ground seed	27	24	43	25	21	11	77	39	52	24
Ground insect	3	11	1	10	2	4	5	9	5	5
Ground mammal	1.5	2	1	1	1	0	0.5	1	2	0
Bark insect	27	24	26	20	17	19	3.5	4	13	8
Foliage seed	11	5	5	6	14	9	4	6	6	7
Foliage insect	3	10	5	14	1	8	1	8	2	15
Air insect	9.5	9	4	9	8	17	1	18	7	26

breeding bird density than those areas with relatively pure cottonwood stands such as RF. In contrast, those areas of CF that had a major valley oak component exhibited density trends comparable to OW (table 2).

The difference between breeding bird populations of the relatively pure cottonwood stands of RF and stands of OW may have been due to the more mesic conditions of the former and subsequent promotion of greater plant growth and higher invertebrate populations than were found in OW or CF. These mesic conditions, if present, also contributed to a more complex, stratified foliage profile. Gaines (1974) arrived at similar conclusions. Carothers et al. (1974), in a study of breeding riparian woodland bird populations in north-central Arizona, determined that those areas of relatively pure cottonwood stands supported the largest breeding bird populations, whereas areas of a mixed deciduous tree and shrub component supported smaller populations of breeding birds.

Breeding bird diversity values in those plant associations surveyed on the study area were consistently higher than the values for wintering birds (tables 1 and 2). This difference was a consequence of the large influx of a relatively few migrant species during the fall/winter period versus the presence of a more evenly distributed population of breeding species.

In contrast to the breeding period census results, the wintering density of OW was similar to that of RF (table 1). This similarity was due in part to the presence of migratory species in the bark insect and ground seed foraging guilds. The relatively open, xeric conditions of OW may have been more conducive to the growth of grasses and other seed-producing plants utilized by wintering species.

The large number of birds utilizing RS1 during the fall and winter was primarily due to seed-eating winter residents such as the White-crowned Sparrow and Golden-crowned Sparrow. This somewhat specialized habitat use by winter visitors has been previously described by Anderson and Ohmart (1977, 1980) for birds in the lower Colorado River Valley. In their study, winter visitors, and to a lesser degree summer visitors, exhibited an increase in specialization with regard to the use of vegetation-types. In addition, Fretwell (1972) predicted that winter residents will exhibit larger populations and a greater degree of habitat specialization than resident species, thus emphasizing the importance of this early seral stage association to wintering birds.

Total Numbers of Birds

It has been generally recognized that there are more birds utilizing the lowlands of California in fall and winter than in spring and summer. There is, however, little documentation of this dichotomy of seasonal utilization. Michny et

al. (1975), in censusing an area of riparian woodland north of Princeton, Colusa County, California, discovered that during the month of August there was a mean of 23.8 birds per ha. Similar results were noted for May and June, with 24.0 birds per ha. However, this same area, when censused in February and March, produced a mean of 40.1 birds per ha. Winter visitor populations were observed to be about twice as dense as breeding bird populations in a south central Louisiana mature hardwood bottomland (Dickson 1978). Monthly winter populations varied between 1400 and 2000 birds per km^2.

In contrast, other researchers have noted a higher level of avian use in riparian systems during the breeding period, for example, Anderson and Ohmart (1976) in several communities on the lower Colorado River; and Gavin and Sowls (1975) for a mesquite bosque (fide Szaro 1980). Factors influencing this disparity in use may include census technique, location of study area in relation to migratory pathways, habitat structure and condition, and suitability of adjacent areas.

During this study, a mean of 26.8 birds per ha. was found over the five associations surveyed during the fall/winter period, versus 7.7 birds per ha. during the spring/summer period. This three-fold increase in bird numbers during the fall and winter period may be due to a combination of several factors. During the wintering period there is a breakdown of territoriality among many members of the avian community. This facilitates an increase in gregariousness among many species and a consequent increase in number of birds inhabiting an area during the non-breeding period. The presence of young-of-the-year in resident species also contributes to the size of the early fall population.

Nevertheless, the most important contribution to the fall/winter population size comes from the arrival of such abundant migrants as the American Robin (Turdus migratorius), Yellow-rumped Warbler (Dendroica coronata), Ruby-crowned Kinglet (Regulus calendula), Dark-eyed Junco, White-crowned Sparrow, and Golden-crowned Sparrow. The general lack of strongly defended territories as well as the presence of an unpredictable and rigorous environment are considered to be primarily responsible for lower evenness levels exhibited by bird populations in winter than in other seasons (Tramer 1969; Holmes and Sturges 1975).

A number of explanations of the seasonality of bird habitat use are discernible and are of importance to habitat management. Species separated by ecological or geographic factors on wintering and breeding grounds merge during migration and contribute to higher densities along migration routes. Abramsky and Safriel (1980) suggested that the resultant increases in inter-individual contacts and mortality during migration increase the importance of transition habitat. They concluded that migratory birds do not merely commute seasonally between two destinations, but rather occupy a series of transient home ranges where food resources are heavily utilized.

Habitat structure and/or quality also provide a highly significant influence on seasonality of avian use. Anderson and Ohmart (1977) found that bird populations in riparian zones along the Colorado River reacted less in summer than during other seasons to such vegetation structure components as patchiness, foliage height diversity, etc. The importance of habitat quality inherent in riparian systems as it relates to adjacent system types and utilization by migratory birds has been frequently cited. Stevens et al. (1977) considered the importance of riparian systems to migrant birds in central Arizona to be substantial in that riparian systems contained up to 10.6 times the number of migrants per hectare as adjacent non-riparian areas. Similarly, Wauer (1977) suggested that riparian systems of the Rio Grande provide a major migratory route due primarily to the arid country through which these species pass.

The availability of winter food has been suggested by Fretwell (1972) to have marked influence on breeding densities via the maintenance of winter population levels. Species feeding primarily on seeds would, on the average, exhibit higher winter densities due to a more abundant food resource. The large number of wintering birds using seeds as a food source can be expected to occur primarily in the early seral stages of a plant community where such a food resource predominates. This was indeed the case in RS1 and the large number of seed eaters it supported during the wintering period. In addition, species of small body size might also be able to maintain high winter densities (Fretwell ibid.). The abundance of fringillids in this study during the fall/winter period supports the above theory.

Foraging Guilds

A general relationship between substrate, foraging guild, and migratory status can be discerned. It appears that winter residents and summer residents utilize those resources that are available only on a seasonal basis. During the wintering period ground seeds are in abundance and are used to a great extent by migratory species. Resident species dominate the ground insect and bark insect guilds, where the substrate and resource can be utilized on a year-round basis.

Conversely, during the spring/summer period, insectivores replace the granivores of the fall/winter period. The presence of foliage and active insect life provide a seasonal substrate and/or forage resource exploited by a separate group of migratory birds that includes such species as the Western Kingbird (Tyrannus verticalis), Ash-throated Flycatcher (Myiarchus cinerascens), Tree Swallow (Iridoprocne bicolor), Northern Oriole (Icterus galbula), and Brown-headed Cowbird (Molothrus ater).

Similar results by Gaines (1977) showed that those substrates present on a year-round basis were used primarily by resident species, whereas most migratory species utilized seasonal substrates or food resources. Herrera (1978) examined an area dominated by extensive evergreen oak woodlands and concluded that resident species normally depend on the more permanent and less seasonal resources, in contrast to non-resident species whose subsistence is based on seasonally variable food supplies. Karr (1976a) described similar conclusions for a tropical bird community. To summarize, non-resident birds generally exploit an abundant, unpredictable food supply during both breeding and wintering periods (Willis 1966; Leck 1972; Bibby et al. 1976; Karr 1976b).

SUMMARY AND CONCLUSIONS

1. A significantly greater number of birds utilized five plant associations of the study area during the fall/winter period than in the spring/summer season. Winter resident species reached their greatest densities in early seral stage riparian growth.

2. Those forage strata and food sources present on a seasonal basis during the wintering and breeding periods were primarily utilized by migratory species.

The importance of early successional stage riparian vegetation to total bird numbers and overall species diversity on a seasonal level is significant. Recognition of this concept can influence managers to alter potential productivity of riparian systems during the planning and development of riparian reestablishment projects, levee maintenance, and bank protection projects. A number of the latter are capable of protecting birds while at the same time allowing natural riparian vegetation succession on river berms (indirect bank protection or river training devices as described by Keown et al. 1977).

To the casual observer, the breeding habitat of a species appears to be of prime importance. This is due in part to the disproportionate amount of effort by field workers in collecting data for this period. The three-fold increase in bird numbers utilizing riparian plant communities during the wintering and migratory periods as described earlier in this paper supports the concept that this ecosystem is of at least equal importance to the avifauna as a wintering area and migratory corridor.

ACKNOWLEDGMENTS

Research was supported by a stipend from the Sacramento Chapter of the National Audubon Society and California State University, Sacramento. Thanks also go to Drs. Gary and Joan Fellers and Dr. M.D.F. Udvardy for their very helpful suggestions and critical reading of the manuscript. Research was conducted as partial fulfillment of a graduate degree at California State University, Sacramento. Pegi Kelly and Diane Waterhouse typed the final manuscript.

LITERATURE CITED

Abramsky, Z., and U. Safriel. 1980. Seasonal patterns in a Mediterranean bird community composed of transient, wintering and resident passerines. Ornis Scand. 11:201-216.

Anderson, B.W., and R.D. Ohmart. 1976. Wildlife use and densities report of birds and mammals in the lower Colorado River Valley. USDI Bureau of Reclamation, Lower Colorado River Region. 278 p. Boulder City, Nevada.

Anderson, B.W., and R.D. Ohmart. 1977. Vegetation structure and bird use in the lower Colorado River Valley. p. 23-34. In: R.R. Johnson and D.A. Jones (ed.). Importance, preservation and management of riparian habitat: A symposium. [Tucson, Arizona, July 9, 1977]. USDA Forest Service GTR-RM-43, Rocky Mountain Forest and Range Experiment Station, Fort Collins, Colo. 217 p.

Anderson, B.W., and R.D. Ohmart. 1979. Riparian vegetation: an approach to mitigating for a disappearing habitat in the Southwest. p. 481-487. In: G.A. Swanson (tech. coord.). The mitigation symposium: A national workshop on mitigating losses of fish and wildlife habitat. USDA Forest Service GTR-RM-65, Rocky Mountain Forest and Range Experiment Station, Fort Collins, Colo. 695 p.

Anderson, B.W., and R.D. Ohmart. 1980. Designing and developing a predictive model and testing a revegetated riparian community for southwestern birds. p. 434-450. In: R.M. DeGraff (tech. coord.). Management of western forests and grasslands for non-game birds. USDA Forest Service GTR-INT-86, Intermountain Forest and Range Experiment Station, Ogden, Utah. 535 p.

Balda, R.P. 1969. Foliage use by birds of the oak-juniper woodland and ponderosa pine forest in southeastern Arizona. Condor 71:399-412.

Balda, R.P. 1970. Effects of spring leaf-fall on composition and density of breeding birds in two southern Arizona woodlands. Condor 72:325-331.

Bent, A.C. 1923. Life histories of North American wildfowl. US National Museum Bulletin 126. Washington, D.C.

Bent, A.C. 1932. Life histories of North American gallinaceous birds. US National Museum Bulletin 162. Washington, D.C.

Bent, A.C. 1937. Life histories of North American birds of prey. US National Museum Bulletin 167. Washington, D.C.

Bent, A.C. 1939. Life histories of North American woodpeckers. US National Museum Bulletin 174. Washington, D.C.

Bent, A.C. 1940. Life histories of North American cuckoos, goatsuckers, hummingbirds and their allies. US National Museum Bulletin 176. Washington, D.C.

Bent, A.C. 1942. Life histories of North American flycatchers, swallows, larks, and their allies. US National Museum Bulletin 179. Washington, D.C.

Bent, A.C. 1948. Life histories of North American nuthatches, wrens, thrashers, and their allies. US National Museum Bulletin 195. Washington, D.C.

Bent, A.C. 1949. Life histories of North American thrushes, kinglets, and their allies. US National Museum Bulletin 196. Washington, D.C.

Bent, A.C. 1953. Life histories of North American wood warblers. US National Museum Bulletin 203. Washington, D.C.

Bent, A.C. 1958. Life histories of North American blackbirds, orioles, tanagers, and their allies. US National Museum Bulletin 211. Washington, D.C.

Bibby, C.J., R.E. Green, G. Pepler, and P.A. Pepler. 1976. Sedge Warbler migration and reed aphids. British Birds 69:384-399.

Bond, R.R. 1957. Ecological distribution of breeding birds in the upland forests of southern Wisconsin. Ecol. Monog. 27:351-382.

Carothers, S.W., and R.R. Johnson. 1975. Water management practices and their effects on nongame birds in range habitats. p. 210-222. In: D.R. Smith (tech. coord.). Proceedings of the symposium on management of forest and range habitats for nongame birds. USDA Forest Service GTR-WO-1, Washington, D.C.

Carothers, S.W., R.R. Johnson, and S.W. Aitchison. 1974. Population structure and social organization of southwestern riparian birds. Am. Zool. 14:97-108.

Cox, G.W. 1972. Laboratory manual of general ecology. 195 p. Wm. C. Brown Co., Dubuque, Iowa.

Dickson, J.G. 1978. Forest bird communities of the bottomland hardwoods. p. 66-73. In: R.M. DeGraff (tech. coord.). Proceedings of the workshop on management of southern forests for nongame birds. USDA Forest Service GTR-SE-14. 175 p. Southeast Forest Experiment Station, Ashville, North Carolina.

Enemar, A. 1959. On the determination of the size and composition of a passerine bird population during the breeding season. Var Fagelvarld, Suppl. 2:1-114.

Fretwell, S.D. 1972. Populations in a seasonal environment. 217 p. Princeton University Press, Princeton, N.J.

Gaines, D. 1974. A new look at the nesting riparian avifauna of the Sacramento Valley, California. Western Birds 5:61-80.

Gaines, D. 1977. The valley riparian forests of California: their importance to bird populations. p. 57-85. In: A. Sands (ed.). Riparian forests in California: their ecology and conservation. 122 p. Institute of Ecology, University of California, Davis.

Gavin, T.A., and L.K. Sowls. 1975. Avian fauna of a San Pedro valley mesquite forest. J. Ariz. Acad. Sci. 10:33-41.

Herrera, C.M. 1978. Ecological correlates of residence and non-residence in a Mediterranean passerine bird community. Jour. Anim. Ecol. 47:871-890.

Holmes, R.T., and F.W Sturges. 1975. Bird community dynamics and energetics in a northern hardwoods ecosystem. Jour. Anim. Ecol. 45:175-200.

Johnson, R.R., L.T. Haight, and J.M. Simpson. 1977. Endangered species vs. endangered habitats: a concept. p. 68-79. In: R.R. Johnson and D.A. Jones (tech. coord.). Importance, preservation and management of riparian habitat: A symposium. [Tucson, Arizona, July 9, 1977]. USDA Forest Service GTR-RM-43, Rocky Mountain Forest and Range Experiment Station, Fort Collins, Colo. 217 p.

Johnston, D.W., and E.P. Odum. 1956. Breeding bird populations in relation to plant succession in the Piedmont of Georgia. Ecology 37:50-62.

Karr, J.R. 1976a. Seasonality, resource availability, and community diversity in tropical bird communities. Amer. Nat. 100:973-994.

Karr, J.R. 1976b. On the relative abundance of migrants from the north temperate zone in tropical habitats. Wilson Bull. 88:443-458.

Kendeigh, S.C. 1944. Measurement of bird populations. Ecol Monog. 14:67-106.

Keown, M.P., N.R. Oswalt, E.B. Perry, and E.A. Dardeau, Jr. 1977. Literature survey and preliminary evaluation of streambank protection methods. US Army Corps of Engineers TR-H-77-9, US Army Corps of Engineers Waterways Experiment Station, Vicksburg, Miss. 262 p.

Leck, C.F. 1972. The impact of some North American migrants at fruiting trees in Panama. Auk 89:842-850.

Michny, F.J., D. Boos, and F. Wernette. 1975. Riparian habitats and avian densities along the Sacramento River. California Department of Fish and Game, Wildlife Management Branch Administrative Report 75-1. 42 p.

Motroni, R.S. 1979. Avian density and composition of a riparian forest, Sacramento Valley, California. M.S. Thesis, California State University, Sacramento. 172 p.

Motroni, R.S. 1980. The importance of riparian zones to terrestrial wildlife: an annotated bibliography. USDI Fish and Wildlife Service. Division of Ecological Services. 83 p. Sacramento, California.

Palmgren, P. 1930. Quantitative Untersuchungen uber die Vogelfauna in den Waldern Sudfinnlands. Acta Zool. Fennica 7:1-218.

Root, R.B. 1967. The niche exploitation pattern of the Blue-gray Gnatcatcher. Ecol. Monog. 37:317-350.

Siegel, S. 1956. Nonparametric statistics for the behavioral sciences. McGraw-Hill, New York, N.Y.

Stevens, L.E., B.T. Brown, J.M. Simpson, and R.R. Johnson. 1977. The importance of riparian habitat to migrating birds. p. 156-164. In: R.R. Johnson and D.A. Jones (tech. coord.). Importance, preservation and management of riparian habitat: A symposium. [Tucson, Arizona, July 9, 1977]. USDA Forest Service GTR-RM-43, Rocky Mountain Forest and Range Experiment Station, Fort Collins, Colo. 217 p.

Szaro, R.C. 1980. Factors influencing bird populations in southwestern riparian forests. p. 403-418. In: R.M. DeGraff (tech. coord.). Management of western forests and grasslands for non-game birds. USDA Forest Service GTR-INT-86, Intermountain Forest and Range Experiment Station, Ogden, Utah. 535 p.

Tramer, E.J. 1969. Bird species diversity: components of Shannon's formula. Ecology 50:927-929.

Udvardy, M.D.F. 1947. Methods of bird sociological survey, on the basis of some Tihany communities investigated. Arch. Biol. Hung. 17:61-89.

Wauer, H.R. 1977. Significance of Rio Grande riparian systems upon the avifauna. p. 165-174. In: R.R. Johnson and D.A. Jones (tech. coord.). Importance, preservation and management of riparian habitat: A symposium. [Tuscon, Ariz., July 9, 1977]. USDA Forest Service GTR-RM-43, Rocky Mountain Forest and Range Experiment Station, Fort Collins, Colo. 217 p.

Williamson, K. 1964. Bird census work in woodland. Bird Study 11:1-22.

Willis, E.O. 1966. The role of migrant birds at swarms of army ants. Living Bird 5:187-231.

RIPARIAN BIRD COMMUNITY STRUCTURE AND DYNAMICS:

DOG ISLAND, RED BLUFF, CALIFORNIA[1]

Stephen A. Laymon[2]

Abstract.--This 5-year weekly census on an 18-ha. plot documents the seasonal and year to year changes in a riparian bird community. High bird densities were found in all seasons. Species richness and bird density were found to be higher than in other wooded habitats in the West. The community was analysed using the concept of species diversity. Effects of Brown-headed Cowbird parasitism and the "habitat island" nature of the study area are discussed.

INTRODUCTION

"In California, the habitat that most clearly approximates the eastern broadleaved hardwood forests is the riparian woodland. This is so because of the nature of the trees in this woodland, their denseness, and the unparalleled diversity of the bird life." (Small 1974).

"Today, with the last extensive remnants of these forests in jeopardy, it behooves us to weigh the importance of riparian habitat to birds and other wildlife." (Gaines 1977).

These two quotations address both the importance of, and the threat to, lowland riparian systems in California and the West. Statewide, the extensive riparian forests encompassing hundreds of thousands of hectares have been reduced to mere remnants within 100 years.

The forests of the interior of California had not been explored extensively by ornithologists until recent years. The summer heat and winter fog were discouraging factors. One study in Red Bluff and the surrounding area retreated to the mountains in mid-May as the temperatures increased (Grinnell et al. 1930), thus missing many late migrant and nesting birds. It was 1964 before mention was made of the massive numbers of fall migrants using the Sacramento Valley willow thickets (Chase and DeBenedictis 1964). In 1974 when I began this study, the only quantitative evidence of riparian bird populations consisted of eight breeding bird censuses and one winter bird study (Dembosz et al. 1972; Gaines 1973; Ingles 1950; Manolis 1973; Shuford

1973; Tangren 1971; Tangren 1972; Winkler 1973a, 1973b). Nothing quantitative had been published on migration.

Since 1974 much more information on riparian bird populations has appeared. In 1979 and 1980 alone, American Birds (vol. 33 and 34) published seven breeding bird censuses and 10 winter bird population studies from riparian areas in California. Several short-term government agency studies in the Sacramento Valley have resulted in administrative reports[3] and papers of varying quality (Stone 1976; Brumley 1979; Michny et al. 1975; Helnke and Stone 1978; Hurst et al. 1980). Most of these studies suffered due to lack of trained field ornithologists to gather the field data. The most impressive study has been conducted along the lower Colorado River, coordinated by Ohmart and Anderson (e.g. Anderson and Ohmart 1977). Their study area represents a different avifauna than that found in the Central Valley.

The present study was formulated to gather population data on a regular basis, monitor changes in breeding and winter populations from year to year, and document the extent of migratory bird usage of the lowland riparian woodland vegetation.

STUDY AREA

Dog Island City Park is located on the west side of the Sacramento River at the north end of the city of Red Bluff, in central Tehama County, California. Development of the park has been held to a low level with parking lot, restrooms, a few picnic tables, and trails. The area is

[1]Paper presented at the California Riparian Systems Conference. [University of California, Davis, September 17-19, 1981].

[2]Stephen A. Laymon is a Graduate Student in the Department of Forestry and Resource Management, University of California, Berkeley.

[3]Stone, T.B. 1976. Birds in riparian habitat of the upper Sacramento River. The Resources Agency, Department of Fish and Game memorandum report. Sacramento, Calif.

17.7 ha. in extent and consists of a 5.9 ha. island, 9.4 ha. mainland portion and 2.4 ha. of river channel (see fig. 1).

The climate of the study area is moderate Mediterranean, with a wet, cool winter and a long, dry, hot summer. During wet winters, much of the area is inundated, sometimes for several weeks at a time.

The dominant vegetation-type is floodplain riparian woodland. The vegetation is quite diverse with different species being dominant on portions of the area, often forming clumps or bands of a single species.

Vegetation was characterized using a series of 2 m.-wide belt transects through the system. The average canopy closure, determined from the belt transects, was 80% while the average ground-cover was 68%. The mean canopy height was 13.4 m. (range 2-35 m.) and total density was 1,619 trees per ha. The most frequent trees were willow (Salix, seven spp., 300 per ha.), black walnut (Juglans sp., 296 per ha.), box elder (Acer negundo, 288 per ha.), Oregon ash (Fraxinus latifolia, 154 per ha.), white alder (Alnus rhombifolia, 124 per ha.), and Fremont cottonwood (Populus fremontii, 110 per ha.). Percent canopy/understory by species was walnut 21%, cottonwood 20%, box elder 18%, willow 16%, alder 8%, and ash 7%. The ground-cover consisted of mugwort (Artemesia douglasiana), blackberry (Rubus, three spp.) and various grasses. There was a small marsh in the center of the island.

The area is a vegetational island surrounded by blue oak (Quercus douglasii) woodland, urban development, grassland, and orchards. The nearest extensive riparian woodland is 15 km. to the south. Additional information on the area is presented in Laymon (1983).

METHODS

Sampling Methods

The census route was laid out along existing pathways which made loops through the two main portions of the study area. The census route was 3.9 km. in length and gave good coverage of the area. No attempt was made to estimate actual numbers except for breeding pairs, using a supplementary spot-mapping system (Kendeigh 1944) and an extrapolation of migrant populations for selected species.

Censuses were begun between 06:30 and 08:30. Censuses ran an average of 170.5 minutes (range 115 to 270 minutes). Census time averaged longer in spring and fall when migrants were present. Censuses were run weekly except when the area was flooded. When possible, days of high wind or rain were avoided. The census method consisted of walking slowly along the route and stopping at regular spots. All birds both seen and heard were recorded. Birds flying overhead were recorded but a notation to that effect was made.

A total of 238 censuses were conducted between February 1974 and June 1980. Of these only the 197 censuses taken from 1975 through 1979 are used in this presentation.

Data Analysis

A system of numbered weeks, starting 1-7 January was used to organize the data. All censuses taken during each week were pooled to gain the overall trend. Week 2 (8-14 Jan.) was not represented by any censuses so the figures for that week are the average of weeks 1 and 3. A three-number running average was used as a curve-smoothing device on the composite graph.

The total number of individuals (TI) and the frequency of occurrence (F) was calculated for all species seen from 1976 through 1979. The species were then ranked by a composite figure computed by multiplying TI by F (proportion of 1.0).

Species diversity (H') was calculated using the Shannon formula (Shannon and Weaver 1948). The maximum species diversity (H'max) was also calculated for each sample as was evenness (J'= H'/H'max) (Pielou 1966). Foliage height diversity (FHD) was calculated using the same formula based on presence or absence of foliage at three levels (0 to 2 m., 2 to 5 m., 5+ m.) at 700 points.

The nesting pair densities were based on spot-mapping of singing males and located nests.

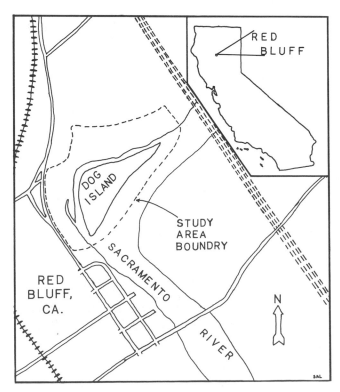

Figure 1.--Dog Island study area and environs.

Density was figured for a hypothetical km^2 of similar habitat. A similar method was used for winter populations but the numbers were based on an average of all censuses from December through mid-February. The migration numbers for selected species were obtained from individual-year census data. The total number of migrants was estimated based on a three-to-four day layover for building up fat stores during migration.[4]

RESULTS

A total of 147 species of birds were recorded during the censuses. The 98 species listed in table 1 occurred regularly. This table shows TI, F, Rank, and nesting, winter, and estimated migrant populations. The two forms of Yellow-rumped Warbler and Dark-eyed Junco are treated as separate taxa. Scientific names of the birds are not included to save space.

Species Diversity

Species diversity (H') is a concept which indicates both the richness and evenness of the members of a plant or animal community. It is mainly used to compare the diversity of one system or area to another.

Robert MacArthur (1972) used this formula to compare bird species diversity (BSD) with foliage height diversity (FHD) (MacArthur and MacArthur 1961). He found that FHD explained BSD better than plant species diversity or any other habitat parameter that he measured. This theory has been widely tested and has held in many cases (Balda 1975).

Table 1.--Frequency (F),[1] abundance (TI),[2] Rank,[3] and season bird densities.

SPECIES	F[1]	TI[2]	TIxF[3] RANK	Nesting density/km^2 76	77	78	79	Winter population/km^2 76-77	77-78	78-79	79-80	Spring migrants/km^2 76	77	78	79	80	Fall Migrant/km^2 76	77	78	79
Great Blue Heron	35.2	65	60					6	6	6	6									
Green Heron	67.0	171	35	+	+	+	+	6	11	6	6									
Mallard	29.1	158	46					–	11	+	17									
Wood Duck	45.6	255	34	6	6	6	6	–	6	6	11									
Turkey Vulture	52.2	147	41					+	+	6	6									
Sharp-shinned Hawk	6.0	12	89					+	+	–	–									
Cooper's Hawk	2.2	4	98					–	–	+	+									
Red-tailed Hawk	12.6	25	79					+	+	–	+									
Red-shouldered Hawk	34.1	76	57	6	6	6	6	–	+	6	6									
American Kestrel	11.5	22	78					+	–	+	–									
California Quail	78.6	1714	5	62	45	28	17	90	40	+	17									
Killdeer	37.9	107	50					6	+	6	6									
Spotted Sandpiper	22.5	48	67					+	6	+	6									
Band-tailed Pigeon	12.6	825	38					–	249	–	+									
Mourning Dove	25.3	68	64	6	6	6	6	–	–	+	–									
Great Horned Owl	4.4	9	92	+	+	+	+	+	+	+	+									
Black-chinned Hummingbird	18.7	50	68	–	6	6	6													
Anna's Hummingbird	94.5	541	21	17	11	11	11	23	17	11	11									
Rufous Hummingbird	11.0	35	77														102	–	124	96
Belted Kingfisher	96.2	234	29	6	6	6	6	6	6	6	11									
Common Flicker	63.2	652	23	11	–	–	–	28	51	40	51									
Acorn Woodpecker	56.6	188	37	11	11	6	6	6	11	+	+									
Lewis Woodpecker	7.7	22	84					–	+	–	–									
Red-breasted Sapsucker	24.7	66	65					6	11	6	6									
Downy Woodpecker	98.4	754	14	28	28	34	34	23	28	23	28									
Nuttall's Woodpecker	100.0	1119	9	34	40	45	45	45	45	28	45									
Western Kingbird	20.9	101	61									85	130	311	198	90				
Ash-throated Flycatcher	30.8	127	52	11	11	17	11													
Black Phoebe	83.5	353	28	–	–	11	11	6	11	11	23									
Willow Flycatcher	17.6	109	62									6	51	40	6	6	395	299	175	112
Hammond's-Dusky Flycatcher	2.7	5	95																	
Western Flycatcher	4.9	9	91																	
Western Wood Pewee	35.7	326	33	23	34	40	40													
Tree Swallow	44.5	777	25	40	34	28	11	6	+	6	+									
Rough-winged Swallow	13.2	60	70																	
Barn Swallow	2.7	7	94																	
Cliff Swallow	33.0	1875	17																	
Steller's Jay	12.1	73	69					–	28	–	–									
Scrub Jay	100.0	2111	3	28	40	51	51	62	90	62	90									
Yellow-billed Magpie	6.0	23	86					+	–	+	+									
Plain Titmouse	96.2	690	16	11	6	6	11	23	23	23	40									
Bushtit	91.8	3641	1	51	68	40	62	130	119	107	113									
White-breasted Nuthatch	95.1	551	20	11	11	11	11	23	23	17	28									
Red-breasted Nuthatch	7.7	18	86					–	–	–	+									
Brown Creeper	14.3	91	66					28	6	–	–									
House Wren	12.1	35	76	–	–	–	6													
Winter Wren	10.4	19	83					+	–	6	–									
Bewick's Wren	100.0	1848	4	73	62	62	57	45	62	34	45									

[4]Stewart, Bob. Point Reyes bird observatory, Stinson Beach, Calif. Personal communication.

Table 1.--Frequency (F),[1] abundance (TI),[2] Rank,[3] and season bird densities (continued).

SPECIES	F	TI	TIxF RANK	Nesting density/km² 76	77	78	79	Winter population/km² 76-77	77-78	78-79	79-80	Spring migrants/km² 76	77	78	79	80	Fall migrants/km² 76	77	78	79
Mockingbird	41.2	106	47					6	6	6	6									
American Robin	92.9	1031	11	11	17	17	34	6	45	51	130									
Varied Thrush	16.5	154	58					−	57	+	+						56	209	23	158
Hermit Thrush	48.9	356	32					11	28	17	40									
Swainson's Thrush	4.4	15	89									−	79	34	−	6				
Golden-crowned Kinglet	20.9	228	45					17	11	34	−						316	169	972	6
Ruby-crowned Kinglet	57.7	2177	7					90	164	124	113						2836	2362	2582	2028
Water Pipit	6.6	88	72					−	−	+	6									
Cedar Waxwing	54.4	4942	2					11	109	90	40									
Starling	94.0	770	15	23	23	17	17	34	34	17	23									
Hutton's Vireo	15.4	37	73					6	+	6	+									
Solitary Vireo	8.2	21	84									23	23	28	45	6				
Black and White Warbler	3.3	6	93																	
Orange-crowned Warbler	80.2	1452	8					17	34	45	28	661	819	582	373	305	1277	2520	1983	1757
Nashville Warbler	25.8	113	55									34	169	153	56	11	192	254	147	102
Yellow Warbler	40.1	958	24	−	−	11	6					136	537	266	181	107	1514	3667	1780	2328
Audubon's Warbler	58.2	1596	12					40	23	45	79	1271	2412	2239	2785	2288	1141	1763	3503	1814
Myrtle Warbler	37.4	193	43					+	6	6	+	254	203	299	34	23	147	198	322	164
Black-throated Gray Warbler	14.8	52	71									6	34	69	−	6	164	68	130	11
Townsend's Warbler	5.5	14	88									40	40	40	−	−				
Hermit Warbler	2.7	5	95									6	11	11	−	−				
MacGillivray's Warbler	28.0	155	48									79	85	113	119	17	294	429	311	232
Common Yellowthroat	20.9	84	63									169	113	45	147	45	102	130	56	51
Yellow-breasted Chat	28.0	140	51	17	23	17	17													
Wilson's Warbler	33.0	634	30									1056	2356	972	1051	571	220	695	322	288
House Sparrow	6.6	35	81																	
Western Meadowlark	6.0	81	74					62	6	+	−									
Red-winged Blackbird	7.7	57	75	−	73	−	−	−	−	+	−									
Northern Oriole	44.5	732	27	17	40	62	51	−	−	+	−									
Brewer's Blackbird	31.9	110	54																	
Brown-headed Cowbird	35.2	280	39	28	17	17	17													
Western Tanager	35.7	320	36									164	469	322	266	186	684	520	395	633
Black-headed Grosbeak	44.0	1360	18	149	141	164	136													
Lazuli Bunting	9.3	24	82	−	6	−	−					6	51	6	23	−				
Evening Grosbeak	11.0	218	59					−	57	−	−									
Purple Finch	8.2	41	78					6	−	−	−	−	356	113	−	740				
House Finch	46.7	156	42	−	−	6	11	6	+	6	+									
Pine Siskin	11.0	372	49					−	57	−	−									
American Goldfinch	73.6	1814	6	17	17	11	−	57	74	55	170									
Lesser Goldfinch	73.1	632	22	−	11	−	6	28	17	34	57									
Rufous-sided Towhee	100.0	973	10	17	28	23	28	28	57	23	45									
Brown Towhee	99.5	822	13	28	34	28	17	23	34	17	23									
Slate-colored Junco	2.2	5	97					−	+	+	−									
Oregon Junco	26.4	78	31					96	74	124	153									
White-crowned Sparrow	56.6	1034	19					23	11	107	23									
Golden-crowned Sparrow	39.0	249	40					6	23	6	6									
Fox Sparrow	31.9	88	56					6	17	6	6									
Lincoln's Sparrow	32.4	166	44					6	+	+	+	299	599	102	220	51	56	90	119	124
Song Sparrow	54.4	624	26					34	51	34	51									
Warbling Vireo	24.7	158	53									232	463	328	277	328	11	68	107	102
TOTAL				740	859	791	751	1198	1932	1311	1640									

Species diversity of the nesting pairs on the study area was figured for each year, 1976 through 1979 (table 2). The average for the four years was 3.00 and the FHD was 1.08. All nesting BSD figures were higher than predicted using MacArthur's graph. This is not at all surprising since the study area was 17.7 ha., as compared to 2-ha. areas used by MacArthur (1972). A larger area will generally have more species nesting, and therefore will have a larger BSD. A sample of three 2-ha. plots was chosen from the 1979 nesting census data. BSD figures of 2.05, 2.40, and 2.70 were calculated for those plots. The latter two figures fit into MacArthur's linear regression, but the first figure falls well below any of his results. It is possible that the FHD was not the same for these small plots as for the whole study area.

Comparison of BSD at different seasons is also possible. When comparing the nesting and wintering population BSD, the wintering BSD was considerably higher, but shows less evenness. This is misleading due to the averaging of 6-12 census dates to obtain the wintering population figures. In order to make valid comparisons between winter and nesting populations, I chose two winter and two summer census weeks and again obtained a higher BSD on the winter samples. This was due mainly to a higher number of species, since the evenness was very similar (table 2).

BSD's for spring and fall census weeks were also calculated. A great deal of difference from week to week for both BSD and evenness was obtained. Overall, summer had the lowest BSD and spring, the highest. This is not surprising

Table 2.--Bird species diversity (BSD).

Year	n	BSD	Max. BSD	Evenness
Nesting bird populations				
1976	27	2.91	3.30	.88
1977	30	3.15	3.40	.93
1978	30	3.95	3.40	.87
1979	31	3.00	3.43	.87
Winter bird populations				
1976-77	55	3.44	4.01	.86
1977-78	68	3.63	4.22	.86
1978-79	69	3.59	4.23	.85
1979-80	62	3.50	4.13	.85

Week	n	BSD	Max. BSD	Evenness
Winter				
52	54	3.17	3.99	.79
3	58	3.42	4.06	.84
Summer				
23	48	3.04	3.87	.79
26	38	3.01	3.64	.83
Spring				
16	77	3.73	4.34	.86
19	77	3.17	4.34	.73
Fall				
33	50	3.38	3.91	.86
37	56	3.13	4.03	.78
42	60	3.09	4.09	.75

since the spring census weeks had the highest number of species and the summer census weeks had the lowest (table 2). When comparing weeks 16 (16-22 April) and 19 (7-13 May), the BSD was much lower during week 19 even though the species total was the same due to the large influx of Cedar Waxwings. Increased numbers of one species will always decrease the BSD.

Seasonal Changes

Figure 2 shows the changes in numbers of birds and in the total and average numbers of species from week to week, averaged over the combined 5-year period of study. The total number of species is a summation of all species found during each week for the five years of the study. The averge number of species is the average number recorded on all censuses during each week over the 5-year period. The peaks and dips in the three lines do not occur in the same places.

Total number of species (species) and average number of individuals (individuals) held relativey constant from the beginning of the year through week 5 (29 Jan.-4 Feb.). In week 6 (5-11 Feb.) and 7 (12-18 Feb.) individuals dropped while species held steady. The drop in individuals was due to a reduction in Band-tailed Pigeons in 1978. During week 8 (19-25 Feb.) individuals began to climb, reaching a peak on week 10 (5-11 Mar.). This peak was due to large increases in swallows, Audubon's Warblers, and American Goldfinches.

Species began to swing upward on week 9 (26 Feb.-4 Mar.) and rose to a peak on weeks 15 to 17 (9-29 Apr.) as spring migration was in full swing. Species dropped from weeks 17 (23-29 Apr.) through 24 (11-17 June) as the wintering species left and migrants passed through, leaving only the summer residents.

On the other hand, individuals dropped from week 10 (5-11 Mar.) through week 14 (2-8 Apr.) as the numerous Band-tailed Pigeons, Audubon's Warblers, and American Goldfinches left the area. Individuals then rose again through week 18 (30 Apr.-6 May) with migrant Cedar Waxwings, Wilson's Warblers, and Black-headed Grosbeaks making large increases. Individuals declined steadily through week 24 (11-17 June) as the migrants and winter residents left.

On week 26 (25 June-1 July) both individuals and species began to rise due to the fledging of young and influx of the first fall migrants. On week 28 (9-15 July), with species still rising, individuals began to fall as the swallows left. Individual continued to fall through week 33 (13-19 Aug.) as the common summer residents (Western Wood Pewee, Northern Oriole, and Black-headed Grosbeak) left. At the same time, species continued to rise as early migrants moved through.

Species peaked from weeks 35 to 37 (27 Aug.-16 Sept.) and then again on week 43 (22-28 Oct.) as the early and late waves of migrants passed

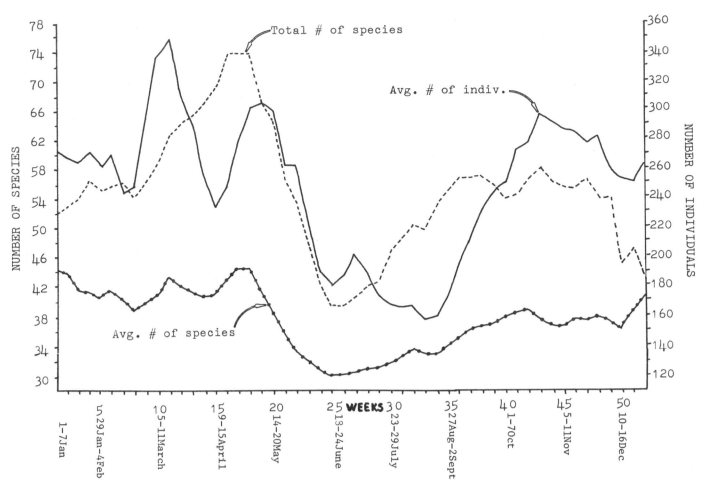

Figure 2.--Variations in numbers of species and individuals
(three-week running average) for 1975 through 1979.

through. Individuals began to rise on week 34
(20-26 Aug.) and continued to go up until a peak
on week 43 (22-28 Oct.) was reached. This was
caused first by large numbers of Orange-crowned
Warbler and Yellow Warbler, and later by an influx of Ruby-crowned Kinglet, Cedar Waxwing, and
Audubon's Warbler. Individuals and species then
dropped gradually to week 50 (10-16 Dec.).

The difference between the average number of
species and total number of species was greatest
during migration, and smallest during winter and
summer. This was caused by a greater chance of
rarities during migration, and differences in
migration timing from year to year. An average
of not more that 45 species was found on any
week, but the chances of new species occurring on
censuses during that week in succeeding years
were greatest during migration.

Nesting Season

The lowland riparian nesting avifauna in
central California is quite rich. A total of 83
species have been documented as nesting in the
riparian areas of the Sacramento Valley in the
past 100 years. Five species (Common Merganser,
Spotted Sandpiper, Western Wood Pewee, Starling,
and Brown-headed Cowbird) have colonized the
area; and 11 species (Double-crested Cormorant,
Cooper's Hawk, Bald Eagle, Long-eared Owl, Willow
Flycatcher, Western Flycatcher, Purple Martin,
Swainson's Thrush, Blue-gray Gnatcatcher, Bell's
Vireo) have become either very rare or extirpated
during that time (Gaines 1974).

Of these 83 species, 35 were found breeding
on Dog Island during the study interval. An
average of 29.5 species nested each year (range
27 to 31). Twenty-five species nested in all
four years, two nested in three years, four
nested in two years, and four nested once. Of
the 10 species not found every year, five (Black-

chinned Hummingbird, Black Phoebe, House Wren, Yellow Warbler, and House Finch) colonized the area during the study. Two species (Common Flicker and American Goldfinch) became extinct as nesting species, and three species (Red-winged Blackbird, Lazuli Bunting, and Lesser Goldfinch) both colonized and became extinct as nesting species during the study.

The most abundant nesting species were the Black-headed Grosbeak, Bewick's Wren, and Bush-tit. The total number of nesting birds averaged 139 pairs in 1977. In most cases, the numbers of nesting pairs of each species varied little from year to year. Notable exceptions were California Quail and Tree Swallow which declined; and Western Wood Pewee, Scrub Jay, American Robin, and Northern Oriole, which increased.

The origin of the nesting pairs was 50% residents, 13% short-distance migrants, and 37% long-distance migrants. The origin of the 35 nesting species was 44% residents, 28% short-distance migrants, and 28% long-distance migrants. Of the unstable species (i.e., those colonizing or becoming extinct), four were long-distance migrants. Only the Black Phoebe was a resident. This indicates a very unstable situation for migrants, with 45% colonizing or becoming extinct in four years.

Nesting guilds were devised on the basis of the type of nesting situation used. The avian community nesting guild composition is presented in table 3. The proportion nesting on the ground was quite low, considering the dense groundcover. This was not surprising however, since ground nesting is dangerous (Skutch 1976). The proportion of tree-hole nesters was high. This was undoubtedly a result of the large number of snags and decadent trees on the plot. These provided sites for woodpeckers to excavate their homes which in turn provided homes for the secondary cavity nesters. Many of the live trees also had natural cavities from broken-off limbs.

Spring and Fall Migration

Each year gave a different overall impression of migration. Much of this impression came from the presence or absence of irruptive species, but much also came from the actual timing and numbers of migrants.

To gain some insight into the spring migration differences over the years, I used two criteria: 1) migration timing; and 2) actual

Table 3.--Avian community nesting guilds on Dog Island, 1975-79.

Guild	% of pairs	% of species
trees	52	40
holes in trees	29	34
shrubs	9	14
ground	9	6
banks	2	6

numbers. The species accounts (Laymon 1981) and estimated spring migrant numbers (table 1) were examined for six categories: 1) record high totals; 2) record low totals; 3) record early arrival date; 4) record late arrival date; 5) record early departure date; and 6) record late departure date. The number of species that set records in any category in any year was recorded (table 4). From a birdwatcher's standpoint, 1977 was clearly the "best", since more species arrived earlier, left later, and set records for numbers. Just as clearly, 1980 was the "worst" spring, with more species arriving later, leaving earlier, and setting record low numbers. The three years 1976 through 1979 all had many early and three late departure dates, indicating a mixed situation.

Fall migration was analysed in the same manner (table 4). Late and early arrival and departure dates seemed to have little relation to the general timing of migration in fall. This was because fall migration is a much more relaxed affair. Migration timing is much less precise than in the spring. As a result, very little pattern was revealed in this portion of the analysis except that 1979 had the most early arrivals and the fewest late arrivals, and 1976 was just the reverse. The record high and low numbers revealed that 1977 had the most highs and no lows, 1976 and 1979 had the least highs and the most lows.

Winter Populations

Winter populations varied from one year to the next, much more so than breeding populations. The difference between the highest and lowest breeding years was only 14%, while the difference between the highest and lowest wintering populations was 38%. The higher totals in 1977-78 were caused almost exclusively by irruptive species such as Band-tailed Pigeon, Steller's Jay, Varied Thrush, Cedar Waxwing, Evening Grosbeak, and Pine Siskin.

Table 4.--Number of species per year with record early and late migration dates and record high and low numbers.

Year	Arrival Early	Late	Departure Early	Late	Record numbers High	Low
			Spring			
1976	4	1	3	3	1	2
1977	6	3	1	6	7	0
1978	6	0	1	1	3	2
1979	4	1	3	3	3	1
1980	2	6	6	1	1	9
			Fall			
1976	5	9	4	4	4	7
1977	4	7	2	0	7	0
1978	6	6	3	5	5	2
1979	9	3	2	2	1	5

Examination of a sample of 25 regularly occurring, non-irruptive species revealed that the winter of 1979-80 actually had the highest wintering population, with an average of 229 individuals per survey. The winter of 1976-77 had 160 individuals, 1977-78 had 198 and 1978-79 had 178 individuals per survey. This was still a 30% difference between the highest and lowest years. Variations in food supply, temperature, rainfall, and floodwaters must have been responsible for some of the variation in bird numbers. Much may also have been caused by nesting success and food supply on the breeding grounds.

DISCUSSION

Yearly Changes in Numbers and Migration Timing

Numbers of migrants, both individuals and species, varied greatly from year to year. The cause of these changes was not readily evident. In some cases, the immediate weather patterns, such as rain or wind, probably grounded many migrants or kept them from leaving an area. In other cases, long-range weather patterns such as a drought, late snows, or a long, severe cold spell probably changed migration patterns. In 1977, many more than average numbers of migrants were found at Dog Island. This was a drought year in which little winter rain and no spring rain fell. It was likely that the spring migrants avoided the foothills which were parched by mid-March, and depended heavily on the lowland riparian forest for a refueling stop. It was also likely that the heavy fall migration that year was caused by the mountain springs and meadows being dry by late summer. The abundant food in the lowland riparian zone seems to be especially important to migrants during drought years.

Another factor leading to changes in numbers of migrants from year to year is nesting and wintering success. The number of birds passing north in the spring is the number which survived the winter. Winter, not breeding season, has been suggested as the season which limits bird population numbers in the temperate zone (Fretwell 1972). It is possible that destruction of riparian woodland to the south and the removal of vast areas of tropical forest may limit nesting and migrant populations here in the future. Removal of riparian woodland here may now be limiting nesting populations to the north. The birds migrating south in the fall are the sum of the surviving adults which went north to breed plus their offspring. In years of good nesting success, the number of migrants could be much higher that in poor years.

Effects of Brown-headed Cowbirds

Brown-headed Cowbirds are a recent immigrant to the Sacramento Valley of California. This bird is a parasitic species which lays its eggs in other birds' nests. The host species then incubates the eggs and raises the young, leaving the cowbird free to look for additional nests and food. The arrival of the cowbird has had a drastic effect on the native avifauna throughout California, particularly in lowland riparian systems adjacent to agricultural areas (Gaines 1974).

Had this study been done prior to the arrival of the Brown-headed Cowbird, a remarkably different avian community would probably have been present. Certain species such as the Willow Flycatcher, Western Flycatcher, Swainson's Thrush, Blue-gray Gnatcatcher, Bell's Vireo, and Warbling Vireo nested in the lowland riparian areas. None of these are now known to nest anywhere in lowland interior California. Other species such as the Yellow-billed Cuckoo, Yellow Warbler, Common Yellowthroat, and Song Sparrow still nest in the Sacramento Valley, but are now found in reduced numbers. With the exception of the Yellow-billed Cuckoo, Western Flycatcher, and Swainson's Thrush, all of the species in both groups are considered to have high to very high susceptibility to cowbird parasitism (Gaines 1974). Evidence implicating the Brown-headed Cowbird in the decline of these species is only circumstantial, since no studies were conducted during the 1940's and 1950's as the decline was occurring. However, no other theory presently explains the decline.

Of all the species which have declined or were extirpated, only the Yellow Warbler nested in the study area during the study. I believe that numbers of nesting individuals, numbers of nesting species, and species diversity were much lower in the study area due to cowbird parasitism. The species which have maintained high populations are either hole-nesters, species which reject cowbird eggs (Rothstein 1971), or species such as the Black-headed Grosbeak, which are large enough to raise a cowbird young along with their own. The small open-cup nesting species which accept cowbird eggs have all declined or disappeared completely.

Effects of the Habitat Island Nature of the Study Area

The study area is an island of riparian vegetation in a sea of farmland, oak woodland, and a river. The theories of island biogeography were developed by studying oceanic islands. These systems have higher extinction rates, lower species diversity, and fewer species than a comparable area of mainland (Diamond 1969). Distinction has been made between oceanic and habitat islands (MacArthur 1972). Habitat islands do not have as marked an effect on avian community structure, but the effect is still evident (Vuilleumier 1970).

Extinctions and colonizations of 10 nesting bird species were recorded in the four summers of the study. This represented almost a third of the nesting species, and seems like a high rate of turnover. BSD figures were at or below the predicted values using MacArthur's FHD linear regression. Both of these findings may be related to the habitat island situation.

As more and more habitat islands are created by conversion of riparian forest to other uses, this study area will become more representative of the valley forests. If the islands are large enough, the effect will not be disastrous since the migrant riparian species in the West have been accustomed to travelling over hundreds of kilometers of desert to nest along the streams. Resident species may not fare as well, and none will fare well if the islands are too small.

An additional topic to consider regarding habitat islands is the concentration of migrants on these islands. This concentration has been documented in desert oases and on coastal islands such as the Farallons on the central California coast. It is very likely that the study area drew a much greater number of migrants because it was surrounded by miles of inhospitable habitat for forest birds than it would if a similar 18-ha. plot was found within a much more extensive stand of forest.

Values of Riparian Systems

The value of a vegetation-type can be measured in a number of ways. Some of the most common methods are bird densities, species richness, and the number of species unique to the system. These figures can be compared from system to system and a relative importance can be derived. Using American Birds breeding bird census and winter bird population studies for 1979 and 1980 I compiled table 5 which compares Dog Island results with other riparian areas and other vegetation-types in the West. No figures for migrant densities are available in the literature, so no comparisons were made.

Table 5.--A comparison of Dog Island breeding and wintering densities with other western vegetation-types.

Vegetation-type	Birds/km^2	Number of species	Sample size
Breeding bird densities			
Dog Island	785	29.5	4
Other riparian	1033	28.6	14
Chaparral	420	19.7	7
Oak woodland	416	17.4	5
Mixed forest	345	16.6	7
Desert scrub	87	6.0	4
Winter bird densities			
Dog Island	1521	63.5	4
Other riparian	1601	26.9	8
Chaparral	640	21.0	1
Oak woodland	650	21.0	2
Mixed forest	228	15.6	3
Pine forest	181	12.0	3
Desert scrub	167	9.6	8

Breeding bird densities were 24% lower at Dog Island than at 14 other riparian sites, while the number of species was slightly higher. When compared to other vegetation-types, however, the Dog Island figures were much higher, with bird densities ranging from 47% higher than chaparral to 89% higher that desert scrub. All other vegetation-types also had fewer species, ranging from 33% less in chaparral to 80% less in desert scrub. The Dog Island winter density figures are comparable to other riparian sites (5% less) and range from 57% higher than oak woodland to 89% higher than desert scrub. Winter bird species numbers were 58% higher than other riparian sites, 67% highr than oak woodland, and 85% higher that desert scrub. None of these other vegetation-types even begin to approach the riparian sites in either density or species richness.

The third category, number of species unique to the vegetation-type, is a harder one to compare. Little information has been gathered on densities of the same species in different vegetation-types, so habitat preferences are usually a matter of subjective judgment. Twenty of the regularly occurring species: Wood Duck, Common Merganser, Red-shouldered Hawk, Spotted Sandpiper, Downy Woodpecker, Black Phoebe, Willow Flycatcher, Tree Swallow, House Wren, Swainson's Thrush, Ruby-crowned Kinglet, Warbling Vireo, Yellow Warbler, Yellow-breasted Chat, Wilson's Warbler, Lazuli Bunting, Black-headed Grosbeak, American Goldfinch, Lincoln's Sparrow, and Song Sparrow are believed to have their highest densities in riparian systems. Of this group, Wood Duck, Red-shouldered Hawk, Willow Flycatcher, Swainson's Thrush, Yellow Warbler, Yellow-breasted Chat, Wilson's Warbler, and American Goldfinch are rarely found away from this vegetation-type. Is is doubtful that other vegetation-types in the West could match these figures.

In this study we have seen that a great many individuals of a great many species of birds use the Dog Island riparian system. This 17.7-ha. plot receives a great deal of avian use throughout the year. It is vital to the nesting, migrating, and wintering success of numerous individuals of many species. When viewed on a larger scale, the riparian systems of the West are vital to the maintenance of many populations, subspecies (Blue Grosbeak, Red-shouldered Hawk, and Yellow-billed Cuckoo), and, in a few cases, species of birds (Willow Flycatcher and Bell's Vireo). These systems have a high species diversity throughout the year. They are an essential link for long-distance migrants from the north and are an important wintering ground for many species.

LITERATURE CITED

Anderson, B.W., and R.D. Ohmart. 1977. Vegetation structure and bird use in the lower Colorado Valley. p. 23-24. In: R.R. Johnson and D.A. Jones (tech. coord.). Importance, preservation and management of riparian habitat: a symposium. [Tuscon, Ariz., July 9, 1977]. USDA Forest Service GTR-RM-43. 217 p. Rocky Mountain Forest and Range Experiment Station, Fort Collins Colo.

Balda, R.P. 1975. Vegetation structure and breeding bird diversity. p. 59-80. In: D.R. Smith (tech. coord.). Management of forest and range habitats for nongame birds: Proceedings of the symposium. [Tuscon, Ariz., May 6-9, 1975]. USDA Forest Service GTR-WO-1. 343 p. USDA Forest Service, Washington, D.C.

Brumley, T.D. 1976. Upper Butte Basin study 1974-75. Wildlife Management Branch administrative report 76-1. The Resources Agency, Department of Fish and Game, Sacramento, Calif.

Chase, T. Jr, and P. DeBenedictis. 1964. Middle Pacific Coast region report. Audubon Field Notes 19:71.

Dembosz, D., K. Ficket, and T. Manolis. 1972. Disturbed floodplain woodland. Amer. Birds 26:978-979.

Diamond, J.M. 1969. Avifaunal equilibria and species turnover rates on the Channel Islands of California. Nat. Acad. Sci., Proc. 64:57-63.

Fretwell, S.D. 1972. Populations in a seasonal environment. Princeton University Press, Princeton, N.J.

Gaines, D. 1973. Floodplain riparian woodland. Amer. Birds 27:995.

Gaines, D.A. 1974. A new look at the nesting riparian avifauna of the Sacramento Valley, California. Western Birds 5:61-80.

Gaines, D.A. 1977. The valley riparian forests of California: their importance to bird populations. p. 57-85. In: A. Sands (ed.). Riparian forests in California: Their ecology and conservation. Institute of Ecology Pub. 15. University of California, Davis. 122 p.

Grinnel, J., J. Dixon, and J.M. Linsdale. 1930. Vertebrate natural history of a section of Northern California through the Lassen Peak region. University of California Publ. in Zool. 35(1).

Hehnke, M., and C.P. Stone. 1978. Values of riparian vegetation to avian populations along the Sacramento River system. p. 228-235. In: R.R. Johnson and J.F. McCormick (tech. coord.). Strategies for protection and management of floodplain wetlands and other riparian ecosystems: Proceedings of the symposium. [Callaway Gardens, Ga., December 11-13, 1978]. USDI Forest Service GTR-WO-12. 410 p. Washington, D.C.

Hurst, E., M. Hehnke, and C.C. Goude. 1980. The destruction of riparian vegetation and its impact on the avian wildlife in the Sacramento River Valley, California. Amer. Birds 34:8-12.

Ingles, L. 1950. Nesting birds of the willow-cottonwood community in California. Auk 67:325-332.

Kendeigh, S.C. 1944. Measurement of bird populations. Ecol. Monogr. 14:67-106.

Laymon, S.A. 1981. Avifauna of an island of lowland riparian woodland: Dog Island City Park, Red Bluff, California. Unpublished masters thesis, California State University, Chico.

Laymon, Stephen A. 1983. Photodocumentation of vegetation and landform change on a riparian site, 1880-1980: Dog Island, Red Bluff, California. In: R.E. Warner and K.M. Hendrix (ed.). California Riparian Systems. [University of California, Davis, September 17-19, 1981]. University of California Press, Berkeley.

MacArthur, R.H. 1972. Geographical ecology. Harper and Row, Inc. New York, New York.

MacArthur, R.H.; and J.W. MacArthur. 1961. On bird species diversity. Ecology 42:594-598.

Manolis, T. 1973. Disturbed floodplain woodland. Amer. Birds 27:994-995.

Michny, F.J., D. Boos, and F. Wernette. 1975. Riparian habitats and avian densities along the Sacramento River. The Resources Agency, Department of Fish and Game, Wildlife Management Branch administrative report 75-1.

Pielou, E.C. 1966. Species diversity and pattern diversity in the study of ecological succession. J. Theoret. Biol. 10:370-383.

Root, R.B. 1967. The niche exploitation pattern of the Blue-gray Gnatcatcher. Ecol. Monogr. 37:317-350.

Rothstein, S.I. 1971. Observation and experiment in the analysis of interactions between brood parasites and their hosts. Amer. Natur. 105:71-74.

Shannon, C.E., and W. Weaver. 1948. The mathematical theory of communication. University of Illinois Press. Urbana, Ill.

Shuford, D. 1973. Disturbed riparian stream border. Amer. Birds 27:1005.

Skutch, A.F. 1976. Parent birds and their young. University of Texas Press. Austin, Texas.

Small, A. 1974. The birds of California. Winchester Press. New York, New York.

Tangren, G. 1971. Riparian oak woodland. Amer. Birds 25:967-969.

Tangren, G. 1972. Riparian oak woodland. Amer. Birds 26:977-978.

Vuilleumier, F. 1970. Insular biogeography in continental regions. The northern Andes of South America. Amer. Nat. 104:373-388.

Winkler, D. 1973a. Riparian oak woodland. Amer. Birds 27:689.

Winkler, D. 1973b. Riparian oak woodland. Amer. Birds 27:996.

AVIAN USE OF MARSHES ON THE LOWER COLORADO RIVER[1]

Bertin W. Anderson, Robert D. Ohmart, Julie K. Meents,

and William C. Hunter[2]

Abstract.--Vegetation composition and structure was used in designating eight types of marshes along the lower Colorado River. Marsh-types that had high densities of cat-tail (Typha latifolia) and bulrush (Scirpus acutus), supported more wading birds (including Yuma Clapper Rail [Rallus longirostris yumanensis]) and insectivores. Waterbirds and shorebirds favored more open marsh situations. The interface between marsh and terrestrial riparian habitat was more important to terrestrial birds than to marsh birds.

INTRODUCTION

Marshes are an important component of wild-life habitat in riparian systems. In the lower Colorado River valley, marshes frequently occur adjacent to terrestrial and aquatic habitats and may support avian species characteristic of both habitats, such as the endangered Yuma Clapper Rail (Rallus longirostris yumanensis), which occurs primarily in marsh vegetation.

In the lower Colorado River valley, marshes differ in vegetation composition and structure; these differences are reflected in the avian species which inhabit them. In this paper, we describe the different types of marshes and their dominant vegetation characteristics. Marsh use by granivores (GR), shorebirds (SB), insectivores (I), waterbirds (WB), and wading birds (WA) is evaluated by marsh-type and by season.

METHODS

A total of 30 transects was established in representative marsh vegetation along the Colorado River between Davis Dam, Arizona/Nevada border and the United States/Mexico International Boundary (fig. 1). Each transect was censused three times per month between May 1976 and July 1978, using a modified variable transect method

[1] Paper presented at the California Riparian Systems Conference. [University of California, Davis, September 17-19, 1981].

[2] Bertin W. Anderson is Faculty Research Associate; Robert D. Ohmart is Associate Director; Julie K. Meents is Research Biologist; William C. Hunter is Field Biologist; all are at the Center for Environmental Studies, Arizona State University, Tempe, Arizona.

(Emlen 1971; Anderson and Ohmart 1977). Results of all censuses on a transect in a particular season were averaged to obtain seasonal densities. Seasons, designated to coincide with changes in avian population, included winter (December-February), spring (March-April), summer (May-July), late summer (August-September), and fall (October-November). Bird species found in marshes were combined into groups or guilds on the basis of similarity in feeding behavior and general habitat use (table 1).

Foliage height diversity (FHD) and foliage density were measured by the method of MacArthur and MacArthur (1961). Percent dominance of each plant species was evaluated by determining the number of times each species was included in foliage density measurements. Principal components analysis (PCA) (Nie et al.) was used to determine which vegetation variables were highly intercorrelated; the PCA also provided a series of new, noncorrelated variables based on the original data. Each transect was given a score representing its relative position on the continuum represented by each of these derived variables. These scores were used in grouping transects into general marsh-types.

RESULTS AND DISCUSSION

Vegetation

The PCA indicated that several of the vegetation variables measured were highly correlated. Cat-tail (Typha latifolia) and bulrush (Scirpus acutus) tended to occur together, but neither coexisted with phragmites (Phragmites australis). These three variables were combined into a derived variable; the relative amounts of these plant species are represented by the score of each transect (Fig. 2). On the

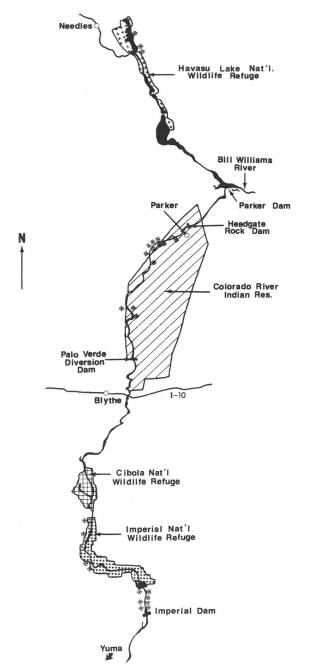

Figure 1.—Map of marsh transects along the lower
Colorado River. ⊚ indicates locations of
transects.

first principal component or derived variable,
positive scores indicate increasing amounts of
cat-tail or bulrush; negative scores indicate
increasing amounts of phragmites. Structural
differences, derived from FHD measurements, indicated that cat-tail/bulrush tends to be short
(below 1.5-m. height) and dense, whereas phragmites is taller (above 1.5-m. height) and more
spatially heterogeneous.

Table 1.—Species composing guilds.

Common name	Scientific name
Wading birds	
Great Blue Heron	Ardea herodias
Green Heron	Butorides striatus
Great Egret	Casmerodius albus
Snowy Egret	Egretta thula
Black-crowned Night Heron	Nycticorax nycticorax
Least Bittern	Ixobrychus exilis
White-faced Ibis	Plegadis chihi
Roseate Spoonbill	Ajaia ajaja
Sandhill Crane	Grus canadensis
Clapper Rail	Rallus longirostris
Virginia Rail	Rallus limicola
Sora	Porzana carolina
Black Rail	Laterallus jamaicensis
Common Gallinule	Gallinula chloropus
Common Snipe	Capella gallinago
Waterbirds	
Common Loon	Gavia immer
Eared Grebe	Podiceps nigricollis
Western Grebe	Aechmophorus occidentalis
Pied-billed Grebe	Podilymbus podiceps
Brown Pelican	Pelecanus occidentalis
White Pelican	Pelecanus erythrorhynchos
Double-crested Cormorant	Phalacrocorax auritus
Canada Goose	Branta canadensis
Snow Goose	Chen caerulescens
Mallard	Anas platyrhynchos
Gadwall	Anas strepera
Pintail	Anas acuta
Green-winged Teal	Anas crecca carolinensis
Blue-winged Teal	Anas discors
Cinnamon Teal	Anas cyanoptera
American Widgeon	Anas americana
Northern Shoveler	Anas clypeata
Wood Duck	Aix sponsa
Redhead	Aythya americana
Ring-necked Duck	Aythya collaris
Canvasback	Aythya valisineria
Greater Scaup	Aythya marila
Lesser Scaup	Aythya affinis
Common Goldeneye	Bucephala clangula
Bufflehead	Bucephala albeola
Ruddy Duck	Oxyura jamaicensis
Hooded Merganser	Mergus cucullatus
Common Merganser	Mergus merganser
Red-breasted Merganser	Mergus serrator
American Coot	Fulica americana
Herring Gull	Larus argentatus
California Gull	Larus californicus
Ring-billed Gull	Larus delawarensis
Bonaparte Gull	Larus philadelphia
Shorebirds	
Semipalmated Plover	Charadrius semipalmatus
Snowy Plover	Charadrius alexandrinus
Killdeer	Charadrius vociferus
Black-bellied Plover	Mniotilta varia
Long-billed Curlew	Numenius americanus

Table 1.--Continued.

Common name	Scientific name
Whimbrel	Numenius phaeopus
Spotted Sandpiper	Actitis macularia
Solitary Sandpiper	Tringa solitaria
Willet	Catoptrophorus semipalmatus
Greater Yellowlegs	Tringa melanoleuca
Lesser Yellowlegs	Tringa flavipes
Pectoral Sandpiper	Calidris melanotos
Baird Sandpiper	Calidris bairdii
Least Sandpiper	Calidris minutilla
Dunlin	Calidris alpina
Western Sandpiper	Calidris mauri
Sanderling	Calidris alba
Long-billed Dowitcher	Limnodromus scolopaceus
Marbled Godwit	Limosa fedoa
American Avocet	Recurvirostra americana
Black-necked Stilt	Himantopus mexicanus mexicanus
Wilson Phalarope	Steganopus tricolor
Northern Phalarope	Lobipes lobatus

Permanent Resident Insectivores

Belted Kingfisher	Megaceryle alcyon
Verdin	Auriparus flaviceps
Bewick Wren	Thryomanes bewickii
Yellow-headed Blackbird	Xanthocephalus xanthocephalus
Red-winged Blackbird	Agelaius phoeniceus
Great-tailed Grackle	Quiscalus mexicanus
Abert Towhee	Pipilo aberti
Song Sparrow	Melospiza melodia

Visiting Insectivores

Marsh Hawk	Circus cyaneus
Forster Tern	Sterna forsteri
Common Tern	Sterna hirundo
Caspian Tern	Sterna caspia
Black Tern	Chlidonias niger
Ash-throated Flycatcher	Myiarchus cinerascens
Black Phoebe	Sayornis nigricans
House Wren	Troglodytes aedon
Long-billed Marsh Wren	Cistothorus palustris
Ruby-crowned Kinglet	Regulus calendula
Water Pipit	Anthus spinoletta
Orange-crowned Warbler	Vermivora celata
Yellow-rumped Warbler	Dendroica coronata
Common Yellowthroat	Geothlypis trichas

Granivores

Brown-headed Cowbird	Molothrus ater
American Goldfinch	Carduelis tristis
Rufous-sided Towhee	Pipilo erythrophthalmus
White-crowned Sparrow	Zonotrichia leucophrys
Lincoln Sparrow	Melospiza lincolnii

The PCA also showed that trees (mostly salt cedar [Tamarix chinensis]) and grasses tend to occur together. A transect's score on this derived variable reflects its measured density of trees and grasses (fig. 3). A negative score indicates few or no trees and grasses and a positive score indicates above-average amounts of trees and grasses.

Marsh-Type

The relative scores of the transects on these two derived variable suggested that there were basically six types of marshes on the lower Colorado River. Two additional marsh-types, an open (water) marsh and a geographically isolated marsh, were compared with the original six types. The types were:

Type I--nearly 100% cat-tail/bulrush, small amounts of phragmites and open water;
Type II--nearly 75% cat-tail/bulrush, many trees and grasses interspersed;
Type III--about 25-50% cat-tail/bulrush, some phragmites, open water, some trees and grass;
Type IV--about 35-50% cat-tail/bulrush, many trees and grasses interspersed;
Type V--about 50-75% cat-tail/bulrush, few trees and grasses interspersed;
Type VI--nearly 100% phragmites, little open water;
Type VII--open marsh (75% water), adjacent to sparse marsh vegetation; includes sandbars and mudflats when Colorado River is low; and
Type VIII--Topock Marsh near Needles, California; vegetatively similar to Type I, but with even denser stands of bulrushes. This marsh-type was kept separate for purposes of analysis as it was censused for only five months and is geographically isolated from the rest of the study area.

Avian Occurrence in Marshes

Granivores

Highest densities of granivores occurred in most marsh-types during fall, winter, and spring (table 2). Occurrence of granivores in marshes was related to the occurrence of trees and grasses. Marsh-type II, having high occurrences of both cat-tail and bulrush and trees and grasses, would be expected to supply the largest food source for granivores. This type supported the highest density of granivores. Type IV, with average densities of cat-tail/bulrush and above-average densities of trees and grasses, and Type III, with average cat-tail/bulrush and average trees and grasses, had the second and third highest granivore densities, respectively. The lowest densities of granivores occurred in Type VI (phragmites), which had few cat-tails, bulrushes, trees, or grasses, and thus provided limited food sources. However, in Type VI, highest densities of granivores occurred during summer. Upon reviewing the species composition for this season and type, the Brown-headed Cowbird (Molothrus ater) was the sole species involved and

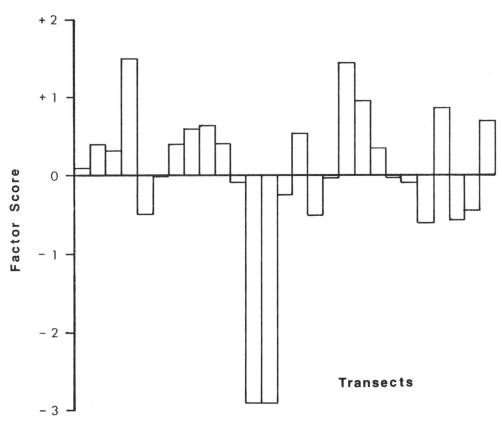

Figure 2.--Factor score of each transect on a derived variable representing the amount of cat-tail, bulrush, and phragmites. Positive scores indicate increasing amounts of cat-tail and bulrush; negative scores indicate increasing amounts of phragmites.

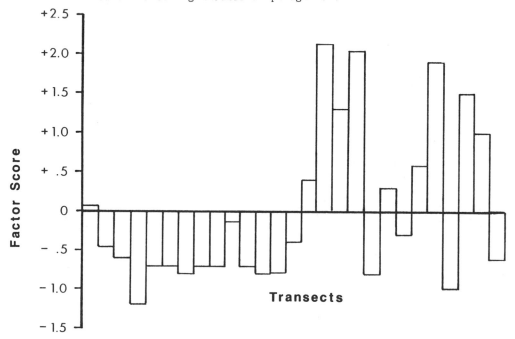

Figure 3.--Factor score of each transect on a derived variable representing density of trees and amount of grass. Positive scores indicate above-average amounts of trees and grasses; negative scores indicate few or no trees and grasses.

probably acted as a nest parasite rather than actually foraging on seeds.

Shorebirds

Shorebirds were most numerous during fall, winter, and spring (table 2). The highest densities occurred in open marsh (Type VII) where exposed sandbars and mudflats facilitated shorebird use. All other marsh-types had low densities; practically no shorebirds occurred in the most vegetationally dense types (I, II, V, and VI).

Insectivores

Insectivore analysis was complex due to the large number of species and the high niche separation of these species. However, the following trends were evident (table 2). Seasonally, the majority of marsh-types supported highest densities of insectivores in fall and winter. Dense and intermediately dense cat-tail/bulrush (Types I and V) did not follow this trend; highest densities of insectivores in these types occurred during summer.

Cat-tail/bulrush marshes of Types II and III had the highest insectivore densities at all seasons (especially fall and winter for Type II; see table 2). Type III had remarkably even numbers of insectivores at all seasons. These consisted mostly of Red-winged Blackbird, Song Sparrow, Common Yellowthroat, and Long-billed Marsh Wren during all seasons. Cat-tail/bulrush marshes of Type I and marshes with trees and grasses interspersed (Type V) had lower insectivore densities and followed Type III in being even at all seasons.

Though only censused during spring and summer, the very dense Type VIII marsh had very high total densities, consisting primarily of Long-billed Marsh Wren, Common Yellowthroat, and Song Sparrow. Overall for breeding insectivores, as cat-tail/bulrush became very dense, densities of Long-billed Marsh Wren, Common Yellowthroat, and Song Sparrow increased (noted in Types VIII and I). As cat-tail/bulrush approached average density, numbers of Red-winged Blackbird increased (note especially Type III; table 2). Overall, large numbers of Yellow-rumped Warbler contributed to the high fall, winter, and spring insectivore densities in most marsh-types. In open marsh (Type VI), however, high densities were accounted for by large numbers of the Water Pipit, which requires more open areas for foraging.

Waterbirds

Seasonally, waterbirds were most numerous during fall, winter, and spring in all marsh-types. Waterbirds reached their highest densities in open marsh (Type VII; table 2). Marsh-types with trees and grasses interspersed (V) and those consisting of phragmites (VI) had very low waterbird densities. The most obvious

Table 2.--Seasonal breakdown of guilds in each marsh-type. WA--wading birds; WB--waterbirds; SB--shorebirds; PRI--permanent resident insectivores; VI--visiting insectivores; GR--granivores; W--winter; SP--spring; S--summer; LS--late summer; and F--fall. X--not censused.

Marsh-type	Season	Birds per 40 ha					
		WA	WB	SB	PRI	VI	GR
I	W	10	119	1	41	112	47
	SP	21	59	1	36	115	42
	S	39	30	1	52	144	56
	LS	13	61	0	27	90	40
	F	29	50	1	42	138	106
II	W	7	115	2	105	302	251
	SP	17	165	9	51	143	129
	S	22	44	3	115	76	43
	LS	30	53	5	35	48	52
	F	10	46	1	52	232	307
III	W	3	161	15	190	166	195
	SP	8	173	17	127	105	111
	S	32	71	3	187	103	50
	LS	26	45	8	151	113	65
	F	3	75	16	178	163	130
IV	W	8	145	9	52	174	152
	SP	7	155	27	30	94	61
	S	12	67	2	80	63	66
	LS	19	56	14	73	87	79
	F	20	34	25	51	170	205
V	W	13	14	2	37	97	56
	SP	31	16	1	94	114	31
	S	47	8	0	94	112	16
	LS	44	10	0	44	111	23
	F	20	15	1	49	167	47
VI	W	15	18	0	10	181	9
	SP	34	8	0	6	189	13
	S	36	6	0	6	82	45
	LS	39	9	0	0	179	0
	F	4	11	0	0	88	0
VII	W	5	294	76	69	170	102
	SP	5	234	73	35	165	57
	S	18	38	8	77	59	33
	LS	14	43	64	105	63	29
	F	6	133	105	78	122	83
VIII	W	X	X	X	X	X	X
	SP	16	114	0	59	181	13
	S	43	53	0	4	238	11
	LS	X	X	X	X	X	X
	F	X	X	X	X	X	X

trend was for waterbirds to avoid densely vegetated areas.

However, Type VIII, a dense cat-tail/bulrush marsh, had unexpectedly high waterbird densities during spring. The American Coot was the overwhelmingly most numerous species. Though the apparent trend for denser vegetation to have lower waterbird densities is probably realistic, it must be tempered with the realization that detectability of species in this guild is difficult due to visibility problems and the lack of highly vocal species (with the exception of the American Coot). More open vegetation would facilitate easier feeding for most species, while denser vegetation would provide cover when species in this guild were not feeding.

Wading Birds

Since the collective total for wading birds was much less than that for any other guild, alterations of marshlands could cause a severe decline in their numbers (table 2). Thus, wading birds may provide an accurate gauge for ascertaining the health of marshlands along the lower Colorado River. One species from this group, the Yuma Clapper Rail, will be analyzed in detail in the following section.

Seasonally, wading birds were most numerous in spring, summer, and late summer (table 2). Most wading birds moved out of marshland after breeding, as indicated by differences between breeding (spring and summer) and wintering seasons in most marsh-types. During summer, cat-tail/bulrush marshes of Types V, VIII, and I, and phragmites marshes of Type VI, in that order, were the most important types of vegetation for breeding. For wading birds collectively, the species comprising the vegetation do not appear to be as important as its density. Open marsh (Type VII) had the lowest density of wading birds. Although not taken into account in this paper, the presence or absence of tall, dead trees should be considered for any studies on habitat use for breeding herons and cormorants, as they use the dead trees for nesting platforms.

Yuma Clapper Rail

The Yuma Clapper Rail is endemic to the marshes of the lower Colorado River from Needles, California south to the Colorado Delta of Mexico, including immediate drainage areas (Salton Sea, Gila River, and Salt River). An analysis of marsh use of the Yuma Clapper Rail was necessary because of its close relationship with marshes and because of the threatened status of this subspecies. The analysis covered only spring, summer, and late summer, as the majority of the Colorado River population is migratory (Smith 1975).

Clapper Rail densities were compared for each of the defined marsh-types by month (table 3). The importance of the different marsh-types was determined by ranking. During each month, the marsh-type with the highest rail density received the highest score; the marsh-type with the lowest density received the lowest score. Scores for each marsh-type were then added across months and compared directly.

Type V was by far the marsh-type most highly used by the rails. Type I ranked one-half as high as Type V, but was nearly double the rank of

Table 3.--Clapper Rail densities (per 40 ha.) in spring, summer, and late summer in each marsh-type along the lower Colorado River. *--indicates not censused.

Marsh-type	Mar	Apr	May	Jun	Jul	Aug	Sep
I	6	9	9	16	18	7	4
II	0	0	0	0	6	18	13
III	0	3	18	6	22	11	0
IV	0	0	5	4	7	4	0
V	8	13	22	19	21	20	10
VI	9	12	3	10	5	0	0
VII	0	0	1	2	4	5	6
VIII	0	0	22	11	3	*	*

Types II, III, VI, and VIII. Marsh-types with trees and grasses interspersed (Type IV) and very open marshes (Type VII) consistently ranked low. Of interest, Type VI (mostly phragmites) had relatively high ranking during spring when rails arrive to breed, and Type VII (above-average density of cat-tail/bulrush and above-average density of trees and grasses) had very high ranking during late summer when rails dispersed from the breeding areas. But during summer breeding, these marsh-types were not used extensively by rails. Even though rails appear to select certain marsh-types for actual breeding, nonbreeding marginal areas may still be important.

CONCLUSIONS

Among the six avian categories or guilds considered, five occurred in significantly greater densities in at least one marsh-type, relative to the density in the marsh-type with the lowest density. Thus, the first conclusion is that the species within these guilds have definite habitat preferences. Among the six guilds, peak populations were reached in four different marsh-types. Thus, the second conclusion is that to maximize densities and diversities of birds using marsh as habitat, it is necessasry to have a variety of marsh-types available.

A third conclusion is that among the marsh-types studied, dense stands of phragmites supported the lowest avian densities and diversities. But even this marsh-type was potentially valuable to the Yuma Clapper Rail in the prebreeding season and to granivorous species, especially in winter, spring, and late summer.

Unrestricted vehicular traffic has been found to reduce the use of marsh and open-water areas by waterfowl (Ohmart and Anderson 1978; Anderson and Ohmart 1981). One simple means of habitat improvement would be to close roads adjacent to at least some marshes during periods of avian peak use, i.e., winter.

603

While man has created a large portion of the existing marshes along the lower Colorado River (Ohmart et al. 1975), we hasten to point out that channelization and riprapping activities, in general, reduce the quality of marshes (ibid.). Riprapping and channelization activities should be undertaken only if the creation of marsh habitat is part of a mitigation proposal.

Immediate action must be taken to support the mesquite (Prosopis glandulosa) skeletons in Topock Marsh to ensure a nesting area for the heron and cormorant rookery, which may well be the largest remaining rookery along the lower Colorado River.

Channelization projects usually result in destruction of sandbars and mudflats. Our final conclusion is that when these operations occur, an assertive stance must be taken to ensure that mitigation includes plans for creation of new sandbars and mudflats in the general areas.

ACKNOWLEDGMENTS

We would like to thank Helen Wood for presenting this paper. Susan M. Cook and Jane R. Durham provided editorial assistance and Marcelett Ector typed the various drafts of the manuscript. Cindy D. Zisner typed the final draft. Judy Huff, Janet Jackson, Ann Kasprzyk, and Helen Wood constructed the tables and graphs. Rodney H. Ohmart and Elaine Hassinger prepared the final figures. We wish to give special acknowledgment to Alton Higgins who was instrumental in conducting the field work. This study was supported by USDI Bureau of Reclamation Contract Number 7-07-30-V0009.

LITERATURE CITED

Anderson, B.W., and R.D. Ohmart. 1977. Climatological and physical characteristics affecting avian population estimates in Southwestern riparian communities. p. 193-200. In: R.R. Johnson and D.A. Jones (tech. coord.). Importance, preservation and management of riparian habitats: a symposium. [Tucson, Ariz., July 9, 1977]. USDA Forest Service GTR-RM-43, Rocky Mountain Forest and Range Experiment Station, Fort Collins, Colo. 217 p.

Anderson, B.W., and R.D. Ohmart. 1981. Vegetation management. Final report to USDI Bureau of Reclamation, Boulder City, Nevada. In preparation.

Emlen, J.T. 1971. Population densities of birds derived from transect counts. Auk 88:323-342.

MacArthur, R.H., and J.W. MacArthur. 1961. On bird species diversity. Ecology 42:594-598.

Nie, N.H., J.G. Jenkins, K. Steinbrenner, D.H. Bent. 1975. Statistical package for the social sciences. McGraw-Hill, Inc., New York, N.Y. 675 p.

Ohmart, R.D., and B.W. Anderson. 1979. Wildlife use values of wetlands in the arid southwestern United States. p. 278-295. In: P.E. Greeson, J.R. Clark, and J.E. Clark (ed.). Wetland functions and values: the state of our understanding. Proceedings of the national symposium on wetlands. [Minneapolis, Minn., November 1978]. American Water Resources Association, Minneapolis, Minn. 674 p.

Ohmart, R.D., W.O. Deason, and S.J. Freeland. 1975. Dynamics of marshland formation and succession along the lower Colorado River and their importance and management problems as related to wildlife in the arid Southwest. p. 240-251. In: Transactions of the 40th North American Wildlife and Natural Resources Conference. Wildlife Management Institute, Washington, D.C.

Smith, P.M. 1975. Habitat requirements and observations on the Clapper Rail (Rallus longirostris yumanensis). Unpublished M.S. Thesis, Arizona State University, Tempe, Ariz. 35 p.

RIPARIAN FOREST AS HABITAT FOR THE LEAST BELL'S VIREO[1]

M. Violet Gray and James M. Greaves [2]

Abstract.--Data are presented on vegetation structure in Least Bell's Vireo (_Vireo bellii pusillus_) breeding habitats. A discussion of vegetation and several other factors relevant to breeding success of this endangered species is presented. Recommendations are made for actions to ensure the future of the subspecies as a breeding inhabitant of riparian forests.

INTRODUCTION

The purposes of this paper are to present data and a discussion of the use of riparian forest by the Least Bell's Vireo (_Vireo bellii pusillus_), its breeding success over two seasons, and an assessment of the features in the habitat which are important to breeding success. The data are the results of a study initiated in 1979 and continued through the 1980 and 1981 breeding seasons in Gibraltar Reservoir watershed in Santa Barbara County, California.

The Least Bell's Vireo (referred to here as vireo) has undergone a rapid decline in California in both numbers and breeding range over the last several decades. Once present as far north as Chico, California (Cogswell 1958), and numerous enough to be considered a common summer resident (Grinnell 1928), the species' present known northern breeding range limit is Santa Barbara County. Only about 200 pairs are thought to still breed in the state (Wertz 1981). The species is considered to be heavily parasitized by the Brown-headed Cowbird (_Molothrus ater_) (McCaskie 1975), with a rate as high as 58% (Goldwasser 1978). The cowbird has been blamed for the vireo's decline in California (Tate 1981). However, we believe that the cowbird problem is merely a symptom of a more crucial problem--the loss or degradation of habitat suitable to sustain healthy breeding riparian bird communities.

Over the past 100 years, the riparian zones of many rivers have been heavily grazed; major

cities have diverted water supplies from watercourses supplying riparian areas; flood control districts have channelized, denuded of vegetation, and often concrete-lined, streambeds; and overuse of water for irrigation has depleted the water tables in many of the state's richest river valleys. As the many prime riparian forests have disappeared, the vireos have disappeared as well, and now survive mostly in remote areas where riparian systems are relatively unaltered; or they attempt to breed (often with no success) in areas where the vegetation has been highly degraded. In these latter areas, cowbirds are often abundant and thus have significant negative effects on the reproductive capacities of most breeding song birds, including the vireo. As the most obvious agent of breeding failure, cowbirds receive an undue portion of the blame.

The riparian vegetation of the Gibraltar Reservoir study area was relatively undisturbed and supported the largest known population of the California subspecies of the vireo--about 60 pairs. By providing data on the use of this unaltered vegetation by the vireo, we hope to aid in establishing guidelines for habitat rehabilitation throughout the bird's breeding range in the state.

DESCRIPTION OF STUDY AREA

The study area comprises 243 ha. (600 ac.) and consists of four sections, each approximately 1.6 km. (1 mi.) in length, containing similar degrees of forestation. The Santa Ynez River, for 1.6 km. (1 mi.) to the southeast and 1.6 km. (1 mi.) west of its confluence with Mono Creek, makes up half the study area. Southeast of the Mono Creek confluence, the river extends for about 11.3 km. (7 mi.) upstream to Juncal Dam (Jameson Lake). Only the lower 1.6 km. of this reach of river is used regularly by the vireo, although a few have been found nesting in thickets above the study area. West of the confluence is the silted-in eastern third of Gibraltar Reservoir (on the Santa Ynez River) which, over the

[1] Paper presented at the California Riparian Systems Conference. [University of California, Davis, September 17-19, 1981].

[2] M. Violet Gray is a field biologist presently contracted to the USDA Forest Service, Santa Barbara District, Calif. James M. Greaves is a biologist presently contracted to the USDA Forest Service, Santa Barbara District, Calif., and Curatorial Assistant, Museum of Natural History, Santa Barbara, Calif.

past 40 years, has developed into a broad silt floodplain with a narrow creek channel bordered by lush riparian forest. This area contains the habitat for approximately one-third to one-half of the vireo population (hereafter Gibraltar Reservoir population).

Mono Creek joins the Santa Ynez River at the east end of the reservoir and has approximately the same flow as the river. The creek is obstructed about 1.6 km. (1 mi.) above the confluence by a debris dam built in the 1930s. Above this dam is the broad bowl of Mono Debris Basin, fed by Mono Creek, Indian Creek, and Little Caliente Creek. One-quarter of the vireo population breeds in the 1.3-sq. km. (0.5-sq. mi.) basin.

The study area is surrounded by rugged mountains with slopes often exceeding 40°. The slopes are very dry; many have open rocky patches that support little or no vegetation. Chaparral communities dominate the majority of the slopes, except where intense fires have recently burned, promoting the growth of grasslands.

There are several plant communities that can be classified as riparian vegetation which are not necessarily dominated by willow/cottonwood forest, and which are associated with vireo breeding. The Gibraltar/Mono study area contains at least four of these communities: oak woodland; willow/cottonwood forest; shrubby thicket; and dry wash. Each of these communities is dependent upon the regular flow of water through canyons, and its stability is determined by the river's flow and flood levels.

Oak Woodland

This is the most permanent of the four communities. It occupies the drier sites in the study area and is transitional between the mesic willow/cottonwood forest and the xeric chaparral-scrub communities. Coast live oak (Quercus agrifolia), squaw bush (Rhus trilobata), poison oak (R. diversiloba), elderberry (Sambucus mexicana), and snowberry (Symphoricarpos mollis) are common elements of this community. There is a great deal of intrusion by species more typical of chaparral communities, such as Ceanothus spp., chaparral honeysuckle (Lonicera johnstonii), and basin sagebrush (Artemisia tridentata).

This community is the only one of the four in which grasses predominate as the primary herbaceous groundcover. Introduced species of brome grass (Bromus spp.) and wild oats (Avena fatua), as well as native mugwort (Artemisia douglasiana) form the major groundcover species. In openings between the oaks or in less shaded areas beneath oaks, thickets of shrubby species have developed. These thickets seldom reach 1.8 m. (6 ft.) in height and are usually limited to about 1.2 m. (4 ft). Wild blackberry (Rubus ursinus) and California wild rose (Rosa californica) are occasional components of these areas and seem to occupy the ecotone

between oak woodland and willow/cottonwood forest as well as being regular associates of the latter community. Tall shrubs and young trees do not generally form a continuous layer here. Young oaks, buck brush (Ceanothus cuneatus), red heart (C. spinosus), elderberry, and coyote bush (Baccharis pilularis) appear as salients from the more continuous lower layer of shrubs. Thus, there is an open aspect to this community which is accentuated by the sparsely foliated habit of many of the dominant taxa. Mature oaks in this area are commonly 15.2 m. (50 ft.) high, with particularly large individuals exceeding 21.3 m. (70 ft.).

Willow/Cottonwood Forest

This community occurs in two basic forms. The first is that of a dense-canopied forest with little or no vegetation below the canopy level. The second form has the same canopy structure, but is also rich in shrubby and/or herbaceous undergrowth. The canopy generally consists of a mixture of Fremont cottonwood (Populus fremontii) and red willow (Salix laevigata), often growing to heights of 9.1-18.3 m. (30-60 ft.). The majority of the willows are not much greater than 229 mm. (9 in.) diameter-at-breast-height (DBH), many having little girth despite their great heights. In a few areas, most notably in the Mono Debris Basin, both willow and cottonwood are found with trunk diameters approaching 1.2 m. (4 ft.). The cottonwood grows in smaller numbers, but to slightly greater size, scattered among the willow. Where cottonwood exist to the exclusion of willow, it takes the form of either evenly distributed gallery forest or large trees growing in grove-like clusters of six to 12 trees, in an open woodland arrangement.

Another common species, arroyo willow (S. lasiolepis), does not generally grow to sufficient size to become a part of the forest canopy layer, but some rather slender trees mixed in with red willow have been found with heights up to 13.7 m. (45 ft.). Other taxa found in this lower canopy, but to a lesser degree, are: western sycamore (Platanus racemosa), black cottonwood (Populus trichocarpa), black willow (S. gooddingii), yellow willow (S. lasiandra), and white alder (Alnus rhombifolia).

The low shrub layer consists partially of taxa which are herbaceous, such as mugwort, but which have the habit of growing in shrub-like clumps and which function (with respect to several nesting bird species) as low shrubs. This layer also contains shrubs which do not attain heights greater than 1.2 m. (4 ft.) or which are at a stage of intermediate growth. Nearly all the plants from the other layers, except those forbs and grasses which usually do not attain heights of 0.6 m. (2 ft.), can be found in the low shrub layer.

The structure of the high shrub layer differs from that of the low shrub layer in that the lower 0.6-1.2 m. (2-4 ft.) of the plants in the high shrub layer are generally devoid of dense foliage. Unless it occurs in conjunction with the low shrub layer or groundcover, the absence of foliage at the lower level in the high shrub layer makes high shrubs of little use to nesting vireos in the study population. All of the willow species contribute to the high shrub layer, either as young or adult trees or in the form of shoots from downed larger trees. Narrowleaf willow (Salix exigua) is a major element of this layer, along with wild blackberry, California wild rose, snowberry, and seep-willow (Baccharis glutinosa). Immature trees of all the above-mentioned species are occasional components of the high shrub layer.

The groundcover in these forested areas is generally composed of only one or two species, with white sweet-clover (Melilotus albus) and mugwort predominating. Many moisture-requiring forbs, such as peony (Paeonia californica), speedwell (Veronica anagallis-aquatica), and hedge-nettle (Stachys albens), were present at several survey sites.

Shrubby Thicket

The thicket is the simplest vegetative community in the study area. It generally possesses neither a canopy nor much groundcover and often is composed solely of one plant species, the most common of which are narrowleaf willow and black willow. The thicket presents an outer aspect which appears to be a solid wall from the ground to the top of the stand, often reaching 6.1 m. (20 ft.) when mature. The wall of vegetation is formed by a combination of low and high shrub layers growing at the edge of the thicket. The interior, which is usually the most mature section, is seldom as dense as the exterior. This community usually occupies loose sandy or rocky ground which is not stable enough to support the larger forest types.

Dry Wash

These areas are generally useless to vireos for breeding, except when thickets establish themselves and are sufficiently large to provide foraging habitat or nest sites. On occasion a tree or small thicket has grown in such a way in a dry wash to withstand the heavy flooding of winter runoff, and vireo nests have been found in such sites. These areas produce cover very slowly because they are heavily washed and scoured every year. There is some encroachment at the edges by thickets of narrowleaf or arroyo willow, which seem to combine rapid maturing rates with strong tolerance for unstable sandy or gravelly soils.

There is some groundcover in the dry washes each year, depending on how heavily scoured they have been and how high the previous winter runoff was. Wild mustard (Brassica campestris), white sweet-clover, and cocklebur (Xanthium strumarium) usually dominate, with some chaparral and oak woodland plants interspersed throughout.

Large piles of debris have created other major open spaces in the study area. These are found scattered within riparian woodlands and consist of matter ranging from large cottonwood and willow trunks to mats of dry foliage mixed with silt. They seldom support much vegetation other than introduced weeds such as curly dock (Rumex crispus) or heliotrope (Heliotropium curassavicum).

METHODS

Before 1979, no in-depth breeding data existed for the Least Bell's Vireo, and there was little information about its habitat requirements. In 1979, the authors began a study of the Gibraltar Reservoir population, banding and color-banding young birds as groundwork for a long-term population study. In 1980 and 1981, we continued these studies and began gathering data on vegetation at individual nest sites and along transect lines established in 243 ha. (600 ac.) of forest comprising the study area.

Because the vireo was the focus of this study, intense field work was required to locate nest sites, determine the number of pairs, and conduct the banding studies. We developed methods in the field for the search-and-find part of the project, walking throughout the habitat, following natural courses as much as possible, listening and looking for vireos. Whenever a male or a pair was encountered, we searched its territory until a nest was located or it was determined that it was not nesting. Adults were mistnetted when practicable, preferably prior to incubation of eggs, and young were banded between the ages of 6 and 10 days (10 to 12 days nestling life). We monitored each nest for success or failure and cause of failure; measured parameters for possible reasons for success; and recorded numbers of eggs, hatchings, and fledgings.

The vegetation study consisted of two parts: a habitat description taken from observation in the field (see DESCRIPTION OF STUDY AREA), and a quantitative analysis of transect data and nest-site surveys. To determine in detail what features of the vegetation are important to vireos in the study area, we surveyed sample plots at 0.04-ha. (0.1-ac.) circles around nest sites (James 1971, modified), and at 161 sites along 11 transect lines arranged across streamcourses. Transect plots were spaced 10 m. apart, each plot alternating to the right or left of the line and having an area of 3 m. square. All data were gathered over each square meter within each transect plot. These transects covered a total length of 2,093 m. Data collected at all sites included: frequency or absence of cover by class; frequency of plant species; and density of shrubs. Four cover-classes were used: groundcover (less than 60 cm. height), low shrub (60-120 cm.), high shrub (greater than 120 cm.), and canopy (greater than 6 m. and stems greater than 7.6 cm. [3 in.] DBH).

RESULTS AND DISCUSSION

Vireo Breeding

Arrival and Territory

Most males and some females arrived in the study area in mid-April. Males initiated nest building immediately upon their arrival, with the females apparently deciding whether to use the nest as is, complete it, or build elsewhere. The remainder of the population drifted in over the following two to four weeks. Territories ranged in size from 0.2 ha. to 1.6 ha. (0.5 ac. to 4.0 ac.), the size usually dependent on availability of food and water, and sufficient vegetation for at least several nest sites.

Nest Location

Nest heights averaged 64 cm. (range 33-133 cm.) aboveground, with successful nests about 8 cm. lower than failed nests. Most nests were placed near or at the edges of thickets, or at the edges of woods and open fields or washes, in low shrub or upper groundcover levels. A few nests were placed in full sun adjacent to, but not protected by, abundant cover. Some nests were built in galleried forests and were usually placed in tangles of groundcover or low shrubs at the bases of large trees. Most nests were hidden well behind a screen of leaves, limbs, or dead material, or combinations of live and dead material. However, high contrast (light and shadow moving across the nest during the day) seems to have contributed more to nesting success than either frequency of occurrence or density of vegetation around the nests. With only a few exceptions, nests were suspended: a) from forks or parallel stems or twigs of live woody material under 5 mm. in diameter; b) from dead twigs of willow or cottonwood; or c) from dead stems of mugwort or white sweet-clover under a cover of live material, usually mugwort.

Nesting and Production

Every known vireo pair nested at least once, usually exploring several sites before settling on a suitable one. Most pairs built a least two nests; as many as six nests were located in one territory. Several pairs built only two nests, successfully rearing young in both, and one pair built a third nest after its second fledging (table 1).

Several successful pairs were able to raise only one nestling in 1981 from each of two successful nests in their territories, in contrast to the normal three or four young raised per nest by most of the population. In 1979 and 1980, the only one-chick nests were the result of cowbird activity, or were begun late in the season when food and water stress would be expected to be higher. Thus, the lower fledgling number per pair, in spite of a higher nesting success rate, may have been the result of a higher-than-normal amount of nonpredation nestling mortality.

Table 1.--Breeding data of Gibraltar Reservoir Least Bell's Vireo population.

	1980	1981
Males present (estimated)	50	61
Nesting pairs (study population)	43	48
Successful pairs	26	32
Percent pairs successful	60%	67%
Vireo eggs produced (minimum)	238	262
Vireo eggs hatched (minimum)	147	147
Vireo young fledged (minimum)	85	91
Average young/successful pair	3.27	2.84
Nesting attempts (nests built)	95	103
Nests used (known minimum)	77	86
Nests successful (minimum)	29	36
Percent nests successful	38%	42%
Average young/successful nest	2.93	2.53
Nests parasitized (known)	14	11
Cowbird eggs produced	14	11
Cowbird eggs hatched[1]	3	2
Nests destroyed by cowbirds[2]	11	10
Nests deserted after parasitism	3	3
Percent parasitized and destroyed	32%	23%

[1] In 1980, cowbird eggs were left in nests until vireo response was ascertained; thereafter, eggs were removed. One cowbird was successfully raised before it could be found and removed. Two nests successfully raised three vireos after a cowbird egg and a chick were removed. In 1981, all cowbird eggs and chicks were removed as they were found. Three nests raised seven vireos after cowbird eggs were removed. One cowbird was successfully raised before its nest was found.

[2] Eggs pierced or dumped, chicks killed in the nest or dumped out, nest cup broken from limb after eggs dumped. Nests deserted after being visited by cowbirds but prior to vireo egg-laying were not included as cowbird-destroyed nests, but rather as straight failures.

Feeding Patterns

As the 1981 season progressed, vireos were seen foraging farther into the chaparral, often traveling several hundred yards to obtain food for their nestlings. This pattern of activity was apparent to a greater extent in 1979 and 1981, indicating the possibility of cyclic food shortages. We and others observed that the vireo does not leave its brood exposed during the 14- to 16-day incubation period (Hensley 1950). During the 1981 season, however, many nests were left unattended for long periods of time with neither adult present nearby. We suspect the reason for this was a combination of extremely high temperatures and low food availability which necessitated the absence from the nest for long periods by both adults because neither was able to obtain enough food for its own sustenance during its turn away from the nest. High daytime temperatures aided in incubation, but humidity was insufficiently maintained around the eggs, and, as a result, many freshly hatched young were weakened and unable to survive the rigors of life outside the egg.

Departure from the Study Area

Adult birds departed the study area as early as mid-July, and all were gone by the beginning of September. Most young birds left or were not seen in their natal territories after the fourth week from fledging. However, in 1981 many first-clutch young were present during second breeding attempts and disappeared from their territories at the time the second brood was ready to fledge, often found over 1.6 km. (1 mi.) away in another vireo's territory. Generally, females and young left the study area before males.

Use of Habitat

The vireo behaves both as a specialist and a generalist within separate and particular elements of the habitat. One major constraint is that the species nests solely in California's southern riparian zones. Since these vireos often raise two clutches of four young each and food is therefore a primary consideration during the breeding season, they would be expected to breed in areas of high humidity and insect productivity such as the riparian zones.

The Vireo as Specialist

As mentioned, nests are placed in a narrow range of heights, rarely higher than 1.8 m. (6 ft.). Since such higher placements are generally reactions to radical environmental disturbances (e.g., sudden removal of lower vegetation layers),[4] they do not appear to reflect a trend toward use of diverse nesting levels.

Nests are usually near the edge of a thicket, or, if in a small shrub or thicket, they may be in the middle. Usually all nests are within 1 m. (3 ft.) of an opening. This arrangement allows at least one unobstructed flight path to the nest, easy visibility of predators, and good foliage cover for nest safety. For small birds incapable of much actual defense at the nest (Best and Stauffer 1980), all of these factors contribute to successful nesting attempts. The branching arrangement of the immediately supporting nest substrate is usually a horizontal or down-sloping fork, or horizontally parallel stems.

The Vireo as Generalist

Within the constraints of the above-stated requisite elements, the vireo is a generalist. Nest substrate, in terms of plant species, seems to correlate fairly closely to those plant taxa available and abundant, with a few notable exceptions. California wild rose and coast live oak

were both used more often than they were encountered in the study area transect lines. This may be because they associate closely with other species (willows and mugwort, respectively) which are abundant and widespread (table 2). The vireo is also a generalist in its selection of plant life forms, using forbs, shrubs, and trees for both nest support and cover. It generalizes more broadly in nest cover, often preferring large-leaved plants, or mixtures of leaf size-classes.

Table 2.--Percent frequency of occurrence and percent use by vireos for nest cover substrate, of plant species available and liable to be used. B--percent frequency of occurrence data from transect plots, n = 161. C1--percent total nests per species, species used for cover, n = 227. C2--percent total nests per species, species used for nest support, n = 216. Dashes are used where combinations did not occur but were possible within the study area.

Plant species	B	C1	C2
Trees			
Salix laevigata	9.4	23.3	15.3
Populus fremontii	5.6	7.0	5.1
Salix gooddingii	0.6	0.9	1.4
S. lasiandra	0.5	--	--
Quercus agrifolia	0.5	4.4	3.2
Platanus racemosa	0.4	--	--
Tamarix sp.	0.1	--	--
Populus trichocarpa[1]	--	0.9	0.9
Alnus rhombifolia	--	--	--
Shrubs			
Salix exigua	18.0	22.5	20.8
S. lasiolepis	11.5	7.9	9.3
Rubus ursinus	3.7	12.8	11.1
Rhus trilobata	1.0	2.6	2.3
Rhus diversiloba	1.0	0.4	0.5
Baccharis glutinosa	--	4.4	1.4
B. pilularis	0.8	0.9	0.5
Rosa californica	0.8	7.0	7.4
Symphoricarpos mollis	0.6	3.5	3.2
Sambucus mexicana	0.1	0.4	0.5
Prunus ilicifolia	0.1	--	--
Eriodictyon sp.	--	0.9	0.5
Salvia apiana	--	--	--
S. leucophylla	--	0.4	0.5
S. mellifera	--	--	--
Potentilla glandulosa	--	--	--
Artemisia californica	--	--	--
A. tridentata	--	--	--

[1]Some species were recorded in the study area but not on transect plots; these are included as possible nest cover and substrate, but no data were gathered on frequency in the study area.

---

[4]Goldwasser, Sharon. Personal communication.

609

Table 2.--Continued.

Plant species	B	C1	C2
Forbs			
Melilotus albus	16.4	17.6	3.2
Artemisia douglasiana	15.0	26.9	10.2
Baccharis douglasii	1.2	0.4	0.5
Conyza canadensis	0.6	1.4	0.9
Ambrosia psilostachya	0.5	-	-
Helenium puberulum	0.5	0.9	0.5
Xanthium strumarium	0.3	-	-
Brassica campestris	0.3	1.8	-
Penstemon heterophyllum	0.3	-	-
Urtica holosericea	0.1	1.3	-
Verbena lasiostachys	0.1	1.8	-
Stachys albens	0.1	0.4	0.5
Elymus condensatus	-	0.4	-
Marah fabaceus	-	-	-
Centaurea solstitialis	-	0.9	0.5

Shrub density at nest sites seems to correspond to density throughout the forest, indicating that the vireos do not seek out any unusually dense stand of vegetation for nesting. There is an extremely broad range of densities both at nest sites and at transect plots, so density is apparently not of importance to the bird in nest-site selection (table 3).

Table 3.--Mean shrub density compared at 0.04 ha. (0.1 ac.) nest circles and line transect plots. Range from raw data figures.

Sampling	Density (stems/ha.)	Range (stems/ha.)
Nest circles	17,070	620-72,200
Transect plots		
All plots	10,280	0-90,000
Excluding open ground	21,100	1,110-90,000

Cover-type frequencies were generally similar in both samplings (nest site and transect plots) (table 4), so presence of a particular

Table 4.--Cover-type frequencies compared for nest sites and the general study area, as interpreted from nest-circle and transect-plot data respectively.

Cover-type	Nest sites (%)	Study area (%)
Canopy	40.1	47.8
High shrub	41.8	40.4
Low shrub	29.4	36.2
Groundcover	35.6	32.2
Open ground	25.5	3.7

cover-type such as canopy does not appear to be a consideration in nest site selection.

Although no data were recorded indicating time allotments in any one level or community, the vireos were observed foraging in all levels and communities in and adjacent to the study area during all parts of the breeding season. However, they seemed to spend a major portion of their time gleaning insects from leaves in the willow and cottonwood forests at and below the middle levels of the canopies. Early to mid-season feeding activity was limited generally to areas near nest sites, while later season feeding encompassed all communities, including a good portion of time in adjacent chaparral.

RECOMMENDATIONS

These recommendations are made for general management of Least Bell's Vireo breeding habitat and for rehabilitation of historical or degraded sites.

1. Prohibit removal of groundcover and low shrubs.

2. If non-native plant species are removed, they should be replaced immediately (within one season) with a suitable native of comparable form.

3. Limit or eliminate recreation and grazing or other agricultural uses in sensitive riparian systems or critical habitat.

4. Replanting of denuded areas should include a diversity of species and should include species which provide all cover-type layers.

ACKNOWLEDGMENTS

This research was sponsored by USDA Forest Service, Santa Barbara District, Calif.; California Department of Fish and Game, Non-game Management Branch; Santa Barbara Audubon Society; USDI Fish and Wildlife Service, Office of Endangered Species. We thank Alan Craig, Maeton Freel, and Sanford Wilbur for their personal aid in obtaining funding. We also thank contributing Audubon Society chapters: Altical, Los Angeles, Morro Coast, and Santa Barbara.

LITERATURE CITED

Best, Louis B., and Dean F. Stauffer. 1980. Factors affecting nesting success in riparian bird communities. Condor 82:149-158.

Cogswell, H.L. 1958. Middle Pacific Region. Audubon Field Notes 12:379-384.

Goldwasser, Sharon. 1978. Distribution, reproductive success and impact of nest parasitism by Brown-headed Cowbirds on Least Bell's Vireos. 27 p. California Department of Fish and Game, Sacramento.

Goldwasser, Sharon, David Gaines and Sanford R. Wilbur. 1980. The Least Bell's Vireo in California: a de facto endangered species. Am. Birds 34:742-745.

Grinnell, J. 1928. A distributional summation of the ornithology of Lower California. Univ. California Publ. Zool. 32(1):1-300.

Hensley, M.M. 1950. Notes on the breeding behavior of the Bell's Vireo. Auk 67:243-244.

James, F.C. 1971. Ordinations of habitat relationships among breeding birds. Wilson Bull. 83:215-236.

McCaskie, G. 1975. Southern Pacific Coast Region. Am. Birds 29:1029-1036.

Tate, James, Jr. 1981. The blue list for 1981. Am. Birds 35:3-10.

Wertz, Paul. 1981. Update on endangered species. Outdoor California 42:1-6.

IMPORTANCE OF RIPARIAN SYSTEMS TO NESTING
SWAINSON'S HAWKS IN THE CENTRAL VALLEY OF CALIFORNIA[1]

Ronald W. Schlorff and Peter H. Bloom[2]

Abstract.--Once a common breeding bird of the Central Valley and elsewhere in California, the Swainson's Hawk (Buteo swainsoni) has experienced a severe population decline due to, among other things, loss of the riparian systems that provided trees for nest sites. The pattern of land use prevalent over the past 130 years has reduced riparian systems of the Central Valley to a tiny fraction of their former extent. It will be necessary to maintain and restore stands of vegetation in riparian systems if the Swainson's Hawk is to continue as a breeding species in the Central Valley.

INTRODUCTION

The Swainson's Hawk (Buteo swainsoni) (fig. 1) was once assumed to be so common in California that most historical reporters felt it did not warrant special mention (Bloom 1980). It was variously described as the most abundant hawk in the southern Transverse Ranges (Sharp 1902) and common in spring, summer, and fall from the foothills to the ocean (Willett 1912). Willet (ibid.) also reported a population of Swainson's Hawks breeding on Santa Catalina Island. Historic accounts provide some qualitative data on the former abundance of the species, but no quantitative studies of Swainson's Hawk population size or breeding distribution in California were published from the late nineteenth and early twentieth centuries. Thus, today, it is difficult to assess the status when quantitative data on the historic population are lacking. Fortunately, however, early records of the egg-collectors do provide useful information on historic distribution of the species.

Bloom (1980) used a combination of factors to arrive at a historic statewide nesting population estimate of between 4,300 and 17,100 pairs of Swainson's Hawks. The method involved taking observed nesting densities in relatively undisturbed habitat at the present and extrapolating backward to include all suitable nesting and

[1] Paper presented at the California Riparian Systems Conference. [University of California, Davis, September 17-19, 1981].

[2] Ronald W. Schlorff is Wildlife Biologist, Nongame Wildlife Program, California Department of Fish and Game, Sacramento, Calif. Peter H. Bloom is Raptor Biologist, Santa Cruz Predatory Bird Research Group, University of California, Santa Cruz.

Figure 1.--Adult male dark-phase Swainson's Hawk marked with colored leg band and USDI Fish and Wildlife Service band.

foraging habitat assumed to be available to the species historically. By comparing estimated historic population levels with that observed today, it is evident that the Swainson's Hawk has suffered a population decline of enormous proportions, perhaps greater than a 90% statewide decline since 1900 (Bloom ibid.).

Comparison of historic and present range reveals the species is now absent from many regions of California where it once was a common breeding bird (figs. 2 and 3). Historic population estimates for the Central Valley ranged from 1,656 to 6,624 pairs. During 1979, a breeding population of 280 pairs was estimated inhabiting the area from 40 km. (25 mi.) south of Fresno in the San Joaquin Valley north to the vicinity of Chico in the Sacramento Valley.

Valley populations of Swainson's Hawks frequently nested in valley oaks (Quercus lob-

Figure 2.--Historic range of the Swainson's Hawk in California. This is the approximate range during the late nineteenth and early twentieth centuries (shaded area).

Figure 3.--Current range of the Swainson's Hawk in California. This range was delineated from results of surveys conducted during 1979-81 (shaded area).

ata) and Fremont cottonwoods (_Populus fremontii_) historically and at the present time. Often, trees chosen as nest sites are within 90 m. (100 yd.) of a major Valley stream, creek, or slough in the riparian zone. Today, remnants of riparian vegetation exist along portions of the Sacramento, American, and Feather Rivers and their tributaries in the Sacramento Valley, and along the San Joaquin River and tributaries in the San Joaquin Valley (fig. 4) (Thompson 1977; Conard _et al_. 1977). Additional riparian vegetation suitable for nesting Swainson's Hawks may be found along the many miles of creeks, sloughs, and canals that crisscross the agricultural and grazing fields of the Central Valley. These habitats often support the only trees in a local agricutural area, and therefore are vital to Swainson's Hawks for nest sites.

The 1979 Swainson's Hawk study (Bloom 1980) provided the basis for subsequent investigations into the species' dependence on riparian systems for nesting in the Central Valley. Monitoring of nest sites in 1980 and 1981 confirmed the initial indication of the importance of riparian systems to Swainson's Hawks. Unfortunately, a pattern of destruction and degradation has characterized much of man's relationship with this vegetation-type in the Central Valley and elsewhere (Thompson 1977; Smith 1977). Smith (_ibid._) estimated that about 314,000 ha. (775,000 ac.) of riparian vegetation existed in the Central Valley in 1850. By 1977, only 4,900 ha. (12,000 ac.)--1.5%-- remained. This loss is continuing and there are plans to remove more vegetation along the Sacramento River and other riparian ecosystems in order to effect "bank protection" and for "flood control" (Jannssen 1976). If species such as Swainson's Hawks are to survive, the trend of destruction must be reversed.

METHODS

Study Area

During 1979, the entire state was surveyed for nesting Swainson's Hawks. For purposes of this paper, the habitat relationships of the species in the Central Valley were investigated. An area corresponding to the Valley floor and extending from 40 km. (25 mi.) south of Fresno to the vicinity of Chico, approximately 47,700 km^2 (18,400 mi^2) constituted the study area (fig. 3). There are still significant riparian systems available to nesting Swainson's Hawks within this area. A 219 km. (135 mi.) section of the Sacramento River, from Colusa south to the Sacramento Delta, served as a riparian study area and was surveyed to determine nesting density and habitat quality. Additional riparian areas consisting of large and small streams, sloughs, and canals also provided study areas.

Habitat Description

Historic and present Central Valley riparian systems have been described in detail (Conard _et al_. 1977; Michny _et al_. 1975; Roberts _et al_. 1977; Thompson 1977). Wildlife studies document habitat relationships of the

Figure 4.—Typical Swainson's Hawk nesting habitat in a Central Valley riparian system. Similar stands of vegetation exist along portions of the Sacramento River.

various species dependent on riparian systems (Brumley 1976; Gaines 1977).

The riparian zone of major Valley streams has been described as a continuum of plant communities following the topographic line from the stream channel through the low and high terrace deposits of the floodplain (Conard et al. 1977). Cottonwoods, oaks, sycamores (Platanus racemosa), and large willow trees (Salix sp.) form the dominant overstory vegetation in the zones most important to Swainson's Hawks. Cottonwoods typically dominate the lower terrace deposits closer to the stream bank while sycamores and valley oaks are found on higher terrace deposits and cut banks along the outside of meanders (Conard et al. 1977). Several species of woody and herbaceous plants comprise the understory in this riparian forest. Historically, and to a lesser extent today, a native grassland community, including oat (Avena sp.), brome-grass (Bromus sp.), ryegrass (Elymus sp.), barley (Hordeum sp.), and ryegrass (Lolium sp.) provided foraging habitat for Swainson's Hawks beyond the valley oak component of the riparian system.

Survey Techniques

Techniques used in the 1979 Swainson's Hawk survey are described in Bloom (1980). Subsequent surveys in 1980 and 1981 were made employing these same methods for automobile surveys of riparian vegetation along major watercourses and smaller streams and sloughs. Systematic search of areas known or suspected to support Swainson's Hawks provided nesting data for the two years following the 1979 survey.

In 1981, a 219 km. (136 mi.) portion of the Sacramento River was surveyed by motorboat to record sightings, territories, and nest sites of

Swainson's Hawks. The boat survey was conducted over three days with approximately 64 to 80 km. (40 to 50 mi.) surveyed per day. In addition to recording data on the hawks, notes and maps were made of habitat availability and quality along the survey route. These maps and notes were compared against past and recent aerial photographs made in the study area. Automobile surveys in areas near to the boat survey route were made to ensure more complete coverage, and the automobile surveys better facilitated assessments of foraging areas near the river.

An analysis of habitat characteristics was made from nesting survey reports made during 1979-81. Data were pooled for the three years and information was summarized on the proximity of territories to riparian systems, and tree species and heights chosen for nesting by Swainson's Hawks.

RESULTS

Review of 1979 Survey

Providing details on habitat association was not a primary objective of the 1979 Swainson's Hawk survey but it was an important secondary goal. The first evidence of the importance of riparian systems to nesting Swainson's Hawks was apparent during the portion of the study involving the Central Valley. Elsewhere in the State, the Klamath Basin for instance, Swainson's Hawks do not appear to be dependent on riparian vegetation because nest trees were located away from the few streams in the area (Bloom 1980).

In the Central Valley, there are also many suitable nest trees available away from riparian systems; however, their continued existence is threatened in many cases. Where these trees grow in the midst of agriculture fields, regeneration is severely hampered due to land use activities. Sometimes livestock grazing prevents regeneration, and always there is the threat of removal if the space trees occupy and the water they use is required in order to expand agricultural activities. Therefore, it is important to preserve nesting habitat in riparian systems. As noted during the 1979 survey, severe destruction of habitat already has occurred in the riparian systems and is continuing at an alarming rate.

A majority of all nests and territories recorded for the Central Valley were close to riparian systems (figs. 5, 6, and 7). Nests were found most often in cottonwoods and oaks (table 1). Cottonwoods were considered an important nest tree because they provide an excellent nest site at the present and, due to rapid growth rate, will be an ideal species for restoration work. Oaks also are important; however, regeneration time will be much longer in areas where oaks are to be restored.

Tree height was an important parameter affecting nesting, and Swainson's Hawks appeared to choose relatively tall trees for nest sites.

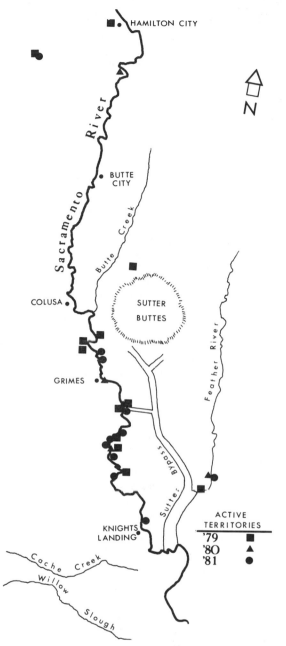

Figure 5.--Location of Swainson's Hawk nest sites in the Central Valley of California, northern section. Data derived from surveys conducted during 1979-81.

Tree heights ranged from 6-30 m. (20-100 ft.) with a mean of 12 m. (41 ft.) (N = 36). Nests were built near the tops of oaks and cottonwoods that provided shade for the nest and also afforded a good view of the surrounding terrain.

Subsequent Surveys

During 1980 and 1981, results of surveys continued to show the importance of riparian systems to Swainson's Hawks (figs. 5, 6, and 7). Occasional nests were found a mile or more away from riparian zones, but a greater proportion

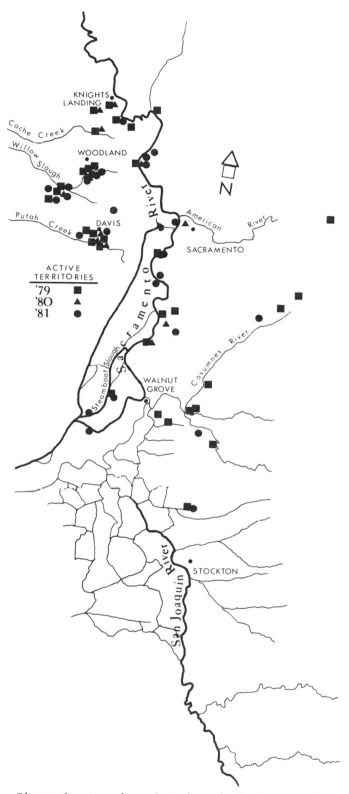

Figure 6.--Location of Swainson's Hawk nest sites in the Central Valley of California, middle section. Data derived from surveys during 1979-81.

615

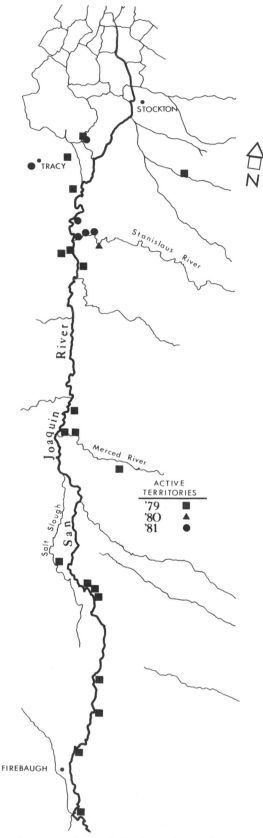

Table 1.--Trees used by Swainson's Hawks for nesting in the Central Valley of California, 1979-81.

Nest tree species	Number	Percent
Valley oak	25	50.0
Quercus lobata		
Fremont cottonwood	21	42.0
Populus fremontii		
Willow	1	2.0
Salix spp.		
Eucalyptus	3	6.0
Eucalyptus spp.		
Totals	50	100.0

were within streamside vegetation (table 2). There is a built-in bias concerning the search for nest trees. Since most suitable trees are in riparian systems in the Valley, it naturally follows that these areas supported the most nesting of Swainson's Hawks. Results of the 1981 boat survey revealed extensive habitat loss along both banks of a 219 km. (136 mi.) stretch of the Sacramento River from Colusa to the Sacramento Delta. It was estimated that 85% of the stream bank was either entirely devoid of vegetation or the vegetation that did remain was unsuitable for nesting Swainson's Hawks.

Where suitable habitat did remain and prerequisites for nesting seemed to be met, Swainson's Hawks often were found (fig. 4). Results indicate that the hawks nested in or near the riparian zone at a frequency of one pair per 13.7 river km. (8.5 river mi.); this is considerbly lower than Bloom's estimate of one territory per 6.4 km. (4.0 mi.) of suitable nesting habitat for Central Valley watercourses (Bloom 1980). The greatest nesting frequency was recorded in 1979 when three active territories were located along a 1.1 km. (0.7 mi.) stretch of Willow Slough in Yolo County. This indicates the abundance of Swainson's Hawks possible given optimum habitat conditions.

Table 2.--Proximity of Swainson's Hawk nesting territories to riparian systems in the Central Valley of California, 1979-81.

Distance from riparian zone	Number of territories[1]	Percent
Within zone	107	71.0
Less than 30 m. (100 yd.)	4	2.5
Less than 0.4 km. (0.25 mi.)	6	4.0
Less than 1.6 km. (1.0 mi.)	7	4.5
Greater than 1.6 km. (1.0 mi.)	27	18.0
Totals	151	100.0

[1]Nest trees not located in every instance.

Figure 7.--Location of Swainson's Hawk nest sites in the Central Valley of California, southern section. Data derived from surveys conducted during 1979-81.

DISCUSSION

It has been noted that the Swainson's Hawk, although not an obligate riparian species, nevertheless is closely associated with riparian systems in certain situations (Bent 1963). The Central Valley appears to be such a situation. Elsewhere in North America, the species is often found nesting in juniper (Juniperus sp.)/sagebrush (Artemesia sp.) and prairie habitats of the Great Basin (Olendorff 1975; Dunkle 1977; Fitzner 1978). The northern California population of Swainson's Hawks exists in such habitat in the Klamath Basin (Bloom 1980).

Land use patterns prevalent over the past 125 years have destroyed the once vast riparian forests that existed. Where gallery forests 6.4- to 8.1-km. (4- to 5-mi.) wide existed there are now kilometers of riprapped banks denuded of even brushy vegetation. The loss came about as a result of man's activities to obtain fuel, building material, and farmland in an earlier era and, in recent decades, to provide for agricultural expansion, "bank protection" and "flood control" (Smith 1977; Gaines 1977; Sands 1978).

Corresponding with the time of riparian vegetation loss in the Central Valley, the Swainson's Hawk population declined catastrophically. The decline has been on the order of 80-90% of the estimated historic level, a decline equal in severity to that suffered by the endangered American Peregrine Falcon (Falco peregrinus anatum) (Bloom 1980; Herman et al. 1970). Indeed, the Swainon's Hawk is a candidate for inclusion on the State's list of endangered species.

Besides habitat loss, other factors, such as problems relating to their migration route and wintering grounds, may have contributed to the species' decline in California. However, it seems clear that the tremendous loss of the riparian vegetation, that today appears so important to the Swainson's Hawk in the Central Valley, must have had a correspondingly tremendous impact on the population.

The solution to the problem of a declining wildlife population is never easy. There are many factors over which we may have little or no control. However, it is clear that we do have an opportunity to affect one critical factor in the Central Valley. A vigorous program to maintain and enhance remaining riparian systems may go a long way to help restore Swainson's Hawks to a more viable status. By maintaining a large and healthy Swainson's Hawk population in the Central Valley, which will serve as the core from which some of the former range may once again be repopulated, it is hoped we can mitigate for those mortality factors which we cannot control (i.e. problems on the wintering grounds in South America). Maintaining suitable nesting habitat in the Central Valley may be the key to saving the Swainson's Hawk from extirpation in California.

LITERATURE CITED

Bent, A.C. 1963. Life histories of North American birds of prey: Part one. Dover Publications, New York, New York. p. 222-236.

Bloom, P.H. 1980. The status of the Swainson's Hawk in California, 1979. Federal Aid in Wildlife Restoration, Project W-54-R-12, Nongame Wildl. Invest. Job Final Report 11-8.0. 24 p. + appendix.

Brumley, T.D. 1976. Upper Butte Basin study 1974-1975. California Department of Fish and Game, Wildlife Management Branch, Administrative report no. 76-1. 30 p. + appendix.

Conard, S.G., R.L. MacDonald, and R.F. Holland. 1977. Riparian vegetation and flora of the Sacramento Valley. p. 47-55. In: A. Sands (ed.). Riparian forests in California: Their ecology and conservation. Institute of Ecology Pub. 15. University of California, Davis. 122 p.

Dunkle, S.W. 1977. Swainson's Hawks on the Laramie Plains, Wyoming. Auk 94:65-71.

Fitzner, R.E. 1978. Behavioral ecology of the Swainson's Hawk (Buteo swainsoni) in Washington. Ph.D. Thesis. Washington State University, Pullman. 194 p.

Gaines, D.A. 1977. The valley riparian forests of California: their importance to bird populations. p. 57-85. In: A. Sands (ed.). Riparian forests in California: Their ecology and conservation. Institute of Ecology Pub. 15. University of California, Davis. 122 p.

Herman, S.G., M.N. Kirven, and R.W. Risebrough. 1970. Peregrine Falcon decline in California. Audubon Field Notes 24(4):609-613.

Jannssen, R. 1976. Army Corps of Engineers projects on the Sacramento River. In: Gaines, D.A. Abstracts from the conference on the riparian forests of the Sacramento Valley. Davis Audubon Society. 25 p.

Michny, F.J., D. Boos, and F. Wernette. 1975. Riparian habitats and avian densities along the Sacramento River. California Resources Agency, Department of Fish and Game. Administrative Report No. 75-1. March 1975. 42 p.

Olendorff, R.R. 1975. Population status of large raptors in northwestern Colorado, 1970-1972. In: J.R. Murphy, C.M. White, and B.E. Harrell (ed.). Population status of raptors. Raptor Res. Rep. No. 3:185-205.

Roberts, W., J.G. Howe, and J. Major. 1977. A survey of riparian forest flora and fauna in California. p. 3-19. In: A. Sands (ed.). Riparian forests in California: Their ecology and conservation. Institute of Ecology Pub. 15. University of California, Davis. 122 p.

Sands, A. 1978. Public involvement in riparian habitat protection, a California case history. p. 216-227. In: R.R. Johnson and J.F. McCormick (tech. coord.). Strategies for protection and management of floodplain wetlands and other riparian ecosystems: Proceedings of the symposium. [Callaway Gardens, Georgia, Dec. 11-13, 1978]. USDA Forest Service GTR-WO-12. USDA Forest Service, Washington, D.C. 410 p.

Sharp, C.S. 1902. Nesting of Swainson's Hawk. Condor 4:116-118.

Smith, F. 1977. Short review of the status of riparian forests in California. p. 1-2. In: A. Sands (ed.). Riparian forests in California: Their ecology and conservation. Institute of Ecology Pub. 15. University of California, Davis. 122 p.

Thompson, K. 1977. Riparian forests of the Sacramento Valley, California. p. 35-38. In: A. Sands (ed.). Riparian forests in California: Their ecology and conservation. Institute of Ecology Pub. 15. University of California, Davis. 122 p.

Willett, G. 1912. Birds of the Pacific Slope of Southern California. Pac. Coast Avifauna 7:47.

SENSITIVITY OF RIPARIAN BIRDS TO HABITAT LOSS[1]

Julie K. Meents, Bertin W. Anderson, and Robert D. Ohmart[2]

Abstract.--The extent and composition of riparian plant
communities in the lower Colorado River valley have historically been altered, primarily by man. Some of these communities are disappearing (cottonwood and mesquite), and others
are expanding (salt cedar and arrowweed). We examined the
avian community associated with riparian vegetation and
identified avian habitat specialists. Nearly all of these
specialists are concentrated in cottonwood/willow or honey
mesquite communities. Salt cedar generally supported no
avian species with narrow habitat breadth.

INTRODUCTION

Riparian vegetation of the Southwest desert
serves as habitat islands for many species of
wildlife. The lush vegetation and water along
riparian corridors is generally surrounded by
relatively sparse, dry uplands that are not suitable for most riparian birds. Within riparian
vegetation there are various plant communities
dominated by one or more plant species. Along
the lower Colorado River, we have identified six
major communities. The plant communities vary in
their areal extent and distribution throughout
the valley (Anderson and Ohmart 1976). Some,
such as the cottonwood/willow and mesquite communities, have become increasingly restricted to
small areas over the past 100 years because of
harvesting for fuel, clearing for agriculture and
urban development, wildfires, and changes in
water cycles (Ohmart et al. 1977). Many of
the factors that have led to the decline of
native communities have promoted the establishment and spread of the exotic salt cedar; salt
cedar-dominated vegetation is one of the few
communities that is stable or expanding in the
lower Colorado River valley.

Many avian species found in riparian vegetation are ubiquitous, but some species occur in
only one or a few plant communities. Restriction
to a few plant communities may limit an avian
population's persistence in an area if the
favored plant communities are rare or require a

very long time to redevelop after disturbance.
Dependence on a limited variety of plant communities may be a particular problem if an avian
species always occurs in low densities. Such
species typically have low tolerance for even
short-term habitat loss or alteration.

In this paper we examine the avian communities of the lower Colorado River valley and identify those species that may be considered plant
community specialists. The current status and
future potential of the plant communities in
which these specialists are found are also
discussed.

METHODS

Major vegetation-types were defined according to the dominant tree or shrub (table 1).
Cottonwood and willow trees frequently co-occur-
red, so they were combined as one vegetation-
type. Salt cedar occurred with other tree
species throughout the study area, but was
considered a separate type only where it was
relatively homogeneous. Salt cedar/honey mesquite was considered a separate vegetation-type
because there were extensive areas that supported
an approximately equal mix of the two species.
Each vegetation-type was further divided into as
many as six structural types based on the vertical distribution of the foliage. Structural Type
I was tallest and was multi-layered (fig. 1).
Vegetation structural-types are referred to as
communities throughout this paper.

The study area included the riparian floodplain of the Colorado River, from Davis Dam on
the Arizona/Nevada border south to the Mexican
border. Two to 11 transects, each 800-1,600 m.
long, were established in stands of each community roughly in proportion to their occurrence in
the valley. Birds were censused three times per

[1]Paper presented at the California
Riparian Systems Conference. [University of
California, Davis, September 17-19, 1981].
[2]Julie K. Meents is Field Biologist;
Bertin W. Anderson is Faculty Research Associate;
Robert D. Ohmart is Associate Director; all are
at the Center for Environmental Studies, Arizona
State University, Tempe, Arizona.

Table 1.--Classification of vegetation-types in the lower Colorado River valley.

Vegetation-type	Criteria
Cottonwood (Populus fremontii)/willow (Salix gooddingii)	Cottonwood and/or willow constituting at least 20% of the total trees
Screwbean mesquite (Prosopis pubescens)/salt cedar (Tamarix chinensis)	Screwbean mesquite constituting at least 20% of trees
Honey mesquite (Prosopis glandulosa)/salt cedar	Approximately equal numbers of each species
Salt cedar	Constituting 95-100% of total trees
Honey mesquite	Constituting 95-100% of total trees
Arrowweed (Tessaria [Pluchea] sericea)	Constituting 95-100% of total vegetation in area

month between May 1976 and July 1979 along these transects, using a modified variable transect method (Emlen 1971, 1977; Anderson et al. 1977). Seasonal averages of avian densities were calculated from all censuses taken in summer (May-July) and winter (December-February). Bird species considered in this paper include those whose occurrence and relative density were fairly predictable and stable between years. This group included most residents, as well as summer and winter visitors. Scientific names of all birds considered are listed in table 2.

Habitat breadth (HB) was calculated using the equation:

$$HB = - \Sigma p_i \log_{10} p_i$$

where p_i equals the proportion of a species' population occurring in community i. Evenness (J) is the percent of maximum HB:

$$J = HB/\log_{10} N$$

where N equals the number of communities and reflects how evenly the members of a species are distributed throughout the available habitat. We arbitrarily chose J = 0.75 as a dividing point between habitat specialists (J < 0.75) and habitat generalists (J > 0.75), based on results of censuses and our knowledge of each species.

RESULTS AND DISCUSSION

Summer Birds

Eighteen bird species were considered common breeding species in the lower Colorado River valley; seven of these are resident throughout the year. The majority (71%; table 3) of the summering species were found to be relatively evenly distributed throughout the plant communities and were considered habitat generalists. Because these species usually occur in all community-types, it seems likely that loss of one or a few plant communities would not constitute a serious threat to their respective populations.

Species with relatively narrow habitat breadth (habitat specialists) are discussed in greater detail below.

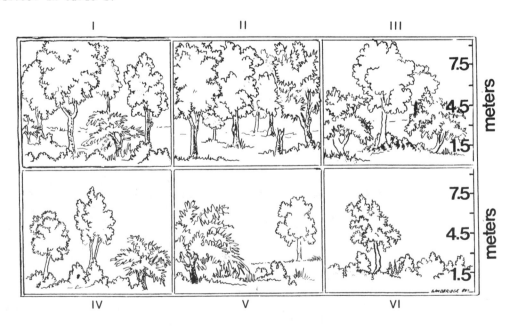

Figure 1.--Illustrations of relative densities of trees and understory shrubs in each of the vegetation-structural types. See Anderson et al. (1977) for details.

620

Table 2.--Common and scientific names of birds species associated with riparian vegetation.

Common Name	Scientific Name
Abert Towhee	Pipilo aberti
Ash-throated Flycatcher	Myiarchus cinerascens
Bell's Vireo	Vireo bellii
Black Phoebe	Sayornis nigricans
Black-tailed Gnatcatcher	Polioptila melanura
Blue Grosbeak	Guiraca caerulea
Brown Creeper	Certhia familiaris
Crissal Thrasher	Toxostoma dorsale
Cactus Wren	Campylorhynchus brunneicapillus
Gambel Quail	Lophortyx gambelii
Gila Woodpecker	Melanerpes uropygialis
House Wren	Troglodytes aedon
Ladder-backed Woodpecker	Picoides scalaris
Lucy Warbler	Vermivora luciae
Mourning Dove	Zenaida macroura
Northern Oriole	Icterus galbula
Orange-crowned Warbler	Vermivora celata
Phainopepla	Phainopepla nitens
Ruby-crowned Kinglet	Regulus calendula
Sage Sparrow	Amphispiza belli
Summer Tanager	Piranga rubra
Verdin	Auriparus flaviceps
Wied Crested Flycatcher	Myiarchus tyrannulus
White-crowned Sparrow	Zonotrichia leucophrys
White-winged Dove	Zenaida asiatica
Yellow-billed Cuckoo	Coccyzus americanus
Yellow-rumped Warbler	Dendroica coronata

Gila Woodpecker

The Gila Woodpecker is fairly common in southern Arizona, where it nests primarily in saguaro cactus (Carnegiea gigantea) (Phillips et al. 1964). In the lower Colorado River valley, the Gila Woodpecker is most frequent in cottonwood/ willow and Type III honey mesquite communities (table 3). This species is a primary cavity nester and, because of its relatively large size, requires large trees for hole excavation and as a foraging substrate (Brush et al.[3]).

---

[3]Brush, T., B.W. Anderson, and R.D. Ohmart. Habitat selection related to resource availability among cavity-nesting birds. 15 p. Unpublished manuscript.

Wied Crested Flycatcher

The population of Wied Crested Flycatcher breeding in the lower Colorado River valley is peripheral to the species' major distribution in Mexico. This flycatcher is primarily found in cottonwood/willow and mesquite communities (table 3). It is a secondary cavity nester and requires excavations or holes in fairly large trees.[3]

Summer Tanager

The Summer Tanager in the lower Colorado River region is also peripheral to the species' major range of distribution. It is mostly found in cottonwood/willow Types I-IV and salt cedar Type I (table 3); these are all communities with a large amount of vegetation at higher levels.

Yellow-billed Cuckoo

The Yellow-billed Cuckoo in the Southwest is limited to cottonwood, willow, or mesquite along rivers (Phillips et al. 1964). The birds in the Colorado River valley are concentrated in cottonwood/willow Types I-III, but are also found occasionally in honey mesquite Type III and screwbean mesquite Type II (table 3).

Bell's Vireo

The Bell's Vireo had a very narrow habitat breadth as well as a very low total population (table 3). Birds were generally found only in Type III or IV vegetation, but there was no association with a particular tree species. Although the Bell's Vireo probably has specific vegetation structure requirements, these do not appear to be limiting its population size, because Types III and IV vegetation are the most widespread types in the valley. Alternatively, the population appears to be most influenced by the rate of cowbird parasitism (Phillips et al. 1964; Serena 1981). The Brown-headed Cowbird (Molothrus ater) has become increasingly common in the valley as agriculture has expanded; this has led to increased parasitism of such birds as the Bell's Vireo. In riparian systems of the Rio Grande River, Bell's Vireo occurs both in greater numbers and in a wider variety of communities (Anderson and Ohmart unpublished data); cowbird populations are also lower and agricultural land is less widespread in this area. Thus it appears that Bell's Vireo in the lower Colorado River valley is probably not primarily limited by habitat availability. The Yellow Warbler (Dendroica petechia) has also been scarce or absent as a breeding bird in recent years in the lower Colorado River valley because of cowbird parasitism (Phillips et al. 1964).

Winter Birds

Five of 18 wintering bird species examined were habitat specialists (table 4).

Table 3.—Average densities (birds/40 ha.) and habitat breadth of summer bird species in riparian communities of the lower Colorado River valley. AR = arrowweed, SH = salt cedar/honey mesquite.

Bird Species	Cottonwood/willow						Screwbean mesquite					Salt Cedar					
	I	II	III	IV	V	VI	II	III	IV	V	VI	I	II	III	IV	V	VI
Resident																	
Abert Towhee	46	110	56	34	39	25	18	26	24	16	9	30	38	39	21	17	19
Black-tailed Gnatcatcher	0	0	7	7	2	2	3	8	18	14	7	7	4	5	4	7	2
Crissal Thrasher	0	2	9	8	5	6	3	5	9	7	8	1	7	7	4	4	3
Cactus Wren	2	1	9	3	1	7	4	4	3	1	3	1	1	2	1	1	2
Gambel Quail	1	2	11	20	27	16	31	11	32	18	34	36	27	22	17	27	27
Gila Woodpecker	35	16	8	4	3	3	2	0	0	1	1	0	2	1	0	0	1
Ladder-backed Woodpecker	26	31	21	13	5	4	15	5	6	3	10	3	5	3	2	1	4
Mourning Dove	21	236	146	80	67	27	436	145	102	28	47	79	129	112	84	35	129
Verdin	9	34	21	21	12	18	17	40	33	26	20	14	15	12	9	10	12
Nonresident																	
Ash-throated Flycatcher	5	11	17	12	12	9	20	13	12	7	19	6	8	6	6	3	10
Blue Grosbeak	4	14	16	12	19	13	4	7	10	8	6	8	13	23	11	6	7
Bell's Vireo	0	0	3	3	0	0	5	0	0	1	0	0	0	0	0	0	0
Lucy Warbler	1	28	15	17	15	5	16	17	19	19	16	43	44	8	13	5	5
Northern Oriole	30	19	29	20	9	15	13	7	13	6	5	6	15	12	6	2	6
Summer Tanager	17	10	8	2	0	0	0	0	0	0	0	13	0	1	0	0	0
Wied Crested Flycatcher	20	18	10	3	4	1	16	6	2	1	5	2	0	1	0	0	1
White-winged Dove	46	93	65	34	24	25	376	75	46	12	22	47	276	99	106	13	20
Yellow-billed Cuckoo	9	5	5	1	1	˙0	2	0	1	0	0	0	0	1	1	0	0

Bird Species	Honey mesquite				AR	SH	Habitat breadth	Percent of maximum habitat breadth
	III	IV	V	VI	VI	IV		
Resident								
Abert Towhee	36	47	9	12	20	24	1.28	0.94
Black-tailed Gnatcatcher	12	15	10	11	4	13	1.28	0.94
Crissal Thrasher	12	7	7	6	4	8	1.30	0.96
Cactus Wren	13	8	6	8	2	0	1.20	0.88
Gambel Quail	26	38	45	45	24	22	1.30	0.96
Gila Woodpecker	8	1	1	0	0	0	0.95	0.70
Ladder-backed Woodpecker	13	6	5	6	1	4	1.20	0.88
Mourning Dove	147	109	44	55	11	78	1.23	0.90
Verdin	31	26	20	22	12	23	1.32	0.97
Nonresident								
Ash-throated Flycatcher	24	16	10	9	4	11	1.31	0.96
Blue Grosbeak	2	2	0	0	8	9	1.33	0.98
Bell's Vireo	1	0	0	0	0	0	0.62	0.46
Lucy Warbler	46	24	13	14	2	26	1.26	0.93
Northern Oriole	29	11	3	6	2	10	1.26	0.93
Summer Tanager	0	0	0	0	0	0	0.66	0.49
Wied Crested Flycatcher	5	0	0	0	0	0	0.98	0.72
White-winged Dove	130	26	9	9	7	41	1.12	0.82
Yellow-billed Cuckoo	3	0	0	0	0	0	0.86	0.63
Mean							1.137	
Standard deviation							0.226	

Table 4.—Average densities (birds/40 ha.) and habitat breadth of winter birds in riparian communities of lower Colorado River valley (abbreviations in table 3).

Bird Species	Cottonwood/willow						Screwbean mesquite					Salt Cedar					
	I	II	III	IV	V	VI	II	III	IV	V	VI	I	II	III	IV	V	VI
Resident																	
Abert Towhee	26	39	13	18	13	12	6	8	7	6	7	12	24	17	6	9	6
Black-tailed Gnatcatcher	0	1	4	5	2	5	2	6	10	7	7	1	3	3	3	9	4
Crissal Thrasher	2	1	3	2	2	2	1	1	3	2	1	2	0	3	1	3	3
Cactus Wren	5	1	1	1	0	1	0	1	2	1	0	0	2	1	0	1	0
Gambel Quail	0	0	7	1	2	3	16	5	6	5	4	0	38	3	3	1	4
Gila Woodpecker	14	13	7	3	2	0	0	0	0	0	1	0	0	1	0	0	0
Ladder-backed Woodpecker	18	18	14	8	1	2	6	4	4	2	6	0	6	4	1	2	2
Mourning Dove	0	8	29	14	4	2	13	18	30	14	15	0	5	4	3	1	107
Verdin	2	8	7	8	5	7	5	8	9	3	8	0	5	11	3	6	4
Nonresident																	
Brown Creeper	6	7	4	1	0	0	0	0	0	0	0	0	0	0	0	0	0
Black Phoebe	2	1	7	3	0	4	0	0	1	0	1	0	0	0	0	0	0
House Wren	14	6	2	5	1	1	0	2	2	1	0	2	4	4	2	2	0
Orange-crowned Warbler	63	46	27	9	9	8	0	3	4	1	5	7	11	8	2	4	4
Phainopepla	0	0	0	0	0	0	1	7	6	1	1	0	1	0	0	0	0
Ruby-crowned Kinglet	138	140	105	50	35	26	13	22	20	12	18	39	25	37	13	14	19
Sage Sparrow	0	0	0	0	0	0	0	0	0	0	0	0	0	0	0	0	0
White-crowned Sparrow	0	1	8	9	8	21	6	8	14	7	17	1	33	21	3	40	17
Yellow-rumped Warbler	140	266	77	32	33	24	10	17	17	13	52	66	113	22	9	17	66

Bird Species	Honey mesquite				AR	SH	Habitat breadth	Percent of maximum habitat breadth
	III	IV	V	VI	VI	IV		
Resident							**Resident**	
Abert Towhee	20	13	5	7	6	9	1.29	0.95
Black-tailed Gnatcatcher	9	13	10	8	9	8	1.25	0.92
Crissal Thrasher	7	4	4	4	2	4	1.28	0.94
Cactus Wren	3	2	2	2	0	0	1.11	0.87
Gambel Quail	48	20	11	11	7	5	1.07	0.79
Gila Woodpecker	5	1	1	0	0	1	0.83	0.61
Ladder-backed Woodpecker	6	4	3	3	0	3	1.07	0.79
Mourning Dove	9	33	15	10	0	2	1.16	0.85
Verdin	12	15	9	11	8	4	1.30	0.96
Nonresident							**Nonresident**	
Brown Creeper	0	0	0	0	0	0	0.53	0.39
Black Phoebe	0	0	0	0	0	0	0.69	0.51
House Wren	2	1	0	0	1	0	1.08	0.79
Orange-crowned Warbler	4	2	1	0	1	2	1.12	0.82
Phainopepla	26	66	45	60	0	10	0.75	0.55
Ruby-crowned Kinglet	17	23	12	14	11	28	1.20	0.88
Sage Sparrow	3	13	5	2	0	0	0.49	0.36
White-crowned Sparrow	5	45	41	45	5	7	1.12	0.82
Yellow-rumped Warbler	8	15	7	8	11	9	1.11	0.82
Mean							1.025	
Standard deviation							0.255	

Gila Woodpecker

The Gila Woodpecker was the only resident species that was a habitat specialist; this was consistent in both seasons. As in summer, it was primarily limited to cottonwood/willow and honey mesquite Type III communities (table 4), where large trees suitable for cavity excavation and foraging were available.

Phainopepla

The Phainopepla was concentrated in honey mesquite communities and had a very narrow habitat breadth (table 4). Anderson and Ohmart (1978) have shown that the association between Phainopepla and mesquite is secondary; the birds rely heavily on the berries from mistletoe (Phoradendron californicum) that infests mesquite trees. Mistletoe berries provide a major source of food for Phainopepla during winter and early in the breeding season.

Sage Sparrow

The Sage Sparrow had the narrowest habitat breadth of the wintering species considered and was confined to honey mesquite communities (table 4). This relationship also appears to be secondary, because the Sage Sparrow is usually found associated with inkweed (Suaeda torreyana), a shrub that grows in patches in mesquite communities (Meents et al.[4]).

Brown Creeper

The Brown Creeper occurred exclusively in cottonwood/willow communities with tall, mature trees. This species is on the verge of extinction in the valley.

Black Phoebe

The Black Phoebe seldom occurred outside of cottonwood/willow communities. Peak densities occurred in stands that were moderately open in the layer >7 m. Usually there was water in the immediate vicinity.

CONCLUSIONS

Most habitat specialists in the lower Colorado River valley are found in cottonwood/ willow or honey mesquite communities. These plant communities were formerly widespread in the valley (Ohmart et al. 1977), and it is probable that the bird species that now have narrow habitat breadths were once much more abundant. Salt cedar is not favored by most bird species in the area (Cohan et al. 1978; Anderson and Ohmart

1981a). The avian species with narrow habitat breadth that we studied were rarely found in salt cedar vegetation or occurred only in the most mature stands. The first conclusion is that the continued spread of salt cedar will have a negative effect on these species. Arrowweed is another plant community that appears to be stable or spreading because it is common in disturbed areas; it is also little used by most bird species. Some bird species in the lower Colorado River valley have benefited or at least partially adapted to recent changes in proportions and composition of the local plant communities (Conine et al. 1978; Anderson and Ohmart 1981a,b). This is also demonstrated by those species with habitat breadths approaching 100% of maximum. But populations of at least six of the species discussed here are potentially threatened by the continuous decline or removal of cottonwood, willow, and mesquite vegetation. The second conclusion is that efforts should be made to revegetate areas with these plant species.

Because food resources for birds appear to be superabundant in summer (Anderson and Ohmart unpublished data), it is likely that summer habitat specialists select vegetation primarily on the basis of nesting requirements. Wintering birds are more likely to be limited by food resources, and their habitat selection probably reflects food availability. Phainopepla feeds on mistletoe which is found almost exclusively in honey mesquite communities. There is also indirect evidence that the Sage Sparrow's association with inkweed is food related (Meents et al.[4]). The third conclusion is that habitat requirements of wintering as well as breeding populations must be studied. Secondary species of vegetation known to have high value, such as mistletoe and inkweed, should be planted in revegetation efforts.

It should be noted that avian species that require large, mature trees (Gila Woodpecker, Wied Crested Flycatcher) may be especially sensitive to habitat loss because even artificial replacement of vegetation may require many years. The Bell's Vireo and other species are hurt directly as riparian vegetation is converted to agricultural uses. Agricultural areas provide habitat for species such as the Brown-headed Cowbird. As this nest parasite increases in numbers, the number of fledged young of parasitized species, such as the Bell's Vireo, will decrease further.

ACKNOWLEDGMENTS

Numerous field biologists helped collect the data. Susan M. Cook and Jane R. Durham provided editorial assistance, and Cindy D. Zisner typed the final copy. Brian Woodridge prepared the figure. We thank Ron Haywood for presenting the paper. We want to thank all of the above people for their tremendous dedication and help. This study was supported by USDI Bureau of Reclamation Contract No. 7-07-30-V0009.

---

[4]Meents, J.K., B.W. Anderson, and R.D. Ohmart. In review. Vegetation relationships and food of Sage Sparrows wintering in honey mesquite habitat.

LITERATURE CITED

Anderson, B.W., R.W. Engel-Wilson, D.G. Wells, and R.D. Ohmart. 1977. Ecological study of southwestern riparian habitats: techniques and data applicability. p. 146-155. In: R.R. Johnson and D.A. Jones (tech. coord.). Importance, preservation and management of riparian habitat: A symposium. [Tucson, Arizona, July 9, 1977.] USDA Forest Service GTR-RM-43, Rocky Mountain Forest and Range Experiment Station, Fort Collins, Colo. 217 p.

Anderson, B.W., and R.D. Ohmart. 1976. Vegetation type maps of the lower Colorado River from Davis Dam to the southerly International Boundary. 4 p. plus 23 maps. USDI Bureau of Reclamation, Lower Colorado Region, Boulder City, Nevada.

Anderson, B.W., and R.D. Ohmart. 1978. Phainopepla utilization of honey mesquite forests in the Colorado River valley. Condor 80:334-338.

Anderson, B.W., and R.D. Ohmart. 1981a. Vegetation management final report. USDI Bureau of Reclamation, Boulder City, Nevada. In preparation.

Anderson, B.W., and R.D. Ohmart. 1981b. Agricultural final report. USDI Bureau of Reclamation, Boulder City, Nevada. In preparation.

Cohan, D.R., B.W. Anderson, and R.D. Ohmart. 1978. Avian population responses to salt cedar along the lower Colorado River. p. 371-381. In: R.R. Johnson and J.F. McCormick (tech. coord.). Strategies for protection and management of floodplain wetlands and other riparian ecosystems: Proceedings of the symposium. [Callaway Gardens, Georgia, December 11-13, 1978.] USDA Forest Service GTR-WO-12, Washington, D.C. 410 p.

Conine, K.H., B.W. Anderson, R.D. Ohmart, and J.F. Drake. 1978. Responses of riparian species to agricultural habitat conversions. p. 248-262. In: R.R. Johnson and J.F. McCormick (tech. coord.). Strategies for protection and management of floodplain wetlands and other riparian ecosystems: Proceedings of the symposium. [Callaway Gardens, Georgia, December 11-13, 1978.] USDA Forest Service GTR-WO-12, Washington, D.C. 410 p.

Emlen, J.T. 1971. Population densities of birds derived from transect counts. Auk 88:323-342.

Emlen, J.T. 1977. Estimating breeding bird densities from transect counts. Auk 94:455-468.

Ohmart, R.D., W.O. Deason, and C. Burke. 1977. A riparian case history: the Colorado River. p. 35-47. In: R.R. Johnson and D.A. Jones (tech. coord.). Importance, preservation and management of riparian habitat: A symposium. [Tucson, Arizona, July 9, 1977.] USDA Forest Service GTR-RM-43, Rocky Mountain Forest and Range Experiment Station, Fort Collins, Colo. 217 p.

Phillips, A., J. Marshall, and G. Monson. 1964. The birds of Arizona. 212 p. University of Arizona Press, Tucson.

Serena, M. 1981. Distribution, habitat requirements, and reproductive success of Arizona Bell's Vireo (Vireo bellii arizonae) along the lower Colorado River. California Department of Fish and Game, Nongame Wildlife Investigations Final Report.

AVIAN USE OF REVEGETATED RIPARIAN ZONES[1]

Bertin W. Anderson and Robert D. Ohmart[2]

Abstract.--We reintroduced native riparian vegetation on three plots located along the lower Colorado River. Vegetational growth and avian colonization of the areas occurred rapidly. Fremont cottonwood (_Populus fremontii_), willow (_Salix gooddingii_), and quail bush (_Atriplex lentiformis_) were important to increased avian use. Selectively clearing salt cedar (_Tamarix chinensis_) and leaving native vegetation, including dead trees, resulted in further enhancement.

INTRODUCTION

We have studied riparian vegetation and its associated wildlife along the lower Colorado River since 1972. These studies were conducted in two phases. In the first phase, we classified the riparian vegetation (Anderson and Ohmart 1976) and determined the avian densities and diversities associated with each vegetation-type. The second phase of our work included the reintroduction of native plant species and the replacement of exotic vegetation with native vegetation. In this report we address three major questions: 1) at what rates do birds begin using a revegetated area?; 2) what combinations of native vegetation have the greatest enhancement value?; and 3) how much wildlife is lost when salt cedar is cleared? We will not provide complete answers here, but we do provide significant data pertaining to these questions.

METHODS

Our revegetation efforts were conducted on three sites ranging in size from 10-30 ha. Two sites were established on barren dredge-spoil. The third initially consisted of a mixed stand of salt cedar and willow. The latter site was selectively cleared, leaving the willow intact.

An avian census transect was established on each site. Transects 1,050 m. long were censused three times each month using a modified version (Anderson and Ohmart 1977) of the line transect

technique developed by Emlen (1971). Foliage density estimates were obtained with the board technique (MacArthur and MacArthur 1961). The number of trees greater than 3 m. tall was ascertained. The number of shrubs was estimated by counting all shrubs within 15 m. of either side of the transect.

Foliage height diversity (FHD) was calculated using $- \Sigma\, p_i \ln p_i$, where p_i was the proportion of foliage density in one of four layers. Layers used were 0 to 0.6 m., 1.5 to 3.0 m., 4.6 to 6.1 m., and ≥ 7.6 m. Each transect was divided into units 150 m. long. An index to horizontal foliage diversity (patchiness) for each of the four layers was calculated as the variance in foliage density at each level. Total patchiness was the sum of the variances (patchiness) at each of the four layers (Anderson et al. 1978). Quantified vegetation variables found on the revegetation sites were compared to the average for all of the riparian vegetation-types we recognized in the lower Colorado River Valley.

Avian use of revegetated areas was determined by comparing avian densities and diversities on revegetated areas with the average for all the riparian vegetation-types we recognized along the lower Colorado River. Vegetation development and avian use were expressed in standard units: the mean for riparian vegetation assumed a value of zero; values greater than the mean had positive values; and those less than the mean had negative values. In our study of the riparian vegetation, transects were established on all of the recognized vegetation-types approximately in proportion to their occurrence in the Valley.

The effect of clearing salt cedar was determined by comparing average densities and diversities found over a 3-year period (108 censuses) on the third plot, which was subsequently cleared. We studied the area for two years after it was cleared (72 censuses) before

[1]Paper presented at the California Riparian Systems Conference. [University of California, Davis, September 17-19, 1981].

[2]Bertin W. Anderson is Faculty Research Associate, Center for Environmental Studies, Arizona State University, Tempe, Arizona. Robert D. Ohmart is Associate Director, Center for Environmental Studies, Arizona State University, Tempe, Arizona.

it was revegetated. We recognized five seasons on the basis of climatic changes and major changes in the avifauna. According to our criteria, March and April were spring; May, June, and July--summer; August and September--late summer; October and November--fall; and December, January, and February--winter. Thus the pre-clearing study encompassed 15 seasons and the postclearing study conducted spanned 10 seasons.

RESULTS

The vegetation and avian variables studied are listed in table 1. Averages for vegetation variables found for all riparian vegetation are presented in table 2, and averages for avian variables are presented in table 3.

Foliage Development of Revegetated Sites

Means of the standardized variable (habitat quality index) were not significantly different between any two of the revegetation sites or from the mean for riparian vegetation in the Colorado River Valley (table 4). This is misleading because similar means can result from fundamentally different structural configurations. For example, total foliage densities were similar on the revegetation sites, and these were similar to the mean for riparian vegetation. However, on the revegetated sites this was due to above-average foliage density at low levels, whereas in the riparian vegetation in general there was above-average density at higher levels. The FHD was above average before clearing but was markedly below average on the revegetation sites. The

dredge-spoil sites had above-average numbers of cottonwood and willow trees greater than 3 m. by the end of the second year. The cleared site had above-average numbers of cottonwood and willow trees from the beginning as a result of the selective clearing. Shrubs were above average by the end of the first year on all three revegetation sites. The number of shrubs was below average on the cleared site before clearing.

Table 2.--Mean value for vegetation variables for the years 1975 to 1979 across all riparian vegetation-types along the lower Colorado River. Transformation of variable in parentheses.

Variable	Mean	Standard deviation
Foliage density		
0-0.6 m	0.529	0.165
1.5-3.0 m	1.250	0.270
Total	1.630	0.599
FHD	0.904	0.219
Horizontal foliage diversity ($\sqrt{}$)		
0-0.6 m	0.161	0.088
1.5-3.0 m	0.151	0.061
Total	0.276	0.135
Shrub density ($\log_{10}[N + 1]$)	0.647	0.847
Cottonwood and willow trees ($\log_{10}[N + 1]$)	0.691	0.417

Table 1.--Vegetation and avian variables used for evaluating revegetation sites.

Vegetation	Avian
Foliage density	Number of species
0-0.6 m	present in
1.5-3.0 m	densities $\geq 1/40$ ha
>4.5 m	
Total	
	Number of species of
	permanent resident
Foliage diversity	insectivores (SPRI)
Foliage height	
diversity (FHD)	Number of species of
Horizontal foliage	visiting
diversity	insectivores (SVI)
(Patchiness index =	
PI)	
0-0.6 m	Number of species of
1.5-3.0 m	granivores (SEE)
≥ 4.5 m	
Total	Densities
	Doves (D)
	Gambel Quail (GQ)
Number of cottonwood	Total (TD)
and willow trees/0.4 ha	Permanent resident
	insectivores
	(DPRI)
Number of shrubs/0.4 ha	Visiting
	insectivores (DVI)
Number of salt cedar	Granivores (DSE)
trees/0.4 ha	

Table 3.--Avian species richness and density expressed as mean values for 1978 seasons. SP = spring, SU = summer, LS = late summer, FA = fall, WI = winter. All riparian vegetation-types along the lower Colorado River are included. Densities are expressed as $\log_{10}(N + 1)$. VI = visiting insectivores, PRI = permanent resident insectivores, GR = granivores, GQ = Gambel Quail. Standard deviation in parentheses.

	Number of species	VI	PRI	GR	Doves	GQ
				Density		
SP	24.1	1.84	1.74	1.20	1.27	0.95
	(6.4)	(0.27)	(0.23)	(0.47)	(0.34)	(0.39)
SU	21.3	1.98	2.01	-	1.94	1.31
	(5.0)	(0.24)	(0.19)	-	(0.34)	(0.49)
LS	24.1	1.71	2.13	1.14	1.49	1.52
	(6.4)	(0.47)	(0.16)	(0.51)	(0.35)	(0.54)
FA	23.5	1.69	1.91	1.27	0.53	1.16
	(4.9)	(0.30)	(0.21)	(0.45)	(0.45)	(0.60)
WI	19.3	1.74	1.77	1.29	0.71	0.74
	(5.4)	(0.47)	(0.19)	(0.44)	(0.68)	(0.54)

Table 4.--Foliage characteristics found on three revegetated sites and on one of the sites before clearing. Data are presented in standardized units based on the mean for riparian vegetation along the lower Colorado River. CW = cottonwood/willow.

	East dredge spoil	West dredge spoil	Cleared area After clearing	Cleared area Before clearing
Months after revegetation	25	25	12	—
Foliage density				
0-0.6 m	1.19	2.13	2.78	-0.76
1.5-3.0 m	-1.58	0.00	0.93	0.92
Total	-0.78	-0.14	0.14	-0.19
Patchiness				
0-0.6 m	0.79	1.22	0.96	-1.35
1.5-3.0 m	1.32	-0.10	-0.47	0.63
Total	-0.21	0.23	0.03	0.15
FHD	-3.33	-1.32	-1.71	0.55
Density				
CW	1.29	1.23	1.10	1.08
Shrubs	1.58	1.79	2.18	-0.76
Habitat Quality Index				
Mean	0.03	0.56	0.65	0.21
SD	1.20	1.10	1.36	0.80

The herbaceous vegetation on the revegetated plots, classified as shrubs, was composed of different species, and the total number of shrubs varied among the plots (table 5). The east dredge-spoil site had the smallest amount of herbaceous vegetation; this was almost exclusively Russian thistle (Salsola iberica). On the west dredge-spoil site the total density of herbaceous vegetation was about 50% greater than on the east dredge-spoil site; there was more smotherweed (Bassia hyssopifolia) and quail bush on the west dredge-spoil site. The greatest number of shrubs occurred on the cleared site; smotherweed, inkweed (Suaeda torreyana), and quail bush were the numerically dominant species.

Table 5.--Densities (number/0.4 ha.) of several plant species characterized as shrubs on three revegetation sites. Mos. = months after planting.

Plot	Mos.	Number Russian thistle	Number Smother- weed	Number Ink- weed	Number Quail bush	Total
East dredge spoil	49	95	0	0	2	97
West dredge spoil	25	55	45	2	42	144
Cleared area	12	0	216	70	335	621

Bird Use of Revegetated Sites

On the dredge-spoil sites, bird use, expressed as standard units, was above the average for riparian systems in the Colorado River Valley for almost all categories in fall, winter, and spring, but below average at other seasons (table 6). Insectivorous birds and doves were the last bird groups to colonize revegetated sites. Granivorous bird species reached above-average densities earlier than other groups and densities of insectivores tended to remain lower than average over the first two years. Bird species richness and densities were greater in winter and fall than at other seasons. Granivorous birds reached greatest densities on the west dredge-spoil and cleared sites. In general, birds used the cleared site to a greater extent a year earlier than the dredge-spoil sites. Summer densities were below the riparian average on all sites.

Impact of Clearing Salt Cedar

Clearing salt cedar resulted in removal of more than 90% of the vegetation present on the site. Cottonwood, willow, screwbean mesquite (Prosopis pubescens), and dead trees remained; their aggregate density was about 30 per ha. The site remained in this condition for two full years. The only change during that time was invasion by a few annuals, inkweed, and quail bush. By fall of the second year there was a total of 15 inkweed and quail bush on the site. Leveling, installing the irrigation system, and augering holes were activities largely responsible for keeping vegetation from developing on the site before planting.

In spite of the removal of most of the vegetation, total species richness, species richness, and densities of passerine granivores, and densities of doves were all significantly higher (P< 0.05) than before clearing (table 7). The density of insectivorous species dropped significantly for visiting insectivores but not for permanent resident birds.

DISCUSSION

Avian colonization of sites revegetated with native vegetation was rapid, reaching average or above-average densities and diversities in less than two years. Revegetation efforts on dredge-spoil sites progressed more slowly than on the site from which salt cedar had been cleared, and the pattern of avian use reflected this. There are at least three reasons for this. First, because selective clearing was done, there were mature trees on the cleared site from the beginning. On the dredge-spoil sites there was less than one mature tree per hectare when planting began. It was not until the second year that an equal number of trees reached a height of 3 m. Second, on the cleared site we made an extensive effort to establish inkweed and quail bush. The avian data collected after clearing, but before shrubs were planted, revealed that these two shrubs are very important in attracting birds.

Table 6.--Avian community characteristics found on three revegetated sites. The data are presented in standard units based on the mean for riparian vegetation studied along the lower Colorado River. Mos. = months after revegetation, abbreviations as in table 3. Passerine granivores were not present in summer.

Plot/ season	Mos.	No. species	Densities VI	PRI	GR	GQ	Doves	Mean	SD
East dredge spoil									
LS	17	−0.18	−1.02	−4.04	−0.05	−0.68	−0.81	−1.23	1.41
FA	19	0.10	−0.48	−1.25	3.00	−1.92	−0.12	−0.11	1.71
WI	21	0.86	−0.21	1.36	2.07	−0.25	−1.05	0.46	1.17
SP	23	0.14	0.22	−0.77	1.89	−0.90	−0.20	0.06	1.01
SU	26	−0.46	−1.91	−3.60	−	−0.73	−0.56	−1.45	1.33
West dredge spoil									
LS	17	−0.17	−0.59	−3.87	0.02	1.07	1.56	−0.33	1.91
FA	19	0.51	−0.75	0.75	2.73	−1.92	2.39	0.62	1.79
WI	21	2.16	0.21	−0.48	2.79	1.61	−0.61	0.95	1.44
SP	23	0.41	−0.77	−1.94	1.84	1.07	−0.28	0.01	1.34
SU	26	−0.66	−2.28	−3.69	−	0.35	0.64	−1.13	1.83
Cleared site									
LS	5	1.08	−0.29	−0.49	1.52	−0.15	2.79	0.74	1.29
FA	7	3.16	−2.30	2.15	4.00	1.38	0.16	1.43	2.26
WI	9	2.53	0.12	2.64	3.92	2.88	−0.16	1.99	1.63
SP	11	1.08	0.80	0.75	3.03	3.49	−0.37	1.46	1.48
SU	14	0.14	−0.17	−2.07	−	−0.06	−0.32	−0.50	0.90

Table 7.--Avian community composition before and after clearing salt cedar from a 20-ha. site. Number of seasons (N) before clearing = 15; after clearing N = 10. Densities calculated as $\log_{10}(N + 1)$. Abbreviations as in table 3. TO = total.

	Before clearing Mean	SD	SE	After clearing Mean	SD	SE	P
Species richness							
TO	16.8	5.8	1.54	21.1	3.7	1.23	<0.025
VI	6.5	3.2	0.85	7.0	1.6	0.53	>0.05
PRI	6.7	1.7	0.47	6.8	2.4	0.81	>0.05
GR	0.8	0.8	0.22	2.2	2.2	0.72	<0.05
Densities							
VI	1.69	0.30	0.08	1.40	0.14	0.05	<0.01
PRI	1.58	0.19	0.05	1.45	0.29	0.10	>0.05
GR	0.51	0.48	0.13	1.00	0.50	0.17	<0.025
GQ	0.57	0.65	0.17	0.84	0.68	0.23	>0.05
Doves	1.03	0.87	0.23	1.49	0.49	0.16	>0.05

We have presented additional data elsewhere in support of this claim (Anderson et al. 1978). Herbaceous vegetation, primarily Russian thistle and smotherweed, developed rapidly on the dredge-spoil sites. Granivorous, but not insectivorous, bird species were attracted to this vegetation. Insectivorous birds were attracted to the cleared site to a greater extent than to the dredge-spoil sites where quail bush was abundant. Finally, several trees with large dead snags were among the trees left on the cleared site, consequently attracting greater numbers of those bird species which use dead limbs and cavities. In areas where trees were planted, but no dead trees were present, it will be years before large dead snags develop naturally. This disadvantage might be overcome by putting up nest boxes and by girdling a few 4-year-old trees. Girdling, of course, will kill the tree unless it is done in the winter, when new growth will develop from suckers at the base of the tree.

Because avian densities and diversities increased after clearing, but before planting, it seems that merely clearing salt cedar results in some enhancement. We have presented additional data elsewhere indicating the negative value of salt cedar to most riparian birds (Anderson et al. 1977; Cohan et al. 1978). After clearing, the areas became more attractive to birds such as the Lesser Nighthawk (Chordeiles acutipennis) and Loggerhead Shrike (Lanius ludovicianus), which typically occur in more open areas. Granivorous bird species were probably attracted to the area after clearing because of the annuals and the few scattered shrubs which developed. Annuals and shrubs were totally absent before clearing. Doves were more abundant during the breeding season before the area was cleared, but they were less abundant at other seasons. Some species of permanent resident birds decreased significantly in numbers after clearing (e.g. Abert Towhee (Pipilo aberto)), but several species (e.g. Roadrunner (Geococcyz californianus)) came into the area (Anderson and Ohmart 1981).

If quail bush, inkweed, cottonwood, and willow are planted, frugivorous species, such as the Phainopepla (Phainopepla nitens), will not use the area. This species, and frugivorous species in general, exist mainly on the fruit of mistletoe (<u>Phoradendron californicum</u>) (Anderson and Ohmart 1978). In the Colorado River Valley mistletoe infests honey mesquite (<u>Prosopis glandulosa</u>) to a far greater extent than any other vegetation. If honey mesquite is not planted in a revegetated area, little use by frugivores can be anticipated.

Colorado River water is perhaps the most sought-after water on the North American continent. Riparian vegetation uses water through evapotranspiration; water which, theoretically, could otherwise be used by man. In addition, there is concern that the vegetation in the floodplain of the lower Colorado River could obstruct the passage of floodflows. The numerically dominant species of vegetation along the lower Colorado River is the exotic salt cedar (Anderson and Ohmart 1976). In this report we have shown that, at least under certain circumstances, a great deal of salt cedar can be cleared without having a negative impact on birds in general. It follows that if salt cedar is replaced with native riparian shrubs and trees, avian populations as well as the native riparian vegetation can be enhanced while total foliage density decreases. Theoretically, the clearing would therefore result in water salvage through reduced evapotranspiration and an increased capacity for the floodplain to carry floodwater.

CONCLUSIONS

We conclude that avian populations can be rapidly enhanced by revegetating riparian zones with native riparian species of vegetation. The native trees and shrubs grow rapidly. Trees will grow 2-3 m. annually, and shrubs will mature and fruit the first year under appropriate conditions. Careful planning will ensure almost immediate use of the area by a large and diverse avian population during most seasons. Plant species used in revegetation efforts should include honey mesquite, cottonwood, willow trees, quail bush, and inkweed. Clearing should be done selectively so that all native trees and all dead trees or trees with large dead snags are left intact. This will make the area attractive to bird species which use snags as perches and cavities for nesting.

Since clearing salt cedar from an area has little deleterious impact on avian communities, we encourage it, provided that at least 25% of the cleared salt cedar is replaced with native vegetation. We must emphasize, however, that native vegetation cannot be expected to thrive by simply planting it anywhere. Autecological conditions such as soil layering and soil density, depth from the surface to the water table, and salinity conditions should be carefully assessed first. Site preparation requirements, such as leveling, extent of tillage, and irrigation system design, must be carefully considered.

Revegetation can be implemented to restore native plant species and enhance wildlife. Water salvage through reduction of evapotranspirative losses and increased streambed capacity to carry floodwater, as a result of overall reduction in the total vegetation, are potential ancillary benefits of revegetation efforts.

ACKNOWLEDGMENTS

We wish to thank Marcelett Ector and Cindy D. Zisner for typing the various drafts of the manuscript. Susan M. Cook, Jane R. Durham, Cindy D. Zisner, and Chuck Hunter reviewed the manuscript and provided editorial suggestions. We are grateful to the many field biologists who assisted in collecting field data. The project was jointly funded by the USDI Bureau of Reclamation and the USDI Fish and Wildlife Service through Contract Number 7-07-30-V0009.

LITERATURE CITED

Anderson, B.W., R.W. Engel-Wilson, D. Wells, and R.D. Ohmart. 1977. Ecological study of southwestern riparian habitats: techniques and data applicability. p. 146-155. In: R.R. Johnson and D.A. Jones (ed.). Importance, preservation and management of riparian habitat: a symposium. [Tucson, Ariz., July 9, 1977]. USDA Forest Service GTR-RM-43. 217 p. Rocky Mountain Forest and Range Experiment Station, Fort Collins, Colo.

Anderson, B.W., and R.D. Ohmart. 1976. Vegetation type maps of the lower Colorado River from Davis Dam to the southerly International Boundary. USDI Bureau of Reclamation, Lower Colorado Region. 27 p. Boulder City, Nev.

Anderson, B.W., and R.D. Ohmart. 1977. Climatological and physical characteristics affecting avian population estimates in Southwestern riparian communities using transect counts. p. 193-200. In: R.R. Johnson and D.A. Jones (ed.). Importance, preservation and management of riparian habitat: a symposium. [Tucson, Ariz., July 9, 1977]. USDA Forest Service GTR-RM-43. 217 p. Rocky Mountain Forest and Range Experiment Station, Fort Collins, Colo.

Anderson, B.W., and R.D. Ohmart. 1978. Phainopepla utilization of honey mesquite forests in the Colorado River valley. Condor 80:334-338.

Anderson, B.W., and R.D. Ohmart. 1981. Revegetation efforts along the lower Colorado River. Final Report to the USDI Bureau of Reclamation, in review, Boulder City, Nev.

Anderson, B.W., R.D. Ohmart, and J. Disano. 1978. Revegetating the riparian floodplain for wildlife. p. 318-331. In: R.R. Johnson and J.F. McCormick (tech. coord.). Strategies for protection and management of floodplain wetlands and other riparian ecosystems: Proceedings of the symposium. [Callaway Gardens, Georgia, Dec. 11-13, 1978]. USDA Forest Service GTR-WO-12. 410 p. Washington, D.C.

Cohan, D.R., B.W. Anderson, and R.D. Ohmart. 1978. Avian population responses to salt cedar along the lower Colorado River. p. 371-382. In: R.R. Johnson and J.F. McCormick (tech. coord.). Strategies for protection and management of floodplain wetlands and other riparian ecosystems: Proceedings of the symposium. [Callaway Gardens, Georgia, Dec. 11-13, 1978]. USDA Forest Service GTR-WO-12. 410 p. Washington, D.C.

Emlen, J.T. 1971. Population densities of birds derived from transect counts. Auk 88:323-342.

MacArthur, R.H., and J.W. MacArthur. 1961. On bird species diversity. Ecology 42:594-598.

GIANT TREE

CIRCUMFERENCE   53 FEET
DIAMETER   17 FEET
OF TREE

PROTECTION OF RIPARIAN SYSTEMS
IN THE CALIFORNIA COASTAL ZONE[1]

John Zentner[2]

Abstract.--Protection of riparian systems is a major concern in coastal California. The Coastal Plan, written in 1975, advocates riparian protection through watershed management plans. The Coastal Act, passed in 1976, contained strong riparian corridor protection policies but deleted the concept of watershed management. This paper explores past actions of the California Coastal Commission to protect riparian systems and discusses the contradiction between strong riparian protection and relatively weak watershed regulation.

INTRODUCTION

Despite the efforts of many federal, state, and local agencies, private organizations, and concerned citizens, riparian vegetation continues to disappear at an alarming rate in California (Beer 1978). Although no separate data are available for coastal areas, subjective observations indicate that this loss also holds true in the state's coastal watersheds.

The California Coastal Commission, a state agency within the Resources Agency, is charged with protecting coastal resources, and is concerned about continued degradation of riparian systems. Through its power to regulate development, the Commission, in conjunction with local government, has the ability to guide much of the growth and change in the coastal zone. This paper discusses the genesis of the Commission, what it has done to protect riparian systems, and what the future may hold.

BACKGROUND

A Governor's Panel recommended in 1936 that a coastal commission be established. However, it was not until 1969 that the first legislation

toward that end was introduced.[3,4] When the Legislature failed to pass a coastal bill, activists gathered enough signatures to place an initiative on the ballot. The initiative, Proposition 20, passed by a 55.1% margin in November, 1972. Proposition 20 established the predecessor of the Coastal Commission, the California Coastal Zone Conservation Commission (CCZCC). The CCZCC was charged with writing a coastal plan in three years and regulating development in the coastal zone. Under Proposition 20 the coastal zone extended landward to the "highest elevation of the nearest coastal mountain range" except in Los Angeles, Orange, and San Diego Counties where it extended to the highest elevation or 8 km. (5 mi.) inland, whichever was less. However, the permit zone only went about 900 m. (1,000 yds.) inland. Thus the "coastal zone" included most coastal watersheds but CCZCC permit authority over development extended only a relatively short distance inland.

In 1975, the CCZCC adopted the California Coastal Plan and submitted it to the Legislature. In addition to an inventory of coastal resources and policies on coastal planning issues, the Plan contained several provisions on protection and management of riparian systems as follow:

> Coastal streams are vital to the
> natural system of the coast;

[1]Paper presented at the California Riparian Systems Conference. [University of California, Davis, September 17-19, 1981].

[2]John Zentner is Resource Ecologist for the California Coastal Commission, San Francisco, Calif. Opinions expressed by the author do not necessarily reflect views of the California Coastal Commission.

[3]Marsh, Linda. 1978. The California Coastal Commission: Who's minding the shore? South Bay Tribune, Manhattan Beach, Calif. 12 July, 1978.

[4]In 1965, the Legislature created the Bay Conservation and Development Commission (BCDC) to regulate development in San Francisco Bay. BCDC became an important precedent for creation of a coastal commission. See Odell (1972) for a history of BCDC.

coastal streams directly affect the coastal environment;

they are vital to anadromous fish that live in both salt and fresh water;

they collect and transport sand from the watershed to supply coastal beaches;

they are valuable to the aesthetic and recreational enjoyment of coastal waterways; and

they are interrelated with the estuarine systems that in turn are essential to the productivity of the marine environment.

Coastal streams also significantly influence flooding, natural ecosystems, agricultural water supply, and groundwater recharge within the coastal land environment. Watershed areas are thus an ideal focus for developing management techniques to maximize utilization and preservation of natural resources of the coastal zone. (California Coastal Zone Conservation Commission 1975)

These findings linked riparian system protection with watershed management. Thus, basic policy for CCZCC riparian system protection would be establishment of comprehensive watershed management. Policy 22 provided the guidance and detail on development of these plans:

Prepare and implement comprehensive watershed management plans:

a. Procedure for Preparation and Implementation of the Plans. A lead agency at the State level designated by the Legislature (e.g., the Resources Agency, Department of Conservation, or Water Resources Control Board) shall coordinate watershed planning and work closely with affected local governments, other State agencies, and Federal agencies. The coastal agency shall participate in an advisory role in the overall watershed planning program and watershed plans beyond the coastal resource management area.

b. Content and Goals of the Plans. The watershed management plans shall relate upland and shoreline land use management to the protection and restoration of the marine environment; use consistent assumptions, standards, and criteria for determining appropriate future population levels and land uses

within each coastal watershed; consider statewide interbasin interests (e.g., true costs of water importation); and otherwise assure that allowable development conforms to the Coastal Plan. The plans shall stress the protection of coastal groundwater resources, streams, wetlands, and estuaries, and shall prevent significant adverse impacts on these resources ... (ibid.)

Watershed management is used by many state water resource departments for water supply planning. However, these departments have rarely considered themselves land-use planning agencies, and have generally tried to simply manage water supply to meet demand (White 1969). It was partially the failure to resolve the increasingly complex conflicts between riparian and watershed protection and water regulation that led to an outcry for more land-use oriented watershed planning (see Howe 1978; Burke and Heaney 1975).

The Coastal Plan reflected this concern by incorporating resource protection and the concept of limiting growth to the level of available resources. However, the land-use planning aspect of these plans provoked substantial concern among local governments. Opposition to further state control was so great that when the Coastal Plan was modified and adopted by the Legislature as the Coastal Act of 1976, the watershed management policies of the Plan were not included in the Act.

Clearly, including coastal watersheds in the coastal zone makes good sense. Upstream developments affecting downstream areas, especially wetlands, could be regulated and the multitude of different governmental bodies coordinated—but the political effort would be considerable. The amount of land which would have been added to the coastal zone was enormous, especially in the north state. This factor alone made it politically infeasible to include watershed management in the Coastal Act.[5]

The Act is, however, very protective of the riparian corridor. Section 30236 states:

Channelizations, dams, or other substantial alterations of rivers and streams shall incorporate the best mitigation measures feasible, and be limited to (1) necessary water supply projects, (2) flood control projects where no other method for protecting existing structures in the flood plain is feasible and where such protection is necessary for public safety or to protect existing development, or (3) developments where the primary function

---

[5]Douglas, Peter. April, 1981. Personal conversation. California Coastal Commission, San Francisco, Calif.

is the improvement of fish and wildlife habitat.

Section 30240 states:

(a) Environmentally sensitive habitat areas shall be protected against any significant disruption of habitat values, and only uses dependent on such resources shall be allowed within such areas.

(b) Development in areas adjacent to environmentally sensitive habitat areas and parks and recreation areas shall be sited and designed to prevent impacts which would significantly degrade such areas, and shall be compatible with the continuance of such habitat areas (California Coastal Act of 1976).

Other portions of the Act established six Regional Commissions, defined development broadly, gave the Commission the power to approve, deny or condition development permits, and directed each local jurisdiction to develop a local coastal plan, which, when certified by the Commission, would give the jurisdiction permit authority over coastal development. In addition, the Act seeks to minimize flood and other hazards and to assure that, in case of policy conflicts, decisions will seek a balance which is most protective of natural resources. The definition of coastal zone also underwent some changes. The coastal zone now extends 4.8 km. (3 mi.) seaward and averages 915 m. (1,000 yds.) inland from the mean high tide line. This distance is reduced in some built-up areas, such as parts of San Francisco, Los Angeles, and San Diego, but can be expanded up to 8 km. (5 mi.) where necessary to protect significant coastal resources.

The remainder of this paper discusses pertinent Commission actions on permits, local coastal plans, and other areas which have affected riparian systems.

PERMITS AFFECTING PROTECTION OF RIPARIAN SYSTEMS

As indicated above, the Commission has permit authority over a wide range of activities within the coastal zone. For this paper, a brief survey was made of permits which were appealed to the state Commission after a regional commission decision, and which were concerned with protection of riparian systems. These are presented below by the issue which seems to characterize each best. Unless otherwise noted, these appeals are referenced by their Commission appeal number.

Development in a Riparian Corridor

The Los Virgenes Municipal Water District sought a permit to expand its handling facility in Monte Nido Valley in the Santa Monica Mountains. The applicant wished to grade and channelize a portion of a small creek to construct a new shop and maintenance building in proximity to the other structures. The Commission approved the permit but required, as a condition of approval, that no grading and channelizing be done in the riparian corridor and that the shop be relocated.

A second major issue which surfaced with this permit concerned impact of the wastewater discharged to Malibu Creek from the facility. The Water District collected data on its discharge for an entire year, and collaborated with the Regional Water Quality Control Board in a report which concluded that the discharge had no effect on algae, fish, or macroinvertebrates in the creek. Based on that report, the Commission concluded that the discharge was not harming the biological productivity of the stream and approved the permit (Appeal 39-80).

The Orange County Flood Control District applied for a permit to remove from a channelized portion of San Juan Creek in Orange County 280,000 cubic yards of sediment deposited by a storm. The Commission aproved the permit on the condition that the flood control district use the excavated material for beach replenishment, thereby avoiding potential shoreline erosion problems. In this case, the Commission made extensive findings showing that removing creek sediments would deplete sand replenishment of downcurrent beaches (Appeal 200-80).

Cumulative Impact of Incremental Developments

A private landowner applied for a permit to divide a four-acre parcel into two parcels for residential development in Cold Creek Canyon in Malibu. Much of the site is either within the Cold Creek Significant Ecological Area (SEA) or the SEA buffer zone as designated in the Commission's Malibu/Santa Monica Mountains Area Plan. The Commission's interpretive guidelines contain policies recognizing the cumulative impacts of new development in Cold Creek Canyon and recommend against new land divisions in the area. The Commission denied the permit, finding that the project would set a precedent by allowing more land divisions in the canyon, thereby severely undercutting the guidelines. The Commission decided that the cumulative impacts of the buildout in the canyon would have significantly degraded the creek's riparian systems (Appeal 360-80).

The Commission has not blocked all development in this area, however. Another applicant was granted a permit for terracing a hillside above Cold Creek for orchard and vineyard planting. The Commission found that this low-intensity use, if properly buffered, was compatible with protection of the biological productivity of the creek (Appeal 53-79).

Setbacks for Development

A private landowner applied for a permit to construct a single-family residence on a narrow lot in Los Flores Canyon in Los Angeles County. The lot was not wide enough for a 50-ft. setback between the septic tank and the stream. The Commission denied the permit, noting that some riparian vegetation would have been destroyed by the riprap needed to protect the house during moderate floodflows. In addition, the Commission found there was not enough room for an adequate stream buffer (a minimum of 30 m. (100 ft.)) from the house (Appeal 61-80).

Timber Harvesting Along Riparian Corridors

Prior to passage of the Coastal Act, the Masonite Corporation applied for a permit to cut timber on 170 ha. (420 ac.) of land along the Albion River in Mendocino County. The lumber company proposed to leave 30-m. (100-ft.) natural buffers along the edge of the river in accordance with the Forest Practices Act, although the company indicated it would harvest the trees left in the buffer after the rest of the trees had been cut. Several local residents spoke in opposition to the permit, requesting that at least 60- to 90-m. (200- to 300-ft.) buffers be required to protect local salmon spawning grounds and blue heron rookeries. The Commission approved the permit but required 60-m. buffers along the river (Healy 1977).

Under the Coastal Act, the Commission was not given the authority to regulate commercial timber operations larger than 1.2 ha. (3 ac.). The Legislature determined that the Forest Practices Act and the Board of Forestry should have sole jurisdiction over larger operations. However, the Coastal Act directed the Commission to submit to the Board of Forestry a list of forest special treatment areas where logging could adversely affect rivers or streams. The Board later adopted these special treatment areas and certain other changes in forestry practices also suggested by the Commission (Blumenthal 1979).

In another case, after the Act was passed, a private landowner applied for a permit to harvest timber, about five cords per year, on a 1-ha. (2.5-ac.) parcel near the Eel River Delta in Humboldt County. The Department of Fish and Game raised concerns about the permit, fearing it could set a precedent for logging other parcels in that area. The Department, the Commission and Humboldt County had been working extensively with local landowners to develop riparian protection measures for the delta. The Commission denied the permit and made the finding that, in order to fully protect the riparian system, no cutting could be allowed until a detailed, comprehensive management plan for the area could be developed (Appeal 68-81).

LOCAL COASTAL PROGRAMS

Each city or county with jurisdiction in the coastal zone is required to prepare a Local Coastal Plan (LCP) under the Coastal Act. An LCP is composed of the Land Use Plan (LUP) and zoning ordinances implementing the LUP. The Commis-

sion reviews each LCP and decides on its conformity with the Coastal Act. The following section discusses two LCPs submitted by the County of San Mateo and the City of Oceanside.

San Mateo County

The San Mateo County LCP, approved 5 December, 1980, was the first county LCP to be certified by the Commission. As one of the earliest plans, it has often been held up as a model for its resource protection policies. The riparian protection policies are especially strong:

Definition of Riparian Corridors

Define riparian corridors by the "limit of riparian vegetation" (i.e., a line determined by the association of plant and animal species normally found near streams, lakes and other bodies of freshwater: red alder, jaumea, pickleweed, big leaf maple, narrowleaf cattail, arroyo willow, broadleaf cattail, horsetail, creek dogwood, black cottonwood, and box elder). Such a corridor must contain at least a 50% cover of some combination of the plants listed.

Designation of Riparian Corridors

Establish riparian corridors for all perennial and intermittent streams and lakes and other bodies of freshwater in the Coastal Zone. Designate those corridors shown on the Sensitive Habitats Map and any other riparian area meeting the definition of Policy 7.7 as sensitive habitats requiring protection, except for man-made irrigation ponds over 2,500 square feet surface area.

Permitted Uses in Riparian Corridors

a. Within corridors, permit only the following uses: (1) education and research, (2) consumptive uses as provided for in the Fish and Game Code and Title 14 of the California Administrative Code, (3) fish and wildlife management activities, (4) trails and scenic overlooks on public land(s), and (5) necessary water supply projects.

b. When no feasible or practicable alternative exists, permit the following uses: (1) stream dependent aquaculture provided that non-stream dependent facilities locate outside of corridor, (2) flood control projects where no other method for protecting existing structures in the flood plain is feasible and where protection is necessary for public safety or to protect existing development, (3) bridges when supports are not in significant conflict with corridor resources, (4) pipelines, (5) repair or maintenance of roadways or road crossings, (5) logging operations which are limited to temporary skid trails, stream crossings, roads and landings in accordance with State and County timber harvesting regulations, and (7) agricultural uses, provided no existing riparian vegetation is removed, and no soil is allowed to enter stream channels (San Mateo County 1980).

The plan also contained extensive policies on performance standards in riparian corridors, establishment of buffer zones, and permitted uses and performance standards in buffer zones. These policies form the basis of the County's LCP ordinances and are now being applied to new development in the coastal portion of San Mateo County.

City of Oceanside

Oceanside's LUP was a different situation. On 8 December, 1981, the Commission determined after two public hearings that several sections of the LUP were not in conformity with Coastal Act policies. One of the sections concerned development in the San Luis Rey River system. The Commission staff reported:

The City's LCP proposes the construction of State Highway 76 through the San Luis Rey River Valley. The proposed construction would include the removal of previously deposited spoils banks, grading of valley slopes, removal of approximately 4.4 acres of old growth riparian habitat, and construction of the expressway.

The currently proposed Route 76, as included in the City's LUP presents serious questions as to impacts on the habitat values of the valley. LCP policies to protect the sensitive resources of the river would require the City to:

a. Post signs at appropriate locations noting regulations on littering, off-road vehicles, use of firearms, and leash laws.

b. Encourage the California Department of Fish and Game to actively enforce the Fish and Game Code in the river area.

c. Require property owners to remove debris from their properties when fire or health hazards exist.

d. Monitor future public use of the river area to identify areas of overuse. If such areas are identified, take steps to restrict access commensurate with the carrying capacity of the resources.

e. Encourage CALTRANS to buy and restore the spoil bank on the south side of the river west of I-5 as a first priority. Acquisition of habitat for the endangered plant _Dudleya viscida_ shall be a second order priority.

f. Continue police and code enforcement against litterers, trespassers, off-road vehicles, and other violators.

The general nature of these policies would not adequately protect the habitat values of the area as is required by the Coastal Act. Major development in the area would disrupt endangered plant/animal species and result in an overall reduction in the resource values of the area.

The San Luis Rey River area, as detailed in the CALTRANS biological Resource Analysis has biological significance in several respects: "As a natural ecosystem with great diversity surrounded by a highly urbanized area; as an important locality for rare and endangered species and utilization by a diverse assemblage of animals. The various plant communities have inter-relationships that tend to indicate that the canyon is a single functioning ecosystem."

As the only publicly accessible coastal riparian stream corridor in San Diego County, the area has significant resource value. In testimony before the State Commission, the representative from the State Department of Fish and Game stated: "The systematic destruction of nearly every coastal river valley in Southern California confers _added_ importance to the maintenance of this and the one or two other remaining river valleys where enough differing and contiguous habitats exist to function at an ecosystem level."

The San Luis Rey River, wetlands, and riparian areas are environmentally sensitive habitat as defined in Section 30107.5 of the Coastal Act. The expressway would be located in and/or adjacent to wetland riparian areas and in this location the project would have to be found consistent with Sections (a) and (b) of Section 30240. Section (a), discussed earlier, addresses the appropriate uses in an environmentally sensitive habitat area. Clearly a road is not a resource dependent use. The Commission has previously described and defined resource dependent uses in its certification of the County of Humboldt North Coast Area Land Use Plan. The Commission considered a variety of interpretations of resource dependent:

"(1) Resource dependent uses are those requiring the use of the ecosystem that led the area to be designated as environmentally sensitive habitat; (2) resource dependent uses may depend on one aspect of the total habitat, but that particular aspect must in turn relate to the functioning of the whole or be an integral part of the habitat value of an area; and (3) any use that relies on the existence of a resource that is simply present in the habitat area". In the North Coast Plan, the Commission considered whether timber harvesting and firewood removal in riparian corridors were resource dependent. Timber harvesting was clearly dependent upon trees as an available, renewable resource. However, locating a road in a riparian corridor is not dependent on any of the renewable/non-renewable resources of the San Luis Rey River area and therefore conflicts with Coastal Act policies regarding sensitive habitat.

As currently proposed, the project has adverse impacts on the environmentally sensitive habitat of the valley (noise, water pollution, air pollution, destruction of sensitive habitat, loss of endangered plants, isolation of remaining riparian areas from coastal sage scrub hillside, etc.) and would therefore require extensive mitigation. Such required mitigation measures have not been adequately identified by either the City or Caltrans. City policies would require transplantation of the endangered Dudleya viscida, and Caltrans proposed to remove the spoils banks as mitigation for the removal of 4.4 acres of old growth riparian habitat, but other project impacts have not been addressed. In the absence of detailed mitigation proposals, the project would conflict with recommendations by the State Department of Fish and Game and the U.S. Fish and Wildlife Service that the whole river area should be afforded protection due to the uniqueness of its ecosystem.

In order to protect the integrity of the river and maintain the functional capacity of related habitat areas, the Commission finds that the policies proposed by the City of Oceanside are not in conformity with the policies of Chapter 3 of the Coastal Act (California Coastal Commission 1981a).

This LUP was an important test case for the riparian protection policies of the Coastal Act. The Commission subsequently approved the remainder of the City's LUP leaving the San Luis Rey River portion uncertified. This meant the Commission retains permit jurisdiction until the plan is revised and approved.

Special Guidelines

The Commission adopts interpretive guidelines primarily for use in reviewing coastal permit applications. These help interpret the Coastal Act and explain Commission precedent to insure consistency. The Statewide Interpretive Guideline for Wetlands and Other Wet Environmentally Sensitive Habitat Areas include considerable guidance on riparian habitat protection (California Coastal Commission 1981b).

Statewide Interpretive Guideline for Wetlands and Other Wet Environmentally Sensitive Habitat Areas

The wetland guideline was adopted February 4, 1981 after almost two years of public hearings and numerous revisions. It represents a major effort on the part of the Commission to protect wet environmentally-sensitive habitat areas. Although the guideline focuses primarily on wetlands, it also addresses riparian areas: defining rivers and streams, riparian habitat, permittable development in streams and rivers, and criteria for establishing buffer areas. Because buffer width can vary depending on the circumstances, the guideline requires the following factors be considered in an analysis: 1) biological significance of adjacent lands; 2) sensitivity of species to disturbance; 3) susceptibility of parcel to erosion; 4) use of natural topographic features to locate development; 5) use of existing cultural features to locate buffer zones; 6) lot configuration and location of existing development; and (7) the type and scale of development proposed.

The guideline has proven very useful in permit analysis. It provides solid, technical criteria for regulating development. This type of guidance is necessry to implement a complex statute, particularly when political and economic pressure are present.

CONCLUSIONS

This report demonstrates that the Coastal Commission has had considerable experience in protecting riparian systems in the coastal zone. Although not discussed as part of this report, other agencies, particularly the Department of Fish and Game, deserve a great deal of credit for this achievement. Their assistance and technical recommendations to the Commission have been greatly appreciated.

However, several gaps exist in this protection network. First, only riparian corridors in the coastal zone are protected. The riparian zone is part of a system which includes upstream headwaters and the surrounding watershed. Degradation of upstream areas is eventually reflected in downstream changes, ultimately in the coastal zone. Most of the watersheds are outside the coastal zone; without good upstream protection it is somewhat futile to discuss long-term downstream regulation.

Second, watershed concerns such as erosion are complex and difficult to address issues. Development within a stream or river corridor is relatively easy to regulate because the resource is identifiable and the impacts direct. Sedimentation from an upslope development, for example, is difficult to trace; its impact difficult to assess. To complicate matters further, effects of sediment in the riparian corridor may be adverse or beneficial (beach replenishment, for example, versus silting of spawning beds).

In addition, under the Coastal Act, removal of vegetation for agricultural purposes is not considered development--and therefore not regulated by the Commission. This problem is especially apparent in Santa Barbara and Ventura Counties where conversion of native vegetation to avocado production is drastically increasing the rate of sedimentation in coastal streams. Local governments are attempting to grapple with this problem with varying degrees of success.

Finally, the Commission itself has a very heavy workload and is subject to some political pressure. In accordance with state law, the regional commissions, which absorbed a large amount of work, were dissolved on 1 July, 1981. The Commission meets only eight days each month. Members of the public, seeking to speak to issues on the Commission's agenda are often limited to two to three minutes per item due to the large number of speakers. Given this situation, it could become easy to ignore the complexities of each issue and forego substantive discussions. This would jeopardize resource protection policies of the Coastal Act and the clear precedents the Commission has set to date.

RECOMMENDATIONS

It would be easy to simply recommend that watershed plans be prepared for all areas. The political pressure against such a measure would be overwhelming. It is more fashionable presently to talk about decreasing the role of government in our lives. On the other hand, who else will be concerned with an entire watershed and the riparian and instream systems it feeds? A neo-classical economic approach, such as advocated by Ostrom and Ostrom (1972), would place each watershed within the control of one user group, on the theory that someone who owns a resource will take better care of it than many individuals who have no incentive to safeguard the resource.

Instead, I would suggest an alternative. All jurisdictions within the state, whether in the coastal zone or not are required to prepare land use plans. I would recommend requiring them, through statute, to include a watershed element in such a plan. This could also

include membership in a watershed planning program as suggested in the Coastal Plan.

Second, education on watershed and riparian issues needs to be greatly expanded. The effort which went into disseminating information on the importance of wetlands was enormous and began over a decade ago; issues of riparian protection are only beginning to become a subject of debate.

Riparian system protection in the coastal zone is a reality. The California Coastal Act assures protection of our rivers and streams within the coastal zone. However, that protection does not extend outside the coastal zone, nor does it adequately protect watersheds inside or out of the coastal zone. These limitations should be changed to insure adequate protection of riparian systems throughout California.

LITERATURE CITED

Beer, Jack. 1978. Identifying habitat types and disappearance rates. p. 38-54. In: Proceedings of the instream use seminar. 178 p. California Department of Water Resources, Sacramento.

Blumenthal, Robert. 1979. Vegetation management report. California Coastal Commission special report. 68 p. California Coastal Commission, San Francisco, Calif.

Burke, Roy, and James Heaney. 1975. Collective decision making in water resources planning. 238 p. Lexington Books, New York, New York.

California Coastal Zone Conservation Commission. 1975. California Coastal Plan. December, 1975. State Documents and Publications Branch, Sacramento.

California Coastal Commission. 1981a. Staff report to the California Coastal Commission from Bob Brown, Chief Planner, and Michael Buck, Staff Analyst. 44 p. California Coastal Commission, San Francisco.

California Coastal Commission. 1981b. Statewide interpretive guideline for wetlands and other wet environmentally sensitive habitat areas. 46 p. California Coastal Commission, San Francisco.

Healy, R.G. 1977. An economic interpretation of the Californi Coastal Commissions. 270 p. Conservation Foundation, Washington, D.C.

Howe, C.W. 1977. Comparative analysis and critique of the institutional framework for water resources planning and management. 106 p. Office of Water Research and Technology, Washington, D.C.

Odell, Rice. 1972. The saving of San Francisco Bay. 115 p. Conservation Foundation, Washington, D.C.

Ostrom, Vincent, and Elinor Ostrom. 1972. Legal and political conditions of water resource development. Land Economics 48(1):1-14.

San Mateo County. 1980. Local coastal plan. 368 p. County of San Mateo, San Mateo, California.

White, Gilbert. 1969. Strategies of American water management. 288 p. University of Michigan Press, Ann Arbor, Michigan.

PLANT SPECIES COMPOSITION AND LIFE FORM SPECTRA

OF TIDAL STREAMBANKS AND ADJACENT RIPARIAN WOODLANDS

ALONG THE LOWER SACRAMENTO RIVER[1]

John W. Willoughby and William Davilla[2]

Abstract.--Flora and life forms of the tidal streambank plant community along the Sacramento River near Collinsville, Solano County, California are compared to those of adjacent plant communities. The tidal streambank flora has a significantly smaller non-native component than the floras of adjacent riparian woodland and annual grassland communities. All three communities have developed in historically disturbed habitats. Rhizomatous herbs represent the predominant life form of the tidal streambank community. In contrast, the riparian woodland community has a much lower percentage of rhizomatous herbs and higher percentages of annual and woody species. Reasons for these differences are discussed.

INTRODUCTION

Plants growing in the intertidal zones of river systems are subjected to rather rigorous growing conditions. Regular, periodic inundation by fresh to brackish waters makes establishment and subsequent growth of vascular plants difficult. Relatively few plant taxa are capable of coping with such conditions. Some plant taxa, however, are totally restricted to intertidal areas of major river systems and are often rare (Ferren and Schuyler 1980).

In some river tidal areas, water salinity (and resultant soil salinity) may be a limiting factor to plant establishment and survival. This is especially true of riverine systems near oceans and bays where substantial volumes of salt water mix with the fresh water of the rivers.

This study examines the life form strategies of the vascular plants in the intertidal zone along the lower Sacramento River (herein referred to as the "tidal streambank" community). This community is compared to the adjacent riparian woodland community. Floristic composition and richness of these two communities and the adjacent annual grassland community are compared.

---

[1]Paper presented at the California Riparian Systems Conference. [University of California, Davis, September 17-19, 1981].

[2]John W. Willoughby is Botanist/Range Conservationist, USDI Bureau of Land Management, Sacramento, Calif. William Davilla is Senior Botanist, BioSystems Analysis, Inc., San Francisco, Calif.

STUDY AREA

The study area is located on the northern banks of the lower Sacramento River east of Collinsville, Solano County, California. The river at this point becomes part of the Sacramento/San Joaquin estuary. Study plots were located at the mouth of Marshall Cut, extending a distance of 1.0 km. east and 0.3 km. west of the cut along the bank of the Sacramento River. Riverbanks in this area were artificially created by levee construction designed to reclaim natural tidal marshland between 1900 and 1940 (Atwater et al. 1979). Tidal streambank and riparian woodland vegetation has developed on the levees during the short period since their construction. Inland of the levees, artificial landfill has resulted in displacement of former natural tidal marshlands. These recent fill areas now support a disturbed cover of annual grassland composed almost entirely of introduced plant species. An artificially flooded marsh behind the levee east of Marshall Cut is presently managed as a duck club. The flora and elevational zonation of vascular plants in this marsh/grassland mosaic have been considered elsewhere (BioSystems Analysis, Inc. 1979).

METHODS

Tidal streambank, riparian woodland, and annual grassland plant communities were subjectively delineated using primarily physiognomic criteria. The riparian woodland community was identified by the presence of tree and shrub strata. In the few cases where these strata were poorly developed or lacking, this community was identified by the presence of herbaceous species commonly associated with the riparian woodland community.

The criteria used to identify the tidal streambank community were: 1) its position between the river and the riparian woodland community; 2) the absence (with two exceptions) of woody species; and 3) the presence of species which flower in late summer to early fall. Upper limits of the tidal streambank community correspond roughly to the upper level of the levee banks inundated by maximum high tides.

The annual grassland community was recognized by its inland location, the absence of woody species, and the predominance of annual grass and forb species which flower in the spring.

A complete species list was compiled for each of these three plant communities. The life forms of each species were determined using available literature (e.g., Munz 1959; Mason 1957; Robbins et al. 1951) and field observations. Five life forms were recognized: annual, perennial herb (including biennials), rhizomatous perennial herb (including herbs spreading by stolons and creeping root systems), shrub, and tree. In a few cases a species may function as either an annual or a perennial. These facultative species were scored under both the annual and perennial herb categories. Suffrutescent (only obscurely or very modestly woody) plants were scored as perennial herbs. Woody plants which exhibit both a tree and shrub habit (e.g., Salix spp.) were scored as either shrubs or trees based on the principal life form exhibited in the study area.

RESULTS AND DISCUSSION

The major environmental variables controlling the distribution of vascular plants in tidal marshes of the northern San Francisco Bay estuary are elevation and water salinity (Atwater and Hedel 1976). Elevation of marsh surfaces relative to tide levels determines the soil moisture content and frequency, duration, and depth of submergence, whereas the salinity of the water flooding a marsh determines the soil salinity (ibid.). Water salinity is an important influence in the regional distribution of tidal marsh plants; high soil salinity causes many plants to disappear toward San Francisco Bay, resulting in tidal marsh communities composed of only 13 or 14 native plant species (Atwater et al. 1979). Where water salinities are rather low, as in the Sacramento/San Joaquin Delta, tidal marsh communities are more diverse, containing some 40 plant species, most of which are relatively salt-intolerant—largely the same species that occur in freshwater marshes in California (ibid.).

Water salinities in the vicinity of the study area vary both seasonally and annually in response to the amount of freshwater flow from the river systems. Figure 1 shows the varia-

tion in mean monthly water salinities at Collinsville. Judging from the salinity data for Collinsville, water salinity is probably not a major limiting factor for plants in the intertidal zone there. Except in unusual circumstances (such as the drought of 1976–77) the water in this area varies from essentially fresh to only slightly brackish. Because of the regular flushing action of the tides and the rapid runoff from riverbanks at low tides, soil-salt concentrations resulting from evaporation would not be expected to be significantly higher than the water salinity of the river. That soil salinities are not high in the intertidal zone of this area can be inferred from the absence of salt-tolerant plants such as Distichlis spicata and Frankenia grandifolia from the upper reaches of the intertidal zone.

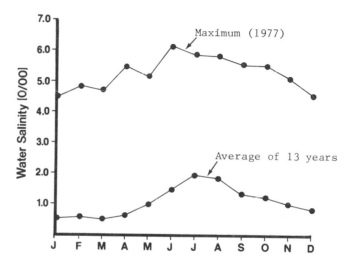

Figure 1.--Mean monthly water salinities (in parts per thousand) of the Sacramento River at Collinsville, California. The bottom line averages monthly means over the period 1967-80. The top line represents monthly means for 1977, the year with the highest salinities on record (from USDI Bureau of Reclamation, Tracy Field Division).

The major ecological factor influencing the distribution of plants in the intertidal zone of the study area is considered to be elevation with respect to tide levels. Tidal heights (in decimeters) at the confluence of the Sacramento and San Joaquin Rivers (near the study area) are as follows (based on data in Simpson et al. 1968; definitions from Atwater et al. 1979):

    10.1--mean higher high water (average height
        of the higher of the daily high
        tides);
    -3.4--mean lower low water (average height
        of the lower of the daily low tides);
    18.3--estimated maximum high water;
    -7.6--estimated minimum low water.

Plants tolerant of relatively long periods of submergence (e.g., Scirpus acutus, S.

californicus, and _Typha_ spp.) occupy lower sites along the river (below mean higher high water), whereas species less tolerant of long submergence (e.g., _Carex barbarae_, _Hydrocotyle verticillata_ var. _triradiata_, and _Lythrum californicum_) occur at higher elevations in the intertidal zone (at or above mean higher high water).

A complete list of the vascular plants of the three plant communities considered in this study (tidal streambank, riparian woodland, and annual grassland) is found in Appendix A.

A tabulation of the flora of the three communities is given in table 1. The riparian woodland community contains the largest number of species (78) followed by the tidal streambank (49) and annual grassland (38) communities. The annual grassland community is included here primarily to illustrate the highly disturbed nature of the site. The low total number of species present (38) and the very high percentage of introduced species (82%) attests to its disturbed condition.

Table 1.--Tabulation of the flora of three plant communities east of Collinsville, California. TSB--tidal streambank; RW--riparian woodland; and G--annual grassland.

	Plant Community		
	TSB	RW	G
Total number of species[a]	49	78	38
Number of introduced species	8	29	31
Percent of flora contributed by introduced species	16.3	37.2	81.6

[a]The term "species" as used here includes infraspecific taxa.

The riparian woodland community also supports a large non-native component (29 species). Over 30% of species are introduced plants, the majority of which also occur in the adjacent annual grassland community.

The tidal streambank community supports the smallest number of introduced species (8), only 16% of the total species. This figure compares favorably with the proportion of introduced species in the California flora as a whole, but is low compared to most California cismontane areas (table 2). Only the floras of Mount Diablo and Mount Hamilton Range have similar non-native components. The published floras of these two areas, however, are almost 40 years old; the percentages of introduced taxa present in both areas are almost certainly higher today.

The percentage of introduced species present in the tidal streambank community is especially low given the disturbed nature of the site. As previously indicated, this community has developed since the construction of levees between 1900 and 1940. The riparian woodland and an-

Table 2.--Relative importance of introduced taxa to the floras of California and several areas of central California with pronounced Mediterranean climates. Introduced species--percent of the flora consisting of introduced species (includes infraspecific taxa except for Marin County and Mount Hamilton Range).

Area	Introduced species (%)
California (a)	15.3
Santa Cruz County (b)	30.7
Vaca Mountains (c)	26.7
Marin County (d)	23.5
Mount Diablo (e)	14.4
Mount Hamilton Range (f)	9.0

(a) Smith and Noldenke (1960); Howell (1972).
(b) Thomas (1961).
(c) Willoughby (unpublished data).
(d) Howell (1970).
(e) Bowerman (1944).
(f) Sharsmith (1945).

nual grassland communities have also developed during this same time period. Their floras, however, exhibit a significantly higher percentage of introduced plant species. Annuals comprise a large percentage of the introduced species in the annual grassland (59%) and riparian woodland (42%) communities. An additional 32% of the introduced species of the annual grassland and 35% of those in the riparian woodland are perennial, non-rhizomatous herbs. Both of these life forms, especially the annuals, appear to be at a competitive disadvantage in the tidal streambank environment. Fifty-eight percent of the tidal streambank flora consists of rhizomatous herbs (fig. 2). Of the 29 species of rhizomatous herbs present in the tidal streambank community, only three (10%) are introduced.

It thus appears that the primary reason for the low number of introduced species in the tidal streambank community (relative to the other two communities) is the restricted capability of introduced plants (most of which are annuals or non-rhizomatous perennials) to establish under conditions of periodic or prolonged inundation. This fact is further emphasized by the relative paucity of introduced species in areas within the intertidal zone which have been more recently disturbed by riprapping. Although cover and density in riprapped areas are far lower than on undisturbed levees, the species which are found in these areas are predominantly native.

The life form spectra of the tidal streambank and riparian woodland plant communities (fig. 2) highlight several differences between these two communities. Almost 25% of the species present in riparian woodland are woody species, as opposed to 4% (2 species) of the total species found in the tidal streambank community. Twenty-five percent of the riparian woodland species are annuals--62% are introduced--while 14% (6 species) of the intertidal flora are annuals--43%

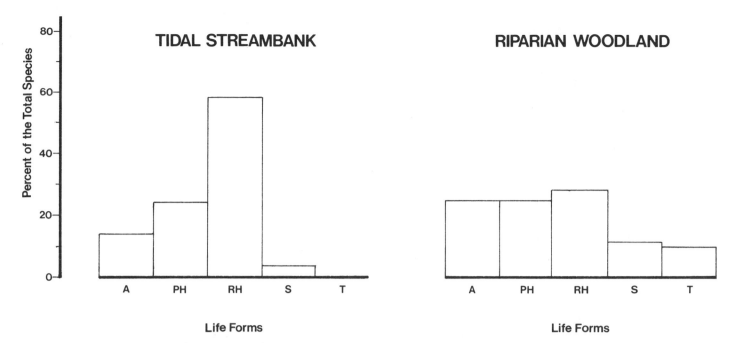

Figure 2.--Life form spectra of the tidal streambank and riparian woodland plant communities. Height of the bars corresonds to the percentage of the total species in the community represented by each of the five life forms. A--annual; PH--perennial herb (including biennials); RH--rhizomatous perennial herb (including herbs spreading by stolons and creeping root systems); S--shrub; and T--tree.

are introduced. The percentage contribution of perennial, non-rhizomatous herbs to the floras of both communities is almost identical, 24% for the tidal streambank community and 25% for the riparian woodland (the absolute species numbers are 10 and 21, respectively). Perhaps the most significant difference between these two communities is the much greater proportion of rhizomatous herbs in the flora of the tidal streambank plant community (58% of the total species compared with 28% for riparian woodland community).

Certain life forms enjoy an apparent competitive advantage in the tidal streambank community. Perennials account for 86% of the total flora, suggesting that one major limiting factor is the difficulty of seedling establishment under the ebb and flow of tidal waters. This would put annuals at a distinct disadvantage. The annual strategy may also be a handicap in another way: in an azonal community where water is not limiting, dry season dormancy is not only unnecessary but is probably detrimental. Rhizomatous species are more successful than non-rhizomatous species, a fact which may be at least partially explained by the greater ability of the former to apomictically spread once established. Even the two woody species present in the intertidal zone, _Salix lasiolepis_ and the introduced _Rubus discolor_, are capable of extensive vegetative reproduction. Thus 63% of the tidal streambank flora is capable of vegetative reproduction.

In terms of floristic composition and life form spectra, the tidal streambank community in this rather disturbed area is remarkably similar to that of other, less disturbed areas in the Sacramento/San Joaquin estuary (compare the species list for Browns Island in Knight 1980). However, the plant cover and density of the tidal streambank community of the study area are certainly lower relative to less disturbed examples of this community elsewhere, although this fact is yet to be quantitatively documented.

Many of the species of the tidal streambank community (e.g., _Typha latifolia_, _Scirpus acutus_) have very wide distributions and occur in several types of moist to wet habitats. However, a few of the tidal streambank species in the study area exhibit restricted distributions and occupy only the intertidal habitat. _Aster chilensis_ var. _lentus_ and _Lilaeopsis masonii_ are both recognized as rare and endangered by the California Native Plant Society (Smith _et al._ 1980). Both of these taxa and a third, _Grindelia paludosa_, formerly considered rare and endangered, are entirely restricted to intertidal areas in the Sacramento/San Joaquin estuary. Although these plants are not particularly rare in the habitats in which they occur, their continued existence may be threatened by human alterations of their narrow habitats. The practice of riprapping streambanks results in a significant loss of habitat; potential increases in water salinity of the estuary as a result of proposed future freshwater diversions may have deleterious effects on these plants.

SUMMARY

The flora of the tidal streambank plant community along the lower Sacramento River near Collinsville is markedly different from the floras of adjacent riparian woodland and annual grassland communities. Non-native plant components of the latter two communities are significantly larger than that of the tidal streambank community, although all three communities have developed within the last 40 to 80 years. The proportion of introduced plants in the tidal streambank community is low even in areas more recently disturbed by riprapping. Introduced species, most of which are annuals or non-rhizomatous perennials, appear to be at a competitive disadvantage in the tidal streambank zone.

The life form spectra of tidal streambank and riparian woodland communities illustrate several significant differences between these two communities. Rhizomatous herbs are the most important life form of the tidal streambank community, apparently because of their facility to spread under conditions unfavorable to seedling establishment. Annuals are at a competitive disadvantage probably for the same reason, and also due to the handicap resulting from dry season dormancy in an azonal habitat where water is not limiting. In contrast, the riparian woodland community has a much lower proportion of rhizomatous herbs and higher percentages of annual and woody species.

In terms of floristic composition and life form spectra, the tidal streambank community that has developed in this disturbed area is similar to that of other, less disturbed areas. Three rare plant species occur in the intertidal zone of the study area, and are restricted in distribution to the intertidal zone of the Sacramento/San Joaquin estuary. Although not currently rare where they occur, they appear to be very narrowly adapted to this habitat. Additional human alterations of their habitat may threaten their continued existence.

LITERATURE CITED

Atwater, B.F., S.G. Conard, J.N. Dowden, C.W. Hedel, R.L. MacDonald, and W. Savage. 1979. History, landforms, and vegetation of the estuary's marshes. p. 347-385. In: T.J. Conomos (ed.). San Francisco Bay: the urbanized estuary. Pacific Division, American Assoc. Adv. Sci., San Francisco, California.

Atwater, B.F., and C.W. Hedel. 1976. Distribution of seed plants with respect to tide levels and water salinity in the natural tidal marshes of the northern San Francisco Bay estuary, California. USDI Geological Survey Open File Report 76-389.

BioSystems Analysis, Inc. 1979. Potential for mitigation of salt marsh losses and associated adverse impacts on salt marsh harvest mice at the proposed Montezuma powerplant site. Unpublished report prepared for Pacific Gas and Electric Co. 51 p.

Bowerman, M.L. 1944. The flowering plants and ferns of Mount Diablo, California. 290 p. Gillick Press, Berkeley, California.

Ferren, W.R., Jr., and A.E. Schuyler. 1980. Intertidal vascular plants of river systems near Philadelphia. Proc. Acad. Nat. Sciences of Philadelphia 132:86-120.

Howell, J.T. 1970. Marin flora. Second edition with supplement. 366 p. University of California Press, Berkeley.

Howell, J.T. 1972. A statistical estimate of Munz' Supplement to a California Flora. Wasmann Journal of Biology 30:93-96.

Knight, W. 1980. The story of Browns Island. Four Seasons 6(1):3-10.

Mall, R.E. 1969. Soil-water salt relationships of waterfowl food plants in the Suisun Marsh of California. California Department of Fish and Game, Wildlife Bulletin No. 1. 59 p.

Mason, H.L. 1957. A flora of the marshes of California. 878 p. University of California Press, Berkeley.

Mueller-Dombois, D., and H. Ellenberg. 1974. Aims and methods of vegetation ecology. 547 p. Wiley and Sons, New York, New York.

Munz, P.A., and D.D. Keck. 1959. A California flora. 1681 p. University of California Press, Berkeley.

Robbins, W.W., M.K. Bellue, and W.S. Bell 1951. Weeds of California (1970 reprint). 547 p. Documents and Publications, State of California, Sacramento.

Sharsmith, H.K. 1945. Flora of the Mount Hamilton Range of California. Amer. Midl. Nat. 34:289-367.

Simpson Stratta and Associates, and K.H. Baruth. 1968. Suisun Soil Conservation District Master Plan Study II. Suisun Soil Conservation District, Dixon, California.

Smith, G.L., and A.M. Noldenke. 1960. A statistical report on A California Flora. Leaflets of Western Botany 9:117-123.

Smith, J.P. Jr., R.J. Cole, and J.O. Sawyer, Jr. 1980. Inventory of rare and endangered vascular plants of California (in collaboration with W.R. Powell). Special Publ. No. 1 (second edition). 115 p. California Native Plant Society, Berkeley.

Thomas, J.H. 1961. Flora of the Santa Cruz Mountains of California. 434 p. Stanford University Press, Stanford, California.

Appendix A.--Vascular plants of three plant communities east
of Collinsville, California, and the life form classes
to which they belong. Introduced plants are marked
with asterisks.

Family Scientific Name	Common Name	Life Form[1]	TSB	RW	G
Anacardiaceae					
Toxicodendron diversilobum					
Greene	poison-oak	S		X	
Apiaceae					
*Conium maculatum L.	poison hemlock	PH		X	
Eryngium articulatum Hook.	blue-flowered				
	coyote-thistle	PH	X		
Hydrocotyle verticillata Thunb.					
var. triradiata (A. Rich.)					
Fern.	whorled marsh-pennywort	RH	X		
Lilaeopsis masonii Math. & Const.		RH	X		
Oenanthe sarmentosa Presl	water parsley	RH	X		
Sium suave Walt.	hemlock water parsnip	PH	X		
Apocynaceae					
Apocynum cannabinum L.					
var. glaberrimum DC.	Indian hemp	RH		X	
Asclepiadaceae					
Asclepias fascicularis	narrow-leaved milkweed	PH		X	X
Asteraceae					
Achillea millefolium L. var.					
californica (Pollard) Jeps.	yarrow	RH		X	
Ambrosia psilostachya DC.	western ragweed	RH	X	X	X
*Anthemis cotula L.	mayweed	A			X
Artemisia douglasiana Bess.	mugwort	RH		X	
Aster chilensis Nees					
var. lentus (Greene) Jeps.	Suisun aster	RH	X		
Aster exilis Ell.	slim aster	A	X	X	
Baccharis douglasii DC.	salt marsh baccharis	PH		X	
Baccharis pilularis DC. var.					
consanguinea (DC.) Kuntze	coyote brush	S		X	
Baccharis viminea DC.	mule fat	S		X	
Bidens laevis (L.) B. S. P.	bur marigold	PH	X		
*Centaurea solstitialis L.	yellow star thistle	A			X
*Cirsium vulgare (Savi) Ten.	bull thistle	PH		X	X
*Conyza bonariensis (L.) Cronquist	South American conyza	A		X	
Gnaphalium chilense Spreng.	cotton-batting plant	A or PH		X	X
*Gnaphalium luteo-album L.	weedy cudweed	A		X	
Grindelia paludosa Greene		PH	X		
Helenium bigelovii Gray	Bigelow's sneezeweed	PH	X		
Heterotheca grandiflora Nutt.	telegraph weed	A or PH			X
*Hypochoeris glabra L.	smooth cat's-ear	A			X
*Lactuca serriola L.	prickly lettuce	A			X
*Picris echioides L.	bristly ox-tongue	A or PH		X	X
Pluchea camphorata (L.) DC.	salt marsh fleabane	A	X		
Senecio hydrophilus Nutt.	alkali marsh butterweed	RH	X		
*Silybum marianum (L.) Gaertn.	milk thistle	A or PH			X
Solidago occidentalis (Nutt.)					
T. & G.	western goldenrod	RH	X	X	

648

Family Scientific Name	Common Name	Life Form[1]	Occurrence in Plant Community[2]		
			TSB	RW	G
*Sonchus asper (L.) Hill	prickly sow-thistle	A		X	
*Sonchus oleraceus L.	common sow-thistle	A		X	X
*Tragopogon porrifolius L.	salsify	PH			X
Xanthium strumarium L. var. canadense (Mill) T. & G.	cocklebur	A		X	
Betulaceae					
Alnus rhombifolia Nutt.	white alder	T		X	
Boraginaceae					
Heliotropium curassavicum L. var. oculatum (Heller) Jtn.	heliotrope	RH			X
Brassicaceae					
*Brassica geniculata (Desf.) Ball	Mediterranean mustard	PH		X	X
*Lepidium latifolium L.	perennial pepper-grass	RH	X	X	
*Sisymbrium officinale (L.) Scop.	hedge mustard	A			X
Caprifoliaceae					
Lonicera involucrata (Richards.) Banks ex Spreng.	twinberry	S		X	
Chenopodiaceae					
*Atriplex semibaccata R. Br.	Australian saltbush	PH			X
Chenopodium ambrosioides L.	Mexican tea	A or PH		X	
*Salsola australis R. Br.	Russian thistle	A			X
Convolvulaceae					

Calystegia sepium (L.) R. Br.
    ssp. limnophila (Greene)
    Brummitt
	hedge bindweed	RH	X	X	

*Convolvulus arvensis L.	bindweed	RH			X
Cucurbitaceae					
Marah fabaceus (Naud.) Greene	wild cucumber	PH		X	
Cyperaceae					
Carex barbarae Dewey	Santa Barbara sedge	RH	X	X	
Cyperus eragrostis Lam.		RH		X	
Scirpus acutus Muhl. ex Bigel.	tule	RH	X		
Scirpus californicus (C.A. Mey.) Steud.	California bulrush	RH	X		
Scirpus cernuus Vahl var. californicus (Torr.) Beetle	low club-rush	A	X		
Scirpus olneyi Gray	Olney's bulrush	RH	X		
Equisetaceae					
Equisetum arvense L.	common horsetail	RH		X	
Equisetum hyemale L. var. affine (Engelm.) A.A. Eat.	western scouring rush	RH		X	
Fabaceae					
Lathyrus jepsonii Greene ssp. californicus (Wats.) Hitchc.	buff pea	PH		X	
*Lotus corniculatus L.	bird's-foot trefoil	PH	X	X	X
Lotus purshianus (Benth.) Clem. & Clem.	Spanish clover	A		X	X
Lotus scoparius (Nutt.) Ottley	deerweed	S			X
*Melilotus alba Desr. ex Lam.	white sweet-clover	A	X	X	
*Melilotus indica (L.) All.	Indian melilot	A		X	

Family Scientific Name	Common Name	Life Form[1]	Occurrence in Plant Community[2]		
			TSB	RW	G
Psoralea macrostachya DC.	leather root	RH	X	X	
*Trifolium repens L.	white clover	RH	X		
Trifolium tridentatum Lindl. var. tridentatum	tomcat clover	A		X	
Trifolium wormskioldii Lehm.	cow clover	RH	X		
Gentianaceae					
Centaurium floribundum (Benth.) Rob.	June centaury	A	X	X	
Geraniaceae					
*Erodium botrys Bertol.	long-beaked filaree	A			X
*Erodium cicutarium (L.) L'Her.	red-stemmed filaree	A			X
Juglandaceae					
Juglans hindsii (Jeps.) Jeps.	California black walnut	T		X	
Juncaceae					
Juncus balticus Willd.	Baltic rush	RH	X		
Juncus phaeocephalus Engelm. var. paniculatus Engelm.	brown-headed rush	RH	X	X	
Juncaginaceae					
Triglochin striata R. & P.	three-ribbed arrow-grass	RH	X		
Lamiaceae					
Lycopus americanus Muhl.	cut-leaved water-horehound	RH	X	X	
*Marrubium vulgare L.	common horehound	PH			X
*Mentha citrata Ehrh.	bergamot mint	RH	X	X	
Stachys albens Gray	white hedge-nettle	RH		X	
Liliaceae					
*Asparagus officinalis L.	garden asparagus	RH		X	X
Lythraceae					
Lythrum californicum T. & G.	California loosestrife	RH	X	X	
Lythrum hyssopifolia L.	grass poly	A or PH		X	
Moraceae					
*Ficus carica L.	common fig	T		X	
Oleaceae					
Fraxinus latifolia Benth.	Oregon ash	T		X	
Onagraceae					
Epilobium ciliatum Raf. ssp. ciliatum	California willow-herb	PH	X	X	
Ludwigia peploides (HBK) Raven	yellow water weed	RH	X		
Plantaginaceae					
Plantago australis Lam. ssp. hirtella (HBK) Rahn	Mexican plantain	PH	X	X	
Poaceae					
*Agrostis semiverticillata (Forsk.) C. Chr.	water bent	PH		X	
*Arundo donax L.	giant reed	RH		X	
*Avena fatua L.	wild oat	A			X
*Bromus diandrus Roth.	ripgut grass	A		X	X
*Bromus mollis L.	soft chess	A		X	X

Family / Scientific Name	Common Name	Life Form[1]	Occurrence in Plant Community[2]		
			TSB	RW	G
*Cynodon dactylon (L.) Pers.	Bermuda grass	RH		X	X
Deschampsia caespitosa (L.) Beauv. ssp. holciformis (Presl.) Lawr.	California hairgrass	PH	X		
*Echinochloa crusgalli (L.) Beauv.	barnyard grass	A	X	X	
Elymus triticoides Buckl.	alkali ryegrass	PH		X	
*Hordeum geniculatum Allioni	Mediterranean barley	A			X
*Hordeum leporinum Link	farmer's foxtail	A			X
*Lolium multiflorum Lam.	Italian ryegrass	PH		X	X
*Paspalum dilatatum Poir.	dallis grass	PH		X	
*Polypogon monspeliensis (L.) Desf.	rabbit's-foot grass	A		X	X
*Setaria geniculata (Lam.) Beauv.	knotroot bristle grass	PH		X	
*Vulpia myuros (L.) K.C. Gmelin var. hirsuta Hack.	rattail fescue	A			X
Polygonaceae					
*Polygonum aviculare L.	common knotweed	A			X
Polygonum punctatum Ell.	water smartweed	RH	X	X	
*Rumex conglomeratus Murr.	green dock	PH		X	
*Rumex crispus L.	curly dock	PH	X	X	X
Primulaceae					
Centunculus minimus L.	false pimpernel	A		X	
Samolus parviflorus Raf.	water pimpernel	PH	X		
Rosaceae					
Potentilla anserina L. ssp. pacifica (Howell) Rousi	Pacific silverweed	RH	X		
Rosa californica Cham. & Sch.	California rose	S		X	
*Rubus discolor Weihe & Nees	Himalaya-berry	S[3]	X	X	
Rubus ursinus Cham. & Sch.	California blackberry	S[3]		X	
Rubiaceae					
Cephalanthus occidentalis L. var. californicus Benth.	California buttonbush	S		X	
Salicaceae					
Populus fremontii Wats.	Fremont cottonwood	T		X	
Salix gooddingii Ball var. variabilis Ball	black willow	T		X	
Salix hindsiana Benth.	sandbar willow	S		X	
Salix laevigata Bebb	red willow	T		X	
Salix cf. lasiandra Benth.	yellow willow	T		X	
Salix lasiolepis Benth.	arroyo willow	S	X	X	
Scrophulariaceae					
Limosella australis R. Br.		RH	X		
Mimulus guttatus Fisch. ex DC.	common monkey-flower	RH	X	X	
Solanaceae					
*Solanum nodiflorum Jacq.	small-flowered nightshade	A or PH	X	X	X
Typhaceae					
Typha angustifolia L.	narrow-leaved cattail	RH	X		
Typha latifolia L.	broad-leaved cattail	RH	X		

[1]Life forms: T=tree; S=shrub; RH=rhizomatous perennial herb (including herbs spreading by stolons and creeping root systems); PH=perennial herb (including biennials); A=annual.

[2]Plant communities: TSB=tidal stream banks; RW=riparian woodland; G=annual grassland. See text for characterizations of these communities.

[3]Although shrubs, these plants spread extensively by trailing stems which root at the nodes.

SEDIMENT CONTROL CRITERIA FOR AN URBANIZING AREA

IN SAN DIEGO COUNTY, CALIFORNIA[1]

James S. Jenks, Thomas C. MacDonald, and James P. McGrath[2]

Abstract.--Studies were conducted to develop criteria and methodologies to mitigate the effects of urbanization on sedimentation processes at North City West in San Diego County. A sediment control plan was developed and adopted to mitigate these effects using on-site erosion controls and detention basins.

INTRODUCTION

The urbanization of undeveloped land can cause many environmental, social, and legal problems, many of which are associated with changes in the hydrologic and sedimentation regimes of the area. The California Coastal Commission has been concerned with these problems in the coastal zone and, in the case of the Los Penasquitos Lagoon-North City West (NCW) area (San Diego County), has been instrumental in developing policies and solutions to urbanization problems. The following paragraphs present the background leading to these policies and solutions and describe the Los Penasquitos Lagoon and NCW areas.

Background

When the voters in California passed Proposition 20 in 1972, they established the Coastal Commission for the purpose of planning for the preservation of the coast of California for all the people of the state. The Commission made recommendations for long-term management of the coastline which are embodied in the California Coastal Plan. Recognizing that changes in coastal streams and wetlands are closely associated with changes in the watershed, the plan recommended that watershed management be required for coastal watersheds.

In 1976, when the Legislature established a permanent agency and body of legislation to carry out the goals of the Coastal Plan, it did not require watershed management plans, although Section 30231 of the Coastal Act did provide a

general policy that runoff should be regulated and managed.

In the legislative mapping of the coastal zone, particularly in urbanizing areas, the coastal zone boundaries are generally too narrow to allow meaningful watershed management. However, there are exceptions to this in various areas along the coast. In Southern California, there are three major exceptions: the Santa Monica Mountains, where the coastal zone boundary included virtually the entire coastal watershed of the proposed national recreation area; the Aliso and Wood Canyon areas in southern Orange County, where the coastal zone included much of the proposed Laguna Greenbelt; and the Los Penasquitos Lagoon area in the northern part of the city of San Diego, where a significant portion of the watershed tributary to the lagoon is within the coastal zone.

The need for protecting the State-owned wetland was clearly evident in Los Penasquitos Lagoon. However, even there, political reality tempered the concept of watershed management. Only the floors and slopes of Carmel Valley, Penasquitos Canyon, and Lopez Canyon were included in the coastal zone. Carroll Canyon and much of the undeveloped area proposed to be developed in the city's NCW community were excluded. In exchange for this mapping of the coastal boundaries, the City of San Diego (and through its influence, the League of Cities), tempered its position on pending bills. In addition, the planning director pledged the city's cooperation in mitigating potential adverse effects of the highly controversial NCW development.

The Coastal Commission's experience in San Diego County under Proposition 20 had clearly revealed that urban development resulted in increased rates of sedimentation. The causes and mechanisms of these problems were less clear, so the Commission authorized a "special study" of the lagoon and watershed by a geologist/ hydrologist. The resulting study, by Karen Prestegaard

[1] Paper presented at the California Riparian Systems Conference. [University of California, Davis, Sept. 17-19, 1981].

[2] James S. Jenks and Thomas C. MacDonald are Principal Engineers with Leeds, Hill and Jewett, Inc., San Francisco, Calif. James P. McGrath is Coastal Analyst, California Coastal Commission, San Francisco, Calif.

provided some of the answers. The study recommended: 1) preservation of the natural areas of sediment storage (largely the undeveloped floodplains); and 2) mitigation of the increased storm flows associated with urbanization to prevent scour of sediment from the stream-beds and banks and increased downstream movement of sediment associated with such scour and increased flow.

The city of San Diego and local developers began further studies to implement these recommendations in the detailed planning of individual developments. The most successful effort was, ironically, in NCW. One of the major developers of the area authorized the detailed hydrologic analyses needed to carry out the recommendations of the Prestegaard study. The resulting study by Leeds, Hill and Jewett, Inc.[3], was successful enough to be incorporated as an element of the city's Local Coastal Program (LCP).

Los Penasquitos Lagoon

Los Penasquitos Lagoon is a coastal lagoon about 1.6 km. (1 mi.) long and 0.8 km. (0.5 mi.) wide, located in San Diego County. It consists of flat marshlands laced with deep tidal channels and interspersed with occasional tidal and salt flats (California Department Fish and Game 1974). The size of the lagoon is being slowly reduced by inflows of sediment from the Los Penasquitos watershed. Reports indicate that before 1888, the lagoon was continuously connected to the ocean. Railroad and highway construction through the lagoon in the 1920s drastically changed drainage patterns in the lagoon area and led to intermittent blockages of the mouth of the lagoon.

Removal of the beach and cobble littoral drift material that collects at the outlet of the lagoon to the ocean was first tried in 1966 to re-establish tidal flushing. It was believed that improved tidal flows would encourage the restoration of a healthy marine fauna to the lagoon. However, maintenance of the outlet to the ocean has been sporadic since 1966 and generally not successful.

One important factor involved in keeping the mouth of the lagoon clear is the volume of water which passes through the opening during one tide cycle. This volume is called the tidal prism. Accumulations of sediment in the lagoon reduce the tidal prism, which reduces the natural sediment-removing mechanism of the lagoon. It has been noted that in recent years there has been a net accumulation of sediment in the upstream areas of the lagoon.

---

[3]Leeds, Hill and Jewett, Inc. 1980. North City West drainage study. Report to Pardee Construction Company, San Francisco, Calif. 44 p.

North City West

In 1975 the North City West Community plan[4] was prepared by the City of San Diego for a new community to be located near the north city limits. The boundaries of NCW encompass about 1,740 ha. (4,300 ac.), most of which are tributary to Los Penasquitos Lagoon. The community will consist of a variety of housing types, commercial developments, and public facilities, including recreational areas and open spaces. The areas associated with each type of development are presented in table 1.

The estimated total number of dwelling units planned for NCW is 13,970, sufficient to house a population of about 40,000. The community will have an employment center and town center. It will also have small commercial centers scattered throughout the area which will contain a variety of light industry, commercial establishments, and offices to serve the needs of future residents and to provide employment opportunities. Open space areas consist of parks, floodplains, areas of hazardous geology, and slopes greater than 25%. The NCW community will be developed by various developers and property owners.

As described in the Community Plan,[4] the NCW area will be developed as nine separate units. More than one of these units may be under development at any one time.

TECHNICAL PRINCIPLES AND CRITERIA FOR SEDIMENT CONTROL

Technical Principles

Development of NCW will have significant impacts on the sedimentation regime of the area which, if not regulated, could increase the rate of sediment accumulation in Los Penasquitos Lagoon.

Table 1.--Type of development, area, and percent of total area planned for North City West.

Development	Area	
	Acres	Percent
Residential (dwelling units per net residential acre)		
Very low density (5)	1,470	34
Low density (10)	444	11
Low medium density (20)	128	3
Medium density (40)	52	1
Commercial	202	5
Public facilities	308	7
Freeways and major streets	296	7
Open space	1,386	32
Total	4,286	100

---

[4]City of San Diego, 1975. North City West Community Plan. 147 p. San Diego, Calif.

Currently most of the NCW area is undeveloped, with the predominant vegetative cover being annual grasses and open brush. Some of the land is used for agricultural and grazing purposes. Soils in the area are fine-grained and cohesionless and are predominately in hydrologic soil group D, which has a very low infiltration rate. This soil-type, along with the minimal vegetative cover and, in some areas, overgrazing, makes the area subject to the erosive forces of rainfall and runoff. This situation is aggravated by point discharges into the unprotected drainage channels in the western part of NCW of urban runoff from areas on the west side of Interstate Highway 5. During the recent wet years, these point discharges have, in at least one place, eroded a huge gully and transported several thousand cubic yards of sediment downstream, some of which has been deposited in the lagoon.

When NCW is developed, the potential for sediment runoff will initially increase when vegetative cover, which tends to hold the soil in place, is removed by grading operations. Sediment runoff during this period must be controlled to avoid clogging the downstream channels and lagoon with sediment.

After NCW is developed, sediment production from the area will be less than currently occurs. Sediment production will decrease as a result of open space and developed areas being protected by roof tops, streets, lawns, and other erosion-resistant groundcovers.

Also after development, rainfall over much of the area will be collected in non-erosive roadbeds, gutters, and storm drains and conveyed to the stream channels, thereby avoiding concentrated flows over sediment-producing areas. Other sediment control devices in NCW, such as berms, downdrains, etc., will protect against local sedimentation damages to other portions of the development.

Although sediment production from NCW will be less after the area is developed and the vegetation is well established, the amount and rate of runoff will increase. The amount of runoff will increase because there will be less infiltration loss in the impervious areas of the development. The rate of runoff will increase because runoff will be collected and conveyed to the downstream channels in a more rapid manner than occurs naturally. Because of this more rapid drainage, runoff from larger areas during the most intense periods of precipitation will be more nearly simultaneous than normal.

The increased volumes and rates of rainfall-runoff and the reduced amount of sediment production after NCW is developed will, if not controlled, have long-term effects on the sediment regime of channels downstream from the development. The increased rates and volumes of runoff will have a greater capacity to transport sediment than the flows that now occur and the watershed will not supply as much sediment to the

flows. Thus, if drainage controls are not provided, erosion of the bed and banks of stream channels can be expected downstream of points where runoff is discharged from NCW.

From the foregoing, it is apparent that both short-term and long-term drainage control plans are needed for NCW to protect against sediment damages to downstream areas.

Drainage Control Criteria

During the construction period, the most effective control plan for a proposed development is to provide on-site controls to reduce the amount of sediment that would otherwise run off the construction slopes. Such controls include vegetating bare slopes, constructing low berms and drains, and other short-term measures.

Reduction of sediment erosion by means of protecting land surfaces can effectively eliminate sediment runoff from many areas. However, it may not be possible to protect all areas or the protection used may not be completely effective at all times. In these cases, it will be necessary to provide additional backup controls. These backup controls have the function of collecting the sediment that does run off before it can cause any downstream damage.

For the long-term, drainage control facilities must be provided that regulate outflows from the development such that the ability of the outflow to erode sediment from the downstream channels is reduced. For a constant rate of flow, the amount of sediment that can be transported is directly proportional to the duration or the volume of flow. However, in most cases it is not practical to try to reduce the volume of stormwater runoff. The sediment transport capacity of the flow increases disproportionately faster than increasing flow rate. Thus, to protect against erosion of downstream channels, it is more important to regulate the rate of runoff.

It is also important that the facilities that provide the long-term control of sedimentation problems allow passage of sediment from the developed watershed. Sediment from the developed watershed will satisfy part of the sediment transport capacity of the downstream flows. To the extent that outflows from an area contain less sediment than the flow's capacity to transport sediment, the flow will try to make up the sediment deficiency by eroding the bed and banks of the downstream channel. Thus, it is important that sediment runoff from the watershed pass through the control facilities and into the downstream channels.

In implementing the recommendation that increased storm flows be mitigated, a number of difficult technical issues had to be resolved. First, the design storm event to be the basis of analyses needed to be selected. Second, methods for estimating and comparing runoff had to be established.

The field work done for the Prestegaard study indicated that the storm event with a recurrence interval of from one to two years did not appear to be the channel-forming event for this Mediterranean-type climate. Also, five-year storm flows are not substantially greater than the two-year flows. However, storms in 1978 and 1979-80 had an approximate 10-year recurrence frequency and indicated that significant channel-forming processes do occur with such storms. Thus, the 10-year storm was selected as the design storm of the analyses. Subsequent analyses showed that the controls developed to regulate runoff from a 10-year event also effectively attenuated runoff from the 25-year storm event—further strengthening arguments for use of the 10-year storm as an analytical base.

The "Rational Formula" for estimating rainfall-runoff is commonly used for subdivision drainage design in the county. This formula estimates the peak rate of rainfall-runoff as the product of the watershed area, rainfall intensity, and an empirical rainfall-runoff coefficient. In general this formula tends to overestimate flow rates. If controls are to be provided to regulate flow rates to natural levels for the purpose of sediment control, that purpose may be defeated by analytical tools that overestimate flow rates. An overestimation of flows from undeveloped lands, if used as a criterion for design of control facilities, would lead to a strategy that did not sufficiently attenuate flows in the developed condition—and thus, failure of the mitigation strategy.

A methodology was developed by Leeds, Hill and Jewett, Inc., for analyzing rainfall-runoff from the 1,740+ ha. (4,300+ ac.) of land tributary to Los Penasquitos Lagoon to be occupied by NCW. This methodology, which utilizes the US Army Corps of Engineers (CE) HEC-1 computer program, provides accurate estimates of runoff hydrographs from relatively small drainage areas for both developed and undeveloped land-use conditions. The methodology and its verification are described below.

NORTH CITY WEST SEDIMENT CONTROL PLAN

Methodology

Several methods to control stormwater runoff from developed areas were investigated, and detention basins were found to be the most effective. These detention basins can also be used, on a temporary basis, to protect against potential erosion during construction when slopes will be bare.

Preparation of an effective drainage control plan utilizing detention basins requires determination of stormwater runoff characteristics for existing and future land-use conditions. Estimates of peak runoff under existing conditions are needed to establish the level of regulation that should be provided. Estimates of increases in runoff under future developed conditions are needed to locate and determine the size of detention basin facilities that would regulate future flows to less than those that would occur under existing conditions.

The CE's HEC-1 computer program was used to analyze stormwater runoff. This program is capable of generating estimated runoff hydrographs from precipitation using very small time intervals in the hydrograph calculation. Because the drainage areas used in the analyses are generally small, and therefore have short times of concentration, a method of analysis that uses even smaller time intervals in the hydrograph calculation is necessary to accurately estimate peak discharges. The HEC-1 program provides a cost-effective method of obtaining these estimates.

The HEC-1 program estimates the amount and rate of rainfall-runoff based on the drainage area size, land use, types of soils, intensity of precipitation, and antecedent moisture conditions. These characteristics can be estimated from soil, groundcover, and topographic maps, photographs of the study area, and information gathered during field inspections. Precipitation intensities and antecedent moisture conditions can usually be obtained from local agencies.

During the initial construction period detention basins can be fitted with a temporary riser so that they function as both sediment traps and as detention basins. Once development is complete and slopes are stabilized by vegetation, the temporary riser can be removed. After the riser is removed, the basin outlet would be at the low point of the basin floor such that much of the subsequent inflow of sediment can pass through the basin and into the downstream channel. As previously noted, allowing sediment to pass through the basin will minimize the tendency of the downstream channel to degrade due to a reduction of sediment inflow. Temporary desilting basins can be provided to protect those areas that do not have a downstream detention basin. Use of both desilting basins and modified detention basins during the construction period is considered a backup to the primary on-site controls of vegetation and avoidance of grading during the runoff season.

Verification

The reliability of the methodology used to estimate runoff characteristics of developed and undeveloped areas was verified by calculating runoff from the drainage areas of Pomerado and Beeler creeks, for which actual precipitation and runoff data are available, and by comparing the measured and calculated runoff hydrographs. These creeks are tributary to Los Penasquitos Lagoon and are about 8 km. (5 mi.) east of the NCW area. Stream gauge measurements on these two creeks are available for a short period of record, so the choice of past storms that can be studied is limited.

A storm which occurred on 4 December 1972, was selected for verification. This was an isolated storm which produced fairly uniform and equal amounts of rainfall over both drainage areas. The drainage areas were divided into urbanized and nonurbanized subareas. The Pomerado Creek area is 10.6 sq. km. (4.1 sq. mi.) in size, of which about 15% is urbanized by medium-density residential housing. About 1.6 km. (1 mi.) of the creek channel is concrete-lined. Beeler Creek drainage area is 14.2 sq. km. (5.5 sq. mi.) in size and, except for a very small development, not urbanized.

The measured precipitation data from nearby rain gauging stations along with hydrologic characteristics of the subareas, estimated from soil and topographic maps and aerial photographs, were used in the HEC-1 computer program. The runoff hydrographs from each of the subareas were calculated, routed through the stream channels, and then combined to obtain the total runoff hydrograph from the drainage areas of the two creeks. These hydrographs were then compared with measured flow rates as shown in figure 1. This comparison indicates that the methodology produced reasonable estimates of runoff from Pomerado and Beeler Creek drainage areas and can be used to produce reasonable estimates of runoff for both urbanized and undeveloped areas.

North City West Analyses

Following verification of the methodology, hydrologic characteristics of each drainage subarea in NCW (fig. 2) were determined and are presented in table 2. Future conditions were estimated using the NCW Community Plan.[4]

Precipitation intensities having recurrence frequencies of 10 and 25 years were used in the analyses for sizing detention basins and analyzing their performance. Peak rates of discharge were computed at the potential basin sites shown in figure 2 for existing and ultimate land-use conditions for the two storm events. These peak discharge rates are presented in table 3 for selected locations.

Alternative basin locations, sizes, and outlet works were then examined to develop a plan which would meet Coastal Commission requirements. It was found that a minimum of three detention basins are needed to meet the requirements but that several alternative combinations of basin locations could be used. Regulated peak outflow rates for one of the alternative plans are presented in table 3.

Hydrographs of stormwater runoff for the 10-year storm under existing and ultimate land-use conditions with and without detention basins are shown in figure 3 for the location where Carmel Creek flows into Los Penasquitos Lagoon. The peak discharge at this location is 554 cubic feet per second (cfs) under existing conditions, 917 cfs under future conditions without detention basins, and 539 cfs with detention basins for the alternative plan that provides detention basins at locations E, R, and H.

In addition to providing for regulation of stormwater runoff under ultimate land-use conditions, the plan requires on-site controls during the interim construction period. These controls provide that no grading be done during the five-month period from October 5 to March 15 of each year. It further provides for planting of exposed construction slopes before November 1 of each year to minimize erosion during the rainy winter season. Although this program should be adequate, the plan also provides backup controls by fitting the detention basins with risers during the interim construction period so that they can act as sediment traps.

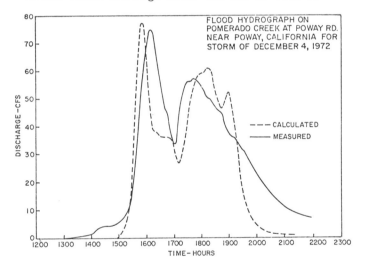

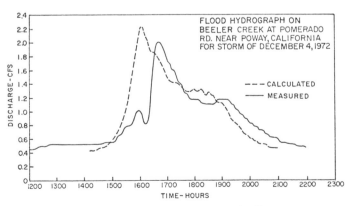

Figure 1.--Calculated and measured discharge for December 4, 1972 storm.

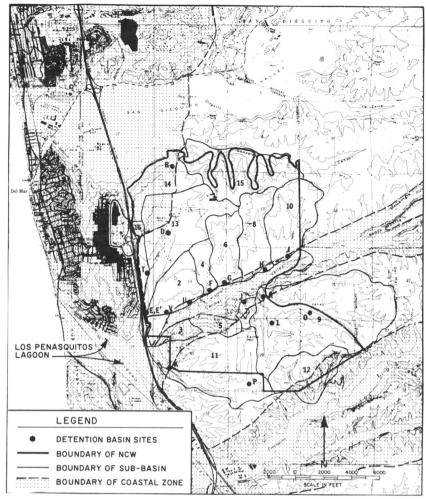

Figure 2.--North City West drainage areas and detention basin sites.

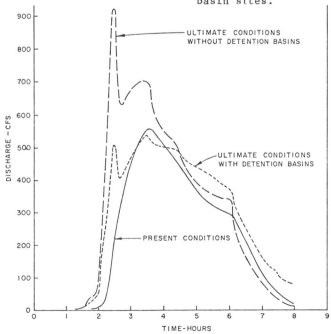

Figure 3.--Discharges from NCW in Carmel Creek at Los Penasquitos Lagoon-10-year storm.

CONCLUSION

The concept of watershed management through stormwater management used in NCW poses great potential for urbanized areas where development goals include minimizing increases in downstream flooding, preserving natural riparian corridors, and/or controlling sediment movement. Although the side canyons of the watershed will be substantially altered through urbanization, the main stem of the stream will be preserved and managed in a state similar to its natural condition. Thus, sediment transport capabilities of the channel will be maintained, although sediment production from the watershed will decrease somewhat after development activities are completed.

The stream's main stem will be capable of maintaining riparian vegetation because flows will not be channelized and stream-bed erosion will be controlled through regulation of runoff rates.

Table 2.--Hydrologic characteristics of the NWC development.

Subareas	Area (Acres)	Mean Slope (Ft/mi)	Shape Factor S[1]	Sediment Delivery Ratio	EXISTING CONDITIONS				FUTURE CONDITIONS			
					Roughness n[2]	Lag Time Hours[3]	% Area Developed	SCS Curve No.[4]	Roughness n[2]	Lag Time Hours[3]	% Area Developed	SCS Curve No.[4]
1	416	55	3.4	.32	.05	.89	0	70	.04	.71	40	73
2	248	165	.17	.34	.20	.94	0	88	.015	.07	100	93
3	74	698	.006	.40	.10	.20	0	75	.05	.10	40	76
4	102	175	.31	.38	.06	.35	0	77	.015	.09	100	83
5	99	508	.17	.38	.08	.30	0	77	.05	.19	50	83
6	253	283	.52	.34	.06	.38	0	76	.02	.13	90	77
7	52	532	.04	.42	.06	.13	0	80	.015	.03	70	90
8	295	54	.60	.33	.05	.46	0	83	.015	.14	70	85
9a	134	60	.14	.37	.04	.21	0	81	.04	.21	[5]	81
9b	110	593	.04	.38	.06	.13	0	83	.06	.13	[5]	83
9c	510	150	.78	.31	.05	.42	0	81	.05	.42	[5]	81
9d	118	140	.41	.38	.05	.33	0	84	.04	.27	30	84
9e	328	203	.17	.33	.05	.22	0	84	.04	.18	40	85
10a	264	138	.47	.34	.05	.35	0	81	.02	.14	80	83
10b	111	138	.47	.33	.05	.35	0	81	.04	.28	[5]	81
11a	282	156	1.6	.34	.05	.55	0	76	.05	.55	[5]	76
11b	144	292	.55	.37	.05	.32	20	75	.02	.13	90	83
11c	196	327	.47	.35	.06	.30	0	79	.02	.10	70	80
11d	101	391	.29	.38	.06	.29	0	72	.04	.19	75	82
12	319	286	.45	.33	.06	.36	0	85	.05	.30	20	85
13a	297	178	.20	.33	.05	.25	20	72	.015	.07	80	87
13b	199	183	.65	.35	.05	.32	0	74	.015	.09	70	87
13c	119	132	1.6	.38	.05	.57	0	65	.015	.17	100	76
14a	119	724	.03	.38	.20	.22	0	82	.015	.22	10	84
14b	114	286	.21	.38	.06	.26	0	82	.02	.09	100	84
15	537	352	.28	.30	.06	.29	0	78	.05	.24	25	79
16a	50	229	.11	.42	.06	.22	0	71	.015	.06	100	90

[1]/ Distance, in miles, from outlet of basin to most remote point in basin times distance, in miles, from outlet of basin to the centroid of the basin.
[2]/ Mean roughness coefficient of basin for Manning's equation for open channel flow.
[3]/ Time between the beginning of excess rainfall and the centroid of runoff.
[4]/ Curve number based on soil and vegetation and gives estimate of precipitation infiltration losses.
[5]/ Sub-basins outside NCW or open-space - it was assumed that development of these lands would not be of a density to affect existing hydrological conditions.

Table 3.--Summary of peak discharge rates at various locations (cubic feet per second).

	10-Year Flood			25-Year Flood		
	Existing Conditions	Ultimate Conditions w/o Basins	Ultimate Conditions w/ Basins	Existing Conditions	Ultimate Conditions w/o Basins	Ultimate Conditions w/ Basins
Basin E	111	424	66	172	590	75
Basin R	283	307	173	436	467	197
Basin H	71	145	44	107	207	52
Carmel Creek Total	554	917	539	858	1329	742
Los Penasquitos Creek	110	120	120	159	174	174
Los Penasquitos Lagoon Total	664	1037	659	1017	1503	916

The issues of long-term maintenance of storm-water detention basins, and to a lesser extent, the questions of liability, are unresolved at the present time. To date, the costs and liabilities of a drainage program which incorporates detention basins have not been compared to those of a conventional drainage system. Thus, it is unclear whether overall costs and liabilities will be higher, lower, or comparable to such facilities. However, the advantages to the riparian system are clear.

The drainage studies for NCW and the resulting drainage control plan were accepted by the City of San Diego and submitted as an element of its LCP. The City is also requiring, as part of the environmental impact report process, implementation of these controls in other developments as an element of subdivision design. Thus, developers can integrate these controls into their initial designs, rather than adding them on late in the development planning process when the LCP is reviewed by the Coastal Commission.

LITERATURE CITED

California Department of Fish and Game. 1974. Natural resources of Los Penasquitos Lagoon. California Department of Fish and Game, Sacramento, Calif. 75 p.

Prestegaard, Karen A. No date. Stream and lagoon channels of the Los Penasquitos watershed, California, with an evaluation of possible effects of proposed urbanization. Coastal Commission Special Studies Series, San Francisco, Calif. 75 p.

MANAGEMENT OF RIPARIAN VEGETATION IN THE NORTHCOAST REGION OF CALIFORNIA'S COASTAL ZONE[1]

Dan Ray, Wayne Woodroof, and R. Chad Roberts[2]

Abstract.--Riparian vegetation has important habitat and economic values. The Coastal Act requires protection of both of these sets of values. Local coastal plans have attempted to resolve this policy conflict by protecting riparian corridors and habitat patches. Protection of large areas of riparian vegetation by land-use regulation has proven difficult.

INTRODUCTION

Northwestern California riparian systems include a complex of biological and economic resources seldom surpassed in richness. Riparian systems provide nesting and foraging areas for a diverse wildlife fauna, protect water quality essential to anadromous fisheries, hold substantial commercial timber, and affect floodwaters and sediment movement in ways essential to local agriculture. State and local policies encourage protection of all of these values--a policy mandate requiring government officials to balance competing goals. Developing policies which can be implemented and are technically sound and politically acceptable is a difficult task.

RIPARIAN SYSTEMS IN THE NORTHCOAST REGION

The northcoast region of California's coastal zone includes the seaward portions of Del Norte, Humboldt, and Mendocino counties. The coastal zone's inland boundary, established by the Coastal Act of 1976, is typically 914 m. (1,000 yd.) inland from the mean high tide. The boundary runs inland in four large bulges to include significant estuarine, habitat, and recreational areas at Lakes Earl and Talawa in the Smith River delta; Freshwater, Stone, and Big lagoons near Redwood National Park; the Eel River delta, and the Ten Mile estuary and dunes complex in Mendocino County. The largest of these bulges, the Eel River delta, extends inland almost 8 km. (5 mi.) above the river's estuary

and up to 18 km. (11 mi.) from Pacific Ocean beaches.

Riparian systems within the northcoast region of the coastal zone are located along most minor streams and all of the major rivers. Their vegetation is characterized by an overstory typically dominated by red alder (Alnus rubra), Sitka spruce (Picea sitchensis), and redwood (Sequoia sempervirens). Black cottonwood (Populus trichocarpa) is commonly dominant on the floodplains of the Mad and Eel rivers. Pacific wax-myrtle (Myrica californica), bigleaf maple (Acer macrophyllum), California-laurel (Umbellularia californica) and Pacific red elder (Sambucus callicarpa) are also common trees and shrubs in mature riparian areas. Willows (Salix spp.) are typical pioneers in disturbed areas. In mature associations, these species are joined by vines, epiphytes, and other herbaceous and woody plants to form a diverse, vertically stratified plant community. For a more complete description of riparian flora, see Roberts et al. (1977) or Proctor et al. (1980).

Wildlife populations in northcoast riparian areas have not been thoroughly surveyed, but lists from comparable areas in inland forests (Marcot 1979; Thomas 1979), coastal Oregon and Washington (Proctor et al. 1980), and other sources (Harris 1973; Monroe 1974) suggest that up to 140 species of birds and 37 species of mammals utilize northcoast riparian forests at some time during the year. Many of these species (wading birds such as egrets, cavity nesters, and some raptors, warblers, and mammalian predators) depend upon mature riparian forest for some portion of their nesting or feeding habitat requirements. The importance of riparian forests may be increased in the northcoast region due to the relatively poor habitat status of upland redwood forest (Leipzig 1972; Harris 1973).

Riparian forests on smaller coastal streams also protect water quality by shading stream

---

[1]Paper presented at the California Riparian Systems Conference. [University of California, Davis, September 17-19, 1981].
[2]Dan Ray and Wayne Woodroof are Coastal Analysts, North Coast District, California Coastal Commission, Eureka, Calif. R. Chad Roberts is Environmental Analyst, Oscar Larson and Associates, Eureka, Calif.

channels and intercepting and filtering runoff from adjacent uplands. This water quality protection is critical in maintaining aquatic species, including anadromous fish, in coastal rivers and streams (Thompson et al. 1972).

Riparian zones in the northcoast also hold a number of economically important resources. Redwood, Sitka spruce, and red alder are important to local timber processors as sources of lumber, plywood, wood chips, and pulp. With the advent of biofuel-thermoelectric power plants, other riparian species such as black cottonwood may become economically important. Beyond the standing timber value, riparian zones are preferred sites for long-term timber production because of their soil quality and the beneficial effects of periodic flooding. For example, annual growth of commercial redwoods in riparian zones of the Big, Albion, and Navarro rivers of Mendocino County is from 1.2 to 1.4 times that of adjacent upland forest sites (USDA Forest Service 1965). Agricultural uses also benefit from productive riparian soils. Flood-borne sediment deposition on the alluvial valleys of the Garcia, Eel, Mad, and Smith rivers has created highly productive soils more than 1.8 m. (6 ft.) deep. These bottomland soils are up to twice as productive as other local farmlands on diked wetlands or upland terraces (McLaughlin and Harradine 1965). Agricultural land owners also use riparian vegetation as a source of firewood for domestic use.

Use of riparian land in the northcoast region has been dominated by the exploitation of these economic resources at the expense of fish and wildlife habitats. Riparian forests were typically among the first used for commercial timber harvest because of the very high lumber volumes they held and the easy access to rivers and estuaries they offered. Level streambeds were modified to allow construction of cordoroy roads or narrow-gauge railroads used to transport sawlogs. Large expanses of Sitka spruce/black cottonwood forest were cleared for agricultural use. An estimated 6,900 ha. (17,000 ac.) of riparian forest were converted to grazing land in the coastal zone of Humboldt and Del Norte counties. The major floods of 1955 and 1964 caused substantial damage to forested riparian lands on the Smith, Klamath, and Eel rivers. Subsequent construction of flood control projects on the Smith River and at Redwood Creek caused additional losses of riparian vegetation.

Existing northcoast riparian forests are a remnant of this history of development. Relatively large riparian areas remain along Elk Creek and the Klamath River in Del Norte County and the Eel River in Humboldt County. Cutover riparian forests in many small forested watersheds and commercial timberlands along the Ten Mile, Big, Albion, and Navarro rivers in Mendocino County have gone through succession to progressively more diverse second growth forests with high habitat values. Riparian woodland patches can still be found scattered in narrow bands along most streams and in unused portions of farms

or residential areas.

COASTAL COMMISSION POLICY FOR MANAGEMENT OF RIPARIAN SYSTEMS

The Coastal Act of 1976 (Public Resources Code 30000 et seq.) created the California Coastal Commission and six regional commissions and charged them with regulating development to protect coastal resources. The Act requires local governments to prepare local coastal plans implementing these policies and authorizes the regional coastal commissions to review local plans and regulate development within the coastal zone until local coastal plans are approved. The Act grants the Commission power to regulate most development affecting riparian systems. The Act does not authorize the Commission to regulate logging operations under timber harvest plans approved by the State Board of Forestry. Instead, the Act empowers the Commission to designate unique coastal resource sites as "special treatment areas" within which timber harvests are carefully regulated under the California Forest Practices Act. Coastal Act policies require protection of sensitive habitat areas and commercial forest lands and encouragement of coastal agriculture. Section 30240(a) of the Coastal Act states: "Environmentally sensitive habitat areas shall be protected against any significant disruption of habitat values, and only uses dependent on such resources shall be allowed within such areas."

Sections 30241 and 30242 require that: "the maximum amount of prime agricultural land shall be maintained in agricultural production to assure the protection of the areas' agricultural economy"; and "... lands suitable for agricultural use shall not be converted to non-agricultural uses unless (1) continued or renewed agricultural use is not feasible, or (2) such conversion would preserve prime agricultural land or concentrate development.... Any such permitted conversion shall be compatible with continued agricultural use on surrounding lands."

Section 30243 provides that: "long term productivity of soils and timberlands shall be protected and conversions of coastal commercial timberlands in units of commercial size to other uses or their division into units of non-commercial size shall be limited to providing for necessary timber processing and related facilities."

These policies express desirable objectives for state and local action but their application in specific areas may lead to conflicts. Purchase of extensive areas along the Big River in Mendocino County was proposed by the USDI Fish and Wildlife Service (FWS) in 1979 to assure protection of its sensitive estuarine and riparian systems. However, the purchase would convert commercial timberlands to non-commercial use. Installation of riprap or other devices along eroding Eel River banks is essential to the protection of prime agricultural lands, yet the bank protection would impede the natural erosion and accretion processes that have been essential to the maintenance of Eel River riparian systems.

Local farmers assert that Coastal Act policies provide priority to the agricultural economy and so should permit clearing of riparian vegetation for pasturelands. The California Department of Fish and Game (DFG) argues that the same policies require riparian systems be protected against even removal of domestic firewood. Industrial foresters believe the Coastal Act policies permit conversion of deciduous hardwood vegetation to commercial conifers.

Anticipating such conflicts among Coastal Act policies, the Legislature found in Section 30007.5 of the Act that: "...such conflicts should be resolved in a manner which on balance is the most protective of significant coastal resources...broader policies which, for example, serve to concentrate development in close proximity to urban and employment centers may be more protective overall than specific wildlife habitat and other similar resource policies."

Based upon this guide, northcoast region staff biologists have turned to conservation ecology theory to formulate policies which identify and protect significant resources of the region's riparian systems.

CONSERVATION ECOLOGY

In the past decade, ecologists have gained insights relating to conservation problems generated when development occurs in or adjacent to relatively undisturbed natural systems. An important work on this subject is that of Pickett and Thompson (1978), which builds upon the theoretical base formed in MacArthur and Wilson (1967). Pickett and Thompson began with concepts from island biogeography, broadened them to include habitat islands in seas of different habitat, and applied the results to conservation issues.

Their basic conceptual conclusion is that if a particular area of undisturbed habitat is reduced in size, the effect is qualitatively like that upon "land-bridge" islands (especially if the "connections" to other, similar habitat patches are severed). The remnant habitat islands are "supersaturated" with species, a phenomenon due to a predictable relationship between island areas and species richness. Reducing the habitat area **always** leads to a reduction in the number of species that a habitat patch will support; this is an empirical result, verified many times. After developing this point, the authors made several recommendations for habitat conservation. Habitat patches should be large, undisturbed, more-or-less round, and either close to or connected to other, similar patches. In addition, the ecology of the patch should be taken into consideration, including such factors as within-patch successional processes, "patch longevity," and patch replacement rate.

Wilcox (1980) developed these arguments further. By focusing on "insular ecology" Wilcox pointed out that habitat patches should be as large as possible. Since any "habitat" has fewer species than a larger, nearby habitat area (an empirical result), the larger the island, the fewer the missing species. Species typically added with greater patch size are the less common species which are usually the management target. Wilcox presented a technique for calculating species number reductions, given a reduction in patch size. That technical discussion is beyond the scope of this report, but the conclusion drawn is that the greater the habitat area reduction, the greater the magnitude of species lost, and the faster their rate of disappearance.

The relationship between habitat patch area and species diversity has been studied by other investigators. Galli et al. (1976) studied bird species diversity in New Jersey forest islands surrounded by other habitat. Thirty islands were studied ranging in size from 0.008 to 24.3 ha. (0.02 to 60 ac.). Bird species diversity increased in the predicted fashion, and the significant variable was shown to be island area. Until a minimum size threshold was crossed, only "edge" species were present. As the area increased further, "interior" bird species were added, though they tended to be present at low densities. A follow-up study in New Jersey by Forman et al. (1976) concluded that diversity continued to increase with patch size up to the 40 ha. (100 ac.) point. In fact, Forman et al. concluded that the highest bird species diversity would not be reached until areas in excess of 40 ha. were sampled.

Forman et al. (ibid.) also concluded: a) over half of all species encountered were "minimum-area" species, found in larger patches; b) larger patches contained more species than an equal areas of smaller patches; c) most of the increase in diversity in patches larger than about 2.8 ha. (7.0 ac.) was due to insectivorous species; and d) large mammal-eating birds were only present on the larger patches. As management considerations, these authors recommended that patches be as large as possible, and that many smaller "stepping-stone" islands be maintained.

The relationship between body size and geographic range size was discussed by Schoener (1968). He showed that, in general, larger birds required larger territories. Apparently the relative densities of the kinds of food eaten by large (especially predatory) birds decrease as bird body weights increases. This is apparently why such species as Pileated Woodpeckers and Buteo hawks have large territories and, conversely, why there are relatively few of these birds (disregarding the basic question of distribution of their required habitats). Schoener's empirical result dovetails with the field results of Forman et al. (1976), adding credence to the recommendation for large habitat patches.

Further, Gates and Gysel (1978) found that forest edge-nesting bird species were more subject to both predation and cowbird parasitism than interior-nesting species. Forest edges acted as a guide to both predators and cowbirds; nesting success increased in proportion to the distance of the nest from the forest edge. There may be a minimally acceptable patch size which ensures availability of enough area for edge-nesting species to avoid nest losses from predators and cowbird parasitism.

Based upon this analysis, we believe that a premium value should be placed on large expanses of undisturbed riparian vegetation. Such large, undisturbed areas will fulfill "minimum-area" requirements of those large and/or uncommon species which require conditions in patch interiors. A second priority should be for smaller areas of undisturbed riparian vegetation in preference to larger areas of disturbed vegetation. These "stepping-stone island" patches can answer the needs of some smaller "interior" species; if population densities randomly fluctuate to low levels, they can help dispersing individuals recolonize larger patches. Finally, retention of some riparian vegetation along all watercourses is essential. While a narrow strip is not in itself satisfactory habitat, it can help in dispersal, and adds minor foraging area for species in nearby, larger patches.

POLICIES FOR RIPARIAN MANAGEMENT

North Coast District local coastal plans being prepared by local governments or already approved by the Coastal Commission generally include riparian vegetation management policies consistent with these recommendations. Where commercial timber use is planned for riparian areas, the conflict between timber production and habitat protection has been resolved through the forest practices rules for special treatment areas. The rules provide protection for many components of riparian systems. Riparian vegetation management policies and their applications in typical riparian systems within the region are discussed below.

RIPARIAN MANAGEMENT ON SMALL COASTAL STREAMS

The northcoast region includes about 240 small coastal streams and their tributaries. Typically, these streams drain watersheds from 1.6 to 6.4 km. (1 to 4 mi.) inland from the coastal zone and would be considered first- and second-order streams under Strahler's (1964) stream ordering rules. Their channels are usually contained within well-defined gorges cutting through the coastal terrace. Riparian vegetation is best developed and most diverse immediately adjacent to the stream channel, although Sitka spruce, redwood, or red alder may extend from riparian zones to adjacent uplands in an undifferentiated forest overstory. Wildlife populations include most typical riparian passerines, but raptors, wading birds, and other avian components of larger

riparian systems are absent. Cutthroat (Salmo clarkii) and steelhead (S. gairdneri) trout and silver salmon (Oncorhynchus kisutch) are common spawners within the streams and their tributaries (Humboldt County Planning Department 1978). Most riparian systems have been altered by timber harvest or fire, but many have gone through succession to relatively diverse second-growth forests.

Local coastal plans propose delineation of riparian corridors by assigning fixed distances from stream channels. For example, Humboldt County's southcoast area plan states:

> Riparian corridors on all perennial and intermittent streams shall be, at a minimum, the larger of the following: (i) 100 feet, measured as the horizontal distance from the stream transition line on both sides; (ii) 50 feet plus four times the average percent of slope, measured as a slope distance from the stream transition line on both sides; (iii) where necessary, the width of riparian corridors may be expanded to include significant areas of riparian vegetation adjacent to the corridor, slides, and areas with visible evidence of slope instability, not to exceed 200 feet. (Humboldt County Planning Department 1981a)

Identification of riparian areas by vegetation analysis has not been proposed in any local coastal plan in the region because of the similarity of riparian and upland forest vegetation along these streams. Local agencies usually lack personnel trained in the vegetation identification and sampling techniques needed to differentiate riparian and upland systems based on hydrophytic understory components. In addition, the fixed distance riparian corridors proposed in these local coastal plans are familiar to most local residents and public officials because of their use in state and federal forest practices standards.

Uses in riparian corridors are usually limited to minor facilities and resource production, such as timber harvest, under standards designed to protect tree canopies and minimize erosion. Humboldt County's southcoast area plan provides that:

> New development within riparian corridors shall be permitted when there is no less environmentally damaging feasible alternative, where the best mitigation measures feasible have been provided, and shall be limited to the following uses: (a) Timber management activities, provided that heavy equipment shall be excluded from the riparian corridor and where feasible, at least fifty percent of the existing tree canopy shall be left standing; (b) Timber harvests smaller than three acres of merchantable timber 18 inches

DBH or greater and non-commercial removal of trees for firewood provided that timber harvest practices shall be consistent with those permitted under the forest practices rules for stream protection zones in Coastal Commission special treatment areas. Where feasible, unmerchantable hardwoods and shrubs should be protected from permanent damage; (c) Maintenance of flood control and drainage channels; (d) Wells in rural areas; (e) Road and bridge replacement or construction, provided that the length of the road within the riparian corridor shall be minimized, where feasible, by rights of way which cross streams at right angles and do not parallel streams within the riparian corridor; (f) Removal of trees for disease control, or public safety purposes. Mitigation measures for development within riparian corridors shall, at a minimum, include replanting disturbed areas with riparian vegetation, retaining snags within the riparian corridor unless felling is required by CAL-OSHA regulation, and retaining live trees with visible evidence of current use as nesting sites by hawks, owls, eagles, osprey, herons, or egrets. (ibid.)

The riparian corridors protected by these policies can maintain habitats which provide "bridges" for wildlife movement between larger stepping stones and riparian islands. Protecting vegetation adjacent to streams can help protect water quality essential to anadromous fisheries. Because of the size of the areas protected and because some activities, such as logging under an approved timber harvest plan, are not regulated by these policies, such policies cannot be relied upon to protect all the riparian components necessary to maximize species diversity.

Policies to protect riparian corridors have met little resistance from landowners and local governments within the area. Most landowners can identify the fixed-distance corridor on their parcels and locate sites outside the corridor which are suitable for development. Local government officials can relate the protection of riparian corridors to local goals of protecting anadromous fisheries and domestic water quality, and so find them politically acceptable

RIPARIAN MANAGEMENT
IN REMNANT VEGETATION PATCHES

Many local coastal programs propose protection of larger patches of riparian vegetation which may be located outside designated corridor areas. These patches are typically undisturbed old-growth forests with a diverse riparian flora and a vertically stratified physiognomy. Wildlife diversity within them may be limited because of their size or location adjacent to other developed uses. They play only a minor role in

water quality or anadromous fisheries protection because they are typically located on broad alluvial plains and may be separated from the stream channel by other development. Many of these areas are located in state or federal parklands. Protection of these riparian areas is typically provided by public agencies which manage them.

Protecting similar patches on private lands has proven more difficult. The affected areas may be relatively large (2-10 ha.) and may seem unrelated to public goals for protecting fisheries or water quality. Consequently local officials have been reluctant to regulate such activities as timber harvests or conversion to agricultural use which may affect the habitat value of the area.

A patch of riparian vegetation at Redwood Creek in Humboldt County, of approximately 10 ha. (25 ac.), is typical of these sites (fig. 1). It includes a dense Sitka spruce/red alder stand which is the last remnant of Redwood Creek's old growth riparian forest. It has had little use as agricultural land and remained unharvested when adjacent riparian areas were converted to pasture. The Redwood Creek flood control project separated the site from the creek and provided access to it along the project's levees. Half of the patch is within Redwood National Park. Approximately 5 ha. (12 ac.) in its eastern half are owned by a local cattleman as part of a larger ranch.

Figure 1.--Remnant patches of riparian vegetation, Redwood Creek, Humboldt County, California.

The local coastal plan (Humboldt County Planning Department 1980a) designated the area for agricultural use and only proposed protection of vegetation within the 30.5 m. (100-ft.) riparian corridor. The owner had no plans to develop or convert the remainder of the site, but resisted land-use policies which required its protection for habitat use. The regional commission did not approve the plan, but stated that it would approve a revised plan which designated the site for natural resources use and limited new development on it to habitat management and tree removal for firewood purposes under certain conditions. The protection plan for the site recommended by the regional commission will probably be accepted by the landowner and the local government because of the parcel's isolation and its relatively small size. By permitting firewood harvesting, traditional woodlot uses of the stand were maintained, providing some economic return to the property owner.

Patches of riparian vegetation such as this site can provide the stepping stones to connect larger habitat islands. The areas themselves provide habitat for wading birds and cavity nesters which are not common inhabitants of the narrower riparian corridors along small coastal streams. These patches are probably not large enough to accommodate minimum area species such as large raptors or to sustain sufficient numbers of individuals to maintain healthy breeding populations of many smaller riparian species. Those species which depend on such specific conditions as dense canopies or dead or dying wood in snags or on the forest floor may be displaced in the future if firewood harvesting reduces these habitat components. Nonetheless, both types of birds could use the area for resting or foraging while traveling between larger riparian areas.

MANAGEMENT OF LARGE RIPARIAN SYSTEMS

Preparing local coastal plans for large riparian systems--the habitat islands for riparian-dependent species--has proven to be one of the most difficult tasks facing local governments and the Coastal Commission.

Protecting these riparian areas is particularly troublesome because of the need to maintain the areas in a virtually undisturbed state in order to retain unique habitat components such as dense canopies or dead and down trees. While state and federal wildlife refuges, parks, conservation areas, and wilderness areas provide large blocks of relatively undisturbed wetland, upland forest, or montane vegetation, there are no comparable publicly-owned riparian reserves within the coastal zone in the northcoast region. Protecting these areas will require either public purchase or extensive regulation of substantial amounts of private land. Public purchase is unpopular because of agency financial constraints, effects on local tax bases, and resentment over the already large public land holdings in the region. Local governments are generally unwilling to adopt the strict regulations necessary to protect these areas because the regulations may affect landowners who are frequently representatives of important segments of the local economy.

Constitutional issues (including questions of taking land without compensation) have not been extensively litigated in cases involving riparian vegetation, and most local governments are hesitant to expose themselves to potential legal and financial liabilities. Finally, because most data on riparian system values are from areas other than the northcoast and are not well understood by the general public, local support for protecting large riparian systems is limited.

Three areas provide examples of the problems presented to local governments and the Coastal Commission in managing these large riparian systems.

Elk Creek, Del Norte County

Elk Creek is located immediately northeast of Crescent City, and has a drainage basin covering approximately 1,670 ha. (4,120 ac.). It originates in the upland forests of Jedediah Smith Redwoods State Park and flows into the Crescent City harbor.

Approximately half of the watershed and almost all of the private lands within the Elk Creek basin, are within the coastal zone. About 225 ha. (550 ac.) of the coastal zone portion of the watershed are forested riparian zones, characterized by Sitka spruce, redwood, western hemlock (_Tsuga heterophylla_), red alder, and Pacific wax-myrtle (fig. 2). These forests meet freshwater marshes along the creek in an ecotone dominated by willows, Douglas spirea (_Spiraea douglasii_), and twinberry (_Lonicera involucrata_). Wildlife within the area includes such riparian-dependent species as Red-shouldered Hawk (_Buteo lineatus_), Snowy Egret (_Leucophoyx thula_), and Great Blue Heron (_Ardea herodias_) (Del Norte Planning Department 1980). The area has been logged, and approximately 15% of its forested lands has been converted to pastureland. Major portions of its basin, including many riparian areas, have been subdivided to parcels of 2 to 8 ha. (5 to 20 ac.) for rural residential use. However, soil moisture has permitted succession of both second-growth forests and abandoned fields to well-developed riparian vegetation. With the extensive clearing of

Figure 2.--Riparian vegetation on Elk Creek, Del Norte County, California.

riparian vegetation along Smith River and at Earl and Talawa lakes, Elk Creek is the principal alluvial riparian system remaining in Del Norte County.

The local coastal plan designated riparian zones in the Elk Creek drainage for a mix of agricultural general, timberland, and woodlot uses.[5] Those portions of the riparian areas which are frequently flooded were identified as wetlands. The plan included the following policies affecting riparian systems in the Elk Creek watershed:

(1) The filling, dredging or diking of any portion of the Elk Creek wetlands shall be prohibited except where necessary for flood control purposes; or when such activity enhances the biological productivity of the marshland; or when compatible with other policies of the coastal program and a specific finding is made which cites that policy;

(2) A buffer strip shall be maintained in natural conditions around the Elk Creek wetlands;

(3) No permanent structures shall be constructed within the identified portions of the Elk Creek wetlands including any delineated buffer zone;

(4) New development adjacent to the Elk Creek wetlands shall not result in adverse levels or additional sediment, runoff, noise, wastewater or other disturbances;

(5) Snags shall be maintained within the Elk Creek wetland for their value to wildlife;

(6) Riparian vegetation along the course of Elk Creek and its branch streams shall be maintained for their qualities of wildlife habitat and stream buffer zones;

(7) Vegetation removal in the Elk Creek wetland shall be limited to that necessary to maintain the free flow of the drainage courses;

(8) The County should encourage and support educational programs in schools, park programs and community organizations which seek to increase public awareness and understanding of sensitive habitats and the need for their protection. (ibid.)

The regional commission did not approve the land-use plan because of the designation of sensitive riparian lands for potential development,

even though at low densities, and the absence of a specifically defined buffer zone. The regional commission stated that it would approve the land-use plan if the county redesignated riparian zones as resource conservation areas, within which residential development was prohibited and parcels in contiguous ownership were merged, and adopted a minimum 100-ft. buffer zone around these lands.

As approved, the land-use plan prohibits development (including removal of vegetation except for flood control) on all riparian lands. Commercial timber harvests are not regulated by the plan; thus protection of riparian vegetation relies in large part on the designation of areas adjacent to riparian areas for rural residential use and other development at 1 unit per 8 ha. or more. The subdivision of these lands makes intensive forestry less feasible due to the loss of economics of scale necessary for long-term commercial timber production. This solution was acceptable to the county--the county relies primarily on public forest lands for its timber production (Proctor et al. 1980)--and was approved by the Coastal Commission because it reflected existing development trends in the area without jeopardizing the habitat values of the creek. Constitutional questions were minimized by merging adjacent parcels to provide larger lots where development could be sited on uplands beyond the buffer zone. The plan relies in large part on the inaccessibility, high water table, and lack of development pressure at Elk Creek to protect its riparian elements.

Eel River, Humboldt County

The Eel River flows from Mendocino and Humboldt County to enter the Pacific Ocean approximately 19 km. (12 mi.) southwest of Eureka. It enters the coastal zone near its junction with the Van Duzen River, and has a drainage basin of 923,000 ha. (2.28 million ac.). About 8,100 ha. of its watershed are within the coastal zone (fig. 3). Approximately 1,000 ha. of this area are forested riparian systems dominated by red alder, willow, and black cottonwood. Dense willow stands are common in areas with high water tables or subject to frequent high velocity water flows. Typical wildlife in the area includes all species previously identified plus additional species of cavity-nesting ducks, and raptors such as the White-tailed Kite (Elanus leucurus) and Peregrine Falcon (Falco peregrinus), which hunt over adjacent farmlands. Winter raptor populations in the area are particularly high--as little as 1.3 km. of transect per bird[6]--due in large part to the availability of riparian, wetland, and pasture vegetation in the area. Over 110 bird species dependent on riparian areas for some portion of their habitat requirements have been identified in the area.

---

[5]Agricultural general use provisions permit residential development at 1 unit per 8 ha. (20 ac.) and related development for grazing use, such as barns. Timberlands are intended for commercial timber use. Divisions to 1 unit per 8 ha. are permitted. Woodlot areas are forested rural residential lands with development permitted at 1 unit per 0.8 ha. (2 ac.).

---

[6]Pierce, H. 1981. Personal correspondence. California Department of Fish and Game, Eureka.

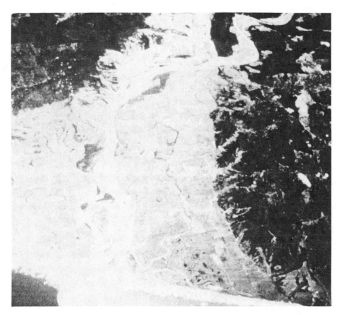

Figure 3.--Eel River delta, Humboldt County, California. Riparian vegetation is located adjacent to the main stem of the river (photo courtesy of NASA).

These riparian lands are a small remnant of the approximately 4,000 ha. (10,000 ac.) of the redwood/Sitka spruce/black cottonwood forest that occupied the Eel River delta floodplain at the advent of human settlement. Most of these lands were converted to grazing use because of their highly productive soils. Together with pasturelands on diked tidal marshes, they account for over half the cultivated agricultural land in Humboldt County's coastal zone and are the heart of the county's dairy industry (Humboldt County Planning Department 1979). Where forested riparian zones remain along the river, they are restricted to either the immediate channel corridor or to one of three large vegetation blocks located on oxbows, islands, or major turns in the river. Within these areas, conifers, which show clearly in historic photos of the same locations, are scarce. Portions of these areas were highly disturbed by flooding in 1955 and 1964. Aerial photos of the area show that mature red alder/ black cottonwood forests occupy 33% of its riparian systems, followed by young black cottonwood/red alder stands occupying 23%, mixed red alder/willow stands occupying 32%, and grassland/ forb pastures with scattered willows and red alder occupying 12%.

The retention of this vegetation pattern is in large part due to deliberate decisions by riparian landowners in response to past experience with flood damage and bank erosion. Eel River farmers have stated that most areas of black cottonwood/red alder vegetation have been retained because of their value in controlling flood-borne drift and coarse sediments which damage adjacent agricultural lands and structures. Most young red alder/willow patches are flood-damaged pastures abandoned after the

1955 or 1964 floods. Landowners of these sites may lack sufficient capital to reclaim the land. Where floodwaters deposit coarse sediments, property owners rely on riparian vegetation to slow the floodwaters, allowing them to drop finer soil particles. Some landowners have retained or even planted willow areas to retard bank erosion.

Most landowners have resisted policies which require retention of existing riparian vegetation. Increased wood chip or pulp wood prices may entice some owners of black cottonwood/red alder stands to harvest their riparian forest lands, even at the risk of increased flood damage. If the owners do not farm on valley pasturelands, there is little incentive to maintain mature forest stands. Where mixed red alder/willow stands occupy flood-damaged areas, property owners may anticipate additional silt deposition, or capital savings may permit reclamation of the site for agriculture. Local farmers have stated that several of these areas have gone through successive cycles of flood damage, forest growth, and clearing since the 1900s. Where construction of bank protection or changes in the river channel have reduced erosion hazards, property owners may decide to clear willow stands. Few landowners are willing to forego such uses as selective timber harvest or firewood removal, which retain riparian woodland stands but damage some habitat components essential to the area's diverse wildlife populations. Finally, almost all landowners wish to retain maximum flexibility of land use to respond to the dynamics of an area where, as one farmer stated: "The Eel owns the first mortgage and the bank gets the second" (Humboldt County Planning Department 1980b).

The Humboldt County Planning Department (1981b) recommended a local coastal plan focused on protecting old-growth black cottonwood/red alder stands, restoring degraded riparian systems, potentially converting some willow/alder stands, and retaining a forested riparian corridor along the river channel. The policies provided:

(1) The total acreage of the riparian corridor shall be established as a minimum base line for riparian vegetation on the Eel River; (2) Three areas of older age class riparian vegetation, comprised of old cottonwoods and alders, are designated Natural Resource. These areas are significant wildlife habitats and are critical to flood protection of adjacent prime agricultural lands and maintenance of the present river channel locations. To insure long term protection of these resources, the County encourages the purchase of these lands in fee title or through easements from willing sellers. Permitted uses within the Natural Resources designation include management for fish and wildlife, development of hunting blinds and similar minor facilities, and removal of trees for

firewood, disease control, or public safety purposes. (3) Removal of riparian vegetation outside the three Natural Resource areas is subject to the following policies: (A) The total acreage of the riparian vegetation shall be maintained by: (i) Encouraging the replanting of riparian vegetation from the stream transition line to the river channel; (ii) Planting of riparian vegetation as part of bank protection projects; (iii) Prohibiting conversions of riparian woodlands to other uses which would decrease the total amount of riparian vegetation below the minimum base line amount, or which would clear riparian vegetation within 200 feet of the stream transition line; and (iv) Limiting removal of vegetation, other than conversions, to timber management, selective timber and firewood harvests, and other minor or incidental uses. (ibid.)

The proposed land-use plan would protect the principal riparian systems from conversion to agricultural use. By encouraging replanting of unvegetated riparian areas and permitting conversion of some younger stands of riparian vegetation only if the total acreage of riparian vegetation on the river increased above existing levels, the plan provides incentives for restoring riparian woodlands on underutilized farmlands or flood-damaged river bars. These policies and those which tie riparian corridors to the river's stream transition line, permit adjustment of protected riparian areas with changes in either the river channel or vegetation patterns. The plan maintains traditonal use of mature riparian stands, including firewood cutting, and identifies additional economic uses such as commercial timber management and harvest in other riparian areas.

The proposed plan has not gained the approval of either fish and wildlife agencies or local agricultural interests and their representatives on the County's Planning Commission. The DFG has criticized the plan for permitting such uses as firewood harvests or timber management, which may remove important habitat components or change the composition of tree species in riparian areas. The DFG pointed out the uncertainty of long-term maintenance of restored riparian systems due to damage by high velocity floodflows or erosion, arguing that conversion of existing stands in exchange for restoring damage-prone areas may result in a long-term reduction in riparian acreage.

Agricultural interests, on the other hand, believe that restricting large areas to natural resource use deprives them of reasonable economic returns from their land holdings. They point out that neither the county nor other agencies have identified funding sources for public purchase of the Natural Resource areas. Most farmers realize the difficulty of any riparian restoration

program, and their own limited ability to reclaim riparian areas for agricultural use. Lands suitable for restoration may not even be located on parcels in the same ownership as those proposed for conversion, necessitating a complex process of land acquisition, leaseholdings, etc.

The plan's potential to protect riparian systems is also undermined by the county's limited responsibility under the Coastal Act to control commercial timber harvests. Commercial timber harvests approved by the Department of Forestry (DF) are not subject to regulation by local coastal programs, and large expanses of riparian vegetation may be harvested for woodchips.[7]

Because the Coastal Commission did not anticipate the effect of chip price increases on the value of the Eel River's riparian woodlands, it did not designate the river's riparian systems as special treatment areas (see discussion of Big River below). Present timber harvest rules offer little protection for the area's riparian values.

Important information necessary to the plan's implementation is lacking. Sites suitable for restoration of riparian vegetation, successful restoration techniques, or funding sources for restoration programs have not been identified. Standards for commercial timber management or firewood harvests which can provide both economic uses and habitat protection have not been identified. Timber management techniques from European or eastern hardwood stands may be applicable (e.g., see Stewart 1981). However, local residents, foresters, and biologists are unfamiliar with these techniques, and their likely impact on wood production or habitat protection is not known.

The Eel River lacks the components which led to agreement on riparian protection for Elk Creek. The Eel River's riparian systems hold resources important to local interest groups and for which substitutes are not available. High soil productivity and exposure to flood hazards make protection of riparian areas as part of residential development infeasible. The absence of special treatment area standards for timber harvest plans leaves the area exposed to significant habitat damage during commercial logging. It appears that a plan lacking a substantial

_____

[7] Red alder may be considered a commercial species in timber harvest plans at the option of the professional forester preparing the plan. Black cottonwood and willow are not subject to timber harvest plans. Because of these administrative guidelines and local government's absence of jurisdiction over logging under timber harvest plans, the county can assure protection of only some components of the riparian systems. The degree of protection will be in large part determined by landowners' decisions to file timber harvest plans for red alder stands, or to manage them for other uses consistent with the county's plan.

public funding committment for purchase of riparian woodlands will not ensure protection of the Eel River's habitat values.

Big River, Mendocino County

Big River, with a drainage basin area of approximately 42,500 ha. (105,000 ac.), is located in central Mendocino County and drains into the ocean through an estuary extending up to 13 km. (8 mi.) above the river's entrance to Mendocino Bay. Approximately 1,500 ha. of the drainage basin are located within the coastal zone. Big River is a drowned river valley rather than a broad alluvial flat.

Riparian systems at Big River are characterized by dense, mature second-growth redwood forests with an understory of grand fir (Abies grandis), red alder, California nutmeg (Torreya californica, and tanoak (Lithocarpus densiflorus). Red alder dominates riparian areas on natural levees between the estuary and the redwood forest (fig. 4). Willows, Oregon ash (Fraxinus latifolia), and cascara (Rhamnus purshiana) are common in alder-dominated forests. Adjacent uplands are coniferous forests with Douglas fir (Pseudotsuga menziesii), redwood, and western hemlock (Warrick and Wilcox 1981).

Figure 4.--Riparian vegetation on Big River, Mendocino County.

Seacat, Seymour, and Marcus (Warrick and Wilcox 1981) identified 10 bird species in mature redwood forest and 23 species in harvested redwood forests. Species lists for the Big River area include most wading birds and waterfowl which nest or roost in riparian systems, but lack the diverse raptor populations found at Elk Creek and Eel River.

Timber has been harvested at least once in most of the river's watershed. Warrick and Wilcox (ibid.) reported that red alder-dominated riparian forests have increased along the river channels, in what were previously estuarine systems, due to accretion of sediments generated by upriver timber harvests.

Mendocino County's local coastal plan designates alder-dominated forests as riparian vegetation. Redwood forests, together with upland redwood/Douglas-fir communities are designated for forest use. Policies for their development include:

(1) Development within 100-foot wide riparian corridors adjoining perennial and intermittent streams and riparian vegetation shall be regulated by Policy 2. Riparian corridors shall be measured from the landward edge of riparian vegetation, or, if no vegetation exists, from the top edge of the stream bank; (2) No structure or development, including dredging, filling and grading, which could degrade the riparian area or detract from its value as a natural resource shall be permitted in the riparian corridor except for: measures necessary for flood control; pipelines, utility lines and road crossings; timber harvesting operations, as regulated by the Forest Practices Act; and collection of firewood, if not more than 25 percent of the forest canopy is lost to cutting over a ten year period; (3) The implementation phase of the LCP shall include preparation of performance standards and/or recommendation of mitigation measures applicable to allowable development within riparian corridors. These standards and measures shall minimize potential development impacts such as increased run-off, sedimentation, biochemical degradation, increased stream temperatures and loss of shade caused by development. When development activities require removal or disturbance of riparian vegetation, replanting with appropriate native plants shall be required; (4) Where riparian vegetation exists away from stream corridors, development shall be minimized; (5) In timberland units of commercial size, permitted uses shall be limited to timber production and related harvesting and processing activities; seasonal recreational uses not requiring permanent structures; management of land for watershed maintenance, grazing and forage, and fish and wildlife habitat; construction and maintenance of gas, electric, water or communication transmission facilities; and residential uses as described in Policy 6; (6) Parcels entirely occupied by timberlands of commercial size shall have not more than one housing unit per 160 acres or 4 units per parcel. (Blayney-Dyett 1980)

Riparian systems of Big River are located entirely on unroaded floodplains with high water tables, and residential development on them is improbable. In this regard, they are much like riparian areas at Elk Creek. Unlike Elk Creek, however, Big River's riparian systems are extraordinarily productive commercial timberlands which provide a significant portion of the coastal Mendocino County sawlog resources. They are owned by a major timber company whose Fort Bragg sawmills provide a substantial percentage of employment in the area.

All riparian forests and some of the adjacent uplands at Big River were designated as forestry special treatment areas. Commercial timber production is the most likely use of this riparian vegetation, and the California Board of Forestry's timber practice rules for Coastal Commission special treatment areas will be central to protecting habitat values of this vegetation. In addition to the practices prescribed for all timber harvests in the Coast Forest District, the rules generally require: (1) protection of live trees with visible evidence of current nesting by endangered species, raptors, waterfowl, or wading birds. Forest practice rules outside of special treatment areas only require protection of endangered species nesting sites, and encourage protecting trees used as nesting sites by eagles and osprey; (2) stream protection zones 46 m. (150 ft.) wide on each side of perennial streams and 30 m. (100 ft.) on each side of intermittent streams. Within these stream protection zones, 50 to 70% of the total tree canopy and 50% of all other vegetation must be left standing. Forest practice rules outside of Coastal Commission special treatment areas require stream protection zones 30 m. (100 ft.) wide on perennial streams and 15 m. (50 ft.) on intermittent streams, within which 50% of the stream-shading canopy must be left standing; (3) a 4 ha. (10 ac.) maximum limitation on clear-cut size. Clear-cuts outside of special treatment areas are limited to a maximum 32 ha. (80 ac.) size.

These timber practice rules can mitigate harvest impacts on many components of Big River and other coastal riparian forests. Rules which protect nesting sites or tree canopies and other vegetation adjacent to the river and its tributaries can maintain feeding, nesting, and roosting sites for riparian wildlife. Limiting clear-cut size can reduce the effects of timber removal outside the stream protection zones, providing a variety of habitat-types as large timberland areas are rotated through successive cycles of harvest and forest growth. However, the rules cannot ensure protection of old-growth vegetation or long-term maintenance of such unique habitat components as snags, which are essential to some riparian wildlife. Nor can they protect riparian systems from the adverse impacts of timber harvests beyond the boundaries of the special treatment area.

Protecting riparian systems at Big River by acquisition is unlikely. In 1979, the USDI Fish and Wildlife Service (FWS) proposed acquiring up to 610 ha. (1,500 ac.) of the Big River watershed including both red alder and redwood riparian

areas (USDI Fish and Wildlife Service 1979). Acquisition was not supported by the Coastal Commission which, in its comments on the proposal, cited Coastal Act policies preventing conversion of commercial timberlands to other uses. The acquisition proposal was opposed by the landowner and Mendocino County, both of which feared adverse effects on sawlog supplies for the company's Fort Bragg mill. The proposal was eventually withdrawn by the FWS due to this local opposition and, perhaps, the rapid escalation of redwood timberland prices following the Redwood National Park expansion.

CONCLUSION

These examples demonstrate the potentials and limitations of regulatory land-use controls in protecting riparian systems. Even an agency with the broad regulatory authority of the Coastal Commission is limited in its ability to protect riparian areas. The limitations are due in part to conflicting objectives—a problem which besets most resource management agencies. The Coastal Commission's limited jurisdiction over timber harvests has presented both opportunities and constraints to the Commission's ability to protect northcoast riparian forests. The Commission has been relatively successful in protecting riparian corridors along small coastal streams and larger patches of riparian vegetation. In the northcoast region, however, its ultimate ability to maintain large riparian systems is in doubt, partly due to limited public understanding of these values and partly to the reluctance of local government to restrict large areas to wildlife habitat use. This reluctance is attributable both to goals of increased economic development and concerns about constitutional protection of property rights. Protecting large, coastal riparian systems through land-use regulation may be successful where these limitations can be overcome. In some areas, effective protection can be achieved only through public purchase. However, even when acquisition funding is available, other social goals may make protection of large riparian systems infeasible.

What do these lessons from the coastal zone suggest for others interested in protecting riparian systems? First, protection must begin with improved information about habitat processes in riparian areas. That information must be effectively transferred to the public. Current developments in wetland protection, for example, are the result of decades of research and public education through sportsmen, conservationists and public information programs. Similar efforts for riparian ecosystems are only beginning.

Second, land-use regulation can successfully protect small riparian areas, but can rarely do more than mitigate impacts in large systems. With effective land-use policies and adequate agency jurisdiction, large riparian areas can be protected from conversion. Forest practice rules can be effective in mitigating the impacts of timber harvest on many components of riparian systems. Extending forest practice rules to cover harvesting of riparian hardwoods and incorporating features of the harvest standards for Coastal Commission special treatment areas into the management of all riparian woodlands would reduce damage to habitat values. In addition, amendment of the forest practice rules to take into consideration critical riparian habitat features by providing, for example, adequate long-term snag recruitment and maintenance of dead and down wood, would help protect wildlife populations dependent on these special habitat components.

Third, a long-term acquisition program for critical riparian systems will be necessary to protect areas where regulation is infeasible or inadequate. Any acquisition program should be based on a statewide or regional assessment of long-term habitat protection objectives, rather than a response to immediate "brushfires". The FWS concept plan for waterfowl wintering habitat preservation is a good example of a long-term program for habitat protection.

Finally, you can't win them all. Some important riparian systems will not be protected despite strong land-use planning and well-planned acquisitions. Wildlife agencies should begin planning to restore degraded riparian areas, to compensate for these unavoidable losses. Potential restoration sites should be identified and restoration activities begun. Within the north-coast region, degraded riparian areas suitable for habitat restoration are located on many existing public lands. Such a restoration program may prove more effective in compensating for unavoidable damage to riparian ecosystems than recommendations for extensive mitigation as part of development projects and could take advantage of funding from a variety of sources, including in-lieu fees collected from projects which degrade riparian areas.

ACKNOWLEDGMENTS

The authors wish to thank Herbert Pierce, Thomas Stone, and Gary Monroe, California Department of Fish and Game; Bruce Fodge, California Coastal Commission; and Donald Tuttle and Patricia Dunn, Humboldt County Public Works and Planning departments, for their interest and assistance in the development of the data, concepts, and land-use policies discussed in this report.

LITERATURE CITED

Blayney-Dyett. 1980. Coastal element, Mendocino County general plan. 191 p. California Coastal Commission, San Francisco, Calif.

Del Norte County Planning Department. 1980. Local coastal program land use plan. 384 p. Del North County Planning Department. Crescent City, Calif.

Forman, R.T.T., A.E. Galli, and C.F. Leck. 1976. Forest size and avian diversity in New Jersey woodlots with some land use implications. Oecologia 26:1-8.

Galli, A.E., C.F. Leck, and R.T.T. Forman. 1976. Avian distribution patterns in forest islands of different sizes in central New Jersey. Auk 93:356-364.

Gates, J.E., and L.W. Gysel. 1978. Avian nest dispersion and fledging success in field-forest ecotones. Ecology 59:871-883.

Harris, S.W. 1973. Birds and their habitats in the mid-Humboldt region. 22 p. Unpublished report. On file at Humboldt State University, Arcata, Calif.

Humboldt County Planning Department. 1978. Habitats sensitivity technical study. 103 p. Humboldt County Planning Department. Eureka, Calif.

Humboldt County Planning Department. 1979. Agriculture technical study. 23 p. Humboldt County Planning Department. Eureka, Calif.

Humboldt County Planning Department. 1980a. North-coast area plan. 75 p. Humboldt County Planning Department. Eureka, Calif.

Humboldt County Planning Department. 1980b. Eel River area plan. 100 p. Humboldt County Planning Department. Eureka, Calif.

Humboldt County Planning Department. 1981a. South-coast area plan. 74 p. Humboldt County Planning Department. Eureka, Calif.

Humboldt County Planning Department. 1981b. Staff recommendation--Eel River area plan. 16 p. Unpublished report. On file at Humboldt County Planning Department, Eureka, Calif.

Leipzig, P. 1972. Wildlife inventory, mid-Humboldt County area. Unpublished report. 15 p. On file at Humboldt State University, Arcata, Calif.

Mac Arthur, R.H., and E.O. Wilson. 1967. The theory of island biogeography. Princeton monogr. in Pop. Biol. No. 1, Princeton University Press, Princeton, J.J. 203 p.

Marcot, B.G. (ed.). 1979. California wildlife/habitats relationships programs--North Coast/Cascades zone. Vol. 1-5. 1136 p. Six Rivers National Forest, USDA Forest Service, Eureka, Calif.

Monroe, G.W. 1974. Natural resources of the Eel River delta. California Department of Fish and Game, Coastal Wetlands series No. 9, Sacramento, Calif. 108 p.

McLaughlin, J., and F. Harradine. 1965. Soils of western Humboldt County. 84 p. Department of Soils and Plant Nutrition, University of California, Davis.

Pickett, S.T.A., and J.N. Thompson. 1978. Patch dynamics and the design of nature reserves. Biol. Conserv. 13:27-37.

Proctor, C.M., J.C. Garcia, D.V. Gaulin, T. Joyner, G.B. Lewis, L.C. Loehr, and A.M. Massa. 1980. An ecological characterization of the Pacific Northwest coastal region. Vol. 1-5. USDA Fish and Wildlife Service, Biological Services Program. FWS/OBS-79/11 through 79/15. Washington, D.C.

Roberts, W.G., J.G. Howe, and J. Major. 1977. A survey of riparian forest flora and fauna in California. p. 3-20. In: A. Sands (ed.). Riparian forests in California--their ecology and conservation. Institute of Ecology Pub. No. 15. 122 p. University of California, Davis.

Schoener, T.W. 1968. Sizes of feeding territories among birds. Ecology 49:123-141.

Stewart, P. 1981. Coppicing with standards. Coevolution Quarterly 30:56-61.

Strahler, A.N. 1964. Quantitative geomorphology of drainage basins and channel networks. Section 4.2. In: Ven to Chow (ed.). Handbook of applied hydrology. McGraw-Hill, New York, N.Y.

Thomas, J.W. (ed.). 1979. Wildlife habitats in managed forests--the Blue Mountains of Oregon and Washington. USDA Forest Service Agricultural Handbook No. 553, Washington, D.C. 512 p.

Thompson, K.E., A.K. Smith, and J.E. Lauman. 1972. Fish and wildlife resources of the southcoast basin, Oregon, and their water requirements (revised). Oregon State Game Commission, Portland, Oregon.

USDA Forest Service. 1965. Soil-vegetation survey of Mendocino County. Pacific Southwest Forest and Range Experiment Station, USDA Forest Service, Berkeley, Calif.

USDI Fish and Wildlife Service. 1979. An environmental assessment of the Big River estuary, Mendocino County, California. 52 p. USDI Fish and Wildlife Service. Sacramento, Calif.

Warrick, S.F., and E.D. Wilcox (ed.). 1981. Big River--the natural history of an endangered northern California estuary. Environmental Field Program Pub. No. 6. 296 p. University of California, Santa Cruz, Calif.

Wilcox, B.A. 1980. Insular ecology and conservation. p. 95-117. In: M.E. Soulé and B.A. Wilcox (ed.). Conservation Biology. 305 p. Sinauer Associates, Sunderland, Mass.

PRESERVING RIPARIAN VEGETATION

ALONG CALIFORNIA'S SOUTH CENTRAL COAST[1]

Mark H. Capelli and Stephen J. Stanley[2]

Abstract—California's south central coast contains over 400 km. (250 mi.) of riparian vegetation within the Coastal Zone, concentrated principally in narrow corridors bordering short coastal streams. A great deal of this vegetation has been disturbed or destroyed by urban, agricultural, and related flood control activities. The South Central Region Coastal Commission and the State Coastal Commission have utilized their regulatory authority to reduce or avoid further disturbance of selected coastal riparian systems and have provided an example to local jurisdictions to follow in preparing of local coastal programs. The effectiveness of continued protection of riparian vegetation under local coastal programs, however, remains uncertain.

INTRODUCTION

In 1976, the California Legislature passed the California Coastal Act[3] in response to a growing concern over the impacts of development on the natural and cultural resources of the California coast. The legislation was the immediate outgrowth of a voter initiative, Proposition 20,[4] passed in 1972, which set up six regional commissions and one state commission. These commissions had interim authority to regulate development along the coast while a master coastal plan was being readied for submission to the California Legislature. The plan prepared by the original commission (California Coastal Zone Conservation Commission 1975) formed the basis for the Coastal Act of 1976 (the Act).

The Act re-established the regional and state commissions with interim authority over most types of development along the coast while local jurisdictions prepared local coastal programs (LCPs), consisting of a land-use plan and a zoning or implementation element. The LCPs were to be based on the environmental and development standards of Chapter 3 of the Act. The regional commissions were terminated after July 1981, leaving the State Commission with the responsibility of reviewing interim permit applications and LCPs.

The policies of the Act address planning issues ranging from protection and provision of affordable visitor facilities to maintenance of biological productivity of environmentally sensitive habitats. Included in the Act are strong policies regarding the protection and restoration of coastal streams and riparian vegetation. The most important of these include the following:

The biological productivity and the quality of coastal waters, streams, wetlands, estuaries, and lakes appropriate to maintain optimum populations of marine organisms and for the protection of human health shall be maintained and, where feasible, restored through, among other means, minimizing adverse effects of waste water discharges and entrainment, controlling runoff, preventing depletion of groundwater supplies and substantial interference with surface waterflow, encouraging waste water reclamation, maintaining natural vegetation buffer areas that protect riparian habitats, and minimizing alteration of natural streams (emphasis added).[5]

(a) The diking, filling, or dredging of open coastal waters, wetlands, estu-

---

[1] Paper presented at the California Riparian Systems Conference. [University of California, Davis, September 17-19, 1981].

[2] Mark H. Capelli and Stephen J. Stanley are Coastal Analysts, South Central Coast Region, California Coastal Commission, Santa Barbara, Calif.

[3] Public Resources Code (PRC) Section 30000-30900.

[4] Coastal Zone Conservation Act. 4 p. State of California, Sacramento.

[5] PRC 30231.

aries, and lakes shall be permitted in accordance with other applicable provisions of this division, where there is no feasible less environmentally damaging alternative, and where feasible mitigation measures have been provided to minimize adverse environmental effects, and shall be limited to the following:

(4) In open coastal waters, <u>other than wetlands, including streams, estuaries, and lakes,</u> [PRC 30233] (emphasis added).

Channelization, dams, or other substantial alterations of rivers and streams shall incorporate the best mitigation measures feasible, and be limited to (1) necessary water supply projects, (2) flood control projects where no other method for protecting existing structures in the floodplain is feasible and where such protection is necessary for public safety or to protect existing development, or (3) developments where the primary function is the improvement of fish and wildlife habitat [PRC 30236].

(a) Environmentally sensitive habitat areas shall be protected against any significant disruption of habitat values, and only uses dependent on such resources shall be allowed within such areas [PRC 30240].

To further clarify the intent of these policies, the State Commission in February 1981 adopted a set of "Statewide Interpretive Guidelines for Wetlands and Other Wet Environmentally Sensitive Habitat Areas" (California Coastal Commission 1981). These guidelines provide a working definition of riparian vegetation and standards for development adjacent to streams. Generally, a buffer area of at least 30 m. (100 ft.) is recommended for small projects such as a single-family residence; criteria for modifying setbacks from riparian vegetation and other environmentally sensitive areas are also provided. Additionally, before being terminated individual regional commissions adopted regional interpretative guidelines which addressed planning issues, including setbacks from identified environmentally sensitive areas located within their jurisdictions.

This paper provides a survey of the riparian resources within the South Central Region and the experience of the South Central Regional Commission (the Regional Commission) and the State Coastal Commission (the State Commission) in protecting these resources through the regulatory process established by the passage of the Act.

REGIONAL SETTING

The jurisdiction of the Regional Commission encompasses the coastal portions of San Luis Obispo, Santa Barbara, and Ventura counties with a combined coastline of 412 km. (256 mi.) (fig. 1). The Coastal Zone boundary line generally runs 914 m. (1,000 yds.) inland from the mean high-tide line. Notable exceptions to this boundary include portions of northern San Luis Obispo County from the Monterey County line south to Villa Creek, the Morro Bay watershed, the Guadalupe and Nipomo Dunes in southern San Luis Obispo and northern Santa Barbara counties, the Hollister and Bixby ranches also in northern Santa Barbara County, the Carpinteria Valley in southern Santa Barbara County, and portions of the Santa Monica Mountains in southern Ventura County to the Los Angeles County line. In these areas the Coastal Zone extends inland 4.8-8.0 km. (3-5 mi.).

Figure 1.--South Central Coast Regional Commission jurisdiction (counties).

Geology and Hydrology

The topography of the South Central Region is dictated principally by the eastward-trending Transverse Ranges which stretch across Ventura, Santa Barbara, and southern San Luis Obispo counties (Oakeshott 1978). The topography of north San Luis Obispo County is shaped by the north-south trending Santa Lucia Mountains of the South Coast Ranges. Both of these ranges are made up of recently uplifted, highly folded and fractured marine and terrestrial sediments. The inland portions of these ranges extend up to 3,050 m. (10,000 ft.), but average only about 760 m. (2,500 ft.) immediately adjacent to the coast. Alluvial and wave-cut terraces have been formed and exposed by the recent uplift of the ranges, creating the setting for much of the modern human development which has occurred during the last 100 years.

The ranges of the Coast and Transverse Provinces have been dissected by faults, broadly alluviated synclinal valleys, and steep, narrow stream canyons (Norris and Webb 1976). The climate of the South Central Region is classified as Mediterranean, with two distinct seasons--a long dry summer and a short mild winter, with most of the precipitation occurring between December and March. The average annual rainfall varies from 1,016 mm. (40 in.) in the mountainous areas to less than 380 mm. (15 in.) along the coast (Bailey 1966).

Four major coastal river systems drain the South Central Region: the Santa Maria and Santa Ynez rivers in Santa Barbara County; and the Ventura and Santa Clara rivers in Ventura County. There are, however, approximately 100 smaller coastal streams and creeks distributed throughout the three counties. Because of the short rainfall season, most of these rivers, streams, and creeks maintain year-round surface flows only along portions of their length, though groundwater is commonly present near the surface in sufficient quantity to support riparian vegetation. Altogether there are approximately 417 km. (259 mi.) of perennial, intermittent, or interrupted watercourses within the South Central Region. In addition, the coastal terraces at sea level contain numerous lagoons and estuaries which are bordered by stands of riparian vegetation. The largest and most productive are: Morro Bay in San Luis Obispo County; the Santa Maria and Santa Ynez river mouths; Goleta Slough and Carpinteria Slough in Santa Barbara County; and the Santa Clara River mouth and Mugu Lagoon in Ventura County.

Vegetation

The highest elevations of the Coast and Transverse ranges are vegetated with scattered stands of conifers (Latting 1976), including Coulter pine (Pinus coulteri), digger pine (Pinus sabiniana), and big cone spruce (Pseudotsuga macrocarpa). Most of both ranges, however, is covered with a dense mixture of chaparral species such as big pod ceanothus (Ceanothus megacarpus), chamise (Adenostoma fasciculatum), east wood manzanita (Arctostaphylos glandulosa), laurel sumac (Rhus laurina), toyon (Heteromeles arbutifolia), and white sage (Salvia apiana). These shrub-like species sometimes assume a tree-like habit and are associated with numerous herbaceous species, including perennial and introduced annual grasses.

Riparian plant communities are generally restricted to narrow bands adjacent to perennial, intermittent, or interrupted watercourses at the bottom of canyons (Sands 1977). Although these riparian corridors constitute less than 2% of the total vegetative cover, they provide habitat for more than 50% of the indigenous species. At the higher elevations, the riparian community may include an overstory of tree species such as western sycamore (Platanus racemosa), black cottonwood (Populus trichocarpa), California bay (Umbellularia californica), coast live oak (Quercus agrifolia), and white alder (Alnus rhombifolia). In the lower reaches of the watercourses, which are the portions most often encompassed within the Coastal Zone, the dominant riparian species are arroyo willow (Salix lasiolepis), and yellow willow (Salix lasiandra).

These lower reaches are also characterized by a variety of herbs and emergent aquatics, including coyote bush (Baccharis pilularis), wild blackberry (Rubus ursinus), nettle (Urtica holosericea), and sedges (Juncus spp.). Near the mouths of most coastal streams, the riparian species begin to be replaced by more salt-tolerant wetland species such as salt bush (Atriplex patula), salt grass (Distichlis spicata), cattail (Typha latifolia), bulrushes (Scirpus spp.), and pickleweed (Salicornia virginica) (Mason 1969; Munz 1974; Barbour and Major 1977; Hoover 1970; Smith 1976).

THREATS TO RIPARIAN RESOURCES

The South Central Region has the third highest growth rate of the six coastal regions (California Coastal Commission 1980). This rate of development has generated conflicts between the Coastal Commission's legal obligation to protect environmentally sensitive habitats, such as riparian vegetation, and the pressure to convert, encroach upon, or otherwise disturb such areas to accommodate development. Urban developments include such diverse activities as land divisions creating marketable or usable building sites; single-family or multi-family residential development; public and private recreational developments such as day-use and recreational vehicle parks; public utilities such as wastewater treatment plants; and commercial and industrial developments including energy facilities. Agricultural developments include greenhouses; floodplain areas cleared for vegetable and flower row crops; tree crops on steep slopes from which the native vegetation has been removed; and cattle grazing.

These developments can result in the modification of adjacent riparian vegetation and of the watercourses themselves. Aside from the actual encroachment of development into the riparian system, flood control projects designed to protect development adjacent to watercourses have also had a major impact on riparian systems. The most common flood control activities include clearing vegetation from channels; realigning and straightening meandering watercourses; and lining channel banks with concrete, riprap, or gabions. Surface diversions and private wells sunk into aquifers have also adversely affected riparian vegetation. Some of the ways these activities and developments have been handled by the Regional Commission and the State Commission through the interim permit process and review of LCPs in the three counties are discussed below.

REGIONAL AND STATE COMMISSION EXPERIENCE

San Luis Obispo County

Setting and Issues

San Luis Obispo County has a coastline of approximately 160 km. (100 mi.). Within the Coastal Zone, there are 48 named streams with a total length of 262 m. (163 mi.) of riparian vegetation. Some of the most important riparian vegetation is found along San Carpoforo, Arroyo de la Cruz, San Simeon, Santa Rosa, Cayucos, Morro, Little Morro, Chorro, Pismo, Arroyo Grande, and Los Osos creeks (fig. 2). Riparian vegetation is also found along portions of the Morro Bay estuary and the freshwater lakes within the Guadalupe and Nipomo Dunes.

Riparian systems along the north county coast have been affected by livestock grazing activities. Public and private commercial developments to serve visitors in the communities of San Simeon, Cambria, and Cayucos have encroached upon stream corridors near their mouths. Proposed private recreational developments requiring the exploitation of local groundwater supplies also pose a potential threat to riparian vegetation which is undisturbed at present. In the southern half of the county, riparian systems have been affected by a variety of residential, recreational, commercial, and public works developments.

Figure 2.--Lagoon and lower reaches of Arroyo de la Cruz, San Luis Obispo County.

The Regional Commission and the State Commission have had occasion to deal with a number of these issues on a case-by-case basis, through their interim permitting process and through review of LCPs prepared by the county and the cities of Morro Bay, Pismo Beach, and Grover City. Some examples of these and their dispositions are presented below.

Permits

Charles Bagwell.--The applicant, Charles Bagwell, had proposed the creation of four lots of 0.4 ha (1 ac.) each for detached, single-family residential development from a 3.9-ha. (9.6-ac.) parcel situated adjacent to the southern border of the Pismo Lake Ecological Reserve.[8] The reserve, which is owned and managed by the California Department of Fish and Game (DFG), is fed by Meadow Creek and is bordered by thick stands of arroyo willow. The subject parcel consisted primarily of a steep slope, dipping toward the reserve, vegetated with coast live oak and having a strand of riparian vegetation on the north side. The applicant had proposed locating the building sites on the back side of the ridge, away from the reserve, but incorporated most of the oak and riparian woodland into one of the building sites.

The Regional Commission found that the proposed development, which the land division would have facilitated, posed a serious potential threat to the oak and riparian woodlands and the adjacent Pismo Lake Ecological Reserve. Accordingly, the Regional Commission approved the land division with the condition that the applicant offer to Grover City, or if the city refused, the DFG, a 2-ha. (5-ac.) portion of the parcel containing all of the oak and riparian woodland, for the purpose of protecting the woodlands and adjoining reserve in perpetuity. The land was ultimately accepted by the city, with the further requirement that it be managed as an integral part of the Pismo Lake Ecological Reserve and subject to the regulatory provisions governing all state ecological reserves.

Aqueduct Farms, Inc.--In a project related to the above development, the applicant proposed dividing 12.6 ha. (31 ac.) of land on the north side of the Pismo Lake Ecological Reserve into three parcels (4.5 ha. [11 ac.], 5.3 ha. [13 ac.], and 2.0 ha. [5 ac.]) to accommodate general commercial and recreational developments.[9] Portions of the original parcel had been disturbed by filling and grading. The remainder consisted of gently rolling swales and ravines dipping down toward the reserve. These portions of the property were vegetated with a combination of coastal sage scrub species and a variety of herbs and other introduced grasses; the area adjacent to the reserve was dominated by arroyo willow. The Regional Commission allowed the creation of the building sites on the already disturbed areas and a small portion of the site with the shallowest gradient (less than 20%), but required the applicant to offer to the DFG the remaining 6.1 ha. (15 ac.) to be incorporated into the Pismo Lake Ecological Reserve.

---

[8]South Central Coast Regional Commission. 1978. Application and permit 133-08: Charles Bagwell. On file with the South Central Coast District Office, Santa Barbara, Calif.

[9]South Central Coast Regional Commission. 1979. Application and permit 205-15: Aqueduct Farms, Inc. On file with the South Central Coast District Office, Santa Barbara, Calif.

California Department of Parks and Recreation/San Luis Obispo County Flood Control District.--The applicants proposed clearing 2,748 cu. m. (3,600 cu. yd.) of sediment from 396 m. (1,300 ft.) of Los Osos Creek, which discharges into the southern end of the Morro Bay estuary. The purpose of the channel clearing was to increase the floodflow capacity of the channel and protect an adjacent local road from flooding.[10] The project as proposed would have entailed the use of a drag-line bucket from the adjacent frontage road. This technique would require removal of the mature riparian canopy, consisting of arroyo willow, on the west bank and trimming back of willows on the east bank so that the drag-line bucket could be drawn along the channel.

While recognizing the need to alleviate the periodic flooding of the adjacent road, the Regional Commission sought to reduce the impacts of the channel clearing by requiring the applicants to submit an alternative plan which did not require the removal of any mature willows and minimized any necessary trimming. One possible alternative method of clearing out sediment and instream vegetation would utilize a "clamshell" dredge, which can be operated more selectively and only requires minimal trimming of the riparian canopy. Because removal of any vegetation, whether instream or riparian, would result in increased sedimentation of the Morro Bay estuary, the Regional Commission also recommended that future applications for stream modifications of Los Osos Creek be accompanied by an erosion control plan which identified the sources of sediments in Los Osos Creek and provided mitigation measures designed to eliminate excess stream sedimentation.

Local Coastal Plans

Within San Luis Obispo County, LCPs are being prepared by Morro Bay, Pismo Beach, Grover City, and the County for their respective jurisdictions. These plans are in various stages of completion and have undergone review by either the Regional Commission or the State Commission or their staffs. To date, however, only Grover City has received certification of both its land-use plan and implementing zoning ordinances. Nevertheless, a brief review of the proposed plan policies regarding the protection of riparian vegetation indicates the range of interpretation of the policies of the Act developed by local jurisdictions.

Morro Bay.--The principal riparian resources within the jurisdiction of the city of Morro Bay are found along Morro, Little Morro, and Chorro creeks (Morro Bay 1981). In response

to Coastal Commission staff review of the draft LCP Land Use Plan, the city staff proposed policies to provide protection of these resources. Several of these policies are summarized below.

Policy 11.14 establishes buffer strips along all streams. The minimum buffer must be 100 ft. in rural areas and 50 ft. in urban areas. These requirements can be adjusted on a case-by-case basis, taking into consideration conditions in the stream corridor, including: 1) soil types and stability; 2) how surface water filters into the ground; 3) slope of the land on either side of the stream; and 4) location of the 100-year floodplain. Riparian vegetation within the buffer is to be protected, and where vegetation has been previously removed the buffer should allow for its re-establishment.

Policy 11.15 prohibits all structures within stream corridors. There are exceptions to this prohibition, including public trails, flood control projects (only where no other method of protection of existing development is feasible), and improvements of fish and wildlife habitat. All development permitted in the stream corridor must incorporate mitigation measures for any impacts on the stream corridor.

Policy 11.16 prohibits any dredging, filling, or grading within the stream corridor, except as a part of the construction activities specified above. If riparian vegetation must be removed, revegetation is required except where undesirable for flood control purposes.

Pismo Beach.--Pismo Creek (fig. 3) and Meadow Creek (including the Pismo Lake Ecological Reserve) support the most important riparian systems in the city (Pismo Beach 1980). The city proposed a set of policies to protect these resources.

After carefully reviewing these policies, the State Commission found that they did not meet the requirements of the Act and denied certification of the Pismo Beach Land Use Plan. The State Commission staff recommended specific and stringent standards for development adjacent to stream and riparian systems. These recommendations included: 1) designation of all wetland and riparian areas as environmentally sensitive habitat; 2) buffer zones for all environmentally sensitive habitat areas, including specific recommendations of buffer size in various areas, mitigation measures where buffer sizes do not meet minimum criteria, and permitted activities within the buffer zone; 3) impact assessment for any development adjacent to the buffer area; 4) prohibition of land division within the environmentally sensitive areas; and 5) specific activities which may be permitted within the stream, and conditions to and limitations on those activities.

Grover City.--The riparian vegetation along the south bank of Meadow Creek and the Pismo Lake Ecological Reserve constitute the major riparian resources within Grover City

---

[10] South Central Coast Regional Commission. 1981. Application and permit 424-01: California Department of Parks and Recreation and San Luis Obispo County Flood Control District. On file with the South Central Coast District Office, Santa Barbara, Calif.

Figure 3.--Lagoon and lower reaches of Pismo Creek, San Luis Obispo County.

(Grover City 1981). After considering policies proposed by the City to protect these resources, the State Commission certified Grover City's Land Use Plan with several site-specific policies that addressed: 1) erosion control; 2) development near and/or disturbance or removal of shagbark manzanita and coast live oak; and 3) the buffer area for Meadow Creek.

San Luis Obispo County.--San Luis Obispo County has jurisdiction over most of the riparian resources within the county (San Luis Obispo (County 1981). This includes over 258 km. (160 mi.) of streams, primarily situated on rural or undeveloped lands in the northern portion of the county, north of Morro Bay. Consequently, the county's policies have a major influence on the future protection of riparian resources. The county has approved its Land Use Plan and submitted it to the State Commission staff for review. The principal policies proposed by the county provide for streamside buffer zones (size requirements, types and intensities of use, and mitigation measures to protect the stream), permitted types of and required procedures for streambed alteration, and protection of riparian vegetation.

The State Commission had not reviewed the San Luis Obispo County LCP at the time of writing [September 1981]; however, the riparian policies proposed by the county do differ in several important respects from those approved by the State Commission for Santa Barbara County (see discussion below).

Santa Barbara County

Setting and Issues

The Santa Barbara coastline is approximately 182 km. (113 mi.) long and is characterized by moderate to steep coastal ranges. The Mussel Rock and Vandenberg Dune areas, as well as the Carpinteria Valley, are exceptions to this general pattern (Dibblee 1950, 1966). As a result of the proximity of steep mountain ranges, the county's coastal area contains a high percentage of steep gradient streams and creeks. There are 72 streams with a total length of 134 km. (83 mi.) in the county's Coastal Zone. Of these watercourses, 25 are perennial and 47 are intermittent or ephemeral. There is only one stream with a perennial flow in the Coastal Zone east of the unincorporated community of Goleta, the most urbanized portion of the Santa Barbara County Coastal Zone. The balance of the perennial streams are located up-coast in the rural portion of the county.

Coastal streams of particular note in the county, from north to south, include the Santa Maria and Santa Ynez rivers, and San Antonio, Jalama, Tecolote, Toro Canyon, Santa Monica, Franklin, Carpinteria, and Gaviota creeks. In addition, there are several short coastal streams with perennial or intermittent flows on the Hollister and Bixby ranches in northern Santa Barbara County. Important coastal wetlands with bordering riparian vegetation include the mouths of the Santa Maria and Santa Ynez rivers (fig. 4), and Goleta and Carpinteria sloughs (see also fig. 5). There are also a number of vernal pools in the Goleta area whose location and floral composition has been cataloged by the University of California at Santa Barbara.

As in other coastal counties, agricultural and urban developments, including energy facilities, are encroaching upon and destroying riparian systems. Several streams, such as Franklin and Santa Monica creeks in eastern Santa Barbara County, have been lined with concrete, resulting in the elimination of all riparian vegetation. Additionally, removal of native chaparral vegetation in the upper watersheds of Carpinteria and Goleta sloughs has resulted in an increased rate of sedimentation within these wetlands and their tributaries. Some Regional Commission and State Commission experiences dealing with threats to riparian resources in Santa Barbara County are presented below.

Permits

Union Oil of California.--The applicant proposed to drill 125 oil wells from multiple well sites and to install appurtenant facilities, including pipelines, storage tanks, and roads on land encompassing existing agricultural fields and portions of the Guadalupe Dunes and Santa Maria River mouth in San Luis Obispo and Santa Barbara counties.[11] The drilling sites would have affected both riparian vegetation and pocket wetlands adjacent to the Santa Maria River. The Regional Commission determined that the development had the potential for causing a serious oil spill, as well as converting an existing degraded

[11]South Central Coast Regional Commission. 1981. Application and permit 314-09: Union Oil of California. On file with the South Central Coast District Office, Santa Barbara, Calif.

Figure 4.--Lower reaches and upper lagoon of the Santa Maria River, border between San Luis Obispo and Santa Barbara counties.

wetland with associated riparian vegetation to an industrial use.

To avoid or mitigate these impacts, the Regional Commission required the applicant, prior to issuance of the permit, to offer for dedication a habitat protection easement over 32 ha. (80 ac.) of riparian vegetation and freshwater marsh. The agency (public or private) accepting the dedication was required to submit a habitat protection plan acceptable to the Regional Commission. In addition to this dedication, Union Oil was required to:
1) relocate wells outside the Santa Maria River riparian zone;
2) submit plans for the storage facilities, which were required to be set back from the creek to minimize biological impacts, the setback requirements to be determined in consultation with DFG;
3) develop, in consultation with DFG, plans for a proposed creek crossing which minimize biological impacts to the creek and surrounding area;
4) minimize the impact of the development on riparian vegetation by removing as little as possible during construction, submitting and carrying out a revegetation plan to restore the vegetation to its previous native state, and monitoring the area (using a qualified biologist) to assess the progress of the revegetation effort.

A feature of particular note in the Regional Commission's decision was the habitat easement which was designed to run the life of the oil-drilling operations. The limited easement condition was applied because mitigation conditions could only be imposed as long as potential or actual impacts associated with the permitted development were present. Since oil developments are by their nature dependent upon a finite resource and it was expected that the operation would terminate at some future date, the easement itself was designed to be limited to the life of the development. The easement could not, however, be removed until the oil-production operation had ceased, and the owner of the underlying land had petitioned the Regional Commission or its successor and the third party holding the easement for reconveyance of the areas covered by the easement, based upon the following stipulations: 1) all oil and gas facilities permitted under the permit were removed; and 2) all landforms were returned to grades existing at the time of the original issuance of the permit. In the interim, the landowner and applicant would be bound by a legal responsibility endorsed by a third party who had a vested interest in protecting the sensitive habitats.

Figure 5.--Soloman Creek, Santa Barbara County.

Edgewood Estates.--The applicant proposed to divide 65 ha. (161 ac.) into nine lots for the purpose of developing eight detached single-family residences.[12] The original parcel consisted of rolling hills traversed by a small coastal stream. The stream was bordered by 10 ha. (25 ac.) of riparian oak woodland consisting of sycamore, coast live oak, and several introduced exotics.

The Regional Commission determined that future development of the sites could affect the riparian woodland and therefore required that a minimum building setback be established and a deed restriction be recorded for the 10 ha. portion of the parcel containing the riparian woodland. In addition, before the permit was issued the developer was required to submit a map, prepared by a qualified biologist, with boundaries of and location of a buffer around the riparian woodland and monarch butterfly habitat, and to prohibit all development within sensitive areas and the buffer. Once deeds to the lots were recorded, the development restriction was to run with the land and could only be excepted by way of a permit from the Regional Commission or its successor.

_____

[12]South Central Coast Regional Commission 1981. Application and permit 315-12: Edgewood Estates. On file with the South Central coast District Office, Santa Barbara, Calif.

In attempting to protect riparian vegetation in Santa Barbara County, the Regional Commission has employed two legal instruments not normally used to provide habitat protection: easement dedications and deed restrictions. Deed restrictions and easements can be applied to individual properties and be designed to run with the land (i.e, a change in ownership does not cancel any restrictions). If executed properly, these restrictions may provide more lasting protection of environmentally sensitive areas than traditional zoning designations which may be changed in accordance with shifting political conditions.

Habitat easement dedications can provide a particularly effective alternative means of protecting large tracts of lands containing habitat values, when the land is too expensive to be purchased outright. Despite the protection afforded by easement dedications, their effectiveness can be limited as a result of the following drawbacks:

1) execution of effective offer-to-dedicate documents requires a great deal of costly legal staff time;

2) the effectiveness of habitat easements depends in part on the cooperation of the underlying landowner and/or leaseholder, and the enforcement capability of the accepting party or regulatory agency;

3) courts may set aside habitat dedications and deed restrictions if it can be shown that there was a "taking" of land without providing the owner or leaseholder an adequate or reasonable use of the land at the time the legal restrictions were imposed; and

4) implementation of the habitat easement restrictions depends upon a public or private agency accepting the dedication and the responsibility for managing dedicated areas.

Deed restrictions have proven to be an effective means of protecting habitat values on smaller parcels located in more urbanized areas. Deed restrictions to developments within a riparian area offer the advantage over land-use designation, which is subject to change, of long-term protection which runs with the title of the land; their principal limitation is that their enforcement is dependent upon the availability of staff time and the initiative of the regulatory agency enforcing the restrictions.

Despite these shortcomings, the Regional Commission has found that few other methods, short of outright public ownership, protect large or medium-sized environmentally sensitive areas, such as riparian systems, as effectively over the long-term as easement dedications and deed restrictions.

Local Coastal Plans

Within Santa Barbara County, LCPs are being or have been prepared by the cities of Santa Barbara and Carpinteria and by the county for their respective jurisdictions. At the time of this writing, only Carpinteria had had its complete LCP certified. The following presents a summary of the riparian protection policies which have been proposed and/or certified by the Regional Commission and the State Commission.

Santa Barbara.--The principal riparian resources within the jurisdiction of the city of Santa Barbara are found along Arroyo Burro, Mission, and Sycamore creeks (Santa Barbara 1981). The State Commission certified the city's Land Use Plan (excepting the airport segment) with policies which are to supplement the policies of the city's existing General Plan Conservation Element. Several of the policies are summarized below.

Policy 6.8 states that the riparian resources, biological productivity, and water quality of the city's Coastal Zone creeks "shall be maintained, preserved, enhanced, and where feasible, restored." The use of reclaimed waste water to enhance creek flow is suggested. The city is to attempt to fund projects: to purchase the Coastal Zone section of Arroyo Burro Creek, to be retained in its natural state upon acquisition; to restore, enhance, and maintain Coastal Zone sections of the city's creeks; and to restore, enhance, and maintain the Andree Clark Bird Refuge.

Policy 6.9 requires the city to support programs, plans, and policies of governmental agencies to further best management practices in the city's watersheds and urban areas. Policy 6.10 establishes the requirements for setback buffers for native vegetation between the bank top and any proposed development. Policy 6.11 outlines procedures for and limitations on channelizations, dams, and other substantial alterations to watercourses.

In addition to the creeks within the contiguous portion of the city of Santa Barbara, Tecolote and Los Caneros creeks, which discharge into the Goleta Slough, are under the jurisdiction of the city. These creeks and the slough will be treated in a separate airport segment of the city's LCP. There are a number of policies proposed in the draft airport segment which relate to the portion of Goleta Slough and its tributary streams which are within the Coastal Zone. Notable among these policies are:

1) Policy C-2, which requires cooperation between the city and the Goleta Valley Mosquito Abatement District to limit mosquito abatement practices to the minimum, in an effort to protect wildlife, including the endangered Light-footed Clapper Rail and Belding's Savannah Sparrow;

2) Policy C-3, which forbids grazing and all other agricultural practices within the slough; and

3) Policy C-6, which requires the maintenance of tidal action to support optimum populations of marine organisms.

There are also a number of policies and proposed actions relating to future development of the airport and its effect upon the slough and its stream tributaries.

The proposed land-use policies for the airport segment of the city's LCP have not been reviewed by the State Commission at the time of this writing; however, a staff-level review of these policies has identified a number of elements which conflict with the requirements of the Act's protection policies. Specifically, the policies do not limit the removal of riparian vegetation from the tributaries to Goleta Slough; ongoing flood control operations which have resulted in the periodic clearing of channels for the purpose of maintaining floodflow capacities would be allowed to continue. Also, the possible realignment of creek channels to accommodate expansion or modification of the existing airport facilities would be permitted, in conflict with Act requirements.

Carpinteria.--The principal riparian resources within the jurisdiction of Carpinteria are located along Santa Monica, Franklin, and Carpinteria creeks (fig. 6) (Carpinteria 1980). Policies for protecting riparian and stream systems have been certified by the State Commission as part of the city's LCP Land Use Plan. Several of these policies are summarized below.

Figure 6.--Franklin Creek, Santa Barbara County.

Policy 9.15 establishes the standards for and methods of determining the size of streamside buffer strips. Policy 9.16 prohibits structures within the stream corridor and lists exceptions to the prohibition, including structures whose

primary function is improvement of fish and/or wildlife habitat and flood control structures. Policy 9.19 forbids "cultivated agriculture and the installation of septic tanks" within the stream corridor. And Policy 9.20 limits stream channelization or other major alteration to those projects presently approved and/or funded.

With the exception of Carpinteria Creek, the other major creeks within the city's portion of the Coastal Zone have been channelized; the remaining undisturbed portion of Carpinteria Creek within the city's portion of the Coastal Zone is scheduled to be acquired by the California Department of Parks and Recreation.

Santa Barbara County.--As with San Luis Obispo County, Santa Barbara County has jurisdiction over most of the riparian resources within the county's Coastal Zone. The most important resources are found along 105 km. (65 mi.) of streams, primarily situated on rural or undeveloped land in the northern portion of the county, north of the unincorporated community of Goleta. The county's resource protection policies will therefore play a major role in the preservation of its riparian systems within the Coastal Zone. The Land Use Plan of the county's LCP has been certified by the State Commission. The policies affecting riparian systems are summarized below.

Policy 9.37 establishes the standards for minimum buffer strips for streams in rural and urban areas and the conditions whereby those minimum conditions can be altered. The buffer strip will be determined in consultation with DFG and the Regional Water Quality Control Board, to protect biological productivity and water quality of the stream. Riparian vegetation, regardless of its distance from the stream itself, is protected and included in the buffer, and provision for reestablishment of previously removed or disturbed vegetation is required.

Policy 9.42 limits developments within the stream corridor involving dredging, filling, and grading to those necessary for flood control, bridge construction, water supply projects, trail construction, and pipeline laying, when no alternate to the proposed development outside the stream corridor is feasible. Policy 9.44 forbids grazing, cultivated agriculture, pesticide application, and installation of septic tanks within the stream corridor.

Until the passage of AB 385 (Hannigan) in 1981, permitting authority was not transferred from the Regional Commission to the local jurisdiction until the certification of the entire LCP (land use element and implementing ordinances). Consequently, prior to its termination in July 1981, the Regional Commission had an opportunity to apply the county's land-use policies to specific developments. In both cases the Regional Commission utilized site-specific restrictions to implement the general resource protection policies summarized above. The county's Land Use Plan policies, however, do not specifically require the use of such implementing techniques as habitat easements or deed restrictions to secure protection of riparian resources.

Ventura County

Setting and Issues

The coastline of Ventura County is approximately 66 km. (41 mi.) long. Within the Coastal Zone there are eight streams, with 21 km. (13 mi.) of riparian vegetation. The most important stands of riparian vegetation occur along the Ventura and Santa Clara rivers (fig. 7), Calleaguas Creek (fig. 8), and Big and Little Sycamore creeks draining the Santa Monica Mountains.

Riparian vegetation has been eliminated as a result of agricultural expansion on the floodplains of the Ventura and Santa Clara rivers, and urban encroachments, including residential developments, public works facilities, and recreational park developments. Flood control facilities, including levees, realigned channels, and concrete box channels, have also reduced the amount of riparian vegetation along watercourses.

Figure 7.--Lagoon and lower reaches of the Santa Clara River, Ventura County.

As with San Luis Obispo County, the Regional Commission has had occasion to deal with some of the potential threats to riparian vegetation on a case-by-case basis through the permitting process. Some of these permit decisions are briefly discussed below.

Permits

Ventura County Flood Control District.-- The Ventura County Flood Control District proposed widening the lower portion of Calleguas Creek (referred to as the Revlon Slough) which discharges into Mugu Lagoon (fig. 9); the Revlon Slough had been previously channelized between earthen levees.[13] The proposed flood control project included excavating 178,000 cu. m. (233,000 cu. yd.) of sediment along a 1.2-km. (0.75-mi.) reach of the Revlon Slough, erecting a new levee on the east bank, and restructuring and enlarging the levee on the west bank to protect adjoining farm lands, the Point Mugu Naval Air Station, and the existing Highway 1 bridge above Mugu Lagoon.

The project also entailed the removal of a dense stand of riparian vegetation, including salt bush (Atriplex lentiformis), which had been established in the Revlon Slough. Furthermore, the proposed periodic maintenance of the channel by the flood control agency would have prevented the re-establishment and maturation of the riparian vegetation after the initial disturbance from construction. While granting the

Figure 8.--Calleaguas Creek/Revlon Slough, Ventura County.

Figure 9.--Mugu Lagoon, Ventura County.

[13]South Central Coast Regional Commission. 1980. Application and permit 212-26: Ventura County Flood Control District. On file with the South Central Coast District Office, Santa Barbara, Calif.

permit to construct the proposed flood control facilities, the Regional Commission imposed conditions on the project which would alleviate the impacts on riparian vegetation stemming directly from the construction of the facilities and subsequent ongoing maintenance activities.

During construction, the Ventura County Flood Control District was required to maintain a pond, the width of the channel and outside the temporary construction dike, for wildlife feeding. When construction was completed, tidal action was to be returned to the the lower portion of the Revlon Slough. The flood control agency was required to revegetate the outer bank of the western levee using salt bush. The Regional Commission also limited the conditions under which maintenance activities could be undertaken, to reduce the adverse impacts of the maintenance procedures on the vegetation. Maintenance activities were prohibited from 15 July to 15 September to protect the Least Tern feeding in the area. The removal of any riparian vegetation from the channel was forbidden once the initial construction was completed; the use of herbicides to control the growth of vegetation in the channel was also prohibited.

Southern Pacific Railroad.--The Southern Pacific Railroad had previously diverted the flow of the lower Ventura River below the Main Street bridge to allow the repair of a portion of a railroad bridge and abutment which had been damaged by floodflows.[14] The Regional Commission granted an emergency permit for the rediversion of the base flow back into the natural low-flow channel, which was lined with riparian vegetation. The Regional Commission imposed several conditions to minimize disruption of the riparian vegetation and associated aquatic resources. 1) The work performed was to be limited to breaching the temporary gravel dike to the degree necessary to redivert the entire flow of the Ventura River back to its original (pre-project) channel on the west river bank. 2) The work was to be supervised by DFG. There was also a time limitation placed on the work.

Local Coastal Plans

Within Ventura County, LCPs are being prepared by the cities of San Buenaventura, Oxnard, and Port Hueneme and by the county for their respective jurisdictions. At the time of this writing, only the Port Hueneme LCP and the Harbor segment of the San Buenaventura LCP have been certified; the other LCPs are in various stages of completion and review. The approaches to protecting riparian systems taken by two of these jurisdictions are summarized below:

[14] South Central Coast Regional Commission. 1978. Application and permit 168-22: Southern Pacific Railroad Company. On file with the South Central Coast District Office, Santa Barbara, Calif.

San Buenaventura.--The principal riparian resources within San Buenaventura are located along the west bank of the lower Ventura River (fig. 10) (San Buenaventura 1981). The State Commission certified the city's Land Use Plan with the several provisions regarding development adjacent to the Ventura River.

1) Environmentally sensitive areas are identified and located, and the requirements for buffer strips around these areas are established.

2) Uses allowed within the buffer areas are listed. No structures are permitted in these areas. Access to the beach from recreational developments on a specific property is limited, and fences and signs are required to restrict access to the buffer and sensitive areas.

3) A Ventura River floodway is defined, and uses permitted within the floodway, including passive recreation, education, and scientific research, are established.

4) A floodway fringe is established, and conditions under which development will be allowed in this area are listed. Developments may not degrade the environmentally sensitive areas or adversely affect flood control facilities.

Figure 10.--Lagoon and lower reaches of the Ventura River, Ventura County.

5) "In order to protect the anadromous fish run in ... and the biological productivity of the Ventura River lagoons and sensitive habitats, the City shall consider the effects of ... its actions ... in order to assure the maintenance of adequate flows within the river to maintain instream flows as well as stream productivity within the Coastal Zone. Developments shall not adversely impact the water supply, groundwater levels, or water quality of the river within the Coastal Zone."

Oxnard.--The east bank of the Santa Clara River and Magrath Lake contain the most significant riparian resources within Oxnard's portion of the Coastal Zone (Oxnard 1981). The mouth of the Santa Clara River and portions of Magrath

Lake have been incorporated into Magrath Beach State Park. Both of these areas have been designated natural preserves within the State Park System. The general policies summarized below regarding development adjacent to environmentally sensitive areas have been certified by the State Commission as part of Oxnard's LCP Land Use Plan:

1) New development adjacent to sensitive or resource protection areas must be sited and designed to mitigate any adverse impacts to the wetlands. Resource protection areas are protected by a buffer strip 30 m. (100 ft.) wide, although the buffer can be reduced in width if an applicant can demonstrate that a larger buffer is unnecessary.

2) No use may significantly disrupt the habitat values of the sensitive areas.

3) Any proposed development within 30 m. (100 ft.) of a sensitive or resource protection area must be accompanied by an assessment by a qualified biologist of the area's resources, any potential impact from the development, and proposed mitigation measures.

4) Evaluations and recommendations of use adjacent to these areas will be made in cooperation with DFG.

5) Restoration of damaged habitat areas may be a condition of permit approval.

Summary

The Commission permit decisions and LCP policies presented in this paper will serve as the principal guides to local governments along the South Central Coast in their efforts to preserve, and where feasible, restore their diminishing coastal riparian resources. It should be recognized, however, that in many cases other public agencies with regulatory powers, such as DFG, the US Army Corps of Engineers, the Regional Water Quality Control Boards, and the State Water Resources Control Board will also share the responsibility of protecting threatened riparian resources.

CONCLUSIONS

The South Central Coast Region contains significant riparian resources distributed along a large number of short coastal rivers and streams. Disturbance and destruction of riparian systems have been most extensive along the lower reaches of these coastal watercourses where residential, industrial, recreational, and agricultural development (and their related flood control facilities) have been most intensive. This is the result of the equable climate, fertile soils, and recreational opportunities found along the coast.

The strong resource protection policies of the Act have provided a legal basis for regulating development which adversely impacts riparian vegetation. During its five-year tenure under the Act, the South Central Coast Regional Commission has on numerous occasions exercised its authority to modify proposed projects in order to alleviate or eliminate their potential adverse impacts on selected riparian systems. In doing so, a wide variety of techniques have been employed. Some of the most effective have been site relocation, setbacks or buffers, special construction techniques, offers-to-dedicate, and deed restrictions.

A review of the Regional Commission's overall record in dealing with riparian resources indicates, however, that the policies of the Act have not always been applied with equal rigor. As a result, projects have been permitted which have either directly or indirectly damaged or eliminated coastal riparian vegetation. There are many reasons for the uneven application of the resource protection policies of the Act, but perhaps the most important have been the imposition of local political pressures (or the lack of active political support) and the changing composition of the Regional Commission membership over its five-year life.

Despite inconsistencies in the application of the resource protection policies of the Act relating to riparian vegetation, the permit history of the Regional Commission provides an important example and guide to local governments preparing LCPs based upon the policies of Chapter 3 of the Act. LCPs prepared to date reflect this permit history in many land-use policies. However, many LCP policies have built in, either as a matter of necessity or expediency, language which allows a wide latitude for interpretation. The presence of such terms (e.g., "wherever feasible," the non-mandatory "may") can be used to undermine initial declarations of intent.

Perhaps more importantly, the decisions of local jurisdictions will be influenced by the composition of individual boards of supervisors or city councils and local political exigencies. The element of a strong statewide perspective which was brought to the decision-making process by selecting Commissioners from a broad spectrum of local and general public interests will not be replicated at the local level. To a greater degree, the preservation of riparian vegetation will depend upon the effectiveness of local constituencies to influence the local political process. The future of riparian vegetation under this new, or more accurately, re-established regulatory arrangement remains uncertain.

AUTHOR'S UPDATE

Since the initial preparation of this paper (in September 1981), California has undergone a change of administrations which has had, and will continue to have, a profound effect on the state's coastal management program.

The newly elected Governor made the abolition of the Coastal Commission a highly visible plank in his campaign platform. While the direct elimination the the Commission has not been possible because of its initial authorization by the California Legislature, the Governor has exercised other constitutional prerogatives in expressing his fundamental opposition to the Commission and the resource protection policies embodied in the Coastal Act of 1976. Most important have been his control over the Commission's budget and the appointment of Commission members.

The Commission's 1983-84 budget, as approved by the legislature, has been reduced by the Governor from $7.8 million to $6.4 million. This new budget is $3 million less than the previous year's budget, a reduction of 32%. Of the $1.4 million cut from the budget by the Governor, over half (or $782,000) was federal matching Coastal Zone management funds--this money does not represent a savings to the state. The most direct impact of the reduced budget is a reduction in the number of staff positions, from 171 authorized in 1982-83, to 115 for fiscal year 1983-84. Many of these reductions will be made in critical areas such as the Commission's technical and legal services departments, which have in the past enabled the Commission to deal effectively in controversial situations.

The Governor's appointments to the Commission have also had a noticeable effect on the operation of the agency. New members appointed to the Commission have gone on record as opposing the Commission's charge and have actively opposed its basic positions on resource protection. Significantly, the Governor has replaced the highly respected representative of the DFG, who sat as an _ex officio_ member and provided the Commission with technical advice on resource issues, with an individual with no resource management experience.

The changing composition of the Commission has been reflected in its decisions on resource issues, including the protection of riparian vegetation. In a recent action, for example, the Commission approved a major LCP which contained policies allowing the construction of roads in riparian corridors, with a minimum setback from the watercourse of only 25 ft. The decision ran counter to the Commission's previously established standard which required a minimum setback from the landward extent of any riparian vegetation of 100 ft., with only passive uses allowed within the buffer area.

Aside from the formal control exercised over the Commission's operations, the Governor has exercised his ability to substantially affect the climate in which the Commission and its staff operate. This includes applying pressure on individual Commission members, encouraging political and legal challenges to the Commission's decisions, directly intervening at the staff level in the professional review process, and endorsing legislation which would undermine the basic policies of the Act.

Some of the effects of these activities have already become apparent. For example, senior staff members have begun to leave the agency in significant numbers, thus depriving the agency of vital expertise and experience. Junior staff members have quickly learned that tough positions on resource issues may not receive support from supervisors or may be modified by the agency's managers for political reasons, without regard to technical or policy considerations.

While the basic policies of the Act remain in force as of this writing [August 1983], the enormously complex and time-consuming bureaucratic apparatus necessary to implement and enforce those policies is being effectively dismantled, if not completely abolished, in order to better conform to the political preferences of the new administration.

LITERATURE CITED

Bailey, H.P. 1966. The climate of southern California. 87 p. University of California Press, Berkeley.

Barbour, M.G. and J. Major (ed.). 1977. Terrestrial vegetation of California. 1,002 p. John Wiley and Sons, New York, N.Y.

California Coastal Zone Conservation Commission. 1975. California coastal plan. 443 p. California Coastal Zone Conservation Commission, San Francisco.

California Coastal Commission. 1980. Biennial report, 1979-80. 32 p. California Coastal Commission, San Francisco.

California Coastal Commission. 1981. Statewide interpretive guideline for wetlands and other wet environmentally sensitive habitat areas. 46 p. California Coastal Commission, San Francisco.

Carpinteria. 1980. Local coastal program, land use plan and zoning ordinances. 97 p. City of Carpinteria, Carpinteria, Calif.

Dibblee, T.W., Jr. 1950. Geology of southwestern Santa Barbara County. Bulletin 150, California Division of Mines and Geology, San Francisco. 87 p.

Grover City. 1981. Local coastal program, land use plan and zoning ordinances. 381 p. City of Grover City, Grover City, Calif.

Hoover, R.F. 1970. The vascular plants of San Luis Obispo County, California. 350 p. University of California Press, Berkeley.

Latting, J. (ed.). 1976. Plant communities of southern California. Special Publication No. 2, California Native Plant Society, Berkeley, Calif. 164 p.

Mason, H.L. 1969. A flora of the marshes of California. 878 p. University of California Press, Berkeley.

Morro Bay. 1981. Local coastal plan, land use plan. 188 p. City of Morro Bay, Morro Bay, Calif.

Munz, P.H. 1974. A flora of southern California. 1,086 p. University of California Press, Berkeley.

Norris, R.M., and R.W. Webb. 1976. Geology of California. 365 p. John Wiley and Sons, New York, N.Y.

Oakeshott, G.B. 1978. California's changing landscapes: A guide to the geology of the state. 379 p. McGraw-Hill Book Company, New York, N.Y.

Oxnard. 1981. Local coastal program, land use plan. 89 p. City of Oxnard, Oxnard, Calif.

Pismo Beach. 1980. Local coastal plan, land use plan. 265 p. City of Pismo Beach, Pismo Beach, Calif.

San Buenaventura. 1981. Local coastal program, land use plan. 228 p. City of San Buenaventura, San Buenaventura, Calif.

San Luis Obispo County. 1981. Local coastal program, land use plan. 384 p. County of San Luis Obispo, San Luis Obispo, Calif.

Sands, Anne (ed.) 1977. Riparian forests in California: their ecology and conservation. Institute of Ecology Pub. No. 15, University of California, Davis. 122 p.

Santa Barbara. 1981. Local coastal program, land use plan: component 9 airport. 63 p. City of Santa Barbara, Santa Barbara, Calif.

Smith, C.F. 1976. A flora of the Santa Barbara region, California. 331 p. Santa Barbara Museum of Natural History, Santa Barbara, Calif.

TEMPORAL DESERT RIPARIAN SYSTEMS--

THE MOJAVE RIVER AS AN EXAMPLE[1]

Louis A. Courtois[2]

Abstract.--During years of high precipitation, temporal riparian zones form on the dry lake playas within the Mojave River drainage and can exist for several years. This is followed by establishment of pioneer aquatic species which eventually give way to halophytes as surface waters recede. Once surface waters evaporate the alkali sink vegetation becomes reestablished.

INTRODUCTION

Riparian systems are usually associated with permanent water such as lotic (rivers, streams or springs) or lentic (lakes, ponds or seeps) habitats. Riparian vegetation may also be found in areas of intermittent flow such as arroyos. In each situation, riparian systems occupy the moist transition (riparian) zones between the wet aquatic and the dry upland zones (Thomas et al. 1979). Water is the major limiting factor upon which riparian vegetation is totally dependent.

A temporal desert riparian system is also dependent upon water and only becomes established during years of high precipitation. Flash floods, which result from high precipitation, carry water through the drainage until it ultimately reaches dry lake playas (e.g., flat floored bottom of an undrained basin) where it becomes impounded. Inundation of these alkali playas kills the existing plants and provides the necessary water source for establishment of a temporal riparian system. The word temporal best defines this system because, as the surface waters evaporate, the riparian zone slowly advances down into the basin, continually establishing itself along the dry shoreline. Immediately above the riparian zone the drier upland zone allows the alkali sink plant community to become reestablished.

The extent of a temporal desert riparian system is dependent upon the amount of seasonal runoff reaching the old lake basin. The temporal system, like a vernal pool, is filled by seasonal runoff. The vernal pool, however, is a much

shorter-lived system, lasting several weeks to a few months. The temporal desert riparian system may last much longer, several months to a few years. The physical characteristics of the soil in these systems are also similar--both are common to older soils which have either a dense claypan or hardpan some depth below the surface. This permits an aquatic habitat to become established, since water cannot seep away into the lower soil column (Holland and Griggs 1976). Vernal pools in California form only during the spring, but temporal riparian systems can form during the winter, spring, or as a result of summer storms.

The Mojave River drainage has both lotic and lentic riparian zones, as well as temporal riparian systems. To better understand these temporal riparian systems we must first understand the drainage characteristics which allow them to form and perpetuate.

HISTORIC DRAINAGE

During the Pleistocene a major portion of the Mojave River drainage consisted of three large lakes, Little Lake Mojave, Lake Mojave, and Lake Manix, which eventually drained into the Colorado River (fig. 1). Buwalda (1914) was one of the first to study Lake Manix and based its pre-existence upon lacustrine deposits, fossils, and ancient shorelines. The outflow from Lake Manix eventually carved out Afton Canyon, which flowed into Little Lake Mojave and Lake Mojave. Little Lake Mojave, the smallest of the three lakes, was intermittent and relatively short-lived. This lake included what today is known as East and West Cronese lakes (fig. 2). Lake Mojave was extensive, covering the present day playas of Soda and Silver lakes (fig. 2). Thompson (1921, 1929) studied the wave-cut cliffs, terraces, beach ridges, sand bars, and lacustrine deposits of Lake Mojave. He also found an "unmistakable outlet channel" which

[1]Paper presented at the California Riparian Systems Conference. [University of California, Davis, September 17-19, 1981].
[2]Louis A. Courtois is Associate Fishery Biologist for California Department of Fish and Game, Rancho Cordova, California.

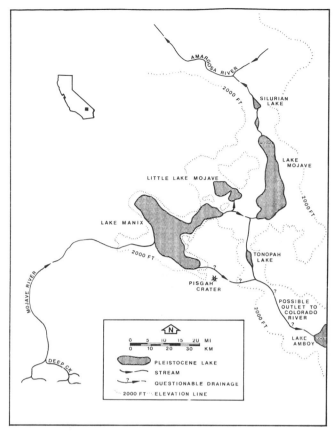

Figure 1.--Historic lakes present within the Mojave River drainage.

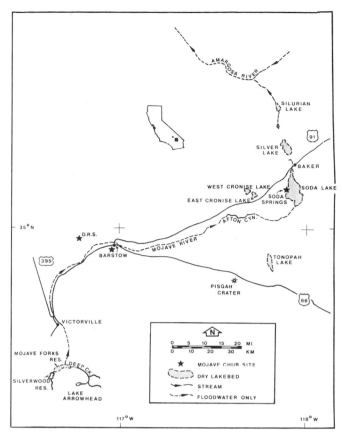

Figure 2.--Present features of the Mojave River drainage.

suggested the Mojave River at one time flowed northward meeting the Amargosa River.

As the climate became more arid, the lakes receded, and a more riverine habitat became established (Hubbs and Miller 1943). Today the Mojave River is an intermittent system of surface and subsurface flows draining into several inland basins. The basin which is the subject of this paper is East Cronese Lake, San Bernardino County, California (fig. 3). Periodic visits were made to this site during 1980-81 to determine what fish species occupied the impounded water. The basin flooded in 1978 following approximately 10 years of desiccation. The narrative which follows describes existing physical characteristics of the drainage and the gradual change in the structure of the plant community following inundation.

PRESENT DRAINAGE

The Mojave River drainage is fed by two headwater streams which originate in the San Bernardino Mountains (fig. 2): the west fork of the Mojave River, which drains 182.1 km^2 (70.3 mi^2); and Deep Creek, which drains 352 km^2 (136 mi^2). Flows from the two tributaries combine at an area known as "the forks"

Figure 3.--East Cronese Lake basin filled with water (April 1981).

approximately 9.6 km. (6 mi.) southeast of Hesperia (fig. 2). From there the river flows underground to Victorville where a granite shelf forces it to the surface. Flows at Victorville and in Afton Canyon are nearly permanent and, at a minimum, supply standing pools of water during low-flow years. Afton Canyon (fig. 4) has a permanent riparian community modified only by periodic floods which scour and rearrange the

689

Figure 4.--Afton Canyon has a permanent riparian biotic community.

streamcourse. During periods of high runoff, water flows from Afton Canyon into East and West Cronese lakes and also into Soda and Silver lakes which are the termini for the drainage. When flooded, the surface area of East Cronese Lake is estimated at 517 ha. (analysis of dry lake contours on Cave Mountain, California, 1:62,500 USDI Geological Survey topographic map). Historic records indicate that both Silver Lake and the Cronese Lake basin have previously flooded (1916) to depths of over 3 m. (10 ft.) (Blanc and Cleveland 1961).

Annual rainfall in the Mojave River drainage varies from 876.1 mm. (34.5 in.) at Deep Creek to 145 mm. (5.7 in.) at Victorville and less than 101 mm. (4 in.) for Cronese Valley (California Department of Water Resources 1964). Flow records which go back to 1930 recorded runoff at Victorville varying between 16,600 acre-feet (AF) (1975) and 290,000 AF (1969) per year (USDI Geological Survey 1930-1979). Runoff at Barstow was 0.3 AF and 146,000 AF per year for those years.

Analysis of surfacewater flow records (ibid.) reveals some interesting factors about the lower Mojave River drainage. During wet years the bulk of the runoff passes through the system over a period of a few days to several weeks (table 1). Victorville and Afton Canyon both had base surface flows recorded every year, but Barstow had no appreciable flow during most years. The system appears to fit an all-or-none flow pattern for Barstow--when seasonal runoff exceeds 150,000 AF at Victorville, the surface flow is continuous from Victorville past Barstow through Afton Canyon and into the Cronese Lake basin. The Cronese Lake basin has flooded at least five times in the past 65 years: 1916, 1922, 1938, 1969, and 1978 (California Department of Water Resources 1964; USDI Geological Survey

Table 1.--Total flow, monthly flow, percent of total flow, and time to reach 50% of total flow (days) at locations within lower Mojave River drainage during high-flow years (from USDI Geological Survey 1930-1979).

Month & Year	Location	Total flow (cfs)	Monthly flow (cfs)	% total flow	Time to reach 50% total flow (days)
Mar. 1978[1]	Afton	23,566	12,854	54.5	18
	Barstow	25,439	15,524	61.0	20
	Victorville	105,427	46,460	44.0	23
Feb. 1969[1]	Afton	36,668	19,752	53.8	4
	Barstow	73,910	36,040	48.8	6
	Victorville	146,758	56,045	38.1	36
Mar. 1943[2]	Barstow	45,865	18,617	40.6	25
	Victorville	64,177	20,147	31.4	47
Mar. 1941[2]	Barstow	48,401	22,880	47.3	25
	Victorville	72,263	25,982	35.9	10
Mar. 1938[1,2]	Barstow	69,622	60,807	87.3	11
	Victorville	94,802	69,103	72.8	13
Mar. 1937[2]	Barstow	52,372	23,870	45.6	36
	Victorville	75,749	26,645	35.1	53

[1]Cronese basin flooded.

[2]No records for Afton Canyon.

1979). Besides these periodic floods, the only other surface flow to the Cronese basin is runoff from the surrounding mountains.

Elapsed time for peak flows to move from Victorville to Barstow range between seven (1969) and 23 hours. Corresponding times from Barstow to Afton Canyon range between six (1969) and 24 hours. Elapsed times appear to depend upon the amount of runoff moving through the system at that particular time.

FLORAL ASSOCIATIONS

Establishment of a distinct riparian plant community following the filling of the lake playa is a progressive process. The gentle slope of the lake basin provides a shallow littoral zone which, when warmed by the sun, allows the planktonic community to bloom. Green filamentous algae are common to this zone. As the impounded waters slowly evaporate, the water surface recedes, leaving filamentous algal mats along the shoreline. East Cronese Lake had a large amount of filamentous algae hanging from the mesquite (Prosopis sp.) trees. These trees had been originally covered by water in 1978. The algal mats were approximately 1.8 m. (6 ft.) above ground level when observed in early 1981 (fig. 5). These mats appeared to form a continuous ring around the lakebed. Where there were no trees, algae was deposited on the playa, possibly providing a nutrient source for the subsequent plant community. The remains of smaller desert shrubs (creosote bush, sage, and desert holly) were evident on the damp soils near the lake surface. Small mounds of alkali sand covered by leaf litter at the base of these plant skeletons were all that remained (fig. 6).

Figure 6.--Skeleton of desert shrub on the lake playa.

Zones of riparian growth were evident around the basin, each in a concentric pattern equidistant from the evaporating water surface (fig. 7). Later that summer (1981) many plant seedlings had grown sufficiently to produce a lush meadow-like area in the desert (fig. 8). Salt cedar (Tamarix sp.), heliotrope (Heliotropium curassavicum) (fig. 9) and sea-purslane (Sesuvium verrucosum) (fig. 10) were the dominant species. These plants commonly grow in alkali sinks but are apparently limited by water availability, especially the heliotrope.

Once the surface water is gone, the vegetation slowly reverts to the pre-flood alkali sink community (Brown 1968).

Figure 5.--Dry algal mats hanging in dead mesquite on the lake playa.

Figure 7.--Concentric growth zones within the lake basin appear as surface waters recede.

Figure 8.--The lake playa resembles a lush meadow
   following establishment of a temporal
   riparian system.

Figure 9.--Heliotrope (Heliotropium curassavicum).

Faunal Associations

There was much evidence of wildlife use of
this area--wild horses and cattle were observed
grazing on surface vegetation. Bird life, including Brown Pelican (Pelecanus occidentalis),
Western Bluebird (Sialia mexicana), Dark-eyed
Junco (Junco hyemalis), Common Crow (Corvus
brachyrhynchos) and Robin (Turdus migratorius), utilized the trees, shoreline, and lake
for feeding and nesting. There were also signs
of coyote (Canis latrans) in the area. The
only amphibians noted were the Pacific tree frog
(Hyla regilla) and the bullfrog (Rana
catesbeiana). They were observed either living
in the cracks of the drying lake surface or desiccated on the dry lake playa. Black bullhead

Figure 10.--Sea-purslane (Sesuvium verrucosum).

(Ictalurus melas), fathead minnow (Pimephales promelas), green sunfish (Lepomis
cyanellus), mosquitofish (Gambusia affinis), and arroyo chub (Gila orcutti),
washed into the basin from upstream sources, were
collected from surface waters.

The temporal desert riparian system provides
an area where impounded fish species rapidly
grow, reproduce, and eventually die once surface
waters evaporate. The author observed numerous
skulls and skeletons of Ictalurus melas and
Lepomis cyanellus along the shoreline. Historical records (Thompson 1929) indicate this to
be a common cycle--windrows of fish "mummies"
being found around the playa once the lake surface totally desiccates. Their loss provides
additional nutrient input to the soils.

THE FUTURE

The temporal desert riparian system has some
interesting physical and biological features
which have been briefly examined in this paper.
More study of this type of system is needed to
provide a clearer understanding of the interrelationships among the various components. The ultimate fate of this system depends upon an awareness of its unique properties and how they
influence the desert community.

Future management of the drainage will most
certainly include increased demands for water.
Already three flow-regulating dams have been con-

692

structed within the drainage: Lake Arrowhead Dam in 1923; Mojave Forks Dam in 1970; and Cedar Springs Dam in early 1972. Each of these structures was build to provide for increased water-related activities such as recreation, flood control, groundwater recharge, and irrigation. Construction of a diversion structure in Afton Canyon by the railroad during the mid-1900s has also modified historic flow patterns. This structure diverts most of the high-water flow into the Cronese Lake basin except during extremes in run-off when water reaches the Soda Lake basin.

Should agricultural development occur in areas downstream from Afton Canyon, the existing ecological balance of the temporal system would be upset. Certainly any permanent agricultural runoff into the Cronese Lake system would provide conditions for establishment of a permanent riparian community. Currently the spread of the exotic salt cedar into the basin has been limited. A more permanent water source, whether surface flow or unbound subsurface water, could provide conditions for the expansion of salt cedar as well as other plants common to permanent riparian communities. One consequence of such vegetation expansion would be the loss of the temporal system. The impact of this loss cannot be fully understood at the present time because of limited biological information. More intensive field surveys and biological studies of this system need to be completed before further modifications occur.

LITERATURE CITED

Blanc, R.P., and G.B. Cleveland. 1961. Pleistocene lakes of southeastern California. California Division of Mines, Mineral Information Service. Vol. 14(4): 1-8.

Brown, G.W., Jr. (ed.). 1968. Desert biology: Special topics on the physical and biological aspects of arid regions. Volume 1. 635 p. Academic Press, New York, N.Y.

Bulwalda, J.P. 1914. Pleistocene beds at Manix in the eastern Mojave Desert region. University of California, Department of Geology Bull. 7: 443-464.

California Department of Water Resources. 1964. Ground water occurence and quality, Lahontan Region. Bull. 106-1.

Holland, R.F., and F.T. Griggs. 1976. A unique habitat--California's vernal pools. Fremontia 4(3): 3-6.

Hubbs, C.L., and R.R. Miller. 1943. Mass hybridization between two genera of cyprinid fishes in the Mohave Desert, California. Pap. Mich. Acad. Sci., Arts and Letters 28(1942): 343-378.

Thomas, J.W., C. Maser and J.E. Rodiek. 1979. Wildlife habitats in managed rangelands--the great basin of southeastern Oregon. Riparian zones. USDA Forest Service CTR-PNW-80, Portland, Ore. 18 p.

Thompson, D.G. 1921. Pleistocene lakes along Mohave River, California. J. Wash. Acad. Sci. 11(17): 423-424.

Thompson, D.G. 1929. The Mohave Desert region California: a geographic, geologic, and hydrologic reconnaissance. USDI Geological Survey Wat. Sup. Pap. 578.

USDI Geological Survey. 1930-1979. Water resources data for California. Water years 1930-1978. Vol. 1: the Great Basin.

COMPOSITION AND ABUNDANCE OF BIRD POPULATIONS

IN RIPARIAN SYSTEMS OF THE CALIFORNIA DESERTS[1]

A. Sidney England, Larry D. Foreman,
and William F. Laudenslayer, Jr.[2]

Abstract.--Avian population diversity, density, and species richness in desert riparian systems were analyzed using
73 breeding bird surveys, 62 winter bird-population studies,
and biweekly surveys at 15 sites. Breeding bird surveys
indicated that cottonwood/willow vegetation-types had the
highest number of breeding and visiting species and the highest bird diversity among desert vegetation-types. Willow
had the highest bird density. Winter bird-population
studies showed that cottonwood/willow also had the highest
species richness and diversity during winter, but palm and
palo verde/ironwood had higher bird densities. All population variables were higher in desert riparian systems than
in non-riparian desert vegetation-types during winter and
breeding seasons. Results from desert riparian systems were
compared with 27 breeding bird surveys and 18 winter population studies in cismontane California riparian systems.
Avian density, diversity, and species richness generally
were greater in cismontane riparian systems. A small number
of resident ground granivorous bird species were found to
comprise a large proportion of all individuals using desert
riparian systems especially during summer. Biweekly surveys
showed species richness varied considerably during the year;
the 15 sites surveyed fell into four general patterns.
Ecological factors such as size of riparian zone, presence
of overstory and shrub vegetation, availability of water,
visibility, and geographic location may affect total and
breeding species numbers. Results are discussed with
respect to ecological factors and land management implications.

INTRODUCTION

In 1976, the United States Congress charged
the USDI Bureau of Land Management (BLM) with
responsibility for preparing a comprehensive
management plan for public lands in the deserts
of California. As part of this effort, the
California Desert Plan Program conducted extensive inventories and studies of many resources
and uses found in the planning area. The wildlife staff began the inventory by compiling existing data including museum records, checklists, unpublished field notes and BLM sight records, and
published articles. It was soon realized that
little quantitative information existed on birds
in the California deserts. Most publications
prior to 1970 were primarily annotated species
accounts confined to specific areas (e.g., Clark
Mountain [Miller 1940]; Providence Mountains
[Johnson et al. 1948]; Joshua Tree National
Monument [Miller and Stebbins 1964]) and did not
cover many of the widely distributed vegetation-
types. Data collected by bird watchers were also
restricted to a few sites (e.g., Morongo Valley,
Furnace Creek Ranch) during selected seasons, and
frequently only unusual species were recorded.

A twofold inventory design was used to collect basic descriptive data on the distribution,
abundance, and seasonal variation of birds in
California desert vegetation-types. First, per-

[1]Paper presented at the California Ripar-
ian Systems Conference. [University of Califor-
nia, Davis, September 17-19, 1981].
[2]A. Sidney England is Wildlife Biologist,
Larry D. Foreman is District Wildlife Biologist;
both are with the Bureau of Land Management,
California Desert District, Riverside, Calif.
William F. Laudenslayer, Jr. is Regional Wildlife
Ecologist, USDA Forest Service, Tahoe National
Forest, Nevada City, Calif.

manent study plots were established throughout the deserts and were censused during the breeding and winter seasons using standard spot-mapping techniques. The advantages of this method included compatibility with similar surveys conducted by others, relative repeatability, and accessibility to results by others through publication in "American Birds."

The second approach was a yearlong survey of selected desert riparian sites. This concentrated effort was warranted by the rarity of these sites in the California deserts, general knowledge of the importance of riparian systems to birds and other desert wildlife, and management concern arising from competing land uses. This year-round approach at specific sites allowed investigation of temporal changes in species richness and abundance not practical with spot-mapping techniques. It also permitted comparison of several vegetation-types of various sizes including very small oases which are typical of most desert riparian areas but are seldom addressed in riparian studies.

This paper presents inventory findings relevant to avian use of desert riparian systems. The following specific questions are discussed.

1. How do abundance and species richness vary by season and between desert riparian vegetation-types?

2. How important are desert riparian systems relative to non-riparian desert sites?

3. How do avian use patterns in desert riparian systems compare to those of cismontane California riparian systems?

4. What factors affect species richness in desert riparian systems?

Answers to questions such as these are needed for management of riparian systems in the California deserts.

METHODS

Study Area

For the purposes of this analysis, California deserts include all of the Mojave and Colorado deserts within California and that portion of the Great Basin Desert within California east of the White and Inyo mountains. Riparian systems along the Colorado River and the perimeter of the Salton Sea are excluded.

Breeding and Winter Bird Surveys

Quantitative data on breeding and winter birds were collected using the spot-mapping techniques prescribed by the National Audubon Society for breeding bird censuses (Svensson 1970; Van Velzen 1972a) and winter bird-population studies (Kolb 1965). From 1976 through 1978, BLM employees and contractors conducted 62 winter bird-population studies and 73 breeding bird censuses in a wide variety of desert sites. Findings from these surveys were combined with other published studies using standardized National Audubon Society techniques in California desert and cismontane California riparian systems.

Avian diversity, population density, and species richness values were calculated for each survey. Diversity was computed using the Shannon-Wiener Index (Shannon and Weaver 1949):

$$H' = - \sum_{i=1}^{s} (p_i \ln p_i)$$

For comparisons among desert riparian vegetation-types, between riparian and non-riparian desert vegetation-types, and between desert and cismontane riparian vegetation-types, surveys were grouped into the following 11 vegetation-types based on the visually dominant plant(s) occurring on each study plot.

Vegetation-type	Visually dominant plants
Cottonwood/willow	Desert: Fremont cottonwood (Populus fremontii), willow (Salix spp.) Cismontane: Fremont cottonwood, willow, valley oak (Quercus lobata)
Willow	Willow
Palm	California fan palm (Washingtonia filifera)
Mesquite	Mesquite (Prosopis glandulosa), screwbean (P. pubescens)
Palo verde/ironwood	Palo verde (Cercidium floridum), desert ironwood (Olneya tesota), smoketree (Dalea spinosa)
Catclaw	Catclaw (Acacia greggii), black-banded rabbit brush (Chrysothamnus paniculatus)
Sycamore/live oak	Sycamore (Platanus racemosa), coast live oak (Quercus agrifolia)
Desert woodland	Single-leaved pinyon (Pinus monophylla), limber pine (P. flexilis), Utah juniper (Juniperus osteosperma), turbinella oak (Q. turbinella)
Desert scrub with overstory	Joshua tree (Yucca brevifolia), Mojave yucca (Y. schidigera), desert ironwood, ocotillo (Fouquieria splendens)
Desert scrub	Creosote bush (Larrea tridentata), burrobush (Ambrosia dumosa), shadscale (Atriplex confertifolia)

Average number of breeding and wintering species, average density, and average species diversity were computed for each vegetation-type. Breeding bird density and diversity values used only breeding males. Average number of species visiting census plots during the breeding season also was calculated; these data were not available for all censuses. Overall density, diversity, and species richness were also averaged for all desert vegetation-types, all "perennial" desert riparian systems, all "ephemeral" desert riparian systems, and cismontane riparian systems. For the purposes of this paper, the continuum of riparian system types present in the California deserts has been divided into two types: 1) "perennial"; and 2) "ephemeral". "Perennial" riparian systems typically have water at or near the surface throughout the year (e.g., springs, seeps, streams, etc.). "Ephemeral" riparian systems occur in washes where surface water typically is available for relatively short periods following storms.

Biweekly Surveys

Data on avian temporal and habitat use patterns were collected at 15 locations selected to represent the wide range of perennial riparian vegetation-types and sizes found in the California deserts (table 1). Study sites were established at each location; sites ranged in size from 0.2 ha. to 36.4 ha. One feature common to all sites was year-round presence of surface water. Censuses were conducted by systematically walking through each site recording all birds detected; individuals seen in riparian vegetation were recorded separately from individuals in adjacent non-riparian vegetation. Two plots were visited per day, one during the three-hour period following dawn and one during the three-hour period preceding sunset. Length of visit varied with the size of study site and the number of birds found. Each study site was visited approximately biweekly during the following periods: 6 November 1977 to 28 January 1978; 9 April 1978 to 17 June 1978; and 16 July 1978 to 3 January 1979.

Table 1.--Location and description of 15 "perennial" desert riparian study sites surveyed between November 1977 and January 1979. S--shrub; SO--shrub with tree overstory; SOP--shrub with tree overstory and pond(s). S.B.--San Bernardino County.

Study site	Location	County	Elev. (m.)	Size (ha.)	Vegetation Structure	Vegetation-type[1]	General Landform
Cottonwood Creek	White Mtns.	Mono	1,600	5.1	SO	Cottonwood/willow	montane
Sam Spring	Deep Spgs. Valley	Inyo	1,700	1.8	SO	Willow/locust	valley
Darwin Falls	Argus Mtns.	"	900	5.6	SO	Willow	montane
Chris Wicht Camp	Panamint Mtns.	"	900	2.9	SO	Cottonwood/willow	montane
Limekiln Spring	Panamint Mtns.	"	1,200	3.0	S	Willow	montane
Brewery Spring	Panamint Mtns.	"	1,400	4.6	S	Willow	montane
Kane Spring	Newberry Mtns.	S.B.	975	2.1	S	Mesquite/catclaw	valley
Old Woman Springs	Johnson Valley	"	975	36.4	SOP	Cottonwood/willow[2]	valley
Salt Creek	Salt Spring Hills	"	160	9.8	SO	Mesquite/salt cedar	valley
Horse Thief Springs	Kingston Range	"	1,400	1.0	SO	Cottonwood/willow	montane
Dove Spring	New York Mtns.	"	1,450	0.8	S	Dwarf ash/hackberry	montane
Cottonwood Spring	Granite Mtns.	"	1,300	0.2	SO	Cottonwood/willow	montane
Bonanza Spring	Clipper Mtns.	"	600	1.8	S	Arrowweed/salt cedar	valley
Mopah Spring	Turtle Mtns.	"	670	0.8	S	Palm/mesquite	valley
Iron Mtn. Pump. Stn.	Iron Mtns.	"	290	24.8	SOP	Suburban woodland[2]	valley

[1]Cottonwood (_Populus fremontii_), willow (_Salix_ spp.), locust (_Robinia pseudoacacia_), catclaw (_Acacia greggii_), mesquite (_Prosopis glandulosa_), salt cedar (_Tamarix_ sp.), dwarf ash (_Fraxinus anomala_), hackberry (_Celtis douglasii_), arrowweed (_Pluchea sericea_), palm (_Washingtonia filifera_).
[2]Consists primarily of man-created system with numerous ornamentals.

Biweekly survey results and literature review were used to assign each species at each site to one or more of eight seasonal status designations. Year-round, summer, and winter residents described species found throughout these time periods. Spring and fall migrants passed through the sites relatively quickly. Summer and winter transients included species that moved through the site, but unlike migrants, remained for extended periods on the way to or from breeding areas (e.g., Great Blue Heron), and species that occurred widely in the desert but were irregular in riparian systems (e.g., Red-tailed Hawk, Roadrunner). Vagrants differed from migrants because they were well outside their normal distributions (e.g., Brown Thrasher, Rose-breasted Grosbeak).

Breeding status at a study site was considered "confirmed" if nesting activity was observed or recently fledged young of species not found in the adjacent desert were seen. Breeding was considered "probable" if the species was known from literature or from other study sites to breed in desert riparian systems and was present at the site throughout the breeding season.

Total number of species observed at each site on all visits (species richness) and total number of breeding species (confirmed plus probable) at each site were plotted against study site size. Sites with shrubs only, shrubs with tree overstory, and shrubs with tree overstory and ponds were examined separately to determine the effects of vegetation structure on species richness and number of breeding species.

Temporal species richness patterns were analyzed by plotting number of species observed per visit at each site against time. If more than one visit occurred at a site in a single biweekly sampling period, the average number of species observed was used. Species richness:time curves for each site were inspected visually and combined into groups with similar patterns. Characteristic curves for each group were constructed by averaging the total number of species observed in each sampling period.

Total number of individuals counted on each visit to each site was plotted against time to show temporal abundance patterns. If multiple visits occurred at a site in one sampling period, the average number of individuals counted was used. Abundance curves were inspected visually to determine gross abundance patterns. Common bird names are those found in the "Checklist of North American Birds" (American Ornithologists' Union 1957), as amended by supplements (1973, 1976).

RESULTS

Breeding and Winter Bird Surveys

Distribution of surveys among vegetation-types and results of the analysis are presented in tables 2 (breeding birds) and 3 (winter birds). Ninety-nine breeding bird censuses and 80 winter bird-population studies were compiled for use in this analysis. Of these 179 surveys, 134 were in California desert (45 riparian and 89 nonriparian) and 45 were in cismontane California.

Among desert riparian vegetation-types, cottonwood/willow, willow, and palo verde/ironwood supported the highest numbers and greatest densities of breeding species. Diversity of breeding species also was highest in these vegetation-types. Cottonwood/willow supported approximately two to five times more breeding species than any other. The number of visiting species counted during breeding bird censuses was higher in perennial than in ephemeral desert riparian systems.

Results from winter bird-population studies indicated that cottonwood/willow, palm, and palo verde/ironwood supported more species than other desert riparian vegetation-types. Winter densities were highest in willow, palm, and palo verde/ironwood. With the exception of visiting species during the breeding bird censuses, all values for palo verde/ironwood, an ephemeral desert riparian vegetation-type, fell within the ranges of values for vegetation-types within perennial riparian systems. Comparisons between catclaw and other vegetation-types were complicated by the lack of replicate samples.

Comparing desert riparian and non-riparian systems data from tables 2 and 3 showed that density, diversity, and species richness of wintering birds were higher in desert riparian systems. Breeding bird densities were higher in all desert riparian systems than in non-riparian areas. The number of breeding species in desert woodland was comparable to that in willow and palo verde/ironwood and exceeded that in palm and mesquite. Desert scrub with overstory supported approximately the same number of breeding species as mesquite; palm supported a smaller number. Breeding species richness was higher in all desert riparian systems than in desert scrub. Only desert woodland was comparable to desert riparian vegetation-types in number of visiting species during the breeding season.

Cismontane riparian vegetation-types generally supported greater numbers of species as well as greater densities than desert riparian vegetation-types (table 2 and 3); diversity values were greater in cismontane vegetation-types during both seasons. Breeding bird surveys indicated only desert cottonwood/willow supported breeding species numbers comparable to cismontane riparian vegetation-types. Only in desert cottonwood/willow and willow were breeding densities similar to

697

Table 2.--Avian diversity, population density, and species richness for breeding bird censuses[1] in riparian and non-riparian desert sites and in cismontane riparian sites (mean $\pm$ 1 standard error). Sample size = number of surveys per site; sample size applies only to residents, values for visitors are smaller.

| | | | Resident | | Visitor |
System/ Vegetation-type	Sample size	Number of species	Density (♂♂/40 ha.)	Diversity (H')	Number of species
Desert riparian	24	16.1+2.1	295.2+ 63.4	2.08+0.12	31.1+ 6.1
Perennial	16	16.7+3.0	332.2+ 89.0	2.04+0.17	34.7+ 7.0
Cottonwood/willow	5	30.0+5.3	349.8+143.6	2.66+0.34	36.0+25.3
Willow	5	13.4+2.9	574.2+211.7	2.04+0.20	34.4+ 7.4
Palm	2	5.5+0.5	133.0+ 38.0	1.36+0.03	19.5+ 0.5
Mesquite	4	9.8+1.7	107.5+ 32.3	1.61+0.15	41.3+ 8.6
Ephemeral	8	14.9+1.8	221.0+ 67.0	2.16+0.14	13.3+ 3.7
Palo Verde/ ironwood	7	15.3+2.0	237.3+ 75.1	2.22+0.14	13.3+ 3.7
Catclaw	1	12.0	107.0	1.74	–
Cismontane riparian	27	26.6+1.3	456.5+ 61.4	2.78+0.07	12.9+ 2.0
Cottonwood/willow	17	26.4+1.9	419.1+ 94.5	2.73+0.11	15.4+ 2.5
Sycamore/live oak	10	27.0+1.4	520.0+ 41.7	2.86+0.05	8.2+ 2.4
Other desert					
Woodland	5	13.4+0.8	72.2+ 14.9	2.19+0.10	24.0+ 3.8
Scrub with overstory	20	10.0+0.9	36.6+ 5.3	1.64+0.11	7.8+ 1.4
Scrub	23	3.4+0.4	20.5+ 4.1	0.68+0.13	7.9+ 1.4

[1]Sources: Loery (1967); Van Velzen (1972b, 1973, 1974, 1977, 1978, 1979, 1980, 1981); Gaines (1974, 1977); USDI Bureau of Land Management (1977, 1978, unpublished field data, Riverside, California); Tomoff (1977); Franzreb (1978).

cismontane riparian vegetation-types. However, the numbers of visiting species were greater in nearly all desert riparian vegetation-types than in cismontane riparian vegetation-types. Cismontane cottonwood/willow exceeded all desert riparian vegetation-types in species richness and density in winter; sycamore/live oak was comparable to several desert riparian vegetation-types.

Biweekly Surveys

A grand total of 190 bird species was observed at all sites on all visits combined. The total number seen at each site ranged from 41 at Brewery Spring to 122 at Old Woman Springs (table 4). Considerably more species were seen at the two large, man-created sites (Old Woman Springs and Iron Mountain Pumping Station) than at any other site. More species were recorded at sites supporting shrub vegetation with tree overstory than at sites with shrub vegetation only (fig. 1). The total number of species observed at sites having shrub vegetation with tree overstory increased with plot size (fig. 1); sites with

ponds were included in this regression after excluding species dependent on open water. An analysis using average number of species per visit in place of total number of species produced similar results.

The number of confirmed breeding species ranged from zero at Dove and Cottonwood springs to nine at Old Woman Springs and Darwin Falls (table 4). Total number of breeding species (total breeding species), which included both confirmed and probable, ranged from two at Cottonwood Spring to 17 at Old Woman Springs. Sites having shrub vegetation with tree overstory generally supported more total breeding species than sites with shrub vegetation only (fig. 2). However, Cottonwood Spring, a site with shrub vegetation and tree overstory, had the lowest total breeding species. This may have been because it had the smallest area of all sites, and consisted of only three cottonwood trees with almost no shrub understory. Mopah Spring was classified as a site with shrub vegetation only, but fell within the range of breeding species for sites with tree overstory. The vegetation at this site was predominantly shrubs but included five palm trees and a number of large palo verde.

Table 3.--Avian diversity, population density, and species richness for winter bird-population studies[1] in riparian and non-riparian desert sites and in cismontane riparian sites (mean ± 1 standard error). Sample size = number of surveys per site.

System/ Vegetation-type	Sample size	Resident Number of species	Density (birds/40 ha.)	Diversity (H')
Desert riparian	21	25.3± 2.4	537.9±164.0	2.05±0.11
Perennial	13	23.7± 3.1	438.5±125.9	1.95±0.15
Cottonwood/willow	2	39.0±13.0	239.5± 72.5	2.37±0.33
Willow	5	18.4± 2.6	588.4±278.3	2.01±0.24
Palm	2	34.0± 3.0	794.0±289.0	2.27±0.31
Mesquite	4	17.5± 1.9	172.8± 42.7	1.51±0.25
Ephemeral	8	27.9± 3.9	699.5±389.1	2.22±0.15
Palo verde/ironwood	7	29.6± 4.0	775.1±440.7	2.31±0.14
Catclaw	1	16.0	170.0	1.58
Cismontane riparian	18	40.4± 3.1	779.2±117.4	2.76±0.08
Cottonwood/willow	8	51.4± 4.2	978.5±229.5	3.01±0.12
Sycamore/live oak	10	31.6± 1.9	619.7± 87.8	2.57±0.07
Other desert				
Woodland	5	13.8± 0.4	107.6± 44.8	1.48±0.21
Scrub with overstory	15	13.4± 1.5	69.1± 10.3	1.35±0.19
Scrub	21	9.4± 1.0	81.6± 21.1	1.19±0.12

[1]Source: Ryder (1972, 1973, 1974); Ryder and Ryder (1975, 1976, 1978, 1979); Gaines (1977); Boyd and Cink (1980); Cink and Boyd (1981).

A seasonal status summary for avian species found at each site is shown in table 4. The largest group of species observed during the bi-weekly surveys was migrants. At 10 of 15 sites, more species were present during fall migration. The number of spring migrant species approximately equalled or exceeded fall migrants at the other five. Year-round resident species were uncommon at nearly all sites. Only Old Woman Springs and Iron Mountain Pumping Station, both large and diverse man-created systems, supported a significant proportion of year-round residents relative to the number of summer and winter residents. Summer residents were more common than winter residents at nine of 15 sites and approximately equal at the remaining six sites.

Species richness graphs for each site were classified into one of four general species richness patterns (table 4; fig. 3) based on shape (i.e., relative position and height of peaks). Five sites were classified as pattern A, summer and winter lows with nearly equivalent spring and late summer/fall peaks. Three sites were pattern B, high spring peak and relatively low late summer/fall peak. Cottonwood Creek and Dove Spring were the only examples of pattern C, with a spring high declining steadily to a winter low. The remaining five sites were pattern D, similar to pattern A except that the spring species rich-ness peak was distinctly lower than the late summer/fall peak. Patterns A, B, and D, with late summer/fall peaks, reached highest values between mid-August and late October. These same patterns reached spring peaks from mid-April to early May; pattern C reached the spring peak in late May. All patterns reached winter lows from late December to early January and began to increase in mid-January.

Figure 4 shows the results from three study sites selected to represent the range of avian abundance patterns. Abundance was considerably more erratic than species richness because abundance was affected by time of survey, weather conditions, and encounters with large flocks. Highest abundances were reached in summer and fall at 13 of 15 sites (e.g., Cottonwood Creek and Horse Thief Springs). Nine were highest from mid-July to late August (e.g., Cottonwood Creek); six of these had peak abundances two to six times greater than any other time of year. The curves for the remaining four sites with highest abundances in summer/fall also had peaks from mid-July to late August, but these were exceeded by peaks from early September to mid-October (e.g., Horse Thief Springs). Kane Springs and Darwin Falls had lows in summer and peak abundances in early December.

699

Table 4.--Breeding and seasonal status summary for avian species found at 15 perennial desert riparian sites surveyed between November 1977 and January 1979.

		Number of Species								No. Breeding Species[2]			Species Richness Pattern[3]
		Resident			Transient		Migrant						
Study Site	Overall	Su	W	Yr[1]	Su	W	Sp	F	Vagrant	Total	C	P	
Cottonwood Creek	75	19	6	(1)	10	17	32	30	1	15	8	7	C
Sam Spring	74	15	5	(2)	9	12	21	44	0	11	4	7	A
Darwin Falls	75	13	14	(3)	6	10	31	40	4	10	9	1	A
Chris Wicht Camp	59	9	4	(0)	5	9	23	29	3	6	5	1	A
Limekiln Spring	42	7	4	(0)	5	4	6	22	2	4	2	2	D
Brewery Spring	41	6	6	(0)	7	3	11	19	0	4	2	2	D
Kane Spring	43	8	5	(2)	9	11	22	16	0	3	2	1	B
Old Woman Springs	122	19	22	(10)	11	20	48	75	4	17	9	8	A
Salt Creek	80	10	8	(1)	9	18	31	46	4	7	3	4	A
Horse Thief Springs	82	15	8	(2)	11	9	33	45	2	12	5	7	D
Dove Spring	44	8	4	(1)	9	5	17	15	1	5	0	5	C
Cottonwood Spring	64	7	3	(0)	22	10	21	28	3	2	0	2	D
Bonanza Spring	46	7	5	(3)	6	8	29	20	0	3	2	1	B
Mopah Spring	50	10	3	(2)	7	12	20	18	0	7	4	3	B
Iron Mtn. Pump. Stn.	121	14	14	(7)	14	24	33	80	8	13	4	9	D

[1]Yr = Year-round resident species. These numbers are included in both summer (Su) and winter (W) resident totals.

[2]C = Confirmed; P = Probable.

[3]See figure 3 for graphs describing four (A-D) species richness patterns.

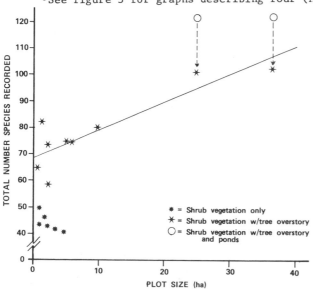

Figure 1.--Total number of species observed (species richness) as a function of plot size and vegetation structure at 15 perennial desert riparian study sites surveyed between November 1977 and January 1979. Data points for sites with ponds adjusted to exclude species dependent on open water before computing the regression equation for plots with overstory trees ($y = 1.05x + 69$).

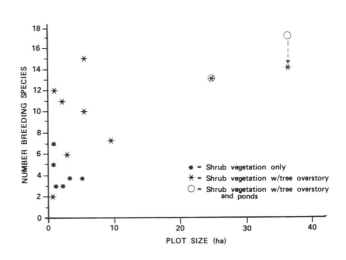

Figure 2.--Total number of breeding species (confirmed and probable) as a function of plot size and vegetation structure at 15 perennial desert riparian study sites surveyed between November 1977 and January 1979 (results from study sites with ponds are shown with and without species dependent on open water).

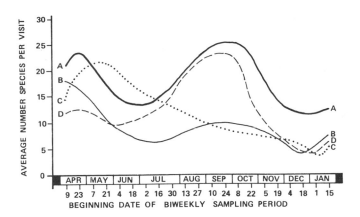

Figure 3.—Avian species richness patterns at 15 perennial desert riparian study sites surveyed between November 1977 and January 1979. Pattern A—nearly equivalent peaks in spring and late summer/fall. Pattern B—high spring peak and relatively low late summer/fall peak. Pattern C—peak in spring declining steadily to winter low. Pattern D—low spring peak and relatively high late summer/fall peak.

Most major abundance peaks were due to large numbers of summer, winter, or year-round resident ground granivores (i.e., California Quail, Gambel's Quail, Mountain Quail, Chukar, Mourning Dove, Horned Lark [at Old Woman Springs only], House Sparrow, House Finch, Black-throated Sparrow, Dark-eyed Junco, Brewer's Sparrow [at Cottonwood Creek only], White-crowned Sparrow, and Golden-crowned Sparrow). These species accounted for 50-90% of the height of summer/fall abundance peaks (fig. 4A and 4B). Most sites showed a small increase in bird numbers during spring migration. Generally this peak was not dominated by resident ground granivores and was more evident when these species were removed (fig. 4). Late fall/early winter populations varied in the proportion of resident ground granivores. The White-crowned Sparrow, a ground granivore, was a common winter resident (fig. 4C). However, two foliage insectivores, the Ruby-crowned Kinglet and the Yellow-rumped Warbler, frequently were more abundant than resident ground granivores (fig. 4A and 4B).

DISCUSSION

Importance of Desert Riparian Systems

The presence of trees or arborescent shrubs in riparian and non-riparian desert systems is an important variable influencing the breeding avifauna. Although quantitative data on vegetation-type structure are not provided, increasing breeding bird diversity, density, and species richness

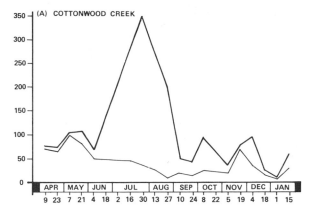

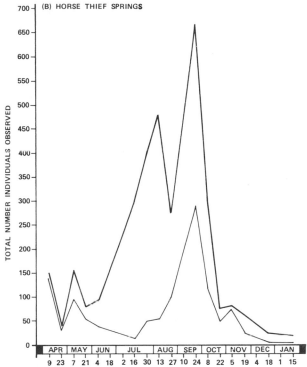

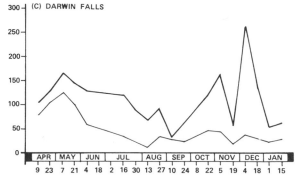

Figure 4.—Avian abundance patterns at three perennial desert riparian study sites surveyed between November 1977 and January 1979. Upper line on each graph includes all species; lower line excludes selected ground granivores (e.g., California Quail, Gambel's Quail, Mountain Quail, Chukar, Mourning Dove, House Sparrow, House Finch, Black-throated Sparrow, Dark-eyed Junco, White-crowned Sparrow, Golden-crowned Sparrow).

are related with increasing amounts of trees and arborescent shrubs. Among desert riparian vegetation-types, cottonwood/willow, willow, and palo verde/ironwood typically have the greatest overstory canopy and thus have a wider availability of perches, nest sites, and foraging substrates. These vegetation-types support more breeding species at higher densities and have higher breeding species diversities than vegetation-types with less overstory (table 2). California fan palms supply a vertical habitat component but do not have the dense canopy provided by trees and arborescent shrubs. To a lesser degree, desert scrub with overstory, dominated by Joshua tree or ocotillo, also has a vertical component, but lacks much of the structural complexity that provides foraging and nesting substrate.

Overstory canopy is also important in non-riparian desert vegetation-types during the breeding season. Overstory vegetation decreases in amount from desert woodland to desert scrub with overstory to desert scrub. The number of breeding species and their density and diversity decline in a similar manner (table 2).

During the winter, birds are less dependent on trees and arborescent shrubs for perching and nesting. At that time, density, diversity, and species richness in riparian and non-riparian systems are not as well correlated with presence or absence of overstory canopy. Among riparian vegetation-types, palm had the highest bird densities in winter; species richness values there were comparable to cottonwood/willow and exceeded all other desert vegetation-types. This observation may be explained by the fact that California fan palms are restricted to the Colorado Desert, which is warmer in the winter than the Mojave and Great Basin deserts. Among non-riparian vegetation-types, desert woodland and desert scrub with overstory supported nearly equal numbers of species; bird densities in desert scrub exceeded desert scrub with overstory.

In addition to the frequent presence of trees or arborescent shrubs, riparian conditions generally result in a total vegetation that is denser than that found in non-riparian desert areas. This denser vegetation contributes to the higher bird densities found in desert riparian systems during breeding and winter seasons by augmenting the food and cover provided by trees and arborescent shrubs.

Surface water is also an important habitat component influencing bird use, especially during the summer months. Smyth and Coulombe (1971) have shown that granivorous birds, including Gambel's Quail, Mourning Dove, White-winged Dove, House Finch, and Black-throated Sparrow, drank regularly at Upper Carrizo Spring in the Santa Rosa Mountains of southern California. Insectivorous and frugivorous birds were seen drinking less regularly or not at all. Our study found that 13 species of summer, winter, or year-round resident ground granivores accounted for a large majority of birds seen at 15 perennial riparian

areas (fig. 4). Nine of these species were present during the summer, but only two (House Sparrow and House Finch) nested almost exclusively in riparian vegetation. The rest of these birds presumably were drawn to the spring largely for water during the hot, dry summer months.

The importance of desert riparian systems to birds is not limited to large sites. Relatively small sites are used by many species over the course of a year (fig. 1); this is especially true for sites with tree overstory. Small sites with tree overstory generally support more breeding species than sites with shrub vegetation only (fig. 2). However, the number of breeding species does not show the correlation with plot size found for total number of species (fig. 1). Cottonwood Spring, the smallest site with overstory vegetation, almost completely lacked shrub cover under its three cottonwoods and supported fewer breeding species than any other site. However, Horse Thief Springs, the next larger site with overstory, had numerous large cottonwoods and patches of tall dense shrubs. It supported among the highest numbers of breeding birds.

Small sites also can support large numbers of individuals. The Cottonwood Creek site is approximately five times larger than Horse Thief Springs (table 1). However, Horse Thief Springs supported numbers of birds comparable to Cottonwood Creek during spring and winter and considerably more in summer and fall (fig. 4). Local factors including surrounding habitat, geographic location, topography, and availability of water in adjacent areas may explain why some sites support more birds than would be expected considering size alone.

The species composition of bird populations in desert riparian systems is extremely dynamic. This is reflected in the species richness patterns illustrated in figure 3. The typical pattern has peaks in spring and fall with lows in summer and winter. Relatively few species are resident in desert riparian systems; most are either transients, migrants, or vagrants (table 4). Breeding species typically are present only during the spring when food and water are most available and temperatures are relatively mild. However, the peak in number of individuals frequently is composed of relatively few species (fig. 4). At nine of 15 sites, sampled biweekly, peak abundance preceded peak species by approximately one month.

Explanations for variations in species richness patterns (fig. 3, table 4) must be tentative since they are based on the data for one year collected at biweekly intervals. Four of five sites with lower species richness in the spring than in the late summer/fall were at high-elevation montane locations. These sites remain colder and less productive later in the spring and may be cooler and more moist, and support food longer than lower elevation and valley sites in the late summer/fall. These reasons could explain the observed pattern. However, two high-elevation montane sites, Cottonwood Creek and Dove Spring, had the highest species richness in the spring and declined throughout the year to winter lows. The reasons for this pattern are less obvious, especially since the number of migrant species recorded at each site was nearly the same in spring and fall (table 4). Iron Mountain Pumping Station, a low-elevation valley site, also showed a low spring peak relative to the fall. However, this site had an extremely high fall peak which may have been due to migrants being attracted to this large, highly visible site for food and water.

Medium to large sites in valleys and low-elevation montane sites had nearly equal species richness peaks in late summer/fall and spring. Small, low-elevation sites situated in valleys had high spring peaks and relatively low fall species richness peaks. Low species richness in the late summer/fall may have been due to lack of resources at very small, hot sites and lower probability that migrating birds could find these oases. Elevation, size, and visibility appear to be variables affecting the number of bird species using desert riparian systems during migration.

In the breeding season, more visiting species are found in desert riparian systems than in cismontane riparian systems (table 2). This pattern probably is due to the isolated nature of desert riparian sites and the relative unsuitability of adjacent desert areas for many birds. Water, cover, and food usually are more available in areas surrounding cismontane sites than those surrounding desert riparian sites. In the desert, many species found in adjacent areas must visit riparian sites. In addition, most studies of birds at desert riparian sites census the entire vegetation at the site. In cismontane locations, the riparian vegetation frequently is more widely distributed; study plots usually include only part of the available vegetation. Therefore, a greater percentage of the species utilizing riparian vegetation may be censused at desert sites than at cismontane sites at any given time.

Management Implications

Riparian systems associated with permanent water are very limited in the desert. However, washes, which are included in the preceding analysis, are more numerous. As we and others have shown, riparian habitats play a vital role in the desert ecosystem by providing water, food, and cover for resident and transient riparian birds, migrating birds, and non-riparian birds, such as quail and doves.

There are, in addition to the intensive use made of these high-value, low-quantity desert riparian systems by wildlife, numerous common high-intensity non-wildlife uses. For example, livestock and feral burros often congregate or linger in riparian habitats to take advantage of shade, forage, and drinking water. Recreationists are attracted to riparian systems in the desert by the shade and high visual quality. Washes are used as vehicular thoroughfares because they lack major obstacles. Mining operations frequently use the water associated with riparian systems in mining or mineral processing. They are also focal points of cultural resources, such as historic and native American sites.

Many of these uses are potentially in conflict with wildlife or maintenance of the riparian community. Riparian systems are generally recognized as vital to desert resident and migrant birds. Understanding the importance of riparian systems is vital to land managers as they attempt to resolve use conflicts. Resolution of these conflicts should take into consideration the breadth of resources which are critical to birds. Among these are the availability of surface water and the presence of a tree overstory and dense groundcover. Proper management should be aimed at maintaining or enhancing all of the individual components making up the riparian zone.

The geographic distribution of riparian systems should also be taken into account when assessing conflicts. Species such as Brown Towhee and Lazuli Bunting breed only in riparian vegetation in the Mojave and Great Basin deserts. Others, including Verdin, Abert's Towhee, and Black-tailed Gnatcatcher, generally are restricted to riparian systems in the Colorado Desert. An adequate distribution of well-managed riparian systems is essential, especially to the maintenance of species with limited distributions in the California deserts.

Results from biweekly surveys indicate that late December and early January is the time of lowest species richness (fig. 3) and bird abundance (fig. 4) at desert riparian sites. Winter bird-population studies conducted primarily in January and February show that midwinter to late winter species richness and abundance is higher. Thus, if it is necessary to create a disturbance such as building a fence or installing a management facility, construction during late December and early January is likely to have less of an impact than at other times. Of course, activities which damage habitat will be harmful to birds regardless of the season.

Human development and artificial habitats can be beneficial to the avifauna. Results of biweekly surveys (table 4) show that the two sites with the highest overall species occurrence (Old Woman Springs and Iron Mountain Pumping Station) are to a large degree man-made systems. Old Woman Springs (122 species recorded) includes a reservoir, residences, gardens, and ornamental trees mixed with native vegetation. Iron Mountain Pumping Station (121 species recorded) is an entirely artificial site with residential areas, parks, and a reservoir. These two sites were also especially high in number of year-round resident, fall migrant, and vagrant species. In addition to their structural diversity, with tall trees, buildings, dense shrubbery, and open water, these sites were exceptionally large (36.4 ha. and 24.8 ha. respectively). Their low elevation (975 m. and 290 m. respectively) made both sites conducive to winter residents and winter transients. Thus, if properly mixed with native vegetation, artificial components can create structural diversity and provide nest and perch sites otherwise not available.

There are a few sites in the desert which are unusually rich in bird species. These frequently become focal points for birdwatchers (e.g., Morongo Valley, Furnace Creek Ranch). Such sites are normally large and diverse and support a substantial tree overstory. However, as knowledge of these sites increases, the importance of smaller, less well-known riparian sites can become obscured. Large sites have special management significance not only for the rarity of some of the birds found in them but also for the high level of public interest in their integrity. However, these sites and their contributions should not overshadow the importance of numerous other riparian sites and the contribution they make to supporting the desert avifauna.

ACKNOWLEDGMENTS

We thank the many biologists who conducted and published breeding bird surveys and winter bird-population studies used in this report. Scott P. Horton developed the biweekly data collection methodology, selected study sites, and conducted initial surveys. Steven W. Cardiff performed biweekly surveys at one site. Kristin H. Berry supervised the wildlife program of the BLM California Desert Plan Staff. The final and several draft manuscripts were typed by Tracy Cortez. Figures were prepared by Clara Stapp.

LITERATURE CITED

American Ornithologists' Union. 1957. Checklist of North American birds. 691 p. American Ornithologists' Union, Baltimore, Md.

American Ornithologists' Union. 1973. Thirty-second supplement to the American Ornithologists' Union checklist of North American birds. Auk 90:411-419.

American Ornithologists' Union. 1976. Thirty-third supplement to the American Ornithologists' Union checklist of North American birds. Auk 93:875-879.

Boyd, R.L., and C.L. Cink (ed.). 1980. Thirty-second winter bird-population study. No. 29, 42. Am. Birds 34:25-41.

Cink, C.L., and R.L. Boyd (ed.). 1981. Thirty-third winter bird-population study. No. 23, 28, 29, 41. Am. Birds 35:21-45.

Franzreb, K.E. 1978. Breeding bird densities, species composition, and bird species diversity of the Algodones Dunes. West. Birds 9:9-20.

Gaines, D. 1974. A new look at the nesting riparian avifauna of the Sacramento Valley, California. West. Birds 5:61-80.

Gaines, D.A. 1977. The valley riparian forests: Their importance to bird populations. p. 57-85. In: A. Sands (ed.). Riparian forests in California: Their ecology and Conservation. Institute of Ecology Pub. 15, University of California, Davis. 122 p.

Johnson, D.H., M.D. Bryant, and A.H. Miller. 1948. Vertebrate animals of the Providence Mountains area of California. Univ. Calif. Publ. Zool. 48:221-376.

Kolb, H. 1965. The Audubon winter bird-population study. Aud. Field Notes 19:432-434.

Loery, G. (ed.). 1967. Thirty-first breeding bird census. No. 35. Am. Birds 21:611-675.

Miller, A. H. 1940. A transition island in the Mohave Desert. Condor 42:161-163.

Miller, A.H., and R.C. Stebbins. 1964. The lives of desert animals in Joshua Tree National Monument. 452 p. University of California Press, Berkeley.

Ryder, R.A. (ed.). 1972. Twenty-fifth winter bird-population study. No. 23. Am. Birds 26:658-688.

Ryder, R.A. (ed.). 1973. Twenty-sixth winter bird-population study. No. 40. Am. Birds 27:666-703.

Ryder, R.A. (ed.). 1974. Twenty-seventh winter bird-population study. No. 45, 46, 48, 49. Am. Birds 28:695-733.

Ryder, R.A., and A. Ryder (ed.). 1975. Twenty-eighth winter bird population study. No. 35. Am. Birds 29:751-788.

Ryder, R.A., and A. Ryder (ed.). 1976. Twenty-ninth winter bird-population study. No. 48-52, 54-57, 67. Am. Birds 30:1040-1075.

Ryder, R.A., and A. Ryder (ed.). 1978. Thirtieth winter bird-population study. No. 48-51. Am. Birds 32:22-48.

Ryder, R.A., and A. Ryder (ed.). 1979. Thirty-first winter bird-population study. No. 23-27, 39-42, 47-55, 58-61, 63-66, 68-94. Am. Birds 33:18-53.

Shannon, C.E. and W. Weaver. 1949. The mathematical theory of communication. 117 p. University of Illinois Press, Urbana, Ill.

Smyth, M. and H.N. Coulombe. 1971. Notes on the use of desert springs by birds in California. Condor 73:240-243.

Svensson, S. 1970. An international standard for a mapping method in bird census work recommended by the International Bird Census Committee. Aud. Field Notes 24:722-726.

Tomoff, C.S. 1977. The spring avifauna of the Colorado Desert of southeastern California. 12 p. plus appendix. USDI Bureau of Land Management, Riverside, Calif.

Van Velzen, W.T. 1972a. Breeding-bird census instructions. Am. Birds 26:1007-1010.

Van Velzen, W.T. (ed.). 1972b. Thirty-sixth breeding bird census. No. 58-60. Am. Birds 26:937-1006.

Van Velzen, W.T. (ed.). 1973. Thirty-seventh breeding bird census. No. 79-82, 100. Am. Birds 27:955-1019.

Van Velzen, W.T. (ed.). 1974. Thirty-eighth breeding bird census. No. 107, 108, 110, 111, 129. Am. Birds 28:987-1054.

Van Velzen, W.T. (ed.). 1977. Fortieth breeding bird census. No. 111, 113, 125, 128, 129. Am. Birds 31:24-93.

Van Velzen, W.T. (ed.). 1978. Forty-first breeding bird census. No. 94-98, 108, 110, 111, 116, 125, 128-130, 134-142, 145-147. Am. Birds 32:49-125.

Van Velzen, W.T. (ed.). 1979. Forty-second breeding bird census. No. 119, 120, 132-136, 139, 140, 142-157. Am. Birds 33:54-114.

Van Velzen, W.T. (ed.). 1980. Forty-third breeding bird census. No. 121, 133, 134, 142-145, 148, 149, 152. Am. Birds 34:41-106.

Van Velzen, W.T. (ed.). 1981. Forty-fourth breeding bird census. No. 161, 174, 175. Am. Birds 35:46-112.

MANAGEMENT ASPECTS OF RELICT POPULATIONS

INHABITING THE AMARGOSA CANYON ECOSYSTEM[1]

Jack E. Williams, Gail C. Kobetich, and Carl T. Benz[2]

Abstract.--Amargosa Canyon is one of three areas within the 264-km. Amargosa River drainage of Nevada and California which contains permanently flowing water. The remainder of the river has desiccated since pluvial times and is now a dry wash. The extensive riparian community and associated habitats of Amargosa Canyon contain a large number of relict populations, including invertebrates (insects and molluscs), fishes (Amargosa pupfish and speckled dace), an amphibian (Amargosa toad), birds (Yellow-billed Cuckoo and Least Bell's Vireo), and mammals (Amargosa pocket gopher and Amargosa vole). Although the USDI Bureau of Land Management has designated Amargosa Canyon a roadless area, the ecosystem is threatened by illegal off-road vehicle use, exotic species, upstream urbanization, and mining of groundwater aquifers. Surveys are needed to determine the status of certain resident invertebrates, amphibians and mammals.

INTRODUCTION

The Great Basin and Mojave Desert are large physiographic congeries comprised of numerous basins and ranges. These geological and biological provinces are products of a complex history spanning hundreds of millions of years. Although much of the pluvial flora and fauna of the area undoubtedly has been lost, where relict ecosystems have persisted some of these species remain. One such relict ecosystem is the Amargosa River drainage, of which Amargosa Canyon is a unique and fragile segment.

Amargosa Canyon lies approximately 65 km. north of the town of Baker, San Bernardino County, California. At the head of the canyon is the small community of Tecopa (fig. 1). At the southern extremity the canyon opens onto a large alluvial plain bordered on the east by Dumont Dunes. The Amargosa Canyon ecosystem includes the Amargosa River from Tecopa Hot Springs to Sperry; springs near Tecopa Hot Springs and Tecopa; and Willow Creek (fig. 2). The canyon varies in width from about 122 m. in the northern portion to approximately 610 m. as it opens up to the south. It is about 20 km. in length. The

[1]Paper presented at the California Riparian Systems Conference. [University of California, Davis, September 17-19, 1981].

[2]Jack E. Williams is Staff Ichthyologist, Gail C. Kobetich is Field Supervisor, and Carl T. Benz is Staff Mammalogist at the Endangered Species Office, USDI Fish and Wildlife Service, Sacramento, California.

Figure 1.--The Amargosa Canyon ecosystem from Tecopa Hot Springs to Sperry, Inyo and San Bernardino Counties, California.

depth of the canyon is variable with a maximum near the nexus of Willow Creek and the Amargosa River, where canyon walls are approximately 293 m. high.

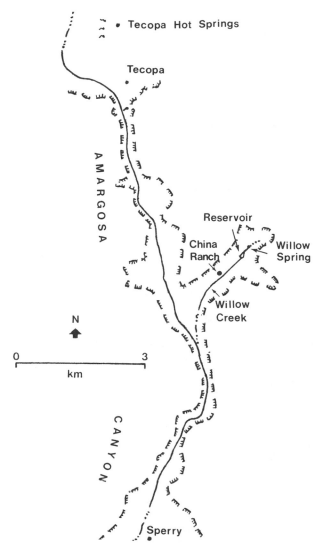

Figure 2.--The Amargosa River drainage, south-western Nevada and southeastern California.

The Amargosa Canyon ecosystem is an "ecological island". Isolated by geographical and climatic factors within the heart of the Mojave Desert, the extant flora and fauna have survived by adapting to the unique environmental conditions of their restricted habitats.

Tecopa Hot Springs is situated on lacustrine deposits of Pleistocene Lake Tecopa (Mason 1948). These spring waters flowing across the alkaline flat support a riparian vegetation characterized by bulrush (Scirpus olneyi) and salt grass (Distichlis spicata).

At the head of the canyon, and throughout it to the old mining site of Sperry, the native floral assemblage is representative of recent pluvial periods. Willow (Salix gooddingii) and mesquite (Prosopis spp.) characterize thickets along the banks of the river. Cattail (Typha latifolia), bulrush, salt grass, rushes (Juncus spp.), and arrowweed (Pluchea sericea) create a moderate to dense vegeta-

tive barrier through which the river flows. The xeric upper slopes parallel to the river support salt bush (Atriplex spp.), buckwheat (Eriogonum spp.), creosote bush (Larrea tridentata), and others. Sawgrass (Cladium mariscus) is found around many of the springs and seeps. Tamarisk (Tamarix spp.) is a major exotic component of the flora at the north end of the canyon and along Willow Creek.

Willow Creek is characterized by the richest botanical complex in the canyon system. Stands of cottonwood (Populus fremontii) and thickets of mesquite, willow, and tamarisk dominate the visual scene, particularly along the creek and around Willow Spring and Willow Creek Reservoir. The spring and reservoir appear to be nearly overgrown with cattail.

Climate

The average annual precipitation during 1973 to 1980 was only 11.5 cm., with peaks occurring during winter and late summer months, as determined from a rain gauge at Shoshone. Extended periods with virtually no precipitation have been recorded during every season of the year.

During the period 1941 to 1970, January temperatures averaged 7.3°C., while July averaged 31.6°C. High summer temperatures, high rates of wind movement, and low humidity all interact to promote high rates of evapotranspiration. A maximum monthly evaporation rate of 502 mm. was recorded at Silver Lake, approximately 40 km. south of Amargosa Canyon (Pupfish Habitat Preservation Committee 1972).

Paleohydrology

The climate of western North America fluctuated widely during later Pleistocene and pluvial times. Pluvial periods were 4-8°C. cooler than at present and appreciably hydric. During these cooler and wetter periods, large lakes and extensive river systems occupied most basins, providing dispersal mechanisms for many aquatic and semi-aquatic organisms (Hubbs and Miller 1948; Mifflin and Wheat 1979; Miller 1946, 1948; Snyder et al. 1964).

The connections and extent of the Amargosa River drainage during later Pleistocene and pluvial times have been extensively studied; however, some differences of opinion still exist. In his studies of the fishes inhabiting southeastern California and southwestern Nevada, Miller (1946, 1948) proposed the name "Death Valley system" for what he believed was a large drainage system including the Amargosa, Mojave, and Owens Rivers, which all drained into Death Valley. Taylor (1980) disputed the existence of a Death Valley system based on his studies of the molluscan fauna. However, it appears clear that the current Amargosa River drainage at one time was occupied by three lakes, Lake Ash Meadows (16 km^2), Lake Tecopa (254 km^2), and Lake Manly (1,601 km^2) (Snyder et al. 1964). At its maximum size, Lake Tecopa extended from north of

707

Shoshone through the Amargosa Canyon area. Lake Manly occupied most of the Death Valley floor, extending south to Saratoga Springs. Paleohydrographic evidence also indicates an occasional connection between the Mojave River and Amargosa River drainages near the vicinity of Silver Lake (ibid.). Wave-cut terraces, gravelbars, and deltas of pluvial origin provide easily visible evidence of the former water systems. The present Amargosa River drainage is but a shadow of its extent during late Pleistocene and pluvial times.

Hydrology

The headwaters of the Amargosa River occur in Oasis Valley north of the old mining town of Beatty, Nye County, Nevada (fig. 2). The Amargosa River drainage is anomalous in that the river flows southward from Oasis Valley, turns westward after flowing through Amargosa Canyon, and finally northward into Death Valley. The final sink of the 264-km. long river is at Bad Water, Death Valley. Much of the river flow is subterranean most of the year, particularly in summer. Three sections of the river wash—Oasis Valley, Amargosa Canyon, and a small (1.2-km.) section just northwest of Saratoga Springs—have perennial flows.

The largest permanent flow occurs through the Amargosa Canyon area (fig. 3). The river surfaces just north of Tecopa and continues through Amargosa Canyon for about 19 km. to the vicinity of Sperry. The entire ecological balance of the canyon, with few exceptions, depends on the natural surface water flows.

The flow entering the canyon emanates from subterranean flows updrainage and springs in and adjacent to the community of Tecopa Hot Springs. The average discharge of the river at Tecopa during 1961 to 1968 was 2.21 cfs (USDI Geological Survey 1968). The Amargosa drainage occasionally experiences torrential floods, as in a 1965 storm that caused a maximum flow of 950 cfs.

In the northern half of the canyon, several minor springs and seeps feed the river. Willow Spring, the headwater of Willow Creek, flows all year. The surface flow of Willow Creek varies seasonally, and is often dry near its confluence with the Amargosa River during summer.

Total dissolved solids (TDS in milligrams per liter) vary considerably within the river because of differing water qualities of inflow springs. During a May 1981 survey, TDS varied from approximately 1,400 at the head of the canyon to 3,850 in the Amargosa River just above the inflow of Willow Creek.[3] The water quality

Figure 3.--Aerial view of Amargosa Canyon looking north. Willow Creek is the tributary canyon to the right.

---

[3]Cindy Williams. California State University, Sacramento. Personal communication.

of Willow Creek is good; TDS is typically 700. The pH of the river water and inflow springs ranges from 8.0 to 8.4. Dissolved oxygen is high, approaching saturation throughout the river.

Geology

The geologic history of Amargosa Canyon is not totally understood. The canyon formed as a result of the Amargosa River cutting through an east-west trending uplift along the major axis of Sperry Hills. A Pleistocene lake, Lake Tecopa, was an ephemeral feature just north of the canyon. The outflow channel of Lake Tecopa is presumably the present-day Amargosa Canyon.

Various geological formations, the result of past geologic processes, are presently visible in Amargosa Canyon. At the north end, lacustrine deposits of Lake Tecopa, with associated vertebrate fossils, are visible (Mason 1948). Further down the canyon, erosional forces have exposed very coarse gravel and cobble (fanglomerates), thought to have been deposited contemporaneously with or after the Lake Tecopa sediments (ibid.). Upstream of the mouth of Willow Creek, rocks of volcanic origin such as tuffs, breccias, and undifferentiated volcanic flows of later tertiary origin have been exposed (Troxel 1961). South of the volcanics lie the China Ranch Beds, a series of light-colored, mainly white to brilliantly pink saline claystones with some interbedded gypsum layers. To the south of Willow Creek the geological sequence is reversed.

Downcutting by the river near the inflow of Willow Creek has exposed Precambrian rock, which is the probable basement for much of the canyon. From Tecopa to approximately 4.5 km. south of the Willow Creek confluence, moderate amounts of water flow at the surface throughout the year. Downstream of this area, water usually flows on the surface throughout the winter and spring months and occasionally during the summer. This suggests that the relatively impervious Precambrian rocks lie very close to the surface throughout the northern reaches of the canyon and are responsible for raising the subterranean water flow.

RELICT POPULATIONS

Aquatic habitats in the desert obviously provide a special environment for plants and animals. Species diversity in such oases is often several times that of the surrounding desert. For example, a weekend bird count during April 1972 yielded 86 species within Amargosa Canyon (Pupfish Habitat Preservation Committee 1972). Since that time the number of bird species utilizing the canyon area has been found to be over 240.[4] The avifauna of the surrounding Mojave Desert is depauperate by comparison.

---

[4]Tarble, Jan. Los Angeles Audubon Society. Personal communication.

In addition to the great number of species utilizing desert riparian systems, the isolated nature of such systems as well as their relative scarcity often result in a biota containing species with greatly restricted ranges. A high degree of endemism often characterizes the fauna of isolated aquatic systems in the desert.

The fauna of the Amargosa Canyon ecosystem is notable in possessing many taxa of rare occurrence. These animals were often present over a much greater range during recent geologic history (e.g., the range of the pupfish has decreased from pluvial times) or their ranges have recently been reduced by habitat alteration (e.g., the range of the Yellow-billed Cuckoo has been reduced by destruction of riparian vegetation). These animal populations, which we refer to as relicts, are well represented in the canyon ecosystem, and include various invertebrates (insects and molluscs), three fishes (speckled dace and pupfishes), one amphibian (Amargosa toad), two birds (Yellow-billed Cuckoo and Least Bell's Vireo), and two mammals (Amargosa pocket gopher and Amargosa vole). Any management activities in the canyon area should consider the welfare of these representatives of the Amargosa Canyon fauna. The following population accounts provide information on identification, distribution within the canyon area, and any special considerations, such as the need for surveys, on the relict populations.

Invertebrates

A large degree of endemism occurs in the invertebrates of the Amargosa River drainage in Nevada and California. Endemism is especially notable in tiger beetles (Cicindelidae), creeping water bugs (Naucoridae), giant water bugs (Belostomatidae), assimineid snails (Assimineidae), hydrobiid snails (Hydrobiidae), and littoridinid snails (Littoridinidae). Members of these invertebrate families are either aquatic or restricted to water-related environments and have therefore been subjected to long periods of isolation from related species in other parts of the Amargosa River drainage and elsewhere. This isolation, and subsequent adaptation to the available habitat-types, has resulted in increased speciation and endemism.

The invertebrate fauna of Amargosa Canyon has not been as thoroughly scrutinized as that of the upper Amargosa River near Beatty, Nevada, or of Saratoga Springs. However, enough information is available to elucidate the distinctive nature of the fauna within the Amargosa Canyon area. The works of Rumpp (1956, 1957) have identified a variety of localized tiger beetles in the Amargosa River including Cicindela denverensis propinqua, C. nevadica nevadica, and C. haemorrhagica haemorrhagica, all from Tecopa and Tecopa Hot Springs. Cicindela willistoni praedicta was described from the Amargosa River bed 5.6 km. south of Shoshone and may occur further downstream (Rumpp 1956). The Cicindela are colorful beetles usually found on damp sand or alkali beds along flowing stretches of rivers, or in nearby grasses. The tiger beetles within the Amargosa River drainage are notable in their extreme reduction in maculation (spots and markings) (Rumpp 1956).

The most localized species of creeping water bugs in the California and Nevada region are _Ambrysus funebris_, recorded only from Cow Creek in Death Valley, and _A. amargosus_, known only from Point-of-rocks Springs in Ash Meadows, Nevada (La Rivers 1953). So far neither of these species has been recorded from Tecopa or Amargosa Canyon. However, a more widespread naucorid waterbug, _A. californicus_, has been found in Willow Creek (Pupfish Habitat Preservation Committee 1972). _Lethocerus angustipes_, a giant water bug otherwise known only from Mexico, has been recorded from Saratoga Springs, just downstream from Amargosa Canyon (Usinger 1956).

The molluscan fauna of the Amargosa River drainage is diverse and includes a high proportion of localized endemics (67%) (Taylor 1980). The known fauna of 35 species within the California portion of the Amargosa River drainage represents approximately one-quarter of the entire freshwater molluscan fauna in California. Taylor (_ibid._) reported two undescribed snails in the Tecopa area, the minute Amargosa spring snail, _Fontilicella_ sp. (Hydrobiiddae), from Shoshone Springs and springs near Tecopa, and the Amargosa tryonia snail, _Tryonia_ sp. (Littoridinidae), in the lower Amargosa River drainage from Ash Meadows to Saratoga Springs.

The primary threats to the Amargosa Canyon area invertebrate fauna include dewatering of the springs, surface alteration of spring and river habitats, and water pollution. Surveys are needed to document the invertebrate fauna and to assist in taxonomic investigations.

Fishes

Speckled dace and two subspecies of Amargosa pupfish are native to the Amargosa Canyon ecosystem. The speckled dace (_Rhinichthys osculus_) occurs in a wide variety of habitats throughout most drainage basins in the western United States. Several isolated populations in the Great Basin and elsewhere have been described as subspecies (Hubbs _et al._ 1974). The population inhabiting Amargosa Canyon has been referred to as the subspecies _nevadensis_, originally described from specimens taken in Ash Meadows, Nevada (Gilbert 1893). However, the speckled dace in Amargosa Canyon are readily distinguishable from the small dace in Ash Meadows and probably deserve a new subspecific designation. The speckled dace also occurs in the upper Amargosa River near Springdale and Beatty, Nevada, but is absent from the Amargosa system below Amargosa Canyon.

Within Amargosa Canyon, the speckled dace occurs in Willow Creek, Willow Creek Reservoir, and sporadically throughout the Amargosa River.

Recent surveys have found it to be rare throughout the canyon, comprising only 1.3% of the fish fauna.[3] The exotic mosquitofish (_Gambusia affinis_ is partly responsible for low numbers of speckled dace.

Two subspecies of Amargosa pupfish (_Cyprinodon nevadensis_) are native to the Amargosa Canyon area. The Tecopa pupfish (_C. n. calidae_) is endemic to springs near Tecopa Hot Springs. The subspecies occurred in crenons, of approximately 32 to 40°C., below thermal springs that can exceed 42°C. at their sources (Miller 1948). Unfortunately, mining of underground aquifers and surface alteration of habitats caused the extirpation of the Tecopa pupfish during the 1970s. The second subspecies, _C. n. amargosae_, is known only from the Amargosa River near Tecopa and Tecopa Hot Springs, the Amargosa Canyon, and from the small perennial stretch of the Amargosa River northwest of Saratoga Springs. No pupfish are known from the Amargosa River near Springdale and Beatty, Nevada. Surveys conducted in 1980 and 1981 found the Amargosa pupfish in abundance--58% of the 11,485 fish sampled--throughout the canyon, but absent in Willow Creek.[3] The Amargosa pupfish occurs in a variety of river habitats within the canyon and often reaches a large size (greater than 60 mm. total length).

The primary threat to the Amargosa pupfish within the canyon area is the establishment of exotic species. The introduced mosquitofish probably competes with the pupfish for food, cover, and other requirements. The bullfrog (_Rana catesbeiana_) often preys on pupfish within the canyon.

Amphibians

The Amargosa toad (_Bufo nelsoni_) is a small toad (maximum total length 72.5 mm.) about one-half the size of the western toad (_Bufo b. boreas_) (Linsdale 1940). Distinctive features of the Amargosa toad include a narrow, wedge-shaped head, especially when viewed from below; smooth skin with weakly developed warts; and small feet with reduced webbing (_ibid._). The preferred habitat of the species is freshwater marshes and areas along rivers in otherwise arid regions. The known distribution of the Amargosa toad includes the upper Amargosa River near Springdale and Beatty, Nevada, as well as the White River area of eastern Nevada. In his original description of _B. nelsoni_, Stejneger (1893) also recorded specimens from Resting Springs, northeast of Tecopa, and from Morans and Lone Pine in Owens Valley, California. Since that time no specimens have been recorded from California; however, we suspect that the species also occurs in the Amargosa Canyon area based on the abundance of available habitat and the proximity of recorded populations. A survey is needed to document the Amphibia of the area.

710

Birds

Localized breeding populations of Yellow-billed Cuckoo and Least Bell's Vireo occur in the Amargosa Canyon area. The historical breeding range of the Yellow-billed Cuckoo (Coccyzus americanus occidentalis) in California extended along the coastal areas from the Mexican border through the San Francisco Bay area, throughout the Sacramento and San Joaquin valleys, along the Colorado River, and in isolated areas of eastern California (Gaines 1974). However, the destruction of riparian vegetation has severely decreased the breeding range of this species. Gaines (ibid.) reported on the extensive tracts of riparian vegetation that appear to be requisite to nesting. These requirements include riparian vegetation at least 300 m. long and 100 m. wide, open water within 100 m., and dense understory vegetation and thickets of willows. Due to the removal of this essential habitat, the primary remaining breeding areas of the Yellow-billed Cuckoo occur along the Sacramento River between Red Bluff and Sacramento, and along the Colorado River (ibid.). The Yellow-billed Cuckoo has also fared well in Amargosa Canyon. Individuals typically arrive in the canyon in June. Breeding pairs have been observed at the north end of the canyon, at China Ranch, 0.8 km. west of Willow Spring, and at the confluence of Willow Creek and the Amargosa River (Gaines 1977; Tarble[4]). The preferred habitat appears to be willows and cottonwoods within extensive areas of riparian vegetation.

The decline of the Least Bell's Vireo (Vireo bellii pusillis) is even more dramatic than that of the Yellow-billed Cuckoo. Until about 1930 the Least Bell's Vireo was common throughout a large portion of California including the Sacramento and San Joaquin valleys, coastal valleys, the entire southwestern part of the state, and the Owens Valley (Grinnel and Miller 1944). In 1944 Grinnell and Miller still considered the bird common although they noticed a considerable decline in numbers throughout southern California and in the Sacramento and San Joaquin valleys (ibid.). This decline continued throughout the known range of the Least Bell's Vireo. Goldwasser et al. (1980) determined that no other passerine in California has declined so dramatically and attributed the decline to a loss of riparian vegetation and to parasitism by Brown-headed Cowbirds (Molothrus ater). Least Bell's Viroes are often seen in the China Ranch area of Amargosa Canyon, especially near Willow Spring.[4] Sightings have also been made near the north end of Amargosa Canyon. The vireos always appear to nest near running water within the canyon area.[4]

Mammals

Two subspecies of mammals are endemic to the Amargosa River area near Shoshone and Tecopa. The Amargosa pocket gopher (Thomomys bottae amargosae) is known only from the Amargosa River near Shoshone and Tecopa. The type specimen was collected from the Amargosa River at Shoshone (Hall 1981). However knowledge of the subspecies near Tecopa is sparse. Annie Alexander's field notes, housed at the Museum of Vertebrate Zoology, University of California, Berkeley, indicated the presence of pocket gophers in sandy washes near Tecopa during a 1936 study. The Amargosa pocket gopher was one of 18 species of mammals recorded from the Amargosa Canyon area during a 1972 survey (Pupfish Habitat Preservation Committee 1972). The occurrence was presumed by the presence of distinctive mounds, rather that by trapping. Jim Patton[5] has trapped Amargosa pocket gophers near Shoshone High School and believes that they occur throughout the Amargosa Canyon area. However, a survey is needed to document the distribution and current status of the Amargosa pocket gopher. This subspecies burrows into moist sand within riparian vegetation which provides suitable cover and forage.

The Amargosa vole (Microtus californicus scirpensis) was described from specimens collected in 1900 from a spring near Shoshone. Habitat destruction was thought to have caused the extinction of this small marsh-dwelling rodent until a small population was discovered during the 1930s (Allen 1942; Bleich 1979). Subsequent surveys during 1978 and 1979 documented the presence of Amargosa voles just southwest of Tecopa Hot Springs and near Tecopa (Bleich 1980). The populations near Tecopa Hot Springs and Tecopa may be substantial; however, they are restricted to very small areas and are therefore susceptible to habitat changes. The primary threats to the vole are continued mining of underground water supplies and destruction of Scirpus marshes. Amargosa voles occur in bulrush marshes on flat (0% slope) to steep (20% slope) areas usually containing open water (ibid.). Marsh habitats within Amargosa Canyon proper need to be investigated to determine the presence of the vole.

MANAGEMENT

Management of any ecosystem should consider its fragility, its uniqueness, and its past, present, and future uses. The Amargosa Canyon ecosystem with its perennial water supply, its fragile soils, and its isolation, as well as its long history of human use, demands special treatment by modern man because of his ability and proclivity to inadvertently or intentionally destroy such natural treasures. Special protective status should be the first management strategy in any efforts to protect the Amargosa Canyon ecosystem.

Past Uses

This ecosystem has been in constant use by man for almost 10,000 years (Rogers 1939). Several types of lithic tools that represent at

---

[5]Jim Patton. University of California, Berkeley. Personal communication.

least four separate cultural groups are evident in Amargosa Canyon and its immediate vicinity. These cultures existed in sequential order from about 10,000 B.C. to the advent of Caucasian man. This is the only area in the Mojave Desert where these four cultures overlapped (ibid.). This, among other things, points out the uniqueness and importance of the Amargosa Canyon area. Even today the archeological work has not been thorough—much remains to be done. Any management scheme should be especially cognizant of the necessity to preserve this significant archeological study area.

The effects of prehistoric cultures on the Amargosa Canyon ecosystem can only be surmised from the scant clues left behind. We presume from their artifacts that the people were hunter/gatherers. We can surmise that they might have engaged in primitive agriculture, though there is no direct evidence for this. The "metates" and "manos" found in the area probably were used to grind seeds gathered from the wild. There are remains of sleeping circles, circle houses, trails, and figures and arrangements in the desert pavement. Regardless of the evidence for use of the Amargosa Canyon by prehistoric man, his influence on the ecosystem was minimal.

This unobtrusive use came to an abrupt end in the early nineteenth century when a route from the Rio Grande Valley in New Mexico (to become known as the Old Spanish Trail) was pioneered by Antonio Armijo. The trail was developed for the purpose of trading woolen goods to the California missions while donkeys and other livestock were driven back to New Mexico. On both legs of the trip, Amargosa Canyon, with its water and forage for livestock, was a welcome stopping place after the rigors of the surrounding desert.

The effects on the ecosystem of a large number of grazing animals is not known, but it must have been considerable. One herd of animals driven along the Old Spanish Trail numbered 4,150. As more people became familiar with Amargosa Canyon and the surrounding area, some mining activities began. No mines of any consequence were ever worked in Amargosa Canyon, though several small mines still exist on some of the drainages into the canyon. The major effect of this mining was indirect, though no less dramatic.

With the advent of the discovery of gold at Tonopah and Goldfield, Nevada, and borax in Death Valley, the economics of developing a transportation system to move materials to and from these mining centers improved sufficiently to allow for the construction of a railroad. Therefore, in 1905 Francis Marion Smith considered the task of constructing a railroad which would run from Tonopah to San Diego and become known as the Tonopah and Tidewater Railroad. Eventually Smith constructed the T & T Railroad from Ludlow, California, to Tonopah, Nevada. At Ludlow the T & T joined the Atchinson, Topeka, and Sante Fe Railroad. The route of the T & T from Ludlow to Tonopah was through Fort Soda, Silver Lake,

Amargosa Canyon, Death Valley Junction, Beatty, and Goldfield. One of the major problem areas during construction of the T & T was Amargosa Canyon. The route through the canyon required much grading and building of several major trestles. The T & T operated profitably for some 25 years, but as the mines and ore bodies failed, so did the economics of running the T & T. In the late 1930s the T & T ceased operation, and near the beginning of World War II the Defense Department confiscated the rails and the T & T ceased to exist.

During its existence however, the railroad probably brought to Amargosa Canyon the most abrupt change that had ever occurred there. The grading of the route through the canyon, the building of the trestles, and the concomitant increase in general use of the area, especially during the construction phase, probably resulted in increased siltation, overgrazing of pasturage, and depletion or localized extirpation of larger animals. It was to be many years before the effects of this enterprise began to be ameliorated, and will be many more years before all vestiges of it will be gone. While there are some who may regret the passing of the T & T, the closing of the railroad and subsequent removal of the rails was undoubtedly one of the best de facto management decisions that could have been made for the good of Amargosa Canyon. That decision, if we can follow through with future wise management, signalled the end of intensive and disruptive use of the canyon.

Present Uses

Other human uses, beyond building and operation of the T & T Railroad, arose in the later nineteenth and early twentieth centuries. China Ranch was established in 1903 along Willow Creek. While the ranch is small and not terribly disruptive of the natural system, it represents a level of use not present before. The establishment of settlements in the vicinity of Tecopa Hot Springs and Shoshone brought downstream disruption from siltation associated with land disturbance and from decreased water flows associated with water use. These communities, according to the U.S. Bureau of Census (1973), accounted for approximately 1,000 people in the Amargosa Canyon area. However, these figures represent only the permanent residents—they do not indicate the significant increase in population during the winter when relatively large numbers of transients arrive to escape harsh northern winters and relax in the hot mineral baths at Tecopa Hot Springs. The effects of these winter visitors are not known, but could be considerable due to their additional demand on the limited water supply.

Human population in the area is likely to increase in the future. A large residential and industrial development is planned for the Ash Meadows area, upstream on the Amargosa River drainage. It is not known what effects this development will have on Amargosa Canyon, but we can surmise that the first effect could be a decrease in subterranean water flows down the Amargosa River drainage, evidenced in decreased surface flows in Amargosa Canyon. For this reason, monitoring water quantity and quality will be of particular importance. Increased use from a larger human population will have to be scruti- nized for its effects on the canyon. Use of privately-owned lands within the canyon will also have to be monitored.

Altogether, there are four inholdings, totalling 623 ha. (1,538 ac.), of privately-owned property in Amargosa Canyon. Two inholdings, a 437-ha. (1,080-ac.) parcel and a 32-ha. (80-ac.) parcel, are owned by mining companies. The other two, the 88-ha. (218-ac.) China Ranch and a 65-ha. (160-ac.) parcel, are owned by local interests. To date the mining companies have not begun to develop their holdings. The owners of China Ranch and the 65-ha. inholding are managing these properties as they have in the past, with minimal disturbance to the natural system. How- ever, if management of private lands should change or if extraction of minerals becomes economically feasible, the delicate riparian systems of the Amargosa Canyon could be dis- rupted. Therefore, as a sensible management tool, these private inholdings should be preser- ved in their present state by cooperative agree- ments, conservation easements, or any other mutually agreeable method.

Other than the 622 ha. of privately-owned land, the canyon is held in public trust by the USDI Bureau of Land Management (BLM). The BLM is therefore the major land manager within the canyon. In 1973, after being petitioned by interested conservationists, the BLM set aside its part of Amargosa Canyon as a roadless natural area. The resultant closure of the canyon to vehicular traffic has allowed the damage incurred from indiscriminate vehicular use to begin to be ameliorated. Access to the north end of the canyon and the canyon at China Ranch is effec- tively barricaded. However, at the more open southern end of the canyon, access is still possible, and off-road vehicle use, with its concomitant damage, is still occurring. However, the management provided by BLM should, with minor modifications, result in preservation of most of the canyon, and BLM is to be commended for its concern.

Future Use

The future for the relatively undisturbed nature of that part of Amargosa Canyon in public ownership appears to be good. The closure of the area to vehicular traffic by BLM must be main- tained. There is always the possibility of dis- ruptive use of resources on private land in the canyon. Continued increases in the population of the area will have an impact if there is exces- sive use of groundwater. Most of the adverse impacts generated by these possible uses can be held at to an acceptable level by proper manage- ment.

Management Recommendations

The management of an area such as Amargosa Canyon would be relatively simple if all land were in public ownership and if all upstream activities that could affect the system were controllable. Barring those desired circum- stances, management recommendations will have to be formulated that will, if implemented, help safeguard the system. With that in mind, the following recommendations are offered for manage- ment of the Amargosa Canyon ecosystem. It is hoped that these recommendations would contribute significantly to the long-term protection of this beautiful desert aquatic/riparian system.

1. Erect an effective barrier to vehicular access at the south end of the canyon. This is a recommendation that needs immediate attention, as recent vehicular use is evident from tire tracks extending several miles northward from where the canyon opens onto the alluvial plain.

2. Secure the safety of the canyon by pre- venting the development and use of resources on the private land which would adversely impact the natural ecosystem. This could be done by cooper- ative agreement, conservation easement, purchase of mineral rights, fee acquisition, or other available mutually agreeable means.

3. Institute a water monitoring program to track on a regular schedule the flows of water in Amargosa Canyon at a point that would give the most meaningful data on water flows. A USDI Geological Survey stream flow monitoring station would be ideal for this purpose.

4. Monitor the quality of the water on a regular basis. Samples should be taken at least every two years. The frequency could be in- creased if samples indicated a significant devia- tion from the expected results or if increased use of the resources is evident.

5. Status surveys are needed to determine the presence and distribution of invertebrates, Amargosa toad, Amargosa pocket gopher, and Amar- gosa vole in the canyon.

6. Population status surveys of the two remaining fishes, the speckled dace and the Amargosa pupfish, should be conducted at two-year intervals to detect any long-term decline. These surveys should be carried out annually if water monitoring programs show significant changes or if other habitat changes, such as introduction of exotic species, occur.

7. A breeding bird survey should be conduc- ted at two-year intervals to detect any change in population levels. Surveys could be carried out annually if there is reason to suspect a dele- terious change.

8. BLM should maintain the status of Amar- gosa Canyon as a "natural area" and should main- tain the closure to vehicular use. The added protection of declaring Amargosa Canyon an "Area

of Critical Environmental Concern" under the Desert Protective Plan is a welcome addition to the protective management decisions made by BLM.

ACKNOWLEDGMENTS

The authors would like to gratefully acknowledge the help and cooperation of the following individuals: Ted Rado, BLM, Barstow; Jan Tarble, Los Angeles Audubon Society; Jim Patton, University of California, Berkeley; Chris Nagano, Los Angeles County Museum of Natural History; Bernie Troxel, University of California, Davis; Judy Maudlin, USDI Fish and Wildlife Service, Sacramento; and Larry Foreman, BLM, Riverside. Phil Pister, California Department of Fish and Game, Bishop, graciously let us use his photograph of Amargosa Canyon. We would especially like to express our appreciation to Cindy Williams, California State University, Sacramento, for typing the manuscript, but most especially for her scientific and editorial comments and her freely contributed data on the aquatic ecosystem of Amargosa Canyon.

LITERATURE CITED

Allen, G.M. 1942. Extinct and vanishing mammals of the Western Hemisphere with the marine species of all the oceans. Am. Comm. Int. Wild. Prot. Spec. Publ. 11:1-620.

Bleich, V.C. 1979. *Microtus californicus scirpensis* not extinct. J. Mammalogy 60:851-852.

Bleich, V.C. 1980. Amargosa vole study. Final report to the California Department of Fish and Game. 8 p.

Gaines, D. 1974. Review of the status of the Yellow-billed Cuckoo in California: Sacramento Valley populations. Condor 76:204-209.

Gaines, D. 1977. Current status and habitat requirements of the Yellow-billed Cuckoo in California. Unpublished manuscript. 94 p.

Gilbert, C.H. 1893. Report on the fishes of the Death Valley expedition collected in southern California and Nevada, with descriptions of new species. No. Am. Fauna 7:229-234.

Goldwasser, S., D. Gaines, and S.R. Wilbur. 1980. The Least Bell's Vireo in California: a de facto endangered race. American Birds 34:742-745.

Grinnell, J, and A.H. Miller. 1944. The distribution of the birds of California. Pacific Coast Avifauna 27. 608 p.

Hall, E.R. 1981. The mammals of North America. Volumes I, II. 1181 p. Wiley-Interscience Publications.

Hubbs, C.L., and R.R. Miller. 1948. The zoological evidence: correlation between fish distribution and hydrographic history in the desert basins of western United States. p. 17-166. In: The Great Basin with emphasis on glacial and postglacial times. Bull. Univ. Utah Vol. 38.

Hubbs, C.L., R.R. Miller, and L.C. Hubbs. 1974. Hydrographic history and relict fishes of the north-central Great Basin. Calif. Acad. Sci 7:1-259.

La Rivers, I. 1953. New gelastocorid and naucorid records and miscellaneous notes, with a description of the new species *Ambrysus amargosus* (Hemiptera:Naucoridae). Wassman J. Biol. 11:83-96.

Linsdale, J.M. 1940. Amphibians and reptiles of Nevada. Proc. Am. Acad. Arts Sci. 73:197-257.

Mason, J.F. 1948. Geology of the Tecopa area, southeastern California. Geol Soc. Amer Bull. 59:333-352.

Mifflin, M.D., and M.M. Wheat. 1979. Pluvial lakes and estimated pluvial climates of Nevada. Nevada Bur. Mines Geol. 94:1-57.

Miller, R.R. 1946. Correlation between fish distribution and pleistocene hydrography in eastern California and southwestern Nevada, with a map of the Pleistocene waters. J. Geol. 54:43-53.

Miller, R.R. 1948. The cyprinodont fishes of the Death Valley system of eastern California and southwestern Nevada. Misc. Publ. Mus. Zool., Univ. Mich. 68:1-155.

Pupfish Habitat Preservation Committee. 1972. Amargosa Canyon-Dumont Dunes proposed natural area. Report to the USDI Bureau of Land Management. 118 p. plus appendices.

Rogers, M.J. 1939. Early lithic industries of the lower basin of the Colorado River and adjacent desert areas. San Diego Mus. Pap. No. 3.

Rumpp, N.L. 1956. Tiger beetles of the genus *Cicindela* in southwestern Nevada and Death Valley, California, and descriptions of two new species. Bull. So. Calif. Acad. Sci. 55:131-144.

Rumpp, N.L. 1957. Notes on the *Cicindela praetextata-californica* tiger beetle complex. Description of a new subspecies from Death Valley, California (Coleoptera: Cicindelidae). Bull So. Calif. Acad. Sci. 56:144-154.

Snyder, C.T., G. Hardman, and F.F. Zdenek. 1964. Pleistocene lakes in the Great Basin. USDI Geological Survey, Misc. Geol. Investigation, Map I-416.

Stejneger, L. 1893. Annotated list of the reptiles and batrachians collected by the Death Valley expedition in 1891, with descriptions of new species. No. Am. Fauna 7:220-221.

Taylor, D.W. 1980. Endangered and threatened freshwater mollusks of Amargosa drainage, California-Nevada. Proposal submitted to USDI Fish and Wildlife Service. 18 p.

Troxel, B.W. 1961. Reconnaissance geologic maps of parts of the Leach Lake, Quail Mountains, and Silurian Hills quadrangles, California, scale 1:62,500. California Division of Mines and Geology.

U.S. Bureau of Census. 1973. Census of population, 1970. Volume I: characteristics of the population. Part 6: California, Section 1. U.S. Government Printing Office, Washington, D.C.

USDI Bureau of Land Management. 1980. The California desert conservation area. Final environmental impact statement and proposed plan. 173 p. California State Office, Sacramento.

USDI Geological Survey. 1969. Water resources data for California. Part I: surface water records. Volume 1: Colorado River Basin, Southern Great Basin, and Pacific Slope Basins excluding Central Valley. 498 p. USDI Geological Survey, Menlo Park, California.

Usinger, R.L. 1956. Aquatic Hemiptera. p. 182-228. In: R.L. Usinger (ed.). Aquatic insects of California. University of California Press, Berkeley.

THE DECLINE OF ASH MEADOWS, A UNIQUE DESERT ECOSYSTEM[1]

Cynthia D. Williams[2]

Abstract.--Ash Meadows is a unique hydric ecosystem of the Amargosa Desert located in southwestern Nye County, Nevada, and southeastern Inyo County, California. The approximately 162-km^2 area is dominated by over 30 springs and seeps that support a wide variety of plant and animal life, including nearly 30 endemics. Ash Meadows was apparently heavily used by several Indian cultures and later mined for peat and clay around 1910 to 1930. Since the late 1960s, the area has been subjected to a variety of agricultural, industrial, residential, and mineral development schemes, the most recent of which threatens to cause the demise of the ecosystem.

INTRODUCTION

Ash Meadow is a unique and biologically rich ecosystem, consisting of approximately 16,200 ha. in southwestern Nevada and southeastern California. It is located in the Amargosa Desert about 64 km. east of Death Valley and 145 km. northwest of Las Vegas (fig. 1). More than 30 springs and seeps discharge a total of 17,000-20,000 acre-feet of water annually in the Ash Meadows area, creating an oasis in the otherwise arid Amargosa Desert. Many of the springs are large, with headwater pools 6-10 m. in diameter (fig. 2). Water temperatures range from 26°C. to 38°C. The large spring discharge creates significant marsh areas for waterfowl and other migrating birds. At least 20 of the springs contain native fish, and most, if not all, contain endemic species of molluscs or insects. Additionally, several rare plants depend on the moist areas surrounding the springs for their survival.

As with much of the Great Basin, the Ash Meadows area was considerably wetter during the late Pleistocene, supporting Lake Ash Meadows as an ephemeral feature (Snyder et al. 1964). Because of elevational differences, the springs of Ash Meadows were isolated in three stages by the post-pluvial desiccation of Lake Ash Meadows. Devil's Hole, at approximately 732 m., was the first aquatic habitat to become isolated as the waters of Lake Ash Meadows receded. The period of isolation has been estimated at upwards of 30,000 years.[3] The mid-level springs, including Scruggs, Indian, Marsh, School, and Mexican springs, became isolated 4,000-10,000 years before present (YBP). Isolation of the lower elevation springs, including Big, Point-of-Rocks, Jack Rabbit, Forest, Bradford 1, Bradford 2, Bradford 3, Crystal, Longstreet, Rogers, and Fairbanks springs, occurred more recently and is still somewhat tenuous.

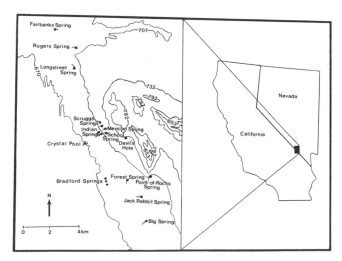

Figure 1.--Location of Ash Meadows, Nye County, Nevada, and Inyo County, California (modified from Soltz and Naiman 1978).

[1] Paper presented at the California Riparian Systems Conference. [University of California, Davis, September 17-19, 1981].

[2] Cynthia D. Williams is Graduate Teaching Assistant, Department of Biological Sciences, California State University, Sacramento.

[3] Deacon, J.E. Professor of Biology, University of Nevada, Las Vegas. Personal communication.

Figure 2.—Crystal Spring is one of the largest springs in the Ash Meadows area, with a discharge rate of 10,741 LPM (Mifflin 1968). Note the extensive riparian zone surrounding the spring.

SPECIES ACCOUNTS

Ash Meadows has the highest amount of biological endemism of any area in the United States. More than 25 organisms—including eight plants, two insects, 10 or more molluscs, five fishes, and one mammal—are endemic to Ash Meadows (table 1). Only one other arid region of North America, the Cuatro Cienegas Basin of northeastern Mexico, supports a greater diversity of endemic organisms (Minckley 1969).

Three of the endemic plants, Astragalus phoenix, Mentzelia leucophila, and Nitrophila mohavensis, are official candidates for inclusion on the federal list of threatened and endangered species. An additional two species and several varieties of plants are also endemic to the Ash Meadows area.

There are more than 10 snail species, including four species of an undescribed "Nevada Spring Snail" genus and approximately six species of Tryonia, endemic to springs in Ash Meadows. These snails are all candidates for federal listing. Ambrysus amargosus, a naucorid restricted to Ash Meadows, is also a candidate species.

Five fishes are endemic to Ash Meadows. The Ash Meadows killifish, Empetrichthys merriami, was last seen in 1948 (Soltz and Naiman 1978). Apparently, E. merriami was a casualty of competition and predation by exotic organisms. Historically, this species occupied most of the large, lower-elevation springs. Three pupfish are endemic to Ash Meadows. The Devil's Hole pupfish, Cyprinodon diabolis, is restricted to Devil's Hole, a disjunct part of Death Valley National Monument, which encompasses 1.6 ha. (4 ac.) of the Ash Meadows system. This species of pupfish has undergone significant evolutionary changes (e.g., loss of pelvic fins) during its long period of isolation and is very distinct from its closest relative. In recognition of the precarious existence of C. diabolis, it is listed as endangered by the USDI Fish and Wildlife Service (FWS). The two Ash Meadows subspecies of Amargosa pupfish, Cyprinodon nevadensis pectoralis and C. n. mionectes, inhabit the mid-level and lower springs, respectively. Cyprinodon n. pectoralis is listed as endangered by the FWS, and C. n. mionectes is an official candidate. A form of speckled dace, Rhinichthys osculus nevadensis, which inhabits many of the lower-

717

Table 1.--Status of the endemic biota of Ash Meadows according to current federal and state regulations. Recommended classifications are also provided. C--candidate: taxon is a candidate to the Federal list of threatened and endangered species. T--threatened: taxon likely to become endangered within the foreseeable future. E--endangered: taxon in danger of extinction throughout all or a significant portion of its range. SC--special concern: taxon could become threatened or endangered by relatively minor disturbances to its habitat; or requires additional information is required before the status of the taxon can be determined.

Taxon	Federal	State	Recommended
Plants			
Nitrophila mohavensis	C	–	E
Astragalus phoenix	C	E	E
Mentzelia leucophila	C	–	–
Ivesia eremica	–	–	E
Grindelia fraxino-pratensis	–	–	T
Centarum namophilum var. namophilum	–	–	T
Enceliopsis nudicaulis var. corrugata	–	–	T
Cordylanthus tecopensis	–	–	T
Insects			
Stenelmis calidae calidae	–	–	T
Ambrysus amargosus	C	–	E
Molluscs			
Tryonia (6+ species)	C	–	E, T, SC
"Nevada Spring Snail" (4 species)	C	–	E, T, SC
Fishes			
Cyprinodon diabolis	E	E	E
C. nevadensis mionectes	C	R	E
C. n. pectoralis	E	R	E
Rhinichthys osculus nevadensis	C	–	E
Empetrichthys merriami	–	–	Extinct
Mammals			
Microtus montanus nevadensis	–	–	Extinct (?)

elevation springs is also a candidate to the list of federally protected species.[4]

The flora and fauna of Ash Meadows represent a unique and threatened biota, including two extinct and over 25 extant endemics. Many of the extant endemics have received official recognition of their precarious status, and such recognition is pending for many more.

THREATS TO THE ECOSYSTEM

Prior to the coming of the white man, Ash Meadows was apparently heavily utilized by several Indian cultures. This unobtrusive use of Ash Meadows came to an abrupt end at the beginning of

the twentieth century. The first detrimental use of the area by man occurred from 1910 to 1930 when Carson Slough, an extensive marsh system in the western part of Ash Meadows, was drained for mining peat and clay. The mid-1940s saw man's continuing impact on the Ash Meadows ecosystem in the introduction of bullfrogs and crayfish to springs in Ash Meadows. Several shifts in abundance of native fishes at that time have been attributed to those introductions (Miller 1948). Since the 1940s a variety of tropical fish and a snail, Melanoides tuberculatum, have been added to the growing list of exotic species in the area (Hardy 1980).

During the late 1960s, Spring Meadows Ranch began extensive groundwater pumping for irrigation, and the water level in Devil's Hole began to decline, reaching an all-time low in 1972. The USDI National Park Service (NPS) began formal court proceedings in 1971 in an effort to protect both the Devil's Hole pupfish and the special geologic character of the limestone cavern in

[4]By emerging rule, the FWS declared Ash Meadows pupfish and the Ash Meadows speckled dace to be endangered species on 10 May 1982. This temporary ruling is in force for 240 days.

which the species resides. A preliminary injunction in 1973 established a minimum level below which water in Devil's Hole could not fall. The case was finally heard in the US Supreme Court, which, on 7 June 1976, established a minimum water level that is considered consistant with the continued survival of the pupfish (Deacon and Deacon 1979).

Subsequent to the Supreme Court decision the Spring Meadows Ranch was put up for sale, and was purchased by Preferred Equities Corporation. Preferred Equities currently owns about 5,665 ha. in the heart of Ash Meadows and most of the water rights. Plans have been completed for three major developments that include parcels for high density trailer lots, single family residences, and commercial areas.

In addition to the current threat from Preferred Equities Corporation, Ash Meadows is now facing pressure from mineral development. In 1980, Anaconda Copper Company purchased property near Big Spring with plans to expand a zeolite mining operation. The zeolite deposit extends northward from the currently worked area toward the center of Ash Meadows. Further to the northwest, Tenneco is mining and processing borax.

MANAGEMENT

Without a doubt, the recent industrial, residential, and mineral development schemes threaten to bring about the demise of the Ash Meadows ecosystem. The planned developments would greatly increase the number of people living and working in the area. In 1980, approximately 15 people lived in Ash Meadows. Preferred Equities' plans for 33,000 homes, and a high density trailer court would dramatically increase that number.

Increased population would result in a variety of direct and indirect impacts. A large amount of land would have to be cleared and leveled to provide homesites and many new roads would have to be built. Several springs would be physically altered for recreational purposes. Plans exist to build a health spa around Crystal Spring and a reservoir over Point-of-Rocks Springs. The incidence of exotic species introduction can be expected to increase with the growing human population. Similarly it can be expected that the native aquatic organisms will be transferred from spring to spring without regard to their historical ranges. Groundwater depletion could once again become a critical problem. Development of the magnitude envisioned by Preferred Equities Corporation would require vast amounts of water for which an adequate supply is questionable.

Ash Meadows presents the opportunity for one of the very few "all or nothing" management decisions. We must make the philosophical decision of whether or not Ash Meadows and its inhabitants are worth saving. If we decide that the Ash Meadows ecosystem should be preserved in perpetuity, federal or state acquisition and subsequent incorporation into a federal or state refuge becomes the only alternative. A vehicle for this action exists in the form of Senate Bill 41, introduced in the ninety-seventh Congress by Senator Alan Cranston. If passed this bill would authorize the establishment of a Desert Pupfish National Wildlife Refuge in Ash Meadows. Sound management of a refuge thus established could allow for protection of the ecosystem with leeway for some mineral development. Regardless of the outcome of S.B. 41, the protections, inherent in the National Monument System, which are now being applied to Devil's Hole should continue to be fully applied.

ACKNOWLEDGMENTS

The manuscript was reviewed by Jack E. Williams of the FWS, who is thanked for his most helpful comments. James E. Deacon of the University of Nevada, Las Vegas, provided information on paleohydrology, but perhaps more importantly instilled in me an appreciation of the Ash Meadows ecosystem.

LITERATURE CITED

Deacon, J.E., and M.S. Deacon. 1979. Research on endemic fishes in the National Parks with special emphasis on the Devils Hole pupfish. USDI National Park Service Trans. and Proc. Ser. 5:9-19.

Hardy, T. 1980. The Inter-basin area report-- 1979. Proc. Desert Fishes Council 11:5-21.

Mifflin, M.D. 1968. Delineation of ground-water flow systems in Nevada. Desert Res. Inst., Center for Water Resources Research Tech. Rep. H-W, No. 4. University of Nevada, Reno. 110 p.

Miller, R.R. 1948. The cyprinodont fishes of the Death Valley system of eastern California and southwestern Nevada. University of Michigan, Mus. Zool. Misc. Publ. 68:1-155.

Minckley, W.L. 1969. Environments of the bolson of Cuatro Cienegas, Coahuila, Mexico. University of Texas, El Paso Sci. Ser. 2:1-65.

Snyder, C.T., G. Hardman, and F.F. Zdenek. 1964. Pleistocene lakes in the Great Basin. USDI Geological Survey, Misc. Geol. Investigations, Map I-416.

Soltz, D.L., and R.J. Naiman. 1978. The natural history of native fishes in the Death Valley system. Nat. Hist. Mus. of Los Angeles Co., Sci. Ser. 30:1-76.

A MANAGER'S PERSPECTIVE OF RIPARIAN AREAS

IN THE CALIFORNIA DESERT[1]

Bruce Ottenfeld[2]

Ask 12 different people what riparian areas mean to them, and one will more than likely get 12 different answers. Even though riparian areas make up less than 19% of the desert and often have known names, people's perceptions will vary according to their interests. Here are a few of my perceptions. Riparian areas are:

1. areas of conflict;
2. rich in cultural values;
3. of religious significance to native Americans;
4. often found along historic transportation routes;
5. essential for survival;
6. areas of critical environmental concern;
7. essential to the livestock industry;
8. often essential for mining;
9. home for many rare plants, animals, and fish;
10. essential for a good share of human habitation in the desert;
11. vital to some agricultural development;
12. centers which attract the recreational user;
13. washes which provide routes of travel;
14. vital for the survival of the burro.

Are my perceptions anything like yours?

I wanted to point out my perceptions to show the many conflicts that arise almost daily in the riparian areas of the California desert. Riparian areas, more than any other zone in the desert, play a key role in its multiple use and management. By law they must be protected, and by law certain uses must be permitted. I believe these precious resources can be managed to permit uses and preserve their assets.

Let me give you an example. Corn Springs is a riparian area in eastern Riverside County for which a management plan has been prepared to give protection to a unique assemblage of resource values. Resource values present are vegetative, wildlife, cultural, scenic, and overall heavy recreational use. The plan provides for protection of these important resources while permitting a quality recreation experience. Some of the major proposed actions of the plan include:

1. move portions of existing camping areas away from critical vegetative and wildlife zones. This will directly benefit wildlife, vegetation, and scenic resource values;

2. remove one evergreen tamarisk and monitor the effect on the spring. This is intended to benefit wildlife, vegetation, and scenic quality;

3. install a sign and barrier in front of petroglyphs and nominate Corn Springs to the National Register. This will benefit cultural values;

4. increase USDI Bureau of Land Management (BLM) presence by rangers and other personnel. This will affect all resource values;

5. control vehicle use;

6. install nesting boxes and wildlife drinkers away from redesigned camping facilities.

7. institute a monitoring program to measure the effects of the management plan on the health of Corn Springs.

Corn Springs is but one riparian area in the desert for which we plan to develop a management plan. Each area will have a plan developed through interdisciplinary approval, and each plan will be unique depending on the conflicts. All plans will be implementable and will reflect the BLM's multiple-use mission.

---

[1]Paper presented at the California Riparian Systems Conference. [University of California, Davis, September 17-19, 1981.]
[2]Bruce Ottenfeld is Assistant District Manager, California Desert District, USDI Bureau of Land Management, Riverside, Calif.

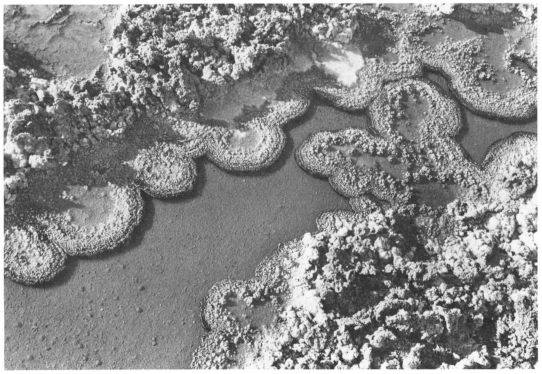

PRODUCTIVITY IN NATIVE STANDS OF PROSOPIS GLANDULOSA,

MESQUITE, IN THE SONORAN DESERT OF SOUTHERN CALIFORNIA

AND SOME MANAGEMENT IMPLICATIONS[1]

E.T. Nilsen, P.W. Rundel, and M.R. Sharifi[2]

Abstract.--Species of Prosopis, in particular, Prosopis glandulosa, form the dominant woody elememt of
wash woodlands over 30 million hectares of the desert and
semiarid communities of southwestern United States. During
1980-81, productivity and biomass were measured in a Prosopis glandulosa stand near the Salton Sea in southern
California. Total stand production was 3,650 kg. per ha.
per year, and the aboveground standing crop was 14,000 kg.
per ha. These values are similar to those found for a
desert wash dominated by the same species in Baja California. Such production rates are remarkably high for desert
ecosystems particularly in relation to the low annual rainfall of 70 mm. per year. These high levels of productivity
for mesquite are possible because the mesophytic nature of
Prosopis and its ability to fix nitrogen allow these
plants to be decoupled from normal limiting water and nitrogen resources in desert ecosystems. Our productivity and
related studies have considerable significance for managed
stands of Prosopis and the influence of managed Prosopis
stands on wash woodland ecosystems.

INTRODUCTION

In the hot deserts of southern California,
wash woodlands are the major riparian systems.
To date, only a few of the many ecosystem and
community investigations carried out in the
southern deserts have concerned themselves with
wash woodland environments. The few available
published data on productivity of plantations in
Chile and Pakistan indicate that remarkably high
productivity rates can be maintained for Prosopis species in arid lands. The paucity of
information concerning native stands of Prosopis stimulated our research investigation on
productivity of Prosopis glandulosa in the
Sonoran desert of southern California.

Wash woodlands support many life forms but
the most dominant are leguminous trees. Prosopis, mesquite, is probably the most abundant
leguminous tree inhabiting wash woodlands in both
southern California and northern Mexico. P.
glandulosa accounts for the dominant woody

woody element in wash woodlands in over 30 million ha. of the desert and semiarid plant communities of the southwestern United States. Even
though mesquite has widespread ecological and
economic importance, few data are available which
characterize the stand biomass and productivity
of mesquite woodlands (Klemmedson and Barth 1975;
Sharifi et al. in press).

Quantification of productivity and biomass
of Prosopis is very desirable for several
reasons. First, as stated above, wash woodland
ecosystems have not been previously studied
extensively, despite their importance to desert
fauna and desert water resources. Second, the
few available published data on Prosopis net
primary production from plantations in Chile and
Pakistan suggest that remarkably high production
rates can be maintained in desert communities
(Salinas and Sanchez 1971; Ahmed 1961). Third,
there has recently been increasing interest in
the importance of energy and food production of
arid zone plants such as Prosopis species,
particularly in many third world countries.

In this investigation we quantified biomass
and production in a P. glandulosa wash woodland riparian system in the Sonoran Desert of
California. We also investigated the influence
of normal desert environmental parameters, which
limit the aboveground production of this Prosopis stand. These data were then used to

[1]Paper presented at the California
Riparian Systems Conference. [University of
California, Davis, September 17-19, 1981].
[2]E.T. Nilsen, P.W. Rundel, and M.R.
Sharifi are associated with the Department of
Ecology and Evolutionary Biology, University of
California, Irvine, California.

project the possible ramifications of managing such a _Prosopis_ stand for biomass and/or fodder production.

SITE DESCRIPTION

The research site was Harper's Well, located 10 km. west of the southern tip of the Salton Sea near the base of the Fish Creek Mountains, Imperial County. Elevation of the site is -30 m. msl. Its age can be dated back 500 years when the site was covered by a larger Salton Sea (Lake Cahuilla). Climatic conditions at Harper's Well are extreme (fig. 1). There is a large year-round evaporative loss of water while precipitation is low (65-70 mm. annually). Temperatures reach a maximum in July, averaging 45C., while temperatures below 5C. are extremely rare. Soil texture is variable, ranging from a sandy loam beneath trees to clay between trees. Water is constantly available as groundwater is at a depth of about 5 m. There are occasional short periods of surface flooding of the wash area by runoff from the Fish Creek Mountains. Tropical storms occasionally create sheet flow over the impermeable clay soil.

METHODS

Biomass and Productivity

Prosopis biomass and productivity were measured by the dimension analysis techniques (Whittaker and Marks 1975). Regressions were formulated between productive branch basal diameter and biomass components. Trunks were measured to determine volume, which was multiplied by wood density to determine trunk weight. Biomass and production were determined as dry weight. The biomass components investigated were trunk weight, productive branch wood, current twigs, leaves, inflorescences, and pods.

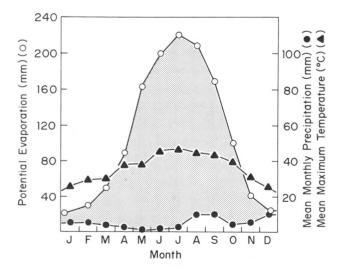

Figure 1.--Climatic conditions at Harper's Well in the Sonoran Desert of southern California.

Productivity was calculated as the sum of the clipping production and the woody increment. Clipping production was measured as the sum of maximum leaf, inflorescence, pod, and current twig biomass. Annual woody increment was determined by measuring the average of five years wood growth as per Whittaker and Marks (_ibid._).

Ten trees were measured carefully to determine total biomass and production for all biomass components on a canopy area and volume basis. Canopy volume per ground area was then determined in 30 0.1-ha. quadrats on two transects which best represented the _Prosopis_ stand. The canopy volume per ground area was multiplied by the biomass and production per canopy volume to yield biomass and productivity per ground area.

Water Use

Several measurements of water use were made during 1980-81. Diurnal cycles of transpiration per leaf area were determined monthly on four representative trees using a steady state porometer (Licor, model 1600). Seasonal variability in total leaf area was ascertained by labeling 20 branches on each tree, determining the number of leaves per branch, and multiplying by the mean leaf area per leaf (determined seasonally for each tree) to give mean leaf area per branch.

These data, when converted to a percent of seasonal maximum basis, were used to adjust maximum leaf area per tree, yielding seasonal leaf area per tree. The monthly diurnal cycles of transpiration per tree were multiplied by the seasonal leaf biomass to yield monthly water use. Soil moisture determinations were made to a depth of 5 m. by the use of neutron activation technique.[3] Relative environmental plant water stress was determined by measuring pre-dawn xylem pressure potential seasonally by the pressure chamber technique.

Nitrogen

Nitrogen concentrations were measured in the soils and in plant tissues by co-workers.[3] These nitrogen values were combined with the productivity values to produce a nitrogen budget for this stand of _Prosopis_.

RESULTS AND DISCUSSION

Biomass and Production

Regressions which were formulated between basal diameter and biomass or production components were quite accurate, with correlation coefficients greater than 0.95 for all components except fruit and flower production ($r^2 = 0.80$). This resulted in an accurate determination of biomass per tree, which was found to be within 5%

---

[3]Data collected by University of California, Riverside co-workers Dr. Wes Jarrell and Dr. Ross Virginia.

of the harvested biomass of a sample tree. Average biomass and production values for aboveground components are shown in table 1 on a stand and canopy area basis.

Total stand biomass was close to 14,000 kg. per ha. on a stand basis and 42,000 kg. per ha. on a canopy area basis. A majority of biomass (85%) was retained in trunk and productive branch wood. Productivity was high in relation to biomass (biomass accumulation ratio = 3.84), indicating that this stand is still actively growing. Fruit production accounted for 21% of the total production and leaf production was 33% of the total.

Table 1.--Aboveground biomass and production for Prosopis glandulosa, at Harper's Well, Sonoran Desert, southern California,

Component	Canopy Biomass	Stand Biomass	Canopy Production	Stand Production
	kg./ha.		kg./ha./year	
Trunk	15,893	5,245	2,706	893
Productive branch	21,470	7,085	2,933	968
Leaves	3,658	1,207	3,658	1,207
Inflorescence	440	145	440	145
Fruit	2,312	763	2,312	763
Total	42,339	3,973	11,015	3,635

There was a considerable variability in stand production and biomass (table 2). Near the wash watercourse itself biomass and production were twice as high as the average. On the outer edges of the stand biomass and production decreased to 25% of the average. The highest stand value for a 0.1-ha. plot was found in the proximity of the wash with 77% cover of P. glandulosa.

Table 2.--Variability in aboveground biomass and production in a Prosopis glandulosa stand at Harper's Well, Sonoran Desert, southern California.

	Biomass (kg./ha.)	Production (kg./ha./yr.)
Stand average	13,973	3,635
Highest value	30,614	7,973
Near wash	21,703	5,655
Stand fringe	3,448	898

These biomass and production values are very high in relation to those of other desert communities. This Prosopis stand at Harper's Well has a biomass and production which far exceeds that measured for other Prosopis stands in New Mexico and Arizona (fig. 2), but is very similar to that measured in Baja California. The Baja California Prosopis stand is older than that of Harper's Well, therefore the biomass is larger

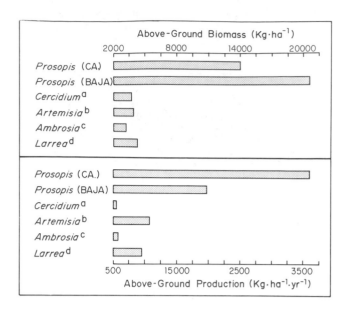

Figure 2.--Biomass and production for several desert communities. a = Whittaker and Neiring 1975; b = Turner and McBrayer 1974; c = Balph et al. 1974; d = Chew and Chew 1975.

and productivity is less. In comparison to other desert shrub communities, Prosopis biomass and production at Harper's Well is by far the largest (fig. 2 and 3).

Based on these comparative data, the Harper's Well Prosopis wash woodland has a higher biomass and production than that measured for any other American desert community. While both biomass and productivity of this Prosopis stand are small in comparison to other California riparian plant communities, aboveground productivity of Prosopis is large in relation to rainfall (fig. 3). This is unusual when compared to other desert ecosystems, and is a clear reflec-

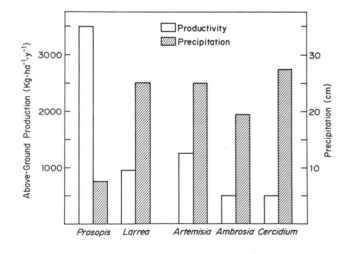

Figure 3.--The relationship of productivity to rainfall in several desert communities.

tion of the riparian character of this wash woodland. It is particularly interesting because moisture is a limiting factor for most growth in desert environments.

Moisture Availability

Several measurements of moisture availability were made at this site during 1980-81 (fig. 4). Soil moisture at 4 m. depth stayed constant throughout the year while soil moisture at 0.3 m. depth increased during the period of rainfall from January through March. Pre-dawn xylem pressure potential gives an indication of the general environmental water availability to the plants. Water is slightly more available during January through March when surface soil moisture increases, although throughout the rest of the year there is no significant water deficit in the plants. This is unusual considering the extreme evaporative demand in July (fig. 1), and can only be the result of a deep tap root system which utilizes the available deep groundwater (Nilsen et al. 1981).

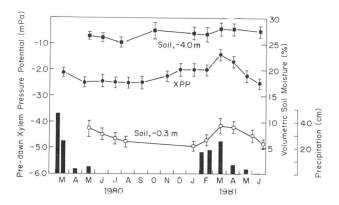

Figure 4.--Measurements of environmental and plant water relationships for _Prosopis glandulosa_ at Harper's Well, Sonora Desert, southern California.

Water Use

Water use per individual plant was considerable, partly due to constant available water at depth, large leaf area, and minimal diurnal water stress. Figure 5 is a representative diurnal curve of transpiration rate for one tree in July, 1981. Most water use occurs in the morning and early afternoon when water stress is minimal and temperatures are moderate.

Such diurnal cycles of transpiration, when summed over each month, produce a measure of monthly water use (fig. 6). A majority of seasonal water use occurred during late spring and summer when leaf evaporative demand was the highest.

Seasonal leaf area, multiplied by monthly water use per leaf area, results in stand and plant water use characteristics. Maximum water

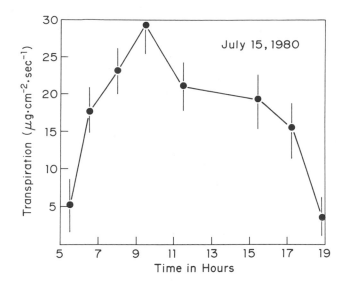

Figure 5.--Diurnal cycle of transpiration for _Prosopis glandulosa_ at Harper's Well, Sonoran Desert, southern California.

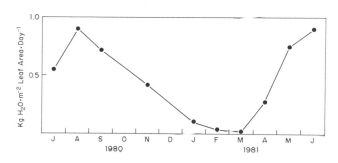

Figure 6.--Average monthly water use per leaf area for a population of _Prosopis glandulosa_ at Harper's Well, Sonoran Desert, southern California.

use occurred in June and August when up to 700 kg. of water were transpired per tree per day. Total seasonal water use on a stand basis and a canopy area basis are shown in table 3.

Table 3.--Aboveground net primary production, annual water use, and transpiration ratio for _Prosopis glandulosa_ at Harper's Well, Sonoran Desert, southern California. NPP--aboveground net primary production; TR--transpiration rate.

	NPP	Water Use	TR
Average individual (kg./yr.)	39	11,353	291
Largest individual (kg./yr.)	177	142,608	805
Average/canopy area (kg./ha./yr.)	11,015	3,440,300	312
Average/stand area (kg./ha./yr.)	3,635	1,135,299	312

It is clear that Prosopis uses tremendous quantities of water per year, far greater than the annual input by precipitation (70 kg. per ha. per year). Despite the large volume of water transpired, there was little change in the availability of groundwater (fig. 4) which served as the major water resource. On a yearly basis approximately 11,353 kg. of water were transpired per tree which results in a transpiration ratio (water transpired/net primary production) of 300. Such a transpiration ratio is similar to that of forested and riparian plant communities with ample water supplies. Therefore, these trees are not water conservative by any means and groundwater availability may be a critical limiting factor for management of a Prosopis wash woodland site in the Sonoran Desert.

Nitrogen

Nitrogen is another limiting factor for production in desert ecosystems. This may be especially true in wash woodlands, where the soils are often sandy and frequently flushed by flooding, commonly resulting in low inorganic and organic nitrogen availability. Table 4 represents the soil nitrogen characteristics in general for the upper 30 cm. at Harper's Well in comparison to other communities. It is clear that organic nitrogen is much higher under the trees than between the trees outside the stand. This is the result of the build-up of decomposed litter and humus under these deciduous trees. The nitrate values under these trees are extremely high for any ecosystem; particularly in relation to the organic nitrogen content. The very high nitrate content is the result of low denitrification rates (Virginia et al. in review), infrequent soil leaching by rainfall, and high deposition rates of nitrogen in abscissed leaves.

Table 4.--Concentrations of nitrate nitrogen, total nitrogen, and percent nitrate nitrogen in soil of a Prosopis stand at Harper's Well, Sonoran Desert, southern California, in comparison to other systems.

Community	Nitrate (NO_3) $(gm./m^2)$	Total nitrogen $(gm./m^2)$	Nitrate nitrogen (%)
Prosopis (under trees)	253	1,020	25
Prosopis (between trees)	55	160	34
Conifer forest[1]	0.2	450	0.04
Grassland[2]	0.01	352	0.01
Mojave Desert[3]	3.0	99	3

[1] from Johnson 1979
[2] from Woodmansee et al. 1981
[3] from West and Skojins 1978

The flux rates of nitrogen through this Prosopis stand indicate considerable accumulation (52 gm. per m^2 per year). Translocation from storage tissues accounted for 8% of accumulation, and uptake from deep groundwater could account for only less than 1% of total accumulation. Thirty percent of accumulated nitrogen was deposited through litter fall. The accumulated nitrogen for the most part (>80%) must be derived from the upper soil layers or nitrogen fixation (Rundel et al. 1981). Clearly, the large amount of nitrogen in surface soils must have been derived from nitrogen fixation in the past since the surrounding areas are very low in nitrogen, as are the lower soil layers. The question still remains whether present nitrogen accumulation in biomass is derived from nitrogen fixation or soil uptake in a recycling manner (presently under investigation). Yet it is apparent that nitrogen fixation must be very important in maintaining such high productivity rates, whether or not the fixation is presently continuing.

Production Potentials

The potential biomass and production of a managed Prosopis stand can be estimated by extending the percentage cover of canopy to 90%. In this case, total production would be 9,900 kg. per ha. per year, and component production would be: leaves 3,300 kg. per ha. per year; fruits 2,080 kg. per ha. per year; wood 5,075 kg. per ha. per year. This is considerably lower than the leaf and pod production (15,000 kg. per ha. per year) found for Prosopis tamarugo in Chile (Salinas and Sanchez 1971), but this would be an extremely high production for North American desert ecosystems. This high pod and leaf production is a potential resource for animal fodder, and the large wood production is a potential resource for biomass fuel, particularly because of the high wood density. However, it is also important to ask: what influence would such a managed stand have on the wash woodland ecosystem?

There is a considerable number of bird, reptile, insect, and mammal species which inhabit and utilize Prosopis for food and shelter (Mares et al. 1977). Increasing the density of the native Prosopis species to 90% should only increase the resources for the wash woodland fauna. The physical environment would also be influenced, particularly in relation to water and nitrogen availability. Clearly, an increased density of Prosopis would increase the upper soil nitrate and total nitrogen contents. Increasing nitrogen availability in upper soil layers could only benefit the nutritional stability of the community. Water resources used by a stand with density of 90% would be three times that presently transpired, or 3×10^6 kg. per ha. per year, yet there was no significant change in groundwater availability. Even though there seems to be a considerable groundwater recharge potential, a non-irrigated, managed stand of 90% cover could conceivably reduce groundwater resources, particularly from June through August.

This problem of groundwater recharge ability could become critical in other desert washes which have ephemeral water tables.

Conclusion

This study indicates that the *Prosopis glandulosa* stand of Harper's Well has extremely high productivity rates in relation to other desert plant communities. These high productivity rates are possible because *Prosopis* fixes nitrogen and is mesophytic, which decouples this taxon from productivity limitation by rainfall and soil nitrogen availability. Even though productivity is decoupled from rainfall, large quantities of groundwater are required for growth. It seems that the major ecosystem disruption as a result of managing a *Prosopis* stand for biomass fuel production and fodder production may be a reduction in groundwater availability. This may be critical in wash woodlands with ephemeral water tables. *Prosopis* has considerable potential for biomass fuel production and fodder production in arid ecosystems, with limited disruption of ecosystem stability.

LITERATURE CITED

Ahmed, G. 1961. Evaluation of dry zone afforestation plots. Pakistan J. of Forestry 168.

Balph, D.T., R.S. Shinn, R.D. Anderson, and C. Gist. 1974. Curlew Valley validation site. US/I.B.P. desert biome research memorandum 74-1. 61 p. Ecology Center, Utah State University, Logan.

Chew, R.M., and A.E. Chew. 1975. The primary productivity of a desert shrub (*Larrea tridentata*) community. Ecol. Monog. 35: 355-375.

Johnson, D.W. 1979. Some nitrogen fractions in two forest soils and their changes in response to urea fertilization. Northwest Science 53(1):22-32.

Klemmedson, J.O., and R.C. Barth. 1975. Distributional balance of biomass and nutrients in desert shrub ecosystems. US/I.B.P. desert biome research memorandum 75-5. 18 p. Ecology Center, Utah State University, Logan.

Mares, M.A., F.A. Enders, J.M. Kingsolver, J.L. Neff, and B.B. Simpson. 1977. *Prosopis* as a niche component. p. 123-149. In: B.B. Simpson (ed.). Mesquite, its biology in two desert ecosystems. Dowden, Hutchinson and Rass, Inc., Stroudsburg, Penn.

Nilsen, E.T., P.W. Rundel, and M.R. Sharifi. In press. Summer water relations of the desert phreatophyte *Prosopis glandulosa* in the Sonoran Desert of southern California. Oecologia.

Rundel, P.W., E.T. Nilsen, M.R. Sharifi, R.A. Virginia, W.M. Jarrell, D.H. Kohl, and G.B. Shearer. In press. Seasonal dynamics of nitrogen cycling for a *Prosopis* woodland in the Sonoran Desert. In: Nitrogen cycling in ecosystems in Latin America and the Caribbean, Cali, Columbia.

Salinas, H.E., and S.C. Sanchez. 1971. Estudio del tamarugal como productor de alimento del grande hanan en la Pampa del Tamarugo. Informe Tecnico Institutio Forestal Section Silvicultura (Santiago, Chile) 38:1-35.

Sharifi, M.R., E.T. Nilsen, and P.W. Rundel. In press. Biomass and net primary production of *Prosopis glandulosa* (Fabaceae) in the Sonoran Desert of California. Am. J. of Botany.

Turner, F.B., and J.F. McBrayer. 1974. Rock Valley validation site report. US/I.B.P. desert biome research memorandum 74-2. 64 p. Ecology Center, Utah State University, Logan.

Virginia, R.A., W.M. Jarrell, and E. Franco-Vizcaino. In review. Direct measurement of denitrification in a *Prosopis* (mesquite) dominated Sonoran Desert ecosystem. Oecologia.

West, N.E., and J. Skojins. 1978. The nitrogen cycle in the North America cold-winter semi-desert ecosystems. Oecologia Plantarum 12:45-53.

Whittaker, R.H., and P.L. Marks. 1975. Methods of assaying terrestrial productivity. p. 55-118. In: H. Leith and R.H. Whittaker (ed.). Primary production of the biosphere. Springer-Verlag, Heidelberg.

Whittaker, R.M., and W.A. Neiring. 1975. Vegetation of the Santa Catalina Mountains, Arizona. V. Biomass, production, and diversity along an elevational gradient. Ecology 56:771-790.

Woodmansee, R.G., I. Vallis, and J.J. Mott. 1981. Grassland nitrogen. p. 443-462. In: F.E. Clark and T. Roswell (ed.). Terrestrial nitrogen in cycles. Ecological Bulletin (Stockholm) 33.

RIPARIAN WOODLAND REGULATION: PROS AND CONS[1]

David E. Pesonen[2]

Abstract.--The Forest Practice Act could be applied to riparian woodlands by action of the Board of Forestry. The act does not, however, apply to non-commercial timber cutting, and it provides little leverage to prevent conversion of such lands to other uses. The situation could change as stumpage values increase. Other laws should be explored for solutions.

INTRODUCTION

In recent years, it has been suggested that the Z'berg-Nejedly Forest Practice Act of 1973[3] might be used to facilitate riparian woodland management. The issue has often been discussed within the California Department of Forestry (DF), and it has come before the Board of Forestry ("Board") on at least one occasion.

At first glance the Forest Practice Act would appear ideally suited to at least prevent abuse of riparian woodlands. The act has done a great deal of good in regulating and preventing the more destructive practices of timber operators in upland timber areas, and the process is continuing to be improved under the impetus of Section 208 of the Federal Water Pollution Control Act.[4] Interestingly enough, the primary motivation for these efforts has been the need to prevent damage to water quality, an important factor in the discussions at this conference.

Nevertheless, the Forest Practice Act may not provide the protection to riparian woodland that it appears to offer. To be sure, nothing in the act prevents its application to any area "... which is available for, and capable of, growing a crop of trees of any commercial species used to produce lumber and other forest products..." (PRC 4526). This provision goes on to assign the determination of "commercial species" to the Board. The Board could determine that riparian woodland species are commercial species, thus placing riparian woodlands under the act. The absence of steady markets for such species might

cause some hesitation in making this determination, but technically it could be done.

The question of "adequate protection," however, is quite another thing. It is actually very doubtful whether the act, as written, could provide any meaningful protection or facilitate the management of bottomland riparian vegetation.

The act has as its main thrust the "maximum sustained production of high quality timber" (PRC 4513). A clear underlying presumption is that the timber involved has a relatively high value and that the underlying land has value primarily for timber production. This assumption, which permeates the act, assumes an economic incentive to manage the timber for its own sake. Thus, the land must be protected from damage during the harvesting process, so as to maintain its capacity to produce timber.

A different situation exists in the riparian woodland. There, the land is typically valued primarily for agriculture, and the pressure to remove the trees comes from a desire to clear the land to make it available for agriculture. If the owner can sell the trees to help pay for the cost of clearing, well and good, but the existence of a market for these trees is not the only incentive for conversion. If he cannot sell the trees, the owner will often simply bulldoze and bunch them for burning.

The Forest Practice Act and the rules adopted under the act apply only to timber that goes into commerce (PRC 4527). If the owner chooses to bunch and burn his riparian trees, or to use them for his own non-commercial purposes, none of the rules will apply. The act deprives the Board of jurisdiction over such operations.

Stumpage values (the value of standing timber) of riparian woodlands are on the increase, however. Eventually, the value of retaining the land in timber may come to be seen by landowners. In such event, the Forest Practice Act may come to have more relevance in preventing improper har-

---

[1]Paper presented at the California Riparian Systems Conference. [University of California, Davis, September 17-19, 1981].
[2]David E. Pesonen is Director of Forestry, State of California, Sacramento, Calif.
[3]Section 4511-4628, Public Resources Code (PRC) Section 4511-4628.
[4]PL 92-500, as amended by the Clean Water Act of 1977, PL 95-217.

vesting practices where sustained yield becomes a recognized goal. The act itself would still do little to prevent conversion of such lands to other uses, however.

Conversion of timberlands to non-timber-growing uses is covered by the Forest Practice Act (PRC 4621 et seq.). These sections require a permit from DF, acting on behalf of the Board, before timberland can be converted to non-timber-growing uses. Currently, of course, such permits are not required on riparian woodlands because the Board has not included these lands in the timberland category.

The Board would have to change still another of its regulations to make this permitting process effective in the riparian areas. Through the definition of "Timberland Conversion" (14 CAC [California Administrative Code] 1102), conversion of non-Timberland Preserve Zone (TPZ) lands can be done without permit where commercial timber operations are not involved. None of the bottomland riparian woodlands are in TPZs. Thus, if the owner carries out conversion by the bunch-and-burn technique, he would not need a conversion permit. The Board would need to amend this regulation to require a permit for any timberland conversion, including many thousands of acres in upland timber not included in a TPZ.

Nevertheless, even if these two things were done, DF could rarely justify the denial of applications for permits to convert riparian woodland. The grounds for denial listed in PRC 4624 are quite limited for non-TPZ lands. Denials may be for only the following reasons:

a) the applicant is not the real person in interest;
b) there is material misrepresentation or false statement in the application;
c) the applicant does not have a bona fide intention to convert the land; and
d) there is a failure or refusal of the applicant to comply with the rules and regulations of the board and the provisions of the chapter.

California Environmental Quality Act[5] requirements might allow DF to impose strict mitigation measures to discourage unwise conversions, but outright denial would be vulnerable to serious legal challenge.

To summarize, nothing in the act prevents the Board from including riparian woodlands under the Forest Practice Act. This could stem abusive harvesting practices. The act would, however, provide little or no relief from conversion of such areas to agriculture or other uses. Owners could evade the Forest Practice rules by non-commercial disposal of the trees. DF lacks authority to deny conversion permits on all non-TPZ lands for any except technical reasons. Therefore, meaningful protection for riparian wood

lands under the Forest Practice Act, as it is currently written, is very unlikely.

Two changes in the act could make meaningful protection possible: 1) amend PRC Section 4527 to extend the act to all timber-cutting and removal operations, not just commercial operations; and 2) amend PRC Section 4621.2 to require the findings now necessary to allow conversion of TPZ lands to apply also to conversion of non-TPZ timberlands. Thus, application for conversions could be denied for more than merely technical reasons.

Such change could require considerable augmentation of DF staff. An estimate of the exact amount is impossible, but it could easily require double the present staff. DF would need additional inspectors not only to inspect known operations, but also to ferret out conversions where no commercial tree harvesting is involved. This would involve more than just riparian woodlands; non-timber harvesting conversion of non-TPZ lands everywhere would come under the regulations as postulated. The kinds of detective work needed to keep track of these conversions could become staggering, and provision for the resources to accomplish the task in an era of tight money—not to mention the spectre of massive regulation of agricultural land—could be politically unpalatable.

Other factors threaten the riparian woodlands beside timber harvesting or conversion to agriculture. Such developments as bank protection and flood control works, power developments, water storage, water diversions and drainage, and recreational developments are just a few that come to mind. Such developments have in the past had devastating effects on riparian woodlands, and none would come under the Forest Practice Act.

Two other areas of law might offer protection. The Wild and Scenic Rivers Act[6] might be used in its present form to guarantee protection of riparian vegetation along portions of the Klamath, Trinity, Smith, Eel, and American rivers. Every effort should be made to assure that valuable stretches of river frontage on these rivers are included in management plans or are recognized for their unique values in Special Treatment Area rules by the Board of Forestry if AB 1600 were to pass in its present form.

Moreover, the act could be amended to include important stretches of river not now included. Riparian woodlands certainly add to the scenic value of the river, to say nothing of their other values.

The Native Species Conservation and Enhancement Act and the Native Plant Protection Act[7]

---

[5]PRC Section 21000-21178.

[6]PRC 5093.50-5093.65.
[7]California Fish and Game Code Sections 1750-1913.

should also be explored for their applicability. These acts offer the possibility of habitat protection for rare and endangered species of plants and animals. Not every riparian woodland serves as habitat for a rare or endangered species, but those that do require the most urgent protection.

I am not unmindful of the political sensitivity of these suggestions. The American farmer has a traditional abhorrence of governmental regulation, and much of the land in question belongs to farmers. Adding this to the more recent generalized backlash against regulation, it seems to me that the times are not propitious for a move toward greater regulation. I cannot help but think that an all-out educational effort, coupled with the increasing value of riparian areas for wood products, could do a lot to reduce destructive conversions.

Perhaps, too, there is a place for a "Riparian Woodland Improvement Program" similar to our California Forest Improvement Program already in place. Such a program could provide incentive payments to maintain the woodlands. Less than 25 years ago, Douglas-fir timber on the North Coast was still being regarded as a weed. It was being slashed, girdled, and burned in wholesale quantities for conversion to grazing land. Very few such conversions are being made today, and much of the stipped land is being allowed to revert; some is being actively reforested. The turn-around occurred when landowners finally realized the true worth of their resources.

I don't say this to minimize damage done in the interim. Not at all. The damage in many instances is irreparable. I offer it only to point out that all is not lost. What was lacking on the North Coast 25 years ago was an effective educational effort or incentive program to take advantage of rapidly improving markets.

DF maintains a keen interest in the issue of riparian system protection and enhancement, even though the resource is not traditionally within our lead agency responsibility. We look forward to creative solutions that will surely emerge from this very timely conference, and we hope to have a significant part in carrying the theme of the conference forward into the next decade.

ECONOMIC VALUES OF THREE FURBEARERS INHABITING

CALIFORNIA RIPARIAN SYSTEMS[1]

Lauren B. Scott[2]

Abstract.--Information on the monetary value of sustained harvest of beaver, mink, and muskrat from California riparian systems is not readily available to planners and decisionmakers developing management plans for these systems. This paper summarizes an effort to establish some basic information on the economic value of sustained harvest to California. The effort was focused on answering three questions: 1) What is the relative economic value of each county's fur harvest? 2) What is the relative importance of each species to each county? 3) What is the direct economic value to California of harvesting the three species? Summaries of rankings of counties and species are presented.

INTRODUCTION

When man interacts with an ecological system, using it to satisfy his wants and needs, he tends to assign his values to it, comparing it to other systems and evaluating the components making up the system. These values can be both monetarily and non-monetarily based.

Knowledge of these values is important to those involved in making management decisions for an ecological system in today's world of conflicting wants and needs. Whether a management plan includes proposals to change or to not change a system, the evaluation used to determine the relative merit of each proposal is often based on trade-offs among components of a system, measured in terms of economic and non-economic values. The value of a particular component can often determine whether a management plan will favor, disfavor, or not consider that component.

This paper presents information on the economic values of three fur-bearing animals--furbearers--inhabiting California riparian systems. Although furbearers are a component of riparian systems, the author has found that their values often are not considered in riparian management plans.

Several reasons can be cited for omitting detailed consideration of these values. Three are listed below.

1. Current analyses of existing data on values of furbearers are not readily available to planners and decisionmakers.

2. The number of individuals knowledgeable about or participating in activities directly associated with furbearers is small.

3. Furbearers are characterized as "cautious animals that are mainly active at night" (Kellert 1979) and are thus difficult for most people to observe.

Kellert (ibid.) rated "attitudes people have toward wildlife as well as the knowledge they have in the area of animals: bird watchers are rated to be most knowledgeable, followed closely by trappers..." or fur harvesters. However, when he measured the "percentage of the general public" participating in "one of the animal activities groups," 78% consisted of people who watched "Wild Kingdom," 25.2% were bird watchers, and 1.7% of the population consisted of trappers. In California, less than 1% of the population buys a trapping license.

Species

The species considered in this study were chosen because they are, for the most part, exclusively riparian species and are known to have direct and indirect economic values. They are beaver (Castor canadensis), mink, (Mustela vison), and muskrat (Ondatra zibethicus). Other species considered were the raccoon (Procyon lotor) and the gray fox (Canis (Urocyon) cinereoargenteus). They were not included because although they may spend some of their time feeding or resting in riparian

---

[1]Paper presented at the California Riparian Systems Conference. [University of California, Davis, September 17-19, 1981].

[2]Lauren B. Scott is Civil Engineer, USDI Bureau of Reclamation, Sacramento, Calif.

systems, they do not depend on riparian systems for most of their life requisites. The terms "species" and "animals" in this paper, therefore, refer to beaver, mink, and muskrat.

These species have several chracteristics in common (Nelson and Hooper 1976). Beavers need water several feet deep in which to live. In small rocky streams or shallow waters, they construct dams to create pools. The water backed up by the dam provides a safe travel way from lodge to food supply and a storage place for winter food (beavers do not hibernate). Along deep rivers and sloughs, beavers prefer to live in dens they dig in the banks. The beaver feeds at night on the bark and twigs of willows, cottonwoods, aspen, and other trees. It also eats roots, bulbs, leaves, and grasses found near water. Beavers can create problems by cutting down too many trees, blocking drainage ditches, and damming streams. These activities often result in flooded agricultural land and timberland, as well as damaged irrigation systems.

Mink are also found near water, preferring riverbanks and streams that have dense growths of vegetation. They live in old logjams, under the roots of trees near the water's edge, and in old muskrat burrows. Mink are nocturnal. They are good swimmers and often catch and kill their prey in the water. They eat mice, rabbits, muskrats, fish, crayfish, frogs, clams, birds, and other small animals and insects found near the water. They often kill more than they are able to eat. Mink may cause trouble because of their fondness for poultry.

Muskrats are always found in or near the water. They prefer the still or slow-moving waters of marshes, ponds, streams, and irrigation canals. They live in burrows dug in banks along the water's edge. In shallow, marshy areas, they build dome-shaped homes of tules, twigs, and mud. The muskrat is mainly nocturnal, although it is sometimes active during the day. It is primarily a vegetarian that feeds on aquatic plants, although it sometimes eats snails, mussels, insects, fish, and crayfish found near or in the water. Its burrowing habits make it a nuisance in areas where it may damage dams and ditches in irrigation systems by burrowing into the banks of these structures.

Values

This study examines the economic values of these three furbearers. The economic values of furbearers can be realized in many ways and are classified in this study as either direct or indirect. The economic value of a furbearer is realized in a direct manner when the animal is harvested and the pelt is sold. In California, this activity is regulated by the California Department of Fish and Game (DFG) and the California Fish and Game Commission. The term "harvest" or "take," as used in this paper, is defined under Title 14 of the Fish and Game Code (California Department of Fish and Game 1981-82). In

addition, in this paper a sustained yield harvest is assumed. This assumption is based on an examination of nearly 60 years of DFG records.

The indirect economic value of furbearers is realized when:

1. these animals provide food, clothing, sport, education, or other needs and wants of man;

2. damage to irrigation and flood control systems and to timber- and cropland by these animals is reduced or prevented;

3. jobs and revenue are created by the fur industry's tanning, fur dressing, manufacturing, and retailing establishments; and

4. jobs and revenue are created by industries supporting and supplying fur-harvesting activities.

Of the two methods by which economic values can be realized, this paper addresses only the direct method.

Data Availability and Organization

The time period covered in this study is the 11 years from the 1969-70 to the 1979-80 fur harvesting seasons, designated the study period. Fur harvesting seasons generally run from November of one year through March of the following year. A season is designated by the year in which it begins, e.g., the 1969-70 season is designated as 1969.

The data in the annual licensed trappers' report (California Department of Fish and Game 1969-80), required by DFG, and in other sources (California Department of Fish and Game 1981) are compiled by county. This paper follows that same format for presenting and analyzing data.

Of the 58 counties in California, only Marin and Ventura counties are not included in this study. No take of beaver, mink, or muskrat was recorded for these counties during the study period, and thus they are considered to realize no direct economic value.

To organize and derive information on the direct economic value to California of the sustained yield harvest of these three furbearers, three questions were posed:

1. What is the relative economic value of each county's fur harvest?

2. What is the relative importance of each species to each county?

3. What is the direct economic value to California of harvesting the three species?

The information acquired by answering these questions is presented here.

METHODS

County Values

The following methods were used to determine the relative economic value of each county's fur harvest. The value of each county's harvest is represented by the average annual value, measured in dollars, of the animals taken in each county during the study period.

The average annual values were calculated using equation 1:

$$\frac{\sum\limits_{y=1}^{11} bB_y N_y}{11} + \frac{\sum\limits_{y=1}^{11} mM_y N_y}{11} + \frac{\sum\limits_{y=1}^{11} rR_y N_y}{11} = V$$

where:

$$b = \frac{\sum\limits_{y=1}^{4} \frac{b'_y}{B_y}}{4} \quad m = \frac{\sum\limits_{y=1}^{4} \frac{m'_y}{M_y}}{4} \quad r = \frac{\sum\limits_{y=1}^{4} \frac{r'_y}{R_y}}{4}$$

and:

y is a number from 1 to 11 where 1 represents data for 1969, 2 for 1970, etc.;

B is the statewide average value of a beaver pelt for a particular year;[3]

M is the statewide average value of a mink pelt for a particular year;[3]

R is the statewide average value of a muskrat pelt for a particular year;[3]

N is the total number of pelts reported taken of a particular species for a county and year;[3]

V is the average value of all species for a particular county;

b is the countywide average value for a beaver pelt for a particular year;

m is the countywide average value for a mink pelt for a particular year; and

r is the countywide average value for a muskrat pelt for a particular year.

After the average value (V) of each county's fur harvest was calculated, the counties were ranked by these values, revealing the relative importance and the degree to which one county is more or less important than another in terms of their fur harvests. Degree is measured by the absolute difference and percent difference between the value of any two counties' fur harvests.

The 10 counties with the highest value of fur harvest are listed in table 1. The total average annual value for all counties is $208,335. However, because of large fluctuations in the raw fur market, this value may not reflect future values. It reflects only the average for the 11-year study period.

---

[3]Calculated by DFG each year from the number of a species sold divided into the total revenue from the species.

Table 1.--Economic value of beaver, mink, and muskrat harvest to California counties.

Rank	County	Average annual value ($)
1	Shasta	20,271
2	Butte	19,141
3	Siskiyou	17,041
4	Colusa	15,690
5	Glenn	14,140
6	San Joaquin	13,853
7	Sacramento	11,949
8	Solano	10,758
9	Merced	10,220
10	Yolo	10,837

Species' Value to Counties

The following method was used to determine the relative importance of each species to each county. For each county, the average annual value of the fur harvest calculated for the species in equation 1 was used to determine their relative importance. This determination was made by calculating each species' percentage contribution to the total average annual value (V) of a county's fur harvest. The species were then ranked by their percentages. The most important species, that species with the highest percentage, was assigned a rank of 1, the second most important a rank of 2, and the third, or least important, a rank of 3. In the case where two species' values contributed the same percent and were less than the third species, they were both assigned a rank of 3. The results of the ranking are shown in table 2.

Economic Value to California

To determine the direct economic value to California of harvesting the three species, the value of this harvest to California was examined in three ways: 1) the value contributed by each species; 2) the value realized by individuals engaged in fur harvest; and 3) any relationship between fur harvest to the extent of riparian systems.

Value Contributed by Each Species

Absolute values and percent contributions of the species' values to each county are summarized in table 3.

Value Realized by Individuals

To determine the value of the fur harvest to individuals, the average annual income of a California trapper resulting from harvest of these species and the percent of the trapper's mean annual income it represented were calculated using information from Boddicker (1980).

Table 2. Relative importance of beaver, mink, and muskrat to fur harvest in counties in California.

| County | Rank of species | | |
	Beaver	Mink	Muskrat
Alameda	2	3	1
Alpine	1	2	3
Amador	1	3	2
Butte	2	3	1
Calaveras	1	3	3
Colusa	2	3	1
Contra Costa	2	3	1
Del Norte	1	3	2
El Dorado	2	3	1
Fresno	2	3	1
Glenn	2	3	1
Humboldt	1	2	3
Imperial	2	3	1
Inyo	1	2	3
Kern	1	3	2
Kings	3	3	1
Lake	3	2	1
Lassen	2	3	1
Los Angeles	3	3	1
Madera	3	2	1
Mariposa	2	3	1
Mendocino	3	2	1
Merced	3	2	1
Modoc	3	2	1
Mono	1	3	2
Monterey	2	3	1
Napa	2	3	1
Nevada	1	3	2
Orange	2	3	1
Placer	2	3	1
Plumas	1	3	2
Riverside	2	3	1
Sacramento	2	3	1
San Benito	3	2	1
San Bernardino	3	3	1
San Diego	3	3	1
San Francisco	2	3	1
San Joaquin	2	3	1
San Luis Obispo	1	3	3
San Mateo	3	2	1
Santa Barbara	1	3	3
Santa Clara	3	3	1
Santa Cruz	3	3	1
Shasta	2	3	1
Sierra	2	3	1
Siskiyou	3	2	1
Solano	2	3	1
Sonoma	3	1	2
Stanislaus	2	3	1
Sutter	2	3	1
Tehama	2	3	1
Trinity	2	3	1
Tulare	1	3	2
Tuolumne	3	3	1
Yolo	2	3	1
Yuba	2	3	1

Table 3.--Relative importance of beaver, mink, and muskrat fur harvest to California.

Rank	Number of counties reporting	% of total counties	Average annual value ($)	% of total value
		Muskrat		
1	43	77	188,483.64	99.6
2	8	14	620.55	0.3
3	6	9	23.22	0.01
		Mink		
1	1	2	9.12	0.2
2	11	19	2,503.04	54.7
3	45	79	2,061.22	45.1
		Beaver		
1	13	23	3,586.48	24.5
2	28	47	9,887.87	67.6
3	16	30	1,159.69	7.9

The mean 1980 income (State of California 1980), the number of licensed trappers during 1980 (California Department of Fish and Game 1981), and the average annual value of the fur harvest for each county was used to calculate the importance of this harvest to the income of individual trappers. The ten counties where trapping of the species made the greatest contribution to a trappers annual income are listed in table 4. The value of the annual harvest of these species appears by inspection to be low for all counties and for California as a whole.

Economic Value and Extent of Riparian Systems

After the counties were ranked according to the value of the harvested species to individual incomes, correlations between the extent of riparian systems in each county and the county's

Table 4.--Average annual value ($) of California trappers' income from harvest of beaver, mink, and muskrat.

County	Average annual value per trapper ($)	Percent of mean 1980 income
Solano	827	6
Colusa	713	7
Yolo	387	4
Glenn	362	3
San Joaquin	261	2
Yuba	243	2
Sutter	235	2
Merced	222	2
Contra Costa	211	1
Butte	179	2
Lassen	85	1
Stanislaus	75	1

rank in terms of average annual value of the fur harvest were examined. Those counties with similar habitats produce fur harvests of similar economic value. These high-ranking counties contain large areas of riparian systems as would be expected.

Information on the extent of riparian systems was available from Katibah et al. (1980) for 41% of the counties considered in this study. The areal extent of all vegetation/coverage classifications except urban and agricultural were summed. These values do not necessarily include all of the riparian vegetation occurring in the county. Nonetheless, an attempt was made to rank the counties, based on this information, according to the number of "riparian" acres found in the county. These ranks were compared with those for economic value (from equation 1), adjusted to the same scale. The average difference in ranks between these two values for all counties was 4.3 positions, with the maximum of 14 for Tehama County and a minimum of 0.

DISCUSSION

The Value of Fur Harvest to Counties

Equation 1 was developed to account for those factors in the fur harvest for which data are available. These factors are the number of animals taken and the quality of fur (reflected in the value). Although this equation accounts for the number of animals taken and the average value of the animals, other variables not accounted for in the equation are known to affect fur harvest. They include:

1. the number and skill of people trapping in a county;

2. the availability of animals;

3. the accessibility and weather conditions of a region;

4. the types and cycles of animal diseases, including rabies, bubonic plague, leptospirosis, tularemia, and distemper; and

5. the seasons set for taking animals.

Data on the number of each species taken in each county, and the statewide average value for each species are available for the 11-year study period. However, if only these data were entered into equation 1, (and variables b, m, and r were set to 1) the equation would account for and the counties would be ranked according to only the differences in the number of animals taken, because the average value data would be the same for each county. The quality of fur would not be taken into account.

The quality of fur is related to the animals' habitat, including such factors as temperature (duration of low temperature), elevation, rainfall, type of food available, and density of animals in an area.[4] Because of the wide range of climates and terrains in which California riparian systems are found, from low desert washes to high mountain meadows, the quality of fur may vary widely enough throughout the state to affect the importance or rank of a county. Thus, equation 1 takes into account differences in the quality of fur between counties. This quality variable is assumed to be independent of the number of animals taken; thus, a county's rank is based on two independent variables: number of pelts taken and the quality of fur.

The quality of a fur is measured in dollars. Higher quality fur is worth more, with the fur market generally controlling demand for the particular species. The standards of quality are defined by the fur market in general and the fur buyer, to whom the pelts are sold, specifically. Standards are defined for each species; species are not judged against each other. The quality of fur produced by a county is measured by an annual county-wide average value.

Data from the DFG on these county-wide average values were available for only 4 years, the 1969 to 1972 seasons. Thus, county-wide average values for 1973 to 1979 seasons had to be derived. First, a ratio was calculated of the average value of the harvest in a county to the statewide average value. Ratios were calculated for each county, species, and year that data were available. The average of these ratios was then calculated. Table 5 shows the ratios for Siskiyou and Plumas counties.

It was expected that the annual ratios would stabilize around a particular point, but this did not necessarily happen. Siskiyou County average values were consistently above the statewide average; the ratios are greater than 1.00. However, Plumas County ratios are consistently above and below the statewide average for beaver and muskrat respectively, and inconsistent for mink.

Assuming that with additional data, the annual ratios would stabilize around a number close to the average of values for 1969 to 1972, these averages were used to derive the annual average values for 1973 to 1979. The average values, as shown in table 5 for Siskiyou and Plumas counties, are represented by variables b, m, and r in equation 1 and are referred to as average value factors.

Several counties reported no harvest of one or more of the species during the 11-year study period. The average value factor for these counties was assigned a value of 0. Other counties

---

[4]Rether, Roger. Certified New York trapper training instructor. Personal conversation.

Table 5.--Sample of factors used to derive average value factors.

	Siskiyou County	Plumas County
Beaver		
1969	1.308	1.045
1970	1.220	1.447
1971	1.301	1.075
1972	1.295	1.092
Average	1.281	1.165
Mink		
1969	1.368	0.893
1970	1.158	1.647
1971	1.289	1.508
1972	1.192	0.946
Average	1.252	1.249
Muskrat		
1969	1.041	0.825
1970	1.081	0.505
1971	1.107	0.893
1972	1.098	0.736
Average	1.082	0.740

reported no harvest during the 1969 to 1972 period but did report during later years. They were assigned the average value factor of a county most alike in terrain and vegetative cover, determined by examining the Aero relief map of California.[5]

The product of an average value factor and a statewide average value for a particular county, species, and year yields the county-wide averge value used in equation 1.

If the fur quality was not accounted for, the values and ranks of some of the counties would not be the same as those obtained in equation 1. Shasta County would, for example, trade places with Butte County. This is not considered significant, as they changed only one position in rank and the degree that Shasta is more important than Butte is only $1,129.83 or 5.6%. However, other counties shifted rank more dramatically. The shift in rank occurred for more than 30% of the counties. Accounting for fur quality in the value and rank of a county is thought to more closely represent the true relative value of a county than if the number of animals taken was the only variable.

---

[5]Aero Service Corporation. 210 E. Courtland Street, Philadelphia, Pennsylvania. Aero relief map of California.

Economic Importance of Species to Counties

The information in table 3 suggests that statewide, muskrat is the most important, beaver is the second most important, and mink is the least important of the three species, although they are not necessarily ranked in that order for each county. Although the average annual value of the species was used to determine their relative importance, it was found that the relative importance of the species is the same whether determined by average value (including fur quality) or by number of animals taken, for all but 14 counties.

A variable not taken into account in determining the relative importance of a species was legal restrictions on fur harvest in a given county. For example, the Fish and Game Code (California Department of Fish and Game 1980-81) lists 14 counties where beaver cannot be taken; however, this restriction was not necessarily in force in these counties during the entire study period. The effects this and other possible legal restrictions have on county and species rank is not known. However, of the 14 counties with restrictions in 1981, beaver ranked third for only nine counties, second for four counties, and first for one county, Santa Barbara.

The information in table 3 also suggests that determining the rank of a county is not necessarily dependent on knowing the value of all animals harvested, but perhaps only the value of the most important animal for that county. To determine if a county's rank is dependent only on the most important species, the counties were ranked according to average annual value, species by species. These rankings were then compared with the ranking shown (for the 10 highest-ranking counties only) in table 1 to identify similarities.

The ranks determined by the average annual value of each species can vary considerably, as shown in table 6 (San Mateo County, which had a rank of 27). It was found that when a county's rank was determined by the species of highest relative importance and when the relative importance was the same regardless of whether or not it was measured by value or number of animals taken, the rank of a county according to that species corresonded within one or two positions of the rank from equation 1 for: Shasta, Butte, Glenn, San Joaquin, Solano, Sutter; Modoc, Yuba, Lassen, Contra Costa, Fresno, Other, Placer, Tehama, Nevada, and Santa Barbara.

Table 6. Rank by value of fur harvest for beaver, mink, and muskrat for San Mateo County.

Rank	Determing factor	Average value
43	Value of beaver	$1.55
36	Value of mink	$2.55
23	Value of muskrat	$440.18

It should be noted that these ranks are determined by an average for an 11-year period. Graphs were prepared for each county which had a continuous harvest for nine or more years, showing number of animals taken and the average annual value for the study period. These graphs were analyzed to better understand the importance of each species to each county, in terms of number of animals, frequency of take, county-wide average value, and number of successful trappers (statewide), to answer the question of what determines its relative importance. An example is presented in figure 1.

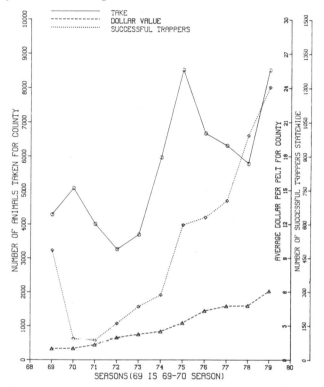

Figure 1.--Plot of fur harvest trends for Shasta County muskrat, 1969-79.

Importance of Harvest to Individuals

The characteristics of an average trapper compiled from a nationwide survey of trappers conducted by Boddicker (1980) at Colorado State University during 1978 and 1979 were examined. Although this was a nationwide survey, I assumed, after consultation with Boddicker, that the results would apply to California. This assumption was verified to the extent the existing data allowed. The results of this survey did not distinguish between those people taking riparian species and those taking other species; however, data could be adjusted to cover only riarian species. This information was used to obtain the average annual value to California trappers of the fur harvest, by county. Some of these values are shown in table 4.

FINDINGS AND CONCLUSIONS

1. Harvest of beaver, mink, and muskrat has been and can continue to be an economically and biologically viable sustained-yield harvest. This harvest has been largely overlooked by conservationists and planners because of: a) lack of information; b) lack of involvement in the harvest by a large segment of the population; and c) lack of interest in conserving these species by a large segment of the population, in part because of the damage they can cause and their nocturnal habits.

Protection of riparian systems can be based in part on economic values of the fur resource component of the system. When planning for conservation of riparian systems, sustained harvest of furbearers should be considered.

2. The rank of a county based on the economic value of fur harvested can, for some counties, be determined by examining only the value of the three species.

3. The economic importance of trapping and fur resources has wide-ranging implications. On a local level, trapping provides residents with additional income, often making a substantial contribution to an individual's livelihood in both an economic and non-economic sense. Fur harvesting of these species has provided up to 7% of an individual's income.

4. Statewide, harvesting beaver, mink, and muskrat is not economically important. It is, however, important to individuals in counties with a lower mean annual income.

5. Statewide, muskrat is the most important, beaver the second, and mink the least important species of the three, in terms of monetary values.

6. Counties with riparian systems of similar extent produce fur harvests of similar economic value. The greater the extent of riparian system, the higher the economic value of the fur harvest.

7. The quality of fur and thus the quality of furbearer habitat does influence the economic value of the fur harvest produced by a county.

LITERATURE CITED

Boddicker, M.L. 1980. Profiles of American trappers and trapping. Proceedings of the first worldwide fur bearers conference. [Frostburg, Maryland, August 1980]. In press.

California Department of Fish and Game. 1969-80. Licensed trappers' report. California Department of Fish and Game, Sacramento, Calif.

California Department of Fish and Game. 1981-82. Fish and Game Code, Section 462.463, 2251.5, 465 Title 14. California Department of Fish and Game, Sacramento.

California Department of Fish and Game. 1981. List of 1981 licensed trappers, Department of Fish and Game, Sacramento.

Katibah, E.F., N.E. Nedeff, and K.J. Dummer. 1980. Areal and linear extent of riparian vegetation in the Central Valley of California. Final report to the California Department of Fish and Game, Sacramento. Remote Sensing Research Program, University of California, Berkeley.

Kellert, S.R. 1979. Public attitudes toward critical wildlife and natural habitat issues. Phase I (final report). 148 p. Yale University, School of Forestry and Environmental Studies, New Haven, Conn.

Nelson, Lewis, Jr., and Jon K. Hooper. 1976. California fur bearers and their management. Leaflet 2721, Cooperative Extension, University of California, Berkeley.

State of California. 1980. California Statistical Abstract.

New York Department of Environmental Conservation. About fur bearers and trapping in New York. Albany, N.Y.

US Department of Commerce. 1981. Facts about the United States fur industry. Voice of the Trapper July 1981.

USDI Fish and Wildlife Service. 1971. Fur catch in the United States, 1970 wildlife. Leaflet 497, USDI Fish and Wildlife Service, Washington, D.C.

COMPATIBILITY OF BIOFUEL PRODUCTION
WITH WILDLIFE HABITAT ENHANCEMENT[1]

John Disano, Bertin W. Anderson, Julie K. Meents,

and Robert D. Ohmart[2]

Abstract.--A stand of native cottonwood trees (Populus fremontii) with hedges of quail bush (Atriplex lentiformis) would attract high avian densities and diversities. Densities and diversities of birds and rodents reached above-average levels for riparian vegetation in the lower Colorado River valley within two years from planting on two experimental plots and within one year on a third plot. The rapid growth rate of native trees and the acceptance of revegetated areas by wildlife, in conjunction with the current demand for wood as fuel, suggests that the two objectives are compatible and the latter can be economically productive.

INTRODUCTION

Since 1977 we have been studying the feasibility of reintroducing native riparian vegetation along the lower Colorado River. Previously, there was virtually no information about the environmental conditions necessary for growth or survival rates of native plant species used in revegetation. We have also studied the densities and diversities of wildlife species associated with the reintroduced vegetation.

The objectives of this report are to discuss: 1) environmental conditions which lead to greatest productivity of trees; 2) the economic potentials of tree farming; and 3) a planting and harvest rotation design which would be compatible with wildlife enhancement.

FACTORS AFFECTING GROWTH AND SURVIVAL OF TREES

We planted about 2,000 trees of four species in February 1979 on a riparian zone dredge-spoil site along the Colorado River about 16 km. south of Blythe (Riverside County), California. The ensuing discussion is based on generalizations

---

[1]Paper presented at the California Riparian Systems Conference. [University of California, Davis, September 17-19, 1981].

[2]John Disano is Research Biologist, Bertin W. Anderson is Faculty Research Associate, Julie K. Meents is Research Biologist, and Robert D. Ohmart is Associate Director; all are at the Center for Environmental Studies, Arizona State University, Tempe, Arizona.

drawn from data collected from growth of those trees. Details of this study have been presented elsewhere (Anderson and Ohmart 1981a). Anderson and others will present details concerning the growth of cottonwood (Populus fremontii) elsewhere in these proceedings (Anderson et al. 1983).

Importance of Tillage

Tillage is defined as breaking up and mixing the soil. In this case tillage was provided with a power auger or backhoe at each tree planting site. When planted in sandy soil, cottonwood and willow (Salix gooddingii) trees grew to an average height of 5 m. within 680 days of planting if the saplings were provided with tillage to a depth of 3 m. (fig. 1). With no tillage, growth averaged less than 2 m. The advantage of deep tillage is that it permits rapid root penetration to the water table. The effect of deep tillage was not pronounced during the first six months, but thereafter saplings with deep tillage rapidly outgrew those without tillage (fig. 1). Tillage also affected survival of the trees. Among 112 trees planted with no tillage, 43 (38%) died by the end of the second growing season; among 772 trees provided with tillage to 3 m., 20 (<3%) died. Tillage to 3 m. was the single most important factor affecting growth and survival in our study.

Other Factors Affecting Growth

Competition

Competition from other vegetation, which invaded tree planting sites as a result of irriga-

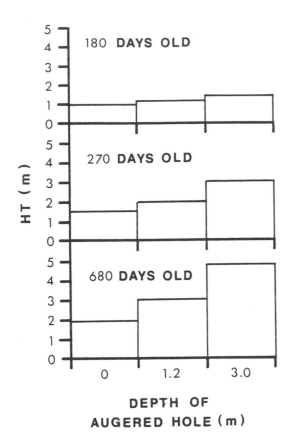

Figure 1.--Effect of tillage on growth of cotton-wood trees at three time intervals after planting in sandy soil along the lower Colorado River.

tion, seriously affected growth and survival of trees. Among 77 willow and honey mesquite (Prosopis glandulosa) trees planted with tillage to 3 m. which received moderate to severe competiton from Bermuda grass (Cynodon dacty-lon), Russian thistle (Salsola iberica), and smotherweed (Bassia hyssopifolia), 35 (45%) had died after two growing seasons, and growth of the survivors was significantly less than in areas where trees had little competitive interference.

Control of weeds potentially involves one of the greatest expenses associated with tree farming. This can be minimized if trees are planted in areas where the surface soil is very sandy, at least to a depth of 1 m. Competing species have difficulty becoming established because of the high temperatures and extremely dry conditions typical of surface sand.

Soil Density

Tree growth decreased as soil density in-creased below a depth of 1 m., even when tillage was to 3 m. and competitive vegetation was absent (Anderson and Ohmart 1981a). As the soil inclu-ded more clay, tree mortality also increased. We recommend that tree farming not be attempted in dense soils, especially those containing significant amounts of clay.

Length of Irrigation Period

Growth rates were maximum and survival approached 100% when planting was in sandy soil, tillage was to 3 m., and irrigation was continued for 150 days at 30-40 l. of water per day. As soil density and competition from other vegeta-tion increased, longer periods of irrigation were necessary (ibid.).

AVIAN USE OF RIPARIAN VEGETATION

Value of Trees

In our studies of avian use of riparian vege-tation along the lower Colorado River, we found that high avian density and species richness were consistently associated with stands of cottonwood and willow trees (Anderson and Ohmart 1981a,b; 1983). This was especially true for insectivor-ous bird species (fig. 2). Doves were attracted more to stands of mesquite trees (fig. 2). Frugi-vorous birds were virtually absent in stands of cottonwood and willow, but were primarily asso-ciated with honey mesquite. This, however, was not because of any intrinsic value of mesquite iself. Honey mesquite is parasitized by mistle-toe (Phoradendron californicum) to a greater extent than other species of trees along the lower Colorado River. Frugivorous birds eat main-ly mistletoe fruit (Anderson and Ohmart 1978).

Value of Shrub-like Vegetation

The term shrub-like refers to herbaceous vegetation such as Russian thistle, smotherweed, inkweed (Suaeda torreyana), and quail bush (Atriplex lentiformis). To examine the value of shrubs and shrub-like vegetation to birds, we compared three revegetation sites with varying shrub densities and composition. On one site shrub density was about one shrub per ha. Rus-sian thistle and smotherweed reached densities of about 1,500 mature plants per ha. on a second site; quail bush and inkweed reached a combined density of 1,500 plants per ha. on a third site. All three areas had cottonwood and willow trees 3-7 m. tall, planted at a density of about 20 trees per ha. The combined density of all other tree species was less than one per ha.

Densities (number per 40 ha.) of various groups of birds on the revegetation sites were compared with the average bird densities in natu-ral riparian vegetation along the lower Colorado River. These densities are expressed in standard units; thus, the average density for riparian vegetation is zero; positive and negative numbers indicate values above and below average, respec-tively.

When herbaceous vegetation was sparse, all avian groups except passerine granivores had below-average densities (fig. 3A). When herba-

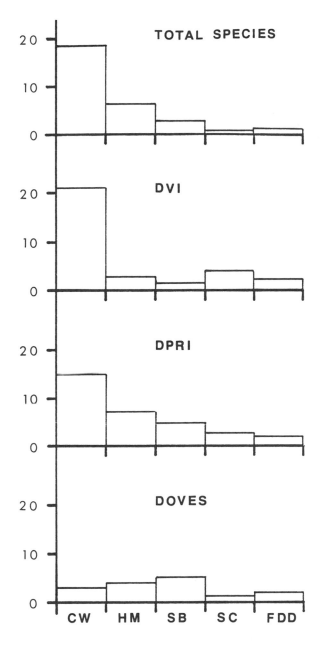

VEGETATION VARIABLES

Figure 2.—Number of times various vegetation variables were included as a step in a significant multiple linear regression equation (Y-axis). Maximum value possible for Y-axis is 25 (5 seasons for 5 years). DVI—density of visiting insectivores; DPRI—density of permanent resident insectivores; CW—number of cottonwood/willow trees; HM—honey mesquite; SB—screwbean mesquite; and SC—salt cedar per 0.4 ha; FDD—foliage density and diversity at 0-0.6 m.

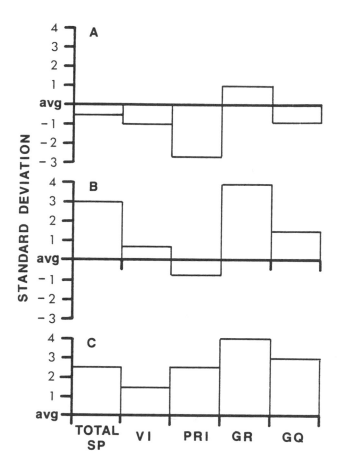

Figure 3.—Populations of various avian groups associated with various kinds and densities of shrubs, other variables being equal. A. Very low density. B. Shrubs abundant, primarily Russian thistle and smotherweed. C. Shrubs abundant, primarily quail bush and inkweed. Avian densities are expressed in standard deviation units where the mean was for all riparian vegetation-types found in the lower Colorado River valley. TOTAL SP—total species; VI—density of visiting insectivores; PRI—density of permanent resident insectivores; GR—density of passerine granivores; and GQ—density of Gambel Quail.

ceous vegetation consisted of Russian thistle and smotherweed, avian species richness and densities of passerine granivores and Gambel Quail (_Lophortyx gambelii_) were above average, but densities of insectivores were about average (fig. 3B). When herbaceous vegetation consisted of quail bush and inkweed, all bird groups were above average, although visiting insectivores were near average (fig. 3C).

We conclude from these data that an area can be maximally enhanced for birds if cottonwood and willow trees, and shrubs such as quail bush and inkweed are planted. Dove densities would probably be somewhat below average, and frugivores would be absent unless honey mesquite with mistletoe was also present. Cavity-nesting bird species, including woodpeckers, Lucy's Warbler (_Vermivora luciae_), Ash-throated Flycatcher (_Myiarchus cinerascens_), and Wied Crested Flycatcher (_Myiarchus tyrannulus_) would be present in very low densities.

PROFITS FROM FARMING

It has been shown that the trees grow rapidly and that tree farms could be attractive to wildlife, especially birds. By the end of the fourth growing season, trees grown in relatively sandy soil with tillage to 3 m. and competitive vegetation controlled will yield about one cord of wood per tree. In the Colorado River area one cord of wood sells for $80-$100 per cord (Fairbank 1980). We estimate a total production cost of $60 per tree, not including land rental or purchase. This estimate includes expenditures for management, labor and secretarial needs, moderate clearing and leveling requirements, irrigation system purchase, installation, and maintenance for 150 days, as well as harvest and transportation costs. An area planted with trees centered at 6 m., a 10% mortality rate, no harvest until the fourth year, which is then harvested at a rate of 40-60 ha. annually would yield a profit approaching $1 million in 12 years of operation if the wood was sold at $80 per cord (fig. 4). We believe our cost and mortality estimates are somewht high and the value per cord conservative. Our cost-income estimates are based on the design in figure 5.

Honey mesquite wood is valued at twice as much per cord as cottonwood and willow (_ibid._), but honey mesquite trees grow much more slowly.

Nonetheless, because of their economic value, honey mesquite trees would be an important species in a tree-farming operation.

After first cutting, trees will sucker at the root crown without additional irrigation if the water table is 4.6 m. or less from the surface. We assume that biomass production in the four years after the first cutting will be decreased by 50%. This may be a conservative estimate because we have obtained greater growth rates after trees have been harvested than from initial plantings. However, our data are for only one year. If this high growth rate continued for four years, the profits indicated here might also prove conservative. The main disadvantages of tree farming are the high initial costs and the relatively long period until first returns on the investment.

ROTATION OF HARVEST

A large variety of planting and harvest schemes are possible. We present only one for the purposes of discussion.

It is desirable to develop a tree farm so that the entire area is not harvested at one time. This would increase the diversity of vegetation height and foliage density on the area. If habitat values for wildlife are to be enhanced, it is also desirable to plant shrubs. Planting shrubs introduces extra costs, but will greatly enhance the area for wildlife.

Shrubs also have practical value. For example, it is desirable to have fire lanes;

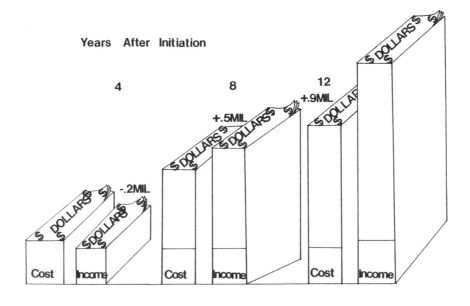

Figure 4.--Profit estimates for a tree farm encompassing 160 ha. over a 12-year period. See text for assumptions concerning expenses and income. Mil = millions of dollars.

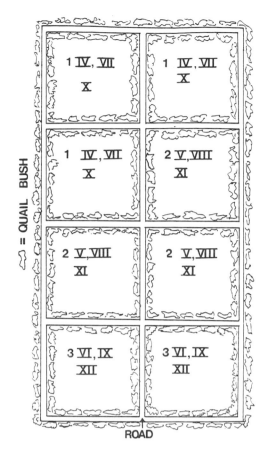

= QUAIL BUSH

ROAD

Figure 5.--A plan for planting and harvesting trees on a 160-ha. plot. The plot is divided into eight subplots of 20 ha. each. Arabic numerals represent year of planting; Roman numerals represent the year of harvest; e.g., 1, IV, VII, and X in one block mean that the first block would be planted the first year and harvested the fourth, seventh, and tenth years after planting.

these can include roads bounded by hedges of quail bush. Quail bush is an evergreen species and is fire resistant. Once established, quail bush is a vigorous competitor and will reduce costs associated with controlling invasion by salt cedar (Tamarix chinensis) and annual weeds (fig. 5). Dried annuals and the large volume of litter produced by the deciduous salt cedar greatly increase fire hazards.

The cottonwood community development envisioned includes planting trees on 38% of the area each of the first two years and 24% the third year. In the fourth year the first trees would be harvested (fig. 5). With this rotation there would be four-year-old trees 10-15 m. tall with relatively open areas, attractive to quail and doves. On our revegetation sites, trees of this height attracted, among others, Northern Orioles (Icterus galbula) and breeding Yellow-billed Cuckoos (Coccyzus americanus), a species listed as endangered in California. The combination of trees and quail bush would attract above-

average densities and diversities of birds in all seasons. If some trees four or five years of age were not harvested but were killed by girdling, the area would also become attractive to at least a few cavity-nesting species.

ACKNOWLEDGMENTS

We wish to thank Jeannie Anderson, Susan M. Cook, Jane R. Durham, Dr. Julie K. Meents, and Cindy D. Zisner for editorial assistance. Marcelett Ector and Cindy D. Zisner typed the numerous drafts of the manuscript. Elaine Hassinger and Julie Huff prepared the illustrations. We are grateful to Dr. F. Aljibury, Les Ede, and Jule Meyer, University of California Agricultural Extension Service, Riverside California, for their advice and cooperation. Ronald Gass, Mountain States Wholesales Nursery, Phoenix, Arizona, kindly provided many trees. The work was jointly funded by the USDI Bureau of Reclamation and the USDI Fish and Wildlife Service Contract No. 7-07-30-V0009.

LITERATURE CITED

Anderson, B.W., J. Disano, D.L. Brooks, and R.D. Ohmart. 1983. Mortality and growth of cottonwood on dredge-spoil. In: R.E. Warner and K.M. Hendrix (ed.). California Riparian Systems. [University of California, Davis, September 17-19, 1981.] University of California Press, Berkeley.

Anderson, B.W., and R.D. Ohmart. 1978. Phainopepla utilization of honey mesquite forests in the Colorado River valley. Condor 80:334-338.

Anderson, B.W., and R.D. Ohmart. 1981a. Vegetation management final report. In preparation. USDI Bureau of Reclamation, Boulder City, Nevada.

Anderson, B.W., and R.D. Ohmart. 1981b. Agricultural final report. In preparation. USDI Bureau of Reclamation, Boulder City, Nevada.

Anderson, B.W., and R.D. Ohmart. 1983. Avian use of revegetated riparian zones. In: R.E. Warner and K.M. Hendrix (ed.). California Riparian Systems. [University of California, Davis, September 17-19, 1981.] University of California Press, Berkeley.

Fairbank, W.C. 1980. On biofuel for air conditioning: a preliminary evaluation of using mesquite for powering residential and small commercial air conditioning systems in the Colorado River Desert. 9 p. Cooperative Extension, University of California, Riverside, Calif.

CONSIDERATIONS OF RIPARIAN BIOMASS

FOR MANAGEMENT AS AN ENERGY SOURCE[1]

Gary Brittner[2]

Abstract.--The biomass resource of riparian zones has potential for management for production of many products including energy. Riparian zones have been too long ignored for this potential. More intensive management of this important resource is needed to realize these benefits. A balanced approach is needed; environmental concerns need to be addressed.

INTRODUCTION

As described in the Conference announcement, the State's riparian systems are productive in many ways, but there is much we still need to find out about them. Our knowledge of the systems could tolerate improvement. Our current management, or as some may insist, mismanagement, of riparian systems could be better organized. Better management would bring about greater benefits from all resource areas.

Riparian systems are particularly important from the standpoint of renewable resources. Throughout much of California, the limiting factor for vegetation growth is water. Water is one common denominator among riparian systems and is the primary element that makes these systems so productive. From the forest production standpoint, riparian environments are especially important. These sites are usually most productive since the moisture requirements of fast-growing mesic plants are satisfied.

RIPARIAN WOOD PRODUCTS

Fiber

The fiber resource of riparian areas outside of commercial timberland is not well documented. These sites have great potential for wood production, but little effort has been focused in this direction. Wood demand is constantly rising in California; demand for wood products will triple in 50 years. The land base for commercial timber is constantly shrinking due to conversion to other uses: residential expansion, road construction, parks, and power line rights-of-way.

To meet the increasing demand we will have to grow more fiber on fewer acres, look for alternative products, and recycle. Another solution to ease the problem is to manage our productive riparian zones more intensively. Getting more wood from these underutilized sites would ease some of the pressures on commercial timberlands.

The fiber resource of riparian zones is not only important for traditional products like lumber and chips for pulp, but also has great value for energy production. Plants are solar energy collectors and this energy can be harnessed through combustion.

Fuel

In California, there are over 124 megawatts of wood-fired power generated yearly, or enough power to meet the needs of a city of 75,000. By 1985, the figure is expected to jump to 625 megawatts. By the year 2000 we expect over 1140 megawatts to be produced in this way.[3] According to the American Pulpwood Association, on a national scale wood supplies more energy now than does nuclear power.[4]

Use of wood has many beneficial aspects. It is clean-burning and, unlike petro-fuels, does not produce noxious compounds; is a renewable resource; decreases our demand for foreign oil imports; stimulates local economies; and helps us to conserve our own finite resources.

MANAGEMENT POTENTIALS

To develop the wood resource, there are a number of management schemes that can be

---

[1]Paper presented at the California Riparian Systems Conference. [University of California, Davis, September 17-19, 1981].

[2]Gary Brittner is Forrester II, California Department of Forestry, Sacramento, Calif.

[3]California Department of Forestry. 1981. Wood energy in California. 150p. Sacramento, Calif.

[4]American Pulpwood Association. August, 1981. Pulpwood highlights.

employed, depending upon the needs and desires of the owner or manager. One new approach is termed short-rotation intensive silviculture. Trees are essentially farmed for fiber in a short period of time, 2-8 years. This is a marked contrast to the longer rotations commonly associated with saw timber with a minimum rotation of about 40 years. Short-rotation intensive silviculture planting stocks are usually exotics, hybrids, or superior phenotypes that have been selected for breeding. Fertilizers, herbicides, and cultivation are used to accelerate crop growth. This management technique is one extreme of the spectrum and it is doubtful it should become a common practice in riparian zones. The other extreme is to totally ignore the resource and let the trees grow in a totally unmanaged state. This would be wasteful, and in a world of increasing demand on dwindling resources, is unacceptable. A balanced system between these two approaches is needed.

Manipulation of the fiber resource of riparian zones would provide many benefits. Increased planting on stream banks and flood-plains can have positive effects on erosion control and stream bank protection, and make a contribution to the wood supply. Hardwoods are the main component in most riparian vegetation outside of commercial timberland zones. In California, the hardwood manufacturing industry is largely undeveloped and is likely to grow in coming years. Hardwood products include lumber for cabinets, furniture, pallets, ties, dunnage, chips for pulp, hog fuel for energy production, and firewood.

Clearing dense riparian growth can improve access to rivers and lakes for the benefit of recreationists for fishing, camping, swimming, and other activities. Planting and harvesting operations can be coordinated with wildlife managers to alter habitats for the improvement of animal populations. Also, more intensive management of the fiber should include fuel management activities to decrease potential for the spread of wildfire.

A well-orchestrated management plan for the riparian fiber resource would have many positive impacts on a variety of resources as I have briefly outlined. Implementation of this type of management does not require any exotic techniques or untried schemes. Application of existing methods would result in better utilization of the fiber resource.

THE WOOD ENERGY PROGRAM

The California Department of Forestry's Wood Energy Program is actively seeking ways to improve utilization of wood for the production of energy. Some of the pilot programs offer various means to improve the quality of the riparian fiber resource, and ways to utilize it.

Biomass Demonstration Projects

We are in the process of selecting sites for a number of biomass tree farming demonstration projects. This program was established by the Legislature to locate lands suitable for biomass farming, and determine which trees and plants are most suitable for high net energy yields. Care must be taken not to interfere with efficient use of forest and food crop lands. We will be researching the silvicultural techniques necessary to produce tree crops and identify and resolve problem areas in order to facilitate implementation of biomass farming by the private sector. Other products besides fiber and fuel will be identified. The program will be administered statewide, so we should be able to gather management information that will have applicability to many different covertypes. This information will be extremely valuable for management on all California lands.

Mobile Wood Densifier

In response to needs for better fuel management and utilization of wood waste, such as logging slash, precommercial thinnings, and cull trees, the Department has begun construction of a mobil wood densifier. The densifier will produce densified wood cubes at a rate of 1.5 tons per hour. The wood cubes can be substituted for charcoal briquets in barbeques and campfires, and for logs in fireplaces and wood heaters, and provide an excellent fuel for biomass burners and gasification.

Any clean woody substance is acceptable raw material for densification. The material is processed first by reduction through a tub-grinder. The shredded material is then passed through a modified hay cuber to produce the briquets. The Department of Forestry has contracted with the Papakube Corporation of San Diego to build the unit. Field testing should begin in the first quarter of 1982. This machine will be able to utilize woody material that has in the past been wasted, and turn it into a useable product. The machine will be valuable because it can consume as raw material, lower quality trees that are frequently associated with riparian zones. This project should help demonstrate the importance of looking at all biomass forms as potential resources.

Biomass Processing Technology

Technology to process biomass into more useful energy forms such as alcohol, fuel, and chemicals is proceeding at a rapid pace, yet the vast biomass resource remains largely untapped. Development of the resource is hindered by the need for economical harvesting methods. Currently there is no economical way to cut, collect, and transport biomass resources, such as logging slash, chaparral, and small hardwood species. To expedite a solution to the problem, the Department of Forestry proposes to work with university engineers and private industry, to fund research to develop machinery for the job.

The Department will take a leadership role in this field to make sure development takes into consideration the environmental impacts which can result from harvesting. Mechanical equipment will be designed to have minimum impact on the land. This is a very worthwhile project. It will shorten the length of time needed for technology and the resource to mesh and will lessen the demand for the other energy sources upon which we now rely. These biomass harvesting systems to be developed could be useful for harvesting in sensitive riparian zones.

ENVIRONMENTAL CONCERNS

Before we plunge headlong into widespread harvesting of biomass, many environmental concerns must be addressed. Thorough studies of the environmental consequences of our proposed activities should be undertaken on a variety of natural system types. Such studies will help us avoid deleterious impacts. This is especially true for the fragile and fertile riparian zones. It is important to analyze what effects harvesting will have on nutrient cycling, plant succession, bank stability, wildlife populations, recreation, and other resources. These considerations are important aspects of a coherent management system. The Department will consider these items as we work together to provide management for this important productive resource.

RECREATION PLANNING AS A TOOL TO RESTORE AND PROTECT

RIPARIAN SYSTEMS[1]

Kenneth E. Martin[2]

Abstract.--This paper examines planning strategies which assure the protection of riparian systems while providing for recreation use. A riparian forest adjacent to a densely populated area and subject to intensive recreation use is investigated. The popular recreation activities that occur in connection with a riparian system are identified and methods for controlling recreation use are discussed.

INTRODUCTION

Recreation suppliers at all levels of government can successfully provide facilities and opportunities while minimizing adverse impacts on especially susceptible resource elements such as riparian forests and wildlife populations. These protections can only be provided when planners and managers are sensitive to the fragility of natural systems and use proven or innovative visitor control techniques.

Jurisdictions and agencies must remain committed to protecting riparian areas while also providing for recreation opportunities. Agency commitment will occur when there is public support (Smith 1977). Such public support will only be gained if the public has an opportunity to experience and enjoy riparian areas. An example of this was recently described in an article by Marjie Lambert on the South Fork of the American River (SOFAR) project. "A half dozen groups including the American River Recreation Association and the State Department of Boating and Waterways filed protests [over the proposed project] with the [State] Water Resources Control Board because of the impact reduced flows [on the South Fork of the American River] could have on recreation and aesthetics".[3] This example demonstrates that as more people have a greater awareness of riparian areas and their values, the greater will be their indignation at the destruction of our remnant riparian forests.

RIPARIAN SYSTEMS ARE ATTRACTIVE RECREATION SITES

California riparian systems provide a variety of recreation opportunities, are physically attractive, have a diverse set of plants and animals, have convenient access, and in summer these areas are generally cooler and more pleasant than the adjacent uplands (Roberts et al 1977). Because of this, large numbers of people are attracted to these areas to participate in many of California's most popular recreation activities. Riparian systems are found in many different settings; those most accessible to urban areas receive the greatest recreation use (Geidel and Moore 1981). Therefore, a portion of the American River Parkway that is highly accessible to people in the Sacramento area was chosen as a case study. Observations were made by the author over a period of three months, from June through August 1981.

INTENSIVE RECREATION USE

There are two major recreation access points to the American River in the vicinity of Howe and Watt avenues. The areas adjacent to these access points contain sections of riparian forest that are in easy reach of over 1,020,000 people.[4] Of these, 84,000 live within a two-mile radius of these two sites. The popularity of these areas is revealed in an on-site use survey conducted by the County of Sacramento. Together, both access points accommodated in excess of 300,000 visitor days from March 1978 to March 1979 (table 1). Interviews with park personnel and my personal observations reveal that the greatest amount of this use takes place within 46-91 m. (50-100 yd.)

[1]Paper presented at the California Riparian Systems Conference. [University of California, Davis, September 17-19, 1981].
[2]Kenneth E. Martin is Supervisor, Statewide Comprehensive Outdoor Recreation Planning Unit, California Department of Parks and Recreation, Sacramento.
[3]Sacramento Bee. August 18, 1981. River project sponsors seek accord with foes.

[4]California Department of Finance, Population Research Unit. Population estimates for Counties, Report 80 E-2.

of the access points and parking areas.[5] This, of course, does not consider instream uses such as rafting, canoeing, and kayaking or the use of the bicycle trail; it describes the land-based recreation use generated by a typical occupant entering the area by vehicle. Even though there is heavy recreation use, the adjacent riparian forest remains attractive.

RIPARIAN VEGETATION AND WILDLIFE

Beyond 46-91 m. of the Howe and Watt Avenue access points, the full diversity of riparian plant and animal associations can be found. Cottonwood, ash, and willows in combination with wild grape, blackberry, wild rose, and other vegetation are essentially in an undisturbed condition. Wildlife is abundant. Beaver, muskrat, and waterfowl can be observed throughout the Howe and Watt Avenue portion of the American River Parkway[6] (fig. 1).

Some access points along the river do show impacts resulting from recreation use. Obvious erosion is in evidence at the popular put-in and take-out sites for boaters particiating in rafting, canoeing, and kayaking. Because these are essentially instream uses, the impact on the shoreside terrestrial areas is minimal and limited to launching and retrieval areas (fig. 2). Popular trails have exposed soil, but this is a localized condition and frequently involves no more than a narrow footpath through a portion of the riverside vegetation.

Table 1.--American River Parkway, Sacramento County, visitor use survey: survey period March 1978 to March 1979.

	Cars	People per car	Total people entering by car	Entry other than vehicle	Total number of visitors
Ancil Hoffman Park					
(San Lorenzo Way)	92,760	1.91	177,172	14,798	191,970
(Tarshes Way)	185,357	1.96	363,300	15,491	378,791
Discovery Park	238,789	2.12	506,233	14,256	520,489
Goethe Park	115,115	2.43	279,729	21,931	301,660
Watt Avenue	83,009	2.04	169,338	18,062	187,400
Lower Sunrise	81,318	2.20	178,900	4,216	183,116
Howe Avenue	65,457	2.01	131,569	11,467	143,036
Sacramento Bar	56,764	2.28	129,422	17,727	147,149
Sailor Bar					
(Illinois Avenue)	33,710	1.84	62,026	3,191	65,217
(Olive Avenue)	18,375	1.90	34,913	7,430	42,343
Upper Sunrise	34,599	1.93	66,776	16,998	83,774
Hazel Avenue	28,250	1.87	52,828	15,664	68,492
El Manto	26,642	2.10	55,948	15,351	71,299
Roosmoor Bar	21,160	2.00	42,320	8,135	50,455
Sarah Court	18,920	1.80	34,056	11,456	45,512
Ambassador	4,542	1.29	5,859	7,523	13,382
Totals	1,104,767		2,290,389	203,696	2,494,085

[5]Rominger, Gary, 1981. Personal conversation. Chief Ranger, American River Parkway, Sacramento County Park Department, Sacramento, California.
[6]Ingles, Steve, 1981. Personal conversation. Manager, Effie Yeaw Interpretive Center, American River Parkway, Sacramento County Park Department, Sacramento, California.

Figure 1.--Resident and migratory waterfowl along with other
wildlife on the American River can be found within easy
access of over 1 million people.

VISITOR CONTROL THROUGH DESIGN

Sensitivity to the need for protection of the riparian resource along with the application of good design techniques can be effective in reducing the impact of recreation facilities and use (fig. 3). A key element in the development of that sensitivity comes from interest exhibited by elected officials; and their interest will be stimulated when there is public support.

Before protecting of resource, however, planners should consider it essential to complete a comprehensive resource inventory. Such inventories are presently compiled by the California Department of Parks and Recreation (DPR). Areas extremely sensitive to recreation use should be mapped and recommended for protection; areas more tolerant to recreation use should also be identified. The intensity of recreation use that can be accommodated should be established. The level of demand that exists for certain activities should also be determined, and an assessment of facilities to accommodate those activities should be made. If deficiencies exist, then a planner should develop alternative ways of providing for the projected use. Techniques are available to

the site planner for minimizing the impact of use on a sensitive resource (Geidel and Moore 1981). Some subtle and direct controls are discussed below.

Subtle Controls

Among the subtle controls available to the planner to minimize use impact on a sensitive site are the following.

1. Route trails away from sensitive resources.
2. Place vehicle parking lots and access points away from environmentally sensitive areas which are to be preserved.
3. Establish natural barriers between sensitive resources and areas planned for intensive use.
4. Determine carrying capacity of an area and control use by collecting fees, issuing permits, use permits, and limiting the size of visitor facilities.

Direct Controls

Among the direct controls available to the planner are the following.

Figure 2.--Intensive use at popular access points prevents
natural restoration of riparian vegetation.

1. Encourage desired behavior through interpretive facilities and signs that describe acceptable limits of use, e.g., "Boats 5 MPH," "No
Motor Vehicles Beyond This Point."

2. Place physical barriers such as gates and
fencing which can be effective and in some cases
unobtrusive, in controlling those who ignore
signs.

FUTURE RECREATION DEMAND

California's population will continue to
grow. Increased pressure from recreationists
will affect recreation areas statewide, and riparian systems will not escape that additional pressure (ibid.) (fig. 4).

Those responsible for managing the recreational use of riparian systems must remain aware
of those activities that have the least impact on
the riparian zone. These include such water-
dependent uses as rafting, kayaking, and canoeing
which occur most frequently on weekends and holi-
days during the summer. Other than at access and
take-out points, these uses do little or no
damage to the riparian vegetation.

Passive recreation activities that are considered water-enhanced, such as nature study, sight-
seeing, fishing, hiking, sunbathing, and swimming, often have little or no permanent impact on
the riparian forest. Speedboating, jet skiing,
and off-road vehicle use are more intensive uses
and have caused some erosive damage to shoreline
and other riparian forest areas.

Figure 3.--The proper location of access points and parking lots can restrict the related intensive use without adversely affecting the riparian vegetation. (Photo courtesy of Sacramento County Park Department.)

The initial findings of the recently completed Statewide Needs Analysis conducted by DPR reveal that participation in the recreation activities described above and considered water-dependent will increase by 17% by 1990. Participation in those activities considered water-enhanced will increase by 21% (fig. 5, table 2).

Richard Warner has pointed out that the "...needs of riparian systems have been seriously 'neglected' by federal, state, and local agencies in the past.... Indeed, some agency programs are so designed that riparian system destruction is inevitable, either a) deliberately (e.g., the so-called 'phreatophyte control' schemes), or b) incidentally (dams, diversion schemes, structural bank protection, channelization, 'clean' farming" (Warner 1979).

A significant portion of California's remaining riparian systems exist today because they have been designated and managed as a recreation resource.

POLICY CONSIDERATIONS

No single agency or level of government is responsible for protecting riparian systems. Integrated programs that reinforce sound policies must be encouraged among all agencies having land-managing responsibilities. Some policies successful in the past or recently enacted are discussed below.

Figure 4.--Instream recreation use is becoming increasingly popular on the lower American River. (Photo courtesy of Sacramento County Park Department.)

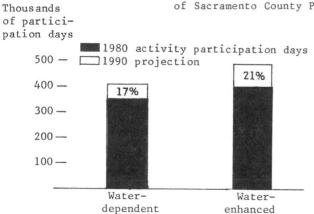

Figure 5.--Projected increases in water-dependent and water-enhanced recreation activities. (Source: Recreation patterns study, Statewide Recreation Needs Analysis, DPR.)

Federal Policies

At the federal level, the USDI National Park Service (NPS), USDI Bureau of Land Management (BLM), USDA Forest Service (FS), USDI Fish and Wildlife Service (FWS), and others with responsibility for providing recreation opportunities all have policies supporting the preservation and rehabilitation of unique environments while utilizing them for recreation.

The NPS policy for preserving natural zones states that "natural resources and processes remain largely unaltered by human activity except for approved developments essential for management, use and appreciation of the park" (USDI National Park Service 1975). The NPS is guided in the rehabilitation of natural zones by the following policies:

Table 2.--Statewide projections for selected individual recreation activities. (Source: Recreation patterns study, Statewide Recreation Needs Analysis, DPR).

	1980	1990
Water-dependent		
Swimming and beach-related	256,823	297,153
Fishing	53,719	64,186
Boating	47,082	58,727
Waterfowl hunting	1,706	1,877
	359,330	421,943
Water-Enhanced		
Nature appreciation	70,460	85,197
Visiting scenic areas	58,862	72,490
Picnicking	97,529	114,864
Camping	61,652	76,476
Hiking and backpacking	61,803	74,189
Sunning	57,278	68,245
	407,584	491,461

Removal of man-made features, restoration of natural gradients, and revegetation with native park species on acquired inholdings and sites from which park development is to be removed.
Rehabilitation and maintenance of areas impacted by visitor use including, if necessary, the redesign, relocation, removal--or the provision--of facilities to avoid or to ameliorate adverse visitor impacts.
Restoration to a natural appearance of areas disturbed by fire control activities.
Restoration of landscapes, altered by human activities before park establishment, to a natural appearing state (ibid.).

Further, in developed areas of the National Park System, landscape and vegetation are planned and managed to "the greatest extent possible with the purpose of a given park. The landscape and vegetation should be managed to effect the transition between park development and the terrain, biota, and physical appearance of surrounding management zones commensurate with the requirements and impacts of visitor use" (ibid.).

The NPS strategy for river use, including riparian shorelines, is to be in accordance with the following:

In order to enhance visitor enjoyment and safety, and to preserve environmental quality, the National Park Service will regulate the use of rivers, as necessary, within units of the National Park System.
Using scientific research, the Service will establish the level of boating and related use that each river system can sustain without causing unacceptable changes in the ecosystem or degradation of the environment or the park experience.
A river management plan will be developed for each appropriate unit of the National Park System as an integral part of the resources management plan...(ibid.)

Federal policy support for the protection of natural systems and their use for recreation and other purposes is also found in the FS draft Regional Land and Resource Management Plan (USDA Forest Service 1981), individual FS land-use plans, specific resource area plans, and published proceedings; US Army Corps of Engineers (CE) resource development guidelines, rules and regulations, and site-specific plans; and several BLM plans and guidelines such as the California Desert Area Conservation Plan (USDI Bureau of Land Management 1980), and Recreational Carrying Capacity in the California Desert (USDI Bureau of Land Management 1978).

State Policies

Although California has developed a basic wetlands protection policy, there is currently no comprehensive state policy for riparian area rehabilitation and preservation. However, there are numerous state policies guiding the recreation use of natural areas (riparian systems and other unique or sensitive environments).

Among the state policies for recreation are:

Policy No. 3--It is state policy that, in meeting the recreation needs of people, their experience shall be enhanced through the appropriate and sensitive use of natural, historic, and human resources and environments that serve as the source or backdrop for recreation activity. Such resources shall be enhanced, conserved, and protected for the enjoyment and appreciation of present and future generations.

Policy No. 6--It is state policy that lands in public ownership that have recreation potential be considered for availability and accessibility to the people for their recreation, use, and enjoyment, when such activities do not unduly impair the quality of the natural and cultural resources.

Policy No. 9--It is state policy that the interpretation of natural, historic, and archeological resources as recreation resources shall be given high priority in all appropriate state-operated and state-influenced programs (California Department of Parks and Recreation 1982).

More specific natural systems protection policy is found in the Resources Management Directives for the DPR (California Department of Parks and Recreation 1979) [Appendix A], and the 1980 State Park System Plan (California Department of Parks and Recreation 1980) [Appendix B]. Additional policies and guidelines have been made by the California State Park and Recreation Commission, the DPR, California Department of Boating and Waterways, California Department of Fish and Game, and the California Department of Water Resources.

Local Policies

Many local governments also protect riparian zones for recreation and other values with policies established through zoning ordinances such as the Napa County's Watercourse Obstruction-Riparian Cover Ordinance.

The General Plan for the City of Davis contains many policies that enhance protection of natural systems while permitting appropriate recreation uses. For example, to achieve the preservation and conservation of natural features, the following two policies are listed in the Open Space Element:

1. Preservation of open lands in their natural state in order to ensure their maintenance as wildlife and fish habitats, natural drainage areas, and areas of passive recreation and outdoor education.
2. Preservation and enhancement of the community's natural resources in acquiring and planning parks and other open spaces (City of Davis 1977).

The Biological Resources Conservation portion of the city's Conservation Element has similar objectives such as:

Objective no. 1: Protection and preservation of the habitats and ecosystems of existing natural areas.
Objective no. 2: Restoration and enhancement of natural areas (ibid.).

Each of these objectives contains policies that form a solid base from which a land-use planner can develop concepts for the protection as well as the use of riparian systems.

The examples of riparian protection through recreation development and management policies given here are but a small sample. Literally hundreds of policy statements at all levels of government may be interpreted to accomplish such protection.

CONCLUSIONS

Land-managing agencies should approach the protection and preservation of riparian systems with a sensitivity to the provision of recreation opportunities.

Recreation development and use of riparian systems can help in the protection of the systems. Careful development located in already disturbed areas will cause minimal impact, and managed public recreation use can enlighten people to the value of protecting these important resources. The impact from providing acceptable recreation activities is a small sacrifice when the end result can be the development of a constituency that will support the protection of the larger system. Careful planning is essential, with a sensitivity to existing and future recreation impacts along with a sensitivity to the protection and preservation of the riparian systems. Before recreation planning is started, a comprehensive resource inventory should be completed. Based on the inventory, decisions can be made on the areas which have the highest and lowest tolerance for use. These designations aid in determining the types of development, types of recreation use, and carrying capacity of each area.

Recreation demand information should be used in conjunction with resource information to develop a general or master plan. The plan should follow policy guidelines which incorporate the need to protect the riparian system and provide for recreation use. The interest and support of recreationists is an excellent tool to protect riparian systems as an alternative to their destruction from industrial, governmental, residential, and agricultural sources.

LITERATURE CITED

California Department of Parks and Recreation. 1982. Recreation in California issues and actions: 1981-1985. 95 p. California Department of Parks and Recreation, Sacramento.

California Department of Parks and Recreation. 1979. Resource management directives for the California Department of Parks and Recreation, Section 1801-1832.4, Operations Manual, Department of Parks and Recreation, Sacramento.

California Department of Parks and Recreation. 1980. California state park system plan 1980. Department of Parks and Recreation, Sacramento. 239 p.

City of Davis. 1977. City of Davis General Plan (as updated 1978 and 1981). City of Davis, Davis, Calif. 79 p. plus addendum.

Geidel, Marcia, A., and Susan F. Moore. 1981. Delta recreation concept plan. 296 p. California Department of Water Resources, Sacramento, California.

Roberts, W.J., G. Howe, and J. Major. 1977. A survey of riparian forest flora and fauna in California. p. 3-19. In: A. Sands (ed.). Riparian forests in California: their ecology and conservation. Institute of Ecology Pub. 15, University of California, Davis. 122 p.

Smith, Felix. 1977. A short review of the status of riparian forests in California. p. 1-2. In: A. Sands (ed.). Riparian forests in California: their ecology and conservation. Institute of Ecology Pub. 15, University of California, Davis. 122 p.

USDA Forest Service. 1981. Draft regional plan. USDA Forest Service, Pacific Southwest Region, San Francisco, Calif. 108 p.

USDI Bureau of Land Management. 1978. Recreational carrying capacity in the California desert. 115 p. USDI Bureau of Land Management, Sacramento, Calif.

USDI Bureau of Land Management. 1980. The California desert conservation area plan, 1980. 173 p. US Government Printing Office, San Francisco, Calif.

USDI National Park Service. 1975. Management policies 1975. Washington, D.C.

Warner, Richard E. 1979. California riparian study program: background information and proposed study design. 177 p. California Department of Fish and Game, Planning Branch, Sacramento, California.

APPENDIX A

The following are specific policies selected by the author from the resource management directives of the California Department of Parks and Recreation to illustrate points made in the foregoing discussion (California Department of Parks and Recreation 1979).

(5) Development in State Parks is to be located and designed to protect and enhance enjoyment of the primary resources. In State Parks, the primary purpose for development is to place visitors in an optimal relationship with the resources, for recreational enjoyment and understanding of those resources. In State Parks, resources may not be managed or manipulated to enhance recreational experiences.

(6) Development in State Reserves is limited to facilities required to enable visitors to see, enjoy, and understand the resources. These generally consist of perimeter access, interpretive facilities, trails, and overlooks. In State Reserves, resources may not be manipulated or managed to enhance recreational experiences. Facilities not required for daytime public use and enjoyment of the primary resources are not appropriate.

(7) The Department shall analyze the major resources of each State Park and State Reserve, both existing and proposed, and will recommend boundaries that preserve the integrity of and provide full protection to the natural and scenic resources involved, while assuring the safety of existing or potential developments beyond the boundaries. Every effort will be made to secure funds for acquisition of lands or waters to establish such boundaries.

(15) When important natural, or cultural values are recognized in a State Recreation Unit, procedures to identify and protect such values will be the same as those in State Parks or State Historical Units.

(26) It is an objective of the Department to identify the total framework of environmental and ecological factors influencing the lands of the State Park System, including those arising from human activities, and to promulgate and apply resource management techniques required to negate deleterious human influences, and to achieve the environmental objectives established for the system.

(27) Wherever natural elements are recognized in the State Park System as being of special significance requiring protection and preservation, and regardless of the classification of the units in which they occur, the Department shall recommend the establishment of natural preserves (PRC Section No. 5019.71), to embrace these elements, and to emphasize their recognition and protection.

(29) In the State Park System, perpetuation of values in today's environment may require purposeful guiding of dynamic ecological factors that are constantly undergoing a successional trend through the interaction of natural and extraneous forces. This guidance may not always involve simply the static protection of the features or elements that happen to be a part of the existing environment in any particular period of time.

(32) In order to assure a continuity of effort in management and preservation of resources, it shall be an objective of the Department to prepare for each unit of the State Park System a resource management program or programs, identifying the field management actions required to achieve unit purpose(s) in relation to resources. When approved by the Director, the resource management program or programs for each unit will form the basis for resource management activities at that unit.

(46) In each State Park System unit, environmental quality shall be such that visitors are aware of being in a place of special quality because of their surroundings. Manmade features and their maintenance will have special qualities which, in total, express a feeling of environmental quality that differs from areas where degrad-

ing and undesirable features and intrusions are commonplace.

APPENDIX B

The following are specific operations policies selected by the author from the State Park System Plan (California Department of Parks and Recreation 1980) to illustrate points made in the foregoing discussion.

Goal 14: Ensure the adequate and proper management and protection of resources within all units of the State Park System.

Policy A—Clearly state the resource management objectives for each unit in the resource element of the General Plan.

Policy B—Monitor and evaluate the ability of unit resources to withstand the impact of visitor use; when necessary, take corrective measure to reduce the intensity of use.

Policy C—Implement appropriate educational and control mechanisms to protect the unit's resource values.

Policy D—Maintain natural habitats where possible and regulate wildlife populations in accordance with the resource management objectives of each unit.

Policy E—Prevent the destruction, deterioration, loss, or other misuses of the geologic, vegetative, or other resources in the natural areas of the State Park System.

Policy F—Protect significant cultural resources (including archeological and historic resources) and their environs from damaging or degrading influences.

Policy G—Minimize environmental degradation of intensively used recreation resources.

Policy H—Permit the use of unit resources by private enterprises for commercial activities, such as films and fairs, only if such uses do not disturb the integrity, and are in accordance with, resource management objectives.

MANAGEMENT AND PROTECTION OF RIPARIAN ECOSYSTEMS

IN THE STATE PARK SYSTEM[1]

W. James Barry[2]

Abstract.--Preserving California's natural heritage is one of the California Department of Parks and Recreation's three primary missions. As part of the planning process of the department, California's natural ecosystems are systematically identified, classified, and evaluated for statewide significance. Riparian and wetland ecosystems are given a high priority when a parcel of land is being considered for inclusion into the State Park System.

After a project is formulated and the land acquired, an "inventory of features" is prepared. The project is classified as "state reserve", "state park", "state recreation area", etc., depending upon the values identified.

A unit carrying capacity is determined prior to planning or developing recreational facilities. A resource management policy document, the "resource element" of the unit's "general plan", is approved by the Director before substantial recreational facilities planning is done. The general objectives of policies formulated for riparian ecosystems are to restore, protect, and maintain riparian ecosystems in as near a natural state as possible. On- and off-site impacts are discussed with specific examples of resource management problems, policies, and programs.

INTRODUCTION

Although managing and protecting riparian ecosystems is not a specific mandate of the California Department of Parks and Recreation (DPR), it is inferred from various legislation incorporated into the California Public Resources Code (PRC) and the California Administrative Code (AC). The three primary missions of DPR are: 1) to preserve California's natural heritage; 2) to preserve California's cultural heritage; and 3) to provide Californians with significant recreational opportunities (Troy et al. 1980). The first two missions often conflict with the third.

Conflicts that cannot be resolved at the staff level are resolved at the administrative level, that is by the Director of DPR or the State Park and Recreation Commission.

The DPR planning process, policies, rules, and regulations pertaining to the management and protection of riparian ecosystems within the State Park System are outlined below. Specific examples of protection efforts and management problems and programs are then given for the State Park System, which comprises more than 250 units totaling around 404,900 ha. (1,000,000 ac.).

RESOURCE PROTECTION AND THE PLANNING PROCESS

The planning process begins with an analysis of recreation and preservation deficiencies within the state. In the case of natural values, areas considered to be outstanding or representative examples of natural "landscapes" are considered for acquisition. The state was divided up into nine landscape provinces (Mason 1970). These areas were identified in landscape province studies conducted by DPR over the last 10 years. Unfortunately, in these studies, scenic landscape features were lumped with geologic and biotic features. Recreation potential was a heavily weighted factor in choosing "natural landscape areas" for acquisition. In this planning scheme, one riparian forest biotic community within the Great Valley Landscape Province and one in the Sierra Landscape Province, etc. would be considered adequate to preserve the "riparian landscape," whether it be a riparian community domina-

---

[1] Paper presented at the California Riparian Systems Conference. [University of California, Davis, September 17-19, 1981].
[2] W. James Barry is State Park Plant Ecologist, California Department of Parks and Recreation, Sacramento.

ted by Fremont cottonwood (<u>Populus</u> <u>fremontii</u>) or one dominated by California sycamore (<u>Platanus</u> <u>racemosa</u>).

Since this broad-brush approach eliminated many natural plant and animal communities from consideration, I began devising a multi-hierarchical classification system for California ecosystems, for use in choosing 1980 bond act projects, as well as for the inventory and management of ecosystems in the State Park System (Barry 1979 and in preparation). Using this system, California's natural ecosystems are being systematically identified, classified, and evaluated for statewide significance and preservation status.

Regrettably, the project selection process becomes quite diluted during project evaluation, due to political factors, funding limitations and allocations, etc. Project size is also important. A few larger units are more economical to operate than numerous small, scattered units.

Once a project is selected for acquisitions by DPR, it must be approved by the State Park and Recreation Commission and plans are submitted to the Legislature for approval.[3] The Department of General Services (DGS) appraises the land. Funding of projects and, if necessary, condemnation[4] must then be approved by the Public Works Board. Condemnation proceedings often take years; most acquisitions are settled out of court and usually for more than the fair market value of the parcel(s) (fig. 1). This of course, puts willing sellers at a disadvantage. During condemnation proceedings, more than one unwilling seller has clear-cut riparian forests, leveled vernal pools, etc., to spite the State. With the primary natural values of the land in question gone, the State likely will abandon the project.

During negotiations, DGS, generally not being environmentally sensitive, may establish long-term agricultural leases, life estates, etc. with landowners. These leases are often detrimental to the very values the project was meant to protect. When the land is acquired, years may pass before the DGS turns the land over to DPR.

Figure 1.--San Louis Island Project, Merced County, contains significant valley oak riparian forests, native grasslands, and vernal pools. Condemnation proceedings were necessary on some parcels.

---

[3]Sections 5017, 5018 PRC.
[4]Section 5074.3 PRC.

759

During this interim period many resource values may be exploited. For example, in the riparian zone of Burton Creek State Park, Placer County, the trees were cut for firewood while the state park rangers stood by, helplessly, with no jurisdiction over state-owned land that was to become a natural preserve!

Once land is turned over to DPR, an "inventory of features"[5] is required for classification of the new unit. DPR staff submits an inventory of features report and recommendations for classification and naming the unit[6] to the State Park and Recreation Commission. The four basic categories of classification are state reserves, state parks, state recreation units, and state historical units.[7] Riparian ecosystems can occur in all of these classifications; more important examples are set aside in subunits such as natural preserves or state wildernesses.[8] State reserves, state wildernesses, and natural preserves are the most restrictive use classifications. Examples of units designated especially for protection of riparian ecosystems include Burton Creek and Woodson Bridge (Tehama County) natural preserves. Other areas are currently being considered (fig. 2).

Figure 2.--The Miller Creek watershed in Salt Point State Park (Sonoma County) has been recommended for natural preserve status (Michaely et al. 1976). This watershed contains Oregon alder (Alnus oregona), riparian forests and the southernmost population of pygmy cypress (Cupressus pygmaea).

Classification establishes, in broad terms, the kind and intensity of recreational use and development allowed within a unit. Attendance is

to be held within limits established by a carrying capacity survey, established prior to any developmental plan.[9] The survey shall include such factors as soil, moisture, and natural cover.[10] Unfortunately, these mandates have been largely ignored, or carrying capacity has been determined by the size of the land area available for potential recreation development (the size of the parking lot rather than ecologic sensitivity has often determined unit carrying capacity).

The most important phase of the planning process for a unit is the general plan phase. Following classification or reclassification of a unit and prior to the development of any new facilities, DPR must prepare a general plan or revise any existing plan. The general plan consists of elements that evaluate and define proposed land use, facilities, operation, environmental impact, management of resources, and any other matter deemed appropriate.

With respect to the protection of riparian ecosystems, the resource element of the general plan is the most important document of the planning process since it evaluates the unit:

> based upon historical and ecological research of plant-animal and soil-geological relationships, and shall contain a declaration of purpose, setting forth specific long-range management objectives for the unit consistent with the unit's classification...and a declaration of resource management policy, setting forth the precise actions and limitations required for the achievement of the objectives established in the declaration of purpose" (Section 5002.2 PRC).

"In order that it shall act as a guide and constraint, the resource element will be prepared, made available for public comment, and approved by the Director before substantial work is done on the other elements of the plan" (Section 4332 AC).

However, substantial work is usually done on the development of units prior to the general plan. Time and budgeting constraints seldom allow adequate research to make wise, indepth resource management policies. Further, the implementation of resource management policies is often costly and difficult, if not impossible. This is especially true where off-site impacts are present. Once the general plan is approved by the State Park and Recreation Commission, resource management policy is implemented through specific resource management programs which must be budgeted for two years in advance. Current funding for the statewide resource management program amounts to between $0.50 and $0.60 per acre per year of State Park System lands. In con-

---

[5] Section 5002.1 PRC.
[6] Section 5019.50 PRC.
[7] Sections 5019.65, 5019.53, 5019.56, and 5019.59 PRC, respectively.
[8] Sections 5019.7 and 5019.68 PRC.

---

[9] Section 5001.96 PRC.
[10] Section 5019.5 PRC.

trast, the approximate equivalent $500,000 has been approved for working drawings for the recreational development of a single unit (Salt Point State Park). Working drawings are not done by DPR, rather they are contracted out to the Office of State Architect, which is less sensitive to environmental constraints and cultural or natural preservation.

MANAGEMENT OF RIPARIAN ECOSYSTEMS

Resource management problems encountered in riparian ecosystems are due to a number of on- and off-site impacts. Off-site impacts are generally the more serious and less controllable of the two. Critical off-site impacts include watershed and hydrologic disturbances such as logging, stream or lake modification (dams, channelization and controlled flow), wildfire, urbanization, off-road vehicular activity, and cultivation.

Off-Site Impacts

The most tragic and dramatic example of off-site impacts is the ongoing destruction of the Bull Creek watershed within Humboldt Redwoods State Park, Humboldt County. At the confluence of Bull Creek and the South Fork of the Eel River is one of the most magnificent stands of coast redwoods in the world--the 3,640-ha. (9,000-ac.) Rockefeller Forest. Prior to the recent discovery of a tree slightly taller in the Redwood Creek watershed the world's tallest tree was thought to be in this pristine grove. In the first part of this century the grove was purchased by DPR with funding provided by private sources (John D. Rockefeller). Meanwhile, logging was occurring in the upper watershed. The entire watershed, with the exception of the state park property, was clear-cut and the slash burned.

The winter of 1955-56 brought heavy rains and flooding to northern California; severe erosion and stream channel destruction resulted. The riparian alder and willow thickets along the stream channel were completely washed out, and the magnificent riparian redwood giant forests of the alluvial flats were undercut; numerous ancient trees toppled into the stream, clogging the channel, which caused further undercutting. The stream channel area was completely devastated, quadrupling in size. The 1964 floods further widened the channel (fig. 3).

DPR began a massive cleanup, erosion control, and stream channelization project. The channel was riprapped and a long-term resource protection program was initiated which included various types of research (fig. 4). Volunteers replanted trees in the watershed and riprapped banks were revegetated with riparian species (willows and alders stuck or planted between the rocks). To date more than $2.28 million has been spent on the Bull Creek Project.

Figure 3.--Bull Creek "shoofly" in Humboldt Redwoods State Park, February 1965.

We are now beginning to look at similar, although less critical, riparian forest losses along the South Fork of the Eel River; however, the upper Bull Creek watershed is still unstable, with massive slides occurring each winter (fig. 5). No feasible solution to these slides has been suggested.

Channelization of the Sacramento River has caused serious bank erosion problems in Woodson Bridge State Recreation Area. The stream channel is undercutting streamside riparian vegetation and has cut through the levee. The channel upstream has been riprapped in such a way that the current is directed into an unriprapped bend within the unit. Further, if this bank is riprapped to protect the valley oak riparian woodland, the current will be deflected to the opposite bank where a fine cottonwood riparian forest is located in Woodson Bridge Natural Preserve. The preserve is a nesting area for the rare Yellow-billed Cuckoo. Various bank protection measures are currently being investigated.

Wildfire has caused numerous types of damage to streamside riparian ecosystems. The combination of an extremely hot wildfire (the Molera Fire of August 1972) and heavy rainfall caused mudflows in the Big Sur River watershed (Cleveland 1973). Between mid-October 1972 and mid-February 1973, mudflows were generated by heavy and occasionally intense winter rains falling on steep, fire-denuded slopes of the Santa Lucia Range. Damage from mudflows and floodwater was predominantly confined to riparian zones along the lower courses of Pheneger, Juan-Higuera, and Pfeiffer-Redwood creeks. Although extensive damage occurred to property and to the coast redwood riparian forests, investigations of coast redwood root systems have shown mudflows to be a recurring natural phenomenon (fig. 6). Thus, from an ecosystem management standpoint no action would be taken; however, burned-over watersheds

Figure 4.--Riprap in Bull Creek, Humboldt Redwoods State Park, October 1971.

Figure 5.--Slide area in the upper Bull Creek watershed, Humboldt Redwoods State Park, October 1971.

Figure 6.--Mudflow material in Pfeiffer-Redwood Creek, Pfeiffer Big Sur State Park, January 1973.

were reseeded and gabions installed in the Big Sur River to try to protect the town of Big Sur, where extensive damage occurred.

Wildfire followed by flash flooding has caused obliteration of desert riparian ecosystems (fig. 7).

Among California's coastal dune systems are fine riparian ecosystems located in moist-dune swales and adjacent to dune-formed lakes. These micro-ecosystems are characteristically dominated by willow thickets in dune swales and alder thickets along lake banks.

Figure 7.--Sedimentation and erosion in Hell Hole Canyon, Anza-Borrego Desert State Park, San Diego County, following wildfire and flash flood, April 1978.

The Ten-Mile River dune system is located in MacKerricher State Park (Mendocino County). Prior to acquisition, the dune system was open to off-road vehicles. Also, by the turn of the century most of the Ten-Mile River had been logged. With the heavy erosion that followed, through the process of littoral drift, sediments from the watershed caused a great increase in sand supply to the dune system. In the 1920s, Highway 1 was inundated with sand and had to be realigned. By the 1950s the dunes were in a relatively stable condition. Off-road vehicles gradually became popular, however, and by the 1970s a great deal of off-road vehicle use and renewed dune movement was evident. Numerous riparian swales were inundated. In some cases the willows were able to grow faster than they were being covered with were being covered with sand, eventually ending up on dune crests and helping halt the inward movement of sand (fig. 8). DPR is currently conducting studies of the impact of off-road vehicles on the dune system and methods to restore the fragile dune vegetation. Of special interest is the unique riparian ecosystem adjacent to Sand Hill Lake. This fen-carr ecosystem is the only one of its kind known in California (Barry and Schlinger 1977).

The most critical off-road vehicular impacts occur at Pismo Dunes State Vehicular Recreation Area, San Luis Obispo County. Here, extremely heavy use has destroyed hundreds of acres of dune vegetation.

Figure 8.--Willow riparian area being inundated by active dunes, Ten-Mile Dunes, MacKerricher State Park.

As a result, most swale riparian ecosystems have been covered up within the first 1.6 to 2.4 km. (1 to 1.5 mi.) of the beach. Oso Flaco Lake, which is surrounded by riparian vegetation and numerous rare endemic, endangered, or otherwise threatened species, is slowly being inundated with sand. A massive dune revegetation program has just been initiated to the windward side of the lake. Revegetation is to be with native dune vegetation; seed collections and cutting stock are being taken from within the dune system. Remaining examples of dune plant communities are being described, mapped, and analyzed through a series of permanent plots. Fencing will be installed to keep vehicles out of the windward dunes. Although DPR plans to spend $160,000 per year on this restoration project, it may be too late to save this unique dune lakes area, which separates the dune system from the rich agricultural lands to the east.

On-Site Impacts

On-site impacts to riparian ecosystems encountered in the State Park System include livestock grazing, cultivation, exotic species invasion, off-road vehicle damage, equestrian trampling, and human trampling, roughly in that order of importance.

With the recent passage of SB 2469,[11] the otherwise inviolate natural resource of the State Park System[12] now may be leased for agriculture purposes. It has long been known that cultivation, grazing, and the interruption of natural flooding and fire cycles have threatened the existence of the magnificent valley oak savannas, woodlands, and forests of California.

---

[11] Section 5069 PRC.
[12] Section 5001.65 PRC.

More subtle but just as critical is the impact of grazing on the understory of riparian communities. Native grasses and palatable native forbs are eliminated and replaced by thistles and other alien weedy species. A once very widespread riparian native understory grass, blue wildrye (Elymus glaucus), has all but been eliminated from these ecosystems. Relict stands of blue wildrye occur associated with valley oak and cottonwood communities on the floor of Yosemite Valley (Tuolumne and Mariposa Counties), in Hungry Valley State Vehicular Recreation Area (Ventura County), and Malibu Creek State Park (Los Angeles County). Grazing of riparian ecosystems also affects the water quality of adjacent waterways. Ahjumawi Lava Springs State Park (Shasta County), illustrates this problem. The springs, rivers, ponds, and lakes in and adjacent to this unit show phosphorus and nitrate loading, with algae blooms turning much of the water green. Cattle roam freely in and out of the aquatic wetland and terrestrial ecosystems of the unit (fig. 9).

The invasion of alien species is almost universal in riparian ecosystems. Alien species from the Mediterranean region are common in the understories of riparian communities throughout the state. Blue gum (Eucalyptus globulus) and other Eucalyptus species have displaced native riparian vegetation at Mt. Tamalpais (Marin County), Montana de Oro (San Luis Obispo County), and Annadel (Sonoma County) state parks. When resource management programs are planned or initiated to eliminate these alien, low-diversity communities and replace them with native riparian species, considerable local opposition has usually all but stopped the efforts.

At Point Mugu State Park, a prime example of a California sycamore riparian woodland ecosystem occurs (fig. 10). However, over 100 years of grazing has eliminated of most native herbs in the understory. The understory is made up largely of milk thistle (Silybum marianum), an alien species which needs disturbance of the soil surface for germination and soil compaction to compete with native species; both factors are provided by the hooves of domestic livestock. To date, a control method for milk thistle has not been found, but biological control methods are being investigated.

In Anza-Borrego Desert State Park many native riparian ecosystems are being invaded by salt cedar (Tamarix gallica), an alien species of Euroasia which not only is out-competing native riparian species, but is also causing springs which the desert big horn sheep and other wildlife rely on for summer and fall water supply to dry up. The problem concerns the California Department of Fish and Game (DFG) as well as DPR. To date, no method has been found to eradicate salt cedar. The problem has been investigated by the National Park Service (NPS) with no satisfactory results. The answer will likely be found in the natural habitat of salt cedar. Somewhere in Eurasia a biological control may exist.

Figure 9.--Cattle grazing in the riparian zone at Ahjumawi Lava Springs State Park. Domestic grazing animals have become a serious ecosystem management problem.

Figure 10.--California sycamore riparian woodland in Point Mugu State Park being grazed. Most native understory herbs have been replaced by alien weeds.

The off- and on-site impacts of off-road vehicles at Pismo State Vehicular Recreation area have been covered. Severe on-site impacts due to off-road vehicles are well illustrated at Hungry Valley State Vehicular Recreation Area (fig. 11), Anza-Borrego Desert State Park, and Red Rock Canyon State Park (Kern County).

Only Hungry Valley State Vehicular Recreation Area will be covered here. The understory of a Fremont cottonwood riparian forest has been about 90% destroyed in the informal staging and camping area at the northern end of the unit (fig. 12). Unique valley oak woodland and savanna ecosystems are threatened with similar devastation. The understory of the valley oak woodland here contains more native grass species than known from any other area in the state. Here blue wildrye (Elymus glaucus), deer grass (Muhlenbergia rigins), purple needle grass (Stipa pulchra), nodding needlegrass (Stipa cernua), and giant squirreltail grass (Sitanion jubatum) occur along with willows (Salix sp.) and California wild rose (Rosa californica).

This unique riparian ecosystem, along with the largest and most diverse native grassland ecosystem within the foothills region of the state, was proposed for natural preserve status at the October 1981 State Park and Recreation Commission hearing in Los Angeles. The proposed natural preserve status for the small valley oak woodland has not been opposed by the off-road vehicle special interest group. However, the proposed natural preserve status for a larger, 567-ha. (1,400-ac.) native grassland has met strong opposition; the grassland is likely doomed to off-road vehicular use and ultimate destruction.

Figure 11.--Sedimentation in riparian woodland, Canada de Los Alamos, Hungry Valley State Vehicular Recreation Area. Off-road vehicle use upstream is causing siltation.

765

Figure 12.--Off-road vehicular staging area has caused destruction of understory and groundcover in Fremont cottonwood riparian woodland, Hungry Valley State Vehicular Recreation Area.

CONCLUSIONS AND RECOMMENDATIONS

Resource management objectives in riparian ecosystems of the State Park System are focused around alleviating a number of long-term problems, some of which may have no satisfactory solutions. Others have expensive long-term solutions.

Wise and sensitive planning is necessary to ensure the perpetuation of high-quality riparian ecosystems. A long-term ecological monitoring program with good baseline data (permanent plots, transects, etc.) is needed to adequately manage riparian ecosystems.

Special interest legislation which allows grazing, logging, mining, commercial fishing, hunting, etc., within the State Park System is, and will remain, a serious problem. Such legislation circumvents the objectives of the State Park System. Perhaps a constitutional amendment, to the effect that the State Park System and the DFG Ecological Reserve System are inviolate and must not be commercially exploited, is necessary.

LITERATURE CITED

Barry, W.J. 1979. Proposed natural heritage program for California, partial draft. 113 p. California Department of Parks and Recreation, Sacramento.

Barry, W.J. and E.I. Schlinger (ed.). 1977. Inglenook Fen, a study and plan. 212 p. California Department of Parks and Recreation, Sacramento.

Cleveland, G.B. 1973. Fire + rain = mudflows, Big Sur, 1972. California Geology 26(6): 127-135.

Mason, H.L. 1970. The scenic, scientific, and educational values of the natural landscape of California. 36 p. California Department of Parks and Recreation, Sacramento.

Michaely, R.D., J. Cochran, J. Barry, and R. Batha. 1976. Salt Point State Park resource management plan and general development plan. 55 p. California Department of Parks and Recreation, Sacramento.

Troy, R.E., R.D. Treece, and H.F. Hallett, Jr. 1980. California State Park System Plan 1980, an element of the California outdoor recreation plan. 239 p. California Department of Parks and Recreation, Sacramento.

PLANNING RECREATION DEVELOPMENT AND WILDLIFE ENHANCEMENT IN

A RIPARIAN ENVIRONMENT AT ORESTIMBA CREEK[1]

Robert H. Morris[2]

Abstract.--This paper summarizes the proposed project for wildlife enhancement and recreation development at Orestimba Creek (Stanislaus County) and discusses problems involved. Some of the problems are especially important because they are common in other riparian environments where public recreation is proposed. This paper deals more with questions than answers. However, an examination of problems is an important phase of productive management of riparian systems.

INTRODUCTION

The proposed recreational development and wildlife enhancement project at Orestimba Creek is a reflection of the concern the California Department of Water Resources (DWR) has for restoration and management of our remaining riparian resources. It is justified by the DWR's legal requirement to include planning for recreation and wildlife habitat enhancement in all appropriate activities involving construction and operation of the State Water Project. The remnant riparian environment at Orestimba Creek, located adjacent to the California Aqueduct, makes it an ideal site for such planning.

This paper is based on a critical examination of some of the problems involved in the project. This does not mean the writer is not in favor of the proposal. On the contrary, the proposed plan could be an effective method of conserving and managing the remaining riparian resources at the creek--if development and operation are carefully implemented. The critical approach is taken to emphasize problems that are pertinent to management of California's riparian systems.

DESCRIPTION OF THE SITE

Orestimba Creek is an intermittent stream which flows eastward into the San Joaquin River, draining the Diablo Range of the Coast Ranges.

In an average year, flow in the creek occurs only during the winter and spring, mostly from January through April. Except for runoff from adjacent irrigated orchards, the creek is dry for the rest of the year. However, the presence of large sycamores (_Platanus racemosa_) (fig. 1) attests to the perennial presence of abundant near-surface water.

The project site is located on a 2.4-km. (1.5-mi.) length of the creek in the western part of the San Joaquin Valley in Stanislaus County. The upstream and downstream limits of the site are defined by the California Aqueduct and the Delta-Mendota Canal, respectively. Both the aqueduct and the canal are siphoned under the bed of the creek to allow the stream to maintain its natural flow. Interstate 5 crosses the creek about 0.8 km. (0.5 mi.) upstream from the Delta-Mendota siphon.

A marshy basin with excellent potential for enhancement as wildlife habitat has formed at the downstream end of the project. Many kinds of wildlife are present throughout the year, both along the creek and in the marsh. Some of these are deer, rabbits, squirrels, ducks, pheasants, herons, quail, doves, and a large variety of smaller birds. Indian Rocks is an additional important amenity. It is a sedimentary outcrop located less than 0.8 km. (0.5 mi.) south of the upstream end of the project area (fig. 2). The site has historical value as a wayside camping area used by early Indian tribes in the valley (Napton 1980).

The part of Orestimba Creek involved in this project is an excellent example of one of California's remnant riparian environments. In addition to a lush growth of other riparian plant species, there are over 300 native sycamores clustered within the limits of the site (fig. 1). These

---

[1]Paper presented at the California Riparian Systems Conference. [University of California, Davis, September 17-19, 1981].

[2]Robert H. Morris is Recreation Planner, California Department of Water Resources, Sacramento.

Figure 1.—Large California sycamore on the floodplain of Orestimba Creek. (Photograph by
R.E. Warner.)

are among the finest specimens of the species remaining in the San Joaquin Valley. Surrounded by
orchards, plowed fields, angular water canals,
and concrete traffic lanes, the site stands out
like an oasis from the past, a remnant of another
time. Although the valley surrounding it has
changed, the appearance of this short length of
creekbed with its sycamores (many dating back hundreds of years) is quite similar to that when the
Miume Yokuts used it as a wayside resting area
that provided shade and relief from the scorching
summer heat of the valley. The principal difference today is the lack of ground- and shrubcover,
and the absence of young trees, because of long-
term cattle grazing in the riparian zone (fig.
3).

The riparian site at Orestimba Creek with
its magnificent sycamores has excellent potential
for recreation development and wildlife enhancement. The 2.4-km length of creek has gently sloping banks that are ideal for installing recreation facilities with minimum disturbance to existing topography. Indian Rocks at the upstream end
of the site is within easy hiking distance of the
creek. An intensive investigation by the Institute of Archeological Research, California State
College, Stanislaus, indicated these attractive
geological features have good potential for development as an outdoor museum displaying the important historical and archeological significance of
the area. The marshy basin at the downstream end
of the project area has fine potential for enhancement as wildlife habitat. This could include a program for public observation and nature
study. The adjacent bikeway along the California
Aqueduct would provide easy access to and from
the creek. No other location along the 113-km.
(70-mi.) length of bikeway provides access to a
creekside environment like the one at Orestimba
Creek. Finally, Interstate 5 and other existing
roads provide excellent access for public recreation use.

PROJECT SUMMARY

Proposals for development and enhancement at
Orestimba Creek fully utilize the excellent potentials that exist there. Perhaps the most important aspect of the plan is the conversion of the
existing intermittent creek into a stream with
year-round flow. This would be accomplished by
gravity releases of water into the creek from the
California Aqueduct at the upstream end of the
site. The releases would be made during summer
months when the creek is normally dry. They
would be carefully planned and controlled to enhance the 2.4-km. downstream site for both recreation and wildlife without causing erosion or
other problems. The amount of water released
would be determined by the flow required to flush
and maintain adequate water quality in a swimming
pond to be excavated in the creekbed. The flow
would also link a chain of fishing ponds created
along the stream by carefully deepening and widening the existing channel at appropriate locations. Excess water would pond in the marshy
basin at the downstream end of the site.

On a long-term basis, the summer water releases would modify the existing riparian environment. Some of these changes would be beneficial,
but others may be less desirable. Because of
this, an important part of the proposed project
is a management plan to control and direct
changes that would occur. A major concept of
operation and management at the site is to limit
recreational use to a level that would assure
long-term conservation of this remnant riparian
environment. Entry control, limitation of parking and other facilities, and appropriate supervision of on-site activities are three important
parts of productive management that would assure
conservation.

Both the creekbed and the marsh would be
modified to improve habitat for a year-round fishery. In addition to deepening and widening exist-

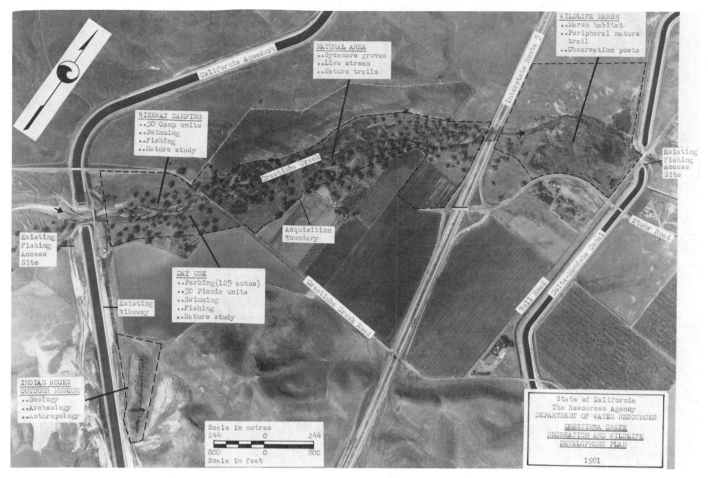

Figure 2.--Orestimba Creek recreation and wildlife development plan.

Figure 3.--California sycamores on Orestimba
Creek floodplain. Note absence of ground-
and shrubcover and sycamore reproduction due
to cattle grazing. (Photograph by R.E.
Warner.)

ing pools, this modification would include a carefully managed planting program to establish new
plant species that would provide shade and escape
cover beneficial to fish reproduction. The planting program would also add new species to provide
additional food and cover for wildlife. Planners
hope this will attract new animals which have a
greater tolerance for coexistence with people to
the site, to replace those species that leave
when initial development and public recreation
use begins.

In conjunction with the year-round stream
concept, the following facilities are proposed as
part of the plan for Orestimba Creek (see fig. 2
for specific locations).

A day-use area would be carefully constructed under the canopy of an existing sycamore
grove. The area would provide access to an instream swimming pond, a picnic area, the chain of
fishing pools along the creek, and a streamside
hiking trail linking the upstream and downstream
ends of the site.

A small wayside camping area for cyclists using the California Aqueduct Bikeway would be located adjacent to the day-use area, but on the opposite side of the creek. The two areas would share basic facilities and be linked by a pedestrian bridge across the creek.

An outdoor museum is proposed at the Indian Rocks site to display for public viewing the historical and archeological significance of the area. The museum would emphasize the area's importance as a campsite of early nomadic Indian tribes of San Joaquin Valley. An appropriate access trail would be provided.

A shoreline interpretive trail would be constructed around the periphery of the downstream marsh, with observation posts to point out important natural features. This interpretive trail would be linked to the creekside hiking trail extending the length of the site.

The remainder of the riparian environment within the project area, including most of the existing sycamores, would remain in its present undisturbed condition. The plan would not deplete or infringe upon agricultural production in the surrounding area. The only land taken for recreation development and wildlife enhancement would be the rocky bed of the creek, the marshy downstream basin, and the outcrop at Indian Rocks. The project could result in a net increase in productive land if the State can trade its adjacent landholdings with agricultural potential for some of the property required to implement the plan.

IS PUBLIC OR PRIVATE OWNERSHIP BEST?

Anyone with a sincere concern for future conservation of the riparian environment at Orestimba Creek must consider the relative merits of public and private ownership. Is it in the best long-term interests of the site to remove it from private ownership? Will government ownership proposing public use and more productive management provide better assurances for future preservation? To answer these questions, the nature of existing private ownership must be considered.

Three landowners are involved. The first is a local family whose ancestors came to the valley as pioneers many years ago. The family has strong ties to the land and a sincere interest in retaining ownership and preserving the site. They have owned their part of the creekbed for as long as anyone can remember, and they maintain a "barbwire" stewardship that has effectively protected the remnant riparian land by excluding all public access. Although there has been no "productive management" to enhance the creekbed, there can be no doubt that many of the sycamores and much of the other riparian vegetation has survived only because of the protection provided by this private ownership. The family is against any proposal to take the land for public use.

The second landowner does not date back to pioneer days, but he also has held his land at the creek for many years. His interests are more commercially oriented. He owns and manages extensive orchard developments along the north and south sides of the creekbed. To protect his orchards, this owner practices the same land stewardship that excludes all public access. Although his motives are different, the results have been the same. The riparian system has survived because of the effective protection provided by the existing private ownership. This landowner is also against the plan to take his holdings at the creek for public use, even though none of his orchard property would be involved.

The third owner is very different. It is a nonresident corporation; the property along the creek is a recent acquisition. The corporation proposes major new commercial developments that include facilities for travelers using Interstate 5. If these plans are implemented, they will attract large numbers of people to the area adjacent to the creek. The corporation is in favor of the plan to open the site for public recreation, primarily because the owners believe it will positively affect their proposed developments. They are willing to sell their part of the creekbed needed by the State if they can benefit by the sale. They do not believe their proposed traveler facilities will have any adverse effects on survival of the adjacent riparian environment of Orestimba Creek.

Approximately 80% of all riparian systems in our country are presently in private ownership and have not been subjected to governmental management (Warner 1979). The remnant site at Orestimba Creek is part of this 80%. Although the land surrounding it has been changed substantially for agricultural uses, the creekbed has remained relatively unchanged. It has survived primarily because of its lack of value for development and the exclusion of the public by private owners. In consideration of this, is it in the long-term interest of the site to substitute governmental management which proposes public use?

New corporate ownership at the creek proposes changes that may threaten the survival of the adjacent riparian system. On the other hand, the limited funds available may not assure appropriate governmental operation to control public uses. We are all familiar with the damage that an unsupervised public can inflict on a fragile riparian environment like the one at Orestimba Creek. Public ownership may be the best way to go, but only if governmental management can assure that this remnant site has at least as much protection in the future as it has had in the past under private stewardship.

ARE PUBLIC RECREATION AND WILDLIFE PRESERVATION COMPATIBLE?

Riparian systems are as attractive and useful to people as they are to dependent fish and wildlife populations (ibid.). This is surely true for the section of Orestimba Creek involved in the proposed plan. As indicated, the site is located adjacent to the California Aqueduct and has excellent potentials for both recreation development and wildlife enhancement. However, the question of compatibility must be considered. Is it logical to assume that these two uses can occur simultaneously at a small, fragile site such as Orestimba Creek?

Remnant riparian environments often constitute the only available roosting, nesting, and escape habitat for many wildlife species (ibid.). This is undoubtedly the case at Orestimba Creek. As the surrounding valley has been modified for agricultural production, the creek and adjacent riparian system have become an escape site for many indigenous species that at one time were present in much greater numbers. Most (if not all) of these remaining animals have definite territorial needs that must be met. In consideration of this, is it good planning to infringe on this remaining sanctuary by trying to combine public recreation use and wildlife enhancement at the same small location?

The summer water releases from the Aqueduct will significantly improve the riparian environment along the creek and in the downstream marsh. This, in conjunction with the planting program to provide additional food and cover resources, should attract new species to the site. However, is it reasonable from a biological point of view to assume most of these animals will be able to adjust their territorial needs to coexist with people in a public recreation setting? At a larger site with adequate room for separation and buffers, the two conflicting uses could probably be managed effectively. Space restrictions at Orestimba Creek may be the limiting factor that will preclude long-term survival for many of the remaining wildlife species in the presence of recreational development.

If the proposed plan, including effective management and operation, is carefully implemented, the creek site can be enhanced for both recreation and wildlife. Limiting public use and maintaining on-site control are two important parts of effective operation. They are necessary if the riparian system is to remain a viable environment for most species. Changes will inevitably occur—to the detriment of some species and the advantage of others—but long-term preservation can be reasonably assured. This preservation will probably involve compromises for recreation and/or wildlife.

DOES EXISTING ENVIRONMENTAL LAW PROVIDE ADEQUATE PROTECTION?

It is probably safe to assume that most people involved with the issue generally agree that existing environmental laws (National Environmental Policy Act and California Environmental Quality Act) provide important protections for the conservation and management of our remaining riparian systems. The environmental investigation and analysis required under these laws assure consideration of significant impacts and long-term preservation. This is especially important because in America over the last 150 years, between 70% and 90% of indigenous riparian resources have been destroyed (ibid.). Adequate legal protections must be provided if the remaining riparian environment is to survive. However, if we take a closer look at specific ways in which environmental laws are interpreted and applied, some serious doubts arise concerning their adequacy. The project described in this paper provides one example of contradictions that can occur.

The plan to develop recreation and enhance wildlife at Orestimba Creek requires completion of a full environmental impact report (EIR) before any final decision for the project can be made. The EIR must evaluate all significant impacts of the proposal and consider mitigation measures and alternatives to the project to minimize adverse impacts. A draft of the report must be available for review by all interested parties, and comments received from reviewers must be given adequate consideration. These are all requirements under the California Environmental Quality Act, and they provide important protections for the remnant riparian site at the creek. This is an example of an appropriate application of the law.

Another recent activity at the Orestimba Creek site presents a different interpretation of the law. A gravel extraction operation just a few hundred feet upstream from the proposed project has been in process for some time and has already produced significant adverse impacts. A large area of the creekbed has been graded clean to excavate gravel material. This has removed protective vegetative cover important in reducing erosion damage during winter floodflows. In addition, a temporary road was constructed across the creek to provide access for gravel trucks. The loose material used to construct the crossing will produce a substantial increase in downstream siltation during winter flows. If the gravel operation continues, it will create serious erosion and siltation problems for downstream recreation use and wildlife enhancement. Even without the proposed project, gravel removal will adversely affect the existing downstream riparian site.

Considering these obvious impacts that surely could have been predicted, why and by what authority was this type of commercial activity permitted? In apparent compliance with the provisions of the California Environmental Quality Act, Stanislaus County officials reviewed the project and granted it full environmental clearance under a Negative Declaration that states the activity will not have significant effect on the environment at the creek. Mitigation measures were not made a condition of the approval, and apparently the extraction operation will be permitted to continue as long as it is economically feasible.

This contradictory application of environmental law raises doubts about is efficacy for preserving at least some of our remaining riparian resources. Based on individual interpretation, the legal "protection" represents a two-edged sword. Those of us concerned with preserving what we have left must be vigilant in our efforts to assure that the cut is for, not against, our cause.

WHO WILL PAY FOR CONSERVING AND MANAGING OUR REMAINING RIPARIAN RESOURCES?

The Orestimba Creek project involves another problem pertinent to management of riparian systems. The proposed site has excellent potentials for recreation use and wildlife enhancement. It is equally important that the remaining riparian system be conserved and managed effectively, but who will assume responsibility for doing the work and where will the required funds come from? Despite its excellent potentials, there is significant doubt that a capable operator with adequate funds will be found to develop and operate the proposed creekside site.

Conservation and productive management of our remaining riparian resources must involve a coordinated multi-agency approach that includes federal, state, county, municipal, and private owner stewardship (ibid.). This is the most effective approach to the problem. However, considering the financial bind that governmental and private agencies are facing (with the compounding effects of rising costs and declining revenues), is it reasonable to expect that large sums of money will be available to do the work required? With the recent cutbacks in many vital services, is it logical that governmental agencies at any level will give a riparian resources program high priority when allocating limited funds? If government participation will be difficult to obtain, is it any more reasonable to expect private ownership, faced with the same revenue and inflationary problems, to invest large sums of money in conserving and managing riparian land when there will be no dollar profit obtained from the investment?

Answers to these questions must be realistically considered before we begin to develop a program to preserve our remaining riparian resources. No matter how valid our motivations, our programs will be meaningless if adequate funding is not available for implementation. This is true for the Orestimba Creek project specifically and other proposals to preserve riparian systems in general.

LITERATURE CITED

Napton, L. K. 1980. Cultural investigations of the proposed Orestimba Creek wayside park, Stanislaus County, California. 142 p. California State College, Stanislaus, Institute of Archeological Research, Department of Anthropology, Turlock, Calif.

Warner, R.E. 1979. The California riparian study program. 177 p. Planning Branch, California Department of Fish and Game, Sacramento.

MANAGEMENT OF CULTURAL RESOURCES IN RIPARIAN SYSTEMS[1]

Patricia Mikkelsen and Greg White[2]

Abstract.--Prehistoric inhabitants of California's North Coast Ranges utilized riparian systems in patterns reflecting cultural and natural environments. Archaeological investigations seek to define these prehistoric cultures and paleo-environments and preserve their remains. The status of archaeology under federal and state legislation can help preserve and protect both cultural and natural resources.

INTRODUCTION

Cultural resources are broadly defined as "districts, sites, buildings, structures, and objects, significant in American history, architecture, archaeology, and culture."[3] They are important non-renewable features of scientific, social, and historic value that often occur within riparian systems. Prehistoric archaeological sites are among the cultural resources found there and are the primary concern of this paper.

An archaeological site (the location of past cultural activities) contains evidence of adaptation to a local environment. Archaeological data in California, along with ethnographic information (gathered from living people), have revealed complex native American cultures with settlement patterns and land-use practices that gave an integral role to the abundant riparian vegetation, wildlife, and water supplies (fig. 1). From this perspective, studies of the component aquatic and riparian systems comprising these ecosystems are important for archaeological interpretation, as native Americans were an integral part of such systems.

The management of cultural resources has become an important part of the land-use planning process; resource conservation is the ideal and the primary goal. Excavation of a site for mitigation of impact when the site is threatened is a form of destruction of that site. Though artifacts kept buried in the ground have little appeal to the public (which can be a vital force in preservation efforts), it is only by slowing

Figure 1.--Native American activities in a riparian system.

the rate of loss of cultural material that we will be able to utilize the new information and techniques that will inevitably be discovered in the future. The preservation of archaeological sites and their context is therefore vital for archaeology. In turn, the management of cultural resources, as a result of various federal and state laws, can be a factor in helping to manage and preserve riparian systems.

SETTLEMENT PATTERNS AND RIPARIAN RESOURCES

The following discussion will show how there is some degree of patterning and hence predictability in the location of archaeological resources, specifically with regard to riparian systems.

[1] Paper presented at the California Riparian Systems Conference. [University of California, Davis, September 17-19, 1981].

[2] Patricia Mikkelsen is a Graduate Student in Cultural Resource Management; Greg White is Staff Archaeologist; both are at Sonoma State University, Rohnert Park, Calif.

[3] 36 CFR 60.2.

In California's North Coast Ranges, most native American groups were characterized by a sociopolitical organization known as the tribelet. The tribelet was composed of a large nuclear village and several smaller hamlets. Within the tribelet territory were many sites that served as camps for those acquiring resources, as well as sites that were the locations for resource processing. Although native Americans of the North Coast Ranges practiced no formal agriculture, complex systems of maintenance and management of the resource-rich habitat were employed. For present purposes, native American resource management can be divided into two kinds: 1) direct alteration of the environment, such as the use of deliberate fires (Lewis 1973), altering streamcourses (Kroeber 1925), or preparing root beds for basketry material (Peri and Patterson 1976); and 2) indirect alteration of the environment, such as limiting the intensity and area of hunting, establishing fishing intensity and privileges along certain streams, or social divisions of labor that responded to the seasonal availability of many resources.

The Lake Miwok tribe, whose territory included Anderson Marsh in southeastern Clear Lake (Lake County), California, followed an annual cycle of population dispersal and re-consolidation that conformed with availability of food resources (Callaghan 1978). During winter months, the Lake Miwok stayed in permanent villages and hamlets that were located along year-round watercourses. Large villages such as these often were established at the confluences of major streams or rivers. During the stay in villages, people relied upon stored foodstuffs, although deer, tule elk, and especially waterfowl hunting were productive. In the spring, Lake Miwok continued to inhabit the villages and hamlets, but small parties went out to collect young, tender greens, and to fish for stream-run suckers and pike. In the summer and fall, most of the population of the village and hamlet communities would move to small family campsites in the hinterland. Nearly always, hinterland sites were located next to permanent water sources. Expeditions for resource collecting from the summer campsites were similar to those conducted from the main village, although a great deal of the collecting of materials for tools and goods took place during the summer and fall. The principal activities of hunting and fishing were also replaced in the fall by acorn collecting and processing (fig. 2).

As the Lake Miwok example shows, year-round water sources were used as locations of settlements, and riparian resources were utilized in each season. Archaeological research seeks to document land-use patterns, their changes through time, and the stimulus for these changes, and must recognize that sites within riparian systems were simply a part of a larger system that excluded few of whatever resources were present within the territory of a given tribelet.

SUPPORTIVE LEGISLATION FOR ARCHAEOLOGICAL RESEARCH

The value of archaeological research and knowledge has been increasingly recognized, beginning with the Antiquities Act in 1906[4] when an attempt was first made to legally protect artifacts. Since then, not just single artifacts, but archaeological sites have come under the protection of federal and state law and have taken their place along with other environmental resources considered for protection when development is to take place. Therefore, the presence of archaeological sites adds to the environmental evidence that urges protection for riparian systems.

The Historic Preservation Act of 1966[5] created the National Register of Historic Places. The Code of Federal Regulations (CFR) set out the functions of the Register to "identify the nation's cultural resources and indicate what properties should be considered for protection from destruction and impairment".[6] Executive Order 11593 attempted to tie together the legislation affecting cultural resources, requiring an inventory to determine eligibility to the National Register. The National Register serves only as a planning document; a listed site is not ensured of preservation. The site will, however, be taken into consideration early in any design plan with federal funding, permit, or land. Also, sites not on the register cannot be excluded from protection if they warrant it. The National Environmental Policy Act of 1969 (NEPA),[7] and the 1970 California Environmental Quality Act (CEQA),[8] directly involved cultural resources in the planning process. CEQA was formulated in part to preserve "...examples of the major periods of California history".[9] To clarify the phrase, the California Secretary of Resources and the California Superior Court stated that environmental impact reports should include a section on archaeological significance (King et al. 1973) and "history" has since been defined to include prehistory, or pre-European periods.

ARCHAEOLOGY IN THE PLANNING PROCESS

Cultural resource management should ideally come at the earliest stages of the planning process for proposed developments. In this way it can work towards avoiding threatened sites rather than permitting any destructive impacts or requiring mitigation. Archaeological site inventories and mapping can be especially useful to

---

[4] Antiquities Act of 1906; PL 59-209, 34 Stat. 225; 16 U.S.C. 431-433.
[5] PL 89-665; 80 Stat. 915; 16 U.S.C. 470 et seq.
[6] 36 CFR 60.2b.
[7] PL 91-190; 83 Stat. 852; 42 U.S.C. 4321-4347.
[8] PRC Section 21000-21176.
[9] Section 21001 Public Resources Code.

774

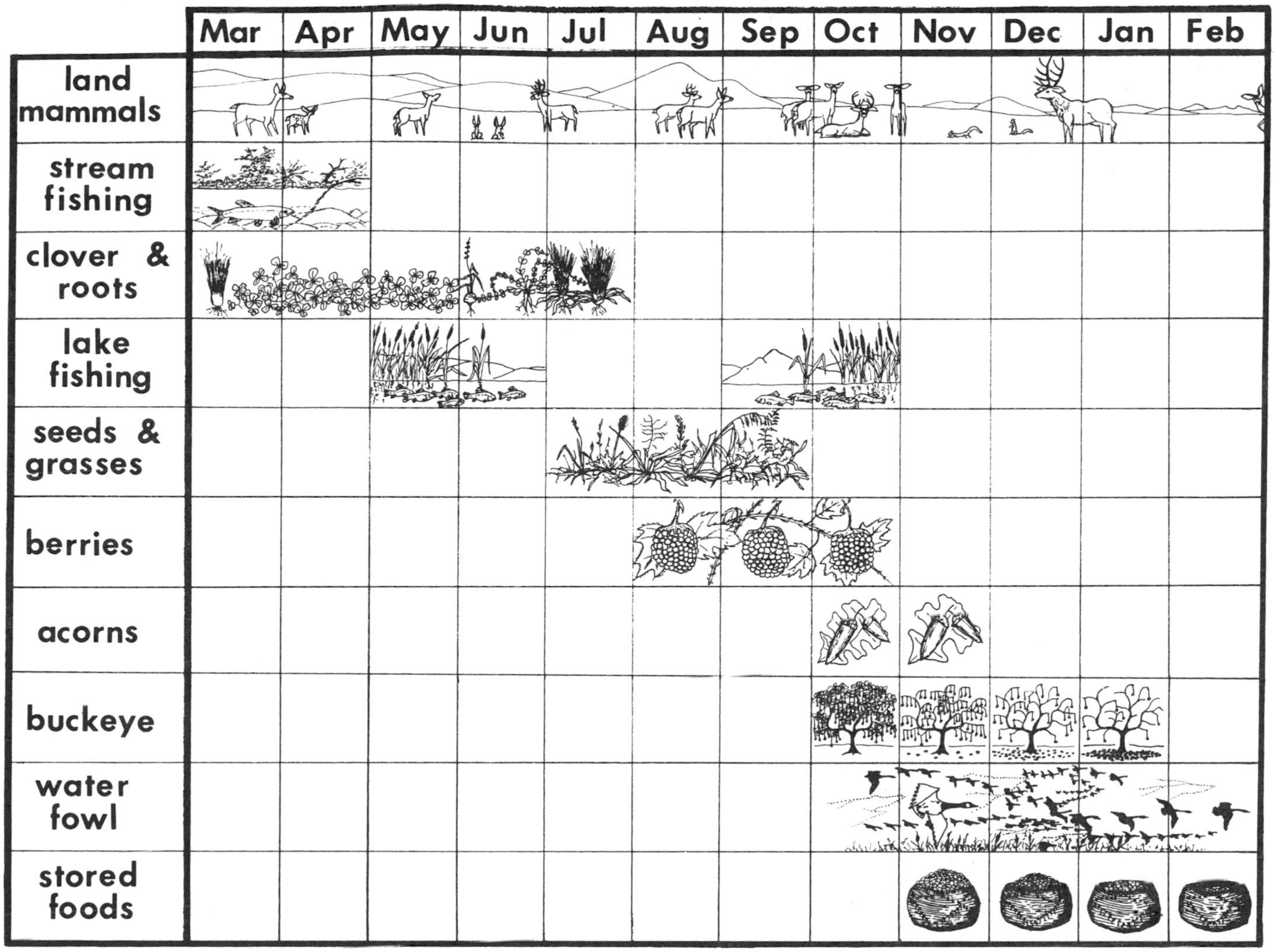

	Mar	Apr	May	Jun	Jul	Aug	Sep	Oct	Nov	Dec	Jan	Feb
land mammals												
stream fishing												
clover & roots												
lake fishing												
seeds & grasses												
berries												
acorns												
buckeye												
water fowl												
stored foods												

Figure 2.--Seasonal resource calendar of the Lower Lake District.

many areas of study, as they supply updated information on archaeological site distribution and can be used for advance planning and research.

The Northwest Information Center of the California Archaeological Inventory, located at Sonoma State University, is an outgrowth of the California Archaeological Survey of the University of California, Berkeley, (established by R. Heizer and now under the control of Department of Parks and Recreation [DPR]) and the Regional Clearinghouse (established by the Society for California Archaeology for the purpose of processing archaeological impact reports and serving as archives for archaeological papers). The document review section is an outreach program for Sonoma and other counties; it reviews applications for development by evaluating archaeological sensitivity and making recommendations for preservation and protection of archaeological resources. Not only does this office, and others throughout California, provide information early in the planning process, they are also able to generate predictive models for site distribution in various regions.

Two of the basic criteria used by the Northwest Information Center for evaluating archaeological sensitivity are proximity of the proposed project to water and/or the existence of ecotones. If a proposed project is along or near a water system, especially one with pronounced ecotones, a survey is generally recommended, unless the terrain is too steep for habitation or use, or other negative criteria exist. Such environments have been found to be archaeologically sensitive. Another source for determining archaeological sensitivity is the ethnographic maps and records of anthropologists and other researchers who worked among native Americans in the late 1800s and early 1900s and recorded the locations of their villages and campsites. As noted in fig-

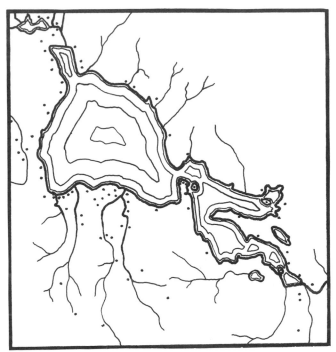

Figure 3.--Distribution of village sites at Clear Lake (Lake County), California (after Barrett, 1908).

ure 3, the sites were often heavily concentrated around lakes and along rivers and streams.

In addition to site-specific review, archaeological sensitivity studies have been developed for districts and regions. One such study in the North Sonoma Valley, Sonoma County, found, as expected, that riparian zones were particularly archaeologically sensitive (Mikkelsen 1980).

According to maps and literature on file at the Northwest Information Center of the California Archaeological Inventory, 47 surveys have been conducted in the 20,240-ha. (50,000-ac.) North Sonoma Valley, covering 10% of the study area. Approximately 80% of the sites discovered in the valley were along streamcourses. Although the surveys have concentrated on riparian zones and other areas have not been thoroughly studied, riparian corridors were clearly shown to be archaeologically sensitive areas. Also, information from Barrett's ethnographic map (1908) revealed villages at the headwaters of two major creeks in the valley. Kroeber's (1925) settlement map showed four villages spread along the banks of one of the creeks.

On the basis of this evidence, it was recommended that 304-m. (1,000-ft.) boundaries along streams be marked as particularly sensitive for archaeological purposes. This rating would not necessarily save a site in a riparian zone, but it would give planners advance knowledge of the recommendations pertaining to archaeology, and archaeological sensitivity could be taken into consideration when plans are formulated. This

would avoid costly mitigation efforts and perhaps result in the preservation of an archaeological site and its riparian context.

ARCHAEOLOGY AND RIPARIAN PRESERVATION

An example of an archaeological investigation that was able to contribute significantly to halting the decline of riparian resources occurred near Clear Lake. An archaeological survey was performed along Cache Creek in Anderson Marsh, along the route of a proposed levee construction planned by the Sacramento District, US Army Corps of Engineers (CE). Cache Creek is the only outlet for Clear Lake in recent history; it flows through the marsh at the southern end of the lake. This marsh/lakeshore environment supports tule, cattail, and bulrush as well as numerous birds and other wildlife (fig. 4).

Figure 4.--Aerial view of Cache Creek, Anderson Marsh, and Clear Lake.

The area also contains numerous archaeological sites: native American villages, campsites, and specific-task sites. Ten prehistoric sites were observed along the proposed levee route during the archaeological survey (Fredrickson and Parker 1977). Artifacts such as milling stones, handstones, mortars and pestles, and projectile points were identified. The significance of the sites to the understanding of local, regional, and state prehistory resulted in their being listed in the National Register of Historic Places. As all sites would be adversely affected by the CE project, the primary recommendation was that the areas of the project containing sites be avoided.

The marsh, surrounding lakeshore and watershed, and three islands have recently been acquired by the State as a cultural and natural preserve. The archaeological sensitivity of the area played an important part in the decision, with 15% of the allocated funds proposed for a cultural heritage preserve.[10] By assessing all environmental variables concurrently, a major case was made for protection of endangered cultural and natural resources.

ARCHAEOLOGICAL RESEARCH AND RIPARIAN SYSTEM STUDIES

Many research questions identified and addressed by archaeologists are developed with data that would be of interest to riparian system researchers. Of particular interest are archaeological efforts to reconstruct extinct local and regional biotic communities. Not only has the changing environment of the prehistoric North Coast Ranges influenced the logistics of settlement patterns, as for example in the shifting of a base camp location to follow a migrating ecotone, but changing environments may have greatly influenced departures from tradition to implement new diets, technologies, and social and cultural systems among the native peoples. The reconstructions of paleo-environments have become a valuable explication and independent test of archaeological inferences.

An example of the research potential for interdisciplinary study of archaeological data comes from D.A. Fredrickson's analysis of CCO-308, a prehistoric native American site near Alamo in Contra Costa County. The investigation of that site was undertaken in 1963 and served as the basis for Fredrickson's Masters Thesis (Fredrickson 1966). Excavations at the site were for salvage purposes. The site was in the path of a rechannelling of San Ramon Creek. The new channel had been dug, exposing a site on the surface

and two deeper cultural strata, each separated by culturally sterile soils. The view of stratigraphy along the channel trench wall, though of regrettable origin, provided a depositional history in the archaeological site locale.

Figure 5 shows a schematic of stratigraphy of the channel's north wall. The overall stratigraphy of the western part of the profile exhibited diagonal sediments, indicating that each of the ancient settlements had been on a terrace adjacent to the streambank and that the creek had steadily migrated to the west while depositing sediments on its east bank. The stratigraphy of the eastern part of the profile shows alternate layers of silts, loam, and gravel, indicating that the terrace on which the old settlements had been located was an occasional floodplain and that the floodplain had contained meandering overflow channels.

In addition to this depositional history, Fredrickson's excavations in an undisturbed portion of the site provided an excellent cultural history. From each cultural stratum, tools implying how vegetation in the locale was used by the succeeding cultures were recovered. The preserved skeletal remains of the faunal species that those groups had exploited were also found.

For a second example of the utility of interdisciplinary study of archaeological research questions, we can turn again to the Lake Miwok Anderson Marsh example. In historic times, the Lake Miwok spoke a language not related to their immediate neighbors, but to languages of groups occupying the San Francisco Bay and Sacramento/ San Joaquin Delta areas. Careful linguistic analysis has found the Lake Miwok to be most

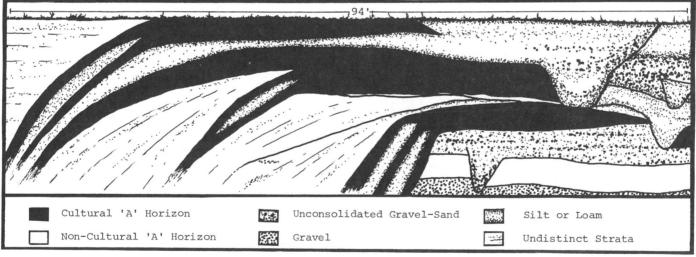

| ■ Cultural 'A' Horizon | ▨ Unconsolidated Gravel-Sand | ▨ Silt or Loam |
| □ Non-Cultural 'A' Horizon | ▨ Gravel | ▨ Undistinct Strata |

Figure 5.--Stratigraphic profile of native American site near Alamo (Contra Costa County).

[10]Hanchett, Roberta. 1980. Anderson Marsh; preserve or develop? Clear Lake Observer, June 5, 1980.

closely related to the Miwok of the Marin (County) coast and that the languages of those two groups split at about the same time-depth as the romance languages, around 2,000 years ago (fig. 6).

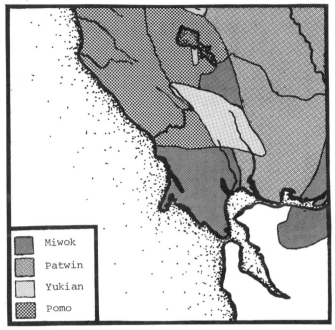

Figure 6.--Native American language groups of north San Francisco Bay.

Legend:
- Miwok
- Patwin
- Yukian
- Pomo

Archaeological analysis has supported the linguistic hypothesis and added the further dimension that the Miwok movement was probably from the south to the north (Fredrickson 1973). The Lake Miwok arrival apparently displaced a semisedentary hunting and collecting culture, and, while adopting some of the earlier traits, the Lake Miwok brought in a radically different technology and social organization. These data have raised research questions that can only be answered by examinations of interest to both the archaeologist and riparian systems researcher.

Apparently, in the bay and delta areas the Miwok had developed adaptations for living along the shores of a large body of water. There is an obvious difference between bayshore and lacustrine (lakeshore) biotic communities. However, it may have been the traditional technology and labor roles of the Miwok that influenced their settlement in riparian communities. One potential indicator of the Lake Miwok carrying on their old bayshore traditions in the new environment is the abundance of freshwater mussel (Anadonta spp.) in some of their early Clear Lake sites (White and Fredrickson 1981). Sites of the early Miwok along the bayshore are characterized by heaps of mussel (Mytilus spp.) and clam (Macoma spp.) dietary debris, while pre-Miwok sites at Clear Lake have not evidenced an importance of freshwater shellfish in the diet.

One of the dramatic differences between Lake and Coast Miwok sites is the much greater inventory of terrestrial-faunal dietary debris present in the Lake-area sites, so some adjustments to the new environment must have taken place in the Lake Miwok culture. Future study of these adjustments may find that entering the new area put strains upon not only the Lake Miwok, by way of new sources of energy and different organizations of labor, but upon the environment as well, because initial Miwok adaptation probably was not in a tradition balanced with local ecology. We might expect that during the period just after arrival, a special strain would be placed upon those species in riparian systems that were identical or similar to traditional sources of food along the coast, simply because the number of traditional foods in the new area was limited and ways of procuring and processing new foods had to be learned. Thus, for example, the early Lake Miwok use of freshwater clams might have made substantial inroads upon the population and ecology of that species, especially since the previous Clear Lake cultures apparently did not make any significant use of the clam in their diet.

These questions about Lake Miwok prehistory cannot be answered without detailed reconstruction of the paleo-environment and, particularly, the early riparian environments. Individuals from Sonoma State University will be conducting an excavation on an early Lake Miwok site in the Anderson Marsh area in the summer of 1982. The plan is to to use not only the available data for early Clear Lake environments (Adam 1979; Casteel et al. 1977), but to obtain one or two pollen cores from Anderson Marsh. It is hoped that this research will provide the detail needed to understand a single period about 2,000 years ago. In addition, the faunal and floral fossil content of the site (which is adjacent to Cache Creek) will be examined in detail. Even if this investigation sheds no light upon Lake Miwok prehistory, it should result in some findings of interest to riparian systems research.

CONCLUSION

Cultural resources are non-renewable; once destroyed they are irreplaceable. They provide data on an extensive stretch of time and are the primary sources of information about the people who lived in California before the arrival of Europeans. The threat to their preservation and the preservation of their environmental context is imminent.

When any development or preservation plans are formulated, the presence of cultural resources should be considered. Information on archaeological sensitivity is available to developers and researchers; this information should be utilized to prevent costly holdups or adjustments in development and to aid in the management of California's natural systems.

LITERATURE CITED

Adam, Dave. 1979. Raw pollen counts from core 4, Clear Lake, Lake County, California. USDI Geological Survey open file report 79-663, Menlo Park, Calif. 7 p.

Barrett, S.A. 1908. The entho-geography of the Pomo and neighboring Indians. University of California Publications in American Archaeology and Ethnology 6(1). 332 p.

Callaghan, Catherine. 1978. Lake Miwok. p. 264--273. In: W. Steurtevant and R. Heizer (ed.). Handbook of North American Indians. Vol. 8: California. 800 p. Smithsonian Institution, Washington, D.C.

Casteel, Richard W., David P. Adam, and Joan D. Sims. 1977. Late-Pleistocene and Holocene remains of Hysterocarpus Traski (tule perch) from Clear Lake, California, and inferred Holocene temperature fluctuations. Quarternary Research 7:133-143.

Fredrickson, David A. 1966. CCO-308: The archaeology of a middle horizon site in interior Contra Costa County, California. Unpublished M.A. Thesis, University of California, Davis. 202 p.

Fredrickson, David A. 1973. Early cultures of the North Coast Ranges, California. Unpublished Ph.D. Thesis. University of California, Davis. 277 p.

Fredrickson, David A. and John Parker. 1977. An archaeological survey of the Cache Creek basin project, Lake County, Calif. Report S-586, on file at the Northwest Information Center of the California Archaeological Inventory, California State University, Sonoma, Rohnert Park, Calif. 45 p.

King, Thomas, Michael Moratto, and Nelson Leonard III. 1973. Recommended procedures for archaeological impact evaluation. Report on a study by the Society for California Archaeology in cooperation with the Archaeology Survey, University of California, Los Angeles. 19 p.

Kroeber, A.L. 1925. Handbook of the Indians of California. Bureau of American Ethnology, Bulletin No. 78, Smithsonian Institution, Washington, D.C. 995 p.

Lewis, Henry. 1973. Patterns of Indian burning in California ecology and ethnohistory. Ballena Press Anthropological Papers, No. 1. 101 p. Ballena Press, Ramona, Calif.

Mikkelsen, Pat. 1980. Archaeological sensitivity study of the North Sonoma Valley. North Sonoma Valley Specific Plan. 137 p. Sonoma County Department of Planning, Sonoma, Calif.

Peri, David, and Scott Patterson. 1976. The basket is in the roots, that's where it begins. Journal of California 3(2):17-32.

White, Greg, and David A. Fredrickson. 1981. Archaeological investigation at CA-LAK-510, near Lower Lake, Lake County, California. Report S-2166 on file at the Northwest Information Center of the California Archaeological Inventory, California State University, Sonoma, Rohnert Park, Calif. 148 p.

WARM SPRINGS DAM-LAKE SONOMA ETHNOBOTANICAL PRESERVE:

AN ATTEMPT TO MITIGATE FOR A CULTURAL LOSS[1]

David K. Tripp[2]

Abstract.--This paper focuses on the importance of riparian systems to native Americans, and the compatibility of native American riparian resource use with the resource base itself. Studies have shown collection techniques for basket materials also enhance the growth and spread of these plants.

INTRODUCTION

The Lake Sonoma project area consists of over 6,880 ha. (17,000 ac.) of federal land about 18 km. (11 mi.) northwest of the city of Healdsburg in Sonoma County, approximately 113 km. (70 mi.) northwest of San Francisco, California. The project, managed by the US Army Corps of Engineers (CE), includes the construction of the earthfill Warm Springs Dam, forming a 1,460-ha. (3,600-ac.) reservoir for water supply and flood control, recreational areas, fish and wildlife facilities, and a cultural resource interpretation program.

The Ethnobotanical Preserve Project is the direct outgrowth of two previous CE-sponsored studies: The Ethnobotanical Element[3] of the Vegetative Management Plan (US Army Corps of Engineers, San Francisco District 1979) undertaken by the firm of Elgar Hill Environmental Planning and Analysis of Sausalito, California, and ethnobotanical research conducted by the Ethnographic Component[4] of the Warm Springs Cultural Resources Study of Sonoma State University, Rohnert Park, California (Peri et al. 1981).

Downstream of the Warm Springs Dam, an ethnobotanical preserve is being established by the San Francisco District, CE, to mitigate for the project-induced loss of long-used sites of certain riparian species of sedge and willow. These sites are some of the last remaining sources of materials essential for the manufacture of Pomo baskets. These ethnobotanically important plants have been transplanted to new locations on federal land, out of the danger from inundation.

Over 34,000 sedge plants have been transplanted to new locations within the ethnobotanical preserve. Existing willow tracts within the preserve are being enhanced through cultivation and limited transplanting.

POMO BASKETRY - A CULTURAL EXPRESSION

Dr. Samuel Barrett, an anthropologist who devoted much of his life to studying California Indians, made the statement that Pomo basketry stands among "the very best examples of aboriginal art anywhere" (Barrett 1908), and certainly it is the most widely acclaimed of the basketry arts in California.

Figure 1.--An example of Pomo basketry.

[1]Paper presented at the California Riparian Systems Conference. [University of California, Davis, September 17-19, 1981].

[2]David K. Tripp is Environmental Protection Specialist, San Francisco District, US Army Corps of Engineers, Geyserville, Calif.

[3]Contract No. DACW07-87-C-0040.

[4]Contract No. DACW07-78-C-0043.

Other anthropologists have stated about native California basketry:

The creative inventiveness with which plant resources were shaped to human cultural purposes in California found its ultimate expression in the extensive, elaborate, and varied utilization of plant fibers in basketry... In short, basketry was an artform in which color of materials, shape, design, texture, and fineness of weave were manipulated for purely aesthetic as well as practical ends. (McLendon and Holland 1979)

Pomo basketry is an integral element in the essence of Pomo cultural expression. Encompassed in the learning process of basketry are entwined myths, legends, and religious values. These qualities of the Pomo people are learned by the young and transmitted to the society at large. Clearly, basketry is a cornerstone of modern Pomo society; its continuity means continuity for the Pomo people themselves. With the destruction of the sedge- and willow-gathering areas (materials that are essential to the construction of Pomo baskets), basketry is also in danger of extinction as an artform.

BASKET SEDGE

The rootstocks of sedge (Carex barbarae) provided the Pomo with basket fibers. The genus Carex, whose members are commonly referred to as sedges, is the largest genus of flowering plants in California and, with its more than 1,000 species, is one of the largest in the world. A total of 144 species has been reported in California. Within the state, the distribution of Carex is remarkably diverse and widespread.

Within the project area, on the upper reaches of Dry and Warm Springs creeks, two species of Carex, C. barbarae and C. nudata, predominate. The former species provides the most desirable of the rootstocks used for Pomo basketry. The latter species, although relatively widespread, typically occupies the more gravelly portions of streams and possesses root development unsuitable for basketry.

Carex barbarae occupies a fairly wide range of substrates and topographical zones in the project area. Most of the populations occupy primary creek terraces, sandy rises, and banks away from flowing water, but the species is occasionally found immediately adjacent to the water's edge and upon sloping hillsides.

"Basket sedges" are "everlasting plants" (perennials), with grass-like triangular stems, that reproduce both by flowers and spreading rhizomes. The mature or parent plant has two separate root systems: one consisting of rootlets or foundation roots that grow vertically into the soil, supplying water and minerals; the other comprising the reproductive rhizomes or runners that grow to form a lateral root network to anchor the plant, reducing erosional effects of the rivers and streams where it commonly grows.

The new season's growth is "spring roots" and is recognized by sharply pointed root tips or spurs. The second season's roots are called ripe roots, referring to their maturity for basketry purposes. After the second season, the rhizomes will then sprout and come to the surface, each eventually growing a mature crown of foliage, foundation roots and its own rhizomes. In later years, if not collected, these original rhizomes turn black with age and rot away completely.

Field reconnaissance determined that in the project area Carex barbarae grows in diverse substrates--from the edges of creeks to the base of adjacent hillsides. The rootstock produced by this species is profoundly affected by the type and condition of the soil in which it grows. Only if a number of specific environmental criteria are met are the roots suitable for basketry purposes.

Basket weavers divide root beds into four subdivisions which are designated by terms that describe their soil conditions: sand beds; dirt beds; heavy clay beds; and sand and gravel beds. The sand root beds contain light sand mixed with silt. The dirt root beds contain soil with a light to moderate clay content which tends to become quite compacted. The heavy clay beds contain a thick, highly compacted soil which becomes almost impossible to dig when dry. Gravel beds consist primarily of sand and gravel of varying sizes.

The most desired of the basket sedge tracts are sand root beds which occur in loosely compacted, highly friable, silty sand. In these beds the rhizomes grow longer before the end of their growing season, since they can easily penetrate the loose soil. The rootstocks obtained from these soil conditions commonly reach lengths of 0.9-1.5 m. (3-5 ft.) and, on occasion, will grow as long as 1.8-2.1 m. (6-7 ft.).

Because of extensive destruction of riparian areas in the region during the last century, the most prized of the sand root beds for Pomo basket weavers are those now found along Dry Creek and Warm Springs Creek within the Lake Sonoma project area. It has been determined through consultation with basket weavers that these sedge beds were used at least as early as the 1850s. Other basket weavers remember Dry Creek as being "the most continuously and most extensively used area in the Russian River basin" (Theodoratus et al. 1975).

WILLOW

The remarkably pliable shoots and branches obtained from the sandbar willow (Salix hindsiana), also called the grey or basket willow, provided the Pomo and neighboring peoples with a plant resource which was indispensable to aboriginal daily life. From the great thickets of this willow, which reportedly grew in the creek and river banks throughout Sonoma, Mendocino and Lake counties, Indians annually harvested vast quantities of willow. Its flexible limbs served as a basic building material used in the construction of living, ceremonial and food-storage structures and were also fashioned into a diverse array of tools and household utensils. Of even greater importance now, the long, slender willow wands are used extensively in a wide variety of coiled and twined basketry.

Within the Lake Sonoma project area, basket willow is most frequently encountered along watercourses where the width of the stream channel is great enough to allow alluvial soil build-up. The best development of this willow usually occurs along elevated and well-drained sandy creekbeds and bars, in close proximity to flowing water. Once colonization has taken place, the willow root system spreads and vegetative sprouts are produced which trap additional silt, sand, and organic debris. This process creates and expands the habitat for the willow and allows it to spread into long, linear belts that often form nearly homogeneous stands. The basket willow is almost always found in situations where shade is nearly or completely absent. Its tolerance to high amounts of light results in part from its silvery-tomentose leaves which reflect sunlight.

COMPATIBILITY OF NATIVE AMERICAN USE AND THE PLANT COMMUNITY

An essential ingredient for developing and maintaining sedge root tracts is recognition and maintenance and improvement of environmental conditions vital for yielding the finest roots. In the collection process, collectors are faced with a delicate problem: they must obtain an adequate root supply and at the same time ensure the tract's continued viability. Weavers utilize a collection strategy regulated by supernatural sanctions and taboos that are compatible with the reproductive mechanisms of sedge. For example, sexual and menstrual taboos serve in part to regulate the number of days available for collecting, thereby reducing collection pressure on the tracts (Peri and Patterson 1976).

Before actually collecting sedge roots, weavers carefully remove debris (rocks, branches, other roots, etc.) from the tract. In addition, during harvesting smaller sedge plants and rhizomes are planted back into the tract. These efforts create a well-cultivated tract of sedge. The harvest/cultivation practices, combined with the elimination of competing plant species on the tract, promote improvement and expansion of the sedge tract. As long as sedge beds are cultivated, they supply a predictable and probably permanently renewable resource.

As with the sedge, the collecting process or harvesting of basket willow employed by native Americans is also highly selective. This selection process has been found to be beneficial to willow stand expansion in preferred tracts. Extensive pruning of upper branches stimulates expansion of the root system and encourages the growth of numerous young shoots, resulting in brushy thickets. The seasonal pruning of willow branches during collection prevents the willow plants from becoming tree-like. Expansion of the root system aids in expansion of the actual willow tract. Overall, native American use practices are not only compatible with, but can be viewed as beneficial to the maintenance of certain species of riparian vegetation.

CONCLUSION

When future riparian system restoration, enhancement, or protection plans are being developed, it would seem advantageous to the agency involved to include some critical input of the local native American community. The needs of the native American community and their usage of various riparian plants can be beneficial to the project's overall goals.

LITERATURE CITED

Barrett, S.A. 1908. The Ethno-geography of the Pomo and neighboring Indians. University of California Publications in American Archaeology and Ethnology 6. 245 p. Berkeley, Calif.

McLendon, S., and B. Holland. 1973. The basketmakers; the Pomoans of California. p. 103-129. In: The ancestors, native artisans of the Americas. The Museum of the American Indian, New York, N.Y.

Peri, David W., and Scott M. Patterson. 1976. The basket is in the roots, that's where it begins. Journal of California Anthropology 3(2):17-32.

Peri, David W., Scott M. Patterson, and Susan L. McMurray. 1981. Warm Springs cultural resources study--the Makahmo Pomo. US Army Corps of Engineers, San Francisco District, San Francisco, Calif.

Theodoratus, Dorothea J., et al. 1975. An ethnographic survey of the Mahilkaune (Dry Creek) Pomo. Warm Springs Ethnographic Survey, Sonoma County, Calif. US Army Corps of Engineers, San Francisco District, San Francisco, Calif.

US Army Corps of Engineers, San Francisco District. 1979. Lake Sonoma-vegetation management plan (preliminary), Design Memorandum No. 21, San Francisco District, US Army Corps of Engineers, San Francisco, Calif.

DEVELOPING A LONG-TERM PROTECTION PLAN

FOR THE McCLOUD RIVER, CALIFORNIA[1]

Thomas F. Hesseldenz[2]

Abstract.--The McCloud River drainage in northern California hosts the Dolly Varden char (Salvelinus confluentus), Shasta rainbow trout (Salmo gairdneri), redband trout (S. campi), Shasta salamander (Hydromantes shastae), and Shasta eupatory (Eupatorium shastense). These species and numerous others with rare or threatened status have until recently been indirectly protected by a history of private ownership and inaccessibility of large parts of the drainage. Dam construction, water diversion, road construction, timber harvest, angling pressure, and limestone quarrying now threaten the drainage and have encouraged intensive planning efforts to lessen their impacts. However, integrated planning using a system-wide approach has been complicated by multiple ownership and agency involvement in the drainage. The Nature Conservancy through the McCloud River Preserve is seeking to resolve this problem with its McCloud River Protection Plan. The tentative components of this plan are presented in detail.

INTRODUCTION

Environmental planning has come into its own as a discipline in the last few years. Aiding in this evolution have been various governmental mandates; most notably the National Environmental Policy Act (NEPA) and the California Environmental Quality Act (CEQA). We are finally seeing proposed actions with potential environmental impact being preceded by thorough studies of the affected system. However, the preservation of the integrity of a whole system as an end in itself is rarely the direct object of planning efforts. Achieving such an end is often complicated by multiple ownership and agency involvement. Such is the case on the McCloud River in northern California, where The Nature Conservancy (TNC) owns the McCloud River Preserve (the Preserve).

Ownership in the McCloud drainage includes private individuals, fishing clubs, and timber companies as well as Pacific Gas and Electric Company, USDA Forest Service (FS), and TNC. The California Department of Fish and Game (DFG) is also deeply involved with the wild trout fishery

there. Each entity has its own recognized values of the drainage, its own goals, and its own planning program to achieve these goals. TNC, through its involvement with the Preserve, is in the position of being able to work towards the preservation of the integrity of the McCloud River drainage as its primary goal. With such a goal, the system will come first; the challenge will be to integrate the activities of the other entities involved and direct them towards this goal.

Work has only just begun on this planning effort, known as the McCloud River Protection Plan. The details behind this plan are presented at this incomplete stage so that they will be available at an earlier date to other planners dealing with whole systems. The author hopes this timing will also generate suggestions which may improve the planning efforts of TNC in the McCloud River drainage.

DESCRIPTION OF THE SYSTEM

The McCloud River drainage is located in Shasta and Siskiyou counties in northern California, in a region where the Sierra Nevada, the Cascades, and the Klamath Mountains intersect (fig. 1). The McCloud River originates in the relatively flat volcanic region southeast of Mt. Shasta. From there it flows westward through extensive yellow pine (Pinus ponderosa) forest for about 40.2 km. (25 mi.) as a large stream.

[1]Paper presented at the California Riparian Systems Conference. [University of California, Davis, September 17-19, 1981].
[2]Thomas F. Hesseldenz is Preserve Manager for the McCloud River Preserve of the Nature Conservancy, San Francisco, Calif.

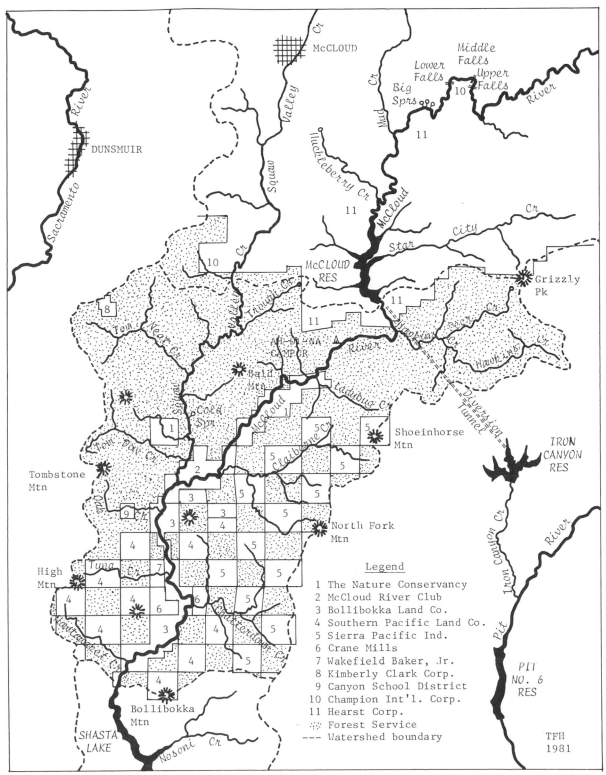

Figure 1.--Map of the portion of the McCloud River drainage being evaluated in the McCloud River Protection Plan, showing significant geographic features and property ownership.

Shortly after descending three large waterfalls, the lowermost being the historic barrier to upstream fish migration, the McCloud greatly enlarges in size due to input from several large springs. These springs, thought to emerge from the collapsed terminus of a lava tube, are a constant 43°F (6.1°C) and have a summer peak flow, in contrast to winter and spring peak flows of the upper McCloud River. The downstream result is a relatively constant flow and large volume of very cold water year-round.[3]

Mud Creek enters the McCloud River about 3.2 km. (2 mi.) below Big Springs, carrying a heavy load of very fine glacial silt and volcanic ash from Mt. Shasta. This imparts a turquoise-gray turbidity to the river. Below Mud Creek, the McCloud River enters a rugged mountainous region of actively uplifting sedimentary and metamorphic rock, considered to be part of the Klamath Mountain geomorphic province.[4] Prior to dam construction, the lower McCloud flowed swiftly through its steep canyon for about 80.5 km. (50 mi.) before joining the Pit River and then, a few miles downstream, merging with the Sacramento River.

Chinook salmon (Oncorhyrchus tshawytscha), silver salmon (O. kisutch), and steelhead trout (Salmo gairdneri) migrated yearly up the McCloud River as far as Lower Falls to spawn. The eggs, young, and carcasses of these species plus the stable large flow of cold water and habitat complexity provided by numerous boulders and deep pools are thought to explain why the interior Dolly Varden char (Salvelinus confluentus) has persisted in the McCloud River as a relict species. The McCloud is the southern limit of its range and the only river in California where the Dolly Varden occurs. The McCloud River strain of rainbow trout, also called the Shasta rainbow (Salmo gairdneri), may be genetically unique and has gained recognition among trout hatcheries and anglers worldwide (Sturgess and Moyle 1978).

Flanking much of the lower McCloud River are large limestone outcrops of the Baird Formation. This limestone formation has gained recognition in scientific circles for the numerous extinct mammal bones found in several of its caves and for two species endemic to both its outcrops and those of the nearby Hosselkus Formation, the Shasta eupatory (Eupatorium shastense) and the Shasta salamander (Hydromantes shastae).

Downstream from Big Springs, the river is joined by numerous tributaries with high channel gradient and cool water shaded by dense riparian vegetation and steep canyons. Squaw Valley Creek is the largest of these and ranks in size among small rivers. This stream originates near Mud Creek on Mt. Shasta and, similar to the upper McCloud, flows through the relatively flat volcanic region around the town of McCloud before entering steep, mountainous terrain and joining the lower McCloud River. Haskins Creek is a large tributary to the lower McCloud which may now play the role of the functional headwaters of the river due to its position as the most upstream tributary below a major diversion dam.

The riparian zones of the McCloud River drainage form a complex assemblage of strips along headwater and tributary streams, vertical borders of waterfalls, lush growth around springs (both volcanic and limestone), oasis-like seeps often high on slopes, "dry" lakes and sinks, and large streamside flats interspersed with narrow gorges along the main river and lower Squaw Valley Creek. These large flats host numerous Wintu Indian archeological sites.

Researchers on the Preserve have noticed a much higher number of plant, avian, and mammalian species in these areas than elsewhere.[5,6,7] Some plant species (e.g., Abies concolor) exhibit a southern range extension here, apparently due to cold air drainage associated with the cold water and steep canyons. Numerous heavily used animal trails link riparian areas to the uplands via the spines of ridges. On the Preserve, the riparian zone along the river has recently been the site for numerous deer kills by mountain lions.

HISTORY OF THE SYSTEM

The Wintu Indians were the original inhabitants of the lower McCloud drainage, relying in part on the anadromous fishery for sustenance. While adjacent drainages were being altered by transportation routes and the search for gold in the late 1800s, the McCloud remained intact.

Central Pacific Railroad acquired the first ownership in the drainage, consisting of a river corridor and surrounding checkerboard ownership of sections. However, construction of a railway along the river never came to pass. By this time the fame of the McCloud River's wild trout fishery had spread to San Francisco, and the river corridor property was quickly bought up by pri-

---

[3]Data on file at the USDI Geologic Survey, Redding, Calif.

[4]Haskins, D.M. 1981. Slope stability hazards and water quality effects: proposed Ah-Di-Na timber sale. Unpublished report. Shasta-Trinity National Forest, Redding, Calif.

[5]Patterson, C. 1975. Vegetation survey: McCloud River Preserve. Unpublished report. The Nature Conservancy, San Francisco, Calif.

[6]Hayes, M. 1975. Report on the avifuana and herpetofauna: McCloud River Preserve. Unpublished report. The Nature Conservancy, San Francisco, Calif.

[7]Hayes, M., and P. Kraai. 1975. Report on the mammals of the McCloud River Preserve. Unpublished report. The Nature Conservancy, San Francisco, Calif.

vate individuals and fly-fishing clubs. Land ownership is shown in figure 1. An egg-taking station was installed a few miles up from the confluence with the Pit River, and the McCloud River rainbow trout was introduced to streams around the world.

The first major change to the McCloud drainage came in the form of Shasta Dam, completed in 1945, which blocked anadromous fish migration and inundated about 24.1 km. (15 mi.) of the lower river. Upstream, the impact was more ecological than visual; the pristine qualities of the McCloud River drainage remained unaltered until its downfall in the early 1960s. At that time Pacific Gas and Electric Company built a reservoir to divert most of the McCloud's flow to the Pit River drainage for hydroelectric production. An extensive system of roads was constructed, and much of the land around the reservoir was logged. The FS subsequently acquired about 8.0 km. (5 mi.) of riverfront property below the reservoir and installed a campground. The new road system and public ownership along the river brought a drastic increase in angling pressure to which DFG responded by stocking the river with hatchery trout. The Dolly Varden char population rapidly declined until it was thought to be extinct in the McCloud River.

Impacts on the riparian zone of the river were substantial. Aside from inundating 8.0 km. (5 mi.) more of river, McCloud Reservoir drastically reduced the annual flow downstream. Most Douglas fir (Pseudotsuga menziesii) and western red cedar (Thuja plicata) trees growing within the riparian zone died, supposedly due to a root rot epidemic.[8] Alders and willows colonized the banks and gravelbars previously scoured by annual floods. The exotic black locust (Robinia pseudoacacia), first introduced at a homesite upstream, likewise responded to this available habitat and spread downstream. The streamside plant Peltiphyllum peltatum began blooming in April instead of June. Beavers began to lodge along the river where they had probably probably been excluded by regular floods in the past.

To complicate this situation, extensive logging and associated road-building increased sediment input. Fortunately, the soils in the McCloud drainage are fairly resistant to mass failure, and the problems found on the Trinity River and Redwood Creek have not yet developed there. However, due to a relatively low channel gradient and reduced flows, the river may not be able to flush out the sediment. This in time could lead to streambed aggradation with associated bank erosion (Seidelman 1980). Fine sediments cloud the river during large rainstorms; this may affect spawning gravels and aquatic invertebrates.

This was the state of affairs when TNC acquired the Preserve in 1973. The McCloud River Club, one of the large private owners, donated 943 ha. (2,330 ac.) of their land, including 10.5

km. (6.5 mi.) of river. The gift was gladly accepted by TNC, which was well aware of the recent and rapid decline in riverine systems throughout the state.

CRITICAL ELEMENTS

Natural diversity may be thought of in terms of the units that comprise it. These are here called "elements" of natural diversity, the building blocks of uniqueness in any natural systems. Many of the elements found in the McCloud River drainage are now considered to be critically threatened. Table 1 lists those critical elements that have been identified to date. Many of these elements do not depend solely on the McCloud region for their continued survival, but since they have been recognized as worthy of concern, they are listed here for the sake of completeness. TNC is primarily concerned with those taxa of proven or potential genetic uniqueness which are restricted in distribution to the McCloud region, as well as those of such critically threatened status as to have received state and/or federal legal recognition.

CURRENT AND POTENTIAL THREATS
TO CRITICAL ELEMENTS

Current and potential threats to the critical elements of the McCloud River drainage include dams, timber harvest, public-use pressure, limestone quarrying, and ignorance. Dams are by far the greatest threat. As mentioned above, these have already resulted in inundation, streamflow and temperature regime alterations, blockage of spawning runs, and to the riparian zone. In the future they may result in stream channel aggradation. The Bureau of Reclamation (BR) and the California Department of Water Resources (DWR) have begun a joint feasibility study to evaluate the proposed enlargement of Shasta Lake's water storage capacity. One proposal is to raise the existing lake by 61 m. (200 ft.). This would inundate 9.7 km. (6 mi.) more of the McCloud River. An alternative to this may be to construct more dams upstream from Shasta Lake, which could involve both the lower McCloud River and lower Squaw Valley Creek.

Timber sales on FS lands in the drainage continue to be planned, and some involve large expanses of old-growth forest adjacent to or near the Preserve. The greatest threat is new road construction which may lead to increased sedimentation, habitat disruption, and undesirable public access. Existing roads in the drainage, especially those adjacent to streams, are already contributing a considerable amount of sediment to the river during storms.

---

[8]Kunkel, G. 1975. Cryptograms of the McCloud River Preserve: a floristic study. Unpublished report. Department of Botany, University of California, Davis.

Table 1.--Critical elements of the McCloud River drainage. Status: CE--California Endangered; CR--California Rare; FE--federal Endangered; DB3--California Natural Diversity Data Base Priority 3;[1] L-#--California Native Plant Society List-# (plus R.E.V.D. Code); DFG--California Department of Fish and Game partial protection. (Note: all animal species listed here as CE, CR, or FE are also listed by the California Natural Diversity Data Base as Priority 1.)

Element Type	Common Name	Scientific Name	Status

Aquatic Environment

Fish	Interior Dolly Varden char	*Salvelinus confluentus*	CE
	McCloud rainbow trout	*Salmo gairdneri*	DFG
	Redband trout	*S. campi*	DB3

(Not found on the Preserve and currently not found in the lower drainage, but proposed to be introduced into Deer Creek by DFG)

General Invertebrates — Unique hydrology of the McCloud River
Possibility of unique species/assemblages
(Aquatic invertebrates need much more study, but preliminary studies indicate some uniqueness)

Riparian Environment

Plants	Howell's lewisia	*Lewisia cotyledon howellii*	L-2 2-2-2-2
	Cantelow's lewisia	*L. cantelowii*	L-2 2-2-2-3
	Purdy's sedum	*Sedum spathulifolium purdyi*	L-Append.

(These three grow primarily on partially shaded rock outcrops immediately along the river and some tributaries since this is the most likely place to find such outcrops, but it also grows well away from the riparian zone on suitable outcrops)

Birds	Bank Swallow	*Riparia riparia*	DB3
	Yellow Warbler	*Dendroica petechia*	DB3
	Yellow-breasted Chat	*Icteria virens*	DB3
	Bald Eagle	*Haliaeetus leucocephalus*	FE,CE
	Osprey	*Pandion haliaetus*	DB3
	Wood Duck	*Aix sponsa*	DB3
	Great Blue Heron	*Ardea herodias*	DB3

(Yellow-breasted Chat, Bald Eagle, Osprey, Wood Duck, and Great Blue Heron have not been observed to breed on the Preserve, but breed elsewhere in the drainage)

Mammals	River otter	*Lutra canadensis*	DB3

Prehistory — Numerous sites on streamside flats
(Sites have significant bearing on FS timber sale planning)

Old-growth Forest Environment

Birds	Spotted Owl	*Strix occidentalis*	DB3

(Not observed breeding on the Preserve, but breeds elsewhere in the drainage; has significant bearing on FS timber sale planning--its nests are given about 1,000 acres of old-growth forest buffer; were located in upper drainages of Ladybug and Hawkins creeks in 1981 by FS personel)

	Goshawk	*Accipiter gentilis*	DB3

(Not observed breeding on the Preserve, but breeds elsewhere in the drainage; has significant bearing on FS timber sale planning)

	Pileated Woodpecker	*Dryocopus pileatus*	DB3

[1]California Natural Diversity Data Base. 1981. Element list. Unpublished report, California Natural Diversity Data Base, Sacramento, Calif.

Table 1.--Continued.

Element Type	Common Name	Scientific Name	Status
Mammals	Wolverine	_Gulo gulo_	CR
	(Sighting was made downstream of the Preserve near Chatterdown Creek by FS personel in 1980)		
	Fisher	_Martes pennanti_	DB3

Baird Formation

Plants	Shasta eupatory	_Eupatorium shastense_	L-3 1-1-1-3
	(Has not been found on the Preserve but occurs nearby)		
Amphibians	Shasta salamander	_Hydromantes shastae_	CR
Mammals	Ringtail	_Bassariscus astutas_	DB3
Invertebates	Cave spiders, pseudo-scorpions, etc.		
	(Cave spiders were observed but not identified in Ringtail Cave; pseudoscorpions were studied in Samwell Cave. Both groups are endemic at the species level to the cave system they are found in.)		
Prehistory	Artifacts found in caves		
	(Cave artifacts include human bone fragments, obsidian chips, freshwater clam shells, marine fossils, and many mammal bones including remains of numerous extinct species.)		
General	Hydrology and geology of the cave system		

General

Plants	Siskiyou corn lily	_Veratrum insolitum_	L-4 1-1-1-1
	(Not yet observed on the Preserve, but abundant on Fisher Ridge and Skunk Hill.)		
Reptiles	Mountain king snake	_Lampropeltis zonata_	DFG
Birds	Sharp-shinned Hawk	_Accipiter striatus_	DB3
	Golden Eagle	_Aquila chrysaetos_	DB3
	(Not observed to breed on the Preserve but breeds elsewhere in the drainage.)		
	Ruffed Grouse	_Bonasa umbellus_	DB3
	Screech owl	_Otus acio_	DB3
Mammals	Ringtail	_Bassariscus astutas_	DB3
	Mountain lion	_Felis concolor_	DFG

The FS has made significant attempts to minimize logging impacts by placing roads high on slopes and ridges, using cable logging on steep slopes, and establishing wide buffer strips along streams and inner gorges. The FS has also been very receptive to TNC concerns and to public input, and is willing to approach timber sale planning as a cooperative effort. Nevertheless, timber values are still ranked higher than ecological and recreational values in the drainage, which makes attempts to establish a sizeable special management area along the river very difficult. One sale has just been approved, another is on the verge of approval, and three more are being planned. One of these latter sales, the Beetle-Dee Sale, could involve up to 48.3 km. (30 mi.) of new roads and the harvest of 50 million board-feet of old-growth timber near the Preserve.

Related to this is the progress of the second FS Roadless Area Review and Evaluation (RARE II). Two large roadless areas were identified along the lower McCloud River, and both have been recommended by the FS for non-Wilderness status. One of the areas, which includes all of lower Squaw Valley Creek drainage, was included in a recent California Resources Agency lawsuit against the FS. This effectively stalled planning on two timber sales, but neither roadless area has been included in any of the pending Congressional wilderness bills.

Timber harvest on private lands has occurred recently both on ridges just upstream from the Preserve and near the river a few miles upstream from Shasta Lake. New roads have been completed for harvesting in two large tributary drainages below the Preserve. Timber harvest plans must be filed with the DFG, but the public review period is both brief and poorly advertised.

Public-use pressure comes mainly from anglers. Impacts on the fishery were significantly reduced between McCloud Dam and the lower boundary of the Preserve by recent inclusion of this section in the state's Wild Trout Stream program. The remaining sections of river between Lower Falls and Shasta Lake are on private land where angling pressure is minimal. Tributaries are not included in the existing Wild Trout Stream section, of which Hawkins Creek and lower Squaw Valley Creek are the main concerns. The former has easy public access and may function as an important spawning area due to McCloud Dam; the latter stream is on FS land where vehicular access may soon become possible. Other forms of public-use pressure include hunting, camping, and hiking (notably along the Pacific Crest Trail which crosses both the lower McCloud River and lower Squaw Valley Creek).

Riparian zones receive the brunt of the traffic from this public use. Wild Trout Stream designation did not alleviate this problem since its regulations only apply to the fishery. On the Preserve, impacts are minimized by limiting the number of visitors to the Preserve at any one time, maintaining well-marked trails, and prohibiting camping.

Limestone is being quarried by the Flintkote Company at the southern tip of the Baird Formation. The Shasta salamander occurs there, and the company has set aside a portion of its land for the salamander's preservation.[9] Flintkote does not anticipate running out of limestone at their present site for many years, but the threat of new mining claims remains.

A very serious threat to the McCloud River drainage is the relative lack of scientific investigation and public knowledge. The Shasta salamander was described in 1953 and the Shasta eupatory in 1958; both dates relatively recent when compared to investigations elsewhere in California. Hayes[6] indicated that an undescribed species of slimy salamander may exist on the Preserve, and Moyle (1976)[10] feels that the taxonomic status of the McCloud strain of rainbow trout is still uncertain. Range extensions for the Shasta salamander and Shasta eupatory have recently been made, and a documented sighting of a wolverine was made in 1980.[11]

Recreational and aesthetic qualities of the drainage, beyond the angling experience, are virtually unknown to most of the public; 70% of the Preserve visitors come to fish and many of the rest are just "tagging along." However, although the drainage is being exploited for its timber and water without much resistance because of this scientific and public ignorance, it stands to suffer the impacts of increased public use should more people learn of its biological and recre-

ational qualities. The latter situation would seem to be the lesser of two evils.

INITIAL PLANNING REPORTS

In the early years of TNC, critically threatened areas were considered protected once they were acquired. Extensive stewardship programs including both restoration and long-term preservation strategies were not developed. Furthermore, no attempt was made to identify and protect whole systems. As the ecological health of many preserves continued to decline from unchecked consumptive public use, lack of restoration, and impacts from surrounding land uses, TNC began to place a greater emphasis on stewardship. This is reflected in the evolution of preserve planning efforts.

The Preserve was acquired at a time when the value of stewardship planning was finally beginning to be recognized. As a result, the first step after acquisition was to make an extensive inventory of the Preserve to determine the presence and status of critical elements and recommend management strategies. Initial action was taken in the form of implementing protective fishing regulations, and a management program including limited public use was begun in 1976. The results of the inventories and inititial management experiences were incorporated into a master plan in 1978, which included a brief introduction to the region, summaries of research findings, and recommendations regarding management.[12]

The management recommendations of the master plan were subsequently implemented, but beyond this the plan had no further practical value. In fact, its title was a misnomer. The need still existed for a long-term, drainage-wide comprehensive plan which described the critical elements and their threats in detail and then proposed specific stewardship strategies which addressed: 1) the protection of the critical elements beyond the existing preserve boundaries; 2) restoration and long-term preservation of these elements on the Preserve; 3) the need for scientific research, baseline studies, and monitoring of long-term changes in the critical elements; 4) public use and education; 5) administrative concerns; and 6) financial support. This need was met by the nation-wide development of preserve preservation plans (PPPs), which were to be renewed on a five-year basis. The 1984 PPP for the McCloud River Preserve was completed in 1979.[13] Each year applicable strategies are taken from this document and included in an annual plan which is the day-to-day guiding tool of preserve management on the McCloud River.

[9]Besecker, R.L. 1979. Personal conversation. Flintkote Company, Calaveras Cement Division, Redding, Calif.
[10]Moyle, P. 1976. McCloud River Preserve: biology and management. Unpublished report. Department of Wildlife and Fisheries Biology, University of California, Davis.
[11]Bacon, M. Personal conversation. USDA Forest Service, Shasta Lake Ranger District Office, Mountain Gate, Calif.

[12]Sheppard, J. 1978. McCloud River Preserve master plan. Unpublished report. The Nature Conservancy, San Francisco, Calif.
[13]Hesseldenz, T., and S. Gordon. 1979. 1984 preserve preservation plan for the McCloud River Preserve. Unpublished report. The Nature Conservancy, San Francisco, Calif.

On the brink of becoming buried under a heap of planning documents, one last plan was found necessary. The 1984 PPP could not adequately address the subject of protection because of lack of sufficient data. The importance and complexity of this subject warranted the development of a separate protection plan for the McCloud River drainage.

THE McCLOUD RIVER PROTECTION PLAN

Although various ideas for protecting the McCloud River drainage have been floating around for several years, actual work on a protection plan was just begun this year. As such, much of what is discussed below is still tentative; it is presented to illustrate the approach being taken. A draft of the plan will be ready for circulation to concerned agencies, clubs, and individuals in mid-1982, and their responses will be incorporated into a final draft by the end of that year.

The McCloud River Protection Plan will consist of three phases: identification, prescription, and implementation. The identification phase, which has already begun, initially involved the establishment of tentative boundaries. In the case of the McCloud River, watershed boundaries from the McCloud Dam to Shasta Lake were initially used to define the major area of concern. The dividing line between logged-over publicly accessible lands and old-growth gated lands roughly coincides with the transition from gentle volcanic to rugged uplifted topography, and provides a useful boundary between lower Squaw Valley Creek and the rest of the drainage, which extends all the way to Mt. Shasta.

The lands around and upstream from McCloud Reservoir have been severely logged, yet the river from Upper Falls to the head of the reservoir is of major concern. Dolly Varden char may extend upstream as far as Lower Falls, and the stretch of river from Big Springs to the reservoir represents the only remaining segment of large unaltered flows. Here the tentative boundary lines define a corridor along and including the river. Gentle topography, extensive logging, limited recreational potential, and lack of many critical elements of the McCloud River above Upper Falls suggest that consideration there be limited to protection of water quality and the redband trout.

Having established tentative boundaries, the pattern of ownership was determined (fig. 1). The majority of the land is owned by the FS. Most of the riverfront property is private. In addition, many sections of land below McCloud Dam are privately owned by large timber companies in a checkboard pattern. Upstream from the dam, most of the land is owned by the Hearst Corporation. Information on private lands obtained at the Shasta County Tax Assessor's Office includes parcel size and location, ownership, assessed value, and ownership of timber or mineral rights. This is the current level of progress made on

development of the protection plan. The next step will be to gather information on each parcel regarding past alterations, presence and status of any critical elements, current and potential threats, and the owner's plans for the property and receptivity to TNC objectives. Similar information will be assembled regarding FS lands.

Once all pertinent information has been gathered in the identification phase, private parcels will be assigned priorities, and alternative protection techniques will be prescribed. Priority will be determined by location, ownership, critical elements, and threats. Parcels closer to the river will probably have higher priority, and those along the river and closest to the existing Preserve will have highest priority. Parcels of land in major tributary drainages will probably rank higher than those along ridgetops away from stream channels. Those parcels strategically located to either maintain the integrity of a large area of native environment or provide a buffer between such an area and disruptive activities will have a higher priority. The distributions of critical elements will play a vital role in establishing priority.

TNC has developed many successful methods of protecting private land. In the McCloud drainage the methods being considered are acquisition by either purchase or donation, conservation easements, management agreements or negotiations, land exchanges, inclusion within protective governmental systems, and no action. Acquisition may in some cases involve mineral or timber rights where the owners of these rights are different than the landowners. In the event that an owner does not wish to sell, an arrangement, termed "rights of first refusal" may be agreed upon, by which TNC is given the opportunity to match any offer made if the owner decides to sell at a later date. A conservation easement is attached to a deed and may apply only to a particular portion of a parcel, such as a river corridor.

A less permanent method of protection is a management agreement, which is made with the present owner and remains in effect until the land changes ownership. If all else fails, specific negotiations can be made regarding land-use activities as they arise. In the case of a timber harvest on private land, the owner must file a timber harvest plan with the state; the plan is then made available for public comment.

From the point of view of the FS, private inholdings, especially those in a checkerboard pattern, present serious management problems. In response, the FS has been exchanging equal or better land on the fringes of national forests with these inholdings. Such land exchanges can be beneficial to TNC as well, by maximizing land-use planning based on ecological/geographic units rather than on often ecologically meaningless property boundaries. TNC may negotiate for direct land exchanges between private owners and the FS or may acquire land and subsequently transfer it to the FS.

Land stewardship philosophy varies sufficiently between TNC and the FS to warrant retention of ownership of the existing Preserve, but in less critical parts of the drainage (e.g., away from the river), the two agencies may be able to negotiate successfully. It is to the advantage of TNC to retain ownership over as little land as possible in order to allow the most efficient use of its limited resources.

Several governmental land status designations could influence activities on private lands and thereby serve as protective methods. Wilderness Area designation would prohibit timber sales and dam construction, but would also drastically increase public-use pressure. The same is true for Wild and Scenic River designation. Furthermore, this status only involves a 0.8-km. (0.5-mi.) wide corridor along the river. Wild Trout Stream status protects the river itself, but has no bearing on the surrounding lands other than requiring angling access. The FS is being actively encouraged to establish a special management area along the river, but this will probably only be a corridor and will only apply to public lands. Of all possibilities preliminarily studied, Research Natural Area (RNA) or Special Interest Area (SIA) designation seem to be the most desirable for appropriate public lands in the drainage.

In cases where timber values, public-use pressures, and/or priority ranking are low, it may prove best to take no action at all. Such areas are under what might be called de facto protection.

After prescribing preferred protection methods for each parcel of private land and evaluating protective land status designations for adjacent public lands, program options must be developed which unify these separate methods into overall strategy options. Development of a protection plan is in itself a unifying force, having one objective and involving one drainage, but when seeking public and government agency support, offering optional "package deals" will help ensure success of the plan. A similar approach was used in developing TNC's California Critical Areas Program; support for the individual critical areas would have been hard to come by without the unifying theme represented by the program. Each alternative package for the McCloud drainage will describe a desired ultimate land ownership pattern, zones of varying degrees of protected status with specific restrictions given (including applicable legal designations), and the costs and time frames necessary to accomplish each alternative. Within the theme of protection for the drainage, the alternatives will range from the "environmentalist's ideal" to the "limits of compromise", such that each one will be viable should it ultimately be the one supported by the public, governmental agencies, and TNC.

As an example, one alternative might be to recommend a university- or Conservancy-operated research field station along the river, surrounded by a RNA. The lower McCloud drainage is ideal for field studies involving fisheries biology, aquatic entomology, old growth forest-related wildlife biology, and studies of the endemic species and artifacts of the Baird Limestone Formation, to name a few. The existing upper portion of the Preserve would continue to be managed under the current public-use system, which could be located on the edge of the RNA and serve as a buffer.

Part of lower Squaw Valley Creek could be included in the RNA and added to the state's Wild Trout Stream system with the upper part being open to reduced-limit fishing as another buffer. Thus, the core of the RNA would be closed to fishing and adequately buffered to ensure undisturbed conditions for ecological protection and scientific study. Since the program would be closely tied with maintaining a high-quality angling stream, substantial financial support on a continuing basis could most likely be achieved from the angling public.

Once options have been developed, the draft protection plan will be circulated among appropriate agencies, clubs, and individuals to determine which alternative is most agreeable to everyone concerned. Once this is completed, TNC will have a fairly accurate idea of how to proceed with implementation of the protection plan.

During the implementation phase, the two most obvious needs will be financial and agency support. TNC has funds for acquisition, but in order to keep these funds available for the most critical of threatened areas, a local fundraising campaign is initiated for every new project. The McCloud is fortunate in having the tremendous support of fly-fishing individuals and clubs across the western United States. Good trout streams are becoming quite rare, and at the same time the sport of fly-fishing is continuing to grow. A new consciousness has been developing along with the sport—an awareness of, and deep concern for, the ecological factors involved in a healthy stream and its surrounding environment. This is what has led to the success of the catch-and-release concept and the continued strong support of the existing Preserve.

Agency support will be much more difficult to achieve. Timber and water values rank very high in the drainage; Warner (1979) indicated that by the year 2000 35% more timber will be required and agricultural and urban uses of water will increase by more than 50%. The federal government is showing a declining interest in environmental concerns. Educational institutions must be convinced of the drainage's scientific value and of a dependable source of continued funding should a research field station be proposed. The "not invented here" attitude towards progressive and aggressive planning efforts could hinder progress with both other agencies and fly-fishing clubs. The solution to this latter problem will be to include all concerned agencies, clubs, and individuals throughout the planning process, such that the protection plan is a product of cooperative effort, as it should be.

OTHER PLANNING EFFORTS

Beyond the in-house reasons for TNC's development of a McCloud River Protection Plan, such a plan is necessary to more effectively coordinate TNC involvement in the planning processes of other agencies in the drainage. To date, interactions with FS and DFG have been on a piecemeal basis, in response to specific threats. Both of these agencies are currently developing management plans affecting the McCloud River drainage.

Involvement in FS planning began in 1975 with the routing of the Pacific Crest Trail through the drainage. Subsequently, as specific timber sales in the drainage were planned, TNC has played an increasingly greater role in seeking minimal harvests, protective techniques, and thorough study of sensitive species and potential water quality impacts. Most recently, TNC has been involved in the development of the Shasta-Trinity National Forest Land and Resource Management Plan in which, it is hoped, a special management area will be established in the drainage and both timber harvest quotas and potential harvest-site suitability ratings will be more realistic. At present, the entire drainage is zoned for timber harvest. Two major drawbacks of this plan, with respect to the McCloud River drainage, are that it will address the whole Shasta-Trinity National Forest, of which the McCloud is only a small part, and it will only deal with public lands in the drainage.

Recent DFG involvement in the drainage began with Wild Trout Stream designation in late 1975, which included the establishment of a Dolly Varden Char Sanctuary within the Preserve. During 1977 and 1978, the river was surveyed from Lower Falls to Shasta Lake with the hope of finding Dolly Varden, and no confirmed sightings were made. It is suspected that the McCloud River population of Dolly Varden char may be genetically distinct, but the lack of sufficient sampling has prevented any progress on this subject, although the DFG is now referring to the population as the California bull trout. At this point the prospect for a rehabilitation project is uncertain, but protective management will nevertheless be encouraged. The most recent efforts to this end have been in the development of a lower McCloud River Wild Trout Area Management Plan. A preliminary position statement was released by DFG early in 1981 for consideration by the FS in their planning efforts.[14]

---

[14]Naylor, A.E. 1981. The lower McCloud River wild trout management area. Position Paper, California Department of Fish and Game, Region 1, Redding, Calif.

These other planning efforts indicate that TNC is in the best position to develop a protection plan for the drainage. However, it must rely upon the support of the users of the drainage (mainly anglers), because the range of values in the drainage extends beyond the strict limits of concern of TNC. To be successful, TNC must focus its limited resources upon the most critical of areas in the nation. With the goal of preserving biological diversity, TNC attempts to identify and protect those species and habitats which are the most threatened and scarce, or as they say, "the last of the least and the best of the rest."

Many of the McCloud's critical elements are represented elsewhere, such that their continued survival is not dependent solely upon this region. Exceptions to this are the possibly genetically distinct McCloud populations of Dolly Varden char and rainbow trout, and the Shasta salamander and eupatory. A very large part of the McCloud River Protection Plan will involve recreational/aesthetic values as well as habitats and species threatened to a lesser extent than those just mentioned. The plan will also address protection of the "essence" of the McCloud River drainage: the product of the river, forests, limestone, etc., which imparts a uniqueness to the region. For these reasons, the public will play a vital role in the development and support of the plan.

CONCLUSION

The ecological/scientific and recreational/aesthetic values of the McCloud River drainage possess enough significance and uniqueness to warrant their protection. The industrial values of the drainage are also significant and, until recently, have greatly outweighed other values. Multiple ownership, multiple agency involvement, and the preoccupation with industrial values have resulted in uncoordinated patterns of resource management and exploitation which are blind to the maintenance of ecological integrity of the system.

The McCloud River drainage is in need of long-term, system-wide, integrated planning. Local planning for national forests now occurs at the individual forest level; the McCloud River drainage is only a small part of the Shasta-Trinity National Forest and as such will probably not receive adequate attention in the soon-to-be-completed Land and Resource Management Plan for the forest. The FS is also not in a comfortable position to emphasize non-consumptive values in the drainage nor to deal with the various private ownerships. The DFG has become increasingly supportive of wild trout programs and would like to develop a plan for this program in the McCloud drainage; however, its approach would be focused on the fishery. TNC has come to recognize the need for appropriate planning in the drainage to both direct its future activities there and to attempt to integrate the activities of other owners and agencies. As such, TNC seems to be the most likely candidate to develop a protection plan for the whole drainage, although it too, in the strict sense, has focused interests.

Recent evolution in TNC's planning efforts has led to the initiation of the McCloud River Protection Plan. By identifying critical elements, threats, ownership patterns, and alternative techniques for protecting land; by prescribing appropriate protection techniques to each geographical unit in the drainage, based upon ownership, critical elements, and threats; by developing viable alternative packaged protection programs ranging from the "environmentalists' ideal" to the "limits of compromise"; by securing public involvement and feedback throughout the planning process, with the goal of discovering the most widely acceptable protection program; and finally by implementing this program through the support of all owners, agencies, organizations, and individuals involved in the McCloud River drainage, TNC's hope is that the McCloud River Protection Plan will satisfy the need for a proper planning perspective here.

Work on the plan has only just begun. As with any environmental planning, it will involve finding a viable path of compromise through the jungle of conflicting interests in the drainage. But without some form of comprehensive planning, a piecemeal approach to protection will continue, jeopardizing the integrity of the magnificent system of the McCloud River.

LITERATURE CITED

Seidelman, P. 1980. Methodology for evaluating cumulative watershed impacts. USDA Forest Service Region 5, San Francisco, Calif.

Sturgess, James A., and Peter B. Moyle. 1978. Biology of rainbow trout (Salmo gairdneri), brown trout (S. trutta), and interior Dolly Varden (Salvelinus confluentus) in the McCloud River, California, in relation to management. Cal-Neva Wildlife 1978:239-250.

Warner, R.E. 1979. California riparian study program. 177 p. Planning Branch, California Department of Fish and Game, Sacramento.

SACRAMENTO RIVER ENVIRONMENT: A MANAGEMENT PLAN[1]

Thomas J. Kraemer[2]

Abstract.--Riparian forest vegetation along the Sacramento River is necessary to control erosion and to promote deposition of sediments. Sedimentation is occurring at rates sufficient to replace some agricultural lands lost to erosion. Money spent on erosion control by riprap would be better spent acquiring a riparian corridor.

INTRODUCTION

In the last 20 years I have been increasingly dismayed by the degradation of the Sacramento River's environment in the upper Sacramento Valley. As a result I have spent the past three years studying the river and its riparian lands. This paper represents a portion of the study submitted as a Master's thesis[3] to California State University, Chico.

EROSION, DEPOSITION, AND RIPARIAN VEGETATION

The presence of significant amounts of riparian forest vegetation along the Sacramento River, to control erosion and to promote deposition of new sediments to replace those soils eroded by the river, is vital to any river system management plan. Riparian vegetation is intimately involved in the sedimentation process. It provides a baffle effect which acts to slow high winter flows enough to allow the deposition of suspended sediments. Furthermore, surface erosion is usually prevented and bank erosion inhibited by the presence of riparian forests. These processes are illustrated in figure 1. The two areas depicted in figure 1 are protected by the same riprap. Note that the river bank has been "stabilized" by the installation of rock riprap, but that the land it was designed to protect has been eroded. The field has eroded and the area of uncleared riparian vegetation has remained stable and, in fact, has caused sediment deposition.

Sedimentation and replacement of eroded soils is thought by some not to be occurring in significant amounts along the Sacramento River since construction of Shasta Dam near Redding. However, significant sedimentation and soil replacement are indeed occurring. Using aerial photos, I have found areas which were shown to be river channel on 1952 maps, and which were subsequently reclassified as prime agricultural land in 1978 by the State of California, Department of Water Resources in the Sacramento River Environmental Atlas (California Resources Agency 1978).

Erosion along the Sacramento River has caused a great deal of damage to agricultural lands. Erosion of agricultural land adjacent to the river is accelerated by forest clearing. Paradoxically, forest clearing and cultivation agriculture immediately adjacent to the river are the causes of accelerated erosion rates at some sites and of related reduction of riverbed sinuosity which has occurred in the last 100 years (Brice 1977). Attempts to control erosion with bank stabilization projects (commonly called riprap) have met with limited success, and are unsuccessful in many instances.

EROSION CONTROL PROJECTS

In 1958-1959 the Federal Government and the State of California authorized the Chico Landing to Red Bluff Project.[4] The Project subsequently spent millions of dollars installing riprap on eroding banks, in an effort to stabilize them.[5] Because of the losses of riparian forest habitat and continuing expenditures by the taxpayers for flood damage, the State of California has withdrawn its support for the Chico Landing to Red Bluff Project, while further

---

[1]Paper presented at the California Riparian Systems Conference. [University of California, Davis, September 17-19, 1981].

[2]Thomas J. Kraemer is a Conservation Ecologist located in Corning, Calif.

[3]Master's thesis "The Sacramento River, Glenn, Butte, and Tehama Counties: a study of vegetation, deposition, and erosion, and a management plan." California State University, Chico. Spring, 1981.

---

[4]US Army Corps of Engineers, Sacramento District, Sacramento, California. Supplement no. 2 to general design memorandum no. 1, Sacramento River, Chico Landing to Red Bluff, California. June 18, 1976. p. 1.

[5]Ibid. Item 25.

Figure 1.--River Mile 220.2, right bank. May 1978. The photo on the left shows uncleared riparian vegetation on the left, and land cleared of riparian vegetation and farmed on the right. The river is to the viewer's back. The photo on the right was taken at approximately the same position as the one on the left, only turned 90° so that the river and formerly farmed lands are visible.

studies are made of alternate approaches.[6] State involvement is necessary for Federal participation in bank protection and, due to this, recent installations of bank protection have been limited to sites where work had been initiated and funded prior to the State's decision.[7] Fiscal year 1978 was the last year the State Reclamation Board recommended State cooperation in the Chico Landing to Red Bluff Project although the Federal agency involved, the US Army Corps of Engineers (CE), continues to study erosion and erosion sites along the Sacramento River.[8]

In 1958 the CE was authorized by Congress

...to provide bank protection and incidental channel improvements between Chico Landing and Red Bluff in Butte, Glenn and Tehama counties at certain sites found to be economically feasible at the time of construction and in the light of conditions then prevailing along the river ...[9]

A 50 year amortization, or economic life, was used when computing the costs and benefits of selected sites.[10]

Average annual benefits... were based on a reduction in the loss of land and improvements which would be prevented at each site by the construction of bank protection... In addition annual benefits were based on a reduction in downstream dredging in the channels and bypasses of the Sacramento River Flood Control project, Sacramento River Deep Water Channel, and San Francisco Bay System Channels.[11]

One of the erosion sites protected in the Chico Landing to Red Bluff Project is located at River Mile (RM) 196.3, near the mouth of Pine Creek, Butte County. Aerial photos dated 1952

[6]James Dufur. "300 mile parkway on big river is dream." Sacramento Bee. April 3, 1979. Sec B, p. 1.

[7]US Army Corps of Engineers, Sacramento District, Sacramento, California. Supplement no. 2 to general design memorandum no. 1, Sacramento River, Chico Landing to Red Bluff, California. June 18. 1976. Item 3.

[8]Gene Anderson. 1981. California State Reclamation Board. Telephone interview.

[9]Sacramento River, Chico Landing to Red Bluff, California. Bank protection project. Final environmental statement. Prepared by US Army Corps of Engineers, Sacramento District, Sacramento, California. January 1975. p. 1.

[10]Ibid. p. 4.

[11]US Army Corps of Engineers, Sacramento District, Sacramento, California. Supplement no. 2 to general design memorandum no. 1, Sacramento River, Chico Landing to Red Bluff, California. June 18, 1976. Item 21.

and 1975 were used to analyze this site. The 1975 photos were chosen because they accurately record the position of the riverbank, minus materials removed during the 1974 construction of bank protection.[12] Site evaluation was undertaken by overlaying a grid on the photos, to determine areal changes during the 22-year period in question. No areal change could be detected; that is, the amount of dry land within the measured area remained the same over the 20-year period. Reference was then made to the USGS 7.5 min. series quadrangles, 1949 edition and 1969 revision.[13] Almost no change in bank position was recorded. Comparison of the 1952 and 1970 aerial photos disclosed that some of the oak trees visible at this site in 1952 were missing in 1970. This was interpreted as evidence of erosion. Finally, on closer examination, and using an engineer's scale referred to a fixed point, measurements indicated that the bank had eroded 25 ft.

Examination of the 1979 aerial photo for this site and comparison with the 1975 aerial photo revealed a change in river channel between 1975 and 1979. During this period a cut-off occurred upstream from the riprap site. By 1980 the entire flow of the river had been diverted into the new cut-off channel and the old channel was completely blocked by alluvium. This change left the bank protection site in a backwater, useless, as it was isolated from the river.

BANK PROTECTION COSTS AND BENEFITS

Construction at the RM 196.3 site was completed in 1974 at an approximate construction cost of $115,000.[14] An additional cost factor of 20% for engineering, design, and administration costs should be added to this to arrive at a total Federal first cost of $138,000.[15] At this particular site State costs are ignored[16] because the land in question was donated.

Prior to the installation of bank protection at this site, the underlying erosion-resistant layer of clay material at and above the water

---

[12]Sacramento River, Chico Landing to Red Bluff, California. Bank protection project. Final environmental statement. Prepared by US Army Corps of Engineers, Sacramento District, Sacramento, Caifornia. January 1975. p. 14, 19.

[13]USDI Geological Survey. Ord Ferry Quadrangle California, 7.5 Minute Series (Topographic) 1949 and Photo Revised Edition 1969.

[14]Construction data, various bank protection sites, Sacramento River, California. Document received from US Army Corps of Engineers, Sacramento District. February 15, 1980.

[15]Don Jones, US Army Corps of Engineers, Sacramento, California. Telephone conversation. April 15, 1980.

[16]Jake Angel, Department of Water Resources, Sacramento, California. Telephone conversation. March 12, 1980.

line was visible.[17] This layer would account for the lack of significant bank movement observed in the aerial photographs between 1952 and 1975.

A 1975 CE document lists a projected cost: benefit ratio for this site of 1.1.[18] The same document uses a 50-year economic life when computing the costs and benefits of a site. However, at this site the river changed course after five years, with no further river flow past this bank protection site. Thus, after but six years of an anticipated 50-year project life, no further benefit was being gained from reduced damages due to potentially eroded land and washed-out structures. Nor will there be a further reduction of dredging costs in the delta for sediments which would have originated at this site in the absence of bank protection. At this site the benefits have ceased after six years but the costs will continue for another 45 years.

This bank protection failure is not an isolated case. I selected 14 riprapped sites for study, five of which were examined in detail. These sites were located between RM 220.5 (near the mouth of Deer Creek, Tehema County) and RM 196.3 (near the mouth of Pine Creek, Butte County). Six of the 14 bank protection sites reviewed have failed completely or are in advanced stages of failure. All six are less than 10 years old. In addition four more sites have potentially serious problems which could lead to a resumption of serious erosion at those sites.

STRUCTURAL BANK PROTECTION VERSUS THE RIVER

The Sacramento River is a dynamic entity, eroding here, depositing there. It is the river's hydrologic nature to form meanders and cut-offs. Indeed, if it were entirely straightened, the river would immediately begin to reform a meandering system (Strahler and Strahler 1978). The management system (rock bank protection) applied for the purpose of controlling river channel movement has been haphazard and expensive, requiring constant maintenance to retain the effectiveness of each site. In an interview with an official of the US Army Corps of Engineers, Sacramento, it was learned that the ultimate goal of that agency is to "freeze" the river in place.[19] In his opinion, this could be done, if economically feasible, by riprapping the outside of every bend in erosion-prone areas. This would necessitate a very large initial expenditure and also require continual maintenance of the channelized system thereafter. In

---

[17]Field observation. June 1969.

[18]Sacramento River, Chico Landing to Red Bluff, California. Bank protection project. Final environmental statement. Prepared by US Army Corps of Engineers, Sacramento District, Sacramento, California. January 1975. p. 5.

[19]Interview with Dave Gundlach, US Army Corps of Engineers, Sacramento office. March 27, 1980.

addition, if this system were implemented, nearly all remaining riparian growth would be eliminated. The loss of this forest and grassland would reduce and probably eliminate the soil formation processes that lead to the prime (high terrace) agricultural land so highly prized by farmers. Erosion would not cease. Overbank erosion would still occur, as would scour at the downstream ends of bank protection sites. Figure 2 illustrates one such scour site. Most wildlife and recreation values would be eliminated. With banks riprapped and the loss of the forest, little would be left of wildland and aesthetic values. This would be very costly indeed.

AN ALTERNATIVE STRATEGY

Acquisition of a Riparian Corridor

A less costly alternative is available. Instead of installing riprap and channelizing most of the Sacramento River, the money which would be spent on such projects could be spent to acquire land, the land which is eroding, if possible.[20]

Figure 2.--River Mile 206.5, left bank looking downstream. August 1979. Scour damage at downstream end of riprap installation. The soil has been eroded from behind the riprap for about 30.5 m. (100 ft.)

----

[20] Indeed, the USDA has suggested that an effort be made to obtain a strip of property adjacent to the river so that riparian vegetation can be reestablished. Sacramento River, Chico Landing to Red Bluff, California. Bank protection project. Final environmental statement. Prepared by US Army Corps of Engineers, Sacramento District, Sacramento, California. January 1975. Appendix C-4.

In addition the Resources Agency, State of California, has proposed a parkway of public easements along the entire length of the Sacramento River. James Dufur, "300 mile parkway on big river is dream." Sacramento Bee. March 4, 1979. sec. B. p. 1.

Farmers would be forewarned that no money would be spent to protect agricultural sites from erosion, but if they should desire to sell the land in question, it would be purchased with public funds. Only those sites where extensive urbanization has occurred and where public structures, such as bridges, have been built would be structurally protected.[21] If the individuals involved chose not to sell their land, other land would be acquired. In this way, over an extended period of time, a corridor of public land adjacent to and on both banks of the river would be acquired.

If a corridor were acquired, erosion would not cut away the land to one man's detriment, only to deposit it further downstream on another's, to that person's benefit. If the meander zone of the river were encompassed by a corridor of public land, there would be only one landowner, the public. The public would not be harmed by erosion here or benefited by deposition there. No single landowner would be hurt by erosion. Landowners would not bring suit against governmental agencies for flood damages, as is presently the case. Riprap would be unnecessary in most instances.

The acquisition of a corridor does not have to be finished tomorrow or even next year, or even in the next 20 years. Only a stated policy by the Federal and/or State government(s) and funding are required. If the corridor is finished in a century it is time enough. Land would not need to be condemned. If the public is willing to wait long enough, all the land in the meander zone will sooner or later be offered for sale.

The money spent on riprap installation and maintenance would be better spent on land acquisition. Many riprap sites have failed or are failing. The money already spent on these particular sites would have been far better spent on the purchase of land. If it had been, the public would now have a resource, instead of a rock pile, sometimes remote from the river.

Cost Comparisons

At RM 211, simple calculations reveal that if the rate of erosion for that site during the 20-year period analyzed were projected for the 50-year economic life of the installation, approximately 23 acres will have been lost. Total first cost at that site was $348,000 in 1976.[22] In 1976 orchard land cost about $3,000

----

[21] It is unlikely that existing bridges would be outflanked by a freely meandering river. In the long term, when such bridges are replaced consideration should be given to a bridge and/or causeway system, such as those at Butte City and Sacramento.

[22] Amortized costs are not included because land purchase also has such costs.

per acre. If the money had been spent on land purchase instead, 116 acres could have been bought.

Corridor Width

The ultimate width of such a riparian corridor, at least in the absence of a public levee system, as is the case north of Ord Ferry Bridge at RM 184.3, should be the width of the recent alluvial soils, or the width of the levee system maintained by public funds. If there is a danger of the river outflanking the existing levee system at its northern terminus, i.e. the river changing course to the outside of the levee, lateral levees could be built across the floodplain, at right angles to the existing levees which are parallel to the river.

Along that portion of the river without a public levee system, particularly north of Ord Ferry Bridge, the corridor ideally should have two management zones. There would be one zone adjacent to the river itself including, initially, all standing riparian forest and a band of perhaps a minimum of 183 m. (200 yd.) wide. This band would be left to revegetate naturally or would be planted to oaks, black walnuts, and whatever riparian species suited the site.[23] The second zone would include the balance of the corridor. In this second zone, agriculture would be practiced on a leasehold basis. The terms of the lease would be such that, if the river did meander or flood into the agricultural zone, the farmer in queston would not be able to make a claim for the financial loss. Flooding and erosion would simply be hazards that the farmer accepted when the lease was signed, as is now the case in the several river bypasses.

Given the development of a meander situation and its attendant erosion of agricultural land, the lease, once expired, would not be renewed. Then the boundaries of the two zones would be redrawn. In like a manner, once lands become suitable for agriculture and, due to river meandering, are found outside the inner riparian zone, they would be leased for agriculture, and forest clearing allowed. In this way a balance between the values of the river environment and the productive usefulness of these soils would be struck.

There is no question that the agricultural potential of the river's alluvial soils is immense. These soils should where possible be used for agriculture. But there are other values to be considered—wildlife, recreation, aesthetic, and, most important to those who consider economics, the cost of efforts to shore up the river's banks. This plan allows for both the needs of agriculture and the retention of wildland along the river. It also guarantees a minimum of expense to the public and the farmer.

---

[23]The proposed dimensions are subject to adjustment, as the needs of the corridor require.

Land Revenues and Maintenance Costs

Many will be concerned about the loss of tax revenues to local government implied in such a plan, but such revenue losses need not occur. Lease monies collected by governmental agencies administering the agricultural zone should be shared with local government. Indeed, the precedent for this already exists. When timber is sold from public lands within the National Forests, the USDA Forest Service is obliged to share the revenues from those sales with the county government where the timber originated.

The public ownership plan, if implemented, would offer many advantages over the channelizing option. The river would be allowed to meander naturally, at least where no publicly maintained levee system exists. The necessity for bank protection would be eliminated, except in those areas where there are structures such as bridges, or where pre-existing urbanization is established, such as the towns of Tehama and Red Bluff. However no further urbanization would be allowed on the floodplain. Farming would be allowed in such a way that production could be maximized. Natural soil building processes would proceed at a maximum rate because of the presence of riparian vegetation, thus replacing soils lost to erosion. Wildlife and wildland values would be conserved and enhanced.

The initial investment for such a plan would be high, but for the channelization option costs are presently high, as are those for maintenance, with no guarantee that the amortized life will be actually achieved. With either option, administration costs will be incurred. However, with the riparian corridor plan, initial outlays are high, but an income-producing resource remains, and a minimum of maintenance is required. Conversely, with the channelization option, money input will be required for installation, maintenance, and reinstallation, so long as the river is to be kept channelized. Benefits are terminal, costs are forever. It is a matter of good economics: with the riparian corridor plan, costs are terminal, benefits are forever.

LITERATURE CITED

Brice, James. 1977. Lateral Migration of the Middle Sacramento River, California. Water Resources Investigations 77-43 (July 1977). USDI Geological Survey.

California Resources Agency. 1978. Sacramento River Environmental Atlas. Prepared for the Upper Sacramento River Task Force by the California Resources Agency. Sacramento.

Strahler, Arthur N., and Alan H. Strahler. 1978. Modern Physical Geography. John Wiley and Sons Inc. New York.

RIPARIAN AREA MANAGEMENT IN

THE PACIFIC SOUTHWEST REGION OF THE FOREST SERVICE[1]

Andrew A. Leven[2]

Abstract.--This paper presents the history and evolution of riparian area management direction for National Forest System lands in California since the early 1960s. Application of national riparian area management direction to Regional and National Forest planning processes along with examples of project plans for improvement and maintenance of riparian areas are presented. Some research needs for management activities to improve and maintain the health of riparian areas are discussed.

HISTORY OF REGIONAL DIRECTION

The USDA Forest Service (FS) has long had a means of recognizing unique management requirements of riparian areas. Since the early 1960s, "water influence zones" have been used in multiple-use plans to designate streams of high recreational value. This value generally was dependent on fishing, scenic, and water sports-related recreational uses. These water influence zones received management direction aimed at protecting their recreational values. Targets for forest commodities were established through multiple-use and resource plans. Many of these targets are still in effect today.

In addition to national water influence zone management direction, in 1966 the FS in California developed a procedure to evaluate a stream channel's ability to accept the impacts from uses such as timber harvesting without the need for special management direction. The process classified streams as "resistant" or "non-resistant." Classification criteria were based mainly on streambank and streambed condition. If streams were resistant to erosional processes accelerated by mechanical disturbance, they were classified as resistant. If erosion would be accelerated by disturbance, the streams were classified as non-resistant. Special clauses were placed in timber sale contracts which called for limited and/or restricted actions in non-resistant streams. The main purpose of these clauses was to protect streams from accelerated erosion caused by direct mechanical disturbance. The criteria were related to physical stream conditions, but the management direction was not closely tied to stream values.

The need remained for specific management direction that was more closely tied to stream values, and conditions. In 1975 the Pacific Southwest Region of the FS developed direction that required the extent of stream protection be tied to stream values. The stream value classification system is still in use today and is based upon an evaluation of the following minimum factors: 1) flow characteristics; 2) present and foreseeable instream and downstream values associated with waters of the stream; and 3) physical and biological characteristics of the stream environment.

Each class establishes the relative importance or significance of a stream or stream segment, based on resource values and beneficial uses. This system is only a step toward the ultimate objective, i.e., a detailed description of the final protection measures needed. The following is a description of each class as taken from a Regional Supplement to the National Forest Service Manual:

Class I, Highly Significant. These are either perennial or intermittent streams, or segments thereof, which meet one or more of the following criteria:
a. Are habitat for large numbers of resident and/or migratory fish for spawning, rearing, or migration.
b. Furnish water locally for domestic or municipal supplies.
c. Have flows large enough to materially influence downstream water quality.
d. Are characterized by major fishing or other water-oriented recreational uses.

---

[1] Paper presented at the California Riparian Systems Conference. [University of California, Davis, September 17-19, 1981].

[2] Andrew A. Leven is Director, Watershed Management Staff, Pacific Southwest Region, USDA Forest Service, San Francisco, Calif.

e. Have special classification or designation, such as wild, scenic, or recreation rivers.

f. Have special visual or distinctive landscape features and are classified as variety class A as defined in "National Forest Landscape Management Volume 2" (Agr. Handbook 462).

g. Are habitat for threatened or endangered animal species, or contain plants which are potential or viable candidates for threatened or endangered classification.

h. Exhibit ethnological, historical, or archeological evidence that makes them eligible for or are included in the National Register of Historical Places.

Class II, Significant. These are either perennial or intermittent streams, or segments thereof, which meet one or more of the following criteria:

a. Are used by moderate numbers of fish for spawning, rearing, or migration.

b. Furnish water locally for industrial or agricultural use.

c. Have enough water flow to exert a moderate influence on downstream quality.

d. Are used moderately for fishing and other recreation purposes.

e. Are of moderate visual quality and meet variety class B as defined in "National Forest Landscape Management Volume 2" (Agr. Handbook 462).

Class III, Moderately Significant. These include perennial or intermittent streams, or segments thereof, which meet one or more of the following criteria:

a. Are habitat for few fish for spawning, rearing, or migration.

b. Are rarely used for fishing or other recreational purposes.

c. Have enough water flow to exert minimum influence on downstream water quality.

d. Are of relatively low visual quality in the landscape and classified as variety class B as defined in "National Forest Landscape Management Volume 2" (Agr. Handbook 462).

Class IV, Minor Significance. These are intermittent or ephemeral streams, or segments thereof, not previously classified (Forest Service 1975).

Land management planning use of the system requires those streams, or segments thereof, which meet the criteria for Class I and II to be shown on land management planning maps; Class III and IV streams may be shown as appropriate. Within project areas all streams and segments must be classified. Management direction and protection measures for the stream zone are then developed for the specific planning unit or project area. This direction is aimed at measures which ensure favorable conditions of water flows and protect the natural environment commonly associated with streamcourses.

The use of buffer strips, areas adjacent to the stream channel, came into use in the early to mid-1970s, to provide protection beyond protecting just the channel. The use of buffer strips was recognized as providing more effective protection to streams and streamside areas during land management activities, by reducing site disturbance and filtering sediment from adjacent upland areas. Buffer strips of a width sufficient to provide such protection are designated during all land management activities which involve land use in close proximity to streams. Resource management activities are permitted within the buffer strips, but are modified so as to safeguard the stream and its natural environment from adverse impacts resulting from such activities.

Some general guidelines for management activities within buffer strips were provided in Regional Forest Service Manual Supplements in 1975 (USDA Forest Service 1976). Several are summarized below.

1. Riparian systems are among the most productive of plant and wildlife diversity in the forest environment. To retain these valuable areas, minimum disturbance from management activities is essential.

2. The shade canopy produced by riparian vegetation overhanging the water surface will be retained in streams where maintenance of proper water temperature is essential for perpetuation of aquatic life. Within timber sales areas, if there are not sufficient hardwoods along the stream to provide this shade, canopy conifers must retained as needed.

3. Adequate protection to the buffer strip must include protection of the soil, litter, and vegetative cover, as well as the streamcourse itself. This may require adjustments in normal operating procedures including appropriate modifications of road locations, silvicultural prescriptions, and uses of heavy equipment.

4. Trees may be removed from the buffer strip if their removal will not adversely affect the watercourse or the buffer strip. Trees to be removed must be individually marked.

5. Heavy equipment and roads, roadfills, and sidecasting must be kept outside of the buffer strip, except at designated crossings and for specifically planned and authorized activities.

Forest Supervisors were given authority to provide management guidelines for streamcourse protection appropriate to their administrative units and to prescribe the method to determine the buffer strip width needed to provide stream protection commensurate with planned land management activities.

In 1975, wildlife and fishery biologists in the Pacific Southwest Regional Office identified a number of goals, objectives, and management activities related to protecting riparian systems.

Goal: To gain recognition and acceptance of the importance of riparian systems to wildlife needs and to implement coordination measures which provide for these needs in land-use planning and resource management activities in national forests.

Objective: To preserve the productivity of riparian systems by maintaining vegetative stratification and integrity. This will result in maintaining wildlife diversity and a stable ecosystem.

Examples of how riparian system management is coordinated with other forest resource management programs are listed below.

1. Recognize riparian systems in timber management planning by establishing protective areas along streams. Coordinate timber harvest activities to avoid damage to riparian systems.
2. Locate campgrounds, access roads, and trails outside of riparian zones.
3. Manage domestic livestock to avoid trampling and overgrazing vegetation in riparian zones.
4. Allow adequate buffer zones when using chemicals to control vegetation near riparian systems.
5. Carefully consider wildlife needs when planning projects to increase water yield through removal of vegetation in the riparian zone.
6. Protect small springs and seeps from trampling and other damaging impacts by fencing the area.

During 1978 and 1979, while participating in Section 208[3] nonpoint pollution abatement water quality planning, the Pacific Southwest Region consolidated its water quality direction into a document describing best management practices (BMPs) for protecting water quality (Pacific Southwest Region, USDA Forest Service 1979). Some of these BMPs included direction for riparian area management because of its relationship to water quality. Twenty different BMPs were described that have some relationship to management of riparian areas for protecting water quality. A few of the subjects and activities addressed were: streamside management zone designation; meadow protection during timber harvesting; minimization of sidecast material; control of in-channel excavation; construction in streamside management zones; exclusion of tractors from wetlands and meadows; control of livestock distribution within allotments.

It is important to note that these BMPs were consolidated from existing manual direction and were not newly developed during or as a result of Section 208 planning. These practices were approved by the US Environmental Protection Agency (EPA) and adopted by the State of California as BMPs for protecting water quality on National Forest System lands. It is also important to note that this was the first introduction of the streamside management zone (SMZ) into a formal FS direction document. Up to that point, direction had related to stream protection. The SMZ introduces the concept that streams must be managed and that protection is only one form of management.

HISTORY OF NATIONAL DIRECTION

In 1976-77, the concern for managing riparian areas to maintain their ability to protect water quality and provide diverse fish and wildlife habitats began to reach national and political levels. The Chief of the FS commissioned a team to review SMZ management on a national scale. This review identified the need for a uniform definition of the SMZ and for criteria to guide overall management of SMZs. These needs were based on review team findings indicating a wide divergence among FS regions in the identification of permitted management activities within SMZs. In general, riparian areas were recognized for their importance in maintaining water quality and wildlife/fisheries habitat; however, there were numerous examples of conflicting uses of these areas. Examples of these uses include: livestock grazing, timber harvest, recreation campsites, and floodplain development.

The Chief's staff began working on national guidance to provide uniform definition of SMZs and policies for their management. While the work was proceeding, Executive Order 11988--Floodplain Management and Executive Order 11990--Protection of Wetlands were signed by President Carter on May 24, 1977. The National Forest Management Act[4] was passed October 22, 1976, providing guidance to the formulation of national Forest Service policy. Several interim directives were written and rewritten to include the Presidential and Congressional direction. Even though work began nationally in 1976, these rewrites delayed finalization of national direction until 1980. (This paper will not discuss the intent of this Presidential and Congressional directive.)

The following national FS policy was published in April 1980:

The Forest Service shall manage riparian areas in relation to various legally mandated requirements, including, but not limited to those associated with floodplains, wetlands, water quality, dredged and fill material, endangered species, wild and scenic rivers, and cultural resources.

Riparian areas must be managed in the context of the environment in which they are located. Specifically, the policy of the Forest Service is to:

---

[3] PL 92-500, Federal Water Pollution and Control Act, as amended. 33 U.S.C. 466.

[4] 16 U.S.C. 1600.

1. Recognize the importance and distinctive values of riparian areas during the land management planning process.
2. Recognize the importance and distinctive value of riparian areas when implementing management activities. Give preferential consideration to riparian area-dependent resources over other resources in cases of unresolvable conflict.
3. Manage riparian areas under the principles of multiple use and sustained yield, while emphasizing protection of soil, water, vegetation, and fish and wildlife resources.
4. Delineate and evaluate riparian areas prior to implementing any project activity (USDA Forest Service 1980).

The 1980 policy and direction also provided the standard agency definition of riparian areas as:

Geographically delineated areas, with distinctive resource values and characteristics, that are comprised of the aquatic and riparian ecosystems, floodplains, and wetlands. They include all areas within a horizontal distance of 100 feet from the edge of perennial streams or other water bodies (ibid.).

The last sentence shows the influence of including National Forest Management Act direction into the definition of riparian areas.

One of the more significant parts of the current national direction deals with a discussion of management activities in riparian areas.

It is important to recognize that timber harvesting, grazing, recreation, wildlife uses, and road construction are examples of activities that are compatible with and may occur within riparian areas. Some resources, however, such as fish, certain wildlife and vegetation, and water are totally dependent upon riparian areas. Other resources, such as timber, forage, minerals, visual and cultural activities, such as transportation and recreation, are not always dependent upon riparian areas.

Actions within or affecting riparian areas will include protection and, where applicable, improvement of dependent resources. Other resource uses and activities will occur to the extent they support or do not adversely affect the maintenance of riparian area-dependent resources. Preferential consideration is given to riparian area-dependent resources over other resources and activities when conflicts occur (ibid.).

In July of 1981, FS national policy and direction was published for the management of floodplains and wetlands, to implement the intent of executive orders 11988 and 11990. The national policy includes the following:

a. Provide opportunity for early public review of plans or proposals for action in floodplains, or for new construction in wetlands... including Federal actions for which the impact is not significant enough to require the preparation of an environmental impact statement...
b. Apply sound floodplain and wetland management to all agency activities, including long-range planning, program reviews, and individual project actions on National Forest System lands, and State and private forestry assistance programs.
c. Avoid, to the extent possible, long- and short-term adverse impacts which may be associated with the occupancy and modification of floodplains and with the destruction, loss, or degradation of wetlands.
d. Avoid direct and indirect support of floodplain development and new construction in wetlands wherever there is a practicable alternative.
e. Reduce the risk of flood loss to minimize the impacts of floods on human health, safety and welfare.
f. Promote the use of nonstructural flood protection methods to reduce the risk of flood hazard and flood loss.
g. Capitalize on opportunities to restore and preserve the natural and beneficial values served by floodplains, and to preserve, enhance and manage the natural and beneficial values of wetlands.
h. Adhere to the objectives of the Unified National Program for Floodplain Management published by the United States Water Resources Council, and provide leadership in applying the conceptual framework and strategies set forth by the Council to Forest Service programs.
i. Promote sound floodplain management, and protection and management of wetlands on non-Federal forest and range lands (USDA Forest Service 1981a).

This national direction also requires the use of the Water Resource Council's eight-step decision-making process for applying for the floodplain executive order (ibid.). The eight steps are given below.

Step 1. Determine whether the proposed action is located in the 100-year floodplain (500-year floodplain for critical actions), or whether it has the potential to affect a floodplain or indirectly support floodplain development. If not, or if an action is of an emergency nature, requirements of the executive order will have been satisfied.

Step 2. Notify the public at the earliest possible time of any plan or proposal to undertake, support, or allow an action which would result in the occupancy, modification, or development in a floodplain, and involve the affected and interested public in the decision-making process.

Step 3. Identify and evaluate practicable alternatives to locating a proposed action in a floodplain, including alternative sites outside the floodplain, alternative actions serving the same purpose as the proposed action, and the "no action" option.

Step 4. Identify the full range of potential direct or indirect adverse impacts associated with the occupancy or modification of floodplain and the potential direct and indirect support of floodplain development that could result from the proposed action.

Step 5. Identify and evaluate mitigation measures that will minimize the potential adverse impacts of the action if avoidance cannot be achieved, and measures that will preserve and restore or enhance the natural and beneficial floodplain values that would be adversely affected by the action.

Step 6. Reevaluate the proposed action. First, determine if it is still practical, even with the application of appropriate mitigating measures, in light of its exposure to flood hazards, and its potential to adversely affect the floodplain. Then determine if the alternatives identified in step 3 are practicable in light of information gained in steps 4 and 5.

Step 7. Prepare and provide the public with a finding and public explanation of any final decision when there is no practicable alternative to locating an action in or adversely affecting a floodplain.

Step 8. Provide ongoing review of implementation and post-implementation phases of the proposed action to ensure that all provisions associated with the action, including appropriate mitigating measures as identified in the environmental assessment, are fully implemented.

The preceding discussion is a synoptic history of the evolution of riparian area management philosophy which has resulted in the current national and regional agency direction to manage riparian areas in the FS. Some examples of how this direction is being applied on National Forest System lands in California follow.

REGIONAL PLANNING

In October 1980, the Pacific Southwest Region began regional planning to implement the National Forest Management Act. Replies to a solicitation for regional issues and concerns indicated a public concern over the intensity of management activities occurring in riparian areas. The concern was also expressed that upland land-use activities were taking place at a rate that could result in a damaging cumulative effect on downstream riparian areas. National Forest managers expressed a concern that historic and current land uses on inholdings could be pre-empting land-use options on National Forest System lands.

To address these public issues and FS concerns, the personnel in national forests were directed to analyze the individual and cumulative effects on riparian and other sensitive areas of producing forest products. National forests could then compare commodity production assigned under multiple-use plans with production under current riparian management direction.

The regional plan is a vehicle for passing national resource production targets for forest commodities assigned to the region down to the individual national forests. The personnel of the individual forests then determine their capability to produce these assigned commodities by developing a forest land and resource management plan. Forest production capacity is aggregated into a regional capability which in turn is aggregated into a national capability. The national capability is used in developing an updated FS program under the Resource Planning Act (RPA)[5]. This is the first real opportunity that personnel of the individual forests, using site-specific information, have had to adjust national targets that may affect riparian area management.

FOREST PLANNING

National forests are scheduled to complete their first forest land and resource management plans by 1983. Draft environmental impact statements and draft forest plans are presently being or will shortly be circulated for public review by the Klamath, Shasta-Trinity, Sierra, and Six Rivers national forests.

Since these are draft documents, and an alternative has not been finalized, it is too early to tell what management changes may result from the riparian area direction that has been established since 1978 (the time at which concern was recognized at the national level). Interested individuals should make a point to review forest planning documents and offer their comments.

PROJECT PLANNING

There are two general types of project plans--plans for improvement and plans for maintenance.

Riparian Area Improvement Plans

Riparian area improvement plans are developed to improve existing conditions in riparian areas. A few of the activities commonly undertaken include structural treatments in stream channels to improve fish-rearing habitat and

---

[5]Forest and Rangeland Renewable Resource Planning Act of 1974, as amended. 16 U.S.C. 1600-1614.

stabilize streambanks to reduce sediment; planting vegetation for shade and soil surface cover; relocating stream crossings, campgrounds, and structures; and fencing to control livestock use.

The following is an extract from Section VIII (Treatment) of "Prescription and Environmental Analysis, Trail Creek" (USDA Forest Service, Inyo National Forest 1979). It is given here as an example of a riparian area improvement plan.

1. Place approximately thirty stream gabions in Trail Creek to slow water velocity and retain moving materials. Gabions are to be made of local rock, with wire and posts as needed. The middle portion of the gabion is to rise 6-10 in. above the original water surface. On approximately seven of these, the streambank is to be reinforced with rock to provide stabilized cattle crossings immediately above the gabions.

2. Evaluate the feasibility of placing approximately three to five stream gabions of "porta-plank" or other interlocking sheet metal in the deep, narrow sections of the stream unsuitable for rock gabions. Proceed if feasible--1979 or 1980.

3. Reroute the present road around three wet meadows that are presently receiving damage. Clear brush on the new roadway. Place enough small boulders on the entrance and exit of the abandoned roadways to discourage further vehicle travel.

4. Rock the road in one wet meadow where it is not possible to reroute. Haul rock locally.

5. Fence the spring located south of Trail Creek in "Camp Meadow." This spring had been fenced at one time but is now being trampled by cattle. Plant aspen shoots inside the approximately 40-foot square enclosure in wet parts. Aspens provide valuable wildlife habitat and are rare in the canyon.

6. Fill the old pipeline trench in Camp Meadow to help raise the water table. Fill in the sump hole on the south side of the creek at the campsite directly below the pond to help raise the water table.

7. Wet area protection--fence the swampy spring area above the pond to exclude cattle from approximately one acre. Plant aspen.

8. Continue the present system of rest-rotation grazing as prescribed in the Trail Canyon Cattle Allotment Management Plan.

9. Continue the program of winter burning in Trail Canyon as proposed in the Trail Canyon EAR for prescribed burning. Thirty-six acres have been burned since 1975. Burning is to be coordinated by the Wildlife Biologist and Resource Officer.

a) Burn a total of 163 acres of mixed woody and meadow vegetation at regular intervals as follows:

	Woody with meadow/ grass understory	Woody
Burn every 5 years	93 acres	
Burn every 15 years		70 acres
Leave unburned		75 acres

Meadow will be increased from 42 to 93 acres by burning former meadow areas being overtaken by woody species. These areas still should have some type of grass understory to be suitable for burning as meadow.
Burn woody areas lacking understory once every 15 years. When convenient, burn invading wildrose patches more often.
Leave 65 acres of woody species along the creek unburned, including the aspen patch below the pond, and local stands of mature woody vegetation immediately adjacent to campspots. (Campspots can be easily identified by the presence of rock campfire rings and adjacent parking spots.)
b) Burn in late fall, winter or early spring to protect nesting or denning wildlife and perennial forage plants. The cost of burning is estimated to be $35 per acre. Fuels management would conduct the actual burning in coordination with wildlife and range management.

10. Apply 2,4-D to sprouting wildrose, willow and rabbitbrush the following growing season after prescribed burning. Spray only to restore areas with grass understory back to meadow habitat. Leave other areas to be used as young browse forage for wildlife and livestock. Complete the necessary application and permits prior to herbicide application and follow established guidelines necessary for safe application. In this case, do not spray within 10 feet of the stream if by hand; or 20 feet if by ground rig. This area should not be sprayed aerially. Spray only with wind less than 5 mph. A supplementary EA [environmental assessment] for herbicide application may be necessary in addition to this document.

In fiscal year 1980, approximately $1,732,000 was obligated to conduct watershed and fishery habitat improvement. These treatments were primarily in riparian areas. In fiscal years 1981 and 1982, it is estimated that national forests in California will use $895,000 and $252,000, respectively, for work in riparian areas.

Riparian Area Maintenance Plans

Maintenance prescriptions are included in environmental assessments (EA) that are developed to provide utilization of forest commodities such as timber and grass. An EA for a timber sale, for example, can include direction for width, location, and treatment in allowable stream management zones. An example follows.

Two swale drainages within unit (Wilcox timber harvest unit 10) will need SMZ protection. Northern drainage is very boggy at upper end and will need SMZ located 25 ft. back from edge. No harvesting should be allowed within bog. Below bog, a 150 ft. SMZ should be sufficient around drainage. Select harvesting can be performed but avoid yarding through zone. Along southern drainage, a 200 ft. SMZ should be retained. Select removal of timber can also be performed if 50% of crown cover is retained. Yarding should again be avoided within the SMZ.

Boundary modification along southern edge of unit (Wilcox timber harvest unit 6) ephemeral drainage from south corner 18+50 to 21+50. Move boundary upslope 50 ft. to avoid impacting adjacent drainage. Allow harvesting of decadents within modified area but retain understory and prohibit equipment (USDA Forest Service 1981b).

The funds devoted to protecting riparian areas are not as easily tracked as are improvement funds. In fiscal years 1980 and 1981, approximately $2,172,000 and $2,845,000, respectively, were obligated for watershed and fish and wildlife assistance in the management of the national forest timber resource in California. This is approximately 21% and 31%, respectively, of their total budgets. A good portion of these funds were probably related to riparian area maintenance.

DISCUSSION

Results of changes in riparian area management direction are slowly being realized. Even though, as early as 1966, the Pacific Southwest Region had begun to recognize that riparian areas needed special management direction, national direction did not emerge until 1980. Prior to 1980, commodity targets for forest products were developed through single-purpose resource management plans, such as forest timber management plans, under coordination requirements outlined in multiple-use plans. Multiple use plans were developed in the 1960s and early 1970s with limited interdisciplinary input. Prior to the current planning emphasis, in only a few cases have these multiple-use plans been updated. Thus, conflicts for use of riparian areas were not uncommon.

FS policy for managing riparian areas allows for management of, as well as protection of, riparian resources. This national direction is being integrated into forest land and resources management plans due for completion in 1983. These plans will determine each national forest's capability to produce forest products while applying this recent national direction. Capabilities will be combined into regional capabilities which in turn are combined into national capabilities. This will be the earliest that recent changes in riparian area management will be reflected in targets assigned to national forests.

How this may effect or change commodities is not clearly known at this time, but an indication may be the preliminary options being considered on the Six Rivers National Forest. Land areas delineated as stream management areas comprise 49,000 ha. (121,000 ac.) or about 13% of the forest not in wilderness. Under previous multiple-use plans, about 8,900 ha. (22,000 ac.) were designated as Water and Travel Influence Zones. Of the 19 billion board feet standing timber volume, 14% occurs in SMZs. Under options being considered, about one million board feet would be scheduled for removal from the SMZ. Under the previous plans, one-half million board feet were scheduled for harvest from the Water and Travel Influence Zone. Thus, areas being delineated for riparian area management have increased, and the rate of removal of timber from these areas has decreased.

FUTURE NEEDS

National forest land and resource management plans will allocate areas for riparian resource management. This management will probably include programming of commodities, such as timber and grazing, to be realized as part of the riparian management prescription. The FS has not had much experience in designing management prescriptions of this type. The agency needs to know what a healthy riparian area should look like and be able to describe this condition in terms familiar to resource personnel applying vegetation management practices, such as silviculturists or range managers. This would allow the design and programming of vegetation manipulation harvests through a systematic, integrated process that is compatible with riparian area management objectives.

Further, monitoring techniques need to be developed to test the results of planning prescriptions, or to verify their design. Research is also needed to develop methods to inventory and assess riparian area resource values. Without a common process to describe the physical and biological character of riparian areas, a standard description of condition and treatment requirements is not feasible.

SUMMARY

The FS in the Pacific Southwest Region has been implementing various intensities of management direction for protecting riparian areas since the mid-1960s. However, targets for commodities are assigned at the national level and have not changed significantly during this time period. Thus, conflicts between competing uses have occurred within riparian areas.

FS direction published nationally, between 1979 and 1981, strengthens regional direction. The national direction provides for protection and improvement of riparian areas while still utilizing commodities, such as timber and grazing, from riparian areas.

National forests are analyzing their capabilities to produce commodities under this direction, as compared to targets determined prior to its issuance. This is the first opportunity to adjust commodity targets since the development of multiple-use plans and single resource plans of the 1960s and early 1970s. Individuals interested in having input to the analysis should make a point to review forest planning documents.

LITERATURE CITED

Pacific Southwest Region, USDA Forest Service. 1979. Water quality management for National Forest System lands in California. USDA Forest Service, Pacific Southwest Region, San Francisco, Calif.

USDA Forest Service. 1975. Classification of streams. R-5 Supplement 15, Forest Service Manual 2536.1. USDA Forest Service, San Francisco, Calif.

USDA Forest Service. 1976. Stream protection measures. R-5 Supplement 17, Forest Service Manual 1521. USDA Forest Service, San Francisco, Calif.

USDA Forest Service. 1979. Prescription and environmental analysis of Trail Creek, Inyo National Forest. USDA Forest Service, Bishop, Calif.

USDA Forest Service. 1980. Riparian areas. Amendment 26, Forest Service Manual 2526. USDA Forest Service, Washington, D.C.

USDA Forest Service. 1981a. Analysis and evaluations for floodplain management and wetland protection. Amendment 31, Forest Service Manual 2527. USDA Forest Service, Washington, D.C.

USDA Forest Service. 1981b. Wilcox timber sale environmental analysis. USDA Forest Service, Shasta-Trinity Natinal Forest, Redding, Calif.

PROTECTING STREAM ENVIRONMENT ZONES
TO PRESERVE WATER QUALITY IN THE LAKE TAHOE BASIN[1]

Judith E. Unsicker, Charles A. White,
Michael R. James, and James D. Kuykendall[2]

Abstract.--Stream environment zones can provide effective natural removal of pollutants in precipitation runoff which would otherwise adversely affect the waters of Lake Tahoe. Human disturbance of some stream environment zones in the Tahoe Basin has drastically reduced their treatment capability. Activities of the California Regional Water Quality Control Board for protecting and restoring stream environment zones are discussed.

INTRODUCTION

Lake Tahoe, located at 1,897 m. elevation on the California-Nevada border (figure 1), is celebrated for its size, purity, clarity, and color. It is one of the largest high-altitude lakes in the world, with a volume of 155 billion cubic meters. The immense volume of the lake, and the relatively small size of its watershed (which discharged very low levels of sediment and nutrients to the lake under natural conditions) account for its outstanding water quality. The watershed includes 63 tributary streams. These streams, together with associated marshes, meadows, and riparian woodlands, are known to local planners as "stream environment zones" (SEZs).

Much of the Lake Tahoe Basin is in public ownership, but development of private lands, including large marsh and meadow areas throughout the basin, has been intensive during the last 25 years. About 10% of the watershed has been urbanized or otherwise disturbed. Increased residential and commercial development has been paralleled by increased phytoplankton productivity in open waters and nearshore periphyton growth. Phytoplankton primary productivity in 1980 was approximately twice that observed in the mid-1960s (Leonard and Goldman 1981).

These changes in productivity are the result of increased nutrient loadings to the lake caused by the increases in erosion and urban runoff flows which accompanied the development. In addition to these direct increases in nutrient loading, the disturbance of SEZs actually causes a reduction or complete loss in the capability of many SEZs to reduce nutrient levels in precipitation runoff through natural filtration, sedimentation, and adsorption processes (Tahoe Regional Planning Agency 1977; California Water Resources Control Board 1980).

The California Water Resources Control Board (State Board) and the California Regional Water Quality Control Board, Lahontan Region (Regional Board) are the state agencies responsible for protecting the water quality of Lake Tahoe and its tributaries through policy making, planning, and enforcement activities. These boards cooperate with a number of federal, state and local agencies, including the bistate Tahoe Regional Planning Agency (TRPA), which recently adopted a bistate water quality plan. This paper summarizes State and Regional Board efforts to protect SEZs in the Lake Tahoe Basin--for their intrinsic value and for the protection of Lake Tahoe.

DEFINITION AND IMPORTANCE OF STREAM ENVIRONMENT ZONES

In 1971, the USDA Forest Service (FS), in cooperation with the TRPA, mapped the soils and geomorphic characteristics of the Lake Tahoe Basin. This information was subsequently used by the FS and TRPA to construct a land capability system. Land capability was defined as: "the level of use an area can tolerate without sustaining permanent damage through erosion and other causes" (Bailey 1974). The system includes seven classes, with Class 1 being those lands which should be kept in their natural state and Class 7 lands rated the most tolerant of distur-

[1] Paper presented at the California Riparian Systems Conference. [University of California, Davis, September 17-19, 1981].

[2] Judith E. Unsicker is Environmental Specialist, Michael R. James is Senior Water Resources Control Engineer, and James D. Kuykendall is Supervising Water Resources Control Engineer; all are with the California Regional Water Quality Control Board, Lahontan Region, South Lake Tahoe, California. Charles A. White is Regional Administrator, Hazardous Material Management, Department of Health Services, Berkeley, California.

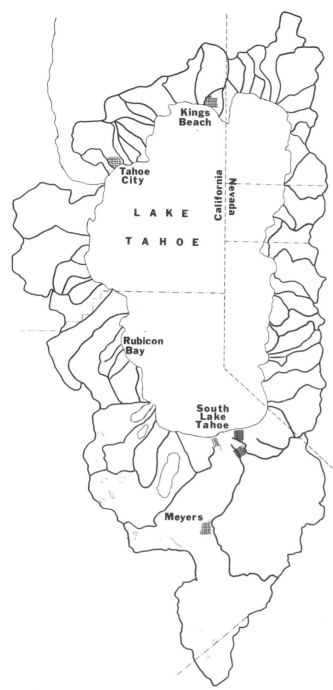

Figure 1.--Map of Lake Tahoe Basin, showing watershed boundaries (after Tahoe Regional Planning Agency 1977).

Table 1.--Allowable coverage in different land capability classes.

Capability Class	Erosion Hazard	Allowable Impervious Surface Coverage (%)
7	low	30
6	low	30
5	low	25
4	moderate	20
3	moderate	5
2	high	1
1	high	1

SEZs, as defined in a later study (Tahoe Regional Planning Agency 1977), are essentially equivalent to Class 1b lands, although the determining criteria have been expanded in some respects. As mapped for the TRPA Water Quality Management Plan (ibid.), SEZs include the broadest of the following limits: streams, lakes, ponds; areas of alluvial soil; the 100-year floodplain; areas of riparian vegetation; a minimum buffer strip (7.5 to 30 m. [25 to 100 ft.]) with width dependent upon stream order (figure 2).

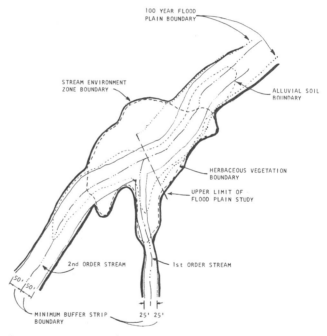

Figure 2.--Idealized stream environment zone (SEZ), showing criteria used in determining boundaries (after Tahoe Regional Planning Agency 1977).

bance (table 1). For each class, a maximum recommended percent coverage from developmental activities (e.g., paving, roof area) was prescribed as part of the land capability system. Class 1 lands were further broken down into three subclasses: 1a--high erosion hazard lands; 1b--lands with poor natural drainage; 1c--lands with fragile flora and fauna. Class 1b lands were defined to include "stream channels, marshes, flood plains, and meadows" (ibid.).

SEZs in the Lake Tahoe Basin are important both as examples of comparatively rare ecosystems (e.g., the quaking bog at Grass Lake), and as fish and wildlife habitat. The Western Federal Regional Council Interagency Task Force (1979) termed SEZs "key wildlife habitats". The ability of SEZs to remove pollutants from precipitation runoff was measured by the TRPA (Tahoe Regional

Planning Agency 1977) and by the Environmental Protection Agency (EPA) (Morris et al. 1980). The TRPA study showed 94% removal of suspended solids, 74% removal of total nitrogen, 86% removal of total phosphorus, and 72% removal of iron as runoff passed through an undisturbed SEZ.

The EPA study compared SEZs having different kinds and amounts of disturbance, and concluded that meadowlands can provide effective treatment of runoff under certain circumstances. Sheet flow, as opposed to channelized flow, results in the best treatment; beaver dams may aid in achieving such flow. Extensive grazing alters the filtration capability of meadow lands, and may accelerate leaching of soil nutrients. The authors emphasized the importance of monitoring during storm events; the most dramatic reductions in sediment and nutrients were associated with storms rather than with monitoring of runoff at regular intervals.

THE HISTORY OF HUMAN INFLUENCE ON STREAM ENVIRONMENT ZONES

The Lake Tahoe Basin provided summer hunting and fishing grounds for the Washoe and Paiute Indians; a number of important archaeological sites are associated with SEZs. Early white settlers pastured their livestock in basin meadows. Much of the basin was logged in the nineteenth and early twentieth centuries. Early resorts were usually associated with riparian zones. All of these activities must have altered SEZs to some extent. However, extensive permanent disturbance began only in the 1950s and 1960s with the development of the Tahoe Basin as a center for winter skiing and casino gaming. These attractions stimulated road construction and residential and commercial development, most intensively at the south shore of the lake. Much of this construction took place in SEZs and included an airport, golf courses, sewerlines, a sanitary landfill, and a quarry, as well as motels, shopping centers, and residential areas on filled SEZ land. The most drastic alteration was the dredging and filling of 140 ha. (340 ac.) of the Truckee Marsh to create the Tahoe Keys subdivision. The Western Federal Regional Council Interagency Task Force (1979) estimates that since 1900, 35% of the riparian streamside zones, 50% of the meadows, and 75% of the marshes in the Lake Tahoe Basin have been lost to development. Between 1969 and 1979 alone, 25% of the marshes were developed.

All of this development produced a variety of disturbances including channelization and rerouting of streams, increased streambank erosion, disturbed soil and vegetation with loss of natural nutrient filtration capability, increases in impervious surface and surface runoff; and additions to surface waters and groundwaters of fertilizers, pesticides, and deicing agents. By the early 1970s over 40,000 dwelling units and an additional 30,000 vacant lots existed in subdivisions which were approved and constructed prior to the development of the land capability system. In some urbanized areas, total coverage exceeded 90%.

As the more level private lands (largely SEZs) were developed, demand grew for construction on steeper slopes (capability classes 1-3). Sewering of the basin by the early 1970s facilitated development on soils which were unsuitable for septic tank/leachfield systems. On many class 1 lands, where land coverage should be limited to 1%, coverage currently exceeds 50%. Development of these fragile lands led to increased sedimentation in SEZs, even when there was no direct encroachment on the SEZ.

Table 2, from the TRPA study (Tahoe Regional Planning Agency 1977), compares the water quality of tributaries of Lake Tahoe with disturbed and undisturbed watersheds. Further documentation of the siltation problem was provided by several other investigators (California Resources Agency 1969; Kroll 1976; Glancy 1976). All of these studies demonstrated that sediment and nutrient discharge was much greater from disturbed than from undistrubed watersheds. Furthermore, these studies provided evidence that sediment and nutrient yields from watersheds undergoing development have a tendency to increase markedly as construction activities encroach on lower capability lands. Present sediment and nutrient loadings to Lake Tahoe are estimated to be equivalent to those from an undisturbed watershed 10 times the size of the Lake Tahoe Basin.

Table 2.--Mean quality of 21 Lake Tahoe tributary streams with disturbed watersheds and 15 tributaries with undeveloped watersheds (Tahoe Regional Planning Agency 1977).

Parameter	Disturbed	Undisturbed
Suspended solids (mg./l.)	8	4
Turbidity (JTU)	5	0.5
Nitrate N (μg./l.)	47	30
Total nitrogen (μg./l.)	300	252
Total iron (μg./l.)	29	15
Algal growth potential (mg./l.)	0.5	0.05

Work by the Tahoe Research Group (e.g., Goldman 1974) showed that suspended sediments could stimulate algal growth both as sources of dissolved nutrients and as substrates for heterotrophs which increase the rate of nutrient cycling.

Two studies by the State and Regional Board staffs contributed to the understanding of the effect of construction on sediment levels. Baker and Davis (1976) sampled benthic invertebrates in streams in and near the Tahoe Basin, above and below disturbed areas including subdivisions, road cuts, ski trails, and a large unpaved parking lot. Compared to reference stations, stations downstream of disturbed areas showed significant decreases in numbers, diversity, and standing crop of benthic macroinvertebrate organisms.

White and Franks (1978) compared sediment and nutrient loadings to streams from the poorly-planned Rubicon Properties subdivision on the west shore of Lake Tahoe with loadings from the carefully planned Northstar-at-Tahoe development just north of the Tahoe Basin. In the former development, roads, driveways and homesites had been graded with little or no attempt at erosion and drainage control. Road cuts at Rubicon were up to 30-40% and 24 m. (80 ft.) high. Full buildout of Rubicon Properties would lead to an eventual 55% land coverage within the subdivision, although the land capability system would restrict development of such high hazard (class 1) lands to only 1% coverage. These disturbances, and later the installation of sewerlines, contributed sediment to Lonely Gulch Creek, which flows through the subdivision. Total sediment loadings were 100 times natural background levels with drastic impacts on benthic invertebrate populations.

At Northstar-at-Tahoe, the ski area and condominiums were located away from SEZs and high erosion hazard lands, and "best management practices" (BMPs) for erosion and drainage control were employed from the beginning. Sediment loadings after construction were estimated to be only two to three times background levels, and there was very little impact on benthic invertebrates of Martis Creek. One of the major conclusions of the work conducted by White and Franks (ibid.) was that the most important BMPs for the protection of water quality in a SEZ are limitation of development activities to conform to land capability and exclusion of significant development activities from the SEZ itself.

HISTORY OF WATER QUALITY PLANNING

In the mid-1960s, concern over the nutrient contribution to Lake Tahoe from domestic waste-water led to negotiations between California and Nevada. These negotiations eventually resulted in the export of sewage and solid waste from the basin, and the creation of the bistate TRPA. The Regional Board's Lake Tahoe Policy (California Regional Water Quality Control Board, Lahontan Region 1967) was concerned mainly with the sewage issue. It recognized the siltation problem, and supported land-use control actions by the State Legislature and local governments. However, it provided relatively little authority for Regional Board enforcement authority. A 1970 addendum to the policy, and the Water Quality Control Plan (Basin Plan) adopted in 1975 included prohibitions on the discharge or threatened discharge of wastes, including earthen materials, to Lake Tahoe and its tributaries, or within their 100-year floodplains. At that time, the land-use planning agencies, the TRPA, and the California Tahoe Regional Planning Agency (CTRPA) enacted ordinances which downzoned many of the SEZs and regulated grading, vegetation disturbance, and shorezone construction. However, the political

situation led to "grandfathering" of development rights, and frequent granting of variances. Encroachment into SEZs continued.

In 1974 the TRPA was designated by California and Nevada as the "Section 208" planning agency for the Tahoe Basin under the Clean Water Act. In 1977 TRPA released a draft Water Quality Management Plan which identified development in SEZs, on high erosion-hazard lands, and in excess of land capability coverage limits as the major sources of water quality problems in Lake Tahoe and its tributaries. This plan recommended strict controls on new development and remedial erosion- and drainage-control projects to remedy impacts of existing development. Unfortunately, the final plan lacked commitment and funding for implementation of these controls. The State Board revoked TRPA's Section 208 planning designation and prepared its own water quality plan for the California portion of the Tahoe Basin (California Water Resources Control Board 1980). The Regional Board was given responsibility for implementing this plan. The major provisions of the State Board plan have been incorporated into the amended bistate plan recently adopted by TRPA. The Regional Board will continue to implement the State Board plan in California.

PROHIBITIONS ON DEVELOPMENT

The State Board plan, pursuant to authority granted by Sections 13170 and 13243 of the Porter-Cologne Act, prohibits discharge of sediment and other waste materials from new subdivisions, and from **any** new development or construction activities which occur in SEZs or exceed land capability coverage limits, or which are not offset by remedial erosion- and urban runoff-control measures for existing problems. The prohibitions effectively preclude development on land capability classes 1, 2, and 3, where coverage limits are 1-5%. Approximately 7,100 lots in California, 2,100 of them in SEZs, are affected by this prohibition. The Regional Board may grant a variance from the prohibitions for projects found to be reasonably necessary for public health, safety, or recreation; or for implementation of the Nonattainment Air Quality Plan (California Air Resources Board 1979). An example of such a variance was granted for a proposed bicycle trail through a SEZ--part of the regional transportation system recommended by the Air Quality Plan. All possible mitigation and offset measures would be required for such projects.

The State Board plan directs local governments, or, alternatively, the Regional Board, to adopt offset policies specifying the amount of correction of existing problems to be required as a condition of approval of new development. The policies could require phasing development each year dependent upon accomplishment of erosion control work to date, and/or collecting an offset fee from each developer. Offset could include financial or institutional contributions toward the restoration of disturbed SEZs. Offset measures are to be over and above the remedial projects required by the State Board plan.

No offset policies have been adopted to date. However the TRPA has recently established a mitigation fee schedule for construction projects in the Lake Tahoe Basin. These fees meet most of the requirements of the offset strategy contained in the Lake Tahoe Basin Water Quality Plan. Mitigation fees for a single family house on high capability land, for example, would be $750. These fees will generate revenues of about $700,000 per year for the construction of erosion and urban runoff control projects in the California portion of the Lake Tahoe Basin.

In practice the development prohibitions in this plan are being enforced mainly by local and regional governments. The Regional Board participates in their development review processes at the staff level, and makes its own findings in the cases of proposed variances and waste discharge requirements.

WASTE DISCHARGE PERMITS

The Regional Board has the authority to issue waste discharge requirements under California law, or National Pollutant Discharge Elimination System (NPDES) permits under federal law for any activity involving potential discharge of wastes into the state's waters. Under the State Board plan, waste discharge requirements may be issued for single family homes as well as for commercial and public projects in the Lake Tahoe Basin. Such permits may prescribe specific erosion and drainage control measures, set limitations for chemical constituents in surface runoff, and/or require reporting of failure of controls to the Regional Board. Lack of compliance with waste discharge requirements may result in cleanup and abatement orders, cease and desist orders, or judicial enforcement by the state Attorney General.

The State Board plan directs the Regional Board to revise discharge permits for sewage agencies in the Tahoe Basin to preclude their serving new development which is in violation of the development prohibitions in the plan. These revisions are in progress. The State Board plan also directs the Regional Board to issue NPDES permits for storm drains into Lake Tahoe.

REMEDIAL EROSION AND DRAINAGE CONTROL PROJECTS

The State Board plan includes a priority list of remedial projects to be undertaken by federal, state, and local agencies over a 20-year period. They include revegetation of areas stripped of vegetation, mechanical stabilization and revegetation of oversteepened and unvegetated roadway slopes, stabilization of eroding dirt roads, roadway shoulders and ditches, and storm drainage controls. The State Board has allocated $10,000,000 for these projects, to be used as matching funds for EPA Clean Lakes Grant money

and local funding sources. To date over $2,000,000 of projects are in the process of being funded. None of the present projects directly affects SEZs. However, all erosion and urban runoff control projects are expected to create substantial reductions in the levels of sediment and nutrient discharges to the SEZs of the watersheds in which the specific projects are located. In the future these funds may be used directly for major SEZ restoration.

MONITORING

The State and Regional Boards are participants in a comprehensive interagency monitoring program which also includes the University of California, Davis, Tahoe Research Group; the California Department of Water Resources; the California Department of Transportation; the FS; and the USDI Geological Survey.

Algal productivity in nearshore and offshore waters of Lake Tahoe, as well as precipitation chemistry, flows, and water quality of tributary streams are being measured in this monitoring effort. Baseline data being collected now will aid in evaluation of the effectiveness of the control measures discussed above.

In 1981 the Regional Board expects to initiate its own surface runoff monitoring program which will include disturbed and undisturbed watersheds, individual commercial discharges, and storm drain systems. This program will be used by the Regional Board to obtain a more accurate assessment of the impacts of development and intense urbanization on the water quality of Lake Tahoe and of the SEZs of the Lake Tahoe Basin.

RESTORATION OF DISTURBED STREAM ENVIRONMENT ZONES

Where encroachments into SEZs have been permitted in the last decade, in most cases some level of mitigation measures have been required to offset the effects of the encroachment. Such measures, as specified in waste discharge requirements adopted by the Regional Board, include stabilization of soils disturbed during construction, and installation and maintenance of facilities to filter virtually all precipitation runoff from man-made impervious surfaces.

The FS has taken the lead in watershed restoration activities in the Lake Tahoe Basin. Significant projects to date have included leachate control at an abandoned landfill in a SEZ, restoration of natural water levels in a partially drained bog, and revegetation and installation of drainage controls in a meadow where casino development had begun.

SEZs will be a high priority for FS acquisition under the Santini-Burton program, which provides money for the buyout of environmentally sensitive lots. Additional money for public acquisition of SEZs and other fragile lands could be available from a proposed California bond issue. The City of South Lake Tahoe is considering buying SEZs with park funds. Acquisition under these proposals would be on a willing seller basis, although it has been suggested that public agencies could acquire SEZs through the power of condemnation.

Other possible means of facilitating preservation and restoration of SEZs include transfer of development rights, easements, and amortization and eventual removal of existing structures (Tahoe Regional Planning Agency 1975).

MAN-MODIFIED STREAM ENVIRONMENT ZONES

The State Board plan recognizes that some SEZs have been so drastically altered that they no longer exhibit the characteristics of SEZs, and that restoration may be impractical. It allows the Regional Board to reclassify such areas, permitting further development provided adequate offset and mitigation measures are undertaken. Such measures would appropriately include restoration of some of the lost SEZ treatment capability through correction of SEZ problems elsewhere in the basin.

In 1982 the Regional Board will be asked to consider whether or not, or under what conditions further development of the Tahoe Keys subdivision should be permitted. If continued development is allowed, mitigation and offset measures might include one or more of the following:

1) continued operation and/or expansion of the existing water treatment and circulation system for the Tahoe Keys lagoon;

2) use of the remaining portions of the Truckee Marsh for natural treatment of surface runoff from developed areas;

3) restrictions on construction, landscaping, and gardening practices to minimize nutrient loadings to surface waters from runoff and groundwater percolation;

4) financial and/or institutional contributions to erosion and drainage control projects elsewhere in the basin--including restoration of sheet flow over meadows in channelized portions of the Upper Truckee River drainage, or correction of runoff problems in the urbanized Tahoe Valley drainage (both drainages were originally tributary to the Tahoe Keys area).

CONCLUSION

State and federal nondegradation regulations require that the existing high quality of Lake Tahoe's water be preserved, and enhanced if possible. Development restrictions and remedial control measures being implemented in the Tahoe Basin are believed to be absolutely necessary to prevent further degradation of water quality in the lake and its tributaries. The State Board plan emphasizes that further restrictions on growth and additional remedial projects are needed to reverse the degradation which has already occurred. The TRPA is now evaluating existing data in order to determine environmental threshold carrying capacities for a number of parameters including water quality. It will revise its regional plan, including land use controls, to reflect the limits. It is to be expected that protection and restoration of SEZs will continue to have high priority.

LITERATURE CITED

Bailey, R.G. 1974. Land capability classification of the Lake Tahoe Basin, California-Nevada. 32 p. USDA Forest Service/Tahoe Regional Planning Agency, South Lake Tahoe, California.

Baker, J.A., and W.E. Davis. 1976. Siltation evaluation investigation for the Lake Tahoe Basin. 58 p. California Regional Water Quality Control Board, Lahontan Region, South Lake Tahoe, California.

California Air Resources Board. 1979. Lake Tahoe Basin control strategy revisions to State of California implementation plan for the attainment and maintenance of ambient air quality standards. 268 p. with appendix. California Air Resources Board, Sacramento.

California Regional Water Quality Control Board, Lahontan Region. 1967. Lake Tahoe water quality control policy. 38 p. California Regional Water Quality Control Board, Lahontan Region, Bishop, California.

California Regional Water Quality Control Board, Lahontan Region. 1975. Water quality control plan, North Lahontan Basin (6A). 533 p. California State Water Resources Control Board, Sacramento.

California Resources Agency. 1969. Sedimentation and erosion in the Upper Truckee River and Trout Creek watershed, Lake Tahoe, California. 50 p. California Department of Conservation, Sacramento.

California State Water Resources Control Board. 1980. Lake Tahoe Basin water quality plan. 378 p. California State Water Resources Control Board, Sacramento.

Glancy, P.A. 1976. A reconnaissance of streamflow and fluvial sediment transport, Incline Village area, Lake Tahoe, Nevada. USDI Geological Survew Water Resources Information Series Report 23, Carson City, Nevada. 47 p.

Goldman, C.R. 1974. Eutrophication of Lake Tahoe emphasizing water quality. EPA 660/3-74-034. 408 p. US Environmental Protection Agency, Corvalis, Oregon.

Kroll, C.G. 1976. Sediment discharge from highway cut slopes in the Lake Tahoe Basin, California. USDI Geological Survey, Water Resources Investigations 76-19. Menlo Park, California. 90 p.

Leonard, R.L., and C.R. Goldman. 1981. Interagency Tahoe monitoring program first annual report, water year 1980. 100 p. Tahoe Research Group, Institute of Ecology, University of California, Davis.

Morris, F.A., M.K. Morris, T.S. Michaud, and L.R. Williams. 1980. Meadowland natural treatment processes in the Lake Tahoe Basin: a field investigation. 180 p. US Environmental Protection Agency, Environmental Monitoring Systems Laboratory, Las Vegas, Nevada.

Tahoe Regional Planning Agency. 1975. TRPA 208 program, draft work element report. 243 p. Tahoe Regional Planning Agency, South Lake Tahoe, California.

Tahoe Regional Planning Agency. 1977. Lake Tahoe Basin water quality management plan (amended 1981). 4 volumes and amending ordinances. Tahoe Regional Planning Agency, South Lake Tahoe, California.

Western Federal Regional Council Interagency Task Force. 1979. Lake Tahoe environmental assessment. 240 p. Western Federal Regional Council, San Francisco, California.

White, C.A., and A.L. Franks. 1978. Demonstration of erosion and sediment control technology, Lake Tahoe region of California. EPA 600/2-78-208. 405 p. US Environmental Protection Agency, Cincinnati, Ohio.

RESOURCE ALLOCATION ISSUES ASSOCIATED WITH

MAINTAINING INSTREAM FLOW FROM WASTEWATER[1]

James R. Vilkitis and Donald R. Woodley[2]

Abstract.--The Chorro Creek study area lacks a comprehensive interagency water management plan. Programs and
policies that relate to the missions of the various institutions and agencies involved in its management appear to be
crisis oriented. The re-allocation of a water resource use
through upgrading of a secondary treatment facility illustrates this approach to planning.

INTRODUCTION

At the inception of this study, the authors
planned to use the Chorro Creek watershed as a
case study area for resource allocation problems
associated with competitive uses of a scarce resource: water. The planned approach was to
review historical and present consumptive uses of
water in the watershed, relative to instream flow
and influence upon the riparian system. Of particular concern were the competing uses of water
among the private and public riparian landowners
during the dry season and the processes by which
these uses were allocated water.

At the time, there appeared to be a plethora
of information available from public agencies
involved with water and its use and from the
numerous reports of the watershed's resource.
These could be used to construct a water management plan and water budget for the watershed.
Upon investigation into the baseline sources, however, it became apparent that much of the information was not available, incomplete, or of poor
quality. As a result, the case study deals only
with factual information gleaned from public documents; hearsay was unsatisfactory and expert opinion was relied upon only when the source could be
documented. Questions related to groundwater
storage and yields have not been addressed, simply because adequate data that may be used for
rational decisions do not exist.

For these reasons, the study concentrated on
Chorro Reservoir (hereafter refered to as the

Reservoir) and the waste water treatment plant at
the California Men's Colony (WWTP), for which
there appear to be enough historical data to give
insight into water management of the study area.

STUDY AREA

The main stream of Chorro Creek flows in a
northwesterly direction. The 122-sq. km. (47-sq.
mi.) watershed is the larger of two basins that
drain into Morro Bay on the central coast of California, San Luis Obispo County. The watershed is
bordered on the northeast by the Santa Lucia
Range and to the southwest by a series of volcanic peaks known as Park Ridge. Two of the peaks
(Black Hill and Cerro Cabrillo) form a narrow,
through which the creek drains (fig. 1.)

The valley, 0.8 km. (0.5 mi.) wide in some
places, varies from rolling hills covered with
range grasses to relatively steep slopes at the
divides. Three categories of land use were identified. 1) Commercial/residential, which includes Camp San Luis Obispo of the California National Guard (CNG), Cuesta College, and the California Men's Colony (CMC), comprised less than 10%
of the area. 2) Agriculture, primarily pasture,
comprised approximately 50% of the area, with
less than 10% devoted to irrigated crops. 3)
Idle land made up the remainder and was in general vegetated, with varying stands of chaparral,
conifers and hardwoods. The denser vegetation
was located on steeper slopes and in the draws of
the basin. There was no urban land (housing
developments) in the valley. The agricultural
land had very high potential for multiple annual
crop production with irrigation. Large landholders included private agriculture ranches, CNG at
Camp San Luis Obispo (1,660 ha. [4,100 ac.]),
national forest (1,730 ha. [4,276 ac.]), and U.S.
General Services Administration (2,374 ha. [5,865

---

[1]Paper presented at the California Riparian Systems Conference. [University of California, Davis, September 17-19, 1981].

[2]James R. Vilkitis, Ph.D., is Natural Resource Manager, and Donald R. Woodley, Ph.D., is
Hydrologist; both are at the School of Agriculture and Natural Resources at California Polytechnic State University, San Luis Obispo, Calif.

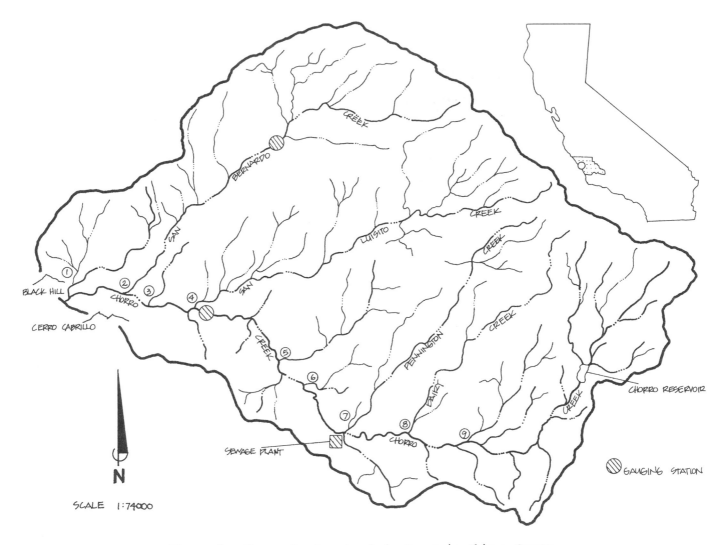

Figure 1.--Chorro Creek watershed, San Luis Obispo County,
California. (K. Frank.)

ac.]). The latter acquired the land some time
after 1963.[3]

Chorro Creek is an intermittent stream with
sections exhibiting no surface flow during the
dry season (Chappell et al. 1976; Central
Coast Regional Water Quality Control Board 1980).
Most sub-basins experience flow during the winter and spring. The flow of the main stream is
modified by consumptive uses during the dry season and continuously by effluent from the CMC's
WWTP located at the junction of Pennington and
Chorro creeks (fig. 1). The extent to which each
of the sub-basins contributes water to the overall flow regime is not known (table 1.)

Streamflow has been monitored at the Canet
Road crossing since November 1978, and on San
Bernardo Creek for nine non-consecutive years
(1960-65 and 1978-present). The data, however,
indicate that the main stream is flashy and irregular. San Bernardo Creek appears to be more
stable in its discharge. The gauging station is
located upstream and not at the confluence of the
San Bernardino with the Chorro (fig. 1). There
are no baseline data for the other feeder stream,
except for the records kept by CMC for the Reservoir and WWTP discharge.

Infiltration of rainfall appears to occur
primarily in the thin residual soil (Henneke
soil) of the headwater canyons. The lower alluviated valley (Salinas soil) generates a greater

[3]Machado, H.W. 1981. Personal communication. CNG, Camp San Luis Obispo, San Luis
Obispo, Calif.

Table 1.—Sub-basin area and stream length, Chorro watershed (M. Barnum). Sub-basin numbers refer to figure 1.

Sub-basin	Area (ha.)	Stream length in km. Main	Feeder
1.	226	2.4	7.9
San Bernardo			
2.	1,187	10.3	21.6
3.	210	1.8	--
San Luisito			
4.	2,616	10.1	25.0
5.	433	3.5	6.8
6.	150	1.8	1.8
Pennington			
7.	502	7.2	8.2
Dairy			
8.	433	7.2	2.7
Chorro			
9.	1,964 (4,852)	19.8 (12.3)	23.0(14.3)
Feeders			
West Bank	4,457(11,009)		
Total	12,178(30,080)	64.2 (39.9)	96.9(60.2)

proportion of the surface runoff due to layers of silts and clays near the surface.[4]

Geologic faults occur in the watershed (Carollo 1977). Their impacts on groundwater and groundwater movement are not known.

PROCEDURES

No baseline data were generated through organized field research. Scientific literature, public agencies and institutions, private professionals, and local experts were consulted as sources of data. Pertinent information was compiled and assessed as to its validity.

Water resource statistics for the Reservoir were calculated from monthly records supplied by the CMC. Data were only assessed from January, 1962 through December, 1980 (study period), since these were the years that water was being imported from Whale Rock Reservoir on Old Creek and utilized by CMC, with subsequent discharge going into Chorro Creek. Whale Rock Reservoir is approximately 21 linear km. (13 mi.) northwest of the Reservoir. Averages in the tables should be approached with caution since in some cases they were calculated using the number of months where water flowed or was used. For example, during January of the study period, water flowed over the spillway 17 years out of the 19-year period; an average was obtained by dividing total flow over the spillway by 17. Results indicate the

average flow for months of flow. Tables present all statistics related to flow and no-flow months.

Statistics for the WWTP were derived from "Repairs and Utilities Operation Log" records supplied by CMC, from July 1966 to June 1975. Reliable data for other time periods were not readily available.[5]

The study area is in a water-deficient region that experiences an average annual rainfall of approximately 560 mm. (22 in.), most of which (75%) falls between 1 December and 31 March. The allocation of water as a resource only becomes a management issue during that portion of the year when water is scarce and demand is great. This is identified as the "dry" period, which extends from May through November. Statistics related to this period are bracketed in the tables by heavier lines.

RESULTS

Comprehensive and/or descriptive baseline data for the natural resources and land-use history of the watershed are not available. The environmental setting was established from information generated from sources specified above.

History

The Reservoir and WWTP are presently operated by CMC and are located within Camp San Luis Obispo, which is the property of the State of California. Established as a National Guard camp in 1928, its control was preempted by the federal government from 1941 to 1946 and from 1951 to 1953. During those periods structures were built that were the property of the federal government. Since 1965, the property has been under state control.

Chorro Dam was completed by the US Army Corps of Engineers (CE) in September 1941 as a device to regulate water imported from Salinas Reservoir (Santa Margarita Lake). Since it was a regulatory device, an appropriation permit from the State Water Resources Control Board (SWRCB), which authorizes construction of projects and uses of water, was not necessary. Over time the use of the Reservoir dam changed from regulation to storage and diversion. On 30 November 1955, the CNG filed an application (16757) for appropriation of water (storage and diversion) to the SWRCB. A permit (11527) was issued in 1958. Subsequently, the CNG made proof (19 July 1963) of a right to use water from Chorro Creek. A license (7844) for diversion and use of water was issued (4 August 1966) for irrigation, domestic, stock-watering, and recreational use. The conditions of the license were as follows:

---

[4]Mann, J.F. 1977. Correspondence. Consulting Geologist and Hydrologist, La Habra, Calif.

[5]Robasciotti, M. 1981. Communications. Waste water treatment plant, California Men's Colony, San Luis Obispo, Calif.

...and that the amount of water to which such right is entitled and hereby confirmed, for the purposes aforesaid, is limited to the amount actually beneficially used for said purposes and shall not exceed one and five-tenths (1.5) cubic feet per second by direct diversion to be diverted from about May 1 to about November 1 of each year for irrigation purposes and throughout the remainder of the year as required for domestic use and one hundred fifty (150) acre-feet per annum by storage to be collected from about October 1 of each year to about May 31 of the succeeding year.

The equivalent of such continuous flow allowance for any thirty-day period may be diverted in a shorter time if there be no interference with other vested rights.

Maximum withdrawal in any one year has been 92 acre-feet.

Licensee shall release or bypass a flow of at least one cubic foot per second into the natural channel of Chorro Creek below the point of diversion whenever the natural flow of the stream entering the Reservoir above the point of diversion is two cubic feet per second or more; and at least one-half of the natural flow into the reservoir shall be bypassed whenever that natural inflow to the Reservoir is less than two cubic feet per second. Releases of water from Licensee's storage will not be required to comply with the foregoing provision.

No devices were available within the Reservoir structure for implementation of the bypass requirement when the Reservoir was less than full. The requirement was met through effluent discharge from the WWTP until 1977, when the conditions of the license were brought to the attention of the California Department of Justice for clarification.

Through mutual understanding among representatives of the California Department of Fish and Game (DFG), CNG, and CMC, a bypass device (syphon) was constructed over the spillway to meet minimum flow requirements when the Reservoir was low. This was implemented during the 1977-78 water year.[6]

The Reservoir is located in the headwaters of Chorro Creek, 4.2 km. (2.6 mi.) upstream from where the creek crosses Highway 1 (fig. 1). Its surface area is approximately 2.8 ha. (7 ac.) with design storage of 150 acre-feet (AF). In 1980 it was estimated that, due to siltation, storage had been reduced to 65 AF. The Operating Engineers Training Trust (Local 12), under license from the CNG, is presently dredging the Reservoir to restore it to its original capacity; the license allows for the training of engineers.[3]

When the US Army preempted its right upon Camp San Luis in 1941, the Salinas Reservoir (approximately 20.9 km. [13 mi.] east) was constructed as the water source. Spent water, upon secondary treatment, was discharged into Chorro Creek (Frank 1963). Information related to the quantity of intake and discharge between 1941 and 1961 was not available. However, during the summer of 1961 the camp drew 500,000 gal. per day (gpd) from Salinas Reservoir to supplement the 300,000 gpd withdrawal from Chorro Reservoir (ibid.). Upon completion and operation of Whale Rock Reservoir in 1962, no water was used from the Salinas watershed.

The secondary WWTP was built on Chorro Creek, 12.9 km. (8 mi.) from Morro Bay, by the US Army at about the same time that the Reservoir was constructed. It was built to serve military purposes and designed to accommodate 1-2 million gallons per day (mgpd) sewage. The effluent discharged directly into Chorro Creek prior to 1 July 1979 was required to meet the following restrictions: 1) average maximum concentration for five-day biochemical oxygen demand (BOD) of 15 mg. per l.; 2) suspended solids of 25 mg. per l.; and 3) total coliform bacteria of 23 MPN per 100 ml.

Chorro Reservoir, the water treatment plant, the storage reservoir, and the sewage plant were leased to the Military Department of California on 1 July 1963; they are currently being operated by CMC under the lease (ibid.). After 20 years of operation through agreement with the former Department of Health, Education and Welfare (HEW), the structures revert to CMC.[7]

By 1969 the Central Coast Region Water Quality Control Board (CCRWQCB) pollution abatement program was being implemented. It was apparent that future effluent discharged at its present quality into Chorro Creek would be unacceptable.[8] As a result, CMC was looking for sources to utilize its effluent. California Polytechnic State University (Cal Poly), recognized the potential for irrigation through a feasibility study conducted in 1970, and, spurred on by the CCRWQBC effluent-recycling scheme, entered into a five-year (January 1972 to December 1976) interagency agreement (ID NO 69) with CMC to utilize the effluent. The nature of usage was not

[6]Younger, E.J. 1977. Correspondence. California Department of Justice, Sacramento.

[7]Salvato, C. 1981. Personal communication. Business Manager, California Men's Colony, San Luis Obispo, Calif.

[8]Gibson, J.C. 1969. Correspondence. California Polytechnic College, San Luis Obispo, Calif.

specified. In August, 1972, Cal Poly constructed a 50-AF storage reservoir to irrigate field crops (sugar beets, silage, corn, and hay). The water was not utilized during that very dry season because downstream landowners were dependent upon the effluent for irrigation. In subsequent years the water was utilized for instructional purposes, through the Agriculture Enterprise Management Program (AEMP) in which students do all of the operations from seedbed preparation to harvesting and marketing. About two-thirds of the field crops are grown on Cal Poly's Chorro Creek Ranch under this program.

The effluent usage arrangement worked so well that it was renewed in toto (ID No. SA69) in January 1977 for another five years, terminating 31 December 1981. In September 1979, a second reservoir (36 AF) was being filled. The philosophy of Cal Poly was to store more water at a time when the creek was high and allow more to go downstream during the dry season. About 100-200 AF of water is stored annually. This irrigates approximately 99 ha. (244 ac.) of land. Effluent is pumped year-round with highest usage occurring between April and September. Approximately 488 AF are used on the Chorro Creek Ranch. Of that amount, 293 AF (60%) comes from effluent; the remainder comes from two shallow wells on the ranch. Since irrigation was brought into the AEMP on Chorro Creek Ranch, 8,596 students spent 215,775 class hours in agricultural instruction.

Chorro Reservoir

Inflow into the Reservoir averages 180 AF per month, most of which (64%) occurs from January through April; 29% occurs during the dry period. The yield for the dry season, based on license restrictions for the average year, is approximately 332 AF. From January 1955 to April 1981, waterflow has been recorded every month. Statistics for the study period are presented by month in table 2.

Of the total flow into the Reservoir, approximately 72% flows over the spillway. Of the amount that spills, 77% occurs from January through April, with 17% occurring between May and November. During the dry period there is no flow over the spillway approximately 44% of the time. In addition, 76% of the no-flow months occur during the dry period (table 2).

Evaporation during the study period totaled approximately 1,097 AF; 72% occurred during the dry period (table 2).

Imported water from Whale Rock Reservoir accounted for 6,762 AF. It was imported 53% of the time. Of the total imported, 83% was brought in during the dry season. The initial safe annual yield for Whale Rock was calculated to be 8,900 AF. Through mutual agreement (1 November 1957), it was proportionally owned for distribu-

Table 2.--Statistics of Chorro Reservoir and imported water from Whale Rock Reservoir (January 1962-1980). Baseline data obtained from CMC.

	Jan	Feb	Mar	Apr	May	June	July	Aug	Sept	Oct	Nov	Dec	Σ
Chorro Reservoir													
Inflow ac ft Σ	6929.3	9026.7	6075.3	4487.5	2989.2	2111.1	1669.8	1371.6	1144.8	1104.0	1602.3	2675.2	41086.8
ȳ ac ft/mo	359.4	475.1	319.8	236.2	157.3	111.11	87.9	72.2	60.3	58.1	84.3	140.8	180.2
cfs	5.9	8.7	5.2	4.0	2.6	1.87	1.4	1.2	1.0	.94	1.4	2.3	3.0
Yield													
cfs					1.6	.9	.7	.6	.5	.47	.7		
ac ft/mo					98.2	53.5	43.0	36.8	29.7	28.8	41.6		
Over spillway													
ac ft Σ	5686.5	8306.5	5265.7	3525.0	1881.0	910.9	457.9	348.5	302.4	364.0	859.4	1681.0	29588.8
Flow	17	15	15	14	13	12	8	9	7	10	15	15	150
No flow	2	4	4	5	6	7	11	10	12	9	4	4	78
ȳ ac ft/mo	334.5	553.8	351.0	251.8	144.7	79.9	57.2	38.7	43.2	36.4	57.3	112.1	197.3
Evaporation													
Σ	50.4	50.5	69.8	92.3	112.4	127.8	142.8	137.0	112.0	92.1	59.6	49.9	1096.6
ȳ ac ft/mo	2.7	2.7	3.7	4.9	5.9	6.7	7.5	7.2	5.9	4.8	3.1	2.6	4.8
Whale Rock													
Σ	20.86	273.56	243.12	338.09	553.38	623.88	939.35	988.99	995.88	868.99	667.03	249.30	6762.43
No import	17	14	14	12	9	9	7	3	4	3	4	11	107
Import	2	5	5	7	10	10	12	16	15	16	15	8	121
ȳ_w	10.43	54.71	46.62	48.30	55.34	62.09	78.28	61.81	66.39	54.31	44.77	31.16	55.89
ȳ_s					29.12	32.83	49.43	52.05	52.41	45.73	35.01		

Legend

Σ	= total for period	ȳ	= ac ft/mo for periods of flow
ȳ	= mean for period	No import	= months with no foreign water
Yield	= requirement of license	Import	= months with foreign water
Flow	= month of flow	ȳ_w	= mean for imported water months
No flow	= months of no flow	ȳ_s	= mean for study period

tion on the following bases: City of San Luis Obispo 4,900 AF (55%); Cal Poly 3,000 AF (34%); and CMC 1,000 AF (11%). Figures presented in table 2 represent the water that is used in the Chorro watershed.[9]

At the 5 June 1974, annual meeting of the Whale Rock Commission, a presentation by California Department of Water Resources (DWR) regarding the Safe Annual Yield Study on the Whale Rock Reservoir led to the lowering of the annual yield. At present it is believed to be 2,300 AF per year.[10]

Waste Water Treatment Plant

Effluent discharge from the WWTP averaged close to 1 cubic foot per second (cfs) throughout the year for the study period. This figure is modified when the minimum and maximum flows are taken into account (table 3). Flow at or above 0.75 cfs generally occurs between the peak hours of 08:00-18:00 throughout the week, rising and falling continuously.[5] Accurate data for hourly flow have not been ascertained, nor are they readily available.

It appears that the effluent discharge has been decreasing through time. In a military report dated 1952, it was stated that low flow of 1 cfs had been reached.[3] Frank (1963) reported that "...the surplus effluent flows into Morro Bay." Surplus refers to water downstream from the sewage plant that has not been used for irrigation. In 1969 Cal Poly correspondence estimated discharge at 1.24 cfs.[11]

Robasciotti[5] states that in the last couple of years discharge has been around 0.77 cfs and has averaged up to 1.01 cfs. He believes that this low figure is due to leakage and that the average flow should be around 1.24 cfs.

Upgrading the Waste Water Treatment Plant

Upgrading of the WWTP was partially brought about by an order (No. 75-50) from CCRWQCB, which prohibited discharge of wastewater into Chorro Creek after 1 July 1977.[12] The quality of the effluent did not come up to the requirements of the 1974 Water Quality Act.[13] The Clean Water

Table 3.--Statistics of effluent discharge from the waste water treatment plant from July 1966 to June 1975. Figures in thousands of gallons unless specified. (Baseline data obtained from CMC Repairs and Utilities Operating Log.)

	Jan	Feb	Mar	Apr	May	June	July	Aug	Sept	Oct	Nov	Dec	
Sewage Plant													
Total flow Σ	208057	147209	177684	183030	162711	164025	143442	191950	176596	180226	176048	197649	2108627
Data	9	7	8	9	8	8	7	9	9	9	9	9	101
No Data	1	3	2	1	2	2	1	1	1	1	1	1	19
$\bar{y}_1$/mo	23117.4	21029.9	22210.5	20336.7	20338.9	20503.1	20491.7	21327.8	19621.8	20025.1	19560.9	21961.0	20877.5
$\bar{y}_2$/day	745.7	751.1	716.5	677.9	656.1	683.4	661.0	688.0	654.1	646.0	652.0	708.4	686.4
$\bar{y}_3$ ac ft/mo	70.9	64.5	68.2	62.4	62.4	62.9	62.9	65.5	60.2	61.5	60.0	67.4	64.1
cfs/day	1.2	1.2	1.1	1.0	1.0	1.1	1.0	1.1	1.0	1.0	1.0	1.1	1.1
Flow cfs													
Max	2.31	2.16	1.89	1.62	1.36	1.29	1.36	1.25	1.20	1.27	1.50	2.16	1.7
Min	.69	.69	.69	.75	.75	.75	.79	.80	.78	.76	.73	.78	.75
Avg	1.15	1.16	1.10	1.04	1.01	1.05	1.02	1.06	1.00	1.00	1.00	1.09	1.06

Legend

Total Flow Σ = Sum of total flow for study period
Data   = Months for which accurate data was available
No data   = Months for which accurate data was not available and deleted.
$\bar{y}_1$ = mean per month = Σ/data
$\bar{y}_2$ = mean per day
$\bar{y}_3$ = mean acre ft/mo

(Flow cfs calculated from max, min and average flow by month in study period.)

[9]Schneider, A. 1981. Communications, California Men's Colony, San Luis Obispo, Calif.
[10]Mayse, R. 1981. Communications. Whale Rock Reservoir, Cayucos, Calif.

[11]Johnson, C. 1969. Correspondence, Cal Poly, San Luis Obispo, Calif.
[12]Jones, K.R. 1976. Correspondence. Central Coast Regional Water Quality Control Board, San Luis Obispo, Calif.
[13]Dupius, R. 1981. Communications, State Water Resources Control Board, Sacramento, Calif.

Grant Program was an opportunity for CMC to up-grade its facility and effectively dispose of effluent within the watershed. Subsequently, procedures to qualify for the grant program were effected. The first two steps in the procedure had been implemented when a major stumbling block was encountered. DFG made known its concern regarding the steelhead trout fishery of Chorro Creek, and its dependence on effluent from the WWTP. Cessation of discharge, one of the alternatives, would allegedly severely alter a considerable portion of the trout's nursery habitat.[13] DFG indicated that at least 0.75 cfs must be maintained to support the fishery.

CCRWQCB staff responded, after review of the CMC draft project report, by considering to revise Order No. 75-50 to permit the discharge of highly treated wastewater to the creek. On 4 March 1977, representatives of DFG, SWRCB, CCRWQCB, and Toups Corporation (responsible for the preparation of an environmental impact report) met in Monterey to define minimum flow requirements necessary to maintain the aquatic habitat of Chorro Creek.[14] It followed that a resolution to the Clean Water Grant Contract regarding the discharge of 0.75 cfs was consumated through agreement of CMC and DFG (30 June 1978). This fulfilled Condition No. 3 of the Concept

Approval letter and authorized payment beyond 50% of the step 2 grant.[15]

Some of the effluent characteristics of the upgraded plant are: 1) average maximum concentration for five-day BOD of 10 mg. per l.; 2) suspended solids of 10 mg. per l.; 3) total coliform bacteria 2.2 MPN per 100 ml.; 4) total phosphorus 0.5 mg. per l.; 5) ammonia 4 mg. per l.; and 6) nondetectable chlorine residual.

Water Balance

Total water input into the Reservoir during the dry period averaged 95 AF per month for the study period. Effluent discharge averaged 62 AF per month. The average loss to the system was 33 AF per month. The minimum flow bypass requirement of 0.75 cfs necessitated an average monthly discharge of 45 AF per month. This assumes that the flow of 0.75 cfs can be maintained throughout the day, which is not the case. The discharge fluctuates above and below this figure. The potential yield to Cal Poly is 17 AF per month. Statistics for the mean for imported water months $(\bar{Y}_w)$ are presented in table 4.

Table 4.--Water balance for Chorro Reservoir and WWTP for dry period. Figures are in AF/month.

	May	June	July	Aug.	Sept.	Oct.	Nov.	Σ
Water Input								
Chorro Reservoir Yield ac ft/mo	98.2	53.2	43.0	36.8	29.7	28.8	41.6	331.3
Whale Rock								
$\bar{y}_w$	55.3	62.1	78.3	61.8	66.4	54.3	44.5	422.7
$\bar{y}_s$	29.1	32.8	49.4	52.1	52.4	45.7	35.0	296.5
Storage Water Intake	5.0	5.0	5.0	5.0	5.0	5.0	5.0	35.0
Total Water in System Using $\bar{y}_w$	158.5	120.3	126.3	103.6	101.1	88.1	91.1	789.0
Total Water in System Using $\bar{y}_s$	132.3	91.0	97.4	93.9	87.1	79.5	81.6	662.8
Effluent Output ($\bar{y}_3$)	62.4	62.9	62.9	65.5	60.2	61.5	60.0	435.4
Loss in System Using $\bar{y}_s$	69.9	28.1	34.5	28.4	26.9	18.0	21.6	227.4
0.75 cfs requirement	46.0	44.6	46.0	46.0	44.6	46.0	44.6	317.8
Yield for Cal Poly Using $\bar{y}_s$	16.4	18.3	16.9	19.5	15.6	15.5	15.4	117.6

Legend

Σ = total
$\bar{y}_w$ = mean for imported water month
$\bar{y}_s$ = mean for study period
$\bar{y}_3$ = mean ac ft/mo

[14]Aleshire, R. Correspondence. Central Coast Regional Water Quality Control Board, San Luis Obispo, Calif.

[15]Rothenbaum, D. 1978. Correspondence. State Water Resources Control Board, Sacramento, Calif.

DISCUSSION

Chorro Creek

It appears that throughout its history Chorro Creek has been an intermittent stream, and that the construction of the Reservoir and WWTP in 1941 created an artificial flow in the creek from water imported initially from Salinas Reservoir and later from Whale Rock. Statements such as:

> We recognize that during dry months, most, if not all of the surface water flowing in the lower portion of the creek is from the Men's Colony. (Toffoli)[16]

> Almost all of the water in Chorro Creek available to Hollister and other properties in the area consisted of treatment plant effluent. (Chesler)[17]

and:

> The California Men's Colony Waste Water Treatment Plant, therefore, constitutes the most significant portion of the Chorro Creek flow during the summer months. (De Falco)[18]

lend strong support to the premise that the fishery may not have been able to survive without the effluent discharge since 1941. It also seems quite feasible that the use of water by Cal Poly through the interagency agreement since 1972 has not destroyed the fishery.

Wastewater

There are some legal restrictions on the ownership of wastewater within the watershed.[13] Basically, if the owner maintains control, as with CMC, it can do as it pleases with the water. When the water is abandoned into the creek, it becomes the property of the people of the state. "Abandoned" is a sticky term, but basically refers to no further intention of use.

Riparial rights deal with the natural flow which exists in the creek. It does not apply to imported water (waste water in this case), water released from storage, or water pumped from underground.[17]

---

[16]Toffoli, E.V. 1977. Correspondence. California Department of Fish and Game, Region 3.

[17]Chesler, A.A. 1977. Correspondence. State Water Control Board, Division of Water Rights, Sacramento, Calif.

[18]De Falco, P. 1977. U.S. Environmental Protection Agency, San Francisco, Calif.

Reservoir Bypass

The bypass license requirement at the Reservoir for maintenance of fish and wildlife habitat commenced 1 October 1977. During that month 750,000 gpd were syphoned over the spillway; the release was lost to evaporation, transpiration and ground infiltration before "...the flow reached Highway 1..."[17] This point is approximately 2.4 km. (1.5 mi.) from the Reservoir.

Waste Water Treatment Plant Minimum Flow

The minimum flow requirement of 0.75 cfs during a dry year would require nearly all the effluent discharged from WWTP.[14]

Water Balance With Cal Poly

Approximately 50% of the water entering the Reservoir is imported (Whale Rock and storage); when the mean for the study period ($\bar{y}_s$) is used in the calculations; this figure increases to 58% when the $\bar{y}$ figure is used (table 4). Effluent output ($\bar{y}_3$) was used as the quantity that had potential for entering Chorro Creek or could be used by Cal Poly through the interagency agreement. The potential quantity available to Cal Poly during the dry season was reduced from 435.4 to 117.6 AF due to grant resolution of 0.75 cfs. In the past, Cal Poly utilized approximately 293 AF of the available effluent through interagency agreement. It appears that if the resolution is enforced, Cal Poly will lose its vested right to the quantity of effluent that it had used for instructional purposes at the Chorro Creek Ranch.

Water Management

A first step to be taken in managing the Chorro Creek watershed should be computation of a water budget. This would allow the manager to determine the relationship between water from precipitation and the outflow of water by streamflow, infiltration, and evapotranspiration. The water balance technique, as developed in the 1940s by C. Warren Thornthwaite, allows planners to utilize commonly available meteorological records to predict variables such as streamflow, groundwater recharge, or the effects of human activities on the ecology of the watershed.

Unfortunately, there are very few "commonly available, meteorological records" and other sources of information necessary for an adequate assessment of the Chorro Creek hydrologic system. No official meteorologic information has been collected in the watershed, although local residents have maintained records on precipitation, wind direction, and associated data on an irregular basis. However, there are over 100 years of precipitation records for the city of San Luis Obispo, and limited meteorological information is available from Cal Poly, the city of Morro Bay, and the San Luis Obispo County Engineer's Office. These data were made available for a preliminary appraisal of the Chorro Creek hydrologic basin.

The precipitation data are important. They are the basis for ascertaining the amount of water available in the drainage basin in a given year. Since recording rain gauges have not been in place in the proximity of Chorro Creek for the past several decades, existing data were used to estimate the average annual precipitation. Both the Theissen-weighted average and isohyetal methods were employed to portray and quantify the spatial patterns of precipitation. The results obtained by the Theissen method were evaluated as most representative of the area. These results, however, are strongly biased by the 110-year records of the San Luis Obispo station; these data commonly are the basis for filling information gaps in the Chorro Creek basin.

Evapotranspiration is the largest debit item in the Chorro Creek hydrologic budget. The evapotranspiration statistics are based on Class A evaporation-pan data collected at the Cal Poly weather station. Coefficients relating water use by each vegetation cover-type to the evaporation-pan information were derived from data developed by the University of California, Davis. The evaporation-pan information also provides the basis for calculated evaporation losses.

Surface runoff is a significant portion of the outflow from the Chorro Creek watershed. The calculated runoff is based on minimal recorded information. Incomplete runoff information was obtained for Chorro Creek and San Bernardo Creek. A gauge recently was placed on Chorro Creek, just downstream from the Camp San Luis Obispo boundary (fig. 1). Significant portions of the record for the 1978-79 and 1979-80 water years are missing. Seven years of discharge records were obtained for San Bernardo Creek. Unfortunately, both the main stream flow and the tributary flow are regulated above the respective gauges. This is important since the gauge information cannot reflect natural stream runoff. Residents of the area report that, prior to the construction of impoundments and other regulating measures, after-the-rainy-season flow in the stream was usually absent. These reports may be verified by well data which appear to place the piezometric surface below the streambed. If this information can be verified, Chorro Creek can be shown to be an effluent stream and intermittent in its natural state.

The available streamflow data were plotted on a precipitation hydrograph to obtain runoff/precipitation relationships. This methodology was used to establish that runoff in an average precipitation year may be expected to range between 18.51 hectare meters (HaM) and 25.49 HaM. The midpoint of the range was selected for the drainage basin hydrologic budget.

Data supplied by DWR, the Whale Rock Commission, and the several municipal and industrial water users were utilized to provide the remaining information presented in table 5.

Table 5.--Average water balance for Chorro Creek hydrologic basin. (Caution is advised when using this table. The data presented are preliminary calculations as derived from often inadequate and incomplete quantitative information. Known hydrologic and metereologic conditions in nearby watersheds provided the basis for interpretive decisions.)

Credit Budget (Inflow)[1]	Hectare meters	Acre feet
Precipitation	62.14	50,376
Whale Rock Reservoir	4.43	3,591
Total	66.57	53,967
Debit Budget (Outflow)		
Evapotranspiration	35.09	28,448
Evaporation and interception	0.79	640
Surface Runoff	22.00	17,836
Consumptive uses[2]		
Agriculture	2.40	1,946
San Luis Obispo	2.50	2,027
Morro Bay	1.36	1,102
Cal Poly	1.23	997
CMC	0.52	422
Cuesta College	0.11	89
Other uses[3]	0.57	462
Total	66.57	53,969

[1]The inflow budget does not include water imported from Santa Margarita Lake since this water is ultimately delivered to the city of San Luis Obispo.
[2]Municipal and institutional consumptive use is based upon information made available by the respective users.
[3]This item includes losses due to groundwater runoff, bedrock infiltration, weathering, and minor out-of-basin appropriations.

Water Budget

As with any budget, the hydrologic income and expenditures should balance. However, the calculated inflow exceeds the outflow in the Chorro Creek budget by about 0.57 HaM. This is a relatively small amount of water in this drainage basin. No attempt was made to "adjust" the respective inflow and outflow items to a balance. The difference is simply allocated as "other uses" on the debit side. This amount of water could be easily absorbed by any of the larger inflows or outflows, or it may be retained in the groundwater.

The questions of groundwater storage and yields were not included in this budget, simply because adequate data do not exist which may be used for rational evaluations. Data which will allow construction of analytical models will promote a better understanding of the groundwater basin, the surface water system, and the relationship between the two. It is impossible to provide competent estimates of the available surface water or groundwater yield without this data.

SUMMARY

The Chorro Creek watershed is a water-deficient area. There is a greater potential demand than natural supply. Conflicts exist among competitive users for imported water--the appropriation of which has not been established. Effective resource management requires sound baseline data to evaluate the resource potential and use. It also necessitates a comprehensive understanding of the integrated needs of the competitive users. At this time there appears to be no movement toward a comprehensive watershed management plan, nor interagency or cooperative agreement for implementation of a management scheme. Mechanisms exist to resolve some of the conflicts among agency users and subsequently allow more flow downstream during the dry season. One approach, through cooperative agreement, is to allow more storage during the rainy season. There is ample public land available for the construction of a storage reservoir. The water could be used for low-flow augmentation of the stream and irrigation. Another approach would be to maintain effluent holding tanks. They could serve as a reservoir to equalize streamflow and for irrigation water.

A third approach would involve interagency and cooperative agreement from local and state governments to utilize effluents from outside the watershed (e.g., Morro Bay, San Luis Obispo) in the development of an aquaculture program. The National Aquaculture Act of 1980 (PL 96-362) could be used as the vehicle for construction of stabilization ponds to be used not only to purify water but to harvest biomass. The water, once polished, could serve for low-flow augmentation, irrigation, and groundwater recharge.

ACKNOWLEDGMENTS

This case study has involved contact with many and diverse agencies, both public and private. As such, scores of individuals supplied much-needed information, some willingly, others not so willingly. We are grateful for all the help we received and apologize for the discomfort we may have, in particular cases, induced. We deeply appreciate all the support and help provided by the SWRCB, the Division of Water Rights, the Division of Water Quality, CMC, the State Clearing House, DFG, Cal Poly, the city of Morro Bay, the city of San Luis Obispo, and all others that we may inadvertently have not mentioned.

LITERATURE CITED

Carollo, J., Engineers. 1977. Draft EIR for Morro Bay-Cayucos Wastewater Facilities. Walnut Creek, Calif.

Central Coast Regional Water Quality Control Board. 1980. Order No. 80-42, NPDES No. CA0047856 adopted 24 November 1980, for California Department of Corrections, California Men's Colony, San Luis Obispo County. 7 p. Central Coast Regional Water Quality Control Board, San Luis Obispo, Calif.

Chappell, P.P., J.L. Lidberg, and M.L. Johnson. 1976. Report to the State Water Resource Control Board summarizing the position of the Department of Fish and Game on Water Application 24120. California Department of Fish and Game Region 3. 39 p.

Frank, A.F.W. 1963. Statement of mission. US Army Garrison, Camp San Luis Obispo, Calif. T/D 6A-6015.

A STATE MANDATE FOR RIPARIAN WETLAND

SYSTEM PRESERVATION[1]

Bruce E. Jones[2]

Abstract.--Management of aquatic and riparian wetlands and floodplain resources generally, is fragmented, uneven, and often contradictory. State programs are reviewed and a sample local ordinance is presented. A California Floodplain Management Act is proposed.

INTRODUCTION

The panel on politics, legislation, and management programs is the most important topic of the California Riparian Systems Conference. Ecology, of course, makes the world go around, but it is politics--and its spawn, legislation--that either saves it or loses it. I will briefly review the highlights of a two-year research project prepared for three state agencies and a book in preparation[3] which includes a critique of federal, state, and local government programs and laws affecting riparian and other wetland resources. Then, based on the insight gained by this study, I will propose state legislation I believe is necessary to create a workable management program in California.

At the federal level, substantial attention has been given to wetlands through the Section 10/404 permit program of the US Army Corps of Engineers (CE) and Presidential Executive Orders 11988 and 11990 of 1977 (floodplain and wetland protection). California has some useful legislative and administrative policies for the more aquatic wetlands, but, except for the Coastal Act,[4] there are no implementable regulations for either aquatic or riparian wetlands and stream systems. At the local government level, it is fairly common to find general plan policies addressing wetlands and even riparian vegetation, usually in brief references, and, interestingly, there are more ordinances for streamside management than for aquatic wetlands. But again, coverage is uneven.

The overall picture is one of a jigsaw puzzle with a few pieces in place but with large gaps throughout.

OVERVIEW OF CALIFORNIA AGENCIES

California does not have anything approaching a watershed resources management program; we do not have comprehensive standards for uses affecting wetlands, riparian zones, hardwood trees (oaks and riparian trees), soil erosion, and floodplain zoning. The Coastal Act provides the only thorough treatment of wetlands/stream/riparian vegetation protection, but the "coastal zone" itself severs many watersheds, which limits thorough treatment. The California Wetlands Preservation Act of 1976[5] provides some state policies, but offers no implementation procedures and penalties. A state executive order on floodplain management (1977) is poorly written and does not mention wetlands or riparian resources. Very briefly, some findings regarding the key agencies (out of over 30 reviewed) are as follows.

Bay Conservation and Development Commission

The Bay Conservation and Development Commission (BCDC), the first coastal management agency in the nation, has been effective in regulating fill intrusions into San Francisco Bay and securing mitigation, often involving restoration of tidal action to diked areas. However, there are important bay wetlands and riparian systems outside of the agency's jurisdiction.

California Coastal Commission

The best wetland and stream policies in any federal or state law are found in the Coastal Act of 1976, especially PRC Section 30231 as follows:

---

[1] Paper presented at the California Riparian Systems Conference. [University of California, Davis, September 17-19, 1981].
[2] Bruce E. Jones is Environmental Consultant, Environmental Projects, Sacramento, Calif.
[3] Jones, Bruce E., and Anne Sands. California marsh and stream conservation zones.
[4] Public Resource Code (PRC) Section 30000-30900.

[5] PRC Section 5810-5818.

The biological productivity and the quality of coastal waters, streams, wetlands, estuaries, and lakes...shall be maintained and where feasible, enhanced through, among other means, minimizing adverse effects of waste water discharges and entrainment, controlling runoff, preventing depletion of ground water supplies and substantial interference with surface waterflow, encouraging waste water reclamation, maintaining natural vegetation buffer areas that protect riparian habitats, and minimizing alteration of natural streams.

Of particular interest is the Commission's document "Interpretive Guidelines for Wetlands and Other Wet Environmentally Sensitive Habitat Areas" (California Coastal Commission 1981). While this is a very useful tool which has improved management of these resources, it is lacking in the important issue of controlling adjacent developments and setting "buffer" zones. Too much emphasis has been put on establishing a 100-ft. nondevelopable buffer, and too little guidance is given on the design and siting of adjacent construction to minimize adverse impacts. The width of a buffer is not the key consideration. Buffers not only will often be compromised for political and economic reasons, but should be, if the design of the use makes it compatible with the adjacent wetland or stream zone. Having missed this key point, the commission's guidelines leave coastal wetlands and streams vulnerable to problems from future encroachments.

California Conservation Corps

A great untapped opportunity exists for applying the skill and energy of the California Conservation Corps (CCC) to an annually scheduled program of wetland and riparian zone restoration.

California Energy Commission

Interestingly, the California Energy Commission (CEC) has some of the best state policies regarding sensitive resource areas. Its organic law and regulations recognize the constraints of the Coastal Commission and BCDC. For the rest of the state, the key provision is PRC Section 25527, which provides protections (against the siting of energy facilities) for parks, reserves, "areas for wildlife protection, recreation, historic preservation, or natural preservation," and undeveloped estuaries. In addition, the commission "shall give the greatest consideration to the need for protecting areas of critical environmental concern."

California Department of Conservation

This agency could be one of the most useful in communicating the values of aquatic and riparian wetlands, but has not yet met this potential. In its useful (but never officially released) "California Soils: An Assessment" (California Department of Conservation 1979), the department

ranks streambed erosion as the third most severe of eleven soil problems in the state, but fails to advocate retention of riparian vegetation as a protective measure. Nor does the otherwise excellent "Erosion and Sediment Control Handbook" (Animoto 1978) offer anything more than: "Vegetative lining reduces the erosion along the channels and provides for the filtration of sediment ...and improves wildlife habitat."

California Department of Fish and Game

The work of the California Department of Fish and Game (DFG) is, of course, oriented toward saving both aquatic and riparian wetlands, but it has precious few tools to do so. Studies in both areas are on-going. Of special note is the DFG authority in Sections 1601-1606 of the California Fish and Game Code to execute Streambed Alteration Agreements for any activity that will divert, obstruct, or change the natural flow or bed of a river, stream, or lake. This is a nearly unique negotiation and mediation process in the nation, but its application to riparian vegetation is limited to what DFG personnel can achieve through negotiation in specific situations.

The DFG has not initiated a vigorous program to solicit land donations of riparian corridors. Nor has it sought to develop a program of restoration of riparian vegetation on public lands. These are two of the most basic elements of any start-up state riparian resources program.

California Department of Forestry

The California Department of Forestry (DF) timber harvesting program is almost exclusively oriented towards conifers. It has reported that only one percent of commercial harvesting is of broad-leafed or hardwood species. However, this figure is misleading because the true amount of cutting of these species cannot be determined since it is not regulated. They are in fact being overharvested and any percentage is immaterial; regulation is needed, either by adoption of administrative rules under the Forest Practices Act of 1973[6] or amendments to it. The DF position is that the act, as it is now written, cannot be used to regulate riparian species. Therefore, amendments to the act should be sought by DF.

California Department of Health

Regulations by this department illustrate the competing interests that must be considered in riparian vegetation management. Thickets of streamside growth, especially blackberry tangles, in urban areas can harbor rats. The department is especially concerned with wetlands restoration and has several sets of guidelines for minimizing mosquitoes.

---

[6] PRC Section 4511-4628.

827

California Department of Parks and Recreation

The California Department of Parks and Recreation (DPR) should develop policies that will classify its wetlands and riparian corridors as "natural preserves" (except those wetlands used for duck hunting), which would prevent intrusions of parking lots, campgrounds, and other intensive uses.

California Department of Water Resources

The California Department of Water Resources (DWR) has in recent years increased its documentation and policy support for preservation of riparian vegetation and instream retention of water (see "Policies and Goals for California Water Management for the Next 20 Years" [California Department of Water Resources 1982]). These policies do not always reach down to the day-to-day operations of DWR. Specifically, the management of DWR's own Maintenance Areas, which include some 300 mi. of waterways, should be redefined to require more sophisticated, selective treatments, including integrated pest management techniques, where possible.

DWR is further constrained by restrictive standards required by CE for so-called "project levees" (where federal funds have been used). There is wide opinion, even within DWR, that these levees can safely retain more vegetation than CE policy currently allows.

Office of Planning and Research

The Office of Planning and Research (OPR) has failed to recognize the existence of wetlands and riparian resources within city limits in its "Urban Strategy Report" (Office of Planning and Research 1978), a situation especially unfortunate since the report is backed up by an executive order to state agencies to implement it. Even more worrisome is the superficial treatment of wildlife habitat preservation in general in the OPR "General Plan Guidelines" (Office of Planning and Research 1980). Detailed appendices for this document should be prepared with DFG to assist local planners in the technicalities of preserving habitat.

The Resources Agency

In September 1977 then-Secretary Huey Johnson released a most useful internal policy on wetlands preservation (amended in July 1980), but no effort has been made to strengthen it through incorporation into an executive order or legislation. Nor has there been equal attention to development of a riparian policy for the agency. The document for the excellent renewable resources program of the agency acknowledges the 91% loss of wetlands statewide but does not specifically mention riparian vegetation. However, it is reported that some of the Energy Resource Funds (ERF) being used to fund the program will go towards stream restoration. It would also be useful for the agency to produce a comprehensive biomass production policy that unifies the work and regulations of the DF, CEC, and DFG, specifically addressing the use and re-establishment of fast-growing riparian trees as a fuel source in selected areas.

State Coastal Conservancy

This agency's Coastal Restoration and Enhancement Projects include several wetlands, but have not included work on streams or riparian zones. Guidelines for Coastal Conservancy projects lack a watershed emphasis that would lead to streamside vegetation restoration for wildlife habitat and erosion control. Further, the agency should not invest public money in wetland restoration until the local jurisdiction offers guarantees that it will establish adequate erosion controls (including establishment of statutorily protected riparian zones) in its watersheds, in an attempt to minimize the sedimentation that could erase the public investment in a restoration project in one wet winter.

State Lands Commission

The State Lands Commission, with its Division, is the guardian of the Public Trust Doctrine, a complex legal concept originating in English common law that protects the public interests in tidal areas. This doctrine is receiving increasing attention by such agencies as the USDI Fish and Wildlife Service (FWS) as a policy justification for the reservation of instream water rights to protect fisheries, riparian vegetation, and many aquatic wetlands.

The Reclamation Board

The Reclamation Board (RB), which is part of DWR, was created as a result of Gold Rush hydraulic mining, which carried massive sediment into Central Valley rivers, changing flood patterns and reducing navigation. Its primary function is to control encroachments on project levees and those within its defined "designated floodways." On 18 February 1981, the RB adopted an important riparian vegetation policy for designated "areas of critical concern" (but which excludes routine maintenance of levees).

State Water Resources Control Board

The State Water Resources Control Board (SWRCB) is involved in many areas of present interest, but two are especially worthy of comment. The "208" area-wide "nonpoint pollutant" control planning process (from Section 208 of the Clean Water Act[7]) has given some attention to the vital importance of vegetated streambanks for erosion control and filtration of sediment-carrying runoff, plus the value of wetlands for sediment and pollution filtration. But the program's emphasis on these natural, cost-effective tools has not been sufficient to secure a state-

---

[7] P.L. 92-500.

wide trend toward their use as "best management practices."

Much more promising is the new program of the SWRCB for retaining instream water flow as part of its water rights program. The regulations are now in place and can be vitally important in protecting the overall health of our streams and many wetlands.

The University System

The revitalization of the Wildlands Resources Center should be expedited to provide a much-needed clearinghouse and "one-stop data retrieval service" for the many university research and reporting services that involve natural resources. The Sea Grant program should be integrated with this center, and a more focussed series of periodic reports should be released to the audience specifically interested in each resources topic.

Wildlife Conservation Board

The Wildlife Conservation Board (WCB) has an active wetland and riparian forest acquisition program.

OVERVIEW OF CALIFORNIA LOCAL GOVERNMENT PROGRAMS

While general plan policies are useful and important as educational tools, it is the ordinances of each local government that must be reviewed to determine the effectiveness of any resource management commitment. Not only are there the occasional watercourse ordinances in some jurisdictions, such as Napa County, but most have grading and drainage ordinances that will usually affect vegetative resources. Even weed control ordinances can have an adverse impact on stream systems (there have been occasions when riparian vegetation has been called "water-sucking weeds"!). Subdivision ordinances may also include provisions for stream setbacks or other resource area protections. In Sacramento County there is a "Special Planning Area" ordinance[8] that can allow specialized attention to specific sites, including natural resource areas.

Perhaps the most underused type of ordinance, one that can produce many benefits, is that for floodplain management (nonstructural land-use measures). Such ordinances should require the scientific determination of the high-velocity floodway, which would be a nondevelopment and nonfill zone; the 100-year flood-risk area wherein development must be "floodproofed" to resist damage during the once-in-a-hundred-years flood; wetlands preservation requirements (for both environmental and fiscal reasons); and can include the riparian preservation corridor provisions often found in separate ordinances (it should be noted

that in this corridor, even farming must be excluded, while in the flood-risk area farming should be encouraged as a desirable, low-risk use).

Example of a Local Watercourse Ordinance

Several counties have watercourse or stream conservation ordinances, but one of the best known and earliest is that of Napa County. Its Ordinance 447[9] addresses:

> ...protecting the riparian cover within specified distances thereof, providing bonding requirements in connection [with] such permit, providing a fee schedule...and abatement as a nuisance such work performed without a permit.

Policy statements in the ordinance acknowledge the interrelationships of flood-hazard areas, public safety, public expenditures for flood protection and emergency relief, riparian vegetation as a "valuable natural resource," and preservation of rural qualities. The preservation of "riparian cover" is specifically declared, to: "preserve fish and wildlife habitats;" "prevent erosion of stream banks;" "maintain cool water temperatures;" and "obtain the wise use, conservation and protection of certain of the County's woodland and wildlife resources according to their natural capabilities."

The ordinance relies on a map on file in the County Office of Engineer to show which watercourses are included, and it states: "There shall be included in the watercourse an area extending laterally outward fifty feet beyond the top of the banks on each side of such channel, except that" a portion of the Napa River shall have a 100-ft. zone. Incorporated cities are excluded from coverage.

A permit is required for the following activities within a watercourse: deposition or removal of material; excavation; construction or alteration of structures; planting or removal of any vegetation; and alteration of embankments. Exceptions to the permit process are given to any public agency; for work in a public right-of-way pursuant to other permits; and for emergency work (which requires a follow-up permit to correct any "impairments"). No application for a permit shall be approved when the Planning Commission finds the proposed work will either substantially impair the water conveyance capacity of the water course or destroy a significant amount of riparian cover."

A final inspection by the County Engineer is required. Any aggrieved person may appeal to the Board of Supervisors. An abatement procedure for violations is established but there is no provision for restoration of vegetation removed in violation of the ordinance.

---

[8] Sacramento County Code, enacted 1978.

[9] Napa County Code, enacted 1973.

Problems in this ordinance include the above-mentioned lack of restoration responsibility, but more important is the absence of a specific directive to public agencies, which are exempted from the permit process, to follow the intent of the law. The undefined reference to removal of a "significant amount" of cover leaves much room for incremental destruction of the resource outside of the permit process. One Napa County resident expressed the opinion that the control of riparian vegetation clearing for farming purposes has not been vigorous.

PROPOSALS FOR STATE LEGISLATION

Comprehensive state legislation is needed to create a consistent, enforceable, effective program for protection of riparian/wetland/ floodplain/watershed resources. I propose the introduction of two acts--one like the Oregon bill, SB 397 of 1981--a voluntary approach of preservation and reduced taxation--and another which establishes a regulatory system for the management of multiple related resources. A "California Floodplain Management Act" would provide a unified approach to management of these resources, at the same time providing: long-needed protections of public safety; reduction of public investments in flood control facilities and emergency bailouts for persons who unwisely locate in flood-risk areas; and equity and certainty of treatment (that is, ensuring that the law is applied evenly and fairly to all persons in similar circumstances). In addition, the comprehensive approach to interrelated problems can have a better chance of political success than a focussed, narrower bill which addresses ecological concerns alone.

Some guidelines which should be followed in preparing the act are listed below.

1. No new state agency would be created (although the expansion of the RB in a modified role throughout the state would be helpful).
2. No new state permits would be required-- and some could be eliminated.
3. Local governments' land-use planning and regulation processes would be the cornerstone of the system, consistent with state policy in the act, with certification of plans and ordinances by the Resources Agency.
4. The primary vehicle would be a Local Floodplain Program (LFP) prepared by each local government in California, similar to the Local Coastal Programs of the Coastal Act, the Local Protection Program of the Suisun Marsh Preservation Act,[10] and the Local Delta Programs of the proposed Delta legislation now being reviewed by the Resources Agency.
5. The State's role would be to fund the LFPs and to certify the end products as consistent with the state law, and to monitor their

implementation and seek judicial recourse where necesssary.
6. Public access to regulated zones would not be appropriate since these would be private lands and the ecology of these areas is sensitive.

Specifically, each LFP would be a combination of amendments to open space/conservation and public safety elements of general plans, land-use maps, and several ordinances. Local governments would be mandated to include the following in their LFPs:

1. Designated floodways for each stream, consistent with federal and state maps (with final arbitration by the RB or DWR);
2. Flood-risk areas covering the 100-year floodplain, with development controls meeting federal and state requirements;
3. Wetland and stream preservation zones, both "primary" and "secondary," as described below.

Setting the Preservation Zone

The definition and mapping of preservation zones for wetlands and riparian corridors is the key issue in the ecological application of the LFP. As suggested by the Coastal Commission review process, it is not as simple as just setting a 100-ft. buffer around a resource area. Multiple considerations should be addressed, including the following:

1. the use of physical features (man-made or natural) to clearly define on the ground the regulatory boundary (especially when the feature can also separate competing uses);
2. controls on the design and siting of uses adjacent to the sensitive resource area (that is, requiring placement of the most neutral activity facing the resource; controlling light and noise from permissible uses; constraining human and pet access with barriers; using landscaping that enhances wildlife values; requiring erosion controls; etc.). In essence, the better the design controls on adjacent uses, the less open buffer is needed;
3. the ecotone or edge considered part of the resource area itself; and
4. the right of the landowner to challenge a boundary by presenting physical evidence (such as soils data) showing the regulatory area to be excessive (as is done in the Connecticut Inland Wetlands Program).

Regarding the last point, for purposes of illustration, consider the result of variably-sized square parcels of land that are edged by a stream. With a 100-ft. non-alteration zone, a one-acre lot is 48% regulated; a 5-acre lot, 21%; a 10-acre lot, 15%; 50 acres, 7%; and 100 acres, 5%. There is no magic percentage at which a "taking" without compensation to the landowner is not a concern, but this kind of evaluation will help planners determine if a narrower zone should be used in specific cases. For a residential or

[10]PRC Section 29000-29612.

commercial lot, the permissible density of any development can be shifted into the area outside the zone, but this is not possible for agricultural lands. Fortunately, most farmlands are large lots, and a 100-ft. band would result in a lower percentage of "taking."

Finally, the different needs for stream and wetland boundaries must be noted; this raises the difference between primary and secondary regulatory zones.

Primary and Secondary Regulatory Zones

In essence, a "Primary Regulatory Zone" involves the actual resource itself--the marsh or the riparian vegetation (and the ecotone) as they are defined by technical or scientific criteria. This is not always easily accomplished and is even more difficult with a riparian zone, where the vegetation has been stripped and the goal is to restore the growth in presently denuded areas.

The "Secondary Regulatory Zone" is, in essence, the "buffer," a term that is often misused. Its purpose is to reduce the adverse impacts of adjacent uses on the resource (within its Primary Regulatory Zone). Therefore, the earlier review of controlling adjacent uses becomes relevant for setting this secondary zone, and again it is to require quality design controls that should be the purpose of setting a buffer.

But there is another complication. For marshes, a further regulatory zone should, ideally, include the entire watershed feeding the wetland, wherein land-use controls would be required to reduce accelerated (human-caused) erosion and sedimentation. Such a third level of regulation could be referred to as the "Watershed Regulatory Zone" for consistency of terminology.

Another point regarding wetlands is that no matter what the size, the "taking" issue should not occur. The public interest in protecting these areas has long been known, as has the poor suitability of wetlands for development. The taking issue in the regulation of wetlands will most frequently arise over the secondary or buffer zone when an agency is attempting to establish a broad non-use area in addition to the marsh itself.

Preferential Assessment

To reduce the concern over the taking issue, it is important that a future act ensure that preferential assessments can be applied to regulatory zones. Such reduction or even exemption from taxation should be left to the discretion of the local government policy board, which can evaluate the request in light of its impact on the jurisdiction's fiscal situation. However, no preferential treatment could occur until the landowner executes a conservation easement in perpetuity. Violation of the terms of the easement should result in at least a penalty of five times the taxes that would have been paid, as is established in the Oregon statute.

The Paradox of Protection Leading to Destruction

Any bill which declares riparian vegetation to be sacred as of the date of its passage will almost ensure the destruction of most of what is left, especially when it occurs on or along farmlands, as landowners rush to remove the cause of more regulation before the law becomes effective. There is no simple means to avoid this, but there must be in the act the use of a date precedent to the bill from which the actual riparian corridor will be measured (prior to the later adjustments, as reviewed above). For instance, in the coastal zone boundaries of all riparian corridors could be drawn to include the vegetation in existence as of 1972, when the voters approved Proposition 20, the Coastal Initiative which included stream protection policies. From that date, it was the State's policy to protect riparian vegetation in this area, and landowners were put on notice. Any cutting of vegetation thereafter would not reduce the width of the regulatory zone. Finding such precedent dates for most of the rest of the state is not as easy, and the provision may have to be hinged upon the general plans of local governments which have riparian policies or other devices (possibly even AB 3147 [Fazio] which mandated the DFG Central Valley and California Desert riparian survey).

The Zones, In Summary

Finally, the major point is that these zones must be variable and subject to change. The primary riparian zone must include: the existing riparian growth; that area which had growth as of a date precedent and shall be set aside for regrowth; the ecotone or edge area; or a 100-ft. band as an interim standard, until the local government can examine each landowner's appeal on the basis of the taking issue, hardship, existing physical intrusions into the zone, and so forth. In the law, the primary wetland zone should be defined by scientific criteria addressing the types of vegetation, type of soil, and the known flow of water. (One clear definition of wetlands must be finally established in California to avoid continuing politically inspired debates!)

The secondary riparian zone should be an area defined by the physical features of the terrain and adjacent uses in which design standards will be required. This would also be the case for the secondary wetland zone. The law can call for the zone to be based on such features, or a 100-ft. band, whichever is greater, as long as it is abundantly clear that this space is not necessarily to remain undeveloped. However, development will only be permitted if the performance requirements can be met.

Finally, for wetlands only a third zone would be required, to permit management of the watershed to reduce erosion and sedimentation.

In fact, California also needs a comprehensive approach to its watersheds and soils. But that is another conference.

Provisions in the Proposed Act for State Agencies

Certain missions of the various state agencies must also be clarified in the new act, including the following.

1. The DWR and the RB process for certifying the LFPs and designated floodplains must be described.

2. All state and local agencies (including special districts) must be directed to conform their plans and programs to the policies of the act and the certified LFPs.

3. The DFG would be directed to plan and implement a statewide site-specific plan for restoration of wetlands and riparian vegetation on state-owned lands.

CONCLUSIONS

The technical and political obstacles in both preparing and enacting such a bill as the "California Floodlain Management Act" are indeed huge. But progress has never been made by experts and advocates prematurely surrendering in the face of anticipated political reactions. We must put forth the most workable and streamlined proposal we can design and then go to work on the politics. Several years may be required, but even the Legislature has a way of coming around on major problems that will not go away, no matter how controversial the solutions.

We must secure legislation such as this. If we do not, then I suggest that we will have to take a lesson from the Friends of the River and chain ourselves to the last willows and the last cottonwoods before they are cut, chipped, or burned.

For it will come to that.

LITERATURE CITED

Animoto, P.Y. 1978. Erosion and sediment control handbook. 197 p. California Department of Conservation, Sacramento.

California Coastal Commission. 1981. Interpretive guidelines for wetlands and other wet environmentally sensitive habitat areas. 58 p. California Coastal Commission, San Francisco.

California Department of Conservation. 1979. California soils: An assessment (draft document). 197 p. plus appendices. California Department of Conservation, Sacramento.

California Department of Water Resources. 1982. Policies and goals for California water management for the next 20 years. Bulletin 4, California Department of Water Resources, Sacramento. 52 p.

Office of Planning and Research. 1978. Urban strategy report. 36 p. Office of Planning and Research, State of California, Sacramento.

Office of Planning and Research. 1980. General plan guidelines. 327 p. Office of Planning and Research, State of California, Sacramento.

PROTECTING URBAN STREAMS--A CASE STUDY[1]

Myra Erwin[2]

Abstract.--The process by which a local government policy regarding urban streams was changed is described. The change was from a policy of channelizing, gunniting, and chain-link fencing to one of minimum modification in the character of the streams and their floodplains.

INTRODUCTION

Since the 1940's the character of Sacramento County has been changing. Urban development in the watersheds and floodplains of rural streams intensified many of the problems caused by agriculture (clearing of riparian vegetation, irrigation runoff, etc.). When it became apparent that damage from flooding might become a hazard, and that the costs of repairing such damage could be substantial, the County commissioned a study of county-wide hydrology. The study was to address the drainage problems associated with urbanization and develop a drainage plan. The result was a Master Drainage Plan (Nolte 1961) which called for the channelization of many streams as a means of allowing the maximum development on land adjacent to the streams; that is, on the floodplains. They were, of course, subject to periodic flooding.

During the 1960's and 1970's many streams were channelized, piped or gunnited in order to facilitate urban development. Substantial riparian vegetation was removed; stream sections bordered with large and attractive oak trees were eliminated, straightened, rerouted, and replaced by concrete-lined ditches with 6-ft. high chain-link fences.

But then came the "ecology movement." People everywhere began to question why such things were happening. Wasn't there a way to remove the flood hazards without destroying the environment? Why should we have to destroy our streams, native vegetation, wildlife habitat, and recreation opportunities; and eliminate the air-cooling and -cleaning effects of the riparian vegetation? There must be a better way.

---

[1] Paper presented at the California Riparian Systems Conference. [University of California, Davis, September 17-19, 1981].

[2] Myra Erwin is a member of the California Regional Water Quality Control Board, Central Valley Region; and Chair, Sacramento County Natural Streams Task Force, Sacramento, Calif.

FINDING A BETTER WAY

The Beginning

It all started when the Sacramento County Department of Public Works proposed concrete lining and chain-link fencing of Chicken Ranch Slough. Certain sections of the slough had drainage problems which also concerned residents, but the Department's solution to the problems-- concrete lining--was an insensitive response to situations where better maintenance or spot solutions (minor channel widening, etc.) would have been appropriate. Property owners along the "slough", which is actually a creek, were incensed. Many of them had, over the years, spent much time and money caring for the native oaks and other vegetation along the stream. Many had beautifully landscaped gardens there. In their view, the proposal would devastate the stream and ruin their gardens. To protect Chicken Ranch Slough, the property owners there banded together and formed the Save Chicken Ranch Slough Association (SCRSA). Figures 1 and 2 illustrate the nature of the problem. Figure 1 is an example of the traditional channelization, gunnite, and chain-link fencing approach. Figure 2 shows the natural character of the streams in question, which residents wanted to protect.

Identifying the Problems

Before long the Environmental Council of Sacramento (ECOS), a coalition of local environmental and civic organizations, joined in and soon took a leading role in the effort to protect not only Chicken Ranch Slough but all the streams threatened by so-called "improvement." Property owners along these other streams had also become aroused. At a very well attended hearing, the Board of Supervisors directed the Department of Public Works to prepare a new plan for the streams. Many thousands of dollars and many months later, their plan, consisting mainly of sets of large-scale aerial photos and water profile maps, was finally presented to the Board and the public. Those in attendance milled around, trying to understand the maps and photos pinned to the walls all around the room. Few, if any, understood. So an accompanying text was

Figure 1.--The channelization, gunnite, chain-link approach on one of the County's streams. Aesthetic, ecological, and recreational values have been destroyed.

Figure 2.--A County stream with native riparian vegetation and floodplain pattern intact. Ecological, recreational, and aesthetic values have been retained.

THE NATURAL STREAMS TASK FORCE

Organization and Structure

The Task Force was indeed structured to involve citizens' groups as well as County staff (see table 1). Certain State and Federal agencies were also invited to attend, which they did initially. However, after giving some input they felt they were no longer needed and no longer attended the meetings.

The Task Force's Coordinator was from the County's Environmental Impact Section. He had a formidable task, faced with the necessity of getting a consensus from mutually suspicious Task Force members with diverse and often conflicting concerns.

demanded. The Board of Supervisors also recognized that recreation and planning considerations had not been included. Not only should existing drainage problems be corrected, but new ones should be prevented. The Board ordered that a comprehensive environmental impact report, to include these considerations, be prepared. The resulting Sacramento County Natural Stream Study (Environmental Impact Section, County of Sacramento 1974) became the explanatory document for the Master Drainage Plan.

However, now that they understood the Plan, and its recommendations for "improving" the streams, neither the SCRSA nor ECOS was satisfied. These organizations insisted that the channelizing and gunniting must stop. The streams must be left as natural as possible. At this point, the ECOS recommended to the Planning Commission that a broad-based task force, comprised of public members representing citizens' groups, and staff members from relevant departments and agencies, be appointed to develop new County policies which would protect the natural character of the 13 designated streams, provide for appropriate recreation, and at the same time prevent flood hazards. To prevent a foreclosure of options while the task force was developing new policies, a moratorium on development adjacent to the streams was recommended. The moratorium was to be effective until the task force's work was completed. The Planning Commission concurred and made these recommendations to the Board of Supervisors. With the Board's adoption of Resolutions 74-1173 and 74-1283, the moratorium went into effect and the Natural Streams Task Force was created.

Table 1.--Composition of the Natural Streams Task Force.

Citizen Groups	County Staff
ECOS	Department of Parks
SCRSA	and Recreation
Audubon Society	Planning Department
Sierra Club	Department of Public
Save the American	Works
River Association	Health Department
Bikeway Action Committee	County Counsel
Streamside residents	Park Districts
Interested citizens	

State and Federal Agencies
State Department of Fish and Game
State Water Resources Control Board
State Reclamation Board
US Army Corps of Engineers

After election of the Chair (the ECOS representative and the only woman), the orientation and education of the Task Force citizen-group members began. There was a great deal to learn about hydrology and existing zoning, grading, and drainage regulations. At the same time, the Task Force Coordinator was developing a work plan to guide the Task Force's efforts in its development of the Natural Streams Plan.

Assignment of Responsibilities

After the work plan was adopted, each citizen-group member was assigned one or more streams as his or her particular responsibility. To gain first-hand knowledge of the problems and opportunities, the members walked the length of "their" streams, often along improvised trails, which were there simply from neighborhood use, often struggling through underbrush and over wire fences. Also, staff members made field inspections of the streams and their environs, for recreation and open space opportunities, and for aquatic and riparian wildlife and vegetation, adding many hours of volunteer time. The Health Department's representative checked for water quality problems, and the Planning Department's member delineated existing zoning districts along the streams.

In due course, public meetings were held, one in the vicinity of each stream, conducted by the appropriate Task Force member. Those individuals who had earlier indicated their interest were kept informed of the Task Force's meetings, and were invited to attend the local meeting on the stream of their concern. In addition, notices were sent to all streamside property owners, and there was good attendance at the meetings. The consensus at all of these stream meetings was: LEAVE THE STREAMS AS THEY ARE!

Administration Problems

As the Task Force proceeded, it became evident to the citizen-group members that responsibility for the administration of uses within the streams' floodplains was fragmented among the participating County departments and that communication and cooperation among the departments had been ineffective or non-existent in the past. It was also noted that some specific recommendations adopted by either of the planning commissions or the Board of Supervisors were not being adequately implemented by the responsible County officials. Further, there was a conspicuous lack of data on existing operations. But most important of all, there was a lack of county-wide comprehensive policy regarding land use within the floodplains. In fact, it was not unusual to find policies calling for the protection of floodplains, while adopted Department of Public Works proposals called for the channelization of those same streams.

A Basic Conflict

Task Force members wrangled interminably, it seemed. Citizen-group members wanted drastic changes in policy and procedures, while the Public Works members held fast to established practices, trying ineffectively to explain why they were necessary. The conflict stemmed primarily from the following diametrically opposed perceptions: the recognition, on the part of most of the citizen-group and some staff members, of the need to stop building in the floodplains; versus the persuasion, on the part of the Public Works member supported by the building industry member, that the only reasonable way to prevent flooding and allow reasonable use of private property was to continue the drainage "improvement" measures of the past.

Figures, formulae, and data supporting different points of view generated reams of reading material for the Task Force.

Floodplain Development Moratorium

All this time, at almost every meeting there were at least one or two proposed development projects near streams to review. Under the moratorium, projects adjacent to the floodplains needed Task Force approval. The Task Force knew it was important to be reasonable rather than arbitrary in order to maintain its credibility with and support from the Board of Supervisors, especially since any decision by the Task Force could be appealed to the Board. Consequently, reaching an agreement on the treatment of the floodplains which was satisfactory to both sides was very time-consuming. Even so, agreement was not always attained.

The first appeal by a developer to the Board was rather frightening to some Task Force members. The project was a subdivision proposal. The small stream or swale which ran through the site was to be piped and houses were to be built over it--at least piping was the choice of the proponent and the recommendation of the Department of Public Works. The case could perhaps be considered borderline: the swale in question was near the headwaters of the stream and in summer carried only a small amount of urban runoff. But the Task Force was concerned that downstream flooding could occur during the winter season as a result of the concentration of flow. Also, a very nice clump of vegetation, plus the rolling nature of the land lent itself to an urban design which could include the stream.

A majority of the Task Force was worried. Would its recommendation to retain the natural character of the stream and incorporate it into the design of the project be upheld, and the request to pipe the stream and fill the floodplain be denied? Or would the developer win and set a precedent which would become a serious obstacle for the protection of other natural streams and floodplains in the future? It was a hard-fought battle--the developer was one of the biggest and most influential in Sacramento, and this kind of stream had always been piped in previous developments. But despite a recommendation in favor of the developer from the Subdivision Review Committee (the County's technical advisory committee), the Planning Commission recommended denial of the piping and adoption of the Task Force recommendations. The Board of Supervisors concurred.

This was a turning point for the Task Force. Henceforth, it was known that the Board's moratorium policy and the Task Force's recommendations were not to be trifled with, and developers would fare better by incorporating the Task Force's recommendations into their projects.

It was a stimulating experience for the Task Force members and they plunged into their work with renewed vigor.

Policy Guidelines

The burden of reviewing projects was made heavier by the need to review those which were located along tributaries as well as along the main channels of the designated streams. To help organize and standardize the review process, the Task Force developed policy guidelines, including a list of information requirements from project proponents, and a map designating the subject tributaries, for consideration by the Board of Supervisors. An enormous amount of work and argument preceded the completion of the Tributary Policy, but it was finally adopted by the Board of Supervisors.[3] From then on projects adjacent to tributaries were administered by staff and the Task Force no longer had to spend precious time on them.

Specific Flooding Problems

One more time-consuming activity which slowed development of the Natural Streams Plan was the need to make recommendations on specific flooding problems. Both the County and the property owners presented proposals relating to stream preservation versus reduction of existing flooding. The Task Force worked hard on these issues and after considerable discussion with all sides, an agreement was generally reached without the need for an appeal to the Board of Supervisors.

Stream Maintenance

Because of the need for data on methods and costs of the County's stream maintenance program, and for information on methods of enforcing existing as well as future ordinances, two Task Force committees were formed. The Maintenance Committee's Chair was an expert at data gathering, and with the assistance of the Public Works staff, he did a professional analysis (all volunteer work) of stream maintenance practices and costs. To the surprise of some, it turned out that the costs of maintaining the streams in their natural state would generally be lower than the total costs for channelized streams if the

---

[3]The Tributary Policy was presented as a report by the Natural Stream Task Force, and adopted by the Board on April 7, 1976.

Task Force recommendations were followed. These recommendations would make the maintenance program self-supporting by improving the revenue system, labor practices, and operational procedures. Ultimately, these recommendations were included in the maintenance element of the Natural Streams Plan.

Enforcement of Existing Regulations

How to enforce regulations prohibiting rubbish dumping, illegal filling, and other modifications of the floodplain was a persistent problem. The Enforcement Committee Chair himself lived near one of the streams and was determined to find solutions to the enforcement problems. The enforcement element of the Natural Streams Plan is mainly the result of his committee's work.

Floodplain Management Element

But of all the elements of the Natural Streams Plan, the floodplain management element was the most controversial and took up a preponderance of the Task Force's time. A basic disagreement among Task Force members was over the "taking" issue: in this case, whether a dedication to the County of floodplain land could be required as a condition of development. Department of Public Works and building industry members argued that floodplains can be filled, thus removing the flood threat on the filled land--there would then be no justification for requiring a dedication. But a majority of Task Force members maintained that filling simply squeezes the water into a narrower channel, raising the water level, increasing its velocity, causing erosion and flooding downstream of the fill, in addition to destroying the riparian vegetation which often is abundant in the floodplains. They argued that the safest, cheapest, and most desirable flood control method was to prohibit any development at all in the floodplains.

The first County Counsel's representative to the Task Force prepared a paper explaining the legal issues and apparently leaving the door open to consideration of prohibitions on floodplain development. But later he was replaced, and his successor prepared a highly critical paper which said that the real purpose of the proposed restrictions on floodplain use was "the protection of aesthetic and recreational values, rather than the protection of public health and safety ..." and therefore they would likely be held unconstitutional as a "taking of private property without compensation."

In the meantime, Federal agencies, in particular the US Army Corps of Engineers, were ordered by the President to prevent development in floodplains partly because of the discovery that enormous expenditures of taxpayers' money were used to rehabilitate floodplain property and reimburse occupants whose property had been flooded. It seemed only prudent to avoid building in floodplains. During the early years of the Task Force's work, the Federal Housing Administration (FHA) was developing rules for Federal flood insurance and the Corps of Engineers was delineating the 100-year floodplain for streams in Sacramento County. The fact that the Federal government was recognizing the hazards and costs of floodplain development gave more credence to the position of the Task Force majority.

In any case, the County Counsel's advice was, in effect, sidestepped when the Task Force adopted recommendations for the Board of Supervisors which included severe restrictions on floodplain development.

The Issue of Cost

Another area of great controversy was the cost issue. The question of maintenance costs has been mentioned above, but there was also the question of costs of the recreation element. There were bicycle trails and recreation areas to be provided--the preliminary cost estimates were clearly beyond the County's capability, even in the long run. However, the Task Force discovered that the figures used to project the costs were based on total purchase of the floodplains and excessive size and construction standards of the bicycle trails. With the inclusion of floodplain dedications, and restriction in the length and construction standards of the bike trails, the costs were brought down to reasonable levels. Recommendations for financing methods as well as a long-range time schedule for implementation of the recreation element were also included.

The Time Factor

Task Force members, during the five years they worked on this Natural Streams Plan, often felt great impatience and frustration with the snail's pace of its progress. There were two or three periods of several months with no meetings and no action at all due to the staff members preemption for higher priorities of the Board of Supervisors. But this long duration worked to the advantage of the goals of the Task Force partly because of the rapidly changing attitudes all over the country regarding environmental issues. Even more important, considerable development occurred in lands adjacent to the floodplains, using the Task Force's preliminary guidelines. That meant that by the time the Natural Streams Plan was ready to present to the Planning Commission and the Board of Supervisors, it had been demonstrated that the floodplain guidelines were not all that onerous, and could result in some very attractive developments with the stream as a sales feature.

The Final Plan

The final Plan, as should be expected, was a compromise. Nevertheless, it was a good compromise from the Task Force majority's point of view.

In preparation for the public hearings on the Plan, a handsome, green and white, glossy brochure was distributed to each streamside property owner. These brochures described the proposed Natural Streams Plan and announced the public hearings to take place over a period of time. Excellent parcel maps were included, showing the stream and the approximate area proposed to be included in the Natural Stream Zone. In addition, the brochures advised residents what to do to protect the streams. Although some Task Force members were apprehensive about possible opposition at the hearings, none materialized, and the Plan was adopted by the Board of Supervisors in July 1980, five and one-half years after the appointment of the Task Force. Seeing the adoption of its recommendations, the Task Force was able to retire with a profound sense of satisfaction and relief.

EPILOGUE

As far as we can tell, one year after adoption of the Natural Streams Plan, the floodplain management aspect of the Plan has been very effective in preventing encroachment on the streams' floodplains, which in turn has eliminated the need for channelization of additional streams. This is due largely to the interest taken in the Plan by the Planning Commission staff and their determination to see that the new regulations are implemented. Their task is made relatively simple by the new Natural Streams Zone established as recommended by the implementation element of the Plan. The County's drainage, grading, and subdivision ordinances were also amended to make them consistent with the Plan's objectives and policies.

Because of financial constraints, the recreation element is in a holding position, but at least the land in the floodplains will be available for recreational uses in the future.

Looking back, it seems quite remarkable that almost all the citizen-group members stuck it out through more than five years of very difficult meetings. Perseverance is perhaps the most needed attribute necessary for the success of citizen action. However, in the final analysis, it was the responsiveness of the Board of Supervisors to the large number of residents who cared about their streams that has made the Natural Streams Plan truly effective.

LITERATURE CITED

Environmental Impact Section, Sacramento County. 1974. Sacramento County natural stream study. PW-74-003. Sacramento County, California.

Nolte, George S. 1961. The County of Sacramento master drainage plan. Part 1--county-wide hydrology. Sacramento County.

SAN DIEGO COUNTY RIPARIAN SYSTEMS:

CURRENT THREATS AND STATUTORY PROTECTION EFFORTS[1]

Gary P. Wheeler and Jack M. Fancher[2]

Abstract.--The effectiveness of present laws in conserving San Diego County riparian systems is examined. Agencies are more effective when several laws apply, when credible statutory authority and enforcement exists, and when public support is generated. Recommendations are made for improvement.

INTRODUCTION

The Mediterranean climate of coastal southern California has induced some obvious and distinct contrasts between mesic and xeric vegetation-types. Coastal sage scrub, chaparral, oak woodland, or California grassland vegetation often ends abruptly at a narrow corridor of riparian vegetation. Woody, perennial wetland vegetation is usually confined to a relatively narrow corridor bordering the enduring, year-round, low-volume water flows and is not directly correlated with the mean annual or ephemeral high-volume storm flows. Consequently, unmodified floodplains in southern California are often relatively wide when compared with the narrow strip of riparian vegetation which frequently occurs only along the path of low flow.

The Mediterranean climate may, in part, have promoted human occupancy of southern California floodplains by fostering the false impression, for decades at a time, that riparian growth delimited the floodplain. Following the rare but inevitable devastating flood, the typical human response has been to "improve" the floodplain to accommodate this rare flood. In doing so, headwaters are dammed, and the natural floodplain usually is constricted into a channelized floodway in order to provide protection for floodplain developments. To maximize hydraulic efficiency, riparian vegetation is typically removed. The trapezoidal, concrete channel of the Los Angeles River is a famous example of such maximized hydraulic efficiency.

---

[1]Paper presented at the California Riparian Systems Conference. [University of California, Davis, September 17-19, 1981].

[2]Gary P. Wheeler and Jack M. Fancher are Biologists with the USDI Fish and Wildlife Service, Laguna Niguel, Calif. The opinions and recommendations offered in this paper are solely those of the authors and do not necessarily reflect the views of the USDI Fish and Wildlife Service.

Since more than half of all Californians live in the four coastal counties of southern California (Ventura, Los Angeles, Orange, and San Diego), unmodified riparian corridors have largely been obliterated. Some significant areas of riparian vegetation do exist, particularly in San Diego County. In some San Diego County rivers, such as the Mission Valley region of the San Diego River, historic sand mining has brought riverbottom elevations nearer to the water table, which facilitated marsh and riparian woodland establishment once mining ceased. Also, the reestablishment of perennial freshwater flows by irrigation and wastewater returns encouraged wetlands redevelopment. However, riparian wetlands continue to be threatened by human actions. Using actual case histories, we will attempt to document the major threats to coastal San Diego County's riparian resources and the effectiveness of agencies in protecting these resources; and we will offer some general observations as to what factors influence the effectiveness of attempts to protect riparian systems.

THE RIPARIAN RESOURCE

San Diego, the southwesternmost county in the mainland United States, encompasses approximately 1.1 million hectares (2.7 million acres) of land ranging from coastal beaches and plains to foothills, mountains, and desert. Riparian systems are extremely limited within the county, occupying somewhere between 0.2% (2,000 ha. [5,000 ac.]) (California Department of Fish and Game 1965) and 0.5% (5,300 ha. [13,000 ac.]) (Oberbauer 1977) of the county's land area.

Riparian vegetation to some degree can be found along most of the coastal region streams; however, the most prominent locations include the mouth of San Mateo Creek, Las Pulgas Creek, the Santa Margarita River, the San Luis Rey River, Las Penasquitos Creek in Sorrento Valley, San Clemente and Rose canyons, the San Diego River, the Sweetwater River, Jamul Creek, Campo Creek, and the Otay River (Goldwasser 1978). Willows (_Salix_ spp.) tend to dominate the riparian vegetation in most areas; however, cottonwoods (_Populus_ _fremontii_ and _P. trichocarpa_), California sycamore (_Platanus racemosa_), and white alder (_Alnus rhombifolia_) are also major components in various areas. Understory vegetation commonly includes mugwort (_Artemesia douglasiana_), mulefat (_Baccharis viminea_), stinging nettles (_Urtica holosericea_), and wild cucumber (_Marah macrocarpus_). Oak woodlands dominated by coast live oak (_Quercus agrifolia_) and canyon live oak (_Q. chrysolepis_) in several areas border or intermix with riparian systems, particularly in the more inland canyons (Oberbauer unpublished).

THREATS

Current threats to San Diego County riparian systems can generally be tied to population pressures and/or pressure for development. Just within the past 10 years, the county's population has increased by approximately 0.5 million people, a 37% increase. The county General Plan Conservation Element (San Diego County 1980) states that vegetation removal is the single most important human action impacting local wildlife. Vegetation removal is not subject to the county environmental review process, and large areas are sometimes cleared for agricultural purposes or residential development prior to filing an environmental impact report. Stream channelization, floodplain filling, and sand and gravel extraction are occurring at a particularly rapid rate along the San Luis Rey River near Oceanside and along the upper San Diego River, and have resulted in major losses of riparian resources along these streams. The proposed construction of two dams and reservoirs on the Santa Margarita River near Fallbrook threatens to inundate over 400 ha. (1,000 ac.) of riparian and oak woodlands.

TOOLS FOR PROTECTION

Several means for countering these threats are available to concerned citizens and public agencies. The National Environmental Policy Act (NEPA)[3] and California Environmental Quality Act (CEQA)[4] constitute disclosure laws which, in themselves, do not directly protect riparian resources, but do require identification of alternatives and assessment of project impacts. Similarly, the Fish and Wildlife Coordination Act (FWCA)[5] mandates consideration of fish and wildlife values in the planning of federal water development projects and issuance of US Army Corps of Engineers (CE) permits, but has no enforcement or implementation provisions. Presidential executive orders such as E.O. 11988,

Floodplain Management, and E.O. 11990, Protection of Wetlands, provide guidance in project planning to federal agencies. State, county, or municipal ordinances and policies generally also provide guidance, but rarely include significant enforcement features. Regrettably, the parochial attitude of most southern California city and county governments has usually resulted in the encouragement of developments which increase the tax base but may result in significant environmental losses.

Two state and two federal laws include enforcement provisions. Because of varying legislative intents and jurisdictions, these laws differ in their effectiveness for protecting riparian resource values.

The California Coastal Act of 1976[6] (CCA) provides emphatic and effective protection of riparian wetlands as environmentally sensitive habitat. Under the CCA, environmentally sensitive habitats are to be protected against any disruption of habitat values which could occur from development within or adjacent to that habitat. Furthermore, only uses dependent upon the sensitive resource are allowed within the area. Removal of riparian vegetation and streambed materials is also controlled by the act. However, the geographic extent of the protection afforded by this strong habitat protection law is severely limited when related to the distribution of riparian systems. The CCA permit process includes public hearing and California Coastal Commission deliberation steps.

Division 2, Chapter 6 of the California Fish and Game Code (California Fish and Game Commission 1979) states: "The protection and conservation of the fish and wildlife resources of this State are hereby declared to be of utmost public interest." The subsequent Fish and Game Code sections 1601 through 1603 have a very broad geographic applicability, covering virtually all streams within the state. These code sections require a Streambed Alteration Agreement between the California Department of Fish and Game (DFG) and any party proposing to alter or modify a streambed, channel, or bank. The major weakness of this regulation, aside from the manpower and time constraints placed upon the DFG, is that an arrangement agreeable to both parties must be reached between the DFG and the developer. The discretion to deny a project which would cause significant damage is not available. In order to reach an agreement, a compromise is normally required, and the existing resource is seldom preserved intact. If agreement is not reached, a three-member arbitration panel is formed to resolve any differences. For various reasons, it is apparently the unstated policy of DFG to refrain from entering arbitration, since fewer than 0.02% of the streambed alteration notifications have been taken to that level of consideration.

---

[3] 42 U.S.C. 4321–4337; 83 Stat. 852.
[4] PRC Section 21000–21151.
[5] 16 U.S.C. 661–666(c); 48 Stat. 401 (as amended).

---

[6] PRC Section 30000–30900.

The federal Endangered Species Act (ESA)[7] as amended, stringently guards listed species against adverse impacts caused by federal actions. However, this act applies only when a listed species and a federal action are involved. Currently there are no federally listed riparian woodland-dwelling species in San Diego County; therefore, the ESA is rarely invoked when riparian woodlands are to be affected. Activities involving certain vernal pools, a rare and unusual riparian system, have been restricted under the ESA due to the presence of the San Diego mesa mint (Pogogyne ambramsii), a federally listed Endangered species.

The federal law most frequently invoked in the protection of riparian resources is the Clean Water Act.[8] Section 404 of the act calls for regulation of the discharge of dredge or fill material into waters of the United States. The permit process, administered by the CE, includes distribution of a public notice and a broad public interest consideration. The Clean Water Act does not restrict excavation within wetlands or clearing of wetland vegetation when no discharge occurs. Jurisdiction requiring individual permits is limited to watercourses, and their adjacent wetlands, conveying an average annual flow of 0.14 cu. m. (5 cu. ft.) per second or greater. Consequently, only major rivers or perennial streams are included, as shown in table 1.

Table 1.--San Diego County rivers and streams over which CE has exercised individual permit authority under the aegis of the Federal Water Pollution Control Act of 1972, later re-enacted as the Clean Water Act of 1977 (US Army Corps of Engineers 1978).

Watercourse	Reach	Miles Within Jurisdiction
Santa Margarita River	Pacific Ocean upstream to 4.0 km. (2.5 mi.) beyond Murietta Creek	34 km. (21 mi.) in San Diego County
San Luis Rey River	Pacific Ocean to Moosa Canyon	21 km. (13 mi.)
San Dieguito River	Pacific Ocean to Lake Hodges	18 km. (11 mi.)
San Ysabel Creek	Lake Hodges to Sutherland Reservoir	27 km. (17 mi.)
San Diego River	Pacific Ocean to Boulder Creek	45 km. (28 mi.) excluding El Capitan Reservoir
Sweetwater River	San Diego Bay to Descanso Creek	60 km. (37 mi.)

[7] 16 U.S.C. 1531-1543; 87 Stat. 884.
[8] 33 U.S.C. 1251-1265, 1281-1292, 1311-1328, 1341-1345, 1361-1376; 86 Stat. 816, 91 Stat. 1566.

CASE HISTORIES

The following four case histories are presented as examples of the threats posed to San Diego County riparian systems and to demonstrate the effectiveness of our current laws in protecting them.

San Diego River

In the fall of 1980, a private developer began to clear and fill an area of riparian woodland within the San Diego River floodplain in the city of San Diego. Approxmately 0.5 ha. (1.2 ac.) of large-stature black willow (Salix gooddingii)-dominated woodland had been leveled, and filling had begun when a DFG warden stopped the work. The developer had obtained neither a streambed alteration agreement with the DFG nor a Section 404 permit from the CE.

The CE would not consider prosecution of this unauthorized act and, instead, expressed a willingness to accept an after-the-fact permit application. The DFG considered prosecution for failure to notify under the Fish and Game Code, but due to limited state resources available for litigation, chose to prosecute an unrelated but similar violation upstream.

As the threat of state and federal prosecution disappeared, the developer's negotiating position significantly improved. The mitigation proposals initially forwarded to the agencies by the developer were minimal and did not offset the loss in riparian values. In the negotiation process, it was revealed that the city had not only required the developer to complete a dedicated street through the subject wetland, but also that the city owned the wetland property. Further, the unauthorized roadway clearing and filling had isolated another 0.4-ha. (1.1-ac.) parcel of wooded wetland owned by the city, which the city ultimately wanted to fill and sell for development. The developer, acting as the city's agent, initiated the agreement procedure with DFG. Apparently because of the time requirements of the agreement procedure, the lack of prosecution, and the unwillingness of the developer to remove the fill, DFG reached an agreement with the developer at a time when the USDI Fish and Wildlife Service (FWS) was still seeking an acceptable mitigation plan.

The city and the developer considered unacceptable any plan which did not allow them to complete 0.9 ha. (2.3 ac.) of fill in the wooded wetland. Under the streambed alteration agreement, the DFG had agreed to this fill provided that 1.9 ha. (4.6 ac.) of adjacent land owned by the city of San Diego were excavated to create wetlands and then revegetated.

The FWS contended that even though 2 ha. of wetland were to be gained for each hectare lost, a loss of habitat values would result. This position was based upon the premise that 1 ha. of mature riparian woodland provides greater habitat

840

values than 2 ha. of open water and early successional wetlands characterized by herbaceous hydrophytes and sapling willows and cottonwoods.
Also, because of the uncertainties of transplant
survival, the modified hydraulic regime of the
river, and the unpredictability of seasonal storm
flows, FWS incorporated a safety factor in its
mitigation recommendations and suggested that 1.6
ha. (4 ac.) of wetlands be created for each 0.4
ha. (1 ac.) of riparian wetland to be filled.

The developers then hired a biological consultant who contradicted the FWS habitat assessment. They also lobbied the CE, as well as the
FWS Washington office, charging that the FWS
recommendations were excessive and unreasonable,
since they went beyond those which had satisfied
the DFG. When the FWS held firm, the developer
and the city recognized that project delays could
result.

Since delay was contrary to the developer's
interests, the developer encouraged the city to
become directly involved and to consider guarantees for the compensating wetlands. Eventually a
mitigation plan was agreed upon which assured
long-term protection of wetland habitat values.

The elements of the mitigation plan, which
offset the loss of 0.9 ha. of forested wetland included: a) creating 1.9 ha. of wetland by excavating a sparsely vegetated upland down to river-
bottom elevations; b) revegetating the newly created wetland with a variety of native riparian
plant species, with maximized edge effect, foliage height diversity, and wildlife cover and food
values given special considerations; c) assurance
by the developer, through a letter of credit,
that for five years the 1.9 ha. transplant effort
will succeed (wetland re-creation success will be
evaluated over the five-year period using avifauna and vegetation monitoring studies); d) an
agreement by the city with FWS, using a deed restriction instrument, to preserve the fish and
wildlife resource values of 4.5 ha. (11 ac.) of
city-owned San Diego River wetlands (1.9 ha. of
compensation area plus an additional 2.6 ha. [6.4
ac.] of contiguous forested wetland); and e) an
agreement whereby the city will not propose any
work in another 2.6-ha. (6.5-ac.) parcel of contiguous forested wetland until a management plan
for preserving San Diego River wetland values is
implemented.

San Luis Rey River #1

A housing development proposed for construction adjacent to the San Luis Rey River in northern San Diego County included a street which was
to encroach upon a riparian wetland composed mainly of giant reed (Arundo donax) and a single
row of large cottonwoods (Populus sp.). Prior
to the public comment period required under Section 404 of the CWA, a streambed alteration agreement requiring no extensive mitigation was signed
by the developer and DFG.

Upon distribution of the CE public notice on
the project, the FWS, DFG, and Environmental Protection Agency (EPA) objected to the issuance of
the permit unless the loss of riparian resource
values would be mitigated. The FWS encouraged
the developer to find an alternative route for
the encroaching roadway, but was informed that a
City-designated street corridor and safety criteria prohibited relocation. At this point the
developer offered to create a new riparian wetland by lowering the elevation of a nearby upland
area of equal size.

Prior to removing its objections to the
issuance of the Section 404 permit, the FWS
requested that the developer prepare a satisfactory revegetation plan. A consulting firm was
employed to develop the plan, which consists of
grading the plot to varying heights above the
riverbed and planting native willows, cottonwoods, sycamores, and a variety of understory
species. A hedgerow of armed vines and shrubs
was included to prevent excessive human intrusion. Irrigation was to be provided if necessary, and a planting survival rate of 80% after
two years will be considered a successful transplanting effort.

San Luis Rey River #2

On the San Luis Rey River near the city of
Oceanside, there is an isolated business and
several residences which could only be reached by
traversing a low, culverted river crossing. This
crossing would typically wash out with any significant floodflows in the river, thereby further
isolating the business and the residents. Consequently, the business owners and area residents
decided to build a bridge across the river. The
bridge was begun prior to notifying Oceanside
city authorities, DFG, or CE to obtain necessary
permits. In the construction process approximately 0.4 ha. (1 ac.) of riparian woodlands were
cleared and filled.

The DFG filed suit against the owner/builder
for failure to notify DFG under Fish and Game
Code Section 1603. In deciding the case, the
judge ruled against the DFG, stating that there
was no substantial alteration of the streambed or
bank and that, in the absence of a definable
riverbank, the ordinary citizen could not be
expected to know that the bank extended to the
outward edge of the riparian vegetation.

Fortunately, this portion of the San Luis
Rey River is also under CE Section 404 jurisdiction. Although the CE would not prosecute the
owner/builder for failure to obtain a permit
prior to construction, it appears that, based
upon recommendations by DFG, FWS, and EPA, the
builder will be required to revegetate the riverbank in order to obtain a CE permit for retaining
the bridge approach fills. The city permit required no mitigation of adverse impacts to San
Luis Rey River riparian resources.

San Luis Rey River #3

In 1966, an industrial manufacturer constructed a plant within the floodplain and an historic channel of the San Luis Rey River. Apparently, his action was based upon the belief that the CE would soon implement a proposed channelization and flood control project along the river. This has not yet occurred, and since construction, floodflows have inundated the facility five times. Due to the delay in construction of the CE flood control project, the developer himself has attempted to protect his plant by rerouting the river north of his plant, constructing a levee along the south bank of the river, clearing the river channel of riparian vegetation, and constructing a ring levee around his plant. With each inundation, greater flood control measures have been implemented and more riparian wetlands have been adversely impacted. On several occasions fill material was placed in wetlands prior to obtaining a CE permit or DFG agreement. The CE has been reluctant to prosecute the developer under the provisions of the CWA, and the developer considers his actions justified, claiming that all actions he has taken have been either under an emergency situation to protect lives and property or have been in the public interest to protect the jobs of his many employees.

The DFG has filed suit against the developer under Section 1603 of the Fish and Game Code for failure to notify the agency prior to altering the stream. This suit is pending and, as yet, no court date has been set.

The developer has indicated his intention to construct a major industrial complex adjacent to his plant in an area currently supporting a lush riparian woodland. His initial step will be to clear and farm this area. Provided there is no addition of fill material, the Clean Water Act does not require a permit for farming of wetlands. It remains to be seen if Section 1603 of the Fish and Game Code will offer any degree of protection for this area. The future of this riparian woodland, however, does not appear to be very promising.

DISCUSSION

Several general points should be considered as one evaluates the relative degree of protection achieved in these cases.

The greatest degree of protection occurs when several agencies have authority for project review under different statutes with similar objectives. This was demonstrated in the San Diego River case and in San Luis Rey #1 and #2. In each of these examples a weaker streambed alteration agreement was backed up by more stringent conditions requested by the DFG, FWS, and EPA on the Section 404 permit. Even though Fish and Game Code sections have protection and conservation of fish and wildlife resources as their

purpose, implementation by DFG is debilitated by the impotent statutory vehicle. Had these actions occurred within the jurisdiction of the California Coastal Commission, it is suggested that wetland values might have been even better conserved.

A greater degree of protection seems to result when opportunity for public review and comment is provided. We have seen on several occasions where public comments provided to the CE have influenced the issuance of a Section 404 permit. The influence of public involvement on private projects, however, can perhaps best be seen in observing the public hearing process of the California Coastal Commission where a multitude of opportunities are provided for meaningful public input.

The effectiveness of protection efforts depends greatly upon the degree of threat which a project sponsor feels the public and an agency posed to his project. In the San Diego River case, the developer initially attempted to weaken the FWS mitigation recommendations and encouraged the CE to issue the Section 404 permit over the agency's objections. The developer had the advantage of knowing prosecution was not likely and that much of the damage to the wetlands had already been accomplished. However, once the developer realized that even if the CE issued the permit over FWS objections costly project delays could still result. The developer and the city were then willing to offer more meaningful mitigation measures.

In the San Luis Rey #3 case the developer has generally ignored the threats of the permit-issuing agencies and simply refused to recognize the authority of the DFG and the CE in regulating his activities in the wetlands on his private property. In addition, he feels that all his actions have been in the public interest; if the DFG and/or the CE don't agree and decide to prosecute, he will be happy to litigate. Fortunately, such flagrant and intentional violations are rare, but they are likely to become more frequent when enforcement is absent or largely bluff.

It is much more difficult to obtain replacement of riparian or wetland values from the developer if a project has been completed by circumventing the permit process than if proper channels are followed from the outset. Obtaining mitigation once the project is completed generally requires the CE or a state agency to litigate against the developer for a violation of Section 404 or the Fish and Game Code.

Because the FWS and the DFG are reviewing agencies under Section 404 and are not the permitting agency, their effectiveness in protecting riparian resources is limited by the actions of the CE. In the past, one of the wildlife agencies' strongest criticisms of the CE regulatory program has been failure to initiate prosecution of violators of Section 404. The apparent low priority of such prosecutions or the insufficient staff in the US Attorney's office are said to contribute to feeble Section 404 enforcement. It is evident that without enforcement the law loses its credibility and offers little protection for the public fish and wildlife values of our nation's waters and wetlands.

The local government level appears, in the authors' opinion, to be the best level at which to protect riparian systems. However, in San Diego County, at this time, the exact opposite seems to be true. Cities and county agencies have promoted the development of riparian areas in fostering the economic growth of their communities. To date, there has been no incentive for local governments to protect their riparian resources.

Under the California Coastal Act, local governments are provided incentives to implement plans and ordinances consistent with the mutually beneficial uses of the coastal zone. The conservation of riparian systems seems clearly in the public interest regardless of whether or not they are found within the coastal zone. Action analogous to the California Coastal Act, i.e., state-wide goals implemented at local government levels, for conservation of riparian systems, therefore, seems appropriate.

RECOMMENDATIONS

With the intention of protecting and conserving the fish and wildlife resources that riparian systems provide, the following actions should be considered.

1. The state should enact a "California Riparian Systems Conservation Act," analagous to the California Coastal Act.

2. Any statutory enactments should have unambiguous statements of purpose, jurisdiction, definitions, and enforcement provisions.

3. Public and private conservation organizations should increase their efforts to foster public awareness of the values of riparian systems.

Other interim or lesser measures could include the following.

4. The state should enact legislation modifying Fish and Game Code Sections 1601-1603 to empower DFG with discretionary permit authority.

5. The three-party arbitration panel outlined in the Fish and Game Code Chapter 6 should be replaced by the existing Fish and Game Commission.

6. To ensure statewide consistency, DFG should produce mitigation guidelines applicable to streambed alteration projects and criteria for referring projects to arbitration.

7. DFG should be allowed to assess an administrative fee for the streambed alteration agreement. Also, the monetary penalty for failure to notify DFG under these code sections should be substantially increased and penalties for noncompliance should be implemented.

8. The state should assume Clean Water Act Section 404 jurisdiction, with DFG or the Resources Agency as the permit-issuing authority, in the event federal authority is abrogated.

9. The opportunity for public comment should be provided in any permitting process established for the conservation of riparian systems.

LITERATURE CITED

California Department of Fish and Game. 1965. California Fish and Wildlife Plan, Vol. III, Part C. 370 p. California Department of Fish and Game, Sacramento.

California Fish and Game Commission. 1979. California Fish and Game Code. 319 p. State of California, Sacramento.

Goldwasser, S. 1978. Distribution, reproductive success and impact of nest parasitism by brown-headed cowbirds on Least Bell's Vireos. Final report to California Department of Fish and Game, Sacramento. 27 p.

Oberbauer, T. 1977. Vegetation communities in San Diego County. Unpublished report for San Diego County Planning Department, San Diego, Calif.

San Diego County. 1980. San Diego County General Plan. Section 1, Part X—Conservation Element. 91 p.

US Army Corps of Engineers. 1978. Revised public notice No. 404 and amendments. Notice of exercise of Section 404 jurisdiction over certain streams and wetlands in California. Department of the Army, Los Angeles District, Corps of Engineers (July 15, 1978).

THE PRESERVATION AND RESTORATION OF RIPARIAN RESOURCES IN CONDUCTING FLOOD CONTROL ACTIVITIES[1]

William M. Lockard and Richard A. Burgess[2]

Abstract.--Flood control activities often require the modification of riparian resources in the interest of public safety. Such activities may do considerable damage to riparian systems. An important goal for those interested in riparian resource preservation is to work with flood control organizations so that necessary flood control activities may be completed in a more environmentally sensitive manner. This paper proposes a five-point program for the riparian resource manager which pursues that goal. The paper concludes that such a program, designed and operated at the local level, is a superior alternative to one generated by a state mandate.

INTRODUCTION

The riparian resource manager is confronted with many of the factors influencing streams and rivers. Where riparian systems are relatively pristine and isolated, the manager's primary goal is to preserve, to the extent possible, natural fluvial processes. More often, however, riparian systems are located within agricultural or urban areas. Normally, in these cases, the riparian system falls within the jurisdiction of a local flood control organization.

The first and foremost responsibility of flood control organizations has been, and continues to be, the protection of life and property. However, does such an organization also have a responsibility as a steward of riparian resources? Not long ago, the universal answer would have been no. However, the environmental movement and certain state mandates, such as the California Environmental Quality Act, have created an environment for change. While some flood control organizations already recognize their responsibility to riparian resources, others may be persuaded.

While a state mandate could be created which would force flood control organizations to preserve and restore riparian systems, this paper

assumes that it is more desirable to instill a conservation ethic in flood control organizations.

We do not suggest that flood control organizations should subjugate their primary responsibilities relating to public safety. We suggest that needed flood control activities can be performed in ways which also preserve and restore riparian systems. This paper, then, presents a program for the riparian resource manager to use when working with flood control organizations. The program is based on the Ventura County experience and contains examples from ongoing programs. The program contains five basic elements as discussed below.

A FIVE-POINT RIPARIAN RESOURCE MANAGEMENT PROGRAM

Establish Political Support

Although this program assumes that a state mandate is not the motivation for riparian resource management, there are other types of state assistance which might be considered appropriate support. These include grants-in-aid to develop the program, technical expertise, educational programs, guidelines and criteria, and the definition of sensitive riparian systems of significance.

However, the most important political support for the program should come from the local decision-making body. Flood control personnel are normally responsible to their board of directors or the county board of supervisors. Since a resource management program involves the expendi-

---

[1]Paper presented at the California Riparian Systems Conference. [University of California, Davis, September 17-19, 1981.]

[2]William M. Lockard is Staff Conservationist, and Richard A. Burgess is Conservationist; both are with Ventura County Flood Control District, Ventura, Calif.

ture of time and money, it must be sanctioned by the decision-making body. Furthermore, flood control personnel need assurances as to what their (new) role as resource manager is. Local political support is not sought as a lever to force the program on unwilling employees. For that reason, policy guidelines should come from the political body. Policy guidelines clarify making body's position and yet allow the manager flexibility.

For example, five important policies were adopted by the Ventura County Board of Supervisors as part of the county's Section 208 Areawide Water Quality Management Plan. These policies can be found in example 1.

Example 1.--Policy guidelines adopted by the
Ventura County Board of Supervisors

A. PUBLIC SAFETY AND WELFARE POLICY
The Board of Supervisors of the Ventura County Flood Control District is committed to responsible flood control activities. Nevertheless, the first and foremost responsibility of the Board of Supervisors, the County staff and all others involved in flood control activities is the protection of life and property. Therefore, it is the policy of the Ventura County Board of Supervisors that no action suggested in this manual shall be accomplished where such action would clearly constitute a threat to life, property or the public welfare.

B. COORDINATION POLICY
The Ventura County Flood Control District will seek, whenever possible, the expertise and advice of the California Department of Fish and Game where flood control activities might have an adverse effect on the County's streams and rivers. During emergency flood conditions, the Deputy Director of Public Works, Flood Control and Water Resources, or his designated representative will provide reports to the Department of Fish and Game and, in accordance with the [California] Fish and Game Code, arrange field meetings to discuss emergency flood control work.

The goal of this policy is to provide the concerned parties with a greater understanding of the physical and economic constraints of flood control activities and basic hydrologic and fluvial processes. It is also the purpose of this policy to cause better understanding of the biological requirements of riparian environments, as well as the ecological relationships of riparian and adjacent habitats. Further, this policy is intended to improve the Flood Control District's ability to perform necessary flood control activities in an environmentally responsible manner.

C. RESTORATION POLICY
It is inevitable that some flood control activities will adversely affect riparian resources in Ventura County. It is not always possible in such a narrow and sensitive habitat to avoid adverse effects with certain flood control activities. Such activities may be necessitated by emergency flood conditions or normal preventative maintenance. Where physical and economic conditions allow, the District may mitigate these effects by utilizing various restoration techniques after the flood control activity is completed. If flood control activities involving such restoration work are to take place in Ventura County, the following policy shall apply: Where physical and budgetary conditions permit, the Ventura County Flood Control District shall initiate restoration programs to mitigate alterations to sensitive or unique riparian resources which have occurred as a result of flood control activities. Such work shall be accomplished pursuant to the criteria defined in the "Operators Manual for Conducting Flood Control Activities in Ventura County Streams and Rivers, April, 1981" [Ventura County Public Works Agency, Flood Control and Water Resources Department 1981] and shall be coordinated with appropriate State and Federal agencies pursuant to the District's Coordination Policy.

D. BEST MANAGEMENT PRACTICES POLICY
It is the policy of the Board of Supervisors of the Ventura County Flood Control District to encourage the use of the Best Management Practices defined in the Operators Manual for Conducting Flood Control Activities in Ventura County Streams and Rivers, April, 1981" [ibid.]

The Best Management Practices herein adopted replace the "Policy Guidelines for Work Conducted in Streams and Rivers During Emergency Conditions" adopted by the Board of Supervisors on September 23, 1980.

Example 1.--Continued.

E. CONTRACTOR'S RESPONSIBILITIES POLICY
The policies and best management practices adopted by the Board of Supervisors as part of the Operator's Manual shall be referenced into any contracts or agreements between the County of Ventura or any of its agencies and any contractor or subcontractor retained by the County. Such contracts shall require that the contractor acknowledge familiarity with the provisions of the Operator's Manual and to assume responsibility for conducting any work performed under such contract in accordance with the policies and best management practices of the Operator's Manual.

The purpose of this policy is to put contractors on notice that it is the policy of the County of Ventura that County-sponsored flood control activities are to be conducted in a manner which protects riparian resources wherever possible.

The following is a hypothetical conversation between two people standing along a lush pristine stream in Ventura County. The first person is Jake, Field Supervisor for the County Flood Control District. The second person is Mike, Biology instructor at a nearby college and member of a local environmental group. A third party, astride a weathered D-8 bulldozer, waits nearby with his engine on an impatient idle.

Mike: What's going on?
Jake: We have to get these lousy bushes out of here!
Mike: Lousy bushes? This is one of the best streams in the county. Those are spawning beds right over there, and there might even be unarmored three-spined stickleback in this stream!
Jake: Unarmored what?
Mike: Unarmored three sp...

Jake interrupts with a disgusted look on his face and wave of his hand.

Jake: Aw, forget it. I have a job to do. We're here to protect people, not fish, and that bulldozer up there is costing the taxpayers money!

Jake looks at the bulldozer operator and points an index finger at the stream. The bulldozer moves quickly forward and begins removing the "lousy bushes."

After the bulldozer has done its work, it doesn't matter if Jake or Mike was right. This situation is relatively easy to imagine. It illustrates the damage that can result from poor communication. Effective communication is essential to a successful riparian management program, and it should be the responsibility of the manager to make it occur. Although we will not go into great detail in discussing the psychology of communication, there are a number of common-sense communication axioms that a resource manager should consider.

1. There is more to communication than the spoken word. Body movements, facial expressions, inflections in the voice, and even inactivity communicate a message (Watzlawick et al 1967).

2. The two basic components of communication are the content (the message) and the relationship (between communicants). A "healthy" communication is one in which the content of the communication predominates. Conversely, a "sick" conversation is characterized by a constant struggle about the nature of the relationship between communicants (ibid.).

3. The relationship component of a communication tends to dominate when an individual feels defensive. Individuals may feel defensive when verbal (or non-verbal) communication tends to suggest that: a) he is being evaluated or judged; b) there is an attempt to control him; c) there is a strategy or "game" going on; or d) the speaker appears uncaring, ungiving, or neutral to the individual's position (Gibb 1961).

The content aspect of communication tends to dominate when an individual feels less defensive and the conversation is more spontaneous and problem oriented. An individual is less defensive when he views the other communicant as an equal, as someone who empathizes with his position and/or wants to know what he has to say (ibid.).

Education Program Design

The orderly mesh of materials, content, and participants is an essential part of any successful program. A structured program design is not only common sense, it usually saves time and money and helps keep participants interested. The education program we suggest is discussed below, with examples provided by ongoing educational programs in Ventura County.

The Need for Dual Education

It is prudent to acknowledge from the beginning that an education program is not one-sided, with the resource manager in the role of teacher and flood control personnel in the role of students. In truth, the resource manager may have a great deal to learn about the flood control organization and its activities. More importantly, the goal of the program--the preservation of riparian resources--will be primarily realized through dialogue in the field, as potential implementation tools are tested and evaluated. In this regard, everyone in the program is a student. In fact, the justification for the education program must be to provide a mutual frame of reference for field dialogue. We suggest that the following subjects should be covered in the education program to achieve that mutual frame of reference.

The Fluvial Process

"Fluvial" is defined in Webster's Dictionary (1971) as that which is "produced by stream action." The term may be unfamiliar to some involved in flood control activities. Other terms may come to mind for them such as "hydraulic" (that which is operated or moved by water) and "hydrologic" (dealing with the properties, distribution and circulation of water). However, these latter terms do not fully describe what is to be defined. The critical point is that streams and rivers are part of a process (defined in Webster's Dictionary as "a natural phenomenon marked by gradual changes that lead toward a particular result"). We suggest that "fluvial process" be defined as: A natural process which results from the dynamic interaction of the hydrologic cycle, the earth's geology, and the living environment.

Process implies movement. The energy sources of the fluvial process are often taken for granted and should be simply defined. These energy sources include gravity, solar energy, and geologic movement (uplifting) of the earth's crust. Other terms which should be defined relate to the with physical effects of these energy sources. These terms include precipitation, transportation, weathering, erosion, and deposition.

A deeper appreciation of fluvial processes comes with an understanding of geologic time and the history of local streams and rivers. Flood control personnel observe from experience that drainage basins differ. One is rugged and rocky, another is flat and sandy. One reason for this probably involves geologic formations. Soil maps of debris-producing soil formations which were once ancient oceans and are now high in elevation could be used to illustrate the forces and time frame involved in the formation of riparian systems. If possible, more recent deposits can be related to existing land features. Figure 1 was used in the "Technical Paper for the Ventura County 208 Water Quality Management Plan" (Lockard and Burgess 1981). The authors pointed out in this example how the Santa Clara River changed course in 1969 from point "b" back to point "a", resulting in considerable damage to the Ventura marina.

The physical elements of a stream or river, which are a result of the fluvial process, provide the medium for the biotic components of the system. The diversity of physical stream elements has permitted a high diversity of wildlife. Each element is part of an interdependent whole. This fact should be stressed as basic stream elements are identified and discussed. Physical stream elements which should be discussed in the education program include: 1) braiding and stream width; 2) pools and riffles; and 3) rapids and falls.

In discussing these elements, it may be convenient to use the description of a "textbook stream" presented in example 2.

Biological Resources and Ecology

A discussion of riparian biology and ecology can be incredibly fascinating or incredibly boring, depending on the presentation and the audience. Realistically, the resource manager should not expect rabid enthusiasm from flood control personnel when the subject of riparian biology is breached. A realistic goal is to keep the topic interesting. The resource manager is faced with the dilemma of deciding what kind and how much of this complex subject to present. It is suggested that this aspect of the education program be broken down into three categories.

1. What are biological resources?
2. How do biological resources interact with the environment (ecology)?
3. What affect do flood control activities have on biological resources?

Biological Resources.--In discussing biological resources of riparian systems, it is convenient to divide them into two areas, aquatic and riparian life. Aquatic is defined as that component of the biota which lives in or on the water. It should be pointed out that aquatic organisms have not only adapted to the medium of water, but also to its movement (see example 3). If local streams provide a significant sports fishery, it is often worth stressing this, since it is a utilitarian value to which people relate strongly (see example 4). Additionally, in discussing aquatic life, it is desirable to accentuate the diversity that exists there. Plants, microorganisms, algae, aquatic insects, reptiles, amphibians, and small aquatic mammals, such as muskrats, should all be discussed briefly.

The importance of the riparian environment as an interface between aquatic and terrestrial environments should be covered. A definition of the plant associations in riparian areas is desirable (fig. 2). A discussion of the diversity of plants and wildlife of riparian systems is most important. The terrestrial wildlife species which use riparian systems for food and cover should also be discussed (example 5).

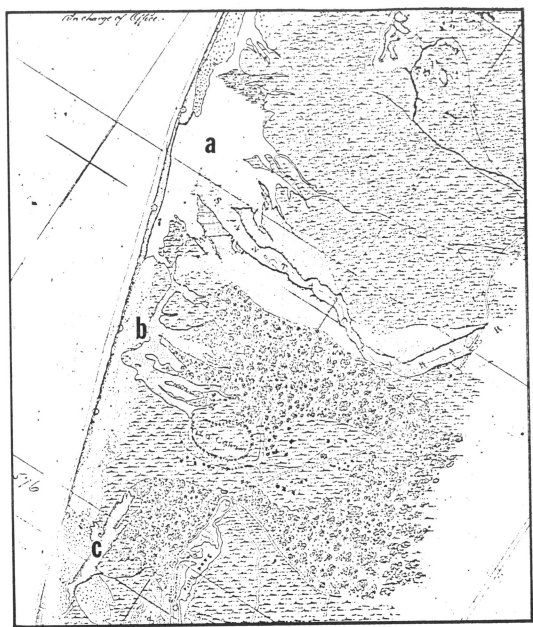

Figure 1.--1855 U.S. Coastal Survey map. Significant
points: a) Santa Clara River mouth and approximate
location of present Ventura Marina; b) approximate location of existing Santa Clara River mouth; c) estuary
and present location of McGrath Lake.

Example 2.--The textbook stream.

The "textbook" stream begins in the highest points of the drainage basin as
surface runoff or groundwater forming small, fast-moving brooks. Precipitation is
greater here than low lying areas, and weathering tends to be greater. These
first brooks are characterized by relatively cold, clear, fast-moving water. The
overall stream gradient is very steep. The stream tends to be quite erosive, but
little deposition occurs. The streambottom is irregular and primarily composed of
large rounded rocks which have been shaped by the turbulent, forceful movement of
water. The turbulence tends to increase the level of dissolved oxygen in the
water.

Example 2.--Continued.

As the brook moves downstream, it joins with other tributaries. The overall stream gradient becomes less steep, but the water continues to be fast-moving and turbulent. Both erosion and deposition are evident. The streambottom begins to be composed of small rocks, pebbles, and sand. The water is not quite as clear and contains some silt and clay particles in suspension.

As the stream moves out of the mountainous and hilly areas into the coastal plain, the gradient decreases even more. The streambottom is smoother and composed of sand, silt, and clay deposits. The volume of water is quite high, but the water moves much slower and with little turbulence. Deposition is much greater, and stream meander and braiding is more pronounced. Precipitation is much lower than in the mountain areas. Bank erosion is reduced considerably.

The "textbook" stream ends as the stream drains into the ocean. The stream may either form an embayment here or flow directly into the ocean. Gradients are very shallow, and deposition is at its greatest. The water often has low levels of dissolved oxygen and high levels of organic matter. There is usually a daily mix of salt water and fresh water (Clapham 1973).

Example 3.--Invertebrate adaption to water movement in streams.

The most conspicuous invertebrates in such situations are frequently aquatic insects which occur as immature forms as well as adults. Insects have been very successful in adapting to aquatic freshwater habitats and may be quite numerous. For example, in a study of a California stream, a single riffle area was found to be inhabited by almost 40 different species of insects (Reid 1961). Insects which live in rapidly moving water tend to be strongly modified so that they are not washed away by the current. They may be firmly attached to rocks, such as black fly larvae (Simulium sp.), or greatly streamlined, such as the naiads of some types of dragonflies (Order Odonata), mayflies (Order Ephemeroptera), and stoneflies (Order Plecoptera). Other insects solve the problem of current by living under or behind objects where the force of water is reduced. The larvae of dobsonflies (Family Corydalidae), caddisflies (Order Trichoptera), as well as a number of mayflies (Order Ephemeroptera) are characteristically found in such protected locations.

Example 4.--Requirements of fisheries.

Many of the streams in Ventura County still support a viable sport fishery. Although game species such as bluegill (Lepomis macrochirus), green sunfish (L. cyanellus), and large mouth bass (Micropterus salmoides) have been introduced and are found with some regularity in county streams, they are more characteristic of lakes. By far the most important game fish in the streams and rivers of Ventura County is the rainbow trout (Salmo gairdneri) and its ocean-going relative, the steelhead rainbow trout (S. g. gairdneri). Both of these fish are native to the county; however, populations of rainbow trout are supplemented with hatchery fish by the California Department of Fish and Game.

Rainbow trout require cool, clear, well-aerated water and are thus found in the larger, less-disturbed watercourses. Depending on the water conditions, trout in Ventura County generally begin spawning in late February (Moore 1979). The female builds a nest in clean gravel where she lays from 200 to 21,000 eggs. These are fertilized by the male, lightly covered with gravel, and abandoned. The young fish begin emerging from the spawning beds in about three weeks and usually reach catchable size within two years (Palmer and Fowler 1975).

Example 4.--Continued.

The steelhead rainbow trout has essentially the same spawning requirements as the rainbow trout, but differs in that it is anadromous. Anadromous fish are those which spend a portion of their life cycle in marine water but must enter fresh water to spawn. Probably because conditions for growth are optimum in the sea, steelhead trout attain a much larger size than do their non-migratory relatives.

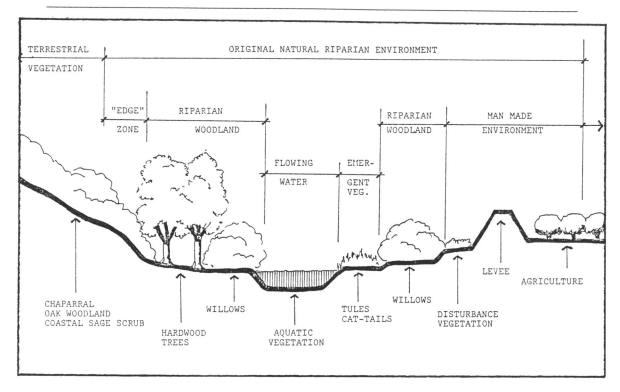

Figure 2.--A definition of plant associations in riparian areas.

Example 5.--Wildlife which use riparian areas.

In addition to providing food and habitat for endemic animals, riparian woodlands are also important to more wide-ranging species. In Ventura County, which experiences a long dry season, water can be a limiting factor to wildlife. The dense riparian plant growth provides cover for animals such as mule deer (Odocoileus hemionus californicus), which may spend most of their time elsewhere, but come to streams to drink. Riparian woodlands also serve as important migration routes for many species of animals, providing corridors with readily available food, water, and cover (Odum 1978).

Riparian Ecology.--The education program should discuss riparian ecology as a subject separate from that of biological resources so that the interdependence of aquatic, riparian, and terrestrial systems can be better understood. In addition to a general discussion of ecology, presenting the concept of energy exchange is useful. Figures 3 and 4 could be used to illustrate the concept of energy exchange.

Effects of Flood Control Activities.--We suggest that flood control organizations be given the stewardship responsibility for preserving and restoring riparian resources. A legitimate step in accomplishing that goal is to make those involved in flood control activities more fully aware of the effects of their actions. This is based on the premise that with understanding goes responsibility.

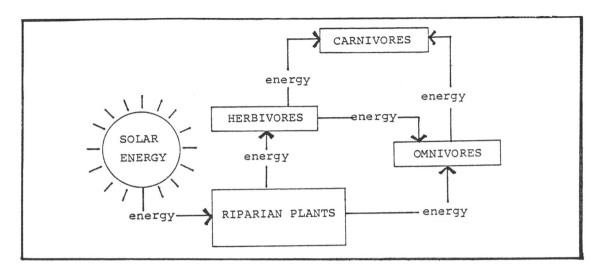

Figure 3.--General diagram of an energy system.

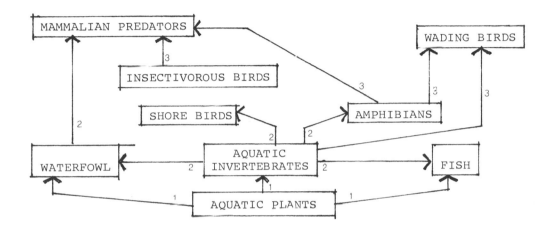

Figure 4.--A highly simplified, generalized food web. The
numbers next to the arrows indicate the trophic level
of the consumer. For example, a wading bird eating a
fish would function as a third-order consumer, while
the same bird eating an aquatic insect would be a second-order consumer. It should be noted that organisms
rarely feed consistently at one trophic level. Indeed,
omnivores such as the raccoon may feed at all levels,
utilizing a variety of plant and animal matter.

It is useful to first discuss the potential
(hypothetical) effects of flood control activities. The most obvious effect of flood control
activities is the confinement of the natural
floodplain. Associated with this are a decrease
in river meandering, reduced deposition of soils
and nutrients, and the separation of riparian systems from each other and from the stream. Other
potential effects are disruption of natural
stream elements and disruption of stream biology
and ecology. Example 6 presents a discussion of
the effects of induced turbidity and sedimentation on fish populations.

Discussions of environmental effects based
on past actions of the flood control organization
may be an effective educational tool, but pose a
threat to friendly open communication. This subject should be presented discreetly, and with a
minimum of personal judgment. As the program progresses, flood control personnel should have a
greater role in evaluating local projects and
their effects. An example of a 1978 emergency
project which weas evaluated during the preparation of the County's 208 Water Quality Management
Plan is contained in example 7.

Example 6.--Effects of turbidity on fish population.

During storm periods, water velocities are usually sufficient to keep sediment in suspension (Shaw and Maga 1943). However, when instream flood control activities take place during periods when the water flow is insufficient to carry the sediment in suspension, the sediments settle out and, in addition to reducing invertebrate populations, cover fish eggs and spawning sites, as well as preventing the emergence of recently hatched young (Cordone and Kelley 1961). Moore found that instream flood control work in the Ventura River and San Antonio Creek, in the spring of 1978, produced heavy sedimentation during the months when juvenile fish were emerging and resulted in depressed numbers of salmonids in subsequent sampling periods (Moore 1980).

Example 7.--Evaluation of the effects of a flood control project.

The diversity and richness of life in riparian systems is well documented throughout the world. They do not, of course, exist in isolation, but are part of the larger natural ecosystem. The "edge" between riparian systems and terrestrial systems becomes extremely important. Therefore, the confinement of natural floodplains, partially through flood control activities, allows the development of urban and agricultural uses immediately adjacent to streams and rivers. This has, in Ventura County, resulted in the separation of riparian vegetation from natural riparian areas and from terrestrial systems. The consequences are: a) loss or reduction of plant and wildlife species which have specifically adapted to the "edge" between riparian and terrestrial systems; b) blocking and loss of vegetative cover used by terrestrial wildlife in migrating to riparian areas for food and water; c) degradation of water quality where rising groundwater is trapped and isolated from the natural stream; and d) isolation of riparian areas from periodic flooding and the related supply of water and nutrients required for riparian plants. Without sufficient water and nutrients, riparian plant communities eventually are replaced by less biologically productive terrestrial vegetation (fig. 5).

Figure 5.--Separation of riparian areas: a) Highway 33; b) isolated area with ponding water and cattails; c) levee built in 1978 in the Ventura River just downstream of its confluence with San Antonio Creek. (Photograph taken in March, 1981).

Flood Control Activities and Equipment

The resource manager must become a student as well. He needs to understand certain basics of flood control activities before meaningful dialogue is possible. These basics include the fundamentals of flood control engineering, watershed management techniques, flood control structures, and maintenance equipment and operations. A grasp of flood control terminology will greatly assist the resource manager in achieving "healthy" communication. Finally, the resource manager will find it highly useful to understand the realities of the fiscal constraints under which the flood control organization operates.

The fundamentals of flood control engineering are primarily related to the principles of hydraulics, since the function of flood control operations is to contain floodwaters. Some important hydraulic principles that should be understood are presented below.

1. The quantity of water ("Q") passing any given point is a function of channel gradient and cross-sectional area and water velocity, and is usually expressed in cubic feet per second (cfs).

2. The ability of water to hold debris (rock, sand, silt, clay and organic materials) in suspension is primarily a function of channel gradient and water velocity. Therefore, water that is carrying near its capacity of suspended solids is less able to erode than water carrying less than its capacity.

3. Surface runoff and the consequent volume of floodflows is a function of the permeability of the land surface. Vegetated land dissipates the energy of rainfall and absorbs water in the soil and plants. Urban areas have a much greater proportion of impervious surfaces (paved surfaces and roofs) and generate a proportionally greater runoff. In fact, areas that are over 80% urban may generate twice the floodflow of a corresponding natural area (Waananen et al. 1977).

4. Water velocity is a function of gradient and the surface resistance of the channel bottom and banks. Rougher, rockier bottoms and sides tend to reduce velocities, while smoother surfaces (such as concrete) increase velocities.

Watershed management involves flood control activities which attempt to reduce runoff and erosion. These practices include revegetating bare soil and encouraging deep-rooted plants. It may also include fuel modification programs which help avoid excessive runoff, which commonly occurs after a large, uncontrollable fire. Most importantly, watershed management should provide for the acquisition of floodplains and their exclusion from agricultural and urban conversion.

Flood control structures range from relatively simple and unobtrusive facilities to those that completely control and subjugate natural processes. Some flood control dams are meant to permanently hold floodflows (reservoirs) or to hold flows temporarily (retention basins), so that peak discharges can be held and released over longer periods of time (fig. 6). Other dams (debris basins) are constructed primarily to reduce the velocity of flows and encourage the deposition of suspended solids behind the dam. This allows "cleaner" water to pass through the dam. While this decreases the deposition of material downstream, it leaves the cleaner water with greater potential energy for erosion. Often, in these cases, energy dissipation or drop structures are placed downstream.

Figure 6.--Flood retention dam, Sycamore Canyon Dam, Simi Valley, California.

Flood control structures which mainly confine the channel (usually called channel improvements) include levees, pilot channels, new earthen channels, trapezoidal channels with rock sideslopes, open concrete channels and concrete conduits (fig. 7).

The resource manager should become familiar with the equipment used in flood control activities. Each type of equipment has a purpose and a unique impact on riparian systems (fig. 8). Flood control maintenance operations often use this equipment to remove earth so that adequate channel capacity is maintained. This is more necessary where the channel is confined by urban or agricultural uses. However, riparian vegetation may also seriously reduce channel capacity by consuming cross-sectional volume and decreasing flow velocities. For this reason, flood control maintenance activities often involve the removal of riparian vegetation.

Figure 7.—Reinforced concrete box conduit under construction, Santa Susana West Drain, Simi Valley, California, 1974.

Figure 8.—Bulldozer and crane clearing debris after January, 1969 flood, Pole Creek, Fillmore, California.

Finally, the resource manager's education is not complete without some insight into the fiscal structure of the flood control organization. Any riparian resource management program will cost money to design and initiate. In the field, some of the best management practices may be more expensive to implement. Additionally, monitoring the program will require time and money. The resource manager should be prepared to answer inevitable questions about the costs of the program and how they relate to the total fiscal structure of the flood control organization. Unfortunately, he may find himself trying to bal-

ance the tangible fiscal costs of the program against the more intangible benefits of riparian resource preservation and restoration.

Define Environmentally Sensitive Management Practices

As already implied, those in flood control activities are, whether they know it or not, involved in riparian resource management. Structural projects, flood control maintenance, and monitoring of private development all require actions which affect riparian resources. The goal of the resource management program is to guide these activities in a more environmentally sensitive direction. The program should, therefore, provide direction to implement new "environmentally sensitive" management practices. Such practices will relate to the organization's own activities as well as those private sector activities over which it has authority.

Best Management Practices

The management practices suggested here are carefully thought out "clay pigeons." They were created out of the experiences and knowledge of the program participants. We expect them to change as their results are monitored and analyzed. The flood control personnel will evaluate the practices' effects on channel hydraulics and capacity, and the potential threat to life or property. The resource manager will evaluate the practices' effects on physical stream elements, biological productivity, etc. All participants in the program will collectively weigh the monetary and environmental cost:benefit relationships of the practices.

Environmentally sensitive mangement practices exerpted from the Ventura County's 208 Water Quality Management Plan, (approved in 1981), are presented in example 8. Most have not yet been applied in the field, so evaluation is difficult. Each is denoted as a best management practice (BMP) and numbered.

Annual Development Plan

The best management practices in example 8 are oriented toward the activities carried out by the flood control organization itself. However, there are similar activities carried out by the private sector over which the flood control organization often has some control. The most common of these private-sector activities is sand and gravel mining. In Ventura County, sand and gravel mining operations are required to obtain a watercourse permit to operate in any channel within the jurisdiction of the Ventura County Flood Control District. The primary purpose of this permit is to ensure that mining operations are not carried out in a manner which would create a potential flood danger.

Example 8.--Best management practices adopted by the Ventura
County Board of Supervisors.

BMP-1. Keep work in streams to an absolute minimum.

Description: Doing the minimum work necessary is, in most cases, something that results from budgetary constraints and good sense. It is, however, the most environmentally sound management practice that can be pursued and is, therefore, worthy of comment here.

Why needed: Streams are the result of millions of years of evolution. Man, however, has the capability of applying great amounts of energy (via earth-moving equipment) in a sudden manner and otherwise disrupting the ecological balance resulting from that evolutionary process.

No amount of money or human effort can result in an exact duplication of nature. Given a million years, certain riparian species may adapt to or even be dependent upon the changes man is able to make through flood control activities. Now, however, the best we can hope to do, even with good management practices, is to assist nature in restoring damaged portions of the ecosystems. Therefore, the best management practice is to disturb this unique, important environmental resource as little as possible.

BMP-2. Where flood control activities are necessary, maintain a portion of the stream in its natural condition and isolate it from the required work.

Description: There are a number of ways in which this management practice can be achieved. Where work must be done in an area where one main channel exists, it may be possible to leave one side of the channel intact. It may be possible to selectively leave portions of the stream vegetation on both sides. In either case, it is essential to maintain the main stream flow adjacent to or through those riparian areas left intact.

Where it is necessary to work in a riparian area that contains more than one channel, it is desirable to leave at least one channel intact with a "buffer zone" of riparian vegetation of at least 50 feet on each side of the flowing water. This normally requires the insertion of a "soft plug" at the upstream terminus of the channels. The "soft plug" should be engineered to maintain low flows in the channel left intact, but allow larger storm flows to wash out the plug.

When there exists a choice of preserving one of several channels, the most environmentally sound choice involves consideration of several factors. These factors include: Proximity to other terrestrial habitats, time of year, existence of unique aquatic resources such as pools, riffle and spawning beds, etc. It is desirable to seek the advice of qualified experts in considering these factors, such as the California Department of Fish and Game and the USDI Fish and Wildlife Service.

Why needed: This management practice will be, in many cases, the fastest, most economical and most environmentally sound technique for preserving riparian resources. Except for the diversion of flows, it does little to the area left intact. During dry periods or when natural flows are being diverted upstream, it may be an "aquatic plus" by concentrating low flows into one channel. If the same low flow channel is used over a period of several years, it allows for the growth of mature riparian plant communities.

BMP-3. Where the earth must be physically moved, store the top two to three feet of material and redistribute after the work is completed.

Description: This practice involves the skimming off of observable nutrient-laden soils, stockpiling them and then redistributing them over finished work areas. This is a desirable practice, particularly near new stream channels. It is extremely important, however, that stockpiled material not be pushed into flowing water. This practice should be employed in rocky sandy stream areas where nutrients (in clay and silts) are scarce. This practice need not be utilized where stream gradients and adjacent soil profiles provide a rich abundance of soil nutrients.

Example 8.--Continued.

Why needed: One of the most basic characteristics of streams and rivers is that they carry materials from upstream areas and deposit them in downstream areas. Some of these materials are nutrients essential to aquatic and terrestrial species along streams and rivers. As flood flows decrease, these nutrients deposit along the receding stream along with native plant seeds and soil dwelling organisms. Since many of the desirable elements do not remain for long, the riparian plant community has adapted by being extremely fast growing and hardy. Nevertheless, even the riparian plants cannot grow well (or at all) without essential nutrients. Unfortunately, many control practices remove or bury nutrient-laden soils. They also remove them from their essential close proximity to the flowing water. This not only results in the reduction (or absence) of riparian plant species, but also promotes higher water temperatures (from less shade), less dissolved oxygen, less wildlife cover, etc.

BMP-4. Where earth work is required, restore natural features such as meanders, pools, turbulence and braiding.

Description: The primary aim of this management practice is not to replace visual aesthetics (although that is a legitimate goal). Rather, the purpose is to assist nature in bringing the disturbed riparian environment back to its desired ecological balance. The manner in which these natural features are restored depends on the previous "natural" circumstances. In a large river system such as the Santa Clara system, it may be appropriate to cut new channels, encourage meander and build pool areas with heavy equipment. In a smaller system such as the Ventura system, it may be appropriate in some areas to create small falls and pools by hand.

In utilizing this management practice, there are no pre-set plans which can be applied to a specific situation. Each stream area will likely have a unique combination of stream elements. A degree of subjective judgment must be used in deciding how to restore natural stream elements. While there is not necessarily a "right" solution, there are "better" solutions. Obviously, the "better" solution is going to result from careful evaluation of the natural stream elements and knowledge of the probable consequences of flood control work. In most situations, the evaluation should be done in the field with input from a qualified maintenance supervisor and a qualified biologist. The primary factors to be covered in the evaluation are found in "Work Sheet for Field Evaluations" [example 9].

Once this evaluation is made, initial decisions can be made as to which natural features are to be restored. Some decisions must be made as work progresses and will require a degree of creativity on the part of the maintenance supervisor. Even though each situation will be unique, there are certain benchmark criteria which can be useful in making field decisions. These "benchmarks" are defined below.

Benchmark Criteria for Restoring Natural Stream Features.

1. Place a 1 to 2-ft. fall at approximately 1/8 mile intervals.
2. Creation of depressions for ponds should be in a ratio of approximately 3:1 with the adjacent stream (i.e., a 3-ft. wide pool would be in proportion to a 1-ft. wide stream).
3. Construct potential stream channels that will meander, rather than flow in a straight line where work exceeds 1/8 mile in length.
4. In all areas except ponds, leave bottoms rough and irregular rather than smooth.
5. Use existing elements, such as large rocks over 4-ft. in diameter and existing falls as much as possible.
6. Use hand methods in creating smaller falls, pools and braiding.

Why needed: The natural features of a stream can be best described as nature's most efficient and diversified molding of the physical environment. The biological environment has evolved to take maximum advantage of these natural features in an evolutionary process which has taken millions of years. Unfortunately man, through flood control activities, has the capacity to disrupt these natural features and therefore place stress on the biological environment. However, some of these features can be replaced or at least assisted back.

856

Example 8.--Continued.

BMP-5. Install culverts, silt curtains and other devices
that control turbidity where work must be conducted in
or adjacent to stream water.

The effects of turbidity on aquatic ecosystems have been discussed. The previous discussion of other best management practices has stressed the need to avoid work in flowing water unless absolutely necessary. If flood control activities are necessary in stream waters, there are a number of ways in which habitat destruction and stream turbidity can be minimized. The following general criteria should be used in applying this management technique.

1. Where equipment must cross flowing water on more than one occasion, install a pipe culvert of sufficient capacity to handle existing flows. The pipe invert should be at or slightly below the existing stream bottom at both ends. Use clean sand and rock to cover the pipe and avoid the use of silts and clays.

2. Where equipment must work adjacent to a stream or pond, establish a barrier to keep equipment and soil from getting in the water. The best barrier is distance and no barrier is necessary if work is in excess of 20-ft. from the edge of water. The next best barrier is native vegetation and no additional barrier is needed if a 20-ft. wide strip of vegetation greater than 6-ft. high remains between the water and the work.

Where work must be conducted closer than 20-ft., a temporary barrier of large rock and sand 2- to 4-ft. high can be constructed. In unique circumstances, a temporary barrier of wood or metal may be used.

3. Where work must be conducted directly in water and flows cannot be diverted, the work should be completed as quickly as possible. In larger water bodies, and where flow velocities permit, plastic silt curtains should be placed down from the work. In faster flowing water, a series of small falls (2- to 3-ft.) can be constructed of larger rock to slow water and encourage the deposition of silts and clays.

Why needed: The primary purpose of this management practice is to avoid the direct and indirect destruction of aquatic systems. Direct effects include the removal of natural stream elements such as pools, falls, rapids, spawning beds, etc. Indirect effects include the disruption of key elements of the overall riparian system and the creation of turbidity which is carried downstream. Increased downstream turbidity may cover spawning beds and benthic (bottom) organisms. It may reduce total dissolved oxygen in the water and otherwise place additional stress on fish, aquatic plants and other aquatic organisms. Finally, turbidity can affect aquatic systems for many miles downstream of the occurrence.

Past experience with watercourse permits indicated that the conditions defined in some permits were not always consistent with those defined in permits required by other agencies. Specifically, it was found that the conditions of the watercourse permit and the Stream Alteration Agreement required by the California Fish and Game Code were sometimes at odds. Therefore, in the interest of better cooperation and resource management, the Ventura County Flood Control District initiated the Annual Development Plan (ADP) process in 1978. A typical annual development plan is developed according to the general schedule defined below.

1. Early spring--The sand and gravel company obtains aerial photographs and topography maps of the proposed excavation site after the winter rains are over.

2. April--The company submits a proposed ADP which includes the aerial photographs, topography and proposed vertical and horizontal extent of excavation for the coming year.

3. May--Meetings are held with the applicant, flood control district engineers, and representatives of the California Department of Fish and Game (DFG). The purpose of these meetings is to identify the concerns of each party and to reach agreement on a plan.

4. May to June--Once a compromise agreement is reached, the ADP is finalized. The final ADP consists of: a) an aerial photograph with horizontal elements identified (for example, see figure 9); b) topography maps, cross sections and profiles defining vertical elements; c) the watercourse permit for the year; d) the DFG permit.

Figure 9.--Aerial photograph indicating typical items agreed
upon for an Annual Development Plan: a) area of potential excavation; b) wildlife corridor from mountainous
area to top of photo; c) soft plug; d) haul road; e)
low-flow corridor.

The Annual Development Plan process has proven to be reasonably successful in preserving
riparian resources. All ADPs issued thus far
have preserved a riparian corridor through excavation areas. A minimum buffer zone of 12-15 m.
(40-50 ft.) on either side of the "low-flow"
stream (fig. 9) has been maintained. Wildlife
migration corridors have been identifed and reserved. Culverts are required at all stream crossings to protect the aquatic environment from
turbidity. Finally, there has been an effort to
create and maintain permanent low-flow areas and
preserve significant mature riparian areas.

Implement and Monitor the Program

Implementation of the best management practices marks the true beginning of the riparian
resource management program. Political commitment, a healthy communication environment, and a
successful education program mean little without
measurable physical improvement in riparian resources. Therefore, in order to evaluate the continued relative value of the program, monitoring
activities are suggested. Areas of the program
which should be monitored are discussed below.

Policy Guidelines

As the resource program progresses, it
should be evaluated periodically for consistency
with the adopted policy guidelines of the local
decision-making body. Lessons learned in the
field may suggest new management practices.
Flood control personnel and the resource manager

may find it prudent to recommend new policies commensurate with the new management practices. In
any case, the decision-making body should receive
annual reports from the staff in order to evaluate for themselves the consequences of their
policy.

Education Program

The education program is an ongoing tool
which allows the participants to make intelligent
decisions about the best management practices and
other field tools. The content of the education
program should be periodically reviewed by the
participants to see if it fits their level of
expertise. New personnel will need to be made
familiar with the background and the goals of the
program.

Best Management Practices

As discussed earlier, the best management
practices listed in example 8 are meant to change
as field experience dictates. The monitoring of
the best management practices should be systematically recorded. Photographs should be taken at
least four times a year to record any changes in
the managed area. Both ground-level and aerial
photographs are desirable. The flood control
personnel may also wish to monitor changes in
stream elevations. This type of information is
usually obtained from stereo-aerial photographs.

Evaluation of the best management practices
should also be recorded in writing. For this pur-

858

Example 9.--Work sheet for field evaluations.

I. PHYSICAL FEATURES

     A. Name of channel _____
     B. Flood Zone _____   C. Location _____
                                                  _____
     D. Stream width _____ E. Approximate flow _____
     F. Braiding?_____   How many? _____
     G. Type of bottom: Rocky_____ Gravels_____ Sand_____
         Silt_____
     H. Water clarity: Clear_____ Turbid_____
     I. Visual appearance of stream (attach pictures if taken)
         _____
         _____

II. BIOLOGICAL FEATURES

     A. Dominant riparian vegetation: Willow_____ Mule Fat_____
         Giant Cain_____   Sycamore_____   Alder_____
         Cottonwood_____   Other _____
     B. Aquatic vegetation: Tules_____   Cattails_____
         Watercress_____   Algae_____   Pond Weed_____
         Other _____
     C. Wildlife observed:
         1. Invertebrates _____
         2. Mammals _____
         3. Birds _____
         4. Fish _____
     D. Apparent biological productivity of area _____
         _____

pose, a "Worksheet for Field Evaluations" was created for the Ventura County 208 Water Quality Management Plan and is shown in example 9. The back of the worksheet provides space for a graphic plan of action and for biological and maintenance comments.

CONCLUSION

Flood control operations have a significant and often severe impact on riparian resources in California. The traditional approach of flood control organizations is to consider public safety as its only function. However, with local political support, improved communication, education, and better management practices, it is possible to assist flood control oganizations in accepting responsibility for the stewardship of riparian resources.

This concept may not be acceptable to some, particularly those more accustomed to bureaucratic combat with flood control organizations. Nevertheless, such a program has been initiated in Ventura County and appears to offer considerable promise. It is suggested that local organizations should be given the responsibility for riparian resource management rather than being burdened by yet another state mandate.

LITERATURE CITED

Clapham, W.B., Jr. 1973. Natural ecosystems. 248 p. Macmillan Company. New York, N.Y.

Cordone, E., and D.W. Kelley. 1961. The influence of inorganic sediments on the aquatic life of streams. Calif. Fish and Game 47(2).

Gibb, J.R. 1973. Defensive communication. p. 284-291. In: C. D. Mortensen. Basic readings in communication theory. 358 p. Harper and Row, New York, N.Y.

Lockard, W.M., and R.A. Burgess. 1981. Technical paper for conducting flood control activities in Ventura County. 71 p. Ventura County Public Works Agency, Flood Control and Water Resources Department, Ventura, Calif.

Moore, M.R. 1979. Stream survey: Ojai Ranger District, Los Padres National Forest. 29+ p. USDA Forest Service.

Moore, M.R. 1980. Factors influencing the survival of juvenile steelhead rainbow trout (Salmo gairdneri gairdneri) in the Ventura River, California. 82 p. M.S. Thesis, Humboldt State University, Arcata, Calif.

Odum, E.P. 1978. Ecological importance of the riparian zone. p. 2-4. In R.R. Johnson and J.F. McCormick (tech. coord.). Strategies for protection and management of floodplain wetlands and other riparian ecosystems: Proceedings of the symposium. [Callaway Gardens, Georgia, December 11-13, 1978.] USDA Forest Service GTR-WO-12, Washington, D.C. 410 p.

Palmer, E.L. 1975. Fieldbook of natural history. Second edition (revised by H.S. Fowler). 779 p. McGraw-Hill Book Company, New York, N.Y.

Reid, G.K. 1961. Ecology of inland waters and estuaries. 375 p. D. Van Nostrand Co., New York, N.Y.

Shaw, P.A., and J.A. Maga. 1943. The effect of mining silt on yield of fry from salmon spawning beds. Calif. Fish and Game 29(1): 29-41.

Ventura County Public Works Agency, Flood Control and Water Resources Department. 1981. Operator's manual for conducting flood control activities in Ventura County streams and rivers. 21 p. Ventura County Flood Control and Water Resources Department, Ventura, Calif.

Waananen, A.O., J.T. Limerinos, and W.J. Kockelman, et al. 1977. Flood-prone areas and land-use planning—selected examples from the San Francisco Bay Region, California. Geological Survey Professional Paper 942. 75 p. U.S. Government Printing Office, Washington, D.C.

Watzlawick, P., J.H. Beavin, and D.D. Jackson. 1967. Pragmatics of human communication. 296 p. W.W. Norton and Company, New York, N.Y.

Webster's Seventh New Collegiate Dictionary. 1971. 1,222 p. G. and C. Merriam Company, Springfield, Mass.

MANAGEMENT OPTIONS FOR DRY CREEK RIPARIAN CORRIDOR

INCLUDING FORMATION OF A LOCAL LAND TRUST[1]

Elgar Hill and Peter Straub[2]

Abstract.--The US Army Corps of Engineers has recognized several administrative options for management of riparian systems which will be affected by operation of Warm Springs Dam, on Dry Creek, Sonoma County, California. This paper presents information and draws preliminary conclusions regarding the viability of the various options.

INTRODUCTION

In 1978, Richard L. Bailey[3] (1978) presented a paper titled: "The Warm Springs Riparian Dilemma." The paper described conflicts relating to riparian issues on Dry Creek, Sonoma County, California. He described the effects of the construction and operation of Warm Springs Dam, by the US Army Corps of Engineers (CE), which would include:

1) inundation of riparian zone above the dam;
2) controlled release of water at the dam, with increase in summer flows;
3) smolts released into the stream from the hatchery below the dam, with adult steelhead and salmon returning to spawn;
4) elimination of severe winter flooding and erosion;
5) clear water release, with increased erosive power.

Secondary effects would include:
1) requirement to mitigate for lost habitat;
2) recreationist use of the stream for canoeing with possible trespass problems;
3) fishermen seeking access to the stream;
4) landowners planting crops closer to the stream;
5) stream degradation with increase in bank erosion.

The "dilemma" was first brought to public attention with the Warm Springs Dam and Lake Sonoma Project Environmental Impact Statement (US Army Corps of Engineers 1973), which included a discussion of impacts relating to inundation of riparian systems, and by a report issued by the USDI Fish and Wildlife Service (FWS),[4] which called for mitigation measures. One of the suggested mitigation measures was Federal purchase of the stream-bed and riparian lands downstream from the dam. In response to this report, the CE made a commitment to consider provision of riparian protection and public access. Strong opposition to fee acquisition from local landowners led to discussion of other administrative options.

Bailey (1978) also discussed the planning process relating to maintenance of the riparian vegetation. He stated that CE policies regarding the public interest in riparian areas downstream from major water resource projects are poorly defined. The extent of CE responsibility for maintenance of present conditions downstream is uncertain (other than for erosion control), despite extensive changes in the environment caused by the dam's operation. He charted the evolution of several administrative/legal tools that could be used to protect the integrity of the riparian zone, including:

1. fee acquisition of the riparian zone;
2. purchase of a conservation easement;
3. an easement held by a local land trust.

These suggestions were made by agency representatives and local landowners during preparation of a Master Plan for Lake Sonoma[5] which included a public participation program. No specific recom-

[1]Paper presented at the California Riparian Systems Conference. [University of California, Davis, September 17-19, 1981].

[2]Elgar Hill (AIA, MLA) is Principal Environmental Planner with Elgar Hill Environmental Analysis and Planning, Sausilito, Calif. Peter Straub (MLA) is a Landscape Architect with the US Army Corps of Engineers, San Francisco District, California.

[3]Richard L. Bailey is a fish and wildlife biologist with the USDI Fish and Wildlife Service, Atlanta, Georgia. He was formerly with the US Army Corps of Engineers, San Francisco District.

[4]Untitled report. July 24, 1978. Sacramento area office, USDI Fish and Wildlife Service.

[5]Royston, Hanamoto, Beck, and Abey. October, 1979. Master plan for Lake Sonoma. Prepared for the US Army Corps of Engineers, San Francisco District.

mendations concerning the extent of government involvement were made in the Master Plan.

The following statement appears in the Master Plan document:

> Proposals for treatment of Dry Creek and its banks from the downstream limits of Corps property to the Russian River have been discussed in a series of workshops held concurrently with the Lake Sonoma master planning process. Based on public input and agency review, there will be no land acquisition for public access to Dry Creek in connection with the project and the streambed will not be acquired by the government. It appears that the protection of existing riparian habitat along the stream is desirable. A committee has been established by local interests to investigate alternative methods for preserving riparian vegetation. Prior to any kind of riparian habitat acquisition by the Corps, it would be necessary to secure Congressional authorization through a post-authorization change report.

Recently, the CE has let a contract for a special study and an environmental impact statement to study alternatives, including those listed above, and to assist in identifying the extent of Federal involvement in the protection of riparian systems.[6] The study has been under way for several months. No decisions regarding a preferred alternative are expected for some time. It is hoped that a consensus will be reached and administrative action will be taken as a result of this study.

As a result of our involvement in this study, it is now possible to add more information and to draw preliminary conclusions relating to administrative approaches.

Several questions arise.

1. Will the riparian systems, following the changes brought about by the Lake Sonoma project, require additional protection and management beyond that which individual landowners are willing and able to give?

2. If so, how effective would be the various administrative procedures which are being proposed?

3. What are some of the requirements for implementation of the various procedures?

4. Can the results of the special downstream report and environmental impact statement, for the Warm Springs Dam-Lake Sonoma Project be extrapolated to other, similar projects?

This paper will endeavor to provide some preliminary answers to these questions. Some further background information will be provided in order to give the reader a better understanding of the special conditions which could affect the decisionmaking process.

SETTING

The Dry Creek Valley is part of the Russian River watershed, and has an economy based on viticulture. The valley is small, 2.4 km. (1.5 mi.) wide and 22.4 km. (14 mi.) long from the dam to the confluence with the Russian River. The moist soil riparian zone extends out beyond the present narrow corridor of remaining riparian vegetation immediately adjacent to Dry Creek itself. It has been largely cleared of its riparian vegetation to permit intensive agricultural use of the rich alluvial soils. It is the remaining narrow streamside corridor of riparian vegetation, rather than the entire riparian zone, that is being considered here.

Land ownerships on both sides of the creek number less than 100. Many of the parcels are small (some less than 4.2 ha. (10 ac.)) but intensively cultivated, because of the present high return on the sale of wine grapes. There is no such thing as a "typical" Dry Creek rancher; tenure ranges from three generations to very recent and from owner-operator to absentee landlord.

It has been estimated that the surrounding region could generate a potential annual visitation at Lake Sonoma of 2,479,000 recreation days. Based on carrying capacity of the lake environs, visitation of 1,520,000 recreation days per year is anticipated. A total of 5,400 vehicle trips per day along Dry Creek Road are predicted for peak recreation periods.[5] All of these visitors will pass through the valley on their way to the dam. Some overflow of recreational activity onto the creek itself could be expected, such as fishing, boating, and off-road vehicle traffic.

Fishing activity can be regulated by the California Department of Fish and Game (DFG). No fishing will be allowed until the dam is completed and the lake filled to capacity, anticipated in 1985. Fishing can be limited to steelhead, the normal season for which is in mid-winter, thus attracting a hardier, more serious angler. The impact of steelhead fishing at prescribed access points would not be as great as would that of summer angling, if it were allowed. Flows in the creek would be high during the winter, and dense vegetation would inhibit streambank use by fishermen, so that access to the stream would be physically limited at this time of year.

---

[6]Elgar Hill Environmental Analysis and Planning. In preparation. Special report and environmental impact statement downstream, Warm Springs Dam-Lake Sonoma Project.

Travel downstream by canoe and raft could have a greater impact than fishing, if access to the upper end of the stream were allowed. Experience on the nearby Russian River shows the popularity of such excursions. At least 750 canoes make the Russian River trip on a peak use day. The recreationists stop for a swim, a picnic lunch, etc., on their way downstream. The riparian vegetation quickly becomes damaged, the soil surface becomes packed, and seedlings are trampled at those points. Unwanted vegetation, such as thistles, find an advantage under such conditions. On Dry Creek, it appears that fences would be required to inhibit recreationists from venturing into the vineyards.

A possible advantage to constant summer flows will be discouragement of 4-wheel-drive vehicle enthusiasts who presently find their way into the Dry Creek bottom. Their vehicles loosen sand and gravel on gravelbars and make it easier for current to shift sediment further downstream. Damage to the vegetation and streambanks from 4-wheel-drive vehicles had been observed.

If administration remains with individual ranchers, no cohesive program of dealing with large scale recreation use can be expected. Each landowner will be responsible for protection of his streambank and crops.

Although many ranchers have stated that they are capable of maintaining their own streambank and riparian vegetation, there is evidence to show that exceptions exist. While it may be true that many of the landowners have sufficient streambank management capability and experience, ownerships in the valley are constantly changing. In the past few years, six to seven parcels each year (5%) have changed hands.[7] There is no way to predict how many of the new owners (for instance, those landowners using the property for tax write-off), will successfully manage their property and be dedicated to preserving the riparian vegetation.

It has been documented (California Division of Mines and Geology 1977) that piecemeal bank protection procedures by individual landowners can lead to destruction of the neighbor's property on the opposite bank. When streamflows are impeded, the stream's energy may be redirected toward the other bank, depending on the type and location of the protection measure with respect to meander potential of the stream. Streamflows in the future will be more constant and the impact of major storms will be dampened by regulation of flows at the dam, so that the erosive energy of the stream should be less. It remains to be seen, however, how much water would have to be released following a major storm (25- to 100-year event) and what would be the effect. It has also been predicted that constant flows will produce a bottom-scouring effect immediately downstream from the dam which could downgrade the channel and cause future bank sloughing.[8]

If no legal/administrative action were taken, it is possible that management practices would continue as before. It is also possible that new owners would be either more or less responsible in riparian management than in the past. It appears that limited access for steelhead fishing would not appreciably damage the riparian zone. On the other hand, potential impacts to the riparian corridor from large-scale boating use would be significant without more cohesive management.

Past experience shows that greatly increased pressure for alternative land use resulting from reservoir construction leads to zoning changes. If the present high return for agricultural investment does not continue, the pressure for zoning changes will further increase.

Without some sort of consistent management of the riparian corridor in the future, there is no guarantee that it will remain in its present condition. The present condition of the Dry Creek riparian system is not of the same quality as it was 25 years ago. The channel has downgraded, streambanks have been eroded, and the channel is much wider than before. Vegetative bank stabilization has included planting of willows and exotic bamboo, resulting in less variety in the vegetation. Higher, steeper banks do not support riparian vegetation as well as the low, sloping contours did in the past.[9] Mature riparian vegetation no longer exists in many places, and a view of what the stream was like 25 years ago can be seen in only a few stretches of the remaining stream. Past farming practices, gravel extraction, and major floods have taken their toll on the quality of streambank riparian vegetation and wildlife habitat potential. However, there is still much habitat value remaining in comparison with other streams in the area.[9] Past bank stabilization efforts have had positive effects. CE channel improvements,[10] combined with controlled releases from Warm Springs Dam, should make future revegetation work feasible. An organized riparian system management program would result in increased habitat value along the stream as well as providing bank stabilization benefits. The results of earlier individual stabilization efforts seem to indicate that well-

_____

[7] Harding, Bruce. 1981. Appraisal report for Dry Creek habitat area, Sonoma County, California. Report to be included in the special report and environmental impact statement.[6]

_____

[8] US Army Corps of Engineers hydrologist. 1981. Personal communication.
[9] McBride, Joe; and Jan Strahan. 1981. Fluvial geomorphic process, bank stabilization, and controlled streamflow effects upon riparian vegetation along Dry Creek, Sonoma County, Calif. Report to be included in the special report and environmental impact statement.[6]
[10] US Army Corps of Engineers, San Francisco District. May, 1981. Design memorandum no. 18, channel improvements, Russian River basin, Dry Creek, Warm Springs Dam and Lake Sonoma project.

planned and implemented revegetation programs could not only stabilize but build up streambanks, depending on future streamflow patterns.

FEDERAL INVOLVEMENT

Three administrative tools involving Federal money or effort have been identified:

1) fee acquisition of all or part of the riparian corridor.
2) conservation easement purchase of the riparian corridor, to be managed by a Federal or State agency.
3) provision of funds for management by a local agency, independent organization (such as a land trust), or farmers group.

Any of these measures would provide consistent management of the entire stream. The first two would carry guarantees of long-term enforcement of regulations and maintenance of riparian vegetation. In the third case, with local management, long-term maintenance would be dependent upon the terms and amounts of the funding. Federal involvement implies, to a degree, removal of local control. The degree of Federal involvement would depend on the details of the specific arrangement. Fee acquisition would obviously imply the greatest shift in control from the current situation; local control would be limited to those rights specifically excluded from the transfer. Whichever agency became responsible for the property would need to implement rules and regulations which best serve the general public. Further maintenance may conflict with those for recreational users and with those of agricultural production. These conflicts may be real (use of land for riparian vegetation vs. crops) or they may only be perceived at this time (will the presence of fishermen or canoeists destroy habitat or crops?). In either case, the conflicts require close attention, since limitations on property and riparian rights will be involved.

Fee Acquisition

This option would transfer all rights to ownership and use of the riparian corridor, with the exception of specifically excluded rights, such as water supply. Special rights to use of the stream would also be forfeited, unless specifically retained by present owners. Some owners have supplemented their incomes through gravel sales; all landowners feel strongly about control of the stream. Some owners do not have stream ownership; others own nothing but stream bottom. Compensation, whether monetary or other, would be of considerable magnitude.

The financial value of the riparian corridor, including the stream channel, would be considerable, depending on how the property is assessed. Values could vary from $500 to $10,000 per acre, depending on the assumptions made during the appraisal.[7] The total would depend on the width of the riparian zone, whether the area above the streambank edge is to be considered agricultural land, and what value is assigned to the gravel resource. Purchase of lands by transfer to a Federal agency would require Congressional approval, a long process with no guarantee of success.

Conservation Easement

A conservation easement limits the use of the land. In order to understand what limits should be set, information regarding the resource and its protection must be acquired. In the case of the Dry Creek riparian corridor, an appraisal of the resource value, as well as the land value, is required. The preferred boundaries of the riparian corridor must be carefully selected, for they will become the basis of the conservation easement. Most of this information has already been compiled for Dry Creek.

Once use limits and the conservation easement (riparian corridor) boundaries are set, and the potential for loss of the resource as a result of management deficiencies is established, management techniques and maintenance procedures can be developed relating to planting; plant succession; monitoring and policing; thinning; selective cutting; pesticide use; and access limitation in terms of types of vehicles, numbers of people, etc.

Although the cost of this option would be much less than that for fee acquisition, Congressional approval would still be necessary. A conservation easement would deed to the Government only those rights deemed necessary for protection of the riparian corridor.

Once the rights have been purchased, and needs relating to management of the riparian corridor have been identified, responsibility for management must be established along with the sources of funds. Management responsibility could be taken over by an agency with experience in wildlife habitat management, such as the DFG. On the other hand, responsibility could be placed with a private organization, a land trust.

Land Trust

A land trust is a mechanism for acquisition of an interest in land for conservation purposes. The formation of a trust takes advantage of current tax laws designed to encourage permanent open space preservation. Taxes affected include income, capital gains, estate, and property taxes. In the case of Dry Creek, most of the landowners are not in a position to greatly benefit from tax breaks. Other advantages, such as streambank protection and limitation of trespassing through consistent management, may prove more important.

Long-term maintenance of open space for wildlife habitat requires not only some form of legal transfer of land or interest in land, but also enforcement of regulations and monitoring of habitat quality. A land trust would need to be endowed with sufficient funds to provide adequate monitoring and enforcement. The money could be held in a legal defense fund, where the interest can be used for normal expenses and the principal drawn upon only in emergencies. Once the decision to transfer the property(ies) has been made (based on management requirements for the protection of the resource), the main duties of the trust would be monitoring and enforcement. In order to monitor the resource, an understanding of the resource is necessary so that it is clear what problems to look for and when to monitor. Regulations affecting the protection of the resource should be fully spelled out, so that enforcement can be adequately carried out.

A trust organization should be independent of local landowner(s). If not, conflicts could occur between management for riparian resource value and management for agricultural resource value. The organization can be any entity capable of handling financial and legal matters involved with maintenance of a contract. The organization should be nonprofit and tax exempt, and incorporated under State and Federal law.

In the case of the Dry Creek riparian corridor, a group of landowners could advise the trust organization in such areas as definition of the resource, and determination of management procedures for processing complaints and suggestions. A presently operating land trust available to handle the protection of the Dry Creek riparian corridor is the Sonoma Land Trust. The Sonoma Land Trust is successfully managing several properties in Sonoma County. Some of these properties were outright gifts; others are the result of conservation easements. None of these properties exhibit the multiplicity of ownership or management complexity inherent at Dry Creek.

CONCLUSION

A consensus has yet to be reached regarding administration of the Dry Creek riparian corridor. Whether one of the options listed above will be chosen remains to be seen. It is unlikely that the riparian corridor will continue to function as a habitat for fish and wildlife with the present multiple ownership and lack of cohesive response to the impending changes. Some of the preceding statements are necessarily speculative at this time; it will be years before the reservoir is filled, and flows in the creek become standardized. It is obvious that significant changes in physical and economic relationships will come about as a result of establishment of the dam and the reservoir. Meanwhile, decisions need to be made regarding the future of the riparian corridor.

Bringing about a consensus will be very difficult. The linear nature of the stream increases the problems involved in reaching a consensus regarding property rights transfer. Most projects managed through a land trust are individual parcels; the transfer has been successful because the original owner was able to financially benefit through tax savings. This would not be the case in many situations at Dry Creek; other ways of compensating landowners, such as direct payments, would probably be necessary. There may be sufficient advantages to the landowners (in terms of protection from trespass, for instance), other than financial, to make the transfer worthwhile. It is hoped that the present process, resulting in an environmental impact statement which lays out the advantages of potentially viable alternatives and includes information from all interested parties, will indicate the correct administrative path to take for riparian system protection.

When the original commitment was made, in 1976, to investigate the potential for mitigation for the loss of riparian system values, the complexity of such an undertaking was not well recognized. In order to successfully prepare a workable plan for the protection of threatened riparian systems in a democratic society, early recognition of the concerns of the affected public and knowledge of the legal complications of land and riparian rights transfer is essential. All interested Federal, State, local, and private organizations need to be contacted and given an opportunity to make their needs and opinions known. Only then can any path be charted to a workable riparian protection plan.

LITERATURE CITED

Bailey, Richard L. 1978. The Warm Springs riparian dilemma. p. 365-369. In: R.R. Johnson and J.F. McCormick (tech. coord.). Strategies for protection and management of floodplain wetlands and other riparian ecosystems: Proceedings of the symposium. [Callaway Gardens, Ga., December 11-13, 1978]. USDI Forest Service GTR-WO-12, 410 p. Washington, D.C.

California Division of Mines and Geology. 1977. Erosion along Dry Creek, Sonoma County, California. Special report 134.

US Army Corps of Engineers. 1973. Final environmental impact statement Warm Springs Dam and Lake Sonoma project, Russian River basin. Office of the Chief, US Army Corps of Engineers, Washington, D.C.

FEDERAL WETLANDS PROTECTION UNDER

THE RIVERS AND HARBORS ACT OF 1899:

AN HISTORICAL OVERVIEW[1]

Kent G. Dedrick[2]

Abstract.--The nation's wetlands, ranging from small streams to major navigation channels, now enjoy protection under Section 404 of the Clean Water Act and Sections 9 and 10 of the Rivers and Harbors Act of 1899. Both acts have increasingly been the subjects of hard-fought court actions and Congressional debate. U.S. Army Corps of Engineers (CE) jurisdiction and historical developments dealing with the 1899 Act are summarized here. Examples of CE jurisdiction and permit and enforcement activities, mainly dealing with the San Francisco Bay estuarine system, are given.

INTRODUCTION

Estuaries and fresh water streams are clearly essential to California's inland and ocean fisheries. In addition, riparian wetlands and forest systems are equally dependent upon adjacent waterways, as they serve both to irrigate riparian vegetation and to provide a food supply for avian, amphibian, and mammalian inhabitants of the riparian system. Because of this, biologists, engineers, and citizens interested in these areas can profit from a basic understanding of the governmental protections that are available to prevent damage to waterways.

In some states, waterways are subject to a number of state and local laws or ordinances. But in all states, the federal Rivers and Harbors Act of 1899 (1899 Act)[3] and the more recent (1972) Section 404 of the Clean Water Act (Section 404)[4] are applicable. These acts establish an important mechanism in which a permit must be issued by the U.S. Army Corps of Engineers (CE) before any "work" can be commenced in ocean waters, estuaries, rivers, streams, lakes,

or in wetlands. The purpose of this paper is to provide a basic introduction to the 1899 Act and give a short history of its administration and enforcement, to review recent attacks upon the CE permit system, and to discuss the extent of CE jurisdiction. In addition, a few comments dealing with Section 404 are appropriate in order to help keep federal wetland protections in perspective.

From the standpoint of environmental protection, the jurisdiction issue is of pivotal importance. The reason for this is simply that the federal Fish and Wildlife Coordination Act[5] requires that the CE "shall first consult" the USDI Fish and Wildlife Service (FWS) and the state wildlife agency (e.g., the California Department of Fish and Game) regarding all applications to the CE for permits in areas of waterways or wetlands under CE jurisdiction. In addition, if the proposed work is deemed sufficiently damaging to the environment, an environmental impact statement (EIS) will be required under the National Environmental Policy Act (NEPA).[6] Neither of these protections is available if the area where the work is proposed lies outside the jurisdictional limits of the CE.

The jurisdiction issue is so clearly recognized that opponents of the 1899 Act and Section 404 have concentrated recent attacks upon both laws at this critical point. In addition, recent litigation concerning application of both laws to specific proposed projects has often centered upon this same point: CE jurisdiction.

[1] Paper presented at the California Riparian Systems Conference. [University of California, Davis, September 17-19, 1981.]
[2] Kent G. Dedrick is Research Program Specialist, State Lands Commission, Sacramento, Calif. The views and opinions expressed are exclusively those of the author and do not necessarily reflect the official policies of the State of California or the State Lands Commission.
[3] Sections 9, 10 et seq. 33 U.S.C. Section 401 et seq. Enacted 1899.
[4] Section 404, 33 U.S.C. Section 1344 (a)-(t). Enacted 1972, with amendments in 1977.

[5] 16 U.S.C. Section 661 et seq.
[6] 42 U.S.C. Section 4321 et seq.

Prior to the 1972 Congressional adoption of Section 404, federal protection of navigable waters was based upon the 1899 Act alone. As will be explained below, the history of administration of the 1899 Act during the first few decades of its existence was almost serene compared with that seen following the end of World War II. During the late 1960s and early 1970s, CE administration of the 1899 Act came under sharp Congressional review. As a result, a number of badly needed reforms were instituted. These reforms exhilarated environmentalists, but a counterattack was not long in coming from a broad range of development interests.

On a separate front, during the 1960s and 1970s wildlife agencies along with hunting, fishing, and environmental groups joined together in pitched battle against federally assisted stream channelization projects (over 21,000 linear miles of natural streams in the United States had been replaced by drainage ditches by 1972). Due to a few quirks in existing law, stream channelization projects received at best only spotty environmental review, and mitigation measures were largely meaningless.

With this background, Congressional passage of Section 404 in 1972 and the court rulings in U.S. v. Holland (1974)[7] and NRDC v. Callaway (1975)[8] provided welcome protection, since these two rulings carried CE permit jurisdiction under Section 404 well into the kind of streams and wetlands that had suffered such severe devastation through stream channelization projects. A revolt against the jurisdiction and apparatus of Section 404 was quickly mobilized, and in 1976-77 the newly won broad CE jurisdiction was nearly lost in Congress; another major attack upon it is now underway. The Section 404 experience has been described in the review by Kramer (1983), and it is recommended that the reader consult this work for further details.

The origins of the 1899 Act, its later history, and CE jurisdiction under it are discussed in the following section, which in the interest of completeness also includes a brief discourse on tidal datums and their relation to CE jurisdiction under this act.

THE RIVERS AND HARBORS ACT OF 1899

Origin and History

For many decades, the CE has been responsible for protecting and improving the waterways of the nation. This responsibility arose as early as 1824 through Congressional action aimed at improving navigation in the Ohio and Mississippi rivers, through the removal of sand bars and snags.[9] At that time, waterways were the primary highways for the young nation's commerce. With no railroads, freeways, or airlines, the CE in effect served the nation's major transportation needs in these waterways almost single-handedly.

"Almost," one should emphasize, for as early as 1795 the Third Congress spelled out the need for hydrographic surveys of the Atlantic seacoast. In 1807, at the recommendation of President Jefferson, Congress adopted a resolution authorizing a "survey of the coast" (Shalowitz 1964). This 1807 Organic Act established the U.S. Coast Survey, which later became the U.S. Coast and Geodetic Survey, and is now the National Ocean Services. Fortunately, the early direction of the U.S. Coast Survey aimed at achieving the highest scientific standards in performing these important tasks. As a result, their early topographic and hydrographic survey maps of United States coasts and navigable waters are today recognized as an invaluable physical and cultural research resource.

Thus the basic governmental tools needed for expanding commercial use of waterways were in place 150 years ago; namely, good navigation charts prepared by the U.S. Coast Survey, and physical improvements to navigation performed by the CE.

Throughout early European and Mediterranean history, the acts of a few often threatened to spoil waterways as pathways for commerce, and in some cases to seize control of them. It was to be no different when the United States became a nation. The matter became critical in 1888, when the U.S. Supreme Court ruled in Willamette Iron Bridge Co. v. Hatch[10] that the federal government had no "common law" authority to protect navigable waters from obstructions. As Koonce explained in 1926 in the Koonce Lecture:

> ...while the Government was expending hundreds of millions of dollars to increase the facilities of navigation, interested parties, including States, Corporations and individuals, were placing obstructions and impediments of all kinds in and across the improved water-

[7] 373 F. Supp. 665 (M.D. Fla. 1974).
[8] 392 F. Supp. 685, 686 (D.D.C. 1975).

[9] See, for example, a lecture by Judge G.W. Koonce, "Federal Laws Affecting River and Harbor Works," Company Officer Class, the Engineer School, Fort Humphreys, Virginia, April 23, 1926 (reprinted in "Hearings on Water Pollution Control Legislation--1971," House Committee on Public Works, 92 Congress, 1st Session 286 [1971]), hereafter referred to as "Koonce Lecture.

[10] 125 U.S. 1 (31 Law Ed. 629)(1888). In this case, the Oregon Legislature in 1878 had authorized construction of a draw bridge across the Willamette River in Portland. Bridge foundations restricted the channel width to 87 ft.--it had formerly allowed passage of seagoing vessels of 2,000 tons for a mile upstream from the bridge.

way. The necessity for Federal legislation to protect these waterways from impairment and ultimate destruction eventually became urgent.

The reaction of Congress was swift. In the Rivers and Harbors Act of 1890 (1890 Act),[11] Congress authorized the basic concepts of the permit authority of the CE.[12] No longer saddled with the Willamette court's refusal to use the common law as the basis for federal authority in navigation disputes, after 1890 this authority became firmly based upon the Commerce Clause of the U.S. Constitution:[13]

> The Congress shall have Power ... To regulate Commerce with foreign Nations, and among the several States, and with the Indian Tribes;

There were problems with the 1890 Act and in 1896, Congress directed the Secretary of War to review existing laws and prepare revisions and amendments that he believed would be in the public interest. As an active participant, Koonce tells us that these recommendations were prepared as a bill that was to be independent of an appropriations bill, adding:

> ... but it slumbered unnoticed for nearly three years, and when we had about concluded it would never receive any attention whatever, it was taken up and passed in the most unexpected manner. (Koonce Lecture)

What happened was that while the 1899 Rivers and Harbors Appropriations Act was being considered by the Senate (it had already passed the House), Senator Frye, then Chairman of the Senate Commerce Committee, introduced what we now know as Sections 9 to 21 of the 1899 Act as an amendment to the appropriations bill.

This important language, said Koonce, was "accepted by Congress without the change of a word and practically without debate or discussion," (Koonce Lecture) apparently in the belief that Sections 9 and 10 did little more than restate existing law. Section 9 of the 1899 Act reads in full as follows:

> It shall not be lawful to construct or commence the construction of any bridge, dam, dike, or causeway over or in any port, roadstead, haven, harbor, canal, navigable river, or other navigable water of the United States until the consent of Congress to the building of such structures shall have

been obtained and until the plans for the same shall have been submitted to and approved by the Chief of Engineers and by the Secretary of the Army: <u>Provided</u>, That such structures may be built under authority of a legislature of a State across rivers and other waterways the navigable portions of which lie wholly within the limits of a single State, provided the location and plans thereof are submitted to and approved by the Chief of Engineers and by the Secretary of the Army before construction is commenced: <u>And provided further</u>, That when plans for any bridge or other structure have been approved by the Chief of Engineers and by the Secretary of the Army, it shall not be lawful to deviate from such plans either before or after completion of the structure unless the modification of said plans has previously been submitted to and received approval of the Chief of Engineers and the Secretary of the Army.

Section 10 of the 1899 Act reads in full as follows:

> The creation of any obstruction not affirmatively authorized by Congress, to the navigable capacity of any of the waters of the United States is prohibited; and it shall not be lawful to build or commence the building of any wharf, pier, dolphin, boom, weir, breakwater, bulkhead, jetty, or other structures in any port, roadstead, haven, harbor, canal, navigable river, or other water of the United States, outside established harbor lines, or where no harbor lines have been established, except on plans recommended by the Chief of Engineers and authorized by the Secretary of the Army; and it shall not be lawful to excavate or fill, or in any manner to alter or modify the course, location, condition, or capacity of any port, roadstead, haven, harbor, canal, lake, harbor of refuge, or inclosure within the limits of any breakwater, or of the channel of any navigable water of the United States, unless the work has been recommended by the Chief of Engineers and authorized by the Secretary of the Army prior to beginning the same.

But much more was involved. Section 9 of the 1899 Act requires Congressional consent and CE approval before construction of any bridge, dam, dike, or causeway "over or in" navigable waters of the United States. (The 1890 Act provided such protection only in the cases of bridges and causeways.) Under Section 10 of the 1899 Act, any structure, excavation, or fill that would "alter or modify the course, location, condition, or capacity" of navigble waters of the

---

[11] Act of Sept. 19, 1890, Ch. 907, Section 7, 26 Stat. 454, as amended by Act of July 13, 1892, Ch. 158, Section 3, 27 Stat. 110.
[12] For a more detailed history, see Barker (1976)
[13] U.S. Constitution, Article I, Section 8.

United States requires a CE permit. (Under the 1890 Act, the CE could regulate only a much-narrower class of activities that would "obstruct or impair navigation, commerce, or anchorage.")

Since 1899, thousands of CE permits under Section 10 have been issued, and important court rulings affirming the validity of the CE permit program are now the classical literature on this subject. Judge Koonce worked for the CE for 40 years, beginning in 1886, and was a key figure in the development of the 1899 Act; he also continued to guide its administration for many years. He concluded his 1926 address noting that the 1899 Act:

> ... has been in force for 27 years, and in all that time there has been no amendment or suggestion of amendment. It has been contested in the courts and the constitutionality of many of its provisions has been questioned, but so far it has withstood all assaults. (Koonce Lecture)

All regulatory programs in government are subject to "assaults," and the CE permit program was no exception. The classic and continual dilemma for an agency regulator is the matter of posture under stress. Does one take a "hard line" and risk the entire program, or does one make accommodation for particular projects where undue political pressures may be exerted upon elected officials and thereby weaken or even cripple the program?

Section 9 of the 1899 Act is a case in point. Its strong language requiring approval by Congress or a state legislature for work that obstructs navigation "over or in" waterways became a case where accommodation prevailed. During his 1926 lecture, Koonce stated that Section 9 applied only "to that class of structures such as bridges and dams which extend entirely across a waterway" (Koonce Lecture)--a considerably restricted interpretation that became the administrative practice of the CE, and recently won favor in a 4th Circuit Court ruling.[14]

Since 1899, on the West Coast at least, some changes in regulatory posture have apparently occurred. For example, since 1905, in south San Francisco Bay nine Section 9 permits for dams across tidal sloughs have been issued; all were issued before 1930. During the 1930s Depression, permit activity was minimal, but, largely after World War II, at least another nine projects involving the damming of many more sloughs were either authorized under Section 10 or completed with no permit whatsoever.[15] The sloughs involved ranged in width from about 100 ft. to well over 500 ft., some have documented histories

of commercial navigation, and most would be suitable for present and future uses in navigation.

Colorful history sometimes appears in CE records. For example, in 1905 CE permission was granted for a dam across Phelps Slough in south San Francisco Bay near Redwood City, and the dam was duly put in place. But unknown to District Engineer Major Wm. M. Harts, former California Governor James H. Budd owned a villa and boat dock on the slough landward of the dam site. CE records show that Governor Budd "made protest and subsequently caused the dam to be blown out." With the dam out of the way, both Budd and the operator of a schooner landing on the slough could again enjoy free navigation into San Francisco Bay. Unfortunately, at some time in the 1950s the slough was again dammed, but no permit for the dam has been located.

Two of these sloughs in San Francisco Bay were declared navigable by statute enacted by the California Legislature,[16] but despite strong citizen protest, they were eventually rendered useless for public navigation. During the years that so many waterways were lost to the public, Section 611 of the California Penal Code was in force and warned that "Every person who unlawfully obstructs the navigation of any navigable stream is guilty of a misdemeanor." Although this section was repealed in 1937, obstruction of navigable waters remains a public nuisance, subject to abatement.[17]

Criticism and Reform

As will become apparent below, an increased attack on the nation's estuaries, streams, and wetlands occurred following World War II. It seems fair to say that the attack peaked during the 1960s, but was arrested in the counterattack of increased environmental awareness in 1970. Congress had strengthened the Fish and Wildlife Coordination Act in 1958, but that action did not prove sufficient to stem losses of irreplacable wetlands.

In 1967, hearings were held by the House Subcommittee on Fisheries and Wildlife Conservation, chaired by Rep. John D. Dingell,[18] at which the extent of estuarine environment losses was

---

[14] Hart and Miller Islands v. Corps of Engineers, etc. 621 F 2d 1281 (1980).
[15] Corps of Engineers records, San Francisco District, San Francisco, Calif.

---

[16] Many California waterways have been declared navigable by statute (see Harbor and Navigation Code, Sections 101 to 106), although a statutory designation is not necessary for their judicial recognition as such (e.g., Churchhill Co. v. Kingsbury, 178 Cal. 554; 174 P. 329 [1918]).
[17] Civil Code Sec. 3479 and Code of Civil Proc. Sec. 731.
[18] Estuarine Areas. Hearings before the Subcommittee on Fisheries and Wildlife Conservation, Committee on Merchant Marine and Fisheries. U.S. House of Representatives, 90th Congress, 1st Session, March 6, 8, 9, 1967. (Hereafter "Dingell Hearings".)

revealed on a nationwide basis. Dr. Stanley A. Cain, then the Assistant Secretary of the Interior for Fish and Wildlife and Parks testified that during the previous 20 years alone, 564,500 ac. of estuarine environment in coastal estuaries had been lost to dredging and filling, while another 4,300 ac. in shoal areas of the Great Lakes were lost as well. The total losses were 7% of the some 8 million acres of estuarine environment in the 26 states considered.

California's losses were cited as greater than the combined losses of the next four most heavily impacted states: Texas, Louisiana, Florida, and New Jersey. According to Cain's figures, 75% of Caifornia's estuarine losses occurred in the San Francisco Bay-Suisun Bay area. In fact, these bay area losses of 300 sq. mi. extended over a period somewhat longer than 20 years. Much of the area is diked (but not filled) and so in principle retains the potential for restoration.

During the Dingell Hearings, scenarios of the loss of many wetland areas were detailed. For example, during a brief six months in 1962, eight projects involving a total of nearly 3 million cubic yards of dredge and fill work in Hempstead Bay (Long Island, N.Y.) had been approved by the CE over strong objections by the FWS and the New York State Conservation Department. Of many other documented examples of Long Island "dredge the bays fill the wetlands" projects noted during the 1960s, some were commenced with no CE permit whatsoever, and some were even approved by the USDI Bureau of Sports Fisheries and Wildlife (BSFW). Between 1936 and 1961, 14,000 ac. of the original 30,000 ac. were lost on the south shore of Long Island alone; while as of 1952, 12.5% had been lost during the preceding five years. Testimony from other states revealed a similarly bleak picture.

Some CE procedures left the Fish and Wildlife Coordination Act as an empty promise. For example, in 1963 public notices for proposed projects published by the Jacksonville District (Florida) CE contained the warning that protests must be "based on the effects on public navigation" alone, and that the federal courts had ruled that CE decisions on the permit must not be based on "considerations having nothing to do with navigation." By 1966, public notice language had improved somewhat, so that issuance of a CE permit "merely expresses the assent so far as the public rights of navigation are concerned," leaving open the door to protests on other grounds.

The Dingell Hearings were ostensibly held to consider nine bills, all containing the language: No person may conduct any dredging, filling, or excavation work within any estuary of the United States or in the Great Lakes and connecting waterways unless a permit for such work is issued by the Secretary of the Interior. That is, these bills would have required dual permits from fed-

eral agencies; one issued by the CE and one by the U.S. Department of the Interior (DI).

In the aftermath of the Dingell Hearings, Secretary of the Army, Stanley Resor, and Secretary of the Interior, Stewart Udall, on 13 July 1967 signed a Memorandum of Understanding setting forth procedures to be followed in treating CE permit applications for work that "will unreasonably impair natural resources ... including fish and wildlife and recreational values." In such cases, the CE will "either deny the permit or include such conditions in the permit" as will be "in the public interest." Because of this action, the dual permit legislation was dropped, and a wait-and-see posture was taken to give this new proposal a chance to prove itself. This important memorandum, and the authority of the CE to deny permits for works that would unreasonably impair natural resources, has since been affirmed in an important court action centered on Florida's west coast.

On the palm-fringed shores of Boca Ciega Bay (an arm of Tampa Bay near St. Petersburg, Florida), two landholders, Alfred Zabel and David Russel, wanted to build a trailer park on the shallow waters of the bay near its shoreline. It would be a dredge and fill operation with the dredged material piled up to form an island, connected to the shore with a dirt berm so that the house trailers could get from shore to the new island.

Zabel and Russel began obtaining local agency permits, ran into a problem, and sued in Florida courts, finally winning in Florida's Supreme Court. They next tackled the federal problem and filed application for a CE permit under the 1899 Act. A public hearing was held in November 1966, where other state and local agencies and numerous citizens protested against the project. A month later, Colonel R.P. Tabb, District Engineer, Jacksonville District, CE, recommended that although "the proposed work would have no material adverse effect on navigation," the "continued opposition of the U.S. Fish and Wildlife Service" as well as the other protests, "convinced me that approval ... would not be in the public interest." Secretary of the Army, Resor, denied Zabel and Russel's application on 28 February, 1967, only a week before the Dingell Hearings commenced.

The two prospective developers and their attorneys set to work and filed a complaint in U.S. District Court a few weeks later on 10 May, 1967. They charged that the CE had no authority to deny the permit, and on 17 February, 1969, District Judge Krentzman agreed, stating that Resor did not have authority to deny a permit in cases "where he has found factually that the construction proposed ... would not interfere with navigation."[19]

---

[19]269 F. Supp. 764 (M.D. Florida, 1969).

The CE appealed Krentzman's ruling before the Fifth Circuit, and that court reversed the ruling on 16 July, 1970, in an opinion in which Judge Brown stated bluntly that "the Corps does not have to wear navigational blinders when it considers a permit request."[20]

"Hallelujah! That is great!" exclaimed Representative Henry S. Reuss on hearing news of the reversal a few days later, while he was conducting the hearings: "Protecting America's Estuaries--The Potomac" before the Subcommittee on Conservation and Natural Resources.[21] "That relieves us of new legislation!" added Representative Paul N. McCloskey, Jr., a member of Reuss' subcommittee.

To no one's surprise, Zabel and Russel appealed the Fifth Circuit's decision to the U.S. Supreme Court, which in 1971 declined to review the case. As a result, the legal apparatus for CE denial of permits on the basis of wildlife concerns (and others not substantively involving navigation) was firmly in place. The 1967 Memorandum of Understanding referred to above and the Zabel v. Tabb decision together formed the foundation that was to make the Fish and Wildlife Coordination Act a powerful tool for environmental protection.

But the euphoria following the 1967 Memorandum of Understanding was to be badly shaken in October of that same year in a case involving landfill at Hunting Creek, along the west shore of the Potomac River and only 7 mi. from the nation's Capitol. The Hunting Creek affair was called a "debacle in conservation".[22]

In this case, a slim wedge of underwater property (36 ac.) jutting one-half mile out into the Potomac was proposed to be filled for apartments and crowned with a drive-in movie at its apex. The Teamsters Union Pension Fund (represented by contractor Howard Hoffman Assoc.) and an apartment firm each claimed ownership of the property, the winter home of thousands of diving ducks. The landfill would be immediately offshore from Jones Point Park (National Park Service), site of an historic (1855) lighthouse that once guided Potomac navigators.

A 1964 CE permit application was vigorously protested by the National Parks Service (NPS), FWS, six Congressmen, a U.S. Senator, and many citizen groups. Interior Secretary Stewart L. Udall asked the CE to deny the permit in the strongest terms, not only on wildlife grounds, but also claiming the fill project would "blight an area of great scenic value."

Udall's statement should have settled the matter. But it didn't. The two firms next scaled down their plans to fill about 10 ac. each initially (20 ac. total) and made new development plans for the full 36 ac. The matter languished until 10 October, 1967, when political considerations coupled with pressures for urgency led to an abrupt withdrawal of DI's objections by Assistant Interior Secretary Cain, who signed a letter on that date prepared by "somebody else." A newspaper item[23] reported that at least two U.S. Senators had intervened for the river-fillers.

The Hoffman firm requested early action for their 9.4 ac. fill, and a CE public hearing was held in February 1968. At the hearing, the chorus of objections became an outcry; even the Daughters of the American Revolution rose up in protest. Now under intense environmental pressure and armed with a new field study, Cain reversed himself on 10 April, 1968, and immediately contacted General Harry Woodbury, Jr. of the CE. A few days later, Woodbury concurred in the CE lower-echelon view that the permit should be granted, and bucked the controversy back to Interior Undersecretary David Black, Cain's superior. On April 26, Black also assented, and the permit was granted on 29 May, 1968.

The House Natural Resources and Power Subcommittee (Representative Robert E. Jones, Chairman) held hearings on the Hunting Creek "debacle" on 24 June and 8-9 July, 1968, and in March 1969 recommended that the CE should issue an order to show cause why the permit should not be revoked as having been "issued in violation of law." Cain resigned after the hearings, and General Woodbury had retired by the end of April 1968. Representative Reuss was later to note that "interests that want to fill and despoil always shop around until they find somebody who will give them a green light. In the Hunting Creek case, ...the U.S. Fish and Wildlife Service to its eternal credit said 'No, this is an outrage, don't fill!'."[24]

In April 1969, the newly appointed Interior Secretary Walter Hickel wrote the Secretary of the Army requesting reconsideration of the Hunting Creek permit, characterizing the landfill proposal as a "needless act of destruction of the environment of the Nation's Capitol." About a year later the CE complied and revoked the permit (Sax 1971).

The wetlands battle was now fully joined. A U.S. Senate Committee held hearings in Seattle on 4 June, 1968, concerning a number of estuary protection bills;[25] but in the meantime, the cri-

[20]430 F. 2d 199 (Fifth Circuit, 1970).
[21]See Appendix A (2).
[22]House Report No. 91-113. The permit for landfill in Hunting Creek: a debacle in conservation. Natural Resources and Power Subcommittee, Committee on Government Operations. 24 March, 1969.

[23]Jackson, R.L. Panel examines land deal with Teamsters Fund. Los Angeles Times, 3 January, 1969.
[24]See Appendix A (1).
[25]Estuaries and their Natural Resources. Hearing before the Committee on Commerce, U.S. Senate. 4 June, 1968.

sis over San Francisco Bay was rapidly coming to a head.

The protections provided by California's San Francisco Bay Conservation and Development Commission (BCDC) were to be terminated late in 1969. The BCDC had submitted its celebrated "Bay Plan" to the California Legislature in January 1969, but the prospect for passage of a bill ensuring a permanent BCDC with strong authority and enforcing the Bay Plan was so remote that BCDC Chairman Melvin B. Lane warned the public early that year of incipient disaster. Lane's alarm gave rise to widespread anxiety among bay area residents.

Environmental leaders met to plan strategy, but disagreed on tactics; nevertheless, an effective two-pronged campaign emerged. East Bay leaders, including the 20,000-member Save San Francisco Bay Association, adopted a major public education and letter-writing campaign. But a hard-hitting group on the San Francisco Peninsula called Save Our Bay Action Committee (SOBAC) used all the tools of a grassroots political campaign (full-page newspaper ads, press attacks upon certain legislators, major fund-raising and volunteer recruitment, bus caravans to Sacramento, etc.). This group distributed over 40,000 "Save Our Bay" bumper strips and obtained 200,000 signatures on petitions. As a result, a satisfactory bill was finally signed by Governor Reagan on 7 August, 1969 (Dolezel and Warren 1971).

After participating in the Hunting Creek affair and learning of the then-impending crisis over San Francisco Bay, Representative Henry Reuss called hearings of his Subcommittee on Conservation and Natural Resources in May 1969. These hearings were to be the first act of a prodigious program lasting through 1973, which resulted in 24 days of hearings, reporting on several thousand pages of hearing records of testimony, reports and correspondence, and dealing with nationwide issues concerning estuaries and streams.[26] This remarkable effort was the product of Reuss and six other Congressmen, assisted by a small, dedicated staff headed by Chief Counsel, Phineas Indritz.

The Reuss Subcommittee has had great impact upon federal protection of the nation's waterways; some examples are given below. Through its oversight function, the subcommittee has managed to revolutionize the administration of the CE permit system. For its part, the CE has made remarkable changes in procedures and efficiency and in cooperating with wildlife agencies and the public.

The concept of "harbor lines" originated in the 1899 Act and represented the limit to which either piers or bulkheads could be built into the nation's harbors and waterways. Permits were not required for work landward of these lines, and large tracts of estuarine lands were lost to landfill as a result. For example, in San Francisco Bay 140 mi. of harbor lines had been established by 1969, with over 19 sq. mi. of baylands shoreward of these lines (see Appendix A [1]). At Reuss' urging, the CE changed its national harbor line policy on 27 May, 1970 to require Section 10 permits in these important shoreland areas.[27]

The Reuss Subcommittee also sought vigorous enforcement of the Refuse Act of 1899, which prohibits deposit of "any refuse matter of any kind" into the navigable waters of the United States.[28] Court rulings have established that a wide variety of industrial pollutants are classified as "refuse," and thus the discharger faces both civil and criminal sanctions under this act.[29] Furthermore, Section 16 of the 1899 Act[30] contains the surprisingly modern idea that a citizen "giving information which shall lead to conviction" may be awarded one-half of the fine imposed on the discharger.

Enforcement of Section 10 of the 1899 Act has always been a difficult matter. Despite the existence of the BCDC and other agencies having enforcement authority in the San Francisco Bay area, illicit filling of the bay continued with disturbing frequency during the early 1970s. Upset with this situation, a handful of citizens became informers and reported many unpermitted bay dumping incidents to the CE and other agencies.[31] The best known example is the case where Mrs. Sylvia Gregory, hospitalized with a broken leg near the San Francisco International Airport, viewed illegal filling in progress at the airport and reported to the CE from her hospital bed.[32] Due to the extensive publicity surrounding these illegal fills, their frequency has decreased. However, eternal vigilance is mandatory to prevent a return of the prior "dump-it-in-the-bay" attitude that had been so destructively commonplace for over a century.

One might ask if the CE permit system that had been strengthened during the early 1970s was prepared to resist a major landfill proposal that would be seriously damaging to ecological values. The answer came in 1976 when the CE under Sections 10 and 404 denied two out of three permits applied for by the Deltona Corporation for dredge and fill work at Marco Island on Florida's south-

---

[26] U.S. House of Representatives, Committee on Government Operations, Conservation and Natural Resources Subcommittee. Representative Henry S. Reuss, Chairman. Hereafter cited as "Reuss Subcommittee." See Appendix A for a list of hearings and reports from 1969 to 1973.

---

[27] See 33 Code of Federal Regulations Part 328. Code of Federal Regulations hereafter "CFR."
[28] Section 13 of the 1899 Act (33 U.S.C. Section 407).
[29] See Appendix A (7), (12), and (16).
[30] 33 U.S.C. Section 411.
[31] Adams, G. The Big Snitchers. California Living, supplement to San Francisco Examiner and Chronicle. 5 March, 1972.
[32] Congressional Record. 21 October, 1971.

ern Gulf coast. The project involved 18.2 million cubic yards of dredge and fill work in more than 2,100 ac. of mangrove wetlands and 70 mi. of waterways, the purpose being to create over 5,600 house lots.

According to testimony by the DI,[33] "the developer continue(d) to sell submerged lots in this tract without the Federal permits necessary to make the submerged lands suitable for the erection of residences." Lt. General William C. Gribble, Jr. (CE Chief of Engineers) said in denying the permits that the proposed filling of the mangrove wetlands would "constitute an unacceptable adverse impact on this aquatic resource" that would be contrary to "overriding national factors in the public interest."[34] The entire project had been started 12 years earlier, and the CE granted the permit for the "Collier Bay" part of the project because, as Gribble pointed out, "a significant amount of destruction has already occurred to the mangrove wetlands" in that area and a number of houses had already been built.[35]

Despite this dramatic victory for environmental interests, nagging problems persist. CE jurisdiction in specific wetland areas has often been removed by Congress through insertion of brief phrases in the language of other bills, such as the Public Works Omnibus Bill. For example, in 1968 the waters and waterfront of a major portion of the port of San Francisco were "declared to be nonnavigable waters" and that "the consent of Congress is hereby given for the filling in of all or any part" of the area.[36] Similarly, in 1976 Congress approved language stating that Lake Coeur d'Alene (Idaho), Lake George (New York), and Lake Oswego (Oregon) "are declared nonnavigable" under the Section 10 permit program.[37] Many other waterways have suffered the same fate; they are listed in Title 33 of the U.S. Code from Section 21 through Section 59p.

San Francisco is a major ocean port, but during the late 1960s a plan was advocated to fill part of the port area for office and commercial use. This project probably triggered Congress' action to declare the area "nonnavigable."

The curious history of the Lake Coeur d'Alene case was revealed during U.S. Senate hearings called by Idaho's Senator James McClure and

held in October 1974.[38] Months earlier in January 1974, the CE had declared the lake to be "navigable waters of the United States" following an extensive investigation which showed the lake had been used for commercial steamboat navigation as early as 1854 and continues to be. In September, McClure introduced a bill to give CE permit authority to the State of Idaho. The bill apparently failed to become law, but only two years later the lake was declared "nonnavigable" as noted above.

In addition to the above "nonnavigable" declarations, some interests have taken complaints of recent CE and FWS actions to Congress. For example, hearings were held in 1975[39] as a forum for officials of Foster City and Redwood City to express their displeasure with FWS, which had requested meaningful mitigation for losses in waterfowl habitat connected with three projects proposed over the prior two years. These projects were continuations of earlier large projects that had created over 3,000 ac. of dry land by filling former San Francisco Bay marshlands; they were substantially financed using tax-exempt bonds. The hearings are of concern as they represented a formal and vigorous protest against a wetlands protection apparatus still in its infancy.

NAVIGABLE WATERS OF THE UNITED STATES

As late as 1972, the definition of navigable waters of the United States published in Title 33 CFR could only be described as narrow.[40] Four U.S. Supreme Court decisions were then used by the CE in defining navigability:

The Steamer Daniel Ball v U.S. (1871);[41]
U.S. v The Steamer Montello (1874);[42]
Economy Light & Power Co. v U.S. (1921);[43]
U.S. v Appalachian Elec. Power Co (1941).[44]

The Daniel Ball and Montello cases provide definitions of navigability that are highly conservative by today's standards, while the Economy and Appalachian cases, coming several decades later, reveal an awareness of the threat to

---

[33] See Appendix A (9).
[34] News release. U.S. Army Corps of Engineers, Jacksonville District, Florida. 16 April, 1976.
[35] For additional information on the saga of Marco Island see Environmental Law Review 6:10117 (1976). Corp. confirms policy against 'unnecessary' development in wetlands. See also Carter (1976).
[36] 33 U.S.C. Section 59h.
[37] 33 U.S.C. Section 59m.

[38] Structures, excavations, or fills in or on certain navigable waters. Hearings before the Subcommittee on Water Resources, Committee on Public Works, U.S. Senate, 93rd Congress, 2d Session. October 7, 1974.
[39] Roles of the Corps of Engineers and U.S. Fish and Wildlife Service in Foster City, Calif. Hearings before Conservation, Energy, and Natural Resources Subcommittee, Committee on Government Operations, U.S. House of Representatives, 94th Congress, 1st Session; 12-13 September, 1975.
[40] See, for example, 1971 edition of 33 CFR Section 209.260.
[41] 77 U.S. (10 Wall.) 557.
[42] 87 U.S. (10 Wall.) 430.
[43] 256 U.S. 113.
[44] 311 U.S. 377.

waterways that is refreshing by contrast.[45] The court's language in the Daniel Ball case may be of help to scientists and engineers seeking historical guidance:

> Those rivers must be regarded as public navigable rivers in law which are navigable in fact. And they are navigable in fact when they are used, or are susceptible of being used, in their ordinary condition, as highways for commerce, over which trade and travel are or may be conducted in the customary modes of trade and travel on water.

The Montello case language noted that "the capability of use" in waterborne commerce is the "true criterion" of navigability, but added:

> It is not every small creek in which a fishing skiff or gunning canoe can be made to float at high water which is navigable, but in order to give it the character of a navigable stream, it must be generally and commonly useful to some purpose of trade or agriculture.

The Economy Light ruling added the important indelible navigability concept that can be paraphrased as "once navigable, always navigable." The court remarked:

> The fact, however, that artificial obstructions exist capable of being abated by due exercise of public authority, does not prevent the stream from being regarded as navigable in law, if, supposing them to be abated, it be navigable in fact in its natural state.

The Appalachian ruling supercedes the prior cases in at least one important area:

> To appraise the evidence of navigability on the natural condition only of the waterway is erroneous. .... A waterway, otherwise suitable for navigation is not barred from that classification merely because artificial aids must make the highway suitable for use before commercial navigation may be undertaken.

On 9 September, 1972, the CE published in the Federal Register an expanded and updated definition of navigable waters of the United States that now appears in Title 33 CFR, Section 329 (first published as Section 209.260). This new material provides the most important guidance available dealing with the CE claim of jurisdiction under the 1899 Act. As such, it is an essential reading assignment for anyone seriously interested in the act. An "Attorney's Supplement" prepared by the Office of General Counsel, CE, provides detailed legal background for the new definition and contains an encyclopedic number of legal references, in sharp contrast to the definitions used before 1972.

At 33 CFR Section 329.4, a general definition of navigable waters of the United States is given:

> Navigable waters of the United States are those waters that are subject to the ebb and flow of the tide and/or are presently used, or have been used in the past, or may be susceptible for use to transport interstate or foreign commerce. A determination of navigability, once made, applies laterally over the entire surface of the waterbody, and is not extinguished by later actions or events which impede or destroy navigable capacity.

For non-tidal waters, the jurisdiction extends to the ordinary high-water mark, which is defined as:

> 'The ordinary high water mark' on nontidal rivers is the line on the shore established by the fluctuations of water and indicated by physical characteristics such as a clear, natural line impressed on the bank; shelving; changes in the character of soil; destruction of terrestrial vegetation; the presence of litter or debris; or other appropriate means that consider the characteristics of the surrounding areas. (33 CFR Section 329.11[1])

It is also stated that private ownership of a river- or lakebed "has no bearing on the existence or extent of the dominant Federal jurisdiction over a navigable waterbody."

The shoreward limit of jurisdiction in coastal areas "extends to the line on the shore reached by the plane of the mean (average) high water," which, if possible, should be based upon 18.6 years of tidal measurements to account for the precession of the moon's orbit in relation to that of the sun.[46] In bays and estuaries, the CE jurisdiction:

> ... extends to the entire surface and bed of all waterbodies subject to tidal action. Jurisdiction thus extends to the edge [as determined by 33 CFR Section 329.12(a)(2) above] of all such waterbodies, even though portions of the waterbody may be extremely shallow, or obstructed by shoals, vegetation, or other barriers. Marshlands are thus considered 'navigable in law,' but only so far as the area is subject to inun-

---

[45] These rulings have been described frequently (e.g., Barker 1976; Leighty 1970).

---

[46] 33 CFR Section 329.12(a)(2).

dation by the mean high waters.... (33
CFR Section 329.12[b])

The 1972 definition (as amended in 1977)
thus includes many areas that had not been specified in prior definitions. Jurisdiction over the
"entire surface" of a waterway arose from the
1961 Supreme Court decision in U.S. v. Virginia Electric and Power Co.,[47] which in turn
cited other cases to the same effect.

During the 1969 Reuss Subcommittee hearings
on San Francisco Bay (Appendix A [1]), Brig. General William M. Glasgow, Jr. testified that "the
Corps has exercised jurisdiction in the Bay based
upon long-established mean higher high water-
lines," and that "the levees constructed by Leslie Salt Co. are shoreward of such lines and no
permits were therefore necessary." In 1970,
objections were made on factual grounds to Glasgow's remark that the mean higher high water
(MHHW) lines were "long established"; it was thus
suggested that the CE did not know the true extent of its jurisdiction in present and former
bay tidal marshlands (see Appendix A [15]).
After considerable debate, the San Francisco District, CE, issued Public Notice No. 71-22(a) in
January 1972 stating that under the 1899 Act:
"Permits are required for all new work in unfill-
ed portions of the interior of diked areas below
former mean higher high water."

As a result, a sizeable but unknown fraction
of the historic 313 sq. mi. of San Francisco-
Suisun Bay marshlands (Nichols and Wright 1971)
was clearly placed under Section 10 protection.
Because Leslie Salt claimed about 70 sq. mi. of
these lands, it was directly affected by the CE
action and, on 20 December, 1973, filed suit
against the CE, arguing that CE jurisdiction was
restricted in both Sections 10 and 404 to the
mean high water (MHW) line. It should be noted
that Pacific Coast tides are of the "mixed" type
in which the two daily high tides usually differ
considerably in height. MHHW is the average of
the higher of the two daily high tides, while MHW
is the average of all high tides. In San Francisco Bay, MHHW is only 7 in. higher than MHW.

District Court Judge William T. Sweigert disagreed with Leslie's contention and set former
MHHW as the jurisdictional limit under Sections
10 and 404.[48] On appeal, the 9th Circuit panel
partially reversed Sweigert, ruling that the 1899
Act jurisdiction "extend(s) to all places covered
by the ebb and flow of the tide to the mean high
water (MHW) mark in its unobstructed natural
state," and that under Section 404 the jurisdiction is not limited to either MHW or MHHW.[49]

---

[47] 365 U.S. 624 (1961).
[48] Sierra Club v Leslie Salt Co. and
Leslie Salt Co. v Froehlke. 412 F. Supp.
1096 (1976).
[49] Leslie Salt Co. v Foehlke and Sierra Club v Leslie Salt Co. 578 F. 2d 742
(1978).

TIDAL PHENOMENA

Anyone involved in coastal and estuary studies needs a good understanding of both the theoretical and practical aspects of tides. For the
most part, the theoretical knowledge needed involves an elementary understanding of astronomy
and the methods of computation of simple averages
in order to establish "mean high water" and other
tidal datums (Marmer 1951; Schureman 1949). It
is also useful to understand the methods used for
obtaining these datums accurately from short series of measurements (Swanson 1974).

In addition to average values, other statistical properties of tides are increasingly being
recognized as important in many scientific and
engineering pursuits in the shorezone. The frequency and height of extreme high tides control
the design of flood control structures and are
critical in determining the dividing line between
upland and aquatic vegetation. At elevations
below these extreme high tides, the frequency of
inundation by tide waters is an important factor
in the survival and propagation of aquatic flora
and fauna, and many opportunities exist for new
multi-disciplinary research that joins land surveying techniques, tidal statistics, and biology
(Hinde 1954; Cameron 1972; Silva 1979).

A statistical analysis of 19 years of predicted high and low tides for 55 stations on all
United States coasts including Alaska and Hawaii
has been prepared by Harris (1981). Tabular
entries and graphs given in this work indicate
the probability that tides higher (or lower) than
a given level will occur, and also provide the
frequencies of high and low tides within small
elements of elevation. Figure 1 was prepared
using Harris' results and shows the probability
densities for high and low tides as functions of
tidal elevation for the Golden Gate, San Francisco Bay. It can be seen that high tides range in
elevation from about 0.2 ft. above mean sea level
(MSL) to nearly 4.0 ft. above MSL. The probability density for high tides has a standard deviation $\sigma = 0.74$ ft., resembles a gaussian error
curve with that value of σ, and is nearly symmetrical about mean high water (MHW). Some 97% of
all high tides fall within the height range from
2σ above MHW to 2σ below MHW.

Also shown in figure 1 is a curve giving the
average number of hours of submergence per solar
day as a function of tide height. The curve
shows an average submergence of about 65 minutes
at the elevation of MHHW, and about 2 hours 45
minutes at the elevation of MHW.

As noted above, the jurisdiction of the CE
under the 1899 Act has been restricted on the
West Coast to the MHW mark in its "natural, unobstructed state." This same mark is also the
limit of state sovereign land title claims (Stevens 1980; Taylor 1972). Yet it is clear that
for a symmetrical high water probability density
function, 50% of all high tides are above MHW,
while the other 50% fall below it. This means

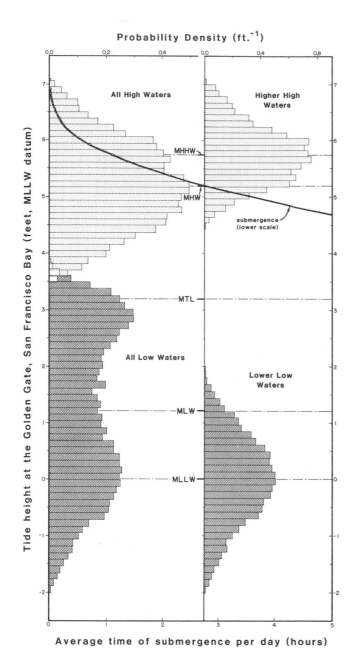

Probability Density (ft.⁻¹)

All High Waters

Higher High Waters

MHHW

MHW

submergence (lower scale)

MTL

All Low Waters

Lower Low Waters

MLW

MLLW

Tide height at the Golden Gate, San Francisco Bay (feet, MLLW datum)

Average time of submergence per day (hours)

Figure 1.—Statistics of predicted tides for the Golden Gate, San Francisco Bay, for the 19-year period: 1963-1981. (Source: Harris 1981.)

that the lands above MHW that are inundated by one-half of all high tides do not receive protection under the 1899 Act or under state sovereign claims, even though these lands are of great importance in marine engineering, flood control, and the general biological health and productivity of an estuary. Fortunately, Section 404 provides regulatory protection for such areas, but only if they satisfy wetlands criteria spelled out in CE and Environmental Protection Agency (EPA) regulations and guidelines.

Finally, a few remarks are in order concerning the natural role of tidal flooding of salt-marsh and other estuarine areas in maintaining navigation channels and reducing the need for maintenance dredging. In 1860, Henry Mitchell, Chief in Physical Hydrography of the U.S. Coast Survey summarized his own studies with the carefully worded statement:

> GENERAL RULE. A river having a bar at its mouth will be injured as a pathway for navigation if the tidal influx is reduced by encroachments upon its basins.[50]

This General Rule makes a direct connection between the goals of estuarine wetlands protection and restoration with the needs of navigation. This basic principle is familiar to students of historic works dealing with harbor design, but is seldom discussed in modern harbor engineering texts and reference works; primarily because harbor water depths needed by increased sizes of freighters and tankships over recent decades can generally be met only by instituting major dredging projects. However, application of Mitchell's General Rule as a guide can spell the difference between high and low maintenance dredging costs for flood channels and small craft harbors.

CONCLUSION

The flow of events—legislative and judicial—leading to the Section 404 wetlands protections has been dramatic, to say the least (see e.g., Kramer 1983). The 1976-77 Congressional debate over the Breaux and Wright amendments to Section 404 (authored by Representatives John Breaux [D-La.] and James C. Wright, Jr. [D-Tex.]) commenced quietly in a House Committee meeting on 13 April, 1976 and rose to a crescendo of head-on confrontations during Senate and conference committee meetings and floor actions lasting well into 1977, when amendments to the Clean Water Act were finally approved.

At the 13 April meeting, Breaux's short (115 word) amendment was adopted on a 22-13 vote of the House Public Works and Transportation Committee, with no input whatsoever from DI, EPA, CE, or the public. Breaux's language[51] would have added two subsections to Section 404:

---

[50]Mitchell, H. On the reclamation of tide-lands and its relation to navigation. Appendix No. 5, Report of the Superintendent, U.S. Coast Survey. House Exec. Doc. No. 206, 41st Congress, 2d Session (1869).

[51]Section 404 of the Federal Water Pollution Control Act amendments of 1972. Hearings held on 27-28 July, 1976 before the Committee on Public Works, U.S. Senate, 94th Congress, 2d Session. Cited hereafter as "404 Hearings".

(d) The term 'navigable waters' as used in this section shall mean all waters which are presently used, or are susceptible to use in their natural condition or by reasonable improvement as a means to transport interstate or foreign commerce, shoreward to their ordinary high water mark, including all waters which are subject to the ebb and flow of the tide shoreward to their mean high water mark (mean higher high water mark on the west coast).

(e) The discharge of dredged or fill material in waters other than navigable waters is not prohibited by or otherwise subject to regulation under this Act, or section 9, section 10, or section 13 of the Act of March 3, 1899.

Public rights in waterways are guaranteed by many state and federal statutes and have been the subject of judicial rulings in the highest courts of both the United States and England. These rights have other precedent through colonial charters of the original thirteen states in English Common Law, which in turn have roots in the Magna Carta of 1215 and the Pandects of Justinian (Roman Law) of far earlier vintage. Subsection (d) of the Breaux amendment curiously tries to replace several hundred years of ruling and precedent by a definition of "navigable waters" merely 76 words long, omits "waters that have been used in the past" for navigation, and omits noting that such waters are to be taken up to the head of navigation. Under Section 404, the Breaux amendment also eliminates vast acreages of adjacent wetlands, vernal pools, prairie potholes, and other vital wetlands from protection. Indeed, one agency in 1976 estimated that only 10 million acres of the 70 million wetland acres remaining in the contiguous 48 states would still be protected. The remaining 60 million acres would be left with no significant federal protection.

Breaux's language was adopted by Representative Wright, and the resulting Wright-Breaux amendment was passed by the full House on 3 June, 1976, after a short, heated debate, on a 234 to 121 vote.

Nearly two months were to pass after the House approval before any public hearings were held on the matter. In two evening sessions on 27-28 July, 1976, the Wright-Breaux language was considered as an amendment to S. 2710 (Hart) by the Senate Committee on Public Works, chaired by Senator Jennings Randolph. The hearings stimulated a massive outpouring of views that led to a 794-page report by the committee.[51] A full description of the testimony presented is far beyond the scope of this review, but supporters of Wright-Breaux included the National Governors Conference and private interest groups associated with coal and other mining, highway construction, forest harvesting, real estate, farming, livestock, reclamation districts, and residential and commercial builders. Opposed to Wright-Breaux were groups and individuals interested in the general environment, sports and commercial fishing, and state and federal wildlife agencies.

Of more than passing interest is the testimony of Peter R. Taft, Assistant U.S. Attorney General, Land and Natural Resources Division. Taft testified that it had been frequently alleged that the CE 404 permit program is "a creation of the courts rather than Congress and transcend(s) the constitutional basis for regulation in navigable waters."[51] Taft sharply claimed this allegation is in error, and in support of his claim provided a brief but pointed history of the public's rights in waterways and of efforts in the United States to halt water pollution, starting with Magna Carta and tracing both the legislative and judicial histories of these concepts in the United States.

Citing a number of examples in the nation, Taft also remarked:

> ...a number of the cases referred to the Justice Department for litigation have involved entities and individuals exhibiting as many characteristics of greed, fraud and outright criminality as I have ever seen in the business world. The worst have involved land developers drawn by the smell of cheap land that can be dredged and filled, often with canals, then subdivided and sold with heavy sales pitches for large front-end profits. Many of them are thinly financed. Most attempt to complete the dredging and make sales before the Corps finds out about the project; they then attempt to avoid restoration of the wetlands on the ground that they will go bankrupt and that innocent purchasers would be stuck with submerged lands they can't use.[51]

Even though the Wright-Breaux amendment was finally defeated in the Senate in 1977, bills with the same thrust have appeared frequently since then. Language identical or substantially similar to Breaux's can be found in the 1980 bills; S. 2970 (Tower), H.R. 7250 (Paul), and others pending before Congress at the time of this writing: S. 777 (Tower and Bentsen), H.R. 3083 (Hall).

The CE permit system has also been weakened in other ways. For example, the 1967 Memorandum of Understanding, referred to above, required "elevation" to Washington for settlement of unresolved differences between local officials of the CE and FWS regarding wildlife impacts of proposed projects. This memorandum was "terminated" on 24 March, 1980 when new language was adopted.[52] On 2 July, 1982 Interior Secretary James

---

[52]Federal Register 45:62768-71 (September 19, 1980).

Watt and others approved yet other language that allows the Assistant Secretary of the Army (Civil Works) to refuse review of contested permits by Washington officials.[53]

In addition, the definition of "fill material" under Section 404 was changed by the CE in 1977 so that it "does not include any pollutant discharged into water primarily to dispose of waste..."[54] This means that garbage disposal in the nation's waters or wetlands is exempt from CE environmental review under Section 404 and requires instead a NPDES (National Pollutant Discharge Elimination System) permit under Section 402 of the Clean Water Act. As a result of this loophole, new garbage dumps are today being created or expanded in diked wetlands of San Francisco Bay, despite the strong admonition by the Reuss Subcommittee in 1970 that "use of the Bay as a refuse dump is inimical to the national policy of preventing the destruction of our estuaries and must be stopped."[55]

Recent developments herald that a new round in the wetlands battle over both Section 10 and 404 has already begun (Mosher 1982). During 1976 and the preceding decade, progress in the development of wetlands protective laws and court rulings--and the defense of them against attack--occurred during both Republican and Democratic administrations, while Presidents Johnson, Nixon, Ford, and Carter served in office; administration support of wetlands protection was the rule during that era. Numerous research investigations conducted during those years also provided a sound scientific, engineering and economic basis that justifies protection of wetlands as a resource of nationwide importance. This factual material coupled with long-term political and judicial support has given great credence to the proposition that the protection of wetlands is a national goal, and clearly in the public interest.

But times have changed, for we now see the administration apparently operating in concert with a substantial Congressional power block bent upon reversing the wetlands protections gained over the past 15 years. Thus stripped to the core, wetlands defense will have to increasingly rely upon informed public opinion.

---

[53]Unpublished Memorandum of Agreement between the Department of the Interior and the Department of the Army. Dated July 2, 1982, and signed by Secretary of the Interior James G. Watt; Secretary of the Army John O. Marsh, Jr.; Assistant Secretary of the Army (Civil Works) Wm. R. Gianelli; Assistant Secretary of the Interior (Fish and Wildlife and Parks) G. Ray Arnett; and USDI Fish and Wildlife Service Director Robert A. Jantzen.
[54]33 CFR Section 323.2(m); (1980 Ed.). First published in the Federal Register 42:37144 et seq. (July 19, 1977).
[55]Appendix A (11).

LITERATURE CITED

Barker, Neil. 1976. Sections 9 and 10 of the Rivers and Harbors Act of 1899: potent tools for environmental protection. Ecol. Law Q. 6:109-159.

Cameron, G.N. 1972. Analysis of insect trophic diversity in two salt marsh communities. Ecology 53:58-73.

Carter, L.J. 1976. Wetlands: denial of Marco permits fails to resolve dilemma. Science 192:641-644.

Dolezel, J.N., and B.N. Warren. 1971. Saving San Francisco Bay: a case study of environmental legislation. Stanford Law Rev. 23: 349.

Harris, D.L. 1981. Tides and tidal datums in the United States. Spec. Rept. No. 7, U.S. Army Corps of Engineers, Coastal Research Engineering Center, Fort Belvoir, Va. 382 p.

Hinde, H.P. 1954. Vertical distribution of salt marsh phanerogams in relation to tide levels. Ecol. Mono. 24:209-225.

Kramer, J.R. 1983. Is there a national interest in wetlands: the Section 404 experience. In: R.E. Warner and K.M. Hendrix (ed.). California Riparian Systems. [University of California, Davis, September 17-19, 1981.] University of California Press, Berkeley.

Leighty, L.L. 1970. The source and scope of public and private rights in navigable waters. Land and Water Law Review 5:391-440.

Marmer, H.A. (ed.). 1951. Tidal datum planes (revised). Special Pub. No. 135, U.S. Coast and Geodetic Survey. U.S. Government Printing Office, Washington, D.C. 142 p.

Mosher, L. 1982. When is a prairie pothole a wetland? When federal regulators get busy. National Journal 14(10):410-414.

Nichols, D.R., and N.A. Wright. 1971. Preliminary map of historic margins of marshland, San Francisco Bay, California. Open file map, USDI Geological Survey, Menlo Park.

Sax, Joseph. 1971. A little sturm and drang at Hunting Creek. Esquire Magazine. February, 1971.

Schureman, P. 1949. Tide and current glossary (revised 1975). Special Pub. No. 228, National Ocean Survey/NOAA. U.S. Government Printing Office, Washington, D.C. 25 p.

Shalowitz, A.L. 1964. Shore and sea boundaries. Vol. 2. Pub. 10-1, U.S. Coast and Geodetic Survey, Government Printing Office, Washington. D.C. 749 p.

Silva, P.C. 1979. The benthic algal flora of central San Francisco Bay. In: T.J. Conomos (ed.). 493 p. San Francisco Bay: the urbanized estuary. Pacific Division, American Association for the Advancement of Sciences, San Francisco, Calif.

Stevens, J. 1980. The public trust: a sovereign's ancient prerogative becomes the people's environmental right. UCD Law Rev. 14: 195-209.

Swanson, L.R. 1974. Variability of tidal datums and accuracy in determining datums from short series of observations. NOAA Technical Report NOS 64, National Ocean Survey/NOAA, U.S. Government Printing Office, Washington, D.C. 41 p.

Taylor, N.G. 1972. Patented tidelands: a naked fee? Calif. State Bar J. 47:420.

APPENDIX A

The following is a list of the hearings and reports of the Committee on Government Operations, Conservation and Natural Resources Subcommittee, U.S. House of Representatives, Representative Henry S. Reuss, Chairman.

HEARINGS

1. The nation's estuaries: San Francisco Bay and Delta, Calif. Part 1: 15 May, 1969, Part 2: 20-21 August, 1969.

2. Protecting America's estuaries: The Potomac. 21-22 July, 1970.

3. The establishment of a national industrial wastes inventory. 17 September, 1970.

4. Refuse Act permit program. 18-19 February, 1971. Senate Commerce Committee with participation by the Reuss Subcommittee.

5. Stream channelization. Parts 1-4: 3-4 May, 3-4, 9, 10, and 14 June, 1971; Part 5: 20 March, 1973.

6. Public access to reservoirs to meet growing recreation demands. 15 June, 1971.

7. Mercury pollution and enforcement of the Refuse Act of 1899. Parts 1 and 2: 1 July, 21 October, and 5 November, 1971.

8. Protecting the nation's estuaries: Puget Sound and the Straits of Georgia and Juan de Fuca. 10-11 December, 1971.

9. Protecting America's estuaries: Florida. Parts 1 and 2: 25-26 May, 1973.

REPORTS

10. Our waters and wetlands: How the Corps of Engineers can help prevent their destruction and pollution. House Report 91-917, March 18, 1970.

11. Protecting America's estuaries: The San Francisco Bay and Delta. House Report 91-1433, August 19, 1970.

12. Qui tam actions and the 1899 Refuse Act: Citizen lawsuits against polluters of the nation's waterways. Committee print, September, 1970.

13. Protecting America's estuaries: The Potomac. House Report 91-1761, December 16, 1970.

14. Public access to reservoirs to meet growing recreation demands. House Report 92-586, October 21, 1971.

15. Increasing protection for our waters, wetlands, and shorelines: The Corps of Engineers. House Report 92-1323, August 10, 1972.

16. Enforcement of the 1899 Refuse Act. House Report 92-1333, August 14, 1972.

17. Protecting America's estuaries: Puget Sound and the Straits of Georgia and Juan de Fuca. House Report 92-1401, September 18, 1972.

VEGETATION OF THE SANTA ANA RIVER

AND SOME FLOOD CONTROL IMPLICATIONS[1]

Ted L. Hanes[2]

Abstract.--The Santa Ana River is the largest drainage system within southern California. Vegetation ranges from alluvial scrub to riparian woodland. The largest willow woodland in southern California occurs in the Prado Dam basin. Composition of vegetation-types and dynamics of vegetation in relation to flooding are discussed. Plans to alter the upper Santa Ana River are evaluated in relation to the existing and future vegetation.

INTRODUCTION

The Santa Ana River is the largest river within southern California. Its watershed covers an area of 6,263 sq. km. (2,418 sq. mi.) from the San Antonio River on the west to the San Jacinto River on the east. Most of the watershed is mountainous or hilly (3,838 sq. km. [1,482 sq. mi.]) with the remaining area being mesas and flat valleys (fig. 1).

The Santa Ana River originates in montane forests above 3,050 m. (10,000 ft.) elevation and terminates in a salt marsh at sea level, where it empties into the Pacific Ocean. Discharges average 322,000 acre-feet (AF) per year, although most of this flow is below ground except during rainstorms. Periodically the Santa Ana River experiences major flooding. During the record flood of 2 March, 1938, the Santa Ana River carried more than one AF per second as it emerged from the mountains. As a consequence, extensive stream channel alteration has been carried out in the lower half of the river below Prado Dam, built in 1941 at the head of Santa Ana Canyon. Current US Army Corps of Engineers (CE) proposals include expansion of the Prado basin by raising Prado Dam and construction of a new flood control dam at Mentone to lessen the impact of an anticipated 100-year storm.

CE alternative 5 calls for raising Prado Dam 13-m. (43-ft.) and the spillway 10.4-m. (34-ft.). The existing reservoir would be increased in size by 2,034 ha. (5,025 ac.), and 592 ha. (1,461 ac.) would be acquired below the dam in the Santa Ana

Canyon to serve as floodplain lands. Alternative 6 calls for the construction of Mentone Dam to control storm runoff from a 673-sq. km. (260-sq. mi.) area. The dam and reservoir area would require 1,376 ha. (3,400 ac.) of land. Prado Dam would be raised 9.1-m. (30-ft.) and the spillway 6-m. (20-ft.). An additional 591 ha. (1,460 ac.) of land would be acquired in the Santa Ana Canyon to serve as floodplain lands.

The vegetation considered in this paper is that located in the reach between Mentone at the foot of the San Bernardino Mountains through the Santa Ana Canyon.

LITERATURE REVIEW

The only published description of the Mentone vegetation is by Ingles (1929). He recognized several plant associations: cottonwood/willow, Salvia/Artemisia, Adenostoma/Ceanothus and Lepidospartum/Croton. In the 1920s, the cottonwood/willow association was found throughout the wash area west of Orange Avenue and included alders (Alnus). This entire association has since been destroyed by the establishment of rock quarries and other urban activities. Ingles considered the Adenostoma/Ceanothus and the Salvia/Artemisia association climax vegetation-types, but proposed that the cottonwood/ willow and Lepidospartum/Croton associations be considered seral (successional). He acknowledged that boundaries of these plant assemblages were not well defined.

The splitting of vegetation into numerous small associations and societies in vogue in the 1920s has been replaced by the practice of designations based upon major plant groupings. Recent studies on alluvial fans in southern California designate the vegetation as alluvial scrub (Andrews 1972; Smith 1978). Smith considered the Lepidospartum/Eriogonum to be a pioneer asso-

---

[1]Paper presented at the California Riparian Systems Conference. [University of California, Davis, September 17-19, 1981].
[2]Ted L. Hanes is Professor of Biology and Director of the Fullerton Arboretum, California State University, Fullerton.

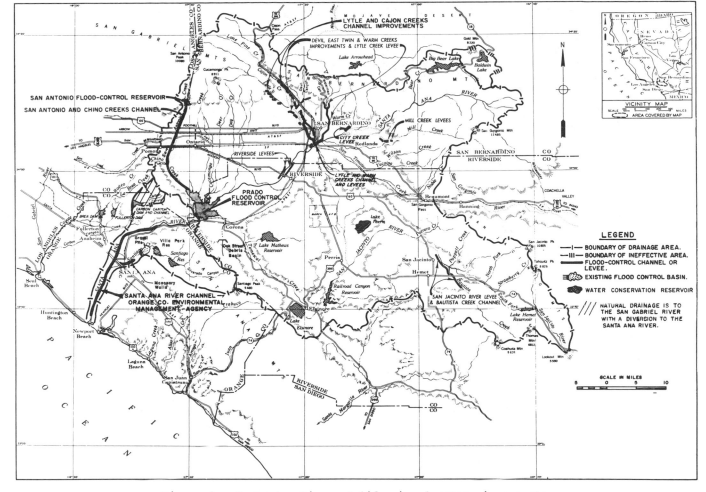

Figure 1.--Santa Ana River, California, largest river system within southern California, showing the 8,100-ha. (200,000-ac.) watershed. Existing flood control improvements are shown. (Source: US Army Corps of Engineers, Los Angeles District.)

ciation and combined numerous half-shrubs and woody sclerophylls into a mature grouping. The fact that the alluvial vegetation contains components of coastal sage scrub (Kirkpatrick and Hutchinson 1977; Mooney 1977) and chaparral (Cooper 1922, Hanes 1976) as well as some plants of the transmontane juniper woodland make the alluvial scrub a unique vegetation-type, difficult to define or describe in ecological terms.

Less definitive treatments of the plant life of the Santa Ana River reach from Mentone to the Prado basin have been prepared. Several natural history guides are helpful, but do not provide any quantitative information (Anderson 1972a; Louis Rubidoux Nature Center 1975; Munns 1977; Riverside County Parks Dept, undated; Tri-County Conservation League 1972). The CE included some information on plant associations and plant species in its draft and final Environmental Impact Statements (US Army Corps of Engineers 1975, 1977).

The existing literature describing the flora of the Santa Ana River through Riverside, Rubidoux, Norco, the Prado basin, and Santa Ana Canyon is generally limited and sketchy in nature. Anderson (1972b) presented a brief account of human impact on the Santa Ana River starting with aboriginal influences. The first vegetation study (Howell 1929) described the woodland in its near-pristine condition. Wieslander (1934) published a detailed vegetation map of the Corona quadrangle showing the Santa Ana River and Chino Creek as naturally wooded areas in the vicinity of what is presently the Prado basin. Little (1979) concluded that the construction of Prado Dam in 1941 did not create an artificial willow/ cottonwood woodland, but simply expanded its previous boundaries by raising and extending the water table. Hanes (1980) presented the first quantitative analysis of the vegetation in the Santa Ana Canyon area.

The riparian woodland in the 6,480-ha. (16,000-ac.) Prado basin is a cottonwood/willow forest-type (Society of American Foresters 1954). Several plant lists have been prepared for the Prado basin (Howell 1929; Marsh and Abbott 1972; URS Research Company 1974). Little (1979) conducted field studies in the Prado basin and combined his findings with previous lists. The combined list contained 232 plant species belonging to 5 families of vascular plants. Of the total, 156 species (67%) were native (indigenous) and 73 (31.5%) were non-native (introduced, exotic). Little (ibid.) speculated that the Santa Ana River should have many rare and endangered species.

Hanes (1980) conducted a study from Mentone to the Santa Ana Canyon during the spring of 1980 and reported 65 families of vascular plants which included 428 species. Of these, 330 (77%) were native and 98 (23%) were non-native species.

METHODS

The Mentone vegetation was sampled extensively using the line-intercept method. Base lines were established every 50-100 m. in major sectors of the alluvial fan. At intervals of 20 m., a 10-m. intercept transect line was placed at right angles to the base line. One transect line was laid to the right and the next line to the left in alternating fashion. The crowns of all perennial shrubs that overlapped or intercepted the transect line were recorded by species, to the nearest 5 cm. crown length. This rapid technique is considered the most efficient and accurate method of sampling full-crowned shrubs (Mueller-Dombois and Ellenberg 1974). The accumulated length occupied by any one species out of the total transect line length used for the sample was expressed as the percent cover for that species.

Riparian woodland vegetation was sampled using 3.3- x 30-m. continuous transects placed at random throughout the woodland stands between Riverside and the Santa Ana Canyon. Trees were recorded by species as alive or dead. Their estimated trunk diameters at breast height (DBH) were placed in one of the following size-classes: 2-6, in., 7-12 in., 13-24 in., 25-48 in. The enumeration of trees by species within the 3.3- x 30-m. plots allowed the calculation of tree density; i.e., the number of each species per unit area (ibid.).

Herbaceous plants were sampled using a 1- x 1-m. quadrat subdivided into 100-dm. squares. Only percent cover by species was determined since individuals in many cases were impossible to determine. Furthermore, percent cover gives a better measure of plant bulk (biomass) than does the number of stems or individuals (ibid.).

Three parameters of vegetation were assessed. These were density (number of plants of a species per plot), cover (size of crown of the plant), and frequency (number of subplots in which a species occurs). Importance value (IV) is a composite of these three vegetation parameters. It was determined by summing the relative density, relative cover, and relative frequency of a species. Relative values for each species were obtained by dividing each vegetation by the total of all species.

VEGETATION STRUCTURE AND FLORISTICS

Mentone

Four vegetation-types were recognized on the Mentone alluvial fan. The most extensive vegetation-type was juniper woodland. A total of 327 line intercepts were established in the woodlands east of Orange Avenue. Juniper (Juniperus californica), by virtue of its size, dominated the vegetation, but smaller shrubs such as Eriogonum fasciculatum, Eriodictyon trichocalyx, Opuntia littoralis, and Gutierrezia sp. were important in terms of percent cover, percent density, and percent frequency. Thirty-two additional shrub species were found in the woodland. Over 43% of the Eriogonum was dead, even though the species had the highest importance value (IV). This was true of the other dominant species except Juniper, which had the lowest dead IV.

The juniper woodland west of Orange Avenue was sampled to compare it with the more extensive woodland east of Orange Avenue. Here the woodland was similar to that east of Orange Avenue in perennial shrub composition and structure, but the IVs were generally lower. This was due in part to the area being used extensively as an unauthorized dump; and perhaps the groundwater supply is lower since it lies between the Santa Ana River and Plunge Creek and the normal drainages from the east have been blocked by Orange Avenue.

Alluvial scrub occupied the younger frequently disturbed sites. This vegetation-type was also dominated by Eriogonum fasciculatum, which had an IV greater than any other shrub species. Other dominant but less frequent shrubs were Adenostoma fasciculatum, Eriodictyon trichocalyx, Lotus scoparius, Artemisia californica, and Rhus ovata. Only 17 shrub species comprised the alluvial shrub vegetation.

The riparian woodland found on the Mentone alluvial fan was poorly developed and a minor component of the vegetation. It was dominated by California sycamore (Platanus racemosa), but these were small, drought-stunted trees that hardly formed a woodland. Other tree species, such as willow or cottonwood, were found only rarely. More commonly, shrubs such as Eriogonum fasciculatum, Yucca whipplei, and Opuntia littoralis, were associated with the sycamore trees along old, as well as active, watercourses.

Herbaceous plants were abundant in the juniper woodlands. The average number of plants was 62 per sq. dm. in the woodland east of Orange Avenue, and 26 per sq. dm. in the woodland west of Orange Avenue. The species number was also higher east of Orange Avenue (25); west of Orange Avenue it was only 18.

Riverside to Norco Reach

Extensive riparian woodlands occur in the Riverside-Norco reach of the Santa Ana River. Gallery cottonwood forests are found in the Riverside-Rubidoux reach. Nearly continuous young riparian woodlands are found in the Rubidoux-Norco reach. These were sampled but the data are not presented in this paper.

Prado Basin

Due to the major flooding of the Prado flood basin during February 1980, a quantitative vegetation analysis could not be performed at the time of the field study.

Qualitative assessments by direct observation from viewing points and other places around the basin perimeter are presented here. About 80% of the Prado basin was covered by extensive areas of riparian woodland, dominated by dense stands of arroyo willow (Salix lasiolepis), black willow (Salix gooddingii), and Fremont cottonwood (Populus fremontii). Other woodland trees dominant by size but scattered in distribution were California sycamore, black cottonwood (Populus trichocarpa), red willow (Salix laevigata var. araquipa), and golden willow (Salix lasiandra).

The riparian woodland trees in the basin had withstood more than 12 weeks of inundation during their dormant (deciduous) stage without apparent ill-effects. While standing in water these trees were developing a full crop of leaves, flowering, and bearing fruit. The trees showing this amazing adaptation to flooding were the willows, cottonwood, and sycamore. Furthermore, fallen trees, broken limbs, and other tree parts left by the eroding action of floodwaters were actively taking root and sprouting vigorously where floodwaters had receded.

Santa Ana Canyon

The vegetation in the upper end of the Santa Ana Canyon was mainly gallery-type riparian woodland. A major stand grew between Prado Dam and the golf course. A second woodland dominated the Featherly Park area. Some isolated riparian shrubs and perennial herbs occurred between Featherly Park and Imperial Boulevard, but in this reach the riverbed was composed of recently deposited sand and other alluvia with limited vegetation.

The woodland composition below Prado Dam is shown in table 1. Willows dominated (91% of the stands); these trees were in the 2-6 in. DBH size-class. Less than 10% of the woodland was composed of Fremont cottonwood; like the willows the majority had small trunks. About 29% of the woodland trees were in the size-class 7-12 in. DBH. The willow density was 1,250 per ha. (506 per ac.) whereas the cottonwood density was 114 per ha. (46 per ac.). Of the trees present, about 20% were dead, standing or fallen. In the woodland below the dam some riparian shrubs such

Table 1.--Tree composition, size-classes, and density of riparian woodland below Prado Dam, including Featherly Park.

Species	Size-class (DBH)				Density	
	2-6 in.	7-12 in.	13-24 in.	Total	trees/ha.	trees/ac.
Willows						
alive	157	57	1	215	977	396
dead	39	21	–	60	273	110
Total	196	78	1	275	1,250	506
Fremont cottonwood						
alive	16	8	–	24	109	44
dead	1	–	–	1	5	2
Total	17	8	–	25	114	46
Black cottonwood						
alive	–	2	–	2	9	4
dead	–	–	–	–	–	–
Total	–	2	–	2	9	4
Grand total	213	88	1	302	1,373	556

as shrub willows and mulefat (Baccharis glutinosa) formed a broken understory. However, these shrubs were found mainly on the woodland margins and were not sampled. Due to the heavy flooding of this woodland stand, the soil surface was either washed or covered with sand and silt deposits to various depths ranging up to 40.6 cm. (16 in.). Little or no herbaceous growth had become established on these recent deposits.

The woodlands in the Featherly Park reach also had considerable shrub understory, making access very difficult. The understory was composed of seedlings of willow with trunks less than 2 in. in diameter and mulefat. The understory was further complicated by dense root sprouts from downed willows and clumps of giant reed (Arundo donax). Natural breaks in the woodland occurred randomly and represented past flooding events of erosion or deposition. These sites were filled with dense stands of mulefat. Over a period of time these shrub areas may succeed to woodlands.

IMPACTS OF PROPOSED FLOOD CONTROL PROJECTS

Construction of Mentone Dam and Reservoir and the realignment of Mill Creek and levee, as proposed by the CE, would have a major impact on the existing vegetation. The borrow pit would destroy over 200 ha. (500 ac.) of native juniper woodland and alluvial scrub vegetation. This would be a significant loss since the Mentone alluvial fan vegetation represents the largest stand of California juniper on the coastal side of the Transverse Ranges in southern California. Further, urban pressures elsewhere have reduced, altered, or destroyed the vegetation on other alluvial fans in coastal southern California. The presence of species such as Lepidospartum squamatum, unique to alluvial fans and washes, and the mixture of coastal sage scrub with chaparral species makes the vegetation unique to southern California. The springtime meadowland created by numerous species of herbaceous plants would be destroyed by inundation. This component of the vegetation is a carpet of herbaceous, annual flowering plants, between the shrubs, that flourishes during the sring months and then dies off with the onset of summer.

The existing percolation basins clearly indicate that junipers, all herbaceous plants, and many of the perennial plants that make up the alluvial scrub vegetation could not tolerate inundation. Plants remaining after grading operations are completed and the dam is operational would be killed if exposed to short episodes of inundation. The proposed recreational area of 121 ha. (300 ac.) would lie partially below the take line and would be subject to infrequent inundation episodes. If the Mentone Dam is constructed, sycamore, other riparian trees, shrubs adapted to the alluvial environment, and shrubs that can withstand inundation should be planted instead of inundation-intolerant species.

Human activity in the remaining natural and recreation areas would not greatly affect the perennial vegetation. However, foot traffic and other uses would have an impact on the annual herbaceous cover.

Within the Prado basin, the impact of flooding on the woodland trees seems minimal. To date they have been able to withstand at least three months of inundation without apparent damage. Whether they can continue to do so is unknown. The riparian shrubs can survive shorter periods of inundation, perhaps several weeks. Herbaceous vegetation and most agricultural crops would be affected by flooding, erosion, siltation, and inundation. The higher the frequency of inundation the greater the impact on herbaceous plants.

If material is taken from the basin for the construction of Mentone Dam, several hundred acres of riparian woodland will be destroyed. The borrow pit may be turned into four small lakes or one large lake for recreational purposes. If shoreline grading is required, this would further destroy riparian woodland vegetation. Small trees replanted to replace mature trees are not equivalent in stature, aesthetics, wildlife habitat value, or time.

Below Prado Dam the impacts of CE alternates 5 and 6 would result from the infrequent releases of volumes of water up to five times that of present release rates. Such high volumes would have major impacts on the riparian woodlands. All types of plants, even mature trees, would suffer from the erosive action and sheer weight and velocity of the water. Existing small channels and riverbanks would be altered or destroyed. Within the more stable woodlands, herbs, shrubs, tree seedlings, and downed dead wood would be swept away. As trees were dislodged and swept downstream, they would become obstructions in the main river channel. Ultimately, they would be swept out to sea.

The above impacts would be accentuated if more water was retained in the basin, since less water would be released in minor storms than at present. This would allow more trees, shrubs, herbs, and other understory plants to establish themselves in the main river channels before they were exposed to the impact of a major release of water. More frequent but less intense flooding would keep the woodland vegetation in a more juvenile stage of develoment; consequently it would show less impact from a major water release.

MITIGATION

1. The loss of prime juniper woodland could be partially mitigated by acquiring the woodland west of Orange Avenue. Although it lacks the richness of that east of Orange Avenue, it does possess the same structure and general physiognomy. This acquisition would insure that this woodland would not be lost to urbanization.

2. Wherever suitable, plantings of ground-cover, shrubs, and trees that are native and otherwise adapted to the site should be used. The present species could be augmented with such species as <u>Alnus</u> <u>rhombifolia</u>, <u>Salix</u> sp., and shrubs found on other alluvial fans in southern California.

3. All plantings around the proposed lake(s) should be species known to be able to withstand the riparian conditions of wet soil, flooding, and inundation.

4. Certain native riparian plants could be introduced to augment the species present. <u>Alnus</u> <u>rhombifolia</u>, <u>Acer</u> <u>macrophyllum</u>, and <u>Umbellularia</u> <u>californica</u> would be suitable additions.

5. Inundation episodes in the upper zones of the Prado Reservoir should not be allowed to last over three weeks, in order to avoid killing off the herbaceous understory plants and agricultural crops.

6. The projected release volumes from Prado Dam should be reduced. This would reduce the impact on the riparian woodlands below the dam and in the Featherly Park reach. Since the reach below the dam is designated as a greenbelt, the devastating effects of massive water release on the riparian woodlands should be reduced or avoided.

LITERATURE CITED

Anderson, E.N. 1972a. Western Riverside County: a natural history guide. 33 p. Anderson Publications, Sunnymead, Calif.

Anderson, E.N. 1972b. Man on the Santa Ana: a brief account of human management of a land. 10 p. Tri-County Conservation League, Riverside, Calif.

Andrews, P.W. 1972. Ecology of a southern California floodplain. Ph.D. Thesis, Claremont Graduate School, Claremont, Calif. 300 p.

Cooper, W.S. 1922. The broad-schlerophyll vegetation of California. An ecological study of chaparral and its related communities. 124 p. Carnegie Inst. Wash. Publ. 319, Washington, D.C.

Hanes, T.L. 1976. Vegetation types of the San Gabriel Mountains. In: Symposium proceedings: plant communities of southern California. Special Publ. Calif. Native Plant Soc., Berkeley, Calif. 164 p.

Hanes, T.L. 1980. Environmental appendix to the final Phase I general design memorandum and the final supplemental environmental impact statement--Santa Ana River main stem including Santiago Creek and Oak Street drainage. U.S. Engineer District, Los Angeles, Calif.

Howell, J.T. 1929. The flora of the Santa Ana Canyon region. Madroño 1:243-253.

Ingles, L.G. 1929. The seasonal and associational distribution of the fauna of the upper Santa Ana River Wash. J. Entomology and Zool. 21:1-45, 57-96.

Kirkpatrick, J.B., and C.F. Hutchinson. 1977. The community composition of California coastal sage scrub. Vegetatio 35(1):21-23.

Little, R.J. 1979. Floristic overview of the Prado Dam flood control basin, Part II--existing biotic environment. 5 p. Santa Ana Watershed Project Authority, by ECOS management criteria, Tustin, Calif.

Louis Rubidoux Nature Center. 1975. Plant communities of the Santa Ana River Regional Park, Rubidoux, Calif. 8 p. Riverside County, Riverside, Calif.

Marsh, G.A., and K.D. Abbott. 1972. Plants and animals of the Santa Ana River, Orange County. Orange County Flood Control District Publ. No. 27, Santa Ana, Calif. 50 p.

Mooney, H.A. 1977. Southern coastal scrub. In: M.G. Barbour and J. Major (eds.). Terrestrial vegetation of California. 1,002 p. Wiley Interscience, New York, N.Y.

Mueller-Dombois, D., and H. Ellenberg. 1974. Aims and methods of vegetation ecology. 541 p. John Wiley and Sons, New York, N.Y.

Munns, Bob. 1977. Flora of the Rubidoux Nature Center. 6 p. Natural Science Section, Angeles Chapter, Sierra Club, Los Angeles, Calif.

Riverside County Parks Dept. Undated. Willow Flats trail, nature trail guide. Prado Basin Regional Park, Norco. 5 p.

Riverside County Parks Dept. Undated. Checklist of the common plants associated with the Santa Ana River Regional Park, Riverside, Calif.

Smith, R.L. 1978. The alluvial scrub vegetation of the San Gabriel River floodplain, California. M.A. Thesis, California State University, Fullerton. 43 p.

Society of American Foresters. 1954. Forest cover types of North America. 67 p. Society of American Foresters, Washington, D. C.

Tri-County Conservation League. 1972. The living Santa Ana River. 31 p. Tri-County Conservation League, Riverside, Calif.

URS Research Company. 1974. Environmental baseline inventory of the Santa Ana River basin. 83 p. Prepared for the Santa Ana Watershed Planning Agency. Santa Ana Calif.

US Army Corps of Engineers. 1975. Draft environmental statement Santa Ana River Basin and Orange County, Los Angeles, Calif. 354 p. U.S. Army Corps of Engineers, Los Angeles, Calif.

US Army Corps of Engineers. 1977. Draft environmental statement. Review report on the Santa Ana River main stem--including Santiago Creek and Oak Street drain for flood control and allied purposes. 126 p. Office of the Chief of Engineers, Department of the Army, Washington. D.C.

Wieslander, A.E. 1934. Vegetation types of California. Corona quadrangle map. From a series of topographic botanical maps: vegetation types by California Forest and Range Experiment Station of the USDA. Forest Service Surveyed 1931 and Revised 1934.

TECHNICAL DELINEATION OF WETLAND BOUNDARIES

WITHIN CALIFORNIA RIPARIAN SYSTEMS[1]

Robert Terry Huffman[2]

Abstract.--Since passage of the Clean Water Act in 1972, significant emphasis has been placed on the need for technology which will enable regulatory personnel to precisely delineate jurisdiction boundaries between wetland and nonwetland ecosystems in the field. To meet this need, the US Army Corps of Engineers and the Environmental Protection Agency have jointly been conducting research directed toward the development of technical standards and field methodology. To date, these efforts have resulted in the development of technical standards and methodology which emphasize an ecosystematic approach whereby wetlands soil, hydrology, and vegetation parameters are jointly assessed when making boundary determinations. By relying on this multiple-parameter approach, the difficulty in making boundary determinations in transitional areas between wetland and upland areas has been substantially reduced. This method is in contrast to traditional techniques which emphasize the use of vegetative indicators.

INTRODUCTION

The primary legislative basis for the US Army Corps of Engineers (CE) regulatory authority in wetlands is Section 404 of the Clean Water Act. This act gives the CE and the US Environmental Protection Agency (EPA) authority to regulate discharge of dredged or fill material in "Waters of the United States". The objective of Section 404 is to maintain and restore the biological, physical, and chemical integrity of the nation's water quality through regulation of the discharge of dredged and fill materials into "Waters of the United States." "Waters of the United States" has a broad meaning, incorporating both aquatic and wetland ecosystems (Federal Register 1977). The purpose of this paper is to summarize the approach developed by the author to technically identify and delineate in the field wetland ecosystems found in association with California riparian zones.

---

[1] Paper presented at the California Riparian Systems Conference. [University of California, Davis, September 17-19, 1981].

[2] Robert Terry Huffman is Senior Project Scientist, Environmental Permitting and Government Relations, Woodward-Clyde Consultants, Walnut Creek, Calif.

JURISDICTION

Definition of jurisdiction in federal environmental regulatory programs has a legal basis that is the result of Congressional action. It is from this point that policy, regulations, and implementation procedures are developed by federal agencies mandated to conduct various regulatory programs.

Prior to enactment of the Clean Water Act, CE jurisdiction, under Section 10 of the Rivers and Harbors Appropriations Act of 1899, was defined as the mean high-tide line for tidal waters and ordinary high-water mark for nontidal waters, as the intent of Section 10 is to protect navigation. Reliance on the boundaries established by Section 10, therefore, proved to be of little value after the enactment of the FWPCA, given the intent of the Act, as water moves in hydrologic cycles, and pollution of this cycle at any point can affect water quality. Regulation of dredge and fill activities that cause water pollution, therefore, cannot rely on artificial boundary lines drawn for administrative purposes. Under Section 404 of the FWPCA, the intent of regulation is to focus on all "Waters of the United States" that together form the entire aquatic ecosystem (ibid.). The term "Waters of the United States" is defined to include:

a. The territorial seas with respect to the discharge of fill material.

b. Coastal and inland waters, lakes, rivers, streams that are navigable waters of the United States, including their adjacent wetlands.
c. Tributaries to navigable waters of the United States, including adjacent wetlands.
d. Interstate waters and their tributaries, including adjacent wetlands.
e. All other waters of the United States not identified above, such as isolated wetlands and lakes, intermittent streams, prairie potholes, and other waters that are not a part of a tributary system to interstate waters or navigable waters of the United States, the degradation or destruction of which could affect interstate commerce (ibid.).

Wetlands are also defined as "those areas that are inundated or saturated by surface or groundwater at a frequency and duration sufficient to support, and that under normal circumstances do support, a prevalence of vegetation typically adapted for life in saturated soil conditions" (ibid.).

These largely technical definitions are the basis from which the jurisdictional limits of Section 404 of the FWPCA must be initially determined. From this point, various exemptions, such as those for normal agricultural and silvicultural practices, come into play in deciding if an activity within the defined limits of jurisdiction would require a permit under the Section 404 regulatory program.

Although the meaning of "Waters of the United States" and wetlands appears to be clearly defined, the on-site determination of the landward limit of jurisdiction has often been difficult to make. This is especially true in areas of gradual gradation from obvious wetlands to obvious nonwetlands (i.e., uplands). These areas are typically under great demand for agricultural and urban development, yet they are vitally important for water quality maintenance and other benefits attributed to wetlands. With this emphasis in mind, it is extremely important that jurisdictional limits be determined with as much technical accuracy and consistency as possible.

DELINEATION OF WETLAND BOUNDARIES

Much emphasis and reliance has been placed on using vegetation as indicators of wetland boundaries. This technique has often proved troublesome for riparian systems, however, especially in areas where man regulates the flow of water within the streamcourse. For example, in the Sacramento River area, management of the river's flows has occurred since the early 1940s. This condition has resulted in a significantly reduced amount of flooding in high-terrace riparian zones, to the point that saturated soil conditions during the growing season are almost non-

existent. Yet vegetation cover-types in these areas largely remain representative of high-terrace wetland systems. If all that was looked for by an investigator was "a prevalence of vegetation typically adapted for life in saturated soil conditions", much of the high-terrace zone along the Sacramento River would technically qualify as being wetlands.

With reference to the above definition of wetlands, two key environmental characteristics are considered essential in the technical delineation of the landward jurisdictional limit of Section 404:

1. inundated or saturated soil conditions that are the result of periodic or permanent inundation by groundwater or surface water; and
2. a prevalence of vegetation typically adapted for life in inundated or saturated soil conditions.

These characteristics are actually general guidelines or concepts rather than specific parameters necessary to identify wetlands within California riparian systems under Section 404 jurisdiction. They alone do not provide solutions to the previously mentioned problem.

It is with these concepts in mind that three distinctive parameters are suggested which, when considered together, significantly increase the investigator's ability to correctly define a wetland boundary. They include wetland hydrology, soil, and vegetation. Each parameter is dependent on the other in an environmental sense, as any one does not uniquely make a wetland. It was from this concept that the "Multiple Parameter Approach to the Field Identification and Delineation of Wetlands" (Huffman 1981) was devised. The technical standard used to define wetlands is based on the following diagnostic environmental characteristics.

1. Hydrology—the area is inundated or saturated by surface water or groundwater either permanently or periodically during the growing season of the prevalent vegetation.

2. Soils—the soils within the root zone become saturated permanently or periodically during the growing season of the prevalent vegetation.

3. Vegetation—the prevalent plant species associated with the plant community are typically adapted for life within habitats that have permanent or alternating dry and inundated and/or saturated soil conditions as characterized by the hydrology and soil conditions given above. Wetland plant species are rooted-emergent organisms that, because of morphological adaptations(s), physiological adaptations(s), and/or reproductive strategies, have the ability to achieve maturity and reproduce in an environment where anaerobic soil conditions occur within the root zone on a permanent or periodic basis during the growing season.

A wetlands determination using the multiple-parameter approach relies upon evidence of a minimum of three positive indicator variables, at least one from each of the three parameters of hydrology, soils, and vegetation, before a positive wetland determination can be made (table 1).

The approach has considerable flexibility from one region to another, as the qualitative variables used to provide positive indication of each parameter can be added or deleted when necessary, given local variations in the environment.

Table 1.--Site inspection form B: Section 404--wetlands determination. See Glossary for definition of terms used in tables 1 and 2. (© Robert Terry Huffman 1981.)

I. WETLANDS INDICATORS FOR SITE #_____ TIME:_____ Date:_____

Mo.   Day   Yr

Wetlands parameter	Positive indicator variables	Indication[1]
1. Wetlands Hydrology	a. Drainage pattern(s)	_____
	b. Drift lines	_____
	c. Sediment deposition on vegetation	_____
	d. Water marks	_____
	e. Ice scars	_____
	f. Erosion features	_____
	g. Active water table within a major portion of the root zone	_____
	h. Stream gauge data	_____
	i. Tidal gauge data	_____
	j. Historical documentation	_____
	k. Visual observation of inundation or saturation	_____
2. Wetlands Soils	a. There is mottling with a chroma (brightness) of 2 or less within a major portion of the root zone	_____
	b. There is a gleyed soil horizon within a major portion of the root zone	_____
	c. If there is not mottling or if mottles present having a chroma greater than 2, the soil below 25 cm. has a chroma of 1 or less	_____
	d. The soil examined has wetness soil characteristics other than a, b, or c above (e.g. fluvent)	_____
	e. Presence of free water within the root zone	_____
	f. Visual observation of soil saturation	_____
3. Wetlands Vegetation	a. The technical literature indicates that the prevalent vegetation is associated with habitat conditions exhibiting any one of the hydrologic/soil-moisture regimes described in Table 2	_____
	b. The presence of morphological or physiological adaptations, or reproductive strategies for survival of the prevalent vegetation in aquatic or wetland habitats is observed or indicated in technical literature	_____
	c. Visual observation of survival of plant species in habitat conditions exhibiting any one of the hydrologic/soil-moisture regimes described in Table 2.	_____

[1]Photograph or describe all positive indicators in detail, reference literature, or other supporting documentation and attach copies where applicable.

Table 1.--Continued.

II. FINAL DETERMINATION

1. Was a positive indication of wetlands hydrology conditions found? ___Yes ___No
2. Was a positive indication of wetlands soil conditions found? ___Yes ___No
3. Was a positive indication of the presence of wetlands vegetation
   found? ___Yes ___No
4. Technical wetlands present (1 + 2 + 3 = technical wetland
   present)? ___Yes ___No

Table 2.--General summary of major vegetation types found
within a study site in relation to relative soil-
moisture habitat regimes. See Glossary for definition
of terms used in tables 1 and 2. (© Robert Terry
Huffman 1981.)

Soil-moisture regime

Prevalent vegetation species or community types

1. Intermittently exposed - Soil inundation or saturation by surface water or groundwater typically exists on a nearly permanent basis throughout the growing season of the prevalent vegetation, except during extreme drought periods.

1._____
_____
_____
_____
_____
_____
_____
_____

2. Semi-permanently inundated or saturated - Soil inundation or saturation by surface water or groundwater occurs periodically[1] for a major portion of the growing season of the prevalent vegetation. Typically occurs during the spring and summer months with a frequency ranging from 51 to 100 years. The total duration of time for the seasonal event(s) typically exceeds 25% of the growing season.

2._____
_____
_____
_____
_____
_____
_____
_____
_____
_____
_____
_____

3. Seasonally inundated or saturated - Soil inundation or saturation by surface water or groundwater typically occurs periodically for 1 to 2 months during the growing season of the prevalent vegetation. Typically occurs up to the beginning of the summer season with a frequency ranging from 51 to 100 years per 100 years. The total duration of time for the seasonal event(s) typically ranges from 12.5% to 25% of the growing season.

3._____
_____
_____
_____
_____
_____
_____
_____
_____
_____

[1]Periodically is used here to describe saturated soil conditions or inundation resulting from ponding from groundwater and/or rainwater, overland flow, stream flooding, or tidal action that occur(s) on a detectable regular or irregular basis with hours, days, weeks, months, or even years between events.

Table 2.--Continued.

Soil-moisture regime	Prevalent vegetation species or community types
4. Temporarily inundated or saturated - Soil inundation or saturation by surface water or groundwater typically occurs periodically for short periods during the growing season but not totaling more than 1 month for the entire growing season of the prevalent vegetation. Typical frequency ranges from 11 to 50 years per 100 years.[2] The total duration of time for the seasonal event(s) typically ranges from 2% to 12.5% of the growing season.	4._____

[2]Certain areas exhibiting this type of hydrologic/ soil-moisture regime are not classified as wetlands because the frequency of soil saturation does not support a prevalence of vegetation typically adapted for life in saturated soil conditions. Reliance on finding indications of each of the environmental parameters of the wetlands hydrology, wetlands soil conditions, and wetlands vegetation is stressed when wetland identification and delineation determinations are being made.

GLOSSARY

Adaptation: Response to selective pressure resulting in an organism (or group of organisms) acquiring characteristics which make the organism better suited to live and reproduce in its environment. A plant adaptation is therefore a peculiarity of morphological structure or physiology that especially aids in fitting the organism to its particular environment.

Aquatic ecosystem: Those areas that are either permanent or periodically flooded by surface water or groundwater and are unsuitable for growth of rooted-emergent vegetation.

Ecosystem: The plant community and the associated nonliving environment (chemical and physical) with which the vegetation interacts.

Flood: The condition that occurs when water overflows the natural or artificial confines of a stream or other body of water or accumulates by drainage over low-lying areas.

Groundwater: Subsurface water including the zone of aeration and zone of saturation.

Growing season: The frost-free period of the year (see US Department of the Interior [1970] for generalized regional delineation).

Habitat: The physical and chemical environment occupied by a particular plant, populations of plants, or a plant community.

Hydrology: The science dealing with the properties, distribution, and circulation of water.

Inundation: A flooded condition created by the rise and spread of surface water or groundwater over a land surface that is not permanently submerged.

Morphological: Pertaining to the structure and form of an organism at any stage of its life cycle.

Periodically: Herein defined to describe saturated soil conditions or inundation resulting from ponding from groundwater and/or rainwater, overland flow, stream flooding, or tidal action that occur(s) on a detectable regular or irregular basis with hours, days, weeks, months, or even years between events.

Physiological: Pertaining to the basic physical and chemical activities that occur in cells and tissues of organisms.

Prevalent vegetation: Herein defined for the purposes of this technical standard as the perennial plant species within all or any given vegetation strata having established relative areal cover, density, basal area, biomass, abundance, dominance value, or importance value per hectare $\geq 50\%$.

Saturated soil condition: Herein defined for the purposes of this technical standard as the soil within the root zone that becomes permeated with water to the extent that detectable anaerobic soil conditions occur.

Submergent plant: A vascular or nonvascular hydrophyte, either rooted or nonrooted, which lies entirely beneath the water surface, except for flowering parts in some species; e.g., wild celery (_Vallisneria americana_ Michx) or the stoneworts (_Chara_ spp.).

Surface water: Water above the substrate.

Typically adapted: Describing a species exhibiting the essential characteristics of a group.

Vegetation: The plant life that occupies a given area.

CONCLUSIONS

In technically defining the landward boundary of federal jurisdiction within wetland ecosystems, much emphasis has traditionally been placed by the CE as well as other federal agencies on using indicator vegetation. However, this technique has historically proven to be quite troublesome. This is because vegetation, considered alone, may both overstate and understate jurisdiction due to the often-broad genetic variability of the plant species encountered.

In contrast to the use of indicator species, wetlands determinations using the multiple parameter approach presented here rely upon evidence of a minimum of three positive indicator variables, at least one from each of the three parameters of hydrology, soils, and vegetation, before a positive wetland determination can be made. This approach has undergone considerable field testing in California and throughout the United States. Results of these tests demonstrate that the approach had considerable flexibility. When moving from one region of the country to another, the qualitative variables used to provide positive indications of each parameter can be added or deleted as necessary, given local variations in the environment. The approach also affords the user the ability to make rapid boundary determinations, thus foregoing lengthy delays while collecting quantitative data, which may take weeks, months, or even years to complete. The multi-parameter approach can also be applied during the winter season. Prior to use of the multiple parameter approach, regulatory jurisdiction determinations could only be made during the spring and summer (approximately three to four months of utility) in snowbound areas such as the Alaskan Arctic.

Training using the above described approach is currently being provided to federal, state, and local governments throughout the United States. The author is currently contemplating offering similar training to private concerns. The multi-parameter approach is easily mastered and does not require that users have an extensive technical background to become proficient in utilizing the approach.

LITERATURE CITED

Federal Register. 1977. Title 33--navigable waters; Chapter II--Corps of Engineers, Department of the Army: regulatory programs of the Corps of Engineers. Vol. 42(138): 37122-37164 (9 July). US Government Printing Office, Washington, D. C.

Huffman, R.T. 1981. Multiple parameter approach to the technical identification and delineation of aquatic and wetland ecosystems: technical standards. US Army Engineer Waterways Experiment Station Technical Report E-81 (in press). Vicksburg, Miss.

US Department of the Interior. 1970. National Atlas 1970:110-111.

RIPARIAN PROTECTION FROM CORPS OF ENGINEERS PROJECTS[1]

Fred Kindel[2]

Abstract.--About 19,800 ha. (49,000 ac.) of riparian vegetation in California can be protected with U.S. Army Corps of Engineers projects. Public support is vital. Some examples are the New Melones Lake project 2,065 ha. (5,100 ac.); Sacramento River Bank Protection project 351 ha. (868 ac.); and Sacramento River and Tributaries Bank Protection and Erosion Control Investigation 11,740 ha. (29,000 ac.).

INTRODUCTION

This paper addresses some work of the US Army Corps of Engineers (CE) in California that has an important influence on riparian systems. It describes the protection, restoration, or improvement of riparian vegetation in connection with 13 projects and investigations in various stages of construction and planning. There are about 19,800 ha. (49,000 ac.) of riparian vegetation that have been, will be, or have the potential of being protected, restored or improved as a part of the CE work within the Sacramento District.

COMPLETED OR NEARLY COMPLETED PROJECTS

New Melones Lake Project

The New Melones Lake Project has been a controversial and widely publicized project. New Melones Dam was completed in 1979. It is located on the Stanislaus River, in the Sierra foothills about 113 km. (70 mi.) east of Stockton (Calaveras and Tuolumne counties). Most people have probably heard the arguments regarding preservation of whitewater in the river versus flood control and development of water resources of the river. But there is a feature of this project that is less widely known--the lower Stanislaus River. The lower Stanislaus runs for about 96.6 km. (60 mi.) from Goodwin Dam, some 16 km. (10 mi.) below New Melones, to its confluence with the San Joaquin River near Caswell State Park.

The CE is acquiring interest in about 2,065 ha. (5,100 ac.) of riparian system along the lower Stanislaus River. This riparian area is

---

[1] Paper presented at the California Riparian Systems Conference. [University of California, Davis, September 17-19, 1981].

[2] Fred Kindel is Chief, Environmental Planning Section, Sacramento District, US Army Corps of Engineers, Sacramento, Calif.

needed for preservation of fish and wildlife habitat, for public recreation, and for passage of floodflows as a part of the overall project. Easements are being acquired for riparian vegetation protection and flowage; fee title is being acquired for a series of small parks for public access and recreation.

Sacramento Bank Protection Project

Another project that many may consider to be controversial is the Sacramento River Bank Protection Project. This is a joint project of the CE and the State of California, with the State paying one-third of the cost. The purpose of the project is to protect the integrity of the Sacramento River Flood Control Project--a system of levees and bypass channels which provides flood protection to about 323,900 ha. (800,000 ac.) of agricultural land and urban areas, including the city of Sacramento.

The first phase of this project was constructed between 1963 and 1974; about 130 km. (81 mi.) of levees was protected with rock bank protection. During the construction work, some riparian vegetation was removed from the levees and replaced with rock. With assistance from the USDI Fish and Wildlife Service (FWS) and agreement by the State of California to pay one-third of the added cost, the CE has prepared a feasibility report which recommends the restoration of 270 ha. (668 ac.) of riparian vegetation that was removed. If Congress authorizes and funds this work, the 270 ha. of riparian vegetation will be restored on berms adjacent to the levees at selected locations along 201 km. (125 mi.) of the Sacramento River upstream from the city of Sacramento.

A similar environmental protection and riparian vegetation restoration program was authorized by Congress in 1974 as an integral part of the next 124 km. (77 mi.) of bank protection, the second phase of the project. In conjunction with the second phase work, the State has acquired environmental easements on over 81 ha. (200 ac.) of land along the Sacramento River Flood Control Project.

Isabella Lake

Isabella Lake is located on the Kern River east of Bakersfield (Kern County). It is a reservoir storing up to 570,000 acre-feet (AF) of water for flood control, irrigation, and hydroelectric power. The project was completed in 1953 and has been recognized as an outstanding fishing lake for many years. In recent years, the wildlife habitat of the lakeshore has been managed and improved. Particular attention has been given to some 526 ha. (1,300 ac.) of riparian vegetation located where the South Fork of the Kern River enters the lake. Protection is being provided for this particular riparian system. The National Audubon Society and other conservation organizations believe it is a significant riparian resource. This area will be discussed more fully in a following section reporting on a current investigation of the CE that may affect it.

AUTHORIZED PROJECTS UNDER STUDY

There are four projects that have been authorized for which the CE has been conducting advanced planning and design studies prior to beginning construction.

Cottonwood Creek Project

The Cottonwood Creek Project includes two large reservoirs in Shasta and Tehama counties. This project will provide an added municipal and industrial water supply. The State of California will repay about 80% of the total cost of the project to conserve and store this water. The two reservoirs will store up to 1,600,000 AF of water and will inundate about 648 ha. (1,600 ac.) of riparian vegetation. The CE, after consulting with the FWS and the California Department of Fish and Game (DFG), has developed plans to restore this riparian vegetation on other lands needed for the project. Lands are needed below the spillways for accommodation of floodwaters and below the dams for management of salmon. The 648 ha. of riparian vegetation would be restored on those lands. In addition, the CE has identified a site of about 1,215 ha. (3,000 ac.) below the dams for riparian vegetation improvement. This is an area of existing riparian vegetation which could be protected and improved to support migratory birds. The FWS has advised that they may recommend the area be purchased to support the migratory bird conservation program which they administer. The two areas together would ensure federal protection and management for about 1,862 ha. (4,600 ac.) of riparian vegetation.

Merced County Streams Project

The Merced County Streams Project includes two existing dams, two dams to be built, and 53 km. (33 mi.) of channel improvements to control flooding in urban and agricultural areas in Merced County. At this project there is a mixture of important vegetation for wildlife, including grasslands, wetlands, and riparian vegetation, that will be protected. In conjunction with the project work, protective easements will be acquired by Merced County on 1,134 ha. (2,800 ac.) of grassland, 61 ha. (150 ac.) of wetlands, and 81 ha. (200 ac.) of existing riparian vegetation. The riparian vegetation is located partially behind the two existing dams which temporarily store floodwaters and partially along the streams below the dams. The design of the flood channels includes protection and restoration of the riparian vegetation while still allowing passage of the floodwaters.

Morrison Creek Project

The Morrison Creek Project is located on the east and south sides of the city of Sacramento (Sacramento County). A small lake would be formed near Mather Air Force Base. About 306 km. (190 mi.) of channel improvements would be provided in the urbanized area south of the Sacramento Army Depot, including the communities of Florin Center and Elk Grove. At the terminus of the channels, near the Sacramento River, floodwaters would be temporarily stored in a 2,834 ha. (7,000 ac.) flood-retardation basin which is also authorized as a national wildlife refuge, to be managed by the FWS. There are about 20 ha. (50 ac.) of riparian vegetation which would be protected at the retardation basin and wildlife refuge; the remainder is wetland and grassland. Additional riparian vegetation improvement may be provided as plans for the small lake, channels, and retardation basin are developed.

Stockton Ship Channel Project

The Stockton Ship Channel Project is an authorized navigation project which will allow larger, fully loaded deep-draft ships to reach the Port of Stockton. The present channel depth is 9.1 m. (30. ft.) deep below mean lower low water. The channel will be deepened to 10.7 m. (35 ft.) to allow ships using the channel to be more fully loaded and not have to leave port only partly loaded as many do now. About 9.2 million cubic meters (12 million cubic yards) of material will be dredged from the channel and deposited at selected sites. Environmental studies have been made in an effort to minimize damage to wetlands and riparian systems along the channel. About 162 ha. (400 ac.) at two flooded islands will be filled with dredged material to create new wetlands and sites for riparian vegetation. About 24 ha. (60 ac.) of riparian vegetation is included in this plan. Since the Sacramento/San Joaquin Delta area has a relatively small amount of riparian vegetation, this will be an important addition.

PREAUTHORIZATION INVESTIGATIONS

There are six investigations underway on possible projects having significant potentials for protecting and improving riparian vegetation.

Sacramento River and Tributaries Bank Protection and Erosion Control Investigation

This study covers 502 km. (312 mi.) of the Sacramento River from Collinsville upstream to Shasta Dam, and lower reaches of major tributaries such as the American and Feather rivers. The investigation is two-thirds complete. The major purpose of the investigation is to study alternatives for controlling streambank erosion and to determine if there is a federal interest in and local support for improved protection from erosion. One of the most promising methods of erosion control appears to be a comprehensive plan involving placement of bank protection at the outside of major river bends. Public recreation, fish and wildlife enhancement, and environmental quality improvement plans are also being studied. Riparian vegetation protection could be an important feature of a federal erosion control project since both fish and wildlife and environmental quality could be improved.

Riparian vegetation could become an important feature of any federal erosion control project that may be developed, if non-federal interests desire it and are willing to participate in the financing. Environmental studies show there are about 10,121 ha. (25,000 ac.) of riparian vegetation along 620 km. (385 mi.) of the Sacramento River and lower reaches of its major tributaries. There are about 1,619 ha. (4,000 ac.) of riparian system along 290 km. (180 mi.) of the smaller tributaries to the Sacramento River within the Sacramento Valley. Important areas of this 11,740 ha. (29,000 ac.) of riparian vegetation could be included in a fish and wildlife management or environmental quality plan to accompany an erosion control plan for the Sacramento River and its major tributaries.

Other Investigations

Five other investigations are underway which do not appear to have significant potential for protecting and improving riparian vegetation, in contrast to that, for example, on the Sacramento River. However, any protection which can be provided to riparian vegetation is useful because of the overall diminished size of this resource. Three of these investigations were completed within the past year, and reports on these investigations are being transmitted to Congress recommending authorization of new projects. The last two investigations are each about two-thirds complete.

Cache Creek Project

The Cache Creek Project would be located partially at the outlet of Clear Lake, to control flooding at the lake, and partially at a sediment control basin near Woodland and the Sacramento River in Yolo County. A new national wildlife refuge would be located on the 1,460 ha. (3,600 ac.) sediment basin and operated by the FWS. This would include about 20 ha. (50 ac.) of riparian vegetation.

Sacramento River Deep Water Ship Channel Project

The Sacramento River Deep Water Ship Channel Project would deepen the Sacramento River Ship Channel from its present 9.1 m. (30 ft.) below mean lower low water to 10.7 m. (35 ft.). Similar to the Stockton Ship Channel, the deeper Sacramento Channel is needed so ships may be more fully loaded at the port, instead of just partly loaded as they often are at the present time. This proposed project includes protection of 61 ha. (150 ac.) of riparian vegetation and about 20 ha. (50 ac.) of wetlands.

Redbank-Fancher Creeks Project

The Redbank-Fancher Creeks Project would be located in the urban area of Fresno (Fresno County). Flood damages in the Fresno metropolitan area would be reduced by providing two small dams and three small detention basins to store floodwaters on the streams that flow through this urban area. Public recreation is included at the larger dam. About 28 ha. (70 ac.) of riparian vegetation would be developed on lands acquired for the larger dam, to mitigate losses resulting from the overall project.

Kern River Investigation

The Kern River Investigation is studying alternatives to determine if additional water should be stored in the existing Isabella Lake, to improve the public recreation and fishery resources. In dry years, when the irrigation interests withdraw their water, the lake is often drawn down below 100,000 AF. Alternatives being studied would provide a minimum pool of 110,000 AF for recreation and fishery improvement.

As mentioned earlier, there is an important riparian vegetation area of 526 ha. (1,300 ac.) in the South Fork area of the existing lake. In cooperation with the FWS, the CE is studying how an enlarged lake would affect this area. This should result in proposals for ways to restore any riparian vegetation that might be lost and improve and increase the amount of existing riparian vegetation. Additional lands could be obtained, or increased water distribution and management could be arranged. Alternately, more intensified management of project lands, or a combination of all these, and perhaps other measures, could be included in a proposal to enlarge the lake, so that the existing riparian vegetation is protected and restored, and the amount is not decreased. A new, added riparian vegetation area of perhaps about 200 ha. (500 ac.) could also be provided as a wildlife enhancement or environmental quality feature if desired.

Sacramento/San Joaquin Delta Investigation

The Sacramento/San Joaquin Delta Investigation is studying alternatives to determine if flood protection, water quality protection, public recreation, fish and wildlife enhancement, and environmental quality improvement can be provided. The CE and the State of California are engaged in joint studies to determine if a solution to these problems and opportunities is feasible and desirable. The CE has prepared an environmental atlas (U.S. Army Corps of Engineers 1979) which shows about 2,874 ha. (7,100 ac.) of riparian vegetation in the Delta. Included in the studies underway are measures for protecting or restoring riparian vegetation which might be affected by new levee construction for flood control. Potential measures for fish and wildlife enhancement and environmental quality improvement are also being studied.

If non-federal interests desire these measures and are willing to participate in the financing, riparian vegetation could become an important feature of any federal plan for protecting the Delta. Important areas of the Delta's riparian vegetation could be included in a fish and wildlife management or environmental quality improvement plan to accompany a flood protection and recreation improvement plan for the Delta.

THE IMPORTANCE OF COOPERATION AND ASSISTANCE

Two additional factors are central to the success of any CE efforts to protect and restore riparian systems on its projects. As a matter of fact, all of the riparian protection initiatives described in this paper would have been or will in the future be impossible to produce without them. These important factors are cooperation and assistance from other agencies, organizations, and the general public.

First, non-federal agencies must sponsor studies and identify needed improvements. The CE looks to these agencies to assist in gathering information and to participate in public meetings and workshops to inform the public and obtain its views. The CE also depends on several federal and non-federal agencies for their expertise in examining the problems and the alternative solutions it evaluates. For example, the FWS is asked to evaluate every project and investigation undertaken by the CE and to develop the means and

measures to protect and improve fish and wildlife resources; riparian vegetation is one of the more important of these resources. In fact, the CE transfers funds to the FWS from project and investigation accounts so that the FWS may accomplish these evaluations.

The CE depends also on citizens groups and individuals to participate in the studies and in meetings to discuss the projects and investigations. The CE depends upon the public's review of its reports and environmental statements. Public participation, cooperation, and assistance is necessary for the CE to prepare project plans which are desirable and will result in riparian protection.

CONCLUSION

Perhaps the best way to conclude is to summarize the figures presented in this paper on the 13 projects and investigations by CE in the Sacramento District. Three completed or almost completed projects will protect about 2,943 ha. (7,268 ac.) of riparian vegetation. Four authorized projects include plans to protect 1,984 ha. (4,900 ac.) of riparian vegetation. Six investigations could result in plans to protect up to 14,939 ha. (36,900 ac.) of riparian vegetation. This is a total of more than 19,838 ha. (49,000 ac.) in the Central Valley of California, a significant protection for riparian vegetation from CE projects.

LITERATURE CITED

U.S. Army Corps of Engineers. 1979. Sacramento-San Joaquin Delta, California, Environmental Atlas. U.S. Army Corps of Engineers, Sacramento District, Sacramento, Calif.

NOTE: The CE has a number of reports concerning the specific projects discussed in this paper. Copies may be obtained by contacting: District Engineer, Sacramento District, U.S. Army Corps of Engineers, 650 Capitol Mall, Sacramento, Calif., 95814.

SECTION 404 JURISDICTIONAL DETERMINATIONS

IN RIPARIAN SYSTEMS[1]

Thomas H. Wakeman and Calvin C. Fong[2]

Abstract.--This paper describes actions at the federal level to protect riparian systems. The emphasis is placed on the regulatory and jurisdictional activities of the US Army Corps of Engineers, San Francisco District, because it operates in California.

INTRODUCTION

It is estimated that 70 to 90% of all original riparian systems in the continental United States has been destroyed (US Council on Environmental Quality 1978). Along the Sacramento, lower Feather, and American rivers and other aggrading streams, it has been estimated there were about 314,000 ha. (775,000 ac.) of riparian vegetation in 1850 and only approximately 4,900 ha. (12,000 ac.) today (Smith 1977). This is a reduction of 98.5%. The importance of riparian systems has become increasingly obvious, particularly with the ecological investigations conducted over the last 10 years (Motroni 1980).

Riparian systems have an especially great value as buffers and filters between man's urban and agricultural activities and critically important freshwater resources (Odum 1978). The purpose of this paper is to explain what has occurred at the federal level to manage these diminishing resources from unnecesssary degradation or loss. Emphasis has been placed on the regulatory activities of the US Army Corps of Engineers (CE), San Francisco District, as it operates in and adjacent to California's riparian systems.

LEGISLATIVE AND JUDICIAL HISTORY

The CE has been involved in regulating certain activities in the nation's waters since 1890. Prior to 1968, the CE regulatory program was primarily directed towards protecting commercial navigation from encroachment. Subsequent to the National Environmental Policy Act of 1969,

the Federal Water Pollution Control Act Amendments of 1972, and the judicial decisions of Zabel v. Tabb,[3] the program evolved from one that considered navigation only to one that protects the full public interest. At this point the foundation of the CE regulatory program became the "public interest balancing process" (Coode 1981). During this process, decisions on permit applications are made only after a balancing of the favorable effects against the detrimental impacts has been concluded. The objective of the program is to ensure that man's uses of the nation's water resources will serve the best interests of society as a whole.

Part of this public interest balancing process is the protection of wetlands from the irresponsible and unregulated discharge of dredged or fill materials that could permanently destroy or alter the character of these valuable resources. The authority for the CE's responsibility to regulate the disposal of dredged or fill material is the Federal Water Pollution Control Act Amendments of 1972, Section 404 (superseded by the Clean Water Act of 1977). Initially, the CE limited its regulatory authority under Section 404 to waters that had been traditionally defined as navigable. In 1975, the limitation of CE authority to these waters was successfully challenged in the Federal District Court for the District of Columbia, in NRDC v. Calloway.[4] The court ordered the CE to expand its legal definition of waters subject to Section 404 jurisdiction to all waters of the United States, including their adjacent wetlands and natural lakes larger than five acres (2 ha.).

As ordered by the court, the CE proceeded to expand its jurisdiction into wetlands. As defined by the Code of Federal Regulations,[5] wetlands are those areas "...that are inundated or saturated by surface or groundwater at a frequen-

---

[1] Paper presented at the California Riparian Systems Conference. [University of California, Davis, September 17-19, 1981].

[2] Thomas H. Wakeman is Chief, South Area Processing Section, Calvin C. Fong is Chief, Regulatory Functions Branch; both are with the US Army Corps of Engineers, San Francisco District, San Francisco, Calif.

---

[3] 430 F. 2d 199 (5th Cir., July 16, 1970).
[4] 392 F. Supp. 685 (D.D.C. 1975).
[5] 33 CFR 323.2(c).

cy and duration sufficient to support, and under normal circumstances do support, a prevalence of vegetation typically adapted for life in saturated soil conditions" (US Department of the Army 1977).

PROBLEMS WITH TERMS AND DEFINITIONS

The CE definition of a wetland, although technical and perhaps narrow in concept, does encompass a variety of wetland types defined by others. Following the wetland classification scheme of Cowardin et al. (1979), their wetland types (emergent wetland, scrub/shrub wetland, forested wetland, moss/lichen wetland) could be considered wetlands under the perview of Section 404 if they meet the three-parameter test of vegetation, soils, and hydrology as defined by Huffman (1983). A riparian system or a portion thereof could also be subject to Section 404 review if the area fits the CE definition of a wetland (using the three-parameter approach). The authors of this paper feel that the wetland definition used by the CE is technical as well as flexible enough to cover most wetland types—although it cannot satisfy everyone's perception of a wetland all the time.

Perception of a wetland is not merely a technical issue; it is very much a subjective one as well. An attempt to make the definition more technical could cause jurisdictional determinations to become bogged (not a pun!) down in details to the point that sight is lost of the important wetland values that are supposed to be protected. On the other hand, to make the definition broader could go beyond the intent of the Clean Water Act. See also the riparian glossary of this volume.

The relationship between the terms "riparian area" and "wetland" is also muddied. Riparian areas could encompass typically non-aquatic wetland areas too, and still be within the "floodplain." Some believe that all three terms—riparian area, wetland, and floodplain—are synonymous. Because of a lack of uniformity in applying these terms nationally, management of the Section 404 program is inconsistent from one region to another. Since the California Riparian Systems Conference is primarily concerned with the Section 404 jurisdiction in riparian areas, for the purpose of this paper, we will use the term "forested wetland" (from Cowardin et al. 1979) as those periodically inundated areas of the California riparian zone typified by "wetland" trees and associated understory that might be regulated under Section 404.

The authors know of no single plant that is an absolute indicator of a forested wetland (i.e., an obligate hydrophyte) along any California watercourse—although there are several good indicator species, especially if they occur together in proximity to a watercourse. This is in contrast to other wetland types that do have at least one absolute indicator of that type wet-

land. For example, emergent wetlands found in both salt water and fresh water have Pacific cordgrass (Spartina foliosa) and cattails (Typha spp.), respectively, that are absolute wetland indicators.

We feel that the plants listed in table 1 are good wetland indicator plants for forested wetlands in California. The more of these plants found in an area adjacent to a lake or tributary, the greater the chances are it would fit the CE's wetland definition and be subject to Section 404 regulations. Table 1 is not a comprehensive list, but rather a provisional one. The CE, San Francisco District, will no doubt add to the list as more information is acquired about the mesic nature of various riparian plants.

Table 1.—Some riparian species that might indicate Section 404 forested wetlands in California.[1]

Common name	Scientific name
Fremont cottonwood	Populus fremontii
Black cottonwood	P. trichocarpa
White alder	Alnus rhombifolia
Red alder	A. rubra
California box elder	Acer negundo
Oregon ash	Fraxinus latifolia
Hind's black walnut	Juglans hindsii
Western sycamore	Platanus racemosa
Arroyo willow	Salix lasiolepis
Yellow willow	S. lasiandra
Sandbar willow	S. hindsiana
Willows	Salix spp.
Western dogwood	Cornus occidentalis
American laurel	Kalmia poliofolia
Western azalea	Rhododendron occidentale
Buttonbush	Cephalanthus occidentalis
California mugwort	Artemisia douglasiana
Cocklebur	Xanthium strumarium
Monkey flower	Mimulus tilingii

[1]Any one species in this table cannot be used as the sole determinant of a forested wetland that would fall under the Section 404 perview. A combination of several of the above species occurring in the same area could indicate a 404 wetland. Soils (degree and length of saturation) and hydrology (source[s] of water) of the area need to be taken into account.

JURISDICTIONAL DETERMINATIONS

Beyond vegetation, wetlands are defined by their soils and hydrology. However, as with vegetation, both the type of soils and the hydrologic characteristics of riparian areas can be ill-defined (O'Brien et al. 1980). This is particularly true of seasonally arid areas of California. According to the CE definition of wetlands, soils have to be periodically inundated or saturated by surface water or groundwater during the growing season. Hydromorphic soils can be identified by temperature, color, oxidation-reduction (redox) potential, and pH (Flint 1980). Hydrologic criteria for determination of CE jurisdiction in riparian areas must also be utilized within the constraints of the terminology used by the authorizing legislation.

Prior to accepting an application for a Department of the Army permit, a determination of the location of the work with respect to the "headwaters" of the stream must be made[6] (US Department of the Army 1977). Work below the headwaters may require an individual permit. The headwaters of a perennial stream has been defined for present purposes as the point above which the average annual flow is less than 5 cu. ft. per second (cfs). For streams that are dry for long periods during of the year, i.e., intermittent streams, the headwaters is that point where flow of 5 cfs is equaled or exceeded 50% of the time. Procedures for making the headwaters determination on streams in the CE, San Francisco District, have been developed (US Army Corps of Engineers 1981).

If work is below the headwaters, the next issue is the determination of whether all or only a portion of the project is in the CE jurisdiction. In the absence of adjacent wetland vegetation, the limit of CE jurisdiction is the "ordinary high-water mark." This mark is the line on the shore established by the fluctuations of the stream and indicated by physical characteristics such as a clear, natural line impressed on the bank; shelving; changes in soil character; the presence of litter and debris; or other appropriate means[7] (US Department of the Army 1977).

Determination of the ordinary high-water mark is made in the CE, San Francisco District, from aerial photographs or on-site field investigations. In some cases, no line on the bank or soil or vegetative changes are identifiable in the stream reach of interest. In such cases, investigations of reaches both upstream and downstream of the project are made, including the presence of discolorations in the concrete at road crossings. Once such locations are identified, it is possible by means of hydraulic water-surface profile calculations to determine the water-surface levels in the reach of interest (US Army Corps of Engineers 1981).

One stream that has been extremely troublesome with regard to establishing CE Section 404 jurisdiction is the Salinas River (fig. 1). The Salinas River system drains a mountain and foothill area of about 10,300 sq. km. (3,950 sq. mi.), exclusive of the Soda Lake watershed, which is a closed interior valley with an area of about 1,550 sq. km. (660 sq. mi.)

[6]33 CFR 323.2(h).
[7]33 CFR 323.2(g).

Figure 1.--Aerial photograph of Salinas River at Texaco's San Ardo oil field showing limits of vegetation in riverbed.

(California Department of Public Works 1946). The main thread of the river is about 270 km. (170 mi.) long; it meanders through the valley in a generally northwesterly course to its mouth in Monterey Bay. Unusually high infiltration and percolation rates exist in the Salinas Valley floor due to porous soil in the alluvial floodplain. It is only during the winter season after moderate to heavy rainfall that these loss rates are reduced. After soil moisture conditions conditions are satisfied, an intense storm of two or more days duration will cause a rapid rise in runoff. There is a large variation in the relationship of peak discharges between the tributaries to the main river channel and channel storage which account for these variations (US Army Corps of Engineers 1970). Because of these runoff and flooding characteristics, determination of the limits of 404 jurisdiction in certain reaches of the Salinas River is very difficult.

One such reach is approximately 8 km. (5 mi.) south of San Ardo (Monterey County), where Texaco, Inc. wanted to construct a two-lane vehicular and pipe bridge. The area is flat and without definitive streambanks from which ordinary high-water can be determined. The soils in the area are a mosaic of Metz Complex, Psamments, and Fluvents in a band more than 1,200 m. (4,000 ft.) wide (US Department of Agriculture 1978). Thus, neither hydrology nor soils classification alone enabled the determination of what portion of the approach fills for the 320-m. (1,060-ft.) box-girder bridge was within the CE jurisdiction. Vegetation in the area included both willows (Salix lasiolepis and S. lasiandra) and valley oak (Quercus lobata). But, as mentioned previously, these species alone are not adequate to establish the limits of Section 404 jurisdiction. However, utilizing discoloration on an upstream bridge to assist in estimating the ordinary high-water mark, on-site analysis of soils, and delineation of the bank boundary using vegetation (see fig. 1), the CE was able to determine that approximately 12,200 cubic m. (16,000 cubic yd.) of material for the approach fills would be within CE jurisdiction.

In other areas the problem of determining jurisdiction becomes even more complex. There are about 80 km. (50 mi.) of non-continuous levees constructed by individual property owners along the Salinas River and its tributaries (US Army Corps of Engineers 1970). The areas behind these levees have had their hydrologic characteristics altered, soil conditions changed, and riparian vegetation removed; this is particularly true if the area is being or has been farmed. Thus, jurisdictional determinations, even with the three-parameter approach, in areas behind levees can be extremely perplexing.

CONCLUSIONS

Section 404 of the Clean Water Act is one of the authorities used by the CE in its process of balancing public interest when issuing a Department of the Army permit. Part of the public interest is the effective management and protection of riparian systems within CE jurisdiction. However, in arid California's intermittent streams, it is often difficult to determine the limits of Section 404 jurisdiction. Assessment of jurisdiction must frequently rely on more than one characterizing parameter (i.e., vegetation, soil, or hydrology). In addition, assessments must be analyzed on a case-by-case basis.

LITERATURE CITED

California Department of Public Works. 1946. Salinas basin investigation. 230 p. State of California, Sacramento.

Cowardin, L.M., V. Carter, F.C. Golet, and E.T. LaRoe. 1979. Classification of wetlands and deep-water habitats of the United States. 103 p. Office of Biological Services, USDI Fish and Wildlife Service, Washington, D.C.

Flint, P.S. 1980. Simple soil testing in the laboratory. 5 p. Harvey and Stanley Associates, Inc., San Jose, Calif.

Goode, B.N. 1981. The public interest review process. National Wetlands Newsletter 3(1): 6-7.

Huffman, R.T. 1983. Technical delineation of wetland boundaries within California riparian systems. In: R.E. Warner and K.M. Hendrix (ed.). California Riparian Systems. [University of California, Davis, September 17-19, 1981.] University of California Press, Berkeley.

Motroni, R. 1980. The importance of riparian zones to terrestrial wildlife. 83 p. Prepared for US Army Corps of Engineers, Sacramento Distict, Calif.

O'Brien, A.L., and W.S. Motts. 1980. Hydrologic evaluation of wetland basins for land use planning. Water Resources Bulletin 16(5): 785-789.

Odum, E. P. 1978. Ecological importance of riparian zone. p. 1-4. In: R.R. Johnson and J.F. McCormick (tech. coord.). Strategies for protection and management of floodplain wetlands and other riparian ecosystems. [Callaway Gardens, Georgia, December 11-13, 1978]. USDA Forest Service GTR-WO-12, Washington, D.C. 410 p.

Smith, F.E. 1977. A short review of the status of riparian forest in California. p. 1-2. In: A. Sands (ed.). Riparian forests in California: their ecology and conservation. Institute of Ecology Pub. 15, University of California, Davis. 122 p.

US Army Corps of Engineers. 1970. Report on January and February 1969 floods, Vol. I. 21 p. US Army Engineer District, San Francisco, Calif.

US Army Corps of Engineers. 1981. Procedures for jurisdictional determinations under Section 404 of the Clean Water Act. 18 p. US Army Engineer District, San Francisco, Calif.

US Council on Environmental Quality. 1978. Environmental quality. Ninth annual report. 599 p. Stock No. 041-011-00040-8, US Government Printing Office, Washington, D.C.

US Department of Agriculture. 1978. Soil survey of Monterey County, California. 228 p. Cartographic Division, USDA Soil Conservation Service, Washington, D.C.

US Department of the Army. 1977. Regulatory program of the Corps of Engineers. Federal Register Part II 42(138): 37122-37164.

RINGTAIL DISTRIBUTION AND ABUNDANCE

IN THE CENTRAL VALLEY OF CALIFORNIA[1]

Linda Belluomini and Gene R. Trapp[2]

Abstract.--The presence of ringtails (_Bassariscus astutus raptor_) in riparian systems of the northern Central Valley is documented in this study, constituting a range extension. Ringtail densities 2.5 to 5 times greater than reported in the literature for other habitats were recorded, _viz._ 10.5 to 20.5 per 100 ha. (26.7 to 52.8 per mi^2). Habitat composition was examined and related to the densities obtained. A direct relationship is suggested between ringtail density and community productivity and structural complexity.

INTRODUCTION

Ringtails (_Bassariscus astutus_) are distributed throughout 11 southwestern states and portions of Mexico (Long and House 1962; Hall 1981). Throughout their range they are typically associated with boulder-strewn chaparral, chaparral interspersed with evergreen woodland, oak woodland, and scrub vegetation of various types (Seton 1929; Grinnell _et al._ 1937; Taylor 1954; Davis 1960; Hall 1981). Within California, ringtails inhabit the "Upper Sonoran Life Zone" on Pacific drainage slopes from the Oregon border to Mexico and the mountain ranges east of the Southern Sierra Nevada (Grinnell _et al._ 1937). Although acknowledging the presence of ringtails (the race _B. a. raptor_) in streamside vegetation to about the 160-m. (500-ft.) elevation, Grinnell _et al._ (_ibid._) apparently found no evidence to suggest that ringtails occurred in this vegetation-type on the floor of the Central Valley. However, they did report ringtail observations for the Sacramento River in southern Tehama County, in the northern end of the Valley. Their belief that ringtails were restricted to the surrounding foothills and mountains is apparent in their distribution map.

The first published report of ringtails occurring on the Valley floor was made by Naylor and Wilson (1956). They observed ringtails in Wood Duck (_Aix sponsa_) nest boxes in Butte Sink, along Butte Creek, 4.8 km. (3 mi.) north-east of Colusa, Colusa County, on the floor of the Sacramento Valley. Notwithstanding the recognized occurrence of ringtails in Butte Sink (Hall and Kelson 1959; Schempf and White 1977; Hall 1981), reviews of ringtail distribution (op. cit.; Ingles 1965) subsequent to Grinnell _et al._ (1937) did not modify the range of ringtails in California relative to the Central Valley.

In December 1971, Dr. Dallas Sutton[3] informed Trapp about the ease of collecting ringtails along the Sacramento River southwest of Chico for his mammal collection at California State University at Chico. Subsequently, two recent mammal inventories suggested that ringtails may occur in riparian vegetation associated with the network of drainages in the Central Valley. Stone (1976) detected an abundance of ringtails at certain sites along the Sacramento River in Tehama County at localities approximating those reported to have ringtails by Grinnell _et al._ (1937). Also, while conducting a mammal census of the Bobelaine Audubon Sanctuary on the Feather River at its confluence with the Bear River in Sutter County, during the spring of 1978, members of the Ecological Research Society of California State University, Sacramento, live-trapped eight ringtails. These data also suggested ringtail densities in riparian vegetation greater than those reported in the literature for other types of systems (_ibid._; Taylor 1954; Trapp 1978).

The present study had three objectives: 1) to refine earlier distribution studies of the ringtail in California with respect to the Central Valley; 2) to verify preliminary observa-

---

[1]Paper presented at the California Riparian Systems Conference. [University of California, Davis, September 17-19, 1981].

[2]Linda Belluomini is Resource Specialist, Natural Resources, Marine Corps Base, Camp Pendleton, Calif. Gene R. Trapp is Associate Professor of Biological Sciences, California State University, Sacramento.

---

[3]Dr. Dallas Sutton, Emeritus Professor, California State University, Chico. Personal conversation.

tions which indicated desities much higher in riparian vegetation of the Central Valley than reported in the literature for other vegetation-types occupied by ringtails; and 3) to examine the composition of the riparian plant community associated with sites occupied by ringtails.

METHODS AND MATERIALS

Ringtail distribution in the Central Valley was evaluated using five methods: 1) a literature review was conducted; 2) a furbearer observation questionnaire was circulated statewide; 3) locality data were gleaned from museum specimens; 4) knowledgeable persons were contacted; and 5) ringtails were captured by livetrapping.

Furbearer observation reports requesting specific information on ringtail sightings were distributed to appropriate Federal, State, and local agencies (e.g., wildlife refuges, sanctuaries, and preserves; California Department of Fish and Game biologists and wardens), as well as licensed trappers throughout California. Letters requesting pertinent locality information were sent to selected college and university museums which might have on deposit ringtail skins and/or skulls collected in the Valley. Personal contact was initiated with persons known to be familiar with wildlife of the Central Valley. Livetrapping was conducted during the summer and fall of 1978 and 1979 at nine sites in the Sacramento Valley to determine if ringtails were present.

Ringtails were easily captured using single-doored 9x9x26-in. and double-doored 6x6x24-in. galvanized, wire mesh livetraps.[4] Several baits (strawberry jam, raisins, muskrat meat) and ringtail lure were used to attract ringtails into the traps. Strawberry jam was the most effective attractant.

Data used for computation of density were collected by livetrapping, tagging, and recapture at five of the nine sites mentioned above. Livetraps were placed in a nonrandom manner (i.e., adjacent to ringtail scats; on, or alongside logs, etc.); throughout a portion of a particular study site. When recaptures indicated that all individuals within the immediate vicinity had been caught, the traps were moved variable distances away from that location until unmarked individuals were captured. This direct count process was repeated until presumably all ringtails within a study site were trapped. Aerial photographs were planimetered to determine the area of each study site, excluding habitats where ringtails were not captured or areas thought to be non-ringtail habitat. The number of ringtails per unit area was determined by dividing the total number captured at a study site by the total area, giving what amounts to an "ecological" density (Odum 1971; Smith 1980).

---

[4]Tomahawk Live Trap Co., P.O. Box 323, Tomahawk, Wisconsin 54487.

To facilitate handling of ringtails, Tranvet 25[5] was used during the early stages of this study. The Tranvet was orally administered using an eyedropper. Dosages ranging from 0.16 ml. to 0.30 ml. were given to individuals weighing from 870 gm. to 1300 gm.

The effect of the Tranvet was not consistent. Hence, an alternative and more effective means of subduing the ringtails was sought. Ketamine hydrochloride,[6] a derivative of phencyclidine, was successfully used. Dosages approximating 0.01 ml. per 100 gm. of body weight were sufficient to sedate ringtails in 1-4 minutes for the 10-20 minutes necessary to tag, measure, weigh, and examine them. Recovery from the drug occurred 30-60 minutes after injection.

Each captured ringtail was weighed (to the nearest 10 gm.) in a burlap sack. Data on the following variables were taken: 1) sex; 2) lengths of tail, body, right hind foot, right ear-to-notch, and right ear-to-crown; 3) circumferences of neck and cranium (all measurements recorded in mm.); 4) pelage condition; and 5) body temperature. A numbered ear tag[7] was fixed to the medial proximal edge of the right ear. Animals were released at the point of capture, after recovery from the drug.

The vegetation on one of the study sites (Site V) was analyzed by the plotless point-quarter and quadrat methods (Cottan and Curtis 1956; Cox 1976). Motroni (1978, 1979) used these techniques to collect data on the composition of riparian vegetation at four of the study sites (Site I, II, III, IV). Overstory, midstory, and understory layers were distinguished (as described by Motroni 1978) and analyzed separately. The plotless point-quarter method was used to collect data on overstory and midstory vegetation. The quadrat method was used to evaluate the understory. In this study, the boundaries of the Central Valley correspond to those of "California Prairie" described by Küchler (1977), excluding that found within Monterey County.

Study Sites

Ringtail densities were determined at five study sites in riparian vegetation of the Sacramento Valley (fig. 1).

Study Site I

Preliminary trapping efforts were conducted at the Bobelaine Audubon Sanctuary, located on the Feather River near its confluence with the Bear River, approximately 3.2 km. (2.0 mi.) north of the town of Nicolaus, Sutter County, Califor-

---

[5]Propio-promazine hydrochloride, 100 mg./ml., Diamond Laboratories, Inc., Des Moines, Iowa.
[6]Vetelar, Parke-Davis & Co., Detroit, Michigan 48232.
[7]No. 1, monel metal, Jiffy wing bands from National Band and Tag Co., Newport, Kentucky.

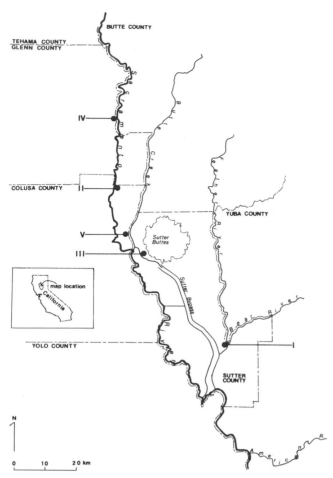

Figure 1.--Ringtail study site locations in the Sacramento Valley, California.

nia (38° 56' 15" north, 121° 35' 45" west). The sanctuary is bordered on the east by the Feather River, on the west by walnut orchards, and on the north and south by riparian woodland. A slough traverses the western edge of the sanctuary and at one point widens into a 4.7 ha. (11.5 ac.) pond.

An extensive vegetation survey of the study site was conducted by Motroni (1979). Five major plant associations were recognized: 1) river grassland; 2) riparian shrub; 3) oak woodland; 4) cottonwood forest; and 5) riparian forest. It was within the last two plant associations and primarily in the riparian forest bordering the slough and pond that the majority of ringtails was livetrapped. These areas comprise approximately 69 ha. (172 ac.). Motroni (ibid.) found the overstory of the riparian forest to be dominated by cottonwood (Populus fremontii). Other species present included box elder (Acer negundo), valley oak (Quercus lobata), and black walnut (Juglans hindsii). The dense midstory was dominated by wild grape (Vitis californica), poison oak (Rhus diversiloba), Mexican tea (Chenopodium ambrosioides). Other species present included blackberry (Rubus vitifolius), coyote bush (Baccharis pilularis var. consanguinea),

and wild rose (Rosa californica). The understory was dominated by bermuda grass (Cynodon dactylon).

Study Site II

This 88-ha. (218-ac.) site is located on the Henry Womble property on the east bank of the Sacramento River 2.4 km. (1.5 mi.) south of Princeton, Colusa County, California (39° 22' 30" north, 122° 00' west). This is virtually a riparian island bordered by the Sacramento River and surrounded on three sides by agricultural fields. There are two small ponds, each less than 0.8 ha. (2 ac.), on the north side of the study site. An oxbow borders the east edge and curves west through the site where it eventually meets the Sacramento River. The vegetation has been described by Motroni (1978). Cottonwood was the dominant overstory tree, with willow (Salix sp.), valley oak, black walnut, and Oregon ash (Fraxinus latifolia) also present. Wild grape, blue elderberry (Sambucus caerulea), black walnut, and box elder formed a dense, often impenetrable midstory. Wild grape dominated the understory much the same as it did the midstory. Also abundant in this layer were blackberry and poison oak.

Study Site III

This 19-ha. (48-ac.) site, the Butte Slough State Wildlife Area, is located in Sutter County 26.4 km. (17 mi.) west of Yuba City (39° 9' north, 121° 53' west). Butte Slough forms the western boundary; agricultural land borders the site to the north and south, and a narrow band of oak woodland savannah was found along the east edge (beyond which is agricultural land). A 1.2-ha. (3-ac.) pond is located near the east edge of the study site.

This site differs markedly in vegetative composition and physiognomy from all other study sites. The riparian forest was a non-contiguous stand. Motroni (1978) found the overstory dominated by cottonwood with some willow and traces of valley oak. The relatively open midstory was dominated by Oregon ash. Buttonbush (Cephalanthus occidentalis var. californicus), valley oak, and box elder were also present in this layer. Poison oak, wild grape, and cocklebur (Xanthium strumarium var. canadense) dominated the understory.

Study Site IV

This 76-ha. (187-ac.) site is on the west bank of the Sacramento River 6.9 km. (4.3 mi.) north of Glenn County, California (39° 35' north, 122° 00' west). It was formerly owned by Louis Heinrich, but now is a state wildlife area, and is bordered by the Sacramento River to the east and by agricultural land on three sides. A slough branches off of the river and borders the west side of the study area. Cottonwood and willow dominated the overstory, with box elder, black walnut, and sycamore (Platanus racemosa) also present in this layer (ibid.).

908

Blue elderberry, willow, box elder, and black walnut combined to form a dense midstory, much like that found at Study Site II. Mugwort (Artemesia douglasiana), box elder seedings, wild cucumber (Marah fabaceus), bed straw (Galium aparine), poison oak, black walnut seedlings, various grasses, wild grape, and blackberry formed the understory. Although not included in the vegetation survey conducted by Motroni (ibid.), approximately one-fourth of the study area was composed of a sparse stand of cottonwood with wild grape forming lianas similar to that described by early explorers of the Sacramento Valley.

Study Site V

This 82-ha. (202-ac.) site is 4.8 km. (3.0 mi.) northeast of Colusa, Colusa County, California (39° 16' north, 121° 57' west). It is adjacent to Butte Lodge Outing Duck Club and adjoins 0.2 km. of Butte Creek. A narrow slough runs the length of this riparian forest. Willow and valley oak dominated the overstory, with cottonwood, Oregon ash, and box elder contributing to form a dense canopy. Density of the midstory, dominated by poison oak, was variable. Oregon ash, box elder, buttonbush, and valley oak were also relatively abundant in this layer. Areas immediately adjacent to water were occupied by extensive stands of wild grape and willow forming a dense, nearly impenetrable midstory similar to Study Sites I, II, and IV. The closed canopy precluded much development of an understory. Poison oak was the dominant understory species, with blackberry, wild grape, mugwort, buttonbush, valley oak seedlings, and various grasses also present.

RESULTS AND DISCUSSION

Ringtails were livetrapped or reported to exist at numerous locations in the Central Valley, including five of the nine sites sampled during this study (table 1; fig. 2, 3). Sightings ranged from the northernmost portion of the Valley near Red Bluff, Tehama County, to Stockton, San Joaquin County. These data represent a range extension, notwithstanding Naylor and Wilson (1956).

With few exceptions, ringtails were found to be associated with remnant stands of riparian forests bordering waterways such as the American River, Sacramento River, Feather River, Butte Creek, and Butte Slough. No ringtails were captured or reported from open, park-like stands of valley oak woodland.

Ringtails were also captured by Trapp in riparian vegetation in the Sutter Buttes, a small, isolated mountain range in the lower central portion of the Scramento Valley. Walt Anderson[8] reported that ringtails or their

_____

[8]Walt Anderson. 1981. Biologist, Colusa, California. Personal communication.

- ● 1 ringtail observation
- ● 2 or more ringtail observations

Figure 2.--Sites at which observations of ringtails have been made within the Central Valley of California, showing spatial relation to the rest of the state.

signs have been seen in other vegetation-types in the Sutter Buttes, including the blue oak woodland.

It is unlikely that ringtails have dispersed into the Valley since the statewide survey by Grinnell et al. (1937). In fact, evidence, apparently overlooked by Grinnell et al., exists in the Museum of Vertebrate Zoology, University of California, Berkeley, from the 1930's which indicates ringtails were present at the Sutter Buttes (table 1, Sutter County). In their discussion of ringtail habitat preference, Grinnell et al. (ibid.) indicated that outside of the preferred "brushy or chaparral type" habitat, ringtails may also be "...found along streams (where) their range extends down to 500

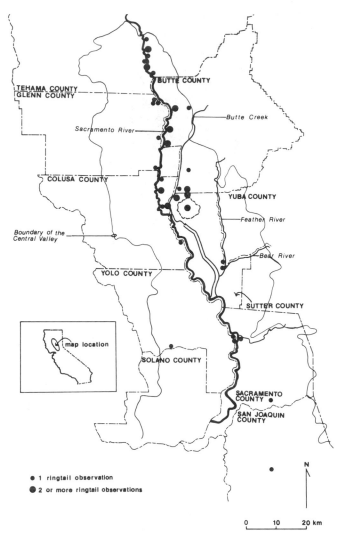

● 1 ringtail observation
● 2 or more ringtail observations

0   10   20 km

Figure 3.--Observation sites of ringtails in the Central Valley of California, showing relation to county boundaries and other local features.

ft. or to the mouths of canyons". Careful examination of the Grinnell range map (ibid.) revealed five ringtail sightings extending from near Red Bluff to the southern border of Tehama County. These sightings, which were just below 160 m. (500 ft.) and within the limit of California Prairie (Küchler 1977, i.e. the Central Valley), appeared to follow the Sacramento River. It is not clear why ringtails were not expected to occur in similar habitat below 160 m. It appears that ringtails were largely overlooked within the Central Valley and that there was simply a lack of effort by other investigators to document their presence prior to the current study.

The lack of sightings for the southern half of the Central Valley could be related to several factors. Historically, there was considerably less riparian vegetation here than in the northern Central Valley (ibid.; Roberts et al. 1977). A large portion of the remaining riparian vegetation has been eliminated in the path of agricultural expansion. Limited habitat availability, coupled with a less intensive survey effort by us in that area may explain why the range appears restricted to the northern portion of the Central Valley.

Trapping efforts undertaken to determine the abundance of ringtails in riparian forests of the Sacramento Valley produced reasonably consistent results where habitat features and trapping efforts were similar (table 2, 3). At study sites II, IV, and V densities of ringtails were 20.5, 17.1, and 19.5 individuals per 100 ha., respectively. Study sites I and II, where habitat features were different or where trapping effort was significantly less, exhibited densities of 11.4 and 10.5 ringtails per 100 ha.

At study site III, trap nights per ha. and trap nights per capture exceeded that of other sites (table 3); however, ringtail density at this site was lowest. There are probably a

Table 1.--Ringtail observations for the Central Valley of California, 1930-1979.

Date	County and Location	Source
	Butte County	
?	Along irrigation ditch between Butte City and Gridley	Joe Tatum
?	Parrot Grant (17 mi. SW of Chico)	CSUC[1]
?	In the Valley along Butte Creek	Lawrence Coleman[2]
1955	Butte Creek, 3 mi. NE of Colusa	Naylor and Wilson (1956)
1964	1 mi. S of Ord Ferry, Llano Seco Ranch (2 sitings)	CSUC[1]
1965	Butte Creek, 3 mi. E of junction of Highway 99E and Skyway	CSUC[1]
1965	Parrot Grant (2 sitings)	CSUC[1]
1969	1/4 mi. E of Sacramento River, NW part of Llano Seco Ranch, slough bank	CSUC[1]
1969	Gray Lodge, Fobestown, Paradise, Sacramento-Colusa Delta	B. Childs[2]
1971	Gray Lodge	Ed Littrell and J. Cowan
1973	Butte Sink, near Sutter Buttes	T. Stone (Schempf and White 1977)
1973	Gray Lodge	H. Moeglin[2]
1977	Sacramento River near Chico	Jerry Penland
1978	Sacramento River, Chico Park area	W.R. Rummell

910

Colusa County

?	Colusa to Princeton	George Seymour
1972	Feather River and Sacramento River, Butte Creek	B. Gossett[2]
1977	Between Colusa and Princeton	Wm. B. Castleberry
1978	Riparian area just S of Glenn County on Sacramento River	L. Belluomini
1979	1 mi. N of Colusa, W of the Sacramento River	CSUS[3]
1979	Along Sacramento River S of Grimes (in day)	John Reysynsky
1979	Butte Lodge Outing Duck Club, between Sacramento River and Butte Creek	L. Belluomini

Glenn County

1965	11 mi. W of Chico	CSUC[1]
1973-1974	1.75 mi. N of Princeton, along Sacramento River	Michny et al. (1974)
1978	2 mi. S of Hamilton City (Highway 32)	Lloyd Powell
1978	2 mi. N of Hamilton City	Lloyd Powell
1979	4.3 mi. N of Glenn on Sacramento River	L. Belluomini

Sacramento County

| 1978 | Continental Can Co., S bank of American River just E of confluence with Sacramento River in Sacramento | Wm. Grenfell |
| 1980 | 0.75 mi. off Hauschildt Rd., N of Twin Cities Road, E of Highway 99 (beside irrigation ditch in blackberry patch) | Bob Hosea |

San Joaquin County

| 1978 | Chapins Shell Station, Stockton | Wm. Grenfell |

Sutter County

1930	3 mi. E of West Butte, Sutter Buttes (5 ringtails)	UCB-MVZ[4]
1962	W side of Feather River near O'Connor Lake at Star Bend	Howard Leach
1971	Sutter Buttes	Walter Frazier[2]
1977	Base of N-face of Sutter Buttes	CSUC[1]
1977	Honolulu Ranch Duck Club, Butte Sink	Jack Grass
1977-1978	Bobelaine Audubon Sanctuary, confluence of Bear River and Feather River on W bank of Feather River	ERS-CSUS,[5] L. Belluomini
1977-1978	Mawson Bridge Sutter Bypass	Walt Anderson
1978	Robert Stack's Duck Club, Butte Sink	Mr. Duffy
1978 (ca.)	Pennington Road, N side of Sutter Buttes	Trent Meyer
1978	Berry Patch Club, N end of Butte Sink	Randall Gray
1978	Brockman Canyon and Twin Peaks, Sutter Buttes	Walt Anderson
1978-1979	Brockman Canyon, Sutter Buttes	G. Trapp, ERS-CSUS[5]
1979	Butte Slough State Wildlife Area	L. Belluomini

Tehama County

1937	Along Sacramento River, S Tehama County (4-5 sitings)	Grinnell et al. (1937)
?	Corning	George Seymour
1965	0.5 mi. E of Woodson Bridge	CSUC[1]
1968	4 mi. N of Woodson Bridge	CSUC[1]
1974-1975	Woodson Bridge State Recreation Area	Tom Stone (1976)
1974-1975	Copeland Bar, 2 mi. N of Woodson Bridge S.R.A.	Tom Stone (1976)
1974-1975	Mooney Island on Sacramento River SE of Red Bluff	Tom Stone (1976)
1976	Along Sacramento River between Red Bluff and Tehama	Jim Duggan
1977	0.5 mi. W of Los Molinos, near Sacramento River	Tyler Young
1978	Sacramento River near Vina	Glenn A. Burke
1978	Along Sacramento River between Red Bluff and Willows	L.T. Dragoo

Table 1.--Ringtail observations for the Central Valley of
California, 1930-1979 (cont.).

Yolo County

1975	6 mi. E of Winters	CSUS[3]
1977	N of Bryte, along Sacramento River	Alan Craig
1978	On Sacramento River where Interstate 880 crosses	Mike Delay

[1]California State University, Chico
[2]California Department of Fish and Game trapper interviews by C. Swick
[3]California State University, Sacramento, Museum of Natural History
[4]University of California, Berkeley, Museum of Vertebrate Zoology
[5]Ecological Research Society, California State University, Sacramento

Table 2.--Ringtail ecological density in the Sacramento Valley, California, 1978-1979.

	Study Site				
	I	II	III	IV	V
Ringtails/ 100 ha.	11.4	20.5	10.5	17.1	19.5
Ringtails/ mi^2	29.8	52.8	26.7	44.5	50.7

Table 3.--Trap nights per unit area and per individual ringtail caught in the Sacramento Valley, California, 1978-1979.

	Study Site				
	I	II	III	IV	V
Trap nights	96	437	164	288	202
Study site size					
ha.	70	88	19	76	41
ac.	172	218	48	187	101
Trap nights/					
ha.	0.2	0.8	1.4	0.6	0.8
ac.	0.6	2.0	3.4	1.5	2.0
Trap nights/ ringtail	12.0	24.3	82.0	22.2	25.3

variety of environmental factors involved in this lower value. This site, which borders Butte Slough, was a relatively narrow, broken stand of riparian forest with little of the grape or poison oak lianas so characteristic of the other sites. A comparison of the vegetation composition revealed a less diverse canopy and midstory. The canopy was composed almost exclusively of cottonwood. The relatively open midstory was dominated by Oregon ash.

Trapp (1972, 1978) documented ringtail anatomical and behavioral adaptations to climbing, as well as their ability to fully utilize all accessible aspects of the terrestrial environment. The ability to exploit the vertical aspect of their environment may allow ringtails to take advantage of a dense midstory, thereby increasing mobility about the forest. During times of winter flooding this could be especially important. A reduction, then, in a potentially critical aspect of their environment such as density of midstory vegetation might manifest itself in a smaller population size. This may partially explain variations in ringtail abundance.

Study sites II, IV, and V had similar ringtail densities and relatively diverse canopy and dense midstory vegetation layers. All three sites contained contiguous stands of riparian forest. Although the vegetation at study site I appeared to be physiognomically similar to that at study sites II, IV, and V, ringtail density was lower. This probably reflects a less intensive trapping effort (table 3).

There are few accounts in the literature on the abundance of ringtails and other procyonids. Grinnell et al. (1937) relied on the observations of W.H. Parkinson for density estimates. On 26 km^2 (10 mi^2) of land near Tollhouse, Fresno County, Parkinson trapped 31 ringtails within a season. Near the same area and over a 0.8-km (0.5-mi.) trail, Parkinson captured 13 ringtails. At 1,067 m. (3,500 ft.) on the western slope of Provo Mountain, near the Tuolumne River, within 0.65 km^2 (0.25 mi^2), he discovered five ringtail nests in blue oak trees. Each was occupied by a single ringtail. With information such as this, Grinnell et al. (ibid.) surmised that there was one ringtail per 13 km^2 (5 mi^2) throughout its range and in a few favored localities there were 2.3 per km^2 (6 per mi^2).

Taylor (1954) reported that J.D. Bankston, a trapper, estimated ringtails at 3.9 per km^2 (10 per mi^2) in suitable broken country of the Edwards Plateau region in Texas.

Using home range data, collected with the use of radio-telemetry, Trapp (1978) estimated the density of ringtails in pinyon/juniper, blackbrush, and riparian vegetation of Zion Canyon, southwest Utah, to be 1.5-2.9 per km^2 (3.8-7.6 per mi^2).

Ringtail densities of 10.5-20.5 per 100 ha. (26.7-52.8 per mi^2) documented during this study are the highest reported in the literature. Assuming that riparian woodland has higher productivity per unit area compared to chaparral and chaparral/woodland vegetations, the variation in ringtail density from shrub-dominated vegetation-types to riparian woodland might be explained on the basis of this factor. A direct relationship may also exist between ringtail density and physiognomic complexity (e.g., stratification) of the riparian plant community. Some evidence exists to support this contention from studies of the coati (Nasua narica), also a procyonid. The coati exploits arboreal aspects of its habitat (Davis 1960). Lanning (1976) reported densities of 1.2-2.0 coatis per 100 ha. in mixed evergreen woodland in and near Chiricahua National Monument, southeast Arizona. Densities of 42 and 26 coatis per 100 ha. have been estimated for tropical forests in Panama (Kaufmann 1962, cited by Lanning 1976). Lanning indicates that such differences in density may be attributed, in part, to ecological differences between the semiarid evergreen woodland and the moist tropical forests.

ACKNOWLEDGMENTS

Special thanks are extended to Paul Laubacher, Randy Gray, Bob Motroni, Linda Heath, and particularly Dennis Messa for assistance in the field. Thanks to Gordon Gould, California Department of Fish and Game, for his cooperation and for arranging for the printing and mailing of the Furbearer Observation Questionnaire. Bob Motroni provided helpful suggestions of the techniques used for vegetational analysis. Larry Salata is gratefully acknowledged for critically reading and providing useful suggestions for this paper.

LITERATURE CITED

Cottam, G., and J.T. Curtis. 1956. The use of distance measures in phytosociological sampling. Ecology 37:451-460.

Cox, G.W. 1976. Laboratory manual of general ecology. 232 p. Wm. C. Brown Co., Dubuque, Iowa.

Davis, W.B. 1960. The mammals of Texas. Texas Game and Fish Commission, Austin. Bulletin No. 41. 252 p.

Grinnell, J., J. Dixon, and J.M. Linsdale. 1937. Furbearing mammals of California. 2 vol., 777 p. University of California Press, Berkeley.

Hall, E.R. 1981. The mammals of North America. 2nd ed., 2 vol. 1181 p. John Wiley & Sons, New York, N.Y.

Hall, E.R., and K.R. Kelson. 1959. The mammals of North America. 2 vol., 1083 p. Ronald Press Co., New York, N.Y.

Ingles, L.G. 1965. Mammals of the Pacific states. 506 p. Stanford University Press, Stanford, Calif.

Kaufmann, J.H. 1962. Ecology and social behavior of the coati, Nasua narica, on Barro Colorado. University of California Publ. Zool. 60:95-222 (cited by Lanning 1976).

Küchler, W.A. 1977. The map of the natural vegetation of California. p. 909. In: M.G. Barbour and J. Major (ed.). Terestrial vegetation of California. 1002 p. John Wiley & Sons, Inc. New York, N.Y.

Lanning, D.V. 1976. Density and movements of the coati in Arizona. J. Mamm. 57(3):609-611.

Long, C.A., and H.B. House. 1961. Bassariscus astutus in Wyoming. J. Mamm. 42(2):274-275.

Michny, F.J., D. Boos, and F. Wernette. 1975. Riparian habitats and avian densities along the Sacramento River. California Department of Fish and Game Administrative Report No. 75-1. 42 p.

Motroni, R.S. 1978. Sacramento Valley critical riparian habitat inventory. California Department of Fish and Game unpublished manuscript. 43 p.

Motroni, R.S. 1979. Avian density and composition of a riparian forest, Sacramento Valley, California. M.S. Thesis, California State University, Sacramento. 172 p.

Naylor, A.E., and G.W. Wilson. 1956. Unusual occurrence of the ring-tailed cat. Calif. Fish and Game 42(3):231.

Odum, E.P. 1971. Fundamentals of ecology. 3rd ed. 574 p. W.B. Saunders Co., Philadelphia, Penn.

Roberts, W.G., J.G. Howe, and J. Major. 1977. A survey of riparian forest flora and fauna. p. 3-19. In: A. Sands (ed.). Riparian forests in California: their ecology and conservation. 122 p. Institute of Ecology, University of California, Davis.

Schempf, P.F., and M. White. 1977. Status of six furbearer populations in the mountains of northern California. 52 p. USDA Forest Service Publications, California Region.

Seton, E.T. 1929. Lives of game animals. Vol. 2, Part I. Doubleday Doran & Co., Inc., Garden City, N.Y.

Smith, R.L. 1980. Ecology and field biology. 3rd ed. 835 p. Harper & Row Pub., New York, N.Y.

Stone T.B. 1976. Observations on furbearers within the riparian habitat of the upper Sacramento River. California Department of Fish and Game Memorandum Report. 12 p.

Taylor, W.P. 1954. Food habits and notes on life history of the ring-tailed cat in Texas. J. Mamm. 35(1):55-63.

Trapp, G.R. 1972. Some anatomical and behavioral adaptations of ringtails, *Bassariscus astutus*. J. Mamm. 53(3):549-557.

Trapp, G.R. 1978. Comparative behavioral ecology of the ringtail and gray fox in southwestern Utah. Carnivore 1(2):3-32.

RARE, THREATENED AND ENDANGERED INVERTEBRATES

IN CALIFORNIA RIPARIAN SYSTEMS[1]

Larry L. Eng[2]

Abstract.--Three California invertebrates dependent upon riparian systems have been listed as Rare, Threatened, or Endangered. These species, the California freshwater shrimp (*Syncaris pacifica*), the valley longhorn beetle (*Desmocerus californicus dimorphus*), and the Trinity bristle snail (*Monadenia setosa*), represent three classes (two phyla) and occupy distinctly different habitats. Other species, not officially listed, are equally or perhaps more endangered; however, available information for official status determination is inadequate. The ultimate listing of all deserving invertebrates is an unlikely, if not impossible, goal given the dearth of data and the sheer number and diversity of species involved. Efforts should be directed at protecting and preserving ecosystems which are threatened rather than expended on individual endangered species which may occupy only a portion of the threatened ecosystem.

INTRODUCTION

Riparian systems support, either directly or indirectly, an abundance and diversity of wildlife (Sands 1978). Many of the species of animals and plants recognized as Rare, Threatened, or Endangered by state and federal agencies are directly or indirectly dependent upon riparian areas for their survival (ibid; Hirsch and Segelquist 1978). The primary reason for the listing of most of these species (and the primary cause for their status) is the substantial loss or degradation of their habitats. Hirsch and Segelquist (1978) estimated that about 70-90% of natural riparian areas have been destroyed or extensively altered.

Recognition of the magnitude of the loss and concern over the continuing assaults on the remnant riparian areas has resulted in several symposia designed to increase awareness not only of the threats to riparian systems, but also of their importance and value. In these symposia and in other forums, emphasis has been placed on plants and vertebrate animals. The invertebrate species in riparian systems have received little consideration. To a degree, this reflects the orientation of the participants, but it also reflects the dearth of information available on invertebrate species dependent on riparian areas.

But even with the emphasis on vertebrates, Bury et al. (1980) expressed concern that "the great bulk of vertebrate species [the nongame species] are not receiving the share of attention that they deserve as interesting and important members of most natural communities." This lack of attention is even more glaring for the invertebrate component of riparian systems.

In this paper I will discuss the officially listed Rare, Threatened, and Endangered invertebrates dependent upon riparian areas in California, the threats to their continued existence, and the need for a different approach in obtaining protection for endangered and rare species.

THREATENED RIPARIAN INVERTEBRATES

Riparian ecosystems are composed of a wide variety of environments and microenvironments, some of which support invertebrate species with very specialized habitat requirements. These specialists, which are unable to compensate or substitute for lost environments are experiencing the most immediate threats as remnant riparian areas continue to shrink.

Within California three species of invertebrates, representing two phyla and three classes, have been officially designated as Endangered, Rare, or Threatened. These species are the California freshwater shrimp (*Syncaris pacifica*),

[1] Paper presented at the California Riparian Systems Conference. [University of California, Davis, September 17-19, 1981].

[2] Larry L. Eng is Invertebrate Biologist, Endangered Species Program, California Department of Fish and Game, Rancho Cordova, Calif.

the Trinity bristle snail (<u>Monadenia setosa</u>), and the valley elderberry longhorn beetle (<u>Desmocerus californicus dimorphus</u>). These species, each of which is dependent upon a markedly different type of habitat, are discussed in more detail below.

California Freshwater Shrimp

The California freshwater shrimp (<u>Syncaris pacifica</u>) (fig. 1), a small freshwater shrimp which lives in lowland streams in Marin, Sonoma, and Napa counties, was designated an Endangered species by the California Fish and Game Commission in 1980 (Eng 1981). It is the only surviving member of the genus <u>Syncaris</u>. Its congener <u>S. pasadenae</u> was extirpated by urban development in southern California. Although an aquatic species, <u>S. pacifica</u> is dependent upon riparian vegetation for food and shelter. During fall and winter months, <u>S. pacifica</u> lives among submerged exposed roots beneath undercut banks, where it is protected from downstream displacement during heavy runoff from winter rains. The tree roots not only provide cover for the shrimp, but also reinforce the streambank enabling the undercuts to persist.

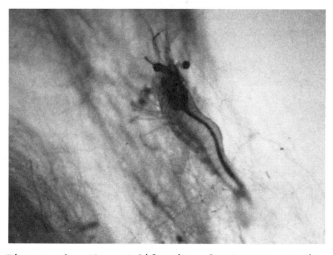

Figure 1.--The California freshwater shrimp (<u>Syncaris pacifica</u>).

The principal riparian plants comprising the shrimps' habitat are alders (<u>Alnus</u>), willows (<u>Salix</u>), blackberries (<u>Rubus</u>), sedges, and ferns. The leafy branches of these plants grow into the water during spring and summer, providing cover and food for the shrimp. The shade provided by the larger trees reduces solar heating of the stream. This shading is especially important during droughts when the shrimp are confined to remnant pools. During spring the shrimp move out from the undercut banks and live on the submerged leafy branches of streamside vegetation. They also utilize the exposed hair-like adventitious roots of alders growing along the stream margin. The submerged leaves and filamentous roots collect detrital material and serve as substrates for bacteria and other decomposers, thus providing a food source for the omnivorous shrimp. Submerged and decomposing leaves may also be consumed by the shrimp.

Habitat degradation has resulted in the extirpation of this species from at least five streams (Hedgpeth 1975). Some longtime residents of the area report that the shrimp once occurred in virtually every stream in the three county area; however, we have records of their existence, historically, in only 10 streams (Eng 1981). Continuing urban and residential development pose threats to streamside vegetation, especially in Sonoma County, one of the fastest-growing counties in the state. Hedgpeth (1968) reported that <u>S. pacifica</u> was extirpated in Santa Rosa Creek by an urban improvement project in Santa Rosa. Livestock grazing continues to be a problem locally, causing loss of riparian vegetation and collapse of streambanks. Construction of summer dams and artificial beaches for recreational purposes has destroyed substantial amounts of shrimp habitat in some streams. Vineyard development has also resulted in the loss of substantial amounts of riparian vegetation. In many cases, the vineyards extend to the stream margin.

Valley Elderberry Longhorn Beetle

The valley elderberry longhorn beetle (<u>Desmocerus californicus dimorphus</u>) (fig. 2) is a rare longhorn beetle, known from only a few localities in the lower Sacramento and upper San Joaquin valleys in California. These beetles are restricted to riparian areas, where the larvae are obligate stem and root borers of elderberry (<u>Sambucus</u> sp.). The adults feed on the foliage of the same plant.

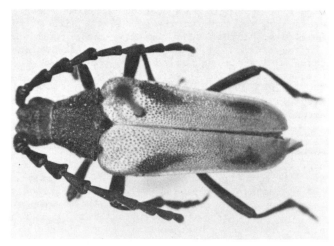

Figure 2.--The valley elderberry longhorn beetle (<u>Desmocerus californicus dimorphus</u>). (Photo by F.G. Andrews.)

The habitat of this longhorn beetle occurs in areas with relatively high human population density and intensive agriculture. Much of the Central Valley riparian vegetation, of which elderberry is a conspicuous component, has al-

916

ready been lost, primarily to urban and agricultural development. Extensive loss of essential habitat for this rare species during historical times and the continuing threats to its remaining habitat were major forces in the decision of the US Department of the Interior to list this species as Threatened in 1980. Loss of elderberry groves continues as agricultural and urban development expand. Construction of industrial parks, bicycle trails, and parking lots all take their toll on the beetle's shrinking habitat. Obviously, some critical density of elderberry plants is required for the maintenance of the beetle's populations; however, studies to determine that necessary density have yet to be undertaken.

Trinity Bristle Snail

The Trinity bristle snail (_Monadenia setosa_) (fig. 3) is a terrestrial snail, living in the riparian zone along several small, primary streams in the Trinity River drainage in Trinity County (Roth and Eng 1980). Adults of this nocturnal species are most commonly found among leaf litter on the forest floor, although they have been observed several feet up in the branches of deciduous trees.[3] Very young snails are apparently dependent upon standing dead trees, spending the first several months of their existence living beneath the loose bark. Trinity bristle snails are active during the moist months of the year, feeding on fungi and decomposing leaves.

Figure 3.--The Trinity bristle snail (_Monadenia setosa_).

The Trinity bristle snail occurs only in the presence of a hardwood understory including bigleaf maple (_Acer macrophyllum_), dogwood (_Cornus_ sp.), and California hazel (_Corylus cornuta_ var. _californica_). In the lower stream reaches, white alder (_Alnus rhombifolia_), California black oak (_Quercus kellogii_) and tanbark-oak (_Lithocarpus densi-_

_____

[3]Roth. Personal communication.

flora) are sometimes interspersed with the above species. The decaying leaf litter from these trees apparently constitutes a major food source for the snail (Roth and Eng 1980). On the dryer upper slopes _M. setosa_ is replaced by its cogener _M. churchi_; it is also absent from lightly shaded areas of exposed hillsides.

The Trinity bristle snail is restricted to sparsely populated, mountainous Trinity County. Much of its habitat is on national forest land. Because of its restricted habitat and very limited range, the California Fish and Game Commission has designated it a Rare species under California law. Threats to this species are logging activities which would encroach on the riparian zone. Fires, road construction, erosion, and removal of standing trees utilized by the juvenile snails would all have substantial deleterious effects on the snail's habitat. Other potential threats come from gold-mining operations and the development of small hydroelectric projects. The USDA Forest Service has responded to the presence of this rare snail and has developed an interim management plan for it (Armijo 1979).

DISCUSSION

Only three invertebrates directly dependent upon riparian systems in California have been legally recognized as Rare, Threatened or Endangered species by the state or federal government. However, these animals come from very different habitats, represent three different classes and two different phyla, and undoubtedly constitute only the tip of the iceberg of threatened invertebrate species. Official recognition of these three species does not mean that they are the only California riparian invertebrates that are threatened. What it means is that enough data and support existed to enable an official determination of their status to be made. A number of other invertebrates dependent upon riparian systems (Roth 1972; Donahue 1975; Hunt and DeMartini 1979; Murphy 1979) have been proposed for federal listing, but the USDI Fish and Wildlife Service considered available information inadequate to make a final determination. Data for most other invertebrate species are even more limited.

We know that many invertebrates are restricted to riparian systems and many others utilize these areas facultatively or as "migration" corridors (Merritt and Cummins 1978; Shapiro 1974). The importance of riparian systems to certain groups was illustrated by Shapiro (1974), who found that 85% of the species comprising the Sacramento Valley butterfly fauna occur along the lower American River.

The riparian systems of California include a wide variety of environments. Many invertebrates inhabiting these areas have highly specialized habitat requirements; others are geographically very localized. Although the continuing loss of riparian systems has resulted in extensive habitat loss for many species, it is an especially urgent threat to those species that are highly specialized and geographically restricted.

The lack of information on invertebrates makes it difficult to demonstrate that the existence of a species is threatened (the minimum requirement for federal listing) or even that it "...exists in such small numbers throughout its range that it may be endangered if its environment worsens" (the minimum requirement for state listing).[4] All this is complicated by a general ignorance of and/or prejudice against invertebrates in general and insects in particular by politicians and the general public. The possibility of a backlash against listing any invertebrate is very real.

The universal threat to riparian systems seems sufficient justification to list those many invertebrate species dependent upon them, especially the rare and highly specialized forms, as Rare, Threatened, or Endangered. The large number of species in this category and the dearth of information on most of them makes the listing of each qualified species unlikely, if not impossible, under present standards of administrative review.

In most cases, a species becomes officially listed as Threatened or Endangered when it can be shown that a substantial loss of its habitat has reduced its abundance to the point where its future survival is threatened. Because the environment which provides this habitat is shared by a variety of other species (in the community sense), some of which are restricted to only portions of that environment, the few listed species should be considered indicators of threatened environments or ecosystems. Planning and management should be directed toward activities which emphasize the protection and preservation of the entire ecosystem which is threatened, rather than focused on a single endangered species which may represent only a portion of the threatened ecosystem. The ultimate success in protecting all species belonging to threatened riparian ecosystems requires the development of a means of protecting these systems without necessitating an official listing of each threatened or endangered component.

ACKNOWLEDGMENTS

I would like to thank Stephen J. Nicola, California Department of Fish and Game, for providing helpful comments on a draft of this paper.

---

[4]California Fish and Game Code Section 2051B.

LITERATURE CITED

Armijó, P. 1979. *Monadenia setosa* (California northern river snail): interim species management plan. 24 p. USDA Forest Service, Shasta-Trinity National Forest, Redding, Calif.

Bury, R.B., H.W. Campbell, and N.J. Scott. 1980. Role and importance of nongame wildlife. Trans. 45th North Amer. Wildl. Nat. Res. Conf. 1980: 197-207.

Donahue, J.P. 1975. A report on the 24 species of California butterflies being considered for placement on the federal lists of endangered or threatened species. 58 p. California Department of Food and Agriculture, Sacramento. Unpublished manuscript.

Eng, L.L. 1981. Distribution, life history, and status of the California freshwater shrimp, *Syncaris pacifica* (Holmes). California Department of Fish and Game, Inland Fish. Endangered Species Program Pub. 81-1, Sacramento. 27 p.

Hedgpeth, J.W. 1968. The atyid shrimp of the genus *Syncaris* in California. Int. Revue Ges. Hydrobiol. 53: 511-524.

Hedgpeth, J.W. 1975. California fresh and brackish water shrimps, with special reference to the present status of *Syncaris pacifica* (Holmes). USDI Fish and Wildlife Service, Office of Endangered Species, Contract 14-16-0008-841, Final Report, Washington, D.C. 27 p.

Hirsch, A., and C.A. Segelquist. 1978. Protection and management of riparian ecosystems: activities and views of the US Fish and Wildlife Service. p. 344-352. In: R. R. Johnson and J. F. McCormick (tech. coord.). Strategies for protection and management of floodplain wetlands and other riparian ecosystems. USDA Forest Service GTR-WO-12, Washington, D.C. 410 p.

Hunt, H., and J.D. DeMartini. 1979. Administrative study of the Karok Indian snail, *Vespericola karakorum*, Talmadge 1962. 20 p. USDA Forest Service, Shasta-Trinity National Forest, Redding, Calif.

Merritt, R.W., and K.W. Cummins. 1978. An introduction to the aquatic insects of North America. 441 p. Kendall/Hunt Publishing Company, Dubuque, Iowa.

Murphy, D.D. 1979. Butterfly survey: Inyo National Forest. USDA Forest Service, Inyo National Forest, Report RFQ R5-04-78-008 (43-91W2-8-747). 37 p. Unpublished manuscript.

Roth, B. 1972. Rare and endangered land mollusks in California. California Department of Fish and Game, Inland Fish. Admin. Rep. 72-10, Sacramento. 21 p.

Roth, B. and L.L. Eng. 1980. Distribution, ecology, and reproductive anatomy of a rare land snail, _Monadenia_ _setosa_ Talmadge. Calif. Fish and Game 66:4-16.

Sands, A. 1978. Public involvement in riparian habitat protection: a California case history. p. 215-227. _In_: R. R. Johnson and J. F. McCormick (tech. coord.). Strategies for protection and management of floodplain wetlands and other riparian ecosystems. USDA Forest Service GTR-WO-12, Washington, D.C. 410 p.

Shapiro, A. M. 1974. The butterfly fauna of the Sacramento Valley, California. J. Res. Lepidoptera 13:73-82, 115-122, 137-140.

GRAY FOX TEMPORAL AND SPATIAL ACTIVITY IN

A RIPARIAN/AGRICULTURAL ZONE IN

CALIFORNIA'S CENTRAL VALLEY[1]

Donald L. Hallberg and Gene R. Trapp[2]

Abstract.--Gray fox (Canis [Urocyon] cinereoargenteus)[3] temporal activity is quantitatively described from 1,094 radio telemetry fixes obtained from two male and two female subjects studied on Putah Creek, near Davis (Yolo County), California, from March through July 1973. The subjects were found to exhibit similar non-random temporal activity. Significant (p ≤ 0.05) increases in diurnal activity occurred one to two hours prior to sunset. Minimum activity began mid-morning and reached a low in late afternoon. Regardless of time, diurnal travel rates were conspicuously lower than nocturnal travel rates. All subjects occupied essentially the same area and had similar home range size (129 ha.). They spent 75.7% of the nocturnal and 91.6% of the diurnal period in riparian zones and the rest of the time on agricultural lands.

INTRODUCTION

The extensive range of the gray fox (Canis [Urocyon] cinereoargenteus), both in Latin America and the contiguous United States, as shown by Hall and Kelson (1959), suggests an ability to adapt readily to widely varying environmental situations. Hence, it is of value to learn how behavior varies in specific parts of its wide range.

Gray fox temporal activity is poorly understood. In 1972, an extensive gray fox literature review was conducted by Trapp and Hallberg (1974). At that time, the number of published references to fox circadian activity were limited to less than a half-dozen (Seton 1929; Grinnell et al. 1937; Taylor 1943; Gander 1966). With the exception of Taylor's (1943) work, little more than passing remarks were made concerning circadian activity.

In Texas, Taylor (ibid.) quantitatively described the activities of four captive animals during one 22-hour period. His conclusions generally agreed with those of Grinnell et al. (1937) in California and Seton (1929), who suggested crepuscular and nocturnal activity is most common.

Howver, Gander (1966), observed that gray foxes visited his southern California feeding station at all hours of the day and night, implying that diurnal as well as nocturnal activity is not unusual. A more recent and somewhat more quantitative investigation conducted from 1967 to 1969 in southwest Utah by Trapp (1978) concluded that: "Foxes, though active mostly at night, also forage diurnally and crepuscularly to a lesser, but important, extent."

Only limited information was available concerning gray fox home ranges. Richards and Hine (1953) in Wisconsin reported home ranges of 13-310 ha., while Lord (1961) in northern Florida estimated gray fox home ranges to be about 770 ha. Using telemetry techniques in southwest Utah, Trapp (1978) determined the mean home range to be 107 ha. It is not clear if the variation in home range size was due to differences in population densities (Trapp and Hallberg 1974), variations in habitat productivity, sampling errors, or other factors.

The present project's objective was to expand upon the temporal aspects of gray fox

---

[1]Paper presented at the California Riparian Systems Conference. [University of California, Davis, September 17-19, 1981.]

[2]Donald L. Hallberg is Associate Data Processing Analyst, California Department of Fish and Game, Sacramento. Gene R. Trapp is Associate Professor of Biological Sciences, California State University, Sacramento.

[3]New genus as suggested by Van Gelder (1977, 1978).

natural history by quantitatively describing circadian activity in relation to habitat utilization. Activity data were secondarily expected to provide information concerning home range and intraspecific interactions.

This paper is based on thesis research undertaken in 1973 (Hallberg 1974).

DESCRIPTION OF STUDY AREA

The study area (fig. 1) is located at 38° 32' N and 121° 41' W, 6.4 km. (4 mi.) southeast of Davis, California. The site is situated on private agricultural land immediately adjacent to the Yolo Bypass. Putah Creek's south fork bisects the study area longitudinally for approximately 4.8 km. (3 mi.) and is paralleled by flood control levees. Putah Creek meanders between the levees and in most cases is bordered by a 0.16- to 0.32-km. (0.1- to 0.2-mi.) wide agricultural belt. During the study period, principal crops associated with the belt included varieties of tomatoes, beans, melons, and wheat.

The area study contained approximately 88 ha. (218 ac.) of stream and riparian zone consisting of approximately 36% tree and shrub cover, 46% open grassland, and 18% covered by water. Fremont cottonwood (Populus fremontii), black walnut (Juglans hindsii), and large willow (Salix laevigata) were plentiful, bordering the creek channel. Less abundant were blue elderberry (Sambucus mexicana), box elder (Acer negundo), tamarix (Tamarisk gallica) and valley oak (Quercus lobata). Dense sandbar willow (Salix hindsiana) thickets were common in low, damp, sandy areas.

Extensive milk thistle (Silybum marianum) stands, some as large as 0.2 ha. (0.5 ac.), were common in early spring. They were usually associated with disturbed areas around the perimeter of open grassy areas. By July, most of the areas of annual grass were overgrown by yellow star thistle (Centaurea solstitialis).

METHODS AND MATERIALS

Field data were obtained primarily by radio-telemetric monitoring (Hallberg et al. 1974) and secondarily by direct observation.

Trapping

Trapping and processing techniques were similar to those employed by Trapp (1978) to capture gray foxes and ringtails (Bassariscus astutus) in Zion National Park, Utah. Nineteen collapsible Tomahawk double-doored livetraps (23 x 23 x 66 cm.) were placed in the field during March 1973 and left for the project's duration. Each was positioned in or near a well-defined trail, camouflaged with surrounding debris, and baited with raisins whenever it was necessary to capture animals.

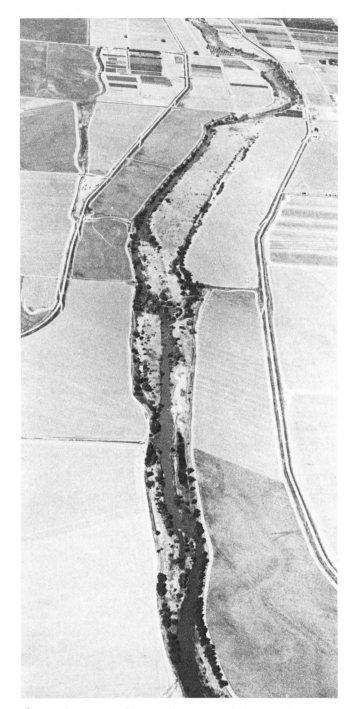

Figure 1.--Gray fox study area along Putah Creek, southeast of Davis, California, as seen from an altitude of approximately 914 m. (3,000 ft.), looking west. Stream and riparian ststem are flanked by agricultural fields and flood control levees. All telemetry fixes were taken from gravel roads on the levees paralleling the narrow agricultural belts.

Telemetry

Four gray foxes, two males and two females, were captured. Each was fitted with a radio-

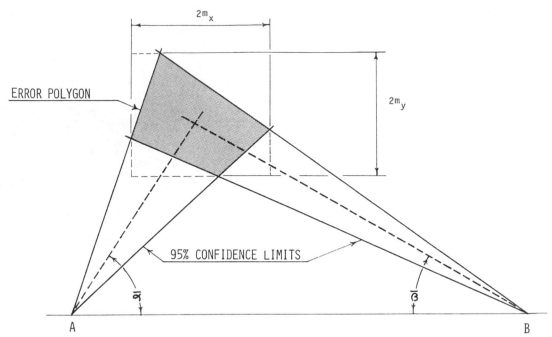

Figure 2.--Error polygons were computed by first calculating
confidence limits (95%) for bearing means ($\overline{\alpha}$, $\overline{\beta}$) and
secondarily deriving the points of confidence limit
intersection. Each fix was then expressed as the inter-
section of bearing means ($\overline{\alpha}$, $\overline{\beta}$) and the location
accuracy as a rectangle circumscribed about the error
polygon. The dimensions $2m_x$ and $2m_y$ represent the
95% confidence range associated with the fix along the
X and Y axes respectively. _____

[4]Source listings of all Fortran IV computer programs are included in Hallberg (1974).

telemetry collar and monitored from 25 March through 27 July 1973. The effective telemetry range varied with atmospheric conditions, but the system usually performed well when within 0.16-0.8 km. (0.1-0.5 mi.) of the subject. Under ideal conditions signals were received from distances exceeding 1.6 km. (1 mi.).

Diurnal resting places were located with a three-element, hand-held yagi antenna and Davidson Model W portable receiver. All triangulation data were collected using a vehicle-mounted broadside array, consisting of two vertically polarized 3-element yagi antennas. The array pivoted from a television mast which also supported a Suunto compass from a projecting arm (Hallberg et al. 1974).

Each subject's location with respect to time was determined from field bearings, recorded to the nearest 0.5° of direction, being determined in the following manner:

1) two to five bearings were made in rapid succession and recorded from a predetermined station in the subject's vicinity;
2) the telemetry vehicle was quickly driven to an adjacent station where a second series of bearings was taken.

The entire procedure required two to five minutes to complete and was similar to the technique employed by Ables (1969) and Trapp (1978). During field observations, an attempt was made to locate two or three subjects every 30 minutes (mean = 34 minutes; range = 4 to 282 minutes; n = 1,094). It was not feasible to locate all subjects every 30 minutes because they were frequently too far apart.

Data Processing

All field bearings were later converted into fix coordinates; their associated error polygons (fig. 2) (Heezen and Tester 1967) were computed in relation to a single (x,y) coordinate system by computer.[4] The error polygons were used to test the significance of the distance between fixes. When successive fixes were shown to be significantly different (ca. p = 0.05), the subject was judged to have moved and therefore determined to be active. When significant movement was not demonstrated, the subject was considered inactive, even though undetectable activity may have occurred. For active subjects, mean travel-rate index values were computed from elapsed time and distance measurements. Rates were considered to be only indices, since there was no reason to suspect foxes moved at a constant rate between fixes or that they traveled in straight lines. All data were related to either sunrise or sunset to correct for variations in day length during the study.

RESULTS AND DISCUSSION

Radio telemetry tracking allowed positive identification of subjects and their location (fix precision: $\overline{x} = \pm 14$ m., $\overline{y} = \pm 8.2$ m., n = 1,094) with respect to time.

No subject was observed to scratch, pull, or otherwise react to the telemetry collar once it was attached. Upon release subjects seemed to have little difficulty negotiating dense vegetation; after recapture several months later no skin chafing was evident. Based upon these observations it was assumed that the telemetry collar had little or no effect upon the subject wearing it.

Temporal Behavior

Statistical independence of subject circadian activity was tested by contingency analysis (Ostel 1963; Adler and Roessler 1972). No substantial evidence was found to suggest that subjects exhibited different circadian activity probabilities, and male:female activity probabilities did not significantly differ (p = 0.05).

The apparent similarity of subject activity probabilities was used to justify lumping all fox data. This in turn provided a larger sample for statistical inference. The pooled data were examined by testing a series of hypotheses. The first assumed the probability of activity to be random with respect to time; that is, the probability of activity equals the probability of inactivity for any given hour. Chi square analysis resulted in the rejection of this hypothesis (p = 0.05) for 19 hours of the day (fig. 3). The five hours where activity was random were the first, second, and sixth hours after sunrise, the first hour prior to sunset, and the seventh hour after sunset. Failure to reject the null hypothesis for the seventh hour after sunset was considered to be due to an inadequate sample (n = 2). Three of the four remaining one-hour intervals appeared random because these intermediate periods occurred while significant increases or decreases (p = 0.001) in activity states were in progress. The remaining period, six hours after sunrise, could not be explained on the basis of these data.

In general, it appeared that gray fox activity periods occurred in non-random fashion, foxes being significantly (p = 0.001) less active during diurnal periods than nocturnal. Statistically significant changes (p = 0.01) in activity appeared during the first two hours after sunrise and the first and third hours prior to sunset. Minimum activity observed was during mid-afternoon, which was significantly less (p = 0.001) than that observed in late morning.

PROBABILITY OF ACTIVITY
(PERCENT)

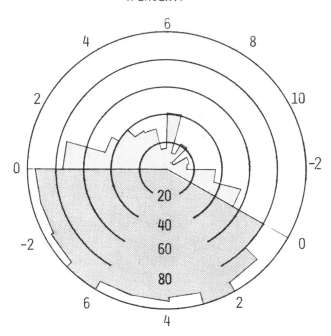

Figure 3.--The probability of activity [(active fixes/total fixes) x 100] is shown for each hour. Hourly polar divisions relate either to sunrise or sunset. The diurnal period is shaded lightly with respect to the nocturnal period.

Gray fox activity probabilities seem to be similar to those observed by Storm (1965) for five red foxes (Vulpes fulva) in Illinois. Storm stated that the daily journeys began as early as two hours before the night and usually continued throughout most of the night; sometimes they continued as late as four hours after dawn. Rymills (1979) found that gray fox activity at Point Reyes National Seashore, California, generally began just before dark and continued until dawn.

Travel Rates

An animal's rate of movement probably depends upon many factors, such as its activity, travel conditions, the weather, and presence of other animals (Sanderson 1966). Since the mean rates, computed for each hour, were influenced greatly when extremes were encountered, no statistical inference was made. However, several interesting trends were apparent. Rates were relatively constant during diurnal periods and considerably lower than nocturnal values (fig. 4). This suggests that the type of activity occurring during diurnal periods was similar for each hour, regardless of activity probability. In contrast, nocturnal rates averaged about twice the diurnal values and exhibited two peak periods, while activity probabilities remained consistently above 80%.

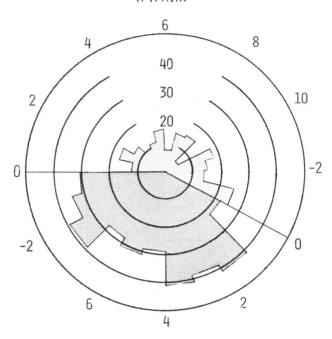

MEAN TRAVEL RATE
(FT/MIN)

Figure 4.--The mean travel rate in feet per minute was calculated for each hour. See figure 3 for description of polar graph.

Rate Indices

Neither activity probabilities nor mean
travel rates seemed to reflect properly the intui-
tive impression of gray fox temporal movement
developed while monitoring the subjects. However, by computing a rate index statistic (rate
index is the product of activity probability and
respective mean travel rate), that took into
account both the probability of activity and mean
travel rate, a more representative graph was constructed (fig. 5). The nocturnal period was
clearly the most active time for each subject.
Animals did not move long distances during diurnal periods, except perhaps just before dusk.

Field observations suggest that three categories of activity may exist; short moves, meanders, and purposeful traverses. Extrapolation
from these assumptions, based upon the available
literature, suggests that a gray fox is likely to
leave its diurnal resting site shortly before sunset and move only short distances while investigating the immediate area before beginning a purposeful traverse toward a foraging area some distance away. Perhaps this was the type of movement observed by Richards and Hine (1953) in Wisconsin when they reported that gray foxes frequently followed fence rows or well-defined
trails. Upon arriving at the foraging area, more
time was spent investigating thickets and crevices.

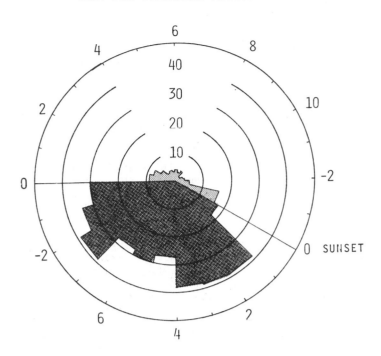

Figure 5.--An index representing the product of
the hourly activity probability from figure
3 and the respective mean travel rate from
figure 4 was calculated for each hour. See
figure 3 for description of polar graph.

During meandering movements, many abrupt
turns and reversals in direction occurred, as was
also observed by Trapp (1978) in southwest Utah.

Two or three hours before sunrise a subject
often made a second purposeful traverse toward
the area in which it would spend the day, before
extensive movement ceased at sunrise. Only short
distances were traversed during diurnal periods
as, perhaps, a fox moved from one resting site to
another to take advantage of varying sun-shade
conditions or pursued a potential meal.

Seasonal Activity

Spring and summer diurnal activity probabilities could not be demonstrated as similar by
contingency analysis (p = 0.05). Spring diurnal
activity was essentially non-existent from mid-
morning through mid-afternoon. During the summer, substantially more activity occurred for the
same period. No tangible evidence was found that
explained this dichotomy. However, it seems reasonable that diurnal activity would be reduced
for secretive carnivores during that portion of
the year when only sparse vegetative cover was
available.

The study area provided little cover during
March and April, since the annual and perennial
grasses were short and deciduous trees and shrubs

did not provide an extensive canopy. The only heavy groundcover available was an occasional brush pile or milk thistle stand. Similarly, certain spring and summer nocturnal activity probabilities could not be demonstrated as being the same, although the differences were not as dramatic as the diurnal differences. This may have been because the concealment afforded by darkness reduced the cover's influence. These assumptions are not supported in the literature since Wood (1954) and Richards and Hine (1953) stated that gray foxes are most active in the fall and winter, presumably when cover is minimal.

Further support for the "availability of cover" hypothesis was shown by the location of diurnal resting sites. In spring, it was not uncommon for a gray fox to return to the same resting area each day for several days in a row. Once the deciduous canopy began to develop, it was more common for subjects to rest in different areas each day. On 26 occasions, actual diurnal resting sites were visually located with the aid of a portable yagi antenna and receiver. In early spring, these sites were always in a dense stand of milk thistle. By late spring, after the vegetative canopy began to develop subjects were found in dense sandbar willow thickets or occasionally in a brush pile or under a tamarisk. None of the sites, except one in a milk thistle stand, appeared to be subterranean.

Reference to computer-drawn maps for each observation period suggested that subjects daily traversed more of their respective home ranges during June and July than in earlier months.

Home Range

Individual gray fox home ranges (fig. 6) were delineated by minimum polygons (Hayne 1949) drawn around the perimeter of fixes from each subject using Ables' (1969) "atypical habitat elimination method." The subjects were found to have a mean home range of 129 ha. (range = 106- 172, n = 4). Fuller (1978), working approximately 6.4 km. (4 mi.) west on Putah Creek in more diverse habitat, calculated four home ranges (30, 132, 142, and 185 ha.) which gives a mean home range size of 122 ha. For eight gray foxes in Zion National Park, Utah, Trapp (1978) calculated a similar mean home range (107 ha.). However, Rymills (1979) computed a smaller mean home range (50 ha.) for three gray foxes at Point Reyes National Seashore, California.

Home ranges for all subjects closely coincided with the riparian zone and adjacent agricultural belts. The importance of the riparian zone as habitat seems evident, since 96.1% of the inactive observations were made within it. Probably less than three hours in any 24-hour period were spent in the bordering agricultural areas, and much of this time undoubtedly was spent travelling the dirt roads that separated riparian and agricultural areas (cf. Richards and Hine 1953; Wood 1954).

The 6-m. high flood-control levees apparently had minimal effect upon lateral movement outside the riparian zone, since the band of lateral activity remained relatively consistent even in the southeastern portion of the study area where no levee existed (fig. 1).

SPATIAL DISTRIBUTION, FOUR GRAY FOX HOME RANGES
25 MAR 73 - 27 JUL 73

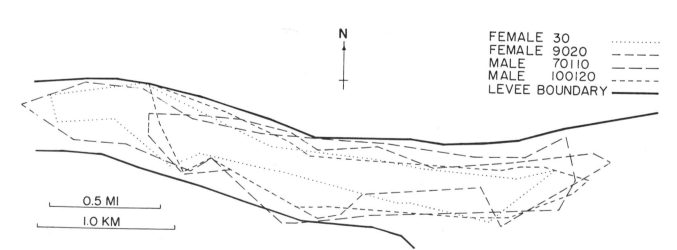

Figure 6.--Individual home ranges of four gray foxes on the Putah Creek study area, Davis, California. Each home range was determined from computer analysis of radio-telemetry data. The levee boundary can be compared with the study area photograph in figure 1.

The home ranges of all four subjects closely coincided (fig. 6). The activity centers (Hayne 1949) were also nearly coincident, suggesting that these animals were not territorial toward each other.

No subject limited its inactive periods to a specific region within the riparian zone, and only 5.9% of the fixes for different subjects appeared to overlap. This suggests that no apparent regional territoriality existed between subjects, although certain inter-individual distances were maintained.

Reducing the number of inactive areas by only counting those locations in which eight or more fixes were recorded reduced the number of inactive sites from 101 to 23 (fig. 7). These 23 sites reflected 60.9% of the inactive observations. Each subject still appeared to rest in various areas throughout the riparian zone, but never was observed at a resting site that had been frequented by another subject.

The apparent solitary diurnal behavior of the subjects did not change appreciably during nocturnal periods. None of the subjects were observed to travel together, although they may have met for brief periods. The frequency of such meetings could not be determined since the subjects often followed what appeared to be erratic paths with many reversals in direction. Presumably, erratic and solitary behavior would allow maximum exploitation of a rather limited range by several gray foxes.

CONCLUSIONS

In a habitat of riparian/agricultural land on Putah Creek, near Davis, California, four gray foxes (two males and two females) were found to exhibit similar temporal and spatial habits. Some temporal movement was observed during all 24 hours of the day. Activity increases began as early as two hours prior to dusk and peaked about three hours after sunset. The probability of activity exceeded 80% for the remainder of the nocturnal period. Although activity probabilities showed a significant reduction two hours following sunrise, minimum activity did not occur until afternoon.

Travel rates suggested that subjects made only local moves during diurnal periods and did not begin longer traverses until an hour after sunset. Although nocturnal travel was extensive, peak travel rates were observed one hour after sunset and again three hours before sunrise. These peak periods seemed to occur as subjects were leaving diurnal resting areas or when returning to them.

Individual gray foxes normally rested in different locations each day, once vegetative cover became abundant in late spring. After dark, activity paths appeared erratic, showing many twists and reversals in direction, particularly during the summer. No differences in circadian rhythms were observed during spring and summer, although the degree of spring activity was reduced. The lower activity probabilities and travel rates in the spring were attributed to sparse vegetative cover.

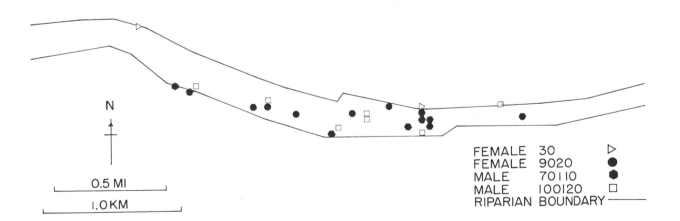

SPATIAL DISTRIBUTION, KNOWN DIURNAL RESTING AREAS

25 MAR 73 – 27 JUL 73

N

0.5 MI

1.0 KM

FEMALE	30	▷
FEMALE	9020	●
MALE	70110	⬡
MALE	100120	□
RIPARIAN	BOUNDARY	——

Figure 7.--The spatial distribution of known diurnal gray fox resting areas as determined from computer analysis of radio-telemetry data taken on the Putah Creek study area, Davis, California.

All subjects appeared to have nearly identical home ranges, since the geographical area and centers of activity were similar. The narrow riparian zone appeared to be the primary influence upon the home range's shape.

The apparent similarity of subject activity was not attributed directly to positive intra-specific co-actions since each subject appeared to exhibit solitary resting and travel habits.

LITERATURE CITED

Ables, E. 1969. Home range studies of red foxes (Vulpes vulpes). J. Mammal. 50(1):108-119.

Adler, H.L., and E.B. Roessler. 1972. Introduction to probability and statistics. 373 p. W.H. Freeman and Co., San Francisco, Calif.

Fuller, T.K. 1978. Variable home-range sizes of female gray foxes. J. Mammal. 59(2):446-449.

Gander, F.F. 1966. Friendly foxes. Pacific Discovery 19(1):28-31.

Grinnell, J., J. Dixon, and J.M. Linsdale. 1937. Fur-bearing mammals of California. 2 volumes, 777 p. University of California Press, Berkeley, Calif.

Hall, E.R., and K.R. Kelson. 1959. The mammals of North America. 2 volumes, 1,083 p. The Ronald Press, New York, N.Y.

Hallberg, D., F. Janza, and G. Trapp. 1974. A vehicle-mounted directional antenna system for biotelemetry monitoring. Calif. Fish and Game 60(4):172-177.

Hallberg, D.L. 1974. A contribution toward the better understanding of gray fox (Urocyon cinereoargenteus) temporal and spatial natural history. M.S. Thesis, California State University, Sacramento. 285 p.

Hayne, D.W. 1949. Calculation of size of home range. J. Mammal. 30(1):1-18.

Heezen, K.L., and J.R. Tester. 1967. Evaluation of radio-tracking by triangulation with special reference to deer movements. J. Wildl. Mgmt. 31(1):124-141.

Lord, R.D. 1961. A population study of the gray fox. Amer. Midl. Nat. 66(1):87-109.

Ostle, B. 1963. Statistics in research. 585 p. Iowa State University Press, Iowa.

Richards, S.H., and R.L. Hine. 1953. Wisconsin fox populations. Wisconsin Conservation Department, Tech. Wildl. Bull. No. 6. 78 p.

Rymills, E.M. 1979. Movements and food habitats of gray fox, Urocyon cinereoargenteus, in Point Reyes National Seashore. M.A. Thesis, San Francisco State University, San Francisco, Calif. 131 p.

Sanderson, G.C. 1966. The study of mammal movements: a review. J. Wildl. Mgmt. 30(1):215-235.

Seton, E.T. 1929. Lives of game animals. Vol. 1, Part 2. pp. 340-640. Doubleday, Doran and Co., Inc., Garden City, N.Y.

Storm, G.L. 1965. Movements and activities of foxes as determined by radio tracking. J. Wildl. Mgmt. 29(1):1-13.

Taylor, W.P. 1943. The grey fox in captivity. Texas Game and Fish 1(10):12-13, 90).

Trapp, G.R. 1978. Comparative behavioral ecology of the ringtail and gray fox in southwestern Utah. Carnivore 1(2):3-32.

Trapp, G.R., and D.L. Hallberg. 1974. Ecology of the gray fox (Urocyon cinereoargenteus: a review. p. 164-178. In: M.W. Fox, ed. The wild canids. 508 p. Van Nostrand Reinhold Co., N.Y.

Van Gelder, R.G. 1977. Mammalian hybrids and generic limits. Amer. Mus. Novitates 2635:1-25.

Van Gelder, R.T., 1978. A review of canid classification. Amer. Mus. Novitates 2646:1-10.

Wood, J.E. 1954. Investigations of fox populations and sylvatic rabies in the Southeast. p. 131-139. In: Trans. 19th North American Wildl. Conf.

FISH SLOUGH: A CASE STUDY IN MANAGEMENT OF

A DESERT WETLAND SYSTEM[1]

E. Philip Pister and Joanne H. Kerbavaz[2]

Abstract.--Fish Slough is a remnant of a once-widespread, shallow aquatic/riparian wetland in the arid Owens Valley (Inyo and Mono counties, California). Fish Slough supports a variety of rare species, including the endangered Owens pupfish. Successes and failures of management efforts at Fish Slough should hold lessons for management of other endangered species and natural areas.

INTRODUCTION AND BACKGROUND

The first recorded observation of the Owens pupfish (Cyprinodon radiosus Miller) (fig. 1) occurred in 1859 when Captain J.W. Davidson of the US Army described vast numbers of pupfish throughout the wetland areas of the Owens Valley (Inyo and Mono counties, California). So abundant were the small cyprinodont fishes that local Indians would seine them with woven baskets and dry them in the sun for winter food (Wilke and Lawton 1976).

Pupfish numbers remained high until at least 1916, when Clarence H. Kennedy, a student from Cornell University, observed large schools of pupfish in the numerous sloughs and swamps between Laws and Bishop (Kennedy 1916). Their time was short, for already severe changes were being effected which would bring about an enormous reduction in the once-abundant wetlands that support this fish. Numbers would be reduced to a point where, when described as a species in 1948, the Owens pupfish would be thought to be extinct (Miller 1948).

The investigations of Carl L. Hubbs and Robert R. Miller during the 1930s and 1940s revealed that because of reduction in surface water supplies, the habitat (and the fish) was progressively becoming reduced in extent. Its remnant habitat was being reduced and confined to the "type locality," that location from which the species was originally collected for official taxonomic description. This locality was de-

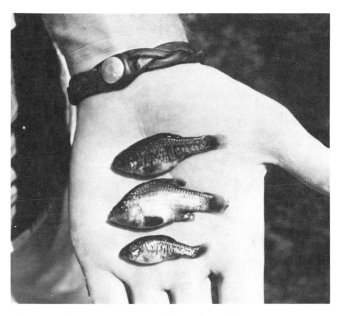

Figure 1.--Owens pupfish (Cyprinodon radiosus Miller). From top to bottom: adult female, adult male, subadult female.

scribed by Miller (ibid.) as: "the northwestern feeder spring of Fish Slough, about 10 miles north of Bishop, California." Today this location is a portion of the Owens Valley Native Fish Sanctuary.

Probably the major factor involved in such severe habitat reduction was the development and export of Owens Valley water to supply burgeoning populations in Los Angeles (Heinly 1910). Then, in later years dams were constructed to retain waters that, during and since the Pleistocene epoch, had periodically covered the Owens River floodplain and created ideal habitat for native fish populations. Nearly as damaging as water development and export, and occurring during this

[1] Paper presented at the California Riparian Systems Conference. [University of California, Davis, September 17-19, 1981.]

[2] E. Philip Pister is Fishery Biologist, California Department of Fish and Game, Bishop, Calif. Joanne H. Kerbavaz is Environmental Planner, California Department of Transportation, Bishop, Calif.

same general time period, was the introduction of predaceous gamefishes and other exotic species, including the western mosquitofish (Gambusia affinis), which preyed upon and competed with a constantly decreasing pupfish population (Pister 1974).

As habitat was reduced and populations of competing and predaceous fishes grew, the pupfish was gradually pushed to its final toehold in the marshlands of Fish Slough (Miller and Pister 1971). It is significant to note that among four native fishes in the Owens River system, two are listed as endangered (Owens pupfish and Owens chub [Gila bicolor snyderi]) and one is threatened (Owens dace [Rhinichthys osculus ssp.]). Only the Owens sucker (Catostomus fumeiventris) remains in substantial numbers (Pister 1981).

PRESERVATION AND MANAGEMENT

Following rediscovery of the Owens pupfish in 1964, thought began to be directed toward its management. Inventories of all fish populations began to be worked into general management plans of the California Department of Fish and Game (DFG), which had up to that time been so completely dedicated to gamefish management that any species not possessing adipose fins or spiny rays became an immediate candidate for eradication (Pister 1976). Suggestions for preserving such things as snails and plants met with derision. Problems of preserving all life forms at that time were more political than biological (Pister 1979).

Changes in the natural character of the Owens Valley continued through the next decade, largely manifested in the loss of spring ecosystems (and their associated flora and fauna) through increased groundwater extraction. This gradual change was accompanied during the 1960s by at least two instances during which pupfish populations in natural habitats thought to be secure were nearly lost.

So on June 26, 1967, when Carl Hubbs, Bob Miller, and Phil Pister met at Fish Slough to consider the possibility of creating refugia for the native fishes of the Owens Valley, their thinking went well beyond that. It was becoming disturbingly clear that the remaining aquatic wetland in Fish Slough was the only area in the entire Owens Valley retaining even a semblance of the magnificent ecosystem that existed before the coming of Europeans. More than fish refugia were needed. Aquifers supplying the springs had to be protected, and private inholdings had to be acquired to minimize further impact on the Fish Slough ecosystem.

The first priority was preservation of the Owens pupfish. Refugia were constructed at two locations in Fish Slough in the early 1970s. Designed to prevent the invasion of introduced predatory fishes that abound in Fish Slough, the

refugia attempted to recreate the conditions under which the native Owens Valley fishes evolved (Miller and Pister 1971). The refugia have been successful in protecting the native fishes, and in 1980 the Owens Valley Native Fish Sanctuary (the first refuge constructed) was expanded to enhance Owens pupfish habitat (fig. 2). Current status and recovery efforts for the Owens pupfish are summarized by Courtois and Tippetts (1979).

Public resistance to the creation of a native fish sanctuary is not widespread, but certainly exists. Fences have been cut, signs torn down, and largemouth bass (Micropterus salmoides) frequently (and illegally) planted into the refuge area. Such actions, although frustrating, only serve to strengthen our resolve to protect the entire ecosystem under a comprehensive management plan.

THE FISH SLOUGH REFUGE

Fish Slough, with its permanent water sources, is an aquatic anomaly in an arid valley and a remnant of a once-widespread shallow wetland. As such it supports a variety of rare species, including the pupfish, an undescribed snail, and at least six rare plants, as well as a dense concentration of cultural sites. It is not just the species and the cultural resources that are rare, it is the wetland with its aquatic and riparian systems.

Ownership boundaries in Fish Slough do not correspond with natural boundaries. As in most of the Owens Valley, much of the actual riparian land is owned by the Los Angeles Department of Water and Power (LADWP). The USDI Bureau of Land Management (BLM) administers land with one of the slough springs and manages most of the surrounding dry shadscale scrublands. There were two private inholdings in Fish Slough. DFG acquired a 64.8-ha. (160-ac.) parcel at the mouth of the Slough in the mid-1970s. The other parcel, 81.8 ha. (202 ac.) about 1.6 km. (1 mi.) southwest of the main slough springs, remains in private hands.

Of the riparian landowners, only DFG has the luxury of managing its lands exclusively for the benefit of the pupfish and the desert riparian system. The LADWP is concerned with developing and maintaining water supplies for export; this concern can conflict with needs for water for instream and riparian uses. BLM labors under a multiple-use mandate and must balance competing human needs and resource values.

Beyond the landowners, additional state and federal agencies and organizations have an interest in Fish Slough. Foremost among them has been the University of California Natural Land and Water Reserves System (NLWRS). The NLWRS, as part of an effort to preserve unique natural systems throughout the state for teaching and research, attempted to purchase the 81.8-ha.

Figure 2.--Prime Owens pupfish habitat, looking west across
Fish Slough to the Sierra Nevada.

private inholding during the 1970s. These
attempts were not successful, but the NLWRS
Systemwide Advisory Committee and staff continue
to support efforts to obtain the inholding and
establish a reserve.

To reconcile varying interests and develop
an effective management program, representatives
of the three landowning agencies and the NLWRS
met in 1975 and drafted a cooperative management
agreement. The agreement recognized the needs
and responsibilities of the various agencies, as
well as the need to manage Fish Slough as an
ecological unit.

The cooperative agreement has allowed the
continuing efforts of DFG to protect and enhance
pupfish populations. But the native fish refugia
and the desert riparian system cannot be consid-

ered secure while there are threats of development and changes in water supply for the slough.

In July 1979, the owners of the 81.8-ha.
private inholding filed Tentative Tract Map 37-23
Zack with Mono County. They proposed creating
the new housing subdivision of Panorama Tuff
Estates, with 49 parcels ranging from 1.2 to 4.3
ha. (3 to 10.6 ac.) in size.

The immediate threat to the integrity of
Fish Slough galvanized support for a refuge among
the landowning agencies and other interested
parties. They convinced the Mono County Board of
Supervisors to defer action on the subdivision
map and concentrated efforts on the acquisition
of the parcel.

The present landowners object to increased government land ownership in the Owens Valley, an area where governmental agencies own an estimated 98% of the land. The owners refused to sell their land, but agreed to exchange the parcel in Fish Slough for developable land somewhere else.

BLM began negotiations to decide on parcels to exchange. Even when both sides agree that an exchange will be mutually beneficial, the exchange process is long and arduous. The process includes a series of agreements, appraisals, and approvals and requires the involvement of several levels of BLM hierarchy.

In the case of Fish Slough, the exchange requires, in addition, the proverbial "Act of Congress." As is the case on much of the public land in the Owens Valley, the parcel selected by the private landowners had been withdrawn for watershed protection for the City of Los Angeles. This withdrawal must be shifted to the parcel in Fish Slough.[3] The necessary legislation, HR 2475, is pending.

Interagency efforts have focused on the prevention of permanent damage to the slough. With the acquisition of the final private inholding, the involved agencies and groups can work towards the creation and management of a reserve to protect all of Fish Slough.

LESSONS DRAWN FROM THE FISH SLOUGH CASE

The unique cooperative management efforts at Fish Slough to save an endangered species and a threatened ecosystem offer the opportunity to assess successes and failures and to draw lessons for the future.

One of the primary lessons taught by this case study is the reaffirmation of one of Murphy's Laws, that anything you try to fix will take longer and cost more than you thought. Attempts to remedy the effects of water diversion, habitat destruction, and unwise species introductions have required a significant investment of time and resources. This seemingly clear-cut case, the effort to preserve a universally recognized significant natural area, has taken almost 20 years to bring towards completion.

This case demonstrates the potential value of vigorous interagency cooperation. For this project, the pathways were primarily informal ones, built from common concern for protection of threatened resources. It would be difficult to

---

[3] Editor note: Although HR 2475 was unopposed, the political process is unpredictable and laborious at best. HR 2475 finally passed on 19 December, 1982, just a few hours before Congress adjourned. Final details of the land exchange are in the process of completion, and no further obstacles are anticipated.

plan in advance for cooperation like that needed for this project; however, it is imperative that land management agencies retain the flexibility to seek innovative, cooperative solutions.

Work to acquire the private inholding shows that we must develop and improve alternatives to fee acquisition in California. Money for land purchases is limited, and some landowners, unwilling to sell, may be interested in other alternatives.

The BLM land exchange process can be a valuable tool, especially in California's desert areas, to both eliminate inholdings and provide land more suited to development in less sensitive areas. The process is time-consuming and cumbersome, however, and many landowners have neither the time nor the patience to work with it.

Many authors have explored the alternatives to fee acquisition for the protection of natural resources (Hoose 1981). We must make it a priority to bring the best of these alternatives to fruition. We can start by making existing options, such as land exchanges, more workable.

CONCLUSION

Never before have the critical relationships between habitat integrity and species existence been brought so sharply into focus as during the 1970s, the decade of the endangered species preservation movement. The near extinction of the Owens pupfish and elimination of its desert wetland is just one example of a situation that is being repeated throughout the world, as natural resources succumb to short-sighted drives for economic development. The forces that reduced the pupfish populations and habitat from abundance to virtual disappearance in only three decades warrant sober and critical reflection.

LITERATURE CITED

Courtois, Louis A., and William Tippetts. 1979. Status of the Owens pupfish, *Cyprinodon radiosus* (Miller), in California. Inland Fisheries Endangered Species Program Special Publication 79-3, California Department of Fish and Game, Sacramento, Calif. 31 p.

Heinly, Burt A. 1910. Carrying water through a desert. National Geographic 21(7):568-596.

Hoose, Phil. 1981. Building an ark: tools for the preservation of natural diversity. 217 p. Island Press, Covelo, Calif.

Kennedy, C.H. 1916. A possible enemy of the mosquito. Calif. Fish and Game 2:179-182.

Miller, R.R. 1948. The cyprinodont fishes of the Death Valley system of eastern California and southwestern Nevada. Miscellaneous Publications of the Museum of Zoology, University of Michigan 68:1-155.

Miller, R.R., and E.P. Pister. 1971. Management of the Owens pupfish, Cyprinodon radiosus, in Mono County, California. Transactions of the American Fisheries Society 100:531-540.

Pister, E.P. 1974. Desert fishes and their habitats. Transactions of the American fisheries Society 103:531-540.

Pister, E.P. 1976. A rationale for the management of nongame fish and wildlife. Fisheries 1:11-14.

Pister, E.P. 1979. Endangered species: costs and benefits. In: The endangered species: a symposium. Great Basin Naturalist Memoir 3:151-158.

Pister, E.P. 1981. The conservation of desert fishes. p. 411-445. In: R.J. Naiman and D.L. Soltz (ed.). Fishes in North American deserts. R. J. Naiman and D. L. Soltz (ed.). 552 p. John Wiley and Sons, Inc., New York, N.Y.

Wilke, P.J., and H.W. Lawton. 1976. The expedition of Captain J. W. Davidson to the Owens Valley in 1859. 55 p. Ballena Press, Socorro, N.M.

GEOGRAPHICAL ECOLOGY OF THE SACRAMENTO VALLEY
RIPARIAN BUTTERFLY FAUNA[1]

Arthur M. Shapiro[2]

Abstract.--The Sacramento Valley butterfly fauna is depauperate and strikingly uniform in the riparian corridor from Redding to the Sacramento-San Joaquin Delta. There are few obvious pre-American relicts and only one taxonomically recognized endemic, Battus philenor hirsuta. Historical reasons for these conditions are discussed along with aspects of the biology of characteristic riparian species.

INTRODUCTION

The Sacramento Valley has the same reputation among Lepidopterists as among weekend recreation-seekers: a hot, dry, flat, uninteresting place between the coast and the Sierra Nevada that should be traversed as quickly and painlessly as possible. To some extent the Lepidopterological reputation, at least, is deserved.

Before 1968 no faunistic or ecological treatment of the Valley butterflies had appeared. In that year Opler and Langston (1968) published a faunistic analysis for Contra Costa County which included part of the Sacramento-San Joaquin Delta, and with it a very significant proportion of the Valley fauna. The entire butterfly fauna of the Valley consists of 65 species, of which only about 50 can be considered permanent residents under present-day conditions (Shapiro 1974, 1975). How rich or poor a fauna is this? It would seem rich to an Englishman; the British Isles, with 243,500 km^2 (94,000 mi^2) and infinitely more topographic and vegetational diversity, have about the same number of species as 19,400 km^2 (7500 mi^2) of Sacramento Valley (Ford 1975). On the other hand, by temperate North American standards this is clearly a poor fauna. A disturbed tidal marsh and adjacent waste ground covering some 104 km^2 (40 mi^2) near Philadelphia boast a fauna of 73 species (Shapiro 1970). Staten Island, New York, has 104 species in 180 km^2 (70 mi^2) (Shapiro and Shapiro 1973). Closer to home, Gates and Mix Canyons on the east slope of the Vaca Hills, Inner Coast Range, Solano County, California, have as many species as the entire Sacramento Valley (Shapiro unpublished). Almost any montane

locality in northern California has more. The Trinity Alps and Mount Eddy have about 112 species (Shapiro et al. 1981); in the Sierra Nevada, Donner Pass (2,130 m. (7,000 ft.)) has over 100 species in about 31 km^2 (12 mi^2), giving it one of the richest butterfly faunas in the North Temperate Zone (Emmel and Emmel 1962; Shapiro unpublished).

Apart from species numbers, a fauna may also be examined by taxonomic composition. An "unbalanced" fauna is one in which one or a few taxonomic groups provide most of the species. When the Valley fauna is compared to others in California, it seems relatively balanced--there is a slight deficit of Lycaenidae, which tend to be specialists, and a corresponding surplus of Hesperiidae, which may be relative generalists (though their ecologies are mostly unstudied).

The reasons for local and regional differences in faunal richness and composition are partly historical and partly ecological.

In Miocene and Pliocene times much of the present Sacramento Valley was a large, shallow inland sea. As noted by Ornduff (1974), one consequence of the emergence of the Valley floor as a habitat for terrestrial plants was the evolution of new and distinctive taxa, mainly ephemeral annuals: "The surrounding upland areas had been occupied by plants for a much longer period of time than the Central Valley and support evolutionarily older plant species and plant communities". The evolution of distinctive plants and communities on the Valley floor was apparently not mirrored in its butterflies.

The pre-American Valley supported three principal community-types: bunchgrass/valley oak savanna, tule/cattail marsh, and riparian forest (Thompson 1961; Sculley 1973). Although the early explorers have left vivid accounts of northern California scenery and wildlife, our knowledge of the butterfly fauna of the pristine Valley is virtually non-existent. A great many

---

[1]Paper presented at the California Riparian Systems Conference. [University of California, Davis, September 17-19, 1981].

[2]Arthur M. Shapiro is Professor of Zoology and Lecturer in Entomology, University of California, Davis.

common California butterflies were described in Europe by J.B.A. de Boisduval, who received them from a Frenchman, Pierre J. Lorquin, who had come during the Gold Rush of 1849. Lorquin's Admiral, (Limenitis lorquini) a common riparian butterfly, is named after him. Nearly all we know of his travels is from the sketchy outline provided in de Boisduval's monograph (1869). He may have followed the Sacramento River north through the Valley to its headwaters (F. Martin Brown, in litt.). De Boisduval says he "explored first all the environs of San Francisco, then the banks of the Sacramento and the Feather, ...made trips into the Sierra Nevada range, even to the forests of the interior, braving the tooth of the bear and the fangs of the rattlesnake." Valley localities are mentioned in the text; for example Pieris protodice is cited as "common enough in the Sacramento [district]".

Lorquin also furnished California butterflies to Felder in Austria and to a Philadelphia entomologist, Tryon Reakirt, who may have described a now-extinct riparian population of the Pieris napi complex from near Stockton (see below). None of the early works gives a good picture of the Valley fauna as a fauna; almost nothing of an ecological nature was published on California butterflies before Tilden's (1959) landmark paper on Tioga Pass! We do know that no species was described from the Valley only to become extinct later, as happened in the San Francisco Bay Area. Whether this reflects a true absence of Valley endemics or only a failure to collect there is another matter. I imagine there was inadequate collecting—of a very limited fauna!

It seems a priori unlikely that the adaptive radiation of ephemeral annuals would have been paralleled in the butterflies. The timing of vernal annual life cycles is largely dependent on rainfall, which is notoriously unreliable and unpredictable. The normal evolutionary response of butterflies to these conditions is long-distance migration (Larsen 1976), as is seen in the Painted Lady (Vanessa cardui) in both the Old World and the New, and in a more disorganized way, in the lowland Orange Sulphur (Colias eurytheme), Checkered White (Pieris protodice), and others.

The surviving vernal-pool communities in the Sacramento Valley have their specialist bees, but no butterflies. The only grassland butterfly associated with a native annual is the Large Marble (Euchloe ausonides), which has a facultatively bivoltine race we infer was originally associated with the mustard, Thelypodium lasiophyllum, but is now "domesticated" on weedy European Brassica. Even here, the Valley population—though phenotypically distinctive—has not been recognized taxonomically, and belongs to a Holarctic complex with vernal phenology in the Old World as well as the New.

The most striking, and rather surprising, absence in the Valley grassland fauna is that of a set of specialist Satyridae or Hesperiidae associated with the native bunchgrasses. The near-extermination of these grasses leaves little hope of finding relicts of a (totally hypothetical) pre-American fauna. Only the endemic California Ringlet (Coenonympha tullia californica), occurs today in disturbed grassland throughout the state, west of the Sierra-Cascade axis. Most of the Hesperiid fauna is weedy, associated with introduced grasses. At least one species, Lerodea eufala, seems to be a recent introduction (since the 1940s). Hesperia juba, otherwise montane, occurs at low densities in the Bay Area and in the Delta.

Equally surprising is the lack of a distinctive fauna in the marshlands. They are older than the grasslands, basically the remnants of the old shallow sea, and better preserved. We have only the Yuma Skipper (Ochlodes yuma), which feeds on a native strain of the common reed (Phragmites communis), and is still numerous in the Delta. There are relict marsh skippers in the montane part of northern California, but they are rare and perhaps in decline. Overall, the marsh fauna in California is poor when compared to those in the East.

The riparian butterfly fauna is the best preserved in the Valley. Although we cannot be absolutely confident that nothing has been lost, the uniformity of the fauna throughout the region suggests that we are seeing most of it. Indeed, it might almost be said that the present Sacramento Valley butterfly fauna is a riparian fauna—albeit one that has expanded into irrigated agricultural and especially urban environments. The remainder of this paper surveys its derivation, distribution, composition, and prospects.

THE RIPARIAN FAUNA TODAY

Sources

As California dried out over several million years, and the present Mediterranean climate became established, many plant species requiring summer moisture contracted their ranges to the banks of the major watercourses. This emerging riparian vegetation included woody taxa, ultimately derived from Axelrod's Arcto-Tertiary Geoflora, which otherwise could not have survived in the absence of summer rain (Raven and Axelrod 1978).

Precisely the same thing seems to have happened to the butterfly fauna. A sizeable proportion of the Valley fauna is of Arcto-Tertiary origin, with strong affinities to the Palearctic. This element is prominent in the riparian faunas. In most lowland California habitats butterfly emergences are concentrated in spring, coinciding with the simultaneous occurrence of good flight weather and lush vegetation. Most species are univoltine and have a summer dormancy, or diapause. This applies not only to Madro-Tertiary derivatives but Arcto-Tertiary ones as well, which may be multivoltine (e.g.,

Pieris napi) or early-summer univoltine (Satyrium spp., Glaucopsyche lygdamus) in more humid climates. Outside the riparian zone there are few multivoltine species, and those that occur are migratory or at least extremely dispersive.

Continuous breeding in summer requires continuous availability of host plants in suitable condition and adult food sources through the long rainless months. Comparing curves representing the number of species flying throughout the year at Valley and foothill locations, the difference in seasonal pattern is striking (fig. 1). It is due to the preponderance of multivoltine species in the riparian zone. These butterflies have no option of summer dormancy, though they do diapause overwinter. They have in effect been sheltered from the summer drought and have never evolved special physiological adaptations to cope with it. They are still doing what their forebearers did in a climate with summer rain.

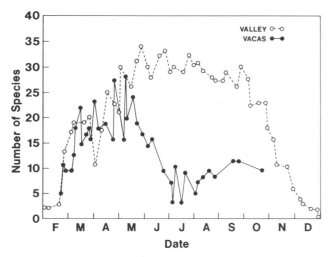

Figure 1.--Number of species flying in the Vaca Hills and adjacent Sacramento Valley during the 1972 season. The spring peak in the hills is due to univoltine species, while most Valley floor species are multivoltine. In the summer, annuals are dried and dead. Perennials and woody plants have ceased to add new growth. Thus both adult nectar and larval food sources are unavailable in the Vaca Hills.

The preadapted character of this riparian fauna contrasts interestingly with the butterfly fauna of another region subjected historically to long-term drying: the Patagonian steppe. Patagonia has been deteriorating climatically since the Tertiary (Menendez 1972; Petriella 1972; Volkheimer 1971). The large rivers coming down from the Andes and crossing the vast treeless plateaus of Patagonia are fringed with a narrow band of riparian forest, but there is essentially no butterfly fauna there. Overall, the Patagonian butterfly fauna is far more depauperate and taxonomically unbalanced than that of the Sacramento Valley. The great majority of species are Satyrids that live not in the moist river bottoms

but on the steppe proper, feeding on the bunchgrasses.

The historical basis for this apparent anomaly is straightforward. Given the past and present geography of the region, where would a riparian fauna be recruited from? Only the cool, humid Tertiary Nothofagus forests of the west slope of the Andes come to mind. But this is a very poor analogue of our Arcto-Tertiary sources. Arcto-Tertiary vegetation covered a vast area in the Northern Hemisphere and was extremely diverse. At that time the Nothofagus forests were already highly insular and much less diverse. Their extreme geographic isolation would have dictated an impoverished butterfly fauna even if the wet, cloudy climate had not. At the same time, an endemic butterfly fauna had differentiated in the treeless puna of the high Andes, and was able to colonize the cool-arid Patagonian steppe with little trouble. Even today, most of the shared taxa are undifferentiated even at the subspecies level. Clearly, the preponderance of riparian butterflies in the Sacramento Valley fauna does not represent a phenomenon inevitable in arid or semi-arid regions.

Although most of the Valley fauna seems to be of Arcto-Tertiary origin, two conspicuous species are not: Atlides halesus and Battus philenor hirsuta. Atlides belongs to a purely Neotropical group. B. philenor has its closest relatives in tropical America but belongs to an old, pan-tropical group of Aristolochia-feeding Papilionidae best developed in southeastern Asia and the Australian region. Both B. philenor and its host plant, Aristolochia californica may be relicts of Axelrod's Neotropical-Tertiary Geoflora, which is extinct at the level of woody plants. Alternately, they and A. halesus might have entered North America quite late in the "Great American Interchange" (Marshall 1981), as Anaea andria, Euptoieta claudia, Eurema mexicana, and some other butterflies found in the eastern and southwestern United States almost certainly did. My own suspicion is that B. philenor, at least, is older.

Distribution

There are no endemic species in the butterfly fauna of the Sacramento Valley, and only one endemic subspecies (Battus philenor hirsuta). The riparian butterflies are largely widespread, generalized mesic species. Like the grassland and marsh faunas, they show little evidence of evolutionary activity. The fauna is extremely uniform from the head of the Valley to the Delta; the species lists for Turtle Bay (Redding) and Discovery Park (Sacramento) are nearly congruent. Nor is there north-south clinal variation or phenotypic differentiation, despite the increase in continentality in the climate of the north Valley.

These facts suggest genetic continuity in the riparian corridors, which have been fragmented only in recent historical time. Even in their present condition, these corridors are still probably adequate to permit the larger, more mobile species to maintain genetic continuity. Many riparian butterflies are excellent dispersers and are often seen as singletons many miles across hostile habitat from their nearest breeding colonies. B. philenor and Phyciodes campestris are good examples. Papilio rutulus has been documented as dispersing 8 km. (5 mi.).[3]

The question of whether these riparian corridors provided continuity across the Valley floor, conecting Coast Range and Sierran foothill populations, remains open. Most species are not phenotypically differentiated in the two foothill systems, and many of them occur in the isolated Sutter Buttes, even though there is no east-west continuity seen today (e.g., Papilio multicaudatus, Battus philenor, Polygonia satyrus, Vanessa atalanta). Shapiro (1977) tells the strange story of Pieris napi castoria, described by Reakirt from Lorquin material possibly collected at or near the Valley town of Castoria (now French Camp, near Stockton); it is not known on the Valley floor today. The Chalcedon Checkerspot (Euphydryas chalcedona) is a riparian/canyon species found in both sets of foothills which does not breed in the Valley today. It is phenotypically differentiated in both larval and adult characters between the two ranges, and has not been collected in the Sutter Buttes. Lorquin's Admiral shows weak phenotypic differentiation in northern California. Valley floor and Sierra populations are less orange below than those of the Coast Range, which resemble Trinity-Siskiyou area residents. Some of this variation may be under environmental control.

Some Distinctive Riparian Butterflies

Surveying the biology of some 50 taxa is beyond the scope of this paper. Readers desiring more complete documentation should consult Shapiro (1974, 1975). The following material presents information on the most distinctive components of the Sacramento Valley fauna.

Battus philenor hirsuta

The Hairy Pipevine Swallowtail, the Valley's only taxonomically recognized endemic entity, is also the most characteristic Valley and foothill riparian butterfly. It occurs everywhere that its sole host plant, Aristolochia californica occurs. The species B. philenor occurs from Baja California and the Arizona desert to the mid-Atlantic coast. This subspecies, though weakly differentiated phenotypically, is unique in being completely disjunct from the rest of the species range. It is also unique in its population biology, sustaining extremely high densities in its larger colonies near Chico and in eastern Sacramento County. Its northern limit is near

Dunsmuir, Siskiyou County. Except for an isolated record at North Bend, Oregon (Dornfeld 1980), it is completely restricted to the Sacramento Valley and adjacent canyons, and a few sites in the Bay Area.

The life-history of B. philenor hirsuta is of great ecological and evolutionary interest. Basically it is multiple-brooded, but part of the pupae in each generation go into diapause. Most of these do not hatch until the following spring, but a few emerge at irregular intervals the same season. The proportion diapausing, and the strength of the diapause, may be functions of the weather[4] rather than daylength, which determines these things in most mid-latitude butterflies.

The adaptive significance of this becomes apparent once the host relations of the butterfly are examined. Although large larvae can and do feed on mature Aristolochia foliage, young ones must begin feeding on the tender shoot tips, and it is here that the eggs are laid. In wet years the plants may put on some new growth all summer, and the butterfly can continue to breed. In very dry years breeding may become impossible as early as late June. The ratio of dormant to nondormant pupae in the very large spring brood thus represents a gamble on the condition of the plants a few weeks hence. The March-April flight is a mixture of adults from all the broods completed in the previous year. We are trying to learn how good this swallowtail is at predicting the condition of its host, and allocating its reproductive effort in different years.

Phyciodes campestris

Not all Sacramento Valley populations of the Field Crescent occur in riparian forests; most are at the edges of such forests or of marshes. Its distribution largely coincides with that of its host plant, Aster chilensis. Aster is a prominent plant in mesic oldfield successions, but is rather rare and local in much of lowland California. Probably many colonies of both plant and butterfly remain undiscovered. In the southern Sacramento Valley (exclusive of the Delta, where it is relatively general), about six colonies are known. One of these (Willow Slough, north of Davis, Yolo County) has been under observation for 10 years. P. campestris is triple-brooded in the Valley and often very abundant where found. It overwinters as a larva, which can somehow survive being flooded for several weeks in winter.

Valley campestris show a distinctive summer phenotype not found elsewhere in the range, but we do not know if other populations would display it if reared under Valley conditions. The nominate subspecies with which our populations are lumped occurs from mesic sites in southern California (rare) north to Arctic Alaska. It also occurs east of the Sierra, as at

---

[3]L. Smith, personal communication.

[4]S.R. Sims, personal communication.

Mono Lake. Intervening between Great Basin and Sacramento Valley populations is a paler-colored entity, montana, endemic to montane and subalpine Sierran meadows. Typical campestris occurs in the same habitats in the Trinity Alps and Eddies. The complicated and often relictual distribution of this species in the far West seems to offer excellent opportunities for biogeographic interpretation, but its high vagility (i.e., potential colonizing ability) mandates caution.

Satyrium californica

The California Hairstreak was not considered a riparian species until 1973, when the author found colonies in north Sacramento and eastern Yolo Counties, using valley oak (Quercus lobata) as a host plant. No more such colonies have turned up, despite an assiduous search of oak groves (Walsh 1977). This may not mean no such colonies occur; Walsh's search was off-season, and the butterfly is easily missed--it spends much of its time in the trees, only coming down to feed around midday.

Although its existence was unsuspected before 1973, a valley oak ecotype of S. californica is hardly surprising. It commonly forms local ecotypes or ecological races, associated with various host plants of the genera Quercus and Ceanothus. At Rancho Cordova, Sacramento County, it is quite common--feeding on interior live oak (Quercus wislizenii) and ignoring valley oak! In the subalpine zone on Packer's Peak in the Trinity Alps, it feeds on tobacco brush (Ceanothus velutinus). It is single-brooded everywhere, overwintering (and in the Valley, oversummering too!) as an egg.

Phenotypically, the valley oak ecotype is distinct from Coast Range foothill specimens, but not from the live oak-feeding Rancho Cordova population. It is not worthy of taxonomic recognition. So little valley oak vegetation remains that no one could be found to write a chapter on it for a major synthesis of California vegetation studies.[5] Even if more than the three original colonies exist, the continuing deterioration of its habitat probably spells doom for this ecotype.

Lycaena xanthoides

The Great Copper presents the greatest mysteries in the Valley riparian fauna. Like Phyciodes campestris, it occurs in riparian broad-leaved vegetation, but also in moist grassland and at the edges of tule marsh. A glimpse at its northern California distribution (fig. 2) suggests that in the Valley it is restricted to the vicinity of the Sacramento River. There is no obvious reason for this. The butterfly is intensely colonial, and absent from a great many

[5]M.J. Barbour, Professor of Botany, University of California, Davis, personal communication.

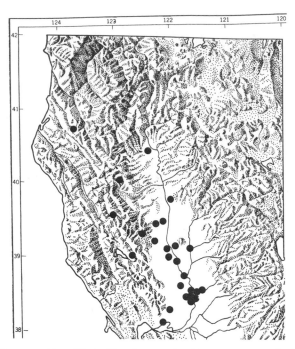

Figure 2.--Distribution of Lycaena xanthoides in and near the Sacramento Valley, north of the Delta. Coastal and Bay Area records, and the populations transitional to L. editha from Dunsmuir to Weed, are omitted (data in part from S.O. Mattoon; base map from California Insect Survey).

suitable-looking sites; yet it persists in the face of great disturbance. Its colonies occur on various soils, from sand to adobe clay; it is associated with at least six species of potential hosts (Rumex species, mostly introduced), none of which occurs in even a majority of its known colonies, except the very weedy R. crispus, whose range far exceeds the butterfly's.

Its distribution in the southern Valley has been carefully traced. It is common near Davis and Dixon (Solano County), and in the Yolo Bypass, West Sacramento, and Broderick (Yolo County). It crosses the Sacramento River at Discovery Park and ascends the American River to just beyond Highway 160, where it stops abruptly. As may be seen from the map, it has isolated (relict?) stations in interior Mendocino and Humboldt Counties, far from the Valley. It is common in the Delta and in vacant lots and marsh edges throughout the Bay Area, and extends to southern California. It is a montane species in the Tehachapis.

The Great Copper is completely unknown in the Sierra foothills and the adjacent east side of the Valley. In the montane and subalpine Sierra it is replaced by the smaller Lycaena editha, which extends northward at progressively lower elevations and appears to intergrade with L. xanthoides along Interstate 5 between Dunsmuir and Weed (Siskiyou County). L. editha is widespread in montane and subarid Oregon, but true L. xanthoides occurs disjunctly in the Willamette Valley (Dornfeld 1980).

As with Phyciodes campestris, this species or species complex seems a good candidate for intensive biogeographic study. It has a single flight in late spring (May to early July). Univoltinism is characteristic of the entire subgenus, and winter is spent as an egg.

Prospects for the Future

Granted the continuing loss and fragmentation of riparian vegetation in the Sacramento Valley, the future of the butterfly fauna can be viewed in two lights. How likely is extinction at the level of populations or species? How are these extinction probabilities related to efforts to preserve riparian systems?

The generalized mesic character of the Valley riparian fauna argues against vulnerability on more than a local, or perhaps ultimately regional, scale. The fact that the fauna is largely derived from an Arcto-Tertiary biota adapted to mild climates with summer rain suggests that many of the species should still be common in such climates. In fact, we find them in the closest analogue available in California— the coastal fog belt. Polygonia satyrus, for example, is very localized and rather rare in the Valley, but common and widespread in both Redwood and Douglas Fir associations coastwide. The Umber Skipper (Paratrytone melane) is an obligate riparian species in the Valley which can be found in every backyard in Berkeley.

Although several species like these might vanish from the Valley if riparian systems continue to disappear, they will leave large, healthy populations elsewhere. Many occur widely in the western half of North America, often with little geographic differentiation. Given the emphasis on endangered taxa (species and subspecies) in Federal conservation legislation, the Sacramento Valley riparian butterflies have little to offer conservationists looking for justifications for saving habitats. This is a pity, because butterflies have received a very favorable response in Washington. The sensitive entities are the colonial, endemic, or quasi-endemic ones discussed in the preceding section. Two of these are not strictly riparian, and only one is a named subspecies.

Richard Arnold, in his Ph.D. dissertation,[6] studied the characteristics of most of the butterflies currently recognized as endangered or threatened. He found that low vagility, close association with a particular host plant and set of adult resources, and increasing fragmentation of the habitable range are attributes shared among them. However, most of the entities listed are Lycaenids, and a great many Lycaenids which are not presently endangered are

local, sedentary, and monophagous. The critical variable is the amount (and contiguity) of breeding habitat. Many Lycaenids are potentially very vulnerable if their habitats become fragmented; other butterflies that resemble Lycaenids in population structure are also potentially in trouble. Let us see how these generalizations apply to the Valley riparian species.

Right now it seems unthinkable that Battus philenor hirsuta might become threatened; its annual population must run into the millions. Still, its reproductive capacity is low and it is completely dependent on a single host plant which is fairly habitat-specific. Notwithstanding these factors, a small colony (actually two colonies 2.4 km. (1.5 mi.) apart) has persisted on a handful of plants along the old channel of Putah Creek in Davis, which is now dry most of the year. These plants are growing in disturbed, mostly unshaded conditions and are subject to exceptional drought stress—yet they and their associated butterflies have remained essentially constant for the decade they have been under observation, even during the 1975-77 drought. In good years, surplus butterflies appear to emigrate from the colony. The Umber Skipper has disappeared from the same area since 1956. The persistence of this presumably relict population suggests that B. philenor can withstand much more fragmentation of habitat than it has yet had to face. However, as our most distinctive, spectacularly colorful, and taxonomically legitimate endemic it should be treated lovingly.

The other three species—Phyciodes campestris, Satyrium californica, and Lycaena xanthoides—are colonial even without human interference. P. campestris fits all of Arnold's criteria for vulnerability except for its high vagility; individuals of both sexes are taken every year at Davis, 4.8 km. (3 mi.) from the nearest colony. They have indeed been taken at 1,525 m. (5000 ft.) on the Sierran west slope, within the range of P. c. montana and at least 80 km. (50 mi.) from the nearest known population in the Valley (Shapiro unpublished). The critical question here is how the spatial pattern of long-range dispersal maps onto the pattern of potentially colonizable sites.

Satyrium californica and Lycaena xanthoides are quite sedentary, especially the former. Strays of xanthoides are recorded 16 km. (10 mi.) from breeding habitat (Shapiro unpublished). Colonies of xanthoides are numerous in the Davis-East Yolo-Sacramento area and gene flow remains likely. The status of the seemingly more isolated northern colonies is unknown. Its apparent rarity in the north Valley may merely reflect spotty collecting.

The long-term survival of the valley oak ecotype of S. californica is very unlikely. It perfectly matches Arnold's profile of an endangered butterfly. Had its phenotypic differentiation progressed to the same degree as the coastal dune endemics he studied, it would have been named and eligible for official Endangered

---

[6]Entomology, University of California, Berkeley, 1981.

status. But it did not. Even if additional colonies are located, the probabilities of inbreeding depression or random extinction are daunting. It requires oak reproduction for its own breeding. This imposes a limit on its tolerance of disturbance in the understory. It seems to be absent from those oak groves with the highest likelihood of preservation and self-renewal. Its known sites are variously zoned for industrial development, and development as a waterfront regional park; and are located in a residential area where relict oaks have a low probability of surviving due to changes in drainage patterns.

The other side of the coin is the successful adaptation of a large part of the riparian butterfly fauna to the ersatz "riparian" systems in urban and suburban environments. Many of the most striking riparian butterflies, including *Papilio rutulus*, *Nymphalis antiopa*, *Vanessa atalanta*, and *Atlides halesus* are breeding in street trees and gardens. I have observed 37 species of butterflies on my lot in one of the older subdivisions in Davis. None of the rarities breeds there, although I do get *Phyciodes campestris* in the garden regularly. So long as man provides mesic vegetation, the generalist multivoltine butterflies will use it.

The hope of finding relicts of the fauna of the pristine Valley has faded. We will probably never know what that fauna was like. Even so, there is plenty to be learned about the distribution and biology of the Valley riparian butterflies, and reason to hope that a few more Lepidopterists crossing the Valley enroute to somewhere else will be sufficiently intrigued to stop and take a look around.

ACKNOWLEDGMENTS

I am indebted above all to Sterling O. Mattoon of Chico, who does collect in the Valley and who has graciously shared his data and perceptions with me. All of the data on figure 2 north of Knight's Landing and Marysville are his. I also thank Gary L. Rominger of the Sacramento County Department of Parks and Recreation for authorizing our ongoing studies of riparian butterflies along the American River Bikeway; everyone whose personal communications were cited in the text; and the Committee on Research and Department of Zoology, UCD, for funding work in the Sacramento Valley when they could have spent the money on research in Amazonia instead. Figure 1 was drawn by Ginny McDonald.

LITERATURE CITED

Boisduval, J.B.A. de. 1869. Lépidoptères de la Californie. Annales de la Société Entomologique de Belgique 12:5-95.

Dornfeld, E. 1980. The butterflies of Oregon. 276 p. Timber Press, Forest Grove, Oregon.

Emmel, T.C., and J.F. Emmel. 1962. Ecological studies of Rhopalocera in a High Sierran community--Donner Pass, California. I: Butterfly associations and distributional factors. Journal of the Lepidopterists' Society 16(1):23-44.

Ford, E.B. 1975. Butterflies. Revised edition. 368 p. Collins-Fontana New Naturalist Series, London, England.

Larsen, T. 1976. The importance of migration to the butterfly faunas of Lebanon, East Jordan, and Egypt. Notulae Entomologicae 56:73-83.

Marshall, L.G. 1981. The Great American Interchange--an invasion-induced crisis for South American mammals. p. 133-230. In: M.H. Nitecki (ed.). Biotic crises in ecological and evolutionary time. 301 p. Academic Press, New York, N.Y.

Menendez, C.A. 1972. Paleofloras de la Patagonia. p. 129-184. In: M.J. Dimitri (ed.). La región de los Bosques Andino-Patagónicos. INTA, Buenos Aires, Argentina.

Opler, P.A., and R.L. Langston, 1968. A distributional analysis of the butterflies of Contra Costa County, California. Journal of the Lepidopterists' Society 22(2):89-107.

Ornduff, R. 1974. Introduction to California plant life. 152 p. University of California Press, Berkeley.

Petriella, B. 1972. Estudio de maderas petrificadas del Terciario Inferior del area de Chubut Central. Revista del Museo de La Plata, nueve serie, Paleontología 6:159-254.

Raven, P.H., and D.I. Axelrod. 1978. Origin and relationships of the California flora. 134 p. University of California Publications in Botany, vol. 72.

Sculley, R. 1973. The natural state. Davis New Review 1(1):3-13.

Shapiro, A.M. 1970. The butterflies of the Tinicum region. p. 95-104. In: Two studies of Tinicum Marsh. 124 p. Conservation Foundation, Washington, D.C.

Shapiro, A.M. 1974. The butterfly fauna of the Sacramento Valley, California. Journal of Research on the Lepidoptera 13:73-82, 115-122, 137-148.

Shapiro, A.M. 1975. Supplementary records of butterflies in the Sacramento Valley and Suisun Marsh, lowland central California. Journal of Research on the Lepidoptera 14:100-102.

Shapiro, A.M. 1977. Photoperiod and temperature in phenotype determination of Pacific Slope Pierini: biosystematic implications. Journal of Research on the Lepidoptera 16:193-200.

Sharpiro, A.M., and A.R. Shapiro. 1973. The ecological associations of the butterflies of Staten Island (Richmond County, New York). Journal of Research on the Lepidoptera 12:65-128.

Shapiro, A.M., C.A. Palm, and K.L. Wcislo. 1981. The ecology and biogeography of the butterflies of the Trinity Alps and Mount Eddy, northern California. Journal of Research on the Lepidoptera 18:69-152.

Thompson, K. 1961. Riparian forests of the Sacramento Valley, California. Annals of the Association of American Geographers 51:294-314.

Tilden, J.W. 1959. The butterfly associations of Tioga Pass. Wasmann Journal of Biology 17:249-271.

Volkheimer, W. 1971. Aspectos paleoclimatológicos del Terciario Argentino. Revista del Museo de Ciencias Naturales "Bernardino Rivadavia," Buenos Aires, serie Paleontológica 1:243-262.

Walsh, J.B. 1977. Report on the distribution and status of Quercus lobata groves in California which may support an ecotype of Satyrium californica. Atala 5:7-12.

THE STATUS OF ECOLOGICAL RESEARCH ON THE MAMMAL FAUNA

OF CALIFORNIA'S CENTRAL VALLEY RIPARIAN COMMUNITIES[1]

Gene R. Trapp, Gail L. Linck, and Edward D. Whisler[2]

Abstract.--An extensive literature search was conducted, and various local authorities questioned, regarding: 1) the species of mammals present in the riparian communities of California's Central Valley; and 2) the status of information on these species in relation to the communities. The result was a realization that the mammal fauna of these riparian communities has been studied very little. A checklist of 55 mammalian species was developed. It appears that about half the species listed have had no ecologically oriented research, and most others have had little.

INTRODUCTION

Each fall semester from 1970 to 1980, the senior author examined the results of comprehensive bibliographic searches on the biology of most species of California mammals. These searches were conducted under his supervision by mammalogy students at California State University, Sacramento (Trapp 1971-80). Much less ecological research has been published on the approximately 173 non-cetacean California species per se than might be expected, considering the relative abundance of research institutions in the state. Less ecologically oriented research had been published on mammals of Central Valley riparian communities than on those of the rest of the state. Riparian communities are rapidly being lost (Gaines 1976; Sands 1977; Warner 1979); those interested in their preservation would be helped by a clarification of the status of our knowledge of the mammal fauna of these communities. Our objectives in this study were: 1) to revise the checklist of mammalian species begun by Roberts et al. (1977) to include all riparian communities of the entire Central Valley; and 2) to determine the status of ecologically oriented research on these species.

PROCEDURE

The expression "riparian communities" is used here according to Warner (1979). We consi-

dered these communities to fall within the boundaries of the Central Valley "California Prairie" according to Küchler (1977).

We used the following sources to construct the checklist: Roberts et al. (1977); Grinnell et al. (1937); Ingles (1965); Williams (1979, 1981); Hall (1981); Elems and Medeiros (1981); and various other reports, e.g., Stone (1976), Brumley (1976), Schempf and White (1977). In addition to drawing upon the senior author's personal experience, we questioned the following authorities about their knowledge of mammals present in the Central Valley or their local areas: Robert Rudd;[3] Robert Schwab, Rex Marsh, Ron Cole;[4] Stan Elems;[5] Howard Leach and William Grenfell;[6] Terry Mansfield;[7] Gary Shook;[8] and Daniel Williams.[9]

---

[3] Robert Rudd. 1981. Personal conversation. Department of Zoology, University of California, Davis.

[4] Robert Schwab, Rex Marsh, and Ron Cole. 1981. Personal conversations. Division of Wildlife and Fisheries Biology, University of California, Davis.

[5] Stan Elems. 1981. Personal conversation. Department of Biology, Modesto Junior College, and Great Valley Museum, Modesto, Calif.

[6] Howard Leach (retired) and William Grenfell. 1981. Personal conversations. Wildlife Investigations Laboratory, California Department of Fish and Game, Sacramento.

[7] Terry Mansfield. 1981. Personal conversation. Big Game Investigations, California Department of Fish and Game, Sacramento.

[8] Gary Shook. 1981. Personal conversation. Woodson Bridge State Recreation Area, Corning, Calif.

[9] Daniel Williams. 1981. Personal communication. Department of Zoology, California State University, Stanislaus, Turlock.

---

[1] Paper presented at the California Riparian Systems Conference. [University of California, Davis, September 17-19, 1981].

[2] Gene R. Trapp is Associate Professor, Gail L. Linck is a Graduate Student, and Edward D. Whisler is a Senior in the Department of Biological Sciences, California State University, Sacramento.

We searched the literature for species on the checklist using two approaches. The first and less productive was a "habitat approach", using key words to search the following sources for the dates indicated:

Zoological Record: 1940-1975 (latest issue) for river, fresh water habitat, riparian habitat, terrestrial habitat, and (in older issues) ecology and habitats;

Wildlife Abstracts: 1935-June 1981 for natural areas and refuges, faunas, communities, and wetlands and wildlife. Prior to 1970-- mammals in general, biotas, faunas, and populations;

Wildlife Reviews: as per Wildlife Abstracts;

Biological Abstracts: 1974-early 1981 for riparian, riverine.

The second and more productive approach was a search for articles about the mammal species on the checklist. We went through the California State University Bibliographies of Selected Mammalian Species (Trapp 1971-80), which generally reach back into the 1930-40 period, and updated each to the dates indicated below with the following sources:

Zoological Record: through 1975;
Wildlife Abstracts: 1935-June 1981;
Wildlife Review: 1935-June 1981;
Mammalian Species: Numbers 1-156 (May 1981);
Journal of Mammalogy indices: through 1980.

Some specialized searches made by others were examined also: Newberry (1973), Trapp and Hallberg (1975), McGrade (1978), and Antonius (1981).

RESULTS AND DISCUSSION

The checklist (table 1) contains 55 species compared to 39 in the initial list begun by Roberts et al. (1977). The amount of evidence for the following species' presence in the natural riparian communities of the Central Valley varies. However, Ingles (1965) shows the following species absent or less widely distributed than reported by the authority indicated in parentheses:

broad-handed mole (Elems 1981[5]);
western (greater) mastiff bat (Hall 1981; Elems 1981[5]);
western gray squirrel (Stienecker 1977[3]);
porcupine (Rudd 1981[3], Shook 1981[8]);
ringtail (Naylor and Wilson 1956; Michny et al. 1975; Stone 1976; Brumley 1976; Belluomini and Trapp, in press);
mountain lion (Brumley 1976; Elems 1981[5]);
black-tailed and California mule deer (Dasmann 1968; Brumley 1976; Mansfield 1981[7]); and
feral hog (Dasmann 1968; Mansfield 1981[7]).

The presence of these species needs to be better documented for the riparian communities of the Central Valley. This is also true for the following species:

Table 1.--A checklist of native and introduced mammals of California's Central Valley riparian communities. Nomenclature after Williams (1979). See text for sources of data. *--San Joaquin Valley only; **--Sacramento Valley only; ?--presence questionable.

Didelphis virginiana Virginia opossum
Sorex ornatus ornate shrew
Scapanus latimanus broad-handed mole
Myotis yumanensis Yuma myotis
Myotis californicus California myotis
Lasionycteris noctivagans silver-haired bat*
Pipistrellus hesperus western pipistrelle
Eptesicus fuscus big brown bat
Lasiurus borealis red bat
Lasiurus cinereus hoary bat
Euderma maculatum spotted bat*
Plecotus townsendii Townsend's big-eared bat
Antrozous pallidus pallid bat
Tadarida brasiliensis Brazilian free-tailed bat
Eumops perotis western mastiff bat*
Sylvilagus bachmani brush rabbit*
Sylvilagus audubonii desert cottontail
Lepus californicus black-tailed hare
Spermophilus beecheyi California ground squirrel
Sciurus griseus western gray squirrel
Sciurus carolinensis gray squirrel
Sciurus niger fox squirrel
Glaucomys sabrinus northern flying squirrel**
Thomomys bottae southwestern pocket gopher
Perognathus inornatus San Joaquin pocket mouse
Dipodomys heermanni Heermann's kangaroo rat*
Dipodomys californicus California kangaroo rat**
Castor canadensis beaver
Reithrodontomys megalotis western harvest mouse
Peromyscus maniculatus deer mouse
Neotoma fuscipes dusky-footed woodrat
Microtus californicus California vole
Ondatra zibethicus muskrat
Rattus norvegicus Norway rat
Rattus rattus black rat
Mus musculus house mouse
Erethizon dorsatum porcupine**
Myocastor coypus nutria?*
Canis latrans coyote
Canis (Vulpes) vulpes red fox
Canis (Urocyon) cinereoargenteus gray fox
Bassariscus astutus ringtail
Procyon lotor raccoon
Mustela frenata long-tailed weasel
Mustela vison mink
Taxidea taxus badger
Spilogale gracilis western spotted skunk
Mephitis mephitis striped skunk
Lutra canadensis river otter
Felis concolor mountain lion
Felis catus feral house cat
Felis (Lynx) rufus bobcat
Sus scrofa wild pig**
Cervus elaphus wapiti, elk
Odocoileus hemionus mule deer and black-tailed deer

brush rabbit
eastern gray squirrel
fox squirrel
San Joaquin pocket mouse
Heermann's kangaroo rat
deer mouse
dusky-footed woodrat
spotted skunk.

The fox squirrel seems to be spreading out into the suburbs from what in the past has been an urban habitat, e.g., in Sacramento suburbs. On 2 July 1981 Michael Lacy and Trapp saw one on the west side of the Sacramento River on the outskirts of Knights Landing (Yolo County).

The nutria (Myocastor coypus), though released in the past at various points in California (Ingles 1965), is thought to have been exterminated by the California Department of Agriculture (Leach 1981;[6] Marsh 1981[4]). However, Williams (1981,[9]) has had reports from ranchers and biologists that nutria are still present in the San Joaquin Valley.

The spread of the black rat, Norway rat, house mouse, and feral hog into natural riparian communities is not well documented. The feral hog occurs along the upper Sacramento River south of Red Bluff in Tehama County; on the Colusa National Wildlife Refuge in Colusa County; and on Grizzly Island in Suisun Marsh, Solano County (Dasmann 1968; Mansfield 1981[7]); it is apparently extending its range.

The tule elk presently exists free-living only on Grizzly Island at the northeast end of Suisun Bay, Solano County. The only other potentially riparian herd of tule elk is in a 308-ha. (761-ac.) enclosure of annual grassland, wooded sloughs, and marsh on the San Luis National Wildlife Refuge along the San Joaquin River in Merced County (Dasmann 1968; USDI Bureau of Land Management 1979; Leach and Grenfell 1981[6]).

The black-tailed deer is found along the Sacramento River and its tributaries, extending south to the Cosumnes River/Stockton region. There its range overlaps and the deer hybridizes with the California mule deer, which occurs along drainages in the San Joaquin system (Mansfield 1981[7]). Dasmann (1968) fails to show these deer in the San Joaquin Valley or in the lower Sacramento Valley.

The following species are not included on the checklist, although they may occur in Central Valley riparian communities. Hall (1981) extrapolates their ranges into the Central Valley, but Ingles (1965) does not. These species are:

    small-footed myotis (Myotis subulatus)
    little brown myotis (M. lucifugus)
    long-legged myotis (M. volans)
    fringed myotis (M. thysanodes)
    long-eared myotis (M. evotis)

The Status of Research

Authoritative contributions to the knowledge of mammalian ecology in the riparian communities of the Central Valley are relatively few, considering the number of species and the number of research institutions in the state. "Furbearing Mammals of California" (Grinnell et al. 1937) still stands as the most important contribution regarding furbearers of the state, though it needs to be updated. The information is largely of a natural history nature with many contributions made by interviewed trappers.

"Mammals of the Pacific States" (Ingles 1965) is another major contribution to mammalogy in California. It contains general information on mammals, a key to the species, distribution maps, and information from the literature and the author's experience summarizing the biology and natural history of the species. This work, however, makes a limited contribution to the riparian mammal ecology in the Central Valley and is in need of revision. Two other helpful works of synthesis, including information collected by game department biologists, are California Department of Fish and Game (DFG) booklets "Big Game of California" (Dasmann 1968), in need of revision, and "Furbearers of California" (Seymour 1977).

Limited information on the distribution of mammals in riparian communities has been included in unpublished reports by the DFG (e.g., Leach 1963, Michny et al. 1975, Stone 1976, and Brumley 1976). Brumley's report is especially useful because it includes a list of 41 mammal species observed in the Upper Butte Basin northeast of Colusa. Schempf and White's (1977) survey of six furbearers in the mountains of northern California makes some brief but useful comments pertaining to the Central Valley on the distribution of ringtail, river otter, and red fox.

Turning to the scientific journals for research papers on Central Valley riparian mammals, we found no information for about half the species on the checklist and very limited amounts for the rest. We found research reports ecologically oriented to riparian communities only for the species mentioned below.

Opossum (Introduced)

Campbell (1981a) reported capturing some albinotic individuals in north San Joaquin County near the Mokelumne River. He also studied activity patterns of captive young Central Valley opossums (kept in outdoor cages in north Sacramento) correlated with elements of weather and photoperiod (Campbell 1981b). Reynolds (1952) reported on reproduction in Central Valley opossums.

Black-tailed Hare

Hardy et al. (1977) reported on natural and experimental arboviral infections in this species along the Sacramento River in Butte County.

California Ground Squirrel

Owings and his associates at the University of California, Davis, have made several contributions to the literature on this species. Owings and Borchert (1975) studied correlates of burrow location; Owings et al. (1977) described general behavior; Coss and Owings (1978) reported on snake-directed behavior by snake-naive and experienced ground squirrels; and Owings et al. (1979) described time budgets of this species during reproduction.

Eastern Gray Squirrel and Fox Squirrel (Introduced)

Byrne (1979) studied distribution and ecology of eastern gray squirrel and fox squirrel in northern California.

Western Gray Squirrel

Ingles (1947) studied several aspects of the life history of western gray squirrel, including food habits, in a Sacramento Valley riparian forest on Big Chico Creek at Bidwell Park in Chico, Butte County. Stienecker (1977) provided an improved range map (cf. Ingles 1965) in his paper on food habits, but had no study sites in the Central Valley. Swift (1977) studied the reproductive cycle of this species in Butte County.

Beaver

For this species, there are only status reports by Tappe (1942); Cram (1951); and Lee (1977).

Deer Mouse

Fuller (1978) mentioned Peromyscus maniculatus as part of the diet of a gray fox at Davis, Yolo County. Biggerstaff (1977) studied swimming behavior of this species and three other mice (Reithrodontomys megalotis, Microtus californicus, and Mus musculus) found in the Sacramento/San Joaquin River delta.

California Vole

Haynie (1974) studied high population density stress and resistance to pasteurellasis in the California vole in outdoor enclosures near Sacramento. Smith (1975) studied the association between small mammal populations and certain plant communities in the Graylodge Wildlife Area of Butte County.

Muskrat (Introduced)

Distribution and status of muskrat were reported on by Twinning and Hensley (1943), Seymour (1954), and Lee (1977). Messa (1981) studied population dynamics and home range of this species along irrigation canals in east Yolo County, northeast of Davis.

Norway Rat and Black Rat (Introduced)

Brooks and Barnes (1972) reported on an outbreak and decline of Norway rat populations in California rice fields. Stroud (1982) studied population dynamics of Norway and black rats in a riparian habitat on Putah Creek in Yolo County. The role of rodents in plague ecology was examined by Nelson (1980).

Coyote

Dow (1975) analyzed four coyote populations in several counties of the Sacramento Valley region. Crellin (1977) related helminths in coyotes to ecological factors in the San Joaquin Valley.

Red Fox (Introduced)

Gray (1977) and Gould (1980) reported on distribution and status of red fox; Roest (1977) examined taxonomic status compared to the native Sierran red fox.

Gray Fox

Lee (1977) reported on status, and Fuller (1978) described variable home-range sizes in four females of this species in relation to habitat on Putah Creek at Davis, Yolo County. Hallberg and Trapp (1981) described temporal behavior and home-range characteristics in two males and two females east of Davis on Putah Creek.

Ringtail

Belluomini and Trapp (1981) summarized earlier ringtail sightings, plus their own work, and reported on distribution and density of this species in the Central Valley, which Grinnell et al. (1937), Ingles (1965), and Hall (1981) indicated was not present to the extent that it is.

Raccoon, Mink, and Badger

Lee (1977) reported on these species' status as furbearers.

Spotted Skunk

Mead (1962) studied several aspects of this species' life history. Orloff (1980) reported on present distribution.

Striped Skunk

Mead (1962) also studied several aspects of striped skunk natural history. Gray (1975) studied home range, movements, activity, and den characteristics; while Peck (1980) studied the family unit's activity patterns, home range, and denning habits, both along Putah Creek, Yolo County. Belluomini (1980) reported on the status of this species.

River Otter

Gould (1977) reported on river otter status; and Grenfell (1978) studied their food habits in Suisun Marsh.

Feral House Cat (introduced)

Hubbs (1951) reported on food habits of the feral house cat in the Sacramento Valley.

Feral Hog (Introduced)

Dasmann (1968) commented on status and distribution of feral hog; and Barrett (1978) studied several aspects of ecology, including movements and food habits, on the Dye Creek Ranch southeast of Red Bluff in Tehama County.

Tule Elk

Dasmann (1968) commented on this species' status and distribution. A more recent report was made by the USDI Bureau of Land Management (1979).

SUMMARY

Roberts et al. (1977) offered their mammal species checklist for the Sacramento Valley riparian forests as a starting point. The checklist presented here has been refined and broadened to include the San Joaquin Valley. It also is offered to interested biologists for further refinement. We have found that the composition of the mammal fauna of the Central Valley's riparian communities is poorly documented.

More research is also needed to improve our knowledge of life histories of riparian mammals, and the ecological relationships between them and the communities they inhabit in the Central Valley. Opportunities for conducting this research have been diminishing with the destruction of natural riparian communities, so we recommend that field biologists turn their attention without delay to the remaining opportunities for research in this poorly understood area.

ACKNOWLEDGMENTS

We would like to thank Daniel F. Williams, Stan W. Elems, Carolyn Stallard, and Jo Ellen Diem for reading the manuscript and offering helpful suggestions. We also thank Richard Warner for suggesting this project and guiding in its preparation, and Gordon Gould for providing information.

LITERATURE CITED

Antonius, D. 1981. Master's thesis bibliography of nongame animals. Nongame Wildlife Investigations Job Final Report, Project No. W-54-R-12, Job III-6. 92 p. California Department of Fish and Game, Sacramento.

Barrett, R.H. 1978. The feral hog on the Dye Creek Ranch, California. Hilgardia 46(9): 283-355.

Belluomini, L. 1980. Status of the striped skunk in California. Nongame Wildlife Investigations Progress Report, Project No. W-54-R-12, Job I-8. 6 p. California Department of Fish and Game, Sacramento.

Belluomini, L., and G.R. Trapp. 1981. Ringtail distribution and abundance in the Central Valley of California. In: R.E. Warner and K.M. Hendrix (ed.). Proceedings of the California Riparian Systems Conference. [University of California, Davis, September 17-19, 1981]. University of California Press, Berkeley.

Biggerstaff, C.E. 1977. A comparison of swimming behavior in four species of mice found in the Sacramento-San Joaquin River delta of California. Unpublished M.S. Thesis. University of the Pacific, Stockton, Calif. 35 p.

Brooks, J.E., and A.M. Barnes. 1972. An outbreak and decline of Norway rat populations in California rice fields. Calif. Vector Views 19(2):5-14.

Brumley, T.D. 1976. Upper Butte Basin study: 1974-75. Admin. Report No. 76-1. 30+ p. California Department of Fish and Game, Wildlife Management Branch, Sacramento.

Byrne, S. 1979. The distribution and ecology of the non-native tree squirrels Sciurus carolinensis and Sciurus niger in northern California. Ph.D. Dissertation. University of California, Berkeley. 196 p.

Campbell, M.R. 1981a. Records of albinotic opossum from central California. Southwest Nat. 25(4):560.

Campbell, M.R. 1981b. Activity patterns of captive opossum young (Didelphis virginiana) correlated with elements of weather and photoperiod. Unpublished M.S. Thesis, California State University, Sacramento. 134 p.

Coss, R., and D.H. Owings. 1978. Snake-directed behavior by snake naive and experienced California ground squirrels in a simulated burrow. Zeit. Tierpsychol. 48(4):421-435.

Cram, D.D. 1951. The status of beavers in the delta area of the San Joaquin River, San Joaquin County, California. Unpublished M.A. Thesis, University of the Pacific, Stockton, Calif. 77 p.

Crellin, J. 1977. Helminths of the coyote in the San Joaquin Valley, California, with some ecological and epidemiological considerations. Unpublished M.A. Thesis. California State University, Fresno. 48 p.

Dasmann, W.P. 1968. Big game of California. 56 p. California Department of Fish and Game, Sacramento.

Dow, R.J. 1975. Analysis of four populations of free ranging coyotes in California. Unpublished M.S. Thesis, University of California, Davis. 54 p.

Elems, S.W. and J. Medeiros. 1981. Flora and fauna of Caswell State Park, Ripon, California. Regional Biota Series No. 1, Great Valley Museum, Modesto, Calif. 20 p.

Fuller, T.K. 1978. Variable home-range sizes of female gray foxes. J. Mamm. 59(2):446-449.

Gaines, D.A. 1976. Abstracts from the conference on the riparian forests of the Sacramento Valley. 25 p. Davis and Altacal Audubon Societies, P.O. Box 886, Davis, Calif.

Gould, G. 1977. Status of the river otter in California. Nongame Wildlife Investigations Status Report. 4 p. California Department of Fish and Game, Sacarmento.

Gould, G. 1980. Status of the red fox in California. Nongame Wildlife Investigations Progress Report, Project No. W-54-R-12, Job I-8. 3 p. California Department of Fish and Game, Sacramento.

Gray, R.L. 1975. Home range, movements, activity, and den ecology of the striped skunk (Mephitis mephitis) in the Sacramento Valley, California. Unpublished M.S. Thesis, California State University, Sacramento. 36 p.

Gray, R. L. 1977. Extensions of red fox distribution in California. Calif. Fish and Game 63(1):58.

Grenfell, W. E., Jr. 1978. Food habits of the river otter in Suisun Marsh, Central California. P. 65-73. In: Proceedings of the Cal-Neva Wildlife Conference. [February 2-4, 1978]. California Department of Fish and Game, Rancho Cordova.

Grinnell, J., J. Dixon, and J.M. Linsdale. 1937. Fur-bearing mammals of California. 2 volumes. 777 p. University of California Press, Berkeley.

Hall, E.R. 1981. The mammals of North America (second edition). 2 volumes. 1181 p. John Wiley and Sons, Inc., New York, N.Y.

Hallberg, D.L., and G.R. Trapp. 1981. Gray fox (Urocyon cinereoargenteus) temporal and spatial activity in a riparian-agricultural habitat in California's Central Valley. In: R.E. Warner and K.M. Hendrix (ed.). Proceedings of the California Riparian Systems Conference. [University of California, Davis, September 17-19, 1981]. University of California Press, Berkeley.

Hardy, J.L., M. Milby, M.E. Wright, A.J. Beck, S.B. Presser, and J.P. Bruen. 1977. Natural and experimental arboviral infections in a population of black-tail jackrabbits along the Sacramento River, Butte County, California (1971-74). J. Wildlife Disease 13(4): 383-392.

Haynie, T. 1974. High population density stress and resistance to pasteurellasis in the California vole, Microtus californicus. Unpublished M.A. Thesis, California State University, Sacramento. 53 p.

Hubbs, E.L. 1951. Food habits of feral house cats in the Sacramento Valley. Calif. Fish and Game 37:177-189.

Ingles, L.G. 1947. Ecology and life history of the California gray squirrel. Calif. Fish and Game 33(3):139-158.

Ingles, L.G. 1965. Mammals of the Pacific States. 506 p. Stanford University Press, Stanford, Calif.

Küchler, W.A. 1977. Map of the natural vegetation of California. p. 909. In: M.G. Barbour and J. Major (ed.). Terrestrial vegetation of California. 1002 p. John Wiley and Sons, Inc., New York, N.Y.

Leach, H.R. 1963. A reconnaissance report on the lower Feather River, with special reference to the effects of water developments on fish, wildlife, and recreation. Report LFR-1063. 97+ p. California Department of Fish and Game, Water Projects Branch, Sacramento.

Lee, R.C. 1977. Status of harvested furbearers in California--badger, beaver, gray fox, mink, muskrat, and raccoon. Nongame Wildlife Investigations Progress Report, Project No. W-54-R-9, Job II-1.0. 29 p. California Department of Fish and Game, Sacramento.

McGrade, H. 1978. Research bibliography: Gray fox, spotted skunk, and striped skunk. Unpublished report, Department of Biological Sciences, California State University, Sacramento. 23 p.

Mead, R.A. 1962. Some aspects of the life histories of the spotted and striped skunks. Unpublished M.A. Thesis, University of California, Davis. 61 p.

Messa, D.J. 1981. Population dynamics of Sacramento Valley muskrats. Unpublished M.S. Thesis, California State University, Sacramento. 66 p.

Michny, F.J., D. Boos, and F. Wernette. 1975. Riparian habitats and avian densities along the Sacramento River. Admin. Report No. 75-1. 42 p. California Department of Fish and Game, Sacramento.

Naylor, A.E., and G.W. Wilson. 1956. Unusual occurrence of the ring-tailed cat. Calif. Fish and Game 42(3):231.

Nelson, B.C. 1980. Plague studies in California--the roles of various species of sylvatic rodents in plague ecology in California. Proc. Vertebr. Pest Conference 9:89-96.

Newberry, D.W. 1973. A contribution toward a bibliography on California furbearers. Special Wildlife Investigations Progress Report, Project W-54-R-5, Job II-5.7. 10 p. California Department of Fish and Game, Sacramento.

Orloff, S. 1980. Spotted skunk distribution study. Nongame Wildlife Investigations Job Final Report, Project No. W-54-R-12, Job IV-1. 13 p. California Department of Fish and Game, Sacramento.

Owings, D.H., and M. Borchert. 1975. Correlates of burrow location in Beechey ground squirrels. Great Basin Nat. 35(4):402-404.

Owings, D.H., M. Borchert, and R. Virginia. 1977. The behavior of California ground squirrels. Animal Behavior 25(1):221-230.

Owings, D.H., R. Virginia, and D. Paussa. 1979. Time budgets of California ground squirrels during reproduction. Southwest. Nat. 24(1): 191-195.

Peck, B. 1980. Activity patterns, home range, denning habits, and observations of the family unit of the striped skunk (Mephitis mephitis) in the Sacramento Valley, California. Unpublished M.S. Thesis, University of California, Davis. 86 p.

Reynolds, H.C. 1952. Studies on reproduction in the opossum (Didelphis virginiana). Univ. Calif. Publ. Zool. 52:223-284.

Roberts, W.G., J.G. Howe, and J. Major. 1977. A survey of riparian forest flora and fauna in California. p. 3-19. In: A. Sands (ed.). Riparian forests in California: their ecology and conservation. Institute of Ecology Pub. 15, University of California, Davis. 122 p.

Roest, A.I. 1977. Taxonomic status of the red fox in California. Nongame Wildlife Investigations Job Final Report, Project No. W-54-R-9, Job II-1.3. 15 p. California Department of Fish and Game, Sacramento.

Sands, A. (ed.). 1977. Riparian forests in California: their ecology and conservation. Institute of Ecology Pub. 15, University of California, Davis. 122 p.

Schempf, P.F., and M. White. 1977. Status of six furbearer populations in the mountains of northern California. 51 p. US Department of Agriculture Publications, Forest Service, California Region.

Seymour, G. 1954. Recent extension of the range of muskrats in California. Calif. Fish and Game 40(4):375-384.

Seymour, G. 1977. Furbearers of California. 53 p. California Department of Fish and Game, Sacramento.

Smith, M.F. 1975. Small mammal populations associated with certain plant communities in Graylodge Wildlife Area. Unpublished M.A. Thesis. California State University, Chico. 39 p.

Stienecker, W.E. 1977. Supplemental data on the food habits of the western gray squirrel. Calif. Fish and Game 63(1):11-21.

Stone, T.B. 1976. Observations on furbearers within the riparian habitat of the upper Sacramento River. Memorandum Report. 12 p. California Department of Fish and Game, Sacramento.

Stroud, D. 1982. Population dynamics of Rattus rattus and R. norvegicus in a riparian habitat. J. Mamm. 63(1):151-154.

Swift, R.J. 1977. The reproductive cycle of the western gray squirrel in Butte County, California. Unpublished M.A. Thesis, California State University, Chico. 78 p.

Tappe, D.T. 1942. The status of beavers in California. Game Bulletin No. 3., California Division of Fish and Game. 59 p.

Trapp, G.R. (ed.). 1971-80. Bibliographies of selected mammalian species. Library, California State University, Sacramento.

Trapp, G.R., and D.L. Hallberg. 1975. Ecology of the gray fox (Urocyon cinereoargenteus): a review. p. 164-178. In: M. W. Fox (ed.). Wild canids. 508 p. Van-Nostrand Reinhold Co., New York, N.Y.

Twinning, H., and A.L. Hensley. 1943. The distribution of muskrats in California. Calif. Fish and Game 29(2):64-78.

USDI Bureau of Land Management. 1979. Third annual report to Congress: the tule elk. 32 p. California State Director, Bureau of Land Management, Sacramento.

Warner, R. E. 1979. The California riparian study program. Phase I: Background studies and program design for Phase II. 177 p. California Department of Fish and Game, Planning Branch, Sacramento.

Williams, D.F. 1979. Checklist of California mammals. Annals of Carnegie Museum 48(23): 425-433.

Williams, D.F. In press. Mammalian species of special concern in California. Nongame Wildlife Investigations Job Final Report, Project No. E-W-4, Job IV-14.1. California Department of Fish and Game, Sacramento.

SENSITIVE, THREATENED, AND ENDANGERED MAMMALS OF
RIPARIAN AND OTHER WETLAND COMMUNITIES IN CALIFORNIA[1]

Daniel F. Williams and Kerry S. Kilburn[2]

Abstract.--Studies of the distribution, habitat requirements, and population status of species and subspecies of mammals in California were conducted in order to identify taxa threatened with extinction. Investigations were limited to taxa without current state or federal Rare, Threatened, or Endangered status. Twenty-one species and subspecies of mammals confined to or dependent upon riparian and other wetland communities were identifed as being especially vulnerable to loss of habitat and facing potential threats of extinction. These taxa are grouped into four categories depending upon the apparent nature and proximity of the threats to their populations. Destruction of riparian and other wetland communities is the principal factor jeopardizing all 21 taxa. Preservation of these and other members of riparian and other wetland communities can probably be accomplished most efficiently by an integrated approach that focuses on preserving biotic communities rather than single species. Herein we outline the elements of such a plan.

INTRODUCTION

Of the 502 recent native species and subspecies of land mammals in California (Hall 1981), approximately 25% (133 taxa) are limited to or largely dependent upon riparian and other wetland communities. No other general type of mammalian habitat in California approaches riparian and other wetland communities in importance to mammals, and none has been so diminished in extent and degraded in quality (Warner 1979). As a result, populations of mammalian species dependent upon freshwater and tidal riparian wetland communities have declined markedly in size in nearly every region within California. White-tailed deer (Odocoileus virginiana ochroura and O. v. couesi) have become extinct in California in this century (Williams in press). Populations of one tideland species, salt marsh harvest mice (Reithrodontomys raviventris raviventris and R. r. halicoetes) and one freshwater wetland species, the Amargosa vole (Microtus californicus scirpensis), are listed as Endangered (California Department of Fish and Game 1980); several other riparian and wetland species are seriously jeopardized by destruction and degradation of their habitats.

Concern over the rapid loss of biotic communities within California and the resulting threats to wildlife prompted the Nongame Wildlife Investigations Unit of the California Department of Fish and Game (DFG) to commission a study of potentially threatened populations of mammals within the state. Williams initiated that study in 1979 and filed the final report to DFG in September 1981 (Williams in press). The investigation was limited to native species of land mammals without state or federal Rare, Threatened, or Endangered status. Populations of 52 species and subspecies were identified as being potentially threatened with extinction; 21 of these are limited to or principally dependent upon riparian and wetland communities.

This report summarizes the investigations into the current population status of those mammalian species confined to or dependent upon riparian and other wetland communities in California.

METHODS

Taxa believed to be extinct and species concurrently being investigated by the DFG were excluded from the investigation. To be included on the final list of concern, the entire California population of a taxon had to be potentially

---

[1] Paper presented at the California Riparian Systems Conference. [University of California, Davis, September 17-19, 1981].

[2] Daniel F. Williams is Professor of Zoology and Kerry S. Kilburn is a student in the Department of Biological Science; both are at California State College, Stanislaus, Turlock.

jeopardized with extinction, given continuation of current trends in diminishment and degradation of habitat, harvest or persecution, or other factors threatening populations. Thus, locally depleted populations of more wide-ranging taxa were excluded, with a single exception: an isolated population of the Sierra Nevada mountain beaver (<u>Aplodontia</u> <u>rufa</u> <u>californica</u>), living in tufa deposits along Lee Vining Creek near where it historically entered Mono Lake (Steele in press), was included because of its unique habitat.

Initially, a working list of 86 candidate species and subspecies was assembled. Information on life history, habitat requirements, past and present distributions, systematic status, probable population status, and the nature of potential threats was gathered for each candidate, from the literature and other sources (see below). Letters and questionnaires requesting information on potentially threatened mammals were sent to all members of the American Society of Mammalogists residing in California, and to other, selected persons in state and federal agencies, universities, and natural history museums. A number of persons were contacted by telephone for inquiries about selected taxa and developments affecting wildlife habitats in certain areas of the state. Williams visited and obtained distribution data from 17 natural history museums which collectively contain the great majority of mammal specimens from California. Distribution data on some taxa were also obtained from 18 other mammal research collections (see Williams in press).

Most areas in the state where loss of habitat was thought to pose a threat to one or more candidate species were visited. Some preliminary field work to determine presence and abundance of candidate species was conducted, but time and funding did not permit detailed or extensive field work. Rather, the objective of the investigations was to develop a list of species, in priority categories, which would be used to determine the disbursement of limited funds for detailed investigations in the field and for other administrative decisions.

Common and scientific names used in this report are from Williams (1979). Vernacular names for subspecies are included because subspecies can be accorded state and federal Rare, Threatened, or Endangered status. These names are from Grinnell (1933), or those coined by the authors of more recently described species and subspecies, or, when no name was available, by Williams (in press). See Williams (<u>ibid</u>.) for detailed remarks on the taxonomy used here.

Refer also to Williams (<u>ibid</u>.) for a detailed account of methods, remarks on systematic status, recommendations for management actions, and documentation of distribution records.

RESULTS

Twenty-one species and subspecies of mammals of riparian and other wetland communities were found to face potential threats of extinction. The major factor jeopardizing each of these populations is loss and degradation of habitat. Each taxon is assigned to one of four categories according to the apparent proximity of the threats to remaining populations (table 1). The categories are described below.

Category 1.--Species are considered to be potentially endangered as defined by the federal Endangered Species Act of 1973.[3] Immediate action to stop loss and degradation of habitat for these species is needed. Field investigations to establish status and baseline population data should be carried out as rapidly as possible.

Category 2.--Species may be threatened or endangered as defined in the federal Endangered Species Act, but the threats of extinction seem less imminent than for species in category 1. Priority in management actions should be given to halting loss and degradation of habitat and establishing baseline data on populations.

Category 3.--Species probably do not warrant Endangered status now and appear not to be under proximate threats of extinction. If current trends in loss and degradation of habitat continue, however, they could quickly become endangered. These species may merit Rare (state) or Threatened (federal) status under current regulations. The principal administrative actions required are to initiate field investigations into population status and to consider the habitat needs of these species in land development and resource management plans.

Category 4.--Species are considered to be sensitive or vulnerable to disturbances, including loss and degradation of habitat, overharvesting, and other factors. Principal administrative actions needed include special considerations for these species in land development and resource management decisions, and protection from overharvest.

Distribution

Table 1 also briefly lists the distribution of each taxon. Note that five species found principally or wholly along the Colorado River in California are considered to be jeopardized. Of the five, only the Yuma mountain lion (<u>Felis</u> <u>concolor</u> <u>browni</u>) probably ranges far beyond the immediate vicinity of the river valley (<u>ibid</u>.), although it appears to be dependent upon the riparian community. Two of the species are restricted to the tidal marshes in the coastal region of the Los Angeles Basin, and two others are confined to the salt marsh communities in the San Francisco Bay area. Four of the poten-

_____

[3]P.L. 93-205.

Table 1.—Categories of concern and distributions of jeopardized species and subspecies of mammals in California. Priority categories are explained in the text.

Species	Priority category	Distribution
Salt marsh wandering shrew (Sorex vagrans halicoetes)	1	South arm of San Francisco Bay
San Bernardino dusky shrew (Sorex monticolus parvidens)	1	San Bernardino and San Gabriel mountains
Buena Vista Lake shrew (Sorex ornatus relictus)	2	Southern floor of San Joaquin Valley
Southern California salt marsh shrew (Sorex ornatus salicornicus)	2	Tidal marshes of Los Angeles Basin
Suisun shrew (Sorex ornatus sinuosus)	1	San Pablo and Suisun bays
Santa Catalina shrew (Sorex willetti)	2	Santa Catalina Island
Arizona myotis (bat) (Myotis occultus)	1	Colorado River valley
Arizona cave myotis (bat) (Myotis velifer velifer)	1	Colorado River valley
Riparian brush rabbit (Sylvilagus bachmani riparius)	1	Lower San Joaquin River
Oregon snowshoe hare (Lepus americanus klamathensis)	2	Mountains of northcentral and northeast California
Sierra Nevada snowshoe hare (Lepus americanus tahoensis)	3	Sierra Nevada
Sierra Nevada mountain beaver (Aplodontia rufa californica)[1]	1	Mono Lake
Point Arena mountain beaver (Aplodontia rufa nigra)	2	Point Arena, Mendocino County
Point Reyes mountain beaver (Aplodontia rufa phaea)	3	Point Reyes, Marin County
Sonora beaver (Castor canadensis repentinus)	4	Colorado River and Imperial valleys
Golden beaver (Castor canadensis subauratus)	4	Sacramento and San Joaquin rivers
Southern marsh harvest mouse (Reithrodontomys megalotis limicola)	2	Tidal marshes of Los Angeles Basin
Colorado River cotton rat (Sigmodon arizonae plenus)	1	Colorado River valley
San Joaquin Valley wood rat (Neotoma fuscipes riparia)	3	Lower San Joaquin valley
White-footed vole (Arborimus albipes)	2	Coastal forests, Del Norte and Humboldt counties
Yuma mountain lion (Felis concolor browni)	1	Colorado River and adjacent areas

[1]Concern is limited to the isolated population in the vicinity of Mono Lake, and not to the subspecies as a whole.

tially jeopardized species are found in the wetland and riparian communities of the San Joaquin Valley. Of these four, only the golden beaver (Castor canadensis subauratus) ranges beyond the San Joaquin Valley. The golden beaver is the only species listed here which may also face a serious threat from overharvesting.

These four areas, the Colorado River Valley, the San Joaquin Valley, and the tidal marshes of the Los Angeles Basin and San Francisco Bay, are viewed as special problem areas in terms of loss and degradation of riparian and wetland commu-

nities. Degradation of riparian and other wetland communities has, however, diminished mammalian habitats throughout all areas of California (table 1).

Jeopardized Species

The habitats of the 21 taxa listed in table 1 are briefly outlined below. In many cases, little or no data were available for the taxa of concern.

952

Salt Marsh Wandering Shrew

The salt marsh wandering shrew (<u>Sorex vagrans halicoetes</u>) occupies the medium-high marsh about 1.8-2.4 m. (6-8 ft.) above sea level and lower marsh areas not regularly inundated, characterized by abundant driftwood and other debris scattered among <u>Salicornia</u>. It requires dense cover, abundant food (invertebrates), suitable nesting sites, and fairly continuous ground moisture (Johnston and Rudd 1957).

San Bernardino Dusky Shrew

The San Bernardino dusky shrew (<u>Sorex monticolus parvidens</u>) is probably similar in its habitat association to the populations in the Sierra Nevada; no information on its specific requirements, however, is available. In the Sierra Nevada, dusky shrews are associated with riparian and wetland communities from the upper mixed conifer zone to the timberline (Williams in press).

Buena Vista Lake Shrew

The Buena Vista Lake shrew (<u>Sorex ornatus relictus</u>) occupied marshes on the perimeter of the historic Lake Buena Vista (Grinnell 1933). It may occupy dense vegetation along streams and sloughs and around the perimeter of tule marshes in the Tulare Basin, although nothing has been recorded about its habitat (Williams in press).

Southern California Salt Marsh Shrew

The Southern California salt marsh shrew (<u>Sorex ornatus salicornicus</u>) occurs in coastal marshes and probably requires fairly dense groundcover, nesting sites above mean high tide and free from inundation, and fairly moist surroundings. Nothing has been recorded about its habitat requirements (<u>ibid</u>.).

Suisun Shrew

The Suisun shrew (<u>Sorex ornatus sinuosus</u>) appears to require dense, low-lying cover where invertebrates are abundant. It typically inhabits tidal marshes characterized, in order of decreasing tolerance to inundation, by <u>Spartina foliosa</u>, <u>Salicornia ambigua</u>, and <u>Grindelia cuneifolia</u>, and brackish marshes dominated by <u>Scirpus californicus</u> and <u>Typha latifolia</u>. Suitability of habitat for shrews is determined by growth forms of the plant community, rather than species composition (Rudd 1955).

Santa Catalina Shrew

The Santa Catalina shrew (<u>Sorex willetti</u>) is probably found at least in the larger, stream-bearing canyons of Santa Catalina Island (von Bloeker 1932) and is possibly widely distributed, at least seasonally. Nothing is recorded about its habitat requirements (Williams in press).

Arizona Myotis (Bat)

The Arizona myotis (<u>Myotis occultus</u>) is most commonly associated with pine forests at 1,800-2,700 m. (6000-9000 ft.) outside California (Barbour and Davis 1969). It is known in California only from the low desert along the Colorado River (Williams in press). In most area, its roosts have been found beneath bridges and in attics of buildings (Barbour and Davis 1969), and it probably also roosts in hollows in trees and protected crevices in rocks (Williams in press).

Arizona Cave Myotis (Bat)

The Arizona cave myotis (<u>Myotis velifer velifer</u>) inhabits arid zones in the southwestern United States (Barbour and Davis 1969). Optimal foraging habitat seems to be the dense, linear stands of mesquite, tamarisk, and catclaw acacia bordering the still water and oxbow ponds along the floodplain of the Colorado River (Vaughan 1959). Preferred roost sites in California appear to be mine tunnels and caves (Stager 1939; Vaughan 1959).

Riparian Brush Rabbit

The riparian brush rabbit (<u>Sylvilagus bachmani riparius</u>) is confined to dense thickets of brush such as wild rose (<u>Rosa</u> sp.), willows (<u>Salix</u> sp.), and blackberries which occur close to the San Joaquin River (Orr 1940).

Oregon Snowshoe Hare

The Oregon snowshoe hare (<u>Lepus americanus klamathensis</u>) is found primarily in riparian areas with thickets of deciduous trees such as willows and alders and in dense thickets of young conifers, particularly young firs (Williams in press).

Sierra Nevada Snowshoe Hare

The Sierra Nevada snowshoe hare (<u>Lepus americanus tahoensis</u>) lives only in boreal zones, typically inhabiting riparian communities with thickets of deciduous trees and shrubs such as willows and alders (Orr 1940).

Sierra Nevada Mountain Beaver

The Sierra Nevada mountain beaver (<u>Aplodontia rufa californica</u>) was recently discovered living along a freshwater seep near where Lee Vining Creek historically entered Mono Lake. Vegetation supported by the seep was characteristic of the herbaceous plants and woody shrubs of the riparian zone of the Great Basin sagebrush-steppe province. The area surrounding the seep predominately supported big sagebrush (<u>Artemisia tridentata</u>) and rabbit bush (<u>Chrysothamnus viscidiflorus</u>) (Steele in press).

Point Arena Mountain Beaver

The Point Arena mountain beaver (Aplodontia rufa nigra) primarily occupies thickets of thimbleberries on north-facing slopes (Camp 1918).

Point Reyes Mountain Beaver

The Point Reyes mountain beaver (Aplodontia rufa phaea) is found in hillsides below 300-m. (1,000-ft.) elevation, in seepage areas overgrown with sword ferns and thimbleberries (Grinnell 1933).

Sonora Beaver

The Sonora beaver (Castor canadensis repentinus) inhabits slow- to moderate-flowing waters of the main channels of the Colorado River and the sloughs, canals, and oxbow lakes along the river and in the Imperial Valley (Williams in press).

Golden Beaver

The golden beaver (Castor canadensis subauratus) inhabits slow- to moderate-flowing streams, ponds, and lakes. Its principal requirement seems to be sufficient food, consisting of roots, bulbs, grasses, cattails, and other herbaceous plants, and bark and twigs of willows, cottonwoods, alders, and other woody plants (Grinnell et al. 1937).

Southern Marsh Harvest Mouse

The southern marsh harvest mouse (Reithrodontomys megalotis limicola) is strictly confined to marshy areas, generally coastal salt marshes dominated by Salicornia. Adjacent weedy areas and marshes in brackish sites may also be inhabited (von Bloeker 1932).

Colorado River Cotton Rat

The Colorado River rat (Sigmodon arizonae plenus) appears to be restricted to "isolated sections of alluvium bottom along the Colorado River" (Goldman 1928). Within this zone, it inhabits areas supporting sedges, rushes, cane, and other grasslike plants (Williams in press).

San Joaquin Valley Wood Rat

The San Joaquin Valley wood rat (Neotoma fuscipes riparia) is strictly confined to riparian communities. Nothing specific has been recorded about the habitat of this subspecies, but dusky-footed wood rats generally occur in areas supporting mixtures of trees and brush (ibid.).

White-footed Vole

The white-footed vole (Arborimus albipes) seems generally to be associated with small streams in forested areas and very small

clearings, created by fallen timber and supporting herbaceous growth (Maser and Johnson 1967). Thickets of alder may be essential habitat for this species (Williams in press).

Yuma Mountain Lion

The Yuma mountain lion (Felis concolor browni) primarily inhabits the dense vegetation of the bottomland along the Colorado River; it has also been found in adjacent, rocky uplands (ibid.). Aside from adequate numbers of deer for food, the habitat requirements for this species are essentially unknown.

DISCUSSION AND CONCLUSIONS

Destruction of riparian and other wetland communities is pandemic in California. This loss and degradation is expected to increase with the increasing human population, unless measures are quickly adopted to protect remaining communities. This will be difficult to accomplish, considering the excessive human competition for limited amounts of water and the many conflicting demands placed upon riparian ecosystems. Loss of riparian and other wetland communities along the Colorado River, the low-elevation segments of the Sacramento and San Joaquin rivers, and the tidal marshes of San Francisco Bay and the Los Angeles Basin poses threats to a number of unique taxa. Biotic communities in these areas should receive priority attention in land development and resource management decisions.

Devising procedures to ensure preservation of biological diversity while permitting needed development of other natural resources is the problem before us. The present approaches are neither efficient nor cost-effective, and efforts are generally fragmented among a plethora of administrative units, resulting in duplication of efforts, gaps in coverage, competition for money and influence, and conflict.

A number of the 21 taxa treated here should be given protection as federally listed Threatened and Endangered species; this would provide for preservation of essential habitat and initiate actions directed at securing and increasing jeopardized populations. Their preservation could be accomplished most efficiently, however, by concentrating conservation efforts on their biotic communities rather than emphasizing single-species management. This would also provide more security to essential members of biotic communities not normally accorded protected status (e.g., lower plants, most invertebrates).

An integrated development/conservation approach which focuses upon preserving representative segments of each unique community while other resource- and land-use goals are being developed is needed. This approach would lessen the need for official listing of most of these species and save much of the money and duplication of effort now expended on management of endangered species on a one-by-one basis. It would also ensure that resource and land development objectives are compatible with national and state goals, including the maintenance of the health and well-being of this and future generations of people.

The state should be divided into management areas based upon known and projected capabilities for resources, rate and degree of projected development, and political and administrative boundaries. We believe that resource management areas based upon major watersheds would be the most efficient approach. A task force consisting of representatives of political and resource management agencies within the management area, USDI Fish and Wildlife Service biologists, conservationists, and development interests should be established to oversee preparation of an integrated conservation/development plan for each management area. The widest possible input from the public should be sought during the formative stage of the resource area management plans.

Guidelines and procedures for implementing conservation/development plans and for amending plans in response to changing resource needs and land conditions should be established. Coordination of activities and development of goals should be accomplished at the state level by a group with a similar composition to that described for the management areas. Federal resource management agencies should set national and regional land- and resource-use goals in cooperation with the state.

Goals for use of land and resources in each management area should be defined. Unique biota and sensitive species should be identifed; resource development goals should include habitat needs of vegetation and wildlife. Harvest and use patterns of renewable resources (timber, grazing, land, wildlife, water, etc.) should be designed to optimize productivity while maintaining community diversity--this would require definition of long-term objectives for land and resource use.

Planning and implementation of long-term management of natural resources, including vegetation and wildlife, could be greatly streamlined and economized by merging land and resource management functions now fragmented among several federal agencies: Department of Agriculture (e.g., forests, soil conservation, environmental quality); Department of Commerce (e.g., marine fisheries, ocean resources, coastal management); Department of Defense (military bases and reservations); Energy Department; Department of the Interior (e.g., rangeland, minerals and mining, national parks, water, fish and wildlife). Sufficient legislation and precedents already exist, however, to implement interagency, multigovernmental programs, such as those proposed without reorganization or new legislation.

Unless actions similar to those proposed here are undertaken immediately, we are confi-

dent that populations of all 21 taxa treated here will diminish, perhaps to the point of extinction for many. These losses alone would be substantial. More alarming, however, is that these species are members of biotic communities which are rapidly diminishing. Riparian and other wetland communities are vital to most wildlife species; their degradation and loss will represent a catastrophic loss of biological diversity.

LITERATURE CITED

Barbour, R.W., and W.H. Davis. 1969. Bats of America. 286 p. University Press of Kentucky, Lexington.

California Department of Fish and Game. 1980. At the crossroads 1980: A report on California's endangered and rare fish and wildlife. 137 p. The Resources Agency, California Department of Fish and Game, Sacramento.

Camp, C.L. 1918. Excavations of burrows of the rodent Aplodontia, with observations on the habits of the animal. University of California Publ. Zool. 18:517-536.

Goldman, E.A. 1928. Three new rodents from western Arizona. Proc. Biol. Soc. Washington 41:203-206.

Grinnell, J. 1933. Review of the recent mammal fauna of California. University of California Publ. Zool. 40:71-284.

Grinnell, J., J.S. Dixon, and J.M. Linsdale. 1937. Fur-bearing mammals of California. 2:377-777. University of California Press, Berkeley.

Hall, E.R. 1981. The mammals of North America (second edition). Volume 1 and 2. 1181 p. John Wiley and Sons, New York.

Johnston, R.F., and R.L. Rudd. 1957. Breeding of the salt marsh shrew. J. Mamm. 38:157-163.

Maser, C., and M.L. Johnson. 1967. Notes on the white-footed vole (Phenacomys albipes). Murrelet 48:24-27.

Orr, R.T. 1940. The rabbits of California. Occas. Papers California Acad. Sci. 19:1-227.

Rudd, R.L. 1955. Population variation and hybridization in some California shrews. Syst. Zool. 4:21-34.

Stager, K.E. 1939. Status of Myotis velifer in California with notes on its life history. J. Mamm. 20:225-228.

Steele, D.T. in press. Mountain beaver (Aplodontia rufa) within the sagebrush-scrub habitat of Mono Basin, California. California Fish and Game.

Vaughan, T.A. 1959. A new subspecies of bat (Myotis velifer) from southeastern California and Arizona. University of Kansas Publ., Mus. Nat. Hist. 7:507-512.

von Bloeker, J.C., Jr. 1932. Three new mammals from salt marsh areas in southern California. Proc. Biol. Soc. Washington 45:131-138.

Warner, R.E. 1979. The California riparian study program. Phase I: Background studies and program design for phase II. 179 p. California Department of Fish and Game, Planning Branch, Sacramento.

Williams, D.F. 1979. Checklist of California mammals. Ann. Carnegie Mus. 48:425-433.

Williams, D.F. in press. Mammalian species of special concern in California. California Department of Fish and Game, Nongame Wildlife Investigations, Final Report, Project E-W-4, IV-14.1. 184 p. (draft copy). Sacramento, Calif.

DEVELOPING MANAGEMENT STRATEGIES FOR

PRIVATELY OWNED RIPARIAN LAND[1]

Lee Fitzhugh[2]

Abstract.--Riparian system management may be defined with preservation or use orientation, depending on the manager's goals. The problem is that goals and values differ. Neither the public values of privately owned riparian lands nor the full extent of private values of those lands are fully recognized. Attitudes and other noneconomic factors are as important as economic factors in determining the management of riparian lands. Changes in attitude will be necessary before major programs can succeed. Educational approaches, however important, should not be the exclusive means to preserve privately owned riparian systems. Incentive programs, changes in taxation, agency budget processes, agency organization, commodity price and market situations, international treaties, and many other factors will determine the outcome of any effort to preserve riparian lands in private ownership.

INTRODUCTION

I have three objectives to meet in this introductory paper: 1) briefly outline how a riparian system needs to be managed in order to preserve it; 2) define the problem we face in preserving riparian sites on private lands; and 3) summarize methods available for resolving riparian preservation problems on private land.

RIPARIAN MANAGEMENT

If riparian systems are defined as the vegetation that would naturally occur in moist situations in the complete absence of man's influence (not always an appropriate definition), then management constitutes maintaining, as nearly as possible, the natural land topography; the flow, volume, and timing of water; and eliminating any of man's impacts. It is absolutely necessary to maintain a representative sample of such undisturbed systems in each region in order to answer land management questions which will arise in the future and which will be unanswerable without reference to undisturbed areas. However, to predicate all riparian system management on such a definition is a practical impossibility, especially on private lands used for other purposes.

A more appropriate definition of riparian management on most private lands would involve maintaining the riparian system with stand structure and plant species composition resembling, to an agreed-upon degree, the undisturbed state. Thus, there would be flexibility in use, volume and timing of water flows; grazing; recreation; logging; and other uses to the extent that the plant community could maintain itself or could recover from such use. The specific nature of uses and community resiliency are site-specific and must be determined at least regionally.

As a generality, riparian management must continually take into consideration the biologic nature of the system, including both its natural resiliency and vulnerabilities, if the riparian vegetation is to be preserved. Consumptive uses are permissible as long as the basic requirements for plant growth and reproduction exist. For example, in desert areas where streams are dry on the surface during summer, upstream water use during periods of flow may not harm the riparian vegetation as long as sufficient flow reaches the riparian zone to recharge the perched water upon which the vegetation depends, and as long as the timing of the flow period is not unduly shortened. In other areas, grazing use may be permissible at proper intensities and during certain times of the year, when it does not change the basic nature of the herbaceous vegetation or shrub structure. Tree removal in logging operations may be permissible as long as the basic natures of the system structure and regeneration are not changed.

---

[1] Paper presented at the California Riparian Systems Conference. [University of California, Davis, September 17-19, 1981].

[2] Lee Fitzhugh is Extension Wildlife Specialist, University of California, Davis.

Another level of riparian management would allow the riparian vegetation to be purposely altered to suit agreed-upon objectives. A site used for recreation and for public educational tours might benefit by periodic grazing designed to open the understory and provide better visibility and access.

Riparian management then can be defined at various levels of intensity. In each of them some resemblance is necessary between the undisturbed and controlled conditions.

THE PROBLEM: RIPARIAN PRESERVATION AND PRIVATE RIGHTS

The basic problem in preserving riparian lands in private ownership is that these lands have different values for different people. Thus, goals for management vary. Differently stated, the problem is in the fact that privately owned riparian lands have certain public values not always recognized by private landowners in decisionmaking, and they have private values to the owners insufficiently recognized by the public.

A few examples will suffice to show that there are public values on these lands. Certainly the game and nongame birds and animals that nest in or otherwise use riparian sites fly off the private land and are harvested by hunters, frequent the bird-feeders in our cities, or provide exciting experiences for vacationing campers. DeGraaf and Payne (1975) reported that birdwatchers alone spent $500 million annually on birdseed, binoculars, and cameras. Riparian vegetation enhances habitat for anadromous fish and thus provides a benefit for the sport and commercial fishing industries. Rafters and fishermen using our waterways certainly benefit and receive value from the natural vegetation of riparian sites along the banks. From a scientific point of view, loss of riparian sites will eliminate gene pools, baseline sites for comparison with treatments, and any hope of knowing what would happen if nothing were done to a certain kind of site. As the number of undisturbed riparian sites diminishes, each site becomes more valuable to the public. Because we now have only about 10% of the original riparian forests in the Central Valley (Katibah 1983), the point of scarcity is already upon us.

Private values of riparian sites are greater than many people realize. The 1981 rice crop in Butte County returned about $130 per acre, including return to management, plus $236 land rent, if the land is owned by the farmer, for a total of $366 per acre per year.[3] The net return on walnuts in 1980 was about $200 per acre.[4] Taxes have been deducted from these figures; to be fair, the taxes should be added back as an item of value to the farmer, since they would have to be paid if the land were not farmed.

Unfarmed riparian lands may have certain negative values for farmers. For example, odd-shaped field boundaries may make machine operation, land leveling, and irrigation more difficult and costly. Unfarmed riparian lands may harbor insect or plant pests, provide roosts for blackbirds, intensify flooding of farmland, and encourage human recreational use against the farmer's wishes. All land owned by a farmer represents capital investment. If a farm can be viewed as a corporation, unfarmed riparian land can be viewed as an unprofitable subsidiary. If the farmer considers public values of riparian land in his decisions it is a matter of personal preference, not of farm economics.

The essence of the problem is not found in the economic facts, however, but in the behavior of people. That people do not always behave according to their best economic interest was demonstrated by Leitch and Danielson (1979) in an analysis of incentives for preserving prairie wetlands. They found that economics was perhaps not even the primary determinant of the future of wetlands. Attitudes, politics, misconceptions, and lack of knowledge were also important factors in determining whether or not farmers preserved wetlands. It is important to recognize, from the Leitch and Danielson research, that landowners with a pro-drainage attitude had a strong commitment to farming, whereas those with pro-preservation attitudes were more interested in retiring than in farm expansion. Each side of the comparison may just be a different way of saying the same thing, but the California agricultural industry is obviously not "interested in retirement." The comparison leads to the conclusion, then, that even with economics on the side of riparian preservation there might be an uphill battle to achieve preservation on private lands. Stated another way, economics is important, but we must not neglect education and other methods of changing attitude.

There is a problem in preserving riparian lands because there is a spectrum of people with different values, attitudes, and economic interests, all concerned about the same piece of land. It is probable that none of these people are thoroughly conversant with the needs or values of the others.

RESOLVING THE PROBLEM

This section is intended only to stimulate thought in the area of broad policy considerations, not to definitively list methods of resolving the problem.

---

[3]Wick, Carl M., Janning D. Kastler, Lynn A. Horel, and Patricia Thomas. 1981 (revised August, 1981). Sample costs of rice production for Butte County. Unpublished report. University of California, Cooperative Extension, Butte County office.

---

[4]Carl Wick. Personal communication.

What Influences Riparian Management on Private Lands?

United States Government programs have been variously designed to influence agriculture. Some have promoted land conversion into agriculture, and some have done the opposite. All of the Government powers of taxation, expenditure, regulation, eminent domain, and direct ownership have been used at one time or another. Some Government programs that have pervasive influence over agricultural expansion are:

1. export markets, including treaty agreements;
2. taxation (tax credits, investment incentives, inheritance taxes, property taxes, etc.);
3. price supports and commodity reserves;
4. pesticide regulation and use;
5. administrative organization (influences policy formation, budgeting);
6. agency budgeting;
7. zoning;
8. health standards, environmental protection, pesticide regulation;
9. credit policies (direct credit, credit guarantees, interest rates);
10. subsidies and incentives;
11. water rights legislation and adjudication;
12. information manipulation (program advertising, news releases, agency policy direction);
13. special governmental bodies (commissions, districts, etc.)
14. regulatory power.

Nongovernmental influences over agriculture include the pervasive influence of custom and religion, very important in forming attitudes. Information transfer through farm bureaus, cattlemen's associations, the Soil Conservation Service, and cooperative extension services can help influence custom and attitude, provide new technology, and influence agricultural management.

In California there are various governmental tools available, intended to influence wildland use generally. These include such programs as the water quality regulations, both Federal and State; US Army Corps of Engineers dredge and fill regulations; and taxation regulations such as the Williamson Act and Timber Preserve Zone legislation.

With all of the above tools, why do we have a riparian problem? One obvious reason is that many of the tools are being used to promote agricultural expansion, rather than to assist in riparian preservation. The reasons discovered by Leitch and Danielson (1979) are not so obvious. They found that the major reasons for landowner nonparticipation in wetland preservation programs were lack of information about the programs, the level of incentive payments, the methods used to tax wetland acreage, and the tax burden of wetland acreage. They found that fee-simple purchases of wetlands by the Government were often blamed for weed control problems and led to a dislike of Governmental interference. Easements were more acceptable when management of the land remained with the landowner. Leitch and Danielson (ibid.) found that the owner's attitude toward drainage and preservation per se was critical to making drainage decisions.

Suggested Programs

It is probably neither desirable nor feasible to change broad national economic and trade policies solely to protect riparian lands. However, people also are increasingly concerned with some of these policies as they influence wildlife, soil protection and conservation, and continued long-term agricultural production. A moderating influence may be developing on broad national economic policies. One interesting suggestion was made by Higbee (1981) for the formation of local "Conservation Banks," funded by low-interest subscription for the purpose of providing low-interest production loans to producers who followed certain conservation procedures.

There are at least four basic approaches for government in resolving the problem of riparian preservation. They are: regulatory, administrative, financial, and psychological.

Regulatory Programs

Certain types of regulation, mentioned above, are designed for application on private land. These include zoning and environmental regulations of different kinds. These types of control over privately owned riparian lands generate antagonism and resistance by landowners. Exercise of this kind of control will require that the agencies enforce regulations on a body that disapproves of them. Prospects for success of such programs are not good. The easiest way for landowners to avoid the adverse impacts of regulation of this nature is to not have riparian land. There have been similar experiences with regulations concerning endangered species. In too many cases, the easiest way to avoid a problem has been to get rid of the animal. In order to be successful, it will be important to work with friends toward a common or at least an acceptable negotiated goal.

Administrative Programs

It may be overly optimistic to expect to realign major state and Federal agency organization to facilitate riparian preservation. However, the formation of committees, task forces, fact-finding bodies, etc., within agencies can focus administrative attention and budgetary allocation on the problem. Suggestions for these types of changes are appropriate.

Financial Programs

Financial solutions to the riparian preservation problem may range from fee-simple purchase of lands, alterations in tax policy, or a variety of incentive or subsidy programs, to alteration of agency budgets. Generally these kinds of programs will be better accepted than most directly regulatory programs. Examples of existing incentive programs in California include the tax programs mentioned previously, the Water Bank programs, the California Forest Improvement Program, wetlands easements, and others.

Alteration of agency budgets involves administrative changes as well as financial changes. The relative status of law enforcement and habitat improvement budgets of two agencies was determined for comparative purposes. In approximate terms, the California Department of Fish and Game budgets 73% as much for habitat improvement as for law enforcement.[5] The USDI Fish and Wildlife Service budget for California allocates only 30% as much to law enforcement as to habitat improvement.[6] The reason for the large habitat improvement budget for the Fish and Wildlife Service is largely the extensive waterfowl refuge system in the state. Other agencies, such as the California Department of Forestry and the US Army Corps of Engineers, can strongly influence riparian management on private lands, and some attention to budgetary allocations in those and other agencies might assist in riparian management.

Psychological Programs

People's attitudes were found to be of major importance in determining their responses to various programs for preserving wetlands (Leitch and Danielson 1979). Attempts to change attitudes are psychological as much as educational. While the term "psychological" may be distasteful when discussing various public programs, using it does allow us to recognize the true nature of the intent and to place appropriate limits on government activity in psychological programs. That there should be limits is clear. What the limits should be is outside the scope of this paper. The major goal of such programs would be to instill a desire among both public and private riparian landowners to preserve riparian lands. Necessary educational steps must include helping landowners recognize and accept their full share of costs involved, and helping the general public recognize and accept their full share of the costs involved.

CONCLUSION

The problem of preserving riparian lands in private ownership is critical and very difficult. Factions have formed, and some of these barriers must be dismantled before cooperation can take place. Federal and State programs varying from multi-national treaties to individual personal contact can have major effects on riparian preservation. Changes in attitude will probably have to occur before any major state-wide program will be successful. Educational approaches will be important but should not be the exclusive means. Incentive programs, changes in taxation, agency budget processes, agency organization, commodity price and market situations, and dozens of other factors will determine the outcome of any effort to preserve riparian lands in private ownership.

LITERATURE CITED

DeGraaf, Richard M., and Brian R. Payne. 1975. Economic values of non-game birds and some urban wildlife research needs. Trans. North Amer. Wildl. and Natural Resources Conf. 40:281-287.

Higbee, Michael. In press. Farmers and wildlife--why is there a rift and how can we bridge it? In: Wildlife management on private lands, symposium proceedings. [Milwaukee, Wisconsin, May 4-6, 1981].

Katibah, Edwin F. 1983. A brief history of riparian forests in the Central Valley of California. In: R.E. Warner and K.M. Hendrix (ed.). California Riparian Systems. [University of California, Davis, September 17-19, 1981.] University of California Press, Berkeley.

Leitch, Jay A., and Leon E. Danielson. 1979. Social, economic, and institutional incentives to drain or preserve prairie wetlands. Economic Report ER79-6, Department of Agricultural and Applied Economics, University of Minnesota Inst. of Agric., Forestry and Home Economics, St. Paul. 78 p.

---

[5]Robert Schulenberg. Personal communication.
[6]Edward J. Collins. Personal communication.

A MANAGEMENT STRATEGY FOR THE
KERN RIVER PRESERVE, CALIFORNIA[1]

Richard P. Hewett[2]

Abstract.--The recently acquired Kern River Preserve has offered The Nature Conservancy an opportunity to design from the ground floor a riparian forest nature preserve. Management plans were formulated, sanctuary areas designated, livestock exclosures constructed, and several research and experimental efforts initiated. Future plans include research, forest restoration, and education.

INTRODUCTION

In July, 1980, The Nature Conservancy acquired the 607-ha. (1,500-ac.) Kern River Preserve. It is located along the South Fork Kern River near Weldon, California. Along its 16-km. length the South Fork Valley contains the single largest remaining stand of riparian forest in the state. The true essence of our sanctuary is the riparian forest. Indeed, it is because of this extremely productive resource that we are in the South Fork Valley at all. The Preserve comprises 105 ha. (260 ac.) of old growth cottonwood/willow woodland that provides habitat for a wealth of flora and fauna, including bear, mountain lion, beaver, and over 200 species of birds, especially the rare Yellow-billed Cuckoo. Scattered around the Preserve are 502 ha. (1,240 ac.) of grazing pasture that are presently leased to a cattle rancher. A resident preserve manager was hired in January, 1981.

DEVELOPING THE STRATEGY

From its inception, the Preserve's primary management goal has been preservation and restoration of the riparian system and adjacent marsh and meadow areas. Beginning in January, 1981, an intensive three-month program was initiated to compile the information necessary to produce an annual operating management plan. Several sources were utilized, including proceedings and technical data from other riparian conferences, Nature Conservancy plans for other preserves with riparian systems, and personal communications with research experts in the field (e.g. Gaines 1976; Johnson and Jones 1977; Laymon 1980; Warner

1979). These sources provided us with the information to answer the question: what is the best procedure for allowing a natural order to return to a disturbed riparian zone?

Typical of many riparian areas throughout the West, our land exhibited moderate to extreme effects from grazing. Few young or medium-age trees were observed and most shrubs were grazed back to a high level, leaving the area in a diminished condition. We identified four separate, noncontiguous parcels of forest and removed them from livestock as of May 1, 1981.

Our present management plan is the result of this three-month search. It focuses on three major categories: 1) preservation and restoration; 2) scientific study; and 3) public visitation and education. Within each category the current situation was assessed and the 1981 goals and objectives were then formulated.

IMPLEMENTING THE STRATEGY

Throughout the implementing process we had two key factors to keep in mind. One was that community involvement was essential to the success of our project. If people in the area were personally involved in our programs then we would have a better foundation upon which to operate. The second factor was that the Nature Conservancy maintains a set of policies and rules for all of its sanctuaries across the country, including the prohibition of fishing, hunting, collecting, wood gathering, or any other blatant form of resource depredation.

Putting plans into action is never an easy, straightforward venture. But at least I had a set of detailed plans from which to work. Here is an example of what the plans required:

1) by April 15 begin and by April 30 complete construction of a 1-km. (.625 mi.) section of barbed wire fence along

---

[1]Paper presented at the California Riparian Systems Conference. [University of California, Davis, September 17-19, 1981].
[2]Richard P. Hewett is Preserve Manager at The Nature Conservancy's Kern River Preserve, Weldon, California.

the north side of riparian grove.

2) by May 1 begin and by December 15 complete a vegetation survey of the Preserve, including species inventory, statement of overall forest condition, and description of trends and threats.

3) by May 1 close off all four riparian tracts to livestock grazing.

This type of management implementation also makes for easy review and evaluation, since it is so specific in the dates and objectives. Supervisory personnel could utilize this system for monitoring the effectiveness of their staff and programs.

Below are listed the highlights of our 1981 management plan.

Preservation and Restoration

The 105 ha. (260 ac.) of riparian forest were posted with official Nature Conservancy signs as of April 1. Fences and gates were finished by May 1, thus excluding livestock from the protected areas. An experimental planting program using native cottonwood and willow saplings was initiated, patterned after the reforestation program begun at the nearby US Army Corps of Engineers South Fork Wildlife Area. Local volunteers were included in these activities and formed an integral part of our work force.

Scientific Study

Our primary goal for this category is to generate scientific information that will better enable us to protect and enhance the Preserve's natural values. Biological monitoring and scientific research are the backbone of this program: the monitoring because it documents over time the biological changes, and the research because it provides us with management-oriented information to accomplish our goals.

In 1981 we contracted for:

1) a flowering plant inventory, including a collection of botanical specimens now located at the California Academy of Sciences, with a duplicate collection at the Preserve;

2) a reptile and amphibian inventory, which produced a brochure, checklist, and set of color slides;

3) a system of permanent bird survey routes and Emlen transects, marked and mapped in the four Preserve areas; and

4) an avifaunal survey of the entire South Fork Valley riparian forest, with special focus on the State-listed rare species Yellow-billed Cuckoo.

In addition to this contract work we initiated a biological monitoring program featuring aerial photographs, permanent photo-points, and resource base mapping.[3]

Selected universities, junior colleges, agencies, and organizations were sent detailed information about this contract work. Interested individuals were encouraged to submit research proposals.

Public Visitation and Education

Several major programs have been initiated this year that give the public information about and access to the Preserve, thereby utilizing the area's inherent educational values. These include:

1) quarterly publication of a Preserve newsletter, the Riparian Rag;

2) a regular schedule of trips, classes, and tours;

3) involvement of a local school in construction and placement of Wood Duck nesting boxes; and

4) refurbishing of old buildings for use as a visitor's center, research lab, and overnight quarters.

Public participation in these programs was encouraged by appeals from myself made at monthly meetings of conservation groups, and radio and newspaper announcements. We also developed a Friends of the Preserve group to enhance the community's involvement. Our public education programs have proven very successful. I would encourage those of you in similar situations to develop this part of your operation, even if it is only to run a couple of articles in your local newspaper or to host some meetings at your preserve.

OTHER CONSIDERATIONS

One of the most important factors affecting our operation is county government. Both the Kern County Planning and Building Inspection Departments have required the lengthy and expensive filing of forms and plans for our project. The delays experienced already have been on the magnitude of four to six months, it is easy to see how crippling these requirements can be.

However, the reverse is also true. We submitted a formal request to the Kern County Wildlife Resources Commission for fencing materials to enclose one of the riparian zones from grazing. The commission granted the request and provided over $1,100 worth of barbed wire, fence posts, and metal T-posts. This public support of a private agency's project was justifiable due to

---

[3]W. Burley. September, 1980. Biological monitoring of Conservancy preserves in California. In-house memorandum. The Nature Conservancy, San Francisco, California.

the inherent educational potential of Nature Conservancy lands and the public's access to them.

LOOKING AHEAD

Our plans for the remainder of 1981 and on into the future will continue to focus on the proper management of our riparian resources. The backbone of our efforts will include forest restoration, native species reintroduction, research, biological monitoring, public education, and resource protection.

The Nature Conservancy hopes to add additional riparian lands to its Preserve in the near future, thereby insuring the continued preservation of one of California's most productive ecosystems.

LITERATURE CITED

Gaines, D. (ed.). 1976. Riparian forests of the Sacramento Valley: Abstracts from the conference. [Chico, California] Davis and Altacal Audubon Societies.

Johnson, R. Roy, and D.A. Jones. 1977. Importance, preservation and management of riparian habitat: a symposium. [July 9, 1977, Tuscon, Ariz.] USDA Forest Service General Technical Report RM-43. 217 p. Rocky Mountain Forest and Range Experiment Station, Fort Collins, Colo.

Laymon, S.A. 1980. Feeding and nesting behavior of the Yellow-billed Cuckoo in the Sacramento Valley.

Warner, R.E. 1979. California riparian study program. 177 p. California Resources Agency, Department of Fish and Game, Sacramento, California.

RIPARIAN SYSTEM RESTORATION BY PRIVATE LANDOWNERS:

AN EXAMPLE OF COORDINATED INTERAGENCY ASSISTANCE[1]

Ronald F. Schultze[2]

Abstract.--An informal task force of private landowners, private organizations, and public agencies has worked together to develop methods and determine programs and funding resources available to help landowners solve erosion, fish and wildlife habitat, and irrigation problems on a man-altered stream. These programs and the coordination technique may assist others in developing a program to reestablish and manage riparian systems.

INTRODUCTION

A major emphasis of the "riparian movement" should be directed toward repairing and reestablishing riparian systems that have been damaged by adverse actions, or inactions, of man. Unfortunately, this task is often extremely expensive and usually beyond the capabilities of private landowners to implement on their own. Most of the values provided by riparian systems benefit the public at large and not just the individual landowner. I think this fact has been amply supported in this conference. It therefore seems appropriate that the general public, through various public agencies and their programs, should accept part of the burden of repairing and re-establishing valuable riparian systems. An example of this cooperation has been the recent efforts to repair damage on Willow Creek, a tributary of Goose Lake, Modoc County, California. Past management, or lack of it, has resulted in devastation of a once-valuable stream and riparian system. A cooperative effort between private landowners, various federal and state agencies, and California Trout has been set in motion to renovate the system.

PROJECT AREA AND HISTORY

Willow Creek is a tributary of Goose Lake, located in northeastern California about 9.7 km. (6 mi.) south of the California/Oregon border. It drains a 90.6-sq. km. (35-sq. mi.) watershed in the Warner Mountain Range. The upper water-

shed consists of ponderosa or yellow pine (Pinus ponderosa) forest with numerous volcanic rock outcrops. The upper 9.7 km. (6 mi.) of Willow Creek transects several mountain meadows with stands of willow (Salix sp.) and quaking aspen (Populus tremuloides). The lower 4.8 km. (3 mi.) of Willow Creek historically meandered over deep alluvial soils covered by mountain meadow with dense stands of willow bordering the creek. In the late 1800s and early 1900s, heavy timber harvesting and livestock overgrazing resulted in diminished resources and serious erosion in the Willow Creek watershed and elsewhere.

In 1904, President Theodore Roosevelt established the Warner Mountains Forest Reserve and Modoc Forest Reserve. These were combined to form the Modoc National Forest in 1908. Conservation measures have been implemented to improve management of timber and range resources on both federal and private lands in the upper watershed.

The lower portions of Willow Creek and adjoining lands are primarily privately owned. In the early 1960s much of the meadow area was converted to irrigated pasture and cropland. Willow Creek was channelized, irrigation diversions and drop structures were installed with planning assistance from the USDA Soil Conservation Service (SCS), and costs were shared with the Agricultural Stabilization and Conservation Service (ASCS).

Not all of the structures required for adequate grade control were installed by the landowners. In addition, extremely high runoff occurred the spring after construction; as a result, deterioration of instream structures and erosion led to failure of some of the structures, followed by accelerated erosion in the channel. Streambank erosion and headcutting threaten remaining structures, as well as the downstream

[1]Paper presented at the California Riparian Systems Conference. [University of California, Davis, September 17-19, 1981.]

[2]Ronald F. Schultze is State Biologist, USDA Soil Conservation Service, Davis, Calif.

apron on the US Highway 395 bridge. The structures have become barriers to upstream migration of fish, including the native Goose Lake redband trout (Salmo sp.). Sediment deposited at the mouth of Willow Creek has further hindered fish migration. Streambank erosion has caused loss of riparian vegetation, destroying fish and wildlife habitat. In addition, erosion is resulting in the loss of valuable cropland and pasture. The area is highly visible from US Highway 395, and its deteriorated condition has thus created an adverse visual impact in the area.

PROJECT PROPOSAL

Private landowners and individuals in various public agencies have been keenly aware of the seriousness of the Willow Creek problem and the threat to various natural resources. There have been numerous attempts at evaluating means of solving this problem. Heretofore, all attempts have been unfruitful. What could be the final effort to arrive at a solution was initiated earlier this year. With the USDA Resource Conservation and Development Program (RC&D) acting as the catalyst, representatives from the landowners, California Trout, and various public agencies were drawn together to evaluate their programs and resources to see what could be done.

The questions raised were: 1) is there something that can be done; and 2) how can it be paid for. Subsequently, a proposal has been developed which we hope will get the job done before it is too late.

The proposed project includes: 1) stabilizing the lowest diversion structure below US Highway 395 and reestablishing the grade of Willow Creek in the portion lying immediately below the structure; 2) repairing the downstream apron of the US Highway 395 bridge; 3) stabilizing diversion and grade structures upstream from US Highway 395; 4) shaping and protecting with natural rock riprap in the main channel and in eroding laterals; 5) revegetating with woody and herbaceous plants; 6) reestablishing fish passage over instream structures; and 7) possibly restocking with Goose Lake redband trout. The project could ultimately reach an estimated cost of $200,000.

Representatives from various public agencies and California Trout, as well as the landowners, have indicated the extent to which their programs and resources can be used to assist in the proposed project. A summary of potential cost-share amounts is shown in table 1.

Stream improvements were placed in three categories for evaluation of agency programs. The general categories included: 1) providing fish passage over instream structures; 2) controlling erosion, stabilizing structures, and providing habitat for fish and wildlife using rock riprap and vegetation (riparian revegetation);

Table 1.—Potential agency/program cost-share percentages and dollar amounts for stream improvement project.

Agency/ program	Fisheries	Habitat Improvement and Erosion Control	Irrigation water
SCS (RC&D)	50%	80%	50%[1]
ASCS (ACP)	0	50-80% $10,000[2]	50-80% $3,500[2]
DF (CFIP)	0	90%	0
DFG (WCB, Dingell-Johnson	WCB 50% WCB 50% D-J 25%	0	0
CAL TRANS	Apron repair 100%	Apron repair 100%	0
Calif. Trout	$5,000[3]		
Private	Cost-share or in-kind	Cost-share or in-kind	50% or in-kind

[1] When benefit:cost ratio is >1:1.
[2] Each owner.
[3] To restock trout (fund or grant).

and 3) re-establishing an irrigation water diversion which washed out.

RC & D Program could have shared costs on all of the proposed work. However, the budget for this program has been severely cut. The future for this program is considered very dim with phase-out proposed in about two years. However, SCS anticipates being able to continue providing technical assistance for planning and installation of improvement measures.

ASCS can share costs on habitat improvement, erosion control, and the irrigation diversion through the Agricultural Conservation Program (ACP). However, budget constraints and program restrictions appear to limit assistance to the agricultural irrigation water development at present.

The California Department of Forestry (DF) administers the California Forest Improvement Program (CFIP). It can pay up to 90% of the cost of fish and wildlife habitat improvement and erosion control measures. In general, this program is restricted to forest lands or lands adjacent to forest lands affected by timber management practices. Prospects for funds through this program for the Willow Creek project look fairly good.

As with other agencies, the resources of the California Department of Fish and Game (DFG) are very limited. Representatives of DFG have indicated the possibility of assisting in design of new fish passage structures and fish screens, and with labor and materials to re-establish passage over existing instream structures. Dingell-Johnson funds (from a federal tax on fishing equipment and supplies) can be a source of money for fish habitat improvement, but they are not being pursued at this time. Theoretically, with the 50% cost-share under RC & D Program, Dingell-Johnson funds could provide an additional 25%. Thus the federal government could fund up to 75% of the cost of fish and wildlife habitat development. Unfortunately, as mentioned earlier, the RC & D Program is slated for termination.

The California Department of Transportation (CAL TRANS) is going to improve the US Highway 395 bridge apron to ensure fish passage.

California Trout, a private, nonprofit organization devoted to the preservation and enhancement of trout and other salmonids, has offered to provide up to $5,000 to help re-establish Goose Lake redband trout in Willow Creek if the stream is ever repaired. The Oregon Department of Fish and Wildlife has offered to cooperate in a re-establishment effort.

The private landowners have expressed a willingness to pay their share of the cost. Some of their cost-share can be made in the form of in-kind services, that is, by providing manpower and equipment to do the work. They have also agreed to provide operation and maintenance services to ensure the system will not fail as it did in the past.

SUMMARY

This brief presentation summarizes various programs and a cooperative approach which can be helpful in restoring riparian resources. I have pointed out that some of these programs are presently limited by guidelines or budget constraints, or even destined to be abolished altogether. A renewal of public support is needed for public cost-sharing programs and adequate funding if cooperative efforts to conserve and restore riparian systems are to grow or even continue to exist.

VECTOR CONTROL IN RIPARIAN/WETLAND SYSTEMS[1]

Don J. Womeldorf[2]

Abstract.--Riparian/wetland systems can support mosquitoes, rodents, ticks, and other animals which may have a deleterious effect upon human health. Proper design and maintenance of developments for waterfowl habitat, recreational facilities, and other onsite activities will reduce vector problems. These provisions should be included during the process of planning riparian development and restoration.

INTRODUCTION

"Environmental protection" means protecting the environment from people. "Environmental health protection" means protecting people from the environment. A problem in managing riparian systems is to maximize the benefits and minimize the risks to both the environment and people. This can be done, and with very little pesticide use.

In California's environmental health usage, the term "vector" is defined to include not only the classic carrier of a disease pathogen from a reservoir animal to man, but also those biting, stinging or venomous organisms that injure people. These have been labeled "vectors of trauma".

Delivery of community-wide vector control services is principally a function of government. In California, special districts and local (primarily county) environmental health entities are involved, with a few cities and other public agencies providing limited vector control services. These local agencies receive training, technical assistance, and laboratory support from the California Department of Health Services, and benefit from research conducted by the University of California.

RIPARIAN VECTOR PROBLEMS

Three major vector problems are identified with riparian/wetland systems. In descending order of frequency of occurrence, they are those associated with mosquitoes, rodents, and ticks. Some problems, minor from the statewide view,

_____

[1]Paper presented at the California Riparian Systems Conference. [University of California, Davis, September 17-19, 1981].
[2]Don J. Womeldorf is Chief, Vector Biology and Control Section, California Department of Health Services, Sacramento.

could be highly important in localized areas. One example is murine typhus; a second is biting gnats such as Leptoconops and Culicoides. This paper discusses the major vector problems and offers suggestions for their mitigation.

Mosquitoes

Mosquitoes are vectors of western equine encephalitis, St. Louis encephalitis, malaria, dog heartworm, and a great deal of trauma. We know of nearly 50 species in the state, including those produced in coastal saltmarshes, those which breed in rain-filled cavities in trees, the many which are associated with irrigated agriculture, and those produced each spring in high mountains in snowmelt water. All these species have in common the need for water in their immature stages. However their habitats vary tremendously. Riparian systems can be highly productive of many of these species.

The principal vector of the encephalitides, Culex tarsalis, and the vectors of malaria, Anopheles spp., are similar in that the female deposits eggs which must remain in the water for a week or more, depending upon temperature, for completion of the life cycle. The water habitat most conducive to reproduction of these species is quiet but not stagnant; not very deep and with "feather edges"; heavily overgrown with emergent vegetation and weedy edges to protect the larvae and pupae from wind and wave action, predators, and mosquito-control people; and relatively permanent to allow several generations to develop. The best way to prevent reproduction is to channelize the water to facilitate its movement and to prevent ponding. If ponding is necessary or desirable, the design and maintenance of the ponds should minimize breeding and encourage predation. Specifically, the water depth should be at least 1.2 m. (4 ft.) deep, side slopes should be steep, and vegetation should be controlled to minimize the water/vegetation interface and reduce the amount of brushy canopy.

Several _Aedes_ spp., injurious and annoying, occur in riparian systems. These mosquitoes differ in habitat from _Culex_ and _Anopheles_ in that the female lays eggs in places where water will be present later. When the area is flooded, the eggs hatch and development begins. The aquatic stages may be completed in only a few days. The simplest way to reduce production of these species is to design and maintain water channels so that floodwater recedes rapidly back into the main channel without being held in temporary puddles, pools, and ponds. If floodwater does become impounded, the same criteria for minimizing reproduction as listed for _Culex_ and _Anopheles_ apply.

Rodents

Riparian systems, with heavy growths of shrubs and vines, are excellent habitats for roof rats, Norway rats, and several species of native wild rodents. Probably the most important rodent-associated disease in these areas is tularemia. Plague is less likely to be found because of the particular rodent species inhabiting the systems. Norway and roof rats are undesirable commensal cohabitants with man. They not only pose the threat of disease, but contaminate food, cause economic damage, and compete with native fauna. Blackberry tangles are especially important in providing food and cover for commensal rats. In the immediate vicinity of human habitation or high-density use, such vegetation should be eliminated entirely. In more remote areas consideration should be given to using other types of vegetation which would enhance wildlife propagation but not support populations of commensal rodents.

Several species of ixodid ticks are common in riparian systems. Tularemia and rickettsial diseases, principally in the Rocky Mountain spotted fever group, present a hazard to day users and campers. While it is not easy to reduce tick populations without drastically disrupting the vegetation, it is possible to cut down on human/tick contact by removing underbrush along trails and in the vicinity of camps. The chances of people being "caught" by ticks waiting for a passing host are thereby diminished.

DISCUSSION

This is a very brief, noncomprehensive discussion of vector problems in riparian/wetland systems and what can be done to mitigate them. None of the mitigating measures suggested for vector control needs to be incompatible with other proposed uses of the systems. In every instance, biological understanding of these problems is basic. This, coupled with sound engineering design and adherence to a maintenance plan, can reduce or preclude riparian systems management from conflicting with vector control concerns.

When, in developing or restoring riparian/wetland systems, should vector concerns be considered? The best answer is, before the problem occurs. If development or restoration is being planned, vector prevention should be one of the considerations in the review and permitting process. Preventing a problem is much simpler and economical than curing it. The California Environmental Quality Act requires full disclosure of all environmental impacts of projects. Many riparian projects may be categorically exempt from the act because they are considered to be for the protection of the environment. But if vector problems are created by development of a riparian system, for example in creating ponds for waterfowl, legal action through the Health and Safety Code may be a recourse. However, it is much better to mitigate a problem during planning and construction than to have a court confrontation after the project is completed. The project planner would be well advised to contact the local vector control agency early in the process.

PEST AND BENEFICIAL INSECTS ASSOCIATED WITH

AGRICULTURE AND RIPARIAN SYSTEMS[1]

Vernon M. Stern[2]

Abstract.--Vast changes have occurred in the California landscape over the past 100 years. In agriculture, many of these changes favor the buildup of pest populations over biological control. The manipulation of pest populations is a complex study in applied ecology.

INTRODUCTION

The species of insects, spider mites, and their close relatives far outnumber all other species of animals in the world. Insects are a complex group, with complicated life histories and interrelationships with other animals and plants. There are more than one million insect species, but only a relatively small number are pests. In the United States there are several thousand such species. These range from those that appear sporadically to major "key" pests that appear annually (Knipling 1979). These pests cause billions of dollars in losses each year in the United States (US Department of Agriculture 1965).

There are also thousands of insect parasites and predators that are natural enemies of pest species. Many crops, such as alfalfa, have a rather large complex of these biological control agents that feed on actual pest species, as well as feeding on an even larger number of potential pests. Often these potential pests can be very important in providing alternative hosts for parasites or food sources for predators. In this way potential pests help to stabilize and maintain populations of natural enemies when the pest population is at a low level, absent, or otherwise unavailable.

There are, of course, many "indifferent" species present in natural and agroecosystems. Their population numbers are not necessarily related to the numbers of pests or natural enemies. These include the scavengers, decomposers, pollinators, and other forms that may provide some useful function in agroecosystems, as well as in riparian and other natural systems. An example of these is the insects that provide food for

birds and fish. However, the precise function of the vast majority of "indifferent" species is generally unknown.

In California, the replacement of natural communities with monocultures of agriculture has caused general faunal impoverishment, while certain species of phytophagous arthropods have become extremely abundant (Smith and Allen 1954). Many of these pest species have developed a high degree of mobility (Southwood 1966). Being good flyers, they often colonize the disrupted agroecosystem ahead of their natural enemies (van den Bosch and Telford 1964).

Burnett (1960), Odum (1971) and many others comment that as biotic complexity increases, particularly with reference to the number and kinds of trophic or feeding interactions, the stability of an agroecosystem will increase. An opposing, although not widely accepted, viewpoint of this ecological "dogma" is taken by van Emden and Williams (1973). They argue that species diversity does not necessarily cause greater stability. However, there are many examples of crop environment diversification which do make it more favorable to natural enemies and less favorable to a pest (Stern et al. 1976).

In general, rich, diverse, biotic complexes should be fostered and maintained. However, the function of the various elements must be understood before they can be intelligently employed or manipulated. The fact that most crop monocultures are threatened annually by pests and the diverse climax vegetation of many natural environments is little harmed has led to a general assumption that maximum diversity is desirable in all agricultural areas. It is thought that this will preserve the continuity, stability, and diversity inherent in the natural environment. There is an element of truth here, but it can be overstressed. In some cases, the "semi-natural" vegetation that adjoins crops can provide overwintering sites, sheltering places, and food for certain crop pests. Such vegetation may also benefit natural enemies if it supports their

[1] Paper presented at the California Riparian Systems Conference. [University of California, Davis, September 17-19, 1981].
[2] Vernon M. Stern is Professor of Entomology, University of California, Riverside.

alternative hosts, but this will not automatically provide a marked increase in biological control. Much depends on whether these benefits to the natural enemies counteract the benefits to the pest population. Once the delicate stability of a climax vegetation has been disturbed by man, even if only slightly, the vegetation, although still complex, may have been sufficiently altered to provide greater benefit to a pest in relation to the natural enemies that previously regulated it (Billiotti et al. 1968). Obviously, the manipulation of insect pest populations is a complex study in applied ecology.

PESTS OF CALIFORNIA AGRICULTURE

The hundreds of insect and spider mite pests attacking California agriculture have come from two sources. These are native species and exotic or introduced species.

Introduced Pests

Introduced pests comprise about 66% of our arthropod pests. Two problems of immediate concern are the Mediterranean fruit fly (Ceratitis capitata) and the gypsy moth (Lymantria dispar). The Mediterranean fruit fly was apparently transported to California in 1979. In some way adults or maggots inside infested fruit escaped detection at quarantine inspection stations. This devastating fly is one of the most serious entomological problems ever encountered by California agriculture. It attacks many crops and will cost many millions of dollars for various types of chemical control and in food loss each year if not eradicated.

On the other hand, the gypsy moth was intentionally brought to the United States by a Professor L. Trouvelot from Harvard. In 1869 he collected gypsy moth egg masses in France and brought them to the United States. His intention was to breed the gypsy moth with the silkworm to overcome a wilt disease commonly plaguing silkworm cultures in France and Italy. For whatever reason, he laid the egg masses on a window ledge, and evidently the wind blew them away.

Professor Trouvelot then published a notice, warning other citizens to be alert for the insect. The incident was forgotten until numerous shade and forest trees in the area were completely defoliated by the voracious caterpillars. Harassed by his irate neighbors, the professor left Harvard and headed west into entomological history.

By 1891 about 518 sq. km. (200 sq. mi.) north and west of Boston were infested. Even though the female moths cannot fly, the insect has steadily spread and now infests nearly all of the New England states and has extended into the Ohio River drainage system.

Through 1972 the gypsy moth had defoliated more than 810,000 ha. (2 million ac.) of forest-land and killed over 5 million trees. The leaves of over 500 species of trees and other plants are eaten by these caterpillars. Important hosts that can be completely defoliated along riparian zones, in and around parks, homes and streets, and in forestland areas include alder, all species of oak, gray birch, basswood, willow, river birch, all species of poplar, box elder, hawthorne and apple. Less defoliation will occur on all species of maple, yellow birch, and elm. The larger caterpillars will also attack all species of pine, hemlock and spruce (Brown 1978).

The first gypsy moth infestation was detected in California in 1976 (Eichlin 1981). Over 400 egg masses were found in Santa Clara County. The California Department of Food and Agriculture (DFA) conducted an apparently successful eradication program against the infestation using two aerial applications of the insect growth regulator diflubenzuron (Hoy 1982).

During 1981, 41 male gypsy moths were trapped in Santa Barbara County. Lesser numbers were trapped in other southern and northern California counties—Los Angeles (3 moths), Marin (7), San Diego (3), Santa Cruz (2), and Ventura (2). Capture of male moths in sex-lure pheromone traps does not prove that the gypsy moth has become established in an area, because they may have developed from eggs or pupae brought into the state from infected areas in the eastern United States. However, intensive surveys in Santa Barbara during the fall and winter (1981-82) revealed four egg masses, indicating that a breeding population of the gypsy moth exists there (ibid.).

Professor Trouvelot's seemingly harmless 1869 venture occurred before the Plant Quarantine Act was passed in 1912. This federal legislative act established regulatory measures dealing with insects and plant diseases. All the states now have regulatory measures in force forbidding the movement of certain plants into or within the state, at least until such plants have been inspected or fumigated, or both. In many cases reinspection is required at the point of destination. Further, it is illegal to ship nursery stock anywhere in the United States unless it is accompanied by a certificate of inspection, stating that it has been found apparently free from certain seriously destructive insect pests and plant diseases.

However, with national and international passenger and cargo aircraft (including military aircraft) constantly entering California, as well as a domestic population coming into California as tourists or to live, it is a monumental task to keep out pests of agriculture and natural ecosystems.

Today, California has hundreds of examples of established exotic insect pests. A few of them are: Egyptian alfalfa weevil, pink bollworm, green peach aphid, codling moth, peach twig borer, Oriental fruit moth, citrus red scale, and olive scale. In addition, there is a wide array of plant pathogens, weeds, and nematode pests that have been inadvertently introduced. The best estimates from some of the author's colleagues are that the vast majority of plant pathogens, nearly all of our weeds, and most of the nematode pests were brought into California from other areas.

The successful establishment of hundreds of exotic pests ties in perfectly with California's wild mosaic of climatic conditions. These range from the hot Imperial Valley, where cotton growers fight the pink bollworm (introduced in 1965) with 10 to 12 spray applications each season, to the cold winters in Modoc County, where cattlemen spray their alfalfa once or twice each spring to control the alfalfa weevil (introduced in the 1930s). The wide array of climates also gives rise to more than 230 commercial crops grown in the state, providing an ample variety of food for pest insects.

Native Pests

When the first Spanish explorers entered the San Joaquin Valley in the late 1700s, they found a large population of Yokut Indians existing on an abundance of elk, antelope, fish, tule roots, acorns, pine nuts, and other seeds. Two huge lakes, Buena Vista (formed by the Kern River) and Tulare (formed by the Tule and Kaweah rivers), and their surrounding tule marshes covered most of the lowlands, at least in the spring months (Kahrl 1979). Large areas of grassland and oak savannah, together with smaller amounts of saltbush desert, chaparral, and riparian communities, were essentially undisturbed by man. A number of insects we know today as crop pests—the western yellow-striped armyworm, alfalfa caterpillar, lygus bug, western spotted cucumber beetle, grape leafhopper, corn earworm, salt marsh caterpillar, several grasshoppers, and a number of other species occurred there, but they could not be considered pests because no agricultural crops existed in the valley.

These insects were greatly influenced by the seasonal occurrence of rain and the limited distribution of native annual vegetation. None of the Mediterranean winter annual herbs and grasses, such as bur clover, filarees, wild oat, and foxtail, were present.

In 1836 the first cattle ranch was established by the Spanish in the northwest fringes of the San Joaquin Valley; animals were produced largely for their hides. The discovery of gold and the rapid influx of settlers from the eastern United states created a demand for beef and other food. The period of 1850-70 was one of huge cattle holdings. Overgrazing began to take its toll, especially in drought years, and the introduction of Mediterranean grasses and forbs changed the composition of the range. The white man had now developed huge pastoral agroecosystems and the indigenous Indian had virtually disappeared.

The discovery in the 1850s that the winter and spring rains were sufficient to produce tremendous crops of wheat brought an era which lasted until about 1890. Huge grainfields displaced extensive areas of native grasslands.

The establishment of railroads also permitted the development of general agriculture along the rivers where water was available. Irrigation systems had small beginnings and were continually threatened by problems involving riparian rights to water, financing, land frauds, large corporate landholdings, and state laws concerning water rights and irrigation districts (ibid).

With the introduction of extensive irrigation systems, using water from snowpack runoff and deep wells, the grasslands and alkali deserts of the San Joaquin Valley were transformed into an intensive irrigated agriculture. Along with grains and alfalfa came tree fruits (deciduous and citrus), grapes, cotton, melons, sugar beets, rice, and vegetables. A variety of native insects found the lush irrigated fields or orchards an ideal haven. An abundant food supply was now available year-round, and their period of increase was no longer confined to the spring.

Indeed, the corn earworm (Heliothis zea) (fig. 1) was just another night-flying moth in the ancient pristine habitat. It undoubtedly dispersed to lay eggs on various annuals germinating from the winter and spring rains. When the rains ceased and the annuals set seed and dried up, there was probably high mortality of the younger larval stages. The moth population emerging from cocoons retracted to riverine and marsh areas to complete two or three summer generations on host plants near water. Undisturbed by today's chemicals, parasites and predators undoubtedly took a heavy toll of the summer generation larvae.

Today, with over 3.6 million hectares (9 million acres) of lush, irrigated farm land and a wide variety of commercial host crops, the native corn earworm is now "King of the Hill;" the scourge of vegetable growers; "number one" agricultural pest in California. It costs growers $80-100 million in chemical control and crop loss annually (California Department of Food and Agriculture 1977).

All of these changes have had an impact on the buildup of insect pest populations in areas of intensified agriculture. There are, of course, many ecological reasons why pest problems are more severe in intensified agriculture than in natural communities (table 1). Indeed, with our intensified production of food, fiber, and forage, we have created our own arthropod competitors.

MAN IN THE ENVIRONMENT

We must recognize that all organisms are subjected to the physical and biotic pressures of

Figure 1.--Corn earworm (<u>Heliothis</u> <u>zea</u>) larva feeding on an immature cotton floral bud.

the environments in which they live, and these factors, together with the genetic makeup of the species, determine their abundance and existence in any given area. Without natural control, a species which reproduces more than the parent stock could increase to infinite numbers. Man is subjected to environmental pressures just as other forms of life are, and he competes with other organisms for food and space.

Utilizing the traits that sharply differentiate him from other species, man has developed a technology permitting him to modify environments to meet his needs. Over the past several centuries, the competition for food and space has been almost completely in favor of man, as is attested by the decimation of vast vertebrate populations, as well as populations of other forms of life. But, while eliminating many species as he changed the environment of various regions to fit his needs for food and space, a number of species became his direct competitors. Today, as the human population continues to increase and civilization to advance, man numbers his arthropod enemies in the thousands of species (Knipling 1979).

Arthropod pests of agriculture are those species present in a crop in sufficient abundance to reduce the quality and/or quantity of food, forage, or fiber. The numbers of a pest may be in balance with their arthropod predators and parasites. However, at various times the pest population level may be sufficiently high to cause crop loss. Some control measure is then required to decrease its numbers. During the period of crop growth, pesticides are often the only way to prevent crop loss or decreased marketability of the product. Fruits and vegetables present the most serious marketability problems because of state and certain federal regulations relating to

Table 1.--Ecological aspects of natural ecosystems versus agroecosystems relating to pest outbreaks.

Natural ecosystems	Agroecosystems
Structure	
1. Many plant and arthropod species with interwoven food chains.	1. Single plant monoculture with few weeds; most crops have few resident arthropods and limited food chains.
2. Wide variation in micro-environments, many niches determined by resident biota of the community.	2. Limited number of niches; cultivation, pesticides, herbicides, harvesting are niche-disturbing; irrigation provides soil moisture.
3. Very stable with minor annual fluctuations of plant and animal species present.	3. Mostly unstable, wide annual fluctuations in plant and animal population composition; arthropod immigrants common.
4. Climax stage of plants and animals persists indefinitely under the prevailing climate.	4. Tree and vine crops relatively long-term; many other crops persist only one season.

Table 1.--Continued.

Productivity

1. No net annual accumulation of organic matter; annual production and import balanced by annual community consumption.
2. Ecosystem is essentially self-sufficient.
3. Input and loss, mainly energy loss, is low; only maintenance is needed in climax stage communities.

1. Food or fiber product removed, biomass sometimes removed (forage crops, some root crops).
2. Agroecosystems are almost totally dependent on man.
3. Large input of chemical energy; irrigation required except for rain-grown cereal crops.

Natural species composition

1. Each species component occupies an available niche, becomes dominant in that niche due to its competitive ability. Arthropods seldom reach pest status. Full population capacity seldom realized because of natural governing mechanisms operating in complex cycles of energy exchange between organisms.

1. First demand is single-species productivity. Uniformity imposed by planting and cultivation with original niches and competitive species suppressed. Arthropods often reach pest status following disruption of natural governing mechanisms.

Space relations

1. Separation of individual plants by other plant species. Spacing may be clumped or more-or-less random.
2. Density of each species is generally low per unit area.

1. Close uniform planting.

2. Concentration of one plant variety in a field, few plant varieties in an area, greatly increases the number of pest arthropods per unit area.

Climate

1. Most favorable conditions for rapid growth are not necessarily those in which a species expresses its competitive ability and capacity for survival.

1. Artificial conditions with plant varieties usually grown in most favorable environment for rapid growth and high productivity. This tends toward monocultures and increases pest arthropods per unit area. Prolonged cropping season favors pest outbreaks.

Genetics of each system

1. Wide genetic variability of plant and arthropod species responding to a variable environment. Natural selection of plants for resistance to arthropods.

1. Plants genetically uniform as possible, responding to a relatively uniform environment. Arthropods tend toward broods and features of homogeneity as influenced by cultural practices, special plant types, and pesticides. Plants often susceptible to attack by pests.

Tolerable degree of pest attack

1. Survival the first consideration; arthropods rarely denude environment; natural control mechanisms regulate population numbers.

1. High yield and quality primary consideration. Potential for crop damage high. Artificial control measures often necessary to suppress pest populations from crop loss or to maintain marketing quality standards.

product quality. Consumers are also involved, because they usually avoid buying food that shows signs of any type of insect damage which spoils the appearance of the product, even though there may be no nutritional loss to the product.

The increase to pest status of a particular species may be the result of a single factor or a combination of factors. The most significant factors of the last century are discussed below (Stern et al. 1959).

First, by changing or manipulating the environment, man has created conditions that permit certain species to increase their population densities. For example, when alfalfa was introduced into California in the 1850s to feed horses, the alfalfa butterfly (Colias eurytheme) (fig. 2), which had previously occurred in low numbers in native legumes, found a widespread and favorable new host plant in its environment. It soon became an economic pest.

A second way in which arthropods have risen to pest status has occurred by their being transported across geographical barriers while leaving their specific predators, parasites, and diseases behind. The increase in importance through such transportation is illustrated by the cottony-cushion scale (Icerya purchasi) (fig. 3). This scale insect was introduced from Australia on acacia in 1868. Within the following two decades, it increased in abundance to the point that it threatened economic disaster for the entire citrus industry. Fortunately, the timely importation and establishment of two of its natural enemies, a lady beetle (Rodolia cardinalis) and a parasitic fly (Cryptochaetum iceryae), resulted in the complete suppression of I. purchasi as a citrus pest.

A third cause for the increasing number of pest arthropods has been the establishment of progressively lower economic thresholds. For example, prior to the discovery of the insecticidal properties of DDT and development of other organic pesticides, the blotches caused by lygus bugs feeding on an occasional lima bean were of little concern. However, with a cheap and readily available method of chemical control of lygus bugs for the first time ever, and with the emphasis on product appearance in the frozen food industry, a demand was created for a near-perfect bean. For this reason, lower economic thresholds were established and lygus bugs came to be considered a serious pest of lima beans.

A fourth cause has been the indiscriminate use of pesticides. As mentioned, the corn earworm (Heliothis zea) is a native insect species and the single most damaging pest in the state. In the late 1950s through the 1960s, cotton was treated widely in the San Joaquin Valley for lygus bug control. Chemical treatments were often started in early June and continued through August. The corn earworm frequently increased to devastating numbers in August and September. From 1967 through 1972, University of California cotton research entomologists demonstrated that lygus bugs were not a pest of cotton after late

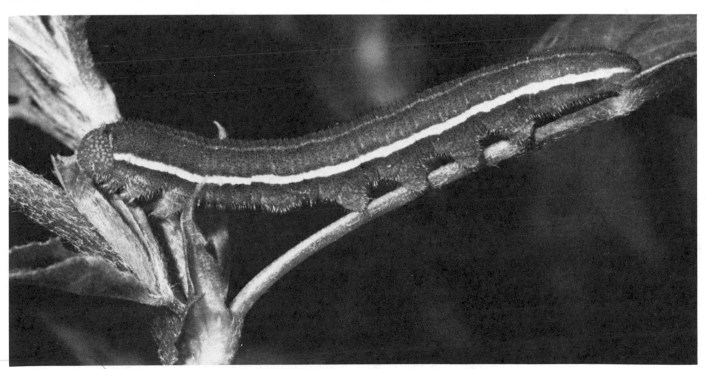

Figure 2.--Alfalfa caterpillar (Colias eurytheme) larva consuming alfalfa. This $800 million forage crop is the main food for California's multi-billion dollar dairy and beef cattle industry.

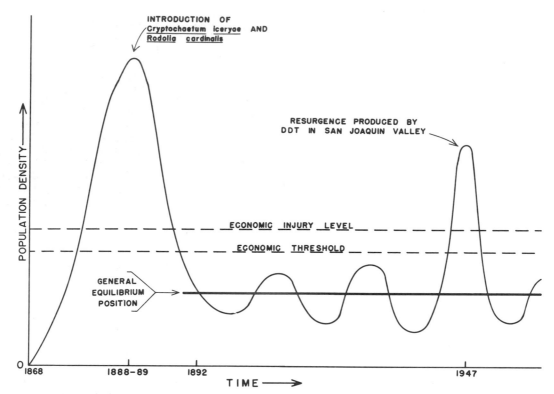

Figure 3.--Schematic graph of fluctuations in population density of the cottony-cushion scale (Icerya purchasi) on citrus from its introduction into California in 1868. Following the successful introduction of two of its natural enemies in 1888, it was reduced to noneconomic status except for a local resurgence produced by DDT treatments.

July. This and other knowledge reduced lygus bug treatments by nearly 50%, and as a consequence, the corn earworm has been reduced to minor pest status on cotton in the San Joaquin Valley.

PEST INTERACTIONS BETWEEN RIPARIAN SYSTEMS AND INTENSIFIED AGRICULTURE

Pierce's Disease

Pierce's disease (PD), which kills grapevines, is caused by a bacterium. This pathogen is spread by a family of leafhoppers known as sharpshooters. The disease had been present in California since the 1880s (Winkler et al. 1949). It initially broke out in southern California, destroying 14,000 ha. (35,000 ac.) of grapes. In the Central Valley the disease was first noted about 1917; from 1933 to 1940 a major outbreak devastated many Central Valley districts. Today the most dramatic vineyard losses to PD occur in the Napa Valley and parts of the San Joaquin Valley. During severe epidemics, losses to PD may require major replanting.

For many years PD was thought to be caused by a virus (ibid.). However, in 1973, University of California researchers, using the elec-

tron microscope, discovered the bacterium in infested grapes. This bacterium infects many different plant species in addition to grapevines. The host plants serve as reservoirs from which the sharpshooter vectors pick up PD bacterium for transmission to grapes. Many host plants of the bacterium also are important food or egg-laying places for the sharpshooter vectors. Some of these include Bermuda grass (Cynodon dactylon), watergrass (Echinochloa crusgalli), blackberry (Rubus vitifolius), willow (Salix spp.), and stinging nettle (Urtica holosericea).

Different grape varieties show different sensitivity to PD. Some of the more sensitive varieties include Mission, Pinot Noir, Pinot Chardonnay, and Barbera. Moderately resistant are Gray Riesling, Petit Sirah, Sauvignon Blanc, Cabernet Sauvignon, and Napa Gamay. Relatively resistant varieties are Thompson Seedless, White Riesling, Chenin Blanc, and Ruby Cabernet. Unfortunately, a number of California's varietal wine grapes are moderately to very sensitive to the disease (Purcell 1981).

Thus, the answer to the PD problem is not quite so simple as ripping out the more sensitive varieties and replanting with resistant varieties. This method of control is often used with field and vegetable crops which are planted for a single season. However, these latter crops are not required by law to carry a varietal label as are varietal wines.

Management of the Disease

Most dispersal of PD seems to develop directly from outside source areas and is then vectored to individual grape vines within vineyards. Studies in both coastal and interior areas have shown that rigorous removal of infected vines is not beneficial in reducing the spread of PD within a vineyard, although removal and replanting may be necessary to keep up vineyard productivity. Therefore, the only way to reduce or prevent PD spread through vector control is to prevent sharpshooters from entering vineyards.

Insect Vectors of Pierce's Disease

The green-headed sharpshooter (Draeculacephala minerva) and red-headed sharpshooter (Carneocephala fulgida) are the primary vectors of PD in the Central Valley. The two sharpshooters feed mainly on grasses, where they pick up the bacterium. These grasses occur commonly along irrigation ditch banks, roadways, pastures, and irrigation drainage sumps. In alfalfa fields, orchards or field-crop areas, it is the grass weeds growing in or at the margins of the crops that result in increased sharpshooter populations. If the PD bacterium is present, vineyards adjacent to such locations may suffer a high incidence of PD (ibid.). Unfortunately, control of weed areas or weedy alfalfa plantings may not be the prerogative of the vineyard owner. However, the owner can eliminate weed grasses on his or her own property to help reduce PD.

Insecticidal treatment is only temporarily effective against adult sharpshooters and of little value overall in the Central Valley. There is a considerable overlap of generations; eggs are present inside protective leaf tissues of host plants from January through the fall.

Coastal Areas--Napa Valley

The blue-green sharpshooter (Graphocephala atropunctata) (fig. 4), unlike the grass-feeding sharpshooters of the Central Valley, will feed and reproduce on many plants. However, it prefers woody or perennial plants such as wild grape, blackberry, elderberry, and stinging nettle. The blue-green sharpshooter is most common along streambanks or in ravines or canyons that have dense growth of trees, vines, and shrubs, where it feeds on succulent new growth in areas of abundant soil moisture and shade. It is seldom found in unshaded dry locations.

Figure 4.--Blue-green sharpshooter (Graphocephala atropunctata), an important vector of Pierce's disease (PD) of grapes in coastal areas of California.

Vineyards in the immediate vicinity of environments favorable to this sharpshooter are frequently PD "hot spots" with a very high incidence of the disease. Unfortunately, removal of the host plants carrying the bacterium is usually impractical because often they provide refuges for wildlife, protect against erosion and flood damage, and contribute substantially to the beauty of the countryside.

To combat the blue-green sharpshooter, which has only one generation per year, insecticide applications of dimethoate have been used in early spring, before the leafhoppers move into the vineyard. At that time, feeding and most flight activity near vineyards is concentrated in relatively small and well-defined locations. Treatment consists of applying the pesticide to a band of native vegetation about 15-30 m. (50-100 ft.) wide along the vineyard edge. At the same time that the natural vegetation is treated, adjacent portions of the vineyard should be treated if new shoot growth is longer than a few centimeters (ibid.).

While blackberry acts as a host to the PD bacterium in the Napa Valley, this riparian plant species can be beneficial in other ways, including its influence on the grape leafhopper.

Grape Leafhopper

The grape leafhopper (Erythroneura elegantuala) (fig. 5) is the most common insect pest of grapes in the San Joaquin, Sacramento, and Napa valleys. Before the development of organic insecticides in the 1940s, severe damage occurred in some years, followed by periods of low populations. Now, with more effective pesticides, losses are primarily due to the cost of treatment plus the side effect of secondary outbreaks of other insect and spider mite pests resulting from the chemical treatment. A good example occurred in the 1960s when the leafhopper developed resistance to DDT and other chemicals. Growers began using the pesticide Sevin for leafhopper control. This material often caused severe outbreaks of spider mites, and in many cases the mites were more damaging to the grapes than the original leafhoppers.

Injury

Both adults and nymphs of the grape leafhopper have piercing mouth parts with which they puncture leaves and suck out the contents. Heavily damaged leaves lose their green color, dry up, and fall off the vine. In addition, in table grapes excessive fruit spotting from the leafhopper excrement can lead to unmarketable fruit before any effect on yield is noted. The crop is then sold for crushing, which is far less profitable than table grapes.

Natural Control

The important natural enemy of the grape leafhopper is a tiny, almost microscopic wasp Anagrus epos (fig. 6). This tiny wasp lays its eggs in the eggs of the grape leafhopper, resulting in the death of the leafhopper egg. These parasitic wasps are particularly valuable because of their amazing ability to locate and attack grape leafhopper eggs. Also, their short life cycle permits them to increase far more rapidly than can leafhopper populations. Their nine to 10 generations during the grape season make them capable of parasitizing 90-95% of all leafhopper eggs that are laid after July (Jensen and Flaherty 1981).

Anagrus epos overwinters on wild blackberries (Rubus spp.) on which it parasitizes the eggs of noneconomic, harmless leafhoppers (Dikrella spp.). These overwintering wasp populations tend to be along rivers that have an overstory of trees sheltering both wild grapes and wild blackberries. When the blackberries leaf out in February, the lush, new foliage apparently stimulates heavy oviposition by the Dikrella leafhoppers. The Anagrus populations increase enormously in these eggs, so that by late March and early April there is widespread dispersal of the newly produced Anagrus adult females. Fortunately, their dispersal occurs at the same time that grape leafhopper females begin to lay eggs. Vineyards located within an 8- to 16-km.

Figure 5.--Grape leafhopper (Erythroneura elegantuala) is the most common and most frequently treated grape pest in central and northern California.

Figure 6.--Adult parasite (Anagrus epos) of
grape leafhopper eggs. The male, shown
above, is blackish-brown, while the female
is straw colored. This microscopic wasp
often reduces the grape leafhopper to non-
pest status in vineyards adjacent to riparian systems.

(5- to 10-mi.) range of an overwintering population will usually benefit immediately from the
immigrant parasites. Vineyards distant from
actual blackberry refuges may not show Anagrus
activity until midsummer or later.

Efforts to establish blackberry refuges near
vineyards in Tulare County have been only partially successful. This is attributed to the lack of
a sheltering overstory of trees as would normally
occur in riparian zones. In full sun, blackberry
plantings gradually become dry thickets, with
only surface foliage that becomes tough and
leathery. Dikrella, wintertime host of Anagrus epos, is a shade- and moisture-loving
insect that breeds on leaves inside blackberry
vines were it is generally cooler and more humid.
Old mature thickets, therefore, become less
desirable Dikrella habitats and are, consequently, poor producers of Anagrus. A vineyard
located within a natural dispersal area will,

therefore, receive early important activity from
the Anagrus parasites.

Where blackberries occur naturally, the commercial vineyards in the vicinity are not seriously troubled by grape leafhopper populations, and
parasitism by Anagrus begins early in the season. This situation was first evident from
studies in the Napa Valley, where blackberries
are common, as well as in vineyards near the
Stanislaus River, in the northern San Joaquin
Valley. Certain locations along the Kings,
Kaweah, and St. Johns rivers are also excellent
sites for Anagrus where blackberries are
common.

By contrast, the vineyards in the southern
San Joaquin Valley are established in locations
that are virtually reclaimed desert. They are
miles from naturally occurring blackberries and
chronically suffer from excessively high leafhopper populations. Parasitism by Anagrus does
not occur until late in the summer, if at all.

Doutt and Nakata (1973) concluded that a
vineyard situated within the predictable early
dispersion range of Anagrus from overwintering
sites can reasonably expect the parasite activity
to be a substantial mortality factor on the first
two broods of leafhoppers. This element is important in pest management programs of vineyards in
the area, and any practice disruptive to this particular host/parasite system should be avoided.

Grapeleaf Skeletonizer

The western grapeleaf skeletonizer (Harrisina brillians) (GLS) is an introduced pest
(fig. 7). It was first found in California in
1941, near San Diego. In canyon areas, wild
grapes (Vitis girdiana) were severely defoliated; in a short time GLS became a serious pest
in commercial vineyards. By 1943, crop loss in
some vineyards reached 90%, but the average was a
loss of about 50%.

A state-imposed eradication program, using
cryolite dust, was tried, but it was not successful. Meanwhile, emphasis was placed on biological control. University of California entomologists at Riverside imported parasites from Mexico
and Arizona. A parasitic wasp, Apanteles
harrisinae, and a parasitic fly, Ametadoria
(==Sturmia) harrisinae, were soon established. A granulosis virus that attacks GLS larvae
was soon found in GLS-rearing laboratories in
Arizona and in San Diego County.

By 1961, GLS was found on backyard grapes at
Kerman (Fresno County). In spite of another try
at eradication, by 1975 devastating infestations
could be found in central and northern California
on wild grapes in riparian systems, on backyard
grapes, and in commercial vineyards. It has
spread slowly in the Central Valley because GLS
adults tend to remain in the area of their larval
development (Stern et al. 1981).

Figure 7.--Larvae of the western grapeleaf skeletonizer (*Harrisina brillians*) feeding on a grape leaf.

To deal with these new infestations, Apanteles and Ametodoria parasites from San Diego County were introduced, and explorations were made for new parasites from outside of California. So far only the parasitic fly appears to have become established, and this only in Siskiyou and Shasta counties where grapes are not commercially important.

Injury

Leaf damage continues to increase through the season in untreated GLS populations. Second and third generations (there are three per year) have defoliated entire vineyards in the central San Joaquin Valley. If vines are heavily or completely defoliated before harvest, fruit maturity can be adversely affected. Heavy defoliation in mid-summer usually destroys the entire crop. Defoliation after harvest is less damaging, but it can affect the food reserves of the vine and weaken it for the following year. At present, biological control is inadeqate and growers have no recourse other than to treat GLS infestations.

Riparian Systems as Biological Controls

When wild grape foliage is abundant, adult GLS moths tend to remain in the area and flitter about in the process of mating and laying eggs. The conspicuous bluish-black moths are caught easily by hand. However, when larvae have defoliated the wild grapes in a spot, adults emerging from the cocoons of these larvae change their flight habits. In seeking out new egg-laying sites, they become very swift fliers. With this unusual flight habit on the part of the moth, wild grapes along riparian zones are a constant source of infestation for commercial vineyards in the area.

On the other hand, the wild grapes along the rivers, streams, and creeks east of Visalia have been extremely beneficial in the attempt to establish biological control agents of GLS. These areas, some in permanent pasture, are never treated with insecticides which would possibly wipe out the released GLS parasites. This author has taken advantage of these riparian systems in cooperation with the private landowners for research projects. None of them grow grapes. One cooperator has walnut groves, another is a dairyman, and still another raises beef cattle and is a descendent of a family that homesteaded and bought property along the Kaweah River in the 1880s.

When the GLS parasites become firmly established in riparian vegetation, they can then spread by themselves into commercial vineyards. It might be noted that about 20% of the vineyards in the Central Valley are never treated with insecticides.

Even more promising, in terms of biological control of GLS, has been the work with the granulosis virus of GLS. During the mid-1950s, Edward Steinhaus, then Professor of Insect Pathology, University of California, Berkeley, purified about one-fourth teaspoon of the GLS virus and placed it in a refrigerator. In 1979 this small bit of virus was sent to the author at Riverside. The virus was tested in Tulare County on single grape leaves containing early larval stages of GLS. The virus proved to be just as potent as when Professor Steinhaus put it in the refrigerator 25 years earlier. Following this, the virus was propagated, and field tests were conducted in 1980. The virus was just as effective on GLS as commercial pesticides. Equally important for these biological control efforts was the effect of the virus at low dosages. These data suggested that the virus could be incorporated as a biological control and could contaminate the GLS population in the San Joaquin Valley. In this study the desired effect is not to kill the GLS larvae outright. Instead, the aim is to apply a sufficiently low virus dosage as to permit the infected larvae to survive so the adults will become carriers of the virus and spread it through the valley.

Adults arising from such larvae are one-half normal size. In 1981, it was found that some of these moths do not lay eggs. About 75% of the eggs that are laid do not hatch. Larvae that do hatch have abnormal feeding habits and eventually all die in the third larval stage. This gives 100% control from exposure to the virus in the previous generation.

During the summer, riparian areas were sprayed with low dosages of the virus. A unique and key feature of the GLS granulosis virus is that it attacks the gut of the larvae. This gives rise to diarrhea which contains millions of virion particles. Other insects crawling over this material will pick it up on their legs and help spread it through the system.

CONCLUSION

In little more than a century, the land- and waterscape of California has been remade through construction of a great network of artificial lakes and rivers. However, the present water system and its domestic, agricultural, and industrial use is far more than these physical elements. It is also constructed of the legal and institutional structures that Californians have erected to govern water use and the social and economic development it has helped to foster. The money invested has led to the transformation of grassland prairie, as well as arid and semi-arid land, into cities, towns, and irrigated cropland and has made California the most populous and agriculturally productive state in the nation.

The past changes as well as current and proposed changes in land use and waterscape are disturbing to a good number of Californians, and rightly so. The original grassland prairie, marshlands, and forests of willow, oak, cotton-wood, and sycamore along rivers and streams, and their accompanying flora and fauna have largely disappeared. To resurrect a portion of the original habitat present when the Spaniards and settlers from the eastern United States arrived would require huge expenditures of public funds. To complicate matters even more is the vast array of public and private agencies (about 3,700) with administrative authority to respond to the political, social, and economic rights of various citizens with respect to water supply, delivery, use, and treatment (Kahrl 1979).

Strict conservation and maintenance of existing riparian areas is certainly needed. Limited restoration of riparian systems is also possible and can be accomplished through the legal process. This mainly concerns private donations in perpetuity of deeded land to an institution, such as the University of California, to remain as or to return to natural riparian habitats. Good examples occur in southern California through the efforts of Dr. William W. Mayhew, Professor of Zoology, University of California, Riverside. At present, donations of deeded land to the University far exceed those that the state legislature and the general public would be willing to purchase outright.

Aesthetic values aside, much remains to be learned of the beneficial as well as adverse effects of crop plant diseases, pest and beneficial arthropods, birds and other flora and fauna associated with riparian and agricultural systems. Riparian areas which harbor specific agents detrimental to adjacent agricultural crops will often have another array of beneficial agents affecting the same or another crop. Long-term ecological studies are needed to elucidate these relationships, and special funding to the University of California from the state legislature for this specific purpose seems most appropriate.

ACKNOWLEDGMENTS

All photographs in this manuscripts are by Jack Kelley Clark, Principal Photographer, Cooperative Extension Service, University of California, Davis.

LITERATURE CITED

Billiotti, E., and V.M. Stern et al. 1968. Report of the second session of the FAO panel of experts on integrated pest control. [Rome, Italy, September 19-24, 1968.] 48 p. Food and Agriculture Organization of the United Nations, Rome, Italy.

Brown, L.R. 1978. Insects of ornamental shrubs, shade trees and turf. p. 535-571. In: R.E. Pfadt (ed.). Fundamentals of applied entomology. 798 p. Macmillan Company, New York, N.Y.

Burnett, T. 1960. Control of insect pests. Proceedings of Federal American Society Experimental Biology 19:557-561.

California Department of Food and Agriculture. 1977. Estimated damage and crop loss caused by insect/mite pests: 1976. 24 p. California Department of Food and Agriculture Publication, Sacramento, Calif.

Doutt, R.L., and J. Nakata. 1973. The Rubus leafhopper and its egg parasitoid: an endemic biotic system useful in grape-pest management. Environmental Entomology 2(3): 381-386.

Eichlin, T.D. 1981. Location of gypsy moth finds in California—1981. p. 81-83. In: Cooperative plant pest report 4(8). California Department of Food and Agriculture, Sacramento, Calif.

Hoy, M. 1982. The gypsy moth—here again. California Agriculture 36(7):4-6.

Jensen, F.L., and D.L. Flaherty. 1981. Grape leafhopper. p. 98-110. In: Grape pest management. University of California Division of Agricultural Sciences Pub. 4105, Berkeley, Calif. 312 p.

Kahrl, W.L. (ed.). 1979. The California water atlas. Prepared by the Governor's Office of Planning and Research in cooperation with the California Department of Water Resources, State of California, Sacramento. 118 p.

Knipling, E.F. 1979. The basic principles of insect populations, suppression and management. US Department of Agriculture Handbook 512, Washington, D.C. 623 p.

Odum, E.P. 1971. Fundamentals of ecology. 574 p. Saunders, Philadelphia, Penn.

Purcell, A.H. 1981. Pierce's disease. p. 62-69. In: Grape pest management. University of California Division of Agricultural Sciences Pub. 4105, Berkeley, Calif. 312 p.

Smith, R.F., and W.W. Allen. 1954. Insect control and the balance of nature. American Science 190:38-42.

Southwood, T.R.E. 1966. Ecological methods. 391 p. Chapman and Hall, London, England.

Stern, V.M., P.L. Adkisson, O. Beingolea, and G.A. Viktorov. 1976. Cultural controls. p. 593-613. In: Theory and practice of biological control. 788 p. Academic Press, Inc., New York, N.Y.

Stern, V.M., W.L. Peacock, and D.L. Flaherty. 1981. Western grapeleaf skeletonizer. p. 140-146. In: Grape pest management. University of California Division of Agricultural Sciences Pub. 4105, Berkeley, Calif. 312 p.

Stern, V.M., R.F. Smith, R. van den Bosch, and K.S. Hagen. 1959. The integrated control concept. In: The integration of chemical and biological control of the spotted alfalfa aphid. Hilgardia 29(2):81-154.

US Department of Agriculture. 1965. Losses in agriculture. US Department of Agriculture Handbook 291, Washington, D.C. 120 p.

van den Bosch, R., and A.D. Telford. 1964. Environmental modification and biological control. p. 459-488. In: P. DeBach (ed.). Biological control of insect pests and weeds. 844 p. Reinhold, New York, N.Y.

van Emden, H.F., and G.F. Williams. 1973. Insect stability and diverstiy in agroecosystems. Annual Review of Entomology 19:455-475.

Winkler, A.J., W.B. Hewitt, N.W. Frazier, and J.H. Frietag. 1949. Pierce's disease investigations. Hilgardia 19(7):207-264.

TIMBER OPERATIONS ALONG CALIFORNIA STREAMS[1]

Jere L. Melo[2]

Abstract.--Commercial forestlands occupy about 16% of California's 100 million acres and about half are managed by private owners. These private lands contribute substantial amounts of forest products and amenities to the state economy. Private operations are controlled by numerous laws; the purpose and results of several important state laws are presented.

INTRODUCTION

Commercial forestlands[3] occupy a substantial portion of California's mountainous terrain. Because these lands receive relatively high amounts of precipitation, streams and riparian areas are common in commercial forests. California's forest industry ranks second in national lumber production, contributing about 12% of the total. Despite this substantial production, consumers in the state annually use about 30% more lumber than is produced and substantially greater quantities of plywood, particle board, poles and piling, and pulp and paper products. Industry estimates that in 1979, 2,458 firms provided direct employment for 100,000 persons in all types of forest product and byproduct manufacturing (California Forest Communicators Council 1979). Commercial forests occupy about 16% of the state's 100 million acres (table 1).

BACKGROUND INFORMATION

Timber lands feature a diverse set of stream and vegetation patterns within relatively small areas on any particular timber harvest unit (fig. 1). Depending on soil and moisture conditions, vegetation near streams can range from dense, redwood groves as found along the North Coast to more open stands of pine and fir as found in the Sierra and Cascade mountains.

---

[1]Paper presented at the California Riparian Systems Conference. [University of California, Davis, September 17-19, 1981].

[2]Jere L. Melo is Division Forester, Northern California Division of Georgia-Pacific Corporation, Fort Bragg, Calif.

[3]Commercial forestlands are generally defined as those capable of producing at least an average of 20 cu. ft. of merchantable wood, per acre per year, during a "rotation" or between timber harvests. Thus, an acre capable of growing 20 cu. ft. for a "rotation" of 100 years will yield 2,000 cu. ft. at harvest of the timber.

Table 1.--Ownership of commercial forestland in California (California Forest Communicators Council 1979).

Ownership Class	Area (acres x 1000)	Percent
National forests (USDA)	8,168	50
Other federal (USDI)	393	2
State and local government	106	1
Forest industry	2,688	17
Other private	4,944	30
Total	16,299	

Figure 1.--Oblique view of forestlands showing stream patterns and developed road system.

Historically, stream routes have served the industry as a logical basis for development of transportation systems. Pioneer lumbermen used water to move logs to the sawmill (fig. 2). Development of roads, railroads, manufacturing sites, and ownership patterns is substantially based on topography, and major streams strongly influence all development. The process of devel-

983

Figure 2.--Pioneer timbermen used streams to move logs to the mill. All summer, logs were piled in front of splash dams. With winter freshets, dams were tripped, and the river drive began. Hell Gate Dam on the South Fork of Big River, Mendocino County. Built in 1902; last used in 1937.

opment on commercial forestlands is quite similar to that for public transportation routes.

COMMERCIAL FOREST USES

From the perspective of a timberland owner, forest uses may be grouped into activities that produce an economic return and those activities that produce no economic return. Economic returns may be stated in positive (profit) or negative (loss) cash flows, depending on market conditions, volume and quality of inventory, and the particular cost structure of individual owners. Activities that produce no economic return are generally those factors where there is an overabundant supply, relative to market demand. Some or all of these non-economic activities may be factors in the business cost of timberland owners, but the consumer enjoys a zero cost for resource or amenity use.

Economic Returns to the Owner

The most obvious economic return to a timberland owner is the harvest and sale of forest pro-

ducts. Today, the largest dollar volume of forest products is for saw logs and veneer logs, but others include posts, poles and piling, split products, burls, greens, Christmas trees, and fuel wood. During the past two decades, substantial gains in timber utilization have been accomplished through increased use of harvested trees. More defective logs are used, given improved manufacturing facilities and marketing efforts. Development of pulp and paper manufacturing and cogeneration of electric power has permitted increased use of mill residue and some specific uses of logging slash.

Timber, similar to agricultural crops, develops best in a good soil with plenty of moisture during long growing seasons. The commercial redwood forest is the most dramatic demonstration in California of the influence of water and deep soils can be demonstrated (table 2).

Table 2.--Mean annual wood yield in cubic feet for sawlogs, young-growth redwood (Lindquist and Palley 1963).

Site Quality	Site Index	60-Year Yield (cu. ft.)
Excellent	200	373
Good	160	215
Average	140	153
Fair	120	97

In the redwood forest, the best soils are the silty deposits along main streams. When rivers reach flood stage, slack water develops above the streambanks, resulting in deposits of fine soil particles. Soil deposits up to 30 ft. are common, and water marks on trees range from 2 ft. to 15 ft. above soil levels. Thus, it is quite common that riparian zones are the most productive commercial timber sites by a substantial margin.

Other economic uses enjoyed by timberland owners include transportation facilities such as roads and railroads, mining of gravel from streambeds for construction and site hardening, and some fee recreation. Where an owner controls a road or railroad, wood products and other freight are subject to tolls. Gravel mining is common in streambeds throughout the state, and some timber owners are able to use gravel on timber operations or for sale for other construction. Fee recreation is not well developed on California timberlands, but some owners have been able to obtain income from railroads, hunting clubs, campgrounds or livestock grazing.

Owner Subsidized Uses

The supply of areas for camping, hunting, fishing, bird watching, and similar activities is so far in excess of demand that these uses have not provided substantial income for most timberland owners. The consumer enjoys a zero cost for resource use, including the capital developments on a property such as roads, bridges, and, perhaps, developed camp sites. A characteristic of most of these types of activities is that the riparian sites are the most desirable areas of use.

A recent development by major timber owners along the North Coast has been to support salmon restoration (fig. 3). Several companies have provided funds for egg-taking facilities and rearing ponds in local streams. This represents a capital investment in fisheries of funds generated from timber harvest.

Figure 3.--Salmon egg-taking station on Hollow Tree Creek in Mendocino County. Station was designed by California Department of Fish and Game (DFG), constructed and installed by timber industry, and operated by commercial fishermen. Eggs taken are hatched by DFG, and fish are raised in rearing ponds on industry lands. Local non-profit groups purchase feed for young fish.

PRIMARY STATE LAWS AND REGULATIONS

The forest products industry is among the most regulated industries in California. Management strategies during the past decade have largely been in the form of responding to legislative and regulatory initiatives. These have been complicated by interpretations of law by various courts and competition among public agencies for regulatory control. Provided below are discussions of several prominent state laws that directly affect timber operations.

Z'Berg-Nejedly Forest Practice Act of 1973

The Z'Berg-Nejedly Forest Practice Act of 1973[4] became effective in 1974. It is administered by the Board of Forestry. The board consists of nine members, five representing the general public (and without financial interests in timber operations or lands), three representing the forest industry, and one representing the range and livestock industry. There are three technical advisory committees representing regional differences in forest conditions and operations. The board is required to consider public and technical advice prior to adopting rules under which timber operations must be conducted.

The act authorizes regulation of timber operations by the use of board-adopted rules for each forest district. Prior to the conduct of a timber operation, a Timber Harvesting Plan must be prepared by a Registered Professional Forester and be approved by the California Department of Forestry (DF) after consulting with other state agencies. Usually, harvest plans are reviewed by DF, DFG and the staff from a Regional Water Quality Control Board (RWQCB).

The board rules are intended to be used as standards for preparing Timber Harvesting Plans and judging the results of logging operations. The act and rules provide standards for several harvest and reforestation systems, operations of logging equipment, road and trail construction, erosion control, stream and lake protection, fire hazard abatement, insect and disease control, and fire prevention and control.

Timber operations described in an approved Timber Harvesting Plan may be conducted during a three-year period following approval. A completion notice must be filed within a month after all work is finished. After completion, the landowner has five years to restock harvested lands with commercial species of trees.

Silvicultural methods allowed include a broad range of cutting intensities, from clearcutting to minor salvage of dead or infested trees. Reforestation may be accomplished by using commercial timber left after a partial harvest; natural or artificial planting of trees and seed is also accepted. The basic requirement is to have 300 seedling trees per acre established within five years after completion of the harvest. If trees larger than seedling size remain after harvest, there are equivalence tables for computing stocking levels.

The act and rules specifically address operations around streams. Essentially, equipment is limited from operating within 50 ft. of streams,

---

[4]Chapter 8 of Division 4, Public Resources Code, Sections 4511-4628, adopted by Statutes of 1973 and amended through 1980.

in an effort to protect streambanks. Vegetation must be left along streams to provide shade and reduce raindrop impact and resulting surface erosion. Erosion control measures include standards for construction of roads and trails, drainage, and winter operations. Most practices are keyed to an erosion-hazard rating system, calculated from soils, slopes, rainfall, and other factors that can be identified on-site.

The concept for administering the act has been revised as a result of a court decision. In 1975, the Humboldt County Superior Court found that the provisions of the California Environmental Quality Act (CEQA) applied to timber operations in addition to the provisions of the act.[5]

Operations within the coastal zone were revised with adoption of the Coastal Act of 1976.[6] Early in 1977, the California Coastal Commission was required to identify specific timberland areas that were designated as "special treatment areas," and in 1978, the Board of Forestry adopted restrictive regulations for the conduct of timber operations (Melo 1979).

Perhaps the most far-reaching revision of the act and the board rules is currently being debated. Silvicultural operations are identified as nonpoint sources of water pollution, and as such they fall under Section 208 of the Federal Water Pollution Control Act of 1972 (as amended by the Clean Water Act of 1977). Each state is required to conduct a planning effort to minimize nonpoint sources of water pollution, and the board has responded by proposing repeal of most existing district rules and major revisions of the Forest Service Act. Numerous regulatory and legislative proposals are now being processed.

The Z'Berg-Nejedly Act is considered the most stringent forest practices act in the nation. Court interpretations and various legislative and regulatory proposals have resulted in some modifications to the program since it became effective.

Professional Foresters Law (1972)

The Professional Foresters Law (1972)[7] provides for professional licensing of individuals who wish to practice forestry. There are minimum requirements for education and experience. The primary influence of this act on timber operations is that only a Registered Professional Forester may prepare a Timber Harvesting Plan.

---

[5] Natural Resources Defense Council vs. Arcata National Corporation (1976) 131 Cal. Rptr. 172, 50 C.A. 3rd 959.
[6] California Coastal Act of 1976, Division 20, Public Resources Code, (SB 1277, Statutes of 1976).
[7] Article 3, Public Resources Code, Sections 750-783 (Statutes of 1972).

Z'Berg-Warren-Keene-Collier Forest Taxation Reform Act of 1976

This complex act[8] made numerous revisions to the assessment and collection of taxes for timber and timberlands. Its primary features include: creation of the Timberland Preserve Zone (TPZ), where only timber production along with certain compatible uses are allowed, and a shift of tax collection of timber taxes by the State (Board of Equalization), based on regional (market area) timber values.

Creation of the TPZ is by contract between a county and an individual timberland owner. Although the owner agrees to restrict his development of forestland to certain limits, the county must then tax the land based on its productive capacity. The "highest and best use" concept of valuation, based on sales of nearby lands, has been abandoned. Abandoning this concept relieves the landowner from the pressures of a tax spiral simply because adjacent owners might sell at a high price.

The tax shift on timber from the standing tree (inventory) to the cut log (yield) allows the timber owner to pay taxes at the time when a cash flow is created. Particularly for private, non-industrial owners, the inventory tax often forced liquidation of timber in order to provide sufficient funds to avoid tax delinquency. Owners can now "play the market" by attempting to sell at perceived high demand (and price) periods while retaining inventory during the low demand periods.

Collection of property taxes has long been a function of local county assessors and tax collectors. The act removed value determination from the local level and placed it with the State Board of Equalization. The Board of Forestry determines average timber values twice yearly, based on transactions within defined market areas of the state. Funds are distributed to counties based on tax collections during past years.

Fish and Game Code, Sections 1600-1606

The Fish and Game Code requires that private and public projects which propose to modify streambed or streambanks or to divert water from streams must have an agreement with DFG before planning construction.[9] Many timber operations have stream crossings on road systems, and numerous applications are made to DFG under Section 1603.

Normally, the process to reach an agreement for work in and around streams can be completed within 30 days. A written application is submitted to DFG describing the proposed work, and after a visit to the site, DFG and the operator

---

[8] AB 1258, Statutes of 1976.
[9] Chapter 6 of Division 2, Public Resources Code, Sections 1600-1606 (AB 2210, Statutes of 1976).

sign a binding agreement. This process features few written rules, and it relies heavily on good will between agency and operator personnel. This regulatory procedure has given minimum difficulty to private operators because it is so simple and its goals are understandable.

Porter-Cologne Water Quality Control Act

The Porter-Cologne Water Quality Control Act[10] provides for regional water quality control under supervision of the State Water Resources Control Board (SWRCB). RWQCBs adopt water quality basin plans which prescribe and define beneficial uses of water, those water standards necessary to maintain the beneficial uses, and an action plan to attain necessary water standards. An interesting feature of the act is that neither a regional board nor the SWRCB may prescribe the method for attainment of water quality goals. In fact, specific practices may not be prescribed.

Staff members of regional boards review timber harvest plans and are advisory to the DF. Up until 1979, the North Coast RWQCB adopted water quality standards (waste discharge requirements) for certain timber operations that were considered controversial. Most of these actions occurred after approval of harvest plans by DF, following objection by the water quality staff. Currently, the major effect on the North Coast of RWQCB action has been a modification of the proposed aerial application of phenoxy herbicides for brush control on timberlands. At the present time, there are proposals before the SWRCB to conduct a study in cooperation with the industry, where standards will be set for application of herbicides.

Food and Agriculture Code

Registration, prescription and application of pesticides statewide is under the control of the Department of Food and Agriculture (DFA). It has registered programs for pesticide dealers, pest control advisors, pest control operators, and agricultural pilots. DFA provides for state registration of pesticides for various uses; county agricultural commissioners represent DFA by issuing permits and inspecting applications.

Application of pesticides in forest management is generally limited to grass and brush control for reforestation or for suppression of undesirable plant species after reforestation. For specific forest types, under epidemic insect attacks, pesticides have been applied as a control effort.

------

[10]Division 7 of the California water code, adopted by Statutes of 1969 (chapter 482) and amended through 1980.

RESEARCH, DEVELOPMENT, EQUIPMENT APPLICATION

Research and development within California's forest industry has been very limited during the past decade. Legislative, regulatory, and legal initiatives have been so frequent and time-consuming that forest managers have not devised many new techniques for operations.

Capital investments in land acquisition, reforestation, and road improvements have been substantial during the past decade. A stable land base, stocked with trees and featuring permanent access roads, is the emphasis of major timber owners today. Given a more stable political and regulatory climate at some point in the future, coupled with fiscal and monetary policies that encourage housing and construction, California timberland owners look forward to production of young timber and amenity benefits from their lands.

During the past decade, particularly for operators in the North Coast area, there has been a shift from moving logs by tractor to cable machine methods. Particularly on steep slopes, cable yarding of logs produces much less soil disturbance, and it allows roads to be located uphill from streams. Although cable yarding methods are more costly than ground-travelling machines, their employment has become quite common in recent years. Log production costs have increased, as has vegetative disturbance, but soil erosion and stream damage risks have been minimized.

LITERATURE CITED

California Forest Communicators Council (CFCC). 1979. California Forest Facts. 12 p. California Forest Communicators Council, Sacramento, Calif.

Lindquist, James and Marshall Palley. 1963. Empirical yield table for young-growth redwood. 47 p. California Agricultural Experiment Station Bulletin 796, University of California, Berkeley.

Melo, Jere L. 1979. California's "Coastal commission special treatment areas." In: Loggers Handbook, Vol. 39. Pacific Logging Congress, Portland, Oregon.

ABELL, Dr. Dana, Consulting Biologist, Aquatic Resources, P.O. Box 711, Davis, CA 95616

ACIETUNO, Mr. Mike, Fishery Biologist, California State Office, USDI Bureau of Land Management, 2800 Cottage Way, Sacramento, CA 95825

ALLEN, Ms. Harriet, Ecologist, 3750 El Canto Drive, Spring Valley, CA 92077

ALLEN, Mr. Hubert A., Jr., Field Biologist, Colorado River Project, 656 Country Lane, Glencoe, IL 60022

ANDERSON, Dr. Bertin W., Director, Colorado River Laboratory, Center for Environmental Studies, 201 S. Palm, Blythe, CA 92225

ANDERSON, Mr. Dave, Attorney, Reclamation Board, California Department of Water Resources, 1416 Ninth Street, Room 1118-6, Sacramento, CA 95814

ANDERSON, Mr. Gene L., Civil Engineer, California Department of Water Resources, 1416 Ninth Street, Sacramento, CA 95814

ARNOLD, J.R., c/o Nona Dennis, ESA/ Madrone, 23-B Pamaron Way, Novato, CA 94947

ANDREWS, Ms. Barbara, Research Assistant, Center for Natural Resource Studies, John Muir Institute, 1016 Grayson Street, Berkeley, CA 94710

BAHRE, Dr. Conrad, Assistant Professor, Department of Geography, University of California, Davis, CA 95616

BALTZ, Dr. Donald M., Postdoctoral Research Associate, Department of Wildlife and Fisheries Biology, University of California, Davis, CA 95616

BARNES, Mr. Robert A., President, California Wilderness Coalition, P.O. Box 269, Porterville, CA 93258

BARRY, Dr. W. James, State Park Plant Ecologist, California Department of Parks and Recreation, P.O. Box 2390 (1416 Ninth Street), Sacramento, CA 95811

BEACH, Mr. Bruce C., Hydraulic Engineer, Reservoir Regulation Unit, U.S. Army Corps of Engineers, Los Angeles District, 300 N. Los Angeles Street, Los Angeles, CA 90053

BELLUOMINI, Ms. Linda, Wildlife Biologist, Natural Resources Office, Marine Corps Base, Camp Pendleton, CA 92083

BENEDICT, Dr. Nathan B., Assistant Professor, Department of Biology, University of Nevada, Reno, NV 89557

BENZ, Mr. Carl T., Staff Mammologist, Office of Endangered Species, USDI Fish and Wildlife Service, 1230 N Street, Sacramento, CA 95814

BERRY, Dr. Kristin, California Desert District, USDI Bureau of Land Management, 1695 Spruce Street, Riverside, CA 92507

BLOOM, Mr. Peter H., Staff Biologist, Condor Research Center, National Audubon Society, 87 N. Chestnut Street, Ventura, CA 93001

BOLLMAN, Dr. Frank, Resources Consultant, 1025 Vanderbilt Way, Sacramento, CA 95825

BOTTORFF, Mr. Richard L., Graduate Student, Department of Land, Air, and Water Resources, University of California, Davis, CA 95616

BRITTNER, Mr. Gary, Forester, Wood Energy Program, California Department of Forestry, 1416 Ninth Street, Room 1342-7, Sacramento, CA 95814

BROCKMAN, Mr. Ronald, Outdoor Recreation Planner, USDI Bureau of Reclamation, 2800 Cottage Way, Sacramento, CA 95825

BRODE, Mr. John, Leader, Amphibian and Reptile Project, Endangered Species Program, California Department of Fish and Game, 1701 Nimbus Road, Rancho Cordova, CA 95670

BROOKS, Mr. Donald L., Research Biologist, P.O. Box 516, Ehrenberg, AZ 85334

BROTHERS, Mr. Timothy S., Graduate Student, Geography Department, University of California, Los Angeles, CA 90024

BROWN, Mr. David, Wildlife Biologist, Arizona Game and Fish Department, 2222 W. Greenway Road, Phoenix, AZ 85023

BULLARD, Mr. Gary, Resource Conservationist, USDA Soil Conservation Service, 2828 Chiles Road, Davis, CA 95616

BURGESS, Mr. Richard, Planning Consultant, 562 S. Rice Road, Ojai, CA 93023

BURNS, Mr. James W., 5130 El Cemonte, Davis, CA 95616

BURY, Dr. R. Bruce, Research Zoologist, USDI Fish and Wildlife Service, 1300 Blue Spruce Drive, Fort Collins, CO 80521

BUSCH, Mr. David E., Wildlife Biologist, USDI Bureau of Reclamation, P.O. Box 427, Boulder City, NV 89005

CAPELLI, Mr. Marc Henri, Coastal Analyst, California Coastal Commission, 735 State Street, Suite 232, Santa Barbara, CA 93101

CAROTHERS, Dr. Steven W., Head, Department of Biology, Museum of Northern Arizona, Flagstaff, AZ 86001

CARTER, Mr. Lee, Supervising Engineer, California Department of Water Resources, 3251 S Street, Sacramento, CA 95816

CAVALLARO, Ms. Janet I., Graduate Student, Department of Forestry and Resource Management, University of California, Berkeley, CA 94720

CHAIMSON, Mr. J. Fred, Senior Engineer, California Department of Water Resources, 1416 Ninth Street, Room 1653-2A, Sacramento, CA 95814

CHANNING, Dr. Ed, 1115 Sierra Drive, Turlock, CA 95380

CLAY, Mr. David H., Agricultural Engineer, Project Coordinator, Northern California-Nevada Resource Conservation and Development, P.O. Box 888, Alturas, CA 96101

COE, Mr. Thomas S., Environmental Specialist, Regulatory Section, U.S. Army Corps of Engineers, Sacramento District, 650 Capitol Mall, Sacramento, CA 95814

COLT, Mr. John, Senior Development Engineer, Department of Civil Engineering, University of California, Davis, CA 95616

COURTOIS, Dr. Louis, Christian Heritage College, 2100 Greenfield, El Cajon, CA 92021

CRAWFORD, Mr. John, Chief, Division of Wildlife, USDI Bureau of Land Management, Washington, D.C. 20240

CRUMPACKER, Dr. David W., Professor, Department of Environmental, Population, and Organismic Biology, University of Colorado, Campus Box B-334, Boulder, CO 80309

CUMMINGS, Mr. Earle W., President, Natural Resource Biologists' Association, 13206 Jackson Road, Sloughhouse, CA 95683

CURRY, Dr. Robert R., Provost, College Eight, University of California, Santa Cruz, CA 95064

DAAR, Ms. Sheila, Project Director, BIRC, Inc., 1307 Acton Street, Berkeley, CA 94706

DAVILLA, Mr. William, Plant Ecologist, BioSystems Analysis, Inc., 530 Howard Street, San Francisco, CA 94105

DAWSON, Dr. Kerry J., Assistant Professor, Department of Environmental Design, University of California, Davis, CA 95616

DEDRICK, Mr. Kent G., Research Program Specialist, State Lands Commission, 1807 Thirteenth Street, Sacramento, CA 95814

DENNIS, Mrs. Nona B., Vice President, ESA/ Madrone, 23-B Pamaron Way, Novato, CA 94947

DISANO, Mr. John, Research Biologist, Center for Environmental Studies, P.O. Box 686, Palo Verde, CA 92266

DUBOIS, Mr. Marc, President, Friends of the River, 3901 San Miguel, Sacramento, CA 95819

DUHNKRACK, Ms. Nancy E., 2321 SW Sherwood Drive, Portland, OR 97201

DUMMER, Mr. Kevin, Staff Research Associate, Department of Forestry and Resource Management, University of California, Berkeley, CA 94720

DUNHAM, Mr. Ray, Division of Water Rights, State Water Resources Control Board, P.O. Box 2000, Sacramento, CA 95810

DUNNING, Mr. Harrison C., Professor, King Hall School of Law, University of California, Davis, CA 95616

EDGAR, Mr. Harold R., Secretary, California Wildlife Federation, P.O. Box 9504, Sacramento, CA 95823

ELLIS, D., c/o Nona Dennis, ESA/ Madrone, 23-B Pamaron Way, Novato, CA 94947

ENDO, Mr. Al, Chief of Resources, California Desert District, USDI Bureau of Land Management, 1695 Spruce Street, Riverside, CA 92507

ENG, Dr. Larry L., Associate Fishery Biologist, California Department of Fish and Game, 1416 Ninth Street, Sacramento, CA 95814

ENGLAND, Mr. A. Sidney, Department of Wildlife and Fisheries Biology, University of California, Davis, CA 95616

ERMAN, Dr. Don C., Professor, Department of Forestry and Resource Management, University of California, Berkeley, CA 94720

ERMAN, Ms. Nancy A., Assistant Specialist—Aquatic Biology, Department of Forestry and Resource Management, University of California, Berkeley, CA 94720

ERWIN, Mrs. Myra, 2450 Marshall Way, Sacramento, CA 95818

FALASCO, Mr. Michael R., Agricultural Specialist, Senate Office of Research, 1100 J Street, Suite 650, Sacramento, CA 95814

FANCHER, Mr. Jack M., Biologist, Division of Ecological Services, USDI Fish and Wildlife Service, 24000 Avila Road, Laguna Niguel, CA 92677

FAYE, Mr. E.M., Jr., Star Route, Knights Landing, CA 95645

FAZIO, Hon. Vic, Congressman, Fourth District, California, U.S. House of Representatives, 1421 Longworth Building, Washington, D.C. 20515

FINCH, Mr. Clarence U., Jr., Area Agronomist, Area 3, USDA Soil Conservation Service, 1130 O Street, Fresno, CA 93721

FITZHUGH, Dr. E. Lee, Extension Wildlife Specialist, Cooperative Extension, University of California, Davis, CA 95616

FLESHMAN, Ms. Carolyn, 1924 S. Salem Drive, Anchorage, AK 99504

FONG, Mr. Calvin C., Chief, Regulatory Functions Branch, U.S. Army Corps of Engineers, San Francisco District, 211 Main Street, San Francisco, CA 94105

FOREMAN, Dr. Larry D., District Wildlife Biologist, USDI Bureau of Land Management, California Desert District, 1695 Sruce Street, Riverside, CA 92507

GAIDULA, Mr. Peter, State Park Forester, California Department of Parks and Recreation, P.O. Box 2390, 1416 Ninth Street, Sacramento, CA 95811

GAINES, Mr. David, Independent Researcher, P.O. Box 29, Lee Vining, CA 93541

GOLDMAN, Dr. Bernard H., Environmental Specialist, Santa Clara Valley Water District, 5750 Almaden Expressway, San Jose, CA 95118

GRAY, Ms. Violet, c/o James Greaves, Santa Barbara Museum of Natural History, 2559 Puesta del Sol Road, Santa Barbara, CA 93105

GRAY, Mr. Randy, Biologist, USDA Soil Conservation Service, 2828 Chiles Road, Davis, CA 95616

GREAVES, Mr. James, Curatorial Assistant, Santa Barbara Museum of Natural History, 2559 Puesta del Sol, Santa Barbara, CA 93105

GRIGGS, Dr. Gary B., Professor of Earth Sciences, University of California, Santa Cruz, CA 95064

HAFENFELD, Mr. Bruce A., Owner, Hafenfeld Ranch, and Manager, Joughlin Ranch, P.O. Box 1006, Lake Isabella, CA 93240

HALL, Mr. Guy, President, Cal-Oak Lumber Company, P.O. Box 689, Oroville, CA 95965

HALLBERG, Mr. Donald L., Associate Data Processing Analyst, California Department of Fish and Game, 1701 Nimbus Road, Rancho Cordova, CA 95670

HANES, Dr. Ted L., Professor, Department of Biology, California State University, Fullerton, 800 N. State College Boulevard, Fullerton, CA 92634

HARRIS, Dr. Richard W., Professor, Department of Environmental Horticulture, University of California, Davis, CA 95616

HECHT, Mr. Barry, Senior Hydrologist/Geomorphologist, HEA, A Division of J.H. Kleinfelder and Associates, 1901 Olympic Boulevard, Walnut Creek, CA 94796

HESSELDENZ, Mr. Thomas F., Preserve Manager, McCloud River Preserve, The Nature Conservancy, P.O. Box 409, McCloud, CA 96057

HEWETT, Mr. Rick, Preserve Manager, Kern River Preserve, The Nature Conservancy, P.O. Box 1662, Weldon, CA 93283

HILL, Mr. Elgar, Principal, Elgar Hill, Environmental Analysis, 65H Gate Five Road, Sausilito, CA 94965

HILLIER, Mr. Gerald E., District Manager, California Desert District, USDI Bureau of Land Management, Riverside, CA 92507

HOLSTEIN, Mr. Glen, Lecturer, Department of Botany, University of California, Davis, CA 95616

HUDDLESTUN, Mr. James R., River Programs Manager, Division of Special Studies, USDI National Park Service, 450 Golden Gate Avenue, San Francisco, CA 94102

HUFFMAN, Dr. Robert Terry, Senior Project Specialist, Woodward and Clyde Consultants, 100 Pringle Avenue, Walnut Creek, CA 94596

HUNTER, W.C., c/o B.W. Anderson, Center for Environmental Studies, 201 S. Palm, Blythe, CA 92225

HUNTER, Ms. Serena, Research Forester, Riverside Fire Laboratory, USDA Forest Service, 4955 Canyon Crest Drive, Riverside, CA 92507

JAMES, Mr. M.R., Senior Water Resources Control Engineer, Water Quality Control Board, Lahontan Region, P.O. Box 14367, South Lake Tahoe, CA 95702

JENKS, Mr. James S., Principal Engineer, Leedshill-Herkenhoff, 1275 Market Street, San Francisco, CA 94103

JENSEN, Ms. Deborah, Plant Ecologist, Natural Diversity Data Base, California Department of Fish and Game, 1416 Ninth Street, Sacramento, CA 95814

JOHNS, Mr. Preston, Lands Coordinator, Wildlife Management Branch, California Department of Fish and Game, 1416 Ninth Street, Sacramento, CA 95814

JOHNSON, Dr. R. Roy, Unit Leader, Cooperative National Park Resources Studies Unit, USDI National Park Service, University of Arizona, 125 Biological Sciences (East) Building 43, Tuscon, AZ 85721

JONES, Mr. Bruce E., Executive Director, The Wildlife Conservancy, P.O. Box 161206, Sacramento, CA 95816

JONES, Mr. Terry, Staff Archaeologist, Sonoma State University, 1801 E. Cotati Avenue, Rohnert Park, CA 94928

JONES, Mr. Thomas T., Engineer, Montecito Sanitary District, 1042 Monte Cristo Lane, Santa Barbara, CA 93108

KAPLAN, Mr. Ken, Past President, Sacramento Valley Landowners Association, P.O. Box 606, Hamilton City, CA 95951

KATIBAH, Mr. Edwin F., 3253 Camino Colorados, Walnut Creek, CA 94596

KATLAS, Mr. Edwin G., Assistant District Manager, USDI Bureau of Land Management, 555 Leslie Street, Ukiah, CA 95482

KAUFMAN, Mr. Darrell, 1924 S. Salem Drive, Anchorage, AK 99504

KELLEY, Mr. Don W., Aquatic Biologist, D.W. Kelley and Associates, P.O. Box 634, Newcastle, CA 95658

KERBAVAZ, Ms. Joanne H., Biologist, California Department of Transportation, 4745 Cape May Avenue, San Diego, CA 92107

KIER, Mr. William M., Environmental Policy Specialist, Senate Office of Research, State Senate, State Capitol, Sacramento, CA 95814

KILBURN, K.S., c/o Daniel F. Williams, Department of Biology, Stanislaus State College, Turlock, CA 95380

KINDEL, Mr. Fred, Environmental Resources Planner, U.S. Army Corps of Engineers, 650 Capitol Mall, Sacramento, CA 95814

KLEBENOW, Dr. Don, Professor, Range, Wildlife, and Forestry, University of Nevada, Reno, NV 89557

KLITZ, Dr. William, Research Scientist, John Muir Institute, 1016 Grayson Street, Berkeley, CA 94710

KNIGHT, Dr. Allen W., Professor, Department of Land, Air, and Water Resources, University of California, Davis, CA 95616

KOBETICH, Ms. Gail C., Field Supervisor, Office of Endangered Species, USDI Fish and Wildlife Service, 1230 N Street, Sacramento, CA 95814

KONDOLF, Dr. G. Matt, Department of Geography and Environmental Engineering, The Johns Hopkins University, Baltimore, MD 21218

KRAEMER, Mr. Thomas J., Geographer/Biologist, Route 2, Box 77C, Corning, CA 96021

KRAMER, Mr. John R., Attorney, California Department of Water Resources, 1416 Ninth Street, Room 1118-11, Sacramento, CA 95814

KULES, Mr. Ken, Ecologist, Environmental Resources Branch, U.S. Army Corps of Engineers, Los Angeles Branch, P.O. Box 2711, Los Angeles, CA 900532

KUNOFSKY, Dr. Judith, Former National President, Zero Population Growth, 2332 Valley Street, Berkeley, CA 94702

KUYKENDALL, Mr. James D., Supervising Engineer, State Water Quality Control Board, Lahontan Region, P.O. Box 14367, South Lake Tahoe, CA 95702

LAROSA, Mr. Ron, Regional Director, Southeast California, Ducks Unlimited, 1976 Willow Street, San Diego, CA 92106

LANGLEY, Mr. Russell, 6387 Mother Lode Drive, Placerville, CA 95667

LAUDENSLAYER, Dr. William F., Jr., Regional Wildlife Ecologist, Tahoe National Forest, USDA Forest Service, Highway 49 and Coyote Street, Nevada City, CA 95959

LAURENCE, Ms. Lee, Writer-Editor, USDI Bureau of Reclamation, 2800 Cottage Way, Sacramento, CA 95825

LAYMON, Mr. Stephen A., Graduate Student, Department of Forestry and Resource Management, University of California, Berkeley, CA 94720

LEISER, Dr. Andrew T., Professor, Department of Environmental Horticulture, University of California, Davis, CA 95616

LEVEN, Mr. Andrew, Director, Watershed Management Staff, Pacific Southwest Region, USDA Forest Service, 630 Sansome Street, San Francisco, CA 94111

LIEBERMAN, Mr. Howard, Environmental Resources Branch, U.S. Army Corps of Engineers, South Pacific Division, 630 Sansome Street, San Francisco, CA 94111

LINCK, G.L., c/o Gene R. Trapp, Department of Biological Sciences, California State University, Sacramento, CA 95819

LOCKHARD, Mr. William M., Staff Conservationist, Ventura County Flood Control District, 800 S. Victoria Avenue, Ventura, CA 93009

LUCOFF, Mr. William O., Scientist, Bechtel Group, Inc., 1745 Beach, #14, San Francisco, CA 94123

LUDWIG, Dr. Robert, Environmental Engineer, Department of Civil Engineering, University of California, Davis, CA 95616

MACDONALD, Mr. Thomas C., Principal Engineer, Leedshill-Herkenhoff, 1275 Market Street, San Francisco, CA 94103

MACIAS, Mr. Phil, Supervisory Civil Engineer, Division of Planning, USDI Bureau of Reclamation, 2800 Cottage Way, Sacramento, CA 95825

MAHONEY, Mr. Donald, 1115 Post Street, # 21, San Francisco, CA 94109

MALCOLM, Kim, Research Assistant, Center for Natural Resource Studies, John Muir Institute, 1016 Grayson Street, Berkeley, CA 94710

MANAGO, Mr. Frank, Ecologist, Environmental Resources Branch, U.S. Army Corps of Engineers, Los Angeles Branch, P.O. Box 2711, Los Angeles, CA 90053

MARQUISS, Ms. Sandra, Report Editor, USDI Bureau of Reclamation, 1303 Darlene Way, #304B, Boulder City, NV 89005

MARTIN, Mr. Kenneth E., Supervisor, SCORP Unit, California Department of Parks and Recreation, P.O. Box 2390, Sacramento, CA 95811

MCBRIDE, Dr. Joe R., Associate Professor, Department of Forestry and Resource Management, University of California, Berkeley, CA 94720

MCGRATH, Mr. James P., Coastal Analyst, California Coastal Commission, 631 Howard Street, Fourth Floor, San Francisco, CA 94105

MCKEVITT, Mr. Jim, Field Supervisor, Ecological Services, USDI Fish and Wildlife Service, 2800 Cottage Way, Sacramento, CA 95825

MEENTS, Dr. Julie K., P.O. Box 4339, Las Cruces, NM 88003

MELO, Mr. Jere, Division Forester, Georgia-Pacific Corporation, 90 W. Redwood Avenue, Fort Bragg, CA 95437

MEYER, Ms. Nancy, 2513 Seville Court, Davis, CA 95616

MEYER, Mr. Philip, Meyer Resources, Inc., P.O. Box 965, Davis, CA 95616

MIKKELSEN, Ms. Patricia, Staff Archaeologist, Sonoma State University, 1801 E. Cotati Avenue, Rohnert Park, CA 94928

MORRIS, Mr. Robert H., Recreation Planner, Central District, California Department of Water Resources, 3251 S Street, Room D-12, Sacramento, CA 95816

MOTRONI, Mr. Robert S., Wildlife Biologist, Plumas National Forest, USDA Forest Service, P.O. Box 7, Blairsden, CA 96103

MOYLE, Dr. Peter, Associate Professor, Department of Wildlife and Fisheries Biology, University of California, Davis, CA 95616

MULLINS, Mr. Chuck, Fish and Wildlife Biologist, USDI Fish and Wildlife Service, P.O. Box 1306, Albuquerque, NM 87103

NEDEFF, Ms. Nicole E., Graduate Student, Department of Geography, University of California, Berkeley, CA 94720

NELSON, Dr. Charles W., Cartographic Technician, Department of Geography, California State University, Chico, CA 95929

NELSON, Mr. James R., Staff Biologist, California Energy Commission, 1111 Howe Avenue, MS-32, Sacramento, CA 95825

NILSEN, Dr. Erik Tallak, Assistant Professor, Department of Biology, Virginia Polytechnic Institute and State University, Blacksburg, VA 24061

NOLAN, Mr. Michael, Civil Engineer, U.S. Army Corps of Engineers, 650 Capitol Mall, Sacramento, CA 95814

OHMART, Dr. Robert D., Professor, Department of Zoology, Arizona State University, Tempe, AZ 85281

OLKOWSKI, Mr. W., c/o Sheila Daar, BIRC, Inc., 1307 Acton Street, Berkeley, CA 94706

PATTERSON, Mr. David W., Biologist, USDA Soil Conservation Service, 1350 N. Main, #1, Red Bluff, CA 96080

PEETERS, Mr. William V., Ecologist, Environmental Resources Branch, U.S. Army Corps of Engineers, Los Angeles District, P.O. Box 2711, Los Angeles, CA 90053

PERKINS, Ms. Deborah, 9768 Medina Drive, Santee, CA 92071

PESONEN, Mr. David, Former Director, California Department of Forestry, 1416 Ninth Street, Sacramento, CA 95814

PISTER, Mr. E. Philip, Fisheries Biologist, California Department of Fish and Game, 407 W. Line Street, Bishop, CA 93517

PLANTICO, Mr. Reuben C., Nerco, Inc., 111 S.W. Columbia, Portland, OR 97201

PLATTS, Dr. William S., Research Fishery Biologist, USDA Forest Service, 316 E. Myrtle Street, Boise, ID 83706

POTTER, Mr. Bob, Civil Engineer/Planner, California Department of Water Resources, 1416 Ninth Street, Sacramento, CA 95814

POWELL, Dr. Doug, Department of Geography, University of California, Berkeley, CA 94720

RAE, Mr. Stephen P., MUSCI, 1130 Cayetano Court, Napa, CA 94559

RAY, Mr. Daniel, Coastal Analyst, California Coastal Commission, P.O. Box 4946, Eureka, CA 95501

RENNING, Mr. John A., Hydraulic Engineer, Division of Planning, USDI Bureau of Reclamation, 2800 Cottage Way, Sacramento, CA 95825

RENSHAW, D.L., c/o Nona Dennis, ESA/ Madrone, 23-B Pamaron Way, Novato, CA 94947

RINEHART, Mr. Eldon E., General Manager, Reclamation Board, California Department of Water Resources, 1416 Ninth Street, Room 335-18, Sacramento, CA 95814

ROBERTS, Mr. Norman, 2810 Hidden Valley Road, La Jolla, CA 92037

ROBERTS, Dr. Robert C., Environmental Analyst, Oscar Larson and Associates, 204 Fourth Street, Eureka, CA 95501

RUCKS, Mr. Michael, Wildlife Biologist, USDI Bureau of Land Management, 425 E. Fourth Street, Safford, AZ 85546

RUGGERONE, Mr. Gregory T., Associate Environmental Planner, District 5, California Department of Transportation, 50 Higuera Street, San Luis Obispo, CA 93401

RUNDEL, Dr. Philip W., Professer, Department of Ecology and Evolutionary Biology, University of California, Irvine, CA 92717

SALWASSER, Dr. Hal, Regional Wildlife Ecologist, Pacific Southwest Region, Tahoe National Forest, USDA Forest Service, Highway 49, Nevada City, CA 95959

SANDS, Ms. Anne, 10 Throckmorton Lane, Mill Valley, CA 94941

SCHADLER, Mrs. Jean, Chairman, Modoc/Washoe Experimental Stewardship Committee, P.O. Box 23, Adel, OR 97620

SCHLORFF, Mr. Ronald W., Wildlife Biologist, California Department of Fish and Game, 1416 Ninth Street, Sacramento, CA 95814

SCHULTZE, Mr. Ronald F., State Biologist, USDA Soil Conservation Service, 2828 Chiles Road, Davis, CA 95616

SCOTT, Ms. Lauren, Civil Engineer, USDI Bureau of Reclamation, 2800 Cottage Way, MP-720, Sacramento, CA 95825

SEINWILL, Mr. Jerry, Acting Director, U.S. Water Resources Council, 2120 L Street, N.W., Washington, D.C. 20037

SHANFIELD, Mr. Allan, 423 N. Palm Drive, #205, Beverly Hills, CA 90210

SHAPIRO, Dr. Arthur M., Professor, Department of Zoology, University of California, Davis, CA 95616

SHARIFI, Dr. M. Rasoul, Post Graduate Research II, UCLA LBES, Division of Environmental Biology, 900 Vernon Avenue, Los Angeles, CA 90024

SHEA, Mr. Kevin, 1719 Poplar Lane, Davis, CA 95616

SHIMAMOTO, Ms. Karen, Forest Ecologist, Modoc National Forest, USDA Forest Service, 441 N. Main Street, Alturas, CA 96101

SIMPSON, Mr. James M., 4249 N. 34th Street, Phoenix, AZ 85018

SLAYBACK, Mr. Robert, Plant Materials Specialist, USDA Soil Conservation Service, 2828 Chiles Road, Davis, CA 95616

SMITH, Mr. Felix, Staff Environmental Specialist, USDI Fish and Wildlife Service, 2800 Cottage Way, Sacramento, CA 95825

SMITH, Mr. Kent A., California Department of Fish and Game, 1416 Ninth Street, Sacramento, CA 95814

SNIECKUS, Mr. Robert, Landscape Architect, USDA Soil Conservation Service, 2828 Chiles Road, Davis, CA 95616

SNYDER, Mr. Bruce W., Terrestrial Ecologist, Engineering Science, Inc., 10 Lakeside Lane, Denver, CO 80212

SOMMERSTROM, Dr. Sari, P.O. Box 538, Covelo, CA 95428

SPETH, Mr. John W., Assistant Chief, Planning Branch, California Department of Fish and Game, 1416 Ninth Street, Sacramento, CA 95814

STANLEY, Mr. John, Harvey and Stanley and Associates, Inc., 906 Elizabeth Street, P.O. Drawer E, Alviso, CA 95002

STANLEY, Mr. Stephen J., Coastal Analyst, California Coastal Commission, 735 State Street, Santa Barbara, CA 93101

STEFAN, Ms. Deborah, Wildlife Biologist, USDA Forest Service, 630 Sansome Street, San Francisco, CA 94111

STEINBLUM, Mr. Ivars, Watershed Management, Region 5, USDA Forest Service, 630 Sansome Street, San Francisco, CA 94111

STERN, Dr. Vernon M., Professor, Department of Entomology, University of California, Riverside, CA 92521

STEVENS, Mr. Jan, Deputy Attorney General, Office of the Attorney General, 1515 K Street, Suite 511, Sacramento, CA 95814

STINE, Mr. Scott, Graduate Student and Lecturer, Department of Geography, University of California, Berkeley, CA 94720

STONE, Dr. Edward C., Professor, Department of Forestry and Resource Management, University of California, Berkeley, CA 94720

STOWELL, Mr. Rich, Graduate Student, Department of Civil Engineering, University of California, Davis, CA 95616

STRAHAN, Ms. Jan, 475 16th Avenue, San Francisco, CA 94118

STRAUB, Mr. Peter, Landscape Architect, U.S. Army Corps of Engineers, 124 Baker Street, San Francisco, CA 94117

STROMBERG, Dr. Larry, Environmental Specialist, Larry Seeman Associates, 2927 Newbury Street, Suite C, Berkeley, CA 94703

SWEENEY, Mr. William D., 4566 Charleston Drive, Carmichael, CA 95608

TCHOBANOGLOUS, Dr. George, Professor, Department of Civil Engineering, University of California, Davis, CA 95616

THOMAS, Dr. Frank H., Assistant Director for Policy, U.S. Water Resources Council, 2120 L Street, N.W., Washington, D.C. 20037

TRAPP, Dr. Gene R., Professor of Biology, Department of Biological Sciences, California State University, Sacramento, CA 95819

TRIPP, Mr. David K., Environmental Protection Specialist, U.S. Army Corps of Engineers, 3333 Skaggs Springs Road, Geyserville, CA 95441

TSCHUDI, Ms. Laura, Ecologist, Environmental Resources, Los Angeles District, U.S. Army Corps of Engineers, P.O. Box 2711, Los Angeles, CA 90053

TURNER, Mr. John L., Environmental Services Supervisor, California Department of Fish and Game, 1416 Ninth Street, Sacramento, CA 95814

UNSICKER, Ms. Judith E., Environmental Specialist, State Water Quality Control Board, Lahontan Region, P.O. Box 14367, South Lake Tahoe, CA 95702

VAN RIPER, Dr. Charles, III, Unit Leader, National Park Service, Cooperative National Park Resources Studies Unit, Institute of Ecology, University of California, Davis, CA 95616

VERKADE, Mr. Robert, Environmental Resource Planner, U.S. Army Corps of Engineers, 650 Capitol Mall, Sacramento, CA 95814

VILKITIS, Dr. James R., Environmental Specialist, Department of Natural Resources Management, California State Polytechnic University, San Luis Obispo, CA 93407

VORTSTER, Mr. Peter, c/o David Gaines, P.O. Box 29, Lee Vining, CA 93541

WAKEMAN, Mr. Thomas H., 4718 Cowell Boulevard, Davis, CA 95616

WARNER, Dr. Richard E., Director, Field Studies Center, P.O. Box 402, Davis, CA 95616

WARNER, Ms. Susan A., Soil Scientist, State Water Quality Control Board, North Coast Region, 1000 Coddingtown Center, Santa Rosa, CA 95401

WARREN, Dr. Charles, 1225 Eighth Street, Suite 285, Sacramento, CA 95814

WEATHERFORD, Mr. Gary D., Senior Research Associate, Center for Natural Resource Studies, John Muir Institute, 1016 Grayson Street, Berkeley, CA 94710

WHEELER, Mr. Gary P., Ecologist, Ecological Services, USDI Fish and Wildlife Service, 24000 Avila Road, Laguna Niguel, CA 92677

WHISLER, E.D., c/o Gene R. Trapp, Department of Sciences, California State University, Sacramento, CA 95819

WHITE, C.A., Senior Water Resources Control Engineer, State Water Quality Control Board, Lahontan Region, P.O. Box 14367, South Lake Tahoe, CA 95702

WHITE, Mr. Greg, Staff Archaeologist, Sonoma State University, 1801 E. Cotati Avenue, Rohnert Park, CA 94928

WHITLOW, Mr. Thomas H., Research Associate, Urban Horticultural Institute, Cornell University, Ithaca, NY 14853

WILCOX, Mr. Glen I., Biologist, USDA Soil Conservation Service, 318 Cayugo Street, Suite 206, Salinas, CA 93901

WILLIAMS, Ms. Cynthia D., Graduate Student, California State University, Sacramento, CA 95819

WILLIAMS, Dr. Daniel F., Professor, Department of Biology, Stanislaus State College, Turlock, CA 95380

WILLIAMS, Mr. Jack E., Staff Ichthyologist, Office of Endangered Species, USDI Fish and Wildlife Service, 1230 N Street, Sacramento, CA 95814

WILLOUGHBY, Mr. John W., Botanist, USDI Bureau of Land Management, 2800 Cottage Way, Sacramento, CA 95825

WOMELDORF, Mr. Don J., Chief, Vector Biology and Control Section, California Department of Health Services, 744 P Street, Sacramento, CA 95814

WOODLEY, Dr. Donald R., Hydrologist, School of Agriculture and Natural Resources, California State Polytechnic University, San Luis Obispo, CA 93407

WOODROOF, Mr. Wayne, Coastal Planner, North Coast Region, California Coastal Commission, P.O. Box 4946, Eureka, CA 95501

ZENTNER, Mr. John, State Coastal Conservancy, 1330 Broadway, Oakland, CA 94612

Ambrosia, 401, 724; dumosa, 695; psilostachya, 610, 648
Ambrysus: amargosus, 710, 717, 718; californicus 710; funebris, 710
Ambystoma, 32; gracile, 32; macrodactylum, 32
Amentiferae, 7, 10
American Fisheries Society, 434
American Forestry Association, 408
American Pulpwood Association, 744
American River (Calif.), 24, 33, 185, 613, 729, 748, 899; Parkway, 748; south fork of, 505-514, 748
American River Canyon Association of West Sacramento, 507
American River Recreation Association, 509, 748
Amerindians, 285, 384, 401, 703, 711-712, 716, 718, 720, 767, 768, 770, 773-779, 786, 883, 929; Asazi, 384; Paiute, 810; Pomo, 780-782; Washoe, 810; Wintu, 786; Yokut, 972
Ametadoria (= Sturmia) harrisinae, 979-980
Ammonia, 497, 821
Amphibians, 30-36, 414
Amphispiza: belli, 207, 621, 623, 624; bilineata, 207, 701
Anacardiaceae, 648
Anadonta, 778
Anaea andria, 936
Anagrius epos, 978-979
Anas: acuta, 205, 493, 599; americana, 205, 599; clypeata, 205, 599; crecca carolinensis, 599; cyanoptera, 205, 493, 599; discors, 205, 599; platyrhynchos, 205, 432, 493, 599; strepera, 205, 599
Andree Clark Bird Refuge (Calif.), 680
Aneides: ferreus, 32; flavipunctatus, 32; lugubris, 32
Anemopsis californica, 517, 521
Angling, 784, 786-787, 789-790, 792. See also Fish
Annadel State Park (Sonoma Co., Calif.), 764
Anniella pulchra, 34
Anopheles, 968, 969
Antelope, pronghorn (Antilocapra americana), 210-213, 972
Anthemis cotula, 648
Anthracnose (Gnomonia platani), 10, 197
Anthus spinoletta, 600, 602
Antilocapra americana, 210-213, 972
Antiquities Act (1906), 774
Anti-regulatory movement, 281-286, 386, 388, 640, 670; and farmers, 730, 960; future of, 282, 284-286
Antrozous pallidus, 943
Anza-Borrego Desert State Park (Calif.), 764, 765
Apanteles harrisinae, 979-980
Aphelocoma coerulescens, 89, 493, 593
Aphid, green peach, 971
Apiaceae, 648
Aplodontia rufa, 951, 952, 953, 954; californica, 952, 953; nigra, 952, 954; phaea, 952, 954
Apocynaceae, 648
Apocynum cannabinum var. glaberrimum, 648
Apodidae, 191
Apple, 971
Applegate Reservoir (Ore.-Calif.), 33
Aquaducts, 80

Aquila chrysaetos, 205, 789
Aravaipa Creek (Ariz.), 97, 101, 103, 105, 107
Arborimus albipes, 952, 954
Arbutus menziesii, 86, 88, 135, 197, 447
Archaeological sites, 338, 712, 773-779, 788, 789, 801, 810; sensitive, criteria for, 775
Archilochus alexandri, 206, 207, 208, 493, 592-593
Arctostaphylos, 364; glandulosa, 675; manzanita, 447; uva-ursi, 448
Arcto-Tertiary Geoflora, 2-3, 15, 89, 935, 936, 939
Ardea herodias, 205, 484, 491, 493, 599, 637, 696, 788
Aristolochia, 936; californica, 23, 48, 348, 936, 937
Arizona Academy of Science, 408
Arizona Department of Game and Fish, 408
Arizona Department of Planning and Development, 408
Arizona Natural Areas Program, 408
Arizona-Nevada Academy of Science, 408
Arizona State Parks Department, 408
Arkansas Act of 1850 (Arkansas Swamp Act), 28, 55, 358
Armyworm, yellow-striped, 972
Arnold v. Mundy (1821), 270
Arrow-grass, three-ribbed (Triglochin striata), 650
Arrowweed (Tessaria/Pluchea sericea), 191, 393, 394, 619, 620, 624, 696, 707
Artemisia, 211, 617, 724, 882; arbuscula, 210, 211, 212; californica, 448, 609, 884; cana, 210, 211, 212; douglasiana, 23, 48, 152, 309, 572, 588, 606, 607, 609, 610, 648, 839, 900, 909; ludoviciana, 98; rothrockii, 93; spinescens, 77, 78; tridentata, 77, 78, 210, 531, 606, 609, 953
Arthropods. See Insects; Mites; Spiders; Ticks
Arundo donax, 445, 573, 650, 841, 886
Ascaphus, 32; truei, 32, 33
Asclepiadaceae, 648
Asclepias fascicularis, 648
Ash (Fraxinus), 6-7, 60, 65, 66, 112; dwarf (F. anomala), 696; Oregon (F. latifolia), 23, 48, 60, 61, 86, 87, 89, 110, 116, 117, 118, 152, 153, 309, 364, 365, 366, 372, 447, 448, 466, 511, 568, 588, 650, 669, 749, 900, 909, 912; velvet (F. velutina), 99, 102, 104, 105, 106, 107
Ash Meadows (Nye Co., Nev.-Inyo Co., Calif.), 716-719
Asio: flammeus, 573; otus, 206, 592
Asparagus, garden (Asparagus officinalis), 650
Aspen (Populus tremuloides), 10, 392, 528, 805, 965
Assimineidae, 709
Associations: faunal, 692; floral, 467-468, 578-579, 619, 620, 691, 847, 882-883, 908
Aster (Aster), 93; slim (A. exilis), 648; Suisun (A. chilensis var. lentus), 645, 648
Aster: alpigenus, 93; chilensis, 645, 648, 937; exilis, 648
Asteraceae, 648
Astragalus phoenix, 717, 718
Athel (Tamarix aphylla), 191, 457

Atlides halesus, 936, 940
Atmospheric circulation, 238
Atriplex, 23, 522, 556, 707; canescens, 77, 78; confertifolia, 77, 78, 695; lentiformis, 48, 448, 524, 626, 628, 629, 630, 682, 683, 739, 740, 741, 743; parryi, 77, 78; patula, 675; polycarpa, 78; semibaccata, 556, 649; torryi 76, 77, 78, 524, 526
Audubon Society. See National Audubon Society
Auriparus flaviceps, 600, 621, 622, 623, 703
Avecennia germinans, 396, 399, 400
Avena, 614; barbata, 71; fatua, 552, 553, 573, 606, 650, 972
Avifauna, riparian, 18-19, 190-195, 203-209, 338, 368, 369, 379, 406, 407, 408, 483, 486, 578-586, 587-597, 598-604, 619-625, 626-631, 695-705
Avocet, American (Recurvirostra americana), 205, 207, 600
Avoyelles Sportsmen's League v. Alexander, 251-252, 256
Aythya: affinis, 599; americana, 599; collaris, 599; marila, 599; valisineria, 599
Azalea, western (Rhododendron occidentale), 900
Azolla, 385; filiculoides, 152

Baccharis, 393, 394; douglasii, 48, 610, 648; glutinosa, 14, 48, 98, 101, 102, 105, 106, 607, 609, 886; pilularis, 349, 351, 364, 365, 445, 447, 448, 449, 556, 606, 609, 648, 675, 908, 909; sarothroides, 98, 102; viminea, 14, 23, 48, 110, 111, 112, 114, 115, 197, 199, 445, 483, 490, 499, 648, 839
Baccharis, salt marsh (Baccharis douglasii), 648
Bacteria, 162, 474, 916, 976; coliform, 497-498, 821
Badger (Taxidea taxus), 943, 945
Baetis, 170
Baird Limestone Formation (Calif.), 786, 789, 792
Baja California (Mexico), 390-403, 722, 724
Baker Creek (Calif.), 80
Bamboo, 549, 863; Phylostachos bambosoides, 48
Bank stabilization, 130, 131, 158, 160, 168, 169, 173, 186, 208, 248, 434, 452-458, 574, 613, 617, 661-662, 729, 745, 746, 752, 761, 795-799, 805, 812, 863, 895, 897, 916, 985; costs of, 458, 574, 797; economic importance of, 452; failure of, 797; physical vs. vegetative, 455-458, 538-565, 571, 574; principles of, 452-454. See also Erosion; Revetment; Riprap
Barberry (Berberis): California (B. dictyota), 447; Japanese (B. thunbergii), 448
Barley (Hordeum), 614; Mediterranean (H. geniculatum), 651
Basin and Range Phytogeographic Province, 211, 425
Bass: black, 257, 572; largemouth (Micropterus salmoides), 849, 930; striped (Morone saxatilis), 185, 225, 572
Bassariscus astutas, 789, 906-914, 921, 943, 945

Bassia hyssopifolia, 78, 439, 628, 629, 740, 741
Basswood, 971
Bat: big brown (Eptesicus fuscus), 943; Brazilian free-tailed (Tadarida brasiliensis), 943; hoary (Lasiurus cinereus), 943; pallid (Antrozous pallidus), 943; red (Lasiurus borealis), 943; silver-haired (Lasionycteris noctivagans), 943; spotted (Euderma maculatum), 943; Townsend's big-eared (Plecotus townsendii), 943; western mastiff (Eumops perotis), 943
Batis maritima, 395, 396, 397, 399, 400
Batrachoseps, 32; aridus, 32, 33; attenuatus, 32; campi, 32, 33; pacificus, 32
Battus philenor, 937; hirsuta, 936, 939
Bay, California (Umbellularia californica), 3, 86, 110, 116, 117, 348, 349, 351, 354, 355, 365, 445, 447, 660, 675, 887
Bay Conservation and Development Commission, 826
Bayou Natchitoches Basin (La.), 251
Bays, 250, 253, 500
Beach, 246, 640
Bear, 962
Bearberry (Arctostaphylos uva-ursi), 448
Bear grass (Nolina microcarpa), 99, 103
Bear River (Calif.), 24
Beaver (Castor canadensis), 80-81, 208, 368, 416, 443, 572, 731-738, 749, 787, 810, 943, 945, 952, 962; mountain (Aplodontia rufa), 951, 952, 953, 954
Bedload, 146, 147
Bedrock. See Substrate
Bed shear stress, 111, 115
Bed straw (Galium aparine), 904
Beeler Creek (San Diego Co., Calif.), 655-656
Bees, 935
Beetles (Coleoptera), 177, 178, 179, 180; lady (Rodolia cardinalis), 975; riffle, 162, tiger, 709; valley elderberry longhorn (Desmocerus californicus dimorphus), 915, 916-917; water penny, 162; western spotted cucumber, 972
Belostomatidae, 709
Benches, 200
Bentgrass, 93, 98, 101, 102
Berberis: dictyota, 447; haematocarpa, 98, 102; thunbergii, 448
Berms, 570, 571, 654, 895
Bethlehem Steel Corporation, 260
Betula, 5-6, 10, 11, 13, 971; fontinalis, 5; glandulosa, 5; occidentalis, 5, 10; papyrifera, 6; pendula, 6; pubescens, 6
Betulaceae, 4, 5, 10, 11, 649
Bidens laevis, 648
Big Chico Creek (Calif.), 24
Bighorn sheep (Ovis canadensis), 764
Big Lagoon (Calif.), 660
Big Reservoir (Calif.), 210
Big River (Mendocino Co., Calif.), 661, 669-670
Big Sur River (Calif.), 135-136, 761
Bikeway Action Committee, 834
Bindweed: field (Convolvulus arvensis), 552, 553, 649; hedge (Calystegia sepium), 649
Bioenergetics, 160-164, 168-169, 183-184
Biogeographic regions, 483

Eisenhower Consortium for Western Environmental
  Forestry Research, 417-419
Elaeagnus angustifolia, 76, 77, 81, 82, 83
Elanus leucurus, 493, 573, 666
Elderberry (Sambucus), 916; S. mexicana,
  48, 61, 116, 117, 118, 152, 153, 348, 459, 606,
  609; blue (S. caerulea), 364, 365, 445,
  447, 449, 908, 909; blue (S. mexicana), 921
Elder, Pacific red (Sambucus callicarpa), 87,
  660
El Dorado Co. (Calif.) Board of Superevisors,
  505, 509, 513
El Dorado Co. (Calif.) Water Agency, 505
El Dorado Irrigation District, 505
El Dorado National Forest, 510
El Dorado Wine Grape Growers, 507
Eleanor Creek (Tuolumne Co., Calif.), 185-186
Electricity. See energy headings
Eleocharis, 560; acicularis, 561;
  coloradoensis, 561; macrostachys, 71, 561;
  palustris, 210, 561; parishii, 521, 522;
  pauciflora, 93
Elevation, tidal, 643
Elk Creek (Del Norte Co., Calif.), 86, 661,
  665-666
Elk (Cervus elaphus), 943, 972; tule (C.
  e. nannodes), 80, 774, 944, 946
Elm, 112, 971
Elymus, 614; cinereus, 525; condensatus,
  610; glaucus, 764, 765; triticoides, 556,
  651
Eminent domain, 283
Empetrichthys merriami, 717, 718
Empidonax: difficilis, 493, 592, 594;
  oberholseri/hammondii, 493; traillii,
  206, 207, 208, 493, 592, 594, 595; wrightii,
  206
Enceliopsis nudicaulis var. corrugata, 718
Encephalitis, 968
Endangered habitat, 323, 325, 404, 533, 718-719
Endangered species, 275, 278, 322-323, 425, 512,
  605-611, 617, 638, 639, 645, 670, 680, 717,
  718, 730, 743, 763, 788, 801, 884, 915-919,
  929, 930, 939, 950-956; criteria for, 323, 617,
  918
Endangered subspecies, 951
Endangered Species Act, 243, 281, 283, 335, 840,
  951
Endemism, 30, 390, 512, 709, 710, 716, 717, 718,
  763, 786, 789, 934, 935, 936
Energy: biofuel, 661, 744-746; combustion, 744;
  conservation, 507; and dissolved organic
  matter, 160, 168, 177, 183; flow, 453, 850-851;
  and fluvial processes, 847; hydraulic, 483;
  hydroelectric, 51, 82, 169, 233, 236, 237, 257,
  260, 267, 330, 333, 334, 379, 384, 484, 505,
  506, 534, 535, 675, 896, 917, 984; nuclear,
  744; photosynthetic, 16, 18, 162, 497, 520,
  522; potential, 110-111; solar, 507, 744, 847;
  wind, 507
Engelhardtia, 7
Enhancement, riparian, 459-464. See also
  Revegetation
Ensatina (Ensatina eschscholtzi), 32, 33
Environmental assessment, 339, 805-806
Environmental Council of Sacramento (Calif.),
  507, 833, 834
Environmental Data System (EDS), 335-339

Environmental design, 460-462, 465-470
Environmental education, 385, 435, 536, 640, 666,
  670, 730, 748, 790, 835, 844, 846-847, 850,
  874, 894, 958, 961
Environmental health protection, 968
Environmental impact, 236, 244, 247, 263, 336,
  339, 459, 500, 506, 514, 636, 639, 677, 693,
  787, 851, 886-887; criteria for, 500, 503;
  mitigation of, 283, 500, 526, 639, 652-659,
  669, 670, 677, 679, 746, 748, 754, 804, 812,
  813, 827, 845, 861, 886-887, 896; off-site vs.
  on-site, 761-765; report, 771, 834, 839;
  socioeconomic, 513; statement, 495, 507, 659,
  803, 804, 861, 868, 883
Environmental Law Institute, 408
Environmental movement, 231-232, 335, 356, 379,
  380, 386, 407, 408-409, 806, 833, 837, 844,
  869, 871, 939, 960; vs. anti-regulatory
  movement, 281-286; future of, 284-286, 880
Environmental planning, 784, 969
Environmental Planning and Information Council
  (El Dorado Co., Calif.), 507
Environmental protection, defined, 968
Environmental quality, 222, 238, 258, 270, 276,
  282, 405, 551, 898
Environmental regulation, 265-268, 274-280,
  281-286; enforcement of, 278-279; future of,
  284-286; inefficiency of, 275, 278, 279, 280;
  recommendations for reform of, 279-280;
  resistance to, 274, 278, 279, 281-286. See
  also Conservation measures; government
  headings; Legislation; Riparian systems, laws
  protecting
"Enviro-obstructionists," 509-510
Ephemeroptera, 162, 177, 180, 849
Epilimnion, 185
Epilobium ciliatum, 650
Epiphytes, 660
Eptesicus fuscus, 943
Equisetaceae, 649
Equisetum: arvense, 649; hyemale, 649
Eremophila alpestris, 493, 701
Erethizon dorsatum, 943
Eriodictyon, 609; trichocalyx, 884
Eriogonum, 93, 365, 522, 707; fasciculatum,
  99, 448, 884
Eriophyllum, 401
Erodium: botrys, 650; cicutarium, 650
Erosion, 9, 38, 52, 56, 59, 66, 83, 84, 88, 89,
  115, 120, 125, 130, 134, 142, 146, 162, 168,
  169-170, 200, 252, 358, 371, 404, 405, 414,
  426, 427, 452, 460, 510, 535, 538, 551, 553,
  555, 640, 751, 761, 763, 771, 781, 787, 795,
  800, 810, 826, 848-849; control of, 130-132,
  148, 166, 177, 226, 227, 261, 275, 276, 469,
  477, 549, 555, 558, 636, 652-659, 667, 745,
  761, 795-796, 827, 829, 897; ecological
  importance of, 662, 808, 917; factors
  increasing, 654, 751, 836; hazard rating
  system, 986; and hydraulic mining, 54; and
  liability, 659; measurement of, 797; and
  vegetation, 124-133, 166, 455-458, 477,
  538-565, 571, 574, 795, 827, 966. See also
  Bank stabilization; Sediment
Eryngium articulatum, 648
Erythrobalanus (subgenus), 11
Erythroneura elegantuala, 978-979
Eschrichtius gibbosus, 396, 397, 398, 399

Flood basin, 24, 52, 896, 897
Flood control, 54, 55-56, 120-123, 131-132,
142-149, 208, 226, 227, 230-232, 233, 236, 237,
239, 243, 257, 266, 330, 356, 371, 379, 393,
405, 406, 446, 447, 465, 484, 495, 534,
538-547, 548-550, 551-557, 558-565, 568, 605,
613, 617, 635, 661, 664, 666, 673, 675, 677,
682, 693, 729, 803, 833, 842, 844-860, 882-888,
895, 896; vs. aesthetics, 546, 548-550, 551,
554-556; costs of, 830, 851, 854; engineering,
853; goals of, 844; impacts of, 844-860,
886-887; limitations of, 143-145, 148, 149,
406, 546; methods of, 406, 534, 803, 836, 853,
896; and vector control, 969
Flood Control Act (1936), 236, 484, 538
Flood gradient, 559
Floodplain, 27, 28, 52, 54, 58, 61, 63, 66,
88-89, 197, 358, 368, 483, 809; human use of,
149, 237, 320, 358, 409, 833, 838; management
of, 237, 275, 278, 375, 386-389, 803-804, 829,
836, 837, 838; 100-year, 145, 446, 803, 809,
829, 837; plant distribution on, 351-355, 614,
838; vs. riparian system, 900; terraces,
110-111, 112, 115-117, 128, 469; vs. wetland,
900; zoning, 375, 379, 826
Flood storage, 233, 236, 238
Flood tolerance, 66, 559, 643-644, 885, 887, 890,
937, 953
Floodway, 683
Floristics, 361, 363, 368-371, 568, 645, 884-886
Fluvial process, 51-53, 58, 59, 60, 66, 110-111,
320, 358, 568, 571, 844, 847
Flycatcher, 484, 572; Ash-throated (Myiarchus
cinerascens), 206, 493, 583, 600, 621, 622,
742; Dusky/Hammond's (Empidonax
oberholseri/hammondii), 493; Gray (E.
wrightii), 206; Olive-sided (Myiarchus
tuberculifer), 493; Western (Empidonax
difficilis), 493, 592, 594; Wied's Crested
(Myiarchus tyrannulus), 493, 621, 622, 624,
742; Willow (Empidonax traillii), 206, 207,
208, 493, 592, 594, 595
Fog belt, California coastal, 939
Folsom Reservoir, 505
Fontilicella, 710
Food chain, 168, 183, 243, 252, 253, 405, 851,
973
Food web, 168, 851
Foothill Woodland, 86
Forbs, 210, 212, 349, 362, 363, 607, 667, 972
Ford, Gerald (President), 880
Forest and Rangeland Renewable Resources Planning
Act (1974), 236, 804
Forestiera neomexicana, 76, 77
Forest products, 984-985. See also Logging;
Silviculture
Forest Service Act, 986
Forni Diversion Dam (Calif.), 505, 510
Fort Hunter Liggett, 196
Fossil record, 466, 709, 786, 789
Fouquieria: diguete, 398; splendens, 695,
702
Fox: gray (Canis/Urocyon cinereoargenteus),
499, 731-732, 920-928, 943, 945; red
(Canis/Vulpes fulva), 924; red (V.
vulpes), 943, 945
Foxtail, 972; farmer's (Hordeum leporinum),
651

Frankenia grandifolia, 643
Frass, 160, 161
Fraxinaster (section), 7
Fraxinus, 6, 7, 17, 65, 66, 112; americana,
7; anomala, 7, 696; cuspidata, 6, 7;
dipetala, 7; excelsior, 7; gooddingii, 7;
latifolia, 7, 8, 23, 48, 60, 61, 86, 87, 89,
110, 116, 117, 118, 152, 153, 309, 364, 365,
366, 372, 447, 448, 466, 511, 568, 588, 650,
669, 749, 900, 908, 909, 912; nigra, 7;
ornus, 6, 7; pennsylvanica, 7;
quadrangulata, 7; velutina, 7, 99, 102,
104, 105, 106, 107
Fremontodendron californicum, 447
Freshwater Lagoon (Calif.), 660
Fresno River (Calif.), 24
Fresno Slough, 25
Friends of the River, 507, 832
Fringillids, 583
Frog, 732; bull- (Rana catesbeiana), 394,
397; Cascades (R. cascadae), 32; foothill
yellow-legged (R. boylei), 32, 35; leopard
(R. pipiens), 32; mountain yellow-legged
(R. muscosa), 32; red-legged (R.
aurora), 32, 33, 35, 394; spotted (R.
pretiosa), 32; tailed (Ascaphus truei),
32, 33. See also Toad; Treefrog
Frugivores, 629-630, 702, 740, 741
Fruitfly, Mediterranean (Ceratitis capitata),
971
Fuchsia, California (Zauschneria
californica), 448
Fuel, 726, 727; bio-, 661, 739-743, 744-746, 828;
petro-, 744. See also Energy; Logging
Fulica americana, 493, 599, 602, 603
Funding: allocation of, 806, 961; reductions in
government, 386, 388, 432, 465, 535, 685, 729,
759, 772, 966; sources of, 671, 792, 796,
811-813, 844, 864, 875, 898, 963, 965, 966-967
Fungi, 10, 162, 197
Fur harvest, 731-738

Gabions, 805
Gadwall (Anas strepera), 205, 599
Galium, 6; aparine, 909
Gallinula chloropus, 599
Gallinule, Common (Gallinula chloropus), 599
Gambusia affinis, 692, 930
Game. See Birds; Fish; Wildlife
Garambullo (Lophocereus schottii), 398
Garcia River (Calif.), 661
Gasterosteus aculeatus, 184; williamsoni,
15
Gavia immer, 599
Gentian, 93
Gentianaceae, 650
Gentianales, 6
Geococcyx californianus, 194, 629, 697
Georyssidae, 180
Geothlypis trichas, 206, 207, 494, 572, 594,
600, 602
Geraniaceae, 650
Geranium pilosum, 71
Germination, 60
Gerrhonotus, 33; coeruleus, 34;
multicarinatus, 34; panamintinus, 34
Gianelli, William (Assistant Secretary of the
Army), 255-256

Gibraltar Reservoir (Santa Barbara Co., Calif.), 605

Gila: bicolor snyderi, 930; orcutti, 692

Gila River (Ariz.), 97, 101, 103-104, 107, 405; valley (New Mexico), 377, 408

Gilliam, Hall, 40-41

Glaciation, 93, 94. See also Pleistocene

Glasswort, 400; Salicornia bigelovii, 395, 396, 397; S. subterminalis, 399

Glaucopsyche lygdamus, 936

Glen Canyon Dam, 405

Glides, 140

Global Resource, Environment, and Population Act (1981), 41

Globe mallow (Sphaeralcea), 99, 102, 103

Glycyrrhiza lepidota, 521, 522

Gnaphalium: chilense, 648; luteo-album, 648

Gnat: biting, 968-969; Leptoconops, 968; Culicoides, 968

Gnatcatcher (Polioptila): Black-tailed (P. melanura), 621, 622, 623, 703; Blue-gray (P. caerulea), 592, 594

Gnomonia platani, 10

Godwit, Marbled (Limosa fedoa), 600

Goldeneye, Common (Bucephala clangula), 599

Goldenrod, western (Solidago occidentalis), 648

Golden State Island, 121

Golden Trout Wilderness, 483

Goldfinch: American (Carduelis tristis), 206, 591, 593, 595, 600; Lawrence's (Spinus lawrencei), 494; Lesser (S. psaltria), 494, 593

Gold Rush, 27, 53, 54, 223, 712, 786, 828, 972

Goleta Valley Mosquito Abatement District, 680

Goodale Creek, 515

Goodwin Dam, 895

Goose: Canada (Branta canadensis), 205, 210, 574, 599; Snow (Chen caerulescens), 599

Gooseberry (Ribes), 348

Goose Lake, 25

Gopher, 544; Amargosa pocket (Thomomys bottae amargosa), 706, 709, 711; pocket (T. bottae), 368; southern pocket (T. bottae), 943

Gordonia lasianthus, 16

Gorton, Slade, 41

Goshawk (Accipiter gentilis), 788

Government, role of, in riparian protection, 226-227, 230-232, 236-237, 267, 269-273, 330, 335, 385, 386-389, 405, 408-409, 430-435, 514, 533, 634-641, 652, 661, 665, 670, 673, 684, 752-755, 758-761, 772, 792, 807, 811-813, 826-832, 864, 868-881, 889-890, 897, 898, 899-903, 955, 960-961; California, 826-829; changing interpretations of, 274, 281-286, 388, 899; future scenarios for, 284; local, 755, 829-830, 843, 844, 859, 864, 897, 963; nonregulatory, 285; state, 388, 754-755, 826-829, 844-845, 955

Governor of California, 231, 232, 684-685

Grackle, Great-tailed (Quiscalus mexicanus), 600

Grade control, 965

Gradient, 127-128, 143, 145-146, 162, 559, 848-849

Grading, 121, 142, 275

Graminae, 490

Graminoids, halophytic, 9

Granivores, 193, 598, 600-602, 627, 628, 629, 694, 701, 702, 740, 741

Grant deeds, 283

Grant Lake Reservoir (Calif.), 528, 529, 531

Grape, 976-980; Arizona wild (Vitis arizonica), 99; California wild (V. californica), 445, 447; wild (= California wild), 23, 48, 61, 71, 72, 309, 364, 365, 372, 511, 579, 749, 908, 909, 978; wild (V. girdiana), 979

Grapeleaf skeletonizer, western (Harrisina brillians), 979-981

Graphocephala atropunctata, 977

Grass, 152, 153, 161, 197, 362, 363, 371, 459, 490, 499, 511, 522, 552, 579, 588, 600; alkali, 519; alkali rye- (Elymus triticoides), 651; annual, 2, 579, 675; barnyard (Echinochloa crusdalli), 651; bear (Nolina microcarpa), 99; Bermuda (Cynodon dactylon), 98, 101, 102, 103, 121, 122, 439, 553, 571, 651, 740, 908, 976; brome (Bromus), 552, 573, 606, 614; bunch-, 934, 935; California hair- (Deschampsia caespitosa), 651; creeping rye (= alkali rye-), 556; dallis (Paspalum dilatatum), 651; deer (Muhlenbergia rigins), 765; ditch (Ruppia maritima), 399; giant squirreltail (Sitanion jubatum), 765; introduced, 644, 935, 972; Italian rye- (Lolium multiflorum), 651; Johnson (Sorghum halopensis), 552; knotroot bristle (Setaria geniculata), 651; lawn, 152; nodding needle- (Stipa cernua), 765; perennial, 23, 579, 675; perennial pepper- (Lepidium latifolium), 649; perla (Phalaris tuberosa 'Hurtiglumis'), 556; purple needle- (Stipa pulchra), 765; rabbit's-foot (Polypogon monspeliensis), 651; reed, 573; ripgut (Bromus diandrus), 650; rye (Elymus), 614; rye- (Lolium), 614; rye (taxon not given), 121, 122, 153; saw- (Cladium mariscus), 707; tropical, 401; tufted hair-, 93; water (Echinochloa crusgalli), 561, 976; wire (Juncus balticus), 521

Grasshopper, 972

Grass Lake (Calif.), 809

Grassland, 12, 16, 23, 68, 72, 79, 80, 164, 197, 211, 288, 310, 358, 414, 466, 483, 642, 643, 667, 765, 838, 896, 921, 938, 972

"Grass roots," 386, 432, 874

Gravel, 9, 59, 111, 112, 113, 114, 117, 128, 130, 134, 141, 151, 223, 427, 517, 607, 781, 849; commercial use of, 204, 257, 266, 275, 276-277, 278, 311, 319, 432, 771, 854, 864, 984; defined, 138

Gravelbar, 58, 60, 61, 63, 65, 66, 88, 158, 310, 469, 499, 708, 787; and salmonids, 136

Grazing, livestock, 38, 65, 80, 92, 94, 101, 104-105, 158, 160, 180, 186, 191, 196, 197, 199-200, 203, 208-209, 210, 212, 227, 314, 318, 356, 358, 361, 363, 366, 371, 384, 404, 407, 413-423, 426-427, 432, 459, 460, 477, 483, 484, 488, 553, 605, 661, 665, 675, 681, 763, 802, 803, 972, 984; benefits of, to pronghorn, 212; impact of, 407, 414-415, 424-428, 483, 763,

764, 805, 810, 916, 962, 965; management options, 415; research on, 415-418, 424-428; restrictions on, 197, 275, 277, 385, 409, 484, 805; and riparian regeneration, 198, 368, 414-415, 958; strategies of, 413, 414-427, 805; suitability of riparian zones for, 320-321, 358, 414, 418, 424, 667, 712, 720, 810
"Great American Interchange," 936
Great Basin Desert, 695, 702, 706
Great Basin Floristic Province, 211
Great Plains region, 413-423
Grebe: Eared (Podiceps nigricollis), 599; Pied-billed (Podilymbus podiceps), 599; Western (Aechmophorus occidentalis), 461, 599
Green Act (1868), 28
Greenbrier (Similax californica), 48
Grevillia, Noel (Grevillia noellii), 556
Greythorn (Condalia), 98, 102
Grindelia: cuneifolia, 953; fraxino-pratensis, 718; paludosa, 645, 648
Grinnell, Josepoh, 529
Grosbeak: Black-headed (Pheucticus melanocephalus), 206, 207, 209, 494, 591, 593, 594, 595; Blue (Guiraca caerulaea), 484, 494, 595, 621, 622; Evening (Hesperiphona vespertina), 593; Rose-breasted (Pheucticus ludovicianus), 484, 494, 697
Groundcover, 61, 65, 359, 362-363, 372
Groundsel, threadleaf (Senecio longilobus), 99, 102
Ground squirrel. See Squirrel, ground
Groundwater, 9, 13, 15, 53, 75, 80, 83, 112, 158, 160, 233, 257, 276, 357, 358, 442-443, 445, 463, 485, 495, 496, 501, 503, 528, 630, 683, 693, 723, 725, 827, 893; pumping, 82, 124, 150, 275, 277, 278, 356, 371, 399, 401, 404, 405, 424, 515-527, 534, 605, 676, 706, 711, 713, 718, 930
Grouse: Ruffed (Bonasa umbellus), 789; Sage (Centrocercus urophasianus), 210, 212
Grover City (San Luis Obispo Co., Calif.), 677-678
Grus: americana, 254; canadensis, 205, 384, 432, 574, 599
Guadalupe Dunes (Santa Barbara Co., Calif.), 678
Gueribo tree (Populus brandegeei), 400
Guilds, 599-600, 603; feeding, 190, 191, 193, 487, 579, 581, 583; nesting, 593
Guiraca caerulea, 484, 494, 595, 621, 622
Gull (Larus), 498; Bonaparte (L. philadelphia), 599; California (L. californicus), 206, 599; Herring (L. argentatus), 206, 599; Ring-billed (L. delawarensis), 206, 599
Gulo gulo, 789, 790
Gum, blue (Eucalyptus globulus), 764
Gutierrezia, 99, 102, 884
Gyrinidae, 179

Habitat: breadth, 620, 621, 624, 645, 646; classification, 566-568; defined, 893; destruction, 322, 385, 487-491, 501, 512, 605, 612, 619-625, 645, 709, 711, 912, 915, 917-918, 929, 938, 939, 950, 951, 955; enhancement, 636, 739-743, 804-805; islands, 594-595, 662-663, 664, 707; manipulation, 486, 554; micro-, 518;

preference, 212, 518, 523, 553, 554, 603; quality, 583, 627, 628; as resource, 566, 829; sensitive, 637, 638, 639, 661, 673, 677, 809, 839; simplification, 89, 405, 970, 973
Hackberry (Celtis douglasii), 696; desert (C. pallida), 98, 102, 378; netleaf (C. reticulata), 98, 102, 106
Hairstreak, California (Satyrium californica), 938, 939
Haliaeetus leucocephalus, 513, 592, 788
Hamamelidae, 7
Hamamelidales, 8, 10
Hardhead, 186
Hardin, Garrett, 258
Hare (Lepus): black-tailed (L. californicus), 943, 944; Oregon snowshoe (L. americanus klamathensis), 952, 953; Sierra Nevada snowshoe (L. a. tahoensis), 952, 953
Harper's Well (Imperial Co., Calif.), 722-727
Harrisina brillians, 979
Harvest: defined, 732; rotation, 742-743, 745
Hatfield, Marc O. (Sen.), 41
Hawk, 572, 662; Cooper's (Accipiter cooperi), 461, 592; Marsh (Circus cyaneus), 205, 207, 208, 461, 600; Red-shouldered (Buteo lineatus), 484, 493, 572, 595, 665; Red-tailed (B. jamaicensis), 205, 493, 572, 697; Sharp-shinned (Accipiter striatus), 461, 789; Swainson's (Buteo swainsoni), 205, 572, 612-618
Hawthorne, 971
Hazel, California (Corylus cornuta var. californica), 917
Headwaters, 88, 173, 901
Heartworm, dog, 968
Heat. See Temperature
Hedera helix, 348
Hedgerows, 326, 841
Helenium: bigelovii, 648; puberulum, 610
Helianthus giganteus, 207
Heliothis zea, 972, 975
Heliotrope (Heliotropium curassavicum), 607, 649, 691
Helodidae, 180
Hemiptera, 177, 178
Hemlock, 971; poison (Conium maculatum), 573, 648; western (Tsuga heterophylla), 665, 669
Hemp, Indian (Apocynum cannabinum var. glaberrimum), 648
Herbaceous cover, 84, 97, 101, 117, 152, 153, 161, 169, 197, 210, 310, 362, 414, 445, 490, 499, 511, 519, 628, 629, 642, 675, 740
Herbicides, 81, 385, 448, 449, 450, 543, 552-553, 683, 745, 802, 805, 973; phenoxy, 987
Heritage Conservation and Recreation Service (HCRS), 329, 330
Heritage programs, 322-323
Heron, 603, 604, 767; Black-crowned Night (Nycticorax nycticorax), 205, 599; Great Blue (Ardea herodias), 205, 484, 491, 493, 599, 637, 665, 697, 788; Green (Butorides striatus), 599
Hesperia juba, 935
Hesperiidae, 934, 935
Hesperiphona vespertina, 593
Heteroceridae, 180
Heterogeneity, 347; genetic, 33

696, 787

Logging, 27, 30, 33, 38, 65, 80, 81, 83, 86, 115,
142, 143, 146, 160, 164-166, 168, 169, 170,
171, 173, 180, 181, 184, 186, 203, 223, 226,
227, 228-229, 235, 237, 239, 251, 252, 266,
273, 275, 276, 277, 278, 310, 330, 356, 361,
366, 384, 385, 393, 432, 459, 483, 484, 488,
510, 619, 630, 637, 660, 661, 663-664, 666,
667, 669, 728, 739-742, 744-746, 761, 763, 784,
787, 802, 803, 810, 827, 958, 985, 983-987
Lolium, 614; multiflorum, 651
Lomboy (Jatropha), 398, 400
Lonely Gulch Creek (Calif.), 811
Long Valley Dam, 82
Lonicera: hispidula var. vacillans, 48;
involucrata, 48, 649, 665; johnstonii, 606
Loon, Common (Gavia immer), 599
Loosestrife, California (Lythrum
californicum), 650
Lophocereus schottii, 398
Lophodytes cucullatus, 205
Lophortyx: californicus, 205, 493, 581, 593,
701; gambeli, 621, 622, 623, 627, 701, 702,
741
Los Angeles Aqueduct, 80, 82-83, 529; Second, 82
Los Angeles (Calif.) Department of Water and
Power, 531, 533, 930
Los Angeles River (Calif.), 838
Los Flores Canyon (Los Angeles Co., Calif.), 637
Los Gatos Creek, 24, 25
Los Osos Creek (San Luis Obispo Co., Calif.), 677
Los Padres Dam, 124, 134
Los Padres National Forest, 134, 196
Los Padres Reservoir, 136
Los Penasquitos Creek, 658
Los Penasquitos Lagoon (San Diego Co., Calif.),
652, 653
Los Vaqueros Reservoir, 33-35
Los Virgenes Municipal Water District, 636
Lotus: corniculatus, 649; purshianus 71,
649; scoparius, 649, 884
Lower San Joaquin River and Tributaries Project,
538, 539
Lowland, 376
Ludwigia peploides, 650
Lutra canadensis, 788, 943, 946
Lycaena: editha, 938; xanthoides, 938-939
Lycaenidae, 934, 939
Lycium, 99, 102
Lycopus americanus, 650
Lygus bug, 972, 975-976
Lymantria dispar, 971
Lythraceae, 650
Lythrum: californicum, 71, 644, 650;
hyssopifolia, 650

Machaerocereus gummosus, 394
MacKerricher State Park (Mendocino Co., Calif.),
763
Maclura pomerifera, 153
Macoma, 778
Macrophytes, aquatic, 160, 161, 164, 169, 177,
183, 184, 517, 520, 521
Madison (Wisc.), 272
Mad River (Calif.), 660, 661
Madrone (Arbutus menziesii), 86, 88, 135,
197, 447
Madro-Tertiary Geoflora, 3, 89, 935

Magna Carta, 879
Magnolia virginiana, 16
Magpie, Black-billed (Pica pica), 206
Magrath Beach State Park (Ventura Co., Calif.),
684
Magrath Lake (Ventura Co., Calif.), 683-684
Mahogany, mountain (Cercocarpus betuloides),
394
Mahonia, red (Berberis haematocarpa), 102
Malaria, 968
Malheur National Wildlife Refuge (Ore.), 432
Malibu Creek (Calif.), 636; State Park, 764
Mallard (Anas platyrhynchos), 205, 432, 493,
599
Mallon v. City of Long Beach (1955), 266
Mallow, globe (Sphaeralcea), 99, 102, 103
Mammals, 166, 414, 491; furbearing, 731-738, 907,
944; riparian, 942-949, 950-956; threatened,
950-956
Mangle, 396; blanco (Laguncularia racemosa),
396; dulce (Tricerma phyllanthoides), 396,
399; negro (Avecennia germinans), 396; rojo
(Rhizophora mangle), 396
Mangrove, 396, 875; black (Avecennia
germinans), 396, 399, 400; button
(Conocarpus erecta), 396, 399; red
(Rhizophora mangle), 396, 397, 399, 400;
white (Laguncularia racemosa), 396, 397,
399, 400
Manzanita (Arctostaphylos), 364; east wood
(A. glandulosa), 675; Parry (A.
manzanita), 447; shagbark, 678
Maple (Acer), 3-4, 971; bigleaf (A.
macrophyllum), 87, 88, 111, 197, 348, 349,
351, 365, 445, 447, 637, 660, 887, 917
Mapping projects, 25-27, 46-48, 307-313, 325-326,
331, 341, 345, 357, 568, 963
Marah: fabaceus, 610, 649, 909;
macrocarpus, 839
Marble, large (Euchloe ausonides), 935
Marble Canyon Dam, 407
Marble-Cone Fire (1977), 130, 134-141
Marigold, bur (Bidens laevis), 648
Marks v. Whitney, 261, 265, 270, 273
Marrubium vulgare, 99, 102, 650
Marsh, 24, 25, 28, 55, 76, 152, 203, 207, 246,
248, 310, 396, 397, 431, 461, 483, 490, 491,
495, 498, 499, 515-527, 528, 558, 571, 598-604,
653, 665, 710, 711, 767, 776, 808, 809, 876,
877, 953; age of, 935; destruction of, 718,
810, 875, 972; faunal richness of, 935; as
habitat, 603-604, 716, 930, 938; manmade, 604,
838; salt, 395, 396, 398, 399, 400, 445, 495,
498-499, 642, 878, 882, 934, 951, 953, 968;
types of, 600
Marsh-pennywort, whorled (Hydrocotyle
verticillata var. triradiata), 648
Marsh-rosemary (Limonium californicum), 401
Marsilea vestita, 71, 72
Martes pennanti, 788, 789
Martin, Purple (Progne subis), 206, 592
Martis Creek (Calif.), 811
Masticophis lateralis, 34
Mathias, Charles, 41
Mating, insect, 178, 179-180
Matsunaga, Spark, 41
Mayflies (Ephemeroptera), 162, 177, 180, 849
Mayweed (Anthemis cotula), 648

McCloskey, Paul N., Jr. (Rep.), 873
McCloud Dam (Calif.), 789, 790
McCloud River (Calif.), 24, 784-794; Preserve, 784
McClure, James (Sen.), 875
Meadow, 92-96, 358, 425, 505, 802, 808, 809, 810; dry, 211; montane, 164, 200, 425, 477-479, 965; restoration of, 477-479, 805; wet, 203, 207, 211, 385, 431, 511, 528, 805
Meadowlark, Western (Sturnella neglecta), 206, 494
Meandering, 52, 55, 59, 66, 111, 113, 118, 120, 208, 216, 228, 452, 797, 849, 965
Meat production, 424-425
Medicago: arabica, 71; sativa, 490
Mediterranean climate, 2, 3, 9, 13-14, 16, 111, 357, 588, 655, 675, 838, 935
Megaceryle alcyon, 206, 493, 573, 600
Megaloptera, 177, 179, 180, 849
Melanerpes: formicivorus, 89; uropygialis, 621, 622, 623, 624
Melanoides tuberculatum, 718
Melilot, Indian (Melilotus indicus,-a), 71, 649
Melilotus, 99; albus (-a), 607, 610, 649; indicus (-a), 71, 649
Melospiza: georgiana, 494; lincolnii, 595, 600; melodia, 207, 209
Mendocino Co. (Calif.), riparian regulations of, 277, 669
Mentha citrata, 650
Mentone Dam (Calif.), 882, 886
Mentzelia, 99, 102, 103; leucophila, 717, 718
Mephitis mephitis, 943, 945
Merced County (Calif.) Streams Project, 896
Merced River (Calif.), 24, 25, 68-74
Merganser: Common (Mergus merganser), 205, 592, 595, 599; Hooded (Lophodytes/Mergus cucullatus), 205, 599; Red-breasted (M. serrator), 599
Mergus: cucullatus, 599; merganser, 205, 592, 595, 599; serrator, 599
Mescal Creek (Ariz.), 97, 101, 104, 107
Mesembryanthemum chilense, 401
Mesoriparian subsystem, 379, 380
Mesquite (Prosopis), 397, 398, 400, 407, 582, 691, 707, 953; P. juliflora, 99, 101, 102, 103, 105, 106, 107; growth rate of, 742; honey (P. glandulosa), 191, 193, 604, 619, 620, 630, 695, 696, 722, 740, 741, 742; screwbean (P. pubescens), 191, 620, 628, 695; velvet (P. velutina), 378; water use by, 725-726
Metabolism, 166
Mexicali Valley, 395
Mexico, government of, 402
Microbes, 162, 183
Microclimate, 319
Micropterus salmoides, 849, 930
Microtus: californicus, 943, 945; c. scirpensis, 711, 950; montanus nevadensis, 718
Midges, 162
Midlevel riparian communities, 88
Midstory, 907, 908, 912
Migration: bird, 191, 194, 582-583, 587, 593, 594, 699; fish, 800, 801, 966; insect, 178
Milkweed, narrow-leaved (Asclepias fascicularis), 648

Milling, 529
Milwaukee v. State (1927), 272-273
Milwaukee (Wisc.), 272-273
Mimosa biuncifera, 99
Mimosa, catclaw (Mimosa biuncifera), 99
Mimulus: guttatus, 99, 103, 490, 651; primuloides, 93; tilingii, 900
Mineral development, 281, 282, 719
Mineral nutrition, 17, 425
Mining, 38, 68-70, 79-80, 160, 227, 257, 311, 319, 330, 384, 404, 529, 703, 712, 713, 716, 718, 719, 720, 854, 879, 917, 984; hydraulic, 53-54, 828; ordinance, 275. See also Quarrying
Mink (Mustela vison), 731-738, 943, 945
Minnehaha Creek (Minn.), 250
Minnehaha Creek Watershed District v. Hoffman, 250-251
Minnows (Cyprinidae), 184; carp, 502; fathead (Pimephales promelas), 692
Mint: bergamot (Mentha citrata), 650; San Diego mesa (Pogogyne ambramsii), 840
Mission Creek (Calif.), 199
Missouri River, 59, 62, 335, 338
Mistletoe (Phoradendron): P. californicum, 624, 630, 740, 741; P. flavescens, 488
Mitchell Creek (Contra Costa Co., Calif.), 12
Mitchell's General Rule, 878
Mites, 971, 978
Mniotilta varia, 599
Models, of ecosystems, 534-535, 558
Modoc Forest Reserve (Calif.), 965
Modoc National Forest, 210, 965
Modoc National Wildlife Refuge, 210
Modoc Wetlands Study, 210
Mojave Desert, 695, 702, 706, 712
Mojave Forks Dam, 693
Mojave River (Calif.), 688-693
Mokelumne River (Calif.), 12, 24, 25
Mole, broad-handed (Scapanus latimanus), 943
Molluscs, 706, 707, 709, 710, 716; clams, 732, 778; mussels, 778; snails, 709, 710, 717, 718, 915-917
Molothrus ater, 19, 206, 494, 583, 592, 594, 600, 605, 608, 621, 663, 711
Monadenia: churchi, 917; setosa, 915-917
Monanthochloe littoralis, 395, 396, 397, 399
Monkeyflower (Mimulus): M. guttatus, 490; M. tilingii, 900; common (M. guttatus), 99, 103, 651
Mono Basin (Calif.), 82, 528
Mono Co. (Calif.), 931
Mono Lake (Calif.), 80, 267, 528-533
Montana de Oro State Park (San Luis Obispo Co., Calif.), 764
Monte Nido Valley (Calif.), 636
Monterey Regional Water Pollution Control Agency, 495
Mooney Island (Tehama Co., Calif.), 370-371
Moraceae, 650
Moretti, Bob, 42-43
Morgan Co. (Colo.), 254
Morone saxatilis, 185
Morrison Creek (Calif.), 231, 896
Morrison Creek Stream Group Project, 231
Morro Bay (San Luis Obispo Co., Calif.), 677
Morse v. Oregon Division of State Lands, 262
Morus, 153; microphylla, 99

Playa, 688, 691
Pleasant Valley Dam, 82
Plecoptera, 162, 166, 177, 180, 849
Plecotus townsendii, 943
Plegadis chihi, 599
Pleistocene, climatic changes during, 689, 707, 716, 935
Plethodon: dunni, 32; elongatus, 32; stormi, 31, 32, 33
Plethodontidae, 32
Pliocene, climatic changes during, 2
Plover: Black-bellied (Mniotilta varia), 599; Semipalmated (Charadrius semipalmatus), 599; Snowy (C. alexandrinus), 599
Pluchea, 393, 394; camphorata, 648; sericea, 191, 619, 620, 624, 696, 707
Plum (Prunus), 153
Poaceae, 650
Podiceps nigricollis, 599
Podilymbus podiceps, 599
Pogogyne ambramsii, 840
Point bars, 63, 65, 112, 113-115, 117
Point Mugu State Park (Calif.), 764
Poison ivy (Rhus radicans), 99
Poison oak. See Oak, poison
Police power, 266, 267, 271
Polioptila: caerulea, 592, 594; melanura, 621, 622, 623, 703
Pollen diagrams, 95
Pollutants, 168, 169-170, 218-219, 229, 235, 242, 245, 257, 258, 259, 262, 271, 272, 639, 710, 808, 809, 810, 811, 821, 874, 889; defined, 245, 246, 250-251, 874; noise, 639, 830; point vs. non-point sources of, 276, 802, 828, 986; and stream environment zone, 809-810
Poly, grass (Lythrum hyssopifolia), 650
Polygonaceae, 651
Polygonia satyrus, 937, 939
Polygonum, 445; aviculare, 651; bistortoides, 178; punctatum, 651
Polypogon monspeliensis, 651
Polystichum lonchitis, 511
Pomerado Creek (San Diego Co., Calif.), 655-656
Ponds, 368, 968, 969
Pools, 140, 166, 184, 186, 453, 847, 916; vernal, 688, 840, 879, 935
Poplar, 971; balsam, 112
Population: age distribution, 197-199, 366-368, 372, 488; control, 41, 42, 80, 970-976; decline, 612-618; density, 190, 191, 193, 194, 361, 368, 427, 486, 488, 489, 498, 499, 578-586, 587, 616, 626, 629, 663, 694-705, 739, 740, 810, 906, 912-913, 937, 945, 972-975; diversity, 486, 694-705; growth of human, 37-43, 534, 712, 839, 973
Populus, 10-11, 17, 63, 65, 66, 112, 153, 186, 193, 203, 310, 367, 368, 406, 407, 408, 414, 464, 469, 499, 571, 574, 578, 606, 614, 749, 761, 841, 882, 883, 962; angustifolia, 10, 11; arizonica, 11; balsamifera, 11; brandegeei, 400; deltoides, 11; fremontii, 4, 9, 10, 11, 12, 13, 15, 23, 48, 60, 61, 64, 65, 70, 71, 76, 77, 86, 89, 99, 102, 103, 104, 105, 106, 107, 110, 114, 116, 118, 152, 191, 196-202, 203, 207, 309, 319, 341, 348, 349, 351, 364, 365, 366, 372, 393, 438-443, 445, 459, 483, 488, 489, 490, 491,

499, 511, 559, 568, 579, 581, 588, 606, 609, 613, 616, 620, 626, 630, 651, 695, 696, 698, 707, 739, 742, 759, 839, 885, 900, 908, 909, 912, 921; monilifera, 207; nigra, 11, sargentii, 10, 11; tremuloides, 10, 398, 528, 805, 965; trichocarpa, 4, 5, 10, 11, 15, 87, 89, 111, 207, 499, 511, 528, 609, 660, 661, 666, 667, 675, 839, 885, 900
Porcupine (Erethizon dorsatum), 943
Porter-Cologne Water Quality Control Act, 276, 462, 811, 987
Port Hueneme (Ventura Co., Calif.), 683
Porzana carolina, 205, 207, 493, 599
Positive law, 268
Potamogeton, 518, 522; crispus, 517; pectinatus, 517, 521, 522
Potentilla: anserina, 651; glandulosa, 609
Power plants, 51, 82, 169, 233, 236, 237, 257, 260, 267, 273, 330, 333, 334, 379, 384, 484, 505, 506, 534, 535, 720. See also energy headings
Prado Dam basin, 882, 883
Prairie Creek (Humboldt Co., Calif.), 4
Preadaptation, 936
Precipitation. See Rain; Snow
Predators, 31, 162, 164, 166, 168, 169, 177, 178, 184, 185, 194, 326, 432, 553, 573, 660, 662, 663, 666, 710, 717, 732, 930, 954, 968, 970, 972, 973, 975. See also Insectivores (birds)
Presa Rodriquez (dam, B. C., Mex.), 393
Preservation. See Conservation measures
President's Environmental Message (1979), 330, 332, 334
Prickly pear (Opuntia), 99
Primulaceae, 651
Princeton (Glenn Co., Calif.), 58
Privet, glossy (Ligustrum lucidum), 448
Procyonids. See Coati; Raccoon; Ringtrail
Procyon lotor, 499, 731-732, 851, 943, 945
Productivity (biol.), 2, 15-19, 160, 162, 385, 497, 510, 520, 636, 661, 666, 673, 808, 812, 906, 974; and biomass, 724; factors influencing, 16, 60, 162, 164, 183, 184, 502, 523, 739, 744; measures of, 170-171, 723; potential, 726; of riparian vegetation, 2, 193, 372, 379, 404, 413, 482, 722-727, 744, 801, 827, 912; and transpiration, 726; of uplands, 379; and valuation of natural systems, 238
Productivity (econ.), 216-220, 221-225, 238, 744-746, 981
Professional Foresters Law (1972), 986
Progne subis, 206, 592
Pronghorn (Antilocapra americana), 210-213, 972
Property rights, 226, 228, 235, 266, 267
Proposition 13 (Calif.), 232, 448
Proposition 20 (Calif.), 634, 652, 673, 831
Prosopis, 397, 398, 400, 407, 691, 707, 953; glandulosa, 191, 193, 604, 619, 620, 630, 695, 696, 722-727, 740, 741, 742; juliflora, 99, 101, 102, 103, 106, 107; pubescens, 191, 620, 628, 695; tamarugo, 726; velutina, 378
Prosopium williamsoni, 425
Protobalanus (subgenus), 11
Prune (Prunus), 60, 65
Prunus, 60, 65, 153, ilicifolia, 609; serotina, 99

pacifica), 915–916
Shrubs, defined, 362, 363
Sialia mexicana, 206, 494, 692
Sialidae, 179
Sialis, 166
Sierra Club, 37, 231, 407, 507, 509, 834
Sierra Club v. Department of the Interior, 273
Sierra Kayak School, 507
Sierra National Forest, 804
Sigmodon arizonae plenus, 952, 954
Silt, 23, 53, 117, 142, 151, 158, 223, 224, 358,
   367, 395, 712, 849; curtains, 857
Silverweed, Pacific (Potentilla anserina),
   651
Silviculture, 242, 247, 745, 801, 985
Silybum marianum, 648, 764, 921, 926
Similax californica, 48
Simuliidae, 180
Simulium, 849
Sinuosity, 127
Siskin, Pine (Spinus pinus), 593
Sisymbrium officinale, 649
Sisyridae, 179
Sitanion jubatum, 765
Sitta: canadensis, 206; carolinensis, 89,
   494
Sium suave, 648
Six Rivers National Forest, 804, 806
Skink (Eumeces): Gilbert's (E.
   gilberti), 33, 34; western (E.
   skiltonianus), 34
Skipper: marsh, 935; umber (Paratrytone
   melane), 939; Yuma (Ochlodes yuma), 935
Skunk: striped (Mephitis mephitis), 943,
   945; western spotted (Spilogale gracilis),
   943, 944, 945
Skunk cabbage (Veratrum californicum), 511
Slider, pond (Chrysemys scripta), 397, 398,
   399
Slough, 52, 207, 228, 253, 310, 871
Sly Park, 506, 509
Smartweed, 572; water (Polygonum punctatum),
   651
Smith River (Calif.), 660, 661, 666, 729
Smoketree (Dalea spinosa), 695
Smotherweed (Bassia hyssopifolia), 439, 628,
   629, 740, 741
Snags (dead trees), ecological importance of,
   603, 604, 629, 630, 665, 666, 670, 671, 743,
   917, 968
Snail, 717; Amargosa spring (Fontilicella),
   710; Amargosa tryonia (Tryonia), 710;
   assimineid, 709; hydrobiid, 709; introduced,
   718; littoridinid, 709; Nevada Spring, 717,
   718; Trinity bristle (Monadenia setosa),
   915–917
Snake, 30; California mountain king-
   (Lampropeltis zonata), 34, 789; checkered
   garter (Thamnophis marcianus), 34; common
   garter (T. sirtalis), 34; common king-
   (Lampropeltis getulus), 34; gopher
   (Pituophis melanoleucus), 34; night
   (Hypsiglena planiceps), 34; northwestern
   garter (Thamnophis ordinoides), 34;
   ringneck (Diadophis punctatus), 31, 33, 34;
   sharp-tailed (Contia tenuis), 33, 34;
   western aquatic garter (Thamnophis couchi),
   34; western black-headed (Tantilla

planiceps), 34; western blind
   (Leptotyphlops humilis), 34; western
   rattle- (Crotalus viridis), 34; western
   terrestrial garter (Thamnophis elegans), 34
Snakeweed (Gutierrezia), 99, 102
Sneezeweed, Bigelow's (Helenium bigelovii),
   648
Snelling (Calif.), 68; dredge field, 68–74
Snipe, Common (Capella gallinago), 599
Snow, 2, 9, 10, 25, 75, 135, 161, 184, 211, 358,
   485, 528
Snowberry (Symphoricarpos), 197; S. mollis,
   606, 607, 609; S. rivularis, 48, 348;
   river, 348
Society for California Archaeology, 775
Society of American Foresters, 41–42, 324
Socioeconomic values, 216–220, 222–223, 226–227,
   233–240, 513, 572, 720, 803
Sodium, 463
SOFAR Project, 505–514
Soil, 59, 72, 140, 151–152, 153, 200, 211, 275,
   358, 439, 442, 630, 781; alluvial, 151, 348,
   404, 452, 569, 661, 799, 809, 862, 984;
   conservation, 855; density, 740; disturbance,
   311, 987; and ecosystem classification, 288,
   325; formation, 798, 799; and grazing, 414;
   hydrologic groups, 654; hydromorphic, 901;
   moisture-holding capacity of, 111, 151–152,
   377, 442–443, 483, 519, 521, 573, 574, 643,
   654, 665, 688, 725, 816–817; permeability of,
   496, 723, 901; riparian-indicator, 26, 216,
   371, 376, 377, 468; salt content of, 442–443,
   498, 642, 643; saturation, as wetland
   criterion, 248, 253, 376, 890, 891, 892–893,
   900–901; and timber production, 661, 984, 987
Solanaceae, 651
Solanum nodiflorum, 651
Solar radiation. See Light
Solidago occidentalis, 648
Sonchus: asper, 649; oleraceus, 649
Sonoma Co. (Calif.), 916
Sonoma State University (Calif.), 775, 780
Sonoran Desert, 722–727
Sora (Porzana carolina), 205, 207, 493, 599
Sorex: monticolus parvidens, 952, 953;
   ornatus, 943; o. relictus, 952, 953; o.
   salicornicus, 952, 953; o. sinuosus, 952,
   953; vagrans halicoetes, 952, 953;
   willetti, 952, 953
Sorghum halopensis, 552
Sound absorption, 226
South Carolina Coastal Plain, 16, 17
South Carolina Wildlife Federation v. Alexander,
   251
South Central Region Coastal Commission (Calif.),
   673, 674, 684
Southern Sierra Power Company, 529
South Valley Coastal Foothills, 315
South Valley Depositional Flatland, 315
South Valley Sierran Foothills, 315
Soybeans, 234, 235, 251
Sparrow, 193; Black-throated (Amphispiza
   bilineata), 207, 701, 702; Brewer's
   (Spizella breweri), 207, 701; Chipping
   (S. passerina), 207; Fox (Passerella
   iliaca), 494; Golden-crowned (Zonotrichia
   atricapilla), 494, 580, 582, 701; House
   (Passer domesticus), 206, 701, 702; Lark

Water bugs: creeping (Naucoridae), 709; giant (Belostomatidae), 709

Watercourses. See Rivers; Streams

Watercress (Rorippa nasturtium-aquatica), 445

Waterfowl, 210, 223, 231, 257, 432, 498, 574, 669, 670, 716, 749, 774, 875, 961

Water grass (Echinochloa crusgalli), 561, 976

Water-horehound, cut-leaved (Lycopus americanus), 650

Water influence zones, 800

Water law, 221, 267, 535, 972, 981

Water Quality Act (1974), 820

Water resource management, 6, 27, 28, 51, 64, 65-66, 82-83, 124, 130, 134, 160, 186, 216-220, 221-225, 233, 240, 260, 262, 267, 282, 333, 384, 386, 405, 460, 465, 482, 485, 498, 505-514, 528-533, 534-536, 635, 800-807, 815-824, 844-860, 929

Water Resources Planning Act, 236

Water rights, 267, 275, 330; Governor's commission to review, 266; state, 253-255, 269, 285

Waters, Norm (Assemblyman), 507, 509

Watershed, 134, 236, 635, 808; management, 635, 652, 826, 831, 852, 955; regulatory zone, 831

Watershed Protection and Flood Prevention Act (PL 83-566), 236

Waterweed, yellow (Ludwigia peploides), 650

Watt, James (U. S. Secretary of Interior), 281, 385, 879-880

Wattle, Sydney golden (Acacia longifolia), 448

Waugh Lake, 528, 529

Wax-myrtle, Pacific (Myrica californica), 14, 86, 448, 660, 665

Waxwing, Cedar (Bombycilla cedrorum), 494, 591, 592, 593

Weasel, long-tailed (Mustela frenata), 943

Weathering. See Erosion

Weeds. See Competition; Introduced species

Weevil, Egyptian alfalfa, 971, 972

Weir, 66, 120, 266, 499, 870

Wells, 82, 124, 130, 150, 235, 310, 356, 358, 396, 399, 401, 471, 496, 503, 506, 517, 534, 675; oil, 678-679

Western Federal Regional Council Interagency Task Force, 809, 810

Western States Water Council, 255n

Wetland(s), 210-213, 358, 635, 678-679, 802, 896, 900; vs. aquatic ecosystems, 246, 889; boundaries of, 889-894; classification of, 375-380, 568, 900; coastal, 226, 247; decline of, 227, 358, 528-533, 828, 871, 872; defined, 376-377, 378, 390, 666, 831, 889, 890, 899-901; desert, 929-933; draining of, 234, 235, 237, 243, 251, 257, 258, 271; vs. drylands, 376-377; easements, 961; eastern vs. western, 378; ecology, 375; emergent, 211, 900; forested, 900; functions of, 252, 378, 380; historic changes in perception of, 271, 871; hydrology, 890, 891; indicator plants, 900; irreplaceability of, 262, 871; laws protecting, 226, 236, 242-256, 257-264, 265-268, 385, 387, 431, 639, 652, 670, 674, 684, 754, 758, 803, 826-832, 868-881; legal significance of, 243, 246, 247, 248, 250, 252-253, 831, 889; management, 929-933; mangrove, 246; and navigation, 878; preservation zones, 830-832;

restoration of, 253, 372, 828, 841, 896; vs. riparian system, 900; simulation of, 575; soil, 248, 253, 376, 890, 891, 892-893; terminology, 893-894, 900; valuation of, 238, 243, 255, 261, 262, 271, 378, 434, 831, 880; and vector control, 968-969; vegetation of, 253, 838, 889, 890, 891, 900; vernal, 211

Whale, gray (Eschrichtius gibbosus), 396, 397, 398, 399

Whale Rock Reservoir (San Luis Obispo Co., Calif.), 817, 818, 819

Wheat, 191, 972

Whimbrel (Numenius phaeopus), 600

White, checkered (Pieris protodice), 935

Whitefish, mountain (Prosopium williamsoni), 425

White River, 24, 25

Whitethorn (Acacia constricta), 98, 102

Widgeon, American (Anas americana), 205, 599

Wild and Scenic Rivers Act, 243, 258, 262, 266, 329, 330, 407, 729, 792

Wilderness Act (1964), 237, 407

Wilderness Area, 792

Wildlands Resources Center, 829

Wildlife: as economic resource, 221, 226, 233, 235, 236, 238, 250, 257, 258, 259, 261, 275, 379, 459, 746; enhancement, 767-772; habitat, 275, 512, 551, 554, 663, 739-743, 809, 839; management, 30, 431, 484-485, 706-715, 745, 803, 896, 951; migration corridors, 858; nongame, 275; refuge, 896; and wetland, 252, 257, 379

Wildlife Management Institute, 408

Wildlife Society, 408

Wildrye, blue (Elymus glaucus), 764, 765

Wild Trout Stream status, 792

Willamette Iron Bridge Co. v. Hatch, 869

Willett (Catoptrophorus semipalmatus), 205, 207, 600

Williamson Act, 960

Willow (Salix), 6, 23, 48, 60, 61, 64, 66, 70, 79, 80, 81, 82, 83, 87, 102, 103, 104, 105, 106, 111, 121, 128, 152, 153, 161, 193, 203, 208, 210, 309, 310, 354, 364, 365, 366, 367, 372, 393, 394, 398, 399, 407, 445, 457, 464, 469, 499, 511, 516, 522, 559, 560, 571, 572, 573, 574, 578, 579, 588, 614, 616, 660, 665, 666, 669, 695, 696, 749, 762, 765, 780, 787, 805, 839, 841, 863, 882, 883, 887, 900, 908, 909, 916, 953, 962, 965, 971, 976; arroyo (S. lasiolepis), 48, 60, 61, 89, 114, 115, 116, 117, 499, 573, 606, 607, 609, 637, 645, 651, 675, 676, 677, 885, 900, 902; basket (= sandbar), 782; black (= Goodding), 488, 489, 606, 607, 609, 651, 885; black (= red), 76, 77; Bonpland (S. bonplandiana), 13, 14, 99; golden (= Pacific), 885; Goodding (S. gooddingii), 48, 60, 71, 106, 191, 309, 483, 561, 573, 620, 626, 630, 651, 707, 739, 740, 742, 840; gray (= sandbar), 782; narrowleaf (S. exigua), 76, 77, 78, 80, 81, 83, 607, 609; Pacific (S. lasiandra), 48, 60, 71, 87, 89, 348, 349, 351, 352, 483; red (S. laevigata), 48, 60, 110, 112, 114, 115, 116, 117, 118, 348, 349, 351, 352, 447, 483, 499, 528, 606, 609, 651, 885, 921; sandbar (S. hindsiana), 48, 60, 63, 66, 71, 110, 112, 114, 115, 116, 117, 459, 499, 573, 651,